The **Rough Gui**

the USA

written and researched by

Samantha Cook, J.D. Dickey,
Nick Edwards and Greg Ward

with additional contributions from

Jeff Benzak, Tim Burford,
Max Grinnell, Charles Hodgkins,
Sarah Hull and Andrew Rosenberg

www.roughguides.com

Contents

◀◀ Leo Carillo State Beach Park ◀ Grand Prismatic Spring, Yellowstone National Park

CANADA
PACIFIC STANDARD TIME
MOUNTAIN STANDARD TIME
Vancouver
Seattle
WASHINGTON
Portland
OREGON
IDAHO
Boise
MONTANA
Helena
Butte
NORTH DAKOTA
Bismarck
SOUTH DAKOTA
Rapid City
MOUNT RUSHMORE
YELLOWSTONE NATIONAL PARK
WYOMING
Cheyenne
NEBRASKA
Reno
Salt Lake City
NEVADA
UTAH
San Francisco
Denver
KANSAS
COLORADO
YOSEMITE NATIONAL PARK
Las Vegas
CALIFORNIA
Wichita
GRAND CANYON NATIONAL PARK
Flagstaff
OKLAHOMA
Los Angeles
ARIZONA
Santa Fe
Amarillo
Albuquerque
Oklahoma City
Phoenix
San Diego
NEW MEXICO
Tucson
TEXAS
Dallas
El Paso
PACIFIC OCEAN
BIG BEND NATIONAL PARK
San Antonio
MEXICO
ALASKA
CANADA
Anchorage
Juneau
ALASKAN STANDARD TIME
HAWAII-ALEUTIAN STANDARD TIME
Kauai
Oahu
Molokai
Honolulu
Maui
HAWAII
Big Island
5
90
15
94
84
90
25
80
80
70
15
70
5
25
40
17
10
8
10
20
35
10

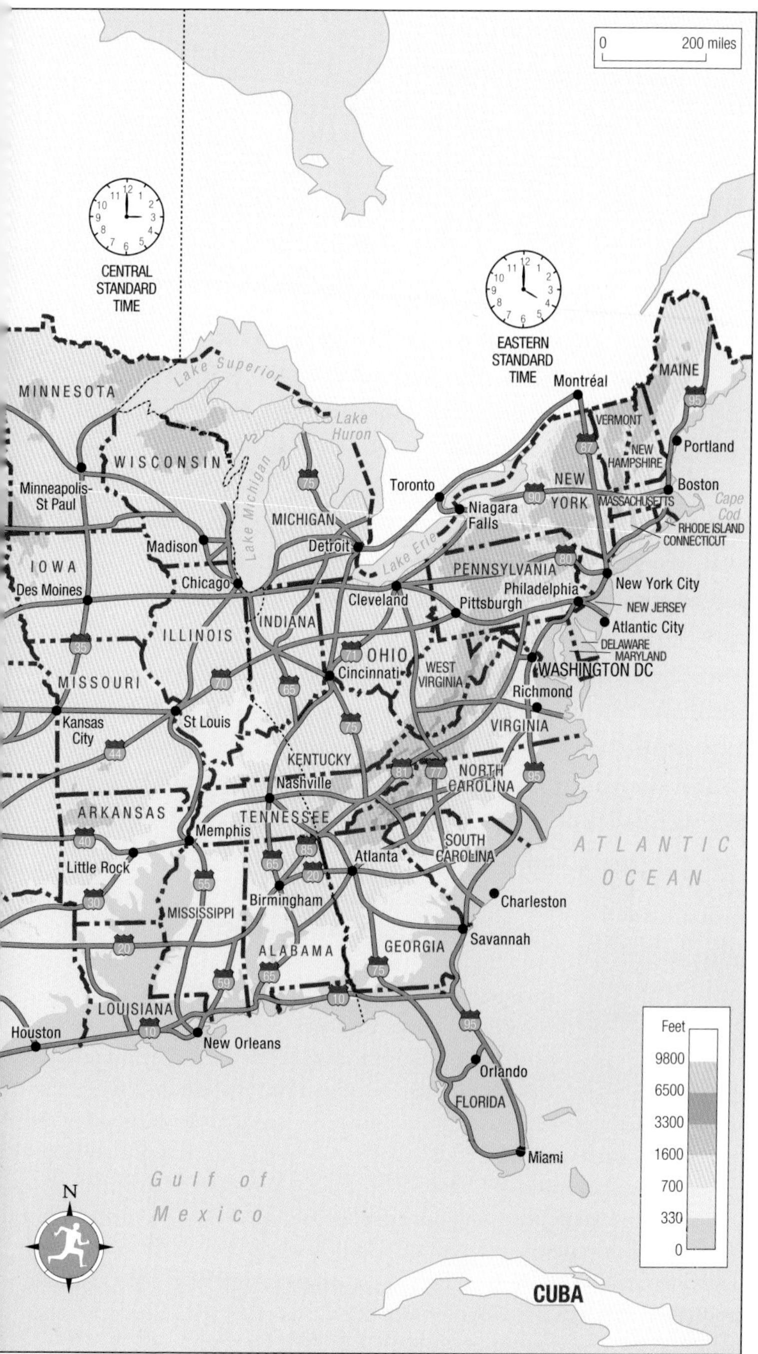
0 200 miles
CENTRAL STANDARD TIME
EASTERN STANDARD TIME
Lake Superior
Lake Huron
Lake Michigan
Lake Erie
MINNESOTA
WISCONSIN
MICHIGAN
IOWA
ILLINOIS
INDIANA
OHIO
MISSOURI
KENTUCKY
TENNESSEE
ARKANSAS
MISSISSIPPI
ALABAMA
GEORGIA
LOUISIANA
FLORIDA
SOUTH CAROLINA
NORTH CAROLINA
VIRGINIA
WEST VIRGINIA
PENNSYLVANIA
NEW YORK
VERMONT
NEW HAMPSHIRE
MAINE
MASSACHUSETTS
RHODE ISLAND
CONNECTICUT
NEW JERSEY
DELAWARE
MARYLAND
Minneapolis-St Paul
Madison
Chicago
Des Moines
Kansas City
St Louis
Detroit
Toronto
Niagara Falls
Montréal
Portland
Boston
Cape Cod
New York City
Philadelphia
Atlantic City
Cleveland
Pittsburgh
WASHINGTON DC
Richmond
Cincinnati
Nashville
Memphis
Little Rock
Atlanta
Birmingham
Charleston
Savannah
New Orleans
Houston
Orlando
Miami
ATLANTIC OCEAN
Gulf of Mexico
CUBA
N
Feet
9800
6500
3300
1600
700
330
0

Introduction to the USA

Lauded as a beacon of freedom, reviled at times as bent on global domination, the United States has many faces, and leaves no one short of opinions. The images of the country that named itself after a continent are embedded in the mind of every traveller: endless highways cutting through bleak deserts; forests of skyscrapers towering over urban jungles; acres of beaches dotted with surfboards and sun worshippers; high mountain peaks and green river valleys; magnificent feats of engineering, from the Brooklyn Bridge to the Hoover Dam. The country's emblems are so familiar that they constitute as much a part of the world's culture as its own – Lady Liberty, the Grand Canyon, the Empire State Building, the US Capitol, the "Hollywood" sign...the list goes on.

For over five hundred years, travellers have brought their hopes and dreams to America. The first European explorers were followed by millions of immigrants, escaping the hidebound societies of the Old World. Eventually, they were joined as free citizens by the Native Americans – the continent's true pioneers – and the slaves who had been shipped over from Africa and the Caribbean. Together they formed a nation that not only offered something genuinely new, but has continued to re-invent itself in the face of each fresh challenge, with a capacity to inspire that remains undiminished. The combination of a shoot-from-the-hip mentality with laissez-faire capitalism and religious fervour can make the US maddening at times, even to its own residents. But what's most surprising, perhaps, is how such an initially daunting land can prove so enticing – its **vibrant mix** of peoples, striking landscapes and city skylines, and rich musical, cinematic and culinary heritage seduce almost every visitor in the end.

The sheer size of the country prevents any sort of overarching statement about the typical American experience, just as the diversity of its people undercuts any notion of the typical American. Many of the stereotypes do hold true – this is a place where you can find real life cowboys, gangsters and other Hollywood standbys – but they are far from widespread. And yet, there are a few common bonds between residents. For one, vigour and passion are animating forces in politics and culture here. While this tendency has deep roots in the country's **religious heritage** (modern evangelism was perfected here), it affects everything from the firm opinions people hold over even trivial matters, to the public stand they make over God, government, guns and other incendiary topics. There is, in short, no such thing as the stiff upper lip in American life – that was left behind a few centuries ago on the voyage west.

▶ Church choir, St Louis

While the US is one of the world's oldest still-functioning democracies and the roots of its European presence go back to the 1500s, the palpable sense

▶ Bryant Park, New York City

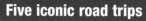

Five iconic road trips

One of the best ways to see the US is to devote several hours, or days, to an in-depth tour of its highways or byways. The old stretch of Route 66 has since been carved up into smaller sections by interstate freeways and these days, the following roads are the finest the country has to offer:

Hwy-1/Pacific Coast Highway This stunning, serpentine road travels from Los Angeles past the surf beaches of the Central Coast and intriguing sights like Hearst Castle up to the foggy reaches of the Bay Area.

Overseas Highway A hundred-mile stretch connecting the major islands of the Florida Keys, you pass countless waysides for fishing, snorkelling, kayaking and scuba diving before arriving at laidback Key West.

Blue Ridge Parkway This route's golden foliage is splendid in the autumn, but you can enjoy excellent year-round hiking in evocative Great Smoky Mountains National Park and take in lively towns like Asheville.

Hwy-100 A perfect rural stretch for experiencing historic small-town America, this Vermont route passes beautiful villages, dazzling autumn trees, vibrant ski resorts and the Ben & Jerry's ice cream factory.

I-40 A memorable transcontinental journey passing the Grand Canyon and Ancestral Puebloan sites, oil-and-cowboy landscapes in the Texas Panhandle, and Tennessee, cradle of blues and country music.

of newness here creates an odd sort of **optimism**, wherein anything seems possible and fortune can strike at any moment. The country's history – from the Gold Rush to the Space Race – testifies to this mentality, and it's still evident whether Americans are constructing towering skyscrapers, transforming their landscape with massive dams and highways or trying to win the jackpot in Las Vegas – or in the stock market. Americans relocate at a rate greater than people of any other society as they try to advance themselves economically and socially, although this wanderlust can create an equal sense of dissatisfaction, as expectations are left unmet and friends left behind in the search for the next golden opportunity.

▲ Gettysburg National Military Park

The **cities** of the US are where foreign visitors often spend the majority of their time, soaking up the high-rise energy of Chicago and New York, the political fervour of Washington DC or the bayside tranquillity of San Francisco. The nation's polyglot character means that any foreigner can find the company of their fellow citizens here, but it's much better to leave the comforts of home behind and dive into the native experience, whether raising heaven with a gospel choir at a Pentecostal church or joining the elated crowds at a baseball game.

The country amounts, however, to much more than the sum of its urban landscapes. While spending time in the cities can be fun, it's seldom as fulfilling as taking a deeper journey into the heart of the continent and its scenic splendours. Indeed, for all of its pride and bluster, the US can be a land of **quiet nuances**: snow falling on a country lane in Vermont, fishermen trolling for their catch on Chesapeake Bay and alligators gliding through the bayou. You could easily plan a trip that focuses on the out-of-the-way hamlets, remote wildernesses, eerie ghost towns and forgotten byways that are every bit as "American" as its showpiece icons and monuments. Putting aside the sheer size of the place, deciding exactly what version of the US you want to see may be the hardest decision of all.

Although we've structured this book regionally, the most invigorating expeditions are those that take in more than one area. Unless you're travelling to and within a centralized location such as New York City, you'll need a **car** – that essential component of life in the US. You do not, however, have to cross the entire continent from shore to shore in order to appreciate its amazing diversity; it would take a long time to see the whole country, and the more time you spend simply travelling, the less time you'll have to savour the small-town pleasures and back-road oddities that may well provide your strongest memories. It will hit you early on that, while there is no such thing as a typical American person or landscape, there can be few places where strangers can feel so confident of a warm reception.

Where to go

For many residents of the country's east and west coasts, the worthwhile parts of the US are strictly found along those urbanized seashores, and everything in between is dismissed as "flyover country". If your itinerary only includes the cities on the water's edge of the continent, you're sure to have an enjoyable time but will miss a great deal of what makes the nation unique and invigorating.

Nevertheless, following the order we've laid out in the Guide, the obvious place to start for most people is **New York City** – international colossus of culture and finance, with a colourful history and numerous skyscrapers to prove its status as the essential American city. While you could easily spend weeks exploring the place, just a little more effort will take you into the deeper reaches of the **Mid-Atlantic** region to the north. Here, whether in upstate New York, New Jersey or Pennsylvania, major cities such as Philadelphia and Pittsburgh border a landscape of unexpected charm and beauty, from the bucolic hamlets of Amish country and the wilderness of the Adirondack Mountains to iconic sights such as Niagara Falls and holiday favourites like the Catskills. Next door, **New England** has a similarly varied appeal; most visitors know it for the muscular Irish-American city of Boston, but there's much to be said for its rural byways, leading to centuries-old villages in Vermont and New Hampshire, bayside Massachusetts and the rugged individualism of the lobster-catching harbours and mountains of Maine – which take up nearly half the region.

▲ Milwaukee Art Museum, Wisconsin

▶ *Setai Hotel*, South Beach, Miami

Seven hundred miles west lie the **Great Lakes**, on the whole the country's most underappreciated region; vigorous cities like Chicago and Minneapolis, isolated and evocative lakeshores in Michigan and Minnesota, and rousing college towns such as Madison, Wisconsin, reward any visitor with more than a few days to explore. Bordering Ohio to the east, the nearby **Capital Region** is the home of Washington DC, capital of the nation and centrepiece for its grandest museums and monuments. Nearby Baltimore is one of the regions few other big cities, and to the south the old tobacco country of Virginia holds a fair share of American history too and coal-mining West Virginia has a scattering of curious natural treasures.

Although Virginia is technically part of **the South**, for the purest experience you'll need to venture even further to get the feel of its charismatic churches, BBQ dinners, country music and lively cities such as Atlanta and Charlotte. The "deepest" part of the South lies in Georgia, Alabama and Mississippi, and in these states – with their huge plantations and long history of slavery – you're sure to get a very different view of American life than anywhere else in the country. Other Southern states have their own unique cultures: **Florida** is a mix of old-fashioned Southern manners and backwater swamps leavened with ultramodern cities like Miami, miles of tempting beaches and the lustrous Keys islands; **Louisiana** offers more atmospheric swamps and "Cajun" culture, with New Orleans one of the few spots in the US with a strongly Catholic, yet broadly indulgent culture of drinking, dancing and debauchery; and **Texas** is the country's capital for oil-drilling, BBQ-eating and right-wing-politicking, with huge expanses of land and equally domineering attitudes.

The **Great Plains**, which sit in the geographical centre of the country, are often overlooked by visitors, but include many of America's most well-known sights, from Mount Rushmore in South Dakota to the Gateway Arch in St Louis and the Wild West town of Dodge City in Kansas. To the west rise the great peaks of **the Rockies**, and with them a melange of exciting cities such as Denver, beautiful mountain scenery like Montana's Glacier National Park and great opportunities for skiing throughout at places like

▲ Cowboys at a rodeo, Fort Worth

Idaho's Sun Valley. Bordering the southern side of the Rockies, the desert **Southwest** region is also rich with astounding natural beauty – whether in the colossal chasm of the Grand Canyon, striking national parks at Zion and Canyonlands or the Native American heart of the Four Corners region – along with a handful of charming towns and less interesting big cities.

The country's most populous state is, of course, **California**, synonymous with the idea of "the West Coast" and its freewheeling culture of surfing, libertine lifestyles and endless navel-gazing and self-worship. However, the further from the water you get, the less the stereotypes hold, especially in the lava beds and redwoods of the far north, the ghost towns of the Sierras and the intriguing deserts of Death Valley. To the state's north, Oregon and Washington – the rain-soaked pair making up the **Pacific Northwest** – offer pleasantly progressive towns such as Seattle and Portland and some of the most striking scenery anywhere in the US: the stunning landscape of the Columbia River Gorge, the pristine islands of the San Juans, the snowy peaks of the Cascades and more.

▲ Grizzly Bear cub, Denali National Park

Beyond the lower 48 states, **Alaska** is a winter wonderland of great mountains and icy spires, with few roads and people, but much to offer anyone with a zest for the outdoors and the unexpected. **Hawaii** is the country's holiday paradise, a handful of splendid islands in the central Pacific with remote jungle settings and roaring volcanoes.

When to go

The US **climate** is characterized by wide variations, not just from region to region and season to season but also day to day and hour to hour. Even setting aside far-flung Alaska and Hawaii, the continental US is subject to dramatically shifting weather patterns, most notably produced by westerly winds sweeping across the continent from the Pacific. As a general rule, however, temperatures tend to rise the further south you go, and to fall the higher you climb, while the climate along either coast is, on the whole, milder and less volatile than inland. What follows is a rough outline of the country's weather patterns from the eastern seaboard to the west.

The **Northeast**, from Maine down to Washington DC, experiences low precipitation as a rule, but temperatures can range from bitterly cold in winter to uncomfortably hot and humid in the summer. Further south, summers get warmer and longer. **Florida**'s air temperatures are not dramatically high in summer, being kept down by the proximity of the sea both east and west, but humidity is also a problem; in the winter, the state is warm and sunny enough to attract many visitors.

The central expanse of the **Great Plains**, which for climatic purposes can be said to extend from the Appalachians to the Rockies, are alternately exposed to seasonal icy Arctic winds streaming down from Canada and humid tropical airflows from the Caribbean and the Gulf of Mexico. Winters around the Great Lakes and Chicago can be abjectly cold, with

▲ *Cloud Gate by Anish Kapoor, Chicago*

▲ Burning Man Festival, Nevada

driving winds and freezing rain. It can freeze or even snow in winter as far south as the Gulf of Mexico, though spring and autumn get progressively longer and milder further south through the Plains. Average rainfall dwindles to lower and lower levels the further west you head across the Plains. In the Midwest tornadoes (or "twisters") are a frequent local phenomenon, tending to cut a narrow swath of destruction in the wake of violent spring or summer thunderstorms.

In the **South** as a whole summer is much the wettest season, with high humidity, and the time when thunderstorms are most likely to strike. One or two hurricanes each year rage across Florida and/or the Gulf of Mexico states from the warm waters to the south between August and October. The winter is mild for the most part and the two shoulder seasons usually see warm days and fresher nights

Temperatures in the **Rockies** correlate closely with altitude, so nights can be cold even in high summer. Beyond the mountains in the south lie the extensive arid and inhospitable deserts of the **Southwest**. Much of this area is within the rain shadow of the California ranges. In cities such as Las Vegas and Phoenix, the mercury regularly soars above 100°F, though the atmosphere is not usually humid enough to be as enervating as that might sound and air conditioning is ubiquitous.

West of the barrier of the Cascade Mountains, the fertile **Pacific Northwest** is the only region of the country where winter is the wettest season, and outside summer the climate is wet, mild and seldom hot. Further south, **California**'s weather more or less lives up to the popular idyllic image, though the climate is markedly hotter and drier in the south than in the north, where there's enough snow to make the mountains a major skiing destination from November to April. San Francisco and the northern coast is kept milder and colder than the inland region by its propensity to attract sea fog, while much of the Los Angeles basin is prone to filling up with smog – though this diminishes the closer you get to the ocean.

All US cities are pretty much year-round destinations, with some exceptions (Fairbanks, Alaska, in winter and Houston, Texas, in summer, for example, can be quite unpleasant), while national parks and mountain ranges tend to be seasonal attractions; this is particularly true of the summer months between Memorial and Labor days, when the majority of domestic tourists visit.

Average temperature (°F) and rainfall

To convert °F to °C, subtract 32 and multiply by 5/9

	Jan	Feb	Mar	Apr	May	Jun	Jul	Aug	Sep	Oct	Nov	Dec
Anchorage												
max/min temp	19/5	27/9	33/13	44/27	54/36	62/44	65/49	64/47	57/39	43/29	30/15	20/6
days of rain	7	6	5	4	5	6	10	15	14	12	7	6
Chicago												
max/min temp	32/18	34/20	43/29	55/40	65/50	75/60	81/66	79/65	73/58	61/47	47/34	36/23
days of rain	11	10	12	11	12	11	9	9	9	9	10	11
Honolulu												
max/min temp	76/69	76/67	77/67	78/68	80/70	81/72	82/73	83/74	83/74	82/72	80/70	78/69
days of rain	14	11	13	12	11	12	14	13	13	13	13	15
Las Vegas												
max/min temp	60/29	67/34	72/39	81/45	89/52	99/61	103/68	102/66	95/57	84/47	71/36	61/30
days of rain	2	2	2	1	1	1	2	2	1	1	1	2
Los Angeles												
max/min temp	65/46	66/47	67/48	70/50	72/53	76/56	81/60	82/60	81/58	76/54	73/50	67/47
days of rain	6	6	6	4	2	1	0	0	1	2	3	6
Miami												
max/min temp	74/61	75/61	78/64	80/67	84/71	86/74	88/76	88/76	87/75	83/72	78/66	76/62
days of rain	9	6	7	7	12	13	15	15	18	16	10	7
New Orleans												
max/min temp	62/47	65/50	71/55	77/61	83/68	88/74	90/76	90/76	86/73	79/64	70/55	64/48
days of rain	10	12	9	7	8	13	15	14	10	7	7	10
New York City												
max/min temp	37/24	38/24	45/30	57/42	68/53	77/60	82/66	80/66	79/60	69/49	51/37	41/29
days of rain	12	10	12	11	11	10	12	10	9	9	9	10
San Francisco												
max/min temp	55/45	59/47	61/48	62/49	63/51	66/52	65/53	65/53	69/55	68/54	63/51	57/47
days of rain	11	11	10	6	4	2	0	0	2	4	7	10
Seattle												
max/min temp	45/36	48/37	52/39	58/43	64/47	69/52	72/54	73/55	67/52	59/47	51/41	47/38
days of rain	18	16	16	13	12	9	4	5	8	13	17	19
Washington DC												
max/min temp	42/27	44/28	53/35	64/44	75/54	83/63	87/68	84/66	78/58	67/48	55/38	45/29
days of rain	11	10	12	11	12	11	11	11	8	8	9	10

29 things not to miss

It's not possible to see everything that the USA has to offer in one trip – and we don't suggest you try. What follows is a selective and subjective taste of the country's highlights: unforgettable cities, spectacular drives, magnificent parks, spirited celebrations and stunning natural phenomena. They're arranged in five colour-coded categories to help you find the very best things to see, do and experience. All highlights have a page reference to take you straight into the Guide, where you can find out more.

01 **Monument Valley, AZ** Page **800** • Massive sandstone monoliths stand sentinel in this iconic southwestern landscape.

02 Chicago's modern architecture, IL Page **285** •

The history of modern architecture is writ large on Chicago's skyline, site of the world's first skyscraper.

03 Skiing in the Rocky Mountains Pages **697, 705** & **744**

• The Rockies make for some of the best skiing anywhere, with their glitzy resorts and atmospheric mining towns.

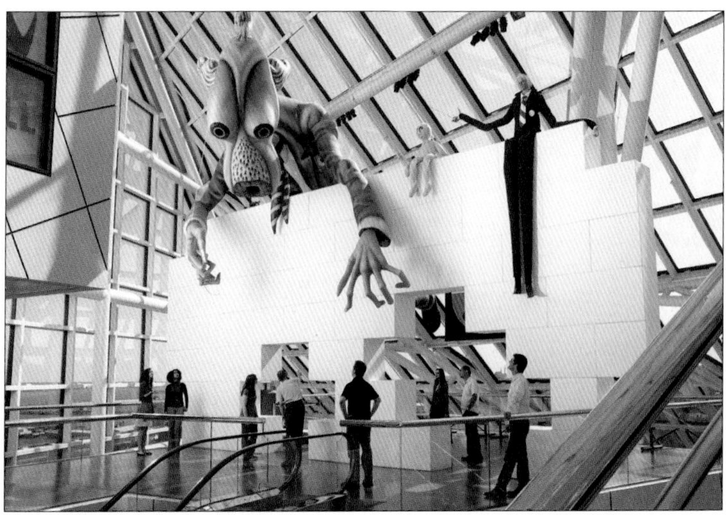

04 Rock and Roll Hall of Fame, OH Page **254**

• Housed inside this striking glass pyramid is an unparalled collection of rock music's finest mementoes, recordings, films and exhibitions.

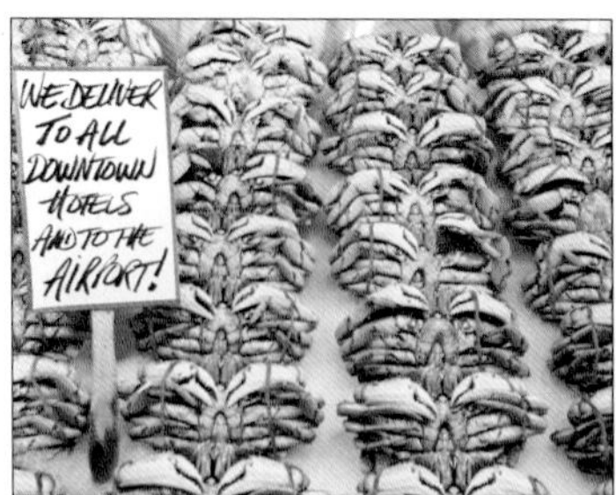

05 Pike Place Market, Seattle, WA Page **953** • Piled high with salmon, lobster, clams and crabs, the oldest public market in the nation is also home to some great seafood restaurants.

06 Savannah, GA Page **436** • Mint juleps on wide verandas, horse-drawn carriages on cobbled streets and lush foliage draped with Spanish moss; this historic cotton port remains the South's loveliest town.

07 Ancestral Puebloan sites Page **762** • Scattered through desert landscapes like New Mexico's magnificent Bandelier National Monument, the dwellings of the Ancestral Puebloans afford glimpses of an ancient and mysterious world.

08 Yellowstone National Park, WY Page **718** • The national park that started it all has it all, from steaming fluorescent hot springs and spouting geysers to sheer canyons and meadows filled with wildflowers and assorted beasts.

09 Going to a baseball game Page **183** & **297** • America's summer pastime is a treat to watch wherever you are, from Chicago's ivy-clad Wrigley Field to Boston's Fenway Park, the oldest in the country.

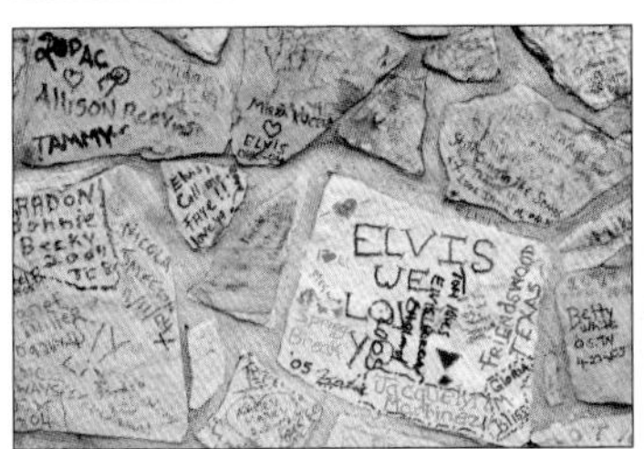

10 Graceland, Memphis, TN Page **456** • Pilgrims from all over the world pay homage to the King by visiting his gravesite and endearingly modest home.

11 Sweet Auburn, Atlanta, GA Page **429** • This historic district holds the birthplace of Dr Martin Luther King Jr and other spots honouring his legacy.

12 Niagara Falls, NY Page **129** • The sheer power of Niagara Falls is overwhelming, whichever angle you view the mighty cataracts from.

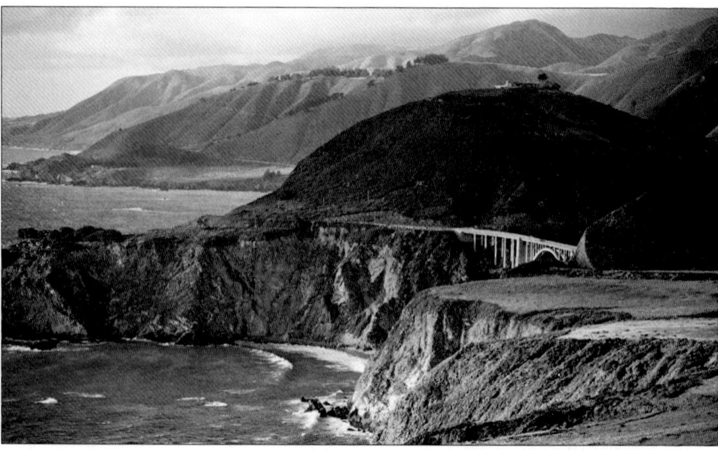

13 **Driving Highway 1, CA** Page **897** • The rugged Big Sur coastline, pounded by Pacific waves, makes an exhilarating route between San Francisco and LA.

14 **Crater Lake, OR** Page **993** • Formed from the blown-out shell of volcanic Mount Mazama, this is one of the deepest and bluest lakes in the world, and offers some of the most evocative scenery anywhere.

15 **Crazy Horse Memorial, SD** Page **673** • A staggering monument to the revered Sioux leader, this colossal statue continues to be etched into the Black Hills of South Dakota.

16 Las Vegas, NV Page **822** • From the Strip's erupting volcanoes, Eiffel Tower and Egyptian pyramid to its many casinos, Las Vegas will blow your mind as well as your wallet.

18 Walt Disney World, Orlando, FL Page **528** • Though each of Orlando's theme parks strives to outdo the rest, Walt Disney World remains the one to beat.

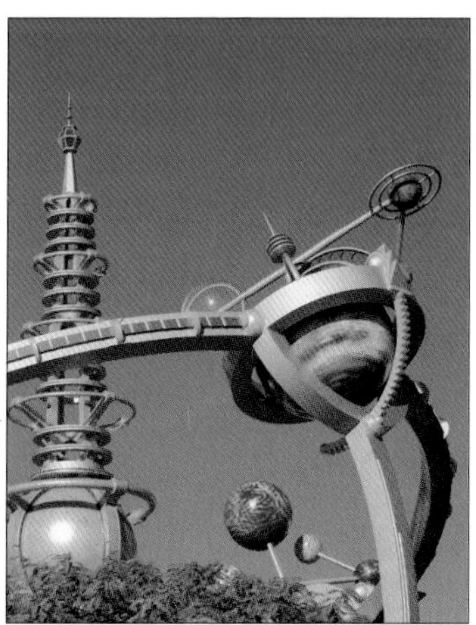

17 Hiking in the Grand Canyon, AZ Page **790** • Explore the innermost secrets of this wondrous spot on many of its superb hiking trails at the heart of one of America's best-loved parks.

19 South by Southwest, TX Page **605** • This thriving ten-day festival in Austin is one of the nation's best music festivals and plays hosts to bands from around the world – and Texas, too.

20 National Aquarium, MD Page **382** • Perhaps the country's finest, this monument to marine biology sits on Baltimore's Inner Harbor and appeals for its many dolphins, sharks, rays, turtles and other seagoing creatures.

21 Glacier National Park, MT Page **740** • Montana's loveliest park holds not only fifty glaciers, but also two thousand lakes, a thousand miles of rivers and the exhilarating Going-to-the-Sun road.

22 San Francisco, CA Page **903** • Enchanting, fog-bound San Francisco remains bohemian and individualistic at heart.

23 Hawaii's volcanoes Page **1043** • Hawaii's Big Island grows bigger by the minute, as the world's most active volcano pours molten lava into the ocean.

24 Yosemite Valley, CA Page **891** • Enclosed by near-vertical, mile-high cliffs and laced with hiking trails and climbing routes, the dramatic geology of Yosemite Valley is among the country's finest scenery.

25 The National Mall, Washington DC Page **339** • From the Lincoln Memorial to the US Capitol by way of the towering Washington Monument – this grand parkway is an awesome showcase of American culture and history.

26 Mardi Gras, New Orleans, LA Page **570** • Crazy, colourful, debauched and historic – this is the carnival to end them all.

27 **New York City, NY** Page **67** • With world-class museums, restaurants, nightlife and shops aplenty, the Big Apple is in a league of its own.

28 **New England in the autumn** Page **165** • The Northeast's breathtaking autumn foliage presents an ever-changing palette of colour and light.

29 **Miami's Art Deco, FL** Page **496** • This flamboyant city is deservedly famed for the colourful pastel architecture of its restored South Beach district.

Basics

Basics

Getting there

Anyone travelling to the US from abroad should start by deciding which area to explore first; the country is so vast that it makes a huge difference which airport you fly into. Once you've chosen whether to hit the swamps of Florida, the frozen tundra of Alaska, the summer heat of the South or the splendor of the Rockies and Southwest, you can then buy a flight to the nearest hub city.

In general, ticket prices are highest from July to September, and around Easter and Christmas. Fares drop during the shoulder seasons – April to June, and October – and even more so in low season, from November to March (excluding Easter, Christmas and New Year). Prices depend more on when Americans want to head overseas than on the demand from foreign visitors. Flying on weekends usually costs significantly more; prices quoted below assume midweek travel.

Flights from the UK and Ireland

More than twenty US cities are accessible by **nonstop** flights from the **UK**. At these gateway cities, you can connect with onward domestic flights. **Direct** services (which may land once or twice on the way, but are called direct if they keep the same flight number throughout their journey) fly from Britain to nearly every other major US city.

Nonstop flights to Los Angeles from London take eleven or twelve hours; the London to Miami flight takes eight hours; and flying time to New York is seven or so hours. Following winds ensure that return flights take an hour or two less. One-stop direct flights to destinations beyond the East Coast add time to the journey, but can work out cheaper than nonstop flights. They can even save you time, because customs and immigration are cleared on first touchdown into the US rather than the final destination, which may be a busy international gateway.

Four airlines run nonstop scheduled services to the US from **Ireland**. Flights depart from both Dublin and Shannon airports, and the journey times are very similar to those from London.

As for **fares**, Britain remains one of the best places in Europe to obtain flight bargains, though prices vary widely. In low or shoulder season, you should be able to find a return flight to East Coast destinations such as New York for around £300, or to California for around £400, while high-season rates can easily double. These days the fares available on the airlines' own websites are often just as good as those you'll find on more general travel websites.

With an **open-jaw** ticket, you can fly into one city and out of another, though if you're renting a car remember that there's usually a high drop-off fee for returning a rental car in a different state than where you picked it up (see p.35). An **air pass** can be a good idea if you want to see a lot of the country. These are available only to non-US residents, and must be bought before reaching the US (see p.33).

Nonstop flights

From London (Heathrow or Gatwick)

Atlanta British Airways, Delta
Baltimore British Airways
Boston American Airlines, British Airways, Virgin Atlantic
Charlotte US Airways
Chicago American Airlines, bmi, British Airways, United, Virgin Atlantic
Cincinnati Delta
Dallas/Fort Worth American Airlines, British Airways
Denver bmi, British Airways, United
Houston bmi, British Airways, Continental, United
Las Vegas Virgin Atlantic
Los Angeles American Airlines, British Airways, United, Virgin Atlantic

Miami American Airlines, British Airways, Virgin Atlantic
New York American Airlines, bmi, British Airways, Continental, Delta, KLM, Kuwait Airways, Virgin Atlantic
Newark United
Orlando British Airways, Virgin Atlantic
Philadelphia British Airways
Phoenix British Airways
Raleigh/Durham American Airlines
San Francisco bmi, British Airways, United, Virgin Atlantic
Seattle British Airways
Washington DC bmi, British Airways, United, Virgin Atlantic

From Manchester

Atlanta Delta
Chicago American Airlines, British Airways
Las Vegas Virgin Atlantic
New York American Airlines, Continental, Delta
Newark United
Orlando Virgin Atlantic
Philadelphia US Airways

From Edinburgh

New York Continental

From Glasgow

Chicago British Airways
New York Continental
Orlando Virgin
Philadelphia US Airways

From Dublin/Shannon

Atlanta Delta
Boston Aer Lingus
Chicago Aer Lingus, American Airlines
New York Aer Lingus, Continental, Delta
Orlando Aer Lingus

Flights from Australia and New Zealand

For passengers travelling **from Australasia** to the US, the most expensive time to fly has traditionally been during the northern summer (mid-May to end Aug) and over the Christmas period (Dec to mid-Jan), with shoulder seasons covering March to mid-May and September, and the rest of the year counting as low season. Fares no longer vary as much across the year as they used to, however.

Five steps to a better kind of travel

At Rough Guides we are passionately committed to travel. We feel strongly that only through travelling do we truly come to understand the world we live in and the people we share it with – plus tourism has brought a great deal of **benefit** to developing economies around the world over the last few decades. But the extraordinary growth in tourism has also damaged some places irreparably, and of course **climate change** is exacerbated by most forms of transport, especially flying. This means that now more than ever it's important to **travel thoughtfully and responsibly**, with respect for the cultures you're visiting – not only to derive the most benefit from your trip but also to preserve the best bits of the planet for everyone to enjoy. At Rough Guides we feel there are five main areas in which you can make a difference:

- Consider the **environment** on holiday as well as at home. Water is scarce in many developing destinations, and the biodiversity of local flora and fauna can be adversely affected by tourism. Try to patronize businesses that take account of this.
- Travel with a purpose, not just to tick off experiences. Consider **spending longer** in a place, and getting to know it and its people.
- Give thought to how often you **fly**. Try to avoid short hops by air and more harmful night flights.
- Consider **alternatives to flying**, travelling instead by bus, train, boat and even by bike or on foot where possible.
- Make your trips "**climate neutral**" via a reputable carbon offset scheme. All Rough Guide flights are offset, and every year we donate money to a variety of charities devoted to combating the effects of climate change.

Packages and tours

Although you can often do things cheaper independently, countless flight and accommodation **packages** to all the major American cities allow you to leave the organizational hassles to someone else. Drawbacks include the loss of flexibility and the fact that you'll probably have to stay in relatively expensive hotels. A typical package might be a return flight plus mid-range Midtown hotel accommodation for three nights in New York City, starting at around £550 per person in low season and more like £800 at peak periods. Pre-booked accommodation schemes, where you buy vouchers for use in a specific group of hotels as you travel around, are not normally good value.

Fly-drive deals, which give cut-rate (sometimes free) car rental when a traveller buys a transatlantic ticket from an airline or tour operator, are always cheaper than renting on the spot, and give great value if you intend to do a lot of driving. They're readily available through general online booking agents such as Expedia and Travelocity, as well as through specific airlines.

Several of the operators listed here go one stage further and book accommodation for **self-drive tours**; some travellers consider having their itineraries planned and booked by experts to be a real boon. Bon Voyage, for example, arranges tailor-made packages in the Southwest; the cost of twelve nights in Arizona, Utah and Nevada, flying into Las Vegas and out from Phoenix, and staying in standard hotels, starts at around £1250 per person.

A simple and exciting way to see a chunk of America's great outdoors, without being hassled by too many practical considerations, is to take a specialist touring and **adventure package**, which includes transportation, accommodation, food and a guide. Companies such as TrekAmerica carry small groups around on minibuses and use a combination of budget hotels and camping. Most concentrate on the West – ranging from Arizona to Alaska, and lasting from seven days to five weeks; cross-country treks and Eastern adventures that take in New York or Florida are also available. Typical rates for a week – excluding transatlantic flights – range from £580 in low season up to £850 in midsummer. Trips to Alaska cost a good bit more. For another touring and adventure package option, see the box on Green Tortoise, p.32.

Instead, fares on the regular Air New Zealand, Qantas and United flights from the eastern states **to Los Angeles**, the main US gateway airport for flights **from Australia**, tend to start at around Aus$1000 in low season, including tax, or more like Aus$1250 in summer. Flying from Western Australia can add around Aus$700, while throughout the year, flying all the way through to New York tends to cost another Aus$250–300 extra.

Similarly, from New Zealand, the cost of flying from Auckland or Christchurch to LA or San Francisco ranges from roughly NZ$1750–2250 across the year, or more like NZ$2500–2800 to New York.

Various add-on fares and air passes valid in the continental US are available with your main ticket, allowing you to fly to destinations across the States. These must be bought before you go.

Airlines and operators

Airlines

Aer Lingus ⓦwww.aerlingus.com
Air Canada ⓦwww.aircanada.com
Air New Zealand ⓦwww.airnz.co.nz
Air Pacific ⓦwww.airpacific.com
air Tran ⓦwww.airtran.com
Alaska Airlines ⓦwww.alaskaair.com
American Airlines ⓦwww.aa.com
bmi ⓦwww.flybmi.com
British Airways ⓦwww.ba.com
Continental Airlines ⓦwww.continental.com
Delta Airlines ⓦwww.delta.com
Frontier Airlines ⓦwww.frontierairlines.com
Great Lakes Airlines ⓦwww.greatlakesav.com
Hawaiian Airlines ⓦwww.hawaiianair.com
Horizon Air ⓦwww.horizonair.com
JAL (Japan Airlines) ⓦwww.jal.com
JetBlue ⓦwww.jetblue.com
KLM ⓦwww.klm.com

Kuwait Airways ⓦwww.kuwait-airways.com
Mesa Airlines ⓦwww.mesa-air.com
Midwest Airlines ⓦwww.midwestairlines.com
Qantas Airways ⓦwww.qantas.com
Scenic Airlines ⓦwww.scenic.com
Singapore Airlines ⓦwww.singaporeair.com
Sky West ⓦwww.skywest.com
Southwest ⓦwww.southwest.com
United Airlines ⓦwww.united.com
US Airways ⓦwww.usair.com
Virgin Atlantic ⓦwww.virgin-atlantic.com
WestJet ⓦwww.westjet.com

Agents and operators

Adventure World Australia ⓦwww.adventureworld.com.au, New Zealand ⓦwww.adventureworld.co.nz
American Holidays Ireland ⓦwww.americanholidays.com
Bon Voyage UK ⓦwww.bon-voyage.co.uk
British Airways Holidays ⓦwww.baholidays.co.uk
Creative Tours Australia ⓦwww.creativeholidays.com.au
Exodus UK ⓦwww.exodus.co.uk
Explore Worldwide UK ⓦwww.explore.co.uk
Funway Holidays UK ⓦwww.funwayholidays.co.uk
Hawaiian Dream UK ⓦwww.hawaiian-dream.co.uk
Jetsave UK ⓣ08712/312 295, ⓦwww.jetsave.com
North America Travel Service UK ⓦwww.northamericatravelservice.co.uk
North South Travel UK ⓦwww.northsouthtravel.co.uk
Titan HiTours UK ⓦwww.titantravel.co.uk
travel.com.au Australia ⓦwww.travel.com.au
Travelsphere UK ⓦwww.travelsphere.co.uk
TrekAmerica UK ⓦwww.trekamerica.co.uk
United Vacations UK ⓦwww.unitedvacations.co.uk
Virgin Holidays UK ⓦwww.virginholidays.co.uk

Getting around

Distances in the US are so great that it's essential to plan in advance how you'll get from place to place. Amtrak provides a skeletal but often scenic rail service, and there are usually good bus links between the major cities. Even in rural areas, by advance planning, you can usually reach the main points of interest without too much trouble by using local buses and charter services.

That said, travel between cities is almost always easier if you have a **car**. Many worthwhile and memorable US destinations are far from the cities: even if a bus or train can take you to the general vicinity of one of the great national parks, for example, it would be of little use when it comes to enjoying the great outdoors.

By rail

Travelling on the national Amtrak network (ⓣ1-800/872-7245, ⓦwww.amtrak.com) is

Historic railroads

While Amtrak has a monopoly on long-distance rail travel, a number of historic or **scenic railways**, some steam-powered or running along narrow-gauge mining tracks, bring back the glory days of train travel. Many are purely tourist attractions, doing a full circuit through beautiful countryside in two or three hours, though some can drop you off in otherwise hard-to-reach wilderness areas. Fares vary widely according to the length of your trip. We've covered the most appealing options in the relevant Guide chapters, such as those on p.120 and p.707.

AMTRAK ROUTES

rarely the fastest way to get around, though if you have the time it can be a pleasant and relaxing experience. As you will see from our map, on p.31, the Amtrak system isn't comprehensive – East Coast states from Virginia northward are well covered with rail routes but some Western states are left out altogether. What's more, the cross-country routes tend to be served by one or at most two trains per day, so in large areas of the nation the only train of the day passes through at three or four in the morning. A number of small local train services connect stops on the Amtrak lines with towns and cities not on the main grid. Amtrak also runs the coordinated, but still limited, Thruway bus service that connects some cities that their trains don't reach.

For any one specific journey, the train is usually more **expensive** than taking a Greyhound bus, or even a plane – the standard rail fare from New York to Los Angeles, for example, starts around $200 one-way with advance online booking – though special deals, especially in the off-peak seasons (Sept–May, excluding Christmas), can bring the cost of a coast-to-coast round trip down to around $300–350. Money-saving **passes** are also available: see box p.33 for details.

Even with a pass, you should always **reserve** as far in advance as possible; all passengers must have seats, and some trains, especially between major East Coast cities, are booked solid. Sleeping compartments start at around $300 per night, including three full meals, in addition to your seat fare, for one or two people. However, even standard Amtrak quarters are surprisingly spacious compared to airplane seats, and there are additional dining cars and lounge cars (with full bars and sometimes glass-domed 360° viewing compartments). Finally, if you want to make your journey in a hurry, hop aboard the speedy Acela service in the Northeast, which can shave anywhere from thirty minutes to an hour off your trip, though tends to cost from $25–100 more than a fare on a standard Amtrak train.

By bus

If you're travelling on your own and plan on making a lot of stops, **buses**, by far the cheapest way to get around, make

Green Tortoise

One alternative to long-distance bus torture is the fun, countercultural **Green Tortoise**, whose buses, complete with foam cushions, bunks, fridges and rock music, mostly ply the West and the Northwest of the country, but can go as far as New Orleans, Washington DC and New York. Highlights include the California Cruiser (11 days; $421), the coast-to-coast USA Explorer (34 days; $1640), and the gung-ho Alaska Expedition (27 days; $1495); food and park admissions cost extra. There are more than 30 seductive options, each allowing plenty of stops for hiking, river-rafting, bathing in hot springs and the like.

Green Tortoise's main office is at 494 Broadway, San Francisco, CA 94133 (Ⓣ415/956-7500 or 1-800/867-8647, Ⓦwww.greentortoise.com).

Pre-trip planning for overseas travellers

Amtrak Passes

The **USA Rail Pass** (15-day/8 segments/$389, 30-day/12 segments/$579, 45-day/18 segments/$749) covers the entire Amtrak network for the designated period, though you are restricted to the respective number of individual journeys. The **California Rail Pass** buys you seven days' travel in a 21-day period within that state for $159. Passes can be bought from the Amtrak website (Ⓦwww.amtrak.com).

Greyhound Discovery Passes

Foreign visitors, especially those inclined to venture beyond the major destinations, can buy a **Greyhound Discovery Pass** either online (give yourself at least 14 days before you leave home) or at any of the major Greyhound terminals and agencies in the States. The pass offers unlimited travel within a set time period. A seven-day pass costs $239; a fifteen-day pass $339; thirty days $439; and sixty days $539. No daily extensions are available.

Each time you travel, you'll need to present your pass at the ticket counter to receive a boarding ticket. For more information go to Ⓦwww.greyhound.com.

Air passes

The main American airlines offer air passes for visitors who plan to fly a lot within the US. These must be bought in advance and are often sold with the proviso that you cross the Atlantic with the same airline or group of airlines (such as Star Alliance). Each deal will involve the purchase of a certain number of flights, air miles, or coupons. Other plans entitle foreign travellers to discounts on regular US domestic fares, again with the proviso that you buy the ticket before you leave home. Check with the individual airlines to see what they offer and the overall range of prices. However you do it, flying within the US is only a wise choice for travel in regions where fares are low anyway; flights within Florida, for example, are very expensive.

sense. The main long-distance operator, **Greyhound** (Ⓣ1-800/231-2222, Ⓦwww.greyhound.com, international customers without toll-free access can also call Ⓣ214/849-8100 from 5am–1am CST), links all major cities and many towns. Out in the country, buses are fairly scarce, sometimes appearing only once a day, if at all. However, along the main highways, buses run around the clock to a full timetable, stopping only for meal breaks (almost always fast-food chains) and driver changeovers.

To avoid possible hassle, travellers should take care to sit as near to the driver as possible, and to arrive during daylight hours – many bus stations are in dodgy areas. It used to be that any sizeable community would have a Greyhound station; now, in some places, the post office or a gas station doubles as the bus stop and ticket office, and in many others the bus service has been cancelled altogether. Reservations can be made in person at the station, online or on the toll-free number. Oddly they do not guarantee a seat, so it's wise to join the queue early – if a bus is full, you may have to wait for the next one, although Greyhound claims it will lay on an extra bus if more than ten people are left behind. **Fares** on shorter journeys average out at about 25¢ per mile, but for longer hauls there are plenty of savings available. Check the website's discounts page – a ticket from New York to San Francisco booked online three weeks in advance can cost only $117.

Other operators include **Trailways** (Ⓣ1-800/776-7581, Ⓦwww.trailways.com), whose regional divisions cover some parts of the country more comprehensively, **Megabus** (Ⓣ1-877/462-6342, Ⓦus.megabus.com), whose low-cost service covers the northeast and midwest, and the alternative **Green Tortoise** (see box above).

Rail and bus contacts

Amtrak US Ⓦwww.amtrak.com
Greyhound US Ⓦwww.greyhound.com
Green Tortoise US Ⓦwww.greentortoise.com

Peter Pan US Ⓦwww.peterpanbus.com
STA Travel US Ⓦwww.statravel.com; UK Ⓦwww.statravel.co.uk

By plane

Despite the presence of good-value discount airlines – most notably Southwest and JetBlue – air travel is a much less appealing way of getting around the country than it used to be. With air fuel costs escalating even faster than gasoline costs, and airlines cutting routes, demanding customers pay for routine services and jacking up prices across the board, the days of using jet travel as a spur to vacation adventuring are long gone. To get any kind of break on price, you'll have to reserve well ahead of time (at least three weeks), preferably not embark in the high season, and be firm in your plans in buying a "non-refundable" fare – which if changed can incur costs of $100 or more. Nonetheless, if you arrange your trip properly, flying can still cost less than the train – especially if you take into account how much you save not paying for food and drink while on the move – though still more than the bus. In those examples where flying can make sense for short local hops, we mention such options wherever appropriate throughout this Guide. Otherwise, phone the airlines or visit their websites to find out routes and schedules.

By car

For many, the concept of cruising down the highway, preferably in a convertible with the radio blasting, is one of the main reasons to set out on a tour of the US. The romantic images of countless road movies are not far from the truth, though you don't have to embark on a wild spree of drinking, drugs and sex to enjoy **driving** across America. Apart from anything else, a car makes it possible to choose your own itinerary and to explore the astonishing wide-open landscapes that may well provide your most enduring memories of the country.

Driving in the cities, on the other hand, is not exactly fun, and can be hair-raising. Yet in larger places a car is by far the most convenient way to make your way around, especially as public transport tends to be spotty outside the major cities. Many urban areas, especially in the west, have grown up since cars were invented. As such, they sprawl for so many miles in all directions – Los Angeles and Houston are classic examples – that your hotel may be fifteen or twenty miles from the sights you came to see, or perhaps simply on the other side of a freeway that can't be crossed on foot. In some centralized cities – mostly in the Northeast, plus Chicago, San Francisco, Portland and Seattle – the main attractions and facilities are concentrated within walking distance of each other.

To **rent a car**, you must have held your licence for at least one year. Drivers under 25 may encounter problems and have to pay higher than normal insurance premiums. Rental companies expect customers to have a credit card; if you don't, they may let you leave a cash deposit (at least $500), but don't count on it. All the major **rental companies** have outlets at the main airports but it can often be cheaper to rent from a city branch. Reservations are handled centrally, so the best way to shop around is either online, or by calling their national toll-free numbers. Potential variations are endless; certain cities and states are consistently cheaper than others, while individual travellers may be eligible for corporate, frequent-flier or AAA discounts.

Driving for foreigners

Foreign nationals from English-speaking countries can drive in the US using their **full domestic driving licences** (International Driving Permits are not always regarded as sufficient). Fly-drive deals are good value if you want to **rent** a car (see below), though you can save up to fifty percent simply by booking in advance with a major firm. If you choose not to pay until you arrive, be sure you take a written confirmation of the price with you. Remember that it's safer not to drive right after a long transatlantic flight – and that most standard rental cars have **automatic transmissions**.

Hitchhiking

Hitchhiking in the United States is a **bad idea**, making you a potential victim both inside (you never know whom you're travelling with) and outside the car, as the odd fatality may occur from hitchers getting a little too close to the highway lanes. At a minimum, in the many states where the practice is illegal, you can expect a steep fine from the police and, on occasion, an overnight stay in the local jail.

In low season you may find a tiny car (a "subcompact") for as little as $150 per week, but a typical budget rate would be more like $35–40 per day or around $200 per week including taxes.

You can get some good deals from strictly local operators, though it can be risky as well. Make reading up on such inexpensive vendors part of your pre-trip planning. Even between the major operators – who tend to charge $50–150 per week more than the local competition – there can be a big difference in the quality of cars. Industry leaders like Alamo, Hertz and Avis tend to have newer, lower-mileage cars and more reliable breakdown services. Always be sure to get **unlimited mileage** and remember that leaving the car in a different city to the one where you rented it can incur a drop-off charge of $200 or more.

When you rent a car, read the small print carefully for details on **Collision Damage Waiver** (CDW), sometimes called **Liability Damage Waiver** (LDW). This form of insurance specifically covers the car that you are driving yourself – you are in any case insured for damage to other vehicles. At $12–20 a day, it can add substantially to the total cost, but without it you're liable for every scratch to the car – even those that aren't your fault. Increasing numbers of states are requiring that this insurance be included in the weekly rental rate and are regulating the amounts charged to cut down on rental-car company profiteering. Some credit card companies offer automatic CDW coverage to customers using their card; contact your issuing company for details. Alternatively, European residents can cover themselves against such costs with a reasonably priced annual policy from Insurance4CarHire (Ⓦwww.insurance4carhire.com).

The **American Automobile Association**, or AAA (Ⓣ1-800/222-4357; Ⓦwww.aaa.com), provides free maps and assistance to its members and to members of affiliated associations overseas, such as the British AA and RAC. If you **break down** in a rented car, call one of these services if you have towing coverage, or the emergency number pinned to the dashboard.

Car rental agencies

Alamo US Ⓣ1-800/462-5266, Ⓦwww.alamo.com
Avis US Ⓣ1-800/230-4898, Ⓦwww.avis.com
Budget US Ⓣ1-800/527-0700, Ⓦwww.budget.com
Dollar US Ⓣ1-800/800-3665, Ⓦwww.dollar.com.
Enterprise US Ⓣ1-800/261-7331, Ⓦwww.enterprise.com
Hertz US Ⓣ1-800/654-3131, Ⓦwww.hertz.com
Holiday Autos US Ⓣ1-866/392-9288, Ⓦwww.holidayautos.com
National US Ⓣ1-800/227-7368, Ⓦwww.nationalcar.com
Thrifty US & Canada Ⓣ1-800/847-4389, Ⓦwww.thrifty.com

Cycling

Typically, **cycling** is a cheap and healthy way to get around the big cities, an increasing number of which have cycle lanes and local buses equipped to carry bikes (strapped to the outside). In country areas, roads have wide shoulders and fewer passing motorists. Bikes can be rented for $15–50 per day, or at discounted weekly rates, from outlets that are usually found close to beaches, university campuses and good cycling areas. Rates in heavily visited areas can be higher. Local visitor centres have details.

The national nonprofit **Adventure Cycling Association**, based in Missoula, Montana (Ⓣ406/721-1776 or 1-800/755-2453, Ⓦwww.adventurecycling.org), publishes maps of several lengthy routes, detailing campgrounds, motels, restaurants, bike shops and sights of interest. Many individual states issue their own cycling guides; contact the tourist offices listed on p.60. Before setting out on a long-distance cycling trip, you'll need a good-quality, multi-speed bike, panniers, tools and spares, maps, padded shorts and a helmet (legally required in many states and localities). Plan a route that avoids interstate highways (on which cycling is unpleasant and usually illegal) and sticks to well-maintained, paved rural roads. Of problems you'll encounter, the main one is traffic – RVs, huge eighteen-wheelers, logging trucks – that screams past creating intense backdraughts capable of pulling you out into the middle of the road.

Backroads Bicycle Tours (Ⓣ1-800/462-2848, Ⓦwww.backroads.com), and the HI-AYH hostelling group (see p.39) arrange multi-day cycle tours, with camping or stays in country inns; we've also mentioned local firms that offer this where appropriate.

Greyhound, Amtrak and major airlines will carry passengers' bikes – dismantled and packed into a box – for a small fee.

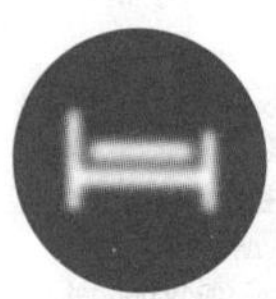

Accommodation

The cost of accommodation is significant for any traveller exploring the US, especially in the cities, but wherever you travel, you're almost certain to find a good-quality, reasonably priced motel or hotel. If you're prepared to pay a little extra, wonderful historic hotels and lodges can offer truly memorable experiences.

Typical room rates in motels and hotels start at $50 per night in rural areas, to around $85 in major cities. Many hotels will set up a third single bed for around $15–20 extra, reducing costs for three people sharing. For lone travellers, on the other hand, a "single room" is usually a double room at a slightly reduced rate at best. A dorm bed in a hostel usually costs $18–29 per night, but standards of cleanliness and security can be low, and for groups of two or more the saving compared to a motel is often minimal.

Accommodation price codes

Throughout this book, **accommodation prices** have been graded with the symbols below, according to the cost of the least expensive double room throughout most of the year. However, except at interstate budget motels, there's rarely such a thing as a set rate for a room. A basic motel in a seaside or mountain resort may quadruple its prices during the summer and on peak weekends, while a big-city, business-oriented hotel that charges "rack rates" of $200 per room during the week will often slash its rate at the weekend. Online rates can throw up considerable savings, and because the high and low seasons for tourists vary widely across the country, astute planning can also save a lot of money. Watch out too for local events – Mardi Gras in New Orleans, the National Cherry Blossom Festival in Washington DC, college football games – which might raise rates far above normal. Only where we say so do these room rates include local **taxes**.

❶ $40 and under
❷ $41–60
❸ $61–80
❹ $81–100
❺ $101–130
❻ $131–160
❼ $161–200
❽ $201–300
❾ $301 and over

In certain parts of the US, camping makes a cheap – and exhilarating – alternative, costing around $10–25 per night.

Wherever you stay, you'll be expected to pay in advance, at least for the first night and perhaps for further nights, too. Most hotels ask for a credit card imprint when you arrive, but some still accept cash or US dollar travellers' cheques. Reservations – essential in busy areas in summer – are held only until 6pm, unless you've said you'll be arriving late.

Hotels and motels

The term **"hotels"** refers to most accommodation in the guide, whereas motels, or "motor hotels", tend to be found beside the main roads away from city centres, and are thus much more accessible to drivers. Budget hotels or motels can be pretty basic, but in general standards of comfort are uniform – each room comes with a double bed (often two), a TV and phone, and an attached bathroom – and you don't get a much better deal by paying, say, $80 instead of $55. Over $80 or so, the room and its fittings simply get bigger and include more amenities, and there may be a swimming pool and added touches such as irons and ironing boards, portable coffeemakers and premium cable TV (HBO, Showtime, etc). Many hotels now offer wi-fi, albeit sometimes in the lobby only.

The least expensive properties tend to be family-run, independent "mom 'n' pop" motels, but these are rarer nowadays, in the big urban areas at least. When you're driving along the main interstates there's a lot to be said for paying a few dollars more to stay in motels belonging to the national chains. These range from the ever-reliable and cheap *Super 8* and *Motel 6* (❷–❹) through to the mid-range *Days Inn* and *La Quinta* (❸–❹) up to the more commodious *Holiday Inn Express* and *Marriott* (❺–❻).

During off-peak periods, many motels and hotels struggle to fill their rooms, and it's worth bargaining to get a few dollars off the asking price. Staying in the same place for more than one night may bring further reductions. Also, look for discount coupons, especially in the free magazines distributed by local visitor centres and Welcome Centers near the borders between states. These can offer amazing value – but read the small print first.

Few budget hotels or motels bother to compete with the ubiquitous diners by offering full breakfasts, although most will provide free self-service coffee, pastries and if you are lucky, fruit or cereal, collectively referred to as "continental breakfast".

B&Bs

Staying in a **B&B** is a popular, sometimes luxurious, alternative to conventional hotels. Some B&Bs consist of no more than a couple of furnished rooms in someone's home, and even the larger establishments tend to have fewer than ten rooms, sometimes without TV or phone, but often laden with potpourri, chintzy cushions and an assertively precious Victorian atmosphere. If this cosy, twee setting appeals to you, there's a range of choices throughout the country, but keep a few things in mind. For one, you may not be an anonymous guest as you would in a chain hotel, but may be expected to chat with the host and other guests, especially during breakfast. Also, some B&Bs enforce curfews, not allowing or appreciating their guests to stumble in long after midnight after a heady night of drunken partying. The only way to know the policy for certain is to check each B&B's policy online – there's often a lengthy list of do's and don'ts.

The price you pay for a B&B – which varies from around $80 to $275 for a double room – always includes breakfast (sometimes a buffet on a sideboard, but more often a full-blown cooked meal). The crucial determining factor is whether each room has an en-suite bathroom; most B&Bs provide private bath facilities, although that can damage the authenticity of a fine old house. At the top end of the spectrum, the distinction between a hotel and a "bed-and-breakfast inn" may amount to no more than that the B&B is owned by a private individual rather than a chain. In many areas, B&Bs have united to form central booking agencies, making it much easier to find a room at short notice; we've given contact information for these where appropriate.

Historic hotels and lodges

Throughout the country, but especially out west, many towns still hold **historic hotels**, whether dating from the arrival of the railroads or from the heyday of Route 66 in the 1940s and 1950s. So long as you accept that not all will have up-to-date facilities to match their period charm, these can make wonderfully characterful places to spend a night or two. Those that are exceptionally well preserved or restored may charge $200 or more per room, but a more typical rate for a not overly luxurious but atmospheric, antique-furnished room would be more like $100–140.

In addition, several **national parks** feature long-established and architecturally distinguished hotels, traditionally known as **lodges**, that can be real bargains thanks to their federally controlled rates. The only drawback is that all rooms tend to be reserved far in advance. Among the best are *El Tovar* and *Grand Canyon Lodge* on the South and North rims, respectively, of the Grand Canyon; the *Old Faithful Inn* in Yellowstone; and *Glacier Park Lodge* in Glacier.

Hostels

Hostel-type accommodation is not as plentiful in the US as it is in Europe, but provision for backpackers and low-budget travellers does exist. Unless you're travelling alone, most hostels work out little cheaper than motels; stay in them only if you prefer their youthful ambience, energy and sociability. Many are not accessible on public transport, or convenient for sightseeing in the towns and cities, let alone in rural areas.

These days, most hostels are independent, with no affiliation to HI-AYH (Hostelling International-American Youth Hostels) network. Many are no more than converted motels, where the "dorms" consist of a couple of sets of bunk beds in a musty room, which is also let out as a private unit on demand. Most expect guests to bring sheets or sleeping bags. Rates range from $18 to about $29 for a dorm bed, and from $35–55 for a double room, with prices in the major cities on the higher end. Those few hostels that do belong to HI-AYH tend to impose curfews and limit daytime access hours, and segregate dormitories by sex.

Youth hostel associations

US and Canada

Hostelling International-American Youth Hostels US ⓣ1-301/495-1240, ⓦwww.hiayh.org
Hostelling International Canada ⓣ613/237-7884, ⓦwww.hihostels.ca

UK and Ireland

Youth Hostel Association (YHA) UK ⓣ01629/592 700, ⓦwww.yha.org.uk
Scottish Youth Hostel Association UK ⓣ0845/ 293 7373, ⓦwww.syha.org.uk
Irish Youth Hostel Association Republic of Ireland ⓣ01/830 4555, ⓦwww.anoige.ie
Hostelling International Northern Ireland Northern Ireland ⓣ028/9032 4733, ⓦwww.hini.org.uk

Australia, New Zealand and South Africa

Australia Youth Hostels Association Australia ⓣ02/9281 9444, ⓦwww.yha.com.au
Youth Hostelling Association New Zealand New Zealand ⓣ0800/278 299 or 03/379 9970, ⓦwww.yha.co.nz

Food and drink

The USA is not all fast food. Every state offers its own specialties, and regional cuisines are distinctive and delicious. In addition, international food turns up regularly – not only in the big cities, but also in more unexpected places. Many farming and ranching regions – Nevada and central California in particular – have a number of Basque restaurants; Portuguese restaurants, dating from whaling days, line the New England coast; and old-fashioned Welsh pasties can be found in the mining towns of Montana. For more on classic American dining and regional cuisine, see the colour section on food.

In the big cities, you can pretty much eat whatever you want, whenever you want, thanks to the ubiquity of restaurants, 24-hour diners, and bars and street carts selling food well into the night. Also, along all the highways and on virtually every town's main street, **restaurants**, fast-food joints and coffeeshops try to outdo one another with bargains and special offers. Whatever you eat and wherever you eat, service is usually prompt, friendly and attentive – thanks in large part to the institution of **tipping**. Waiters depend on tips for the bulk of their earnings; fifteen to twenty percent is the standard rate, with anything less sure to be seen as an insult.

Regional cuisines

Many regions have developed their own cuisines, combining available ingredients with dishes and techniques of local ethnic groups. It's perfectly possible to create a fabulous US road-trip itinerary by tracking the nation's **regional cuisines** – much of it dished up in humble roadside restaurants packed full with locals. Broadly, **steaks** and other cuts of beef are prominent in the Midwest, the Rockies, the South and Texas, while **fish** and seafood dominate the menus in Florida, Louisiana, along the "low country" coast of the Carolinas and Georgia, around Chesapeake Bay in Maryland, and in the Pacific Northwest. **Shellfish**, such as the highly rated Dungeness crab and the Chesapeake's unique soft-shell crab, highly spiced and eaten whole, is the dish of choice on the east coast; Maine lobsters and steamers (clams), eaten whole or mixed up in a chowder, are reason alone to visit New England. Although the Hawaiian islanders consume more than half the **Spam** eaten in the nation, they also dish up delicious fresh fish and sushi as a matter of course, with tasty local varieties including *mahi-mahi* (dorado) and *ono* (which translates as "delicious"). Even in the Deep South, where almost everything will be cooked with some delicious piece of meat, catfish provide a delicious alternative, slathered in butter and "blackened" with spices.

Cajun food, country French-inspired cooking that originated in the bayous of Louisiana as a way to finish up leftovers, uses a lot of pork – chitlins (pork intestines), and

Vegetarian eating

In the big US cities at least, being a **vegetarian** – or even a vegan – presents few problems. However, don't be too surprised in rural areas if you find yourself restricted to a diet of eggs, grilled-cheese sandwiches and limp salads. In the Southeast, most soul-food cafés offer great-value vegetable plates (four different veggies, including potatoes), but many dishes will be cooked with pork fat, so ask before tucking in. Similarly, baked beans in the Rockies, and the nutritious-sounding red beans and rice dished up in Louisiana, usually contain bits of diced pork.

the spicy sausages known as boudin and chaurice abound. Sausages are also prepared with seafood like crawfish, or even alligator. **Creole** cuisine, its urban cousin, found mainly in New Orleans, is the product of a number of cultures: spicy, fragrant jambalayas, po-boys and gumbos are cooked as often in local homes as they are in restaurants (the oft-misunderstood distinction between Cajun and Creole cooking is explained in our "Louisiana" chapter, on p.568).

Southern cooking, or **soul food**, is delicious and very fattening – everything from grits to collard greens, from crispy fried chicken to teeth-rotting pralines. **BBQ** is also very popular in the South, especially in Tennessee and in particular in Memphis, where every neighbourhood has their own classic 'cue hut, offering anything from dry rub ribs to sweetly smoky BBQ spaghetti (generally, the more ramshackle the restaurant, the better the BBQ). Other BBQ centres outside the South include Kansas City and Chicago. In the Southwest, indigenous **Native American** communities continue to cook their traditional food; you will see Navajo frybread everywhere, a kind of fried taco dished up with minced beef.

At the other end of the spectrum, in a region where butter is despised and raw food diets abound, **California cuisine** is geared toward health and aesthetics. It grew out of French nouvelle cuisine and was pioneered in the 1970s, utilizing a wide mix of fresh, local, seasonal ingredients. Portions are small but beautifully presented, with accompanying high prices: expect to pay $50 a head (or much more) for a full dinner with wine. **New American cuisine** applies the same principles to different regional food, generally presenting healthier versions of local favourites.

Finally, there are also regional variations on **American staples**. You can get plain old burgers and hot dogs anywhere, but for a truly American experience, grab a piping-hot **Philly cheesesteak** sandwich, gooey with cheese and thin-sliced beef from a diner in eastern Pennsylvania, or one of New York's signature **Coney Island hot dogs** – or the LA version of the **frankfurter**, rolled in a tortilla and stuffed with cheese and chili. Almost every Eastern state has at least one spot claiming to have invented the **hamburger**, and regardless of where you go, you can find a good range of authentic diners where the buns are fresh, the patties are large, handcrafted and tasty, and the dressings and condiments are inspired. Needless to say, although we list the better of these locations in the Guide, almost none of them can be found along the interstates, under massive signs advertising their wares for 99 cents.

Other cuisines

In the cities, in particular, where centuries of settlement have created distinctive local neighbourhoods, each community offers its own take on the cuisine of its homeland. San Francisco has its Chinatown, New York its Jewish delis, Boston its Italian restaurants, Miami its Cuban coffeeshops. **Mexican food** is so common it might as well be an indigenous cuisine, especially in border territories of southern California, Texas and the Southwest. The food is different from that found south of the border, however, focusing more on frying and on a standard set of staples. The essentials, however, are the same: lots of rice and black or pinto beans, often served refried (boiled, mashed and fried), with variations on the tortilla, a thin corn or flour pancake that can be wrapped around fillings and eaten by hand (a burrito); folded and filled (a taco); rolled, filled and baked in sauce (an enchilada); or fried flat and topped with a stack of filling (a tostada).

Italian food is widely available, too; the top-shelf restaurants in major cities tend to focus on the northern end of the boot, while the tomato-heavy, gut-busting portions associated with southern Italian cooking are usually confined to lower-end, chequered-tablecloth diners with massive portions and pictures of Frank and Dino on the walls. Pizza restaurants occupy a similar range from high-end gourmet eateries to cheap and tasty dives – New Yorkers and Chicagoans can argue for days over which of their respective cities makes the best kind, either Gotham's shingle-flat "slices" or the Windy City's overstuffed wedges that actually resemble slices of meat pie.

When it comes to **Asian** eating, Indian cuisine is usually better in the cities, though there are exceptions. When found in the Chinatown neighbourhoods of major cities Chinese cooking will be top-notch, and often inexpensive – beware, though, of the dismal-tasting "chop suey" and "chow mein" joints in the suburbs and small towns. Japanese, once the preserve of the coasts and sophisticated cities, has become widely popular, with sushi restaurants in all price ranges and chain teriyaki joints out on the freeways. Thai and Vietnamese restaurants, meanwhile, provide some of the best and cheapest ethnic food available, sometimes in diners mixing the two, and occasionally in the form of "fusion" cooking with other Asian cuisines (or "pan-Asian", as it's widely known).

Drink

New York, Baltimore, Chicago, New Orleans and San Francisco are the consummate **boozing towns** – filled with tales of plastered, famous authors indulging in famously bad behaviour – but almost anywhere you shouldn't have to search very hard for a comfortable place to drink. You need to be 21 years old to buy and consume alcohol in the US, and it's likely you'll be asked for ID if you look under 30.

"Blue laws" – archaic statutes that restrict when, where and under what conditions alcohol can be purchased – are held by many states, and prohibit the sale of alcohol on Sundays; on the extreme end of the scale, some counties (known as "**dry**") don't allow any alcohol, ever. The famous whiskey and bourbon distilleries of Tennessee and Kentucky, including Jack Daniel's (see p.466), can be visited – though maddeningly, several are in dry counties, so they don't offer samples. A few states – Vermont, Oklahoma and Utah (which, being predominantly Mormon, has the most byzantine rules) – restrict the alcohol content in beer to just 3.2 percent, almost half the usual strength. Rest assured, though, that in a few of the more liberal parts of the country (New York City, for one), alcohol can be bought and drunk any time between 6am and 4am, seven days a week, while in the cities of New Orleans and Savannah you are even permitted to drink alcohol on the streets.

Note that if a bar is advertising a happy hour on "**rail drinks**" or "well drinks" that these are cocktails made from the liquors and mixers the bar has to hand (as opposed to top-shelf, higher-quality brands).

Beer

The most popular American **beers** may be the fizzy, insipid lagers from national brands, but there is no lack of alternatives. The craze for microbreweries started in northern California several decades ago, and even today Anchor Steam – once at the vanguard – is still an excellent choice for sampling. The West Coast continues to be, to a large extent, the centre of the microbrewing movement, and even the smaller towns have their own share of decent handcrafted beers. Portland, Oregon, abounds in breweries, with enthusiasts from around the world making the trip to sample draughts. Los Angeles, San Diego, Seattle, the Bay Area, Denver and other Western cities rank up there, too, and you can even find excellent brews in tiny spots such as Whitefish, Montana, where the beers of Great Northern Brewing are well worth seeking out, or Asheville, North Carolina, where the number of excellent craft breweries grows each year.

On the East Coast look for Boston-based Samuel Adams and its mix of mainstream and alternative brews, the top-notch offerings of Pennsylvania's Victory Brewing or stop in at Washington DC's great beer-tasting spot, the Brickskeller, to sample a broad array of the country's finest potables – some eight hundred different kinds. Elsewhere, the Texas brand Lone Star has its dedicated followers, Indiana's best beverages come from Three Floyds Brewing and Pete's Wicked Ales in Minnesota can be found throughout the US. Indeed, microbreweries and brewpubs can now be found in virtually every sizeable US city and college town. Almost all serve a wide range of good-value, hearty food to help soak up the drink. For more on craft beers, see Ⓦwww.craftbeer.com.

Wine

California and, to a lesser extent, Oregon, Washington, and a few other states, are famous for their **wines**. In California, it's the Napa and Sonoma valleys that boast the finest grapes, and beefy reds such as Merlot, Pinot Noir and Cabernet Sauvignon as well as crisp or buttery whites like Chardonnay and Sauvignon Blanc all do very well. Many tourists take "wine-tasting" jags in the California vineyards, where you can sip (or slurp) at sites ranging from down-home country farms with tractors and hayrides to upper-crust estates thick with modern art and yuppies in designer wear. Elsewhere, Oregon's Willamette Valley and other areas in the state are known for excellent vino, especially pinot noir, while Washington state has its prime vineyards in places like the Yakima Valley, Columbia River Gorge and Walla Walla area, among others. Beyond this, a broad variety of states from Arizona to Virginia have established wineries, typically of varying quality, though there are always a few standouts in each state that may merit a taste while you're on your journey. You'll find details of tours and tastings throughout the Guide.

Festivals

In addition to the public holidays listed on p.56 – on July 4, Independence Day, the entire country takes time out to picnic, drink, salute the flag, and watch or participate in fireworks displays, marches, beauty pageants, eating contests and more, to commemorate the signing of the Declaration of Independence in 1776 – there is a diverse multitude of engaging local events in the US: arts-and-crafts shows, county fairs, ethnic celebrations, music festivals, rodeos, sandcastle-building competitions, chili cookoffs and countless others.

Certain festivities, such as Mardi Gras in New Orleans, are well worth planning your vacation around – obviously other people will have the same idea, so visiting during these times requires an extra amount of advance effort. **Halloween** (Oct 31) is also immensely popular. No longer just the domain of masked kids running around the streets banging on doors and demanding "trick or treat", in some bigger cities Halloween has evolved into a massive celebration. In LA's West Hollywood, New York's Greenwich Village, New Orleans's French Quarter and San Francisco's Castro district, for example, the night is marked by colourful parades, mass cross-dressing, huge block parties and wee-hours partying. **Thanksgiving Day**, on the fourth Thursday in November, is more sedate. Relatives return to the nest to share a meal (traditionally, roast turkey and stuffing, cranberry sauce, and all manner of delicious pies) and give thanks for family and friends. Ostensibly, the holiday recalls the first harvest of the Pilgrims in Massachusetts, though Thanksgiving was a national holiday before anyone thought to make that connection.

Annual festivals and events

For further details of the festivals and events listed below, including more precise dates, see the relevant page of the Guide, or access their websites. The state tourist boards listed on p.60 can provide more complete calendars for each area.

January

Cowboy Poetry Gathering Elko, NV Ⓦwww.westernfolklife.org. See p.833.
Sundance Film Festival Park City, UT Ⓦfestival.sundance.org. See p.821.
Winter Carnival St Paul, MN Ⓦwww.winter-carnival.com. See p.320.

February

Daytona 500 Daytona Beach, FL Ⓦwww.daytona500.com. See p.520.

Mardi Gras New Orleans, LA (the six weeks before Lent) Ⓦwww.mardigrasneworleans.com. See p.570.
Groundhog Day Punxsutawney, PA Ⓦwww.groundhog.org.

March

South by Southwest Music Festival Austin, TX Ⓦsxsw.com. See p.605.
World Championship Crawfish Étouffée Cookoff Eunice, LA Ⓦwww.eunice-la.com. See p.576.
Ice Alaska Fairbanks, AK Ⓦwww.icealaska.com. See p.1025.
Academy Awards (the "Oscars") Los Angeles, CA Ⓦwww.oscars.org. See p.859.
St Joseph's Day and the Mardi Gras Indians' "Super Sunday" New Orleans, LA Ⓦwww.mardigrasindians.com. See p.571.

April

Gathering of Nations Pow Wow Albuquerque, NM Ⓦwww.gatheringofnations.com.
Coachella Music & Arts Festival Coachella, CA Ⓦwww.coachella.com.
Festival International de Louisiane Lafayette, LA Ⓦwww.festivalinternational.com. See p.576.
Arkansas Folk Festival Mountain View, AR Ⓦwww.ozarkgetaways.com/folk_festival.html. See p.489.
French Quarter Festival New Orleans, LA Ⓦwww.fqfi.org. See p.571.
Jazz and Heritage Festival (Jazz Fest) New Orleans, LA (into May) Ⓦwww.nojazzfest.com. See p.571.
Fiesta San Antonio San Antonio, TX Ⓦwww.fiesta-sa.org. See p.612.

May

Leaf Festival (also Oct) Black Mountain, NC Ⓦwww.theleaf.com. See p.417.
Crawfish Festival Breaux Bridge, LA Ⓦwww.bbcrawfest.com. See p.576.
Spoleto Festival Charleston, SC (into June) Ⓦwww.spoletousa.org.
Merrie Monoarch Hilo, HI Ⓦwww.merriemonarch.com.
Indianapolis 500 Indianapolis, IN Ⓦwww.indy500.com. See p.282.
Folk Festival Kerrville, TX (into June) Ⓦwww.kerrvillefolkfestival.com. See p.605.
Kentucky Derby Louisville, KY Ⓦwww.kentuckyderby.com. See p.447.
Memphis in May International Festival Memphis, TN Ⓦwww.memphisinmay.org. See p.459.
Tejano Conjunto Festival San Antonio, TX Ⓦwww.guadalupeculturalarts.org.

June

Little Bighorn Days Hardin, MT Ⓦwww.custerslaststand.org. See p.730.
CMA Music Festival Nashville, TN Ⓦwww.cmafest.com. See p.465.
Texas Folklife Festival San Antonio, TX Ⓦwww.texasfolklifefestival.org.
Bluegrass Festival Telluride, CO Ⓦwww.bluegrass.com. See p.709.

July

Cheyenne Frontier Days Cheyenne, WY Ⓦwww.cfdrodeo.com. See p.711.
National Basque Festival Elko, NV Ⓦwww.elkobasque.com. See p.833.
World Eskimo-Indian Olympics Fairbanks, AK Ⓦwww.weio.org. See p.1025.
Hopi Festival of Arts and Culture Flagstaff, AZ Ⓦwww.musnaz.org.
Essence Music Festival New Orleans, LA Ⓦwww.essencemusicfestival.com.
Newport Folk Festival Newport, RI Ⓦwww.newportfolkfest.net. See p.207.
Taste of Minnesota St Paul, MN. See p.320.
National Cherry Festival Traverse City, MI Ⓦvisit.cherryfestival.org. See p.275.

August

Mountain Dance and Folk Festival Asheville, NC Ⓦwww.folkheritage.org.
Burning Man Black Rock City, NV (into Sept) Ⓦwww.burningman.com. See p.833.
Iowa State Fair Des Moines, IA Ⓦwww.iowastatefair.com.
Augusta Festival of Appalachian Culture Elkins, WV Ⓦwww.augustaheritage.com.
Inter-Tribal Indian Ceremonial Gallup, NM Ⓦwww.theceremonial.com. See p.772.
Tribute Elvis Week (Anniversary of Elvis's death) Memphis, TN Ⓦwww.elvis.com. See p.459.
Satchmo SummerFest New Orleans, LA Ⓦwww.fqfi.org. See p.571.
Newport Jazz Festival Newport, RI Ⓦwww.newportjazzfest.net. See p.207.
Maine Lobster Festival Rockland, ME Ⓦwww.mainelobsterfestival.com. See p.236.
Indian Market Santa Fe, NM Ⓦwww.swaia.org. See p.759.

September

Moja Arts Festival Charleston, SC (into Oct) Ⓦwww.mojafestival.com
Bluegrass and Chili Festival Claremore, OK Ⓦwww.claremore.org.
Great American Beer Festival Denver, CO Ⓦwww.greatamericanbeerfestival.com.
Detroit International Jazz Festival Detroit, MI Ⓦwww.detroitjazzfest.com. See p.269.
Mississippi Delta Blues & Heritage Festival Greenville, MS Ⓦwww.deltablues.org. See p.479.
Panhandle South Plains Fair Lubbock, TX Ⓦwww.southplainsfair.com. See p.623.
Monterey Jazz Festival Monterey, CA Ⓦwww.montereyjazzfestival.org.
Southern Decadence New Orleans, LA Ⓦwww.southerndecadence.net. See p.571.
Festa di San Gennaro New York, NY Ⓦwww.sangennaro.org.
Southwest Louisiana Zydeco Festival Opelousas, LA Ⓦwww.zydeco.org. See p.576.
Pendleton Round-Up Pendleton, OR Ⓦpendletonroundup.com. See p.995.
Fiestas de Santa Fe Santa Fe, NM Ⓦwww.santafefiesta.org. See p.759.
Bumbershoot Seattle WS Ⓦbumbershoot.org. See p.960.

October

International Balloon Fiesta Albuquerque, NM Ⓦwww.balloonfiesta.com.
Buffalo Roundup Custer State Park, SD Ⓦwww.southdakota.com. See p.672.
Art & Pumpkin Festival Half Moon Bay, CA Ⓦwww.miramarevents.com/pumpkinfest/.
Arkansas Blues and Heritage Festival Helena, AR Arkansas Ⓦwww.bluesandheritagefest.com. See p.485.
Festivals Acadiens et Créoles Lafayette, LA Ⓦwww.festivalsacadiens.com. See p.576.
Voodoo Fest New Orleans, LA Ⓦthevoodooexperience.com. See p.571
Helldorado Days Tombstone, AZ Ⓦwww.helldoradodays.com. See p.781.
Puyallup Fair

November

Ozark Folk Festival Eureka Springs, AR Ⓦwww.ozarkfolkfestival.com. See p.490.

The outdoors

Coated by dense forests, cut by deep canyons and capped by great mountains, the US is blessed with fabulous backcountry and wilderness areas. Even the heavily populated East Coast has its share of open space, notably along the Appalachian Trail, which winds from Mount Katahdin in Maine to the southern Appalachians in Georgia – some two thousand miles of untrammelled woodland. To experience the full breathtaking sweep of America's wide-open stretches, however, head west: to the Rockies, the red-rock deserts of the Southwest or right across the continent to the amazing wild spaces of the West Coast. On the downside, be warned that in many coastal areas, the shoreline can be disappointingly hard to access, with a high proportion under private ownership.

National parks and monuments

The **National Park Service** administers both national parks and national monuments. Its rangers do a superb job of providing information and advice to visitors, maintaining trails and organizing such activities as free guided hikes and campfire talks.

In principle, a **national park** preserves an area of outstanding natural beauty, encompassing a wide range of terrain and prime examples of particular landforms and wildlife.

The Park Service website, Ⓦwww.nps.gov, details the main attractions of the national parks, plus opening hours, the best times to visit, admission fees, hiking trails and visitor facilities.

Thus Yellowstone has boiling geysers and herds of elk and bison, while Yosemite offers towering granite walls and cascading waterfalls. A **national monument** is usually much smaller, focusing perhaps on just one archeological site or geological phenomenon, such as Devil's Tower in Wyoming. Altogether, the national park system comprises around four hundred units, including national seashores, lakeshores, battlefields and other historic sites.

While national parks tend to be perfect places to **hike** – almost all have extensive trail networks – all are far too large to tour entirely on foot (Yellowstone, for example, is bigger than Delaware and Rhode Island combined). Even in those rare cases where you can use public transport to reach a park, you'll almost certainly need some sort of vehicle to explore it once you're there. The Alaska parks are mostly howling wilderness, with virtually no roads or facilities for tourists – you're on your own.

Most parks and monuments charge **admission fees**, ranging from $5 to $25, which cover a vehicle and all its occupants for up to a week. For anyone on a touring vacation, it may well make more sense to buy the **Inter-agency Annual Pass**, also known as the "America the Beautiful Pass". Sold for $80 at all federal parks and monuments, or online at Ⓦstore.usgs.gov/pass, this grants unrestricted access for a year to the bearer, and any accompanying passengers in the same vehicle, to all national parks and monuments, as well as sites managed by such agencies as the US Fish and Wildlife Service, the Forest Service and the BLM (see below). It does not, however, cover or reduce additional fees like charges for camping in official park campgrounds, or permits for backcountry hiking or rafting.

Two further passes, obtainable at any park but not online, grant **free access** for life to all national parks and monuments, again to the holder and any accompanying passengers, and also provide a fifty percent discount on camping fees. The **Senior Pass** is available to any US citizen or permanent resident aged 62 or older for a one-time fee of $10, while the **Access Pass** is issued free to blind or permanently disabled US citizens or permanent residents. While hotel-style **lodges** are found only in major parks, every park or monument tends to have at least one well-organized **campground**. Often, a cluster of motels can be found not far outside the park boundaries. With appropriate permits – subject to restrictions in popular parks – backpackers can also usually camp in the backcountry (a general term for areas inaccessible by road).

Other public lands

National parks and monuments are often surrounded by tracts of **national forest** – also federally administered but much less protected. These too usually hold appealing rural campgrounds but, in the words of the slogan, each is a "Land Of Many Uses", and usually allows logging and other land-based industry (thankfully, more often ski resorts than strip mines).

Other government departments administer wildlife refuges, national scenic rivers, recreation areas and the like. The **Bureau of Land Management** (BLM) has the largest holdings of all, most of it open rangeland, such as in Nevada and Utah, but also including some enticingly out-of-the-way reaches. Environmentalist groups engage in endless running battles with developers, ranchers and the extracting industries over uses – or alleged misuses – of federal lands.

While **state parks** and **state monuments**, administered by individual states, preserve sites of more limited, local significance, many are explicitly intended for recreational use, and thus hold better campgrounds than their federal equivalents.

Camping and backpacking

The ideal way to see the great outdoors – especially if you're on a low budget – is to tour by car and **camp** in state and federal campgrounds. Typical public campgrounds range in price from free (usually when there's no water available, which may be seasonal) to around $20 per night. Fees at the generally less scenic commercial campgrounds – abundant near major towns, and often resembling open-air hotels, complete with shops and restaurants – are more like $20–30. If you're camping in high season, either reserve in advance or avoid the most popular areas.

Backcountry camping in the national parks is usually free, by permit only. Before you set off on anything more than a half-day hike, and whenever you're headed for anywhere at all isolated, be sure to inform a ranger of your plans, and ask about weather conditions and specific local tips. Carry sufficient food and drink to cover emergencies, as well as all the necessary equipment and maps. Check whether fires are permitted; even if they are, try to use a camp stove in preference to local materials. In wilderness areas, try to camp on previously used sites. Where there are no toilets, bury human waste at least six inches into the ground and a hundred feet from the nearest water supply and campground.

Backpackers should never drink from rivers and streams; you never know what acts people – or animals – have performed further upstream. **Giardia** – a waterborne bacteria that causes an intestinal disease characterized by chronic diarrhoea, abdominal cramps, fatigue and weight loss – is a serious problem. Water that doesn't come from a tap should be boiled for at least five minutes, or cleansed with an iodine-based purifier or a giardia-rated filter.

Hiking at lower elevations should present few problems, though near water **mosquitoes** can drive you crazy; Avon Skin-so-Soft or anything containing DEET, are fairly reliable repellents. **Ticks** – tiny beetles that plunge their heads into your skin and swell up – are another hazard. They sometimes leave their heads inside, causing blood clots or infections, so get advice from a ranger if you've been bitten. One species of tick causes **Lyme Disease**, a serious condition that can even affect the brain. Nightly inspections of your skin are strongly recommended.

Beware, too, of **poison oak**, which grows throughout the west, usually among oak trees. Its leaves come in groups of three (the middle one on a short stem) and are distinguished by prominent veins and shiny surfaces. If you come into contact with it, wash your skin (with soap and cold water) and clothes as soon as possible – and don't scratch. In serious cases, hospital emergency rooms can give antihistamine or adrenaline shots. A comparable curse is **poison ivy**, found throughout the country. For both plants, remember the sage advice, "Leaves of three, let it be".

Mountain hikes

Take special care hiking at higher elevations, for instance in the 14,000ft peaks of the Rockies, or in California's Sierra Nevada (and certainly in Alaska). Late snows are common, and in spring avalanches are a real danger, while meltwaters make otherwise simple stream crossings hazardous. Weather conditions can also change abruptly. **Altitude sickness** can affect even the fittest of athletes: take it easy for your first few days above seven thousand feet. Drink lots of water, avoid alcohol, eat plenty of carbohydrates and protect yourself from the sun.

Desert hikes

If you intend to hike in the **desert**, carry plentiful extra food and water, and never go anywhere without a map. Cover most of your ground in early morning: the midday heat is too debilitating. If you get lost, find some shade and wait. So long as you've registered, the rangers will eventually come looking for you.

At any time of year, you'll stay cooler during the day if you wear full-length sleeves and trousers, while a wide-brimmed hat and good sunglasses will spare you the blinding headaches that can result from the desert light. You may also have to contend with **flash floods**, which can appear from nowhere. Never camp in a dry wash, and don't attempt to cross flooded areas until the water has receded.

It's essential to carry – and drink – large quantities of **water** in the desert. In particular, hiking in typical summer temperatures requires drinking a phenomenal amount. Loss of the desire to eat or drink is an

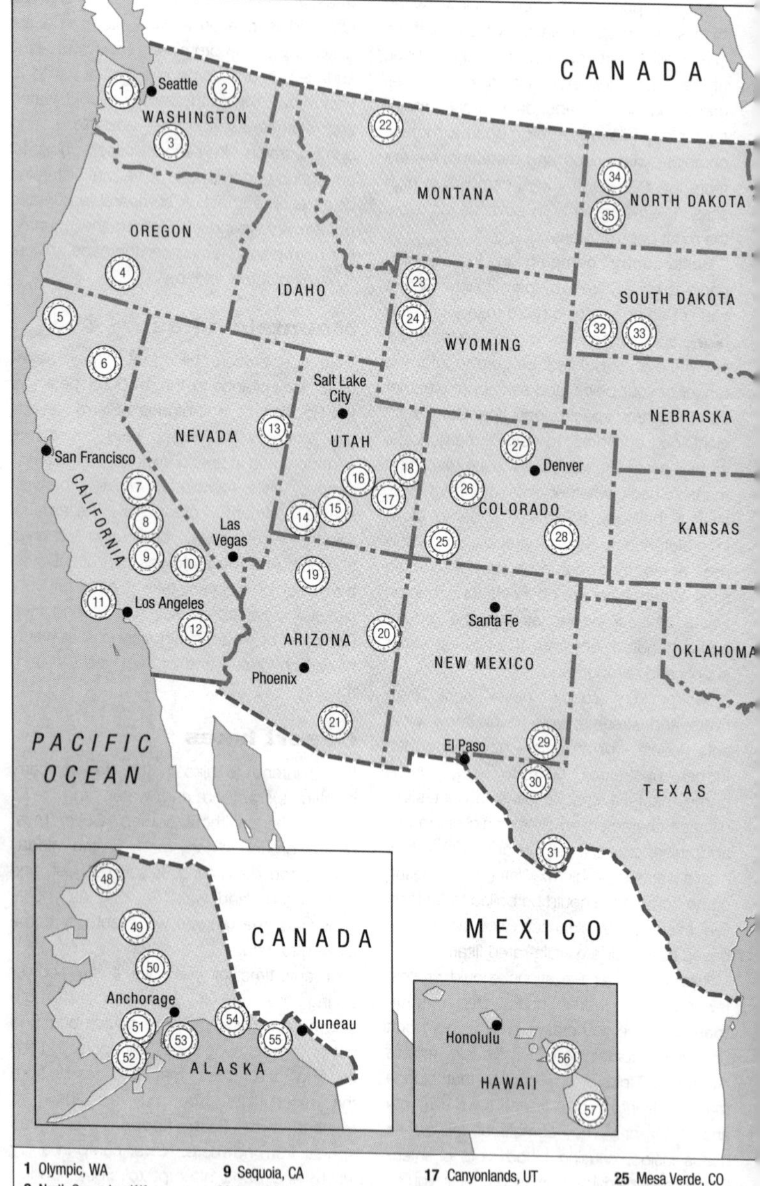

1 Olympic, WA
2 North Cascades, WA
3 Mount Rainier, WA
4 Crater Lake, OR
5 Redwood, CA
6 Lassen Volcanic, CA
7 Yosemite, CA
8 Kings Canyon, CA
9 Sequoia, CA
10 Death Valley, CA
11 Channel Islands, CA
12 Joshua Tree, CA
13 Great Basin, NV
14 Zion, UT
15 Bryce Canyon, UT
16 Capitol Reef, UT
17 Canyonlands, UT
18 Arches, UT
19 Grand Canyon, AZ
20 Petrified Forest, AZ
21 Saguaro, AZ
22 Glacier, MT
23 Yellowstone, WY
24 Grand Teton, WY
25 Mesa Verde, CO
26 Black Canyon of the Gunnison, CO
27 Rocky Mountain, CO
28 Great Sand Dunes, CO
29 Carlsbad Caverns, NM
30 Guadalupe Mtns, TX
31 Big Bend, TX
32 Wind Cave, SD

33 Badlands, SD
34 T. Roosevelt (north), ND
35 T. Roosevelt (south), ND
36 Voyageurs, MN
37 Isle Royale, MI
38 Hot Springs, AR
39 Mammoth Cave, KY
40 Cuyahoga Valley, OH
41 Great Smoky Mtns, TN
42 Congaree, SC
43 Shenandoah, VA
44 Acadia, ME
45 Everglades, FL
46 Biscayne, FL
47 Dry Tortugas, FL
48 Kobuk Valley, AK
49 Gates of the Arctic, AK
50 Denali, AK
51 Lake Clark, AK
52 Katmai, AK
53 Kenai Fjords, AK
54 Wrangell-St Elias, AK
55 Glacier Bay, AK
56 Haleakala, HI
57 Hawaii Volcanoes, HI

early symptom of heat exhaustion, so it's possible to become seriously dehydrated without feeling thirsty. Watch out for signs of dizziness or nausea; if you feel weak and stop sweating, it's time to get to the doctor. Check whether water is available on your trail; ask a ranger, and carry plenty with you even if it is.

When **driving** in the desert, carry ample water in the car, take along an emergency pack with flares, a first-aid kit and snakebite kit, matches and a compass. A shovel, tyre pump and extra gas are always a good idea. If the engine overheats, don't turn it off; instead, try to cool it quickly by turning the front end of the car towards the wind. Carefully pour some water on the front of the radiator, and turn the air conditioning off and the heat up full blast. In an emergency, never panic and leave the car: you'll be harder to find wandering around alone.

Adventure travel

The opportunities for **adventure travel** in the US are all but endless, whether your tastes run towards whitewater rafting down the Colorado River, mountain biking in the volcanic Cascades, canoeing down the headwaters of the Mississippi River, horseback riding in Big Bend on the Rio Grande in Texas or Big Wall rock climbing on the sheer granite monoliths of Yosemite Valley.

While an exhaustive listing of the possibilities could fill another volume, certain places have an especially high concentration of adventure opportunities, such as Moab, Utah (p.815) or New Hampshire's White Mountains (p.218). Throughout the book we recommend guides, outfitters and local adventure-tour operators.

Skiing

Downhill **ski** resorts can be found all over the US. The Eastern resorts of Vermont and New York State, however, pale by comparison with those of the Rockies, such as Vail and Aspen in Colorado, and the Sierra Nevada in California. Expect to pay $40–100 per day (depending on the quality and popularity of the resort) for lift tickets, plus another $25 or more per day to rent equipment.

A cheaper alternative is **cross-country skiing**, or ski touring. Backcountry ski lodges dot mountainous areas along both coasts and in the Rockies. They offer a range of rustic accommodation, equipment rental and lessons, from as little as $20 a day for skis, boots and poles, up to about $200 for an all-inclusive weekend tour.

Wildlife

Watch out for bears, deer, moose, mountain lions and rattlesnakes in the backcountry, and consider the effect your presence can have on their environment.

Other than in a national park, you're highly unlikely to encounter a **bear**. Even there, it's rare to stumble across one in the wilderness. If you do, don't run, just back away slowly. Most fundamentally, it will be after your food, which should be stored in airtight containers when camping. Ideally, hang both food and garbage from a high but slender branch some distance from your camp. Never attempt to feed bears, and never get between a mother and her young. Young animals are cute; their irate mothers are not.

Snakes and creepy-crawlies

Though the deserts in particular are home to a wide assortment of poisonous creatures, these are rarely aggressive towards humans. To avoid trouble, observe obvious precautions. Don't attempt to handle wildlife; keep your eyes open as you walk, and watch where you put your hands when scrambling over obstacles; shake out shoes, clothing and bedding before use; and back off if you do spot a creature, giving it room to escape.

If you are bitten or stung, current medical thinking rejects the concept of cutting yourself open and attempting to suck out the venom. Whether snake, scorpion or spider is responsible, apply a cold compress to the wound, constrict the area with a tourniquet to prevent the spread of venom, drink lots of water and bring your temperature down by resting in a shady area. Stay as calm as possible and seek medical help immediately.

Sports

As well as being good fun, catching a baseball game at Chicago's Wrigley Field on a summer afternoon or joining the screaming throngs at a Steelers football game in Pittsburgh can give visitors an unforgettable insight into a town and its people. Professional teams almost always put on the most spectacular shows, but big games between college rivals, minor league baseball games and even Friday night high-school football games provide an easy and enjoyable way to get on intimate terms with a place.

Specific details for the most important teams in all the sports are given in the various city accounts. They can also be found through the major league websites: Ⓦwww.mlb.com (baseball); www.nba.com (basketball); www.nfl.com (football); www.nhl.com (ice hockey); and www.mlsnet.com (soccer).

Baseball, because the major league teams play so many games (162 in total, usually at least five a week throughout the spring and summer), is probably the easiest sport to catch when travelling. The ballparks – such as Boston's historic Fenway Park, New York's famed Yankee Stadium, LA's glamorous Dodger Stadium or Baltimore's evocative Camden Yards – are great places to spend time. It's also among the cheapest sports to watch (from around $10 a seat for the bleachers), and tickets are usually easy to come by.

Pro football, the American variety, is quite the opposite. Tickets are exorbitantly expensive and almost impossible to obtain (if the team is any good), and most games are played in huge, fortress-like stadiums far out in the suburbs; you'll do better stopping in a bar to watch it on TV.

College football is a whole lot better and more exciting, with chanting crowds, cheerleaders and cheaper tickets, which can be hard to obtain in football-crazed college towns in parts of the South and Midwest. Although New Year's Day games such as the Rose Bowl or the Orange Bowl are all but impossible to see live, big games like USC vs UCLA, Michigan vs Ohio State or Notre Dame vs anybody are not to be missed if you're anywhere nearby.

Basketball also brings out intense emotions. The protracted pro playoffs run well into June. The men's month-long college playoff tournament, called "March Madness", is acclaimed by many as the nation's most exciting sports extravaganza, taking place at venues spread across the country in many small to mid-sized towns.

Ice hockey, usually referred to simply as hockey, was long the preserve of Canada and cities in the far north of the US, but now penetrates the rest of the country, with a concentration around the East Coast and Great Lakes. Tickets, particularly for successful teams, are hard to get and not cheap.

Soccer, meanwhile, remains much more popular as a participant sport, especially for kids, than a spectator one, and those Americans that are interested in it usually follow foreign matches like England's Premier League, rather than their home-grown talent. The good news for international travellers is that any decent-sized city will have one or two pubs where you can catch games from England, various European countries or Latin America; check out Ⓦwww.livesoccertv.com for a list of such establishments and match schedules.

Golf, once the province of moneyed businessmen, has attracted a wider following in recent decades due to the rise of celebrity golfers such as Tiger Woods and the construction of numerous municipal and public courses. You'll have your best access at these, where a round of golf may cost from $15 for a beaten-down set of links to $50 for a nicer, more upmarket offering. Private golf courses have varying standards for allowing non-members to play (check their websites) and steeper fees – over $100 a person for the more elite courses.

The other sporting events that attract national interest involve four legs or four wheels. The **Kentucky Derby**, held in Louisville on the first Saturday in May (see p.447), is the biggest date on the horseracing calendar. Also in May, the NASCAR **Indianapolis 500**, the world's largest motor-racing event, fills that city with visitors throughout the month, with practice sessions and carnival events building up to the big race.

Travel essentials

Costs

When it comes to **average costs** for travelling expenses, much depends on where you've chosen to go. A road-trip around the backroads of Texas and the Deep South won't cost you much in accommodation, dining, or souvenir-buying, but **gas prices** will add to the expense – these vary from state to state, but at the time of writing average less than $3 per gallon. By contrast, getting around a city such as Boston, New York or Chicago will be relatively cheap, but you'll pay much more for your hotel, meals, sightseeing and shopping. Most items you buy will be subject to some form of state – not federal – **sales tax**, anywhere from less than three percent (in Colorado) to more than eight percent (in California). In addition, varying from state to state, some counties and cities may add on another point or two to that rate. (Alaska, Delaware, Montana, New Hampshire and Oregon have no state sales tax, but goods may be liable to some other form of tax from county to county.)

Unless you're camping or staying in a hostel, **accommodation** will be your greatest expense while in the US. Adequate lodging is rarely available for under $60, outside of bare-bones roadside motels and off-season cabins. A halfway decent room will run anywhere from $75–100, with fancier hotels costing much, much more – upwards of $200–350 in many of the big cities. Note that some cities – probably the ones you most want to visit – tack on a **hotel tax** that can raise the total tax for accommodation to as much as fifteen percent.

Unlike accommodation, prices for good **food** don't automatically take a bite out of your wallet, and you can indulge anywhere from the lowliest (but still scrumptious) burger shack to the chicest restaurant helmed by a celebrity chef. You can get by on as little as $20 a day, but realistically you should aim for more like $40.

Where it exists, and where it is useful (which tends to be only in the larger cities), **public transport** is usually affordable, with many cities offering good-value travel passes. **Renting a car**, at around $200 per week, is a far more efficient way to explore the broader part of the country, and, for a group of two or more, it's no more expensive, either. Keep in mind, though, that supplements of $20 per day are liable to be tacked onto rental fees for drivers aged under 25. Drivers staying in larger hotels in the cities should factor in the increasing trend towards charging even for **self-parking**; this daily fee may well be just a few dollars less than that for valet parking.

For attractions in the Guide, prices are quoted for adults, with children's rates listed if they are more than a few dollars less; at some spots, kids get in for half-price, or for free if they're under 6.

Tipping

In the US, waiters earn most of their income from tips, and not leaving a fair amount is seen as an insult. Waiting staff expect tips of at least fifteen percent, and up to twenty percent for very good service. When sitting at a bar, you should leave at least a dollar per round for the barkeeper; more if the round is more than two drinks. Hotel porters and bellhops should receive at least $2 per piece of luggage, more if it has been lugged up several flights of stairs. About fifteen percent should be added to taxi fares; round up to the nearest 50¢ or dollar, as well.

Crime and personal safety

No one could pretend that America is crime-free, although away from the urban centres crime is often remarkably low. Even the lawless reputations of Miami, Detroit or Los Angeles are far in excess of the truth and most parts of these cities, by day at least, are safe; at night, however, some areas are completely off-limits. All the major tourist areas and the main nightlife zones in cities are invariably brightly lit and well policed. By planning carefully and taking good care of your possessions, you should, generally speaking, have few problems.

Car crime

Crimes committed against tourists driving rented cars aren't as common as they once were, but it still pays to be cautious. In major urban areas, any car you rent should have nothing on it – such as a particular licence plate – that makes it easy to spot as a rental car. When driving, under no circumstances should you stop in any unlit or seemingly deserted urban area – and especially not if someone is waving you down and suggesting that there is something wrong with your car. Similarly, if you are accidentally rammed by the driver behind you, do not stop immediately, but proceed on to the nearest well-lit, busy area and call ⓣ911 for assistance. Hide any valuables out of sight, preferably locked in the trunk or in the glove compartment.

Electricity

Electricity runs on 110V AC. All plugs are two-pronged and rather insubstantial. Some travel plug adapters don't fit American sockets.

Entry requirements

Citizens of more than 30 countries – including the UK, Ireland, Australia, New Zealand and most Western European countries – visiting the United States for a period of less than ninety days used to be permitted to enter under what was known as the **Visa Waiver Scheme**. Since 2009, those same people must now apply online for ESTA (Electronic System for Travel Authorization) approval before setting off. This is a straightforward process – simply go to the ESTA **website** (ⓦhttps://esta.cbp.dhs.gov/) fill in your info and wait a very short while (sometimes just minutes, but it's best to leave at least 72 hours before travelling to make sure) for them to provide you with an authorization number. You will not generally be asked to produce that number at your port of entry, but it is as well to keep a copy just in case, especially in times of high security alerts – you will be denied entry if you don't have one. This ESTA authorization is valid for up to two years (or until your passport expires, whichever comes first). When you arrive at your port of entry you will be asked to confirm that your trip has an end date, that you have an onward ticket and that you have adequate funds to cover your trip. The customs official may also ask you for your address while in the USA; the hotel you are staying at on your first night will suffice. Each traveller must also undergo the US-VISIT process at immigration, where both index fingers are digitally scanned and a digital headshot is also taken for file. All passports need to be **machine readable;** any issued after October 2006 must include a digital **chip** containing biometric data (most countries issue these automatically nowadays, but check).

Prospective visitors from parts of the world not mentioned above require a valid passport and a non-immigrant **visitor's visa** for a maximum ninety-day stay. How you'll obtain a visa depends on what country you're in and your status when you apply; check ⓦtravel.state.gov. Whatever your nationality, visas are not issued to convicted felons and anybody who owns up to being a communist, fascist or drug dealer. On arrival, the date stamped on your passport is the latest you're legally allowed to stay. The

Department of Homeland Security (DHS) has toughened its stance on anyone violating this rule, so even **overstaying** by a few days can result in a protracted interrogation from officials. Overstaying may also cause you to be turned away next time you try to enter the US. To get an **extension** before your time is up, apply at the nearest Department of Homeland Security office, whose address will be under the Federal Government Offices listings at the front of the phone book. INS officials will assume that you're working in the US illegally, and it's up to you to convince them otherwise by providing evidence of ample finances. If you can, bring along an upstanding American citizen to vouch for you. You'll also have to explain why you didn't plan for the extra time initially.

Foreign embassies in the US

Australia 1601 Massachusetts Ave NW, Washington DC 20036 ⓣ202/797-3000, ⓦwww.austemb.org
Canada 501 Pennsylvania Ave NW, Washington DC 20001 ⓣ202/682-1740, ⓦcanadianembassy.org
Ireland 2234 Massachusetts Ave NW, Washington DC 20008 ⓣ202/462-3939, ⓦwww.embassyofireland.org
New Zealand 37 Observatory Circle NW, Washington DC 20008 ⓣ202/328 4800, ⓦwww.nzembassy.com
South Africa 3051 Massachusetts Ave NW, Washington DC 20008 ⓣ202/232-4400, ⓦwww.saembassy.org
UK 3100 Massachusetts Ave NW, Washington DC 20008 ⓣ202/588-7800, ⓦukinusa.fco.gov.uk/en/

Gay and lesbian travellers

The gay scene in America is huge, albeit heavily concentrated in the major cities. San Francisco, where between a quarter and a third of the voting population is reckoned to be gay or lesbian, is arguably the world's premier gay city. New York runs a close second, and up and down both coasts gay men and women enjoy the kind of visibility and influence those in other places can only dream about. Gay public officials and police officers are no longer a novelty. Resources, facilities and organizations are endless.

Virtually every major city has a predominantly gay area and we've tried to give an overview of local resources, bars and clubs in each large urban area. In the rural heartland, however, life can look more like the Fifties – homosexuals are still oppressed and commonly reviled. Gay travellers need to watch their step to avoid hassles and possible aggression.

National publications are available from any good bookstore. Bob Damron in San Francisco (ⓣ415/255-0404 or 1-800/462-6654, ⓦwww.damron.com) produces the best and sells them at a discount online. These include the *Men's Travel Guide*, a pocket-sized yearbook listing hotels, bars, clubs and resources for gay men ($22.95); the *Women's Traveler*, which provides similar listings for lesbians ($18.95); the *Damron City Guide*, which details lodging and entertainment in major cities ($22.95); and *Damron Accommodations*, with 1000 accommodation listings for gays and lesbians worldwide ($23.95).

Gayellow Pages in New York (ⓣ212/674-0120, ⓦwww.gayellowpages.com) publishes a useful directory of businesses in the US and Canada ($25, CD-ROM edition $10), plus regional directories for New England, New York and the South. *The Advocate*, based in Los Angeles ($3; ⓦwww.advocate.com) is a bimonthly national gay news magazine, with features, general info and classified ads. Finally, the International Gay & Lesbian Travel Association in Fort Lauderdale, FL (ⓣ1-954/776-2626, ⓦwww.iglta.org), is a comprehensive, invaluable source for gay and lesbian travellers.

Health

If you have a serious accident while in the US, emergency medical services will get to you quickly and charge you later. For emergencies or ambulances, dial ⓣ911, the nationwide emergency number.

Should you need to see a doctor, consult the *Yellow Pages* telephone directory under "Clinics" or "Physicians and Surgeons". The basic consultation fee is $50–100, payable in advance. Tests, X-rays etc are much more. Medications aren't cheap either – keep all your receipts for later claims on your insurance policy.

Foreign visitors should bear in mind that many pills available over the counter at

Rough Guides travel insurance

Rough Guides has teamed up with WorldNomads.com to offer great **travel insurance** deals. Policies are available to residents of over 150 countries, with cover for a wide range of **adventure sports**, 24-hour emergency assistance, high levels of medical and evacuation cover and a stream of **travel safety information**. Roughguides.com users can take advantage of their policies online 24/7, from anywhere in the world – even if you're already travelling. And since plans often change when you're on the road, you can extend your policy and even claim online. Roughguides.com users who buy travel insurance with WorldNomads.com can also leave a positive footprint and donate to a community development project. For more information go to Ⓦ**www.roughguides.com/shop**.

home – most codeine-based painkillers, for example – require a prescription in the US. Local brand names can be confusing; ask for advice at the pharmacy in any drugstore.

In general, inoculations aren't required for entry to the US.

Medical resources for travellers

CDC Ⓦwww.cdc.gov/travel. Official US government travel health site.
International Society for Travel Medicine Ⓦwww.istm.org. Full listing of travel health clinics.

Insurance

In view of the high cost of medical care in the US, all travellers visiting from overseas should be sure to buy some form of travel insurance. American and Canadian citizens should check that they are already covered – some homeowners' or renters' policies are valid on vacation, and credit cards such as American Express often include some medical or other insurance, while most Canadians are covered for medical mishaps overseas by their provincial health plans. If you only need trip cancellation/interruption coverage (to supplement your existing plan), this is generally available at a cost of about six percent of the trip value.

Internet

With most American homes now online, **cybercafés**, where you can get plugged in for around $3–6 per hour on a terminal in the café, are not as common as they were, though many places have wi-fi for web access. Hotels may offer free or cheap **high-speed internet access**, many coffee-shops have wi-fi (though without computers) and nearly all **public libraries** provide free internet access, but often there's a wait and machine time is limited. A useful website – Ⓦwww.kropla.com – has information on how to plug in a laptop when abroad, as well as useful worldwide communications info.

Mail

Post offices are usually open Monday to Friday from 9am to 5pm, and Saturday from 9am to noon, and there are blue mailboxes on many street corners. At time of publication, first-class mail within the US costs 44¢ for a letter weighing up to 28 grams (an ounce), 75¢ for Canada and 98¢ for the rest of the world. Airmail between the US and Europe may take a week.

In the US, the last line of the address includes the city or town and an abbreviation denoting the state ("CA" for California; "TX" for Texas, for example). The last line also includes a five-digit number – the **zip code** – denoting the local post office. It is very important to include this, though the additional four digits that you will sometimes see appended are not essential. You can check zip codes on the US Postal Service website, at Ⓦwww.usps.com.

Rules on sending **parcels** are very rigid: packages must be in special containers bought from post offices and sealed according to their instructions, which are given at the start of the *Yellow Pages*. To send anything out of the country, you'll need a green customs declaration form, available from a post office.

Maps

The free **road maps** distributed by each state through its tourist offices and welcome centres are usually fine for general driving and route planning. In addition, Rough Guides makes rip-proof, waterproof maps for numerous **cities, states and regions** in the US, such as New York, California, New England and many more.

Rand McNally produces maps for each state, bound together in the *Rand McNally Road Atlas*, and you're apt to find even cheaper state and regional maps at practically any gas station along the major highways for around $3–7. Britain's best source for maps is Stanfords, at 12–14 Long Acre, London WC2E 9LP (ⓣ020/7836 1321, ⓦwww.stanfords.co.uk), which also has a mail-order service.

The American Automobile Association, or AAA ("Triple A"; ⓣ1-877/244-9790, ⓦwww.aaa.com) provides free maps and assistance to its members, as well as to British members of the AA and RAC. Call the main number to get the location of a branch near you; bring your membership card or at least a copy of your membership number.

If you're after really **detailed maps** that go far beyond the usual fold-out, try Thomas Guides ($20–40; ⓦwww.thomasguidebooks.com). Highly detailed **park, wilderness** and **topographical maps** are available through the Bureau of Land Management for the West (ⓦblm.gov) and for the entire country through the Forest Service (ⓦwww.fs.fed.us/maps). The best supplier of detailed, large-format map books for travel through the American outback is **Benchmark Maps** (ⓦwww.benchmarkmaps.com), whose elegantly designed depictions are easy to follow and make even the most remote dirt roads look appealing.

Money

The US dollar comes in $1, $5, $10, $20, $50 and $100 **denominations**. One dollar comprises one hundred cents, made up of combinations of one-cent pennies, five-cent nickels, ten-cent dimes and 25-cent quarters. You can check current exchange rates at ⓦwww.xe.com/ucc; at the time of writing one pound sterling will buy $1.45–1.50 and a euro $1.20–1.30.

Bank hours are generally from 9am to 5pm Monday to Thursday, and until 6pm on Friday; the big bank names are Wells Fargo, US Bank and Bank of America. With an **ATM card**, you'll be able to withdraw cash just about anywhere, though you'll be charged $2–4 per transaction for using a different bank's network. Foreign cash-dispensing cards linked to international networks, such as Plus or Cirrus, are also widely accepted – ask your home bank or credit card company which branches you can use. To find the location of the nearest ATM, call AmEx ⓣ1-800/227-4669; Cirrus ⓣ1-800/424-7787; Accel/The Exchange ⓣ1-800/519-8883; or Plus ⓣ1-800/843-7587.

Credit and **debit cards** are the most widely accepted form of payment at major hotels, restaurants and retailers, even though some smaller merchants still do

Opening hours and public holidays

Government offices (including post offices) and banks will be closed on the following national **public holidays**:

Jan 1 New Year's Day
Third Mon in Jan Martin Luther King Jr's Birthday
Third Mon in Feb Presidents' Day
Last Mon in May Memorial Day
July 4 Independence Day
First Mon in Sept Labor Day
Second Mon in Oct Columbus Day
Nov 11 Veterans' Day
Fourth Thurs in Nov Thanksgiving Day
December 25 Christmas Day

Calling home from the USA

For country codes not listed below, dial 0 for the operator, consult any phone directory or log onto ⓦwww.countrycallingcodes.com.

Australia 011 + 61 + area code minus its initial zero.

New Zealand 011 + 64 + area code minus its initial zero.

UK 011 + 44 + area code minus its initial zero.

Republic of Ireland 011 + 353 + area code minus its initial zero.

South Africa 011 + 27 + area code.

not accept them. You'll be asked to show some plastic when renting a car, bike or other such item, or to start a "tab" at hotels for incidental charges; in any case, you can always pay the bill in cash when you return the item or check out of your room.

US **travellers' cheques** are the safest way for overseas visitors to carry money, and the better-known cheques, such as those issued by American Express and Visa, are treated as cash in most shops.

Phones

The US currently has well over one hundred **area codes** – three-digit numbers that must precede the seven-figure number if you're calling from abroad (following the 001 international access code) or from a different area code, in which case you prefix the ten digits with a 1. It can get confusing, especially as certain cities have several different area codes within their boundaries; for clarity, in this book, we've included the local area codes in all telephone numbers. Note that some cities require you to dial all ten digits, even when calling within the same code. Numbers that start with the digits 1-800 – or, less commonly 1-888, 1-877 and 1-866 – are **toll-free**, but these can only be called from within the USA itself.

Unless you can organize to do all your calling online via Skype (ⓦwww.skype.com), the cheapest way to make **long-distance** and **international** calls is to buy a **prepaid phonecard**, commonly found in newsagents or grocery stores, especially in urban areas. These are cheaper than the similar cards issued by the big phone companies, such as AT&T, that are usually on sale in pharmacy outlets and chain stores, and will charge only a few cents per minute to call from the USA to most European and other western countries. Such cards can be used from any touchpad phone but there is usually a surcharge for using them from a payphone (which, in any case, are increasingly rare). You can also usually arrange with your local telecom provider to have a **chargecard** account with free phone access in the US, so that any calls you make are billed to your home. This may be convenient, but it's more expensive than using prepaid cards.

If you are planning to take your **mobile phone** (more often called cell phones in America) from outside of the USA, you'll need to check with your service provider whether it will work in the country: you will need a **tri-band** or **quad-band** phone that is enabled for international calls. Using your phone from home will probably incur hefty **roaming charges** for making calls and charge you extra for incoming calls, as the people calling you will be paying the usual rate. Depending on the length of your stay, it might make sense to rent a phone or buy compatible prepaid SIM cards from USA providers; check ⓦwww.triptel.com or www.planetomni.com. Alternatively, you could pick up an inexpensive pay-as-you-go phone from one of the major electrical shops.

Senior travellers

Anyone aged over 62 (with appropriate ID) can enjoy a vast range of discounts in the US. Both Amtrak and Greyhound offer (smallish) percentage reductions on fares to older passengers, and any US citizen or permanent resident aged 62 or over is entitled to free admission for life to all national parks, monuments and historic sites using a Senior Pass (issued for a one-time fee of $10 at any such site). This free admission applies to all accompanying travellers in the same vehicle and also gives a fifty percent reduction on park user fees, such as camping charges.

For discounts on accommodation, group tours and vehicle rental, US residents aged 50 or over should consider joining the AARP (American Association of Retired Persons; ⓣ1-888/687-2277; ⓦaarp.org) for an annual $16 fee; the website also offers lots of good travel tips and features. Road Scholar (previously known as Elderhostel; ⓣ1-800/454-5768, ⓦwww.roadscholar.org), runs an extensive network of educational and activity programmes for people over 60 throughout the US, at prices broadly in line with those of commercial tours.

Shopping

Not surprisingly, the US has some of the greatest **shopping** opportunities in the world – from the luxury-lined blocks of Fifth Avenue in New York, the Miracle Mile in Chicago and Rodeo Drive in Beverly Hills, to the local markets found in both big cities and small, offering everything from fruit and vegetables to handmade local crafts.

When buying clothing and accessories, international visitors will need to convert their sizes into American equivalents (see box). For almost all purchases, state taxes will be applied (see "Costs", p.52).

Time

The continental US covers four **time zones**, and there's one each for Alaska and Hawaii as well. The Eastern zone is five hours behind Greenwich Mean Time (GMT), so 3pm London time is 10am in New York (see below for the one-week exceptions). The Central zone, starting approximately on a line down from Chicago and spreading west to Texas and across the Great Plains, is an hour behind the east (10am in New York is 9am in Dallas). The Mountain zone, which covers the Rocky Mountains and most of the Southwest, is two hours behind the East Coast (10am in New York is 8am in Denver). The Pacific zone includes the three coastal states and Nevada, and is three hours behind New York (10am in the Big Apple is 7am in San Francisco). Lastly, most of Alaska

Clothing and shoe sizes

Women's clothing

American	4	6	8	10	12	14	16	18	
British	6	8	10	12	14	16	18	20	
Continental	34	36	38	40	42	44	46	48	

Women's shoes

American	5	6	7	8	9	10	11
British	3	4	5	6	7	8	9
Continental	36	37	38	39	40	41	42

Men's shirts

American	14	15	15.5	16	16.5	17	17.5	18
British	14	15	15.5	16	16.5	17	17.5	18
Continental	36	38	39	41	42	43	44	45

Men's shoes

American	7	7.5	8	8.5	9.5	10	10.5	11	11.5
British	6	7	7.5	8	9	9.5	10	11	12
Continental	39	40	41	42	43	44	44	45	46

Men's suits

American	34	36	38	40	42	44	46	48
British	34	36	38	40	42	44	46	48
Continental	44	46	48	50	52	54	56	58

(except for the St Lawrence Islands, which are with Hawaii) is nine hours behind GMT (10am in New York is 6am in Anchorage), while Hawaii is ten hours behind GMT (10am in New York is 5am in Honolulu). The US puts its clocks forward to daylight saving time on the first Sunday in April and turns them back on the first Sunday in November (a week later than the EU in both cases).

Tourist information

Each state has its own tourist office, as listed in the box on p.60. These offer prospective visitors a colossal range of free maps, leaflets and brochures on attractions from overlooked wonders to the usual tourist traps. You can either contact the offices before you set off, or, as you travel around the country, look for the state-run "welcome centres", usually along main highways close to the state borders. In heavily visited states, these often have piles of discount coupons for cut-price accommodation and food. In addition, visitor centres in most towns and cities–often known as the "Convention and Visitors Bureau", or CVB, and listed throughout this book – provide details on the area, as do local Chambers of Commerce in almost any town of any size.

Tourist offices and government sites

Australian Department of Foreign Affairs ⓦwww.dfat.gov.au, ⓦwww.smartraveller.gov.au
British Foreign & Commonwealth Office ⓦwww.fco.gov.uk
Canadian Department of Foreign Affairs ⓦwww.dfait-maeci.gc.ca
Irish Department of Foreign Affairs ⓦwww.foreignaffairs.gov.ie
New Zealand Ministry of Foreign Affairs ⓦwww.mft.govt.nz
US State Department ⓦtravel.state.gov

Travelling with children

Children under 2 years old go free on domestic flights and for ten percent of the adult fare on international flights – though that doesn't mean they get a seat, let alone frequent-flier miles. Kids aged between 2 and 12 are usually entitled to half-price tickets. Discounts for train and bus travel are broadly similar. Car-rental companies usually provide kids' car seats – which are required by law for children under the age of 4 – for around $10 a day. You would, however, be advised to check, or bring your own; they are not always available. Recreational vehicles (RVs) are a particularly good option for families Even the cheapest motel will offer inexpensive two-bed rooms as a matter of course, which is a relief for non-US travellers used to paying a premium for a "family room", or having to pay for two rooms.

Virtually all tourist attractions offer reduced rates for kids. Most large cities have natural history museums or aquariums, and quite a few also have hands-on children's museums; in addition most state and national parks organize children's activities. All the national restaurant chains provide highchairs and special kids' menus; and the trend for more upmarket family-friendly restaurants to provide crayons with which to draw on paper tablecloths is still going strong.

For a database of kids' attractions, shops and activities all over the US, check the useful site ⓦgocitykids.parentsconnect.com.

Travellers with disabilities

By international standards, the US is exceptionally accommodating for travellers with mobility concerns or other physical disabilities. By law, all public buildings, including hotels and restaurants, must be wheelchair accessible and provide suitable toilet facilities. Most street corners have dropped curbs (less so in rural areas), and most public transport systems include subway stations with elevators and buses that "kneel" to let passengers in wheelchairs board.

Getting around

The Americans with Disabilities Act (1990) obliges all air carriers to make the majority of their services accessible to travellers with disabilities, and airlines will usually let attendants of more seriously disabled people accompany them at no extra charge.

Almost every Amtrak train includes one or more coaches with accommodation for handicapped passengers. Guide dogs travel free and may accompany blind, deaf

State tourism information

Alabama ⓣ1-800/252-2262, ⓦwww.alabama.travel
Alaska ⓣ1-800/862-5275, ⓦwww.travelalaska.com
Arizona ⓣ1-866/275-5816, ⓦwww.arizonaguide.com
Arkansas ⓣ1-800/628-8725, ⓦwww.arkansas.com
California ⓣ1-800/TO-CALIF, ⓦwww.visitcalifornia.com
Colorado ⓣ1-800/COLORADO, ⓦwww.colorado.com
Connecticut ⓣ1-888/288-4748, ⓦwww.ctvisit.com
Delaware ⓣ1-866/284-7483, ⓦwww.visitdelaware.com
Florida ⓣ1-888/735-2872, ⓦwww.visitflorida.com
Georgia ⓣ1-800/847-4842, ⓦwww.exploregeorgia.org
Hawaii ⓣ1-800/GO-HAWAII, ⓦwww.gohawaii.com
Idaho ⓣ1-800/VISIT-ID, ⓦwww.visitidaho.org
Illinois ⓣ1-800/226-6632, ⓦwww.enjoyillinois.com
Indiana ⓣ1-888/365-6946, ⓦwww.visitindiana.com
Iowa ⓣ1-800/345-IOWA, ⓦwww.traveliowa.com
Kansas ⓣ1-800/252-6727, ⓦwww.travelks.com
Kentucky ⓣ1-800/225-8747, ⓦwww.kentuckytourism.com
Louisiana ⓣ1-800/99-GUMBO, ⓦwww.louisianatravel.com
Maine ⓣ1-888/624-6345, ⓦwww.visitmaine.com
Maryland ⓣ1-800/634-7386, ⓦwww.visitmaryland.org
Massachusetts ⓣ1-800/227-6277, ⓦwww.massvacation.com
Michigan ⓣ1-888/784-7328, ⓦwww.michigan.org
Minnesota ⓣ1-800/657-3700, ⓦwww.exploreminnesota.com
Mississippi ⓣ1-866/733-6477, ⓦwww.visitmississippi.org
Missouri ⓣ1-800/519-2100, ⓦwww.visitmo.com
Montana ⓣ1-800/847-4868, ⓦwww.visitmt.com
Nebraska ⓣ1-800/228-4307, ⓦwww.visitnebraska.gov
Nevada ⓣ1-800/237-0774, ⓦwww.travelnevada.com
New Hampshire ⓣ1-800/386-4664, ⓦwww.visitnh.gov
New Jersey ⓣ1-800/847-4865, ⓦwww.visitnj.org
New Mexico ⓣ1-800/545-2070, ⓦwww.newmexico.org
New York ⓣ1-800/I-LOVE-NY, ⓦwww.iloveny.com
North Carolina ⓣ1-800/847-4862, ⓦwww.visitnc.com
North Dakota ⓣ1-800/435-5663, ⓦwww.ndtourism.com
Ohio ⓣ1-800/BUCKEYE, ⓦwww.discoverohio.com
Oklahoma ⓣ1-800/652-6552, ⓦwww.travelok.com
Oregon ⓣ1-800/547-7842, ⓦwww.traveloregon.com
Pennsylvania ⓣ1-800/847-4872, ⓦwww.visitpa.com
Rhode Island ⓣ1-800/556-2484, ⓦwww.visitrhodeisland.com
South Carolina ⓣ1-888/727-6453, ⓦwww.discoversouthcarolina.com
South Dakota ⓣ1-800/732-5682, ⓦwww.travelsd.com
Tennessee ⓣ1-800/462-8366, ⓦwww.tnvacation.com
Texas ⓣ1-800/888-8839, ⓦwww.traveltex.com
Utah ⓣ1-800/882-4386, ⓦwww.utah.com
Vermont ⓣ1-800/VERMONT, ⓦwww.vermontvacation.com
Virginia ⓣ1-800/847-4882, ⓦwww.virginia.org
Washington ⓣ1-800/544-1800, ⓦwww.experiencewa.com
Washington DC ⓣ1-800/422-8644, ⓦwww.washington.org
West Virginia ⓣ1-800/225-5982, ⓦwww.wvtourism.com
Wisconsin ⓣ1-800/432-8747, ⓦwww.travelwisconsin.com
Wyoming ⓣ1-800/225-5996, ⓦwww.wyomingtourism.org

or disabled passengers. Be sure to give 24 hours' notice. Hearing-impaired passengers can get information on ⓣ1-800/523-6590 (TTY/TDD).

Greyhound, however, has its challenges. Buses are not equipped with lifts for wheelchairs, though staff will assist with boarding (intercity carriers are required by law to do this), and the "Helping Hand" policy offers two-for-the-price-of-one tickets to passengers unable to travel alone (carry a doctor's certificate). The American Public Transportation Association, in Washington DC (ⓣ202/496-4800, ⓦwww.apta.com), provides information about the accessibility of public transportation in cities.

The American Automobile Association (contact ⓦwww.aaa.com for phone number access for each state) produces the *Handicapped Driver's Mobility Guide*, while the larger car-rental companies provide cars with hand controls at no extra charge, though only on their full-sized (ie most expensive) models; reserve well in advance.

Resources

Most state tourism offices provide information for disabled travellers (see opposite). In addition, SATH, the Society for Accessible Travel and Hospitality, in New York (ⓣ212/447-7284, ⓦwww.sath.org), is a not-for-profit travel-industry group of travel agents, tour operators, hotel and airline management, and people with disabilities. They pass on any inquiry to the appropriate member, though you should allow plenty of time for a response. Mobility International USA, in Eugene, OR (ⓣ541/343-1284, ⓦwww.miusa.org), offers travel tips and operates exchange programmes for disabled people. They also serve as a national information centre on disability.

The "America the Beautiful Access Pass", issued without charge to permanently disabled or blind US citizens, gives free lifetime admission to all national parks. It can only be obtained in person at a federal area where an entrance fee is charged; you'll have to show proof of permanent disability, or that you are eligible for receiving benefits under federal law.

Women travellers

A woman travelling alone in America is not usually made to feel conspicuous, or liable to attract unwelcome attention. Cities can feel a lot safer than you might expect from recurrent media images of demented urban jungles, though, particular care must be taken at night: walking through unlit, empty streets is never a good idea, and, if there's no bus service, take a taxi.

In the major urban centres, if you stick to the better parts of town, going into bars and clubs alone should pose few problems: there's generally a pretty healthy attitude toward women who do so, and your privacy will be respected.

However, small towns may lack the same liberal or indifferent attitude toward lone women travellers. People seem to jump immediately to the conclusion that your car has broken down, or that you've suffered some strange misfortune. If your vehicle does break down on heavily travelled roads, wait in the car for a police or highway patrol car to arrive. You should also rent a mobile phone with your car, for a small charge.

Women – as well as men – should never hitchhike in the US. Similarly, you should never pick up anyone who's trying to hitchhike. If someone is waving you down on the road, ostensibly to get help with a broken-down vehicle, just drive on by or call the highway patrol to help them.

Avoid travelling at night by public transport – deserted bus stations, if not actually threatening, will do little to make you feel secure. Where possible, team up with a fellow traveller. On Greyhound buses, sit near the driver.

Should disaster strike, all major towns have some kind of rape counselling service; if not, the local sheriff's office will arrange for you to get help and counselling, and, if necessary, get you home. The National Organization for Women (ⓣ202/628-8669, ⓦwww.now.org) has branches listed in local phone directories and on its website, and can provide information on rape crisis centres, counselling services and feminist bookstores.

Resources and specialists

Gutsy Women Travel Glenside PA ⓣ1-866/464-8879, ⓦwww.gutsywomentravel.com. International agency that provides practical support and organizes trips for lone female travellers.

Womanship Annapolis MD ⓣ1-800/342-9295, ⓦwww.womanship.com. Live-aboard, learn-to-sail cruises for women of all ages. Destinations may include Chesapeake Bay, Florida, the Pacific Northwest and Mystic, Connecticut.

The Women's Travel Club Bloomfield NJ ⓣ1-800/480-4448, ⓦwww.womenstravelclub.com. Arranges vacations, itineraries, room-sharing and various activities for women.

Working in the USA

Permission to work in the USA can only be granted by the Immigration and Naturalization Service in the USA itself. Contact your local embassy or consulate for advice on current regulations, but be warned that unless you have relatives or a prospective employer in the USA to sponsor you, your chances are at best slim. Students have the best chance of prolonging their stay, while a number of **volunteer** and **work programmes** allow you to experience the country less like a tourist and more like a resident.

Study, volunteer and work programmes

American Field Service Intercultural Programs ⓦwww.afs.org, www.afs.org.au, www.afsnzl.org.nz, www.afs.org/southafrica. Global UN-recognized organization running summer student exchange programmes to foster international understanding.

American Institute for Foreign Study ⓦwww.aifs.com. Language study and cultural immersion, as well as au pair and Camp America programmes.

BTCV (British Trust for Conservation Volunteers) ⓦwww.btcv.org.uk. One of the largest environmental charities in Britain, with a programme of unusual working holidays (as a paying volunteer) – you're looking at £300 for two months wilderness camping while restoring the deserts in Nevada, for example.

BUNAC (British Universities North America Club) ⓦwww.bunac.com. Working holidays in the US for international students.

Camp America Camp America ⓦwww.campamerica.co.uk. Well-known company that places young people as counsellors or support staff in US summer camps, for a minimum of nine weeks.

Council on International Educational Exchange (CIEE) ⓦwww.ciee.org. Leading NGO offering study programmes and volunteer projects around the world.

Earthwatch Institute ⓦwww.earthwatch.org. Long-established international charity with environmental and archeological research projects worldwide.

Guide

Guide

1

New York City

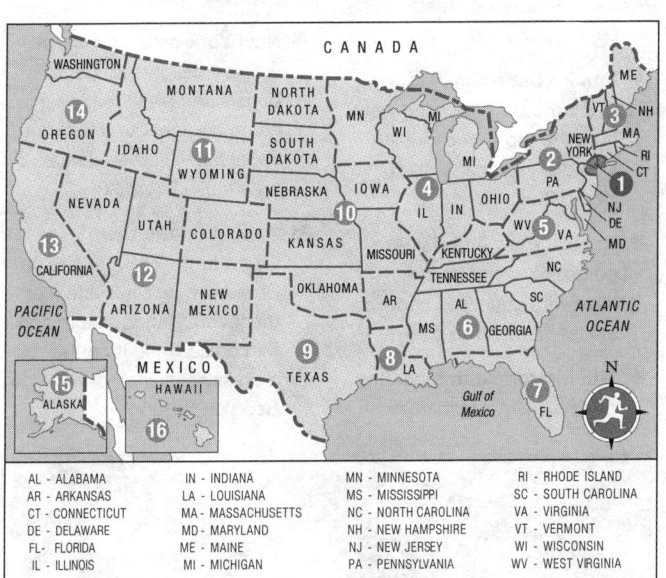

CHAPTER 1

Highlights

* **Ellis Island** Once the first stop for millions of prospective immigrants from all over the world, and now the site of a moving museum. See p.74

* **The High Line** The most innovative walkway around, on a disused railroad line above Chelsea and the Meatpacking District. See p.86

* **Empire State Building** Enjoy the mind-blowing views from the top of the most iconic skyscraper in the city. See p.86

* **Central Park** A massive, gorgeous, green space, filled with countless bucolic amusements. See p.89

* **The Metropolitan Museum of Art** The museum's mammoth collection could keep you busy for days. See p.90

* **Coney Island** Stroll the boardwalk, scream on the Cyclone and savour the most famous hot dogs in America at this beachside amusement park. See p.96

* **New York delis** The city's culinary delights range from bagels and pizza to global haute cuisine, but *Katz's* and *Zabar's* delis are essential New York. See p.98

* **A night on the town** Opera at the Met, theatre on Broadway, jazz in Harlem or the West Village...you're spoilt for choice when it comes to a dressy evening out. See p.103–106

▲ *Zabar's* deli

1

New York City

The cultural and financial capital of the US, if not the world, **New York City** is an adrenaline-charged, history-laden place that holds immense romantic appeal for visitors. Its past is visible in the tangled lanes of Wall Street and tenements of the Lower East Side; meanwhile, towering skyscrapers like the Empire State Building serve as monuments of the modern age. Street life buzzes round the clock and shifts markedly from one area to the next. The waterfront, sometimes salty, sometimes refined, and the landscaped green spaces – notably Central Park – give the city a chance to catch its breath. Iconic symbols of world culture from the neon of Times Square to the sculptures and murals at Rockefeller Center always seem just a stone's throw away. For raw energy, dynamism and social diversity, you'd be hard-pressed to top it; simply put, there's no place quite like it.

New York City comprises the central island of **Manhattan** and the four outer boroughs – **Brooklyn**, **Queens**, the **Bronx** and **Staten Island**. Manhattan, to many, *is* New York; certainly, this is where you're likely to stay and spend most of your time. The island is broadly divided into three areas: **Downtown** (below 14th St), **Midtown** (14th St to Central Park/59th St) and **Uptown** (north of 59th St). Though you could spend weeks here and still barely scratch the surface, there are some key attractions and pleasures that you won't want to miss. These include the different **ethnic neighbourhoods**, like Chinatown, and the more artsy concentrations of Soho and the East and West villages. Of course, there is the celebrated **architecture** of Midtown and the Financial District, as well as many fabulous **museums** – not just the Metropolitan and MoMA, but smaller collections like the Frick and the Morgan Library that afford days of happy wandering. In between sights, you can **eat** just about anything, at any time, cooked in any style; you can **drink** in any kind of company; and enjoy any number of obscure **movies**. The more established arts – **dance**, **theatre** and **music** – are superbly presented. For the avid consumer, the choice of **shops** is vast, almost numbingly exhaustive, in this heartland of the great capitalist dream.

Manhattan is a hard act to follow, and while the four, largely residential **outer boroughs**, inevitably pale in comparison, they do have many virtues. There's the ragged glory of Coney Island, the trim brownstones of Brooklyn Heights and the hip nightlife of Williamsburg, all in **Brooklyn**; the innovative museums of **Long Island City** and **Astoria**, both in Queens; and the renowned **Bronx Zoo** and adjacent botanical gardens in the Bronx. Last but not least, a free trip on the **Staten Island Ferry** is a sea-sprayed, refreshing good time, though there's no reason to do anything on the other side other than turn around and come right back.

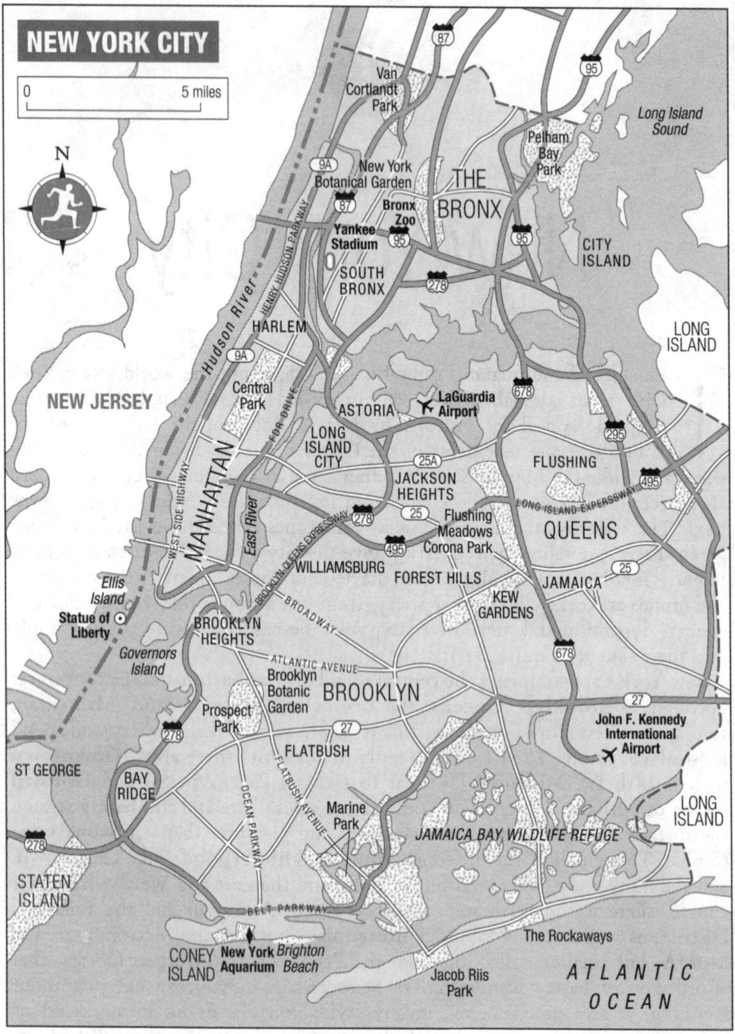

Some history

The first European to see Manhattan Island, then inhabited by the Lenape, was the Italian navigator Giovanni da Verrazano, in 1524. Dutch colonists established the settlement of **New Amsterdam** exactly one hundred years later. The first governor, Peter Minuit, was the man who famously bought the island for a handful of trinkets. Though we don't know for sure who "sold" it (probably a northern branch of the Lenni Lenape), the other side of the story was that the concept of owning land was utterly alien to Native Americans – they had merely agreed to support Dutch claims to use the land. By the time the British laid claim to the area in 1664, the heavy-handed rule of governor **Peter Stuyvesant** had so alienated its inhabitants that the Dutch relinquished control without a fight.

Renamed **New York**, the city prospered and grew, its population reaching 33,000 by the time of the American Revolution. The opening of the **Erie Canal** in 1825 facilitated trade farther inland, spurring the city to become the economic powerhouse of the nation, the base later in the century of **tycoons** such as Cornelius Vanderbilt and **financiers** like J.P. Morgan. The **Statue of Liberty** arrived from France in 1886, a symbol of the city's role as the gateway for generations of immigrants, and the early twentieth century saw the sudden proliferation of Manhattan's extraordinary **skyscrapers**, which cast New York as the city of the future in the eyes of an astonished world.

Almost a century later, the events of **September 11, 2001**, which destroyed the World Trade Center, shook New York to its core. Yet the Financial District bounced back with a comprehensive redevelopment plan to ensure that a new array of glitzy skyscrapers – some completed, some in mid-construction right now – will keep the Downtown skyline as prominent as ever.

Arrival, information and city transport

New York City is served by three major **airports**: **John F. Kennedy**, or **JFK**, in Queens, **LaGuardia**, also in Queens, and **Newark**, in New Jersey.

From JFK, the New York Airport Service (Ⓣ212/875-8200, Ⓦwww.nyairportservice.com) runs **buses** to Grand Central Terminal, Port Authority Bus Terminal and Penn Station (every 15–20min 6.05am–11.10pm; 45–60min; $15 one-way, $27 return). The **AirTrain** (24hr daily; $5; Ⓦwww.panynj.gov/airports/jfk-airtrain.html) runs between JFK and the Jamaica and Howard Beach **subway** stations in Queens; at Jamaica you can connect to the subway lines E, J or Z, and at Howard Beach, to the A subway line, into Manhattan (from both stations: 1hr; $2.25). Alternatively, the Long Island Railroad runs **trains** from the Jamaica station to Penn Station (20min; $5.75 off-peak, $8 peak).

From LaGuardia, New York Airport Service **buses** take 45 minutes to get to Grand Central and Port Authority Bus Terminal (every 15–30min 7.30am–11pm; $12 one-way, $21 return). Alternatively, for $2.25, you can take the #M60 bus to 106th Street in Manhattan, where you can transfer to Downtown-bound subway lines.

From Newark, Newark Airport Express (Ⓣ877/863-9275, Ⓦwww.coachusa.com) runs **buses** to Grand Central Station, Port Authority Bus Terminal and Penn Station (every 20–30min 4.45am–12.45am; $15 one-way, $25 return). You can also use the **AirTrain** service, which runs for free between all Newark terminals, car parks and the Newark Airport Train Station, where you can connect with NJ Transit or Amtrak **trains** into New York Penn Station. It usually takes about twenty minutes, and costs $15 one-way (every 20–30min 6am–midnight).

Taxis are pricey from the airports; reckon on paying $25 to $30 from LaGuardia to Manhattan, a flat rate of $45 from JFK, and $50 to $60 from Newark; you'll also be responsible for the turnpike and tunnel tolls – an extra $5 or so – as well as a fifteen- to twenty-percent tip for the driver. You should only use official yellow taxis that wait at designated ranks – just follow the signs out of the terminal.

Greyhound buses pull in at the Port Authority Bus Terminal, 42nd Street and Eighth Avenue. Amtrak **trains** come in to Penn Station, at Seventh Avenue and 33rd Street. From either Port Authority or Penn Station, various subway lines will take you where you want to go.

Arriving by car, you have multiple options: Rte-495 transects Midtown Manhattan from New Jersey through the Lincoln Tunnel ($6) and from the east through the Queens–Midtown Tunnel ($5.50). From the southwest, I-95 (the New Jersey Turnpike) and I-78 serve Canal and Spring streets (near Soho) via the Holland

City streets and orientation

The first part of Manhattan to be settled was what is now Downtown; this is why the streets here have names (as opposed to numbers) and are somewhat randomly arranged. Often you will hear of places referred to as being either on the **West Side** or the **East Side**; this refers to whether the place lies west or east of **Fifth Avenue**, which begins at the arch in Washington Square Park and runs north to cut along the east side of Central Park. On the East Side above Houston Street (pronounced "Howstun"), and on the West Side above 14th, the streets follow a **grid pattern**, progressing northward one by one. When looking for a specific **address**, keep in mind that on streets, house numbers increase as you walk away from Fifth in either direction; on avenues, house numbers increase as you move north.

Tunnel ($8). From the north, I-87 (New York State Thruway) and I-95 serve Manhattan's loop roads. Be prepared for **delays** at tunnels and bridges. As for **parking**, you might get lucky with street parking depending on where you stay; otherwise, Ⓦnyc.bestparking.com gives garage maps and price comparisons. It won't be cheap.

Information

The best place for information is **NYC & Company**, 810 Seventh Ave at 53rd Street (Mon–Fri 8.30am–6pm, Sat & Sun 9am–5pm; Ⓣ212/484-1222, Ⓦwww.nycgo.com). It has leaflets on what's going on in the arts, bus and subway maps, and information on accommodation – though they can't actually book anything for you.

City transport

Few cities equal New York for sheer street-level stimulation, and **walking** is the most exciting way to explore. However, it's also exhausting, so at some point you'll need to use some form of **public transport**. Citywide subway and bus system **maps** – the subway map is especially invaluable – are available from all subway station booths, tourist information centres (see above), the concourse office at Grand Central or online at Ⓦwww.mta.info.

The subway

The fastest way to get from point A to point B in Manhattan and the boroughs is the **subway** (Ⓦwww.mta.info), open 24 hours a day. A number or letter identifies each train and route; every trip, whether on the **express** lines, which stop only at major stations, or the **locals**, which stop at all stations, costs $2.25. All riders must use a **MetroCard**, available at station booths or credit/debit/ATM card-capable vending machines. MetroCards can be purchased in any amount from a $2.25 single ride to $89; a $20 purchase provides $23 worth of rides. Unlimited rides are available with a 24-hour "Fun Pass" ($8.25), a seven-day pass ($27) and a thirty-day pass ($89).

Buses

New York's **bus system** (again, Ⓦwww.mta.info) is clean, efficient and fairly frequent. The big advantage is that you can see where you're going and hop off more or less when you want; on the downside, it can be extremely slow – in peak hours almost down to walking pace – though it can be your best bet for travelling crosstown. Buses leave their route terminal points at five- to ten-minute intervals, and stop every two or three blocks. The $2.25 fare is payable on entry with a MetroCard (the same one used for the subway) or in cash, but with exact change only; you can **transfer** for free (continuing in the same direction) within two hours of swiping your MetroCard.

Taxis

Taxis are relatively good value for short journeys (fares start at $2.50), convenient and can be caught just about anywhere; there's a maximum of four passengers per cab. You should only use official yellow taxis.

Guided tours

Countless businesses and individuals compete to help you make sense of the city, offering all manner of **guided tours**. One of the more original – and least expensive – ways to get oriented is with Big Apple Greeter, 1 Centre St, suite 2035 (free; ⓣ212/669-8159, ⓦwww.bigapplegreeter.org). This not-for-profit group matches you with a local volunteer and points you to places that interest you.

Gray Line, the biggest operator of guided **bus tours** in the city, have an office at the Port Authority Bus Terminal (ⓣ1-800/669-0051, ⓦwww.newyorksightseeing.com). Double-decker bus tours offer an unlimited hop-on, hop-off service, taking in the main sights of Manhattan, for around $45. If you're not happy with your tour guide (quality can vary), you can hop off the bus and wait another fifteen minutes for the next bus.

A good way to see the city skyline is with the **Circle Line Ferry** (ⓣ212/563-3200, ⓦwww.circleline42.com), which sails from Pier 83 at West 42nd Street and Twelfth Avenue, circumnavigating Manhattan with live commentary; the three-hour tour runs year-round ($34). Alternatively, the **Staten Island Ferry** (p.77) provides a beautiful panorama of the Downtown skyline for free.

For a bird's-eye view, Liberty Helicopter Tours, at the west end of 30th Street (ⓣ212/967-6464, ⓦwww.libertyhelicopters.com), offers **helicopter flights** from around $135 (6–8min) to $230 (16–20min) per person.

Accommodation

Prices for **accommodation** in New York are well above the norm for the US as a whole. Most hotels charge more than $200 a night (although exceptions for under $100 a night do exist), and for anything better than four stars you'll be lucky to pay less than $400. Most of New York's **hotels** are in Midtown Manhattan, though more and more chic spots are being built downtown. **Booking ahead** is strongly advised; at certain times of the year – May, June, September, October and the lead up to Christmas and New Year, for example – everything is likely to be full. The **price codes** given at the end of each review reflect the cost of the cheapest double room during the high season.

Hostels offer savings, and run the gamut in terms of quality, safety and amenities. It pays to do research ahead of time to ensure satisfaction upon arrival. Average hostel rates range from $30 to $60.

Walking tours

Big Onion Walking Tours ⓣ212/439-1090, ⓦwww.bigonion.com. The Onion guides peel off the many layers of the city's history (all guides hold advanced degrees in American history). Tours are $15, though the eating tour costs $20.

Harlem Heritage Tours ⓣ212/280-7888, ⓦwww.harlemheritage.com. Cultural walking tours of Harlem, general and specific (such as Harlem jazz clubs). Reservations are recommended and can be booked online (average $25–40).

Wall Street Experience ⓦwww.thewallstreetexperience.com. Illuminating tours of the Financial District (2hr; Mon, Wed & Fri; $30–45) from Wall Street insiders.

Hotels

414 414 W 46th St, between Ninth and Tenth aves ⓣ1-866/414-HOTEL or 212/399-0006, ⓦwww.414hotel.com. Subway C, E to 50th St. Popular with Europeans but welcoming to all, this guesthouse, which has larger-than-ordinary rooms across two townhouses, makes a nice camp a bit removed from Times Square's bustle. The garden is a wonderful place to enjoy your morning coffee. ❽

Ace 20 W 29th St at Broadway ⓣ212/679-2222, ⓦwww.acehotel.com. Subway N, Q, R to 28th St. Capturing the spirit of old New York yet fully modern, the *Ace Hotel* sets a new standard for bohemian chic. A whole host of different room styles are on offer (including bunks), with retro-style fridges, guitars, muted tones and artwork that can make it feel more expensive than it is. ❾ ($300)

Algonquin 59 W 44th St, between Fifth and Sixth aves ⓣ1/888-304-2047 or 212/840-6800, ⓦwww.algonquinhotel.com. Subway B, D, F, M to 42nd St. New York's classic literary hangout has retained its old-club atmosphere: the decor remains little changed since its Round Table heyday, though the bedrooms have been refurbished to good effect, and the lobby restored. ❾ ($549)

Amsterdam Inn 340 Amsterdam Ave, at 76th St ⓣ212/579-7500, ⓦwww.nyinns.com. Subway #1 to 79th St; B, C to 81st St. Within easy walking distance of Central Park, Lincoln Center and the American Museum of Natural History. Rooms are basic but clean, and the staff are friendly and helpful. ❻

Blue Moon 100 Orchard St, between Delancey and Broome sts ⓣ212/533-9080, ⓦwww.bluemoon-nyc.com. Subway F to Delancey St; J, Z to Essex St. Lower East Side tenement transformed into a luxurious boutique, with rooms named after 1930s and 1940s celebrities and decked out with period iron-frame beds and the odd antique – rooms on the 6th, 7th and 8th floors have fabulous views across the city. ❽

The Chelsea Hotel 222 W 23rd St, between Seventh and Eighth aves ⓣ212/243-3700, ⓦwww.hotelchelsea.com. Subway #1, C, E to 23rd St. One of New York's most noted landmarks, this ageing neo-Gothic building boasts a notorious past (see p.86). Most of the spacious rooms have been renovated but still come with wood floors, log-burning fireplaces and space for a few extra friends. ❼

Chelsea Lodge 318 W 20th St, between Eighth and Ninth aves ⓣ1-800/373-1116 or 212/243-4499, ⓦwww.chelsealodge.com. Subway C, E to 23rd St. A converted boarding house with Early American/Sportsman decor, down a nice block. Normal rooms, which offer in-room showers and sinks (there's a shared toilet down the hall), are a little snug for two, but the few deluxe rooms are great value. ❺

Cosmopolitan 95 W Broadway, at Chambers St ⓣ1-888/895-9400 or 212/566-1900, ⓦwww.cosmohotel.com. Subway #1, #2, #3, A, C to Chambers St. A great Tribeca location, smart, well-maintained rooms and incredibly low prices make the *Cosmopolitan* a steal. ❼

Distrikt 342 W 40th St, between Eighth and Ninth aves ⓣ1-888/444-5610 or 212/706-6100, ⓦwww.distrikthotel.com. Subway A, C, E to 42nd St/Port Authority. With a city neighbourhood theme, the welcoming *Distrikt* has nice-sized rooms done in classy muted browns and beiges; choose one of the upper floors ("Harlem") for the best views. The street, however, is on the unsalubrious side. ❽

Dylan 52 E 41st St, between Park and Madison aves ⓣ212/338-0500 or 1-866/55-DYLAN, ⓦwww.dylanhotel.com. Subway #4, #5, #6, #7 to Grand Central-42nd St. Classy and clever, *Dylan's* rooms have been attentively designed, and the high ceilings make them look quite large. If you can afford it, book the Alchemy Suite, a one-of-a-kind Gothic bedchamber with a vaulted ceiling and unusual stained-glass windows. ❾ ($459)

Edison 228 W 47th St, between Broadway and Eighth Ave ⓣ212/840-5000, ⓦwww.edisonhotelnyc.com. Subway #1, C, E, to 50th St; N, Q, R to 49th St. The most striking thing about the funky 1000-room *Edison*, a good-value establishment for Midtown, is its beautiful Art Deco lobby. ❽

Grace 125 W 45th St, between Sixth and Seventh aves ⓣ212/354-2323, ⓦwww.room-matehotels.com. Subway B, D, F, M to 42nd St. You won't find many hotels like this, with a lobby that more closely resembles a concession stand; a tiny glassed-in pool overlooked by a louche loungey bar; different, funky retro wallpaper on each floor; and ultra modern (and pet-friendly) rooms, with platform beds. ❾ ($399)

Gramercy Park 2 Lexington Ave, at E 21st St ⓣ212/475-4320, ⓦwww.gramercyparkhotel.com. Subway #6 to 23rd St. In a lovely location, this once-bohemian hotel was given a once-over by Ian Schrager, with the help of Julian Schnabel. The entrance is both grand and strange, the rooms bold and luxurious. Guests get a key to the adjacent private park (see p.83). ❾ ($495)

Larchmont 27 W 11th St, between Fifth and Sixth aves ⓣ212/989-9333, ⓦwww.larchmonthotel.com. Subway F, L, M to 14th St. This budget hotel, with a terrific location on a tree-lined street in Greenwich Village, has small but nice, clean rooms – it's a bargain, but the bathrooms are shared. ❺

Mansfield 12 W 44th St, between Fifth and Sixth aves ⓣ1-800/255-5167 or

Bed and breakfasts, guesthouses and apartments

If you're looking for something a bit more personalized, consider a **B&B**, **homestay**, **apartment swap** or **rental**. Agencies for B&Bs include UK-based Colby International (Ⓣ0151/292-2910, Ⓕ292-2911, Ⓦwww.colbyinternational.com) and the local CitySonnet (Ⓣ212/614-3034, Ⓦwww.citysonnet.com) and City Lights (Ⓣ212/737-7049, Ⓦwww.citylightsbandb.com). VRBO (Ⓦvrbo.com) is a nationwide site with vacation rental apartments listed by owners; Ⓦnewyork.craigslist.org also lists vacation rentals and short-term stays.

212/277-8700, Ⓦwww.mansfieldhotel.com. Subway B, D, F, M to 42nd St. One of the nicest little hotels in the city, the *Mansfield* manages to be both grand and intimate. A clubby library lounge and live jazz during the week lends an affable air. Complimentary European breakfast and all-day cappuccino. ❾ ($399)

Milburn 242 W 76th St, between Broadway and West End aves Ⓣ1-800/833-9622 or 212/362-1006, Ⓦwww.milburnhotel.com. Subway #1 to 79th St. This welcoming and well-situated hotel is great for families. ❽

Pod 230 E 51st St, between Second and Third aves Ⓣ212/355-0300, Ⓦwww.thepodhotel.com. Subway #6 to 51st St. This stylish budget hotel is one of the best deals in Midtown, with cramped but extremely hip doubles, singles and bunks set against the glass-enclosed private bathrooms. You get free wi-fi, LCD TVs, and yes, iPod docking stations. ❽

Roger Smith 501 Lexington Ave, at E 47th St Ⓣ212/755-1400, Ⓦwww.rogersmith.com. Subway #6 to 51st St. Lots of personality: individually decorated rooms, a great restaurant, helpful service and artwork on display in public spaces. Breakfast is included. ❾ ($349)

Seventeen 225 E 17th St, between Second and Third aves Ⓣ212/475-2845, Ⓦwww.hotel17ny.com. Subway #4, #5, #6, L, N, Q, R to 14th St-Union Square. *Seventeen*'s rooms have basic amenities and many share baths, but it's clean, friendly and nicely situated on a pleasant tree-lined street minutes from Union Square and the East Village. ❻

Smyth Tribeca 85 West Broadway, between Warren and Chambers sts Ⓣ212/587-7000, Ⓦwww.thompsonhotels.com. Subway A, C, #1, #2, #3 to Chambers St. One of the newest boutiques in this part of town, with plush, contemporary design, furnishings with Classical and Art Deco touches and high-tech gadgets. ❾ ($445)

Wales 1295 Madison Ave, between 92nd and 93rd sts Ⓣ212/876-6000, Ⓦwww.waleshotel.com. Subway #6 to 96th St. Just steps from NYC's "Museum Mile" (see p.89), rooms are attractive with antique details, thoughtful in-room amenities and some views of Central Park. ❾ ($345)

Washington Square 103 Waverly Place, at Washington Square Park Ⓣ212/777-9515, Ⓦwww.washingtonsquarehotel.com. Subway A, B, C, D, E, F, M to W 4th St. Located in the heart of Greenwich Village, a stone's throw from the NYU campus. Don't be deceived by the posh-looking lobby – the rooms are surprisingly simple for the price (the "Deluxe" rooms have a bit more character). ❽

Hostels

Big Apple Hostel 119 W 45th St, between Sixth and Seventh aves Ⓣ212/302-2603, Ⓦwww.bigapplehostel.com. Subway B, D, F, M, N, Q, R, #1, #2, #3 to 42nd St. An unbeatable Times Square location. There's a secure luggage room and even an outdoor deck with BBQ. All rooms have a/c and shared baths. Dorms $45, private double rooms ❺–❻, including tax.

Gershwin 7 E 27th St, between Fifth and Madison aves Ⓣ212/545-8000, Ⓦwww.gershwinhotel.com. Subway N, R to 28th St. This hostel and hotel geared towards young travellers offers pop art decor and dormitories with two, six, or ten beds/room (from $40 a night) and private rooms (❻). Reservations recommended for both room types.

Jazz on the Park 36 W 106th St, at Central Park West Ⓣ212/932-1600, Ⓦwww.jazzhostels.com. Subway B, C to 103rd St. This groovy bunkhouse boasts a TV and games room, a café and lots of activities, including live jazz on weekends. Rooms sleep up to fourteen people, are clean and bright with a/c, and start around $30/night; private doubles (❺). Reserve at least one week in advance.

Whitehouse Hotel of New York 340 Bowery Ⓣ212/477-5623, Ⓦwww.whitehousehotelofny.com. Subway #6 to Bleecker, F to second Ave. The only hostel that offers single and double rooms at dorm rates; a/c, ATMs, cable TV and linens are bonuses. Private singles ❶, private doubles ❷.

Downtown Manhattan

The patchwork of neighbourhoods below 14th Street, **DOWNTOWN MANHATTAN**, runs the gamut from high finance and cutting-edge cool to Old World charm; it's one of the most vibrant, exciting parts of the city. Downtown's interest actually begins in New York Harbor, which holds the compulsory attractions of the **Statue of Liberty** and **Ellis Island**. The southernmost neighbourhood on the mainland is the **Financial District**, with Wall Street at its centre; less than half a mile north, the buildings of the **Civic Center** transition into the jangling streetlife of **Chinatown**, which has encroached upon touristy **Little Italy**. East of Chinatown and Little Italy, the **Lower East Side** marks the traditional point of entry into the city for many different immigrant groups. These days, it's a trendy spot full of chic bars and restaurants.

West of Chinatown and Little Italy, respectively, the one-time industrial area of **Soho** is now an expensive residential and shopping district. The smallish area known as **Nolita** takes in numerous boutiques and hip restaurants in its few well-manicured blocks. North of Houston Street, the activity picks up even more in the **West Village** (also known as Greenwich Village) and **East Village**, two former bohemian enclaves that remain great fun despite ongoing gentrification, the former for its charming backstreets and brownstones, the latter for its energetic nightlife.

The Statue of Liberty and Ellis Island

Standing tall and proud in the middle of New York Harbor, the **Statue of Liberty** (Ⓦwww.nps.gov/stli) has for more than a century served as a symbol of the American Dream. Depicting Liberty throwing off her shackles and holding a beacon to light the world, the monument was the creation of the French sculptor Frédéric Auguste Bartholdi, in recognition of fraternity between the French and American people. The statue, designed by Gustave Eiffel, of Eiffel Tower fame, was built in Paris between 1874 and 1884 and formally dedicated by President Grover Cleveland on October 28, 1886. Three (free) tour options of the statue are available (reserved with ferry ticket); the basic ticket grants entrance to the museum at the base and the pedestal observation deck (168 steps up). It's 354 steps up to the crown; you'll need to book a special ticket for that ($3 for crown entrance, but book well ahead; see contact details for Statue Cruises ferry below). Just across the water, **Ellis Island** was the first stop for more than twelve million prospective immigrants. It became an immigration station in 1892, mainly to handle the massive influx from southern and eastern Europe, and remained open until 1954, when it was left to fall into an atmospheric ruin. In the turreted central building, the **Ellis Island Immigration Museum** (daily 9.30am–5.15pm; free; Ⓣ212/363-3200, Ⓦwww.nps.gov/elis) eloquently recaptures the spirit of the place with artefacts, photographs, maps and personal accounts that tell the story of the immigrants who passed through. The huge, vaulted **Registry Room** on the second floor, scene of so much trepidation, elation and despair, has been left imposingly bare, with just a couple of inspectors' desks and American flags.

To get to Liberty and Ellis islands (no admission fees for either), you'll need to take a **Statue Cruises ferry** from the pier in Battery Park (daily every 30–45min, 8.30am–2.30pm departure, last boat back at 6pm; $12 return, tickets from Castle Clinton, in the park; Ⓣ877/523-9849, Ⓦwww.statuecruises.com); the ferry goes first to Liberty Island, and then continues on to Ellis. It's best to leave as early in the day as possible and to **reserve tickets** in advance, both to avoid long lines and to ensure you get to see both islands; if you take the last ferry of the day, you won't be able to visit Ellis Island. Both islands require at least two hours.

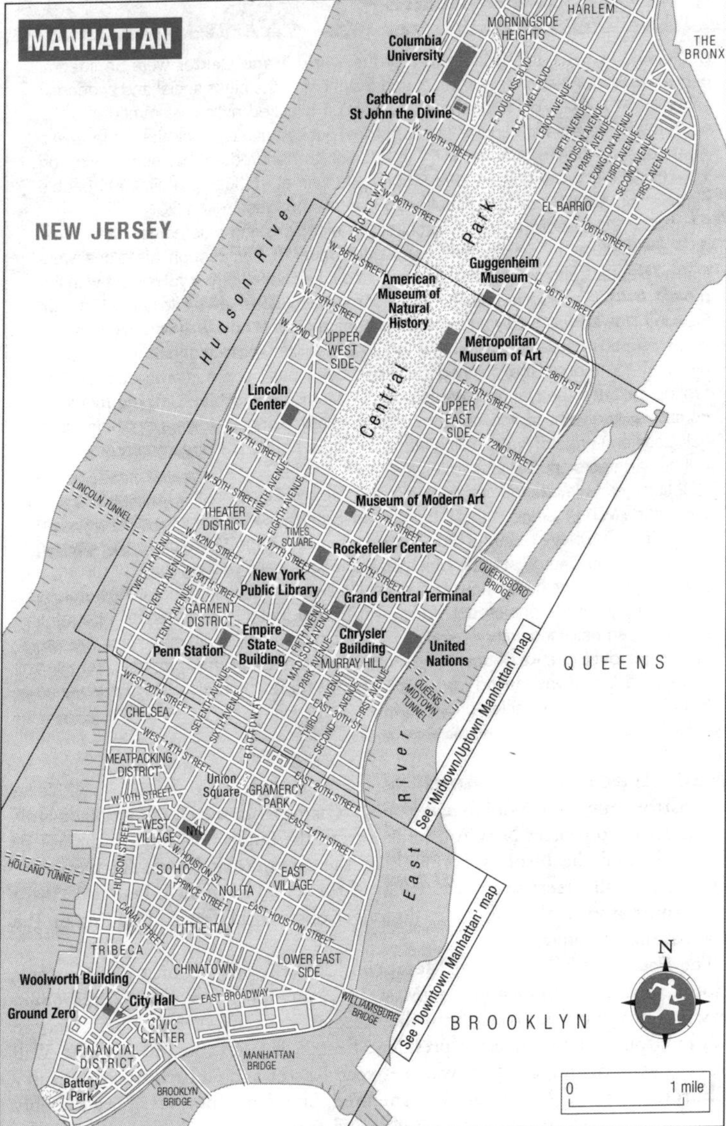

The Financial District

The **Financial District** is synonymous with the Manhattan of popular imagination, its tall buildings and powerful skyline symbols of economic strength. Though the city had an active securities market by 1790, the **Stock Exchange** wasn't officially organized until 1817, when 28 stockbrokers adopted their own constitution. It's been one of the world's great financial centres ever since.

September 11 and its aftermath

Completed in 1973, the Twin Towers of the **World Trade Center** were an integral part of New York's legendary skyline, and a symbol of the city's social and economic success. At 8.46am on September 11, 2001, a hijacked airliner slammed into the north tower; seventeen minutes later another hijacked plane struck the south tower. As thousands looked on in horror – in addition to hundreds of millions viewing on TV – the south tower collapsed at 9.50am, its twin at 10.30am. In all, 2995 people perished at the WTC and the simultaneous attack on Washington DC.

In 2003, Polish-born American architect Daniel Libeskind was named the winner of a competition to design the new World Trade Center, though his plans were initially plagued with controversy and he's had little subsequent involvement with the project. In 2006 a modified design, still incorporating Libeskind's original 1776ft-high Freedom Tower, was finally accepted and construction is now well underway, supervised by architect David Childs. The whole $12-billion scheme should be complete by 2014–15 (though the planned date has been put back numerous times). The project includes the National September 11 Memorial and Museum; the memorial comprises two voids representing the footprints of the original towers, surrounded by oak trees and rings of water falling into illuminated pools. The underground museum will use artefacts and exhibits to tell the story of 9/11.

Until it's completed, you can peek into the Ground Zero construction site and visit the Tribute WTC Visitor Center (Mon & Wed–Sat 10am–6pm, Tues noon–6pm, Sun noon–5pm; $10; ⓣ212/393-9160, ⓦwww.tributewtc.org), 120 Liberty St between Greenwich and Church streets, which also arranges daily walking tours of the site's perimeter ($10). The centre houses five small galleries that commemorate the attacks of 9/11, beginning with a model of the Twin Towers and a moving section about the day itself, embellished with video and taped accounts of real-life survivors. You can also check out St Paul's Chapel (Mon–Sat 10am–6pm, Sun 7am–3pm; free), at Fulton Street and Broadway, dating from 1766; the main attraction inside is "Unwavering Spirit", a poignant exhibition on 9/11.

Wall Street and around

The narrow canyon of **Wall Street** gained its name from the Dutch stockade built in the 1650s to protect New Amsterdam from the English colonies to the north. Today, behind the Neoclassical mask of the **New York Stock Exchange**, at Broad and Wall streets, the purse strings of the world are pulled. Due to security concerns, however, the public can no longer observe the frenzied trading on the floor of the exchange.

The **Federal Hall National Memorial**, 26 Wall St, was once the Customs House, but the exhibits inside (Mon–Fri 9am–5pm; free; ⓣ212/825-6888, ⓦwww.nps.gov/feha) relate to the headier days of 1789, when George Washington was sworn in as president from a balcony on this site. At Wall Street's western end, on Broadway, between Rector and Church streets, **Trinity Church** (Mon–Fri 7am–6pm, Sat 8am–4pm, Sun 7am–4pm; free), is a knobbly neo-Gothic structure erected in 1846, and was the city's tallest building for fifty years. The place has the air of an English church, especially in its sheltered graveyard, which is the resting place of early luminaries including the first Secretary of the Treasury Alexander Hamilton, who was killed in a duel by then-Vice President Aaron Burr.

Broadway comes to a gentle end at **Bowling Green Park**, an oval of turf used for the game by eighteenth-century colonial Brits, in the shadow of Cass Gilbert's 1907 **US Custom House**. The Custom House contains the superb **National Museum of the American Indian** (daily 10am–5pm, Thurs till 8pm; free;

Ⓣ212/514-3700, Ⓦwww.nmai.si.edu), a fascinating assembly of artefacts from almost every tribe native to the Americas, including large wood and stone carvings from the Pacific Northwest and elegant featherwork from Amazonia.

Battery Park and around

Across State Street from the Custom House, Downtown Manhattan lets out its breath in **Battery Park**, where the nineteenth-century Castle Clinton (daily 8.30am–5pm) once protected the southern tip of Manhattan and now sells ferry tickets to the Statue of Liberty and Ellis Island (see p.74). The spruced-up park stretches for blocks up the west side and is dotted with piers and some inventive landscaping.

Further toward the tip of the island, in the adjacent Robert F. Wagner Park and just a few feet from the Hudson River, the **Museum of Jewish Heritage**, 36 Battery Place (Sun–Tues & Thurs 10am–5.45pm, Wed 10am–8pm, Fri 10am–5pm; closed Jewish holidays; $12 or $17 with audio guide; Ⓣ646/437-4200, Ⓦwww.mjhnyc.org) is essentially a memorial of the Holocaust, and has three floors of exhibits on twentieth-century Jewish history. The moving and informative collection features objects from everyday Eastern European Jewish life, prison garb that survivors wore in Nazi concentration camps, photographs, personal belongings and multimedia presentations.

South Street Seaport and the Brooklyn Bridge

North up Water Street from Battery Park stands the partly reconstructed **Fraunces Tavern**, at Pearl and Broad streets (Tues–Sat noon–6pm; $10; Ⓣ212/425-1778, Ⓦwww.fraucestavernmuseum.org). Here, on December 4, 1783, with the British conclusively beaten, a weeping George Washington took leave of his assembled officers, intent on returning to rural life in Virginia. Today there's a quirky museum of Revolutionary artefacts upstairs, including a lock of Washington's hair, preserved like a holy relic. The restaurant/bar downstairs was closed but looking to reopen at the time of writing.

Further up Water Street, at the eastern end of Fulton Street, is the renovated **South Street Seaport Historic District**, formerly New York's bustling sail-ship port and now crammed with pubs, restaurants and well-known chain stores. Wander out to Pier 17, home to a touristy shopping mall and an assembly of restored nineteenth-century boats, for grand views across the East River.

From just about anywhere in the seaport you can see the much-loved **Brooklyn Bridge**, which was the world's largest suspension bridge when it opened in 1883. The beauty of the bridge itself and the spectacular views of Manhattan it offers make a walk across its wooden planks an essential part of any New York trip; you'll find the pedestrian walkway at the top of Park Row, opposite City Hall.

Staten Island Ferry

The **Staten Island ferry** (Ⓣ718/727-2508, Ⓦwww.siferry.com) sails from a modern terminal on the east side of Battery Park, built directly above the South Ferry subway station. Departures are frequent, from every 15–20 minutes during weekday rush hours (7–9am and 5–7pm), to every 60 minutes late at night (the ferry runs 24hr). The 25-minute ride is New York's best bargain: it's absolutely free, offering wide-angle views of the city and the **Statue of Liberty** that become more spectacular as you retreat. Most visitors get the next boat straight back to Manhattan, as there's not much to detain you on **Staten Island** itself.

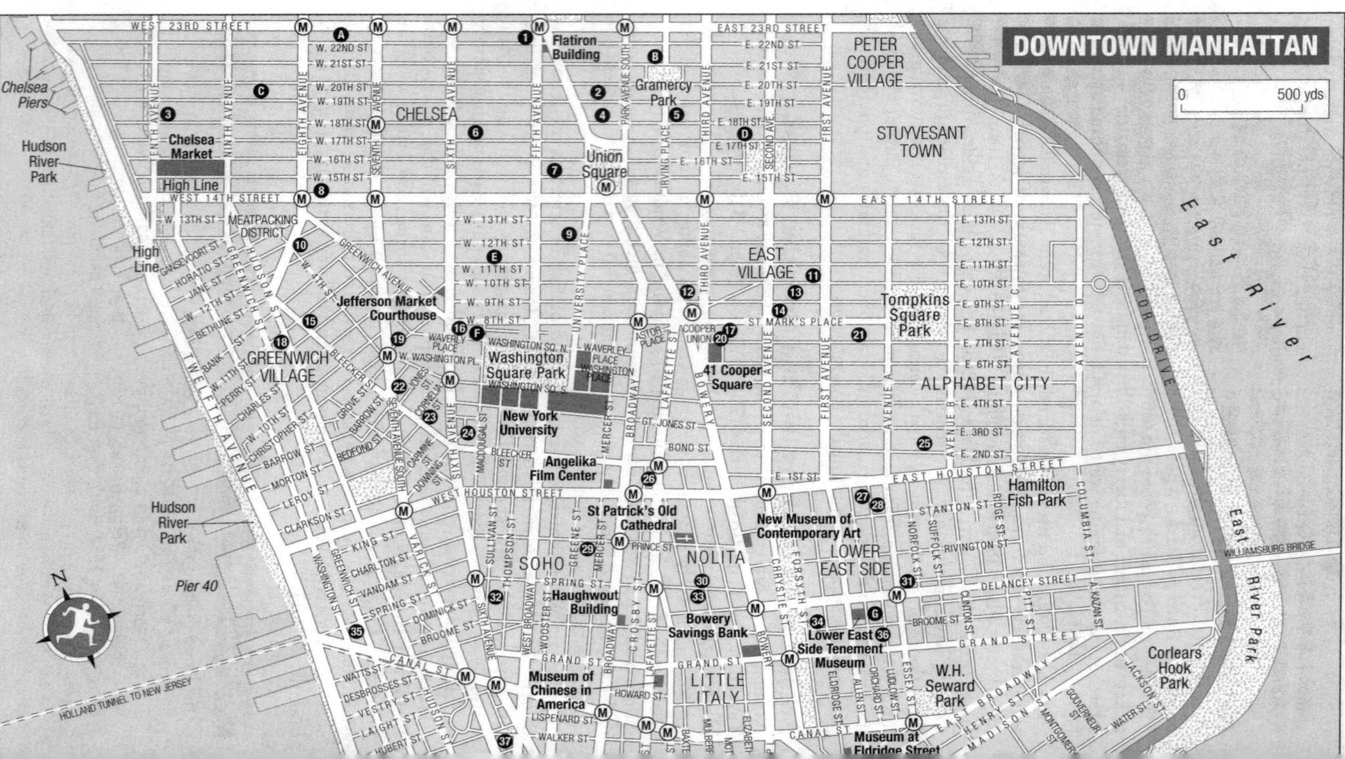
DOWNTOWN MANHATTAN
0 500 yds
East River
FDR DRIVE
East River Park
WILLIAMSBURG BRIDGE
PETER COOPER VILLAGE
STUYVESANT TOWN
Flatiron Building
Gramercy Park
Union Square
CHELSEA
Chelsea Market
High Line
Chelsea Piers
Hudson River Park
MEATPACKING DISTRICT
EAST VILLAGE
Tompkins Square Park
ALPHABET CITY
Jefferson Market Courthouse
GREENWICH VILLAGE
Washington Square Park
New York University
41 Cooper Square
Angelika Film Center
Hamilton Fish Park
St Patrick's Old Cathedral
New Museum of Contemporary Art
LOWER EAST SIDE
NOLITA
SOHO
Haughwout Building
Bowery Savings Bank
Lower East Side Tenement Museum
Museum of Chinese in America
LITTLE ITALY
W.H. Seward Park
Corlears Hook Park
Museum at Eldridge Street
Pier 40
HOLLAND TUNNEL TO NEW JERSEY
WEST 23RD STREET
EAST 23RD STREET
WEST 14TH STREET
EAST 14TH STREET
EAST HOUSTON STREET
WEST HOUSTON STREET
TWELFTH AVENUE
BROADWAY
BOWERY
CANAL ST
DELANCEY STREET
GRAND STREET
ST MARK'S PLACE
FIFTH AVENUE
SIXTH AVENUE
SEVENTH AVENUE
EIGHTH AVENUE
NINTH AVENUE
TENTH AVENUE
FIRST AVENUE
SECOND AVENUE
THIRD AVENUE
AVENUE A
AVENUE B
AVENUE C
AVENUE D
N

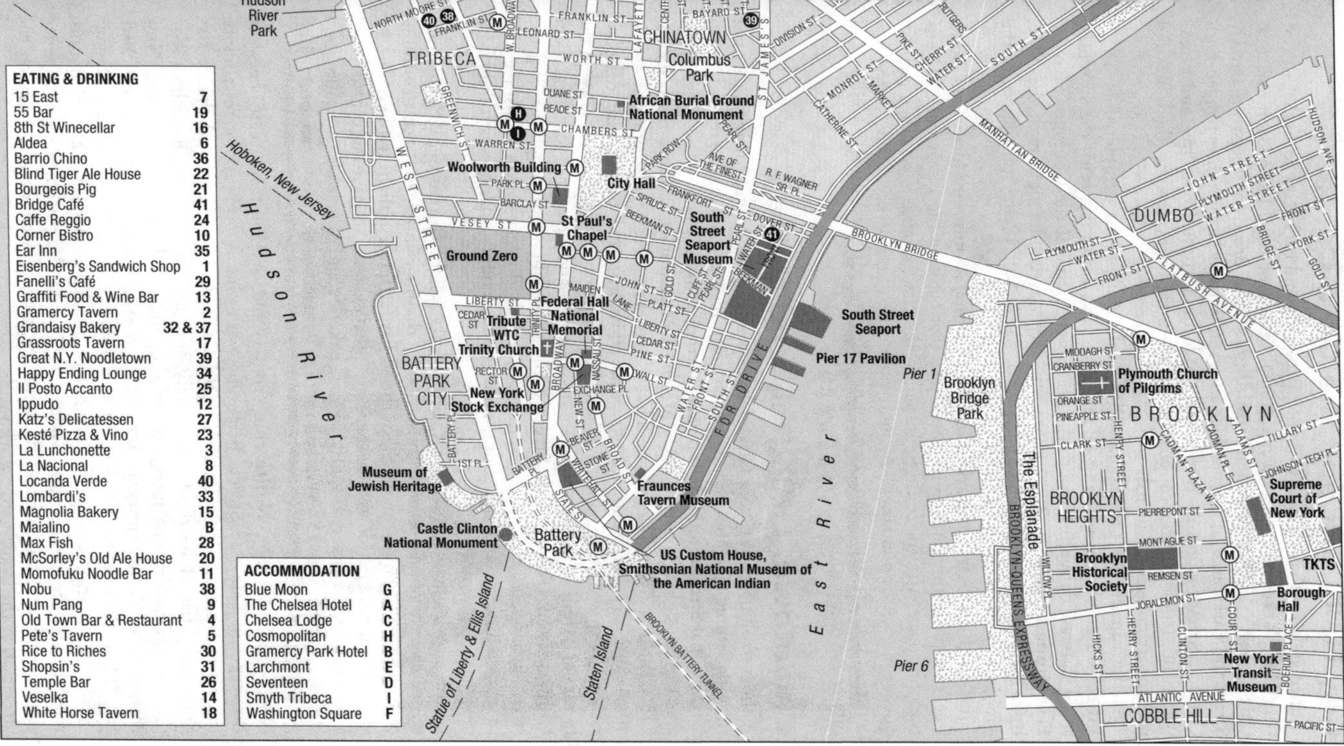
EATING & DRINKING
15 East 7
55 Bar 19
8th St Winecellar 16
Aldea 6
Barrio Chino 36
Blind Tiger Ale House 22
Bourgeois Pig 21
Bridge Café 41
Caffe Reggio 24
Corner Bistro 10
Ear Inn 35
Eisenberg's Sandwich Shop 1
Fanelli's Café 29
Graffiti Food & Wine Bar 13
Gramercy Tavern 2
Grandaisy Bakery 32 & 37
Grassroots Tavern 17
Great N.Y. Noodletown 39
Happy Ending Lounge 34
Il Posto Accanto 25
Ippudo 12
Katz's Delicatessen 27
Kesté Pizza & Vino 23
La Lunchonette 3
La Nacional 8
Locanda Verde 40
Lombardi's 33
Magnolia Bakery 15
Maialino B
Max Fish 28
McSorley's Old Ale House 20
Momofuku Noodle Bar 11
Nobu 38
Num Pang 9
Old Town Bar & Restaurant 4
Pete's Tavern 5
Rice to Riches 30
Shopsin's 31
Temple Bar 26
Veselka 14
White Horse Tavern 18
ACCOMMODATION
Blue Moon G
The Chelsea Hotel A
Chelsea Lodge C
Cosmopolitan H
Gramercy Park Hotel B
Larchmont E
Seventeen D
Smyth Tribeca I
Washington Square F
Hudson River Park
TRIBECA
CHINATOWN
Columbus Park
African Burial Ground National Monument
Woolworth Building
City Hall
St Paul's Chapel
Ground Zero
South Street Seaport Museum
Federal Hall National Memorial
Tribute WTC
Trinity Church
New York Stock Exchange
BATTERY PARK CITY
Museum of Jewish Heritage
Castle Clinton National Monument
Battery Park
Fraunces Tavern Museum
US Custom House, Smithsonian National Museum of the American Indian
South Street Seaport
Pier 17 Pavilion
Hoboken, New Jersey
Hudson River
East River
Statue of Liberty & Ellis Island
Staten Island
BROOKLYN BATTERY TUNNEL
FDR DRIVE
BROOKLYN BRIDGE
MANHATTAN BRIDGE
DUMBO
FLATBUSH AVENUE
Pier 1
Brooklyn Bridge Park
Pier 6
The Esplanade
BROOKLYN-QUEENS EXPRESSWAY
Plymouth Church of Pilgrims
BROOKLYN
BROOKLYN HEIGHTS
Brooklyn Historical Society
Supreme Court of New York
TKTS
Borough Hall
New York Transit Museum
COBBLE HILL

City Hall Park and the Civic Center

Immediately north of St Paul's Chapel, Broadway and Park Row form the apex of **City Hall Park**, a brightly flowered triangle now worthy of its handsome setting. Cass Gilbert's 1913 **Woolworth Building**, at 233 Broadway, between Barclay Street and Park Place, is a venerable onlooker, with its soaring lines fringed with Gothic decoration. Frank Woolworth made his fortune from "five and dime" stores and, true to his philosophy, he paid cash for his skyscraper (the lobby and interior are closed to tourists).

At the top of the park stands **City Hall**, which was completed in 1812. Inside, it's an elegant meeting of arrogance and authority, with the sweeping spiral staircase delivering you to the precise geometry of the Governor's Room. **Free guided tours** (Wed noon) are the only way inside: sign up at the **NYC information kiosk** (Mon–Fri 9am–6pm, Sat & Sun 10am–5pm) opposite the Woolworth Building.

Just north, the **African Burial Ground National Monument** (daily 9am–5pm; free) occupies a tiny portion of a cemetery that between the 1690s and 1794 was the only place Africans could be buried in the city (because it was then actually outside the city boundaries). Around the corner, at 290 Broadway, the visitor centre (Mon–Fri 9am–5pm; free) illuminates the history through a video and interactive exhibits.

Chinatown, Little Italy and Nolita

A short stroll northeast from City Hall leads into **Chinatown**, Manhattan's most thriving ethnic neighbourhood, which over recent years has extended north across Canal Street into Little Italy and northeast into the Lower East Side. There aren't many sights, save the slickly presented **Museum of Chinese in America**, 215 Centre St (Mon 11am–5pm, Thurs 11am–9pm, Fri 11am–5pm, Sat & Sun 10am–5pm; $7, free Thurs; Ⓦwww.mocanyc.org), and some lavish temples; rather, the appeal of the neighbourhood lies simply in its unbridled energy, in the hordes of people coursing the streets all day long – and, of course, for its excellent **Chinese food**. Today, **Mott Street** is the most vibrant thoroughfare, and the streets around – Canal, Pell, Bayard, Doyers and Bowery – host a positive glut of restaurants, tea and rice shops, grocers and vendors selling everything from jewellery to toy robots.

On the north side of Canal Street, **Little Italy** is light years away from the solid ethnic enclave of old. Originally settled by the huge nineteenth-century influx of Italian immigrants, the neighbourhood has far fewer Italians living here now and the restaurants (of which there are plenty), tend to have high prices and a touristy feel. However, some original bakeries and *salumerias* (specialty food stores) do survive, and you can still indulge yourself with a good cappuccino and a tasty pastry.

North of Little Italy, **Nolita** runs from Grand to Houston streets, between Bowery and Lafayette Street. Brimming with chic boutiques and restaurants, the district surrounds **St Patrick's Old Cathedral** (on Mott and Prince sts), once the spiritual heart of Little Italy and the oldest Catholic cathedral in the city. If you're not interested in shopping, at least check out the **New Museum of Contemporary Art**, 235 Bowery, opposite Prince Street (Wed, Sat, & Sun noon–6pm, Thurs & Fri noon–9pm; $12; Ⓣ212/219-1222, Ⓦwww.newmuseum.org), a powerful symbol of the **Bowery**'s rebirth, which until recently was the city's original skid row. The building itself, a stack of seven shimmering aluminium boxes designed by Japanese architects, is as much the attraction as the avant-garde work inside.

The Lower East Side

Below the eastern stretch of Houston Street, the **Lower East Side** began life toward the end of the nineteenth century as an insular slum for roughly half a million Jewish immigrants. Since then it has changed considerably, with many Dominican and Chinese inhabitants, followed by a recent influx of well-off students, artists, designers, and the like. It's all made the neighbourhood quite cool, and a hotbed for trendy shops, bars and restaurants, with **Stanton** and **Clinton streets** as the epicentre.

You can still **buy** just about anything cut-price in the Lower East Side, especially on Sunday mornings, when **Orchard Street** is filled with stalls and stores selling discounted clothes and accessories. Next to this melee is the excellent **Lower East Side Tenement Museum**, 97 Orchard St, between Broome and Delancey streets (visitor centre daily 10am–6pm, tours 10.30am–5pm; can only be seen by tour, $20; Ⓣ212/431-0233, Ⓦwww.tenement.org), which is housed in a nineteenth-century tenement and chronicles the neighbourhood's immigrant and impoverished past; tours begin and end at the visitor centre at 108 Orchard St. To get a feel for the area's Jewish roots, make for the absorbing **Museum at Eldridge Street** (Sun–Thurs 10am–5pm; $10; Ⓣ212/219-0888, Ⓦwww.eldridgestreet.org), just south of Canal Street, at 12 Eldridge St. Built in 1887 as the first synagogue constructed by Eastern European Orthodox Jews in the city (and still a functioning house of worship), half-hourly guided tours take you upstairs to the main sanctuary and provide a thorough introduction to the history of the building.

Soho and Tribeca

Since the early 1980s, Soho, the grid of streets that runs *so*uth of *Ho*uston Street, has been all about fashion chic, urbane shopping and cosmopolitan art galleries. For the first half of the twentieth century, this area was a wasteland of manufacturers and warehouses, but as rising rents drove artists out of Greenwich Village in the 1940s and 1950s, Soho suddenly became "in". In the 1960s, largely due to the area's magnificent cast-iron architecture, Soho was declared a historic district. Following this, yuppification set in, bringing the fashionable boutiques, hip restaurants and tourist crowds that are Soho's signature today. The landmark Apple Store occupies the former post office on the corner of Greene and Prince streets, while the best example of cast-iron architecture, the flamboyant **Haughwout Building**, can be found at the northeast corner of Broome Street and Broadway. You should also check out **72–76 Greene Street**, a neat extravagance whose Corinthian portico stretches the whole five storeys, all in painted metal, and the strongly composed elaborations of its sister building at nos. 28–30.

Tribeca (the *tri*angle *be*low *Ca*nal St), south of Soho and west of City Hall, is a former wholesale-food district that's now an enclave of urban style; mixed in among the spacious loft apartments are upmarket restaurants, tiny parks and the odd gallery.

The West Village

For many visitors, the **West Village** (also known as Greenwich Village, or simply "the Village") is the most-loved neighbourhood in New York, despite having lost any radical edge long ago. Its bohemian image endures well enough if you don't live in the city, and it still sports many attractions that brought people here in the first place: a busy streetlife that lasts later than in many other parts of the city; more restaurants per head than anywhere else; and bars cluttering every corner.

Greenwich Village grew up as a rural retreat from the early and frenetic nucleus of New York City. Refined Federal and Greek Revival townhouses lured some of the city's highest society names, and later, at the start of World War I, the Village proved fertile ground for struggling artists and intellectuals, who were attracted to the area's cheap rents and growing community of freethinking residents. The **Beat movement** flourished here after World War II, laying the path for rebellious, countercultural groups and activities in the 1960s, particularly **folk music**, with Bob Dylan a resident for much of his early career. The natural heart of the Village, **Washington Square Park**, is not exactly elegant, though it does retain its northern edging of red-brick rowhouses – the "solid, honorable dwellings" of Henry James's novel *Washington Square* – and Stanford White's imposing **Washington Arch**, built in 1892 to commemorate the centenary of George Washington's inauguration. The park is also the heart of New York University: in warm weather, it becomes a space for sports, perfomance, protest and socializing. From the bottom of the park, follow **MacDougal Street** south and you hit **Bleecker Street** – the Village's main drag, packed with shops, bars, people and restaurants. Walk right (west) onto Bleecker, then right again (north) on Sixth Avenue, until you see the unmistakable clock tower of the beautiful nineteenth-century **Jefferson Market Courthouse**, at West 10th Street. This imposing High Victorian-style edifice first served as an indoor market, but later went on to be a firehouse, a jail, and finally a women's detention centre before enjoying its current incarnation as a public library.

West of here, in the brownstone-lined side streets off Seventh Avenue, such as Bedford and Grove, you'll glimpse one of the city's most desirable living areas. Bedford Street is particularly attractive, and is the site of the oldest house in the Village, at no. 77 (from 1799), while 17 Grove St (from 1822) is the most complete wood-frame house in the city. Nearby, **Christopher Street** joins Seventh Avenue at **Sheridan Square**, home of the *Stonewall Inn*'s gay bar where, in 1969, a police raid precipitated a siege that lasted the best part of an hour. The **Annual Gay Pride Parade**, typically held on the last Sunday in June (starting at 5th Ave and 52nd St, and ending around Sheridan Square), honours this turning point in the struggle for equal rights.

The East Village

The **East Village**, sandwiched between 14th and Houston streets, to the east of Broadway – though its heart is east of Third Avenue – differs quite a bit from its western counterpart. Once, like the adjacent Lower East Side, the neighbourhood was a refuge for immigrants and solidly working-class people. Home to New York's nonconformist intelligentsia in the early twentieth century, it later became the haunt of **the Beats** – Kerouac, Burroughs, Ginsberg et al – who would get together at Ginsberg's house on East Seventh Street for declamatory poetry readings. Later, Andy Warhol debuted the Velvet Underground here; and Richard Hell, Patti Smith and The Ramones invented punk rock at a hole-in-the-wall club called **CBGB** (closed in 2006, it's now a John Varvatos fashion boutique, where the walls are plastered with punk memorabilia).

Much of the East Village has changed since the economic boom of the mid-1980s and the 1990s; gone is its status as a hotbed of dissidence and creativity. Nevertheless, the area's main drag, the vaudevillian **St Mark's Place** (8th St), is still one of Downtown's more vibrant strips, even if the thrift shops, panhandlers and political hustlers have given way to more sanitized forms of rebellion.

Continuing east on 8th Street takes you to **Tompkins Square Park**, bordered by avenues A and B and 7th and 10th streets. It's long been a focus for the East Village community, and was the scene of the notorious 1988 riots that partly inspired the musical *Rent*. These days things are far more relaxed, and the surrounding area sports some of the most enticing bars and restaurants in the city. In the opposite direction, at Cooper Square, the seven-storey brown mass of the **Cooper Union for the Advancement of Science and Art** is the centre of attention; in 1860, Abraham Lincoln wowed top New Yorkers here with his "right makes might" speech, in which he boldly criticized the pro-slavery South and helped propel himself to the Republican nomination for president. The swooping, fractured building at 41 Cooper Square, a new academic hall finished in 2009, does give it a run for its money.

Midtown Manhattan

MIDTOWN MANHATTAN encompasses everything from the East to the Hudson rivers, between 14th Street and 59th Street, the southern border of Central Park. New York's most glamorous (and most expensive) thoroughfare, **Fifth Avenue**, cuts through Midtown's heart, with the neon theatre strip of **Broadway** running just to the west for much of the way. The character of Midtown is very different whether you're east of Fifth or west of Sixth (between Fifth and Sixth, there's almost a character to itself, from Koreatown up to Rockefeller Center). On Fifth Avenue itself and to the east are corporate businesses and prestigious skyscrapers – including the Empire State, Chrysler and Seagram buildings – as well as Grand Central Station and the UN. Here you'll also find the residential neighbourhoods of **Murray Hill** and elegant **Gramercy Park**. Just below Gramercy's eponymous park, busy **Union Square** is always great for people-watching. Meanwhile, west of Sixth, **Chelsea** is home to art galleries and the new High Line park; north of it, the tiny **Garment District** doesn't have much to see. Around 42nd Street, the **Theater District** heralds a cleaned-up, frenetic area of entertainment that culminates at **Times Square**. West of Broadway in the 40s and low 50s, colourful **Hell's Kitchen** is now more or less wholly gentrified.

Union Square and Gramercy Park

Downtown Manhattan ends at 14th Street, which slices across from the housing projects of the East Side through rows of cut-price shops to the meatpacking warehouses on the Hudson River. In the middle is **Union Square**, its shallow steps enticing passers-by to sit and watch the motley assortment of skateboarders, Whole Foods shoppers and NYU students or to stroll the cool, tree-shaded paths and lawns. The shopping that once dominated the stretch of **Broadway** north of here, formerly known as Ladies' Mile for its fancy stores and boutiques, has been moved to Fifth Avenue, where chain stores now cover virtually every block in the mid-teens through the 20s.

Northeast from here, between 20th and 21st streets, where Lexington Avenue becomes Irving Place, Manhattan's clutter suddenly breaks into the ordered, open space of **Gramercy Park**. This former swamp, reclaimed in 1831, is one of the city's best parks, its centre tidily planted and, most noticeably, completely empty for much of the day – principally because the only people who can gain access are those rich enough to live here and possess keys to the gate (guests at the *Gramercy Park Hotel* are also allowed in; see p.72).

Broadway and Fifth Avenue meet at 23rd Street at **Madison Square**, with a serene, well-manicured **park** to take the edge off, enhanced by the celebrated burgers of *Shake Shack* (see p.99). Most notable among the elegant structures nearby is the **Flatiron Building**, 175 Fifth Ave, between 22nd and 23rd streets; the 1902 Beaux Arts structure is known for its unusual narrow corners and six-and-a-half-feet-wide rounded tip.

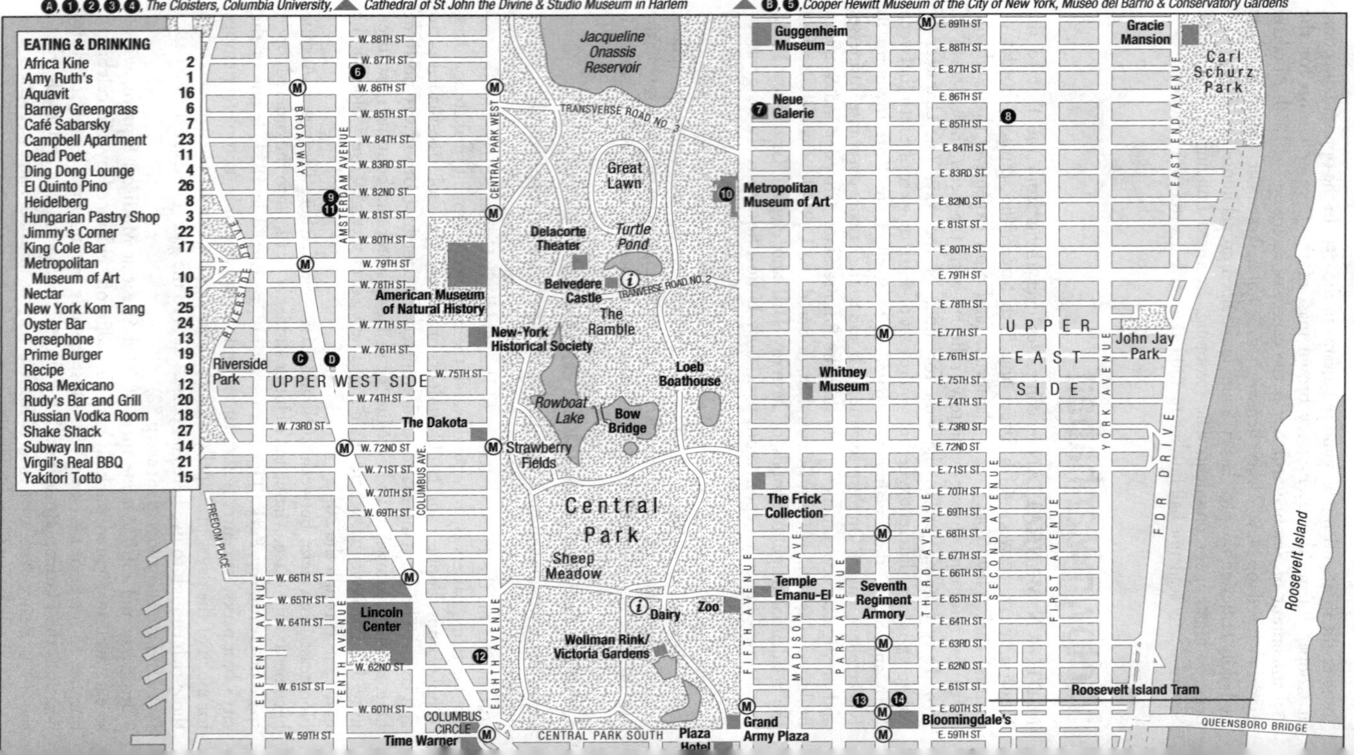
A, 1, 2, 3, 4, The Cloisters, Columbia University, Cathedral of St John the Divine & Studio Museum in Harlem
B, 5, Cooper Hewitt Museum of the City of New York, Museo del Barrio & Conservatory Gardens
EATING & DRINKING
Africa Kine 2
Amy Ruth's 1
Aquavit 16
Barney Greengrass 6
Café Sabarsky 7
Campbell Apartment 23
Dead Poet 11
Ding Dong Lounge 4
El Quinto Pino 26
Heidelberg 8
Hungarian Pastry Shop 3
Jimmy's Corner 22
King Cole Bar 17
Metropolitan Museum of Art 10
Nectar 5
New York Kom Tang 25
Oyster Bar 24
Persephone 13
Prime Burger 19
Recipe 9
Rosa Mexicano 12
Rudy's Bar and Grill 20
Russian Vodka Room 18
Shake Shack 27
Subway Inn 14
Virgil's Real BBQ 21
Yakitori Totto 15
Jacqueline Onassis Reservoir
Transverse Road No. 3
Great Lawn
Turtle Pond
Delacorte Theater
Belvedere Castle
Tranverse Road No. 2
The Ramble
Loeb Boathouse
Rowboat Lake
Bow Bridge
Strawberry Fields
Central Park
Sheep Meadow
Dairy
Zoo
Wollman Rink/ Victoria Gardens
Central Park South
Plaza Hotel
Guggenheim Museum
Neue Galerie
Metropolitan Museum of Art
Whitney Museum
The Frick Collection
Temple Emanu-El
Seventh Regiment Armory
Grand Army Plaza
Bloomingdale's
Gracie Mansion
Carl Schurz Park
John Jay Park
Upper East Side
Roosevelt Island
Roosevelt Island Tram
Queensboro Bridge
FDR Drive
East End Avenue
York Avenue
First Avenue
Second Avenue
Third Avenue
Park Avenue
Madison Ave
Fifth Avenue
E. 89th St
E. 88th St
E. 87th St
E. 86th St
E. 85th St
E. 84th St
E. 83rd St
E. 82nd St
E. 81st St
E. 80th St
E. 79th St
E. 78th St
E. 77th St
E. 76th St
E. 75th St
E. 74th St
E. 73rd St
E. 72nd St
E. 71st St
E. 70th St
E. 69th St
E. 68th St
E. 67th St
E. 66th St
E. 65th St
E. 64th St
E. 63rd St
E. 62nd St
E. 61st St
E. 60th St
E. 59th St
Central Park West
Broadway
Amsterdam Avenue
Columbus Ave.
Eighth Avenue
Tenth Avenue
Eleventh Avenue
Riverside Drive
Freedom Place
Riverside Park
Upper West Side
American Museum of Natural History
New-York Historical Society
The Dakota
Lincoln Center
Columbus Circle
Time Warner
W. 88th St
W. 87th St
W. 86th St
W. 85th St
W. 84th St
W. 83rd St
W. 82nd St
W. 81st St
W. 80th St
W. 79th St
W. 78th St
W. 77th St
W. 76th St
W. 75th St
W. 74th St
W. 73rd St
W. 72nd St
W. 71st St
W. 70th St
W. 69th St
W. 66th St
W. 65th St
W. 64th St
W. 62nd St
W. 61st St
W. 60th St
W. 59th St

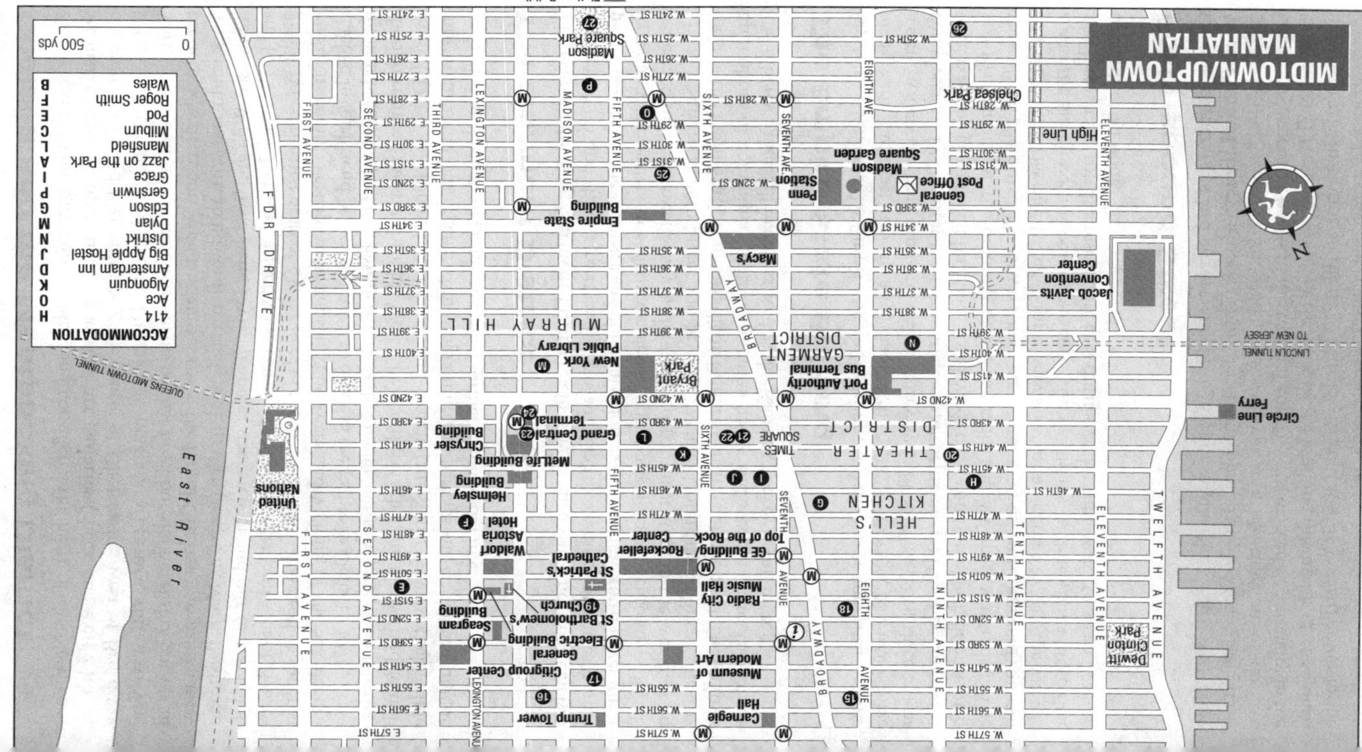
MIDTOWN/UPTOWN MANHATTAN
ACCOMMODATION
414 H
Ace O
Algonquin K
Amsterdam Inn D
Big Apple Hostel J
Distrikt N
Dylan M
Edison G
Gershwin P
Grace I
Jazz on the Park A
Mansfield L
Milburn C
Pod E
Roger Smith F
Wales B
0 500 yds
East River
Queens Midtown Tunnel
FDR Drive
United Nations
Murray Hill
Trump Tower
Citigroup Center
General Electric Building
Seagram Building
St Bartholomew's Church
St Patrick's Cathedral
Waldorf Astoria Hotel
Helmsley Building
MetLife Building
Chrysler Building
Grand Central Terminal
New York Public Library
Empire State Building
Madison Square Park
Flatiron Building
Carnegie Hall
Museum of Modern Art
Radio City Music Hall
GE Building/ Top of the Rock
Rockefeller Center
Bryant Park
Times Square
Broadway
Macy's
Penn Station
Madison Square Garden
General Post Office
Hell's Kitchen
Theater District
Garment District
Port Authority Bus Terminal
Jacob Javits Convention Center
High Line
Chelsea Park
Dewitt Clinton Park
Circle Line Ferry
Lincoln Tunnel to New Jersey
First Avenue
Second Avenue
Third Avenue
Lexington Avenue
Madison Avenue
Fifth Avenue
Sixth Avenue
Seventh Avenue
Eighth Avenue
Ninth Avenue
Tenth Avenue
Eleventh Avenue
Twelfth Avenue

Chelsea and the Meatpacking District

Home to a thriving **gay community**, and considered the heart of the New York art market because of its many renowned **art galleries** (check out West 24th St, between Tenth and Eleventh aves), the centre of **Chelsea** lies west of Broadway between 14th and 23rd streets. During the nineteenth century, this was New York's theatre district. Nothing remains of that now, but the hotel that put up all the actors, writers and attendant entourages – the **Hotel Chelsea** – remains a New York landmark, with an Edwardian grandeur all its own (see p.72). Mark Twain and Tennessee Williams lived here, Dylan Thomas staggered in and out of the hotel, and in 1951 Jack Kerouac, armed with a customized typewriter (and a lot of Benzedrine), typed the first draft of *On the Road* nonstop onto a 120ft-long roll of paper in one of its rooms. Perhaps most famously, however, Sid Vicious, of the Sex Pistols, stabbed his girlfriend Nancy Spungen to death in their suite in October 1978, a few months before he died of a heroin overdose. Beginning in the Meatpacking District, though running mostly through West Chelsea, the **High Line** (daily: mid-March to mid-Dec 7am–10pm, mid-Dec to mid-March 7am–8pm; Ⓦwww.thehighline.org) is an ambitious regeneration programme and perhaps the city's most unique park, slicing through the high-rises on a former elevated rail line.

The Garment District

The ever-diminishing **Garment District**, a loosely defined patch north of Chelsea between 34th and 42nd streets and Sixth and Eighth avenues, produces a high percentage of all the women's and children's clothes in America. You'd never guess it, though; the outlets are strictly wholesale, with no need to woo customers. Retail stores abound, however: **Macy's**, the largest department store in the world, is on **Herald Square** at 34th Street and Seventh Avenue. Dominant landmarks nearby include the **Penn Station** and **Madison Square Garden** complex, which swallows up millions of commuters in its train station below and accommodates the Knicks and Liberty basketball teams, as well as the Rangers hockey team, up top.

The Empire State Building

Up Fifth Avenue is the **Empire State Building**, at 34th Street and Fifth Avenue (daily 8am–2am, last trip up at 1.15am; $20; Ⓣ212/736-3100, Ⓦwww.esbnyc.com), which has been a muscular 102-storey symbol of New York since it was completed in 1931. After the terrorist attacks of September 11th, it became, as it once was, the city's tallest building. An elevator takes you to the 86th floor, which was the summit of the building before the radio and TV mast was added. The views from the outside walkways here are as stunning as you'd expect (you can continue up to the tiny 102nd-floor observatory for an extra $15, but the view is about the same). For the best experience, you should try to time your visit so that you'll reach the top at sunset; note that during peak times, waits to ascend can be upwards of an hour.

Forty-second Street

On the corner of **42nd Street** and Fifth Avenue stands the Beaux Arts **New York Public Library** (Mon & Thurs–Sat 10am–6pm, Tues & Wed 10am–9pm; Ⓣ917/275-6975 or 212/930-0800, Ⓦwww.nypl.org), boasting one of the five largest collections of books in the world. Leon Trotsky worked occasionally in the large coffered Reading Room at the back of the building during his brief sojourn in New York, just prior to the 1917 Russian Revolution. It's worth going inside just to appreciate its reverent, church-like atmosphere.

East on 42nd Street at Park Avenue, the huge bulk of **Grand Central Terminal** was completed in 1913 around a basic iron frame, but features a dazzling Beaux Arts facade; it's immense size is now dwarfed by the **MetLife** Building behind it. Regardless, the main station's **concourse** is a sight to behold – 470ft-long and 150ft-high, it boasts a barrel-vaulted ceiling speckled like a Baroque church with a painted representation of the winter night sky. The 2500 stars are shown back to front – "as God would have seen them", the painter is reputed to have explained. You can explore Grand Central on your own, or take a tour sponsored by the Municipal Arts Society's (Wed 12.30pm, $10 suggested donation; ⓣ212/935-3960, ⓦmas.org) or the Grand Central Partnership (Fri 12.30pm, free; ⓣ212/883-2420, ⓦwww.grandcentralpartnership.org).

The **Chrysler Building**, at 405 Lexington Ave, dates from a time (1930) when architects carried off prestige with grace and style. For a short while, this was the world's tallest building; today, it's one of Manhattan's best-loved structures. The lobby, once a car showroom, with its opulently inlaid elevators, walls covered in African marble and murals depicting airplanes, machines and the brawny builders who worked on the tower, is all you can see inside.

At the eastern end of 42nd Street, the **United Nations** complex comprises the glass-curtained **Secretariat**, the curving sweep of the **General Assembly**, and, connecting them, the low-rising **Conference Wing**. Guided **tours** leave from the General Assembly lobby (Mon–Fri 9.45am–4.45pm, tours last 45min; $16, bring ID; ⓣ212/963-8687, ⓦwww.un.org) and take in the UN conference chambers and its constituent parts. Note that tours may vary depending on official room usage.

Times Square and the Theater District

Forty-second Street meets Broadway at the southern margin of **Times Square**, centre of the **Theater District** and a top tourist attraction. Traditionally a melting pot of debauchery, depravity and fun, Times Square was cleaned up in the 1990s and turned into a largely sanitized universe of popular consumption, with refurbished theatres and blinking signage – best experienced as a rush of neon and energy after dark.

North of Times Square, along Seventh Avenue at 154 West 57th St, **Carnegie Hall** (Sept–June only, tours available Mon–Fri at 11.30am, 2pm & 3pm, Sat 11.30am & 12.30pm, Sun 12.30pm; $10; general info ⓣ212/903-9600, tours ⓣ212/903-9765, tickets ⓣ212/247-7800, ⓦwww.carnegiehall.org) is a world-famous venue for opera and concerts. Tchaikovsky conducted the programme on opening night and Mahler, Rachmaninov, Toscanini, Frank Sinatra and Judy Garland have played here. Even if you don't have time for a show, it's worth taking the tour to admire the vast interior.

Fifth Avenue and around

Fifth Avenue has been a great thoroughfare for as long as New York has been a great city, and its very name evokes wealth and opulence. All who consider themselves suave and cosmopolitan end up here, and the stores showcase New York's most conspicuous consumerism. That the shopping is beyond the means of most people needn't put you off, for Fifth Avenue has some of the city's best architecture, too.

At the heart of the glamour is **Rockefeller Center**, built between 1932 and 1940 by John D. Rockefeller Jr, son of the oil magnate. One of the finest pieces of urban planning anywhere, the Center balances office space with cafés, a theatre, underground concourses and rooftop gardens, which work together with a rare intelligence and grace. The **GE Building** here rises 850ft; the "Top of the Rock" observation deck offers another mesmerizing view of the Manhattan skyline (daily 8am–midnight, last entry 11pm; $21; ⓣ212/698-2000, ⓦwww.topoftherocknyc.com). At its foot, the **Lower Plaza** holds a sunken restaurant in summer, linked visually by Paul Manship's sparkling *Prometheus* statue; in winter, the plaza becomes a small **ice rink**, allowing skaters to show off their skills to passers-by. Inside, the Center is no less impressive: in the GE lobby, José Maria Sert's murals, *American Progress* and *Time*, are a little faded but in tune with the 1930s Art Deco ambience. A leaflet available from the lobby desk details a **self-guided tour** of the Center. Among the GE Building's many offices are the **NBC Studios** (tours Mon–Thurs 8.30am–4.30pm, Fri & Sat 9.30am–5.30pm, Sun 9.30am–4.30pm; reservations at the NBC Experience Store Tour Desk; $19.25, $16.25 for children 6–12; ⓣ212/664-3700). If you're a TV fan, pick up a free ticket for a **show recording** from the mezzanine lobby or out on the street. Keep in mind that the most popular tickets evaporate before 9am. The glass-enclosed **Today Show** studio is at the southwest corner of the plaza at 49th Street, surrounded in the early morning by avid fans waiting to get on TV by way of the cameras that obligingly pan the crowds from time to time.

At 1260 Sixth Ave, at 50th Street, Rockefeller Center's **Radio City Music Hall** (1hr tours daily 11am–3pm; $18.50; ⓣ212/307-7171 or 247/4777, ⓦwww.radiocity.com) is the last word in 1930s luxury. The staircase is regally resplendent, the chandeliers are the world's largest and the huge auditorium looks like an extravagant scalloped shell. Surely, however, Radio City is best known for the Rockettes, whose Christmas shows and kicklines have dazzled the masses since 1932. Almost opposite Rockefeller Center, on 50th Street and Fifth Avenue, **St Patrick's Cathedral**, designed by James Renwick and completed in 1888, seems the result of a painstaking academic tour of the Gothic cathedrals of Europe.

East of Fifth, **Madison Avenue** makes for pleasant strolling, and is filled with expensive galleries, haute couture shops and elegantly dressed Eastsiders. The next avenue east, **Park Avenue**, was said by Collinson Owen in 1929 to be the place "where wealth is so swollen that it almost bursts". Things haven't changed much: corporate headquarters and four-star hotels jostle in triumphal procession, led by the massive New York Central Building (now the **Helmsley Building**) that literally sits above Park Avenue at 46th Street and boasts a lewdly excessive Rococo lobby.

Crouched behind the Art Deco **Waldorf Astoria Hotel**, on Park between 49th and 50th streets, is **St Bartholomew's Church**, a striking, low-slung Byzantine hybrid that adds immeasurably to the street and gives the lumbering skyscrapers a much-needed sense of scale. The spiky-topped **General Electric Building** behind seems like a wild extension of the church, its slender shaft rising to a meshed crown of abstract sparks and lightning bolts that symbolizes the radio waves used by its original owner, RCA. The lobby (entrance at 570 Lexington) is yet another Deco delight and is free to enter.

Overshadowing all this is the **Museum of Modern Art**, at 11 West 53rd St, between Fifth and Sixth avenues, offering the finest collection of late-nineteenth- and twentieth-century art anywhere, and an essential stop. Nineteenth-century highlights include Van Gogh's *Starry Night* and Munch's *Madonna*, while the modern period is represented by works such as Picasso's *Demoiselles d'Avignon*, Jasper Johns' *Flag* and Warhol's soup cans (Mon & Wed–Sun 10.30am–5.30pm, Fri until 8pm; $20, $16 for seniors, free for children 16 and under, also free Fri 4–8pm; ticket includes admission to MoMA PS 1 in Queens, if visited within 30 days; ⓣ212/708-9400, ⓦwww.moma.org).

Uptown Manhattan

UPTOWN MANHATTAN begins above 59th Street, where the businesslike bustle of Midtown gives way to the comfortable domesticity of the Upper East and West sides. In between, people come to **Central Park**, the city's giant backyard, to play, jog and escape Midtown's crowds in a particularly intelligent piece of urban landscaping.

The **Upper East Side** is at its most opulent in the several blocks just east of Central Park, and at its most distinguished in the Metropolitan and other great museums of "Museum Mile", from 82nd to 104th streets along Fifth Avenue. The predominantly residential **Upper West Side** is somewhat less refined, though there are certainly plenty of expensive townhouses and apartment buildings. The northern reaches embrace the monolithic Cathedral of St John the Divine and Columbia University. North and east from here, **Harlem**, the cultural capital of black America, is experiencing a new renaissance. Still further north, in the **Washington Heights** area, you'll find one of the city's most intriguing museums – The Cloisters and its medieval arts collection.

Central Park

Completed in 1876, smack in the middle of Manhattan, **Central Park** extends from 59th to 110th streets, and provides residents (and street-weary visitors) with a much-needed refuge from big-city life. The poet and newspaper editor William Cullen Bryant had the idea for an open public space in 1844 and spent seven years trying to persuade City Hall to carry it out. Eventually, 840 desolate and swampy acres north of the city limits were set aside. The two architects commissioned to design the landscape, **Frederick Law Olmsted** and **Calvert Vaux**, planned a complete illusion of the countryside in the heart of Manhattan – even then growing at a fantastic rate. Despite changes in and around the park, the sense of captured nature largely survives. For general park **information**, call ⓣ212/310-6600, or visit ⓦwww.centralparknyc.org.

One of the best ways to explore the park is to rent a **bicycle** from the Loeb Boathouse, between 74th and 75th streets (April–Nov daily 10am–6pm; $9–15/hour, $45–50/day). Otherwise, it's easy to get around **on foot**, along the many paths that crisscross the park. There's little chance of getting lost, but to know exactly where you are, find the nearest lamppost: the first two figures signify the number of the nearest street. After dark, however, you'd be well advised not to enter on foot.

Most places of interest in the park lie in its southern reaches. At 64th Street and Fifth Avenue, the **Central Park Zoo** tries to keep caging to a minimum and the animals as close to the viewer as possible (April–Oct Mon–Fri 10am–5pm, Sat & Sun 10am–5.30pm; Nov–March daily 10am–4.30pm; $10, $5 ages 3–12; ⓣ212/439-6500). Beyond here, the **Dairy**, once a ranch building intended to provide milk for nursing mothers, now houses a **visitor centre** (Tues–Sun 10am–5pm; ⓣ212/794-6564), which distributes free leaflets and maps, sells books and puts on exhibitions.

Nearby, the Trump-owned **Wollman Rink**, 63rd Street at mid-park (ice skating Nov–April Mon & Tues 10am–2.30pm, Wed & Thurs 10am–10pm, $10.25; Fri & Sat 10am–11pm, Sun 10am–9pm, $14.75; ⓣ212/439-6900, ⓦwww.wollmanskatingrink.com), is a lovely place to skate in winter; in the warmer months it becomes a small amusement park, **Victoria Gardens**. From the rink, swing west past the restored **Sheep Meadow**, a dust bowl in the 1970s, now emerald green; then move north up the formal Mall to the terrace, with the sculptured birds and animals of **Bethesda Fountain** below, edging The Lake. West is **Strawberry Fields**, a tranquil, shady spot dedicated to John Lennon by his widow, Yoko Ono, and the **Imagine mosaic** – both are near where he was killed in 1980 (see p.92). On the eastern bank of the lake, you can rent a **rowboat** from the Loeb Boathouse (daily 10am until dusk weather permitting; ⓣ212/517-2233; $12 for the first hour, $2.50/15min thereafter; $20 refundable cash deposit required) or cross the water by the elegant cast-iron **Bow Bridge**.

Beyond the bridge, the wild woods of **The Ramble** are a maze of paths and bridges. At 81st Street, near the West Side, stands the mock citadel of **Belvedere Castle** (Tues–Sun 10am–5pm), another visitor centre that has nature exhibits and boasts great views of the park from its terraces. Next to the castle, the **Delacorte Theater** is home to **Shakespeare in the Park** performances in the summer (tickets are free, though they go very quickly; visit ⓦwww.publictheater.org for details), while the immense **Great Lawn** is the preferred sprawling ground for many sun-loving New Yorkers. Beginning at 86th Street, the track around the **Jacqueline Onassis Reservoir** is a favoured place for joggers; however, the one can't-miss in the northern part of the park is the lush **Conservatory Garden** (daily 8am–dusk; East 104th–106th sts along Fifth Ave, with entrance at 105th).

The Metropolitan Museum of Art

One of the world's great art museums, the **Metropolitan Museum of Art** (usually referred to as just "the Met") juts into the park at Fifth Avenue and 82nd Street (Tues–Thurs & Sun 9.30am–5.30pm, Fri & Sat 9.30am–9pm; suggested donation $20, seniors $15, students $10; includes same-day admission to The Cloisters; ⓣ212/535-7710, ⓦwww.metmuseum.org). Its all-embracing collection amounts to more than two million works of art, spanning America and Europe as well as China, Africa, the Far East, and the classical and Islamic worlds. You could spend weeks here and not see everything.

If you make just one visit, head for the **European Painting** galleries. Of the early (fifteenth- and sixteenth-century) **Flemish and Dutch paintings**, the best are by Jan van Eyck, who is generally credited with having started the tradition of North European realism. The **Italian Renaissance** is less spectacularly represented, but a worthy selection includes an early *Madonna and Child Enthroned with Saints* by Raphael and Duccio's sublime masterpiece *Madonna and Child*. Don't miss the **Spanish** galleries, which include Goya's widely reproduced portrait of a toddler in a red jumpsuit, *Don Manuel Osorio Manrique de Zuniga*, and a room of freaky, dazzling canvases by El Greco.

The **nineteenth-century galleries** house a startling array of **Impressionist** and **post-Impressionist** art, showcasing Manet and Monet among others, and the compact twentieth-century collection features Picasso's portrait of Gertrude Stein and Gauguin's masterly *La Orana Maria*, alongside works by Klee, Hopper and Matisse. The **Medieval Galleries** are no less exhaustive, with displays of sumptuous Byzantine metalwork and jewellery donated by J.P. Morgan, while the **Asian Art galleries** house plenty of murals, sculptures and textile art from Japan, China, Southeast and Central Asia, and Korea. Other highlights include the imposing **Temple of Dendur** in the Egyptian section, and the **Greek** and **Roman** sculpture galleries, magnificently restored a few years back.

The Upper East Side

A two-square-mile grid, the **Upper East Side** has wealth as its defining characteristic, as you'll appreciate if you've seen any of the many Woody Allen movies set here. The area's stretch of **Fifth Avenue** has been the patrician face of Manhattan since the opening of Central Park attracted the Carnegies, Astors and Whitneys to migrate north and build fashionable residences. **Grand Army Plaza**, at Central Park South and Fifth Avenue, flanked by the extended chateau of the swanky **Plaza Hotel**, and glowing with the gold statue of the Civil War's General William Tecumseh Sherman, serves as the introduction.

On the corner of Fifth Avenue and 65th Street, America's largest Reform synagogue, the **Temple Emanu-El**, strikes a sober tone (on-site museum Sun–Thurs 10am–4.30pm, check site for service times; free; Ⓣ212/744-1400, Ⓦwww.emanuelnyc.org). The brooding Romanesque-Byzantine cavern manages to be bigger inside than it seems from outside, and, as you enter, the interior appears to melt away into darkness, making you feel very small indeed.

At 70th Street, you'll find Henry Clay Frick's house, a handsome spread and now the tranquil home of the **Frick Collection** (Tues–Sat 10am–6pm, Sun 11am–5pm; $18; Ⓣ212/288-0700, Ⓦwww.frick.org). One of many prestigious museums in the area, the Frick is perhaps the most enjoyable of the big New York galleries; it is made up of the art treasures hoarded by Frick during his years as probably the most ruthless of New York's robber barons. The collection includes paintings by Rembrandt, Reynolds, Hogarth, Gainsborough (*St James's Park*) and Bellini, whose *St Francis* suggests his vision of Christ by means of pervading light, a bent tree and an enraptured stare. Opposite *St Francis*, El Greco's *St Jerome* reproachfully surveys the riches all around, looking out to the South Hall, where an early Vermeer hangs – *Officer and Laughing Girl* – a masterful play on light.

Just a few blocks north, over on Madison Avenue at 75th Street, the **Whitney Museum of American Art** (Wed–Thurs, Sat & Sun 11am–6pm, Fri 1–9pm; $18, Fri 6–9pm pay what you wish; Ⓣ1-800/WHITNEY, Ⓦwww.whitney.org) boasts a pre-eminent collection of twentieth-century American art and a superb exhibition locale. Every other year the museum mounts the Whitney Biennial show of contemporary American art, always an exercise in provocation. When that's not on, enjoy the prominent Abstract Expressionists collection, with great works by high priests Pollock and De Kooning, leading on to Rothko and the Colour Field painters, and the later pop art works of Warhol, Johns and Oldenburg. The museum is especially strong on Hopper, O'Keeffe and Calder.

A ten-minute walk north from the Whitney, the **Guggenheim Museum**, Fifth Avenue at 89th Street (Sun–Wed & Fri 10am–5.45pm, Sat 10am–7.45pm; $18, Sat 5.45–7.45pm pay what you wish; Ⓣ212/423-3500, Ⓦwww.guggenheim.org), is better known for the building than its collection. Designed by Frank Lloyd Wright, this unique, curving structure caused a storm of controversy when it was unveiled in 1959. Its centripetal spiral ramp, which wends all the way to the top floor or, alternatively, from the top to the bottom, is still thought by some to favour Wright's talents over those of the exhibited artists. Much of the building is given over to temporary exhibitions, but the permanent collection includes work by Chagall, the major Cubists and, most completely, Kandinsky. Additionally, there are some late-nineteenth- and early-twentieth-century paintings, not least the exquisite Degas' *Dancers*, Modigliani's *Jeanne Héburene with Yellow Sweater* and Picasso's haunting *Woman Ironing*.

Two blocks up, at Fifth Avenue and 91st Street, lies the Smithsonian-run **Cooper-Hewitt, National Design Museum** (Mon–Thurs 10am–5pm, Fri 10am–9pm, Sat 10am–6pm, Sun noon–6pm; $15; Ⓣ212/849-8400, Ⓦcooperhewitt.org). This wonderful institution is the only museum in the US devoted exclusively to historic and contemporary design. Founded in 1897, it's housed in the magnificent mansion once owned by Andrew Carnegie and functions as a research centre as well as museum. North of here, the **Museo del Barrio**, 1230 Fifth Ave at 104th Street (Wed–Sun 11am–6pm; $6 suggested donation;

Ⓣ212/831-7272, Ⓦwww.elmuseo.org), showcases Latin American and Caribbean art and culture. The museum takes its name from **El Barrio** or Spanish Harlem, which collides head-on with the affluence of the Upper East Side around here. Traditionally the centre of a large Puerto Rican community, it remains one of the rougher parts of Manhattan.

About a thirty-minute walk away, at the far eastern end of 88th Street overlooking the East River, **Gracie Mansion** (tours Wed 10am, 11am, 1pm & 2pm; $7; Ⓣ212/570-4751), is one of the best-preserved colonial buildings in the city. Built in 1799, it has been the official residence of the mayor of New York City since 1942, when Fiorello LaGuardia, "man of the people" that he was, reluctantly set up house here – though "mansion" is a bit overblown for what's a rather cramped clapboard cottage.

The Upper West Side

North of 59th Street, Manhattan's West Side transitions from the hustle of Columbus Circle to the grandeur of Lincoln Center's cultural institutions, before morphing into a lively residential area. This is the **Upper West Side**, now one of the city's more desirable addresses, though in truth an area long favoured by artists and intellectuals.

Occupying a four-block plot west of Broadway between 62nd and 66th streets, the **Lincoln Center for the Performing Arts** (Ⓦnew.lincolncenter.org) is a marble assembly of buildings put up in the early 1960s on the site of some of the city's worst slums. Home to the Metropolitan Opera, the New York Philharmonic, the prestigious Juilliard School and a host of other companies (see p.104), the centre is worth seeing even if you don't catch a performance (tours daily 10.30am–4.30pm, leaving from the David Rubinstein Atrium on Broadway between 62nd and 63rd sts; $15; Ⓣ212/875-5350 to reserve). At the centre of the complex, the marble-and-glass **Metropolitan Opera House** showcases murals by Marc Chagall behind each of its high front windows.

The most famous of the monumental apartment buildings of **Central Park West** is the **Dakota**, a grandiose Renaissance-style mansion on 72nd Street, completed in 1884. Over the years, tenants have included Lauren Bacall and Leonard Bernstein, and in the late 1960s the building was used as the setting for Roman Polanski's film *Rosemary's Baby*. Now most people know it as the former home of **John Lennon** – and (still) of his wife Yoko Ono, who owns a number of the apartments. Outside the Dakota, on the night of December 8, 1980, Lennon was shot to death by a man who professed to be one of his greatest admirers (see p.90 to read about the nearby Lennon memorial in Central Park).

North up Central Park West, at 77th Street, the often-overlooked **New-York Historical Society** (Tues–Thurs & Sat 10am–6pm, Fri 10am–8pm, Sun 11am–5.45pm; $12, free Fri 6–8pm; Ⓣ212/873-3400, Ⓦwww.nyhistory.org) is more a museum of American than of New York history. Its collection includes paintings by naturalist James Audubon; a broad sweep of nineteenth-century American portraiture; Hudson River School landscapes; and a glittering display of Tiffany glass. Note that the museum is in the midst of major renovations, and portions will be closed through 2011; call or check the website ahead of your visit.

Up the street looms the **American Museum of Natural History**, on Central Park West at 79th Street (daily 10am–5.45pm; $16, children 2–12 $9; IMAX films, Hayden Planetarium & special exhibits extra; Ⓣ212/769-5100, Ⓦwww.amnh.org). This, the largest such museum in the world, is a strange architectural blend of heavy Neoclassical and rustic Romanesque styles covering four city blocks. The museum boasts superb nature dioramas and anthropological collections, interactive and multimedia displays and an awesome assemblage of bones, fossils and models.

Top attractions include the **Dinosaur Exhibit**, the massive totems in the **Hall of African Peoples**, the taxidermic marvels in **North American Mammals** (including a vividly staged bull and moose fight), and the two thousand gems in the **Hall of Meteorites**. The **Hall of Ocean Life** features a replica of, among other aquatic beings, a 94ft-long blue whale.

The **Rose Center for Earth and Space**, comprising the **Hall of the Universe** and the **Hayden Planetarium**, boasts all the latest technology and an innovative design, with open construction, spiral ramps and dramatic glass walls on three sides of the facility. The Planetarium screens the dramatic 30-minute "Journey to the Stars", narrated by Whoopi Goldberg (every half-hour 10.30am–4.30pm, except Wed from 11am and weekends until 5pm; $24, children $14, prices include museum admission).

After Central Park West, the Upper West Side's second-best address is **Riverside Drive**, which weaves its way from 72nd Street up the western edge of Manhattan, flanked by palatial townhouses put up in the early twentieth century and by **Riverside Park**, landscaped in 1873 by Frederick Law Olmsted, of Central Park fame. Riverside Drive makes the most pleasant route up to prestigious **Columbia University**, whose campus fills seven blocks between 114th and 121st streets and Amsterdam Avenue and Morningside Drive. Regular guided **tours** (Mon–Fri 1pm; free) start from the visitors centre, in room 213 of the stately Low Library, in the heart of the campus.

At Amsterdam Avenue and 112th Street, the **Cathedral Church of St John the Divine** (Mon–Sat 7am–6pm, Sun 7am–7pm; free), rises up with a solid kind of majesty. A curious, somewhat eerie mix of Romanesque and Gothic styles, the church was begun in 1892, though building stopped with the outbreak of war in 1939 and only resumed, sporadically, from the late 1970s into the late 1990s; today, with no ongoing construction, it's barely two-thirds finished.

Harlem

Home to a culturally and historically – if not economically – rich black community, **Harlem** is still a focus of black activism and culture, and well worth seeing. Up until recently, because of a near-total lack of support from federal and municipal funds, Harlem formed a self-reliant and inward-looking community. For many downtown Manhattanites, white and black, 125th Street was a physical and mental border not willingly crossed. Today, the fruits of a co-operative effort involving businesses, residents and City Hall are manifest in new housing, retail and community projects. But while brownstones triple in value, there remain problems of how to deal with the area's evolution and gentrification, as well as the poverty and unemployment still in evidence.

Harlem's sights are very spread out; it's not a bad idea to get acquainted with the area via a **guided tour** (see p.71) and follow that up with further trips. Harlem's working centre is 125th Street, between Broadway and Fifth Avenue, anchored by the famous **Apollo Theater**, 253 West 125th St, for many years the nexus of black entertainment in the Northeast (tours Mon, Tues, Thurs & Fri 11am, 1pm, 3pm; Wed 11am; Sat & Sun 11am & 1pm; $16 Mon–Fri, $18 Sat & Sun; ⓣ212/531-5337). Almost all the great jazz, blues and soul figures played here – James Brown recorded his seminal *Live at the Apollo* album in 1962 – though a larger attraction today is Wednesday Amateur Night, open to all (7.30pm; $17–27; ⓣ212/531-5300). At 144 West 125th St, the **Studio Museum in Harlem**

(Wed–Fri & Sun noon–6pm, Sat 10am–6pm; $7; ⓣ212/864-4500, ⓦwww.studiomuseum.org) is a small but vibrant collection of African and African-American art from all eras.

One avenue block east, the **Schomburg Center for Research in Black Culture**, 515 Malcolm X Blvd at 135th Street (exhibitions Mon–Sat 10am–6pm, other parts open later, call ahead; free; ⓣ212/491-2200, ⓦwww.nypl.org/research/sc), has displays on black history and literally millions of artefacts, manuscripts, artworks and photographs in its archives. Meanwhile, just north, at 132 West 138th St, is the **Abyssinian Baptist Church**, famed for its revival-style Sunday morning services and a gospel choir of gut-busting vivacity. Cross over west to 138th Street, between Powell Boulevard and Eighth Avenue, and you're in what many consider the finest block of rowhouses in Manhattan – **Strivers' Row** – commissioned during the 1890s housing boom and designed by three sets of architects. Within the burgeoning black community at the turn of the last century, this came to be the desirable place for ambitious professionals to reside – hence its moniker.

Washington Heights and the Cloisters

North of Harlem, starting from West 145th Street or so, is the neighbourhood of **Washington Heights**, an area that evolved from poor farmland to highly sought-after real estate in the early part of the twentieth century. Today, the area is home to the largest Dominican population in the US, and while its points of interest are safely accessed during daylight hours, it's advisable to stay clear of the area after dark.

A real surprise lies on 160th Street, between Amsterdam and Edgecombe avenues: the **Morris–Jumel Mansion**, the oldest house in Manhattan (Wed–Sun 10am–4pm; $5; ⓣ212/923-8008, ⓦwww.morrisjumel.org). With its proud Georgian outlines (faced by a later Federal portico), it was built as a rural retreat in 1765 by Colonel Roger Morris and served briefly as George Washington's headquarters. Later, wine merchant Stephen Jumel bought the mansion and refurbished it for his wife Eliza, formerly a prostitute and his mistress. When Jumel died in 1832, Eliza married ex-vice president Aaron Burr, twenty years her senior. The marriage lasted six months; Burr died on the day of their divorce while Eliza battled on to the age of 91. On the top floor you'll find her obituary, a magnificently fictionalized account of a "scandalous" life.

It's worth continuing up to the northern tip of Manhattan for **The Cloisters** in Fort Tryon Park. This reconstructed monastic complex houses the pick of the Metropolitan Museum's (see p.90) medieval collection – take subway A to 190th Street/Fort Washington Avenue (Tues–Sun: March–Oct 9.30am–5.15pm; Nov–Feb 9.30am–4.45pm; suggested donation $20, students $10, includes admission to the Metropolitan Museum on the same day; ⓣ212/923-3700, ⓦwww.metmuseum.org). Among its larger artefacts are a monumental Romanesque Hall made up of French remnants and a frescoed Spanish Fuentidueña Chapel, both from the thirteenth century, as well as the famed "Unicorn Tapestries".

The outer boroughs

Many visitors to New York don't stray off Manhattan, but if you're staying a while, choose to investigate the **outer boroughs** and you'll be well rewarded. **Brooklyn** is certainly worth a trip, primarily for Brooklyn Heights just across the East River, bucolic Prospect Park and the Brooklyn Museum. For inveterate nostalgics, Coney Island and its Russian neighbour, Brighton Beach, lie at the far end of the subway line. Few indeed make it to **Queens**, though the borough holds the bustling Greek community of Astoria, the increasingly hip neighbourhood of Long Island City and the Museum of the Moving Image. The **Bronx**, renowned for the desolate and bleak environs of its southern reaches, which are in fact slowly improving, has the city's largest zoo, Yankee Stadium and another glorious botanical garden. **Staten Island** is primarily a sleepy residential community, with little in the way of sights (see p.77 for the **Staten Island** ferry).

Brooklyn

Until the early 1800s, **Brooklyn** was no more than a group of autonomous towns and villages, but Robert Fulton's steamship service across the East River changed all that, starting with the establishment of a leafy retreat at Brooklyn Heights. What really transformed things, though, was the opening of the Brooklyn Bridge on May 24, 1883. Thereafter, development spread deeper inland, as housing was needed to service a more commercialized Manhattan. By 1900, Brooklyn was fully established as part of the newly incorporated New York City, and its fate as Manhattan's perennial kid brother was sealed.

Brooklyn Heights (#2, #3, #4, #5, R to Court St-Borough Hall, or simply walk from Manhattan over the Brooklyn Bridge), one of New York City's most beautiful neighbourhoods, has little in common with the rest of the borough. Begin your tour at the **Esplanade** – more commonly known as the **Promenade** – with its fine Manhattan views across the water. **Pierrepoint** and **Montague** streets, the Heights' main arteries, are studded with delightful brownstones, restaurants, bars and shops. Below the Esplanade is the still-in-development **Brooklyn Bridge Park**, where Piers 1 and 6 have playgrounds and waterparks looking out on the waterfront. Just north, **DUMBO** is an artsy neighbourhood where the factories have mostly become condos; it boasts galleries, performance spaces and a lovely waterfront strip.

Farther into Brooklyn, Flatbush Avenue leads to **Grand Army Plaza** (#2 or #3 to the eponymous subway station), a grandiose junction laid out by Calvert Vaux (co-designer of Central Park) in the late nineteenth century as a dramatic entry-point to the newly unveiled Prospect Park just beyond. The triumphal **Soldiers and Sailors' Memorial Arch**, a tribute to the Union victory in the Civil War, was added thirty years later.

The enormous swath of green that rolls forth from behind the arch is **Prospect Park**. Landscaped in the early 1890s, the park remains an ideal place for exercise, picnics and family gatherings. During the day it's perfectly safe, but it's best to stay clear of the park at night. The adjacent **Brooklyn Botanic Garden** (March–Oct Tues–Fri 8am–6pm, Sat & Sun 10am–6pm; Nov–Feb Tues–Fri 8am–4.30pm, Sat & Sun 10am–4.30pm; $8, free all day Tues & Sat before noon; ⓣ718/623-7200, ⓦwww.bbg.org), one of the city's most enticing park and garden spaces, is smaller and more immediately likeable than its more celebrated cousin in the Bronx. Sumptuous but not overplanted, its 52 acres comprise a Rose Garden, Japanese Garden, Shakespeare Garden and delightful lawns draped with weeping willows and beds of flowering shrubs.

Though doomed to stand in the shadow of the Met, the **Brooklyn Museum**, 200 Eastern Parkway (#2 or #3 to Eastern Parkway; Wed–Fri 10am–5pm, Sat & Sun 11am–6pm, first Sat of every month 11am–11pm; $10, students $6; ⓣ718/638-5000, ⓦwww.brooklynmuseum.org), is a major museum and a good reason to forsake Manhattan for an afternoon. Highlights include the Egyptian antiquities on the third floor and, on the fourth floor, Judy Chicago's *The Dinner Party* and the American period rooms. A floor up, works by Charles Sheeler and

Georgia O'Keeffe head the American Identities exhibition, but just as fascinating is the Visible Storage section, an array of Americana objects behind glass that are part of the museum holdings but not in normal rotation.

Generations of working-class New Yorkers have come to relax at one of Brooklyn's farthest points, **Coney Island** (Ⓦwww.coneyislandusa.com), reachable from Manhattan on the D, F, N or Q subway lines (45min–1hr). Undeniable highlights include the 1927 wooden roller coaster, the **Cyclone** ($8), and the 90-year-old **Wonder Wheel** ($6). The beach, a broad swath of golden sand, is beautiful, although it is often crowded on hot days and the water might be less than clean. In late June, catch the **Mermaid Parade**, one of the country's oddest and glitziest small-town fancy-dress parades, which culminates here. Meanwhile, the **New York Aquarium** on the boardwalk opened in 1896 and is still going strong, showcasing fish and invertebrates from the world over in its darkened halls, along with open-air displays (April–May & Sept–Oct Mon–Fri daily 10am–5.30pm; June–Aug Mon–Fri 10am–6pm, Sat & Sun till 7pm; Nov–March daily 10am–4.30pm; $13, $9 for kids 3–12; Ⓣ718/265-3474, Ⓦwww.nyaquarium.com).

Further east along the boardwalk, **Brighton Beach**, or "Little Odessa", is home to the country's largest community of Russian émigrés and a long-established, largely elderly Jewish population. Livelier than Coney Island, it's also more prosperous, especially along its main drag, **Brighton Beach Avenue**, which runs underneath the Q subway line in a hodgepodge of food shops and appetizing restaurants. In the evening, the restaurants become a near-parody of a rowdy Russian night out, with loud live music and the frenzied knocking back of vodka.

Queens

Named in honour of the wife of Charles II of England, **Queens** was one of the rare places where postwar immigrants could buy their own homes and establish their own communities (**Astoria**, for example, holds the world's largest concentration of Greeks outside Greece). Other than exploring the ethnic neighbourhoods here, the major attraction in Queens is the **American Museum of the Moving Image**, in the old Paramount complex in Astoria, at 35th Avenue and 36th Street (M or R to Steinway; call or check website for new hours Ⓣ718/784-0077, Ⓦwww.ammi.org). The museum, devoted to the history of film, video and TV, just completed a major renovation that added an adjacent three-storey building with a theatre and education centre. The core exhibit, "Behind the Screen", contains more than 125,000 objects, including old movie cameras and special-effects equipment; early televisions; all kinds of costumes and props, including the chariot from *Ben Hur*; fan magazines, posters and enough *Star Wars* action figures to make an obsessed fan drool with envy. There's a real focus on interactivity, too, as you have the opportunity to create a short animated film, make a soundtrack and see how live television is edited.

Nearby in Long Island City, **MoMA PS1**, 22–25 Jackson Ave at 46th Street (Thurs–Mon noon–6pm; $5, free with a MoMA ticket from the last 30 days; Ⓣ718/784-2084, Ⓦwww.ps1.org), is one of the oldest and biggest organizations in the US devoted exclusively to contemporary art and leading emerging artists.

The Bronx

The city's northernmost and only mainland borough, **The Bronx** was for a long time believed to be its toughest and most crime-ridden district. In fact, it's not much different from the other outer boroughs, though geographically it has more in common with Westchester County to the north than it does with the island regions of New York City: steep hills, deep valleys and rocky outcroppings to the west, and marshy flatlands along Long Island Sound to the east. Settled in the seventeenth century by the Swede Jonas Bronk, it became, like Brooklyn, part of New York proper around the end of the nineteenth century. Its main thoroughfare, **Grand Concourse**, was lined with luxurious Art Deco apartment houses; many, though greatly run-down, still stand. Just off the Grand Concourse, the new **Yankee Stadium**, at 161st Street and River Avenue (Ⓣ718/293-4300, Ⓦnewyork.yankees.mlb.com), is home to the most winning team in professional sports, 27-time World Series champs the New York Yankees.

Further north, the **Bronx Zoo** (April–Oct Mon–Fri 10am–5pm, Sat & Sun 10am–5.30pm; Nov–March daily 10am–4.30pm; $15, kids $11, pay-what-you-wish every Wed; Ⓣ718/220-5100, Ⓦwww.bronxzoo.com) is accessible either by its main gate on Fordham Road or by a second entrance on Bronx Park South. The latter is the entrance to use if you come directly here by subway (#2 or #5 to East Tremont Ave). With over four thousand animals, it's the largest urban zoo in the US, and is better than most; it was one of the first institutions of its kind to realize that animals both looked and felt better out in the open. The "Wild Asia" exhibit is an almost-forty-acre wilderness through which tigers, elephants and deer roam relatively free, visible from a monorail (May–Oct; $4). Look in also on the colobus monkeys and baboons in the innovative "Congo Gorilla Forest", "Himalayan Highlands", with endangered species such as the red panda and snow leopard, and "Tiger Mountain", which allows visitors the opportunity to get up close and personal with Siberian tigers.

Across the road from the zoo's main entrance is the back turnstile of the **New York Botanical Gardens** (Tues–Sun 10am–6pm; $20, gardens only $6; Ⓣ718/817-8700, Ⓦwww.nybg.org), in parts as wild as anything you're likely to see upstate. Don't miss its Enid A. Haupt Conservatory, a turn-of-the-century crystal palace featuring a stunning 90ft dome, beautiful reflecting pool, lots of tropical plants and seasonal displays.

Eating

There isn't anything you can't eat in New York, and New Yorkers take their food very seriously, obsessed with new cuisines, new dishes and new restaurants. Certain areas hold pockets of ethnic restaurants, especially in the outer boroughs, but you can generally find whatever you want, wherever (and whenever) you want.

Downtown Manhattan (below 14th St)

Bridge Café 279 Water St, at Dover St Ⓣ212/227-3344. Subway #4, #5, #6 to Brooklyn Bridge. This is the city's oldest surviving tavern, opening in 1847 (the building is 50 years older), but now an upmarket restaurant. The crabcakes are excellent, as is the list of microbrew beers. Entrees $23–34.

Caffè Reggio 119 MacDougal St, between Bleecker and W 3rd sts Ⓣ212/475-9557. Subway A, B, C, D, E, M to W 4th St. One of the first Village coffeehouses, dating back to 1927, embellished with all sorts of Italian antiques and paintings. Sip an espresso and pretend the bohemian spirit still lives.

Corner Bistro 331 W 4th St, at Jane St Ⓣ212/242-9502. Subway A, C, E, L to 14th St. This down-to-earth tavern serves some of the best burgers and fries in town ($6.75 for burger, couple of bucks for the fries), along with cheap beer. An excellent place to unwind and refuel in a friendly neighbourhood atmosphere, though it can get quite crowded.

Graffiti Food & Wine Bar 244 E 10th St, between First and Second aves Ⓣ212/677-0695. Subway #6 to Astor Place. Chef Jehangir Mehta cooks up a fusion of Chinese,

American and Indian flavours in this artsy space, with just four tables and courses ranging from $7–15: chickpea-crusted skate and cumin eggplant buns grace the menu. Closed Mon.

Grandaisy Bakery 250 W Broadway at Beach St; also 73 Sullivan St near Spring St and 176 W 72nd St ⓣ212/334-9435. Subway: #1 to Franklin St (Tribeca location). The best coffee in Tribeca comes with some fabulous extras; tasty vegetarian pizza slices featuring cauliflower, potato, tomato and zucchini, as well as superb pastries.

Great N.Y. Noodletown 28 1/2 Bowery, at Bayard St ⓣ212/349-0923. Subway B, D to Grand St; #6 to Canal St. Best during soft-shell crab season (May–Aug), when the crustaceans are cooked crispy and salty ($16). The roast meats and other salt-baked seafood are good year round.

Il Posto Accanto 190 E 2nd St between aves A and B. Subway F to Lower East Side-Second Ave. Nab a spot at a high wooden table at this small, intimate wine bar serving a vast array of Italian reds by the glass. You can easily make a meal from the excellent small plates of pasta ($12–15), panini ($8) and the like. Can get crowded, like its popular parent restaurant next door (*Il Bagatto*).

Ippudo 65 Fourth Ave, between 9th and 10th sts. Subway #6 to Astor Place. The first overseas outpost of Fukuoka-based "ramen king" Shigemi Kawahara, this popular Japanese ramen shop offers steaming bowls of classic *tonkotsu*-style noodles for around $13–14 in booths and at communal wooden tables, as well as tasty pork buns and roast chicken appetizers.

Katz's Delicatessen 205 E Houston St, at Ludlow St ⓣ212/254-2246. Subway F to Second Ave. Venerable Lower East Side Jewish deli serving archetypal overstuffed pastrami and corned-beef sandwiches (around $15). Best known as the site of the orgasm scene in *When Harry Met Sally*.

Kesté Pizza & Vino 271 Bleecker St, between Jones and Cornelia sts. Subway A, B, C, D, F, M to W 4th St. Newest pizzeria on the block, stirring things up with its Neapolitan-designed wood-fire oven; try the original Mast'nicola (lardo, pecorino romano and basil; $9) or lip-smacking Pizza de Papa (butternut squash cream, smoked mozzarella and artichoke; $16).

Locanda Verde 377 Greenwich St, at N Moore St ⓣ212/925-3797, ⓦlocandaverdenyc.com. Subway #1 to Franklin St. This casual Italian taverna is a showcase for star chef Andrew Carmellini's exceptional creations; try the porchetta sandwich ($17), stuffed mountain trout ($26) or his fabulous pastas ($17–19).

Lombardi's 32 Spring St, between Mott and Mulberry sts ⓣ212/941-7994. Subway #6 to Spring St. The oldest pizzeria in Manhattan serves some of the best pizzas town (from $19.50) – try the amazing clam topping. No slices, though.

Magnolia Bakery 401 Bleecker St, at W 11th St ⓣ212/462-2572. Subway #1 to Christopher St. There are lots of baked goods on offer here, but everyone comes for the heavenly and deservedly famous multi-coloured cupcakes (celebrated in both *Sex and the City* and *Saturday Night Live*), $2.75 each. Lines can stretch around the block.

Momofuku Noodle Bar 171 First Ave, between E 10th and E 11th sts ⓣ212/777-7773. Subway #6 to Astor Place. Celebrated chef David Chang's first restaurant, where his simplest creations are still the best: silky steamed pork buns, laced with hoisin sauce and pickled cucumbers ($9), or steaming bowls of chicken and pork ramen noodles ($10).

Nobu 105 Hudson St, at Franklin St ⓣ212/219-0500. Subway #1 to Franklin St. Superlative Japanese cuisine such as black cod with miso ($26) and chilled sake served in hollow bamboo trunks. If prices or the difficult-to-get reservations put you off, try the somewhat cheaper *Next Door Nobu*, literally next door.

Num Pang 21 E 12th St at University Place ⓣ212/255-3271. Subway #4, #5, #6, L, N, Q, R to Union Square. Superb Cambodian-style sandwiches served on freshly toasted semolina flour baguettes with chili mayo and home-made pickles; try the pulled duroc pork or peppercorn catfish (both $7.50).

Rice to Riches 37 Spring St, between Mott and Mulberry sts ⓣ212/274-0008. Subway #6 to Spring St. Rice pudding made hip and utterly irresistible, served up in this funky takeaway space, from peanut butter and chocolate chip, to mango and cinnamon flavours. Bowls start at $6.75.

Shopsin's Essex St Market, 120 Essex St (no phone). Subway F to Delancey St; J, Z to Essex St. Something of a New York institution, Kenny Shopsin ran his famously idiosyncratic diner in the West Village for years (no cell phones or parties of five), but was forced down here by high rents. His addictive creations – like peanut-butter-filled pancakes – have a loyal following. Closed Sun & Mon.

Veselka 144 Second Ave, at 9th St ⓣ212/228-9682. Subway #6 to Astor Place. The terrific grilled *kielbasa* (Polish sausage, $14.75), Ukrainian pierogi (stuffed dumplings, $6.75–10.50) and hearty soups ($3.50–4.75) are great for sopping up alcohol and killing hunger pangs at 4am. Daily 24hr.

Midtown Manhattan (14th St to 59th St)

Unless otherwise stated all of the establishments listed below can be found on the map on p.85.

15 East 15 E 15th St between Fifth Ave and Broadway ⓣ212/647-0015, ⓦwww.15eastrestaurant.com. Subway #4, #5, #6, L, N, Q, R to 14th St/Union Square. See map on p.79. The attention given to both cooked dishes like slow-poached octopus ($12) and sea urchin risotto ($24), and the fresh sushi and sashimi (chef's selection of either $55) help elevate this stylish Japanese restaurant to among the top in the city.

Aldea 31 W 17th St between Fifth and Sixth aves ⓣ212/675-7223, ⓦwww.aldearestaurant.com. Subway F, M to 14th St. See map on p.79. In a cool, relaxed dining room, Portuguese-accented dishes come exquisitely prepared and full of flavour – say, duck confit with crisped duck skin and chorizo, or cod with braised chickpeas. Entrees $24–29, three-course *prix-fixe* lunch $24.

Aquavit 65 E 55th St, between Madison and Park aves ⓣ212/307-7311, ⓦwww.aquavit.org. Subway E, M to Fifth Ave/53rd St. Go for a blowout in the main dining room or a more casual, and much less expensive, meal in the bistro of this renowned Scandinavian restaurant. Your best opportunity to try the silky gravlax and herring every which way, though, is probably at the Sunday smorgasbord ($48), a good time to stuff yourself silly. Reserve well ahead.

Eisenberg's Sandwich Shop 174 Fifth Ave, at 22nd St. Subway N, R to 23rd St. See map on p.79. A colourful luncheonette, this shop has been serving cheesy Reubens ($8.50), great tuna sandwiches ($7.25), matzoh-ball soup and old-fashioned fountain sodas at a well-worn counter since 1930. Closes at 8pm weekdays, earlier on weekends.

Gramercy Tavern 42 E 20th St, between Broadway and Park Ave ⓣ212/477-0777. Subway #6 to 23rd St. See map on p.79. Its neo-colonial decor, exquisite New American cuisine and perfect service make for a memorable meal ($86–112 depending on à la carte or tasting menu). The lively front room is a great place to drop in for a drink, or more casual (and cheaper) dining.

La Lunchonette 130 Tenth Ave, at W 18th St ⓣ212/675-0342. See map on p.79. Subway A, C, E, L to 14th St. Understated, real-deal French restaurant, serving lamb sausage with sautéed apples ($15.50), skate wing ($16.50) and steak au poivre ($24), though the specialty is slow-cooked cassoulet (not always available).

La Nacional 239 W 14th St, between Seventh and Eighth aves ⓣ212/243-9308. Subway #1, #2, #3, A, C, E, L to 14th St. See map on p.79. Home of the Spanish Benevolent Society, *La Nacional* retains the feel of a club while being open to all comers. Try *croquetas* ($8), shrimp with garlic sauce ($9) and top-notch paella ($18).

Maialino *Gramercy Park Hotel*, 2 Lexington Ave ⓣ212/777-2410, ⓦwww.maialinonyc.com. Subway #6 to 23rd St. See map on p.79. If a place can be both rustic and refined, Danny Meier's attractive Roman trattoria is it. Much of the focus is on the hog (which gives the place its name) – there's excellent cured salumi ($7–16), tripe ($12), pasta with *guanciale* ($15) or suckling pig ragu ($19), pig's foot ($21) and, as a special, roast suckling pig – but everything's well prepared and desserts are exceptional. Reservations essential.

New York Kom Tang 32 W 32nd St, between Broadway and Fifth Ave ⓣ212/947-8482. Subway B, D, F, M to 34th St–Herald Square. There's fresh sushi or sashimi ($22.95/$39.95) and excellent grill-it-yourself barbecue (*kalbi* $24.99), but the rich, bountiful soups are the stars – everything from oxtail ($13.95) to young chicken with ginseng ($19.95). Good lunch deals. 24hr; closed Sun.

Oyster Bar Lower level, Grand Central Station ⓣ212/490-6650. Subway #4, #5, #6, #7 to Grand Central–42nd St. This wonderfully atmospheric old place, down in the vaulted dungeons of Grand Central, features a staggering menu of daily catches – she-crab bisque ($6.95), steamed Maine lobster (market price by the pound) and sweet Kumamoto oysters ($2.95 each). Prices are moderate to expensive; you can eat more cheaply at the bar.

Prime Burger 5 E 51st St between Madison and Fifth aves. Subway E, M to Fifth Ave/53rd St. This classic coffeeshop makes a nice stopoff before or after a MoMA or Rockefeller Center visit. Fit yourself in one of the retro swivel tables, order one or two of the juicy namesakes ($5.25 and up) and try to save room for a piece of pie.

Shake Shack Madison Square Park. Subway #6, N, R to 23rd St. Wildly popular food kiosk, with long lines for the perfectly grilled burgers and frozen-custard shakes. You can also buy beer and wine to sip outside, with everything around $7 or less. Closes at 7pm in winter; until 11pm the rest of the year.

Virgil's Real BBQ 152 W 44th St, between Sixth and Seventh aves ⓣ212/921-9494. Subway #1, #2, #3, #7, B, D, F, M, N, Q, R to 42nd St. *Virgil's*, one of New York's earliest entries in the BBQ game, is one of the few Times Square eateries that's not just for tourists. All the food groups – Memphis ribs ($24.95), Carolina pulled pork ($20.50), Texas brisket ($22.50), Maryland ham ($18.50) – are well represented, and you'll likely be able to skip breakfast in the morning.

Yakitori Totto 251 W 55th St (second floor), between Broadway and Eighth Ave ⓣ212/245-4555. Subway #1, A, B, C, D to 59th St/Columbus Circle; N, Q, R to 57th St or B, D, E to Seventh Ave. This popular hideaway is perfect for late-night snacking – though by that time some of the more esoteric offerings might be gone. Still, grilled skewers of chicken heart, skirt steak and chicken thigh with scallion, along with some sides and a cold Sapporo draft, make a nice meal.

Uptown Manhattan (60th St and above)

Africa Kine 256 W 116th St between Douglass and Powell blvds ⓣ212/666-9400. Subway B, C to 116th St. Best place on the emerging Little Senegal strip to try authentic West African and Senegalese dishes, such as lamb curry, lamb and peanut butter stew and spicy fish with okra ($10–15). Daily until 2am.

Amy Ruth's 113 W 116th St, between Lenox and Seventh aves ⓣ212/280-8779. The BBQ fried chicken ($13.25), named in honour of President Obama, is reason enough to travel to this casual, family restaurant in Harlem.

Barney Greengrass 541 Amsterdam Ave, between 86th and 87th sts. Subway #1 to 86th St. The "sturgeon king" is an Upper West Side fixture; the deli (and restaurant) have been around since time began. The smoked-salmon section is a particular treat.

Café Sabarsky in the Neue Galerie 1048 Fifth Ave, at E 86th St ⓣ212/288-0665. Subway #4, #5, #6 to 86th St. Sumptuous decor that harkens back to Old Vienna fills the handsome parlour of the former Vanderbilt mansion. The menu includes superb pastries, like *Linzertorte* and strudels ($8), and small sandwiches ($12), many made with cured meats.

Heidelberg 1648 Second Ave, between E 85th and 86th sts ⓣ212/628-2332. Subway #4, #5, #6 to 86th St. At one of the last Yorkville German joints, the food is authentic even if the atmosphere a bit kitsch: excellent liver dumpling soup, Bauernfruestuck omelets and potato pancakes (entrees $16.95–24.95). Have a huge, boot-shaped glass of Weissbier with anything.

Hungarian Pastry Shop 1030 Amsterdam Ave, between W 110th and 111th sts. Subway #1 to 110th St. This simple, no-frills coffeehouse is a favourite with Columbia University affiliates. You can sip your espresso and read Proust all day if you like (madeleines, anyone?); the only problem is choosing among the home-made pastries, cookies and cakes.

Persephone 115 E 60th St, between Park and Lexington aves ⓣ212/339-8363. Subway #4, #5, #6 to 59th St. One of the best Greek tavernas in the city, with salty fried sheep's-milk cheese, rabbit stew, moussaka and grilled lamb ranging from $17–26; the $24.95 *prix-fixe* three-course lunch is a great deal.

Recipe 425 Amsterdam Ave between 81st and 82nd sts ⓣ212/501-7755, ⓦwww.recipenyc.com. Subway #1 to 79th St. The focus is squarely on local farm-fresh ingredients in this slip of a restaurant, with industrial-meets-country decor. The prices are reasonable (entrees $17–24; great *prix-fixe* lunch $11.95), and the dishes, from the foie gras terrine ($10) to the crisp and tender duck ($22) hit the mark with frequency.

Rosa Mexicano 61 Columbus Ave, between W 62nd and 63rd sts ⓣ212/977-7700. Subway #1, A, B, C, D to 59th St-Columbus Circle. Right across from Lincoln Center, it's the perfect location for a post-opera meal. Try the guacamole ($14/order), which is mashed at your table, and their signature pomegranate margaritas ($11).

The outer boroughs

Agnanti Meze 19–06 Ditmars Blvd, Astoria, Queens ⓣ718/545-4554. Subway N, Q to Astoria-Ditmars Blvd. Specializing in Greek meze – small plates for snacking – this restaurant overlooks Astoria Park. Don't miss the "specialties from Constantinople" section of the menu, with goodies like *bekri-meze*, wine-soaked cubes of tender meat. There's a second location in Bay Ridge, Brooklyn.

Café Glechik 3159 Coney Island Ave, between Brighton Beach Ave and 10th St ⓣ718/616-0494, ⓦwww.glechik.com. Subway B, Q to Brighton Beach. A refreshing break from flashier places in the neighbourhood (go to *Primorski* or *Rasputin* if you want the full monty, so to speak), this *tchotchke*-laden Ukrainian restaurant is known for its dumplings – *pelmeni* and *vareniki* ($5–8) – as well as its borscht ($5), stews ($9–15) and stuffed cabbage ($9). Cash only.

Frankies 457 Spuntino 457 Court St, at Luquer St, Carroll Gardens, Brooklyn; another location on Lower East Side ⓣ718/403-0033, ⓦwww.frankiesspuntino.com. Subway F, G to Carroll St. Co-chefs Frank and Frank revive and refine Italian-American favourites on the south side of Carroll Gardens. Home-made pastas ($13–17) are the way to go, coupled with a fresh salad of seasonal greens and a few crostini. Cash only; no reservations except for large groups.

Nathan's 1310 Surf Ave at Schweiker's Walk, Coney Island, Brooklyn ⓣ718/946-2202. Subway D, F, N, Q to Coney Island-Stillwell

Ave. Home of the "famous Coney Island hot dog", served since 1916, *Nathan's* is not to be missed (unless you're a vegetarian). Its annual Hot Dog Eating Contest is held on July 4.

Pies and Thighs 166 S 4th St, at Driggs Ave, Williamsburg, Brooklyn ⓣ347/529-6090. Subway J, Z to Marcy Ave. This once underground institution has found a bright corner location in which to serve its southern-style food: great chicken biscuits ($5), expertly fried chicken ($11 with a side) and a changing rotation of pies (slice $4.50; key lime and rhubarb are a few favourites).

Peter Luger Steak House 178 Broadway, at Driggs Ave, Williamsburg, Brooklyn ⓣ718/387-7400. Subway J, M, Z to Marcy Ave. Catering to carnivores since 1887, *Peter Luger's* may just be the city's finest steakhouse. The service is surly and the decor plain, but the porterhouse steak – the only cut served – is divine (roughly $42.50/person for just the meat). Cash only.

Drinking

New York's best **bars** are, generally speaking, in **Downtown Manhattan** – the West and East villages, Soho and the Lower East Side – and in outer-borough hoods like Williamsburg, Red Hook and Long Island City. Most of the ones listed below serve food of some kind and have happy hours sometime between 4pm and 8pm during the week. See also the bars listed in "Gay New York," p.107.

Downtown Manhattan (to 14th St)

55 Bar 55 Christopher St, between Sixth and Seventh aves ⓣ212/929-9883. Subway #1 to Christopher St. A gem of an underground dive-bar that's been around since the days of Prohibition, with a great jukebox, congenial clientele and live jazz music seven nights a week.

8th St Winecellar 28 W 8th St, between Fifth Ave and MacDougal St ⓣ212/260-9463. Subway A, B, C, D, E, F, M to W 4th St. Simple, clean space with wooden tables and knowledgeable bartenders; fabulous wine selection, with most bottles in the $30–40 range (and 20 by the glass from $8).

Barrio Chino 253 Broome St, at Orchard St ⓣ212/228-6710. Subway B, D to Canal St. Don't be confused by the Chinese lanterns or drink umbrellas here – the owner's specialty is tequila, and there are a dozen brands to choose from. Shots are served with a traditional sangria chaser, made from a blend of tomato, orange and lime juices.

Blind Tiger Ale House 281 Bleecker St, at Jones St ⓣ212/462-4682. Subway A, B, C, D, E, F, M to W 4th St; #1 to Christopher St. This wood-panelled pub is the home of serious ale connoisseurs, with 28 rotating drafts, a couple of casks and loads of bottled beers – they also serve cheese plates from *Murray's* (see p.109). Tends to get packed.

Bourgeois Pig 111 E 7th St, between First Ave and Ave A ⓣ212/475-2246. Subway L to First Ave; #6 to Astor Place. The decadent Versailles theme at this funky wine bar, replete with wall-size mirrors, chandeliers and crimson satin couches, is backed by an extensive cocktail menu (using just wines, beers and champagne).

Ear Inn 326 Spring St, between Washington and Greenwich sts ⓣ212/226-9060. Subway C, E to Spring St; #1 to Houston St. This historic pub, a stone's throw from the Hudson River, opened in 1890 (the building dates from 1817). Its creaky interior is as cosy as a Cornish inn, with a good mix of beers on tap and basic, reasonably priced American food.

Fanelli's Café 94 Prince St, at Mercer St ⓣ212/226-9412. Subway N, R to Prince St. Established in 1922 (the building dates from 1853), *Fanelli* is another of the city's oldest bars. Relaxed and informal, it's a favourite destination of the not-too-hip after-work crowd.

Grassroots Tavern 20 St Mark's Place, between Second and Third aves ⓣ212/475-9443. Subway #6 to Astor Place. This roomy, wooden and wonderful underground den has an extended happy hour, popcorn for a buck and the manager's pets roaming around at all times of the day.

Happy Ending Lounge 302 Broome St, between Eldridge and Forsyth sts ⓣ212/334-9676. Subway J, Z to Bowery; B, D to Grand St. A former erotic massage parlour has been reborn as an exceptionally cool bar and club, with the original tiled sauna rooms downstairs converted to cosy booths. Drinks $8–12.

Max Fish 178 Ludlow St, between Houston and Stanton sts ⓣ212/529-3959. Subway F to Second Ave. Local hipsters come here in droves, lured by the unpretentious but arty vibe, pinball machine, pool table and good jukebox.

McSorley's Old Ale House 15 E 7th St, between Second and Third aves ⓣ212/472-9148. Subway #6 to Astor Place. Yes, it's touristy and often full of local frat boys, but you'll be drinking at a landmark that served its first beer in 1854.

Temple Bar 332 Lafayette St, between Bleecker and Houston sts ⓣ212/925-4242. Subway #6 to Bleecker St. One of the most discreet and romantic spots for a drink anywhere in the city, this sumptuous, dark lounge evokes 1940s glamour. They take their martinis very seriously.

White Horse Tavern 567 Hudson St, at W 11th St ⓣ212/243-9260. Subway #1 to Christopher St. A Greenwich Village institution, opening in 1880: Dylan Thomas supped his last here before being carted off to hospital, while Norman Mailer and Hunter S. Thompson were also regulars.

Midtown Manhattan (14th St to 59th St)

Unless otherwise stated all of the establishments listed below can be found on the map on p.85.

Campbell Apartment Southwest balcony, Grand Central Terminal ⓣ212/953-0409. Subway #4, #5, #6, #7 to Grand Central-42nd St. The former home of businessman John W. Campbell – built to look like a Florentine palace – has been given a snappy refit by designer Nina Campbell and is one of New York's most distinctive cocktail bars. Go early, bring a chunk of cash and don't wear sneakers.

El Quinto Pino 401 W 24th St at Ninth Ave. Subway C, E to 23rd St. There are relatively few seats in this elegant tapas bar, so come early to nibble on pork cracklings ($6) and an uncanny sea urchin sandwich ($15), paired up with a good selection of Spanish wines.

Jimmy's Corner 140 W 44th St, between Broadway and Sixth Ave ⓣ212/221-9510. Subway #1, #2, #3, B, D, F, M, N, R, Q to 42nd St. The walls of this long, narrow corridor of a bar, one of the most characterful dives in the city, are a virtual boxing hall of fame; it's owned by ex-fighter and trainer Jimmy Glenn.

King Cole Bar 2 E 55th St, between Fifth and Madison aves, in the *St Regis* hotel. Subway E, M to Fifth Ave/53rd St. You might want to dress smart and be ready to spend at the reputed home of the Bloody Mary, but sipping a cocktail at a table or under the Maxfield Parrish mural at the bar, you'll surely feel like a million bucks.

Old Town Bar & Restaurant 45 E 18th St, between Broadway and Park Ave ⓣ212/529-6732. Subway #4, #5, #6, L, N, Q, R to 14th St/Union Square. See map on p.79. An atmospheric Flatiron District pub that's popular with publishing types and photographers. Opened in 1892, much of the creaking interior is original.

Pete's Tavern 129 E 18th St, at Irving Place ⓣ212/473-7676. Subway #4, #5, #6, L, N, Q, R to 14th St/Union Square. See map on p.79. This former speakeasy, which opened in 1864, trades unashamedly on its history, having had patrons such as John F. Kennedy Jr and O. Henry. Still, a fun spot to grab a pint near Gramercy Park.

Rudy's Bar and Grill 627 Ninth Ave, between W 44th and 45th sts ⓣ212/974-9169. Subway A, C, E to 42nd St. One of New York's friendliest and liveliest bars, a favourite with local actors and musicians. *Rudy's* offers free hot dogs, a backyard that's great in the summer and some of the cheapest pitchers of beer in the city ($9).

Russian Vodka Room 265 W 52nd St, between Broadway and Eighth Ave ⓣ212/307-5835. Subway #1, C, E to 50th St. They serve more than fifty different types of vodka here, as well as their own fruit-flavoured and sublime garlic-infused concoctions; don't dare ask for a mixer.

Uptown Manhattan (60th St and above)

Dead Poet 450 Amsterdam Ave, between 81st and 82nd sts ⓣ212/595-5670. Subway #1 to 79th St. Happy hour lasts an inordinately long time, and is the best reason to come to this sweet spot; the backroom has armchairs, books and a pool table.

Ding Dong Lounge 929 Columbus Ave, between 105th and 106th sts ⓣ212/663-2600. Subway B, C to 103rd St. A punk bar with a DJ and occasional live bands that attracts a vibrant mix of graduate students, neighbourhood Latinos and stragglers from the nearby youth hostel.

Nectar 2235 Frederick Douglass Blvd at 121st St ⓣ212/961-9622. Subway A, B, C, D to 125th St. Harlem's first wine bar is a smart, bright space offering a decent spread of vintages and varieties for $6–19 by the glass (happy hour daily 5–7pm).

Metropolitan Museum of Art 1000 Fifth Ave at 82nd St ⓣ212/535-7710. Subway #4, #5, #6 to 86th St. It's hard to imagine a more romantic spot to sip a glass of wine and kick off the evening (the bars close 8.30pm Fri & Sat), whether on the *Roof Garden Café* (May–Oct), which has some of the best views in the city, or in the *Balcony Bar* overlooking the Great Hall (Fri & Sat only).

Subway Inn 143 E 60th St, at Lexington Ave ⓣ212/223-8929. Subway #4, #5, #6 to 59th St N, R, Q, to Lexington Ave/59th St. This neighbourhood dive bar, across from Bloomingdale's, has been serving customers since 1937, and is great for a late-afternoon beer.

The outer boroughs

Bohemian Hall and Beer Garden 29–19 24th Ave, at 29th St, Astoria, Queens ⓣ718/274-4925. Subway N, Q to Astoria Blvd. This old-timey Czech bar has a devoted following and serves a good selection of pilsners, along with burgers and sausages. Outside, there's a very large beer garden, complete with picnic tables, tree and a bandshell for polka groups.

Brooklyn Brewery 1 Brewers Row, 79 N 11th St, Williamsburg, Brooklyn ⓣ718/486-7422. Subway L to Bedford Ave. New York's best-known microbrewery, open Fri nights only (6–10pm), for "happy hour" (beers $4).

Brooklyn Inn 148 Hoyt St, at Bergen St, Boerum Hill, Brooklyn ⓣ718/522-2525. Subway F, G to Bergen St. Locals – and their dogs – gather at this convivial favourite with high ceilings and a friendly bar staff. Great place for a daytime buzz or shooting pool in the back room.

L.I.C. Bar 45–58 Vernon Blvd, at 46th Ave, Long Island City ⓣ718/786-5400. Subway #7 to Vernon Blvd/Jackson Ave or 45th Rd/Courthouse Square; G to 21st St. A friendly, atmospheric place for a beer, burger and some free live music (Mon & Wed); hunker down at the old wooden bar or in the pleasant outdoor garden.

Pete's Candy Store 709 Lorimer St, between Frost and Richardson sts, Williamsburg, Brooklyn ⓣ718/302-3770, ⓦwww.petescandystore.com. Subway L to Lorimer St. This terrific little spot, once a real candy store, offers free live music every night, a reading series, Scrabble and Bingo nights, pub quizzes and some well-poured cocktails.

Sunny's 253 Conover St, between Beard and Reed sts, Red Hook, Brooklyn ⓣ718/625-8211. Subway F, G to Smith-9th St, then #B77 bus. Red Hook is off the subway grid, but it's a great place to explore and make an evening of it; if you do, make sure to grab at least one drink at this pub by the river. It's an old-school dive with $4 bottle beers, loyal regulars, erratic opening hours and impromptu jam sessions. Wed, Fri & Sat 8pm–4am.

Nightlife and entertainment

You'll never be at a loss for something fun or culturally enriching to do while in New York. The **live music** scene, in particular, well reflects New York's diversity: on any night of the week, you can hear pretty much any type of music, from thumping hip-hop to raging punk, and, of course, plenty of jazz. There are also quite a few **dance clubs**, where you can move to hard-hitting house or cheesy tunes from the 1970s and 80s.

Home to Broadway and 42nd Street, New York is also one of the world's great **theatre** centres, with productions that range from lavish, over-the-top musicals to experimental productions in converted garages. **Classical music**, **opera** and **dance** are all very well represented, too. As for **film**, you couldn't hope for better pickings: the city has several large indie theatres, assorted revival and arthouse cinemas and countless Hollywood-blockbuster multiplexes. Last but not least, NYC has many excellent **comedy** clubs.

For **listings** of what's on during any particular week, check out *Time Out New York* ($3.99; available from newsstands citywide) or *The Village Voice* (free; available in newspaper boxes and many other spots around town). Useful **websites** include ⓦwww.ohmyrockness.com (for indie rock), ⓦwww.thelmagazine.com and www.timeout.com (for general listings).

Clubs and live music

New York has plenty of great **live music venues**, from tiny rock joints to sublime jazz clubs. **Cover charges** at these smaller places will run you from $10 to $25 or so; at the larger, well-known venues, a ticket can cost anywhere from $25 to $100. If the show's not sold out, tickets are usually available at the door. For advance tickets, go to the venue's box office, or visit **Ticketmaster** (ⓣ212/307-4100 or 1-800/755-4000 outside NY, ⓦwww.ticketmaster.com) or **Ticketweb** (ⓦwww.ticketweb.com).

As for **clubs**, things change at a rapid pace, so be sure to check the listings in *The Village Voice* or *Time Out* before you make any plans. The action is spread out, with the Lower East Side, the East and West villages and Brooklyn offering as many venues as "hot" nightlife hubs like the Meatpacking District. **Cover charges** range from $15 to $50, though most average out at around $20; always bring photo **ID**.

Theatre

Even if you're not normally a **theatre** buff, going to see a play or a musical while in New York is virtually de rigueur. The various theatre venues are referred to as **Broadway**, **Off-Broadway** or **Off-Off Broadway**, representing a descending order of ticket price, production polish, elegance and comfort. Broadway offerings consist primarily of large-scale musicals, comedies and dramas with big-name actors, while Off-Broadway theatres tend to combine high production qualities with a greater willingness to experiment. Off-Off Broadway is the fringe – drama on a shoestring. As for **location**, most Broadway theatres are just east or west of Broadway, between 40th and 52nd streets; the rest are sprinkled throughout Manhattan. Check out *Time Out New York* for the latest shows.

On Broadway, **ticket prices** run $60–200; Off-Broadway, expect to pay $25–75; Off-Off is usually $12–20. The prices of Broadway and Off-Broadway shows can be cut considerably, sometimes down to half-price, if you can wait in line on the day of the performance at the **TKTS** booth in Times Square (Mon, Thurs & Fri 3–8pm, Tues 2–8pm, Wed & Sat 10am–2pm & 3–8pm, Sun 11am–7pm); there are also booths at the Seaport and downtown Brooklyn. Keep in mind that you may have to wait in line for a couple of hours and that the show you want to see may be sold out by the time you get to the front of the line.

If you're prepared to pay **full price**, go directly to the theatre box office or use **Telecharge** (Ⓣ212/239-6200 or 1-800/432-7250 outside NY, Ⓦwww.telecharge.com) or **Ticketmaster**; expect to pay a $7 surcharge per ticket. For Off-Broadway shows, **Ticket Central** (Ⓣ212/279-4200, Ⓦwww.ticketcentral.com) sells tickets online and at its offices at 416 West 42nd St, between Ninth and Tenth avenues (daily noon–8pm; Ⓣ212/279-4200).

Classical music, opera and dance

Lincoln Center (see p.92), located on Broadway between West 62nd and West 66th streets (Ⓣ212/875-5456, Ⓦwww.new.lincolncenter.org), is New York's powerhouse of performing arts. The complex comprises some twenty venues in all, including the **Avery Fisher Hall** (Ⓣ212/875-5030, Ⓦwww.nyphil.org), permanent home of the New York Philharmonic, and the **Metropolitan Opera House** (Ⓣ212/362-6000, Ⓦwww.metoperafamily.org), New York City's premier venue for opera. The soaring theatre hosts the venerable Metropolitan Opera Company from September to April, as well as the American Ballet Theater from May into July. Tickets are outrageously expensive and can be difficult to get, though 175 standing-room tickets ($20) go on sale the morning of the performance.

The **David H Koch Theater**, also in Lincoln Center (Ⓣ212/870-5570) is the springtime home to the **New York City Ballet**, considered by many to be the top dance company in existence. Tickets must be purchased through the company's website (Ⓦwww.nycballet.com), or through Ticketmaster. This accessible venue is also where the New York City Opera (Ⓦwww.nycopera.com) plays David to the Met's Goliath. Seats go for less than half the Met's, and standing-room tickets are available if a performance sells out.

Besides **Lincoln Center**, the most important venue is **Carnegie Hall** (see p.87), where the greatest names from all schools of music have performed.

When it comes to **dance,** Lincoln Center once again serves as a showcase, though a number of other venues regularly host events. The **Brooklyn Academy of Music** (or **BAM**), at 30 Lafayette St in Brooklyn, between Ashland Place and St Felix Street (Ⓣ718/636-4100, Ⓦwww.bam.org), is America's oldest performing arts academy and one of the most daring producers in New York – definitely worth crossing the river for. Meanwhile, back in Manhattan, the **New York City Center**, 131 West 55th St, between Sixth and Seventh avenues (Ⓣ212/581-1212, Ⓦwww.citycenter.org), is home to some of the country's leading dance companies, including Alvin Ailey American Dance Theater (Ⓣ212/405-9000, Ⓦwww.alvinailey.org) and the Paul Taylor Dance Company (Ⓣ212/431-5562, Ⓦwww.ptdc.org). For small and mid-sized companies, the most important space in Manhattan is the **Joyce Theater**, 175 Eighth Ave, at 19th Street (Ⓣ212/242-0800, Ⓦwww.joyce.org). The Joyce hosts companies from around the world, and also has a small Downtown satellite – Joyce SoHo – at 155 Mercer St, between Houston and Prince streets (Ⓣ212/431-9233).

Rock, pop and multi-genre

Arlene's Grocery 95 Stanton St, between Ludlow and Orchard sts Ⓣ212/358-1633, Ⓦwww.arlenesgrocery.net. Subway F to Second Ave. This intimate, erstwhile bodega hosts gigs by local indie talent during the week. Monday is "Punk/Heavy Metal Karaoke" night (free), where you can wail along with a live band to your favourite songs. Cover $8–10.

The Bowery Ballroom 6 Delancey St, at Bowery Ⓣ212/533-2111, Ⓦwww.boweryballroom.com. Subway J, Z to Bowery; B, D to Grand St. A minimum of attitude, great sound and even better sightlines make this a local favourite to see well-known indie-rock bands. Shows $15–50.

Joe's Pub At the Public Theater, 425 Lafayette St, between Astor Place and E 4th St Ⓣ212/539-8778, Ⓦwww.publictheater.org. Subway #6 to Astor Place; N, R to 8th St. The word "pub" is a misnomer for this swanky nightspot, which features music and cabaret nightly. Cover ranges greatly depending on the performer.

Knitting Factory 361 Metropolitan Ave, at Havemeyer St, Wiliamsburg Ⓣ347/529-6696, Ⓦbk.knittingfactory.com. Subway L to Bedford Ave; G, L to Metropolitan Ave. This intimate showcase for indie rock and underground hip-hop moved to Brooklyn in 2009, but has maintained a loyal following and quality acts. Most tickets $5–15.

(Le) Poisson Rouge 158 Bleecker St at Thompson St Ⓣ212/505-3474 Ⓦlepoissonrouge.com. Subway A, B, C, D, E, F, M to W 4th St. Mix of live rock, folk, pop and electronica Thurs at 7pm ($10–15), with dance parties most Fri and Sat (often free).

The Mercury Lounge 217 E Houston St, between Ludlow and Essex sts Ⓣ212/260-4700, Ⓦwww.mercuryloungenyc.com. Subway F to Second Ave. The dark, smallish mainstay hosts a mix of local, national and international pop and rock acts. It's owned by the same crew as *Bowery Ballroom*, which usually gets the better-known bands. Tickets usually $8–15.

Music Hall of Williamsburg 66 N 6th St, between Wythe and Kent aves, Williamsburg, Brooklyn Ⓣ718/486-5400, Ⓦwww.musichallofwilliamsburg.com. Subway L to Bedford Ave. A large performance space with excellent acoustics, set in an old factory. One of Brooklyn's really great venues and another in the *Bowery Ballroom* stable – expect the same kind of acts. Tickets $10–20.

S.O.B.'s 204 Varick St, at W Houston St Ⓣ212/243-4940, Ⓦwww.sobs.com. Subway #1 to Houston St. Short for "Sounds of Brazil", this lively club-restaurant, with regular Caribbean, salsa and world music acts, puts on two performances a night. Ticket prices vary depending on type of performer; no cover, however, for those with dinner reservations pre-7pm.

Southpaw 125 Fifth Ave, between Sterling Place and Douglass St, Park Slope, Brooklyn Ⓣ718/230-0236. Ⓦwww.spsounds.com. Subway #2, #3 to Bergen St; R to Union St. Brooklyn's premier live venue, with 5000 square feet of space and a wide range of acts and DJs from almost every genre. Admission varies, but is rarely more than $10–12, while a cab from lower Manhattan costs around $10–15.

Jazz venues

Birdland 315 W 44th St, between Eighth and Ninth aves Ⓣ212/581-3080, Ⓦwww.birdlandjazz.com. Subway A, C, E to 42nd St. Not the original place where Charlie Parker played, but nonetheless an established jazz club that plays host to some big names. Sets nightly at 9 and 11pm. Music charge of $20–50; at a table, you'll need to spend a minimum of $10 or more on food or drink, while at the bar, the cover includes your first drink.

Lenox Lounge 288 Lenox Ave, at 125th St Ⓣ212/427-0253, Ⓦwww.lenoxlounge.com. Subway #2, #3 to 125th St. Entertaining Harlem since the 1930s, this historic jazz lounge has an over-the-top Art Deco interior (check out the Zebra Room); you're paying for the atmosphere as much as the music. Cover $25, with a two-drink minimum on weekends.

Louis 649 649 E 9th St between aves B and C ⓣ212/673-1190. Subway L to First Ave; #6 to Astor Place. With no cover and live performances seven nights a week, *Louis 649* is a must if you love jazz. Mon and Thurs are lively, and weekends get downright hectic. They serve gourmet bottled beer and a number of excellent vintages, but no cocktails.

St Nick's Pub 773 St. Nicholas Ave, at 149th St ⓣ212/690-7807, ⓦwww.stnicksjazzpub.net. Subway A, B, C, D to 145th St. This small, basic basement venue is one of Harlem's top jazz halls, dating back to 1930, with jumpin' live shows six nights a week from 10pm (7pm weekends). No cover ($3 for a table seat).

Smoke 2751 Broadway, at 106th St ⓣ212/864-6662, ⓦwww.smokejazz.com. Subway #1 to 103rd St. This Upper West Side joint is a real neighbourhood treat; sets start at 9pm, 11pm, & 12.30am. Cover varies.

Village Vanguard 178 Seventh Ave S, between W 11th and Perry streets ⓣ212/255-4037, ⓦwww.villagevanguard.com. Subway #1, #2, #3 to 14th St. This jazz landmark, 75 years young, still lays on a regular diet of big names. Cover $35, plus $10 drink minimum; cash only.

Larger music venues

Beacon Theatre 2124 Broadway, at W 74th St ⓣ212/496-7070. Subway #1, #2, #3 to 72nd St. A beautiful, restored theatre that caters to a more mature rock crowd. Tickets $50–300.

Hammerstein Ballroom 311 W 34th St, between Eighth and Ninth aves ⓣ212/564-4882, ⓦwww.mcstudios.com. Subway A, C, E to 34th St. This grand 1906 building has seen many incarnations: it's been an opera house, a vaudeville hall and a Masonic temple, and it now hosts indie and rock bands. Capacity is 3600, but the sound system and acoustics are of high enough quality that most seats are pretty good. Tickets $50 and up.

Radio City Music Hall 1260 Sixth Ave, at 50th St ⓣ212/247-4777, ⓦwww.radiocity.com. Subway B, D, F, M to 47–50th sts-Rockefeller Center. Although not as prestigious a venue as it once was, the building is a star in its own right (see p.88).

Clubs and discos

Cielo 18 Little W 12th St, between Ninth Ave and Washington St ⓣ212/645-5700, ⓦwww.cieloclub.com. Subway L to Eighth Ave; A, C, E to 14th St. Expect velvet rope-burn at this see-and-be-seen place; Monday's reggae and dub party Deep Space from Francois K is the top night. Cover $20.

Pacha 618 W 46th St ⓣ212/209-7500, ⓦwww.pachanyc.com. Subway A, C, E to 42nd St. New York outpost of the chain of Ibiza superclubs. Sprawling over 30,000 square feet, and featuring a spine-tingling, high-tech sound system, three floors, palm trees and mosaic-mirrors, this is the place for a big, corporate club experience, and a generally non-local clientele. Cover $30–40.

Sapphire Lounge 249 Eldridge St, at Houston St ⓣ212/777-5153, ⓦwww.sapphirenyc.com. Subway F to Second Ave. DJ bar and lounge, with an arty, sexy vibe, created by the dark lights and enhanced by the moody Lower East Side regulars. Expect music of almost every genre on different nights – it's open seven days, and the cover is usually minimal ($5 or so).

Sullivan Room 218 Sullivan St, at Bleecker St ⓣ212/252-2151, ⓦwww.sullivanroom.com. Subway A, B, C, D, E, F, M to W 4th St. Basement club for serious dancing; the only downside: two bathrooms for the whole place. Thurs–Sat 10pm–5am. Cover $10–25.

Film

Angelika Film Center 18 W Houston St, at Mercer St ⓣ212/995-2000, ⓦwww.angelikafilmcenter.com. Subway B, D, F, M to Broadway-Lafayette. Somewhat overhyped arthouse venue, but it's one of the few surviving spots for smaller films in the city.

Film Forum 209 W Houston St, between Varick and Sixth Ave ⓣ212/727-8110, ⓦwww.filmforum.org. Subway #1 to Houston St. Offers the best in independent film and documentary, as well as themed revivals.

Landmark Sunshine Cinema 143 E Houston St, at First Ave ⓣ212/330-8182, ⓦwww.landmarktheatres.com. Subway F to Second Ave. This former synagogue and vaudeville theatre is now one of the plushest art house movie theatres in town, with fun midnight screenings of cult classics.

Comedy

Caroline's on Broadway 1626 Broadway, between W 49th and 50th sts ⓣ212/757-4100, ⓦwww.carolines.com. Subway #1 to 50th St; N, R, to 49th St. Some of the best acts in town (and Hollywood) appear at this glitzy spot. Cover $15–40, with a two-drink minimum.

Gotham Comedy Club 208 W 23rd St, between Seventh and Eighth aves ⓣ212/367-9000, ⓦwww.gothamcomedyclub.com. Subway #1, C, E to 23rd St. A swanky comedy venue, highly respected by New York media types and those who scout up-and-coming comics. Cover $20–30 plus two-drink minimum.

Upright Citizens Brigade Theatre 307 W 26th St, between Eighth and Ninth aves ⓣ212/366-9176,

Ⓦ www.ucbtheatre.com. Subway C, E to 23rd St; #1 to 28th St, Consistently hilarious sketch-based and improv comedy, seven nights a week. You can sometimes catch *Saturday Night Live* cast members in the ensemble. Cover $5–15.

Gay New York

There are few places in America where **gay culture** thrives as it does in New York. **Chelsea** (centred on Eighth Ave, between 14th and 23rd sts), the **East Village** and **Hell's Kitchen** have replaced the **West Village** as the hubs of gay New York, although a strong presence still lingers around Christopher Street. There's Brooklyn's **Park Slope**, too, though perhaps more for women than for men. Up-to-the-minute news can be found in *Gay City News*, *Next* and *GO*, free, provocative weekly papers/magazines.

Resources

Bluestockings 172 Allen St, between Stanton and Rivington sts Ⓣ 212/777-6028, Ⓦ www.bluestockings.com. Subway F, to Second Ave or Delancey St. Collectively run radical bookstore (with a focus on gay and feminist titles) and organic café on the Lower East Side.

Gay Men's Health Crisis (GMHC) 119 W 24th St, between Sixth and Seventh aves Ⓣ 212/367-1000, Ⓦ www.gmhc.org. Despite the name, this organization – the oldest and largest not-for-profit AIDS organization in the world – provides information and referrals to everyone, no matter their sex or sexual orientation.

The Lesbian, Gay, Bisexual & Transgender Community Center 208 W 13th St, at Seventh Ave Ⓣ 212/620-7310, Ⓦ www.gaycenter.org. The Center houses well over a hundred groups and organizations, sponsors workshops, parties, movie nights, guest speakers, youth services, programmes for parents and lots more.

Bars and clubs

Barracuda 275 W 22nd St, between Eighth and Ninth aves Ⓣ 212/645-8613. Subway #1, C, E to 23rd St. A favourite spot in New York's gay scene, though as un-sceney as you'll find in Chelsea. Check out the two-for-one happy hour 4–9pm during the week.

Duplex 61 Christopher St, at Seventh Ave Ⓣ 212/255-5438, Ⓦ www.theduplex.com. Subway #1 to Christopher St-Sheridan Square. This Village cabaret is popular with a gay crowd but entertaining for all. Cover varies, from free to $20, plus two-drink minimum.

Ginger's 363 Fifth Ave, between 5th and 6th sts, Park Slope, Brooklyn Ⓣ 718/788-0924. Subway F, G, R to Fourth Ave/9th St. The best lesbian bar in New York is this dark, laidback Park Slope joint with a pool table, outdoor space and plenty of convivial company.

Marie's Crisis 59 Grove St, between Seventh Ave S and Bleecker St. Subway #1 to Christopher St-Sheridan Square. Well-known cabaret/piano bar popular with tourists and locals alike. Features old-time singing sessions nightly. Often packed, always fun.

Stonewall Inn 53 Christopher St, between Waverly Place and Seventh Ave Ⓣ 212/488-2705. Subway #1 to Christopher St. Sherida Sq. The site of the seminal 1969 riot flies the pride flag like they own it – which, one supposes, they do.

Shopping

When it comes to consumerism, New York leaves all other cities behind. Shopping can be extraordinarily cheap, but move further uptown and it can also be phenomenally expensive. **Midtown Manhattan** is mainstream territory, with the department stores, big-name clothes designers and branches of the larger chains. Downtown plays host to a wide variety of more offbeat stores – **SoHo** is perhaps the most popular shopping neighbourhood in these parts, and generally the most expensive. Affordable alternatives for the young and trendy are available in the **Lower East Side**, and good vintage clothing can be found there, in the East Village and in Williamsburg, Brooklyn.

Bookstores

Book Culture 2915 Broadway at 114th St ⓣ646/403-3000, ⓦwww.booksite.com. Subway #1 to Cathedral Parkway (110th St). The new, main shop of the largest independent bookstore in the city (the first Book Culture, now mostly academic-oriented, remains at 536 112th St) boasts a fine selection of literary (especially international) fiction, children's books and much more.

Books of Wonder 18 W 18th St, between Fifth and Sixth aves ⓣ212/989-3270. Subway #1 to 18th St; F, M to 14th St; #4, #5, #6, N, Q, R to Union Square. A heavenly collection of kid lit.

Complete Traveller Antiquarian Bookstore 199 Madison Ave, at E 35th St ⓣ212/685-9007. Subway #6 to 33rd St. An extensive collection of rare travel tomes, including the entire Baedekers series, WPA Guides, old books on NYC and maps galore. You can also find other (non-travel) first pressings and vintage children's books here.

Housing Works Used Books Café 126 Crosby St, between Houston and Prince sts ⓣ212/334-3324. Subway B, D, F, M to Broadway-Lafayette; N, R to Prince St; #6 to Bleecker St. Very cheap books in a spacious and comfy environment. Proceeds benefit AIDS charities.

Partners & Crime 44 Greenwich Ave, at Charles St ⓣ212/243-0440, ⓦwww.crimepays.com. Subway #1 to Christopher St. Superb, informed shop for devout mystery fans: author signings, a lending library, authoritative staff recommendations and radio play re-enactments the first Sat of every month (6pm & 8pm; $7).

Revolution Books 146 W 26th St, between Sixth and Seventh aves ⓣ212/691-3345, ⓦwww.revolutionbooksnyc.org. Subway #1 to 28th St. New York's major left-wing bookstore and contact point, with a wide range of political and cultural titles and periodicals. Almost every night the store holds screenings, salons or other events (after official closing time).

Strand Bookstore 828 Broadway, at 12th St ⓣ212/473-1452, ⓦwww.strandbooks.com. Subway #4, #5, #6, L, N, Q, R to Union Square. With a stock of more than 2.5 million, this is the largest book operation in the city. Recent review copies and new books show up at half-price; older books are from 50¢ up.

Boutique, designer and vintage shops

Beacon's Closet 88 N 11th St, Williamsburg, Brooklyn ⓣ718/486-0816, ⓦwww.beaconscloset.com. Subway L to Bedford Ave. Vast used-clothing

Sports in New York

Seeing either of New York's two **baseball** teams involves a trip to the outer boroughs. The **Yankees** play in the Bronx, at the new **Yankee Stadium**, between 161st and 164th streets and River Avenue (ⓣ718/293-6000, ⓦwww.yankees.com). Get there on the #4, B or D subway lines direct to the 161st Street station. The **Mets** are based in Queens, at the equally new **Citi Field**, 126th Street and Roosevelt Avenue, Willets Point, Queens (ⓣ718/507-8499, ⓦmets.mlb.com). Take the #7 train, direct to Willets Point. Tickets for games run from $14 (Yankees' bleachers) to $300 (again, for the Yankees).

New York's football teams – the **Jets** and **Giants** – play at the **New Meadowlands Stadium**, East Rutherford, New Jersey (ⓣ201/935-8500, ⓦwww.meadowlands.com). Buses from the Port Authority Bus Terminal, 42nd Street at Eighth Avenue, serve the stadium. Tickets for both teams are always officially sold out well in advance, but you can often get seats (legally) from secondary-broker websites such as ⓦwww.ticketliquidator.com.

Basketball's two New York pro teams are the NBA **Knicks** (ⓦwww.nba.com/knicks) and the WNBA **Liberty** (ⓦwww.wnba.com/liberty). Both play at **Madison Square Garden**, West 33rd Street at Seventh Avenue (ⓣ212/465-6741, ⓦwww.thegarden.com). Tickets for the Knicks are very expensive, and, due to impossibly high demand, available in only limited numbers, if at all. The women's games are fairly exciting and cheaper (starting at $10, though can be much more). Another area team, the **New Jersey Nets**, are scheduled to move to Brooklyn in 2012 but for now, they play at the Izod Center in the Meadowlands Complex; tickets range from $10 to over $200, and are relatively easy to procure. New York's hockey team, the **Rangers** (ⓦrangers.nhl.com), also plays at Madison Square Garden; tickets range from $40 to $254. The area soccer team, the **New York Red Bulls** (ⓣ201/583-7000, ⓦwww.newyorkredbulls.com; tickets $22–50), play over in Harrison, New Jersey.

paradise, specializing in modern fashions and vintage attire. Also in Park Slope.

Comme des Garçons 520 W 22nd St, at Tenth Ave ⓣ212/604-9200. Subway C, E to 23rd St. Japanese designer Rei Kawakubo's avant-garde line has a stunning showcase in this Chelsea store – worth stopping to see even if you don't plan to buy any clothes.

Edith Machinist 104 Rivington St at Ludlow St ⓣ212/979-9992. Subway J, Z to Essex St, F to Delancey St. Treasure-trove of chic vintage women's fashion, especially shoes and leather, for those willing to sift through the massive stock.

Inven.tory Soho 237 Lafayette St at Spring St ⓣ212/226-5292. Subway #6 to Spring St. Inven.tory's store is essentially a curated sample sale made permanent; expect designer items at wholesale prices, serious shoppers and fabulous bargains.

Kirna Zabête 96 Greene St, between Prince and Spring sts ⓣ212/941-9656. Subway R to Prince St. The best of the downtown boutiques, this is a concept store that stocks hand-picked highlights from designers such as Jason Wu, Rick Owens and Proenza Schouler.

Marc Jacobs 163 Mercer St, between Houston and Prince sts ⓣ212/343-1490. Subway R to Prince St. Marc Jacobs rules the New York fashion world like a Cosmopolitan-sipping colossus. Women from all walks of life come here to blow the nest egg on his latest "it" bag or pair of boots.

Prada 575 Broadway, at Prince St ⓣ212/334-8888. Subway R to Prince St. The jaw-dropping flagship store designed by Rem Koolhaas is as much of a sight as Miuccia's deservedly famous clothes.

Department stores

Barney's 660 Madison Ave, at 61st St ⓣ212/826-8900, ⓦwww.barneys.com. Subway N, Q, R to Fifth Ave/59th St. The most fashion-forward of the big NYC department stores and the place to find next season's hot item.

Bergdorf Goodman 754 and 745 Fifth Ave, at 58th St ⓣ212/753-7300, ⓦwww.bergdorfgoodman.com. Subway N, Q, R to Fifth Ave/59th St. Housed in what used to be a Vanderbilt mansion, this venerable department store caters to the city's wealthiest clientele. Even if you can't afford to shop, it's still fun to browse and dream.

Bloomingdale's 1000 Third Ave, between 59th and 60th sts ⓣ212/705-2000, ⓦwww.bloomingdales.com. Subway #4, #5, #6, N, Q, R to 59th St. Perhaps Manhattan's most beloved department store, Bloomingdale's is packed with designer clothes, perfume concessions and the like.

Century 21 22 Cortlandt St, at 61st St ⓣ212/227-9092, ⓦwww.c21stores.com. Subway R to Cortlandt St. One of a chain of designer discount department stores, where you can pick up top labels at bargain prices.

Macy's 151 W 34th St, at Broadway ⓣ212/289-6229, ⓦwww.macys.com. Subway B, D, F, M, N, Q, R to 34th St. The world's largest department store embraces two buildings, two million square feet of floor space and ten floors; the homeware department in the Cellar is a highlight.

Food

Chelsea Market 75 Ninth Ave, between 15th and 16th sts ⓦwww.chelseamarket.com. Subway A, C, E to 14th St. An array of food shops line this former Nabisco factory warehouse's ground floor; go for fresh produce, lobster rolls, chewy breads and kitchenware, or simply to browse.

Mast Brothers Chocolate 105A N 3rd St, Williamsburg ⓣ718/388-2625. Subway L to Bedford Ave. Once you've tried the handmade artisan chocolate here, you'll be utterly hooked; the delicate dark chocolate with almonds and sea salt is a mind-bending treat. Quality comes at a price – it's around $9 a bar. Sat & Sun noon–8pm.

Murray's Cheese Shop 254 Bleecker St, between Sixth and Seventh aves ⓣ212/243-3289, ⓦwww.murrayscheese.com. Subway A, B, C, D, E, F, M to W 4th St; #1 to Christopher St. The city's number-one stop for cheese lovers; go to learn about the cheese-making process, sample the wares, or pick up a pungent panini sandwich.

Russ & Daughters 179 E Houston St, between Allen and Orchard sts ⓣ212/475-4880. Subway F to Second Ave. This small family-run shop has been serving fine Jewish edibles such as smoked whitefish and salmon, chopped liver and pickled herring since 1914. A must-visit.

Union Square Greenmarket In Union Square, at 16th St. Subway #4, #5, #6, N, Q, R to Union Square. A bit of country in the city: an open-air market that offers local seasonal produce and natural goods sold by regional farmers and purveyors (Mon, Wed, Fri & Sat 8am–6pm).

Zabar's 2245 Broadway, at 80th St ⓣ212/787-2000, ⓦwww.zabars.com. Subway #1 to 79th St. The pre-eminent gourmet store; choose from a dizzying selection of cheeses, olives, baked breads, bagel schmears and prepared foods. Fine kitchenware is sold upstairs.

Record stores

Halcyon 57 Pearl St, Dumbo, Brooklyn ⓣ718/260-WAXY, ⓦwww.halcyonline.com. Subway F to York St. A trusted source for dance music, but offers stuff ranging from jazz to techno. Radio shows, listening parties and a general air of music-nerd community make this a top pick.

Generation Records 210 Thompson St, between Bleecker and W 3rd sts ⓣ212/254-1100. Subway A, B, C, D, E, F, M to W 4th St. The focus here is on hardcore, metal and punk, with some indie thrown in. New CDs and vinyl are upstairs, while the used records are downstairs.

Other Music 15 E 4th St, between Broadway and Lafayette ⓣ212/477-8150, ⓦwww.othermusic.com. Subway #6 to Astor Place. This homespun shop is an excellent spot for "alternative" CDs that can otherwise be hard to find. There's less indie on vinyl than before, but the store retains the same friendly, knowledgeable staff as always.

Miscellaneous

Apple Store 103 Prince St at Greene St. Subway R to Prince St. The original Apple gadget store in Manhattan gets extremely crowded, but the latest in laptops, iPads, iPhones and iPods are all here for as cheap as you'll get them anywhere – you can also play with the newest models. Also has equally eye-catching branches at 767 Fifth Ave, 401 W 14th St and 1981 Broadway.

MoMA Design Store 81 Spring St, between Broadway and Crosby ⓣ646/613-1367. Subway R to Prince St; #6 to Spring St. The Museum of Modern Art's retail wing, this shop holds a host of super-stylish housewares, modish knick-knacks and contemporary art books.

2

The Mid-Atlantic

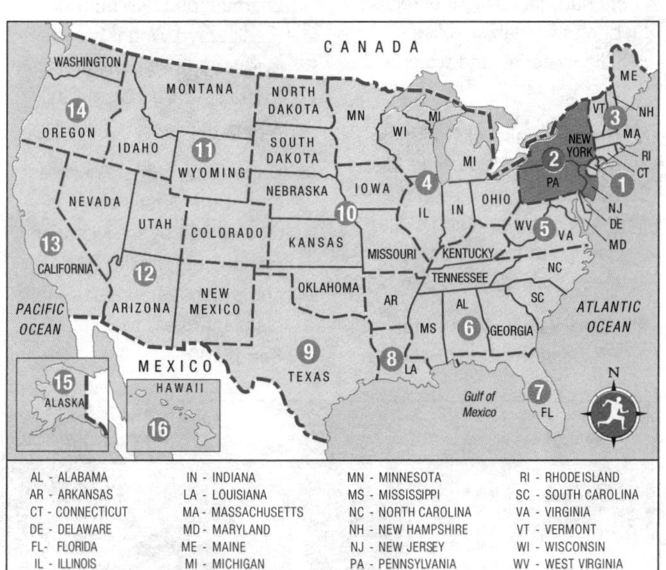

CHAPTER 2 Highlights

* **The Adirondacks, NY** A vast and rugged alpine wilderness offering superb hiking, skiing, fishing and mountain-climbing opportunities. See p.122

* **The Finger Lakes, NY** With charming Ithaca, famed for its Ivy-League university, as its hub, this delightful region brims with lakes, rolling hills, wineries and waterfalls. See p.124

* **Niagara Falls, NY** Take the memorable *Maid of the Mist* boat trip, or visit the Cave of the Winds and stand close enough to feel the spray from these majestic falls. See p.129

* **History in Philadelphia, PA** See the Liberty Bell and trace the steps of Benjamin Franklin in the city of brotherly love, where the Declaration of Independence was signed. See p.132

* **Art and architecture, Pittsburgh, PA** The Warhol Museum, Cathedral of Learning and two outlying Frank Lloyd Wright houses lend a surprising cultural flair to the so-called Steel City. See p.147

* **Cape May, NJ** The cultured end of the Jersey shore is exemplified by the Victorian architecture, quaint B&Bs and swish restaurants of this pleasant resort town. See p.160

▲ Pittsburgh architecture

2

The Mid-Atlantic

The three **MID-ATLANTIC** states – New York, Pennsylvania and New Jersey – stand at the heart of the most populated and industrialized corner of the US. Although dominated in the popular imagination by the grey smokestacks of New Jersey and steel factories of Pennsylvania, these states actually encompass beaches, mountains, islands, lakes, forests, rolling green countryside and many worthwhile small cities and towns.

European settlement here was characterized by considerable shifts and turns: the **Dutch**, who arrived in the 1620s, were methodically squeezed out by the **English**, who in turn fought off the **French** challenge to secure control of the region by the mid-eighteenth century. The Native American population, including the **Iroquois Confederacy** and Lenni Lenape, had sided with the French against the English and were soon confined to reservations or pushed north into Canada. At first, the economy depended on the fur trade, though by the 1730s English **Quakers**, along with **Amish** and **Mennonites** from Germany, plus a few Presbyterian **Irish**, had made farming a significant force, their holdings extending to the western limits of the region.

All three states were important during the **Revolution**: over half the battles were fought here, including major American victories at **Trenton** and **Princeton** in New Jersey. Upstate New York was geographically crucial, as the British forces knew that American control of the Hudson River would effectively divide New England from the other colonies. After the Revolution, industry became the region's prime economic force, with **mill towns** springing up along the numerous rivers. By the mid-1850s the large **coalfields** of northeast Pennsylvania were powering the smoky steel mills of Pittsburgh and the discovery of high-grade **crude oil** in 1859 marked the beginning of the automobile age. Though still significant, especially in the regions near New York City, heavy industry has now largely been replaced by tourism as the economic engine.

Although many travellers to the East Coast do not venture much further than New York City itself, the region offers varied attractions, from the crashing Atlantic surf of **Long Island**, through the wooded **Catskill Mountains** and the imposing **Adirondacks**, occupying a quarter of the state, to the cultured and pastoral **Finger Lakes**. In the northwest corner of the state, beyond the **Erie Canal cities** along I-90, awesome **Niagara Falls** and artsy post-industrial **Buffalo** hug the Canadian border. **Pennsylvania** is best known for the fertile **Pennsylvania Dutch** country and the two great cities of **Philadelphia** and **Pittsburgh**. **New Jersey**, often pictured as one big industrial carbuncle, offers shameless tourist pleasures along the shore – from the boardwalk and casinos of **Atlantic City** to the small-town charm of **Cape May**.

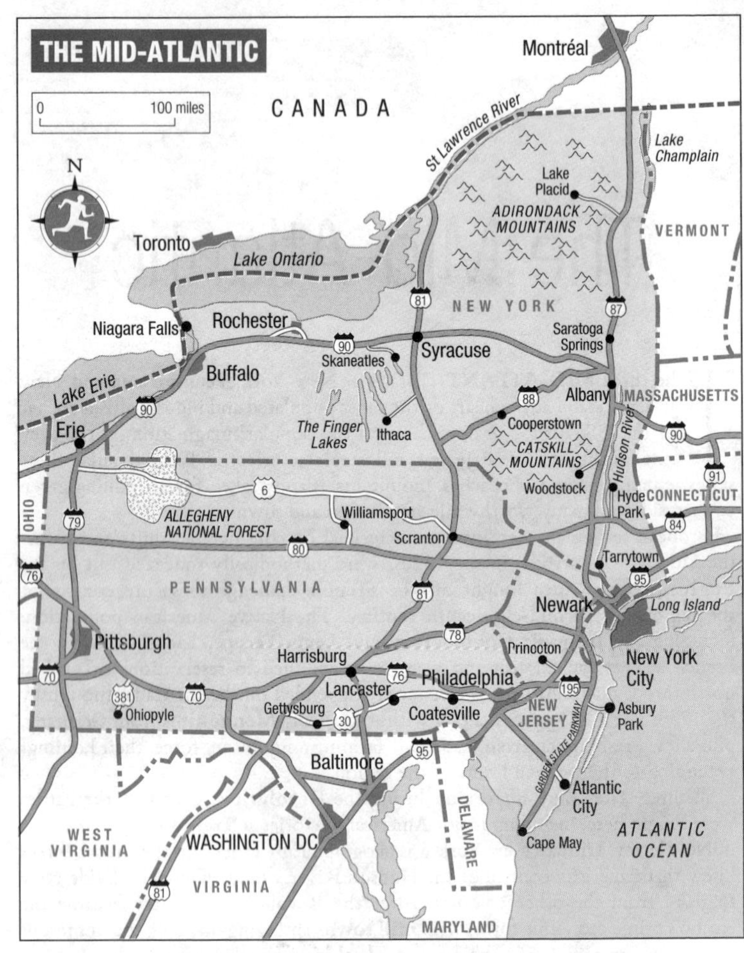

Getting around the Mid-Atlantic

The entire region is well covered by **public transportation**, with New York's JFK, New Jersey's Newark and Philadelphia airports acting as major international gateways, New York's LaGuardia Airport serving domestic flights and another busy hub at Pittsburgh. Amtrak **trains** run routes up and down the Northeast Corridor through New York, New Jersey and Pennsylvania, their services supplemented by New Jersey Transit, Metro-North and the Long Island Railroad. Greyhound **buses** follow the major interstates, with a few subsidiary lines running to more out-of-the-way places. The metropolitan areas have good local transportation systems that radiate out to outlying areas, meaning only the wilder forest and mountain areas really need a car. **Car rental** is expensive out of New York City, so better done from one of the other cities.

New York State

However much exists to attract visitors, the vast state of **NEW YORK** stands inevitably in the shadow of America's most celebrated city. The words "New York" bring to mind soaring skyscrapers and congested streets, not the beaches of **Long Island** to the east or 50,000 square miles of rolling dairy farmland, colonial villages, workaday towns, lakes, waterfalls and towering mountains that fan out north and west from New York City and constitute **upstate New York**. Just an hour's drive north of Manhattan, the valley of the **Hudson River**, with the moody **Catskill Mountains** rising stealthily from the west bank, offers a respite from the intensity of the city. Much wilder and more rugged are the peaks of the vast **Adirondack Mountains** further north, which hold some of eastern America's most enticing scenery. To the west, the slender **Finger Lakes** and endless miles of dairy farms and vineyards occupy the central portion of the state. Of the larger cities, only **Buffalo** and **Rochester** hold much of interest, but some of the smaller towns, like Ivy-League **Ithaca** and the venerable spa town of **Saratoga Springs**, can be quite captivating.

In the seventeenth and eighteenth centuries semi-feudal **Dutch landowning dynasties** held sway upstate. Their control over tens of thousands of tenant farmers was barely affected by the transfer of colonial power from Holland to Britain or even by American independence. Only with the completion of the **Erie Canal** in 1825, linking New York City with the Great Lakes, did the interior start to open up; improved opportunities for trade enabled canal-side cities like Syracuse, Rochester and especially Buffalo to undergo massive expansion.

Long Island

Just east of New York City, **Long Island** unfurls for 125 miles of lush farmland and broad sandy beaches, and is most often explored as an excursion from the metropolis. Its western end abuts the urban boroughs of Brooklyn and Queens but further east the settlements begin to thin out and the countryside gets surprisingly wild. The **north** and **south shores** differ greatly – the former more immediately beautiful, its cliffs topped with luxurious mansions and estates, while the South Shore is fringed by almost continuous sand, interspersed with vacation spots such as **Jones Beach** and **Fire Island**. At its far end, Long Island splits in two, the **North Fork** retaining a marked rural aspect while the **South Fork** includes **the Hamptons**, an enclave of New York's richest and most famous.

The quickest way to reach Long Island is via the reliable **Long Island Railroad** from Penn Station (Ⓣ718/330-1234, Ⓦwww.mta.info/lirr). You can also arrive via **ferry** from New England: Cross Sound Ferry makes the trip from New London, CT to Orient Point, Long Island (Ⓣ860/443-5281 in New England, Ⓣ631/323-2525 on Long Island, Ⓦwww.longislandferry.com). Numerous **bus services** (operated by the usual major companies, as well as Hampton Jitney; Ⓣ1-800/936-0440, Ⓦwww.hamptonjitney.com) cover most destinations. If you are **driving** to Long Island, you'll take the Brooklyn–Queens Expressway (the BQE) to I-495 East. **Parking permits** during summer for most of Long Island's beaches are issued only to local residents. Also be aware that **accommodation** prices all over the island rise dramatically during the summer season, rigidly demarcated by Memorial and Labor days, so visit at other times if possible.

The South Shore and Fire Island

Long Island's **South Shore** merges gently with the wild Atlantic, with shallow, creamy sand beaches and rolling dunes – two of the most popular options are **Long Beach** and **Jones Beach**, which together run along fifty miles of seashore, getting less crowded the further east you go. **Ocean Parkway** leads along the narrow offshore strand from Jones Beach to **Captree**, from where the **Robert Moses Causeway** crosses back to **Bay Shore**, or heads south to pristine **Robert Moses State Park**, at the western tip of Fire Island. This way you can bypass the sprawling mess of **Amityville**, famous for its 1974 "horror"; the house in which a mysterious supernatural force is said to have victimized the occupants still stands as a private residence at 108 Ocean Ave.

A slim spit of land parallel to the South Shore, **Fire Island** is in many ways a microcosm of New York City and on the summer weekends half of Manhattan seems to be holed up in its tiny settlements, including the primarily gay enclaves of **Cherry Grove** and **The Pines**, lively **Ocean Beach**, exclusive **Point O'Woods** and **Sunken Forest** (aka Sailor's Haven), which attracts a mixed crowd. There are various **ferry crossings**, which anybody planning to stay must use, as driving between the two road access points at either end of the island is restricted to island business owners. Ferry schedules are subject to change; Fire Island Ferries (30–45min; $9 one-way; ⓣ631/665-3600, ⓦwww.fireislandferries.com) run from Bay Shore, the Sayville Ferry Service (25–45min; $6.50–12 one-way; ⓣ631/589-0810, ⓦwww.sayvilleferry.com) from Sayville, and Davis Park Ferries (25–35min; $8.50 one-way; ⓣ631/475-1665, ⓦwww.pagelinx.com/dpferry) from Patchogue.

All **accommodation** should be booked well in advance during summer, when rates can rise manifold; options include the hopping *Grove Hotel*, Bayview Walk and Holly Walk, Cherry Grove (ⓣ631/597-6600, ⓦwww.grovehotel.com; ❸); *Cleggs Hotel*, 478 Bayberry Walk, Ocean Beach (open May–Oct; ⓣ631/583-5399, ⓦwww.cleggshotel.com; ❻); and the *Fire Island Hotel & Resort*, at 25 Cayuga Walk, Ocean Bay Park (ⓣ631/583-8000, ⓦwww.fireislandhotel.com; ❽). For a **meal**, try nearby *Matthew's*, 935 Bay Walk (ⓣ631/583-8016), for its terrific fish specials for around $30. At weekends, the *Ice Palace*, at the *Grove Hotel*, and *Flynn's*, at 1 Cayuga St in Ocean Beach (ⓣ631/583-5000), are good for riotous boozing and dancing.

The North Shore and North Fork

Along the rugged **North Shore**, Long Island drops to the sea in a series of bluffs, coves and wooded headlands. The expressway beyond Queens leads straight onto the ultra-exclusive **Gold Coast**, where **Great Neck** was F. Scott Fitzgerald's West Egg in *The Great Gatsby*. In Old Westbury, at 71 Old Westbury Rd, **Old Westbury Gardens** comprise a Georgian mansion with beautiful, well-tended gardens and some pleasant works of art, including a few Gainsboroughs (late April to Oct Wed–Mon 10am–5pm; $10; ⓣ516/333-0048, ⓦwww.oldwestburygardens.org).

Sagamore Hill, on the coast road in Oyster Bay, twelve miles north of Old Westbury, is the heavily touristed former country retreat where **Teddy Roosevelt** lived for thirty-odd years (May–Sept daily, rest of year Wed–Sun 10am–5pm; hourly tours $5; ⓣ516/922-4788, ⓦwww.nps.gov/sahi). Its 23 rooms are adorned with hunting trophies, while the Old Orchard Museum (same days 9am–5pm; free), set within the same gorgeous grounds, recounts Teddy's political and personal life. Nearby **COLD SPRING HARBOR** grew up as a whaling port, and retains some of its looks. A fully equipped whaleboat and a 400-piece assembly of scrimshaw work help its **Whaling Museum** (Tues–Sun 11am–5pm; $6; ⓣ631/367-3418, ⓦwww.cshwhalingmuseum.org) to recapture that era.

After fifty more miles of bluffs and parks, the less touristed **North Fork** – once an independent colony – boasts typical wild Atlantic coastal scenery. In **GREENPORT**, its most picturesque town, a spacious wooden boardwalk encloses a harbour pierced by the masts of visiting yachts. At the west end there's the small **East End Seaport Museum and Marine Foundation** (mid-May to June & Sep Sat & Sun 11am–5pm; July & Aug Mon & Wed–Fri 11am–5pm, Sat & Sun 9.30am–5pm; $2; ⓣ631/477-2100, ⓦwww.eastendseaport.org). Plentiful **accommodation** includes Victorian B&Bs like the ten-room *Bartlett House Inn*, 503 Front St (ⓣ631/477-0371, ⓦwww.bartletthouseinn.com; ❼) and you can get a decent seafood meal at the *Chowder Pot Pub*, 102 3rd St (ⓣ631/477-1345), opposite the ferry terminal. Regular **ferries** connect the North Fork (pedestrians $2 one-way, cars including driver $9 one-way, $13 return; ⓣ631/749-0139, ⓦwww.northferry.com) with pleasant **Shelter Island** (ⓦwww.shelter-island.org) and on to the South Fork (pedestrians $1 one-way, cars including passengers $12 one-way, $15 return; ⓣ631/749-1200, ⓦwww.southferry.com).

The South Fork

The US holds few wealthier quarters than the small towns of Long Island's **South Fork**, where huge mansions lurk among the trees or stand boldly on the flats behind the dunes. Nowhere is consumption as deliberately conspicuous as in **the Hamptons**, among the oldest communities in the state. Long association with the smart set has left **SOUTHAMPTON** unashamedly upper class, its streets lined with galleries, and clothing and jewellery stores. The **Chamber of Commerce** at 76 Main St (Mon–Fri 10am–4pm, Sat & Sun 11am–3pm; ⓣ631/283-0402, ⓦwww.southamptonchamber.com) has lists of pricey **B&Bs**. You can get marvellous fresh seafood in a number of **restaurants**, notably *Barrister's*, at 36 Main St (ⓣ631/283-6206), and the venerable brewpub-restaurant *Southampton Publick House*, at 40 Bowden Square (ⓣ631/283-2800). **EAST HAMPTON** is the trendiest of the Hamptons, filled with the mansions of celebrities like Renée Zellweger, Jerry Seinfeld and Steven Spielberg. To see what's on in the Hamptons, pick up *Dan's Hamptons* (ⓦwww.danshamptons.com).

Historic **SAG HARBOR**, in its heyday a port second only to that of New York, was designated first Port of Entry to the New Country by George Washington; the **Old Custom House** (May & Sep Sat & Sun 10am–5pm; June–Aug Tues–Sun 10am–5pm; $5; ⓣ631/692-4664) dates from this era. The **Whaling Museum** on Main Street (mid-May to Oct Mon–Sat 10am–5pm, Sun 1–5pm; $5; ⓣ631/725-0770, ⓦwww.sagharborwhalingmuseum.org) commemorates the town's brief whaling days with guns and scrimshaw. The windmill where John Steinbeck once lived serves as a **visitor centre** (May–June & Sept–Oct Fri–Sun, July–Aug daily 10am–4pm; ⓣ631/725-0011, ⓦwww.sagharborchamber.com). You can get a luxurious **room** at the *Baron's Cove Inn*, at 31 W Water St (ⓣ631/725-2100, ⓦwww.baronscove.com; ❻), while at the well-heeled *American Hotel* on Main Street (ⓣ631/725-3535, ⓦwww.theamericanhotel.com; ❽) you can also get a splendid French **meal**. There are several good, less expensive restaurants along Main Street, such as the superb sushi bar *Sen* at no. 23 (ⓣ631/725-1774).

Blustery, wind-battered **MONTAUK**, on the furthest tip of Long Island, isn't chic or quaint. Real people actually live here and it provides access to the rocky wilds of **Montauk Point**. A **lighthouse** – New York State's oldest, dating from 1796 – forms an almost symbolic finale to this stretch of the American coast. **Motels** in the town centre, such as *Sands Motel*, as you enter on Rte-27 (ⓣ631/668-5100, ⓦwww.montauksands.com; ❸), offer refreshingly reasonable room prices; for something fancier, try *Gurney's Inn* on Old Montauk Highway (ⓣ631/668-2345, ⓦwww.gurneysinn.com; ❸). The ultimate Montauk **dining** experience is *The Lobster Roll*, halfway back towards East Hampton on Rte-27 (ⓣ631/267-3740), which serves excellent fresh seafood. Other good options include the moderately priced Chinese food at *Shagwong* on Main Street (ⓣ631/668-3050) and the delicious sushi at *West Lake Clam & Chowder House* (ⓣ631/668-6252).

The Hudson Valley and the Catskills

You only need to travel a few miles north of Manhattan before the Hudson River Valley takes on a Rhine-like charm, with prodigious historic homes rising from its steep and thickly wooded banks. A little further on come the forests of the **Catskill Mountains**, whose brilliant autumn colours rival anything to be seen in New England. Few of the cities along the Hudson, including the large but lacklustre state capital of **Albany**, hold much to attract the visitor, though many of the small towns are worth checking out, such as regional historic and culinary mecca **Hyde Park**.

The east bank

A mere 25 miles north of central New York City on US-9, leafy **TARRYTOWN** and the village of **IRVINGTON** were the original settings for Washington Irving's tales of *Rip Van Winkle* and *The Legend of Sleepy Hollow*. You can tour the farm cottage on West Sunnyside Lane, off Broadway/US-9, which the author rebuilt and renamed **Sunnyside** (April–Oct Wed–Mon 10am–5pm, Nov & Dec Sat & Sun 10am–4pm; $12; ⓣ914/591-8763, ⓦwww.hudsonvalley.org). Irvington's riverside **Hudson Park** makes for a scenic picnic. About ten miles north of Tarrytown along US-9, the town of **OSSINING** holds two impressive mid-Victorian creations: one is a huge bridge carrying the **Old Croton Aqueduct**, New York City's first water supply; the other, just south of town, is **Sing Sing Prison**, which for over 150 years has been the place where New York City criminals get sent "up the river".

HYDE PARK, set on a peaceful plateau some forty miles further up the Hudson's east bank, is worth a stop for the homes of **Franklin D.** and **Eleanor Roosevelt**. Well signposted off US-9, these homes, a Vanderbilt mansion (see below) and a couple of minor attractions all come under the aegis of the **Henry A. Wallace Visitor and Education Center** (April–Oct daily 8.45am–6.30pm; Nov–March 8.45am–5.30pm). The house where the "New Deal" president was born and spent much of his adult life is preserved here along with a library and a good **museum** (daily 9am–5pm; museum and guided house tour $14; ⓣ845/486-7770, ⓦwww.nps.gov/hofr), containing extensive letters, photos and artefacts. FDR lies buried in the Rose Garden, beside his wife (and distant cousin) Eleanor, one of the first women to play a prominent role in politics. After FDR's death in 1945, Eleanor moved to **Val-Kill** (May–Oct daily 9am–5pm; Nov–April Thurs–Mon 9am–5pm; tours $8; ⓦwww.nps.gov/elro), the nearby cottage retreat where she carried on her work until her death in 1962. A three-mile-long cliff-top **path** along the Hudson from the Roosevelt complex winds up at the Beaux Arts **Vanderbilt Mansion** (daily 9am–5pm; $8; ⓦwww.nps.gov/vama). This virtual palace is, believe it or not, the smallest of the family's residences. The furnishings are quite garish but the formal gardens are very pretty and offer a fine view of the Hudson River. The grounds to all three homes are open from dawn to dusk at no charge.

Hyde Park has one other huge tourist draw: the excellent restaurants and fascinating campus of the **Culinary Institute of America**, the most prestigious cooking school in the country, which stands along US-9, south of Hyde Park at 1946 Campus Drive. The outstanding restaurants here (lunch and dinner Mon–Sat;

Ⓣ845/471-6608 or Ⓦwww.ciachef.edu for reservations) have trained some of America's best chefs; classes and **tours** (Mon 10am & 4pm, Wed & Thurs 4pm; $5) can also be booked. Bargain **accommodation** in Hyde Park is available at the *Golden Manor Motel* (Ⓣ845/229-2157, Ⓦwww.goldenmanorhydepark.com; ❸), located on US-9 almost opposite the Roosevelt complex.

Six miles north of Hyde Park, **RHINEBECK** is the location of **America's oldest hotel** in continuous operation. The lovely, white colonial *Beekman Arms* on Rte-9 has been hosting and feeding travellers in its warm, wood-panelled rooms since 1766 (Ⓣ845/876-7077, Ⓦwww.beekmandelamaterinn.com; ❻). Among a number of good places to **eat** are the *Calico Restaurant & Patisserie*, 6384 Mill St (Ⓣ845/876-2749; closed Mon & Tues), which has a menu featuring Italian and French influences, and the all-American *Foster's Coachhouse Tavern*, 6411 Montgomery St (Ⓣ845/876-8052). Rhinebeck is also home to the New Agey **Omega Institute for Holistic Studies**, which runs a spa and offers a wide range of health and wellness workshops at a large campus east of town on Lake Drive (Ⓣ1-800/944-1001, Ⓦwww.eomega.org).

The west bank and Catskill Mountains

Rising above the west bank of the Hudson River, the magnificent crests of the **Catskills**, cloaked with maple and beech that turn orange, ochre and gold each autumn, have a rich and absorbing beauty. This dislocated branch of the Appalachians is inspiring country, filled with amenities – campgrounds, hiking, fishing and, especially, skiing.

Woodstock

Around twenty miles northwest of Rhinebeck, on the other side of the Hudson, Hwy-28 meanders into the Catskills, looping past the lovely Ashokan Reservoir where Hwy-375 branches off to **WOODSTOCK**. The village, carved out of the lush deciduous woodlands and cut by fast-rushing creeks, was not actually the venue of the famed **psychedelic picnic** of August 1969. That was some sixty miles southwest in Bethel, where a monument at Herd and West Shore roads marks the festival site on the farm owned by Max Yasgur. However, Woodstock has enjoyed a bohemian reputation since the foundation in 1903 of the **Byrdcliffe Arts Colony** (which runs summer residency courses; Ⓣ845/679-2079, Ⓦwww.woodstockguild.org), and during the 1960s it was a favourite stomping ground for the likes of Dylan, Hendrix and Van Morrison. The town still trades on its **hippie** past with shops selling crystals and tie-dyed T-shirts. Woodstock's galleries and craft shops command a regional reputation and the village is also a hub for the performing arts: the **Maverick Concert** series (late June to Aug; $25–40, students $5; Ⓣ845/679-8217, Ⓦwww.maverickconcerts.org) has played host to some of the world's finest chamber musicians since 1906.

Woodstock is a great base for exploring the Catskills, and the best option for **accommodation** is the cosy *Twin Gables Guest House*, 73 Tinker St (Ⓣ845/679-9479, Ⓦwww.twingableswoodstockny.com; ❹). If this is full, try the equally central *Getaway-on-the-Falls* at 5 Waterfall Way (Ⓣ845/679-2568, Ⓦwww.getawayonthefalls.com; ❻). Between Woodstock and Saugerties, which offers a string of chain motels ten miles northeast, are *Bed by the Stream* (Ⓣ845/246-2979, Ⓦwww.bedbythestream.com; ❻), a lovely rustic B&B, and *Rip Van Winkle* **campgrounds** (May–Oct; sites from $35; Ⓣ845/246-8334, Ⓦwww.ripvanwinklecampgrounds.com), both signposted off Rte-212. Apart from the town's favourite café, *Joshua's*, at 51 Tinker St (Ⓣ845/679-5533), the best **places to eat** are a little way out of the village: the menu at the *New World Home Cooking Company*, towards Saugerties at 1411 Rte-212 (April–Oct; Ⓣ845/246-0900), has Caribbean and Creole-influenced dishes for under $20, while two miles west on Rte-212 in tiny **Bearsville**, the lively *Bear Café* (ⓣ845/679-5555) serves excellent French bistro cuisine. Several daily **buses** take two and a half hours to reach Woodstock from New York City's Port Authority Bus Terminal (Adirondack Trailways; ⓣ1-800/858-8555, ⓦwww.trailwaysny.com). For more **information**, visit the Chamber of Commerce booth on Rock City Road, just off the village green (ⓣ845/679-6234, ⓦwww.woodstockchamber.com).

On through Catskill Park

Seven miles west of Woodstock, in the hamlet of **MOUNT TREMPER**, the **Emerson Place Kaleidoscope** (Sun–Thurs 10am–5pm, Fri & Sat 10am–7pm; $8) claims to be the world's largest, created by a local hippie artist in a 60ft-high converted grain silo. It plays ten-minute sound and light shows on request throughout the day and is part of the constantly expanding, upmarket *Emerson Place Resort & Spa*, 146 Mt Pleasant Rd (ⓣ845/688-2828 or 1-877/688-2828, ⓦwww.emersonplace.com; ❼), which offers spacious suites and soothing holistic treatments.

As you continue along Hwy-28, the picturesque village of **PHOENICIA**, in a hollow to the right of the road, is an ideal resting place and a great base for hiking trails in the area. You can catch the circular **Catskill Mountain Railroad** (late May to late Oct Sat, Sun & holidays 11am, 1pm & 2.50pm; $14 return; ⓣ845/688-7400, ⓦwww.catskillmtrailroad.com) through scenic Esopus Creek. The *Phoenicia Belle*, 73 Main St (ⓣ845/688-7226, ⓦwww.phoeniciabelle.com; ❺), is a very decent-value lodge with optional breakfast. A few doors along is the ever-popular café *Sweet Sue's* (ⓣ845/688-7852), while the *Phoenicia Diner* is another good option back on Hwy-28 (ⓣ845/688-9957).

For a scenic loop back to I-87, continue west on Hwy-49A and return via Hwy-23A and Hwy-23, halting for a breathtaking view of the dramatic **gorge** between the villages of Hunter and Catskill. The area's premier **ski runs** are on Hunter Mountain (ⓣ518/263-4223, ⓦwww.huntermtn.com), where daredevils can try out the exhilarating zip-line during other seasons. Accommodation rates rise significantly during the ski season: *Scribner Hollow Lodge*, half a mile from the mountain on Hwy-23A (ⓣ518/263-4211, ⓦwww.scribnerhollow.com; ❽), boasts deluxe rooms, a fine-dining restaurant with great views and a multi-pool swimming grotto. Rooms in the hamlet of Catskill, such as in the *Red Ranch Motel* at 4555 Rte-32 (April–Dec; ⓣ518/678-3380 or 1-800/962-4560, ⓦwww.redranchmotel.com; ❸), are basic but more affordable.

Albany

Founded by Dutch fur-trappers in the early seventeenth century, **ALBANY** made its money by controlling trade along the Erie Canal, and its reputation by being capital of the state. It's not an unpleasant town, just rather boring, though there are a few livelier areas on the fringes. A good place to start a tour is the **Quackenbush House**, the city's oldest building, built along the river in 1736 and now serving as part of the **Albany Urban Culture Park**. The modern **visitor centre**, next door at Broadway and Clinton (Mon–Fri 9am–4pm, Sat 10am–3pm, Sun 11am–3pm; ⓣ518/434-0405, ⓦwww.albany.org), has free maps and can provide details of **tours** of the imposing Neoclassical **Capitol** and the downtown area, where a number of Revolutionary-era homes survive.

Uphill from the waterfront, the ugly complex of Nelson A. Rockefeller's **Empire State Plaza** has one redeeming feature: the view from **Corning Tower**'s 42nd-floor observation deck (daily 10am–2.30pm; free) looks out far across the state, beyond the twisting Hudson River to the Adirondack foothills, the Catskills and the Berkshires in Massachusetts. It also peers down on the neighbouring

Performing Arts Center, known locally as "**The Egg**" (Ⓣ518/478-1845, Ⓦwww.theegg.org) – which adds the only curves to the Plaza's harsh angularity. The **New York State Museum** (daily 9.30am–5pm; free; Ⓣ518/474-5877, Ⓦwww.nysm.nysed.gov), one level down at the south end of the plaza, reveals everything you could want to know about New York State in imaginative exhibits, including the original set of *Sesame Street*.

The most engaging part of Albany is the few blocks west of the plaza, a neighbourhood full of nineteenth-century brick-built Victorian houses. The **Albany Institute of History and Art**, 125 Washington Ave (Wed–Sat 10am–5pm, Sun noon–5pm; $10; Ⓣ518/463-4478, Ⓦwww.albanyinstitute.org), has a good range of Hudson River School paintings.

Practicalities

Arrive by Greyhound or Adirondack Trailways (see opposite) and it's a short, hilly walk to the heart of downtown; come in via Amtrak and you face a two-mile bus ride across the river. If you intend to **stay** the night, it's mainly a choice between suburban chain motels at $60 a night and downtown standards like the *Hampton Inn & Suites*, 25 Chapelk St (Ⓣ518/432-7000, Ⓦwww.hamptoninn.com; ❺). For more atmosphere, try the *Mansion Hill Inn*, 115 Philip St (Ⓣ518/465-2038 or 1-888/299-0455, Ⓦwww.mansionhill.com; ❺), a lovely B&B in a restored home; it also has a fine restaurant. Other good **places to eat** are located on or near **Lark Street**, a few blocks west of the plaza, which is also the hub of the local gay scene. *Justin's*, at no. 301 (Ⓣ518/436-7008), and *Café Hollywood*, at no. 275 (Ⓣ518/472-9043), serve good, progressive American food at moderate prices, while the welcoming *Mamoun's*, 206 Washington Ave (Ⓣ518/434-3901), has great inexpensive lamb, chicken and vegetarian dishes. Two of the most popular **nightlife** haunts are *Jillian's*, 59 N Pearl St (Ⓣ518/432-1997, Ⓦwww.jilliansofalbany.com), which has live music, as does *Tess' Lark Tavern*, 453 Madison Ave (Ⓣ518/463-7875, Ⓦwww.larktavern.com), an Irish bar. Or head across the river to the college town of **Troy**.

North through the Adirondacks

Mountaineers, skiers and dedicated hikers form the majority of visitors to the vast northern region between Albany and the Canadian border. Outdoor pursuits are certainly the main attractions in the rugged wilderness of the **Adirondack Mountains**, though a few small resorts, especially the former Winter Olympic venue of **Lake Placid** and its smaller neighbour **Lake Saranac**, offer creature comforts in addition to breathtaking scenery; and the elegant spa town of **Saratoga Springs** nestles invitingly in the delicate countryside of the southern foothills.

Saratoga Springs

Saratoga was fast, man, it was real fast. It was up all night long.

Hattie Gray, founder of *Hattie's* restaurant

For well over a century, **SARATOGA SPRINGS**, just 42 miles north of Albany on I-87, was very much the place to be seen for the Northeast's richest and most glittering names. At first, the town's curative waters were the main attraction; then John Morrisey, an Irish boxer, transformed things by opening a **racetrack** and **casino** here during the 1860s. During the August horse-racing season, Saratoga Springs retains the feel of an exclusive vintage resort – but for the rest of the summer it is accessible, affordable and fun.

Broadway, the main axis, and the few blocks just east of it are where you'll find most of the action. The carefully cultivated **Congress Park**, off South Broadway, remains a shady retreat from town-centre traffic. Three of the original mineral springs still flow up to the surface here, funnelled out into drinking fountains. Also here is the original **casino**, which when built formed part of a whole city block. The **racetrack** (late July to early Sept, post time 1pm; $3–5; ⓣ518/584-6200, ⓦwww.nyra.com) still functions in a rather grand, old-fashioned manner, though there is no longer such a strict dress code. There's no such pretension at the **harness track**, aka the Equine Sports Center, on nearby Crescent Avenue (evening races several times a week May–Nov; $2; ⓣ518/584-2110). If you can't get to either, visit the array of paintings, trophies and audiovisual displays at the **National Museum of Racing and Hall of Fame**, on Union Avenue at Ludlow Street (Wed–Sat 10am–4pm, April–Dec also Sun noon–4pm, during race meet daily 9am–5pm; $7; ⓣ518/584-0400, ⓦwww.racingmuseum.org).

On the southern edge of town, green **Saratoga Spa State Park** (daily 8am–dusk; $8/car; ⓣ518/584-2000, ⓦwww.saratogaspastatepark.org) presents opportunities to swim in great old Victorian pools, picnic, hike or even "take the waters", ie, take a hot bath in the tingly, naturally carbonated stuff and receive a variety of spa treatments. The nearby **Saratoga Performing Arts Center** (June to early Sept; ⓣ518/587-3330, ⓦwww.spac.org) – or SPAC – is home to the New York City Ballet in July, the Philadelphia Orchestra in August and hosts other quality festivals.

Practicalities

Central Saratoga Springs is easily explored on foot. **Accommodation** is only a problem during August's race season, or if there's a big gig on at SPAC, when prices can more than double. One good central motel is the *Turf and Spa*, 140 Broadway (April–Oct; ⓣ518/584-2550 or 1-800/972-1229, ⓦwww.saratogaturfandspa.com; ❷). Both the lavishly restored landmark *Adelphi Hotel*, 365 Broadway (May–Oct; ⓣ518/587-4688, ⓦwww.adelphihotel.com; ❺), and the grand *Gideon Putnam Hotel*, located right in Saratoga Spa State Park (ⓣ518/584-3000, ⓦwww.gideonputnam.com; ❽), have more character. The **visitor centre**, 97 Broadway (ⓣ518/584-3255, ⓦwww.saratoga.org), has full lists of accommodation.

Finding somewhere to eat is also easy. One longtime favourite is the soul food at *Hattie's*, 45 Phila St (ⓣ518/584-4790), where huge entrees cost $15–18; another good bet is *Wheat Fields*, 440 Broadway (ⓣ518/587-0534), with good salads and pasta served on an outdoor patio. *Beverly's*, 47 Phila St (ⓣ518/583-2755), serves great but pricey breakfasts. There's usually good Irish **music** at the *Parting Glass Pub*, 40 Lake Ave (ⓣ518/583-1916), and *9 Maple Avenue*, logically enough at 9 Maple Ave (ⓣ518/583-2582, ⓦwww.9mapleavenue.com), offers live jazz and blues until the early hours. Folksy nonprofit *Caffé Lena*, 47 Phila St (ⓣ518/583-0022, ⓦwww.caffelena.org) is where Don McLean first inflicted "American Pie" on the world.

The Adirondacks

The **Adirondacks**, which cover an area larger than Connecticut and Rhode Island combined, are said by locals to be named after an Iroquois insult for enemies they'd driven into the forests and left to become "bark eaters". Until recent decades the area was almost the exclusive preserve of loggers, fur trappers and a few select New York millionaires. For sheer grandeur, the region is hard to beat: 46 peaks reach to over 4000ft; in summer the purple-green mountains span far into the distance in shaggy tiers, in autumn the trees form a russet-red kaleidoscope.

Though Adirondack Trailways buses serve the area, you'll find it hard-going without a **car**. General **information** and some special deals can be had from the Adirondack Region tourist office (ⓣ1-800/487-6867, ⓦwww.visitadirondacks.com), and the Adirondack Mountain Club (Ⓣ518/668-4447, Ⓦwww.adk.org) and Adirondack Park Visitor Interpretive Centers (daily 9am–5pm; Ⓣ518/327-3000, Ⓦwww.adkvic.org), can provide details on **hiking** and **camping**.

Lake Placid

The winter sports centre of **LAKE PLACID**, twice the proud host of the Winter Olympics, lies thirty miles west of I-87 on Hwy-73. In winter there's thrilling alpine skiing at imposing Whiteface Mountain and all manner of Nordic disciplines at Mount Van Hoevenberg; in summer you can watch luge athletes practise on refrigerated runs, freestyle skiers somersaulting off dry slopes into swimming pools and top amateur ice hockey games. The mountain slopes also provide challenging terrain for hikers and cyclists; good **mountain bikes**, maps of local trails, and **guided tours** are available from High Peaks Cyclery, 2733 Main St (Ⓣ518/523-3764). The **Olympic Sites Passport** ($29; Ⓣ518/523-1655, Ⓦwww.whiteface.com) allows you on the chairlift to the top of the 393ft ski jump and eight miles up the sheer Whiteface Mountain toll road and back again, on the Whiteface gondola, and into the Olympic museum (see below). At the **Olympic Sports Complex** on Mount Van Hoevenburg (Ⓣ518/523-4436), you can do a blood-curdling bobsled run ($70) or bike the extensive trail network ($35/day rental; $6 trail pass).

The town itself is set on two lakes: **Mirror Lake**, which you can sail on in summer and skate on in winter, and larger **Lake Placid**, just to the west, on which you can take a narrated **cruise** in summer ($11; Ⓣ518/523-9704). Other attractions include the **Olympic Center** on Main Street, which houses four ice rinks, and the informative **1932 and 1980 Lake Placid Winter Olympic Museum** (self-guided audio tour $5; Ⓣ518/523-1655). Outside the village on Hwy-73, the **John Brown Farm State Historic Site** (May–Oct Wed–Mon 10am–5pm; $2; Ⓣ518/523-3900) was where the famous abolitionist brought his family in 1849 to aid a small colony of black farmers and where he conceived his ill-fated raid on Harper's Ferry in an attempt to end slavery. The house is less interesting than his story (see p.373); the grounds, which include Brown's grave, are open year-round.

Practicalities

Lake Placid's helpful **visitor centre** (Ⓣ518/523-2445 or 1-800/447-5224, Ⓦwww.lakeplacid.com) was due to relocate to the Olympic Sports Complex at the time of writing. **Accommodation** in town ranges from the somewhat economical to the opulent. The casually elegant *Mirror Lake Inn Resort & Spa*, 77 Mirror Lake Drive (Ⓣ518/523-2544, Ⓦwww.mirrorlakeinn.com; ❽), has over 120 rooms, the best of them palatial, and an array of facilities, while the welcoming *Stagecoach Inn*, 3 Stagecoach Way (Ⓣ518/523-9698, Ⓦwww.lakeplacidstagecoachinn.com; ❻) exudes rustic charm. *Edelweiss Motel*, on the east side of town at 2806 Wilmington Rd, has clean if somewhat dated rooms (Ⓣ518/523-3821; ❹). The *Keene Valley Hostel*, around fifteen miles southeast in Keene Valley (Ⓣ518/576-2030, Ⓦwww.keenevalleyhostel.com; dorm beds $25, camping $15), is a great base to be within walking distance of all the best hiking trails.

It's possible to **eat** well, with a view, for relatively little here. *Blues Berry Bakery*, 2436 Main St (Ⓣ518/523-4539), is much loved for its apple strudel, while *Hunan Oshaka* (Ⓣ518/523-1558), nearby at no. 2663, offers a unique choice of Chinese, Japanese and Mexican cuisine. On the east side of town, the *Station Street Bar & Grille*, 1 Station St (Ⓣ518/523-9963), is undoubtedly the friendliest place for a night out with the locals and serves delicious ribs and other dishes. Main Street's buzzing *Zig Zags Pub* (Ⓣ518/523-8221) is the main place for **live music** at the weekend.

Saranac Lake

SARANAC LAKE, ten miles northwest of Lake Placid, is a smaller, more laidback and cheaper base for the region. The tranquil lakeshore is lined with lovely gingerbread cottages, most of them built during the late 1800s, when this was a popular middle-class retreat and spa. **Robert Louis Stevenson** spent the winter of 1888 in a small cottage on the east side of town at 44 Stevenson Lane; it's now preserved as a **museum** (July–Sept Tues–Sun 9.30am–noon & 1–4.30pm; rest of year by appointment; $5; ⓣ518/891-1462, ⓦwww.robertlouisstevensonmemorialcottage.org).

Set in quiet rustic grounds at 371 Park Ave, the *Saranac Club & Inn* (ⓣ518/891-7212 or 1-866/595-9800; ❺) is a spacious B&B that offers far better value than its Lake Placid equivalents. Downtown the *Hotel Saranac*, 100 Main St (ⓣ518/891-2200 or 1-800/937-0211, ⓦwww.hotelsaranac.com; ❸), also has a friendly **bar**. *Eat-n-Meet*, 139 Broadway (ⓣ518/891-3149), is a quirky and laidback little **restaurant**, serving inexpensive home-cooking at very fair prices.

The Finger Lakes

At the heart of the state, southwest of Syracuse on the far side of the Catskills from New York City, are the eleven **Finger Lakes**, narrow channels gouged out by glaciers that have left telltale signs in the form of drumlins, steep gorges and a number of waterfalls. With the exception of progressive, well-to-do **Ithaca** and tiny **Skaneateles**, few towns compete with the lakeshore scenery. That said, the area as a whole is relaxing and enjoys a growing reputation for quality **wineries**.

Skaneateles and Seneca Falls

SKANEATELES (pronounced "Skinny-Atlas"), crouching at the neck of Skaneateles Lake, is perhaps the prettiest Finger Lakes town. It's also the best place to go swimming in the region: just a block from the town centre, and lined by huge resort homes, the appealing bay sports a **beach** (summer daily; $3) and the Skaneateles Marina, where you can rent watersports equipment (ⓣ315/685-5095) and take boat trips, from Mid-Lakes Navigation ($11 for 50min; ⓣ315/685-8500, ⓦwww.midlakesnav.com). **Accommodation** options include the simple *Colonial Motel*, one mile west on Hwy-20 (ⓣ315/685-5751, ⓦwww.colonialmotelonline.com; ❸). Overlooking the lake are the elegant *1899 Lady of the Lake* B&B, 2 W Lake St (ⓣ1-888/685-7997, ⓦwww.ladyofthelake.net; ❼) and the *Sherwood Inn*, 26 W Genesee St (ⓣ315/685-3405, ⓦwww.thesherwoodinn.com; ❺), which features a good dining room and tavern. Cheaper but still scrumptious **meals** can be had at the ever-popular *Doug's Fish Fry*, 8 Jordan St (ⓣ315/685-3288), while the spot for a classy blowout is *Krebs 1899*, 53 W Genesee St (ⓣ315/685-5714), which does an excellent American home-cooking buffet for under $50 per person and has a bar with snacks upstairs.

At **SENECA FALLS**, just west of the northern tip of Cayuga Lake and around 15 miles west of Skaneateles, Elizabeth Cady Stanton and a few colleagues held the first Women's Rights Convention in 1848 – well before female suffrage in 1920. On the site of the **Wesleyan Chapel**, 136 Fall St, where the first campaign meeting was held, is the terrific **Women's Rights National Historical Park** (daily 9am–5pm; ⓣ315/568-2991, ⓦwww.nps.gov/wori), which sets the early and contemporary women's movements in their historical contexts, emphasizing the connection with the African-American civil rights movements. A block east, at 76 Fall St, the **National Women's Hall of Fame** (May–Sept Mon–Sat 10am–5pm, Sun noon–5pm; Oct–April Wed–Sat 11am–5pm, closed Jan; $3; ⓣ315/568-8060, ⓦwww.greatwomen.org), honours about two hundred women, including Emily Dickinson and Sojourner

Truth. If you want to stop over, the best **place to stay** is the *Hubbell House* B&B, at 42 Cayuga St (Ⓣ315/568-9690, Ⓦwww.hubbellhousebb.com; ❻). There are several places to eat, such as *Jeremy's Café*, 77 Fall St (Ⓣ315/568-1614), which offers standard American fare. Hwy-89, between Seneca Falls and Ithaca, has been dubbed the **Cayuga Wine Trail**, with dozens of small wineries operating along the west shore of the largest of the Finger Lakes, such as Sheldrake Point (Ⓦwww.sheldrakepoint.com) and Thirsty Owl (Ⓦwww.thirstyowl.com); both offer tastings for $1.

Ithaca

Cayuga Lake comes to a halt at its southern end at picturesque **ITHACA**, piled like a diminutive San Francisco above the lakeshore and culminating in the towers, sweeping lawns and shaded parks of Ivy-League **Cornell University**. On campus, which is cut by striking gorges, creeks and lakes, the sleek, I.M. Pei-designed **Herbert F. Johnson Museum of Art** (Tues–Sun 10am–5pm; free; Ⓣ607/255-6464, Ⓦwww.museum.cornell.edu), across the street from the gorge-straddling **suspension bridge**, merits a visit more for its fifth-floor view of the town and lake than for the moderate collection of Asian and contemporary art. Adjacent to campus lie the **Cornell Plantations** (daily: dawn–dusk; free; Ⓣ607/255-2400, Ⓦwww.plantations.cornell.edu), the extensive botanical gardens and arboretum run by the university.

The pick of the countless **waterfalls** within a few miles of town are the slender **Taughannock Falls**, ten miles north of town just off Hwy-89 and with a swimming beach; they are taller than Niagara at a height of 215ft. **Buttermilk Falls State Park**, two miles south of town on Rte-13, is a delightful spot and the dangerous-looking Lucifer Falls, at lush **Robert H. Treman State Park**, three miles further south, should not be missed. Parking is $7 for the day, which covers all three parks. Cayuga Lake provides excellent **boating** and **windsurfing** opportunities; boards and boats can be rented from several places.

Practicalities

Greyhound and other **buses** operate out of the terminal at W State and N Fulton. Free **internet** access is available at the huge, partially solar-powered library on Cayuga Avenue next to the Ithaca Commons. The helpful **visitor centre** is at 904 East Shore Drive, off Hwy-34 N (Mon–Fri 9am–5pm, Sat 10am–5pm, Sun 10am–4pm, longer in summer; Ⓣ607/272-1313 or 1-800/284-8422, Ⓦwww.visitithaca.com). **Accommodation** options include the *Inn on Columbia*, a classy B&B at 228 Columbia St (Ⓣ607/272-0204, Ⓦwww.columbiabb.com; ❹), or the luxurious *Statler Hotel*, on East Avenue within the campus proper (Ⓣ1-800/541-2501, Ⓦwww.statlerhotel.cornell.edu; ❽). For a more rural setting, the *Halsey House* B&B, at 2057 Trumansburg Rd (Ⓣ607/387-5977, Ⓦwww.halseyhouse.com; ❼), is in Trumansburg, within walking distance of Taughannock Falls.

Ithaca boasts two **dining** and entertainment zones. **Downtown**, centred on the vehicle-free Commons, is the larger and better of the two. Here DeWitt Mall, on the corner of Cayuga and Seneca streets, features a number of restaurants, such as the top-rated vegetarian *Moosewood* (Ⓣ607/273-9610) of cookbook fame. A block away, *Just a Taste*, 116 N Aurora St (Ⓣ607/277-9463), is a lively wine and tapas bar. Numerous cheap student-oriented places to eat line the streets of **Collegetown**; check out *The Nines*, 311 College Ave (Ⓣ607/272-1888), which serves up the best deep-dish pizza around and has live music. Further afield, at 53 E Main St in Trumansburg, *Hazlenut Kitchen* (Ⓣ607/387-4433) serves delicious and imaginative food fresh from the farm. For news of the lively **music** scene, pick up the free *Ithaca Times* (Ⓦwww.ithacatimes.com); *The Haunt*, 702 Willow Ave (Ⓣ607/275-3477, Ⓦwww.thehaunt.com), is one of the liveliest venues.

The Erie Canal towns

The fertile farming country stretching from Albany at the head of the Hudson to the growing tourist destination of **Buffalo** on Lake Erie, along the route of the **Erie Canal**, comprises the agricultural heartland of New York State. The eastern parts – also known as **Central Leatherstocking**, after the protective leggings worn by the area's first settlers – are well off the conventional tourist trails, with the exception of the lovely village of **Cooperstown**. The industrial college town of Syracuse only merits a visit for the Erie Canal Museum (Mon–Sat 10am–5pm, Sun 10am–3pm; free; ⓣ315/471-0593, ⓦwww.eriecanalmuseum.org), housed in an 1850s weighing station at 318 E Erie Blvd. **Rochester**, however, possesses some worthy attractions and a few exploratory detours en route to Buffalo/Niagara will pay dividends in the shape of quaint canal-side villages and deserted beaches up on Lake Ontario.

Cooperstown

Seventy miles west of Albany, sitting gracefully on the wooded banks of tranquil Otsego Lake, is pleasant **COOPERSTOWN**, christened "Glimmerglass" by novelist James Fenimore Cooper, son of the town's founder. The birth of baseball, said to have originated here on Doubleday Field, is commemorated by the inspired and spacious **National Baseball Hall of Fame**, on Main Street (daily 9am–5pm, summer until 9pm; $16.50; ⓣ607/547-7200, ⓦwww.baseballhalloffame.org), enjoyable even for the uninitiated. The delightful **Fenimore Art Museum**, just north of town on Lake Road/Rte-80 (April to mid-May & mid-Oct to Dec Tues–Sun 10am–4pm; mid-May to mid-Oct daily 10am–5pm; $12; ⓣ1-888/547-1450, ⓦwww.fenimoreartmuseum.org), has innovative special exhibits and a fine collection of folk and (Native North American art. In summer, Cooperstown hosts **classical concerts** and the **Glimmerglass Opera** at Alice Busch Opera Theater, north on Hwy-80 by the lake (ⓣ607/547-5704, ⓦwww.glimmerglass.org).

If you drive here in summer, park in one of the free car parks on the edge of town and take the **trolley** around the various sights (8am–9pm; $3 all-day pass). The helpful **visitor centre** is at 31 Chestnut St (summer daily 9am–6pm, winter Mon–Sat 9am–5pm; ⓣ607/547-9983, ⓦwww.cooperstownchamber.org); their website is an excellent way to arrange **accommodation**. Rooms in the town itself are expensive during summer at classy establishments such as *The Inn At Cooperstown*, 16 Chestnut St (ⓣ607/547-5756, ⓦwww.innatcooperstown.com; ❺), but there's a cluster of clean motels right on pretty Otsego Lake, a few miles north on Rte-80; the *Lake 'N Pines* (ⓣ607/547-2790 or 1-800/615-5253, ⓦwww.lakenpinesmotel.com; ❸; closed Dec–March) offers superb value off-season. Further north on Rte-80, the *Blue Mingo Grill* (ⓣ607/547-7496), where fusion and New American dishes change nightly, is one of the area's best and most creative **restaurants**. For a quick bite in town away from the crowds, try the *Cooperstown Diner*, 136 1/2 Main St (ⓣ607/547-9201), open until 2pm for breakfast and burgers.

Rochester

In contrast to its sprawling suburbs, downtown **ROCHESTER** is a salubrious place, with its central office-block area bordered by well-heeled mansions on spacious boulevards. High-tech companies such as Bausch & Lomb, Xerox and Kodak have created a thriving local economy throughout the years, despite national and regional economic downturns. Kodak's (and its founder, George Eastman's) legacies throughout the metropolitan area include Kodak Park, the Eastman Theater and, above all, the **International Museum of Photography** at George Eastman House, two miles from downtown at 900 East Ave (Tues–Sat 10am–5pm,

Thurs until 8pm, Sun 1–5pm; $10; ⓣ585/271-3361, ⓦwww.eastmanhouse.org). In the modern annexe, a first-rate exhibition of photographic history ranges from high-quality Civil War prints to modern experimental works. There's also a space for temporary exhibitions and an arthouse cinema, but the house itself is surpassed in glory by its superbly maintained gardens. A few blocks back towards downtown at 657 East Ave, the **Rochester Museum & Science Center** (Mon–Sat 9am–5pm, Sun 11am–5pm; $12; ⓣ585/271-4320, ⓦwww.rmsc.org) houses interesting interactive displays on science, natural history, Native Americans and local history. Nearby at 500 University Ave, the **Memorial Art Gallery** (Wed–Sun 11am–5pm, Thurs until 9pm; $10; ⓣ585/473-7720, ⓦwww.mag.rochester.edu) houses a surprisingly extensive collection that includes three Monets and a Rembrandt.

An obsessive collector of anything and everything, local bigwig Margaret Woodbury Strong (1897–1969) bequeathed her estate to the city and today it is the **Strong National Museum of Play** on Manhattan Square (Mon–Thurs 10am–5pm, Fri & Sat 10am–8pm, Sun noon–5pm; $11, kids $9; ⓣ585/263-2700, ⓦwww.strongmuseum.org). Half devoted to a history of the American family and half obsessed with a history of American children's pop culture, it features interactive exhibits such as a history of *Sesame Street* and a fully working 1920s carousel. There's also a stunning indoor butterfly garden. The theme of celebrating former Rochester residents continues at the **Susan B. Anthony House** at 17 Madison St, where this renowned suffragette lived from 1866 to 1906 (Tues–Sun 11am–5pm; $6; ⓣ585/235-6124, ⓦwww.susanbanthonyhouse.org).

Practicalities

Greyhound drops off at Broad and Chestnut streets downtown. The Amtrak station, 320 Central Ave, is on the north side beyond the I-490 inner loop road; it's served by Regional Transit Service (RTS) public **buses** (ⓣ585/288-1700, ⓦwww.rgrta.com). Rochester's **visitor centre** is at 45 East Ave (Mon–Fri 8.30am–5pm, Sat 10am–3pm; ⓣ1-800/677-7282, ⓦwww.visitrochester.com). **Accommodation** is somewhat expensive downtown, where choices include the excellent *428 Mt Vernon B&B* (ⓣ716/271-0792 or 1-800/836-3159, ⓦwww.428mtvernon.com; ❻), at the entrance to lush Highland Park. Among budget options in the south of the city is the standard chain motel *Red Roof Inn*, 4820 W Henrietta Rd, off I-90 exit 46 (ⓣ585/359-1100, ⓦwww.redroof.com; ❸).

Popular **places to eat** downtown include *Aladdin's Natural Eatery*, 646 Monroe Ave (ⓣ585/442-5000), serving inexpensive Middle Eastern food, and *Nick Tahou Hots* at 320 W Main St (ⓣ585/436-0184), famous for its "Garbage Plate" – a local hodgepodge of meats, eggs and vegetables. In the university area *Esan*, 696 Park Ave (ⓣ585/271-2271), is the place for authentically spicy and inexpensive Thai food, while in the up-and-coming area known as South Wedge the *Beale St Café*, 689 South Ave (ⓣ585/271-4650), serves fine heapings of Southern and Cajun cooking, complemented by live blues four nights a week.

Buffalo

As I-90 sweeps down into the state's second largest city, **BUFFALO**, downtown looms up in a cluster of Art Deco spires and glass-box skyscrapers – Manhattan in miniature on Lake Erie. The city's early twentieth-century prosperity is reflected in such architecturally significant structures as the towering 1932 **City Hall** (free observation deck on the top floor) and the deep red terracotta relief of Louis Sullivan's **Guaranty Building** on Church Street. The massive abandoned grain elevators form part of current redevelopment of the **Erie Canal Harbor** into a major entertainment and shopping hub. Renowned as a blue-collar city, Buffalo also loves its professional **sports** teams: football's Bills (Ⓣ1-877/228-4257, Ⓦwww.buffalobills.com) and ice hockey's Sabres (Ⓣ1-888/467-2273, Ⓦwww.sabres.nhl.com) both draw huge crowds.

That Buffalo's wealthy merchants were a cultured lot is apparent in the excellent **Albright-Knox Art Gallery**, 1285 Elmwood Ave (Tues–Sun noon–5pm, Fri until 10pm; $12; Ⓣ716/882-8700, Ⓦwww.albrightknox.org), two miles north of downtown amid the green spaces of the Frederick Law Olmsted-designed **Delaware Park**. One of the top modern collections in the world, it's especially strong on recent American and European art with works by Pollock, Rothko, Warhol and Rauschenberg. Other highlights are a Surrealism collection and pieces by earlier artists such as Matisse, Picasso and Monet. Opposite at 1300 Elmwood Ave, the airy new **Burchfield Penney Art Center** (Tues–Sat 10am–5pm, Thurs until 9pm, Sun 1–5pm; $9; Ⓣ716/878-6011, Ⓦwww.burchfieldpenney.org) displays works by local artists. The area around Delaware Park features several homes designed by **Frank Lloyd Wright**, most notably the Darwin D. Martin House Complex (tour times and lengths vary; $15–30; Ⓣ716/947-9217, Ⓦwww.darwinmartinhouse.org). Between here and downtown lie **Elmwood Village** and **Allentown**, Buffalo's most bohemian neighbourhoods. At 641 Delaware Ave, the **Theodore Roosevelt Inaugural National Historic Site** (Mon–Fri 9am–5pm, Sun noon–5pm; $10; Ⓣ716/884-0095, Ⓦwww.trsite.org) allows you to tour the house where Teddy took the oath of office after President Mckinley's assassination in 1901.

Arrival and information

Greyhound, Metro Bus and Metro Rail, the city's tramway (both Metros Ⓣ716/855-7211, Ⓦwww.nfta.com/metro), all operate from the downtown depot at Ellicott and N Division streets. Several routes go to **Niagara Falls** (see opposite). Amtrak **trains** stop some six blocks away, at Exchange Street, as well as in the eastern suburb of Depew, eight miles from town but close to the **airport** (Ⓣ716/630-6020, Ⓦwww.buffaloairport.com). There's a helpful **visitor centre** at 617 Main St (Mon–Fri 9am–5pm, Sat 10am–2pm; Ⓣ716/852-2356 or 1-800/283-3256, Ⓦwww.visitbuffaloniagara.com), which offers a wealth of information. Taxis can be booked from Buffalo Taxi Cab (Ⓣ716/822-3030, Ⓦwww.buffalotaxicab.com).

Accommodation

Buffalo has no shortage of good **places to stay**, many of which are in the heart of downtown.

Beau Fleuve 242 Linwood Ave Ⓣ716/882-6116 or 1-800/278-0245, Ⓦwww.beaufleuve.com. Extremely comfortable, well-appointed B&B with great breakfasts. ❺

Comfort Inn & Suites 601 Main St Ⓣ716/854-5500, Ⓦwww.comfortsuites.com. A safe bet with smart, spacious suites in the heart of downtown; free breakfasts. ❺

HI-Buffalo Hostel 667 Main St Ⓣ716/852-5222, Ⓦwww.hostelbuffalo.com. Very central hostel with beds for $25 and some private rooms. Best budget option for the Buffalo/Niagara area. No lockout. ❷

Lenox Hotel & Suites 140 North St Ⓣ716/884-1700 or 1-800/825-3669, Ⓦwww.lenoxhotelandsuites.com. Rather drab brick building but centrally located and the simple rooms are good value. ❹

The Mansion on Delaware Avenue 414 Delaware Ave Ⓣ716/886-3300, Ⓦwww.mansionondelaware.com. Centrally located luxury inn, with all modern amenities and gourmet breakfasts. ❼

Eating, drinking and nightlife

The heart of Buffalo's downtown centres on Chippewa and Main streets. For a quick snack, the cheap food stalls and tiny Polish cafés of ancient **Broadway Market**, 999 Broadway, are well worth perusing. The main **nightlife** drag on Chippewa has plenty of sports bars and nightclubs, while the majority of theatres and venues that house the city's burgeoning **arts scene** are handily grouped nearby along Main.

Asbury Hall, inside Ani DiFranco's *Babeville*, 341 Delaware Ave (Ⓣ716/852-3835, Ⓦwww.babevillebuffalo.com), hosts left-field gigs and other events. For details of what's on, pick up the free weekly *Art Voice* (Ⓦwww.artvoice.com) or the gay and lesbian *Outcome* (Ⓦwww.outcomebuffalo.com).

Anchor Bar 1047 Main St Ⓣ716/886-8920, Ⓦwww.anchorbar.com. The city's specialty of buffalo (spicy chicken) wings with blue cheese and celery dressing is said to have been invented here.

Bacchus Wine Bar & Restaurant 54 W Chippewa St Ⓣ716/854-9463. A good late-night bar and restaurant, with jazz, blues, folk and world music.

Cole's 1104 Elmwood Ave Ⓣ716/886-1449. Lively diner-style joint that rustles up a tasty and inexpensive array of appetizers, salads, burgers, wraps and chicken dishes, as well as decent beers.

India Gate 1116 Elmwood Ave Ⓣ716/886-4000. Good, inexpensive Indian restaurant with generous lunch buffet.

Nietzsche's 248 Allen St Ⓣ716/886-8539, Ⓦwww.nietzsches.com. Bar with friendly staff and cheap drinks, hosting a wide variety of live acts seven days a week; there's room for dancing in the back.

Spot Coffee 227 Delaware Ave Ⓣ716/856-2739; 765 Elmwood Ave Ⓣ716/332-5288. Lively, happening neighbourhood institution serving basic food and good drinks.

Niagara Falls

Every second almost three-quarters of a million gallons of water explode over the knife-edge **NIAGARA FALLS**, right on the border with Canada some twenty miles north of Buffalo on I-190. This awesome spectacle is made even more impressive by the variety of methods laid on to help you get closer to it. At night the falls are lit up and the coloured waters tumble dramatically into blackness, while in winter the whole scene changes as the fringes of the falls freeze to form gigantic razor-tipped icicles.

Some visitors will, no doubt, find the whole experience a bit too gimmicky, although the green fringes of the state park provide some bucolic getaways. Don't expect too much from the touristy towns of **Niagara Falls, New York** or even more developed **Niagara Falls, Ontario**. Once you've seen the falls, from as many different angles as you can manage and traced the **Niagara Gorge**, you'll have a better time heading back to Buffalo.

Arrival, information and getting around

Amtrak **trains**, en route between New York City and Toronto, stop two miles from downtown Niagara Falls at 27th Street and Lockwood Road. **Buses** stop downtown at 303 Rainbow Blvd, ten minutes' walk from the falls. Arriving **by car**, follow the signs to one of the National Park car parks, which cost $10 (free off-season), although some street parking is available. **Information** is available at the Niagara Tourism & Convention Corporation, 10 Rainbow Blvd (Ⓣ716/282-8992 or 1-800/325-5787, Ⓦwww.niagara-usa.com), and from the Niagara Falls State Park Visitors' Center (Ⓣ716/278-1796, Ⓦwww.niagarafallsstatepark.com) near the falls. As for **getting around**, local Metro Transit System **buses** ($1.75 base fare, plus 30¢/zone; Ⓣ716/285-9319, Ⓦwww.nfta.com) run to all areas of the city and to Buffalo (see opposite).

Accommodation

Places to stay in central Niagara can be quite expensive if you don't plan ahead, but huge competition keeps rates down overall. US-62 (Niagara Falls Blvd), east of I-190, is lined with dozens of inexpensive motels, some being rather tacky

honeymoon spots. The closest place to **camp** is six miles from downtown at *Niagara Falls Campground & Lodging* at 2405 Niagara Falls Blvd (April–Oct; from $31/site; ⓣ716/731-3434, ⓦwww.niagarafallscampground.net).

Crowne Plaza 300 3rd St ⓣ716/285-3361 or 1-800/953-2557, ⓦwww.crowneplaza.com/niagarafalls. Typical of the chain hotels that dominate downtown and overcharge at peak times. ❺

HI-Niagara Falls 1101 Ferry Ave ⓣ716/282-3700, ⓔniagarahostel@gmail.com. Friendly, well-run hostel with dorm beds from $22, good-value singles from $25 and larger rooms. Preference is given to HI members and reservations are necessary in summer. ❷

Park Place B&B 740 Park Place ⓣ716/282-4626 or 1-800/510-4626, ⓦwww.parkplacebb.com. Comfortable spot near downtown, with full breakfast and afternoon pastries. Good off-season rates. ❸

Red Coach Inn 2 Buffalo Ave ⓣ716/282-1459 or 1-866/719-2070, ⓦwww.redcoach.com. Popular, well-appointed mock Tudor B&B with rooms, suites and views of the falls. ❹

Seneca Niagara Casino & Hotel 310 4th St ⓣ716/299-1100 or 1-877/873-6322, ⓦwww.senecaniagaracasino.com. Luxury pad whose interiors are about as garish as the flashy neon entrance. Rates vary considerably – look out for online promotions. Several highly rated restaurants on the premises. ❼

The Falls

Niagara Falls comprises three distinct cataracts. The tallest are the **American** and **Bridal Veil falls** on the American side, separated by tiny Luna Island and plunging over jagged rocks in a 180ft drop; the broad **Horseshoe Falls** which curve their way over to Canada are far more majestic. Together, they date back a mere twelve thousand years, when the retreat of melting glaciers allowed water trapped in Lake Erie to gush north to Lake Ontario. Back then the falls were seven miles downriver, but constant erosion has cut them back to their present site.

Getting around Niagara Falls State Park is easy, thanks to the convenient but twee **Niagara Scenic Trolley** ($2) which connects all car parks and the major sightseeing points. The best views on the American side are from the **Observation Tower** (daily 10am–5pm; $1, free in winter), and from the area at its base where the water rushes past. In the middle of the river, Terrapin Point on **Goat Island** has similar views of Horseshoe Falls. Near here, the nineteenth-century tightrope-walker Blondin crossed the Niagara repeatedly, and even carried passengers across on his back. The sheer power of the falls is most evident when you approach the towering cascade on the not-to-be-missed **Maid of the Mist** boat trip, which leaves from the foot of the observation tower (May–Oct daily 9.15am–7.30pm every 15 min; $13.50, kids $7.85; ⓣ716/284-8897, ⓦwww.maidofthemist.com). Another excellent way to see the falls is the **Cave of the Winds** tour (mid-May to late Oct daily 9am–5pm, until 9pm July & Aug; $10, kids $7; ⓣ716/278-1730), which leads from Goat Island by elevator down to the base of the falls. A "**Discovery Pass**" for these and other attractions costs $33 for adults, or $26 for children at the visitor centre.

For a bird's-eye view, Rainbow Air Inc **helicopter** tours, 454 Main St (9am–dusk; from $90; ⓣ716/284-2800), are breathtaking but brief. To check out the superior view from Niagara, Ontario, it's a twenty-minute walk across the **Rainbow Bridge** to the Canadian side (free to Canadians, 50¢ to US citizens; passports required). Driving across is inadvisable: discounting the $3.50 toll, parking on the other side is expensive and increased security checks make delays more likely.

Eating and drinking

Though most of the **eating options** in Niagara Falls are fast-food joints of indifferent quality, there are a few decent local bars and restaurants – with some better places over in Canada.

Caffé Lola 507 3rd St ⓣ716/282-5652. Hip new place serving entrees like lobster macaroni and cheese for $12–17, and excellent Italian ices.

Como Restaurant 2200 Pine Ave ⓣ716/285-9341. A good, posh option with huge portions of Italian cuisine and a reasonably priced deli.

The Orchard Grill 1217 Main St ⓣ716/282-8079. Large portions of all-American classics are served at this unpretentious spot with a pleasant outdoor patio.

Sadar Sahib 431 3rd St ⓣ716/282-0444. Authentic and inexpensive curry house with an emphasis on Punjabi dishes.

Top Of The Falls Goat Island, Niagara Falls State Park ⓣ716/278-0340. The food is adequate standard American fare but the setting is unrivalled. Floor-to-ceiling windows ensure everyone gets a great view across the falls. Open April–Oct.

Pennsylvania

PENNSYLVANIA was explored by the Dutch in the early 1600s, settled by the Swedes forty years later, and claimed by the British in 1664. Charles II of England, who owed a debt to the Penn family, rid himself of the potentially troublesome young **William Penn**, an enthusiastic advocate of religious freedom, by granting him land in the colony in 1682. Penn Jr immediately established a "holy experiment" of "brotherly love" and tolerance, naming the state after his father and setting a good example by signing a peaceful cohabitation treaty with the Native Americans. Most of the early agricultural settlers were religious refugees, Quakers like Penn himself and Mennonites from Germany and Switzerland, to be joined by Irish Catholics during the potato famines of the nineteenth century.

"The Keystone State" was crucial in the development of the United States. Politicians and thinkers like **Benjamin Franklin** congregated in Philadelphia – home of both the Declaration of Independence and the Constitution – and were prominent in articulating the ideas behind the Revolution. Later, the battle in Gettysburg, in south Pennsylvania, marked a turning point in the Civil War. Pennsylvania was also vital industrially: Pittsburgh, in the west, was the world's leading steel producer in the nineteenth century, and nearly all the nation's anthracite coal is still mined here.

The two great urban centres of **Philadelphia** and **Pittsburgh**, both lively and vibrant tourist destinations, are at opposite ends of the state. The three hundred miles between them, though predominantly agricultural, are topographically diverse. There are over one hundred state parks, with green rolling countryside in the east and brooding forests in the west. **Lancaster County**, home to traditional Amish farmers, the **Gettysburg** battlefield and the **Hershey** chocolate factory, minutes away from state capital **Harrisburg**, draws visitors by the thousands. Finally, in the far northwest, **Lake Erie** provides the state's only waterfront, centred upon the eponymous town.

Philadelphia

The original capital of the nation, **PHILADELPHIA** was laid out by William Penn Jr in 1682, on a grid system that was to provide the pattern for most American cities. Just a few blocks away from the noise and crowds of downtown, shady cobbled alleys stand lined with red-brick colonial houses, while the peace and quiet of huge Fairmount Park make it easy to forget you're in a major metropolis. Settled by **Quakers**, Philadelphia prospered swiftly on the back of trade and commerce, becoming the second largest city in the British Empire by the 1750s. Economic power fuelled strong revolutionary feeling, and the city was the hub for most of the **War of Independence** and the US capital until 1800, while Washington DC was being built. The **Declaration of Independence** was written, signed, and first publicly read here in 1776, as was the **US Constitution** ten years later. Philadelphia was also a hotbed of new ideas in the arts and sciences, as epitomized by the scientist, philosopher, statesman, inventor and printer **Benjamin Franklin**.

Philadelphia, which means "City of Brotherly Love" in Greek, is in fact one of the most **ethnically mixed** US cities, with substantial communities of Italians, Irish, Eastern Europeans and Asians living side-by-side among the large **African-American** population. Many of the city's black residents are descendants of the migrants who flocked here after the Civil War when Philadelphia was seen as a bastion of tolerance and liberalism. Philly also retains its Quaker heritage, with large "meetings" or congregations of **The Society of Friends**. Once known as "Filthydelphia", the city underwent a remarkable resurgence preparing for the nation's bicentennial celebrations in 1976. Philadelphia's strength today is its great energy in the face of economic adversity – fuelled by history, strong cultural institutions and grounded in its many staunchly traditional neighbourhoods.

Arrival and information

Philadelphia's **International Airport** (ⓣ215/937-6800, ⓦwww.phl.org) is seven miles southwest of the city off I-95. **Taxis** into town cost around $30 (try Yellow Cab; ⓣ215/829-4222), and the South East Pennsylvania Transit Authority (**SEPTA**) runs trains from the airport every thirty minutes (4.30am–11.30pm; $7; see "City transport", below) to five downtown stations. The very grand and busy 30th Street **Amtrak** station is just across the Schuylkill River in the university area (free

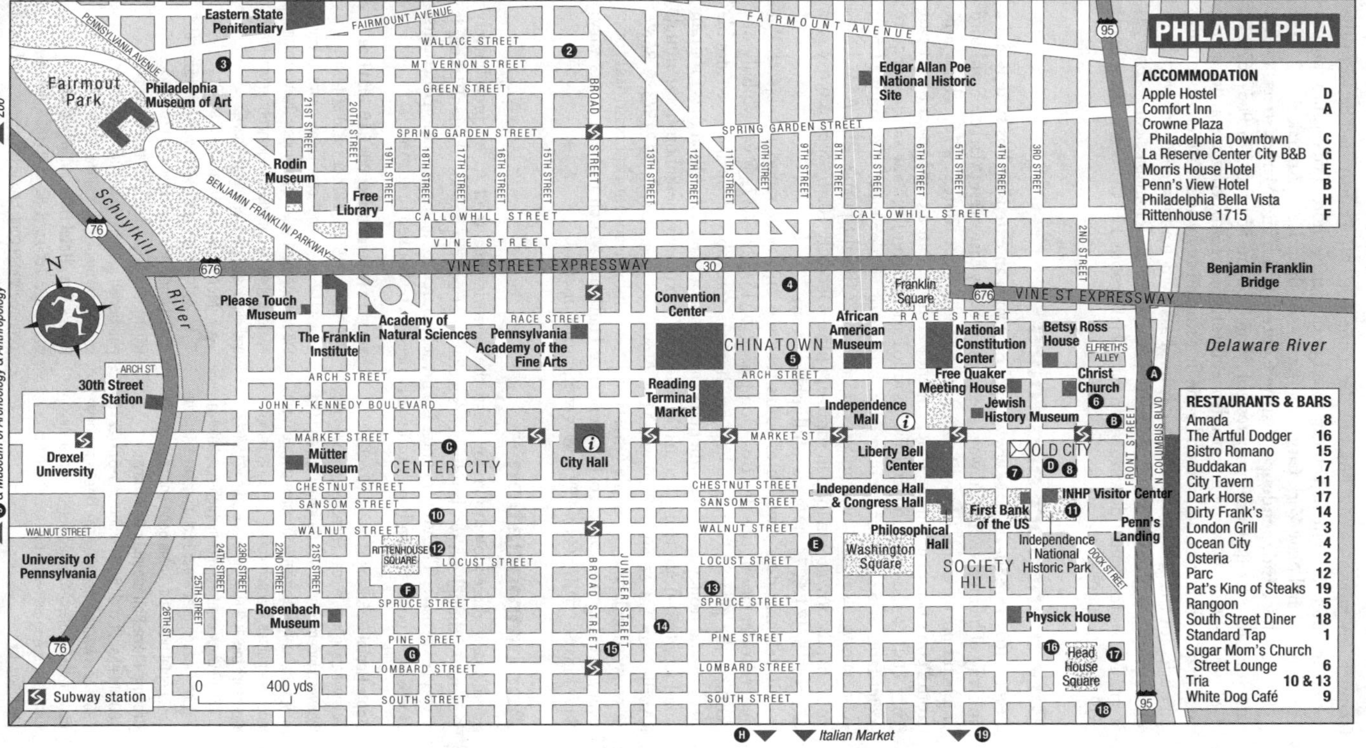
PHILADELPHIA
ACCOMMODATION
Apple Hostel D
Comfort Inn A
Crowne Plaza Philadelphia Downtown C
La Reserve Center City B&B G
Morris House Hotel E
Penn's View Hotel B
Philadelphia Bella Vista H
Rittenhouse 1715 F
RESTAURANTS & BARS
Amada 8
The Artful Dodger 16
Bistro Romano 15
Buddakan 7
City Tavern 11
Dark Horse 17
Dirty Frank's 14
London Grill 3
Ocean City 4
Osteria 2
Parc 12
Pat's King of Steaks 19
Rangoon 5
South Street Diner 18
Standard Tap 1
Sugar Mom's Church Street Lounge 6
Tria 10 & 13
White Dog Café 9
Subway station
0 400 yds
Eastern State Penitentiary
Fairmount Park
Philadelphia Museum of Art
Rodin Museum
Free Library
Please Touch Museum
The Franklin Institute
Academy of Natural Sciences
Pennsylvania Academy of the Fine Arts
Convention Center
CHINATOWN
Reading Terminal Market
City Hall
CENTER CITY
Mütter Museum
Rosenbach Museum
30th Street Station
Drexel University
University of Pennsylvania
Edgar Allan Poe National Historic Site
African American Museum
Franklin Square
National Constitution Center
Free Quaker Meeting House
Independence Mall
Jewish History Museum
Liberty Bell Center
Independence Hall & Congress Hall
Philosophical Hall
Washington Square
First Bank of the US
Independence National Historic Park
SOCIETY HILL
OLD CITY
INHP Visitor Center
Penn's Landing
Betsy Ross House
Elfreth's Alley
Christ Church
Physick House
Head House Square
Benjamin Franklin Bridge
Delaware River
Schuylkill River
Rittenhouse Square
Vine Street Expressway
Vine St Expressway
Benjamin Franklin Parkway
Fairmount Avenue
Pennsylvania Avenue
Wallace Street
Mt Vernon Street
Green Street
Spring Garden Street
Callowhill Street
Vine Street
Race Street
Arch Street
John F. Kennedy Boulevard
Market Street
Chestnut Street
Sansom Street
Walnut Street
Locust Street
Spruce Street
Pine Street
Lombard Street
South Street
Broad Street
Juniper Street
Front Street
N Columbus Blvd
Dock Street
Arch St
2nd Street
3rd Street
4th Street
5th Street
6th Street
7th Street
8th Street
9th Street
10th Street
11th Street
12th Street
13th Street
15th Street
16th Street
17th Street
18th Street
19th Street
20th Street
21st Street
22nd Street
23rd Street
24th Street
25th Street
26th St
95
676
30
76
N
Zoo
9 & Museum of Archeology & Anthropology
1 & Northern Liberties
H
Italian Market
19

transfer downtown on SEPTA). SEPTA connects to **NJ Transit**, and between the two commuter rail systems you can travel to the Jersey shore, Princeton, suburban Pennsylvania and New York City for a fraction of the price of Amtrak.

The excellent **Independence Visitor Center**, at 6th and Market streets (daily: late June to Aug 8.30am–7pm; rest of year 8.30am–5pm; ⓣ215/965-7676 or 1-800/537-7676; ⓦwww.independencevisitorcenter.com), contains a staggering wealth of information and should be the first stop on any visitor's itinerary. It is also an outlet for the good-value **Philadelphia Pass**, which allows entry to over thirty city attractions (valid 1–5 days; $49–103; ⓦwww.philadelphiapass.com). There is a smaller visitor centre downtown in City Hall, room 121 (Mon–Fri 9am–5pm; ⓣ215/686-2840).

City transport and tours

SEPTA (ⓣ215/580-7800, ⓦwww.septa.org) runs an extensive **bus** system and a **subway**. The most useful subway lines cross the city east–west (Market–Frankford line) and north–south (Broad St line); the handiest bus route is **#76**, which runs from Penn's Landing and the Independence Hall area out along Market Street past City Hall to the museums and Fairmount Park. Bus and subway services require exact fares of $2 (tokens, purchased in batches of two or more, cost only $1.55); **day passes**, also good for the airport, go for $7. Bright purple **PHLASH** buses run a handy downtown loop in summer (June–Oct daily 10am–8pm; $2; day pass $5; ⓣ215/474-5274, ⓦwww.phillyphlash.com).

Philadelphia offers a wealth of **tours** focusing on a wide range of subjects. For general orientation, the Big Bus Company (ⓣ215/389-8687, ⓦwww.phillytour.com; 24hr pass $27) runs a hop-on, hop-off tour aboard open-topped double deckers and trolleys, with commentary on the major sites. The Mural Arts Program conducts two-hour trolley tours of the city's extensive neighbourhood murals (April–Nov Sat & Sun 12.30pm, May–Nov Wed 10am; $25; ⓣ215/389-8687, ⓦwww.muralarts.org), while Ghosts of Philadelphia leads morbid historical tours every evening from next to Independence Hall (late March to Nov, hours vary; $17, kids $8; ⓣ215/413-1997, ⓦwww.ghosttour.com).

Accommodation

Hotels anywhere downtown or near the historic area tend to be prohibitively expensive, though on weekends there's a chance of getting a reduced rate. Parking is always expensive. The visitor centre is a great resource for accommodation discounts; B&Bs are a good option here, but usually need to be booked in advance.

Apple Hostel 32 S Bank St ⓣ215/922-0222, ⓦwww.applehostels.com. Friendly hostel wedged between Independence Hall National Park and Old City, with bunk beds from $30, some private rooms and free games, tea and coffee. No curfews. ❸

Comfort Inn 100 N Columbus Blvd ⓣ215/627-7900, ⓦwww.comfortinn.com. High-rise hotel in a good location near Penn's Landing; rates include continental breakfast. Some good online deals. ❻

Crowne Plaza Philadelphia Downtown 1800 Market St ⓣ215/561-7500 or 1-877/227-6963, ⓦwww.crowneplaza.com. One of the best downtown business-oriented hotels, with lush furnishings. A British-style pub is attached to the lobby. ❼

La Reserve Center City B&B 1804 Pine St ⓣ215/735-1137 or 1-800/354-8401, ⓦwww.lareservebandb.com. Lovely rooms, of which the two cheapest share a bathroom. The welcoming owner dishes up a modest-sized gourmet breakfast and dispenses loads of information. ❸

Morris House Hotel 225 S 8th St ⓣ215/922-2446, ⓦwww.morrishousehotel.com. Luxury boutique hotel in a 1787 Society Hill mansion with a lovely courtyard, cleverly refurbished to maintain its historical feel. Ample continental breakfast included. ❼

Penn's View Hotel Front and Market sts ⓣ215/922-7600 or 1-800/331-7634, ⓦwww.pennsviewhotel.com. Exceptional service and clean, comfortable rooms in Old City, some of the best value in central Philly. There's a very fine wine bar next to the lobby. Continental breakfast included. ❻

Philadelphia Bella Vista 752 S 10th St ⓣ215/238-1270 or 1-800/680-1270, ⓦwww.philadelphiabellavistabnb.com. Cute little gaily painted place with comfy, compact rooms that constitute some of the best deals in town. Handy both for downtown and the buzzing South St area. ❹

Rittenhouse 1715 1715 Rittenhouse Sqare St ⓣ215/546-6500 or 1-877/791-6500, ⓦwww.rittenhouse1715.com. Classing itself as a boutique hotel, this centrally located B&B offers a range of rooms, all with marble bathrooms, and a few truly palatial suites. ❽

The City

Central Philadelphia stretches for about two miles from the Schuylkill (pronounced "school-kill") River on the west to the Delaware River on the east; the metropolitan area extends for many miles in all directions, but everything you're likely to want to see is right in the central swath. The city's central districts are compact, walkable and readily accessible from each other; Penn's sensibly planned grid system makes for easy sightseeing.

Independence National Historic Park

Any tour of Philadelphia should start with **Independence National Historic Park**, or **INHP** (ⓣ215/597-8974 or 965-2305, ⓦwww.nps.gov/inde), "America's most historic square mile". Though the park covers a mere four blocks just west of the Delaware River, between Walnut and Arch streets, it can take more than a day to explore in full. The solid red-brick buildings here, not all of which are open to the public, epitomize the Georgian (and after the Revolution, Federalist) obsession with balance and symmetry.

All INHP sites (unless otherwise specified) are open 365 days a year and admission is free; hours are usually 9am to 5pm, sometimes longer in summer. Free **tours** set off from the rear of the east wing of Independence Hall, the single most important site. Throughout the day, costumed actors perform patchy but informative skits in various locations across the site – *The Gazette* free newsletter has listings and a useful map. It's best to reach **Independence Hall** early, to avoid the hordes of tourists and school parties. In peak season, free tickets must be obtained at the Independence Visitor Center. Built in 1732 as the Pennsylvania State House, this was where the Declaration of Independence was prepared, signed and, after the pealing of the Liberty Bell, given its first public reading on July 8, 1776.

The **Liberty Bell** itself hung in Independence Hall from 1753, ringing to herald vital announcements such as victories and defeats in the Revolutionary War. Stories as to how it received its famous crack vary, but it's undisputed that it rang publicly for the very last time on George Washington's birthday in 1846. It later acquired the name Liberty Bell because of its inscription from Leviticus, advocating liberty, which made it an anti-slavery symbol. After the Civil War, the silent bell was adopted as a symbol of freedom and reconciliation and embarked on a national rail tour. The iconic lump of metal now rests in a shrine-like space in the new multimedia **Liberty Bell Center** in INHP.

Next door to Independence Hall, on 6th and Chestnut streets, **Congress Hall**, built in 1787 as Philadelphia County Courthouse, is where members of the new United States Congress first took their places, and where all the patterns for today's US government were established. The **First Bank of the United States**, at 3rd and Chestnut streets, was established in 1797 to formalize the new union's currency. In 1774, delegates of the first Continental Congress – predecessor of the US Congress – chose defiantly to meet at Carpenter's Hall, 320 Chestnut St, to air their grievances against the English king. Today the building exhibits early tools and furniture (Tues–Sun 10am–4pm). Directly north, Franklin Court, 313 Market St, is a tribute to Benjamin Franklin on the former site of his home. An underground museum has hilarious dial-a-quote recordings of his pithy sayings and the musings of his contemporaries, as well as a working printshop. The B Free Franklin Post Office, 316 Market St, sells stamps and includes a small postal museum. Other buildings in the park include the original 1783 **Free Quaker Meeting House**, at 5th and Arch. There's also the still-used **Philosophical Hall**, 104 S 5th St (March–Sept Wed–Sun 10am–4pm; rest of year Thurs–Sun 10am–4pm; free), also founded by Franklin.

Old City

Immediately north of INHP lies **Old City**, Philadelphia's earliest commercial area, above Market Street near the riverfront. Washington, Franklin and Betsy Ross all worshipped at **Christ Church**, on 2nd Street just north of Market, which dates from 1727. The church's official burial ground, two blocks west at 5th and Arch (tour times vary; ⓣ215/922-1695, ⓦwww.christchurchphila.org), includes gravestones of signatories to the Declaration of Independence, among them **Benjamin Franklin**. At 239 Arch St, the **Betsy Ross House** (daily 10am–5pm; $3; ⓣ215/686-1252, ⓦwww.betsyrosshouse.org), by means of unimpressive wax dummies, salutes the woman credited, probably apocryphally, with making the first American flag.

The claim of **Elfreth's Alley** – a pretty little cobbled way off 2nd Street between Arch and Race streets – to be the "oldest street in the United States" is somewhat dubious, though it has been in continuous residential use since 1727; its thirty houses, notable for their wrought-iron gates, water pumps, wooden shutters and attic rooms, date from later in the eighteenth century. At no. 126 is the **Elfreth's Alley Museum** (Tues–Sat 10am–5pm; $3, guided tour $5; ⓣ215/574-0560, ⓦwww.elfrethsalley.org); the house was built by blacksmith Jeremiah Elfreth in 1762.

The area north of Market Street also holds three excellent museums. The must-see **National Constitution Center**, 525 Arch St (Mon–Fri 9.30am–5pm, Sat 9.30am–6pm, Sun noon–5pm; $12; ⓣ1-866/917-1787 or 215/409-6600, ⓦwww.constitutioncenter.org), a modern, interactive and provocative museum dedicated to the nation's best-known document, offers a wealth of information on the venerated document. The **National Museum of American Jewish History**, 55 N 5th St (ⓦwww.nmajh.org), was due to reopen in November 2010 in a completely new five-storey building. Finally, the emotive and politically informed **African American Museum in Philadelphia**, 7th and Arch streets (Tues–Sat 10am–5pm, Sun noon–5pm; $10; ⓣ215/574-0380, ⓦwww.aampmuseum.org) tells the stories of the thousands of blacks who migrated north to Philadelphia after Reconstruction and in the early twentieth century. The Old City is also home to a number of **art galleries**, clustered around N 2nd and 3rd streets, and to September's annual Philadelphia Fringe Festival, a popular experimental theatre series (ⓣ215/413-9006, ⓦwww.pafringe.org).

Penn's Landing

Just east of Old City along the Delaware River, where William Penn stepped off in 1682, spreads the huge and heavily industrialized port of Philadelphia. Along the port's southern reaches, on the river-side of the I-95 freeway, the old docklands have been renovated as part of the **Penn's Landing** development, the most interesting feature of which is the **Independence Seaport Museum** (daily 10am–5pm; $12, donation only Sun 10am–noon; ⓣ215/925-5439, ⓦwww.phillyseaport.org). Admission includes entry onto two **historical ships**: the flagship USS *Olympia* and the World War II submarine *Becuna*. All along the riverfront promenade are food stalls, landscaped pools and fountains; regular outdoor concerts and festivals are held here. The seasonal Riverlink **ferry** crosses the Delaware (May–Sept hourly 10am–6pm; $7 return; ⓣ215/925-5465, ⓦwww.riverlinkferry.org) to the down-at-heel town of **Camden**, where the main attraction is the **Adventure Aquarium** (daily 9.30am–5pm; $21.95; ⓣ856/365-3300, ⓦwww.adventure aquarium.com), only worthwhile with kids in tow.

Society Hill

Society Hill, an elegant residential area west of the Delaware and directly south of INHP, spreads between Walnut and Lombard streets. Though it is indeed Philadelphia's high society that lives here now, the area was named after its first inhabitants, the Free Society of Traders. After falling into disrepair, the Hill itself was flattened in the early 1970s to provide a building site for I.M. Pei's twin skyscrapers, Society Hill Towers. Luckily, the rest of the neighbourhood has been restored to form one of the city's most picturesque districts: cobbled gas-lit streets are lined with immaculately kept colonial, Federal and Georgian homes, often featuring the state's namesake keystones on their window frames. One of the few buildings open to the public is the **Physick House**, 321 S 4th St, home to Dr Philip Syng Physick, "the Father of American Surgery", and filled with eighteenth- and nineteenth-century decorative arts (Thurs–Sat noon–4pm, Sun 1–4pm; $5; ⓣ215/925-7866, ⓦwww.philalandmarks.org).

Center City

Center City, Philadelphia's main business and commercial area, stretches from 8th Street west to the Schuylkill River, dominated by the endearing baroque wedding cake of **City Hall** and its 37ft bronze statue of Penn. Before ascending thirty storeys to the **observation deck** (Mon–Fri 9.30am–4.30pm; $2) at Penn's feet, check out the quirky sculptures and carvings around the building, including the cats and mice at the south entrance. A couple of blocks north at Broad and Cherry streets, the **Pennsylvania Academy of the Fine Arts** (Tues–Sat 10am–5pm, Sun 11am–5pm; $10; ⓣ215/972-7600, ⓦwww.pafa.org), housed in an elaborate, multicoloured Victorian pile, exhibits three hundred years of American art, including works by Mary Cassatt, Thomas Eakins and Winslow Homer.

Beginning at 8th Street, **Chinatown**, marked by the gorgeous 40ft Friendship Gate at 10th and Arch, has some of the best budget food in the city. A few blocks over on 12th Street is the century-old **Reading Terminal Market** (daily 9am–4pm; ⓣ215/922-2317, ⓦwww.readingterminalmarket.org), where many Amish farmers come to the city to sell their produce. It's always good for a lively time and makes a great lunch spot.

Rittenhouse Square

Grassy **Rittenhouse Square**, one of Penn's original city squares, is in a very fashionable part of town. On one side it borders chic Walnut Street, on the other a residential area of solid brownstones with beautifully carved doors and windows. The red-brick 1860 **Rosenbach Museum**, 2010 Delancey Place, holds over thirty thousand rare books, as well as James Joyce's original hand-scrawled manuscripts of *Ulysses* (Tues & Fri noon–5pm, Wed & Thurs noon–8pm, Sat & Sun noon–6pm; $10, including house tour; ⓣ215/732-1600, ⓦwww.rosenbach.org). On summer evenings there are free outdoor jazz and R&B concerts in the square.

Museum Row and Fairmount Park

The mile-long Benjamin Franklin Parkway, known as Museum Row, sweeps northwest from City Hall to the colossal Museum of Art in **Fairmount Park**, an area of countryside annexed by the city in the nineteenth century. Spanning nine hundred scenic acres on both sides of the Schuylkill River, this is one of the world's largest landscaped city parks, with jogging, biking and hiking trails, early-American homes, an all-wars memorial to the state's black soldiers, and the country's first **zoo** at 3400 W Girard Ave (March–Nov 9.30am–5pm; $18; Dec–Feb 9.30am–4pm; $13; ⓣ215/243-1100, ⓦwww.phillyzoo.org). In the late 1960s, local resident **Joe Frazier** and **Muhammad Ali** all but brought the city to a standstill with the announcement one afternoon that they were heading to Fairmount for an informal slug-out.

The steps of the **Philadelphia Museum of Art**, 26th Street and Franklin Parkway (Tues–Sun 10am–5pm, Fri until 8.45pm; $16, donation first Sun of month; ⓣ215/763-8100, ⓦwww.philamuseum.org), were immortalized by **Sylvester Stallone** in the film *Rocky*, an event commemorated by the **Rocky statue**. Inside are some of the finest treasures in the US, with a twelfth-century French cloister, **Renaissance** art, a complete Robert Adam interior from a 1765 house in London's Berkeley Square, **Rubens** tapestries, Pennsylvania Dutch crafts and Shaker furniture, a strong **Impressionist** collection and the world's most extensive **Marcel Duchamp** collection.

A few blocks back towards Center City, at Franklin Parkway and 22nd Street, the exquisite **Rodin Museum** (Tues–Sun 10am–5pm; $5 suggested donation; ⓣ215/763-8100, ⓦwww.rodinmuseum.org), marble-walled and set in a shady garden with a green pool, holds the largest collection of Rodin's Impressionistic sculptures and casts outside of Paris, including *The Burghers of Calais*, *The Thinker* and *The Gates of Hell*. Diagonally across the road, within the vast edifice of **The Franklin Institute**, N 20th Street and Benjamin Franklin Parkway (daily 9.30am–5pm; $15.50, $21 including one IMAX show; ⓣ215/448-1200, ⓦwww.fi.edu), are a Planetarium, the Tuttleman IMAX Theater (film only $9), and the Mandell Futures Center, which concentrates on technological developments. Continuing the educational theme, the nearby **Academy of Natural Sciences**, 1900 Benjamin Franklin Parkway, exhibits dinosaurs, mummies and gems (Mon–Fri 10am–4.30pm, Sat & Sun 10am–5pm; $12; ⓣ215/299-1000, ⓦwww.ansp.org). Among the rare items at the **Free Library of Philadelphia**, 19th and Vine streets (Mon–Wed 9am–9pm, Thurs–Sat 9am–5pm, Sun 1–5pm; tours at 11am; free; ⓣ215/686-5322, ⓦwww.library.phila.gov), are cuneiform tablets from 3000 BC, medieval manuscripts and first editions of Dickens and Poe.

Just a short walk northeast of the museums, occupying two full blocks of Fairmount Avenue between 20th and 22nd streets, stand the gloomy Gothic fortifications of the **Eastern State Penitentiary** (daily 10am–5pm, last entry 4pm; $12; ⓣ215/236-3300, ⓦwww.easternstate.org), one of Philadelphia's most significant historic sites, which embodies a complete history of attitudes toward crime and punishment in the US. After a period of decay following its closure in 1970, the bulk of the Panopticon-style radial prison has been restored. Informative **audio tours** point out the prison's many novel architectural features, as well as its old synagogue and the upmarket cell where Al Capone cooled his heels.

West Philadelphia

Across the Schuylkill River, **West Philadelphia** is home to the Ivy-League **University of Pennsylvania**, where Franklin established the country's first medical school. The compact but extremely pleasant campus has some great museums: the small **Institute of Contemporary Art**, 118 S 36th St (Wed–Fri noon–8pm, Sat & Sun 11am–5pm; free; ⓣ215/898-5911, ⓦwww.icaphila.org) displays cutting-edge travelling exhibitions in an airy space; the intriguing **Arthur Ross Gallery**, 220 S 34th St (Tues–Fri 10am–5pm, Sat & Sun noon–5pm; free; ⓣ215/898-2083, ⓦwww.upenn.edu/ARG) features changing exhibits, particularly of international and colourful, innovative artwork; finally, the superlative **Museum of Archeology and Anthropology**, 33rd and Spruce streets (Tues–Sat 10am–4.30pm; Sun 1–5pm; $10; ⓣ215/898-4000, ⓦwww.museum.upenn.edu)

is the university's top draw. Regarded by experts as one of the world's finest science museums, its exhibits span all the continents and their major epochs – from Nigerian Benin bronzes to Chinese crystal balls. Most astonishing is the priceless twelve-ton granite Sphinx of Rameses II, c.1293–1185 BC, in the Lower Egyptian Gallery.

South Philadelphia

Staunchly blue-collar **South Philadelphia**, centre of Philadelphia's black community since the Civil War, is also home to many of the city's Italians; opera singer **Mario Lanza** and pop stars Fabian and Chubby Checker grew up here. It's also where to come for an authentic – and very messy – **Philly cheesesteak** (see "Eating", below), and to rummage through the wonderful **Italian Market** (another *Rocky* location), which runs along 9th Street south from Christian Street. One of the last surviving urban markets in the US, the wooden market stalls are packed to overflowing with bric-a-brac and various produce – most famously, mozzarella. **South Street**, the original boundary of the city, is now one of Philadelphia's main **nightlife** districts, with dozens of cafés, bars, restaurants and nightclubs lined up along the few blocks west from Front Street; there are also many good book, record and clothing **shops** for browsing by day or evening.

Eating

Eating out in Philadelphia is a real treat: the ubiquitous street stands sell **soft pretzels** with mustard for 50¢, Chinatown and the Italian Market are good for ethnic food, while Reading Terminal Market offers bargain lunches of various cuisines. South Street has plenty of good, if well-touristed, eateries, while pricier, trendier restaurants cluster along S 2nd Street in the Old City. The South Philly **cheesesteak**, a hot sandwich of wafer-thin roast beef topped with melted cheese (aka Cheez Whiz), varies from place to place around town. Philly's growing number of **cafés** are spread all around the city.

Amada 217 Chestnut St ⓣ215/625-2450. A dash of Spanish inspiration in Old City, with over 60 tapas dishes at around $10, great paella and fine red or white sangria.

Bistro Romano 120 Lombard St ⓣ215/925-8880. Quality Italian food is served in a converted eighteenth-century granary, with authentic pastas and other dishes costing around $20. There is a piano bar on Fri & Sat evenings.

Buddakan 325 Chestnut St ⓣ215/574-9440. Delicious pan-Asian fusion entrees cost well over $20. Admire the 10ft gilded Buddha in the modernist interior while dining.

City Tavern 138 S 2nd St ⓣ215/413-1443. Reconstructed 1773 tavern in INHP, originally frequented by John Adams. Chef Walter Staib cooks and costumed staff serve "olde style" food to a harpsichord accompaniment – dinner entrees like braised rabbit are mostly $20 and up.

London Grill 2301 Fairmount Ave ⓣ215/978-4545. This sophisticated establishment in the museum district serves delicious American and European cuisine at fair prices, with dishes such as duck confit going for $21.

Ocean City 234-6 N 9th St ⓣ215/829-0688. Huge Chinatown space specializing in fresh seafood, which is on display in tanks; also excellent dim sum before 3pm. Great value.

Osteria 640 N Broad St ⓣ215/763-0920. Award-winning Italian restaurant with a good selection of pizzas and antipasti, entrees such as wild halibut for $25–30 and delicious desserts.

Parc 227 S 18th St ⓣ215/545-2262. Excellent French bistro right opposite ritzy Rittenhouse Square. Entrees like skate grenobloise go for $20–30 in this touch of Paris ambience. Also a wide wine list, lots of bottled beers and absinthe.

Pat's King of Steaks 1237 E Passyunk Ave ⓣ215/468-1546. At this delightfully decrepit, outdoor-seating-only cheesesteak joint, take care to order correctly or prepare yourself to be sent to the back of the line. The cheesesteaks here are the real deal. Open 24hr.

Rangoon 112 N 9th St ⓣ215/829-8939. Friendly and intimate Burmese joint, serving an authentic selection of curries, rice and noodle dishes at around $10–12; try the cheap lunch specials.

South Street Diner 140 South St ⓣ215/627-5258. Huge menu with great three-course dinner specials well under $10. Open 24hr.

White Dog Café 3420 Sansom St ⓣ215/386-9224. Delicious, creative food in three Victorian brownstones near the universities. Artsy, student crowd; lunch entrees $13–16, dinner around double that; happy hour Sun–Thurs 10pm–midnight.

Bars

The most popular place for bar-hopping is **South Street** and around **2nd Street** in the Old City, although the **Northern Liberties** area, about eight blocks north, beyond the flyovers, now has an established enclave of trendy bars and clubs. Local brews are popular and inexpensive; try any ale by Yards or Yuengling if you prefer lager.

The Artful Dodger 400 S 2nd St ⓣ215/922-1790. Lively bar that gets livelier late on, especially if the 2008 world champion Phillies are playing baseball on TV. Reasonable ales and music too.

Dark Horse 421 S 2nd St ⓣ215/928-9307. Unpretentious British-style boozer with a fine range of beer and the added bonus of soccer on TV for visitors from the old continent.

Dirty Frank's 347 S 13th St ⓣ215/732-5010. Popular with a very mixed crowd, this Philly institution touts itself as "one of the few places in the world where you can drink a $3 pint of Yuengling underneath oil paintings by nationally recognized artists".

Standard Tap 901 N 2nd St ⓣ215/922-0522. Popular Northern Liberties bar, located in a fine house, with a range of beers from regional breweries like Flying Fish and River Horse on tap, as well as filling bar food.

Sugar Mom's Church Street Lounge 225 Church St ⓣ215/925-8219. Popular basement bar where the jukebox ranges from Tony Bennett to Sonic Youth, with a dozen international beers on tap.

Tria 123 S 18th St ⓣ215/972-8742. As the name suggests, this trendy bar-café concentrates on three elements, in this case beer, wine and cheese. Runs educational classes too. There's another location at 1123 Spruce St.

Live music and entertainment

Few reminders are left of the 1970s "Sound of Philadelphia". Instead, in recent times the city has produced the likes of pop starlet Pink, while its active underground scene features psych bands like Bardo Pond and The Asteroid #4. Philadelphia is a good place to see rock bands, as most of the names that play New York perform here for half the price. The world-famous **Philadelphia Orchestra** performs at the smart modern Kimmel Center for the Performing Arts (ⓣ215/790-5800, ⓦwww.kimmelcenter.org). Philadelphia's other great strength is its **theatre** scene, where small venues abound: visit the Theatre Alliance website at ⓦwww.theatrealliance.org, which features the StageTix discount ticket programme. **Listings** for all events can be found in the free *City Paper* (ⓦwww.citypaper.net) or *Philadelphia Weekly* (ⓦwww.philadelphiaweekly.com) newspapers.

Johnny Brendas 1201 N Frankford Ave ⓣ215/739-9684, ⓦwww.johnnybrendas.com. Underground establishment that showcases mostly unknown local and national rock and indie bands. Free to $20.

The Khyber 56 S 2nd St ⓣ215/238-5888, ⓦwww.thekhyber.com. Small rock venue with a gargoyle-lined bar, bluesy jukebox and casual young clientele. Cover is mostly around $10 when bands are on. There is a bar with no cover charge upstairs.

Painted Bride Art Center 230 Vine St ⓣ215/925-9914, ⓦwww.paintedbride.org. Art gallery with live jazz, dance and theatre performances after dark.

Theater of Living Arts 334 South St ⓣ215/922-1011, ⓦwww.thetla.com. Converted movie palace that's one of the best places to catch mid-size rock bands.

Tin Angel 20 S 2nd St ⓣ215/928-0770, ⓦwww.tinangel.com. Intimate upstairs bar and coffeehouse, featuring top local and nationally known folk, jazz, blues and acoustic acts.

Trocadero 1003 Arch St ⓣ215/922-5483, ⓦwww.thetroc.com. Downtown music venue in a converted 1870 theatre, sometimes featuring big-name alternative bands. Cover varies, and ID is essential.

Central Pennsylvania

Central Pennsylvania, cut north to south by the broad **Susquehanna River**, has no major cities – though the state capital, **Harrisburg**, is an excellent base from which to explore sights that include the nearby **Hershey** chocolate empire and the rolling Amish farmlands of **Lancaster County** further east, while the Civil War site of **Gettysburg** nestles on the state's southern border. To the north, lie some mighty forests around Williamsport but the further back east you go leads into the industrial mediocrity of towns like Scranton, whose dullness got it chosen as the setting for the US version of *The Office*.

Lancaster County: Pennsylvania Dutch Country

Lancaster County stretches for about 45 miles from **Coatesville**, which is 40 miles west of Philadelphia on US-30, to the Susquehanna River in the west. Although tiny, uncosmopolitan Lancaster, ten miles east of the river, was US capital for a day in September 1777, the region is famed more for its preponderance of agricultural religious communities, known collectively as the **Pennsylvania Dutch**. They actually have no connection to the Netherlands; the name is a mistaken derivation of Deutsch (German). A touristy place even before it was brought to international fame by the movie *Witness*, most of Lancaster County has maintained its natural beauty in the face of encroaching commercialization. It is a region of gentle countryside and fertile farmlands, eccentric-sounding place names such as **Intercourse**, horse-drawn buggies, tiny roadside bakeries and Amish children wending their way between immaculate, flower-filled farmhouses and one-room schoolhouses.

Indeed, attempting to live a simple life away from the pressures of the outside world has proved too much for many Pennsylvania Dutch. A few (mainly Mennonites) have succumbed to commercial need by offering rides in their buggies and meals in their homes, while members of the stricter orders have moved away to communities in less touristed mid-West states. When visiting, remember that Sunday is a day of rest for the Amish, so many attractions, restaurants and other amenities will be closed.

Arrival, information and getting around

The best route through the concentrated Amish communities is US-30, which runs east–west. **Amtrak** arrives at the train station at 53 McGovern Ave, Lancaster, as do buses from Capital Trailways (Ⓣ717/397-4861) and Greyhound. The bustling **Pennsylvania Dutch Convention and Visitors Bureau**, just off US-30 at 501 Greenfield Rd, Lancaster (daily 9am–4pm, until 6pm in summer; Ⓣ717/299-8901 or 1-800/723-8824, Ⓦwww.padutchcountry.com), does an excellent job of providing orientation and advice on accommodation. Visitors keen to learn about Pennsylvania Dutch culture should head to the **Mennonite Information Center** (April–Oct Mon–Sat 8am–5pm; Nov–March Mon–Sat 8.30am–4.30pm; Ⓣ717/299-0954 or 1-800/858-8320, Ⓦwww.mennoniteinfoctr.com), off US-30 at 2209 Millstream Rd, Lancaster, which shows a short film entitled *Who Are the Amish?* and also organizes lodging with Mennonite families. If you call at least two hours ahead, a guide can take you on a two-hour, $44 tour in your car.

Although a **car** will get you to the quieter backroads that the tour buses miss, it's more fun to ride a **bike**, which gives the benefits of all that fresh air and shows more consideration for the ubiquitous horse-drawn buggies. For self-guided **bike tours**, contact Lancaster Bicycle Club in Lancaster (Ⓦwww.lancasterbikeclub.org). The Amish Experience, on US-340 between Intercourse and Bird-in-Hand at Plain

The Pennsylvania Dutch

The people now known as the Pennsylvania Dutch originated as **Anabaptists** in sixteenth-century Switzerland, under the leadership of Menno Simons. His unorthodox advocacy of adult baptism and literal interpretation of the Bible led to the order's persecution; they were invited by William Penn to settle in Lancaster County in the 1720s. Today the twenty or so orders of Pennsylvania Dutch include the "plain" Old Order **Amish** (a strict order that originally broke away from Simons in 1693) and freer-living **Mennonites**, as well as the "fancy" **Lutheran** groups (distinguished by the colourful circular "hex" signs on their barns). Living by an unwritten set of rules called Amish Ordnung, which includes absolute pacifism, the Amish are the strictest and best-known: the men with their wide-brimmed straw hats and beards (but no "military" moustaches), the women in bonnets, plain dresses (with no fripperies like buttons) and aprons. Shunning electricity and any exposure to the corrupting influence of the outside world, the Amish power their farms with generators, and travel (at roughly 10mph) in handmade horse-drawn buggies. For all their insularity, the Amish are very friendly and helpful; resist the temptation to photograph them, however, as the making of "graven images" offends their beliefs.

& Fancy Farm (Ⓣ717/768-3600 ext 210, Ⓦwww.amishexperience.com), operates, among various attractions, two-hour **bus tours** (Mon–Sat 10.30am & 1.45pm, Sun 11.30am only) for $29.95, though some accommodations (see the *Village Inn* below) offer a similar service for free. AAA Buggy Rides offer lolloping four-mile countryside excursions for $12 (Ⓣ717/989-2829, Ⓦwww.aaabuggyrides.com) from the *Kitchen Kettle Village* in Intercourse.

Accommodation

Accommodation options in Pennsylvania Dutch Country range from reasonably priced **hotels** and **B&Bs**, which can be arranged through a central agency (Ⓣ1-800/552-2632, Ⓦwww.authenticbandb.com), to **farm vacations** (ask at the visitors bureau; see above) and **campgrounds**. *White Oak Campground*, 372 White Oak Rd, Quarryville, four miles north of Strasburg (Ⓣ717/687-6207, Ⓦwww.whiteoakcampground.com; sites from $26), overlooks the heart of the Dutch farmlands.

Cameron Estate Inn & Restaurant 1855 Mansion Lane, Mount Joy Ⓣ717/492-0111 or 1-800/422-6376, Ⓦwww.cameronestateinn.com. Out-of-the-way gay-friendly inn on fifteen acres with sparkling, comfortable rooms (one with jacuzzi), free full breakfast and a restaurant. ❻

Countryside Motel 134 Hartman Bridge Rd, Ronks Ⓣ717/687-8431. Clean and simple place six miles east of Lancaster on Hwy-896. ❸

Historic Strasburg Inn 1400 Historic Drive, Strasburg Ⓣ717/687-7691 or 1-800/872-0201, Ⓦwww.historicinnofstrasburg.com. Over a hundred luxury rooms, plus a hot tub and a sauna, tucked away on sixty rolling acres. Great value. ❹

O'Flaherty's Dingeldein House 1105 E King St, Lancaster Ⓣ717/293-1723 or 1-800/779-7765, Ⓦwww.dingeldeinhouse.com. Friendly rustic eight-room B&B. Rates include a large country breakfast. ❹

Village Inn & Suites 2695 Old Philadelphia Pike, Bird-in-Hand Ⓣ1-800/665-8780, Ⓦwww.bird-in-hand.com/villageinn. Excellent old inn with modern amenities, large breakfast, deck, lawn and back pasture. Price includes 2hr tour of Amish Country and use of the adjacent motel's pool. Book ahead. ❻

Touring Pennsylvania Dutch Country

Though useful for a general overview and historical insight, the attractions that interpret Amish culture tend toward overkill. It's far more satisfying just to explore the countryside for yourself. Here, among the streams with their covered bridges and fields striped with corn, alfalfa and tobacco, the reality hits you – these aren't actors recreating an ancient lifestyle, but real people, part of a living, working community. On Sunday, for example, commercial activities are suspended but you may see a large gathering of buggies outside one of the farms, indicating an Amish church service (in High German) or a "visiting day".

Among the widely spread formal attractions, the **Ephrata Cloister**, 632 W Main St, **Ephrata** (junction of US-272 and 322), recreates the eighteenth-century settlement of German Protestant celibates that acted, among other things, as an early publishing and printing centre (May–Oct Mon–Sat 9am–5pm, Sun noon–5pm, rest of year closed Mon, Jan & Feb also closed Tues; $9; ⓣ717/733-6600, ⓦwww.ephratacloister.org). Further south, about three miles northeast of Lancaster, the **Landis Valley Museum**, 2451 Kissell Hill Rd (Tues–Sat 9am–5pm, Sun noon–5pm; $12; ⓣ717/569-0401, ⓦwww.landisvalleymuseum.org), is a living history museum of rural life, with demonstrations of local crafts. The oldest building in the county, the **Hans Herr House**, 1849 Hans Herr Drive, five miles south of downtown Lancaster off US-222 (April–Nov Mon–Sat 9am–4pm; $5; ⓣ717/464-4438, ⓦwww.hansherr.org), is a 1719 Mennonite church with a pretty garden and orchard, a medieval German facade and exhibits on early farm life.

Eating, drinking and entertainment

Lancaster County **food** is delicious, Germanic and served in vast quantities. There are no Amish-owned restaurants, but Amish roadside stalls sell fresh home-made root beer, jams, pickles, breads and pies. The huge "all-you-care-to-eat" **tourist restaurants** on US-30 and US-340 may look off-putting, all pseudo-rusticism with costumed waitresses, but most serve good meals for under $20 "family-style" – you share long tables with other out-of-towners. Typical fare includes fried chicken, hickory-smoked ham, *schnitz und knepp* (apple, ham and dumpling stew), sauerkraut, pickles, cottage cheese and apple butter, shoo-fly pie and the like. None stays open later than 8pm, though a few regular **diners** in busier areas do open later. Rural Lancaster County is, unsurprisingly, not known for its nightlife – though there are a couple of very friendly **bars** in downtown Lancaster worth checking out. The Fulton Opera House, 12 N Prince St (ⓣ717/394-7425, ⓦwww.fultontheatre.org), is a plush red-and-gold restored Victorian **theatre**, hosting dance, plays and special events.

Central Market Penn Square, Lancaster. Covered market selling fresh local farm produce and lunch to loyal Lancastrians and tourists alike. Tues & Fri 6am–4pm, Sat 6am–2pm.

Good 'n' Plenty East Brook Rd, US-896, Smoketown ⓣ717/394-7111. Not Amish-owned, though Amish women cook and serve food in this, the best of the family-style restaurants. Open early Feb to mid-Dec Mon–Sat.

Lancaster Brewing Co. 302 N Plum St, Lancaster ⓣ717/391-6258. Brewpub serving good bar food and five different microbrews. Tours given Fri & Sat by appointment. Open daily.

Lancaster Dispensing Co. 33–35 N Market St, Lancaster ⓣ717/299-4602. Downtown Lancaster's trendiest, friendliest bar, with live weekend jazz and blues, plus overstuffed sandwiches for around $7.

Lapp's 2270 Lincoln Hwy E (US-30), near Lancaster ⓣ717/394-1606. A solid diner with family atmosphere and ample Germanic food typical of Lancaster County; open daily.

Molly's Pub 253 E Chestnut St, Lancaster ⓣ717/396-0225. Neighbourhood bar with lively atmosphere and good burgers. Closed Sun.

Plain and Fancy 3121 Old Philadelphia Pike (Rte-340), Bird-in-Hand ⓣ717/768-4400. Standard family-style restaurant; only one in the area open on Sun.

Harrisburg and Hershey

HARRISBURG, Pennsylvania's capital, lies on the Susquehanna River thirty or so miles northwest of Lancaster. It's a surprisingly attractive small city, its lush waterfront lined with shuttered colonial buildings, and is amusingly complemented by its kitschy Chocolatetown neighbour **Hershey**. Harrisburg is also known as the site of the **Three Mile Island** nuclear facility, which suffered a famous meltdown in the 1970s and stands along the river on the east side of town.

The ornate, attractive Italian Renaissance **capitol** at Third and State streets has a dome modelled after St Peter's in Rome (tours Mon–Fri 8.30am–4pm; Sat & Sun 9am, 11am, 1pm & 3pm; free; ⓣ1-800/868-7672, ⓦwww.pacapitol.com). The complex includes the four-floor **State Museum of Pennsylvania** at Third and North (Thurs–Sat 9am–5pm, Sun noon–5pm; $5; ⓣ717/787-4980, ⓦwww.statemuseumpa.org), a cylindrical building that holds a planetarium (Sat & Sun only), archeological and military artefacts, decorative arts, tools and machinery. Undoubtedly the real attraction is the excellent **National Civil War Museum**, roughly two miles east of downtown at the summit of hilly Reservoir Park (Mon–Sat 10am–5pm, Sun noon–5pm, Wed until 8pm; $9; ⓣ717/260-1861 or 1-866/258-4729, ⓦwww.nationalcivilwarmuseum.org), with fine city views. Almost 730,000 Americans were killed in the Civil War – more than in all other conflicts since the Revolution combined – and the museum offers an intelligent analysis of the reasons for, and results of, the war. Especially evocative are the fictionalized monologues, playing on video screens in every gallery, which focus on the human cost of the conflict.

HERSHEY, ten miles east, was built in 1903 by candy magnate Milton S. Hershey for his chocolate factory – so it has streets named Chocolate and Cocoa avenues and streetlamps in the shape of Hershey's Chocolate Kisses. **Hershey's Chocolate World** (daily 9am–5pm, later in summer months; ⓣ717/534-4900, ⓦwww.hersheyschocolateworld.com) offers a free mini-train ride through a romanticized simulated chocolate factory, a 3-D chocolate show ($5.95), and a cheesy musical/historical trolley ride around town ($12.95). Nearby **Hersheypark** (mid-May to Sept, hours vary; $52.95; ⓣ717/534-3090 or 1-800/437-7439, ⓦwww.hersheypark.com) is a hugely popular amusement park, with stomach-churning roller coasters and various other rides; cheaper special events take place for Halloween and Christmas. The adjacent **Hershey Story** (daily 9am–5pm, later in summer months; $10; ⓣ717/534-3439, ⓦwww.hersheystory.org) has exhibits on the Pennsylvania Dutch and tells the Milton S. Hershey story.

Practicalities

Amtrak **trains** share the central station at Fourth and Chestnut streets with Greyhound, whose **buses** also stop in Hershey at 337 W Chocolate St. Harrisburg's **visitor centre** (ⓣ717/231-7788, ⓦwww.visithhc.com) is not open to walk-ins, but can be contacted for good local and regional information. In leafy Camp Hill, just across the river from Harrisburg, the *Radisson Penn Harris* (ⓣ717/763-7117, ⓦwww.radisson.com; ❹) has good-value rooms in relaxing surroundings. Options in Hershey include the standard *Howard Johnson Inn*, 845 E Chocolate Ave (ⓣ717/533-9157, ⓦwww.howardjohnsonhershey.com; ❹), which has a decent restaurant, while luxury lodging is available at the palatial *Hotel Hershey*, Hotel Road (ⓣ717/533-2171, ⓦwww.thehotelhershey.com; ❽), complete with an on-site spa offering chocolate-based beauty treatments. The best **campground** in the region is *Hershey Highmeadow Campground*, 1200 Matlack Rd, Hummellstown, on the Harrisburg side of Hershey (ⓣ717/534-8999 or 1-800/437-7439, ⓦwww.hersheycamping.com), which has sites from $35 off-season to $41 in summer. Budget **restaurants** line Second Street in downtown Harrisburg, the best being *Fisaga's*, at Locust and N Second streets (ⓣ717/441-1556), which serves good basic sandwiches and pasta. *Scott's*, 212 Locust St (ⓣ717/234-7599), is a popular bar and grill, with live music some nights.

Gettysburg

The small town of **GETTYSBURG**, thirty miles south of Harrisburg near the Maryland border, gained tragic notoriety in July 1863 for the cataclysmic **Civil War** battle in which fifty thousand men died. There were more casualties during these three days than in any American battle before or since – a full third of those who fought were killed or wounded – and entire regiments were wiped out when the tide finally turned against the South.

Four months later, on November 19, Abraham Lincoln delivered his **Gettysburg Address** at the dedication of the National Cemetery. His two-minute speech, in memory of all the soldiers who died, is acknowledged as one of the most powerful orations in American history. Gettysburg, by far the most baldly commercialized of all the Civil War sites, is overwhelmingly geared toward **tourism**, relentlessly replaying the most minute details of the battle. Fortunately, it is perfectly feasible to avoid the crowds and commercial overkill and explore for yourself the rolling hills of the battlefield (now a national park) and the tidy town streets with their shuttered historic houses.

Information and getting around

Gettysburg **Convention & Visitors Bureau**, 102 Carlisle St (daily 8.30am–5pm; ⓣ717/334-6274, ⓦwww.gettysburg.travel), is housed next door to the tiny historic train depot where Lincoln disembarked in November 1863. Though the town is compact and easy to walk around, there is no public transportation, and a car helps when touring the huge battlefield. Two-hour double decker **Battlefield Bus Tours**, running through the town and making numerous stops, depart from 778 Baltimore St (up to eight tours daily; $24.95 for audio, $27.95 for live guide; ⓣ717/334-6296, ⓦwww.gettysburgbattlefieldtours.com).

Accommodation

There is plenty of lodging in and around Gettysburg, including many **B&Bs**. The most central place to **camp** is at *Artillery Ridge Resort*, 610 Taneytown Rd (ⓣ717/334-1288, ⓦwww.artilleryridge.com; sites from $34; open April–Oct).

Baladerry Inn 40 Hospital Rd ⓣ717/337-1342, ⓦwww.baladerryinn.com. Historic hospital turned B&B, with nine en-suite rooms. ❻

Doubleday Inn 104 Doubleday Ave ⓣ717/334-9119, ⓦwww.doubledayinn.com. A very welcoming, memorabilia-packed luxury B&B – the only one within the battlefield itself. ❺

Gettysburg Travelodge 613 Baltimore St ⓣ717/334-9281, ⓦwww.travelodge.com. Standard motel between downtown and the battlefield. ❸

HI-Gardners 1212 Pine Grove Rd, Gardners ⓣ717/486-7575, ⓦwww.hiusa.org. Located on the Appalachian Trail in remote Pine Grove Furnace State Park, over 20 miles away. Busiest during ski season. Beds from $15.

Historic Farnsworth House Inn 401 Baltimore St ⓣ717/334-8838, ⓦwww.farnsworthhouseinn.com. An 1810 townhouse, used as Union HQ in the war and still riddled with bullet holes. Includes 10 rooms, a tavern and a theatre. ❻

The battleground

It takes most of a day to see the 3500-acre **Gettysburg National Military Park**, which surrounds the town (daily 6am–10pm; free; ⓦwww.nps.gov/gett). The stunning new **visitor centre**, just over a mile south of downtown at 1175 Baltimore Pike (daily: summer 8am–7pm, rest of year 8am–6pm; ⓣ717/334-1124) now rivals Harrisburg's (see p.143) as the best Civil War **museum** in the state, possibly the country. It is beautifully designed, with tons of memorabilia such as photos, guns, uniforms, surgical and musical instruments, tents and flags, as well as exhaustive written information. Five repeating ten-minute videos, insterspersed throughout the chronological sequence of the museum, chronicle the early part of the war, the three days of the battle and the war's conclusion. The star exhibit is the moving **Cyclorama**, a 356ft circular painting of Pickett's Charge, the suicidal Confederate thrust across open wheatfields in broad daylight. This is also the place to pick up details of a self-guided **driving route**, or a **guide** will join you in your car for a personalized two-hour tour ($55).

Not far from the visitor centre, the **Gettysburg National Cemetery** contains thousands of graves arranged in a semicircle around the Soldiers' National Monument, on the site where Lincoln gave the Gettysburg Address. Most stirring of all are the hundreds of small marble gravestones marked only with numbers. A short walk away, the battlegrounds themselves, golden fields reminiscent of an English country landscape, are peaceful now except for their names: **Valley of Death**, **Bloody Run**, **Cemetery Hill**. Uncanny statues of key figures stand at appropriate points, while heavy stone monuments honour different regiments.

Other attractions

Star billing in the town centre goes to the impressive new 800-square-foot 3-D **diorama** of the battle at the **Gettysburg History Center**, 241 Steinwehr Ave (Sun–Thurs 9am–8pm, Fri & Sat 9am–9pm, until 10pm in summer; $5; ⓣ717/334-6408, ⓦwww.gettysburgdiorama.com). The only other sight worth a peek in town, at 528 Baltimore St, is the **Jennie Wade House** (daily: June–Aug 9am–7pm, Sept–Nov & March–May 9am–5pm; $7.25; ⓣ717/334-4100), the former home of the only civilian to die in the battle, killed by a stray bullet as she made bread for the Union troops in her sister's kitchen. To the west of the park, President Eisenhower, who retired to Gettysburg, is commemorated at the **Eisenhower National Historic Site** (daily 9am–4pm; $7.50; ⓣ717/338-9114, ⓦwww.nps.gov/eise), where his Georgian-style mansion holds an array of memorabilia. The site is accessible only on shuttle-bus tours from the National Park Visitor Center (see p.145).

Eating and entertainment

Evenings in Gettysburg tend to be quiet once the tour buses have gone home. However, there are some good **restaurants**, many in historically important buildings.

Blue Parrot Bistro 35 Chambersburg St ⓣ717/337-3739. Pasta and steaks with a good choice of sauces. Like most restaurants in town, things wind down soon after 8.30pm.

Dobbin House Tavern 89 Steinwehr Ave ⓣ717/334-2100. The oldest house in the city, a former hideout for escaped slaves dating from 1776. Lunch from $10; candlelit dinners are more expensive, with entrees around $25. Food veers between Pennsylvania Dutch, early American and contemporary.

Garryowen Irish Pub 126 Chambersburg St ⓣ717/337-2719. This is the town's liveliest spot, which hosts open mic and other live music nights, some trad Irish, which you can sip a Guinness to.

Gettysbrew Restaurant & Brewery 248 Hunterstown Rd ⓣ717/337-1001. Also a pub and historic site. Brews five beers, plus its own root beer and soda.

Mayflowers 533 Steinwehr Ave ⓣ717/337-3377. Huge modern Chinese restaurant that does a high-quality evening buffet for $9.99 and à la carte sushi.

Western Pennsylvania

Western Pennsylvania, a key point for frontier trade and an important thoroughfare to the West, was the focus of the fighting between the English and the French in the seven-year French and Indian War for colonial and maritime power (1756–63). This region grew to industrial prominence in the nineteenth century, with the exploitation of its coal and oil resources gathering pace after the Civil War.

Today, tourism in western Pennsylvania is concentrated around the surprisingly appealing city of **Pittsburgh**. To the south of the city, the **Laurel Highlands** features Frank Lloyd Wright's not-to-be-missed architectural masterpiece, **Fallingwater**, as well as nearby **Ohiopyle State Park**. In the overwhelming rural northwest corner of the state, another great wilderness area to explore is the lush **Allegheny National Forest**, which begins twenty miles north of I-80. The region's only major conurbation, **Erie**, is located on the eponymous great lake and includes **Presque Isle State Park**, well worth a visit for its sandy lake beaches and wooded hiking trails.

Pittsburgh

The appealing ten-block district known as the **Golden Triangle**, at the heart of downtown **PITTSBURGH**, stands at the confluence of the Monongahela, Allegheny and Ohio rivers; this area was once bitterly fought over as the gateway to the West. The French built Fort Duquesne on the site in 1754, only for it to be destroyed four years later by the British, who replaced it with **Fort Pitt**. Industry began with the development of iron foundries in the early 1800s and by the time of the Civil War, Pittsburgh was producing half of the iron and one third of the glass in the US. Soon after, the city became the world's leading producer of steel, thanks to the vigorous expansion programmes of **Andrew Carnegie**, who by 1870 was the richest man in the world. Present-day Pittsburgh is dotted with his cultural bequests, along with those of other wealthy forefathers, including the Mellon bankers, the Frick coal merchants and the Heinz food producers.

The city has gradually ditched its Victorian reputation for dirt and pollution since its transformation began in the 1960s and has now established itself as one of America's most attractive and most liveable cities. The face-lift involved large-scale demolition of abandoned steel mills, which freed up much of the downtown waterfront to make way for sleek skyscapers and green spaces. Each of Pittsburgh's close-knit neighbourhoods – the **South Side** and **Mount Washington**, across the Monongahela River from the Golden Triangle, the **North Side** across the Allegheny River and the **East End** – has a distinct flavour.

Arrival, information and city transport

Greyhound **buses** pull in downtown at 55 11th St, bang opposite the attractive Amtrak **train** station at 1100 Liberty Ave. From the modern, efficient **Pittsburgh International Airport**, fifteen miles west (Ⓣ412/472-3525, Ⓦwww.pitairport.com), several shuttle services run to Pittsburgh. More frequent and significantly cheaper, the excellent PAT bus #28X runs roughly every twenty minutes between the airport and twelve downtown and Oakland locations (daily 5am–midnight; $2.25).

Pittsburgh's main **welcome centre** is downtown on Liberty Avenue, adjacent to the Gateway Center (Mon–Fri 8am–4pm, Sat 9am–5pm, Sun 10am–3pm; Ⓣ412/281-7711 or 1-800/366-0093, Ⓦwww.visitpittsburgh.com), with subsidiary branches at the airport and at the Senator John Heinz Pittsburgh Regional History Center.

Transportation between Pittsburgh's various districts is simple. **Buses** through town (free–$2.75), the Monongahela and Duquesne Heights trolley inclines ($1.75) and the small "T" **subway** system (free downtown; up to $3.25 further out) are all excellent transportation options. **PAT**, the combined transit authority (Ⓣ412/442-2000, Ⓦwww.portauthority.org), has a downtown service centre at 534 Smithfield St (Mon–Thurs 7.30am–5.30pm, Fri 7.30am–5pm), where you can pick up timetables. For **taxis**, call Yellow Cab (Ⓣ412/665-8100).

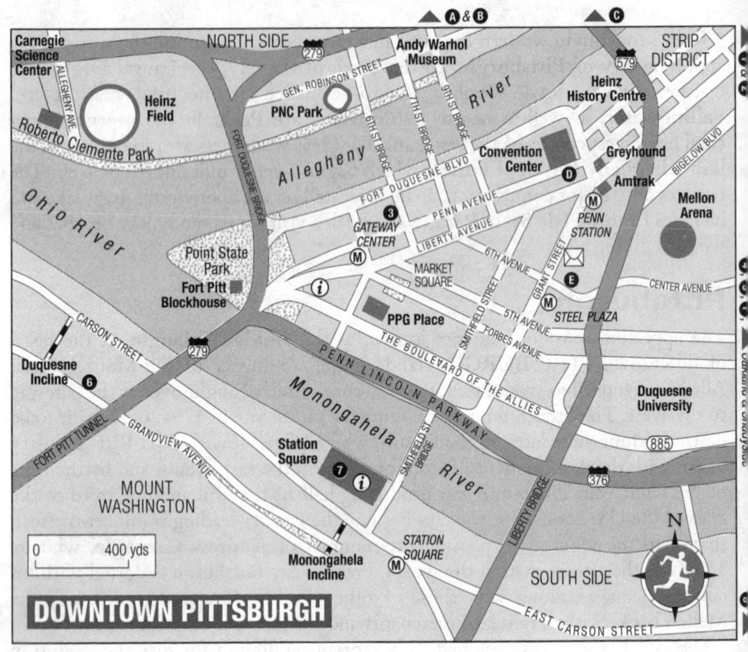

ACCOMMODATION				RESTAURANTS			
Doubletree Hotel Pittsburgh City Center	E	The Priory – A City Inn	A	The Church Brew Works	2	La Feria	4
The Inn on Negley	F	Valley Motel	C	Grand Concourse	7	Lemon Grass Café	3
The Inn on the Mexican War Streets	B	The Westin Convention Center Pittsburgh	D	Grandview Saloon	6	Mallorca	8
				Kaya	1	Yumwok/Lulu's Noodles	5

Accommodation

Pittsburgh's **hotels** and few **B&Bs** are generally pricey, although weekend packages at luxury downtown hotels can bring rates down to not too much above $100. You can check out all of the Pittsburgh area's B&Bs at Ⓦwww.pittsburghbnb.com.

Doubletree Hotel Pittsburgh City Center One Bigelow Square Ⓣ412/281-5800 or 1-800/225-5858, Ⓦwww.doubletree.com. Convenient downtown high-rise chain hotel offering suites with kitchens; look for advance internet rates. ⑦

The Inn on Negley 703 S Negley Ave, Shadyside Ⓣ412/661-0631, Ⓦwww.theinnsonnegley.com. Friendly, upmarket establishment with eight elegantly furnished rooms and suites, several with jacuzzi. As well as the complimentary gourmet breakfasts, quality teas and sweets are served noon–4pm. ⑦

The Inn on the Mexican War Streets 604 W North Ave Ⓣ412/231-6544, Ⓦwww.innonthemexicanwarstreets.com. Eight tastefully refurbished rooms in one of the North Side's trendiest areas. The less expensive rooms are great value. ⑥

The Priory – A City Inn 614 Pressley St Ⓣ412/231-3338, Ⓦwww.thepriory.com. Restored 1880s inn, originally built to house travelling Benedictine monks; now, it's the North Side's nicest B&B. Room rates include continental breakfast, evening wine, weekday limo service and use of fitness room. ⑤

Valley Motel 2571 Freeport Rd, Harmarville Ⓣ412/828-7100, Ⓦwww.valleymotel.net. Basic motel with low rates, located eleven miles northeast of downtown. A fair option if you have a car. ②

The Westin Convention Center Pittsburgh 1000 Penn Ave Ⓣ412/281-3700 or 1-800/937-8461, Ⓦwww.westin.com. Flashy downtown tower with pool, gym and other top amenities. ⑧

Downtown: the Golden Triangle

The *New York Times* once described Pittsburgh as "the only city with an entrance" – and, true enough, the view of the **Golden Triangle** skyline on emerging from the tunnel on the Fort Pitt Bridge is undeniably breathtaking. Surrounded by water and steel bridges, the Triangle's imaginative contemporary architecture stands next to Gothic churches and red-brick warehouses. Philip Johnson's magnificent postmodern concoction, the black-glass Gothic **PPG Place** complex, looms incongruously over the old **Market Square**, lined with restaurants and shops. **Point State Park**, at the peak of the Triangle, is where it all began. The site of five different forts during the French and Indian War, it still contains the 1764 **Fort Pitt Blockhouse**, the city's oldest structure. The park itself is now a popular gathering area, boasting a 150ft fountain with a pool, and is a great place to view sunsets and an excellent venue for the city's free outdoor festivals.

History is most apparent on the faded buildings along Liberty Avenue, with 1940s and 1950s fronts left in place during successive interior renovations. At the flat end of the Triangle, the modernist new steel and glass edifice of the **Consol Energy Center** hosts large concerts and exhibitions and is home to the **Pittsburgh Penguins** ice hockey team (Ⓣ412/642-7367, Ⓦpenguins.nhl.com). Northeast of downtown, along Penn Avenue past the vast new Convention Center, the characterful **Strip District** has a bustling early-morning fresh produce market, as well as bargain shops by day and lively night-time venues. The seven-floor **Senator John Heinz Pittsburgh Regional History Center**, at 1212 Smallman St (daily 10am–5pm; $10; Ⓣ412/454-6000, Ⓦwww.pghhistory.org), does a good job of telling the city's story, paying particular attention to immigrants of various eras.

The South Side

In the nineteenth century, 400ft **Mount Washington**, across the Monongahela River, was the site of most of the city's coal mines. No longer dominated by belching steel mills and industry, the **South Side**, banked by the green "mountain", is an area of many churches, colourful houses nestled on steep hills and old neighbourhoods. The 1877 **Duquesne Incline**, from 1197 W Carson St to 1220 Grandview Ave, is a working cable-car system ($2 one-way; Ⓣ412/381-1665, Ⓦwww.incline.cc) whose upper station contains a small **museum**. The outdoor observation platform is a prime spot for **views** over the Golden Triangle and beyond, especially awesome after dark.

The best way to get to the South Side is across the 1883 blue-and-cream **Smithfield Street Bridge**, the oldest of fifteen downtown bridges and notable for its elliptical "fisheye" truss. Just to the west of the bridge stands red-brick **Station Square**, a food and shopping complex converted from old railroad warehouses. In front stands the jetty for the enjoyable hour-long narrated Just Ducky Tours **river cruises** (April–Oct daily 10.30am–6pm; Nov Sat & Sun 10.30am–6pm, $19, kids $15; tours every 90min; Ⓣ412/402-3825, Ⓦwww.justduckytours.com).

Heading east along the banks of the Monongahela, **East Carson Street** is the main commercial drag of South Side, where a long-standing community of Polish and Ukrainian steelworkers has gradually absorbed an offbeat mix of artsy residents, along with the attendant cafés and bars, making it far and away Pittsburgh's most vibrant **nightlife** centre (see p.152).

The North Side

The star attraction on the **North Side** is undoubtedly the **Andy Warhol Museum**, 117 Sandusky St, just over the Seventh Street Bridge from downtown (Tues–Sun 10am–5pm, Fri until 10pm; $15, Fri 5–10pm $7.50; Ⓣ412/237-8300,

The guru of pop art

Born in Pittsburgh in 1928, **Andy Warhol** (born Andrew Warhola, the youngest son of working-class Slovakian immigrants) moved to New York City at the age of 21, after graduating from Carnegie-Mellon University. After a decade as a successful commercial artist, by the early 1960s he was leading the vanguard of the new pop art, shooting 16mm films such as *Chelsea Girls*, and by 1967 had developed the "Exploding Plastic Inevitable" multimedia show, featuring erotic dancers and music by The Velvet Underground, whom he managed. After founding *Interview* magazine in 1969, Warhol became transfixed with the rich and famous and, up until his death in 1987, was perhaps best known for his celebrity portraits and his appearances at society events. Ironically, he always disowned his gritty hometown, which didn't fit with NYC cool, and would probably turn in his grave that his main shrine is located back there, as are his mortal remains, in Bethel cemetery, Bethel Park (Ⓣ412/835-8538).

Ⓦwww.warhol.org). The museum documents the life and work of Pittsburgh's most celebrated son (see box, above) over seven floors of a spacious Victorian warehouse; it claims to be the largest museum in the world devoted to a single artist. Although the majority of Warhol's most famous pieces are in the hands of private collectors, the museum boasts an impressive and ever-changing selection of over five hundred exhibits, including iconic pop art and portraiture. It pays equal attention to archival material, there are informative **self-guided tours** and occasional workshops take place. At any given time, two or three non-Warhol exhibits show work related in some way to Warhol themes. During "**Good Fridays**" (5–10pm) there is free entrance to the lobby, which has a cash bar, and often buzzes with live bands or other performance arts.

Elsewhere on the North Side, revitalization centres around the intriguingly named **Mexican War Streets**, on the northern edge of Allegheny Commons, a tree-lined area of nineteenth-century grey-brick and limestone terraces. The excellent and highly unusual **Mattress Factory**, 500 Sampsonia Way (Tues–Sat 10am–5pm, Sun 1–5pm; $10; Ⓣ412/231-3169, Ⓦwww.mattress.org), has contemporary installations by top mixed-media artists, and is a must on any visit to the city. The **National Aviary**, Allegheny Commons West (Mon–Sat 10am–5pm, Sun noon–5pm; $12; Ⓣ412/323-7235, Ⓦwww.aviary.org), is a huge indoor bird sanctuary with over two hundred species, including foul-mouthed parrots, fluttering inside a thirty-foot glass dome. Nearby, **The Children's Museum of Pittsburgh**, 10 Children's Way, Allegheny Square (Mon–Sat 10am–5pm, Sun noon–5pm; $11, kids $10; Ⓣ412/322-5058, Ⓦwww.pittsburghkids.org), offers a plethora of games, events and special exhibitions.

Heading northwest along the river, the huge, state-of-the-art **Carnegie Science Center**, 1 Allegheny Ave (daily 10am–5pm, Sat until 7pm; $17.95, kids $9.95; Ⓣ412/237-3400, Ⓦwww.carnegiesciencecenter.org), is also predominantly aimed at children, with an interactive engineering playspace, a miniature railroad and a planetarium. The centre contains an impressive OMNIMAX theatre ($8 for one show, $13 for two). Admission also includes entry to the **USS Requin**, a 1945 submarine out beside the river. Next door, the gargantuan edifice of **Heinz Field** is home to football's **Pittsburgh Steelers** (Ⓣ412/323-1200, Ⓦwww.steelers.com), the only team with six Superbowls, most recently in 2009. Further along the river toward the Sixth Street Bridge is **PNC Park**, the home of the **Pittsburgh Pirates** baseball team (Ⓣ1-800/289-2827, Ⓦwww.pirates.com). Beautifully constructed so that from most seats you get a sweeping view of the Allegheny and downtown, it's a real treat to watch a game here on a balmy summer night, even though the team is a laughing stock.

Oakland and the East End

Oakland, Pittsburgh's university area, is totally dominated by the campuses of **Carnegie-Mellon University**, the **University of Pittsburgh** (always known as "Pitt"), and several other colleges. At Fifth Avenue and Bigelow Boulevard, the 42-storey, 2529-window Gothic Revival **Cathedral of Learning** is a university building with a difference: among its classrooms the 26 **Nationality Rooms** are furnished with antiques and specially crafted items donated by the city's different ethnic groups, from Lithuanian to Chinese. These can be visited on ninety-minute **guided tours** (Mon–Sat 9am–2.30pm, Sun 11am–2.30pm; $3; ⓣ412/624-6000, ⓦwww.pitt.edu/~natrooms). On the grounds behind the Cathedral of Learning is the French Gothic **Heinz Memorial Chapel** (Mon–Fri 9am–5pm, Sun 1–5pm; free), notable for its long, narrow, stained-glass windows depicting political, literary and religious figures.

Across from the cathedral at 4400 Forbes Ave, the **Carnegie** cultural complex holds two great museums – the **Museum of Natural History**, famed for its extensive dinosaur relics and sparkling gems, and the **Museum of Art**, with Impressionist, post-Impressionist and American regional art, as well as an excellent modern collection (both museums Tues–Sat 10am–5pm, Thurs until 8pm, Sun noon–5pm; $15; ⓣ412/622-3131, ⓦwww.carnegiemuseums.org). Nearby, Schenley Park includes the colourful flower gardens of **Phipps Conservatory** (daily 9.30am–5pm, Fri until 10pm; $12; ⓣ412/622-6814 ⓦwww.phipps.conservatory.org) and wild wooded areas beyond.

The stretch of Fifth Avenue from the Cathedral of Learning up to **Shadyside** is lined with important and architecturally beautiful academic buildings, places of worship and the former mansions of the early industrialists. Other buildings of note include the exquisite external mural of the Byzantine Catholic **Church of the Holy Spirit** and the humble broadcasting complex of **WQED** opposite, notable for being the first publicly funded TV station when it opened in April 1954. Shadyside itself is an upmarket, trendy neighbourhood containing the particularly chic commercial section of Walnut Street. Continuing along Fifth Avenue, the **Pittsburgh Center for the Arts**, at no. 6300, in the corner of Mellon Park, showcases innovative Pittsburgh art in various media (Tues–Sat 10am–5pm, Thurs until 7pm, Sun noon–5pm; suggested donation $5; ⓣ412/361-0873, ⓦwww.pittsburgharts.org). A short way to the southeast, **Squirrel Hill** is another lively area, housing a mixture of students and the city's largest Jewish community, with a fine selection of shops and restaurants lining Murray and Forbes avenues.

Further east, the most notable feature at the **Frick Art and Historical Center** complex, 7227 Reynolds St (Tues–Sun 10am–5pm; free; ⓣ412/371-0600, ⓦwww.frickart.org), is the **Frick Art Museum**, which displays Italian, Flemish and French art from the fifteenth to the nineteenth centuries, as well as two of Marie Antoinette's chairs. Three miles north, bordering the Allegheny River, the green expanse of **Highland Park** contains the nicely landscaped and enjoyable **Pittsburgh Zoo and PPG Aquarium** (daily: summer 9.30am–6pm; spring & autumn 9am–5pm; winter 9am–4pm; April–Nov $13, Dec–March $9; ⓣ412/665-3640, ⓦwww.zoo.pgh.pa.us), which has the distinction of owning a Komodo dragon and having successfully bred two baby elephants.

Eating

Eating downtown can prove expensive, and the area is rather deserted at night; it's better to head for the **Strip District** or along and around **East Carson Street** on the South Side. **Station Square** and **Mount Washington** are more upmarket, while **Oakland** is home to various cheap student hangouts. The other **East End** neighbourhoods have a number of good cheap and mid-priced places.

The Church Brew Works 3525 Liberty Ave ☎412/688-8200. Vast establishment 2 miles east of downtown (and Bloomfield), serving American cuisine and fine ales brewed on site. Housed in a grand, converted old church where vats have replaced the organ.

Grand Concourse 1 Station Square ☎412/261-1717. Pricey, plush seafood restaurant in a gorgeous setting, where you can feast on delights such as coconut macadamia-encrusted shrimp. Expect to pay at least $50 per head.

Grandview Saloon 1212 Grandview Ave ☎412/431-1400. Relaxed Mt Washington restaurant, where you can enjoy $10 burgers at lunchtime or much more expensive American dinner entrees. Arrive early for a deck table with a view.

Kaya 2000 Smallman St ☎412/261-6565. Stylish Caribbean restaurant in the Strip District with a varied vegetarian selection, as well as a huge range of beers, rums and cocktails.

La Feria 5527 Walnut St ☎412/682-4501. Colourful upstairs Peruvian shop-cum-restaurant in Shadyside, offering a limited but tasty selection of inexpensive specials from the Andes. BYOB.

Lemon Grass Café 124 6th St ☎412/765-2222. Excellent, authentic and cheerful Thai restaurant, serving delightful curries, stir-fries and salads for under $10. One of the best downtown options. BYOB.

Mallorca 2228 E Carson St ☎412/488-1818. This smart South Side restaurant serves excellent paella and Mediterranean dishes, as well as fine sangria. Ask if they have the delicious goat in red-wine sauce – at under $30 it's enough for two.

Yumwok/Lulu's Noodles 400 S Craig St ☎412/687-7777. Combined Oakland establishment serving filling noodles and good standard pan-Asian cuisine at bargain prices. Justifiably popular with students. BYOB.

Nightlife and entertainment

Pittsburgh's **nightlife** offers rich pickings in everything from the classics to jazz and alternative rock. The nationally regarded City Theatre, 1300 Bingham St (☎412/431-4400, Ⓦwww.citytheatrecompany.org), puts on groundbreaking productions in a converted South Side church. The widely travelled **Pittsburgh Symphony Orchestra** plays at the Heinz Hall, 600 Penn Ave (☎412/392-4900, Ⓦwww.pittsburghsymphony.org) and the city's ballet, dance and opera companies perform at the downtown **Benedum Center for the Performing Arts**, 719 Liberty Ave (☎412/456-6666, Ⓦwww.pgharts.org). The *City Paper*, a free weekly newspaper published on Wednesdays (Ⓦwww.pghcitypaper.com), has extensive **listings**.

Brillobox 4104 Penn Ave ☎412/621-4900, Ⓦwww.brillobox.net. Two prodigal Pittsburghers returning from New York have created a unique bar that's both chic and a fun local spot for watching sports. There's a good jukebox downstairs and a performance space for mostly obscure acts above.

Club Café 56–58 S 12th St ☎412/431-4950, Ⓦwww.clubcafelive.com. Laidback South Side club with regular live music, including rock, folk and salsa.

Kelly's 6012 Penn Circle S, E Liberty ☎412/363-6012. Just east of Shadyside, this popular bar offers good beer such as East End Big Hop and eclectic recorded music.

Mr Small's Funhouse 400 Lincoln Ave, Millvale ☎1-800/594-8499, Ⓦwww.mrsmalls.com. Several miles northeast of downtown off US-28, this converted church hosts most of the mid-sized US and foreign indie rock acts.

Piper's Pub 1828 E Carson St ☎412/431-6757, Ⓦwww.piperspub.com. One of the South Side's most convivial bars and the place for soccer, rugby and Gaelic football on TV. Imported and US beers are available and the food is decent, especially the breakfasts.

Rex Theater 1602 E Carson St ☎412/381-6811, Ⓦwww.rextheater.com. This former cinema hosts mainly rock shows, often of national and international standing.

Around Pittsburgh

Just over an hour southeast of Pittsburgh, the **Laurel Highlands** takes in seventy miles of rolling wooded hills and valleys. The main reasons to come this way down Hwy-381 are to see one of Frank Lloyd Wright's most unique creations, **Fallingwater** and to take advantage of some prime outdoor opportunities around the small town of **Ohiopyle**.

Fallingwater

You do not need to be an architecture buff to appreciate Wright's **Fallingwater** (mid-March to late Nov Thurs–Tues 10am–4pm; Dec & early March Fri–Sun 11.30am–3pm; tour $18; ⓣ724/329-8501, ⓦwww.fallingwater.org), which was built in the late 1930s for the Kaufmann family, owners of Pittsburgh's premier department store. Signposted off Hwy-381, some twenty miles south of I-70, it is set on Bear Run Creek in the midst of the gorgeous deciduous forest of Bear Run Nature Reserve. It is the only one of Wright's buildings to be on display exactly as it was designed, which makes sense as it's built right into a set of cliffside waterfalls. Wright used a cantilever system to make the multi-tiered structure "cascade down the hill like the water down the falls". The house's almost precarious position is truly stunning, and it is remarkable how well its predominantly rectangular shapes blend in with nature's less uniform lines. Among the house's pioneering features is a lack of load-bearing walls, which gives an extra sense of space, and natural skylights.

Ohiopyle

Five miles south of Fallingwater, tiny **OHIOPYLE** is the most convenient base from which to enjoy the wilds of **Ohiopyle State Park** or activities like white-water rafting on the **Youghiogheny River**. The park fans out around the town and river, offering a maze of trails for hiking or biking, and natural delights such as **Cucumber Falls** and the unique habitat of the **Ferncliff Peninsula**, known for its wildflowers. A small **visitor centre on Hwy-381** dispenses local information (daily 10am–4.30pm; ⓣ724/329-8591). Just beyond it the *Ohiopyle House Café*, 144 Grant St (ⓣ724/329-1122), serves up tasty dishes like lobster ravioli and caramel pudding. The *Yough Plaza Motel* on Sherman Street (ⓣ1-800/992-7238, ⓦwww.youghplaza.com; ❹) has reasonable standard units and studio apartments; even better for budget travellers is camping or renting a cabin in the park itself (ⓣ1-888/727-2757). For **rafting**, White Water Adventurers at 6 Negley St (equipment rental $23; ⓣ1-800/992-7238, ⓦwww.wwaraft.com) is one of several outfits that rent equipment and give instruction.

Allegheny National Forest

Occupying over half a million acres and a sizeable portion of four counties, the pristine **Allegheny National Forest** affords a bounty of opportunities for engaging in outdoor pursuits like hiking, fishing, snowmobiling and, best of all, admiring the **autumn foliage**, which rivals any in New England. In the north, there are several points of interest within easy access of Hwy-6, the major route through the forest. Just north of the highway, it is worth a stop to admire the views from the **Kinzua Viaduct** railroad bridge, the highest and longest in the world when constructed in 1882. The dominant feature of the forest's northern section is the huge **Kinzua Reservoir**, created by a dam at the southern end. Swimming is possible at **Kinzua** and **Kiasutha beaches** or you can enjoy a picnic at **Rimrock Overlook** or at **Willow Bay** in the very north. The summer-only Kinzua Point **Information Center** on Hwy-59 (ⓣ814/726-1291) has details on trails, private cabins and campgrounds around the forest, or you can **camp** in any of the twenty state-run campground (ⓣ1-877/444-6777, ⓦwww.reserveusa.com).

Erie

The focal point of Pennsylvania's forty-mile slice of Lake Erie waterfront is the pleasant city of **ERIE** itself. It bears no resemblance to the major urban centres of Pittsburgh or Philadelphia, being entirely low-rise and extremely leafy. There are several places of cultural interest in the city, all within walking distance of the square, including the Neoclassical **Court House** and several **museums** devoted to history, art and science. Better than these, the **Erie Maritime Museum** at 150 E Front St in the Bayfront Historical District (April–Oct Mon–Sat 9am–5pm, Sun noon–5pm; Nov–March closed Mon–Wed; $8; ⓣ814/452-2744, ⓦwww.flagshipniagara.org) has a fascinating display on the geological and ecological development of the Great Lakes, and also focuses on warships of different periods; the elegant **US Flagship Niagara**, usually moored outside, is part of the museum.

Undoubtedly, Erie's main attraction is the elongated comma-shaped peninsula of **Presque Isle State Park**, which bends east from its narrow neck three miles west of downtown until it almost touches the city's northernmost tip. The park is maintained as a nature preserve and has wide sandy **beaches** good for swimming, backed by thick woods offering a series of trails. Those without a vehicle can hop on the Port of Erie **water taxi** (late May to mid-Oct Mon noon–6pm, Tues–Sun 10am–6pm; $6 return; ⓣ814/881-2502, ⓦwww.porterie.org) from Dobbins Landing on the Erie Bayfront.

Practicalities

Erie has frequent Greyhound **bus** connections to Pittsburgh, Cleveland and Buffalo from the Intermodal Transit Terminal, at 208 E Bayfront Drive. The **Visit Erie office**, within the same complex (Mon–Fri 8.30am–5pm; ⓣ814/454-1000 or 1-800/524-3743, ⓦwww.visiteriepa.com), is the place to go for general information, while Presque Isle's **Stull Interpretive Center and Nature Shop** (spring & autumn 10am–4pm; summer 10am–5pm; ⓣ814/836-9107, ⓦwww.presqueisle.org) disseminates knowledge about the peninsula.

Accommodation is often twice as expensive in the summer as in the off-season. The *Bayfront Inn*, 2540 W 8th St (ⓣ814/838-2081, ⓦwww.bayfrontinnerie.com; ❷), provides great off-season bargains but the elegant *Boothby Inn B&B*, at 311 W 6th St (ⓣ814/456-1888 or 1-866/266-8429, ⓦwww.theboothbyinn.com; ❺), is more central and makes for a far more pleasant stay. Numerous functional **motels** also line Peninsula Drive. The well-sited *Sara's Campground*, 50 Peninsula Drive (ⓣ814/833-4560, ⓦwww.sarascampground.com; from $23), is just before the entrance to Presque Isle. Nearby in Sara Coyne Plaza, *Sally's Diner* (ⓣ814/833-1957) serves up hearty breakfasts and meals. Back downtown, try *The Pufferbelly*, 414 French St (ⓣ814/455-1557), for classy entrees such as steak Madagascar, or the inexpensive Chinese food at *Happy Garden*, 418 State St (ⓣ814/452-4488).

New Jersey

The skinny coastal state of **NEW JERSEY** has been at the heart of US history since the Revolution, when a battle was fought at **Princeton**, and George Washington spent two bleak winters at Morristown. As the Civil War came, the state's commitment to an industrial future ensured that, despite its border location along the Mason–Dixon Line, it fought with the Union.

That commitment to industry has doomed New Jersey in modern times; most travellers only see "the Garden State", so called for the rich market garden territory at the state's heart, from the stupendously ugly New Jersey Turnpike toll road, which is always heavy with truck traffic. Even the songs of **Bruce Springsteen**, **Asbury Park**'s golden boy, paint his home state as a gritty urban wasteland of empty lots, grey highways, lost dreams and blue-collar heartache. The majority of the refineries and factories actually hug only a mere fifteen-mile-wide swath along the turnpike, but bleak cities like **Newark**, home to the major airport, and Trenton, the forgettable capital, reinforce the dour image. But there is more to New Jersey than factories and pollution. Alongside its revolutionary history, the northwest corner near the Delaware Water Gap is traced with picturesque lakes, streams and woodlands, while in the south, the town of **Princeton** adds architectural elegance to the interior with the grand buildings of its Ivy League university. Best of all perhaps, the Atlantic shore offers many bustling resorts, from the compelling tattered glitz of **Atlantic City** to the old-world charm of **Cape May**.

Inland New Jersey

Visitors most often travel from New York to northern New Jersey for the great **shopping**: from huge malls and designer outlet stores to ethnic emporia like Mitsuwa Marketplace, the Japanese shopping centre in Edgewater (Ⓣ201/941-9113, Ⓦwww.mitsuwa.com), both prices and taxes are lower than across the Hudson River. The well-off towns, such as Englewood and Rockleigh, along the river also contain some fine Italian and Asian restaurants, while Hoboken offers a spillover of Manhattan subculture just west of the island itself. Travelling southwest on the interstates from the shore or from New York City, however, visitors see the New Jersey of popular imagination: a heavily industrialized cultural desert peppered with run-down cities like Trenton, Paterson and Newark. The one place that holds interest in inland New Jersey is **Princeton**, an Ivy-League town that makes a pretty afternoon stop-off.

Princeton

Self-satisfied **PRINCETON**, which began its days inauspiciously as Stony Brook in the late 1600s, lies on US-206 eleven miles north of Trenton. It rose to fame as home to **Princeton University**, the nation's fourth oldest, which broke away from overly religious Yale in 1756. In January 1777, a week after Washington's triumph against the British at Trenton, the **Battle of Princeton** occurred southwest of town, another turning point in the Revolutionary effort. After the war, in 1783, the **Continental Congress**, fearful of potential attack from incensed unpaid veterans in Philadelphia, met here for four months; the leafy, well-kept town was then left in peace to follow its academic pursuits. Alumni of Princeton University include actor James Stewart, Jazz-Age writer F. Scott Fitzgerald, actress Brooke Shields and presidents Wilson and Madison.

Arrival, information and getting around

A shuttle **bus**, the Olympic Airporter, makes the run from Newark airport to town (daily: times vary; 1hr 30min trip; $24–38 one-way; Ⓣ609/587-6600, Ⓦolympic-limo.com). On their New York–Philadelphia runs, Amtrak and NJ Transit **trains** stop at Princeton Junction, three miles south of Princeton. You can buy a transfer in advance for the SEPTA shuttle (Ⓣ215/580-7800, Ⓦwww.septa.com) from downtown to Princeton's train terminal, on campus at University Place. Coach USA **buses** from New York's Port Authority bus station (Ⓣ1-800/222-0492, Ⓦwww.suburbantransit.com) run every thirty minutes to Palmer Square.

Information is available from the Frist Campus Center at the university (Ⓣ609/258-1766, Ⓦwww.princeton.edu/frist) or from the **Chamber of Commerce** at 9 Vandeventer Ave (Mon–Fri 8.30am–5pm; Ⓣ609/924-1776, Ⓦwww.princetonchamber.org). The **Historical Society Museum**, 158 Nassau St (Tues–Sun noon–4pm; Ⓣ609/921-6748, Ⓦwww.princetonhistory.org), organizes **walking tours** through town (Sun 2pm; $7) and also provides **maps** so you can do it yourself. Central Princeton is easily **navigable on foot**, but weather extremes in the winter and summer, as well as the distance of accommodation, may make you glad to have a **car**.

The town and the university

Mercer Street, the long road that sweeps southwest past the university campus to Nassau Street, is lined with elegant colonial houses, graced with shutters, columns and wrought-iron fences. The **Princeton Battlefield State Park**, a mile and a half out, includes the **Thomas Clarke House**, 500 Mercer St, a Quaker farmhouse that served as a hospital during the battle. The simple house at 112 Mercer, back toward town, is where **Albert Einstein** lived while teaching at the Institute of Advanced Study. Unfortunately, the house is not open to the public.

Princeton University's tranquil and shaded campus is a beautiful place for a stroll. Just inside the main gates on Nassau Street, **Nassau Hall**, a vault-like historic building containing numerous portraits of famous graduates and one of King George II, was the largest stone building in the nation when constructed in 1756; its 26in-thick walls, now patterned with plaques and patches of ivy placed by graduating classes, withstood American and British fire during the Revolution. It was also the seat of government during Princeton's brief spell as national capital in 1783. The 1925 **chapel**, based on one at King's College, Cambridge University, in England, has stained-glass windows showing scenes from works by Dante, Shakespeare and Milton, as well as the Bible. Across campus, the **Prospect Gardens**, a flowerbed in the shape of the university emblem, are a blaze of orange in summer. Somewhat smug student-led **tours** (during term Mon–Sat 10am, 11am, 1.30pm & 3.30pm, Sun 1.30pm & 3.30pm; hours vary during holidays; free; Ⓣ609/258-1766) take you around to all of these sights, leaving from the Frist Campus Center.

In the middle of the campus, fronted by the Picasso sculpture *Head of a Woman*, the **University Art Museum** is well worth a look for its collection from the Renaissance to the present, including works by Modigliani, Van Gogh and Warhol, as well as Asian and pre-Columbian art (Tues–Sat 10am–5pm, Sun 1–5pm; free; Ⓣ609/258-3788, Ⓦwww.princetonartmuseum.org).

Accommodation, eating and drinking

The only **hotels** in the centre of Princeton are the ersatz-colonial *Nassau Inn* on Palmer Square (Ⓣ609/921-7500 or 1-800/862-7728, Ⓦwww.nassauinn.com; ❽) and the *Peacock Inn* (Ⓣ609/924-1707, Ⓦwww.peacockinn.com; ❽), tucked in a quieter spot at 20 Bayard Lane. Budget **motels** can be found along US-1 and in the suburb of **Lawrenceville** a few miles south of town; one such is the functional *Red Roof Inn*, 3203 Brunswick Pike (Ⓣ609/896-3388, Ⓦwww.redroof.com; ❸).

Despite its affluence, Princeton is by no means the culinary capital of New Jersey. You'll find cheap diner-type **food** along Witherspoon Street. *Teresa's*, 19–23 Palmer Square E (Ⓣ609/921-1974), serves creative, good-value Italian food; and *Elements*, at 163 Baynard Lane (Ⓣ609/252-9680), serves upmarket fish and meat dishes such as Griggstown guinea hen. **Nightlife** is limited, especially when school is out, but the *Triumph Brewery*, 138 Triumph St (Ⓣ609/942-7855), has good, home-brewed beers and is popular with a mixed crowd; meanwhile, the old *Yankee Doodle Tap Room* bar, downstairs at the *Nassau Inn*, is usually full of ancient revellers drinking, reminiscing and enjoying live jazz.

The New Jersey shore

New Jersey's Atlantic coast, a 130-mile stretch of almost uninterrupted **resorts** – some rowdy, some run-down, some undeveloped and peaceful – has long been reliant on farming and tourism, in the absence of a major port. The beaches, if occasionally somewhat crowded, are safe and clean: sandy, broad and lined by characteristic wooden **boardwalks**, some of them charge admission during the summer, in an attempt to maintain their condition. The rowdy, sleazy glitz of **Atlantic City** is perhaps the shore's best-known attraction, though there are also quieter resorts like **Spring Lake** and Victorian **Cape May**.

Spring Lake and Asbury Park

SPRING LAKE, an elegant Victorian resort about twenty miles down the Jersey coast, is one of the smallest, most uncommercial communities on the shore, a gentle respite on the road south to Atlantic City. You can walk the undeveloped two-mile **boardwalk** and watch the crashing ocean from battered gazebos, swim and bask on the white beaches (in summer, compulsory beach tags cost a small fee), or sit in the shade by the town's namesake, **Spring Lake** itself. Wooden footbridges, swans, geese and the grand St Catharine Roman Catholic Church on the banks of the lake give it the feel of a country village. What little activity there is centres on the upmarket shops of Third Avenue.

Bruce Springsteen fans can use the town as a base for visiting nearby **ASBURY PARK**, a decaying old seaside town where The Boss lived for many years and played his first gigs. Almost nothing remains of the carousels and seaside arcades that Springsteen wrote about on early albums such as his debut, *Greetings from Asbury Park*. The **Stone Pony**, 913 Ocean Ave (ⓣ732/502-0600, ⓦwww.stoneponyonline.com), where Springsteen played dozens of times in the mid-1970s and has returned occasionally since, has survived and is the one obligatory stop for devotees.

Practicalities

Spring Lake is accessible by US-34 from the New Jersey Turnpike and served by New Jersey Transit from New York. The Chamber of Commerce is at 302 Washington Ave (Mon–Sat 11am–3pm; ⓣ732/449-0577, ⓦwww.springlake.org) and can help with lodging, especially on summer weekends. There are no cheap **motels** and rates at **B&Bs** can triple in summer; the *Chateau Inn*, 500 Warren Ave (ⓣ732/974-2000 or 1-877/974-5253, ⓦwww.chateauinn.com; ❺), is typical. Adjacent to Asbury Park, in the less exclusive Victorian resort of **Ocean Grove**, friendly *Lillagaard B&B*, 5 Abbot Ave (ⓣ732/988-1216, ⓦwww.lillagaard.com; ❺), is right on the beach.

Most of Spring Lake's **restaurants** are in the elegant Victorian hotels along the seafront and can be pricey. *Who's On Third*, 1300 Third Ave (ⓣ732/449-4233), is a no-nonsense café serving breakfast and lunch. For a blowout, *Whispers*, 200 Monmouth Ave (ⓣ732/974-9755), serves superb fresh fish and quality cuts of meat. In Asbury Park, *Red Fusion* (ⓣ732/775-1008), at 660 Cookman Ave, serves excellent Asian/American fusion food in a unique space that is part art gallery, part sports bar.

Atlantic City

What they wanted was Monte Carlo. They didn't want Las Vegas. What they got was Las Vegas. We always knew that they would get Las Vegas.

Stuart Mendelson, *Philadelphia Journal*

ATLANTIC CITY, on Absecon Island just off the midpoint of the Jersey shoreline, has been a tourist magnet since 1854, when Philadelphia speculators created it as a rail terminal resort. In 1909, at the peak of the seaside town's popularity, Baedeker wrote "there is something colossal about its vulgarity" – a glitzy, slightly monstrous quality that it sustains today. The real-life model for the modern version of the board game **Monopoly**, it has an impressive **popular history**, boasting the nation's first **boardwalk** (1870), the world's first **Ferris wheel** (1892), the first colour **postcards** (1893) and the first **Miss America Beauty Pageant** (1921 – it only moved to Las Vegas in 2006). During Prohibition and the Depression, Atlantic City was a centre for rum-running, packed with speakeasies and illegal gambling dens. Thereafter, in the face of increasing competition from Florida, it slipped into a steep decline, until desperate city officials decided in 1976 to open up the decrepit resort to legal **gambling**, now its mainstay. The city also has a huge **Latino** population.

Arrival, information and city transport

The **bus terminal** at Atlantic and Michigan is served by NJ Transit and Greyhound. NJ Transit trains stop at the **train station** next to the Convention Center, at 1 Miss America Way, and are connected by free shuttle service to all casinos. **Atlantic City International Airport** in Pomona (Ⓣ609/645-7895, Ⓦwww.acairport.com) has direct flights to Philadelphia, as well as some flights further afield; cabs cost around $30 to downtown. For maps and information, head for the helpful **Boardwalk Visitors Center** inside Boardwalk Hall at 2314 Pacific Ave (summer Mon–Fri 9.30am–5.30pm, Thurs–Sun until 8pm; winter Thurs–Mon 9.30am–5.30pm; Ⓣ609/449-7130 or 1-888/228-4748, Ⓦwww.atlanticcitynj.com). Atlantic City is easy to **walk** around, though it's unwise to stray further from the five-mile boardwalk along the ocean than the parallel Pacific, Atlantic and Arctic avenues, as other parts of the city can be **dangerous** at night and are not that savoury by day. Ventnor and Margate, to the south on Absecon Island, are served by **buses** along Atlantic Avenue. Pale blue Jitneys ($2.50, exact change required; Ⓣ609/344-8642, Ⓦwww.jitneys.net) offer a 24-hour minibus service the length of Pacific Avenue. Along the boardwalk, various **bike rental** stands and rickshaw-like **rolling chairs** (Ⓣ609/347-7148) provide alternative means of transportation. Atlantic City Cab Service (Ⓣ609/822-7900) operates a reliable service.

Accommodation

Though you will not find the same bargains as Las Vegas, the recession has forced **accommodation** rates at the casinos down for most of the year, although they still rise at weekends and in summer. Advance online booking is likely to yield good discounted **package deals** even then, with $200 suites going for around half-price. Alternatively, cheap **motels** line the main highways into town such as US-30 in Absecon, six miles northwest, and hotel prices are cheaper in quiet Ocean City, a family resort around ten miles south.

Bally's Atlantic City Park Place and Boardwalk Ⓣ609/340-2000, Ⓦwww.harrahs.com. One of the big midtown theme casinos, *Bally's* offers a full-service spa, fifteen restaurants and four bars, not to mention multiple gambling opportunities, all under one roof. ❹

EconoLodge Beach & Boardwalk 3001 Pacific Ave Ⓣ609/344-2925, Ⓦwww.econolodge.com. Standard chain motel behind the boardwalk and close to the *Trump Taj Mahal* casino. ❸

The Irish Pub Inn 164 St James Place Ⓣ609/344-9063, Ⓦwww.theirishpub.com. Basic, cheap rooms above one of the town's best bars. Great single rates from $25. Hotel closed Oct–April. ❷

Resorts Atlantic City Casino Hotel 1133 Boardwalk ⓣ1-800/336-6378, ⓦwww.resortsac.com. The most pleasant and most reasonably priced of the huge casino hotels, with pool and spa. ❷

Rodeway Inn 124 S North Carolina Ave ⓣ609/345-0155, ⓦwww.choicehotels.com. Clean, basic, reasonably priced rooms close to the boardwalk. ❸

The Town

Atlantic City's wooden **boardwalk** was originally built as a temporary walkway, raised above the beach so that vacationers could take a seaside stroll without treading sand into the grand hotels. Alongside the brash 99¢ shops and exotically named palm-readers, a few beautiful Victorian buildings that survived the wrecking ball invoke past elegance, despite the fact that many now house fast-food joints. The **Central Pier** offers all the fun of a fair, with rides and old-fashioned games. A few blocks south, another pier has been remodelled into an ocean-liner-shaped shopping centre. The small and faded **Atlantic City Arts Center** (summer daily 10am–4pm, closed Mon off-season; free; ⓣ609/347-5837, ⓦwww.acartcenter.org), on the Garden Pier at the quiet northern end of the boardwalk, has a free collection of seaside memorabilia, postcards, photos and a special exhibit on Miss America, and also hosts travelling art shows. A block off the boardwalk, where Pacific and Rhode Island avenues meet, and at the heart of some of the city's worst deprivation, stands the **Absecon Lighthouse**. Active until 1933, it's now fully restored and offers a terrific view from its 167ft tower (July & Aug daily 10am–5pm; rest of year Thurs–Mon 11am–4pm; $7; ⓣ609/449-1360, ⓦwww.abseconlighthouse.org).

Atlantic City's **beach** is free, family-filled and surprisingly clean considering its proximity to the boardwalk. Beaches at well-to-do **Ventnor**, a Jitney ride away, are quieter, while three miles south of Atlantic City, New Jersey's beautiful people pose on the beaches of **Margate** (both beaches charge a nominal fee), watched over by **Lucy the Elephant** at 9200 Atlantic Ave. A 65ft wood-and-tin Victorian oddity, Lucy was built as a seaside attraction in 1881 and used variously as a tavern and a hotel. Today, her huge belly contains a museum (June to early Sept Mon–Sat 10am–8pm, Sun 10am–5pm; $5; ⓣ609/823-6473, ⓦwww.lucytheelephant.org) filled with Atlantic City memorabilia, as well as photos and artefacts from her own history.

The casinos of Atlantic City

Each of Atlantic City's dozen **casinos**, which also act as luxury hotels, conference centres and concert halls, has a slightly different image, though you might not guess it among the apparent uniformity of vast, richly ornamented halls, slot machines, relentless flashing lights, incessant noise, chandeliers, mirrors and a disorienting absence of clocks or windows. The casinos are divided into four areas: **uptown**, **midtown** and **downtown** occupy the north, central and south sections of the boardwalk respectively, while the **marina** enclave towers over a spit of land in the northwest of the city.

The most outwardly ostentatious, unsurprisingly, is Donald Trump's **Taj Mahal**. Occupying nearly twenty acres and over forty storeys high, dotted with glittering minarets and onion domes, this gigantic but oddly anticlimactic piece of Far Eastern kitsch stands uptown, opposite the arcade-packed Steel Pier. **Bally's** charmingly garish midtown Wild West Casino is much more outlandish and fun, and also offers complete access to the games and memberships of adjacent Roman-themed **Caesar's**, the smaller **Showboat** uptown and **Hilton** downtown, although garish **Tropicana** is the more amusing of the two casinos down at that end. All casinos are **open 24 hours**, including holidays, and have a strict minimum **age requirement**, so be prepared to show ID that proves you're 21 or older. Oddly, the slot machines now only take notes (minimum $5).

Eating

One effect of Atlantic City's rabid commercialization is an abundance of **fast food**. The boardwalk is lined with pizza, burger and sandwich joints, while the diners on Atlantic and Pacific avenues serve soul food and cheap breakfasts. All the large casinos boast several restaurants, ranging in price and menu but all of average quality, as well as all-you-can-eat **buffets** – most cost around $15 for lunch, and around $20 for dinner. If money's running low after bad luck in the casino, there are bargain buffets on the boardwalk for around $5 – but inevitably, you get what you pay for.

Dune 9510 Ventnor Ave, Margate ⓣ609/487-7450. Specializing in tasty and fresh, if a little pricey, seafood. Entrees of quality fish like grouper, black bass and Arctic char run around $25–30.
Hunan Chinese Restaurant 2323 Atlantic Ave ⓣ609/348-5946. Reasonably priced Chinese food two blocks from the boardwalk. Combination plates cost $8–12.
Los Amigos 1926 Atlantic Ave ⓣ609/344-2293. Great for cheap, late-night food, this pleasant but average Mexican restaurant and bar across from the bus station is open until 3am Fri and Sat.
Pappa T's Pizza 445 Boardwalk ⓣ609/348-5030. One of the better cheap boardwalk joints, with pizza and breakfast from $5.
White House Sub Shop 2301 Arctic Ave ⓣ609/345-1564. This bright and super-efficient Atlantic City institution is where the submarine sandwich was born; definitely worth a visit.

Entertainment and nightlife

Atlantic City sells itself as the fun night-time city, but the **nightlife** centres on the casinos and boardwalk amusements. Once you get bored with slot machines there is little else to do. Big-name entertainers perform regularly at the casinos, but you'll be lucky to find tickets much under $100 – the free *Atlantic City Weekly* (ⓦwww.acweekly.com) has listings. For cheaper informal fun, try the friendly, dark-panelled *Irish Pub* (see Accommodation listings, p.158), which serves extremely cheap food and often has live Irish music.

Cape May

CAPE MAY was founded in 1620 by the Dutch Captain Mey, on the small hook at the very southern tip of the Jersey coast, jutting out into the Atlantic and washed by the Delaware Bay on the west. After periods as a whaling and farming community, in 1745 the first advertisement for Cape May's restorative air and fine accommodation appeared in the Philadelphia press, heralding a period of great prosperity through tourism.

The Victorian era was Cape May's finest, when Southern plantation owners flocked to the fashionable boarding houses of this genteel "resort of Presidents". Nearly all its gingerbread architecture dates from a mass rebuilding after a severe fire in 1878. Today, the whole town is a National Historic Landmark, with over six hundred **Victorian buildings**, tree-lined streets, beautifully kept **gardens** and a lucrative B&B industry. The town also boasts good **beaches**.

Arrival, information and getting around

New Jersey Transit runs an express **bus** to Cape May from Philadelphia and the south Jersey coast, as well as services from New York and Atlantic City. Greyhound also stops at the terminal, opposite the corner of Lafayette and Ocean Street. **Ferries** connect the town to Lewes, Delaware ($8–10/person, $30–44/car; schedules on ⓣ1-800/643-3779, ⓦwww.capemaylewesferry.com). Maps, **information** and help with accommodation are available from the **Welcome Center** (daily 9am–4.30pm; ⓣ609/884-9562, ⓦwww.capemaynj.com), attached to the bus terminal.

Though Cape May itself is best enjoyed on foot, to venture out a bit further rent a **bike** from the Village Bike Shop near the bus terminal, at 609 Lafayette ($5/hr, $15/day; ⓣ609/884-8500). The Cape May Whale Watcher, at Second Avenue and Wilson Drive (ⓣ609/884-5445 or 1-800/786-5445, ⓦwww.capemaywhalewatcher.com), offers three trips (daily March–Dec) around Cape May Point: two **dolphin-watches** (2hr; 10am & 6.30pm; $28) and a **whale & dolphins voyage** (3hr; 1pm; $38).

Accommodation

Many of Cape May's pastel Victorian homes have been converted to pricey **B&Bs** or **guesthouses** and the resort is so popular that choice plummets on summer weekends. During July and August even old motor inns can command over $100 a night; June and September rates are often around half that. Standard **hotels** front the ocean on Beach Drive and you can **camp** at the very expensive *Seashore Campsites*, 720 Seashore Rd (sites from $53 in summer, $25 off-season; ⓣ609/884-4010 or 1-800/313-2267, ⓦwww.seashorecampsites.com).

Cape Harbor Motor inn 715 Pittsburgh Ave ⓣ609/884-0018, ⓦwww.capeharbormotorinn.com. Comfortable motel, situated in a residential street seven blocks from the beach; cheaper than most places but rates soar in summer. ❸–❼

The Chalfonte 301 Howards St ⓣ609/884-8409, ⓦwww.chalfonte.com. The oldest continually operating B&B, set in an 1876 mansion, with wraparound verandas, three blocks from the beach. ❹–❽

Inn of Cape May 7 Ocean St ⓣ609/884-5555 or 1-800/582-5933, ⓦwww.innofcapemay.com. This once-fashionable Victorian shorefront hotel now has a small adjoining modern motel wing. The cheapest rooms are those with shared baths in the main building. Open daily April–Oct, weekends only late Oct to Dec. ❸–❽

Queen Victoria 102 Ocean St ⓣ609/884-8702, ⓦwww.queenvictoria.com. Twenty-one rooms in four buildings, including a cottage and a carriage house. Rates include bicycle loans, beach chairs, breakfast (in bed, if desired) and afternoon tea. ❺–❾

Summer Cottage Inn 613 Columbia Ave ⓣ609/884-4948 or 1-866/392-5600, ⓦwww.summercottageinn.com. 1867 inn with verandas and a cupola. Wide range of rates including good-value deals. ❹–❽

The town and the beaches

Cape May's brightly-coloured houses were built by nouveau riche Victorians with a healthy disrespect for subtlety. Cluttered with cupolas, gazebos, balconies and "widow's walks", the houses follow no architectural rules except excess. They were known as "patternbook homes", with designs and features chosen from catalogues and thrown together in accordance with the owner's taste. The Victorian obsession with the Near East is everywhere: Moorish arches and onion domes sit comfortably next to gingerbread- and Queen Anne-style turrets. The **Emlen Physick Estate**, 1048 Washington St (tour hours vary; $10; ⓣ609/884-5404, ⓦwww.capemaymac.org), was built by the popular Philadelphia architect Frank Furness. It has been restored to its 1879 glory, with whimsical "upside-down" chimneys, a mock-Tudor half-timbered facade and much original furniture. West of town, where the Delaware Bay and the ocean meet, the 1859 **Cape May Lighthouse**, visible from 25 miles out at sea, offers great views from a gallery below the lantern (199 steps up) and a small exhibit on its history at ground level (daily April–Nov, winter weekends, hours vary; $7; ⓣ609/884-8656, ⓦwww.capemaymac.org). Three miles north of town on US-9, **Historic Cold Spring Village**, 720 Rte-9 (late May to mid-June & Sept Sat & Sun 10am–4.30pm; June–Aug Tues–Sun 10am–4.30pm; $8; ⓣ609/898-2300, ⓦwww.hcsv.org), depicts a typical nineteenth-century south Jersey farming community. Restored buildings from the region house a jail, school, inn and shops, plus there are various craft shows and special events.

Cape May's excellent **beaches** literally sparkle with quartz pebbles. Beach tags ($5/day, $13/week, $25 for a seasonal pass purchased before Memorial Day) must

Wildwood

The traditionally blue-collar resort of nearby **Wildwood**, on a barrier island east of Rte-47, offers a counterpoint to the pretty but often pretentious olde-worlde charm of Cape May. Its 1950s architecture, left lovingly intact, includes dozens of gaudy and fun-looking hotels with names like *Pink Orchid*, *Waikiki* and *The Shalimar*, all still featuring plastic palm trees, kidney-shaped swimming pools and plenty of aqua, orange and pink paint. To best appreciate the town's brash charm, take a stroll along the boardwalk and stop along the wide, throbbing, free beaches. Additionally, check out the local amusement rides and water parks, such as Morey's Piers, Raging Waters and Splash Zone.

be worn from 10am until 6pm in the summer and are available at the beach, from official vendors or from **City Hall**, 643 Washington St (Ⓣ609/884-9525, Ⓦwww.capemaycity.com).

Eating

Cape May lacks the usual boardwalk snack bars, but it has plenty of cheap **lunch** places. **Dinner**, however, is far more expensive. Cape May's liquor laws are stringent, which means that many restaurants are BYO – call to check.

Depot Market Café 409 Elmira St Ⓣ609/884-8030. Opposite the bus terminal, offering filling sandwiches, salads and hoagies; dinners around $10.

Gecko's Carpenter's Lane Ⓣ609/898-7750. A good lunch stop with a tasty Southwestern menu and great desserts. Patio seating available.

Le Verandah 107 Grant St Ⓣ609/884-5868. The French chef here makes sure that his creations such as gravlax in a mustard dill sauce and seafood bouillabaisse ($27) are the real thing.

The Lemon Tree 101 Liberty Way Ⓣ609/884-2704. The cheesesteaks at this cheap, cheerful deli are Philly-quality; a nice antidote to the coffeeshops along the street.

Mad Batter 19 Jackson St Ⓣ609/884-5970. Splash out on meat and fresh fish dishes, served by candlelight in the garden. Lunch is $10–15, dinner $20–30. Live jazz and blues some nights.

Nightlife and entertainment

Cape May is a friendly and laidback place to be after dark; the day-trippers have gone home and the **bars** and **music venues** are enjoyed by locals and tourists alike. If you're after something a bit more lively, head a few miles north to the raucous nightclubs of **Wildwood**, such as *H2O*.

Cabanas 429 Beach Ave Ⓣ609/884-4800. Two-level bar that often hosts live music downstairs; upstairs is a low-key cocktail lounge.

Carney's 401 Beach Ave Ⓣ609/884-4424. Spacious and relaxed Irish bar, with raucous live music.

Ugly Mug Washington St Mall and Decatur St Ⓣ609/884-3459. This friendly bar is a local favourite and serves chowder, sandwiches and seafood.

3

New England

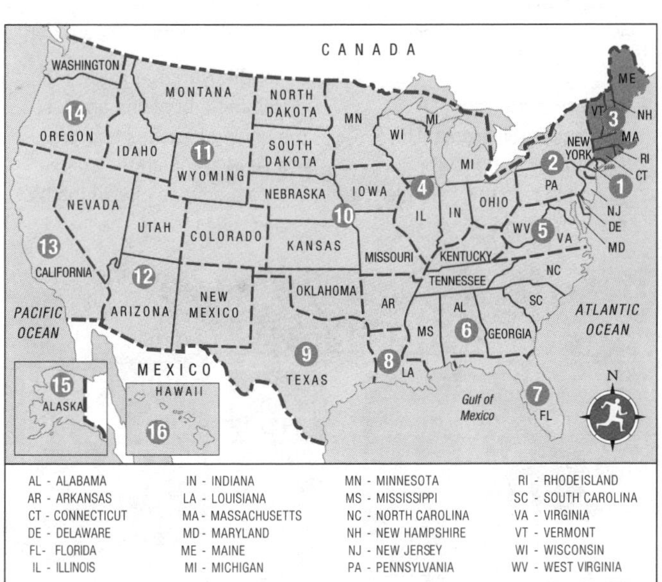
CANADA
WASHINGTON
MONTANA
NORTH DAKOTA
MN
WI
MI
ME
VT
3
NH
MA
NEW YORK
RI
CT
14
OREGON
IDAHO
11
WYOMING
SOUTH DAKOTA
MI
2
PA
1
NEBRASKA
IOWA
4
NEVADA
10
IL
IN
OHIO
NJ
DE
UTAH
COLORADO
KANSAS
WV
5
VA
MD
13
CALIFORNIA
MISSOURI
KENTUCKY
NC
12
TENNESSEE
OKLAHOMA
NEW MEXICO
AR
AL
SC
PACIFIC OCEAN
ARIZONA
MS
6
GEORGIA
ATLANTIC OCEAN
9
8
LA
MEXICO
TEXAS
15
ALASKA
HAWAII
16
Gulf of Mexico
7
FL
N
AL - ALABAMA
AR - ARKANSAS
CT - CONNECTICUT
DE - DELAWARE
FL- FLORIDA
IL - ILLINOIS
IN - INDIANA
LA - LOUISIANA
MA - MASSACHUSETTS
MD - MARYLAND
ME - MAINE
MI - MICHIGAN
MN - MINNESOTA
MS - MISSISSIPPI
NC - NORTH CAROLINA
NH - NEW HAMPSHIRE
NJ - NEW JERSEY
PA - PENNSYLVANIA
RI - RHODE ISLAND
SC - SOUTH CAROLINA
VA - VIRGINIA
VT - VERMONT
WI - WISCONSIN
WV - WEST VIRGINIA

CHAPTER 3 Highlights

* **Boston, MA** Revolutionary history comes to life around every charming corner, in one of America's most chronicled, walkable cities. See p.168

* **Provincetown, MA** Wild beaches, lovely flower-filled streets, and an alternative vibe on the outer reaches of Cape Cod. See p.190

* **Historic "summer cottages", Newport, RI** Conspicuous consumption gone crazy in this yachtie resort. See p.206

* **White Mountains, NH** Ski, hike or just soak up the scenery on Mount Washington or Franconia Notch. See p.218

* **Montpelier, VT** Relaxed, friendly, and relatively tourist-free, pretty Montpelier is bounded by rivers and a forest of tall trees. See p.225

* **Acadia National Park, ME** Remote mountains and lakes, stunning beaches and the chance to catch the sunrise before anyone else in the US. See p.241

▲ Lobster shack, Cape Cod

3

New England

To visitors and residents alike, the six **NEW ENGLAND** states of Massachusetts, Rhode Island, Connecticut, New Hampshire, Vermont and Maine conjure up nostalgic images of landscapes studded with ageing clapboard houses, Revolutionary War sites and white-spired churches set upon immaculate rolling greens. And while nostalgia does play a role in New England's marketing, this is still undeniably one of the most historic parts of the United States. Boston especially is celebrated as the birthplace of American independence – so many of the seminal events of the Revolutionary War took place here – and the region was home to, and inspiration for, some of the pre-eminent figures of American literature, from Mark Twain and Henry Thoreau, to Emily Dickinson and Jack Kerouac.

The **Ivy League** colleges – Harvard, Yale, Brown, Dartmouth et al – are the oldest in the country and remain hugely influential, continually channelling new life into towns like Cambridge and Amherst, attracting vast numbers of bright students from all over the world and setting a decidedly liberal tone throughout the region; though New Hampshire is something of a swing state, New England has voted solidly for Democratic presidential candidates since the 1980s.

The best time to visit New England is in late September and October, when visitors flock to see the magnificent **autumn foliage**. Particularly vivid in Vermont, autumn in New England is not an event to be underrated, and though hotel rates go up during this time, the region's magnificent display of crimsons and hues, when it seems someone has flipped the light switch on underneath entire swaths of countryside, is an event that's not to be missed.

To the east, the peninsula of **Cape Cod** flexes off of **Massachusetts** like a well-tanned arm. Here you will find innumerable sunbathing opportunities amid 300 miles of shoreline, fragrant sea roses and tumbling sand dunes. In the western part of the state, the tranquil **Berkshires** offer the best in summer festivals as well as fascinating and funky art museums, good for a diversion. The sights of **Connecticut** and **Rhode Island** tend to be urban, but away from I-95 you'll find plenty of tranquil pockets, particularly in the way of Newport and Block Island, fifty miles south of Providence. **Boston** is a vibrant and stimulating city from which to set off north, where the population begins to thin out (and the **seafood** gets better as you go). The rest of **Massachusetts** is rich in historical and literary sights, while further inland, the lakes and mountains of **New Hampshire** and **Maine** offer rural wildernesses to rival any in the nation. Maine is also known for its coastline, appealingly corrugated and dotted with lighthouses and wild blueberry bushes. The beloved country roads of **Vermont** offer pleasant wandering through rural towns and serene forests; while in the neighbourhood, be sure to pick up some handcrafted maple syrup for your pancakes back home.

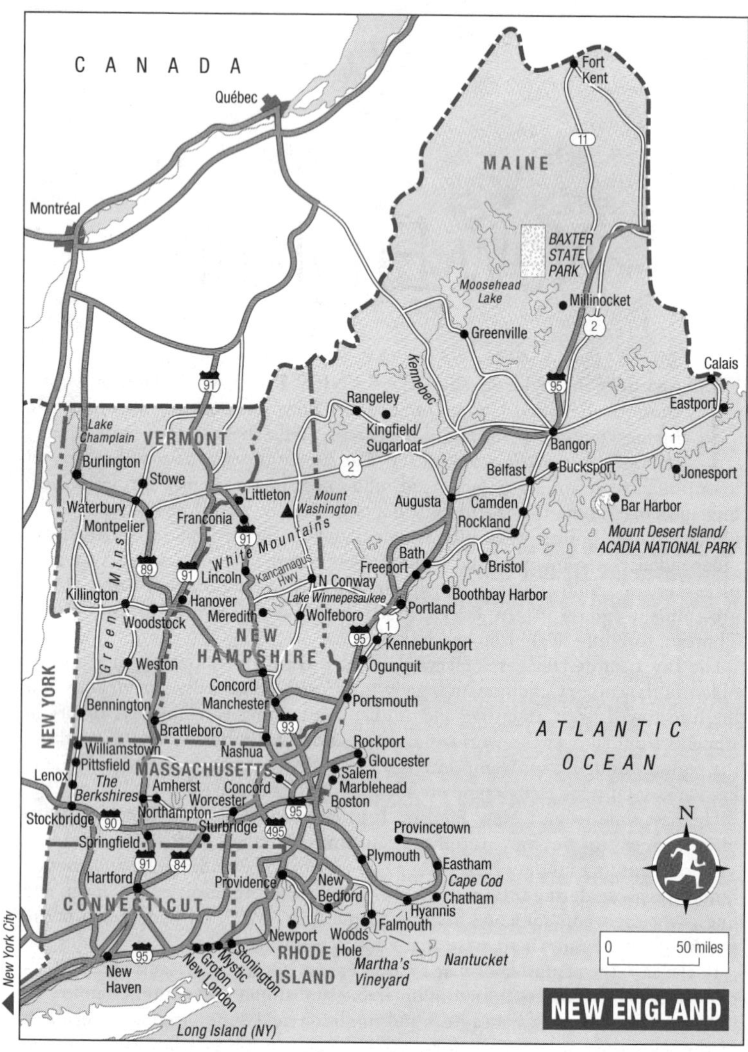

Getting around New England

Planes, trains and buses all radiate out from Boston, Massachusetts, the heart of New England. If you really want to explore the area in-depth, you should plan to have your own set of wheels, as public transport thins considerably outside of the major towns. Boston, however, is the one exception to this – having a car in that city, with its limited parking, confusing roads and crazy drivers, is almost an adversity.

Frequent Amtrak **trains** connect Boston with Providence, Hartford, New York, Philadelphia and Washington DC, while the *Vermonter* gives access to Vermont and Connecticut, and (via Springfield) Chicago and Toronto. Also in

Connecticut, Metro North (ⓣ212/532-4900) **trains** carry passengers between New Haven and New York City. The *Downeaster* follows a scenic route that links Boston to Portland, Maine, stopping in New Hampshire at the sleepy towns of Exeter, Durham and Dover.

Buses from Boston are plentiful, including services to Cape Cod. In Rhode Island, it is possible to get around on **public transport**, with local RIPTA **buses** and **ferries** connecting Providence and Newport (ⓣ401/781-9400, ⓦwww.ripta.com). Connecticut's Greyhound and Peter Pan **buses** run to most of the main towns and while New Hampshire has regular bus service along the Nashua–Concord corridor or the coast, it should be noted that only a few services on Concord Coach Lines continue north to the Lakes Region and the White Mountains. In Vermont, Greyhound **buses** connect towns such as Burlington, Montpelier and Brattleboro with their national network.

A visit to sprawling Maine really requires a car, but there are three helpful daily Greyhound **buses** from Boston to Portland; Greyhound also accesses Bath, Rockland, Camden and Fort Kent as well as a number of other mid to northern Maine towns. Concord Coach Lines (which makes it all the way down east to Bangor; ⓣ1-800/639-3317, ⓦwww.concordcoachlines.com) has the best access to the **coast**. The CYR bus lines (ⓣ207/827-2335) trek up to the far north (culminating at Fort Kent) via Bangor.

Massachusetts

To the first colonists of the **Massachusetts Bay Company**, their arrival near the site of modern Salem in 1629 marked a crucial moment in history. **Puritans** who had decided to leave England before it was engulfed by civil war saw their purpose, in the words of Governor John Winthrop, as the establishment of a utopian "**City upon a hill**". Their new colony of **MASSACHUSETTS** was to be a beacon to the rest of humanity, an exemplar of sober government along sound spiritual principles. This clarity of thought and forcefulness of purpose can be traced from the foundation of Harvard College in 1636, through the intellectual impetus behind the Revolution and the crusade against slavery, to the nineteenth-century achievements of **writers** such as Melville, Emerson, Hawthorne and Thoreau.

Spending a few days in **Boston** is strongly recommended. While its history is often visible, there's a great deal of modern life and energy besides, thanks in part to the presence of **Cambridge**, the home of Harvard University and MIT (Massachusetts Institute of Technology), just across the river. Several historic towns are within easy reach – **Salem** to the north, **Concord** and **Lexington** just inland, and **Plymouth** to the south. **Provincetown**, a ninety-minute ferry ride across the bay at the tip of Cape Cod, is great fun to visit, and the rest of the Cape offers old towns and lovely beaches. **Western Massachusetts**, home to a handful of college towns such as **Amherst**, is much quieter; its settlements are naturally concentrated where the land is fertile, such as along the Connecticut River Valley and in the **Berkshires** to the west.

Boston

Although the metropolitan area of **BOSTON** has long since expanded to fill the shoreline of **Massachusetts Bay**, and stretches for miles inland as well, the seventeenth-century port at its heart is still discernible. The tangled roads (former cow paths) clustered around **Boston Common** are a reminder of how the nation started out, and the city is enjoyably walkable in scale.

Boston was, until 1755, the biggest city in America; as the one most directly affected by the whims of the British Crown, it was the natural birthplace for the opposition that culminated in the **Revolutionary War**. Numerous evocative sites from that era are preserved along the downtown **Freedom Trail**. As the third busiest port in the British Empire (after London and Bristol), Boston stood on a narrow peninsula. What is now Washington Street provided the only access by land, and when the British set off to Lexington in 1775 they embarked in ships from the Common itself. During the nineteenth century, the Charles River marshlands were filled in to create the posh Back Bay residential area. Central Boston is now slightly set back from the water, and until recently, was divided by the unsightly John Fitzgerald Expressway that carried I-93 across downtown. In 2006 the city successfully routed the traffic underground and disposed of this eyesore – a project more than a decade in the making, known as "the **Big Dig**".

Echoes of the "Brahmins" of a century ago can be seen in the stately brick enclaves and purple windowpanes of the city's posher districts. But this is by no means just a city of WASPs: the Irish who began to arrive in large numbers after the Great Famine had produced their first mayor as early as 1885, and the president of the entire nation within a hundred years. The liberal tradition that spawned the Kennedys remains very much alive, fed in part by the presence in the city of more than one hundred universities and colleges, the most famous of which – **Harvard University** – is actually in the contiguous city of Cambridge, just across the Charles River.

The slump of the Depression seemed to linger in Boston for years – in the 1950s, the population was actually dwindling – but these days the place has a bright, rejuvenated feel. The aesthetic effects of the Big Dig have completely reshaped the city – most notably with the elegant, skyline-boosting Zakim Bridge, the Rose Kennedy Greenway and the beautification of the HarborWalk. With its busy street life, imaginative museums, eminent architecture and palpable history, Boston is one destination in New England there's no excuse for missing.

Arrival and information

Boston is the centre of New England's transportation networks. It provides many visitors arriving by air from Europe with their first taste of America, while efficient rail and bus services from New York, Chicago and further afield make this an obvious starting point.

By air

Logan Airport (Ⓣ617/561-1800 or 1-800/23-LOGAN), busy with both international and domestic services, is a mere three miles from downtown Boston. A **taxi** into town costs around $35; trips to Downtown take about twenty to thirty minutes. Between 4am and 1am, free **shuttle buses** run every few minutes from all airport terminals to the airport **subway** station on the MBTA Blue line (see "City transport and tours", opposite), from where it's an easy fifteen-minute ride to the city centre.

By train

Amtrak (Ⓣ1-800/USA-RAIL, Ⓦwww.amtrak.com) trains along the Northeast Corridor from Providence, Washington DC and New York, and from Chicago and Canada via Springfield, arrive a short walk from downtown Boston near the waterfront at **South Station**, on Summer Street and Atlantic Avenue. The station houses information booths, newsstands, restaurants and a fantastic old clock, though no currency exchange. The Red subway line inside the station can whisk you to the centre of town or out to Cambridge. Some Amtrak services also make an extra stop at **Back Bay Station**, 145 Dartmouth St, on the Orange subway line near Copley Square. **North Station** is used by northerly MBTA commuter trains as well as the amiable *Downeaster*, which connects Boston to Portland, Maine and a number of Maine and New Hampshire stops along the way.

By bus

Several **bus** companies provide direct links between the rest of New England and Boston. Greyhound (Ⓣ1-800/231-2222, Ⓦwww.greyhound.com) covers western Massachusetts, New Hampshire's White Mountains, Vermont and Montréal in addition to a nationwide service; while Concord Coach (Ⓣ1-800/639-3317, Ⓦwww.concordcoachlines.com) runs to New Hampshire and up the Maine coast; it also has a shuttle service to Logan Airport. Heading south, Peter Pan Bus Lines (Ⓣ1-800/343-9999, Ⓦwww.peterpanbus.com) connects Providence and Newport, Cape Cod and New York City, as well as western Massachusetts. The Bolt Bus (Ⓣ1-877/BOLTBUS, Ⓦwww.boltbus.com) takes you from South Station to midtown Manhattan for around $20 and has the added benefit of wireless internet (reserve your seat in advance as this is a very hot ticket). The popular Fung Wah bus offers an hourly service to Canal Street in New York City (Ⓣ617/345-8000, Ⓦwww.fungwahbus.com) for a mere $15 dollars each way. Plymouth and Brockton Bus Co. (Ⓣ508/746-0378, Ⓦwww.p-b.com), serves Cape Cod, provides access to Martha's Vineyard and Nantucket, and has buses that leave from Logan Airport as well as South Station (see "By train", above).

Information

The most convenient place to get advice and maps is the **Visitor Information Center** (daily 9am–5pm; Ⓣ617/426-3115 or 1-888/SEE-BOSTON, Ⓦwww.bostonusa.com) near the Park Street subway stop on the Tremont Street side of Boston Common. Across the street from the Old State House, at 15 State St, is an excellent information centre maintained by rangers from the National Park Service (daily 9am–5pm; Ⓣ617/242-5642), as well as bathrooms and a bookstore. There are also information kiosks in **Quincy Market** and at the **Prudential Center** (in Back Bay).

City transport and tours

Much of the pleasure of visiting Boston comes from being in a city that was built long before cars were invented. Walking around town can be a joy; conversely, driving is an absolute nightmare. There's no point renting a car in Boston until the day you leave, since the city's public transport is good and the local drivers notoriously crazy.

Subways and trolleys

The Massachusetts Bay Transportation Authority (MBTA, known as the "**T**") is responsible for Boston's **subway** system and **trolleys**. The subway, which opened in 1897, is the oldest in the US; its first station, **Park Street**, remains its centre (any train marked "inbound" is headed here). Four lines – Red, Green, Blue and Orange – operate daily from 5am until 12.30am, although certain routes begin to shut down earlier. The four lines are supplemented by a bus rapid transit (BRT) route, the **Silver Line**, which runs aboveground along Washington Street, cutting through the heart of the South End, with additional access to the airport and the Seaport District. While maps are posted at each station, it's a good idea to pick up the widely available transport maps for reference. Trains are fast and safe; only some parts of the Orange line might be said to be unsafe after dark.

Boston has recently installed a new and somewhat confusing system for subway fares. Within the city, the standard fare is $2, payable by the purchase of a "CharlieTicket", which can be purchased at any of the ATM-like machines in the station. If you pick up a "CharlieCard" – with more of a credit card thickness and a longer lifespan – from a station attendant – your fare begins at only $1.70 per ride. Your safest (and simplest) bet is the **LinkPass** which seamlessly covers all subway and local bus journeys (as well as the ferry to Charlestown) at a cost of $9 a day or $15 a week. For MBTA **information** call ⓣ617/222-3200, or visit ⓦwww.mbta.com.

Buses

The normal fare on MBTA's **local buses** is $1.50 (exact change or CharlieTicket, $1.25 with CharlieCard), but longer distances, such as out to Salem or Marblehead, cost $3.50 one-way. MBTA also runs **commuter rail lines**, extending as far as Salem, Concord and Providence, Rhode Island, some with wi-fi on board; destinations north leave from **North Station** (ⓣ617/222-3200) on Causeway Street, under the TD Banknorth Garden; destinations south leave from (you guessed it) **South Station** (ⓣ617/222-3200) on Summer Street and Atlantic Avenue, by the waterfront.

Cycling

In and around Boston are some eighty miles of **bike trails**. Bicycles can be rented from Urban AdvenTours, in the North End at 103 Atlantic Ave (ⓣ617/670-0637, ⓦwww.urbanadventours.com), Community Bicycle Supply, 496 Tremont St (ⓣ617/542-8623, ⓦwww.communitybicycle.com), and from Back Bay Bicycles at 366 Commonwealth Ave (ⓣ617/247-2336, ⓦwww.backbaybicycles.com). Rentals are around $30 per day.

City tours

It's easy enough to get to know Boston on foot by following the **Freedom Trail** (see p.174). The National Park Service, 15 State St (ⓣ617/242-5642, ⓦwww.nps.gov/bost), conducts free, ranger-led tours centring on a number of Freedom Trail hotspots as well as the Black Heritage Trail (see box, p.176). Other standout walking tours include those offered by North End Market Tours ($50–65; ⓣ617/523-6032, advance tickets required, ⓦwww.northendmarkettours.com), which conduct tasting tours of the North End and Chinatown neighbourhoods.

If you prefer to see the city while comfortably seated, nothing is as popular (or as novel) as a Boston Duck Tour (adults $31, kids 3–11 $21; ⓣ617/267-DUCK, ⓦwww.bostonducktours.com) or its newbie rival Super Duck Tours (adults $35, kids 3–11 $23; ⓣ1-877/34DUCKS, ⓦwww.superducktours.com), entertaining romps by land and by sea aboard a real WWII amphibious landing vehicle or Hydra-Terra. The former departs from the Prudential Center as well as the Museum of Science, while the latter leaves from Gate 1 of the Charlestown Navy Yard, March to November.

More conventional are the **bus excursions** to Lexington, Concord, Salem and Plymouth with Brush Hill Tours/Gray Line (ⓣ1-800/343-1328, ⓦwww.beantowntrolley.com or www.grayline.com). Urban Adventours (ⓣ617/670-0637, ⓦwww.urbanadventours.com) can take you around for a couple of fun and easy-going hours by bike.

Accommodation

Good-quality, inexpensive **accommodation** is hard to find in Boston – any hotel room within walking distance of downtown for under $200 has to be considered a bargain. Room rates range wildly depending on the season and the day – if the rates below seem high, it's worth calling to check the current price. On the plus side, the city has a number of good hostels, and there are some well-priced B&Bs in the area as well.

Hotels, motels and B&Bs

Back Bay Hotel 350 Stuart St ⓣ617/266-7200, ⓦwww.doylecollection.com; Arlington **T**. A modern hotel with an historic (it's housed in the former Boston police headquarters), Irish bent, the Back Bay features stylish rooms equipped with wi-fi, Kiehl's soap, heated towel racks, a fitness centre and the swanky *Stanhope Grille*. ⑨

Beacon Hill Hotel 25 Charles St ⓣ617/723-7575 or 1-888/959-BHHB, ⓦwww.beaconhillhotel.com; Charles **T**. Pampered luxury in the heart of Beacon Hill; the thirteen sleek chambers come with flat-screen televisions, high-speed internet access and wi-fi, and great views onto Charles St. The hotel is also home to a fantastic bistro and fireplace bar. ⑧–⑨

Charlesmark Hotel 655 Boylston St ⓣ617/247-1212, ⓦwww.charlesmarkhotel.com; Copley **T**. Forty smallish, contemporary rooms in Back Bay with cosy beechwood furnishings, good rates, a lively bar and modern accoutrements like wi-fi and a hooked-up speaker system that lets you sing in the shower. ⑤–⑧

Encore B&B 116 West Newton St ⓣ617/247-3425, ⓦwww.encorebandb.com; Back Bay **T**. On a pleasant South End side street, this well-loved B&B has contemporary decor, wi-fi and a sitting area or balcony in each of their three rooms. ⑥–⑧

Green Turtle Floating B&B Shipyard Quarters Marina, 13th St, Charlestown ⓣ617/337-0202, ⓦwww.greenturtlebb.com; North Station **T**. A special place: two well-appointed rooms situated on a peaceful marina in scenic Charlestown. Wake up to fresh pastries, your own private harbourfront patio and the sound of waves lapping at your door. ⑧

Harborside Inn 185 State St ⓣ617/723-7500, ⓦwww.harborsideinnboston.com; Aquarium **T**. Cosy hotel featuring exposed brick, hardwood floors and cherry furniture in a renovated 1890s mercantile warehouse; across from Quincy Market and the Custom House. ⑤–⑧

Hotel 140 140 Clarendon St ⓣ617/585-5600, ⓦwww.hotel140.com; Back Bay **T**. Appealing, affordable accommodation in the heart of Back Bay. A self-proclaimed "boutique hotel", the amenities won't blow your mind, but the hotel does have a sense of style, and it's tough to beat the price for its location. ⑦

Hotel Commonwealth 500 Commonwealth Ave ⓣ617/933-5000, ⓦwww.hotelcommonwealth.com; Kenmore **T**. This spacious Kenmore Square crowdpleaser has something for everyone: stylish decor, views of Fenway Park, imported Italian linens and fancy bathrobes, flat-screen TVs with digital cable, wi-fi and the fabulous *Eastern Standard* bar and *Foundation Lounge*. ⑧–⑨

Inn @ St. Botolph 99 St Botolph St ⓣ617/236-8099, ⓦwww.innatstbotolph.com; Back Bay **T**. On a quiet side street on the western cusp of the South End, this stylish hideaway features sixteen oversized suites with kitchenettes, bold houndstooth patterns and black and brown striped furniture, wi-fi, an on-site laundry room and gym and continental breakfast. ⑦

Irving House 24 Irving St, Cambridge ⓣ617/547-4600, ⓦwww.cambridgeinns.com; Harvard **T**. No-frills, endearing, friendly option near Harvard Square with (coin-operated) laundry facilities and tasty breakfast included; both shared and private baths. ⑤–⑦

John Jeffries House 14 David G. Mugar Way ⓣ617/367-1866, ⓦwww.johnjeffrieshouse.com; Charles **T**. A little gem with some of the best prices in town, and clean and tasteful rooms to match. This mid-scale hotel at the foot of Beacon Hill features Victorian-style decor, cable TV, wi-fi and kitchenettes in most rooms; singles start at $115 in summer. ⑤–⑦

La Cappella Suites 290 North St ⓣ617/523-9020, ⓦwww.lacappellasuites.com; Haymarket **T**. Accommodation has opened up in the North End with this lovely newbie – three cosy, modern

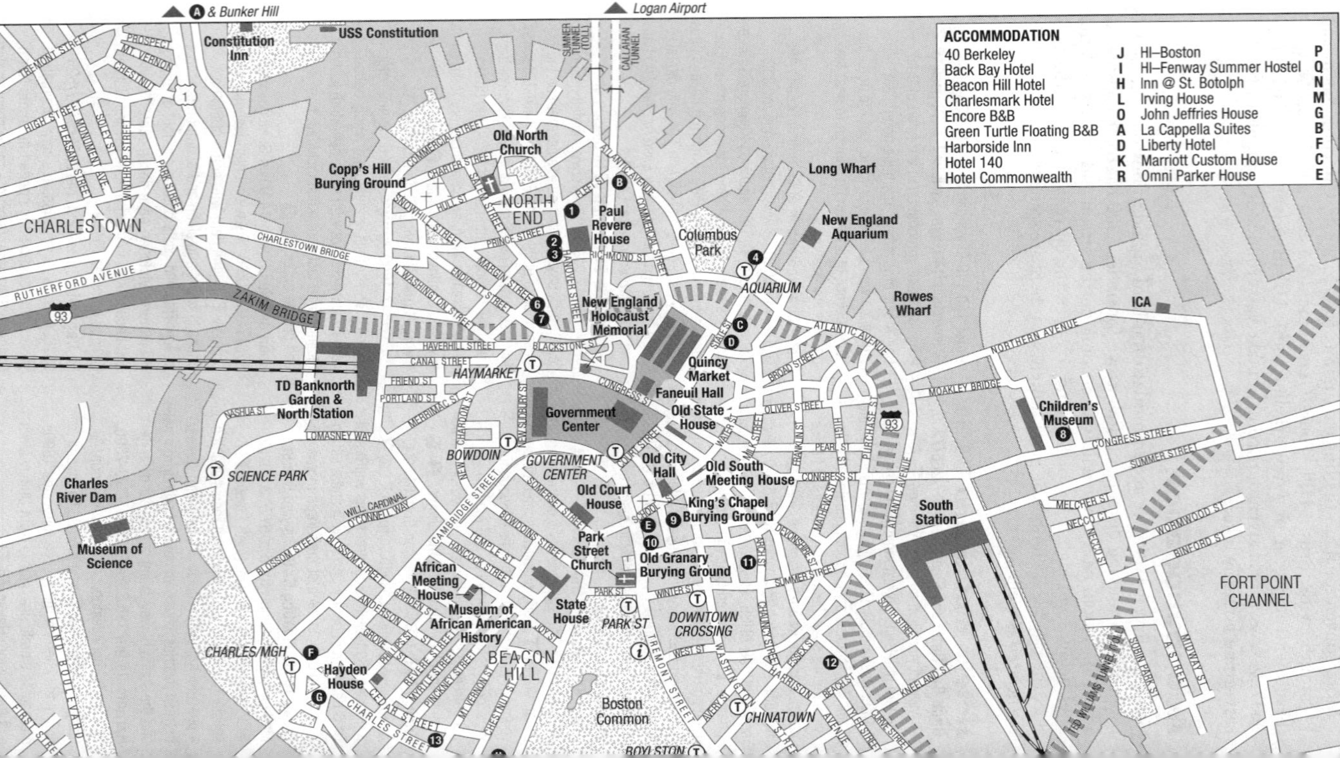

& Bunker Hill
Logan Airport
Bankorth Garden
ACCOMMODATION
40 Berkeley J
Back Bay Hotel I
Beacon Hill Hotel H
Charlesmark Hotel L
Encore B&B O
Green Turtle Floating B&B A
Harborside Inn D
Hotel 140 K
Hotel Commonwealth R
HI–Boston P
HI–Fenway Summer Hostel Q
Inn @ St. Botolph N
Irving House M
John Jeffries House G
La Cappella Suites B
Liberty Hotel F
Marriott Custom House C
Omni Parker House E
Constitution Inn
USS Constitution
CHARLESTOWN
Copp's Hill Burying Ground
Old North Church
NORTH END
Paul Revere House
Columbus Park
Long Wharf
New England Aquarium
AQUARIUM
Rowes Wharf
ICA
ZAKIM BRIDGE
New England Holocaust Memorial
Quincy Market
Faneuil Hall
HAYMARKET
TD Banknorth Garden & North Station
Government Center
Old State House
Children's Museum
BOWDOIN
GOVERNMENT CENTER
Old City Hall
Old South Meeting House
SCIENCE PARK
Charles River Dam
Old Court House
King's Chapel Burying Ground
South Station
Museum of Science
Park Street Church
Old Granary Burying Ground
African Meeting House
Museum of African American History
State House
PARK ST
DOWNTOWN CROSSING
FORT POINT CHANNEL
CHARLES/MGH
BEACON HILL
Hayden House
Boston Common
CHINATOWN
BOYLSTON

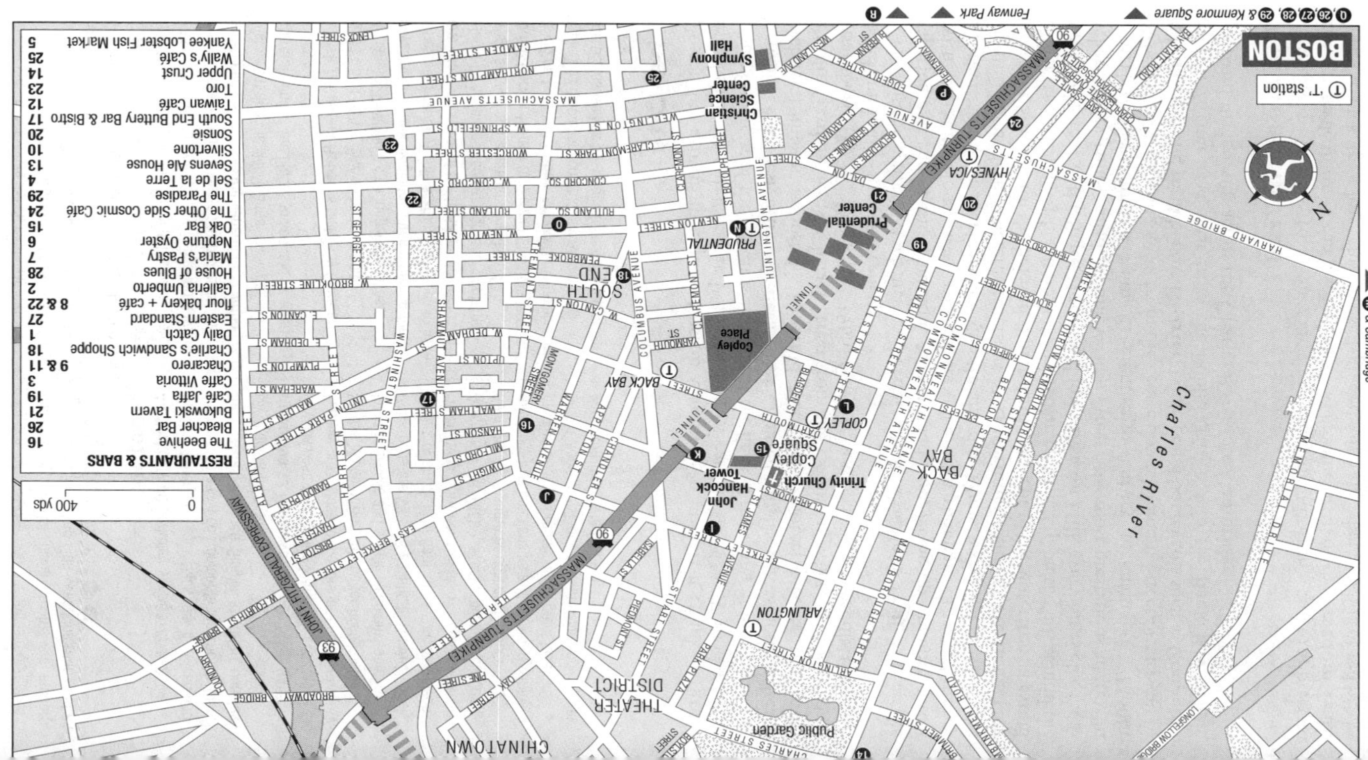
BOSTON
T 'T' station
0, 26, 27, 28, 29 & Kenmore Square
Fenway Park
R
M & Cambridge
0 400 yds
RESTAURANTS & BARS
The Beehive 16
Bleacher Bar 26
Bukowski Tavern 21
Café Jaffa 19
Caffe Vittoria 3
Chacarero 9 & 11
Charlie's Sandwich Shoppe 18
Daily Catch 1
Eastern Standard 27
flour bakery + café 8 & 22
Galleria Umberto 2
House of Blues 28
Maria's Pastry 7
Neptune Oyster 6
Oak Bar 15
The Other Side Cosmic Café 24
The Paradise 29
Sel de la Terre 4
Sevens Ale House 13
Silvertone 10
Sonsie 20
South End Buttery Bar & Bistro 17
Taiwan Café 12
Toro 23
Upper Crust 14
Wally's Café 25
Yankee Lobster Fish Market 5
CHINATOWN
THEATER DISTRICT
BACK BAY
SOUTH END
Public Garden
ARLINGTON
Trinity Church
Copley Square
John Hancock Tower
COPLEY
Copley Place
PRUDENTIAL
Prudential Center
HYNES/ICA
Christian Science Center
Symphony Hall
Charles River
JOHN F. FITZGERALD EXPRESSWAY
(MASSACHUSETTS TURNPIKE)
TUNNEL
HARVARD BRIDGE
JAMES J. STORROW MEMORIAL DRIVE
MEMORIAL DRIVE
LONGFELLOW BRIDGE
COMMONWEALTH AVENUE
BOYLSTON STREET
HUNTINGTON AVENUE
COLUMBUS AVENUE
TREMONT STREET
WASHINGTON STREET
SHAWMUT AVENUE
HARRISON STREET
ALBANY STREET
MASSACHUSETTS AVENUE

rooms with great views, wi-fi, cable TV and a nice public seating area. Two of the rooms have private balconies. Be prepared for a five-floor walk up. ❺–❽

Liberty Hotel 215 Charles St ⓣ617/224-4000, ⓦwww.libertyhotel.com; Charles **T**. The *Liberty Hotel* has taken over the labyrinthine digs of an 1851 prison in Beacon Hill and fashioned it with contemporary furnishings and lush details. This swish pad also houses the venerable *Scampo* restaurant and the *Alibi* lounge; the latter is currently one of the places to see and be seen In Boston. ❾

Marriott Custom House 3 McKinley Square ⓣ617/310-6300, ⓦwww.marriott.com; Aquarium **T**. While it's no longer the tallest skyscraper in New England (a title it held in the nineteenth century), this *Marriott* continues to have jaw-dropping views of the harbour, historic, elegantly appointed rooms, high-speed internet, great service and a fantastic location. ❾

Omni Parker House 60 School St ⓣ617/227-8600 or 1-800/843-6664, ⓦwww.omnihotels.com; Park **T**. The oldest continuously running hotel in the US (as well as the originators of Boston cream pie), the *Omni Parker House* features a gorgeous gilded lobby, smallish, historic rooms with modern renovations (including high-speed internet), and an unbeatably central location. ❽–❾

Hostels

40 Berkeley 40 Berkeley St ⓣ617/375-2524, ⓦwww.40berkeley.com; Back Bay **T**. Clean and simple rooms in a convenient South End location; full breakfast included. Singles are ($58), doubles ($70) and triples ($105).

HI-Boston 12 Hemenway St ⓣ617/536-9455, ⓦwww.bostonhostel.org; Hynes **T**. Located in the Fenway area, close to the funkier end of Newbury St, this is one of Boston's better hostel options. Internet access and a safe, clean environment. Dorm beds are $32–48 a night. In summer, book ahead, or check in at 8am, to be sure of a place.

HI-Fenway Summer Hostel 575 Commonwealth Ave ⓣ617/267-8599, ⓦwww.bostonhostel.org; Kenmore **T**. A summer-only hostel (June 1 to mid-Aug) that functions as a BU dorm in winter months. Spacious rooms and a great location within walking distance of nightclubs and Fenway Park. Non-members $39–48.

The City

Boston has grown up around **Boston Common**, a utilitarian chunk of green established for public use and "the feeding of cattell" in 1634. A good starting point for a tour of the city, it is also one of the links in the string of nine parks (six of which were designed by Frederick Law Olmsted, America's foremost landscape architect) known as Boston's **Emerald Necklace**. Another piece is the lovely **Public Garden**, across Charles Street from the Common, where Boston's iconic swan boats ($2.75; ⓣ617/522-1966, ⓦwww.swanboats.com), paddle the main pond amid tulip-strewn greenery.

The visitor centre, which marks the start of the **Freedom Trail**, is near the tapering east end of the Common. As you stand here, facing up Tremont Street with the State House away to your left, the main shopping district, **Quincy Market**, and the **waterfront** are slightly ahead (a 12min walk) and down to the right. The modern concrete structures of **Government Center** are straight up Tremont Street, with the beloved **North End** (adjacent to the waterfront) beyond – first Irish, then Jewish and now a very Italian enclave. Up on the hill behind the visitor centre rises the **State House** and lofty **Beacon Hill**, every bit as elegant as when Henry James called Mount Vernon Street "the most prestigious address in America" (far removed from its eighteenth-century nickname of "Mount Whoredom"). Heading away from the centre down Tremont Street brings you to **Chinatown** and the **Theater District**, while grand boulevards such as Commonwealth Avenue lead west from the Public Garden into the **Back Bay**, where Harvard Bridge runs across the Charles River into **Cambridge**.

The Freedom Trail

Probably the best way to orient yourself in downtown Boston – and to appreciate the city's role in American history – is to walk some or all of the **Freedom Trail**. You can pick up or leave this easy self-guided route anywhere – a line of red bricks (or red paint) marking the trail is embedded in the pavement – but technically it begins on Boston Common at the **Visitor Information Center**.

From here, head for the golden dome of the **Massachusetts State House** (free tours Mon–Fri 10am–3.30pm); a Charles Bulfinch design completed in 1798. It remains the seat of Massachusetts' government; its most famous fixture, a carved fish dubbed the "Sacred Cod", symbolizes the wealth Boston accrued from maritime trade. Politicos take this symbol so seriously that when Harvard pranksters stole it in the 1930s the House of Representatives didn't reconvene until it was recovered.

Though **Park Street Church**, on the corner of Park and Tremont Street, (July & Aug Tues–Sat 8.30am–3.30pm; rest of year by appointment; free) is by no means "the most interesting mass of bricks and mortar in America", as Henry James once claimed, its ornate white steeple is undeniably impressive. It was here, on July 4, 1829, that orator William Lloyd Garrison delivered his first public address calling for the nationwide abolition of slavery. Just around the corner, the atmospheric **Old Granary Burying Ground** (daily 9am–5pm; free) includes the Revolutionary remains of Paul Revere, Samuel Adams and John Hancock, as well as those of the so-called Mother Goose, née Elizabeth Vergoose (or Vertigoose), said to have collected nursery rhymes for her grandchildren. A block or so north on Tremont is the ethereal **King's Chapel Burying Ground** (summer Mon–Sat 10am–4pm; winter Sat till 4pm; free), final resting place for seventeenth-century luminaries such as Mary Chilton, woman of the *Mayflower*, and Boston's first governor, John Winthrop. Nearby on School Street, a statue of Benjamin Franklin marks the site of **Boston Latin School**, America's first public school, attended by Franklin (who later dropped out) and Samuel Adams. Malcolm X and Ho Chi Minh are both former employees of the **Omni Parker House** hotel (not officially on the Trail, see opposite), the longest continuously operating luxury hotel in the nation and home of the first-ever Boston cream pie.

Next come two of the Trail's more striking and significant buildings. The **Old South Meeting House** (daily: April–Oct 9.30am–5pm; Nov–March 10am–4pm; $6) is where Samuel Adams pronounced "this meeting can do nothing more to save the country" – the signal that triggered the Boston Tea Party on December 16, 1773. Considered to be the first major act of rebellion preceding the Revolutionary War, it was a carefully planned event wherein one hundred men, some dressed in Indian garb, solemnly threw enough British tea into the harbour to make 24 million cuppas. The elegant **Old State House**, built in 1712, was the seat of colonial government, and from its balcony the Declaration of Independence was first publicly read in Boston on July 18, 1776; two hundred years later, Queen Elizabeth II made a speech from that same balcony. Inside is a neat **museum** of Boston history that includes a dapper jacket belonging to John Hancock (daily 9am–5pm; $7.50). Outside, a circle of cobblestones set on a traffic island at the intersection of Devonshire and State streets marks the site of the **Boston Massacre** on March 5, 1770, when British soldiers fired on a crowd that was pelting them with stone-filled snowballs, and killed five, including Crispus Attucks, a former slave.

Lively **Quincy Market** and **Faneuil Hall Marketplace** (a 5min walk northeast from here; Mon–Sat 10am–9pm, Sun noon–6pm; free) is a popular place to refuel, with restaurants and takeaway food stalls or shop for souvenirs. The market is a pioneer example of successful urban renewal (by the same developer who transformed London's Covent Garden). Faneuil Hall (daily 9am–5pm; free) was, however, once known as the "Cradle of Liberty", a meeting place for revolutionaries and, later, abolitionists. Nearby on Union Street, step off the Freedom Trail to visit **The New England Holocaust Memorial** – lofty, hollow glass pillars etched with six million numbers recalling the tattoos the Nazis gave their victims. Its smokestack design is particularly striking at night, when the steam that rises from the pillars is lit up from within.

Passing over pleasant parkland and the splashy fountains of the new Rose Kennedy Greenway (formerly a massive, aboveground highway) and into the **North End**, you reach **Paul Revere House**, 19 North Square, Boston's last surviving seventeenth-century house (mid-April to Oct daily 9.30am–5.15pm; Nov to mid-April daily till 4.15pm; Jan, Feb, March closed Mon; $3.50; ⓣ617/523-2338, ⓦwww.paulreverehouse.org), built after the Great Fire of 1676, and home to Paul Revere – patriot, silversmith, Freemason and father of sixteen children – from 1770 until 1800. When Revere embarked upon his famous **ride** of April 18, 1775, to warn Samuel Adams and John Hancock (as well as the residents of Lexington, MA) that the British were assembling for an attack, two lanterns were hung from the belfry of **Old North Church**, 193 Salem St (Jan–Feb Tues–Sun, 10am–4pm; March–May daily 9am–5pm, June–Oct daily till 6pm, Nov–Dec daily 10am–5pm; free; ⓣ617/523-6676; ⓦwww.oldnorth.com), to alert Charlestown in case he got caught. Up the hill on Hull Street, from **Copp's Hill Burying Ground** (daily 9am–5pm; free), you can see across the harbour to Charlestown; as indeed could the British, who planted their artillery here for the Battle of Bunker Hill. As you exit the cemetery, keep an eye out for the **narrowest house** at 44 Hull St; a private residence merely ten feet in width.

Next, the Freedom Trail crosses the Charlestown Bridge, a fairly long – but scenic – walk. Its final two sites are also reached by the frequent **ferries** from Long Wharf to Charlestown Navy Yard (Mon–Fri every 15–30min 6.30am–8pm, Sat & Sun every 15min 10am–6pm; $1.70 each way).

The Black Heritage Trail

Massachusetts was the first state to declare slavery illegal, in 1783 – partly as a result of black participation in the Revolutionary War – and a large community of free blacks and escaped slaves swiftly grew in the North End and on Beacon Hill. Very few African Americans live in either place today, but the **Black Heritage Trail** traces Beacon Hill's key role in local and national black history – perhaps the most important historical site in America devoted to pre-Civil War African-American history and culture.

Pick up the Trail at 46 Joy St, where the **Abiel Smith School** contains a **Museum of African American History** (Mon–Sat 10am–4pm; $5), and rotates a number of well-tailored exhibits centred on abolitionism and African-American history. Built in 1806 as the country's first African-American church, this became known as "Black Faneuil Hall" during the abolitionist campaign; Frederick Douglass issued his call here for all blacks to take up arms in the Civil War. Among those who responded were the volunteers of the **Massachusetts 54th Regiment**, commemorated by a monument at the edge of Boston Common, opposite the State House, which depicts their farewell march down Beacon Street. Robert Lowell won a Pulitzer Prize for his poem, "For the Union Dead", about this monument, and the regiment's tragic end at Fort Wagner was depicted in the movie *Glory*.

From the monument, the Trail winds around Beacon Hill, and includes a stop at the **Lewis and Harriet Hayden House**. Once a stop on the famous "Underground Railroad", the Haydens sheltered hundreds of runaway slaves from bounty-hunters in pursuit.

While it's easy enough to traverse it on your own, the best way to experience the Trail is by taking a National Park Service **walking tour** (June–Aug Mon–Sat 10am, noon & 2pm, rest of year Mon–Sat 2pm; free; call to reserve ⓣ617/742-5415 or 617/720-2991, ⓦwww.nps.gov/boaf).

The celebrated **USS Constitution**, also known as "Old Ironsides", is the oldest commissioned warship still afloat in the world. Launched in Boston in 1797, she earned her nickname during the War of 1812, when advancing cannonballs bounced off her hull; she subsequently saw 33 battles without ever losing one. Free tours of the ship are led every half-hour (April – Oct Tues–Sun 10am–6pm; Nov – March Thurs–Sun till 4pm). Across the way, the **USS Constitution Museum** (April – Oct daily 9am–6pm; Nov – March daily 10am–5pm; free) houses well-tailored displays on the history of the ship; upstairs is more fun-oriented, with hands-on sailorly exhibits testing your ability to balance on a footrope and helping to pinpoint whether your comrades have scurvy or gout. Beyond the museum, the **Bunker Hill Monument** (July & Aug daily 9am–5.30pm; rest of year daily till 4.30pm; free) sits on Breed's Hill, the actual site of the battle fought on June 17, 1775, which, while technically won by the British, invigorated the patriots, whose strong showing felled nearly half the British troops. A spiral staircase of 294 steps leads to sweeping views at the top; a new **museum** (July & Aug daily 9am–6pm; rest of year daily till 5pm; free) at the base has interesting exhibits on the battle as well as the history of Charlestown. In summer there's usually an ice-cream truck to reward your hike to the top, and the park makes a nice spot for picnicking.

The waterfront and Seaport District

Boston's **waterfront** has recently seen major revitalization efforts – inviting fountains, well-maintained green spaces and historic signage have all started popping up – making it a great spot for a warm-weather stroll. Wisteria-laden **Columbus Park**, next to the *Marriott Long Wharf Hotel*, is a pretty place to lounge and picnic. Faneuil Hall originally stood at the head of **Long Wharf**, which stuck out nearly two thousand feet into the harbour; it also served as the site of the final British evacuation on March 17, 1776. Later, a 1000ft expanse of the waterfront was filled in, and the **Custom House Tower**, 3 McKinley Square (free; ⓣ617/310-6300), once the tallest skyscraper in New England, was erected to mark the end of the wharf. It too now finds itself inland; although its observation deck offers terrific harbour views.

Close by on Central Wharf, the **New England Aquarium** (July–Aug Sun–Thurs 9am–6pm, Fri & Sat till 7pm; Sept–Jun Mon–Fri till 5pm, Sat & Sun 9am–6pm; $21, kids $13; ⓣ617/973-5200) has an outdoor pool of basking sea otters. Inside, a colossal, three-storey glass cylindrical tank is packed with giant sea turtles, moray eels and sharks as well as a range of other ocean exotica that swim by in unsettling proximity. Scuba divers hand-feed the fish five times a day, and sea lion shows are held in a floating amphitheatre alongside. The Aquarium also runs excellent **whale-watching** trips (early April to late Oct call for times; $40, kids $32; ⓣ617/973-5206; 3–4hr).

The waterfront is also the base for **ferries** to Provincetown, MA on Cape Cod (see p.190; ⓣ617/227-4321), Salem, MA (see p.184; ⓣ978/741-0220) and day-trips to the Harbor Islands, including Spectacle and George's Island (ⓣ617/223-8666). All of these trips are highly recommended.

It's hard to miss the newly updated **Boston Children's Museum**, 300 Congress St (daily 10am–5pm, Fri till 9pm; $12, kids $9, Fri 5–9pm $1; ⓣ617/426-6500) marked as it is by a whimsical Boston icon: a forty-foot-tall Hood **milk bottle** (it doubles as a food stand). The museum's three floors of educational exhibits are craftily designed to trick kids into learning about a huge array of topics, from musicology to the engineering of a humongous bubble. Before leaving, check out the Recycle Shop where industrial leftovers are transformed into appealing craft-fodder.

Looking like a glamorous glass ice cube perched above a chilly Boston Harbor, the glimmering facade of the **Institute of Contemporary Art**, located in the Seaport District at 100 Northern Ave (Tues & Wed 10am–5pm, Thurs & Fri till 9pm, Sat & Sun till 5pm, closed Mon; $15, kids free, Thurs 5–9pm free, free for families the last Saturday of the month; ⓣ617/478-3100, ⓦwww.icaboston.org; Courthouse Station **T**) puts on a show before you've even crossed the museum's threshold. Complementing the museum's collection of contemporary artworks is the building's dramatic cantilever shape that extends 80ft into the water's edge. From the interior, this extended section functions as the "Founders Gallery", a meditative, enclosed ledge where, if you look down from the gallery's wall of glass, you'll find yourself standing directly above a jellyfish-laden Boston Harbor.

The Museum of Science

At the northern end of the waterfront, clear across the Boston peninsula from the Children's Museum, the beloved **Museum of Science** (July to early Sept Sat–Thurs 9am–7pm, Fri till 9pm, mid-Sept to June Sat–Thurs 9am–5pm, Fri till 9pm; $20, kids $17; ⓣ617/723-2500, ⓦwww.mos.org) has several floors of interactive exhibits illustrating basic principles of natural and physical science. An impressive IMAX cinema takes up the full height of one end of the building, and the museum's **3D Theater** provides a chance to wear those retro-cool 3-D glasses.

Back Bay and beyond

Beginning in 1857, the spacious boulevards and elegant houses of **Back Bay** were fashioned along gradually filled-in portions of former Charles River marshland. Thus a walk through the area from east to west provides an impressive visual timeline of Victorian architecture. One of the most architecturally significant of its buildings is the Romanesque **Trinity Church**, 206 Clarendon St (Mon–Fri 9am–5pm, Sun 1–6pm; $6), whose stunning interior was built to feel like "walking into a living painting". Towering over the church is Boston's signature skyscraper, the **John Hancock Tower**, an elegant wedge designed by I.M. Pei. Nearby **Newbury Street** is an atmospheric and inviting stretch of swanky boutiques, cafés and art galleries.

The **Christian Science Center** at Huntington and Massachusetts avenues is the "Mother Church" of the First Church of Christ, Scientist, and the home of the *Christian Science Monitor* newspaper; Nelson Mandela made a point of paying a personal visit in 1990 to thank the paper for its support of his release from prison. The complex houses the marvellous **Mapparium** (Tues–Sun 10am–4pm; $6), a curious, 30ft stained-glass globe through which you can walk on a footbridge. The globe's best feature is its lack of sound absorption, which enables a tiny whisper spoken at one end of the bridge to be easily heard by someone at the other.

Further south, beyond the boundaries of Back Bay and a long enough walk to warrant taking the "**T**'s" green line (take the train marked "E" to the "Museum" stop), is the **Museum of Fine Arts** at 465 Huntington Ave (Mon, Tues, Sat & Sun 10am–4.45pm, Wed–Fri till 9.45pm; $20, which includes a free repeat visit within 30 days; Wed after 4pm suggested donation only; ⓣ617/267-9300, ⓦwww.mfa.org). From its magnificent collections of Asian and ancient Egyptian art onwards, the MFA (as it's known) holds sufficient marvels to detain you all day – but be forewarned, the museum is currently undergoing a major expansion (including the addition of a new wing and central courtyard); even the best-loved galleries have been known to close down for periods of time. High points include Renoir's *Dance at Bougival*; Gauguin's sumptuous display of existential angst *Where do we come from? What are we? Where are we going?*; a saxophone made by Adolphe Sax himself (Musical Instruments room); and Botero's voluptuous *Venus* sculpture.

Less broad in its collection, but more distinctive and idiosyncratic than the MFA, is the **Isabella Stewart Gardner Museum**, just down the road at 280 The Fenway (Tues–Sun 11am–5pm; $12; free admission for those named "Isabella"; ⓣ617/566-1401, ⓦwww.gardnermuseum.org). Styled after a fifteenth-century Venetian villa, the Gardner brims with a dazzling collection of works meant to "fire the imagination". While it's best known for its spectacular central courtyard, the museum's greatest successes are its show-stopping pieces by John Singer Sargent, including a stunning portrait of Isabella herself. Weekend concerts are held on select Friday nights as well as on Sunday afternoons from January to May; tickets $23 (includes museum admission).

Cambridge

The excursion across the Charles River to **Cambridge** merits at least half a day, and begins with a fifteen-minute ride on the Red **T** line to **Harvard Square**. This is not so much a square as a number of interlocking streets, filled with small shopping malls and bookstores, at the point where Massachusetts Avenue runs into JFK and Brattle streets. It's an exceptionally lively area, filled with students from nearby Harvard University and MIT, and in the warm weather, street musicians are a common sight. The **Cambridge Visitor Information Booth** right by the Harvard **T** (Mon–Sat 9am–5pm; ⓣ617/441-2884) sporadically organizes walking tours in summer, and offers local maps and guides. Additional info (as well as free internet access) is available from the **Holyoke Center**, 1350 Massachusetts Ave (Mon–Sat 9am–5pm; ⓣ617/495-1573), which also arranges student-led tours of the campus.

Feel free to wander into **Harvard Yard** and around the core of the university, founded in 1636; its enormous Widener Library (named for a victim of the *Titanic*) boasts a Gutenberg Bible and a first folio of Shakespeare. Five minutes' walk west along Brattle Street (at no. 105) is the best known of the Brattle Street mansions, the **Longfellow House** (May Thurs–Sat 10am–4pm, June–Sept Wed–Sun till 4.30pm, tours hourly 10.30–11.30am & 1–4pm; $3; ⓣ617/876-4491), named after the author of *Hiawatha*, who lived here until 1882. Its halls and walls are festooned with Longfellow's furniture and art collection, best of which are the stunning pieces culled from the Far East. Dexter Pratt, immortalized in Longfellow's "Under the spreading chestnut tree, the village smithy stands", lived at 56 Brattle St; a marker on the corner of Brattle and Story streets commemorates the exalted tree.

Cambridge has several first-class museums, with a few engaging exhibits of note. Unfortunately, the **Harvard University Art Museums** are currently closed for a major renovation and are slated to reopen as a single museum in 2013. Once open, the new **Harvard Art Museum** will encompass over 150,000 works of art, including highlights of Harvard's substantial collection of Western art, a small yet excellent selection of German Expressionists and Bauhaus works, and sensuous buddhas and gilded bodhisattvas from its Asian and Islamic art collection. During the renovation, you can check out a selection of the museum's holdings at 485 Broadway, the former home of the **Arthur M. Sackler Museum** (Mon–Sat 10am–5pm, Sun 1–5pm; $9; ⓣ617/495-9400). The stellar **Harvard Museum of Natural History**, 26 Oxford St (daily 9am–5pm; $9), features a number of freakishly huge dinosaur fossils as well as a visually stunning collection of flower models constructed entirely from glass.

A couple of miles southeast of Harvard Square is the **Massachusetts Institute of Technology** (MIT), whose very cool **MIT Museum**, 265 Massachusetts Ave (daily 10am–5pm; $7.50; ⓣ617/253-5927) is filled with hypnotizing mini-machines, like a walking wishbone that swaggers forward, pulling along a mass of wiry wheels.

Eating

Boston offers a hearty range of culinary options. Above all, there's **seafood** – lobsters (boiled red or hand-picked into lobster rolls), scrod (a generic term for young, white-fleshed fish), clams (served steamed and dipped in butter, or as creamy chowder), and oysters (some of the world's best come fresh daily from Wellfleet and other Cape Cod spots). You could base a day's tour of the different neighbourhoods around the foods on offer: breakfast in the cafés of **Beacon Hill**; lunch in the food plazas of **Quincy Market** or **The Garage** on JFK Street in Cambridge, or dim sum in **Chinatown**; for dinner, a budget **Indian** restaurant in Cambridge, an **Italian** place around Hanover Street in the North End, one of the South End's stylish foodie hangouts or seafood overlooking the Harbor.

Chinatown, where restaurants stay open until 2 or 3am, is the best place for **late-night dining**.

Boston

Cafe Jaffa 48 Gloucester St ⓣ617/536-0230; Hynes **T**. One of Back Bay's best inexpensive dining options, with great Middle Eastern fare served up in an inviting space. They're known for their falafel and locally famous lamb chops, but you can't really go wrong here.

Chacarero 26 Province St ⓣ617/367-1167, 101 Arch St ⓣ617/542-0392; Downtown Crossing **T**. Fabulous and fresh, the *chacarero* is a Chilean sandwich built upon warm, soft bread and filled with avocado, chicken, green beans, muenster cheese and hot sauce. Closed weekends, cash only.

Charlie's Sandwich Shoppe 429 Columbus Ave ⓣ617/536-7669; Back Bay **T**. Open since 1927, this historic greasy spoon serves up great eggs and famous turkey hash from a delightful vintage diner environs. No bathrooms, closed Sun, cash only.

Daily Catch 323 Hanover St ⓣ617/523-8567 Haymarket **T**. Ocean-fresh seafood, notably calamari and shellfish – Sicilian-style, with megadoses of garlic – draws big lines to this tiny storefront restaurant.

flour bakery + cafe 1595 Washington St ⓣ617/267-4300; Back Bay **T**; 12 Farnsworth St ⓣ617/338-4333; South Station **T**; in Cambridge at 190 Mass Ave ⓣ617/225-2525; Central **T**. A well-loved South End institution, now with two offshoots, this casual café bursts with fantasticly fresh pastries, sandwiches and salads; they're best known for their unimpeachable BLTs and home-made raspberry seltzer. Top it off with a home-made peanut butter Oreo cookie. The Farnsworth location makes for a great post-Children's Museum treat.

Galleria Umberto 289 Hanover St ⓣ617/227-5709; Haymarket **T**. North End nirvana. There are fewer than a dozen items on the menu, but the lines are consistently to the door for *Umberto's* perfect pizza slices and *arancini*. Lunch only, and get there early – they always sell out. Cash only; very inexpensive.

Maria's Pastry 46 Cross St ⓣ617/523-1196; Haymarket **T**. The best pastries in the North End, and inexplicably underrated; the chocolate cannoli with fresh ricotta filling will make your day.

Neptune Oyster 63 Salem St ⓣ617/742-3474; Haymarket **T**. Snazzy little raw bar filled with devotees who swoon over the shucked shellfish and notable lobster rolls

The Other Side Cosmic Café 407 Newbury St ⓣ617/536-8437; Hynes **T**. This ultra-casual hipster hangout on "the other side" of Newbury St offers gourmet sandwiches, tasty salads and fresh juices. They also have pitchers of good beer. Open late.

Sel de la Terre 255 State St ⓣ617/720-1300; Aquarium **T**, 774 Boylston St ⓣ617/266-8800; Copley **T**. *Sel de la Terre* serves up rustic Provençal fare like hearty bouillabaisse and roasted lamb and eggplant, as well as what are perhaps the best french fries in town.

Silvertone 69 Bromfield St ⓣ617/338-7887; Park **T**. Nostalgia runs high at this bustling basement bar and eatery with standout comfort foods like mashed potatoes and meatloaf, and a super-cheesy mac and cheese. Good beers on tap. Closed Sun.

Sonsie 327 Newbury St ⓣ617/351-2500, Hynes **T**. This Newbury St staple is good for contemporary bistro fare, particularly the swanky sandwiches, pastries and chocolate bread pudding.

South End Buttery Bar & Bistro 314 Shawmut Ave ⓣ617/482-1015, Back Bay **T**. Impossible to resist, this adorable neighbourhood café offers egg sandwiches on home-made biscuits, fresh soups and sandwiches, and terrific cupcakes named for the owner's dogs. The *Buttery* additionally now offers swanky bistro fare at suppertime.

Taiwan Café 34 Oxford St ⓣ617/426-8181; Chinatown **T**. Locals swoon over this busy, authentic Taiwanese eatery which serves up mustard greens with *edamame* (soybeans) and steamed pork buns done just right. Open late. Cash only.

Toro 1704 Washington St ⓣ617/536-4300; Back Bay **T**. A hip and lively tapas bar brimming with white and red sangria and inventive tapas plates such as the grilled corn with lime and aged cheese, or the citrus and soy tuna. Get there early for dinner or risk a highly unreasonable wait time.

Upper Crust 20 Charles St ⓣ617/723-9600; Charles/MGH **T**. Popular pizza joint with excellent thin-crust pizzas; there's generally a slice of the day (such as spinach with pesto and tomato, $3). Keep your eyes peeled for the other outposts around town.

Yankee Lobster Fish Market 300 Northern Ave ⓣ617/345-9799; World Trade Center **T**. Right by the water in the Seaport District, this low-key fried fishery serves up fresh seafood (the lobster roll is particularly noteworthy) from its counter space. It's a hike from downtown – you might want to hop on the Silver Line.

Cambridge

Darwin's Ltd 148 Mt Auburn St ⓣ617/354-5233; 1629 Cambridge St ⓣ617/491-2999; both Harvard **T**. Two locations, both housing fantastic delis with wonderfully inventive sandwich combinations. Cash only.

East Coast Grill 1271 Cambridge St, Inman Square ⓣ617/491-6568; Harvard or Central **T**. A festive and funky atmosphere – think shades of *Miami Vice* – in which to enjoy fresh seafood and Caribbean side dishes. The Sunday serve-yourself *Bloody Mary* bar is reason enough to visit.

Emma's Pizza 40 Hampshire St ⓣ617/864-8534; Kendall **T**. Consistently listed at or near the top of Boston's "best of" lists, this local pizzeria has signature thin pies and slices with fun toppings like roasted sweet potatoes and ricotta.

Hungry Mother 233 Cardinal Medeiros Ave ⓣ617/499-0090; Kendall **T**. A great special occasion spot famed for its south of the Mason-Dixon line cuisine, accompanied by sweet tea served in mason jars and salty boiled peanuts as starters. Mains, like the cornmeal catfish with dirty rice ($18), are culinary perfection; come dessert, you'll be offering up an "amen" for the *Mother*.

Mr Bartley's Burger Cottage 1246 Massachusetts Ave, ⓣ617/354-6559; Harvard **T**. A Cambridge must-visit. Perhaps the best burgers on the planet, washed down with raspberry lime rickeys. Served amid Americana-festooned environs and menus making fun of politicians of the hour. Good veggie burgers, too. Cash only, closed Sun.

Bars, clubs and live music

Boston has a lively **nightlife** scene that offers the best of both old and new, from tried-and-true neighbourhood taverns to young, trendy lounges. The **live music** circuit in Boston and Cambridge is dominated by the very best local and touring indie bands. The free weeklies *Boston Phoenix* (ⓦwww.thephoenix.com) and *Boston's Weekly Dig* (ⓦwww.weeklydig.com) are the foremost source for up-to-date **listings**. Key nightlife zones include **Lansdowne Street**, an entire block of nightclubs next to Fenway Park; **Boylston Street**, on the south side of Boston Common; and Cambridge's **Central Square** district. Note that most establishments are unusually officious in demanding **ID**.

Boston

The Beehive 541 Tremont St ⓣ617/423-0069; Back Bay **T**. With chandeliers dripping from the ceiling, a red-curtained stage and knock-you-down cocktails, the *Beehive* exudes a vaudeville vibe, complete with jazz, cabaret or burlesque shows playing nearly every night of the week.

Bleacher Bar 82A Landsdowne St ⓣ617/262-2424; Kenmore **T**. Beneath the bleachers in dead centre field is the newest addition to Fenway Park, and you don't need a ticket to get in. Here, you'll find a vintage pub setting, the highlight of which is the window that looks directly onto the diamond – quite thrilling on game night.

Bukowski Tavern 50 Dalton St ⓣ617/437-9999; Hynes **T**. Boston's best dive bar, this parking garage watering hole has views over the MassPike and a beer selection so vast it prompted a home-made "wheel of indecision" – spun by the waitstaff for indecisive patrons.

Caffe Vittoria 296 Hanover St ⓣ617/227-7606; Haymarket **T**. A Boston institution, the *Vittoria's* atmospheric original section, with its dark wood panelling, pressed-tin ceilings and Sinatra-blaring Wurlitzer, is vintage North End. It's also a subterranean cigar bar.

Eastern Standard 528 Commonwealth Ave ⓣ617/532-9100; Kenmore **T**. Set inside a gorgeous, spacious dining room, this Boston favourite pulls in a nice mix of clientele, both age-wise and style-wise. The bartenders really know what they're doing, and are just as quick to make a swanky highball as they are to pour a pint. There's also a nice patio in the summer.

House of Blues 15 Lansdowne St ⓣ1-888/693-BLUE; Kenmore **T**. This former Boston icon has returned, hosting big-name acts like Cyndi Lauper, BB King and She & Him in a glossy new venue right by Fenway Park.

Oak Bar In the Fairmont Copley Plaza, 138 St James Ave ⓣ617/267-5300; Copley **T**. Rich wood panelling, high ceilings and excellent martinis are the highlights of this ultra-swanky Back Bay drinkery.

The Paradise 967–969 Commonwealth Ave, Allston ⓣ617/562-8800; Pleasant Street **T**. One of Boston's classic rocking venues (many greats have played here), and it's still happening after 25 years.

Sevens Ale House 77 Charles St, Beacon Hill ⓣ617/523-9074; Charles **T**. This unpolished gem of a neighbourhood pub provides local flavour in the midst of smart Beacon Hill; far more authentic than the nearby *Bull and Finch Pub*.

Wally's Café 427 Massachusetts Ave ⓣ617/424-1408; Massachusetts Ave **T**. Founded in 1947, this is one of the oldest jazz clubs around, and some folks think it's one of Boston's best assets.

Cambridge

Charlie's Kitchen 10 Eliot St ⓣ617/492-9646; Harvard **T**. Marvellously atmospheric local hangout in the heart of Harvard Square, with red vinyl booths, an outdoor beer garden and great cheeseburger specials. The bar upstairs is equally cool, particularly during Tuesday's karaoke nights.

Enormous Room 567 Massachusetts Ave ⓣ617/491-5550; Central **T**. Walking into this comfy, tiny lounge is tantamount to entering a swanky slumber party – the clientele lounges along myriad couches, and sways to the tune of a local DJ.

Lily Pad 1353 Cambridge St ⓣ617/395-1393; Central **T**. This bare-bones space covers the musical spectrum: everything from early jazz to rock, electro-acoustic, chamber music and even (very popular) yoga classes can be found here.

Lizard Lounge 1667 Massachusetts Ave ⓣ617/547-0759; Harvard or Porter **T**. An intimate rock and jazz venue, and one of Boston's best. Fairly nominal cover charges.

Middle East 472 Massachusetts Ave ⓣ617/864-EAST; Central **T**. Local and regional progressive rock acts regularly stop in at this Cambridge institution. Downstairs hosts bigger bands; smaller ones ply their stuff in a tiny upstairs space.

Miracle of Science 321 Massachusetts Ave ⓣ617/868-ATOM; Central **T**. Surprisingly hip despite its status as an MIT hangout. There's a Table of Elements-minded decor and a laidback, unpretentious crowd. The bar stools will conjure up memories of high school chemistry class.

Regattabar In the *Charles Hotel*, 1 Bennett St ⓣ617/661-5000; Harvard **T**. The *Regattabar* draws top national jazz acts, although, as its location in the swish *Charles Hotel* might suggest, the atmosphere is a bit sedate. Dress nicely and prepare to pay around a $25 cover.

Shay's 58 JFK St ⓣ617/864-9161; Harvard **T**. Unwind with grad students over wine and quality beer at *Shay's*, right in the heart of Harvard Square. Appealing burgers and burritos are also on offer here.

T.T. the Bear's 10 Brookline St ⓣ617/492-BEAR; Central **T**. Highly esteemed, intimate, divey venue, showcasing live music (mainly rock) seven nights a week.

Western Front 343 Western Ave ⓣ617/492-7772; Central **T**. This former jazz and blues club is now dedicated to reggae, with live music Fri and Sat nights, cheap drinks, and delectably authentic Jamaican food served up on the weekends.

Performing arts

Mainstream Boston's pride and joy, the **Boston Symphony Orchestra** is based at Symphony Hall, 301 Massachusetts Ave (ⓣ617/266-1200, ⓦwww.bso.org), which Stravinsky called the best auditorium in the world. The orchestra's winter season is supplemented by the **Boston Pops** concerts in May and June, as well as its signature show on July 4.

The city's **theatre** scene divides into the traditionally mainstream productions of the Theater District (often Broadway offshoots) and more experimental companies in Cambridge. The **BosTix** ticket kiosks (ⓣ617/482-BTIX, ⓦwww.artsboston.org) at Faneuil Hall marketplace and in Copley Square sell tickets for all major events – as well as tours, **T** passes and so on – with some half-price same-day tickets (cash only). They're open Tuesday to Saturday 10am to 6pm and Sunday 11am to 4pm; the Copley Square location is also open on Monday 10am to 6pm.

Sports

Baseball is treated with reverence in Boston, so it's fitting that the Red Sox play at historic Fenway Park (Kenmore subway stop on the Green **T** line; tickets $12–325; information ⓣ1-877/REDSOX9, tickets ⓣ617/482-4769, ⓦwww.redsox.com). Built in 1912 and squeezed into an odd-shaped plot just off Brookline Avenue, the stadium is famed for its crazy dimensions and awkward quirks, particularly the 37ft wall in left field known as the "**Green Monster**". The very popular Fenway Park **tours** (ⓣ617/226-6666; $12) are well recommended.

Basketball's Celtics and **hockey**'s Bruins both play at the TD Banknorth Garden, 150 Causeway St near North Station; Celts tickets will run you $10–700, Bruins tickets $10–176 (box office Mon to Fri 10am–5pm; call Ticketmaster for tickets by phone ⓣ1-800/745-3000, ⓦwww.tdbanknorthgarden.com).

Every October features the annual **Head of the Charles** river regatta crew race (ⓣ617/868-6200, ⓦwww.hocr.org) that draws thousands of exuberant, picnicking fans to the shorelines.

Lexington and Concord

On the night of April 18, 1775, **Paul Revere** rode down what is now Massachusetts Avenue from Boston, racing through Cambridge and Arlington on his way to warn the American patriots gathered at **Lexington** (eleven miles to the west) of an impending British attack. Close behind him was a force of more than seven hundred British soldiers, intent on seizing the supplies that they knew the local militia had hoarded at **Concord**, further north.

Although much of Revere's route has been turned into major thoroughfares, the various settings of the first military confrontation of the Revolutionary War – "the shot heard 'round the world" – remain much as they were then. The triangular **Town Common** at Lexington was where the British encountered their first opposition. Captain John Parker ordered his 77 American "**Minutemen**" to "stand your ground. Don't fire unless fired upon, but if they mean to have a war let it begin here". No one knows who fired the first shot, but the eight soldiers who died are buried beneath a surprisingly affecting memorial at the northwestern end of the park. Guides in period costume lead tours of the **Buckman Tavern** (April–Oct daily 10am–4pm; $6; ⓣ781/862-5598), where the Minutemen waited for the British to arrive; the **Hancock-Clarke House**, a quarter of a mile north, where Samuel Adams and John Hancock were awakened by Paul Revere, is now a museum (April–Oct daily 10am–4pm).

By the time the British soldiers marched on Concord, on the morning after the encounter in Lexington, the surrounding countryside was up in arms, and the Revolutionary War was in full swing. In running battles in the town itself, and along the still-evocative **Battle Road** leading back toward Boston, 73 British soldiers and 49 colonials were killed over the next two days. The relevant sites now form the **Minuteman National Historic Park**, with visitor centres at the scenic North Bridge, 174 Liberty St, in Concord (daily: end March to end Oct 9am–5pm; end Oct to Nov till 4pm; Dec–March 11am–3pm), and at 250 North Great Rd (Rte-2A), in Lincoln (daily: end March to end Oct 9am–5pm; end Oct to Nov till 4pm; Dec–March closed; ⓣ978/318-7832).

After a morning spent denouncing eighteenth-century British rule, it's customary to indulge in a quintessential British activity – high tea – at the historic *Concord Inn* (Sat & Sun 3–5pm, there is also an informal tea Mon to Fri; $10.95–24.95; ⓣ978/369-2373; reservations recommended). Just outside Concord, the area's rich **literary heritage** is the focus at **Orchard House** (April–Oct Mon–Sat 10am–4.30pm, Sun 1–4.30pm; Nov–March Mon–Fri 11am–3pm, Sat 10am–4.30pm, Sun 1–4.30pm; closed Jan 1–15; entry by guided tour only, $9; ⓣ978/369-4118, ⓦwww.louisamayalcott.org), 399 Lexington Rd, where Louisa May Alcott lived from 1858 to 1877 and wrote *Little Women*.

South of Concord on Rte-126, **Walden Pond** was where Henry David Thoreau conducted the experiment in solitude and self-sufficiency described in his 1854 book *Walden*. The site where his log cabin once stood is marked with stones, and at dawn you can still watch the pond "throwing off its nightly clothing of mist" (at midday, it's a great spot for swimming and hiking). Thoreau is interred, along with Ralph Waldo Emerson, Nathaniel Hawthorne and Louisa May Alcott, atop a hill in **Sleepy Hollow Cemetery**, just east of the centre of Concord.

As well as guided bus tours from Boston (see p.171), **buses** (25min) run to Lexington from Alewife Station (15min; $1.50), at the northern end of the Red **T** line, and **trains** to Concord run from North Station (40–45min; $6.25). Once in the area, **Liberty Ride**, run by the Lexington Chamber of Commerce, offers great trolley bus tours along the area's literary and historical circuit (June–Oct daily 10am–4pm; the $25 fee includes access to nearly all area sites; ⓣ781/862-0500 ext 702, ⓦwww.libertyride.us).

The north shore

As you head northward out of Boston, you pass through a succession of rich little ports that have been all but swallowed up by the suburbs. **Salem** makes for an enticing day-trip, and if you have the time, the atmospheric old fishing ports of **Gloucester** and **Rockport**, further out on Cape Ann, are also worth a look. This area is the best place on the East Coast for **whale-watching** trips. Cape Ann Whale Watch (ⓣ1-800/877-5110, ⓦwww.seethewhales.com) offers trips from Gloucester (May–Oct; 3–4hr; $45).

Salem

SALEM is remembered less as the site where the colony of Massachusetts was first established than as the place where, sixty years later, Puritan self-righteousness reached its apogee in the horrific **witch trials** of 1692. Nineteen Salem women were hanged as witches (and one man, Giles Corry, was pressed to death with a boulder), thanks to a group of impressionable teenage girls who reported as truth a garbled mixture of fireside tales told by a West Indian slave, Tituba, and scare stories published by Cotton Mather, a pillar of the Puritan community. That this unpleasant history is now the basis of a child-oriented tourist industry – all black hats and broomsticks – is a bit unsettling. However, if you can overlook the sometimes contrived witchy vibe (and the shops selling corsets and fairy clothing) this pretty, historic town proves to be quite an enjoyable visit.

The **Salem Witch Museum** in Washington Square (daily: July & Aug 10am–7pm; Sept–June till 5pm; $8.50; ⓣ978/744-1692) draws parallels with modern racism and political persecution, but is at its heart a rather tacky show of illuminated dioramas and pre-recorded commentary. Innumerable other witch-related attractions in town are best ignored. Salem's crown jewel is the **Peabody Essex Museum** at 161 Essex St (Tues–Sun 10am–5pm; $15; ⓣ978/745-9500), whose vast, modern space incorporates more than thirty galleries filled with remarkable *objets* brought home by voyaging New Englanders, as well as standout collections devoted to contemporary art and photography. Founded by a ship captain in 1799, the museum has stellar Asian and Oceanic displays, most notably the **Yin Yu Tang** ($5 extra), a stunning sixteen-room Qing dynasty merchant's house reassembled here in Salem.

The remnants of Salem's original waterfront have been preserved as the **Salem Maritime National Historic Site** (visitors' centre at 174 Derby St; ⓣ978/740-1650). The chief sights – opulent Derby House and the imposing Customs House, where Nathaniel Hawthorne once worked as a surveyor – can only be visited on daily one-hour tours ($5). The nearby **House of Seven Gables** at 115 Derby St, the star of Hawthorne's eponymous novel, is a rambling old mansion beside the sea (daily: July–Oct 10am–7pm, Nov–June till 5pm, closed first half of Jan; $12.50; ⓣ978/744-0991). Hour-long guided tours of the complex also take in the author's birthplace, moved here from its original site on Union Street.

Practicalities

Regular MBTA **buses** run to Salem from Boston's Haymarket station (every 30min; $3.50). Frequent **trains** also leave from North Station (weekdays 2–3 an hour, weekends hourly; $5.25). For **accommodation**, the historic and well-run *Hawthorne Hotel*, 18 Washington Square W (ⓣ978/744-4080, ⓦwww.hawthornehotel.com; ❻–❽) is right in the heart of things, while *Morning Glory Bed and Breakfast*, 22 Hardy St (ⓣ978/741-1703 or 1-800/446-2995, ⓦwww.morninggloryb.com; ❻–❼), has home-made goodies in the morning and great views of the water. The atmospheric *A and J King Bakery*, 48 Central St (ⓣ978/744-4881), features impeccable walnut sticky buns and fresh, overstuffed sandwiches, while the *Sixty2 on Wharf*, 62 Wharf St (ⓣ978/744-0062), is an upmarket trattoria with home-made pastas and *arancini* (entrees $22–24). Heading south out of town on Rte-1A, *Salem Diner,* 70 Loring Ave (1A) (ⓣ978/741-7918), is a must-visit for road-trip aficionados, housed in an original 1941 Sterling Streamliner car, one of only four remaining in the US.

The south shore

Heading south, it can take a while to get clear of Boston, especially on summer weekends, when the traffic down to Cape Cod can be horrendous. Two historic towns, one north and one west of the Cape, are worth exploring: **Plymouth** and **New Bedford**.

Plymouth

"America's Hometown", little **PLYMOUTH**, on the south shore of Massachusetts Bay, forty miles south of Boston, is given over to commemorating, in various degrees of taste, the landing of the 102 **Pilgrims** in December of 1620.

By the sea, a solemn pseudo-Greek temple encloses the nondescript **Plymouth Rock**, where the Pilgrims are said to have first touched land. Given that the rock was only identified in 1741, and that the Pilgrims had already spent two months on Cape Cod before settling here, it is of symbolic importance only.

Two worthier memorials make no claim to authenticity, but meticulously reproduce the experience of the Pilgrims. Both the replica of the **Mayflower** in town (the *Mayflower II*), and **Plimoth Plantation** three miles south, are staffed by costumed "interpreters", each of whom acts out the part of a specific Pilgrim, Wampanoag or sailor (both attractions: April–Nov daily 9am–5pm; *Mayflower II* alone $10, Plantation alone $24, together $28; ⓣ508/746-1622, ⓦwww.plimoth.org). The charade visitors are obliged to perform – pretending to have stepped back into the seventeenth century – can be a little tiresome, but ultimately the sheer depth of detail in both endeavours makes them fascinating. At the Plantation, everything you see in the Pilgrim Village of 1627, and the Wampanoag Settlement, has been created using traditional techniques.

Practicalities

Plymouth's **Visitor Information Center** is on the waterfront at 130 Water St (daily: summer 8am–8pm; winter 9am–5pm; ⓣ508/747-7525 or 1-800/USA-1620, ⓦwww.visit-plymouth.com). Plymouth & Brockton provides a regular **bus** service to and from Boston ($14 one-way, $25 return; ⓣ508/746-0378, ⓦwww.p-b.com). There are also express ferries from Plymouth to Provincetown (see p.190). A good standard **motel** option is the clean and comfortable *Best Western Cold Spring*, 188 Court St (closed late Nov to early March; ⓣ508/746-2222 or 1-800/678-8667, ⓦwww.bwcoldspring.com; ❻). *A White Swan B&B*, 146 Manomet Pond Rd (ⓣ508/224-3759, ⓦwww.whiteswan.com; ❻–❼), is set in a 200-year-old historic farmhouse that's a pleasant walk from delightful White Horse Beach. America's hometown has a few favourable **food** options. Right on the waterfront, *Blue-Eyed Crab*, 170 Water St (ⓣ508/747-6776), offers fresh cuts of seafood, great cocktails and a bright outdoor patio, while *Martha's Stone Soup*, 517 Old Sandwich Rd (ⓣ508/224-8900) serves chicken breast picatta ($18) and salads mixed with pumpkin seeds from inside an eighteenth-century tavern building.

New Bedford

The old whaling port of **NEW BEDFORD**, 45 miles due south of Boston, was immortalized at the start of Herman Melville's *Moby Dick*, and is still home to one of the nation's most prosperous fishing fleets. Much of the downtown and working waterfront area is preserved within the **New Bedford Whaling National Historic Park**, (visitor centre at 33 Williams St, daily 9am–5pm; ⓣ508/996-4095), the centrepiece of which is the impressive **New Bedford Whaling Museum** at 18 Johnny Cake Hill (daily 9am–5pm, every second Thurs of the month till 9pm; $10), featuring a 66ft blue whale skeleton, collections of scrimshaw and harpoons, and an evocative half-sized whaling vessel replica. More affecting is the **Seamen's Bethel** directly opposite the museum; the chapel really does have the ship-shaped pulpit described in *Moby Dick*, though this one was rebuilt after a fire in 1866.

One good place to **stay** is the *Orchard Street Manor*, 139 Orchard St (ⓣ508/984-3475, ⓦwww.the-orchard-street-manor.com; ❺–❻), a nineteenth-century whaling captain's home that's festooned with marble fireplaces and Moroccan accoutrements. A favourite local place to **eat** is the Portuguese *Antonio's*, 267 Coggeshall St (ⓣ508/990-3636), where long lines often stretch out the door (cash only). Close to the museum, *No Problemo*, at 813 Purchase St (ⓣ508/984-1081) is the place to go for whale-sized burritos, tasty *taquitos* and sangria (cash only; open late).

Cape Cod and the islands

One of the most celebrated slices of real estate in America, **Cape Cod** boasts a dazzling, three-hundred-mile coastline with some of the best beaches in New England. Unsurprisingly, this means that the Cape's main haunts are packed in the summer. If you're planning on driving in during June or August, try to start your trip on a weekday or a Sunday night. If that's just not possible, and a weekend jaunt

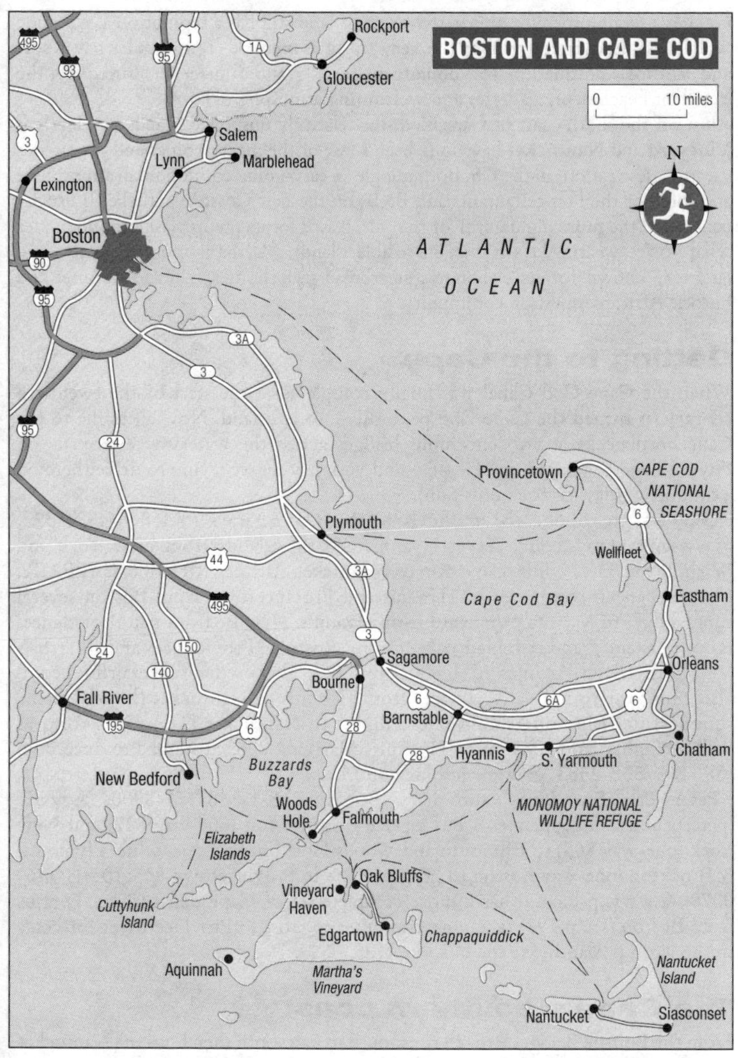

is what you're hankering after, aim to the leave the Boston area by 2pm on Friday, so as to avoid rush hour and the hordes of sun-worshippers clamouring to get over the Sagamore Bridge. Alternatively, a visit to the Cape midweek during May or September will find lower hotel prices, thinned crowds and quite pleasant (albeit cooler) weather.

Cape Cod was named by Bartholomew Gosnold in 1602, on account of the prodigious quantities of cod caught by his crew off Provincetown. Less than twenty years later the Pilgrims landed nearby, before moving on to Plymouth. Today, much of the land on the Cape, from its salt marshes to its ever-eroding dunes, is considered a fragile and endangered ecosystem, and once you head north to the **Outer Cape**, past the spectacular dunes of **Cape Cod National Seashore**, you get a feeling for why this narrow spit of land still has a reputation as a seaside wilderness. **Provincetown**, at the very tip of Cape Cod, is a popular gay resort and summer destination for bohemians, artists and fun-seekers lured by the excellent beaches, art galleries and welcoming atmosphere.

Just off the south coast of Cape Cod, the relatively unspoiled islands of **Martha's Vineyard** and **Nantucket** have long been some of the most popular and prestigious vacation destinations in the US. Both mingle an easy-going cosmopolitan atmosphere and some of the best restaurants and B&Bs on the East Coast. Nantucket is usually considered the more highfalutin' of the pair, teased for its preppy fashions (no matter what you're wearing, it's still an incredible island); Martha is more expansive and laidback, known for its elaborate gingerbread-style houses, vintage carousel and historic African-American community.

Getting to the Cape

When the Cape Cod Canal was finally completed at the start of the twentieth century, it turned the Cape Cod peninsula into an island. Now all traffic to the Cape bottlenecks at two enormous bridges across the waterway – Bourne on Hwy-28 and Sagamore on Hwy-6 – and you may regret trying to drive there on a summer Friday (or back on a Sun).

One way to dodge the traffic is to fly. US Airways (Ⓣ1-800/428-4322, Ⓦwww.usairways.com), serves Hyannis and the islands from New York and Washington DC, while Cape Air & Nantucket Airlines (Ⓣ1-866/CAPEAIR, Ⓦwww.capeair.com), flies to Hyannis and Provincetown from Boston several times a day; to Martha's Vineyard from Hyannis, New Bedford and Providence, Rhode Island; and to Nantucket from Boston, Providence and Martha's Vineyard. Island Airlines (Ⓣ1-800/248-7779, Ⓦwww.nantucketairlines.com) also runs year-round daily services from Hyannis to Nantucket (hourly in the summer). Jet Blue offers convenient flights to Nantucket from New York, as well as flights from Boston to Hyannis, Martha's Vineyard and Provincetown (Ⓣ1-800/538-2583, Ⓦwww.jetblue.com).

Peter Pan Bus Lines' subsidiary Bonanza (Ⓣ1-888/751-8800, Ⓦwww.peterpanbus.com) operates a bus service from Boston (one-way $27) and New York (one-way $65) to Falmouth and Woods Hole on the Cape, while Plymouth & Brockton (one-way Boston to Hyannis $25, to Provincetown $35; Ⓣ508/746-0378, Ⓦwww.p-b.com) has a more complete set of Cape destinations. **Ferries** from Boston (see p.192) take ninety minutes to cross to Provincetown; for boats to the various islands, see the box on p.195.

The Cape's southern coast

From the Bourne Bridge, **Rte-28** runs south to Falmouth then hugs the Nantucket Sound until it merges with routes 6 and 6A in Orleans. Pleasant Falmouth makes a diverting jump-off point for ferries to Martha's Vineyard. Further up, Hyannis, the commercial hub of Cape Cod, is quite commercialized and ferry-oriented, although it does have a number of great beaches and watering holes. All the way at the lower tip of the peninsula (the "elbow" of the Cape's arm), affluent Chatham charms with its fancy guesthouses, renowned pie shop (*Marion's*), and the blissfully quiet **Monomoy National Wildlife Refuge.**

Falmouth and Woods Hole

One obvious base for catching a **ferry** to the islands is **FALMOUTH**, where cosy accommodation includes the *Inn on the Sound*, 313 Grand Ave (Ⓣ508/457-9666, Ⓦwww.innonthesound.com; ⑦–⑨), a classic sea-shingled home with ten stylish beach-toned rooms that peer out onto the Vineyard Sound, or the *Woods Hole Passage*, at 186 Woods Hole Rd (ⓣ508/548-9575, ⓦwww.woodsholepassage.com; ❼), with brightly painted chambers equipped with wireless internet. The *Sippewissett Campground & Cabins*, a couple of miles out at 836 Palmer Ave (ⓣ508/548-2542, ⓦwww.sippewissett.com; peak season $31; off-season $26; plus $10 for each additional adult year-round), gets crowded, but it has a great location, allows campfires and offers a free shuttle service to the ferries and beaches.

Restaurants, such as *Betsy's Diner*, 457 Main St (ⓣ508/540-0060), an authentic 1950s diner beckoning you to "eat heavy", abound in Falmouth; you might also want to try the assorted moderately-priced seafood places along the waterfront at **WOODS HOLE**, four miles southwest. The *Fishmonger's Café*, 56 Water St (ⓣ508/540-5376), is a natural-foods restaurant that serves eggs, granola and the like at breakfast, with seafood specials at lunch and dinner. As for sights, the **Woods Hole Oceanographic Institution's exhibit centre**, at 15 School St, near Little Harbor (May–Oct Mon–Sat 10am–4.30pm; Nov & Dec Tues–Fri till 4.30pm; $2; ⓣ508/289-2663, ⓦwww.whoi.edu), focuses on the Institution's underwater research, including their sensational finding of the *Titanic* in 1986. If you're looking to get out on the water, Ocean Quest runs informative, hands-on **ocean cruises** in summer (July & Aug Mon–Fri 10am, noon, 2pm & 4pm, Sat noon & 2pm; $22; ⓣ1-800/37-OCEAN, ⓦwww.oceanquest.org).

Hyannis

It stands to reason that **HYANNIS** – the largest port on the Cape, and its main commercial hub – would be a little less charming than Falmouth and Woods Hole. Nevertheless, it still sparkles a bit from the glamour it earned when the **Kennedy compound** at Hyannisport placed it at the centre of world affairs. Hence the existence of the **John F. Kennedy Museum**, 397 Main St (mid-April to mid-May Mon–Sat 10am–4pm, Sun noon–4pm; mid-May to late Oct Mon–Sat 9am–5pm, Sun noon–5pm; Nov, Dec & mid-Feb to mid-April Thurs–Sat 10am–4pm, Sun noon–4pm; $5; ⓣ508/790-3077), which shows photographs, news clippings and film footage of the days JFK spent on the Cape.

If you have a boat to catch and need to stay in Hyannis, options include the friendly, neat and affordable *Sea Beach Inn*, 388 Sea St (ⓣ508/775-4612, ⓦwww.capecodtravel.com/seabeach; ❹–❻), the motel-style *Sea Coast Inn*, with kitchenettes and helpful innkeepers, 33 Ocean St (ⓣ1-800/466-4100, ⓦwww.seacoastcapecod.com; ❺–❻), or the brand-new, sea-shingled *HI-Hyannis* hostel, across the street from the ferry at 111 Ocean St (ⓣ508/775-7990, ⓦcapecod.hiusa.org, dorm beds $29–39). For **food** and entertainment stick to Main Street: *Brazilian Grill*, at no. 680 (ⓣ508/771-0109), is carnivore heaven, with mouthwatering meats delivered straight from the skewer and onto your plate; *Spanky's Clam Shack*, right by the ferry at 138 Ocean St (ⓣ508/771-2770), features fresh broiled and fried seafood, while *Four Seas*, in Centerville at 360 S Main St (ⓣ508/775-1394), has been serving up enormously fantastic ice-cream cones beside Craigville beach since 1934.

The Mid-Cape

The middle stretch of Cape Cod holds some of its prettiest, most unspoiled places. Timeworn fishing communities like Wellfleet and Chatham, along with dozens of carefully maintained, mildly touristy hamlets along the many winding roads, are what most people hope to find when they come to the Cape. Cutting across the middle, the **Cape Cod Rail Trail** follows a paved-over railroad track from Dennis to Eastham, through forests and cranberry bogs. It makes a good **cycling** trip; bikes can be rented in all the main towns.

The whitewashed old town of **CHATHAM** is tucked away in a protected harbour between Nantucket Sound and the open Atlantic Ocean. Hang out at the **Fish Pier** on Shore Road and wait for the fleet to come in during the mid-afternoon, or head a mile south on Hwy-28 to **Chatham Light**, one of many lighthouses built to protect mariners from the treacherous shoals. Tour **maps** are available from the information booth at 533 Main St (May–Oct Mon–Sat 10am–5pm, Sun noon–5pm; ⓣ508/945-5199, ⓦwww.chathaminfo.com). Good **seafood** and good times abound at the *Chatham Squire*, 487 Main St (ⓣ508/945-0945), a low-key, local institution. Also, be sure to stop by ★ *Marion's Pie Shop*, 2022 Main St (Rte-28) (ⓣ508/432-9439), for a life-changing bumbleberry pie (note that "misbehaving children will be made into pies"). If you're going to **stay** in chic Chatham, you might as well indulge; the fantastic *Captain's House Inn*, 369–371 Old Harbor Rd (ⓣ508/945-0127, ⓦwww.captainshouseinn.com; ❽–❾), is a gorgeous old whaling captain's home with rambling gardens and afternoon tea, while the *Pleasant Bay Village Resort*, 1191 Orleans Rd (ⓣ508/945-1133, ⓦwww.pleasantbayvillage.com; ❼–❽) has lovely grounds and more affordable digs.

The **place to stay** in the resort community of **EASTHAM** is the romantic *Whalewalk Inn*, at 220 Bridge Rd (ⓣ508/255-0617 or 1-800/440-1281, ⓦwww.whalewalkinn.com; ❽–❾). Rates for the secluded B&B rooms include use of their fabulous spa facilities. Right around the corner is the *Mid-Cape American Youth Hostel*, 75 Goody Hallet Drive, (ⓣ508/255-2785; open May–Sept; $32 dorm beds), a collection of woodsy cabins (the hostel up the road in Truro may be more appealing, however; see below).

For **food**, join those obsessed with the onion rings at *Arnold's Lobster and Clam Bar*, 3580 Rte-6 (ⓣ508/255-2575), a popular seafood **restaurant** and beer garden. *Sam's Deli*, 100 Brackett Rd (ⓣ508/255-9340) is the place to go for bulging beach sandwiches.

Cape Cod National Seashore

After the bustle of Cape Cod's towns, the **Cape Cod National Seashore** really does come as a proverbial breath of fresh air. These protected lands, spared by President Kennedy from the rampant development further south, take up virtually the entire Atlantic side of the Cape, from Chatham north to Provincetown. Most of the way you can park by the road, sometimes for a fee, and strike off across the dunes to windswept, seemingly endless beaches – though in places parking is limited to local residents. A programme of grass-planting helps to hold the whole place together: three feet of the sands south of the National Seashore are washed away each year.

Displays and movies at the main **Salt Pond Visitor Center**, on US-6 just north of Eastham (daily 9am–4.30pm, till 5pm in summer; ⓣ508/255-3421, ⓦwww.nps.gov/caco), trace the geology and history of the Cape. A road and a hiking and cycling trail head east to the sands of **Coast Guard Beach** and **Nauset Light Beach**, both of which offer excellent swimming. Another fine beach is the **Head of the Meadow**, halfway between Truro and Provincetown, on the northeast shore (beach parking $15). The inviting *HI-Truro* **hostel**, at 111 North Pamet Rd in Truro (ⓣ508/349-3889, ⓦcapecod.hiusa.org; closed late Sept to early May), has dorms beds for $29–39 in a breezy former Coast Guard station with spectacular views of the seashore and the dunes.

Provincetown

The compact fishing village of **PROVINCETOWN** (or, as it's popularly known, "P-Town") is a gorgeous place, with silvery clapboard houses and gloriously unruly gardens lining the town's tiny, winding streets. Bohemians and

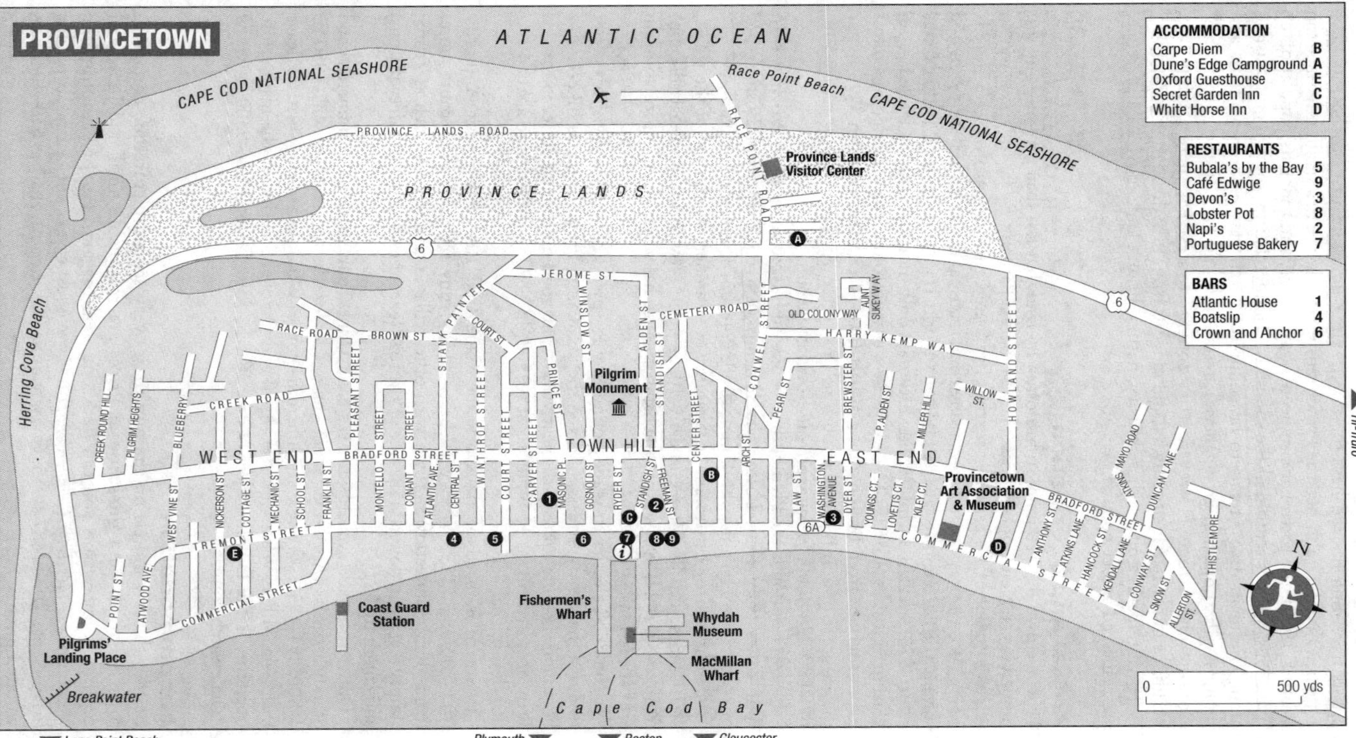
PROVINCETOWN
ATLANTIC OCEAN
CAPE COD NATIONAL SEASHORE
Race Point Beach
CAPE COD NATIONAL SEASHORE
ACCOMMODATION
Carpe Diem B
Dune's Edge Campground A
Oxford Guesthouse E
Secret Garden Inn C
White Horse Inn D
RESTAURANTS
Bubala's by the Bay 5
Café Edwige 9
Devon's 3
Lobster Pot 8
Napi's 2
Portuguese Bakery 7
BARS
Atlantic House 1
Boatslip 4
Crown and Anchor 6
PROVINCE LANDS ROAD
RACE POINT ROAD
Province Lands Visitor Center
PROVINCE LANDS
6
JEROME ST
WINSLOW ST
ALDEN ST
CEMETERY ROAD
CONWELL STREET
OLD COLONY WAY
AUNT SUKEY WAY
HARRY KEMP WAY
HOWLAND STREET
RACE ROAD
BROWN ST
SHANK PAINTER
COURT ST
PRINCE ST
Pilgrim Monument
STANDISH ST
CENTER STREET
PEARL ST
BREWSTER ST
P. ALDEN ST
MILLER HILL
WILLOW ST.
MAYO ROAD
DUNCAN LANE
ATKINS
CREEK ROAD
CREEK ROUND HILL
PILGRIM HEIGHTS
BLUEBERRY
PLEASANT STREET
STREET
STREET
WINTHROP STREET
COURT STREET
CARVER STREET
TOWN HILL
ARCH ST
WEST END
BRADFORD STREET
EAST END
Provincetown Art Association & Museum
WEST VINE ST
NICKERSON ST
COTTAGE ST
MECHANIC ST
SCHOOL ST
FRANKLIN ST
MONTELLO
CONANT
ATLANTIC AVE.
CENTRAL ST
MASONIC PL
GOSNOLD ST
RYDER ST
STANDISH ST
FREEMAN ST
LAW ST
WASHINGTON AVENUE
DYER ST
YOUNGS CT.
LOVETTS CT.
KILEY CT.
6A
BRADFORD STREET
ANTHONY ST
ATKINS LANE
HANCOCK ST
KENDALL LANE
CONWAY ST
SNOW ST
ALLERTON ST.
THISTLEMORE
COMMERCIAL STREET
TREMONT STREET
POINT ST
ATWOOD AVE
COMMERCIAL STREET
Herring Cove Beach
Pilgrims' Landing Place
Breakwater
Coast Guard Station
Fishermen's Wharf
Whydah Museum
MacMillan Wharf
Cape Cod Bay
N
0 500 yds
Hi-Truro
Long Point Beach
Plymouth
Boston
Gloucester

artists have long flocked here for the dazzling light and vast beaches; in 1914 Eugene O'Neill established the Provincetown Playhouse in a small hut. Since the Beatnik 1950s, the town has also been a **gay** centre, and today its population of five thousand rises tenfold in the summer. Commercialism, though quite visible along the main drags, tends to be countercultural: gay, environmentalist and feminist gift shops join arty galleries, restaurants and bars on the aptly named **Commercial Street**. However, strict zoning ensures that there are few new buildings in town. Albeit crowded and raucous from July through to September, P-Town remains a place where history, natural beauty and, above all, difference, are respected and celebrated.

Arrival and information

Provincetown lies 120 miles from Boston by land, but less than fifty miles by sea, nestled in the New England coast's largest natural harbour. By far the nicest way to arrive is on one of the passenger **ferries**. Bay State Cruise Company (Ⓣ1-877/783-3779, Ⓦwww.baystatecruisecompany.com) runs a daily express ferry in the summer three times per day from Boston's World Trade Center pier (90min express return $79), and a standard ferry on Saturdays only (return $44; 3hr), while Boston Harbor Cruises (Ⓣ617/227-4321, Ⓦwww.bostonharborcruises.com), offers express service from Boston's Long Wharf (May–Oct; 90min; return $79). By far the cheapest option is the Plymouth to Provincetown ferry (90min; return $40; Ⓣ1-800/225-4000, Ⓦwww.provincetownferry.com).

A slower option is the Plymouth & Brockton **bus**, which runs to Provincetown four times daily from Boston via Hyannis ($35 one-way from Boston; $25 one-way from Hyannis; 3hr 45min; Ⓣ508/746-0378, Ⓦwww.p-b.com).

The tiny **visitor centre**, in the Chamber of Commerce at the end of the wharf, 307 Commercial St (May–Oct daily 10am–4pm; Nov–April Mon–Sat till 3pm; Ⓣ508/487-3424, Ⓦwww.ptownchamber.com), has a wealth of information on area attractions.

It couldn't be easier to **walk** around tiny P-Town, though many visitors prefer to **cycle** the narrow streets, hills and the undulating Province Lands Bike Trail, a beguiling six-mile route with great vistas. One good bike rental outlet in town is Provincetown Bikes, 42 Bradford St (Ⓣ508/487-8735); they charge about $22 a day (less for half-days).

If you're in need of transport, the Cape Cod Regional Transit Authority (Ⓣ1-800/352-7155, Ⓦwww.thebreeze.info) runs frequent Flex route buses (6am–8pm) connecting P-Town with other villages on the Cape such as Truro; simply flag them down on the side of the road (except for Rte-6, for safety reasons) and cough up $2.

Dunes **tours** are available at Art's Sand Dune Tours, based at Commercial and Standish streets (April–Oct 10am–dusk; $26 for 1hr tours; Ⓣ508/487-1950 or 1-800/894-1951, Ⓦwww.artsdunetours.com). **Whale-watching cruises** leave from MacMillan Wharf between April and October 31; one of the main cruise operators is the Dolphin Fleet Whale Watch; $39 (Ⓣ1-800/826-9300, Ⓦwww.whalewatch.com).

Accommodation

Besides the few motels on the outskirts, every second picturesque cottage in town seems to be a **guesthouse**. Prices are reasonable until mid-June, and during the off-season you can find some real bargains. As for **camping**, the welcoming *Dunes' Edge Campground*, on Hwy-6 just east of the central stoplights (May–Sept; Ⓣ508/487-9815, Ⓦwww.dunes-edge.com), charges $30–40 for its wooded pitches.

Carpe Diem 12 Johnson St ⓣ508/487-4242, ⓦwww.carpediemguesthouse.com. Wonderful innkeepers, beautifully-appointed rooms, horseback riding and spa services at this lovely B&B on a quiet side street. ❽

Oxford Guesthouse 8 Cottage St ⓣ508/487-9103, ⓦwww.oxfordguesthouse.com. Seven elegantly styled rooms and suites, with classical drapes and patterned wallpaper adding to the Victorian ambience – you get fresh, continental breakfast, cookies in the afternoons and a civilized "wine hour" every evening. CDs, DVDs and w-fi available. ❼–❽

Secret Garden Inn 300a Commercial St ⓣ1-866/766-9646, ⓦwww.secretgardenptown.com. This is a relative bargain; seven quaint rooms in an 1830s sea captain's house with a veranda done up in country furnishings with a beautiful garden out the front. Big breakfast included. ❺

White Horse Inn 500 Commercial St ⓣ508/487-1790. A whimsical, colourful, art-strewn space; some rooms have shared baths. There are also family-sized apartments with kitchens. Beach access, and a beatnik vibe. ❹–❻

The town and the beaches

Provincetown's tiny core is centred on the three narrow miles of **Commercial Street**. **MacMillan Wharf**, always busy with charters, yachts and fishing boats (which unload their catch each afternoon), splits the town in half. Somewhat out from the centre, on Commercial Street, are scores of quaint art galleries, as well as the delightful **Provincetown Art Association and Museum**, at no. 460 (mid-May to Sept Mon–Thurs 11am–8pm, Fri till 10pm, Sat & Sun till 5pm; Oct to mid-May Thurs–Sun noon–5pm; $7; ⓣ508/487-1750), with displays of local artists.

Looming above the centre of P-Town, the **Pilgrim Monument and Provincetown Museum** on High Pole Hill (daily: April to mid-June & mid-Sept to Nov 9am–5pm, mid-June to mid-Sept till 7pm; $7; ⓣ508/487-1310), has permanent exhibits giving a fairly romantic account of the Pilgrim story and subsequent history of the town, along with a 252ft granite tower with an observation deck (only accessible by 116 stairs) that looks out over the whole of the Cape.

A little way beyond the town's narrow strip of sand, undeveloped **beaches** are marked only by dunes and a few shabby beach huts. You can swim in the clear water from the uneven rocks of the two-mile breakwater, where the sea bed crunches with soft-shell clams, or head through scented wild roses and beach plums to find blissful isolation on undeveloped beaches nearby. West of town, **Herring Cove Beach**, easily reached by bike or through the dunes, is more crowded, but never unbearably so. In the wild **Province Lands**, at the Cape's northern tip, vast sweeping moors and bushy dunes are buffeted by Cape Cod's deadly sea, the site of one thousand known shipwrecks. The **visitor centre** (May–Oct daily 9am–5pm; ⓣ508/487-1256), in the middle of the dunes on Race Point Road, has videos and displays highlighting the exceptionally fragile environment here.

Eating

Great **food** options abound in P-Town. Portuguese bakeries, relics of early settlement, can be found along Commercial Street.

Bubala's By the Bay 183 Commercial St ⓣ508/487-0773. Perhaps the freshest seafood in P-Town at a fun hangout right on the water; good non-fish fare as well; open all day.

Café Edwige 333 Commercial St ⓣ508/487-2008. Breakfast's the thing at this popular second-floor spot; try the home-made Danish pastries and fresh fruit pancakes. Creative bistro fare at dinnertime. Closed Tues.

Devon's 40 1/2 Commercial St ⓣ508/487-8200. This cute fishing shack has been converted into a fine dining outpost with just 37 seats and an open kitchen. The menu features French/American fusion cuisine; desserts and breakfast are also spectacular.

Lobster Pot 321 Commercial St ⓣ508/487-0842. Its landmark neon sign is like a beacon for those who come from far and wide for the ultra-fresh crustaceans. Affordable and family-oriented, with a great outdoor deck. Closed Dec–March.

Napi's 7 Freeman St ⓣ508/487-1145. Popular dishes at this art-strewn spot include pastas and its celebrated soups: thick Portuguese fish stews and clam chowders (from $5.95). They have a less expensive menu on week nights.

Portuguese Bakery 299 Commercial St ⓣ508/487-1803. This old standby is the place to come for cheap baked goods, particularly the tasty fried *rabanada*, akin to portable French toast.

Nightlife and entertainment

Each weekend, boatloads of revellers from the mainland seek out P-Town's notoriously wild **nightlife**. Heavily geared towards a **gay** clientele, resulting in ubiquitous tea dances, drag shows and video bars, some establishments have terrific waterfront locations and terraces to match, making them ideal spots to sit out with a drink at sunset.

Atlantic House 6 Masonic Place, behind Commercial St ⓣ508/487-3821. The "A-House" – a dark drinking hole favoured by Tennessee Williams and Eugene O'Neill – is now a trendy gay club and bar.

Boatslip 161 Commercial St ⓣ508/487-1669. The tea dances at this resort are legendary (every afternoon from 4–7pm); you can either dance away on a long wooden deck overlooking the water, or cruise inside under a disco ball and flashing lights.

Crown and Anchor 247 Commercial St ⓣ508/487-1430, ⓦwww.onlyatthecrown.com. A massive complex housing several bars, including *The Vault*, a leather bar, *Wave*, a video-karaoke bar, and *Paramount*, the town's largest nightclub.

Martha's Vineyard

The largest offshore island in New England, twenty-mile-long **MARTHA'S VINEYARD** encompasses more physical variety than Nantucket, with hills and pastures providing scenic counterpoints to the beaches and wild, windswept moors on the separate island of **Chappaquiddick**.

Martha's Vineyard's most genteel town is **Edgartown**, all prim and proper with its freshly painted, white clapboard colonial homes, museums and manicured gardens. The other main settlement, **Vineyard Haven**, is more commercial and one of the island's ferry ports. **Oak Bluffs**, in between the two (and the other docking point for ferries), has an array of whimsical wooden gingerbread cottages and inviting eateries. Be aware of island terminology: heading "Up-Island" takes you southwest to the cliffs at **Aquinnah** (formerly known as Gay Head); conversely, "Down-Island" refers to the triumvirate of easterly towns mentioned above.

The island has an increasingly frequent and reliable **bus** system that connects the main towns and villages, from around 7am to 12.45am daily (ⓣ508/639-9440, ⓦwww.vineyardtransit.com); tickets cost $1 per town, one way, or $7 per day. Bringing a car over is expensive and generally pointless, as the island is jam-packed with vehicles throughout the summer, and you can easily get around by bus or **bike**; pick one up at the rental places lined up by the ferry dock ($25/day). The best bike ride is along the State Beach Park between Oak Bluffs and Edgartown, with the dunes to one side and marshy Sengekontacket Pond to the other; purpose-built cycle routes continue to the youth hostel at West Tisbury.

Trips around the west side of the island are decidedly bucolic, with nary a peep of the water beyond the rolling hills and private estates; however, you do eventually come to the **lighthouse** at **Aquinnah**, where the multicoloured clay was once the main source of paint for the island's houses – now, anyone caught removing any clay faces a sizeable fine. From Moshup beach below, you can get great views of this spectacular formation.

Martha's Vineyard is clustered with beautiful **beaches**. Highlights include the secluded, gorgeous Wasque, at the end of Wasque Road in Chappaquiddick, and South Beach, at the end of Katama Road south of Edgartown, known for its "good waves and good bodies". The gentle State Beach, along Beach Road between Oak Bluffs and Edgartown, is more family-oriented.

Ferries to Martha's Vineyard and Nantucket

Unless otherwise specified, all the **ferries** below run several times daily in midsummer (mid-June to mid-Sept). Most have fewer services from May to mid-June, and between mid-September and October. There is at least a skeleton service to each island year-round, though not on all routes. To discourage clogging of the roads, round-trip costs for cars are prohibitively high in the peak season (mid-May to mid-Sept; Woods Hole ferry only), while costs for bikes are just $6 each way. Be sure to call in advance for reservations as spaces do sell out.

To Martha's Vineyard

Falmouth to Oak Bluffs (about 35min): pedestrians, bikes ($6) or kayaks ($12) only; $18 return (cash or cheque only); the *Island Queen* ferry ⓣ508/548-4800, ⓦwww.islandqueen.com.

Falmouth to Edgartown (1hr): pedestrians only; $50 return; Falmouth Ferry Service ⓣ508/548-9400, ⓦwww.falmouthferry.com.

Falmouth to Vineyard Haven (45min): pedestrians only; $25 return; Falmouth Ferry Service ⓣ508/548-9400, ⓦwww.falmouthferry.com.

Hyannis to Oak Bluffs (about 1hr 35min; fast ferry about 55min): pedestrians only; $43 return, fast ferry $69 return; Hy-Line ⓣ1-800/492-8082, ⓦwww.hy-linecruises.com.

New Bedford to Oak Bluffs or Vineyard Haven (1hr): pedestrians only; $70 return; New England Fast Ferry ⓣ1-866/683-3779, ⓦwww.nefastferry.com.

Quonset Point, Rhode Island, to Oak Bluffs (1hr 30min): pedestrians only; $69 return; Vineyard Fast Ferry (ⓣ401/295-4040, ⓦwww.vineyardfastferry.com). Shuttles provided to Kingston Amtrak train station ($18) and Providence airport ($15).

Woods Hole to Vineyard Haven and Oak Bluffs (45min): pedestrians $15 return; May–Oct vehicles $135 return; off-season vehicles $85 return; Steamship Authority ⓣ508/477-8600, ⓦwww.steamshipauthority.com.

To Nantucket

From Hyannis: pedestrians $33 return (2hr journey); pedestrians $65 return (1hr journey); May–Oct vehicles $380 return; off-season vehicles $260 return; Steamship Authority ⓣ508/477-8600 for auto reservations, ⓣ508/495-3278 for pedestrians, ⓦwww.steamshipauthority.com. Also Hy-Line Cruises, pedestrians only; 2hr journey $43 return; 1hr journey $75 return; ⓣ1-800/492-8082, ⓦwww.hy-linecruises.com.

In summer, the Hy-Line ferry company also runs a **connecting service** between Oak Bluffs, Martha's Vineyard and Nantucket (one departure daily; pedestrians only; $34 one-way; ⓣ1-800/492-8082). The trip takes 1hr 10min.

Accommodation

If accommodation is booked up, as is very likely, the main **Chamber of Commerce** office, at 24 Beach Rd in Vineyard Haven (Mon–Fri 9am–5pm, Sat 10am–4pm; ⓣ508/693-0085, ⓦwww.mvy.com), may be able to help. There is a **campground** in Vineyard Haven, at 569 Edgartown Rd (May–Oct; ⓣ508/693-3772, ⓦwww.campmv.com); tent pitches cost $48 per day for two people and include water and electricity hook-ups.

Crocker House Inn 12 Crocker Ave, Vineyard Haven ⓣ1-800/772-0206, ⓦwww.crockerhouseinn.com. Elegant and accommodating, the *Crocker House* features pretty rooms, free wi-fi, good proximity to shops and lots of home-made goodies. ❾

HI-Martha's Vineyard 525 Edgartown–West Tisbury Rd ⓣ508/693-2665, ⓦcapecod.hiusa.org. A cheerful hostel in an appealing setting at the forest's edge and away from town; near the island's main bike path, and right on the bus route. Free wi-fi. Open April to mid-Nov. Dorm beds $29–39 a night.

Menemsha Inn & Cottages and Beach Plum Inn North Rd, Menemsha ⓣ508/645-9454 or 1-800/901-2087, ⓦwww.menemshainn.com and ⓦwww.beachpluminn.com. These adjacent properties are beautifully maintained. Within walking distance of the Menemsha beach, they also include private beach access. ❾

Nashua House Hotel 30 Kennebec Ave, Edgartown ⓣ508/693-0043, ⓦwww.nashuahouse.com. Small rooms, some with shared baths, but this friendly, central hotel is an easy walk from the ferry, and with rates starting at $69 in low season, it's one of the less expensive choices on the island. It can get loud at night. ❸–❽

Oak Bluffs Inn 64 Circuit Ave, Oak Bluffs ⓣ508/693-7171, ⓦwww.oakbluffsinn.com. One of the most alluring hotels on the island, with a convenient location, cosy, clean Victorian-style rooms, wi-fi, wide porch, free cookies and a great host. ❽–❾

The Winnetu Inn & Resort South Beach, south of Edgartown ⓣ508/627-4747, ⓦwww.winnetu.com. This family-friendly resort hotel is just a short walk from a private stretch of South Beach, but you really need a car to stay here; very well-appointed rooms, many with kitchenettes. ❽–❾

Eating and drinking

Eating is one of the principal pleasures of Martha's Vineyard; fresh lobster, quahogs (large clams) and fresh fish are particularly abundant. Only in Edgartown and Oak Bluffs can you order alcohol with meals, but you can bring your own elsewhere.

ArtCliff Diner 39 Beach Rd, Vineyard Haven ⓣ508/693-1224. Perfect for a pre-ferry send-off breakfast with the likes of almond-crusted French toast and chorizo, egg and pepperjack sandwiches. Open 7am–2pm, closed Wed.

The Bite 29 Basin Rd, Menemsha ⓣ508/645-9239. Roadside, seaside nirvana. Some of the juiciest fried belly clams you'll ever taste (from $13.95), served up in a tiny seafood shack. Good chowder, too. Cash only.

The Black Dog Bakery 11 Water St, Vineyard Haven ⓣ508/693-4786. Skip the overrated *Black Dog Tavern* next door and stock up on delicious muffins and breads for the ferry ride back.

Chilmark Chocolates 19 State Rd, Chilmark ⓣ508/645-3013. People line up for *Chilmark's* island-grown berries dipped in unbelievably tasty organic chocolate. Closed Mon, Tues, Wed.

Chilmark Store 7 State Rd, Chilmark ⓣ508/645-3739. Another island institution, but not for sweets or seafood; lines form here for the perfectly fired slices of pizza ($3.95), which come in four flavours with freshly made olive oil and pesto bases – try the wholewheat.

Détente Nevin Square, off Winter St (between N Water St and N Summer St), Edgartown ⓣ508/627-8810. Of the fancier restaurants on the island, this one's your best bet for a great dinner. Seasonal menus showcase local ingredients, ranging from halibut to lamb shank.

Larsen's Fish Market 56 Basin Rd, Menemsha ⓣ508/645-2680. For about $20 you can pick out your very own lobster and then eat it on low-key flats overlooking the harbour. Good lobster rolls, too ($11).

Offshore Ale Company 30 Kennebec Ave, Oak Bluffs ⓣ508/693-2626. Local brewpub with wooden booths, toss-on-the-floor peanut shells and lots of live shows. If you're there at night, be sure to stop by *Back Door Donuts* (via the "back door" of *Martha's Vineyard Gourmet Café* (ⓣ508/693-3688; daily 9pm–12.30am) for one of its life-changing apple fritters or warm honey-dipped donuts – it's a Martha's Vineyard must-do.

Nantucket

The thirty-mile, two-hour sea crossing to **NANTUCKET** may not be an ocean odyssey, but it does set the "Little Gray Lady" apart from her larger, shore-hugging sister, Martha. Nantucket's smaller size adds to its palpable sense of identity, as does the architecture; the "gray" epithet refers not only to the winter fogs, but to the austere grey clapboard and shingle applied uniformly to buildings across the island.

The tiny cobbled carriageways of **Nantucket Town** itself, once one of the largest cities in Massachusetts, were frozen in time by economic decline 150 years ago. Today, this area of delightful old restored houses – the town has more buildings on the National Register of Historic Places than Boston – is very much the island hub. Surrounding the ferry exit are a plethora of bike rental places and tour companies.

Straight Wharf leads directly onto **Main Street**, with its shops and restaurants; the **information office** – which has a daily list of accommodation vacancies, but doesn't make reservations – is nearby at 25 Federal St (April–Dec 9am–6pm; Jan–March Mon–Sat till 5pm; ⓣ508/228-0925, ⓦwww.nantucket.net). The **Chamber of Commerce**, Zero Main St, 2/F (Mon–Fri 9am–5pm; ⓣ508/228-1700, ⓦwww.nantucketchamber.org), carries the best range of island information.

The excellent **Whaling Museum**, 13 Broad St, at the head of Steamboat Wharf (late May to mid-Oct daily 10am–5pm; $17; ⓣ508/228-1894, ⓦwww.nha.org), houses an outstanding collection of seafaring exotica, including a gallery of delicately engraved scrimshaw and a 46ft sperm whale skeleton that washed ashore in 1998. Look for the rotted tooth on its jaw; officials believe a tooth infection brought on the whale's demise.

Beyond the town, Nantucket remains surprisingly wild, a mixture of moors, marshes and heathland, though the main draw remains its untrammelled sandy **beaches**. One of the best can be found at **Siaconset** (pronounced 'Sconset'), seven flat, bike-friendly miles east of the town, where venerable cottages stand literally encrusted with salt; meander back across the heaths and moorland via Polpis Road. **Bikes** can be rented from Young's Bicycle Shop, 6 Broad St (around $25 for a full day, can also be rented by the half-day; ⓣ508/228-1151). **Buses** also link Nantucket Town and 'Sconset: NRTA (ⓣ508/228-7025) runs shuttles from late May through to early October ($2 one way).

Accommodation

But for the youth hostel, accommodation on Nantucket is expensive; most **B&Bs** and **guesthouses** charge well over $200 in the summer.

HI-Nantucket Surfside Beach 31 Western Ave ⓣ508/228-0433, ⓦcapecod.hiusa.org. Dorm beds ($29–39 a night) a stone's throw from Surfside Beach, just over three miles south of Nantucket town. Open mid-May to Sept.

Martin House Inn 61 Centre St ⓣ508/228-0678, ⓦwww.martinhouseinn.com. Thirteen lovely rooms (some for singles) offer good value in this 1803 seaman's house; close to shops and ferries. ❺–❾

Union Street Inn 7 Union St ⓣ888/517-0707, ⓦwww.unioninn.com. This luxurious B&B boasts a central location, hearty breakfasts and dazzling rooms, with stylish rugs, drapes and patterned wallpaper – it's pricey, and is thus much better value off-season. ❾

Veranda House 3 Step Lane ⓣ508/228-0695, ⓦwww.theverandahouse.com. This boutique hotel adds a refreshingly contemporary take on the island's traditional Victorian-style B&Bs; rooms are stylishly designed, most with harbour views and come with a bevy of luxurious amenities (Frette linens, wi-fi, flat-screen TVs and Simon Pearce lamps). ❾

Eating and drinking

Nantucket abounds in first-rate **restaurants**, most of them located in or around Nantucket Town. Dinner can be exceptionally expensive, however, easily costing $30 to $40 for an entree. You'll find a bevy of cheaper takeaway options on Broad Street near Steamboat Wharf.

Black Eyed Susan's 10 India St ⓣ508/325-0308. Beloved little brunch spot with inventive egg scrambles and delectable buttermilk pancakes. Get there early to avoid a long line. Cash only.

Chicken Box 16 Dave St ⓣ508/228-9717. Every summer night, people of all stripes pack into "the Box" for great live shows and casual drinking environs. Shuffleboard and pool tables, too. Cash only; ATM inside.

Downyflake 18 Sparks Ave ⓣ508/228-4533. The island's best diner, a bit out of the way on the edge of town, but worth a visit for the reasonably-priced plates of comfort food and the freshly made donuts (get them to go).

Juice Bar 12 Broad St ⓣ508/228-5799. The fresh juices are the healthiest options on offer at this small takeaway shop, but in summer expect long lines for the luscious home-made ice cream (try "crantucket"), served in cups or giant waffle cones ($3.30–4.50).

Sayle's Seafood 99 Washington St Extension ⓣ508/228-4599. Breezy, very casual seafood shack serving chowder ($3.25), fried shellfish, fresh lobster and fried clams (at market prices) – get it to go for a picnic or munch on the veranda. **Something Natural** 50 Cliff Rd ⓣ508/228-0504. Bulging sandwiches, enormous cookies; this charming deli is a great stopover on the way to Madaket beach. Alternatively, linger outside on one of their readily available picnic blankets.

Central and western Massachusetts

The 150 miles of Massachusetts that stretch inland to the west of Boston are known best to vacationers for the beautiful **Berkshires,** which host the celebrated **Tanglewood** summer music festival and boast museum-filled towns such as **North Adams** and **Williamstown** – both in the far northwest corner of the state, at the end of the incredibly scenic **Mohawk Trail**. **Amherst** and **Northampton** are stimulating college towns in the verdant **Pioneer Valley**, with all the cafés, restaurants and bookstores you could want.

Amherst and Northampton

North of Springfield, the Pioneer Valley is a verdant corridor created by the Connecticut River, home to the college towns of **AMHERST** and **NORTHAMPTON**, both good places to kick back for a few days, hang out in cafés, and browse bookstores in one of New England's most liberal and progressive areas.

Amtrak **trains** stop in Amherst at 13 Railroad St, while you can catch Peter Pan Trailways **buses** at 1 Roundhouse Plaza in Northampton (ⓣ1-800/343-9999) and at Amherst Books at 8 Main St in Amherst (ⓣ1-800/343-9999). Good **accommodation** is available at the *Allen House Victorian Inn*, 599 Main St, Amherst (ⓣ413/253-5000, ⓦwww.allenhouse.com; ❹–❼), a quintessentially New England inn. Among the numerous places to **eat**, *Sylvester's*, 111 Pleasant St (ⓣ413/586-5343), serves up tasty fare, including delightful breakfast treats such as banana-bread, French toast and waffles, while *Herrell's Ice Cream*, 8 Old South St (ⓣ413/586-9700) is the home base of a small but irresistible chain of ice-cream stores. *Hangar Pub and Grill*, 55 University Drive, Amherst (ⓣ413/549-9464), serves the best wings around in a small, fun, but rather divey college bar.

The Berkshires

A rich cultural history, world-class summer arts festivals and a bucolic landscape of forests and verdant hills make the **Berkshires**, at the extreme western edge of Massachusetts, ideal for warm weather exploration.

While you're in the area, try to visit the excellent **Berkshire Visitors Bureau**, 3 Hoosac St (Rte-8) in Adams (Mon–Fri 8.30am–5pm; ⓣ413/743-4500, ⓦwww.berkshires.org), the best source for information on the area.

Old Sturbridge Village

Halfway between Worcester and Springfield on US-20, near the junction of I-90 and I-84, the restored and reconstructed **Old Sturbridge Village** (April to late Oct daily 9.30am–5pm, late Oct to March Tues–Sun till 4pm; $20; ⓣ508/347-3362 or 1-800/SEE-1830, ⓦwww.osv.org), made up of preserved buildings brought from all over the region, gives a somewhat idealized but engaging portrait of a small New England town of the 1830s. Costumed interpreters act out roles – working in blacksmiths' shops, planting and harvesting vegetables, tending cows, and the like – but they pull it off in an unusually convincing manner. The 200-acre site itself, with mature trees, ponds and dirt footpaths, is very pretty, and worth a half-day visit.

The Mohawk Trail: North Adams and Williamstown

In the northwest corner of the region, the **Mohawk Trail** passes through **NORTH ADAMS** and **WILLIAMSTOWN**, following the scenic route the Native Americans used to travel between the valleys of the Connecticut and Hudson rivers. North Adams is home to the glorious **Mass MoCA** (Massachusetts Museum of Contemporary Art), 1040 Mass MoCA Way (July & Aug daily 10am–6pm; Sept–June Mon & Wed–Sun (closed Tues) 11am–5pm; $15; ⓣ413/662-2111, ⓦwww.massmoca.org), a sprawling, neo-funhouse collection of modern art installations, contemporary videos and upside-down trees gathered in a captivating old mill site. Williamstown has two worthy art museums: the highlight of the **Sterling and Francine Clark Art Institute**, 225 South St (Tues–Sun 10am–5pm, July & Aug daily till 5pm; $12.50 June–Oct, rest of year free; ⓣ413/458-2303, ⓦwww.clarkart.edu), is the thirty-strong collection of Renoir paintings, while the **Williams College Museum of Art**, 15 Lawrence Hall Drive (Tues–Sat 10am–5pm, Sun 1–5pm; free; ⓣ413/597-2429, ⓦwww.wcma.org), has good exhibits of ancient Middle Eastern and modern American art in a beautiful Neoclassical space. The ultramodern *Porches Inn*, 231 River St, right around the corner from Mass MoCA (ⓣ413/664-0400, ⓦwww.porches.com; ❼–❾), is *the* place to **stay** in the area, with stylish rooms in a converted rowhouse formerly occupied by mill workers. The *Topia Inn*, at 10 Pleasant St in Adams (right by the visitor's bureau) has eight artful, eco-friendly rooms, each one designed by an individual of a creative persuasion, such as an artist, cinematographer or dancer (ⓣ413/664-0400, ⓦtopiainn.com; ❼–❽). For **food**, head to *Mezze*, at 16 Water St in Williamstown (ⓣ413/458-0123), for outstanding New American flavours in a gracious, airy space.

Stockbridge

STOCKBRIDGE, just south of I-90 and fifty miles west of Springfield, looks like the archetypal New England small town (most of all when there's snow on the ground). This is probably due in part to the artist **Norman Rockwell**, who lived here for 25 years until his death in 1978. Many of his *Saturday Evening Post* covers, whose sentimentality was shaped by an intelligent wit, featured the town; a collection of covers can be seen at the **museum** at no. 9 Rte-183 (May–Oct daily 10am–5pm; Nov–April Mon–Fri till 4pm, Sat & Sun till 5pm; $15; ⓣ413/298-4100, ⓦwww.nrm.org). Some of the tour guides modelled for Rockwell as children and recall that for every few minutes they managed to hold still he'd slip them a coin from his large pile of nickels.

Magnificent houses in the hills around Stockbridge include **Chesterwood**, half a mile south of the Norman Rockwell Museum at 4 Williamsville Rd (May–Oct daily 10am–5pm; $15; ⓣ413/298-3579, ⓦwww.chesterwood.org), the luxurious home and studio of Daniel Chester French, sculptor of the Lincoln Memorial, and **Naumkeag**, on Prospect Hill Road, Rte-7 (late May to mid-Oct daily 10am–5pm; $15; ⓣ413/298-3239), which was the first modernist garden estate in the country.

The slightly frou-frou *Red Lion Inn* is one of the grander edifices on Main Street (ⓣ413/298-5545, ⓦwww.redlioninn.com; ❺–❼); their **restaurant** has big portions of reliable American cuisine, with standout burgers and steaks, in a charming old dining room with a fireplace, while the rooms (some with shared baths) are charmingly old-fashioned and furnished with antiques and vintage wallpaper.

Lenox and around

Roughly five miles north of Stockbridge on US-7, well-heeled tourists flock to **LENOX** each year for the summer season of the Boston Symphony Orchestra at **Tanglewood**, 297 West St (for ticket info, call ⓣ413/637-1666 or visit ⓦwww.bso.org). Open-air orchestral concerts are held on weekends from July to late

August, with chamber music and recitals given on other days; covered seats are pricey and often hard to get, but you can sit and picnic on the lush lawns for an admission fee of around $17. Some midweek rehearsals are also open to the public, and there's a **jazz** festival on Labor Day weekend (the first weekend of Sept). On Rte-20 between Becket and Lee, **Jacob's Pillow** (June–Aug; ⓣ413/243-0745, ⓦwww.jacobspillow.org) puts on one of the best contemporary dance festivals in the country.

Further north on US-7, **Arrowhead** (late May to Oct daily 9.30am–4pm; $12; ⓣ413/442-1793, ⓦwww.mobydick.org), in Pittsfield, was Herman Melville's home while he wrote *Moby Dick*; declining sales of his books eventually forced him to sell his house and move to New York. The **Hancock Shaker Village**, five miles west of Pittsfield (daily: April–Oct 10am–5pm; $17, ⓣ413/443-0188, ⓦwww.hancockshakervillage.org), was a going concern from 1783 to 1960. Its legacy includes the large dwelling-place, in which almost one hundred people slept and ate, and a round stone barn for their cattle. You can **stay** in total luxury at *Blantyre*, Blantyre Road (ⓣ413/637-3556, ⓦwww.blantyre.com; ⑨), one of the country's most plush (and expensive) resorts. *Hampton Terrace*, 91 Walker St (ⓣ1-800/203-0656, ⓦwww.hamptonterrace.com; ⑧) was originally the site of Lenox's blacksmith, then its twentieth-century owners were featured in the *Age of Innocence* (Edith Wharton lived next door); it currently houses a posh 14-room B&B. For **food**, head over to *Church Street Café,* 65 Church St in Lenox (ⓣ413/637-2745) for standout New England fare, or linger over a martini at the atmospheric *Bistro Zinc*, around the corner at 56 Church St (ⓣ413/637-8800). *Berkshire Bagel*, 18 Franklin St, just off Rte-7A (ⓣ413/637-1500) is a rare budget option in the centre of town, with a huge range of bagels and cream cheese spreads ($2–5).

Rhode Island

A mere 48 miles long by 37 miles wide, **RHODE ISLAND** is the smallest state in the Union, yet it had a disproportionately large influence on national life: it enacted the first law against slavery in North America; it was the first of the thirteen colonies to declare independence from Britain; it helped to foster the nation's tradition of religious freedom; and it also saw the beginning of the **Industrial Revolution** in America. Today, Rhode Island is a prime tourist destination, boasting nearly four dozen National Historic Landmarks and four hundred miles of spectacular coastline.

Over thirty tiny islands make up the state, including Hope, Despair and the bay's largest, Rhode Island (also known by its Native American name "Aquidneck"), which gives the state its name. **Narragansett Bay** has long been a determining factor in Rhode Island's economic development and strategic military importance, as the **Ocean State** developed through sea trade, whaling and smuggling before shifting to manufacturing in the nineteenth century. Today, the state's principal destinations are its two original ports: the colonial college town of **Providence**, and well-heeled **Newport**, yachting capital of the world, with lavish mansions along its gorgeous shores.

Providence

Spread across seven hills on the Providence and Seekonk rivers, **PROVIDENCE** was Rhode Island's first settlement, founded in 1636 "in commemoration of God's providence" on land granted to Roger Williams by the Narragansett Indians.

The state's capital since 1901, Providence is today one of New England's three largest cities. Ivy League **Brown University** and the **Rhode Island School of Design** (RISD, or "Rizdee") give the place a certain cultural pizazz, while the many original colonial homes on **Benefit Street** and around **College Hill** emanate a charming historic feel. The city's ethnic diversity is showcased west of downtown by the large Italian community on **Federal Hill**, with bustling restaurants and traditional appeal.

Arrival, information and city transport

T.F. Green Airport in Warwick, nine miles south of Providence, connects to all major US cities. The **Amtrak station** (☎1-800/USA-RAIL) is in a domed building at 100 Gaspee St; here you can also catch the commuter rail to Boston (1hr; ☎617/222-3200). Greyhound (☎1-800/231-2222) and Peter Pan (☎1-888/343-9999) **buses** stop downtown at the Kennedy Plaza hub.

The well-stocked **Visitors' Center**, in the rotunda lobby of the Rhode Island Convention Center, 1 Sabin St (Mon–Sat 9am–5pm; ☎401/751-1177 or

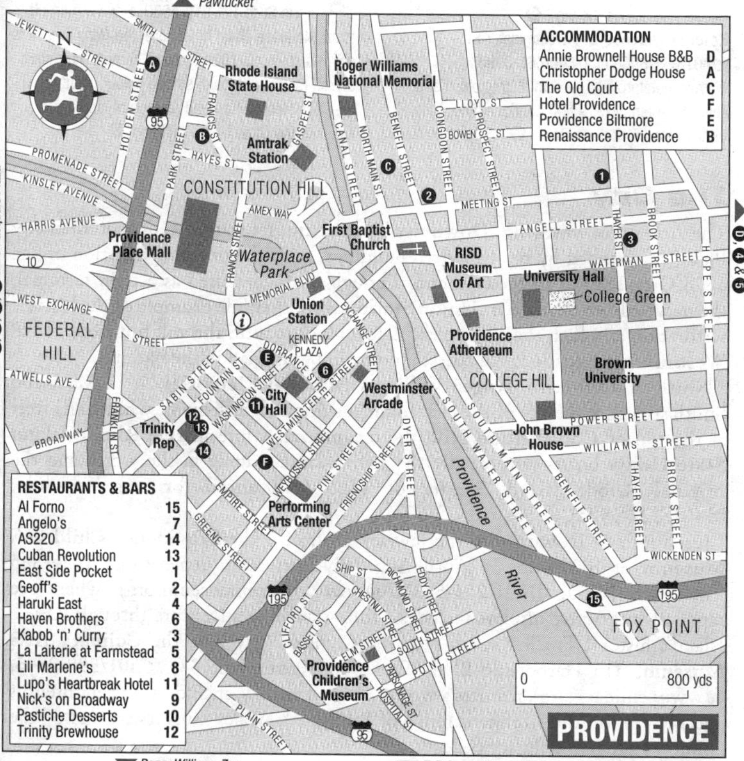

1-800/233-1636), provides maps and brochures. The **Rhode Island Historical Society**, 110 Benevolent St (Ⓣ401/331-8575, Ⓦwww.rihs.org) leads walking tours through the city.

There is good **bus transport** within the city, provided by RIPTA ($1.75, tickets sold on board; Ⓣ401/781-9400, Ⓦwww.ripta.com), which has a hub at Kennedy Plaza.

Accommodation

Downtown Providence is largely geared to the business traveller and has few budget rooms, but **B&Bs** are a viable option. Motorists can take advantage of the mid-priced **motels** along I-95 north towards Pawtucket, and south near the airport at Warwick.

Annie Brownell House B&B 400 Angell St Ⓣ401/454-2934, Ⓦwww.anniebrownellhouse.com. A handful of guest rooms in an 1899 Colonial Revival house near Thayer St. Full hot breakfasts and a nice pup on the premises. ❺

Christopher Dodge House 11 West Park St Ⓣ401/351-6111, Ⓦwww.providence-hotel.com. Sunny, eight-room Italianate B&B with early American reproduction furniture and plenty of home-made cookies on offer. Expect a three-floor walk up. They also run the *Mowry-Nicholson House*, just across the way. ❻

Hotel Providence 311 Westminster St Ⓣ401/861-8000 or 1-800/861-8990, Ⓦwww.hotelprovidence.com. Eighty plush and colourful rooms in RI's first boutique hotel, with a trendy restaurant downstairs. ❽

The Old Court 144 Benefit St Ⓣ401/751-2002, Ⓦwww.oldcourt.com. Appealing ten-room Victorian B&B in an old rectory near RISD. ❻–❽

Providence Biltmore 11 Dorrance St Ⓣ401/421-0700 or 1-800/294-7709, Ⓦwww.providencebiltmore.com. Although the *Biltmore's* lobby looks like a set for the *Godfather*, the rooms in this 1922 Providence landmark are plush, contemporary and recently renovated. Here you'll find Old World charm and good rates in the heart of downtown. ❻

Renaissance Providence 5 Avenue of the Arts St Ⓣ401/919-5000, Ⓦwww.marriott.com. No blasé chain hotel here, the *Renaissance* is set in a spacious 1929 Masonic Temple that offers stylish rooms with bold, striped colour palettes, an on-site fitness centre and restaurant, and great views of the State House building. ❼

The City

The hub of downtown (“**Downcity**”) is the transportation centre at Kennedy Plaza, surrounded by new, modern buildings, with the notable exception of the 1878 **City Hall** at its western end. Though no longer used as a train terminal, the nearby 1898 Beaux Arts **Union Station** is another fine example of the historic restoration at which the city excels. A few blocks south, the still functional 1828 **Westminster Arcade** is the oldest indoor shopping mall in the nation.

North of Downcity, **Roger Williams National Memorial**, at N Main and Smith streets, is the site of the city-founder's original settlement, while to its west at the top of **Constitution Hill**, the magnificent white-marble **Rhode Island State House** boasts purportedly the fourth-largest dome in the world and the original Rhode Island Charter of 1663 (call ahead for tour schedule; Ⓣ401/222-3983).

Just south of Downcity in the Jewelry District is the **Providence Children's Museum**, at 100 South St (April–Aug daily 9am–6pm, Sept–March Tues–Sun 9am–6pm; $8.50; Ⓣ401/273-5437, Ⓦwww.childrenmuseum.org), where the range of interactive displays includes a time-travelling adventure through Rhode Island's history. Further south near the Cranston city line, the **Culinary Arts Museum**, 315 Harborside Blvd (Tues–Sun 10am–5pm; $7; Ⓣ401/598-2805, Ⓦwww.culinary.org), features a wealth of food history, including ancient utensils and recipes, on the satellite campus of Johnson & Wales University, one of the country's premier culinary colleges.

Two miles south of downtown, the 430-acre **Roger Williams Park** is home to the marvellous **Roger Williams Zoo**, the third oldest zoo in the country with 130 species of animals and imaginative exhibits (daily 9am–4pm; $12; ⓣ401/785-3510, ⓦwww.rogerwilliamsparkzoo.org).

College Hill and Federal Hill

Across the river from Downcity, laidback **College Hill** is an attractive district of colonial buildings and museums. The white clapboard **First Baptist Meeting House**, at the foot of the hill at 75 N Main St, dates from 1638, and testifies to the state's origins as a "lively experiment" in religious freedom. Nearby **Benefit Street** is Providence's "**mile of history**", lined with beautifully restored former homes of merchants and sea captains. The street was once a dirt path leading to graveyards until it was improved in the nineteenth century for the "benefit of the people of Providence" – hence its name. One of the few homes open to the public, the elegant **John Brown House**, 52 Power St, at Benefit Street (call for tours; $8; ⓣ401/273-7507), was the first house built on the hill and home to the patriot and entrepreneur (also uncle to the man the university is named after) who prospered from the slave trade and trade with China.

The leafy, historic campus of Ivy League **Brown University** sets the tone for this three-centuries-old district; for free tours, contact the admissions office, 45 Prospect St (ⓣ401/863-2378, ⓦwww.brown.edu). In the same area, the smaller RISD campus is home to the **RISD Museum of Art**, 224 Benefit St (Tues–Sun 10am–5pm; $10; ⓣ401/454-6500, ⓦwww.risd.edu), featuring 45 galleries, including superb European and American decorative arts collections and an outstanding Asian collection with more than six hundred Japanese woodblock prints and a Heian Buddha. Also here, the Greek Revival **Providence Athenaeum**, 251 Benefit St (Mon–Thurs 9am–7pm, Fri & Sat till 5pm, Sun 1–5pm; closed Sun in summer; free; ⓣ401/421-6970, ⓦwww.providenceathenaeum.org) is one of America's oldest libraries, where Edgar Allan Poe once courted Sarah Whitman. East and south of College Hill, **Thayer** and **Wickenden streets** buzz with an assortment of bookstores and cafés.

Federal Hill, west of Downcity, is Providence's **Little Italy**, greeting visitors with the traditional symbol of welcome, a bronze pine cone, on the entrance arch on Atwells Avenue; note the avenue's median line, a stripe of red, white and green that's a charming homage to the Italian flag. This is one of the friendliest areas in the city, alive with cafés, delis, bakeries and bars, and with a lively piazza around the Italianate fountain in **DePasquale Square** (in DePasquale Plaza).

Eating

Providence boasts excellent **food** options. **Thayer Street** is lined with inexpensive eateries popular with students, while nearby **Wickenden Street** has a more mature clientele. Or head to **Federal Hill**, where you can find great Italian food at reasonable prices. Also, keep an eye out for coffee milk (milk flavoured with coffee syrup) or Del's Lemonade (a slushy frozen lemonade), two regional Rhode Island treats.

Al Forno 577 S Main St ⓣ401/273-9760. Famed wood-grilled pizzas, meats and other treats at one of the best restaurants in the state (mains hover around $30). Dinner only, closed Sun & Mon.

Angelo's 141 Atwells Ave ⓣ401/621-8171. A staple in Federal Hill since 1924, with homey, no-frills, affordable Italian cooking.

East Side Pocket 278 Thayer St ⓣ401/453-1100. Bulging falafel sandwiches ($5) and other Middle Eastern "pockets" served hot, fresh and cheap at this beloved student standby.

Geoff's 163 Benefit St ⓣ401/751-2248. A quirky, casual sandwich spot with an enormous menu of ingenious bread-and-filling combinations, many with humorous names; try the "Chicken George": chicken salad, bacon, melted Swiss, hot spinach and Shedd's sauce ($7.49).

Haruki East 172 Wayland Ave ⓣ401/223-0332. Known as one of the best Japanese places around, with mid-priced, finely presented dishes.

Haven Brothers Diner-on-wheels since 1893, with classic hot dogs, burgers and fries. Parked outside City Hall every night 4.30pm–5am.

Kabob 'n'Curry 261 Thayer St ⓣ401/273-8844. Above-average Indian meals on lively Thayer St, with fun twists like "naninis" ($6–8).

La Laiterie at Farmstead 184 Wayland Ave ⓣ401/274-7177. Locally sourced, bistro-style dinners in a rustic-yet-chic little dining room adjacent to a glorious cheese shop.

Nick's on Broadway 500 Broadway ⓣ401/421-0286. A fair hike from anything else (it's in the West End), brunch lovers flock to *Nick's* for his best-in-town black beans and eggs ($10) and brioche French toast ($8). Also open for lunch and dinner; closed Mon and Tues.

Pastiche Desserts 92 Spruce St ⓣ401/861-5190. Exquisite cakes, cookies and pastries served from an adorable little blue house in Federal Hill.

Nightlife and entertainment

Providence has a rich and varied **performing arts** and **film** scene. The Avon Rep Cinema at 260 Thayer St (ⓣ401/421-3315) shows independent and art **films**, as does the love-seat-filled Cable Car Cinema at 204 S Main St (ⓣ401/272-3970). In Downcity, **Trinity Rep**, 201 Washington St (ⓣ401/351-4242, ⓦwww.trinityrep.com) is one of America's foremost regional theatres, while the **Providence Performing Arts Center**, 220 Weybosset St (ⓣ401/421-2787, ⓦwww.ppacri.org), hosts **musicals** in a grand old Art Deco movie house. On Gallery Night (March–Nov, third Thurs of the month, 5–9pm; ⓣ401/490-2042, ⓦwww.gallerynight.info), free Art Buses leave from the Regency Plaza (diagonally opposite the rear of the library) and stop along many of the city's **galleries** and museums, where admission is also free for the evening.

In the warmer months, the unusual event known as **WaterFire** (several times a month, May–Oct; ⓦwww.waterfire.org) sees nearly one hundred small bonfires set at sunset in the centre of the Providence River starting at Waterplace Park, tended by gondoliers and accompanied by rousing music. Complete entertainment listings can be found in the free weekly *Providence Phoenix* and the *Providence Journal*'s Thursday edition.

The city's **nightlife** bustles around Empire and Washington streets, south of Kennedy Plaza in Downcity, and along **Thayer Street** near Brown University during term-time.

AS220 115 Empire St ⓣ401/831-9327. Hip, lively, anti-establishment venue that operates as a café/bar/gallery, showcasing vibrant local art and diverse nightly performances.

Cuban Revolution 50 Aborn St ⓣ401/331-8829. Cuban beer and tropical cocktails amid candlelight and revolutionary posters of Marilyn Monroe and Malcolm X; you can also munch on assorted tapas, sushi and Che fries while vintage fans spin overhead.

Lili Marlene's 422 Atwells Ave ⓣ401/751-4996. Dark, spacious yet intimate venue with burgundy

Block Island

Twelve miles off Rhode Island's southern coast, Block Island makes a great detour from the mainland. Somehow, this little gem continues to preserve its melancholy, seductive charm: inhabited by only nine hundred year-round residents, it's a small bump of gently rolling hills and broad expanses of moorland, surrounded by a sometimes angry sea. The island bustles with tourist activity in the summertime, but attracts little of the accompanying scene; there are plenty of free beaches in addition to thirty miles of walking trails. To get here, hop on the ferry at Fort Adams State Park in Newport ($10.85; 2hr trip; ⓣ401/783.7996; ⓦwww.blockislandferry.com).

booth enclaves, a pool table and late-night snacks, tucked out of the way in Federal Hill.

Lupo's Heartbreak Hotel 79 Washington St ⓣ401/272-5876. This is the spot in town to see nationally recognized bands rock out. Tickets around $10–40, cheaper in advance.

Trinity Brewhouse 186 Fountain St ⓣ401/453-2337. The interior of this hip brewhouse-meets-sports-bar feels a bit like the dining hall for a Harry Potter prep school – all high ceilings, oversized chandeliers, wooden walls and church-style windows. It's a great spot, with fresh brews on tap and a bit of dinosaur decor.

Newport

NEWPORT, nicknamed "America's First Resort", is a place out of a picture book, distinct for its polished yacht fleets, rose-coloured sunsets and long-time association with America's fine and fabulous. The Kennedys were married here (Jackie was a local girl); and during his presidency Eisenhower spent time at the Naval War College, which continues to introduce a uniformed presence to the lively streets. Tourists come today for the opulent *fin-de-siècle* mansions that line Bellevue Avenue – huge tree-lined estates and ornate palaces, former summer homes of the likes of the Astors and Vanderbilts.

Stroll beyond the extravagant facades, though, and you'll find much more, including many original eighteenth-century homes that sit among downtown's restaurants, boutiques and shops. The town's prime seaside location also means that the views are often, if not always, free – a short drive and you're greeted by unrivalled shores, with rugged seascapes and long swaths of sand.

Arrival and information

There are three towns on Aquidneck Island: **Portsmouth**, **Middletown** and **Newport**. The mainland (and I-95) is connected to the island by US-138, which passes over the scenic **Jamestown Bridge** to Jamestown, and from there by the **Newport Bridge** to Newport.

Newport is easy to **walk** around, with Thames (pronounced "Thaymz") Street as the main thoroughfare. Just north of downtown, at 23 America's Cup Ave, the **Gateway Visitor Center** is a hub of information (daily: June to early Sept 9am–5pm; ⓣ401/845-9123 or 1-800/976-5122, ⓦwww.gonewport.com). It also serves as the terminal for **Bonanza** (ⓣ401/846-1820) and **RIPTA** buses, as well as an **airport shuttle**.

Bikes are available for rent at Ten Speed Spokes, 18 Elm St ($7/hr, $35/day; ⓣ401/847-5609). On foot, the Newport Historical Society and Newport Restoration Foundation organize walking **tours** through downtown, departing from the Brick Market Museum, 127 Thames St ($12; ⓣ401/841-8770, ⓦwww.newporthistorytours.org). Alternatively, you could cruise around town on one of the popular Segway of Newport tours ($75; ⓣ401/619-4010, ⓦwww.segwayofnewport.com). But easily the most relaxing way of seeing Newport is on one of a number of **cruises**; try the beautiful schooner *Madeleine* (ⓣ401/847-0298, ⓦwww.cruisenewport.com), with ninety-minute tours in the summer departing from Bannister's Wharf ($27).

Accommodation

Accommodation in Newport, mostly inns and B&Bs, is not cheap, and prices skyrocket during summer weekends. Chain motels and **campgrounds** can be found just a few miles north in Middletown and Portsmouth.

The Almondy 25 Pelham St ⓣ401/848-7202 or 1-800/478-6155, ⓦwww.almondyinn.com. 1890s B&B, with harbour views, jacuzzi baths and gourmet breakfasts. ❽

Chart House Inn 16 Clarke St ⓣ401/846-5676, ⓦwww.charthouseinn.com. Eight sunlit, airy rooms in centrally located B&B. All rooms with private bath, but some in hallway. ❼

Hilltop Inn 2 Kay St ⓣ1-800/846-0392, ⓦwww.hilltopnewport.com. Pamper yourself in this historic five-room B&B with Italian linens, Bose CD players, marble showers and jacuzzis. ❽–❾

Ivy Lodge 12 Clay St ⓣ401/849-6865, ⓦwww.ivylodge.com. Boasting a stunning 33ft Gothic entry hall with wraparound balconies, this B&B beauty has eight rooms filled with antique reproduction furniture and modern amenities like flat-screen TVs, DVR and whirlpool tubs. Come in the off-season, when prices drop precipitously. ❾

Newport Beach Hotel & Suites One Wave Ave, Middletown ⓣ1-800/655-1778, ⓦwww.newportbeachhotelandsuites.com. Situated on Newport Beach, this recently renovated hotel has two massive properties, one brand new and filled with luxurious suites, the other a historic property with smaller rooms and prices. Great for families, they often have noteworthy specials online. ❻–❾

William Gyles Guesthouse 16 Howard St ⓣ401/369-0243, ⓦwww.newporthostel.com. Welcoming hostel in the heart of downtown. Private accommodation also available. Summer dorm beds $35–69/night.

The Town

Newport's palatial nineteenth-century **mansions** are its main draw; when you tire of the opulence, head to the shoreline to enjoy some spectacular **beaches**.

The mansions

When sociologist Thorstein Veblen visited Newport at the turn of the twentieth century, he was so horrified by the extravagance that he coined the phrase "conspicuous consumption". Beginning in the 1870s, Newport was an arena for the New York elite, where the industrial magnates and their families competed to outdo each other in building lavish estates. Many of the mansions fell to bleak fates just a few decades later; the **Preservation Society of Newport County**, 424 Bellevue Ave (mansions open April–Jan; ⓣ401/847-1000, ⓦwww.newportmansions.org) maintains the bulk of the dozen or so houses open for public viewing today.

The mansions each boast their own version of Gilded Age excess: **Marble House**, with its golden ballroom and adjacent Chinese teahouse; **Rosecliff**, with a colourful rose garden and heart-shaped staircase; the ornate French **The Elms**, known for its gardens; and Cornelius Vanderbilt's **The Breakers**, an Italian Renaissance palace overlooking the ocean and the grandest of the lot. Besides those, a number of earlier, smaller houses, including the quirky Gothic Revival cottage **Kingscote**, may well make for a more interesting excursion. Admission to the Breakers is $19; visit with one other property and it's $24; and a combo ticket to three plus a behind the scenes tour with lunch is $49. Note that many houses operate on hourly tours; unless you're a mansion nut, viewing one or two should suffice to get a glimpse of the opulence.

One way to see the mansions on the cheap is to peer in the back gardens from the **Cliff Walk**, which begins on Memorial Boulevard where it meets First (Easton) Beach. This spectacular three-and-a-half-mile oceanside path alternates from pretty stretches lined by jasmine and wild roses to rugged rocky passes.

The beaches

The attraction of Newport's shoreline, with its many coves and gently sloping sands, is indubitably its beaches. Small **Gooseberry Beach** is surrounded by grand houses, while **First Beach** is the lively town beach at the eastern end of Memorial Boulevard; further out, **Second (Sachuest) Beach**, with its quiet, long sandy swaths, is where you really want to go, while calmer waters can be found at **Third**

Beach. Most beaches have summer parking fees of $10–20 per car. If you want spectacular views without getting wet, bike along the several miles of **Ocean Drive**, leading to **Brenton Point State Park** (open daily sunrise–sunset; free), a great sunset spot where you'll find panoramic views of Narragansett Bay.

Eating

Many of Newport's **restaurants** are geared to tourists and are overpriced, though with a little hunting you can find some marvellous exceptions. Note that many of the restaurants listed below have seasonal hours.

The Black Pearl Bannisters Wharf ⓣ401/846-5264. Newport institution famous for its chunky clam chowder; informal patio as well as formal dining available.

Belle's Cafe 1 Washington St, in Newport Shipyard ⓣ401/619-0634. Right in the Newport Shipyard (you'll have to walk past a guard to get in), *Belle's* has diner-style breakfast and lunches best enjoyed on its outdoor picnic tables, which are surrounded by an impressive collection of elegant yachts.

Cafe Zelda 528 Thames St ⓣ401/849-4002. Right in the heart of downtown, *Zelda* serves fairly-priced salads, sandwiches and steak frites and has a great little bar and classy striped blue wallpaper. Lunch weekends only, dinner seven days.

Flo's Clam Shack 4 Wave Ave, Middletown ⓣ401/847-8141. Hugely popular joint across from First Beach, famed for cheap chowder and the usual clam shack faves.

Mamma Luisa's 673 Thames St ⓣ401/848-5257. At the quiet end of Thames St, *Mamma* serves up Italian favourites in a cosily elegant dining room set inside a quaint green house. Dinner only.

Pasta Beach 7 Memorial Blvd ⓣ401/847-2222. Irresistible, affordable, authentic Italian fare in casual environs. Open for lunch and dinner.

Salvation Café 140 Broadway ⓣ401/847-2620. Funky spot off the main drag, with exotic concoctions like Moroccan chicken and Thai shrimp cakes, at reasonable prices. Dinner daily.

Scales & Shells 527 Thames St ⓣ401/846-3474. Casual but pricey restaurant known for its standout fresh seafood – raw, broiled or mesquite-grilled. Dinner only, cash only.

Festivals

There is always something afoot in Newport, particularly in the summer for the **Newport Folk Festival** (where Bob Dylan got his start in 1963; ⓣ401/848-5055; ⓦwww.newportfolkfest.net) as well as the high-profile **Jazz Festival** (ⓦwww.newportjazzfest.net). The **Newport Music Festival** (ⓣ401/849-0700; ⓦwww.newportmusic.org) boasts classical music performed at the mansions, while the **Irish Waterfront Festival** is one of the region's biggest Irish events (ⓦwww.newportwaterfrontevents.com).

Connecticut

New England's southernmost state, **CONNECTICUT**, was named *Quinnehtukqut* ("great tidal river") by the Native Americans after the river that bisects it and spills into Long Island Sound. First settled by white settlers in the 1630s, Connecticut is one of the oldest colonies of the Union, playing crucial roles during the Revolutionary War (hence named "**the provisions state**") and in the country's founding – its original 1639 charter helped to inspire the American Constitution (hence also named "**the Constitution state**"). During the eighteenth and nineteenth centuries, the state prospered from steady industrialization and lucrative whaling along the coast. Today, much of the old industry has withered away, leaving areas of green countryside and idyllic villages that typify New England's quaint image.

While predominantly rural, Connecticut is densely populated along the coast, with a vibrant southwestern corner exuding the cosmopolitan air of neighbouring New York City, and the at once industrial and intellectual **New Haven**, home to Yale University. Further east, **Mystic** and **New London** still maintain intimate ties to their maritime past, while inland, the old architecture scattered around the state capital of **Hartford** tells of the city's more glorious days.

Southeastern Connecticut

The much-visited **southeastern coast** of Connecticut spans 25 miles from Stonington in the east to Niantic in the west. The old whaling port of **Mystic** is a big draw with its restored nineteenth-century seaport and huge aquarium, while **New London** is home to the US Coast Guard Academy. Further east is the picturesque seaside village of **Stonington**.

Mystic

As purists will tell you, the town of **MYSTIC**, right on I-95, does not really exist; **Old Mystic** comprises a couple of quaint streets north of the highway, while tourists are drawn to the maritime recreations at **Mystic Seaport**, a couple of miles south, and its bustling downtown just across the Mystic River. The drawbridge leading downtown is still raised hourly and on request for some magnificent taller ships sailing through.

The area's biggest draw is the **Mystic Aquarium & Institute for Exploration**, exit 90 off I-95 (daily Jan & Feb 10am–5pm, March 9am–5pm, April–Oct till 6pm, Nov till 5pm; adults $28, children 3–17 $20; ⓣ860/572-5955, ⓦwww.mysticaquarium.org), home to over twelve thousand weird and wonderful marine specimens, including penguins, sea lions, piranhas and the only beluga whales in New England.

Whether you think it's authentic or tacky, **Mystic Seaport**, also known as the Museum of America & the Sea (daily: April–Oct 9am–5pm, Nov 10am–4pm, closed rest of year; $24, children $15; ⓣ860/572-5315, ⓦwww.mysticseaport.org), is the area's other big draw, where more than sixty buildings house old-style workshops and stores reflecting life in a nineteenth-century seafaring village. In the **Preservation Shipyard**, watch the restoration and maintenance of a vast collection of wooden ships, among them the 1841 *Charles W. Morgan*, the last wooden whaling ship in the world.

Practicalities

Mystic's main **information office** lies in the tacky Olde Mistick Village Shopping Mall (Mon–Sat 9am–5pm, Sun 10am–5pm; ⓣ860/536-1641), with a smaller branch office (daily 10am–4pm, ⓣ860/572-1102) at the Amtrak **train station** (ⓣ1-800/872-7245). **Accommodation** options include the *Steamboat Inn*, 73 Steamboat Wharf (ⓣ860/536-8300, ⓦwww.steamboatinnmystic.com; ❽), overlooking the water with eleven elegant rooms in the heart of downtown. Near I-95 are a handful of chain motels, including the pet-friendly *Hampton Inn & Suites Mystic*, 6 Hendel Drive (ⓣ860/536-2536; ❼); the *Harbour Inne & Cottage*, 15 Edgemont St (ⓣ860/572-9253; ❸–❻) has simple, clean, wood-panelled rooms right on the water, and is walkable to town and the train station. The

Seaport **campground**, off Rte-184 in Old Mystic (ⓣ860/536-4044, ⓦwww.morganrvresorts.com; $45/pitch), has 130 pitches.

Mystic's excellent **restaurants** include *Bravo Bravo*, 20 E Main St (ⓣ860/536-3228), serving inspired pastas and fine Italian classics in an unpretentious space, and *S&P Oyster Company*, 1 Holmes St (ⓣ860/536-2674), serving fine seafood on the waterfront. The small, family-run *Mystic Pizza*, at 56 W Main St (ⓣ860/536-3700), unruffled by its movie-title status, serves huge pizzas for $10–16.

Stonington

STONINGTON, just south of I-95 near the state's eastern border, is a pretty old fishing village, originally settled in 1649 and still very much a New England enclave with its whitewashed cottages and peaceful waterfront. Its main road, **Water Street**, is dotted with restaurants and shops. At no. 7, the **Old Lighthouse Museum** (May–Oct daily 10am–5pm; $8; ⓣ860/535-1440), relays fine textures of town life through the last centuries in six small rooms of exhibits. The view from the top, as from the entrance, is endless on a sunny day. Museum admission includes access to the Italianate **Captain Nathaniel B. Palmer House**, 40 Palmer St (May–Oct Wed–Sun 1–5pm; $8; ⓣ860/535-8445), at the north end of town, celebrating Stonington's premier seafarer credited with one of the earliest sightings of Antarctica.

For **accommodation**, the *Orchard Street Inn*, 41 Orchard St (ⓣ860/535-2681, ⓦwww.orchardstreetinn.com; ❼–❽) has five rooms in a quiet cottage. In neighbouring Pawcatuck, the *Cove Ledge Inn & Marina*, on Rte-1 at Whewell Circle (ⓣ860/599-4130, ⓦwww.coveledgeinn.com; ❹–❺), offers twenty rooms close to the water. For **food**, try *Noah's*, 113 Water St (ⓣ860/535-3925; closed Mon), known for fine home-style cooking, featuring eclectic choices ranging from Korean pancakes to fresh local catch. Alternatively, *Skipper's Dock*, 66 Water St (ⓣ860/535-0111), offers mid-priced seafood dishes complemented by fantastic water views.

New London

NEW LONDON, on the west side of the Thames River, is the most populated city along this stretch of the coast, spreading over six square miles. Originally settled in 1646, it was a wealthy whaling port in the nineteenth century. Today, it's home to the **US Coast Guard Academy**, off I-95 at 31 Mohegan Ave, on an attractive sloping campus overlooking the Thames. Visitors are welcome to take a self-guided tour (daily 9am–4.30pm; ID required; free), with walking maps available from the admissions office in Waesche Hall (ⓣ860/444-8500). Here, the **US Coast Guard Museum** (call for hours as its schedule is tied to Academy breaks; free; ⓣ860/444-8511) explores two centuries of coastguard history, and you can also visit the USS *Eagle* when it's docked here (ⓣ860/444-8595).

From the info centre at the Trolley Station on Eugene O'Neill Drive (ⓣ860/444-7264), you can pick up a self-guided walking tour map of downtown, and continue down the formerly prosperous Huntington Street, past the Greek Revival mansions known as **Whale Oil Row**. The city boasts a number of historic houses open to the public, among them the **Shaw-Perkins Mansion**, 11 Blinman St (Wed–Fri 1–4pm, in summer Sat 10am–4pm; $5; ⓣ860/443-1209), a stone house built in 1756 for wealthy shipowner and trader Nathaniel Shaw, and the **Monte Cristo Cottage**, 325 Pequot Ave (June–Sept Tues–Sat 10am–5pm, Sun 1–3pm; $7; ⓣ860/443-0051), childhood home of boozy, Nobel-winning playwright **Eugene O'Neill**. The Eugene O'Neill Theater Center, 305 Great Neck Rd (exit 82 off I-95) in nearby **Waterford**, is an acclaimed testing-ground for emerging playwrights and actors (Ⓣ860/443-5378, Ⓦwww.oneilltheatercenter.org).

South of downtown, **Ocean Beach Park**, at 1225 Ocean Ave, has a sugar-sand beach and huge saltwater pool, as well as a wooden boardwalk, mini-golf and arcade (open summer daily till late; $14–18 parking; additional fees for activities; Ⓣ860/447-3031).

Practicalities

You can arrive in New London by **ferry** from Orient Point on Long Island (via Cross Sound Ferry, 2 Ferry St, Ⓣ860/443-5281, Ⓦwww.longislandferry.com; reservations recommended). The city is also served well by Amtrak **trains** and Greyhound **buses**.

Information is available at the **Trolley Station**, on Eugene O'Neill Drive (May & Oct Fri–Sun 10am–4pm, June–Sept daily till 4pm; Ⓣ860/444-7264). A number of motels are scattered along I-95. For a more atmospheric stay, try *The Kirkland House Bed and Breakfast*, 51 Glenwood Ave (Ⓣ860/437-1500, Ⓦwww.kirklandhouse.com; ❻), with two endearing rooms in a nineteenth-century Italianate "summer villa", known for its great breakfasts and expansive porch. Downtown, the French café *Mangetout*, 140 State St (Ⓣ860/444-2066) offers fresh, organic breakfasts and lunches and delicious desserts, while *Captain Scott's Lobster Dock*, tucked away on 80 Hamilton St (Ⓣ860/439-1741), is the place to go for hot lobster rolls, fried oysters and water views.

Hartford

The town that Mark Twain once described as "the best built and handsomest…I have ever seen" is today hardly recognizable as such. Rather, the modern capital of Connecticut, **HARTFORD**, is best known as the insurance centre of the United States. Though the city itself has fallen on rather hard times, the old architecture scattered around town continues to tell many a history. Highlights include the gold-domed **State Capitol** in Bushnell Park (free tours hourly Mon–Fri 9.15am–1.15pm, July & Aug additional tour at 2.15pm; also April–Oct Sat 10.15am–2.15pm), an 1878 mixture of Gothic, Classical and Second Empire styles, emanating an ecclesiastical ambience. Also in the park, the 1914 antique wooden merry-go-round still gives jangling rides for a mere $1 (mid-May to Oct, closed Mon).

Hartford's pride and joy is the Greek Revival **Wadsworth Atheneum**, at 600 Main St (Wed–Fri 11am–5pm, Sat & Sun 10am–5pm; $10; Ⓣ860/278-2670, Ⓦwww.wadsworthatheneum.org), founded by Daniel Wadsworth in 1842 and the nation's oldest continuously operating public art museum. The world-class collection, spanning over five thousand years, includes a distinguished collection of American paintings and sculpture, Renaissance and Baroque masterpieces, and a significant contemporary collection.

A mile west of downtown, the hilltop community known as Nook Farm was home in the 1880s to next-door neighbours **Mark Twain** and **Harriet Beecher Stowe**. Their Victorian homes, furnished much as they were then, are both open for tours. Twain lived at 351 Farmington Ave from 1874 until 1891, writing many of his classic works in this ornate house, complete with elaborate brickwork and Tiffany interiors (April–Dec Mon–Sat 9.30am–5.30pm, Sun noon–5.30pm; rest of year closed Tues; $15; Ⓣ860/247-0998, Ⓦwww.marktwainhouse.org).

Next door, the much less flamboyant **Harriet Beecher Stowe Center**, 77 Forest St (May–Oct Wed–Sat 9.30am–4.30pm, Sun noon–4.30pm; open Tues in June from 9.30am–4.30pm ; $9; ⓣ860/522-9258, ⓦwww.harrietbeecherstowecenter.org), celebrates one of America's most important female activists. The white Victorian Gothic home is a fine example of the nineteenth-century "cottage", with a hint of the romantic villa, and you can see Stowe's writing table.

Other town highlights include the beautiful campus of **Trinity College**, at 300 Summit St, located on a hundred acres at the highest point in the city. Founded in 1823, the college hosts an array of stunning Victorian Gothic architecture, including its magnificent college **chapel**. West on Prospect and Asylum avenues, **Elizabeth Park** (daily dawn–dusk; free; ⓦwww.elizabethpark.org) is the first municipal rose garden in the nation. June is the best time to visit to see the more than eight hundred varieties of roses in bloom, but in addition there are rock gardens, greenhouses and miles of tranquil walking paths.

Practicalities

Hartford, which lies at the junction of I-91 and I-84, is easily accessible by car. Greyhound, Peter Pan and Bonanza **buses**, and Amtrak **trains**, all pull into Union Station, just north of Bushnell Park. Twelve miles north of town lies Connecticut's **Bradley International Airport** (ⓣ860/292-2000, ⓦwww.bradleyairport.com), served by a CT Transit **shuttle** ($1.25) to the Old State House in downtown. For **information**, visit the Greater Hartford Welcome Center, 45 Pratt St (Mon–Fri 9am–5pm; ⓣ860/244-0253, ⓦwww.hartford.com).

Hartford has a limited range of **lodging** options, with a handful of pricey downtown hotels catering mainly to business travellers, with weekend deals, including the *Hartford Marriott Downtown*, 200 Columbus Blvd (ⓣ860/249-8000; ⑥–⑧), a freshly renovated 401-room hotel a short walk from the Atheneum. Budget motels can be found along I-91, a half-mile from downtown, but note that this area is a bit dodgy; you may want to take a look around before you book your room. More charming options are available in Farmington, just a few miles from town – try the spacious, elegant *Farmington Inn*, 827 Farmington Ave (ⓣ860/677-2821, ⓦwww.farmingtoninn.com; ⑤–⑥).

Hartford's classic **restaurant** is *Trumbull Kitchen*, 150 Trumbull St (ⓣ860/493-7417), which offers a cross-cultural menu in a modern setting, while *Firebox*, 539 Broad St (ⓣ860/246-1222), serves tempting, locally-sourced New American food at lunch and dinner. For an exotic touch, visit the *Abyssinian*, 535 Farmington Ave (ⓣ860/218-2231), offering authentic Ethiopian stews, salads, fish and breads, with plentiful vegetarian options. Road-trippers will want to make the pilgrimage to *Rein's Deli*, 435 Hartford Turrpike, 11 miles north in Vernon (exit 65 off I-84, open till midnight, ⓣ860/875-1344), where the bulging pastrami sandwiches and home-made pickles have nourished road-weary souls since 1973.

New Haven

Don't be put off by the grubby initial impression you get when you arrive in **NEW HAVEN**. Tucked away among the grimy factories and architecturally nondescript office blocks are some of the best restaurants, most exciting nightspots, and most diverting cultural activities in all of New England. Founded in 1638 by a group of wealthy Puritans from London, New Haven became the seat of Yale University in 1716, the third oldest college in the nation. Today, its leafy campus and magnificent Gothic architecture continue to exert a veritable historic presence. The tensions between the city's two very different facets (tension-ridden urbanity and Ivy League idyll) once made New Haven an uneasy place, though an active symbiosis has thrived since the early 2000s. Easily accessed from New York City, New Haven is home to one of the finest college art museums in the country (as well as some of the world's most legendary pizza), and makes a particularly enjoyable stop for any pizza lover in search of a memorable slice.

Arrival, information and city transport

New Haven lies where interstates I-91 and I-95 fork, and is well served by Greyhound **buses** and Amtrak **trains**. **Union Station**, on Union Avenue six blocks southeast of the Yale campus downtown, is the main terminal. From New York, the Metro-North Commuter Railroad (Ⓣ1-800/638-7646) is a better deal than Amtrak. If you arrive at night, you may want to grab a **taxi**; try Metro Taxi (Ⓣ203/777-7777).

Public transport is provided by Connecticut Transit, 470 James St ($1.25; Ⓣ203/624-0151, Ⓦwww.cttransit.com), which also runs a daytime **shuttle** between Union Station and Temple Plaza, across from the *Omni Hotel* downtown. An **INFO New Haven** office is located just off the Green at 1000 Chapel St (Mon–Thurs 10am–9pm, Fri & Sat till 10pm, Sun noon–5pm; Ⓣ203/773-9494, Ⓦwww.infonewhaven.com), with helpful staff.

Accommodation

New Haven has a good selection of **accommodation**, but make sure to book well in advance if you intend to visit around Yale graduation in June, around the start of term in late August or during Parents' Weekend in October.

Farnam Guesthouse 616 Prospect St Ⓣ203/562-7121 or 1-888/562-7121, Ⓦwww.farnamguesthouse.com. Seven charming rooms (including some priced for singles) close to Yale Divinity School. ❹

Hotel Duncan 1151 Chapel St Ⓣ203/787-1273. Although its dark rooms are in desperate need of a renovation, the centrally located *Duncan* still enchants with its old-fashioned building, dating to 1894. $60 for singles, $80 for two. ❹

La Quinta Inn & Suites 400 Sargent Drive Ⓣ203/562-1111 Ⓦwww.lq.com. Basic yet appealing rooms with complimentary breakfast and wi-fi in a location that's easily accessed from I-95. A free shuttle whisks guests into downtown New Haven. ❸–❹

New Haven Hotel 229 George St Ⓣ203/498-3100 Ⓦwww.newhavenhotel.com. Pleasant downtown rooms, all of which have been recently renovated. ❺

Omni New Haven Hotel at Yale 155 Temple St Ⓣ203/772-6664, Ⓦwww.omnihotels.com. Over three hundred deluxe units in New Haven's plush downtown landmark. ❽–❾

Study at Yale 1157 Chapel St Ⓣ203/503-3900. A welcome newcomer to downtown, this contemporary dreamboat has all the right fixings: luxe linens, free wi-fi, an appealing restaurant serving locally-sourced food, and great coffee and reading material on hand. Guest rooms feature postcard-perfect views of the Yale campus, deftly framed by oversized windows. ❼

The City

Downtown, centred on the **Green**, retains a historic atmosphere. Laid out in 1638, the Green was the site of the city's original settlement and also functioned as a meeting area and burial ground. In its centre, the crypt of the 1812 **Center Church** (Ⓣ203/787-0121) holds tombs dating back to 1687. Surrounding the Green are a number of stately government buildings, including the 1861 High Victorian **City Hall**. Bordering the Green, lively, student-filled **College Street** and **Chapel Street** are lined with bookstores, shops, cafés and bars.

At the opposite end of the Green, Yale University's 1750 **Connecticut Hall** is the oldest surviving building in New Haven, guarded by a statue of Yale alum and Revolutionary War hero Nathan Hale. The nearby 1895 **Phelps Gate** allows access to the cobbled courtyards of Yale's **Old Campus**. While you're free to wander at will, you may want to consider the free hour-long student-led **tours** setting off daily (Mon–Fri at 10.30am & 2pm, Sat & Sun at 1.30pm) from the

Yale Visitor Information Center at 149 Elm St (Ⓣ203/432-2300, Ⓦwww.yale.edu/visitor), as many of the key sights have restricted access. Tour highlights include the magnificent, modern Gothic-style **Sterling Memorial Library**, the university's largest library.

Among Yale's notable museums, the modernist **Yale Center for British Art**, 1080 Chapel St (Tues–Sat 10am–5pm, Sun noon–5pm; free; Ⓣ203/432-2800) boasts the most comprehensive collection of British art outside of the UK. Opposite, the **Yale University Art Gallery**, 1111 Chapel St (Tues–Sat 10am–5pm, Sun 1–6pm; free; Ⓣ203/432-0600) holds the nation's most venerable university art collection, with more than 100,000 objects from around the world, ranging from Etruscan vases and African masks to Baroque masterpieces and contemporary art. North at 170 Whitney Ave, the huge **Peabody Museum of Natural History**, 170 Whitney Ave (Mon–Sat 10am–5pm, Sun noon–5pm; $7; Ⓣ203/432-5050, Ⓦwww.peabody.yale.edu) holds an impressive collection of artefacts from the natural world, including a brontosaurus skeleton.

Another source of New Haven affection and pride is its close-knit **Italian District**, based since 1900 within the well-kept brownstones and colourful window boxes of **Wooster Square** (just beyond Crown Street southeast of the Green). This was where the city's original Italian immigrants settled when they came to work on the railroad. Here, you'll find some incredibly popular restaurants, including two pizzeria rivals (*Pepe's* and *Sally's Apizza*) that have been vying for the city's "best pizza" title since 1938.

Eating

New Haven offers a rich and eclectic range of **restaurants**, many located around the Green and on Chapel and College streets. Savour this university town's intellectual atmosphere at one of many fine downtown **cafés**, and don't leave town without trying the **pizza**, available at the family-run Italian restaurants in Wooster Square.

Caseus 93 Whitney Ave Ⓣ203/6CHEESE. *Caseus* means cheese in Latin, and this popular fromagerie and bistro zealously exalts its moniker. A little pricey, head here for organic meat and salad dishes, cheese plates and artisanal charcuterie. There's also a nice outdoor patio, and good wine and beer on offer.

Frank Pepe's Pizzeria 157 Wooster St Ⓣ203/865-5762. A Wooster St institution since 1925, drawing crowds with its coal-fired pizzas.

Ibiza 39 High St Ⓣ203/865-1933. Upmarket Spanish restaurant serving traditional specialties, with a fine list of Spanish wines.

Louis'Lunch 261 Crown St Ⓣ203/562-5507. Small, brick, tasty burger institution which claims to have served America's first hamburger, circa 1895. No ketchup; cash only.

Mamoun's Falafel 85 Howe St Ⓣ203/562-8444. Cheap, lovingly prepared Middle Eastern fare (the falafel sandwich is $3) in a no-frills dining room four blocks from the Green. Open 11am–3am, 365 days a year. Cash only.

Pacifico 220 College St Ⓣ203/772-4002. Fun, seafood-centred, "nuevo Latino" spot, with signature dishes like lobster ravioli and caramelized salmon. They also do a mean mojito.

Pantry 2 Mechanic St Ⓣ203/787-0392. Beloved brunch spot nearly always accompanied by a long wait. Once inside, croon over their eggs Benedict and scallion-studded home fries. Cash only, closed Mon.

Union League Café 1032 Chapel St Ⓣ203/562-4299. Expensive French bistro, known as one of the finest restaurants around.

Vendors Intersection of York and Cedar sts, by the Yale-New Haven Hospital. A gastronomic rainbow (Thai, Italian, Chinese, Greek, Mexican, soul food, cupcakes) of over forty food carts sets up shop here in warm weather months.

Performing arts and nightlife

New Haven's rich **cultural scene** is especially strong in **theatre**. The Yale Repertory Theatre, 1120 Chapel St (Ⓣ203/432-1234, Ⓦwww.yalerep.org), which boasts among its eminent past members Jodie Foster and Meryl Streep, turns out consistently good shows during term-time. The Shubert Performing

Arts Center, 247 College St (Ⓣ203/562-5666, Ⓦwww.shubert.com) is known for musicals.

As you'd expect with such a large student population, there are plenty of excellent **bars** and **clubs**, mostly concentrated around Chapel and College streets. The *New Haven Advocate*, a free weekly news and arts paper, has detailed **listings**.

Anna Liffey's 17 Whitney Ave Ⓣ203/773-1776. Off-the-beaten path bar, this subterranean Irish pub offers great fish and chips and pours pints for a happy mix of town and gown.

Bar 254 Crown St Ⓣ203/495-8924. A simple name for a not-so-simple spot that's a combination pizzeria, brewery, bar and nightclub.

Café Nine 250 State St Ⓣ203/789-8281. Dive bar with live music every night, from punk to jazz and R&B. Cover $5–10.

Owl Shop 268 College St Ⓣ203/624-3250. Smoky, old school cigar bar (it dates to 1934) enhanced by good scotch and frequent jazz.

Prime 16 172 Temple St Ⓣ203/782-1616. Temple St hot spot with creative gourmet burgers and two dozen beers on tap.

Rudy's 372 Elm St Ⓣ203/865-1242. A favourite local dive bar with a great soundtrack and legendary frites. Cash only.

Toad's Place 300 York St Ⓣ203/562-5589, Ⓦwww.toadsplace.com. Mid-sized live music venue where Bruce Springsteen and the Stones used to "pop in" to play impromptu gigs. Some shows 21 and over.

New Hampshire

Long after sailors, fishermen and agricultural colonists had domesticated the entire coastline of New England, the glacier-marked interior of **NEW HAMPSHIRE**, with its dense forests and forbidding mountains, remained the exclusive preserve of the Abenaki. Only the few miles of seashore held sizeable seventeenth-century communities of European settlers, such as the one at **Portsmouth**.

Even when the Native Americans were driven back, the settlers could make little agricultural impact on the rocky terrain of this "granite state", and it wasn't until the Industrial Revolution made possible the development of water-powered **textile mills** that the economy took off. For a while, **timber** companies looked set to strip all northern New Hampshire bare, but they were brought under control when the state recognized that the pristine landscape of the **White Mountains** might turn out to be its greatest asset. Large-scale **tourism** began towards the end of nineteenth century; at one time fifty trains daily brought travelers up to Mount Washington.

Ever since becoming the first American state to declare independence, in January 1776, New Hampshire has been proud to go its own idiosyncratic way. The absence of a sales tax, or even a personal income tax, is seen as a fulfilment of the state motto, "Live Free or Die". The state has long gained inordinate political clout as the venue of the first **primary election** of each presidential campaign, with its villages well used to playing host to would-be world leaders.

Beyond the charming coastal town of Portsmouth, the major destinations are **Lake Winnipesaukee**, **Conway**, **Lincoln** and **Franconia Notch** in the White Mountains. To see the bucolic rural scenery more usually associated with New England, take a detour off the main roads up the Merrimack Valley, to **Canterbury Shaker Village** near Concord or the **Robert Frost Farm** close to Nashua.

The coast

Of all the US states with ocean access, New Hampshire has the shortest coastline – just eighteen miles. Skip the tacky family-oriented resort of **Hampton Beach**, and keep driving on Rte-1A to **NORTH HAMPTON BEACH**, which is far more pleasant. The beach here is usually quieter, with abundant metered parking, though it still catches a bit of the slough from its brash neighbour. Popular with surfers and families alike, **Jenness State Beach**, a few miles north in Rye, has a long, curving stretch of sand with a smallish car park ($1.50/hr). Finally, beyond Rye Harbor, lies **Wallis Sands State Beach** ($15/car), even more serene and the best place for swimming and sunning. **Portsmouth**, further north (indeed, it's only separated from Maine by the Piscataqua River) has a renowned restaurant scene and some of the state's liveliest streetlife.

Portsmouth

New Hampshire's oldest community, **PORTSMOUTH** blends small-town accessibility with the enthusiasm of a rejuvenated city. Its position at the mouth of the Piscataqua River has always made it an important port – it was the state capital until 1808 – but it still has the feel of a New England village, with the spire of **North Church** in the central **Market Square**, dating from 1854, remaining the tallest structure in town. Nowadays, Portland attracts artists, musicians and, most notably, gourmet chefs, who have opened up a number of outstanding restaurants alongside the chic boutiques and nineteenth-century brewery buildings that line **Market Street**.

Portsmouth is home to eight carefully restored **colonial homes**, which are open to the public during the summer. The 1758 gambrel-roofed, boxy, yellow **John Paul Jones House**, 43 Middle St, at State Street (daily late May to mid-Oct 11am–5pm; $6, self-guided tours only; Ⓣ603/436-8420), is the most distinctive, home to the Portsmouth Historical Society's museum (Ⓦwww.portsmouthhistory.org). Jones, America's first great naval commander, stayed here in 1777 while his ships were being outfitted in the harbour. You should also check out the **Moffatt-Ladd House**, a grand old mansion at 154 Market St (mid-June to Oct Mon–Sat 11am–5pm, Sun 1–5pm; $6; Ⓦwww.moffattladd.org), completed in 1763 and particularly notable for its Great Hall.

Strawbery Banke

Although historic buildings can be found all over Portsmouth, for a more concentrated look at American architecture over the last three centuries, visit the **Strawbery Banke Museum**, 64 Marcy St (May–Oct daily 10am–5pm; Nov by guided tour only, offered on the hour Sat & Sun 10am–2pm; $15; tickets good for two consecutive days; Ⓣ603/433-1100, Ⓦwww.strawberybanke.org), a fenced-off, ten-acre neighbourhood of forty meticulously restored and maintained old wooden buildings (though some can only be viewed from the outside). The area began life as the residence of wealthy shipbuilders, and was successively the lair of privateers and a red-light district before turning into respectable – and, in the 1950s, decaying – suburbia. Restoration began in 1958, starting with the removal of all newer buildings, and the museum opened in 1965.

Each building is shown in its most interesting former incarnation, whether that be 1695 or 1955. The 1766 **Pitt Tavern** holds the most historic significance, having served as a meeting place during the Revolution for patriots and loyalists. Traditional crafts can be viewed in the **Dinsmore Shop**, where an infinitely patient cooper manufactures barrels with the tools and methods of 1800.

Practicalities

Greyhound **buses** (Ⓣ603/433-3210) run from Boston twice daily, stopping outside 55 Hanover St, a short walk from Market Square. You can pick up **information** from the **visitor centre** at 500 Market St, a fifteen-minute walk from Market Square (June–Sept Mon–Fri 8.30am–5pm, Sat & Sun 10am–5pm; Oct–May Mon–Fri 8.30am–5pm; Ⓣ603/436-1118, Ⓦwww.portsmouthchamber.org), or from the kiosk in Market Square (May–Oct daily 10am–5pm). Portsmouth Harbor Cruises (Ⓣ603/436-8084 or 1-800/776-0915, Ⓦwww.portsmouthharbor.com) is one of several operators offering **boat trips**, from $13.

Accommodation in the town centre is restricted to expensive places such as the grand *Sise Inn*, 40 Court St (Ⓣ603/433-1200 or 1-877/747-3466, Ⓦwww.siseinn.com; ❼–❽), a beautifully preserved Queen Anne-style house with large rooms; the peaceful, rambling seven-room *Inn at Strawbery Banke*, 314 Court St (Ⓣ603/436-7242 or 1-800/428-3933, Ⓦwww.innatstrawberybanke.com; ❼); and the hip *Ale House Inn*, 121 Bow St (Ⓣ603/431-7760, Ⓦwww.alehouseinn.com; ❼–❽), a remodelled former brewery on the waterfront. Cheaper motels near the traffic circle, where I-95 and Rte-1 intersect, include the good-value *Port Inn*, Rte-1 Bypass South (Ⓣ1-800/282-PORT, Ⓦwww.theportinn.com; ❺).

Portsmouth bills itself as the "food capital of New England". Of the in-town **restaurants**, *Jumpin' Jay's Fish Café*, 150 Congress St, (Ⓣ603/766-3474), offers the best seafood in town. *Ristorante Massimo*, 59 Penhallow St (Ⓣ603/436-4000), is a gourmet Italian restaurant with a strong wine list (reservations a must), and funky *Friendly Toast*, 121 Congress St (Ⓣ603/430-2154), makes for an inexpensive breakfast and lunch spot, with generous portions.

At night, the *Portsmouth Brewery*, 56 Market St (Ⓣ603/431-1115, Ⓦwww.portsmouthbrewery.com), serves up exceptional microbrews and occasional live music, while *The Press Room*, 77 Daniel St (Ⓣ603/431-5186, Ⓦwww.pressroomnh.com), has jazz, blues, folk or bluegrass performances every night. Those searching for caffeine rather than alcohol will be happy at *Breaking New Grounds* (Ⓣ603/436-9555) in Market Square.

The Merrimack Valley

The financial and political heartland of New Hampshire is the **Merrimack Valley**, which – first by water and now by road – has always been the main thoroughfare north to the White Mountains and Québec. Nowadays, there are a few detours off its country roads that are notable to travellers.

About twenty miles north of state capital Concord, off I-95, exit 18, **Canterbury Shaker Village**, 288 Shaker Rd (May–Oct daily 10am–5pm; Nov to early Dec Fri–Sun same hours; $17, good two consecutive days; Ⓣ603/783-9511, Ⓦwww.shakers.org), was founded in 1774, and was three-hundred-strong by 1860; three different hour-long tours explain the Shaker way of life. There are craft demonstrations (such as basket-making) and even frequent all-day craft workshops if you're so inclined. The *Shaker Table* near the village entry serves delicious and imaginative Shaker-inspired food. South of Concord, 122 Rockingham Rd, in Derry just off Rte-28 (take exit 4 from I-93), the **Robert Frost Farm** (May–June & Sept to mid-Oct Wed–Sun 10am–4pm; July & Aug daily same hours; entry free, tour $5; Ⓣ603/432-3091, Ⓦrobertfrostfarm.org) has been evocatively restored to its condition when New England's poet laureate lived here from 1900 to 1911. Displays in the barn highlight his work, and a half-mile "poetry nature trail" leads past the sites that inspired many of his best-known poems.

From burger bars to bistros

Food is big in America – a country where a deli sandwich can be a meal for two and where all-you-can-eat buffets are destinations in themselves. Still, it's not all about quantity. There's something irresistible about sitting in a vintage diner, munching on a simple grilled-cheese sandwich while a gum-chewing waitress with big hair pours endless coffee refills and calls you darlin'. Such quintessentially American experiences are there for the taking, along with a host of other intriguing dining opportunities, and – those buffets notwithstanding – some of the finest food in the world.

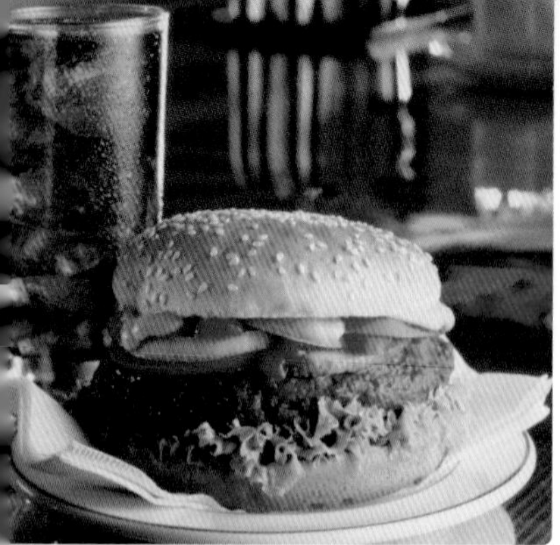

A classic hamburger ▲

Home-made BBQ sign ▼

Lobsters ▼

Burgers, BBQ and seafood

No one knows who invented the **burger**, but it's an American staple that's set to stay. Fans of the Golden Arches may not recognize the infinitely tastier home-made versions served in regional restaurants – a Big Mac will never seem the same again. Famous **hot dog** spots include New York City, where every July 4 *Nathan's* in Coney Island holds a hot-dog-eating contest, and Chicago, where the dog is served in a poppy-seed bun and *never* with ketchup. Other meaty takeout treats include the **Philly cheesesteak**, a dripping sandwich of hot sliced beef and rich melted cheese born on the streets of Philadelphia, and New Orleans's **muffuletta**, in which spicy Italian cured meats are combined with piquant olives and cheese and crammed into a colossal bun.

Emotions run high when it comes to **BBQ** – smoked pork or beef shredded and drenched in tangy sauces – with the southern states and the cities of Memphis, Kansas City and Chicago hotly claiming to serve the world's best. Texas is where you'll find the best **chili** – and scores of passionately fought chili cookoffs. If you fancy a really big **steak** head for Texas or Western states like Montana and Wyoming. This is cattle-rearing country, so the slab of beef on your plate couldn't be fresher – or bigger.

Crab is king along the Mid-Atlantic shore, with steamed blue crabs and spicy soft-shells around Chesapeake Bay, and stone-crab claws abounding in Florida. New Englanders feast on giant Maine **lobsters** and **steamers** (clams), perhaps in a creamy **chowder**, while any trip to Louisiana should see you slurping back raw **oysters** and mounds of juicy mudbugs (**crawfish**) boiled with spices. Florida offers **conch**, a meaty mollusc, while the firm-fleshed, tasty **catfish** is a staple in the south. Hawaii, meanwhile, is home to some of the world's finest **Pacific Rim** restaurants, fusing Asian, Pacific and Californian cuisine and centring on local fish like **mahi mahi** (dorado).

▲ Cajun food sign

Regional cuisine

The complex pattern of immigration in the US is writ large in its food. In the soggy swamplands of southern Louisiana, for example, the French-speaking population cooks up a spicy stew called **gumbo** – made with okra, garlic and bell peppers and filled out with anything from chicken or pork sausage to crawfish – that was heavily influenced by the cooking of West African slaves. This **Cajun** cooking, as rustic as it is, has similarities with **Creole cuisine**, its urban cousin, and you'll find gumbos served in grand New Orleans restaurants alongside shrimp *étouffé* ("smothered" in a flavourful sauce).

▼ Oyster bar

Southern cooking, or **soul food**, is the perfect comfort food, if often quirkily named. Take unappetizing-sounding grits, for example (in fact a tasty, steaming hot gloop of ground corn cooked with butter and salt) – not to mention collard greens (cabbage), chitlins (pork sweetmeats), Hoppin' John (black-eyed beans and rice) and hush puppies (fried corn balls).

▼ Chicken tacos

Tex-Mex, spicier than Mexican food, adds guacamole, melted cheese and chopped tomatoes with cilantro to staples like pinto beans and tortillas. Originally Mexican, **tamales**, wads of soft crumbly corn dough filled with shredded pork and chicken, cheese and vegetables steamed in a cornhusk, have spread throughout the southern states. In the health-conscious 1980s, California created its own take on

Katz's Delicatessen ▲

Maui Wowie Salad, *Roy's Poipu Bar & Grill* ▼

Chez Panisse ▼

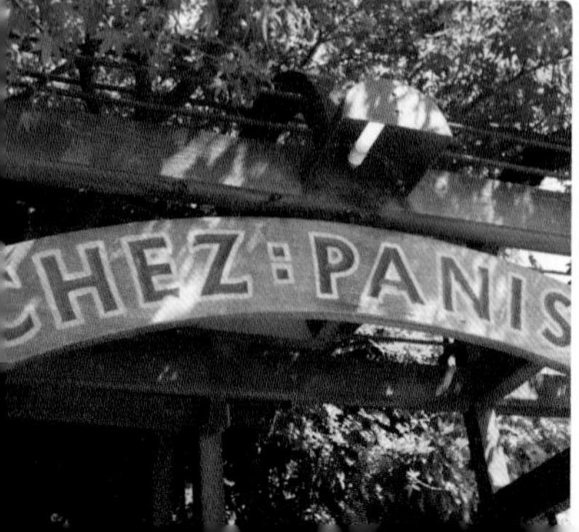

nouvelle cuisine, producing tiny plates of highly designed, healthy food. This fad spread nationwide, evolving into **New American Cuisine** – a style of cooking that can be applied to any regional dish with a modern edge. In the **Southwest**, local ingredients – chili peppers, *jicama*, *piñons* – give Tex-Mex a creative twist. Another Southwestern staple is **Navajo frybread**, which is similar to a taco, served with minced beef and chili, or, in New Mexico, with honey butter.

The best...

For the very best food in the US, pay a visit to one of the following restaurants:

▸▸ **All-you-can-eat buffet** *The Bellagio*, Las Vegas, NV (p.825)

▸▸ **BBQ** *Fresh Air Barbecue*, Jackson, GA (p.436)

▸▸ **Cajun** *Prejean's*, Lafayette, LA (p.580)

▸▸ **California cuisine** *Chez Panisse*, Berkeley, CA (p.925)

▸▸ **Crab** *Obrycki's*, Baltimore, MD (p.384)

▸▸ **Creole** *Galatoire's*, New Orleans, LA (p.568)

▸▸ **Delicatessen** *Katz's*, New York, NY (p.98)

▸▸ **Diner** *Moody's Diner*, Waldoboro, ME (p.236)

▸▸ **Hot dog** *Nathan's*, Brooklyn, NY (p.101)

▸▸ **Lobster** *Lobster Shack at Two Lights*, Cape Elizabeth, ME (p.233)

▸▸ **New American** *Alpenglow Stube*, Keystone, CO (p.695)

▸▸ **Pacific Rim** *Roy's Poipu Bar & Grill*, Poipu, HI (p.1050)

▸▸ **Soul food** *Four Way Grill*, Memphis, TN (p.459)

▸▸ **Southern** *Mrs Wilkes'*, Savannah, GA (p.440)

▸▸ **Southwestern** *Turquoise Room*, Winslow, AZ (p.786)

▸▸ **Steak** *Cattleman's Steak House*, Fort Worth, TX (p.620)

▸▸ **Tex-Mex** *Boudro's*, San Antonio, TX (p.612)

The Lakes Region

Of the literally hundreds of lakes occupying the state's central corridor, the biggest by far is **Lake Winnipesaukee**, which forms the centre of the holiday-oriented Lakes Region. Long segments of its three-hundred-mile shoreline, especially in the east, consist of thick forests sweeping down to waters dotted with little islands, which are disturbed only by pleasure craft. The most sophisticated of the towns along the shoreline is **Wolfeboro**; the most fun has to be **Weirs Beach**.

Ideally, you would bring your own small boat here and get thoroughly lost in the maze of small channels and islets. Failing that, the **cruise ship** M/S *Mount Washington*, a 230ft monster of a boat, departs from the dock in the centre of Weirs Beach several times a day to sail to Wolfeboro, on the western side of the lake (mid-May to Oct; from $25; ⓣ603/366-5531 or 1-888/843-6686, ⓦwww.cruisenh.com). The ship also sets sail for dinner and dance cruises several times per week (from $43). The same company offers cruises from Weirs Beach on the smaller M/V *Doris E* (late June to early Sept daily; $15) and the US mailboat, M/V *Sophie C* (mid-June to mid-Sept Mon–Sat; $22), from which you can view some of the lake's many islands as the boat delivers the mail.

Wolfeboro

Because Governor Wentworth of New Hampshire built his summer home nearby in 1768, tiny **WOLFEBORO** claims to be "the oldest summer resort in America". Sandwiched between lakes Winnipesaukee and Wentworth, it's a relaxing place to spend a few hours, especially along the short but bustling main street, next to the quay where the *Mount Washington* (see above) comes in.

For **accommodation**, the 1812 *Wolfeboro Inn*, 90 N Main St (ⓣ603/569-3016 or 1-800/451-2389, ⓦwww.wolfeboroinn.com; ⑧), stands in a dignified waterfront position just a few yards from the town proper. The *123 North Main B&B*, 123 N Main St (ⓣ603/569-9191; ⑦), is a cosy, friendly place to stay, close to both the town and lake. *Wolfeboro Campground* is at 61 Haines Hill Rd (ⓣ603/569-9881, ⓦwww.wolfeborocampground.com; $26–30), and is open from mid-May to mid-October. For **food**, *Full Belli Deli*, at 15 Mill St (ⓣ603/569-1955) serves enormous and tasty sub sandwiches in a little subterranean spot just off Main Street; while *Bailey's Bubble*, on Railroad Avenue (ⓣ603/569-3612), serves luscious local ice cream to enjoy on the quayside; *Lydia's Café*, 33 N Main St (daily until 2.30pm; ⓣ603/569-3991), is an excellent, veggie-oriented place for breakfast, lunch or smoothies.

Weirs Beach

The short boardwalk at **WEIRS BEACH**, the very essence of seaside tackiness (even if it is fifty miles inland), is the social centre of the Lakes Region in the summer. Its little wooden jetty throngs with vacationers, the amusement arcades jingle with cash and there's even a neat little crescent of sandy beach, suitable for family swimming. A quieter diversion here is the **Winnipesaukee Railroad** (late May to early June & Sept–Oct weekends; mid-June to Aug daily; $13 for 1hr, $14 for 2hr; ⓣ603/279-5253, ⓦwww.hoborr.com), which operates scenic trips along the lakeshore between Weirs Beach and Meredith.

Meredith

Four miles north of Weirs Beach, **MEREDITH** enjoys a peaceful location and has an upmarket character, making it the best place to stay on the lake's western shore. The *Inns at Mill Falls*, which is actually four separate hotels (Ⓣ1-800/622-6455, Ⓦwww.millfalls.com), are the best choice for **accommodation**. Choose from the *Inn at Mill Falls* (❺) and the *Chase House* (❽), both on the hill overlooking the lake, or the *Inn at Bay Point* (❽) or the new *Church Landing* (❽–❾), directly on the water and offering unrivalled lake views. *Town Docks*, on US-3 just south of the intersection with Rte-25 (Ⓣ603/279-3445), is a reliable choice for seafood.

The White Mountains

Thanks to their accessibility from both Montréal to the north and Boston to the south, the **White Mountains** have become a year-round tourist destination, popular with both summer hikers and winter skiers. Commercialized they may be, but the great granite massifs retain most of their majesty and power. **Mount Washington**, the highest peak in the northeast, can claim some of the most severe weather in the world, and conditions are harsh enough for the timberline to lie at four thousand feet (compared to the Rockies' norm of ten thousand).

Just a few high passes – here called "**notches**" – pierce the range, and the roads through these gaps, such as the **Kancamagus Highway** between Lincoln and Conway, make for enjoyable driving (compulsory **parking permits** are $3 for the day, $5 for the week, or $20 for the season). However, you won't really have made the most of the White Mountains unless you also set off, on foot or on skis, across the long expanses of thick evergreen forest that separate them, with snowcapped peaks poking out in all directions. The best sources of **information** in the region are the White Mountains Visitor Center, at I-93 exit 32, in North Woodstock (July–Sept 8.30am–6pm; Oct–June 8.30am–5.30pm; Ⓣ603/745-8720 or 1-800/FIND-MTS, Ⓦwww.visitwhitemountains.com), and the Pinkham Notch Visitor Center on Rte-16 (daily 6.30am–10pm; Ⓣ603/466-2721, Ⓦwww.outdoors.org), north of Jackson.

Hiking, skiing and cycling in the White Mountains

Hiking in the White Mountains is coordinated by the **Appalachian Mountain Club** or "AMC" (Ⓦwww.outdoors.org), whose chain of information centres, hostels and huts along the Appalachian Trail, traversing the region from northeast to southwest, is detailed below. Call Ⓣ603/466-2721 for trail and weather information before you attempt any serious expedition.

Downhill and cross-country **skiers** can choose from several resorts that double up as summertime activity centres. The Waterville Valley Resort (Ⓣ603/236-8311 or 1-800/468-2553, Ⓦwww.waterville.com) and Loon Mountain (Ⓣ603/745-8111 or 1-800/229-LOON, Ⓦwww.loonmtn.com), both just east of I-93, are good for downhill, while Jackson (Ⓣ603/383-9355, Ⓦwww.jacksonxc.org), about fifteen miles north of Conway on Rte-16, has some of the finest cross-country skiing trails in the northeast. General information on the skiing centres is available from Ski NH (Ⓣ603/745-9396 or 1-800/88SKI-NH, Ⓦwww.skinh.com).

In the summer, the cross-country skiing trails can make for strenuous but exhilarating **biking** (you can take lifts up the slopes and ride back down). Both Waterville and Loon have bikes for rent on site for around $32 per day; Loon also runs a zip line ($25), horseback riding ($50/person) and a bungee trampoline and climbing wall area ($18).

Accommodation

Thanks to the influx of young hikers and skiers to the White Mountains, there's a relative abundance of **budget** accommodation in the area. Keep in mind, too, that rates vary dramatically between seasons, and even from weekday to weekend.

Along the Appalachian Trail itself, there are eight **Appalachian Mountain Club huts**, which can only be reached on foot. In summer, each hut provides meals and bedding for between forty and ninety people. Prices range from $27–98 a night, according to the amount of privacy, luxury and food you're after (and depending on whether or not you're an AMC member; individual membership is $50; see ⓦwww.outdoors.org for details). **Reservations** are strongly recommended (call ⓣ603/466-2727, or visit the website), and you'll be expected to pay in full when you book the accommodation.

Campers can pitch their tents anywhere below the treeline and away from the roads in the White Mountains National Forest, provided they show consideration for the environment. There are also numerous official campgrounds ($19–31/night), particularly along the Kancamagus Highway.

The AMC runs two scheduled **shuttle van services** ($19, reservations recommended, ⓣ603/466-2727) for hikers between major trailheads and the lodges daily from June to mid-September, with weekend-only service from late Sept to mid-October.

AMC lodges

Highland Center US-302, Crawford Notch ⓣ603/466-2727, ⓦwww.outdoors.org. This innovatively designed and environmentally friendly building offers a bunk in a shared room for $100 or private rooms (❽), breakfast and dinner included (peak season rates). Open year-round.

Joe Dodge Lodge Hwy-16, Pinkham Notch ⓣ603/466-2727, ⓦwww.outdoors.org. Filled with hikers, this second AMC lodge-cum-hostel has bunks ($75) or double rooms (❹) with shared bath and meals. Near the Mount Washington Auto Rd. Open year-round.

Motels, hotels and B&Bs

Adair Country Inn 80 Guider Lane, Bethlehem ⓣ603/444-2600 or 1-888/444-2600, ⓦwww.adairinn.com. Deluxe antique-furnished rooms, with sweeping views of the landscaped grounds and impeccable staff, all reflected in the steep prices. ❼–❽

Balsams Dixville Notch ⓣ1-800/255-0800 in NH or 1-800/255-0600 outside NH, ⓦwww.thebalsams.com. Like the *Mount Washington*, *Balsams* is another of the last grand, red-roofed resort hotels. Opened in the 1860s (under a different name and since expanded in 1918), the hotel has year-round activities (skiing, golf, tennis, boating), light and airy rooms, and delicious meals (cooking classes are available). ❾

Boulder Motor Court 5 Harmony Hill Rd, Rte-302 (junction with US-3), Twin Mountain ⓣ603/846-5437, ⓦwww.bouldermotorcourt.com. Bargain one- and two-bedroom cottages with kitchens, fireplaces and other amenities. ❸

Eagle Mountain House 179 Carter Notch Rd, Jackson ⓣ603/383-9111 or 1-800/966-5779, ⓦwww.eaglemt.com. Highly atmospheric inn with a roaring fireplace in the lobby and a wraparound porch filled with rocking chairs, far above the bustle of North Conway. Has its own nine-hole golf course. ❺–❼

Omni Mount Washington Resort Rte-302, Bretton Woods ⓣ603/278-1000 or 1-800/314-1752, ⓦwww.mountwashingtonresort.com. Beautiful hotel dating from 1902, with a quarter-mile terrace, stellar views, indoor pool and a complete range of activities (including a zip line, golf, horseback riding and skiing) and pricing packages. Also runs the less-fancy *Bretton Arms*, on the same property, which is a bit cheaper (❼), though rooms are still spacious. ❽

Sugar Hill Inn 116 Route 117, Sugar Hill ⓣ603/823-5621, ⓦsugarhillinn.com. Nicely sited by Franconia Notch State Park, this charming B&B is settled into a 200-year-old farmhouse and boasts a well-executed restaurant on the premises to boot. ❺–❽

Thayer's Inn 111 Main St, Littleton ⓣ603/444-6469 or 1-800/634-8179, ⓦwww.thayersinn.com. Creaky but comfortable and classy old inn since 1850, which has hosted guests such as Ulysses S. Grant and Richard Nixon. ❹–❺

Franconia Notch

Ten miles beyond **Lincoln,** I-93, which speeds up towards northern Vermont, briefly merges with the more leisurely US-3, to pass through **Franconia Notch State Park**. **Franconia Notch** itself is a slender valley crammed between two great walls of stone. From the Flume Visitor Center (May to late Oct daily 9am–5pm; ⓣ603/745-8391), you can walk along a two-mile boardwalk-cum-nature trail to the Pemigewasset River as it rages through the narrow, rock-filled Flume gorge (entry $13). Alternatively, take a $13 cable-car ride up the sheer granite face of Cannon Mountain (late May to mid-Oct daily 9am–5pm; ⓣ603/823-8800, ⓦwww.cannonmt.com), or hike the various, well-marked trails up to panoramic views for free.

Further on, one mile south of the friendly village of **FRANCONIA**, the **Frost Place** on Ridge Road (late May to early July Sat & Sun 1–5pm; early July to early Oct Wed–Mon 1–5pm; $5 suggested donation; ⓣ603/823-5510, ⓦwww.frostplace.org) is another former home of poet Robert Frost, memorable largely for an inspiring panorama of unspoiled mountains. Each summer the poet-in-residence will often give poetry readings during visiting hours.

Mount Washington

From the awe-inspiring peak of 6288ft **Mount Washington** you can, on a clear day, see all the way to the Atlantic and into Canada. But the real interest in making the ascent lies in the extraordinary severity of the weather up here, which results from the summit's position right in the path of the principal storm tracks and air-mass routes affecting the northeastern US. The wind here exceeds hurricane strength on more than a hundred days of the year, and in 1934 it reached the highest speed ever recorded anywhere in the world – 231mph. At the top, you'll see the remarkable spectacle of buildings actually held down with great chains; many have been blown away over the years, including the old observatory, said to be the strongest wooden building ever constructed. Up here you'll also find a **visitor centre** (mid-May to mid-Oct 8.30am–6pm; ⓣ603/466-3347), the new observatory with small museum (daily 9am–6pm; $3), a large viewing platform and **Tip Top House**, once a hotel for wealthy travellers and now a basic museum (June–Oct daily 10am–4pm; free).

On the way to the top, you pass through four distinct climatic zones, starting with century-old fir and ash trees so stunted as to be below waist-height and ending with Arctic tundra. The drive up the **Mount Washington Auto Road** (early May to late Oct, weather permitting 8am–4pm; ⓣ603/466-3988 for weather conditions, ⓦwww.mtwashingtonautoroad.com) isn't as hair-raising as you might expect, though the hairpin bends and lack of guardrails certainly keep you alert. There is a $23 **toll** for car and driver (plus $8 for each additional adult and $6 for kids), which comes with an audio tape or CD detailing the road's history. You can also take a **narrated tour** in a specially adapted minibus (daily 8.30am–5pm; $29).

Last but far from least, you can also ride to the top on the coal-fired steam train of the **Mount Washington Cog Railway**, which noisily climbs the exposed flank of the mountain, ascending grades of up to 38 degrees on a track completed in 1869. It's truly a unique experience, as you inch up the steep wooden trestles while trying to avoid descending showers of coal smut. The three-hour round trip costs $62 ($39 for kids), and trains leave hourly (weekends only in May, June to early Nov daily, weather permitting; ⓣ603/278-5404 or 1-800/922-8825 for other dates and times and to reserve, ⓦwww.thecog.com) from a station off Rte-302 six miles northeast of Bretton Woods.

North Conway

A few miles south of Mount Washington, US-302 and Hwy-16 enter **NORTH CONWAY** by first passing through a hodgepodge of shopping malls, fast-food joints and kiddie theme parks such as Story Land (Ⓣ603/383-4186; $27). More useful is the **White Mountain National Forest Saco Ranger Station**, 33 Kancamagus Hwy near Rte-16 in Conway (daily 8am–4.30pm; Ⓣ603/447-5448), which sells books, maps and the mandatory National Forest parking permits ($3 for one day, $5 for seven consecutive days). It also provides a ton of resources for area planning and handles backcountry cabin rentals.

The Kancamagus Highway

The **Kancamagus Highway** (Hwy-112), connecting North Conway and Lincoln, is the least busy road through the mountains, and makes for a very pleasant 34-mile drive. Several campgrounds are situated in the woods to either side, and various walking trails are signposted. The half-mile hike to **Sabbaday Falls**, off to the south roughly halfway along the highway, leads up a narrow rocky cleft in the forest to a succession of idyllic waterfalls. If you plan on a picnic, though, take note: there is no food or gas available along the highway.

Eating and drinking

Family **restaurants** and fast-food joints line the main drags of major centres such as North Woodstock and North Conway. The best places are in less conspicuous areas and worth rooting out. Some of the hotels and B&Bs recommended on p.219 also serve food.

Chef's Market of North Conway 2724 Main St, North Conway Village Ⓣ603/356-4747. A dazzling display case of fancy picnic fixings (such as Angus beef medallions or chicken marsala); there are also tasty soups and sandwiches on offer. Open til 6pm, closed Tues.

Beal House Inn 2 W Main St, Littleton Ⓣ603/444-2661. Intimate bistro and piano bar serving a mix of classic cuisines with contemporary flair, such as lobster sauté with wide noodles and spring vegetables.

Miller's Cafe and Bakery 16 Mill St, Littleton Ⓣ603/444-2146. Fresh home-made soups, salads and sandwiches enjoyed on a deck overlooking the Ammonoosuc River.

Polly's Pancake Parlor I-93 exit 38, Rte-117, Sugar Hill Ⓣ603/823-5575. Yes, it's in the middle of nowhere, but it's a scenic nowhere and well worth the trip if you love pancakes ($6.99 for three). Open early May to Oct 7am–2pm (till 3pm on weekends).

Thompson House Eatery 193 Main St, Jackson Ⓣ603/383-9341. Atmospheric old farmhouse with inventive salad and sandwich creations at lunchtime (think breaded eggplant with basil olive mayonnaise); there are equally ingenious entrees served for dinner.

Vermont

VERMONT comes closer than any other New England state to realizing the quintessential image of small-town America, with its white churches and red barns, covered bridges and clapboard houses, snowy woods and maple syrup. The largest city is **Burlington** and the chief tourist attraction is **Ben & Jerry's** ice-cream factory in Waterbury. Though rural, Vermont's landscape is not all that agricultural – much of it is covered by mountainous forests (the state's name derives from the French *vert mont*, or "green mountain").

This was the last area of New England to be settled, early in the eighteenth century. The leader of the New Hampshire settlers, the now-legendary **Ethan Allen**, formed his **Green Mountain Boys** in 1770, and during the Revolutionary War, this all-but-autonomous force helped to win the decisive Battle of Bennington. In 1777, Vermont declared itself an independent republic, with the first constitution in the world explicitly forbidding slavery and granting universal (male) suffrage; in 1791 it became the first state admitted to the Union after the original thirteen colonies. A more recent example of Vermont's progressive attitude occurred in 2000, when former governor Howard Dean signed the **civil union** bill into law, making the state first in the US to sanction marital rights for same-sex couples.

With the occasional exception, such as the extraordinary assortment of Americana at the **Shelburne Museum** near Burlington, there are few specific goals for tourists. Visitors come in great numbers during two well-defined seasons: to see the **autumn foliage** during the first two weeks of October, and to **ski** during the heart of winter, when resorts such as **Killington** and **Stowe** (former home to *The Sound of Music*'s Von Trapp family) spring into life. For the rest of the year, you might just as well explore any of the state's minor roads, confident that some picturesque village will appear around the next corner.

The Green Mountains

The weather in the **Green Mountains**, which form the backbone of Vermont, is not as harsh as in New Hampshire's White Mountains – though its forests are usually buried in snow for most of the winter, and local roads at high elevations may be blocked due to snowfall. Routes north from **Bennington**, **Brattleboro** and along scenic **Hwy-100** offer unspoiled mountain views and the best of small-town New England.

In summer, hikers take up the challenge of the **Long Trail** along the central ridge, leading 273 miles from the Massachusetts border all the way to Québec. Built between 1910 and 1930, the trail served as inspiration for the Appalachian Trail; today, the two trails follow the same path for 100 miles north of the Massachusetts border. The Long Trail is maintained by the **Green Mountain Club** (Ⓣ802/244-7037, Ⓦwww.greenmountainclub.org), whose *Long Trail Guide* ($18.95) is an invaluable resource for hikers.

Bennington

In the past two hundred years, little has happened in **BENNINGTON** to match the excitement of the days when Ethan Allen's Green Mountain Boys were based here. A 306ft hilltop obelisk (mid-April to Oct daily 9am–5pm; $2) commemorates the 1777 **Battle of Bennington**, in which the Boys were a crucial factor in defeating the British under General Burgoyne (though the battle itself was fought just across the border in New York). You should also check out the **Bennington Museum**, 75 Main St (daily except Wed 10am–5pm; $10; Ⓣ802/447-1571, Ⓦwww.bennington museum.org), which contains a memorable array of Americana and the largest collection of paintings by folk artist Grandma Moses. For fine hand-crafted ceramics visit **Bennington Potters**, 324 County St (Mon–Sat 9.30am–6pm, Sun 10am–5pm; Ⓣ1-800/205-8033, Ⓦwww.benningtonpotters.com).

The *Hampton Inn Bennington*, 51 Hannaford Square (Ⓣ802/448-9862, Ⓦwww .hamptoninn.com; ❻), is the best of several downtown **motels** on this stretch. A cosy B&B alternative is the *Alexandra Inn* at 916 Orchard St, just off 7A

(T802/442-5619, Wwww.alexandrainn.com; 6–7). As for **food**, students from the small and arty Bennington College crowd into the *Madison Brewing Company*, 428 Main St (T802/442-7397) or the *Blue Benn Diner*, 314 North St (US-7; T802/442-5140).

North from Brattleboro

Driving north from **BRATTLEBORO**, noted for its lively local arts scene and student-driven nightlife, routes 30 and 35 offer a less-travelled alternative into central Vermont. Few places come closer to the iconic image of rural New England than **GRAFTON**, a truly gorgeous ensemble of brilliant white clapboard buildings, shady trees and a bubbling brook in the centre. Stop in at the **Grafton Village Cheese Company** at 55 Townshend Rd (daily 10am–6pm; T802/843-2221 or 1-800/472-3866, Wwww.graftonvillagecheese.com). Further north, sleepy **CHESTER** blends prototypical Vermont clapboard houses with more ornate, Victorian architecture, laid out charmingly where Rte-11 runs along a narrow green. Here you can jump aboard the **Green Mountain Flyer** (1 departure Fridays at 11am, May to mid-Oct; $21; T1-800/707-3530, Wwww.rails-vt.com), a sightseeing train that runs two-hour return trips from Chester Depot down to Bellows Falls and back.

Practicalities

The most popular place to **stay** in Brattleboro is the Art Deco *Latchis Hotel*, 50 Main St (T802/254-6300, Wwww.latchis.com; 5). In Grafton, try the upmarket *Old Tavern*, 92 Main St (T1-800/843-1801, Wwww.old-tavern.com; 8), which has an excellent **restaurant**. The best place in Chester is *Inn Victoria*, 321 Main St (T802/875-4288 or 1-800/732-4288, Wwww.innvictoria.com; 5–9).

In Brattleboro you'll find decent **eating** at the *Riverview Café*, 36 Bridge St (T802/254-9841), which has a nice view overlooking the Connecticut River. The best **beer** resides at the *Flat Street Brew Pub*, inside the *Latchis Hotel*, 6 Flat St (T802/257-1911). The vintage 1938 *Chelsea Royal Diner*, just west of town at 487 Marlboro Rd (Rte-9; T802/254-8399), has standout diner fare and authentic Mexican food served Tuesday to Saturday evenings (hours: 6am–9pm). For coffee, join the queue at the beloved *Mocha Joe's Café*, 82 Main St (T802/257-7794).

Hwy-100 Scenic Drive: Weston

One of the prettiest villages along Rte-100 is **WESTON**, which spreads out beside a little river and centres on a perfect green. The **Vermont Country Store**, south of the green, is larger than it looks from its modest facade. For all its seeming quaintness, this Vermont institution is actually part of a chain. Opposite, the **Weston Village Store** is more authentic – and cheaper – with a range of vaguely rural and domestic articles, such as local maple syrup and cheeses.

Weston's best **accommodation** is the lovely *Inn at Weston*, on Hwy-100, near the village green (T802/824-6789, Wwww.innweston.com; 7–8), with homey rooms, an orchid-filled gazebo, an excellent **restaurant** and a cosy pub. The basic yet appealing *Colonial House*, at 287 Rte-100, has both a motel property and B&B on site, with a full breakfast included in the price (T802/824-6286, Wwww.cohoinn.com; 4–5). A small but magnificent soda fountain dominates the 1885 mahogany bar of the *Bryant House* restaurant, next door to the Vermont Country Store on Main Street (dinner daily; T802/824-6287), whose lunch menu includes country fare, such as "johnnycakes". The best bet for **entertainment** is the attractive Weston Playhouse, which offers summer and autumn performances (Tues–Sun; $24–52; T802/824-5288, Wwww.westonplayhouse.org).

Killington

The ski resort of **KILLINGTON** (ⓣ802/422-6200 for the resort or 1-800/621-6867 for other area reservations; ⓣ802/422-3261 for 24-hour taped skiing information, ⓦwww.killington.com), in the centre of the Green Mountains, thirty miles north of Weston, has grown exponentially since 1958. The resort sprawls over seven mountains (Pico Mountain is the best for skiers of mid-range ability), and is notorious for its rowdy nightlife. For hikers, the Long and Appalachian trails meet just north of here. In summer and autumn, you can still take the **K-1 Gondola** ($10 one-way, $15 return) up to the observation deck and cafeteria on Killington Peak (4241ft). Choose your way back down: hike or mountain bike (rentals are available at the base).

In winter, the Killington Road up from US-4 is humming with crowded **bars** and **restaurants**: *Wobbly Barn Steakhouse* (Nov–April; ⓣ802/422-6171) is good for beef in all forms, and lively entertainment, and the *Pickle Barrel* (ⓣ802/422-3035) is a rowdy bar that gets crazier on winter weekends. The cosy and clean *Killington Motel*, 1946 Rte-4 (ⓣ802/773-9535, ⓦwww.lodgingkillington.com ❹), is nicely situated for ski access, and has friendly owners and great breakfasts; the *Inn at Long Trail*, on Sherburne Pass (ⓣ802/775-7181 or 1-800/325-2540; ⓦwww.innatlongtrail.com; ❺), is perfectly situated for Long Trail hikers (see p.222).

Woodstock

Since its settlement in the 1760s, beautiful **WOODSTOCK**, a few miles west of the Connecticut River up US-4, has been one of Vermont's more refined centres (not to be confused with Woodstock, New York, namesake of the 1969 music festival). Its distinguished houses cluster around an oval green, now largely taken over by art galleries and tearooms.

Woodstock's main paying attraction is the **Billings Farm and Museum**, Rte-12, at River Road (May 1 to Oct 31, daily 10am–5pm; Nov–Feb weekends 10am–3.30pm; $12; ⓣ802/457-2355, ⓦwww.billingsfarm.org). Part museum of late-nineteenth-century farm life, part working dairy farm, it features demonstrations of antiquated skills and an Academy Award-nominated film of the farm's history. **Hiking trails**, accessible from the town centre, are great for a leisurely stroll; they join up with forest trails of the nearby **Marsh-Billings-Rockefeller National Historical Park** (year-round; visitor centre open late May to Oct daily 10am–5pm; trails free, $8 for a guided tour of the mansion, alternatively, there's a $17 combo ticket that includes admission to Billings Farm; ⓣ802/457-3368, ⓦwww.nps.gov/mabi), which are groomed for winter skiing and snowshoeing (see the excellent National Park Service map for details).

The friendly staff at the centrally located **Woodstock Welcome Center** on Mechanic Street (daily 9am–5pm; ⓣ802/432-1100, ⓦwww.woodstockvt.com) has extensive information on lodging, dining and other area attractions. Options include the well-refurbished *Shire Riverview*, 46 Pleasant St (ⓣ802/457-2211, ⓦwww.shiremotel.com; ❹–❼), the upmarket, newly renovated *Woodstock Inn and Resort*, 14 The Green, US-4, in the centre of the village (ⓣ802/457-1100 or 1-800/448-7900, ⓦwww.woodstockinn.com; ❾), and the cosy *Applebutter Inn*, four miles east of town on US-4, in Taftsville (ⓣ802/457-4158, ⓦwww.applebutterinn.com; ❹–❽). For an excellent B&B experience, it's difficult to beat ✱ *October Country Inn* (located 10 miles west of Woodstock, ⓣ802/672-3412, ⓦwww.vermontinns.net; ❼) for charm and comfort, especially during the autumn foliage season.

Of the several places to **eat** in Woodstock, *Bentley's*, 3 Elm St (ⓣ802/457-3232), has a range of microbrews and smart versions of traditional bistro food, and the *Osteria*

Pane e Salute, 61 Central St (Ⓣ802/457-4882), serves locally-sourced Italian food paired with great wine in an intimate, romantic dining room. Comfort food breakfasts, lunches and ice cream are on offer at *Mountain Creamery*, 33 Central St (daily 7am–3pm; Ⓣ802/457-1715), while *Wasp's Snack Bar*, 57 Pleasant St (Ⓣ802/457-3334), is a no-frills local institution, specializing in home-cooked breakfasts.

Quechee

Six miles east of Woodstock, **QUECHEE** is off the main US-4 highway, a combination of quaint Vermont village and expensive new condos. The main highlight here lies on US-4 itself, **Quechee Gorge State Park**, which preserves the splendours of the **Quechee Gorge**. A delicate bridge spans the 165ft chasm of the Ottauquechee River, and hiking trails lead down from the **visitor centre** (daily 9am–5pm; Ⓣ802/295-6852). You can **camp** at the Quechee State Park campground ($16–25/night; Ⓣ802/295-2990 or 1-888/409-7579), or if you'd rather not rough it, the *Quality Inn* (Ⓣ802/295-7600 or 1-800/732-4376, Ⓦwww.qualityinnquechee.com; ❻) on US-4, between the gorge and tourist shops of the Quechee Gorge Village, offers the best-value **accommodation**.

The river spins the turbines of the **Simon Pearce Glass Mill** (daily 10am–9pm; Ⓣ802/295-2711, Ⓦwww.simonpearce.com), housed in a former wool mill along Main Street back in Quechee. Here, you can watch glass bowls and plates being blown (10am–5pm), and then eat from them at the superb on-site **restaurant** (overlooking a waterfall) which serves, among other dishes, horseradish-crusted blue cod, sesame-seared tofu and crispy roast duck ($22–30 dinner entrees, about $15 for lunch); reservations are recommended (Ⓣ802/295-1470).

Montpelier

Some fifty-five miles north of Quechee on I-89, **MONTPELIER** is the smallest state capital in the nation, with fewer than ten thousand inhabitants. Surrounded by leafy gardens, the golden-domed **State House** (Mon–Fri 8am–4pm) is well worth a free tour for its marble-floored and mural-lined hallways (guided tours on the half-hour July to mid-Oct Mon–Fri 10am–3.30pm, Sat 11am–2.30pm; Ⓣ802/828-2228). Copious information on accommodation, here and throughout the state, is available from the **Capitol Region Visitors Center**, opposite the State House at 134 State St (Mon–Fri 6am–6pm, Sat & Sun 9am–5pm; Ⓣ802/828-5981 or 1-800/VERMONT, Ⓦwww.vermontvacation.com). Good **B&B** rooms can be had at the central yet quiet *Inn at Montpelier*, 147 Main St (Ⓣ802/223-2727, Ⓦwww.innatmontpelier.com; ❻).

For **food**, students from the local New England Culinary Institute run the *Main St Grill & Bar* at 118 Main St (closed Mon; Ⓣ802/223-3188), serving excellent, inexpensive, experimental dishes from all over the world. *Coffee Corner*, on Main Street at State (Ⓣ802/229-9060), has been serving dirt-cheap diner food for over sixty years.

There are several options for live music; *Langdon Street Café*, 4 Langdon St (Ⓣ802/223-8667, Ⓦwww.langdonstreetcafe.com), has a homey feel, with live music nightly and beer, wine and coffee, while *Black Door Bar and Bistro*, 44 Main St (closed Sun; Ⓣ802/223-7070, Ⓦwww.blackdoorvt.com), is a bit fancier, with jazz, zydeco or comedy ($3 cover) and a great restaurant on the second floor.

Waterbury

Few people paid much attention to **WATERBURY** before 1985, when Ben Cohen and Jerry Greenfield (whose ice-cream-making history began in 1978, in a renovated

Burlington gas station) decided to locate their new manufacturing facility in the tiny town. Today, **Ben & Jerry's Ice Cream Factory**, one mile north of I-89 on Rte-100 in the centre of Waterbury, has become the number-one tourist destination in Vermont. Half-hour tours (daily: July to mid-Aug 9am–9pm; late Aug to mid-Oct till 7pm; late Oct to June 10am–6pm; $3, under 12 free; every 30min; ⓣ802/882-1240 or 1-866/BJ-TOURS, ⓦwww.benjerry.com) include a short film, a view of the workforce from an observation platform (weekdays only) and a free mini-scoop of the stuff that made it all possible – you can buy more at the counter outside.

Stowe

At the foot of Vermont's highest mountain, the 4393ft **Mount Mansfield**, lies the popular summer- and wintertime resort of **STOWE**. There is still a beautiful nineteenth-century village at the town's heart – with a white-spired meeting house and a pretty green – though a century's worth of catering to skiers and outdoor enthusiasts has swamped the approach road to the main ski area with equipment stores, resort spas and sprawling condo complexes. Nevertheless, Stowe's setting remains spectacular.

Stowe's **visitor centre** on Main Street, near the intersection with Mountain Road (Mon–Sat 9am–8pm, Sun till 5pm; ⓣ802/253-7321 or 1-877/GO-STOWE, ⓦwww.gostowe.com), provides information on skiing conditions and accommodation. **Bikes** for the Recreation Path, a paved trail that twists through 5.3 miles of scenery, can be rented from the Skier Shop, 580 Mountain Rd ($25/day; ⓣ802/253-7919, ⓦwww.skiershop.com).

Hwy-108 – **Mountain Road** – leads up to the main Stowe Mountain Resort (ⓦwww.stowe.com) and beyond, through the dramatic **Smugglers' Notch** pass (closed during winter). The Smugglers' Notch Resort on the other side (ⓣ1-800/451-8752, ⓦwww.smuggs.com) is a less crowded, more family-orientated alternative to Stowe. Weather permitting, you can get to the top of Mount Mansfield either by driving four and a half miles up the **Toll Road**, which begins seven miles up Mountain Road (late May to mid-Oct daily 9am–4pm; $25/car), or by taking the **Gondola Skyride** (mid-June to mid-Oct daily 10am–5pm; $18 one-way, $24 return; ⓣ802/253-7311) up to the *Cliff House Restaurant* (lunch only, elevation 3660ft).

In 1941, after fleeing Austria, the **Von Trapp family**, of *The Sound of Music* fame settled in Stowe, where they established the *Trapp Family Lodge* at 700 Trapp Hill Rd (ⓣ802/253-8511 or 1-800/826-7000, ⓦwww.trappfamily.com; ❾). The original lodge, where Maria von Trapp held singing camps, burned down in 1980; it has since been replaced by a luxurious resort, home to 62 miles of groomed trails suitable for hiking, cross-country skiing and snowshoeing; along with numerous amenities.

Practicalities

The best of the plentiful accommodation (save the lodge above) includes the sumptuous *Stowe Mountain Lodge*, 7412 Mountain Rd (ⓣ1-888/478-6938 or ⓣ802/253-3560, ⓦwww.stowemountainlodge.com; ❾), right next to the Spruce Peak ski area; and the historic *Green Mountain Inn*, 18 Main St (ⓣ802/253-7301 or 1-800/253-7302, ⓦwww.greenmountaininn.com; ❻–❼). Cheaper rooms are available at the *Riverside Inn*, 1965 Mountain Rd (ⓣ802/253-4217 or 1-800/966-4217, ⓦwww.rivinn.com; ❹). *Gold Brook Campground* is two miles south on Hwy-100 (ⓣ802/253-7683; $23).

There are plenty of places to **eat** on Mountain Road. *McCarthy's* (ⓣ802/253-8626), at no. 2043, is best for breakfast; the *Shed Restaurant & Brew Pub*, at no. 1859

(☎802/253-4364), has moderately-priced American food and good beer; and the always-crowded *Piecasso*, at no. 1899 (☎802/253-5100), serves excellent pizza and pasta dishes. A more upmarket option for dinner is the *Blue Moon Café*, at 35 School St in the main village (☎802/253-7006), which offers an innovative menu including Vermont rabbit and venison, as well as a good wine list.

Burlington and around

Lakeside **BURLINGTON**, Vermont's largest "city", with a population near forty thousand, is one of the most enjoyable towns in New England. Renowned for its liveability and green development, Burlington is a hip, eclectic community that fuses urbanism with rural Vermont values. The city faces 150-mile-long **Lake Champlain**, which forms the natural boundary between Vermont and New York. Burlington's founders included Revolutionary War hero Ethan Allen and his family; Ethan's brother Ira founded the University of Vermont. Home to five colleges and universities, Burlington is a youthful and outward-looking college town. Its downtown area is easily strolled by foot, notably around the **Church Street Marketplace**.

Arrival, information and getting around

Greyhound **buses** stop in downtown Burlington, at 219 S Winsooki St. The Amtrak **train** station is an inconvenient five miles northeast, in the small community of Essex Junction (connecting buses $1.25). The **airport**, Vermont's largest, is a few miles east of town along US-2.

Information and help with accommodation is available from the **Lake Champlain Regional Chamber of Commerce**, 60 Main St (July–Sept Mon–Fri 8.30am–5pm, Sat & Sun 9am–5pm; Oct–June Mon–Fri 8.30am–5pm; ☎802/863-3489 or 1-877/686-5253, ⓦwww.vermont.org).

The local CCTA **bus** company (☎802/864-2282, ⓦwww.cctaride.org) runs a free shuttle (every 15–30min Mon–Fri 6.45am–9.30pm; Sat 9am–6.15pm, no Sun service) connecting the university campus, downtown and the waterfront.

Accommodation

Burlington has no shortage of moderately priced **accommodation**, especially along Shelburne Road between Burlington and Shelburne, while for **camping** the lakeside *North Beach Campground* (☎802/862-0942 or 1-800/571-1198; $25–34) is less than two miles north on Institute Road.

Courtyard Burlington Harbor 25 Cherry St ☎802/864-4700, ⓦwww.marriott.com. Best hotel downtown, with a fabulous location near the waterfront and new, luxurious rooms and amenities; buffet breakfast, indoor pool and LCD TVs included. ❽

G.G.T. Tibet Inn 1860 Shelburne Rd, South Burlington ☎802/863-7110, ⓦwww.ggttibetinn.com. Popular motel run by amiable Tibetan émigrés; rooms, though small and simple, are a great value (each with cable TV, fridge and microwave), but it's the extra touches, including arts and crafts, a Tibetan library and prayer flags, that make it so memorable. ❹

Howard Street Guest House 153 Howard St ☎802/864-4886, ⓦwww.howardstreetguesthouse.com. Two charming suites – one with a bright colour palette, the other with a beachhouse feel – equipped with wi-fi, air conditioning and kitchenettes in a quiet carriage house a mile outside of town. ❼

Willard Street Inn 349 S Willard St ☎802/651-8710, or 1-800/577-8712, ⓦwww.willardstreetinn.com. A few blocks south of the town centre, this gorgeously restored home comes with a relaxing garden, pantry and sweet and savoury breakfasts served in its antique solarium. ❼–❾

The City

The pedestrianized **Church Street Marketplace**, commercial and cultural centre of historic Burlington, features cafés, a farmer's market (during spring and summer) and frequent live street performances.

In the summertime, locals and visitors alike stroll leisurely along the pedestrian boardwalks that line Burlington's **waterfront**, taking in gorgeous views of the Adirondack Mountains (in wintertime, they may be strolling *on* Lake Champlain, which often freezes over during February). The highly interactive **ECHO Lake Aquarium and Science Center** (Ⓣ802/864-1848 or 1-877/864-6386, Ⓦwww.echovermont.org), situated at the water's edge, is an excellent place to bring young children. Burlington's annual waterfront **Winter Festival** (during the first week in February) boasts fabulous ice sculptures, carved on the premises. For a tour of the lake itself, the convivial *Spirit of Ethan Allen III* ($14.49 narrated tour, $19.25–47 lunch and evening theme and lobster dinner cruises; Ⓣ802/862-8300, Ⓦwww.soea.com) sets off from the dock at the end of College Street.

Biking opportunities abound: the 7.6 mile **Burlington Bike Path** follows the lake shoreline, linking six major waterfront parks. Bikes are easily rented ($28+/day) from North Star Sports, 100 Main St (Ⓣ802/863-3832), and Skirack, 85 Main St (Ⓣ802/658-3313). Elevated **Battery Park** (located at the top of Battery Street) is also an ideal spot for watching the sun set over the Adirondacks. For opportunities to swim and kayak, Burlington's pristine **North Beach** is the go-to spot (May 1 to Labor Day; $8/vehicle parking for non-residents 9am–9pm).

For a diversion off the beaten track, follow Rte-127 north to the **Ethan Allen Homestead** (May–Oct Thurs–Mon 10am–4pm; $7; Ⓣ802/865-4556, Ⓦwww.ethanallenhomestead.org), which offers a multifaceted look at Vermont's controversial founding father, as well as scenic walking trails.

Eating, drinking and entertainment

Thanks in part to the presence of ten thousand students, Burlington features many good, inexpensive **restaurants**, as well as some raucous nightspots.

American Flatbread 115 St Paul St Ⓣ802/861-2999. Wildly popular place with all-natural and organic pizzas, many baked with locally-farmed produce.

Farmhouse Tap & Grill 160 Bank St Ⓣ802/859-0888. Satisfyingly built on the heap of a former *McDonald's* (it's the local-foodie that could!), *Farmhouse* boasts a scenic beer garden with on-the-premises brews and a restaurant with gourmet burgers and locally-sourced pub grub. Fun tip: check out the old *McD's* tiles on the dining room floor.

Leunig's Bistro 115 Church St Ⓣ802/863-3759. A Burlington institution, this authentic French bistro buzzes at all hours with patrons hungry for Parisian classics prepared with a Vermont twist.

Muddy Waters 184 Main St Ⓣ802/658-0466. Eclectic woody interior and colourful clientele distinguish this popular coffeehouse.

Penny Cluse Café 169 Cherry St Ⓣ802/651-8834. This funky brunch spot has an all-day breakfast touting biscuit & eggs and famed gingerbread pancakes; lunchtime offerings include beer-battered fish tacos and warm orzo salad.

Trattoria Delia 152 St Paul St Ⓣ802/862-5253. Pricey, exquisite Italian fare, served in a rustic, romantic dining room that evokes the belly of a ship.

Shelburne

It takes a whole day – if not more – to fully appreciate the remarkable fifty-acre collection of unalloyed **Americana** gathered at the **Shelburne Museum**, on US-7 in Shelburne, three miles south of Burlington (May–Oct daily 10am–5pm; $20, valid for two successive days; Ⓣ802/985-3346, Ⓦshelburnemuseum.org). More than thirty structures – including an authentic general store, apothecary, railroad station and 220-foot **paddlewheel steamboat** *Ticonderoga* – invite a first-hand look at two centuries of everyday American life, all centred around heiress Electra Webb's French Impressionist paintings.

Just west of the Shelburne Museum, **Shelburne Farms** (Ⓦ www.shelburnefarms.org; Ⓣ 802/985-8686), a multi-use farm education centre, features scenic walking trails and a "children's farmyard" (open early May to mid-Oct) where educators teach about caring for farm animals and activities include milking cows, collecting eggs and rabbit-petting.

Maine

Celebrated as "the way life should be", spectacular **MAINE** lives up to its laurels. As large as the other five New England states combined, Maine has barely the population of Rhode Island. In theory, therefore, there's plenty of room for its exuberant influx of summer visitors; in practice, the majority of these head for the extravagantly corrugated **coast**. You only really begin to appreciate the size and space of the state, however, farther north or inland, where vast tracts of mountainous forest are dotted with lakes and barely pierced by roads. This region is ideal territory for hiking and canoeing (and spotting moose), particularly in **Baxter State Park**, home to the northern terminus of the Appalachian Trail.

North America's first agricultural **colonies** took root in Maine: de Champlain's **French** Protestants near Mount Desert Island in 1604, and an **English** group that survived one winter at the mouth of the Kennebec River three years later. At first considered part of Massachusetts, Maine became a separate entity only in 1820, when the Missouri Compromise made Maine a free, and Missouri a slave, state. Today, the **economy** remains heavily centred on the sea. Thanks to careful planning among Maine's hearty lobstering community, lobster fishing in particular has defied gloomy predictions and boomed again, as evidenced by the many thriving **lobster pounds** (seaside shacks where patrons choose their very own lobster to be steamed and served to them on a plate).

Maine's climate is famously harsh. In **winter**, the state gets quite snowy and the landscape is marked by buzzing snowmobiles and the crisscrossing of skis. Officially, summer is spread between two long weekends: Memorial Day, the last Monday in May, and Labor Day, the first Monday in September. This is Maine's most popular season, heralded by sweetcorn and lobster shacks; its end is marked by wild blueberry crops – ninety percent of the nation's harvest comes from Maine – and the cheery blue berries show up in everything from pies to pancakes to chicken dishes. Brilliant **autumn colours** begin to spread from the north in late September – when, unlike elsewhere in New England, off-season prices apply – and the sweater weather is great for apple picking, leaf peeping and curling up with a book.

The Maine coast

Although the water is chilly, the **beaches** of southern Maine are unequivocally beautiful, and there are plenty of rocky coastal footpaths and harbour villages to explore. The liveliest destinations are **Portland** and **Bar Harbor** (at the edge of

Acadia National Park**); there's a wide choice of smaller seaside towns, such as **Wiscasset** and **Blue Hill**, if you're looking for a more peaceful base. **Beaches** are more common (and the sea warmer) further south, for example at **Ogunquit**.

The best way to see the coast itself is by **boat**: ferries and excursions operate from even the smallest harbours, with major routes including the ferries to Canada from Portland and Bar Harbor, shorter trips to **Monhegan** island via Port Clyde, Boothbay Harbor and New Harbor, and **Vinalhaven** via Rockland.

South of Portland

I-95 crosses from Portsmouth, New Hampshire (see p.215) into an area of Maine so dense with little communities that Mark Twain alleged one couldn't "throw a brick without danger of disabling a postmaster". Three miles over the Maine border, at the intersection with Rte-1, an **information centre** at **Kittery** provides copious details on the whole state (late May to early Sept Mon–Thurs 8am–6pm, Fri & Sat till 8pm; rest of year daily 9am–5.30pm; ⓣ207/439-1319). For a fun fish dinner overlooking the water, stop into the *Chauncey Creek Lobster Pier* (ⓣ207/439-1030), 16 Chauncey Creek Rd in Kittery Point, while you're here.

If you want to avoid the tolls on the interstate and follow more scenic Rte-1 instead (both head north, but Rte-1 hugs the coast), you'll soon find yourself in pleasant **YORK**, which was in 1642 the first English city to be chartered in North America. Its seventeenth-century **Old Gaol** now serves as a museum, commemorating its colourful, criminal past – dating from 1653, it was used as Maine's primary prison until the Revolutionary War. As well as its historical attractions, York is home to several fine beaches, a vintage arcade (the endearing "Fun-O-Rama") and a number of invigorating cliff walks. Head beyond Old York, for example, towards **Nubble Light**, at the end of Shore Road, off Rte-103, at York Beach, where you'll find one of Maine's most striking lighthouses, situated on an island of its own and observable from a rocky promontory. People love to line up for *Flo's* **hot dogs**, just north of here in Cape Neddick, Rte-1 across from Mountain Road (closed Wed), a crowd-pleasing institution since 1959, while *Stonewall Kitchen's* flagship *Company Store*, 2 Stonewall Lane, right behind the Chamber of Commerce just off Rte-1 (ⓣ207/351-2712) has fresh lobster BLTs and salads to take to the beach alongside its signature displays of mustards, jams and chocolate sauces.

Ogunquit and around

The three-mile spit that shields gay-friendly **OGUNQUIT** from the open ocean is one of Maine's finest **beaches**, a long stretch of sugary sand and calm surf that is ideal for leisurely strolls. In town the summer season at the **Ogunquit Playhouse** (ⓣ207/646-5511) usually attracts a few big-name performers. The late director of the Met Museum in New York called the **Ogunquit Museum of American Art** ($8; ⓣ207/646-4909) "the most beautiful little museum in the world". Its tiny space is blessed with a strong collection of seascapes, enhanced by the museum's sweeping ocean views.

One great place to **stay** in Ogunquit is the *Terrace by the Sea*, 11 Wharf Lane (ⓣ207/646-3232, ⓦwww.terracebythesea.com; ❺–❽) with lovely gardens and a location right on the water's edge. The *Beachmere Inn*, Shore Road (ⓣ207/646-2021, ⓦwww.beachmereinn.com; ❼–❾), has newly refurbished rooms in a quirky, turreted old wooden hotel that overlooks the ocean. The nearest campground, *Pinederosa*, is north of town at 128 North Village Rd (May–Sept; $30 for two adults; ⓣ207/646-2492, ⓦwww.pinederosa.com); it operates a free shuttle to Ogunquit Beach in July and August. Back downtown, the misnamed Marginal Way, a scenic clifftop path, leads from central Ogunquit to pretty

Perkins Cove, a mile south. *Barnacle Billy's*, 50 Perkins Cove (ⓣ207/646-5575) could probably be labelled a "tourist trap", but even the locals keep heading back here for the straight-ahead **seafood** dishes and outstanding water views; *Joshua's Restaurant*, 1637 Rte-1 (ⓣ207/646-3355) just north in **Wells**, has the best dinners in the area; many of the dishes use ingredients from their own local farm.

Kennebunkport

There's a reason former presidents **George Herbert Walker Bush** (known locally as "41") and **George "W" Bush** summer in **Kennebunkport** – it's beautiful, historical and full of eats even Barbara applauds. The best **beach** in town is Goose Rocks, about three miles north of the centre on King's Highway (off Dyke Rd via Rte-9). It's a premium stretch of expansive sand, though you will need a parking permit to park here ($12 daily, $50 weekly; call the Kennebunkport police to snag one (ⓣ207/967-2454). After a day in the sun, get some nightlife in at *The Ramp*, a lively bar with water views; the interior evokes the belly of a ship (below *Pier 77 Restaurant*, 77 Pier Rd, Cape Porpoise; ⓣ207/967-8500). A fun place to hang out and eat seafood is *Alisson's*, downtown at 8 Dock Square (ⓣ207/967-4841), or the low-key *Clam Shack*, just before the bridge into town (ⓣ207/967-3321).

An intriguing diversion is the tiny Tom's of Maine outlet store at 52 Main St, Kennebunk (ⓣ207/467-4005; closed Sun–Wed); the pleasantly aromatic space sells slightly dented toothpaste "seconds" for only $2.

Portland

The largest city in Maine, **PORTLAND** was founded in 1632 in a superb position on the Casco Bay Peninsula, and quickly prospered, building ships and exporting great inland pines for use as masts. A long line of wooden **wharves** stretched along the seafront, with the merchants' houses on the hillside above.

From its earliest days, Portland was a cosmopolitan city. When the **railroads** came in the 1840s, the Canada Trunk Line had its terminus right on Portland's quayside, bringing the produce of Canada and the Great Plains one hundred miles closer to Europe than it would have been at any other major US port. **Custom House Wharf** remains much as it must have looked when Anthony Trollope passed through in 1861 and said, "I doubt whether I ever saw a town with more evident signs of prosperity".

Grand Trunk Station was torn down in 1966, and downtown Portland appeared to be in terminal decline – until, that is, a group of committed residents undertook the energetic redevelopment of the area now known as the **Old Port**. Their success has revitalized the city, keeping it at the heart of Maine life – though you shouldn't expect a hive of energy. Portland is quite simply a pleasant, sophisticated and very attractive town, where one can experience the benefits of a large city at a lesser cost and without the hassle of crowds.

Arrival, information and getting around

Both I-95 and Rte-1 skirt the promontory of Portland, within a few miles of the city centre, while I-295 runs directly through it and offers access to downtown. **Portland International Jetport** is next to I-95, and is connected with downtown by regular city buses. Concord Coach Lines (ⓣ207/828-1151, ⓦwww.concordcoachlines.com) and Greyhound are the principal **bus** operators along the coast, with frequent service to Boston, as well as north to Bangor (and, in summer, Bar Harbor). Greyhound also runs to Montréal, New Hampshire and Vermont, as well as destinations within Maine; the station is at 950 Congress St, on the eastern edge of downtown. The **visitor centre** is in the Gateway building at 94 Commercial St (Mon–Sat 9am–4pm; ⓣ207/772-5800, ⓦwww.visitportland.com), and friendly staffers can help you with the city's ins and outs.

Congress Street is the main central thoroughfare, while Commercial Street is prettier and runs along the harbour. Though served by public **buses** ($1.50), downtown Portland is compact enough to stroll or bike around; Cycle Mania, at 59 Federal St (ⓣ207/774-2933), rents **bicycles** for $25 a day. You can also take a **land & sea tour** of the city with the affable Portland Discovery Land & Sea Tours, 170 Commercial St ($33; ⓣ207/774-0808), or the amphibious Downeast Duck Adventures, at 94 Commercial St ($24; ⓣ207/774-DUCK), which whisks you through historical Old Port and then takes you into Casco Bay to view the Calendar Islands.

Accommodation

Finding a room in Portland is no great problem, although it's highly advised that you book in advance for summer and autumn. A number of **budget motels** cluster around exit 48 off I-95. The closest **campground** is *Wassamki Springs*, west of Portland off Rte-22 towards Westbrook (May to mid-Oct only; $41; ⓣ207/839-4276).

The Chadwick 140 Chadwick St ⓣ207/774-5141, ⓦwww.thechadwick.com. Tucked away in Portland's West End, this delightful B&B has four cosy rooms decked out in warm tones, a welcoming innkeeper, excellent breakfasts, wi-fi and happy guests. ❻–❼

Hilton Garden Inn 65 Commercial St ⓣ207/780-0780, ⓦwww.hiltongardeninn.com. Fitness centre, saltwater pool and wireless internet, all in a snappy location that overlooks the harbour. A bit overpriced, but a good spot. ❾

Inn at Park Spring 135 Spring St ⓣ207/774-1059 or 1-800/437-8511, ⓦwww.innatparkspring.com. A charming B&B from 1835 in the Arts District and convenient to the restaurant and shops of Old Port. Friendly innkeepers and delicious breakfasts. ❻–❼

Inn at St John 939 Congress St ⓣ207/773-6481 or 1-800/636-9127, ⓦwww.innatstjohn.com. Located just outside of downtown in a slightly dodgy area, this elegant but somewhat creaky Victorian mainstay offers reasonably priced, comfortable rooms, some with shared baths. No elevator. ❺–❼

Marriott Residence Inn 145 Fore St ⓣ207/761-1660, ⓦwww.marriott.com. A slinky, brand-new *Marriott* garnering rave reviews for its smart waterfront location and 179 suites well stocked with a fridge, microwave and dishwasher. On-site laundry facilities, fancy linens and a free continental breakfast are among the litany of other perks. ❽

Morrill Mansion B&B 249 Vaughan St ⓣ207/774-6900, ⓦwww.morrillmansion.com. Well-appointed, West End B&B with cosy, stylish rooms, refrigerators, DVD players, free internet access and a helpful, well-informed innkeeper. ❻–❽

Portland Harbor Hotel 468 Fore St ⓣ207/775-9090 or 1-888/798-9090, ⓦwww.theportlandharborhotel.com. Pretty rooms with particularly nice bathrooms, in a great location near the waterfront; many units overlook the English garden. ❽–❾

The City

Thanks to several fires, not much of old Portland survives, though grand mansions can be seen along Congress and Danforth streets. The **Wadsworth-Longfellow House/Maine Historical Society**, at 485–489 Congress St (guided tours May–Oct Mon–Sat 10.30am–4pm, Sun noon–4pm; tours 45min on the hour; $8 includes museum; ⓣ207/774-1822), was Portland's first brick house when built in 1785 by Peleg Wadsworth. However, the house owes its fame primarily to Wadsworth's grandson, the poet Henry Wadsworth Longfellow, who spent his boyhood here. Next door, the **Historical Society Museum** (Mon–Sat 10am–5pm, Sun noon–5pm; free with admission to W-L House, above, otherwise $5) has changing displays of state history and art.

The **Portland Museum of Art** at 7 Congress Square, was built in 1988 by the renowned I.M. Pei partnership (Tues–Thurs, Sat & Sun 10am–5pm, Fri till 9pm; June to mid-Oct Mon till 5pm; $10, free Fri 5–9pm; ⓣ207/775-6148, ⓦwww.portlandmuseum.org). It's a stellar exhibition space, filled with maritime pieces such as Winslow Homer's *Weatherbeaten* and other affecting seascapes.

The restored **Old Port** near the quayside, between Exchange and Pearl streets, can be quite entertaining, with all sorts of red-brick antiquarian shops, bookstores, boutique clothing spots (especially on Exchange Street) and other esoterica. Several companies operate **boat trips** from the nearby wharves: The Portland Schooner Co. (daily in summer; 2hr trip $35, overnight trips $240; ⓣ207/766-2500 or 1-87/SCHOONER, ⓦwww.portlandschooner.com) has two vintage schooners that sail around the harbour and to the Casco Bay islands and lighthouses from the Maine State Pier, adjacent to Casco Bay Lines on Commercial Street. With Lucky Catch Cruises, at 170 Commercial St ($25; ⓣ207/761-0941, ⓦwww.luckycatch.com) shellfish fans don a pair of lobsterman overalls and head out to catch their very own lobster. Casco Bay Lines runs a twice-daily mailboat all year, and additional cruises in summer, to seven of the innumerable **Calendar Islands** in Casco Bay, from its terminal at 56 Commercial St at Franklin (return fares to one island $7.70–11.55, scenic cruises $12.75–24; ⓣ207/774-7871, ⓦwww.cascobaylines.com). **Long** and **Peaks islands** have accommodation or camping facilities.

If you follow Portland's waterfront to the end of the peninsula, you'll come to the **Eastern Promenade**, a remarkably peaceful two-mile harbour trail that connects to East End Beach, below the headland. Above the promenade, at the top of Munjoy Hill, at 138 Congress St, is the eight-sided, shingled 1807 **Portland Observatory** (June to mid-Oct daily 10am–5pm; $8; ⓣ207/774-5561); you can climb its 103 steps for an exhilarating view of the bay.

Eating

Portland is stuffed with outstanding **restaurants**, and most of its bars (see p.234) serve good food as well. The bountiful **Farmer's Market**, in Monument Square (May–Nov Wed, 7am–2pm) offers the perfect opportunity to sample local produce.

Bar Lola 100 Congress St ⓣ207/775-5652. Off the beaten path in Portland's East End, this whimsical tapas gem utilizes lots of local ingredients in a tasty seasonal menu with Greek undertones. Open Wed–Sat; dinner only.

Becky's Diner 390 Commercial St ⓣ207/773-7070. A vintage Maine breakfast spot with a newly-expanded upper deck serving hearty American portions, including home-made muffins and pies, from 4am (for the fishermen) until 9pm.

Flatbread Company 72 Commercial St ⓣ207/772-8777. Tasty pizza, made with flatbread dough, their own sauce and all-natural ingredients, in a hip waterfront location.

Lobster Shack at Two Lights 225 Two Lights Rd, in Cape Elizabeth ⓣ207/799-1677. Perhaps the best seafood-eating scenery in all of Maine – lighthouse to the left, unruly ocean to the right and a scrumptious lobster roll on the plate in front of you.

Market Street Eats 36 Market St ⓣ207/773-3135. You won't find any frou-frou juice drinks on the menu at this subterranean sandwich joint. Instead, there's awesome lunch fare like the Red Rooster wrap (chicken, bacon, provolone, spicy Thai mayo and red onions, $6.75).

Miyake 129 Spring St ⓣ207/871-9170. This teeny West End sushi spot garners a worthy buzz for dishes such as fresh *uni*, and seared tuna sashimi with truffle oil. Plus it's run by a chef-owner so devoted that he even harvests his own clams. BYOB, but there's a liquor store next door.

Street and Co. 33 Wharf St ⓣ207/775-0887. A great special-occasion seafood spot where the cuts are grilled, blackened or broiled to perfection amid an intimate, noisy dining room. There are a few good non-fish items as well. Reservations recommended.

Walter's 2 Portland Square (on Union St) ⓣ207/871-9258. New American cuisine in a sophisticated, high-ceilinged dining room near the Old Port. Entrees are $19–24; lunch is less expensive and just as good.

Nightlife and entertainment

Performing arts in town include chamber music, opera, dance and touring theatre, some as part of PCA Great Performances held at City Hall's Merrill Auditorium (tickets ⓣ207/842-0800, ⓦwww.pcagreatperformances.org); larger productions are put on by the Portland Stage Company at the Portland Stage Co, 25A Forest Ave (ⓣ207/774-0465). Portland Parks and Recreation (ⓣ207/756-8275, ⓦwww.ci.portland.me.us) sponsors free outdoor noontime and evening **jazz** and **blues concerts** throughout the city during the summer. The free *Portland Phoenix* has weekly **listings** of events.

Portland's **bar scene** is rowdier than you might expect, with pubs packed on the weekend with beer-drinking fun seekers.

Gritty McDuff's 396 Fore St ⓣ207/772-2739. Portland's first brewpub, making Portland Head Pale Ale and Black Fly Stout. Food, folk music, long wooden benches and a friendly atmosphere, which can get rowdy on Sat nights.

Novare Res Bier Café 4 Canal Plaza, Suite 1 (enter through alleyway on lower Exchange St, by Keybank sign) ⓣ207/761-2437. A little tricky to find, this Old Port beer spot sports over 200 brews (fifteen on tap), outdoor and indoor picnic tables, and tasty meat and cheese accompaniments.

The Port Hole 20 Custom House Wharf ⓣ207/780-6533. Right on the water, this sea-breezy Portland fixture has all sorts of cool features, including a great daily breakfast. Their summertime Sun reggae shows, held on a sunny deck in the harbour, are seriously bumping.

RiRa 72 Commercial St ⓣ207/761-4446. Lively, authentic Irish pub with great food and an inviting waterfront location.

SPACE Gallery 538 Congress St ⓣ207/828-5600, ⓦwww.space538.org. Cool, artsy space which displays contemporary artworks and always has something interesting going on, whether it's films, music, art shows or local bands.

North from Portland: the mid-coast

The coastal towns immediately north of Portland are no less commercialized than those to the south; **Freeport**, for example, is basically just an outdoor mall (albeit a good one). However, soon after **Brunswick**, I-95 veers inland toward Augusta, and Rte-1 is left to run on alone, parallel to the ocean. From here, things become much less frenetic, and prices a whole lot lower; even on the main road you'll find pleasant communities such as **Bath**; the many headlands can be even more peaceful.

Freeport

Much of the current prosperity of **FREEPORT**, fifteen miles north of Portland, rests on the invention by Leon L. Bean, in 1912, of a funky-looking rubber-soled fishing boot. That original boot is still selling (there's now an enormous replica at the entrance), and **L.L. Bean** has grown into a multinational clothing conglomerate, with an enormous clothing store on Main Street that literally never closes. Originally, this was so pre-dawn hunting expeditions could stock up; all the relevant equipment is available for rent or sale, and the store runs regular workshops to teach backcountry activities and survival skills. In practice, though, the late-night hours seem more geared toward high school students, who attempt to fall asleep in the tents without being noticed by store personnel. L.L. Bean is now more of a fashion emporium (it's Maine's most-visited destination) and Freeport has expanded to include a mile-long stretch of top-name **factory outlets** (such as Gap, Banana Republic and Cole Haan), most of which do give genuine reductions on the standard retail prices.

Freeport is not an ideal place to stay – everything falls quiet once the shoppers have gone home – but if you need **accommodation**, the *Harraseeket Inn* at 162 Main St (ⓣ207/865-9377 or 1-800/342-6423, ⓦwww.harraseeketinn.com; ❽–❾) is a wonderful clapboard B&B inn with some eighty rooms. There is also the *Applewood Inn*, 8 Holbrook St (ⓣ207/865-9705, ⓦwww.applewoodusa.com; ❼–❾), an eleven-room B&B stretching between two properties; Mr L.L. Bean himself used to live next door to one of the homes. A few miles north of town, the lovely *Maine Idyll*

Motor Court, at 1411 Rte-1 N (Ⓣ207/865-4201, Ⓦwww.maineidyll.com; ❸–❺), provides basic but romantic cottages in a pretty, woodsy setting.

The best **food** in Freeport is actually south of town at *Conundrum Wine Bistro*, 117 Rte-1 S (Ⓣ207/865-0303); most people come for the swanky martinis, then they get hooked on the fresh, eclectic seasonal entrees, such as butternut squash ravioli with sage cream sauce. Right downtown, the *Mediterranean Grill*, 10 School St (Ⓣ207/865-1688) has really good authentic Lebanese food (like *gyro* kebabs) at lunch and dinner. For a scenic change of pace, head a mile south of Freeport (on Rte-1) to the sea, where the *Harraseeket Lunch & Lobster Co* (Ⓣ207/865-4888), at 36 Main St in South Freeport, extending on its wooden jetty into the peaceful bay, makes a great outdoor lunch spot. The very green promontory visible just across the water is **Wolfe's Neck Woods State Park**. In summer, for $4.50, you can follow hiking and nature trails along the unspoiled fringes of the headland (daily 9am–sunset; Ⓣ207/865-4465).

Bath

Eight miles on, the charming small town of **BATH** has an exceptionally long history of **shipbuilding**: the first vessel to be constructed and launched here was the *Virginia* in 1607, by Sir George Popham's short-lived colony. **Bath Iron Works**, founded in 1833, continues to produce ships – during World War II, more destroyers were built here than in all Japan. At the superb **Maine Maritime Museum**, 243 Washington St, (daily 9.30am–5pm; $12 for two days; Ⓣ207/443-1316), you can take a tour of the Iron Works (reservations recommended, $30), explore several visiting historic vessels or browse the museum's intriguing collection of ship-related paintings, photographs and artefacts. There's even a mini-pirate ship for little buccaneers to climb around on.

The *Inn at Bath*, 969 Washington St (Ⓣ207/443-4294 or 1-800/423-0964, Ⓦwww.innatbath.com; ❼), is an eight-room **B&B** with beautiful gardens and all the amenities, while the serene *Kismet Inn*, 44 Summer (Ⓣ207/443-3399, Ⓦwww.kismetinnmaine.com; ❽–❾), has bright rooms, luxurious soaking tubs, body scrubs and yoga classes.

Places to **eat** in the area include *Solo Bistro Bistro*, 128 Front St (Ⓣ207/443-3373) which serves hip, tasty fare in contemporary environs and hosts live jazz Friday nights; and *Beale Street Barbecue & Grill*, at 215 Water St (Ⓣ207/442-9514), offering slow-smoked chicken, pulled pork and ribs, to stay or to go. *The Cabin*, 552 Washington St (Ⓣ207/443-6224) has great pizza. *The Sea Basket*, right on Rte-1 N in Wiscasset (Ⓣ207/882-6581), has craveable fried seafood; while eating at *Red's Eats* (Ⓣ207/882-6128), just further on Rte-1 N (in Wiscasset), is a bit of a culinary rite of passage – people line up and down the block to get their hands on one of his justly famous lobster rolls.

Boothbay Harbor

BOOTHBAY HARBOR, at the southern tip of Hwy-27, twelve miles south from Rte-1, is a crowded, yet undeniably pretty, resort town that's right on the water. The town lays on boat trips of all kinds, including Balmy Days Cruises (Ⓣ207/633-2284 or 1-800/298-2284), which offers all-day trips to Monhegan Island for $32, and harbour tours for $15. The Coastal Maine Botanical Gardens (call for directions, it's a little tricky to find; daily 9am–5pm; $10; Ⓣ207/633-4333, Ⓦwww.mainegardens.org) has bloom-filled trails that wind along the Sheepscot River.

If you want to **stay** in Boothbay, look no further than the stylish *Topside Inn*, 60 McKown St (Ⓣ207/633-5404, Ⓦwww.topsideinn.com; ❺), with pleasant rooms in an old sea captain's house and great views of the harbour from its location up on a hill.

The *Lobster Dock* **restaurant**, across the footbridge at 49 Atlantic Ave (ⓣ207/633-7120), dishes up ultra-fresh lobster rolls and seafood dinners at low prices (with a beer-and-picnic-table vibe), while the *Boathouse Bistro*, 12 By-Way on Pier 1 (ⓣ207/633-0400), has excellent tapas and a sunny rooftop deck and bar. Lastly, *The Thistle Inn*, 55 Oak St, serves up stellar New American fare at dinner-time and also has lovely rooms (ⓣ207/633-3541, ⓦwww.thethistleinn.com; ❻). Back on Rte-1 N (about ten miles north of Boothbay) in Waldoboro, the legendary *Moody's Diner* (ⓣ207/832-7785) has been a Maine institution for more than eighty years. *Moody's* is the real deal, open late and oozing nostalgia, with vinyl booths, inexpensive daily specials and fourteen types of freshly made pie – their four-berry is a must-have.

Rockland and Monhegan Island

ROCKLAND, where Rte-1 reaches Penobscot Bay, has historically been Maine's largest distributor of **lobsters**, boasting one of the busiest working harbours in the state, and more recently, it has grown into one of Maine's hippest, most liveable places. The town is home to the annual Maine Lobster Festival (held on the first weekend of Aug; ⓣ1-800/LOB-CLAW, ⓦwww.mainelobsterfestival.com) as well as the North Atlantic Blues Festival (held mid-July; ⓣ207/596-6055, ⓦwww.northatlanticbluesfestival.com) and its cultural centrepiece is the outstanding **Farnsworth Art Museum**, 352 Main St (late May to mid-Oct daily 10am–5pm; rest of year Tues–Sun same hours; $12; ⓣ207/596-6457, ⓦwww.farnsworthmuseum.org). The collection spans two centuries of American art, much of it Maine-related, and spreads over several buildings; the **Wyeth Center**, a beautiful gallery in a converted old church, holds two floors' worth of works by Jamie and N.C. Wyeth. Rockland's other star attraction is the lush Art Deco **Strand Theatre**, 345 Main St (tickets $8.50; ⓣ207/594-0070, ⓦwww.rocklandstrand.com), showing film classics as well as contemporary indie fare.

For **dining**, one of the best of the area's traditional lobster pounds (where a lobster is boiled freshly for its patrons) is *Miller's* (ⓣ207/594-7406), on the shore of Wheeler's Bay in an isolated cove at Spruce Head on Hwy-73, open from 10am until 7pm in season. The *Brass Compass Café*, 305 Main St (ⓣ207/596-5960), does a standout breakfast and lunch, and the best dinners in town can be had at funky and perennially crowded *Café Miranda*, tucked away at 15 Oak St, just off Main Street (ⓣ207/594-2034), with an array of moderately priced international entrees. *Primo*, 2 S Main St (ⓣ207/596-0770), serves some of the best food in the state (for less moderate prices) from inside a restored Victorian home. A great place to **stay** is the turreted *LimeRock Inn*, 96 Limerock St (ⓣ207/594-2257, ⓦwww.limerockinn.com; ❻–❽), with fantastic innkeepers, flat-screen cable TVs and a wraparound porch, while the bright, petite *Ripples Inn*, 16 Pleasant St (ⓣ207/594-5771, ⓦwww.ripplesinnattheharbor.com; ❻–❽) is another appealing option.

Monhegan Island

South of Rockland, the pretty **St George Peninsula**, in particular the village of Tenants Harbor, inspired writer Sarah Orne Jewett's classic Maine novel *Country of the Pointed Firs*. At the tip of the peninsula, boats leave from the hamlet of Port Clyde for tiny **Monhegan Island**, eleven miles off the coast and with a year-round population of less than a hundred residents. The island makes a great day-trip away from the tourist bustle of the mainland; you can get there (in about an hour) via Monhegan Boat Lines (May–Oct daily; Nov–April Mon, Wed & Fri; three sailings a day in summer, fewer at other times; $32 return; ⓣ207/372-8848, ⓦwww.monheganboat.com).

On this rocky outcrop, **lobsters** are the main business, though the stunning cliffs and isolated coves have long attracted artists as well – including Edward Hopper. Fifteen miles of **hiking trails** twist through the wilderness and past a magnificent 1824 lighthouse. **Accommodation** – such as the *Island Inn*, well sited overlooking the harbour right by the ferry dock (ⓣ207/596-0371, ⓦwww.islandinnmonhegan.com; ❻–❾) – is generally pricey; you may want to try the simple comforts of *Trailing Yew* (ⓣ207/596-0440, ⓦwww.trailingyew.com; ❺).

Camden and Rockport

The adjacent communities of **CAMDEN** and **ROCKPORT** split into two separate towns in 1891, in a dispute over who should pay for a new bridge over the Goose River between them. Rockport is now a quiet working port, among the prettiest on the Maine coast, home to lobster boats, pleasure cruisers and little else; Camden, while also quite pretty, has clearly won the competition for visitors. One essential stop in the area is **Camden Hills State Park**, two miles north of Camden ($4.50), where you can hike or drive up to a tower that affords one of the best views of the Maine coastline; on a clear day it's possible to see as far as Acadia National Park.

Camden and Rockport specialize in organizing sailing expeditions of up to six days in the large schooners known as **windjammers**. Expeditions sail from late May into mid-October. Vessels include the *Appledore* (ⓣ207/236-8353), which does two-hour cruises for $35 from Camden. Contact the Maine Windjammer Association (ⓣ1-800/807-WIND) for information and schedules for longer three- to six-day trips out of the area. Maine Sport Outfitters in Rockport (ⓣ207/236-7120, ⓦwww.mainesport.com) rents **kayaks** and **bikes**, and the Camden-Rockport **information** office is at the Public Landing (ⓣ207/236-4404, ⓦwww.camdenme.org).

Don't underestimate the magnetism of the Belted Galloway cows at **Aldermere Farm**, on Russell Avenue in Rockport (ⓣ207/236-2739, ⓦwww.aldermere.org). These quirky, endearing "Oreo cookie cows" (so named for the funny white stripe of fur that's sandwiched between their black front and back) have been amusing passers-by for ages. The farm doesn't currently have any public programming, per se, but the cows are nearly always in plain view of their fans.

A great **place to stay** in town is the beautiful *Camden Maine Stay Inn*, 22 High St (ⓣ207/236-9636, ⓦwww.camdenmainestay.com; ❼–❽), a cosy 1813 white-clapboard inn. *The Belmont*, 6 Belmont Ave, Camden (ⓣ1-800/238-8053, ⓦwww.thebelmontinn.com; ❼–❽), has a lovely porch and grounds and is decked out in conservative elegance. The *Ducktrap Motel*, just north on Hwy-1 in Lincolnville (ⓣ207/789-5400 or 1-877/977-5400; ❹), is a cute budget option.

Among busy **eating** and **drinking** spots in Camden are the *Camden Deli*, 37 Main St (ⓣ207/236-8343), with gourmet, bulging sandwiches and harbour views from

The Bucksport Observatory

Named after founder Colonel Jonathan Buck, who's buried at the Bucksport Cemetery near the Verona Bridge, quiet yet up-and-coming **BUCKSPORT** was first settled as a trading post in 1762. These days, it's known for its **Penobscot Narrows Observatory** (just across the river from Bucksport, get tickets at nearby Fort Knox on Rte-174; daily 9am–5pm, summer 9am–6pm; $5; ⓣ207/469-7719), which whisks gleeful viewers up inside a 420-foot viewing station. On a clear day you can see out to Mount Desert Island and Katahdin, but even if it's cloudy, it's still a thrill to look down and see the traffic moving on the bridge 400ft below.

the upstairs patio. Tea-lit *Francine*, 55 Chestnut St (☎207/230-0083), serves excellent French bistro fare amid romantic environs. The *Lobster Pound Restaurant*, Rte-1 N in Lincolnville (☎207/789-5550) is a wildly popular seaside restaurant serving heaps of the bright-red crustaceans.

The Blue Hill Peninsula

It used to be that the **Blue Hill Peninsula**, reaching south from Bucksport, was a sleepy expanse of land, too far off the primary roads to attract much attention. But word is slowly getting out about this beautiful area, blanketed with fields of wild blueberries and their pinkish-white flowers, and dotted with both dignified towns like **Blue Hill** and hardcore fishing villages like **Stonington** and **Deer Isle**. Even farther off the established tourist trail, **Isle au Haut** is a remote outpost accessible only by mailboat. As you might expect, the main draw down here is the quiet tranquillity that comes with isolation, and while the area presents ample opportunities for exploration, you might find yourself content with a good book, an afternoon nap and a night in a posh B&B.

Accommodation

If you need help finding **accommodation**, the Blue Hill Peninsula Chamber of Commerce, at 28 Water St, (☎207/374-3242), can point you in the right direction.

Blue Hill Inn 40 Union St, Blue Hill ☎207/374-2844 or 1-800/826-7415, Ⓦwww.bluehillinn.com. Romantic 1830 inn with inviting rooms and decor. Guests are treated to outstanding gourmet breakfasts and a tasty evening wine hour. A small apartment, Cape House, is available in winter for $185/night, two-night minimum. Closed Dec–April ❼–❽

Boyce's Motel 44 Main St, Stonington ☎207/367-2421 or 1-800/224-2421. Centrally located, basic, clean rooms complemented by a very cool owner. They also have full apartments available with kitchens and living rooms. ❸–❺

Deer Isle Homestead Hostel 65 Tennis Rd, Deer Isle ☎207/348-2308, Ⓦwww.deerislehostel.com. This is a beautiful hostel, set amidst spruce trees and organic gardens. Crafted from scratch by the owners, it's a no-frills lodging in a beautiful location, with a woodstove for cooking, solar showers and an indoor composting toilet; it also gives access to 3–4 miles of walking trails on the shore and nearby canoeing launch spots. Dorm beds $25 a night.

Inn on the Harbor Main St, Stonington ☎1-800/942-2420. Stonington's fanciest (and priciest) place to stay, with beautiful rooms and good amenities (wi-fi, TVs, binoculars) throughout. It also has the best location, with a fine view of the harbour. Breakfast included. ❻–❽

Pres du Port B&B W Main St at Highland Ave, Stonington ☎207/367-5007. Brightly wallpapered, whimsically furnished B&B, with a great view from the rooftop deck – literally on the peak of the roof. Also has one endearing little room for only $40. No credit cards. June to Oct only. ❷–❺

Blue Hill

Plenty of folks come to **BLUE HILL**, at the intersection of routes 172, 176 and 15 adjacent to the Blue Hill Harbor, simply to relax in the quietude. Still, there are lively activities available, such as the chamber music festival that takes place here every summer (Ⓦwww.kneisel.org); Blue Hill is also the "Steel Drum Capital of Downeast Maine" (Ⓦwww.flashinthepans.org). The best time to visit is Labor Day weekend (the last weekend in Aug), when oxen pulling, sheepdog trials, fireworks and carnival rides are all in effect at the Blue Hill Fair ($5; Ⓦwww.bluehillfair.com). The fairground was the basis for the fictional county fair featured in E.B. White's *Charlotte's Web* – White was a longtime resident of the area.

It's a 30 to 45 minute walk up to the top of **Blue Hill Mountain**, from which you can see across the Blue Hill Bay to the dramatic ridges of Mount Desert Island. The trailhead is not difficult to find, halfway down Mountain Road between Rte-15 and Rte-172. South on Rte-175, **Blue Hill Falls** is a good spot to give kayaking a try: the Activity Shop in Blue Hill at no. 61 Rte-172 (Ⓣ207/374-3600, Ⓦwww.theactivityshop.com) has canoe and kayak rentals that they'll even deliver to your door ($25 a day and up; reservations recommended). In summer, the Marine Environmental Research Institute (**MERI**) at 55 Main St (Ⓣ207/374-2135) runs 4-hour island excursions ($60 for adults, $40 for kids) where you might spot a seal or pull a lobster trap from a people-free shoreline.

Stonington and Isle au Haut

The **Deer Isle** peninsula is one of the most beautiful regions in a state that's known for beauty. Clear down at the end of Rte-15, it doesn't get much more remote than seaside **STONINGTON**, a working fishing village whose residents have long had a reputation for superior seamanship (many pirates and smugglers reputedly made port here in the late nineteenth century). Over the past hundred years, the place has found hard-earned prosperity in the sardine canning and granite quarrying businesses; now it has turned to lobstering. Old Quarry Ocean Adventures (Ⓣ207/367-8977, Ⓦwww.oldquarry.com) runs excellent kayaking, boating and camping trips as well as the highly recommended Puffin Boat Trip. For nightlife, the restored, more than one-hundred-year-old Opera House (Ⓣ207/367-2788, Ⓦwww.operahousearts.org) always has something cool to see, be it a jazzfest, Shakespeare performance or contemporary film.

Mailboats headed for **ISLE AU HAUT** ("I'll ah hoe") depart from the Stonington landing several times daily (Ⓣ207/367-5193; $18 one-way). On this lonely island, you can explore the trails of the less-visited part of **Acadia National Park** – highlighted by the rocky shoreline, bogs and dense stands of spruce trees. If you are looking to spend more time here, there is one place to **stay** on the island: the *Inn at Isle au Haut*, an endearing B&B that whisks you up from the ferry dock and transports you the 2.5 miles east to the inn (all meals included; Ⓣ207/335-5141, Ⓦwww.innatisleauhaut.com; ⑨).

Eating and drinking

There's a lot of good **food** to be had on the peninsula, but keep in mind that distances between towns are deceptively large. The appealing Blue Hill **farmer's market** is held Saturday mornings at the Blue Hill Fairgrounds (Rte-172), on Fridays in summer.

El El Frijoles 41 Caterpillar Hill Rd (Rte-15), Sargentville Ⓣ207/359-2486. Worth visiting for the name alone (it's a riff on "L.L. Bean"), this casual, California-style taqueria serves up wicked good tacos, burritos and home-made *agua fresca*. Open Wed–Sun 11am–8pm.

Fish Net 162 Main St, Blue Hill Ⓣ207/374-5240. Soft-serve ice cream and really good lobster rolls, right in the middle of town.

Lily's Café and Wine Bar 450 Airport Rd at Rte-15, Stonington Ⓣ207/367-5936. The sunny, flower-filled gardens welcome you in to this local lunch and breakfast spot where you can munch on fresh sandwiches and home-made soups on tabletops constructed out of windows. Closed weekends.

Mount Desert Island

Considering that five million visitors come to **MOUNT DESERT ISLAND** each year; that it contains most of New England's only national park; and that it boasts not only a genuine fjord but also the highest headland on the entire Atlantic coast north of Rio de Janeiro, it is an astonishingly small place, measuring just sixteen miles by thirteen. It is, of course, simply one among innumerable rugged granite islands along the Maine coast; the reason to come here is that it is the most accessible, linked to the mainland by bridge since 1836, and has the best facilities.

The island was named *Monts Deserts* (bare mountains) by Samuel de Champlain in 1604 and fought over by the French and English for the rest of the century. Although all existing settlements date from long after the final defeat of the French, the name remains, still pronounced in French (more like *dessert*, actually).

The social centre, **Bar Harbor**, has accommodation and restaurants to suit all wallets, while you'll find lower-key communities all over the island. **Acadia National Park**, which covers much of the island, offers active travellers plenty of outdoor opportunities, including camping, cycling, canoeing, kayaking and birdwatching.

Getting there and getting around

Mount Desert is easy to reach by **car**, travelling along Hwy-3 off Rte-1. In high summer, though, roads on the island get congested – the horse-drawn tours don't help – and the 55 miles from Belfast seem much longer.

There are a number of ways to get around Mount Desert via **public transport**. Before setting out, check out the excellent Island Explorer services (Ⓣ207/667-5796, Ⓦwww.exploreacadia.com/guide.html), which include the free **shuttle buses** that travel through Acadia to Bar Harbor, and even out to the airport. Nearby Hancock County/Bar Harbor Airport (Ⓣ207/667-7329) has a limited service run by Colgan Air (reservations via US Airways Ⓣ1-800/428-4322); Bangor International Airport, 45 miles away, is served by Delta, US Airways and Allegiant Air, and there is a **shuttle bus** that links Bar Harbor and Bangor ($30 and up, cash only; Ⓣ207/479-5911).

Accommodation

Hwy-3 into and out of Bar Harbor (which becomes Main Street on the way south) is lined with budget **motels** to satisfy the enormous demand for accommodation. Many places are open May to October only, and rates increase drastically in July and August; anywhere offering sea views will cost a whole lot more, as well. If possible, make your reservations in advance.

Bar Harbor Hostel 321 Main St, Bar Harbor Ⓣ207/288-5587, Ⓦwww.barharborhostel.com. Clean, safe hostel right near the centre of town. Dorm beds $25 a night (linens included), private rooms ❹. They also have three tent platforms for $15/person.

Coach Stop Inn 715 Acadia Highway, Bar Harbor Ⓣ207/288-9886 or 1-800/927-3097, Ⓦwww.coachstopinn.com. Lovely innkeepers, slightly frilly rooms and lots of outstanding food – including life-changing blueberry fritters. ❺–❻

Emery's Cottages on the Shore Sand Point Rd, five miles north of Bar Harbor Ⓣ207/288-3432 or 1-888/240-3432, Ⓦwww.emeryscottages.com. Sweet little cottages with kitchenettes (many with wi-fi) on a private pebble beach just off Hwy-3. Weekly stays in high season cost $570 and up. ❹

Lindenwood Inn 118 Clark Point Rd, Southwest Harbor Ⓣ207/244-5335 or 1-800/307-5335, Ⓦwww.lindenwoodinn.com. This first-class inn, built in 1904, offers tastefully decorated rooms and African accents in a stylish former sea captain's home. ❻–❾

Ullikana B&B 16 The Field, Bar Harbor Ⓣ207/288-9552, Ⓦwww.ullikana.com. Sited on a secluded byway just off Main St, this is the place to go in town for a romantic splurge; nicely decorated rooms and sumptuous breakfasts on a terrace overlooking the water. They also own the *Yellow House*, just across the way. ❼–❾

Bar Harbor

The town of **BAR HARBOR** began life as an exclusive resort, summer home to the Vanderbilts and the Astors; the great fire of October 1947 that destroyed their opulent "cottages" changed the direction of the town's growth. It's now firmly geared towards tourists, though it's by no means downmarket.

Bar Harbor's main **tourist information** office is on Rte-3 right before you cross into Mount Desert Island (ⓣ207/288-5103). In summer, there's another in the Municipal Building at 93 Cottage St. Both offices offer many free and comprehensive maps of the area. In high season, up to 21 different **sea trips** set off each day, ranging from deep-sea fishing to cocktail cruises. Among the most popular are the **whale-watching**, puffin and seal cruises offered by Bar Harbor Whale Watch Company, 1 West St (June–Oct at least twice daily; ⓣ207/288-2386, ⓦwww.barharborwhales.com), and the two-hour cruises on the impressive **four-masted schooner** *Margaret Todd* from the *Bar Harbor Inn* (daily June–Oct; $35; ⓣ207/288-4585, ⓦwww.downeastwindjammer.com). Lulu Lobster Boat Rides ($30; ⓣ207/963-2341, ⓦwww.lululobsterboat.com) offers authentic **lobstering** trips wherein Captain John raises his lobstering traps and woos riders with seafaring folklore and lighthouse sightings.

The native Wabanaki heritage is preserved in the **Abbe Museum**, 26 Mount Desert St (mid-May to Oct daily 10am–6pm; rest of year Thurs–Sat till 4pm; $6, admission includes entrance to the original Sieur de Monts location; ⓣ207/288-3519, ⓦwww.abbemuseum.org), which has gorgeously constructed exhibit spaces full of light and pale wood panelling. Although the opening displays on Wabanaki culture are well put together, the Abbe's knockout piece is the "Circle of the Four Directions", a contemplative, circular space built of cedar panels. The museum even has an original piece from glass wizard Dale Chihuly, his personal gift to the institution. The museum's original location, just off Park Loop Road, relates its history and is included in the admission price (daily mid-May to mid-Oct 9am–4pm).

Acadia National Park

ACADIA NATIONAL PARK, sprawled out over most of Mount Desert Island, the Schoodic Peninsula to the east and Isle au Haut to the south, is the most visited natural place in Maine. It's visually stunning, with all you could want in terms of mountains and lakes for secluded rambling, and **wildlife** such as seals, beavers and bald eagles. The two main geographical features are the narrow fjord of **Somes Sound**, which almost splits the island in two, and lovely **Cadillac Mountain**, 1530ft high, which offers tremendous ocean views. The summit can be reached either by a moderately strenuous climb or by a very leisurely drive, winding up a low-gradient road.

Open all year, the park has the Hulls Cove **visitor centre** near the entrance to the Loop Road north of Bar Harbor (mid-April to Oct daily 8am–4.30pm; July & Aug till 6pm; ⓣ207/288-3338), and its headquarters at Eagle Lake (daily 8am–4.30pm; same number as above). The entrance fee is $20 per vehicle or $5 per motorcycle or bike; good for seven days. There are two official **campground**: *Blackwoods*, five miles south of Bar Harbor, off Rte-3 ($20/pitch; reserve through the National Park Service at ⓣ1–800/365-2267 or ⓦwww.reservations.nps.gov), and *Seawall* on Hwy-102A, four miles south of Southwest Harbor ($14–20/pitch; ⓣ207/288-3338). Both are in woods, near the ocean, and have full facilities in summer; only *Blackwoods* is open in winter, with minimal facilities.

Once here, the free Island Explorer (ⓦwww.exploreacadia.com) **shuttle buses** travel through Acadia to Bar Harbor. However, the most enjoyable way to explore the park is to ride a rented **bicycle** around the fifty miles of gravel-surfaced "**carriage roads**", built by John D. Rockefeller to protest the 1913 vote allowing "infernal combustion engines" onto the island. Three Bar Harbor companies rent mountain bikes at less than $30 a day: Bar Harbor Bicycle Shop, at 141 Cottage St, on the edge of town (ⓣ207/288-3886), Acadia Bike & Canoe, across from the post office at 48 Cottage St (ⓣ1-800/526-8615), and Southwest Cycle, on Main Street in Southwest Harbor (ⓣ207/244-5856). All outlets provide excellent **maps**. Be sure to carry water, as there are very few refreshment stops inside the park. You can take a 4-hour guided **kayak tour** ($48) from mid-May to mid-October with National Park Sea Kayak Tours, 39 Cottage St (ⓣ1-800/347-0940, ⓦwww.acadiakayak.com). Another popular tour operator, Coastal Kayaking Tours (ⓣ207/288-9605, ⓦwww.acadiafun.com), has the same location as Acadia Bike.

The one and only sizeable beach, five miles south of Bar Harbor, is a stunner: called simply **Sand Beach**, it's a gorgeous strand bounded by twin headlands, with restrooms, a car park and a few short hiking trails. The water, sadly, is usually arctic.

Eating, drinking and nightlife

Mount Desert's most memorable **eating** experiences are to be found near the many **lobster pounds** all over the island. For nightlife (such as it is), Bar Harbor is where the people are. Cottage Street is a much more promising area to look for food and evening atmosphere than the surprisingly subdued waterfront. The Art Deco **Criterion Theater** at 35 Cottage St (ⓣ207/288-3441) shows current films, while ImprovAcadia at 15 Cottage St, 2nd floor ($15; ⓣ207/288-2503) has nightly comedy shows in summer.

Beal's Lobster Pier 182 Clark Point Rd, Southwest Harbor ⓣ207/244-7178. Fresh seafood for under $10, on a rickety wooden pier. You can pick out your own lobster from a tank, or choose from a small menu of other seafood choices.

Café This Way 14 ½ Mt Desert St, Bar Harbor ⓣ207/288-4483. Fresh, creative breakfast options like the café Monte Cristo (a French toast sandwich with eggs, ham, cheddar cheese and syrup on the side). Very busy in summer. They also serve dinner.

Jordan Pond Park Loop Rd, Acadia National Park ⓣ207/276-3316. Light meals, ice cream and popovers (light, puffy egg muffins). Afternoon tea, a longtime Acadia tradition, is served in the beautiful lakeside garden from 11.30am–6pm; reservations recommended.

Lompoc Café & Brewpub 36 Rodick St, Bar Harbor ⓣ207/288-9392. A healthy Middle Eastern menu for $14–20 with local microbrews on draft, complemented by a woodsy outdoor dining area and bocce ball court. Live music every Fri and Sat night, Open 11.30am–1am.

Morning Glory Bakery 39 Rodick St, Bar Harbor ⓣ207/288-3041. Fabulous fresh-baked breads, coffee and pastries served at a purple-trimmed cottage. Good lunch options, too. Closed Sun.

XYZ Restaurant 80 Seawall Rd (Rte 102-A), at the end of Bennett Lane, Manset ⓣ207/244-5221. Slamming Mexican entrees served in a bright, folk-artsy interior that will make you long for the southlands. Reservations (and the margaritas) strongly recommended. Dinner only, closed Sun.

Downeast Maine: the coast to Canada

Few travellers venture into the hundred miles of Maine lying east beyond Acadia National Park, mainly because it is almost entirely unpopulated, windswept and remote. In summer, though, the weather is marked by mesmerizing fogs, and the coastal drive is exhilarating – it runs next to the Bay of Fundy, home to the highest tides in the nation. **Downeast Maine** is also characterized by its wild **blueberry** crops – ninety percent of the nation's harvest comes from this corner of the state.

A short way northeast of Acadia, a loop road leads from Rte-1 to the rocky outcrop of **Schoodic Point**, which offers good birdwatching, great views and a splendid sense of solitude. Each village has one or two B&Bs and well-priced restaurants, such as Machias, known for its best-in-state blueberry pie from *Helen's Restaurant* on Rte-1 (ⓣ207/255-8433). Close to Canada, you'll find the salt-of-the-earth communities of **Lubec** and **Eastport**, tiny enclaves with jaw-dropping ocean scenery.

West Quoddy Head and around

With a distinctive, candy-striped **lighthouse** dramatically signalling its endpoint, **WEST QUODDY HEAD** is the easternmost point of the US, jutting defiantly into the stormy Atlantic. Just beyond the turn-off for Quoddy Head, tiny **LUBEC** was once home to more than twenty sardine-packing plants. They're all gone now, but the restored McCurdy's Fish Company, on Water Street, now gives tours ($3); you might spot a seal as you stroll the main drag. Lubec also hosts the dynamic adult music summer camp The Summer Keys (Ⓦwww.summerkeys.com) and is the gateway to **Campobello Island**, in New Brunswick, Canada, where President Franklin D. Roosevelt summered from 1909 to 1921, and to which he occasionally returned during his presidency. His barn-red cottage (mid-May to mid-Oct daily 9am–5pm; free) is now open to the public, furnished just as the Roosevelts left it – although keep in mind you will need a birth certificate or valid passport to make the border crossing. The rest of **Roosevelt Campobello International Park** (daily sunrise–sunset; free; Ⓦwww.fdr.net), located on Canadian soil but established jointly with the United States, is good for a couple of hours of wandering – the coastal trails and the drive out to **Liberty Point** are worth the effort. The *Peacock House*, 27 Summer St (Ⓣ207/733-2403, Ⓦwww.peacockhouse.com; ❹–❻) is a fantastic place to **stay**; it offers friendly B&B accommodation that are at once stylish and cosy.

The border between the United States and Canada weaves through the centre of Passamaquoddy Bay; the towns to either side get on so well that they refused to fight against each other in the War of 1812, and promote themselves jointly to tourists as the **Quoddy Loop** (Ⓦwww.quoddyloop.com). It's perfectly feasible to take a "two-nation vacation", but each passage through customs and immigration between **Calais** (pronounced "callous") in the States (fifty miles north of Lubec) and **St Stephen** in Canada does take a little while – and be aware, also, that the towns are in different time zones. If you have the driving stamina, **Eastport**, some forty miles up the road, is one of the most spectacular places you'll ever see, with an edge-of-the-earth seaside feel and stunning views of the Canadian shoreline. Eastport has some good **eats**, particularly at the *Pickled Herring*, 32 Water St (Ⓣ207/853-2323) and the *Eastport Chowderhouse*, 169 Water St (Ⓣ207/853-4700). *Katie's on the Cove* (Ⓣ207/454-8446), a Maine institution north of town on Rte-1, doles out unbelievably good confections from a little canary-yellow house. *The Commons*, 51 Water St (Ⓣ207/853-4123, Ⓦwww.thecommonseastport.com; weekly rentals $975/week, sometimes they'll do a shorter stay for you if it's not filled up) offers two inviting, year-round suites above an art gallery, and is one of the best **stays** in Maine; each comes with two bedrooms, a kitchen, dining room, internet access, laundry and a front porch with BBQ set-up and jaw-dropping views of the harbour into Canada.

Inland and western Maine

The vast expanses of the **Maine interior**, stretching up into the cold far north, consist mostly of evergreen forests of pine, spruce and fir, interspersed with the white birches and maples responsible for the spectacular autumn colours.

Distances here are large. Once you get away from the two largest cities – **Augusta** and **Bangor** – it's roughly two hundred miles by road to the northern border at **Fort Kent**, while to drive between the two most likely inland bases, **Greenville** and **Rangeley**, takes three hours or more. Driving (there's no public transportation) through this mountainous scenery can be a great pleasure – it smells like Christmas trees as you go – but be aware that beyond Millinocket some roads are tolled access routes belonging to the lumber companies, with gravel surfaces and vulnerable to bad weather.

This is great territory in which to **hike** – the **Appalachian Trail** culminates its two-thousand-mile course up from Georgia at the top of Mount Katahdin, and in August you'll often run into hikers celebrating with champagne at the terminus – or raft on the **Allagash Wilderness Waterway**. Especially around **Baxter State Park**, the forests are home to deer, beaver, a few bears, some recently introduced caribou – and plenty of **moose**. These endearingly gawky creatures are virtually blind and tend to be seen at early morning or dusk; you may spot them feeding in shallow water. They can cause major havoc on the roads, particularly at night, and each year several drivers (and moose) are killed in collisions; try to get to your destination while it's still light out.

Baxter State Park and the far north

About seventy miles from Bangor, **MILLINOCKET** is a genuine company town, built on a wilderness site by the Great Northern Paper Company in 1899–1900. The hundred-year-old manufacturing facilities still churn out nearly twenty percent of the newsprint produced in the United States. The real draw here though is the 200,000 acre, serenely unspoiled **BAXTER STATE PARK** ($14/car; ⓣ207/723-5140). On a clear day the 5268ft peak of **Katahdin** (or "greatest mountain", in the language of the local Penobscot tribe) is visible from afar. The area's **chamber of commerce** resides in Millinocket at 1029 Central St (Rte-11/157) (ⓣ207/723-4443, ⓦwww.katahdinmaine.com); the **Baxter State Park Authority** is at 64 Balsam Drive next to *McDonald's* (ⓣ207/723-5140).

Next to **Millinocket Lake**, the splendidly ramshackle old *Big Moose Inn* (ⓣ207/723-8391, ⓦwww.bigmoosecabins.com; ❷) makes a great place to stay, with cabins and an inn, and a wide range of activities. There's also an adjacent campground ($10/person). A more standard place to stay is the jacuzzi-enhanced *Baxter Park Inn*, 935 Central St (Rte-11) (ⓣ207/723-9777, ⓦwww.baxterparkinn.com; ❹), or the clean *Gateway Inn*, Rte-11/157 just off I-95 at the Medway exit (ⓣ207/746-3193, ⓦwww.medwaygateway.com; ❸), where many rooms have decks with views of Katahdin. New England Outdoor Center (ⓣ1-800/634-7238, ⓦwww.neoc.com) conducts day **rafting** and **canoeing** expeditions, as well as "**moose safaris**" and snowmobile vacations and rentals, according to the season. Head over to the *Appalachian Trail Café*, 210 Penobscot Ave (ⓣ207/723-6720) for a hot **meal** before heading into the park.

The Great Lakes

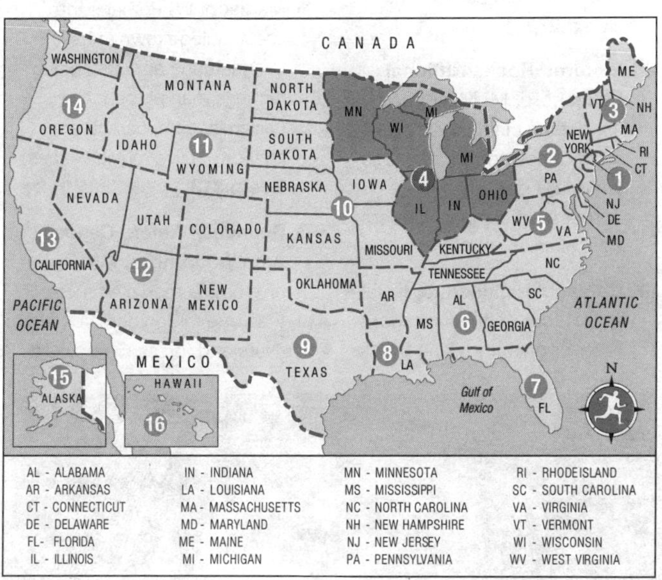

CHAPTER 4

Highlights

* **Rock and Roll Hall of Fame and Museum, Cleveland, OH** From rockabilly to Motown to punk – it's all here inside this striking museum. See p.254

* **The Henry Ford Museum, Detroit, MI** Home to such oddities as the car JFK was riding in when he was shot. See p.270

* **Pictured Rocks National Lakeshore, MI** Multi-hued sandstone cliffs, spectacular sand dunes and picturesque waterfalls dot this remote corner of Michigan's Upper Peninsula. See p.278

* **Chicago architecture, IL** Take a boat tour on the Chicago River or plan a walking tour to see the Second City's diverse architectural heritage. See p.285

* **Wrigley Field, Chicago, IL** Soak in the sun with a cold beer and a hot dog at this historic ivy-covered ballpark. See p.297

* **Madison, WI** Perhaps the finest college town in the US, featuring an outstanding farmer's market, beautiful university campus and a plethora of live music venues. See p.313

* **Boundary Waters Canoe Area Wilderness, MN** Canoe, hike or just marvel at more than one million acres of lakes, rivers and forest. See p.324

▲ Chicago

The Great Lakes

Swept by tumultuous storms and traversed by fleets of oceangoing tankers, the interconnected **Great Lakes** form the largest body of fresh water in the world; Lake Superior alone is more than three hundred miles from east to west. The shores of these inland seas can rival any coastline: Superior and the northern reaches of Lake Michigan offer stunning rocky peninsulas, craggy cliffs, tree-covered islands, mammoth dunes and deserted beaches. However, for lengthy stretches along Lake Erie, and the bottom lips of lakes Michigan and Huron, sluggish waters lap against large cities and decaying ports.

To varying degrees, the principal states that line the American side of the lakes – **Ohio**, **Michigan**, **Indiana**, **Illinois**, **Wisconsin** and **Minnesota** – share this mixture of natural beauty and ageing industry. Cities such as **Chicago** and **Detroit**, for all their pros and cons, do not characterize the entire region, although the former's magnificent architecture, museums, music and restaurants make it a worthy destination. Within the first hundred miles or so of the lakeshores, especially in Wisconsin and Minnesota, tens of thousands of smaller lakes and tumbling streams are scattered through a luxuriant rural wilderness; beyond that, you are soon in the heart of the **Corn Belt**, where you can drive for hours and encounter nothing more than a succession of crossroads communities, grain silos and giant barns.

Some history

The first foreigner to reach the Great Lakes, the French explorer Champlain, found the region in 1603 inhabited mostly by tribes of Huron, Iroquois and Algonquin. France soon established a network of military forts, Jesuit missions and fur-trading posts here, which entailed treating the native people as allies rather than subjects. After the **French and Indian War** with Britain from 1754 to 1761, however, the victorious British felt under no constraints to deal equitably with the Native Americans, and things grew worse with large-scale American settlement after independence. The **Black Hawk War** of 1832 put a bloody end to traditional Native American life.

Settlers from the east were followed to Wisconsin and Minnesota by waves of **Scandinavians** and **Germans**, while the lower halves of Illinois and Indiana attracted **Southerners**, who attempted to maintain slavery here and resisted Union conscription during the Civil War. These areas still have more in common with neighbouring Kentucky and Tennessee than with the industrial cities of their own states.

The demands of the Civil War encouraged the growth of **industry** in the region, with its abundant supplies of ores and fuel, as well as efficient transportation by water and rail. As lakeshore cities like Chicago, Detroit and Cleveland grew, their

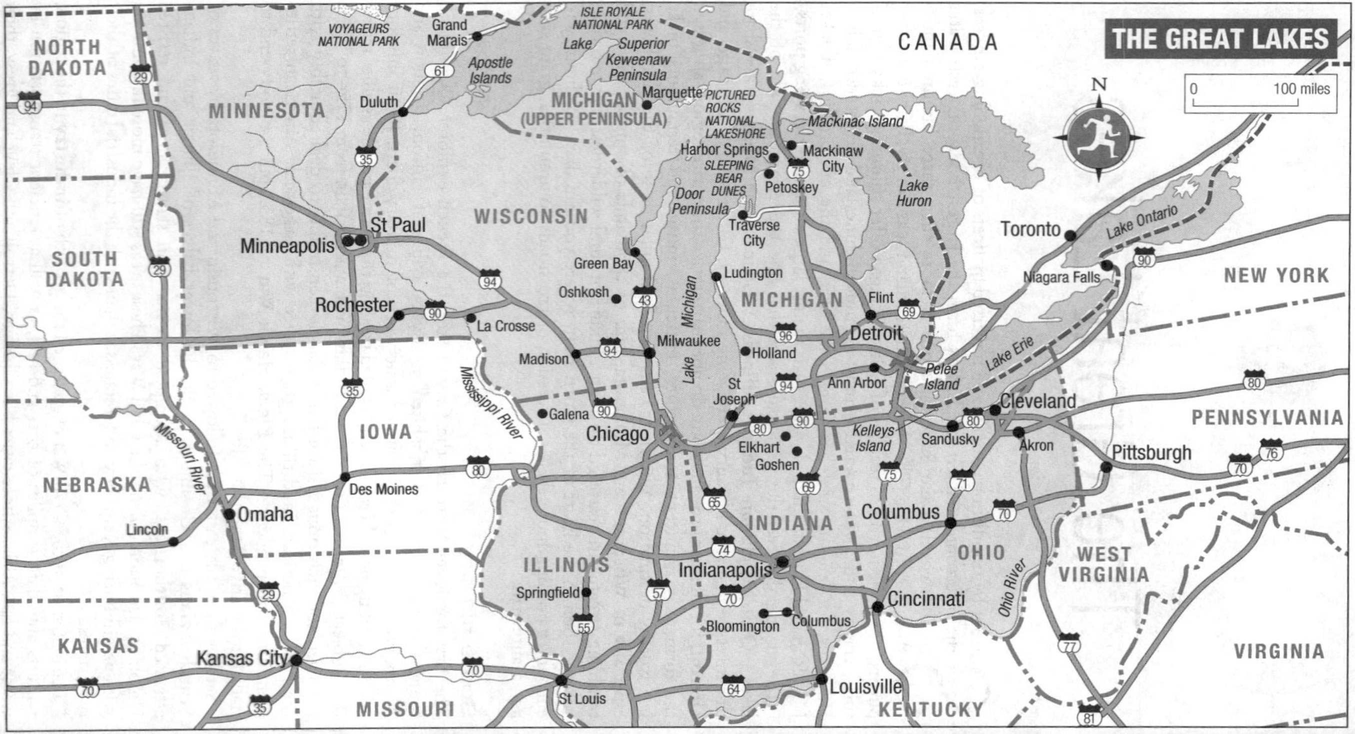

THE GREAT LAKES

populations swelled with hundreds of thousands of poor blacks who migrated from the Deep South in search of jobs. But a lack of planning, inadequate housing and mass layoffs at times of low demand bred conditions that led to the riots of the late 1960s and continuing inner-city deprivation. Depression in the 1970s ravaged the economy – especially the **automobile** industry, on which so much else depended – and gave the area the unwanted title of "**Rust Belt**". Since then, cities such as **Cleveland** have revived their fortunes to some degree, although the current economic crisis has hit the region especially hard.

Getting around the Great Lakes

Moving through the Great Lakes region can be a challenge without a private automobile, but with a little planning, it can be fairly manageable. Airplane service is frequent and almost omnipresent, but the price of airline travel in the United States has continued to rise as of late. The Greyhound and Megabus **bus** companies travel frequently between major cities in the area, including Chicago, Milwaukee, St Louis, Indianapolis, Columbus and Madison. Finally, Amtrak **train** services connect many of the major cities throughout the Midwest, but a lot of places are only served by one train daily.

Ohio is well served by Greyhound and Megabus buses, and there are major airports at Cleveland and Cincinnati. I-71 is the major interstate linking Cincinnati, Columbus and Cleveland, while I-70 bisects the state from west to east, passing through Columbus as well. The 325-mile Ohio to Erie biking trail (Ⓦwww.ohiotoerietrail.org), following former railroad and canal routes, is slowly nearing completion; when finished, it will link the three "C" towns.

In **Michigan**, Greyhound buses run regularly throughout Michigan's south, but services elsewhere are less frequent, and the few buses that serve the remote Upper Peninsula do so at night. Amtrak trains from Chicago stop at Detroit, Dearborn, Ann Arbor and Grand Rapids. Michigan's principal airport is just outside Detroit. Cycling is both feasible and rewarding, particularly with the abundance of bike paths in and around Traverse City; the League of Michigan Bicyclists in Lansing (Ⓣ1-888/642-4537, Ⓦwww.lmb.org) organizes tours and provides info.

Travelling south to **Indiana**, nine interstates crisscross the state, five of which slice through Indianapolis, and provide boring but fast ways to traverse Indiana via automobile, Greyhound and Megabus. Indianapolis, Michigan City and South Bend are the major stops on the state's three different Amtrak routes. Flights from most Midwestern and Eastern cities land at Indianapolis International Airport.

West in **Illinois**, Chicago is the site of O'Hare and Midway Airports and the hub of the national Amtrak train network. If you plan to spend time in the rest of Illinois, Amtrak, numerous commuter railroads, and, to a lesser extent, Greyhound and Megabus, provide a range of public transport options. Cycling is also generally easy on these endless flat plains. Half a dozen interstates fan out across the country from Chicago to all corners of the Great Lakes region and beyond.

Travel in the northern sections of **Wisconsin** and the Door peninsula (the "thumb" of the state) can be difficult without a vehicle; public transport is better in the south. Madison is served by Greyhound, Megabus and the Van Galder Coach line, and five **trains** daily connect Milwaukee and Chicago (a ninety-minute journey), while one crosses the state in the south en route for Seattle, via Columbus (near Madison), Portage, Wisconsin Dells, Tomah and La Crosse.

Over in **Minnesota**, travelling by road is fairly easy, and three major interstate highways cross the state on their way north to Duluth, east to Madison and south to Iowa. One Amtrak train route connects the Twin Cities and select cities in the state to Chicago and points west all the way to Seattle. The Twin Cities are also served by Megabus and Greyhound buses, which provides services to Milwaukee,

Chicago and Madison. Finally, the state's major airport hub is Minneapolis-St. Paul International Airport, which is in Minneapolis; there are light rail and bus services from the airport into the heart of Minneapolis.

Ohio

OHIO, the easternmost of the Great Lakes states, lies to the south of shallow Lake Erie. This is one of the nation's most industrialized regions, but the industry is largely concentrated in the east, near the Ohio River. To the south the landscape becomes less populated and more forested.

Enigmatic traces of Ohio's earliest inhabitants exist at the **Great Serpent Mound**, a grassy state park sixty miles east of Cincinnati, where a cleared hilltop high above a river was reshaped to look like a giant snake swallowing an egg, possibly by the Adena Indians around 800 BC. When the French claimed the area in 1699, it was inhabited by the **Iroquois**, in whose language Ohio means "something great". In the eighteenth century, the territory's prime position between Lake Erie and the Ohio River made it the subject of fierce contention between the French and British. Once the British acquired control of most land east of the Mississippi, settlers from New England began to establish communities along both the Ohio River and the Iroquois War Trail paths on the shores of the lake.

During the Civil War, Ohio was at the forefront of the struggle, producing two great Union generals, **Ulysses Grant** and **William Tecumseh Sherman**, and sending more than twice its quota of volunteers to fight for the North. Its progress thereafter has followed the classic "Rust Belt" pattern: rapid industrialization, aided by its natural resources and crucial location, followed by 1970s post-industrial gloom and a period of steady revitalization that has been stopped in its tracks by the current credit crunch.

Although the state is dominated by its triumvirate of "C" towns (**Cleveland**, **Columbus** and **Cincinnati**), the **Lake Erie Islands** are its most visited holiday destination, attracting thousands of partying mainlanders. Cincinnati and Cleveland have both undergone major face-lifts and are surprisingly attractive, as is the comparatively unassuming state capital of Columbus.

Cleveland

Today, the great industrial port of **CLEVELAND** – for so long the butt of jokes after the heavily polluted Cuyahoga River caught fire in 1969 – is no longer the "Mistake on the Lake". Although parts of the city have been hit by the latest recession, areas like **the Warehouse District**, **East Fourth Street** and **University Circle** remain hubs of energy. Cleveland boasts a sensitive restoration of the Lake Erie and Cuyahoga River waterfront, a superb constellation of museums, a growing culinary scene and modern downtown super-stadiums. Add to that the now well-established **Rock and Roll Hall of Fame** and there's an unmistakable buzz about the place.

Founded in 1796, thirty years later Cleveland profited greatly from the opening of the **Ohio Canal** between the Ohio River and Lake Erie. During the city's heyday, which began with the Civil War and lasted until the 1920s, its vast iron and coal supplies made it one of the most important **steel** and **shipbuilding centres** in the world. **John D. Rockefeller** made his billions here, as did the many others whose restored old mansions line "Millionaires' Row".

Arrival, information and city transport

Cleveland Hopkins International Airport is ten miles southwest of downtown. The twenty-minute **taxi** ride into town costs around $20, but the Regional Transit Authority (RTA; ⓣ216/621-9500, ⓦwww.gcrta.org) **train** is only $2.25 and takes just ten minutes longer. Greyhound arrives at 1465 Chester Ave, at the back of Playhouse Square, while the Amtrak station is on the lakefront at 200 Cleveland Memorial Shoreway NE.

Maps and **information** can be ordered or picked up from **Positively Cleveland**, suite 100, 100 Public Square (summer daily 9am–5pm, rest of year Mon–Fri 9am–5pm; ⓣ216/875-6680 or 1-800/321-1001, ⓦwww.positivelycleveland.com); or try the booth on the baggage level of the airport (hours vary).

Cleveland is generally safe, though its size makes getting around easiest by **car**. The RTA runs an efficient **bus** service ($1.75 single or $3.50 for an unlimited day pass) and a small train line ($1.75), known locally as "the Rapid", until about 12.30am. A **light rail** system – the Waterfront Line – connects Terminal Tower, the Flats, the Rock and Roll Hall of Fame and other downtown sights (every 15min, 6.15am– midnight; $1.75). There are also two **free trolleys**, the B-Line and the E-Line that cover different parts of downtown (Mon–Fri 7am–7pm).

Accommodation

Travellers without cars tend to stay at the downtown **hotels**, whose room-only prices are not cheap, but most offer packages that include admission to the Rock and Roll Hall of Fame or other attractions. **B&Bs** can be booked through ⓦwww.positivelycleveland.com.

Cleveland Marriot Downtown at Key Center 127 Public Square ⓣ216/696-9200, ⓦwww.marriot.com. This 25-storey hotel has comfortable rooms with superb views and touches of sophistication in their decor, plus a pool, fitness centre and plush lobby. ❽

Doubletree Cleveland Downtown 1111 Lakeside Ave ⓣ216/241-5100 or 1-800/222-8733, ⓦdoubletree1.hilton.com. Good online deals, great lake views and proximity to the Rock and Roll Hall of Fame make this a popular choice. ❺

Glidden House 1901 Ford Drive ⓣ216/231-8900 or 1-800/759-8358, ⓦwww.gliddenhouse.com. Sixty rooms and suites are housed in a Gothic mansion situated in University Circle. Large continental breakfast is included. ❻

Hyatt Regency at The Arcade 420 Superior Ave, University Circle ⓣ216/575-1234, ⓦwww.cleveland.hyatt.com. Set behind the imposing facade of The Arcade, a historic landmark, this hotel provides all the usual upscale comforts and services. ❽

Wyndham Cleveland at Playhouse Square 1260 Euclid Ave ⓣ216/615-7500 or 1-800/996-3426, ⓦwww.wyndham.com. The best option in the downtown theatre district, Playhouse Square, providing luxury accommodation at mid-range prices. ❺

The City

The main streets in Cleveland lead to the stately nineteenth-century Beaux Arts **Public Square**, at the very centre of downtown, and dominated in its south-western corner by the landmark **Terminal Tower**. **Ontario Street**, which runs north–south through the Square, divides the city into east and west. Cleveland's

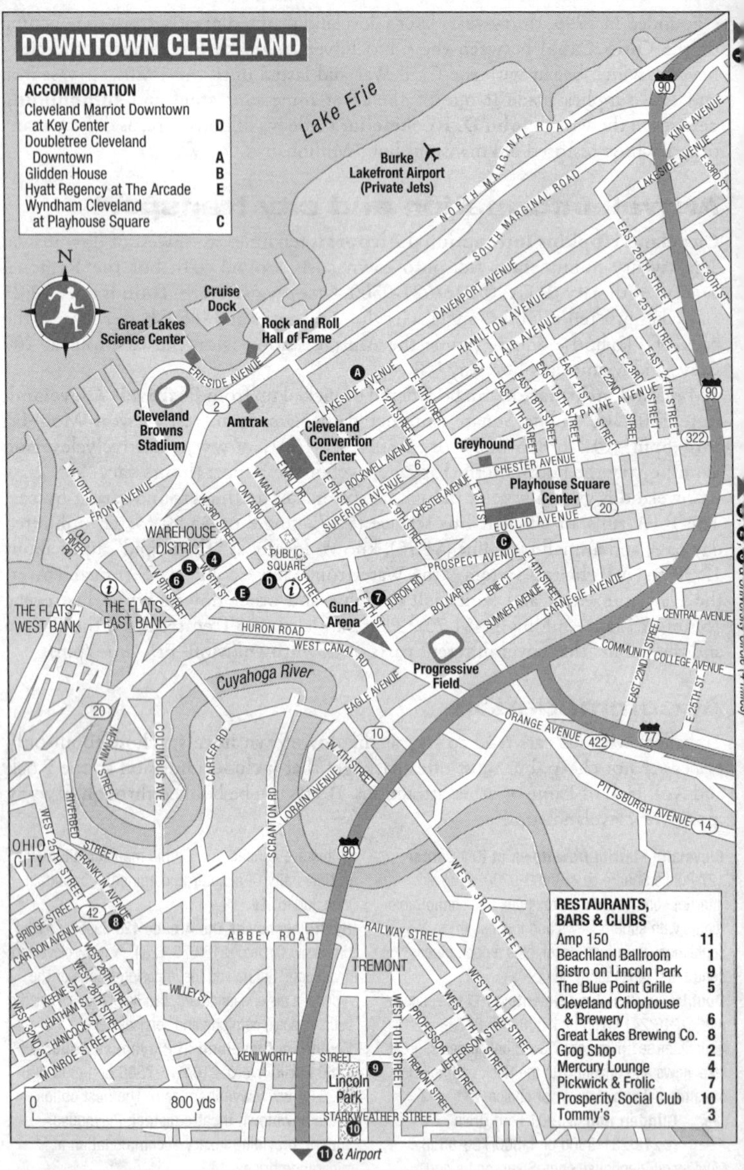

most interesting areas are at two opposite ends of the spectrum: the revived industrial romance of the **Flats** and **Warehouse District** in the northwest and the cultural institutions of **University Circle,** east of the river.

Downtown and around

Downtown Cleveland is a bustling place and its redevelopment has seen the emergence of several distinct subsections. In its traditional heart, among the banks and corporate headquarters, stand a couple of glamorous shopping malls. One, the **Avenue at Tower City**, is located in the Terminal Tower. Another, the **Arcade**, is a skylit hall built in 1890. Twelve blocks away, at 1501 Euclid Ave, the **Playhouse Square** (see p.255) is an impressive complex of four renovated old theatres; the small Ohio Theater, with its gorgeous starlit-sky lobby ceiling, is worth a look.

Just to the southwest is the **Gateway District**, where new restaurants and bars surround **Progressive Field** stadium, home of the Indians baseball team (ⓣ216/420-4200, ⓦwww.indians.com), and the equally modern, multipurpose **Quicken Loans Arena** (ⓣ216/420-2000, ⓦwww.theqarena.com), aka "The Q", which hosts the Cavaliers basketball team, along with major sporting and entertainment events.

Northwest of The Q, at the riverfront, one of the nation's busiest waterways shares space with excellent bars, clubs and restaurants, all strung out along a boardwalk. On the west bank of the Cuyahoga River, the Flats, long known for its nightlife, has an atmospheric, still industrial setting, set among some remaining grimy buildings and no less than fourteen bridges.

A short but steep walk back up from the river leads to the historic **Warehouse District**, a pleasant stretch of nineteenth-century commercial buildings between West Third and West Ninth streets, given over to shops, galleries, cafés and trendy restaurants. North of here, on the other side of the busy Cleveland Memorial Shoreway (Hwy-2), the waters of Lake Erie lap gently into **North Coast Harbor**, a showpiece of Midwest regeneration. To see the city from the water, try a two-hour cruise on the *Goodtime III* ($15; ⓣ216/861-5110) from the dock at East Ninth Street Pier, just beyond the **Rock and Roll Hall of Fame** (see box, p.254). Next door to the Rock Hall – as Clevelanders refer to it – is the giant **Great Lakes Science Center** (daily 10am–5pm; $9.95, $14.95 OMNIMAX combo-ticket; ⓣ216/696-4941, ⓦwww.greatscience.com), one of America's largest interactive science museums, which cleverly outlines the interdependency of science, technology and the environment, with emphasis on the lakes region. Across the road, the futuristic, 72,000-seat **Cleveland Browns Stadium** is the home of the Browns pro football team (ⓣ440/891-5000, ⓦwww.clevelandbrowns.com).

To the west of the river, **Ohio City** is one of Cleveland's more hip neighbourhoods, with junk stores, exotic eateries, Victorian clapboard houses and the busy **West Side Market**, at Lorain Avenue and West 25th Street (Mon & Wed 7am–4pm, Fri & Sat 7am–6pm), which sells all manner of ethnic foods. It's easily spotted by its red-brick clock tower. Nearby **Tremont** is another up and coming area.

Out from downtown

Four miles east of downtown, **University Circle** is a cluster of more than seventy cultural and medical institutions and is also home to several major performing arts companies (see p.255), as well as Frank Gehry's twisted-steel Weatherhead School of Management building at Case Western University. The eclectic **Museum of Art**, fronted by a lagoon at 11150 East Blvd (Tues, Thurs, Sat & Sun 10am–5pm, Wed & Fri 10am–9pm; free; ⓣ216/421-7340, ⓦwww.clevelandart.org) has a collection that ranges from Renaissance armour to African art, with a good café. Also notable is the **Museum of Natural History**, Wade Oval (Mon–Sat 10am–5pm, Sun noon–5pm; Wed until 10pm; $10, planetarium $4; ⓣ1-800/317-9155, ⓦwww.cmnh.org), with exhibits on dinosaurs and Native American culture. The **Cleveland Botanical Garden**, 11030 East Blvd (Tues–Sat 10am–5pm, Sun noon–5pm; May–Sep Wed until 9pm; April–Oct $8.50; Nov–March $7.50; ⓣ1-888/853-7091, ⓦwww.cbgarden.org), has a glass house that features a cloud forest, a desert ecosystem, free-roaming chameleons and butterflies, a waterfall and a treetop walkway. Meanwhile, dotted along East

The Rock and Roll Hall of Fame

Cleveland, not the most obvious candidate, convincingly won a hotly contested bid to host the **Rock and Roll Hall of Fame** largely because **Alan Freed**, a local disc jockey, popularized the phrase "rock and roll" here back in 1951. Since then, Cleveland has hardly produced a roll call of rock icons – Joe Walsh, Pere Ubu and Nine Inch Nails are the biggest names. Ignoring criticism that it bought victory by stumping up most cash, the city embraced the idea of the museum with enthusiasm and few now argue with the choice.

The museum's octogenarian architect – **I.M. Pei** – wanted the building "to echo the energy of rock and roll". A trademark Pei tinted-glass pyramid (he also did the larger Louvre one), this white structure of concrete, steel and glass strikes a bold pose on the shore of Lake Erie, especially when illuminated at night. The base of the pyramid extends into an impressive entrance plaza shaped like a turntable, complete with a stylus arm attachment.

The museum is much more than an array of **mementos** and artefacts. Right from the start, with the excellent twelve-minute **films** *Mystery Train* and *Kick Out the Jams*, the emphasis is on the contextualization of rock. The exhibits chart the art form's evolution and progress, acknowledging influences ranging from the blues singers of the Delta to the hillbilly wailers of the Appalachians. Elsewhere in the subterranean main exhibition hall, there's an in-depth look at seven crucial **rock genres** through the cities that spawned them: rockabilly (Memphis), R&B (New Orleans), Motown (Detroit), psychedelia (San Francisco), punk (London and New York), hip-hop (New York) and grunge (Seattle). Much space is taken up by exhibits on what the museum sees as the key rock artists of all time, including Elvis Presley, the Beatles, Jimi Hendrix, the Rolling Stones and U2. All inductees to the hall are selected annually by an international panel of rock "experts", but only performers who have released a record 25 years prior to their nomination are eligible.

Escalators lead to a level devoted to Freed, **studio techniques** and a great **archive** of rare live recordings, which you can listen to on headphones. The third floor houses the **Hall of Fame** itself, where an hourly video presentation of all inductees unfolds on three vast screens; the upper storeys contain the museum's **temporary exhibitions** and a **3-D film** of U2 in concert (extra $3).

The museum is at North Coast Harbor (daily 10am–5.30pm, Wed & summer Sat until 9pm; $22; reservations ⓣ216/781-7625 or 1-800/493-7655, ⓦwww.rockhall.com). Weekends get very crowded and are best avoided.

and Martin Luther King Jr boulevards in Rockefeller Park, 24 small landscaped cultural **gardens** are dedicated to and tended by Cleveland's diverse ethnic groups, including Croatians, Estonians and Finns. Adjacent to University Circle, **Murray Hill** is Cleveland's Little Italy; beyond this attractive area of brick streets, small delis and galleries is the trendy neighbourhood of **Coventry Village**.

Five miles southwest of downtown via I-71 (exit at W 25th or Fulton Rd), the **Cleveland Metroparks Zoo**, 3900 Wildlife Way (daily 10am–5pm; summer Sat & Sun 10am–7pm; $10; ⓣ216/661-6500, ⓦwww.clemetzoo.com), features a "Wolf Wilderness", while the spectacular 164-acre rainforest building is populated by some seven thousand plants and 118 species of animals, including orang-utans, American crocodiles and Madagascan hissing cockroaches. During summer, the RTA runs special **buses** from downtown to the zoo.

Eating

The city has a range of culinary delights, many of them ethnic. The excellent **West Side Market** (Mon & Wed 7am–4pm, Fri & Sat 7am–6pm) in Ohio City abounds with cheap, unusual picnic food, while there are some excellent fine-dining restaurants around town. Little Italy and Coventry Village are worth exploring for authentic Italian food and coffee bars, respectively.

Amp 150 4277 W 150th St ⓣ216/706-8787. The airport *Marriot Hotel* might seem an unlikely location but it's worth the trip for top chef Ellis Cooley's fabulously imaginative creations such as white truffle coleslaw and braised lamb with artichoke, and chili-spiced grapes. 4-course dinner $30.

Bistro on Lincoln Park 2391 W 11th St ⓣ216/862-2969. This enchanting spot in upcoming Tremont serves a mixture of French, Italian and Spanish cuisine, as well as great wines and ales. Try the Tuscan pork for $17.

The Blue Point Grille 700 W St Clair Ave ⓣ216/875-7827. Warehouse District favourite, serving the best seafood in town, with specials such as Nag's Head grouper with lobster mashed potatoes for $32.

Cleveland Chophouse and Brewery 824 W St Clair ⓣ216/623-0909. Try the mashed potatoes at this spacious, casual and moderately priced brewery and steakhouse – they're fantastic.

Pickwick & Frolic 2035 E 4th St ⓣ216/241-7425. Cavernous restaurant with champagne lounge and martini bar. You can enjoy cabaret and stand-up comedy while dining on a huge range of pizza, rustic American cuisine and oddities like Cheddar Ale Soup.

Tommy's 1824 Coventry Rd ⓣ216/321-7757. Great-value food, much of it Middle Eastern and vegetarian, dished up in a trendy, bright setting in lively Coventry Village. Try the famous shakes and check out the adjoining used-book store.

Nightlife and entertainment

The **Warehouse District** and **E 4th Street** boast the greatest conglomeration of drinking, live music and dancing venues, although those in the know head across the river to more bohemian **Tremont**. Under five miles east, both **University Circle** and youthful **Coventry Village** have good bars.

For more refined entertainment, **Playhouse Square** (ⓣ216/241-6000, ⓦwww.playhousesquare.com) is home to the **Cleveland Opera** and **Ballet**, as well as comedy, musicals, concerts and the Great Lakes Theatre Festival. The well-respected **Cleveland Orchestra** (ⓣ216/231-1111, ⓦwww.clevelandorchestra.com) is based in University Circle at Severance Hall, 11001 Euclid Ave, close to the leading regional theatre of the **Cleveland Play House** (ⓣ216/795-7000, ⓦwww.clevelandplayhouse.com). For **listings** information, the free weekly, the *Cleveland Scene* (ⓦwww.clevescene.com), is the place to look for alternative music, cinema and other events.

Beachland Ballroom 15711 Waterloo Rd ⓣ216/383-1124, ⓦwww.beachlandballroom.com. Over ten miles east of downtown, but this buzzing venue still draws the top indie and rock bands.

Great Lakes Brewing Co. 2516 Market Ave, Ohio City ⓣ216/771-4404. At this famous old joint, Cleveland's best brewpub, the huge mahogany bar still bears the bullet holes made during a 1920s shoot-out involving lawman Elliot Ness.

Grog Shop 2785 Euclid Heights Blvd, Cleveland Heights ⓣ216/321-5588. Near Coventry Village, the *Grog Shop* is a fun, sweaty, collegiate punk and alternative venue.

Mercury Lounge 1392 W 6th St ⓣ216/566-8840. In the Warehouse District, this hip martini lounge tends to attract Cleveland's fashionable set.

Prosperity Social Club 1109 Starkweather Ave ⓣ216/937-1938, ⓦwww.prosperitysocialclub.com. Located in a 1938 ballroom in Tremont, this is a hip hangout, with a great jukebox, live music and a huge range of beers.

The Lake Erie Islands

The **LAKE ERIE ISLANDS** – **Kelleys Island** and the three **Bass Islands** further north – were early stepping stones for the **Iroquois** on the route to what is now Ontario. French attempts to claim the islands in the 1640s met with considerable hostility, and they were left more or less in peace until 1813, when the Americans established their control over the Great Lakes by destroying the entire English fleet in the **Battle of Lake Erie**. A boom in **wine production** brought the islands prosperity in the 1860s but last century they were hit successively by Prohibition, the emergence of the California wineries, an increase in motoring vacations and the lake's appalling pollution. Thankfully, the cleanup of recent decades has worked; today the islands are again a popular summer destination, with fishing, swimming and partying as the main attractions. **Sandusky** and nearby **Port Clinton** act as the main jump-off points to the islands.

The mainland

The large coal-shipping port of **SANDUSKY**, fifty miles west of Cleveland on US-2, is probably the most visited of the lakeshore towns, thanks to **Cedar Point Amusement Park**, five miles southeast of town (early May to Aug daily hours vary; Sept to early Nov weekends only; $45.99; ⓣ419/627-2350, ⓦwww.cedarpoint.com). The largest ride park in the nation – and considered by many to be the best in the world – Cedar Point boasts no less than seventeen roller coasters. The neighbouring **Soak City** water park (June–Aug daily 10am–8pm; $29.99) provides a good way to cool off, with eighteen acres of water slides and a wave pool. Aquatic fun continues through the winter a few miles further southeast at **Kalahari Waterpark** (daily 10am, closing times vary; $39–42, after 5pm $29–32; ⓣ1-877/525-2477, ⓦwww.kalahariresorts.com), America's largest indoor water park; there's even a surf-making pool. The smaller resort town of **PORT CLINTON**, twelve miles west across the Sandusky Bay Bridge, is another departure point for the islands. Its pleasant lakefront is dotted with decent cafés and jet-ski rental outlets.

Practicalities

Amtrak **trains** pass through Sandusky once daily en route between Chicago and the east coast. The unstaffed station, at North Depot and Hayes avenues, is in a dodgy area. Greyhound **buses** stop way out at 6513 Milan Rd (US-250). Sandusky's **Visitors Center** is at 4424 Milan Rd (summer Mon–Fri 8am–8pm, Sat 9am–8pm, Sun 10am–4pm; rest of year Mon–Fri 8.30am–5.30pm; ⓣ419/625-2984 or 1-800/255-3743, ⓦwww.shoreislands.com).

Accommodation prices in Sandusky shoot up in high season, with simple motel rooms costing $200-plus on peak weekends. Along the main drag of Cleveland Road (US-6), the *Best Western Cedar Point*, no. 1530 (ⓣ419/625-9234, ⓦwww.bestwestern.com; ❺), has a pool. **Camping** is available at *KOA*, 2311 Cleveland Rd (ⓣ419/625-7906 or 1-800/962-3786, ⓦwww.mhdcorp.com; from $24.45).

Getting to the islands

Ferries to Kelleys Island are operated by Kelleys Island Ferry Boat Line from Main Street in **Marblehead** year-round, when weather permits, as frequently as every half-hour at peak times ($9 one-way, bikes $4, cars $15; ⓣ419/798-9763, ⓦwww.kelleysislandferry.com). Jet Express runs summer **catamaran** services from their dock at 101 West Shoreline Drive, Sandusky (ⓣ1-800/245-1538, ⓦwww.jet-express.com) to Kelleys Island ($28 return) and **South Bass Island** ($36 return), and to the latter only from 5 N Jefferson St, Port Clinton ($28 return). South Bass Island is also served by Miller Ferry (ⓣ1-800/500-2421, ⓦwww.millerferry.com; $6.50 one-way, bikes $2, cars $15) from late March to late November. **Flights** to both Kelleys Island and South Bass Island leave daily from Sandusky and Port Clinton and cost $50 one-way. Contact Griffing Flying Service (ⓣ419/626-5161, ⓦwww.griffingflyingservice.com).

Port Clinton has the *Sunnyside Tower*, 3612 NW Catawba Rd (Ⓣ419/797-9315 or 1-888/831-1263, Ⓦwww.sunnysidetower.com; ④), a Victorian-style B&B. For a good **meal** and **live music** in fun surroundings (there's an on-site waterfall), head for *Margaritaville* in Sandusky, at the junction of highways 6 and 2 (Ⓣ419/627-8903).

Kelleys Island

About nine miles north of Sandusky, **KELLEYS ISLAND** (Ⓦwww.kelleysisland.com) lies in the western basin of Lake Erie. Seven miles across at its widest, it's the largest American island on the lake, but it's also one of the most peaceful and picturesque, home to under two hundred permanent residents. With few buildings less than a century old, the whole island is a National Historic District. Its seventy-plus archeological sites include **Inscription Rock**, a limestone slab carved with 400-year-old pictographs; you can find it east of the dock on the southern shore. The **Glacial Grooves State Memorial**, on the west shore, is a 400ft trough of solid limestone, scoured with deep ridges by the glacier that carved out the Great Lakes.

Settled in the 1830s, Kelleys was initially a working island, its economy based on lumber, then wine, and later limestone quarrying. All but the last have collapsed, though a steady **tourist industry** has developed.

Practicalities

The Kelleys Island **Chamber of Commerce** is on Division Street, straight up from the dock (summer daily 10am–5pm; Ⓣ419/746-2360, Ⓦwww.kelleysislandchamber.com). Getting around the island is easy; cars are heavily discouraged and most people, when not strolling, use **bikes** ($3.50/hr or $15/day) or **golf carts** ($15/hr or $80/day), available from Caddy Shack Square, also on Division Street (Ⓣ419/746-2221). The Chamber of Commerce can help with **accommodation** such as the comfortable *The Inn on Kelleys Island*, 317 W Lakeshore Drive (Ⓣ1-866/878-2135, Ⓦwww.kelleysisland.com/theinn; ④), a restored nineteenth-century Victorian home with a great lake view and a private beach. You can **camp** for $18 at the first-come, first-served state park on the north bay near the beach. The jovial *Village Pump*, 103 W Lakeshore Drive (Ⓣ419/746-2281), serves good homestyle **food and drink** until 2am, while the menu at the *Kelleys Island Brewery*, 504 W Lakeshore Drive (Ⓣ419/746-2314), includes several choices for vegetarians.

South Bass Island

SOUTH BASS ISLAND is the largest and southernmost of the Bass Island chain, three miles from the mainland and northwest of Kelleys Island; the islands' name derives from the excellent bass fishing in the surrounding waters. Also referred to as **Put-in-Bay** after its one and only village, this is the most visited of the American Lake Erie Islands, its permanent population of 450 growing tenfold in the summer.

Just a year after its first white settlers arrived, British troops invaded the island during the War of 1812. The Battle of Lake Erie, which took place off the island's southeastern edge, is commemorated by **Perry's Victory and International Peace Memorial**, set in a 25-acre park. You can see the distant battle site from an observation deck near the top of the 352ft stone column (May–Oct daily 10am–7pm; $3). All this history is well documented at the **Lake Erie Islands Historical Society**, 441 Catawba Ave (May–Oct daily 10am–5pm, until 6pm July & Aug; $2; Ⓣ419/285-2804, Ⓦwww.leihs.org), which features dozens of model ships, memorabilia and exhibits on the shipping and fishing industries.

Practicalities

Put-in-Bay's **Visitor Center** on Harbor Square, is just next to the northern dock (summer daily 9am–6pm; rest of year hours vary; ⓣ419/285-2832, ⓦwww.visitputinbay.com). Most people rent either **golf carts** from Baycarts Rental, Harbor Square ($10–20/hr; ⓣ419/285-5785), or **bikes** from Island Bike Rental, at both docks ($10/day; ⓣ419/285-2016). A **shuttle bus** runs between the northern dock and the state park ($1).

Accommodation gets heavily booked at weekends and during the summer, with **B&Bs** often requiring a two-night stay. The *Arbor Inn B&B*, 511 Trenton Ave (ⓣ419/285-2306, ⓦwww.arborinnpib.com; ❹), and the *Commodore Resort*, 272 Delaware Ave (ⓣ419/285-3101, ⓦwww.commodoreresort.com; ❸), which has a pool, offer some of the most competitive rates. You can **camp** for $18 in the state park or at the *Fox's Den Campground*, on the southern shore (ⓣ419/285-5001; $30).

Food on the island is expensive, including the grilled seafood sandwiches at *The Boardwalk* (summer only; ⓣ419/285-3695), the only downtown restaurant directly on the water. Just across the street, *Frosty's* (ⓣ419/285-3278) does good pizza. Put-in-Bay's famously raucous nightlife pulls in partiers from the other islands and the mainland. Numerous live music venues include the *Beer Barrel Saloon* (ⓣ419/285-2337, ⓦwww.beerbarrelpib.com) – said to have the longest uninterrupted bar in the world, complete with 160 bar stools – and the appropriately named *Round House* (ⓣ419/285-4595, ⓦwww.theroundhousebar.com).

Columbus

Ohio's largest city, state capital and home to the massive Ohio State University, **COLUMBUS** is a likeable place to visit. Its position in the rural heart of the state also makes it the only centre of culture for a good two-hour drive in any direction. Ohio became a state in 1803 and legislators designated this former patch of rolling farmland, on the high east bank of the Scioto River, its capital in 1812. The fledgling city was built from scratch, and its considered town planning is evident today in broad thoroughfares and green spaces.

Though Columbus has more people, it always seems to lag behind Cincinnati or Cleveland in terms of public recognition. As such, the place is best enjoyed for what it is – a lively college city with some good **museums**, gorgeous Germanic **architecture** and a particularly vibrant **nightlife**. Surprisingly, it boasts one of the country's most active **gay scenes**. The spacious, orderly and easy-going **downtown** area holds several attractions, along with the new **Arena District** entertainment zone. The main nightlife areas – bohemian **Short North Arts District** and more mainstream **Brewery District** – are on the north and south fringes of the centre, respectively.

Arrival, information and city transport

Port Columbus International Airport is seven miles northeast of downtown. Central Ohio Transit Authority's (COTA; ⓣ614/228-1776, ⓦwww.cota.com) express route bus #52 runs from there through downtown for $2.50, while **taxis** cost around $25. **Greyhound** stops at 111 East Town St. The most central **visitor centre** is at 90 N High St (Mon–Fri 9am–5pm; ⓣ614/221-2489 or 1-800/345-4386, ⓦwww.experiencecolumbus.com). COTA's good, citywide **bus service** connects all points of interest; a day pass costs $4.

Accommodation

Compared with other cities in the region, Columbus offers a good choice of convenient mid-range places to **stay**. Downtown rates are good, while even more savings can be had by staying in the German Village area.

Drury Inn and Suites Convention Center 88 E Nationwide Blvd ⓣ614/221-7008, ⓦwww.druryhotels.com. Smart and comfortable chain hotel which offers a decent breakfast and happy hour. Within walking distance of downtown and Short North. ❻

German Village Inn 920 S High St ⓣ614/443-6506, ⓦwww.germanvillageinn.net. This family-run motel, on the south edge of the German Village/Brewery District, is one of the best deals going. ❸

The Lofts Hotel 55 E Nationwide Blvd ⓣ614/461-2663, ⓦwww.55lofts.com. Luxury New York-style loft conversions, within easy walking distance of the Arena and the downtown areas. Great online deals. ❺

Short North B&B 50 E Lincoln St ⓣ614/299-5050 or 1-800/516-9664, ⓦwww.columbus-bed-breakfast.com. Enjoy a warm welcome and lavish furnishings in one of the seven rooms of this grand Short North house. ❺

The Westin Great Southern 310 S High St ⓣ614/228-3800 or 1-888/627-7088, ⓦwww.westincolumbus.com. Columbus's grand downtown Victorian hotel, with surprisingly moderate rates for some rooms. ❺

Downtown

As good a place as any to start a walking tour of downtown is the **Ohio Statehouse**, pleasantly set in ten acres of park at the intersection of Broad and High streets, the two main downtown arteries (Mon–Fri 7am–6pm, Sat & Sun 11am–5pm; hourly tours Mon–Fri 10am–3pm, Sat & Sun noon–3pm; free; ⓣ1-888/644-6123, ⓦwww.statehouse.state.oh.us). Highlights of this 1839 Greek Revival structure – one of the very few state capitols without a dome – are the ornate Senate and House chambers.

From here, most places of interest lie a few blocks east and west along Broad Street. **COSI**, housed in a streamlined structure across the river at 333 W Broad St (Mon–Sat 10am–5pm, Sun noon–6pm; $13.75, kids $8.75; ⓣ614/228-2674 or 1-877/257-2674, ⓦwww.cosi.org), boasts more than 300,000 square feet of exhibit space, most of it geared toward familiarizing children with science. It shows related movies ($7.50), as well as live shows (prices vary).

About a mile east, a giant Henry Moore sculpture stands at the entrance to the inviting **Columbus Museum of Art**, 480 E Broad St (Tues–Sun 10am–5.30pm, Thurs until 8.30pm; $10, free Sun; ⓣ614/221-6801, ⓦwww.columbusmuseum.org). Indoors, this airy space holds particularly good collections of Western and modernist art.

In the northwest corner of downtown, the area surrounding the impressive Nationwide Arena, home to NHL's Columbus Blue Jackets (ⓣ1-800/645-2637, ⓦbluejackets.com), dubbed the **Arena District**, has attracted a number of restaurants and nightspots. Just above it, left off High Street, is the restored Victorian warehouse of **North Market** (see "Eating" p.260), while on the right side the strikingly deconstructivist **Greater Columbus Convention Center** is a massive pile of angled blocks designed by Peter Eisenman and completed in 1993.

German Village and Brewery District

Just six blocks south of the Statehouse, I-70 separates downtown from the delightful **German Village** neighbourhood. During the mid-nineteenth century, thousands of German immigrants settled in this part of Columbus, building neat red-brick homes, the most lavish of which surround the 23-acre **Schiller Park**. Their descendants gradually dwindled in numbers by the 1950s and the area became increasingly run-down until it won a place on the National Register of Historic

Places. The best way to explore its brick-paved streets, corner bars, old-style restaurants, Catholic churches and grand homes is to stop in at the German Village Meeting Haus, 588 S 3rd St (Mon–Fri 9am–4pm, Sat 10am–2pm; ⓣ614/221-8888, ⓦwww.germanvillage.com), where popular walking tours ($12) run by the German Village Society start with a twelve-minute video presentation. The Society also oversees the immensely popular Haus und Garten Tour on the last Sunday in June, and the Oktoberfest celebrations in late September. Book-lovers will adore the Book Loft, 631 S 3rd St (daily 10am–11pm; ⓣ614/464-1774), whose books, many of them discounted, are crammed into 32 rooms of one grand building.

Just across High Street (US-23) are the warehouses of the **Brewery District**, where, until Prohibition, the German immigrants brewed beer by traditional methods. Many of the original buildings still stand, but today the beer is produced by just a couple of microbreweries. These brewpubs are typical of the area's more mainstream **nightlife**.

North of downtown

Across Nationwide Boulevard at the top end of downtown is the **Short North Arts District** (ⓦwww.shortnorth.org), a former red-light district that's now Columbus's most vibrant enclave. Standing on either side of High Street – the main north–south thoroughfare – its entrance is marked by the iron gateways of The Cap at Union Station. Thereafter starts the trail of galleries, bars and restaurants that makes the area so popular with locals; it is also the heart of the gay community. The first Saturday of each month sees the **Gallery Hop**, when local art dealers throw open their doors – complementing the artworks with wine, snacks and occasional performance pieces – and the socializing goes on well into the evening.

Businesses become a little more low-rent for a mile before High Street cuts through the **university campus** and suddenly sprouts cheap eating places and funky shopping. For bargain vinyl, head to Used Kids Records, 1980 N High St (ⓣ614/421-9455). On the other side of the road, the **Wexner Center for the Arts**, North High Street at 15th Avenue (Tues, Wed, & Sun 11am–6pm, Thurs–Sat 11am–8pm; free; ⓣ614/292-3535, ⓦwww.wexarts.org), is another Eisenman construction, even more extreme than the Convention Center (p.259).

Eating

The Short North and German Village neighbourhoods are crammed with places to **eat**, be they bottom-dollar snack bars or stylish and adventurous bistros. For a wide range of ethnic and organic snacks during the day, try the **North Market**, downtown at 59 Spruce St (Tues–Fri 9am–7pm, Sat 8am–5pm, Sun noon–5pm; ⓣ614/463-9664), which also sells fresh produce.

Haiku 800 N High St, Short North ⓣ614/294-8168. Excellent Japanese restaurant with a huge range of sushi, noodle and rice dishes for $10–15. Also hosts art and entertainment events.

Katzinger's 475 S 3rd St, German Village ⓣ614/228-3354. A mesmerizing range of sandwiches, Jewish delicacies and cheesecakes, though prices are high for a deli.

Marcella's 615 N High St, Short North ⓣ614/223-2100. Buzzing Italian restaurant with a lively bar. The food is a range of moderately upmarket pizzas, pasta, salads and main dishes like veal saltimbocca ($21.95).

Schmidt's 240 E Kossuth St, German Village ⓣ614/444-6808. This Columbus landmark (since 1886) serves a range of sausages, schnitzel, and strudel in a former slaughterhouse, served by waitresses in German garb.

Surly Girl Saloon 1126 N High St, Short North ⓣ614/294-4900. Heapings of Tex-Mex, Cajun and other cuisines only cost around $10 in this quirky joint where Western bordello meets *Pirates of the Caribbean*. Fine microbrews on tap help the place get rowdy late on.

Nightlife

This youthful university town has a rich source of local **bands**, from country revivalists to experimental alternative acts. The **gay scene** is concentrated in the Short North, with a few additional bars and clubs downtown – the weekly *Outlook* (Ⓦwww.outlookweekly.net) has complete listings. The *Other Paper* (Ⓦwww.theotherpaper.com) provides fuller free details of what's happening around town.

Axis Night Club 775 N High St Ⓣ614/291-4008. Very popular gay nightspot that gets steamier as the night wears on, as people gyrate to the latest disco and trance vibes.

Basement 391 Neil Ave, Arena District Ⓣ614/461-5483. One of the city's hottest new music venues, where you are likely to hear upcoming bands of different genres. Good sound system.

Oldfield's On High 2590 N High St Ⓣ614/784-0477, Ⓦwww.oldfieldsonhigh.com. Campus bar with live music across a broad range of genres. No cover.

Short North Tavern 674 N High St, Short North Ⓣ614/221-2432. The oldest bar in the neighbourhood, with live bands playing at the weekend German garb.

Skully's Music-Diner 1151 N High St, Short North Ⓣ614/291-8856, Ⓦwww.skullys.org. Classic 1950s-style diner whose happy hour (4–9pm) is often followed by cool indie-rock shows.

Sloppy Donkey Sports Bar 2040 N High St Ⓣ614/297-5000. Another popular student hangout with cheapish drinks, large screens and bar games.

Cincinnati

CINCINNATI, just across the Ohio River from Kentucky, is a dynamic commercial metropolis with a definite European flavour and a sense of the South. Its tidy centre, rich in architecture and culture, lies within walking distance of the attractive **riverfront**, the lively **Over-the-Rhine** district to the north and arty **Mount Adams**.

The city was founded in 1788 at the point where a Native American trading route crossed the river. Its name comes from a group of Revolutionary War admirers of the Roman general Cincinnatus, who saved Rome in 458 BC and then returned to his small farm, refusing to accept any reward. Cincinnati quickly became an important supply point for pioneers heading west on flatboats and rafts, and its population skyrocketed with the establishment of a major steamboat **riverport** in 1811. Tens of thousands of **German** immigrants poured in during the 1830s.

Loyalties were split by the **Civil War**. Despite the loss of some important markets, the city decided that its future lay with the Union. In the prosperous postwar decade, Cincinnati acquired Fountain Square and the country's first professional baseball team, the **Reds**; they, along with the **Bengals** football team, remain a great source of pride.

Arrival, information and city transport

Cincinnati–Northern Kentucky International Airport is twelve miles south of downtown, in Covington, Kentucky. **Taxis** to the city centre (Ⓣ859/586-5236) cost $32. The **Greyhound** station is on the eastern fringe of the city centre, just off Broadway, at 1005 Gilbert Ave. Amtrak **trains** arrive a mile northwest of downtown at the Union Terminal museum complex, which is on the daytime, citywide SORTA/Metro **bus** network ($1.75; Ⓣ513/621-4455, Ⓦwww.sorta.com). Buses on the Kentucky side are run by TANK ($1.50; Ⓣ859/331-8265, Ⓦwww.tankbus.org), including shuttle buses across to Cincinnati. Until the proposed riverfront tourist booth is built next to the suspension bridge, **info** can be obtained by phone or online from the Cincinnati USA Regional Tourism Network (Ⓣ859/589-2260, Ⓦwww.cincinnatiusa.com).

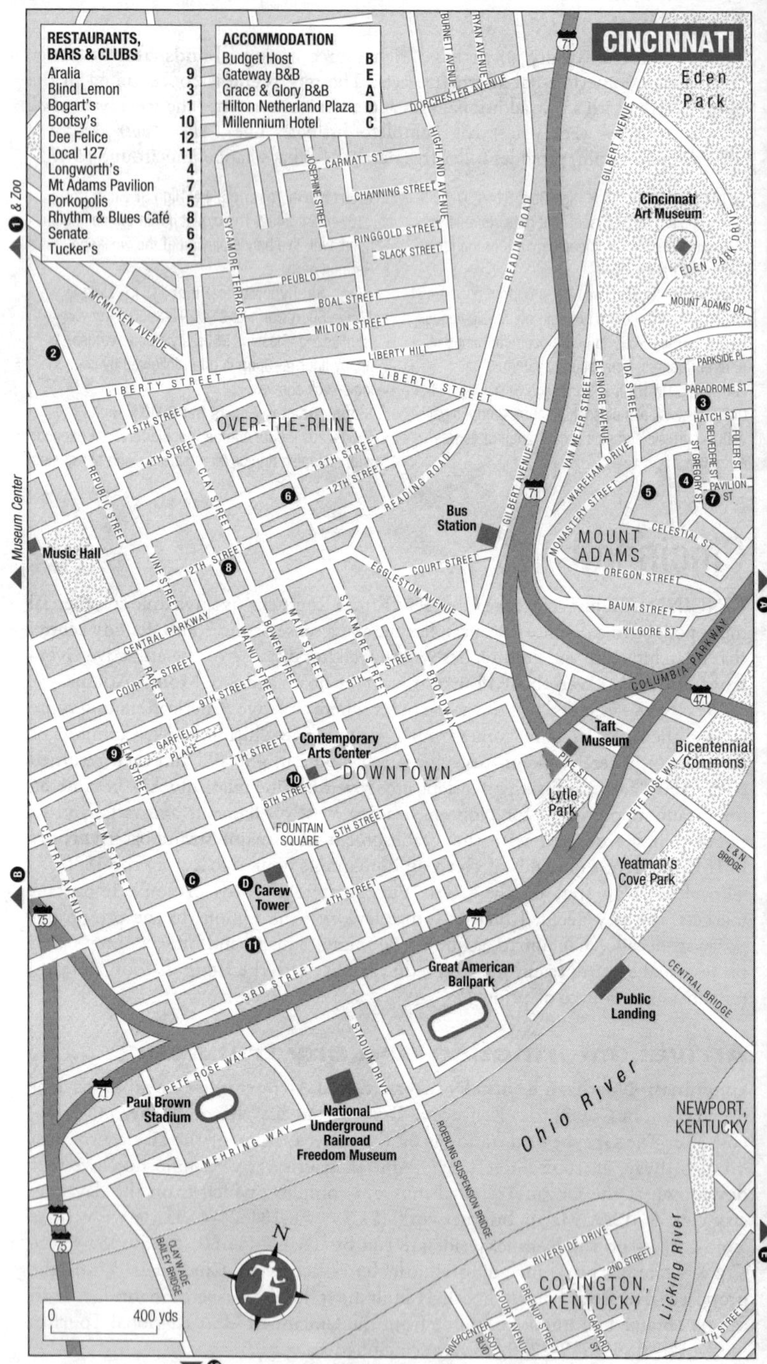
CINCINNATI
RESTAURANTS, BARS & CLUBS
Aralia 9
Blind Lemon 3
Bogart's 1
Bootsy's 10
Dee Felice 12
Local 127 11
Longworth's 4
Mt Adams Pavilion 7
Porkopolis 5
Rhythm & Blues Café 8
Senate 6
Tucker's 2
ACCOMMODATION
Budget Host B
Gateway B&B E
Grace & Glory B&B A
Hilton Netherland Plaza D
Millennium Hotel C
Eden Park
Cincinnati Art Museum
OVER-THE-RHINE
MOUNT ADAMS
Bus Station
Music Hall
Contemporary Arts Center
DOWNTOWN
FOUNTAIN SQUARE
Carew Tower
Taft Museum
Lytle Park
Bicentennial Commons
Yeatman's Cove Park
Great American Ballpark
Public Landing
Paul Brown Stadium
National Underground Railroad Freedom Museum
Ohio River
NEWPORT, KENTUCKY
COVINGTON, KENTUCKY
Licking River
Museum Center
& Zoo
0 400 yds

Accommodation

Although Cincinnati's quality **hotels** are reasonable by big-city standards, budget travellers may have problems finding affordable downtown rooms. Uptown **motels** – about two miles north – are much cheaper, but you'll need a car to get around safely at night.

Budget Host 3356 Central Parkway ⓣ513/559-1600 or 1-800/283-4678, ⓦwww.budgethost.com. Just about the cheapest place in uptown Cincinnati, though doubles vary greatly in price. Three miles from downtown. ❷

Gateway B&B 326 E 6th St, Newport, Kentucky ⓣ859/581-6447, ⓦwww.gatewaybb.com. Comfortable, affordable Victorian place, five minutes from downtown Cincinnati and Covington, Kentucky. ❺

Grace & Glory B&B 3539 Shaw Ave ⓣ513/321-2824, ⓦwww.graceandglorybb.com. This small cosy place in a safe area, five miles east of downtown, is a good option if you have a car. The Glory Suite Extension room is a super bargain. ❷

Hilton Netherland Plaza 35 W 5th St ⓣ513/421-9000 or 1-800/445-8667, ⓦwww.hilton.com. One of the classier Hilton franchises, located in a National Historic Landmark building, with a sumptuous Art Deco lobby, gym and well-furnished rooms. ❼

Millennium Hotel 150 W 5th St ⓣ513/352-2188, ⓦwww.millenniumhotels.com. Another luxury option right downtown, with a vast lobby, smart rooms and great views from the upper storeys. ❻

Downtown

Downtown Cincinnati rolls back from the Ohio River to fill a flat basin area ringed by steep hills. During the city's emergent industrial years, the filth, disease and crime drove the middle classes from downtown en masse. Nowadays, however, attractive stores, street vendors, restaurants, cafés, open spaces and gardens occupy the area. The city's rich blend of architecture is best appreciated **on foot**. Over, among and even right through the hotel plazas, office lobbies and retail areas, the **Skywalk** network of air-conditioned passages spans sixteen city blocks.

At the geographic centre of downtown, the **Genius of the Waters** in **Fountain Square** sprays a cascade of hundreds of jets, meant to symbolize the city's trading links. Surrounded by a tree-dotted plaza and all but enclosed by soaring facades of glass and steel, it's a popular lunch spot and venue for daytime concerts, as well as the second largest **Oktoberfest** in the world, after Munich, in late September. Looming above Fifth and Vine streets, the 48-storey, Art Deco **Carew Tower** has a viewing gallery on its top floor that gives a wonderful panorama of the tight bends of the Ohio River and the surrounding hillsides (Mon–Thurs 9.30am–5.30pm, Fri & Sat 9.30am–9pm, Sun 11am–5pm; $2).

Just east of Fountain Square are the Art Deco headquarters of the detergents and hygiene-product giant **Procter & Gamble**. The company was formed in 1837 by candle-maker William Procter and soap-maker James Gamble, to exploit the copious supply of animal fat from the slaughterhouses of "Porkopolis", as Cincinnati was then known. By sponsoring radio's *The Puddle Family* in 1932, the company created the world's first **soap opera**.

Nearby, the left-field, multimedia art exhibitions at the superb **Contemporary Arts Center**, housed in a stunning new building designed by Iraqi-born British architect Zaha Hadid, at Sixth and Walnut streets (Mon 10am–9pm, Wed–Fri 10am–6pm, Sat & Sun 11am–6pm; $7.50; free after 5pm Mon; ⓣ513/345-8400, ⓦwww.contemporaryartscenter.org), lead to continual run-ins with the city's more conservative citizens. By contrast, the **Taft Museum**, just east of downtown in an immaculate 1820 Federal-style mansion, at 316 Pike St (Wed–Sun 11am–5pm; $8, free on Sun; ⓣ513/241-0343, ⓦwww.taftmuseum.org), contains a priceless collection of works by Rembrandt, Goya, Turner and Gainsborough.

South across I-71, Paul Brown Stadium, home of the Bengals, and the Reds' Great American Ballpark, are giant cement additions on the Cincinnati side of the

Ohio River. In between the two stands the engaging **National Underground Railroad Freedom Museum** (Tues–Sat 11am–5pm; $12; ⓣ513/333-7500, ⓦwww.freedomcenter.org), whose light and airy space chronicles the city's role in the emancipation of slaves as well as other worldwide struggles for freedom. A mile-long **riverside walk** begins at **Public Landing**, at the bottom of Broadway, and stretches east past painted showboats and the **Bicentennial Commons**, a 200th-birthday present from the city to itself in 1988.

North of downtown

Just over a mile northeast from downtown, the land rises suddenly and the streets start to conform to the contours of **Mount Adams**. Here, century-old townhouses coexist with avant-garde galleries, stylish boutiques, international restaurants and trendy bars. To explore these and enjoy unparalleled views of the river, take a taxi or the #49 bus from downtown.

Adjacent to this tightly packed neighbourhood are the rolling lawns, verdant copses and scenic overlooks of **Eden Park**, where you will find the delightful **Krohn Conservatory** at 1501 Eden Park Drive (daily 10am–5pm; free; ⓣ513/421-5707). A loop road at the western end of the park leads to the **Cincinnati Art Museum**, on Art Museum Drive (Tues–Sun 11am–5pm; free; ⓣ513/639-2984, ⓦwww.cincinnatiartmuseum.org). Its one hundred labyrinthine galleries span five thousand years, taking in an excellent Islamic collection as well as a solid selection of European and American paintings by the likes of Matisse, Monet, Picasso, Edward Hopper and Grant Wood.

Meanwhile, northwest from downtown, Cincinnati's three-in-one **Museum Center** is housed in the magnificent Art Deco **Union Terminal**, approached via a stately driveway off Ezzard Charles Drive (Mon–Sat 10am–5pm, Sun 11am–6pm; museums $8.50 each, all three $12.50, OMNIMAX $7.50, discount with museum entry; ⓣ513/287-7000, ⓦwww.cincymuseum.org). Highlights of the **Museum of Natural History** are dioramas of Ice Age Cincinnati and "The Cavern", which houses a living bat colony. The **Historical Society** holds a succession of well-presented, short-term exhibitions, and the **Cinergy Children's Museum** has a two-storey treehouse and eight other interactive exhibit areas.

Covington and Newport, Kentucky

Covington, directly across the Ohio River on the Kentucky side, is regarded as the southern side of Cincinnati. It can be reached from downtown Cincinnati by walking over the bright blue, 1057ft-long **John A. Roebling Suspension Bridge**, at the bottom of Walnut Street, which was built in 1867 and served as a prototype for the Brooklyn Bridge. A ten-minute walk southwest of the bridge brings you to the attractive, narrow, tree-lined streets and nineteenth-century houses of **MainStrasse Village**. It's a Germanic neighbourhood of antique shops, bars and restaurants that plays host to the lively **Maifest** on the third weekend of each May and is the centrepiece of the citywide **Oktoberfest** on the weekend after Labor Day. At 6th and Philadelphia streets, 21 mechanical figures accompanied by glockenspiel music toll the hour on the German Gothic **Carroll Chimes Bell Tower**. Further south, en route to the airport off I-275, one of the area's newest attractions is the multi-million-dollar **Creation Museum** (Mon–Fri 10am–6pm, till 9pm summer Fri, Sat 9am–6pm, Sun noon–6pm; $21.95; ⓣ1-888/582-4253, ⓦwww.creationmuseum.org). A truly "only in America" experience, the state-of-the-art dioramas, video show and planetarium ($7) argue an uncompromising creationist case and make Darwin out to be little short of Lucifer himself.

Across the Licking River from Covington, the subdued town of **Newport** has gotten a lot livelier since the opening of a large shopping complex and the impressive **Newport Aquarium**, One Aquarium Way (daily 9am–7pm; $22; ⓣ859/261-7444 or 1-800/406-3474, ⓦwww.newportaquarium.com). Clear underwater tunnels and see-through floors allow visitors to be literally surrounded by sharks and snapping gators.

Eating

Cincinnati boasts excellent home-grown gourmet and continental **restaurants**. It's also famous for fast-food **Cincinnati chili**, a combination of spaghetti noodles, meat, cheese, onions and kidney beans, served at chains such as *Skyline Chili*, open all day at more than forty locations, including one at Vine and 7th streets, downtown.

Aralia 815 Elm St ⓣ513/723-1217. Excellent Sri Lankan curries, including plenty of veggie options, in a convenient downtown location.

Dee Felice 529 Main St, Covington, Kentucky ⓣ859/261-2365. This small and atmospheric spot specializes in Cajun cuisine, with lots of fresh seafood dishes, and doubles as a jazz venue.

Local 127 127 W 4th St ⓣ513/721-1345. Excellent restaurant serving New American cuisine in chic surroundings. Duck breast with sweet potato, arugula and mustard fruits goes for $25. Live music in the attached bar.

Longworth's 1108 St Gregory St, Mount Adams ⓣ513/651-2253. Good hamburgers, sandwiches, salads and pizzas at attractive prices in a delightful garden setting. Food is served all day until midnight, with music until 2.30am.

Porkopolis 1077 Celestial St, Mount Adams ⓣ513/721-5456. Steaks and sandwiches are served in the building that once produced the city's celebrated pottery.

Senate 1212 Vine St ⓣ513/421-2020. Pristine diner-style spot which dishes up gourmet hot dogs such as Korean or Japanese-style, as well as oysters, mussels and other delights for around $10. Great draught ales too.

Tucker's 1637 Vine St ⓣ513/721-7123; also 18 E 13th St, Over-the-Rhine ⓣ513/241-3354. Get a perfect start on your day with traditional and gourmet breakfasts in a 1950s setting.

Nightlife and entertainment

After dark, the hottest area with the widest appeal is the **Over-the-Rhine** district, which fans out from Main Street around 12th and 14th streets, and buzzes every night – though be careful where you park or walk, as it backs onto some unsafe areas. The next liveliest areas are ritzier **Mount Adams** and more collegiate **Corryville**, a five-minute drive northwest from downtown. Entertainment **listings** for the whole city can be found in the free *Cincinnati CityBeat* (ⓦwww.citybeat.com).

For classical music and the like, **Music Hall**, 1243 Elm St (ⓣ513/744-3344, ⓦwww.cincinnatiarts.org), an 1870s conglomeration of spires, arched windows and cornices, is said to have near-perfect acoustics. Home to Cincinnati's Opera and Symphony Orchestra, it also hosts the May Festival of choral music. The **Cincinnati Playhouse in the Park**, in Eden Park (ⓣ513/421-3888, ⓦwww.cincyplay.com), puts on drama, musicals and comedies, with performances throughout the year.

Blind Lemon 936 Hatch St, Mount Adams ⓣ513/241-3885, ⓦwww.theblindlemon.com. Beyond the intimate, low-ceilinged bar, you'll find a relaxed patio crowd. Music (mostly acoustic) nightly at 9.30pm.

Bogart's 2621 Vine St, Corryville ⓣ513/281-8400, ⓦwww.bogarts.com. Established indie acts play this mid-sized venue a couple of miles north of downtown.

Bootsy's 631 Walnut St ⓣ513/241-0707. Owned by Parliament/Funkadelic legend Bootsy Collins, the nightclub above the restaurant contains memorabilia and a lively vibe for late-night cocktails.

Mt Adams Pavilion 949 Pavilion St, Mount Adams ⓣ513/744-9200. From its terraced outdoor deck, you'll have great views of the city and the Ohio River. Great Bloody Marys.

Rhythm & Blues Café 1142 Main St, Over-the-Rhine ⓣ513/684-0080. Good food and great atmosphere. Nightly live rock, blues and various genres Wed–Sat.

Michigan

The very mention of **MICHIGAN** to most people will have them thinking of the automotive industry and the grittiness of Detroit. Those who have visited before will also know of its diverse beaches, dunes and cliffs which are scattered along the 3200-mile shoreline of its two vividly contrasting **peninsulas**.

The mitten-shaped **Lower Peninsula** is dominated from its southeastern corner by the industrial giant of **Detroit**, surrounded by satellite cities heavily devoted to the automotive industry. In the west, the scenic 350-mile Lake Michigan shoreline drive passes through likeable little ports before reaching the stunning **Sleeping Bear Dunes** and resort towns such as **Traverse City**, in the peninsula's balmy northwest corner. The desolate, dramatic and thinly populated **Upper Peninsula**, reaching out from Wisconsin like a claw to separate lakes Superior and Michigan, is a far cry indeed from the cosmopolitan south.

In the mid-seventeenth century, **French explorers** forged a successful trading relationship with the Chippewa, Ontario and other Native American tribes. The **British**, who acquired control after 1763, were far more brutal. Governor Henry Hamilton, the "Hair Buyer of Detroit", advocated taking scalps rather than prisoners. Ever since, Michigan's economy has developed in waves, the eighteenth-century fur, timber and copper booms culminating in the state establishing itself at the forefront of the nation's manufacturing capacity, thanks to its abundant raw materials, good transport links and the genius of innovators such as **Henry Ford**. Today the state is attempting to reinvent itself as a "creative hub" for new technologies, as the automotive industry continues to decline.

Detroit and around

DETROIT is the poster child for urban blight in the United States, despite many attempts to overcome this negative imagery, and in some cases, a rather stark reality. It is a city which boasts a billion-dollar downtown development, ultramodern motor-manufacturing plants, some excellent museums and one of the nation's biggest art galleries – but since the 1960s, media attention has dwelt instead on its huge tracts of urban wasteland, where for block after block there's nothing but the occasional heavily fortified loan shop or unpleasant-looking grocery store. As of late, it is a city on the mend, and local business promoters point to the bustle around Greektown at night and the Motown Historical Museum as signs of a renaissance of sorts.

Founded in 1701 by **Antoine de Mothe Cadillac**, as a trading post for the French to do business with the Chippewa, Detroit was no more than a medium-sized port two hundred years later. Then **Henry Ford**, **Ransom Eli Olds**, the **Chevrolets** and the **Dodge** brothers began to build their automobile empires. Thanks to the introduction of the mass assembly line, Detroit boomed in the 1920s, but the auto barons sponsored the construction of segregated neighbourhoods and shed workers during times of low demand. Such policies created huge ghettos, resulting, in July 1967, in the bloodiest **riot** in the US in fifty years. More than forty people died and thirteen hundred buildings were destroyed. The **inner city** was left to fend for itself, while the all-important motor industry was rocked by the oil crises and Japanese competition. Today, though scarred and bruised, Detroit is not the mess some would have it, and suburban residents have started to return to the city's festivals, theatres, clubs and restaurants.

As for orientation, it makes sense to think of Detroit as a region rather than a concentrated city – and, with some planning and wheels, it holds plenty to see and do. For the moment, **downtown** is not so much the cultural or social heart of the giant as just another segment. Other interesting areas include the huge **Cultural Center**, freewheeling **Royal Oak**, posh **Birmingham**, the Ford-town of **Dearborn**, nearby **Windsor, Ontario** and the college town of **Ann Arbor**, a short drive west.

Arrival, information and getting around

Flights come into **Detroit Metropolitan Wayne County Airport** in Romulus, eighteen miles southwest of downtown and a hefty $41-plus taxi ride (Metro Airport Taxi ⓣ1-800/745-5191 cost $41 while Checker Sedan Taxis ⓣ800/351-5466 are $55), though SMART ($1.50; ⓣ866/962-5515, ⓦwww.smartbus.org) bus #125 goes downtown from Smith terminal.

The main Greyhound (1001 Howard Ave) **bus** and Amtrak (11 W Baltimore Ave) **train** terminals are in areas where it's inadvisable to walk around at night. Amtrak also stops ten miles out at 16121 Michigan Ave, Dearborn, near the Henry Ford Museum and several mid-range motels, and at unstaffed suburban stations at Birmingham, Pontiac and Royal Oak.

Detroit's main **visitor centre** is downtown at 211 W Fort St, on the tenth floor (Mon–Fri 9am–5pm; ⓣ313/202-1800 or 1-800/338-7648, ⓦwww.visitdetroit.com). The main **post office** is at 1401 W Fort St, at Eighth Street (Mon–Fri 8.30am–5pm, Sat 8am–noon).

Downtown, the People Mover elevated **railway** loops around thirteen art-adorned stations (Mon–Thurs 6.30am–midnight, Fri till 2am, Sat 9am–2am, Sun noon–midnight; 50¢). Further out, public transport is just about adequate. SMART serves the entire metro region, while DDOT **buses** ($1.50; ⓣ313/933-1300, ⓦwww.detroitmi.gov/ddot) run a patchier inner-city service. Getting around in the Motor City is much easier with a car.

Accommodation

Downtown Detroit caters well for expense-account travellers – its top-range **hotels** are as secure as any city's – but if your budget is restricted it's harder to find lodging that is both cheap and safe at night.

The Atheneum 1000 Brush St ⓣ313/962-2323 or 1-800/772-2323, ⓦwww.atheneumsuites.com. At this upmarket hotel In Greektown, visitors can look out at the skyline from their rooms, or just use their luxurious In-room soaking tubs. ❻–❾

Detroit Marriott Renaissance Center Renaissance Center ⓣ313/568-8000 or 1-800/228-9290, ⓦwww.marriotthotels.com. A fun place to stay, it towers over the city by the river – ask for a room on the upper floors. ❻

Hilton Garden Inn Detroit 351 Gratiot Ave ⓣ313/967-0900, ⓦhiltongardeninn.hilton.com. Smack in the centre of downtown life, near Commercial Park. Warm and relaxed atmosphere and is pet friendly. Safe, full service hotel with free internet access. ❻

Inn on Ferry Street 84 East Ferry St ⓣ313/871-6000, ⓦinnonferrystreet.com. This fine hotel over in the Midtown neighbourhood is made up of four Victorian homes, with a total of 40 rooms. A nice place to spend a bit of time away from downtown proper, and it's close to the Detroit Institute of Arts and other cultural attractions. ❺

MGM Grand Hotel and Casino 1777 Third St ⓣ877/888-1212 or 1-888/MGM-DETR, ⓦwww.mgmgranddetroit.com. A bit at odds with its surroundings, this swanky new resort is dripping with luxury and loaded with amenities. ❻–❽

Shorecrest Motor Inn 1316 E Jefferson Ave ⓣ313/568-3000 or 1-800/992-9616, ⓦwww.shorecrestmi.com. Friendly, family-run place in lively Rivertown, with clean rooms and specials for Greyhound passengers. ❹

Westin Book Cadillac Detroit 1114 Washington Blvd ⓣ313/442-1600, ⓦwww.bookcadillacwestin.com. Listed on the National

Registry of Historic Places, the *Book Hotel* was renovated and taken over by the Westin chain. Elegant rooms and a full range of amenities. 7–9

Woodbridge Star Bed and Breakfast 3985 Trumbull Ave ⓣ 313/831-9668. Friendly, more affordable option, with good-value rooms just west of the Theater District. 4–6

Downtown

Futuristic glass-box office buildings and a tastefully revamped park overlook the glass-green **Detroit River**, but for the most part downtown seems rather empty, even in the middle of the day. One reason is that most offices and stores are squeezed into the six gleaming towers of the **Renaissance Center**, a virtual city within a city. Zooming up 73 storeys from the riverbank, the towers offer a great view of the metropolis from their free observation deck (open as part of the free

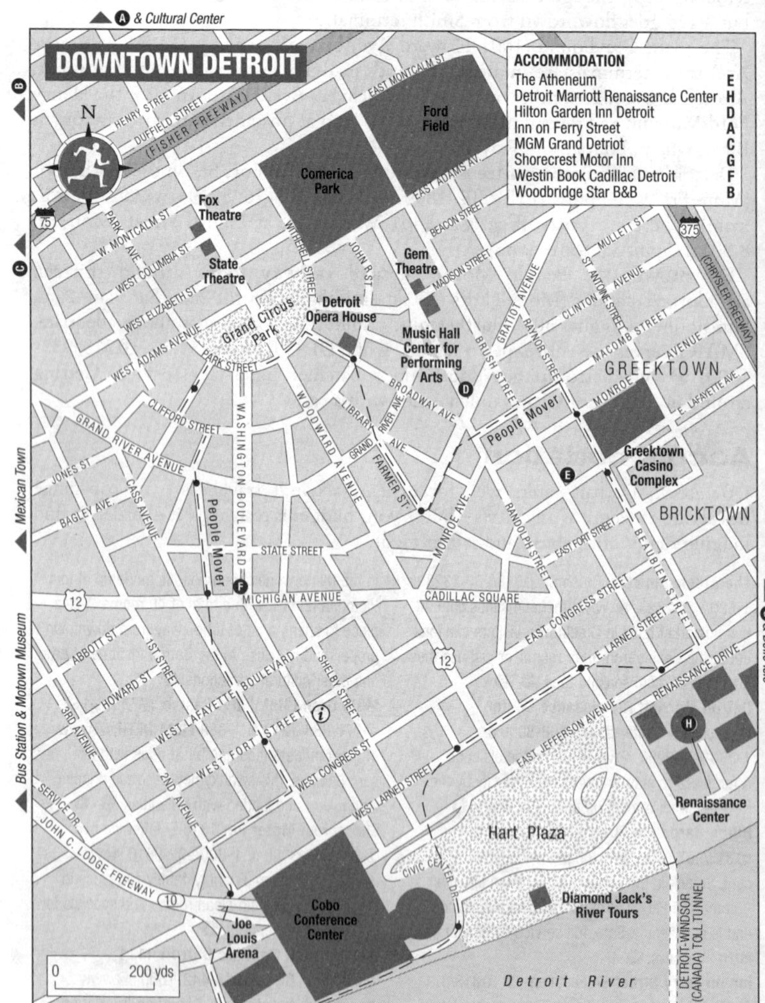

tours which start from the PURE DETROIT/GM Collection Store; Mon–Fri 12pm & 2pm). This giant business, convention and retail centre, known locally as the RenCen, was one of many complexes developed by **Detroit Renaissance** (a joint public/private sector project) to rejuvenate downtown in the aftermath of the 1967 riot, although it was criticized for forcing out small businesses. Nevertheless, it's an attractive public space and the soaring glass atrium known as the "Winter Garden" is particularly impressive.

Rare greenspace is found among the fountains and sculptures of **Hart Plaza**, which rolls down to the river in the shade of the RenCen. The plaza hosts free lunchtime concerts and lively weekend ethnic festivals all summer long. The US leg of the annual **Detroit International Jazz Festival**, the largest free jazz festival in the world, takes place here over Labor Day weekend and now spreads up to the Campus Martius square. Across the plaza from the RenCen is the Cobo Convention Center; next to this is **Joe Louis Arena**, home of the beloved Red Wings hockey team (see p.273).

Ten blocks north of the RenCen up Woodward Avenue is the **Theater District**, downtown's prime nightlife spot. Highlights are the magnificently restored Siamese-Byzantine **Fox Theatre** (see p.273) a huge old movie palace that is the city's top concert, drama and film venue, and the grand Italian Renaissance **State Theatre** next door. This area is at the centre of the city's massive **Columbia Street** redevelopment project, home to Ford Field and Comerica Park (see p.273), as well as microbreweries, coffeehouses and the inevitable themed restaurants.

Three miles east of the RenCen, **Belle Isle Park** is an inner-city island retreat with twenty miles of walkways, sports facilities, a marina and free attractions including an aquarium, a Great Lakes Museum and elaborate gardens. It is quiet during the week but can attract crowds on the weekend. Belle Isle Park is also home to the annual **Detroit Grand Prix** Indy car race. To see the island, use Diamond Jack's River Tours (early June to early Sept; $17; Ⓣ313/843-9376, Ⓦwww.diamondjack.com), which depart from Hart Plaza downtown, last two hours, and loop round Belle Isle, or just take DOT bus #25 and transfer at MacArthur Bridge to the #12.

The Detroit Cultural Center

Three miles northwest of downtown, next to Wayne State University, the top-class museums of the **Detroit Cultural Center** are clustered within easy walking distance of one another; you can easily spend a whole day here.

One of America's most prestigious art museums and newly refurbished, the colossal **Detroit Institute of Arts**, 5200 Woodward Ave (Wed & Thurs 10am–4pm, Fri 10am–10pm, Sat & Sun till 5pm; $8; Ⓣ313/833-7900, Ⓦwww.dia.org), traces the history of civilization through one hundred galleries, most notably Chinese, Persian, Egyptian, Greek, Roman, Dutch and American collections – not to mention the largest Italian collection outside of Italy. The museum has masterpieces such as a Van Gogh self-portrait and Joos Van Cleeve's *Adoration of the Magi*, as well as Diego Rivera's enormous, show-stealing, 1933 *Detroit Industry* mural. The DIA also presents live music every Friday from 6–10pm (free with museum admission).

The impressive Charles H. Wright **Museum of African American History**, 315 E Warren St (Tues–Sat 9am–5pm, Sun 1–5pm; $8; Ⓣ313/494-5800, Ⓦwww.maah-detroit.org), is the largest African-American museum in the world. Its massive core exhibit covers six hundred years of history in eight distinct segments, starting with a chilling sculpture of a slave boat, before moving through the Civil War, the Great Depression and the work of Dr Martin Luther King Jr and Malcolm X. Also in

The Motown sound

The legend that is Tamla Motown started in 1959 when Ford worker and part-time songwriter **Berry Gordy Jr** borrowed $800 to set up a studio. From his first hit onward – the prophetic "Money (That's What I Want)" – he set out to create a cross-over style, targeting his records at white and black consumers alike.

Early Motown hits were pure formula. Gordy softened the blue notes of most contemporary black music in favour of a more danceable, poppy beat, with **gospel**-influenced singing and clapping. Prime examples of the early approach featured all-female groups like the **Marvelettes** ("Needle in a Haystack"), the **Supremes** ("Baby Love") and **Martha Reeves and the Vandellas** ("Nowhere to Run"), as well as the all-male **Miracles** ("Tracks of My Tears"), featuring the sophisticated love lyrics of lead singer **Smokey Robinson**. Gordy's "Quality Control Department" scrutinized every beat, playing all recordings through speakers modelled on cheap transistor radios before the final mix.

The Motown organization was an intense, close-knit community: **Marvin Gaye** married Gordy's sister, while "Little" **Stevie Wonder** was the baby of the family. The label did, however, move with the times, utilizing such innovations as the wah-wah pedal and synthesizer. By the late 1960s its output had acquired a harder sound, crowned by the acid soul productions of Norman Whitfield with the versatile **Temptations**. In 1968 the organization outgrew its premises on Grand Avenue; four years later it abandoned Detroit altogether for LA. Befitting the middle-of-the-road tastes of the 1970s, the top sellers were then the high-society soul of **Diana Ross** and the ballads of the **Commodores**. This saw many top artists, dissatisfied with Gordy's constant intervention, leave the label, although the crack songwriting team of Holland-Dozier-Holland, responsible for most of the **Four Tops**' hits, stayed in Detroit to produce the seminal **Chairmen of the Board** ("Gimme Just A Little More Time"), along with **Aretha Franklin** and **Jackie Wilson**. Today, Motown is owned by the giant **Universal Music Group**.

the Cultural Center, the **Detroit Historical Museum**, 5401 Woodward Ave (Wed–Fri 9.30am–3pm, Sat 10am–5pm, Sun noon–5pm; $6; ⓣ313/833-1805, ⓦwww.detroithistorical.org), interprets the city's past through its **"Streets of Old Detroit"** display of reconstructed shops dating from the 1840s to the 1900s.

The Motown Museum

Unlike cities such as Memphis, Nashville and New Orleans, Detroit is devoid of the bars, clubs and homes of its musical heroes. The golden age of Motown was very much confined to a specific time and a place, and, disappointingly, only at the **Motown Museum**, 2648 W Grand Blvd (Tues–Sat 10am–6pm; $10; ⓣ313/875-2264, ⓦwww.motownmuseum.com), can Tamla fans pay homage to one of the world's most celebrated record labels. The museum, run as a not-for-profit organization, is housed in the small white-and-blue clapboard house, Hitsville USA, which served as Motown's recording studio from 1959 to 1972. On the ground floor, Studio A remains just as it was left: battered instruments stand piled up against the nicotine-stained acoustic wall-tiles, and a well-scuffed Steinway piano all but fills the room. Upstairs are the former living quarters of label founder **Berry Gordy**, while in the adjoining room record sleeves, gold and platinum discs, and other memorabilia are displayed.

The Henry Ford Museum, Greenfield Village and the Automotive Hall of Fame

The enormous **Henry Ford Museum**, ten miles from downtown at 20900 Oakwood Blvd, Dearborn (daily 9.30am–5pm; $15; ⓣ313/271-6001 or 1-800/835-5237,

Ⓦwww.thehenryford.org; accessible on SMART bus routes #200 and #250), pays fulsome tribute to its founder, an inveterate collector of Americana, as a brilliant industrialist and do-gooder. The former is certainly true. The hero of the "second industrial revolution" and inventor of the assembly line didn't succeed by being a philanthropist. His Service Department of 3500 private policemen prompted the *New York Times* in 1928 to call him "an industrialist fascist – the Mussolini of Detroit". Despite considering unions "the worst things that ever struck the earth", Ford was forced to let the United Auto Workers (UAW) into his factories in 1943, after only 34 out of 78,000 workers voted against joining. Ford also bowed to the economic necessity of employing blacks, though he banned them from the model communities he built for his white workers. Instead, the company constructed a separate town, which he sardonically named Inkster.

In addition to the massive **"The Automobile in American Life"** exhibit ranging from early Ford models and postal carriages to NASCAR vehicles and electric cars, the twelve-acre museum amounts to a giant curiosity shop, holding planes, trains, and row upon row of domestic inventions and non-technological collectibles. Real oddities include the chair Lincoln was sitting in and the car Kennedy was riding in when each was shot, the bus Rosa Parks was riding when she refused to give up her seat, and even a test tube holding Edison's last breath. One pertinent item not on view is the Iron Cross that Hitler presented to Ford (a notorious anti-Semite) in 1938. Down the street from the main museum complex, **Greenfield Village** is a collection of homes owned by famous Americans, relocated from across the country to this site by Ford (same hours as museum; $22). Among the 240 buildings, you'll find Ford's own birthplace, the Wright Brothers' cycle shop, Edison's laboratory and Firestone's farm. Costumed hosts demonstrate everything from weaving to puncture-repairing.

Directly next door to the Ford sprawl, the **Automotive Hall of Fame**, 21400 Oakwood Blvd (Sept–April: Wed–Sun 9am–5pm; May–October: Mon–Sun, 9am–5pm; $8; Ⓣ313/240-4000, Ⓦwww.automotivehalloffame.org), is more interesting than it might at first sound. In paying homage to the innovators and inventors of the global (not just the Detroit) auto industry, the interactive exhibits let visitors see how they would have handled problems encountered by Buick, Honda and the like. It's not just for mechanical types, either – there's a chance to pit your wits against the dealmakers who set up General Motors.

Windsor, Ontario

Across the Detroit River from the Motor City sits the Canadian city of Windsor, which offers pleasant views of its larger neighbour's skyline. Like Detroit, Windsor's main industry is auto manufacturing, but it's much smaller and more relaxed, and makes a good place simply to hang out. The newly renovated **Caesars Casino** (Ⓦwww.caesarswindsor.com) brings shows and a touch of Vegas to town, while the **Hiram Walker Distillery** provides a diverting booze-oriented attraction. Here, Canadian Club whiskey is distilled and stands just a short stroll from downtown at Riverside and Walker (free tours and samplings Mon–Sat 10am–6pm; Ⓣ519/255-9192).

Transit Windsor **buses** (Ⓣ519/944-4111) connect the downtowns of Detroit and Windsor for $2.75 each way. Bring proper identification/passports for customs and immigration officials. To **drive**, take the Windsor Tunnel ($3.75 toll) or the less claustrophobic Ambassador Bridge ($3.75 toll). Windsor has two **visitor centres**, one across the Ambassador Bridge at 1235 Huron Church Rd, and one at 110 Park St E in the city centre (both open daily 8.30am–4.30pm; Ⓣ519/973-1338 or 1-800/265-3633, Ⓦwww.visitwindsor.com).

Eating

Detroit's **ethnic** restaurants dish up the best (and least expensive) food in the city. **Greektown**, basically one block of Monroe Avenue between Beaubien and St Antoine streets, is crammed with authentic Greek places. Less commercial, but offering just as high a standard, are the bakeries, bars and cantinas of **Mexican Town**, five minutes west of downtown. **Royal Oak**, ten miles north, has a wide range of vaguely alternative wholefood places and is the liveliest suburban hangout in this sprawling metropolis.

Atwater Block Brewery 237 Joseph Campau St ⓣ313/393-2073. This spacious Rivertown brewpub serves up excellent beer-battered fish, mushrooms, mussels, wings and whatever else the chefs can think of.

Fishbone's Rhythm Kitchen Café 400 Monroe Ave, Greektown ⓣ313/965-4600. This noisy, fun and often-packed, chain restaurant is a Cajun joint with whiskey ribs, crawfish, gumbo, sushi and lots more.

Golden Fleece 525 Monroe St, Greektown ⓣ313/962-7093. Laidback Greek diner serves the most authentic gyros in town, complete with reasonable prices.

Rattlesnake Club 300 River Place ⓣ313/567-4400. Owned by creative Detroit master chef Jimmy Schmidt, the *Rattlesnake Club* has a setting in Rivertown to match the exquisite food. Dinner will set you back $30–40 per main course, lunch a lot less. Closed Sun & Mon.

SaltWater In the *MGM Grand* (see p.267) ⓣ313/465-1777. Casual, chic and quiet dining tucked amid the lively casino gamblers. Dishes like miso-glazed sea bass are a tad expensive but well worth it.

Slows Bar BQ 2138 Michigan Ave ⓣ313/962-9828. A lively, affordable restaurant and bar that brings the Southern flavour north. Located in Corktown, it has the best mac and cheese around.

Xochimilco 3409 Bagley Ave ⓣ313/843-0179. The cornerstone restaurant of Detroit's authentic Mexican Town, bustling *Xochimilco* delivers on huge portions, great service and superb value. Open till 2am.

Nightlife

There's a lot to do at night in Detroit – the city where the **techno** beat originated and is still going strong. The bars and clubs of the **Theater District** are ever popular, while the **Rivertown** area is renowned for its chic bistros and funky jazz and blues bars. The suburbs of upmarket **Birmingham** and youthful **Royal Oak** are good places to hang out, while there are a couple of fun establishments in the blue-collar neighbourhood of **Hamtramck**. Way up on the northern fringe, once-deserted **Pontiac** now has a range of well-attended rock venues, clubs and lounges. Canadian **Windsor** also has some good nightlife, with a drinking age of 19 as opposed to Michigan's 21. For event **listings** in Detroit and Ann Arbor, pick up the free weekly *Metro Times*.

Baker's Keyboard Lounge 20510 Livernois Ave, Royal Oak ⓣ313/345-6300. Mostly local jazz musicians jam in what claims to be the world's oldest jazz club.

Gusoline Alley 309 S Center St, Royal Oak ⓣ248/545-2235. Cramped and dark with a loaded jukebox, this is a legend among Detroit bars serving beers from all over the globe. Go early for a seat; the wildly mixed crowd is a people-watcher's dream.

Magic Stick 4120 Woodward Ave ⓣ313/833-9700, ⓦwww.majesticdetroit.com/stick.asp. This great venue incorporates billiards, bands and, of course, alcoholic beverages. It's part of the Majestic Theater complex, a venue for big rock shows and huge techno nights.

Saint Andrew's Hall/Shelter 431 E Congress St ⓣ313/961-6358. This cramped downtown club promotes top bands on the alternative circuit. It only holds 800 people, so get a ticket in advance. Downstairs is the *Shelter* club, with lesser-known touring bands followed by dance music.

Tonic 29 S Saginaw St, Pontiac ⓣ248/334-7411, ⓦwww.tonicdetroit.com. Open Fri–Sun until 2am, the over-18 crowd *Tonic* bills itself as the premier concert after-party: three levels of dancing and all the DJ vibe you can handle. Hip dress code.

The performing arts

Most of Detroit's major arts venues are conveniently grouped together in the northwest section of downtown. A sweeping staircase and giant chandeliers are part of the splendour at the **Detroit Opera House**, 1526 Broadway (ⓣ313/237-SING, ⓦwww.detroitoperahouse.com). Close by, the **Music Hall Center for Performing Arts**, 350 Madison Ave (ⓣ313/887-8500, ⓦwww.musichall.org), is the primary venue for **dance** in the city; it also hosts rock concerts, youth theatre and Broadway shows. In the Theater District, the gorgeous Fox Theatre, 2211 Woodward Ave (ⓣ313/983-6611, ⓦwww.olympiaentertainment.com), is the biggest draw, hosting big Broadway shows, while the cosy 450-seater **Gem Theatre**, 333 Madison Ave (ⓣ313/963-9800, ⓦwww.gemtheatre.com), is also worth a visit. A little further on toward the Cultural Center, the **Detroit Symphony Orchestra** performs at the **Max M Fisher Music Center**, 3711 Woodward Ave (ⓣ313/576-5111, ⓦwww.detroitsymphony.com).

Sports

Detroit is one of the few cities with franchises competing at the professional level in all four major team sports. **Hockey**'s Red Wings are arguably the town favourites, and tickets are hard to get; they play downtown at the Joe Louis Arena (ⓣ313/983-6606, ⓦwww.detroitredwings.com). **Baseball**'s Tigers (ⓣ313/962-4000, ⓦ.detroit.tigers.mlb.com) call the snazzy Comerica Park, or COPA, home, while the Lions play **football** at adjacent Ford Field (ⓣ313/262-2003, ⓦwww.detroitlions.com). Lastly, the Pistons (ⓣ248/377-0100, ⓦwww.nba.com/pistons) play **basketball** in the Palace of Auburn Hills, twenty-five miles north.

Ann Arbor

Although its population just tops 114,000, **ANN ARBOR**, 45 minutes' drive west of Detroit along I-94, offers a greater choice of restaurants, live music venues and cultural activities than most towns ten times its size. The **University of Michigan** has shaped the economy and character of the town ever since it was moved here from Detroit in 1837, providing the city with a very conspicuous radical edge.

The best thing to do in Ann Arbor is to stroll around downtown and the campus, which meet at South State and Liberty streets. Downtown's twelve blocks of brightly painted shops and street cafés offer all you would expect from a college town, with forty bookshops and more than a dozen record stores.

Practicalities

Frequent **Greyhound** services from Detroit stop at 116 W Huron St; **Amtrak** is on the north edge of downtown at 325 Depot St; and the **visitor centre** is at 120 W Huron St (Mon–Fri 8.30am–5pm; ⓣ734/995-7281 or 1-800/888-9487, ⓦwww.annarbor.org). There are dozens of national **hotel** chains as well as cosy intimate options. The choice place to stay is the *Campus Inn*, right downtown at 615 E Huron St (ⓣ734/769-2200 or 1-800/666-8693, ⓦwww.campusinn.com; ❻). A good central B&B is the *Burnt Toast Inn*, 415 W William St (ⓣ734/669-6685, ⓦwww.burnttoastinn.com; ❹–❺) and bargain *Eighth Street Trekkers' Lodge*, 120 Eighth St (ⓣ734/369-3107, ⓦwww.ofglobalinterest.net; ❸), run by an inveterate trekker.

Restaurants worth seeking out include *The Original Cottage Inn*, 512 E William St (ⓣ734/663-3379) for delicious pizza and *Zingerman's*, 422 Detroit St (ⓣ734/663-DELI), an excellent (if expensive) deli. A more fine-dining experience can be had at *Gandy Dancer*, 401 E Depot St (ⓣ734/769-0592).

Ann Arbor's **live music** scene enjoys a nationwide reputation. Unlike many college towns, the place doesn't go to sleep during the summer, either. For news of gigs, grab a copy of *Current*, a free monthly. Likely venues include the *Blind Pig*, 208 S First St (Ⓣ734/996-8555, Ⓦwww.blindpigmusic.com), the best place to watch live rock, alternative and blues, while *The Ark*, 316 S Main St (Ⓣ734/761-1451, Ⓦwww.a2ark.org), is an important venue for folk, acoustic and roots music. From time to time there are also live bands at the beautiful Art Deco Michigan Theater, 603 E Liberty St (Ⓣ734/668-TIME, Ⓦwww.michtheater.org), otherwise a great place to watch movies on the cheap.

Festivals are also a key part of Ann Arbor life. In June, the orchestral Summer Festival kicks off activities with music and film (Ⓦwww.annarborsummer festival.org); July sees the hectic Ann Arbor Art Fairs with hundreds of stalls; and mid-September brings the recently revived Ann Arbor Blues and Jazz Festival.

The rest of the Lower Peninsula

From Ann Arbor, you will travel a little over 150 miles west along I-94 before you reach Lake Michigan and the quaint town of St Joseph, just the first of many small ports along the lake's 350-mile eastern shoreline. North from St Joseph along Hwy-31, the northwest reaches of the lower peninsula attract sportspeople and tourists from all over the Midwest. Here, out on the unspoiled **Leelanau Peninsula** you'll find the beautiful **Sleeping Bear Dunes**, as well as the charming towns of **Harbor Springs** and **Petoskey**; all are within striking distance of larger **Traverse City**. At the northern tip of the lower peninsula, revitalized **Mackinaw City** is the departure point for the state's major tour-bus attraction, Old-World **Mackinac Island**.

Along Lake Michigan

Less than thirty miles north of Indiana, **ST JOSEPH** lies just north of "Harbor Country" – a string of adorable small towns offering good swimming, boating and fishing opportunities. St Joseph's tidy and compact downtown perches on a high bluff, from which steep steps lead down to sandy Silver Beach and two lighthouses atop two piers. You can enjoy great **food** such as nachos, steak salad and pasta on the waterfront at *Clementine's Too*, 1235 Broad St (Ⓣ269/983-0990). Places to **stay** include the stately lakeside *Boulevard Inn*, 521 Lake Blvd (Ⓣ269/983-6600, Ⓦwww.theboulevardinn.com; ❺), where all the rooms are suites, and the good-value *Holiday Inn Express*, at 3019 Lakeshore Drive (Ⓣ269/982-0004, Ⓦwww .hiexpress.com; ❸–❹). For general information on the area, stop in at the **welcome centre**, just off I-94 exit 29 (summer Mon–Sat 9am–5pm; rest of year closed Sat; Ⓣ269/925-6301).

Fifty miles north, **HOLLAND** was settled in 1847 by Dutch religious dissidents. Today's residents lose no opportunity to let visitors know of their roots: tens of thousands of tulips brighten the town in early summer, while the Holland museum, a Dutch village, a clog factory and the inevitable windmill all attract tourist dollars. You can **stay** in the Hope College favourite *Haworth Inn* (Ⓣ616/395-7200 or 1-800/903-9142, Ⓦwww.haworthinn.com; ❹), 225 College Ave, and go for a pint of fine ale at *The Curragh* (Ⓣ616/393-6340), 73 E 8th St, which also serves up bar **food**. Twenty miles farther up the shoreline, **GRAND HAVEN** boasts one of the largest and most appealing sandy beaches on the Great Lakes, best seen on a leisurely stroll along the one-and-a-half-mile largely concrete boardwalk.

Just under one hundred miles farther north, a string of pleasant small villages starts with **LUDINGTON**, where a long stretch of public beach precedes **Ludington State Park**, eight miles north on Hwy-116, which offers great hiking and sightseeing amid sweeping sand dunes and virgin pine forests; admission is $8 per car. **Camping** in some beautiful sites cost around $29 a night, though sites for the summer tend to fill up a year in advance (Ⓣ301/784-9090 or 1-800/447-2757). The **visitor centre** is on the east side of town at 5827 US-10 (Mon–Fri 8am–5pm; Ⓣ231/845-0324 or 1-800/542-4600, Ⓦwww.visitludington.com). From downtown, the **Lake Michigan Car Ferry** departs for Manitowoc, Wisconsin ($69/adult, $59/car, not including driver; Ⓣ231/845-5555 or 1-800/841-4243, Ⓦwww.ssbadger.com) – worth it to avoid Chicago traffic. There are countless places to **stay overnight**, from national chains to cottage rentals; a great option is *Snyder's Shoreline Inn*, 903 W Ludington Ave (May–Oct Ⓣ231/845-1261 or 1-800/843-2177, Ⓦwww.snydersshoreinn.com; ❹), the only downtown property with uninterrupted views of the lakeshore. *House of Flavors*, 402 W Ludington Ave (Ⓣ231/845-5785), is a chrome-heavy **diner** with breakfasts, burgers and a huge range of ice cream.

Surrounded by forest 32 miles to the north, **MANISTEE** boasts an attractive Victorian downtown and a mile-long **boardwalk** that runs alongside the Manistee River onto Lake Michigan. One of several pretty lakeside areas is **Douglas Park** – with a good sandy beach, small marina and picnic area. The **Chamber of Commerce** is at 11 Cypress St (Mon–Fri 9am–5pm; Ⓣ231/723-2575, Ⓦwww.manistee.com).

The Leelanau Peninsula

The southwestern edge of the heavily wooded **Leelanau Peninsula** is occupied by the **Sleeping Bear Dunes National Lakeshore** (Ⓦwww.sleepingbeardunes.com), a constantly resculptured area of towering dunes and precipitous 400ft drops; admission is $10 per car. The area was named by the Chippewa, who saw the mist-shrouded North and South Manitou islands as the graves of two drowned bear cubs, and the massive mainland dune, covered with dark trees, as their grieving mother. Fierce winds off Lake Michigan cause the dunes to edge inland, burying trees that reappear years later stripped of foliage, while the continual attack of high water undercuts the massive sandbanks, occasionally sending huge chunks into the lake. Stunning overlooks can be had along the hilly, nine-mile loop of the **Pierce Stocking Scenic Drive**, off Hwy-109. You can also clamber up the strenuous but enjoyable **Dune Climb**, four miles farther north on Hwy-109.

The **visitor centre**, south of the dunes at 9922 Front St (Hwy-72) in Empire (daily: summer 8am–6pm; rest of year 8.15am–4pm; Ⓣ231/326-5134, Ⓦwww.nps.gov/slbe), provides details on trails, campgrounds and beaches.

Traverse City

Smooth beaches and striking bay views help make lively **TRAVERSE CITY**, the favourite in-state resort for Michigan natives. A town of fifteen thousand year-round residents, it was saved from the stagnation that overtook many communities when their lumber mills closed down, because the stripped fields proved to be ideal for fruit-growing. Today, the area's claim to be **"Cherry Capital of the World"** is no idle boast. Thousands of acres of cherry orchards envelop the town, their wispy, pink blossoms bringing a delicate beauty each May. At the **National Cherry Festival**, held during the first full week in July, visitors can watch parades, fireworks and concerts, while sampling every imaginable cherry product.

Traverse City's neat **downtown** rests along the bottom of the west arm of **Grand Traverse Bay**, below the Old Mission Peninsula. This slender seventeen-mile strip of land, which divides the bay into two inlets, makes for a pleasant short driving tour along narrow roads with tremendous simultaneous views of the bay on either side. Five sandy public beaches and a small harbour can be found around the town itself. Various companies offer boat, windsurfer, jet-ski and mountain bike rental. There are 36 **golf courses** in the immediate area, as well – some of them among the most beautiful in the country.

Practicalities

Greyhound **buses** stop near downtown at 3233 Cass Rd. The **visitor centre**, downtown at 101 Grandview Parkway (Mon–Fri 9am–5pm, Sat till 3pm; ⓣ231/947-1120 or 1-800/872-8377, ⓦwww.visittraversecity.com), can help with finding **accommodation**, though prices anywhere near downtown soar in summer. For a taste of the good life along the nice beaches in the area, the *Sugar Beach Resort*, 1773 U.S. 31 North (ⓣ231-938-0100, ⓦwww.tcresorts.com; ❺) is an excellent choice. For a bit of a splurge, the *Grand Traverse Resort & Spa*, 100 Grand Traverse Village Blvd (ⓣ1-800/236-1577, ⓦwww.grandtraverseresort.com; ❻) has excellent restaurants and a bit of a secluded feel. Finally, the *Old Mission Inn* B&B, 18599 Mission Rd (ⓣ231/231-7770, ⓦwww.oldmissioninn.com; ❻) is located in a distinguished building built in 1869. There's **camping** at Traverse City State Park, just outside town at 1132 US-31 N (ⓣ231/922-5270; $27/night).

Affordable places to **eat** in Traverse City are easy to find. Big breakfasts with home-baked bread are served at *Mabel's*, 472 Munson Ave (ⓣ231/947-0252), while *Mode's Bum Steer*, 125 E State St (ⓣ231/947-9832), is a ribs joint. The best bet for a meal, though, particularly in the evening, is to drive north onto the Old Mission Peninsula where the *Boathouse*, 14039 Peninsula Drive (ⓣ231/223-4030), dishes up fresh seafood, pasta and vegetarian food right by the lake. The *North Peak Brewing Company*, 400 W Front St (ⓣ231/941-7325), is a fine downtown **bar** that serves up excellent salmon and burgers.

North to Mackinaw City

On its way north from Traverse City, scenic Hwy-31 skims along Lake Michigan through **Charlevoix** and other pretty lakeside towns. The northern tip of the peninsula is occupied by **Mackinaw City**, where ferries take excursionists to much-hyped **Mackinac Island** – billboards advertise its attractions for fifty miles before you arrive.

Petoskey

In **PETOSKEY**, high above Lake Michigan sixteen miles north along US-31, grand Victorian houses encircle the downtown's nicely restored **Gaslight District**. Ernest Hemingway spent many of his teenage summers here and alludes to the town in his novel *The Torrents of Spring*. The **visitor centre** is at 401 E Mitchell St (Mon–Fri 8am–5pm, Sat 10am–4pm, summer Sun noon–4pm; ⓣ1-800/845-2828, ⓦwww.boynecountry.com). For an affordable **place to stay**, try the *Comfort Inn*, 1314 US 31 North (ⓣ231/347-3220 or 1-877/228-5150, ⓦwww.comfortinn.com/hotel/mi412; ❺), or the venerable *Stafford's Perry Hotel*, centrally located at Bay and Lewis streets (ⓣ231/347-4000 or 1-800/737-1899, ⓦwww.staffords.com; ❹); its *Noggin Room Pub* has good snacks and pizza. Other options for something to eat include a Hemingway haunt, *Jesperson's*, 312 Howard St (ⓣ231/347-3601), which still does great pies and sandwiches (closed during winter). *Roast & Toast Café & Coffee*, 309 Lake St (ⓣ231/347-7767) an eclectic coffeeshop and café serves soups and sandwiches and home-made potpies.

Twelve miles up Hwy-119, **HARBOR SPRINGS** is a favourite with the Midwestern elite. The charming Main Street and small shaded beach of this "Cornbelt Riviera" resort are certainly captivating. The comfy *Colonial Inn*, at 210 Artesian Ave (ⓣ231/526-2111; ❹–❺), has the only reasonably affordable rooms in town; much pricier is the new and luxurious *Hotel Janelle*, 266 Main St (ⓣ231/526-2537, ⓦwww.hoteljanelle.com; ❾). From Harbor Springs, the "**Tunnel of Trees**" scenic drive follows a section of Hwy-119 to Mackinaw City. Along this narrow winding road, occasional breaks in the overhanging trees afford views of Lake Michigan and Beaver Island.

Mackinaw City

Forty miles northeast of Petoskey, **MACKINAW CITY** has long enjoyed a steady tourist trade as the major embarkation point for Mackinac Island and, though the streets have been landscaped and visitors flock to **Mackinaw Crossings**, a mall-cum-entertainment zone on South Huron Street, that remains its real *raison d'être*, as well as being the last stop en route to the Upper Peninsula.

The **visitor centre** is located at 10800 S US-23 (Mon–Fri 8am–5pm; ⓣ800/666-0160, ⓦwww.mackinawcity.com). Several mid-priced **hotels** have been built alongside the shore, among them the *Best Western Dockside Waterfront,* 505 S Huron Ave (ⓣ231/436-5001, ⓦwww.bestwestern.com; ❺). More rooms can be found at the *Clarion Hotel Beachfront*, 905 S Huron (ⓣ231/436-5539, ⓦwww.clarionhotel.com; ❺–❻). The hotel features a 300ft private sandy beach, a free hot breakfast bar and rooms with a view of Mackinac Island.

To reach Mackinac Island, contact Arnold Transit (May–Oct, schedule varies; $26 for pedestrians, $8 for bikes; ⓣ906/847-3351 or 1-800/542-8528, ⓦwww.arnoldline.com) or Shepler's Ferry (late April to mid-Oct, schedule varies; $21 and $8 for bikes; ⓣ231/436-5023 or 1-800/828-6157, ⓦwww.sheplersferry.com); both companies offer **high-speed catamaran crossings** from the Ferry Terminal in Mackinaw City, and do not require reservations.

Mackinac Island

Viewed from an approaching boat, the tree-blanketed rocky limestone outcrop of **MACKINAC ISLAND** (pronounced "Mackinaw"), suddenly thrusting out from the swirling waters, is an unforgettable sight. As you near the harbour, large Victorian houses come into view, dappling the hillsides with white and pastel. The most conspicuous is the imposing, $300-a-night *Grand Hotel* (ⓣ906/847-3331 or 1-800/334-7263, ⓦwww.grandhotel.com; ❾), where just to enter the foyer costs $10. On disembarking, you'll see rows of horses and buggies (all motorized transportation is banned from the island, except for emergency vehicles) and inhale the omnipresent smell of fresh manure. Also ubiquitous on the island is **fudge**, relentlessly marketed as a Mackinac "delicacy".

Mackinac's crowded **Main Street** can get irritating, but the island is worth visiting, not least for the ferry ride over and the chance to cycle along the hilly backroads. Underneath the tourist trimmings is a rich history. French priests established a mission to the Huron Indians here during the winter of 1670–71. The French built a fort here in 1715, but within fifty years had lost control of the island to the British. The government acknowledged the island's beauty by designating it as the country's second national park, two years after Yellowstone in 1875, though it was handed over to the state of Michigan twenty years later. To get a feel for the history, hike or cycle up to the whitewashed stone

Fort Mackinac, a US Army outpost until 1890. Its ramparts afford a great view of the village and lake below, though admission is a steep $10.50 (May to mid-Oct 9.30am–4.30pm).

On Main Street, an **information kiosk** (daily 9am–5pm; ⓣ906/847-3783, ⓦwww.mackinac.com) provides full details of accommodation and other facilities. The less costly **hotel** is *Murray Hotel* (ⓣ906/847-3360 or 1-800/462-2546, ⓦwww.4mackinac.com; ⑤), which serves a large continental breakfast buffet. Unpretentious **B&Bs** dot the island. Places to **eat** include *Pink Pony Bar & Grill* (ⓣ906/847-3341), which has a great harbour view and lively atmosphere, and *Horn's Gaslight Bar* (ⓣ906/847-6154), which also has nightly live music.

The Upper Peninsula

From the map, it would seem logical for Michigan's **Upper Peninsula**, separated from the rest of the state by the **Mackinac Straits**, to be part of Wisconsin. However, when Michigan entered the Union in 1837, its legislators, eyeing the peninsula's huge mineral wealth, incorporated it into their new state before Wisconsin existed.

Previously the "UP" (pronounced "You-p"), as it's commonly known, figured prominently in French plans to create an empire in North America. Father Jacques Marquette and other missionaries made peace with the native people and established settlements, including the port of Sault Ste Marie in 1688. The French hoped to press further south, but before they could get much past Detroit, the British inflicted a severe military defeat in 1763.

Vast, lonesome and wild, the Upper Peninsula is full of stunning landmarks, exemplified by the **Pictured Rocks National Lakeshore**. Most of the eastern section is marked by low-lying, sometimes swampy land between softly undulating limestone hills. Infamous for its bitter winters the northwest corner is the most desolate, especially the rough and broken **Keweenaw Peninsula** and **Isle Royale National Park**, fifty miles offshore. The UP's only real city is **Marquette**, a college town with a quiet buzz and a good base for exploration. Until 1957 you could get to the UP from lower Michigan only by ferry. Today, the five-mile **Mackinac Bridge** ($3.50 toll), lit up beautifully at night, stretches elegantly across the bottleneck Mackinac Straits.

Pictured Rocks National Lakeshore

The 42 miles between the attractive fishing villages of Grand Marais and Munising form the **Pictured Rocks National Lakeshore**, a splendid array of multicoloured cliffs, rolling dunes and secluded sandy beaches. Rain, wind, ice and sun have carved and gouged arches, columns and caves into the face of the lakeshore, all stained different hues. Hiking trails run along the clifftops, and Hwy-58 takes you close to the water, but the best way to see the cliffs is by **boat**. Pictured Rocks Cruises offers a three-hour narrated **tour** that leaves from the City Pier in Munising (late May to early Oct 2–8 trips daily; $34; ⓣ906/387-3386, ⓦwww.picturedrocks.com). Less than a mile farther along the lake, at 1204 Commercial St, Shipwreck Tours gives two-hour narrated cruises in a glass-bottomed boat, with surprisingly clear views of three shipwrecks – one intact (June to early Oct 2–3 trips daily; $28; ⓣ906/387-4477, ⓦwww.shipwrecktours.com). Those in a hurry can get a glimpse of the cliffs by visiting the **Miners Castle Overlook**, twelve miles east of Munising, or **Munising Falls**, one of a half-dozen nearby waterfalls, near the village's well-signposted **visitors bureau** (Mon–Fri 9am–5pm; ⓣ906/387-2138, ⓦwww.munising.org). In Munising, *Scotty's Motel*,

415 Cedar St (ⓣ906/387-2449; ❸), and the *Munising Motel*, 332 E Onota St (ⓣ906/387-3187; ❹), are fairly comfortable places to stay. At 101 E Munising Ave, *The Navigator* (ⓣ906/387-1555) is the only **restaurant** in Munising with a view of Lake Superior, and serves breakfast any time along with steaks, seafood, pizza and burgers.

Marquette

Forty miles west of Munising is the unofficial capital of the UP, the low-key college town of **MARQUETTE**, also the centre of the area's massive ore industry. The helpful **state welcome centre**, just south of town at 2201 US-41 S (daily: summer 9am–6pm; rest of year till 5pm; ⓣ906/249-9066, ⓦwww.marquettecountry.org), has vouchers for local hotel discounts and lots of information about Marquette's sights. Premier among them is rugged **Presque Isle Park**, north of town on Lakeshore Boulevard, almost completely surrounded by Lake Superior and with stunning views of the lake. Back in town, at East Ridge Street and Lakeshore, the **Marquette Maritime Museum** (mid-May to late Oct daily 10am–5pm; $4; ⓣ906/226-2006, ⓦwww.mqtmaritimemuseum.com) has exhibits on the fishing and freighting industries, as well as a video about the fabled Superior wrecking of the *Edmund Fitzgerald*. The area's most curious sight is the **Superior Dome**, on Northern Michigan University's campus at 1401 Presque Isle Ave, the largest wooden dome in the world.

By far the nicest place to **stay** is the grand *Landmark Inn*, 230 N Front St (ⓣ906/228-2580, ⓦwww.thelandmarkinn.com; ❺), which has rooms overlooking the lake, although a host of cheaper motels cluster west of town on US-41. You can **camp** at the *Tourist Park Campground* on Sugarloaf Avenue (ⓣ906/228-0465; $15). *JJ's Shamrock*, downtown at 113 S Front St (ⓣ906/226-6734), serves basic bar **food** along with occasional live music. For a more formal dining experience, locals favour the *Northwoods Supper Club*, just west of town off US-41 (ⓣ906/228-4343), with a meat-and-potatoes menu in a rustic setting. One popular watering hole is *Remie's Bar*, 111 Third St (ⓣ906/226-9133), with a rowdy local crowd and live music on Wednesdays.

Isle Royale National Park

Much closer to Canada than the US, the 45-mile sliver of **Isle Royale National Park**, fifty miles out in Lake Superior, is in a double sense as far as you can get in Michigan from Detroit. All cars are banned and, instead of freeways, 166 miles of hiking trails lead past windswept trees, swampy lakes and grazing moose. Aside from other outdoors types, the only traces of human life you're likely to see are ancient mineworks, possibly two millennia old, shacks left behind by commercial fishermen in the 1940s, and a few lighthouses and park buildings. Hiking, canoeing, fishing and scuba-diving among shipwrecks are the principal leisure activities.

The park is open from mid-May until the end of September. **Camping** is free, though you should visit the **park headquarters** at 800 E Lakeshore Drive in Houghton (Mon–Fri 8am–4.30pm; ⓣ906/482-0984, ⓦwww.nps.gov/isro) before you leave the mainland, for advice on water purity, mosquitoes and temperatures that can drop well below freezing even in summer. Aside from camping, you can stay in a self-catering cottage or a luxury lodge room at the *Rock Harbor Lodge* (ⓣ906/337-4993, Oct–April ⓣ866/644-2003, ⓦwww.isleroyaleresort.com; ❻–❾). The lodge rents canoes and motorboats for $39 and $76 per day, respectively, and offers cruises for $37.75.

Ferries to Isle Royale leave from Copper Harbor ($75 one-way; ⓣ906/289-4437, ⓦwww.isleroyale.com), Houghton ($60 one-way; ⓣ906/482-0984,

Ⓦwww.nps.gov/isro) and Grand Portage, Minnesota ($63 one-way; Ⓣ715/392-2100, Ⓦwww.grand-isle-royale.com). If you are in a hurry, you can hop over by **plane** with the Isle Royale Seaplane Service in Houghton ($290 return; Ⓣ906/482-8850, Ⓦwww.royaleairservice.com).

Indiana

Thanks to an influx of northward migrants early in the nineteenth century – including the family of Abraham Lincoln, who lived for fourteen years near the present village of Santa Claus before moving to Illinois – much of **INDIANA** bears the influence of the easy-going South. Unlike the abolitionist Lincolns, many former Southerners brought slaves to this new territory, and thousands rioted against being drafted into the Union army when the Civil War broke out. However, massive industrialization throughout the northwest corner of the state since the late nineteenth century firmly integrated Indiana into the regional economy. On a national level, this sports-happy state is best known these days for automobile racing and high school basketball.

Despite some beautiful dunes and beaches, the most lasting memories provided by Indiana's fifty-mile **lakeshore** (by far the shortest of the Great Lakes states) are of the grimy steel mills and poverty-stricken neighbourhoods of towns like Gary and East Chicago. In northern Indiana, the area in and around Elkhart and Goshen contains one of the nation's largest **Amish settlements**. The central plains are characterized by small market towns, except for the sprawling capital, **Indianapolis**, which makes a nice enough stopover. **Bloomington** is the home of Indiana University (and their perennial standout college basketball team), and it is the state's premier college town. Hilly southern Indiana, at its most appealing in the fall, is a welcome contrast to the central cornbelt, boasting several quaint towns such as Nashville, while thriving Columbus exhibits a great array of contemporary architecture for such a small city.

Indianapolis and around

INDIANAPOLIS began life in 1821, when a tract of barely inhabited marshes was designated the state capital. While its location in the middle of Indiana's rich farmland bore immense commercial advantages, the absence of a navigable river prohibited the transportation of bulky materials such as coal and iron to sustain heavy industry. Though home to more than sixty car manufacturers by 1910, the city never seriously threatened Detroit's supremacy. Today the city's economic well-being is centred around the food, paper and pharmaceutical industries, including the giant Eli Lilly Corporation.

Although Indianapolis continues its focus on sports – in recent years, it has constructed several world-class sports arenas, including the retro-styled **Conseco Fieldhouse** downtown – there is more to the city than could perhaps once be said. Along with new hotels, a gaggle of fine museums and a zoo, its old downtown landmarks have become cultural, shopping and dining complexes. No longer is it (quite) true that nothing happens here except for the glamorous **Indianapolis 500 car race** each May.

Arrival and information

Indianapolis International Airport is ten miles southwest of downtown, on the #8 IndyGo bus route ($1.75; ⓣ317/635-3344) – IndyGo's Green Line Downtown/Airport Express route provides nonstop service from the airport to downtown and the Convention Center (daily 5am–9pm; $7). A **taxi** into the centre costs around $35; try Yellow Cabs (ⓣ317/487-7777). Both Greyhound **buses** and Amtrak **trains** arrive at 350 S Illinois St (ⓣ317/267-3071), next to the fairly central Union Station complex. Useful **visitor centres** can be found at 201 S Capitol St, beside the RCA Dome (Mon–Fri 8.30am–5.30pm; ⓣ1-800/323-4639, ⓦwww.indy.org), and in the glass pavilion at 100 W Washington St (Mon–Sat 10am–9pm, Sun noon–6pm; ⓣ317/624-2563).

Accommodation

Indianapolis has plenty of quality **places to stay**, with budget options about five miles from downtown. Prices can double during the race months of May, August and September.

Canterbury Hotel 123 S Illinois St ⓣ317/204-2569 or 1-877/866-0837, ⓦwww.canterburyhotel.com. Much the classiest downtown option, this landmark hotel was rebuilt in 1928 and offers a hundred opulent and expensive rooms. ⑦–⑧

Crowne Plaza Union Station 123 W Louisiana St ⓣ317/631-2221 or 1-877/227-6963, ⓦwww.crowneplaza.com/ind-downtown. Regular hotel rooms plus some much more exciting suites in converted railway carriages. ⑥–⑦

Indy Hostel 4903 Winthrop Ave ⓣ317/727-1696, ⓦwww.indyhostel.us. Appealing small-scale hostel in a former family home, located in a friendly neighbourhood six miles from downtown. Dorm beds for $25 weekdays, $29 weekends, plus basic private rooms (②). Bike hire available.

Staybridge Suites 535 S West St ⓣ317/536-7500, ⓦwww.ichotelsgroup.com. This hotel is right next to Lucas Oil Stadium, and it features a complimentary hot breakfast buffet, an afternoon cocktail reception during the week and free laundry services. ④

The Villa Inn 1456 N Delaware St ⓣ317/916-8500 or 1-866/626-8500, ⓦwww.thevillainn.com. Castellated six-room luxury B&B inn with the feel of a hotel, two miles north of downtown, and offering a spa and restaurant. The same owners run two other local B&Bs. ⑧

Downtown

The nerve centre of Indianapolis's spacious, relaxed downtown is the reasonably tasteful **Circle Centre** shopping and entertainment complex. Suspended over the busy Washington and Illinois intersection, the spectacular **Indianapolis Artsgarden** is an eight-storey glass rotunda illuminated with twinkling lights. A performance and exhibition space, it doubles as a walkway to Circle Centre and several downtown hotels. One block north, streets radiate from **Monument Circle**, the starting point for a lengthy series of memorials and plazas dedicated to war veterans. Many visitors climb the 330 steps of the renovated 284ft **Soldiers and Sailors Monument** (daily 10am–7pm; walk up free, elevator $2) – the tiny elevator can seldom cope with the demand – but in truth the view of the city from the top is nothing special.

Five blocks east, starting at New York and East streets, the serene tree-shaded **Lockerbie Square Historic District** is a small enclave of picturesque residences that were home to nineteenth-century artisans and business leaders. Small wood-frame cottages line the cobblestone streets, many of them painted in bright pinks, blues and yellows, and fronted by ornately carved porches.

Several blocks west of Monument Circle, the **Indiana State Museum**, 650 W Washington St (Mon–Sat 9am–5pm, Sun 11am–5pm; $7; ⓣ317/232-1637,

The Indianapolis 500

Seven miles northwest of downtown, the **Indianapolis Motor Speedway** stages three events each year; one is the legendary **Indianapolis 500**, held on the last Sunday in May, the others are July's prestigious NASCAR Brickyard 400 and August's Red Bull Indianapolis GP.

The Indy 500 is preceded by two weeks of qualification runs that whittle the hopeful entrants down to a final field of 33 drivers, one of whom will scoop the million-dollar first prize. The two-and-a-half-mile circuit was built as a test track for the city's motor manufacturers. The first 500-mile race – held in 1911 and won in a time of 6hr 42min, at an average speed of 74.6mph – was a huge success, vindicating the organizers' belief that the distance was the optimum length for spectators' enjoyment. Cars now hit 235mph, though the official times of the winners are reduced by delays caused by accidents. While the technology is marvellous, the true legends in the eyes of their fans are such championship drivers as A.J. Foyt, Mario Andretti and members of the Unser dynasty. The big race crowns one of the nation's largest festivals, attended by almost half a million spectators. Seats for the race usually sell out well in advance ($70–90; ⓣ1-800/822-4639, ⓦwww.imstix.com), but you may gain admittance to the infield ($20), for a tailgate-style, rowdy atmosphere and limited viewing.

ⓦwww.indianamuseum.org), gives a useful insight into the state's history through exhibits on everything from geology to sport. The **Eiteljorg Museum of American Indians and Western Art** is nearby at 500 W Washington St, on the western edge of downtown (Mon–Sat 10am–5pm, Sun noon–5pm; tours at 1pm; $8; ⓣ317/636-9378, ⓦwww.eiteljorg.org). Harrison Eiteljorg, an industrialist who went West in the 1940s to speculate in minerals, fell so deeply in love with the art of the region that he brought as much of it back with him as possible, especially from Taos, New Mexico. On display are works by Frederic Remington, Charles M. Russell and Georgia O'Keeffe, as well as tribal artefacts from all over North America and a 38ft Haida totem pole. There are also superb touring exhibits and a gorgeous gift shop. The Eiteljorg stands amid the rolling greenery of **White River State Park**, which is also home to the sizeable **Indianapolis Zoo** (summer Mon–Thurs 9am–5pm, Fri–Sun till 6pm; rest of year daily till 4pm; $14.50; ⓣ317/630-2001, ⓦwww.indyzoo.com). In the park's southeast corner stands the superb **Victory Field**, home of the Indianapolis Indians (ⓣ317/269-3545), the feeder team for baseball's Cincinnati Reds.

Out from downtown

Although the bodies of former president Benjamin Harrison and Hoosier poet James Whitcomb Riley lie in the enormous **Crown Hill Cemetery**, at 38th Street and Michigan, the most visited grave belongs to 1930s bank robber **John Dillinger**, at Section 44 Lot 94. Designated Public Enemy Number One, Dillinger completed thirteen bank raids – killing four policemen, three FBI agents, one sheriff and an undetermined number of innocent bystanders – in a single-year career. Something of a folk hero, he escaped from jail twice, but was eventually ambushed by the FBI outside a Chicago theatre in 1934 (see p.297) – that said, some researchers allege that another man was killed in his place.

Opposite the cemetery at 1200 W 38th St, more than 150 lush wooded acres accommodate the capacious **Indianapolis Museum of Art** (Tues, Wed, & Sat 11am–5pm, Thurs & Fri till 9pm, Sun noon–5pm; ⓣ317/923-1331, ⓦwww.imamuseum.org). The main building is surrounded by a lake, botanical garden, sculpture courtyard and a concert terrace. Inside, the exceptional displays include the largest collection of Turner paintings outside Britain and an array of paintings and prints from Gauguin's Pont Aven school.

The **Children's Museum of Indianapolis**, 3000 N Meridian St, four miles north of downtown off I-65 (daily 10am–5pm; closed Mon late Sept to late Feb; $15.50, under-18s $10.50; ⓣ317/334-3322, ⓦwww.childrensmuseum.org), is arguably the best of its kind in the country. Its most popular exhibit is the Dinosphere, in which visitors can dig for genuine fossils, while All Aboard! is an entertaining romp through the Age of Steam.

Eating

The swish **Circle Centre** mall houses dozens of **places to eat**, but most are chains. You'd do better to stick to the more established restaurants downtown or head up to **Broad Ripple Village** (bus #17) at College Avenue and 62nd Street, which is packed with bars and cafés (along with galleries and shops).

3 Sisters Café 334 N Guilford Ave ⓣ317/257-5556. Stop in for a laidback atmosphere and a healthy dose of vegetarian fare.

Bazbeaux 6360 Massachusetts Ave, downtown ⓣ317/636-7662 and 811 E Westfield Blvd, Broad Ripple Village ⓣ317/255-5711. The best (thin-crust) pizzas in town, with a range of exotic toppings.

Elbow Room 605 N Pennsylvania St ⓣ317/635-3354. This pub serves specialty sandwiches and lots of import beers.

H20 Sushi 1912 Broad Ripple Ave ⓣ317/254-0677. This restaurant and sushi bar has successfully married a traditional mix of sushi with a more modern choice of savoury combos. Closed Sun & Mon.

Shapiro's 808 S Meridian St ⓣ317/631-4041. Landmark deli just a few blocks off downtown, where you can fill up on lox, tongue and other specialties in an old-style cafeteria atmosphere for around $8. Leave room for the huge desserts.

Yat's Cajun and Creole 659 Massachusetts Ave ⓣ317/686-6380; also at 5463 N College Ave ⓣ317/253-8817. Wildly popular Louisiana-flavoured cafeteria, offering a changing menu of inexpensive daily specials in two locations (entrees $4.50–6.50).

Nightlife and entertainment

The **nightlife** area in downtown is Massachusetts Avenue, where along with some good bars and restaurants, the 3000-seat **Murat Centre**, a former Masonic shrine at 502 N New Jersey St (ⓣ317/231-0000, ⓦwww.murat.com), hosts headliners and Broadway musicals. Otherwise, head north to chic **Broad Ripple Village**. Check the free weekly *NUVO* (ⓦwww.nuvo.net) "Indy's alternative voice", for full details of gigs and events.

On the **performing arts** scene, the 1927 Spanish Baroque Indiana Repertory Theatre, 140 W Washington St (ⓣ317/635-5252, ⓦwww.irtlive.com), puts on dramatic productions between September and May, while the Indianapolis Symphony Orchestra has weekly concerts at the equally elaborate 1916 Hilbert Circle Theatre, 45 Monument Circle (ⓣ317/639-4300, ⓦwww.indyorch.org).

Broad Ripple Brew Pub 842 E 65th St ⓣ317/253-2739. Atmospheric brewpub located six miles north of downtown Indianapolis.

Chatterbox 435 Massachusetts Ave ⓣ317/636-0584, ⓦwww.chatterboxjazz.com. Ever-busy local bar, hosting live jazz nightly for the past 25 years.

Madame Walker Theatre Center 617 Indiana Ave ⓣ317/236-2099, ⓦwww.walkertheatre.com. Black cultural and heritage centre putting on "Jazz on the Avenue" every 4th Friday, plus regular dance events, plays and concerts.

Rathskeller Restaurant 401 E Michigan St ⓣ317/636-0396. German beer hall in the basement of the historic Athenaeum building, which also serves food. Live music and a biergarten.

Slippery Noodle 372 S Meridian St ⓣ317/631-6974. Indiana's oldest bar, established in 1850, is next to Union Station. Cheap beer Mon and Tues, and live blues every night starting at 8.15pm.

Vogue 6259 N College Ave ⓣ317/259-7029, ⓦwww.thevogue.ws. Popular Broad Ripple rock and indie venue in a former movie theatre, also featuring retro club nights.

Bloomington

BLOOMINGTON, a college town, is by far the liveliest small city in Indiana, just 45 miles southwest of Indianapolis on Hwy-37. It owes its vibrancy to the main campus of Indiana University, east of downtown. The I.M. Pei-designed **Indiana University Art Museum** on East Seventh Street (Tues–Sat 10am–5pm, Sun noon–5pm; free) holds a fine international collection of painting and sculpture. Across the street from the pastoral campus, Indiana native and law student, Hoagy Carmichael composed the TinPan Alley gem *Stardust* on the piano of a popular hangout. The architecturally rich downtown also features a host of good shops.

Practicalities

Bloomington Shuttle, 3200 Venture Blvd, (Ⓣ812/332-6004 or 1-800/589-6004), runs a **bus** service to Indianapolis. Bloomington's friendly **visitor centre** can be found at 2855 N Walnut St (Mon–Fri 8.30am–5pm, Sat 9am–4pm; Ⓣ812/334-8900, Ⓦwww.visitbloomington.com).

If you need to **stay**, the conveniently located *Hampton Inn*, 2100 N Walnut St (Ⓣ812/334-2100; ④–⑤), is a friendly, clean choice. The cosy and also very central Victorian *Grant Street Inn*, 310 N Grant St (Ⓣ812/334-2353 or 1-800/328-4350, Ⓦwww.grantstreetinn.com; ⑥–⑦), offers more luxury. Among student bars and cafés lining Kirkwood Avenue is the vegetarian *Laughing Planet*, at no. 322 E Kirkwood (Ⓣ812/323-2233), renowned for its burritos, while local **restaurant** *FARMbloomington*, 108 E Kirkwood Ave (Ⓣ 812/323-0002), offers real food right from the farm. The *Brewpub at Lennie's*, 1795 E Tenth St (Ⓣ812/339-2256), is the liveliest drinking spot around.

Illinois

While there is plenty more to **ILLINOIS** than just the Windy City, much of the cultural and social identity of this state revolves around **Chicago**, the largest and most exciting city in the Great Lakes region. Perched in the state's northeastern corner, on the shores of **Lake Michigan**, Chicago has a fabulous skyline, plus top-rated museums, restaurants and cafés, and dozens of nightspots that send forth blues, jazz and rock into the night. Seventy-five percent of the state's twelve-million-strong population lives within commuting distance of the Windy City. The contrast between Illinois' quiet rural hinterlands and its buzzing urban centre could hardly be greater.

Illinois was first explored and settled by the French, though in 1763 the territory was sold to the English. Granted statehood in 1818, Illinois remained a distant frontier until the mid-1830s; only once the native **Sauk** were subjugated, after a series of uprisings, did settlers arrive in sizeable numbers. Among them were the first followers of Joseph Smith, founder of the Mormon Church, who established a large colony along the Mississippi at Nauvoo. The **Mormons** met with suspicion and persecution and, after Smith was murdered by a lynch mob in 1844, fled west to Utah. Other early immigrants included the young **Abraham Lincoln**, who practised law from 1837 onward in **Springfield**. Now the state capital, it is home to a wide range of Lincolniana, including his restored home, his law offices and various other period buildings and artefacts, as well as his monumental tomb and a new Presidential Library and Museum. Despite the claims of other nearby states, Illinois maintains that it is truly the "Land of Lincoln".

Chicago

CHICAGO is in many ways the nation's last great city. Sarah Bernhardt called it "the pulse of America" and, though long eclipsed by Los Angeles as the nation's second most populous city after New York, Chicago really does have it all, with less hassle and fewer infrastructural problems than its coastal rivals.

Founded in the early 1800s, Chicago had a population of just fifty in 1830. Its expansion was triggered first by the opening of the Erie Canal in 1825, and then

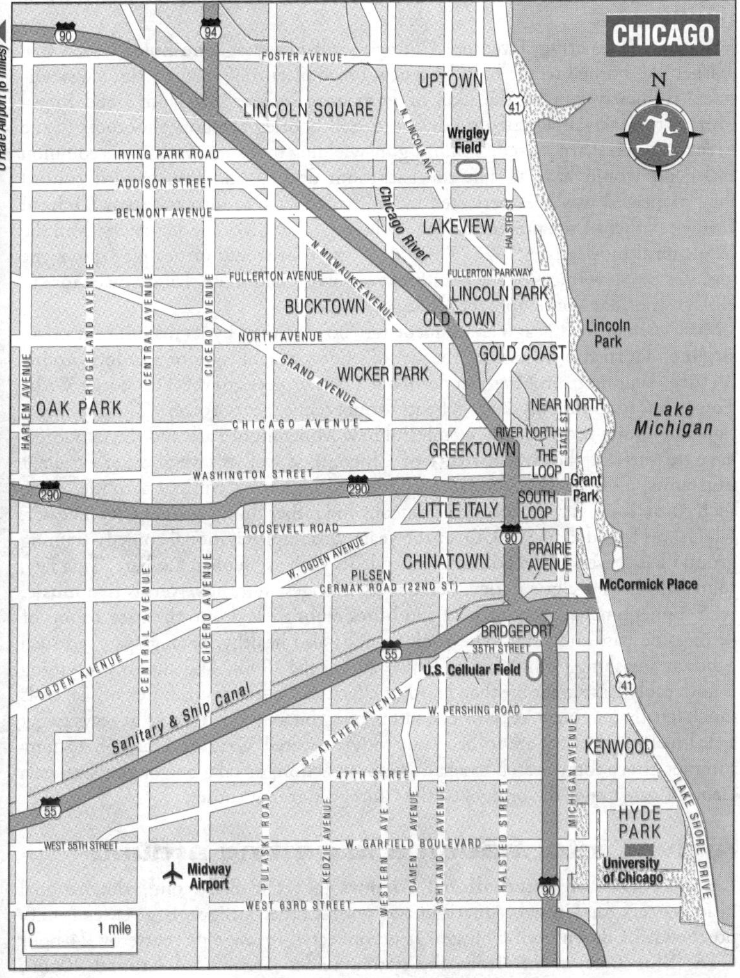

by the arrival of the first locomotive in 1848; by 1860 it was the largest railroad centre in the world, serving as the main connection between the established East Coast cities and the frontier that stretched over 2000 miles west to the Pacific Ocean. That position on the sharp edge between civilization and wilderness made it a crucible of innovation. Many aspects of modern life, from skyscrapers to suburbia, had their start, and perhaps their finest expression, here on the shores of Lake Michigan.

Despite burning to the ground in 1871, Chicago boomed thereafter, doubling in population every decade and by 1900 the city was home to over two million people, many of whom made their way on crowded ships from Ireland and Eastern Europe. In the early years of the twentieth century, it cemented its reputation as a place of apparently limitless opportunity, with jobs aplenty for those willing and not averse to strenuous physical labour and largely monotonous tasks. The attraction was strongest among **blacks** from the Deep South: African-Americans poured into the city, with more than 75,000 arriving during the war years of 1916–18 alone.

During the Roaring Twenties, Chicago's self-image as a no-holds-barred free market was pushed to the limit by a new breed of entrepreneur. Criminal syndicates, ruthlessly run by the likes of **gangsters** such as Al Capone and Bugsy Moran, took advantage of Prohibition to sell bootleg alcohol. Shootouts in the street between sharp-suited, Tommy-gun-wielding mobsters were not as common as legend would have it, but the backroom dealing and iron-handed control they pioneered was later perfected by politicians such as former mayor **Richard Daley** – father of the present mayor – who ran Chicago single-handedly from the 1950s until his death in 1976. These days, the tourist authorities play down the mobster era; few traces of the hoodlum years exist, and those that do owe more to Hollywood than contemporary Chicago.

Most visitors to Chicago are immediately bowled over by its magnificent urban **skyline**, adorned with one of the world's finest assemblages of **modern architecture**, ranging from Mies van der Rohe's masterpieces to the 110-storey **Willis Tower** (more commonly known by its former name, Sears Tower). The city is also rightfully quite proud of the wonderful new Millennium Park and the extraordinary treasures of the **Art Institute of Chicago**, as well as several other excellent **museums**, along with restaurants, sports and highbrow cultural activities. One such cultural activity of note is the raucous and rather funny Second City Theater, which was founded in 1959. Over the years, this improvisational comedy training ground has served as the incubator for talents such as Stephen Colbert, Tina Fey, John Belushi and Chris Farley. Perhaps its strongest suit, however, is **live music**, with a phenomenal array of **jazz** and **blues** clubs packed into the back rooms of its amiable bars and cafés. The **rock** scene is also healthy, having spawned such bands as Smashing Pumpkins and Wilco during the 1990s. And almost everything is noticeably less expensive than in other US cities – **eating out**, for example, costs much less than in New York or LA, but is every bit as good. Two great ways to get a real feel for the city are to head out to ivy-covered **Wrigley Field** on a sunny summer afternoon to catch baseball's Cubs in action, or take one of the Wendella Cruise Boats under the bridges of the Chicago River at sunset.

Arrival, information and getting around

Chicago's **O'Hare International Airport** (Ⓦwww.ohare.com), the national headquarters for United, American and several other airlines, is seventeen miles northwest of downtown Chicago. It is connected to the city centre by 24-hour CTA (Blue Line) **trains** from the station under Terminal 4 (around 40min;

$2.25). **Midway Airport** is smaller than O'Hare and primarily used by domestic airlines. Midway is eleven miles southwest of downtown, and you can take one of CTA's Midway (Orange Line) trains from right outside of the terminal (30min; $2.25). **Taxis** into town from O'Hare cost up to $40 (there's also a ride-share programme with a flat rate of $22), and take thirty minutes to an hour. From Midway the fare is about $30 and the journey time is twenty to forty minutes. Another option is Airport Express's **express bus and van service** between the airports and downtown hotels (around $28 from O'Hare, $23 from Midway; Ⓣ1-888/284-3826, Ⓦwww.airportexpress.com).

Chicago is the hub of the nationwide **Amtrak** rail system, and almost every cross-country route passes through **Union Station**, west of the Loop at Canal and Adam streets. Greyhound and a number of regional bus companies pull into the large 24-hour **bus station** at 630 W Harrison St (Ⓣ312/408-5800), three blocks southwest of Union Station.

Arriving in Chicago **by car**, racing towards the gleaming glass towers of the Loop, can be memorable. Bear in mind, though, that traffic on the expressways to and from downtown can be bumper-to-bumper during rush hours. **Parking** can also be a problem. Recently the city decided to contract with a private company for parking meters, and the fare boxes now accept credit cards, which is helpful. Check street signs for additional restrictions, which are rigidly enforced – violations may result in your car being towed and impounded. Perhaps the best place to leave a car in the downtown area is in the garage under Grant Park, at Columbus Street and Monroe Drive, close to the east side of the Art Institute ($29 for 24hr).

Information

Pick up information and maps from the **Chicago Office of Tourism**, in the lobby of the Chicago Cultural Center, 77 E Randolph St (Mon–Thurs 8am–7pm,

Guided tours

The best **guided tours** of Chicago have to be the wide range offered by the **Chicago Architecture Foundation**, based in the Archicenter in the Santa Fe Building at 224 S Michigan Ave (Ⓣ312/922-3432, Ⓦwww.architecture.org). Expert guides point out the city's many architectural treasures and explain their role in Chicago's history and development. Most popular of all are the superb Architecture River Cruises, ninety-minute **boat trips** along the Chicago River that leave from Michigan Avenue and Lower Wacker Drive (late April to early June Mon–Fri 3 departures, Sat & Sun 5 deps; early June to Sept Mon–Fri 10 deps, Sat & Sun 13 deps; Oct Mon–Fri 5 deps, Sat & Sun 6 deps; Nov Fri–Sun 3 deps; $32). The Foundation also runs several **walking tours** of the Loop, departing from the Archicenter on a complicated schedule of at least two different 2-hour tours daily throughout the year ($16 for one tour), and a daily 45-minute, $5 lunchtime tour of downtown landmarks at 12.15pm. Their longer-range **bus tours** operate mainly in summer, focusing principally on the works of Frank Lloyd Wright ($52) and the "Bungalow Belt" tour ($40), though the three-and-a-half-hour "highlights" tour ($40) leaves at 9.30am on Saturdays and Wednesdays all year.

For a free and personalized tour, the Chicago Greeter programme (Ⓦwww.chicagogreeter.com) is an excellent choice. Tours leave from the lobby of the Chicago Cultural Center and visitors can set up their tour beforehand by contacting the website listed above several weeks in advance. Alternately, visitors can just show up and take advantage of the "Instagreeter" programme. The tours are led by a trained greeter, and visitors can learn about 25 different neighbourhoods or pick one of the 40 popular interest areas, such as "Ethnic Chicago" or "Public Art".

CityPass

For significant **discounts** at five of the city's major tourist and cultural attractions – the Hancock Observatory (or Skydeck Chicago at the Willis Tower), the Field Museum, Shedd Aquarium, Adler Planetarium & Astronomy Museum and the Museum of Science and Industry – you can purchase a **CityPass** ($69, ages 4–11 $59; ⓣ1-888/330-5008, ⓦwww.citypass.com). Valid for nine days, it allows you to skip most lines and save money (up to $65, if you visit all five sights). CityPasses are sold at each of the attractions, or via the website.

Fri till 6pm, Sat 9am–6pm, Sun 10am–6pm; ⓣ1-800/877-CHICAGO, ⓦwww.explorechicago.org). There are also **information centres** in the Historic Water Tower, 800 N Michigan Ave on the Magnificent Mile (Mon–Thurs 8am–7pm, Fri till 6pm, Sat 9am–6pm, Sun 10am–6pm) and in the Northwest Exelon Pavilion at Millennium Park (daily 10am–4pm).

Chicago's main **post office**, the largest in the world, is at 433 W Harrison St (open 24hr). There's a downtown branch at 211 S Clark St (Mon–Fri 7am–6pm).

City transport

Getting around Chicago is simple and quick, thanks to buses and the "L", a system of elevated trains operated 24 hours a day by the Chicago Transit Authority (CTA; ⓣ312/836-7000, ⓦwww.transitchicago.com). Pick up a CTA System Map, available at most subway stations and visitor centres, or from CTA headquarters west of the Chicago River at 567 W Lake St. **Buses** run every five to fifteen minutes during rush hours and every eight to twenty minutes at most other times. **Rapid transit trains** run every five to fifteen minutes during the day and every fifteen to sixty minutes all night. Lines are colour-coded and denoted by route rather than destination. The Howard–Dan Ryan is the Red Line; Lake–Englewood–Jackson Park is the Green Line; the O'Hare–Congress–Douglas is the Blue Line; the Ravenswood is the Brown Line (whose trains circle the Loop, giving the area its name); the Evanston Express is the Purple Line; the Midway–Loop is the Orange Line; the Pink Line runs from the Loop to the suburb of Cicero, and the Skokie Swift is the Yellow Line.

CTA riders will need to purchase a "**Chicago card**" (available in all "L" stations) and add value to it. One ride costs $2.25; two more rides within two hours costs just 25¢. Passes good for one ($5.75), three ($14) or seven ($23) days of unlimited rides on both buses and the "L" are sold at O'Hare and Midway airports as well as Union Station, the visitor centre and other locations. In addition, **Metra Commuter Trains** run from various points downtown to and from the suburbs and outlying areas, including Oak Park and Hyde Park. One ride is $2.25.

Chicago's **taxis** cost $2.25 at the drop of the flag, and $1.80 per mile. They can be hailed anytime in the Loop and other central neighbourhoods; otherwise call Yellow (ⓣ312/829-4222) or Checker taxis (ⓣ312/243-2537).

Finally, **bicycles** are available for rent ($30/day) at Millennium Park's multi-level bike park at 239 E Randolph St.

Accommodation

Most central **accommodation** is oriented toward business and convention trade rather than tourism, but there are still plenty of moderately priced rooms in and around the Loop, to say nothing of the myriad of establishments that are scattered alongside major interstates. Even top-class downtown hotels are, comparatively, not that expensive. Note, however, that a **room tax** of 15.4 percent is added to all

ACCOMMODATION

Allegro	G	Hampton Inn & Suites	E	Palmer House Hilton	H
Comfort Inn & Suites Downtown	D	HI-Chicago	I	Trump International Hotel & Tower	F
The Drake	B	Holiday Inn Express Mag Mile-Hotel Cass	C	Wheeler Mansion	J
Gold Coast Guest House	A				

bills, while overnight **parking** can cost $25 at a modest downtown hotel, and as much as $45 at a fancy one.

If you're stuck, Hot Rooms is a reservation service offering hotel rooms at discount rates (ⓣ773/468-7666 or 1-800/468-3500, ⓦwww.hotrooms.com). While they're not as prominent as elsewhere, **bed-and-breakfast** rooms are available from around $80 per night; the Chicago B&B Association maintains full listings (ⓦwww.chicago-bed-breakfast.com).

Allegro 179 W Randolph St ⓣ312/236-0123 or 1-800/643-1500, ⓦwww.allegrochicago.com. With a colourful, updated Art Deco design, this boutique hotel is sure to delight. Luxury amenities throughout, and a wine reception in the afternoon ❽

Chicago Getaway Hostel 616 W Arlington Place ⓣ773/929-5380 or 1-800/467-8355, ⓦwww.getawayhostel.com. Easy-going hostel close to loads of good bars and Wrigley Field, with segregated dorms ($25–31) and private rooms (❶–❸) with and without en-suite facilities. Open 24hr.

Comfort Inn & Suites Downtown 15 E Ohio St ⓣ312/894-0900 or 1-888/775-9223, ⓦwww.chicagocomfortinn.com. This high-rise chain hotel is given considerable charm by its restored Art Deco lobby. The rooms are well equipped, and complemented by fitness and sauna facilities. Rates include continental breakfast. ❻

Days Inn Lincoln Park North 644 W Diversey Parkway at Clark ⓣ773/525-7010 or 1-888/576-3287, ⓦwww.lpndaysinn.com. This good, friendly motel is popular with visiting musicians and a convenient base for North Side nightlife. Free continental breakfast. ❺

The Drake 140 E Walton Place ⓣ312/787-2200 or 1-800/553-7253, ⓦwww.thedrakehotel.com. Chicago's society hotel, just off the Magnificent Mile, has been modernized without sacrificing its sedate charms. Its well-appointed rooms feature high-speed internet access and jacuzzis. You can always just pop in for a drink at the elegant *Palm Court Lounge*. ❽–❾

Gold Coast Guest House 113 W Elm St ⓣ312/337-0361, ⓦwww.bbchicago.com. Inconspicuous 1870s rowhouse that's been beautifully converted to offer four high-class en-suite B&B rooms, with a friendly atmosphere and plenty of useful advice from the knowledgeable hostess. ❺

Hampton Inn & Suites 33 W Illinois Ave ⓣ312/832-0330, ⓦwww.hamptoninnchicago.com. Clean high-rise chain hotel (built in 1988 but "Frank-Lloyd-Wright-inspired") in a good River North location, four blocks east of the Magnificent Mile. ❻

HI-Chicago – The J. Ira & Nicki Harris Family Hostel 24 E Congress St ⓣ312/360-0300 or 1-800/909-4776 code 244, ⓦwww.hichicago.org. Huge, very central hostel, where beds in the clean and spacious dorms cost $29–35 for members, $32–38 for non-members. Open 24hr, with internet access, full kitchen laundry facilities and free continental breakfast. ❶

Holiday Inn Express Mag Mile-Hotel Cass 640 N Wabash Ave ⓣ312/787-4030 or 1-800/799-4030, ⓦwww.casshotel.com. Budget hotel with complimentary wi-fi and a breakfast buffet. Basic, but a reliable lodging option. ❹

House of Two Urns 1239 N Greenview Ave, Wicker Park ⓣ773/235-1408 or 1-877/896-8767, ⓦwww.twourns.com. This rambling, artist-owned B&B, three blocks from the El and close to Wicker Park, is filled with contemporary art; the five guest rooms have a quirky flair, but some share facilities. Three- and four-room apartments are also available. Rooms ❹, apartments ❼–❾.

Palmer House Hilton 17 E Monroe St ⓣ312/726-7500 or 1-800/445-8667. ⓦwww.chicagohilton.com/hotels_palmer.aspx. One of the city's most historic hotels, the *Palmer House* is in the centre of the Loop, and perfect for visits to Millennium Park and the Art Institute of Chicago. ❻

Trump International Hotel & Tower 401 N Wabash Ave ⓣ312/588-8000 or 1-877/458-7867, ⓦwww.trumpchicagohotel.com. New York's favourite real estate developer has made his mark in the Windy City with this 92-storey hotel. Every room has floor-to ceiling windows, and there are a number of kid-friendly amenities, such as in-room video game systems and children's robes. ❽

Wheeler Mansion 2020 S Calumet Ave ⓣ312/945-2020, ⓦwww.wheelermansion.com. A very grand mansion that's been converted into a plush, formal, but romantic B&B that's a hit with business travellers. In the Prairie Avenue Historic District, in close proximity to Soldier Field. ❽

The City

Chicago's visitor-friendly street grid is numbered from **State Street** – "that great street" in Sinatra's song – at zero east and west, and **Madison Street** at zero north and south. **Lake Michigan**, which gives the city some of its most attractive open space (twenty miles of lakeshore lie within the city limits), makes a clear point of reference to the east of the urban grid. **Michigan Avenue** is the main thoroughfare, running between the lakeside museums and parklands, the densely packed skyscrapers of downtown and the diverse low-rise neighbourhoods that spread to the north, south and west. The nickname "**Windy City**" was coined by a New York newspaper editor describing the boastful claims of the city's promoters when attempting to lure investors from the eastern United States. The **Chicago River**, which cuts through the heart of downtown, separates the business district from the shopping and entertainment areas of the North Side, including the upmarket **Near North** and **Gold Coast** neighbourhoods; the artists' lofts and galleries of **River North**; the modestly charming area of **Old Town**; and the young professional enclaves of **Lincoln Park**, **Wrigleyville** and **Lakeview**, as well as hip **Wicker Park**.

In contrast to the wealth and prosperity of the North Side, the **South Side** contains some very stark contrasts between the very wealthy and the tremendously poor. A few of its corners are well worth visiting – particularly the Gothic and well-landscaped campus of the **University of Chicago** which sits in **Hyde Park**, site of the **Museum of Science and Industry**. Other than **Oak Park** to the west, which holds the childhood home of **Ernest Hemingway** and more than a dozen well-maintained examples of the influential architecture of **Frank Lloyd Wright**, suburban Chicago has little to offer.

Millennium Park

Until the late 1990s, the area that is downtown's **Millennium Park** was a rather poorly used bit of dreary looking real estate, albeit well located. Now, however, thanks to a highly ambitious (and hugely expensive, to the tune of almost $500 million) renovation project that long overran its original 2000 completion date, it's a showcase for all that's best in the city. Its twin artistic centrepieces are equally compelling. First is a stunning, seamless, stainless-steel sculpture officially titled **Cloud Gate** but universally known as "The Bean", by the Indian-born, British-based artist Anish Kapoor. Inspired by liquid mercury, it invites viewers to walk around, beside and even underneath it to enjoy spectacular and endlessly intriguing reflections of both the city and the sky above it. Nearby, **Crown Fountain** consists of two glass-brick towers set to either side of a black granite plaza; giant video images of the faces of ordinary Chicagoans play across them both, and water spurts from them in summer at unexpected intervals to form a lake that's usually filled with playing children. Further back, the **Jay Pritzker Pavilion** is an amazing open-air auditorium designed by Frank Gehry, who used mighty swirls and flourishes of steel to improve its acoustics. If you're heading for the lakefront, follow Gehry's sinuous, intriguing, wood-and-steel BP Pedestrian Bridge across Columbus Drive.

Downtown Chicago: The Loop

Downtown Chicago puts on what is perhaps the finest display of **modern architecture** in the world, from the prototype skyscrapers of the 1890s to Mies van der Rohe's "less is more" modernist masterpieces, and the fourth tallest building in the world, the quarter-of-a-mile-high **Willis Tower**.

The compact heart of Chicago is known as **the Loop**, because it's circled by the elevated tracks of the CTA "L" trains. The best way to get your bearings downtown is on one of the many excellent **city tours** detailed on p.287; whether you take a river cruise, ride the "L", or join a walking tour, you'll get a sense of the major architectural landmarks and their assorted histories.

Once you're ready to explore by yourself, start by calling in at the **Chicago Cultural Center** at 77 E Randolph St, which not only holds the city's main visitor centre (as described on p.287), but is worth admiring in its own right. Built in 1897 as the original Chicago Public Library, it's a splendid Beaux Arts palace filled with opulent detail, including the 38ft Tiffany Dome on the fourth floor; it also stages all manner of temporary exhibitions.

The Loop holds two of Chicago's grandest century-old **department stores**. The best looking, the 1899 **Carson Pirie Scott** building (the store went out of business in 2007), at 1 S State St, boasts a magnificent ironwork facade that blends botanic and geometric forms in an intuitive version of Art Moderne. Its architect, Louis Sullivan, was also responsible for the gorgeous spherical bronze clocks suspended from the corners of the **Macy's** department store (Mon–Thurs 9am–9pm, Fri & Sat till 9pm, Sun 11am–6pm), two blocks north at State and Washington. The comparatively bland exterior masks one of the world's great stores, with seven floors of merchandise. Make sure you pop in to see the elaborate Tiffany ceiling, which is made up of over one million pieces of iridescent glass.

Half the world's wheat and corn (and pork-belly futures) are bought and sold amid the cacophonic roar of the **Chicago Board of Trade**, housed in a gorgeous Art Deco tower, appropriately topped by a 30ft stainless steel statue of Ceres, the Roman goddess of grain. It's no longer possible to watch the action inside, but if you're interested in learning more about the similarly energetic ballet that goes on within the **Chicago Mercantile Exchange**, three blocks away at 30 S Wacker Drive, a high-tech visitor centre in the lobby explains all (Mon–Fri 8am–4.30pm; free). Precious metals, currencies and commodities are bought and sold here to the tune of some $50 billion a day.

Half a block from the Board of Trade, **The Rookery**, 209 S LaSalle St, built in 1886 by Burnham and Root, is one of the city's most celebrated and photographed edifices. Its forbidding Moorish Gothic exterior gives way to a wonderfully airy lobby, decked out with cool Italian marble and gold leaf during a major 1905 remodelling by Frank Lloyd Wright; the spiral cantilever staircase rising from the second floor must be seen to be appreciated. A couple of doors down toward the Board of Trade, check out the **Continental Illinois Bank** lobby, with its 28 Ionic marble columns and intricate murals.

Looking up at the proud facade of the **Reliance Building**, 32 N State St, you'd be forgiven for thinking it dates from the Art Deco Thirties, but it was in fact completed way back in 1895 by Daniel Burnham, who did much to shape the face of Chicago through his buildings. His **Fisher Building**, with its tongue-in-cheek, aquatic-inspired ornamental terracotta, stands at 343 S Dearborn St. A block farther south, the 1890 **Manhattan Building** was the world's first tall all-steel-frame building, and is generally acknowledged as the progenitor of the modern curtain-walled skyscraper. Now converted into luxury apartments, it preserves some noteworthy exterior ornament.

A resurrected stretch of the riverfront walk follows the west bank of the river, with open-air cafés and gardens. Farther south, and back on the Loop side at South Wacker Drive and Adams Street, is the 1468ft **Willis Tower** (formerly the Sears Tower), which was the tallest building in the world until 1998, when Malaysia's Petronas Towers nudged it from the top by the length of an antenna; both have since been eclipsed by further construction projects in Southeast Asia and Taiwan. Various companies occupy the tower (Sears moved out in the early 1990s), and it's so huge that it has more than one hundred elevators. Two ascend, in little more than a minute, from the ground-level shopping mall to the 103rd-floor **Skydeck Observatory** (daily: May–Sept 10am–10pm, Oct–April till 8pm; $15.95), for breathtaking views that on a clear day take in four states – Illinois, Michigan, Wisconsin and Indiana. And visitors can also peer down onto the city from one of the elaborate glass boxes that hang off the side of the Skydeck as part of the experience here. Look east for the distinctive triangular **Metropolitan Detention Center**, where prisoners exercise on the grassy roof beneath wire netting to ensure they don't get whisked away by helicopter.

The Chicago River

The Loop is usually said to end at the "L" tracks, but the blocks beyond this core, to either side of the Chicago River, hold plenty of interest. Broad, double-decked **Wacker Drive**, parallel to the water, was designed as a sophisticated promenade, lined by benches and obelisk-shaped lanterns, by Daniel Burnham in 1909. Though never completed, and despite the almost constant intrusion of construction works, it makes for a nice extended walk. The direction of the river itself was reversed a century ago, in an engineering project more extensive than the digging of the Panama Canal. As a result, rather than letting its sewage and industrial waste flow east into Lake Michigan, Chicago now sends it all south into the Corn Belt.

A **boat tour** from beneath the Michigan Avenue Bridge gives magnificent views of downtown (see p.287). However, half an hour's walk, especially at lunchtime when the office workers are out in force, will do the trick nearly as well. Burnham's promenade runs along both sides of the river, crossing back and forth over the twenty-odd drawbridges that open and close to let barges and the occasional sailboat pass. The **State Street Bridge** makes a superb vantage point. On the south bank, at 35 E Wacker Drive, the elegant Beaux Arts **Jewelers Building** was built in 1926 and is capped on the seventeenth floor by a domed rotunda that once housed Al Capone's favourite speakeasy. Across the river stands what's commonly considered Ludwig Mies van der Rohe's masterpiece – the 1971 **330 North Wabash building** (formerly known as the IBM Building), 330 N Wabash Ave. The gentle play of light and shadow across the detailed bronze and smoked-glass facade has been the model for countless other less considered copies worldwide. The building is so huge that it acts as a funnel for winter winds off Lake Michigan, and heavy ropes sometimes must be tied across the broad plaza at its base to protect people from getting blown away.

Perhaps Chicago's most successful and acclaimed building of recent years stands four blocks west at **333 W Wacker Drive**. Towering over a broad bend in the river, and bowed to follow its curve, the green glass facade reflects the almost fluorescent green of the river (now upgraded from "toxic" to merely "very polluted"). On the lower floors, a more classically detailed stone base actively addresses its stalwart elder neighbours.

The Art Institute of Chicago

The **Art Institute of Chicago** ranks as one of the greatest art museums in the world, thanks to a magnificent collection that includes, and extends way beyond, Impressionist and Post-Impressionist paintings, Asian art, photography and architectural drawings (Mon–Wed & Fri 10.30am–5pm, Thurs till 8pm, Sat & Sun 10am–5pm; suggested donation $12, free Thurs from 5–8pm; ⓣ312/443-3600, ⓦwww.artic.edu). While the Neoclassical facade of the main entrance, on the lake side of South Michigan Avenue, does its best to look dignified, the numerous added-on wings can make it hard to find your way around inside. In 2009, the museum also opened its new Modern Wing, designed by "starchitect" Renzo Piano.

Most visitors head straight upstairs to the Impressionist works, which include a wall full of Monet's *Haystacks* captured in various lights, next to Seurat's immediately familiar pointillist *Sunday Afternoon on La Grande Jatte*. A handful of Post-Impressionist masterpieces by Van Gogh, Gauguin and Matisse are arrayed nearby. Beyond that, the rooms seem to stretch away forever; it takes at least half a day to get even a basic sense of what's here and where it is. Specific highlights include the pitchfork-holding farmer of Grant Wood's oft-parodied *American Gothic*, which he painted as a student at the Art Institute school, and sold to the museum for $300 in 1930; El Greco's 1577 *Assumption of the Virgin*; Edward Hopper's lonely *Nighthawks*; and Pablo Picasso's melancholy *Old Guitarist*, one of the definitive masterpieces of his Blue Period; a tortured, tuxedoed self-portrait that was Max Beckmann's last Berlin painting before fleeing the Nazis; canvases by Jackson Pollock and Mark Rothko; and several works by Georgia O'Keeffe, such as a 1926 depiction of New York's *Shelton Hotel*, where she was living.

Be sure to look for the beautiful pre-Columbian ceramics from what's now the Southwest USA; the ornate carved stone used for the coronation of the Aztec ruler Moctezuma II on July 15, 1503; and the delightful seventh-century Indonesian-sculptured stone monkeys in the Southeast Asia collections, displayed around the McKinlock Court Garden, which in summer is employed as an **open-air café**. Also here, in the east end of the complex, is the immaculately reconstructed Art Moderne trading room of the Chicago Stock Exchange, designed by Louis Sullivan in 1893 and moved here in the 1970s.

The graceful lines of the Modern Wing include contemporary arts and early-twentieth-century European masterworks, including Picasso's *The Old Guitarist*. Finally, the Art Institute's delightful store is worth perusing, and the quality of goods here is on a par with the masterworks on the walls inside.

Grant Park

East of the Art Institute toward Lake Michigan, **Grant Park** is an urban oasis that's become a bit overshadowed by the high-profile Millennium Park (see p.291) immediately northwest. In any case, wandering through the park requires traversing some busy roads, so casual rambling can be frustrating.

The major attractions are gathered in its landscaped southern half, known as the **Museum Campus**. The extensive and engaging **Field Museum of Natural History**, 1200 S Lake Shore Drive, at Roosevelt Road (June daily 8am–5pm; July & Aug Mon–Thurs till 5pm, Fri–Sun 7.30am–5pm; Sept–May daily 9am–5pm; last admission always 4pm; $15, plus extra for temporary exhibitions; Ⓦwww.fieldmuseum.org), is ten minutes' walk south of the Art Institute, in a huge, marble-clad, Daniel Burnham-designed Greek temple. It's quite an erratic sort of institution, in which the exhibits vary enormously in their age and sophistication; as a rule, its temporary exhibitions tend to be the most compelling, but cost a hefty additional premium on the already high entrance fee. "Natural history" is taken to include anything non-white and non-European, so as well as a hall of stupendous dinosaurs, including "Sue", the most complete *T.rex* fossil ever found, the permanent collection ranges from Egyptian tombs – the entire burial chamber of the son of a Fifth Dynasty pharaoh was brought here in 1908 – to the man-eating lions of Tsavo and some fascinating displays on the islands of the Pacific. Best of all for young kids is the "Underground Adventure", a simulated environment that "shrinks" visitors to a hundredth of their normal size and propels them into a world of giant animatronic spiders and crayfish.

Just across busy Lake Shore Drive, on the shores of Lake Michigan, the **John G. Shedd Aquarium** (first three weeks of June daily 9am–6pm; late June to Aug Mon–Wed & Fri till 6pm, Thurs till 10pm; Sept–May Mon–Fri till 5pm, Sat & Sun till 6pm; $26.95 for all of the exhibits, $2 additional for the aquatic show; Ⓣ312/939-2438, Ⓦwww.sheddaquarium.org) proclaims itself the largest indoor aquarium in the world. The 1920s structure is rather old-fashioned, but the light-hearted and often tongue-in-cheek displays – some use *Far Side* cartoons – are informative and entertaining. The central exhibit, a 90,000-gallon recreation of a coral reef, complete with sharks (who are fed at 11am and 2pm daily), turtles and thousands of tropical fish, is surrounded by more than a hundred lesser tanks. Highlights include the new wild reef exhibit, which features floor-to-ceiling living reefs, tropical fish, sharks and rays. The **Oceanarium** provides an enormous contrast, with its modern lake-view home for marine mammals such as Pacific dolphins and beluga whales. Designed to replicate a rocky Alaskan coastline, it's a carefully disguised amphitheatre for demonstrations of the animals' "natural behaviour", such as jumping out of the water and fetching plastic rings. Performances are four times daily; at other times, watch from underwater galleries as the animals cruise around the tank, and listen to the clicks, beeps and whistles they use to communicate with each other. Get to the Shedd early to beat the long lines and school groups.

At the tip of the Museum Campus peninsula, the **Adler Planetarium** (late May to early Sept daily 9.30am–6pm, rest of year daily till 4.30pm, first Fri of month always till 10pm; $10–25, determined by exhibits entered; ⓣ312/922-STAR, ⓦwww.adlerplanetarium.org) has an interactive 360-degree movie theatre and offers one of the best views of the city skyline.

The Near North Side

While Chicago's **Near North Side** has few showstopping attractions, it's great for simply wandering around, chancing upon odd **shops**, neighbourhood bars and historic sites in a generally low-rise tangle containing some of the city's most characteristic corners.

When the Michigan Avenue Bridge was built over the Chicago River in 1920, the warehouse district along its north bank quickly changed into one of the city's most upmarket quarters, now known as the **Magnificent Mile**, famed for its fashionable shops and department stores. Throughout the Roaring Twenties one glitzy tower after another was thrown up along Michigan Avenue. At the north end, the opulent **Drake Hotel** rose off Lincoln Park. To the south, the white terracotta, wedding-cake colossus of the **Wrigley Building** was put up just over the river at no. 400; it's spectacularly lit up at night. Built by the Chicago-based chewing-gum magnate, it was eclipsed almost immediately by the "Mag Mile's" most famous structure, the **Tribune Tower**. Still housing the editorial offices of Chicago's morning newspaper, as well as, on the ground floor, the studios of its main AM radio station, WGN (you can peer in from the street and watch the DJs in action), the tower was completed in 1925. Its flying buttresses and Gothic detailing turn their back on the then-prevalent Moderne style. Look closely at its lower floors and you'll see embedded chunks of historic buildings – like the Parthenon and the Great Pyramid – pilfered from around the world by *Tribune* staffers.

While the Tribune Tower anchors its southern end, the Mag Mile's northern reaches are dominated by the cross-braced steel **John Hancock Center** at 875 N Michigan Ave. Though it's about 325 feet shorter than the Sears Tower, the 360-degree panorama on a clear day from its 94th-floor **Skydeck Observatory** (daily 9am–11pm; $15) is unforgettable. It's worth pointing out that taking the elevator to the swanky *Signature Lounge* on the 96th floor costs nothing, and you can use that extra money to buy a cocktail of your choice. If you prefer quality over quantity, the Hancock Observatory is a better, less trafficked experience than the Sears.

Back at ground level, you're right at the heart of Chicago's prime **shopping district**. Stores like Neiman-Marcus and Tiffany & Co front onto Michigan Avenue, but most of the shops are enclosed within multistorey complexes, or "vertical shopping malls". The oldest of these – and still the best – is **Water Tower Place**, 835 N Michigan Ave, with more than a hundred stores on seven floors, plus a bustling food court. The **900 N Michigan Avenue** mall offers a less-cramped space and more upmarket shops, anchored by Bloomingdale's.

Across from Water Tower Place, at the centre of this consumer paradise, stands the **Historic Water Tower** – a whimsically Gothic stone castle, topped by a 100ft tower, that was built in 1869 and is one of the very few structures to have survived the 1871 fire. Inside the Water Tower is a tiny, yet compelling gallery that features rotating photographic exhibits by Chicago-based artists. The **Museum of Contemporary Art**, one block east at 220 E Chicago Ave (Tues 10am–8pm, Wed–Sun 10am–5pm; free on Tues, $12; ⓣ312/280-2660; ⓦwww.mcachicago.org), is a spare space that holds photography, video and installation works, as well as a permanent collection featuring pieces by Calder, Nauman, Warhol and others. At the rear is a lake-view patio where a Wolfgang Puck café serves good coffee and bistro food; additionally, the museum store is well worth a browse. Away from the Magnificent Mile, the area along the river between Michigan Avenue and the lake has seen dramatic redevelopment since **Navy Pier**, at East Illinois Street (ⓦwww.navypier.com), was reopened to the general public in 1995. The pier attracts more than eight million visitors annually to its shops, chain restaurants, IMAX theatre, and fifteen-storey Ferris wheel. Three floors are taken up by the imaginative interactive exhibits of the **Chicago Children's Museum** (Sun–Wed & Fri 10am–5pm, Thurs & Sat till 8pm; also Fri 5–8pm mid-June to Aug; $10, no reduction for children; free Thurs 5–8pm; ⓣ312/527-1000, ⓦwww.chichildrensmuseum.org). The pier also serves as a venue for concerts and weekend festivals in summer, and an embarkation point for several boat tours.

The Gold Coast and Old Town

As its name suggests, the **Gold Coast**, stretching north from the Magnificent Mile along the lakeshore, is one of Chicago's wealthiest and most desirable neighbourhoods. This residential district is primarily notable for Chicago's most central (and style-conscious) beach. The broad strand of **Oak Street Beach** is accessible via a walkway under Lake Shore Drive, across from the *Drake Hotel*. After dark, the summertime crowds are apt to be found in the myriad bars of Rush and Division streets. The more northerly reaches of the Gold Coast, approaching Lincoln Park, are also its most exclusive, especially in the stretch of Astor Street running south from the park. **Old Town**, west of LaSalle Street to either side of North Avenue, has a much more lived-in look. Originally a German immigrant community based around the 1873 **St Michael's Church**, it now boasts a broad ethnic and cultural mix. **Wells Street**, the main drag, emerged in the late 1960s as a mini-Haight-Ashbury. Although almost all signs of that era have vanished, at least one survivor, the *Second City* comedy club (see p.303), is still going strong. The rest of the neighbourhood is packed with bars, galleries and BBQ joints, and makes for a diverting afternoon's wander. Especially noteworthy is the House of Glunz, 1206 N Wells St, a wine shop dating to 1888 that is known for its wine-tasting programmes.

Lincoln Park and Wrigleyville

In summer, Chicago's largest greenspace, **Lincoln Park**, gives visitors and locals a much-needed respite from the gridded pavements of the rest of the city. Unlike Grant Park to the south, Lincoln Park is packed with leafy nooks and crannies, monuments and sculptures, and has a couple of friendly, family-oriented **beaches**, at the eastern ends of North and Fullerton avenues. Near the small **zoo** at the heart of the park (late May to Oct Mon–Fri 9am–6pm, Sat & Sun till 7pm; Nov–March daily till 5pm; free), renowned for its menagerie of African apes, you can rent paddleboats or bikes. If the weather's bad, head for sauna-level conditions at the **conservatory**, 2400 N Stockton Drive (daily 9am–5pm; free), or bone up on Chicago's captivating past at the **Chicago History Museum**, at the south end of the park at 1601 N Clark

St (Mon–Wed and Fri & Sat 9.30am–4.30pm, Thurs till 8pm, Sun noon–5pm; $14, free on Mon; ⓣ312/642-4600, ⓦwww.chicagohistory.org), with comprehensive displays on regional and national history.

The Lincoln Park neighbourhood, inland from the lake, centres on **Lincoln Avenue** and **Clark Street**, which run diagonally from near the Historical Society Museum; **Halsted Street**, with its blues bars and nightclubs, runs north–south through the neighbourhood's heart. Any of these main roads merits an extended stroll, with forays into the many book and record stores. Look for the **Biograph Theatre** movie house (now a live theatre stage), 2433 N Lincoln Ave, where **John Dillinger** was ambushed and killed by the FBI in 1934, thanks to a tip from his companion, the legendary Lady in Red.

Chicago spreads north from Lincoln Park for block after low-rise block of houses and shops, many of which date from the late 1800s, when thousands of German immigrants settled in what was then the separate enclave of Lakeview. This area is now called **Wrigleyville** in honour of **Wrigley Field**, 1060 W Addison St at N Clark Street, the ivy-covered 1920s stadium of baseball's much-loved Cubs, and one of the best places to get a real feel for the game – the club is so traditional that it fought the installation of floodlights (for night games) until 1988. There are few more pleasant and relaxing ways to spend an afternoon than drinking beer, eating hot dogs and watching a ballgame in the sunshine, among the Cubs' faithful; see p.304 for ticket information. Two-hour **Field tours** run from May through September on select days every half-hour from 10am to 4pm, and cost $25.

Wicker Park and Bucktown

Three miles northwest of the Loop, **Wicker Park/Bucktown** is Chicago's newest neighbourhood. Once a Polish and German community referred to as the "Polish Gold Coast", it is now a trendy, upmarket enclave of shopping, clubbing and Victorian mansions. Stylish health-food cafés, galleries, tattoo parlours, smoky clubs, boutiques and alternative bookstores follow Damen Street north to Bucktown.

The West Side and Oak Park

West of the Chicago River, Chicago's **West Side** was where the **Great Fire of 1871** started – supposedly when Mrs O'Leary's cow kicked over a lantern. The flames spread quickly east to engulf the entire central city, which was built of wood and fed the fire for three full days. Appropriately enough, the O'Leary cottage is now the site of the Chicago Fire Department training academy. The West Side also saw 1886's **Haymarket Riots**, when striking workers assembled at the old city market at Desplaines and Randolph streets; after a peaceful demonstration, as police began to break up the crowd, a bomb exploded, killing an officer. Six more policemen and four workers died in the resulting panic. Four labour leaders were later found guilty of murder and hanged, although none had been present at the event. Today the West Side of the city remains plagued with poverty and socio-economic problems, though the Little Italy community (anchored by the University of Illinois at Chicago) remains stable.

Nine miles west of the Loop, the affluent and attractive nineteenth-century suburb of **Oak Park** is easily accessible by public transport: take the Green Line west to the Harlem Avenue stop. The area's **visitor centre**, just over two blocks east of the station at 158 N Forest Ave (daily 10am–3.30pm; ⓣ708/848-1500, ⓦwww.visitoakpark.com), provides an excellent architectural **walking tour map**.

Ernest Hemingway was born and raised in Oak Park, editing his high school newspaper and living a normal middle-class life. His birthplace at 339 N Oak Park Ave, where he lived until the age of six, is now preserved as a shrine to the author, and is run in conjunction with a museum of his life two blocks south at 200 N Oak Park Ave (Sun–Fri 1–5pm, Sat 10am–5pm; $10; ⓣ708/848-2222, ⓦwww.ehfop.org).

In 1889, a decade before Hemingway's birth, an ambitious young architect named **Frank Lloyd Wright** arrived in Oak Park, which he used for the next twenty years as a testing ground for his innovative design theories. Most of the 25 buildings he put up here are in keeping with conventional Victorian design, and few are open to the public; fortunately, however, his most interesting and groundbreaking edifices are maintained as monuments. His ideal of an "organic architecture", in which all aspects of the design derive from a single unifying concept – quite at odds with the fussy "gingerbread" style popular at the time – is exemplified by the **Unity Temple** at 875 Lake St (Mon–Fri 10.30am–4.30pm, Sat & Sun 1–4pm; $8; ⓣ708/383-8873, ⓦwww.unitytemple-utrf.org). Though the simplicity of this angular, reinforced-concrete structure was largely dictated by economics, its unembellished surfaces contribute to a masterful manipulation of space, especially in the skylit interior, where the subtle interplay of overlapping planes creates a dynamic spatial flow.

Wright built his small, brown-shingled **home and studio** nearby at 951 Chicago Ave at Forest, aged 22 in 1889, and remodelled it repeatedly for the next twenty years. It shows all his hallmarks: large fireplaces to symbolize the heart of the home and family; free-flowing, open-plan rooms; and the visual linking of interior and exterior spaces. The furniture of the kitchen and dining rooms is Wright's own design; he added a two-storey studio in 1898, with a mezzanine drafting area suspended by chains from the roof beams. You can see the house itself on a 45-minute guided tour (Mon–Fri 11am, 1pm & 3pm, Sat & Sun every 20min 11am–3.30pm; $15; ⓣ708/848-1976, ⓦwww.wrightplus.org). Lengthier, self-guided audio walking tours ($15) take in the dozen other Wright-designed houses within a two-block radius.

The South Side

The **South Side** of Chicago has always had a raw deal, cursed with the presence of bad-neighbour heavy industries like the sprawling **Chicago Stockyards**, the slaughterhouses and meatpackers that Upton Sinclair exposed in his 1906 novel *The Jungle*, and whose oppressive odours covered most of the South Side until the 1950s. Parts of the South Side failed to benefit from the economic uplift of the 1990s, but there remain a number of thriving districts: not just the **Prairie Avenue** and **Hyde Park** districts described below, but also the buzzing **Chinatown** around Wentworth Avenue and 22nd Street; the artsy, predominantly Mexican **Pilsen** district, a few blocks north and west; and the largely Irish, blue-collar **Bridgeport**, formerly known by the evocative name "Hardscrabble", which was the nucleus of Mayor Daley's old fiefdom, along with serving as the home of baseball's White Sox (see p.304).

Two blocks east of Michigan Avenue, a mile from the Loop and only a quarter of a mile from the lake, **Prairie Avenue** started life as an exclusive suburb. It's best reached by taxi, bus or train, as the walk south from the Loop just isn't that interesting. As the one part of Chicago to remain unscathed in the Great Fire of 1871, this area had a brief moment of glory as the city's finest address. However, by 1900 the railroads had cut it off from Lake Michigan, and the wealthy fled back to their traditional North Side haunts. One of the few structures to have survived is the Romanesque 1887 **Glessner House**, Chicago's only surviving H.H. Richardson-designed house, standing sentry at Prairie Avenue and 18th. Behind the forbidding stone facade, the house opens onto a garden court, its interior filled with Arts and Crafts furniture, and swathed in William Morris fabrics and wall coverings. The

Chicago Architecture Foundation gives guided tours (Wed–Sun 1pm and 3pm; $10; ⓣ312/326-1480, ⓦwww.glessnerhouse.org).

Six miles south, **Hyde Park**, the most attractive and sophisticated South Side neighbourhood, is also one of Chicago's more racially integrated areas. Of course, these days, the neighbourhood has received additional attention for being the home of President Barack Obama prior to his arrival in the White House. The **University of Chicago**, endowed by Rockefeller in 1892, has encouraged a college-town atmosphere, with bookshops and cafés surrounding its compact campus, especially along East 57th Street. On the campus itself, two buildings are well worth searching out: the massive Collegiate Gothic pile of the **Rockefeller Memorial Chapel**, 59th Street and Woodlawn Avenue (daily 9am–4pm; free), and the Prairie-style, Frank Lloyd Wright-designed **Robie House**, two blocks north at 5757 S Woodlawn Ave (tours Sat, 11am–3pm; $15; ⓦwww.wrightplus.org).

Washington Park wraps around the south side of the campus to join the long green strip of the **Midway** – one of the few reminders that Chicago was the site of the **World's Fair Columbian Exposition**. Attracting some thirty million spectators in the summer of 1893 (at the time, 45 percent of the US population), the Midway was then filled with full-sized model villages from around the globe, including an Irish market town and a mock-up of Cairo, complete with belly dancers. These days it's used mainly by joggers and students tossing Frisbees.

A short stroll east, in Jackson Park, the cavernous **Museum of Science and Industry**, 57th Street at Lake Shore Drive (Mon–Sat 9.30am–4pm, Sun 11am–4pm; $15; ⓣ773/684-1414, ⓦwww.msichicago.org), was Chicago's single most popular tourist destination until it started charging admission in 1991. Besides interactive computer displays, the best of which explores the inner workings of the brain and heart, exhibits include a captured German U-boat, a trip down a replica coal mine, the Apollo 8 command module and a simulated space-shuttle journey. It's fun for kids, but adults may not feel like staying very long. The complex also hosts a giant OMNIMAX movie dome; admission is $8 extra.

East of the museum, **Promontory Point** juts into Lake Michigan, giving great views of the Chicago skyline, including a close-up look at Mies van der Rohe's first high-rise, the Promontory Apartments at 5530 S Lake Shore Drive.

Eating

Chicago's cosmopolitan make-up is reflected in its plethora of ethnic restaurants. **Italian** food, ranging from hearty **deep-dish pizza** (developed in 1943 at *Pizzeria Uno*; see p.300) to delicately crafted creations presented at stylish trattorias, continues to dominate a very dynamic scene. In recent years there's been a surge of popularity for **New American** cuisine. **Thai** restaurants still thrive, as do ones with a broad **Mediterranean** slant, many of which serve tapas; and there are still plenty of opportunities to sample more long-standing Chicago cuisines – Eastern European, German, Mexican, Chinese, Indian, even Burmese and Ethiopian. Of course, a number of establishments serve good old-fashioned **BBQ ribs**, a legacy of Chicago's days as the nation's meatpacker. And no visit is complete without sampling a messy Italian beef sandwich, or a Chicago-style hot dog, laden with tomatoes, onions, celery salt, hot peppers and a pickle.

The largest concentration of restaurants is found north and west of the **Loop**. To the west, **Greektown**, around Halsted Street at Jackson Boulevard, and **Little Italy**, on and around Taylor Street, are worth a look, while the **Near North** and **River North** areas harbour a good number of upmarket places.

The Loop

Billy Goat Tavern 430 N Michigan Ave at Kinzie ⓣ312/222-1525. This legendary journalists' haunt opens early and closes late, serving the "cheezborgers" made famous by John Belushi's comedy skit. Very reasonable.

Italian Village 71 W Monroe St at Clark ⓣ312/332-7005. Three Italian establishments flourish under one roof. *The Village* has traditional Italian-American food and a world-class wine cellar; the basement *Cantina Enoteca* serves chicken Vesuvio, a Chicago creation, among its reasonably priced dishes; and the expensive *Vivere* has an adventurous menu, a mesmerizing wine list and a large pre-theatre crowd (meaning it's best to arrive after 8pm). *The Village* is open daily, but the other two establishments are closed Sun.

Lou Mitchell's 565 W Jackson Ave at Clinton ⓣ312/939-3111. Near Union Station, *Lou's* has been around since 1923, serving terrific omelets, waffles and hash browns all day long. Try the pecan-laden cookies.

Russian Tea Time 77 E Adams St at Michigan ⓣ312/360-0000. This Midwestern nod to New York's *Russian Tea Room* offers a (pricey) sampling of authentic fare from the former Soviet empire.

Trattoria No. 10 10 N Dearborn St ⓣ312/984-1718. This charming surprise, in a series of underground rooms, serves up delicious ravioli, grilled sea scallops and risotto. Closed Sun.

The West Side: Greektown and Little Italy

Francesca's on Taylor 1400 W Taylor St ⓣ312/829-2828. Assorted Francesca-family restaurants dot Chicago. This relatively subdued example offers some of the best Italian food in the city, at moderate prices. Don't be surprised to find a crowd here all day.

Parthenon 314 S Halsted St at Jackson ⓣ312/726-2407. One of the oldest places in Greektown, but still deservedly popular: *saganaki* (fried cheese doused with Metaxa brandy and ignited) was invented here.

Pegasus 130 S Halsted St at Adams ⓣ312/226-3377. Lively Greek option, where true hospitality and evocative wall murals add to the appeal. Stuffed squid and *pastitsio* (macaroni, meat and cheese casserole) are recommended. During the summer the rooftop garden has a superb view of the Loop skyline.

Santorini 800 W Adams St at Halsted ⓣ312/829-8820. The decor recreates a Greek island village, and the food is beguiling, too; grilled octopus and lamb *exohiko* (wrapped in filo pastry and fried) are highlights.

South Loop and the South Side

Gioco 1312 S Wabash Ave at 13th ⓣ312/939-3870. Immensely popular (and somewhat expensive) place, whose classic, meticulously prepared Italian cuisine is drawing a hip crowd to the rapidly gentrifying South Loop district.

The Medici 1327 E 57th St ⓣ773/667-7394. Hyde Park institution close to the University of Chicago that serves up a mix of salads, pizza and quality hamburgers.

Opera 1301 S Wabash Ave at 13th ⓣ312/461-0161. High-class, high-concept, high-priced but very funky new-Chinese restaurant, housed in an opulent former film studio in the South Loop that holds a few private dining booths.

Near North Side and River North

Bistrot Zinc 1131 N State St at Elm ⓣ312/337-1131. Very friendly, intimate neighbourhood bistro, offering a quintessential French menu prepared and served just the way it should be, at good prices.

Club Lago 331 W Superior St at N Orleans ⓣ312/337-9444. Best described as a post-World War II American take on Northern Italian, this low-key restaurant is a good place for a drink or a plate of baked clams.

Frontera Grill & Topolobampo 445 N Clark St at Illinois ⓣ312/661-1434. Wildly imaginative Mexican food: *Frontera Grill* is crowded and boisterous; *Topolobampo* is more refined and pricier. The front door and bar are shared between the two. Closed Sun & Mon.

Gino's East 633 N Wells St at Ontario ⓣ312/943-1124. Despite its relocation into larger but meticulously aged premises, this remains a Chicago tradition, with huge deep-dish pizzas and graffiti-covered walls. Expect a considerable wait to get in, and at least 40 minutes for your pizza to cook.

Le Colonial 937 N Rush St at Walton ⓣ312/255-0088. This atmospheric evocation of some colonial outpost in Indochina, with its palm trees and rattan furniture, serves zestful French-influenced Vietnamese food at reasonable prices, and has outdoor seating in summer.

Pizzeria Uno 29 E Ohio St at Wabash ⓣ312/321-1000. The original outlet of the chain that put Chicago deep-dish pizza on the map.

Portillo's 100 W Ontario St at La Salle ⓣ312/587-8930. Much-loved local chain that serves delicious Chicago hot dogs and the best Italian beef sandwich in the city.

Star of Siam 11 E Illinois St at State ⓣ312/670-0100. Terrific Thai food served in a spacious, inviting setting. The tom yum soup, pad thai and curries are top-notch.

Lincoln Park and Old Town

Boka 1729 N Halsted St near Willow ⓣ773/337-6070. Stylish option close to the Steppenwolf Theatre, serving inventive and tasty dishes from around the world on a changing weekly menu that offers small ($8–12) and large ($21–37) portions, depending on your appetite.

Charlie Trotter's 816 W Armitage Ave at Halsted ⓣ773/248-6228. Prepare for a superb experience: Chef Trotter is a true artist, and his daring creations, such as caviar-stuffed quail eggs or Maine salmon with blood sausage, are constantly evolving. The prices are appropriately high; you can only choose between two set menus, at $135 (vegetarian) or $165. Closed Sun & Mon.

Hema's Kitchen II 2411 N Clark St ⓣ773/529-1705. Bustling Indian restaurant that's well regarded for its garlic naan, curried fish and tandoori chicken. As an added bonus, you can bring your own beer or wine.

Old Jerusalem 1411 N Wells St at Evergreen ⓣ312/944-3304. This long-time favourite serves reasonable Middle Eastern dishes; the falafel is great. BYO beer or wine.

RJ Grunts 2056 Lincoln Park W at Clark ⓣ773/929-5363. Check out the great burgers and a top-notch salad bar – purported to be the nation's first – in a casual neighbourhood atmosphere.

Wicker Park

Café Absinthe 1954 W North Ave at Milwaukee ⓣ773/278-4488. Fine French dining in a romantic, casual setting. One of the city's best restaurants, with prices to match.

Earwax Cafe 1561N Milwaukee Ave at North ⓣ773/772-4019. Bustling, inexpensive coffeehouse in a happening neighbourhood, with an extensive menu of light vegetarian meals as well as meaty deli sandwiches.

Hot Chocolate 1747 N Damen Ave near St Paul ⓣ773/489-1747 Priding themselves on a mix of "sweet" and "savoury" offerings, the weekend brunch is a good bet, and their chocolate desserts are miniature masterpieces.

Irazu 1865 N Milwaukee Ave near Armitage ⓣ773/252-5687. Very cheap but wonderful Costa Rican diner, serving great burritos plus a small selection of authentic main courses. Closed Sun.

Drinking

Chicago is a consummate boozer's town, and is one of the best US cities for **bars**, catering to just about every group and interest, with many open until 3, 4 or even 5am. The city's drinking areas include the touristy **Division Street**, the post-college melange that is **Wrigleyville**, and a clutch of places in scholarly **Hyde Park**. **Wicker Park** is the trendiest hangout zone, while Halsted Street between Belmont and Addison is known as **Boystown** for its gay bars and clubs.

The hundred-plus **cafés and coffeehouses** across the city may not have taken the place of the traditional taverns, but they're a growing alternative.

Saloons, pubs and bars

Delilah's 2771 N Lincoln Ave ⓣ773/472-2771. Choose from a great selection of beers (150) and whiskeys at this dimly lit bar (playing underground records – from rock to alt-country – at night).

Goose Island Brewing Co. 1800 N Clybourn Ave ⓣ312/915-0071. Forty ales and lagers, including the popular Honker's Ale, are brewed on the premises at this lively Lincoln Park haunt, which ranks as Chicago's best brewpub.

Green Door Tavern 678 N Orleans St ⓣ312/664-5496. In an unlikely spot near the galleries of River North, this historic place is chock-full of Chicago memorabilia: some pure kitsch, others genuine antiques. Drink at the long bar or settle into a cosy back room to sample home-style cooking.

John Barleycorn 658 W Belden Ave ⓣ773/348-8899. A dimly-lit Lincoln Park pub dating to 1890. This former speakeasy and John Dillinger haunt has retained many of its original nautical-themed fixtures. The lovely garden is open in summer.

Matchbox 770 N Milwaukee Ave ⓣ312/666-9292. All kinds of Chicago characters squeeze into this phenomenally narrow little neighbourhood hangout on the West Side.

Old Town Ale House 219 W North Ave ⓣ312/944-7020. An eclectic crowd of scruffy regulars and yuppies mingle in this convivial haunt, complete with a pinball machine and a library of paperbacks.

Rainbo Club 1150 N Damen Ave ⓣ773/489-5999. Busy Wicker Park bar and hangout for indie-rock types.

Twin Anchors 1655 N Sedgwick St at North ⓣ312/266-1616. You'll wait for a seat in this neighbourhood spot, famed for its BBQ ribs, but the interesting clientele and 1950s-style bar make it worthwhile.

Woodlawn Tap 1172 E 55th St at Woodawn ⓣ773/643-5516. In the centre of Hyde Park, this place features cheap cold beer and conversation that alternates between the White Sox and Wittgenstein.

Gay and lesbian bars

Big Chicks 5024 N Sheridan Rd, Andersonville ⓣ773/728-5511. A friendly place for a mixed crowd, with a no-charge jukebox and free BBQs outside on summer Sundays.

Gentry 440 N State St ⓣ773/836-0933. Cabaret and piano bar popular with corporate types after work.

Sidetrack 3349 N Halsted St ⓣ773/477-9189. One of the most popular bars along Halsted's gay strip in Lakeview. Theme nights include Sun, which is dedicated to showtunes.

Nightlife and entertainment

From its earliest frontier days, Chicago has had some of the best **nightlife** in the US. Blues fans who celebrate Chicago as the birthplace of Muddy Waters' **urban blues** will be disappointed that the original South-Side headquarters of Chess Records, at 2120 S Michigan Ave (immortalized in a Rolling Stones song recorded on site), has yet to become a museum. However, the city remains proud of its blues traditions, and continues to innovate in other genres, such as the energetic dance beat of 1980s **house music** as well as the groundbreaking **jazz** of the Art Ensemble of Chicago.

Nightclubs aplenty can be found all over town, especially along Halsted Street, Lincoln Avenue and Clark Street on the North Side. **Uptown**, at the intersection of North Broadway and Lawrence, has a couple of excellent venues for jazz and rock. The best **gay clubs** congregate in the Boystown area, which is a mile north of Lincoln Park. Highbrow pursuits are also well provided for: Chicago's **classical music**, **dance** and **theatre** are world-class.

For **what's-on information**, Chicagoans pick up free weeklies like the excellent *Chicago Reader* (available Thurs afternoon and online at ⓦwww.chicagoreader.com), the *New City*, and the gay and lesbian *Windy City Times*. Full listings also appear in the Friday issues of the *Chicago Sun-Times* and the *Chicago Tribune*, while *Time Out Chicago* has useful arts, music, theatre and movie listings.

Blues

B.L.U.E.S. 2519 N Halsted St ⓣ773/528-1012, ⓦwww.chicagobluesbar.com. Opened in the 1970s, *B.L.U.E.S.* is still going strong, though it's a bit touristy. The tiny stage has been graced by all the greats.

Buddy Guy's Legends 700 S Wabash Ave ⓣ312/427-0333, ⓦwww.buddyguys.com. South Loop club owned by veteran bluesman Buddy Guy, with great acoustics and atmosphere, aims to present the very best local and national acts. Not as touristy as other downtown blues clubs.

Kingston Mines 2548 N Halsted St ⓣ773/477-4646. Top-notch local and national acts on two stages play to an up-for-it, partying crowd.

Rosa's Lounge 3420 W Armitage Ave ⓣ773/342-0452, ⓦwww.rosaslounge.com. Run by Mama Rosa and her son, this West-Side club is undoubtedly the friendliest blues joint around. For real aficionados. Closed Sun & Mon.

Jazz

Andy's 11 E Hubbard St ⓣ312/642-6805. Very popular with the after-work crowd; informal with moderate prices.

Green Dolphin Street 2200 N Ashland Ave ⓣ773/395-0066, ⓦwww.jazzitup.com. This swanky, pricey restaurant and jazz club offers a solid line-up of regular performers. Closed Mon.

The Green Mill 4802 N Broadway ⓣ773/878-5552. One of the best – and most beautiful – rooms for local and national talent. Located in the Uptown neighbourhood, and proud of its chequered Prohibition-era past.

Jazz Showcase 806 S Plymouth Court ⓣ312/360-0234, ⓦwww.jazzshowcase.com. A classy, dressy room that hosts premier jazz by top names.

Velvet Lounge 67 E Cermak Rd ⓣ312/791-9050. Avant-garde and free jazz are the usual sounds at this South Side mainstay.

Rock

Double Door 1572 N Milwaukee Ave ⓣ773/489-3160, ⓦwww.doubledoor.com. Former biker bar turned hip music venue in the Wicker Park/Bucktown neighbourhood. Indie bands play almost every night.

Elbo Room 2871 N Lincoln Ave ⓣ773/549-5549, ⓦwww.elboroomchicago.com. Easy-going venue specializing in emerging bands, whether indie, pop, funk or ska.

Empty Bottle 1035 N Western Ave ⓣ773/276-3600, ⓦwww.emptybottle.com. Loud hole-in-the-wall club where you might hear just about anything: experimental jazz, alternative rock, hip-hop, house, dub and progressive country.

Metro 3730 N Clark St ⓣ773/549-0203, ⓦwww.metrochicago.com. Arguably the top spot in the city, this club, in an old cinema building, regularly hosts young British bands trying to break the States, plus DJ mixes.

Folk, country and world music

Fitzgerald's 6615 W Roosevelt, Berwyn ⓣ708/788-2118, ⓦwww.fitzgeraldsnightclub.com. In the western suburb of Berwyn, an excellent venue for alt-country, Americana, Cajun and zydeco. Accessible by the CTA's Blue Line.

Old Town School of Folk Music 4544 N Lincoln Ave. Established in 1959, this place presents about eighty concerts a year, including just about every type of folk and world music, and also offers great classes.

Schubas Tavern 3159 N Southport Ave, Lakeview ⓣ773/525-2508, ⓦwww.schubas.com. A quirky roster of up-and-coming acts, from rock to alt-country or roots, appear at this intimate, all-but-perfect neighbourhood venue.

Dance

Excalibur 632 N Dearborn St ⓣ312/266-1944. City institution blasting out rock and R&B on several floors to a predominantly out-of-town crowd.

Funky Buddha Lounge 728 W Grand Ave ⓣ312/666-1695, ⓦwww.funkybuddha.com. Small West-Side club where the resident DJs attract a devoted young crowd.

Smartbar 3730 N Clark St, underneath the *Metro* (see opposite) ⓣ773/549-0203, ⓦwww.smartbarchicago.com. Great techno and house on the weekend in post-industrial Wrigleyville surroundings. Weekdays see a mix of punk, goth and Eighties. The whole complex is open late – until 5am Fri and Sat.

Theatre and comedy

While it was once every Chicago actor and playwright's ambition to end up in New York, many are now perfectly happy to remain here. The city supports numerous **theatre** companies, several of which boast reputations as good as any in the US. Best known of all is Steppenwolf, with alumni like John Malkovich and Gary Sinise, based at 1650 N Halsted St (ⓣ312/335-1650, ⓦwww.steppenwolf.org), while others include the Court Theatre, 5535 S Ellis St (ⓣ773/753-4472, ⓦwww.courttheatre.org) and the Goodman Theatre, 170 N Dearborn St (ⓣ312/443-3800, ⓦwww.goodman-theatre.org). **Comedy**, too, is particularly vibrant; Chicago's improvisational scene is considered the best in the nation, with the troupe at **Second City** – who now spread their activities across three separate auditoriums centred on 1616 N Wells St (ⓣ312/337-3992, ⓦwww.secondcity.com) – especially heralded.

Classical music, opera and dance

The world-famous **Chicago Symphony Orchestra** is based at Symphony Center, 220 S Michigan Ave (ⓣ312/294-3000, ⓦwww.chicagosymphony.org), but spends part of the year on tour. The 186-member **Symphony Chorus** performs both classical and contemporary choral works with the CSO, specifically in summer at the open-air **Ravinia Festival**, 25 miles north of downtown Chicago (ⓦwww.ravinia.org). Home for the **Lyric Opera of Chicago** is the beautiful Civic Opera House, 20 N Wacker Drive (ⓣ312/332-2244, ⓦwww.lyricopera.org); its season is from mid-September to early February, and most performances end up being sold out. Chicago can also boast two world-class dance companies: the classically oriented **Joffrey Ballet**, based at 70 E Lake St (ⓣ312/739-0120, ⓦwww.joffrey.com), and the more contemporary **Hubbard Street Dance Chicago**, 1147 W Jackson Blvd (ⓣ312/850-9744, ⓦwww.hubbardstreetdance.com).

Sports

Staunchly blue-collar Chicago must be among the best US cities for watching **sports**, as Chicagoans are, for better or worse, loyally supportive of their teams. The city's most successful outfit in recent memory was the Michael Jordan-led **Bulls** basketball team, winner of six NBA championships in the 1990s (ⓣ312/559-1212, ⓦwww.nba.com/bulls). Now, though, with the Jordan era long gone, Bulls fans have little to cheer about, though the team's fortunes have improved in recent years. The team plays in the ultramodern United Center, 1901 W Madison St, as do hockey's **Blackhawks**, who triumphed in 2010 to become the Stanley Cup champions (same phone, ⓦwww.chicagoblackhawks.com). The **Bears** football team (ⓣ312/295-6600, ⓦwww.chicagobears.com) can be seen at the 61,000-capacity Soldier Field, 425 E McFetridge Drive, at the south end of Grant Park. As for baseball, neither Chicago team had won a World Series since 1917 until the **White Sox** finally broke the streak in 2005. Their rather bland home, US Cellular Field stadium, sits at 333 W 35th St on the South Side, and it has a distinctly non-descript feel (ⓣ312/831-1SOX, ⓦchicago.whitesox.mlb.com). The long-suffering **Cubs** still call grand old Wrigley Field home (ⓣ312/831-CUBS, ⓦchicago.cubs.mlb.com).

Central Illinois

Interstates 55 and 57 slice south through the Corn Belt of **central Illinois** from Chicago. Parallel to I-55, the legendary **Route 66** began its run here, cutting through the state before running all the way to the Pacific Coast – you might try to catch a glimpse of it, as some old-time diners and other Americana still stand. One worthwhile stop, reachable by either interstate, is the state capital, **Springfield**, which commemorates president and former resident **Abraham Lincoln**. Otherwise, if you're on your way south, the college towns of **Bloomington-Normal** and **Champaign-Urbana** are the only good urban stops, while if you're heading west from Chicago spare the time to pause at the delightful Civil War river town of **Galena**.

Springfield

Two hundred miles south of Chicago, the Illinois state capital of **SPRINGFIELD** spreads out from a neat, downtown grid. Abraham Lincoln honed his legal and political skills here, and tourists flock to his old homes, haunts and final resting place. What they find is neither tacky nor pompous, but rather sites that illuminate not only the life of the sixteenth president of the USA, but also the uncertainty and turmoil of a nation on the brink of civil war.

The number one Lincoln attraction is the only house he ever owned, and which he shared with his wife, Mary Todd from 1844 to 1861. For a free narrated tour, pick up tickets at the **Lincoln Home Visitor Center**, 426 S Seventh St (daily 8.30am–5pm; ⓣ217/492-4241, ⓦwww.nps.gov/liho). Assorted displays and a brief film help to pass the time while you wait for the next available tour.

Four blocks north, at 212 N Sixth St, the **Abraham Lincoln Presidential Library and Museum** (daily 9am–5pm; Library is free, Museum $12; ⓣ217/782-5764, ⓦwww.alplm.org) is a state-of-the-art new facility that covers Lincoln's career in exhaustive detail, with fascinating original documents and interactive displays, as well as some simple mock-ups aimed largely at kids.

In the restored Greek Revival **Old State Capitol**, at Sixth and Adams nearby (mid-April to Aug daily 9am–5pm; Sept to mid-April Tues–Sat same hours; free;

☎217/785-7960), Lincoln attended at least 240 Supreme Court hearings, and proclaimed in 1858, "A house divided against itself cannot stand. I believe this government cannot endure permanently, half slave and half free". Objects, busts and papers relating to Lincoln and the Democrat Stephen A. Douglas, whom he debated (and subsequently lost to) in Illinois' 1858 US Senate election, and whom he defeated in the 1860 presidential race, can be found throughout the building. At the tastefully renovated **Lincoln Depot** on Tenth and Monroe streets (April–Aug daily 10am–4pm; free), the newly elected president said goodbye to Springfield in February 1861 and boarded a train for his inauguration in Washington DC (a video illustrates the twelve-day journey). The next time he returned was in his funeral train. **Lincoln's Tomb**, an 117ft-tall obelisk, stands in beautiful Oak Ridge Cemetery on the north side of town. The vault, adorned with busts and statuettes, is open to the public (March–April Tues–Sat 9am–5pm; May–Aug Mon–Sun same hours; Sep–Nov Tues–Sat same hours; Dec–Feb, Tues–Sat till 4pm; free). Inside are inscribed the words, "Now he belongs to the ages".

The **Illinois State Museum**, at 502 South Spring and Edwards on the south side of the complex of the current Illinois State Capitol, is crammed with natural history and Native American and contemporary art exhibits. (Mon–Sat 8.30am–5pm, Sun noon–5pm; free). Just south of Springfield, along Springfield Lake sits **The Lincoln Memorial Gardens**, 2301 E Lake Drive (daily; free; ☎217/529-1111, Ⓦwww.lmgnc.org). Designed by famous landscape architect Jens Jensen, the hundred-acre site is home to hordes of arbour, plant and bird life, all native to the states where Lincoln spent his young life. Completed in 1904, the **Dana-Thomas House**, 301 E Lawrence Ave (tours given every 20 minutes, 9am–4pm, Wed–Sun, $5; ☎217/782-6776), survives as the best-preserved and most completely furnished example of **Frank Lloyd Wright**'s early Prairie houses, with more than four hundred pieces of glasswork, original art and light fixtures. A museum ripe for amateur photographers is just north of town, at 2075 Peoria Rd, where Bill Shea proudly displays fifty years' worth of road signs, gas pumps and Route 66 memorabilia at **Shea's Gas Station Museum** (Tues–Fri 7am–4pm, Sat 8am–noon; free).

Practicalities

Abraham Lincoln Capital Airport (☎217/788-1060, Ⓦwww.flyspi.com) currently has two major airlines serving Springfield (United Airlines and American Airlines). Amtrak **trains** from Chicago and St Louis roll in at Third and Washington streets downtown, at manageable times. Greyhound **buses** drop off two miles east of downtown at 2351 S Dirksen Parkway. The **Convention and Visitors Bureau**, 109 N Seventh St (Mon–Fri 8.30am–5pm; ☎217/789-2360 or 1-800/545-7300, Ⓦwww.visit-springfieldillinois.com), has brochures and maps.

The best selection of **accommodation** includes the full-service *President Abraham Lincoln Hotel and Convention Center*, 701 East Adams St (☎217/544-8800 or 1/866-7888-1860, Ⓦwww.presidentabrahamlincolnhotel.com; ❹). *The Inn at 835*, 835 S Second St (☎217/523-4466, Ⓦwww.innat835.com; ❺), is a charming ten-room B&B converted from a 1909 downtown apartment block.

Springfield's **cafés** are the origin of a phenomenon known as the **Horseshoe** – simply said, a meat sandwich, but fried, covered in melted cheese and very tasty. *D'Arcy's Pint Restaurant*, 661 W Stanford Ave. (☎217/492-8800) serves up the ultimate Horseshoe, however, first timers should steer toward the smaller Ponyshoe version ($6.50). The *Cozy Dog Drive-In*, 2935 S Sixth St (☎217/525-1992) claims to be the birthplace of the **Cozy Dog** (also known as the corn dog), a deep-fried, batter-drenched hot dog on a stick (closed Sun). At the other end of the health spectrum, *Augie's Front Burner*, 109 S Fifth St (☎217/544-6979), serves up good California-style and vegetarian meals.

Galena

The charming town of **GALENA**, a few miles short of both Iowa and Wisconsin in the far northwest corner of Illinois, has changed little since its nineteenth-century heyday. Thanks to its sheltered location just a few miles up the Galena River, it was a major port of call for Mississippi River steamboats. These days, the main foot traffic comes from weekend travellers who step back in time strolling along the gentle crescent of Main Street. Its impeccable red-brick facades and graceful skyline of spires and crosses place it among the most attractive river towns in the US.

Galena boasts of having contributed nine generals to the Union army during the Civil War, the most significant of whom was **Ulysses S. Grant**. Grant moved to the town in 1860, working with his brothers as a clerk in a leather store owned by his father. His West Point education encouraged the townspeople to appoint him as colonel when they raised the 21st Illinois regiment on the outbreak of war. When he came home, in August 1865, it was as overall commander of the victorious Union army.

The grateful citizens of Galena presented Grant with a **house**, a couple of blocks up Bouthillier Street on the far side of the river (Wed–Sun 9am–4.15pm; suggested donation $3; ⓣ815/777-0248; it is best to phone before arriving). It was there, in the drawing room that Grant received the news of his election as president in 1868. Although he went on to serve two terms, he is commonly agreed to have been a better general than president. His administrations were plagued by scandal, and he lost all his own money through unwise investments. The family fortunes were restored just before his death in 1885, when Mark Twain first persuaded Grant to write, and then published, his bestselling *Memoirs*.

Practicalities

The 1857 Railroad Museum, across the river from the town proper at 101 Bouthillier St, serves as the local **visitor centre** (daily 9am–5pm; ⓣ815/777-4390 or 1-877/464-2536, ⓦwww.galena.org). The gracefully restored 1850's *Victorian Mansion*, 301 High St (ⓣ815/777-0675, ⓦwww.victorianmansion.com; ❺), is an elegant eight-room B&B where President Grant gave his farewell speech to the town before heading off to the White House. If your budget won't stretch that far, the *Grant Hills Motel*, a mile east on highway 20 (ⓣ815/777-2116 or 1-877/421-0924, ⓦwww.granthills.com; ❷), makes a good-value option. As for a local spot to **eat**, *Railway Café'*, 100 Bouthillier St (ⓣ815/777-0047) serves organic breakfasts and lunches and has live music. *Backstreets Steak and Chophouse*, 216 S Commerce St (ⓣ815/777-4800) serves up the delicious meats the Midwest makes famous or try *Fried Green Tomatoes*, 213 N Main St (ⓣ815/777-3938), a reliable Italian alternative.

Wisconsin

Nearly as many cows as humans call **WISCONSIN** home; over five million of each reside in this rich, rolling farmland. However, America's self-proclaimed "Dairyland" is more than just one giant pasture. Beyond the massive hills, red barns and silvery silos lie endless pine forests, some fifteen thousand sky-blue lakes, postcard-pretty valleys and dramatic bluffs. The state, whose Ojibway name means "gathering of the waters", is bordered by Lake Michigan to the east, Lake Superior in the north and, to the west, the Mississippi and St Croix rivers.

The **history** of Wisconsin exemplifies the standard formula for westward expansion. Seventeenth-century French and British explorers began by trading with the Native Americans and soon ousted them from their land. The European settlers who followed – predominantly Germans, Scandinavians and Poles – tended to be liberal and progressive; such major national social programmes as labour laws for women and children, assistance for the elderly and the disabled, and unemployment compensation found their first manifestation in the US right here.

Wisconsin today is best known for its liquids. The **milk** from all those cattle yields cheeses of all kinds, while the **beer**, as the song says, is what made **Milwaukee** famous. Sparkling Madison apart, Wisconsin's other cities – **La Crosse**, **Green Bay**, **Oshkosh** – can veer toward the quiet and tame side, but they're also clean, safe and amiable, while the smaller towns can be distinctive and charming.

Milwaukee

Just ninety miles north of Chicago, bustling **MILWAUKEE** is the largest city in Wisconsin and is a combination of the rural Midwest and its stylish urban counterparts. Known for its lakeside and ethnic **festivals** and huge **breweries**, Milwaukee is reshaping its image. Visually it's a mix of elegant architecture, rambling Victorian warehouses and revamped waterfront developments. Its prime position on the shores of Lake Michigan, at the confluence of three rivers, made it a meeting place for Native American groups long before white settlers moved in, while the opulent mansions lining the lake commemorate the industrialists who helped make this Wisconsin's economic and manufacturing capital. By 1850, less than two decades old and with a population of twenty thousand, Milwaukee already had a dozen breweries and 225 saloons.

Arrival, information and city transport

Milwaukee is well served by air, rail and bus. Mitchell **airport**, eight miles south of downtown at 5300 S Howell Ave, is connected with the city centre by bus #80 ($2.25), and by shared-ride van service ($15). A taxi will set you back about $30. Amtrak is at 433 W St Paul Ave, while Greyhound (ⓣ414/272-2156) which has several locations and Wisconsin Coach (ⓣ262/542-8864; ⓦwww.wisconsincoach.com), serving southeastern Wisconsin, operate out of the same terminal at 606 N James Lovell Drive. Badger Bus (ⓣ414/276-7490, ⓦwww.badgerbus.com), across the street at no. 635, runs to Madison and points between (six daily; $38 return).

Milwaukee's **Visitor Center** is at Discovery World, at Pier Wisconsin (daily 8am–5pm; ⓣ414/273-7222 or 1-800/554-1448, ⓦwww.visitmilwaukee.org), and has details on such **festivals** as the eleven-day Summerfest (late June to early July), also known as "The Big Gig", and the Wisconsin State Fair (early Aug).

Getting around Milwaukee is easy and inexpensive via the county's extensive **transport system** (flat fare $2.25; 24hr info ⓣ414/344-6711; ⓦwww.ridemcts.com). The Milwaukee Loop is a special trolley service connecting 25 stops in the city centre (June–Aug, Wed–Sat 11am–10pm; free).

Accommodation

Accommodation in Milwaukee runs the gamut from low-budget motels to upmarket chains and luxury hotels. Staying a few miles outside of town will reduce your rates drastically.

Aloft Hotel 1230 N. Old World Third St ⓣ414/226-0122; ⓦwww.aloftmilwaukee downtown.com. With its close proximity to some of Milwaukee's storeyed "Old World" brew pubs and its modish jet-set-style interiors, this hotel is a good bet for those who want to be close to the nightlife. ⑤

Brumder Mansion 3046 W Wisconsin Ave ⓣ414/342-9767 or 866/793-3676; ⓦwww .brumdermansion.com. Fabulously decorated, enormous B&B with an in-house theatre, just minutes from downtown. Rooms include antiques, marble, rich draperies and stained glass. ④

Comfort Inn & Suites Downtown Lakeshore 916 E State St ⓣ414/276-8800 or 1-800/328-7275, ⓦwww.comfortinn.com. Clean, very comfortable rooms in a nice part of downtown. ④

Hotel Metro 411 East Madison St ⓣ414/272-1937 or 1-877/638-7620; ⓦwww.hotelmetro.com. This retro Art Deco hotel has an historic feeling with a modern twist. Updated and eco-friendly, it's worth the extra cash you might need to lay down for the fireplace and jacuzzi that sit in the centre of the room. A little forward planning might secure a discounted package. ⑦

The Pfister Hotel 424 E Wisconsin Ave ⓣ414/273-822, ⓦwww.pfisterhotel.com. This hotel sits nestled like a Victorian Grande Dame in the heart of downtown. Replenish yourself in the spa or visit the 23rd floor martini lounge. There is even a world-class Victorian art collection. It will cost a bit more, but often you can grab a special package for considerably less. ⑦–⑨

The City

Downtown Milwaukee, split north to south by the Milwaukee River, is only a mile long and a few blocks wide. Handsome old buildings and gleaming, modern steel-and-glass structures are comfortably corralled together on three sides by spaghetti-like strands of freeway, with Lake Michigan forming the fourth boundary. To bolster the allure of downtown, the city has successfully poured millions into its **Riverwalk** development along the Milwaukee River, now something of a nightlife centre and the site of many public entertainment events. East of the river on the lakefront, the **Milwaukee Art Museum**, 700 N Art Museum Drive (Tues & Wed and Fri–Sun 10am–5pm, Thurs till 8pm; $12; ⓣ414/224-3200, ⓦwww.mam.org), contains works by European masters and twentieth-century Americans. One wing – with stunning views of the lake – is devoted to a comprehensive collection of Post-Impressionist paintings. Architect Santiago Calatrava's spectacular expansion is an attraction in itself, the white wings of the building flapping up and down three times each day to reduce heat gain and glare. Close by, **Discovery World at Pier Wisconsin**, 500 N Harbor Drive (Tues–Sun 9am–5pm; $15.95; ⓣ414/765-9966, ⓦwww.discoveryworld .org), features popular hands-on exhibits and the S/V *Denis Sullivan* schooner. Downtown at 800 W Wells St are the **Milwaukee Public Museum** (Mon–Sat 9am–5pm, Sun 10am–6pm; $12; ⓣ414/278-2702 or 1-888/700-9069, ⓦwww .mpm.edu), where the intertwined histories and mysteries of the earth, nature and humankind are imaginatively presented through dioramas such as "A Sense of Wonder", and the **Humphrey IMAX Dome Theater**, which has a giant, wraparound screen (show times vary; $8–10, $17 for a combo ticket; ⓣ414/319-4629, ⓦwww.mpm.edu/imax).

West of downtown, the 37-room **Pabst Mansion**, at 2000 W Wisconsin Ave (Feb–Oct Mon–Sat 10am–4pm, Sun noon–4pm; closed Mon mid-Jan to Feb; $5–9; ⓣ414/931-0808, ⓦwww.pabstmansion.com), was completed in 1893 as the castle of a local beer baron and is a knockout example of ornate Flemish Renaissance architecture, featuring exquisite wood-, glass- and ironwork. Although the Pabst Brewery here has shut down, the **Miller Brewing Company**, five miles west of downtown at 4251 W State St, still offers free behind-the-scenes tours (Mon–Sat, usually 10.30am–3.30pm but times change frequently; ⓣ414/931-2337 or 1-800/931-BEER), culminating in generous samples for over-21s. The shiny new museum responsible for Milwaukee's other legendary brand name,

Harley-Davidson, located at 400 Canal St, (May–Oct Mon–Fri 9am–6pm, Nov–April Mon–Fri 10am–5pm, Sat & Sun 9am–6pm; $16 ⓣ877/436-8738, ⓦwww.hdmuseum.com) is geared squarely toward Harley devotees; for those more interested in Harley chic, there's ample opportunity to purchase all kinds of merchandise at the shop or throughout Milwaukee.

Eating

The Germans who first settled in Milwaukee determined its **eating** style – heavy on bratwurst, rye bread and beer. Subsequent immigrants threw the collective kitchen wide open, making for a culinary cornucopia. With Lake Michigan lapping the city's feet, freshwater fish can hardly be overlooked, especially on a Friday night when legendary fish fries break out all over the place. Wherever you go, portions tend to be big.

Bacchus 925 E Wells ⓣ414/765-1166. Located in the historic Cudahy Tower and featuring fresh seafood and handmade pastas, this place drips with taste and style.

Carnevor 724 N Milwaukee St ⓣ414/223-2200. The art of fine dining and outstanding cuts of meat are in full swing at this chic and contemporary steakhouse. Closed Sun.

Eddie Martini's 8612 W Watertown Plank Rd ⓣ414/771-6680. Highly energetic atmosphere with inventive takes on American classics.

Rudy's 1122 N Edison St ⓣ414/223-1122. Family-friendly and affordable Mexican from 11am–11pm daily. Try the house special combo platters.

Trocadero 1758 N Water St ⓣ414/272-0205. Parisian-styled eastside spot that serves small plates and great continental dishes like grilled tuna and saffron shrimp.

Nightlife and entertainment

The concept of neighbourhoods is vital to Milwaukee's nightlife. On the east side, **Brady Street**, a counterculture haven in the 1960s, is now filled with Italian restaurants and bars. **Walker's Point**, on the edge of downtown, has all sorts of watering holes, while the Polish locals can be found farther south. Downtown gets busy on the weekend, especially either side of the river on **Water** and **Old World Third** streets between Juneau and State.

Live theatre and high culture in downtown Milwaukee revolves around the **Marcus Center for the Performing Arts**, 929 N Water St (ⓣ414/273-7121 or 1-888/612-3500, ⓦwww.marcuscenter.org). The plush, historic **Pabst Theater**, 144 E Wells St (ⓣ414/286-3663) and the **Riverside Theater**, 116 W Wisconsin Ave (ⓣ414/286-3663), host well-known bands, while the **Milwaukee Repertory Theater**, 108 E Wells St (ⓣ414/224-9490, ⓦwww.milwaukeerep.com), has a reputation for staging risk-taking productions in addition to classics like "A Christmas Carol". The **Third Ward**, a restored warehouse district on the edge of downtown full of shops and cafés, is also worth checking out.

Milwaukee Ale House 233 N Water St ⓣ414/226-BEER. Milwaukee's sole all-grain, old-style brewpub serves filling food and its own beer.

Old German Beer Hall 1009 N Old World Third St ⓣ414/226-2728. This Old-World favourite is distinguished by its excellent hot pretzels, sausages and a charming game in the back room that involves pounding nails into a massive tree stump. It should not be missed.

Safe House 779 N Front St ⓣ414/271-2007, ⓦwww.safe-house.com. This unique, tongue-in-cheek nightclub seems to come straight out of a spy film. Hint: enter through the "International Exports Ltd" office.

Up and Under Pub 1216 E Brady St ⓣ414/276-2677. Milwaukee's top blues bar.

Von Trier 2235 N Farwell Ave ⓣ414/272-1775. Black Forest decor and lots of imported beers – the Weise is a house specialty.

Wisconsin's eastern shores

North of Milwaukee, **eastern Wisconsin** is a melange of the industrial and the maritime, shaped by its proximity to **Lake Michigan** and the smaller **Lake Winnebago**. Of its towns, **Green Bay**, home to the legendary Packers, is best seen as a prelude to idyllic **Door County**.

Green Bay

GREEN BAY was an important location for seventeenth-century French explorers, but for the past nine decades, it has been most well known for the Green Bay Packers, one of the United States' most beloved professional football teams. **The Green Bay Packer Hall of Fame**, 1265 Lombardi Ave (daily 8am–9pm; $10; ⓣ920/569-7500), celebrates the dynastic years of the 1960s when the Pack won Superbowls I and II, as well as more recent stars such as Antonio Freeman and Brett Favre. Stuffed with hands-on displays, movie theatres and memorabilia, the museum offers more than enough to satisfy any football fan. The Hall of Fame is located in an atrium inside the Packers' **Lambeau Field** stadium, which you can also tour (times vary; $11, or $19 combination ticket with Hall of Fame; ⓦwww.packers.com).

The city's **Convention & Visitor's Bureau** (ⓣ920/494-9507 or 1-888/867-3342; ⓦwww.greenbay.com) sits in the shadow of the football stadium, off Lombardi Avenue, at 1901 S Oneida St. Nearby, the *Best Western Midway Hotel*, 780 Armed Forces Drive (ⓣ920/499-3161 or 1-800/528-1234, ⓦwww.bestwestern.com; ❹–❺), has standard rooms and an indoor pool. *Titletown Brewing Company*, 200 Dousman St (ⓣ920/437-2337), has a great setting for drinks in a former railroad depot downtown, while *Brett Favre's Steakhouse*, 1004 Brett Favre Pass (ⓣ920/499-MVP4), is an upmarket family restaurant/sports bar serving Southern cuisine.

Door County

From Sturgeon Bay, 140 miles north of Milwaukee, **Door County** sticks into Lake Michigan like a gradually tapering candle for 42 miles. A charming collection of small towns, tiny villages and an island, its 300 miles of shoreline smacks more of New England than the Midwest. Prices can be a little steep in the summer, but you get what you pay for – a small sliver of America devoid, for the most part, of crude billboards, sloppy diners, bland chain motels and tacky amusements. Activities include browsing around galleries and attending arts festivals, as well as hiking, fishing and boating. Renting a **bicycle** gives you the chance to follow an excellent **cycle trail**; try Fish Creek's Nor Door Cyclery (ⓣ920/868-2275, ⓦwww.nordoorsports.com), on Hwy-42 just north of the entrance to Peninsula State Park (see below), which has the best models. Winter is considerably quieter, with ice fishing, cross-country skiing and snowmobiling being the predominant outdoor activities.

Pick up road and trail maps at the **visitor centre** on Hwy-42/57 upon entering Sturgeon Bay (lobby open 24 hours; staffed times vary; ⓣ920/743-4456 or 1-800/52-RELAX, ⓦwww.doorcounty.com), where you can also phone local lodgings for free.

Exploring Door County

Door County's only sizeable town, **Sturgeon Bay**, is a pleasant enough shipbuilding community, if not exactly abundant in small-town splendour. Ten miles north on Hwy-57 you find one of five state parks, the rolling **Whitefish Dunes State Park**, with its wispy sand dunes and popular mile-long beach (daily;

$7/car, $10 with out-of-state plates). A short trail beginning at the park's Nature Center leads to the spectacular rocky **Cave Point County Park** (free), studded with wind- and wave-sculptured caves that are particularly dramatic in winter. In general beaches are better this side of the peninsula; you can also swim in several placid inland lakes.

Over on the western side, biking and hiking trails traverse the thickly forested hills of **Peninsula State Park** (situated between tiny Fish Creek and enchanting **Ephraim**, with its picturesque white-clapboard architecture). Peninsula Park is one of the most popular parks in Wisconsin and summer camping reservations usually book up in January. Just outside it on Hwy-42, the old-fashioned Skyway Drive-In movie theatre (T920/854-9938) offers a couple of hours' diversion on a warm night. Northeast of Ellison Bay near the peninsula's tip, **Newport State Park** is one of Wisconsin's least visited parks, with hiking, mountain biking, cross-country skiing and camping opportunities.

Washington Island, off the peninsula's northern tip, is a tiny dollop of land that offers a different cultural perspective. During Prohibition, the Icelandic community here convinced authorities that (40 percent alcohol) bitters were an ancient cure for rheumatism and dyspepsia. Cases of the stuff were shipped in, and the habit stuck; drop into the historic *Nelsen's Hall Bitters Pub and Restaurant* (T920/847-2496), about two miles from the Detroit Harbor dock for a taste. **Motel rooms** are available on Washington, but there's no such luxury on the primitive neighbouring 950-acre **Rock Island**. Once the private estate of a millionaire, it's dotted with stark, stone buildings; no cars are allowed, so see it by foot or bike.

The islands are served by the Washington Island Ferry from Northport at the tip of the peninsula (daily; $11.50 return, cars $25, bikes $4; T920/847-2546 or 1-800/223-2094, Wwww.wisferry.com) and the Rock Island Ferry out of Jackson Harbor (May to early Oct daily; $9 return for foot traffic only; T920/847-3322).

Accommodation

Door County has a full range of **accommodation**, including some overpriced resorts. Prices given are for off-peak seasons (the best time to come); expect to pay up to 25 percent extra at the grander hotels in July and August, and a small weekend premium. Camping is idyllic. State park sites cost $12–17 (plus $10 reservation fee and $7 daily admission or $10 for out-of-state residents; T1-888/947-2757). Among the best of the private campgrounds is the pet-friendly *Path of Pines*, County Road F off Hwy-42, near Fish Creek (mid-May to mid-Oct; $20; T920/868-3332 or 1-800/868-7802).

Birchwood Lodge 337 Hwy-57, Sister Bay T920/854-7195, Wwww.birchwoodlodge.com. A pleasant lodge with a variety of accommodation options. European-designed suites with a modern touch 5–7

French Country Inn 3052 Spruce Lane, Ephraim T920/854-4001. This charming B&B close to the water offers seven rooms (two with private baths) in the summer and four in the winter. Breakfast features organic, local produce when possible. 3–4

Settlement Courtyard Inn & Lavender Spa 9126 Hwy-42, Fish Creek T920/868-3524 or 1-877/398-9308, Wwww.settlementinn.com. The *Settlement*'s location on a 200-acre estate makes it an ideal year-round destination with four miles of trails for biking, hiking or cross-country skiing. Clean and comfortable, breakfast included. 5

White Gull Inn 4225 Main St, Fish Creek T920/868-3517 or 1-888/364-9542, Wwww.whitegullinn.com. The county's crown jewel, this elegant old inn, next to delightful Sunset Park, was built in 1896. Rooms are decorated in antiques, and some have fireplaces and double whirlpools. The inn is also known for its good restaurant (breakfast is included) and fish boil (see below) every night in summer. 6–9

Eating

One reward of a midsummer visit to Door County is the chance to sample the cherry in all its guises. Another traditional treat is the **fish boil**, a delicious outdoor ritual involving whitefish steaks, potatoes and onions cooked in a cauldron over a wood fire. Rounded off with coleslaw and cherry pie, it's widely available for between $12 and $18.

Al Johnson's Swedish Restaurant Hwy-42, Sister Bay ⓣ920/854-2626. Swedish pancakes, meatballs and other fine Scandinavian dishes make this spot worth a look. Be sure and look up to see goats grazing atop the sod roof.

C & C Supper Club Hwy-42, Corner of Spruce and Main St ⓣ920/868-3412. Get your supper club fix at *C & C's* and set aside room for the delicious apple cobbler.

Square Rigger Galley 6332 Hwy-57, Jacksonport ⓣ920/823-2408 or 1-866/439-4578. This cocktail lounge and restaurant, on a private sandy beach, serves one of the county's best fish boils.

Northern Wisconsin

Sparsely settled **northern Wisconsin** has no large cities (and few small ones) and no interstates to speak of. It's a lake-studded wilderness, covered by enormous tracts of forest. Canoe its rivers, fish for record-breakers, or ski or snowmobile cross-country trails without having to fight for space. **Bayfield, Madeline Island** and the **Apostle Islands** in the northwest are the obvious destinations.

The Apostle Islands

All but one of the 22 islands scattered off **Bayfield Peninsula** in Lake Superior are part of the **Apostle Islands National Lakeshore** – a prized preserve for outdoors enthusiasts seeking to recharge depleted spiritual batteries.

The jumping-off point for the islands, **BAYFIELD**, once a lumbering and fishing village, is now a pleasant soft-sell tourist trap. Its sumptuous *Old Rittenhouse Inn*, 301 Rittenhouse Ave (ⓣ715/779-5111 or 1-800/779-2129, ⓦwww.rittenhouseinn.com; ❺–❻), offers gourmet meals and well-appointed **rooms**. *Tree Top House*, 225 N Fourth St (ⓣ715/779-3293; ❷), features clean, simple doubles. Lodges and cottages are the centrepiece for the thirty gorgeous lakeside acres of *Rocky Run* (ⓣ715/373-2551; ❹), a resort outside **Washburn** eleven miles south. Bayfield's **visitor centre** is at 42 S Broad St (ⓣ715/779-3335 or 1-800/447-4094; ⓦwww.bayfield.org). Campers heading for the islands require permits from the visitor centre (ask about permit fees) at 415 Washington Ave (summer daily 10am–5pm; winter Mon–Fri 10am–4pm; ⓣ715/779-3397). Getting around the islands is straightforward: Apostle Island's Cruise Services boats ($32.95; ⓣ715/779-3925, ⓦwww.apostleisland.com) wend their way past all of the islands, and will set down and pick up campers.

Madeline Island

By the fifteenth century **Madeline Island** was known to the Ojibway as Moningwunakauning – home of the golden-shafted woodpecker. Frenchman Michel Cadotte founded a fur-trading post there for the British in 1793, and subsequently married Equaysayway, daughter of a tribal leader, who took the name the island bears today. Madeline is now the only commercially developed Apostle Island, but it remains pretty low-key. Cadotte is buried in an overgrown cemetery in its sole town, **LA POINTE**.

La Pointe is accessible in summer via the twenty-minute ride on the Madeline Island Ferry Line from Bayfield (every 30min in peak season; cars $12 one-way,

$24 return; passengers $5.75, $11; bikes $2.75, $5.50; ⓣ715/747-2051, ⓦwww.madferry.com). Its 180 year-round residents maintain an interesting little **historical museum** (May–Oct daily 10am–5pm; $7), and assorted sandy beaches, wide bays, scenic points and forests can also be explored along 45 miles of sometimes rough road in the area. The Ferry Line conducts two-hour bus tours of the island (July & Aug, Mon–Sat, 1.30pm; $11).

The **visitor centre** on Main Street (ⓣ715/747-2801 or 1-888/475-3386, ⓦwww.madelineisland.com) can offer advice on **places to stay**; the *Madeline Island Motel* (ⓣ715/747-3000; ❹) and *The Island Inn* (ⓣ715/747-2000; ❺), both near the ferry dock, are probably the best value. A wooden footbridge from La Pointe across the lagoon leads to **Big Bay State Park** where the campgrounds share a splendid mile-long beach. Camping sites, on top of a bluff and close to caves in the park (ⓣ1-888/947-2757), cost $10–17, plus a $10 reservation fee and a $7–10 vehicle fee. **Eating** options include the pub in *The Inn on Madeline Island* resort (ⓣ715/747-6322 or 1-800/822-6315, ⓦwww.madisland.com; ❹–❻) where homes, cottages and condominiums can also be rented along a private beach.

Southern Wisconsin

Assorted highways and backroads lace up **southern Wisconsin**, passing over rolling hills and deep dales. The main urban centre of Wisconsin's most populated region is the immensely likeable lakeside college town of **Madison**, which is also the state capital. Cosy Madison-area communities like New Glarus or Mount Horeb, and historic settlements like Little Norway have cute, walkable downtowns. Further north, a kid's dream town, Wisconsin Dells has a picturesque setting, but may appeal only to those who revel in tacky attractions and T-shirt shops. Undulating down the state's western border, alongside the Mississippi River, the scenic highway designated as **The Great River Road** runs from near Canada to the Gulf of Mexico.

Madison and around

The history books record that **MADISON**, just over an hour west of Milwaukee, was little more than a wooded, mosquito-infested swamp when it was selected to be the political nucleus of the Wisconsin Territory in 1836. The University of Wisconsin was chartered shortly thereafter in 1848, and today this stimulating, youthful metropolis is one of the most beautifully set cities in the US, with a handful of diverting museums, great restaurants and a student-fuelled nightlife scene.

Arrival, information and accommodation

Greyhound **buses** run regularly to Milwaukee, Green Bay and beyond, while Badger Coaches makes six trips daily from downtown Milwaukee ($19 one-way, $38 return; ⓣ608/255-6771, ⓦwww.badgerbus.com). Both operate out of the terminal at 2 S Bedford St. Van Galder/Coach USA buses depart from the Memorial Union to Chicago's O'Hare Airport (10 daily; $27 one-way, $54 return; ⓣ608/752-5407 or 1-800/747-0994, ⓦwww.coachusa.com/vangalder). Madison also has a recently renovated airport (ⓣ608/246-3380), offering flights all over the Midwest and further afield. The **visitor centre** is at 21 N Park St (Mon–Fri 9am–4.30pm, Sat 11am–2pm, closed Sun; ⓣ608/262-4636, ⓦwww.visitmadison.com).

Accommodation can be found throughout the city, though the budget chains lie to the east, off I-90/94. *Madison Concourse Hotel*, 1 W Dayton St (Ⓣ608/257-6000 or 1-800/356-8293, Ⓦwww.concoursehotel.com; ❺–❻) has spacious, well-appointed rooms steps from State Street. Right on Capitol Square, you can stay in one of the comfortable rooms at *The Best Western Inn on the Park*, 22 S Carroll St (Ⓣ608/257-8811 or 1-800/279-8811; ❺). The *Mansion Hill Inn*, 424 Pinckney St (Ⓣ608/255-0172 or 1-800/798-9070; Ⓦwww.mansionhillinn.com; ❽) close to campus provides a bit more relaxed setting within a restored 1857 Romanesque Revival mansion. There's also a Hostelling International location at 141 S Butler St (Ⓣ608/441-0144, Ⓦwww.madisonhostel.org), with 28 beds ($22 members/$25 non-members), 5 private rooms ($49 members, $52 non-members), and all the usual amenities: kitchen, laundry, internet access, storage and lockers.

The Town

Downtown is neatly laid out on an isthmus between lakes Mendota and Monona, with the white-granite **State Capitol** (tours Mon–Sat 9am–3pm excluding noon, Sun 1–3pm; Ⓣ608/266-0382) sitting on a hill at its centre, surrounded by shady trees, lawns and park benches. The State Capitol square is the site of a nationally renowned **farmers' market** (late April to early Nov Sat 6am–2pm), where you can browse the local produce and arts-and-crafts. Nearby, the brand-new, glassy **Overture Center**, 201 State St, hosts touring musicians, Broadway plays and other cultural events (box office Ⓣ608/258-4141, Ⓦwww.overturecenter.com); inside, the **Madison Museum of Contemporary Art** 227 State St (Tues & Wed 11am–5pm, Thurs & Fri till 8pm, Sat 10am–8pm, Sun noon–5pm, closed Mon; free; Ⓣ608/257-0158; Ⓦwww.mmoca.org), features touring exhibits.

Frank Lloyd Wright designed the **Unitarian Meeting House**, 900 University Bay Drive, in the late 1940s. Its sweeping, dramatically curved ceiling and triangle motif are definitely worth a look (May–Oct Mon–Fri 10am–4pm, Sat 9am–noon; $3). The lakeside **Monona Terrace Community and Convention Center**, 1 John Nolen Drive, is a more recently realized example of Wright's grand vision (daily tours at 1pm; $3). Surprisingly intimate and full of architectural detail, the Center, with its curves, arches and domes, echoes the State Capitol building just a few blocks away.

If the Capitol is the city's governmental heart, the 46,000-student **University of Wisconsin** is its spirited, liberal-thinking head, now mellowed since its protest heyday in the late 1960s. The **Memorial Union**, 800 Langdon St (Ⓣ608/262-1583), holds a cafeteria and pub, the *Rathskeller*, with tables strewn beneath huge, vaulted ceilings and live music most nights. Outside, the spacious **UW Terrace** offers beautiful sunset views over Lake Mendota. Capitol and campus are arterially connected by State Street, eight tree-lined, pedestrianized blocks of restaurants, cafés, bars and funky stores.

Eating, drinking and entertainment

State Street is a veritable smorgasbord of food and drink, and the **Capital Square** and **King Street** areas have also seen a spate of great new restaurants open in recent years. For details of what's on, check the free weekly *Isthmus* (Ⓦwww.thedailypage.com), which comes out on Thursdays and carries full listings.

Great Dane Pub & Brewing Co 123 E Doty St Ⓣ608/284-0000. Billiards and brews complement fresh hearty fare in this inviting pub.

Marigold Kitchen 118 S Pinckney St Ⓣ608/661-5559. Charming, sunny spot serving delicious, creative breakfast and lunch dishes – such as *challah* French toast and chili poached eggs – focusing on local, organic ingredients.

Oceans Grille 117 Martin Luther King, Jr. Blvd Ⓣ608/285-2582. Terrific seafood and an extensive wine list in a lively, festive atmosphere.

The Old Fashioned 23 N Pinckney St ⓣ608/310-4545, ⓦwww.theoldfashioned.com. Named for the state's signature brandy cocktail, this homey restaurant serves the traditional food that made Wisconsin famous, like fried cheese curds and a killer version of its eponymous cocktail.

Spring Green

During his seventy-year career, Wisconsin-born architect and social philosopher **Frank Lloyd Wright** designed such monumental structures as New York's spiralling Guggenheim Museum and Tokyo's earthquake-proof *Imperial Hotel*. Three miles south of **SPRING GREEN**, itself forty miles west of Madison on Hwy-14, stand more intimate examples of his work: Wright's magnificent former residence, **Taliesin**, and his **Hillside Home School**. His studio is imposing, and there's also a theatre space on the estate. Extensive and varied tours are available of the house and the school (May–Oct daily; reservations recommended; $16–75). Tours leave from the **Frank Lloyd Wright Visitor Center** (ⓣ608/588-7900 or 1-877/588-7900, ⓦwww.taliesinpreservation.org), which was designed by Wright in 1953 as a restaurant; it now features displays, a café and a bookstore. Among numerous other Wright-influenced buildings in Spring Green are the bank and the pharmacy.

From 1944 onward, Alex Jordan built the **House on the Rock**, six miles south of Taliesin on Hwy-23, on and out of a natural, 60ft, chimney-like rock – for no discernible reason. He certainly never lived in it, nor did he intend it to become Wisconsin's number one tourist attraction (mid-March to Oct daily 9am–dusk, $12.50 per section or $28.50 for all three; Nov & Dec Christmas tours Thurs–Mon 9am–5pm; $19.95; ⓣ800/947-2799, ⓦwww.thehouseontherock.com). Only the first section of this multi-level series of furnished nooks and chambers bears any resemblance to a house of any kind. With its low ceilings, indirect lighting, indoor pools, waterfalls, trees and pervasive shag carpeting, the style brings to mind Frank Lloyd Wright meets *The Flintstones*. The rest of the house is a logic-free labyrinth, containing Jordan's astounding collection of collections (antiques, an enormous carousel and pneumatic music machines, miniature circuses, dolls and dolls' houses, maritime memorabilia, armour and firearms, ad infinitum). The net effect is overwhelming and disorienting, alternately great fun and ghastly.

Practicalities

Spring Green is a pretty place to stay, but prices can be high in summer. If you're looking to **stay** overnight in the area, a great bet is the *Castle of Spring Green*, 2247 State Rd 133 in nearby Blue River. Built to resemble a French chateau and set on 500 acres, the *Castle* doesn't disappoint with its ornate furnishings and luxurious rooms. Full castle and grounds rentals available as well as nightly rates (ⓣ847/543-1452; ❹–❽). For a **bite to eat**, follow the locals to *The Shed* (ⓣ608/588-9049), an easy-going diner and bar at 123 N Lexington St in downtown Spring Green.

Minnesota

Though **MINNESOTA** is more than a thousand miles from either coast, it's virtually a seaboard state, thanks to **Lake Superior**, connected to the Atlantic via the St Lawrence Seaway. The glaciers that, millions of years ago, flattened all but its southeast corner also gouged out more than fifteen thousand **lakes**, and major **rivers** run along the eastern and western borders. Ninety-five percent of the population lives within ten minutes of a body of water, and the very name Minnesota is a Sioux word meaning "land of sky-tinted water".

French explorers in the sixteenth century encountered prairies to the south and, in the north, dense forests whose abundant waterways were an ideal breeding ground for beavers and muskrats. **Fur trading**, **fishing** and **lumbering** flourished, and the Ojibway and Sioux were eased out by waves of French, British and American immigrants. Admitted to the Union in 1858, the new state of Minnesota was at first settled by Germans and Scandinavians, who farmed in the west and south. Other ethnic groups followed, many drawn by the massive **iron ore** deposits of north central Minnesota, which are expected to hold out for two more centuries.

More than half of Minnesota's hardy inhabitants, who endure some of the fiercest winters in the nation, live in the southeast, around the so-called Twin Cities of **Minneapolis** and **St Paul**. Together these two cities function as the Midwest's great civic double act for their combined cultural, recreational and business opportunities. Smaller cities include the northern shipping port of **Duluth**, the gateway to the Scenic Hwy-61 lakeshore drive, and **Rochester**, near pretty river towns like Red Wing and Winona. The tranquil waters of **Voyageurs National Park** lie halfway along the state's boundary with Canada.

Minneapolis and St Paul

Commonly known as the **Twin Cities**, **MINNEAPOLIS** (a hybrid Sioux/Greek word meaning "water city") and **ST PAUL** are competitive yet complementary. Fraternally rather than identically twinned, they may be even better places to live than they are to visit, thanks to their cleanliness, cultural activity, social awareness and relatively low crime rates

Only a twenty-minute expressway ride separates the respective downtowns, but each has its own character, style and strengths. **St Paul**, the state capital – originally called Pig's Eye, after a scurrilous French-Canadian fur trader who sold whisky at a Mississippi River landing in the 1840s – is the staid, slightly older sibling, careful to preserve its buildings and traditions. The compact but stately downtown is built, like Rome, on seven hills: the **Capitol** and the **Cathedral** occupy one each, both august monuments that keep the city mindful of its responsibilities.

Minneapolis, founded on money generated by the Mississippi's hundreds of flour-and sawmills, is livelier, artier and more modern, with up-to-date architecture and an upbeat attitude. The residents are spread over wider ground than in St Paul, and dozens of lakes and parks underscore the city's appeal.

Arrival, information and getting around

Twin Cities International Airport lies about ten miles south of either city in suburban Bloomington. Super Shuttle Minneapolis (T 612/827-7777) takes travellers between the airport and major hotels for around $16, while some lodgings provide their own transport. **Taxis** to Minneapolis will set you back close to $40, and to St Paul $30. You can also take the new Hiawatha **light rail system** (T 612/373-3333; W www.metrotransit.org) into Minneapolis (daily 4am–1am: $1.75–2.25), or bus #54 to St Paul (same hours: $1.75–2.25). The 12-mile-long Hiawatha Light Rail line is a nice way to explore the city and it includes stops at the Mall of America, Target Field and Nicollet Mall. The Amtrak **train** station is rather inconveniently located midway between the cities at 730 Transfer Rd, off University Avenue. The Greyhound **bus** terminals, both in convenient downtown locations, are at 950 Hawthorne Ave (ⓣ612/371-3325) in Minneapolis and the less-used 166 W University Ave location (ⓣ651/222-0507) in St Paul. Metro Transit **buses** (ⓣ612/341-4287 or 612/373-3333) make both cities relatively easy to explore without a car.

In Minneapolis, the **visitor centre** is at 250 Marquette Ave (Mon–Fri 8am–5pm; ⓣ612/767-8000 or 1-888/676-MPLS, ⓦwww.minneapolis.org). In St Paul, it's at 175 W Kellogg Blvd, suite 502 (ⓣ651/265-4900 or 1-800/627-6101, ⓦwww.visitsaintpaul.com).

Accommodation

You're likely to pay more for lodgings downtown than in the suburbs, where dozens of cheap **motels** line I-494 near the airport, though some of the pricier central hotels offer reduced rates and special package deals on weekends. The pretty riverside community of **Stillwater**, 25 miles from St Paul via I-35 N and Hwy-36 E, has many grand old B&Bs and motels (ⓣ651/439-4001 for information). For **B&B** options in the Twin Cities, consult ⓦwww.bedandbreakfast.com, as many B&Bs do not have their own websites.

Minneapolis

The Depot 225 Third Ave S ⓣ612/375-1700, ⓦwww.thedepotminneapolis.com. The historic *Depot* building recently underwent massive renovations and now boasts an enormous indoor water park, luxury accommodation, dining and even an ice rink. It is best to check for any packages or specials to keep the cost down. 6–7

Evelo's B&B 2301 Bryant Ave S ⓣ612/374-9656, ⓦwww.bedandbreakfast.com/minnesota-minneapolis-evelosbedbreakfast.html. Three comfortable rooms in a well-preserved Victorian home near bus lines, lakes and downtown. Non-smoking only. 4

Hilton Minneapolis 1001 Marquette Ave ⓣ612/376-1000, ⓦwww.minneapolis.hilton.com. Elegant downtown spot with a great gym and pool. Weekend rates are considerably less. 6–8

Minneapolis International House 2400 Stevens Ave ⓣ612/874-0407, ⓦwww.minneapolishostel.com. This conveniently situated independent hostel has private rooms (1–3) and $27 dorm beds.

Nicollet Island Inn 95 Merriam St ⓣ612/331-1800, ⓦwww.nicolletislandinn.com. Pricey, mid-river establishment with the edge on other downtown hotels because of its delightful location and excellent restaurant. 8–9

St Paul

Best Western Bandana Square 1010 Bandana Blvd W ⓣ651/647-1637, ⓦwww.bestwestern.com. Straightforward rooms and a nice indoor pool and sauna housed in a former railroad car repair shop. 5

The Covington Inn Pier 1, Harriet Island ⓣ651/292-1411, ⓦwww.covingtoninn.com. A one-of-a-kind B&B in a converted towboat facing downtown. 6–8

Embassy Suites 175 E 10th St ⓣ651/224-5400 or 1-800/EMBASSY, ⓦwww.embassystpaul.com. The tropical atrium is the outstanding feature of this comfortable chain hotel on the edge of downtown. 6

The Saint Paul Hotel 350 Market St ⓣ651/292-9292 or 1-800/292-9292, ⓦwww.stpaulhotel.com. This grand, 1910 establishment is Minnesota's top hotel. Rooms tend to be smaller than those of other luxury hotels, but the staff and atmosphere make up for it. The *St Paul Grill*, in the hotel, provides some of the city's finest dining, while the classy bar has tons of great scotches and cognacs. 6

Exploring Minneapolis

Downtown Minneapolis is laid out on a simple grid. The riverfront, dubbed the **Mississippi Mile**, continues to be developed as a place for strolling, dining and entertainment. The vast Third Avenue Bridge makes an ideal vantage point for viewing **St Anthony Falls**, a controlled torrent in a wide stretch of the river. The missionary Father Hennepin discovered the falls in 1680, but it wasn't until the early nineteenth century that the first permanent settlement of present-day Minneapolis was begun nearby.

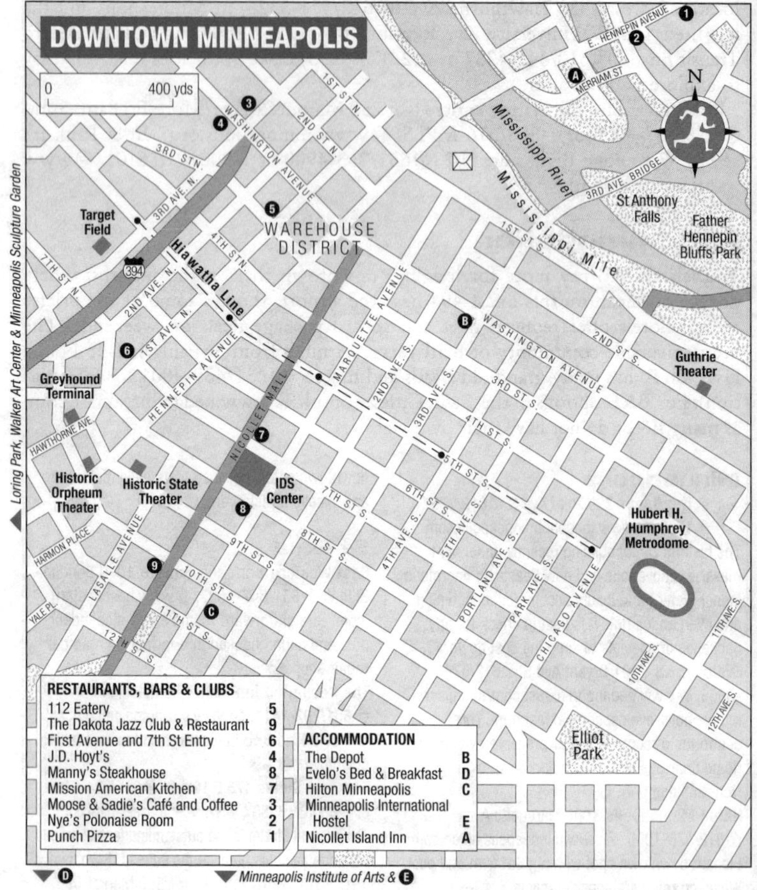

Downtown's major stores line up along the pedestrianized **Nicollet Mall**, which runs along Nicollet Avenue between Washington Avenue S and 13th Street S Hennepin Avenue, the other main drag, is a block west. It has been revitalized as an entertainment district in recent years thanks, in part, to the beautifully restored **Orpheum** and **State theatres**, twin hosts to top-quality Broadway shows and concerts. The ultramodern **Guthrie Theater**, 818 S Second St (Ⓣ612/377-2224 or 1-877/44-STAGE; Ⓦwww.guthrietheater.org), opened in 2006 on the riverfront. Even if you can't make it to one of the classic or brand-new stage productions, presented on one of the venue's three stages, the building itself is still worth a look.

Culturally, Minneapolis would be poorer without the **Walker Art Center**, 1750 Hennepin Ave S (Tues–Sun 11am–5pm, Thurs till 9pm; $10, free Thurs 5–9pm and first Sat of month; Ⓣ612/375-7622, Ⓦwww.walkerart.org). This multipurpose contemporary art and performance space underwent an expansion in 2005, nearly doubling its exhibition area. The museum balances its permanent collection of sculpture and paintings (such as German Expressionist Franz Marc's *Blue Horses*) with exciting temporary exhibitions. The eleven-acre outdoor **Sculpture Garden** (free) is a work of collective genius featuring pieces by Calder, Louise Bourgeois and Frank Gehry. Its most striking piece is the gigantic, whimsical *Spoonbridge and Cherry* by Claes Oldenburg and Coosje van Bruggen. One mile south from downtown, at 2400 Third Ave S, the huge **Minneapolis Institute of Arts** has a thoroughly comprehensive collection of art from 2000 BC to the present (Tues, Wed, Fri & Sat 10am–5pm, Thurs till 9pm, Sun 11am–5pm; free; ⓣ612/870-3200 or 888/MIAARTS, ⓦwww.artsmia.org). Arctic winters aside, hordes of Minneapolitans flock to the shores of lakes **Calhoun** and **Harriet** and also **Lake of the Isles**, all in residential areas within two miles south of downtown. The **Hubert H. Humphrey Metrodome**, 900 S Fifth St (ⓣ612/332-0386), squats on the eastern edge of downtown like a giant white pincushion; the dome is home to the state's pro football team, the Vikings. Back downtown the Twins baseball team controls the diamond within the brand-new Target Field, 1 Twins Way (ⓣ1-800/338-9467). **Minnehaha Falls**, south of downtown, was featured in Longfellow's 1855 poem "*Song of Hiawatha*" without his ever having laid eyes on it. The adjacent park is a favourite spot for hikes and picnics.

Exploring St Paul

St Paul, Minnesota's capital city, reached along I-94, has more expensive old homes and civic monuments than Minneapolis. The city has its own landing site on Harriet Island for narrated summertime **paddleboat** cruises (summer Tues–Sun noon and 2pm; $16; ⓣ651/227-1100 or 1-800/543-3908, ⓦwww.riverrides.com). Here, as well as in Minneapolis, downtown buildings are linked via skyways. Call in at the jazzy Art Deco lobby of the **City Hall & Courthouse**, Fourth and Wabasha streets, to see Swedish sculptor Carl Milles' revolving 36ft *Vision of Peace*, carved in the 1930s from white Mexican onyx. The castle-like **Landmark Center**, a couple of blocks away at Fifth and Market streets, and the glittering **Ordway Center for the Performing Arts** both overlook Rice Park, probably the prettiest little square in either city. A sculpture garden with characters from Charles Schulz's "Peanuts" comic strip, the artist himself a St Paul native, has been added to **Schulz Park** next to the Landmark Center. A few blocks east, **Town Square Park** is a lush, multi-level indoor garden in a shopping complex at Minnesota and Sixth streets. The gorgeous granite and limestone **Minnesota History Center**, 345 W Kellogg Blvd (Tues 10am–8pm, Wed–Sat till 5pm, Sun noon–5pm; open Mon in summer; $10; ⓣ651/259-3000 or 888/727-8386, ⓦwww.mnhs.org), with its extensive research facilities and some inventive exhibits for the more casual visitor, is the best place to grasp the state's story. An immense steel iguana is the doorkeeper at the exciting hands-on **Science Museum of Minnesota**, 120 W Kellogg Blvd (Mon–Sun 9.30am–9.30pm; $17; ⓣ651/221-9444, ⓦwww.smm.org), which also has a domed Omnitheater (entry included in ticket) where you can see giant-screen films.

A well-preserved five-mile Victorian boulevard, Summit Avenue, leads away from downtown. **F. Scott Fitzgerald**, who was born close by, finished his first success, *This Side of Paradise*, in 1918 while living in a modest rowhouse at no. 599. He disparaged the avenue as a "museum of American architectural failures". Look for the coffin atop no. 465, once the home of an undertaker, and visit the **James J. Hill House** at no. 240, a railroad baron's sumptuous mansion from around 1891 (tours every half-hour Wed–Sat 10am–3.30pm and Sun 1–3.30pm; $8; reservations recommended; ⓣ651/297-2555). Minnesota's first territorial governor **Alexander Ramsey**'s house, nearby at 265 S Exchange St, remains a showcase of

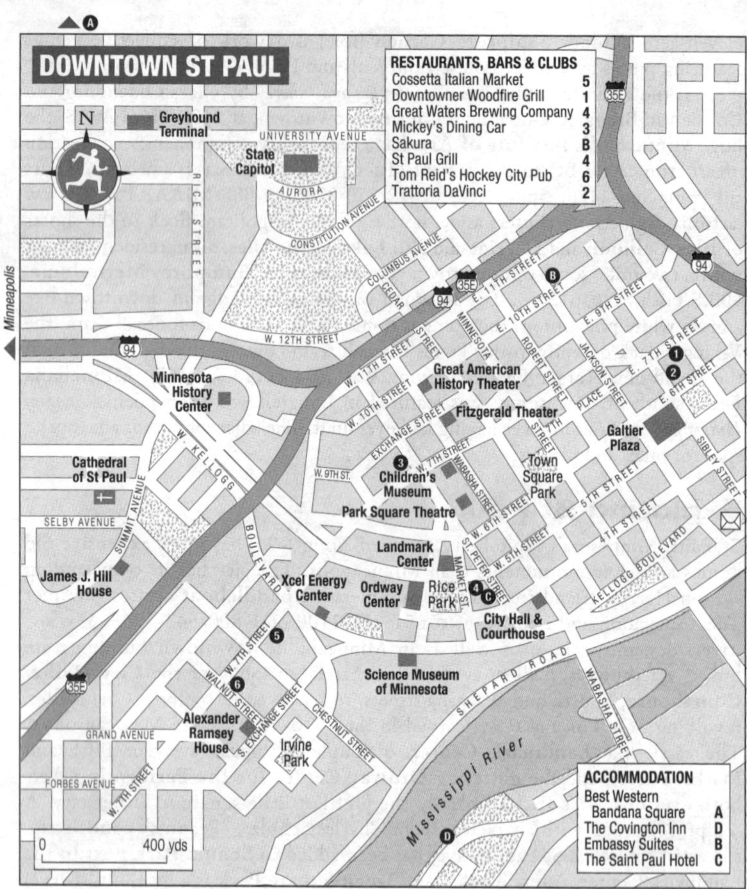

Victorian high style (tours on the hour Fri & Sat 10am–3pm, summer also Tues–Thurs 1pm; $8; ⓣ651/296-8760; reservations recommended).

Another good bet is the venerable and picturesque **Como Park Zoo and Marjorie McNeely Conservatory**, reached by taking I-94 to the Lexington Avenue exit, then continuing north on Lexington for about three miles (daily: April–Sept 10am–6pm; rest of year till 4pm; $2 donation requested; ⓣ651/487-8200). Annual celebrations in St Paul include the **Taste of Minnesota** (tons of food, live entertainment, rides and fireworks) running from late June to July 4 on Harriet Island and the nation's largest **State Fair** (end of Aug to early Sept). The **Winter Carnival** (late Jan to early Feb) is a frosty gala designed to make the most of the season with ice and snow sculpturing, hot-air ballooning, team sports, parades and more.

The Mall of America

Shopping addicts make the pilgrimage to the **Mall of America** (Mon–Sat 10am–9.30pm, Sun 11am–7pm; ⓣ952/883-8800; ⓦwww.mallofamerica.com) from all over the Midwest – and far beyond, including parties from as far away as Japan. Opened in 1992, this mind-boggling 4.2-million-square-foot, four-storey monument to consumerism tallied 42 million visits in a recent year. It incorporates more than five hundred stores, with a seven-acre Nickelodeon Universe theme park. Featured rides include **UnderWater Adventures** ($18.99), with 1.2 million gallons of water and amazing Gulf of Mexico and Caribbean aquariums. Evidence of the Mall's all-under-one-roof convenience is provided by the **Chapel of Love** retail store, where more than five thousand couples have legitimately tied the knot.

The Mall is twenty minutes south of the cities on I-494 at 24th Avenue, Bloomington. Take bus #54M from St Paul's West Sixth Street at Cedar, the #5E bus or the light rail from downtown Minneapolis; catch the train from 5th Street on Nicollet Mall.

Eating

Preconceptions of Midwestern blandness are swiftly put to rest by an almost bewildering array of **restaurants** in the Twin Cities. In **Minneapolis**, head for the downtown warehouse district, the southerly Nicollet neighbourhood, the funky Uptown and Lyn-Lake areas, or the university's Dinkytown. In **St Paul**, try Galtier Plaza downtown, the Asian restaurants on University Avenue or the horde of ethnic options all along Grand Avenue.

Minneapolis

112 Eatery 112 N 3rd St ⓣ612/343-7696. This small, upscale café serves an inventive mix of American and Continental dishes, from pork tenderloin to sautéed sweetbreads.

Bryant-Lake Bowl 810 W Lake St ⓣ612/825-3737. Bowling and fantastic food rarely go hand-in-hand, but this Lyn-Lake institution manages to do both well, turning out such creative dishes as organic chicken wings and a bison Philly sandwich.

Emily's Lebanese Deli 641 University Ave NE ⓣ612/379-4069. Friendly, low-cost local place for Lebanese staples.

Fugaise 308 E Hennepin Ave ⓣ612/436-0777. An exceptional French dining experience in the Old St Anthony neighbourhood.

J.D. Hoyts 301 Washington Ave N ⓣ612/338-1560. A traditional supper club serving down-home food at good prices.

Manny's Steakhouse 821 Marquette Ave ⓣ612/215-3700. Dry-aged, hand-trimmed and every other master butcher delicacy you can imagine at this local favourite.

Mission American Kitchen 77 S 7th St ⓣ612/339-1000. This great lunch and dinner spot serves delicious and creative starters like Truffle Cream Cheese Wontons and Deviled Eggs.

Moose & Sadie's Café and Coffee 212 3rd Ave ⓣ612/371-0464. This great breakfast and lunch spot in the warehouse district has yummy baked goods and soups like coconut milk curry.

Punch Pizza 210 Hennepin Ave ⓣ612/3623-8114. Stylish wood-fired ovens produce these popular Neapolitan pizzas.

St Paul

Acropol Inn 748 Grand Ave ⓣ651/312-1299. Mom-and-pop-styled diner serving authentic Greek fare.

Downtowner Woodfire Grill 253 W 7th St ⓣ651/228-9500. Great neighbourhood restaurant if you plan to catch a Wild game or just dinner. Weekends have live jazz music starting at 8pm.

Mickey's Dining Car 36 W 7th St ⓣ651/698-0259. Landmark 24hr diner in a 1930s dining car.

St Paul Grill 350 Market St ⓣ651/224-7455. Traditional American fare in a classic downtown hotel.

Trattoria DaVinci 400 Sibley St ⓣ651/222-4050. Exceptional Northern Italian cuisine served in an Italian Renaissance-inspired setting.

Sakura 350 Saint Peter St ⓣ651/224-0185. Fresh sushi in a relaxing environment. Great long sushi bar and smooth vibe perfect the dining experience.

W.A. Frost 374 Selby Ave and Western Ave ⓣ651/224-5715. This former pharmacy and F. Scott Fitzgerald hangout has been converted into a plush restaurant with a garden patio. The menu spans Mediterranean, Asian and Middle Eastern cuisines and features dishes like mushroom Wellington and squash ravioli; the wine cellar stocks some 3000 bottles.

Entertainment and nightlife

The Greater Twin Cities have been dubbed a "cultural Eden on the prairie", where 2.5 million people support upwards of one hundred **theatre** companies, more than forty **dance** troupes, twenty **classical music** ensembles and more than a hundred art galleries. Sir Tyrone Guthrie began the theatrical boom back in 1963, enrolling large-scale local assistance to establish the classical repertory company named for him. The cities now have more theatres per capita than anywhere in the US apart from New York City.

Unusually, **nightlife** in Minneapolis (and, to a lesser extent, St Paul) hasn't been siphoned off by suburbia – one hundred thousand students ensure a vibrant club scene. For complete entertainment information and **listings**, check out the ubiquitous free weekly *City Pages*.

Minneapolis and St Paul theatres

Chanhassen Dinner Theater 501 W 78th St, Chanhassen (24 miles west of Minneapolis) ⓣ952/934-1525 or 1-800/362-3515. Mainstream musicals, popular comedies and drama on four stages, plus meals. Thirty minutes from downtown.

Fitzgerald Theater 10 E Exchange St, St Paul ⓣ651/290-1200, ⓦwww.fitzgeraldtheater.org. Best known as the venue for Garrison Keillor's weekly *A Prairie Home Companion* performance, it also hosts other concerts and lectures.

Great American History Theater 30 E 10th St, St Paul ⓣ651/292-4323, ⓦwww.historytheatre.com. Original plays deal with events and personalities from the region's past.

Park Square 20 W 7th Place, St Paul ⓣ651/291-7005, ⓦwww.parksquaretheatre.org. The venue for well-executed classic and contemporary plays.

Penumbra 270 N Kent St, St Paul ⓣ651/224-3180, ⓦwww.penumbratheatre.org. African-American theatre company focusing on works by African-American playwrights.

Minneapolis bars and clubs

The Dakota Jazz Club and Restaurant 1010 Nicollet Mall ⓣ612/332-1010, ⓦwww.dakotacooks.com. Gourmet Midwestern food and great local and national jazz acts downtown.

First Avenue and 7th St Entry 701 1st Ave ⓣ612/338-8388 or 332-1775, ⓦwww.first-avenue.com. The landmark rock venue where Prince's *Purple Rain* was shot still packs them in with top bands and dance music.

Muddy Pig 162 N Dale St ⓣ651/254-1030. A hip neighbourhood joint with good bar food and a wide selection of microbrews.

Nye's Polonaise Room 112 E Hennepin Ave ⓣ651/379-2021. Experience old-European atmosphere at the piano and polka bars and in the Polish-American restaurant.

Tom Reid's Hockey City Pub 258 W 7th St ⓣ651/292-9916. This pre- and post-game hangout is where locals gather to honour the state's favourite sport.

Northern and southern Minnesota

Minnesota's substantial **northern** half, covered with forested lakes, remains much as it was when the Europeans first traded with the Native Americans. The northeast – **the Arrowhead**, poking into Lake Superior – holds the greatest charm: most visitors choose secluded outdoor vacations centred on fishing, canoeing and snowmobiling, but there's infinite potential for driving tours in a wilderness comparable to the Alaskan interior.

The Arrowhead is anchored by busy **Duluth**. From here, **Scenic Hwy-61** skirts the clifftops around Lake Superior, passing waterfalls, state parks and neat little towns on the way northeast to the Canadian border. Sleepy **Grand Marais** is poised at the edge of the wild **Boundary Waters Canoe Area Wilderness** and the **Gunflint Trail**, while inland, the **Iron Range** makes a scenic route north to the idyllic **Voyageurs National Park**. To the southwest, in **Itasca State Park**, the Mississippi River begins its great roll down to the Gulf of Mexico; you can cross the headwaters on stepping stones. Everywhere you'll find campgrounds and wholesome lakeside **resorts**, havens of homey simplicity dedicated to soothing urban-ravaged souls.

Southern Minnesota is split between high plains, timbered ravines and slow-flowing Mississippi tributaries in the east, and the drier, flatter prairie and chequerboard farmland of the west. In the scenic **southeast**, spared a grinding-down by the last glacial advance, attractive small towns sit along the Mississippi, or on bluffs above it, in the ninety-mile **Hiawatha Valley**. Mississippi shipping helped sustain easy-going communities like Winona, Red Wing, Lake City and Wabasha, all of which share well-preserved old homes and hotels. **Rochester** occupies the rolling farmland to the west.

Duluth

DULUTH, at the western extremity of Lake Superior, 150 miles north of Minneapolis and St Paul, forms a long crescent at the base of the Arrowhead. Named for a seventeenth-century French officer, Daniel Greysolon, Sieur du Luth (1636–1710), the town cascades down from the granite bluffs surrounding **Skyline Drive** (an exhilarating thirty-mile route) to a busy **harbour**, shared with Superior, Wisconsin. Together these "twin ports" constitute the largest inland harbour in the US.

In the 1980s, Duluth went through a rebuilding period and began to encourage tourism. The main drawback is that it's bitingly **cold** here. The seaway is frozen through the winter, and even spring and autumn evenings can be chilly. Temperatures are always significantly cooler near the lake – the location of nearly all the attractions and activities.

From the Convention and Visitors Bureau (see below), a short walk down Lake Avenue leads to the free **Marine Museum** (June to early Oct daily 10am–9pm; rest of year times vary; ⓣ218/727-2497, ⓦwww.lsmma.com) in Canal Park, a vantage point for watching big boats from around the world pass under the delightfully archaic Aerial Lift Bridge. Originating at Canal Park, Duluth's **Lakewalk** is the free way to take in the view, though in summer you can also take ninety-minute **harbour cruises** ($14; ⓣ218/722-6218 or 1-877/883-4002; ⓦwww.vistafleet.com). Also worthwhile is a visit to the stately lakeside Jacobean Revival mansion **Glensheen**, 3300 London Rd (May–Oct daily 9.30am–4pm; Nov–April Sat & Sun 11am–2pm; $15; ⓣ218/726-8910 or 1-888/454-GLEN). The vast interior features finely crafted original furnishings, and the grounds are immaculate.

Rail excursions along the Superior shoreline to the busy harbour community **Two Harbors** run from **The Depot** complex at 506 W Michigan St (early May to mid-Oct; ⓣ218/722-1273 or 1-800/423-1273, ⓦwww.lsrm.org). The Depot (summer 9.30am–6pm; winter 10am–5pm; $12) also houses the Lake Superior Railroad Museum, a children's museum, cultural heritage centre and art museum; at night, it's home to performing arts companies.

Practicalities

Greyhound **buses** pull into town four miles south of town just off I-35 at 4426 Grand Ave. The **Convention and Visitors Bureau** is at 21 W Superior St suite 100 (Mon–Fri 8.30am–5pm; ⓣ218/722-4011 or 1-800/4-DULUTH, ⓦwww.visitduluth.com). For a **place to stay**, the *Charles Weiss Inn*, 1615 E Superior St (ⓣ218/724-7016 or 1-800/525-5243, ⓦwww.acweissinn.com; ❺–❻), is a nice Victorian-styled **B&B**, while better **motels** include the *Edgewater Resort and Waterpark*, 2400 London Rd (ⓣ218/728-3601 or 1-800/777-7925; ⓦwww.duluthwaterpark.com; ❹–❺), which has a new indoor water park. Keep in mind that accommodation rates and availability fluctuate in summer. *Indian Point* **campground**, west off Hwy-23 at 75th Street and Grand Avenue (Ⓣ218/624-5637), has summer bayside tent sites for $21; full hook-ups are also available for $32.

Two of the best **dining** options in town are the revolving *Top of the Harbor*, which serves American cuisine atop the *Radisson Hotel* at 505 W Superior St (Ⓣ218/727-8981) and the lovely *Bennett's on the Lake*, 600 E Superior St (Ⓣ218/722-2829), where you can dine on steaks and seafood with a superb view of the lake.

Highway 61

Memorialized on vinyl by Minnesota native Bob Dylan, stunning **Scenic Highway 61** follows Lake Superior for 150 miles northeast from Duluth to the US/Canadian border, its precipitous cliffs interspersed with pretty little ports and picture-postcard picnic sites.

At **Gooseberry River State Park**, forty miles along from Duluth, the river splashes over volcanic rock through waterfalls and cascades to its outlet in Lake Superior. Like all but one of the seven other state parks along Hwy-61, it provides access to the rugged three-hundred-mile **Superior Hiking Trail** (Ⓣ218/834-2700), divided into easily manageable segments for day-trekkers. To camp at any of the state parks, reserve at Ⓣ1-866/857-2757.

Just beyond **Cascade River State Park**, the road dips into the somnolent little port of **GRAND MARAIS**, where a walk around the photogenic Circular Harbor will soon cure car-stiff legs. The **visitor centre**, 13 N Broadway (Ⓣ218/387-2524 or 1-888/922-5000, Ⓦwww.grandmarais.com), has lists of **outfitters** for those going into the Boundary Waters Canoe Area Wilderness (see below). The town of **GRAND PORTAGE**, just below the Canadian border, is at the lake end of the historic 8.5-mile portage route – so vital to the nineteenth-century fur trade – now preserved in the form of **Grand Portage National Monument**, where a clutch of fur-trade-era buildings has been superbly reconstructed. In town, residents of the Grand Portage Indian Reservation operate a **casino**. In summer, ferries run daily to remote **Isle Royale National Park** (see p.279).

Boundary Waters Canoe Area Wilderness and the Gunflint Trail

The huge **Boundary Waters Canoe Area Wilderness**, west of Grand Marais, is one of the most heavily used wilderness areas in the country. It's accessible from Tofte, Cook and especially from easy-going **Ely**, home of the intriguing **International Wolf Center** (hours vary; $8.50; Ⓣ218/365-4695). The wilderness is a paradise for canoeing, backpacking and fishing. Overland trails, or "portages", link more than a thousand lakes; in winter you can ski and dogsled cross-country. The unpaved sixty-mile **Gunflint Trail** from Grand Marais cuts the wilderness in two; otherwise there are no roads in this outback, let alone electricity or telephones. Most lakes remain motor-free, and stringent rules limit entry to the wilderness: in summer you need a date-specific **permit** that local outfitters can issue. If you visit again the following year, permit applications may be submitted by website, fax or mail. Phone reservations are accepted ($12 reservation fee and a $20 deposit; Ⓣ1-877/550-6777, Ⓕ518/885-9951, Ⓦwww.bwcaw.com). For those who don't want to rough it, several rustic lodges lie strung out along the trail; the **Gunflint Trail Association** (Ⓣ218/387-3191 or 1-800/338-6932, Ⓦwww.gunflint-trail.com) can offer good advice.

The Iron Range

In the **Iron Range**, a few miles west of Ely, which is itself about one hundred miles west of Grand Marais, a number of fabulously rich mines continue to function more than a century after their construction. If you're interested in surveying old workings, it's possible to descend 2300ft at the **Soudan Underground Mine State Park** on Hwy-169 (summer daily 10am–4pm; admission and vehicle fee).

Voyageurs National Park

Set along the border lakes between Minnesota and Canada, **VOYAGEURS NATIONAL PARK** is like no other in the US national park system. To see it properly, or indeed to grasp its immense beauty at all, you need to leave your car behind and venture into the wild by boat. Once out on the lakes, you're in a great, silent world. Kingfishers, osprey and eagles swoop down for their share of the abundant walleye; moose and bear stalk the banks.

The park's name comes from the intrepid eighteenth-century French-Canadian trappers, who needed almost a year to get their pelts back to Montréal in primitive birch bark canoes. Their "customary waterway" became so established that the treaty of 1783 ending the American Revolution specified it as the international border.

You can't do Voyageurs justice on a day-trip, though daily cruises from the **Rainy Lake visitor centre** (open daily mid-May to Sept 9am–5pm, Oct to mid-May Wed–Sun same hours; from $12–20 for a range of tours; ⓣ218/286-5258 ⓦwww.nps.gov/voya) do at least allow a peek at the lake country. If you're here for a few days, rent a **boat** (figure on $50 a day) and camp out. It's easy to get lost in this maze of islands and rocky outcrops, and unseen sandbanks lurk beneath the surface. If you're at all unsure, hire a guide from one of the resorts for the first day (around $250/8hr day). During **freeze-up** – usually from December until March – the park takes on a whole new aura, as a prime destination for skiers and snowmobilers.

Practicalities

Most travellers access Voyageurs from Hwy-53, which runs northwest from Duluth. After just over one hundred miles, at Orr, Hwy-53 intersects with Rte-23, which runs northeast toward **Crane Lake**, at the eastern end of the park. About 28 and 31 miles past Hwy-53's junction with Rte-23, highways 129 and 122 lead, respectively, to the **visitor centres** at **Ash River** (May–Sept daily 9am–5pm; ⓣ218/374-3221) and **Kabetogama Lake** (same hours; ⓣ218/875-2111). Another prime visitor centre is at **Rainy Lake**, at the westernmost entrance, 36 miles farther on via International Falls.

Once inside the park, you need to take a few **precautions**. Check (natural) mercury levels in fish before eating them, don't pick wild rice (only Native Americans may do this), be wary of Lyme Disease (a tick-induced gastric illness), boil drinking water and watch out for bears. Discuss such matters along with customs procedures, in case you plan to paddle into Canadian waters, with a ranger before venturing out.

The definitive way to experience the park is to **camp** on one of its many scattered islands, most plentiful around Crane Lake (if you don't have your own boat, cruise operators can drop you off and pick you up at a later date). There are also first-come, first-served state-owned campgrounds on the mainland at Ash River and Woodenfrog, near Kabetogama. However, most visitors stay in one of more than sixty **resorts**. Basically family-run cottages, these usually cater for weekly stays, with all meals, though you can rent rooms nightly. Kayak in or take a boat taxi to *Kettle Falls Hotel*, a perfectly rustic way to experience Voyageurs. They have a wide range of lodging options and day-trips (Ⓦwww .kettlefallshotel.com; open seasonally ❷–❽).

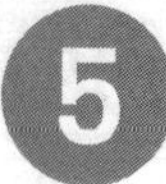

The Capital Region

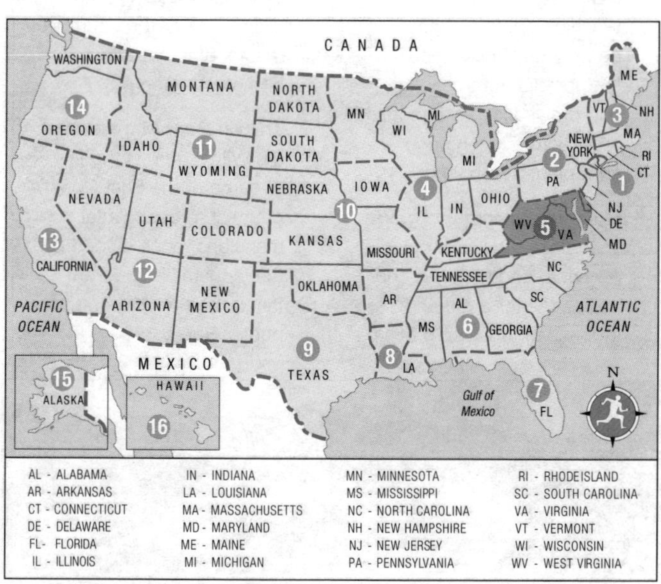

CHAPTER 5

Highlights

* **National Gallery of Art, Washington DC** One of the country's premier Institutions for art and culture, laid out in spacious, elegant surroundings on the National Mall. **See p.341**

* **Georgetown, Washington DC** Though now part of Washington, this eighteenth-century neighbourhood long predates the capital and draws visitors with its architecture, dining and shopping. **See p.347**

* **Colonial Williamsburg, VA** This close replica of colonial America, apothecaries and all, makes for a fun and interesting trip. **See p.361**

* **Monticello, VA** Thomas Jefferson's home is as much an architectural icon as it is a symbol of democracy. **See p.368**

* **New River Gorge, WV** A spectacular river canyon with a 1000ft chasm carved in steep-walled limestone cliffs – one of the country's outstanding natural attractions. **See p.377**

* **The du Pont Mansions, DE** Wilmington is the site of some of the East Coast's greatest, most palatial mansions, once owned by the industrialist du Pont family, and now open to the public. **See p.392**

▲ New River Gorge

The Capital Region

The city of Washington, in the District of Columbia, and the four surrounding states of Virginia, West Virginia, Maryland and Delaware are collectively known as the **CAPITAL REGION**. Since the days of the first American colonies, US history has been shaped here, from the Jamestown landings to agitation for independence, to the battles of the Revolutionary and Civil wars to 1960s Civil Rights milestones and protest movements on issues including war, abortion and gay rights.

Early in the seventeenth century, the first British settlements began to take root along the rich estuary of the **Chesapeake Bay**; the colonists hoped for gold but found their fortunes in tobacco. Virginia, the first settlement, was the largest and most populous. Half of its people were **slaves**, brought from Africa to do the backbreaking work of harvesting the "noxious weed" of tobacco. Despite its central position on the East Coast, almost all of the region lies below the Mason-Dixon Line – the symbolic border between North and South, drawn up in 1763 to resolve a border dispute, but which became the symbolic boundary between free and unfree states. Slaves helped build the Capitol, and until the Civil War one of the country's busiest slave markets was just two blocks from the White House.

Tensions between North and South finally erupted into the **Civil War**, of which traces are still visible everywhere. The hundred miles between the capital of the Union – Washington DC – and that of the Confederacy – Richmond, Virginia – were a constant and bloody battleground for four long years.

Washington DC, itself, with its magnificent monumental architecture and terrific museums, is an essential stop on any tour of the region, or of the country in general. **Virginia**, to the south, is home to hundreds of historic sites, from the estates of revolutionary leaders and early politicians to the Colonial capital of **Williamsburg**, as well as the narrow forested heights of **Shenandoah National Park**, along the crest of the Blue Ridge Mountains. Much greater expanses of wilderness, crashing whitewater rivers and innumerable backwoods villages await you in far less-visited **West Virginia**. Most tourists come to **Maryland** for the maritime traditions of Chesapeake Bay, though many of its quaint old villages have been gentrified by weekend pleasure-boaters. **Baltimore** is full of character, enjoyably unpretentious if a bit ramshackle, while **Annapolis**, the pleasant state capital, is linked by bridge and ferry to the Eastern Shore. **New Castle**, across the border in **Delaware**, is a well-preserved colonial-era town; nearby are some of the East Coast's best and least crowded beaches.

Getting around the Capital Region

The relative ease of getting around the Capital Region depends on the state. **Driving** is the first choice if you want to see the greatest number of sights. Routes

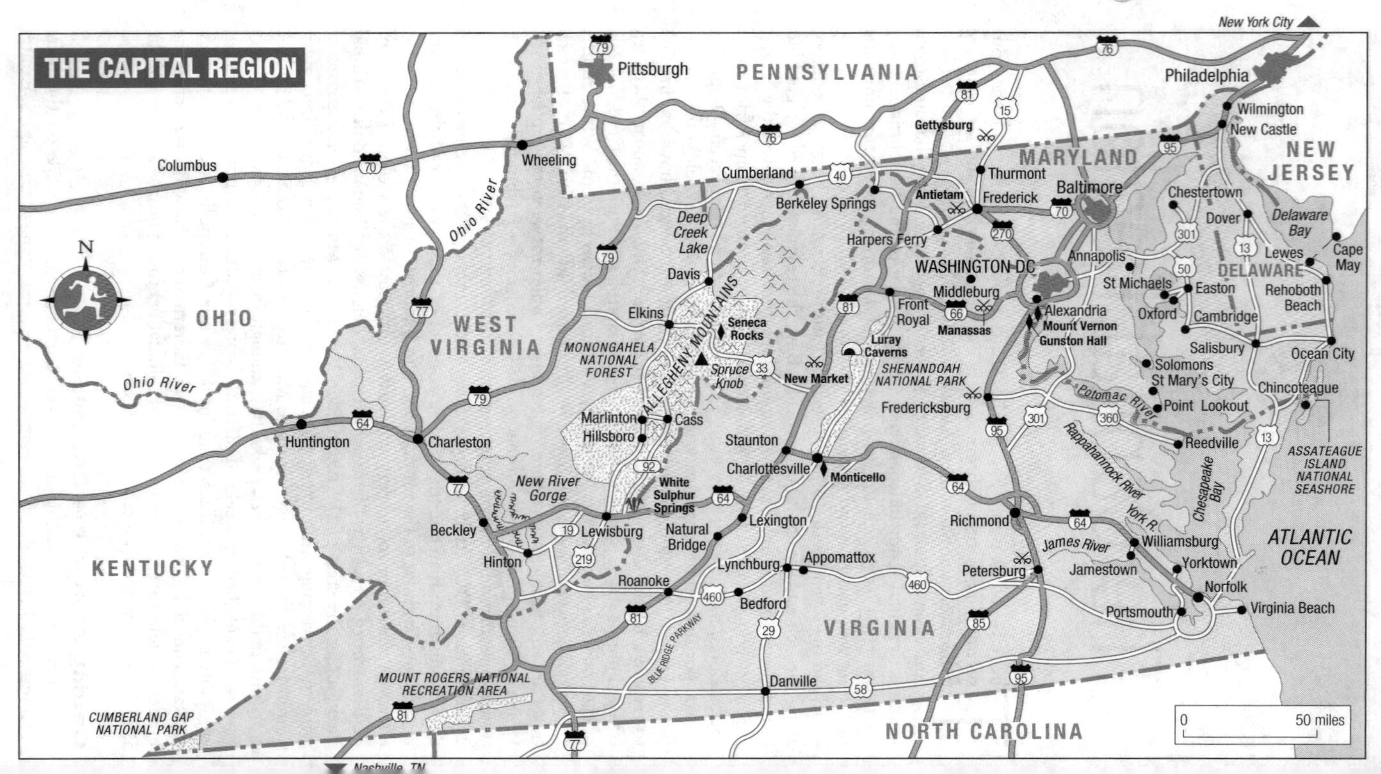
THE CAPITAL REGION
New York City
Pittsburgh
PENNSYLVANIA
Philadelphia
Wilmington
New Castle
NEW JERSEY
Gettysburg
MARYLAND
Thurmont
Baltimore
Frederick
Antietam
Columbus
Wheeling
Ohio River
Cumberland
Berkeley Springs
Chestertown
Dover
Delaware Bay
Deep Creek Lake
Harpers Ferry
Annapolis
Lewes
Cape May
WASHINGTON DC
DELAWARE
Davis
St Michaels
Easton
Rehoboth Beach
Middleburg
Elkins
Front Royal
Manassas
Alexandria
Mount Vernon
Gunston Hall
Oxford
Cambridge
Seneca Rocks
OHIO
WEST VIRGINIA
MONONGAHELA NATIONAL FOREST
ALLEGHENY MOUNTAINS
Luray Caverns
Salisbury
Ocean City
Solomons
St Mary's City
Spruce Knob
New Market
SHENANDOAH NATIONAL PARK
Potomac River
Chincoteague
Ohio River
Point Lookout
Fredericksburg
Marlinton
Cass
Hillsboro
Huntington
Charleston
Staunton
Reedville
ASSATEAGUE ISLAND NATIONAL SEASHORE
Rappahannock River
Chesapeake Bay
Charlottesville
Monticello
New River Gorge
White Sulphur Springs
York R.
Richmond
ATLANTIC OCEAN
Beckley
Lewisburg
Lexington
Natural Bridge
Williamsburg
James River
Appomattox
Lynchburg
Petersburg
Jamestown
Yorktown
KENTUCKY
Hinton
Roanoke
Norfolk
Bedford
Portsmouth
Virginia Beach
BLUE RIDGE PARKWAY
VIRGINIA
Danville
MOUNT ROGERS NATIONAL RECREATION AREA
CUMBERLAND GAP NATIONAL PARK
NORTH CAROLINA
0
50 miles
Nashville, TN
N

such as the stunning Blue Ridge Parkway along the Appalachians can make for incredibly scenic drives, with numerous waysides to explore as you go. In West Virginia, which is wholly built around mountains and rivers, straight, flat roads are virtually nonexistent and you should plan on allowing plenty of time to traverse the narrow, serpentine roads up and down. In Delaware, you'll also be hard-pressed to get around without a car.

For public transit in Virginia, five north–south Amtrak **train** routes cross the central and eastern side of the state, and Greyhound **buses** reach dozens of smaller towns. In Maryland, Baltimore is on the main Amtrak route between New York and Washington DC, and it and other cities are linked by regular buses. West Virginia options are more limited: Greyhound mostly travels the western side of the state along Hwy-77, while Amtrak's Cardinal line crosses the southeast part and the Capitol Limited goes from DC via Harpers Ferry on to the Great Lakes. In Delaware, Wilmington is on the main East Coast **train** and **bus** routes, and Greyhound stops only at Wilmington and Dover.

As for alternative transport options, one of the more evocative ways to get around Maryland and Virginia is by **boat**, sailing around the gorgeous Chesapeake Bay. If you've got the time, there is also ample opportunity for **cycling** in the region, whether on quiet country roads or up in the mountains, and **hiking** or **walking** are compelling choices — especially on the Eastern Shore of Maryland and Virginia, where the roads are wide-shouldered and sparsely travelled.

Washington DC

WASHINGTON, DISTRICT OF COLUMBIA (the boundaries of the two are identical) can be unbearably hot and humid in summer, and bitterly cold in winter. It was chosen as the site of the **capital** of the newly independent United States of America because of a compromise between the northern and southern states and, basically, because George Washington wanted it there – 16 miles upstream from his Mount Vernon estate. The other side of DC, with a majority black population, is run as a virtual colony of Congress, where residents have only non-voting representation and couldn't vote in presidential elections until the 23rd amendment was passed in 1961 – the city's official license plate reads "Taxation Without Representation".

The best times to come are during April's National Cherry Blossom Festival and the more temperate months (May–June and Sept). The nation's showcase puts on quite a display for its guests, and, best of all, admission to all major attractions on the **National Mall** is free; the most famous sites include the White House, memorials to four of the greatest presidents and the superb museums of the Smithsonian Institution. In recent years, even the once-blighted area known as **Old Downtown** (north of the eastern side of the Mall), has had a dramatic uptick in visitors and nightlife around its **Penn Quarter**, centred around 7th and F streets. Still, you're more likely to spend your evenings in the hotels and restaurants of the city's most vibrant neighbourhoods: historic **Georgetown**, arty **Dupont Circle** and funky **Adams Morgan**.

Some history

Once the site of the national capital was chosen, Maryland and Virginia ceded sovereignty of a diamond-shaped tract to the federal government (though a half-century later Virginia demanded its land back). Although George Washington's baroque, radial plan of the city was laid out in 1791 by a Frenchman, **Pierre L'Enfant**, few buildings were put up, apart from the actual houses of government, until well into the next century. Charles Dickens, visiting in 1842, found "spacious avenues that begin in nothing and lead nowhere". After the **Civil War**, thousands of Southern blacks arrived in search of a sanctuary from racial oppression; to some extent, they found one. By the 1870s African-Americans made up more than a third of the 150,000 population, but as poverty and squalor became endemic, official **segregation** was reintroduced in 1920. After **World War II**, the city's economy and population boomed. Segregation of public facilities was declared illegal in the 1950s, and Martin Luther King Jr gave a famous 1963 speech on the steps of the Lincoln Memorial. When King was killed five years later, large sections of the city's ghettos burned, and are only now being rebuilt, as gentrified, high-rent neighbourhoods. Indeed, the revitalized downtown, with its chic restaurants, and cultural and sporting events, has begun to attract visitors once again to an area once considered an urban wasteland.

Arrival and information

Washington DC is served by three major **airports**, two on the outskirts and one right in the city centre. **Dulles International Airport**, 26 miles west in northern Virginia (IAD; ⓣ703/572-2700, ⓦwww.mwaa.com/dulles), and **Baltimore-Washington International Airport** (BWI), halfway between DC and Baltimore (BWI; ⓣ410/859-7111, ⓦwww.bwiairport.com), get the majority of the international traffic. By far the most convenient, **Ronald Reagan Washington National Airport**, west across the Potomac River from the Mall (DCA; ⓣ703/417-8000, ⓦwww.metwashairports.com), is mostly used by domestic flights.

You can take a **taxi** downtown from BWI or Dulles ($60), while SuperShuttle (ⓣ1-800/BLUE-VAN, ⓦwww.supershuttle.com) offers **door-to-door** service from Dulles (45min; $29) and National (15min; $12). Cheaper are the express **buses** that run every half-hour from both airports to nearby Metro subway stations. From Dulles, take the Washington Flyer Express Bus (ⓣ1-888/WASH-FLY, ⓦwww.washfly.com) to the West Falls Church Metro station (30min; $10, return $18), from which you can access downtown. From BWI, a free shuttle service connects the airport with the BWI rail terminal (10–15min). The most economical choice is the southbound Penn Line of the **Maryland Rail Commuter Service** (MARC; $6 one-way ⓣ410/539-5000, ⓦmta.maryland.gov), providing frequent peak-hour departures to Washington's Union Station, a forty-minute trip. The station is also reached from BWI by the quicker daily **Amtrak** trains; $10 regular, $34 express (ⓦwww.amtrak.com), which take 30 minutes, with regular services. National Airport conveniently has its own subway stop and is just a short ride from the city centre. A **taxi** downtown from National costs around $20.

By **train**, you arrive amid the gleaming, Neoclassical spectre of **Union Station**, 50 Massachusetts Ave NE, three blocks north of the US Capitol and with a connecting Metro station. Greyhound and other **buses** stop at a modern terminal at 1005 First St NE, in a fairly dodgy part of the city, a few blocks north of the Union Station Metro; take a cab, especially at night. **Driving** into DC is a sure way to experience some of the worst traffic on the East Coast – the main I-95 and I-495 freeways circle Washington on the **Beltway** and are jammed eighteen hours a day.

Once in the city, stop at the **DC Chamber of Commerce Visitor Center**, 1213 K St NW (Mon–Fri 9am–4.30pm; ⓣ1-866/324-7386, ⓦwww.dcchamber.org), which can help with maps, tours, bookings and information. The **White House Visitor Information Center**, not located at the president's mansion, but downtown at 1450 Pennsylvania Ave NW (daily 7.30am–4pm; ⓣ202/208-1631, ⓦwww.nps.gov/whho), supplies free maps and handy guides to museums and attractions.

The **Benjamin Franklin Post Office**, 1200 Pennsylvania Ave NW (Mon–Fri 9am–5pm, Sat 11am–1pm; ⓣ202/842-1444), is one of the most central post offices.

City transport

Getting around DC is easy. The most prominent sights, including the museums, monuments and White House, are within walking distance of each other, and an excellent **public transit** system reaches outlying sights and neighbourhoods. The expansive **Metro subway** (ⓣ202/637-7000, ⓦwww.wmata.com) is clean and efficient (trains run Mon–Thurs 5am–midnight, Fri 5am–3am, Sat 7am–3am, & Sun 7am–midnight). Single fares start at $1.45; during rush hours the fare is $1.75 (5am–9.30am & 3–7pm); and if you're going out to the suburbs the one-way fare can be up to $4.50. **Day passes** cost $8.30 and are valid weekdays (from 9.30am) and all day on weekends. **Weekly passes** are $27.90 – good for fares of up to $2.65 during weekday rush hours and all fares at other times. The standard fare on the extensive **bus** network is $1.45, or $3.20 for express buses. **Taxis** are a good alternative: if travelling in the downtown core, most journeys are around $10 and most cross-town fares are no more than $20. There are taxi stands at major hotels and transportation terminals (like Union Station). For more information, call the **DC Taxicab Commission** at ⓣ202/645-6018 or visit ⓦdctaxi.dc.gov. There's also the special "**DC Circulator**" (ⓣ202/962-1423, ⓦwww.dccirculator.com), which covers major sights on five routes via shuttle bus. During the day, **Tourmobiles** (daily 8.30am–4.30pm; $30–32; ⓣ202/554-5100, ⓦwww.tourmobile.com) connect the major museums and sights, allowing you to stop for as long as you choose at fifteen to twenty different locations.

Accommodation

Washington DC is one of the most expensive places to **stay** in America outside of New York. Most DC **hotels** cater to business travellers and political lobbyists, and during the week are quite expensive. At weekends, however, many cut their rates by up to fifty percent, or up to $100 or so. Alternatively, if you really want to save money, numerous chain hotels on the suburban outskirts have affordable rates and Metro access. For a list of vacancies, call WDCA Hotels (ⓣ1-800/554-2220, ⓦwww.wdcahotels.com), which provides a hotel reservation and travel-planning service.

Similarly, a number of **B&B** agencies offer comfortable doubles starting from $60 in the low season: try Capitol Reservations (ⓦwww.capitolreservations.com) or Bed & Breakfast Accommodations, Ltd (ⓣ1-877/893-3233, ⓦwww.bedandbreakfastdc.com). Wherever you go, make sure the facility has **air conditioning**; DC can be unbearably stifling in the summer without it.

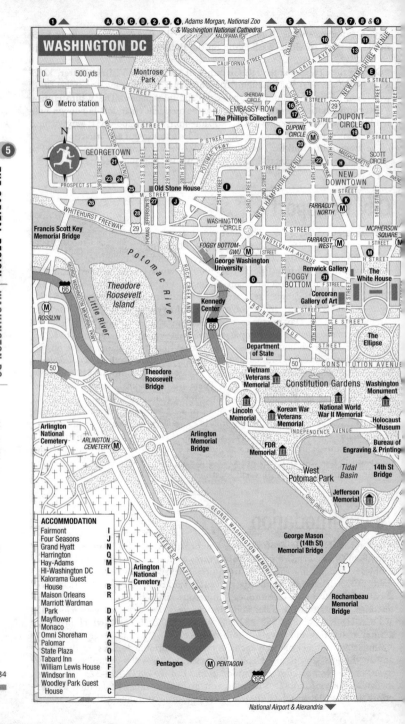

WASHINGTON DC

1 ▲ A, B, C, D, 2, 3, 4, Adams Morgan, National Zoo & Washington National Cathedral ▲ 5 ▲ ▲ 6, 7, 8 & 9

0 500 yds

M Metro station

N

GEORGETOWN
Montrose Park
EMBASSY ROW
The Phillips Collection
DUPONT CIRCLE
SHERIDAN CIRCLE
SCOTT CIRCLE
NEW DOWNTOWN
FARRAGUT NORTH
FARRAGUT WEST
MCPHERSON SQUARE
Old Stone House
WASHINGTON CIRCLE
FOGGY BOTTOM-GWU
George Washington University
Renwick Gallery
The White House
FOGGY BOTTOM
Corcoran Gallery of Art
Kennedy Center
Department of State
The Ellipse
Francis Scott Key Memorial Bridge
Potomac River
Theodore Roosevelt Island
Little River
ROSSLYN
Theodore Roosevelt Bridge
Vietnam Veterans Memorial
Constitution Gardens
Washington Monument
Lincoln Memorial
Korean War Veterans Memorial
National World War II Memorial
Holocaust Museum
Arlington National Cemetery
ARLINGTON CEMETERY
Arlington Memorial Bridge
FDR Memorial
Bureau of Engraving & Printing
West Potomac Park
Tidal Basin
14th St Bridge
Jefferson Memorial
George Mason (14th St) Memorial Bridge
Rochambeau Memorial Bridge
Pentagon
PENTAGON

ACCOMMODATION	
Fairmont	I
Four Seasons	J
Grand Hyatt	N
Harrington	Q
Hay-Adams	M
HI-Washington DC	L
Kalorama Guest House	B
Maison Orleans	R
Marriott Wardman Park	D
Mayflower	K
Monaco	P
Omni Shoreham	A
Palomar	G
State Plaza	O
Tabard Inn	H
William Lewis House	F
Windsor Inn	E
Woodley Park Guest House	C

National Airport & Alexandria ▼

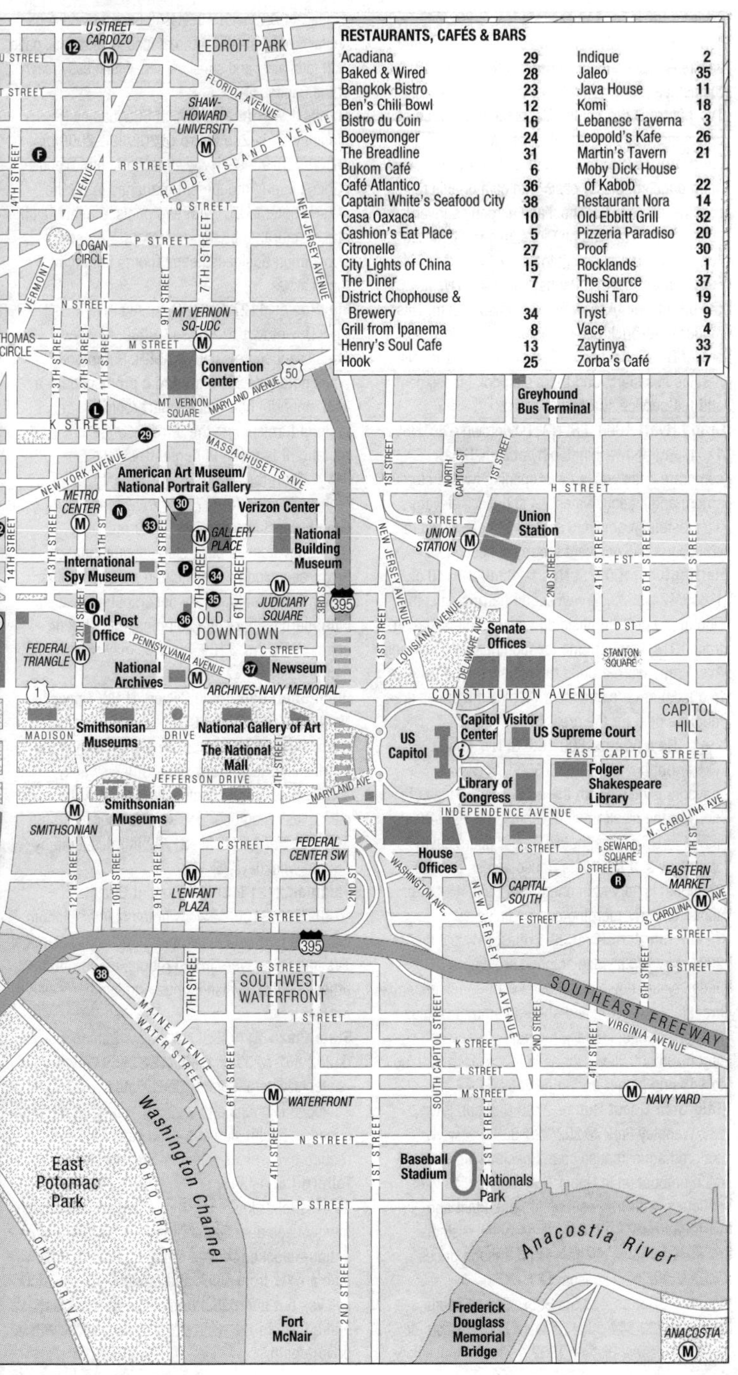

RESTAURANTS, CAFÉS & BARS

Acadiana	29	Indique	2
Baked & Wired	28	Jaleo	35
Bangkok Bistro	23	Java House	11
Ben's Chili Bowl	12	Komi	18
Bistro du Coin	16	Lebanese Taverna	3
Booeymonger	24	Leopold's Kafe	26
The Breadline	31	Martin's Tavern	21
Bukom Café	6	Moby Dick House of Kabob	22
Café Atlantico	36	Restaurant Nora	14
Captain White's Seafood City	38	Old Ebbitt Grill	32
Casa Oaxaca	10	Pizzeria Paradiso	20
Cashion's Eat Place	5	Proof	30
Citronelle	27	Rocklands	1
City Lights of China	15	The Source	37
The Diner	7	Sushi Taro	19
District Chophouse & Brewery	34	Tryst	9
Grill from Ipanema	8	Vace	4
Henry's Soul Cafe	13	Zaytinya	33
Hook	25	Zorba's Café	17

Adam's Inn 1744 Lanier Place NW ⓣ202/745-3600 or 1-800/578-6807, ⓦwww.adamsinn.com. Three adjoining Victorian townhouses with simple B&B rooms near the zoo in Adams Morgan. No in-room TVs, but free wi-fi, continental breakfast, garden patio and laundry. Sharing a bath saves you $30. ❺

Fairmont 2401 M St NW ⓣ202/429-2400, ⓦwww.fairmont.com. Classy oasis with comfortable rooms, pool, health club, whirlpool and garden courtyard. Just north of Washington Circle, midway between Foggy Bottom and Georgetown. ❾

Four Seasons 2800 Pennsylvania Ave NW ⓣ202/342-0444, ⓦwww.fourseasons.com. This modern red-brick pile in eastern Georgetown is one of DC's most luxurious and expensive hotels. Service is superb, and there's a pool, fitness centre and full-service spa. ❾

Grand Hyatt 1000 H St NW, Downtown ⓣ202/582-1234, ⓦgrandwashington.hyatt.com. Smart corporate hotel with an eye-opening twelve-storey atrium and lagoon, waterfalls and glass elevators, plus tasteful rooms and an on-site café, restaurant and sports bar. Adjacent Metro connection. ❾

Harrington 1100 E St NW ⓣ202/628-8140 or 1-800/424-8532, ⓦwww.hotel-harrington.com. One of the old and basic downtown hotels, dating from 1914, with a prime location near Pennsylvania Ave. Pretty worn around the edges, rooms (singles to quads) are a/c and have TV, plus the prices are tough to beat for the area. ❺

Hay-Adams 800 16th St NW, Foggy Bottom ⓣ202/638-6600, ⓦwww.hayadams.com. From the gold-leaf and walnut lobby to the sleek modern rooms, the *Hay-Adams* is one of DC's finest hotels. Upper floors have great views of the White House across the square. Breakfast is served in one of the District's better spots for early-morning power dining. ❾

HI-Washington DC 1009 11th St NW ⓣ202/737-2333, ⓦwww.hiwashingtondc.org. Large (270 beds), clean, downtown hostel with free continental breakfast and wi-fi, and shared bathrooms, plus kitchen, lounge, laundry, luggage storage and organized activities. Dorms in low season $29, up to $45 and higher during peak travel. ❶

Kalorama Guest House 2700 Cathedral Ave NW, Woodley Park ⓣ202/328-0860, ⓦwww.kaloramaguesthouse.com. Spacious Victorian accommodation in Upper Northwest, filled with antiques, with free continental breakfast and wi-fi (but no TV). Booking is essential – single rooms can be as cheap as $85, though prices spike in the high season. ❺

Maison Orleans 414 5th St SE, Capitol South Metro ⓣ202/544-3694, ⓦwww.bbonline.com/dc/maisonorleans. Historic 1902 rowhouse that's now a pleasant B&B with wireless net access and continental breakfast, plus a trio of functional rooms, patio with fountains, and small garden, within easy reach of the Capitol. ❻

Marriott Wardman Park 2660 Woodley Rd NW, Woodley Park–Zoo Metro ⓣ202/328-2000 or 1-800/228-9290, ⓦwww.marriott.com. Woodley Park's historic monument manages to be the largest hotel in DC, with two pools, a health club and restaurants bristling with cracking staff. Convention business keeps rooms full most of the year. ❾

Mayflower 1127 Connecticut Ave NW, New Downtown ⓣ202/347-3000, ⓦwww.renaissancehotels.com/WASSH. Sumptuous Washington classic featuring a promenade – a vast, imperial hall – and smart rooms with subtle, tasteful furnishings; the terrific *Café Promenade* restaurant is much in demand. ❾

Monaco 700 F St NW, Downtown ⓣ202/628-7177, ⓦwww.monaco-dc.com. Grand, Neoclassical former post office that today houses ultra-chic accommodation. Features include sophisticated modern rooms, minimalist contemporary decor, public spaces with marble floors and columns, and striking spiral stairways. $189, but weekday rates can double. ❼–❾

Omni Shoreham 2500 Calvert St NW, Upper Northwest ⓣ202/234-0700, ⓦwww.omnihotels.com. Plush institution bursting with history and overlooking Rock Creek Park. Offers swanky, comfortable rooms, many with a view of the park, plus an outdoor pool, tennis courts and the *Marquee Bar* for drinks. $179 but rates jump by $80 on weekdays. ❼–❽

Palomar 2121 P St NW, Dupont Circle ⓣ202/293-3100, ⓦwww.hotelpalomar-dc.com. Excellent boutique accommodation with flat-panel TVs and CD players in the rooms, an on-site pool, fitness centre, stylish lounge and location close to the Circle. ❽

State Plaza 2117 E St NW, Foggy Bottom ⓣ202/861-8200 or 1-800/424-2859, ⓦwww.stateplaza.com. Commodious suites with fully equipped kitchens and a dining area, plus a rooftop sundeck, health club and good café. Peak periods require three-night minimum stay. ❺–❼

Tabard Inn 1739 N St NW ⓣ202/785-1277, ⓦwww.tabardinn.com. Three converted Victorian townhouses near Dupont Circle, with forty unique, antique-stocked rooms. Old fixtures and furnishings are far from sleek and modern (no elevators or TVs), but affordable rates include breakfast and a pass to the nearby YMCA. ❺, or ❻ with private bath.

William Lewis House 1309 R St NW ⓣ202/462-7574 or 1-800/465-7574, ⓦwww.wlewishous.com. Elegantly decorated, gay-friendly B&B set in two century-old townhouses north of Logan Circle. All ten antique-filled rooms have shared bath and net access. Outside there's a roomy porch and a garden with a hot tub. Rates include breakfast. It's ultra-cheap for what you get, so reservations are essential. ❹

Windsor Inn 1842 16th St NW ⓣ202/667-0300 or 1-800/423-9111, ⓦwww.windsor-inn-dc.com. Not too far from Dupont Circle, with units in twin, brick, 1920s houses and spacious suites. Some rooms have fridges and ground-floor rooms look onto a terrace. Free wi-fi access and continental breakfast. ❻

Woodley Park Guest House 2647 Woodley Rd NW, Upper Northwest ⓣ202/667-0218 or 1-866/667-0218, ⓦwoodleyparkguesthouse.com. Sixteen cosy rooms (the cheapest share facilities) that come with free continental breakfast. Close to the zoo, the Metro and plenty of good restaurants. ❺, add $30 for double occupancy with private bath.

The City

With the US Capitol as the centre of the street grid, the District is divided into four **quadrants** – northeast, northwest, southeast and southwest. Dozens of broad **avenues**, named after states, run diagonally across a standard grid of **streets**, meeting up at monumental traffic circles like Dupont Circle. Almost all the most famous sights are on **Capitol Hill** or, running two miles west, the broad, green **National Mall**, which holds monuments to famous presidents, as well as the **White House**, official home of the current president. Also here are the bulk of the city's many fine museums, including the peerless collections of the **Smithsonian Institution**.

Between the Mall and the main spine of **Pennsylvania Avenue** – the route connecting Capitol Hill to the White House – the Neoclassical buildings of the **Federal Triangle** are home to agencies forming the hub of the national bureaucracy. North and east of here, **Old Downtown** features splashy new plazas, galleries and restaurants, while west of the White House, **Foggy Bottom** is another cornerstone of the federal bureaucracy. Further northwest is the city's oldest area, **Georgetown**, where popular bars and restaurants line M Street and Wisconsin Avenue above the **Potomac River**. Other neighbourhoods to check out – especially for hotels, restaurants and bars – are **Dupont Circle** at Massachusetts, Connecticut and New Hampshire avenues, and the gentrifying community of **Adams Morgan**, a favoured destination of the weekend party crowd. More gung-ho visitors may also want to follow the Red Line Metro out to the genteel precinct of **Upper Northwest**, which offers some interesting historical neighbourhoods, along with the National Zoo. Most tourists also walk or take the short Metro ride to **Arlington** in Virginia to see the National Cemetery, burial place of John F. Kennedy.

Capitol Hill

Although there's more than one hill in Washington DC, when people talk about what's happening on **"The Hill"**, they mean **Capitol Hill** – an 88ft knoll topped by the giant white edifice and dome of the US Capitol. Home of both the legislature – **Congress** – and the judiciary – the **Supreme Court** – this is the place where the law of the land is made and interpreted; in addition, it's the site of the esteemed **Library of Congress** and **Folger Shakespeare Library**.

US Capitol

The **US Capitol**, at the east end of the National Mall, between Constitution and Independence avenues (ⓣ202/226-8000, ⓦwww.visitthecapitol.gov), is the most prominent sight in Washington DC and the most essential stop to visit for most newcomers to town.

George Washington laid the building's cornerstone in 1793 in a ceremony rich with Masonic symbolism, and though the Capitol was torched by the British during the War of 1812, it was later rebuilt and repeatedly expanded over the ensuing centuries. Ten presidents – most recently Gerald Ford – have lain in state in the impressive **Rotunda**, which, capped by a massive cast-iron dome 180ft high and 96ft across, links the two halves of the Capitol – the **Senate** in the north wing, the **House of Representatives** in the south. When the "Tholos" lantern above the dome is lit, Congress is in session. The Rotunda is decorated with massive frescoes and paintings of national heroes, and other highlights include the esteemed casts of famous personages in **National Statuary Hall**; the **historic chambers** for the US Senate and Supreme Court; and the **Crypt** where George Washington was supposed to be buried, but which now serves as an exhibition hall. **Tours** of the building or visits to the House and Senate require prior arrangement: for American citizens, through the office of their US senator or representative; for foreign visitors, through their embassy.

Most visitors' first look inside the building will come via the recently opened **Capitol Visitor Center** (Mon–Sat 8.30am–4.30pm; free; no reservation needed), a $600 million underground showpiece that took more than eight years to finish and contains around half a million square feet for exhibitions, meeting halls and dining facilities. In addition to offering access to the Capitol, the Center features a massive **Emancipation Hall** that, among other things, contains a plaster cast of the Statue of Freedom, two skylights offering you a chance to experience a magisterial view of the dome and around two dozen statues that state governments have donated to National Statuary Hall, but which have ended up here instead, in the overflow space, among them the figures of Sacagawea and Helen Keller. The **Exhibition Hall** is where you can find out all about the building – including an 11ft model of the dome – and the role it played in the nation's democracy, including biographies and information about some of the key figures in congressional history, and the various inaugurations that have taken place.

Library of Congress

With 140 million books, manuscripts, microfilm rolls and photographs kept on 530 miles of shelves, the **Library of Congress** is the largest library in the world. Housed east of the Capitol in the Jefferson, Madison and John Adams buildings between 1st and 3rd streets SE and E Capitol and C streets SE (hours vary; often Mon–Sat 8.30am–4.30pm or until 9.30pm; free; ⓣ202/707-8000, ⓦwww.loc.gov), the library was set up to serve members of Congress in 1800. In 1870, the library became the national copyright repository, and in time it outgrew its original home. The exuberantly eclectic **Thomas Jefferson Building** opened in 1897, complete with a domed octagonal **Reading Room** and hundreds of mosaics, murals and sculptures in its stunning Great Hall. The library's huge collection is showcased on the second floor in the **main gallery**, where periodic exhibitions are based around broad subjects. You must sign up to do **research** in the collection, since this is a non-circulating library; also, free **tours** depart Monday to Saturday at 10.30am, 11.30am, 1.30pm, 2.30pm and 3.30pm (with the latter tour time not available on Sat).

Supreme Court

The **Supreme Court**, across from the US Capitol, at 1st St NE and Maryland Avenue NE (Mon–Fri 9am–4.30pm; free; ⓣ202/479-3211, ⓦwww.supremecourtus.gov), is the nation's final arbiter of what is and isn't legal. The federal judiciary dates to 1787, but the court didn't receive its own building until 1935, when Cass Gilbert – architect of New York's Woolworth Building – designed this Greek Revival masterpiece. The Court is in session from October to June.

Between the beginning of October and the end of April, oral arguments are heard every Monday, Tuesday and Wednesday from 10am to noon, and 1pm to 3pm on occasion. The sessions, which almost always last one hour per case, are open to the public on a first-come, first-served basis. Arrive by 8.30am if you really want one of the 150 seats.

Folger Shakespeare Library

The renowned **Folger Shakespeare Library**, 201 E Capitol St (Mon–Sat 10am–5pm; tours Mon–Fri 11am & 3pm, Sat 11am & 1pm; free; Ⓦwww.folger.edu), on the south side of the Supreme Court, was founded in 1932 and today holds more than 600,000 items including books, manuscripts, paintings and engravings, many of them related to Shakespeare's work and background – although most are off-limits unless you're a registered researcher. The dark-oak Great Hall – with its carved lintels, stained glass, Tudor roses and sculpted ceiling – displays public exhibitions about the playwright and Elizabethan themes, and the reproduction Elizabethan Theater hosts lectures and readings as well as medieval and Renaissance music concerts. An Elizabethan garden on the east lawn grows herbs and flowers common in the sixteenth century.

The National Mall - monuments

The elegant, two-mile-long **National Mall** stretches from the Capitol to the Lincoln Memorial and is DC's most popular green space, used for summer softball games and Fourth of July concerts. When there's a protest gesture to be made, the Mall is the place to make it. What the Mall is perhaps best known for, however, is its quartet of presidential **monuments**, along with the **White House** and the powerful **memorials** to veterans of the twentieth century's various wars.

Washington Monument

The Mall's most prominent feature, the **Washington Monument**, is an unadorned marble obelisk built in memory of George Washington. At 555ft, it's the tallest all-masonry structure in the world, towering over the city from its hilltop perch at 15th Street NW and Constitution Avenue (daily 9am–5pm, summer until 10pm; free; Ⓣ202/426-6841, Ⓦwww.nps.gov/wamo). To visit the monument pick up a ticket from the 15th Street kiosk, just south of Constitution Avenue on Madison Drive (8am–4.30pm), which allows you to turn up at a fixed time later in the day. The kiosk is first-come, first-served; tickets run out early during the peak season. You can also book a ticket in advance with the National Park Service ($1.50; Ⓣ1-877/444-6777). Once you gain access, a seventy-second **elevator ride** whisks you past the honorary stones in the (closed) stairwell and deposits you at a level where the views are, of course, tremendous (though the windows could use some cleaning).

The White House

For nearly two hundred years, the **White House** has been the residence and office of the president of the United States. Standing at the edge of the Mall, due north from the Washington Monument at America's most famous address, 1600 Pennsylvania Ave NW, this grand, Neoclassical edifice was completed in 1800 by Irish immigrant James Hoban, who modelled it on the Georgian manors of Dublin. Security at the White House is tight but somewhat looser than during the lockdown years of the Bush administration. Self-guided **tours** (Tues–Thurs 7.30–11am, Fri 7.30am–noon, Sat 7.30am–1pm; free; Ⓣ202/456-7041, Ⓦwww.whitehouse.gov) are offered at least one month in advance (and no more than six) on a first-come, first-served system. US citizens should submit a request through their Congressional representative (foreign visitors should consult their embassy). If you're interested in the history of the place and its occupants, walk a few blocks southeast to the **visitor centre** at 1450 Pennsylvania Ave (daily 7.30am–4pm; ⓣ202/208-1631, ⓦwww.nps.gov/whho).

Lincoln Memorial

The **Lincoln Memorial**, with its stately Doric columns, anchors the west end of the Mall (daily 24hr, staffed 9.30am–11.30pm; free; ⓦwww.nps.gov/linc), a fitting tribute to the sixteenth US president, who preserved the Union through the Civil War, and provided the first step towards ending slavery in the country with his Emancipation Proclamation in 1863. During the Civil Rights March on Washington in 1963, Martin Luther King Jr delivered his epic "I Have a Dream" speech here, and on-site protests against the Vietnam War in the 1960s fuelled the growing anti-war feeling in the country. Inside the monument, an enormous, craggy likeness of Lincoln sits firmly grasping the arms of his throne-like chair, deep in thought. Inscriptions of his two most celebrated speeches – the Gettysburg Address and the Second Inaugural Address – are carved on the south and north walls.

Other monuments and memorials

Just west of the Washington Monument, the **National World War II Memorial**, 17th Street SW at Independence Avenue (daily 24hr, staffed 9.30am–11.30pm; free; ⓣ202/426-6841, ⓦwww.nps.gov/nwwm), comprises two arcs around a fountain with a combined 56 stone pillars (representing the number of US states and territories at the time of the war) decorated with bronze wreaths. Quotes from FDR and Eisenhower are chiselled on the walls, and a concave wall of four thousand golden stars reminds you of the 400,000 fallen US soldiers. Even more moving is the striking wedge of black granite slashed into the green lawn of the Mall at Constitution Avenue and 21st Street NW, where the **Vietnam Veterans Memorial** (daily 24hr, staffed 9.30am–11.30pm; free; ⓦwww.nps.gov/vive) serves as a sombre and powerful reminder of the 58,000 US soldiers who died in Vietnam. The pathway that slopes down from the grass forms a gash in the earth, its increasing depth symbolizing the increasing involvement of US forces in the war. The polished surface is carved with the names of every soldier who died, in chronological order from 1959 to 1975, and you can often find family members taking paper rubbings of the names of the departed. On the opposite side of the Vietnam memorial, southeast of the Lincoln Memorial, the **Korean War Veterans Memorial** (daily 24hr, staffed 8am–11.45pm; free; ⓦwww.nps.gov/kwvm) has as its centrepiece a Field of Remembrance, featuring nineteen life-sized, armed combat troops sculpted from stainless steel.

To the south, several memorials honour past presidents, starting with the **Jefferson Memorial**, just south of the Mall near 14th Street SW and Ohio Drive (daily 24hr, staffed 9.30am–11.30pm; free; ⓦwww.nps.gov/thje), whose shallow dome hovers over a huge bronze statue of Thomas Jefferson, the author of the Declaration of Independence and the third US president. Just outside the front, the picturesque **Tidal Basin** stretches up to the Mall and offers one of the best places in town to take a break from sightseeing (or view the bright blooms of **Japanese cherry trees** in early to mid-April). Across the Tidal Basin, the **FDR Memorial**, West Basin Drive SW at Ohio Drive (daily 24hr, staffed 9.30am–11.30pm; free; ⓦwww.nps.gov/fdrm), spreads across a seven-acre site made up of a series of interlinking granite outdoor galleries – called "rooms" – punctuated by waterfalls, statuary, sculpted reliefs, groves of trees, shaded alcoves and plazas.

The National Mall – museums

In contrast to the memorials and monuments of its western half, the **National Mall**'s eastern side is dominated by museums, most of which are part of the spectacular **Smithsonian Institution**. The Smithsonian was endowed in 1846 by Englishman James Smithson; the Institution's original home, the 1855 fantasy-medieval structure known as **The Castle**, 1000 Jefferson Drive SW, is in the centre of the Mall's south side and now acts as the main **visitor centre** (daily 8.30am–5.30pm; ⓣ202/633-1000). Unless otherwise stated below, all Smithsonian museums and galleries are **open daily** all year (except Dec 25) from 10am until 5.30pm, with summer hours until 7.30 or 8pm, and admission is **free**. For details on current exhibitions and events, call the visitor centre or visit the Smithsonian's website at ⓦwww.si.edu.

National Museum of American History

One of the prime repositories of US cultural artefacts is the **National Museum of American History**, located at 14th Street NW and Constitution Avenue (ⓣ202/633-1000, ⓦwww.americanhistory.si.edu), which recently reopened to high praise after a lengthy renovation. A wide common area off the lobby is lined with new "**artefact walls**" that show off some of the items that the museum previously had to keep in storage – anything from 200-year-old tavern signs and toy chests, to the **John Bull**, the nation's oldest functioning steam locomotive, dating from 1831. Elsewhere in the museum, you're apt to find anything from George Washington's wooden teeth to Jackie Kennedy's designer dresses to Judy Garland's ruby slippers from *The Wizard of Oz*. You could easily spend a full day poking around the displays, but three to four hours would be a reasonable compromise – and to stick to this time frame, you'll have to be selective. The museum's biggest draw is the battered red, white and blue flag that inspired the US national anthem – the **Star-Spangled Banner** itself, which survived the British bombardment of Baltimore Harbor during the War of 1812.

National Museum of Natural History

Continuing eastward toward the Capitol, on the north side of the Mall, at 10th St NW and Constitution Avenue, lies the imposing, three-storey entrance rotunda of the **National Museum of Natural History** (ⓣ202/633-1000, ⓦwww.mnh.si.edu), which traces evolution from fossilized four-billion-year-old plankton to dinosaurs' eggs and beyond. In fact, the "Dinosaurs" section is the most popular part of the museum, with hulking skeletons reassembled in imaginative poses. The museum also boasts a truly exceptional array of gemstones, including the legendary 45-carat Hope Diamond, which once belonged to Marie Antoinette, and the **Gem and Mineral Hall**, which features natural and reconstructed environments, interactive exhibits and hands-on specimens. Elsewhere, the **z** has some three hundred replicas focusing on mostly fur-wearing, milk-producing creatures, and the 25,000-square-foot **Ocean Hall** uses hundreds of displays and specimens – among them, a 50ft-long whale model – to explain the world of the sea. All this makes the museum an incredible educational institution, so be prepared to handle the hundreds of children scampering about almost any hour the museum is open.

National Gallery of Art

The visually stunning **National Gallery of Art**, just east on Constitution Avenue, between 3rd and 9th streets NW (Mon–Sat 10am–5pm, Sun 11am–6pm; free; ⓣ202/737-4215, ⓦwww.nga.gov), is one of the most important museums in the US, though not part of the Smithsonian per se. The original Neoclassical gallery, opened in 1941, is now called the **West Building** and holds the bulk of the permanent collection. Galleries to the west on the main floor display major works by early- and high-Renaissance, and Baroque masters, arranged by nationality: half a dozen Rembrandts fill the **Dutch** gallery, including a glowing, mad portrait of *Lucretia*; Van Eyck and Rubens dominate the **Flemish**; and El Greco, Goya and Velázquez face off in the **Spanish**. In the voluminous **Italian** galleries, there's the only da Vinci in the Americas, the 1474 *Ginevra de' Benci*, painted in oil on wood; Titian's vivid image of *Saint John the Evangelist on Patmos* and *Venus with a Mirror*; and Raphael's renowned *Alba Madonna* (1510). The other half of the West Building holds an exceptional collection of **nineteenth-century paintings** – a couple of Van Goghs, some Monet studies of Rouen Cathedral and water lilies, Cézanne still lifes, and the like. For **British art**, you can find genteel portraits by Gainsborough and Reynolds, but even more evocative hazy land- and waterscapes by J.M.W. Turner. Augustus St Gaudens' magisterial battle sculpture *Memorial to Robert Gould Shaw and the Massachusetts 54th Regiment* takes up a whole gallery to itself.

The National Gallery's **East Building** (same hours and admission) was opened in 1978 with an audaciously modern I.M. Pei design, dominated by a huge atrium. **European** highlights of the permanent collection include Pablo Picasso's Blue Period pieces *The Tragedy* and *Family of Saltimbanques*, along with his Cubist *Nude Woman*; and Henri Matisse's exuberant *Pianist and Checker Players*. Andy Warhol's works are as familiar as they come, with classic serial works *32 Soup Cans*, *Let Us Now Praise Famous Men* and *Green Marilyn*. Notable **Abstract Expressionist** works include large, hovering slabs of blurry colour by Mark Rothko, *The Stations of the Cross* by Barnett Newman and Jackson Pollock's *Number 1, 1950 (Lavender Mist)*. There's also Robert Rauschenberg's splattered, stuffed-bird sculpture known as *Canyon*, and Jasper Johns's *Targets*, among his most influential works.

National Air and Space Museum

The **National Air and Space Museum**, across the Mall between Fourth and Seventh streets SW (Ⓣ202/633-1000, Ⓦwww.nasm.si.edu), is DC's most popular attraction, and a huge draw for families of all ages. Here you can see all kinds of flying machines, rockets, satellites and assorted aeronautic gizmos, highlighted by Charles Lindbergh's **Spirit of St Louis**. Elsewhere, the "Space Race" exhibit traces the development of space flight, including an array of spacesuits from different eras, while nearby, "Rocketry and Space Flight" outlines the history of rocketry. The whimsically labelled "Wright Cycle Co." is devoted to the siblings who pioneered aeronautics; the focus is the handmade Wright Flyer, in which the Wrights made the first powered flight in December 1903. However, "Apollo to the Moon" is the most popular and crowded room in the museum, centring on the **Apollo 11** (1969) and **17** (1972) missions, the first and last US flights to the moon.

Other Mall museums

Just east of the Air and Space Museum, skirting the Capitol Reflecting Pool along Jefferson Drive, the Smithsonian's **National Museum of the American Indian** (Ⓣ202/633-1000, Ⓦwww.nmai.si.edu) has undulating walls the colour of yellow earth, and a collection that reaches back thousands of years and incorporates nearly a million objects from nations spread out from Canada to Mexico – featuring fascinating ceramics, textiles and other artefacts from civilizations such as the Olmec, Maya and Inca.

West of the Air and Space Museum, the **Hirshhorn Museum**, Independence Avenue at 7th Street SW (Ⓣ202/633-4674, Ⓦwww.hirshhorn.si.edu), with its concrete facade and monumental scale, is strongest for its modern sculpture:

bronzes by Henri Matisse, masks and busts by Pablo Picasso and Brancusi's *Torso of a Young Man*, resembling a cylindrical brass phallus. The Hirshhorn's cache of modern paintings has several strengths (de Kooning, Bacon) and starts with figurative paintings from the late nineteenth and early twentieth centuries, winding its way toward Abstract Expressionism and pop art.

Further on, the domed **National Museum of African Art**, 950 Independence Ave SW (Ⓣ202/633-4600, Ⓦwww.nmafa.si.edu), holds more than six thousand sculptures and artefacts from sub-Saharan Africa. The permanent collection ranges widely and there are plenty of rotating exhibits, which may include headrests, mostly carved from wood using an adze (cutting tool), as well as assorted ivory snuff containers, carved drinking horns, combs, pipes, spoons, baskets and cups.

Continuing west, the two buildings that make up the **National Museum of Asian Art** are also consistently fascinating. The angular and pyramidal **Arthur M. Sackler Gallery**, 1050 Independence Ave SW (Ⓣ202/633-4880, Ⓦwww.asia.si.edu), features 3000-year-old Chinese bronzes, ritual wine containers decorated with the faces and tails of dragons, intricate jade pendants, remarkably well-preserved carved wooden cabinets and book stands, and Qing imperial porcelain embellished with symbolic figures and motifs. Hindu temple sculpture from India includes bronze, brass and granite representations of Brahma, Vishnu and Shiva; there's also a superb thirteenth-century stone carving of the elephant-headed Ganesha. The companion **Freer Gallery**, Jefferson Drive at 12th Street NW (same info as above), also offers a fine array of Asian art – Chinese jades and bronzes, Byzantine illuminated manuscripts, Buddhist wall sculptures and Persian metalwork. The highlight, though, is the collection of more than one thousand prints, drawings and paintings by London-based American artist James McNeil Whistler – the largest collection of his works anywhere – featuring the magnificent **Peacock Room**, with a ceiling covered with imitation gold leaf and walls painted with blue and gold peacocks. Among other works are pieces by Whistler's contemporaries, Winslow Homer and John Singer Sargent.

Other attractions near the Mall

Just off the Mall, the most important institution is the sizeable **United States Holocaust Memorial Museum**, just south at 100 Raoul Wallenburg Place SW (daily 10am–6.30pm; free; Ⓣ202/488-0400, Ⓦwww.ushmm.org), which recalls the persecution and murder of six million Jews by the Nazis and personalizes the suffering of individual victims. Newspapers and newsreels documenting Nazi activities from the early 1930s through to the "Final Solution" are on display, plus replicas and, in many cases, actual relics, of Warsaw Ghetto streets, railroad cattle-cars and other artefacts on the top floors. **Tickets** for specific entry times are available free of charge from 10am each day at the 14th Street entrance. You can also reserve in advance. Just south, the **Bureau of Engraving and Printing**, 14th and C streets SW (access by tour only; free; Ⓣ202/874-2330, Ⓦwww.moneyfactory.gov), is the federal agency for designing and printing all US currency, government securities and postage stamps; it's also host to one of DC's most popular tours, netting half a million visitors annually. Between May and August you must pick up **tickets** in advance for tours from 9am to 2pm; you can, and should, start waiting in line at 8am, as tickets are often gone by 11.30am. The rest of the year, you can just show up without tickets, though you'll still have to wait in line. Finally, just north of the Mall, the **Corcoran Gallery of Art**, 17th Street NW and New York Avenue (Wed–Sun 10am–5pm, Thurs closes 9pm; $10; Ⓦwww.corcoran.org), is one of the oldest and most respected art museums in the US, featuring masterpieces by Frederic Edwin Church and Albert Bierstadt, and portraits by John Singer Sargent, Thomas Eakins and Mary Cassatt, among others. The mid-level paintings by Degas, Renoir, Monet, Sisley and Pissarro, however, aren't as eye-catching as the **Salon Doré** (Gilded Room), an eighteenth-century Parisian interior that's been re-created to stunning effect, with floor-to-ceiling hand-carved panelling, gold-leaf decor and ceiling murals.

Downtown and around

Those whose patience grows thin with the hordes of people on the Mall may enjoy a trip through Washington DC's **downtown** district, which in the last fifteen years has seen new boutiques, restaurants and hotels spring up in the so-called **Penn Quarter**. Adjacent to Downtown is the wedge-shaped **Federal Triangle**, home to countless government agencies and the National Archives, while, to the northwest, the **New Downtown** area, known for its lobbyist-rich K Street, has swanky shops and restaurants.

National Archives

On display at the **National Archives**, 700 Pennsylvania Ave NW (daily 9am–5pm, closes Wed–Fri 9pm; free; Ⓣ202/501-5205, Ⓦwww.archives.gov), are the three short texts upon which the United States was founded: the **Declaration of Independence**, the **Constitution** and the **Bill of Rights** – three original sheets of parchment secured in bomb-proof, argon-filled, glass-and-titanium containers. The impressive Neoclassical Greek building also houses temporary exhibitions with fascinating documents such as the Louisiana Purchase, the Marshall Plan, Nixon's resignation letter, the Emancipation Proclamation and the Japanese surrender from World War II. As the official repository of all US national records – census data, treaties, passport applications – the Archives also attracts thousands of visitors who come here each year in search of their own genealogical, military or other records. Among the holdings are seven million pictures; 125,000 reels of film; 200,000 sound recordings; eleven million maps and charts; and a quarter of a million other artefacts.

National Portrait Gallery and American Art Museum

In the centre of the Penn Quarter, the **Old Patent Office** – a Neoclassical gem dating from 1836 – houses two of the city's major art displays: the Smithsonian's **National Portrait Gallery** and **American Art Museum** (both daily 11.30am–7pm; free; Ⓣ202/633-8300, Ⓦwww.npg.si.edu). In the Portrait Gallery, striking images of figures from the performing arts include Paul Robeson as Othello; photographs of Gloria Swanson and Boris Karloff; and a rough-hewn wooden head of Bob Hope. Also worth a look are the presidential portraits – one for every man to occupy the office, from Gilbert Stuart's George Washington, an imperial study of an implacable leader, to Norman Rockwell's overly flattering portrait of Richard Nixon.

The other major museum to occupy the Old Patent Office building, the **American Art Museum** (daily 10am–5.30pm; free; Ⓣ202/633-7970, Ⓦamericanart.si.edu), holds one of the more enduring of the city's art collections, which dates back to the early nineteenth century. The museum contains almost four hundred paintings by George Catlin, who spent six years touring the Great Plains, painting portraits and scenes of Native American life as well as lush landscapes. There are also notable twentieth-century modern pieces – items by Robert Motherwell, Willem de Kooning, Robert Rauschenberg, Clyfford Still, Ed Kienholz and Jasper Johns – but none more vibrant than Nam June Paik's jaw-dropping **Electronic Superhighway**, a huge, neon-outlined map of the US. Another branch of the American Art Museum, the **Renwick Gallery**, located near the White House, at 17th Street and Pennsylvania Avenue (daily 10am–5.30pm; free; ⓣ202/633-2850), offers overflow space for the museum's treasures, as well as rotating exhibits focusing on the decorative arts.

International Spy Museum

The **International Spy Museum**, 800 F St NW (hours vary, usually summer daily 9am–7pm; rest of year daily 10am–6pm; $15; ⓦwww.spymuseum.org), is a hugely popular DC attraction – tickets sell out days in advance during the high season – celebrating espionage in all forms, from feudal Japan's silent and deadly ninjas, to surveillance pigeons armed with cameras from World War I, to infamous modern-day CIA moles like Aldrich Ames. The museum's standouts are undoubtedly its artefacts from the height of the Cold War in the 1950s and 1960s, including tiny pistols disguised as lipstick holders, cigarette cases, pipes and flashlights; oddments like invisible-ink writing kits and a Get Smart!-styled shoe phone; a colourful and active model of James Bond's Aston Martin spy car; and a rounded capsule containing a screwdriver, razor and serrated knife – ominously marked, "rectal tool kit".

Ford's Theatre National Historic Site

Ford's Theatre National Historic Site, 511 Tenth St NW (daily 9am–5pm, closed during rehearsals and matinees; free; ⓣ202/347-4833, ⓦwww.nps.gov/foth), is a beautiful restoration of the nineteenth-century playhouse, which continues to stage regular productions of contemporary and period drama (see p.351). It was here, on April 14, 1865, a mere five days after the end of the Civil War, that **Abraham Lincoln** was shot by the actor and Confederate zealot John Wilkes Booth during a performance of *Our American Cousin*. A grand new renovation has brought the site back to vivid life, and you can see the damask-furnished presidential box, in which Lincoln sat in his rocking chair, and eye-opening items like the actual murder weapon (a .44 Derringer), a bloodstained piece of Lincoln's overcoat, and Booth's knife, keys, compass, boot and diary. Free advance tickets are required for entry; either turn up when the site opens to reserve them, or call ⓣ202/397-SEAT. After he was shot, the mortally wounded president was carried across the street to the **Petersen House**, where he died the next morning. That, too, is open to the public (daily 9.30am–5.30pm; free; ⓣ202/426-6924), who troop through its gloomy parlour rooms to see a replica of Lincoln's deathbed.

Other Downtown attractions

Housed in a converted Masonic Temple at 1250 New York Ave NW, the **National Museum of Women in the Arts** is the country's only major museum dedicated to female artists (Mon–Sat 10am–5pm, Sun noon–5pm; $10; ⓣ202/783-5000, ⓦwww.nmwa.org). The collection is arranged chronologically, starting with works from the Renaissance, on to twentieth-century works that include the classical sculpture of Camille Claudel, the paintings of Georgia O'Keeffe and Tamara de Lempicka, linocuts by Hannah Höch, and, most boldly, a cycle of prints depicting the hardships of working-class life by the socialist Käthe Kollwitz. Less appealing but much more popular, the **Newseum**, on 6th Street at Pennsylvania Avenue (daily 9am–5pm; $20; ⓦwww.newseum.org), is an "edutainment" colossus that provides a flashy look at the greatest hits of the news biz, spread over 250,000 square feet and seven levels. On the various levels, you'll see how modern news is gathered and transmitted, witness pivotal moments in journalism through re-enactments, bone up on the freedoms of speech and press, and get a look at the history of news as provided by the News Corporation, owner of controversial **FOX News**. Finally, the **National Building Museum**, 401 F St NW (Mon–Sat 10am–5pm, Sun 11am–5pm; $5; Ⓦwww.nbm.org), is a stirring museum of architecture. Its best feature of the museum, though, is the majestic **Great Hall**, one of the most impressive interior spaces anywhere in DC. The eight supporting columns are 8ft across at the base and more than 75ft high; each is made up of 70,000 bricks, plastered and painted to resemble Siena marble.

Dupont Circle to Upper Northwest

Washington's other key attractions are spaced out among various neighbourhoods, but they are nevertheless worth taking the time to visit. Many lie near Connecticut Avenue, running from the swanky shopping and dining area of **Dupont Circle** up to the elite precinct of **Upper Northwest** – both areas conveniently accessed by subway. Less convenient, just to the northeast, is the funky urban district of **Adams Morgan**– a draw for its diners, clubs and bars.

Phillips Collection

The oldest part of the Georgian Revival brownstone housing the **Phillips Collection**, just northwest of Dupont Circle, at 1600 21st St NW (Tues–Sat 10am–5pm, Thurs until 8.30pm, Sun 11am–6pm; free admission weekdays, $10 weekends, $12–15 special exhibitions; Ⓣ202/387-2151, Ⓦwww.phillipscollection.org), is one of DC's key museums, and has expanded considerably in the last several years. On display are works by everyone from Renoir to Rothko (and several by non-modern artists like Giorgione and El Greco). Highlights include signature pieces by Willem de Kooning and Richard Diebenkorn, Blue Period Picassos, Matisse's *Studio, Quai St-Michel*, a Cézanne still life, and no fewer than four van Goghs, including the powerful *Road Menders*. Top billing generally goes to *The Luncheon of the Boating Party* by Renoir, where straw-hat-wearing dandies linger over a feast.

Embassy Row

An intriguing strip that is unique to Washington DC among American cities, **Embassy Row** starts in earnest a few paces northwest up Massachusetts Avenue from Dupont Circle, where the **Indonesian Embassy** at no. 2020 (closed to the public) occupies the magnificent Art Nouveau Walsh-McLean House, built in 1903 for gold baron Thomas Walsh. It's a superb building – with colonnaded loggia and intricate, carved windows – and saw regular service as one of Washington society's most fashionable venues. Nearby, the **Anderson House**, no. 2118 (free admission and guided tours Tues–Sat 1.15pm, 2.15pm, & 3.15pm; Ⓣ202/785-2040), was finished in 1905 with a grey-stone exterior sporting twin arched entrances, heavy wooden doors and colonnaded portico. Inside there's a grand ballroom, and original furnishings include cavernous fireplaces, inlaid marble floors, Flemish tapestries and diverse murals.

The National Zoo

Continuing well north, into the hilly district of Upper Northwest, at 3001 Connecticut Ave NW (luckily a short walk from the Metro), the Smithsonian's **National Zoo** (buildings: daily April–Oct 10am–6pm; Nov–March 10am–4.30pm; grounds: daily April–Oct 6am–8pm; Nov–March 6am–6pm; free; parking $10; Ⓦwww.natzoo.si.edu) was founded back in 1889, and provides plenty of interest to animal enthusiasts. **Amazonia** is a re-creation of a tropical river and rainforest habitat – piranhas included – while the **Small Mammal House** showcases some of the zoo's lovable oddballs like golden tamarind monkeys, armadillos, meerkats and porcupines. Further along, orang-utans are encouraged to leave the confines of the **Great Ape House** and commute to the "**Think Tank**", where scientists and four-legged primates come together to hone their communication skills. If all else fails, there's always the **giant pandas**, who have been amusing visitors since their arrival in 1972. Nearby, the **Asia Trail** displays such curious beasts as the sloth bear, a fishing cat, a somewhat grotesque Japanese giant salamander and the formidable clouded leopard.

Washington National Cathedral

The twin towers of **Washington National Cathedral**, the world's sixth-largest cathedral, are visible long before you reach the heights of Mount St Alban where the church sits, a good walk from the subway line in Upper Northwest (Mon–Fri 10am–5.30pm, Sat 10am–4.30pm, Sun 8am–5pm; $5 donation; Ⓦwww.cathedral.org/cathedral). Built from Indiana limestone in the medieval English Gothic style, the Episcopal cathedral took 83 years to build and measures more than a tenth of a mile from the west end of the nave to the high altar at the opposite end. Among other things, you'll find the sarcophagus of **Woodrow Wilson**, the only president to be buried in the District – though presidents including Ford and Reagan have lain in state here – and the **Space Window** commemorating the flight of Apollo 11, whose stained glass incorporates a sliver of moon rock.

Georgetown

Although it is a mile from the nearest subway stop (taking the DC Circulator helps; see p.333), **Georgetown** is the quintessential DC neighbourhood, enlivened by a main drag – M Street – where chic restaurants and boutiques are housed in 200-year-old buildings, and the historic **C&O Canal** runs parallel to the south (tour info at Ⓦwww.nps.gov/CHOH). The **Old Stone House**, 3051 M St (daily noon–5pm; free; Ⓦwww.nps.gov/olst), is the only surviving pre-Revolutionary home in the city. Built in 1765 by a Pennsylvania carpenter, it retains its rugged, rough-hewn appearance, the craggy rocks used for the three-feet-thick walls being quarried from blue fieldstone.

In the hillier part of the district, there are two spots that definitely merit a visit: Tudor Place and Dumbarton Oaks. **Tudor Place**, 1644 31st St NW (tours on the hour Tues–Sat 10am–3pm, Sun noon–3pm; $8; Ⓦwww.tudorplace.org), was once the estate of Martha Washington's granddaughter, and with its Federal-style architecture and Classical domed portico, has remained virtually untouched since it was built in 1816. At R Street NW at 31st Street, **Dumbarton Oaks** (gardens: mid-March to Oct Tues–Sun 2–6pm; Nov to early March Tues–Sun 2–5pm; $8; Ⓦwww.doaks.org) encompasses a marvellous red-brick Georgian mansion surrounded by gardens and woods. In 1944, this was the site of a meeting that led to the founding of the United Nations the following year. Its **museum** (Tues–Sun 2–5pm; free) is excellent for its pre-Columbian gold, jade and polychromatic carvings, sculpture and pendants, as well as ceremonial axes, jewellery made from spondylus shells, stone masks of unknown significance and sharp jade "celts", possibly used for human sacrifice.

Arlington National Cemetery and around

Across the Potomac River west of the National Mall, the vast sea of identical white headstones on the hillsides of Virginia's **Arlington National Cemetery** (daily: April–Sept 8am–7pm; Oct–March 8am–5pm; free; Ⓦwww.arlingtoncemetery.org) stands on land that once belonged to Confederate general **Robert E. Lee**. Some 350,000 US soldiers and others – from presidents to Supreme Court justices – now lie here. An eternal flame marks the grave of **President John F. Kennedy**, who lies next to his wife, Jacqueline Kennedy Onassis, and a short distance from his brother, Robert (the only grave marked with a simple white cross). At the **Tomb of the Unknowns**, visitors can watch a solemn Changing of the Guard ceremony (every thirty minutes April–Sept; hourly Oct–March). The cemetery's prominent Neoclassical **Arlington House** (same hours as cemetery; free) is Lee's modest mansion, which his family was forced to sell after the war as the proximity of the nation's war dead created a less than ideal setting for the country home.

Unless you have strong legs and lots of time, the best way to see the vast cemetery is by Tourmobile (see p.333), which leaves from the visitor centre at the entrance. You can also walk here from the Lincoln Memorial, across the Arlington Bridge, or take the Blue Line Metro. Finally, beyond the gates of the cemetery are notable **memorials** to the **Marine Corps**, on Arlington Boulevard at Meade Street (daily 24hr; ⓦ www.nps.gov/gwmp/usmc.htm), based around the Iwo Jima Statue, commemorating the bloody World War II battle where 6800 lives were lost; and to the **Air Force**, on Columbia Pike off Washington Boulevard (daily: April–Sept 8am–11pm; Oct–March 8am–9pm; ⓦ www.airforcememorial.org), recognizable by its three giant steel arcs, which twist 270ft out into the sky.

Eating

Restaurants come and go more quickly in Washington DC than in similarly sized cities in the US. Certain neighbourhoods – Connecticut Avenue around Dupont Circle, 18th Street and Columbia Road in Adams Morgan, M Street in Georgetown, and downtown's Seventh Street and Chinatown – always seem to hold a satisfying range of dining options. Otherwise, the **cafés** in the main museums are good for downtown lunch breaks. Likewise, you'll find convenient food courts in Union Station and at the Old Post Office.

Downtown

Acadiana 901 New York Ave NW ⓣ 202/408-8848. Chic Cajun spot that serves up mid-priced muffaletta, poboys and crawfish for lunch, then saves the big-ticket scallops and bacon, veal medallions with grits, and grilled swordfish for dinner.

Café Atlantico 405 8th St NW ⓣ 202/393-0812. Upmarket nuevo Latino treat with spicy spins on traditional cuisine, but really best for its *minibar*, a six-seat counter famed for the likes of beet "tumbleweeds", olive oil bon bons and familiar dishes put in quotes to indicate the subversive strategy at work. Reserve a month in advance and expect to pay $120 a head.

Captain White's Seafood City 1100 Maine Ave SW ⓣ 202/484-2722. South of downtown at the Fish Wharf, a fine vendor hawking catfish, oysters, crab and other delicious choices, which you can get fresh to go or fried up in a tasty platter or sandwich.

Jaleo 480 7th St NW ⓣ 202/628-7949. Smart tapas bar-restaurant with tempting selections such as sautéed shrimp, chicken fritters and patatas bravas, plus supreme paella. Limited reservation policy makes for long waits during peak hours.

Old Ebbitt Grill 675 15th St NW ⓣ 202/347-4801. One of DC's biggest-name eateries: a plush re-creation of a nineteenth-century tavern, with mahogany bar (serving microbrews), gas chandeliers, leather booths and gilt mirrors. Offers everything from burgers to oysters.

Proof 775 G St NW ⓣ 202/737-7663. A delicious, upper-end grab bag of flavours and styles, with a fine wine selection to boot. Try the charcuterie plates to start, then move on to a huge range of cheeses, sashimi, ceviche and salmon or sablefish.

The Source 575 Pennsylvania Ave NW ⓣ 202/637-6100. LA-based wunder-chef Wolfgang Puck takes DC by the lapels with this expensive fusion eatery – doling out curiosities from pork-belly dumplings to "lacquered" Chinese duckling – and attracts a range of celebrities, including President Obama himself.

Zaytinya 701 9th St NW ⓣ 202/638-0800. Stylish mid-priced Turkish and Middle Eastern eatery that serves a range of inventive meze plates, ranging from Lebanese beef tartare to pork-and-orange-rind sausage and veal cheeks. Good cheeses, too.

Dupont Circle

Bistrot du Coin 1738 Connecticut Ave NW ⓣ202/234-6969. Classic bistro with a superb bar, boisterous atmosphere and genuine, affordable French food – goat cheese salad, foie gras, tartines and rabbit stew, among other offerings.

Java House 1645 Q St NW ⓣ202/387-6622. A local favourite serving the neighbourhood's best coffee. A good spot to read a book, have an afternoon chat, or fire up the laptop for wi-fi access. Desserts, bagels, salads and sandwiches are on offer, too.

Komi 1509 17th St NW ⓣ202/332-9200. One of the city's top restaurants, for which you should reserve well in advance. Enjoy pricey, rotating, fixed-price ($90 and $120) selections that may include suckling pig, pasta and spanakopita – though you really never know.

Moby Dick House of Kabob 1300 Connecticut Ave NW ⓣ202/833-9788. Delicious and cheap Middle Eastern fare featuring spicy and savoury gyros, chicken and lamb sandwiches, boneless chicken in pomegranate sauce, braised beef with eggplant and other cheap delights.

Pizzeria Paradiso 2003 P St NW ⓣ202/223-1245. Supreme pizzeria, with famously tasty pizzas such as the enormous Siciliana, potato-and-pesto Genovese, and ultra-peppery, spicy Atomica. Expect to wait in line.

Restaurant Nora 2132 Florida Ave NW ⓣ202/462-5143. Top-notch eatery with prices to match. The all-organic fare includes Spanish octopus, Amish pork roast and veal osso bucco.

Sushi Taro 1503 17th St NW ⓣ202/462-8999. Plenty of fine sushi, sashimi, tempura and teriyaki, with moderate to expensive prices. If raw fish isn't your thing, choose from the selection of steak and pork cutlets.

Adams Morgan and Shaw

Amsterdam Falafelshop 2425 18th St NW ⓣ202/234-1969. Among the finest falafel spots in the country, this unassuming eatery doles out piping-hot, seriously yummy falafel with a broad range of garnishes, and pretty good brownies and fries, too.

Ben's Chili Bowl 1213 U St NW, Shaw ⓣ202/667-0909. Another favourite of the president's, and well worth the trip for the legendary chili dogs, milkshakes and cheese fries.

Bukom Café 2442 18th St NW, Adams Morgan ⓣ202/265-4600. Serves delicious West African dishes like spicy "beer meat", oxtail or okra soup, *egusi*, a broth of goat meat with ground melon seeds and spinach, and chicken *yassa*, with onions and spices, for $10–12.

Casa Oaxaca 2106 18th St NW ⓣ202/387-2272. Not as flashy as some other Latin joints in the area, but among the best – great for its wide range of mole dishes, grilled steak and sautéed shrimp, for mid-range prices.

Cashion's Eat Place 1819 Columbia Rd NW, Adams Morgan ⓣ202/797-1819. New Southern cuisine, offering hickory-smoked lamb, rabbit meatloaf, corn cakes, grits, sweet potatoes and fruit and nut pies – at mid- to high prices. Brunch dishes are about half-price.

Grill from Ipanema 1858 Columbia Rd NW, Adams Morgan ⓣ202/986-0757. Brazilian staples highlighted by meat stews, shrimp dishes and a scrumptious weekend brunch. Try the mussels and watch your caipirinha intake.

Henry's Soul Cafe 1704 U St NW, Shaw ⓣ202/265-3336. Authentic soul food: the chicken wings, fried trout, meatloaf, ribs, beef liver and sweet-potato pie give a savoury and heavy taste of the Deep South for $10.

Georgetown

Baked & Wired 1052 Thomas Jefferson St NW ⓣ202/333-2500. Among the city's finest bakeries, where you can sample great pies, coffee cakes, brownies, cookies and especially delicious cupcakes, plus a good selection of coffee and tea.

Bangkok Bistro 3251 Prospect St NW ⓣ202/337-2424. In its often-crowded dining room, this mid-priced gem has old favourites (tom yum, pad thai, shrimp cakes and satay) offered alongside coconut shrimp, duck noodles, spicy curries and fish in chili sauce.

Booeymonger 3265 Prospect St NW ⓣ202/333-4810. Crowded deli-coffeeshop, excellent for its inventive sandwiches like the Gatsby Arrow (roast beef and brie) and the Patty Hearst (turkey and bacon with Russian dressing).

Citronelle In the *Latham Hotel*, 3000 M St ⓣ202/625-2150. Huge player on the DC dining scene, serving up French-inspired cuisine and set-price food and wine pairings starting at $350. Reserve in advance, dress chic and bring plenty of snooty attitude.

Hook 3241 M St NW ⓣ202/625-4488. Hard to do better for the catch of the day than this centrally located seafood favourite, which serves up a mean tuna tartare, porchetta and king salmon at upper-end prices.

Leopold's Kafe 3315 M St NW ⓣ202/965-6005. European café that features mid- to high-priced Continental fare like sweet onion tarts, veal schnitzel, bratwurst, smoked fish and delicious desserts and pastries. Breakfast can be particularly good here.

Rocklands 2418 Wisconsin Ave NW ⓣ202/333-2558. A bit north of the main action, but still worth the trek to enjoy some of DC's best pork sandwiches, ribs, beans, sausages and other staples of the barbecue scene, all for cheap prices.

Upper Northwest

Indique 3512 Connecticut Ave NW ⓣ202/244-6600. Recipes from all over India come together with a modern twist at this stylish and affordable restaurant. Don't miss the tasty curries including seafood masala and a piquant lamb vindaloo.

Lebanese Taverna 2641 Connecticut Ave NW ⓣ202/265-8681. Solid Middle Eastern joint with an assortment of kebabs, grilled-meat platters and leg of lamb. Part of a local chain.

Morty's Deli 4620 Wisconsin Ave NW ⓣ202/686-1989. Jewish deli-diner that's a long way from anywhere, but devotees consider the trek worth it for the corned beef, lox and bagels, whitefish and sablefish platters, stuffed cabbage, pastrami, chicken or matzoh-ball soup and the rest.

Vace 3315 Connecticut Ave NW ⓣ202/363-1999. Grab a slice of the excellent designer or traditional pizzas – some of DC's best – and tasty sub sandwiches, focaccia and pasta, or pack a picnic from the selection of sausages, salads and olives, then head to the zoo.

Nightlife and entertainment

Peak times for **drinking** in DC tend to be during rush hour, but for solid late-night imbibing, the well-worn haunts of collegiate **Georgetown**, yuppified **Dupont Circle** and boisterous **Adams Morgan** will do nicely – and in the suit-and-tie spots on **Capitol Hill**, you can even spy a politician or two. For clubs, expect to pay a cover of $5 to $25 (highest on weekends); ticket prices for most gigs run to the same amount, unless you're seeing a major name. Check the free weekly **CityPaper** (ⓦwww.washingtoncitypaper.com) for up-to-date **listings** of music, theatre and other events, in addition to alternative features and reporting. **Gay** and **lesbian** life is centred on Dupont Circle.

Bars

Birreria Paradiso 2029 P St NW ⓣ202/223-1245. Downstairs at Dupont Circle's *Pizzeria Paradiso* (see p.349) this is a supreme touchstone for beer lovers, who come to sample US and European brews, among them excellent Belgian ales, lambics, stouts and porters.

Brickskeller 1523 22nd St NW, Dupont Circle ⓣ202/293-1885. Renowned brick-lined basement saloon serving "the world's largest selection of beer" – though only a fraction are typically available. Still worth it to get a sense of the convivial atmosphere.

Bullfeathers 410 First St SE ⓣ202/543-5005. Politician-watchers just may catch a sighting at this old-time Hill favourite, a dark and clubby spot with affordable beer, that was named for one of Teddy Roosevelt's favourite euphemisms during his White House years.

Capitol City Brewing Co 2 Massachusetts Ave NE ⓣ202/842-2337. Prominent microbrewing spot near Union Station, highlighted by a good range of ales and porters, but only adequate food. Part of a small local chain.

Capitol Lounge 231 Pennsylvania Ave SE ⓣ202/547-2098. Signature brick-walled saloon on the Hill for drinking and partying, with pool tables, inexpensive beer, three bars on two levels and a bevy of Congressional staffers looking to get plastered.

The Dubliner 520 N Capitol St NW, in the *Phoenix Park Hotel* ⓣ202/737-3773. A wooden-vaulted, good-time Irish pub with draft Guinness, boisterous conversation and live Irish music. The patio is a solid summer hangout.

Fox and Hounds 1537 17th St NW, Dupont Circle ⓣ202/232-6307. This easy-going bar draws a diverse crowd, all here to enjoy the stiff and cheap rail drinks and the solid jukebox.

Hawk 'n' Dove 329 Pennsylvania Ave SE ⓣ202/543-3553. Iconic, well-worn DC pub that attracts Hill interns for its cheap food, half-price food and football.

Nanny O'Brien's 3319 Connecticut Ave NW, Upper Northwest ⓣ202/686-9189. An authentic Irish pub with live music from (or in the style of) the Emerald Isle, several nights a week.

RFD Washington 810 7th St NW ⓣ202/289-2030. The leader in Downtown DC microbreweries, with hundreds of bottled beers and dozens of locally crafted brews on tap. Centrally located near the Verizon Center, so watch for heavy post-game crowds.

Clubs and live music venues

9:30 Club 815 V St NW, Shaw ⓣ202/265-0930. Top musicians love to play at this spacious yet intimate club, deservedly famous as DC's best venue for live acts, from indie rock and pop to reggae and rap.

The Black Cat 1811 14th St NW, Shaw ⓣ202/667-7960. One of the top venues in town, part-owned by Dave Grohl, this indie institution provides a showcase for rock, punk and garage bands, and veteran alternative acts alike.

Blues Alley 1073 Wisconsin Ave NW (rear) ⓣ202/337-4141. Small, celebrated Georgetown jazz bar, in business for over forty years, which attracts top names. Cover can run up to $45. Book in advance.

Bohemian Caverns 2003 11th St NW, Shaw district ⓣ202/299-0800. Legendary DC jazz supper club, set in a basement grotto below the stylish ground-level restaurant. A limited number of reserved tickets for bigger acts.

Chief Ike's Mambo Room 1725 Columbia Rd NW, Adams Morgan ⓣ202/332-2211. Ramshackle mural-clad bar that draws the college crowd for live bands playing rock, reggae and r'n'b, or DJs hosting theme nights.

Habana Village 1834 Columbia Rd NW ⓣ202/462-6310. Intoxicating Latin dance joint (tango and salsa lessons are available) infused with an eclectic spirit. A good downstairs bar serves a fine mojito.

HR-57 1610 14th St NW, Logan Circle ⓣ202/667-3700. Small but authentic club where jazz in various manifestations – classic, hard bop, free and cool – is performed by ardent professionals as well as up-and-comers. Cover usually around $10.

IOTA 2832 Wilson Blvd, Arlington, VA ⓣ703/522-8340. Fine warehouse-style music joint with nightly performances by local and national indie, folk, and blues bands. Has a great bar, and attached restaurant, too.

Madam's Organ 2461 18th St NW ⓣ202/667-5370. Funky spot known for showcasing a variety of driving live blues, grinding, raw funk and the odd bluegrass band, plus some solidly rib-sticking soul food and generous cocktails.

Rumba Café 2443 18th St NW, Adams Morgan ⓣ202/588-5501. This Latin oasis is a good bet for a night of sipping caipirinhas and grooving to live Brazilian bossa nova and Afro-Cuban rhythms.

Performing arts

The **performing arts** heavyweight in town, the **Kennedy Center**, 2700 F St NW (ⓣ202/467-4600, ⓦwww.kennedy-center.org), hosts most of the capital's highbrow cultural events, including National Symphony Orchestra and Washington National Opera performances. Otherwise, some of the more notable arts venues are noted below.

Arena Stage ⓣ202/488-3300, ⓦwww.arenastage.org. Highly regarded, often pioneering site that puts on contemporary pieces, though check ahead since the current facility is being renovated (opening 2011) and performances take place in Arlington, Virginia.

Ford's Theatre 511 Tenth St NW, Downtown ⓣ202/347-4833, ⓦwww.fordstheatre.org. Historic and recently renovated venue with a family-friendly programme of mainstream musicals and dramas, frequently historical in nature.

Shakespeare Theatre 450 Seventh St NW, Downtown ⓣ202/547-1122, ⓦwww.shakespearetheatre.org. Celebrated troupe stages six productions per year of work by the Bard and others, plus free summer performances in Rock Creek Park.

National Theatre 1321 Pennsylvania Ave NW, Downtown ⓣ202/628-6161, ⓦwww.nationaltheatre.org. Offers big-name touring musicals and other crowd-pleasers.

Wolf Trap Farm Park 1624 Trap Rd, Vienna, Virginia ⓣ703/255-1868 or 1900, ⓦwww.wolftrap.org. Great spot to see American music in all its native forms, like bluegrass, jazz, ragtime, Cajun, zydeco etc. Enquire about public transit to and from performances.

Woolly Mammoth Theatre 641 D St NW, Downtown ⓣ202/289-2443, ⓦwww.woollymammoth.net. Experimental theatre showcasing budget and mid-priced contemporary, and off-the-wall plays.

Spectator sports

Tickets to Washington Redskins **football** games at FedEx Field in Landover, Maryland (ⓣ301/276-6050, ⓦwww.redskins.com), are almost impossible to get unless you have a connection. Much easier to obtain are tickets to DC's Washington Nationals **baseball** team, which plays at Nationals Park on the Anacostia waterfront; tickets $5–170 (ⓣ202/675-NATS, ⓦnationals.mlb.com). East of Capitol Hill, at RFK Stadium, is the DC United **soccer** squad; tickets $15–50 (ⓣ202/587-5000, ⓦwww.dcunited.com), which plays in the pro MLS league. The huge downtown Verizon Center (ⓦwww.verizoncenter.com) hosts home games of the men's pro **basketball** Washington Wizards; tickets $15–120 (ⓣ202/661-5050, ⓦwww.nba.com/wizards) and women's Mystics; tickets $10-75 (ⓣ202/397-SEAT, ⓦwww.wnba.com/mystics), as well as the pro **hockey** Capitals (tickets $15–100; ⓣ202/397-SEAT, ⓦcapitals.nhl.com).

Virginia

VIRGINIA is the oldest American colony and its recorded history famously began at **Jamestown**, just off the Chesapeake Bay, with the establishment in 1607 of the first successful British colony in North America. Though the first colonists hoped to find gold, it was **tobacco** that made their fortunes – as Native Americans were driven off their land and **slaves** were imported from Africa to work the plantations. Many of the wealthy Virginian planters had an enormous impact on the foundation of the United States: Thomas Jefferson, George Washington and James Madison among them. Later, as the confrontation between North and South over slavery and related issues grew more divisive, Virginia was caught in the middle, but joined the Confederacy when the **Civil War** broke out, providing the Confederate capital, Richmond, and its military leader, Robert E. Lee. Four long years later, Virginia was ravaged, its towns and cities wrecked, its farmlands ruined and most of its youth dead.

Richmond itself was largely destroyed in the war; today it's a small city with some good museums, the best ones historical in nature. The bulk of the colonial sites are concentrated just east, in what is known as the **Historic Triangle**, where **Jamestown**, the original colony, **Williamsburg**, the restored colonial capital, and **Yorktown**, site of the final battle of the Revolutionary War, lie within half an hour's drive of each other on the Colonial Parkway. Another historic centre, **Charlottesville** – famously home to Thomas Jefferson's Monticello – sits at the foot of the gorgeous **Blue Ridge Mountains**, an hour west of Richmond. It's also within easy reach of the natural splendour of **Shenandoah National Park** and the little towns of the western valleys. **Northern Virginia**, a short hop from Washington DC, features a number of restored historic homes, the antique architecture of **Alexandria**, and **Manassas**, the scene of two important Civil War battles.

Northern Virginia

Despite its conservative pedigree, **Northern Virginia** has in recent years become one large suburban enclave with a decidedly liberal bent, due to the number of former inhabitants of Washington DC taking residence there, including a high proportion of US senators. **Alexandria**, nestled on the Potomac River just beyond the limits of the nation's capital (but not beyond its Metro system), seems at least two centuries removed from the modern political whirl. Further afield, this heartland of the landed gentry holds well-preserved estates, cottages, churches, barns and taverns tucked away along the quiet backroads. It's all very popular with tourists, and nowhere more so than **Mount Vernon**, the longtime home of George Washington, while **Manassas** to the west was the site of the two bloody battles of Bull Run.

Alexandria

Extending a good half-mile west of the Potomac, the Old Town of **ALEXANDRIA** was originally an important colonial trading post and a busy port named after the pioneer John Alexander. The town was part of the District of Columbia in 1800, but Virginia demanded it and the surrounding land back in 1846.

In earlier days, George Washington maintained close ties with Alexandria, owning property here and attending gatherings at the famous **Gadsby's Tavern**, 134 N Royal St (tours: April–Oct Tues–Sat 10am–5pm, Sun & Mon 1–5pm; Nov–March Wed–Sat 11am–4pm, Sun 1–4pm; $5; ⓣ703/838-4242, ⓦwww.gadsbystavern.org), which occupies two stately Georgian buildings dating from 1792 and 1785. Downstairs, there's a working restaurant, complete with colonial food and costumed staff. Among other restored buildings open to the public are **Carlyle House**, 121 N Fairfax St (tours Tues–Sat 10am–4pm, Sun noon–4.30pm; $5; ⓣ703/549-2997, ⓦwww.carlylehouse.org), a 1752 sandstone manor that was home to five royal governors, and **Lee-Fendall House**, 614 Oronoco St (Wed–Sat 10am–4pm, Sun 1–4pm; $5; ⓣ703/548-1789, ⓦwww.leefendallhouse.org), a splendid clapboard mansion built in 1785 by Phillip Fendall, a cousin of Robert E. Lee's father. South of King Street, the **Lyceum**, 201 S Washington St (Mon–Sat 10am–5pm, Sun 1–5pm; $2; ⓣ703/838-4994, ⓦwww.alexandriahistory.org), houses the town's history museum in a magisterial, 1839 Greek Revival building, designed to be a centrepiece for the town's cultural affairs. Another eye-catcher is the **Stabler-Leadbeater Apothecary Shop**, 105 S Fairfax St (April–Oct Tues–Sat 10am–5pm, Sun & Mon 1–5pm; Nov–March Wed–Sat 11am–4pm, Sun 1–4pm; $5; ⓣ703/838-3852, ⓦwww.apothecarymuseum.org), which was founded in 1792 and remained in business until the 1930s. It still displays herbs, potions and medical paraphernalia – some eight thousand items in all.

Down on the waterfront, a former munitions factory houses the **Torpedo Factory Art Center**, 105 N Union St (daily 10am–5pm; free; ⓣ703/838-4565, ⓦwww.torpedofactory.org), where you can watch artists at work in their studios and browse numerous galleries. In the same building, the **Alexandria Archaeology Museum** (Tues–Fri 10am–3pm, Sat 10am–5pm, Sun 1–5pm; free; ⓣ703/838-4399, ⓦwww.alexandriaarchaeology.org) displays aspects of 250 years of the town's history and prehistory.

Next to the Amtrak and King Street subway station stands the 333ft obelisk of the **George Washington National Masonic Memorial**, 101 Callahan Drive (Mon–Sat 10am–4pm, Sun noon–4pm; free; ⓣ703/683-2007, ⓦwww.gwmemorial.org), where there's a 17ft bronze **statue** of the founding father, sundry Masonic memorabilia and dioramas depicting events from his life.

Practicalities

The **Metro** station for Old Town Alexandria is King Street (25min from downtown DC; yellow and blue lines), a mile or so from most of the sights; alternatively, you can pick up the local DASH **bus**; $1.25 (ⓣ703/746-DASH, ⓦwww.dashbus.com), which runs down King Street and throughout Old Town; or, if you prefer, you can make the twenty-minute walk from the station instead. The friendly **visitor centre** is located in **Ramsay House**, the town's oldest, at 221 King St (daily 10am–8pm, Jan–March closes 5pm; ⓣ703/746-3301, ⓦwww.funside.com), where you can get the usual tourist information as well as details on walking tours.

Good places to **stay** include *Best Western Old Colony Inn*, 1101 N Washington St (ⓣ703/739-2222, ⓦwww.bestwestern.com; ❻), with free breakfast and high-speed internet access; *Morrison House*, 116 S Alfred St (ⓣ703/838-8000, ⓦwww.morrisonhouse.com; ❽), a Federal-style townhouse (built in 1985) with modern boutique comforts like free wi-fi and designer furnishings; and *Hotel Monaco*, 480 King St (ⓣ703/549-6080, ⓦwww.monaco-alexandria.com; ❽), boasting stylish decor, free wi-fi, wine tastings and chic rooms and suites that variously offer jetted tubs, flat-screen TVs and in-room bars.

There's a great range of **places to eat**. Try the elite *Restaurant Eve*, 110 S Pitt St (ⓣ703/706-0450), a nouveau American bistro offering expensive multi-course meals drawn from a rotating menu of seafood, game and beef ($110–150); *The Majestic*, 911 King St (ⓣ703/837-9117), whose upmarket diner offerings include chowder, ribs, chops, meatloaf and calf's liver; or, on the cheaper end of the spectrum, the *Hard Times Café*, 1404 King St (ⓣ703/837-0050), doling out four styles of fiery chili, from classic Texas to spicy-as-hell Terlingua, plus a veggie option. Good wings, rings, fries and savoury microbrews, too.

Mount Vernon

Set on a bluff overlooking the Potomac River, eight miles south of Alexandria, at 3200 George Washington Memorial Parkway, **Mount Vernon** (daily: April–Aug 8am–5pm; March, Sept, & Oct 9am–5pm; Nov–Feb 9am–4pm; $15; ⓣ703/780-2000, ⓦwww.mountvernon.org) is **George Washington**'s five-hundred-acre country estate, which has been restored to the year 1799, the last year of the general's life. Fifteen miles from downtown DC, it can be reached as a day-trip on the Tourmobile ($30; see p.333), or by the Fairfax Connector bus #101 from the Huntington metro station (hourly; $1.45; ⓦwww.fairfaxcounty.gov/connector).

In the house itself, the furnishings and decoration reflect Washington's sense of simple, spartan style. The items on display include a reading chair with a built-in fan and a key to the destroyed Bastille, presented by Thomas Paine on behalf of Lafayette. The four-poster bed upon which Washington died stands in an upstairs bedroom. Outside are the renovated **slave quarters**, built to house the ninety slaves who lived and worked on the grounds. Washington and his wife, Martha, are buried in a simple tomb on the south side of the house. For the full background on Mount Vernon, the fancy modern **Reynolds Museum** on the plantation site, has interactive displays, models of Washington and assorted short films. It also traces Washington's ancestry and displays porcelain from the house, medals, weapons, silver and a series of striking miniatures.

Three miles away stands the restored **grist mill**, Route 235 S (April–Oct daily 10am–5pm; $4, or $2 extra with Mount Vernon admission), that Washington built as a water-powered testament to the future of American industry. Today colonial re-enactors go about the laborious work of crushing grain into flour and cornmeal. A **distillery** features copper stills, a boiler and mash tubs, and a short movie about Washington's role in the whiskey-making process.

Manassas National Battlefield Park

Manassas National Battlefield Park extends over grassy hills at the western fringes of the Washington DC suburbs, just off I-66. The first major land battle of the Civil War – known in the North as the **Battle of Bull Run** – was fought here on the morning of July 21, 1861. Expecting an easy victory, some 25,000 Union troops attacked a Confederate detachment that controlled a vital railroad link to the Shenandoah Valley. But the rebels proved powerful opponents, and their strength in battle earned their commander, his famous nickname. (See p.371) He and General Lee also masterminded a second, even more demoralizing Union loss here in late August 1862, the battle of "Second Manassas", that came close to the high point of Confederate ascendancy. The **visitor centre** at the entrance, at 6511 Sudley Rd (daily 8.30am–5pm; $3 park admission; ⓣ703/361-1339, ⓦwww.nps.gov/mana), describes how the battles took shape, and details other aspects of the war.

Richmond and the tidewater

At the very heart of Virginia, **Richmond** and the **Chesapeake Bay tidewater** make up a fairly compact area that holds some of the country's most important surviving colonial- and Civil War-era sites. The greatest interest is to be found in the fascinating **Historic Triangle**, east of Richmond, and in **Fredericksburg**, to the north, site of several crucial battles.

Fredericksburg

Only a mile off the I-95 highway, halfway to Richmond from Washington DC, **FREDERICKSBURG** is one of Virginia's prettiest historic towns, where elegant downtown streets are backed by residential avenues lined with white picket fences. In colonial days, this was an important inland port, in which tobacco and other plantation commodities were loaded onto boats that sailed down the Rappahannock River. Dozens of stately early-American buildings along the waterfront now hold antique stores and boutiques.

In the 1816 town hall, the **Fredericksburg Area Museum**, 907 Princess Anne St (Mon & Thurs–Sat noon–5pm, Sun 1–5pm; $7; ⓣ540/371-3037, ⓦwww.famcc.org), has a range of displays tracing local history, from Native American settlements to the wartime era. The **Rising Sun Tavern**, 1304 Caroline St, was built as a home in 1760 by George Washington's brother, Charles. As an inn, it became a key meeting place for patriots and a hotbed of sedition. It is now a small **museum** (March–Oct: Mon–Sat 10am–5pm, Sun noon–4pm; Nov–Feb: Mon–Sat 11am–4pm, Sun noon–4pm; $5; ⓣ540-373-1776;), showcasing antique decor and a collection of pub games and pewter. Guides are also on hand to explain eighteenth-century medicine at **Hugh Mercer's Apothecary Shop**, 1020 Caroline St (same hours as above; $5), which often involved treating patients with the likes of leeches and crab claws. If you're more interested in George Washington, you can venture out to his family's **Ferry Farm**, 268 Kings Hwy (daily: March–Oct 10am–5pm, Jan & Feb 10am–4pm; $5; ⓣ540/370-0732, ⓦwww.kenmore.org), where he grew up and which still maintains a bucolic setting and gardens appropriate for the era. For information about the dozens of other key historical and cultural treasures in the region, visit **Preservation Virginia** (ⓦwww.apva.org).

Fredericksburg's strategic location made it vital during the **Civil War**, and the land around the town was heavily contested. More than 100,000 men lost their lives in the major battles and countless bloody skirmishes. The **visitor centre**, 702 Caroline St (daily: summer 10am–6pm; rest of year 10am–5pm; ⓣ540/373-1776, ⓦwww.visitfred.com), has informative exhibits and can lead you out to **Fredericksburg and Spotsylvania National Battlefield Park** (hours vary, often Mon–Fri 9am–5pm, Sat & Sun 9am–6pm; free; ⓦwww.nps.gov/frsp), south of town. Contact the centre or the above website for information on the other major battlefields, **Wilderness** and **Chancellorsville**, both west of town, as well as the various manors and shrines in the area.

Practicalities

The Amtrak **train** station is at 200 Lafayette Blvd and the Greyhound **bus** station at 1400 Jefferson Davis Hwy. Fredericksburg has many good, old-fashioned **B&Bs**, including the *Richard Johnston Inn*, 711 Caroline St (Ⓣ540/899-7606 or 877-557-0770, Ⓦwww.therichardjohnstoninn.com; ❻), an elegant, eighteenth-century establishment with plush rooms and some jetted tubs. One worthwhile motel to try is the *Inn at the Olde Silk Mill*, 1707 Princess Anne St (Ⓣ540/371-5666, Ⓦinnattheoldesilkmill.com; ❺), known for its rooms stocked with antiques, plus free wi-fi. The town has several good places to **eat** and **drink**. *Sammy T's*, 801 Caroline St (Ⓣ540/371-2008), is a popular bar and diner with substantial sandwiches, salads, wraps and pastas, and a good range of bottled beers; *Balisco*, west of the centre at 2577 Cowan Blvd (Ⓣ540/370-0355), is a fine Italian deli with rib-stuffing pizzas, pastas and sandwiches; and the *Colonial Tavern*, 406 Lafayette Blvd (Ⓣ540/373-1313), is the place to fill up on Irish food, music and beer.

Richmond and around

Founded in 1737 at the farthest navigable point on the James River, **RICHMOND** remained a small outpost until Virginians, realizing that their capital at Williamsburg was open to British attack, shifted it fifty miles further inland. When war broke out it was named the **capital of the Confederacy**. After the war, Richmond was devastated, but today's town maintains an extensive inventory of architecturally significant older buildings alongside its modern office towers, while **tobacco** is still a major industry.

Arrival, information and city transport

Two hours by car from Washington DC, via I-95, which cuts through the east side of downtown, Richmond is also served by Amtrak; **trains** pull into 1500 E Main St (further out of town, there's another station at 7519 Staples Mill Rd). The Greyhound **bus** station, just off I-64 at 2910 N Blvd, is a good way from the centre of town. The **airport**, ten miles east of downtown, is served by a half-dozen national carriers and has a small **visitor centre** (Mon–Fri 9.30am–4.30pm; Ⓣ804/236-3260; Ⓦwww.flyrichmond.com) in the arrivals terminal. Much of Richmond is compact enough to walk around, but to get to outlying places you can take a GRTC **bus**; $1.25, $1.75 express routes (Ⓣ804/358-GRTC, Ⓦwww.ridegrtc.com).

Accommodation

Finding well-priced **accommodation** in Richmond isn't difficult, with plenty of chain hotels downtown catering to the business and government trade. If you prefer to get a feel for the old city, stay the night in a **B&B** in one of the historic quarters.

The Berkeley 1200 E Cary St Ⓣ804/780-1300 or 1-888/780-4422, Ⓦwww.berkeleyhotel.com. Elegant small hotel with boutique touches and suites with private terraces, on the historic Shockoe Slip. ❽

Grace Manor Inn 1853 W Grace St Ⓣ804/353-4334, Ⓦwww.thegracemanorinn.com. Stately B&B housing three tasteful suites in a grand 1910 building. Rooms are rich with antique decor; some have fireplaces and claw-foot tubs. Breakfast can be quite good, too. ❻

Henry Clay Inn 114 N Railroad Ave, Ashland, Virginia Ⓣ804/798-3100, Ⓦwww.henryclayinn.com. Though eleven miles out of town, this pleasant B&B has fourteen antique-filled rooms with wi-fi. Some are suites with jacuzzis and fridges. ❹

The Jefferson 101 W Franklin St Ⓣ804/788-8000 or 1-800/424-8014, Ⓦwww.jeffersonhotel.com. Grand hotel with touches like a marble-columned lobby, marble baths, high-speed internet access and stylish rooms. Smart and sizeable suites also available. ❽

Linden Row Inn 100 E Franklin St Ⓣ804/783-7000 or 1-800/348-7424, Ⓦwww.lindenrowinn.com. A chic row of red-brick Georgian terraced houses converted into a comfortable modern hotel with antique furnishings and high-speed internet access. However, unless you get a swanky Parlor Suite, the rooms can be on the drab side. ❺

William Catlin House 2304 E Broad St ⓣ804/780-3746. B&B dating from 1845 that offers a mix of seven antebellum and Victorian rooms and suites, sited in the Church Hill district, not too far from downtown and the Shockoe Slip. ❺

Downtown Richmond

Richmond's **downtown** centres on a few blocks rising up from the James River to either side of Broad Street. Up the hill in the **Court End District**, dozens of well-preserved antebellum homes provide a suitable backdrop for some important museums and historic sites.

The **Virginia State Capitol**, 910 Capitol St (tours Mon–Sat 9am–4pm, Sun 1–4pm; free; ⓣ804/698-1788, ⓦlegis.state.va.us), houses the oldest legislative body still in existence in the US; the site has been in continuous use since 1788 as the state (and, briefly, Confederate) legislature. Thomas Jefferson had a hand in the design, and the domed central rotunda holds the only marble statue of George Washington modelled from life (by master sculptor Jean-Antoine Houdon), as well as busts of Jefferson and the seven other Virginia-born US presidents line the walls.

Also on Capitol Square is the Federal-style **Governor's Mansion**, 901 E Grace St, which, like the Capitol, is the oldest of its kind in the US, dating to 1813 (Tues–Thurs 10am–noon & 2–4pm; free; ⓣ804/371-2642). Much less reserved, across from Capitol Square, is the huge Victorian artefact of **Old City Hall**, 1001 E Broad St, designed in 1894 in a Gothic Revival style and so visually busy it makes your head spin. Just two blocks north of the Capitol, the **Museum of the Confederacy**, 1201 E Clay St (Mon–Sat 10am–5pm; Sun noon–5pm; $9; ⓦwww.moc.org), covers the history of the Civil War through weapons, uniforms and personal effects of Confederate leaders, including J.E.B. Stuart's plumed hat, the tools used to amputate Stonewall Jackson's arms at Chancellorsville (he died regardless), and Robert E. Lee's revolver and the pen he used to sign the surrender. Next door, the **White House of the Confederacy** (Mon–Sat 10am–5pm, Sun noon–5pm; $9, $12 combo ticket with museum), is an 1818 Neoclassical mansion where Jefferson Davis lived as Confederate president. After he absconded when the South fell in 1865, Abraham Lincoln famously visited the house and even sat briefly in Davis's office chair.

Two blocks west, the 1812 **Wickham House** now forms part of the excellent **Valentine Richmond History Center**, at 1015 E Clay St (Tues–Sat 10am–5pm, Sun noon–5pm; $8; ⓣ804/649-0711, ⓦwww.richmondhistorycenter.com). This Federal-style monolith houses a small local history museum focusing on the experience of working-class and black Americans, as well as an extensive array of furniture and pre-Civil War clothing such as whalebone corsets and other **Victorian** apparel.

Jackson Ward

West of the Convention Center on Sixth Street is a neighbourhood of early-nineteenth-century houses, **Jackson Ward**, filling a dozen blocks around First and Clay streets. This National Historic Landmark District has been the centre of Richmond's African American community since well before the Civil War, when Richmond had the largest free black population in the US. As well as covering local history, the **Maggie L. Walker House**, 110 E Leigh St (Mon–Sat 9am–5pm; free; ⓣ804/771-2017, ⓦwww.nps.gov/mawa), traces the working life of the physically disabled, black Richmond woman who, during the 1920s, was the first woman in the US to found and run a bank, now the Consolidated Bank and Trust. Nearby, the **Black History Museum**, at 00 Clay St (Tues–Sat

10am–5pm; $5; Ⓦwww.blackhistorymuseum.org), includes a well-presented gallery of artefacts of the Civil Rights movement as well as textiles from different peoples in Africa and America.

Canal Walk and around

A nice example of urban revitalization is the landscaping of a 1.25-mile stretch of waterfront into **Canal Walk**, which runs between downtown and Shockoe Bottom. **Canal boat rides** depart from around 14th and Virginia streets (hours vary, often Fri & Sat noon–7pm, Sun noon–5pm; $5; Ⓣ804/649-2800), providing a leisurely and pleasant half-hour jaunt. For insight into the Confederate period, you can start or end your stroll at the **American Civil War Center**, 490 Tredegar St (daily 9am–5pm; free; Ⓣ804/771-2145, Ⓦwww.nps.gov/rich), at the refurbished **Tredegar Iron Works**, a munitions plant whose foundry churned out tons of Confederate materiel. The centre has multimedia presentations about Civil War history and three floors of compelling exhibits. Tredagar is also the main visitor centre for **Richmond National Battlefield Park**, which describes the dozens of Civil War sites in the area that can be accessed on an eighty-mile drive. Four other local visitor centres are also in operation, the most interesting being the **Chimborazo Medical Museum**, a few miles east at 3215 E Broad St (daily 9am–5pm; free; Ⓣ804/226-1981), which has disturbing displays on the medicine and technology available (or not) to help wounded soldiers of the era. Those who weren't so lucky ended up just west of Tredagar at **Hollywood Cemetery**, 412 S Cherry St (daily 8am–5pm; free tours April–Oct Mon–Sat 10am; Ⓣ804/648-8501, Ⓦwww.hollywoodcemetery.org), where a 90ft-tall granite **pyramid** commemorates the 18,000 Confederate troops killed nearby.

Shockoe Bottom, the Poe Museum and Church Hill

Split down the middle by the raised I-95 freeway, the gentrified riverfront warehouse district of **Shockoe Bottom** still holds a few reminders of Richmond's industrial past among the restaurants and nightclubs on its cobblestone streets. From **Shockoe Slip**, an old wharf rebuilt in the 1890s after being destroyed in the Civil War, Cary Street runs east along the waterfront, lined by a wall of brick warehouses – many of which have been converted into lofts and condos – known as **Tobacco Row**.

Nearby, Richmond's oldest building, an appropriately gloomy 250-year-old flagstone house, holds the **Edgar Allan Poe Museum**, 1914 E Main St (Tues–Sat 10am–5pm, Sun 11am–5pm; $6; Ⓣ804/648-5523, Ⓦwww.poemuseum.org), commemorating the dark poet who grew up here, and showcasing memorabilia and relics such as his walking stick and a lock of his hair, plus a model of Richmond as it was in Poe's time.

Church Hill, a few blocks northeast, is one of Richmond's oldest surviving districts, its decorative eighteenth-century houses looking out over the James River (it's also the site of the Chimborazo Museum; see above). Capping the hill at the heart of the neighbourhood, the 1741 **St John's Church**, 2401 E Broad St (tours Mon–Sat 10am–3.30pm, Sun 1–3.30pm; $6; Ⓦwww.historicstjohnschurch.org), is best known as the place where, during a 1775 debate, future state governor and firebrand **Patrick Henry** proclaimed, "Give me liberty or give me death!". His speech, along with the debate itself, is re-created by actors in period dress every Sunday at 2pm in summer.

The Fan District

The **Fan District**, so named because its tree-lined avenues fan out at oblique angles, spreads west from the downtown area, beyond Belvidere Street (US-1), and its centrepiece, **Monument Avenue**, which is lined with garish Victorian and historic-revival mansions from the turn of the twentieth century. South of Monument Avenue, at 2800 Grove Ave, stands the **Virginia Museum of Fine Arts** (daily 10am–5pm; $5 donation; ⓦwww.vmfa.museum), newly remodelled into a grand and inspiring modern space to house its extensive collection of Impressionist and post-Impressionist paintings, among them American works ranging from Charles Willson Peale's acclaimed portraits, to George Catlin's romantic images of Plains Indians to the pop art creations of Roy Lichtenstein and Claes Oldenburg. Other galleries contain such items as Frank Lloyd Wright furniture, Lalique jewellery, Hindu and Buddhist sculpture from the Himalayas and jewel-encrusted Fabergé Easter eggs, crafted in the 1890s for the Russian tzars.

Eating and drinking

Richmond has a good choice of **eating** options at both ends of the price spectrum, with barbecue and the higher-priced New Southern cuisine being specialities.

The Black Sheep 901 W Marshall St, near Jackson Ward ⓣ804/648-1300. Prime eclectic restaurant whipping up fantastic hashes and French toast for breakfast, as well as chicken and dumplings, mushroom bucatini and lamb kebabs – a hodgepodge of flavours and prices.

Border Chophouse 1501 W Main St, Fan District ⓣ804/355-2907. Mid-priced Western-style spot that serves up pasta, veal and lamb dishes, but whose specialty is barbecue, be it beef ribs, pork or chicken, and some lip-smacking Bloody Marys.

Julep's 1719 E Franklin St, Shockoe Bottom ⓣ804/377-3968. New Southern dining at its best, with many great mid-priced to expensive dishes, among them onion-crusted salmon, sweetwater crab soup and duck breast with pancetta.

Mamma Zu 501 S Pine St, south of Downtown ⓣ804/788-4205. Italian food in the South can often be awful, but this is one big exception: a terrific upper-end restaurant that serves up delicious oyster soup, veal marsala and calamari, among other savoury choices.

Millie's Diner 2603 E Main St ⓣ804/643-5512. Worth a trip out beyond Shockoe Bottom to enjoy expensive but delicious seafood and steak, plus rack of lamb and molasses-braised breast, and there's also a nice range of brews.

Penny Lane Pub 421 E Franklin St, Downtown ⓣ804/780-1682. British-style joint with substantial grilled food and other affordable pub grub, including a mean steak-and-Guinness pie, plus a full range of English and other beers, and European soccer on TV.

Strawberry Street Café 421 N Strawberry St ⓣ804/353-6860. Casual and comfortable Fan District café offering mainly inexpensive quiches, pasta and salads, but also mid-priced jambalaya and crab cakes, and a salad bar nestled in an old bathtub.

Nightlife

Richmond's main **nightlife** spots are concentrated around the **Shockoe Slip** and **Shockoe Bottom** areas, just east of downtown. A good bet for mainstream **theatre** is the Barksdale Theatre, 1601 Willow Lawn Drive (ⓣ804/282-2620, ⓦwww.barksdalerichmond.org), while the Chamberlayne Actors Theatre, 319 N Wilkinson Rd (ⓣ804/262-9760, ⓦwww.cattheatre.com), offers fringe works that are more daring and contemporary. For details on music and events, check the free **Style Weekly** newspaper or ⓦwww.arts.Richmond.com.

The Historic Triangle

Along with Massachusetts, the **Historic Triangle**, on the peninsula that stretches southeast of Richmond between the James and York rivers, holds the richest concentration of colonial-era sites in the US. **Jamestown**, founded in 1607, was Virginia's first settlement; **Williamsburg** is a detailed replica of the colonial capital; and **Yorktown** was the site of the climactic battle in the Revolutionary War. All are within a scenic hour's drive from Richmond, and Williamsburg is accessible by Amtrak **train**.

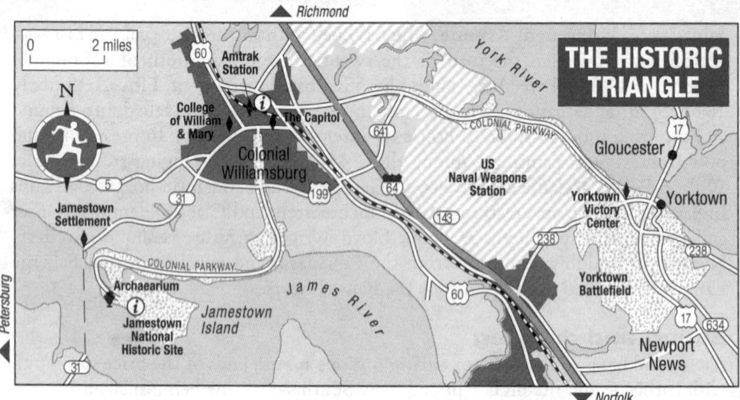

Although I-64 is the quickest way to cover the fifty miles from Richmond to Williamsburg, a far more pleasing drive along US-5 rolls through **plantation** country, where many eighteenth-century mansions are open to the public. Once you're in the Historic Triangle, the best way to get around is along the wooded **Colonial Parkway**, which winds west to Jamestown and east to Yorktown, twenty miles in all. Most of the area's numerous tourist facilities are to be found around Williamsburg; a few suggestions are listed under "Historic Triangle practicalities" on p.362.

Jamestown

Jamestown was England's first successful stab at a New World colony, after earlier efforts to the south failed. Built as a trading and military outpost, its lore and legend are still being celebrated four hundred years later, with recent archeological discoveries adding new insights and perspectives. You'll want to visit both the original location and the re-created site by taking the scenic Colonial Parkway, or highways 5 and 31 from Williamsburg. Protected within the **Jamestown National Historic Site** on Jamestown Island, the one bit of seventeenth-century Jamestown to survive the ravages of time and a 1698 fire is the 50ft tower of the first brick church, built around 1650 – one of the oldest extant English structures in the US.

The area is roughly divided into two sections: the **New Towne** is where the colonists relocated after the 1620s to erect businesses, establish permanent residences, build livestock pens and so on. Much of what's visible are replicas of the original brick foundations buried below (to protect from weather damage). More interesting is the site of the **Old Towne**, which includes ruins from the original triangular 1607 fort. Here you'll see dozens of archeologists working behind a perimeter, and you can also drop in on the **Archaearium**, where some of the many treasures discovered here – everything from glassware to utensils, to the skeleton of a colonist who died a violent death – are on display (also online at Ⓦ www.historicjamestowne.org).

At the end of the Colonial Parkway, the **visitor centre** (daily 9am–5pm; seven-day pass $10/car, includes Yorktown battlefield; Ⓣ 757/229-1733, Ⓦ www.nps.gov/jame; see opposite), features drawings and audiovisual exhibits that conjure up the past, and, closer to the park entrance, you can watch artisans making old-fashioned **glasswork** and purchase some of their creations, as well as see the brick remnants of a seventeenth-century kiln.

If looking at dusty artefacts isn't enough for you, head to the adjacent **Jamestown Settlement** (daily 9am–5pm; $14, $19.25 with Yorktown Victory

Center; ⓣ757/253-4838, ⓦwww.historyisfun.org), for a more family-friendly, somewhat simplified look at the early colony. This complex of museums and full-size replicas provides a colourful view of what went on here, its reconstructed buildings staffed by guides in period costume weaving, making pottery and so on. Replicas of the three **ships** that carried the first settlers are moored on the James River.

Colonial Williamsburg

The splendid re-creation of **Colonial Williamsburg** is an essential tourist experience for anyone with a flair for American history. While you have to buy a pricey ticket to look inside the restored buildings, the grounds are open all the time, and you can wander freely down the cobblestone streets and across the green commons.

From the Wren Building on the William and Mary campus, separated from Colonial Williamsburg by a mock-historic shopping centre, **Duke of Gloucester Street** runs east through the historic area to the old Capitol. The first of its eighteenth-century buildings, a hundred yards along, is the Episcopalian **Bruton Parish Church**, where all the big names of the revolutionary period were known to visit, and which has been serving as a house of worship for nearly 300 years. Behind the church, the broad **Palace Green** spreads north to the Governor's Palace (see below). West of the church, the 1771 **courthouse** and the octagonal **powder magazine**, protected by a guardhouse, face each other in the midst of Market Square. Further along, **Chowning's Tavern**, a reconstruction of an alehouse that stood here in 1766, is a functioning pub with lively entertainment.

The real architectural highlight is the **Capitol**, a monumental edifice at the east end of Duke of Gloucester Street. The current building, a 1945 reconstruction of the 1705 original, has an open-air ground-floor **arcade** linking two keyhole-shaped wings. One wing housed the elected, legislative body of the Colonial government, the **House of Burgesses**, while the other held the chambers of the **General Court** – where alleged felons, including thirteen of Blackbeard's pirates, were tried.

The "merchants" of Duke of Gloucester Street have been done up as eighteenth-century apothecaries, cobblers and silversmiths, and the docents inside are an excellent source of historical information on their respective crafts; taking part in a casual conversation or working demonstration can be an excellent way to get into the spirit of things – learning about anything from making bullets and saddles, to printing presses and wigs. The **Raleigh Tavern** along Gloucester Street was where the independence-minded colonial government reconvened after being dissolved by the loyalist governors in 1769 and again in 1774; the original burned down in 1859. Finally, the imposing two-storey **Governor's Palace**, at the north end of Palace Green, has a grand ballroom and opulent furnishings, and must have served as a telling declaration of royal power, no doubt enforced by the startling display of swords, muskets and other deadly weaponry interlaced on the walls of the foyer.

Yorktown

YORKTOWN, along the York River on the north side of the peninsula, gave its name to the decisive final major battle of the **Revolutionary War**, when, on October 18, 1781, overwhelmed and besieged British (and German mercenary) troops under the command of Charles, Lord Cornwallis, surrendered here to the joint American and French forces commanded by George Washington. At the heart of the namesake battlefield that surrounds the town, a **visitor centre** (daily 9am–5pm; $10/car for seven-day pass, good also for admission to Jamestown National Historic Site ⓣ757/898-2410; ⓦwww.nps.gov/yonb) has interpretive displays, including a replica, walk-through fighting ship and military artefacts, and also provides several guided tours of the area. A dozen original buildings

Tickets for Colonial Williamsburg

Although it's pleasant enough to stroll about the open spaces of Colonial Williamsburg, to set foot inside any of the buildings that have been restored or rebuilt you need to buy a ticket, either from the main **visitor centre** (daily 9am–5pm; ⓣ1-800/HISTORY, ⓦwww.history.org), north of the centre off the Colonial Parkway, or from a smaller office at the west end of Duke of Gloucester St. Most buildings in the park are open daily from 9am to 5pm, but about a third of them may have special hours and days they're open; check the website for details. Day-pass **tickets** are $36 (kids $18) and include access to the merchant shops and the Capitol, and admission to on-site museums devoted to folk art and the decorative arts, or $46 (kids $23) to include a Governor's Mansion tour and an extra day. Aside from these, there are additional charges for the special programmes and events offered by Colonial Williamsburg, such as staged courthouse trials, holiday spectacles and candlelit walking tours.

survive from the era, along with the earthworks. The **Siege Line Overlook** (at the visitor centre) has good views of strategic points, while maps and an audio tour are available if you want to explore in detail.

Note that, as at Jamestown, the state of Virginia and National Park Service have constructed a mini theme park nearby – this time a re-created Continental Army encampment – as part of the **Yorktown Victory Center** (daily 9am–5pm; $9.50, $19.25 with Jamestown Settlement, see p.360; ⓦwww.historyisfun.org), west of the battlefield on US-17. The museum covers both sides of the conflict, and two outdoor museums portray life on a middle-class farm and in a Revolutionary War camp.

Historic Triangle practicalities

Of the three main sites, only Williamsburg is easily reached without a car, and it's the hub of accommodation and dining. Amtrak **trains** and Greyhound **buses** stop at 468 N Boundary St, two blocks from the Governor's Palace. The Colonial Parkway makes an excellent, scenic cycling route to Jamestown (12 miles away) or Yorktown (14 miles); rent a **bike** from Bikes Unlimited at 759 Scotland St in Williamsburg ($15–20/ day; ⓣ757/229-4620, ⓦwww.bikewilliamsburg.com). In Colonial Williamsburg, ticket-holders can use the hop-on, hop-off **shuttle buses** (daily 9am–10pm) that leave from the visitor centre and stop at convenient points in the historic area. You can also pick up the **Historic Triangle Shuttle**, which is free and stops at all the major attractions (mid-March to Nov daily every 30min, 9.30am–4pm).

For **accommodation**, the Williamsburg Hotel/Motel Association (ⓣ757/220-3330 or 1-800/221-7165, ⓦwww.gowilliamsburg.com) can find you a bed at no extra charge. West of the centre, US-60 is lined with endless motels, and there are also several cheap options just a few blocks east of the Capitol, including the basic but clean and well-sited *Bassett Motel*, 800 York St (ⓣ757/229-5175, ⓦwww.bassettmotel.com; ❷). The pricier *Duke of York Motel*, 508 E Water St in Yorktown (ⓣ757/898-3232, ⓦwww.dukeofyorkmotel.com; ❻), has beachfront units, some with kitchenettes, fridges and jacuzzis, along the York River. Even better, *Marriott's Manor Club at Ford's Colony*, 101 St Andrews Drive (ⓣ757/258-5705, ⓦwww.marriott.com; ❻), is four miles outside of town and has expensive villas as well as entry-level units with DVD players, fireplaces and patios. Finally, there are several **campgrounds** along US-5 and US-60, west of Williamsburg ($25–35/tent).

The various **restaurants** and taverns along Duke of Gloucester Street in Colonial Williamsburg feature good (if overpriced) pub food; some operate on a seasonal basis only (often April–Oct) and all except *Chowning's Tavern* should be reserved in advance (ⓣ1-800/HISTORY). West of the historic area, in the Merchants Square shopping mall, the excellent *Trellis Café* (ⓣ757/229-8610) serves pricey seafood and steak entrees for dinner, but affordable sandwiches and burgers for lunch, and across the street the *Cheese Shop* (T757/220-0298) has great deli sandwiches – try the Virginia ham – but expect a wait during peak hours. There is also a clutch of solid restaurants near the William and Mary campus, including the *Green Leafe Café*, 765 Scotland St (T757/220-3405), offering solid chili, burgers, pizza and pasta, and dozens of brews on tap. Finally, Yorktown isn't the place to have a fine-dining experience, but for serviceable pub grub, burgers and chowder, the *Yorktown Pub*, 540 Water St (T757/886-9964), will do in a pinch.

The Atlantic coast

One of the busiest of the East Coast ports, **Norfolk** sits midway along the coast at the point where the Chesapeake Bay empties into the Atlantic Ocean. As Virginia's only heavy industrial centre, it's not pretty, but it does have a rich maritime and naval heritage, as well as the Chrysler Museum, one of the region's best art galleries, and access to historic **Portsmouth**, a short ferry ride away. Fifteen miles east of Norfolk, along the open Atlantic, **Virginia Beach** draws summer sun-seekers to the state's busiest seashore.

The rest of Virginia's Atlantic coast is on its isolated and sparsely populated **Eastern Shore**, where the attractive little island town of **Chincoteague** serves as the headquarters of a wildlife refuge that straddles the Maryland border as part of the Assateague Island National Seashore.

Norfolk

Along with Hampton Roads and Newport News on the north side of the James River, **NORFOLK** is home to the largest US naval base, with all manner of grey-steel behemoths cruising past regularly. The waterfront features Norfolk's premier attraction, **Nauticus: The National Maritime Center** (daily 10am–5pm; $11; T757/664-1000, Wwww.nauticus.org), which has oceanography displays, shallow pools for touching tidal creatures and horseshoe crabs, bigger aquariums, large-screen films, interactive naval exhibits and a deep-sea submersible. On the second floor, the **Hampton Roads Naval Museum** (Tues–Sat 10am–5pm, Sun noon–5pm; free; Wwww.hrnm.navy.mil) documents historical naval operations in the area; across from the centre, you can tour the decks of the **USS Wisconsin** (daily 10am–4.45pm; included in Nauticus admission).

An extraordinary array of Asian antiquities is displayed in the intimate Tudor-style home, now known as the **Hermitage Foundation Museum**, by the Lafayette River at 7637 N Shore Rd (45min guided tours only; Mon–Sat 10am–5pm, Sun 1–5pm; $5; T757/423-2052, Wwww.hermitagefoundation.org). It's really a hodgepodge, encompassing everything from Persian rugs, medieval tapestries and ancient Chinese ceremonial vessels, to European Christian icons and hand-painted stained glass. There are also tours of the gardens ($6) and of some of the related buildings on the site (summer, by reservation only; $40).

The city's biggest-name institution, the **Chrysler Museum**, half a mile north of the Norfolk waterfront, 245 W Olney Rd at Mowbray Arch (Wed 10am–9pm, Thurs–Sat 10am–5pm, Sun noon–5pm; free; T757/664-6200, Wwww.chrysler.org), holds another eclectic collection, this one belonging to car magnate Walter Chrysler Jr, comprising ancient Greek statuary, French Impressionist paintings, Franz Klein abstractions and Maya funerary objects, as well as world-class Tiffany and Lalique glassware. For a glimpse of bourgeois life in the area c.1800, check out the museum's **Moses Myers House**, on Bank Street at E Freemason Street (tours on the hour Wed–Sat 10am–3pm, Sun 1–3pm, no tours at 2pm; free), the elegant home of one of Norfolk's most prominent Jewish residents, adorned with portraits by Gilbert Stuart and Thomas Sully, and carefully restored to its early-nineteenth-century flair. The Chrysler's associated **Norfolk History Museum**, 601 E Freemason St (tours only, on the hour Wed–Sun noon & 2pm; free; ⓣ757/441-1526), has a predictable array of historical objects and antiques but is most interesting for the sturdy 1794 Georgian manor it's housed in.

Practicalities

Norfolk Airport Shuttle (ⓣ757/963-0433, ⓦwww.onetransportationsolution.com) connects downtown Norfolk with **Norfolk International Airport** ($21), five miles northeast. Amtrak **bus** connections from Newport News, across the James River on the north shore, stop at W Bute Street at York Street, and Greyhound stops at 701 Monticello Ave. Norfolk's convenient **visitor centre**, at exit 273 off I-64, is at 9401 Fourth View St (daily 9am–5pm; ⓣ757/441-1852). Free **NET buses** provide transportation to major sites (Mon–Fri 6.30am–11pm, Sat noon–midnight, Sun noon–8pm; ⓦwww.norfolk.gov/Visitors/net.asp).

With far better **accommodation** options available nearby in Virginia Beach (see below), there should be no need to resort to the usual chain hotels in Norfolk. Two exceptions are the pleasant *Freemason Inn*, 411 W York St (ⓣ757/963-7000, ⓦwww.freemasoninn.com; ❻), a four-unit B&B whose rooms offer fireplaces and jacuzzi tubs, with free on-site wine and cheese, and the good-value *Governor Dinwiddie*, 506 Dinwiddie St (ⓣ757/392-1330, ⓦwww.governordinwiddiehotel.com; ❺), in Portsmouth, whose rooms and suites variously offer DVD players, kitchens and in-room bars.

For **dining**, there's inexpensive seafood with an Asian edge – seared tuna, ginger dumplings and fried shrimp – at *Bardo*, 430 W 21st St, (ⓣ757/622-7362), and for a cheap taste of Americana, stop by *Doumar's*, a 1950s-era drive-in restaurant at 1919 Monticello Ave, (ⓣ757/627-4163), where white-hatted waitstaff bring the food to your car; it's tops for barbecue, burgers and waffle-cone ice cream. Finally, in downtown Norfolk, the ornate 1913 Wells Theater, 110 E Tazewell St (ⓣ757/627-1234, ⓦwww.vastage.com) puts on plays, musicals and the odd vaudeville show.

Portsmouth

A small **paddlewheel ferry** (hours vary, often weekdays 7.15am–11.30pm, weekends 10.15am-11.45pm; $1.50; ⓦwww.hrtransit.org) shuttles from Waterside Park in **Norfolk** across the harbour to the historic city of **PORTSMOUTH**. Here, if you're sufficiently fired up by all the military hardware on view, drop by the **Norfolk Naval Shipyard Museum**, 2 High St, on the waterfront (Tues–Sat 10am–5pm, Sun 1–5pm; $3; ⓣ757/393-8591, ⓦwww.portsnavalmuseums.com), whose tourable highlight is a century-old **lightship** (same hours, but closed Dec–Feb), which once acted as a floating lighthouse for the harbour. Away from the docks, Portsmouth's brick-lined streets are flanked by charming early-American houses and the fetching 1846 Colonial Revival **courthouse**, on High and Court streets (Tues–Sat 9am–5pm, Sun 11am–5pm; $5; ⓦwww.courthousegalleries.com), now an art gallery.

Virginia Beach

The massive resort of **VIRGINIA BEACH** has grown to become the largest city in the state, with nearly half a million people. Although the oceanfront commercial activity can be a monument to tackiness, the relaxed atmosphere actually leads some to stay longer than planned.

The city's focus is its long, sandy **beach**, lined with hotels and motels, and backed by a boardwalk strip of bars, restaurants and nightclubs. Virginia Beach is also a major **surf centre**, hosting the **East Coast Surfing Championships** in late August (Ⓣ1-800/861-SURF, Ⓦwww.surfecsc.com). The beach is the site of dozens of high-spirited annual **festivals**, few better than the **American Music Festival** (Ⓣ757/491-SUNN, Ⓦwww.beachstreetusa.com), which draws big-name artists to jam on the sands over Labor Day weekend. Away from the beach, most of the action is along Atlantic Avenue, the main drag.

High-tech exhibits and an IMAX theatre are featured at the **Virginia Aquarium and Marine Science Center**, 717 General Booth Blvd (daily 9am–5pm; $17, $23 with IMAX show; Ⓣ757/385-FISH, Ⓦwww.virginiaaquarium.com), which explores all things aquatic, including tanks devoted to sharks, rays, sea turtles and jellyfish in different climatically themed environments, a short, pleasant nature trail through the **Owls Creek salt marsh** and an aviary displaying dozens of native species. The museum also organizes **dolphin-watching** expeditions (April–Oct; $19; 90min) and **whale-watching** cruises (late Dec to mid-March; $28; 2hr 30min), for which you should reserve in advance.

Heading north, the eccentric Association for Research and Enlightenment, 215 67th St at Atlantic Avenue (Mon–Sat 10am–8pm, Sun noon–6pm; free; Ⓦwww.edgarcayce.org), focuses on **Edgar Cayce** (1877–1945), known as "the sleeping prophet" because of his alleged ability, while in a trance, to diagnose and heal the ailments of individuals anywhere in the world. Willing visitors can use an enormous metaphysical library, take in a lecture on various New Age subjects or test their own personal ESP. With an entrance five miles west off Hwy 60/Shore Drive, the woodland of **First Landing State Park** was the site where the first English settlers touched land in 1607 before moving on to Jamestown; it's Virginia's most popular state park, good for boating, cycling and campgrounds ($24, or $30 with electricity; Ⓣ1-800/933-PARK), with a beach on the Chesapeake Bay. About eight miles inland from the park is one of the city's many historic relics (for the various others, enquire at the visitor centre), the **Adam Thoroughgood House**, 1636 Parish Rd (Tues–Sat 9am–5pm, Sun 11am–5pm; $4; Ⓣ757/460-7588), the squat brick home of a man who came to the New World as a servant and ended up as a colonial leader and militiaman; his story, and that of the era, is told through the 1636 house's antiques and displays.

A few miles up and down the coast are some beautiful and peaceful stretches of golden sand. To the south lies the 9000-acre, four-mile-long **Back Bay National Wildlife Refuge** (daily dawn–dusk; $5/car, $2/hiker or cyclist; Ⓦwww.fws.gov/backbay), an avian preserve for snow geese, sea turtles, falcons and bald eagles, where you can walk, bike or fish (but not swim), and **False Cape State Park**, a mile-wide barrier spit that connects to North Carolina and is one of the region's last undisturbed coastlines – though you'll have to arrive by foot, bike or boat (cars are banned to False Cape), and only primitive camping is available ($11/night; Ⓣ1-800/933-PARK).

Practicalities

Greyhound stops at 1017 Laskin Rd, off 31st Street, while the Amtrak **bus** connection from Newport News train station arrives at 19th Street and Pacific Avenue. The **visitor centre**, 2100 Parks Ave (daily 9am–5pm, summer until 7pm; Ⓣ1-800/822-3224, Ⓦwww.vbfun.com), is at the east end of I-264, half a mile west of the beach at 21st Street. Beach **trolleys** called The Wave (May–Sept daily 8am–2am; $1.50; Ⓣ757/222-6100, Ⓦwww.hrtransit.org) are the easiest way to get around (buses cost the same price); the most useful route is up and down Atlantic Avenue (#30).

Virginia Beach has good **accommodation** for a range of budgets, though typical rates at the seafront hotels tend to approach \$200 in summer. Otherwise, *Barclay Cottage*, 400 16th St (ⓣ757-422-1956, ⓦwww.barclaycottage.com; ❹–❻ by season), is a tasteful B&B in a century-old homestead, whose rooms offer the usual quaint Victorian decor, with some jetted tubs; *The Capes Ocean Resort*, 2001 Atlantic Ave (March–Oct; ⓣ757/428-5421, ⓦwww.capeshotel.com; ❹–❻), offers a broad range of rooms, though all come with oceanfront balconies and fridges; and the *Four Sails*, 3301 Atlantic Ave (ⓣ757/491-8100, ⓦfoursails.com; ❹–❽ by season), is a seaside tower with amenities such as sauna, pool and sundeck, in a central location, with widely varying rates depending on the season.

The town also offers some great **restaurants**. Among the best are ★ *Terrapin*, 3102 Holly Rd (ⓣ757/321-6688), a moderate to upper-end eatery with delicious specialties such as veal shank, truffle mac and cheese, and spicy sea scallops, and the elite *One Fish-Two Fish*, 2109 W Great Neck Rd (ⓣ757/496-4350), which has a fine range of seafood, as well as steak and rack of lamb. On the main drag, the choices are inconsistent, but *Catch 31*, 3001 Atlantic Ave (ⓣ757/213-3472), does have decent burgers and surf-and-turf, with a waterside view, and *Baja Cantina*, 206 23rd St (ⓣ757/437-2920), is a friendly bar featuring serviceable Mexican food at cheap prices.

The Eastern Shore

Virginia's longest and least-visited stretch of Atlantic coastline, the **Eastern Shore**, lies separated from the rest of the state on the distant side of the Chesapeake Bay, and with its fishing and farming culture, has developed fairly independently from the rest of the state over the centuries. Only the southernmost segment of what's known as the Delmarva Peninsula belongs to Virginia, by which point it has narrowed to become a flat spit of sand protected by a fringe of low-lying islands.

US-13, which runs down the centre of the peninsula and provides a handy short cut from Philadelphia or points north, crosses seventeen miles of open sea at the mouth of the Chesapeake Bay via the **Chesapeake Bay Bridge-Tunnel** (\$12/car single, \$17 single within 24hr; ⓦwww.cbbt.com). For most of its 23-mile length, the roadway runs just a few yards above the water, twice burrowing beneath the surface, before reaching its southern extremity halfway between Norfolk and Virginia Beach. To either side of US-13, a few hamlets and fishing harbours such as Nassawadox, Assawoman and Accomac are tucked away on rambling backroads.

Chincoteague and Assateague Island National Seashore

The most appealing destination on the Eastern Shore, **Chincoteague** occupies a beautiful seven-mile-long barrier island just south of the Maryland border. Little more than a village, the town is attracting new migrants, but still makes a relaxed base for exploring **Assateague Island National Seashore** (hours vary, often 6am–8pm; \$15 week-long vehicle pass, \$5/day, walkers and cyclists free; ⓣ757/336-6577, ⓦwww.nps.gov/asis), whose northern half holds several good hiking trails and can only be reached from Maryland; there are several types of first-come, first-served **campgrounds** available on the Maryland side, on the bay- or oceanfront (mid-Oct to mid-April; \$16; ⓣ410/641-3030). The southern half of the seashore, just a mile onwards from Chincoteague, is taken up by the 14,000-acre **Chincoteague National Wildlife Refuge** (daily: May–Sept 5am–10pm; March, April & Oct 6am–8pm; Nov–Feb 6am–6pm; \$10 seven-day vehicle pass, daily pass \$5; ⓦwww.fws.gov/northeast/chinco), notable for fine birdwatching and a range of animals from bats and otters to wild ponies. Call in at the **visitor centre** (Ⓣ757/336-6122) for information on the fifteen miles of trails through the dunes and marshes, or the pleasant beach at **Tom's Cove**. If you're in Chincoteague on the last Wednesday and Thursday of July, don't miss the annual **Pony Swim**, when the 150 wild ponies that roam Assateague Island to the north are herded together and directed on a swim through the channel to Chincoteague Memorial Park. Here the foals are sold by auction to help the local community. Note that it is only possible to cross the island's state border on foot – you must return to the mainland for vehicular access.

Reasonable **accommodation** options in Chincoteague include the grand *Island Manor House*, 4160 Main St (Ⓣ1-800/852-1505, Ⓦwww.islandmanor.com; ❺), a smart, antique-furnished B&B with eight quaint rooms; the *Refuge Inn*, 7058 Maddox Blvd (Ⓣ757/336-5511, Ⓦwww.refugeinn.com; ❺), providing an assortment of charming rooms and suites with patios and balconies, plus a swimming pool (though rates double in summer); and the *Cedar Gables Seaside Inn*, 6095 Hopkins Lane (Ⓣ1-888/491-2944, Ⓦwww.cedargable.com; ❼), a homey B&B whose four suites have fireplaces, jacuzzis, CD players and fridges, with excellent breakfasts, too. The best of the seafood eateries, *Bill's Seafood*, 4040 Main St (Ⓣ757/336-5831), is a fine **restaurant** serving delicious crab, oysters, clams and shrimp at moderate prices, plus steaks and chops. Just as good, the *Island Creamery*, 6243 Maddox Blvd (Ⓣ757/336-6236), is known for its broad range of tasty ice-cream flavours.

Charlottesville and the Shenandoah Valley

The densely forested but fairly low peaks of the **Blue Ridge Mountains** are nonetheless the highest on the East Coast, reaching 6600ft in places, and forming the eastern front of the four-hundred-mile-long crest of the **Appalachian Mountains**. At the geographical centre of the state sits the friendly college town of **Charlottesville**, which holds two monuments to Thomas Jefferson. South of here, **Appomattox Court House** is where Robert E. Lee surrendered his Confederate army, while to the west, **Shenandoah National Park** culminates in the 5729ft Mount Rogers. On the far side of the mountains, the lush **Shenandoah Valley** was once a vital and heavily contested Civil War battleground.

The main highway through the Shenandoah Valley, I-81, can be reached in the north via I-66 from Washington DC, and in the middle via I-64 from Richmond through Charlottesville. Numerous scenic routes are slower but more worthwhile, such as **Skyline Drive** and the **Blue Ridge Parkway** – both weave along the mountain crest, which averages 4000ft or so. You'll need a car to get the most out of the region, though cycling is a good option along the many backroads and, for hikers, the **Appalachian Trail** runs right down the middle.

Charlottesville

Seventy miles west of Richmond, **CHARLOTTESVILLE** holds some of the finest examples of early-American architecture, set around a compact, low-rise centre, crisscrossed by magnolia-shaded streets, which make for a pleasant stroll along the pedestrianized blocks of **Main Street**. The most compelling attraction is Thomas Jefferson's home and memorial, **Monticello**, which sits atop a hill just east of town, overlooking the beautiful Neoclassical campus of the University of Virginia, which he also designed.

The University of Virginia

Though he wrote the Declaration of Independence and served as the third US president, Thomas Jefferson took more pride in having established the **University of Virginia** than in any of his other achievements, as he designed every building down to the most minute detail, planned the curriculum and selected the faculty.

The centrepiece of the campus, called by Jefferson an "academical village", is the red-brick, white-domed **Rotunda**, modelled on the Pantheon and completed in 1826 to house the library and classrooms. A basement gallery tells the history of the university, while upstairs a richly decorated central hall links three elliptical classrooms. A staircase winds up to the **Dome Room**, where paired Corinthian columns rise to an ocular skylight. From the Rotunda, 45-minute guided tours of the campus begin (daily 10am, 11am, 2pm, 3pm & 4pm, except during holidays; free). Twin colonnades stretch along either side of a lushly landscaped quadrangle – **The Lawn** – linking single-storey student apartments with ten taller pavilions in which professors live and hold tutorials.

Monticello

One of America's most familiar buildings – it graces the back of the nickel – **Monticello**, three miles southeast of Charlottesville on Hwy-53, was the home of Thomas Jefferson for most of his life. Its symmetrical brick facade, cantered upon a white Doric portico, is surrounded by acres of beautiful hilltop grounds, which once made up an enormous plantation, with fine views out over the Virginia countryside.

You can see Monticello on one of several **guided tours** (daily: March–Nov 9am–5pm; Dec–Feb 10am–4pm; ⓣ434/984-9822, ⓦwww.monticello.org), each of which covers a different aspect of the site, though taking in more than one can get quite expensive. Options include the furnishings and gadgets of the "House" tour (30min; March–Oct $22, Nov–Feb $17), the more in-depth "Architecture" tour (1hr 15min; $27), and the kid-oriented "Family" tour (30min; $22). Evening "Signature" tours (1hr; May to early Sept $45) provide a broad overview with fewer people in tow. Each tour requires a timed ticket, for which you must reserve ahead.

From the outside, Monticello looks like an elegant, Palladian-style country estate, but as soon as you enter the domed entrance hall, with its animal hides, native craftworks, and fossilized bones and elk antlers (from Lewis and Clark's epic 1804 journey across North America, which Jefferson sponsored as president), you begin to see a different side of Jefferson. His love of gadgets is evidenced by an elaborate dual-pen device he used to make automatic copies of all his letters, and a weather vane over the front porch, connected to a dial so he could measure wind direction without stepping outside. In his **private chambers**, he slept in a cramped alcove that linked his dressing room and his study, and would get up on the right side of the bed if he wanted to make some late-night notes, on the left if he wanted to get dressed.

With the price of a tour ticket you can also visit the **gardens**, in which extensive flower and vegetable gardens spread to the south and west, and other parts of the plantation site focus on the remains of **Mulberry Row**, Monticello's slave quarters. Despite calling slavery an "abominable crime", he owned almost two hundred slaves and recent research indicates he probably had one or more children with one of them, Sally Hemings. At the south end of Mulberry Row, a grove of ancient hardwood trees surrounds Jefferson's gravesite, marked by a simple stone **obelisk**; the epitaph, which lists his major accomplishments, does not mention his having been president.

Practicalities

Amtrak **trains** from DC stop at 810 W Main St, and Greyhound **buses** pull in at 310 W Main St. Once you arrive, you can get to everything on foot, including the downtown **visitor centre**, 610 E Main St (daily 9am–5.30pm; ⓣ434/293-6789 or 1-877/386-1102, ⓦwww.charlottesville.org). Charlottesville has a good range of **accommodation**. Most places are of the familiar chain variety, but for better digs, try the *English Inn*, 2000 Morton Drive (ⓣ434/971-9900, ⓦwww.englishinncharlottesville.com; ❺), a large, mock-Tudor motel with clean and functional rooms, some of which have fridges and microwaves, plus a pool, sauna and gym. Good-value **B&B** rooms are available at the two restored, antique-laden houses of the *200 South Street Inn*, 200 South St (ⓣ434/979-0200, ⓦwww.southstreetinn.com; ❼), some of whose two dozen units have fireplaces and whirlpool tubs. Similar amenities are available at the handsome *Inn at Court Square*, 410 E Jefferson St (ⓣ434/295-2800, ⓦwww.innatcourtsquare.com; ❻), which has nine rooms in two houses as well as excellent Southern cuisine on offer. You can also arrange a stay in a B&B through Guesthouses (ⓣ434/979-7264, ⓦwww.va-guesthouses.com).

The best **eating** and **drinking** can be found near the university and the downtown mall, just north of which the upmarket *Tastings*, 502 E Market St (ⓣ434/293-3663), offers upper-end steak, fricassees, crab cakes and lobster bisque, plus a fine selection of wine – including many from local vineyards. The *Bluegrass Grill & Bakery*, 313 2nd St SE (ⓣ434/295-9700), makes a good morning stop for tasty pancakes, hash, biscuits and blintzes, while the *C&O Restaurant*, 515 E Water St (ⓣ434/971-7044), housed in an old railroad engineers building, offers high-end cuisine from braised veal to pan-fried trout, on a rotating menu of New Southern favourites.

Appomattox Court House

Set amid the rolling hills of central Virginia, some sixty miles south of Charlottesville on US-460 and Hwy-24, the village of **APPOMATTOX COURT HOUSE** was the site where Ulysses S. Grant blocked Robert E. Lee's retreating Confederate army and forced a surrender, on April 9, 1865, that effectively ended the Civil War after four bloody years. Final papers were signed in the home of the **McLean family**, who, ironically, had moved here to get away from the war after the first major battle – Bull Run – was fought on their property in Manassas. Details of the surrender are given in **Appomattox Court House National Historical Park** (daily 8.30am–5pm; $3–5/person by season; ⓦwww.nps.gov/apco). The village has been handsomely restored and the McLean home is now a museum.

Shenandoah National Park

The dark forests, rocky ravines and lovely waterfalls of **SHENANDOAH NATIONAL PARK**, far from being untouched wilderness, were created when hundreds of small family farms and homesteads were condemned by the state and federal governments during the Depression, and the land was left to revert to its natural state. With this history, it's no surprise that Shenandoah, meaning "river of high mountains", has one of the most scenic byways in the US, **Skyline Drive**, a thin, 105-mile ribbon of pavement curving along the crest of the Blue Ridge Mountains. It starts just off I-66 near the town of **Front Royal**, 75 miles west of DC, and winds south through the park, giving great views over the area. However, the road was constructed using the latest in 1930s technology and its width can be quite narrow at points for modern vehicles. Some of the vertiginous slopes alongside, combined with wildlife such as deer and smaller mammals that cross over the road, also make a trip on the Drive a bit hazardous in places – so a 35 mph limit is in force throughout the route.

Week-long **admission** to the park is $15 for cars and $8 for pedestrians ($10 for cars and $5 for pedestrians during the winter). Any time of year you can get the best of what the park has to offer by following one of the many **hiking trails** that split off from the ridge; most are two to six miles long. One begins near Byrd visitor centre and winds along to tumbling **Dark Hollow Falls**; another trail, leaving Skyline Drive at mile marker 45, climbs up a treacherous incline to the top of **Old Rag Mountain** for panoramic views out over the whole of Virginia and the Allegheny Mountains in the west. More ambitious hikers, or those who want to spend the night out in the backcountry, head for the **Appalachian Trail**. Details on any of these hikes, and free overnight camping permits, can be picked up at the following **visitor centres**: Dickey Ridge, milepost 4.7, Harry F. Byrd Sr, milepost 51, and Loft Mountain, milepost 79 (daily 8.30am–5pm; ⓣ540/999-3500, ⓦwww.nps.gov/shen).

Park **accommodation** (ⓣ1-888/896-3833, ⓦwww.visitshenandoah.com) includes the 1894 *Skyland Resort*, at milepost 41.7, with cabins and hotel rooms (❻), as well as a large restaurant with panoramic views; *Big Meadows Lodge*, at milepost 51.2, with similar facilities (❻); and *Lewis Mountain Cabins*, at milepost 57.5, with cosy, rustic accommodation (❹). There are also four **campgrounds** in the park ($15–20/night); reserve online at ⓦwww.recreation.gov or by calling ⓣ1-877/444-6777.

The Shenandoah Valley

Many of the small towns of the **SHENANDOAH VALLEY**, below Skyline Drive, were left in ruins after the Civil War – the region changed hands over seventy times at a cost of some 100,000 dead or maimed – but have since been restored to their original appearance. Numerous monuments and cemeteries line the backroads, surrounded by horse farms and apple orchards. Some eight major battlefields can be found here, and the region is marked as an official **National Historic Area**; for more details on following the military campaigns on foot or by car, see ⓦwww.shenandoahatwar.org.

Besides its martial history, the northern Shenandoah Valley also holds half a dozen of Virginia's many **limestone caverns**, which tend to be privately owned and touristy, and cost between $15–25 to explore. One of the largest is **Luray Caverns**, twelve miles east of New Market off Hwy-211 (hours vary, often daily 9am–6pm; $22; ⓦwww.luraycaverns.com), featuring an underground "organ" with stalagmites as "pipes", which you can see on the one-hour guided tours.

Further south, off Hwy-250 northwest of the town of **STAUNTON**, the **Frontier Culture Museum** (daily: winter 10am–4pm; rest of year 9am–5pm; $10; ⓦwww.frontiermuseum.org) showcases eight different kinds of immigrant farms, including buildings that were mostly imported from Europe. It's more a historic theme park than an authentic cultural experience, but still worth a look to see how backbreaking it must have once been to live the rural life. Finally, the **Woodrow Wilson Presidential Library**, 18–24 N Coalter St (daily: March–Oct 9am–5pm; Nov–Feb 10am–4pm, opens at noon Sun; $12, kids $3; ⓦwww.woodrowwilson.org), commemorates the 28th president of the US with exhibits on how he led the country into World War I and into various moral crusades, with a look at his chic Pierce-Arrow presidential limousine and his birthplace next door.

Lexington

With horse-drawn carriages moving along its quiet, brick-lined streets, the small valley town of **Lexington** offers a few key historical sites. The sombre **Lee Chapel and Museum** (Mon–Sat 9am–5pm, Sun 1–5pm, closes an hour earlier in winter; free; Ⓦchapelapps.wlu.edu), is on the colonnaded campus of **Washington and Lee University**, north of the town centre. Robert E. Lee taught here after the war – when it was known as Washington University – and, along with his family, is interred in the chapel's crypt; his famed horse, Traveler, is buried just outside. East of the chapel, on the far end of the parade ground of the arch **Virginia Military Institute**, the **George C. Marshall Museum** (Tues–Sat 9am–5pm, Sun 1–5pm; $5; Ⓣ540/463-7103, Ⓦwww.marshallfoundation.org) documents the life of World War II US General, and later Secretary of State, George C. Marshall, whose Marshall Plan helped rebuild Europe after the war.

In the town centre, the **Stonewall Jackson House**, 8 E Washington St (March–Dec Mon–Sat 9am–5pm, Sun 1–5pm; $8; Ⓦwww.stonewalljackson.org), is where the Confederate general and VMI professor lived before he rode off to war, and died at the battle of Chancellorsville. His spartan 1801 brick townhouse is furnished as it was when he lived there. Nearby, Jackson is buried, with 144 other Confederates, in the **Stonewall Jackson Memorial Cemetery**, on S Main Street at White Street (daily dawn–dusk; free).

For a break from military history, take a trip fifteen miles north of town, off Rte-606, to **Cyrus McCormick's Farm** (daily 8.30am–5pm; free; Ⓣ540/377-2255), where the famed inventor of the industrial reaper is honoured in an antique setting that includes a gristmill, blacksmith's forge, smokehouse and museum. For a further taste of the bucolic life, the **Virginia Horse Center**, a few miles north of town on Rte-39 (hours vary; Ⓣ540/464-2950, Ⓦwww.horsecenter.org), sits on six hundred acres, with eight barns and eighteen rings and arenas for displays of equine gallantry. Some are free, others cost between $5 and $20 and require advance tickets (Ⓣ540/464-2956 to reserve).

Twenty miles south of Lexington on US-11 is the spectacular **Natural Bridge** (daily 8am until dark; $18; Ⓦwww.naturalbridgeva.com), a 215ft limestone arch slowly carved by a creek; George Washington allegedly carved his initials into the rock (though it takes a keen eye to see them) and Thomas Jefferson was so impressed that he bought the site to preserve it and owned it for fifty years.

Practicalities

Lexington is also a good place to visit for its dozens of fine old homes; pick up a walking-tour map at the **visitor centre**, 106 E Washington St (Ⓣ540/463-3777, Ⓦwww.lexingtonvirginia.com). For distinctive **accommodation**, Historic Country Inns operates some of the most appealing B&Bs, spread over three stately old structures with 31 rooms and 12 suites, some with fireplaces, jacuzzis and in-room bars (Ⓣ1-877/283-9680, Ⓦwww.lexingtonhistoricinns.com; ❹). The *1868 Magnolia House Inn*, 501 S Main St (Ⓣ540/463-2567, Ⓦwww.magnoliahouseinn.com; ❻), was built by the architect of the Lee Chapel and has five comfortable units with tasteful furnishings and free wi-fi in a pleasant garden setting. Just a few miles north of town, the *Hummingbird Inn*, 30 Wood Lane (Ⓣ540/997-9065, Ⓦwww.hummingbirdinn.com; ❻), has five quaint rooms, with the added appeal of a renovated c.1780 farmhouse with fine dining, a solarium, veranda and wi-fi.

For **dining**, the *Southern Inn Restaurant*, right in the centre of town, at 37 S Main St (Ⓣ540/463-3612), has good, affordable sandwiches, steak and seafood, with pricier New Southern offerings such as shad roe and roasted guinea hen.

The similarly priced 🏃 *Sheridan Livery Inn*, 35 N Main St (Ⓣ540/464-1887), offers some of the best food around, from the barbecued shrimp and crab cake sandwiches to the succulent strip steak and chili-braised pork shoulder. For delicious shrimp-and-grits, catfish and duck breast at moderate prices, the *Bistro on Main*, 8 N Main St (Ⓣ540/464-4888), is also a reliable choice.

Along the Blue Ridge Parkway

Once it wends its way out of Shenandoah National Park, Skyline Drive becomes the **Blue Ridge Parkway**, a beautiful route heading southwest along the crest of the Appalachians. However, **I-81**, sweeping along the flank of the mountains, is a more efficient way of getting from Virginia to North Carolina and on to the Great Smoky Mountains (see p.417). Call Ⓣ828/271-4779 or visit Ⓦwww.nps.gov/blri for information on the various **campgrounds** ($16) and **visitor centres** along the Parkway. From May to November, the *Rocky Knob Cabins* (Ⓣ540/593-3503, Ⓦwww.blueridgeresort.com; ❸), on milepost 174, offers a memorable stay in the idyllic Meadows of Dan, with units dating from the Depression now featuring kitchenettes and fireplaces. Alternatively, the handsome *Peaks of Otter Lodge*, twenty miles north of Roanoke, VA, at milepost 86 (Ⓣ1-800/542-5927, Ⓦwww.peaksofotter.com; ❺), is open year-round, with clean, simple rooms and a view overlooking a lake.

Roanoke

Of the nearby towns, **ROANOKE**, between I-81 and the Parkway, is the largest in western Virginia. It's known for its historic **farmers' market**, dating from 1882, on Campbell Avenue at Market Street (Mon–Sat 8am–5pm, Sun 10am–4pm; Ⓣ540/342-2028), along with the new site of the **Taubman Museum**, 110 Salem Ave SE (Tues–Sat 10am–5pm, Sun noon–5pm; $10.50; Ⓣ540/342-5760, Ⓦwww.taubmanmuseum.org), whose sweeping, ultramodern steel-and-glass structure was designed by an associate of Frank Gehry; the art is no less interesting, focusing on oddball folk and outsider art, local artists and eye-opening conceptual and minimalist pieces. Fascinating castoffs are on view at the **History Museum of Western Virginia**, 1 Market Square (Tues–Fri 10am–4pm, Sat 10am–5pm, Sun 1–5pm; $3; Ⓦwww.history-museum.org), which records settlement of the region and holds everything from Victorian fashions to documents signed by Thomas Jefferson and war relics, and at the **Virginia Museum of Transportation**, 303 Norfolk Ave (Mon–Sat 10am–5pm, Sun 1–5pm; $8; Ⓦwww.vmt.org), home to the South's largest collection of diesel locomotives, plus antique buggies, buses and fire trucks. The **visitor centre**, 101 Shenandoah Ave NE (daily 9am–5pm; Ⓣ540/342-6025 or 1-800/635-5535, Ⓦwww.visitroanokeva.com), has walking-tour maps of the town and information on historic homes, plantations and other tourable sites. Finally, for sweeping views of the valley, make the fifteen-minute drive from the farmers' market up Mill Mountain to the **Roanoke Star**, an 89ft, neon-lit star built in 1949 (ask at the visitor centre for directions), which gives the town its nickname, "Star City".

Unlike many towns in the region, Roanoke boasts one fine **hotel**, the 🏃 *Hotel Roanoke*, 110 Shenandoah Ave (Ⓣ540/985-5900, Ⓦwww.hotelroanoke.com; ❻), an upmarket, mock-Tudor structure built in 1882, whose units now feature smart decor, flat-screen TVs and high-speed net access, plus there are on-site pools and a fitness centre. For cheaper digs, the *Sheraton Roanoke*, 2801 Hershberger Rd (Ⓣ540/563-9300, Ⓦwww.starwoodhotels.com; ❺), has a pool, gym and sauna, and quality rooms with high-speed internet. Check the visitor centre for details on local **B&Bs**.

You'll find a number of appealing **restaurants** in Roanoke, including the *Texas Tavern*, 114 W Church Ave (ⓣ540/342-4825), a longtime diner favourite where you can load up on gut-stuffing egg and ham sandwiches, burgers, and of course, great chili; *202 Market*, 202 Market Square (ⓣ540/343-6644), a sizeable spot for drinking and live music that also boasts fine high-class cuisine such as seafood, ribs and some Asian offerings; and *Grace's Place*, 1316 Grandin Rd (ⓣ540/981-1340), which has a savoury array of pizzas, pastas and sandwiches for affordable prices.

West Virginia

Mostly poor and rural, **WEST VIRGINIA** is known for its timber and coal mining industries, which thrive thanks to the state's rich natural resources. Rightly called "the Mountain State", it boasts the longest whitewater rivers and most extensive wilderness in the eastern US; for these reasons, the state has become a popular destination for hikers and outdoors enthusiasts, as the moonshiners of old have been replaced by ski instructors and mountain-bike guides.

Back when the state was part of Virginia proper, the small-plot farmers here had little in common with the slave-holding tidewater planters of eastern Virginia. When the Civil War broke out, the area voted to set up a rival Virginia government, loyal to the Union. **Statehood** was formalized by Congress in 1863, and then eight years later by the Supreme Court. But mostly the state's been known for its **mining**, with one of America's most powerful unions, the United Mine Workers, developing here, and the companies responsible for resource extraction despoiling much of the landscape – the latest depredation being the "mountaintop removal" that has rendered much of the majestic scenery into a cleaved and scarred wasteland.

The state's most popular destination, the restored 1850s town of **Harpers Ferry**, is barely in West Virginia at all, standing just across the broad rivers that form its Maryland and Virginia borders. To the west, the **Allegheny Mountains** stretch for over 150 miles, their million-plus acres of hardwood forest rivalling New England's for brilliant autumnal colour. West Virginia's oldest town, **Lewisburg**, sits just off I-64 at the mountains' southern foot, while the capital, **Charleston**, lies in the comparatively flat Ohio River Valley of the west.

Harpers Ferry

The ruggedly sited eighteenth-century town of **HARPERS FERRY** has been restored as a **national historic park**, clinging to steep hillsides above the rocky confluence of the Potomac and Shenandoah rivers. After suffering the ravages of the Civil War and torrential floods, the town was all but abandoned, but has since been reconstructed.

The place is most identified, of course, with **John Brown**, the zealous antebellum-era abolitionist and possible lunatic who seized a federal arsenal here in 1859 in hopes of raising a national black insurrection against slavery. It didn't work, and Brown's scattered forces were routed by US troops commanded by none other than Robert E. Lee. The town is still redolent of the era, and kept that way as a national historical park. Parking is virtually banned in the central area, though you can arrive via the shuttle buses that run from the large park **visitor centre** on US-340 (park and centre daily 8am–5pm; park entry $4/person, $6/car; ⓣ304/535-6029, ⓦwww.nps.gov/hafe).

Shuttle buses drop off at the end of gas-lit Shenandoah Street in the heart of the restored **Lower Town**, or Old Town, whose buildings include a blacksmith's shop, clothing and dry-goods stores, tavern and boarding house – as well as the **Master Armorer's House**, once occupied by the chief gunsmith. Museums housing exhibits on the Civil War and black history line both sides of High Street as it climbs away from the river. In the vicinity, a set of stone steps leads to the 1782 **Harper House**, the oldest in town.

A footpath continues uphill, past overgrown churchyards hemmed in by dry-stone walls, to **Jefferson Rock**, a huge grey boulder affording a great view over the two rivers. For a longer hike, several trails lead onwards into the surrounding forest: the **Appalachian Trail** – linking Maine to Georgia – continues from Jefferson Rock across the Shenandoah River into the Blue Ridge Mountains of Virginia, while the **Maryland Heights Trail** makes a six-mile round-trip around the headlands of the Potomac River. You can also float down the Shenandoah in a **raft** or inner-tube provided by one of the many outfitters along the rivers east and south of town.

Practicalities

Harpers Ferry makes a popular excursion from Washington DC and is served by several trains daily on the Maryland Rail Commuter network ($11 one-way; ⓣ1-800/325-7245, ⓦwww.mtamaryland.com) and by one daily Amtrak service, the Capitol Limited. Otherwise, you'll need to drive here.

If you want to spend the night, appealing **B&Bs** are sprinkled throughout the area, among them the *Ledge House*, 280 Henry Clay St (ⓣ304/582-2443, ⓦwww.theledgehouse.com; ❺), whose simple, pleasant units have balconies and wireless internet. The cosy *Laurel Lodge*, 844 E Ridge St (ⓣ304/535-2886, ⓦwww.laurellodge.com; ❺), is a charming Craftsman bungalow with three rooms featuring wireless internet and smart antique decor. The *Angler's Inn*, 867 W Washington St (ⓣ340/535-1239, ⓦwww.theanglersinn.com; ❻, save $30 on weekdays), an 1880 Victorian dwelling, provides the requisite B&B amenities, plus the opportunity to go on a full-day fishing expedition on local rivers (combo packages start at $540). Another option is the *Harpers Ferry Hostel*, seven miles east at 19123 Sandy Hook Rd in Knoxville, Maryland (ⓣ301/834-7652, ⓦwww.harpersferryhostel.org; dorm beds from $21, private rooms ❷). The park's visitor centre and the **Jefferson County tourist bureau**, 37 Washington Court (ⓣ304/535-2627, ⓦwww.hello-wv.com), have details on area camping.

Eating choices in town are limited, though the *Canal House*, 1225 W Washington St (ⓣ304/535-2880), is a reliable option for its coffee and sandwiches.

Around Harpers Ferry

CHARLES TOWN, four miles south of Harpers Ferry on US-340, is where John Brown was tried and hanged; the **Jefferson County Museum**, at Washington and Samuel streets (March–Dec Tues–Sat 11am–4pm; $3; ⓣ304/725-8628, ⓦjeffctywvmuseum.org) tells the story of his trial, which took place at the still-functional, 1836 Greek Revival gem of the **Jefferson County Courthouse**, 100 E Washington St (Mon–Fri 9am–5pm), as well as his conviction and execution, which deepened animosity between North and South, and helped lead to the Civil War in 1861. Drop by the museum for walking tours of the town's fetching antique homes, which include a half-dozen owned by the family of George Washington. **SHEPHERDSTOWN**, a cosy village along the Potomac, ten miles to the north, is even better for wandering, with quaint shops and cafés looking across the river to Maryland's infamous **Antietam Battlefield** (see p.386), casualties from which lay scattered throughout the town during and after the fighting. Sited in a 1786 red-brick edifice with plenty of Victorian furnishings and antiques, the **Historic Shepherdstown Museum**, 129 E German St (April–Oct Sat 11am–5pm, Sun 1–4pm; $4; Ⓦwww.historicshepherdstown.com), displays war relics and a replica of the 1787 steamboat that James Rumsey designed as a prototype, two decades before Robert Fulton got the official credit.

Further afield, **BERKELEY SPRINGS** (also known as Bath) is preserved as a state historic park, thirty miles west of Harpers Ferry on Hwy-9 and seven miles south of I-70, and was a favourite summer retreat of George Washington. Assorted massage and steam-bath treatments are still available. You can take a soak in the old **Roman Baths**, 2 S Washington St (daily 10am–6pm; $25/30min soak or $45 with massage; Ⓣ304/258-2711 for reservations, Ⓦwww.berkeleyspringssp.com), in active use since 1815; the spring's waters are 74°F year-round but heated to 102°F for bathers. The town's leafy and green **central square** has footpaths fanning out in all directions; one of these climbs the hill up to the medieval-looking **Berkeley Castle**, a private estate built in 1885. Among the better **B&Bs** here are the *Highlawn Inn*, 171 Market St (Ⓣ304/258-5700 or 1-888/290-4163, Ⓦwww.highlawninn.com; ➎), spread over four buildings, including some rooms with whirlpool tubs featuring the area's famed waters, and the *Manor Inn*, 234 Fairfax St (Ⓣ304/258-1552, Ⓦwww.bathmanorinn.com; ➍), where the three simple rooms are affordable and quaint.

The Allegheny Mountains

The **Allegheny Mountains**, West Virginia's segment of the Appalachian chain, are spread along a 140-mile crest protected as part of the **Monongahela National Forest**, within which numerous state parks contain the most spectacular sights and a variety of wildlife, including deer, turkey, bear and otters. There are no cities and few towns, and public transportation is nonexistent, but if you like to backpack, hike, cycle, climb or canoe, the Alleghenies merit a lengthy visit. For maps and more detailed information, contact the state tourist office (see p.60) or the Monongahela National Forest Supervisor, 200 Sycamore St, Elkins, West Virginia (Mon–Fri 8am–4.45pm; Ⓣ304/636-1800, Ⓦwww.fs.fed.us/r9/mnf).

The Northern Monongahela

Some of the most beautiful stretches of the Monongahela National Forest are in the **northern** part of the state, where the thundering torrents of the **Blackwater Falls**, near the town of Davis, pour over a 60ft limestone cliff before crashing down through a steeply walled canyon, its water amber from the presence of tannins. South from here spreads the dense forest of broad **Canaan Valley**, while to the east rise the highlands of the **Dolly Sods Wilderness**, vividly marked with rocky topography and murky bogs.

Rising up at the south end of the Canaan Valley, the state's highest point, 4861ft **Spruce Knob**, stands out over the headwaters of the Potomac River – you can actually drive all the way to the summit, which is crowned with a squat observation tower. Even more impressive views can be had from the top of the notched and craggy **Seneca Rocks**, some twenty miles to the northeast, whose 1000ft cliffs offer the most challenging rock climb on the East Coast. If you want to take the easy way up, a good trail leads in around the back of the North Peak, and takes well under an hour to the top. Get more information at the **Seneca Rocks Discovery Center**, near the junction of highways 33 and 55 (April–Oct daily

9am–4.30pm; free; ⓣ304/567-2827). Of the limited **lodging** options, the *Smoke Hotel Resort*, 10min north of the rocks on Hwy-55 (ⓣ1-800/828-8478, ⓦwww.smokehole.com) is the most reliable, with modern log cabins (❻), cottages (❻) and motel rooms (❸). Nearby is **Smoke Hole Canyon**, whose river has cut a nearly half-mile-deep chasm into the sheer rock walls, out of which sometimes rise mist and fog for a truly spellbinding sight. For the hardy, the **North Fork Mountain Trail** follows the canyon for 24 miles, and the *Big Bend Campground* is available seasonally (April–Oct; ⓣ304/257-4488 or 1-877/444-6677; $16).

The Southern Monongahela

The **southern half** of the Monongahela National Forest is, like most of the Alleghenies, a mountainous, semi-inaccessible region – two roads, US-219 and Hwy-92, wind north to south, with a handful of minor roads twisting between them – offering outstanding recreation as well as great scenic vistas. The **visitor centre** in Marlinton, 708 2nd Ave (ⓣ1-800/336-7009; ⓦwww.pocahontascountywv.com), has maps of the area and information on recreational guides and outfitters.

One signature sight is the state-run **Cass Scenic Railroad**, a restored, steam-powered logging railroad built in 1902, which carries visitors on a five-hour trip up to the top of 4842ft Bald Knob (schedule varies; $24–27; ⓣ304/456-4300 or 1-800/CALL-WVA, ⓦwww.cassrailroad.com), starting at the old lumber-mill-company town of **CASS**, five miles west of Hwy-28 (near the town of Green Bank), now preserved in its entirety as a historic park. You can **stay the night** in one of thirteen rail-employees' two-storey cottages built in 1902; the cottages have been converted into self-service accommodation and sleep four to ten people (ⓣ1-800/CALL-WVA; by season ❹–❻). You can also rent a historic 1920s train carriage, with basic furnishings, for a trip up the mountain ($85–119/person), or an overnight stay as well (❺ plus train fare).

A rigorous five-mile walk downhill from Cass leads along the tracks to the start of the bicycle-friendly **Greenbrier River Trail** (ⓦwww.greenbrierrivertrail.com), which follows the river and the railroad for 79 miles, coming out near Lewisburg (see below). You can also rent a **mountain bike** or take part in a fishing, cycling or skiing tour, from Elk River Touring Center (ⓣ1-866/572-3771, ⓦwww.ertc.com), fifteen miles north of Marlinton, off US-219 in the hamlet of **Slatyfork**. It also operates basic **lodging** in an inn (❹), farmhouse (❸) and four cabins with more amenities (❻); weekends require a two-night stay.

Five miles west of the junction between the Cass Scenic Road and exquisite Highland Scenic Highway (Rte-150), is **Cranberry Glades Botanical Area**, where a half-mile boardwalk is set out around a patch of peat bog swamp – one of four such bogs occupying 750 acres. Further information can be obtained from the Cranberry Mountain Nature Center (late April to Oct Thurs–Mon 9am–4.30pm; ⓣ304/653-4826) at the junction of highways 39 and 55. Further along, the **Highland Scenic Highway** (April–Oct only) merits a leisurely trip to explore its 43 miles of eye-catching views, several fine **campgrounds** and 150 miles of hiking trails that branch off from it. Contact the Marlington Ranger District (ⓣ304/799-4334) for more information on access and activities.

Lewisburg and the Greenbrier Resort

Just off I-64, south of the Monongahela National Forest, **LEWISBURG** offers a collection of handsome, brick-faced, early-nineteenth-century houses and makes for pleasant wandering, especially along **Washington Street**. It's also known for its somewhat touristy **Lost World Caverns**, off Fairview Road outside of town (hours vary, often daily 9am–5pm; $12; ⓦwww.lostworldcaverns.com), which provides 45min self-guided tours through dramatic cave formations, as well as a guided, four-hour spelunking tour ($70) into the darker, more claustrophobia-inducing recesses of the site. The **visitor centre**, 540 N Jefferson St (T 1-800/833-2068, W www.greenbrierwv.com), hands out walking tour maps and can suggest driving tours around Greenbrier Valley. It can also put you in touch with various cosy **hotels**, such as the *General Lewis Inn*, 301 E Washington St (T 304/645-2600 or 1-800/628-4454, W www.generallewisinn.com; 6), which has two dozen comfortable Victorian rooms and a fine, moderately priced **restaurant** serving all-American cuisine.

Just east of Lewisburg, **WHITE SULPHUR SPRINGS** is a historic resort town mainly known for its *Greenbrier Hotel and Resort*, 300 W Main St (T 304/536-1110 or 1-800/453-4858, W www.greenbrier.com; 8), the grandest hotel in the state, with a pillared entrance hall, 6500 lush acres, 850 units, golf courses and fine restaurants. Two dozen US presidents have stayed here, perhaps thanks in part to the hotel's extensive, deep-underground Cold War-era **bunker**, which, having been decommissioned, is now open for fascinating 90min tours (hours vary; $30; T 304/536-7810).

The New River Gorge

One of West Virginia's most spectacular river canyons, the **NEW RIVER GORGE** (24hr; free; W www.nps.gov/neri), lies just thirty miles west of Lewisburg along I-64. Stretching for over fifty miles, and protected as a national park, the thousand-foot chasm was carved through the limestone mountains by the New River – ironically one of the oldest in North America. Apart from one daily Amtrak **train**, there's no easy access to most of the gorge; to see it in full, you have to get out on the water. For details on the cycling, climbing, hiking and rafting options available, visit the gorge's southern **Sandstone Visitor Center**, located where Hwy-64 crosses the river (daily 9am–5pm; T 304/466-0417), or the **Canyon Rim visitor centre**, seven miles north of Oak Hill on Hwy-19 (June–Aug 10am–5pm; T 304/574-2115), which sits near the **New River Gorge Bridge**, dramatically rising 900ft above the river.

HINTON, on the southern end of the gorge (and another Amtrak stop), is an almost perfectly preserved company town, beautifully sited, with brick-lined streets angling up from the water, lined by dozens of grand civic buildings as well as rows of old worker housing. A walking tour map is available from the **visitor centre**, 206 Temple St (Tues–Sat 10am–2pm; T 304/466-5420, W www.threeriverswv.com), also the site of a railroad museum. There are the usual budget **motels**, highlighted by the *New River Falls Lodge*, 110 Cliff Island Drive (T 304/466-5710, W www.newriverfallslodge.com), offering basic B&B rooms (4) and four two-bedroom cottages with kitchens and fireplaces (6).

Charleston

CHARLESTON, West Virginia's capital and largest city, holds few major attractions, but does have a nice selection of Victorian-era buildings, which you can see on a walking tour provided by the **visitor centre**, 200 Civic Center Drive (Mon–Fri 9am–5pm; T 1-800/733-5469, W www.charlestonwv.com). The riverfront **State Capitol,** 1900 Kanawha Blvd (Mon–Fri 7am–7pm, Sat & Sun 11am–7pm; T 304/558-4839), designed by Lincoln Memorial and US Supreme Court architect Cass Gilbert, is a stately Renaissance Revival structure from 1932 that has an impressively large, gold-leafed dome. The **West Virginia Cultural Center** (Tues–Sat 9am–5pm, Sun noon–5pm; free; T 304/558-0220, W www.wvculture.org), in the same complex, has useful displays on coal mining, geology, forestry, war and state history, but much more extensive is the unexpectedly modern **Clay Center for the Arts & Sciences of West Virginia**, One Clay Square (Wed–Sat

10am–5pm, Sun noon–5pm; $13.50; ⓣ304/561-3570, ⓦwww.theclaycenter.org), a huge one-stop shop for everything scientific and artistic, with kid-friendly science-exhibit halls, a planetarium, concert stages for theatre and musical performances, an art gallery for regional artists and various cafés and gift shops. Finally, the town hosts the **Vandalia Festival**, Appalachia's largest celebration of arts and crafts, held on Memorial Day weekend and featuring lively bluegrass and folk music as well as tall-tale contests.

If you want distinctive **accommodation** in Charleston, try the *Brass Pineapple*, 1611 Virginia St E (ⓣ304/344-0748, ⓦbrasspineapple.com; ❺), a Victorian-styled B&B with plenty of antique, flowery decor. Other lodging choices are of the chain variety, of which the *Embassy Suites*, 300 Court St (ⓣ304/347-8700, ⓦwww.embassysuites.com; ❻), is among the most reliable, with a gym, pool and business centre. For **dining**, the *Bluegrass Kitchen*, 1600 Washington St E (ⓣ304/346-2871), has top-notch, mid-priced New Southern fare such as bourbon trout & grits, butternut-squash pasta and a nice brisket reuben, while the Art Deco *Blossom Deli and Soda Fountain Cafe*, 904 Quarrier St (ⓣ304/345-2233), has tasty sandwiches, burgers and sundaes for lunch, and more expensive steak, seafood and regional fare for dinner.

Maryland

Founded as the sole Catholic colony in strongly Protestant America, and, in the nineteenth century, one of the most contentious slave states in the Union, **MARYLAND** has always been unique. Within its small, irregularly shaped geometry, its attractions range from the frantic boardwalk beaches of **Ocean City**, to the sleepy fishing villages of the **Chesapeake Bay** and the little-known hamlets of the **Eastern Shore**. The Chesapeake Bay's legendary **blue crabs** and sweet rockfish are another highlight, served by roadside eateries in the Bay's colonial-era towns.

Maryland's largest city is the busy port of **Baltimore**, a quirky metropolis with a revitalized urban waterfront, thriving cultural scene and eclectic neighbourhoods. **Western Maryland** stretches over a hundred miles to the Appalachian foothills, its rolling farmlands notable chiefly for the Civil War killing grounds at **Antietam**. Just twenty miles south of Baltimore, picturesque **Annapolis** has served as Maryland's capital since 1694 and is best known for its national naval academy. Some of the state's most worthwhile spots are across the Chesapeake Bay on the Eastern Shore, connected to the rest of the state by the US-50 bridge but still a world apart.

Baltimore

Thanks to TV's potent *The Wire*, **BALTIMORE** has a reputation as a city in deep decline, its glory days of port industry now distant, and its various criminals fighting desperate wars of survival. While it's true that there are crime-ridden places in town worth avoiding, Baltimore is still among the more enjoyable stops on the East Coast, and its closely knit neighbourhoods and historic quarters provide an engaging backdrop to many diverse attractions, especially those along its celebrated **waterfront**. The city also boasts top-rated **museums**, which cover everything from fine arts to black history, to urban archeology, and has been home to everyone from writers Edgar Allan Poe and H.L. Mencken, to civil rights icons Frederick Douglass and Thurgood Marshall.

Arrival and information

Baltimore-Washington International Airport (BWI; ⓣ410/859-7111, ⓦwww.bwiairport.com) is ten miles south of the city centre and also serves as a key airport for Washington, DC. The cheapest way to get into the city is on the **MTA commuter rail system**; 25min; $1.60 (ⓣ410/539-5000 or 1-800/RIDE-MTA, ⓦmta.maryland.gov), which connects BWI to the restored **Pennsylvania Station**, half a mile north of downtown, at 1515 N Charles St. Penn Station is also the arrival point of Amtrak **trains** (ⓣ1-800/USA-RAIL); because it's in a dicey neighbourhood, you should either take a cab downtown or get on the Penn-Camden **light-rail shuttle** (Mon–Sat 6am–11pm, Sun 11am–7pm; $1.60 single), which stops downtown. **Shuttle vans** from the airport go to downtown Baltimore, including Super Shuttle; 20min; $13–23 single (ⓣ1-800/BLUE VAN, ⓦwww.supershuttle.com). Greyhound **buses** stop south of downtown, at 2110 Haines St, though this is in a grim area, too; take a taxi downtown.

Pick up free **maps** and **guides** at the **Baltimore Area Convention and Visitors Association**, 401 Light St, near the Maryland Science Center (Mon–Fri 8.30am–5pm; ⓣ410/837-7024 or 1-877/BALTIMORE, ⓦwww.baltimore.org), or from its booths at the airport and train station.

City transport

Because the city is compact, you can cover a lot of territory on foot. The **MTA**'s bus, subway and light-rail lines ($1.60, day-pass $3.50; ⓣ410/539-5000, ⓦmta.maryland.gov) cover many locations, though the subway and light rail are limited to one main route each, connecting at Lexington Market. On buses, have exact change ready. **Water taxis** link the Inner Harbor and sixteen citywide attractions, including the National Aquarium, Fell's Point and Fort McHenry (daily: schedule varies, often high season 10am–11pm, low season 11am–6pm; $9 all-day pass; ⓣ410/563-3901 or 1-800/658-8947, ⓦwww.thewatertaxi.com).

Accommodation

Baltimore has the usual chain **hotels** available downtown, along with a few local institutions, while the **B&Bs** clustered around the historic waterfront area of Fell's Point make for a pleasant alternative. The Convention and Visitors Association (see above) can help with reservations.

Admiral Fell Inn 888 S Broadway ⓣ410/522-7377 or 1-866/583-4162, ⓦwww.harbormagic.com. Chic historic hotel spread over seven buildings (some dating from the 1770s) in the heart of Fell's Point. Rooms have vaulted ceilings and fireplaces, with free internet access; some have jacuzzis and balconies as well. ⑦

Brookshire Suites 120 E Lombard St ⓣ410/625-1300, ⓦwww.harbormagic.com. Arty boutique rooms define this stylish establishment at the Inner Harbor, with modern decor in its suites, a business centre, drinks in the *Cloud Club* and fine waterside views. ⑦

Henderson's Wharf Inn 1000 Fell St ⓣ410/522-7087, ⓦwww.hendersonswharf.com. Prominent harbourside spot with modern rooms that include boutique furnishings, refrigerators and internet access. Continental breakfast and on-site gym as well. ⑧

HI-Baltimore 17 W Mulberry St ⓣ410/576-8880 ⓦwww.baltimorehostel.org. Set in a sturdy 1850s

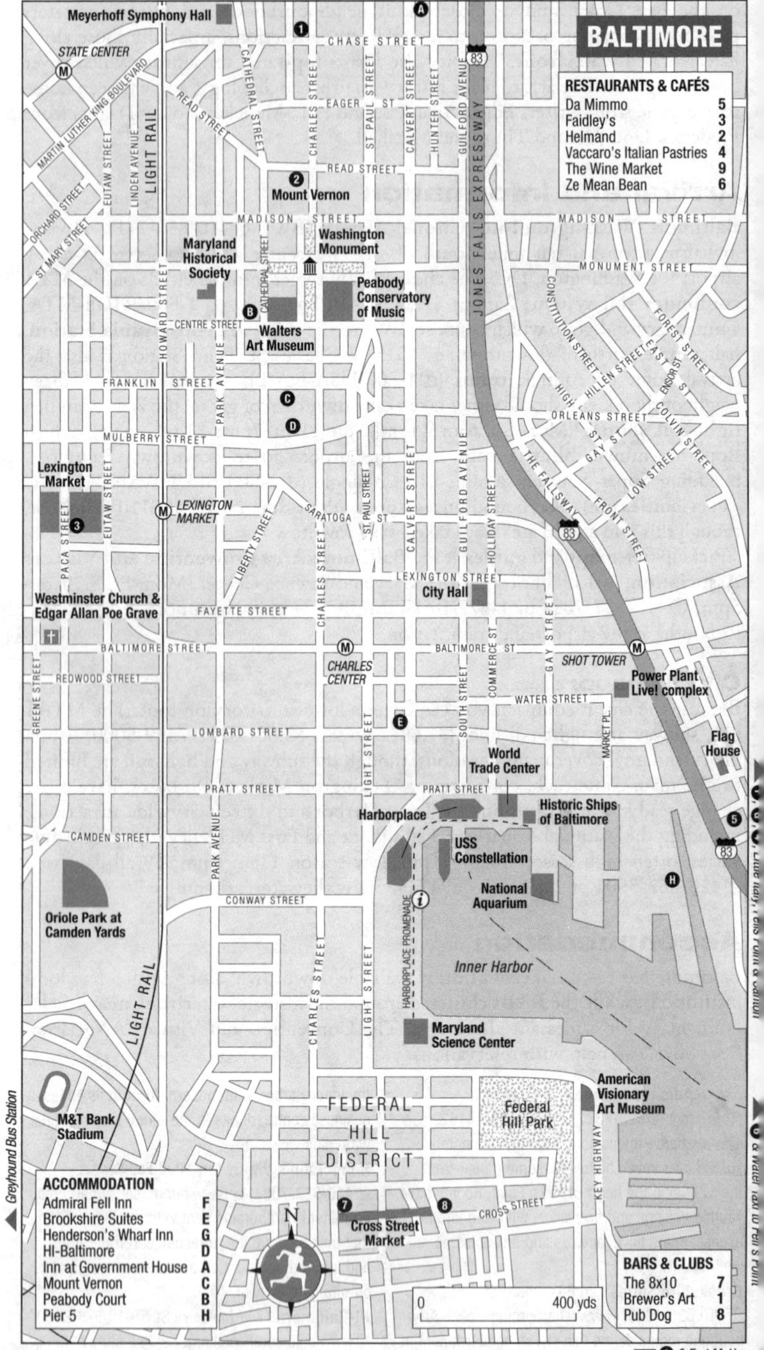
Pennsylvania Station & Baltimore Museum of Art
BALTIMORE
RESTAURANTS & CAFÉS
Da Mimmo 5
Faidley's 3
Helmand 2
Vaccaro's Italian Pastries 4
The Wine Market 9
Ze Mean Bean 6
ACCOMMODATION
Admiral Fell Inn F
Brookshire Suites E
Henderson's Wharf Inn G
HI-Baltimore D
Inn at Government House A
Mount Vernon C
Peabody Court B
Pier 5 H
BARS & CLUBS
The 8x10 7
Brewer's Art 1
Pub Dog 8
Meyerhoff Symphony Hall
STATE CENTER
Mount Vernon
Washington Monument
Maryland Historical Society
Peabody Conservatory of Music
Walters Art Museum
Lexington Market
LEXINGTON MARKET
Westminster Church & Edgar Allan Poe Grave
City Hall
CHARLES CENTER
SHOT TOWER
Power Plant Live! complex
Flag House
World Trade Center
Historic Ships of Baltimore
Harborplace
USS Constellation
National Aquarium
Inner Harbor
Oriole Park at Camden Yards
Maryland Science Center
American Visionary Art Museum
Federal Hill Park
FEDERAL HILL DISTRICT
M&T Bank Stadium
Cross Street Market
Greyhound Bus Station
9 & Fort McHenry
LIGHT RAIL
JONES FALLS EXPRESSWAY
HARBORPLACE PROMENADE
CHASE STREET
EAGER ST
READ STREET
MADISON STREET
MONUMENT STREET
CENTRE STREET
FRANKLIN STREET
MULBERRY STREET
SARATOGA ST
LEXINGTON STREET
FAYETTE STREET
BALTIMORE STREET
BALTIMORE ST
REDWOOD STREET
WATER STREET
LOMBARD STREET
PRATT STREET
CAMDEN STREET
CONWAY STREET
CROSS STREET
ORLEANS STREET
CATHEDRAL STREET
CHARLES STREET
ST PAUL STREET
CALVERT STREET
HUNTER STREET
GUILFORD AVENUE
HOLLIDAY STREET
COMMERCE ST
SOUTH STREET
GAY STREET
MARKET PL.
LIGHT STREET
PARK AVENUE
HOWARD STREET
EUTAW STREET
LINDEN AVENUE
PACA STREET
GREENE STREET
LIBERTY STREET
MARTIN LUTHER KING BOULEVARD
ORCHARD STREET
ST MARY STREET
CONSTITUTION STREET
HIGH ST
HILLEN STREET
FOREST STREET
EAST ST
ENSOR ST
COLVIN STREET
GAY ST
LOW STREET
THE FALLSWAY
FRONT STREET
KEY HIGHWAY
0 400 yds
N

brownstone, this boasts four dozen dorm beds, with antiques, deck and patio, free wi-fi access, karaoke and laundry, plus movie screenings. Dorm beds $25, private rooms $50+ (❷).

The Inn at Government House 1125 N Calvert St ⓣ410/539-0566. City-government-run 1889 Victorian mansion with antique-filled, somewhat worn rooms, grand music and dining rooms, and breakfast and parking included. ❺

Mount Vernon 24 W Franklin St ⓣ410/727-2000 or 1-800/245-5256, ⓦwww.mountvernonbaltimore.com. Ultra-cheap hotel has clean rooms with free high-speed net access and complimentary breakfast, plus a central location. ❹

Peabody Court 612 Cathedral St ⓣ410/727-7101, ⓦwww.peabodycourthotel.com. Classy lodging in a handsome, converted 1928 apartment building set in a historic neighbourhood. Has marble bathrooms and tasteful decor, plus internet access. Pet-friendly. ❺

Pier 5 711 Eastern Ave ⓣ410/539-2000, ⓦwww.harbormagic.com. Centrally located, upmarket boutique hotel with plenty of snazzy style, offering smart rooms with CD players, and suites with fridges, microwaves and in-room bars. ❾

Downtown Baltimore

The re-emergent core of **downtown Baltimore** makes for a pleasant stroll along the brick-lined waterfront and features a bevy of nautical and science-oriented attractions. It's also within walking distance of the two sports stadiums, which makes it a convenient spot for fans to meet for dinner or a drink.

The main cluster of **restaurants and cafés** is found west of **Charles Street**, in Baltimore's original shopping district. One Baltimore landmark here, dating from 1782, is the oldest and loudest of the city's covered markets, **Lexington Market**, 400 W Lexington St (Mon–Sat 8.30am–6pm; ⓣ410/685-6169, ⓦwww.lexingtonmarket.com), with more than a hundred food stalls, including **Faidley's** (see p.384). Safe during the day, the area can become more dicey after dark.

Just south of the market, **Westminster Church**, 519 W Fayette St, was built in 1852 atop the main Baltimore cemetery. The most famous resident here is **Edgar Allan Poe**, who lived in town for three years in the 1830s before moving on to Richmond, Virginia. In 1849, while passing through Baltimore, Poe was found incoherent near a polling place and died soon after. In 1875, his remains were moved from a pauper's grave and entombed within the stone memorial that stands along Green Street on the north side of the church. Despite the notoriety of the Poe site, most visitors come to visit **Oriole Park at Camden Yards** ($9–60 tickets; ⓣ1-888/848-BIRD, ⓦwww.theorioles.com), five blocks south, the baseball stadium of the Baltimore Orioles. Open-faced and city-oriented, the park was one of the first to reintroduce a historic flair to stadium design, in contrast to the concrete boxes that had dominated pro sports for a generation. Just next door, resembling a newly landed alien spaceship, is the 68,400-seat **M&T Bank Stadium**, home to the **Baltimore Ravens** football team, who were named after Edgar Allan Poe's most (in)famous character ($50–175 tickets; ⓣ410/547-SEAT, ⓦwww.baltimoreravens.com).

The Inner Harbor

The **Inner Harbor** is a success story of urban revitalization. The rotting wharves and derelict warehouses that stood here through the 1970s have been replaced by the sparkling steel-and-glass **Harborplace** shopping mall (Mon–Sat 10am–9pm, Sun noon–6pm; ⓣ410/332-4191, ⓦwww.harborplace.com), though the businesses inside aren't too different from what you'll find in any other consumer zone. Sweeping views of the entire city and beyond can be admired from the 27th-storey Top of the World observation deck at Baltimore's **World Trade Center**, on the north pier (hours vary, often Wed & Thurs 10am–6pm, Fri & Sat 10am–7pm, Sun 11am–6pm; $5; ⓣ410/837-VIEW, ⓦwww.viewbaltimore.org). Nothing in the Inner Harbor dates from before its rebuilding, but to lend an air of authenticity, a handful of historic ships have floated here, as part of the Baltimore Maritime Museum's rebranding as **Historic Ships of Baltimore** (hours vary, often daily 10am–4.30 or 5.30pm; one-ship tour $10, two ships $14, four ships $18; ⓣ410/539-1797, ⓦwww.historicships.org). Although the four boats on view are rather eclectic – a Coast Guard cutter that survived Pearl Harbor, a Chesapeake Bay lightship and a World War II diesel submarine – the highlight for most is the USS *Constellation*, the only Civil War-era vessel still afloat and the last all-sail warship built by the US Navy. It was constructed in 1854 and restored in 1999.

Far and away the biggest tourist attraction in Baltimore, the **National Aquarium**, 501 E Pratt St (hours vary, often Sun–Thurs 9am–5pm, Fri 9am–8pm, Sat 9am–6pm; $25, or $28 with dolphin show; ⓣ410/576-3800, ⓦwww.aqua.org), is an essential sight for anyone with an affection for jellyfish, sharks, rays, sea turtles and other oceanic creatures, which dart around before visitors in their own enclosed tanks and pools. It is, of course, as much theme park as scientific institution, so it's no surprise the aquarium's **Dolphin Amphitheater** is very much in the style of SeaWorld, where you can see the playful cetaceans cavorting to the delight of the crowd.

Federal Hill and around

A short walk south of the Inner Harbor, the **Federal Hill** district is a great place to escape from the crowds. Lined with interesting shops, restaurants and galleries, its main thoroughfare, **Light Street**, leads to the indoor **Cross Street Market**, which opened in 1875 and has two blocks of open-air markets boasting some excellent delis, seafood bars and fruit vendors. **Federal Hill Park** in the northeast is a quiet public space with fine views over the harbour and the downtown cityscape.

In the northern part of the area, by the harbour at 601 Light St, the glass, steel and concrete **Maryland Science Center** (Mon–Fri 10am–5pm, Sat 10am–6pm, Sun 11am–5pm; $15, kids $12, IMAX show $8; ⓣ410/685-5225, ⓦwww.mdsci.org) is mainly aimed at kids, with interactive displays on themes ranging from dinosaurs to space travel. More interesting is the **American Visionary Art Museum**, east of Federal Hill Park at 800 Key Hwy (Tues–Sun 10am–6pm; $16; ⓣ410/244-1900, ⓦwww.avam.org), devoted to the works of untrained or amateur artists, with thousands of pieces by American "visionaries", crafted with everything from glass and porcelain to toothpicks and tinfoil. Some of the more notable pieces include an obsessively intricate sculpture of Coney Island's boardwalk and eerie Bosch-like paintings of alien abductions.

Mount Vernon

Baltimore's most elegant quarter is just north of downtown on the shallow rise known as **Mount Vernon**. Adorned with eighteenth-century brick townhouses, this district takes its name from the home of George Washington, whose likeness tops the 178ft marble column of the central **Washington Monument** (Wed–Fri 10am–4pm, Sat & Sun 10am–5pm; $1), where 228 steps lead to a great view over the city. It's located in a small park next to the spire of the sham-Gothic Mount Vernon Methodist Church at Charles Street and Monument Place.

Across the street, a solemn stone facade of the **Peabody Conservatory of Music**, part of Johns Hopkins University, hides one of the city's best interior spaces: the beautiful, skylit atrium of the **Peabody Library**, 17 E Mount Vernon Place (Mon–Thurs 8am–10pm, Fri 8am–6pm, Sat 10am–5pm, Sun 1–10pm; ⓣ410/659-8179, ⓦwww.peabody.jhu.edu/library), an 1878 Victorian delight rich with cast-iron balconies, soaring columns and glass skylights. The ground floor features displays of various history books, among them a wonderful illustrated 1555 edition of Boccaccio's *Decameron*, and a 1493 printing of the *Nuremburg Chronicles*. Two blocks west, the **Maryland Historical Society** museum, 201 W Monument St (Thurs–Sun 10am–5pm; $4; ⓣ410/685-3750, ⓦwww.mdhs.org), traces the path of local history through portraits of the old Maryland elite and their clothing, jewels, toys and household amenities, and its antique-filled chambers give a sense of the maritime wealth created here through nineteenth-century trade.

A block south of the Washington Monument, the beautiful hodgepodge of international treasures at the **Walters Art Museum**, 600 N Charles St (Wed–Sun 11am–5pm; free; ⓣ410/547-9000, ⓦwww.thewalters.org), is well deserving of a lengthy visit. The site is set around a large sculpture court, modelled on an Italian Renaissance palazzo, beyond which modern galleries show off Greek and Roman antiquities, European illuminated manuscripts, Islamic ceramics, Byzantine silver, pre-Columbian artefacts and French Impressionist works. You're apt to see anything from Ethiopian Christian icons to medieval suits of armour, Egyptian jewellery and sarcophagi, including an intact mummy.

The Flag House and Star-Spangled Banner Museum, and Little Italy

A quarter of a mile east of downtown and the Inner Harbor is the **Flag House and Star-Spangled Banner Museum**, 844 E Pratt St (Tues–Sat 10am–4pm; last tour at 3.30pm; $7; ⓣ410/837-1793, ⓦwww.flaghouse.org), where in 1813 Mary Pickersgill sewed the 30ft-by-45ft US flag, whose presence at the British attack on Baltimore Harbor the following year inspired Francis Scott Key to write "The Star-Spangled Banner". The house is full of patriotic tributes, as well as various antiques from the era, and there's a less interesting **War of 1812 Museum** (same hours and admission) that covers that conflict with costumes and military relics.

The densely tangled streets of **Little Italy**, still a strongly Italian neighbourhood with dozens of good restaurants and cafés, spread to the east of downtown and hold plenty of Baltimore's trademark stone-fronted **rowhouses**, almost all with highly polished steps quarried from local marble, the same also used to construct the stone monuments of Washington DC.

Fell's Point, Canton and Greektown

Southeast of Little Italy stands Baltimore's oldest and liveliest quarter, **Fell's Point**, once the heart of the city's extensive shipbuilding industry. The shipyards are long gone, but many old bars and earthy pubs have hung on to form one of the better nightlife districts on the East Coast, set in and around handsome nineteenth-century buildings. To pick up a healthy snack, the area's **Broadway Market**, 610 S Broadway (Mon–Sat 7am–6pm; ⓣ410/675-1466), is always a favourite stopping point. The Fell's Point **visitor centre**, 808 S Ann St (daily noon–4pm; ⓣ410/675-6750), provides good self-guided walking maps and tours of the 1765 **Robert Long House**, the oldest surviving urban residence in Baltimore.

East of Fell's Point and two miles southeast of downtown, **Canton** is another district full of historic rowhouses, some of which date back to the Civil War, and is being revitalized with new restaurants and nightlife. A mile east, **Greektown** is still a thriving Hellenic community, after almost a century, and boasts its share of authentic bakeries, diners and groceries.

Fort McHenry

Linked by water taxi from Fell's Point, but on the opposite side of the harbour, **Fort McHenry National Monument**, 2400 E Fort Ave (summer daily 8am–8pm; rest of year daily 8am–5pm; $7 seven-day pass; ⓣ410/962-4290, ⓦwww.nps.gov/fomc), is a star-shaped fort that the British bombed during the War of 1812 to penetrate the harbour and attack Baltimore. The attack failed, and when he saw "the bombs bursting in air", Francis Scott Key was moved to write the poem *The Star-Spangled Banner*, first known as "The Defense of Fort McHenry". Over the next century, the fort was used as a prison for Confederate soldiers and political prisoners. You can tour the fort's old barracks, officers' and enlisted men's quarters, and guardhouse, and see military hardware and relics of different eras. The Banner itself, however, is housed in the National Museum of American History (see p.341) in Washington, DC.

Baltimore Museum of Art

Two miles north of downtown, the **Charles Village** district is enjoyable for its early-twentieth-century rowhouses and walkable streets. Here you can find the **Baltimore Museum of Art**, 10 Art Museum Drive (Wed–Fri 10am–5pm, Sat & Sun 11am–6pm; free ⓣ443/573-1700, ⓦwww.artbma.org), as good a value as you're likely to find for viewing classic art in the area. As well as Italian and Dutch works by Botticelli, Raphael, Rembrandt and Van Dyck, the museum holds Chardin's *A Game of Knucklebones*, played by a smiling scamp, drawings by Dürer and Goya, and photographs from Weston, Stieglitz and others. The highlight is the **Cone Collection** of works by Delacroix, Degas, Cézanne and Picasso, as well as over a hundred drawings and paintings by Matisse, among them his signature *Large Reclining Nude* and *Seated Odalisque*.

Eating

Baltimore's restaurants tend to be good value and reasonably priced, with particularly appealing fresh **seafood** places offering top-notch **steamed crabs**, as well as the usual diners and more than a dozen good restaurants side by side in Little Italy. Fell's Point boasts numerous vegetarian, seafood and other types of eateries.

Bertha's 734 S Broadway ⓣ410/327-5795. Classic, affordable seafood restaurant, tucked away behind a tiny Fell's Point bar. Known for its delicious mussels, crab cakes and high tea, and nightly live blues, jazz, and Dixieland.

Black Olive 814 S Bond St, Fell's Point ⓣ410/276-7141. Expensive but succulent Mediterranean restaurant that has affordable meze (small plates) like grilled octopus salad and calamari, as well as pricier entrees like rack of lamb, crab cake platters and lobster tail.

Da Mimmo 217 S High St ⓣ410/727-6876. Intimate, upmarket Little Italy café, with a wide-ranging menu that includes clams, *saltimbocca*, gnocchi and lobster tettrazzini. Live piano music and a romantic ambience.

Faidley's 203 N Paca, downtown ⓣ410/727-4898. Located in Lexington Market, the best and cheapest of many outlets serving oysters, clams and other catches from the Chesapeake Bay, including terrific crab cakes – a business dating back to 1886. Stand-up dining only.

Helmand 806 N Charles St ⓣ410/752-0311. Mid-priced, dinner-only Afghan restaurant in Mount Vernon, with savoury dishes such as *aushak* (leek-filled vegetarian ravioli), *koufta challow* (lamb and beef meatballs) and the delicious *kaddo borawni* (a fried-pumpkin appetizer).

Matthew's Pizza 3131 Eastern Ave, west of Greektown ⓣ410/276-8755. Old-style hole in the wall that still boasts the city's best slices – rich and tangy, with a solid crust and traditional ingredients, or toppings like crab and home-made meatballs.

Obrycki's 1727 E Pratt St, just north of Fell's Point ⓣ410/732-6399. Baltimore's longest-established seafood restaurant, with delicious steamed, soft-shell and broiled crabs at premium prices, as well as other excellent seafood. Closed in winter.

Peter's Inn 504 S Ann St, Fell's Point ⓣ410/675-7313. Top-notch restaurant with a fine, rotating menu, where you can get anything from shrimp grits to mushroom risotto, to veal cheeks, for moderate to expensive prices. Also has an enjoyable bar on site.

Vaccaro's Italian Pastries 222 Albemarle St, Little Italy ⓣ410/685-4905. Great spot to load up on cheesecakes, cannoli, cookies and other sweets, and to indulge in the kind of delicious gelato they make in the Old Country. Part of a local chain.

The Wine Market 921 E Fort Ave, south of Federal Hill ⓣ410/244-6166. Innovative, mid- to upper-end cuisine that throws together a melange of curious dishes – anything from Korean short ribs and potstickers to mac and cheese and fried oysters – often successfully.

Ze Mean Bean 1739 Fleet St, Fell's Point ⓣ410/675-5999. Rib-stuffing Slavic eatery where you can get your fill of rich and tasty potato dumplings, pierogi, goulash and even chicken Kiev, most for affordable prices, though the service can be spotty.

Drinking and nightlife

Baltimore has plenty of places to **drink** and **Fell's Point** may well have the most. One bar after another lines up along Broadway and the many smaller side streets, and almost all feature some sort of entertainment. The Power Plant Live! complex, next to the Inner Harbor, at 34 Market Place (ⓣ410-727-LIVE, ⓦwww.powerplantlive.com), offers dining and mainstream entertainment. The city's highbrow culture is concentrated northwest of the centre, in the **Mount Royal Avenue area**, centered around **Meyerhoff Symphony Hall**, 1212 Cathedral St (ⓣ410/783-8000, ⓦwww.bsomusic.org). For a rundown of what's on, pick up a copy of the excellent and free **City Paper** (ⓦwww.citypaper.com) or check out ⓦwww.Baltimore.org.

The 8x10 10 E Cross St, Federal Hill ⓣ410/625-2000. Enjoyable bar and live music venue that features good beer and cocktails, and an eclectic mix of bands, from jazz to indie rock and electronica, often for a cover charge of, $5–15, as with other venues in town.

Brewer's Art 1106 N Charles St, Mount Vernon ⓣ410/547-9310. The place anyone with a yen for microbrews must visit – a local landmark for beer-making that's tops for its Belgian-style "Ozzy", dark "Proletary Ale" and good old "Charm City Sour Cherry".

Cat's Eye Pub 1730 Thames St, Fell's Point ⓣ410/276-9085. Cosy, crowded bar, offering forty beers on tap and live music nightly, from blues and rock, to jazz, bluegrass and folk.

Max's Taphouse 735 S Broadway ⓣ410/675-6297. Huge corner venue with a very long bar known for its prime domestic and European ales –with some 500 kinds in bottles, and up to 100 on tap – pool tables, and, upstairs, a leather-upholstered cigar lounge.

Pub Dog 200 E Cross St, Federal Hill ⓣ410/727-6077. Baltimore has countless places to drink and this is among the best, with a great atmosphere, doling out a range of handcrafted brews from the Irish stout Black Dog to the various fruity Berry Dogs, and some serviceable burgers and pizza as well.

Sláinte 1700 Thames St ⓣ410/563-6600. Free-spirited Irish pub in Fell's Point where you can knock back the requisite Guinness and indulge in hearty fare such as bangers and mash, potato pancakes and fish and chips.

Wharf Rat Bar 801 S Ann St, Fell's Point ⓣ410/276-9034. This friendly bar, well stocked with English ales, other European imports and regional microbrews, packs in a trendy and discerning crowd.

Western Maryland

Western Maryland stretches for some two hundred miles east to west, but is in places only two miles north to south. The further west you go the more hilly and rural it becomes, similar to West Virginia.

Apart from the Civil War battlefield at **Antietam**, west of the only sizeable town, **Frederick**, the best reason to come to this part of the state is to cycle or hike the footpath of the restored **Chesapeake and Ohio Canal**, which winds along the Maryland side of the Potomac River from Washington DC for over 180 miles to **Cumberland** in the western mountains. Even further west is the state's largest fresh water lake, **Deep Creek Lake**, which has more than 70,000 acres of public parks and forests surrounding it, some of which make for nice cross-country skiing.

Frederick and around

One of the first towns settled in northwestern Maryland, **FREDERICK**, less than an hour west of Baltimore, at the junction of I-70 and I-270, was laid out in 1745 by German farmers and grew to become a main stopover on the route west to the Ohio Valley; the bulk of today's tidy town survives from the early 1800s. Frederick is also a good base for exploring Antietam (see below) and Harpers Ferry (see p.373).

The **visitor centre**, 19 E Church St (Ⓣ301/600-2888 or 1-800/999-3613, Ⓦwww.fredericktourism.org), has walking-tour maps of the town highlights, some of which include the **Schifferstadt House**, just off US-15 (April to mid-Dec Tues–Sun noon–4pm; $3; Ⓣ301/668-6088), a stone-walled farmhouse built in 1756 and largely unaltered since; the **Roger Taney House**, 121 S Bentz St (Sat 10am–4pm, Sun 1–4pm; $6; Ⓣ301/663-1188), owned by the US Supreme Court chief justice best known for presiding over the infamous **Dred Scott** case, which helped lead to the Civil War; and the **Barbara Fritchie House**, 154 W Patrick St (tours by appointment at Ⓣ301/698-8992), the place where 95-year-old Barbara Fritchie was said to have defiantly waved the US flag while Confederate soldiers marched past. Although this story is mythical, the house is a well-preserved piece of Americana, with a historic flag still hanging from the pitched roof. A short walk east, the **National Museum of Civil War Medicine**, 48 E Patrick St (Mon–Sat 10am–5pm, Sun 11am–5pm; $7; Ⓦwww.civilwarmed.org) offers intriguing exhibits on mid-nineteenth-century military medicine, including grisly amputation tools and battlefield triage.

In the outskirts north of Frederick, **Cunningham Falls State Park** (8am–sunset) and the **Catoctin Mountain Park** (dawn–dusk; free) hold seemingly endless hardwood forests – great for autumn colour – in the midst of which are preserved remnants of early homesteads and industrial operations such as a sawmill, ironworks and whiskey still. Pick up details on hiking and camping at the main **visitor centre**, off Hwy-77 two miles west of US-15 (Mon–Thurs 10am–4.30pm, Fri 10am–5pm, Sat & Sun 8.30am–5pm; Ⓣ301/663-9330, Ⓦwww.nps.gov/cato). You can also **camp** here ($20/night), and **rent cabins** of various size ($50–70).

There are **motels** along both I-70 and US-15, but the town's major **B&Bs** are better options: the *Hill House*, 12 W Third St (Ⓣ301/682-4111, Ⓦwww.hillhousefrederick.com; ❺), has rooms artfully decorated in Victorian and early-American design that feature antiques and balconies, and *Hollerstown Hill*, 4 Clarke Place (Ⓣ301/228-3630, Ⓦwww.hollerstownhill.com; ❻), has four pleasant rooms in historic buildings from the late nineteenth century. If you plan on visiting Antietam, try the excellent *Jacob Rohrbach Inn*, 138 W Main St, Sharpsburg (Ⓣ301/432-5079, Ⓦwww.jacob-rohrbach-inn.com; ❻), with four well-appointed rooms and suites, and one detached cottage, all decorated in a style appropriate for a 200-year-old homestead.

For a bite to **eat**, try *Monocacy Crossing*, 4424 Urbana Pike (Ⓣ301/846-4204), for its fine sandwiches and seafood at lunchtime, or somewhat expensive ribs, crab cakes, duck étouffée and other top-shelf cuisine for dinner. Also worthwhile are the cheaper sandwiches and surf-and-turf entrees at *Barley & Hops*, 5473 Urbana Pike (Ⓣ301/668-5555), with good microbrewed pale ales and stouts, and a nice range of handcrafted beer on tap, from Kolsch to oatmeal stout, at **Brewer's Alley**, 124 N Market St (Ⓣ301/631-0089).

Antietam National Battlefield

The site of the single bloodiest battle in the Civil War – causing more American deaths than any other single day in US history – **Antietam National Battlefield** spreads over unaltered farmlands outside the village of **Sharpsburg**, fifteen miles west of Frederick. Here, on the morning of September 17, 1862, forty thousand troops faced a Union army twice that number. Hours later, 23,000 men from both sides lay dead or dying. The fiercest fighting, and the worst bloodshed, occurred in cornfields to the north.

For all the carnage, the battle wasn't tactically decisive and the South would invade the North the following year, but the Confederates' lack of success lost them the support of their would-be ally Great Britain, while the Union performance encouraged Lincoln to issue the Emancipation Proclamation. Pick up a brochure and driving-tour map of the park at the **visitor centre**, a mile north of Sharpsburg off Hwy-65 (hours vary, usually daily 8.30am–5pm; $4 three-day pass; ⓣ301/432-5124, ⓦwww.nps.gov/anti).

Cumberland and the C&O Canal

The only large town in the far west of Maryland, sandwiched between West Virginia and Pennsylvania in a part of the state only eight miles wide, **CUMBERLAND** was a very important town in early-American life. It started life as a coal-mining centre in the late 1700s, before becoming the eastern terminus of the **National Road**, one of the country's first graded, modern **turnpikes** (for horse-drawn cargo), and was later made the terminus of the **C&O (Chesapeake & Ohio) Canal**, an impressive engineering feat begun in 1813 and completed in 1850.

There are six **visitor centres** along the canal: the westernmost is in Cumberland, at 13 Canal St (daily 9am–5pm; entry to National Park $3/pedestrian, $5/car for three days; ⓣ301/722-8226, ⓦwww.nps.gov/choh). All centres provide information on hiking, cycling, canoeing and camping, which can prove valuable if you're interested in travelling the entire 184.5 miles along the **canal towpath**, one of the longest and loveliest contiguous trails in the US. In summer, the historic trains of the **Western Maryland Scenic Railroad** leave from here to make the three-hour trip to Frostburg, to the west, through the surrounding mountains (hours vary; $30; ⓣ301/759-4400 or 1-800/872-4650, ⓦwww.wmsr.com). Look for the tiny black-and-white log cabin where George Washington served his first commission in the 1750s, standing directly opposite the station on the other side of the canal.

The Cumberland Amtrak **train station** is at E Harrison Street at Queen City Street. **Accommodation** in Cumberland is limited, but one good choice is the *Bruce House Inn*, 201 Fayette St (ⓣ301/777-8860, ⓦwww.brucehouseinn.com; ❺), an 1840 charmer that appeals for its fine breakfasts and four B&B rooms with stylish modern and early-American furnishings and high-speed net access.

Annapolis

Maryland's capital since 1694, **ANNAPOLIS** has changed little in size and appearance over the centuries, its charmingly narrow, time-worn streets making it among the more engaging small US cities. At the centre of **annapolis**, overlooking the town's dense web of streets, stands the stately Georgian beauty of the **Maryland State House** (Mon–Fri 9am–5pm, Sat & Sun 10am–4pm; free tours by request at ⓣ410/974-3400). The structure was completed in 1779, and for six months between 1783 and 1784, it served as the official Capitol of the US, and remains the nation's oldest statehouse still in use. The **Old Senate**

Chamber, off the grand entrance hall, is where the Treaty of Paris was ratified in 1784, officially ending the Revolutionary War. A statue of George Washington stands here on the spot where, three weeks before the treaty signing, he resigned his commission as head of the Continental Army. Also on the grounds of the State House is the cottage-sized **Old Treasury**, built in 1735 to hold colonial Maryland's currency reserves.

Many grand post-revolutionary brick homes line the streets of Annapolis. Among the best are the red-brick **Hammond-Harwood House**, two blocks west of the State House at 19 Maryland Ave, off King George Street (April–Oct Tues–Sun noon–5pm, last tour 4pm; $6; Ⓦwww.hammondharwoodhouse.org), which was built in 1774 and is notable for its beautiful woodwork and intricate front doorway; the 1774 **Chase-Lloyd House**, 22 Maryland Ave (donation; by appointment at Ⓣ410/263-2723), a three-storey Georgian brick townhouse with grand stairway, interior Ionic columns and intricate ornamentation; and the 1765 **William Paca House**, 186 Prince George St (hours vary, tours often hourly 10.30am–3.30pm; $8 including tour; Ⓣ410/267-7619), named for one of the state's governors and signers of the Declaration of Independence. Its splendid formal garden has French-styled geometry and lovely topiary and boasts a nice viewing pavilion. Besides such elite manors, dozens of eighteenth-century clapboard cottages and warehouses fill the narrow streets that run down to the waterfront. The **Historic Annapolis Foundation**, housed in a c.1715 tavern at 18 Pinkney St (Ⓣ410/267-7619, Ⓦwww.annapolis.org), can provide information on self-guided tours of many of them. Finally, for a different insight into Maryland history, stop by the **Banneker-Douglass Museum**, 84 Franklin St, a few blocks northeast of the Capitol (Tues–Sat 10am–4pm; free; Ⓣ410/216-6180, Ⓦwww.bdmuseum.com), named after two of the most prominent black figures of early America and home to the state's largest holding of African-American art and artefacts.

The waterfront and US Naval Academy

Few historic sites survive on the **Chesapeake Bay waterfront**, save the 1850s dockside **Market House**, 25 Market Place (Mon–Thurs 8am–7pm, Fri & Sat 8am–9pm, Sun 10am–5pm; Ⓦwww.annapolismarkethouse.com), a replacement of a colonial warehouse that was used by the Revolutionary army but today is home to a handful of food vendors. Among the boat-supply shops and harbourside bars, the grey-stone walls of the **US Naval Academy** house four thousand "plebes" who spend four rigid years here before embarking on careers as naval officers. Superb guided tours leave from **Armel-Leftwich Visitor Center** ($9.50; call for hours at Ⓣ410/293-8687, Ⓦwww.navyonline.com) in Halsey Field House, through Gate 1 at the end of King George Street, and take in the elaborate crypt and marble sarcophagus of early-American naval hero John Paul Jones, as well as cannons, a space capsule and other oddments.

Practicalities

Annapolis is easy to reach: Greyhound **buses** stop at 308 Chinquapin Round Rd, and you can access Amtrak and MARC trains (Ⓣ1-800/RIDE-MTA; Ⓦmta.maryland.gov) at BWI Airport via the North Star (C-60) Route on Annapolis's ADOT bus system; $4 (Ⓣ410/263-7964). By road, it's only about half an hour from Washington DC (via US-50) or Baltimore (via I-97). Central, historic Annapolis is very walkable, and the city's **visitor centre**, 26 West St (Ⓣ410/280-0445, Ⓦwww.visit-annapolis.org), can provide free maps and information about walking, bus and water tours.

Finding a **place to stay** is not usually a problem. Playing off their charms, the city's **B&Bs** are expensive; the best value are the four rooms and one suite of the *Flag House Inn*, 26 Randall St (ⓣ410/280-2721 or 1-800/437-4825, ⓦwww.flaghouseinn.com; ❼), and the *Royal Folly*, 65 College Ave (ⓣ410/263-3999, ⓦwww.royalfolly.com; ❽), whose sizeable modern suites variously come with fireplaces, jacuzzis, patios, flat-screen TVs and iPod docks. Also, the three supremely elegant suites of the *Annapolis Inn*, 114 Prince George St (ⓣ410/295-5200, ⓦwww.annapolisinn.com; ❾), and the three stylish buildings of the *Historic Inns of Annapolis*, 58 State Circle (ⓣ410/263-2641, ⓦwww.historicinnsofannapolis.com; ❻), all provide smart accommodation options in classic Georgian structures.

Worthwhile **dining** options include the no-frills *Chick and Ruth's Delly*, 165 Main St (ⓣ410/269-6737), good for an energy boost with its gut-busting breakfasts and huge sandwiches; *Sam's on the Waterfront*, 2020 Chesapeake Harbour Drive E (ⓣ410/263-3600), a primo marina-side eatery with a range of delicious offerings from lamb sirloin and lobster-rice noodles to tuna tartare; and the exquisite Atlantic fare of the *Wild Orchid Cafe*, 909 Bay Ridge Ave (ⓣ410/268-8009), featuring fine crab cakes, rack of lamb, steak and other favourites.

The Eastern Shore

The rambling backroads of Maryland's **Eastern Shore** cross over half of the broad Delmarva (**Del**aware, **Mar**yland, **V**irgini**a**) peninsula that protects the Chesapeake from the open Atlantic, its country lanes passing the odd wooden farmhouse or dilapidated tobacco barn. It's accessible via the US-50 bridge, built across the Chesapeake Bay in the early 1960s. Branching off from US-50 as the highway races down to the beach resort of **Ocean City**, quiet country lanes lead to 200-year-old bayside towns like **Chestertown** and **St Michaels**.

Chestertown

A prime Chesapeake port in colonial days, **CHESTERTOWN** stretches west along High Street from the Chester River, hosting fine old riverfront homes and a courthouse square lined with ornate wooden cottages. Although the town is rich with historic edifices, like the grand 1769 Georgian mansion **Widehall**, 101 N Water St, the only house regularly open to the public is the contemporaneous **Geddes-Piper House**, 101 Church Alley (Tues–Fri 10am–4pm; tours May–Oct Sat 1–4pm; $4; ⓣ410/778-3499), a Federal-style brick structure that has a good collection of kitchen tools and eighteenth-century furnishings.

Many of the old houses have been converted into charming **B&Bs**, like the *Widow's Walk Inn*, 402 High St (ⓣ410/778-6455 or 1-888/778-6455, ⓦwww.chestertown.com/widow; ❺), with its five dainty, rather twee rooms; the more refined and elegant, but more expensive, rooms of *Great Oak Manor*, 10568 Cliff Rd (ⓣ1-800/504-3098, ⓦwww.greatoak.com; ❽), some of which come with fireplaces and antique decor; and the *Imperial Hotel*, 208 High St (ⓣ410/778-5000, ⓦwww.imperialchestertown.com; ❻), which has a central location with eleven rooms and a pair of suites, plus wi-fi access, along with the *Front Room* restaurant, serving fine steak and seafood. Also good, the *Brooks Tavern*, 870 High St (ⓣ410/810-0012), has a mean crab cake sandwich, plus upper-end seafood, steak, duck ragu and BBQ crepes. The **visitor centre**, Hwy-213 at Cross St (Mon–Fri 9am–5pm, Sat & Sun 10am–4pm (2pm in autumn & winter); ⓣ410/778-9737, ⓦwww.chestertown.com), has information on the town's historic features, walking and cycling tours, and a two-hour cruise on the **Sultana**, a replica eighteenth-century schooner, (April–Sept, hours vary; $30; ⓣ410/778-5954, ⓦwww.sultanaprojects.org).

St Michaels

The fetching harbour of **ST MICHAELS**, twelve miles west of US-50 on Hwy-33, is one of the Chesapeake Bay's oldest ports. Founded during the mid-1600s, it grew into one of colonial America's prime shipbuilding centres. Since the 1960s, it has been revitalized, its old buildings now gentrified into art galleries, boutiques and cosy B&Bs.

The old town green, **St Mary's Square**, sits a block east of Talbot Street on Mulberry Street, while north along the docks is the extensive and modern **Chesapeake Bay Maritime Museum** (hours vary, often daily 10am–5pm; $13; ⓦwww.cbmm.org), which hosts a number of restored old vessels on its premises, and exhibits on steamboats, the oyster industry and the working-class life of the Bay. The complex also focuses on the restored 1879 **Hooper Strait Lighthouse** (which you can tour), a squat structure perched on iron pilings, at the foot of which float several Chesapeake Bay sailboats, designed to make the most of the bay's shallow waters.

There are a number of very nice **B&Bs** in town, including the 1883 Victorian splendour of the *Parsonage Inn*, (ⓣ410/745-8383, ⓦwww.parsonage-inn.com; ❼), whose rooms have graceful period decor, and some have fireplaces; and the excellent *Cherry Street Inn*, 103 Cherry St (ⓣ410/745-6309, ⓦwww.cherrystreetinn.com; ❼), whose two lovely suites are well appointed, with a tasty breakfast on offer, too. Among local **restaurants**, *Bistro St Michaels*, 403 S Talbot St (ⓣ410/745-9111), has some of the best steamed mussels, salmon and shrimp around, at a premium price, while the *Key Lime Cafe*, 207 N Talbot St (ⓣ410/745-3158), is tops for its succulent clams, oysters, duck salad and ribs, with a nice selection of fresh fish, too.

Ocean City

With more than ten miles of broad Atlantic beach and hordes of visitors, **OCEAN CITY** is Maryland's number one summer resort, accessible across the Eastern Shore via US-50. There's a lively, three-mile-long **beach boardwalk**, along which are numerous fast-food and trinket vendors hawking their wares, and a pair of amusement parks with the usual carnival-style thrill rides.

The Greyhound **bus** stop is at 12848 Ocean Gateway, and the city has two helpful **visitor centres**: the Chamber of Commerce, on US-50 as you approach the city (ⓣ410/213-0552, ⓦwww.oceancity.org), and another at 4001 Coastal Hwy (ⓣ1-800/626-2326, ⓦwww.ococean.com); both have the usual brochures and can help with accommodation.

Places to **stay** are plentiful except on summer weekends, and off-season rates are at least half the prime-time ones. The *Crystal Beach Hotel*, 2500 N Baltimore Ave (ⓣ1-866/BEACH-21, ⓦwww.crystalbeachhotel.com; ❼), has rooms with wi-fi access, kitchenettes and balconies, while cheaper are the clean and reliable units of the *Sea Hawk Motel*, 12410 Coastal Hwy (ⓣ1-800/942-9042, ⓦwww.seahawkmotel.com; ❺), with some fridges and microwaves, and those of the *Commander Hotel*, boardwalk at 14th Street (ⓣ410/289-6166, ⓦwww.commanderhotel.com; ❼), with its variety of rooms, suites and apartments.

Good **eating** options amid the national chains include the *PGN Crab House*, 2906 Philadelphia Ave (Ⓣ410/289-8380), for its succulent crab cakes, and the seafood, shepherd's pie and burgers at *Shenanigan's*, 4th and Boardwalk (Ⓣ410/289-7181), an Irish pub with a full menu and live music.

Delaware

Founded in 1631, **DELAWARE** was once part of neighbouring Pennsylvania – Philadelphia is only ten miles north – until separating in 1776. In 1787 it was the first former colony to ratify the Constitution and become a state. Much of Delaware's fortunes can be traced to its lax corporate laws that have allowed countless multinational corporations to take up official residence here, and to the **du Pont family**, who, fleeing the wrath of revolutionary France, set up a gunpowder mill that became the main supplier of conventional explosives to the US government. The family built huge mansions in the **Brandywine Valley** north of Wilmington, near the perfectly preserved old colonial capital, **New Castle**, on the Delaware Bay, five miles south of I-95. Further south, **Dover**, the capital, may not detain you long, but beyond it, the small and amiable resorts of **Lewes** and **Rehoboth Beach** mark the northern extent of over twenty miles of mostly unspoiled Atlantic beaches.

Wilmington and around

Pleasant **WILMINGTON** boasts decent art museums and some pretty waterside parks, and the surrounding Brandywine Valley holds the manor homes and gardens (and factories) of the du Ponts. Amtrak **trains** pull in at 100 S French St, and Greyhound **buses** at 101 N French St, both on the dicey south side of the city. From here, the two main streets, Market and King, run north for about a mile to the Brandywine River, lined with stores and other businesses, as well as a handful of restored eighteenth-century structures, including the **Old Town Hall**, 500 Market St (special events only; Ⓣ302/655-7161 for details), a graceful 1798 Federal mansion. Nearby is the **Delaware History Museum**, 504 Market St (Wed–Fri 11am–4pm, Sat 10am–4pm; $4, free Fri; Ⓦwww.hsd.org/dhm.htm), offering three storeys of exhibits on the history, life and folk art of the state. A short walk north of the downtown commercial district, at the top end of Market Street, **Brandywine Park** is filled with grassy knolls lining both banks of the Brandywine River. The nearby **Delaware Art Museum**, 2301 Kentmere Parkway (Wed–Sat 10am–4pm, Sun noon–4pm; $12, free Sun; Ⓦwww.delart.org), focuses on Pre-Raphaelites such as Dante Rossetti, and on American artists from the nineteenth and twentieth centuries like Frederic Church, Winslow Homer, Edward Hopper and Augustus Saint Gaudens. For those with a yen for the archly modern, the **Delaware Center for the Contemporary Arts**, downtown at 200 S Madison St (Tues & Thurs–Sat 10am–5pm, Wed & Sun noon–5pm; free; Ⓦwww.thedcca.org), is best known for its dozens of yearly rotating exhibits that showcase regional and national artists.

Most of Wilmington's colonial sites are hidden away amid the shambling, industrialized waterfront east of downtown. These include the **Hendrickson**

House Museum, at 606 Church St, a c.1690 pinewood residence with furnishings from various eras, and **Old Swedes Church**, one of the oldest houses of worship in the US, built in 1698 (both Wed–Sat 10am–4pm; $2 ⓣ302/652-5629). Several miles north, near I-95 in Rockwood Park, the Gothic Revival **Rockwood Mansion**, 610 Shipley Rd (park and gardens daily 6am–10pm, mansion tours Wed–Sun 10am–3pm; $5 tours; ⓦwww.rockwood.org), was built in 1854 in the style of a rural English estate, its elegant rooms now restored to their resplendent Gilded Age appearance.

Practicalities

The downtown **Convention & Visitors Bureau**, 100 W 10th St (Mon–Fri 9am–5pm; ⓣ1-800/489-6664, ⓦwww.VisitWilmingtonDe.com), has walking and driving tour maps and practical information. The DART **bus** system runs around the county; tickets $1.15 (ⓣ1-800/652-3278, ⓦwww.dartfirststate.com). Easily the best **lodging** choice is the splendidly ornate 1913 *Hotel du Pont*, 100 W 11th St (ⓣ302/594-3100 or 1-800/441-9019, ⓦwww.hoteldupont.com; ❾), which has well-appointed rooms and suites that are the height of contemporary chic. Other options are far less appealing, though the *Inn at Wilmington*, 300 Rocky Run Parkway (ⓣ302/479-7900, ⓦwww.innatwilmington.com; ❺), does offer affordable rooms and suites with CD players and microwaves. A good choice for **eating** is the happening Trolley Square area northwest of downtown, where *Moro*, 1307 N Scott St (ⓣ302/777-1800), has upmarket Atlantic cuisine like wine-braised rabbit, veal chops and pan-seared scallops, plus several fixed-price menus. Elsewhere, the *Washington Street Ale House*, 1206 Washington St (ⓣ302/658-2537), has serviceable pasta and seafood, but the main draw is its copious microbrew selection.

The du Pont mansions

A short distance up I-95 from the Rockwood Mansion, the first of the **du Pont mansions** is accessible in **Bellevue State Park**, 800 Carr Rd (daily 8am–dusk; free). William du Pont Jr converted a Gothic Revival mansion into his own version of James Madison's Neoclassical home and called it **Bellevue Hall**. You can't get inside, but can visit the grounds and see the charming ponds, woodlands, gardens and tennis courts.

Twenty minutes northwest of Wilmington, members of the du Pont family built opulent homes in the rural Brandywine Valley. The **Hagley Museum**, off Hwy-141 just north of Wilmington (mid-March to Dec daily 9.30am–4.30pm; $11; ⓦwww.hagley.org), showcases their 1802 founding of a small water-powered gunpowder mill, which grew over the next century to include larger steam- and electricity-powered factories – most of which are still in working order. Be sure to tour the luxurious du Pont mansion, Eleutherian Mills, the centrepiece of the 235-acre estate.

The enormous, dusty-pink **Nemours Mansion**, just a mile away at 1600 Rockland Rd (tours Tues–Sat 9am, noon & 3pm, Sun noon & 3pm; $15; ⓣ1-800/651-6912, ⓦwww.nemoursmansion.org), was built by Alfred du Pont in 1910 and named for the family's ancestral home in France, and is surrounded by a three-hundred-acre, French-style garden. Inside the mansion, you'll find plenty of lavish rooms including those devoted to fitness, bowling and ice-making, and a collection of early-twentieth-century automobiles. Two miles northwest, off Hwy-52, the one-time du Pont family estate of **Winterthur** (March–Nov Tues–Sun 10am–5pm; tours $18–40; ⓦwww.winterthur.org) now displays American decorative arts from 1640 to 1860, each of its 175 rooms showcasing styles ranging from a simple Shaker cottage to a beautiful three-storey elliptical staircase taken from a North Carolina plantation. Separately, the estate galleries present a selection of furniture, textiles, ceramics, paintings and glass in a museum setting.

New Castle

Delaware's original capital, **NEW CASTLE**, fronts the broad Delaware River, just six miles south of Wilmington via Hwy-141. Founded in the 1650s by the Dutch and taken over by the British in 1664, New Castle has managed to survive intact, its quiet cobbled streets and immaculate eighteenth-century brick houses shaded by ancient hardwood trees.

The heart of New Castle is the tree-filled **town green** that spreads east from the shops of Delaware Street, and dominated by the stalwart tower of the **Immanuel Episcopal Church**, on Harmony Street at The Strand, built in 1703 and bordered by tidy rows of eighteenth-century gravestones. On the west edge of the green, the **Old Court House**, 211 Delaware St (Wed–Sat 10am–3.30pm; free), was built in 1732 and served as the first state capitol until 1881. Its dainty cupola provided the vista from which surveyors determined the state's arcing northern border, drawn up when Delaware seceded from Pennsylvania (and Great Britain) in 1776.

Fine colonial houses fill the blocks around the town green. The largest is the **George Read II House**, two blocks south along the river at 42 The Strand (winter Sat 10am–4pm & Sun 11am–4pm; rest of year Tues–Fri & Sun 11am–4pm, Sat 10am–4pm; $5; Ⓦwww.hsd.org/read.htm), a sumptuous replica of a c.1800 house, with marble fireplaces, elaborately carved woodwork, Federal-style plaster ornament and picturesque gardens. A collection of classic edifices lies several blocks north along Third and Fourth streets: the **Amstel House**, 2 E Fourth St (April–Dec Wed–Sat 10am–4pm, Sun noon–4pm; $4; Ⓦwww.newcastlehistory.org), a 1730 early-Georgian mansion that hosted prominent Revolutionary-era figures; the hexagonal brick **Old Library Museum**, 40 E Third St (March–Dec Sat & Sun 1–4pm; free), housing the historical society's collection; and the **Dutch House**, 32 E Third St (April–Dec: Wed–Sat 10am–4pm, Sun noon–4pm; $4), a simple c.1700 residence with decor and artefacts including a cherry-wood cupboard, duck-footed wooden chairs and polychromed Delft ceramics.

Practicalities

To pick up the self-guided **walking tour** map, drop by the **visitor centre** at 211 Delaware St, in the Old Court House (Ⓣ302/323-4453). There's only one **B&B** left in New Castle, and it's just as well that it's the *Terry House*, 130 Delaware St (Ⓣ302/322-2505, Ⓦwww.terryhouse.com; ④), a stately townhouse dating from the Civil War with four simple, tastefully decorated rooms; otherwise, there's the usual array of clean, budget **motels**. The better **restaurants** serve colonial-style food, such as crabs, clams and shepherd's pie, as at the popular *Jessop's Tavern*, 114 Delaware St (Ⓣ302/322-6111). There are also savoury dishes like salmon tarragon and grilled lamb chops at the *Arsenal at Old New Castle*, next to the Episcopal Church at 30 Market St (Ⓣ302/328-1290).

Dover

Located in Delaware's mostly agricultural centre, just west of US-13, the capital **DOVER** is a small town hemmed in by suburbia. South of **Lockerman Street**, the main route through town, the 1791 **Old State House**, 25 The Green, is the state's one-time judicial and legislative chambers, now a museum furnished with early-American antiques (Wed–Sat 9am–4.30pm; free; ⓣ302/744-5055). To the west, around the oval **town green**, lawyers and corporations have taken over a number of eighteenth- and nineteenth-century buildings.

In the same building as the **visitor centre** (Tues–Sat 9am–4.30pm, Sun 1.30–4.30pm; ⓣ302/739-4266), at the corner of Duke of York and Federal streets next to the Old State House, the impressive **Biggs Museum of American Art** (same hours; free; ⓦwww.biggsmuseum.org) has a wealth of historical and decorative art, including colonial-era furniture, paintings by the likes of Benjamin West and Gilbert Stuart, silver and porcelain services, and heroic landscapes from Albert Bierstadt and Thomas Cole. Nearby, **First State Heritage Park**, 102 S State St (ⓦwww.destateparks.com), not only hosts the current statehouse and state archives, but includes a smattering of museums that are either open only on the first Saturday of the month or closed for renovation. Visit the **Welcome Center** (Mon–Fri 8am–4.30pm, Sun 1.30–4.30pm; free; ⓦhistory.delaware.gov), to find out more about building hours and tours, along with rotating exhibits on state history.

For more than fifty years, **Spence's Bazaar**, 550 S New St (Tues & Fri 7.30am–6.30pm; free; ⓣ302/734-3441), has hosted a **flea market** that all of Dover turns out for, including dozens of local **Amish**, who ride here in their old horse-drawn buggies, often from southeastern Pennsylvania, to sell home-grown fruits and vegetables.

A few miles outside town, the eighteen-acre **John Dickinson Plantation**, off Rte-9 at 340 Kitts Hummock Rd (Wed–Sat 10am–3.30pm; free; ⓣ302/739-3277), is where costumed re-enactors of colonial residents, including slaves, go about farming, cooking and gardening; both the estate's grounds and 1740 brick mansion are viewable on various tours, lasting ninety minutes to two hours.

Practicalities

Greyhound **buses** pull in at 716 S Governors Ave. Appealing **B&Bs** include the *Little Creek Inn*, 2623 N Little Creek Rd, off Hwy-8 (ⓣ302/730-1300, ⓦwww.littlecreekinn.com; ❺), an attractive 1860 estate, with five rooms (some with jacuzzis) featuring period appointments, as well as a pool, gym and bocce court; and the similar amenities of the *State Street Inn*, 228 N State St (ⓣ302/734-2294, ⓦwww.statestreetinn.com; ❺), more centrally located, but with rooms that are a bit smaller. As for **eating**, *Franco's*, 1708 E Lebanon Rd (ⓣ302/677-1946), is good for affordable pizza and pasta dishes; further out, *Kirby and Holloway*, 656 N Dupont Hwy (ⓣ302/734-7133), is known for its filling steaks, burgers, chicken and dumplings, and turkey platters, most below $10.

The Delaware coast

The thirty-mile-long **Delaware coast** is one of the little-known jewels of the East Coast, aside from the brash summer resort of **Rehoboth Beach**. The historic fishing community of **Lewes** is an attractive stopover, but what sets the area apart are the long, isolated stretches of sand. Much has been preserved as open space, most extensively at **Delaware Seashore State Park**, which stretches south to the Maryland border.

Lewes

Accessible via Hwy-1, the natural harbour at the mouth of Delaware Bay at **LEWES** has attracted seafarers ever since a Dutch whaling company set up a small colony here in 1631, a history outlined in the mock-Dutch **Zwaanendael**

Museum, Savannah Road at Kings Highway (Tues–Sat 10am–4.30pm, Sun 1.30–4.30pm; free; ⓣ302/645-1148). The **tourist office** next door (Mon–Fri 9am–5pm, Sat 10am–2pm; ⓣ302/645-8073, ⓦwww.leweschamber.com), housed inside a gambrel-roofed 1730s farmhouse, has walking-tour maps of the town and its numerous eighteenth-century homes. Don't miss the **Lewes Historic Complex**, three blocks north at 110 Shipcarpenter St (mid-June to mid-Sept Mon–Sat 11am–4pm; $5; ⓣ302/645-7670, ⓦwww.historiclewes.org), twelve classic properties dating from the early-colonial to late-Victorian eras, including a crude plank-house, doctor's office, store and boathouse. On Front Street, 1812 **Memorial Park** is decorated by an array of cannons, and commemorates a British attack that resulted in spotty cannonball damage around town.

There's a popular, extensive **beach** along the Delaware Bay at the foot of town, while three-thousand-acre, four-mile-long **Cape Henlopen State Park** (daily 8am–dusk; ⓣ302/645-8983), where the bay meets the open ocean just a mile east of the town centre, offers the chance to **camp** ($30–32/night) beside the biggest sand dunes north of Cape Hatteras, and hike appealing trails, including one to a World War II-era observation tower. You can also ride the **ferry** across Delaware Bay from beside the state park to Cape May, New Jersey (times vary by day and season; 1hr 20min; $30–44/car, $7.50–10/person; ⓣ1-800/64-FERRY, ⓦwww.cmlf.com; see also p.160).

Practicalities

You can walk to most places in town, or **rent a bike** from Lewes Cycle Sports, 526 Savannah Rd ($25/day; ⓣ302/645-4544). Due to its proximity to Rehoboth Beach, in summer **accommodation** prices can be steep. There are cheap motels along Savannah Road, but try instead *Hotel Blue*, 110 Anglers Rd (ⓣ302/645-4880, ⓦwww.hotelblue.info; by season ❻–❽), whose modern rooms and suites come with flat-panel TVs, boutique decor, fireplaces and internet access. Continuing the azure theme, the *Blue Water House*, 407 E Market St (ⓣ302/645-7832, ⓦwww.lewes-beach.com; ❸, two-night minimum), is a B&B with eight stylish rooms and a suite, all with net access and watersports rentals. For **dining**, *Cafe Azafran*, 109 Market St (ⓣ302/644-4446), has a nice assortment of tapas (including seafood items) for a range of prices, and *The Buttery*, 2nd Street at Savannah Road (ⓣ302/645-7755), is a fine French bistro that has mid-priced crab cakes, burgers, and seafood sandwiches for lunch, and pricey steak and rack of lamb for dinner.

Rehoboth Beach

A nonstop parade of motels and malls along the six miles of Hwy-1 links Lewes with **REHOBOTH BEACH**, Delaware's largest beach resort, which merges into **Dewey Beach** at its southern end. The resort's wooden **boardwalk** is one of the last ones left on the East Coast, stretching along the Atlantic to either side of Rehoboth Avenue – "**The Avenue**" – which acts as the main drag. With its novelty and trinket shops, carnival-style amusements and various tourist traps, the town has no particularly important sights, but it can be enjoyable if you just want to mingle with the crowds or worship the sun on the beach.

The **tourist office** is at 501 Rehoboth Ave (ⓣ302/227-2233 or 1-800/441-1329, ⓦwww.beach-fun.com). The best of Rehoboth's **motels** (very pricey in July and Aug) is the *Crosswinds*, three blocks from the beach at 312 Rehoboth Ave (ⓣ302/227-7997, ⓦwww.crosswindsmotel.com; ❸–❽), whose clean rooms have fridges and wireless internet. Among area **B&Bs**, try the *Corner Cupboard Inn*, 50 Park Ave (ⓣ302/227-8553, ⓦwww.cornercupboardinn.com; ❹–❽), with clean and tasteful units, or the gay-friendly *Rehoboth Guest*

House, 40 Maryland Ave (Ⓣ302/227-4117, Ⓦwww.rehobothguesthouse.com; ❹–❻), with porch and shaded backyard, and basic rooms (add $35 for private bath). Most of the **restaurants** are concentrated on the boardwalk, but the better ones include the *Planet X Cafe*, 35 Wilmington Ave (Ⓣ302/226-1928), which has appealing, expensive Asian fusion cuisine such as ahi tuna fillets, peanut-crusted shrimp and, of course, lump crab cakes, and 7, 320 Rehoboth Ave (Ⓣ302/226-2739), which is best for its fine microbrews, weekend live bands and an on-site distillery.

South of Rehoboth, **Delaware Seashore State Park** (daily 8am–dusk; Ⓣ302/227-2800, Ⓦwww.destateparks.com) stretches for miles along a thin, sandy peninsula, split by Hwy-1 and bounded by the ocean and freshwater marshlands, and good for its fishing and surfing.

6

The South

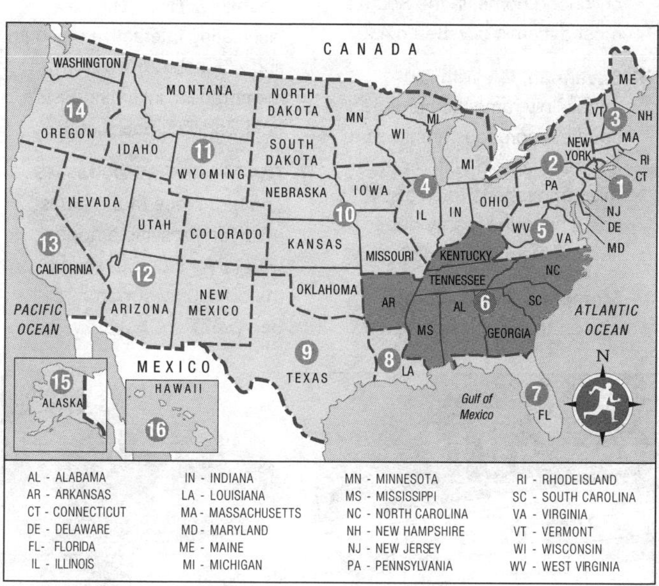
CANADA
WASHINGTON
MONTANA
NORTH DAKOTA
MN
WI
MI
ME
VT
NH
MA
NEW YORK
RI
CT
OREGON
IDAHO
WYOMING
SOUTH DAKOTA
MI
PA
NEBRASKA
IOWA
NJ
DE
MD
NEVADA
UTAH
COLORADO
KANSAS
IL
IN
OHIO
WV
VA
CALIFORNIA
MISSOURI
KENTUCKY
NC
TENNESSEE
OKLAHOMA
AR
ARIZONA
NEW MEXICO
AL
SC
PACIFIC OCEAN
MS
GEORGIA
ATLANTIC OCEAN
MEXICO
TEXAS
LA
HAWAII
ALASKA
Gulf of Mexico
FL
N
1
2
3
4
5
6
7
8
9
10
11
12
13
14
15
16
AL - ALABAMA
AR - ARKANSAS
CT - CONNECTICUT
DE - DELAWARE
FL- FLORIDA
IL - ILLINOIS
IN - INDIANA
LA - LOUISIANA
MA - MASSACHUSETTS
MD - MARYLAND
ME - MAINE
MI - MICHIGAN
MN - MINNESOTA
MS - MISSISSIPPI
NC - NORTH CAROLINA
NH - NEW HAMPSHIRE
NJ - NEW JERSEY
PA - PENNSYLVANIA
RI - RHODE ISLAND
SC - SOUTH CAROLINA
VA - VIRGINIA
VT - VERMONT
WI - WISCONSIN
WV - WEST VIRGINIA

CHAPTER 6

Highlights

✱ **Blue Ridge Parkway, NC** A tortuous but exhilarating wilderness highway that makes a destination in itself. **See p.414**

✱ **Martin Luther King Birth Home, Atlanta, GA** Engaging tours take you around King's childhood home, in the South's most dynamic city. **See p.430**

✱ **Savannah, GA** With its impossibly romantic garden squares, gorgeous architecture and bustling old waterfront, this atmospheric town also has a hip edge, partly due to its art school. **See p.436**

✱ **Memphis, TN** This sleepy city on the Mississippi is especially thrilling for music fans: you could spend days checking out Beale Street, Sun Studio, the Stax Museum, Al Green's church and, of course, Graceland. **See p.450**

✱ **Country Music Hall of Fame, Nashville, TN** At once a fascinating interactive museum and a treasure-trove of memorabilia, including Elvis's gold Cadillac. **See p.463**

✱ **The Mississippi Delta, MS** The birthplace of the blues holds an irresistible appeal, with funky little Clarksdale as the obvious first port of call. **See p.477**

▲ Stax in Memphis

6

The South

Mark Twain put it best, as early as 1882: "In the South, the [Civil] war is what AD is elsewhere; they date everything from it." Several generations later, the legacies of slavery and "The War Between the States" remain evident throughout the southern heartland states of **NORTH CAROLINA, SOUTH CAROLINA, GEORGIA, KENTUCKY, TENNESSEE, ALABAMA, MISSISSIPPI** and **ARKANSAS**. It's impossible to travel through the region without experiencing constant jolting reminders of the two epic historical clashes that have shaped its destiny: the **Civil War**, and the **civil rights** movement of the 1950s and 1960s.

Although enough white Southerners continue to identify with the Confederate past to make it debatable whether the much-vaunted "New South" has truly come into being – outside the major cities, at least – the last decades have unquestionably seen dramatic change. The inspirational campaigns that finally secured black participation in Southern elections resulted not only in the prominence of black political leaders but also in the emergence of liberal white counterparts including Jimmy Carter and Bill Clinton. High-tech industries have moved in, luring considerable inward migration, while urban centres such as **Atlanta**, the birthplace of Dr Martin Luther King Jr, are booming.

That said, it's misleading in any case to generalize too much about "the South". Even during the Civil War there were substantial pockets of pro-Union support, particularly in the mountains, while during the long century of segregation that followed, certain states, such as Mississippi and Alabama, were far more brutally oppressive than others. These days, inequities within the South, between for example the industrialized "Sun Belt" centres of North Carolina and northern Alabama and the poorer rural backwaters of southern Georgia, Mississippi or Tennessee, are just as significant as those between the South and the rest of the nation, and are no longer so clearly demarcated along racial lines. For many travellers, the most exciting aspect of a visit to the South has to be its **music**. Fans flock to the homelands of Elvis Presley, Hank Williams, Robert Johnson, Dolly Parton and Otis Redding, heading to the country and blues meccas of **Nashville** and **Memphis**, or seeking out backwoods barn dances in Appalachia and blues juke joints in the Mississippi Delta.

The Southern experience is also reflected in a rich regional **literature**, documented by the likes of William Faulkner, Carson McCullers, Eudora Welty, Margaret Mitchell and Harper Lee. Other major destinations include the elegant coastal cities of **Charleston** and **Savannah**, college towns like **Athens** and **Chapel Hill**, and the historic Mississippi River ports of **Natchez** and **Vicksburg**. Away from the urban areas, the classic Southern scenery consists of fertile but sun-baked farmlands, with undulating hillsides dotted with wooden shacks and rust-red barns, and broken by occasional forests. Highlights include the misty Appalachian **mountains** of Kentucky, Tennessee and North Carolina; the subtropical **beaches** and tranquil **barrier islands** along the Atlantic and Gulf coasts of Georgia and South Carolina; and the river road through the tiny, time-warped settlements of the flat **Mississippi Delta**. In July and August, the daily high **temperature** is mostly a very humid 90°F, and while almost every public building is air-conditioned, the heat can be debilitating. May and June are more

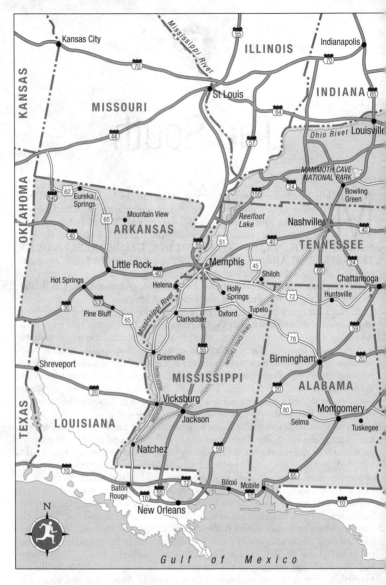

bearable, and tend to see a lot of local festivals, while the autumn colours in the mountains – just as beautiful and a lot less expensive and congested than New England – are at their headiest during October.

Motels are everywhere, while abundant **B&Bs** offer a chance to sample the much-vaunted Southern hospitality – though unless you share a broadly Confederate view of history, these can occasionally be socially uncomfortable. The region's varied **cuisine**, much of it dished out at simple roadside shacks, ranges from the ubiquitous grits (maize porridge) to highly calorific, irresistible **soul food**: fried chicken, wood-smoked BBQ and the like, along with turnip greens, spinach, macaroni and all manner of tasty vegetables. Fish is also good, from catfish to the wonderful **Low Country Boils** – seafood stews served with rice, traditionally prepared on the sea islands of the Carolinas and Georgia.

Getting around the South

Atlanta (GA) has the world's biggest passenger **airport** (Savannah, GA, also has a reasonable connections, but fares between the two are high), while Charlotte (NC), is a major hub for direct transatlantic flights. Other key airports include Charleston (SC), which has flights to and from major towns on the east coast; Memphis (TN), Nashville (TN) and to a lesser extent Little Rock (AK). **Amtrak** crosses much of the region, apart from Kentucky: in North Carolina, Charlotte, Raleigh and Durham are served by train, as are Charleston, Atlanta, Memphis and Little Rock, though not all on the same route. In Alabama, Birmingham and Mobile have train service, with Amtrak buses connecting the two cities via Montgomery. As a rule, however, **public transport** in rural areas is poor and you will see far more, and be able get out to the backwaters – the Blue Ridge Parkway, the Outer Banks of North Carolina, the Ozarks and the Mississippi Delta to mention but a few – if you **rent a car**. In any case, it's best to take things at your own pace – you'll find things to see and do in the most unlikely places. Incidentally, if you harbour fantasies of travelling through the South by **boat** along the Mississippi, note that only luxury craft make the trip these days.

Some history

The Spanish and French constructed settlements along the southern coastline of North America during the sixteenth century. However, it was the British who dominated the region from the seventeenth century onwards, establishing increasingly successful agricultural colonies in the Carolinas and Georgia. Both climate and soil favoured staple crops, and massive labour-intensive plantations sprang up, predominantly growing tobacco prior to independence, and then increasingly shifting to cotton. No self-respecting European would cross the Atlantic to toil on a plantation, so the big landowners turned to slavery as the most profitable source of labour. Millions of blacks were brought across from Africa, most arriving via the port of Charleston.

Although the South prospered until the middle of the nineteenth century, there was little incentive to diversify its economy. As a result, the Northern states began to surge ahead in both agriculture and industry; while the South grew the crops, Northern factories monopolized the more lucrative manufacturing of finished goods. So long as there were equal numbers of slave-owning and "free" states, the South continued to play a central role in national politics, and was able to resist **abolitionist** sentiment. However, the more the United States fulfilled its supposed "Manifest Destiny" to spread across the continent, the more new states joined the Union for which plantation agriculture, and thus slavery, was not appropriate. Southern politicians and plantation owners accused the North of political and economic aggression, and felt that they were losing all say in the future of the nation. The election of **Abraham Lincoln**, a longtime critic of slavery, as president in 1860 brought the crisis to a head. South Carolina **seceded** from the Union that December, and ten more southern states swiftly followed. On February 18, 1861, Jefferson Davis was sworn in as president of the **Confederate States of America** – an occasion on which his vice president proudly proclaimed that this was the first government in the history of the world "based upon this great physical and moral truth... that the Negro is not equal to the white man".

During the resultant **Civil War**, the South was outgunned and ultimately overwhelmed by the vast resources of the North. The Confederates fired the first shots and scored the first victory in April 1861, when the Union garrison at Fort Sumter (outside Charleston) surrendered. The Union was on the military defensive until mid-1862, when its navy blockaded Georgia and the Carolinas and occupied key ports. Then Union forces in the west, under generals Grant and Sherman, swept through Tennessee, and by the end of 1863 the North had taken Vicksburg, the final Confederate-held port on the Mississippi, as well as the strategic mountain-locked town of Chattanooga on the Tennessee–Georgia border. Grant proceeded north to Virginia, while Sherman captured the transportation nexus of Atlanta and began a bloody and ruthless march to the coast, burning everything in his way. With 258,000 men dead, the Confederacy's defeat was total, and General Robert E. Lee **surrendered** on April 9, 1865, at Appomattox in Virginia.

The war left the South in chaos. A quarter of the South's adult white male population had been killed, and two-thirds of Southern wealth destroyed. From controlling thirty percent of the nation's assets in 1860, the South was down to twelve percent in 1870, while the spur the war gave to industrialization meant that the North was booming. For a brief period of **Reconstruction**, when the South was occupied by Union troops, newly freed Southern blacks were able to vote, and black representatives were elected to both state and federal office. However, unrepentant former Confederates, spurred in part by allegations of profiteering by incoming Northern Republican "carpetbaggers", thwarted any potential for change, and by the end of the century the Southern states were firmly back under white Democratic control. As Reconstruction withered away, "**Jim Crow**" segregation laws were imposed, backed by the not-so-secret terror of the **Ku Klux Klan**, and poll taxes, literacy tests and property qualifications disenfranchised virtually all blacks. Many found themselves little better off as **sharecroppers** – in which virtually all they could earn from raising crops went to pay their landlords – than they had been as slaves, and there were mass migrations to cities like Memphis and Atlanta, as well as to the North.

Not until the landmark 1954 Supreme Court ruling in **Brown vs Topeka Board of Education** outlawed segregation in schools was there any sign that the federal authorities in Washington might concern themselves with inequities in the South. Even then, individual states proved extremely reluctant to effect the required changes. In the face of institutionalized white resistance, non-violent black protestors coalesced to form the **civil rights movement**, and broke down segregation through a sustained programme of mass action. After tackling such issues as public transportation – most famously in the Montgomery bus boycott and the Freedom Rides – and segregated dining facilities, with lunch-counter sit-ins reaching their apex in Greensboro, the campaign eventually culminated in restoring full black voter registration – not without the loss of many protestors' lives. One fulfilling itinerary through the Southern states today is to trace the footsteps of **Dr Martin Luther King Jr**, from his birthplace in Atlanta, through his church in Montgomery, to the site of his assassination in Memphis.

The dispossession of the **Native Americans** is often the forgotten chapter of Southern history. After the Revolution, pressure from plantation owners and small farmers led to the forced removal in the 1830s of the "five civilized tribes" – the Cherokee, Creek, Choctaw, Chickasaw and Seminole – to malarial Oklahoma. Today only a few thousand Native Americans live in the South.

North Carolina

NORTH CAROLINA, the most industrialized of the Southern states, breaks down into three distinct areas – the coast, the Piedmont and the mountains. The **coast** promises stunning beaches, beautiful landscapes and a fascinating history. The inner coast consists largely of the less developed **Albemarle Peninsula**, with colonial **Edenton** nearby. The central **Piedmont** is less appealing, dominated by manufacturing cities and the academic institutions of the prestigious "Research Triangle": **Raleigh**, the state capital, is home to North Carolina State University; Durham has Duke; and the University of North Carolina is in trendy **Chapel Hill**. **Winston-Salem** combines tobacco culture and Moravian heritage, while the boomtown of **Charlotte** is distinguished by little but its downtown skyscrapers. In the **Appalachian Mountains**, alternative **Asheville** makes a hugely enjoyable stop along the spectacular **Blue Ridge Parkway**; **Great Smoky Mountains National Park** overlaps the border with Tennessee.

The North Carolina coast

The **North Carolina coast**, which ranges through salt marshes, beaches, barrier islands and estuaries, holds most of the state's more interesting **historic sites**. The continent's earliest English colonists vanished inexplicably from **Roanoke Island** in 1590; just over three centuries later, the Wright brothers achieved the first powered flight a few miles up the road. The **Outer Banks**, the long reef of barrier islands that stretches down from Virginia, are in parts beautifully unspoiled and elsewhere downright tacky.

Edenton and the Albemarle

The huge **Albemarle Peninsula** remains largely unexploited. Local towns try to make much of their **colonial history** – but often there's not a lot left to see. The area is rewarding to explore if you like to travel off the beaten path, its sleepy old towns and remote plantations set in wide swathes of rural farmland and endless marshes that eventually give way to water in a ragged pattern of sounds and lakes.

Edenton

EDENTON, set along the majestic Albemarle Sound waterfront, was established as North Carolina's first state capital in 1722 and was a major centre of unrest in the American Revolution. Nowadays, it makes a nice, peaceful little base for explorations of the coast, with some good B&Bs and restaurants, and a nostalgic small-town ambience.

Strolling along the town's main road, **Broad Street**, lined with Victorian facades and old-fashioned stores, brings you to the **visitor centre** at 108 N Broad (Mon–Sat 9am–5pm, Sun 1–5pm; ⓣ252/482-2637, ⓦwww.nchistoricsites.org/iredell/); you can take a **guided tour** from here, or pick up a walking tour map. Among other important figures, Edenton was home to **Harriet Jacobs**, a runaway slave who hid for seven years in her grandmother's attic. In 1842, she finally escaped to the North through such ruses as disguising herself as a sailor, and was eventually reunited in Boston with the two children she had with a white man in Edenton. She wrote her autobiography as *Incidents in the Life of a Slave Girl*, one of the most famous published slave narratives of the nineteenth century.

Luxurious **B&Bs** include the peaceful *Trestle House Inn*, set in seven acres overlooking a nature refuge on a lake; it's five miles south of town, off Hwy-32, at 632 Soundside Rd (Ⓣ252/482-2282, Ⓦwww.trestlehouseinn.com; ❺). A few minutes' walk from the waterfront, the friendly *Governor Eden Inn*, 304 N Broad St (Ⓣ252/482-2072; ❹), offers appealing rooms and a huge veranda. *Chero's*, 112 W Water St (Ⓣ252/482-5525), is a colourful **restaurant** serving Mediterranean and regional food; for seafood, head for the *Waterman's Grill*, 427 S Broad St (Ⓣ252/482-7733).

Exploring the Albemarle

Albemarle **plantation life** is brought alive in the informed, illuminating tours of **Hope**, the home of David Stone, a state governor and US senator of the Revolutionary and Federal periods. It's a remote place set in the sleepy fields of the rural heartland; you'll find it off Hwy-308, a few miles west of **Windsor**, about 25 miles southwest of Edenton (Mon–Sat 10am–4pm, Sun 2–5pm; $8; Ⓦwww.hopeplantation.org).

At Creswell, 25 miles southeast of Edenton on US-64, a vivid picture of slave life is painted by **Somerset Place State Historic Site** (April–Oct Mon–Sat 9am–5pm, Sun 1–5pm; Nov–March Tues–Sat 10am–4pm, Sun 1–4pm; free; Ⓦwww.nchistoricsites.org/somerset). The museum here tells the history of the plantation, from its origins in the 1780s to its growth by 1860 into a 2000-acre enterprise, and its demise after the Civil War. Exhibits detail the accumulation of more than 300 enslaved Africans and the work they did; in the grounds, a sweeping vista of lowland fields and huge oaks dissolving into marshland beyond, you can walk through reconstructions of the plantation hospital and two typical slave houses. The southern shore of the Albemarle Peninsula holds less to see, though the marshy country roads make for a pleasant drive. **Lake Mattamuskeet Wildlife Refuge** (Ⓦwww.fws.gov/mattamuskeet) is an amazing sight in winter, when thousands of swans migrate here from Canada. The entrance is on Hwy-94, about a mile north of its intersection with US-264. South of Mattamuskeet, you can catch a **ferry** from **Swan Quarter** to Ocracoke on the Outer Banks (see p.408).

The Outer Banks

The **OUTER BANKS**, a string of skinny barrier islands, the remnants of ancient sand dunes, stretch about 180 miles from the Virginia border to Cape Lookout. This is a great region to meander, with wonderful wild beaches, otherworldly marshes and attractive small towns. There is **no public transportation** other than the ferries between islands and to the mainland.

If you come in on the main road from the north, US-158, stop at the well-stocked Cape Hatteras National Park Service **visitor centre** (daily: June–Aug 9am–6pm, Sept–May 9am–5pm; Ⓦwww.nps.gov/caha). South along US-158 and the parallel shoreline Beach Road, the coastal towns of **Kitty Hawk**, **Kill Devil Hills** and **Nags Head** nestle closely together where the **beaches** are lined with motels, restaurants and huge vacation "cottages". Arriving from the west on Hwy-64, you'll come to another **visitor centre** (daily 9am–5pm; Ⓣ252/473-2138, Ⓦwww.outerbanks.org) on **Roanoke Island**. The island, site of the first English settlement in the US, has obvious historical interest; its village, **Manteo**, is perhaps the nicest on the Outer Banks.

Kill Devil Hills and Nags Head

The main feature of the **Wright Brothers National Memorial** (daily: June–Aug 9am–6pm, Sept–May 9am–5pm; $4; Ⓦwww.nps.gov/wrbr), just off the main road at **KILL DEVIL HILLS**, is the Wright Brothers Monument, a 60ft granite fin atop a 90ft dune (which is in fact *the* Kill Devil Hill). The memorial commemorates Orville Wright's **first powered flight**, on December 17, 1903. (Most histories say the flight took place at **Kitty Hawk**, a town eight miles north, but that was just the name of the nearest post office.) A boulder next to the memorial's **visitor centre** marks where Orville's first aircraft hit the ground, and numbered markers show the distance of each of his three subsequent flights. Exhibits in the visitor centre record the brothers' various outlandish experiments. A few miles south, in **NAGS HEAD**, at Mile 12 on Hwy-158, **Jockey's Ridge State Park** (Ⓦwww.jockeysridgestatepark.com) boasts the largest sand dunes on the east coast – beautiful at sunset.

Motels line the beaches north of Oregon Inlet, which separates Bodie Island and Cape Hatteras National Seashore. The luxurious *First Colony Inn*, 6720 S Virginia Dare Trail, Nags Head (Ⓣ252/441-2343, Ⓦwww.firstcolonyinn.com; ❺), is housed in a 1930s beach hotel, with wraparound verandas and a pool. The standard of **food** varies; good bets in Kill Devil Hills include the

Roanoke: The Lost Colony

According to popular myth, the first English attempt to settle in North America – Sir Walter Raleigh's colony at Roanoke – remains an unsolved mystery, in which the "Lost Colony" disappeared without trace. Sir Walter himself never visited North America. The original patent to establish a colony was granted by Queen Elizabeth I to his half-brother, Sir Humphrey Gilbert, but Gilbert died following an abortive landfall in Newfoundland in 1583. Raleigh directed subsequent explorations further south; a 1584 expedition pinpointed Roanoke Island, behind the Outer Banks of North Carolina and thus hidden from the view of the Spanish, who were by now jealously patrolling the Atlantic seaboard from their bases in Florida. The English named the region **Virginia**, in honour of the Virgin Queen.

A party led by Ralph Lane in 1585 was interested in gold; their hopes of finding a fortune were quickly dashed, however, and the following year they sailed home with Sir Francis Drake, who visited on his way up from the West Indies. In 1587, 117 more colonists set off from England, intending to farm a more fertile site beside Chesapeake Bay; but, fearing Spanish attack, the ships that carried them dumped them at Roanoke once again. Their leader, **John White**, who went home to fetch supplies a month later, was stranded in England when war broke out with Spain, and the Spanish Armada set sail. When he finally managed to persuade a reluctant sea captain to carry him back to Roanoke in 1590, he found the island abandoned. Even so, he was reassured by the absence of the agreed distress signal (a carved Maltese cross), while the word "**Croatoan**" inscribed on a tree seemed a clear message that the colonists had moved south to the eponymous island. However, fearful of both the Spanish and of the approaching hurricane season, White's crew refused to take him any further. There the story usually ends, with the colonists never seen again. In fact, during the next decade, several reports reached the subsequent, more durable colony of Jamestown (in what's now Virginia), of English settlers being dispersed as slaves among the Native American tribes of North Carolina. Rather than admit their inability to rescue their fellow countrymen, and thus expose a vulnerability that might deter prospective settlers or investors, the Jamestown colonists seem simply to have written their predecessors out of history. In a little-known footnote, Roanoke Island gained and lost another colony during the **Civil War**. After it was captured by Union forces in February 1862, so many freed and runaway slaves made their way here through Confederate lines that the federal government formally declared it to be a "**Freedmen's Colony**". Around 4000 blacks were living on Roanoke by the end of the war, and many of the men served in the Union army. During Reconstruction, the government returned all land to its former owners, and the colony was disbanded. Roanoke retains a substantial black population to this day.

Flying Fish Café, 2003 S Croatan Hwy (Ⓣ252/441-6894; dinner only), which serves Mediterranean-influenced cuisine, and the retro **Kill Devil Grill**, 6720 S Virginia Dare Trail (Ⓣ252/449-8181; closed Mon) for seafood, burgers and amazing desserts. In Nags Head, the tiny *Blue Moon Grill*, in Surf Side Plaza, an unprepossessing mall at Mile 13 (Ⓣ252/261-BLUE; Tues–Sat), is renowned for its seafood and pasta.

Roanoke Island and Manteo

ROANOKE ISLAND, between the mainland and Bodie Island, is accessible from both by bridges. This was the **first English settlement** in North America, founded in 1585, and makes much of its status as Sir Walter Raleigh's so-called "Lost Colony" (see opposite). Nothing authentic survives of the settlement, though **Fort Raleigh National Historic Site**, three miles north of Manteo off US-64, contains a tiny reconstruction of the colonists' earthwork fort, set in a wooded glade (daily: June–Aug 9am–6pm, Sept–May 9am–5pm; free; Ⓦwww.nps.gov/fora). A museum covers the history of the expeditions and colonization, and an outdoor amphitheatre on the ocean hosts performances of *The Lost Colony* (June–Aug Mon–Sat 8.30pm; $12–24; Ⓦwww.thelostcolony.org). Outside, a simple monument commemorates the Underground Railroad and the **Freedmen's Colony** that formed here during the Civil War. Adjacent to the fort, the **Elizabethan Gardens** are elegantly landscaped with walkways and statues (daily, times vary with season; $8; Ⓦwww.elizabethangardens.org).

Just across from the waterfront at **Manteo**, the **Roanoke Island Festival Park** has a slew of historical attractions (end Feb to Dec daily 9am–5pm; $8 tickets valid for two consecutive days; Ⓦwww.roanokeisland.com). Highlights include the **adventure museum**, an interactive exhibit on the history of the Outer Banks, the **settlement site**, a living museum peopled with "Elizabethan" soldiers and craftsmen and the *Elizabeth II*, a reconstruction of a sixteenth-century English ship. The breezy *Outdoors Inn*, 406 Uppowoc Ave (Ⓣ252/473-1356, Ⓦwww.theoutdoorsinn.com; ⑤), has two stylish, colourful **B&B** rooms in an airy home. For **eating**, the casual, friendly *Full Moon Café*, across from the waterfront at the corner of Sir Walter Raleigh and Queen Elizabeth streets (Ⓣ252/473-6666), serves chowder, gourmet sandwiches, shrimp and grits and the like.

Cape Hatteras National Seashore

CAPE HATTERAS NATIONAL SEASHORE stretches south from South Nags Head on Bodie Island to **Hatteras** and **Ocracoke** islands, with forty miles of unspoiled beaches on its seaward side. Even in high season you can pull off the road and walk across the dunes to deserted beaches. The salt marshes on the western side are also beautiful. At the northern end of Hatteras Island, the **Pea Island National Wildlife Refuge** (Ⓦwww.fws.gov/peaisland) offers guided canoe tours (Ⓣ252/475-4180), trails and observation platforms for birdwatching.

Around a thousand ships have been wrecked along this treacherous stretch of coast since the sixteenth century. At the south end of Hatteras Island, near the early-nineteenth-century black-and-white-striped **Cape Hatteras Lighthouse**, a **visitor centre** (daily: summer 9am–6pm; rest of year 9am–5pm; Ⓦwww.nps.gov/caha) has exhibits on the island's maritime history; you can climb the 208ft (around 12-storey) lighthouse (mid-April to mid-Oct; $7). Further south at the village of **Frisco**, the **Native American Museum** is a loving collection of arts and crafts from around the US, including a drum from a Hopi *kiva*. It also offers several acres of forested nature **trails** (Tues–Sun 11am–5pm, $5; Ⓦwww.nativeamericanmuseum.org). In **Hatteras**, next to the Ocracoke ferry landing,

Ocracoke ferries

In summer, free **ferries** run **between Hatteras and Ocracoke** (40min). There's room for only thirty cars, and it's loaded on a first-come, first-served basis. Ferries **from Ocracoke** also head south down the coast to **Cedar Island** on the mainland (2hr 15min; $1 pedestrian, $15 car) and to **Swan Quarter** on the Albemarle Peninsula (2hr 30min; same fares). Both require **reservations** in summer, preferably a day or two in advance. For **further information** contact ⓣ1-800/BY-FERRY or ⓦwww.ncferry.org.

the **Graveyard of the Atlantic Museum** (Mon–Fri 10am–4pm; free; ⓦwww.graveyardoftheatlantic.com) tells the stories of the explorers, pirates and Civil War blockade-runners who perished along this wild stretch of coast.

Motels, grocery stores and **restaurants** are scattered through the fly-blown settlements along Hwy-12. In **Buxton**, the faded *Cape Hatteras Motel* right on the beach, a mile from the lighthouse (ⓣ252/995-5611, ⓦwww.capehatterasmotel.com; ❹), has simple oceanfront rooms and a pool, while *Diamond Shoals*, 46843 Hwy-12 (ⓣ252/995-5217) serves good breakfasts and seafood (try the clam chowder). The NPS operates first-come, first-served **campgrounds** (ⓦwww.nps.gov/caha; $20/night) at Frisco and Oregon Inlet on Bodie Island (early April to mid-Oct); and at Cape Point near Buxton (late May to Sept).

Ocracoke Island

Peaceful **OCRACOKE ISLAND** a 16-mile ribbon of land forty minutes by free ferry from Hatteras, is even more beautiful. Despite the tourist crowds in the tiny village of **Ocracoke**, the southern tip of the island has hung onto its atmosphere and it's easy to find yourself a deserted patch of beach.

Hotels and **B&Bs** in the village fill up in summer and are fairly expensive; as elsewhere on the Outer Banks, rates drop come September. One good option is the low-key *Edward's*, 226 Old Beach Rd (ⓣ1-800/254-1359, ⓦwww.edwardsofocracoke.com; ❸), which offers simple rooms and cottages with outdoor space. For **eating** and **drinking**, the airy *Flying Melon*, 804 Irvin Garrish Hwy (ⓣ252/928-253) serves tasty Southern brunches and fresh **seafood** with a Creole twist, while *Howard's Pub*, a mile north of the village on Hwy-12 (ⓣ252/928-4441), offers more than two hundred beers. Ocracoke's Park Service **campground** tends to be the first of the Outer Banks sites to fill up; unlike the others, it accepts reservations (April–Oct; $23; ⓣ1-877/444-6777, ⓦwww.nps.gov/caha).

Cape Lookout National Seashore

The mainland between Cedar Island and Beaufort is a rural backwater, sparsely settled and barely touched by tourists. There are no hotels, and the most likely reason to pass through is to get to the all-but-deserted **CAPE LOOKOUT NATIONAL SEASHORE**, a narrow ribbon of sand stretching south of Ocracoke Island along three Outer Banks with no roads or habitation. The seashore is only accessible by **ferry** (mid-March to early Dec) or private boat, and its few visitors share a total of around 56 miles of beach along all three islands. The **visitor centre** is at the eastern end of the mainland settlement of **Harker's Island** (daily 9am–5pm; ⓣ252/728-2250, ⓦwww.nps.gov/calo).

At the northern tip of the first island, **North Core Banks**, stand the eerie ruins of the abandoned village of **Portsmouth**, whose last two residents left in 1971. Ferries arrive here from Ocracoke (call Austin Boat Tours on ⓣ252/928-4361). The ferry from **Atlantic**, south of Cedar Island on the mainland (call Morris Marina on ⓣ252/225-4261), lands at **Long Point**, seventeen miles south of Portsmouth, which you can only reach on foot. **Cabins** on the island are operated by Morris Marina (starting at $100/night for up to six people); otherwise there's only primitive **camping**. **South Core Banks** is served by private ferry from **Davis**, south of Atlantic on the mainland, Beaufort and Harker's Island; see Ⓦwww.nps.gov/calo/planyourvisit/ferry.htm. To get to the peaceful **Shackleford Banks**, inhabited by wild mustangs since the early 1500s, when they are thought to have swum ashore from shipwrecks, you can catch ferries from Beaufort (see below).

Beaufort and the beaches

BEAUFORT, about 150 miles southeast of Raleigh, is probably the nicest of North Carolina's coastal towns. A good base for visiting the nearby beaches, it has an attractive waterfront that's lively at night. North Carolina's third-oldest town, Beaufort also has an appealing twelve-block **historical district**, centring on Turner Street, off the waterfront. Here you'll find handsome old houses, an apothecary and the city jail.

Ferries (15min; $15) to **Shackleford Banks** (see above) are run by Island Ferry Adventures (Ⓦwww.islandferryadventures.com) and Outer Banks Ferry Service (Ⓦwww.outerbanksferry.com), both of which are on the waterfront. The nearby Beaufort Inlet Watersports, (Ⓦwww.beaufortwatersports.com), offers **parasailing** ($50) and kayaking.

South of Beaufort, the **beaches** along the twenty-mile offshore **Bogue Bank** are always pretty crowded, especially **Atlantic Beach** at the east end, with **Emerald Isle**, to the west, marginally less so. On **Bear Island** to the south – reached from **Swansboro** by boat taxi or ferry (May–Sept Wed–Sun, April & Oct Fri–Sun, hours vary; $5; Ⓦwww.ncparks.gov) – the stunning **Hammocks Beach State Park** has high dunes, a wooded shore and perfect beaches. To **camp** ($13), register first at the small park centre (daily: Sept–May 8am–5pm; June–Aug 8am–6pm; Ⓣ910/326-4881). Camping isn't permitted in turtle season (March/April), when **loggerhead sea turtles** come ashore to lay their eggs.

Practicalities

Among the many historic **B&Bs** on the leafy streets off Turner, *Langdon House*, 135 Craven St (Ⓣ252/728-5499, Ⓦwww.langdonhouse.com; ❻), is relaxed, with delicious breakfasts. The *Inlet Inn*, a waterfront hotel at 601 Front St (Ⓣ252/728-3600, Ⓦwww.inlet-inn.com; ❺), has large, plain, balcony rooms and rocking chairs on the deck.

Beaufort's waterfront is vibrant at night, with yachties and vacationers strolling, drinking and listening to **music** at the *Dock House* (Ⓣ252/728-4506). Decent bars and restaurants line the **boardwalk**, with other good options a block or so inland. The *Beaufort Grocery Co*, 117 Queen St (closed Tues; Ⓣ252/728-3899), prides itself on inventive Southern food made from superbly fresh ingredients, while the buzzy *Aqua*, 114 Middle Lane (Ⓣ252/728-7777; dinner only, closed Sun & Mon), offers Modern American "small plates" and wines by the glass.

Wilmington and the beaches

Though it's the largest town on North Carolina's coast, **WILMINGTON**, set back along the **Cape Fear River**, fifty miles short of the state's southern border, is a laidback, attractive place. The location for a number of movies and TV shows (including, notably, *Dawson's Creek* and *One Tree Hill*), it has earned the nickname "Wilmywood", and the influx of creative types has led to a certain gentrification that feels very different from the rest of the coast. It's particularly lively after dark, when the tiny riverfront downtown takes on an edgy energy that belies the town's size.

While Wilmington's extravagant houses, ornate **City Hall** and lovely **Thalian Hall theatre** demonstrate its former wealth as a port – and the **Cape Fear Museum**, 814 Market St (summer Mon–Sat 9am–5pm, Sun 1–5pm; rest of year closed Mon; $6) gives a lively account of local history – the three or four blocks parallel to the river, and in particular the weathered, boardwalked **waterfront**, dotted with bars and restaurants, are the real draw. At the foot of Market Street, at the small **Riverfront Park**, you can pick up a horse-drawn **carriage tour** ($12; ⓦwww.horsedrawntours.com); a **harbour cruise** (from $15; ⓦwww.cfrboats.com); or a **water taxi** ($5 return) to the battleship USS *North Carolina* (daily: summer 8am–8pm; rest of year 8am–5pm; $12) which participated in every naval offensive in the Pacific during World War II. Wilmington makes a great base for a number of **beaches**: broad and bustly Wrightsville Beach, just six miles east; Carolina Beach, ten miles north, which is also good for hiking; and the laidback white sands of Kure Beach, a popular fishing destination. Local celebs and starlets hang out on rarefied and lovely **Bald Head Island**, around an hour's drive from Wilmington south on Hwy-17.

Practicalities

The **bus station** is at 201 Harnett St, a mile north of downtown off Third Street. Wilmington's main **visitor centre** is in the old courthouse at 24 N Third St (Mon–Fri 8.30am–5pm, Sat 9am–4pm, Sun 10am–4pm; ⓣ1-877/406-2356, ⓦwww.capefearcoast.com); there's also an information booth at the foot of Market Street by the water.

Chain motels line Market Street; lavish **B&Bs** include the romantic *Graystone Inn* on Third and Dock (ⓣ910/763-2000, ⓦwww.graystoneinn.com; ❼). The non-smoking *Best Western Coastline Inn* has a prime location on the riverfront at 503 Nutt St (ⓣ1-800/617-7732, ⓦwww.coastlineinn.com; ❺). Wilmington is an unexpected foodie destination. You'll find stylish **restaurants** around the waterfront, which is buzzing on weekend evenings. *Deluxe* at 114 Market St (ⓣ910/251-0333) offers French- and Pacific-Rim-inspired entrees for around $26, while the cosy *Circa 1922*, 8 N Front St (ⓣ910/762-1922) is a reliable, reasonably priced bet with a varied menu and good, organic ingredients. The casual *Dock Street Oyster Bar*, 12 Dock St (ⓣ910/762-2827), specializes in raw oysters, crab claws and seafood. If you're after a glass of wine and a small plate, try *Catalan* (ⓣ910/815-0200), a little French-style café/wine bar in a great spot on the boardwalk at 224 S Water St. The hip young crowd enjoying all that delicious food tends to make a night of it; for **listings**, pick up a copy of the free weekly *Encore* (ⓦwww.encorepub.com). The *Soapbox*, 255 N Front St (ⓦwww.thesoapboxlive.com), hosts indie music, stand-up and hip-hop, while the *Barbary Coast*, 116 S Front St (ⓣ910/762-8996), is a hole-in-the-wall bar with a certain grungy cachet.

The North Carolina Piedmont

North Carolina's **PIEDMONT** is an industrialized area of textile and tobacco towns, many of them in decline. The main area of interest is the **Research Triangle** trio of neighbouring college towns: **Raleigh**, the state capital; relaxed **Durham**, with its strong **African-American heritage**; and hip college town **Chapel Hill**. **Winston-Salem**, famous for its tobacco industry, boasts Old Salem village, while **Charlotte**'s international airport is the point of arrival for many European visitors.

Raleigh

Founded as North Carolina's capital in 1792, **RALEIGH** focuses around the central **Capitol Square**, where the **North Carolina Museum of History**, 5 E Edenton St (Mon–Sat 9am–5pm, Sun noon–5pm; free; Ⓦncmuseumofhistory.org), provides a far-reaching chronology. Opposite, the **North Carolina Museum of Natural Sciences**, 11 W Jones St (same hours and admission; Ⓦnaturalsciences.org), looks at local geology, as well as animal and plant life back to the dinosaur age.

South of the capitol, the four-block **City Market**, a lamplit, cobbled enclave at Blount and Martin streets, holds a number of good shops and restaurants. Check out the local artists at work in **Artspace**, 201 E Davie St (Tues–Sat 10am–6pm; Ⓦwww.artspacenc.org).

A little way to the northwest via I-40, the **North Carolina Museum of Art**, 2110 Blue Ridge Rd (Tues–Thurs, Sat & Sun 10am–5pm, Fri 10am–9pm; free; Ⓦncartmuseum.org), has an eclectic display from the ancient world, Africa, Europe and the US, along with a smart restaurant, *Iris*.

Practicalities

Raleigh-Durham **airport** is off I-40, fifteen minutes northwest of town. A **taxi** into town costs around $30, while a circuitous **shuttle service** will set you back $25. Amtrak stops at 320 W Cabarrus St, while the Greyhound station is in a seedy area at 314 W Jones St. The **visitor centre**, 500 Fayetteville St (Mon–Sat 9am–5pm; Ⓣ919/834-5900, Ⓦwww.visitraleigh.com), has the usual maps and leaflets.

Chain **hotels** abound near the airport and around exit 10 of I-440. For **food**, *Big Ed's*, in the City Market at 220 Wolfe St (closed Sun; Ⓣ919/836-9909), serves huge Southern breakfasts. The *42nd St Oyster Bar*, downtown at 508 W Jones St (Ⓣ919/831-2811), has been a popular spot for fresh fish and seafood since the 1930s. **Hillsborough Street**, lined with bars and restaurants, is the epicentre of Raleigh's student **scene**. *Neomonde*, nearby at 817 Beryl Rd, is a great Middle Eastern diner with lots of veggie options (Ⓣ919/828-1628), while *The Brewery*, 3009 Hillsborough St (Ⓣ919/838-6788, Ⓦwww.brewerync.com), hosts regional rock and alternative bands.

Durham

Twenty miles northwest of Raleigh, **DURHAM** found itself at the centre of the nation's tobacco industry after farmer Washington Duke came home from the Civil War with the idea of producing cigarettes. By 1890 he and his three sons had formed the **American Tobacco Company**, one of the nation's most powerful businesses. The **Duke Homestead Historical Site**, north of I-85 at 2828 Duke Homestead Rd (Tues–Sat 9am–5pm; free; Ⓦwww.nchistoricsites.org), is an absorbing living museum covering the social history of tobacco farming, with demonstrations of early farming techniques and tobacco-rolling. In 1924, the Duke family's $40 million endowment to the Trinity College enabled it to expand into a world-respected medical research facility that became **Duke University**. On campus, the **Nasher Museum of Art** at 2001 Campus Drive (Tues, Wed, Fri & Sat 10am–5pm, Thurs 10am–9pm, Sun noon–5pm; $5; Ⓦwww.nasher.duke.edu) has good African, pre-Columbian, medieval and Asian collections.

Seven miles north of town, in rural Treyburn Park, the fascinating **Historic Stagville** (hourly tours Tues–Sat 10am–4pm; free; Ⓦwww.historicstagvillefoundation.org) illustrates North Carolina plantation life, in particular the slave experience, from the early 1800s to Reconstruction. Around 100 enslaved Africans worked on the Stagville plantation; you can see the small two-storey houses they lived in, four families (one per room) per dwelling, as well as the plantation owners' house and a colossal barn built by slave carpenters.

Practicalities

Greyhound **buses** stop at 412 W. Chapel Hill St. Pick up maps and information from the Durham **visitor centre**, 101 E Morgan St (Mon–Fri 8.30am–5pm, Sat 10am–2pm; ⓣ919/687-0288, ⓦwww.durham-nc.com). The *Arrowhead Inn*, 106 Mason Rd (ⓣ919/477-8430, ⓦwww.arrowheadinn.com; ❻), which dates back to 1775, offers lovely **B&B** rooms, a cute cottage and a rustic log cabin in the pretty garden.

For **food**, try places around **Brightleaf Square**, an upbeat shopping area of restored tobacco warehouses at Gregson and Main streets: stylish *Parker & Otis*, 112 S Duke St (ⓣ919/683-3200), serves organic gourmet sandwiches, salads and breakfasts using local ingredients, while *Anotherthyme*, 109 N Gregson St (dinner only; ⓣ919/682-5225), specializes in creative seafood, Asian fusion and tapas.

Chapel Hill

CHAPEL HILL, on the southwest outskirts of Durham, is a liberal little college town with a strong music scene – having given birth to bands like Southern Culture on the Skids and Archers of Loaf, and musicians including Ben Folds and Ryan Adams, not to mention James "Carolina on My Mind" Taylor, it's a regular on the indie band tour circuit. It's a pleasant place to hang out, joining the students in the bars and cafés along **Franklin Street**, which fringes the north side of campus. Franklin continues west into the community of **Carrboro**, where it becomes **Main Street**; bars and restaurants here have a slightly hipper, post-collegiate edge.

The **University of North Carolina**, dating from 1789, was the nation's first state university. On campus, the splendid **Morehead Planetarium**, E Franklin Street (Tues–Thurs 10am–3.30pm, Fri & Sat 10am–3.30pm & 6.30–9pm, Sun 1–4.30pm; $7.25; ⓦwww.moreheadplanetarium.org), served as an early NASA training centre, while the **Ackland Art Museum**, 101 S Columbia St (Wed, Fri & Sat 10am–5pm, Thurs 10am–8pm, Sun 1–5pm; free; ⓦwww.ackland.org) is strong on Asian art and antiquities.

Practicalities

The **visitor bureau** is at 501 W Franklin (Mon–Fri 9am–5pm, Sat 10am–2pm; ⓣ1-888/968-2060, ⓦwww.chocvb.org). There are few places to **stay** downtown; one of the most popular is the historic, university-owned *Carolina Inn*, on campus at 211 Pittsboro St (ⓣ919/933-2001, ⓦwww.carolinainn.com; ❺). On the outskirts, chain motels line N Fordham and E Franklin streets.

Foodies – and vegetarians – will find a lot to like in Chapel Hill, especially along W Franklin. *Sandwhich*, no. 407 (ⓣ919/929-2114; closed Mon) offers flavoursome, Moroccan-influenced Southern fusion food, with gourmet sandwiches and tagines. *Lantern*, no. 423 (dinner only, closed Sun; ⓣ919/969-8846) is an upmarket option for Asian and Pacific Rim, while *Crooks Corner*, no. 610 (closed Mon; ⓣ919/929-7643) offers stylish Southern cooking. In Carrboro, *Elmo's Diner*, Carr Mill Mall, 200 N Greensboro St (ⓣ919/929-2909), does great breakfasts and daily lunch specials, with lots of veggie choices.

For **nightlife**, stay on Franklin and Main streets. *Orange County Social Club*, 108 E Main St, Carrboro (ⓣ919/933-0669), is a hip, laidback **bar** with vintage decor, a pool table, a great jukebox and a garden. Most **music** venues have an eclectic booking policy: *Local 506*, 506 W Franklin St (ⓣ919/942-5506, ⓦwww.local506.com), features indie bands, open-mic and hip-hop, while over in Carrboro, the *Cat's Cradle*, 300 E Main St (ⓣ919/967-9053, ⓦwww.catscradle.com), books local and national indie and hip-hop. Check **listings** in the free *Independent Weekly* (ⓦwww.indyweek.com).

Winston-Salem

Though synonymous with the brand names of its cigarettes, **WINSTON-SALEM**, eighty miles west of Chapel Hill, owes its spot on the tourist itinerary to **Old Salem**, a well-preserved twenty-block area that honours the heritage of the city's first Moravian settlers. Escaping religious persecution in what are now the Czech and Slovak republics, the first Moravians settled in the Piedmont in the mid-seventeenth century. They soon established trading links with the frontier settlers and founded the town of Salem on a communal basis – they permitted only those of the same religious faith to live here. Demand for their crafts helped establish the adjacent community of Winston, which, accruing tremendous wealth from tobacco, soon outgrew the older town. The two merged in 1913 to form Winston-Salem.

Old Salem is a living history museum, with costumed craftspeople demonstrating original skills, including paper-cutting and pottery, in a number of **restored buildings** (Tues–Sat 9.30am–4.30pm, Sun 1–4.30pm; $21, $24 for two days, $14 for two buildings of your choice) and various seasonal gardens growing Moravian crops. Start at the huge **visitor centre** at 900 Old Salem Rd (Tues–Sat 9am–5pm, Sun 12.30–5pm). Admission includes entrance to the far-reaching **Museum of Early Southern Decorative Arts**, 924 S Main St (Tues–Sat 9.30am–5pm, Sun 1–5pm; $10 if not bought as part of general admission). Large meals and beer are served at the *Old Salem Tavern*, 736 S Main (Ⓣ336/748-8585), where costumed waiters carry Moravian chicken pie and meatloaf to diners on the spacious patio.

Practicalities

Winston-Salem's **visitor centre** is three blocks from Old Salem, at 200 Brookstown Ave (Ⓣ336/728-4200, Ⓦwww.visitwinstonsalem.com). Next door, the *Brookstown Inn* (Ⓣ336/725-1120, Ⓦwww.brookstowninn.com; ❺), is a quirky, historic small **hotel** in a former textile mill.

By far the best place to **eat** is cosy *Fabian's*, northwest of downtown at 1100 Reynolda Rd, which serves a delicious five-course *prix-fixe* menu of locally sourced, farm-fresh Modern American food (Wed–Sat, one seating at 7.30pm, reservations essential; Ⓣ336/723-7700).

Charlotte

The prosperous banking centre of **CHARLOTTE**, where I-77 and I-85 meet near the South Carolina border, is the largest city in the state. It's also a transportation hub, with direct flights from Europe, and some fine museums to divert anyone in transit. Downtown (more commonly called "uptown" or "center city"), an unlovely mass of skyscrapers and commerce focused on **Tryon Street**, boasts the kids-oriented **Discovery Place**, 301 N Tryon St, with an aquarium and an IMAX theatre (Mon–Fri 9am–5pm, Sat 10am–6pm, Sun noon–5pm; $12; Ⓦwww.discoveryplace.org) and the **Bechtler Museum**, 420 S Tryon St (Mon & Wed–Sat 10am–5pm, Sun noon–5pm; $8; Ⓦwww.bechtler.org) whose quality collection of mid-twentieth-century art includes pieces by Picasso, Warhol and Miró. Arts, crafts and modern design are displayed at the stylish new **Mint Museum Uptown**, 500 S Tryon St (Tues 10am–9pm, Wed–Sat 10am–6pm, Sun noon–5pm; $10; Ⓦwww.mintmuseum.org), while the **Gantt Center**, 551 S Tryon St, focuses on African-American art and photography (Tues–Sat 10am–5pm, Sun 1–5pm; $8; Ⓦwww.ganttcenter.org). A few blocks away, the excellent **Museum of the New South**, 200 E Seventh St (Mon–Sat 10am–5pm, Sun noon–5pm; $6; Ⓦwww.museumofthenewsouth.org), looks at the growth of the region from Reconstruction onwards.

Practicalities

Charlotte/Douglas International Airport, seven miles west of town, is a $25 **taxi ride from uptown**. Greyhound stops at 601 W Trade St, while Amtrak pulls in at 1914 N Tryon St. The huge **visitor centre** is at 330 S Tryon St (Mon–Fri 8.30am–5pm, Sat 9am–3pm; ⓣ704/331-2700, ⓦwww.charlottesgotalot.com); there are smaller branches in the Museum of the New South and at the airport.

In addition to the usual highway **motels** and business hotels, uptown's 1929 *Dunhill Hotel*, 237 N Tryon St (ⓣ704/332-4141, ⓦwww.dunhillhotel.com; ❻), possesses a faded, old-fashioned charm. There's more retro at 2900 Wilkinson Blvd (Hwy-74) west of town, where the drive-in *Bar-B-Q King* (ⓣ704/399-8344; closed Sun & Mon) dishes up delicious **BBQ** and soul food to eat in your car. For **nightlife listings** check the free weekly *Creative Loafing* (ⓦcharlotte.creativeloafing.com).

The North Carolina mountains

The best way to see the **mountains** of North Carolina is from the exhilarating **Blue Ridge Parkway**, which runs across the northwest of the state from Virginia to the **Great Smoky Mountains National Park**. It's a delight to drive; the vast panoramic expanses of forested hillside, with barely a settlement in sight, may astonish travellers fresh from the crowded centres of the east coast. This rural region has been a breeding ground since the early twentieth century for **bluegrass** music, which you will still find performed regularly; laidback, liberal **Asheville** is a good place to see the edgier stylings of "newgrass". The North Carolina High Country Host, 1700 Blowing Rock Rd in Boone (ⓣ1-800/438-7500, ⓦwww.mountainsofnc.com) is a helpful **visitor centre** that services most of the mountain area.

The peak tourist season for the **BLUE RIDGE PARKWAY** is October, when the leaves of the deciduous trees turn vivid shades of yellow, gold and red. Year-round, however, this twisting mountain road – largely built in the 1930s by President Roosevelt's Civilian Conservation Corps volunteers – is a worthwhile vacation destination in itself, peppered with state-run campgrounds, short hiking trails and dramatic overlooks. Although the Parkway is closed to commercial vehicles, the constant curves make it hard to average anything approaching the 45mph speed limit.

The Blue Ridge Parkway Mountain activities

Organized **outdoor pursuits** available along the Blue Ridge Parkway include **white-water rafting** and **canoeing**, most of it on the Nolichucky River near the Tennessee border, south of Johnson City, Tennessee, but also on the Watauga River and Wilson Creek. Companies running trips include Nantahala Outdoor Center (ⓣ1-888/905-7238, ⓦwww.noc.com) and High Mountain Expeditions (ⓣ1-800/262-9036, ⓦwww.highmountainexpeditions.com), who also offer biking, hiking and caving trips. Expect to pay around $85 per person for a full day of rafting.

Winter sees **skiing** at a number of slopes and resorts, particularly around **Banner Elk**, twelve miles southwest of Boone. Resort accommodation is expensive, ski passes less so. Appalachian Ski Mountain (ⓦwww.appskimtn.com) is near Blowing Rock and Ski Beech (ⓦwww.skibeech.com), the highest ski area in the east, is at Beech Mountain. You can pick up full listings at visitor centres, or check ⓦwww.skithehighcountry.com.

Boone

Friendly **BOONE** is the most obvious northern base for exploring the mountains. Corny family entertainments dot US-321, while pretty backroads hold offbeat settlements such as **Valle Crucis**, off US-194, where the 1883 Mast General Store (summer Mon–Sat 7am–6.30pm, Sun noon–6pm; winter hours vary; Ⓦwww.mastgeneralstore.com) is worth a look for its cast-iron cookware, fresh coffee beans, rustic furniture and outdoor gear.

Boone's **visitor centre** is downtown at 208 Howard St (Ⓣ828/262-3516, Ⓦwww.visitboonenc.com). You'll get clean, comfortable **rooms** at the wonderfully friendly mom-and-pop *Hidden Valley Motel*, west of town at 8725 Hwy-105 S (Ⓣ828/963-4372, Ⓦwww.hiddenvalleymotel.com; ❷); good **B&Bs** include the *Lovill House Inn*, 404 Old Bristol Rd (Ⓣ1-800/849-9466, Ⓦwww.lovillhouseinn.com; ❺), set in wooded grounds. King Street yields the best **eating** and **drinking** options, with a couple of locavore gems. The lovely *Vidalia*, no. 831 (Ⓣ828/263-9176), serves inventive New Southern food using fresh local produce, while most dishes on the long, globally influenced menu at *Hob Nob Farm Café*, no. 506, are organic and/or locally sourced (Wed–Sun; Ⓣ828/262-5000).

South along the Parkway

Eight miles south of Boone, **BLOWING ROCK** is a pleasant, if touristy, resort just south of the Blue Ridge Parkway. The "Blowing Rock" itself, a high cliff from which light objects thrown over the side will simply blow back up, is nowhere near as impressive as photos suggest. The three-mile steam-driven **Tweetsie Railroad**, now the centre of a family theme park on Hwy-321, is all that remains of a train line that used to cross the mountains to Johnson City, Tennessee (June–Aug daily 9am–6pm; May, Sept & Oct Fri–Sun 9am–6pm; $32; Ⓦwww.tweetsie.com).

Blowing Rock's **visitor centre** (Mon–Sat 9am–5pm; Ⓣ828/295-4636; Ⓦwww.blowingrock.com) is at 7738 Valley Bvd. On Main Street you'll find **motels** such as the cosy *Boxwood Lodge* at no. 671 (Ⓣ828/295-9984, Ⓦwww.boxwoodlodge.com; ❸) and the *Village Café* (take the stone path beyond no. 1103; closed Mon; Ⓣ828/295-3769), which serves tasty breakfasts, salads, crepes and sandwiches in a lovely garden setting. *Woodlands* (Ⓣ828/295-3651), on the Hwy-321 bypass, dishes up pork **BBQ**, beer and live bluegrass. The privately owned nature preserve of **Grandfather Mountain** (5964ft), fifteen miles south of Blowing Rock, with access at milepost 305 (daily: spring & autumn 8am–6pm; summer 8am–7pm; winter 9am–5pm; $15; Ⓦwww.grandfather.com), offers nature trails and alpine hiking paths, as well ranger-led programmes. The price may be high, but the owners make a genuine attempt to protect this unique environment.

Rough Ridge, near milepost 301, is one of several access points to the 13.5-mile **Tanawha Trail**, which runs along the ridge above the Parkway from Beacon Heights to Julian Price Park, looking out over the dense forests to the east. Another good hiking destination is the **Linville Gorge Wilderness**, near milepost 316 a couple of miles outside Linville Falls village. There are two main trails; one is a steep, 1.6-mile round-trip climb to the top of the high and spectacular **Linville Falls** themselves. Breathtaking views from either side of the gorge look down 2000ft to the **Linville River** below. An easier walk leads to the base of the falls. You can also climb **Hawksbill** or **Table Rock** mountains from the nearest forest road, which leaves Hwy-181 south of the village of Jonas Ridge (signposted "Gingercake Acres", with a small, low sign to Table Rock). The amiable **Linville Falls village** has a friendly **campground** (Ⓣ828/765-2681, Ⓦwww.linvillefalls.com; $20/night) and the peaceful *Linville Falls Lodge*, Hwy-221 (Ⓣ828/756-2658, Ⓦwww.linvillefallslodge.com; ❹); *Spears Grill*, at the lodge (ⓣ828/765-0026), serves microbrews and good country cooking, including fresh trout and hickory-smoked pork BBQ.

The views from the Parkway in the **Mount Mitchell State Park** (ⓦwww.ncparks.gov) area, south toward Asheville, are tremendous. Sadly, however, this is largely because the trees around the summit of Mount Mitchell – the highest peak in the eastern US, at 6684ft – have been ravaged by acid rain from coal-burning industries and the barren patches leave the horizon clear.

Asheville

Relaxed **ASHEVILLE**, in a pretty spot roughly 100 miles southwest of Boone, is both an outdoors sports hub and a vibrant arts community, with a strong student presence from UNC and superb restaurants, galleries, vintage shops and live music venues. Retaining an appealing 1920s downtown core, it's a nice place to walk around, with handsome **Art Deco** buildings and some genuinely interesting local crafts. Quirky **Woolworth Walk**, 25 Haywood St, exhibits more than one hundred local artists in a vintage Woolworth store, while the friendly **Malaprop's Bookstore**, 55 Haywood, has a great selection. **Mast's**, 15 Biltmore Ave, is a homey general store dating from the 1940s and little changed since then. For a madcap, but informed, historical overview, join a LaZoom comedy **bus tour**, which depart from 90 Biltmore Ave (June–Oct; $22; ⓦwww.lazoomtours.com). Twentieth-century novelist Thomas Wolfe memorialized the town in the autobiographical novel, *Look Homeward, Angel*. **Wolfe's childhood home**, a yellow Victorian pile that also served as a boarding house called Old Kentucky Home, has been preserved at 52 N Market St (tours Tues–Sat 9am–5pm, Sun 1–5pm, $1, ⓦwww.wolfememorial.com).

Asheville's big attraction, however, two miles south of town, is the **Biltmore Estate**, the largest private mansion in the US, with 250 rooms (hours and prices vary: typically Sun–Fri; $50, Sat $55; ⓦwww.biltmore.com). Built in the late nineteenth century by George Vanderbilt – the youngest son of the wildly wealthy industrialist family – and loosely modelled on a Loire chateau, it's a wild piece of nouveau riche folly, from the Victorian chic of the indoor palm court to the gardens designed by Frederic Law Olmsted, he of New York's Central Park. At the time it was built it took a week simply to travel the estate on horseback; today you can easily fill a day or more taking a tour, enjoying tastings at the winery, renting a bike to explore the 250 acres of grounds, hopping on a river raft or a kayak and eating at its restaurants; there's even a 213-room "inn" (ⓣ1-800/411-3812; ❽).

Practicalities

Asheville's **Greyhound** terminal is two miles out of downtown at 2 Tunnel Rd, a highway lined with motels. The comfortable *Days Inn Asheville Mall*, 201 Tunnel Rd (ⓣ828/252-4000, ⓦwww.daysinnashevillemall.com; ❸) is excellent, with a free breakfast buffet featuring unusual items like lassi drinks and roast sweet potatoes. Set in glorious forest ten minutes north of Asheville, *Campfire Lodgings*, 116 Appalachian Village Rd (ⓣ828/658-8012, ⓦwww.campfirelodgings.com) offers **campsites** ($30), cabins sleeping up to six ($150), and luxurious **yurts** (two-night minimum; ❺). There's a **visitor centre** at 36 Montford Ave, reached via exit 4C off I-240 (daily 9am–5pm; ⓣ828/258-6101, ⓦwww.exploreasheville.com).

Asheville has by far the best **restaurants** in the region, with lots of ethnic, vegetarian and organic food and a lively café society downtown. The fabulous ★ *Laughing Seed Café*, 40 Wall St (ⓣ828/252-3445; closed Tues off-season), dishes up healthy global vegetarian cuisine, while the vaguely Moorish *Zambra*, 85 Walnut St (ⓣ828/232-1060) offers excellent Mediterranean-inspired dishes and tapas in a buzzy, cosy cellar. *Doc Chey's*, 37 Biltmore Ave (ⓣ828/252-8220; closed Wed) is the place for zingy, fresh Asian fusion. There's a lively **nightlife** scene, too, with lots of places to drink craft beers and listen to live music and even a few good gay bars. Check **listings** in the free *Mountain Xpress* (Ⓦwww.mountainx.com). *Jack of the Wood*, an enjoyable bar with hand-brewed beers at 95 Patton Ave (Ⓣ828/252-5445), features regular live **bluegrass**, folk and newgrass; for national acts check out the *Orange Peel*, 101 Biltmore Ave (Ⓦwww.theorangepeel.net).

Black Mountain and Chimney Rock

Laidback **BLACK MOUNTAIN**, fourteen miles east of Asheville on I-40, hosts the hugely enjoyable **Leaf Festival** (Ⓦwww.theleaf.org), a folk music and arts and crafts gathering, held in mid-May and October. Showcasing Appalachian and world folk music, it attracts major European and African musicians. There's little to do in peaceful Black Mountain otherwise, but it has a few good local **music** venues, including the *Watershed*, 207 W State St (Ⓣ828/669-0777) and the *White Horse*, 105 Montreat Rd (Ⓣ828/669-0816, Ⓦwww.whitehorseblackmountain.com). *Dripolator*, 221 W State St (Ⓣ828/669-0999), offers **coffee**, desserts and free wi-fi.

Twenty-five miles southeast of the Parkway on US-64/74A, the natural granite tower of **Chimney Rock** protrudes from the almost-sheer side of Hickory Nut Gorge (daily: hours vary; $14; Ⓦwww.chimneyrockpark.com). After taking the elevator 26 storeys up through the body of the mountain, you can walk along protected walkways above the impressive cliffs. Many of the climactic moments of *The Last of the Mohicans* were filmed here; you may recognize the mighty **Hickory Nut Falls**, which tumble 400ft from the western end of the gorge.

Great Smoky Mountains National Park

West of Asheville, **GREAT SMOKY MOUNTAINS NATIONAL PARK** is the most visited national park in the US. It straddles the border with **Tennessee** and is covered in more detail – with a map – in our Tennessee section on p.467. The **Oconaluftee visitor centre**, the headquarters of the North Carolina side of **the park**, is two miles north of **Cherokee** on US-441 (daily: June–Aug 8am–6pm; Sept & Oct 8.30am–6pm; Nov–April 8.30am–4.30pm; May 8.30am–5pm; Ⓣ828/497-1904).

CHEROKEE itself is the largest base for touring the park. Here a few Cherokee Indians managed to hang on when the tribe was "removed" along the Trail of Tears to Oklahoma in 1838 (see p.450). Now known as the "Eastern Band of the Cherokee Nation", they have a small reservation on the edge of the park, which derives its main income from tourism. Though the colossal *Harrah's* casino resort now dominates – rapidly squeezing out the local mom-and-pop motels – its presence is controversial: small local businesses and tribal activists battle against the strain the ever-growing resort is placing on the local environment and its draining of visitors away from the park toward the gaming tables.

Ironically, many of Cherokee's old-fashioned and hokey-themed stores, which were generally owned by non-tribal entrepreneurs, are disappearing as the casino swells, while a number of genuine Cherokee attractions remain; the impressive **Museum of the Cherokee Indian**, Hwy-441 at Drama Road (June–Sept Mon–Sat 9am–7pm, Sun 9am–5pm, Oct–May daily 9am–5pm; $10; Ⓦwww.cherokeemuseum.org), has archeological and interactive displays on Cherokee arts and history – including Sequoyah's invention of a syllabary in 1821, to preserve the oral Cherokee culture in writing. Qualla Arts and Crafts, across the street, is a splendid Cherokee-owned co-op selling quality traditional **crafts** (Ⓣ828/497-3103, Ⓦwww.quallaartsandcrafts.com). Nearby, the **Oconaluftee Indian Village** (mid-May to late Oct daily 9am–5.30pm; $15) is a reconstruction of a mid-eighteenth-century Cherokee village, where amid the log cabins, Cherokee demonstrate such skills as dugout canoe construction and basket-weaving. The **visitor centre** (daily 8am–5pm; ⓣ1-800/438-1601, ⓦwww.cherokee-nc.com), on Hwy-441 by the river, has information on the National Park and the Parkway.

The prettily situated *River's Edge Motel*, 1026 Tsali Blvd (ⓣ828/497-7995, ⓦwww.riversedgecherokee.com; ❷), offers clean **rooms** with balconies over the Oconaluftee River; you can enjoy delicious country breakfasts and plate lunches at the nearby *Peter's Pancakes*, 1384 Tsali Blvd (ⓣ828/497-5116), an iconic old **diner**. For some authentic Cherokee culture with your **coffee**, head for the friendly *Tribal Grounds Coffee*, 938 Tsalagi Rd (ⓣ828/497-0707), a community hub that also hosts live local **music**; try the Sequoyah cappuccino, its foam inscribed with the syllabary for the word "Cherokee".

Fifteen miles east, the small community of **MAGGIE VALLEY** boasts a string of mom-and-pop motels with peaceful views – the cosy *Valley Inn*, 236 Soco Rd/Hwy-19 (ⓣ1-800/948-6880, ⓦwww.thevalleyinn.com; ❷), has comfortable creekside rooms. Tourism focuses on hillbilly theming, with lots of hoedowns and the like; the nearby **Ghost Town in the Sky** is a kitsch piece of fun, with a chairlift that sweeps you up into a Wild West-style theme park (summer daily; autumn Fri–Sun only; $30; discounts available online; ⓦwww.ghosttowninthesky.com). At the end of July, Maggie Valley hosts North Carolina's **International Folk Festival** (ⓦwww.folkmootusa.org).

South Carolina

The relatively small state of **SOUTH CAROLINA** remains, with Mississippi, one of the poorest and most rural in the US; there are no big cities to speak of and though the pockets of prime real estate along its coast have been developed into exclusive golf courses and tennis clubs, these are self-contained enclaves that make little impression on the rest of the state. **Politics** in the first state to secede from the Union in 1860, have traditionally been conservative. Reconstruction was mired in Klan violence, while demagogues openly espoused lynching and enforced "Jim Crow" laws with frightening zeal. Today, the state is home to a surprising number of universities, among them Christian Bob Jones University in Greenville, a training-ground for the fundamentalist right.

South Carolina's main fascination lies in the subtropical coastline, also called the **Low Country**, and its **sea islands**. Wild beaches, swampy marshes and lush palmetto groves preserve traces of a virtually independent black culture (featuring the unique patois, "Gullah"), dating back to when enslaved Africans escaped here from the mainland plantations. There are no interstates along the coast, so journeys take longer than you might expect, the views are pretty and the pace of life definitely feels slower. Beyond the grand old peninsular port of **Charleston** – one of the most elegant towns in the nation with its pastel-coloured old buildings, appealing waterfront and Caribbean ambience – restored plantations stretch as far north as **Georgetown**, en route toward tacky **Myrtle Beach**. Inland, the rolling Piedmont and flat coastal plain hold little to see.

The north coast

MYRTLE BEACH is an unmitigated stretch of commercial seaside development twenty miles down the coast from the North Carolina border. Predominantly a family resort, it's packed during mid-term vacations with students drinking and partying themselves into a frenzy. Fans of elaborate mini-golf, water parks, factory outlet malls, funfairs and parasailing will be in heaven. The widest stretch of sand is at **North Myrtle Beach**, a chain of small communities centring on Ocean Boulevard. South of Myrtle Beach lies **Murrells Inlet**, a fishing port with lots of good seafood restaurants and **Pawleys Island**, a secluded resort once favoured by plantation owners and today retaining a slower pace than its neighbours.

South to Charleston: Georgetown and the plantations

The peaceful waterfront community of **GEORGETOWN** – the first town in forty miles beyond Myrtle Beach that's anything more than a resort – makes a nice contrast (though when the wind is blowing in the wrong direction, the fragrance from the monstrous paper works on the opposite bank can be off-putting). It's hard to imagine today, but in the eighteenth century Georgetown was the centre of a thriving network of Low Country rice plantations; by the 1840s the area produced nearly half the rice grown in the United States. While Front Street, the main street, has a time-warped, late-1950s feel, Georgetown's 32-block **historic district** features many fine eighteenth-century and antebellum houses; the **visitor centre**, 531 Front St (Mon–Sat 9am–5pm; ⓣ843/546-8436, ⓦwww.georgetownchamber.com), has maps. The **Rice Museum**, in the Clock Tower at 633 Front St (Mon–Sat 10am–4.30pm; $7; ⓦwww.ricemuseum.org), tells of the Low Country's long history of rice cultivation and its dependence on a constant supply of enslaved Africans brought over from the Windward coast for their expertise. Hop on the *Carolina Rover* (3 daily Mon–Sat; $30; ⓦwww.rovertours.com; 3hr) for a cruise of the coast, including a spell shelling on a nearby barrier island.

The *Jameson Inn*, near the water at 120 Church St (ⓣ843/546-6090, ⓦwww.jamesoninns.com; ❸) is a good **motel** with marsh views. There are a number of places to **eat** on Front Street, many of which have patios overlooking the water. One of the most laidback, *Pita Rolz* at no. 725 (ⓣ843/485-4215) has a flower-filled deck and healthy veggie wraps and smoothies; the funky *Old Fish House*, no. 807 (ⓣ843/546-1045) specializes in fresh seafood. For breakfasts, light lunches and pastries, head to the nearby *Kudzu Bakery*, 120 King St (ⓣ843/546-1847; closed Sun).

Hopsewee Plantation, the grand 1740 mansion home of Thomas Lynch, a signatory of the Declaration of Independence, is set in Spanish-moss-draped grounds, twelve miles south of Georgetown on US-17 (Feb–Nov Tues–Fri 10am–4pm, Sat noon–4pm; $15; ⓦwww.hopsewee.com). Tours of the less manicured **Hampton Plantation State Historic Site**, further south, two miles off US-17 on Hwy-857, concentrate on the history of slavery. The grounds are lovely, but the house (Sat–Tues 1pm, 2pm & 3pm; $4) is most impressive. An eighteenth-century Neoclassical monolith built by Huguenots, the inside is relatively bare. The plantation itself is isolated in the heart of the dense **Francis Marion National Forest**, a heavily African-American area particularly known for its sweetgrass basket-weaving, which originated with the slaves in West Africa.

Charleston

CHARLESTON, one of the finest-looking towns in the US, is a compelling place, its **historic district** lined with tall, narrow houses of peeling, multicoloured stucco, adorned with wooden shutters and wide piazzas (porches). The palm trees and tropical climate give the place a Caribbean air, while the hidden gardens, leafy patios and ironwork balconies evoke the romance of New Orleans.

Founded by a group of English aristocrats in 1670, Charles Towne swiftly boomed as a **port** serving the rice and cotton plantations. It became the region's commercial and cultural centre with a mixed population of French, Germans, Jews, Italians and Irish, as well as the English majority. One-third of the nation's **enslaved Africans** passed through Charleston, sold at the riverfront market and bringing with them their ironworking, building and farming skills. The town had a sizeable **free black** community too. Nevertheless there was still slave unrest, culminating in the abortive Veysey revolt of 1823, after which the city built the Citadel armoury and later the military university to control future uprisings. Charleston was practically ruined by the **Civil War**, which started on its doorstep, at **Fort Sumter** in the harbour. Fire swept through in 1861 and Union bombardment was relentless until it was finally taken in February 1865. The decline of the plantation economy and slump in cotton prices led to an economic crash after the war, worsened by a catastrophic earthquake in 1886. As the upcountry industrialized, capital steadily deserted the city, and it only really recovered when World War II restored its importance as a port and naval base. Since then, a steady programme of preservation and restoration has made **tourism** Charleston's main focus. Downtown there's a genteel air about the place and prices tend to be high; nonetheless, Charleston has kept its charm without turning into a theme park. The traditions of the sea islands are a tangible presence: "basket ladies" still weave their sweetgrass baskets at the market and many residents – both black and white – speak the distinctive **Gullah** dialect.

Arrival, information and city transport

Charleston International Airport is twelve miles north of downtown, off I-526 (Ⓦwww.chs-airport.com); the airport **shuttle** (Ⓣ843/767-1100) costs $12, while a Yellow Cabs **taxi** (Ⓣ843/577-6565) costs around $30. The **Amtrak** station is in a dodgy area at 4465 Gaynor Ave, eight miles north of downtown, as is the **Greyhound** station, 3610 Dorchester Rd, out near I-26. CARTA **buses** ($1.50; Ⓦwww.ridecarta.com) cover most areas, including nearby beaches and there are four useful **trolley** routes, the Downtown Area Shuttles (DASH; $1.50). **Passes** (one-day $5, three-day $11, ten-rides $12) cover both.

Charleston is a lovely place to stroll around; the huge **visitor centre**, 375 Meeting St (daily: March–Oct 8.30am–5.30pm; Nov–Feb 8.30am–5pm; Ⓣ843/853-8000, Ⓦwww.explorecharleston.com), has details of **walking tours** covering everything from pirates through architecture to black history, as well as discount coupons, maps and bus/trolley passes. **Horse and carriage rides** provide a lively and leisurely overview; Old South Carriage Co leaves regularly from 14 Anston St (1hr; $21/$15 children; Ⓦwww.oldsouthcarriagetours.com).

Accommodation

To enjoy the best of Charleston it's worth budgeting to stay within walking distance of downtown, where many homes in the historic district serve as pricey **B&Bs**. Further out, the usual **motels** cluster around US-17 in West Ashley and Mount Pleasant and along I-26 in North Charleston.

Andrew Pinckney Inn 40 Pinckney St ⓣ843/937-8800, ⓦwww.andrewpinckneyinn.com. Stylish, Caribbean-style rooms in this boutique hotel located beside the historic market. Continental breakfast served on the rooftop terrace overlooking the city. Free wi-fi. ❺

Days Inn Historic District 155 Meeting St ⓣ843/722-8411, ⓦwww.the.daysinn.com. This two-storey motel lacks the charm of the B&Bs, but rooms are spacious and comfortable, with attractive wrought-iron balconies and the location can't be beat. The pool and free off-street parking are a bonus. ❹

Merhaven Bed no Breakfast 16 Halsey St ⓣ843/577-3053, ⓦwww.virtualcities.com/ons/sc/z/scz6801.htm. Two simply elegant rooms, with shared bath and, obviously, no breakfast, in an artist-owned Arts and Crafts home with a pretty, shady courtyard. No credit cards. ❹

Mills House Hotel 115 Meeting St ⓣ843/577-2400, ⓦwww.millshouse.com. Large, smart, very central hotel, in business since 1853. Guest rooms combine elegant period furnishings with modern comfort. ❻

Not So Hostel 156 Spring St ⓣ843/722-8383, ⓦwww.notsohostel.com. Appealing, very friendly hostel in a double-porched 1850 house on the northern edge of downtown. Rates include wi-fi and full breakfast. Dorms $23/night. An annexe a few blocks away has simple rooms from $60. ❶/❸

Vendue Suites 30 Vendue Range ⓣ843/723-2228, ⓦwww.venduesuites.com. Three stylish, spick-and-span suites and a friendly atmosphere at this lovely, superbly located boutique hotel. Free snacks and in-room breakfast provided. ❻

The City

Charleston's **historic district** is a predominantly residential area of leaning lines, weathered colours and exquisite hidden courtyards bounded by Calhoun Street to the north and East Bay Street by the river. The further south of Broad you head, the posher and more residential the streets become. The district is best taken in by strolling at your own pace – though that pace can get pretty slow in high summer, when the heat is intense. Attractive spots to pause in the shade include the exquisitely landscaped **Waterfront Park**, a piazza with fountains and boardwalks leading out over the river and **White Point Gardens**, by the Battery on the tip of the peninsula, where the breezy, flower-filled lawns have good views across the water.

Most of the city's fine **houses** are private and can only be admired from the outside; some, however, are available for **tours**. The late-nineteenth-century **Calhoun Mansion**, 16 Meeting St, is fabulously over-the-top, with ornate plaster and woodwork and hand-painted porcelain ballroom chandeliers (11am–5pm every 30min; $15; ⓦwww.calhounmansion.net). Nearby, the antebellum **Edmonston-Alston House**, one of the first houses built on the Battery in 1825, overlooks the harbour at 21 E Battery St (Tues–Sat 10am–4.30pm, Sun & Mon 1.30–4.30pm; $10; ⓦwww.middletonplace.org). The elegant Neoclassical **Nathaniel-Russell House**, 51 Meeting St (Mon–Sat 10am–5pm, Sun 2–5pm; $10, $16 with the Aiken-Rhett House; ⓦwww.historiccharleston.org), is noted for its flying staircase, which soars unsupported for three floors.

The Charleston Museum's $22 combination ticket (see below) gets you into the 1803 **Joseph Manigault House**, a lovely Neoclassical structure built by descendants of Huguenot settlers and the 1772 **Heyward-Washington House**, at the south end of the peninsula at 87 Church St, which was built by Thomas Heyward, a rice baron and signatory of the Declaration of Independence. Admission to each separately is $10 (Mon–Sat 10am–5pm, Sun 1–5pm; ⓦcharlestonmuseum.org). North of downtown, the antebellum urban plantation **Aiken-Rhett House**, 48 Elizabeth St, retains not only its original decor and furnishings but also the work-yard and slave quarters (Mon–Sat 10am–5pm, Sun 2–5pm; $10, $16 with the Nathaniel-Russell House; ⓦwww.historiccharleston.org).

Built in 1771 as the Customs House and used as a prison during the Revolutionary War, the **Old Exchange and Provost Dungeon**, 122 E Bay St (daily 9am–5pm; $8; ⓦwww.oldexchange.com), is a hugely significant Colonial structure. The upper floors feature exhibits on the history of the building and of Charleston; the tone changes in the dank confines below, however, where spotlit dummies recount tales of revolutionaries, gentlemen pirates and all manner of derring-do. Nearby, at 6 Chalmers St, the **Old Slave Mart** was built in 1859 for the express purpose of buying and selling African slaves (Mon–Sat 9am–5pm; $7). The few exhibits in this underfunded, haunting place include rare personal footage from ex-slaves.

Charleston's **market area** runs from Meeting Street to East Bay Street, focusing on a long, narrow line of enclosed, low-roofed, nineteenth-century sheds. Undeniably touristy, packed with hard-headed "basket ladies", this is one of the liveliest spots in town, selling junk, spices, tacky T-shirts, jewellery and rugs. The intriguing **Gibbes Museum of Art**, a couple of blocks south at 135 Meeting St (Tues–Sat 10am–5pm, Sun 1–5pm; $9; ⓦwww.gibbesmuseum.org), places a strong emphasis on Charleston itself, providing a quick history of the city through art.

The vast **Charleston Museum**, opposite the visitor centre at 360 Meeting St (Mon–Sat 9am–5pm, Sun 1–5pm; Ⓦwww.charlestonmuseum.org; $10, $16 with the Joseph Manigault House or the Heyward-Washington House, $22 with both), is filled with a wealth of city memorabilia, with videos on subjects from rice-growing to the Huguenots and strong sections on Native Americans, architecture and the devastation of the Civil War. At the end of Calhoun Street, overlooking the harbour, you'll find Charleston's splendid **Aquarium** (daily: March–Aug 9am–5pm, Sept–Feb 9am–4pm; $17.95; Ⓦscaquarium.org). With a 40ft-deep tank at the core, its open, eye-level exhibits recreate South Carolina's various watery habitats – including the Piedmont, swamps, salt marshes and ocean – and their indigenous aquatic, plant and animal life. The porch-like terrace, with giant rocking chairs, is a nice place to catch the river breezes; watch out for schools of dolphins playing in the water below.

Fort Sumter National Monument

The first shots of the Civil War were fired on April 12, 1861, at **Fort Sumter**, a redoubtable federal garrison that entirely occupied a small artificial island at the entrance to Charleston Harbor. After secession, the federal government had to decide whether to reprovision its forts in the south. When a relief expedition was sent to Fort Sumter, Confederate General Pierre Beauregard demanded its surrender. After a relentless barrage, the garrison gave in the next day.

Fort Sumter may only be seen on regular **boat tours** that leave from alongside the Aquarium at the eastern end of Calhoun Street (2–3 daily; $16; Ⓣ843/722-BOAT, Ⓦwww.fortsumtertours.com). Just one of the fort's original three storeys is left, thanks not to the assault that started the war, but to its subsequent siege and bombardment by Union troops, who finally recaptured it on Good Friday 1865, the very day Lincoln was assassinated. Exhibits in the **Fort Sumter visitor centre** on the mainland at 340 Concord St cover not only the fort but also the history of Charleston and the build-up to the conflict (daily 8.30am–5pm; free; Ⓦwww.nps.gov/fosu).

Eating

Historic Charleston's elegant ambience lends itself very well to classy **New Southern cooking** served up in a variety of innovative restaurants. There are also plenty of ethnic restaurants and cafés along Market and King streets.

Cru Café 18 Pinckney St Ⓣ843/534-2434 Cosy, pretty restaurant in an eighteenth-century house with a porch, dishing up satisfying, well-executed food that puts a modern global twist on local staples. Try the pan-roasted local trigger fish with green tomatoes. Lunch & dinner Tues–Sat.

FIG 232 Meeting St Ⓣ843/805-5900. Minimalist, smart and unpretentious neighbourhood bistro with a firm emphasis on fresh Low Country ingredients. Menus change seasonally, but the fish stews, green garlic soup and shrimp with polenta are good bets and the farm-fresh veggies are all wonderful.

Hominy Grill 207 Rutledge Ave Ⓣ843/937-0930. This neighbourhood restaurant has built up such a reputation for its comforting Low Country cooking that it's almost impossible to get a place for lunch. Come for dinner instead and try the purloo – a kind of local pilau, or paella – the tomato pudding, or trigger fish with fava bean hummus. Closed Sun eve.

Jestine's Kitchen 251 Meeting St Ⓣ843/722-7224. Black Low Country cooking, served in a simple, tourist-filled dining room in the heart of downtown. Go for the fried chicken, meat loaf, or fried green tomatoes and finish off with Coca-Cola cake. Closed Mon.

Slightly North of Broad 192 E Bay St Ⓣ843/723-3424. One of the smart, buzzy nouvelle Southern bistros that Charleston specializes in – crab-stuffed flounder, crispy chicken livers with grits and the like. It's lively at lunchtime (Mon–Fri only), when they offer a $10 *prix-fixe* menu.

Nightlife and entertainment

Charleston has a vibrant **nightlife**, though downtown bars tend to be touristy. For listings, see the free weekly *City Paper* (Ⓦwww.charlestoncitypaper.com).

Chief among the city's many **festivals** is **Spoleto** (Ⓦwww.spoletousa.org), an extraordinarily rich extravaganza of international arts held in late May/early June.

Blind Tiger 38 Broad St Ⓣ843/577-0342. Popular downtown drinking hole with hidden entrance, busy deck, good bar food and regular live music.

The Griffon 18 Vendue Range Ⓣ843/723-1700. Cosy tavern, serving craft ales as well as tasty English-style fish and chips.

Music Farm 32 Ann St Ⓦwww.musicfarm.com. This warehouse-like building alongside the visitor centre is the best place in Charleston to see regional and national touring bands.

Rooftop Bar at the Vendue Inn 19 Vendue Range Ⓣ843/577-32767970. Enjoyable and elegant cocktail bar and restaurant with dramatic views over the harbour and the historic district and live music nightly.

Squeeze 213 E Bay St Ⓣ843/837-6210. Tiny bar (thus the name) with an unpretentious, friendly atmosphere.

Around Charleston

The **river road**, Hwy-61, leads **west** from Charleston along the Ashley River, past a series of opulent **plantations**. **Drayton Hall**, closest to Charleston at 3380 Ashley River Rd (daily: March–Oct 8.30am–5pm; Nov–Feb 9.30am–4pm; $15; Ⓦwww.draytonhall.org), is an elegant Georgian mansion with handcarved wood and plasterwork; there is little furniture on show, and the hourly guided tours of the house concentrate on the fine architecture. However, at 11.15am, 1.15pm and 3.15pm, talks, backed up by photographs and artefacts, emphasize the role of **African-Americans** in the Low Country, tracing the story of slavery and emancipation and how it related to Drayton Hall.

The nearby **Magnolia Plantation and Gardens** is famed for its stunning ornamental gardens, particularly in spring when the azaleas are blooming (daily March–Oct 8am–5.30pm; Nov–Feb hours vary; $15; Ⓦwww.magnoliaplantation.com). Admission gives you access to the gardens, which include a tropical greenhouse, a petting zoo, a maze and a wildlife observation tower, but you have to pay extra ($7 each) for **house tours**, the "**Slavery to Freedom**" tour, a "nature train" tour of the grounds or a "nature boat" tour of the swamp. You don't have to pay the general admission charge to explore the **Audubon Swamp** ($7), complete with alligators and lush plant life.

Across the Ashley River, on Hwy-171, west of the Ashley River Bridge, **Charles Towne Landing** is a 663-acre state park on the site where in 1670 the English colonists established the first permanent settlement in the Carolinas (daily 9am–5pm; $7.50; Ⓦwww.charlestowne.org). As well as the landing site itself, you can see a living history settlement, a replica of a seventeenth-century merchant ship and a zoo, home to species the colonists would have encountered when they landed here – pumas, bison, alligators, black bears and wolves.

East of Charleston, **beaches** such as **Isle of Palms** and **Sullivan's Island** are heavily used by locals on weekends. The further from town, the more likely you are to find a peaceful stretch. On Isle of Palms, the breezy *Sea Biscuit*, 21 J.C. Long Blvd (Ⓣ843/886-4079; closed Mon), serves great Southern breakfasts and lunches, while on Sullivan's Island, *Poe's Tavern*, 2210 Middle St (Ⓣ843/883-0083) is good for beer, burgers and fish tacos.

The sea islands

South of Charleston toward Savannah, the coastline dissolves into small, marshy islands. On pretty **Edisto Island**, south of US-17 on Hwy-174, live oaks festooned with drapes of Spanish moss form canopies over the roads, bright green marshes harbour rich birdlife and fine beaches line the seaward side. There are no motels, but **Edisto Beach State Park** (daily 8am–6pm; Ⓦwww.southcarolinaparks.com) has a **campground** ($19) near a beach lined with palmetto trees and other semitropical plants. They have a few air-conditioned cabins that fill up months in advance (❹).

The largest town in the area, **BEAUFORT** (pronounced "Byoofert"), has a lovely historic district – offset somewhat by racial tensions and the baleful proximity of the Parris Island US Marine Base, notorious for the brutality of its training regime. Think *The Big Chill* meets Kubrick's *Full Metal Jacket*; both movies are set here. The **Greyhound** station is two miles north of town on US-21. The **visitor centre**, 713 Craven St (Mon–Sat 9am–5pm, Sun noon–5pm; Ⓣ843/525-8500, Ⓦwww.beaufortsc.org) has details of local tours and discount coupons for the **motels** out on US-21. In town, the *Best Western Sea Island Inn*, near the water at 1015 Bay St (Ⓣ843/522-2090, Ⓦwww.bestwestern.com/seaislandinn; ❻), has nice rooms with an old-fashioned feel. For a luxurious **B&B**, head for the *Beaufort Inn*, 809 Port Republic St (Ⓣ1-888/522-0250, Ⓦwww.beaufortinn.com; ❻). Breakfasts and **lunches** are tasty at *Blackstone's Deli*, 205 Scott St (Ⓣ843/524-4330), while the friendly *Sgt White's*, 1908 Boundary St (Ⓣ843/522-2029; cash only) is a local favourite for BBQ, fried chicken and soul food.

St Helena Island and Hunting Island Beach

Across the bridge southeast of Beaufort, **ST HELENA ISLAND**, dotted with small shrimp- and oyster-fishing communities, is among the least spoiled of the eastern sea islands. The further south you go the more gorgeous the **landscape** gets: amazing Spanish moss hangs from ancient oaks, while enormous, wide views stretch out across bright green marshes patterned with small salt creeks.

This is an area of strong **black communities**, descended from slaves, who were given parcels of land when they were freed by the Union army in February 1865; their Gullah dialect is an Afro-English patois with many West African words. The **Gullah Institute**, in the **Penn Centre Historic District** off US-21 (Mon–Sat 11am–4pm; Ⓦwww.penncenter.com), houses the **school** started for freed slaves by Charlotte Forten, a black Massachusetts teacher. The school was an important retreat for civil rights leaders in the 1960s. Nearby, off US-21, the ruined black **Chapel of Ease**, with seashell-adorned interior walls, was built in 1742.

There are some great **places to eat** around here. On Sea Island Parkway, *Gullah Grub* at no. 877 (noon–5pm; Ⓣ843/838-3841) and *Ultimate Eating*, no. 859 (Ⓣ843/838-1314), serve nourishing Low Country and Gullah dishes, while at no. 1929, before the bridge across to Hunting Island, the tiny *Shrimp Shack* (March–Dec Mon–Sat from 11am; Ⓣ843/838-2962), is a fresh **seafood** joint serving fat, juicy shrimp burgers at trestle tables.

St Helena's main **beach**, at **Hunting Island State Park** on the east shore (daily dawn–dusk; $5; Ⓦwww.huntingisland.com), can get crowded, but it's ravishing: soft white sand, wide and gently shelving, scattered with shards of pearly shells and fringed with a mature maritime forest of palmettos, palm trees and sea oats. Pelicans come here to feed, particularly in the early morning; it's also a turtle-nesting site. You can **stay** near the lighthouse in one weather-beaten cabin, although you need to reserve well in advance (Ⓣ843/838-2011; ❺). There's also the larger *Hunting Island* campground: head first to the **park office** (Mon–Fri 9am–5pm, Sat & Sun 11am–5pm).

Georgia

Compared to the rest of **GEORGIA**, the largest of the Southern states, the bright lights of its capital **Atlanta** are a wild aberration. Apart from some beaches and towns on the highly indented coastline, this rural state is composed of slow, easy-going settlements where the best and sometimes the only, way to enjoy your time is to sip iced tea and have a chat on the porch.

Settlement in Georgia, the thirteenth British colony (named after King George II), started in 1733 at Savannah, intended as a haven of Christian principles for poor Britons, with both alcohol and slavery banned. However, under pressure from planters, **slavery** was introduced in 1752 and by the time of the **Civil War** almost half the population were black slaves. Little fighting took place on Georgia soil until Sherman's troops marched in from Tennessee, burned Atlanta to the ground, and, in the infamous "March to the Sea", laid waste to all property on the way to the coast.

Today, bustling **Atlanta** stands as the unofficial capital of the South. The city where **Dr Martin Luther King Jr** was born, preached and is buried bears little relation to *Gone With the Wind* stereotypes and its forward-thinking energy is upheld as a role model for the "New South". Atlanta's main tourist destination, though, is the **Georgia coast**, stretching south from beautiful old **Savannah** via the **sea islands** to the semitropical **Okefenokee Swamp**, inland near Florida. In the **northeast**, the **Appalachian foothills** are fetching in autumn, while the college town of **Athens** is known for its offbeat rock heroes R.E.M. and the B-52s.

Atlanta

ATLANTA is a relatively young city. It only came into being in 1837, when an almost random dot on the map was named "Terminus" during plans for railroad construction. The Chattahoochee River here is not navigable and the land poor for agriculture, but after the railroads duly arrived, the re-named Atlanta proved to be a crucial transportation centre in the Civil War. In 1864 Sherman's army **burned** the entire city, an act immortalized in *Gone with the Wind*, but postwar recovery was speedy: Atlanta was the archetype of the aggressive, urban, industrial "New South", championed by "**boosters**" – newspaper owners, bankers, politicians and city leaders. Industrial giants who based themselves here included **Coca-Cola**, source of a string of philanthropic gifts to the city. Heavy **black** immigration increased its already considerable black population and led to the establishment of the thriving African-American community, centred around **Auburn Avenue**, that was to produce **Martin Luther King, Jr**.

Today's Atlanta is at first glance a typical large American city and one that suffers particularly badly from urban sprawl: the population of the entire metropolitan area now exceeds 5.5 million. It is also undeniably upbeat and progressive, with

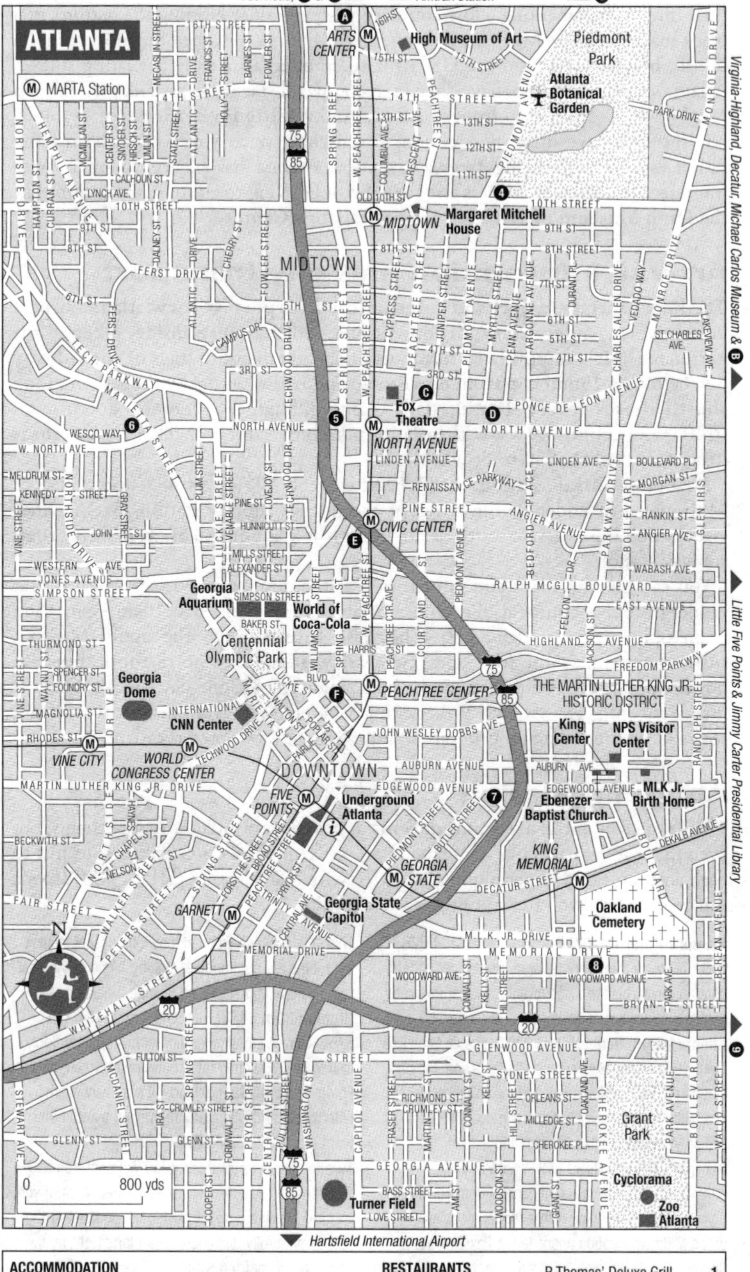

ACCOMMODATION			
Artmore Hotel	A	Hampton Inn and Suites Downtown	F
Atlanta International Hostel	D	Highland Inn	B
Georgian Terrace Hotel	C	Twelve Centennial Park	E

RESTAURANTS			
Ann's Snack Bar	9	R Thomas' Deluxe Grill	1
Colonnade	2	Ria's Bluebird	8
Fat Matt's Rib Shack	3	Sweet Auburn Curb Market	7
Flying Biscuit	4	Thelma's Kitchen	6
		The Varsity	5

little interest in lamenting a lost Southern past, and since electing the nation's first black mayor, the late Maynard Jackson, in 1974, it has remained the most conspicuously **black-run** city in the US. As if to counterbalance the alienating sprawl, Atlanta's neighbourhoods have distinct, recognizable identities; swanky **Buckhead** is only a short drive away from grungier, punky **Little Five Points**, for example, but the two have little in common. Meanwhile, once you accept the driving distances and the roaring freeways, upbeat Atlanta has plenty to offer, with must-see attractions from sites associated with Dr King to cultural institutions like the **High Museum of Art and Atlanta History Center**.

Arrival, information and city transport

The huge **Hartsfield-Jackson International Airport** (Ⓦwww.atlanta-airport.com) is ten miles south of downtown Atlanta, just inside I-285 ("the perimeter"). It's the southern terminus of the north/south lines of the **subway** (see below), a 15min trip from downtown and is also served by the Atlanta Link **shuttle buses** (every 15min, daily 6am–midnight; $16.50 to downtown; Ⓣ404/524-3400, Ⓦwww.theatlantalink.com) and Checker Cab **taxis** (Ⓣ404/351-1111; $30 to downtown).

Atlanta's **Amtrak** station, 1688 Peachtree St NW, is at the north end of Midtown, just under a mile north of the nearest subway station, Arts Center. Greyhound **buses** arrive south of downtown at 232 Forsyth St, near the Garnett subway station.

You can pick up maps and information at the downtown **visitor centre**, near Underground Atlanta at 65 Upper Alabama St (Mon–Sat 10am–6pm, Sun noon–6pm; Ⓦwww.atlanta.net). They also have maps of the useful MARTA **subway** system, whose four lines, two east/west and two north/south, intersect downtown at Five Points (daily 5am–1am; single fare $2, one-day pass $8; Ⓦwww.itsmarta.com). The Atlanta Preservation Center leads lively historical **walking tours** of different neighbourhoods (90min; $10; Ⓦwww.preserveatlanta.com).

Accommodation

The most economical **accommodations** in **downtown** Atlanta are the chains, but even these aren't particularly inexpensive; weekend rates can be better, but just to park costs at least $18 per night (and up to twice that for valet parking). **Midtown** can be cheaper, and puts you nearer the nightlife.

Artmore Hotel 1302 W Peachtree St Ⓣ404/876-6100, Ⓦwww.artmorehotel.com. Cool independent hotel in a refurbished historic building, with a pretty candlelit courtyard, near the High Museum. ❺

Atlanta International Hostel 223 Ponce de Leon Ave Ⓣ404/875-9449, Ⓦwww.hostel-atlanta.com. Around a hundred beds in single-sex and mixed dorms ($27), in a Midtown location near the North Ave MARTA station. Also a pool table, kitchen and laundry. ❶

Georgian Terrace Hotel 659 Peachtree St NE Ⓣ404/897-1991, Ⓦwww.thegeorgianterrace.com. Stylish century-old hotel, with a rooftop pool, in a prime Midtown location opposite the Fox Theatre. Rooms – some are circular, offering great views – could do with updating, but a good choice overall. ❺

Hampton Inn and Suites Downtown 161 Spring St NW Ⓣ404/589-1111, Ⓦhamptoninn.hilton.com. This downtown chain hotel may look unspectacular, but rooms are comfortable, making it one of the best-value central options. Rates include breakfast. ❺

Highland Inn 644 N Highland Ave Ⓣ404/874-5756, Ⓦwww.thehighlandinn.com. Hipsters flock to this funky, slightly tatty, hotel near Little Five Points and Virginia Highlands. It's a lively place, with music and DJs many nights, so avoid if you want peace and quiet. ❹

Twelve Centennial Park 4000 W Peachtree St Ⓣ404/418-1212, Ⓦwww.twelvehotels.com. If you want to live like a (moneyed) local, book one of these beautifully designed urban lofts right by the Civic Center metro downtown. The suites are vast, modern and well equipped, with balconies, while the good sushi/steak restaurant, *Room* and lively bar downstairs help the buzzy atmosphere. ❼

The City

Atlanta's layout is confusing, with its roads following old Native American trails rather than a logical grid. An unbelievable number of streets are named "Peachtree"; be sure to note whether you're looking for Avenue, Road or Boulevard and pay special attention to whether it's "NW", "W" or so forth. The most important, **Peachtree Street**, cuts a long north–south swath through the city. Sights are scattered, but relatively easy to reach by car or on the subway. Most neighbourhoods, including **downtown**, the Martin Luther King Jr Historic District along **Auburn Avenue** and trendy **Little Five Points**, are easy to explore on foot.

Downtown Atlanta

Downtown Atlanta centres on the railroad terminus for which the city was founded. During the late nineteenth century, its original core was effectively buried by the construction of railroad viaducts; businesses moved their commercial activities up to the new street level and used their former premises as cellars. An underground labyrinth of cobbled streets used as an entertainment, shopping and dining complex known as **Underground Atlanta** (or "the Underground"), it is today a gimmicky mall.

Far more successful is the nearby **Centennial Olympic Park**. Created when several downtown blocks were razed prior to the 1996 Olympics, the park was forced into temporary closure by the pipe-bombing that killed two people. Now relandscaped, it's the city's most popular open space. On the north side, the **Georgia Aquarium**, 225 Baker St (summer Sun–Thurs 9am–6pm, Fri 9am–10pm, Sat 9am–9pm; rest of year Sun–Fri 10am–5pm, Sat 9am–6pm; $26, various passes available; Ⓦwww.georgiaaquarium.org), is a state-of-the-art facility that is so popular you should probably book in advance. Highlights include the biggest tank in the world, filled with sharks and manta rays and recreations of Georgia habitats; it's also the only aquarium outside Asia to have whale sharks. East of the aquarium, the **World of Coca-Cola** is a shiny, happy slice of modern Americana. Pushed by its relentlessly smiley guides as an "entertainment experience", it's stuffed with high-tech displays and hokey memorabilia illustrating the iconic brand's extraordinary journey from Atlanta soda fountain to world domination. Above all, it's an eye-opening study of genius marketing, peaking in the "Tastes" room, where kids and parents alike excitedly slurp Coke drinks from around the world – best avoid Italy's bitter "Beverly" – a hyper feeding frenzy that pumps visitors full of sugar before siphoning them off to the gift store (Mon–Sat from 9am, Sun from 10am, hours vary, $15; Ⓦwww.worldofcoca-cola.com). The **CNN Center**, 190 Marietta St, is the head quarters of the largest news broadcaster in the world. A variety of adrenaline-fuelled guided tours (daily 9am–5pm; $12, reservations essential; Ⓦcnn.com/tour) rush you past frazzled producers and toothy anchorpersons.

Sweet Auburn

A half-mile east of downtown, **Auburn Avenue** stands as a monument to Atlanta's black history. During its heyday in the 1920s, **"Sweet Auburn"** was a prosperous, progressive area of black-owned businesses and jazz clubs, but it went into a decline with the Depression from which it has never truly recovered. Several blocks have been designated as the **Martin Luther King Jr National Historic Site**, in honour of Auburn's most cherished native son. This short stretch of road is the most visited attraction in all Georgia and it's a moving experience to watch the crowds of school kids waiting in turn to take photographs. Head first for the park service's **visitor centre**, 450 Auburn Ave (daily: mid-June to mid-Aug 9am–6pm; mid-Aug to mid-June 9am–5pm;

Ⓦ www.nps.gov/malu) where an exhibition covers King's life and campaigns. If you're looking for a broader account of the civil rights years, the museum at Memphis is much more comprehensive (see p.454), but this provides a powerful summary, culminating with the mule-drawn wagon used in King's funeral procession in Atlanta on April 9, 1968.

You should register here for a free tour of King's **Birth Home**, a short walk east at 501 Auburn (same hours). As only fifteen people can visit at a time and school groups often visit en masse, you may have to settle for a "virtual tour", using the computers at the visitor centre. The house itself is a 14-room Queen Anne-style shotgun, restored to its prosperous 1930s appearance. Home to King until he was 12, it remained in his family until 1971. Across from the visitor centre, the **King Center**, 449 Auburn Ave NE (daily 9am–5pm; Ⓦ www.thekingcenter.org), is privately run by King's family. Chiefly a research facility, it features artefacts such as King's Bibles and travelling case, as well as tiny rooms devoted to Mahatma Gandhi and Rosa Parks. King's mortal remains, along with those of his wife, Coretta, who died in 2006, are held in a plain marble **tomb** inscribed with the words "Free at last, free at last, thank God Almighty I'm free at last", which stands, guarded by an eternal flame, in the shallow Reflecting Pool outside. Next door, the **Ebenezer Baptist Church**, where King's funeral took place – and where his mother was assassinated while playing the organ in 1974 – is now only used for special occasions, despite rumours that it is to be opened as a museum; its congregation has decamped to a much larger church alongside the visitor centre.

Rev. Martin Luther King, Jr (1929–68)

Martin Luther King, Jr was born at 501 Auburn Avenue, Atlanta, on January 15, 1929. The house was then home to his parents and his grandparents; both his maternal grandfather, Rev A. D. Williams, and his father, Martin Luther King, Sr, served as pastor of **Ebenezer Baptist Church** nearby. Young Martin was ordained at 19 and became co-pastor at Ebenezer with his father, but continued his studies at Crozer Theological Seminary in Pennsylvania, where he was profoundly influenced by the ideas of Mahatma Gandhi, and at Boston University. Returning to the South, King became pastor of Dexter Avenue Baptist Church in **Montgomery**, Alabama, in 1954, where his leadership during the bus boycott a year later (see p.473) brought him to national prominence. A visit to India in 1957 further cemented his belief in non-violent resistance as the means by which racial segregation could be eradicated. He returned to Atlanta in 1960, becoming co-pastor at Ebenezer once more, but also taking on the presidency of the **Southern Christian Leadership Conference**. As such, he became the figurehead for the civil rights struggle, planning strategy for future campaigns, flying into each new trouble spot, and commenting to the news media on every latest development. His apotheosis in that role came in August 1963, when he addressed the **March on Washington** with his "I Have a Dream" speech. He was awarded the **Nobel Peace Prize** in 1964. Despite King's passionate espousal of non-violence, J. Edgar Hoover's **FBI** branded him "the most dangerous and effective Negro leader in the country", and persistently attempted to discredit him over his personal life. King himself became more overtly politicized in his final years. Challenged by the stridency of Malcolm X and the radicalism of urban black youth, he came to see the deprivation and poverty of the cities of the North as affecting black and white alike, and only solvable by tackling "the triple evils of racism, extreme materialism, and militarism". In the South, he had always been able to appeal to the federal government as an (albeit often reluctant) ally; now, having declared his opposition to the war in **Vietnam,** he faced a sterner and lonelier struggle. In the event, his **Poor People's Campaign** had barely got off the ground before King was assassinated in Memphis on April 4, 1968.

Midtown

Midtown stretches from Ponce de Leon Avenue to 26th Street. Nestled among the glass skyscrapers, the flamboyant Art Deco **Fox Theatre**, 660 Peachtree St NE, with its strong Moorish theme, is a rare and gorgeous remnant of old Atlanta. If you're not attending one of its fairly mainstream shows, you can see the lovely interior on an organized tour (Mon, Wed & Thurs 10am, Sat 10am & 11am; $10; Ⓦwww.foxtheatre.org).

Three blocks north of the theatre, the only brick home left on Peachtree Street, at no. 990, is the **Margaret Mitchell House** (Mon–Sat 10am–5.30pm, Sun noon–5.30pm; $13; Ⓦwww.gwtw.org). Mitchell and her husband lived in the small apartment she called "the dump" during the ten years she took to write the best-selling novel of all time *Gone With the Wind*. Published in 1936, it took just six weeks to sell enough copies to form a tower fifty times higher than the Empire State Building; the 1939 movie scaled further peaks of popularity. Lively guided tours tell the fascinating tale. Further up Peachtree, at no. 1280, Atlanta's splendid **High Museum of Art** (Tues, Wed, Fri & Sat 10am–5pm, Thurs 10am–8pm, Sun noon–5pm; $18; Ⓦwww.high.org), in stunning, airy premises designed by Renzo Piano and Richard Meier, is world-class. Permanent collections include idiosyncratic folk art by Howard Finster and Mose Tolliver, some fabulous mid-century American furniture and extensive European galleries covering five centuries from Renaissance Italy to the French Impressionists. A few blocks east of Peachtree Street, the highlight of **Piedmont Park** is the wonderful landscaped **Atlanta Botanical Garden** (Tues–Sun: May–Oct 9am–7pm; Nov–March 9am–5pm; $15; Ⓦwww.atlantabotanicalgarden.org). In addition to its landscaped gardens and vast conservatories of gorgeous tropical and desert plants, the garden hosts summer-long sculpture exhibitions and hosts big-name concerts.

Buckhead

North of Midtown, where Peachtree meets Paces Ferry Road, the affluent **Buckhead** neighbourhood is the preserve of glitzy malls and swanky hotels, expensive restaurants and swish nightclubs. Tucked away in the west, the **Atlanta History Center**, 130 W Paces Ferry Rd (Mon–Sat 10am–5.30pm, Sun noon–5.30pm; $16.50; Ⓦwww.atlantahistorycenter.com) offers a superb run-through of the factors that lead to the city's relentless growth and is good on black and women's history. A Civil War exhibit features an extraordinary number of artefacts; even if the military minutiae don't captivate you, the human stories will, and the whole combines to provide a clear history of the war, albeit with a tangible lean towards the Confederate cause. You can also tour two houses on the pretty grounds: the 1920s mock-classical mansion **Swan House** and the antebellum **Tullie Smith Farm**.

The West End

Historically a black residential area, **West End**, southwest of downtown, remains so today: a more upbeat counterpoint to Sweet Auburn. The **Wren's Nest**, 1050 R.D. Abernathy Blvd, is the former home of Joel Chandler Harris, the white author of *Br'er Rabbit* (Tues–Sat 10am–2.30pm; $8; Ⓦwww.wrensnestonline.com). The house remains much as Harris left it upon his death in 1908, while a short film explains that he first heard the Uncle Remus stories from slaves when he trained as a printer on a plantation newspaper. On Saturday afternoon, storytelling sessions take place in the peaceful, untamed garden.

Grant Park

A mile southeast of downtown, in **Grant Park** – named for a Confederate defender of Atlanta, not the victorious Union general – a theatre houses the **Cyclorama**

(Tues–Sat 9.15am–4.30pm, Sun 12.15–3.30pm; $10; Ⓦwww.atlantacyclorama.org), a huge circular painting, executed in 1885–86, depicting the Battle of Atlanta. Cycloramas were popular entertainments in the days before movies; you sit inside the circle of the painting while the whole auditorium slowly rotates. In part to mask deterioration of the canvas, a 3-D diorama has been built in front that makes it hard to see where the painting ends and the mannequins begin. The accompanying **museum** treats the war from the viewpoint of the average soldier, interspersing distressing statistics with photos and memorabilia. Next door, **Zoo Atlanta** (Mon–Fri 9.30am–5.30pm, Sat & Sun 9.30am–6.30pm; $19.99; Ⓦwww.zooatlanta.org) features a pair of giant pandas from Chengdu, gorillas and several orang-utans, plus recreations of various habitats.

Nearby, **Oakland Cemetery** (Ⓦwww.oaklandcemetery.com), the largest and oldest in the city, is the resting place of famous Atlanta citizens including Margaret Mitchell; walking tours are available.

Little Five Points to Emory University

Northeast of Auburn Avenue, around Euclid and Moreland avenues, the youthful, if gentrifying, **Little Five Points** district is a tangle of thrift stores, funky restaurants, body-piercing parlours, bars and clubs. By way of contrast, just a few blocks north at 441 Freedom Parkway, on the hill where Sherman is said to have watched Atlanta burn, the **Jimmy Carter Presidential Library and Museum** (Mon–Sat 9am–4.45pm, Sun noon–4.45pm; $8; Ⓦwww.jimmycarterlibrary.org) is devoted to the peanut farmer who rose to become Georgia state governor and the 39th president of the USA; look out for twelve-year-old Jimmy's school essay on health, in which he earnestly urges readers to keep their teeth clean.

Northeast, beyond the yuppie **Virginia-Highland** restaurant district, the trek to **Emory University**'s campus is rewarded by the lovely **Michael C. Carlos Museum**, 571 S Kilgo Circle (Tues–Sat 10am–4pm, Sun noon–4pm; $8; Ⓦcarlos.emory.edu), which hosts a splendid collection of fine art and antiquities from all six inhabited continents.

Eating

Atlanta has scores of good **restaurants** to suit all budgets and tastes. Most downtown options are upmarket, while Buckhead is even glitzier. Southern **soul food** is best around Auburn Avenue.

Colonnade 1879 Cheshire Bridge Rd NE Ⓣ404/874-5642. This Atlanta institution, a respectable old place incongruously set in a stretch of girlie bars and sex shops northeast of downtown, is full of old-timers and regulars feasting on Southern fried chicken made the way it's supposed to be. Cash only.

Fat Matt's Rib Shack 1811 Piedmont Ave NE Ⓣ404/607-1622. Atlanta's best BBQ, between Midtown and Buckhead, plus live blues nightly. It makes little difference if you choose a plateful of juicy pork or chicken, or a "sandwich" (a slab of ribs piled on a slab of bread) – everything is delicious.

Flying Biscuit 1001 Piedmont Ave Ⓣ404/874-8887. A pleasing diner at a lively Midtown intersection. Renowned locally for its healthy/organic breakfasts, it also serves reasonably priced New American lunches and dinners, all with a Southern twist. Four other Atlanta outposts exist.

R Thomas' Deluxe Grill 1812 Peachtree St NW Ⓣ404/872-2942. Friendly, funky 24hr Midtown place where you dine, sheltered from the street by rattan screening, among flowers, parrots and colourful Chinese lampshades. The varied, healthy menu ranges from Thai stir-fries with quinoa to fish tacos and the giant breakfasts are delicious.

Ria's Bluebird 421 Memorial Drive Ⓣ404/521-3737. Lines snake out of the door for *Ria's* hearty and healthy daily breakfast and lunch specials – buttermilk pancakes, overfilled burritos, tempeh Reuben sandwiches – in this cosy, friendly diner opposite Oakland Cemetery.

Sweet Auburn Curb Market 209 Edgewood Ave Ⓣ404/659-1665. Bustling indoor fresh produce market, with counter diners serving cheap soul food, Caribbean and African meals, healthy smoothies, deli sandwiches and fresh coffee. Closed Sun.

Thelma's Kitchen 302 Auburn Ave ⓣ404/688-5855. Inexpensive Sweet Auburn soul-food joint; try the salmon and grits, the BBQ plates, the veggie sides and, of course, fried chicken.

The Varsity 61 North Ave NW ⓣ404/881-1706. The world's largest drive-in diner on the fringes of downtown and Midtown: a true Fifties throwback, with chilli dogs and fried apple pies for under $2.

Nightlife

The main nightlife areas are **Virginia-Highland**, **Little Five Points** and **Midtown**, the centre of Atlanta's thriving **gay and lesbian** scene. **Buckhead** can be fun if you are prepared to spend a lot of money. For **listings**, check the free weekly *Creative Loafing* (ⓦwww.creativeloafing.com). **AtlanTIX** (ⓦwww.atlantaperforms.com), with a booth in the visitor centre (see p.428), sells half-price (usually same-day) tickets for local events and performances.

Apache Café 64 3rd St NW ⓣ404/876-5436, ⓦwww.apachecafe.info. Busy downtown café serving Latin, Caribbean and Southwestern-influenced food, as well as a stimulating nightly programme of live R & B and soul singers, jazz funk and hip-hop dance nights and spoken-word performances.

Blind Willie's 828 N Highland Ave NE ⓣ404/873-2583, ⓦwww.blindwilliesblues.com. One of the more casual joints in Virginia-Highland, this laidback blues bar has live music, strong drinks and a small dancefloor. Occasional big-name acts.

The Drunken Unicorn 736 Ponce de Leon Ave NE, no phone, ⓦwww.thedrunkenunicorn.net. This unsigned, all-ages basement music venue hosts hot indie bands and DIY. dance parties. Closed Sun.

Manuel's Tavern 602 N Highland Ave NE ⓣ404/525-3447. Memorabilia lines the walls of this classic neighbourhood bar in the West End, a favourite watering hole for journalists, writers and politicians. Jimmy Carter announced his run for governor here in 1970. Superb pub food served until late.

Star Community Bar 437 Moreland Ave NE ⓣ404/681-9108, ⓦwww.starbar.net. Enjoyable, hip Little Five Points bar, in a former bank bursting with Elvis memorabilia, offering live Americana, funk, ska and rockabilly Wed–Sat. Thurs nights no cover.

North from Atlanta: the mountains

Spectacular **Appalachian mountain scenery** – at its best in October, when the leaves turn a brilliant red and gold – lies just a short drive from Atlanta, a region that abounds in **state parks**. Secondary roads lead you through endless hairpins and narrow passes; Hwy-348 ascends a particularly impressive pass at the White County line, crossed at the top by the **Appalachian Trail**. Of the towns, attractive **Dahlonega** makes the best base; the rest – like **Helen**, a pseudo-Bavarian village 35 miles northeast – are pretty kitschy.

Dahlonega

DAHLONEGA, in the Appalachian foothills fifty miles northeast of Atlanta on US-19, owes its origins to the first-ever **Gold Rush** in the US. Benjamin Parks discovered gold at Auraria, six miles south, in 1828; Dahlonega was established five years later as the seat of Lumpkin County. Soon enough gold had been excavated for Dahlonega to acquire its own outpost of the US Mint, which, by the time production was terminated by the Civil War, had produced over $6 million of gold coin. The story is recounted in the lively **Gold Museum** on the main square (Mon–Sat 9am–5pm, Sun 10am–5pm; $5). Summer Saturday afternoons see bluegrass jams on the museum grounds; the town also hosts one of Appalachia's biggest annual **bluegrass** festivals in late June and **Gold Rush Days**, a down-home hoedown, in October.

The *Smith House*, near the museum at 84 S Chestatee St (Ⓣ706/867-7000), is a classic Southern **restaurant**, serving all-you-can-eat meals; **rooms** can be had at the hospitable *Cedar House* eco-lodge (Ⓣ706/867-9446, Ⓦwww.georgiamountaininn.com; ④), which also has rustic yurts and serves a delicious veggie breakfast.

Amicalola Falls State Park

Twenty miles west of Dahlonega on Hwy-52, **Amicalola Falls State Park** (daily 7am–10pm; $3/vehicle, $25 to camp; Ⓦwww.gastateparks.org/Amicalola) focuses on a dramatic waterfall that cascades down a steep hillside. After driving to the overlook, continue another half-mile to the park's modern **lodge** (Ⓣ1-800/864-7275; Ⓦwww.amicalolafalls.com; ④), which has comfortable rooms and a restaurant with panoramic views. For even more seclusion, hike five miles toward the start of the **Appalachian Trail**, to reach the *Hike Inn* (reservations essential; Ⓣ1-800/581-8032, Ⓦwww.hike-inn.com; ③), accessible only on foot, which offers basic rooms with family-style breakfast and dinner included.

Athens

Appealing **ATHENS**, almost seventy miles east of Atlanta, is home to the 30,000-plus students of the University of Georgia and has a liberal feel. Its compact downtown, north of campus, is alive with clubs, bars, restaurants, galleries and – of course – record stores; **Broad Street** in particular is lined with tables, but the town holds few tourist sights. It's probably best known as the home of rock groups such as R.E.M., the B-52s and the Drive By Truckers, and remains one of the top college music towns in the nation.

Practicalities

From Atlanta, Greyhound arrives at 220 W Broad St. The **visitor centre**, near campus at 280 E Dougherty St (Mon–Sat 10am–5pm, Sun noon–5pm; Ⓣ706/353-1820, Ⓦwww.athenswelcomecenter.com) has details of tours covering everything from historic buildings to music heritage.

Lodging can be a problem during football games and other big university functions. Downtown choices include the good-value *Holiday Inn*, 197 E Broad St (Ⓣ706/549-4433, Ⓦwww.holidayinn.com; ④), and the hip *Indigo*, 500 College Ave (Ⓣ706/546-0430, Ⓦwww.indigoathens.com; ⑤), with comfortable rooms. R.E.M. fans head straight for *Weaver D's* soul-food **café**, whose motto, "**Automatic for the People**", inspired the band's 1992 album. A short walk east of downtown at 1016 E Broad St (Ⓣ706/353-7797), it serves delicious fried chicken and veggies. *The Grit*, also near downtown on the northwest side at 199 Prince Ave (Ⓣ706/543-6592), offers eclectic vegetarian food from around the globe, while *Mama's Boy*, south of downtown at 197 Oak St (Ⓣ706/548-6249), serves good breakfasts. As for the **bar** scene, *The Globe,* 199 Lumpkin St (Ⓣ706/353-4721) is a friendly Athens institution that also does tasty food. For craft beer (try the excellent local brews from Terrapin Brewery), head to *The Georgia Bar*, a classic dive at 159 W Clayton St (Ⓣ706/546-9884). You'll want to catch some **live music** in Athens. R.E.M. started out playing at the eclectic *40 Watt Club*, though it has moved from its original location to 285 W Washington St (Ⓣ706/549-7871, Ⓦwww.40watt.com); the *Melting Point*, 295 E Dougherty St (Ⓣ706/254-6909, Ⓦwww.meltingpointathens.com) is a more intimate venue for Americana and roots bands. Until fire gutted it in 2009, the Georgia Theatre, a lovely old movie house at 215 N Lumpkin St (Ⓦwww.georgiatheatre.com), was one of Athens' top music venues; it is currently being rebuilt. Up-and-coming bands can be heard at the *Caledonia Lounge*, 256 W Clayton St (Ⓣ706/549-5577, Ⓦwww.caledonialounge.com), or *Tasty World*, 312 E Broad (Ⓣ706-543-0797). For full **listings**, check the free weekly *Flagpole* (Ⓦwww.flagpole.com).

Central Georgia

South of Atlanta, **central Georgia** is famous more for its people than places. **Otis Redding**, **James Brown**, **Little Richard** and the **Allman Brothers** were all born or grew up here, while former president **Jimmy Carter** came from little Plains, 120 miles south of the capital. The largest communities are Columbus, a dull army centre and likeable, appealingly old-fashioned **Macon**. The small towns hold little in the way of conventional sights, although dozy **JULIETTE**, twenty miles north of Macon, is where the weathered clapboard *Whistle Stop Café*, by the old railroad tracks, dishes up the (delicious) fried green tomatoes of book and chick-flick fame to a friendly Southern crowd straight out of Central Casting (ⓣ478/992-8886; Sun–Fri 11am–4pm, Sat 11am–8pm).

Macon

MACON (rhymes with "Bacon"), set along the **Ocmulgee River** eighty miles southeast of Atlanta, makes an attractive stop en route to Savannah, especially when its 280,000 **cherry trees** erupt with frothy blossoms, celebrated by a ten-day festival in late March. Founded in 1823, and once a major cotton port, this sleepy place is permeated with music history: home to **Little Richard**, **Otis Redding** and the **Allman Brothers**, it was also where **James Brown** recorded his first smash, the epoch-making "Please Please Please", in an unlikely-looking antebellum mansion at 830 Mulberry St. Otis is commemorated by a bronze statue beside the Otis Redding Memorial Bridge; the Dreams to Remember store, 339 Cotton Ave (ⓣ478/742-5737) sells a nice line in memorabilia. Duane Allman and Berry Oakley, killed here in motorcycle smashes in 1971 and 1972 respectively, are buried in **Rose Hill Cemetery** on Riverside Drive, the inspiration for several of the band's songs. These lives and many more are celebrated in the **Georgia Music Hall of Fame**, 200 Martin Luther King Jr Blvd (Tues–Sat 9am–5pm; $8; ⓦwww.georgiamusic.org). A huge roster of Georgian musicians are recalled by interactive displays including a gospel chapel and a rock'n'roll soda shop. As well as admiring Redding's trademark black sweater and the B-52s' wigs, you can watch Ray Charles singing *Georgia on My Mind* to the state legislature, see a photo of James Brown confiding to the pope that he feels like a sex machine and listen to 75 years' worth of jukebox tunes.

The **Tubman African American Museum**, 340 Walnut St (Mon–Fri 9am–5pm, Sat noon–4pm; $6; ⓦwww.tubmanmuseum.com), named for Underground Railroad leader Harriet Tubman, is dedicated to African-American arts, culture and history. Exhibits range from African drums and textiles through to intricate quilts and angry, dazzling avant-garde work.

Ocmulgee National Monument

Between 900 and 1100 AD, a Native American group migrated from the Mississippi Valley to a spot overlooking the Ocmulgee River a couple of miles east of modern downtown Macon, where they levelled the site that is now **Ocmulgee National Monument** (daily 9am–5pm; free; ⓦwww.nps.gov/ocmu). Their settlement of thatched huts has vanished, though two grassy mounds, each thought to have been topped by a temple, still rise from the plateau. Near the visitor centre, you can enter the underground chamber of a ceremonial **earthlodge**, the clay floor of which holds a ring of moulded seats and a striking bird-shaped altar.

Practicalities

Greyhound pulls into town at 65 Spring St, where Little Richard wrote "Tutti Frutti" while washing dishes. Macon's friendly **visitor centre**, 450 Martin Luther

King Jr Blvd (Mon–Sat 9am–5.30pm; ⓣ478/743-1074, ⓦwww.maconga.org), can advise on everything from discount museum admission packages to guided **trolley tours**. Though the interstate chains are cheaper, it's nicer to **stay** downtown: the luxurious antebellum *1842 Inn*, 353 College St (ⓣ877/452-6599, ⓦwww.1842inn.com; ❼), offers a full Southern breakfast in its lovely courtyard. The *Macon Marriott City Center*, just across the river from downtown at 200 Martin Luther King Jr Blvd (ⓣ478/621-5300, ⓦwww.marriott.com; ❺) is comfortable and clean.

Cherry Street, which looks little changed since Redding's day, is downtown's main commercial strip, with a number of cafés. For traditional **soul food**, head for the nearby *H & H*, 807 Forsyth St (ⓣ478/742-9810), an unmarked brick hut famed for its fried chicken and baked hams. There's authentic Southern **BBQ** a 45 minute drive away, north of town on US-23: *Fresh Air Barbecue*, near Jackson (ⓣ478/775-3182) is a roadside shack serving pork that's been hickory-smoked for 24 hours.

Savannah

American towns don't come much more beautiful than **SAVANNAH**, seventeen miles up the Savannah River from the ocean. The ravishing **historic district**, arranged around Spanish-moss-swathed garden squares, formed the core of the original city and boasts examples of just about every architectural style of the eighteenth and nineteenth centuries, while the cobbled **waterfront** on the Savannah River is edged by towering old cotton warehouses.

Savannah was founded in 1733 by **James Oglethorpe** as the first settlement of the new British colony of Georgia. His intention was to establish a haven for debtors, with no Catholics, lawyers or hard liquor – and, above all, no slaves. However, with the arrival of North Carolina settlers in the 1750s, plantation agriculture, based on slave labour, thrived. The town became a major export centre, at the end of important railroad lines by which **cotton** was funnelled from far away in the South. Sherman arrived here in December 1864 at the end of his March to the Sea; he offered the town to Abraham Lincoln as a Christmas gift, but at Lincoln's urging left it intact and set to work apportioning land to freed slaves. This was the first recognition of the need for "reconstruction", though such concrete economic provision for slaves was rarely to occur again. After the Civil War, the plantations floundered, cotton prices slumped and Savannah went into decline. Not until the 1960s did local citizens start to organize what has been the successful restoration of their town. In the last two decades, the private **Savannah College of Art and Design** (SCAD) has injected even more vitality, attracting young artists and regenerating downtown by buying up a number of wonderful old buildings. Today it's a prosperous, relaxed place, more raffish than Charleston, less rowdy than New Orleans, but sharing their faded, melancholy beauty. Savannah acquired notoriety in the mid-1990s thanks to its starring role in John Berendt's best-selling *Midnight in the Garden of Good and Evil*; a compelling mix of cross-dressing, voodoo and murder that sums up this rather louche, very lovable place to a tee.

Arrival, information and city transport

Savannah's **airport** is eight miles west of the city; a taxi to downtown costs around $28. The **bus station** is on the western edge of downtown at 610 W Oglethorpe Ave, while trains pull in about three miles southwest, at 2611 Seaboard Coastline Drive.

The historic district is best explored on foot, though Chatham Area Transit (CAT; ⓦwww.catchacat.org) operates the free **CAT Shuttle** service between downtown,

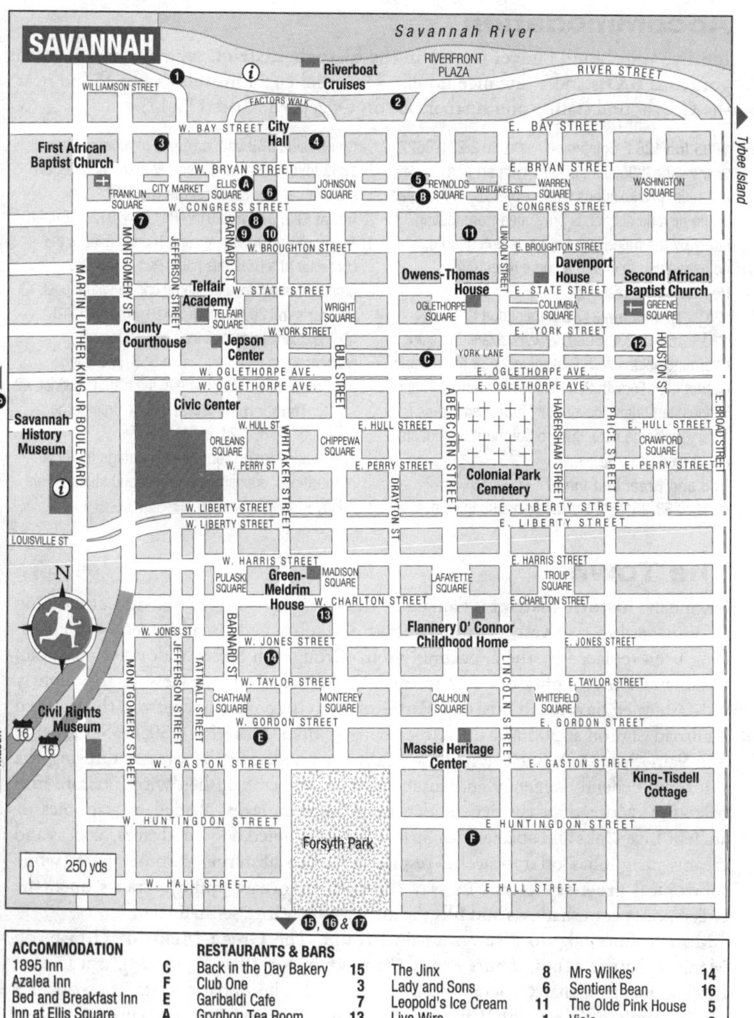

ACCOMMODATION	
1895 Inn	C
Azalea Inn	F
Bed and Breakfast Inn	E
Inn at Ellis Square	A
Planter's Inn	B
Thunderbird Motel	D

RESTAURANTS & BARS	
Back in the Day Bakery	15
Club One	3
Garibaldi Cafe	7
Gryphon Tea Room	13
Hang Fire	10
Jazz'd Tapas Bar	9
The Jinx	8
Lady and Sons	6
Leopold's Ice Cream	11
Live Wire	1
Local 11 Ten	17
Moon River Brewing Co	4
Mrs Wilkes'	14
Sentient Bean	16
The Olde Pink House	5
Vic's	2
Wall's	12

the visitor centre, the waterfront and City Market, and a number of buses for destinations further afield ($1.50). Savannah's **visitor centre**, 301 Martin Luther King Jr Blvd (Mon–Fri 8.30am–5pm, Sat & Sun 9am–5pm; ⓣ912/944-0455, ⓦwww.savannahvisit.com) has details of countless **walking tours**, and serves as the starting point for several different **trolley tours**, costing from around $20. There's another small **tourist office** at River Street on the waterfront (daily 10am–10pm). Relaxing **horse-and-carriage tours** set off from the *Hyatt Regency*, next to City Hall on W Bay Street ($20; ⓣ912/443-9333, ⓦwww.savannahcarriage.com), and you can buy tickets for lazy **riverboat cruises** at 9 E River St ($18.95; ⓦwww.savannahriverboat.com).

Accommodation

Ideally, you should budget to stay in the **historic district**, which is packed with gorgeous **B&Bs** and a few nice hotels. The usual chain **motels** can be found near the Greyhound station and further out on Ogeechee Road (US-17).

1895 Inn 126 E Oglethorpe Ave ⓣ912/231-8822, ⓦwww.the1895inn.net. Filled with art and antiques, this luxurious four-room B&B, in the heart of the historic district, is prevented from feeling stuffy by the friendliness of hosts Bob and Ed, who do everything to create a home from home. Delicious breakfasts. ❼

Azalea Inn 217 E Huntingdon St ⓣ912/236-6080, ⓦwww.azaleainn.com. Charming, laidback B&B at the edge of the historic district near Forsyth Park, complete with adorable Yorkies, ten bright, delightfully furnished rooms and a very welcome pool. Superb Southern breakfasts are served daily. ❼

Bed and Breakfast Inn 117 W Gordon St ⓣ912/238-0518, ⓦwww.savannahbnb.com. Great-value B&B with a variety of rooms in two 1853 townhouses and some carriage houses, on shady Chatham Square. Free wi-fi. ❺

Inn at Ellis Square 201 W Bay St ⓣ912/236-4440, ⓦwww.innatellissquare.com. Though it lacks the character of a B&B, this hotel, part of the *Days Inn* group, is an affordable, central choice with a pool. ❹

Planter's Inn 29 Abercorn St ⓣ1-800/544-1187, ⓦwww.plantersinnsavannah.com. A formal, welcoming, hotel rather than a B&B, in a lovely position on Reynolds Square in the historic district. ❺

Thunderbird Motel 611 W Oglethorpe ⓣ1-866/324-2661, ⓦwww.thethunderbirdinn.com. Quirky vintage motel with retro fittings, opposite the Greyhound station. Free Krispy Kremes and wi-fi. ❹

The Town

Savannah's **historic district** is flanked by the river to the north, Martin Luther King Jr Boulevard to the west, Gaston Street to the south and Broad Street – which has long been replaced by the appealingly retro Broughton Street as downtown's main commercial thoroughfare – to the east. You can get an overview at the slightly old-fashioned **Savannah History Museum**, next to the visitor centre in the restored Railroad Station at 303 Martin Luther King Jr Blvd (Mon–Fri 8.30am–5pm, Sat & Sun 9am–5pm; $5), but the main appeal is in wandering the streets admiring the shuttered Federal, Regency and antebellum houses, embellished with intricate iron balconies. More than twenty residential **garden squares**, shaded by canopies of ancient Live Oaks and ablaze with Spanish-moss-tangled dogwood trees, azaleas and creamy magnolias offer peaceful respite from the blistering summer heat, while subtropical **greenery** creeps its way through the ornate railings, cracks open the streets, casts cool shadows and fills the air with its warm, sensual scent.

Most visitors take in a few **mansion tours**. The **Green-Meldrim House**, on Madison Square (Tues, Thurs & Fri 10am–4pm, Sat 10am–1pm; $7), is a Gothic Revival mansion that General Sherman used as his headquarters. Its ironwork is a rare example of pre-Civil War craftsmanship; most iron in Savannah was melted down during the Civil War. Literature fans will appreciate the **Flannery O'Connor Childhood Home** at 207 E Charlton St (daily except Thurs 10am–4pm; $5), where the legendary Southern Gothic writer lived from her birth in 1925 until 1938.

The **Telfair Academy** (Mon noon–5pm, Tues–Sat 10am–5pm, Sun 1–5pm), a Regency mansion designed by English architect William Jay on Telfair Square at 121 Barnard St, forms the original core of the venerable **Telfair Museum of Art**, which now spreads across three sites ($15 for entry to all three; ⓦwww.telfair.org). Its collection of nineteenth- and twentieth-century American and European art is missable. More interesting are the Telfair's **Jepson Centre**, also on Telfair Square at 207 W York St – a deliciously cool, light and airy modern structure that hosts changing contemporary exhibitions from photography to sculpture (Mon & Wed–Sat 10am–5pm, Thurs 10am–8pm, Sun 1–5pm) – and the **Owens-Thomas House**, 124 Abercorn St (same hours as Academy) – designed by Jay when he was just 23. Tours here tell the history of the town through the history of the Regency-influenced building, which, rather than being all gussied up, reveals fascinating glimpses of its structure and workings.

At the southern edge of the historic district, on Calhoun Square, the **Massie Heritage Center**, 207 E Gordon St (Mon–Fri 9am–4pm; $5; Ⓦ www.massieschool.com), is housed in Savannah's first public elementary school. Today it's a simple, effective museum, illuminating Savannah's architecture with displays on its city plan, its neighbourhoods and growth, and tracing influences from as far away as London and Egypt. Though the city squares are redolent of the Old South, Savannah's **waterfront**, at the foot of a steep little bluff below Bay Street and reached by assorted stone staircases and alleyways, resembles more an eighteenth-century European port and offers a rare evocation of early America.

The main thoroughfare, **River Street**, loomed over by five-storey brick cotton warehouses, is cobbled with the ballast carried by long-vanished sailing ships. It's now a touristy stretch, lined with seafood restaurants and salty bars filled with partying crowds, but well worth a stroll. Savannah also has a rich **black history**; two blocks south of the visitor centre, at 460 Martin Luther King Jr Blvd, the small but fascinating **Civil Rights Museum** (Tues–Sat 9am–5pm; $8; Ⓦ www.savcivilrights.com) is a must-see. With a sustained programme of sit-ins, "wade-ins" at whites-only Tybee Island beaches, and a fifteen-month boycott of local department store Levy's – the longest-running store boycott in the history of the movement – Savannah was active in the campaigns of the 1960s; by 1964, Dr King called it "the most integrated city south of the Mason-Dixon Line". Artefacts include an original burnt cross and a Klan robe; visitors should decide for themselves whether to follow the signs on the separate "Colored" and "White" restrooms. The 1775 **First African Baptist Church**, 23 Montgomery St (Tues–Sat 11am & 2pm; $5; Ⓦ www.theoldestblackchurch.org), is the oldest black church in North America, built by slaves. The superbly informative tours point out the tribal carvings on the sides of the pews upstairs, and, downstairs, the diamond shapes made by holes in the floor – ventilation holes for slaves hiding in the four-foot subterranean crawl spaces while waiting to escape to safe havens via the Underground Railroad. At the **Second African Baptist Church**, 123 Houston St, General Sherman read the Emancipation Proclamation in December 1864, and issued the famous **Field Order #15**, which granted each freed slave forty acres and a mule.

Eating

Savannah has lots of **restaurants**. Most places on the **waterfront** are unremarkable, though the lively and upmarket *Vic's*, 26 E Bay St (Ⓣ 912/721-1000, is the exception, serving modern Southern seafood. **City Market** – four blocks of restored grain warehouses a few blocks back from the river – is downtown's prime restaurant and nightlife district; restaurants on the historic district squares are a little classier. Bustling **Broughton Street** also has a number of options, many of them in lovely restored Deco buildings.

Back in the Day Bakery 2403 Bull St Ⓣ 912/495-9292. Artisan bakery where everything is made from scratch, including moist red velvet cupcakes. Plus savoury treats like the jambon royal panini, light lunches and espresso drinks. Tues–Fri 9am–5pm, Sat 8am–3pm.

Garibaldi Cafe 315 W Congress St Ⓣ 912/232-7118. This atmospheric, upmarket City Market restaurant, all gold mirrors and pressed-tin ceiling, serves great Northern Italian pasta and seafood.

Gryphon Tea Room 337 Bull St Ⓣ 912/525-5880. There's a nice mix of art students, lecturers and ladies-that-lunch in this sweet tearoom, housed in an old pharmacy with its original counter, tiled floor and mirrors. Hundreds of special teas, genteel gourmet lunches and mouthwatering cakes; high tea is served 4–6pm. Closed Sun.

Lady and Sons 102 W Congress St Ⓣ 912/233-2600. Thanks to heavy TV exposure, the outrageous Paula Deen's Southern restaurant sees lines around the block for its fried chicken and veg buffets

(\$13.99 lunch, \$17.99 dinner), and à la carte dishes (crab cakes, chicken pot pie, fried green tomatoes and the like). What's amazing, given that in effect this is mass catering, is just how good the food is. No phone reservations; turn up early (from 9.30am) to put your name on a list in order to secure a same-day table.

Leopold's Ice Cream 212 E Broughton St ⓣ912/234-4442. Hollywood producer Stratton Leopold has revamped his family's traditional ice-cream parlour, originally opened in 1919, and serves home-made ices, plus a full menu of sandwiches, salads and burgers.

Local 11 Ten 1110 Bull St ⓣ912/790-9000. A hip, buzzy interpretation on Low Country, Italian and French food (pastas are made from scratch), with a small, seasonal menu using the freshest local ingredients and a thorough wine list. Dinner nightly.

Mrs Wilkes' 107 W Jones St ⓣ 912/232-5997. This local institution offers a real Southern experience, serving all-you-can-eat lunches for \$16. Diners sit around communal tables helping themselves to delicious mounds of fried chicken, sweet potatoes, spinach, beans and pickled beets. There's no sign and no reservations; arrive early and join the line. Mon–Fri 11am–2pm. Cash only.

The Olde Pink House 23 Abercorn St ⓣ912/232-4286. With its pink Regency facade and effortlessly elegant upstairs dining room, the romantic *Pink House* is perfect for relaxed, special-occasion dining. You can also order their delicious Low Country food – crispy scored flounder, she-crab soup, Southern "sushi" – in the cheery, high-spirited tavern downstairs. Dinner nightly, lunch Tues–Sat.

Sentient Bean 13 E Park Ave ⓣ912/232-4447. This spacious, slightly scruffy, alternative coffeehouse overlooking Forsyth Park serves great veggie food and fair-trade coffee and hosts regular movie nights, open mic and live music.

Wall's 515 E York Lane ⓣ912/232-9754. Tiny, spick-and-span cue hut, tucked away down a little lane, dishing up delicious devilled crab as well as succulent ribs, pulled pork and the like, with red rice and stewed okra offering lighter alternatives to the usual soul food staples. Thurs–Sat 11am–9pm.

Entertainment and nightlife

Savannah's **nightlife** is decidedly laidback, given energy by its large student population. Almost uniquely in the US (New Orleans is another exception) you can drink **alcohol** on the streets in open cups. For **listings**, pick up the free weekly *Connect* newspaper (ⓦwww.connectsavannah.com).

St Patrick's Day (March 17) is a big deal in Savannah, with its large Irish population. Around a million visitors descend here to guzzle copious amounts of Guinness; many permanent residents choose this weekend to leave town.

Club One 1 Jefferson St ⓣ912/232-0200, ⓦwww.clubone-online.com. Decadent gay club, where drag acts include Lady Chablis, from *Midnight*; everyone is welcome.

Hang Fire 37 Whitaker St ⓣ912/443-9956. A friendly, refreshingly ungrungy, little hipster bar downtown, where PBR (Pabst Blue Ribbon) flows freely and folk art lines the walls. It gets packed late on with a jovial 20-and-30-something crowd. Occasional DJs.

Jazz'd Tapas Bar 52 Barnard St ⓣ912/236-7777, ⓦwww.jazzdsavannah.com. Industrialist decor meets splashy folk art cheer at this buzzy basement martini bar/restaurant which has live, no-cover jazz or blues Tues–Sun. The "tapas" (think Southern-style appetizer plates) are tasty and inexpensive.

The Jinx 127 W Congress St (the sign says *Velvet Elvis*) ⓣ912/236-2281, ⓦwww.thejinx.net. Savannah's premier rock club, in City Market, also puts on rock'n'roll bingo, karaoke and dance nights.

Live Wire 307 W River St ⓣ912/233-1192, ⓦlivewiremusichall.com. Local and Southerm bands, with some national acts, play this friendly venue with three bars and two stages.

Moon River Brewing Co. 21 W Bay St ⓣ 912/447-0943. Popular brewpub near the waterfront.

Beaches near Savannah

Tybee Island, an attractive enclave of colourful raised cottages eighteen miles east of Savannah on US-80, has the area's best **beach**, as well as a 154ft **lighthouse** from 1736 (daily except Tues 9am–5.30pm; \$7). **Accommodation** includes the 1930s oceanfront *DeSoto Beach Hotel*, 212 Butler Ave (ⓣ912/786-4542, ⓦwww.desotobeachhotel.com; ❺). *The Crab Shack*, 40 Estill Hammock

Rd (Ⓣ912/786-9857), serves **Low Country boils**, crabs and shrimp in a casual setting by the creek. Take a right off the main road to the beach, about two miles before the lighthouse turn-off.

Fort Pulaski National Monument, off US-80 E en route to Tybee (daily 9am–5pm; $3; Ⓦwww.nps.gov/fopu), is the most interesting of several local forts and a nice place for a walk. An impressive Confederate stronghold, set on its own idyllic, if buggy, little island and ringed by an alligator-inhabited moat, it was nevertheless taken by Union troops, the first masonry fortress to be pierced by cannon fire. Much of the Georgia coast consists of a string of **National Wildlife Refuges**, on the small marshy islands of the **barrier island chain**. It's well worth backtracking along the quiet side roads to cross to **Blackbeard Island**, **Wolf Island**, **Pinckney** or **Wassaw**, where tranquil swamps are filled with nesting birds and offer great fishing.

Brunswick and the southern coast

BRUNSWICK, the one sizeable settlement south of Savannah, is a hop-off point for the offshore **sea islands**. The town in itself is industrial, though the shrimp docks can be quite interesting when the catch is brought in. The **visitor centre**, 4 Glynn Ave (daily 8.30am–5pm; Ⓣ912/265-0620, Ⓦwww.bgivb.com), has lists of **motels** and **B&Bs**. A more unusual alternative is the wonderful *Hostel in the Forest*, a couple of miles west of I-95 exit 6, reached via a muddy driveway on the south side of US-82 (Ⓣ912/264-9738, Ⓦwww.foresthostel.com; ❶; 3 nights max; no credit cards). For $25 per person you'll get a rustic room in one of nine treehouses and a communal vegetarian dinner; guests are expected to perform a small daily chore. At the *Georgia Pig* smokehouse, a tumbledown shack next to a gas station at exit 29 on I-95 (Ⓣ912/264-6664), you'll get smoky **BBQ** with Brunswick stew, coleslaw and honey-flavoured baked beans.

The sea islands

Like those of South Carolina, several of Georgia's **sea islands** were divided among freed slaves after the Civil War. They remained poor, agricultural communities, however, and today, with few tourist sights, simply make handy alternatives to Florida as seashore break destinations for inlanders.

Jekyll Island

The **southern islands** are the most developed, thanks largely to **Jekyll Island** (reached by $5 toll road), which was originally bought in 1887 for use as an exclusive "club" by a group of millionaires including the Rockefellers, the Pulitzers, the Macys and the Vanderbilts. Their opulent residences, known as "cottages", are still standing, in varying states of repair. A small **Welcome Center** stands on the causeway (daily 9am–5pm; Ⓣ912/635-3636, Ⓦwww.jekyllisland.com); the **Jekyll Island Museum**, in the old club stables on Stable Road (daily 9am–5pm) provides a good overview of the island's history and runs seasonally changing tours (daily 11am, 1pm & 3pm; $16). The island's historic district centres on the rambling old original club building, which, as the *Jekyll Island Club Hotel*, now offers elegant **accommodation** (Ⓣ 912/635-2600, Ⓦwww.jekyllclub.com; ❸). There's a **campground** a little further north (Ⓣ912/635-3021; starting at $23), near the nesting sites of loggerhead turtles.

St Simon's Island and Cumberland Island

Most of **St Simon's Island**, reached via toll road across a green marsh inhabited by wading birds, is still an evocative landscape of palms and live oaks covered with

Spanish moss. The village is pleasantly quiet and the nearby beach is nice for strolling, but fierce currents render **swimming** unsafe: head instead for the east side of the island, where the sand stretches for miles. Southeast Adventure Outfitters, 313 Mallory St (Ⓣ912/638-6732, Ⓦwww.southeastadventure.com), rents **kayaks** and runs bird- and dolphin-watching tours. **Fort Frederica National Monument**, seven miles north of the causeway (daily 9am–5pm; $3; Ⓦwww.nps.gov/fofr/), was built by General Oglethorpe in 1736 as the largest British fort in North America; it's now an atmospheric ruin. Among the luxury **resorts**, *Saint Simon's Inn*, 609 Beachview Drive, a block from the beach near the village (Ⓣ912/638-1101, Ⓦwww.stsimonsinn.com; ❺) is a good-value condo hotel. Relaxed, buzzy *Blackwater Grill*, 260 Redfern Village (Ⓣ912/634-6333), dishes up delicious contemporary Low Country **food**.

To the south, **Cumberland Island** ($4) is a stunning wildlife refuge of marshes, beaches and semitropical forest roamed by wild horses, with the odd deserted planter's mansion. You can get here by ferry from the village of **St Mary's**, back on the mainland near the Florida border (9am & 11.45am: March–Nov daily; Dec–Feb Thurs–Mon; 45min; $17 return; Ⓦwww.stmaryswelcome.com).

Okefenokee Swamp

The dense **Okefenokee Swamp** stretches over thirty miles down to Florida from a point roughly thirty miles southwest of Brunswick. Tucked away in its astonishing profusion of luxuriant plants and trees are some 20,000 alligators and over thirty species of snake, as well as bears and pumas. The entrance is at the **Okefenokee Swamp Park**, a private charity-owned concession at the northeast tip, on Hwy-177 off US-23/1 (daily 9am–5.30pm; $15; Ⓦwww.okeswamp.com). Admission grants access to a wildlife interpretive centre, observation tower and reconstructed pioneer buildings; $12–30 extra will get you **boat tours** through the swamp (slick yourself with bug repellent). Nearby accommodation in unlovely **Waycross**, ten miles north, includes the *Best Western Bradbury Inn*, 2570 Memorial Drive (Ⓣ912/284-0095; ❸).

Kentucky

Both of the rival presidents during the Civil War, Abraham Lincoln and Jefferson Davis, were born in **KENTUCKY**, where acute divisions existed between slave-owning farmers and the merchants who depended on trade with the nearby cities of the industrial North. While the state remained officially neutral, more Kentuckians joined the Union army than the Confederates; after the war, however, Kentucky sided with the South in its hostility to Reconstruction and has tended to follow southern political trends.

Kentucky's rugged beauty is at its most appealing in the mountainous **east** and the small historic towns of the **Bluegrass Downs**, home to bluegrass, bourbon and thoroughbred horses. Most of these are within reach of reserved **Lexington**, a major horse-breeding market, while hipper **Louisville**, home of the **Kentucky Derby**, lies eighty miles west. Western Kentucky, where the Ohio River meets the Mississippi, is flat, heavily forested and generally less attractive.

Lexington, Bluegrass Country and eastern Kentucky

The fertile **Bluegrass Downs**, just eighty miles across, form the base of America's thoroughbred racing industry, with **Lexington** quietly prospering at its heart. The name comes from the unique steel-blue sheen of the buds in the meadows, only visible in early morning during April and May. Kentucky's first white pioneers, who trekked in the 1770s through the 150 miles of wilderness now called the **Daniel Boone National Forest**, were amazed to find this "Eden" deserted while the Native Americans lived in much less attractive terrain. Archeologists later discovered this was due to mineral deficiencies in the soil that caused fatal bone diseases. The area around Lexington holds some of the oldest towns west of the Alleghenies, while eastern Kentucky suffers from acute rural poverty despite the fine scenery of the **Natural Bridge** and **Cumberland Gap** regions.

Lexington and around

Although the lack of a navigable river has always made its traders vulnerable to competition from Louisville, the productivity of the **bluegrass** fields has kept **LEXINGTON**'s economy ticking over since 1775, especially after its emergence as the world's largest **burley tobacco** market following World War I. However, its most conspicuous activity these days is the **horse** trade, with an estimated 450 farms in the vicinity.

Arrival and information

Lexington's **airport** is six miles west of town on US-60 W, near Keeneland Racetrack. **Greyhound** drops off about a mile northeast from downtown at 477 New Circle Rd, opposite the local bus station (bus #3 goes downtown). The **visitor centre**, 301 E Vine St (Mon–Fri 8.30am–5pm, Sat 10am–5pm, plus Sun May–Aug noon–5pm; ⓣ859/233-7299, ⓦwww.visitlex.com), gives out handy walking- and driving-tour maps. Check the free *ACE Weekly* (ⓦwww.aceweekly.com) for local **listings**.

Accommodation

Lexington has limited downtown accommodation, though there are budget **motels** around I-75. The best **campground** is north of downtown at the Horse Park (ⓣ859/233-4303, ⓦwww.kyhorsepark.com; from $15).

Gratz Park Inn 120 W Second St ⓣ859/231-1777 or 1-800/752-4166, ⓦwww.gratzparkinn.com. Downtown's oldest and most prestigious hotel, with rooms decorated in nineteenth-century style and a gourmet restaurant. ❼

Holiday Inn North 1950 Newtown Pike ⓣ859/233-0512, ⓦwww.hilexingtonnorth.com. Vast upscale *Holiday Inn* northeast of downtown, with a covered "Holidome" holding a swimming pool, sports hall and gym. ❹

La Quinta 1919 Stanton Way, junction I-64 & I-75, exit 115 ⓣ859/231-7551 or 1-800/531-5900. Handily placed motel with comfortable rooms and free continental breakfast. ❸

Swann's Nest B&B 3463 Rosalie Lane ⓣ859/226-0095, ⓦwww.swannsnest.com. An appealing rural retreat, offering five comfortable guest suites on a thoroughbred farm. ❻

Downtown Lexington

The glass office blocks, skywalks and shopping malls of Lexington's city centre, set in a dip on the Bluegrass Downs, crowd in on fountain-filled **Triangle Park**. There are few attractions beyond the **University of Kentucky Art Museum**, in

Lexington's horses

Along **Paris** and **Ironworks pikes**, northeast of Lexington in an idyllic Kentucky landscape, sleek thoroughbred horses cavort in bluegrass meadows, often penned in by immaculate white-plank fences. To the west, you can watch the horses' early-morning workouts at **Keeneland** racetrack (April–Oct daily dawn–10am; $5; ⓣ859/254-3412, ⓦwww.keeneland.com). Dark-green grandstands emphasize the crisp white rails around the one-mile oval track, where **meetings** are held for three weeks in April (Wed–Sun 7.30pm) and three weeks in Oct (Wed–Sun 1pm). General admission is $5 and seats cost $8–20. There is a great canteen too.

The easiest way to see a farm is to take a guided bus tour out of Lexington; **Blue Grass Tours** (daily 9am & 1.30pm; $30; ⓣ859/252-5744, ⓦwww.bluegrasstours.com) offer a three-hour, fifty-mile itinerary that includes a stop at **Old Friends Farm** (ⓦwww.oldfriendsequine.org), plus a visit to Keeneland. One of the few farms conducting its own tours is **Three Chimneys** ($10; book on ⓣ859/873-7053 ⓦwww.threechimneys.com) on Old Frankfort Pike, about fifteen minutes west of downtown. The **Thoroughbred Center**, 3380 Paris Pike (9am: April–Oct Mon–Sat; Nov–March Mon–Fri; $10; ⓣ859/293-1853, ⓦwww.thethoroughbredcenter.com), allows you to watch trainers at work. The enjoyable 1032-acre **Kentucky Horse Park**, a little further along at 4089 Ironworks Parkway (mid-March to Oct daily 9am–5pm; Nov to mid-March Wed–Sun 9am–5pm; $9–16; ⓦwww.kyhorsepark.com), features over thirty different equine breeds, a working farm and guided **horseback rides** ($22); its fascinating **International Museum of the Horse** traces the use of horses throughout history. In nearby Georgetown, at **Whispering Woods**, experienced equestrians can canter unsupervised, while novices ride with a guide ($25 for 1hr, up to $90/day; ⓦwww.whisperingwoodstrails.com).

the Singletary Center for the Arts, at Rose Street and Euclid Avenue (Tues–Sun noon–5pm, Fri until 8pm; free; ⓦwww.uky.edu/ArtMuseum), which displays contemporary American art and Native American artefacts.

Eating, drinking and nightlife

Lexington's large student population means it has several lively **places to eat** besides the steakhouses catering to the horse crowd and conventioneers. The streets around the junction of Broadway and Main Street hold a few lively bars, such as the *Horse & Barrel*.

Alfalfa Restaurant 141 E Main St ⓣ859/253-0014. Hippyish café featuring wide range of international food, mostly under $10, with an emphasis on vegetarian dishes and famous buckwheat pancakes. Regular art exhibitions.

Atomic Café 265 N Limestone St ⓣ859/254-1969. Fun Caribbean ambience, with good spicy food (mains around $15) and potent cocktails. Live reggae Fri & Sat and a pleasant outdoor space.

Le Deauville 199 N Limestone St ⓣ859/246-0999. Enjoy a touch of Paris at this delightful bistro with pavement seating. Dishes such as bouillabaisse Marseillaise or filet mignon cost around $30–35.

Ramsey's Diner 496 E High St ⓣ859/259-2708. Very popular and atmospheric diner, with three other outlets around town, all serving tasty sandwiches, burgers and meals for $6–15. Open until 1am.

Bluegrass Country

Other than the horse farms directly to the north, most places of interest near Lexington lie southwards, including the fine old towns of Danville and Harrodsburg, the restored **Shaker Village** at Pleasant Hill and **Berea College**. After about forty miles, the meadows give way to the striking **Knobs** – random lumpy outcrops, shrouded in trees and wispy low-hanging clouds, that are the eroded remnants of the Pennyrile Plateau.

The Shaker Village at Pleasant Hill

The utopian settlement of **PLEASANT HILL**, hidden among the bluegrass hillocks near Harrodsburg, 26 miles southwest of Lexington, was established by **Shaker missionaries** from New England around 1805. Within twenty years, nearly five hundred villagers here were producing seeds, tools and cloth for sale as far away as New Orleans. During the Civil War, the pacifist Shakers were obliged to billet Union and Confederate troops alike. Numbers declined until the last member died in 1923, but a nonprofit organization has since returned the village to its nineteenth-century appearance.

The Shaker values of celibacy (they maintained their numbers through conversion and adoption of orphans), hygiene, simplicity and communal ownership have left their mark on the thirty-four grey and pastel-coloured dwellings, which women and men entered via different doors. Visitors can watch demonstrations of traditional handicrafts including broom-making and weaving (daily: April–Oct 10am–5pm; $15; Nov–March 10am–4.30pm; $7). An on-site **inn** offers good-value rooms and also houses a superb **restaurant** specializing in boiled ham, lemon pie and other Kentucky favourites (Ⓣ859/734-5411, Ⓦwww.shakervillageky.org; ❹); reserve in advance to either eat or sleep.

Berea

BEREA, thirty miles south of Lexington, just off I-75 in the foothills where Bluegrass Country meets Appalachia, is home to unique **Berea College**, which gives its 1500 mainly local students free tuition in return for work in crafts ranging from needlework to wrought ironwork. It was founded in 1855 by abolitionists as a vocational college for the young people of East Kentucky – both white and black, making it for forty years the only integrated college in the South. The college's reputation has attracted many private art and craft galleries to little Berea; for details on these and a chance to buy local goods, visit the **Kentucky Artisan Center** at exit 77 off I-75 (daily 8am–8pm; free; Ⓦwww.kentuckyartisancenter.ky.gov). Free tours of the campus and student craft workshops leave from the sumptuous *Boone Tavern Inn*, a student-run inn and restaurant at 100 Main St N (Ⓣ859/985-3700, Ⓦwww.boonetavernhotel.com; ❺).

Eastern Kentucky

Almost the entire eastern length of Kentucky is taken up by the steep slopes, narrow valleys and sandstone cliffs of the unspoiled **Daniel Boone National Forest**. Few Americans can have been so mythologized as **Daniel Boone**, who first explored the region in 1767 and thus ranks as one of Kentucky's earliest fur-trapping pioneers. Sadly, Boone failed to legalize his land claims and was forced to press further west to Missouri, where he died in 1820 at the age of 86. *Twin Knobs,* in Salt Lick at the north end of the forest, is a good **campground** (mid-March to Oct; Ⓣ1-877/444-6777; $16).

The geological extravaganza of the **Red River Gorge**, sixty miles east of Lexington via the Mountain Parkway, is best seen by driving a thirty-mile loop from the **Natural Bridge State Resort Park** (Ⓦwww.parks.ky.gov) on Hwy-77, near the village of Slade. Natural Bridge itself is a large sandstone arch surrounded by steep hollows and exposed clifflines; for those reluctant to negotiate the half-mile climb, there is a chairlift ($7 return). As well as hiking trails, canoeing, fishing, rock climbing and camping, there's **accommodation** at the secluded *Hemlock Lodge* (❹), where weekends can be reserved a year in advance.

Toward the south

In 1940, "Colonel" Harland Sanders, so titled as a member of the Honorable Order of Kentucky Colonels, opened a small clapboard diner, the *Sanders Café*, alongside his motel and gas station in tiny **Corbin**, ninety miles south of Lexington on I-75. His **Kentucky Fried Chicken** empire has since spread all over the world. The original 100-seat restaurant, near the junction of US-25 E and US-25 W, has been restored with 1940s decor and an immense amount of memorabilia. The food served is the usual *KFC*, but it's an atmospheric little spot.

On the tristate border of Kentucky, Tennessee and Virginia, the **Cumberland Gap National Historic Park**, a natural passageway used by migrating deer and bison, served as a gateway to the West for Boone and other pioneers. **Pinnacle Overlook**, a 1000ft lookout over the three states, is near the **visitor centre**, on US-25 E in Middlesboro (daily 8am–5pm; Ⓦwww.nps.gov/cuga).

Louisville and central Kentucky

Lively **Louisville,** with its cultural and racial mix, stands out in such a heavily rural state. Beyond, however, in the **southern** hinterland, numerous small towns retain their tree-shaded squares and nineteenth-century townhouses – and their strict Baptist beliefs – while the endless caverns of **Mammoth Cave National Park** attract spelunkers and hikers in the thousands.

Louisville and around

LOUISVILLE, just south of Indiana across the Ohio River, is firmly embedded in the American national consciousness for its multimillion-dollar **Kentucky Derby**. Each May, the horse race attracts over half a million fans to this cosmopolitan industrial city, which still bears the traces of the early French settlers who came upriver from New Orleans. Louisville also produces a third of the country's **bourbon**.

Besides a vibrant arts and festivals scene, the city boasts an excellent network of public parks. One native son who took advantage of the recreation facilities was three-times world heavyweight boxing champion **Muhammad Ali**, who would do his early-morning training in the scenic environs of Chickasaw Park.

Arrival and information

Most major US airlines fly into **Louisville International Airport**, five miles south on I-65; it's an $18 cab fare into town. The **Greyhound** terminus is fairly central at 720 W Muhammad Ali Blvd. Downtown, you can hop on a TARC **trolley** (Mon–Fri 7.30am–8pm/10pm, Sat 7.30am–6pm; 50¢, free June–Aug; Ⓦwww.ridetarc.org). The **visitor centre**, Fourth and Jefferson streets (Mon–Sat 10am–6pm, Sun noon–5pm; Ⓣ502/379-6109, Ⓦwww.gotolouisville.com), offers discounts on some of the attractions. Check **listings** in the free *LEO* (*Louisville Eccentric Observer*; Ⓦwww.leoweekly.com) and *Velocity* (Ⓦlouisville.metromix.com).

Accommodation

Louisville's **accommodation** is plentiful, though not especially cheap and solidly booked up for the Derby. You can **camp** just over the river in Clarksville, Indiana at the central *KOA*, 900 Marriott Drive (Ⓣ812/282-4474, Ⓦwww.koa.com).

21C Museum Hotel 700 West Main St ⓣ502/217-6300, ⓦwww. 21chotel.com. This boutique hotel also houses an art museum and top-notch restaurant. Look out for the red penguins dotted around the property. ❻

Central Park B&B 1353 S Fourth St ⓣ502/638-1505, ⓦwww.centralparkbandb.com. Opulent seven-room Victorian B&B in the heart of the Historic District. ❺

Econo Lodge 401 S Second St ⓣ502/583-2841, ⓦwww.econolodge.com. About as cheap as you'll find right downtown. Most rooms are simple but perfectly adequate, while the priciest have hot tubs. ❹

Hampton Inn Downtown Louisville 101 E Jefferson St ⓣ502/585-2200, ⓦwww.louisvilledowntown.hamptoninn.com. Comfortable rooms plus free buffet breakfast, indoor pool and fitness centre. ❺

Downtown Louisville

Downtown Louisville rolls gently toward Main Street, then abruptly lunges to the river. **Riverfront Plaza**, between Fifth and Sixth streets, is a prime observation point for the natural **Falls of the Ohio** on the opposite side of the river. In summer, two sternwheelers, the *Belle of Louisville* and the *Spirit of Jefferson*, conduct lunchtime and dinnertime cruises from the wharf at Fourth Street and River Road (schedules vary; $18; ⓦwww.belleoflouisville.org). The town's star attraction is the excellent **Muhammed Ali Center**, beside the river at 144 N Sixth St (Tues–Sat 9.30am–5pm, Sun noon–5pm; $9; ⓦwww.alicenter.org), which, apart from chronicling the local hero's boxing career with entertaining multimedia displays, provides insight into his political activism and Muslim faith, refreshingly presented in a positive light.

Even non-baseball fans will likely be impressed by the **Louisville Slugger Museum**, 800 W Main St (Mon–Sat 9am–5pm, Sun noon–5pm; $10; ⓦwww.sluggermuseum.com), which is actually the factory of the country's prime baseball bat manufacturer. All visitors receive a souvenir miniature bat. On the university campus, **Speed Art Museum**, 2035 S Third St (Wed, Thurs & Sat 10am–5pm, Fri 10am–9pm, Sun noon–5pm; $4; ⓦwww.speedmuseum.org), hosts travelling exhibits and has a small collection of art and sculpture from medieval to modern times, featuring works by Rembrandt, Monet, Rodin and Henry Moore.

The Kentucky Derby

The **Kentucky Derby** is one of the world's premier horse races; it's also, as Hunter S. Thompson put it, "decadent and depraved". Derby Day itself is the first Saturday in May, at the end of the two-week **Kentucky Derby Festival**. Since 1875, the leading lights of Southern society have gathered at **Churchill Downs**, three miles south of downtown, for an orgy of betting, haute cuisine and mint juleps in the plush grandstand, while tens of thousands of the beer-guzzling proletariat cram into the infield. Apart from the $40 infield tickets available on the day – offering virtually no chance of a decent view – all seats are sold out months in advance. The actual race, traditionally preceded by a mass drunken rendition of "My Old Kentucky Home", is run over a distance of one and a quarter miles, lasts barely two minutes and offers around a million dollars in prize money. The excellent hands-on **Kentucky Derby Museum** (mid-March to Nov Mon–Sat 8am–5pm, Sun 11–5pm; Dec to mid-March Mon–Sat 9am–5pm, Sun 11am–5pm; $12; ⓦwww.derbymuseum.org), next to Churchill Downs at 704 Central Ave, will appeal to horseracing enthusiasts and neophytes alike. Admission includes a magnificent audiovisual display that captures the Derby Day atmosphere on a 360° screen; you can take a Behind the Scenes tour of the stables and racecourse for an extra $10.

Eating, drinking and entertainment

Louisville's **restaurants** cater to all tastes, though downtown prices are fairly high. Fronted by several outlandish sculptures, the **Kentucky Center for the Arts**, 501 W Main St (Ⓦwww.kentuckycenter.org), is the main venue for high culture, while the **Actors' Theatre of Louisville**, 316 W Main St (Ⓦwww.actorstheatre.org), has a national reputation for its new productions. The two-mile strip around Bardstown Road and Baxter Avenue is punctuated by fun **bars**; the best **gay** clubs are on the eastern edge of downtown.

Restaurants and cafés

Cumberland Brews 1576 Bardstown Rd Ⓣ502/458-8727. Welcoming microbrewery that makes fine ales, as well as decent appetizers, salads and sandwiches, all under $10.

Lynn's Paradise Café 984 Barrett Ave Ⓣ502/585-5966. Nationally acclaimed chef Lynn Winter serves up home-style cooking in an offbeat, friendly atmosphere.

Mayan Café 813 E Market St Ⓣ502/566-0651. Traditional Mayan dishes ($15–20) with the likes of rabbit in a corn-ginger sauce and salmon in creamy Mexican mushroom sauce, served in a bright dining room.

Ramsi's Café on the World 1293 Bardstown Rd Ⓣ502/451-0700. Atmospheric café open nightly until late and offering eclectic, tasty selections from around the world. A downtown branch, 215 S Fifth St, opens for weekday cafeteria-style lunches only.

Bars and clubs

Connections 130 S Floyd St. The pick of Louisville's gay scene. At weekends, this giant club, complete with terrace garden, holds over 2000.

Headliners 1386 Lexington Rd Ⓦwww.headlinerslouisville.com. Lively club that showcases local, national and even international indie bands.

Phoenix Hill Tavern 644 Baxter Ave Ⓦwww.phoenixhill.com. Big bar with four separate areas; occasionally hosts national touring acts.

Stevie Ray's 230 E Main St Ⓦwww.stevieraysbluesbar.com. As the name suggests, a loud, rocking blues bar.

South of Louisville

South from Louisville to Tennessee, **central Kentucky** offers great scope for a driving tour. There's small-town charm and well-aged bourbon in **Bardstown** and Abraham Lincoln's birthplace of **Hodgenville**, while the top natural attraction is the amazing **Mammoth Cave National Park**, the largest underground cave system in the world. Legendary **Fort Knox**, surrounded by security fences, machine-gun turrets, patrol guards and huge floodlights, straddles 100,000 acres on either side of US-31 W, thirty miles southwest of Louisville.

Bardstown and bourbon country

Forty miles south of Louisville on US-31 E, attractive **BARDSTOWN** is the place to get acquainted with Kentucky **bourbon whiskey**, created in early pioneer days, so the story goes, when Elijah Craig, a Baptist minister, added corn to the usual rye and barley. Named after Bourbon County near Lexington, Kentucky's whiskey soon gained a national reputation, thanks to crisp limestone water, strict laws concerning ingredients and the skills of small-scale distillers. Ironically, you can't drink the stuff in many counties, as they are **dry**.

A good starting point is Bardstown's **Oscar Getz Museum of Whiskey History** in Spalding Hall, 114 N Fifth St (May–Oct Mon–Fri 10am–5pm, Sat 10am–4pm, Sun noon–4pm; Nov–April Tues–Sat 10am–4pm, Sun noon–4pm; free; Ⓦwww.whiskeymuseum.com). Fourteen miles northwest at **Clermont**, the **Jim Beam American Outpost** (Mon–Sat 9am–4.30pm, Sun 1–4pm; free; Ⓦwww.jimbeam.com) has an informative museum and offers a free tour of the Beam family home, followed by a tasting. At **Maker's Mark Distillery**, twenty miles south of Bardstown on Hwy-49 near **Loretto**, whiskey is still hand-crafted in an out-of-the-way collection of beautifully restored black, red and grey plankhouses (Mon–Sat 10.30am–3.30pm, plus Sun March–Dec 1.30–3.30pm; free; Ⓦwww.makersmark.com).

Abraham Lincoln's birthplace

On February 12, 1809, **Abraham Lincoln**, the sixteenth president of the US, was born in a one-room log cabin in the frontier wilds, son of a wandering farmer and, if some accounts are to be believed, an illiterate and illegitimate mother. Three miles south of Hodgenville, on US-31 E, the **National Historic Site** (daily summer 8am–6.45pm; rest of year closes 4.45pm; free; Ⓦwww.nps.gov/abli) has a symbolic cabin of his birth, enclosed in a granite and marble Memorial Building with 56 steps, one for each year of Lincoln's life. You can stay on site in one of the three rustic *Nancy Lincoln Inn Cabins* (Ⓣ270/358-3845; ❸). The family moved ten miles northeast in 1811 to the **Knob Creek** area, where Lincoln's earliest memory was of slaves being forcefully driven along the road. Here you can visit another recreation of his boyhood home (daily April–Oct varying hours; free).

Mammoth Cave National Park

The 365 miles of labyrinthine passages (with an average of five new miles discovered each year) and domed caverns of **MAMMOTH CAVE NATIONAL PARK** lie around ninety miles south of Louisville. Its amazing geological formations, carved by acidic water trickling through limestone, include a bewildering display of stalagmites and stalactites, a huge cascade of flowstone known as **Frozen Niagara** and **Echo River**, 365ft below ground, populated by a unique species of colourless and sightless fish. Among traces of human occupation are Native American artefacts, a former saltpetre mine and the remains of an experimental tuberculosis hospital, built in 1843 in the belief that the cool atmosphere of the cave would help clear patients' lungs. You can take a limited-access self-guided tour, but by far the best way to appreciate the caves is to join a lengthy **ranger-guided tours** (2–6hr; $5–48). Tickets are available from the **visitor centre** (daily: mid-April to Nov 8am–6.15pm; Dec to mid-April 9am–5pm; Ⓦwww.nps.gov/maca). Make reservations (Ⓦwww.recreation.gov) in advance especially in summer, and keep in mind that the temperature in the caves is a constantly cool 54°F.

The park's attractions are by no means all subterranean. You can explore the scenic **Green River**, as it cuts through densely forested hillsides and jagged limestone cliffs, by following hiking trails or renting a canoe from Green River Canoeing (Ⓣ270/597-2031). **Camping** is free in the backcountry, though you'll need a permit from the visitor centre; the rustic *Mammoth Cave Hotel* (Ⓣ270/758-2225, Ⓦwww.mammothcavehotel.com; ❷) has cottages and motel **rooms**. The privately owned caves all around and the "attractions" in nearby Cave City and Park City, are best ignored.

Tennessee

A shallow rectangle, just one hundred miles from north to south, **TENNESSEE** stretches 450 miles from the Mississippi to the Appalachians. The marshy **western** third of the state occupies a low plateau edging down toward the Mississippi. Only in the far southwest corner do the bluffs rise high enough to permit a sizeable riverside settlement – the exhilarating port of **Memphis**, the birthplace of urban **blues** and long-time home of **Elvis**. The plantation homes and dull, tidy towns of **middle Tennessee**'s rolling farmland reflect the comfortable lifestyle of its pioneers; smack in the heart of it sprawls **Nashville**, synonymous with **country**

music. The mountainous **east** shares its top attraction with North Carolina – the peaks, streams and meadows of **Great Smoky Mountains National Park**.

Tennessee's first white settlers, most of them British Protestants, arrived across the mountains in the 1770s to settle in the hills and hollows of the Appalachians. Initially relations with the **Cherokee** were good. However, demand for land increased and confrontations throughout the state culminated in 1838 with the forced removal of the Native Americans on the "Trail of Tears". When the **Civil War** came, the plantation owners of the west manoeuvred Tennessee into the Confederacy, against the wishes of the non-slaveholding farmers in the east. The last state to secede became the primary battlefield in the west, site of 424 battles and skirmishes. Despite economic development to rival any in the country, soil erosion and farm mechanization led to a mass migration to the cities in the years before World War I. The fundamentalist beliefs of these transplanted hill-dwellers (whose folk and fiddle music sparked Nashville's country scene) influenced a **prohibition** movement that kept Tennessee bone-dry until 1939 and still sees many "dry" counties forbidding the sale of alcohol. The New Deal of the 1930s brought significant changes; in particular, the **Tennessee Valley Authority**, created in 1933, which harnessed the flood-prone **Tennessee River**, providing much-needed jobs and cheap power and ignited the transition from an agricultural to an industrial economy.

Memphis

Perched above the Mississippi River, **MEMPHIS** is perhaps the single most exciting destination in the South – especially for music-lovers. Visitors flock to celebrate the city that gave the world **blues**, **soul** and **rock'n'roll**, as well as to chow down in the unrivalled **BBQ** capital of the nation. Memphis is both deeply atmospheric – with its faded downtown streets dotted with retro stores and diners and the sun setting nightly across the broad Mississippi – and invigorating, with a cluster of superb museums and fantastic restaurants. If it's the **Elvis** connection that appeals, you won't leave disappointed – let alone empty-handed – but even the King represents just one small part of the rich musical heritage of the home of Sun and Stax studios.

Culturally and geographically, Memphis has always had more in common with the delta of Mississippi and Arkansas than with the rest of Tennessee. Founded in 1819 and named for Egypt's ancient Nile capital, its fortunes rose and fell with **cotton**. The Confederate defeat that ended slavery briefly plunged the city into economic chaos, but thanks to its potential for river and rail transportation it soon bounced back. The nation's second largest inland port became a major stopping-off point for **black migrant** farmers and sharecroppers escaping the poverty of the Delta and many stayed, significantly shaping the city's identity.

In the 1950s and 60s, the vibrant musical metropolis had a confidence that belied its size. The city reached its lowest ebb, however, when **Dr Martin Luther King Jr** was **assassinated** here in 1968, and for a couple of decades thereafter it tottered on the brink of terminal decline, with downtown blighted by white flight. In the 1990s money was poured into tourism projects like **Mud Island** and the colossal stainless-steel **Pyramid**, while the new millennium brought the huge **Peabody Place** mall to downtown. Those lofty schemes are white elephants today, hit by recession and the draining of tourism away from the city by the big Mississippi casinos, but a handsome minor league baseball stadium – **Autozone Field**, home of the Redbirds – and a major performance arena, the **FedEx Forum**, as well as the fabled **blues** corridor of **Beale Street** keep Memphis's downtown far livelier and more appealing, than most, while the **Rock'n'Soul Museum**, **Sun Studio** and **Stax Museum** keep

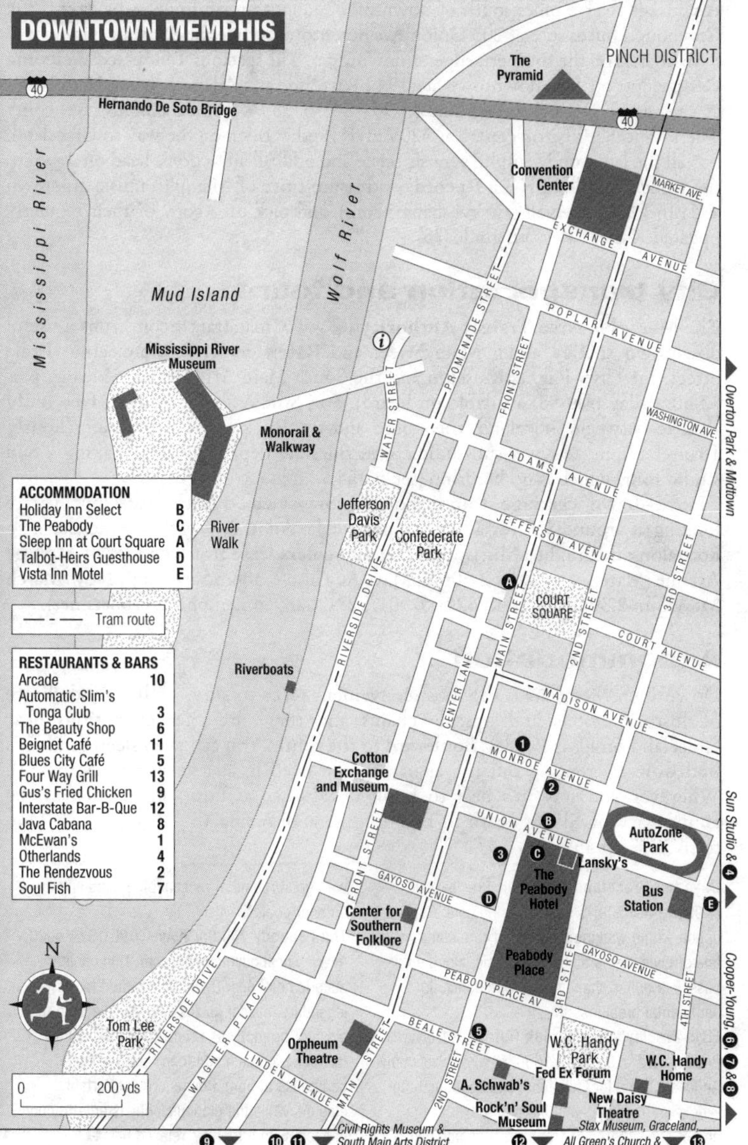

true to the city's astonishing musical heritage. Then there is **Graceland,** a warm and witty tribute that provides an intimate glimpse of the city's most famous son.

Arrival and information

Memphis is on I-40 as it runs east–west and I-55 from the south. Both join I-240, which loops around the city and cross the Mississippi River. **Memphis International**

Airport is twelve miles south of downtown – about fifteen minutes by **taxi** ($30). Greyhound **buses** stop at 203 Union Ave downtown, while the **Amtrak** station, 545 S Main St, is on the southern edge of downtown. The spacious **Tennessee Welcome Center**, just off I-40 downtown at 119 N Riverside and Adams – facing Mud Island at river level – is open 24 hours (T 901/543-5333, W www.memphistravel.com). There's another **visitor centre** at 3205 Elvis Presley Blvd, on the way to Graceland. For all the latest on Memphis's music scene and oddball attractions, head on down to the wonderful **Shangri-La Records**, a treasure-trove of Memphis music, midtown at 1916 Madison Ave (W www.shangri.com), and pick up a copy of their regularly updated *Kreature Komforts* guide ($5).

City transportation and tours

The **Memphis Area Transit Authority** (W www.matatransit.com) runs a useful downtown **trolley** along Main Street and Riverside Drive, connecting Beale Street, the Civil Rights Museum and the South Main Arts District ($1, day pass $3.50, 3-day pass $8, available on board). Sun Studio also provides a **free daily shuttle** between Graceland, the studio and the Rock 'n' Soul Museum (hourly 10am–6.30pm; W www.sunstudio.com); rides are dependent upon taking a Sun studio tour, which is no hardship (see p.454).

Horse-drawn **carriage tours** abound downtown – prices vary but you're looking at around $50 for a thirty minute ride. Another way to see the city is to float along the mighty Mississippi: **sternwheelers** leave from the foot of Monroe Avenue (March–Oct daily 2.30pm, May–Aug also 4.30pm Sat & Sun; Nov–March Sat & Sun 2.30pm; 90min; $22; T 901/527-2628, W memphisriverboats.net).

Accommodation

Downtown Memphis is the most convenient place to **stay**, with a good choice of historic hotels and upscale chains and there are cheaper options near Graceland on Elvis Presley Boulevard to the south. You can even sleep in **Elvis's bedroom** by renting out the apartment he lived in as a teenager (see p.456). Wherever you stay, it's best to book in advance at busy times, such as the anniversary of Elvis's death in mid-August and during the **Memphis in May** festival (see p.459).

Days Inn Graceland 3839 Elvis Presley Blvd T 901/ 346-5500, W www.daysinn.com. Good option within walking distance of Graceland, with lots of Elvis memorabilia and music, along with – bliss! – a guitar-shaped pool. Rates include continental breakfast. ❸

Elvis Presley's Heartbreak Hotel 3691 Elvis Presley Blvd T 901/332-1000, W www.elvis.com. An ideal choice for Elvis fans, this boutique hotel – next to Graceland, and literally "down at the end of Lonely Street" – features a (small) heart-shaped pool, kitschy Elvis decor and peanut butter sandwiches in the Jungle Room lounge. Lavish Elvis-themed suites sleep up to eight (and start at around $550/night). Free downtown shuttle and breakfast. ❺

Holiday Inn Select 160 Union Ave T 901/525-5491, W www.hisdowntownmemphis.com. In an unbeatable location opposite the *Peabody*, with good rooms at reasonable prices and an outdoor pool. ❺

The Peabody 149 Union Ave T 901/529-4000, W www.peabodymemphis.com. This opulent historic hotel near Beale St is famed for its legendary mascot ducks, who waddle from the elevator promptly at 11am, spend the day in the lobby fountain and then return to their penthouse at 5pm. Rooms are comfortably elegant, while the glorious lobby is an attraction in itself, with a friendly, relaxed bar. ❽

Sleep Inn at Court Square 40 N Front St T 901/522-9700, W www.sleepinn.com. Upscale, good-value motel facing the river and backing onto Main St and the trolley line. Rates include continental breakfast and free wi-fi. ❹

Talbot-Heirs Guesthouse 99 S Second St T 901/527-9772, W www.talbotheirs.com. Characterful, friendly and comfortable family-run place near Beale St. Each of the eight themed suites has a kitchenette, CD player and internet access. Rates include continental breakfast. ❻

Vista Inn Motel 265 Union Ave ⓣ901/527-4305, ⓦwww.vistarez.com. Central motel just off Beale St with well-kept basic rooms and good rates. ❹

The City

Laidback and oddball, melancholy and determinedly nostalgic, Memphis has a friendly scale that's uncommon in cities of comparable size. **Downtown** still retains a healthy ensemble of buildings from the cotton era – best admired either along the riverfront or from the trolley down **Main Street** – along with a number of places that look unchanged since Elvis's day. Tourist activity downtown is concentrated around the enormous **Peabody Place** mall – which could really be anywhere in the US – and the nearby bars and clubs of **Beale Street**; the **Civil Rights** and **Rock'n'Soul** museums just beyond that; and **Sun Studio** to the east. Elsewhere, **Mud Island** on the river itself merits half a day, as does the **Stax** museum, while **Graceland**, ten miles south, should not on any account be missed.

Beale Street and around

Beale Street began life in the mid-nineteenth century as one of Memphis's most exclusive enclaves; within fifty years its elite residents had been driven out by yellow fever epidemics and the ravages of the Civil War to be replaced by a diverse mix of blacks, Greeks, Jews, Chinese and Italians. But it was **black culture** that gave the street its fame. Beale Street was where black roustabouts and travellers passing through Memphis immediately headed. In the Jim Crow era, Beale served as the centre for black businesses, financiers and professionals. As the black Main Street of the mid-South, Beale in its Twenties' heyday was jammed with vaudeville theatres, concert halls, bars and juke joints (mostly white-owned). Along with the frivolity came a reputation for heavy gambling, voodoo, murder and prostitution. Although Beale still drew huge crowds in the Forties, the drift to the suburbs and, ironically, the success of the **civil rights** years in opening the rest of Memphis to black businesses, almost killed it off. The **bulldozers** of the late Sixties spared only the grand Orpheum Theatre, at 203 S Main St and a few commercial buildings between Second and Fourth streets.

Beale Street has now been restored as a handsome **Historic District**. Its souvenir shops, music clubs, bars and cafés are bedecked with retro facades and neon signs, while a sidewalk Walk of Fame honours musical greats such as B.B. King and Howlin' Wolf. Blues fans in particular will be drawn to its music venues, which showcase top regional talent. At Beale's western end, no. 126 – the former home of the iconic **Lansky's**, tailor to the Memphis stars – has been remodelled to become a restaurant; if you're looking to buy any of their gorgeous rock'n'roll threads, including Elvis's favourite pink shirts, Lansky's continues to thrive in the historic *Peabody* hotel (see opposite).

A. Schwab's Dry Goods Store, 163 Beale (closed Sun) looks much as it must have done when it opened in 1876, with an incredible array of such voodoo paraphernalia – best-sellers include Mojo Hands and High John the Conqueror lucky roots – as well as 99¢ neckties and Sunday School badges. Further east, at no. 352, the tiny former home of **W.C. Handy** – moved here from its original site in south Memphis – offers another evocative sense of old Memphis (Tues–Sat: June–Aug 10am–5pm; Sept–May 11am–4pm; $3). In 1910, Handy was the first man to publish blues tunes (often blues in name only; see p.478). One block south of Beale, in the plaza of the enormous FedEx Forum, the appealing **Rock'n'Soul Museum** (daily 10am–7pm, last admission 6.15pm; $10; ⓦwww.memphisrocknsoul.org) presents the story of the city's musical heritage scrapbook-style, making connections between migration, racism, civil rights and youth culture, with artefacts ranging from Elvis's stage gear and one of B.B. King's "Lucille" guitars to Al Green's Bible. The tiny **Centre for Southern Folklore**, meanwhile, a couple of blocks north of Beale at 123 S Main St (Mon–Fri 11am–5pm, Sat & Sun 11am–6pm; Ⓦwww.southernfolklore.com) celebrates the culture of the South, with a café, a store full of books, folk art and CDs and a stage for live performances.

The National Civil Rights Museum

The **National Civil Rights Museum**, which provides the most rewarding and comprehensive history of the long and tumultuous struggle for civil rights to be had anywhere in the South, is a few blocks south of Beale at 450 Mulberry St (June–Aug Mon & Wed–Sat 9am–6pm, Sun 1–6pm; Sept–May closes 5pm; $13; Ⓦwww.civilrightsmuseum.org). It's built around the shell of the former *Lorraine Motel*, where **Dr Martin Luther King Jr** was assassinated by James Earl Ray on April 4, 1968. Dr King was killed by a single bullet as he stood on the balcony, the evening before he was due to lead a march in Memphis in support of a strike by black sanitation workers.

The *Lorraine* itself was one of the few places where blacks and whites could meet in Memphis during the segregation era; thus black singer Eddie Floyd and white guitarist Steve Cropper wrote soul classics such as "Knock on Wood" here, and Dr King was a regular guest. The facade of the motel is still all too recognizable from images of King's death, but once inside visitors are faced with a succession of galleries that recount the major milestones of the movement, from A. Philip Randolph of the Brotherhood of Sleeping Car Porters, who originally called for a march on Washington in 1941, through to the Nation of Islam and the Black Panthers. There is some horrifying and very emotional footage, but by far the most affecting moment comes when you reach King's actual room, Room 306, still laid out as he left it, and see the spot where his life was cut short. Another wing, across from the motel, completes the story by incorporating the rooming house from which the fatal shot was fired. The bedroom rented that same day by James Earl Ray, and the sordid little bathroom that served as his sniper's nest, can be inspected behind glass, with the death site clearly visible beyond. King's own family remain highly sceptical as to whether Ray acted alone, and detailed panels lay out all sorts of conspiracy theories.

The South Main Arts District

A block west of the National Civil Rights Museum, the once flyblown South Main Street has been given a new lease of life. Spanning the nine or so blocks along Main between Vance and St Paul avenues, the **South Main Arts District** is a burgeoning stretch of galleries, stores and restaurants, complete with a crop of condos and lofts. It's particularly buzzing on the last Friday of the month, when the free "Art Trolley" (6–9pm) runs along Main and stores offer complimentary snacks and drinks.

Sun Studio

Second only to Graceland, Memphis's principal shrine to the memory of Elvis is the hip little **Sun Studio**, east of Beale Street at 706 Union Ave. The studio where, in 1953, the shy eighteen-year-old trucker from Tupelo turned up with his guitar, claiming "I don't sound like nobody", went on to introduce rock'n'roll to the world with not only the King but also artists like Jerry Lee Lewis and Carl Perkins. Though Sun Records moved out of the building in 1959, the soundproofing remained in place through a variety of incarnations – including a brief, unlikely period as a scuba-diving store – making possible its restoration as a functioning studio in 1987, and retaining the eerie, almost spiritual atmosphere of the place. Every hour on the half-hour, lively forty-minute tours (daily 10.30am–5.30pm; $13; Ⓦwww.sunstudio.com) start in an upstairs room where you can see B. B. King's chair and Elvis's high school diploma, before heading down into the studio. Measuring just eighteen by thirty feet, the shabby room fills with music as enthusiastic rockabilly guides play wild rock'n'roll recordings and tell choice anecdotes. Few visitors leave unmoved – or without posing for a photo with Elvis's original mic stand.

The Stax Museum of American Soul Music

In 1960, one of Memphis' most famous addresses, 926 E McLemore Ave, was occupied by the Capitol Theatre, a landmark in a neighbourhood where blacks had just started to outnumber whites. The theatre became the headquarters of the **Stax** record label, a veritable powerhouse of funky soul where over the next fifteen years artists such as Otis Redding, Isaac Hayes, Albert King and the Staples Singers cut fifteen US number-one hits and achieved 237 entries in the top 100. By the early 2000s, however, with Stax long since defunct, 926 E McLemore was just a derelict lot in a sketchy neighbourhood.

The sound of Memphis

Since the start of the twentieth century, Memphis has been a meeting place for black musicians from the Delta and beyond. During the Twenties, its downtown pubs, clubs and street corners were alive with the sound of the blues. **Jug bands**, in which singers were given a bass accompaniment by a musician blowing across the neck of a jug, were a specialty. Several songs by **Gus** Cannon's Jug Stompers – such as *Walk Right In* – became hits for white artists during the folk revival of the Sixties. Bukka White, Memphis Slim and guitarist Memphis Minnie appeared at nightspots like *Mitchell's Hotel* and *Pee Wee's Saloon*, all long since defunct. After World War II, young musicians and radio DJs such as Bobby Bland and B.B. King experimented by blending the traditional blues sound with jazz, adding electrical amplification to create rhythm'n'blues. White promoter Sam Phillips started Sun Records in 1953, employing Ike Turner as a scout to comb the Beale Street clubs for new talent. Among those whom Turner helped introduce to vinyl were his own girlfriend, Annie Mae Bullock (later Tina Turner), Howlin' Wolf and Little Junior Parker, whose *Mystery Train* was Sun's first great recording. In 1953, the 18-year-old Elvis Presley hired the studio to record *My Happiness*, supposedly as a gift for his mother, and something prompted Phillips' assistant Marion Keisker to file away his details. The next summer, Phillips called Elvis back to the studio to cut *That's All Right*, and thereby set out towards proving his much-quoted conviction that "If I could find a white man who had the Negro sound and the Negro feel, I could make a billion dollars". Phillips swiftly dropped his black artists and signed other white rockabilly singers like Carl Perkins and Jerry Lee Lewis to make classics such as *Blue Suede Shoes* and *Great Balls of Fire*. Elvis – who in the words of Carl Perkins had the advantage that he "didn't look like Mr Ed, like a lot of the rest of us" – was soon sold on to RCA (for just $35,000), and didn't record in Memphis again until 1969, when at Chips Moman's American Studios he produced the best material of his later career, including *Suspicious Minds*. In the Sixties and early Seventies, Memphis's Stax Records provided a rootsy alternative to the poppier sounds of Motown. This hard-edged southern soul was created by a multiracial mix of musicians, Steve Cropper's fluid guitar complementing the blaring Memphis Horns. The label's first real success was *Green Onions* by studio band Booker T and the MGs; further hits followed from Otis Redding (*Try A Little Tenderness*), Wilson Pickett (*Midnight Hour*), Sam and Dave (*Soul Man*) and Isaac Hayes (*Shaft*). The label eventually foundered in acrimony; the last straw for many of its veteran soulmen was the signing of the British child star Lena Zavaroni for a six-figure sum. For **gospel music** in Memphis, see p.460.

Now Stax has resurfaced, reconstructed larger than ever, with a music academy sitting next to the fabulous **Stax Museum of American Soul Music**, or **Soulsville** (April–Oct Mon–Sat 10am–5pm, Sun 1–5pm; Nov–March closed Mon; $12; Ⓦwww.staxmuseum.com). Visits start with a film history of the label, using stunning footage to illuminate the triumphs and the tensions that arose from its all-but-unique status as a joint black-white enterprise in the segregated South. The first exhibit beyond, emphasizing soul music's gospel roots, is an entire Episcopal Church, transported here from Mississippi. Among the wealth of footage and recordings, showpiece artefacts include Isaac Hayes's peacock-blue and gold Cadillac. The studio has been recreated in detail, featuring the two-track tape recorder used by Otis Redding to record "Mr Pitiful" and "Respect". A map of the neighbourhood, still largely run-down, shows what an amazing assembly of talent lived nearby; Aretha Franklin was born at 406 Lucy Ave, while other locals included Booker T, David Porter and Memphis Slim.

The riverfront

The northern boundary of downtown Memphis is marked by the astonishing 32-storey, 321ft **Pyramid** glinting in the sun over the mighty river. Completed in 1991, at two-thirds the size of Egypt's Great Pyramid, it was created to make a symbolic link with Egypt's Nile Delta. After years hosting major exhibitions and shows, it has since been overshadowed by downtown's FedEx Forum and lain empty since 2005. While it remains to be seen what is to become of this marvellous folly, its symbolism is undeniable. The surrounding neighbourhood, the **Pinch District**, is named for the impoverished – "pinched" – Irish immigrants who settled here in the mid-1800s. The young **Elvis Presley** lived nearby from 1949 until 1953, in an apartment at 185 Winchester Ave (now named Uptown Square). Thrillingly, it's available for rent at around $250 a night – except during Elvis week in August (Ⓣ901/523-8662; Ⓦwww.lauderdalecourts.com; ❾).

From Riverside Drive, which runs south from the Pyramid, **monorail trains** and a walkway head across the Mississippi's Wolf Channel to **Mud Island** (Tues–Sun: April, May, Sept & Oct 10am–5pm; June–Aug 10am–6pm; park free, monorail $4 or free with $10 museum admission; Ⓦwww.mudisland.com). Highlights of the island's slightly old-fashioned but enjoyable **Mississippi River Museum** include a full-sized reconstructed steam packet, a morbidly fascinating "Theatre of Disasters", and salty tales of characters like keelboatman Mike Fink, who in 1830 styled himself "half horse, half alligator". **River Walk**, which runs to the southern tip of the island, is a scale replica of the lower Mississippi River; at the end, you can rent canoes and kayaks for a leisurely paddle around the nearby "Gulf of Mexico".

Mud Island hosts a variety of concerts and events: in summer, you can even bring a sleeping bag and join a mass campout where the tent, dinner, breakfast and entertainment is laid on. On the mainland, a walk via the riverfront Jefferson Davis and Confederate parks brings you to **Tom Lee Park**, a venue for major outdoor events including **Memphis in May** (see p.459). Stretching a mile along the river, it commemorates a black boatman who rescued 32 people from a sinking boat in 1925 – despite not being able to swim.

Graceland

In itself, Elvis Presley's **Graceland** was a surprisingly modest home for the world's most successful entertainer – it's certainly not the "mansion" you may have imagined. And while Elvis was clearly a man who indulged his tastes to the fullest, Graceland has none of the pomposity that characterizes so many other showpiece Southern residences. Visits are affectionate celebrations of the man; never exactly tongue-in-cheek, but not cloyingly reverential either.

American music

Some of the world's greatest musical genres took root in cities across America: Chicago, birthplace of the blues; New Orleans, with unrivalled jazz and R&B scenes; Nashville, synonymous with country; and Memphis, home to seminal record labels and the ultimate rock'n'roll shrine, Graceland. Outside the cities, rural Appalachia brims with backwoods fiddlers; Louisiana's sleepy bayous are alive with Cajun and zydeco; and Mississippi Delta juke joints enrapture blues purists.

Bluegrass fiddle player ▲

Tootsie's Orchid Lounge, Nashville ▼

Patsy Cline ▼

Rural beginnings

American **folk music** can be traced back to the Europeans – particularly those from England and the Celtic lands – who settled in the Appalachian mountains. Over the centuries, traditional ballads mixed with influences from other parts of the world and evolved into the guitar-twanging **country** music that is today associated with the American South. It wasn't until the mid-twentieth century, however, that country music broke into the mainstream, with the plain cowboy style of Roy Rogers, the sweet harmonies of the Carter Family, and the raw honky-tonk tearjerkers of Hank Williams.

The banjo- and fiddle-based sound of **bluegrass** has enjoyed a revival recently, with popularity for traditionalists like Ralph Stanley and fresh indie takes on the genre from young "new grass" or "jam grass" bands.

The Mississippi sounds

Jazz and the blues grew out of African-American culture, with the latter inextricably linked to the experiences of slavery and poverty. Forged from a combination of African and gospel sounds into a simple twelve-bar form during the late nineteenth century, by the 1930s the **blues** had gained widespread popularity, spreading along a path that followed the Mississippi River through Memphis, then on to northern urban centres (especially Chicago). Thanks to icons like Leadbelly, Muddy Waters and BB King, the genre not only solidified its stature but – as the saying goes – had a baby and named it rock'n'roll. You can still catch Mississippi blues in Delta juke joints, and electrified urban blues in the gritty clubs of Chicago.

Jazz, meanwhile, took root in the Creole culture of New Orleans. Blending African traditions with western techniques, with a heavy emphasis on brass and drum, it's a distinctly American art form. Jazz is still dance music in New Orleans; cooler urban stylings can be enjoyed in clubs in New York and other major cities.

From rock to rap

Rock has come a long way since its blues-based infancy, when young trucker Elvis Presley shook up white country with raw R&B in 1950s Memphis and changed the world forever. Before long, Chuck Berry told Beethoven it was time to roll over and super-coiffed Little Richard showed him how it was done. The amorphous new form would absorb a host of influences, from Bob Dylan's folk protest songs to the pop that followed the Beatles-led British invasion, and the drug- and sitar-tinged psychedelic revolution of bands like the Grateful Dead in the late 1960s. Spiky New York punk, quirky Ohio industrial, furious LA hardcore, slacker Seattle grunge, and spaced-out neo-psychedelia are but a few of the rock genres that continue to thrive in the USA.

As the black social experience diversified over the course of the twentieth century, various forms of music sprang up to give it voice. In the 1960s, the heartfelt soul of masters like Otis Redding preceded the explosion of talent that came to define the Motown era, born in Detroit. As soul went mainstream in the 1970s, progressive mavericks like Parliament and Funkadelic paved the way for the transition to 1980s rap: loaded with attitude, street-style and political savvy, rappers from Run DMC to NWA, mostly based in New York and LA, stood at the forefront of a dynasty that gave birth to hip-hop and r'n'b. Today

▲ Miles Davis

▼ Bob Dylan in concert

▼ Yeasayer play the Guggenheim

any city with a major black population has a distinctive rap scene, including in the so-called "Dirty South", where rappers play on the raw call-and-response stylings of early blues.

Red Rocks Amphitheater ▲

Maple Leaf ▼

Rosa's Lounge ▼

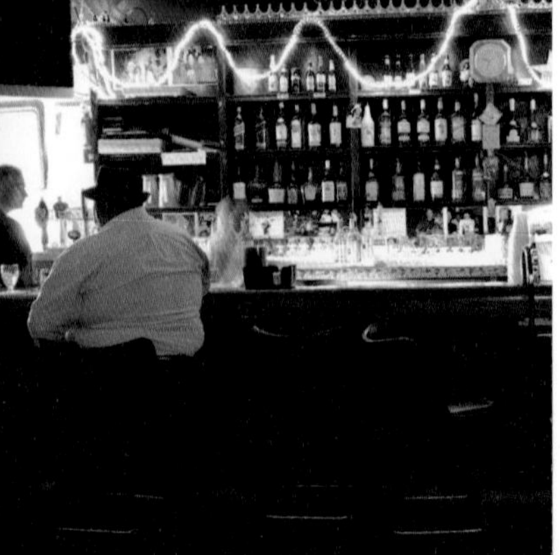

Iconic venues

▶▶ **The Blue Worm** Memphis, TN. While you can catch live blues in the bars along touristy Beale Street, head out to this friendly locals' club for a more authentic experience. p.460

▶▶ **Bohemian Caverns** Washington DC. Famed cellar where cool cats play sophisticated soul jazz to an appreciative crowd. p.351.

▶▶ **Continental Club** Austin, TX. Laidback place for interesting country, folk and Americana acts in the music capital of Texas. p.605

▶▶ **The Fillmore** San Francisco, CA. This venerable hippy landmark, lined with groovy 60s posters, still hosts rock and alt-rock acts. p.921

▶▶ **Maple Leaf** New Orleans, LA. Funky brass-hop band the Rebirth play a legendary weekly gig at this wonderful old neighbourhood bar. See p.575.

▶▶ **Preservation Hall** New Orleans, LA. Quite simply the nation's best venue for red-hot trad jazz. p.574

▶▶ **Red Rocks Amphitheater** Denver, CO. Spectacular arena carved out of glowing red sandstone. p.688.

▶▶ **Rosa's Lounge** Chicago, IL. Intimate and welcoming blues club that offers a variety of great local talent. p.302

▶▶ **Ryman Auditorium** Nashville, TN. This classic seated theatre is one of Nashville's top spots for great country music. p.464

▶▶ **The Stone Pony** Asbury Park, NJ. The down-and-dirty bar that helped launch Bruce Springsteen maintains its tradition of promoting local talent. p.197

▶▶ **Whisky-a-Go-Go** Los Angeles, CA. The former stomping ground of the Doors now tends to showcase harder-edged outfits. p.873

Graceland practicalities

Graceland is ten miles from downtown Memphis, at 3734 Elvis Presley Blvd. The mansion and Graceland Plaza are open March–May, Sept & Oct Mon–Sat 9am–5pm, Sun 10am–4pm; June–Aug Mon–Sat 9am–5pm, Sun 9am–4pm; Nov daily 10am–4pm. From Dec–Feb the house is open Wed–Mon 10am–4pm, Graceland Plaza daily 10am–4pm. The ticket office opens 30min before the first tour; the last house tour starts when the ticket office closes. Combined "Platinum" ticket to all attractions (allow three hours) is $34; house tours alone $30; parking $10. The $69 VIP tour is barely worth it, only granting access to a room with a few extra personal items and allowing you to bypass queues. Reservations are recommended, especially in Aug, but not essential (Ⓣ901/332-3322 or 1-800/238-2000, Ⓦwww.elvis.com).

Elvis was just 22 when he paid $100,000 for Graceland in 1957. Built in 1939, the stone-clad house was then considered one of the most desirable properties in Memphis, though today the neighbourhood is distinctly less exclusive, its main thoroughfare – **Elvis Presley Boulevard** – lined with discount liquor stores, ancient beauty parlours, used car lots and surprisingly few Elvis-related souvenir shops. Tours start opposite the house in **Graceland Plaza**; excited visitors, kitted out with headphones, are ferried across the road in minibuses, which depart every few minutes and sweep through the house's famous "musical gate", etched with musical notes and Elvis's silhouette. No stops are made at the perimeter "Wall of Love", scrawled with tens of thousands of messages from fans, but you are free to walk back there after the tour.

Audio tours, peppered with spoken memories from Priscilla Presley and Elvis's daughter, Lisa Marie, and rousing choruses from the King himself, allow you to spend as long as you wish, although upstairs is out of bounds. The interior is a jubilant tribute to the taste of the Seventies, each room reflecting Elvis's personal passions; highlights include the Hawaiian-themed **Jungle Room**, with its waterfall, Tiki ornaments and green shag-carpeted ceiling, where Elvis recorded "Moody Blue" and other gems from his latter years, the **Pool Room**, whose walls and ceiling are covered in heavily pleated, paisley fabric suggesting a little-documented psychedelic phase and the navy-and-lemon **TV Room**, mirrored and fitted with three screens that now show classic 1970s TV shows and Elvis's favourite movies.

In the **trophy building**, you parade past Elvis's platinum, gold and silver records, some of his wilder Vegas stage costumes and cases of intriguing clippings, photos and memorabilia; footage of early TV performances offers breathtaking reminders of just how charismatic the young Elvis was. The tour of the interior ends with the **racquetball building**, where he played on the morning he died. In the attached lounge, the piano where he sang for the last time (apparently "Unchained Melody") stands eerily silent, while in the court itself his resplendent, bejewelled capes and jumpsuits stand sentinel beneath a huge monitor showing a late performance of "American Trilogy". Here, perhaps more than anywhere else, you can feel the huge presence of the man who changed the face of music forever. Elvis (Jan 8, 1935–Aug 16, 1977), his mother, Gladys, his father, Vernon, and his grandmother, Minnie Mae, lie buried in the **meditation garden** outside, their graves strewn with flowers and soft toys sent from fans. Elvis's body was moved here two months after his death, when security problems at the local cemetery became unmanageable. There's often a log-jam here, as visitors crane to read the messages sent by fans, take moments to offer their own prayers, and snap photos of the bronze memorial plaques. Graceland Plaza, resounding with nonstop Elvis hits, holds several extra attractions.

Don't miss **Sincerely Elvis**, in which exhibits on each of his 31 movies trace the sad story of how his attempts to be a dramatic actor where thwarted by the demands of the studios; and Elvis's personal **airplanes**, including the *Lisa Marie*, customized with 24-carat-gold washroom sink and blue suede furnishings. Quite apart from his many cars – among them a Harley-Davidson golf cart and super-sleek powder-pink 1955 Cadillac – the enjoyable **Elvis Presley Automobile Museum** shows a wittily edited film of action-packed and vaguely car-related clips from his movies. The Plaza's many **gift stores** will keep you occupied for hours, whether you're after an Elvis toothbrush or a pair of blue suede shoes – you can even pose with the King for a photo, movie poster, or music DVD.

Graceland Crossing, the mall next door, has a couple of related attractions: the small but fascinating **Fashion King**, which covers the King's inimitable style and **Elvis 68**, which is little more than an add-on to the neighbouring gift store. While Graceland Plaza has a clutch of themed **diners**, you'll eat better on Elvis Presley Boulevard (*A&R*, no. 1802, and *Payne's*, no. 1393, are classic **BBQ** huts; *Piccadilly* at no. 3968 is an old-style Southern diner). If you can't drag yourself away from Graceland, though, go for the *Chrome Grill* where you can settle down in a 1950s Cadillac to eat tasty BBQ.

Midtown and East Memphis

The centrepiece of wooded **Overton Park**, three or so miles east of downtown on Poplar Avenue, is the **Memphis Zoo** (daily: March–Oct 9am–6pm; Nov–Feb 9am–5pm; last admission 1hr before closing; $15, $5 parking; Ⓦmemphiszoo.org). If the usual array of gorillas, orang-utans and giraffes doesn't satisfy you, you can visit a pair of giant pandas. The park also holds the impressive **Memphis Brooks Museum of Art** (Wed & Fri 10am–4pm, Thurs 10am–8pm, Sat 10am–5pm, Sun 11am–5pm; $7; Ⓦwww.brooksmuseum.org), whose array of fine art features a strong collection of medieval and Renaissance works.

A mile south of the park, the **Cooper-Young** intersection boasts a handful of funky restaurants and vintage stores, as well as an outstanding bookstore, **Burke's** at 936 S Cooper (Ⓦwww.burkesbooks.com). It's a lively yet laidback neighbourhood, quite different from downtown but still distinctly Memphis, where blues and BBQ rub along with poetry readings and yard sales. A couple of miles further southeast, the **Pink Palace,** 3050 Central Ave (Mon–Sat 9am–5pm, Sun noon–5pm; $8.75; Ⓦwww.memphismuseums.org) centres on the marble mansion of Clarence Saunders, who founded America's first chain of self-service **supermarkets**, Piggly-Wiggly, in 1916. Saunders went bankrupt in 1923 and never actually lived here; instead, the building became an appealingly old-fashioned and quirky museum of Memphis history.

Eating

Memphians love their food and proclaim their city to be the **pork BBQ** capital of the world. In addition to checking the places listed below and scores of other corner joints in town, fans should head for the Memphis in May festival (see p.459), when hundreds of teams compete in the World Championship Barbecue Contest. **Soul food** fans, too, will be delighted at the choice and quality on offer. You'll have no problem finding somewhere good to eat **downtown**, from dives to sophisticated bistros (note that several of the Beale Street clubs also serve food), along **South Main**, or in the eclectic restaurants of **Cooper-Young**.

Arcade 540 S Main St ⓣ901/526–5757. Open since 1919, this landmark vintage diner – Elvis ate here! – in the South Main District was featured in Jim Jarmusch's movie *Mystery Train*, among many others. Come for big Southern breakfasts, pizzas and home cooking and heaps of atmosphere. Daily 8am–3pm.

Automatic Slim's Tonga Club 83 S Second St ⓣ901/525-7948. A hip Memphis institution in the heart of downtown, where you can eat modern Southern fusion food – sassafras chicken, for example – in a comfortably stylish space that stays open late. It's also good for a glass of wine and simple bar food.

Beignet Café 124 G.E. Patterson Ave ⓣ901/527-1551. A happy combo of comfort food (fried mac and cheese balls, shrimp and grits) and gourmet sandwiches (roast salmon BLT) with more than a touch of New Orleans flair (po-boys, beignets) at this cosy South Main restaurant. Closed Mon; brunch only on Sun.

The Beauty Shop 966 S Cooper Ave ⓣ901/272-7111. The witty fittings – glass brick partitions, mismatched crockery, pastel-coloured hairdryer chairs – in this renovated 1940s salon are perfectly in tune with Cooper-Young's funky vintage-store flair, while the eclectic fusion food (lunch, dinner and Sun brunch) is tasty and creative.

Blues City Café 138 Beale St ⓣ901/526-3637, ⓦwww.bluescitycafe.com. Popular Beale St BBQ joint, all retro chrome and formica, booths and banquettes, where bluesmen dine on ribs, catfish, skillet shrimp and tamales in an authentic, high-spirited atmosphere. Live music nightly in the adjoining *Band Box* bar. Daily 11am–3am (5am at weekends).

Four Way Grill 998 Mississippi Blvd ⓣ901/507-1519. Convenient for the Stax museum, this spotless little soul food joint – a favourite haunt of Martin Luther King Jr – dishes up unbeatable blue plate specials, including catfish, smothered chicken, green tomatoes and the like at low prices. Closed Mon.

Gus's Fried Chicken 310 S Front St ⓣ901/527-4877. This tiny place near the South Main Arts District has caught the attention of the national press for its delicious, crackling-crisp and spicy chicken.

Interstate Bar-B-Que 2265 S Third St ⓣ901/775-2304. Legendary, always buzzing BBQ restaurant, in a poor area south of downtown (leave I–55 at exit 7) on the way to the Delta. Try the sweetly smoky BBQ spaghetti. Closed Sun.

Java Cabana 2170 Young Ave ⓣ901/272-7210. Friendly, funky Cooper-Young coffeehouse, with vintage clothes and local art for sale plus poetry readings and live music. Closed Mon.

McEwan's 122 Monroe Ave ⓣ901/527-7085. At the heart of downtown, four blocks north of Beale, upscale *McEwan's* feels like a cosy neighbourhood bistro, serving inventive and delicious modern Southern fusion in a brick-walled room. The laidback adjoining bar is also a local favourite. Closed Sun.

Otherlands 641 S Cooper Ave ⓣ901/278-4994. Hip Midtown coffeehouse that's good for espresso, juices, breakfast and fresh sandwiches. The laidback crowd hangs out for hours in the spacious warren of rooms, with their jumble of tatty sofas, armchairs and even desks. Free wi-fi and occasional live music. Till 8pm Mon–Sat, 7pm Sun.

The Rendezvous General Washburn Alley, 52 S Second St ⓣ901/523-2746. Tucked away in a back alley, this touristy downtown pork BBQ joint – famed for its herby dry-rub ribs rather than sloppy "wet" BBQ with sauce – is colossal and always very crowded.

Soul Fish 562 S Cooper Ave ⓣ901/725-0722. This big, stylishly bare-bones Cooper-Young hotspot effortlessly combines trad and contemporary, dishing up phenomenal catfish and Southern sides (try the Cajun cabbage) to a mixed, friendly crowd.

Nightlife and entertainment

Memphis's thriving **music** scene can be tasted during the city's many **festivals**, especially **Memphis in May** (ⓦwww.memphisinmay.org), where big-name performances share space with BBQ contests, August's **Elvis Week** (ⓦwww.elvisweek.com), and the free **Memphis Music and Heritage festival**, staged downtown over Labor Day weekend. While the best **blues clubs** are beyond downtown and usually open at weekends only, at other times even touristy **Beale Street** has things to offer – especially *B.B. King's*, where B.B. himself appears once or twice a year, the Morgan Freeman-owned **Ground Zero**, or the lower-key **Rum Boogie Café** – though it can all get horribly crowded at weekends. At the other end of the spectrum, the city's vibrant alternative scene sees garage **bands** playing holes-in-the-wall; head **Midtown** for the hippest underground happenings and

Memphis gospel: Al Green's Church

Memphis has been renowned for its **gospel** music since the Thirties, when Rev Herbert Brewster wrote **Mahalia Jackson**'s *Move On Up a Little Higher*. Following a religious revelation, the consummate soul stylist **Al Green**, who achieved chart success for **Hi Records** with hits like *Let's Stay Together* and *Tired of Being Alone*, has since the early 1980s ministered at his own **Full Gospel Tabernacle**, at 787 Hale Rd in the leafy suburb of Whitehaven. Visitors are welcome at the 11am Sunday services; continue a mile south of Graceland, then turn west (phone ahead to check he's in town; ⓣ901/396-9192; ⓦwww.algreen.com). While they're very much church services rather than concerts, Green remains a charismatic performer and he does sing, backed by a smoking soul band. For more on Memphis music, see p.455.

check out the **Goner Records festival** of garage and rock music in September (ⓦwww.goner-records.com). And on a Sunday, the **Rev. Al Green's** gospel service is unmissable (see above).

The best source of **listings** is the free weekly *Memphis Flyer* (ⓦwww.memphisflyer.com). You could also simply ask the in-the-know crowd at **Shangri-La Records** (see p.452), Sun Studio, Stax or the **Center for Southern Folklore** (see p.454).

The Blue Worm 1405 Airways Blvd ⓣ901/327-7947, ⓦwww.freewebs.com/theblueworm. Enormous old live music venue where vintage bluesmen – don't miss the Fieldstones – play to an enthusiastic, local crowd at the weekend.

Buccaneer Lounge 1368 Monroe Ave ⓣ901/278-0909. This grungy midtown venue – with a kind of pirate-themed junk store ambience – is one of the city's best places to see local underground bands.

Earnestine and Hazel's 531 S Main St ⓣ901/523-9754, ⓦwww.earnestineandhazels.com. A legendary brothel-turned-juke joint, this spot was the haunt of everyone from Elvis to the Stax musicians. It's especially good late at night, when the Memphis juke box blasts and the famed burgers start sizzling.

Executive Inn 3222 Airways Blvd ⓣ901/332-3800. Old-fashioned lounge at a mom-and-pop motel out by the airport. Make sure to be here for Sunday nights to see drummer-singer Big Don Valentine, a true Memphis entertainer.

HiTone Café 1913 Poplar Ave ⓣ901/278-8663, ⓦwww.hitonememphis.com. From Memphis garage bands to indie rock to Elvis impersonators, this eclectic Midtown bar/club is always worth checking out.

Hollywood Disco 115 Vance St ⓣ901/528-9313, ⓦwww.hollywooddisco.com. Most definitely a disco and not a club, this old-school downtown hotspot – with a light-up dancefloor, dry ice, disco-balls, 40oz beers and a free limo service – is a Memphis institution, where hipsters of all persuasions get down after hours to the funkiest jams.

New Daisy Theater 330 Beale St ⓣ901/525-8981, ⓦwww.newdaisy.com. Restored movie theatre at the east end of Beale that attracts a young, pierced crowd for its punk, metal and rock.

Wild Bill's 1580 Vollintine Ave ⓣ901/726-5473. Juke joint three miles northeast of downtown where in-the-know tourists join locals at the long tables for live blues and soul on Fri & Sat. $10 cover.

Young Avenue Deli 2118 Young Ave ⓣ901/278-0034, ⓦwww.youngavenuedeli.com. Misleadingly named Cooper-Young favourite, featuring local and national blues, folk, punk and garage bands.

Nashville

Set on a bluff by the Cumberland River amid the gentle hills and farmlands of central Tennessee, sprawling **NASHVILLE** attracts millions of visitors each year. The majority come for the **country music**, whether at mainstream showcases like the **Country Music Hall of Fame** and the **Grand Ole Opry**, or in the funkier honky-tonks found not only downtown but also in Nashville's many neighbourhoods.

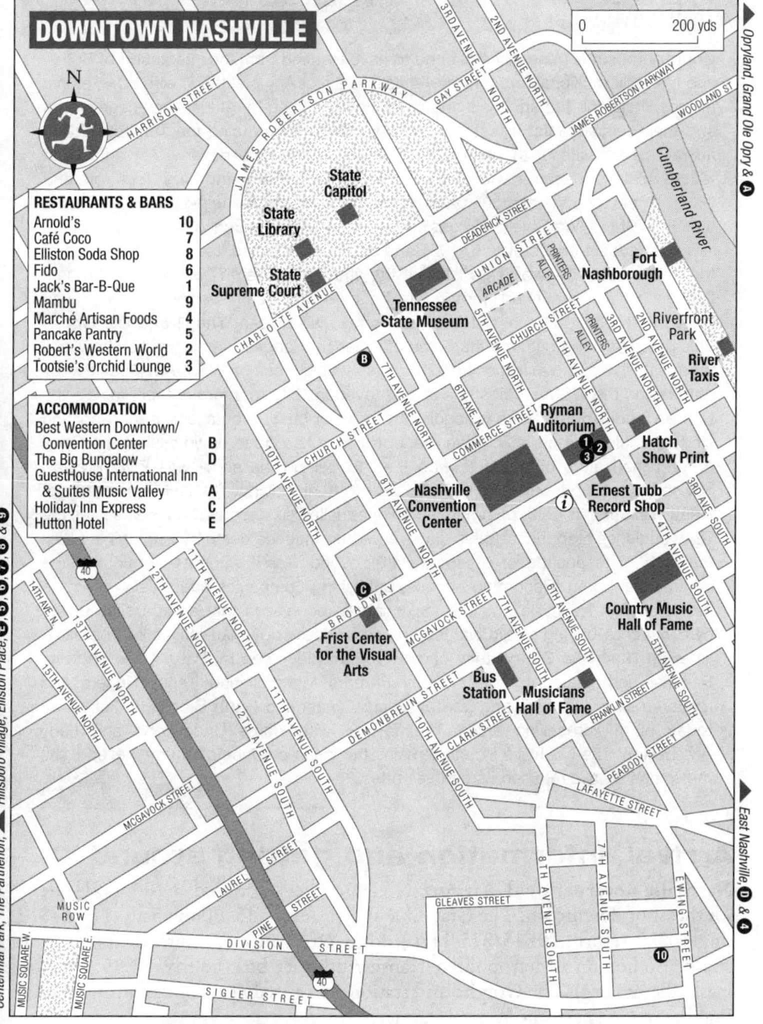

Behind the rhinestone glitter and showbiz exists a conservative, hard-working city; one that for the visitor is less immediately accessible than those other great music cities, Memphis and New Orleans. Nashville has been the leading settlement in middle Tennessee since **Fort Nashborough** was established in 1779, and state capital since 1843. It is now a major **financial** and **insurance** centre and a seriously **religious** place: there are more churches per head here than anywhere else in the nation. Rapid development since World War II has transformed the town into a maze-like conurbation, stretching out in all directions along the undulating roads known as **pikes**. While there are hip little neighbourhoods ripe for discovery, most visitors will enjoy themselves most by launching full-tilt into what "Nash Vegas" is best known for: the flash and fun of country music.

Nashville Country

Country music is generally reckoned to have resulted from the interaction of British and Irish folk music, as brought by Tennessee's first Anglo settlers, with other ethnic musics, including the spirituals and gospel hymns sung by African-American slaves and their descendants. It first acquired its current form during the 1920s, with the arrival in **Nashville** of thousands of migrants fleeing rural poverty. As radios and record players became widely available, the **recording industry** took off and Nashville became the obvious base for the musicians of the mid-South. Local radio station **WSM** – "We Shield Millions", the slogan of its insurance-company sponsor – first broadcast on October 5, 1925 and swiftly established itself as a champion of the country sound. Two years later, at the start of his *Barn Dance* show, compere George D. Hay announced "for the past hour we have been listening to music taken largely from Grand Opera, but from now on we will present **The Grand Ole Opry**". This piece of slang became the name of America's longest-running radio show, still broadcast live out to millions two to three nights per week on WSM-AM (650). Swiftly outgrowing the WSM studios, the show moved in 1943 to a former tabernacle – the **Ryman Auditorium**. There it acquired a make-or-break reputation; up-and-coming singers could only claim to have made it if they had gone down well at the Opry. Among thousands of hopefuls who tried to get on the show was Elvis Presley, advised by an Opry official in 1954 to stick to truck-driving. The first appearance of **Hank Williams**, in 1949, commanded an unequalled six encores. Four years later, the Opry audience responded to his drink- and drug-induced death by singing his *I Saw the Light*. The decade of prosperity after World War II witnessed country's first commercial boom. Recording studios, publishing companies and artists' agencies proliferated in Nashville and the major labels recognized that a large slice of the (white) record-buying public wanted something less edgy than rockabilly. The easy-listening **Nashville Sound** they came up with, pioneered by Patsy Cline and Jim Reeves, perpetuated by the likes of Barbara Mandrell and Kenny Rogers and rendered even further twang-free by Shania Twain and Garth Brooks, is kept alive today by million-selling artists like Taylor Swift, Carrie Underwood and Lady Antebellum. The Nashville Sound remains the clean-cut face of country, even if the music has always retained its earthier side.

Arrival, information and getting around

Nashville International Airport is eight miles – around a $25 **taxi** ride – southeast of downtown. The Gray Line shuttle (every 15–20min 5am–11pm; $12 single, $20 return; ⓣ615/275-1180) drops off at most downtown hotels; you could also hop on a Metropolitan Transit Authority **bus** (hourly; $1.35; ⓦwww.nashvillemta.org). The **Greyhound** station is in a seedy part of downtown at 200 Eighth Ave S. There's no Amtrak service.

In addition to its superb pre-planning website, the huge **visitor centre**, downtown at Fifth and Broadway (Mon–Sat 8am–5.30pm, Sun 10am–5pm; ⓣ615/259-4747, ⓦwww.visitmusiccity.com) has free wi-fi and features live music; the second branch, 150 4th Ave N (Mon–Fri 8am–5pm; ⓣ615/259-4730), is also good. If you like your country music laid on with lots of campy fun, hop aboard the "Big Pink Bus" and let the singing Jugg Sisters of **Nash-Trash Tours** dish the dirt on all your favourite stars (Mon–Sat, 90min; $29.50; reservations essential, as far in advance as possible; ⓣ615/226-7300, ⓦwww.nashtrash.com).

Accommodation

Nashville has plenty of big-name chain hotels all around town and budget **motels** along the interstates and along Briley Parkway in Music Valley. Note that rates increase during the CMA Music Festival in June (see p.465), and that the city's **hotel tax** is above 14 percent.

Best Western Downtown/Convention Center 711 Union St ⓣ615/242-4311 or 1-800/627-3297, ⓦbestwestern.com/downtownconventioncenter. Reasonably priced motel on the north side of downtown. Rates include continental breakfast. ❹

The Big Bungalow 618 Fatherland St ⓣ615/256-8375, ⓦwww.thebigbungalow.com. Friendly and progressive three-room B&B in the heart of funky East Nashville. Amenities include on-site massage and occasional live local music. ❹

GuestHouse International Inn & Suites Music Valley 2420 Music Valley Drive ⓣ615/885-4030, ⓦwww.guesthouseintl.com. Clean, comfortable and good-value option near the Grand Ole Opry. Rates include continental breakfast. ❸

Holiday Inn Express 920 Broadway ⓣ615/244-0150, ⓦwww.holidayinnexpress.com. A good downtown option with a pool and free breakfast buffet. ❺

Hutton Hotel 1808 West End Ave ⓣ615/340-93333, ⓦwww.huttonhotel.com. It's all about style at this hip, independent hotel, well placed for the restaurants and bars of the West End. ❻

The City

In addition to the venerable structures you'd expect in a state capital, such as the Capitol building itself, **downtown Nashville** boasts the city's premier attraction, the **Country Music Hall of Fame**. Further afield, **Music Row**, which centres on Demonbreun Street a mile southwest of downtown, forms the heart of Nashville's recording industry, with companies like Warner Bros., Mercury and Sony operating out of plush office blocks – there's little of interest to tourists, however. Beyond, the **West End** is a trendy area of students, hopeful musicians and yuppies, with a few tourist attractions. Nashville gets hipper across the river in gentrifying **East Nashville**, a left-leaning neighbourhood of aspiring musicians and young families where funky galleries share space with vintage stores and hip restaurants. Nine or so miles northeast of downtown along **Music Valley Drive**, you'll find not only the **Grand Ole Opry** – which still hosts its famed live shows – but also several old-fashioned country music-related sights and the colossal **Opryland** hotel resort.

The Country Music Hall of Fame

Everyone's first stop should be the superb **Country Music Hall of Fame**, 222 5th Ave S (daily 9am–5pm, closed Tues in Jan & Feb; $19.99, $29.99 including Studio B; ⓦwww.countrymusichalloffame.org). A wealth of paraphernalia from countless stars, including all manner of gowns, guitars and battered leather boots, not to mention Elvis's gold Cadillac – combine with video footage, photos and, of course, lots and lots of music, to create a hugely enjoyable account of the genre from its earliest days. Songwriters and musicians give regular live performances and masterclasses.

The Hall of Fame also offers short **bus tours** (10.30am–2.30pm) of RCA's legendary **Studio B** on Music Row. Between 1957 and 1977, forty gold records were cut here, including Dolly Parton's "Jolene", but it's probably most famous for a thirteen-year run of Elvis hits. Restored and rewired, it's open for business again, but only the most dedicated of fans will find any thrill in walking through these bare rooms.

Downtown Nashville

While most of **downtown Nashville**, spread along the Cumberland River, looks much like any other regional business centre, the "District", along **Broadway** between 2nd and 5th avenues, is prime country music territory, lined with honky-tonks, bars, restaurants and gift stores. In business since 1879, the unmissable **Hatch Show Print**, 316 Broadway (Mon–Fri 9am–5pm, Sat 10am–5pm;

Ⓦwww.hatchshowprint.com), prints and sells posters from the early days of country and rock 'n' roll, using the original blocks, and continues to produce new work. Opposite, another institution, **Ernest Tubb Record Shop** (Ⓦwww.etrecordshop.com), has been selling vintage and rare country, gospel and bluegrass music for more than sixty years and displays Grand Ole Opry costumes. Nearby, the original home of the Grand Ole Opry, the **Ryman Auditorium**, 116 5th Ave, was built as a religious revival house (daily 9am–4pm; $13; Ⓦwww.ryman.com). A church-like space, its wooden pews illuminated by stained glass, it beautifully evokes the heyday of traditional country, with small exhibits on everything from Johnny and June to Hatch Show Print. It's also a great venue for live gigs and musicals.

Downtown also has some non-music-related diversions. Housed in a gorgeous Art Deco building, the **Frist Center for the Visual Arts**, 919 Broadway (Mon–Wed & Sat 10am–5.30pm, Thurs & Fri 10am–9pm, Sun 1–5.30pm; $8.50; Ⓦwww.fristcenter.org), features everything from sculpture and photography to ancient art. At the other end of Broadway, **Riverfront Park** dips down to the **Cumberland River**. Immediately north, a replica of the wooden **Fort Nashborough** serves as a monument to the city's founders of 1779. A few blocks north again, **Tennessee State Museum**, 505 Deaderick St (Tues–Sat 10am–5pm, Sun 1–5pm; free; Ⓦwww.tnmuseum.org), is strongest on Civil War history, highlighting the hardships suffered by the soldiers on both sides, of whom 23,000 out of 77,000 died at Shiloh.

The West End and Fisk University

In 1897, Tennessee celebrated its Centennial Exposition in **Centennial Park**, two miles southwest of downtown at West End and 25th avenues. Nashville honoured its nickname as the "Athens of the South" by constructing a full-sized wood-and-plaster replica of the **Parthenon**. That proved so popular that it was replaced by a permanent structure in 1931, which is now home to a minor **museum** of nineteenth-century American art (Tues–Sat 9am–4.30pm; June–Aug also Sun 12.30–4.30pm; $6). The upper hall is dominated by a gilded 42ft replica of Phidias's statue of the goddess Athena – said to be the largest indoor statue in the Western hemisphere.

East of Centennial Park, across West End Avenue, the campus of **Vanderbilt University** abuts the colourful **Hillsboro Village**, a four-block radius sliced through by 21st Ave South and abounding in cafés, restaurants and funky vintage stores. Between downtown and the West End, **Fisk University** is one of the nation's oldest black colleges. The excellent **Van Vechten Gallery**, on campus at Jackson Street and 18th Avenue N (Tues–Sat 10am–5pm; donation), holds works by Picasso, Cézanne and O'Keeffe.

Eating

Though **downtown** does have some down-home southern joints, there are few good places to eat in **the District** itself. **East Nashville** is fast becoming a foodie destination, while the studenty **Hillsboro Village** and **Elliston Place** in the **West End** are the domain of funky, inexpensive cafés. Many live music venues (see opposite) also serve food.

 **Arnold's** 605 8th Ave S ⓣ615/256-4455. Classic canteen, south of downtown, where locals wait in line for tasty meat-and-threes (meat, three veggies and buttery cornbread). The delicious soul food includes fried chicken, ham or pork chops with sides for around $7. Get there early; weekday lunch only.

Café Coco 210 Louise Ave, West End ⓣ615/321-2620. Open 24hr, this offbeat, tumbledown old frat house near Elliston Place has a shady garden and lots of nooks where a mixed, laid-back crowd enjoy salads, paninis, pastas and desserts, with all-day breakfasts, coffee happy hours, alcoholic drinks and live music most nights. Free wi-fi.

Elliston Soda Shop 2111 Elliston Place, West End ⓣ615/327-1090. This vintage soda fountain – leatherette booths, counter seating, tabletop jukeboxes – not only looks great, but serves tasty retro food: big Southern breakfasts, meat-and-threes and home-made banana pie. Mon–Sat 7am–3pm.

Jack's Bar-B-Que 416 Broadway ⓣ615/254-5715. Across the street from Ernest Tubb's, friendly *Jack's* dishes up moist pork shoulder, ribs and mac and cheese, piled high on a Styrofoam plate.

Loveless Café 8400 Hwy-100, 20 miles south of town ⓣ615/646-9700. This vintage roadhouse is a local institution for its country cooking. The fried chicken is amazing and breakfast superb: hunks of salty ham with gravy, eggs, toast and fluffy, secret-recipe biscuits. Reservations recommended.

Mambu 1806 Hayes St, West End ⓣ615/329-1293. An unexpected little oasis in this upscale hotel-lined stretch: *Mambu* dishes up a changing menu of modern American and Mediterranean-influenced food in a lovely old house, which, decked with fairy lights and funky retro bric-a-brac, has a casual, friendly and relaxing atmosphere. Dinner only.

Marché Artisan Foods 1000 Main St, East Nashville ⓣ615/262-1111. Impeccably fresh European-style food in a modern, airy space with artisanal meats, cheeses and antipasti to go; the home-made brioche and croissants make brunch particularly satisfying. All day Mon–Fri, brunch only Sat & Sun. The same people run the more upscale and equally wonderful *Margot* bistro (ⓣ615/227-4668; dinner Tues–Sat; brunch Sun) around the corner at 1017 Woodland St.

Pancake Pantry 1796 21st Ave ⓣ615/383-9333. With more than 20 pancake choices, this cheery Hillsboro Village institution is a popular breakfast spot – expect to wait for a table at the weekend.

Nightlife and entertainment

The two obvious ways to experience **live country music** in Nashville are either to head for the cluster of **honky-tonks** in the District or to buy a ticket for a **Grand Ole Opry** show, which will feature a mix of stars and newcomers (Thurs–Sat, sometimes Tues; ⓦwww.opry.com). However, it's worth making the effort to catch up-and-coming or more specialized acts at places like the *Bluebird Café* and the *Station Inn*; look out, too, for special events, including bluegrass nights, at **Ryman Auditorium** (see opposite). In the West End, studenty little **Elliston Place** boasts an inordinate number of nightlife options for its size, while musician-packed **East Nashville** is building a strong local scene. With its tacky clubs and vacant storefronts, **Printers Alley**, north of Broadway, is best avoided. For **listings**, check the free weekly *Nashville Scene* (Thurs; ⓦwww.nashvillescene.com).

In June, the huge four-day **CMA Music Festival** is one of country music's major events, packed with big-name concerts and opportunities to meet the stars (ⓦwww.cmafest.com).

The Basement 1604 8th Ave S ⓣ615/254-8006, ⓦwww.thebasementnashville.com. Alt-country, rock and raw indie rule the roost in this tiny, rough-round-the-edges, smoke-free venue south of downtown.

Bluebird Café 4104 Hillsboro Rd ⓣ615/383-1461, ⓦwww.bluebirdcafe.com. Having launched the careers of superstars like Garth Brooks and Taylor Swift, this intimate café, six miles west of downtown in the Green Hills district, is *the* place to see the latest country artists. The first of the two nightly shows tends to be open mic or up-and-coming songwriters. Cover varies.

Douglas Corner Café 2106 8th Ave S ⓣ615/298-1688, ⓦwww.douglascorner.com. The *Bluebird's* main competitor has live music – Americana, rock, country, open mic – six nights a week, often with no cover.

Ernest Tubb Record Store Midnight Jamboree Texas Troubadour Theatre, 2414 Music Valley Drive ⓦwww.etrecordshop.com. Old-time radio show, recorded every Sat at 10pm, and broadcast from midnight to 1am, in a theatre adjoining the Music Valley branch of the Tubb store (the main store is on Broadway). Features promising newcomers as well as major Opry stars. Free.

Exit/In 2208 Elliston Place ⓣ615/321-3340, ⓦwww.exitin.com. Venerable venue for rock, reggae and country, with the occasional big name.

Family Wash 2038 Greenwood Ave, East Nashville ⓣ615/226-6700, ⓦwww.familywash.com. A friendly neighbourhood hub – part tavern, part café, part live music venue – with comfort food and eclectic unplugged music

(from bluegrass through to folk and jazz) on the menu. Tues–Sat only.
Robert's Western World 416 Broadway ⓣ615/244-9552, ⓦwww.robertswesternworld.com. Some of the best country music on Broadway, plus rockabilly and Western swing, in a lively honky-tonk that doubles as a cowboy boots store.
Station Inn 402 12th Ave S ⓣ615/255-3307, ⓦwww.stationinn.com. Long-standing bluegrass, swing and acoustic venue near Music Row. To reserve for Tuesday night's cult *Doyle and Debbie* show (ⓦdoyleanddebbie.com), about two washed-up country stars, call ⓣ615/887-5680. Shows 9pm nightly.
Tootsie's Orchid Lounge 422 Broadway ⓣ615/726-0463, ⓦwww.tootsies.net. Touristy, enjoyable downtown honky-tonk, with a raucous atmosphere and good, gutsy live performers.

South from Nashville

The change-resistant village of **LYNCHBURG**, 75 miles southeast of Nashville, is home to **Jack Daniel's Distillery** (daily 9am–4.30pm; free; ⓦwww.jackdaniels.com). Founded in 1866, this is the oldest registered distillery in the country. **Tours** lead you through the sour-mash whiskey-making process; ironically, you can't actually sample the stuff, as this is a dry county. Lynchburg itself is tiny, laid out around a neat town square with a red-brick courthouse and a number of old-fashioned stores. One enjoyable throwback is *Miss Mary Bobo's Boarding House*, behind a white picket fence on Main Street, which serves enormous **Southern lunches** (fried chicken, turnip greens and the like, along with delicious stewed apples laced with Jack Daniel's) at group tables in an 1805 home (closed Sun; reservations essential; ⓣ615/759-7394; cash only).

Eastern Tennessee

Until the creation of the Tennessee Valley Authority, the opening of **Great Smoky Mountains National Park** and the construction of the interstates, life had remained all but unchanged in the remote hills and valleys of **eastern Tennessee** since the arrival of the earliest pioneers. Now visitors flock here for the natural beauty; and as a result, especially in the autumn, the Smokies can get clogged with traffic. Most communities are small and either unbearably touristy or just bland. Of the two main cities – modern **Knoxville** and **Chattanooga**, both of which have benefited from considerable industrial growth thanks to cheap TVA power – only Chattanooga holds much appeal for tourists.

Smoky Mountain gateway towns

Most visitors who approach the Smokies from the north or west leave I-40 twenty miles east of Knoxville, or two hundred miles east of Nashville and sweep south on **Hwy-66** and **US-441** through the 25-mile procession of heavily commercialized **"gateway towns"** that leads to the national park. This is Tennessee's most conspicuously touristed area, with its endless motels and expensive novelty "attractions" geared toward vacationing families.

Pigeon Forge and Gatlinburg

For anyone who loves kitschy themed **attractions**, there's plenty to do on the double-lane highway that makes up **Pigeon Forge** – ranging from Dollywood (see opposite) through to "Jurassic Jungle" boat rides and the Black Bear Jamboree; anyone else should arrive with low expectations. If you want to stay overnight, you'll do better in **GATLINBURG**, squeezed amid the foothills of the Smokies another five miles south on US-441. As well as being a fraction more upmarket, it's more compact, with a walkable centre; that said, it's also bursting with

Dollywood

Born in 1946, one of twelve children, **Dolly Parton** grew up in several modest homes around Pigeon Forge, the most isolated of them two miles from the nearest neighbour and over four miles from the mailbox. As a child she sang every week on local radio, before leaving for Nashville on the day she finished at Sevier County High School. Her first success, duetting with Porter Wagoner, came to an acrimonious end in the early Seventies, but she scored a major country hit in 1976 with "Jolene". She then crossed over to a poppier sound, and, with her charismatic presence, was a natural in Hollywood films like *9 to 5* and *The Best Little Whorehouse in Texas*. Her songs have been acclaimed for their readiness to address issues like rural poverty, and as a woman, a singer, and a songwriter she has always been a strong-minded and inspirational figure. **Dollywood**, Parton's "homespun fun" theme park at 700 Dollywood Lane in Pigeon Forge (April–Dec; schedules vary; April–Oct $55.90, children 4–11 $44.70; cheaper in Nov & Dec; Ⓦwww.dollywood.com), blends ersatz mountain heritage with the glamour of its celebrity shareholder. One section showcases Appalachian **crafts**; a museum looks at Dolly herself in entertaining detail; music shows are constantly on the go and the thrill rides offer plenty for adrenaline-junkies and kiddies alike. A water park, **Dolly's Splash Country** (late May to mid-Sept; $45.80, children $40.25; Ⓦwww.dollywoodssplashcountry.com), is adjacent.

overpriced, gimmicky tourist attractions. A couple of chairlifts sweep you up the surrounding peaks, one of them to the year-round Ober Gatlinburg **ski resort** and **amusement park** (Ⓦwww.obergatlinburg.com).

Gatlinburg's three **visitor centres**, all on Parkway/US-441 (Ⓣ1-800/588-1817, Ⓦwww.gatlinburg.com), can provide discount coupons for the competing attractions. This being the closest town to the park, **accommodation** is relatively expensive. The good-value, old-fashioned *Sidney James Mountain Lodge*, slightly up from the mayhem at 610 Historic Nature Trail (Ⓣ1-800/876-6888, Ⓦwww.sidneyjames.com; ❸), has comfortable rooms, some of them creekside, and two pools. *Dolce Uva Wine Bar*, 463 Parkway/US-441 (Ⓣ865/277-7585; Wed–Sun), is one of the classiest places to eat, serving salads, wraps and pastas plus wine by the glass.

Townsend

A less frenetic approach to the Smokies, if you're driving in from the east, is to follow the Foothills Parkway and then take US-321 for the final seven miles to **TOWNSEND**, twelve miles west of Pigeon Forge. There's no town to speak of, just a peaceful strip where the motels are laidback and the air is clear. The *Highland Manor*, 7766 E Lamar Alexander Parkway (Ⓣ865/448-2211, Ⓦwww.highlandmanor.com; ❸), has nice grounds and a pool. You can **eat** fresh trout, tilapia with grits, or a gourmet sandwich at the nearby *Miss Lily's Café*, 1116 Carr's Creek Rd (Ⓣ865/448-9895).

Great Smoky Mountains National Park

The northern boundary of **GREAT SMOKY MOUNTAINS NATIONAL PARK**, which stretches for seventy miles along the Tennessee–North Carolina border (see also p.417), lies just two miles south of Gatlinburg on US-441. Don't expect immediate tranquillity, however: the roads, particularly in the autumn, can be lined almost bumper-to-bumper, and if you're not staying in Gatlinburg it's best to use the bypass rather than drive through the town.

Located within a day's drive of the major urban centres of the east coast and the Great Lakes – and of two-thirds of the entire US population – the Smokies attract

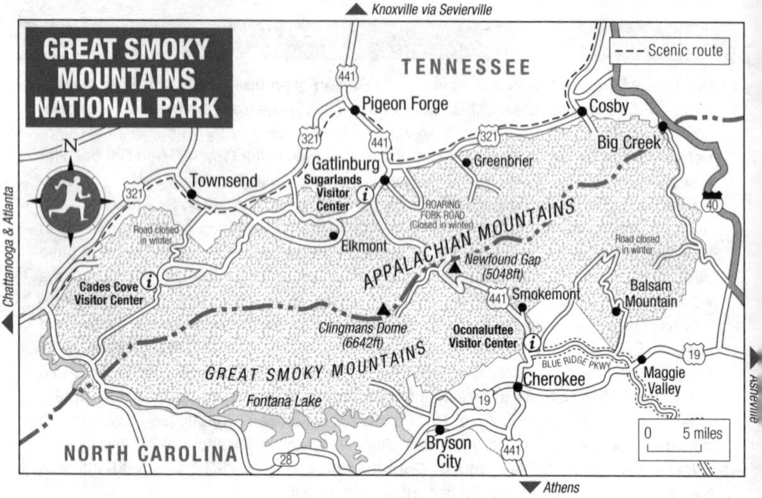

GREAT SMOKY MOUNTAINS NATIONAL PARK

over ten million visitors per year, more than twice as many as any other national park. These heavily contorted peaks are named for the **bluish haze** that hangs over them, made up of moisture and hydrocarbons released by the lush vegetation. Since the Sixties, however, **air pollution** has been adding sulphates to the mix, which has cut back visibility by thirty percent. Sixteen peaks rise above 6000ft, their steep elevation accounting for dramatic changes in climate. While late March to mid-May is a great time to visit for spring flowers, the **busiest periods** are midsummer (mid-June to mid-Aug), and, especially, October, when the hills are shrouded in a canopy of red, yellow and bronze. During June and July, rhododendrons blaze fiercely in the sometimes stifling summer heat. The best way to escape the crowds is to sample the park's eight hundred miles of **hiking** trails. Just inside the park on US-441, **Sugarlands Visitor Center** (daily: March 8am–5pm; April, May, Sept & Oct 8am–6pm; June–Aug 8am–7pm; Dec–Feb 8am–4.30pm; Ⓣ865/436-1200, Ⓦwww.nps.gov/grsm) has details of trails, driving tours and various ranger-led tours and activities. Many visitors, however, do no more than follow **US-441**, here known as the Newfound Gap Road, all the way to North Carolina. From the gap itself, ten miles along on the state line, a spur road to the right winds for seven more miles up to **Clingman's Dome**, at 6643ft the highest point in Tennessee. A spiral walkway on top affords a panoramic, though hazy, view of the mountains, rather spoiled by the fact that virtually all the mature balsam firs in the area have been killed off by insect infestation.

If you want to stay longer, the main focus of visitor activity is in the **Cades Cove** area, which can be reached either by branching west at Sugarlands along the scenic **Little River Road**, or directly from Townsend via **Rich Mountain Road** (closed in winter). The eleven-mile driving loop here, jam-packed with cars in summer and autumn, passes deserted barns, homesteads, mills and churches that stand as a reminder of the farmers who carved out a living from this wilderness, before they were forced to move out when National Park status was conferred in 1934. Halfway along, there's another **visitor centre** (daily: April–Aug 9am–7pm; March, Sept & Oct 9am–6pm; Nov & Feb 9am–5pm; Dec & Jan 9am–4.30pm). The loop is reserved for **cyclists** on Saturday and Wednesday mornings in summer; bikes can be rented at the *Cades Cove Campground* (Ⓣ865/448-9034). For more on **camping** in the Smokies, check Ⓦwww.recreation.gov.

Chattanooga

Few places are so identified with a single song as **CHATTANOOGA**, in the southeast corner of Tennessee. Though visitors expecting to see Tex Beneke's and Glenn Miller's "Chattanooga Choo-Choo" will be disappointed (the town is not even served by Amtrak), the place has a certain appeal, not least its beautiful location on a deep bend in the **Tennessee River**, walled in by forested plateaus on three sides. This setting led John Ross, of Scottish and Cherokee ancestry, to found a trading post here in 1815 and its strategic importance made it a prize during the Civil War.

The Town

The centrepiece of Chattanooga's twenty miles of reclaimed riverfront is **Ross's Landing** (the town's original name), a park at the bottom of Broad Street. Here the five-storey **Tennessee Aquarium** traces the aquatic life of the Mississippi from its Tennessee tributaries to the Gulf of Mexico (daily 10am–8pm; last admission 6pm; $24.95; Ⓦwww.tnaqua.org). They also offer **catamaran cruises** into the Tennessee River Gorge (2–3hr; $29), while more sedate *Southern Belle* **riverboat cruises** (from $13.50; Ⓦwww.chattanoogariverboat.com) leave from Pier 2.

Perched above the river, the **Bluff View Art District**, where High meets Second, comprises a handful of galleries, museums and cafés in lovely old buildings. The **Hunter Museum of American Art** is worth a look, with a changing roster of exhibitions covering photography, painting, sculpture, folk art and crafts from the nineteenth century to the present (Mon, Tues, Fri & Sat 10am–5pm, Wed & Sun noon–5pm, Thurs 10am–8pm; $9.95; Ⓦwww.huntermuseum.org). Keep walking to find grand century-old buildings in the lively **business district**, such as the Tivoli Theatre at 709 Broad St; as a general rule, however, the further you get from the river, the more run-down Chattanooga becomes. To ride a Chattanooga choo-choo, the authentic **steam trains** of the **Tennessee Valley Railroad** offer a variety of trips, from 55-minute local jaunts to a stunning six-mile ride, crossing the river, running through deep tunnels and turning round on a giant turntable (from $15; Ⓦwww.tvrail.com).

Lookout Mountain and Rock City

The name Chattanooga comes from a Creek word, meaning "rock rising to a point"; the rock in question, the 2215ft **Lookout Mountain** (Ⓦwww.lookoutmountain.com), looms six miles south of downtown. To reach the top, either drive the whole way along a poorly signed road or catch the world's steepest **incline railway**, which grinds its way up through a narrow gash in the forest from 3917 St Elmo Ave, near the foot of the mountain, tackling gradients of up to 72.7 percent (daily: April, May, Sept & Oct 9am–6pm; June–Aug 8.30am–9.30pm; Nov–March 10am–6pm; $14 return, combination tickets available, see below).

At the top, a short steep walk through **Point Park** brings you to **Point Lookout**, which commands a view of the city and the Tennessee River below. This forms part of the **Chickamauga and Chattanooga National Military Park**, covering several sites around the city and in nearby Chickamauga, Georgia, that witnessed fierce Civil War fighting in 1863. Among the many memorials in Point Park is the only **statue** in the country to show Union and Confederate soldiers shaking hands. For a true chunk of roadside Americana, join generations of road-trippers and "See Rock City" – the iconic sign, painted on roadside barns as far away as Georgia and Texas, was the result of an aggressive 1930s marketing campaign. **Rock City** (Ⓦwww.seerockcity.com) itself is basically a walking trail along the top of Lookout Mountain that offers not only the pleasure of scrambling through narrow gaps and swinging on rope bridges, but also the weird

Fairyland Caverns, carved into the rock and populated by grotesque characters that will delight kids and terrify adults. Inside the mountain itself, **Ruby Falls**, a 145ft waterfall, is heralded by a mock-medieval castle entrance; a treetop obstacle course ($32; Ⓦwww.rubyfallszip.com) provides adrenaline-fuelled thrills (Rock City $17.95; Ruby Falls $16.95; combination ticket $31.90, combination with Incline Railway $44.90).

Practicalities

Greyhound connections with Nashville and Atlanta arrive on Broad Street, downtown. The **visitor centre** (daily 8.30am–5.30pm; Ⓣ1-800/322-3344, Ⓦwww.chattanoogafun.com) is next to the aquarium at 2 Broad St. **Motels** line the interstates; more central is the *Bluff View Inn*, 412 E 2nd St (Ⓣ423/265-5033; 6x), which offers a variety of rooms – some with lovely views – spread across three restored houses in the Bluff View Art District. For creative New Orleans-influenced **cuisine** try the upmarket *Easy Bistro*, 203 Broad St (Ⓣ423/266-1121; dinner daily, brunch Sat & Sun), whose menu depends on the freshest produce and seafood. The touristy *Big River Grille & Brewing Works*, 222 Broad St (Ⓣ423/267-2739), is a cavernous brewpub and restaurant nearby.

Alabama

Just 250 miles from north to south, **ALABAMA** ranges from the fast-flowing rivers, waterfalls and lakes of the **Appalachian foothills** to the bayous and beaches of the **Gulf Coast**. Industry is concentrated in the **north**, around **Birmingham** and **Huntsville**, first home of the nation's space programme, while the farmlands of middle Alabama envelop **Montgomery**, the state capital. Away from the French-influenced coastal strip around the pretty little town of **Mobile**, fundamentalist Protestant attitudes have traditionally backed right-wing demagogues, such as **George Wallace**, the four-time state governor who received ten million votes in the 1968 presidential election, and, more recently Alabama Chief Justice **Roy Moore**, who in the summer of 2003 was suspended for not obeying a federal court order to remove a monument of the Ten Commandments from the rotunda of the state judicial building in Montgomery. While times have moved on since the epic **civil rights** struggles in Montgomery, Birmingham and **Selma** – monuments and civic literature celebrate the achievements of the campaigners, and even Wallace renounced his racist views – a visit to Alabama offers a crucial reminder of just how recently those bloody struggles were fought.

Northern Alabama

Northern Alabama, on the trailing edges of the Appalachians, is brightened by the mountain lakes, rivers and canyons of the **Tennessee River Valley**. The area's first white settlers were small farmers who had little in common with plantation owners further south, and attempted to dissociate from the Confederacy during the Civil War. Substantial mineral finds led to an industrial boom that peaked in the early Thirties.

In World War II the army consolidated **rocket and missile research** efforts in **HUNTSVILLE**, a hundred miles south of Nashville, just inside the Alabama border. Heading the project were **Dr Wernher von Braun** and 118 other German scientists, who came here after a token period of rehabilitation. Von Braun's contribution to the Nazi war effort is ignored by the city, which prefers to laud his later Space Age achievements, such as **Explorer I**, the nation's first satellite and the **Saturn V** rocket, which you can see at the giant **US Space and Rocket Centre**, five miles west of downtown off I-65 (daily 9am–5pm; $20, $25 with IMAX; Ⓦwww.spacecamp.com/museum).

Birmingham

The rapid transformation of farmland into **BIRMINGHAM** began in 1870, with speculators attracted not by the scenery, but what lay under it – a mixture of iron ore, limestone and coal, perfect for the manufacture of iron and steel. The expansion of heavy industry was finally brought to an abrupt halt by the Depression and today iron and steel production account for only a few thousand jobs.

During the **civil rights** era Birmingham was renowned for the brutality of its police force. An intense civil rights campaign in 1963 was a turning point, setting Birmingham on the road to smoother race relations, and after 1979, under five-term black mayor Richard Arrington, the city slowly began to turn itself around. Today, the **Civil Rights Institute** near downtown memorializes the city's turbulent history of race relations, but even a short stroll around town leaves the impression that much remains to be done.

Arrival, information and accommodation

Birmingham Airport is four miles from downtown; call Yellow Cabs (around $22) on Ⓣ205/252-1131. The Greyhound station lies on 19th Street N, between Sixth and Seventh avenues – a rough area – while **Amtrak** pulls in downtown at 1819 Morris Ave. The **visitor centre** is just off I-20/59 at 2200 Ninth Ave N (Mon–Fri 8.30am–5pm; Ⓣ205/458-8000, Ⓦwww.birminghamal.org). Birmingham has two free **listings** magazines: *The Birmingham Weekly* (Ⓦbirminghamweekly.com) and the *Black and White* (Ⓦwww.bwcitypaper.com). Although downtown **hotels** are pricier than the chains near the highway, they're more characterful and many offer special rates at the weekend, when downtown gets deserted.

Hampton Inn Downtown – Tutwiler 2021 Park Place N Ⓣ205/322-2100, Ⓦwww.thetutwilerhotel.com. Luxurious restored 1920s hotel near the Civil Rights Institute. Each room has a unique layout, with huge dark-wood framed windows. ❺

Hotel Highland at Five Points South 1023 20th St S Ⓣ205/933-9555, Ⓦwww.thehotelhighland.com. Modern boutique hotel within walking distance of Five Points South, offering luxury suites, free continental breakfast and complimentary airport shuttle. ❻

Redmont Hotel 2101 5th Ave N Ⓣ205/324-2101, Ⓦwww.theredmont.com. Fading historic hotel with a 1920s feel and affordable rooms a few blocks northeast of Amtrak. ❹

The City

Downtown Birmingham extends north from the railroad tracks at Morris Avenue to Tenth Avenue N, between 15th and 25th streets. The main interest is the powerful **Civil Rights Institute** and the **16th St Baptist Church** (see p.472). Call in too at the **Carver Theatre for the Performing Arts**, 1631 4th Ave N, where the **Alabama Jazz Hall of Fame** (Tues–Sat 10am–5pm; $2; Ⓦwww.jazzhall.com) is a fond memorial to legends ranging from boogie-woogie maestro Clarence "Pinetop" Smith to jazzy space cadet Sun Ra. **Five Points South**, its narrow streets

Civil rights in Birmingham

In the first half of 1963, civil rights leaders chose Birmingham as the target of "Project C" (for confrontation), aiming to force businesses to integrate lunch counters and employ more blacks. Despite threats from Police Chief **"Bull" Connor** that there would be "blood running down the streets of Birmingham", pickets, sit-ins and marches went forward, resulting in mass arrests. Over 2000 protesters flooded the jails; one was Dr Martin Luther King Jr, who wrote his *Letter from a Birmingham Jail* after being branded as an extremist by local white clergymen. Connor's use of high-pressure hoses, cattleprods and dogs against demonstrators acted as a potent catalyst of support. Pictures of snarling German shepherds sinking their teeth into the flesh of schoolkids were transmitted around the world, and led to an agreement between civil rights leaders and businesses that June. Success in Birmingham sparked demonstrations in 186 other cities, which culminated in the 1964 Civil Rights Act prohibiting racial segregation. The headquarters for the campaign, the **16th Street Baptist Church**, on the corner of Sixth Avenue, was the site of a sickening Klan bombing on September 15, 1963, which killed four young black girls attending a Bible class. Two of the three murderers were eventually jailed in 2000. Across the road, run-down Kelly Ingram Park, the site of many huge rallies during the Sixties has a Freedom Walk, lined with several sculptures of protestors, but is mainly populated by panhandlers and homeless men. Nearby, the admirable **Civil Rights Institute**, 520 16th St (Tues–Sat 10am–5pm, Sun 1–5pm; $12; Ⓦwww.bcri.org), is an affecting attempt to interpret the factors that led to such violence and racial hatred in the US. Exhibits re-create life in a segregated city, complete with a burned-out bus and heart-rending videos of bus boycotts and the March on Washington.

packed with bars and restaurants a mile or so south of the tracks on 20th Street and 11th Street S, is livelier than downtown thanks to the presence of the university.

Northwest of downtown, the Birmingham-Jefferson Civic Center, 22nd St and 10th Ave N, houses the **Alabama Sports Hall of Fame** (Mon–Sat 9am–5pm; $5; Ⓦwww.ashof.org), a tribute to greats like 1936 Olympic hero **Jesse Owens**, legendary Negro League pitcher **Le Roy "Satchel" Paige** and boxer **Joe Louis**. The nearby **Museum of Art**, 2000 Rev Abraham Woods, Jr Blvd (Tues–Sat 10am–5pm, Sun noon–5pm; free; Ⓦartsbma.org), is strong on American landscapes, decorative arts, African and African-American works. The chimney stacks of **Sloss Furnaces** (Tues–Sat 10am–4pm, Sun noon–4pm; free; Ⓦwww.slossfurnaces.com), which produced pig iron to feed the city's mills and foundries from 1882 until 1971, loom east of downtown, at 1st Avenue N and 32nd Street. Self-guided **tours** through the boilers, stoves and casting areas vividly highlight the harsh working conditions endured by the ex-slaves, prisoners and unskilled immigrants who laboured here.

Eating, drinking and nightlife

Birmingham is great for **BBQ** joints; for something a little more upmarket, head for **Five Points South**.

Bottega 2240 Highland Ave S Ⓣ205/939-1000. Elegant 1920s clothing store in Five Points South that houses one of the city's classiest restaurants, serving luscious, garlic-rich Italian cuisine with entrees at around $25; prices are lower in the adjoining café.

Bottle Tree Cafe 3719 3rd Ave S Ⓣ205/533-6288, Ⓦwww.thebottletree.com. Catch the hottest indie bands at this gallery /club/bar/café decked out with comfy retro couches. Closed Sun & Mon.

Chez Fonfon 2007 11th Ave S Ⓣ205/939-3211. Good French-influenced food in a romantic, Five Points South bistro.

Dreamland Barbecue 101 Tallapoosa St Ⓣ205/273-7427. Enjoy a big plate of ribs or pulled pork with sliced white bread and *Dreamland's* famous sauce. Lots of beers on tap, too, and occasional live music. It's part of a small local chain.

Garage Cafe 2304 10th Terrace S ⓣ205/332-3220, ⓦwww.garagecafe.us. A converted garage turned ephemera-strewn hip nightspot. Cash only.

South central Alabama

Southern Alabama – memorably depicted in Harper Lee's child's-eye view of racial conflict, *To Kill a Mockingbird* – still consists mostly of small, sleepy, God-fearing rural communities. Only state capital **Montgomery** achieves metropolitan status; it lies in the heart of the **Black Belt**, originally named for the rich loamy soil, but now usually taken to refer to the region's ethnic make-up. Cotton was the major earner until the boll weevil infestation of 1915; it has now been supplanted by soybeans, corn and peanuts.

Montgomery

MONTGOMERY's Black Belt location, 90 miles south of Birmingham and 160 west of Atlanta, made it a natural political centre for the plantation elite, leading

Civil rights in Montgomery

In the Fifties, Montgomery's **bus system** was a miniature model of segregated society – as was the norm in the South. The regulation ordering blacks to give up seats to whites came under repeated attack from black organizations, culminating in the call by the Women's Political Council for a mass boycott after seamstress **Rosa Parks** was arrested on December 1, 1955, for refusing to give up her seat, stating that she was simply too tired. Black workers were asked to walk to work, while black-owned taxis carried those who lived further away for the same 10¢ fare as buses. The protest attracted huge support and the Montgomery Improvement Association (MIA), set up to coordinate activities, elected the 26-year-old pastor **Dr Martin Luther King Jr** as its chief spokesperson. Meanwhile, the laid-off white bus drivers were employed as temporary police officials. Despite personal hardships, bomb attacks and jailings, protestors continued to boycott the buses for eleven months, until in November 1956 the US Supreme Court declared segregation on public transportation to be illegal.

King remained pastor at the small brick **Dexter Avenue King Memorial Baptist Church**, in the shadow of the capitol at 454 Dexter Ave, for a few years. The upstairs sanctuary, left much as it was during his ministry, contains his former pulpit, and you can also tour the Parsonage where King lived with his family until their move back to his hometown of Atlanta in 1960 (book tours via the website ⓦwww.dexterkingmemorial.org).One block away at the corner of Washington Avenue and Hull Street, in front of the Southern Poverty Law Center (which specializes in helping victims of racial attacks), the moving **Civil Rights Memorial**, designed by Maya Lin, consists of a cone-shaped black granite table. It's inscribed with a timeline of events structured around the deaths of forty martyrs murdered by white supremacists and police; the circle ends with the assassination of Dr King. You can run your hands through the cool water that pumps evenly across it, softly touching the names while being confronted with your reflection. The wall behind, also running with water, is engraved with the quotation employed so often by Dr King: "(We will not be satisfied) until justice rolls down like waters and righteousness like a mighty stream." Displays in the **Civil Rights Memorial Centre** (Mon–Fri 9am–4.30pm, Sat 10am–4pm; $2; ⓦwww.splcenter.org) tell the story of the campaigns. A few blocks west of the memorial, the **Rosa Parks Museum**, 252 Montgomery St (Mon–Fri 9am–5pm, Sat 9am–3pm; $6; ⓦmontgomery.troy.edu/rosaparks/museum/), commemorates "the mother of the civil rights movement". Exhibits cover her life, the bus boycott and other major civil rights figures.

to its adoption as state capital in 1846 and temporary capital of the Confederacy fifteen years later. Despite its monumental buildings, downtown is strangely quiet, many of its businesses having relocated to the suburbs. Most neighbourhoods are either exclusively white or totally black; an irony in the city that saw the first successful mass **civil rights** activity in 1955.

Arrival, information and accommodation

Dannelly Field Airport is fifteen miles from downtown on US-80; the Greyhound station is at 950 W South Blvd. The **visitor centre**, in the old train station at 300 Water St (Mon–Sat 9am–5pm, Sun noon–4pm; ⓣ334/262-0013, ⓦwww.visitingmontgomery.com), can provide a civil rights audio tour. As for accommodation, there are a couple of homey **B&Bs** in town, plus the usual **motels** alongside the highways; with a few exceptions, hotels downtown tend to be run-down.

Hampton Inn & Suites Downtown 100 Commerce St ⓣ334/265-1010, ⓦhamptoninnhilton.com. Clean, comfortable rooms and a substantial continental breakfast in a newish hotel in a historic building. ❹

Lattice Inn 1414 S Hull St ⓣ334/262-3388. Lovingly restored 1906 house offering relaxed B&B, a pool, hot tub and lovely gardens a mile or so southeast of downtown in the Cloverdale neighbourhood. ❹

Red Bluff Cottage 551 Clay St ⓣ334/264-0056, ⓦwww.redbluffcottage.com. Friendly B&B near the capitol, with comfortable rooms, a big porch and delicious food. ❺

The City

Although 1993 saw Alabama's state flag finally replace the Confederate flag over the **State Capitol** at the top of Dexter Avenue, downtown Montgomery still bears reminders of its white-supremacist past. Inside the Capitol (Mon–Fri 9am–5pm, Sat 9am–4pm; free), a bronze star marks the spot where Jefferson Davis was sworn in as president of the Confederacy on February 18, 1861 (see p.402) – a hundred years later Governor George Wallace stood here and proclaimed "Segregation forever!" As an "attraction" it sits uneasily with **Dr Martin Luther King's church**, the **Civil Rights Memorial** and the **Rosa Parks Museum** (see p.473).

On a different note, Montgomery was jammed with mourners in 1954 for the funeral of 29-year-old country star **Hank Williams**, who died of a heart attack on his way to a concert on New Year's Eve 1953. An Alabama native, Williams was as famous for his drink- and drug-fuelled lifestyle as he was for writing classics like "I'm So Lonesome I Could Cry". The **Hank Williams Memorial** dominates the Oakwood Cemetery Annex, 1304 Upper Wetumpka Rd, near downtown, and there's also the **Hank Williams Museum**, at 118 Commerce St (Mon–Fri 9am–4.30pm, Sat 10am–4pm, Sun 1–4pm; $8; ⓦwww.thehankwilliamsmuseum.com), complete with the 1952 Cadillac in which he made his final journey. Just off Woodmere Boulevard, ten miles southeast of the city, **Blount Cultural Park** is home to the acclaimed **Alabama Shakespeare Festival** (ⓦwww.asf.net) and the slick **Montgomery Museum of Fine Arts** (Tues, Wed, Fri & Sat 10am–5pm, Thurs 10am–9pm, Sun noon–5pm; free; ⓦwww.mmfa.org), which spans more than two hundred years of American art and has an impressive collection of European masters.

Eating and drinking

Downtown Montgomery has some good soul food, but is quiet at night. A few minutes' drive southeast, suburban **Cloverdale** offers a selection of fancier restaurants and, with its bars and jazz clubs, is the place for **nightlife**.

Derk's Filet and Vine 431 Cloverdale Rd ⓣ334/262-8463. Very popular neighbourhood deli/grocery/wine store serving hearty, varied lunches including grilled fish or potato casserole, deli sandwiches, wraps and salads.

Farmers' Market Café 315 N McDonough St ⓣ334/262-1970. Montgomery's best spot for Southern breakfasts and "meat-and-three" lunches, just off downtown, next to the busy marketplace. Mon–Fri 5.30am–2pm.

Lek's Railroad Thai 300b Water St ⓣ334/269-0708. Next to the visitor centre, this elegant downtown anomaly serves tasty pad Thai, sushi, noodles and soups, along with lots of veggie options. Closed Sun.

Martha's Place 458 Sayre St ⓣ334/263-9135. Superb Southern food, from collard greens to fried chicken, with a fine red velvet cake for dessert. Lunch only Mon–Fri.

Selma

The market town of **SELMA**, fifty miles west of Montgomery, became the focal point of the civil rights movement in the early Sixties. Black demonstrations, meetings and attempts to register to vote were repeatedly met by police violence, before the murder of a black protester by a state trooper prompted the historic **march from Selma to Montgomery**, led by, among others, **Rev Martin Luther King Jr**. On "Bloody Sunday", March 7, 1965, six hundred unarmed marchers set off across the steep incline of the imposing, narrow **Edmund Pettus Bridge**. As they went over the apex, a line of state troopers fired tear gas without warning, lashing out at the panic-stricken demonstrators with nightsticks and cattle prods. This violent confrontation, broadcast all over the world, is credited with having directly influenced the passage of the **Voting Rights Act** the following year. The full story is told in the **National Voting Rights Museum**, beside the bridge at 1012 Water Ave (Mon–Fri 9am–5pm, Sat 10am–3pm; $6; ⓦwww.nvrm.org), which is packed with personal testimony.

Broad Street is the town's main thoroughfare, running into the wide riverfront **Water Avenue**, with its frontier-style storefronts and garages.

Practicalities

Selma's **visitor welcome centre**, 132 Broad St (Mon–Fri 10am–4pm, Sat 11am–3pm; ⓣ1-800/45-SELMA, ⓦwww.selmaalabama.com), has details of a Martin Luther King Jr walking tour. Downtown is short on inexpensive **places to stay**. Jesse James slept at the historic *St James Hotel*, near the Pettus Bridge at 1200 Water Ave (ⓣ334/872-3234, ⓦwww.historichotels.org; ④), which has rooms with balconies and river views. The best of several soul-food **restaurants** is the *Downtowner*, 1114 Selma Ave (Mon–Fri 7am–2.30pm; ⓣ334/875-5933).

Alabama's Gulf Coast

Alabama's narrow **Gulf coastline** is blessed with white sand beaches, lapped by clear blue waters. The coast veers sharply inward to the faded port city of **Mobile**, which features antebellum buildings in a tree-shaded centre. Away from the water's edge, agriculture, dominated by pecans, peaches and watermelons, flourishes on the gently sloping coastal plain.

Mobile

MOBILE (pronounced "Mo-beel") traces its origins to a French community founded in 1702 by Jean-Baptiste Le Moyne, who went on to establish the cities of Biloxi and Nouvelle Orleans. These early white settlers brought with them **Mardi Gras**, which has been celebrated here since 1704, several years before New Orleans was even dreamed of. With its early-eighteenth-century Spanish and colonial-style buildings, parallels with New Orleans are everywhere, from wrought-iron balconies to French street names, but there the comparisons end. It's a pretty place – especially in spring, when ablaze with delicate azaleas, camellias and dogwoods – but there's little to actually do.

A good starting point is **Fort Condé**, 150 S Royal St (daily 8am–5pm; free), a reconstruction of the city's 1724 French fort. Dioramas cover local history; don't miss the atmospheric old photos of carnival, the old city and local African-American figures. North of the fort is the **Church Street Historic District**, full of pre-Civil War buildings. Head for the **Museum of Mobile**, 111 S Royal St (Tues–Sat 9am–5pm, Sun 1–5pm; $5; Ⓦwww.museumofmobile.com), which tells the story of the town from its earliest days and the **Carnival Museum**, 355 Government St (Mon, Wed, Fri & Sat 9am–4pm; $5; Ⓦwww.mobilecarnivalmuseum.com) with quirky exhibits covering carnival's arcane rituals. You can also tour the World War II battleship **USS Alabama** (daily: April–Sept 8am–6pm; Oct–March 8am–4pm; $12).

Practicalities

Downtown Mobile lies under the shadow of I-10. The **Greyhound** station is centrally located at 2545 Government St. Mobile's **visitor centre**, in Fort Condé (see above), has a number of discount coupons (daily 8am–5pm; Ⓣ251/208-7569, Ⓦwww.mobile.org). Cheap **motels** cluster at exit 3 of I-65; it's nicer to stay downtown. The *Malaga Inn*, made up of two townhouses at 359 Church St (Ⓣ251/438-4701, Ⓦwww.malagainn.com; ❹), has large rooms around a pretty courtyard.

Wintzell's Oyster House, 605 Dauphin St (Ⓣ251/432-4605), serves fresh **oysters**; to add water views to the mix, take Hwy-98 across the bridge, where the *Original Oyster House*, on the bay (Ⓣ251/626-2188) specializes in fried blue-crab claws. Back on Dauphin, at no. 661, there's a good Mexican restaurant, *Dauphin Street Taqueria*, in the *OK Bicycle Shop*, 661 Dauphin St, a laidback **pub**. Bands play at *Grand Central*, 256 Dauphin (Ⓦgrandcentraldauphin.com); *Soul Kitchen*, no. 219 (Ⓦwww.soulkitchenmobile.com), hosts rock, blues and reggae on the weekends. For **listings**, check the free weekly *Lagniappe* (Ⓦwww.lagniappemobile.com).

Mississippi

Before the Civil War, when cotton was king and slavery remained unchallenged, **MISSISSIPPI** was the nation's fifth wealthiest state. Since that war, it has consistently been the poorest, its dependence on cotton a handicap that leaves it victim to the vagaries of the commodities market. From Reconstruction onwards, it was also renowned as the greatest bastion of segregation in the South. It witnessed some of the most notorious incidents of the **civil rights** era, from the lynching of Chicago teenager Emmett Till in 1955 to the murder of three activists during the "Freedom Summer" of 1964, which exposed the intimate connections between the Ku Klux Klan and the state's law enforcement officers. Not until the Seventies did the church bombings and murders end.

The legalization of gambling in the 1990s stimulated the economy somewhat, with the hulking **casinos** of Biloxi and Tunica sucking considerable revenues across the state line from Tennessee and Alabama. The Gulf shoreline suffered appalling devastation from Hurricane Katrina in 2005, however, and though most of the casinos had re-opened, the coast was still undergoing reconstruction when hit by the BP oil spill in 2010. Mississippi's **poverty**, hidden down rural backroads – or clearly visible just across the railroad tracks – can be truly shocking for visitors, but the state has an undeniable pull, also – especially for **blues** fans, drawn to sleepy **Delta settlements** such as Alligator or Yazoo City. **Clarksdale** is heaven for music fans, with its juke joints, festivals and atmospheric accommodation lending it a vibrancy rare in these parts. The largest city is the capital, **Jackson**, but there's little reason to stop here when you could stay in historic river towns like **Vicksburg** and **Natchez** instead. In the north, literary **Oxford** has a lively college scene; Elvis fans should make a beeline for **Tupelo** and the King's humble birthhome.

The Delta

That Delta. Five thousand square miles, without any hill save the bumps of dirt the Indians made to stand on when the River overflowed.

William Faulkner, *Sanctuary*

"That Delta" is not in fact a delta at all; technically it's an alluvial flood plain, a couple of hundred miles short of the mouth of the Mississippi. The name stems from its resemblance to the fertile delta of the Nile (which also began at a city named Memphis); the extravagant meanderings of the river on its way to **Vicksburg** deposit enough rich topsoil to make this one of the world's finest cotton-producing regions.

The Delta is a land of scorching sun, parched earth, flooding creeks and thickets of bone-dry evergreens, best seen at dawn or dusk, when the glassy-smooth Mississippi reflects the sun and the foliage along the banks. Though the main thoroughfare south is the legendary **Hwy-61**, exploring is best on the backroads, characterized by huge, silent empty views interrupted only by roadside shacks, tiny churches and the sound of the blues.

Clarksdale

CLARKSDALE, the first significant town south of Memphis, has an unquestionable right to claim itself the **home of the blues**. Its phenomenal roll call of former residents – stretching from Son House, Muddy Waters, John Lee Hooker, Howlin' Wolf and Robert Johnson up to Ike Turner and Sam Cooke – is celebrated in the superb **Delta Blues Museum**, housed at 1 Blues Alley (March–Oct Mon–Sat 9am–5pm, Nov–Feb Mon–Sat 10am–5pm; $7; Ⓦwww.deltabluesmuseum.org) in the restored passenger depot of the Illinois Central Railroad, where many black Mississippians started their migration to the cities of the north.

Make time to drop into **Cat Head**, 252 Delta Ave (Mon–Sat 10am–5pm; Ⓦwww.cathead.biz), a hub for the local blues scene, selling folk art, DVDs and books, and producing CDs; they can advise on where to catch live blues. Also worth a look is the **Rock and Blues Museum**, 113 E 2nd St (Thurs & Sun 1–5pm, Fri, Sat & Mon 11am–5pm; $5; Ⓦwww.blues2rock.com) a treasure-trove of rare blues and rock memorabilia.

Clarksdale's music festivals are a major draw, among them the free **Sunflower River Blues and Gospel Festival** (Ⓦwww.sunflowerfest.org) in August, and the **Juke Joint festival** in April (Ⓦwww.jukejointfestival.com); you'll need to book accommodation months in advance.

The Delta blues

As recently as 1900, much of the Mississippi Delta remained an impenetrable **wilderness** of cypress and gum trees, roamed by panthers and bears and plagued with mosquitoes. Bit by bit land was cleared for cotton plantations, but, though the soil was fertile, white labourers could not be enticed to work in this godforsaken backcountry. After emancipation, the economy came to depend on black **share-croppers**, who would work a portion of the land on a white-owned plantation in return for a share (often pitifully small) of the eventual crop. As a rule, this lifestyle ensured long periods of poverty and debt interspersed with occasional windfalls; but in the Delta the returns tended to be greater than elsewhere, and blacks moved here from all over Mississippi. In 1903, **W.C. Handy**, often rather spuriously credited as "the Father of the Blues" (see p.453) but at that time the leader of a vaudeville orchestra, found himself waiting for a train in Tutwiler, 15 miles southeast of Clarksdale. At some point in the night, a ragged black man carrying a guitar sat down next to him and began to play what Handy called "the weirdest music I had ever heard". Using a pocketknife pressed against the guitar strings to accentuate his mournful vocal style, the man sang that he was "Goin' where the Southern cross the Dog'.

This was the **Delta blues**, characterized by the interplay between words and music, with the guitar aiming to parallel and complement the singing rather than simply provide a backing. Though a local, place-specific music – the "Southern" and the "Dog" were railroads that crossed a short way south at Moorhead – it did not simply appear from nowhere, but combined traditional African instrumental and vocal techniques with the "field hollers" chanted by slaves and the reels and jigs then at the basis of popular entertainment.

The blues started out as young people's music; the old folk liked the banjo, fife and drum, but the younger generation were crazy for the wild showmanship of bluesmen such as **Charley Patton**. Born in April 1891, Patton was the classic itinerant bluesman, moving from plantation to plantation and wife to wife, and playing Saturday-night dances with a repertoire that extended from rollicking dance pieces to documentary songs such as *High Water Everywhere*, about the bursting of the Mississippi levees in April 1927. Another seminal artist, the enigmatic **Robert Johnson** was rumoured to have sold his soul to the Devil in return for a few brief years of writing songs such as *Love in Vain* and *Stop Breakin' Down*. His *Crossroads Blues* spoke of being stranded at night in the chilling emptiness of the Delta; themes carried to metaphysical extremes in *Hellhound on My Trail* and *Me and the Devil Blues* – "you may bury my body down by the highway side/So my old evil spirit can catch a Greyhound bus and ride."

Both Patton and Johnson died in the 1930s. However, within a few years the Delta blues had been carried north to **Chicago** by men such as **Muddy Waters** and **Howlin' Wolf**, whose electrified urban blues was the most immediate ancestor of rock 'n' roll.

In addition to towns such as Clarksdale and Helena (in Arkansas, see p.484), blues enthusiasts may want to search out the following rural sites:

Stovall Plantation Stovall Road, 7 miles northwest of Clarksdale. Where tractor-driver Muddy Waters was first recorded; a few cabins remain, though Muddy's own is now in the Clarksdale blues museum.

Sonny Boy Williamson II's grave Outside Tutwiler, 13 miles southeast of Clarksdale.

Parchman Farm Junction US-49 W and Hwy-32. Mississippi State penitentiary, immortalized by former prisoner Bukka White.

Dockery Plantation Hwy-8, between Cleveland and Ruleville. One of Patton's few long-term bases, also home to Howlin' Wolf and Roebuck "Pops" Staples.

Charley Patton's grave New Jerusalem Church, Holly Ridge, off US-82 6 miles west of Indianola.

Robert Johnson's grave Payne Chapel, Quito, off Hwy-7, roughly 6 miles southwest of Greenwood, where he was poisoned.

Practicalities

Clarksdale has some quirky **places to stay**. Chief among them, two miles south on US-49, the *Shack Up Inn* (ⓣ662/624-8329, ⓦwww.shackupinn.com; ❸) on the former Hopson cotton plantation, offers six old sharecroppers' cabins with kitchenette and porch, along with ten slightly plusher rooms in the cotton gin. It's hard to imagine a more evocative place to stay in the Delta. Another is the iconic *Riverside Hotel*, 615 Sunflower Ave (ⓣ662/624-9163, ⓦwww.cathead.biz/riverside.html; ❷), which offers basic, clean rooms (shared bath) in the old hospital building where **Bessie Smith** died after a car crash in 1937. The owner, local legend Frank "Rat" Ratliff, the son of the original owner, will happily recount to you the "true history of the blues". More upmarket, the funky *Big Pink Guest House*, near the blues museum at 312 Yazoo Ave, offers huge, stylishly shabby-chic rooms in a converted icehouse (ⓣ601/431-4961, ⓦwww.bigpinkguesthouse.com; ❺).

As for **eating**, *Abe's*, 616 S State St, at the iconic blues crossroads of Hwy-61 and 49 (ⓣ662/624-9947), is a famed BBQ joint. The more upscale *Madidi*, 164 Delta Ave (ⓣ662/627-7770; closed Sun & Mon), offering a classy French take on Southern cuisine, is part-owned by Morgan Freeman, who also owns the nearby *Ground Zero Blues Club*, Blues Alley (ⓣ662/621-9009, ⓦwww.groundzerobluesclub.com). Otherwise, catching **live blues** takes a bit of luck, as long-standing juke joints find it hard to compete with the Tunica casinos. Most gigs are at weekends. Ask at the Blues Museum or Cat Head about upcoming events at authentic venues like the funky *Sarah's Kitchen*, Sunflower Ave (ⓣ662-627-3239), which serves soul food (Thurs–Sat lunchtime) as well as hosting young blues bands and *Red's* juke joint, Sunflower Ave and MLK Drive (ⓣ662/627-3166).

Delta towns

Some 70 miles south of Clarksdale, **GREENVILLE**, the largest town on the Delta and an important riverport, hosts the **Mississippi Delta Blues & Heritage Festival** (ⓦwww.deltablues.org) in mid-September. The *Greenville Inn*, 211 Walnut St (ⓣ662/332-6900; ❸) has clean, comfy rooms, while for a **meal**, stop by *Doe's Eat Place*, 502 Nelson St (ⓣ662/334-3315), a great spot in a sketchy neighbourhood which serves arguably the best down-home cooking in the Delta – go for steaks and tamales.

Every summer **INDIANOLA**, 23 miles east of Greenville on US-82, has a "Homecoming" celebration for its most famous son, **B.B. King**, who plays along with other local blues bands. The **B.B. King Blues Museum** 400 2nd St (Mon–Sat 10am–6pm, Sun 1–5pm; $10; ⓦwww.bbkingmuseum.org) tells a story of the blues by tracing King's sixty-year career from sharecropper in the cotton fields via Memphis to international success. The *Crown* serves delicious new Southern **cuisine**, including catfish, in a gallery at 12 Front St (ⓣ662/887-4522); friendly **juke joints** include King's *Club Ebony*, 404 Hannah Ave (ⓣ662/887-9915) and *308 Blues*, 308 Depot Ave (ⓣ662/887-7800, ⓦwww.milewis.com/blues). Sleepy **GREENWOOD**, on the shady Yazoo River forty miles east of Indianola, is the country's second largest cotton exchange after Memphis. It has an odd atmosphere nowadays, the huge, aseptic surrounds of the Viking kitchen goods corporation and its associated **Alluvian** resort creating a wealthy enclave entirely out of keeping with the rest of the Delta. Robert Johnson died here; you can find out more about him in the **Blues Heritage Museum,** 222 Howard St (ⓦwww.threedeuces.net). In the same building, *Veronica's* serves delicious home-baked pastries, while the *Blue Parrot Café* (ⓣ662/451-9430) is a friendly Latin **restaurant**. For yet another quirky Delta experience, try the Italian/Cajun cuisine at *Lusco's*, on the wrong side of the tracks at 722 Carrolton Ave (ⓣ662/453-5365; closed Sun & Mon). Each table in this eccentric old place is hidden away in a small booth, veiled by curtains – an arrangement dating from the days of Prohibition, when *Lusco's* was the haunt of cotton barons who came here to drink moonshine. You can **stay** in one of six renovated, appealingly dilapidated old Delta shacks at the *Tallahatchie Flats* (ⓣ662/453-1854; ⓦwww.tallahatchieflats.com; ❸), three miles north of town on County Road 518; porches look out over the river and nothing disturbs the peace but the whistle of the lonesome railroad. Greenwood hosts an annual **Cotton Capital Blues Festival**.

Northeastern Mississippi

Cutting its way south through Mississippi, I-55 acts as a boundary between the Delta and the luscious forests of the **northeast**. Dotted with small, old-fashioned towns, this corner of the state has a couple of highlights: the college town of **Oxford** and blue-collar **Tupelo**, birthplace of **John Lee Hooker** and, famously, **Elvis Presley**.

Oxford

Twelve thousand residents and 11,000 students enable **OXFORD**, an enclave of wealth in a predominantly poor region, to blend rural charm with a vibrant cultural life. Its central square is archetypal smalltown America, but the leafy streets have a vaguely European air – the town named itself after the English city as part of its (successful) campaign to persuade the **University of Mississippi**, known as Ole Miss, to locate its main campus here.

An appealing place today, in 1962 this idyllic little town was the site of one of the bitterest displays of racial hatred seen in Mississippi – events that Bob Dylan responded to with his contemptuous "Oxford Town". After eighteen months of legal and political wrangling, federal authorities ruled that **James Meredith** be allowed to enrol as the first black student at Ole Miss. The news that Meredith had been "sneaked" into college by federal troops sparked a riot that left three dead and 160 injured. Despite constant threats, Meredith graduated the following year, wearing a "NEVER" badge, the segregationist slogan of Governor Ross Barnett, upside down. A memorial commemorating his achievement was finally unveiled in September 2002, on the fortieth anniversary of his admission. From Ole Miss, a ten-minute walk through lush Bailey's Woods leads to secluded **Rowan Oak**, the former home of novelist **William Faulkner**, preserved as it was on the day he died in July 1962 (Tues–Sat 10am–4pm, Sun 1–4pm; $5). The fictional Deep South town of Jefferson in Yoknapatawpha County, where the Nobel Prize-winner set his major works, was based heavily on Oxford and its environs. The University holds a **Faulkner and Yoknapatawpha Conference** each July (ⓦfaulknersociety.com). East of the campus, in town, life revolves around the central **square**. Here you'll find Neilson's, the oldest department store in the south – little changed since 1897. You can pick up a piece of quirky Mississippi folk art in one of the gift stores, have a quick lunch or join students sipping espressos on the peaceful balcony of the splendid **Square Books**.

Practicalities

Oxford's **visitor centre** (Mon–Fri 8am–5pm, Sat 10am–4pm, Sun 1–4pm; ⓣ662/232-2367, ⓦwww.oxfordcvb.com), with lots of information on William Faulkner and local events, has offices in the courthouse and an adjoining cottage on the town square. **Accommodation** includes the *Downtown Oxford Inn*, just off the square at 400 N Lamar Blvd (Ⓣ662/234-3031, Ⓦwww.downtownoxfordinn.com; ❹). There's a great selection of places to **eat** on the square, from the huge plates of soul food at the *Ajax Diner* (Ⓣ662/232-8880; closed Sun), to the more sophisticated Southern cuisine at the buzzy *City Grocery* (Ⓣ662/232-8080; closed Sun), which has a balcony and upstairs bar. The friendly, funky little *Bottletree Bakery*, just off the square at 923 Van Buren Ave (Ⓣ662/236-5000; closed Mon), serves healthy breakfasts, scrumptious home-baked pastries – including their trademark humble pie – soups and sandwiches. Fifteen minutes' south of Oxford, in tiny **Taylor**, *Taylor's Grocery* (Ⓣ662/236-1716), on Hwy-338, is a rickety old shack dishing up amazing catfish to a raucous crowd. Oxford has the lively **nightlife** scene that you'd expect from a progressive college town. On the square, *Rooster's Blues* (Ⓦroostersblueshouse.com) offers live blues at the weekend, while *Proud Larry's*, nearby at 211 S Lamar Blvd (Ⓣ662/236-0050, Ⓦwww.proudlarrys.com) hosts indie, rock and Americana bands.

Tupelo

On January 8, 1935, **Elvis Presley** and his twin brother Jesse were born in **TUPELO**, an industrial town in northeastern Mississippi. Jesse died at birth, while Elvis grew up to be a truck driver. Their parents, Gladys and Vernon Presley, who lived in poor, white East Tupelo, struggled to survive. The financial strain was bad enough that Elvis' sharecropper father, in a desperate attempt to raise cash, resorted to forgery and was jailed for three years. Their home was repossessed and the family moved to Memphis in 1948.

Surprisingly, for most of the year Tupelo doesn't go in for Elvis overkill; Main Street is a long, placid stretch of nondescript buildings, with nary a gift shop to be seen. The Tupelo **CVB**, at 399 E Main St (Mon–Fri 8am–5pm; Ⓣ1-800/533-0611, Ⓦwww.tupelo.net), has details of the enjoyable three-day Elvis Festival, held in June, when the town fills with jumpsuited tribute artists. The actual **Elvis Presley Birthplace**, a little east of the CVB at 306 Elvis Presley Drive (May–Sept Mon–Sat 9am–5.30pm, Sun 1–5pm; Oct–April Mon–Sat 9am–5pm, Sun 1–5pm; house $4, museum $8, church $6, $12 for all three; Ⓦwww.elvispresleybirthplace.com), is fascinating. A two-room shotgun house, built for $150 in 1934, it's been furnished to look as it did when Elvis was born; it's an undeniably moving experience to stand in this tiny building that the Presley family struggled so hard to keep. Equally poignant is the adjacent family **church**, moved here from nearby; you sit in the pews as wraparound movie screens recreate the kind of barnstorming services that Elvis grew up with, ringing with speechifying, testifying and the emotional gospel music that the King always kept close to his heart. An unmissable small **museum** puts Elvis' early years in fascinating context, illustrating life in the prewar South with lots of old photos and memorabilia. **Motels** are concentrated along Gloster Street and McCullough Boulevard north of Main Street. The *Comfort Inn*, 1190 Gloster St (Ⓣ662/842-5100, Ⓦwww.comfortinn.com; ❸) is a good choice. Locals can be found chowing down on ribs and Southern plate lunches at *BBQ by Jim*, near the CVB at 203 Commerce St (Ⓣ662/840-8800; closed Sun).

South central Mississippi

South of the Delta, the rich woodlands and meadows of **central Mississippi** are heralded by steep loess bluffs, home to engaging historic towns such as **Vicksburg** and **Natchez**. Driving is a pleasure, especially along the unspoiled **Natchez Trace Parkway** – devoid of trucks, buildings and neon signs. State capital **Jackson**, meanwhile, holds little to take you away from the backroads.

Vicksburg

The historic port of **VICKSBURG** straddles a high bluff on a bend in the Mississippi, 44 miles west of Jackson. During the Civil War, its domination of the river halted Union shipping and led Abraham Lincoln to call Vicksburg the "key to the Confederacy". It was a crucial target for General Ulysses S. Grant, who eventually landed to the south in the spring of 1863, circled inland and attacked from the east. After a 47-day siege, the outnumbered Confederates surrendered on the Fourth of July – a holiday Vicksburg declined to celebrate for the next hundred years – and Lincoln was able to rejoice that "the Father of Waters again goes unvexed to the sea".

Entered via Clay Street (US-80) just northeast of town, **Vicksburg National Military Park** preserves the main Civil War battlefield (daily: summer 8am–7pm, rest of year 8am–5pm; $8/vehicle; ⓦwww.nps.gov/vick). A sixteen-mile loop drive through the rippling green hillsides traces every contour of the Union and Confederate trenches, punctuated by statues, refurbished cannon and over 1600 state-by-state monuments. Nearby, in the **Vicksburg National Cemetery**, 13,000 of the 17,000 Union graves are simply marked "Unknown". As the Mississippi has changed course since the 1860s, it's now the slender, canalized Yazoo River rather than the broad Mississippi that flows alongside the battlefield and most of downtown Vicksburg. The core of the city, a bare but attractive place of precipitous streets, steep terraces and wooded ravines, has changed little, however, despite the arrival of permanently moored riverfront **casinos**. Downtown is being restored to its original late-Victorian appearance, though most of its finest buildings were destroyed during the siege. The fascinating **Old Court House Museum**, 1008 Cherry St (summer Mon–Sat 8.30am–5pm, Sun 1.30–5pm; rest of year closes 4.30pm; $5; ⓦwww.oldcourthouse.org), covers the Civil War era in depth, even selling genuine minié balls (bullets), but also holds displays on Vicksburg's first settlement, Nogales, which was founded in 1796, as well as the postwar years. A small museum at the **Biedenharn Candy Company**, 1107 Washington St (Mon–Sat 9am–5pm, Sun 1.30–4.30pm; $3; ⓦwww.biedenharncoca-colamuseum.com), marks the spot where Coca-Cola was first bottled, with vivid displays on how it all came about.

Practicalities

Vicksburg has two major **visitor centres**, both just off I-20: the Mississippi Welcome Center, at exit 1A beside the river (daily 8am–6pm), and the town's own tourist information centre near exit 4, opposite the battlefield entrance on Clay Street (daily: summer 8am–5.30pm; winter 8am–5pm; ⓣ601/636-9421, ⓦwww.visitvicksburg.com).

The military park is the prime area for **motels**; the comfortable, mom-and-pop *Deluxe Inn*, at 2751 I-20 Frontage Rd (ⓣ1-800/546-4167; ❸) offers clean, quiet rooms. Among appealing **B&Bs** is *Anchuca*, housed in the town's first colonnaded mansion, at 1010 First East St (ⓣ1-888/686-0111, ⓦwww.anchucamansion.com; ❻); it boasts a pool and a very good **restaurant** with outdoor seating. Other eating options include the superb all-you-can-eat "round table" lunches of fried chicken and other Southern delicacies at *Walnut Hills*, 1214 Adams St (ⓣ601/638-4910; Mon–Sat 9am–11pm, Sun 11am–2pm); they also do à la carte. *Hwy 61 Coffeehouse*, in the **Attic** folk art gallery downtown at 1101 Washington St (ⓣ601/638-9221; closed Sun) is an arty little place for espresso.

Natchez

Sixty miles south of Vicksburg – at the end of the pretty Natchez Trace Parkway, the old Native American path that ran from here to Nashville – the river town of **NATCHEZ** is the oldest permanent settlement on the Mississippi River. By the time it first flew the Stars and Stripes in 1798, it had already been home to the Natchez people (see below) and their predecessors, as well as French, British and Spanish colonists. Unlike its great rival, Vicksburg, Natchez was spared significant damage during the Civil War, ensuring that its abundant Greek Revival antebellum mansions remained intact, complete with meticulously maintained gardens. Interspersed among them are countless simpler but similarly attractive white clapboard homes, set along broad leafy avenues of majestic oaks, making Natchez one of the prettiest towns in the South. **Horse and carriage** tours (see below) explore downtown, while a number of individual mansions are open for tours. Fans of HBO's *True Blood* will recognize the elaborate, octagonal **Longwood**, 140 Lower Woodville Rd, with its huge dome, snow-white arches and columns, as the home of the vampire king of Mississippi. The mansions can also be seen during the twice-yearly **Natchez Pilgrimage** (March & Oct; $10/house or $24 for 3; ⓣ601/446-6631, ⓦwww.natchezpilgrimage.com), on tours led by hapless women trussed up in massive hoopskirts.

While Natchez proper perches well above the river, a small stretch of riverfront at the foot of the bluff constitutes **Natchez Under-the-Hill**. Once known as the "Sodom of the Mississippi", it now houses a handful of bars and restaurants, plus the 24-hour *Isle of Capri* riverboat **casino**. Natchez takes its name from the Natchez Indians, regarded as one of the most significant flowerings of the widespread Mississippian culture. They survived here in strength until 1729, when they rose en masse against French plans to replace one of their villages with a tobacco plantation. Joined by African slaves, they killed 250 colonists before the French and their Choctaw allies crushed the rebellion. The former Natchez spiritual centre known as the **Grand Village**, home to a leader revered as the "Great Sun", can be explored at 400 Jefferson Davis Blvd (Mon–Sat 9am–5pm, Sun 1.30–5pm; free; ⓦwww.nps.gov). It's an atmospheric place, holding an informative visitor centre and some reconstructed dwellings as well as a large park-like area with an imposing ceremonial mound at either end. Another Natchez site, the much larger **Emerald Mound**, stands just off the Natchez Trace northeast of town (free 24hr access). Natchez's rich **African-American** heritage – Richard Wright, the author of *Native Son*, was born nearby and lived in the town as a boy – is chronicled with a small display at the **Forks of the Road monument**, a mile east of downtown on Liberty Road at St Catherine (ⓦwww.forksoftheroads.net), on the site of the second largest slave market in the South.

Practicalities

Natchez's vast **Visitor Reception Center**, overlooking the river at 640 S Canal St by the Mississippi River bridge (Mon–Sat 8.30am–5pm, Sun 9am–4pm; ⓣ601/446-6345, ⓦwww.visitnatchez.com), is the starting point for various **trolley and bus tours** along with **carriage rides** (around $15).

This is **B&B territory**. The *Stone House Music Room B&B*, 804 Washington St (ⓣ601/445-7466, ⓦwww.josephstonehouse.com; ❺), offers something a little different from the other grand mansions; owned by a professional musician who gives free piano recitals to guests, it also features a billiards room and a store selling antique maps and prints. Of the hotels, the historic *Natchez Eola*, downtown at 110 N Pearl St (ⓣ601/445-6000, ⓦwww.natchezeola.com; ❺), has a certain faded charm. For **food**, *Pig Out Inn*, 116 S Canal St (ⓣ601/422-8050) is *the* place for pulled pork BBQ; *Fat Mama's Tamales*, 500 S Canal St (ⓣ601/442-4548), offers tamales and Margaritas; and *Cock of the Walk* is a touristy, fun catfish restaurant on the bluff at 200 N Broadway (ⓣ601/446-8920). The *Marketplace Café*, 613 Main

St (☎601/304-9399; closed Mon), serves good breakfasts, lunches and espressos. Every April, the **Natchez Bluff Blues Fest** celebrates an eclectic mix of regional blues styles.

Arkansas

Historically, Arkansas belongs firmly to the South. It sided with the Confederacy during the Civil War and its capital, Little Rock, was, in 1957, one of the most notorious flashpoints in the struggle for **civil rights**. Geographically, however, it marks the beginning of the Great Plains. Unlike the Southern states on the east side of the Mississippi River, Arkansas (the correct pronunciation, following a state law from 1881, is "Arkansaw") remained sparsely populated until the late nineteenth century. Westward expansion was blocked by the existence of the Indian Territory in what's now Oklahoma, and not until the railroads opened up the forested interior during the 1880s did settlers stray in any numbers from their riverside villages. Only once the Depression and mechanization had forced thousands of farmers to leave their fields did Arkansas begin to develop any significant industrial base. In 1992 local boy **Bill Clinton's** accession to the presidency catapulted Arkansas to national prominence.

Though Arkansas encompasses the **Mississippi Delta** in the east, oil-rich timber lands in the south, and the sweeping **Ouachita** ("Wash-ih-taw") **Mountains** in the west, the cragged and charismatic **Ozark Mountains** in the north are its most scenic asset, abounding with parks, lakes, rivers and streams, and a couple of alternative little towns that make welcoming places to stay.

Eastern Arkansas

What's surprising about the eastern Arkansas delta lands is that they are far from totally flat: **Crowley's Ridge**, a narrow arc of windblown loess hills, breaks up the uniform smoothness, stretching 150 miles from southern Missouri to the sleepy river town of **Helena**, which is an important stop for **Delta blues** enthusiasts.

Helena

The small Mississippi port of **HELENA**, roughly sixty miles south of Memphis, was once the shipping point for Arkansas' cotton crop, when Mark Twain described it as occupying "one of the prettiest situations on the river". A compact **historic district** bordered by Holly, College and Perry streets reflects that brief period of prosperity, before the arrival of the railroad left most of the river towns obsolete, but nowadays it feels the strain of living in the shadow of the enormous casinos across the river. Most activity takes place along run-down **Cherry Street** on the levee.

In 1941, the town was the birthplace of the celebrated **King Biscuit Time Show**, broadcast on radio station KFFA (1360 AM). The first radio show in the nation to broadcast live Delta blues, it featured performances from legends like boogie pianist Pinetop Perkins and harmonica great **Sonny Boy Williamson II**

("Rice" Miller) – the local boy who featured Helena in intimate detail in many of his (usually extemporized) recordings. With a huge influence that belies its tiny size – musicians from B.B. King to Levon Helm quote it as a major inspiration – the show is the longest running in history, having been on air continuously ever since and hosted since 1951 by living legend "Sunshine" Sonny Payne. Broadcasts (Mon–Fri 12.15–12.45pm; Ⓦwww.kingbiscuittime.com) are recorded from the foyer of the excellent **Delta Cultural Center**, 141 Cherry St (Tues–Sat 9am–5pm; Ⓦwww.deltaculturalcenter.com); observers are welcome. If you miss the show, make sure to stop by the centre's **music exhibit**. Blues fans can also buy a thrilling assortment of records at **Bubba Sullivan's Blues Corner**, in the mall at 105 Cherry St (Ⓣ870/338-3501). Bubba is a mine of information on local music, not least the town's superb **Arkansas Blues and Heritage Festival** (Ⓦwww.bluesandheritagefest.com), which held every autumn, attracts more than 60,000 visitors annually for its big-name blues, acoustic and gospel. The **Delta Cultural Center** has another site a block south of the visitor centre, in a restored train depot at 95 Missouri St (Tues–Sat 9am–5pm; free). Exhibits cover all aspects of the region's history, from the first settlers of this soggy frontier to contemporary racism, with, of course, lots of good stuff about local musical heritage.

Practicalities

The 1904 *Edwardian Inn*, 317 Biscoe St, north of the Mississippi Bridge (Ⓣ870/338-9155, Ⓦwww.edwardianinn.com; ❹), is an opulent, reasonably priced **B&B** with large oak-panelled rooms, slightly marred by its views over a chemical plant. On Cherry Street, *Granny Dee's*, no. 426 (Ⓣ870/817-0200), serves Southern **food**, while *Roadkill Grill*, no. 523 (Ⓣ870/995-2881) is good for burgers, BBQ and enchiladas. For **live blues** check out *Sonny Boy's Music Hall*, no. 301 (Ⓣ870/338-3501), or *Fonzie's*, no. 400 (Ⓣ870/817-7736).

Central Arkansas

Little Rock sits in the centre of the state, just fifty miles west of the quirky spa town of **Hot Springs**, which marks the eastern gateway to the remote **Ouachita Mountains**. The rippling farmland of the **Arkansas River Valley** is sandwiched by the Ouachita crests on the south side and the craggy ridges of the Ozarks to the north. Mining and logging communities dot the east–west roads in the hill country, while the fastest growing region in the state is the I-540 corridor between the college town of **Fayetteville** and Wal-Mart's company town, **Bentonville**.

Little Rock

The geographical, political and financial centre of Arkansas, **LITTLE ROCK** is at the meeting point of the state's two major regions, the northwestern hills and the eastern Delta. Site of one of the key flashpoints of the civil rights era (see p.486), the town today has a relaxed, open feel and maintains a certain cachet from the election of William J. Clinton to the presidency in 1992. Bill is celebrated in the dazzling **William J. Clinton Presidential Library and Museum**, an elevated, glass-and-metal building glinting above the Arkansas River east of downtown at 1200 President Clinton Ave (Mon–Sat 9am–5pm, Sun 1–5pm; $7; Ⓦwww.clintonlibrary.gov). Spearheading the revitalization of a once-depressed district of abandoned warehouses, the environmentally friendly structure is now part of a campus of federally certified "green" buildings.

Confrontation at Central High

In 1957, Little Rock unexpectedly became the battleground in the first major conflict between state and federal government over **race relations**. At the time, the city was generally viewed as progressive by Southern standards. All parks, libraries and buses were integrated, a relatively high thirty percent of blacks were on the electoral register and there were black police officers. However, when the Little Rock School Board announced its decision to phase in **desegregation** gradually – the Supreme Court having declared segregation of schools to be unconstitutional – James Johnson, a candidate for governor, started a campaign opposing interracial education. Johnson's rhetoric began to win him support, and the incumbent governor, **Orval Faubus**, who had previously shown no interest in the issue, jumped on the bandwagon himself.

The first nine black students were due to enter **Central High School** that September. The day before school opened, Faubus, "in the interest of safety", reversed his decision to let blacks enrol, only to be overruled by the federal court. He ordered state troopers to bar the black students anyway; soldiers with bayonets forced Elizabeth Eckford, one of the nine, from the school entrance into a seething crowd, from which she had to jump on a bus to escape. As legal battles raged during the day, at night blacks were subject to violent attacks by white gangs. Three weeks later, President Eisenhower reluctantly brought in the 101st Airborne Division, and, amid violent demonstrations, the nine entered the school. That year, they experienced intense intimidation; when one retaliated, she was expelled. The graduation of James Green, the oldest, seemed to put an end to the affair, but Faubus, up for re-election, renewed his political posturing by closing down all Little Rock's public schools for the 1958–59 academic year – and thereby increased his majority. Today Central High School – an enormous brown, crescent-shaped structure at 1500 S Park Ave, bearing no little resemblance to a fortress – is on the National Register of Historic Places and has been designated as a National Park site. Across the street, at 2125 Daisy L. Gatson Bates Drive, the **Central High Visitor Centre** (daily 9am–4.30pm, Sun 1–4.30pm; free; Ⓦwww.nps.gov/chsc/), on the spot from which reporters filed stories on the only public payphone in the neighbourhood, has a good exhibition about the crisis.

The library forms an anchor for the vibrant **River Market District**, with its splash of restaurants and bars, farmers' market and eclectic food hall. At 610 President Clinton Ave, the **museum store** (Ⓦwww.clintonmuseumstore.com) sells marvellous gifts – from Socks the cat mousepads to compilation CDs of the former president's favourite music. The **Museum of Discovery**, 500 President Clinton Ave, is a hit with kids (Mon–Sat 9am–5pm, Sun 1–5pm; $8; Ⓦwww.amod.org), while, along the river, **Riverfront Park** runs for several blocks. A commemorative sign here marks the "little rock" for which the city is named (not particularly striking, but then the name gives that away). Surrounded by smooth lawns and shaded by evergreens, the **Old State House Museum** (Mon–Sat 9am–5pm, Sun 1–5pm; free; Ⓦwww.oldstatehouse.com), in the old capitol building at 300 W Markham St, backs onto the river. The displays – everything from Civil War battle flags to African-American quilts – do an admirable job of covering Arkansas history. The **Historic Arkansas Museum**, 200 E 3rd St (Mon–Sat 9am–5pm, Sun 1–5pm; $2.50; Ⓦwww.historicarkansas.org), a living museum of frontier life, includes the 1827 Hinderliter Grog Shop, Little Rock's oldest standing building. In MacArthur Park, the elegant **Arkansas Arts Centre** (Mon–Sat 10am–5pm, Sun 11am–5pm; free; Ⓦwww.arkarts.com), has high-profile rotating shows, drawings dating from the Renaissance and a nice selection of contemporary crafts.

Practicalities

Greyhound arrives at 118 E Washington Ave in North Little Rock, across the river. **Amtrak** has a more central location at Markham and Victory streets. The **visitor centre** is at 615 E Capitol Ave (Mon–Fri 8.30am–4.30pm; Ⓣ501/376-4781, Ⓦwww.littlerock.com).

Bill Clinton was a regular visitor at the luxurious *Rosemont B&B*, 515 W 15th St (Ⓣ501/374-7456, Ⓦwww.rosemontoflittlerock.com; ❹), which offers home comforts; the *Comfort Inn & Suites Downtown*, near the Clinton Center at 707 I-30 (Ⓣ501/687-7700; Ⓦwww.comfortinnlittlerock.com; ❹) has large rooms, a pool and a hearty free breakfast. In the River Market District, the bustling market hall **food court** (Mon–Sat 7am–6pm) provides a wealth of places to **eat**, with stalls dishing up organic soups, Middle Eastern salads, BBQ, pad Thai, artisan breads and coffee. Unpretentious *Doe's Eat Place*, 1023 W Markham St (Ⓣ501/376-1195), a branch of the Greenville, Mississippi, restaurant (see p.479), serves excellent steak and tamales; it's a longtime favourite of Clinton and still a hotspot for hungry politicos. The fanciest restaurant in town, though, is *Brave New Restaurant*, just outside downtown at 2300 Cottondale Lane (Ⓣ501/663-2677), which serves delicate combinations of fresh meats and seafood on a deck overlooking the river. *Rumba Revolution*, in the River Market District at 300 President Clinton Ave (Ⓣ501/823-0090, Ⓦwww.rumbarevolution.com) is an eclectic **music** venue with a Mexi-Cuban restaurant attached. There's more music at *Vino's*, 923 W 7th St (Ⓣ501/375-8466, Ⓦwww.vinosbrewpub.com), a friendly brewpub/pizza joint with live indie and rock after dark. For **listings**, check the free weekly *Arkansas Times* (Ⓦwww.arktimes.com).

Hot Springs

Fifty miles southwest of Little Rock, the low-key, historic and somewhat surreal spa town of **HOT SPRINGS** nestles in the forested Zig Zag Mountains on the eastern flank of the Ouachitas. Its **thermal waters** have attracted visitors since Native Americans used the area as a neutral zone to settle disputes. Early settlers fashioned a crude resort out of the wilderness, and after the railroads arrived in 1875 it became a European-style spa; its hot waters are said to cure rheumatism, arthritis, kidney disease and liver problems. The resort reached its glittering heyday during the Twenties and Thirties, when the mayor reputedly ran a gambling syndicate worth $30 million per annum, and players included Al Capone and Bugsy Siegel. Movie stars and politicians, aristocrats and prizefighters flocked to "quaff the elixir", and Hot Springs became *the* place to see and be seen. The resort's popularity waned when new cures appeared during the Fifties; today its faded grandeur and small-town sleepiness give it a distinctive appeal.

Downtown Hot Springs threads through a looping wooded valley, barely wide enough to accommodate the main thoroughfare of Central Avenue. Eight magnificent buildings behind a lush display of magnolia trees, elms and hedgerows make up the splendid **Bathhouse Row**. Between 1915 and 1962, the grandest of them all was the **Fordyce Bathhouse**, at the 300 block of Central, which reopened in 1989 as the **visitor centre** for **Hot Springs National Park** – the only national park to fall within city limits. Apart from the Buckstaff (see below), this is the only bathhouse you can actually enter: the interior, restored to its former magnificence, is an atmospheric mixture of the elegant and the obsolete. The heavy use of veined Italian marble, mosaic-tile floors and stained glass lend it a decadent feel, while the gruesome hydrotherapy and electro-therapy equipment, including an electric shock massager, seem impossibly brutish (Feb–Dec daily 9am–5pm; free; Ⓦwww.nps.gov/hosp).

It's still possible to take a "**bath**" – an hour-long process involving brisk rubdowns, hot packs, a thorough steaming and a needle shower – on Bathhouse Row. The only establishment still open for business is the 1912 **Buckstaff**, 509 Central Ave, where a thermal mineral bath in a municipal, rather prosaic, atmosphere costs $24 (Ⓦwww.buckstaffbaths.com). Full bathing facilities are also available at several hotels. Hot Springs' water lacks the sulphuric taste often associated with thermal springs; fill a bottle at any of the drinking fountains near Central Avenue. Most of them pump out warm water – if you prefer it cold, head for the Happy Hollow Spring on Fountain Street.

Behind the Fordyce, two small **springs** have been left open for viewing. The **Grand Promenade** from here is a half-mile brick walkway overlooking downtown. Trails of various lengths and severity lead up the steep slopes of **Hot Springs Mountain**. To reach the summit, take a short drive or any of several different trails, including a testing two-and-a-half-mile hike through dense woods of oak, hickory and short-leafed pine.

Quite apart from its waters, Hot Springs prides itself on its small **galleries**, plenty of which line Central Avenue, along with some wonderfully weird Americana.

Practicalities

Most places of interest, including hotels, are within easy distance of **Central Avenue**, the city's main thoroughfare. **Greyhound** pulls in at no. 1001. Though rates can rise during the lengthy high season (Feb–Nov), accommodation is surprisingly inexpensive, ranging from bathhouse hotels to chain motels and B&Bs. Dominating the centre, the quirky 1920s *Arlington Resort/Spa*, 239 Central Ave (Ⓣ501/623-7771, Ⓦwww.arlingtonhotel.com; ❹), oozes faded grandeur – Al Capone rented the entire fourth floor and President Clinton attended his junior and senior proms in the ballroom. At the other end of the scale, the *Alpine Motel*, a mile or so from Bathhouse Row at 741 Park Ave, is a kitschy, clean mom-and-pop place (Ⓣ501/624-9164, Ⓦwww.alpineinnhotsprings.com; ❸). The nearest place to **camp** is the first-come, first-served *Gulpha Gorge Campground* in the national park, two miles northeast on Hwy-70 B (Ⓦwww.nps.gov/hosp; $10).

Hidden among the family **restaurants** along Central Avenue, *Rolando's* at no. 210 is a festive Nuevo Latino place serving up tasty, creative food (Ⓣ501/318-6054). At *McClard's Bar-B-Q*, three miles south of downtown at 505 Albert Pike (Ⓣ501/624-9586; closed Sun & Mon; cash only), the mouthwatering ribs, slaw, beans and tamales are all prepared by hand; it's so good that Bill and Hillary stopped by on their wedding day.

Hot Springs' **nightlife** is marvellously cheesy, ranging from variety and magic shows to jamborees and *The Witness*, an outdoor musical of Christ's life as sung by the Apostle Peter. On a different note, there's a prestigious **documentary film festival** each October (Ⓦwww.hsdfi.org), and a well-known classical **music festival** in June (Ⓦwww.hotmusic.org).

The Ozark Mountains

Although the highest peak fails to top 2000ft, the **Ozark Mountains**, extending beyond northern Arkansas into southern Missouri, are characterized by severe steep ridges and jagged spurs. Hair-raising roads weave their way over the precipitous hills, past rugged lakeshores and pristine rivers. When speculators poured into Arkansas in the 1830s, those who missed the best land etched out remote hill farms, much like those they'd left behind in Kentucky or Tennessee, and lived in isolation until the second half of the twentieth century. A massive tourism boom, while bringing much-needed cash, also created a string of cookie-cutter American towns; the Ozarks are now the fastest-growing rural section of the US.

The word "Ozark" is everywhere, used to entice tourists into music shows, gift emporia and fast-food restaurants. With all the hype, it's difficult to tell what's genuine – a good reason to visit **Mountain View**, where traditional Ozark skills and music are preserved. The region's most visited town, **Eureka Springs**, just inside the Missouri border, is a pretty Victorian spa resort with a rootsy, bohemian scene.

Mountain View and around

Roughly sixty miles north of Little Rock, the state-run **Ozark Folk Centre**, two miles north of the town of **MOUNTAIN VIEW** on Hwy-14, is a good living history museum that attempts to show how life used to be in these remote hills, not reached by paved roads until the Fifties. Homestead skills are displayed in reconstructed log cabins, and folk musicians and storytellers perform throughout. In the evenings you can see Ozark and roots music **concerts** (mid-April to end Sept Wed–Sat, Oct Tues–Sun; crafts $10, concerts $10; combination ticket $17.50; Ⓦwww.ozarkfolkcenter.com).

Mountain View's **visitor centre**, 107 N Peabody Ave (April–Oct Mon–Fri 9am–5pm, Sat 10am–4pm; Nov–March Mon–Fri 10am–4pm, Sat 10am–2pm; Ⓣ870/269-8068, Ⓦwww.ozarkgetaways.com), can help with **accommodation**; there is plenty of choice, particularly if you like B&Bs and rustic mountain cabins. The Folk Center offers quiet, comfortable cabins year-round (Ⓣ870/269-3851; ❸), while the friendly *Inn at Mountain View*, 307 W Washington St (Ⓣ870/269-4200, Ⓦwww.innatmountainview.com; ❹), is a pretty B&B owned by folk musicians; they serve a full country breakfast (minimum stay required at weekends and festivals). Good **restaurants** include the Folk Center's *Iron Skillet* (Ⓣ870/269-3851) and *Tommy's Famous*, a funky little place at 205 Carpenter St, four blocks west of the town square, that dishes up good pizza, ribs and BBQ (Ⓣ870/269-3278; dinner only). Mountain View is dry. For entertainment, it's hard to beat the friendly **jam sessions** in the town square, and there are also a number of good music **festivals**. Reserve a room well in advance for the venerable **Arkansas Folk Festival** (music, crafts, food stalls, parades; Ⓦwww.ozarkgetaways.com/folk_festival.html), in April, and the **Bean Festival** (beans, cornbread, music, outhouse races; Ⓦwww.ozarkgetaways.com/beanfest_outhouse.html), in late October.

In the **Ozark National Forest**, fifteen miles northwest of Mountain View off Hwy-14, you can tour the **Blanchard Springs Caverns** (times vary; $10; Ⓦwww.blanchardcavetours.com), an eerily beautiful underground cave system with a crystal-clear swimming hole surrounded by towering rock bluffs. The **Buffalo River** – a prime destination for whitewater canoeing – flows across the state north of Mountain View. In the sweet little settlement of Gilbert, off Hwy-65 at the end of Hwy-333 E, **Buffalo Camping and Canoeing** (Ⓣ870/439-2888, Ⓦwww.gilbertstore.com) rents canoes for trips on the mid-section of the river, at its most spectacular around **Pruitt Landing**. A few log **cabins**, most of which sleep at least four, are available (Ⓦwww.buffalorivercabin.com; ❹).

Eureka Springs

Picturesque **EUREKA SPRINGS**, set on steep mountain slopes in Arkansas' north-western corner, began life in the nineteenth century as a health resort. As that role diminished, its striking location turned it into a tourist destination, filled with

Victorian buildings and streets linked by flights of stone stairs. Today it's a cool, progressive spot, with kitsch outdoor movie events (Ⓦwww.lucky13cinema.org), diversity weekends (Ⓦwww.eurekapride.com), and plenty of places offering alternative therapies. Take a ride on the **Eureka Springs and North Arkansas Railway**, whose rolling stock includes a magnificent "cabbage-head" wood-burning locomotive; trips depart from the depot at 299 N Main St (April–Oct Tues–Sat 10.30am, noon, 2pm & 4pm; $13; Ⓦwww.esnarailway.com).

Three miles east of town on US-62 E, a seven-storey **Christ of the Ozarks** – a statue of Jesus with a 60ft arm span – sets the tone for a jaw-dropping religious complex known as the **Great Passion Play** (April–Oct), the brainchild of Elna M. Smith, who, worried that the holy sites of the Middle East would be destroyed by war, decided to build replicas in the Ozarks. The play itself re-enacts Christ's last days on earth with a cast of 250, including live animals, in a 4100-seat amphitheatre (May–Oct; $26; Ⓦwww.greatpassionplay.com).

Practicalities

In town, US-62 becomes Van Buren. The **visitor centre**, 2000 E Van Buren (daily 9am–5pm; Ⓦwww.eurekasprings.com) has information on everything from reiki practitioners to gay-friendly restaurants. Eureka Springs has lots of appealing places to **stay**; log cabins and B&Bs abound, many with staggering views. The friendly *Sherwood Court,* 248 W Van Buren, offers individually decorated cottages around flower-filled courtyards (Ⓣ479/253-8920, Ⓦwww.sherwoodcourt.com; ❹ including continental breakfast), while at *Treehouse Cottages* (Ⓣ479/253-8667, Ⓦwww.treehousecottages.com; ❻) you can hide away in one of seven luxury cabins on stilts, set deep in the forest.

For **food**, the artsy *Mud Street Café,* 22 S Main St, serves good espresso, light lunches and desserts (Ⓣ479/253-6732; closed Wed), while *Local Flavor*, 71 S Main St (Ⓣ479/253-9522) dishes up tasty modern American cuisine and has balcony seating. The friendly local institution *Chelsea's Corner*, 10 Mountain St, off Spring Street (Ⓣ479/253-6723, Ⓦwww.chelseascornercafe.com), features **live music** most evenings. Eureka Springs holds the fine **Ozark folk festival** in autumn (Ⓦwww.ozarkfolkfestival.com), and the acclaimed **blues festival** in June (Ⓦwww.eurekaspringsbluesfestival.com).

Florida

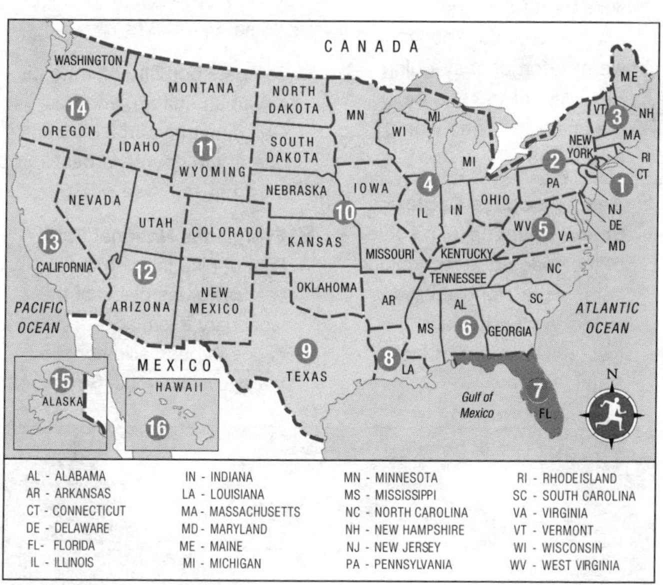
CANADA
WASHINGTON
MONTANA
NORTH DAKOTA
MN
WI
MI
MI
ME
VT
NH
NEW YORK
MA
RI
CT
OREGON
IDAHO
WYOMING
SOUTH DAKOTA
NEBRASKA
IOWA
IL
IN
OHIO
PA
NJ
DE
MD
NEVADA
UTAH
COLORADO
KANSAS
MISSOURI
KENTUCKY
WV
VA
CALIFORNIA
ARIZONA
NEW MEXICO
OKLAHOMA
AR
TENNESSEE
NC
SC
AL
MS
GEORGIA
PACIFIC OCEAN
ATLANTIC OCEAN
TEXAS
LA
FL
Gulf of Mexico
MEXICO
ALASKA
HAWAII
N
1
2
3
4
5
6
7
8
9
10
11
12
13
14
15
16
AL - ALABAMA
AR - ARKANSAS
CT - CONNECTICUT
DE - DELAWARE
FL- FLORIDA
IL - ILLINOIS
IN - INDIANA
LA - LOUISIANA
MA - MASSACHUSETTS
MD - MARYLAND
ME - MAINE
MI - MICHIGAN
MN - MINNESOTA
MS - MISSISSIPPI
NC - NORTH CAROLINA
NH - NEW HAMPSHIRE
NJ - NEW JERSEY
PA - PENNSYLVANIA
RI - RHODE ISLAND
SC - SOUTH CAROLINA
VA - VIRGINIA
VT - VERMONT
WI - WISCONSIN
WV - WEST VIRGINIA

CHAPTER 7 Highlights

* **Ocean Drive, Miami** South Beach's finest Art Deco showpiece, buzzing with cosmopolitan cafés, flashy vintage cars and beautiful people. See p.500

* **Florida Keys** Dive, snorkel or just admire the flaming sunsets off this chain of enticing islands. You won't want to forget easy-going Key West at the end of the chain, but who would? See p.508

* **Kennedy Space Center, Space Coast** Take In some of the space-age technology here, just a stone's throw from the Merritt Island National Wildlife Refuge. See p.519

* **St Augustine** Sixteenth-century Spanish town packed with historic homes, an impressive living history museum and several nice beaches.See p.521

* **Walt Disney World** Pure entertainment, planned down to the last detail, for better or worse. See p.528

* **Tampa** Ybor City offers a bit of Cuban culture, and this Gulf coast favourite also has one of the country's best steakhouses. See p.535

* **Everglades National Park** Bike or hike through the vast sawgrass plains of the legendary Everglades, or canoe through alligator-filled mangrove swamps. See p.543

▲ Islamorada, Florida Keys

7

Florida

Brochure images of tanning tourists and Mickey Mouse give an inaccurate and incomplete picture of **FLORIDA**. Although the aptly nicknamed "Sunshine State" is indeed devoted to the tourist trade, it's also among the least-understood parts of the US. Away from its overexposed resorts lie forests and rivers, deserted strands filled with wildlife, vibrant cities and primeval swamps. Contrary to the popular retirement-community image, new Floridians tend to be a younger, more energetic breed, while Spanish-speaking enclaves provide close ties to Latin America and the Caribbean.

By far, the essential stop is cosmopolitan, half-Latin **Miami**. A simple journey south from here brings you to the **Florida Keys**, a hundred-mile string of islands known for sports fishing, coral-reef diving and the sultry town of **Key West**, legendary for its sunsets and liberal attitude. Back on the mainland, west from Miami stretch the easily accessible **Everglades**, a water-logged sawgrass plain filled with alligators, a symbol of the state that can be found on college campuses (as a college mascot) and on innumerable business billboards. Much of Florida's **east coast** is heavily built-up – a not-so-small side effect of powerful migration flows of so-called "sunbirds" seeking to escape the cold climes of the northeast USA. The residential stranglehold is loosened further north, where the **Kennedy Space Center** launches NASA shuttles. Further along, historical **St Augustine** stands as the longest continuously occupied European settlement in the US, and at its urban core, its dense street pattern gives it a vaguely European flavour.

In **central Florida** the terrain turns green, though it's no rural idyll, thanks in the most part to **Orlando** and **Walt Disney World**, which sprawl out across the countryside. From here it's just a skip west to the towns and beaches of the **Gulf Coast**, and somewhat further north to the forests of the **Panhandle**, Florida's link with the Deep South.

Weather-wise, warm sunshine and blue skies are almost always the norm. The state does, however, split into two **climatic zones**: subtropical in the south and warm temperate in the north. Orlando and points south have a mild season from October to April, with warm temperatures and low humidity – this is the **peak tourist season**, when prices are at their highest. Conversely, the southern summer (May to Sept) brings high humidity and afternoon storms; the rewards for braving the mugginess are lower prices and fewer tourists.

North of Orlando, winter is the off-peak period, even though daytime temperatures are generally comfortably warm (although snow has been known to fall on the Panhandle). During the northern Florida summer, the crowds arrive, and the days and nights are hot and very humid. Keep in mind that June to November is **hurricane season**, and there is a strong possibility of major storms throughout the entire state.

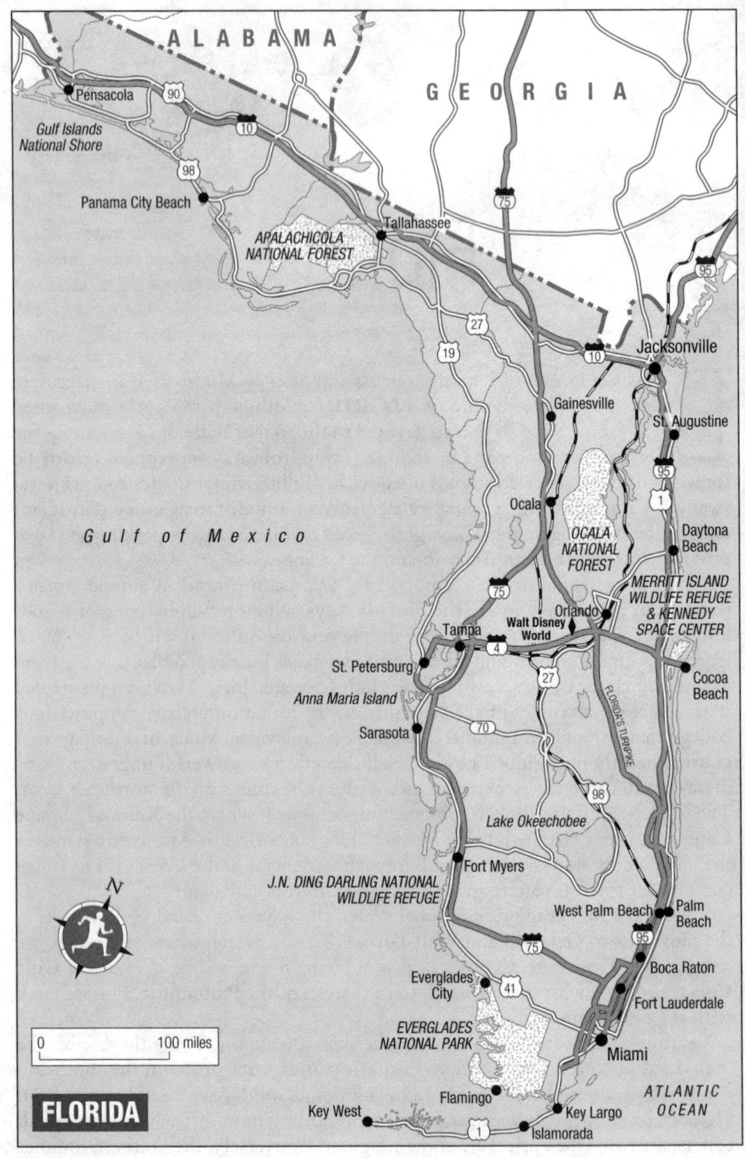

Some history

The **first European sighting** of Florida, just six years after Christopher Columbus reached the New World, is believed to have been made by John and Sebastian Cabot in 1498, when they spotted what is now Cape Florida, on Key Biscayne in Miami. At the time, the area's one hundred thousand inhabitants formed several distinct **tribes**: the Timucua across northern Florida, the Calusa around the southwest and Lake Okeechobee, the Apalachee in the Panhandle and the Tequesta along the southeast coast.

In 1513, a Spaniard, **Juan Ponce de León**, sighted land during *Pascua Florida*, Spain's Easter celebration; he named what he saw *La Florida*, or "Land of Flowers". Eight years later he returned, the first of several Spanish incursions prompted by rumours of gold hidden in the north of the region. When it became clear that Florida did not harbour stunning riches, interest waned, and it wasn't until 1565 that conquistador Pedro Menéndez de Avilés founded **St Augustine** – site of the longest continuous European habitation in North America. In 1586, St Augustine was razed by a British naval bombardment led by Francis Drake. The ensuing bloody confrontation for control of North America was eventually settled when the British captured the crucial Spanish possession of Havana, Cuba; Spain willingly parted with Florida to get it back. By this time, indigenous Floridians had been largely wiped out by disease. The area's Native American population now largely comprised disparate tribes that had arrived from the north, collectively known as the **Seminoles**, who were generally left undisturbed in the inland areas.

Following American independence, Florida once more reverted to Spain. In 1814, the US general (and future president) Andrew Jackson – on the pretext of subduing the Seminole, but with the actual intention of taking the region – marched south from Tennessee, killing hundreds of Native Americans and triggering the **First Seminole War**. Following the war, in 1819, Spain **ceded Florida** to the US, in return for American assumption of $5 million of Spanish debt. Not long after, Jackson was sworn in as Florida's first American governor, and Tallahassee was selected as the new administrative centre.

Eleven years later, the **Act of Indian Removal** decreed that all Native Americans in the eastern US should be transferred to reservations in the Midwest. Most Seminole were determined to stay and, as a result, the **Second Seminole War** broke out, with the Native Americans steadily driven south, away from the fertile lands of central Florida and into the Everglades, where they eventually agreed to remain. Florida became the **27th state** on March 3, 1845, coinciding with the prosperity brought by the railroads. As a member of the Confederacy during the **Civil War**, Florida's primary contribution was the provision of food – a foretaste of its postwar economic role after being re-admitted to the Union.

At the beginning of the twentieth century, the country's newspapers extolled the curative virtues of Florida's climate, and northern speculators began to invest in the state. These early efforts to promote Florida as a **tourist destination** brought in the wintering rich: the likes of Henry Flagler and Henry Plant extended their railroads and opened luxury resorts on the east and west coasts respectively. After World War I, it seemed that everyone in America wanted a piece of Florida, and chartered trains brought in thousands of eager buyers. But, most deals were on paper only, and in 1926 the banks began to default. The **Wall Street Crash** then made paupers of the millionaires whose investments had helped shape the state.

What saved Florida was **World War II**. During the war, thousands of troops arrived to guard the coastline, providing them with a taste of Florida that would entice many to return; postwar, the government expanded their facilities in and around Jacksonville, Tampa and Pensacola, bringing in thousands of new residents and billions of dollars in investment. Furthermore, in the mid-Sixties, the state government bent over backwards to help the Disney Corporation turn a sizeable slice of central Florida into **Walt Disney World**, the biggest theme park ever. Its enormous commercial success helped solidify Florida's place in the international tourist market: directly or indirectly, tourism now makes up twenty percent of the total state economy.

Behind the optimistic facade, however, lie many **problems**. There's a broadening gap between the relative liberalism of the big cities and the arch-conservatism of the northern Bible Belt. Gun laws remain notoriously lax, and the multimillion-dollar **drug trade** shows few signs of abating – at least a quarter of the cocaine entering the US is said to arrive via Florida. Increased protection of the state's **natural resources** has been a more positive feature of the last decade and impressive amounts of land are under state control – overall, wildlife is less threatened now than at any time since white settlers first arrived. Most recently, the environment along Florida's Gulf Coast has been threatened by the Deepwater Horizon oil spill, which occurred in April 2010. While initial reports from the west coast of Florida are fairly encouraging, visitors should consult local sources before any major outings.

Getting around Florida

Getting around Florida is a time-consuming affair, even by automobile; flights between major cities are pricey, and visitors should allot ample time for driving. Getting around by **public transportation** requires ample advance planning. Major towns and cities are linked by Greyhound **buses** and Amtrak **trains** run along the east coast and west to Orlando and Tampa. However, many of the state's rural areas and some of the most enjoyable sections of the coast are not served by any reasonable type of public transportation. Although inadvisable in the cities, **cycling** is a great way to see large parts of Florida – miles of cycle paths follow the coasts, and long-distance bike trails cross the state's interior.

Miami

MIAMI is an often intoxicatingly beautiful place, with palm trees swaying in the breeze and South Beach's famous Art Deco buildings stunning in the warm sunlight. Away from the beaches and the tourists, the gleaming skyscrapers of downtown herald Miami's proud status as the headquarters of many US corporations' Latin American operations. Even so, it's the people, not the climate, the landscape or the cash, that makes Miami so noteworthy. Two-thirds of the two-million-plus population are Hispanic, the majority of whom are **Cuban,** and Spanish is the predominant language in the cafés, the beachfronts and the cocktail lounges.

Just over a hundred years ago Miami was a swampy outpost of mosquito-tormented settlers. The arrival of Henry Flagler's railroad in 1896 gave the city its first fixed land-link with the rest of the continent, and cleared the way for the Twenties property boom and subsequent bust after 1924. In the Fifties, Miami Beach became a celebrity-filled resort area, just as thousands of Cubans fleeing the regime of Fidel Castro began arriving here as well. The Sixties and Seventies brought decline, and Miami's dangerous reputation in the Eighties was well deserved – in 1980 the city had the highest murder rate in America.

Since then, with the strengthening of Latin American economic links and the gentrification of South Beach – which helped make tourism the lifeblood of the local economy again in the early Nineties – Miami is enjoying a surge of affluence and optimism.

Arrival and information

Miami International Airport (Ⓣ305/876-7000, Ⓦwww.miami-airport.com) is six miles west of the city. A cab from the airport costs $22–52, depending on your destination. You can opt for one of the 24-hour SuperShuttle minivans, which will deliver you to any address in Miami for $15–20 per person (Ⓣ305/871-2000, Ⓦwww.supershuttle.com). Via **public transportation**, take the #7 Metrobus (Ⓣ305/770-3131) to downtown, a trip of 40 to 50 minutes ($2; every 30min), or the #J Metrobus ($2; every 20–40min) to Miami Beach farther on. Shuttle buses also leave from the airport to the nearby **Tri-Rail** (Ⓣ1-800/TRIRAIL) train station, with onward services to West Palm Beach.

A short taxi ride ($10) from the airport will deliver you to the Miami Greyhound **bus** station, at 4111 NW 27th St (Ⓣ305/871-1810). The **Amtrak** station, at 8303 NW 37th Ave, is seven miles northwest of the city centre. Three blocks south lies the Tri-Rail Metrorail Station at 1125 E 25 St (coming from Amtrak take a taxi, as this area can be unsafe), where Tri-Rail connects with **Metrorail** services to downtown Miami. Bus #L also makes a stop here. By 2011, all trains and buses should arrive at the new Miami Intermodal Center, next to the airport.

For **tourist information** head to the Downtown Welcome Center in the lobby of the Olympia Theater, 174 E Flagler St (Mon noon–5pm, Tues–Sat 10am–5pm; Ⓣ305/379-7070, Ⓦwww.downtownmiami.com); otherwise, try the Miami Beach Chamber of Commerce, 1920 Meridian Ave (Mon–Sun 10am–4pm; Ⓣ305/672-1270, Ⓦwww.miamibeachchamber.com), which is crammed with leaflets and staffed by helpful locals. Also in South Beach, the Art Deco Welcome Center, 1001 Ocean Drive (Mon–Sun 9.30am–7pm), is a great source of information on the historic Art Deco hotels in the area and walking tours (see below) offered by the Miami Design Preservation League (Ⓣ305/672-2014, Ⓦwww.mdpol.org).

City transport and tours

Downtown and South Beach, the two main tourist areas, are eminently walkable – and, indeed, are best enjoyed **on foot**. However, if you want to see more of the city, **driving** is the most practical option. An integrated **public transportation network** run by Metro-Dade Transit (Ⓣ305/770-3131, Ⓦwww.miamidade.gov/transit) covers Miami, making the city easy – if time-consuming – to get around, at least by day (night-time services are quite limited). **Metrorail** trains ($2) run along a single line between the northern suburbs and South Miami; useful stops are Government Center (for downtown), Vizcaya, Coconut Grove and Douglas Road or University (for Coral Gables). Downtown Miami is also ringed by the **Metromover** (free), a monorail that doesn't cover much ground but gives a great bird's-eye view. **Metrobuses** ($2, with a 50¢ surcharge for transfers) cover the entire city, but services dwindle at night.

Taxis are abundant in Miami (**meters** start at $2.50); either hail one on the street or call Central Cab (Ⓣ305/532-5555) or Metro Taxi (Ⓣ305/888-8888). If you want to rent a **bike**, try the Miami Beach Bicycle Center, 601 5th St, South Beach (Mon–Sat 10am–7pm, Sun till 5pm; $8/hr, $24/24hr; Ⓣ305/674-0150, Ⓦwww.bikemiamibeach.com).

For an informed stroll, take one of **Dr Paul George's Walking Tours** from the Historical Museum of Southern Florida (call for schedule; no tours July & Aug; prices start at $20; Ⓣ305/375-1621, Ⓦwww.hmsf.org). In South Beach, don't miss the ninety-minute **Art Deco Walking Tour** (Mon–Sun 10.30am, Thurs 6.30pm; $20; ⓣ305/672-2014), which starts at the Art Deco Welcome Center. The shop also offers a self-guided audio walking tour of the district (available daily 9.30am–5pm; 90min; $15).

Accommodation

Accommodation is rarely a problem in Miami – though you should expect **rates** to go up on weekends, holidays and in the main winter tourist season (Dec–April), when you'll pay $120–150 (or upwards of $250 in the swankier places) per night. Though it can be great fun to stay in one of the numerous Art Deco **South Beach** hotels, note that they were built in a different era, and, as such, rooms can be tiny. Most visitors will want to be close to the lively beachfront, but good offers can be had at hotels near Miami International Airport.

Albion Hotel 1650 James Ave, South Beach ⓣ1-877/RUBELLS, ⓦwww.rubellhotels.com. A sensitive conversion of a classic Nautical Deco building, this is one of the best-value hotels on the beach. Rooms are hip but simple; the raised pool – with portholes cut into its sides – is also a big draw. ❹

Cadet Hotel 1701 James Ave ⓣ305/672-6688, ⓦwww.cadethotel.com. Tranquil boutique hotel, with a peaceful patio that is redolent of a Jane Austen novel, in the South Beach fashion; the fresh strawberries and chocolate in the rooms upon arrival are nice touches. ❺

Clay Hotel Hostel 1438 Washington Ave, South Beach ⓣ1-800/379-2529, ⓦwww.clayhotel.com. This beautiful converted monastery serves as the city's best budget hotel and youth hostel. Private rooms (with and without bath) ❸; dorm rooms $22, with rates dropping to $20 in the summer.

The Clifton Hotel 801 Collins Ave ⓣ305/455-1630, ⓦwww.cliftonsouthbeach.com. With its custom bamboo furniture and overall "green" feng-shui and design measures, this Art Deco property is a pretty good find along Collins Avenue. *The Clifton* also has a small, yet serviceable, bar where fellow guests can meet and greet. ❻

Daddy O Hotel 9660 East Bay Harbor Drive ⓣ305/868-4141, ⓦwww.daddyohotel.com. Ensconced in the relative tranquillity of Bay Harbor Islands, north of Miami Beach, this boutique hotel offers a pleasant respite from the pulse of the Collins Avenue/A1A corridor. It also has a nice breakfast spread, and the bagels are top-notch. ❻

The Hotel 801 Collins Ave ⓣ305/531-2222 or 1-877/843-4683, ⓦwww.thehotelofsouthbeach.com. Designer Todd Oldham oversaw every element in the renovation of this hotel, and his colourful yet thoughtful makeover makes it one of the best luxury options on the beach. Don't miss the rooftop pool, shaped like a gemstone in honour of the hotel's original name, *The Tiffany*. ❻

Miami Beach International Travelers Hostel 236 9th St, South Beach ⓣ305/534-0268, ⓦwww.hostelmiamibeach.com. Friendly hostel with beds in four-person dorms starting at $23, as well as private singles (from $99) and doubles ($49/person, double occupancy obligatory). Offers free breakfast, internet facilities, kitchen, laundry, a movie-lounge and free English and Spanish classes once a week.

Pelican 826 Ocean Drive, South Beach ⓣ1-800/7-PELICAN, ⓦwww.pelicanhotel.com. Each room at this campy, quirky hotel is individually themed and named – try the "Power Flower" room, which is two parts Age of Aquarius, one part *Rosemary's Baby*. ❼

The Shore Club 1901 Collins Ave, South Beach ⓣ305/695-3100, ⓦwww.shoreclub.com. Ultra-trendy hotel on the beach, with minimalist, brightly coloured rooms and several swanky bar-restaurants, like the poolside *Sky Bar* (see p.508). ❾

The Standard Miami 40 Island Ave, South Beach ⓣ305/673-1717, ⓦwww.standardhotels.com. The Miami outpost of hip hotelier André Balazs's Standard chain has transformed a forlorn hotel on Belle Isle into spa accommodation complete with Turkish baths and a yoga centre. ❻

Townhouse Hotel 150 20th St, South Beach ⓣ1-877/534-3800, ⓦwww.townhousehotel.com. Small but stylish white rooms, great staff, free breakfast and squishy rooftop waterbeds – all at a fraction of most boutique hotel prices. ❺

The City

Like an elaborate layer cake, Miami has a range of districts that mirror its variegated cultural, economic and social divisions. Separated from the mainland by Biscayne Bay, the most popular is **Miami Beach**, which is defined largely by the bacchanalian pursuits along **South Beach**. In addition to an enticing stretch of sand, this is where many of the city's famed Art Deco buildings can be found, draped in pastels, neon and wavy lines.

Back on the mainland, **downtown** has a few good museums, though the district is being transformed by one of the largest concentrations of residential skyscrapers in the US. To the north, the art galleries and showrooms of **Wynwood** and the **Design District**, and even the Caribbean enclave known as **Little Haiti** are gradually starting to attract more visitors. Meanwhile, southwest of downtown, there's nowhere better for a Cuban lunch than **Little Havana**, which spreads out along 8th Street, which is also known as Calle Ocho. Immediately south, the spacious boulevards and ornate public buildings of **Coral Gables** are as impressive now as they were in the 1920s, when the district set new standards in town planning. Lastly, sun-worshippers should make time for **Key Biscayne**, a smart, secluded island community with some beautiful beaches, an easy five miles off the mainland by causeway. **Virginia Key** is right in this area, and it is the home to the legendary *Jimbo's* (see p. 000). The Key has a unique place in Miami history, as it had a "colored-only" beach in the pre-civil rights era, and it is a significant site in local African American history. Today, the beach has been restored after decades of neglect, and it includes the largest mangrove wetland area in the state.

Miami Beach

A long slender arm of land between Biscayne Bay and the Atlantic Ocean, **MIAMI BEACH**, three miles off the mainland, has been a headline-grabbing resort town for almost a hundred years, from its first heyday in the Art Deco-dominated 1920s, to a slick-as-Vegas era in the 1950s and the hip hedonism of today. Until the 1910s – when its Quaker owner, John Collins, formed an unlikely partnership with a flashy entrepreneur, Carl Fisher – it was nothing more than an ailing fruit farm. With Fisher's money, Biscayne Bay was dredged, and the muck raised from its murky bed was used as landfill to transform this wildly vegetated barrier island into a carefully sculptured landscape of palm trees, hotels and tennis courts. After a hurricane in 1926 devastated Miami (and especially the beach), damaged buildings were replaced by grander structures in the new Art Deco style, and Miami Beach as we know it appeared. More recently, the 1990s saw a renaissance spearheaded by a few savvy hoteliers and Miami's gay community.

Miami beaches

With twelve miles of calm waters, clean sands, swaying palms and candy-coloured lifeguard towers, you can't go wrong with Miami's cornucopia of **beaches**. The young, beautiful and recently beautiful soak up the rays between 5th and 21st streets, a convenient hop from the juice bars and cafés on Ocean Drive. From 6th to 14th streets, **Lummus Park** – much of whose sand was shipped in from the Bahamas – is the heart of the South Beach scene; there's an unofficial gay section roughly around 12th Street. North of 21st, things are more family-oriented, with a **boardwalk** running between the shore and the hotels up to 46th. To the south, **First Street Beach** and **South Pointe** are favoured by Cuban families, and are quite busy on weekends. For good **swimming**, head up to 85th, a quiet stretch that's usually patrolled by lifeguards.

South Beach

Occupying the southernmost three miles of Miami Beach is gorgeous **SOUTH BEACH**, with its hundreds of dazzling pastel-coloured 1920s and 1930s Art Deco buildings. By day, the sun blares down on sizzling bodies on the sand – though it's worth braving an early-morning wake-up call to catch the dawn glow, which bathes the Deco hotels in pure, crystalline white light. By night, the ten blocks of Ocean Drive become one of the liveliest stretches in Miami, as terrace cafés spill across the specially widened sidewalk and crowds of tourists and locals saunter by the beach.

Loosely bordered north/south by 5th and 20th streets, and west/east by Lenox Avenue and the ocean, the area referred to as the **Deco District** actually incorporates a variety of styles: take one of the informative walking tours offered by the **Miami Design Preservation League** (see p.497) to learn the difference between Streamline, Moderne and Florida Deco, not to mention Mediterranean Revival.

If the tourist hordes get to be too much, head a block west to **Collins Avenue**, lined with more Deco hotels and fashion chains, or on to **Washington Avenue**, which tends more toward funky thrift stores and cool coffee bars. At 1001 Washington Ave, the Mediterranean-Revival **Wolfsonian-FIU** (Mon, Tues, Sat & Sun noon–6pm, Thurs & Fri till 9pm; $7; students and children under 12 $5; free after 6pm on Fri; ⓣ305/531-1001, ⓦwww.wolfsonian.fiu.edu) houses an eclectic collection of decorative arts from the late nineteenth century to 1945. Throughout Miami Beach's history, one group that has kept a constant presence is its sizeable Jewish population, which includes many Holocaust survivors and their families. This contingent is the reason for the moving **Holocaust Memorial**, near the north tip of South Beach, at 1933–1945 Meridian Ave (daily 9am–9pm; $2 suggested donation for brochure; ⓣ305/538-1663, ⓦwww.holocaustmmb.org). A complex, uncompromising reminder to their experience, the monument depicts a defiant hand punching into the sky.

A few blocks northeast is the **Bass Museum of Art**, 2121 Park Ave (Tues–Sat 10am–5pm, Sun 11am–5pm; $8; ⓣ305/673-7530, ⓦwww.bassmuseum.org). The only fine art museum on the beach, the Bass is housed in a 1930s building designed by Russell Pancoast, the architect son-in-law of beach pioneer John Collins. The white box grafted onto the original building along Park Avenue was designed by Japanese architect Arata Isozaki. The museum's permanent collection consists of fine, if largely unremarkable, European paintings, although its temporary exhibitions are often lively and worth visiting.

Biscayne Bay's million-dollar mansions

America's rich and famous have been coming to Miami for years, hiding away within ostentatious palm-smothered mansions on the cays that lie between the city and Miami Beach; the only way to get a good look is to take a **boat tour** from Bayside Marketplace. These are unashamedly touristy, but provide fabulous views of the city, and include a narrated jaunt around some of the most exclusive areas. Guides will point out the opulent mansions of Shaquille O'Neal, Sean Combs (aka P Diddy or Puff Daddy) and Oprah Winfrey, among numerous others.

Operators include Island Queen Cruises (ⓣ305/379-5119, ⓦwww.islandqueencruises.com), which runs daily 1.5hr tours (10.30am–7pm, on the hour) for $26. You can also tour the same islands by **kayak**, though it pays to take the boat tour first so you know which celebrity backyard you're paddling past. Try South Beach Kayak (Wed–Sat 10.30am–sunset, Sun & Mon 11am–sunset; $25/2hr, $70/day; ⓣ305/332-2853, ⓦwww.southbeachkayak.com), 1771 Purdy Ave, Miami Beach, near the Venetian Causeway.

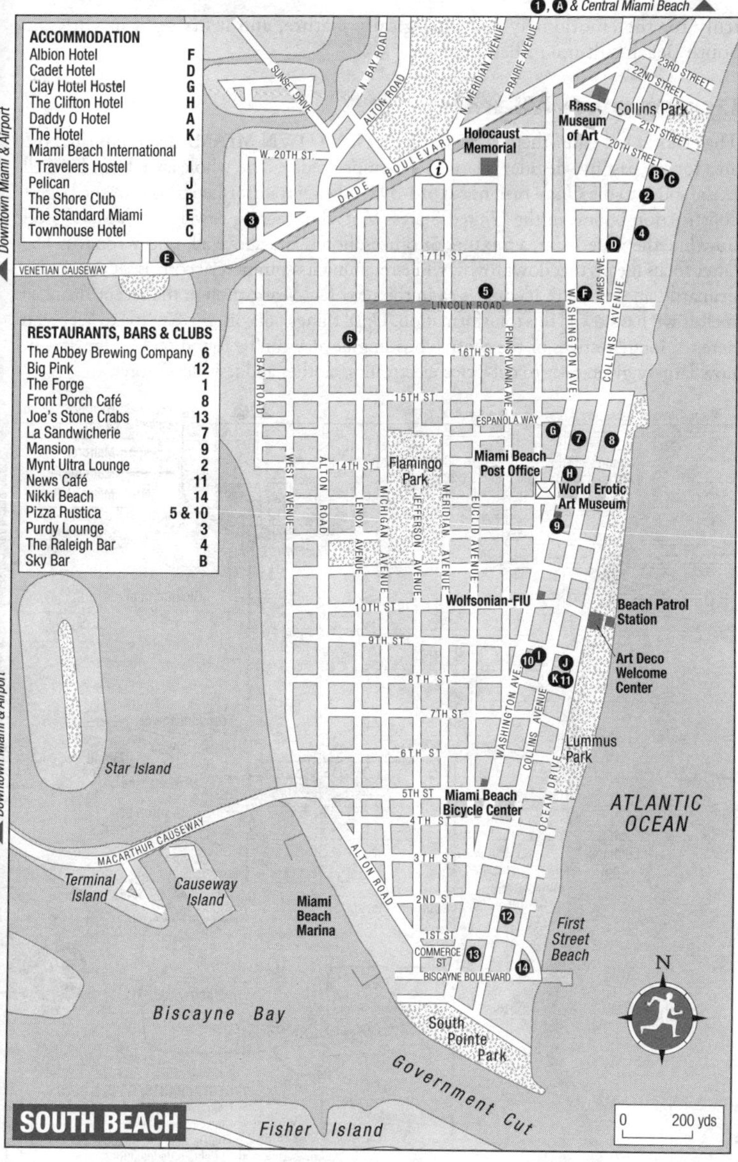

Tucked into a rather innocuous looking storefront back on Washington Avenue is the **World Erotic Art Museum**, 1205 Washington Ave (Mon–Thurs 11am–10pm, Fri–Sun till 12am; $15, students $13.50; ⓣ305/532-9336 or 1-866/969-WEAM, ⓦwww.weam.com). The collection here includes thousands of posters, statues, paintings and decorative items that document the erotic art traditions throughout North America. Unusual items include the phallus chair/sculpture from the film *A Clockwork Orange* and other one-of-a-kind items. It is truly for the emotionally and biologically mature, and it fits right in with the South Beach cultural milieu.

Downtown Miami

The chaotic and Latin-themed bustle of **DOWNTOWN MIAMI** that dominated the area for the past five decades is largely a memory today. The whole area, from Brickell in the south to the Omni mall north of I-395, is being transformed by one of the largest construction booms in the United States. Vast, shimmering towers of glass and steel now line the waterfront, a mixture of offices, hotels and above all, pricey condos. The latter focus means that downtown, while retaining its commercial core, is set to become primarily an upscale residential area in the next few years, though the recent financial meltdown has slowed this transformation. Until things take off, there's little to keep you here for long; vestiges of the centre's bustling heyday can be found on **Flagler Street**, now largely given over to cut-price electronics, clothes and jewellery stores.

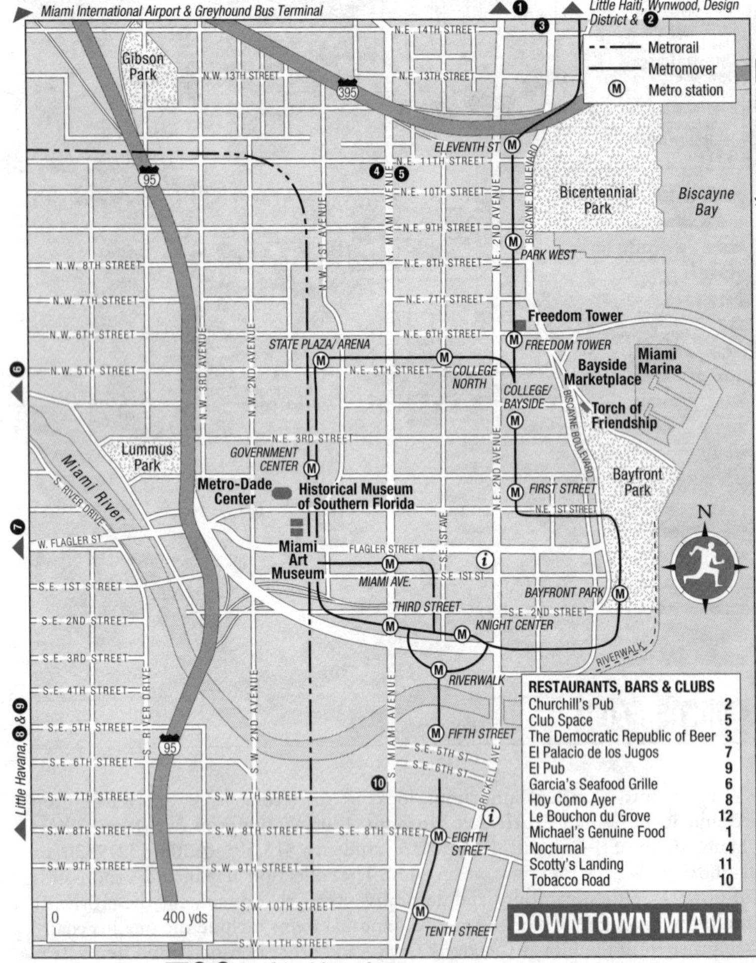

Cubans in Miami

During the mid-Fifties, when opposition to Cuba's Batista dictatorship began to assert itself, a trickle of Cubans started arriving in a predominantly Jewish section of Miami that was then called Riverside. The trickle became a flood when Fidel Castro took power in 1959, and the area became **Little Havana**, populated by the affluent Cuban middle classes who had the most to lose under communism.

These original immigrants were joined by a second influx in May 1980, when the **Mariel boatlift** brought 125,000 islanders from the port of Mariel to Miami in only a few days. These arrivals were poor and uneducated, and a fifth of them were fresh from Cuban jails – incarcerated for criminal rather than political crimes. Bluntly, Castro had dumped his misfits on Miami. The city reeled and then recovered from this mass arrival, but it left Miami's Cuban community utterly divided. Even today, older Cuban-Americans claim that they can pick out a *Marielito* from the way he or she walks or talks.

That said, local division gives way to fervent agreement when it comes to Castro: he's universally detested. In Miami, Cubans have been killed for being suspected of advocating dialogue with Castro. Despite failing to depose the dictator, Cuban-Americans have been far more successful at influencing the US government. Since the 1980s, Cubans have been vociferous supporters of the Republican Party in what has traditionally been a crucial swing state – and therefore one of the main reasons that the US embargo of Cuba (imposed in 1962), remains in place, for now at least.

At the western end of NE 1st Street, the **Metro-Dade Cultural Center** contains the **Historical Museum of Southern Florida** (Tues–Fri 10am–5pm, Sat & Sun noon–5pm, 3rd Thurs of each month 10am–9pm; $8; ⓣ305/375-1492, ⓦwww.hmsf.org), which provides a comprehensive look at the region's history and includes two shockingly small genuine refugee rafts.

On the east side of the plaza, the **Miami Art Museum** (Tues–Fri 10am–5pm, Sat & Sun noon–5pm, 3rd Thurs of each month 10am–9pm; $8, free every second Sat; ⓣ305/375-3000, ⓦwww.miamiartmuseum.org) houses a well-laid-out collection of post-1940 art, and showcases outstanding international travelling exhibits. The museum is expected to relocate to a waterfront space close to I-395, to be called Museum Park, sometime in early 2013; call or check the museum website for details.

The eastern edge of downtown is bounded by Biscayne Boulevard, near which is the **Bayside Marketplace**, a large pink shopping mall with pleasant waterfront views from its terrace – take a **boat tour** of Biscayne Bay from here (see box, p.500). Across the boulevard, the striking **Freedom Tower**, built in 1925 and modelled on a Spanish bell tower, earned its name by housing the Cuban Refugee Center in the 1960s. It is now owned by nearby Miami-Dade Community College, and in recent years, they have had special exhibitions on the work of Cuban artists living in Miami.

Wynwood and the Design District

North of downtown and 20th Street, the **Wynwood Art District** is home to one of the largest and most dynamic concentrations of **art galleries** in the nation. Though it's relatively safe to explore, the area remains sketchy at night, and galleries are spread out, so this is one part of Miami best experienced by car. Highlights include **Locust Projects**, 155 NE 38th Street #100 (Thurs–Sat noon–5pm; ⓣ305/576-8570, ⓦwww.locustprojects.org), a warehouse crammed with tantalizing multimedia installations, and the **Rubell Collection**, 95 NW 29th St (Wed–Sat 10am–6pm, second Sat of each month 10am–10pm;

$10; ⓣ305/573-6090, ⓦwww.rfc.museum), a massive modern art collection housed in an old warehouse. Further north, the **Design District** (ⓦwww.miamidesigndistrict.net), hemmed in by 36th and 41st streets between Miami Avenue and Biscayne Boulevard, is also worth a wander, crammed with hip restaurants and designer furniture stores.

Little Haiti

Continuing north along NE 2nd Avenue, you'll cruise into **LITTLE HAITI**, an immigrant area filled with Caribbean colours, music and smells, its trilingual shop signs making sales pitches in English, French and Creole. In its former incarnation as Lemon City, this neighbourhood was the oldest inhabited European settlement in the area, alongside Coconut Grove. Today, the best place to soak up the atmosphere is 54th Street, which is lined with stores known as *botánicas*, providing supplies for the voodoo-like religion **Santería**.

Little Havana

The initial home of Miami Cubans was a few miles west of downtown in what became **LITTLE HAVANA**, whose streets, parks, memorials, shops and food all reflect the Cuban experience in all its diversity. Note, though, that streets are much quieter than those of South Beach (except during the Little Havana Festival in early March), and today, many successful Cuban-Americans have moved elsewhere in the city, to be replaced by immigrants from parts of Central America, especially Nicaragua.

Make a beeline here for lunch at one of the many small restaurants on SW 8th Street, or Calle Ocho, the neighbourhood's main drag. Check out also **Cuban Memorial Boulevard**, the stretch of SW 13th Avenue just south of Calle Ocho, where a cluster of memorials underscores the Cuban-American presence in Miami. Here, the simple stone **Brigade 2506 Memorial** remembers those who died at the Bay of Pigs on April 17, 1961, during the abortive invasion of Cuba by US-trained Cuban exiles.

Coral Gables

All of Miami's constituent neighbourhoods are fast to assert their individuality, though none does it more definitively than **CORAL GABLES**, located southwest of Little Havana. Twelve square miles of broad boulevards, leafy side streets and Spanish and Italian architecture form a cultured setting for a cultured community.

Coral Gables's creator was a northern transplant born in Pennsylvania, **George Merrick**, who raided street names from a Spanish dictionary to plan the plazas, fountains and carefully aged stucco-fronted buildings here. Unfortunately, Coral Gables was taking shape just as the Florida property boom ended. Merrick was wiped out, and died as Miami's postmaster in 1942. But Coral Gables never lost its good looks, and it remains an impressive place to explore. Merrick wanted people to know they'd arrived somewhere special, and as such, eight grand **entrances** were planned on the main approach roads (though only four were completed). Three of these stand along the western end of Calle Ocho as you arrive from Little Havana.

The best way into Coral Gables is along SW 22nd Street, known as the **Miracle Mile**. Long dominated by fusty, no-name ladieswear boutiques, it's been redeveloped to attract some funkier, livelier tenants. Note the arcades and balconies, and the spirals and peaks of the **Omni Colonnade Hotel**, at 180 Aragon Ave, one block north, completed in 1926 to accommodate George Merrick's office. Further west, along Coral Way, the **Merrick House** (by 45min tour only on Sun & Wed

1pm, 2pm & 3pm; $5; ⓣ305/460-5361) was George's boyhood home. In 1899, when he was twelve, his family arrived here from New England to run a 160-acre farm, which was so successful that the house quickly grew from a wooden shack into an elegant dwelling of coral rock and gabled windows (thus inspiring the name of the future city).

While his property-developing contemporaries left ugly scars across the city after digging up the local limestone, Merrick had the foresight to turn his biggest quarry into a sumptuous swimming pool. Opened in 1924, the **Venetian Pool**, 2701 De Soto Blvd (June–Aug Mon–Fri 11am–7.30pm; April, May, Sept & Oct Tues–Fri 11am–5.30pm; Nov–March Tues–Fri 10am–4.30pm; year-round Sat & Sun 10am–4.30pm; May–September $10.50, October–April $6.75; ⓣ305/460-5356, ⓦwww.venetianpool.com), is an essential stop on a steamy Miami afternoon. Its pastel stucco walls hide a delightful spring-fed lagoon, with vine-covered loggias, fountains, waterfalls, coral caves and plenty of room to swim.

Wrapping its broad wings around the southern end of De Soto Boulevard, Merrick's crowning achievement was the fabulous **Biltmore Hotel**, 1200 Anastasia Ave (ⓣ1-800/727-1926, ⓦwww.biltmorehotel.com). With a 26-storey tower visible across much of low-lying Miami, everything about the *Biltmore* is over-the-top: 20ft-tall fresco-coated walls, vaulted ceilings, immense fireplaces, custom-loomed rugs and a massive swimming pool, which hosted shows by such bathing belles and beaux as Esther Williams and Johnny Weissmuller. Today, it costs upward of $200 a night to stay here, but a fascinating free tour leaves from the lobby every Sunday at 1.30pm, 2.30pm and 3.30pm; meet at the birdcages. You can also take **afternoon tea** in the lobby for $17 (Mon–Fri 2pm & 4.30pm sittings).

Vizcaya Museum & Gardens

In 1914, south of downtown, farm-machinery mogul James Deering dropped $15 million on recreating a sixteenth-century Italian villa within the tropical jungle. A thousand-strong workforce completed his **Villa Vizcaya**, 3251 S Miami Ave (daily 9.30am–4.30pm; free house tours every hour 11.30am–2.30pm, subject to availability of voluntary tour guides; $15; ⓣ305/250-9133, ⓦwww.miamidade.gov/vizcaya), in just two years. Deering's madly eclectic art collection, and his desire that the villa should appear to have been inhabited for four hundred years, result in a thunderous clash of Baroque, Renaissance, Rococo and Neoclassical fixtures and fittings. The fabulous landscaped **gardens**, with their many fountains and sculptures, are just as excessive.

Key Biscayne

A compact, immaculately manicured community, **KEY BISCAYNE**, five miles off mainland Miami, is a great place to live – if you can afford it. The only way onto the island is along the four-mile **Rickenbacker Causeway** ($1.50 one-way toll), which runs from SW 26th Road just south of downtown.

Crandon Park Beach, a mile along Crandon Boulevard (the continuation of the main road from the causeway), is one of the finest landscaped beaches in the city, with crystal-clear waters, BBQ grills and sports facilities (daily 8am–sunset; $5/car; ⓣ305/361-5421). Three miles of yellow-brown beach fringe the park, and give access to a sand bar enabling knee-depth wading far from the shore. Before you get to Crandon Park Beach, look out for the collection of worn-out buildings, tubs of beer and smoked fish known as *Jimbo's* on Duck Lake Road (see p.507). Crandon Boulevard terminates at the entrance to the **Bill Baggs Cape Florida State Recreation Area**, four hundred wooded acres covering the southern extremity of Key Biscayne (daily 8am–sunset; $8/car, pedestrians and cyclists $2;

☎305/361-5811). An excellent swimming **beach** lines the Atlantic-facing side of the park and a boardwalk cuts around the wind-bitten sand dunes towards the 1820s **Cape Florida lighthouse**. Climb the 95ft-high structure for mesmerizing views of the whole island and downtown Miami. For more detailed information, take a ranger-led tour (Thurs–Mon 10am & 1pm; free; contact details as above) and check out the exhibits and video in the nearby **keeper's cottage**.

Eating

Cuban food is what Miami does best, and it's not limited to the traditional haunts in **Little Havana**. The hearty comfort food – notably rice and beans, fried plantains and shredded pork sandwiches – is found in every neighbourhood, and you'll also want to try Cuban coffee: choose between *café cubano*, strong, sweet and frothy, drunk like a shot with a glass of water; *café con leche*, with steamed milk, and particularly good at breakfast with *pan cubano* (thin, buttered toast); or *café cortadito*, a smaller version of the *con leche*. Cuban cooking is complemented by sushi bars, American home-style diners, as well as Haitian, Italian and New Floridian (sometimes known as Floribbean: a mix of Caribbean spiciness and fruity Florida sauces) restaurants, among a handful of other ethnic cuisines.

Coral Gables, **South Beach** and the **Design District** are best for upmarket cafés and restaurants. **Seafood** is abundant: succulent grouper, yellowfin tuna and wahoo, a local delicacy, are among five hundred species of fish that thrive offshore. **Stone-crab claws**, served from October to May, are another South Florida specialty.

Big Pink 157 Collins Ave, South Beach. Prodigious portions of comfort food rule the menu here: mashed potatoes, ribs, macaroni and cheese and classic "TV dinners", all served at long communal tables.

David's Café 1058 Collins Ave. Eat deep-fried delicacies and daily Cuban specials like chicken with rice and beans ($6) on the tables outside, wedged between businessmen and teens, or grab a *café Cubano* (95¢) at the takeaway window. There's dining room-style seating at the second branch, 1654 Meridian Ave, just off Lincoln Rd: try staples like Cuban sandwiches ($7.95) and pork chops ($12.45). Open 24hr.

El Palacio de los Jugos 5721 W Flagler Ave, Little Havana. A handful of tables at the back of a Cuban produce market, where the pork sandwiches and shellfish soup from the takeaway stand are the tastiest for miles. Also serving refreshing *jugos* (juices) from $2.

El Pub 1548 SW 8th St, Little Havana. Comfortable Cuban restaurant that serves up a mighty fine *café con leche*. Sit awhile and try the shrimp and garlic, or the roast pork. Hard to miss with the colourful rooster statue out front.

The Forge 432 41st St, Miami Beach ☎305/538-8533. A memorable, upmarket dining spot where the hearty traditional food and huge wine cellar combine appealingly with a vibrant atmosphere and eclectic clientele. Prices for entrees here range from $31–50.

Front Porch Café 1418 Ocean Drive, South Beach This local hangout is refreshingly low-key considering its location: the delicious, dinner-plate-sized pancakes will easily take care of both breakfast and lunch.

Garcia's Seafood Grille 398 NW N River Drive, downtown ☎305/375-0765. Wonderful waterfront café with ramshackle wooden benches and superb, fresh fish dishes for around $15. Usually closes at 9.30pm.

Joe's Stone Crabs 11 Washington Ave, South Beach ☎305/673-0365. Specializing in succulent stone crabs and always packed – if you're impatient, do as the locals do and head to the takeaway window. Crabcakes ($19), fresh fish and the crispy fried chicken basket ($10) are also good. Open Oct–May.

La Sandwicherie 229 W 14th St, South Beach. Gigantic sandwiches stuffed with gourmet ingredients such as prosciutto and imported cheeses and starting at $5.20. It's open until 6am on the weekend, so it's a good choice for a post-clubbing refuel.

Le Bouchon du Grove 3430 Main Highway, Coconut Grove ☎305/448-6060. Along the tree-lined main street of Coconut Grove sits *Le Bouchon du Grove*. They serve lunch and dinner here, but you'll really want to come for breakfast and people-watch. The cajun omelet ($11) is quite fine, and on weekends, a mimosa is included with breakfast.

Michael's Genuine Food 130 NE 40th St, Design District ⓣ305/573-5550. One of the hottest restaurants in town, with seasonal, local ingredients whipped into eclectic creations by lauded chef Michael Schwartz; sizes range small to extra large (medium and large entrees $11–36). Favourites include the steak au poivre ($36) and the sweet & spicy pork belly ($14).

News Café 800 Ocean Drive, South Beach This mid-priced street café has front-row seating for the South Beach promenade – although the food's undistinguished. Open 24hr.

Pizza Rustica 863 Washington Ave, South Beach Mouthwateringly fresh gourmet pizza, with slab-like slices costing around $5. Also at 667 Lincoln Rd.

Scotty's Landing 3381 Pan American Drive, Coconut Grove. Tasty, inexpensive seafood and fish 'n' chips consumed at marina-side picnic tables. It's tucked away on the water by City Hall, and so can be hard to find – ask if you get lost.

Tap Tap 819 5th St, South Beach. Tasty, attractively presented and reasonably priced Haitian food. Most dishes are less than $10 – the goat in a peppery tomato broth is a knockout. Dinner only.

Nightlife and entertainment

Miami's **nightlife** is still unsurpassed in Florida. Almost every dancefloor is attached to a restaurant or a bar, so you could end up dancing anywhere. At the fully-fledged **clubs**, house and techno beats are most popular, followed by salsa or merengue played by Spanish-speaking DJs. Most of the action is centred in South Beach, and **cover charges** are around $20. Door policies are notoriously fierce at current in-spots; the places listed below include laidback local haunts as well as some of the hotter bars and clubs. The free *New Times* magazine, published every Thursday, offers **listings** of what's going on where and when – including **gay and lesbian** info.

If you want to try out the local **sports** scene, the Marlins major league baseball team and the Dolphins, Miami's pro football team, play at Dolphin Stadium, 2269 Dan Marino Blvd, sixteen miles northwest of downtown Miami (ⓣ305/623-6100, ⓦwww.dolphinstadium.com; take bus #27 from the main bus station). Note that the Marlins are due to move to a new stadium in 2011, at 1400 NW 4th St, Little Havana.

Bars and live music venues

The Abbey Brewing Company 1115 16th St, South Beach ⓣ305/538-8110. Beer-lovers congregate here for the best beers on South Beach. Try the creamy Oatmeal Stout – their best and most popular brew. Open until 5am.

Churchill's Pub 5501 NE 2nd Ave, Little Haiti ⓣ305/757-1807, ⓦwww.churchillspub.com. A touch of Britain within Little Haiti, with soccer and rugby matches on TV, UK beers on tap and live rock music. Check website for schedule.

The Democratic Republic of Beer 255 NE 14th St, ⓣ305/372-4161, ⓦwww.drbmiami.com. With well over 400 beers available, this is truly one of the best places for a pint in all of South Florida. The whole place is a bit indie-rock, and as a bonus (for some) it is a non-smoking establishment.

Hoy Como Ayer 2212 SW 8th St, Little Havana ⓣ305/541-2631, ⓦwww.hoycomoayer.us. Despite the city's sizeable Cuban population, this dark, smoky joint is about the only place in Miami to hear decent Cuban music. Check website for schedule.

Jimbo's Inside the park at Virginia Key Beach, Virginia Key ⓣ305/361-7026, ⓦwww.jimbosplace.com. Renowned ramshackle bar where you can help yourself to a beer from a wheelbarrow filled with ice. A good place to chat with old-timers.

Purdy Lounge 1811 Purdy Ave, South Beach ⓣ305/531-4622. An unheralded beachside gem, this large neighbourhood bar avoids clogging crowds of out-of-towners by its location on the less-touristed western side of South Beach. Open until 5am.

The Raleigh Bar Inside the *Raleigh Hotel*, 1775 Collins Ave, South Beach ⓣ305/534-6300. This elegant 1940s hotel bar, with its lushly restored wood panelling, is a throwback to the heyday of cocktail culture.

Sky Bar Inside the *Shore Club* hotel, 1901 Collins Ave, South Beach ⓣ786/276-6772. Sprawling outdoor bar draped around the hotel pool, with giant overstuffed square seats: dress up and expect a tough door unless you're staying at the hotel. Check out the smaller, attached *Sandbar*, with its view of the beach and ocean.

Tobacco Road 626 S Miami Ave, downtown ⓣ305/374-1198, ⓦwww.tobacco-road.com. This friendly dive bar – Miami's oldest, from 1912 – is a favourite with locals for its exceptional live r'n'b. Come early (it's packed after 7pm), and check website for the schedule of live acts.

Nightclubs

Club Space 34 NE 11th St, downtown ⓣ305/375-0001, ⓦwww.clubspace.com. This downtown pioneer has a rough-around-the-edge decor, with a type of illicit elegance: most people migrate here when the other venues shut down, for after-hours dancing until dawn – expect a friendly, loved-up, youngish crowd and big-name DJs.

Mansion 1235 Washington Ave, South Beach ⓣ305/531-5535, ⓦwww.mansionmiami.com. Sprawling nightclub complex with six VIP areas, nine bars and five dancefloors, each with its own style of music, hip-hop being the most popular.

Mynt Ultra Lounge 1921 Collins Ave, South Beach ⓣ786/276-6132, ⓦwww.myntlounge.com. Lounge/dance club, washed in green light, with an enormous bar and large, black leather sofas. Beautiful people abound here, and they are picky at the door.

Nikki Beach 1 Ocean Drive ⓣ305/538-1111, ⓦwww.nikkibeach.com/miami. Located right on the beach, this massive club features loungers, beds and palm trees, offering a real iconic South Beach experience. The food In the restaurant Is passable, and the dance tunes provided by a host of international and local DJs is the main reason to show up.

Nocturnal 50 NE 11th St, downtown ⓣ305/576-6996, ⓦwww.nocturnalmiami.com. The spaced-out will enjoy the trippy images projected on the rooftop terrace's 360-degree IMAX-style screen as the deep house music thumps in their ears.

The Florida Keys

Folklore, films and widespread hearsay have given the **FLORIDA KEYS** – a hundred-mile chain of islands that runs to within ninety miles of Cuba – an image of glamorous intrigue they don't really deserve; at least, not now that the go-go days of the cocaine cowboys in the 1980s are long gone. The Keys can more accurately be described as an outdoor-lover's paradise, where fishing, snorkelling and diving dominate. Terrific untainted natural areas include the **Florida Reef**, a great band of living coral just a few miles off the coast. But for many, the various keys are only stops on the way to **Key West**. This self-proclaimed "Conch Republic" has vibrant, Caribbean-style streets with plenty of convivial bars in which to while away the hours, watching the spectacular **sunsets**.

Wherever you are on the Keys, you'll experience distinctive **cuisine**, served for the most part in funky little shacks where the food is fresh and the atmosphere laidback. **Conch**, a rich meaty mollusc, is a specialty, served in chowders and fritters. There's also **key lime pie**, a delicate, creamy concoction of special Key limes and condensed milk, that bears little resemblance to the lurid green imposter pies served in the rest of the US.

Getting around the Keys could hardly be easier, provided you have a car. Fortunately, Greyhound does run a shuttle **bus** three times a day from the Fort Lauderdale and Miami airports all the way to Key West. There's just one route all the way through to Key West: the **Overseas Highway** (US-1). The road is punctuated by **mile markers** (MM), starting with MM127 just south of Miami and finishing with MM0 in Key West, at the corner of Whitehead and Fleming streets. As per Keys convention, addresses are given by the closest mile marker, along with the appellation of either "Oceanside" or "Bayside", depending on whether the place in question faces the Atlantic Ocean or Florida Bay.

Key Largo

The first and largest of the keys, **KEY LARGO**, is a bric-a-brac mix-up of filling stations, shopping plazas and fast-food outlets. The town does, however, provide a fine opportunity to visit the Florida Reef, at the **John Pennekamp Coral Reef State Park**, at MM102.5-Oceanside (daily 8am–sunset; $8/car and up to 8 passengers, or $4 for a single-occupant vehicle, pedestrians and cyclists $2; ⓣ305/451-1202, ⓦwww.pennekamppark.com). This protected 78-square-mile section of living coral reef is rated as one of the most beautiful in the world. If you can, take the **snorkelling tour** (9am, noon & 3pm; 2hr 30min; $29.95, plus $7 for equipment), or the **guided scuba dive** (9.30am & 1.30pm; 1hr 30min; $60; diver's certificate required). The **glass-bottom boat tour** (9.15am, 12.15pm & 3pm; 2hr 30min; $24) is less demanding. For information and to make reservations for all of these tours, call ⓣ305/451-6300. On any of them, you're virtually certain to spot lobsters, angelfish, eels and jellyfish along the reef, and shoals of silvery minnows stalked by mean-looking barracuda. The reef itself is a delicate living thing, comprising millions of minute coral polyps extracting calcium from the sea water and growing from one to sixteen feet every thousand years.

Practicalities

Key Largo has some of the widest selections of reasonably priced **accommodation** in the Keys, with many of the motels offering diving packages. Among the cheaper options, there's the basic but clean *Ed & Allen's Lodgings*, MM103.5-Oceanside (ⓣ1-888/333-5536, ⓦwww.ed-ellens-lodgings.com; ❸–❹), or the gloriously quirky, adult-only *Largo Lodge*, MM101.5-Bayside (ⓣ1-800/468-4378, ⓦwww.largolodge.com; ❺–❻). For something a bit more luxurious, try the huge, stylish chalets at the *Kona Kai Resort*, MM97.8-Bayside (ⓣ1-800/365-7829, ⓦwww.konakairesort.com; ❾), which is also distinguished by its lovely orchid house and rather unique art gallery. Delicious, fresh **seafood** – as well as chunks of alligator served like chicken nuggets – is available at *Snapper's*, 139 Seaside Ave, at the end of Ocean View Avenue off US-1 at MM94.5-Oceanside (ⓣ305/852-5956), while *Harriette's*, MM95.7-Bayside (ⓣ305/852-8689, open till 2pm) serves good breakfasts.

Islamorada

Comprising a twenty-mile strip of separate islands, including Plantation, Windley and Upper and Lower Matecumbe keys, **ISLAMORADA** (pronounced "eye-lah-more-RAH-da) is a much more welcoming place to dawdle than Key Largo. Most visitors come here to **fish** (you'll see charter boats advertised all along the highway), but you can also explore **Indian Key Historic State Park**, one of many small, mangrove-skirted islands off Lower Matecumbe Key. Once a thriving settlement founded by wrecker Jacob Houseman, it now boasts a riot of exotic plants and evocative ruins. Kayak rentals ($20/hr, $50/day) are available from **Robbie's Marina** (ⓣ305/664-9814) at MM78.5-Oceanside (there are no ferries).

Good-value **accommodation** in Islamorada includes the very cheap *Key Lantern/Blue Fin Inn*, MM82-Bayside (ⓣ305/664-4572, ⓦwww.keylantern.com; ❸) – ask for a room at the *Blue Fin* (same price), since these were more recently renovated – and the rather tranquil *Casa Morada* MM82-Bayside (Ⓣ1-888/881-3030, Ⓦwww.casamorada.com; ➎). As for **eating**, *Hungry Tarpon*, MM77.5-Bayside (Ⓣ305/664-0535), serves excellent fresh fish as well as tasty breakfasts, while the pricier – and often packed – *Islamorada Fish Company*, MM81.5-Bayside (Ⓣ1-800/258-2559), is also good for seafood.

The Middle Keys

Once over Long Key Bridge, you're into **THE MIDDLE KEYS**. At the not-for-profit **Dolphin Research Center**, MM59-Bayside (daily 9am–4.30pm; Ⓣ305/289-1121, Ⓦwww.dolphins.org), you can swim with the dolphins for $189 (reservations at Ⓣ305/289-0002).

The largest of several islands in the Middle Keys, **Key Vaca** holds the nucleus of the area's major settlement, **Marathon**. Here you'll find great **fishing** and **water-sports** opportunities, as well as a couple of small beaches. **Sombrero Beach**, along Sombrero Beach Road (off the Overseas Highway near MM50-Oceanside), has good swimming waters and shaded picnic tables.

Opposite the turning to the beach is the entrance to the 64-acre tropical forest of **Crane Point** (Mon–Sat 9am–5pm, Sun noon–5pm; $12; Ⓣ305/743-9100, Ⓦwww.cranepoint.net). This includes the **Museum of Natural History of the Florida Keys**, which presents an excellent introduction to the history and ecology of the area. Follow the 1.5-mile **nature trail** past the hammock forest, an area of dense hardwood trees characteristic of the Keys, until you reach the end. Here, you'll find the hundred-year-old **Adderley House Historic Site**, established by settlers from the Bahamas.

Marathon has some well-equipped **resorts**, such as the lush *Banana Bay*, MM49.5-Bayside (Ⓣ1-866/-689-4217, Ⓦwww.bananabay.com; ➎), which has a private beach. The best **budget option** is the *Flamingo Inn*, MM59.3-Bayside (Ⓣ1-800/439-1478, Ⓦwww.theflamingoinn.com; ➍–➏), a lovingly maintained retro motel with large rooms. For **eating**, there's terrific seafood – including succulent beer-steamed shrimp – at *Castaway*, 15th Street near MM47.5-Oceanside (Ⓣ305/743-6247). The tiny, laidback *Seven Mile Grill*, by the bridge of the same name at MM47.5-Bayside (Ⓣ305/743-4481), serves delicious conch chowder ($3.25) and creamy key lime pie to locals, sea salts and tourists alike. For good, cheap Cuban food and fresh snapper, try *Taino*'s, MM53-Oceanside (Ⓣ305/743-5247).

The Lower Keys

Starkly different from their neighbours to the north, **THE LOWER KEYS** are quiet, covered in dense vegetation and predominantly residential. Built on a limestone rather than a coral base, these islands have a flora and fauna all their own, most notably the elusive **Key deer** (see opposite).

The first place of consequence you'll hit after crossing Seven Mile Bridge is one of the Keys' prettiest spots: **Bahia Honda State Park**, at MM37-Oceanside (daily 8am–sunset; $8/car; pedestrians and cyclists $2; Ⓣ305/872-2353, Ⓦwww.bahiahondapark.com). It has the best stretch of sand in the Keys by far, and pristine, two-tone ocean waters, which can be enjoyed on a leisurely **kayak ride** ($10/hr, $30/day). You can also take snorkelling trips out to the **Looe Key Marine**

Sanctuary from here (daily 9.30am and 1.30pm; $29.95, $7 for equipment; ⓣ305/872-3210), a five-square-mile protected reef, easily the equal of the John Pennekamp Coral Reef State Park (see p.509). If you want to spend more time in the water, drive on to **Ramrod Key** and the Looe Key Dive Center (ⓣ1-800/942-5397, ⓦwww.diveflakeys.com), which offers daily 5-hour scuba ($70) and snorkelling ($30) excursions to the sanctuary.

Delightfully tame Key deer can be found ambling around the **National Key Deer Refuge** on Big Pine Key. Visit the refuge centre (Mon–Fri 8am–5pm, park open daily sunrise–sunset; ⓣ305/872-2239, ⓦnationalkeydeer.fws.gov), tucked away in a shopping mall off Key Deer Boulevard, just north of US-1 at MM30, to get a map of the best viewing spots.

Big Pine Key is the main Lower Keys settlement. Nearby you'll find most of the **accommodation** in these parts – which is generally more limited and expensive than in the Middle and Upper Keys. *Looe Key Reef Resort*, MM27.5-Oceanside (ⓣ1-800/942-5397, ⓦwww.diveflakeys.com; ❹–❺), is an ideal base for visiting the marine sanctuary, while for a real splurge, stay at the idyllic, adult-only *Little Palm Island*, MM28.5-Oceanside, Little Torch Key (ⓣ1-800/343-8567, ⓦwww.littlepalmisland.com; ❾), a private islet whose thatched cottages are set in lush gardens a few feet from the beach.

For **food**, the dollar-bill-decorated *No Name Pub*, a mile or so from MM30-Bayside down North Watson Boulevard (ⓣ305/872-9115) is known for its superb thin-crust pizza. Further on down the Overseas Highway, on Sugarloaf Key at MM20-Bayside, the friendly *Mangrove Mama's* (ⓣ305/745-3030; closed Sept) serves stupendous local cuisine in a cheery shack with a tropical garden; for pork lovers, the hog roast every Saturday night ($8.95) will be quite a hit.

Key West

Closer to Cuba than to mainland Florida, **KEY WEST** has a culture that is a bit contrary to the rest of the mainland US. Famed for their tolerant attitudes and laidback lifestyles, the thirty thousand islanders seem adrift in a great expanse of sea and sky, and – despite a million tourists a year – the place resonates with an individual spirit. In particular, liberal attitudes have stimulated a large gay influx, estimated at two out of five of the population. Although Key West today has been heavily transformed for tourists, the town has retained some of its offbeat character, especially away from the main drag of Duval Street.

Arrival and information

The **airport** (ⓣ305/296-5439) is four miles east of town, with the Greyhound **bus** station (ⓣ305/296-9072) adjacent to its entrance. There are no shuttle buses into town; a **taxi** (ⓣ305/296-6666) costs around $18.

The best place to head for **information** is the Greater Key West Chamber of Commerce, in the centre of town next to Mallory Square at 402 Wall St (Mon–Fri 8.30am–6.30pm, Sat & Sun 9am–6pm; ⓣ305/294-2587, ⓦwww.keywestchamber.org). The Chamber can give precise dates for Key West's annual **festivals**, the best of which are the Conch Republic Celebration in April and Fantasy Fest in late October, which feels like a gay Mardi Gras crossed with Halloween. A good source of **GLBT information** on celebrations and festivals is the Key West Business Guild, 513 Truman Ave (daily 9am–5pm; ⓣ305/294-4603, ⓦwww.gaykeywestfl.com).

It's best to explore the narrow streets of the mile-square Old Town – which contains virtually everything that you'll want to see – **on foot**. You could do it in

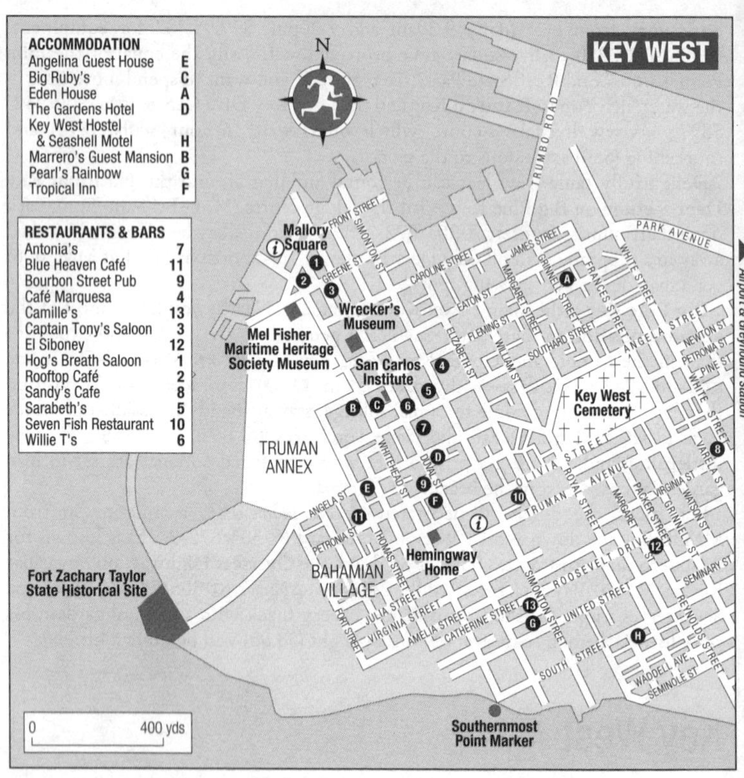

little more than a day, though dashing about isn't the way to enjoy the place, and the humidity might get in the way of sprinting everywhere. Cycling is another good way of getting around: **bikes** can be rented from Adventure Scooter & Bicycle Rentals, with locations at 1 Duval St ($15/day; ⓣ305/293-0441) and 617 Front St (same price; ⓣ305/293-9955).

Accommodation

During the winter, it's essential to make a **reservation** for accommodation in Key West; the Fantasy Fest festival at the end of October is another extremely busy time. In summer, competition for rooms is less fierce, and prices drop by up to thirty percent.

Angelina Guest House 302 Angela St ⓣ1-888/303-4480, ⓦwww.angelinaguesthouse.com. This charming guesthouse, tucked away in the backstreets of the Bahamian Village, has a cool, Caribbean feel, and is one of the best deals in town. Room with shared bath ❸–❹, room with private bath ❹–❺

Big Ruby's 409 Applerouth Lane ⓣ1-800/477-7829, ⓦwww.bigrubys.com. Gay guesthouse with stylish rooms clustered round a lagoon pool and a patio that's perfect for peaceful lounging. ❼

Eden House 1015 Fleming St ⓣ305/296-6868, ⓦwww.edenhouse.com. Here, a grotty lobby hides one of the city's best deals – large rooms, free parking, free happy hour every night and a shaded pool. Room with shared bath from ❹–❻, with private bath from ❻–❼

The Gardens Hotel 526 Angela St ⓣ1-800/526-2664, ⓦwww.gardenshotel.com.

One of the swishest hotels in town, this graceful inn has only 17 suites decked out in an airy Malaysian style with flat-screen TVs, fresh flowers and enormous beds. Groves of greenery and orchids envelop the building and hide it from prying eyes. ❼–❾

Key West Hostel & Seashell Motel 718 South St ⓣ305/296-5719, ⓦwww.keywesthostel.com. The hostel has cheap dorm beds ($44), a sunny patio and no curfew, while the *Seashell Motel* (❸) offers standard rooms ($75, low season) at the lowest rates in the neighbourhood.

Marrero's Guest Mansion 410 Fleming St ⓣ305/294-6977 or 1-800/459-6212, ⓦwww.marreros.com. Antique-filled old mansion that's supposedly haunted; room 18 is where most of the paranormal activity has been reported. Cheapest room ❻, room 18 ❼

Pearl's Rainbow 525 United St ⓣ1-800/749-6696, ⓦwww.pearlsrainbow.com. The lone women-only guesthouse on the island, this attractive former cigar factory serves breakfast and has two pools and two jacuzzis. ❺

Tropical Inn 812 Duval St ⓣ1-888/611-6510, ⓦwww.tropicalinn.com. The large, airy rooms in this charming restored "conch" house are at the centre of the action. Most rooms sleep three, and the more expensive ones have balconies. ❻–❼

The Town

Anyone who visited Key West two decades ago would now barely recognize the Old Town's main promenade, the mile-long swath of **Duval Street**. Much of the street has been transformed into a well-tended tourist strip of boutiques and beachwear shops, although it's still a pleasant place for a leisurely stroll. For a sense of the locals' town, take time to explore the side streets, where gnarled banyans, tall skinny palms, creeper and unruly, exotic blooms threaten to overtake the faded wooden houses. Make sure to visit the **Bahamian Village**, centred on Thomas and Petronia streets. Originally settled by Cubans and African-Bahamians, this relatively unrestored, untouristy corner of town is an atmospheric patchwork of single-storey cigar-makers' cottages, Cuban groceries and ramshackle old churches, all covered by a rich green foliage.

Numerous **museums** in town concern themselves with "wrecking", or the salvaging of cargo from sunken vessels; it's the industry on which Key West's earliest good times were based. The friendly little **Wreckers Museum**, 322 Duval St (also known as the Oldest House; daily 10am–4pm; free; ⓣ305/294-9502), illuminates the lives of the wreckers, portraying them as brave, uninsured heroes who risked all to save cargoes, ships and lives. Judging by the choice furniture that fills the house – lived in by the wrecker Captain Watlington during the 1830s – they did pretty well for their pains.

Farther up Duval, at no. 516, the **San Carlos Institute** (Fri–Sun noon–6pm; ⓣ305/294-3887) has played a leading role in Cuban exile life since it opened in 1871. Financed by a grant from the Cuban government, the present building dates from 1924; Cuban architect Francisco Centurion designed the two-storey building in the Cuban Baroque style of that period. Soil from Cuba's six provinces covers the grounds, and a cornerstone was taken from the tomb of Cuban independence campaigner José Martí. Don't forget to pick up the free Cuban Heritage Trail pamphlet here, which details sites of interest around town.

The **southernmost point** in Key West, and consequently in the continental US, is at the intersection of Whitehead and South streets. A daft-looking buoy marks the spot, and it is constantly mobbed by tourists. Back up and just west from the northern end of Duval Street is **Mallory Square**. In the early 1800s, thousands of dollars' worth of salvage was landed at the piers, stored in the warehouses and flogged at the auction houses here. At night there is usually some type of live music, which is really the main draw here.

Head rather to the nearby **Mel Fisher Maritime Heritage Society Museum**, 200 Greene St (Mon–Fri 8.30am–5pm, Sat & Sun 9.30am–5pm; $12; ⓣ305/294-2633, ⓦwww.melfisher.org), which showcases the diamonds, pearls and daggers, as well as countless vases, an impressive emerald cross and the obligatory cannon, that Fisher pulled up from two seventeenth-century shipwrecks in the 1980s – a haul said to be worth at least $200 million. Finally, further down Whitehead Street, you'll find Key West's most popular tourist attraction: the **Ernest Hemingway Home & Museum**, at no. 907 (daily 9am–5pm; $12, tours leave every 10–30min and last approximately 30min; ⓣ305/294-1136, ⓦwww.hemingwayhome.com). Hemingway owned this large, vaguely Moorish house for thirty years, but lived in it for barely ten, and most of the time he was occupied with fishing, writing and drinking. Some of his most acclaimed novels, including *A Farewell to Arms* and *To Have and Have Not*, were written in the study (the hayloft of a carriage house, which the author entered by way of a rope bridge). Divorced in 1940, Hemingway boxed up his manuscripts and moved them to a back room at the original *Sloppy Joe's* (see opposite), before heading off for a house in Cuba with his new wife, journalist Martha Gellhorn. Today, some sixty cats – many of them with six toes, traditionally employed as ships' mascots – pad contentedly around the gardens. Whatever the guides say, Hemingway kept his feline harem while living in Cuba, not Key West, so it's unlikely that these cats are in any way related to Papa's pets.

Eating

There's no shortage of chic venues for fine French, Italian and Asian cuisine in Key West, but most menus, not surprisingly, feature fresh **seafood**, and you should sample **key lime pie** and **conch fritters** – Key West specialties – at least once.

Antonia's 615 Duval St ⓣ305/294-6565. Expensive but excellent northern Italian cuisine served in a formal but friendly environment. Sit in the old front room rather than the characterless modern extension at the back. Open for lunch and dinner.

Blue Heaven Café Corner of Thomas and Petronia sts ⓣ305/296-0867. Sit in a dirt yard and enjoy yellowtail snapper, jerk chicken and fabulous lobster Benedict breakfasts as chickens peck around your feet.

Café Marquesa Inside the *Marquesa Hotel* at 600 Fleming St ⓣ305/292-1244. This chichi restaurant with its imaginative and pricey New American menu is the town's best fine dining spot. Entrees here range from $25–38.

Camille's 1202 Simonton St ⓣ305/296-4811. Great, affordable breakfasts and brunches – menu options in the past have included yellow corn cashew nut waffles and elaborate French toast with Godiva chocolate sauce. The dinner menu changes every night, but usually features fresh fish and fancy steaks.

El Siboney 900 Catherine St ⓣ305/296-4184. Come to this no-frills family diner for copious, inexpensive and good-quality Cuban dishes like grilled pork tenderloin ($14.95) and breaded shrimp ($11.95).

Rooftop Café 310 Front St ⓣ305/294-2042. This is the insider's choice for key lime pie; it's served with a top layer of fluffy meringue and a gooey graham cracker crust, which oozes with a tangy syrup made with lime juice and traces of melted butter. Slices are $7.

Sandy's Cafe Inside the M&M Laundry, 1026 White St ⓣ305/295-0159. Dingy café offering cheap and excellent Cuban sandwiches and the best *café con leche* this side of Miami.

Sarabeth's 530 Simonton St ⓣ305/293-8181. Satisfying home-style cooking served in the appropriately welcoming setting of an old wooden clapboard house. Specials here include the poached salmon salad ($14.95) and the chicken pot pie ($19.50).

Seven Fish Restaurant 632 Olivia St ⓣ305/296-2777. This little-known mid-priced bistro, easy to miss in its tiny white corner building, serves some of the best food – shrimp scampi, meatloaf and the like – in town. There are just over a dozen tables, so it pays to call ahead.

Nightlife and entertainment

The anything-goes nature of Key West is exemplified by the convivial **bars** that make up the bulk of the island's **nightlife**. Gregarious, rough-and-ready affairs, many stay open as late as 4am and feature regular **live music**. The most popular places are grouped around the northern end of Duval Street, and they are merely a conch toss away from each other.

Bourbon Street Pub 724 Duval St ⓣ305/296-1992. This huge pub complex is the largest gay-friendly place to drink in the centre of town; there's a pleasant garden out the back, complete with a large hot tub.

Captain Tony's Saloon 428 Greene St ⓣ305/294-1838. This rustic saloon was the original *Sloppy Joe's*, where Hemingway hung out (see opposite). Today, it's one of the less cheesy choices for live music and the offerings are diverse.

Hog's Breath Saloon 400 Front St ⓣ305/292-2032, ⓦwww.hogsbreath.com. This bar's one of the best places to catch live music in town, mostly for a nominal cover – just don't be put off by the boozed-up patrons circling its entrance.

Willie T's 525 Duval St ⓣ305/294-7674, ⓦwww.williets.com.com. There's food here, but their selection of mojitos (over 30) is what distinguishes this Duval Street watering hole. The people-watching is fine, and on Monday nights two mojitos can be had for $12.

The East Coast

Florida's **East Coast** presents a tremendously built-up mix of hotels, resorts, beaches and affluent developments north of Miami all the way to St Augustine. This is not to say this section of Florida is not without merit, but it's a lot less laidback than the state's Gulf Coast. **Fort Lauderdale**, no longer the party town of popular imagination, is today a sophisticated cultural centre with a bubbling, increasingly upmarket social scene. To the north, **Boca Raton** and **Palm Beach** are quiet, exclusive communities, their Mediterranean Revival mansions inhabited almost entirely by multimillionaires. Beyond Palm Beach, the coast is less developed; even the **Space Coast**, anchored by the extremely popular **Kennedy Space Center**, is smack in the middle of a nature preserve. Just north, **Daytona Beach** attracts race car- and motorcycle-enthusiasts with its festivals and the Daytona International Speedway. Before reaching Georgia, **St Augustine** is the spot where Spanish settlers established the first permanent European foothold in North America.

By car, the scenic route along the coast is **Hwy-A1A**, which sticks to the ocean side of the **Intracoastal Waterway**, formed when the rivers dividing the mainland from the barrier islands were joined and deepened during World War II. When necessary, Hwy-A1A turns inland and links with the much less picturesque **US-1**. The speediest road in the region, **I-95**, runs about ten miles west of the coastline, and is only worthwhile if you're in a hurry.

Fort Lauderdale

Following the 1960 teen-exploitation movie *Where the Boys Are*, **FORT LAUDERDALE**, with its seven miles of palm-shaded white sands, instantly became the number-one Spring Break destination in the US. However, having fuelled its economic boom on underage drinking and lascivious excess, the city promptly turned its back on the revellers. By the end of the 1980s, it had imposed enough restrictions on boozing and wild behaviour to put an end to the bacchanal. Since then, Fort Lauderdale has transformed itself into a thriving pleasure port, catering to individual yacht-owners and major cruise liners alike. It's also one of the fastest-growing residential areas in the country, and has for years been known as one of **gay** America's favourite holiday haunts.

Arrival and information

Both of Fort Lauderdale's public transit terminals are in or close to downtown. Greyhound **buses** pull in at 515 NE 3rd St, while the Amtrak and Tri-Rail **train** station (Ⓣ1-800/TRI-RAIL, Ⓦwww.tri-rail.com) is two miles west at 200 SW 21st Terrace – take bus #22 into town ($1.50). The main local **visitor centre** is at 100 E Broward Blvd, Suite 200 (Mon–Fri 8.30am–5pm; Ⓣ1-800/22-SUNNY, Ⓦwww.sunny.org).

Local bus #11 runs twice hourly along Las Olas Boulevard between downtown and the beach. You can also use the **water taxi** (all-day pass $15; Ⓣ954/467-6677, Ⓦwww.watertaxi.com), which can take you almost anywhere along Fort Lauderdale's many miles of waterfront.

Accommodation

Although Fort Lauderdale is moving inexorably upmarket, plenty of **motels** near the beach still offer a reasonable room for around $45 in summer (more like $85 in winter).

The Atlantic Resort & Spa 601 North Fort Lauderdale Beach Blvd Ⓣ954/567-8020, Ⓦwww.theatlantichotelfortlauderdale.com. The first of a projected series of luxury residence properties facing the ocean, this Mediterranean-style hotel features elegant rooms and suites, a spa, an oceanfront pool and a superb restaurant. ❾

Backpackers Beach Hostel 2115 N Ocean Blvd Ⓣ954/567-7275, Ⓦwww.fortlauderdalehostel.com. Clean, well-equipped hostel with free parking, internet and local calls. Dorm beds $20, private rooms $55 ❸

Tropi Rock Resort 2900 Belmar St Ⓣ1-800/987-9385, Ⓦwww.tropirock.com. Funky, family-owned hotel a block from the beach, where the good-value rates include use of tennis courts and a small gym. ❹–❺

Downtown Fort Lauderdale

Downtown Fort Lauderdale focuses on a few blocks between E Broward and E Las Olas boulevards, which cross US-1 a couple of miles east of I-95. Heavily prettified with parks and promenades, it's a pleasant place for a stroll, especially if you follow the mile-long pedestrian **Riverwalk** along the north shore of the New River into the **historic district**. Las Olas Boulevard itself, the main **shopping district**, remains busy day and night, with boutiques, galleries, restaurants, bars and street cafés in abundance. It's also home to the stimulating **Museum of Art**, 1 E Las Olas Blvd (daily 11am–5pm, closed Mon June–Sept; $10; Ⓣ954/525-5500, Ⓦwww.moafl.org), whose largely modern collection features the emotionally powerful expressionistic work of the CoBrA movement of artists from Copenhagen, Brussels and Amsterdam. Not far west, the simulators and interactive displays at the **Museum of Discovery & Science**, 401 SW 2nd St (Mon–Sat 10am–5pm, Sun noon–6pm; $11, $16 includes one IMAX film; Ⓣ954/467-6637, Ⓦwww.mods.org), includes the largest living Atlantic coral reef in captivity and a set of cockpit simulators for those who pine for aviator-themed thrills.

The beach

Although downtown has its charms and attractions, most visitors come to Fort Lauderdale for its broad, clean and undeniably beautiful **beach**. You'll find it by crossing the arching Intracoastal Waterway Bridge, about two miles along Las Olas

Boulevard from downtown. Stretching out along the seafront, Fort Lauderdale Beach Boulevard once bore the brunt of Spring Break partying, though only a few beachfront bars suggest the carousing of the past. Today, an attractive promenade draws a healthier crowd of joggers, in-line skaters and cyclists.

Eating and drinking

The two main drags for **eating** and **drinking** in Fort Lauderdale are Las Olas and Sunrise boulevards.

Casablanca Café 3049 Alhambra St ⓣ954/764-3500. An American piano bar in a Moroccan setting, serving a good, eclectic and moderately priced menu of Mediterranean-influenced American fare. Live music Wed–Sun nights.

The Floridian 1410 E Las Olas Blvd ⓣ954/463-4041. Retro decor and outstanding diner food – especially the mammoth breakfasts – at rock-bottom prices. Open 24hr.

Seasons 52 2428 E Sunrise Blvd at the Galleria Mall ⓣ954/537-1052. Health-conscious regional restaurant chain where every one of the fresh and tasty seasonal dishes has less than 475 calories.

Southport Raw Bar 1536 Cordova Rd ⓣ954/525-2526. South of downtown, near Port Everglades, this boisterous local bar specializes in succulent crustaceans and well-prepared fish dishes.

Taverna Opa 3051 NE 32nd St ⓣ954/567-1630. A raucous good time can be had at this fun Greek establishment, complete with flowing ouzo, crashing plates and belly dancing. Dinner only.

Boca Raton

BOCA RATON (literally, "the mouth of the rat"), twenty miles north of Fort Lauderdale, is noteworthy mostly for its abundance of **Mediterranean Revival architecture**. This style, prevalent here since the 1920s, has been kept alive in the downtown area by strict building codes. New structures must incorporate arched entranceways, fake bell towers and red-tiled roofs whenever possible, ensuring a consistent and distinctive "look".

The roots of this approach to architectural design originated with architect Addison Mizner, who swept into Boca Raton on the tide of the Florida property boom in 1925. Mizner was influenced by the medieval architecture he'd seen around the Mediterranean, and the few public buildings he completed (along with close to fifty homes) left an indelible mark on Boca Raton (Mizner also shaped the look of nearby Palm Beach). His million-dollar *Cloister Inn*, for example, grew into the present **Boca Raton Resort**, 501 E Camino Real, a pink palace of marble columns, sculptured fountains and carefully aged wood (ⓣ1-888/491-BOCA, ⓦwww.bocaresort.com; ➐–➒). Mizner's spirit is also invoked at **Mizner Park**, off US-1 between Palmetto Park Road and Glades Road, a stylish open-air shopping plaza adorned with palm trees and waterfalls. The park is home to the **Boca Raton Museum of Art**, 501 Plaza Real (Tues–Fri 10am–5pm, Sat & Sun noon–5pm; $8; ⓣ561/392-2500, ⓦwww.bocamuseum.org), worth a stop for its drawings by modern European masters – Degas, Matisse and Picasso – and a formidable collection of West African tribal masks.

A mile north of Hwy-798 (which links downtown Boca Raton with the beach), at 1801 N Ocean Blvd/Hwy-A1A, the **Gumbo Limbo Nature Center** (Mon–Sat 9am–4pm, Sun noon–4pm; $5 donation; ⓣ561/338-1473, ⓦwww.gumbolimbo.org) covers twenty acres inhabited by osprey, brown pelicans and sea turtles. Reserve well in advance for the night-time turtle-watching tours offered between May and July.

A couple of miles north of downtown, Boca Raton's most explorable **beachside** area is **Spanish River Park** (daily 8am–sunset; cars $16 weekdays, $18 weekends, pedestrians and cyclists free). Most of these fifty acres of lush vegetation and high-rise greenery are only penetrable on trails through shady thickets.

Practicalities

Greyhound does not serve Boca Raton. Tri-Rail **trains** stop off I-95, at 680 Yamato Rd (Ⓣ1-800/TRI-RAIL); there's a connecting shuttle to the town centre. The **Chamber of Commerce** is at 1800 N Dixie Hwy (Mon 9.30am–5pm, Tues–Fri 8.30am–5pm; Ⓣ561/395-4433, Ⓦwww.bocaratonchamber.com). The *Townplace Suites by Marriott*, 5110 NW 8th Ave (Ⓣ561/994-7232, Ⓦwww.towneplacebocaraton.com; ❺), and *Ocean Lodge*, 531 N Ocean Blvd (Ⓣ561/395-7772, Ⓦwww.oceanlodgeflorida.com; ❸), are two **hotels** providing reasonable value for money. For **eating**, the upscale *Max's Grill*, 404 Plaza Real, Mizner Park (Ⓣ561/368-0080), has appealing American dishes with Asian influences, while the *Whale's Rib*, 2033 NE 2nd St (Ⓣ954/421-8880) keeps the rock shrimp, raw oysters and conch chowder coming with a vengeance.

Palm Beach

A small island town of palatial homes and gardens, **PALM BEACH** has been synonymous with new and old money of all sorts. The nation's wealthy began wintering here in the 1890s, after Henry Flagler brought his East Coast railroad south from St Augustine, building two luxury hotels on this then-secluded, palm-filled island. Since then, the rich and famous have flocked here to become part of the Palm Beach elite.

Lined with designer stores and high-class art galleries, **Worth Avenue**, close to the southern tip of the island, is a good place to see some of the town's Addison Mizner-inspired **architecture**: stucco walls, Romanesque facades, passageways leading to small courtyards and spiral staircases climbing to the upper levels.

To the north, just off Cocoanut Row, white Doric columns front Whitehall, also known as the **Flagler Museum** (Tues–Sat 10am–5pm, Sun noon–5pm; $18; Ⓣ561/655-2833, Ⓦwww.flagler.org). This, the most overtly ostentatious home on the island, was a $4 million wedding present from Henry Flagler to his third wife, Mary Lily Kenan. As in many of Florida's first luxury homes, the interior design was lifted from the great buildings of Europe: among the 73 rooms are an Italian library, a French salon and a Louis XV ballroom.

Practicalities

In keeping with the upper-crust atmosphere, **public transportation** options around Palm Beach are limited. The West Palm Beach Amtrak (Ⓣ1-800/USA-RAIL), Tri-Rail (Ⓣ1-800/TRI-RAIL) and Greyhound (Ⓣ561/833-8534) stations are all located at 205 S Tamarind Ave in West Palm Beach on the mainland. To get to Palm Beach from here, take any PalmTran **bus** ($1.50; Ⓣ561/841-4BUS) terminating at Quadrille Boulevard, and transfer to the #41 or the #42 (no Sun service). The **Convention and Visitors' Bureau** is at 1555 Palm Beach Lakes Blvd, Suite 800 (Mon–Fri 9am–5pm; Ⓣ561/233-3000, Ⓦwww.palmbeachfl.com).

You'll need plenty of money to **stay** here: prices of $200 a night are not uncommon (rates are cheapest between May and Dec). The elaborate, antique-furnished *Palm Beach Historic Inn*, 365 S County Rd (Ⓣ561/832-4009, Ⓦwww.palmbeachhistoricinn.com; ❼), offers some of the best rates in town, but you'll need to reserve early. The equally opulent *Chesterfield*, 363 Cocoanut Row (ⓣ561/659-5800, ⓦwww.chesterfieldpb.com; ⓻), is another good choice. *Charley's Crab*, 456 S Ocean Blvd (ⓣ561/659-1500), is the place to go for reasonably priced **seafood**, while the lunch counter at *Hamburger Heaven*, 314 S County Rd (closed Sun; ⓣ561/655-5277), has been serving its delicious **burgers** since 1945.

The Space Coast

About two hundred miles north of Palm Beach, the so-called **Space Coast** is the base of the country's space industry, with a focus on the government-sponsored endeavours in this area of exploration. The focal point is the much-visited **Kennedy Space Center**, which occupies a flat, marshy island bulging into the Atlantic. In stark contrast, the rest of the island is taken over by a sizeable nature preserve, the **Merritt Island National Wildlife Refuge**, offering great opportunities for seeing wildlife, especially birds.

The Kennedy Space Center

The **Kennedy Space Center** is the nucleus of the US space programme: it's here that space vehicles are developed, tested and blasted into orbit. **Merritt Island** has been the centre of NASA's activity since 1964, when the launch pads at Cape Canaveral US Air Force base, across the water, proved too small to cope with the giant new Saturn V rockets used to launch the Apollo missions.

To reach the **Visitor Complex** (daily 9am–6pm; $38 adults, $28 children; ⓣ321/449-4444, ⓦwww.kennedyspacecenter.com), take exit 212 off I-95 to Hwy-405, and follow the signs; you can also get here by connecting with Hwy-3 off Hwy-A1A. The best **times to visit** are on weekends and in May and September, when crowds are thinner – but at any time, you should still allow an entire day for everything the Space Center has to offer. Check the weather, too, as thunderstorms may force some attractions to close.

The various exhibits in the Visitor Complex – mission capsules, spacesuits, lunar modules, a mock-up Space Shuttle flight deck – will keep anyone with the slightest interest in space exploration interested for a couple of hours. Afterwards, be sure to watch the two impressive IMAX movies dealing with some space theme or other and take a stroll around the open-air **Rocket Garden**, full of deceptively simple rockets from the 1950s, cleverly illuminated to show how they looked at blast-off. The newest attraction is the **Shuttle Launch Experience**, a simulation ride, where passengers get to see what it's like to be an astronaut, vertically "launching" into space and orbiting Earth aboard the Space Shuttle. The remainder of the visit is comprised of a two-hour guided **bus tour**. The bus passes the 52-storey Vehicle Assembly Building (where Space Shuttles are prepared for launch), stops to view the launch pad and winds up with an opportunity to inspect a Saturn V rocket and witness a simulated Apollo countdown. For the dates and times of **real-life launches**, call ⓣ321/449-4444 or check the website listed above.

Near the Space Center, on Hwy-405 in Titusville, the **Astronaut Hall of Fame** (included with regular $38 admission) is one of Florida's most entertaining interactive museums, where exhibits allow you to experience G-force and a bumpy ride along the surface of Mars.

Practicalities: Cocoa Beach

The closest **motels** to the Kennedy Space Center are on the mainland along US-1 (in Titusville, for example) – or, if you're looking for a more picturesque location, in **COCOA BEACH**, a few miles south on a ten-mile strip of shore washed by some of the biggest surfing waves in Florida. Options include the *Luna Sea*, 3185 N Atlantic Ave (Ⓣ1-800/586-2732, Ⓦwww.lunaseacocoabeach.com; ❹), *Days Inn*, 5500 N Atlantic Ave (Ⓣ321/784-2550, Ⓦwww.daysinncocoabeach.com; ❹), and *Fawlty Towers*, 100 E Cocoa Beach Causeway (Ⓣ321/784-3870, Ⓦwww.fawltytowersresort.com; ❸–❹). For great oysters and super riverfront views, head for *Sunset Café*, 500 W Cocoa Beach Causeway (Ⓣ321/783-8485) – but go early, as it's frequently mobbed.

Merritt Island National Wildlife Refuge

NASA doesn't have Merritt Island all to itself: the agency shares it with the **Merritt Island National Wildlife Refuge** (daily sunrise–sunset; free). Alligators, armadillos, raccoons, bobcats and an extravagant mix of birdlife live right up against some of the human world's most advanced hardware. Winter (Oct–March) is the best time to visit, when the skies are alive with birds migrating from the frozen north and mosquitoes aren't part of the equation. At any other time, especially in summer, the island's Mosquito Lagoon is worthy of its name: bring repellent.

Eight miles off I-95's exit 220, Hwy-406 leads to the seven-mile **Black Point Wildlife Drive**, which gives a solid introduction to the basics of the island's ecosystem; pick up the free leaflet at the entrance. Be sure to walk in the refuge, too: off the Wildlife Drive, the five-mile **Cruickshank Trail** weaves around the edge of the Indian River. Drive a few miles further east along Hwy-402 – branching from Hwy-406 just south of the Wildlife Drive and passing the **visitor centre** (Mon–Fri 8am–4.30pm, Sat & Sun 9am–5pm, closed Sun Nov–March; Ⓣ321/861-0667) – and then hike the three-quarters-of-a-mile **Oak Hammock Trail** or the two-mile **Palm Hammock Trail**, both accessible from the visitor centre car park.

Daytona Beach

The consummate Florida beach town, with its T-shirt shops, amusement arcades and wall-to-wall motels, **DAYTONA BEACH** owes its existence to twenty miles of enticing light-brown sands. Once a favourite Spring Break destination, Daytona Beach has been trying to cultivate a more refined image in recent years. In a strange twist of fate, partying students have been replaced by bikers and race-car fanatics. The town hosts three major annual events: the legendary **Daytona 500** stock-car race in February (tickets from $79; call Ⓣ877/306-RACE or visit Ⓦwww.daytonainternationalspeedway.com); **Bike Week**, in early March, which attracts tens of thousands of leather-clad bikers; and the relatively new **Biketoberfest**, in October, a scaled-down, more family-orientated version of Bike Week.

The origin of Daytona's race-car and motorcycle obsession goes back to the early 1900s, when pioneering auto enthusiasts including Louis Chevrolet, Ransom Olds and Henry Ford came to Daytona's firm sands to race prototype vehicles beside the ocean. In fact, the world land speed record was smashed here five times by the British millionaire Malcolm Campbell. As increasing speeds made racing on the sands unsafe, the **Daytona International Speedway**, an ungainly configuration of concrete and steel holding 150,000 people, was opened in 1959 three miles west of downtown along International Speedway Boulevard (buses #9, #10 and #60).

Though they can't capture the excitement of a race, **guided trolley tours** (daily except race days 9.30am–5.30pm, every half-hour; included in general admission) do provide a first-hand look at the remarkable gradients that help make this the fastest racetrack in the world. Occupying a large building next to the Speedway, the interactive exhibits that comprise the **Daytona 500 Experience** (daily 9am–5pm; $24; ⓣ386/947-6800; ⓦwww.daytona500experience.com) let you have a virtual try at jacking a race-car off the ground during a pit stop and commentating on a race, while an engaging wide-screen film complete with excellent 3-D effects tells you all about NASCAR (National Association of Stock Car Auto Racing).

For all the excitement that racing generates, the best thing about Daytona is the seemingly limitless **beach**: it's five hundred feet wide at low tide, and fades dreamily off into the heat haze. Daytona is also one of the few beaches in Florida you can drive on, which is perhaps a dubious environmental activity. Pay $5 (Feb–Nov only) at the various entrances and follow the posted procedures.

Practicalities

US-1 (called, in town, Ridgewood Avenue) ploughs through mainland Daytona Beach, passing the Greyhound **bus** station at 138 S Ridgewood. **Trolleys** ($1.25) run the length of the beach until midnight from mid-January to early September. The **visitor centre** is at 126 E Orange Ave (Mon–Fri 9am–5pm; ⓣ1-800/854-1234, ⓦwww.daytonabeach.com). If you're going to be in Daytona during any of the big events, **accommodation** should be booked at least six months ahead; and expect minimum stays and prices to at least double. Any of the **motels** along the oceanfront Atlantic Avenue makes a good beach base: there's the *Cove Motel*, 1306 N Atlantic Ave, right on the beach (ⓣ1-800/828-3251, ⓦwww.themathorgroup.com/motelcove/home.htm; ❹–❺); or the welcoming, British-run *Ocean Court*, 2315 S Atlantic Ave (ⓣ386/253-8185, ⓦwww.oceancourt.com; ❸). Away from the beach, and close to lively Beach Street, the *Coquina Inn*, 544 S Palmetto Ave (ⓣ386/254-4969; ⓦwww.coquinainndaytonabeach.com; ❺), is a cosy B&B.

Atlantic Avenue is lined with the predictable fast-food outlets, but for more inspiring **eating** options head to Beach Street on the mainland, where the Fifties-style *Daytona Diner* at no. 290 1/2 N (ⓣ386/258-8488) dishes up huge breakfasts for around $6 and *Angell & Phelps Café* at no. 156 S (ⓣ386/257-2677) offers creative American-style gourmet cuisine in an informal setting. For fresh fish and seafood, head south towards Ponce Inlet, where you'll find the equally good *Lighthouse Landing*, beside the Ponce Inlet Lighthouse at 4940 S Peninsula Drive (ⓣ386/761-9271), and *Inlet Harbor*, overlooking a marina at 133 Inlet Harbor Rd (ⓣ386/767-5590).

St Augustine

Forty miles north of Daytona Beach, US-1 passes through the heart of charismatic **ST AUGUSTINE**. With a densely packed city centre and an eminently walkable Mediterranean feel, it bucks the sprawling feel of much of Florida's East Coast. The oldest permanent settlement in the US, with much from its early days still intact along its narrow streets, it also offers two alluring lengths of **beach** just across Matanzas Bay.

Though Ponce de León touched ground here in 1513, European settlement didn't begin until half a century later, when Spain's Pedro Menéndez de Avilés put ashore on St Augustine's Day in 1565. The town developed into a major social and administrative centre, soon to be capital of east Florida. Subsequently, Tallahassee (see p.546) became the capital of a unified Florida, and St Augustine's

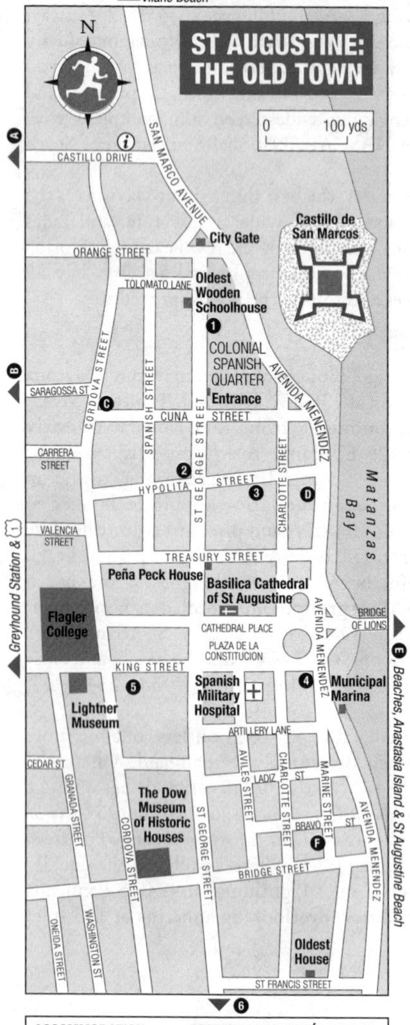

ACCOMMODATION		RESTAURANTS, CAFÉS & BARS	
Carriage Way	A	95 Cordova	5
Casa Monica	C	A1A Aleworks	4
Casablanca Inn	D	Casa Maya	3
Kenwood Inn	E	Columbia	2
Pirate Haus Inn	F	Mill Top Tavern	1
The Saragossa Inn	B	The Oasis	6

fortunes waned. Since then, expansion has largely bypassed the town – a fact inadvertently facilitating the restoration programme that has turned this quiet community into a fine historical showcase.

Arrival and information

The Greyhound **bus** station, 1711 Dobbs Rd, is a couple of miles from the centre of town. The **visitor centre**, 10 Castillo Drive (daily 8.30am–5.30pm; Ⓣ1-800/653-2489, Ⓦwww.visitoldcity.com), shows a film on the history of the town, has recommendations for a variety of tours (see below) and information on numerous local festivals, including torchlit processions and a Menorcan Fiesta.

St Augustine is best seen **on foot**, though two **sightseeing trains** tour the main landmarks (daily 8.30am–5pm; $19; tickets available from visitor centre or at many B&Bs and hotels – discount if you purchase online; Ⓣ1-800/824-1906, Ⓦwww.redtrains.com). There's **no public transportation**, so if you want to get to the beaches two miles away and you don't have a car you'll have to take a **taxi** (Ancient City Cabs; Ⓣ904/824-8161). The Old Town Trolley sightseeing train (daily 8.30am–4.30pm; Ⓣ1-888/910-8687, Ⓦwww.trolleytours.com/st-augustine) weaves its way around St Augustine, offering up a mix of compelling narration as it stops at 22 different sites around town. Visitors are welcome to jump on and off the trolley at any of the sites, and a three-day unlimited pass for adults is $23, children $10. As for organized **tours**, harbour cruises by Scenic Cruise ($16.75; Ⓣ904/824-1806) leave four to six times a day from the Municipal Marina, near the foot of King Street. The well-organized and informative Tour St Augustine ($12; Ⓣ1-800/797-3778) leads historical walking tours, while various spooky sites are visited during the A Ghostly Experience" evening walking tour ($12; Ⓣ904/461-1009).

Accommodation

The Old Town has many excellent restored **inns** offering bed-and-breakfast, and there are cheaper chain **hotels** outside the centre of town along San Marco Avenue and Ponce de León Boulevard. Note that rates generally rise by $20–60 on weekends.

Carriage Way 70 Cuna St ⓣ1-800/908-9832, ⓦwww.carriageway.com. Canopy and four-poster beds, claw-foot tubs and antiques add to the period feel of this 1880s house. ❺–❻

Casa Monica 95 Cordova St ⓣ1-800/648-1888, ⓦwww.casamonica.com. Elegant, beautifully restored Spanish-style hotel that has hosted the king and queen of Spain. The rooms have wrought-iron beds and a certain sumptuous seaside charm. ❼–❽

Casablanca Inn 24 Avenida Menendez ⓣ904/829-0928, ⓦwww.casablancainn.com. This inn features many rooms with jacuzzis, whirlpool baths and a delightful cosy martini bar with live music. A good choice for those who want to be right in the mix of things. ❻

Kenwood Inn 38 Marine St ⓣ904/824-2116, ⓦwww.thekenwoodinn.com. Peacefully situated near the waterfront, this charming B&B has a pretty pool and offers complimentary use of bikes for guests. ❺

Pirate Haus Inn 32 Treasury St ⓣ904/808-1999, ⓦwww.piratehaus.com. The town's only hostel accommodation, near the Plaza, is popular with backpackers. It has a giant kitchen and a common room stuffed with guidebooks. Beds in a/c dorms are $20; five private rooms are available from $50. And there's also an all-you-can-eat free pancake breakfast. ❷

The Saragossa Inn 34 Saragossa St ⓣ904/808-7384 or 1-877/808-7384, ⓦwww.saragossainn.com. This lovely little pink cottage began life in 1924 as a Sears Craftsman bungalow and now holds four comfortable guest rooms and two suites, just a bit west of the beaten path. ❺–❻

The Old Town

Bordered on the west by St George Street, and on the south by Plaza de la Constitución, St Augustine's **Old Town** holds the well-tended evidence of the town's Spanish period. It may be small, but there's a lot to see: an early start, around 9am, will give you a lead on the tourist crowds, and should allow a good look at almost everything in one day.

Given the fine state of the **Castillo de San Marcos National Monument**, on the northern edge of the Old Town beside the bay (daily 8.45am–4.45pm; $6; ⓦwww.nps.gov/casa), it's difficult to believe that the fortress was built in the late 1600s. Its longevity is due to its design: a diamond-shaped rampart at each corner maximized firepower, and 14ft-thick walls reduced its vulnerability to attack. Inside, there are a number of great demonstrations (including a historic weapons demonstration) and venturing along the 35ft-long ramparts gives good views across the city and the bay.

A hundred yards west of the monument, the eighteenth-century **City Gate** marks the entrance to **St George Street**, once the main thoroughfare and now a tourist-trampled, though genuinely historic, pedestrianized strip. You'll find a bunch of places called "The oldest..." in St Augustine; the **Oldest Wooden Schoolhouse**, set in lush gardens at 14 St George St (daily 9am–5pm; $3.50), is one of the most atmospheric – a restored wooden shack with speaking wax dummies portraying nineteenth-century schoolchildren. It's perhaps unintentionally camp, but it all seems to work.

Heading south on St George Street, a fair-sized plot between Tolomato Lane and Cuna Street is taken up by the excellent **Colonial Spanish Quarter** (daily 9am–5.30pm, last ticket sold at 4:45pm; $7). In its nine reconstructed homes and workshops, volunteers dressed as Spanish settlers go about their business at anvils and foot-driven wood lathes. Don't forget to stop by the Taberna del Gallo here for a glass of beer and good conversation about this interpretive site.

For a more intimate look at local life during a slightly later period, head a little further south to the **Peña Peck House**, 143 St George St (Mon–Fri 10.30am–5pm, Sun 12.30–5pm; donation requested; ⓣ904/829-5064). Thought to have originally been the Spanish treasury, by the time the British took over in 1763 this was the home of a physician and his gregarious spouse, who turned the place into a high-society rendezvous.

In the sixteenth century, the Spanish king decreed that all colonial towns must be built around a central plaza; thus, St George Street runs into the **Plaza de la Constitución**, a marketplace from 1598. On the plaza's north side, the **Basilica Cathedral of St Augustine** (daily 7am–5pm; donation) adds a touch of grandeur, although it's largely a Sixties remodelling of the late eighteenth-century original.

Tourist numbers lessen as you cross **south of the plaza** into a web of quiet, narrow streets, all just as old as St George Street. West of the plaza along King Street, opposite Flagler College, the opulent **Lightner Museum** (daily 9am–5pm, last admission 4pm; $10; ⓣ904/824-2874) displays fine and decorative arts in the former building of one of the most fabulous resorts of the late nineteenth century. A more substantial exploration of local history is available a ten-minute walk southeast from here, at 14 St Francis St, in the form of the fascinating **Oldest House** (daily 9am–5pm, last admission 4.30pm; $8), which is indeed the oldest house in town, dating from the early 1700s. Its rooms are furnished to show how the house – and people's lives – changed as new eras unfolded.

The beaches

Some fine **beaches** – busiest at weekends – lie just a couple of miles east from the Old Town. Crossing the bay via the Bridge of Lions, and continuing east on Hwy-A1A will bring you to the **Anastasia State Recreation Area**, on Anastasia Island (daily 8am–sunset; cars $8, cyclists and pedestrians $2), which offers a thousand protected acres of dunes, marshes and scrub, linked by nature walks. A few miles further south, **St Augustine Beach** is family terrain, with some good restaurants and a fishing pier.

Eating, drinking and entertainment

Eating in the Old Town can be expensive, and a number of its cafés and restaurants are closed in the evening. Of those that stay open, several double as **drinking** spots and **live music venues**.

A1A Aleworks 1 King St ⓣ904/829-2977. Nice brewpub that features fried lobster bites ($12) and mango BBQ shrimp skewers ($15). The beers are quite good, and the A Strange Stout and Porpoise Point Ale are both highly recommended.

95 Cordova At the *Casa Monica* hotel, 95 Cordova St ⓣ904/810-6810. This luxurious and elegant restaurant's menu features expensive but masterful nouvelle continental cuisine. Entrees range from $19–33.

Casa Maya 17 Hypolita St ⓣ904/823-1739. Pleasant and healthy Mayan-influenced food here, including corn tortilla mahi-mahi tacos and excellent brunch.

Columbia 98 St George St ⓣ904/824-3341. Enjoy paella, tapas and other traditional Spanish/Cuban food in a sumptuous setting of fountains and candlelight.

Mill Top Tavern 19 1/2 George St ⓣ904/829-2329. There's a terrific, funky atmosphere at the top of this nineteenth-century mill, where you'll hear live music and get a great, open-air view of the Castillo.

The Oasis 4000 Ocean Trace Rd, St Augustine Beach ⓣ904/471-3424. This beach bar is famous for its burgers with their multitude of tasty toppings.

Jacksonville

Hunkered down between the great double loop of the St Johns River, **JACKSONVILLE** struggled for years to throw off its long-standing reputation as a dour industrial port city with a deeply conservative population. During the 1990s, the city began to gain standing as a new service industry centre, bringing a spate of construction projects and new homebuyers to the area. The sheer size of the city – at 841 square miles, the largest in the US – serves to dilute its easy-going character, and it is quite difficult to get around without a car.

The most noteworthy building in the downtown area, which occupies the north bank of the St Johns River, is the **Florida Theater**, 128 E Forsyth St (box office ⓣ904/355-2787, ⓦwww.floridatheatre.com). The theatre's interior has been restored with a dazzling gold proscenium arch, and today it's used for a variety of performances. Five minutes' walk from the theatre, at 333 N Laura St, the **Museum of Contemporary Art** (Tues, Weds, Fri & Sat 10am–4pm, Thurs till 8pm, Sun noon–4pm; $8, free Wed 5–9pm; ⓣ904/366-6911, ⓦwww.mocajacksonville.org) has paintings, sculptures and photography of surprising scope and depth, including large Ed Paschke and James Rosenquist canvases.

Just south of the Fuller Warren River bridge (I-95), the **Cummer Museum of Art and Gardens**, 829 Riverside Ave (Tues 10am–9pm, Wed, Thurs, Fri 10am–4pm, Sun noon–5pm; $10, free Tues after 4pm; ⓣ904/356-6857, ⓦwww.cummer.org), has spacious rooms and sculpture-lined corridors containing works by prominent European and American masters. The two acres of lovely Italianate and English gardens that overlook the river are an added bonus.

Practicalities

From the Greyhound **bus station** downtown at 10 N Pearl St, it's an easy walk to the **Convention and Visitors Bureau**, 550 Water St, suite 1000 (Mon–Fri 8am–5pm; ⓣ904/798-9111 or 1-800/733-2668, ⓦwww.visitjacksonville.com). The **train station** is an awkward six miles northwest of downtown at 3570 Clifford Lane; one local reputable **taxi** company is Yellow Cab (ⓣ904/355-8294). The cheapest **accommodation** can be found at the chain hotels on the city's perimeter, such as *Comfort Suites*, 1180 Airport Rd (ⓣ904/741-0505; ❺). Downtown, the *Hyatt Regency Jacksonville Riverfront*, 225 Coastline Drive (ⓣ1-800/233-1234, ⓦwww.jacksonville.hyatt.com; ❼), has a great riverfront location. Alternatively, head to the Riverside-Avondale residential neighbourhood (near the Cummer Museum) for a choice of good B&Bs, including the riverfront *The House on Cherry Street*, 1844 Cherry St (ⓣ904/384-1999, ⓦwww.houseoncherry.com; ❹–❺). For **eating**, you'll find several places for a quick and filling lunch at the Jacksonville Landing mall, downtown between Water Street and the river. On the south bank, the *River City Brewing Co.*, 835 Museum Circle (ⓣ904/398-2299), offers great steaks, home-brewed beer and river views, while Riverside-Avondale has some appealing cafés such as *Biscotti's*, 3556 St Johns Ave (ⓣ904/387-2060).

Jacksonville's beaches

Travelling south from Jacksonville on I-95, then east on Hwy-202, you'll first hit **Ponte Vedra Beach**, whose crowd-free sands and million-dollar homes form one of the most exclusive communities in northeast Florida. A few miles north from here on Hwy-A1A is the much less snooty **Jacksonville Beach**. Two miles north of Jacksonville Beach's old pier, the more commercialized **Neptune Beach** blurs into the identical-looking **Atlantic Beach**; both are more family-oriented, and are best visited for eating and socializing.

Practicalities

A pleasant place to stay for a few days is the *Pelican Path Bed and Breakfast By the Sea*, 11 19th Ave N, Jacksonville Beach (Ⓣ904/249-1177, Ⓦwww.pelicanpath.com; ❼–❽), Down the street is the *Sea Horse Oceanfront Inn*, 120 Atlantic Blvd, Neptune Beach (Ⓣ904/246-2175, Ⓦwww.seahorseoceanfrontinn.com; ❺). Good **eating options** at the beaches are *Ragtime Tavern Seafood Grill*, 207 Atlantic Blvd, Atlantic Beach (Ⓣ904/241-7877), with its extensive seafood menu; *Sun Dog Diner*, 207 Atlantic Blvd, Neptune Beach (Ⓣ904/241-8221), offering above-average, creative diner fare; and *Beach Hut Café*, 1281 S 3rd St, Jacksonville Beach (Ⓣ904/249-3516), serving huge, delicious breakfasts.

Central Florida

Encompassing a broad and fertile expanse between the east and west coasts, most of **Central Florida** was farming and ranching country when vacation-mania first struck the state's beachside strips. From the 1970s on, this picture of tranquillity was shattered: no section of the state has been affected more dramatically by modern tourism. As a result, the most visited part of Florida can also be one of the ugliest. A clutter of highway interchanges, motels and billboards arch around the sprawling city of **Orlando**, where a tourist-dollar chase of Gold Rush magnitude was sparked by **Walt Disney World**, the biggest and cleverest theme-park complex ever created. The rest of central Florida is quiet by comparison, though visitors may wish to take in some of the quietude around Ocala, which is known for its horse ranches.

Orlando and the theme parks

Once a quiet farming town, **ORLANDO** now welcomes more visitors than any other place in the state. The reason, of course, is **Walt Disney World**, along with **Universal Orlando**, **SeaWorld Orlando** and a host of other attractions. Most of the hotels are found along International Drive, Hwy-192 or in and around Disney World, all of which lie several miles south of the downtown area, which has the city's best nightlife.

Arrival and information

The **international airport** is nine miles south of downtown Orlando; local buses (see below) link the airport with downtown (#11 or #51) and International Drive (#42). Alternatively, **shuttle buses** operated by Mears Transportation (24hr; Ⓣ407/423-5566) charge a flat fee of $16 to any hotel in downtown; $17 to International Drive; and $19 to Hwy-192. Those staying at Disney can take advantage of the free airport transfer offered by **Disney's Magical Express Transportation** (Ⓣ1-866/599-0951). **Taxis** to these destinations cost between $30 and $60. **Buses** and **trains** arrive, respectively, downtown at the Greyhound terminal, 555 N John Young Parkway (Ⓣ407/292-3424), and the Amtrak station,

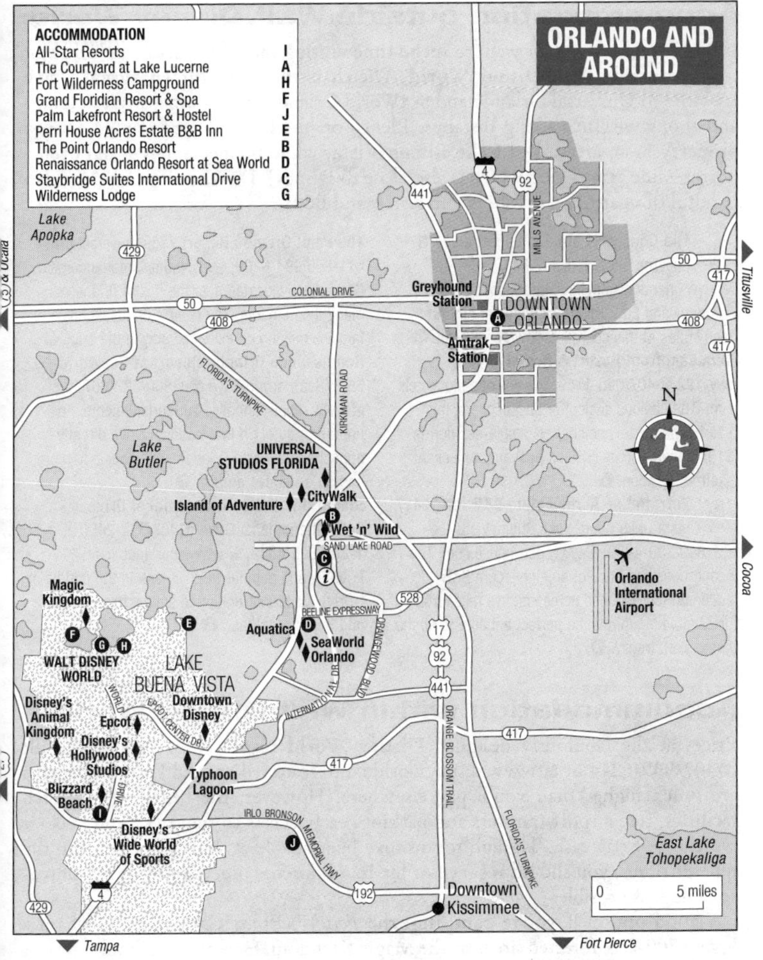

1400 Sligh Blvd (Ⓣ407/843-7611). The efficient **Official Visitor Center**, 8723 International Drive (daily 8.30am–6.30pm; Ⓣ407/363-5872, Ⓦwww.orlandoinfo.com) has a plethora of brochures and discount coupons.

Getting around

You have to be determined to get to the theme parks without a car, but it can be done. Local Lynx **buses** (Ⓣ407/841-5969, Ⓦwww.golynx.com) converge at the downtown Orlando terminal, 455 N Garland Ave. Route #50 heads to Walt Disney World, while route #8 or the limited stop #38 go to International Drive (all rides are $2). Along International Drive (including SeaWorld Orlando), the **I-Ride Trolley** (Ⓣ1-866/243-7483, Ⓦwww.iridetrolley.com) operates every twenty minutes daily from 8am to 10.30pm, costing $1.25 one-way. **Taxis** are the best way to get around at night – try Diamond Cab (Ⓣ407/523-3333). All the main **car rental** firms have offices at or close to the airport.

Accommodation outside Walt Disney World

If you're on a budget, or want to spend time visiting the other parks, you'd do best to stay **outside Walt Disney World**. The chain hotels on **International Drive** are close to Universal Orlando and SeaWorld Orlando, with numerous restaurants and shops within walking distance. Plenty of hotels are dotted around Disney property in an area called **Lake Buena Vista**, while budget hotels – and even a hostel – line **Hwy-192** (which is also close to Disney). **Downtown** Orlando has a handful of charming, privately run hotels and B&Bs.

The Courtyard at Lake Lucerne 211 N Lucerne Circle E ⓣ407/648-5188, ⓦwww.orlandohistoricinn.com. Choose from Victorian- and Edwardian-era rooms or airy Art Deco suites at this charming downtown hotel. ❺

Palm Lakefront Resort & Hostel 4840 W Hwy-192 ⓣ407/396-1759, ⓦwww.orlandohostels.com. The obvious choice for backpackers, this resort-style hostel has six-bed, single-sex dorms ($19), private rooms ($36), a pool and a pleasant lakefront location. ❷

Perri House Acres Estate B&B Inn 10417 Vista Oaks Court, Lake Buena Vista ⓣ1-800/780-4830, ⓦwww.perrihouse.com. The incongruous presence of an eight-room B&B hidden on four wooded acres just five miles from the Magic Kingdom is the perfect antidote to all the theme-park frenzy. ❺

The Point Orlando Resort 7389 Universal Blvd ⓣ1-866/994-6309, ⓦwww.thepointorlando.com. Conveniently located near the mix of Orlando's many theme parks, *The Point* is an ideal choice for families making an extended stay in the area. ❽

Renaissance Orlando Resort at SeaWorld 6677 Sea Harbor Drive ⓣ1-800/327-6677, ⓦwww.renaissanceseaworldorlando.com. An upmarket hotel off International Drive directly opposite Sea World Orlando, with spacious rooms and an attractive atrium. ❼

Staybridge Suites International Drive 8480 International Drive ⓣ407/352-2400 or 1-800/866-4549, ⓦwww.sborlando.com. Friendly and popular hotel smack in the middle of I-Drive, with well-equipped suites, free internet and buffet breakfast. ❻

Accommodation within Walt Disney World

Prices at the fabulously designed **Disney World resorts** (reservations for all: ⓣ407/939-6244 or ⓦwww.disneyworld.com) scattered around Disney property are much higher than you'll pay elsewhere. However, the benefits (top-notch facilities, free airport transfers and parking, early access to the parks) can make it worth the extra cash. Though rooms may be available at short notice during the quieter times, you should **reserve as far in advance** – nine months is not unreasonable – as possible.

A good option if you're **camping**, the *Fort Wilderness Campground* is set on a lovely 700-acre forested site near the Magic Kingdom. Here you can hook up your RV or pitch your tent from $44, or rent a six-berth cabin from $270, and still enjoy the privileges of being a Disney guest.

All-Star Resorts Three resorts near the Blizzard Beach water park, with themes based on sports, music and movies. The most affordable options in Disney by far.

Animal Kingdom Lodge Wake up to see African wildlife grazing outside your window at one of Disney's most spectacular and luxurious resorts. ❽

Grand Floridian Resort & Spa Gabled roofs, verandas, crystal chandeliers and a full-service spa make this Disney's most elegant – and expensive – resort. ❾

Wilderness Lodge This convincing recreation of a frontier log cabin features a wood-burning fire in the lobby and welcoming rooms. ❽

Walt Disney World

As significant as air conditioning in making the state what it is today, **WALT DISNEY WORLD** turned a wedge of Florida farmland into one of the world's most lucrative holiday destinations. The immense and astutely planned empire also pushed the state's media profile through the roof: from being a down-at-heel mixture of cheap motels, retirement homes and alligator zoos, Florida became a showcase of modern international tourism overnight.

Disney World is the pacesetter among theme parks. It goes way beyond Disneyland (see p.867), which opened in Anaheim, California, in 1955, delivering escapism at its most technologically advanced and psychologically brilliant, across an area twice the size of Manhattan. Its four main theme parks are quite separate entities and, ideally, you should allow at least a full day for each. The **Magic Kingdom** is the Disney park of popular imagination, where Mickey mingles with the crowds – very much the park for kids, though at its high-tech best capable of captivating even the most jaded of adults. Known for its giant, golfball-like geosphere, **Epcot** is Disney's celebration of science, technology and world cultures; this sprawling area involves a lot of walking, and young children may grow restless here. The smaller **Disney's Hollywood Studios** takes its inspiration from movies, TV and music, offering some good thrill rides and live shows that will appeal to adults and kids alike. The newest of the four, **Disney's Animal Kingdom Park**, brings all manner of African and Asian wildlife to the theme-park setting.

Along with the main parks, other forms of entertainment have been created to keep people on Disney property for as long as possible. There are two excellent water parks, **Blizzard Beach** and **Typhoon Lagoon**, a sports complex called **Disney's Wide World of Sports** and **Downtown Disney**, where you can eat, drink and shop to your heart's content.

The Magic Kingdom

The **Magic Kingdom**, dominated by **Cinderella's Castle**, a stunning pseudo-Rhineland palace, follows the formula established by California's Disneyland, dividing into several themed sections: **Tomorrowland**, **Frontierland**, **Fantasyland**, **Adventureland**, **Liberty Square** and **Mickey's Toontown Fair**. Fantasyland and Mickey's Toontown Fair are very much for the kids, while the other lands, and in particular Tomorrowland and Frontierland, have the edgier rides. In Tomorrowland, the old favourite **Space Mountain** is in essence an ordinary roller coaster, although its total darkness still manages to terrify younger riders. **Splash Mountain** employs water to great effect, culminating in a stunning 52ft drop guaranteed to get you wet. **Big Thunder Mountain Railroad** puts you on board a runaway train, which trundles through Gold Rush California at a moderately fast pace.

Away from the thrill rides, many of the best attractions in the park rely on "Audio-Animatronics" characters – impressive vocal robots of Disney invention – for their appeal. Some of the finest are seen in **Stitch's Great Escape**, where the mischievous monster wreaks havoc on the audience, who feel, hear and smell strange things in the dark. A large cast of Audio-Animatronics characters is also used to good effect in the **Haunted Mansion**, a mildly spooky ghost ride memorable for its spectacular holograms; the leisurely **Jungle Cruise** down the Amazon, Nile, Congo and Mekong, past ferocious animals and cannibal camps; and **Pirates of the Caribbean**, the classic boat ride around a pirate-infested Caribbean island, which inspired several recent big-budget CGI-enhanced films.

Fantasyland is mainly full of rather dated, juvenile rides, but does have the superb **Mickey's PhilharMagic**, an enchanting 3-D journey with Daffy Duck and other well-known characters, set to classic Disney soundtracks. Equally magical is the **Wishes** firework display, which takes place at park closing time, and which brings out even the most cynical visitors.

Epcot

Even before the Magic Kingdom opened, Walt Disney was developing plans for **Epcot** (Experimental Prototype Community of Tomorrow), conceived in 1966 as a real community experimenting with the new ideas and materials of the technologically advancing US. However, the idea failed to shape up as Disney had envisioned: Epcot didn't open until 1982, when global recession and ecological concerns had put a dampener on the belief in the infallibility of science. One glaring drawback of this park is simply its immense size: it's twice as big as the Magic Kingdom, and very sapping on the feet.

The Epcot Center is dominated by a 180ft geosphere that sits in the heart of **Future World**, which keeps close to Epcot's original concept of exploring the history and researching the future of agriculture, transport, energy and communication. Future World is divided into several pavilions (including the geosphere, with its classic, recently modified **Spaceship Earth** ride), each corporate-sponsored and featuring its own rides, films, interactive exhibits and games. The best of the attractions are **Soarin'**, using the latest flight-simulator and IMAX movie technology to sweep you off on a breathtaking hang-glider ride over California; **Mission: SPACE**, a realistic recreation of a mission to Mars, including real G-force on take-off; **Test Track**, a roller-coaster-style ride where you test a high-performance car; and the **3-D** cinematic thrill of **Honey, I Shrunk the Audience**.

Occupying the largest area in the park is **World Showcase**, with eleven different countries represented by recognizable national landmarks or stereotypical scenes. The **restaurants** here are among the best in Disney World; and it's a great place to watch the spectacular night-time sound-and-light show, **IllumiNations: Reflections of Earth**.

Information, tickets and how to beat the crowds

For general Disney World **information**, call ⓣ407/939-6244 or visit ⓦwww.disneyworld.com. **Tickets** cost $79 (children aged 3–9 $68), and allow unlimited access to all shows and rides in one park only, for that day only. The **Magic Your Way** ticket saves money if you spread your visit over a number of days – for example, a seven-day ticket would cost $234 (children 3–9 $201). You can buy a Magic Your Way ticket for a maximum of ten days and you can only visit one park per day. If you want to move from park to park in the same day, you must add the **Park Hopper** option for an additional flat fee of $60. The **Water Park Fun & More** option allows you to add from two to ten extra admissions (the exact number depends on the length of your basic Magic Your Way ticket) to Blizzard Beach, Typhoon Lagoon, DisneyQuest and Disney's Wide World of Sports for a flat fee of $60. The **car parks** cost $14 a day, but are free if you're staying at a Walt Disney World resort.

Each park is generally **open** daily from 9am to between 6pm and 10pm, depending on the time of year; pick up the current schedule when you arrive. Note that Disney's Animal Kingdom Park closes at 5pm year-round. At their worst, waiting times for the most popular rides can be well over an hour. The best way to **beat the crowds** is to use Disney's FASTPASS system. Place your admission ticket into a machine at the entrance of the attraction; the machine returns it with another ticket that gives you a time to return to the attraction, usually about two hours later. When that time arrives, you can join the FASTPASS line, which gets you in to the attraction with little or no wait. Another good tactic upon arrival is to rush to the far end of the park and work backwards, or to head straight for the big rides, getting them out of the way before the crowds arrive. Lines are pretty much a given any time of the year, and traditional holidays in the US bring increased traffic to the parks.

The world of Walt Disney

When the brilliant illustrator and animator Walt Disney devised the world's first theme park, California's **Disneyland** (see p.867), he left himself with no control over the hotels and restaurants that quickly engulfed it, preventing growth and erasing profits Disney felt were rightly his. Determined not to let that happen again, the Disney corporation secretly bought up 27,500 acres of central Florida farmland, acquiring by the late Sixties a site a hundred times bigger than Disneyland. With the promise of a jobs bonanza for Florida, the state legislature gave the corporation the rights of any major municipality (via a special jurisdiction called the Reedy Creek Improvement District) – empowering it to lay roads, enact building codes and enforce the law with its own security force.

Walt Disney World's first "land", the Magic Kingdom, which opened in 1971, was a huge success. Unveiled in 1982, the far more ambitious Epcot represented the first major break from cartoon-based escapism – but its rose-tinted look at the future received a mixed response. Partly due to this, and to some bad management decisions, the Disney empire (Disney himself died in 1966) faced bankruptcy by the mid-1980s. Since then, the corporation has sprung back from the abyss, and despite being subject to a (failed) hostile takeover bid by Comcast in 2004, steers a tight and competitive business ship. It may trade in fantasy, but when it comes to money, the Disney Corporation's nose is firmly in the real world.

Disney's Hollywood Studios

After signing an agreement in the 1980s with Metro-Goldwyn-Mayer (MGM) to exploit MGM's many movie classics, Disney had an ample source of instantly recognizable images to mould into rides suitable for adults as much as for kids. The park opened in 1989 as Disney-MGM Studios, but since then, the addition of attractions encompassing music, television and theatre led to the decision to rename the park **Disney's Hollywood Studios** to reflect the broader focus on "entertainment".

Most of the things to do at Disney's Hollywood Studios take the form of rides or shows, and there are fewer exhibit-style attractions when compared with the other Disney parks. Thrill-seekers will enjoy the gravity-defying drops (including moments of weightlessness) in the outstanding **The Twilight Zone Tower of Terror** or the slightly more ordinary **Rock 'n' Roller Coaster** with its breakneck-speed launch.

Don't miss the half-hour behind-the-scenes **Backlot Tour**, climaxing with the dramatic special effects on the *Catastrophe Canyon* movie set; the funny **Muppet Vision 3-D** show; and **The Great Movie Ride**, where Audio-Animatronics figures from famous movies interact with real-life actors.

Disney's Animal Kingdom Park

Disney's Animal Kingdom Park was opened in 1998 as an animal-conservation theme park with Disney's patented over-the-top twist. The park is divided into six "lands" – **Africa, Asia, Discovery Island, Camp Minnie-Mickey, DinoLand U.S.A.** and **Rafiki's Planet Watch** – with Africa and Asia being the most visually impressive, each recreating the natural landscapes and exotic flavors of these two continents with admirable attention to detail.

The best-realized attraction is Africa's **Kilimanjaro Safaris**, where a jeep takes you on what feels very much like a real African safari, to view giraffes, zebras, elephants, lions, gazelles and rhinos, as well as take part in anti-poacher manoeuvres. Elsewhere in Africa, the troop of lowland gorillas at the **Pangani Forest Exploration Trail** are definitely worth a look. Crossing over to **Asia**, you'll get an astoundingly up-close look at the healthiest-looking tigers in captivity at the **Maharajah Jungle Trek.** DinoLand U.S.A.'s **DINOSAUR** is a slower but still exciting ride full of small drops and short stops in the dark while scary dinosaurs pop out of nowhere.

Universal Orlando

For some years, it seemed that TV and film production would move away from California to Florida, which, with its lower taxes and cheaper labour, was more amenable. The opening of Universal Studios in 1990 appeared to confirm that trend. So far, though, for various reasons, Florida has not proved to be a fully realistic alternative. Even so, this hasn't stopped the Universal enclave here, known as **Universal Orlando**, off I-4, half a mile north of exits 74B or 75A (park opens daily at 9am, closing times vary; one-day, one-park ticket $79, children 3–9 $69, under-3s free; two-day, two-park ticket $109.99/$99.99; parking $12; ⓣ1-407/363-8000, ⓦwww.uescape.com), from becoming a major player in the Orlando theme-park arena. Though Disney World still commands the lion's share of attention, Universal has siphoned off many visitors with **Universal Studios**' high-tech movie-themed attractions and the excellent thrill rides at **Islands of Adventure**. And with all the nightclubs at Disney now closed, **CityWalk** has become the main competition to downtown Orlando for nightlife dollars (see "Nightlife and entertainment", p.534). Furthermore, Universal has achieved full-fledged resort status with its three luxurious on-site **hotels**: *Loews Portofino Bay*, *Hard Rock* and *Loews Royal Pacific Resort* (all three ⓣ1-888/273-1311, ⓦwww.uescape.com; ❾). By purchasing **Universal Express Plus** ($19.99–59.99 depending on the time of year), you can enter the Universal Express line whenever and wherever you like for the whole day in both parks.

Universal Studios

Like its competitor Disney's Hollywood Studios, the four-hundred-acre Universal Studios is a working production studio. The newest attraction, **The Simpsons Ride**, combines cutting-edge flight-simulator technology with the irreverent humour of *The Simpsons*. The park's only roller coaster, **Revenge of the Mummy**, takes you on a medium-paced journey through scenes from the most recent iteration of this hoary tale. Don't miss **Shrek 4-D**, a delightful 3-D presentation brought even more to life by an overdose of superb "feelies" (including a few too many water sprays). Also worthwhile, **Disaster** gives you an intensely claustrophobic two minutes of terror as you experience what it's like to be caught on a subway train when an 8.0 Richter-scale quake hits.

Islands of Adventure

Islands of Adventure is Orlando's leader in state-of-the-art, edge-of-your-seat thrill rides: though there are plenty of diversions for the less daring, these rides are what brings the crowds. The park is divided into six sections – **Marvel Super Hero Island**, **The Lost Continent**, **Jurassic Park**, **Toon Lagoon**, **Seuss Landing** and the latest addition, which opened in June 2010: **The Wizarding World of Harry Potter**.

After five years of planning and consultation with author J.K. Rowling on all elements of the park it is an immersive experience, with permanent snow-cover on the gift shops, which feature postcards with Potter-themed stamps, magic wands and black school robes. Overall, the effect is to give visitors a very real-life version of the world that one might experience in the Harry Potter books.

The real meat and potatoes of the Wizarding World are the rides though, and they do not disappoint. They are the **Dragon Challenge**, **The Flight of the**

Hippogriff and **Harry Potter and the Forbidden Journey**. The Dragon Challenge sends two speeding trains in close proximity to each other, while The Flight of the Hippogriff is a fairly tame wicker-covered roller coaster that resembles the magical beast. For those willing to wait (and you will wait) in line for a time, the Forbidden Journey is a kaleidoscope of virtual reality and extremely advanced **robotic technology** based around a recreation of Hogwarts school. Along the way, you will swoop around perilious mountain peaks, encounter giant spitting spiders and so on – you'll be sitting in a four-person roller-coaster car the whole time, though the motion is quite intense.

The queues are a bit less intense over at **The Amazing Adventures of Spider-Man**, which uses every trick imaginable – 3-D, sensory stimuli, motion simulation and more – to spirit you into Spider-Man's battles with villains. **Dueling Dragons** is the park's scariest ride: twin roller coasters ("Fire" and "Ice" – separate lines for each) engineered to provide harrowing head-on near misses with one another; for this reason, the front-row seats are especially sought after. Other park offerings for kids include **Dudley Do-Right's Ripsaw Falls** and **Popeye & Bluto's Bilge-Rat Barges**, both good for getting a midday drenching; and the whole of **Seuss Landing**, where everything is based on Dr Seuss characters. There's one **live performance** offered throughout the day: **The Eighth Voyage of Sindbad Stunt Show**, where the set, stunts and pyrotechnics are as good as the jokes are bad.

SeaWorld Orlando and Discovery Cove

SeaWorld Orlando, at Sea Harbor Drive, near the intersection of I-4 and the Beeline Expressway, is the cream of Florida's sizeable crop of marine parks, and should not be missed; allocate a full day to see it all (park opens daily at 9am, closing times vary; $78.95, children 3–9 $68.95; Ⓣ407/351-3600, Ⓦwww.seaworld.com). The big event is *Believe* – thirty minutes of tricks performed by playful killer whales (you'll get drenched if you're sitting in the first fourteen rows of the stadium). Also, try not to miss the kid-orientated sea lion extravaganza, Clyde and Seamore Take Pirate Island. The **Wild Arctic** complex, complete with artificial snow and ice, brings you close to beluga whales, walruses and polar bears, while a flight-simulator ride takes you on a stomach-churning helicopter flight through an Arctic blizzard.

The park's first thrill ride, **Journey to Atlantis**, travels on both water and rails, and has a sixty-foot drop (be prepared to get very wet). Much more exhilarating, however, is **Kraken**, a roller coaster that flings you around at speeds of up to 65 miles per hour, free-flying and looping-the-loop at great heights. The newest addition to their stable of rides is the Manta, which quite literally takes visitors on a steel roller coaster that emulates the movements of a manta ray.

With substantially less razzmatazz, plenty of smaller aquariums and displays offer a wealth of information about the underwater world. Among the highlights, **Penguin Encounter** recreates Antarctica, with scores of the waddling, flightless birds scampering over an iceberg; **Manatee Rescue** gives you a close-up look at

The Orlando Flexticket

Universal Orlando, Sea World Orlando, Islands of Adventures and two water parks – Wet 'n Wild and Aquatica – have teamed together to create a pass that permits access to each park over a period of fourteen consecutive days. The **Orlando Flexticket** costs $259.95 (children 3–9 $239.95), or $299.95/$279.95, including Tampa's Busch Gardens, with a free shuttle from Orlando to Busch Gardens.

these endangered mammals; and **Shark Encounter** includes a walk through an acrylic-sided and -roofed tunnel.

Orlando's water parks

Disney World has two excellent **water parks**. **Blizzard Beach**, north of the *All-Star Resorts* (see p.528) on World Drive (daily 9am–7pm; $46, children 3–9 $40; ⓣ407/560-3400), is based on the fantasy that a hapless entrepreneur has opened a ski resort in Florida and the entire thing has started to melt. The star of the show is **Summit Plummet**, which shoots you down a 120ft vertical drop at more than fifty miles per hour. Gentler rides include toboggan-style slalom courses and raft rides. As well as the slides, **Typhoon Lagoon**, just south of Downtown Disney (daily 9am–7pm; $46, children 3–9 $40; ⓣ407/560-4141), features a huge surfing pool and a shark reef where you can snorkel amongst tropical fish. Keen to get in on the act, SeaWorld Orlando has recently opened **Aquatica**, across the road from SeaWorld on International Drive (daily 9am–5pm, longer hours in summer; $47.95, children 3–9 $41.95; ⓣ1-888/800-5447, ⓦwww.aquaticabyseaworld.com), which combines live animal attractions with wave pools, slides and beaches. Finally, **Wet 'n Wild**, 6200 International Drive (daily 10am–5pm, longer hours in summer; $47.95, children 3–9 $41.95; ⓣ1-800/992-9453, ⓦwww.wetnwildorlando.com), defends itself admirably in the face of the stiff competition, with a range of no-nonsense slides including the almost vertical **Der Stuka**.

Eating in the Orlando area

Downtown and its environs hold the pick of the locals' **eating** haunts; most visitors, however, head for International Drive's inexpensive all-day buffets and gourmet restaurants. You are not allowed to take food into any of the theme parks, where the best restaurants are in **Epcot's World Showcase** – particularly the French- and Mexican-themed establishments.

Bahama Breeze 8849 International Drive ⓣ407/248-2499. Decent Caribbean food ($15–20) and the entrees include a nice lobster and shrimp quesadilla. Dinner only.

Café Tu Tu Tango 8625 International Drive ⓣ407/248-2222. Original, imaginative dishes here include spicy crap chopsticks ($8) and pumpkin pizza ($10).

Dexter's of Thornton Park 808 E Washington St, downtown ⓣ407/648-2777. Trendy yet informal eatery in downtown's hip Thornton Park neighbourhood. Moderately priced.

The Globe 25 Wall St Plaza, downtown ⓣ407/849-9904. Inexpensive snacks and light meals with an Asian twist; the tables outside are ideal for people-watching.

Ming Court 9188 International Drive ⓣ407/351-9988. An exceptional Chinese restaurant, with dim sum and sushi available. Not as costly as you might expect.

New Punjab 7451 International Drive ⓣ407/352-7887. Reasonably priced vegetable curries from $10.95–18.95.

Roy's 7760 W Sand Lake Rd, near International Drive ⓣ407/352-4844. Founded in Hawaii, *Roy's* specializes in Hawaiian fusion cuisine. Try the $35 three-course menu for a mix of potstickers, meats and a dessert.

White Wolf Café 1829 N Orange Ave, downtown ⓣ407/895-9911. Down-to-earth café/antique store known for creative salads and sandwiches.

Nightlife and entertainment

The closure in 2008 of the nightclubs at Disney's shopping and entertainment complex, **Downtown Disney**, means that Orlando's **nightspots** are now concentrated in two main areas, each offering a quite different atmosphere.

For wholesome, packaged and somewhat sterile entertainment, head to Universal Orlando's **CityWalk**, 6000 Universal Blvd ($11.95 for all-night access to every club, plus free parking after 6pm; ⓣ407/363-8000, ⓦwww.citywalkorlando.com), thirty acres of restaurants, dance clubs and shops wedged between Universal Studios and Islands of Adventure. Away from the theme parks, **downtown Orlando** has a large, eclectic and much more appealing crop of bars, lounges and clubs. Most of the after-dark action focuses along **Orange Avenue**: *The Social*, no. 54, is a well-known venue for live alternative rock, grunge and the like; *The Independent Bar* no. 68, is a dance club/bar that isn't afraid to mix it up musically; and *Pulse*, no. 1912, a mile or so south of downtown, is a popular **gay** nightspot.

The West Coast

In the three hundred miles from the state's southern tip to the junction with the Panhandle (see p.546), Florida's **West Coast** embraces all the extremes. Buzzing, youthful towns rise behind placid fishing hamlets; mobbed holiday strips are just minutes from desolate swamplands and world-class art collections vie with glitzy theme parks. Surprises are plentiful, though the coast's one constant is proximity to the Gulf of Mexico – and sunset views rivalled only by those of the Florida Keys.

The west coast's largest city, **Tampa**, has more to offer than its corporate towers initially suggest – not least the lively nightlife scene in the Cuban enclave of **Ybor City**, and the Busch Gardens theme park. For the mass of visitors, though, the Tampa Bay area begins and ends with the **St Petersburg beaches**, whose miles of sea and sand are undiluted vacation territory. South of Tampa, a string of barrier-island beaches run the length of the Gulf (including those on beautiful Anna Maria Island), and the mainland towns that provide access to them – such as Sarasota and Fort Myers – have enough to warrant a stop. Inland, the wilderness of the **Everglades** can be navigated by simple walking trails, canoe, kayak or an overnight stay at a campground.

Tampa

A small, stimulating city with an infectious, upbeat mood, **TAMPA**, the business hub of the west coast, is well worth a stop. As one of the major beneficiaries of the flood of people and money into Florida, Tampa boasts an impressive cultural infrastructure envied by many larger rivals. In addition to its fine **museums** and **Busch Gardens**, one of the most popular theme parks in the state, the city holds, in the Cuban-influenced **Ybor City**, just northeast of the city centre, the west coast's hippest and most culturally eclectic quarter.

Tampa began as a small settlement beside a US Army base that was built in the 1820s to keep an eye on the Seminoles. In the 1880s, the railroad arrived, and the Hillsborough River, on which the city stands, was dredged to allow seagoing vessels to dock. Tampa became a booming port, simultaneously acquiring a major tobacco industry as thousands of Cubans moved north from Key West to the new cigar factories of neighbouring Ybor City. The Depression ended the economic surge, but the port remained one of the busiest in the country and tempered Tampa's postwar decline. Today, Tampa continues to draw on the strengths of its local universities and historically minded tourist attractions, and a few that are just attractions.

Arrival and information

Tampa's **airport** (Ⓣ813/870-8700, Ⓦwww.tampaairport.com) is five miles northwest of downtown: local HART bus #30 is the least costly connection ($1.75; see below). **Taxis** (try United Ⓣ813/253-2424) to downtown or a Busch Boulevard motel cost $28–52; to St Petersburg or the beaches, $45–75. Greyhound **buses** arrive downtown at 610 Polk St (Ⓣ813/229-2174); trains at 601 N Nebraska Ave (Ⓣ813/221-7600).

The downtown **Visitor Information Center**, 615 Channelside Drive, suite 108A (Mon–Fri 9.30am–5pm, Ⓣ1-800/44-TAMPA, Ⓦwww.visittampabay.com), and the **Ybor City Visitor Information Center**, 1600 E 8th Ave, suite B104 (Mon–Fri 10am–5pm, Sat 11am–6pm, Sun noon–6pm; Ⓣ813/241-8838, Ⓦwww.ybor.org), give out useful leaflets and maps.

Although both downtown Tampa and Ybor City are easily covered on foot, to travel between them without a car you'll need to use the HART **local buses** ($1.75, one-day pass $3.75; Ⓣ813/254-4278, Ⓦwww.hartline.org) or the TECO Line **Streetcar System** ($2.50; Ⓣ813/254-4278, Ⓦwww.tecolinestreetcar.org), a vintage replica streetcar which runs between downtown and Ybor several times an hour. Useful HART bus routes are #8 to Ybor City, #5 to Busch Gardens and #6 to the Museum of Science and Industry.

Accommodation

Tampa is not generously supplied with low-cost **accommodation** right in town; you'll almost certainly save money by staying in St Petersburg (see p.539) or at the beaches (see p.540). There are some good deals, though, at the motels near Busch Gardens and the airport.

Best Western All Suites 301 University Center Drive, behind Busch Gardens Ⓣ813/971-8930 or 1-800/780-7234. A reasonable base for seeing the city by car, and so close to Busch Gardens that the parrots escape into their trees. Features a happy hour every afternoon and free breakfast. ❺

Don Vincente de Ybor Historic Inn 1915 Avenida Republica de Cuba Ⓣ1-866/206-4545, Ⓦdonvicenteinn.com. A luxurious B&B option in Ybor City. Features sixteen beautifully restored suites and swing dancing on Tuesday nights. ❻

Gram's Place 3109 N Ola Ave Ⓣ813/221-0596, Ⓦwww.grams-inn-tampa.com. This funky motel-cum-hostel offers both private rooms – all themed in different musical styles – and rather tatty youth-hostel-style accommodation. $23 for a dorm bed; private rooms $60 ❸

Sheraton Tampa Riverwalk 200 N Ashley Drive Ⓣ813/223-2222, Ⓦwww.sheratontampariverwalk.com. Very convenient downtown location, nicely situated on the banks of the Hillsborough River. ❼

Wingate by Wyndham 3751 E Fowler Ave Ⓣ813/979-2828, Ⓦwww.wingatetampa.com. With a free shuttle bus to Busch Gardens (5min away), great free breakfast, clean rooms and solicitous staff, you can't go wrong here. ❺–❻

Downtown Tampa

The highly regarded **Tampa Museum of Art** at 120 W Gasparilla Plaza Ave (Mon–Wed & Fri 11am–7pm, Thurs till 9pm, Sat & Sun till 5pm; $10; Ⓣ813/274-8130, Ⓦwww.tampamuseum.org), moved into a new facility at the Curtis Hixon Waterfront Park in the autumn of 2009, with 66,000 square feet of gallery space, making it 150 percent larger than the former location. The museum specializes in classical antiquities and twentieth-century American art, and it also plays host to travelling exhibits such as noted collections of works by American Impressionists. From the river, you'll see the silver minarets and cupolas on the far bank, sprouting from the main building of the University of Tampa. These neo-Moorish architectural ornaments adorn what was formerly the 500-room **Tampa Bay Hotel**, financed by steamship and railroad magnate Henry B. Plant. To reach it, walk across the river on Kennedy Boulevard and descend the steps into Plant Park.

The structure is as bizarre a sight today as it was when it opened in 1891. Since the Civil War, Plant had been buying up bankrupt railroads, steadily inching his way into Florida to meet his steamships unloading at Tampa's harbour. Eventually, he became rich enough to put his fantasies of creating the world's most luxurious hotel into practice. However, lack of care for the fittings and Plant's death in 1899 hastened the hotel's transformation from the last word in comfort to a pile of crumbling plaster. The city bought it in 1904 and leased it to the University of Tampa in 1933. In one wing, the **Henry B. Plant Museum**, 401 W Kennedy Blvd (Tues–Sat 10am–4pm, Sun noon–4pm; $5; ⓣ813/254-1891, ⓦwww.plantmuseum.com), holds what's left of the hotel's original furnishings. In Tampa's dockland area, a mile or so southeast of the Tampa Bay Hotel, the splendid **Florida Aquarium**, 701 Channelside Drive (daily 9.30am–5pm; $19.95; ⓣ813/273-4000, ⓦwww.flaquarium.org), houses lavish displays of Florida's fresh- and saltwater habitats, from springs and swamps to beaches and coral reefs. Animal residents include an impressive variety of fish, birds, otters, turtles and alligators.

Ybor City

In 1886, as soon as Henry Plant's ships had ensured a regular supply of Havana tobacco into Tampa, cigar magnate Don Vincente Martínez Ybor cleared a patch of scrubland three miles northeast of present-day downtown Tampa and laid the foundations of **YBOR CITY**. About twenty thousand migrants, mostly Cuban, settled here and created a Latin American enclave, producing the top-class, hand-rolled cigars that made Tampa the "**Cigar Capital of the World**" for a time. However, mass production, the popularity of cigarettes and the Depression proved a fatal combination for skilled cigar-makers: as unemployment struck, Ybor City's tight-knit blocks of cobbled streets and red-brick buildings became surrounded by drab, low-rent neighbourhoods.

Ybor City today buzzes with tourists, and at night the atmosphere can get raucous, especially on the weekends. The town is trendy and culturally diverse, yet its Cuban roots are immediately apparent, and explanatory background texts adorn many buildings. The **Ybor City State Museum**, 1818 9th Ave (daily 9am–5pm; $4; ⓣ813/247-1434, ⓦwww.ybormuseum.org), helps you grasp the main points of Ybor City's creation and its multi-ethnic make-up. The museum also offers cigar-rolling demonstrations (Fri–Sun 11am–1pm) and historic walking tours (Sat 10.30am; $6).

Busch Gardens and the Museum of Science and Industry

Busch Gardens, located two miles east of I-275, or two miles west of I-75, exit 54, at 3000 E Busch Blvd (opening hours vary day to day but generally daily 10am–6pm; $74.95, children $64.95; parking $11; ⓣ1-888/800-5447, ⓦwww.buschgardens tampabay.com) is one of Florida's most popular theme parks, based on a recreation of colonial-era Africa and offering some of the fastest and most nerve-jangling roller coasters in the country. A sedate pseudo-steam-train or cable-car journey allows inspection of a variety of African wildlife, but by far the most popular of the twenty-odd rides are the roller coasters: **Sheikra**, with its terrifying 200ft, 90-degree dive; **Montu**, where your legs dangle precariously in midair; **Gwazi**, a giant wooden coaster; and **Kumba**, with plenty of high-speed loop-the-loops. After this excitement, retire to the Hospitality House for two free cups of Budweiser beer.

Eating

There are plenty of good places to **eat** in Tampa, with a good mix of lively restaurants in Ybor City.

Bernini 1702 7th Ave, Ybor City ⓣ813/248-0099. An Italian joint serving up wood-fired pizza and pasta in the lovely old Bank of Ybor City.

Bern's Steak House 1208 S Howard Ave Hyde Park ⓣ813/251-2421. An institution in Tampa, this high-end steakhouse has a farm where they grow their own vegetables, fruits and other items. Other than that, they also have one of the world's largest wine cellars. Have dinner here and you'll feel like royalty and they'll give you a tour of the kitchen. Impeccable service and the dessert room upstairs is an experience as well.

Café Dufrain 707 Harbour Post Drive, Harbour Island, ⓣ813/275-9701. This great, moderately priced place overlooking the water on Harbour Island serves a variety of contemporary cuisine with both mouthwatering meat and seafood dishes – try the gingered tuna ($25) or the flat iron steak ($28).

Cephas 1701 E 4th Ave, Ybor City ⓣ813/247-9022. A funky Jamaican restaurant offering jerk chicken and curried goat, chicken and fish.

La Creperia Café 1729 E 7th Ave, Ybor City ⓣ813/248-9700. A wide choice of delicious sweet and savoury crepes, plus free wi-fi internet access.

Taco 913 E Hillsborough Ave ⓣ813/232-5889. This is quite literally a parked bus where great tacos are made and served 24 hours a day. The ingredients are fresh, and prices range from $2.75 to $7.50

Nightlife and entertainment

Ybor City's renowned **nightlife** tends to be younger and more raucous than the city's other entertainment areas of Channelside, downtown next to the Florida Aquarium, and the International Plaza and Bay Street, near the airport at the junction of West Shore and Boy Scout boulevards. The free *Weekly Planet* (ⓦwww.weeklyplanet.com) has **listings**, as does Friday's *Tampa Tribune*.

Green Iguana 1708 E 7th Ave, Ybor City ⓣ813/248-9555. Rock bands play nightly, and DJs keep the young crowd very much in the party mood.

New World Brewery 1313 E 8th Ave, Ybor City ⓣ813/248-4969. A very solid microbrew selection, and a patio for enjoying the beers as the sun sets.

Side Splitters 12938 N Dale Mabry Hwy ⓣ813/960-1197. One of the best comedy clubs in the area.

Skipper's Smokehouse 910 Skipper Rd ⓣ813/971-0666. Blues and reggae rule at this family-oriented live music venue that includes a regular Grateful Dead tribute band.

Tampa Theatre 711 Franklin St ⓣ813/274-8981. Foreign-language, classic and cult films shown in an atmospheric 1920s theatre. Tickets $9.

St Petersburg

Situated on the eastern edge of the Pinellas Peninsula, a bulky thumb of land poking between Tampa Bay and the Gulf of Mexico, **ST PETERSBURG** is a world away from Tampa, even though the two cities are just twenty miles apart. Declared the healthiest place in the US in 1885, St Petersburg wasted no time in wooing the recuperating and the retired, at one point putting five thousand green benches on its streets to take the weight off elderly feet. Today, St Petersburg's diverse selection of museums and plethora of art galleries have contributed to its emergence as one of Florida's richest cultural centres. The **Salvador Dalí Museum**, corner of Bayshore Drive SE and 5th Avenue SE (Mon–Wed & Sat 9.30am–5.30pm, Thurs till 8pm, Fri till 6.30pm, Sun noon–5.30pm; $17, Thurs after 5pm $5; ⓣ727/823-3767, ⓦwww.salvadordalimuseum.org), has brand-new digs, designed by noted architect Yann Weymouth. This impressive museum stores more than a thousand paintings from the collection of a Cleveland industrialist, A. Reynolds

Morse, who struck up a friendship with the artist in the 1940s. Hour-long **free tours** that run continuously throughout the day trace a chronological path around the works, from the artist's early experiments with Impressionism and Cubism to the seminal Surrealist canvas *The Disintegration of the Persistence of Memory*.

Once you've done Dalí, the quarter-of-a-mile-long **pier**, jutting from the end of 2nd Avenue North, is the town's focal point. The pier often hosts arts-and-crafts exhibitions, and the inverted-pyramid-like building at its head holds five storeys of restaurants, shops and fast-food counters. At the foot of the pier, the **Museum of History**, 335 2nd Ave NE (Wed–Sat 10am–5pm, Sun 1–4pm; $9; ⓣ727/894-1052, ⓦwww.spmoh.org), recounts using modest displays St Petersburg's early-twentieth-century heyday as a winter resort. Nearby, the **Museum of Fine Arts**, 255 Beach Drive NE (Tues–Sat 10am–5pm, Sun 1–5pm; $12, including free guided tour; ⓣ727/896-2667, ⓦwww.fine-arts.org), holds a superlative collection ranging from pre-Columbian art through to Asian and African and the European Old Masters, as well as rotating exhibits in the airy and modern Hazel Hough wing, which more than doubles the museum's space.

Practicalities

The Greyhound **bus** station is downtown at 180 9th St N (ⓣ727/898-1496). The **Chamber of Commerce** is at 100 2nd Ave N (Mon–Fri 8am–7pm, Sat 9am–7pm; ⓣ727/821-4715, ⓦwww.stpete.com). **Accommodation** in St Petersburg can be less costly than at the beaches (see p.540). The area is also rich in charismatic B&Bs, such as *Dickens House*, 335 8th Ave NE (ⓣ1-800/381-2022, ⓦwww.dickenshouse.com; ❻). For sheer luxury, stay at *Renaissance Vinoy Resort*, 501 5th Ave NE (ⓣ1-888/303-4430, ⓦwww.renaissancehotels.com/tpasr; ❽). Hearty, economical Cuban **food** (try the Ybor City-style Cuban sandwich) can be had at *Tangelo's Grill*, 226 1st Ave N (ⓣ727/894-1695). Alternatively, try *Moon Under Water*, 332 Beach Drive NE (ⓣ727/896-6160); overlooking the waterfront, this inexpensive British tavern is well known for its cocktails and curries.

The St Petersburg beaches

Framing the Gulf side of the Pinellas Peninsula, a 35-mile chain of barrier islands forms the **St Petersburg Beaches**, one of Florida's busiest coastal strips. When the resorts of Miami Beach lost some of their allure during the 1970s, the St Petersburg beaches grew in popularity with Americans and have since evolved into an established destination for package-holidaying Europeans. The beaches are beautiful, the sea warm and the sunsets fabulous.

All **buses** ($1.75; ⓣ727/540-1900, ⓦwww.psta.net) to the beaches originate in St Petersburg, at the Williams Park terminal, on 1st Avenue North and 3rd Street North; an **information booth** there has route details. **Route #35** runs daily to St Pete Beach on Gulf Boulevard, which links all the St Petersburg beach communities. At St Pete Beach, you can change for the **Suncoast Beach Trolley** ($1.75), which links Passe-a-Grille in the extreme south to Sand Key in the north.

The southern beaches

In twenty-odd miles of heavily touristed coast, only **Pass-a-Grille**, at the very southern tip of the barrier island chain, has the look and feel of a genuine community – two miles of tidy houses, cared-for lawns, small shops and a cluster of bars and restaurants. During the week, the town is blissfully quiet, while on weekends informed locals come here to enjoy one of the area's liveliest stretches of sand.

A mile and a half north of Pass-a-Grille, the painfully luxurious **Don CeSar Hotel**, 3400 Gulf Blvd (ⓣ727/360-1881 or 1-866/728-2206, ⓦwww.doncesar.com; ❾), is a grandiose pink castle, filling seven beachside acres. Opened in 1928, and briefly busy with the likes of Scott and Zelda Fitzgerald, it enjoyed a short-lived glamour. During the Great Depression, part of the hotel was used as a warehouse, and later as the spring training base of the New York Yankees baseball team.

The northern beaches

Much of the northern section of **Sand Key**, the longest barrier island in the St Petersburg chain, and one of the wealthier portions of the coast, is taken up by stylish condos and time-share apartments. The island terminates in the pretty **Sand Key Park**, where tall palm trees frame a silky strip of sand. The park occupies one bank of **Clearwater Pass**, across which a belt of sparkling white sands marks the holiday town of **CLEARWATER BEACH**, where a recent condo boom has all but obliterated the small-town feel. The staff at the family-run *Barefoot Bay Motel*, 401 East Shore Drive (ⓣ727/447-1016, ⓦwww.barefootbayresort.com; ❹) couldn't be friendlier. The rooms are clean and well-kept, and the beach is a five- minute walk. Regular **buses** (#80) provide links to the mainland town of Clearwater, across the two-mile causeway.

Beach practicalities

The **motels** that line mile after mile of Gulf Boulevard tend to be cheaper than the **hotels** – typically $80–110 in winter, $15–20 less in summer. You'll pay $5–10 extra for a room on the beach side of Gulf Boulevard compared with an identical room on the inland side. At the southern beaches, good, cheap accommodation can be found at the peaceful *Lamara Motel*, 520 73rd Ave, St Petersburg Beach (ⓣ1-800/211-5108, ⓦwww.lamara.com; ❸), while the pick of the hotels at the northern beaches is the *Sheraton Sand Key*, 1160 Gulf Blvd, Sand Key (ⓣ727/595-1611, ⓦwww.sheratonsandkey.com; ❽). Visitors should also think about making a trip a few miles down the road on I-75 to stay at the *Tortuga Inn and Beach Resort*, 1325 Gulf Drive N, Bradenton Beach (ⓣ941/778-6611, ⓦwww.tortugainn.com). The rooms here are nice, there's a well-kept pool and there's good access to Anna Maria Island. It's easy to find a decent place to **eat** around the beaches: overlooking the sea, *Hurricane*, 807 Gulf Way, Pass-a-Grille (ⓣ727/360-9558), has a well-priced menu of the freshest seafood; *Fetishes*, 6690 Gulf Blvd, St Pete Beach (ⓣ727/363-3700), is ideal for a more upmarket and intimate dining experience, serving expensive American cuisine. In Clearwater Beach, *Frenchy's Café*, 41 Baymont St (ⓣ727/446-3607), cooks up good grouper sandwiches and seafood gumbo.

Sarasota

Rising on a gentle hillside beside the blue waters of Sarasota Bay, **SARASOTA**, 35 miles south of St Petersburg, is one of Florida's better-off and better-looking towns. It's also one of the state's leading cultural centres, home to numerous writers and artists, and the base of several respected performing arts companies. The community is far less stuffy than its wealth might suggest, and Sarasota is fairly lively, with cafés, bars and restaurants complementing the excellent grouping of bookstores around the charming St Armand's Circle, located across the John Ringling Causeway.

The Ringling Museum Complex

John Ringling, one of the owners of the fantastically successful Ringling Brothers Circus, who started their complex train-powered stops across the US from the 1880s, acquired during his lifetime a fortune estimated at $200 million. Recognizing Sarasota's investment potential, he built the first causeway to the barrier islands and made this the winter base for his circus. His greatest gift to the town, however, was a Venetian Gothic mansion and an incredible collection of European Baroque paintings.

The **Ringling Museum Complex**, which includes the mansion (daily 10am–5pm; $25; ⓣ941/359-5700, ⓦwww.ringling.org), is at 5401 Bay Shore Rd, three miles north of downtown beside US-41. Begin your exploration by walking through the gardens to the former winter residence of John and Mable Ringling, **Cà d'Zan** ("House of John", in Venetian dialect), built in 1926 for $1.5 million, and furnished with New York estate sale castoffs for an additional $400,000. A gorgeous piece of work and a triumph of taste and proportion, it's serenely situated beside the bay. The artwork is displayed in the spacious **museum**, built around a mock fifteenth-century Italian palazzo. Five enormous paintings by Rubens, commissioned in 1625, and the painter's subsequent *Portrait of Archduke Ferdinand*, are highlights, though there's also a wealth of talent from Europe's leading schools of the mid-sixteenth to mid-eighteenth centuries. Free guided **tours** depart regularly from the entrance. If you visit one of the grand palatial homes in Florida, this should be it.

The Sarasota beaches

Increasingly the stamping ground of European package tourists spilling south from the St Petersburg beaches, the white sands of the **Sarasota beaches** are worth a day of anybody's time. The beaches are located on Lido Key and Siesta Key, and they are both accessible from the mainland, though there is no direct link between them. A third island, Longboat Key, is primarily residential.

The Ringling Causeway crosses the yacht-filled Sarasota Bay from the foot of Sarasota's Main Street to **Lido Key**. The causeway flows into **St Armands Circle**, a roundabout ringed by upmarket shops and restaurants dotted with some of Ringling's replica classical statuary, including some that pay homage to great circus stars of the past. Continuing south along Benjamin Franklin Drive, you come to the island's most accessible beaches, ending after two miles at the attractive **South Lido Park** (daily 8am–sunset; free).

The bulbous northerly section of tadpole-shaped **Siesta Key**, reached by Siesta Drive off US-41, about five miles south of downtown Sarasota, attracts a younger crowd. The soft sand at the pretty but busy **Siesta Key Beach** (beside Beach Rd) has a sugary texture due to its origins as quartz (not the more usual pulverized coral). To escape the crowds, continue south past Crescent Beach and follow Midnight Pass Road for six miles to **Turtle Beach**, a small, secluded stretch of sand.

Practicalities

In downtown Sarasota, **Greyhound buses** stop at 575 N Washington Blvd (ⓣ941/955-5735). The **Amtrak bus** from Tampa pulls in at 1993 Main Street. The local bus terminal is a few blocks west at 1565 1st St (at Lemon St): catch buses here for the Ringling estate or the beaches ($0.75). Call at the **Information and History Visitor Center**, 701 N Tamiami Trail (Mon–Sat 10am–4pm, ⓣ1-800/522-9799, ⓦwww.sarasotafl.org), for discount coupons and leaflets.

On the mainland, **motels** run the length of US-41 (N Tamiami Trail) between the Ringling estate and downtown Sarasota, typically charging around $60–90 a night: try the *Best Western Midtown*, 1425 S Tamiami Trail (T941/955-9841, Wwww.bwmidtown.com; 3). Green-friendly types might do well to check out the *Hampton Inn Sarasota*, 5995 Cattleridge Blvd, Sarasota (T941/371-1900, Wwww.hamptoninnsarasota.com) as it has several eco-friendly features, including the use of green cleaning supplies and fluorescent light features.

Eating options along Main Street include the reasonably priced sandwiches at *Main Bar Sandwich Shop*, no. 1944 (T941/955-8733), as well as the excellent Tex-Mex favourites at *Two Señoritas*, no. 1355 (T941/366-1618). On Siesta Key, check out *The Broken Egg*, 140 Avenida Messina (T941/346-2750), popular with locals for the all-American breakfasts and lunches.

Fort Myers

Fifty miles south, **FORT MYERS** may lack the élan of Sarasota, but it's nonetheless one of the up-and-coming communities of Florida's southwest coast. Fortunately, most of its recent growth has occurred on the north side of the wide Caloosahatchee River, which the town straddles, allowing the traditional centre, along the waterway's south shore, to remain relatively unspoiled.

Once across the river, US-41 strikes **downtown** Fort Myers, picturesquely nestled on the water's edge. For a thorough insight into the town's history, head to the **Southwest Florida Museum of History**, 2300 Peck St (Tues–Sat 10am–5pm, Sun noon–5pm; $12.50; T239/332-5955), which has an eye-catching 84ft-long Pullman rail car and a series of exhibits on the local Calusa and Seminole peoples.

In 1885, six years after inventing the light bulb, **Thomas Edison** collapsed from exhaustion and was instructed by his doctor to find a warm working environment or face an early death. Vacationing in Florida, the 37-year-old Edison bought fourteen acres of land on the banks of the Caloosahatchee and cleared a section of it to spend his remaining winters. This became the **Edison Winter Estate**, 2350 McGregor Blvd, a mile west of downtown (daily 9am–5.30pm; $20 for homes and gardens tour, every 30min; T239/334-3614, Wwww.efwefla.org). Tours begin in the gardens, planted with such exotics as African sausage trees and wild orchids. However, the house, which you can glimpse only through the windows, is anticlimactic – its plainness probably due to the fact that Edison spent most of his waking hours inside the **laboratory**, attempting to turn the latex-rich sap of *Solidago edisonii* (a strain of goldenrod weed he developed) into rubber. However, when the tour reaches the engrossing **museum**, the full impact of Edison's achievements becomes apparent: you'll see several examples of the phonograph that Edison created in 1877, as well as some of the ungainly cinema projectors derived from Edison's Kinetoscope – which brought him a million dollars a year in royalties from 1907. Next door, you can also traipse through the plain **Ford Winter Estate**, bought by Edison's close friend Henry Ford in 1915. Much more awe-inspiring is the enormous banyan tree outside the ticket office – the largest of its kind in the continental US.

The Fort Myers beaches

The **Fort Myers beaches** on **Estero Island**, fifteen miles south of downtown, are appreciably different in character from the west coast's more commercialized beach strips, with a cheerful seaside mood. Accommodation is plentiful on and around Estero Boulevard – reached by San Carlos Boulevard – which runs the seven-mile length of the island. Most activity revolves around the short fishing pier and the **Lynne Hall Memorial Park**, at the island's north end.

Estero Island becomes increasingly residential as you press south, Estero Boulevard eventually swinging over a slender causeway to **Lovers Key State Recreation Area** (daily 8am–sunset; $8/car, $2 for pedestrians and cyclists; ⓣ239/463-4588), where a footpath picks a trail over a couple of mangrove-fringed islands and several mullet-filled creeks to **Lovers Key**, a secluded beach. If you don't fancy the walk, a free trolley will transport you between the park entrance and the beach.

Reached only by crossing a causeway (with a $6 toll), the islands of **Sanibel** and **Captiva**, 25 miles southwest of Fort Myers, are virtually impossible to visit unless you have a car. However, if you have a spare day, these islands offer a wildlife refuge, mangroves and shell-strewn beaches – for which they are widely renowned. In contrast with the smooth beaches along the gulf side of Sanibel Island, the opposite edge comprises shallow bays and creeks, and a vibrant wildlife habitat under the protection of the **J.N. "Ding" Darling National Wildlife Refuge** (daily except Fri 7.30am–sunset; cars $5, cyclists and pedestrians $1; ⓣ239/472-1100). The main entrance and **information centre** are just off the Sanibel–Captiva Road. If you intend to stay here for a night or two, contact the Fort Myers visitor centre beforehand for lodging ideas. By doing so, you'll be treated to a beach experience unlike those in most of Florida – lovely, yet with an acute sense of isolation.

Practicalities

Greyhound buses pull in at the Rosa Parks Transportation Center, 2250 Peck St, while daily **Amtrak buses** from Tampa arrive at 6050 Plaza Drive, about six miles east of downtown. The **Chamber of Commerce** is at 2310 Edwards Drive (Mon–Fri 9am–4.30pm; ⓣ1-800/366-3622, ⓦwww.fortmyers.org). Distances within Fort Myers, and from downtown to the beaches, are large, and you'll struggle without a car, though it is possible – just – to reach the beaches on local **LeeTran buses**; $1.25 (ⓣ239/533-8726, ⓦwww.rideleetran.com). You can pick up most LeeTran services at the Greyhound terminal.

Accommodation costs in and around Fort Myers are low between May and December, when 30–60 percent gets lopped off the standard rates. However, in high season, prices skyrocket, and spare rooms are rare. For a truly unique and offbeat experience, drive on over to *The Sun and the Moon Inn*, 3962 NW Pine Island Rd, Matlacha (ⓦwww.sunandmoon.net); owner Curt Peer is a true character and this B&B is a perfect place to relax and wander around the nearby mangroves via kayak. At the beaches, Estero Boulevard is your best bet: the *Outrigger Beach Resort*, no. 6200 (ⓣ239/463-3131, ⓦwww.outriggerfmb.com; ❸), and *Casa Playa*, no. 510 (ⓣ1-800/569-4876, ⓦwww.casaplayaresort.com; ❹–❼), are both clean and reliable. Of the **campgrounds**, only *Red Coconut*, 3001 Estero Blvd (from $40; ⓣ239/463-7200, ⓦwww.redcoconut.com), is right on the beach.

For downtown **food**, try *The Veranda*, 2122 Second St (ⓣ239/332-2065), where the Old South lives on in two houses dating to 1902 and a lush courtyard of mango trees, or *Oasis Restaurant*, 2260 Dr Martin Luther King Jr Blvd (ⓣ239/334-1556), for large, cheap breakfasts and lunch specials.

Everglades National Park

One of the country's most celebrated natural areas, the **EVERGLADES NATIONAL PARK** is a vast, tranquil wildlife reserve, with a subtle, raw appeal that makes a stark contrast to America's more rugged national parks. The most dramatic sights are small pockets of trees poking above a completely flat sawgrass plain, yet these wide-open spaces resonate with life, forming part of an ever-changing ecosystem, evolved through a unique combination of climate, vegetation and wildlife.

Though it appears to be flat as a table-top, the limestone on which the Everglades stands actually tilts very slightly towards the southwest. For thousands of years, water from summer storms and the overflow of nearby Lake Okeechobee has moved slowly through the Everglades towards the coast. The water replenishes the sawgrass, which grows on a thin layer of soil formed by decaying vegetation. This gives birth to the algae at the base of a complex food chain that sustains much larger creatures – most importantly **alligators**. After the floodwaters have reached the sea, drained through the bedrock, or simply evaporated, the Everglades are barren except for the water accumulated in ponds – or "gator holes" – created when an alligator senses water and clears the soil covering it with its tail. Besides nourishing the alligator, the pond provides a home for other wildlife until the summer rains return. Sawgrass covers much of the Everglades, but where natural indentations in the limestone fill with soil, fertile tree islands – or "**hammocks**" – appear, just high enough to stand above the floodwaters.

In the nineteenth century, the Seminole and Miccosukee **Native American tribes** were forced to live hunter-gatherer existences in the Everglades, and still maintain a sizeable presence here. By the late 1800s, a few towns had sprung up, peopled by settlers who, unlike the Native Americans, looked to exploit the land. As Florida's population grew, the damage caused by hunting, road building and draining for farmland gave rise to a significant **conservation** lobby. In 1947, a section of the Everglades was declared a national park, which today bestows federal protection to a comparatively small area at the southern tip of the Florida peninsula. The Everglades' boundaries have been steadily pushed back by urban development over the last century, and unrestrained commercial use of nearby areas continues to upset the region's natural cycle. The 1200 miles of canals built to divert the flow of water away from the Everglades and toward the state's expanding cities, the poisoning caused by agricultural chemicals from local farmlands and the broader changes wrought by global warming could yet turn Florida's greatest natural asset into a wasteland.

Arrival and information

There are **three entrances** to the park: Everglades City, at the northwestern corner; Shark Valley, at the northeastern corner; and the one near the Ernest Coe Visitor Center, at the southeastern corner. **US-41** skirts the northern edge of the park, providing the only land access to the Everglades City and Shark Valley entrances. There is **no public transportation** along US-41, or to any of the park entrances.

Park entry is free at Everglades City, although from here you can travel only by boat or canoe. At the other entrances it's $10 per car and $5 for pedestrians and cyclists. Entry tickets are valid for seven days.

The park is **open year-round**, but the most favourable time by far to visit is **winter**, when the receding floodwaters cause wildlife to congregate around gator holes, ranger-led activities are frequent and the mosquitoes are bearable. In **summer**, afternoon storms flood the prairies, park activities are substantially reduced and the mosquitoes are a severe annoyance. Visiting between seasons is also a good bet. Before trekking out to the park, you might want to pick up Michael Grunwald's excellent book, *The Swamp: The Everglades, Florida, and the Politics of Paradise* to learn about the good, bad and the ugly regarding the interactions between humans and this unique corner of the world.

Accommodation

There are a handful of places to stay in the towns just outside the park's perimeter. In Everglades City, try the charming and clean *Ivey House*, 107 Camellia St (Ⓣ239/695-3299, Ⓦwww.iveyhouse.com; ❹), or head five miles south to the

Chokoloskee Island Resort (Ⓣ239/695-2881), where you can rent an **RV** by the night for $69–89. Ten miles east of the park, you'll find plenty of **motels** in Homestead and Florida City, as well as the *Everglades International Hostel*, 20 SW 2nd Ave, off Palm Drive, Florida City (Ⓣ1-800/372-3874, Ⓦwww.evergladeshostel.com); this is the best option for budget-minded travellers who don't want to camp. Beds go for $25–28 a night and there are also some private rooms (❷–❸). The hostel rents canoes ($30/day) and bikes ($15/day); bike rental plus return transport to the park entrance is $30 total. They also offer excellent tours (minimum 4 people; $80). There are well-equipped **campgrounds** (both $16/night; reservations at Ⓣ1-800/365-CAMP or Ⓦwww.nps.gov) at Flamingo and Long Pine Key, six miles from the Coe entrance. There are also many free backcountry spots on the longer walking and canoe trails (permits are issued at the visitor centres for $10, plus $2/person).

Everglades City and around

Purchased and named in the 1920s by an advertising executive dreaming of a subtropical metropolis, **EVERGLADES CITY**, three miles south off US-41 along Route 29, now has a population of just under five hundred. Most who visit are solely intent on diminishing the stocks of sports fish living around the mangrove islands – the aptly titled **Ten Thousand Islands** – arranged like scattered jigsaw-puzzle pieces around the coastline.

For a closer look at the mangroves, which safeguard the Everglades from surge tides, take one of the park-sanctioned **boat trips**. Try either the Everglades National Park Boat Tours; from $26.50 (Ⓣ239/695-2591), which depart from the visitor centre, or Everglades Rentals and Eco Adventures (Ⓣ239/695-3299, Ⓦwww.evergladesadventures.com), at the *Ivey House* (see above). The dockside **Gulf Coast Visitor Center** (daily: May–Oct 9am–4.30pm, Nov–April 8am–4.30pm; Ⓣ239/695-3311) provides details on the cruises, as well as the excellent ranger-led **canoe trips**.

Shark Valley and the Miccosukee Indian Village

Around forty miles east of Everglades City, **Shark Valley** (entrance open daily 8.30am–6pm) epitomizes the Everglades' "River of Grass" moniker. From here, dotted by hardwood hammocks, the sawgrass plain stretches as far as the eye can see. Aside from a few simple walking trails close to the **visitor centre** (daily: May–Oct 9.15am–5.15pm, Nov–April 8.45am–5.15pm; Ⓣ305/221-8776), you can see Shark Valley only from a fifteen-mile loop road, ideally covered by renting a **bike** from the visitor centre ($6.50 an hour; must be returned by 4pm). Alternatively, a highly informative two-hour **tram tour** (daily; $17.25; reservations on Ⓣ305/221-8455) stops frequently to view wildlife, but won't allow you to linger in any particular place, as you'll certainly want to do.

You'll pass real Native American villages all along US-41, with most belonging to the **Miccosukee tribe**, descendants of the survivors of the last Seminole War (1858). Today the tribe runs a small but relatively prosperous reservation in the heart of the Everglades, though the kitschy souvenirs and displays at the **Miccosukee Indian Village** (daily 9am–5pm; $10; Ⓣ305/223-8380) are rather contrived – grab some home-made chili instead at nearby *Billie's Restaurant*.

Pine Island and Flamingo

The **Pine Island** section of the park – from the Coe Visitor Center entrance to Flamingo, perched at the end of the park road on Florida's southern tip – holds virtually everything that makes the Everglades tick. Spend a day or two in this southerly portion of the park and you'll quickly grasp the fundamentals of its complex ecology.

Route-9336 (the only road in this section of the park) leads past the comprehensive **Ernest Coe Visitor Center** (daily: May–Oct 9am–5pm, Nov–April 8am–5pm; ⓣ305/242-7700) to the main park entrance. A mile further on, the **Royal Palm Visitor Center** (open 24hr) usually features ranger activities and events (but little information). The large numbers of park visitors who simply want to see an alligator are usually satisfied by walking the half-mile **Anhinga Trail** here: the notoriously lazy reptiles are easily seen during the winter, often splayed near the trail, looking like plastic props. All manner of birdlife can also be spotted, from snowy egrets to the bizarre, eponymous anhinga, an elegant black-bodied bird resembling an elongated cormorant. To beat the crowds, go early to the Anhinga Trail; after that, peruse the adjacent, but very different, **Gumbo Limbo Trail**, a hardwood jungle hammock packed with exotic subtropical growths.

The Panhandle

Rubbing hard against Alabama in the west and Georgia in the north, the long, narrow **Panhandle** has much more in common with the states of the Deep South than with the rest of Florida. Hard to believe, then, that just over a century ago, the Panhandle *was* Florida. At the western edge, **Pensacola** was a busy port when Miami was still a swamp. Fertile soils lured wealthy plantation owners south, helping to establish **Tallahassee** as a high-society gathering place and administrative centre – a role which, as the state capital, it retains. But the decline of cotton, the chopping-down of too many trees and the coming of the East Coast railroad eventually left the Panhandle high and dry. Much of the inland region still seems neglected, and the **Apalachicola National Forest** is perhaps the best place in Florida to disappear into the wilderness. The **coastal Panhandle**, on the other hand, is enjoying better times: despite rows of hotels, much is still untainted, boasting miles of blinding white sands.

Tallahassee and around

State capital it may be, **TALLAHASSEE** is nevertheless a provincial city of oak trees and soft hills that won't take more than two days to explore in full. Around its small grid of central streets – where you'll find plenty of reminders of Florida's formative years – briefcase-clutching bureaucrats mingle with some of Florida State University's 35,000 students, who brighten the mood considerably and keep the city awake at night.

Tallahassee was built on the site of an important prehistoric meeting place, and takes its name from the Apalachee: *talwa* meaning "town", and *ahassee* meaning "old". The city's **history** really begins, though, with Florida's incorporation into the US, and Tallahassee's selection as the state's administrative base; the first Florida government convened here in 1823. Today, in contrast to the lightning-paced development of south Florida, Tallahassee has a slow tempo and a strong sense of the past, evoked in its historic buildings and museums.

Arrival and information

Tallahassee's Greyhound **bus terminal** is at 112 W Tennessee St (Ⓣ850/222-4249), within short walking distance of downtown, which can easily be explored on **foot**. For stacks of background information, drop by the **Visitor Information Center**, 106 E Jefferson St (Mon–Fri 8am–5pm, Sat 9am–1pm; Ⓣ1-800/628-2866, Ⓦwww.visittallahassee.com).

Accommodation

Accommodation in Tallahassee is in short supply only during the sixty-day sitting of the state legislature, from early March, and on fall weekends during home football games of the Florida State Seminoles and Florida A&M Rattlers. **Hotels** and **motels** on N Monroe Street, about three miles from downtown, are far cheaper than those downtown.

Comfort Suites 1026 Apalachee Parkway Ⓣ850/224-3200, Ⓦwww.comfortsuites.com. The beds are heavenly at this comfortable, spotless motel, within walking distance of the capital. There's also a delicious, free continental breakfast. ❻

Governors Inn 209 S Adams St Ⓣ1-800/342-7717, Ⓦwww.thegovinn.com. Every room in this splendid downtown inn is decorated with antique furniture reflecting the period of the governor each is named after. ❽–❾

Super 8 2801 N Monroe St Ⓣ850/386-8286. A good option for the budget traveller, this motel offers simple rooms with basic amenities. ❸

The Town

A $50 million eyesore dominates the square mile of **downtown Tallahassee**: the vertical vents of the towering **New Capitol Building**, at Apalachee Parkway and Monroe Street (Mon–Fri 8am–5pm; free). Florida's growing army of bureaucrats had previously been crammed into the more attractive **Old Capitol Building** dating from 1845 (Mon–Fri 9am–4.30pm, Sat 10am–4.30pm, Sun noon–4.30pm; free), which stands in the shadow of its replacement.

For easily the fullest account of Florida's past anywhere in the state, visit the **Museum of Florida History**, 500 S Bronough St (Mon–Fri 9am–4.30pm, Sat 10am–4.30pm, Sun noon–4.30pm; free; Ⓣ850/245-6400, Ⓦwww.museumofloridahistory.com). Detailed accounts of Paleo-Indian settlements, and the significance of their burial and temple mounds, some of which have been found on the edge of Tallahassee, are valuable tools in comprehending Florida's prehistory. The colonialist crusades of the Spanish are outlined with copious finds, though there's little on the nineteenth-century Seminole Wars – one of the bloodier skeletons in Florida's closet. Railroads get ample attention, and this makes sense, given the role they played in early tourism efforts and general boosterism throughout the state.

The **Black Archives Research Center and Museum**, in the nineteenth-century Union Bank Building, along Apalachee Parkway from the Old Capitol's entrance (Mon–Fri 9am–5pm; free; Ⓣ850/599-3020), holds one of the largest and most important collections of African-American artefacts in the nation, with oral histories and music stations, as well as some chilling Ku Klux Klan memorabilia.

Eating

With so many politicos and students, there's plenty of good **food** for all budgets in Tallahassee.

Andrew's Capital Grill & Bar/Andrew's 228 228 S Adams St Ⓣ850/222-3444. Casual grill and bar serving a variety of sandwiches and burgers all day; the chic downstairs *Andrew's 228* prepares delicious nouveau Italian dishes like gorgonzola cheesecake and grouper piccata.

Barnacle Bill's 1830 N Monroe St ☎850/385-8734. Inexpensive fresh fish and seafood served in a riotous atmosphere.

La Fiesta 2329 Apalachee Pkwy ☎850/656-3392. The very best Mexican food in the city.

Mom and Dad's 4175 Apalachee Pkwy ☎850/877-4518. Delicious home-made Italian food. Closed Sun & Mon.

Po' Boys Creole Café 224 E College Ave ☎850/224-5400. A range of Creole delights; also one of Tallahassee's most popular live music venues.

Wakulla Springs State Park

Fifteen miles south of Tallahassee, off Route-61 on Route-267, **Wakulla Springs State Park** (daily 8am–sunset; cars $6, pedestrians and cyclists $2; ☎850/926-0700) holds what is believed to be one of the biggest and deepest natural springs in the world. It pumps up half a million gallons of crystal-clear pure water from the bowels of the earth every day – though you'd never guess it from the calm surface.

It's refreshing to **swim** in the cool pool (in a small roped-off area – this is gator territory), but to learn more about the spring, take the thirty-minute **glass-bottom boat tour** ($8), and peer down to the swarms of fish hovering around the 180ft cavern through which the water flows. Forty-minute **river cruises** ($8) let you glimpse some of the park's inhabitants: deer, turkeys, turtles, herons, egrets and the inevitable alligators. Built in 1937 beside the spring, the lovely wooden *Wakulla Lodge* (☎850/926-0700; ❹–❺) is a serene hotel, with an excellent **restaurant** serving home-cooked country food for breakfast, lunch and dinner.

The Apalachicola National Forest

With swamps, savannahs and springs dotted liberally about its half-million acres, the **Apalachicola National Forest**, which fans out southwest of Tallahassee, is the inland Panhandle at its natural best. Several roads enable you to drive through a good-sized chunk, with many undemanding spots for a rest and a snack. To see deeper into the forest you'll need to make more of an effort, by following one of the hiking trails, canoeing on the rivers or simply spending a night under the stars at one of the basic campgrounds. On the forest's southern edge, the large and forbidding **Tate's Hell Swamp** is a breeding-ground for the deadly water moccasin snake; you're well advised to stay clear.

The main **entrances** to the forest (free) are off Hwy-20 and Hwy-319; three minor roads, routes 267, 375 and 65, form cross-forest links between the two highways. **Accommodation** is limited to camping; apart from *Camel Lake* and *Wright Lake* ($10/night for both; hot showers available), all the campgrounds are free (except for a $3 daily vehicle charge), with very basic facilities (no running water). For more information, call the **ranger stations** at Apalachicola (☎850/643-2282) or Wakulla (☎850/926-3561).

Panama City Beach

Follow Hwy-98 fifty miles west from Apalachicola and you'll hit the orgy of motels, go-kart tracks, mini-golf courses and amusement parks that is **PANAMA CITY BEACH**. Entirely without pretension, the area capitalizes blatantly on the appeal of its 27-mile stretch of white sand. The whole place is as commercialized as can be, but with the shops, bars and restaurants all trying to undercut one another, there are some great bargains to be found. That said, throughout the lively summer (the so-called "100 Magic Days"), accommodation costs are high and reservations essential. In winter, prices drop and visitors are fewer; most are Canadians and – increasingly – Europeans, many of whom have no problem sunbathing and swimming in the cool temperatures.

Getting a tan, running yourself ragged at beach sports and going all out on the nightlife are the main concerns in Panama City Beach, one of the country's foremost Spring Break destinations. Go-karting, jet-skiing and parasailing are all available at many locations along the coastal strip; otherwise, splash around at the water park ($35 for a go-on-everything day-ticket). For scuba-divers, several accessible shipwrecks litter the area; get details from any of the numerous dive shops.

Practicalities

Places to stay, while plentiful, fill with amazing speed, especially at weekends. As a general rule, **motels** at the east end of the beach are smarter and slightly pricier than those in the centre. Those at the west end are quieter and more family-oriented. The *Sugar Sands Motel*, 20723 Front Beach Rd (Ⓣ1-800/367-9221, Ⓦwww.sugarsands.com; ❺–❻), is an excellent-value oceanfront motel away from the noise. The cheapest places to **eat** are the buffet restaurants on Front Beach Road, which charge $9–14 for all you can manage. Alternatively, try one of the regular lunch or dinner restaurants: *Shuckum's Oyster Pub & Seafood Grill*, 15614 Front Beach Rd (Ⓣ850/235-3214); *Mike's Diner*, 17554 Front Beach Rd (Ⓣ850/234-1942), which is also open for breakfast, and until late at night; or the *Boatyard*, 5323 N Lagoon Drive (Ⓣ850/249-9273), for alfresco dining beside a lagoon. **At night**, party-goers congregate at *Club La Vela*, 8813 Thomas Drive (Ⓣ850/235-1061), or *Spinnaker*, 8795 Thomas Drive (Ⓣ850/234-7892), each with dozens of bars, several discos and a young crowd.

Pensacola and around

You might be inclined to overlook **PENSACOLA**, tucked away as it is at the western end of the Panhandle. The city, on the northern bank of the broad Pensacola Bay, is five miles inland from the nearest beaches, and its prime features are a naval aviation school and some busy dockyards. Pensacola is, however, worth a visit, and the city centre has expressed something of a renaissance in the past few years. The nearby white beaches are relatively untouched, and it boasts a rich history, having been occupied by the Spanish as early as 1559. The town repeatedly changed hands between the Spanish, the French and the British before becoming the place where Florida was officially ceded by Spain to the US in 1821.

Pensacola was already a booming port by 1900, when the opening of the Panama Canal was expected to boost its fortunes still further. The many new buildings that appeared in the **Palafox District**, around the southerly section of Palafox Street, in the early 1900s – with their delicate ornamentation and attention to detail – reflect the optimism of the era.

In earlier times, Native Americans, pioneer settlers and seafaring traders had gathered to swap, sell and barter on the waterfront of the **Seville District**, just east of Palafox Street. Those who did well took up permanent residence here, and many of their homes remain in fine states of repair, forming – together with several museums – the **Historic Pensacola Village** (Mon–Sat 10am–4pm; $6; Ⓣ850/595-5985, Ⓦwww.historicpensacola.org). Tickets are valid for one week, and allow access to all of the museums and former homes in an easily navigated four-block area. Inside the US naval base on Navy Boulevard, about eight miles southwest of central Pensacola, the **Museum of Naval Aviation** (daily 9am–5pm;

free, IMAX movie $8; ⓣ1-800/327-5002, ⓦwww.navalaviationmuseum.org) exhibits US naval aircraft. They range from the first flimsy seaplane, acquired in 1911, to the Phantoms and Hornets of more recent times.

Another unsung gem in the area is the **Gulf Islands National Seashore** (ⓦwww.nps.gov/guis), which contains historic fortifications (Fort Pickens), sumptous white-sand beaches and ample wildlife-viewing opportunities. The park stretches across the states of Alabama and Florida, and the best access to the park from Pensacola proper is via FL-292. The entrance fee is $8 for automobiles, and the Fort Barrancas Visitors Center (March–Oct 9.30am–4.45pm, Nov–Feb 8.30am–3.45pm) contains an informative short film, a gift shop and free brochures about what to see in this corner of the park.

Pensacola Beach

On the other (south) side of the bay from the city, glistening beaches and windswept sand dunes fringe the fifty-mile-long **Santa Rosa Island**. On the island directly south of Pensacola, **PENSACOLA BEACH** has everything you'd want from a Gulf Coast beach: fine white sands, watersports rental outlets, a busy fishing pier and a sprinkling of motels, beachside bars and snack stands.

Practicalities

The Greyhound **bus station** is seven miles north of the city centre, at 505 W Burgess Rd (ⓣ850/476-8199); ECAT buses #50 and #45 ($1.75; ⓣ850/595-3228, ⓦwww.goecat.com) link it to Pensacola proper. A good local **taxi** firm is Yellow Cab (ⓣ850/433-3333). ECAT **buses** serve the city, while #61 goes to the beach twice daily; the main terminal is at 1515 W Fairfield Drive. At the foot of the city side of the three-mile Pensacola Bay Bridge, the **visitor centre**, 1401 E Gregory St (Mon–Fri 8am–5pm, Sat 9am–4pm and Sun 11am–4pm; ⓣ1-800/874-1234, ⓦwww.visitpensacola.com), has the usual worthwhile handouts.

Plenty of budget chain **hotels**, charging $55–70 per night, line North Davis and Pensacola boulevards, the main approach roads from I-10. Central options are the *Days Inn*, 710 N Palafox St (ⓣ850/438-4922; ❸), and *Noble Manor*, 110 W Strong St (ⓣ850/434-9544, ⓦwww.noblemanor.com; ❺), a charming B&B. At Pensacola Beach, try the downright fun and occasionally raucous (they have a fun bar with live music every night of the week) *Paradise Inn*, 21 Via De Luna Drive (ⓣ850/916-5087 ❼–❽). For **eating** in town, *Fish House*, 600 S Barracks St (ⓣ850/470-0003), has sushi and steaks along with the seafood. For beachside dining, *Peg Leg Pete's*, 1010 Fort Pickens Rd (ⓣ850/932-4139), is known for its Cajun food and varied half-dozen oyster selections ($5.99–12.99).

8

Louisiana

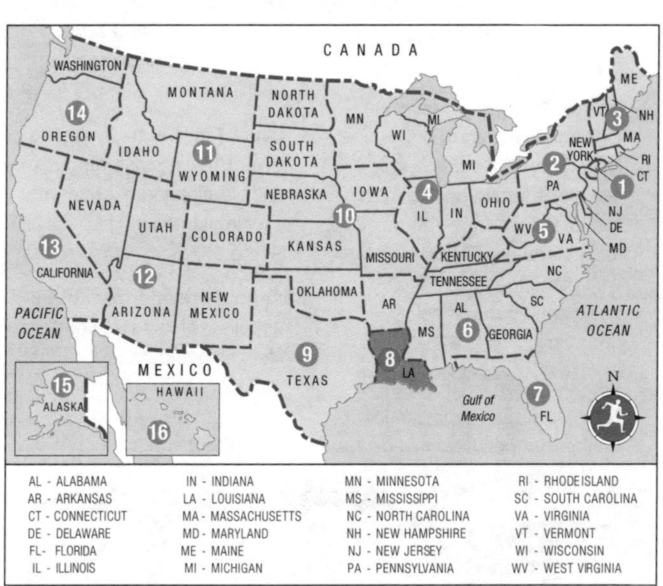
CANADA
WASHINGTON
MONTANA
NORTH DAKOTA
MN
WI
MI
ME
VT
NH
MA
RI
CT
NEW YORK
14
OREGON
IDAHO
11
WYOMING
SOUTH DAKOTA
MI
3
2
PA
1
NJ
DE
MD
NEVADA
NEBRASKA
IOWA
4
IL
IN
OHIO
WV
5
VA
UTAH
COLORADO
10
KANSAS
MISSOURI
KENTUCKY
13
CALIFORNIA
12
TENNESSEE
NC
OKLAHOMA
AR
AL
SC
PACIFIC OCEAN
ARIZONA
NEW MEXICO
MS
6
GEORGIA
ATLANTIC OCEAN
8
LA
9
TEXAS
MEXICO
15
ALASKA
HAWAII
16
7
Gulf of Mexico
FL
N
AL - ALABAMA
AR - ARKANSAS
CT - CONNECTICUT
DE - DELAWARE
FL- FLORIDA
IL - ILLINOIS
IN - INDIANA
LA - LOUISIANA
MA - MASSACHUSETTS
MD - MARYLAND
ME - MAINE
MI - MICHIGAN
MN - MINNESOTA
MS - MISSISSIPPI
NC - NORTH CAROLINA
NH - NEW HAMPSHIRE
NJ - NEW JERSEY
PA - PENNSYLVANIA
RI - RHODE ISLAND
SC - SOUTH CAROLINA
VA - VIRGINIA
VT - VERMONT
WI - WISCONSIN
WV - WEST VIRGINIA

CHAPTER 8

Highlights

* **Swamp tours** Watch out for alligators lurking in the ghostly, Spanish-moss-shaded bayous. See pp.559 & 582

* **Mardi Gras** From the masking and dancing of New Orleans's urban spectacular, to Cajun country's pagan rituals, Louisiana's Fat Tuesday is unlike any other. See pp.570 & p.576

* **Napoleon House, New Orleans** Steeped in old New Orleans elegance, this gorgeous family-owned bar has stayed the same for generations, complete with flickering lamps and a romantic subtropical courtyard. See p.572

* **Vaughan's on a Thursday, New Orleans** Kermit Ruffins on the trumpet, beans and rice on the stove, and riotously happy music fans tearing the roof off this tiny tumbledown neighbourhood bar. See p.574

* **Cajun and Creole festivals** Celebrating anything from sweet potatoes to world music, these country festivals offer superb opportunities to enjoy Cajun and zydeco music, crafts and lots of delicious food. See p.576

* **Laura Plantation** By far the River Road's most intriguing and illuminating account of Creole plantation life. See p.577

* **Angola prisoner rodeo** An unbelievable spectacle, with lifers slugging it out for guts and glory in this notorious maximum-security prison. See p.583

▲ *Napoleon House*

Louisiana

Swathed in the romance of pirates, voodoo and Mardi Gras, **LOUISIANA** is undeniably special. Its history is barely on nodding terms with the view that America was the creation of the Pilgrim Fathers; its way of life is proudly set apart. This is the land of the rural, French-speaking **Cajuns** (descended from the Acadians, eighteenth-century French-Canadian refugees), who live in the prairies and swamps in the southwest of the state, and the Creoles of jazzy, sassy **New Orleans**. (The term **Creole** was originally used to define anyone born in the state to French or Spanish colonists – famed in the nineteenth century for their masked balls, patois and distinct culture – as well as native-born, French-speaking slaves, but has since come to define anyone or anything native to Louisiana, and in particular its black population.) Louisiana's distinctive, spicy **cuisine**, **festivals**, and, above all, its **music** (**jazz**, **R&B**, **Cajun**, and its bluesy black counterpart, **zydeco**) draw from all these cultures and more. Oddly enough, **northern Louisiana** – Protestant Bible Belt country, where old plantation homes stand decaying in vast cottonfields – feels more "Southern" than the marshy bayous, shaded by ancient cypress trees and laced with wispy trails of Spanish moss, of the Catholic south.

The **French** first settled Louisiana in 1682, braving treacherous swamps and plagues to harvest the abundant cypress. Its first permanent settlement, the trading post of **Natchitoches**, was established in 1714, followed by New Orleans in 1718. In 1760, Louis XV secretly handed New Orleans, along with all French territory west of the Mississippi, to his **Spanish** cousin, Charles III, as a safeguard against British expansionism. Louisiana remained Spanish until it was ceded to Napoleon in 1801, under the proviso that it should never change hands again. Just two years later, however, Napoleon, strapped for cash to fund his battles with the British in Europe, struck a bargain with President Thomas Jefferson known as the **Louisiana Purchase**. This sneaky agreement handed over to the US all French lands between Canada and Mexico, from the Mississippi to the Rockies, for just $15 million. The subsequent "Americanization" of Louisiana was one of the most momentous periods in the state's history, with the port of New Orleans, in its key position near the mouth of the **Mississippi River**, growing to become one of the nation's wealthiest cities. Though the state seceded from the Union to join the Confederacy in 1861, there were differences between Louisiana and the rest of the slave-driven South. The **Black Code**, drawn up by the French in 1685 to govern Saint-Domingue (today's Haiti) and established in Louisiana in 1724, had given slaves rights unparalleled elsewhere, including permission to marry, meet socially and take Sundays off. The black population of New Orleans in particular was renowned as exceptionally literate and cosmopolitan, with a significant number of **free people of colour** who owned businesses, property and even slaves.

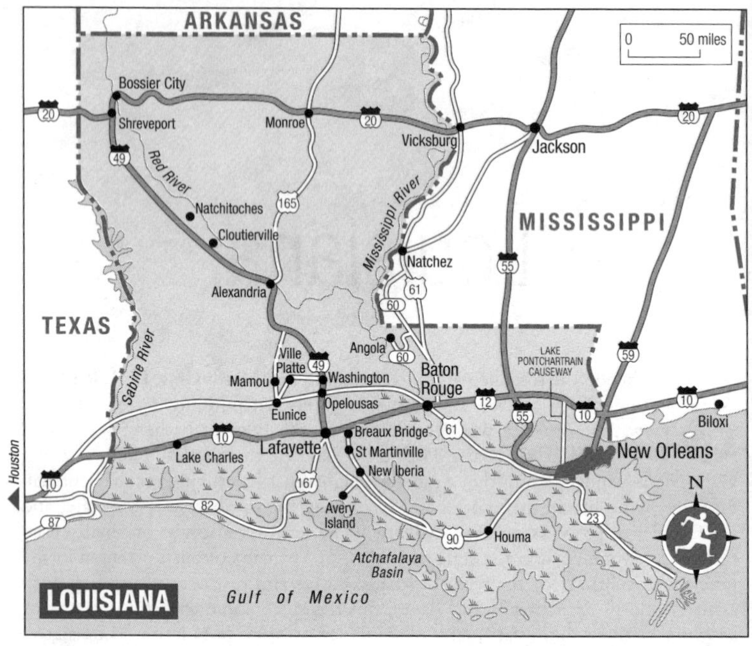

Economically and socially ravaged by the Civil War, Louisiana was almost brought to its knees by **Reconstruction,** with the once great city of New Orleans suffering a period of unprecedented lawlessness and racial violence. In time, the economy, at least, recovered, benefiting from the key importance of the mighty Mississippi and the discovery of offshore oil in the 1950s – but during the twentieth century Louisiana came to rely heavily upon **tourism**.

In August 2005, the double whammy of **Hurricane Katrina**, which swept in through the coastal wetlands, and the horrific after-effects of the levee breaks in New Orleans, seemed as if it might put an end to all that. Slowly but surely, however, recovery continued and Louisiana, although diminished, returned to some normality – until the disastrous **BP oil spill** of May 2010 dealt the region, and its all-important seafood industry, another blow. Today, though no thinking person can visit southern Louisiana without feeling a sense of loss, the state has an enormous amount to offer. Whether you're canoeing along a cypress-clogged bayou, dining on spicy crawfish in a crumbling Creole cottage, or dancing on a steamy starlit night to the best live music in the world, Louisiana remains unique, a state that will get under your skin and stay there.

Getting around Louisiana

Louisiana is crossed east–west by two major **interstates**, I-20 in the north and I-10 in the south. New Orleans is the hub, traversed by I-10 and served by I-55 and I-59 from Mississippi. I-49 sweeps across the state southeast to northwest, connecting Cajun country with the north.

The international **airport** is in New Orleans; regional airlines serve the rest of the state and surrounding areas. Amtrak **trains** link New Orleans with New York,

Chicago and Memphis, as well as Los Angeles, via Lafayette. Greyhound **buses** connect the major towns with the rest of the country, and are supplemented by smaller local lines.

New Orleans

Infused with a dizzying jumble of cultures and influences, **NEW ORLEANS** is a bewitching place. Here, people dance at funerals and hold parties during hurricanes; world-class musicians make ends meet busking on street corners and hole-in-the-wall dives dish up gourmet Creole cuisine. There's a wistfulness here too, along with its famed *joie de vivre* – not only in the ghostly devastation of the flood-wracked Ninth Ward, but also in the peeling facades of the old French Quarter, in its filigree cast-iron balconies tangled with ferns and fragrant jasmine, and in the cemeteries lined with crumbling above-ground marble tombs. New Orleans's melancholy beauty – along with its ebullient spirit – has always come with an awareness of the fragility of life, due at least in part to its perilous geography.

It has become painfully clear to the rest of the world, too, since the events of August 2005, that there's a lot more to the "Big Easy" than its image as a nonstop party town. Even at the best of times this was a contradictory city, repeatedly revealing stark divisions between rich and poor (and, more explicitly, between white and black); years after **Katrina**, with the emotional and physical scars slowly healing, those contradictions remain. While you can still party in the French Quarter and the Faubourg Marigny till dawn, dancing to great jazz and gorging on garlicky Creole food, just fifteen minutes away entire neighbourhoods struggle to rebuild. That's not to say that enjoying life is inappropriate in today's New Orleans – while it was let down not only by nature but also by federal and local government after Katrina, the city's vitality, courage and stubborn loyalty remain strong. The melange of cultures and races that built the city still gives it its heart; not "easy", exactly, but quite unlike anywhere else in the US – or the world.

Some history

New Orleans began life in 1718 as a **French-Canadian** outpost – an improbable, swampy setting in a prime location near the mouth of the **Mississippi River**. Development was rapid, and with the first mass importation of African **slaves**, as early as the 1720s, its unique demography took shape. Despite early resistance from its francophone population, the city benefited greatly from its period as a **Spanish** colony between 1763 and 1800: by the end of the eighteenth century, the **port** was flourishing, the haunt of smugglers, gamblers, prostitutes and pirates. Newcomers included Anglo-Americans escaping the American Revolution and aristocrats fleeing revolution in France. The city also became a haven for refugees – whites and **free blacks**, along with their slaves – escaping the slave revolts in Saint-Domingue (Haiti). As in the West Indies, the Spanish, French and free people of colour associated and formed alliances to create a distinctive **Creole** culture with its own traditions and ways of life, its own patois, and a **cuisine** that drew influences from Africa, Europe and the colonies. New Orleans was already a many-textured place when it experienced two quick-fire changes of government, passing back into French control in 1801 and then being sold to **America** under the Louisiana Purchase two years later. Unwelcome in the Creole city – today's French Quarter – the Americans who migrated here were forced to settle in the areas now known as the **Central Business District** (or **CBD**) and, later, in the **Garden District**.

New Orleans's antebellum **golden age** as a major port and finance centre for the cotton-producing South was brought to an abrupt end by the Civil War. The economic blow wielded by a lengthy Union occupation was compounded by the ravages of **Reconstruction**: particularly disastrous for a city once famed for its large, educated, free black population. As the North industrialized and other Southern cities grew, the fortunes of New Orleans slipped.

Jazz exploded into the bars and the bordellos around 1900, and, along with the evolution of **Mardi Gras** as a tourist attraction, breathed new life into the city. And though the Depression hit here as hard as it did the rest of the nation, it also – spearheaded by a number of local writers and artists – heralded the resurgence of the **French Quarter**, which had disintegrated into a slum. Even so, it was the less romantic duo of **oil** and **petrochemicals** that really saved the economy – until the slump of the 1950s pushed New Orleans well behind other US cities. The oil crash of the early 1980s gave it yet another battering, a gloomy start for near on two decades of high crime rates, crack deaths and widespread corruption.

By the turn of the millennium things were improving, until **Hurricane Katrina** and its subsequent floods (see box, opposite) ripped the place apart. In 2010 the Saints, amazingly, won the **Superbowl** (see p.566); so deeply emotional was this victory that the election of **Mitch Landrieu**, the black-majority city's first white mayor in thirty years, went barely noticed in even the local newspapers. A few months later,

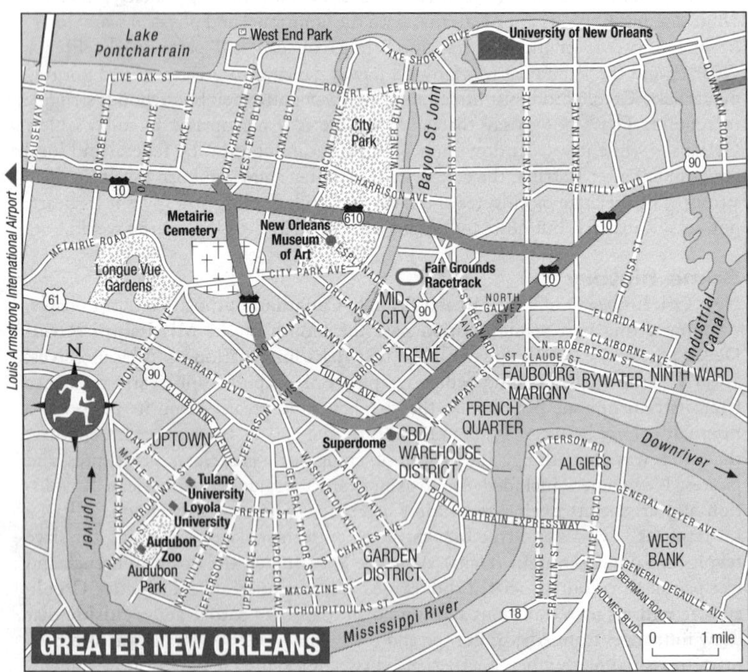

The Federal Flood

When **Hurricane Katrina** hit ground in 2005, it seemed at first as though the city had done relatively well in light of the full-scale damage wrought along the Mississippi coast. On August 29, however, New Orleans's **levees** were breached, and rising floodwaters soon covered eighty percent of the city, destroying much of it in their wake. Most damage was sustained by residential areas – whether in the suburban homes around the lakeside, from where most residents had been evacuated, to the less affluent neighbourhoods of the east, like the **Ninth Ward** and Gentilly, where those too poor or ill or old to move were trapped in attics and on rooftops for days. The French Quarter, which, as the oldest part of the city was built on the highest ground, was physically unhurt by the flooding, although the economic blow – not least the loss of a huge number of the neighbourhood's workforce – was tremendous.

Despite being referred to in shorthand as Katrina, the devastation of New Orleans was no natural disaster: in November 2009, a federal judge declared the Corps of Engineers, the government body responsible for building New Orleans' levees, as **guilty of negligence**, ruling that "The Corps' lassitude and failure to fulfil its duties resulted in a catastrophic loss of human life and property in unprecedented proportions...Furthermore, the Corps not only knew, but admitted by 1988, that the Mr-Go [navigation channel] threatened human life... and yet it did not act in time to prevent the catastrophic disaster that ensued". The Corps appealed on a technicality, and the finding may still be overturned, but for most people, the case has been amply proven: the worst engineering disaster in American history could have been avoided.

the sense of new beginnings was dealt a savage blow from the disastrous **BP oil spill** in the Gulf of Mexico and its long-term implications for the economy; if ever a city knew how to hold on and to fight back, however, New Orleans is it.

Arrival and information

Louis Armstrong New Orleans International Airport (**MSY**; Ⓦwww.flymsy.com), eighteen miles northwest of downtown on I-10, has an information booth (daily 8am–6pm) in its baggage claim area, along with hotel courtesy phones. Flat-rate **taxi** fares into town (20–30min) are $33 for up to two people, or $14 each for three or more; **shuttles** can also take you to your hotel (every 10min; tickets sold 8am–11pm in the baggage claim area or from the driver otherwise; $20 to downtown, $38 return; Ⓣ504/522-3500; Ⓦwww.airportshuttleneworleans.com).

Drivers approaching from either direction on I-10 should make sure not to stray onto I-610, which bypasses downtown altogether. For the CBD take exit 234C, following signs for the Superdome; for the French Quarter take 235B (signs for Vieux Carré), and for the Garden District take the St Charles Street exit. Using I-12 hooks you up with the Lake Pontchartrain Causeway – at 23 miles, the longest bridge in the world – which enters the city from the northwest and connects with I-10. **Greyhound** buses arrive next to **Amtrak** at the Union Passenger Terminal, 1001 Loyola Ave, near the Superdome. This area, beneath the elevated Pontchartrain Expressway, is not great; book a **cab** in advance to take you to your lodgings. United Cabs is the best firm (Ⓣ504/522-9771).

Before you leave home, check Ⓦwww.neworleanscvb.com; once you've arrived, you can pick up self-guided walking tours, free **maps** and discount vouchers at the helpful **Welcome Center** on Jackson Square at 529 St Ann St in the French Quarter (daily 9am–5pm; Ⓣ504/566-5031).

Staying safe in New Orleans

Although the heavily touristed French Quarter is comparatively safe, to wander unwittingly beyond it – even just a couple of blocks – can place your **personal safety** in serious jeopardy. While walking from the Quarter to the Marigny is usually safe enough during the day, it's not a good idea to stray far from the main drag of Frenchmen Street. Wherever you are, take the usual common-sense precautions, and at night always travel by cab when venturing any distance beyond the Quarter.

City transport

Though New Orleans's most-visited neighbourhoods are easy to **walk** around, getting between them is not always easy on foot, and if you're travelling anywhere outside the Quarter after dark you should call a **cab** (see above). The Regional Transit Authority (RTA) runs a network of **buses** and **trolleys** ($1.25, exact fare; Ⓦwww.norta.com). VisiTOUR **passes**, valid on all services, cost $5 for one day, $12 for three and $20 for five; the RTA website lists vendors.

The most useful **bus routes** include "Magazine" (#11), which runs between Canal Street in the CBD and Audubon Park uptown, and "Jackson-Esplanade" (#91), from Rampart Street on the edge of the Quarter to City Park. Far more romantic is the handsome sage-green **St Charles streetcar** (a National Historic Monument, dating back around one hundred years) that rumbles a thirteen-mile loop from Carondelet Street at Canal, along St Charles Avenue in the Garden District, past Audubon Park to Carrollton uptown. Service is limited after dark. There are also two **Canal Street streetcars**: the **City Park** service (#48, "City Park/Museum") starts by Harrah's casino on Canal Street, turns off at Carrollton and heads to City Park. The **Carrollton Avenue** line (#47, "Cemeteries") travels the length of Canal Street to where it meets City Park Avenue; if you're heading to City Park, make sure to get off at Carrollton and transfer onto the #48. There's also a **riverfront** trolley between the Convention Center and Esplanade Avenue.

Accommodation

New Orleans has some lovely **places to stay**, from rambling old guesthouses seeping faded grandeur to stylish boutique hotels. **Room rates**, never low (you'll be pushed to find anything half decent for less than $75 a night), increase considerably for Mardi Gras and Jazz Fest, when prices can go up by as much as two hundred percent and rooms are reserved months in advance.

Most people choose to stay in the **French Quarter**, in the heart of things. Many accommodations here are in atmospheric **guesthouses**, most of them in old Creole townhouses. In any one place, rooms can vary considerably in size, comfort and amenities, so be specific if you have certain preferences – and ask for a room away from the street if you want peace and quiet. Outside the Quarter, the **Lower Garden District** offers a couple of budget options, while the **Faubourg Marigny** specializes in B&Bs, and the **Garden District** proper has a couple of gorgeous old hotels. The **CBD** is the domain of the city's upmarket chain and business hotels.

French Quarter

Bourgoyne Guest House 839 Bourbon St ⓣ504/524-3621, ⓦwww.bourgoynehouse.com. Good-value guesthouse in an 1830s Creole mansion. Five worn but cosy studios are set around a subtropical courtyard; fancier options include the lovely Green Suite, accessed by a sweeping staircase, and boasting two bedrooms, a kitchen, parlour and Bourbon St balcony. ❹

Hotel Monteleone 214 Royal St ⓣ504/523-3341, ⓦwww.hotelmonteleone.com. This handsome French Quarter landmark is the oldest hotel in the city, owned by the same family since 1886, and hosting a fine array of writers and luminaries since then. At sixteen storeys, it's something of a gentle giant on genteel Royal St, with an elegant Baroque facade, marble lobby, comfy rooms, a splendid revolving bar and a rooftop pool. ❼

Hotel Provincial 1024 Chartres St ⓣ504/581-4995, ⓦwww.hotelprovincial.com. This sprawling – yet somehow intimate – place is in a quiet part of the Quarter, with rooms around five peaceful, gaslit courtyards. Some rooms are filled with antiques, others are more ordinary. Plus two nice outdoor pools, a bar and a fancy restaurant, *Stella!*, on site. ❹

Olivier House 828 Toulouse St ⓣ504/525-8456, ⓦwww.olivierhouse.com. Though a bit dark in places, this atmospheric, quintessentially New Orleans guesthouse offers real character. The 42 rooms (all with bath) vary widely, but most have funky antique furniture and tall shuttered windows. There's a tropical courtyard, and a tiny pool. ❻

Le Richelieu 1234 Chartres St ⓣ504/529-2492, ⓦwww.lerichelieuhotel.com. Handsome hotel in a restored factory and neighbouring townhouse. Though the old-world ambience of the lobby is not continued in the rather ordinary rooms, they are comfortable and clean. There's a small (unheated) outdoor pool, a small café, and, uniquely, free on-site self parking. Free wi-fi. ❺

Ursuline Guest House 708 Ursulines St ⓣ504/525-8509, ⓦursulineguesthouse.com. The laidback *Ursuline* is sociable and occasionally noisy, with impromptu parties in the courtyard. Sixteen rooms, all with bath (and one budget option with bunks), open onto a gallery or courtyard (which has a clothing-optional jacuzzi). Continental breakfast and nightly wine and cheese included. ❷–❺

Outside the French Quarter

AAE Bourbon House 1660 Annunciation St ⓣ1-304/268-8981, ⓦbourbon.aaeworldhotels.com. This friendly hostel in the Lower Garden District has mixed and same-sex dorms ($16) and rooms sleeping one to eight. It's scruffy but clean enough, with a decent pancake breakfast and free daytime pick-up and drop-off to the

City tours and river cruises

Walking tours are especially popular in New Orleans, with its wealth of gorgeous hidden courtyards and fine architectural details. The **Jean Lafitte National Historic Park Service** offers scholarly and accessible overviews of the Quarter (daily 9.30am; 45min; free; collect tickets from the NPS visitor centre, 419 Decatur St, at 9am). Many visitors, especially with kids in tow, take a narrated trot through the Quarter ⓣ504/589-2636; in one of the **mule-drawn carriages** that wait behind Jackson Square on Decatur. These can be fun, though you should take the "historic" commentary with a grain of salt (30–45min; $13–16/person).

Another lazy way to while away a steamy afternoon is on a **river cruise**. Leaving from the Toulouse Street wharf behind the Jackson Brewery mall, the *Natchez* steamboat heads seven miles or so downriver before turning back. The captain gives a running commentary while a jaunty Dixieland band plays in the dining room (daily 2.30pm, plus 11.30am at busy times; 2hr; $24.50, $34.50 with lunch; evening cruise 7pm, $40, $64.50 with dinner; ⓣ504/586-8777, ⓦwww.steamboatnatchez.com). Tickets are sold at booths behind Jackson Brewery and the aquarium.

New Orleans's local **swamps** – many of them protected areas just a thirty-minute drive from downtown – are otherworldly enclaves that provide a wonderful contrast to the city itself. Dr Wagner's Honey Island Swamp Tours, based ten miles north of Lake Pontchartrain, venture onto the delta of the Pearl River, a wilderness occupied by nutrias, black bears and alligators, as well as ibis, great blue herons and snowy egrets. (Wildlife most abundant April–May & Sept–Nov; 2hr; $25, not including transport from downtown; ⓣ985/641-1769, ⓦwww.honeyislandswamp.com).

train/bus stations (email in advance). At busy times, like Mardi Gras, they add airbeds in the dorms ($42) and offer limited tent space ($35). Free wi-fi. ❶

Chimes B&B 1146 Constantinople St ⓣ504/899-2621, ⓦwww.chimesneworleans.com. You're in a pretty part of the Garden District at this peaceful, casually stylish B&B. Each of the five rooms – all with their own entrance from the gorgeous courtyard – is light, airy and full of intriguing period detail. Great breakfast, too. Free off-street parking. ❺

Columns Hotel 3811 St Charles Ave ⓣ504/899-9308, ⓦwww.thecolumns.com. Deliciously atmospheric uptown hotel in a stately 1883 mansion on the streetcar line. The whole place seeps louche bordello glamour, especially the faded Victorian bar (see p.573); the porch, with its namesake columns, is one of the nicest places in the city for a drink. Some rooms come with a balcony, some are bordering on shabby; none have TV. Rates include full breakfast, but it's not great. ❺

India House Hostel 124 S Lopez St ⓣ504/821-1904, ⓦwww.indiahousehostel.com. The Mid-City location of this funky, run-down hostel is excellent for Jazz Fest and Voodoo Fest, and the Canal St streetcar is close by. It's the most sociable, and booziest, of the hostels, with the occasional jam session, crawfish boils and rowdy pool parties. Dorms ($17–20) plus a few basic rooms, some with bath. The area isn't great at night. Free wi-fi. ❷

Royal Street Inn 1431 Royal St ⓣ504/948-7499, ⓦwww.royalstreetinn.com. Hip Faubourg Marigny lodging footsteps from Frenchmen St above the *R-Bar* (see p.573), and run by the same people. Quirky New Orleans style meets big-city boutique hip in the five suites (all with bath, and some with balcony) with their stripped floors, bare brick walls and leather sofas; all have DVD players, iPod docks and free wi-fi. It's favoured by a young crowd who hang out in the bar, and can be noisy at weekends, but the comfort, location and price can't be beat. ❸

The City

New Orleans is called the **Crescent City**, because of the way it nestles between the southern shore of Lake Pontchartrain and a horseshoe bend in the Mississippi River. This unique location makes the city's layout confusing, with streets curving to follow the river, and shooting off at odd angles to head inland. Compass points are of little use – locals refer instead to **lakeside** (toward the lake) and **riverside** (toward the river), and, using Canal Street as the dividing line, **uptown** (or upriver) and **downtown** (downriver).

The French Quarter

The beautiful **French Quarter** is where New Orleans began in 1718. Today, battered and bohemian, decaying and vibrant, it remains the spiritual core of the city, its cast-iron balconies, hidden courtyards and time-stained stucco buildings exerting a fascination that has long caught the imagination of artists and writers. It's a wonderful place simply to wander; early morning, in the pearly light from the river, is a good time to explore.

The Quarter is laid out in a grid, unchanged since 1721. At just thirteen blocks wide – smaller than you might expect – it's easily walkable, bounded by the Mississippi River, Rampart Street, Canal Street and Esplanade Avenue, and centring on lively **Jackson Square**. Rather than French, the **architecture** is predominantly Spanish Colonial, with a strong Caribbean influence. Most buildings date from the late eighteenth century; much of the old city was devastated by fires in 1788 and 1794. Shops, restaurants and bars are concentrated between Decatur and Bourbon streets, while beyond Bourbon, up toward Rampart Street, and in the Lower Quarter, downriver from Jackson Square, things become more peaceful. Here, you'll find quiet, residential streets where the Quarter's **gay** community lives side by side with elegant dowagers, condo-dwellers and scruffy artists.

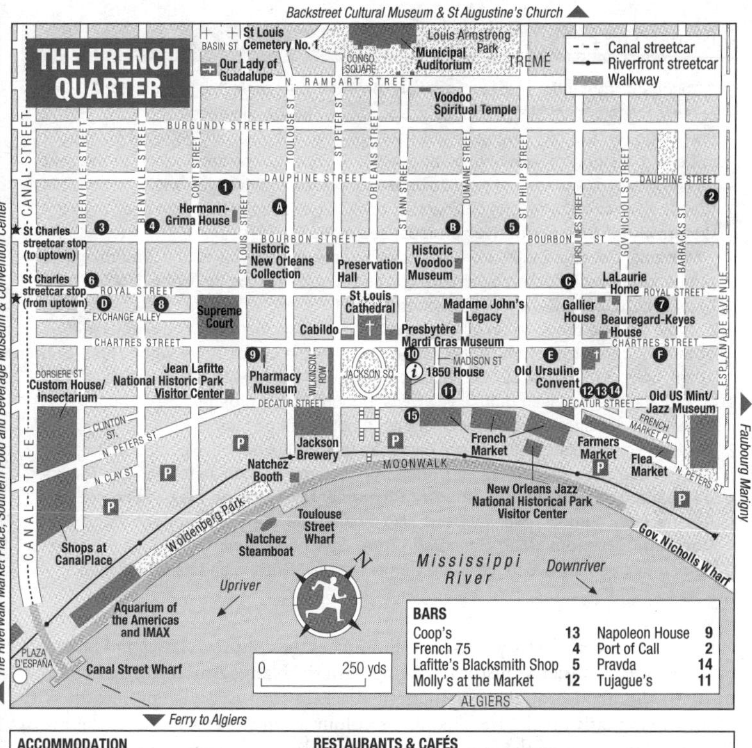

ACCOMMODATION				RESTAURANTS & CAFÉS					
Bourgoyne Guest House	B	Olivier House	A	Bayona	1	Galatoire's	3	Stanley	10
Hotel Monteleone	D	Le Richelieu	F	Bennachin	7	Green Goddess	8	Tujague's	11
Hotel Provincial	E	Ursuline Guest House	C	Café du Monde	15	Mr B's	6		
				Coop's	13	Napoleon House	9		

Jackson Square

Ever since its earliest incarnation as the Place d'Armes, a dusty parade ground used for public meetings and executions, **Jackson Square** has been at the heart of the Quarter. Presiding over it, an **equestrian statue** – the first in the nation, constructed by Clark Mills in 1856 – shows Andrew Jackson, the general whose victory in the 1815 **Battle of New Orleans**, the final battle in the War of 1812, finally secured American supremacy in the States. Portrayed here in uncharacteristically jaunty mode, waving his hat, Jackson went on to become US president. The hectoring inscription, "The Union Must and Shall be Preserved", was added by Union General "Beast" Butler during the Civil War occupation.

During the day, everyone passes by at some time or another, weaving their way through the tangle of artists, hot-dog vendors, palm readers and shambolic brass bands. A postcard-perfect backdrop for the Jackson statue, the 1794 **St Louis Cathedral** is the oldest continuously active cathedral in the United States. Dominated by three tall slate steeples, the facade, which marries Greek Revival symmetry with copious French arches, is oddly two-dimensional, like an elaborate stage prop for the street drama below.

On the upriver side of the cathedral, the **Cabildo** (Tues–Sun 10am–4.30pm; $6) was built as the Casa Capitular, seat of the Spanish colonial government. Inside the building – which cuts a dash with its colonnade, fan windows and wrought-iron

The Mississippi River

A resonant, romantic and extraordinary physical presence, the **Mississippi River** is New Orleans's lifeblood and its *raison d'être*. In the nineteenth century, as the port boomed, the city gradually cut itself off from the river altogether, hemming it in behind a string of warehouses and railroads. But, as the importance of the port has diminished, a couple of downtown parks, plazas and riverside walks, accessible from the French Quarter, the CBD and uptown, have focused attention back onto the **waterfront**. For details of **river cruises**, see p.559.

Crossing Decatur Street from Jackson Square brings you to the **Moonwalk**, a promenade where buskers serenade you as you gaze across the water. Upriver from here, **Woldenberg Park** makes a good place for a picnic, watching the river traffic drift by; it's also the location of a number of free music festivals. At the upriver edge of the park, the **Aquarium of the Americas**, near the Canal Street wharf (Tues–Sun 10am–5pm; $18, IMAX $9, combination tickets available with the Insectarium [see p.566] and the Zoo [see p.567]; ⓦwww.auduboninstitute.org), features a huge glass tunnel where visitors – rampaging infants, mostly – come face to face with rays and sawfish. There's also a Mississippi River habitat – complete with Spots, a white gator – an Amazonian rainforest, and an IMAX theatre. Beyond here, via the **Piazza d'España**, you can enter the touristy **Riverwalk Marketplace** mall, which not only has its own outdoor riverwalk but also boasts the superb **Southern Food and Beverage Museum** (Mon–Sat 10am–7pm, Sun noon–6pm; $10; ⓦsouthernfood.org), a wonderfully evocative love letter to old New Orleans and its foodie quirks.

balconies – a superb history **museum** illuminates the cultures, classes and races that bind together Louisiana's history, starting with the Native Americans and winding up with the demise of Reconstruction. Black history is well represented, with as much emphasis on the free people of colour as on the city's role as the major slave-trading centre of the South; there's also a gloomy section devoted to disease, death and mourning. Forming a matching pair with the Cabildo, the **Presbytère** (Tues–Sun 10am–4.30pm; $6), on the other side of the cathedral, was designed in 1791 as a rectory, went on to serve as a courthouse, and today holds an unmissable **Mardi Gras museum**, covering carnival from every conceivable angle. Full of odd treasures – jewel-encrusted costumes, primitive masks, posters, bizarre dance cards – it also features videos, interactive themed rooms and music stations.

Decatur Street and Esplanade Avenue

Something of an anomaly among Upper Decatur's brassy T-shirt shops and theme restaurants, the **Jean Lafitte National Historical Park Visitor Center**, 419 Decatur St (daily 9am–5pm; ⓦwww.nps.gov/jela/french-quarter-site.htm), is not only a starting point for excellent **walking tours** (see p.559), but also a great one-room introduction to Louisiana's delta region. Panels outline local history, architecture, cultural traditions, cuisine and ecology, while listening stations let you eavesdrop on natives expounding, in a variety of accents, on the meaning of local expressions. Touch-screen monitors feature classic footage of Louis Armstrong, Mahalia Jackson and Professor Longhair, among others.

Downriver along Decatur Street, the specialty shops of the restored **French Market** – said to be on the site of a Native American trading area and certainly active since the 1720s – sell tourist knick-knacks; for stalls, head toward the old **Farmers' Market**, just off Decatur on N Peters Street, where fresh produce, spices, hot sauce and the like are sold around the clock. Next door, a flea market abounds in trashy tack and bargain oddities; for vintage curiosities, head instead to the cavernous thrift stores across the way on Decatur. The **New Orleans Jazz National Historical**

Park Visitor Center (Tues–Sat 10am–5pm; free; Ⓦwww.nps.gov/jazz), tucked away between the French Market and the river at 916 N Peters St, is a must for any music fan. Light, airy and intimate, it's a superb, informal place to attend regular free jazz concerts, talks, movies and workshops; afterwards, check out the photo displays, self-guided jazz walking tour brochures and bookstore.

Continuing downriver, you'll come to the outer boundary of the Quarter, **Esplanade Avenue**, an exquisite, oak-shaded boulevard lined with crumbling nineteenth-century Creole mansions. Pre-Katrina, the **Old US Mint** (Tues–Sun 10am–4.30pm; $6), on the 400 block near the river, housed a fascinating **Jazz Museum** – featuring old instruments, sheet music, photos and personal effects – that has yet to reopen. In the meantime, the Mint hosts small shows of local interest (recent highlights have included a Napoleon exhibition and another on early jazz).

Across Esplanade from the Quarter, the funky **Faubourg Marigny** is an appealingly mixed, low-rent area of Creole cottages and shotgun houses. Though the neighbourhood is gentrifying, and its gaggle of music venues, coffeeshops, bars and restaurants increasing, it's best **not to wander** too far away from the blocks around **Frenchmen Street**, the district's main drag. Even Elysian Fields – where Stanley and Stella lived in Tennessee Williams's *A Streetcar Named Desire* – can feel distinctly dodgy, despite its heavenly name.

Chartres and Royal streets

Built between 1745 and 1750, the tranquil **Old Ursuline Convent**, 1112 Chartres St (Mon–Sat 10am–4pm; $5), is the only intact French Colonial structure in the city, and quite possibly the oldest building in the Mississippi valley. Established by nuns from Rouen, it's one of the many places in the Quarter that are said to be haunted, its corridors roamed by spectres of the "casket girls" – white virgins shipped over in the early days of the colony, who were kept here before being sold off as wives in an attempt to stop the increasing number of couplings between French settlers and African or Native American women. Inside, the hushed rooms are lined with wordy old information panels explaining the history of the convent and the gruelling existence of the nuns who lived here; the real interest, however, is in the time-worn rooms and the lovely working herb garden at the back.

At 1132 Royal St, the handsome 1857 **Gallier House** is a fascinating little place (hourly tours Mon & Fri 10am–2pm, Sat noon–3pm; $10, $18 with the Hermann-Grima House; Ⓦwww.hgghh.org; see p.564). Prominent architect James Gallier Jr designed the house for himself, combining classic Creole features – a carriageway leading to a courtyard – with an Americanized enclosed hall and indoor bathroom. Innovations included a cooling system and a flushing toilet, while the filigree cast-iron galleries would have been the last word in chic. Tours are superb, focusing as much on social history as fine furniture.

A rare example of the Quarter's early West Indies-style architecture, **Madame John's Legacy**, off Royal at 628 Dumaine St (Tues–Sun 10am–4.30pm; free), was rebuilt after the fire of 1788 as an exact replica of the 1730 house that had previously stood on the site. Raised on stucco-covered pillars, it also features a distinctive, deep wraparound gallery that, cooler and airier than the indoor rooms, provided extra living space. There never was a real Madame John – the name was given to the house by nineteenth-century author George Washington Cable in his tragic short story *'Tite Poulette*, and it simply stuck, attracting hundreds of tourists to the city and spawning a nice line in Madame John souvenirs.

Standing proud among the antique stores and chichi art galleries is the splendid **Historic New Orleans Collection**, 533 Royal St. Entry to the streetfront gallery (Tues–Sat 9.30am–4.30pm, Sun 10.30am–4.30pm; Ⓦwww.hnoc.org), which holds excellent temporary exhibitions, is free, but to see the bulk of the collection you'll need to take a guided tour (Tues–Sat 10am, 11am, 2pm, & 3pm; $5). Tours might take in the galleries upstairs, where fascinating exhibits – including old maps, drawings and early publicity posters – fill a series of themed rooms, or they might venture into the neighbouring **Williams House**. The Williamses, prominent citizens in the 1930s, filled their home with unusual, exotic objects, and the house is a must for anyone interested in design and decorative arts.

The quirky **Pharmacy Museum,** in an old apothecary at 514 Chartres St (in theory Tues–Sat 10am–5pm, but hours change, so check website; $5; Ⓦwww.hnoc.org), offers great insights into the history of medicine. Huge hand-carved rosewood cabinets are cluttered with *gris-gris*, a fine range of Creole "tonics" used to cure "all the various forms of female weakness", dusty jars of leeches for blood-letting ("to remove irritability"), and various unpleasant-looking drills and corkscrews. Upstairs is mostly devoted to **women's medicine**, with a nineteenth-century sick room.

Bourbon Street and above: toward Rampart Street

Though you'd never guess it from the hype, there are two faces to world-renowned **Bourbon Street**. The tawdry, touristy, booze-drenched stretch spans the seven stinky blocks from Canal to St Ann: a frat-pack cacophony of trashy daiquiri stalls, novelty shops and tired girlie bars. This enclave is best experienced after dark, when a couple – though by no means all – of its **bars** and **clubs** are worth a look, and the sheer mayhem takes on a bacchanalian life of its own. When the attraction of fighting your way through crowds of weekending drunks palls, however, it's easy to dip out again into the quieter parallel streets. If you do manage to make it as far as St Ann, you come to a distinct crossroads, marked by a gaggle of raucous gay clubs, beyond which Bourbon transforms into an appealing, predominantly gay, residential area.

Above Bourbon Street, tourists are outnumbered by locals walking their dogs, jogging or chatting on stoops. Half a block above Bourbon, at 820 St Louis St, the 1832 **Hermann-Grima House** (hourly tours Mon & Fri 10am–2pm, Sat noon–3pm; $10, $18 with the Gallier House; Ⓦwww.hgghh.org; see p.563) does a nice job illustrating the lifestyle of middle-class Creoles in antebellum New Orleans; otherwise, although these quiet streets are fringed by some of the Quarter's finest **vernacular architecture**, "sights" as such are few.

Rampart Street, the run-down strip separating the Quarter from **Tremé**, is a boundary rarely crossed by tourists. Though it's home to a good little jazz club (*Donna's*, see p.573), which is just a short walk from the heart of the Quarter, it can feel hairy at night. **Louis Armstrong Park**, meanwhile, is best avoided altogether except during its occasional **music festivals**, many of which, continuing its long tradition of black music and celebration, are held in **Congo Square**, the small paved area to the left of the entrance arch.

Tremé and Mid-City

In the 1800s, Tremé, the historic African-American neighbourhood where **jazz** was developed in the bordellos of Storyville – long since gone – was a prosperous area, its shops, businesses and homes owned and frequented by New Orleans's free black population. By the late twentieth century, however, blighted by neglect and crime, Tremé had become a no-go zone. Despite this, its rich tradition of music, **jazz funerals** and **Second Lines** (loose, joyous street parades, led by funky brass bands and gathering dancing "Second Lines" of passers-by as they go) continued, and the turn of the millennium saw signs of gentrification.

While many of its houses remain in bad shape post-Katrina, David *The Wire* Simon's HBO series *Tremé*, which premiered in 2010, brought the area much-appreciated visibility.

The best way to experience this financially poor but culturally rich neighbourhood is to join a Second Line; to find out more about when you might catch one, make for the **Backstreet Cultural Museum**, in an old funeral parlour at 1116 St Claude St (Tues–Sat 10am–5pm; $10; Ⓦwww.backstreetmuseum.org). This labour of love celebrates local street culture, including jazz funerals and the city's unique **Mardi Gras Indians** (see p.575); it also acts as a social hub during the city's many festivals. Across the road, **St Augustine's Church**, 1210 Governor Nicholls St, is the earliest African-American church in the nation, active since 1842. Of major significance to the local black community, St Augustine's was at the centre of a major post-Katrina storm; when the Catholic Church, cash-strapped after the floods, announced St Augustine's closure in 2006, local protests – including an occupation – became national news; in 2009 the church was finally allowed to remain open. Today it welcomes tourists to occasional jazz masses and fundraising events. The spruce, light interior is peaceful, with stained-glass windows portraying French saints, and flags printed with affirmations (Unity, Creativity, Self-Determination, Purpose) in English and Swahili. In the garden, the affecting **Tomb of the Unknown Slave**, a toppled metal cross entwined with balls-and-chains and shackles, honours all African and Native American slaves buried in unmarked graves.

Beyond Tremé, towards the lake, in the vast area known as **Mid-City**, New Orleans's 1500-acre **City Park** is another welcome green space, streaked with lagoons and shaded by centuries-old live oaks. The chief attraction, the excellent **New Orleans Museum of Art** (Wed noon–8pm, Thurs–Sun 10am–5pm; $16; Ⓦwww.noma.org), includes pre-Columbian pieces, African works, Asian ceramics and paintings, and contemporary art and photography. Its five-acre **sculpture garden** (free) is a must-see, its works – by Louise Bourgeois, Barbara Hepworth, Henry Moore and others – dotted among oaks, magnolias and lush gladioli.

The Faubourg Marigny, Bywater and Ninth Ward

Across Esplanade Avenue from the French Quarter, **Faubourg Marigny** (or "the Faubourg") is a happening, mixed and low-rent area of Creole cottages and shotguns populated by artists, musicians and sundry bohemians. Its main drag and nightlife strip is **Frenchmen Street**, where revellers spill out onto the streets, especially at the weekend and during festivals, to create a block party. For now the street keeps its edge, with some of New Orleans's best spots to hear live music, but recently its hipper – and hippier – credentials have been passed onto its neighbour, residential **Bywater**, another low-key, appealing artists' district. Bywater is officially part of the **Ninth Ward**, which, as one of the areas most drastically affected by the levee breaks and flooding, has become a byword for the very worst of Katrina's horrors. The **Lower Ninth** – downriver from the Industrial Canal – was particularly badly hit. Once a bustling neighbourhood, now battling against enormous odds to get back on its feet, the Lower Ninth has become a hauntingly surreal place. The further towards the lake you go, the further behind you the city seems. The silence is palpable; grass grows to six feet high and above; flowering shrubs thrust their way through concrete foundations; egrets balance on fences, and turtles creep dozily along the scarred and potholed roads. Meanwhile, valiant new builds, many of them financed by high-profile nonprofits – including Brad Pitt's Make It Right foundation – stand like sentinels of hope among the devastated landscape, and on a Sunday morning you may hear the hymns of a determined, if depleted, congregation, gathered on garden chairs on a bare concrete foundation, raising their voices in hope.

The CBD and Warehouse District

Mark Twain had a point when he dismissed the foreboding Classical interior of the **Custom House** as "inferior to a gasometer", but the dour granite colossus, in the Central Business District – or **CBD** – at 423 Canal St, was key to New Orleans's grand antebellum building programme, a hymn to the city's optimism and aspirations. In summer 2008, after more than a decade of delays, a similar optimism was in the air with the opening of the **Insectarium** (Tues–Sun 10am–5pm; $15, combination tickets available with the Aquarium [see p.562] and the Zoo [see opposite]; Ⓦwww.auduboninstitute.org) on the ground floor. It's mainly of appeal to kids, but there's genuine interest in the exhibits on local breeds, and some exquisite beauty in the butterfly house.

The lakeside edge of the CBD, a tangle of grey highways, is dominated by the colossal home of the New Orleans Saints NFL team, the **Superdome**. At 52 acres, with 27 storeys and a diameter of 680ft, this is one of the largest buildings on the planet, and has been etched upon the world's consciousness after housing more than 30,000 Katrina evacuees in unthinkable conditions for six days. Though lurid tales of gang rapes, murders and suicides were later discovered to have been urban myths, the Superdome became a byword for the shocking neglect, chaos and human rights atrocities that New Orleans faced in the wake of the floods. Standing sentinel over the battered CBD for a year after Katrina, it finally reopened in autumn 2006 with a star-studded rock concert and a triumphant victory by the Saints over the Atlanta Falcons. The high-profile event marked a turning point in the city's sense of its own recovery; things reached an even higher emotional peak in January 2010 when the Saints defeated the Minnesota Vikings here to win their first-ever place in the **Superbowl**. Even the team's eventual astonishing Superbowl victory over the Indianapolis Colts – which gained the highest TV audience ever in the USA – could not quite match this moment; never had a game, a team, or a stadium, signified quite so much.

The Warehouse District

Spreading upriver from the foot of Canal Street, New Orleans's **Warehouse District**, part of the CBD, has a handful of attractions. Most sights are concentrated in the **Arts District**, the outcrop of galleries concentrated around Julia and Camp streets. The hub of the scene is the **Contemporary Arts Center**, 900 Camp St (Thurs–Sun 11am–4pm; ground-floor galleries free, temporary exhibitions $5; Ⓦwww.cacno.org). Around the corner, the colossal **National World War II Museum**, 945 Magazine St (daily 9am–5pm; $16, $20 with Victory Theater; Ⓦwww.nationalww2museum.org), opened on June 6, 2000, the 56th anniversary of D-Day. Although it has expanded to become the nation's official World War II museum, its core collection still concentrates on the various shoreline assaults that led to the downfall of both Nazi Germany and Japan, all of which it categorizes as D-Days. Though impressive, its gung-ho militarism can feel relentless; the **Victory Theater** sets an uneasy tone with the "Beyond All Boundaries" 4-D movie (hourly 10am–4pm; $9, $20 with museum), a series of irritating super-effects, narrated by Tom Hanks, which disguise propaganda as history. Meanwhile, the nearby **Civil War Museum**, 929 Camp St at Lee Circle (Mon–Sat 10am–4pm; $7; Ⓦwww.confederatemuseum.com) has its own, equally partisan, take on history. A gloomy

Romanesque Revival hulk, designed in 1891 as a place for Confederate veterans to display their mementos, this so-called "Battle Abbey of the South" is a relic from a bygone age, full of bittersweet remembrances of long-lost Confederate generals and their forgotten families. A world away but just next door, at 925 Camp St, the superb **Ogden Museum of Southern Art** (Wed–Sun 10am–5pm, Thurs also 6–8pm with live music; $10; Ⓦwww.ogdenmuseum.org) represents the South in all its complexity, strangeness and melancholy beauty. Its impressive collection runs the gamut from rare eighteenth-century watercolours through to self-taught art, photography and modern sculpture.

The cavernous "dens" of **Blaine Kern's Mardi Gras World** (daily 9.30am–4.30pm; $17.50; Ⓦwww.mardigrasworld.com), 1380 Port of New Orleans Place, beyond the Convention Center, are best reached on a free shuttle from the Canal Street ferry terminal (every 15min). Here you can see artists constructing and painting the overblown, garish papier-mâché floats used in the official carnival parades. It's a surreal experience wandering past piles of dusty, grimacing has-beens from parades gone by.

The Garden District and uptown

Pride of uptown New Orleans, the **Garden District** drapes itself seductively across a thirteen-block area bounded by Magazine Street and St Charles, Louisiana and Jackson avenues. Two miles upriver from the French Quarter, it was developed as a residential neighbourhood in the 1840s by an energetic breed of Anglo-Americans who wished to display their accumulating cotton and trade wealth by building sumptuous mansions in huge gardens. Today, shaded by jungles of subtropical foliage, the glorious houses – some of them spick-and-span showpieces, others in ravishing ruin – evoke a nostalgic vision of the Deep South in a profusion of porches, columns and balconies. While it's a pleasure simply to wander around, you can pick up more details about the individual houses on any number of official or self-guided tours.

The historic **St Charles streetcar** (see p.558) is the nicest way to get to the Garden District and uptown, affording front-row views of "the Avenue" as St Charles is locally known. Just before the streetcar takes a sharp turn at the riverbend, it stops at peaceful **Audubon Park**, a lovely space shaded by Spanish-moss-swathed trees. Its top attraction, **Audubon Zoo**, a ten-minute walk or a free shuttle ride (every 20–30min) from the park's St Charles entrance (Tues–Fri 10am–4pm, Sat & Sun 10am–5pm; $13, combination tickets available with the Aquarium [see p.562] and the Insectarium [see opposite]; Ⓦwww.audubonistitute.org), boasts, among other habitats, a beautifully re-created **Louisiana swamp**, complete with Cajun houseboats, wallowing alligators (including the milky white, blue-eyed gators found in a local swamp), and knobbly cypress knees poking out of the emerald-green water.

You can also approach the Garden District and uptown via **Magazine Street**, a six-mile stretch of funky galleries, restaurants and stores that runs parallel to St Charles riverside.

Eating

New Orleans is a gourmand's dream. Restaurants here are far more than places to eat: from the haughtiest *grandes dames* of Creole cuisine right down to rough-and-ready po-boy shacks, they are fiercely cherished as the guardians of community, culture and heritage. While many restaurants will never return post-Katrina,

New Orleans food

New Orleans **food**, commonly defined as **Creole**, is a spicy, substantial – and usually very fattening – blend of French, Spanish, African and Caribbean cuisine, mixed up with a host of other influences including Native American, Italian and German. Some of the simpler dishes, like red beans and rice, reveal a strong West Indies influence, while others are more French, cooked with long-simmered sauces based on a **roux** (fat and flour heated together) and herby stocks. Many dishes are served **étouffée**, literally "smothered" in a tasty Creole sauce (a roux with tomato, onion and spices), on rice. Although there are some exceptions, what passes for **Cajun** food in the city tends to be a modern hybrid, tasty but not authentic; the "blackened" dishes, for example, slathered in butter and spices, made famous by chef Paul Prudhomme.

The mainstays of most menus are **gumbo** – a thick soup of seafood, chicken and vegetables – and **jambalaya**, a paella jumbled together from the same ingredients. Other specialties include **po-boys**, French-bread sandwiches overstuffed with oysters, shrimp, or almost anything else, and **muffulettas**, the round Italian version, crammed full of aromatic meats and cheese and dripping with garlicky olive dressing. Along with **shrimp** and **soft-shell crabs**, you'll get famously good **oysters**; they're in season from September to April. **Crawfish**, or mudbugs (which resemble langoustines and are best between March and Oct), are served in everything from omelets to bisques, or simply boiled in a spicy stock. Everyone should enjoy a *café au lait* and **beignet** (featherlight donuts, without a hole, cloaked in powdered sugar) at *Café du Monde* in the French Quarter; open around the clock, this historic market coffee-house serves nothing else. And for another only-in-New-Orleans snack, look out for the absurd, giant, hot-dog-shaped **Lucky Dogs** carts set up throughout the Quarter. Featured in John Kennedy Toole's farcical novel *A Confederacy of Dunces*, they've become a beloved institution, though in truth the dogs themselves are nothing great.

others have come back with a vengeance, and, fired with a passion for their city, have raised their game. Gratifyingly, **prices** are not high compared to other US cities – even at the swankiest places you can get away with $40 per head for a three-course feast with wine. **Lunch** can be a real bargain, especially at the more upmarket establishments.

French Quarter

Bayona 430 Dauphine St ⓣ504/525-4455. Splendid, romantic and upmarket restaurant – the lovely courtyard feels more relaxed than the formal dining room. Local staples are given a global twist – the simple garlic soup, sweetbreads and lamb dishes are fantastic – and there's a 250-plus wine list. Lunch is a steal – try the grilled cashew butter, smoked duck and pepper jelly sandwich for just $11. The pricier dinner menu is also well worth it. Closed Sun.

Bennachin 1212 Royal St ⓣ504/522-1230. Historically, New Orleans owes a lot to West Africa, including much of its traditional cuisine. And in this tiny, family-run restaurant, the hefty portions of inexpensive, delicious African food – black-eyed-bean fritters, peanut-infused stews, grilled fish in ginger sauce, spinach with plantains – bring Creole food back to its roots. The iced ginger-honey tea is a treat on a steamy night. Lunch specials (before 3pm, around $8) are a good deal. BYOB; no credit cards.

Coop's 1109 Decatur St ⓣ504/525-9053. A merry fixture on the heavy-drinking, late-night, Lower Decatur bar scene, this dark-wood dive is a great bar, but the amazing surprise is the delicious food. This is gourmet stuff, at ridiculous prices – the "Taste of Coop's" gets you a seafood gumbo packed with fat oysters; shrimp Creole; a fantastic jambalaya; red beans and rice, *and* spicy, crispy fried chicken for an astonishing $13. Open till 2am or later.

Galatoire's 209 Bourbon St ⓣ504/525-2021. This grand Creole establishment – Tennessee Williams's favourite restaurant – is quintessential New Orleans with its mirror-lined dining room, and not at all stuffy. It's best for lunch, on Fri or Sun especially, when you can join the city's old guard (gents in seersucker, Southern belles in pearls) spending long, convivial hours gorging on turtle soup, oysters *en* *brochette*, crabmeat *maison* and *filet mignon*. No reservations (except for the less characterful upstairs room), so expect a wait. Jacket and tie required after 5pm and all day Sun. Closed Mon.

Green Goddess 307 Exchange Alley ☎504/301-3347. Luscious Creole-Mediterranean-Southern fusion food at this gorgeous, teensy, hole in the wall. Menus, using the freshest ingredients, vary seasonally, but don't miss the stupendous garlicky barbecue shrimp with grits or sweet potato biscuits with orange honey butter. It's also a lovely place to come for a glass of wine and an artisan cheese plate.

Mr B's 201 Royal St ☎504/523-6727. Buzzy Creole bistro with dark-wood and etched glass booths, a relaxed, chatty ambience and spectacular food. The garlic chicken is the city's finest; the same accolade could go to the signature barbecue shrimp. It can be pricey, but lunch is good value. Walk-ins are welcome. Closes 9pm.

Stanley 547 St Ann St ☎504/587-0093. Fresh and airy, with huge picture windows on Jackson Square and posies of fresh flowers on the marble-and-iron tables, this modern place with an unfussy retro feel offers a simple, creative menu of all-day breakfasts and brunches, salads and sandwiches. Closes 7pm.

Tujague's 823 Decatur St ☎504/525-8676. With one of the loveliest dining rooms in the city, the beloved "Two Jacks", both relaxed and elegant, is a must-visit. Little has changed here over the last 150 years, not least the five-course *prix-fixe* menu, which always includes shrimp remoulade and tender beef brisket appetizers. If money's tight, simply order the tasty chicken "Bonne Femme" (fried chicken with garlic and parsley) at the beautiful old bar (see p.573).

Outside the French Quarter

Boucherie 8115 Jeannette St ☎504/862-5514. The Krispy Kreme bread pudding may be the headliner here, but all the creative, Southern dishes in this pretty uptown cottage are fabulous, from the pulled pork and "grit fries" to the smoked scallops with smothered green beans. Closed Sun & Mon.

Café Reconcile 1631 Oretha Castle Haley Blvd ☎504/568-1157. Something special: a nonprofit venture, spearheaded by a Jesuit church, where local at-risk teens are trained for jobs in the hospitality industry. The bustling dining room, in the blighted but recovering neighbourhood of Central City, north of the Lower Garden District, is welcoming, prices are ridiculously low, and the food – fried chicken, catfish, pot roast, beans and rice – beyond delicious. Mon–Fri breakfast & lunch only.

Casamento's 4330 Magazine St ☎504/895-9761. Spotless and old-fashioned, this prettily tiled uptown oyster bar serves inexpensive ice-fresh oysters, fried crab claws and overstuffed trout "loaves" (sandwiches) to die for. Closed Sun, Mon & June–Aug. Cash only.

Cochon 930 Tchoupitoulas St ☎504/588-2123. Upscale but unintimidating CBD place, full of blissed-out diners – from businessmen to bearded hipsters – feasting on fine, authentic Cajun food: not spicy and stodgy, but flavoursome and complex. Everything, from the melt-in-the-mouth fried boudin balls to the tangy sweet potato and andouille flan, is utterly delicious. Closed Sun.

Jacques Imo's 8324 Oak St ☎504/861-0886. This cheery, noisy uptown restaurant is the perfect place to fill up before a gig at the *Maple Leaf* (see p.575), and well worth a trip any time. The decor is funky folksy, and the cooking, a delicious Creole-Cajun take on soul food, is great value – from the fried oysters and chicken livers to the ambrosial alligator sausage cheesecake. Dinner only; closed Sun. Reservations only for groups of five or more; you may have to wait awhile at the bar.

The Joint 801 Poland Ave ☎504/949-3232. This tiny yellow Bywater shed hides an amazing barbecue joint with its own smokehouse outside. The combo plate gets you three meats plus one delicious home-made side for $15; fabulous jukebox, too. Expect a wait. Closed Sun; Mon & Tues lunch only.

Mona's 504 Frenchmen St ☎504/949-4115. Its handy Faubourg Marigny location is just part of the appeal of this popular, no-fuss, Middle Eastern restaurant. The food – kebabs, flatbread pizzas, meze, split red lentil soup – is fresh, zingy and inexpensive, with lots of delicious vegetarian options. BYOB.

Entertainment and nightlife

New Orleans has long been one of the best places in the world to hear **live music**. From lonesome street musicians, through shambling, joyous brass bands, to international names like Dr John and the Neville Brothers, music remains the heartbeat and lifeline of the Crescent City. The devastation wrought by

Mardi Gras and other New Orleans festivals

New Orleans's **carnival season** – which starts on Twelfth Night, January 6, and runs for the six weeks or so until Ash Wednesday – is unlike any other in the world. Though the name is used to define the entire season, **Mardi Gras** itself, French for "Fat Tuesday", is simply the culmination of a whirl of parades, parties, street revels and masked balls, all inextricably tied up with the city's labyrinthine social, racial and political structures. Mardi Gras was introduced to New Orleans in the 1740s, when **French** colonists brought over the European custom, established since medieval times, of marking the imminence of Lent with masking and feasting. Their slaves, meanwhile, continued to celebrate **African** and **Caribbean** festival traditions, based on musical rituals, masking and elaborate costumes, and the three eventually fused. From early days carnival was known for cavorting, outrageous costumes, drinking and general bacchanalia – and little has changed. However, although it has become the busiest tourist season, when the city is invaded by millions, Mardi Gras has always been, above all, a party that New Orleanians throw for themselves. Visitors are wooed, welcomed and shown the time of their lives, but without them carnival would reel on regardless.

Official carnival took its current form in 1857, with the appearance of a stately moonlit procession calling itself the "Krewe of Comus, Merrie Monarch of Mirth". Initiated by a group of Anglo-Americans, the concept of the "**krewes**", or secret carnival clubs, was taken up enthusiastically by the New Orleans aristocracy, many of them white supremacists who, after the Civil War, used their satirical float designs and the shroud of secrecy to mock and undermine Reconstruction. Nowadays about fifty official krewes equip colourful floats, leading huge processions with different, often mythical, themes. Each is reigned over by a King and Queen (generally an older, politically powerful man and a debutante), who go on to preside over the krewes' closed, masked balls. There are women-only krewes, "super krewes", with members drawn from the city's new wealth (barred from making inroads into the gentlemen's-club network of the old-guard krewes), and important **black** groups. The best known and most important of these is **Zulu**, established in 1909 when a black man mocked Rex, King of Carnival, by dancing behind his float with a tin can on his head; today the Zulu parade on Mardi Gras morning is one of the most popular of the season. There are also many alternative, or **unofficial krewes**, including the anarchic **Krewe du Vieux** (from *Vieux Carré*, another term for the French Quarter), whose irreverent parade and "ball" (a polite term for a wild party, open to all) is a blast. The **gay** community plays a major part in Mardi Gras, particularly in the French Quarter, where the streets teem with strutting drag divas. And then there's the parade of the **Mystic Krewe of Barkus**, made up of dogs, hundreds of whom, during what is surely the campest parade of the season, can be seen trotting proudly through the French Quarter all spiffed up on some spurious theme.

Tourists are less likely to witness the **Mardi Gras Indians**, African-American groups who, in their local neighbourhoods, organize themselves into "tribes" and, dressed in fabulous beaded and feathered costumes, sewed themselves over the previous year, gather on Mardi Gras morning to compete in chanting and dancing. Made up of poor black men, many of whom lost their homes in the flooding, this is the Mardi Gras group that has been most diminished by the devastation of Katrina; their continued existence against the odds is testament to their cultural importance and the sacred importance of their rituals. For a chance of seeing the Indians, head to the Backstreet Cultural Museum in Tremé (see p.564) on Mardi Gras morning; this is also the meeting place for other black Mardi Gras groups including the "**skeleton**" gangs, who don bloody butcher's aprons and "wake the day" at dawn by beating bones on drums, and the **Baby Dolls**, grown women frolicking around in silky bonnets and bloomers.

Another New Orleans Mardi Gras ritual is the flinging of "**throws**" from the parade floats. Teasing masked krewe members scatter beads, beakers and doubloons (toy coins) into the crowds, who beg, plead and scream for them. Even outside the parades, tourists embark upon a frantic **bead-bartering** frenzy, which has given rise to the famed "Show Your Tits!" phenomenon – women pulling up their shirts in exchange for strings of beads and roars of boozy approval from the goggling mobs. Anyone keen to see the show should head for Bourbon Street.

The two weeks leading up to Mardi Gras are filled with processions, parties and balls, but excitement reaches fever pitch on **Lundi Gras**, the day before Mardi Gras. Some of the city's best musicians play at **Zulu's** free party in Woldenberg Park, which climaxes at 5pm with the arrival of the King and Queen by boat. Following this, you can head to the **Plaza d'España**, where, in a formal ceremony unchanged for over a century, the mayor hands the city to Rex, King of Carnival. The party continues with more live music and fireworks, after which people head off to watch the big **Orpheus** parade, or start a frenzied evening of clubbing. Most clubs are still hopping well into Mardi Gras morning.

The fun starts early on Mardi Gras day, with **walking clubs** striding through uptown accompanied by raucous jazz on their ritualized bar crawls, and the Skeletons (see above) gathering in Tremé. Zulu's big parade, in theory, sets off at 8.30am (but can be as much as two hours late), followed by **Rex**. Across town, the Indians are gathering for their sacred Mardi Gras rituals, while the arty **St Ann walking parade** sets off from the Bywater to arrive in the Faubourg at around 11am. Anyone is welcome to join them, as long as they are wearing something creative and/or surreal. The gay costume competition known as the **Bourbon Street awards** gets going at noon in the Quarter, while hipsters head back to the Faubourg, where **Frenchmen Street** is ablaze with bizarrely costumed carousers. The fun continues until midnight, when a siren wail heralds the arrival of a cavalcade of mounted police that sweeps through Bourbon Street and declares through megaphones that Mardi Gras is officially over. Like all good Catholic cities, New Orleans takes carnival very seriously. Midnight marks the onset of Lent, when repentance can begin.

Other New Orleans festivals

St Joseph's Day (March 19). Sicilian saint's day, at the midpoint of Lent. Altars of food, groaning with bread, fig cakes and stuffed artichokes, are erected in churches all around town, including St Louis Cathedral, and there's a parade. The Sunday closest to St Joseph's ("Super Sunday") is the only time outside Mardi Gras that the Mardi Gras Indians (see above) take to the streets.

French Quarter Festival (early April). Superb free three-day music festival that rivals Jazz Fest for the quality and variety of music – and food – on offer. Ⓦ www.fqfi.org.

Jazz Fest (two weekends, Fri–Sun & Thurs–Sun, end April/early May). Enormous festival at the Fairgrounds Race Track, Mid-City, with stages hosting jazz, R&B, gospel, African, Caribbean, Cajun, blues and more, with evening performances in clubs all over town. Also features crafts and phenomenal food stands. Ⓦ www.nojazzfest.com.

Satchmo SummerFest (end July/early Aug). Enjoyable three-day festival, celebrating Louis Armstrong, in the Quarter. Includes talks, local jazz and brass bands, food stalls, Second Lines and a jazz mass at St Augustine's Church. (See p.565) Ⓦ www.fqfi.org.

Southern Decadence (six days around Labor Day weekend). Huge gay extravaganza, bringing around 100,000 party animals to the Quarter and the Faubourg, with a costume parade of thousands on the Sunday afternoon. Ⓦ www.southerndecadence.net.

Halloween (Oct 31). Thanks to its long-held obsession with all things morbid, and the local passion for dressing up, New Orleans is a fabulous place to spend Halloween, with haunted houses, costume competitions, ghost tours and parades all over town.

Voodoo Fest (end Oct). Three-day rock festival held in City Park with 150 acts – from Eminem via The Pogues to Duran Duran and the New York Dolls – plus an eclectic span of local acts performing to a mixed, high-spirited, Halloween-costumed crowd. Ⓦ www.thevoodooexperience.com.

the post-Katrina flooding hit many musicians – among the less wealthy of the population – particularly hard, but the city continues to heal its wounds the best way it knows how: mourning, remembering, celebrating and surviving by making and dancing to music.

While the French Quarter has its share of clubs and bars, there are plenty of good places elsewhere. Visitors who make a beeline for **Bourbon Street**, hoping to find it crammed with cool jazz clubs, will be disappointed. That said, even this tawdriest of streets has a couple of good spots to hear live jazz. A better bet, however, is **Frenchmen Street** in the Faubourg, lined with bars and music venues that get packed on the weekends. Most bars feature music at least one night of the week; those listed below under "Bars" tend not to have live music, but many of the places reviewed as live music venues (see p.574) are great bars in their own right, too. To decide where to go, check the free weekly *Gambit* (Ⓦ www.bestofneworleans.com) and the music monthly *Offbeat* (Ⓦ www.offbeat.com). Fliers can be found in French Quarter **record stores** such as Louisiana Music Factory, 210 Decatur St, and the fabulous local **radio station** WWOZ (90.7 FM) features regular gig information.

Bars

New Orleans's drinking scene, like the city itself, is unpretentious and inclusive: whether sipping Sazeracs in the golden glow of a 1930s cocktail bar or necking an Abita at dawn in a down-and-dirty dive, you'll more than likely find yourself in a high-spirited crowd of bohemian barflies. It is also legal to **drink alcohol in the streets** – for some visitors it's practically de rigueur – though not from a glass or bottle. Simply ask for a plastic **"to go"** cup in any bar and carry it with you. You'll be expected to finish your drink before entering another bar, however.

French Quarter

French 75 *Arnaud's*, 815 Bienville St. Hidden away in one of the city's old French-Creole restaurants, this is something of an in-the-know joint in the Quarter. The epitome of old New Orleans elegance with its dark mahogany walls, bevelled glass doors and etched-glass lamps, it's classy but unintimidating, just the place to dress up, settle back and sip on classic drinks.

Lafitte's Blacksmith Shop 941 Bourbon St. Lively, tumbledown bar that's a favourite for tourists and locals alike. A front for pirate Lafitte's plottings, the building's practically unchanged since the 1700s – despite its exterior sprucing – and retains its beamed ceilings and blackened brick fireplace.

Molly's at the Market 1107 Decatur St. Once famed for being a haunt of politicos and media stars, *Molly's* is a French Quarter institution – remaining open through Katrina, the flooding and subsequent evacuation – and pulls a rowdy crowd of locals, tourists, off-duty waitstaff and grungy street punks. On a stretch known for its dive bars, a couple of doors down, *Coop's* is another friendly joint, which also serves great food (see p.568).

Napoleon House 500 Chartres St. If you visit just one bar in New Orleans, let this ravishing old place – all crumbling walls, classical music and shadowy corners – be it. Exuding a classic, relaxed New Orleans elegance, the eighteenth-century building was the home of Mayor Girod, who schemed with notorious pirate Jean Lafitte to rescue Napoleon from exile, but since 1914 it has been owned and run by the same Italian family. Lamps flickering, its time-stained walls crammed with ancient oil paintings, it's atmospheric in the extreme, and on a warm night its tropical courtyard is one of the best places on earth to be. Bow-tied waiters serve café food, including warm muffulettas, gumbo and Mediterranean salads.

Port of Call 838 Esplanade Ave. Strung with rigging and life rings, this unpretentious drinking hole is haunted by a noisy crowd who put the world to rights around the large wooden bar or the small tables. Great burgers, too, served with mushrooms or cheese and a buttery baked potato.

Pravda 1113 Decatur St. Though the Tzarist boudoir-cum-Social Realist styling is a little chaotic, its dim red lighting, rugs and comfy banquettes make this a nice, relaxed alternative to the down-and-dirty Decatur St bars nearby, especially if you want a quiet drink. They serve quality absinthe and have a pretty courtyard outside.

Tujague's 823 Decatur St. Old guard New Orleans restaurant (see p.569) with an equally atmospheric, stand-up bar. It's particularly lively on Sun afternoons, when regulars gather to catch up and gossip.

Outside the French Quarter

Bacchanal 600 Poland St, Bywater. *Bacchanal* may have the feel of a ramshackle, thrift store-cum-living room – bare brick walls, peeling stucco, wooden barrel seating and ancient, overstuffed bookcases – but it's actually a very good, friendly wine bar in the style of a European bodega. Classy wines available by the glass; simple and delicious food; and occasional live bands in the courtyard.

Columns Hotel 3811 St Charles Ave. This gorgeous hotel bar, on the fringes of the Garden District, seeps faded Southern grandeur; on warm evenings, make for the grand columned veranda, which overlooks the streetcar line.

Ernie K-Doe's Mother-in-Law Lounge 1500 N Claiborne Ave. Since the untimely death of local R&B legend Ernie in 2001, and his formidable wife Antoinette in 2009, Antoinette's daughter has kept their Tremé lounge open as something of a shrine to the self-styled "Emperor of the Universe" – complete with an "Ernie in Heaven" mannequin holding court. Hop in a cab and join the combination of arty hipsters and unimpressed locals that make this place unique.

Mimi's 2601 Royal St. The coolest Faubourg/Bywater hipsters have made this bar a home from home not only for the drinks, the DJs and the live music, but for the cheap and tasty tapas.

R-Bar 1431 Royal St. Hip Faubourg bar with funky thrift-store decor, a pool table and a great jukebox. It's popular with a youngish set, which includes visitors staying at the guesthouse upstairs (see p.560).

Snake and Jake's 7601 Oak St, uptown. Dim, debauched and derelict, strewn with ancient Christmas tree lights, this quintessential New Orleans dive bar has a superb jukebox, with a playlist of New Orleans R&B and classic soul. Go very late.

Jazz

Jazz, especially trad jazz, is **dance music** in New Orleans – inclusive, joyous and sexy. You may or may not get to see world-famous names such as pianist Allen Toussaint or trumpeters Terence Blanchard and Nicholas Payton, but you will discover an astonishing range of local talents – one of the city's best-loved performers, trumpeter **Kermit Ruffins** can always be counted on for a good show. There is an enjoyable **indie trad** scene, incubated on the streets of the Quarter and in the bars of Frenchmen Street, where you'll join a high-spirited mix of gutter punks and slick hipsters, delighted tourists and lindy-hopping locals. Even **Preservation Hall**, the holy grail for trad fans, keeps things fresh with guest musicians and ever-evolving line-ups for its famed house band.

At the heart of it all, though, are the **brass bands**. Although brass bands have been integral to New Orleans's street music and parade culture since the nineteenth century, their resurgence in the 1990s led to an explosion of energy on the local jazz scene. Ragtag groups of musicians, many of them from Tremé, the young brass bands blast out a joyful, improvised and danceable cacophony of horns – a kind of homegrown party music that goes down as much of a storm in the student bars as on the backstreet parades. Favourites include the ReBirth, the Soul Rebels and the Stooges, who mix trad brass stylings with hard funk, hip-hop, carnival music and reggae. The more traditional bands, meanwhile, whose line-up will typically include octogenarian old hands and up-and-coming youngsters, play music that is just as danceable and equally popular.

Though the **venues** reviewed below are best known for, or exclusively devoted to, jazz, New Orleans music endlessly crosses boundaries, and nearly everywhere will feature jazz, in some shape or form, some nights of the week.

Donna's 800 N Rampart St ⓣ504/596-6914. Hosting smooth jazz, trad and blues, this scruffy BBQ joint on the fringe of the Quarter feels like a locals' place but attracts a loyal out-of-town crowd. Cover varies; one-drink minimum.

Le Bon Temps Roulé 4801 Magazine St ⓣ504/895-8117. A convivial mix of drinkers fills this uptown neighbourhood bar, complete with pool tables and good food. The weekly Soul Rebels gig (Thurs) has become an institution. No cover.

New Orleans jazz

Jazz was born in New Orleans, shaped in the early twentieth century by the twin talents of Louis Armstrong and Joe "King" Oliver from a diverse heritage of African and Caribbean slave music, Civil War brass bands, plantation spirituals, black church music and work songs. In 1897, in an attempt to control the prostitution that had been rampant in the city since its earliest days, a law was passed that restricted the brothels to a fixed area bounded by Iberville and Lower Basin streets. The area, which soon became known as Storyville, after the alderman who pronounced the ordinance, filled with newly arrived ex-plantation workers, seamen and gamblers, and, from the "mood-setting" tunes played in the brothels to bawdy saloon gigs, there was plenty of opportunity for musicians, in particular the solo piano players known as "professors", to develop personal styles. After Storyville was officially closed in 1917, there was a mass exodus of musicians to Chicago and New York. Many more jazz artists left the city or gave up playing altogether during the Depression; but in the 1950s, the city fathers literally changed their tune and began to promote jazz as a tourist attraction. Nowadays jazz remains an evolving, organic art form, and you're spoilt for choice for places to hear it, whether in Second Lines (see p.564), at the city's many festivals, in dive bars or sophisticated lounges.

Preservation Hall 726 St Peter St, French Quarter ☎504/522-2841. This tumbledown old building – with no bar, a/c or toilets, and just a few hard benches for seating – has long been lauded as the best place in New Orleans to hear trad jazz. The music is joyous, building steam as the night goes on – lines form well before the doors open. Thurs is brass band night. Nightly sets every 45min 8–11pm. $10 cover.

Snug Harbor 626 Frenchmen St ☎504/949-0696. Sophisticated Faubourg jazz club in an intimate, two-storey space. Regulars include Astral Project, who play cool modern jazz, clarinet maestro Dr Michael White and pianist Ellis Marsalis. Nightly shows 8pm & 10pm, cover $8–25.

Spotted Cat 623 Frenchmen St, Faubourg Marigny ☎504/943-3887. With nightly roots music, the *Spotted Cat* has become the place to see the New Orleans Cottonmouth Kings, whose high-octane twist on jubilant swing and trad is impossible not to dance to. No cover.

Vaughan's 4229 Dauphine St, Bywater ☎504/947-5562. Rickety old neighbourhood bar that fills to bursting point on Thurs, Kermit Ruffins's night. The band is crammed up against the audience – a mixed bunch of locals, students and the players' friends and family; between sets, help yourself to free beans and rice. Take a cab and prepare for a magical New Orleans evening. Cover $10 on Thurs.

Other live music

There's far more to New Orleans than jazz alone. Though the "**New Orleans sound**", an exuberant, carnival-tinged hybrid of blues, parade music and R&B, had its heyday in the early 1960s, many of its stars are still gigging, from Al "Carnival Time" Johnson to Irma "It's Raining" Thomas. Their shows, crowded with devoted locals, make for a quintessentially New Orleans night out. Since the 1960s the city has also been famed for its homegrown **funk** – top acts include Galactic and Dumpstaphunk – while New Orleans's version of hip-hop, known as **bounce**, took the nation by storm in the 1990s. While **Cajun** music is not indigenous to the city, there are a couple of fantastic places to *fais-do-do* (the Cajun two-step) and dance to **zydeco**, its raunchier black relation. Blues fans should look out for the blues/R&B fusion of Walter "Wolfman" Washington, Delta-blues guitarist John Mooney and Washboard Chaz, who sends the indie crowd wild with his *frottoir*-based acoustic swing. New Orleans **rock** is alive and kicking, in its own quirky style: watch out for king and queen of the Ninth Ward Quintron and Miss Pussycat, along with multi-talented bandleader Clint Maedgen and his skewed vaudevillian cabaret *The New Orleans Bingo! Show*.

For something unique, scour the listings for **Mardi Gras Indians** (see p.565) such as the Wild Magnolias, whose rare gigs – you're most likely to catch them around Mardi Gras or Jazz Fest – are the funkiest, most extraordinary performances you're ever likely to see.

Chickie Wah Wah 2828 Canal St ⓣ504/304-4714. An intelligently selected mixed bag – folk, blues, brass and jazz – at this relatively upmarket club with retro folk art-meets-neon decor and a superb jukebox of local music. Unusually, many shows start early, at around 7 or 8pm. Cover varies.

Circle Bar 1032 St Charles Ave ⓣ504/588-2616. Painfully hip bar in a crumbling old house at Lee Circle. With an eclectic booking policy, from alt rock to bluegrass, it's renowned for resurrecting R&B legends from oblivion, and pulls a gorgeous, hard-partying crowd. Cover varies.

Hi-Ho Lounge 2239 St Claude Ave ⓣ504/945-4446. On the fringes of Tremé, the Faubourg and Bywater, this quirky place – vintage booths and an old Deco bar, domino games and table football – attracts a friendly crowd for everything from bluegrass jams to burlesque, hardcore punk, Mardi Gras Indians and old-school R&B. Cover varies.

Maple Leaf 8316 Oak St ⓣ504/866-9359. Legendary uptown bar with pressed-tin walls, a large dancefloor and a patio. It's a New Orleans favourite for really great blues, R&B, funk and brass bands; ReBirth's Tues-night gigs are a must. There's chess and pool, too. Cover varies.

Mid-City Lanes Rock 'n' Bowl 3000 S Carrollton Ave ⓣ504/482-3133. Its Mid-City location may be unprepossessing, but this eccentric and fun bowling alley-cum-music venue is an institution. Though it's especially heaving on Thurs – zydeco night – they also book great local R&B, blues and swing, and the crowd is always lively. Cover varies.

One Eyed Jack's 615 Toulouse St, French Quarter ⓣ504/569-8361. Loosely conceived as a decadent cabaret lounge in old Bourbon St style, this hip bar and club presents a wide range of shows, including burlesque, trad jazz, rap battles, indie rock and punk to a friendly crowd. Cover varies.

Tipitina's 501 Napoleon Ave ⓣ504/895-8477. Venerable uptown venue, named after a Professor Longhair song, with a consistently good funk, R&B, brass, ska and reggae line-up. The Cajun *fais-do-do* (Sun 5–9pm; free lessons available) is fun, too. Cover $7–40.

Cajun country

Cajun country stretches across southern Louisiana from Houma in the east, via **Lafayette**, the hub of the region, into Texas. It's a region best enjoyed away from the larger towns, by visiting the many old-style hamlets that, despite modernization, can still be found cut off from civilization in soupy bayous, coastal marshes and inland swamps.

Cajuns are descended from the French colonists of Acadia, part of Nova Scotia, which was taken by the British in 1713. The Catholic **Acadians**, who had fished, hunted and farmed for more than a century, refused to renounce their faith and swear allegiance to the English king, and in 1755 the British expelled them all, separating families and burning towns. About 2500 ended up in French Louisiana, where they were given land to set up small farming communities, enabling them to rebuild the culture they had left behind. Hunting, farming and trapping, they lived in relative isolation until the 1940s, when major roads were built, immigrants from other states poured in to work in the **oil** business, and **Cajun music**, popularized by local musicians such as accordionist Iry Lejeune, came to national attention. Since then, the history of the Cajuns has continued to be one of struggle. The erosion of coastal wetlands threatens the existence of entire communities; the silting up of the Atchafalaya Basin is having adverse effects on fishing and shrimping; and not only are coastal towns in the firing line of devastating hurricanes, like **Katrina**, that hurtle up from the Gulf of Mexico, but also catastrophic oil spills, like the **BP disaster** of 2010. After Roosevelt's administration decreed that all American children should speak English in schools, French was practically wiped out in Cajun country, and the local patois of the older inhabitants, with its strong African influences, was kept alive primarily by music. Since the 1980s, CODOFIL (the Council for Development of French in Louisiana) has been devoted to preserving the region's indigenous **language** and culture, and today you will find many signs, brochures and shopfronts written in French.

Cajun and zydeco **fais-do-dos** – dances, with live bands, held mostly on weekends – are great fun, and visitors will find plenty of opportunity to dance, whether at a restaurant, a club, or one of the region's many **festivals**. Although

Cajun festivals

Held almost weekly it seems, **Cajun festivals** provide an enjoyable way to experience the food and music of the region. Note that for the larger events, it's a good idea to reserve a room in advance. The following is merely a sampler; for full details, check with any tourist office in the area.

Mardi Gras (Feb/March). Cajun Carnival differs from its city cousin; although there are private balls, parties and formal parades, it is a far more countrified and very family-oriented affair. There's plenty of music and street dancing, of course, and villages like Eunice, Church Point and Mamou are the scene of the mischievous, somewhat surreal *Courir du Mardi Gras*. Ⓦwww.lsue.edu/acadgate/mardmain.htm.

Catfish Festival, Washington, near Opelousas (spring, but dates vary each year, so check the website). A lively weekend festival featuring arts, crafts, parades, catfish cookoffs and lots of zydeco. Ⓦwww.townofwashingtonla.org/catfishfest.html.

World Championship Crawfish Étouffée Cookoff, Eunice (last Sun in March, or the third Sun, if Easter falls on the last one). *The* place to taste the very best mudbugs, accompanied by great local music and a fierce spirit of competition among the scores of teams. Ⓦwww.eunice-la.com/festivals.html.

Festival International de Louisiane, Lafayette (last full week in April). Huge, free five-day festival with big-name participants from all over the French-speaking world, celebrating a wealth of indigenous music, culture and food. Ⓦwww.festivalinternational.com.

Breaux Bridge Crawfish Festival, Breaux Bridge (first full weekend of May, Fri–Sun). Crawfish-eating contests, étouffée cookoffs and mudbug races, along with music, craft stalls and dancing. Ⓦwww.bbcrawfest.com.

Opelousas Spice and Music Festival, Opelousas (June). Three-day extravaganza of zydeco, fiddle jams and cookoffs. Ⓦwww.OpelousasSpiceAndMusicFestival.com.

Southwest Louisiana Zydeco Music Festival, Plaisance, near Opelousas (Sat before Labor Day). A month of zydeco-related events culminates in a full day of top zydeco performers playing turbo-fuelled "black Creole" music. Also regional cuisine, African-American arts and crafts, talks, dancing and workshops. Ⓦwww.zydeco.org.

Mamou Cajun Music Festival, Mamou (Fri & Sat in mid- or late Aug). Traditional live music, food, crafts, beer-drinking and boudin-eating contests. Ⓦwww.mamoucajunmusicfestival.com.

Festivals Acadiens et Créoles, Lafayette (late Sept or early Oct). Huge three-day festival, with Cajun, zydeco and traditional French bands, as well as indigenous crafts and food. Ⓦwww.festivalsacadiens.com.

Louisiana Yambilee, Opelousas (last week in Oct). Opelousas celebrates the sweet potato in a big way, with food stalls, auctions, zydeco music, competitions and the marvellously named Lil' Miss Yum Yum beauty contest. Ⓦwww.yambilee.com.

Baton Rouge, the capital of Louisiana, is not actually in Cajun country, heading out this way from New Orleans, via the **plantations** on the banks of the Mississippi, makes an easy approach.

Plantation country

The fastest roads out from New Orleans toward the west are the major I-10 and US-61; you can also drive along the **River Road**, which hugs both banks of the Mississippi all the way to Baton Rouge, seventy miles upriver. It's not a particularly eventful drive, winding through flat, fertile farmland, but a series of bridges and ferries allows you to crisscross the water, stopping off and touring several restored antebellum **plantation homes** along the way. Before the Civil War, these spectacular homes were the focal points of the vast estates from where wealthy planters – or rather, their slaves – loaded cotton, sugar or indigo onto steamboats berthed virtually at their front doors. Generally, the superb Laura plantation excepted, **tours**, often led by belles in ball gowns, skimp on details about the estates as a whole, and in particular their often vast slave populations, presenting them instead as showcase museums filled with priceless antiques. The cumulative effect can be stultifying, so it's best to pick just one or two. Many of the houses also offer luxurious **B&B**, which allows you to absorb more of the atmosphere of the plantations than is possible on the walk-throughs.

To get to the River Road from New Orleans, take I-10 west to exit 220, turn onto I-310 and follow it to **Hwy-48**, on the east bank (*above* the river on the map). This shortly becomes **Hwy-44**, or the River Road. For the west bank (*below* the river), cross Destrehan Bridge onto **Hwy-18** rather than branching onto Hwy-48. Note that the levee runs the length of the banks, blocking the river from view, and though you'd never guess it from the tourist brochures, hulking chemical plants dominate the River Road landscape. There are rural stretches where wide sugar-cane fields are interrupted only by moss-covered shacks – the prettiest views are around the small town of **Convent**, on the east bank – but you'll more often find yourself driving through straggling communities of boarded-up lounges and laundromats, scarred by scrap piles and smokestacks.

From **Edgard**, 25 miles along on Hwy-18, you can cross the river to the **San Francisco House** (daily: April–Oct 9.30am–4.40pm; Nov–March 10am–4pm; $15; Ⓦwww.sanfranciscoplantation.org), two miles upriver of **Reserve** on Hwy-44. Built in a style dubbed "Steamboat Gothic" by novelist Frances Parkinson Keyes, its rails, awnings and pillars were designed to recreate the ambience of a Mississippi showboat. The elaborate facade is matched by a gorgeous interior – a riot of pastoral trompe-l'oeils, floral motifs and Italian cherubs. Crossing the river at **Lutcher**, the settlement a few miles beyond San Francisco, brings you to Vacherie and the fascinating **Laura plantation** (daily 10am–4pm; $18; Ⓦwww.lauraplantation.com). Rather than dwelling lovingly on priceless antiques, the tours here, which draw upon a wealth of historical documents – from **slave accounts** and photographs to private diaries – sketch a vivid picture of day-to-day plantation life in multicultural Louisiana. Nine miles upriver from Laura, **Oak Alley**, the quintessential image of the antebellum plantation home, is an opulent Greek Revival mansion dating from 1839 – the magnificent oaks that form a canopy over the driveway are 150 years older (Mon–Fri 10am–4pm, Sat & Sun 10am–5pm; $15; Ⓦwww.oakalleyplantation.com). You can **stay** in pretty B&B cottages in the grounds (Ⓣ225/265-2151; ❻). Eighteen miles south of Baton Rouge on the west bank, **Nottoway** (1859) is the largest surviving plantation home in the South, a huge, white Italianate edifice with 64 rooms (daily 9am–4pm; $20, $8 grounds only). The house also has fancy **B&B** rooms (ⓣ225/545-2730, ⓦwww.nottoway.com; ❼).

Also on the west bank, in the small town of **Donaldsonville** at 406 Charles St, the **River Road African American Museum** (Wed–Sat 10am–5pm, Sun 1–5pm; $4) offers an alternative view of the region's history, highlighting its cuisine, music, the Underground Railroad, Reconstruction and the culture of the free blacks.

Baton Rouge

When French explorers came upon the site of **BATON ROUGE** in 1699, they found poles smeared in animal blood to designate the hunting grounds of the Houmas and Bayougoulas Native Americans. The area on these shallow bluffs therefore appeared on French maps as *Baton Rouge* – "red stick". Now capital of Louisiana and a key port, Baton Rouge is a relaxed city for its size. Even the presence of the state's largest **universities**, LSU and Southern, has done surprisingly little to raise the town anywhere much above "sleepy" status.

Surrounded by fifty acres of showpiece gardens, the magnificent Art Deco **Louisiana State Capitol** (daily 8am–4pm; free) serves as a monument to **Huey Long**, the "Kingfish", the larger-than-life populist Democratic governor who ordered its construction in 1931 and was assassinated in its corridors just four years later. Mark Twain referred to Baton Rouge's **Old State Capitol** (in use from 1850 to 1932), 100 North Blvd, as "that monstrosity on the Mississippi". A crenellated, pseudo-Gothic pile on a mound overlooking the river, it's worth a look for the **Museum of Political History** (Mon–Sat 9am–4.30pm, Sun noon–4.30pm; free), which illuminates Louisiana's scandal-ridden political past. The **LSU Rural Life Museum**, 4560 Essen Rd, just off I-10 southeast of downtown (daily 8.30am–5pm; $9; ⓦrurallife.lsu.edu), re-creates pre-industrial Louisiana life through its restored buildings – among them a plantation house, slave cottages and a grist mill – spread over 25 sultry acres.

Practicalities

Greyhound, and connecting **buses** from New Orleans's Amtrak station, come in at 1253 Florida St, fifteen minutes from downtown. For **Yellow Cabs**, call ⓣ225/926-6400. For **visitor information** check ⓦwww.visitbatonrouge.com; the **Convention and Visitors Bureau** is downtown at 359 3rd St, three blocks from the river (daily 8am–4.30pm). There are chain **motels** on and off I-10; *Best Western Richmond Suites*, near LSU at 5668 Hilton Ave (ⓣ225/924-6500, ⓦwww.bestwesternlouisiana.com; ❺) is a cut above many, with a pool, large rooms and a free cooked breakfast.

The simple *Harrington's*, downtown at 329 Florida St (ⓣ225/343-2626), serves tasty Louisiana **lunch** specials (Mon–Fri); in the evening, the nearby *Capital City Grill*, 100 Lafayette St (ⓣ225/381-8140), is more upmarket, specializing in seafood and fish. Most of the city's **bars** and **clubs** are near the **LSU campus**.

Lafayette and around

LAFAYETTE, 135 miles northwest of New Orleans on I-10, is geographically central in Cajun country, and the key city for its oil business. Originally named Vermilionville, after the orangey bayou nearby, it was renamed in 1844 in honour of the Marquis de Lafayette, the aristocratic French hero of the American Revolution.

Today it's a sprawling city with a small-town feel, and is particularly vibrant during the superb **Festival International de Louisiane** and **Festivals Acadiens** (see p.576); at other times, you could use it as a base for exploring the swamps, bayous and dance halls of the region. There are plenty of smaller places nearby, especially in and around **Breaux Bridge**, that offer something a little more personal.

Arrival, information and getting around

Greyhound arrives at 315 Lee Ave; **Amtrak** pulls in a few blocks north at 133 E Grant St at Jefferson Street. The **airport** is south of town on Hwy-90. The website of the Lafayette Parish **visitor centre** at 1400 NW Evangeline Thruway, off I-10 (Mon–Fri 8.30am–5pm, Sat & Sun 9am–5pm; ⓣ1-800/346-1958, ⓦwww.lafayettetravel.com) is full of useful information on Cajun culture.

To get the best from the area you'll need a **car**, as the dance halls, restaurants and hotels are spread out, and the local bus system is of little use to visitors. If you need a **taxi**, try Quality Cab (ⓣ337/235-8993).

Accommodation

Chain **hotels** line Evangeline Thruway just south of I-10, US-90 and Hwy-182 toward New Iberia, but if you are after something with more character you'll need to head further out. The friendly hamlet of **Breaux Bridge**, just eight miles east, makes another appealing base.

Bayou Cabins 100 W Mills Ave/Hwy-94, Breaux Bridge ⓣ337/332-6158, ⓦwww.bayoucabins.com. Thirteen rustic cabins – most of which date from the nineteenth century – backing onto Bayou Teche, a 125-mile long waterway. Run by the owners of *Bayou Boudin and Cracklin'* (see p.580); rates include a free taster of their fantastic Cajun food and breakfast served in the café next door. You're near the highway here, so there is some traffic noise. ❸

Blue Moon Guest House and Saloon 215 E Convent St, Lafayette ⓣ1-877/766-BLUE, ⓦwww.bluemoonhostel.com. Cheerful hostel and guest-house, in a nineteenth-century home on a nice street downtown, with two dorms ($18–21) and four private rooms. The main appeal is the back porch saloon, with regular Cajun, zydeco and bluegrass gigs and a full bar. Rates increase for festivals, when it's a gathering place for local musicians. Free wi-fi. ❶–❸

Juliet Hotel 800 Jefferson St, Lafayette ⓣ337/261-2225, ⓦwww.juliethotel.com. Though it offers nothing distinctively Cajun, this hotel has a nice downtown location and luxurious touches. You can skip the breakfast, though, and head downtown to eat. Free wi-fi. ❺

Pear Tree Inn 126 Alcide Dominique, Lafayette ⓣ1-888/399-2151; ⓦwww.druryhotels.com. Comfortable, clean and friendly motel (part of the Drury chain) off I-10 and convenient to downtown. Free happy hour and a good buffet breakfast. ❹

The Town

In the centre, such as it is, of Lafayette stands the Romanesque **Cathedral of St John the Evangelist**, 914 St John St, and the old **cemetery**, where the crumbling, raised graves include that of Jean Mouton, the town's Cajun founder. Each of the magnificent branches of the five-hundred-year-old **Cathedral Oak**, spreading over 200ft, weighs seventy tons. Three blocks away, the small **Lafayette Museum**, 1122 Lafayette St (Tues–Sat 9am–4.30pm, Sun 1–4pm; $3), was the "Sunday home" – a townhouse used after Mass, before the family returned to their plantation – of Jean's son Alexandre, Louisiana's first Democratic governor. It's now filled with family memorabilia, Civil War relics, and Cajun Mardi Gras costumes.

Lafayette has two excellent reconstructions of early Cajun communities. **Vermilionville**, 300 Fisher Rd across from the airport, is the best, exploring the culture of the early Creoles as well as the Cajuns (Tues–Sun 10am–4pm; $8). Set in 23 attractive acres on the Bayou Vermilion, it's a living history site, filled with authentic old buildings occupied by craftspeople using traditional skills. A large replica of an old cotton gin serves as a **theatre** for noisy *fais-do-dos* and festivals. The **restaurant** serves good Cajun lunches, and they even offer cooking classes.

Next to Vermilionville, at 501 Fisher Rd, the **Acadian Cultural Center**, in the **Jean Lafitte National Historical Park and Preserve** (daily 8am–5pm; free), offers good background on the Cajuns, with regular boat tours of the bayou. Further southwest, Lafayette's other folk-life museum, the smaller **Acadian Village**, 200 Greenleaf Drive (Mon–Sat 10am–4pm; $8), depicts early-nineteenth-century Cajun life along the bayous.

Eating

Eating Cajun food is one of the big appeals of visiting the region. Although it bears resemblances to the Creole cuisine you'll find in New Orleans – lots of seafood, rice, rich tomatoey sauces and gumbos – this is more rustic, often spicy, and using plenty of pork. At lunchtime, takeaway **boudin** (spicy sausage made with rice) is a treat, as are rich pork cracklin' and salty hogshead cheese.

Bayou Boudin and Cracklin' 100 Mills Ave, Hwy-94, Breaux Bridge, exit 109 from I-10 ⓣ337/332-6158. Rustic Cajun cottage on Bayou Teche, serving fantastic home-made boudin – including a seafood variety – hogshead cheese, smothered chicken, crawfish balls, gumbo and beignets. Closed Mon & Tues.

Blue Dog Café 1211 W Pinhook Rd, Lafayette ⓣ337/237-0005, ⓦwww.bluedogcafe.com. Popular, touristy spot for Cajun-Creole food – the crabmeat au gratin is great – surrounded by the distinctive blue dog paintings of Cajun artist George Rodrigue. Lunch Mon–Sat, Sat dinner, & Sun brunch with music.

Café des Amis 140 E Bridge St, Breaux Bridge ⓣ337/332-5273, ⓦwww.cafedesamis.com. This friendly, arty restaurant is a buzzing community hub, and the Cajun/Creole food, with lots of creamy crawfish concoctions, is very tasty. Live music Wed evenings and zydeco breakfasts Sat 8.30–11.30am. Closed Mon; lunch only Tues & Sun.

Dwyer's 323 Jefferson St, Lafayette ⓣ337/235-9364. Downtown diner serving huge, inexpensive breakfasts (try the sweet potato pancakes), plate lunches and local specialties. You'll hear a lot of French spoken here.

Earl's 510 Verot School Rd, Lafayette ⓣ337/237-5501. Though you can get tasty lunches to take away from this grocery/butcher's store, all for around $5, it's the unfeasibly delicious boudin you should go for.

Prejean's 3480 I-49 N, Lafayette ⓣ337/896-3247. Barn-like, touristy restaurant offering delicious, gourmet Cajun food – try the Mardi Gras oyster bake and the gumbos – nightly live music (from 7pm), and dancing.

Robin's 1409 Henderson Hwy, Henderson, Breaux Bridge ⓣ337/228-7594. Innovative Cajun food, with lots of use of Tabasco hot sauce – even in the ice cream – and a killer crawfish étouffée.

Touring Cajun country

You could easily drive through tiny **BREAUX BRIDGE**, eight miles east of Lafayette, and miss it, which would be a shame. Quite apart from its old-fashioned main street, its crawfish-emblazoned steel bridge over the Bayou Teche, and its handful of B&Bs, restaurants and music venues, it also makes an appealing base for **swamp tours** (see p.582), and for exploring the **Lake Martin nature reserve**, three miles south on Hwy-31. There's an end-of-the-earth feel to the reserve, where land turns to water, and it's a great experience to drive – or walk the trails – past vistas of tangled cypress flickering with Spanish moss and encroaching greenery creeping onto the narrow road. From February to June tens of thousands of birds nest at the lake, and there's an abundance of **birdlife** year-round, not to mention busy nutria splashing through the undergrowth and **alligators** dozing

Cajun and zydeco music venues

It's easy to "pass a good time" in Cajun country, especially if you're here at the weekend, when the *fais-do-dos* are traditionally held, or during any of its many festivals (see p.576). **Cajun music** is a jangling, infectious melange of nasal vocals backed by jumping accordion, violin and triangle, fuelled by traces of country, swing, jazz and blues. **Zydeco** is similar, but sexier, more blues-based, and usually played by black Creole musicians. Though songs are in French, the patois heard in both bears only a passing resemblance to the language spoken in France. Music is never performed without space for dancing; everyone can join in. As well as the popular restaurants *Café des Amis* and *Prejean's* (reviewed on opposite), plus the *Blue Moon Guest House* (see p.654), **venues** include record stores, river landings and the streets themselves. Sadly, old-time zydeco dance halls are dying out, but a few still exist. Check the music **listings** in the free weekly *Times of Acadiana* (Ⓦwww.timesofacadiana.com) or *Independent* (Ⓦwww.theind.com); log onto Ⓦwww.zydecoonline.com, or simply look for signs saying "French dance here tonight".

Angelle's Whiskey River Landing 1365 Henderson Levee Rd, Henderson, Breaux Bridge Ⓣ337/228-2277, Ⓦwww.whiskeyriverlanding.net. Lively Cajun and zydeco parties on Sun afternoons (4–8pm).

El Sid O's 1523 N St Antoine St, Lafayette Ⓣ337/235-0647. This old favourite is open for dancing Fri & Sat, with great zydeco and blues bands.

Fred's Lounge 420 6th St, Mamou, 10 miles north of Eunice Ⓣ337/468-5411. Welcoming lounge presided over by the delightful Tante Sue, with music, dancing and lots of drinking. Sat only, 7am–2pm.

Grant Street Dancehall 113 W Grant St, Lafayette Ⓣ337/237-8513, Ⓦwww.grantstreetlive.com. Eclectic music barn in downtown Lafayette hosting hip-hop, swamp pop, New Orleans jazz, brass and blues, as well as Cajun and zydeco.

La Poussière 1215 Grand Point Rd, Breaux Bridge Ⓣ337/332-1721, Ⓦwww.lapoussiere.com. The old folks' favourite, this venerable dance hall – where most people speak French – hosts *fais-do-dos* (Sat night & Sun afternoon).

McGee's Landing 1337 Henderson Levee Rd, Breaux Bridge Ⓣ337/228-2384, Ⓦwww.mcgeeslanding.com. A swamp tour outfit-cum-café-cum-music venue hosting live music on Sat & Sun afternoons.

Pat's Atchafalaya Club 1008 Henderson Levee Rd, Henderson, Breaux Bridge Ⓣ337/228-7512, Ⓦwww.patsfishermanswharf.com. Large dance hall on the levee, linked to *Pat's* seafood restaurant, and hosting Cajun, zydeco and swamp pop bands Fri–Sun.

Rendezvous des Cajuns Liberty Center for Performing Arts, S 2nd St and Park Ave, Eunice Ⓣ337/457-7389, Ⓦwww.eunice-la.com/libertyschedule.html. Family-oriented and hugely popular live Cajun/zydeco radio and TV show, mostly in French. Sat 6–7.30pm. Cover $5.

Savoy Music Center 4413 Hwy-190 E, 3 miles east of Eunice Ⓣ337/457-9563, Ⓦsavoymusiccenter.com. Free jam sessions (Sat 9am–noon) at this Cajun record store and accordion workshop are a local institution. Store closed Sun & Mon.

Slim's Y-Ki-Ki 8393 Hwy-182 N, Opelousas Ⓣ337/942-6242. Famed old locals' venue for zydeco music and dancing. Usually Fri & Sat but call to check.

in the sun. If you fancy paddling a **canoe** through this wilderness, contact Pack and Paddle, 601 E Pinhook Rd, Lafayette (Ⓣ337/232-5854, Ⓦwww.packpaddle.com; closed Sun).

North of Lafayette, the **Cajun Prairie** has been described by folklorist Alan Lomax as the "Cajun cultural heartland". A patchwork of rice and soybean fields scattered with crawfish ponds, the region has a few tiny towns of interest. Sleepy old

OPELOUSAS, twenty miles north of Lafayette on I-49, was capital of Louisiana for a short period during the Civil War, and now has several claims to fame. It was the boyhood home of Jim Bowie, Texas Revolutionary hero and inventor of the Bowie knife; the birthplace of the great zydeco musician **Clifton Chenier**; and is the **yam** capital of the universe. It also hosts some good festivals (see p.576), and is a hub for zydeco music. You can find out more at the quirky **Opelousas Museum**, 315 N Main St (Mon–Sat 9am–5pm; free; ⓦwww.cityofopelousas.com) – which displays such relics of local history as the barber's stool on which outlaw Clyde Barrow got his last shave before being shot dead by the FBI in northern Louisiana. The 1950s *Palace Café*, on the central square at 135 W Landry Ave (ⓣ337/942-2142), offers shrimp, crawfish and gumbo in immaculate **diner** surroundings. Chain **hotels** line I-49; the *Comfort Inn* (ⓣ337/942-4900, ⓦwww.choicehotels.com; ❹), south of town, is a reasonable option.

To learn a little about the Cajun prairie, head for friendly **EUNICE**, about twenty miles west of Opelousas. The **Prairie Acadian Cultural Center** at the **Jean Lafitte National Historical Park**, 250 W Park Ave (Tues–Fri 8am–5pm, Sat 8am–6pm; free; ⓦwww.nps.gov), holds far-reaching displays on local life, with live Cajun music, storytelling and cookery demonstrations. There's more music at the **Cajun Music Hall of Fame**, 240 S C.C. Duson Drive (Tues–Sat: summer 9am–5pm, winter 8.30am–4.30pm; free), which features accordions, steel guitars, fiddles and triangles among its memorabilia. If time is short, choose these two over the **Eunice Museum**, next to the Hall of Fame at 220 S C.C. Duson Drive (Tues–Sat 8am–noon & 1–5pm; free) – though this too has its charms; it's an old train depot crammed with a ragbag of local memorabilia. *Allison's Hickory Pit*, 501 W Laurel Ave (Fri–Sun 11am–2pm; ⓣ337/457-9218), does wonderful home-smoked barbecue, while *Ruby's*, downtown at 221 W Walnut St (closed Sun; ⓣ337/550-7665), dishes up home-cooked soul food in a vintage setting. Eunice is also central to the region's **music scene** (see p.581). *L'Acadie Inn*, a couple of miles east of downtown on Hwy-90 (ⓣ337/457-5211, ⓦwww.hotboudin.com; ❸), is a good-value, friendly **place to stay**.

Swamp tours

Swamp tours are available from many landings in the **Atchafalaya Basin**; you'll pass numerous signs pinned to the old cypress trees along the roadside. The basin is an eerie place: in some places cars cut right across on the enormous concrete I-10 above, and old houseboats lie abandoned. The best tours take you further out, to the backwoods; wherever you go, you'll see scores of fishing boats and plenty of wildlife, including sunbathing alligators. The tours below are conducted by Cajuns who see the basin as more than just a tourist attraction and provide fascinating personal commentaries.

The Atchafalaya Experience 338 N Sterling St, Lafayette ⓣ337/277-4726, ⓦwww.theatchafalayaexperience.com. The son in this father–son team is a geologist; both guides are lifelong explorers of the swamp, and tours are ecologically sensitive. Daily; 3hr 30min (2hr touring the swamp itself); call for schedule and to reserve; $50.

Bryan Champagne Lake Martin Landing, Rookery Rd, Breaux Bridge ⓣ337/230-4068, ⓦwww.champagnesswamptours.com. Champagne navigates a small crawfish skiff through the bird-rich Cypress Island Swamp – lots of opportunity for alligator-spotting. Daily; call for schedules; 2hr; $20.

McGee's Swamp Tours McGee's Landing, 1337 Henderson Levee Rd, near Breaux Bridge ⓣ337/228-2384, ⓦwww.mcgeeslanding.com. This quiet landing offers leisurely tours of the Atchafalaya Basin as well as live music (see p.581). Daily 10am, 1pm & 3pm, plus special tours by arrangement; 90min; $20. They also rent kayaks and canoes.

From here it's twenty miles north to **VILLE PLATTE**, and the fabulous Floyd's Music Store, 434 E Main St (Mon–Sat 8.30am–4.30pm; Ⓦwww.floydsrecordshop.com), owned by Floyd Soileau, the world's chief distributor of **South Louisiana music**, and stocking everything from zydeco reissues to swamp pop. A couple of doors down at the *Pig Stand*, 318 E Main St (Ⓣ337/363-2883), giant plates of fried chicken, smothered sausage and ribs come heaped with delicious Southern side dishes.

South of Lafayette

South of Lafayette, the towns are less immediately welcoming than those in the Prairie, but the surroundings are undeniably atmospheric: this is **bayou country**, a marshy expanse of rivers and lakes dominated by the mighty Atchafalaya swamp, where the soupy green waters creep right up to the edges of the highway. The economy is based on fishing and shrimping, with hunting in the forests and sugar fields, but it's also a semi-industrial landscape, with a web of oil pipelines running beneath the waterways, and refineries and corrugated-iron shacks sharing space with white Catholic churches. The main town of interest is **ST MARTINVILLE**, off US-90 18 miles south of Lafayette. Settled in 1765 on the Bayou Teche, this was a major port of entry for exiled Acadians. The **Museum of the Acadian Memorial** (daily 10am–4pm; $3; Ⓦwww.acadianmemorial.org) pays tribute to the thousands of refugees displaced from Canada to Louisiana between 1764 and 1788; part of the same complex, the **African-American Museum** focuses on the arrival of enslaved Africans into southwest Louisiana during the 1700s, the emergence of free people of colour and the violence of Reconstruction. The *Old Castillo*, 220 Evangeline Blvd, by the bayou (Ⓣ318/394-4010, Ⓦwww.oldcastillo.com; ④) is a B&B with huge rooms; *Le Petit Paris Café*, 116 S Main St (Ⓣ337/342-2606), serves light lunches.

Northern Louisiana

Northern Louisiana is at the heart of the region known as the **Ark-La-Tex**, where the cottonfields and soft vocal drawl of the Deep South Bible Belt merges with the ranches, oil and country music of Texas and the forested hills of Arkansas. Settled by the Scottish and Irish after the Louisiana Purchase, the area is strongly Baptist, with less of a penchant for fun than southern Louisiana, though it does share its profusion of **festivals**.

Angola Prison

Isolated at the end of the long and lonely Hwy-60, hemmed in by the Tunica foothills and the Mississippi River sixty miles northwest of Baton Rouge, **Angola** – or "the farm" as it is commonly known – is the most famous maximum-security prison in the United States, its very name a byword for brutality and desperation. Famous inmates have included blues singer **Leadbelly**, who, as Huddy Ledbetter, served here in the 1930s; today, it holds about five thousand prisoners, 77 percent of whom are black. Most of the men are lifers, and around a hundred of them are on Death Row. Outside the main gate, the **Angola Museum** (Tues–Fri 8am–4.30pm, Sat 9am–5pm; free) offers a fascinating, if uncomfortable, insight into this complex place. Fading photos and newspapers reveal appalling prison conditions; the prodding sticks and belts used to beat convicts bring it closer to home. Since 1970, Angola has staged a **prisoner rodeo** every Sunday in October, an unsettling gladiatorial spectacle which draws thousands (there is also a two-day rodeo in April; both $10; reservations required; Ⓦangolarodeo.com). These are extraordinary affairs, the crowds baying while lifers are flung, gored or trampled in their struggle for glory or just a simple change of scene.

Natchitoches and around

Tiny **NATCHITOCHES** (pronounced "Nakitish"), in the sleepy cottonfields of the Cane River, is the oldest European settlement in Louisiana, having begun life as a French trading post in 1714. With its lovingly restored Creole architecture, Natchitoches's **Front Street**, on the river, bears a passing resemblance to New Orleans's French Quarter – its lacy iron balconies, spiral staircases and cobbled courtyards complemented by old-style stores. Fleurs-de-lis on the **St Denis Walk of Honor** commemorate celebrities with local connections, such as John Wayne, Clementine Hunter (see below) and the cast of the movie *Steel Magnolias*, which was set and filmed here in 1988.

The **Cane River National Heritage Area** (Ⓦwww.caneriverheritage.org), a collection of restored plantation homes, churches and forts, stretches for 35 miles south from Natchitoches. Head first for the fascinating **Melrose Plantation**, on Hwy-119 (daily noon–4pm; $8), which was granted in 1794 to Marie Therese Coincoin, a freed slave, by her owner, Thomas Metoyer – the father of ten of her fourteen children. Coincoin expanded the original grounds into an 800-acre plantation; she was later able to buy freedom for two of her children and one of her grandchildren. Around 1900, enterprising Melrose owner "Miss Cammie" Henry turned the crumbling plantation into an arts community, visited by painters and writers such as William Faulkner and John Steinbeck. In the 1940s, a black Melrose cook, **Clementine Hunter**, began to paint vivid images of life on and around the plantation; her works, many of which are on show here, have since become valuable pieces of folk art.

Natchitoches practicalities

Natchitoches lies 140 miles northeast of Lafayette. This is **B&B** territory: the *Jefferson House*, 229 Second St by the Cane River Lake, is walkable to downtown (Ⓣ318/352-5834, Ⓦwww.jeffersonhousebandb.com; ❹). The **visitor centre**, 781 Front St (daily 9am–5pm; Ⓣ1-800/259-1714, Ⓦwww.historicnatchitoches.com), provides self-guided **walking tours** of historic downtown. The best place to **eat** is *Lasyone's* (Ⓣ318/352-3353), 622 Second St, which specializes in delicious meat pies, cream pies, red beans and sausage, and fresh, crumbly cornbread.

9

Texas

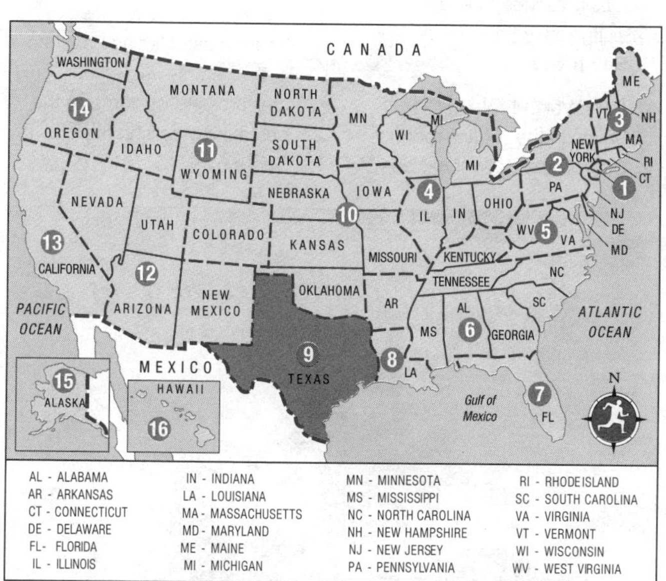
CANADA
WASHINGTON
14
OREGON
MONTANA
NORTH DAKOTA
MN
SOUTH DAKOTA
IDAHO
11
WYOMING
WI
MI
MI
ME
VT
3
NH
MA
NEW YORK
RI
CT
2
1
PA
NEVADA
UTAH
COLORADO
NEBRASKA
IOWA
4
IL
IN
OHIO
10
KANSAS
WV
5
VA
NJ
DE
MD
13
CALIFORNIA
12
ARIZONA
NEW MEXICO
OKLAHOMA
MISSOURI
KENTUCKY
TENNESSEE
NC
AR
SC
AL
MS
6
GEORGIA
PACIFIC OCEAN
ATLANTIC OCEAN
9
TEXAS
8
LA
MEXICO
15
ALASKA
HAWAII
16
Gulf of Mexico
7
FL
N
AL - ALABAMA
AR - ARKANSAS
CT - CONNECTICUT
DE - DELAWARE
FL- FLORIDA
IL - ILLINOIS
IN - INDIANA
LA - LOUISIANA
MA - MASSACHUSETTS
MD - MARYLAND
ME - MAINE
MI - MICHIGAN
MN - MINNESOTA
MS - MISSISSIPPI
NC - NORTH CAROLINA
NH - NEW HAMPSHIRE
NJ - NEW JERSEY
PA - PENNSYLVANIA
RI - RHODE ISLAND
SC - SOUTH CAROLINA
VA - VIRGINIA
VT - VERMONT
WI - WISCONSIN
WV - WEST VIRGINIA

CHAPTER 9

Highlights

* **The Rio Grande Valley** Tiny, historic border towns dot one of the least-visited regions of the state. See p.599
* **Austin** The live-music capital of the US – a hotbed for Americana, outlaw country and the blues, with enough music venues to keep any visitor busy for weeks. See p.600
* **Fort Worth** From cattle drives in the rootin'-tootin' Stockyards, to world-class galleries in the Cultural District, Fort Worth is Texas' best-kept secret. See p.618
* **Marfa** An improbable minimalist arts community in the middle of the West Texas desert. See p.626
* **Big Bend National Park** The Rio Grande rushes through astonishing canyons in this remote wilderness, crisscrossed by some of the best hiking trails in the US. See p.627

▲ Cowboys at Fort Worth rodeo

9

Texas

Still cherishing the memory that it was from 1836 to 1845 an independent nation in its own right, **TEXAS** stands proudly apart from the rest of the United States. While its 25 million residents are firmly bound together by a shared history and culture, the sheer size of Texas – 700 miles from east to west and more than 800 from top to bottom – gives it great geographical diversity.

The swampy, forested **east** is more like Louisiana than the pretty **Hill Country** or the agricultural plains of the northern **Panhandle**, while the tropical **Gulf Coast** has little in common with the mountainous **deserts** of the west. Changes in **climate** are dramatic: snow is common in the Panhandle, whereas the humidity of Houston is often unbearably thick.

There are 28 cities with a population of 100,000 or more, and each of the major tourist destinations is unique. Hispanic **San Antonio**, for example, with its Mexican population and rich history, has a laidback feel absent from commerce-driven **Houston** or **Dallas**, while trendy **Austin** revels in a lively music scene and an underground DIY ethos. One thing shared by the whole of Texas is **state pride**: Texas is a special place and its friendly residents know it.

Some history

Early inhabitants of Texas included the Caddo in the east and nomadic Coahuiltecans further south. The **Comanche**, who arrived from the Rockies in the 1600s, soon found themselves at war when the **Spanish** ventured in looking for gold. In the 1700s, the Spanish began to build **missions** and **forts**, although these had minimal impact on the indigenous population's nomadic way of life. When Mexico won its independence from Spain in 1821, it took Texas as part of the deal. At first, the Mexicans were keen to open up their land and offered generous incentives to settlers. Stephen F. Austin established Anglo-American colonies in the Brazos and Colorado River valleys. However, the Mexican leader, Santa Anna, soon became alarmed by Anglo aspirations to autonomy, and his increasing restrictions led to the eight-month **Texas Revolution** of 1835–36. The romance of the Revolution draws legions of tourists to San Antonio, site of the legendary **Battle of the Alamo**, which, though a military disaster, presaged independence.

The short-lived **Republic of Texas**, which included territory now in Oklahoma, Kansas, New Mexico, Colorado and Wyoming, served to define the state's identity. In 1845, Texas joined the Union on the understanding that it could secede whenever it wished; this antiquated provision has resurfaced in modern-day Texas politics. The influence, especially in the north and east, of settlers from the Southern states and their attendant slave-centred cotton economy resulted in Texas joining the **Confederacy** during the Civil War (1860–65). During

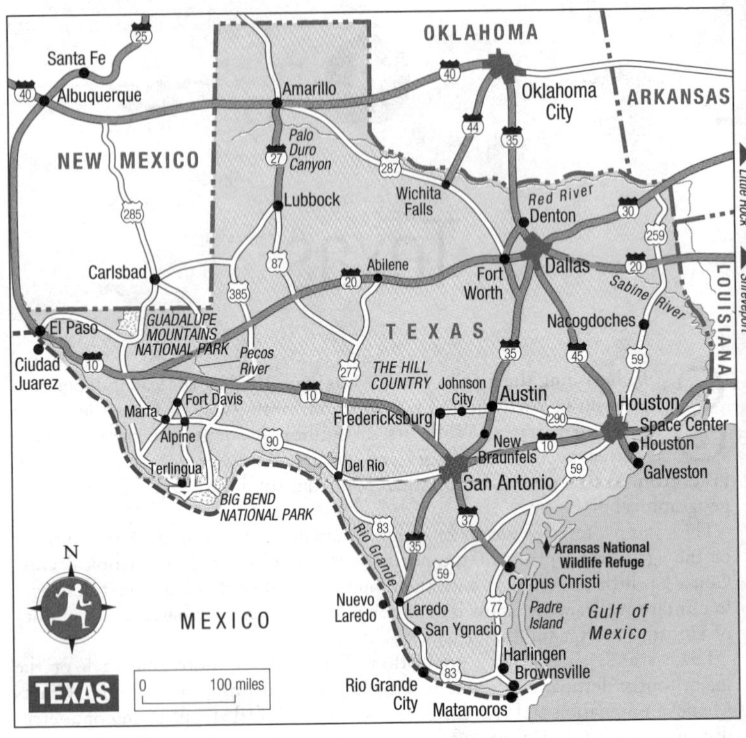

Reconstruction, settlers from both the North and the South began to pour in, and the phrase "Gone to Texas" was applied to anyone fleeing the law, bad debts or unhappy love affairs. This was also the period of the great **cattle drives**, when the longhorns roaming free in the south and west of Texas were rounded up and taken to the railroads in Kansas. The Texan – and national – fascination with the romantic myth of the **cowboy** has its roots in this. Today, his regalia – Stetson, boots and bandana – is virtually a state costume.

Along with ranching and agriculture, **oil** has been crucial. After the first big gusher in 1901, at Spindletop on the Gulf Coast, the focus of the Texas economy shifted almost overnight from agriculture toward rapid industrialization. Boom towns popped up as wildcatters chased the wells and millions of dollars were made as ranchers, who had previously thought their land only fit for cattle, sold out at vast profit. Today, Texas produces one-fifth of all the domestic oil in the United States, and the sight of nodding pump jacks is one of the state's most potent images. Even **George W. Bush** was a West Texas oilman before ascending to the governor's office and then to the presidency. But the state's commitment to renewable energy is becoming a part of the landscape, too, as gleaming white **wind turbines** sprout up like mushrooms in the Panhandle-Plains region.

Getting around Texas

Texas distances are best negotiated by **car**, and in Houston driving is essential. Mass transit has proved impractical in a sprawling state with long commuting distances and gasoline prices that are historically lower than the national average.

Cycling and **walking** still makes sense within cities like Austin and San Antonio though, and rentals are available from bike shops.

Greyhound routes are concentrated between the major cities of the east and the central region, though buses also serve the Gulf Coast, the Rio Grande Valley, West Texas and the Panhandle. Two trains pass through Texas: *The Texas Eagle* travels north–south between Chicago and San Antonio, with stops in Dallas and Austin; while the east–west *Sunset Limited* stops in Beaumont, Houston, San Antonio, Alpine and El Paso on its way between New Orleans and Los Angeles. Given the vast distances, **flying** can save time.

East Texas

The coastline of **Texas** curves southward more than 350 miles from Port Arthur, on the Louisiana border (a petrochemical town and the birthplace of Janis Joplin) to the delta of the Rio Grande, which snakes northwest to form a 900-mile natural border with Mexico. Encompassed in this eastern section of the state is an interesting mix of big-city life and rural, backwoods culture.

Houston, population 2.3 million, dominates the region. It is home to corporate headquarters, renowned medical centres and art museums flush with oil cash – NASA's **Space Center Houston** is also 25 miles south of the city. Outside of Houston are tall pine forests that bear more relation to Louisiana than to the rest of the state. While undeniably Texan, locals here identify themselves culturally and geographically with the adjacent corners of Arkansas and Louisiana – the "**Arklatex**" – and you'll find jambalaya and gumbo in restaurants along with standard Texas dishes. The smaller population centre of Galveston, on the coast outside Houston, offers easy beach access. Galveston was hit hard by **Hurricane Ike** in September 2008. The blow wasn't fatal, though – the city has begun to rebuild its battered downtown and for the most part tourism has returned to pre-hurricane levels.

Houston and around

The fourth-largest city in the United States, **HOUSTON** is an ungainly beast of a place, choked with successive rings of highways and high on humidity. Despite this, its sheer energy, its relentless Texas pride, and, above all, its refusal to take itself totally seriously, lends it no small appeal. For visitors, its well-endowed museums, highly regarded performing arts scene and decent nightlife mean there is always something to do.

They city's very existence has always depended on wild speculation and boom-and-bust excess. Founded on a muddy mire in 1837 by two real estate-booster brothers from New York – their dream was to establish it as the capital of the new Republic of Texas – Houston was soon superseded by the more promising site of Austin, even while somehow developing itself as a commercial centre.

Oil, discovered in 1901, became the foundation, along with cotton and real estate, of vast private fortunes, and over the next century wildly wealthy philanthropists poured cash into swanky galleries and showpiece skyscrapers. That colossal self-confidence helped Houston weather devastating oil crises in the 1980s, and more recently it endured the **Enron** corporate scandal. Houston has also developed a growing workforce eager to bring **alternative energy** to scale. Solar and wind projects offer the most promise in Texas; more than 25 percent of Houston's energy load, for instance, comes from wind.

Several **megachurches** headquartered downtown – with smooth-talking celebrity pastors like Joel Olsteen – have become powerful social, cultural and political forces, drawing as many as 16,000 people to their Sunday services, which are open to the public.

Arrival and information

Downtown Houston lies at the intersection of I-10 (San Antonio–New Orleans) and I-45 (Dallas–Galveston), with most of what you'll want to see encircled by Loop 610. **George Bush Intercontinental Airport** (Ⓣ281/230-3100), 23 miles north, is the main hub for Continental Airlines, while the smaller, domestic **William P. Hobby Airport** (Ⓣ713/640-3000), seven miles southeast of downtown, is a major hub for Southwest. You'll need to **rent a car** to see the best of Houston, particularly since taxis are expensive; all the major companies are represented at the airports. **Taxis** downtown cost about $50 from Intercontinental, $35 from Hobby. The SuperShuttle **van**; starting at $23 from Intercontinental, $19 from Hobby (Ⓣ1-800/BLUE-VAN, Ⓦwww.supershuttle.com) drops off at hotels downtown and near the Galleria mall, west of downtown. **METROBus** (Ⓣ713/635-4000, Ⓦwww.ridemetro.org) also offers routes from both airports. **Amtrak** arrives at 902 Washington Ave, on the western fringe of downtown, while the **Greyhound** terminal is more centrally located at 2121 Main St.

For brochures and maps, visit the **tourist office** on the first floor of City Hall, 901 Bagby St (Mon–Sat 9am–4pm; Ⓣ713/437-5200, Ⓦwww.visithoustontexas.com). There is a library branch on the other side of the plaza. Downtown has free **wi-fi**.

City transport

Houston's **public transit** system is woefully inadequate for a city of its size, but visitors might get use out of the downtown **METRORail tram**, which runs north–south for about eight miles, mostly along Main and Fanin streets, between the University of Houston (UH) and Reliant Park; the Museum District stop is in the middle. Many riders don't bother purchasing $1 honour system tickets. METRO also operates dozens of **bus** routes (Ⓣ713/635-4000, Ⓦwww.ridemetro.org). With Houston's wide shoulders, **bikes** – which can be placed on the front of city buses – are an option. The Houston Bicycle Company at 404½ Westheimer (Ⓣ713/522-4622, Ⓦwww.houstonbicyclecompany.com) rents three-speeds for $25 a day.

Accommodation

Inexpensive hotels are concentrated in three areas: near Reliant Stadium (southwest of downtown), and outside the Loop along either I-45 or I-10. Upmarket, **business-oriented chains** abound downtown and near the Galleria. **B&Bs** offer a welcome alternative in a city as potentially alienating as Houston, and there are a few **budget options**.

Downtown YMCA 1600 Louisiana St ⓣ713/758-9250. Offers clean single rooms with shared shower. A great downtown location if you don't have a car. No dorm rooms available. ❶

Hotel ZaZa 5701 Main St, ⓣ888/880-3244, ⓦwww.hotelzazahouston.com. Trendy decor, with "concept suites" like the space-age Houston We Have a Problem. Fine position near Hermann Park and museums. ❼

Houston International Hostel 5302 Crawford St ⓣ713/523-1009, ⓦwww.houstonhostel.com. This hostel is grubby, but it's in a decent neighbourhood, with the Museum District tram stop six blocks away; dorm beds from $15. ❶

La Colombe d'Or 3410 Montrose Blvd ⓣ713/524-7999, ⓦwww.lacolombedor.com. With just six rooms and an ideal setting near the museums, this quaint but luxurious property is the best hotel in town. If you can't afford a room, sip a cocktail at the small, elegant bar. ❽

The Lancaster 701 Texas Ave ⓣ1-800/231-0336, ⓦwww.thelancaster.com. A sophisticated, old-world option, Lady Bird Johnson's Houston hotel of choice is situated in the heart of the Theater District. ❼

Lovett Inn 501 Lovett Blvd ⓣ713/522-5224, ⓦwww.lovettinn.com. On a leafy avenue on the edge of the Montrose district, this historic house offers large, comfortable rooms, first-class service and a continental breakfast. ❹

Magnolia Hotel 1100 Texas Ave, ⓣ888/915-1110, ⓦwww.magnoliahotelhouston.com. A modern boutique hotel in an excellent downtown location. ❼

The City

Don't try and see too much of Houston in one go. If you have just a short time, concentrate on the superb galleries of the **Museum District** and **Hermann Park**, which are linked to **downtown**, some five miles northeast, by tram. The city's human face is most evident in the **Montrose** area, which lies west of downtown and overlaps with the Museum District.

Uptown, also called the **Galleria** district after its massive upscale mall, is three miles west. Just outside the Loop, the Galleria's 300 or so shops and restaurants spread north along Post Oak Boulevard; there is little to do around here except shop and eat.

Downtown

Houston's skyline remains a dramatic monument to capitalism, ambition and glitz. The observation deck on the 60th floor of **Chase Tower**, 600 Travis St (Mon–Fri 7am–7pm; free), the highest building in the state, offers staggering views of the Texas-sized sprawl. Also notable is the nearby Philip Johnson-designed **Penzoil Place**, 711 Louisiana St, and the lobby of the historic **JP Morgan Chase Building**, 712 Main St, is an Art Deco masterpiece.

Nestled below the skyscrapers, **Sam Houston Park** (Tues–Sat 10am–4pm, Sun 1–4pm) is an appealing green space dotted with restored historic structures from all walks of nineteenth-century life. House tours ($10) leave from 1100 Bagby St. Across the street is a reflecting pool.

The Museum District and Montrose

Five miles southwest of downtown, the quiet oak-lined streets of the **Museum District** are enjoyable to explore on foot – a rarity for Houston. There are two main concentrations of exhibition spaces, with one entire complex dominated by the collections of oil millionaires **John and Dominique de Menil**. The Menil galleries and the Houston Center for Photography are in the **Montrose** district, which spreads west of downtown.

This is one of the hippest neighbourhoods in town and though the forces of gentrification are at work, don't think it's all gone the way of American Apparel. **Westheimer**, the district's main drag, has enough tattoo parlours, vintage clothes stores, experimental art galleries and junk shops to feel refreshingly bohemian. Montrose has also long been the base of a very visible **gay community**, and a high concentration of gay bars and clubs remain.

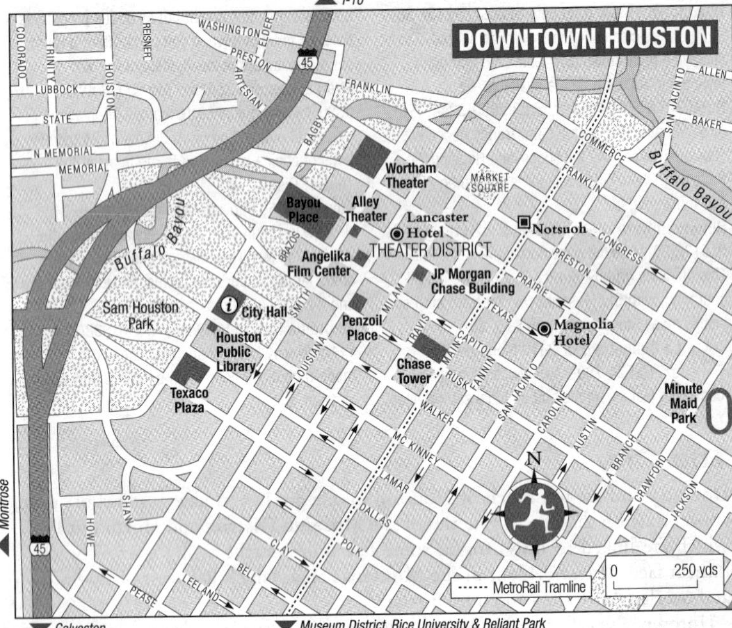

The district also extends south to pleasant **Hermann Park** and the appealing **Rice University** area, both accessible by the tram system. Just beyond **Mecom Fountain**, the park has a Japanese meditation garden and is a nice place to grab an ice cream and go for a stroll

The Menil galleries

At 1515 Sul Ross St, a magnificent purpose-built gallery, designed by Renzo Piano, houses the private **Menil Collection** (Wed–Sun 11am–7pm; free; ⓣ713/525-9400, ⓦwww.menil.org). Displayed in spacious, naturally lit white-walled rooms, the superb works range from Paleolithic carvings to Surrealist paintings. Artists with rooms to themselves include Picasso, Max Ernst and René Magritte. There's also a fine array of Alaskan Tlingit masks and an excellent bookstore, too.

A block east, the minimalist ecumenical **Rothko Chapel**, 3900 Yupon St (daily 10am–6pm; free; ⓦwww.rothkochapel.org), contains fourteen sombre paintings commissioned by the de Menils from Mark Rothko shortly before his death. The artist, who worked with architect Philip Johnson in designing the chapel, considered these to be his most important works and their power in this tranquil space is undeniable. The broken obelisk in the small park outside is dedicated to Dr Martin Luther King Jr. Check the website for talks and events hosted at the chapel, from Sufi dancing to meditations.

Diagonally opposite, the **Byzantine Fresco Chapel Museum**, 4011 Yupon St (Wed–Sun 11am–6pm; free), houses a pair of thirteenth-century Cypriot frescoes – the only intact Byzantine frescoes in the Western hemisphere – in a simple contemporary structure.

Houston Center for Photography

Within walking distance of the Byzantine Fresco Chapel Museum, at the corner of West Alabama and Mulberry, is the **Houston Center for Photography** (Wed &

Fri 11am–5pm, Thurs 11am–9pm, Sat & Sun noon–6pm; free; Ⓦwww.hcponline.org), which features work from emerging American photographers. Although it doesn't have its own collection, the small space exhibits some of the most striking visual art produced in the Southwest.

Museums of Fine Arts and Contemporary Arts

At the intersection of Bissonet and Main streets, the expansive **Museum of Fine Arts** (Tues & Wed 10am–5pm, Thurs 10am–9pm, Fri & Sat 10am–7pm, Sun 12.15–7pm; $7, free Thurs; Ⓦwww.mfah.org) features an eclectic collection from all eras, filling its impressive buildings with everything from Renaissance art to rare African gold, with a couple of wings entirely devoted to decorative arts. Crane your neck upward from the Matisses and Rodins in the pine-shaded **Cullen Sculpture Garden** outside for a view of the downtown skyline.

The **Contemporary Arts Museum**, across Main Street at 5216 Montrose Blvd (Tues, Wed, Fri & Sat 10am–5pm, Thurs 10am–9pm, Sun noon–5pm; free; Ⓦwww.camh.org), is housed in another of Houston's showpiece buildings: a low-slung windowless corrugated-steel parallelogram. It hosts strong temporary exhibitions, with artists sometimes on hand to answer questions.

Houston Museum of Natural Science

At Hermann Park's **Houston Museum of Natural Science** (Mon & Wed–Sun 9am–5pm, Tues 9am–8pm; $15; Ⓦwww.hmns.org), near the Sam Houston monument, most exhibitions are geared toward kids. But at the museum's **Wiess Energy Hall**, you can pour crude oil over a cluster of clear marbles to learn, for example, that Middle Eastern light crude is similar in viscosity to West Texas intermediate crude. You can also decide for yourself what technologies – such as solar, wind and geothermal – are most likely to ease the world's energy crunch. The museum's **Cockrell Butterfly Center** (daily 9am–5pm; $8) is a giant three-storey greenhouse where you can walk among exotic butterflies as they flutter around a muggy rainforest environment. In an automobile-age city built to such an inhuman scale, watching delicate butterflies dance about is a refreshing change of pace.

The Orange Show, Beer Can House and the Port of Houston

The Orange Show (Sat & Sun noon–5pm; $1; Ⓦwww.orangeshow.org), five miles east of Hermann Park at 2402 Munger St, just off I-45 at the Telephone Road exit, is a strange affair. A triumph of folk art, it's not really a show but a suburban house transformed into a paean to the orange by the monomaniacal former postal worker and would-be inventor Jeff McKissack. With one simple purpose – "to get more people to eat more oranges" – McKissack spent 24 years covering his home with celebratory tiles, ironwork and slogans.

Run by the same folks but located on the opposite side of town is the **Beer Can House**, 222 Malone (Sat & Sun noon–5pm; $2, guided tour $5). Retired Southern Pacific Railroad upholsterer John Milkovisch and his friends guzzled some 50,000 beers to help give his home its shiny aluminum siding.

The **Port of Houston**, 7300 Clinton Drive, offers free boat tours of the fourth-largest port in the US (Tues, Wed, Fri & Sat 10am & 2.30pm, Thurs & Sun 2.30pm; Ⓣ713/670-2416, Ⓦwww.portofhouston.com). The boat used in the tour, the M/V *Sam Houston*, was retrofitted in 2010 with a low-emission engine. The vessel also has an outside deck and air conditioning. Security is tight and reservations are essential.

Eating

Houston's mixed population has left its mark on its **cuisine**: look for Mexican and Vietnamese restaurants, as well as steak and BBQ joints that rival any in the state.

Breakfast Klub 3711 Travis St ⓣ713/528-8561. Obama campaign staffers favoured this busy breakfast spot when their office was located across the street. Serves unique dishes like wings and waffles, as well as more traditional morning fare.

Café Annie 1800 Post Oak Blvd ⓣ713/840-1111. If you've got the money, honey, head to the best restaurant in Houston, which plates innovative Southwestern cuisine.

Goode Company 5109 Kirby Rd ⓣ713/522-2530. Good BBQ, with big portions of sliced beef brisket and outdoor seating.

Haven 2502 Algerian Way ⓣ713/522-2530. Certified "green" with locally sourced entrees from about $20. Highly recommended – try the wood-grilled pork loin.

Mi Sombrero 3401 N Shepard ⓣ713/581-6101. An authentic mom-and-pop Tex-Mex joint a few miles north of downtown. It's good value, with dinner plates that start at about $5, and it's been around since 1978.

Pappas Bros. Steak House 5839 Westheimer Rd ⓣ713/780-7352. Leather booths, marble columns, mahogany panelling and brass trim set the stage for you to devour an in-house, dry-aged slab of beef.

Nightlife and entertainment

There's no shortage of things to do in Houston; just check the listings in the free *Houston Press* (ⓦwww.houstonpress.com). Downtown's much-trumpeted **Theater District** (ⓦwww.houstontheaterdistrict.org), a seventeen-block area west of Milam Street between Congress and Capitol streets, includes the **Alley Theatre** at 615 Texas Ave (ⓣ713/220-5700, ⓦwww.alleytheatre.org), which offers various discount seats, and the elaborate **Wortham Theater Center**, 501 Texas Ave (ⓣ713/237-1439, ⓦwww.worthamcenter.org), home to Houston's opera and ballet, among a host of others. The **Angelika Film Center**, 510 Texas Ave (ⓣ713/225-1470, ⓦwww.angelikafilmcenter.com), shows art movies and has a sister screen in New York City.

AvantGarden 411 Westheimer Rd ⓣ832/519-1429, ⓦwww.avantgardenhouston.com. Small, classy bar with a commitment to live music. Listen to local neo-folk bands like the Sideshow Tramps blow the roof off the joint or sit outside by the fountain constructed out of recycled Petron tequila bottles.

Catbird's 1336 Westheimer Rd ⓣ713/523-8000. Laidback creative types swill Lone Star Beer at this convivial bar with a pleasant patio.

Continental Club 3700 Main St ⓣ713/529-9899, ⓦwww.continentalclub.com. Cousin to the original in Austin, a classic live-music venue on the tram line.

Etta's 5120 Scott St ⓣ713/528-2611. Smokin' Sunday blues jams are the stuff of legend at this bar in a predominantly black neighbourhood.

Mugsy's 2239 Richmond Ave ⓣ713/522-7118. Friendly clientele, good bartenders and a pleasant patio.

Notsuoh 314 Main St ⓣ713/409-4750 Young artists and hipsters congregate at this funky downtown bar featuring live music, poetry readings and wi-fi. Look for the old neon sign outside that reads "The Home of EASY CREDIT"./

Space Center Houston

Space Center Houston (Mon–Fri 10am–5pm, Sat & Sun 10am–6pm; $18.95, parking $5; ⓦwww.spacecenter.org) lies 25 miles south of the city, off I-45 at 1601 NASA Parkway. NASA has been controlling space flight from the **Johnson Space Center** here since the launch of Gemini 4 in 1965 – locals love to point out that the first word spoken on the moon was "Houston". A working facility, the nerve centre of the International Space Station, it offers insight into modern space exploration, with tram tours giving behind-the-scenes glimpses into various NASA compounds. The crowds can be overwhelming, however, and with all the kids running around, it feels a bit like Disney World.

San Jacinto Battleground

San Jacinto Battleground (daily 9am–6pm), 22 miles east of Houston off the La Porte Freeway, was the site of an eighteen-minute battle in 1836, when the Texans all but wiped out the superbly trained Mexican army. The fight is commemorated by the tallest stone-column **monument** in the world (570ft, topped by a 34ft Lone Star). For $5, an elevator takes you to the top, which provides views of the battlefield.

Big Thicket National Preserve

The **Big Thicket National Preserve**, 40 miles from Houston on US Hwy-69/287, is a remarkable composite of natural elements from the south-western desert, central plains and Appalachian Mountains, with swamps and bayous to boot. The area once offered refuge for outlaws, runaway slaves and gamblers; now, it just hides a huge variety of **plant and animal life**, including deer, alligators, armadillos, possums, hogs and panthers, and nearly 200 species of birds. Wildflowers, orchids and towering trees share space with cacti and yucca.

Before entering the site, check in at the **visitor centre** (daily 9am–5pm; Ⓣ 409/951-6725, Ⓦ www.nps.gov/bith). There is hiking, canoeing and backcountry camping here.

The Gulf Coast

Look at the number of condo developments along the **Gulf Coast** and you will see that this is a major getaway destination. The climate ranges from balmy at **Galveston** to subtropical at the Mexican border. Devastating hurricanes in 1900 and again in 2008 all but levelled Galveston; recovery from the 2008 storm is ongoing, but the old, salty city still offers history, shopping and low-key relief from Houston. **Corpus Christi** makes the best base to explore the relatively unspoiled northern beaches of **Padre Island National Seashore**.

Galveston

In 1890, **GALVESTON** – on the northern tip of Galveston Island, the southern terminus of I-45 – was a thriving port, far larger than Houston 50 miles northwest; many newly arrived European immigrants chose to stay here in the so-called "Queen of the Gulf". However, the construction of Houston's Ship Canal, combined with the hurricane of 1900 that killed more than 6000 people (as told in Erik Larson's excellent book *Isaac's Storm*), left the coastal town to fade away. But thanks to its pretty historic district and its popularity with Houston residents seeking a summer escape, Galveston underwent a revitalization. Today, its pastel shotgun houses echo New Orleans, while its boozy bars and edgy beach bums bring to mind Jimmy Buffett songs about sailors and smugglers; once again locals have done an admirable job of cleaning up their town after 2008's Hurricane Ike swamped the seawall with a 20ft storm surge.

Arrival and information

Driving from Houston to Galveston is straightforward: once it crosses over to the island, I-45 becomes Broadway, the town's main drag. **Greyhound** arrives at 714 25th St (a $6 taxi ride from downtown). There is no Amtrak service. The main **visitor centre** is at 2328 Broadway (summer: daily 9am–5pm; winter: daily 10am–5pm; ⓣ409-797-5000, ⓦwww.galveston.com). **Trolley** service was suspended after Hurricane Ike.

Accommodation

Hotels in Galveston are pricey in summer and on weekends, but bargains can be found at other times; rates along the coastal strip, Seawall Boulevard, can drop below $50 per night. Within easy walking distance of the Strand, the town's East End historic district has relaxing and luxurious **B&Bs**.

Gaido's Seaside Inn 3828 Seawall Blvd ⓣ409/762-9625, ⓦwww.gaidosofgalveston.com. A clean, friendly, no-frills choice, with two decent fish restaurants attached. ❸

Galveston Island State Park 14901 F.M. 3005 ⓣ409/737-1222, ⓦwww.tpwd.state.tx.us. Six miles from downtown, with only 11 campsites after the hurricane washed away dozens of others. From $20.

Hotel Galvez 2024 Seawall Blvd ⓣ409/765-7721, ⓦwww.galveston.com/galvez. Classy hotel, built in 1911, with a beautiful pool and a grand lobby. ❻

The City

Downtown, the historic **Strand** has been fitted with gaslights, upmarket shops, restaurants and galleries. There are museums, too: the **Texas Seaport Museum**, for instance, in a complex of shops and restaurants on Pier 21, just off Water Street (daily 10am–5pm; $8), focuses on the port's role in trade and immigration during the nineteenth century; admission includes boarding the *Elissa*, an 1877 tall ship.

Between the Strand and the beaches to the south, Galveston boasts a profusion of historic homes open for guided tours. A standout in this architectural nirvana is the ostentatious stone masterpiece **Bishop's Palace**, 1402 Broadway (summer Mon–Sat 11am–4pm, Sun noon–4pm; $10), with its stained glass, mosaics and marble.

With 40,000 trees mortally wounded by Ike's salty storm surge, regional artists have been commissioned to turn the stumps into **sculpture**. As of the middle of 2010, 20 have been completed (a Dalmatian and a geisha were two of the first), but the project has proved popular in a town that appreciates art and nature, and has a good sense of humour.

The downtown **beaches** of Seawall Boulevard are a bit rocky. They are hemmed in by a ten-mile-long seawall, which was constructed 100 years ago to protect Galveston from hurricanes. Slowly pedalling a **beach cruiser bike** along the seawall at sunset is a classic Galveston experience. Contact Island Bicycle Company, 1808 Seawall Blvd, for rentals (ⓣ409/762-2453; $8/hr, $25/day). A few miles from downtown, **Jamaica Beach** is relatively quiet and a locals' favourite.

Touristy **Moody Gardens**, Galveston's biggest attraction – for families, at least – lies on the west side of town, at I-45 off the 61st Street exit. The complex (daily 10am–6pm; day pass $50) centres on three giant glass pyramids, and has an IMAX theatre and an aquarium.

Eating and drinking

Dining out in Galveston will mean either settling in at one of the many low-key seafood restaurants along Seawall Boulevard or strolling the Strand for a more upscale option. As Galveston likes to party, there are several **nightlife** options as well.

MOD 2126 Postoffice St ⓣ409/765-5659. Hipster downtown coffeeshop with free wi-fi. Friendly staff.

Mosquito Cafe 628 14th St ⓣ409/763-1010. A local favourite, this tasty breakfast and lunch joint serves good salads and iced teas.

Old Quarter Acoustic Café 413 20th St ⓣ409/762-9199, ⓦwww.oldquarteracousticcafe.com. A great venue for folk, alt-country and blues; the late Texas singer-songwriter Townes Van Zandt wrote *Rex's Blues* about the café's owner, musician Rex Bell.

Poop Deck 2928 Seawall Blvd ⓣ409/763-9151. Great bar, shitty name. Sunsets are the specialty at this dive named after the nautical term for the roof atop the aft cabin.

The Spot 3204 Seawall Blvd ⓣ409/621-5237. Lively bar and a nice family restaurant. A grilled Gulf shrimp dinner plate costs $14.

Corpus Christi

Laidback **CORPUS CHRISTI** is reached along the coast on the two-lane Hwy-35 from Houston or Galveston, or on I-37 from San Antonio. Originally a rambunctious trading post, it too was hit by a fierce hurricane, in 1919, but recovered, transforming itself into a centre for naval air training, petroleum and shipping.

Much of the population is Hispanic, and the community was devastated in 1995, when 23-year-old singer **Selena** was shot dead in a downtown *Days Inn* car park by the former president of her fan club. Selena was on the verge of becoming the first major crossover star of **Tejano** music, and 50,000 fans attended her funeral. The bizarre **Selena Museum** (Mon–Fri 10am–4pm; $2), 5410 Leopard St, is stuffed with Selena memorabilia, from her extravagant gowns to her red Porsche.

Corpus Christi is an outdoor destination, but apart from fishing, sailing, birding and watersports (mostly located across the channel on Padre Island), there are a few worthy cultural diversions. The impressive collection of the **Art Museum of South Texas**, 1902 N Shoreline Blvd (Tues–Sat 10am–5pm, Sun 1–5pm; $6; ⓦwww.stia.org), focuses on fine arts and crafts of the Americas. The bleach-white, Philip Johnson-designed building, renovated in 2005, is stunning, with bright windows that give close-up views of freighters navigating Corpus Christi Bay; look for dolphins riding the bow wake. The museum also has an excellent small lunch spot called the *Dobson Café*.

Nearby at 1581 N Chaparral is tranquil **Heritage Park** (Tues–Thurs 9am–5pm, Fri 9am–2pm, Sat 11am–2pm; free), a collection of twelve Victorian homes and gardens, which makes a nice place to sit and read a book.

Practicalities

There is a greyhound dog-racing track in Corpus, but don't get that confused with the Greyhound **bus station**, which is downtown at 702 N Chaparral St. The international **airport** is located about ten miles west of the city's centre.

The **visitor centre** is at 1823 N Chaparral (Tues–Sat 9am–5pm; ⓣ1-800/766-BEACH, ⓦwww.corpuschristi-tx-cvb.org). A daytime **trolley** (daily except Sun; 25¢; ⓣ361/289-2600, ⓦwww.ccrta.org) connects the major attractions with area hotels. Other services include a **ferry** from Peoples Street to Corpus Christi Beach ($3 for a daily pass) and a good **metro bus** system.

Motels line kitschy Corpus Christi Beach across the Hwy-181 bridge. Downtown at 601 N Shoreline Blvd, the *Bayfront Inn* (ⓣ1-800/456-2293, ⓦwww.bayfrontinncc.com; ❸) has decent rooms and a good location.

Corpus's main concentration of **restaurants** is downtown on Water Street, and at no. 309 the busy *Water Street Oyster Bar* (ⓣ361/881-9448) serves fresh seafood. But the best place to eat is a few miles away at *The Yardarm*, a bayfront restaurant located in a cute yellow house at 4310 Ocean Drive (ⓣ361/855-8157).

Two worthy downtown **bars** are the *Executive Surf Club*, 309 N Water St, and the *House of Rock*, 511 Starr St, both of which have packed live-music calendars.

Padre Island National Seashore

Operated by the National Park Service, **Padre Island National Seashore** is not as unspoiled as its name suggests, with ranks of condos advancing steadily up the coast and a surprising amount of vehicular traffic on the beach itself. But it remains a good destination for kiteboarding, birdwatching, fishing, windsurfing and camping.

Pick up details at the **visitor centre**, 20420 Park Rd 22 (daily, 9am–5pm; Ⓣ361/949-8068, Ⓦwww.nps.gov/pais). The park is open 24 hours, with a $10 admission charge per vehicle, $5 for pedestrians and cyclists, good for one week. Camping on the beach is free, but permits cost $5 for the primitive *Bird Island Basin* and $8 for the semi-primitive *Malaquite Campground*.

Note that an impassable channel divides the island, meaning that the pricier and much more touristy **South Padre Island** in the south can only be reached from the mainland – it's a three-hour drive from Corpus Christi.

Port Isabel and South Padre Island

The graceful Queen Isabella Causeway, northeast of Brownsville, connects **PORT ISABEL**, home to one of the biggest commercial fishing fleets in Texas, to **SOUTH PADRE ISLAND**, one of the rowdiest Spring Break destinations in the US. As you might expect, much of the island's activities don't extend beyond getting in the water, soaking up the sun's rays and drinking a **beer** or three. If you want to exercise your mind instead of your liver, you can glean local knowledge from the friendly owners of the **Beachcomber's Museum**, 104 W Pompano St (Ⓣ956/761-5231), which is also a bookstore and coffeeshop rolled into one. Ask Kay Lay to tell you about sea beans that wash ashore after drifting north from South American forests.

Though most visitors to the area head straight for the island, you can **stay** in Port Isabel at the elegant *Port Isabel Yacht Club and Hotel*, 700 N Yturria (Ⓣ956/943-1301 Ⓦwww.portisabelyachtclub.com; ❸). On SPI, a good option is the beachfront *Wanna Wanna*, 5100 Gulf Blvd (Ⓣ956/761-7677, Ⓦwww.wannawanna.com; ❻), which also has a friendly bar popular with locals. A more sedate choice is the *South Beach Inn* at 120 E Jupiter (Ⓣ956/761-2471, Ⓦwww.southbeachtexas.com; ❹), which is a few blocks from the beach and has a pool.

Watch the sun set and eat dinner at the secluded *Palm Street Pier* restaurant, at 204 W Palm. Popular with locals, the **restaurant** has west-facing sunset views of the Laguna Madre and serves $10 fresh shrimp dinners (Ⓣ956/772-PALM, Ⓦwww.palmstreetpier.com). After dinner, old salts and bikers belly up to the *Coral Reef Lounge*, 5401 Padre Blvd, to grunt, drink beer and tip the pretty barmaid.

South Texas

At the very southern tip of Texas, near where the Rio Grande flows into the gulf, this is **border country**, where Texan and Mexican cultures swirl together to form one of the most unique cultural regions anywhere in the US. The population here is about ninety-percent **Latino**. Everything from the food to the hip-hop music reflects this inescapable Mexican influence.

Aside from a few manufacturing towns and cities, including **Laredo**, **Brownsville** and **Harlingen**, much of the region is agricultural. Between the population centres is an area called the **Rio Grande Valley** – actually a delta prone to flooding, the 180-mile-long valley is rural, historic country. This is as exotic as Texas gets; few tourists visit the sparsely populated region, and side-trips to small Mexican villages that have so far escaped rampant drug violence are also possible. Tiny downtowns that have barely been touched in 200 years are sprinkled along two-lane Hwy-83, which makes an excellent **driving** or **cycling tour**.

Laredo

LAREDO, population 200,000, is situated at the southern terminus of I-35 (the northern terminus is 1600 miles to the north in Duluth, MN). A busy bridge connects the US to Mexico at the bottom of Convent Avenue, where a major Border Patrol presence exists. As battles between Mexican **drug cartels** have escalated in recent years, Laredo and its sister city across the border have garnered a violent reputation – most of the real risk is in Mexico though.

The focus of Laredo's main square is the pretty St Augustin Cathedral containing a modernist mural of the Crucifixion; there's a pleasant stone grotto outside. Also on the main square is the historic and sprawling three-star *La Posada Hotel*, at 1000 Zaragoza St (Ⓣ956/722-1701, Ⓦwww.laposadahotel.com; ❺), with a lobby bar favoured by martini-drinking businessmen (drug kingpins?) conducting cross-border deals, and two courtyard pools. The young Texas musician Ryan Bingham, who in 2010 won an Oscar for *Crazy Heart*, references the hotel in his song *Bread and Water*. *El Mason*, nearby at 908 Grant St – you have to look hard to find the door – serves the best Mexican food in the state, with a daily menu and $5 meals.

The Rio Grande Valley

Heading southeast from Laredo down US Hwy-83 (called the **Zapata Highway**) travellers pass through the Rio Grande Valley, a rarely visited subtropical slice of South Texas. **San Ygnacio** is a sleepy and friendly hamlet where yapping chihuahuas roam dusty streets. The tiny town was once part of the insurgent Republic of the Rio Grande, and its rich history is a reminder of the fiercely independent streak that contributes to the complexity of this region.

Roma, 55 miles down the highway, has a strong architectural heritage. Its nine-square-block downtown is home to several structures built in the 1800s; some date to Spanish rule in the 1750s. A birdwatching platform constructed on sandstone cliffs near downtown looks across the Rio Grande toward Mexico; try to spot with your field glasses one of 500 species like the groove-billed ani. You can also hear Mexican children playing across the muddy river, which until sixty years ago was plied by steamboats.

Rio Grande City, down the highway another 20 miles, has several motels and the *La Borde House* (Ⓣ956/487-5101; ❸), a nonprofit historic hotel at 601 E Main St. It has clean, comfortable rooms decorated with period furniture and the restaurant *Che's*, which serves breakfast beneath a mural depicting local scenes. Run by the same family for 70 years, *Caro's*, 607 W 2nd St (Ⓣ956/487-2255), dishes up excellent Mexican food.

Further southeast along the highway toward the Gulf of Mexico is a booming **urban region**. With a population of 180,000, **Brownsville** is the biggest city, though smaller **Harlingen**, 25 miles to the northwest, is the most pleasant to visit. Its downtown is walkable and active, with several art galleries, coffeeshops and cafés. The *Rio Grande Grill*, 417 W Van Buren, is a popular local diner, and Chopp Shopp Records, 103 W Jackson St, has a good selection of CDs from local hip-hop artists like Nino.

Central Texas

Central Texas stretches from the prairies of the northeast, through the green and fertile Hill Country, and into the chalky limestone landscape of the west. It includes two of Texas' most pleasant cities: the music-oriented state capital of **Austin**, and eighty miles to the south, Hispanic-flavoured **San Antonio**.

Across much of the landscape, agriculture has been the economic mainstay ever since the resistant Comanche were packed off to reservations in the 1840s. The slave-driven cotton plantations of the south and east are gone, but small communities set up by Polish, Czech, Norwegian, German and Swedish immigrants in the **Hill Country** maintained, even until very recently, the traditions, architecture and languages of their homelands.

Austin

AUSTIN was a tiny community on the verdant banks of the (Texas) Colorado River when Mirabeau B. Lamar, president of the Republic of Texas, suggested in 1839 that it would make a better capital than swampy and disease-ridden Houston. Early building had to be done under armed guard, while angry Comanche watched from the surrounding hills. Despite this perilous location, Austin thrived.

Today the city wears its state capital status lightly. Since the 1960s, the laidback and progressive city – an anomaly in Texas – has been a haven for artists, musicians and writers, and many visitors come specifically for the **music**. And while complacency has crept in, its "alternative" edge being packaged as just another marketing tool, artists hungry for recognition are still attracted to this creative hotbed.

Local musicians are renowned for their innovative reworkings of Texas' country, folk, Tejano and R&B heritage. They use Austin's enthusiastic environment as a springboard to national fame – Spoon and White Denim are recent examples.

Due to a tech-fuelled population leap, brand-new towering condo complexes have shot up to threaten Austin's small-town vibe. Still, it remains the best city in the state for **cycling** (Lance Armstrong lives here), and the presence of the vast and pretty University of Texas campus adds to the pleasant atmosphere. Within the city limits a great park system offers numerous hiking and biking trails, plus a wonderful spring-fed swimming pool. Looking further afield, Austin makes a fine base for exploring the green **Hill Country** that rolls away to the west.

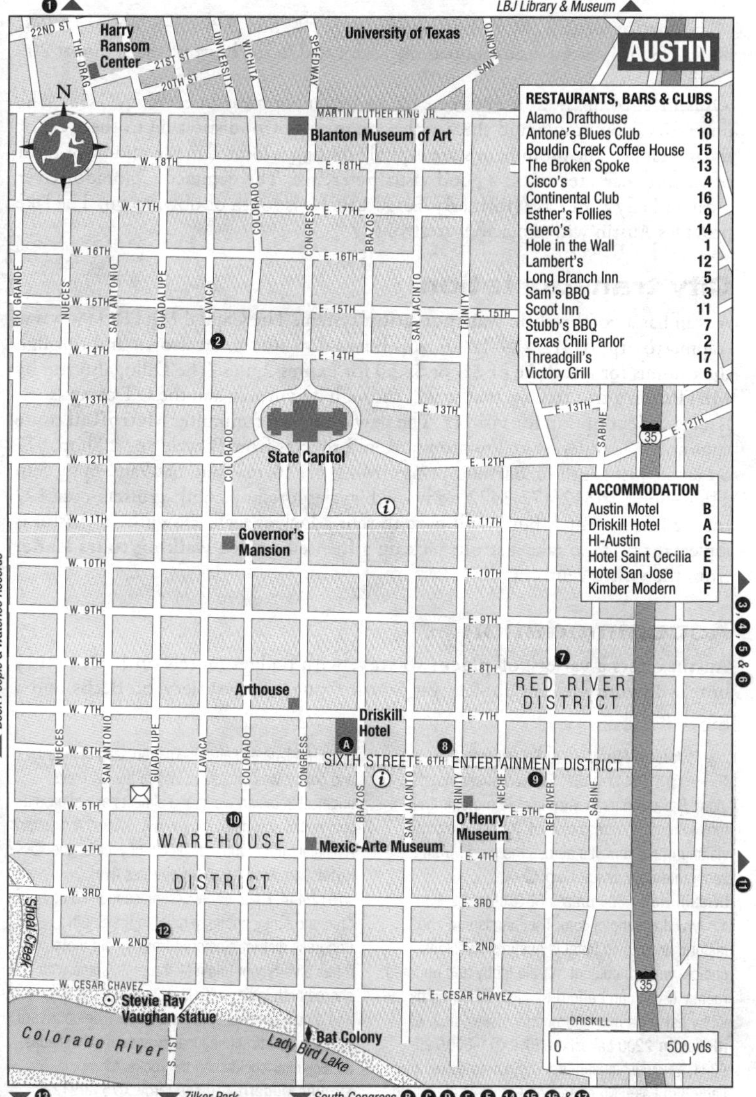

Arrival, information and orientation

Flights arrive at the **Austin-Bergstrom International Airport** (Ⓣ512/530-2242, Ⓦwww.ci.austin.tx.us/austinairport), eight miles southeast of downtown. From here it's about twenty minutes to downtown by **taxi** (Yellow Cab; around $28 Ⓣ512/452-9999) or by SuperShuttle **van**; $12 (Ⓣ512/258-3826, Ⓦwww.supershuttle.com). **Bus** #100 runs every twenty minutes (except late at night and early in the morning) from the airport to downtown. **Car rentals** are available at the airport.

The **visitor centre** (Mon–Fri 9am–5pm, Sat & Sun 9.30am–5.30pm; ⓣ866/GO-AUSTIN, ⓦwww.austintexas.org) is located in the heart of the action at 209 E 6th St.

Austin encompasses an eighteen by twenty mile area, bisected by I-35. The university, downtown and the South Congress (SoCo) district lie to the west of the interstate. The prominent state capital building is located in the middle of most of the popular sites and is a good visual reference. The dammed Colorado River – called Lady Bird Lake (formerly Town Lake) – is south of downtown. The lake provides Austin with a placid waterfront.

City transportation

Austin has a good **public transportation** system. The Capital METRO (ⓦwww.capmetro.org, ⓣ512/474-1200) runs **buses** downtown, crosstown and through the campus for a flat fare of $1, or $2.50 for express buses. The Dillo, also run by METRO, is a free **trolley** that snakes through downtown and the UT campus – it is an excellent option for visitors. The newly opened commuter **MetroRail** route runs north 32 miles from downtown. Rent **bicycles** from Bicycle Sport Shop, 517 S Lamar, just south of Barton Springs (Mon–Fri 10am–7pm, Sat 9am–6pm, Sun 11am–5pm; ⓣ512/477-3472, ⓦwww.bicyclesportshop.com); cruisers cost $22 for a 24-hour rental, but you'll have to rent a lock as well. Downtown Austin is a pleasant place to take a stroll; pick up a free self-guided **walking tours leaflet** from the visitor centre.

Accommodation

Austin offers a variety of **places to stay**, with budget motels on I-35, luxury hotels downtown, hip choices on South Congress, a variety of B&Bs and a good hostel.

Austin Motel 1220 S Congress Ave ⓣ512/441-1157, ⓦwww.austinmotel.com. Basic rooms in a trendy old motel in the funky South Congress district. A favourite with visiting musicians, it's across the street from the venerable *Continental Club*. ❸

Driskill Hotel 604 Brazos St ⓣ800/252-9367, ⓦwww.driskillhotel.com. This handsome and historic downtown hotel is Austin's swankiest choice, with an opulent marble lobby and updated rooms. If you can't afford to stay here, drop by the lobby bar for a mid-afternoon whiskey sour. ❽

HI-Austin 2200 Lakeshore Blvd ⓣ1-800/725-2331, ⓦwww.hiaustin.org. Bargain rates right on Lady Bird Lake. No curfew and most of the young guests head out to 6th St at night. Dorm beds start at $25. ❶

Hotel Saint Cecilia 112 Academy Drive ⓣ512/852-2400, ⓦwww.hotelsaintcecilia.com. This swanky SoCo hotel, named after the patron saint of music and poetry, was created to inspire the best and brightest in the art world. You almost have to pass a cool test to stay here: Are you a rock star? A director? A painter? If not, you may be out of your league. ❽

Hotel San Jose 1316 S Congress Ave ⓣ512/444-7322, ⓦwww.sanjosehotel.com. Chic and funky boutique hotel in the South Congress district. Restored from an old motel, it has a variety of minimalist rooms, some with shared bath, along with lovely gardens, a tiny pool and a cool coffeeshop, *Jo's*, on site. The courtyard happy hour attracts a local crowd for Micheladas, a spicy beer cocktail on the rocks. ❺

Kimber Modern 110 The Circle ⓣ512/912-1046, ⓦwww.kimbermodern.com. A stunning addition to an already thriving South Congress boutique hotel scene. A modern, architecturally significant structure. ❽

The City

The **Texas State Capitol**, at 12th Street and Congress Avenue (Mon–Fri 7am–10pm, Sat & Sun 9am–8pm, free guided tours also available, call ⓣ512/305-8400 for schedule), is over 300ft high, taller than the Capitol in Washington, with a sunset-red granite dome that accents the downtown skyline. The chandeliers, carpets, and even the door hinges of this colossal building are emblazoned with Lone Stars and other Texas motifs.

Congress Avenue, an attractive, walkable stretch of shops and office buildings that slopes south from the Capitol down to the lake, is the heart of downtown. At 700 Congress is the **Arthouse** (Ⓦwww.arthousetexas.org), an excellent space to explore trends in modern art. Temporarily closed for renovations, it's scheduled to reopen in autumn 2010.

Sixth Street crosses Congress one block south of here, and at night it is crowded with bar-hopping party people. If you're touring downtown during the day, cool off in the elegant lobby of the *Driskill Hotel*, at Sixth and Brazos, or visit the tiny **O. Henry Museum**, 409 East Fifth St (Wed–Sun noon–5pm; free; Ⓦwww.ci.austin.tx.us/ohenry), a period home dedicated to one of the literary lions of Texas, William Sydney Porter (note the rosewood piano with mother-of-pearl inlay). West of downtown but within walking distance at the intersection of N Lamar Boulevard and Sixth Street, are **Waterloo Records** and **Book People**, the best music store and bookstore in town. The flagship Whole Foods grocery store is also at this intersection.

Back on Congress at the 400 block, the **Mexic-Arte Museum** has a collection of traditional and contemporary Latin American art (Mon–Thurs 10am–6pm, Fri & Sat 10am–5pm, Sun noon–5pm; $5; Ⓦwww.mexic-artemuseum.org).

If you're visiting between March and November, take a walk at dusk down to where Congress Avenue crosses Lady Bird Lake to watch 1.5 million **Mexican free-tailed bats** – the world's largest urban bat colony – emerge in an amorphous black cloud from their hangout under the bridge. You can smell the guano and the best views are from the tour boats.

Across the bridge, **South Congress** is a hip neighbourhood of funky stores, bars and restaurants. It's easy to whittle away an afternoon or evening in this section of town. Be sure to visit Uncommon Objects for unusual antiques, Allen's Boots for top-end Western wear and Friends of Sound for vintage vinyl. Several trailers parked streetside sell home-made snacks like cupcakes to keep you fuelled; check out Ⓦwww.austinfoodcarts.com for a list.

Southwest of here, 350-acre **Zilker Park** is the best of the city's many fine green spaces, a perfect retreat on sultry Austin afternoons. One of its main attractions is the spring-fed (and deliciously cool) **Barton Springs Pool** (daily 5am–10pm; $3). Another appealing outdoor space, south of the Barton Springs Pool on Robert E. Lee Road, the **Umlauf Sculpture Garden** (Wed–Fri 10am–4.30pm, Sat & Sun 1–4.30pm; $3.50; Ⓦwww.umlaufsculpture.org) is a tranquil, grassy enclave dotted with over 100 works in bronze, terracotta, wood and marble.

The University of Texas

The **University of Texas** – and its fiercely supported Longhorn football team, which plays on autumn Saturdays at 94,000-seat Darrell K. Royal-Texas Memorial Stadium – has a tangible, almost defining, presence in Austin. You'll find most student activity in the inexpensive restaurants, vintage clothing shops and bookstores on the "Drag", the stretch of **Guadalupe Street** that runs along campus north from Martin Luther King Boulevard to 24th.

The campus itself has a number of attractions. Oil has made this one of the world's richest universities and its purchasing power is almost unmatched when it comes to rare and valuable books. The university's collection of manuscripts is available to scholars amid tight security in the **Harry Ransom Center**, in the southwest corner of campus, which houses a gallery (Tues, Wed & Fri 10am–5pm, Thurs 10am–7pm, Sat & Sun noon–5pm; free; Ⓦwww.hrc.utexas.edu) whose permanent collection includes a **Gutenberg Bible** and the **world's first photograph**. A quiet and beautiful place on campus to sit and read a book is **Battle Hall**, which houses UT's architecture library; note the stencilled open-truss ceiling. The best views in Austin are at sunset from the top of the **Texas Tower**, near the corner of 24th and Guadalupe (weekends and evenings only, depending on sunset times; $5 ⓣ1-877/475-6633, ⓦwww.utexas.edu/tower; reservations required).

The **LBJ Library and Museum** (daily 9am–5pm; free; ⓦwww.lbjlibrary.org), on the northeast edge of campus at 2313 Red River St, traces the career of the brash and egotistical Lyndon Baines Johnson from his origins in the Hill Country to the House of Representatives, the Senate and the White House. Forty-five million documents are housed here and it's worth a visit. JFK is said to have made Johnson his vice president to avoid his establishing a rival power base; but in the aftermath of Kennedy's assassination, Johnson's administration (1963–69) was able to push through a radical social programme; indeed, Barack Obama's 2010 healthcare bill was hailed as the most meaningful domestic legislation since the civil rights advancements of the LBJ era. Johnson's nemesis, Vietnam, is presented here as an awful mess left by Kennedy for him to clear up, at the cost of great personal anguish.

Eating

Austin has some of the best **restaurants** in the state and many have a focus on local ingredients. The greatest concentration is on **South Congress** and there are some good spots **downtown**. Budget restaurants popular with students are scattered along the **Drag**.

Bouldin Creek Coffee House 1501 S 1st ⓣ512/416-1601. Breakfast made from scratch is served all day at this spot not far from South Congress. It has reasonable prices (a free-range, three-egg omelet with two sides costs $7) and friendly staff.

Cisco's 1511 E 6th ⓣ512/478-2420. This second-generation Mexican family restaurant is open for breakfast and lunch. Order the *migas* (scrambled eggs and corn tortillas; $7) to chase away your hangover.

Guero's 1412 S Congress Ave ⓣ512/447-7688. *Tacos al pastor* are a specialty (about $9) at this busy, sprawling restaurant located across the bridge, south of downtown.

Lambert's 401 W 2nd St ⓣ512/494-1500. Exercise your taste buds at this self-described "fancy barbeque" restaurant that puts a modern twist on the old Texas staple. Produce and meats are sourced from local farms and ranches.

Magnolia Café 1920 S Congress Ave ⓣ512/445-0000. A 24hr joint that's a local favourite for Tex-Mex and pancake breakfasts. A great place to refuel after a night living it up on South Congress.

Sam's BBQ 2000 E 12th ⓣ512/478-0378. Austin residents may warn you about the neighbourhood, but don't be timid when food like this is on the line – heaping portions of tender beef brisket and big glasses of sweet tea for $8.50.

Texas Chili Parlor 1409 Lavaca St ⓣ512/472-2828. Rub elbows with politicians and their staffers at this venerable lunch spot downtown near the State Capitol.

Threadgill's 6416 N Lamar Blvd ⓣ512/451-5440, ⓦwww.threadgills.com. An Austin institution, north of downtown, established when Kenneth Threadgill was given the first licence to sell beer in the city after Prohibition. Bringing together hippies and rednecks in the 1960s, *Threadgill's* was an incubator for the Austin sound and still features live bands, as well as basic Southern cuisine.

Nightlife and entertainment

Austin's **live music scene** is legendary. Though the clubs and bars of Sixth Street are touristy and jammed with drunken 20-somethings, there are plenty of good places elsewhere downtown, and it's easy enough to hop in a cab to some of the further-flung classic joints. Two newspapers carry listings: the daily *Austin American-Statesman* (ⓦwww.austin360.com) and the alt-weekly *Austin Chronicle* (ⓦwww.austinchronicle.com). Also, the website ⓦwww.billsmap.com pegs

The Austin sound

Although Austin's folk revival in the 1960s attracted enough attention to propel Janis Joplin on her way from Port Arthur, Texas, to stardom in California, the city first achieved prominence in its own right as the centre of **outlaw country** music in the 1970s. **Willie Nelson** and **Waylon Jennings**, disillusioned with Nashville, spearheaded a movement that reworked country and western with an incisive injection of rock'n'roll. Venues like the now-closed *Armadillo World Headquarters*, far removed from the more conservative honky-tonks of the Plains, provided an environment that encouraged and rewarded risk-taking, experimentation and lots of sonic cross-breeding. These days the predominant **Austin sound** is a melange of country, folk and the blues, with strong psychedelic and alternative influences – but the scene is entirely eclectic. The tradition of black Texas bluesmen like Blind Lemon Jefferson and Blind Willie Johnson, as well as the rocking bar blues of Stevie Ray Vaughan, still lives on, with a top-notch **blues** club in the form of *Antone's*.

the venue of each night's shows on an endlessly helpful interactive map. Other nightlife options include excellent **cinema** and **performing arts**.

Live music

Austin's ten-day **SXSW festival** (South by Southwest; ⓦ www.sxsw.com), held in mid-March, has become the pre-eminent music and film conference in the nation. Attending a showcase of the best bands from Texas and around the world, along with tons of movies, is not cheap: passes for all film, music and interactive events cost $850 in advance, increasing to $1200 for a walk-up rate; a music-only pass is $550 ($650 walk-up). Even if you can't afford to attend, the city is an exciting place to be during SXSW, with hundreds of unofficial gigs and events open to all.

Another major event, showcasing folk, bluegrass, acoustic, blues, country, jazz and Americana, is the **Kerrville Folk Festival** (ⓦ www.kerrville-music.com), which lasts nearly three weeks in May and June. It's held on a ranch 100 miles west of Austin in the small town of Kerrville. Here you can camp and listen to live music under the stars.

Antone's Blues Club 213 W 5th St ⓣ 512/320-8424, ⓦ www.antones.net. This old Austin joint is the best blues club in the city, a hot and sweaty haunt showcasing national and local acts. The club helped launch the Fabulous Thunderbirds to fame.

The Broken Spoke 3201 S Lamar Blvd ⓣ 512/442-6189, ⓦ www.brokenspokeaustintx.com. Neighbourhood restaurant (good chicken-fried steak) and foot-stomping honky-tonk dance hall in South Austin. The barn-like dancefloor attracts great country acts; it's a lot of fun.

Continental Club 1315 S Congress Ave ⓣ 512/441-2444, ⓦ www.continentalclub.com. This long-standing classic is the city's premier place to hear hard-edged country or bluesy folk sung the Austin way.

Stubb's Bar-B-Q 801 Red River St ⓣ 512/480-8341, ⓦ www.stubbsaustin.com. Indoor and outdoor stages feature eclectic bands of national repute – including a Sunday gospel brunch – which you can watch while chomping on great Texas-style brisket, sausage and ribs.

Victory Grill 1104 E 11th St ⓣ 512/902-505, ⓦ historicvictorygrill.org. Ike and Tina Turner played here and a Brooklyn artists' collective spray-painted a soulful mural on its main outside wall in 2008. The old building, noted for its heavy blues history, hangs on despite nearby condo development, but its future seems uncertain. BYOB.

Bars

Like some of the restaurants listed, many of Austin's **bars** double as music venues.

Hole in the Wall 2538 Guadalupe St ⓣ 512/477-4747. A dive near the UT campus with pool tables and live Americana music.

Horseshoe Lounge 2034 S Lamar Blvd ⓣ 512/442-9111. This beer joint is a survivor from a not-too-distant, rough-and-tumble

South Austin past. Look for the red and green neon lights.

Long Branch Inn 1133 E 11th St ⓣ512/472-5591. This dark, artsy dive has a small stage, a nice old wooden bar, and slow-turning ceiling fans. It's located smack dab in the middle of a quickly gentrifying neighbourhood.

Scoot Inn 1308 E 4th St ⓣ512/524-1932. Owned by the same folks who run the *Long Branch Inn*, the *Scoot Inn* attracts a similar but slightly younger crowd and has a nice outdoor beer garden.

Other nightlife

The highly recommended **Alamo Drafthouse** (ⓣ512/476-1230, ⓦwww.drafthouse.com) has several locations, including one in the heart of Sixth Street, and offers perhaps the best cinematic experience in the US. The movie theatres feature everything from award-winning documentaries to air guitar competitions – pints of local beer and made-to-order food are served right at your comfy seat. There's usually something to catch on campus, too. Try the **UT Performing Arts Center**, 23rd Street and Robert Dedman Drive (ⓦwww.utpac.org). The **Cactus Café** (ⓦwww.utexas.edu), a bar and folk-oriented live music venue in the student union building, was scheduled to close by 2011 because of budget cuts. But the announcement shocked – and mobilized – Austin's music community, and it's worth checking to see if preservation efforts have saved this classic spot. *Esther's Follies*, 525 E 6th St (ⓦwww.esthersfollies.com) is Austin's hippest **cabaret**, which combines spoofs of local and national politicians with Texas-style singing and dancing.

The Hill Country

The rolling hills, lakes and valleys of the **HILL COUNTRY**, north and west of Austin and San Antonio, were inhabited mostly by Apache and Comanche until after statehood in 1845, when German and Scandinavian settlers arrived. Many of the log-cabin farming communities they established are still here, such as **New Braunfels** (famous for its sausages and pastries, and, more recently, its watersports), **Fredericksburg** and Luckenbach. You may still hear German spoken, and the German influence is also felt in local food and music; *conjunto*, for example, is a blend of Tex-Mex and accordion music. The whole region is a popular retreat and resort area, with some wonderful hill views and lake swimming, and some good places to camp. History buffs will gravitate towards various sites related to the childhood of former US president **Lyndon B. Johnson**.

New Braunfels

NEW BRAUNFELS, just 30 miles north of San Antonio on I-35, was founded by German immigrants – mostly artisans and artists – in 1845 and quickly became a trade centre. Nowadays, the community, along with its equally historic satellite, **Gruene**, just northeast, makes its living from tourism. The town's two rivers – the Comal and the Guadalupe – are ideal for easy **rafting and tubing**, making this a popular weekend destination.

If outdoor activities don't appeal, downtown's historic district has enough antique stores, galleries and restored buildings to fill a couple of hours. New Braunfels' **visitor centre**, exit 187 off I-35 (Mon–Fri 8am–5pm; 1-800/572-2626, ⓦwww.nbjumpin.com), provides a list of accommodations, as well as information on renting rafts and tubes. Should you need a **bed**, the *Heidelberg Lodges* (ⓣ830/625-9967, ⓦwww.heidelberglodges.com; ❹), 1020 N Houston St, are rustic, and their riverfront location makes them a bargain. For **food**, head for

Huisache Grill, 303 W San Antonio St (Ⓣ830/620-9001), for sophisticated, reasonably priced contemporary cuisine, or *Pat's Place*, at 202 South Union, for cheese enchiladas in a more casual setting.

There's good, though touristy, nightlife at the atmospheric clapboard **Gruene Hall**, 1281 Gruene Rd (Ⓣ830/606-1281, Ⓦwww.gruenehall.com), where you can see top country stars perform.

Fredericksburg

On weekends in **FREDERICKSBURG**, crowds of well-heeled day-trippers from San Antonio and Austin throng Main Street's cutesy specialty stores and fancy tearooms. Several original structures make up the **Pioneer Museum** at 325 W Main St, including a church and a store (Mon–Sat 10am–5pm, Sun noon–4pm; $5). A little more incongruous, the **National Museum of the Pacific War**, 340 E Main St (daily 9am–5pm; $12), features a Japanese garden of peace and lays out a historical trail past aircraft, tanks and heavy artillery. Question: why is a World War II museum that commemorates far-off ocean battles located in landlocked Fredericksburg? Answer: the admiral who commanded the US Navy's Pacific fleet was born in the Hill Country.

Practicalities

The **CVB information centre**, one block off Main Street at 302 East Austin St (Mon–Fri 8.30am–5pm, Sat 9am–5pm, Sun noon–4pm; Ⓣ830/997-6523, Ⓦwww.fredericksburg-texas.com), has details on budget **hotels** along E Main Street; of these, the pool-equipped *Sunday House* at no. 501 (Ⓣ830/997-4484, Ⓦwww.sundayhouseinn.com; ❸) is one of the more luxurious. **B&Bs** are another option in the area. The *Full Moon Inn*, 10 miles southeast of Fredericksburg at 3234 Luckenbach Rd (Ⓣ1-800/997-1124, Ⓦwww.luckenbachtx.com; ❻), offers accommodation in rural cottages and cabins in the sleepy musical hamlet of **Luckenbach**, immortalized in song by both Willie Nelson and Waylon Jennings. There's **camping** in the lovely surrounds of Lady Bird Johnson Municipal Park (Ⓣ830/997-7521; $10), three miles to the southwest on Hwy-16.

Restaurants and **bakeries** line Main Street. *Dietz Bakery*, at no. 218, is the oldest family-owned bakery in town. You can eat more substantially at *Friedhelm's Bavarian Inn*, at no. 905 (Ⓣ830/997-6300; closed Mon), which specializes in starchy plates of dumplings and sauerkraut. The Hill Country is also a booming **wine region**, and the best of the bunch is *Becker Vineyards* (Ⓣ830/644-2681; Ⓦwww.beckervineyards.com), located in a stone barn eleven miles east of Fredericksburg, off Hwy-290. A bottle of Becker's "Iconoclast" red wine is a great buy at $10.

The Lyndon B. Johnson National and State Historical Parks

About seventy miles west of Austin on Hwy-290, the **Lyndon B. Johnson National and State Historical Parks** preserve LBJ's birthplace and the ranch house where Lady Bird Johnson continued to live long after her husband's death in 1973. They are technically two different parks – one operated by the federal government, the other by the state. The visitor areas are separated by 14 miles.

In **Johnson City** you'll find LBJ's boyhood home and the land where the future president's grandparents settled (daily 8.45am–5pm; free; Ⓦwww.nps.gov/lyjo). A short drive to the west, near **Stonewall**, is the LBJ Ranch (daily 8am–5pm; free; Ⓦwww.tpwd.state.tx.us). Both parks offer tours. For a good lunch – chicken-fried steak, barbecue catfish and the like – stop off at the *Hill Country Cupboard*, at the junction of Hwy-281 and Hwy-290 (Ⓣ830/868-4625).

San Antonio

With neither the modern skyline of an oil metropolis, nor the tumbleweed-strewn landscape of the Wild West, attractive and festive **SAN ANTONIO** looks nothing like the stereotypical image of Texas – despite being pivotal in the state's history. Standing at a geographical crossroads, it encapsulates the complex social and ethnic mixes of all of Texas. Although the Germans, among others, have made a strong cultural contribution, today's San Antonio is predominantly **Hispanic**. Now the seventh largest city in the US, it retains an unhurried, organic feel and is one of the nicest places in Texas to spend a few days.

Founded in 1691 by Spanish missionaries, San Antonio became a military garrison in 1718, and was settled by the Anglos in the 1720s and 1730s under Austin's colonization programme. It is most famous for the legendary **Battle of the Alamo,** in 1836, when General Santa Anna wiped out a band of ragtag Texas volunteers seeking independence from Mexico. After the Civil War, it became a hard-drinking, hard-fighting "sin city", at the heart of the Texas **cattle and oil empires**. Drastic floods in the 1920s wiped out much of the downtown area, but the sensitive **WPA programme** that revitalized two of

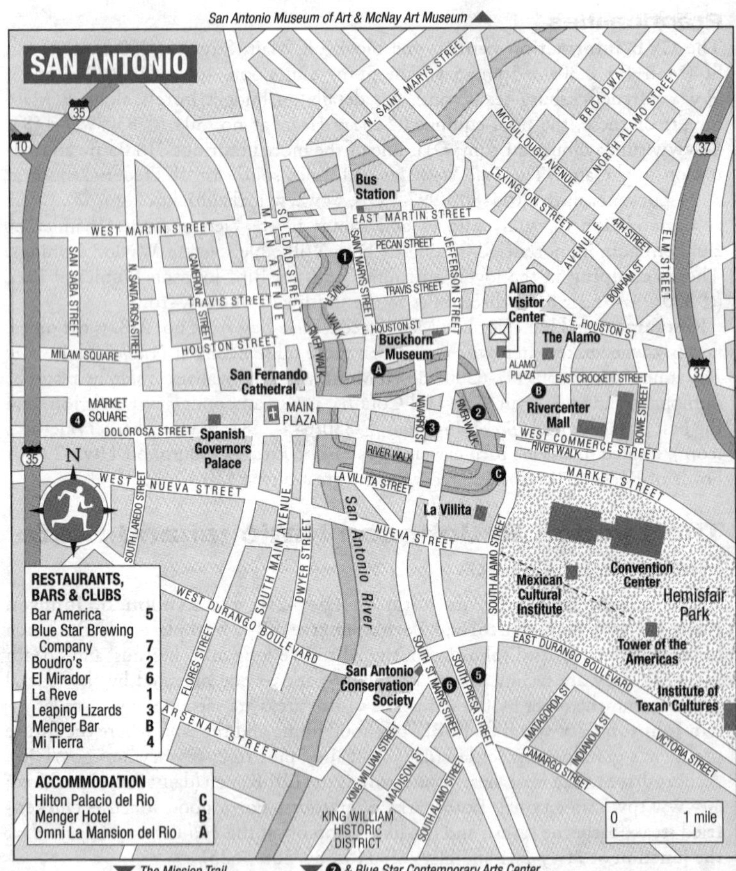

the city's prettiest sites, **La Villita** and the **River Walk**, laid the foundations for its future as a major tourist destination. Recently several massive hotels (think Vegas) have been constructed to accommodate the booming tourism and convention industries. The **military** has a major presence in San Antonio, too, with four bases in the metropolitan area.

Arrival and information

San Antonio International Airport (Ⓣ210/207-3411, Ⓦwww.sanantonio.gov/aviation) is just north of the I-410 loop that encircles most of the sights. **SA Trans Shuttle** (Ⓣ210/281-9900, Ⓦwww.saairportshuttle.com) makes the twenty-minute journey downtown (every 15min, 7am–1.30am; $18 one-way, $32 return), while **taxis** cost about $24 (Yellow Cabs; Ⓣ210/222-2222). **Amtrak** arrives centrally at 350 Hoefgen Ave, while **Greyhound** operates from 500 N St Mary's St. Pick up maps and information from the **visitor centre** at 317 Alamo Plaza (daily 9am–5pm; Ⓣ1-800/447-3372, Ⓦwww.visitsanantonio.com).

City transport

Driving in San Antonio, which is Texas' second largest city, can be stressful and parking is expensive – thankfully, most of the main attractions are within walking distance of each other. Also, in addition to a relatively good bus network, four downtown streetcar routes from Alamo Plaza serve the major attractions (every 10min; $1.10). A one-day pass ($4) available from the VIA Downtown Information Center, 211 W Commerce (Mon–Fri 7am–6pm, Sat 9am–2pm; Ⓣ210/475-9008, Ⓦwww.viainfo.net) can be used on all buses and streetcars. Bikes can be rented from a small shop above the Blue Star Brewing Company at 1414 S Alamo; $25 for 24hr (Ⓣ210/212-5506, Ⓦwww.bluestarbrewing.com) and are an excellent option for exploring neighbourhoods beyond the River Walk.

Boat tours (daily 9am–9pm; $8.25; Ⓣ1-800/417-4139, Ⓦwww.riosanantonio.com) make a 35min circuit of the River Walk, departing from several locations. The same company also runs a **boat taxi**, which costs $5 for a single ride or $10 for a day pass.

Accommodation

The pleasure of a moonlit amble along the River Walk back to your **hotel** is one of the joys of visiting San Antonio, so it's worth paying more to stay in the centre. **Motels** are clustered near Market Square on the west side of downtown; just north of Brackenridge Park on Austin Highway; or on I-35 north toward Austin.

Bullis House Inn and Hostel 621 Pierce St Ⓣ210/223-9426, Ⓦwww.bullishouseinn.com. The cheapest accommodation in town; far from the River Walk but close to a military base (the grounds smell a bit like cat urine). Dorm beds with clean sheets in an old Quonset hut cost $23; rooms at the adjacent inn ❸.

Hilton Palacio del Rio 200 S Alamo St Ⓣ210/222-1400, Ⓦwww.hilton.com. Modularly constructed for the 1968 World's Fair in just nine months, this hotel features balconies overlooking the River Walk. Good value for the prime location. ❻

Menger Hotel 204 Alamo Plaza Ⓣ210/223-4361, Ⓦwww.mengerhotel.com. Bang by the Alamo, this atmospheric historic hotel was a famous destination on the great cattle drives; Teddy Roosevelt recruited his "Rough Riders" here in 1898 for the Spanish–American War. The rooms don't quite live up to the glamour of the lobby, bar and communal areas. ❻

Omni La Mansion del Rio 112 College St Ⓣ210/518-1000, Ⓦwww.omnihotels.com. Rooms at the nicest hotel property on the River Walk come with a full range of amenities and Spanish colonial decor, and some have courtyard access to the pool. ❼

The City

San Antonio is a delight to walk around, as its main attractions, including the pretty **River Walk**, the **Alamo**, **Market Square** and **HemisFair Park**, are all within strolling distance of each other. Slightly further out, but still accessible on foot, is the **King William Historic District** and the neighboring **Blue Star Contemporary Arts Center**.

The River Walk and La Villita

Since mission times, the **San Antonio River** has been vital to the city's fortunes. Destructive floods in the 1920s and subsequent oil drilling reduced its flow, leading to plans to pave the river over. Instead, a careful landscaping scheme, started in 1939 by the WPA, created the Paseo del Rio, or **River Walk**, now the aesthetic and commercial focus of San Antonio. The walk, located below street level, is reached by steps from various spots along the main roads and crossed by humpbacked stone bridges. Cobbled paths, shaded by pine, cypress, oak and willow trees, wind for 2.5 miles beside the jade-green water, with much of the city's dining and entertainment options concentrated along the way.

La Villita ("Little Town"), on the River Walk opposite HemisFair Park, was San Antonio's original settlement, occupied in the mid- to late eighteenth century by Mexican "squatters" with no titles to the land. Only when its elevation enabled it to survive fierce floods in 1819 did this rude collection of stone and adobe buildings become suddenly respectable. It is now a National Historic District, turned over to a dubious "arts community" consisting mostly of overpriced craftshops.

The Alamo

San Antonio's most distinctive landmark, **the Alamo** (Mon–Sat 9am–5.30pm, Sun 10am–5.30pm; free), lies smack in the centre of downtown. Inextricably associated with the battle that took place here in 1836, a defining moment in the Texas struggle for independence against Mexico, the Alamo has been immortalized in movies and songs, and exists now as a rallying cry for Texas spirit.

Its fame, however, has little to do with its original purpose. It was built in the eighteenth century by the Spanish, the first in a trail of **Catholic missions** established along remote stretches of the San Antonio River. Each was laid out like a small fortified town, with the church as aesthetic and cultural focus. The goal was to strengthen Spanish control by "converting" the indigenous Coahuiltecans – in practice, using them as workforce and army. The missions flourished from 1745 to 1775, but couldn't survive the ravages of disease and attack from the Apache and Comanche, and fell into disuse early in the nineteenth century.

The infamous **Battle of the Alamo** occurred on March 6, 1836, when 5000 Mexican troops wiped out 189 rebels dreaming of Texan autonomy. Driven by the battle cry of "Victory or Death!" the besieged band – a few native Hispanic-Texans, adventurers like Davy Crockett and Jim Bowie, and aspiring colonists from other states – held out for thirteen days against the Mexicans before their demise.

Considering its fame, the Alamo is surprisingly small. All that is left of the original complex is its **chapel**, fronted by a large arched sandstone facade, and the **Long Barracks**. A stream of bus tours makes visits crowded and hectic, but for anyone curious about the state's unique brand of pride and stubbornness, the Alamo is unmissable. No response but absolute reverence is permitted – effectively this is a shrine, and a sign insists visitors remove their hats. The grounds, with four acres of lush blooms, palms and cacti, are a haven from the commotion.

Other downtown attractions

For a jaw-dropping slice of kitsch Americana, the **Buckhorn Saloon and Museum**, 318 E Houston St (daily: summer 10am–8pm; winter 10am–5pm; Ⓦwww.buckhornmuseum.com), can't be beat. During San Antonio's heyday as a cowtown, cowboys, trappers and traders would bring their cattle horns to the original *Buckhorn Saloon* in exchange for a drink. The entire bar, a vast and lively Old West-themed space, has since been transplanted to this downtown location, where you can enjoy a mug of beer and a steak in the presence of hundreds of mounted horns and antlers. It is well worth exploring the extra floor ($17.99), which displays a staggering collection of wildlife trophies and includes an informative and entertaining museum of Texas history.

San Antonio's Hispanic heart beats strongly west of the river. At 115 Main Plaza, the handsome **San Fernando Cathedral** is one of the oldest cathedrals in the US, established in 1731. Mariachi Masses are held on Saturday at 5.30pm, when crowds overflow onto the plaza. **Market Square** (daily 10am–6pm), a couple of blocks further northwest on W Commerce Street, dates from 1840. Its festive outdoor restaurants and stalls make it an appealing destination, especially during fiestas like Cinco de Mayo and the Day of the Dead. Fruit and vegetables are on sale early in the morning, while the shops are a compelling mix of colour and kitsch. **El Mercado**, an indoor complex, sells tourist-oriented gifts, jewellery and oddities.

It's a long walk on a hot day through the enormous **HemisFair Park** – a sprawling campus of administrative buildings with scant lawns – to the **Institute of Texan Cultures**, 801 E Durango Blvd (Mon–Sat 9am–5pm, Sun noon–5pm; $8), but it's worth the trip. Mapping the social histories of 26 diverse Texas cultures, this lively museum has especially pertinent African-American and Native American sections. Also in the park, the touristy 750ft **Tower of the Americas** (Mon–Thurs & Sun 10am–10pm, Fri & Sat 10am–11pm) offers big views from its observation deck ($10.95).

The 25-block **King William Historic District**, between the river and S Alamo Street, offers a different flavour, its shady streets lined with the elegant late-nineteenth-century homes of German merchants. It remains a fashionable residential area and has some stylish B&Bs; pick up **self-guided walking tours** outside the headquarters of the San Antonio Conservation Society, 107 King William St. Further south, the grassroots **Blue Star Contemporary Art Center**, 116 Blue Star St (Ⓣ210/227-6960, Ⓦwww.bluestarart.org), makes an appealingly rakish contrast to the rest of the neighbourhood, with its brewpub, workshops, galleries and funky crafts stores. This cool complex is the centre of the San Antonio arts scene and it's a wonderful place to spend a few hours away from the roving packs of corporate conventioneers.

San Antonio Museum of Art and McNay Art Museum

The **San Antonio Museum of Art**, 200 W Jones Ave (Tues 10am–9pm, Wed–Sat 10am–5pm, Sun noon–6pm; $8, free Tues 4–9pm), occupies the old Lone Star Brewery north of downtown. It's full of treasures, with comprehensive Western Antiquity and Latin American collections.

A little further north, the **McNay Art Museum**, 6000 N New Braunfels Ave at Austin Highway (Tues, Wed & Fri 10am–4pm, Thurs 10am–9pm, Sat 10am–5pm, Sun noon–5pm; $8) is another treat. This exquisite Moorish-style villa, complete with tranquil garden, was built in the 1950s to house the art collection of millionaire folk artist Marion Koogler McNay, and includes works from major players like Hopper and O'Keeffe.

The Mission Trail

Any trip to San Antonio will include a visit to the Alamo, but for a real taste of early Spanish influence in Texas, make an effort to see the more distant, less-visited missions. The **Mission Trail** (Ⓦwww.nps.gov/saan) runs eleven miles south along the river from Alamo Street, down S St Mary's Street and onto Mission Road. Missions Concepción and San José are covered on the hop-on, hop-off **Alamo Trolley** tour ($26; Ⓣ210/492-4144, Ⓦwww.sanantoniotrolleytours.com). Both can also be reached via **Bus** #42 down Roosevelt Avenue; to get to the others, you need to drive. Each mission has its own character and acts as an interpretive centre, illustrating some aspect of mission life; the churches themselves still serve active parishes. The main **visitor centre** (daily 9am–5pm; Ⓣ210/932-1001) is at Mission San José.

Eating

San Antonio has good **Tex-Mex** food in all price ranges. Many visitors head straight for the restaurants on the River Walk, but, charming as it is to eat alfresco beside the river, don't be seduced to such an extent that you never venture above ground.

Boudro's 421 E Commerce St Ⓣ210/224-8484. This stylish River Walk Tex-Mex bistro serves creative New American/Southwestern entrees, a wonderful guacamole made at your table and killer prickly-pear margaritas.

Casbeers 1150 S Alamo St and 1719 Blanco Rd. Both locations offer good, cheap eats – enchiladas are a specialty – and happening bars.

El Mirador 722 S St Mary's St Ⓣ210/225-9444. Popular family-owned cantina serving very cheap Mexican breakfasts and lunches, and pricier Southwestern cuisine in the evening.

The Guenther House 205 E Guenther St. Light lunches, cookies and cakes in an airy flour-mill-cum-museum in the King William Historic District.

La Reve 152 E Pecan St Ⓣ210/212-2221. One of the fanciest and best options in town, with an eight-course, $100 tasting menu.

Liberty Bar 328 E Josephine St Ⓣ210/227-1187. This inexpensive restaurant is so old that the building actually leans. Rotating menus feature specials like wild boar sausage.

Mi Tierra 218 Produce Row Ⓣ210/225-1262. With its bedazzlement of *piñatas*, fairy lights and fiesta flowers, this festive 24hr institution is the highlight of Market Square, serving good, inexpensive Tex-Mex staples and delicious sugary cakes at their *panadería*. Great bar, too.

Nightlife and entertainment

With its abundance of picturesque settings, San Antonio is a great city for **festivals**. The year's biggest event is April's 10-day **Fiesta San Antonio** (Ⓦwww.fiesta-sa.org), marking Texas's victory in the Battle of San Jacinto with parades, cookouts and Latin music.

Downtown, the River Walk offers rowdy **bars and clubs**. Somewhat less touristy, Houston Street is fast becoming a party strip with a crop of slick yuppie bars, while S Alamo Street has a smattering of great dives and live music joints. Just a short drive away in the Hill Country you'll find some great old **rural dance halls**, including *Gruene Hall* in New Braunfels (see p.606) and the *John T. Floore Country Store* in Helotes.

Other possibilities are the outdoor **Arneson River Theatre**, on the River Walk opposite La Villita, where you can watch Mexican folk music and dance on a stage separated from the audience by the river, and **Aztec on the River**, 201 E. Commerce St, an opulent Art Deco theatre renovated in 2008.

For **listings**, check the free weekly *Current* (Ⓦwww.sacurrent.com).

Bar America 723 S Alamo St Ⓣ210/223-1285. Three pool tables, two rows of booths with well-worn orange vinyl seating and the best jukebox in town, make this thirty-year-old family-run dive a favourite for a cross section of locals. Lone Star pounders cost $1.50.

Beethoven Beer Garden 422 Pereida St ⓣ210/222-1521. Just off of S Alamo St in the King William District, this private club (regularly open to the public) is devoted to the preservation of German song, music and language. On the first Fri of each month, stop by for cheap beer and heaped portions of delicious potato salad.

Blue Star Brewing Company 1414 S Alamo St ⓣ210/212-5506, ⓦwww.bluestarbrewing.com. Home brews, food and live music – from Texas swing to Latin – in a funky arts complex in the King William District.

John T. Floore Country Store 14492 Old Bandera Rd, downtown Helotes ⓣ210/695-8827, ⓦwww.liveatfloores.com. Old country dance hall 20 miles northwest of San Antonio, with great *tamales* (starchy, corn-based dough cooked in a leaf wrapper) and outdoor dancing on the weekend. The best bands in Texas play here regularly.

Leaping Lizards 302 E Commerce ⓣ210/271-9494. At street level just a few steps up from the River Walk, this rowdy and youthful dive is frequented by local service-industry workers.

Menger Bar 204 Alamo Plaza ⓣ210/223-4361. Cigar-smoking, top-shelf whisky drinkers will feel right at home in this bar attached to the *Menger Hotel*, steps from the Alamo.

North Texas

Early immigration into **North Texas**, during the days of the Republic and following the devastation of the Civil War, was largely from the Southern states. In the 1930s, the oil fields near **Tyler**, east of Dallas, proved to be the richest ever found in the US. In addition to oil, agriculture has become a prime source of commerce, with logging important further east. The grand exception is, of course, the **Metroplex** – the sprawling urban area that includes **Dallas** and **Fort Worth**. The main tourist attractions and cultural life of the region are concentrated here, but if you want to explore small-town America, and you have a car, the region can yield more subtle pleasures in towns like **Denton** and **McKinney**.

Dallas

Contrary to popular belief, there's no oil in status-conscious **DALLAS**. Since its founding in 1841 as a prairie trading post, by Tennessee lawyer John Neely Bryan and his Arkansas friend Joe Dallas, successive generations of **entrepreneurs** have amassed wealth here through trade and finance, using first cattle and later oil reserves as collateral. The power of **money** in Dallas was demonstrated in the late 1950s, when its financiers threw their weight behind integration – potentially racist restaurant owners and bus drivers were pressured not to resist the new policies and Dallas was spared major upheavals. The city's image, however, was tarnished by the **assassination** of President Kennedy in 1963 and it took the building of the Dallas/Fort Worth International Airport in the 1960s, and the twin successes of the *Dallas* TV show and the Cowboys football team in the 1970s, to restore confidence. These days, its occasional stuffiness (**George W. Bush** moved here, to 10141 Daria Place, after vacating the White House) is tempered by a typically Texas delight in self-parody – this is, after all, the city that calls itself "Big D".

Arrival and information

Dallas is served by two major **airports**. **Dallas/Fort Worth** (ⓣ972/574-8888, ⓦwww.dfwairport.com) is exactly midway between the two cities (around 17

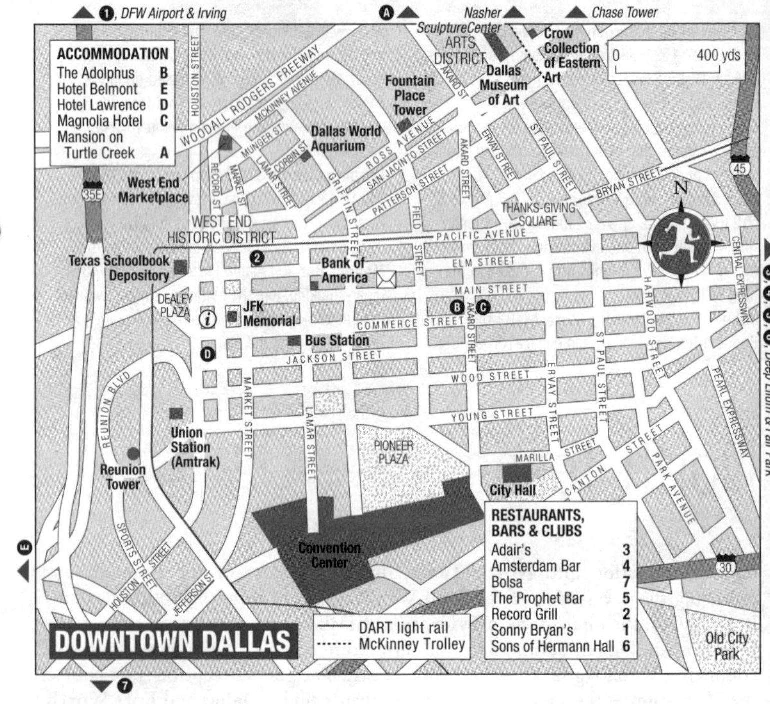

miles from each). You can catch one of a variety of different **shuttle buses**, such as SuperShuttle (ⓣ817/329-2000, ⓦwww.supershuttle.com), which costs $17 to get downtown; **taxis** cost around $45 (Yellow Cab; ⓣ214/426-6262). The other major airport, **Love Field** (ⓣ214/670-6073, ⓦwww.dallas-lovefield.com), used mostly by Southwest Airlines, lies about nine miles northwest of Dallas. **Taxis** to downtown cost around $18, shuttles around $15. **Greyhound** is downtown at 205 S Lamar St, while **Amtrak**'s 1916 Union Station is further west at 400 S Houston St. The **Trinity Railway Express** (ⓣ214/979-1111, ⓦwww.trinityrailwayexpress.org) service runs regular commuter trains to Fort Worth for $3.75.

The downtown **visitor centre** is in the "Old Red" Courthouse, 100 S Houston St, near the Kennedy-related sights (daily 9am–5pm; ⓣ214/571-1000, ⓦwww.visitdallas.com).

City transport

Dallas proper is circled by Inner Loop 12 (or Northwest Highway) and Outer Loop I-635 (which becomes LBJ Freeway). Downtown's main sights are easy to tour on foot. **DART**, the Dallas Area Rapid Transit system (ⓣ214/979-1111, ⓦwww.dart.org), is a **light rail** network that operates downtown and travels further afield to places like Mockingbird Station, a laudable example of New Urbanism. Unlike other cities in Texas, Dallas is investing in light rail and a big expansion of the system is expected to be completed by 2011. Day passes cost $4 and they're also good for the city's **buses**. The **McKinney Trolley** (ⓣ214/855-0006, ⓦwww.mata.org) runs north from the downtown Dallas Museum of Art up McKinney Avenue to the West Village, a complex of restaurants and bars (every 30min, Mon–Fri 7am–midnight, Sat 10am–midnight; free).

Accommodation

Hotels in downtown Dallas are geared towards business travellers. Chain **motels** are concentrated on the freeways; there are lots on LBJ Freeway near the Galleria mall, twelve miles north, and there is a friendly **hostel** in Irving, ten miles west of Dallas.

The Adolphus 1321 Commerce St ⓣ214/742-8200, ⓦwww.hoteladolphus.com. Stunning historic downtown hotel, decorated with antiques. Said to be the most beautiful building west of Venice, Italy, when it was built in 1912, it's a glamorous place to stay. ❼

Dallas Irving Backpackers Guest House 214 W 6th St, Irving ⓣ214/682-9636 or 972/255-9636. Located in Irving, 10 miles west of Dallas. Ivan Ivanov, the owner, is friendly and welcoming, and the hostel is clean enough. From downtown, take the TRE train to South Irving Station. ❶

Hotel Belmont 901 Fort Worth Ave ⓣ1-866/870-8010, ⓦwww.belmontdallas.com. Renovated 1940s motel located a short drive from downtown. Feels more like LA than Dallas, with a hip, casual bar and a pool with stunning city views. ❺

Hotel Lawrence 302 S Houston St ⓣ1-877/396-0334, ⓦwww.hotellawrence.com. Centrally located European-style hotel in a 1920s building. Small, comfortable rooms, a good continental breakfast, and milk and cookies every evening. ❹

Magnolia Hotel 1401 Commerce St ⓣ214/915-6500, ⓦwww.magnoliahoteldallas.com. This downtown 330-room hotel (housed in the former headquarters of Mobil Oil's predecessor) is popular with business travellers. Look for the iconic red neon Pegasus atop the 29-storey building. ❼

Mansion on Turtle Creek 2821 Turtle Creek Blvd ⓣ214/559-2100, ⓦwww.mansiononturtlecreek.com. Situated in a leafy Dallas neighbourhood, this is the most exclusive and expensive hotel property in the city – it also features some fine restaurants, too. ❽

The City

Downtown Dallas is a paean to commerce. Studding the elegant modern skyline, many of its skyscrapers are landmarks themselves. The most noteworthy is **Fountain Place Tower**, 1445 Ross Ave, designed by I.M. Pei, its sharp edges are reminiscent of a blue crystal. At night, two miles of green argon tubing delineate the 72-storey **Bank of America** building at Lamar and Main, while the **Reunion Tower**, 300 Reunion Blvd, on the west side of downtown next to the Amtrak station, looks like a giant 1970s microphone. For big views of the Big D, head to the 40th floor of the **Chase Tower**, at 2200 Ross Ave (Mon–Fri 8am–5pm; free).

One refuge from the downtown hubbub is the Philip Johnson-designed **Thanks-Giving Square** (Mon–Fri 9am–5pm, Sat & Sun 10am–5pm), at the intersection of Akard, Ervay and Bryan streets, and Pacific Avenue, with its fountains, garden and modern spiralling chapel.

The Arts District

On the northern edge of downtown, the surprisingly walkable **Arts District** is Dallas' high-culture headquarters. The **Dallas Museum of Art**, 1717 N Harwood St (Tues–Sun 11am–5pm, Thurs until 9pm; $10, $16 combination ticket with Nasher Sculpture Center; ⓣ214/922-1200, ⓦwww.dallasmuseumofart.org), has an impressive pre-Columbian collection in the Gallery of the Americas, along with artefacts from Africa, Asia and the Pacific, plus works by European artists. Across Harwood Drive, the **Nasher Sculpture Center** (Tues–Sun 11am–5pm; $10, $16 combination ticket with the DMA; ⓦwww.nashersculpturecenter.org) has a few galleries inside, but saves the best of its collection for the garden. Don't miss James Turrell's meditative walk-in installation *Tending (Blue)*. Cross Flora Street to get to the smaller **Crow Collection of Eastern Art**, 2010 Flora St (Tues–Sun 10am–5pm, Thurs until 9pm; free; ⓦwww.crowcollection.com), which fills its very peaceful space with delicately hewn works from China, Tibet, Cambodia and India.

The newest addition to the downtown arts scene, completed in late 2009, is the **AT&T Performing Arts Center**, 2100 Ross Ave (ⓣ214/880-0202, ⓦwww.attpac.org). The modern, four-venue complex, designed by some of the world's pre-eminent architects, is within walking distance from the museums listed above and shows plays and big-name music concerts. This means you can spend the whole day in the Arts District without hopping into a car – a near miracle in Texas.

West End, Dealey Plaza and around

The restored red-brick warehouses of the **West End Historic District**, the site of the original 1841 settlement on Lamar and Munger streets, are filled with specialty stores and theme restaurants; it's a touristy place, thronged on weekends. A few blocks south and west lies **Dealey Plaza**, forever associated with the **Kennedy assassination**. A small green space beside Houston Street's triple underpass, it has become one of the most recognizable urban streetscapes in the world. Whenever you come, you will find tourists snapping pictures. The **Texas Schoolbook Depository** itself, at 411 Elm St, is now the Dallas County Administration Building, the penultimate floor of which houses **The Sixth Floor Museum** (Mon noon–6pm, Tues–Sun 10am–6pm; $13.50 ⓣ214/747-6660). Displays build up a suspenseful narrative, culminating in the infamous juddering 8mm footage of Kennedy crumpling into Jackie's arms; the images remain deeply affecting. The "gunman's nest" has been recreated and, whatever you believe about Oswald's guilt, it's chilling to look down at the streets below and imagine the mayhem the shooter must have seen that day. One block east of Dealey Plaza, in the **Dallas County Historical Plaza** on Main and Market streets, is the striking **John F. Kennedy Memorial**. Walk inside the minimalist, open-air concrete structure and you will feel removed from the city.

Pioneer Plaza and Old City Park

The city's main administrative district, on the south side of downtown, is focused around **City Hall**, a cantilevered upside-down pyramid designed in 1972 by I.M. Pei. The **library** is located near here, while **Pioneer Plaza**, at Young and Griffin streets, holds the world's largest bronze sculpture, a monument to the mighty cattle drives of the West. It depicts forty life-size longhorn steers marching down a natural landscape under the guidance of three cowboys. It is a peaceful space, with an adjacent old cemetery.

Further southeast, across I-30 at 1515 S Harwood St, Dallas's first park, **Old City Park**, is now both a recreational area and home to the **Dallas Heritage Village**, a living museum that charts the history of north Texas from 1840 to 1910. More than thirty buildings have been relocated here from towns across the region, among them a farmhouse, a bank, a train station, a store, a church and a schoolhouse (Tues–Sat 10am–4pm, Sun noon–4pm; $7).

Deep Ellum

Deep Ellum – five blocks east of downtown between the railroad tracks and I-30 at Elm and Main streets – is the city's struggling **alternative district**. Famous in the 1920s for its jazz and blues clubs (and supposedly named by Blind Lemon Jefferson, though it's more likely to stem from the Southern pronunciation of "elm"), the old warehouse district has fallen on tough times in recent years. It is one of the few examples in the US of a gentrifying urban area that began to fail just as it was taking off. Locals say it earned an undeserved violent reputation (partly because of misinformation peddled by the mayor) and people stayed away. It may have reached bottom, though, and its bars, music clubs, galleries and restaurants – including some of the best in the city – are starting to lure the crowds back. It's walkable and not nearly as dangerous as some would lead you to believe.

Fair Park

Not far southeast of Deep Ellum, **Fair Park**, a gargantuan Art Deco plaza bedecked with endless Lone Stars, was built to house the Texas Centennial Exposition in 1936, and now hosts the annual **State Fair of Texas** (Ⓦwww.bigtex.com) for three weeks in October, the biggest event of its kind in the US, with more than three million revellers. Its plethora of fine museums include the lively **Women's Museum** (Tues–Sun noon–5pm; $5; Ⓦwww.thewomensmuseum.org), full of intriguing facts and figures (women smile eight times a day more than men, apparently) and temporary exhibits exploring subjects as varied as Marilyn Monroe, female photographers and the lure of the shoe. The nearby **African-American Museum** (Tues–Fri 11am–5pm, Sat 10am–5pm; free; Ⓦwww.aamdallas.org) is also terrific, with a superb collection of folk art. The **Museum of Nature and Science** (Mon–Sat 10am–5pm, Sun noon–5pm; $9.50; Ⓦwww.natureandscience.org) boasts exhibits on everything from fossils to dental hygiene.

The centrepiece of the park is the magnificent **Hall of State Building**, an Art Deco treasure of bronze statues, blue tiles, mosaics and murals, with rooms decorated to celebrate the different regions of Texas (Tues–Sat 10am–5pm, Sun 1–5pm; free). The park also holds the **Cotton Bowl** stadium, home of the annual Oklahoma vs Texas college football game, and the largest Ferris wheel in the US.

Eating

Dallas has a number of **restaurant** districts. Downtown, the West End Historic District is lively, if touristy, with rowdy chains; in hipper Deep Ellum you can chow down on anything from sushi to Mexican. Uptown, chic West Village, accessible on the McKinney Trolley, is a squeaky-clean cluster of **bars** and eateries catering to youthful loft-dwellers. Northeast of downtown, parallel to I-75, Lower Greenville Avenue has a funkier feel.

All Good Café 2934 Main St Ⓣ214/742-5362, Ⓦwww.allgoodcafe.com. Fresh home-style cooking at this cheery Deep Ellum haunt, which is more evocative of Austin than Dallas and transforms into a live Texas music venue in the evenings.

Bolsa 614 W Davis Ⓣ214/367-9367. Located in the (for Dallas) bohemian neighbourhood of Oak Cliff, this restaurant focuses on fresh, local ingredients and attracts a young, professional crowd.

Local 2936 Elm St Ⓣ214/752-7500. Upscale but unpretentious modern restaurant in a historic Deep Ellum building. The chef is the owner.

Record Grill 605 Elm St Ⓣ214/742-1353. A small downtown greasy spoon wedged between a building and a car park. A double-meat bacon cheeseburger costs $4. Not far from the Sixth Floor Museum.

Sonny Bryan's 2202 Inwood Rd Ⓣ214/357-7120. The original location – it still looks like a shack – of this favourite local BBQ chain lies uptown. Get there in good time as the deliciously tender, smoky meat can be all snapped up by early afternoon.

Entertainment and nightlife

The best **nightlife** destinations in Dallas are Deep Ellum and Lower Greenville, and there is a small cluster of good **bars** on Perry Avenue near Fair Park. The **Dallas Symphony Orchestra** performs at the showpiece Morton H. Meyerson Symphony Center (Ⓣ214/670-0203, Ⓦwww.dallassymphony.com), while the **Dallas Opera** (Ⓣ214/443-1000, Ⓦwww.dallasopera.org) just moved into the bright-red Winspear Opera House in the Arts District.

Full **listings** can be found in Thursday's free *Dallas Observer* (Ⓦwww.dallasobserver.com) or in the *Dallas Morning News* (Ⓦwww.dallasnews.com).

Adair's 2624 Commerce St Ⓣ214/939-9900, Ⓦwww.adairssaloon.com. A Deep Ellum hole in the wall that attracts both old-timers and students with its hard-edged live honky-tonk music, and shuffleboard and pool tables.

Amsterdam Bar 831 Exposition Ave, ⓣ214/827-9933. The best of a cluster of great bars right next door to Fair Park, with occasional live jazz. Also check out the *Meridian Room*, practically next door at 3611 Parry Ave.
Granada Theater 3524 Greenville Ave ⓣ214/824-9933, ⓦwww.granadatheater.com. Lovely old movie theatre hosting big-name acts.
Lee Harvey's 1807 Gould St ⓣ214/428-1555, ⓦwww.leeharveys.com. PBR beer flows like water at this dive situated between downtown and Deep Ellum.
The Prophet Bar 2548 Elm St ⓣ214/742-3667, ⓦwww.theprophetbar.com. Erykah Badu's band plays at this Deep Ellum live-music spot every Wed night.
Sons of Hermann Hall 3414 Elm St ⓣ214/747-4422, ⓦwww.sonsofhermann.com. Delightfully old-school country venue, just beyond Deep Ellum, where the Texas masters come to play, and respectful young outfits pay tribute. Plus swing lessons, open-mic nights and acoustic jams.

Fort Worth

Often dismissed as some kind of poor relation to Dallas, friendly **FORT WORTH** in fact has a buzz largely missing from its neighbour 35 miles to the east. Fort Worth has a distinctly Western character and history. In the 1870s, it was a stop on the great cattle drive to Kansas, the **Chisholm Trail**, and when the railroads arrived it became a livestock market in its own right. Cowboys and outlaws populated the city in its early years and much of that character remains. But while the cattle trade is still a major industry and the **Stockyards** provide a stimulating, atmospheric slice of Old West life, Fort Worth also prides itself on excellent **museums** – the best in the state – and a compact, bustling and walker-friendly **downtown**. Looking toward the future, the city is also undertaking the massive **Trinity River Master Plan**, which will include one of the largest urban parks in the US, and trails and greenways along the Trinity River.

Arrival and information

The main road between Fort Worth and Dallas is **I-30**. It runs east–west through the city, while **I-35W** runs north–south. **Loop 820** encircles all the major sights. The Yellow Checker **shuttle** service (ⓣ817/267-5150, ⓦwww.goyellowcheckershuttle.com) runs to and from DFW International Airport, 17 miles northeast, for about $17. The **Amtrak** (ⓣ817/332-2931) and **Greyhound** (ⓣ817/429-3089) stations are both located southeast of downtown at 1001 Jones St.

There are three **visitor centres** (ⓣ800/433-5747, ⓦwww.fortworth.com): downtown at 508 Main St; in the Cultural District at the Will Rogers Memorial Center, 3401 W Lancaster Ave; and in the Stockyards at 130 E Exchange Ave.

City transport

Fort Worth's public transportation system, **The T** (ⓦwww.the-t.com, ⓣ817/215-8600), operates useful **buses and shuttles** ($1.50), with the **Trinity Railway Express** (ⓣ817/215-8600, ⓦwww.trinityrailwayexpress.org) running a longer commuter service to Dallas for $3.75. The downtown Sundance Square and Stockyard areas are well patrolled and safe to **walk** around after dark; for a **taxi** between the two, call Yellow Checker (ⓣ817/426-6262). Fares are about $12.

Accommodation

The liveliest **places to stay** are around Sundance Square downtown, or in the cowtown atmosphere of the Stockyards; standard motel rooms can be found along I-35.

The Ashton Hotel 610 Main St ⓣ1-866/327-4866, ⓦwww.theashtonhotel.com. Small luxury hotel in a great location, featuring 39 rooms appointed with custom furniture. ❼

Courtyard Fort Worth Downtown/Blackstone 601 Main St ⓣ817/885-8700, ⓦwww.marriott.com. Friendly hotel in a downtown Art Deco building. Rooms on the upper floor have great views, and there's a pool. ❻

Hotel Texas 2415 Ellis Ave ⓣ817/624-2224. Great value on the edge of the Stockyards; you can stumble from the rowdy beer hall to your room. Popular with touring country musicians, but the service is poor. ❹

The City

Fort Worth's main attractions fall tidily into a triangle anchored by downtown, with the Cultural District and the Stockyards two miles away to the west and north respectively. The chief focus of **downtown** Fort Worth is **Sundance Square**, a leafy, red-brick-paved fourteen-block area of shops, restaurants and bars between First and Sixth streets. The square is ringed by glittering skyscrapers and pervaded with a genuine enthusiasm for the town's rich history. Filling the block bounded by Commerce, Calhoun, Fourth and Fifth streets, the **Bass Performance Hall** (see p.620) is a showpiece for the district. It's a breathtaking building that recalls the great opera houses of Europe and is fronted by angels blowing golden trumpets. Elsewhere, notice the **trompe l'oeil murals** – especially the Chisholm Trail mural on Third Street between Main and Houston. Fans of cowboy art should head for the **Sid Richardson Museum of Western Art**, tucked away at 309 Main St (Mon–Thurs 9am–5pm, Fri & Sat 9am–8pm, Sun noon–5pm; free; ⓦwww.sidrichardsonmuseum.org), which has an excellent collection of late works by Frederic Remington, including some of his best black-and-white illustrations, and early elegiac cowboy scenes by Charles Russell; it also hosts temporary exhibitions. If you want to stock up on top-of-the-line **rhinestone Western wear** or cowboy hats, Leddy's Ranch at 410 Houston St dresses some of the biggest acts in country music.

The Cultural District

Fort Worth has the best galleries and museums in Texas, most of them concentrated in the **Cultural District**, two miles west of downtown on the #2 bus. The **Kimbell Art Museum**, 3333 Camp Bowie Blvd (Tues–Thurs & Sat 10am–5pm, Fri noon–8pm, Sun noon–5pm; usually free, but admission sometimes charged for special exhibits; ⓦwww.kimbellart.org), is one of the best small art museums in the US. The vaulted, naturally-lit structure was designed by Louis Kahn, and the impeccable collection includes pre-Columbian and African pieces, with some noteworthy Mayan funerary urns, unusual Asian antiquities and a handful of Renaissance masterpieces.

The most recent addition to the area, the **Modern Art Museum**, 3200 Darnell St (Tues–Sat 10am–5pm, Sun 11am–5pm; $10, free Wed and first Sun of each month; ⓦwww.themodern.org), is a Tadao Ando-designed modernist building whose light-flooded rooms hold the largest collection of modern art in the nation after New York's MoMA. The **Amon Carter Museum**, just up the hill at 3501 Camp Bowie Blvd (Tues, Wed, Fri & Sat 10am–5pm, Thurs 10am–8pm, Sun noon–5pm; free; ⓦwww.cartermuseum.org), concentrates on American art, with stunning photographs of Western landscapes, as well as a fine assortment of Remingtons and Russells, and works by Winslow Homer and Georgia O'Keeffe.

The Stockyards

With its wooden sidewalks, old storefronts, dusty rodeos and beer-soaked honky-tonks, the ten-block **Stockyards** area – centred on Exchange Avenue, two miles north of downtown – offers an evocation of the days when Fort Worth was "the richest little city in the world". There are daily **cattle drives**, a huffing, shuffling cavalcade of fifteen or so Texas Longhorns, that occur, weather permitting, at 11.30am. The cattle drives begin at the corrals behind the Livestock Exchange Building and the herd returns around 4pm.

Along with the saloons and steakhouses, the **stores** in Fort Worth are heaven for Wild West fans. Check out M.L. Leddy's hat, boot and saddle shop on Exchange Avenue. **Stockyards Station** is a bit touristy, but it houses the Ernest Tubb Record Shop, which sells country music CDs.

Museums in the Stockyards have an appealing small-town feel. Try the **Stockyards Museum** (Mon–Sat 10am–5pm; free), in the huge Livestock Exchange Building at 131 E Exchange Ave, offering a lovingly compiled jumble of local memorabilia including steer skulls, pre-Columbian pottery and rodeo posters. Next door the **Cowtown Coliseum** (ticket prices vary; Ⓣ817/625-1025, Ⓦwww.cowtowncoliseum.com), holds rodeos, Wild West shows and country music hoedowns every weekend. It's fronted by a statue of Bill Pickett, the black rodeo star who invented the unsavoury but effective practice of "bulldogging" – stunning the bull by biting its lip.

Eating

If you love **steak**, Fort Worth is for you – especially the Stockyards area, where the many good steakhouses are frequented as much by cattle ranchers as by tourists.

Angelo's Barbecue 2533 White Settlement Rd Ⓣ817/332-0357. Venerable westside BBQ joint, north of the Cultural District. Locals declare the brisket here to be the best in the city.

Cattlemen's Steak House 2458 N Main St Ⓣ817/624-3945. Dim lighting and wall-sized portraits of prize steers set the scene at this Stockyards institution, beloved for its juicy steaks – from T-bones to sirloin – and icy margaritas.

Kincaid's Hamburgers 4901 Camp Bowie Blvd. This place used to be a grocery store, but since 1966 it's served the best eight-ounce hamburgers in Texas.

Paris Coffee Shop 700 W Magnolia Ave. Busy southside breakfast and lunch spot that serves basic, fresh grub.

Reata 310 Houston St Ⓣ817/336-1009. One of the nicest places to eat in downtown's Sundance Square, with a tempting Southwestern menu that ranges from upscale cuisine to home-style comfort food. Named after the ranch in the movie *Giant*, James Dean's last.

Nightlife and entertainment

You'd be hard-pressed not to find something to your taste in after-dark Fort Worth, a city where roustabouts happily down beers next to modern jazz fans and bikers. Bar crawling is fun, and there's a great mix of live music venues. Check the *Fort Worth Weekly* (Ⓦwww.fwweekly.com) or the *Fort Worth Star-Telegram* (Ⓦwww.star-telegram.com) for listings. If you're after a rambunctious Wild West night out, head for the **Stockyards**. For the performing arts, there's the stunning downtown **Bass Performance Hall** (Ⓣ817/212-4325, Ⓦwww.basshall.com), home to the city's orchestra, opera and theatre companies. Big-name touring musicians like Lyle Lovett and k.d. lang also make the rounds here.

Billy Bob's Texas 2520 Rodeo Plaza Ⓣ817/624-7117, Ⓦwww.billybobstexas.com. The jewel in cowtown's crown, this is the largest honky-tonk in the world, down in the Stockyards, with pro bull-riding, pool tables, bars, restaurants, stores, weekly swing and country dance lessons and big-name concerts.

White Elephant Saloon 106 E Exchange Ave Ⓣ817/624-8273, Ⓦwww.whiteelephantsaloon.com. Notoriously wild and authentic old Stockyards saloon with a cowboy-hat hall of fame.

The Panhandle

Inhabitants of the **Panhandle**, the northernmost part of the state, call it "the real Texas". On a map, it appears as a rectangular appendix bordering Oklahoma and New Mexico. A starkly romantic agricultural **landscape** strewn with tumbleweeds and mesquite trees, it fulfils the fantasy of what Texas should look like. When Coronado's expedition passed this way in the sixteenth century, the gold-seekers drove stakes into the ground across the vast and unchanging vista, despairing of otherwise finding their way home – hence the name **Llano Estacado**, or staked plains, which persists today (the Panhandle is the southernmost portion of the Great Plains).

Once the buffalo – and the natives – had been driven away from what was seen as uninhabitable frontier country, the Panhandle in the 1870s began to yield great **natural resources**. Helium, especially in Amarillo, as well as oil and agriculture, have brought wealth to the region, which is also home to large **ranches**.

The Panhandle holds few actual tourist attractions – its real appeal is its barren, rural beauty. But **music** has deep roots in the area, too. Songwriters such as Bob Wills, Buddy Holly, Roy Orbison, Waylon Jennings, Terry Allen, Joe Ely, Jimmie Dale Gilmore and Natalie Maines of the Dixie Chicks all grew up here.

Lubbock

The largest city in the Panhandle, **LUBBOCK**, population 264,000, was built on cotton. In recent years, with farming in decline, the town's economy has come to rely on manufacturing, healthcare and Texas Tech University.

With its faceless block buildings and simple homes, Lubbock is at first glance unremarkable. Dig a little deeper, though, and you will find a complex city, one that accommodates Southern Baptism, the high-scoring Texas Tech Red Raiders football team and a songwriting history unmatched in the state, led by Buddy Holly.

Arrival and information

Loop 289 circles Lubbock proper, with the **airport** (Ⓣ806/775-2044, Ⓦwww.flylia.com) a few minutes north on I-27; taxis to downtown cost around $20 (Yellow Cab; Ⓣ806/765-7777). **Citibus** (Ⓣ806/712-2000, Ⓦwww.citibus.com) runs commuter routes within the Loop, stopping at around 7.45pm (Mon–Sat; $1.50).

The **visitor centre** is on the sixth floor of 1500 Broadway (Mon–Fri 8am–5pm; Ⓣ1-800/692-4035, Ⓦwww.visitlubbock.org).

Accommodation

Prices for **accommodation** are reasonable and rooms are plentiful; Avenue Q has a string of reliable chain **hotels**.

Lubbock Inn 3901 19th St Ⓣ800/545-8226, Ⓦwww.lubbockinn.com. Well-located and recently renovated independent motel with no-frills rooms, a restaurant and a pool with waterfalls. ❹

Woodrow House B&B 2629 19th St Ⓣ806/793-3330, Ⓦwww.woodrowhouse.com. Seven rooms, each with a different theme – there's even one in a restored train carriage – in a mansion-style modern house opposite Texas Tech. ❺

Buddy Holly

Lubbock's claim to world fame is as the birthplace of **Buddy Holly**. Inspired by the blues and country music of his childhood – and a seminal encounter with the young Elvis Presley, gigging in Lubbock at the *Cotton Club* – Buddy Holly was one of rock'n'roll's first singer-songwriters. The Holly sound, characterized by steady strumming guitar, rapid drumming and his trademark hiccupping vocals, was made famous by hits such as *Peggy Sue*, *Not Fade Away* and *That'll Be the Day*. Buddy was killed at 22 in the Iowa plane crash of February 3, 1959 ("The Day the Music Died"), that also claimed the Big Bopper and Ritchie Valens. Don't leave town without visiting the **Buddy Holly Center**, 1801 Crickets Ave (Tues–Sat 10am–5pm, Sun 1–5pm; $5; Ⓦwww.buddyhollycenter.org), an impressive space that holds a collection of Holly memorabilia, including the black glasses he wore on the day he died.

Other sites include the **Buddy Holly Statue** at 8th Street and Avenue Q; it's scheduled to move to a new location in Lubbock by 2011. This 8ft bronze figure currently towers over a **Walk of Fame**, with plaques to local performers like Waylon Jennings, who played bass at Buddy's final concert. **Buddy's grave** is in Lubbock's cemetery at the end of 34th Street; take the right fork inside the gate, and the grave, decorated with flowers and guitar picks, is on the left.

The City

Downtown Lubbock and Texas Tech University are on the northern side of town. Few buildings of interest survive, thanks to the construction boom of the 1950s and a fierce tornado that ripped through Lubbock in 1970, killing 26 people. However, you can get an interesting overview of local history at the university's **Ranching Heritage Center**, 3121 4th St (Mon–Sat 10am–5pm, Sun 1–5pm; free; Ⓦwww.depts.ttu.edu/ranchhc), where 38 original buildings show the evolution of ranch life (but don't think that ranchers were the first to populate the region – humans have lived in the area for 12,000 years).

The **American Wind Power Center**, 1701 Canyon Lake Drive (Tues–Sat 10am–5pm, summer also Sun 2–5pm; $5; Ⓦwww.windmill.com), provides a comprehensive survey of the role wind energy has played, and will continue to play, in Texas. It showcases more than 120 windmills, many collected by Billie Wolf, a Texas Tech home economics faculty member who spent much of her life interviewing Great Plains farmers and purchasing their rare windmill models. The centre also has a towering new turbine: the million-dollar Vestas V47, which powers the museum as well as 75 nearby homes (for more on wind energy in Texas, see box, opposite).

Eating

Lubbock has a variety of **places to eat**, with especially good BBQ and steak joints. Note that many establishments close before 10pm.

Cagle Steaks Corner of W Fourth and F.M. 179 Ⓣ806/795-3879. Classic Texas Plains steak restaurant. A sixteen-ounce ribeye with all the fixings costs $25.

Gardski's 2009 Broadway Ⓣ806/744-2391. Popular American restaurant for Texas Tech students and alumni. Historic photos line the walls. Onion strings are a specialty.

Home Cafe 3131 34th St. A funky new breakfast and lunch spot, with good coffee served all day. Owned and operated by young, friendly Lubbock natives.

Tom and Bingo's 3006 34th St. This tiny eatery churns out the best chopped beef sandwich in Lubbock.

Entertainment and nightlife

Designated the "Music Crossroads of Texas" by the state legislature in 1999, Lubbock exerts surprisingly little energy supporting young local musicians; many decamp to Austin.

The downtown **Depot District**, which spreads out for a few blocks from 19th Street and Hwy-27, has a mix of **bars** and **clubs** popular with students. At the heart of the area, the lovely old **Cactus Theater**, 1812 Buddy Holly Ave (Ⓣ806/762-3233, Ⓦwww.cactustheater.com), features nostalgic musicals and variety shows. **The Strip**, located off the 98th Street exit of the Slaton Highway, is where Lubbock residents buy their booze. It has a rich honky-tonk history. The local *Lubbock Avalanche-Journal* (Ⓦwww.lubbockonline.com) carries listings.

Rodeos are always fun: Texas Tech holds one each year, and every spring there's the **ABC Rodeo** at the Lubbock City Bank Coliseum. In the same spirit, the **Panhandle South Plains Fair** in late September offers bull-riding, big-name country performers and livestock exhibits.

Amarillo and around

AMARILLO may seem cut off from the rest of Texas, up in the northern Panhandle, but it stands on one of the great American cross-country routes – I-40, once the legendary **Route 66**. The city's name comes from the Spanish word for "yellow", the colour of the soil characteristic to these parts. Sitting on ninety percent of the world's helium and hosting a world-class cattle market, Amarillo is a prosperous, laidback city with a nice mix of cowtown appeal, arty eccentricity and mouthwatering steaks.

Arrival, information and accommodation

I-40 cuts through Amarillo, running south of downtown; the old Route 66 (Sixth St) runs parallel, to the north. **Greyhound** arrives downtown at 700 S Tyler St (Ⓣ806/374-5371) and there's a small **airport** (Ⓣ806/335-1671) seven miles east.

Wind energy in Texas

Texas knows economic booms, most famously due to oil following the gusher at Spindletop in 1901. Now the energy industry is supporting another classic American boom cycle, this one in **wind**. Since white settlement in the 1800s, the parched Texas Panhandle-Plains region has relied on windmills to tap the massive subterranean Ogallala Aquifer and pump up to the surface fresh water for livestock, crops and farm families. In fact, though they may seem dated, many of the simple wooden and aluminium windmill structures that dot the landscape are still spinning, albeit a bit creakily. So it seems only natural that with the recent national focus on renewable energy, Texas would once again turn to the wind.

There are more than 5000 modern wind turbines in Texas, more than any other state in the US. The largest collection is found in the Panhandle-Plains region, near Sweetwater. Here motels can't be built fast enough to house workers hired to install the turbines. Convoys of oversized trucks cart the elongated turbine blades, one at a time, down I-10. At West Texas A&M University in Canyon, professors at the **Alternative Energy Institute** will inform you that Texas wind produces energy for almost 2.5 million homes, but inefficiencies in the grid system create energy bottlenecks. Nevertheless, businessmen like billionaire T. Boone Pickens – who despite struggling US credit markets hopes to build the largest wind farm in the world near Pampa – flock to the region for wind that blows at an average annual speed of 15mph.

You can pick up information from the downtown **visitor centre** in the Civic Center, 401 S Buchanan St, Entrance No. 2 (April–Sept Mon–Fri 9am–6pm, Sat & Sun 10am–4pm; Oct–March Mon–Fri 8.30am–5.30pm, Sat noon–4pm; ⓣ806/374-8474, ⓦwww.visitamarillotx.com).

Chain hotels are concentrated along I-40. For cowboy kitsch, you can't beat the *Big Texan Steak House Motel*, 7701 E I-40 at exit 75 (ⓣ806/372-5000, ⓦwww.bigtexan.com; ❸), with its Texas-flag shower curtains, cowhide bedcovers and saloon doors – and a famed restaurant (see below).

The Town

Amarillo's small **"old town"** consists of a few tree-lined streets and some shabby homes. More interesting is the **Route 66 Historic District**, known locally as **Old San Jacinto**, a quirky stretch of restaurants, bars and stores that runs west along Sixth Street (the old Route 66) from Georgia for about a mile to Western Street.

For more classic Americana, drive ten miles west of town on I-40 to exit 60 (Arnot Road) and **Cadillac Ranch**. An extraordinary vision in the middle of nowhere, ten battered cars stand upended in the soil, their tail fins demonstrating the different Cadillac designs from 1949 to 1963. Since the cars were installed in 1974, they have been subject to countless makeovers at the hands of graffiti artists, photographers and members of the public – all encouraged by owner Stanley Marsh 3 (he prefers to use 3 rather than III), eccentric helium millionaire and *bon vivant*, on whose land the cars are planted, and who is also responsible for the wacky signs ("Strong drink!") dotted around Amarillo and the art installation **Floating Mesa** (visible from roads southwest of town).

Amarillo is also host to the world's most stomping, snorting **livestock auction** (ⓣ806/373-7464, ⓦwww.amarillolivestockauction.com), held on Tuesdays in the stockyards at 100 S Manhattan off Third, on the east side of town – it's a great show.

Eating and drinking

Carnivores will be in heaven – this is **steak country** through and through.

Big Texan Steak House 7701 E I-40, exit 75 ⓣ806/372-6000. Rip-roaring Wild Western fun in this famed old restaurant, which as well as serving fried rattlesnake and ostrich burgers, offers the 72oz steak challenge: if you can eat it within an hour, you get it free (losers pony up around $70).

Golden Light Café and Cantina 2908 W 6th Ave ⓣ806/374-9237. Tasty food at good value at this well-located joint. The cantina regularly draws some of the best touring musicians in Texas.

Outlaws Supper Club 10816 SE Third Ave ⓣ806/335-1032. Practically surrounded by ranch land, this friendly, casual restaurant is a must for steak connoisseurs.

Canyon

In the former cattle town of **CANYON**, 15 miles south of Amarillo on I-27, the superb **Panhandle-Plains Historical Museum**, 2503 4th Ave (Mon–Sat 9am–5pm, Sun 1–6pm; $10; ⓦwww.panhandleplains.org), has engaging exhibits on, among other things, Texas ranching, geology, Southern Plains Indians, the automobile and guns. One recent temporary exhibit explored the years Woody Guthrie spent in the region.

Palo Duro Canyon State Park

Palo Duro Canyon, twelve miles east of Canyon and twenty miles southeast of Amarillo, is one of Texas' best-kept secrets. Plunging 1000ft from rim to floor, it splits the plains wide open and offers breathtaking views and colours, especially at sunset and in spring, when the whole chasm is scattered with wildflowers.

The park (daily 8am–8pm; $5; ⓣ806/488-2227, ⓦwww.palodurocanyon.com;) encompasses the most scenic part of the 120-mile canyon. You can explore the depths on **horseback** (1hr guided ride $35, 5hr ride $140; ⓣ806/488-2180), though backpackers and hikers may want to escape the tourist busloads by following the Prairie Dog Town fork into more remote sections of the park. To **camp** ($12), or to stay in one of the rustic **cabins** (prices start at $60), call ⓣ512/389-8900.

You may balk at heart-warming musical extravaganzas, but the outdoor production *TEXAS*, about the settling of the Panhandle in the 1800s, has an undeniable pull in an area not exactly throbbing with nightlife, with the dramatic prairie sky as a ceiling, a 600ft-high cliff as a backdrop, and genuine thunder and lightning (June–Aug Tues–Sun 8.30pm, pre-show steak dinner 6pm; dinner $10, show tickets $10–30; ⓣ806/655-2181 ⓦwww.texas-show.com).

West Texas

West Texas is the stuff of Wild West fantasy: parched deserts, ghost towns, looming mesas and, above all, a sense of utter isolation. Although the area south from the Panhandle down to Del Rio on the Rio Grande is, for convenience, also known as West Texas, the fantasy really begins west of the Pecos River; you can drive for hours without seeing another soul to **El Paso**, Texas' westernmost city. Many travellers venture into the desolation to explore sublime **Big Bend National Park**, nearly 300 miles southeast of El Paso in the bend of the Rio Grande, but the region also boasts several small towns that provide delightfully offbeat stopovers.

Minimal rainfall (as little as eight inches a year!) and harsh land were not the only hindrances to settlement. The **Apache** and **Comanche**, though accustomed in the 1820s to trading with Mexican *comancheros*, were infuriated when hapless white pioneers began to trickle in during the 1830s. With their horsemanship and ability to find scarce water supplies, the Native Americans posed a real threat; upon statehood, a string of cavalry forts was set up by the federal government to protect Mexican and Anglo settlers from attack. As trading posts and cattle ranges sprung up after the Civil War, the paramilitary **Texas Rangers** were sent out on violent vigilante missions. Eventually, as in the Panhandle, a brutal programme of buffalo slaughter, supported by the US Army, starved the natives out. Not long afterward, **oil** was discovered in West Texas and boom towns appeared, with all the attendant gunslinging and brawling. Those lawless days are long gone, but the area remains susceptible to natural resource-based boom-and-bust cycles and has been capitalizing on its Wild West image ever since.

The Davis Mountains

The temperate climate of the verdant **Davis Mountains**, south of the junction of I-10 and I-20, makes them a popular summer destination for sweltering urban Texans, while the glassy, starry nights facilitate the work of the **McDonald Observatory** about twenty miles northwest of Fort Davis on Hwy-118 (daily 10am–5.30pm; free; ⓣ432/426-3640, ⓦwww.mcdonaldobservatory.org).

Nocturnal "star parties" here provide the opportunity to look at the constellations for yourself (Tues, Fri & Sat, time depends on sunset; $10). Be sure to bring a cooler of beer. **Davis Mountains State Park** (open year-round; $5; Ⓣ1-800/792-1112, Ⓦwww.tpwd.state.tx.us), which starts four miles northwest of Fort Davis, offers good hiking. Rooms at its romantic 1930s adobe-style *Indian Lodge* are clean and comfortable – and often booked up, so call in advance (Ⓣ1-800/792-1112). The **Nature Conservancy** also owns 32,000 acres in the area, but public access is limited to one weekend a month (Ⓣ432/837-5954).

Fort Davis itself, a one-street town at the junction of Hwy-118 and Hwy-17, is a peaceful base for exploring the state park. The **visitor centre**, on Memorial Square (Mon–Fri, 9am–5pm; Ⓣ432/426-3015, Ⓦwww.fortdavis.com), offers road maps for the 75-mile scenic loop of the Davis Mountains. The historic *Hotel Limpia* (Ⓣ432/426-3237, Ⓦwww.hotellimpia.com; ❺) is full of character and serves home-cooked dinners in its cosy dining room. There's delightfully little to do in Fort Davis at **night**, though you can buy "membership" to the hotel's bar for $3.

Marfa and around

MARFA, a small ranching town and arts community 21 miles south of Fort Davis on Hwy-17, has three claims to fame. First, James Dean's last film, the 1956 epic, *Giant*, was filmed here; the cast stayed at the historic and swanky **Hotel Paisano** downtown on Hwy-17 (Ⓣ432/729-3669, Ⓦwww.hotelpaisano.com; ❺).

Next, there's the "**Marfa Lights**": mysterious bouncing lights that have been seen in the town's flat fields since the 1880s, attracting conspiracy theorists and alien-hunters. The town's **visitor centre** (varied opening hours), in the *Hotel Paisano*, can give advice on good vantage points to see the ghostly illuminations; if in doubt, head for the viewing centre, nine miles east of town, four hours after sunset.

Marfa's third attraction, just outside town, is the extraordinary **Chinati Foundation** (tours Wed–Sun 10am; $10; Ⓣ432/729-4362, Ⓦwww.chinati.org). Founded by minimalist Donald Judd, the avant-garde works on display here include some of the world's largest permanent art installations, set in dramatic contexts both indoors and out. The **Judd Foundation** at 104 S Highland also has art spaces open to the public (Mon–Fri 9am–5pm; Ⓣ432/729-4406).

There are innumerable, high-end **galleries** in Marfa that wouldn't be out of place in New York or LA, and at affable Marfa Book Co, 105 S Highland St (Wed–Sun 10am–7pm; Ⓣ432/729-3906), you can browse its selection of art, architecture and Texana titles.

Practicalities

Besides the *Paisano*, another **lodging** option is *El Cosmico* (Ⓦwww.elcosmico.com; ❹), where a "magical tribe of dirt wizards" is constructing an avant-garde development of renovated Air Stream trailers and yurts on fifteen acres. You can stay in a vintage trailer for $90 a night; yurts and tent sites are cheaper. Closer to town, the *Thunderbird Hotel*, 601 W San Antonio (Ⓣ1-877/729-1984, Ⓦwww.thunderbirdmarfa.com; ❻) is a renovated motor court turned high-end hipster hotel. Further east, **Marathon** is best known for the luxurious *Gage Hotel*, 101 Hwy-90 W; (Ⓣ432/386-4205, Ⓦwww.gagehotel.com; ❺), which has a nice restaurant and bar on site; try the buffalo burger.

For such a small town, good **eats** abound in Marfa, led by *Maiya's* downtown at 103 N Highland St (Ⓣ432/729-4410, Ⓦwww.maiyasrestaurant.com). The *New York Pizza Foundation*, 102 E San Antonio (Ⓣ432/729-3377, Ⓦwww.pizzafoundation.com), has the best pizza in the Trans Pecos region, while the funky *Food Shark*,

Shade Pavillion, Highland Avenue (ⓣ432/386-6540, ⓦwww.foodsharkmarfa.com) is operated out of an old delivery truck and serves up dishes such as Mediterranean-inspired fatoush salad for $7.50.

Big Bend National Park

The **Rio Grande**, flowing through 1500ft-high canyons, makes a ninety-degree bend south of Marathon to form the southern border of **BIG BEND NATIONAL PARK** – thanks to its isolation, one of the least visited of the US national parks.

The Apache, who forced the Chisos out 300 years ago, believed that this hauntingly beautiful wilderness was used by the Great Spirit to dump all the rocks left over from the creation of the world; the Spanish, meanwhile, called it *terra desconocida*, "strange, unknown land". A breathtaking 800,000-acre expanse of forested mountains and ocotillo-dotted desert, Big Bend has been home to ranchers, miners and smugglers, a last frontier for the true-grit pioneers of the American West. Today, there is camping in designated areas, but much of the park remains barely charted territory. Ruins of primitive Mexican and white settlements are testament to Big Bend's power to defeat earlier visitors. The park's topography results in dramatic juxtapositions of desert and mountain, plant and **animal life**: mountain lions, black bears, roadrunners and javelinas (a bristly, grey hog-like creature with a snout and tusks) all roam free. Despite the dryness, tangles of pretty wildflowers and blossoming cacti erupt into colour each March and April. In the heightened security measures since September 11th, it has become illegal to cross the Rio Grande into **Mexico**.

The most interesting route into Big Bend is from the west. You can't follow the river all the way from El Paso, but Hwy-170 – the **River Road**, reached on Hwy-67 south from Marfa (see opposite) – runs through spectacular desert scenery east from Ojinaga, Mexico, which was practically wiped off the map due to floods in 2008. Before reaching the park boundary just beyond **Study Butte**, you pass through **Big Bend Ranch State Park** and the community of **Terlingua** (see p.628).

Once in the park, unless you're prepared to do some strenuous hiking, there are few opportunities to see the river itself; the main road is obliged to run across the desert, north of the outcrop of the Chisos Mountains. West of park headquarters at **Panther Junction** a spur road leads south for about six miles, up into the **Chisos Basin**, which is ringed by dramatic peaks – the one gap in the rocky wall here is called the **Window**, looking out over the Chihuahuan Desert. A twelve-mile loop hike to the **South Rim** is one of the most popular in the park, and the views deep into the interior of Mexico are humbling. Driving twenty miles southeast of Panther Junction brings you to the riverside **Rio Grande Village** – unless you choose to detour just before, to bathe in the natural **hot springs** that feed into the river.

At three separate stages within the park's boundaries the river runs through gigantic **canyons.** The westernmost, **Santa Elena**, is the most common **rafting trip**; outfitters are available at Terlingua.

For the serious hiker, the thirteen-mile loop hike to the river on the **Marufo Vega trail** is one of the most stunning in the entire National Park Service. It offers views of the Sierra del Carmen mountain range in Mexico and a descent into a rarely visited slick-rock canyon. Feral burros (wild donkeys) sometimes wail here at sunset, and subsistence Mexican farmers set up camps to harvest candelilla across the border. A more accessible trail leads to the **Upper Burro Mesa pour-off**; it's about five mostly flat miles.

Practicalities

The **park headquarters** at Panther Junction (daily 8am–6pm; Ⓣ432/477-2251), where you can pay the $20 per vehicle entrance fee (good for seven days), has recently updated orientation exhibits and a daytime gas station.

Most **camping** at the park's three developed campgrounds (pay at a visitor centre; $14) is first-come, first-served, though some reservations can be made for the high season (Nov–April; Ⓣ1-877/444-6777, Ⓦwww.recreation.gov). **Primitive campgrounds** are scattered along the many marked hiking trails. These have no facilities, and you'll need a wilderness permit ($10) from a visitor centre. The sites at **Juniper Flats** are only about a three-mile hike and are located in a nice meadow. Other stunning sites in the Chisos Mountains are **SE-3**, **SW-3** and **NE-4**.

The **Chisos Basin** has a **visitor centre** and is the site of the park's only roofed accommodation. The *Chisos Mountains Lodge* (reservations essential; Ⓣ432/477-2292, Ⓦwww.chisosmountainslodge.com; ❺) offers motel-style rooms with balconies and a few stone cottages (#102 and #103 are the best). The on-site restaurant has a good all-you-can-eat salad bar for $8. There are additional **visitor centres** at Persimmon Gap and Castolon.

Terlingua

TERLINGUA, a tiny town scattered across the low hills along Hwy-170, used to be populated by the hard-scrabble folks who worked in the mercury mines. But in the 1970s, river guides began moving into the abandoned stone structures and now Terlingua is home to friendly outdoors enthusiasts, artists and miscreants lured by stunning sunsets and remote environs.

For such a small place, Terlingua has a lot to recommend it. Desert Sports (Ⓣ432/371-2727, Ⓦwww.desertsportstx.com) offers a variety of **rafting trips**, from one to twelve days; allow $135 for a full day's guided trip along Santa Elena Canyon. It also leads group hikes, rents rafts and bikes, and provides shuttles into the backcountry. During the first weekend in November, the community hosts its world championship **chili cookoff** (Ⓦwww.chili.org/terlingua.html), when the place turns into the "Redneck Mardi Gras".

La Posada Milagro, at the top of the hill, offers four luxuriously rustic **rooms** (Ⓣ432/371-3044, Ⓦwww.laposadamilagro.net; ❻) in a restored dry-stack stone building, along with a four-bed bunkhouse. Just down the road is *Las Ruinas Camping Hostel* (❶); stop by the *Boathouse* bar for info. Near Terlingua's fly-blown cemetery, set against a backdrop of evocative ruins, an old movie house has been converted into the welcoming *Starlight Theater* (Ⓣ432/371-2326, Ⓦwww.starlighttheatre.com), which in fact is a **bar** and **restaurant**. Just outside, locals linger on the porch to drink beer, gossip and marvel at the mountains. You can buy six-packs and browse a fantastic selection of local books at the Terlingua Trading Company. There's good **food** at *Rio Bravo*, *Kathy's Kosmic Kowgirl Kafe* and the *Ghost Town Café*. For rowdy late-night action, head to ★ *La Kiva* (Ⓣ432/371-2250, Ⓦwww.lakiva.net) on Hwy-170 at Terlingua Creek, or the *Boathouse* in the Ghost Town.

El Paso and around

Back when Texas was still Tejas, **EL PASO**, the second-oldest settlement in the United States, was the main crossing on the Rio Grande. It still plays that role today, its 600,000 residents joining with another 1.7 million across the river in **Ciudad Juarez**, Mexico, to form the largest binational (and bilingual) megalopolis in North

America. At first sight it's not an especially pretty place – massive railyards fill up much of downtown, the belching smelters of copper mills line the riverfront and the northern reaches are taken up by the giant Fort Bliss military base. Its dramatic setting, however, where the Franklin Mountains meet the Chihuahuan Desert, gives it a certain bold pioneer edge, bearing more relation to old rather than new Mexico, with little of the pastel softness of the Southwest US. And while it's tempting to cross the border here into Mexico, remember that escalating **drug wars** have rapidly turned Juarez into one of the most dangerous cities in the world.

Arrival and information

El Paso's **airport** is about five miles east of downtown; a **taxi** to the centre will cost about $22, although many downtown hotels offer free van rides. **Greyhound** buses stop at 200 W San Antonio Ave (Ⓣ915/542-1355), while **Amtrak** (Ⓣ915/545-2247) pulls in at the Daniel Burnham-designed Union Station at 700 San Francisco St.

The **visitor centre** (Mon–Fri 8am–5pm, Sat 10am–3pm; Ⓣ1-800/351-6024, Ⓦwww.visitelpaso.com) is at 1 Civic Center Plaza in the convention centre complex.

Accommodation

Room rates in El Paso tend to be reasonable. The usual cheapie chains line I-10.

Camino Real 101 S El Paso St Ⓣ915/534-3000, Ⓦwww.caminoreal.com. Downtown hotel in a grand old 1912 building. The romantic lobby bar is topped by a colourful Tiffany glass dome and surrounded by rose and black marble. ❻

Gardner Hotel & Hostel 311 E Franklin St Ⓣ915/532-3661, Ⓦwww.gardnerhotel.com. Rooms in this atmospheric hotel – where John Dillinger bedded down in the 1920s – vary from dorms ($22 for a bed), through to singles with shared bath, to simple en-suite doubles furnished with antiques. ❸

The City

Downtown El Paso's character is shaped by the **US–Mexico border**. In times past, outlaws and exiles from either side of the border would take refuge across the river, and today's traffic remains considerable and not entirely uncontroversial. Manual labourers come north to find undocumented jobs, and US companies secretly dump their toxic waste on the south side. Drugs are a major issue, too. The border itself, the **Rio Grande**, has caused its share of disagreements: the river changed course quite often in the 1800s, and it was not until the 1960s, when it was run through a concrete channel, that it was made permanent. An attractive, 55-acre park, the **Chamizal National Memorial**, on the east side of downtown off Paisano Drive, was built to commemorate the settling of the border dispute; it has a small museum (Tues–Sat 10am–5pm; free) and provides a pleasant green space for walks and picnics. The small but engrossing **Border Patrol Museum**, 4315 Transmountain Drive (Tues–Sat 9am–5pm; free), explains the work of the patrollers and highlights the ingenuity of smugglers.

On the river itself, the **Cordova Bridge** – or Bridge of the Americas – heads across **into Mexico**, where there's a larger park and a number of museums; there are no formalities, so long as you have a multiple-entry visa for the US and don't travel more than twenty or so miles south of the border. Crossing here is free; at the three other bridges – two downtown and one near the Ysleta Mission – you have to pay a 35-cent fee. But be warned: Juarez has been a violent place lately, with about 3000 mostly drug-related murders in 2009 alone.

Although El Paso is predominantly Hispanic, there is also a substantial population of **Tigua Indians**, a displaced Pueblo tribe, based in a reservation (complete with the almost statutory casino) on Socorro Road, southeast of downtown. The reservation's arts-and-crafts centre sells pottery and textiles. Adjacent to the reservation, the simple **Ysleta del Sur**, the oldest mission in the United States, marks the beginning of an eight-mile **Mission Trail** (Ⓣ915/534-0630), with three missions – still active churches – set among scruffy cotton, alfalfa, chili, onion and pecan fields.

In **Concordia Cemetery**, just northwest of the I-10 and Hwy-54 intersection, a shambling collection of crumbling stones and plain wooden crosses commemorates assorted pioneers and desperados. Romanticized gunslinger **John Wesley Hardin** is buried here – a black iron jail cell has been constructed above the outlaw's plot, keeping him behind bars for eternity. A few paces away is the Chinese graveyard, a section walled off since the Chinese built the railroads in the 1880s. El Paso is also the home of Tony Lama, makers of top-quality **cowboy boots**, available at substantial discounts at outlets across town.

Eating and nightlife

Dining is, naturally, mostly Mexican. **After dark**, downtown practically expires; try the university area (UTEP), northwest of downtown. Check the free monthly *El Paso Scene* (Ⓦwww.epscene.com) for listings. The gorgeous Plaza Theater downtown hosts big-name acts; Wilco came through in 2009.

Ardovino's Desert Crossing 1 Ardovino Drive, Sunland Park, NM Ⓣ575/589-0653. Just across the state line in New Mexico, this enchanting restaurant serves up pasta dishes and hosts a summer farmers' market.

Casa Juardo 226 Cincinnati Ave Ⓣ915/532-6429. Great Mexican food in a lively, fun neighbourhood – try the tortilla soup.

H&H Coffee Shop & Car Wash 701 E Yandell Drive Ⓣ915/533-1144. Quirky time-warp diner dishing up tasty Tex-Mex – reputed to be a favoured stop for George W. Bush and assorted governors. Stop by in the morning for their *huevos rancheros*.

L&J Café 3622 E Missouri Ave Ⓣ915/566-8418. A good-value joint next to Concordia Cemetery, offering up excellent Mexican food.

Tap Bar and Restaurant 408 E San Antonio St Ⓣ915/532-1848. A diverse local crowd hangs out at this downtown dive, which serves good, cheap food.

Guadalupe Mountains National Park

Roughly one hundred miles east of El Paso, Hwy-62/180 climbs toward Carlsbad Caverns along the southern fringes of the **Guadalupe Mountains**, once a stronghold of the Mescalero Apache. The national park here (park headquarters in Pine Springs; park open year-round; $5; Ⓣ915/828-3251, Ⓦwww.nps.gov/gumo;) is a hiking and camping destination, barely penetrated by roads and without accommodation, food or gas. It's possible to hike right to the top of **Guadalupe Peak**, at 8749ft the highest point in Texas, but most walkers opt instead for the flat trek through **McKittrick Canyon**, passing from bare desert into lush mountain forests beside sheer canyon walls. Camping within the park ($8/night/tent) is allotted on a first-come, first-served basis. Many travellers to this region combine a trip to Guadalupe Mountains National Park with Carlsbad Caverns and White Sands National Monument, both of which are across the state line in **New Mexico**.

10

The Great Plains

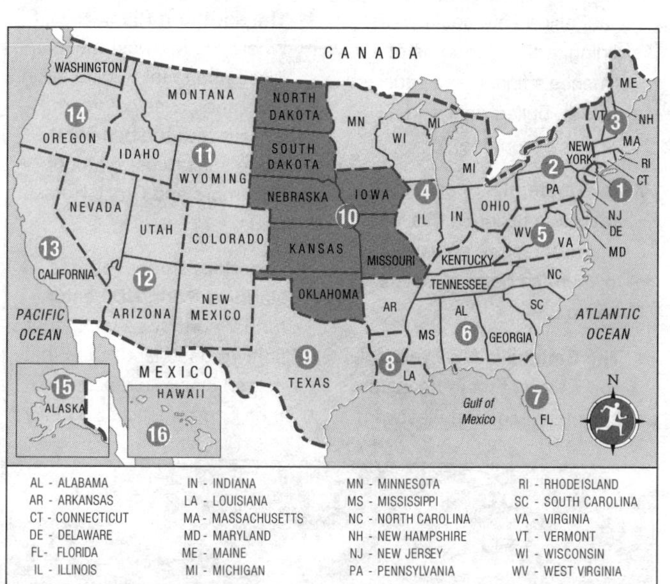

CHAPTER 10 Highlights

* **Gateway Arch, St Louis, MO** Ride the pod-like tram to the top of this iconic monument, or simply admire its majestic symmetry from the lovely riverside park below. See p.637

* **BBQ in Kansas City, MO** Cast aside your healthy dining regime for some of America's finest (and sauciest) brisket, pulled pork and beans. See p.645

* **Lawrence, KS** Spend an afternoon taking in this leafy and progressive college town in the heart of America. See p.654

* **The Sandhills, NE** Every mile seems to get more beautiful as you roll and dip westward along scenic Hwy-2 and through the verdant Sandhills. See p.661

* **Badlands National Park, SD** South Dakota's grassy answer to the Grand Canyon and Death Valley boasts its own austere charms. See p.668

* **The southern Black Hills, SD** Where the Midwest meets the West: abundant wildlife, hiking trails and caves galore, quiet byways and the behemoth stone sculptures of Mount Rushmore and Crazy Horse. See p.671

* **Theodore Roosevelt National Park, ND** Venture further north for a look at the softly eroded landscape that helped inspire a rancher to the US presidency. See p.677

▲ Mount Rushmore National Memorial

The Great Plains

Stretching west of the Mississippi through **Missouri**, **Oklahoma**, **Kansas**, **Nebraska**, **Iowa**, **South Dakota** and **North Dakota**, **THE GREAT PLAINS** are often lumped together in the popular imagination as an expanse of unvaryingly flat prairies, conservative "Middle American" values and boredom – a place to either drive through or escape from. Once, however, this was the **West**, an empty canvas on which outlaws, fur trappers, buffalo hunters and cowboys painted their dreams. In the 1870s, the wide-open range of the lone prairie, which had originally been known as the **Great American Desert**, was suddenly promoted as a bountiful Garden of Eden, inspiring such fascination that famed US Army officer George Custer was moved to call it "the fairest and richest portion of the national domain".

Nonetheless, the Plains share a troubled history. The systematic destruction by white settlers of the awesome herds of **bison** presaged the virtual eradication of the **Plains Indians**. Reservations, agencies and "assigned lands" dwindled as the natural resources of the area attracted white settlement; after 1874, when **gold** was discovered in the Black Hills, the fate of the Native Americans was practically sealed. However, thanks to warriors like **Crazy Horse** and **Sitting Bull**, the struggle for control of the Plains was by no means easy.

The Plains are most comfortable glorying in a romantic myth of the Wild West and flaunting sanitized versions of wicked old cowtowns like **Deadwood** in South Dakota, **Dodge City** (once trumpeted as the Beautiful, Bibulous Babylon of the Frontier) in Kansas, and **St Joseph**, Missouri, the birthplace of the Pony Express. **Calamity Jane**, **Wild Bill Hickok**, **Billy the Kid** and **Annie Oakley** all left their marks when this was truly the wild frontier, and today, in the sandy scrublands of the Plains, working ranches and cattle drives are as common as the region's inevitable summer thunderstorms.

Defining the geographical limits of the Plains is difficult, and the term itself is almost a misnomer – just as there are vast flat expanses and long uninterrupted roads, there are also canyons, forests and splashes of unexpected colour, as well as two of the nation's mightiest **rivers**: the **Missouri**, which begins in Montana and follows a winding southeasterly course through the Dakotas; and the **Mississippi**, the headwaters of which are found in northern Minnesota. The two mammoth rivers eventually meet just north of St Louis.

The woods, caves and springs of the **Ozarks**, the lunar landscapes of South Dakota's **Badlands** and stately **Mount Rushmore** are the region's most visited areas. Drama comes in the form of such unpredictable **weather** as freak blizzards, dust devils, lightning storms and, most notoriously, "twister" tornadoes. Images of the devastating 1930s "Dustbowl" – when topsoil was whisked as far as

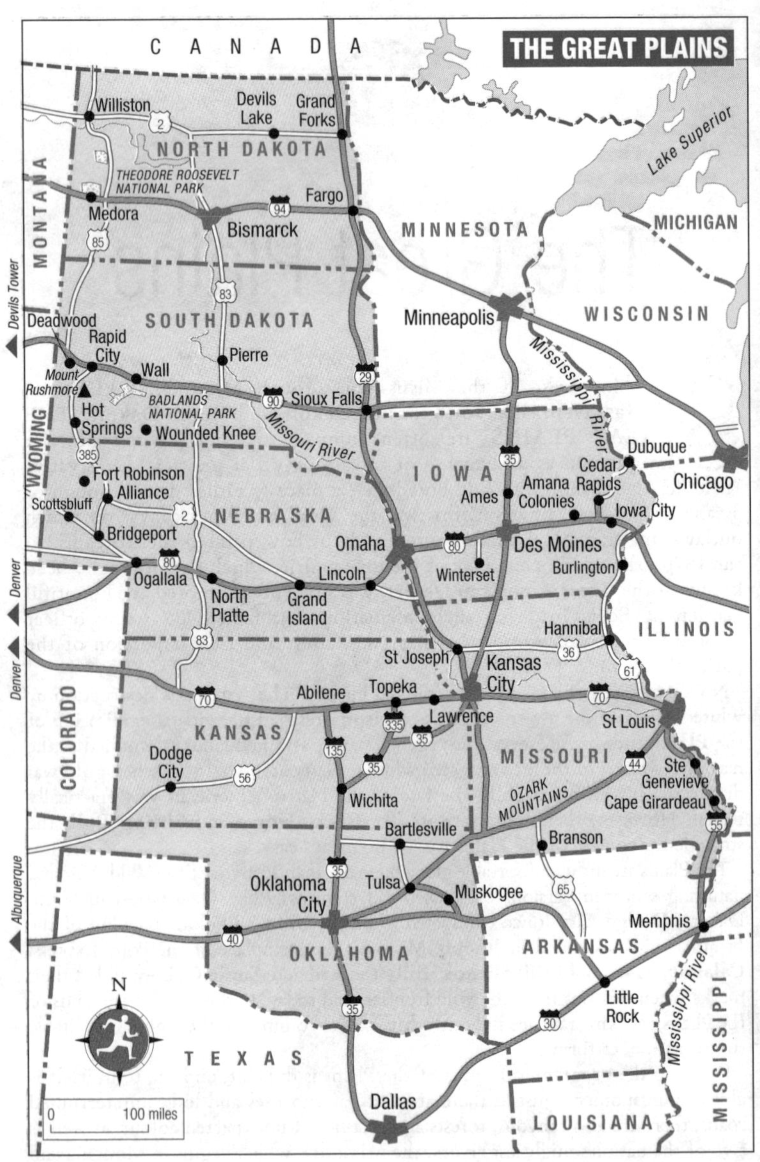

Washington DC – remain as potent as the fantasy of Dorothy and Toto being swept up from Kansas by a tornado to the land of Oz.

Still, the Plains are called the "breadbasket of the world" for a good reason, providing the nation with much of its **wheat** and **corn**, seas of which wave over flat fields from Kansas up to North Dakota. The region's economy has also long been dependent on **oil**, especially in Oklahoma, and **gold** in the Dakotas.

Getting around the Great Plains

Having a **car** is practically imperative to properly see the Great Plains, where distances are long, roads straight and seemingly endless and the population sparse. The main **interstate** routes cross from east to west, while with only a couple exceptions, north–south travel is often limited to country byways. St Louis and Kansas City host the region's major **airports**, while several other sizeable cities – such as Oklahoma City, Wichita and Omaha – act as regional hubs.

It takes Greyhound **buses** about six hours to traverse Missouri's central corridor between St Louis and Kansas City, and they also serve Oklahoma's I-35 and I-40, and visit major cities along I-70 and I-80 in Kansas and Nebraska; routes to smaller cities in these states are supplemented by erratic lesser companies. Iowa sees Greyhound call in from Chicago, and daily buses also run from St Louis to Des Moines and Iowa City. In South Dakota, Jefferson Lines buses trundle across the state and serve points between Sioux Falls and Rapid City; the same company operates in North Dakota, making the eight-hour trip from Minneapolis to Bismarck along I-94 twice daily before continuing along into Montana.

Amtrak **trains**, crossing the region almost exclusively at night, are not a great option for exploring the Great Plains. Still, some helpful daily routes exist, particularly from Chicago to St Louis, where direct connections can be made to points west, including Kansas City. Oklahoma City is served by one train a day from Fort Worth, Texas, while to the north, several cities through the middle of Kansas and Nebraska have stations along Amtrak's cross-continental routes. Iowa and South Dakota suffer from particularly poor train service, with Amtrak missing all of Iowa's major cities in favour of several small communities through the southern part of the state, and South Dakota not served at all. Rail travel possibilities brighten in North Dakota, with one daily train connecting Fargo and Williston via Grand Forks.

For keen **cyclists**, there's Missouri's popular Katy Trail (Ⓦwww.bikekatytrail.com), which stretches 225 miles from the St Louis suburb of St Charles across the state to Clinton; to the north, Iowa's popular seven-day, cross-state ride, the RAGBRAI (Ⓦwww.ragbrai.com) – the Register's Annual Great Bike Ride Across Iowa – attracts thousands of entrants each July, all of whom will exhaustedly testify that the Plains aren't necessarily flat.

Missouri

The "Show Me State" of **MISSOURI** – so called because of the supposed scepticism of the typical Missourian – boasts two significant cities: **St Louis** is midway down the state's eastern fringe along the Mississippi River; **Kansas City**, astride the Missouri River, sits almost directly across on the western border. These mid-size metropolises are linked by I-70, but there's not much to excite visitors in between. In contrast, the southern part of the state features the beautiful hillsides, streams and ragged lakes of the **Ozark Mountains**, as well as the booming tourist haven of **Branson**. In the east, small river towns such as **Hannibal** do their best to brighten the course of the muddy Mississippi; **St Joseph**, about fifty miles north of Kansas City, is one of the state's most richly historical communities.

Although the first French colonists honoured the claims of local Native Americans, once the area was sold to the US in 1803 as part of the **Louisiana Purchase**, the natives were driven west by a great rush of settlers; throughout the 1840s and 1850s, immigrants from Germany and Ireland flooded into eastern Missouri. Although these new residents outnumbered their pro-slavery predecessors – thereby swinging the balance in favour of remaining in the Union during the **Civil War** – Confederate guerrilla forces attracted considerable support among slave-owners in the western part of the state. At the same time, both St Louis and St Joseph established themselves as important gateways to the West.

Eastern Missouri

The Mississippi River defines the state's eastern border, absorbing as major tributaries the Missouri, Ohio, Illinois and Des Moines rivers. Over the years, innumerable towns have sprung up along the "Big Muddy", their aspirations reflected by such classical names as Alexandria, Antioch and Athens. **Hannibal**, the boyhood home of Mark Twain, is the most notable in the northeast, but all of Missouri's riverside communities have decreased in importance with the growing pre-eminence of **St Louis** since the mid-nineteenth century.

St Louis

Perched just below the confluence of the Mississippi and Missouri rivers, three hundred miles south of Chicago and the same distance north of Memphis, **ST LOUIS** (pronounced, despite what any song might suggest, "Saint Lewis") owes its vaguely European air to its history and cultural infrastructure. Any city capable of producing one of the twentieth century's finest poets, as well as one of its greatest rock 'n' rollers – namely, **T.S. Eliot** and **Chuck Berry** – certainly has a lot going for it.

The original riverside port town was founded in 1764 by French fur trader Pierre Laclede; however, the American immigration that followed its sale to the US under the **Louisiana Purchase** all but extinguished the refinement it had gained during French and Spanish rule. St Louis subsequently became crucial as the major gateway for pioneers headed westward on wagon trails, and through the years, **transportation** – first steamboats, then trains, and today, air haulage – has continued to provide an economic foundation for the city's considerable industrial strength.

Although the Mississippi **riverfront**, with the magnificent **Gateway Arch** and the restored warehouses of **Laclede's Landing**, inevitably attracts visitors' attention, the city's **outlying districts** are also worth seeking out. West of downtown you'll find the stately **Central West End** and young, vibrant **University** (or "U") **City**; each neighbourhood is close to prodigious **Forest Park**, with its bevy of free museums and huge fields. **South City** features the markets, antique shops and corner blues pubs of **Soulard**, as well as another excellent public greenspace, **Tower Grove Park**, just east of the inviting Italian shops and cafés of **the Hill**.

Arrival, information and city transport

Medium-sized **Lambert-St Louis International Airport** is a dozen miles northwest of downtown and connected by taxi, bus or MetroLink light rail. Some Greyhound **buses** call at the airport – you can board without a ticket and pay your fare when you arrive in the main terminal downtown at 1450 N 13th St. Amtrak **trains** stops a mile or so west of downtown at 551 S 16th St.

The Bi-State Transit System (Ⓣ314/231-2345) operates **MetroLink**, the St Louis area light-rail system ($2.25). **Buses** ($2) go to all of the city's suburbs, though service can be slow and infrequent.

A number of **visitor centres** operate around town, including two at the airport and others at the America's Center convention complex (Mon–Fri 8.30am–5pm, Sat 9am–3pm; Ⓣ1-800/916-0092) and Kiener Plaza (same hours; Ⓣ314/231-0336). Visit Ⓦwww.explorestlouis.com for information on local sights and accommodation.

Accommodation

Sophisticated **lodging** can be found downtown and in the Central West End, while budget **motels** line I-70 near the airport. Comfortable **B&Bs** are also scattered around many St Louis neighbourhoods.

Chase Park Plaza 212 Kingshighway Blvd Ⓣ314/633-3000, Ⓦwww.chaseparkplaza.com. Overlooking Forest Park, this stately and historic high-rise hotel features richly appointed one- and two-bedroom suites. 7–8

Drury Inn Union Station 201 S 20th St Ⓣ314/231-3900, Ⓦwww.druryhotels.com. Tastefully restored accommodation with a grand lobby and serviceable, albeit small rooms. 5

Hotel Indigo 4630 Lindell Blvd Ⓣ314/61-4900, Ⓦwww.ichotelsgroup.com. Surprisingly affordable boutique lodging in the heart of the Central West End's cafés and shops, a short walk from Forest Park. 5

The Huckleberry Finn Youth Hostel 1904–1908 S 12th St Ⓣ314/241-0076, Ⓦwww.huckfinnhostel.com. Dorms ($25) on the edge of a dodgy area in Soulard, near the Anheuser-Busch brewery.

Millennium Hotel 200 S 4th St Ⓣ314/241-9500, Ⓦwww.millenniumhotels.com. Round tower at the southern edge of downtown with striking views and convenient pedestrian access to the Gateway Arch and Busch Stadium. 6

Park Avenue Mansion 2007 Park Ave Ⓣ314/588-9004, Ⓦwww.parkavenuemansion. Attractive B&B across from Lafayette Square with a lovely private garden and regal dog portraits along the stairwell. Don't miss the innkeeper's extra-sweet pancakes. 5

The riverfront

This one-and-a-half-mile cobbled granite **wharf** along the Mississippi, where roustabouts once handled cargoes of cotton and ores amid a dense tangle of warehouses and factories, underwent a major makeover once river trade decreased. Most structures were ripped down, but those between the Eads and Martin Luther King bridges that survived the wrecking ball now form **Laclede's Landing**, a tourist-baiting clutch of antique shops, restaurants and bars, many fronted by cast-iron facades. Each year in early September, the area hosts the **Big Muddy Blues Festival** (Ⓣ314/241-5875, Ⓦwww.lacledeslanding.org), featuring prominent acts and a boisterous party atmosphere.

Ten minutes' walk south, more than thirty blocks of derelict buildings were cleared away in the mid-twentieth century for the **Jefferson National Expansion Memorial**, dedicated to the US president who negotiated the Louisiana Purchase and thereby opened up the West, as well as to the pioneers who journeyed along the Oregon and Santa Fe trails. The highlight of the expansive greenspace is the gracefully imposing **Gateway Arch** (tram rides daily: summer 8.20am–9.10pm; rest of year 9.20am–5.10pm; $10; Ⓣ1-877/982-1410, Ⓦwww.gatewayarch.com), one of the nation's definitive monuments. Designed by Eero Saarinen and completed in 1965, the 630ft-high stainless-steel parabola is a weighted catenary curve, its outline formed by a heavy cable hanging freely from two points. Provided you're not claustrophobic, it's fun to take the four-minute **tram ride** up the hollow, gently curving arch, as tiny, five-seat capsules carry you to a viewing gallery at the top, where you can linger as long as you like – the views of St Louis,

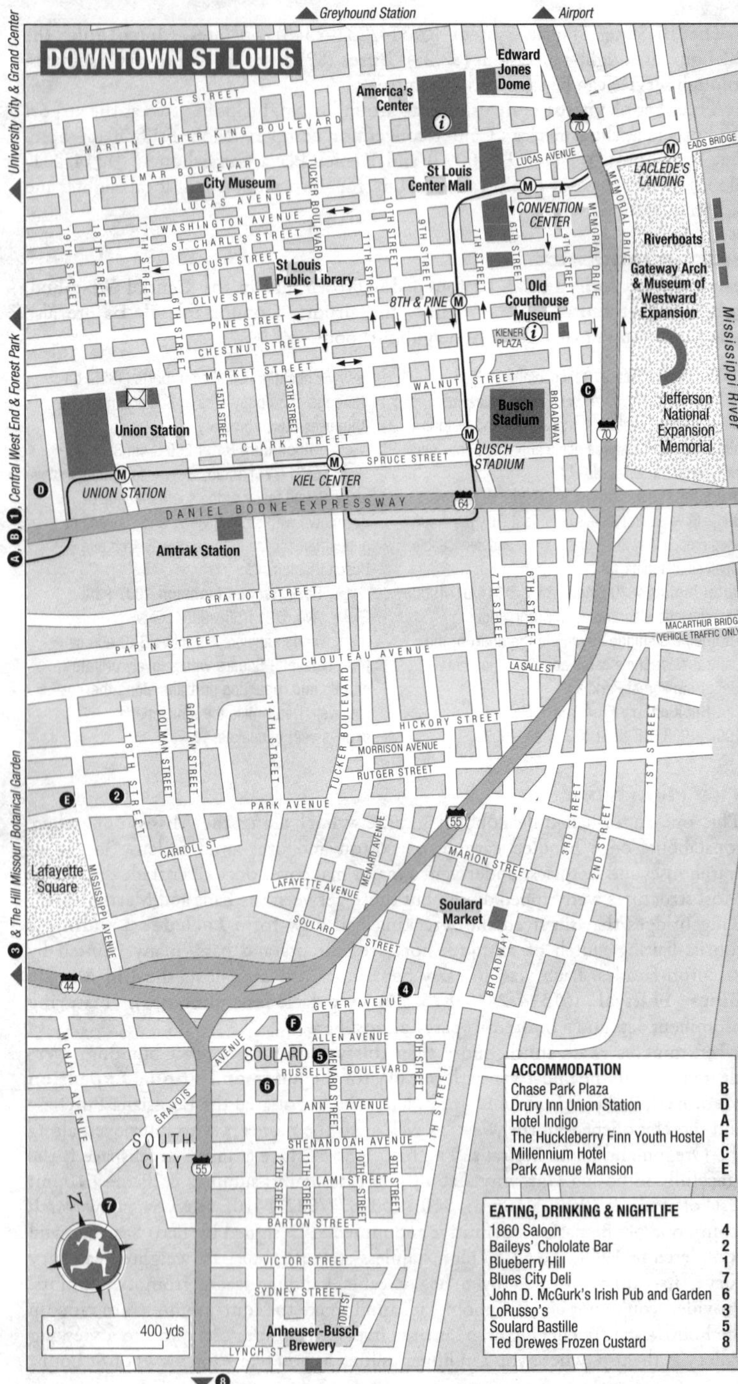
DOWNTOWN ST LOUIS
Greyhound Station
Airport
University City & Grand Center
Central West End & Forest Park
A, B, 1,
3 & The Hill Missouri Botanical Garden
Edward Jones Dome
America's Center
City Museum
St Louis Center Mall
St Louis Public Library
Old Courthouse Museum
Kiener Plaza
Riverboats
Gateway Arch & Museum of Westward Expansion
Mississippi River
Jefferson National Expansion Memorial
Busch Stadium
Union Station
Amtrak Station
Laclede's Landing
Convention Center
8th & Pine
Busch Stadium
Kiel Center
Eads Bridge
MacArthur Bridge (vehicle traffic only)
Daniel Boone Expressway
Cole Street
Martin Luther King Boulevard
Delmar Boulevard
Lucas Avenue
Washington Avenue
St Charles Street
Locust Street
Olive Street
Pine Street
Chestnut Street
Market Street
Walnut Street
Clark Street
Spruce Street
Tucker Boulevard
Memorial Drive
Broadway
Gratiot Street
Papin Street
Chouteau Avenue
La Salle St
Hickory Street
Morrison Avenue
Rutger Street
Park Avenue
Carroll St
Marion Street
Lafayette Avenue
Soulard Street
Mississippi Avenue
Dolman Street
Grattan Street
Menard Avenue
Lafayette Square
Soulard Market
Geyer Avenue
Allen Avenue
Soulard
Russell Boulevard
Ann Avenue
Shenandoah Avenue
Lami Street
Barton Street
Victor Street
Sydney Street
Lynch St
Gravois Avenue
McNair Avenue
South City
Anheuser-Busch Brewery
0 400 yds
ACCOMMODATION
Chase Park Plaza B
Drury Inn Union Station D
Hotel Indigo A
The Huckleberry Finn Youth Hostel F
Millennium Hotel C
Park Avenue Mansion E
EATING, DRINKING & NIGHTLIFE
1860 Saloon 4
Baileys' Chololate Bar 2
Blueberry Hill 1
Blues City Deli 7
John D. McGurk's Irish Pub and Garden 6
LoRusso's 3
Soulard Bastille 5
Ted Drewes Frozen Custard 8

the mighty Mississippi and the surrounding tree-studded plains are spectacular. Lengthy waits are a sure thing in the summer, but you can pick up a numbered ticket earlier in the day and come back at an appointed time. Still, you'll have to wait again for the elevator, so expect an hour round-trip.

Set in a massive bunker beneath the arch, the **visitor centre** (daily: summer 8am–10pm; rest of year 9am–6pm; museum free, films $7) shows a fine **film** about the construction of the monument, and another on the **Lewis and Clark Expedition**, which set off from St Louis in 1804 to explore potential water passages to the Pacific Ocean. Also in the visitor centre complex, the spacious **Museum of Westward Expansion** recounts the Lewis and Clark story, drawing heavily on the pair's eminently readable journals. Down on the waterfront itself, on the levee below the Arch, one-hour **cruises** aboard replica paddle-wheelers depart regularly (March–Nov daily, noon, 2pm & 3pm; $14; same contact information as Gateway Arch). Combination tickets are available for many of the Memorial's attractions.

Downtown and around

A few minutes' walk west from the Gateway Arch and also part of the Jefferson National Expansion Memorial, vintage photographs at the domed **Old Courthouse Museum** (daily 8am–4.30pm; free) record the development of the city and the ensuing settling of the West, as well as the watershed Dred Scott trial that hastened the onrush of the Civil War. Far more hyperactive is the **City Museum** (March–Sept: Mon–Thurs 9am–5pm, Fri–Sat till 1am, Sun 11am–5pm,; rest of year: Wed–Thurs 9am–5pm, Fri–Sat till 1am, Sun 11am–5pm, closed Mon–Tues; $12 ⓣ314/231-2489, ⓦwww.citymuseum.org), possibly the Midwest's finest repository of randomness, at 701 N 15th St. The eleven-storey building is immensely popular with kids and adults alike, containing everything from carnival bric-a-brac (a 6ft-tall set of men's underpants, an extensive spatula collection, vintage corndog adverts) and bug exhibits to a small aquarium ($6 extra) and even a maddening maze of secret passages, slides and artificial caverns. Once you stop trying to make sense of it all, you're in for a terrific time. Thrill seekers will enjoy the Ferris wheel and old school bus perched over a ledge, both on the building's roof (summer only; $5 extra).

A few miles west of downtown, the city's theatre district, called **Grand Center**, is staked out with ornate street lamps along Grand Avenue between Lindell and Delmar boulevards. Posters advertise upcoming concerts and current Broadway shows at the **Fox Theatre**, 527 N Grand Ave (tours available, call for times and prices; ⓣ314/657-5068, ⓦwww.fabulousfox.com), where you can have a look at the magnificent Siamese-Byzantine interior and massive Wurlitzer organ.

Forest Park and the Central West End

The decision to locate **Forest Park** four miles directly west of downtown (served by MetroLink every ten to thirty minutes depending on time of day) aroused much criticism in the 1870s, with opponents claiming that its inaccessibility would make it merely a pleasure ground for the local rich and mobile. Today, its 1293 acres make it larger than more celebrated cousins such as New York's Central Park and San Francisco's Golden Gate Park, and it features no shortage of compelling museums and outdoor attractions – many of which are free, thanks to local taxpayers – as well as open space for roaming.

Standing on **Art Hill** in the central-western section of the park, the striking, Beaux Arts-style **St Louis Art Museum** (Tues–Sun 10am–5pm, Fri till 9pm; free; ⓣ314/721-0072, ⓦwww.slam.org) is the only surviving structure from the park's 1904 World's Fair. Its mission – to cover international art from prehistoric times onwards – is ambitious, but it manages to house one of the world's most extensive collections of German Expressionism; also, its pre-Columbian artworks cover every significant style, medium and culture from Mexico to Peru. In early 2010, the museum started a major expansion but plans to remain open, with no set completion date.

In addition to the animals in its "cageless displays", the well-regarded **St Louis Zoo** (hours vary seasonally; free; ⓣ314/781-0900, ⓦwww.stlzoo.org), set in beautiful grounds in the park, boasts a "Living World" exhibit, in which an animatronic robot of Charles Darwin offers synopses of his theories. In summer, Forest Park's 12,000-seat amphitheatre, **the Muny**, is regularly filled for Broadway-style musical theatre productions (ⓣ314/361-1900, ⓦwww.muny.org).

The main strengths of the **Missouri History Museum**, on the north-central fringe of the park (daily 10am–5pm, Tues till 8pm, extended hours in summer; free, touring exhibits extra; ⓣ314/746-4599, ⓦwww.mohistory.org), are its thematic collections of old photos of St Louis documenting river life, sports and black music in the city, and Charles Lindbergh's 1927 New York to Paris flight in the *Spirit of St Louis* (sponsored by the city's aircraft industry). The kid-friendly **St Louis Science Center** (Mon–Sat 9.30am–4.30pm, Sun 11.30am–4.30pm, extended hours in summer; free, parking and certain attractions extra; ⓣ314/289-4400, ⓦwww.slsc.org) straddles I-64 along the park's southern edge; use one of the radar guns on the covered access bridge to check the speed of cars on the freeway below.

On the edge of Forest Park, trendy shops, wine bars and c.1900 mansions line the leafy thoroughfares of the **Central West End**, ideal for a lazy stroll. A few blocks away at 4431 Lindell Blvd, the Romanesque-Byzantine **Cathedral Basilica of St Louis** houses the world's largest collection of mosaic art (daily 10am–4pm; free; call for tour information; ⓣ314/373-8242).

South City and the Hill

The tens of thousands of Germans who came to St Louis in the mid-eighteenth century settled mostly in **South City**, where the Teutonic influence is noticeable. These immigrants were skilled brewers; only one of the breweries they opened from the 1850s onwards still stands, but it does happen to be the largest in the US. The one hundred intricate red-brick buildings of the **Anheuser-Busch Brewery**, at 12th and Lynch streets, produce a sizeable proportion of the millions of barrels the company makes annually, most notably Budweiser. Locals were fiercely proud of the family-run company until its 2008 sale (some say takeover) by Belgian company InBev. Free eighty-minute **tours** (hours vary seasonally; ⓣ314/577-2626, ⓦwww.budweisertours.com) mostly consist of company PR, but they're still good fun.

A few blocks towards downtown, the colourful **Soulard Market**, at Broadway and Lafayette avenues (Wed–Fri 8am–5pm, Sat 6am–5pm; ⓣ314/622-4180; ⓦwww.soulardmarket.com), is a terrific place to pick up picnic items and fresh fruit, especially on a Saturday. The streets of **Soulard** behind it hold the city's best blues and jazz pubs, with taverns on practically every corner.

Further west, fire hydrants painted in Italian colours let you know you're in the thirty-square-block district known as **the Hill** – a small, neat Italian community three miles from Soulard. At its heart, **St Ambrose Church** displays a statue of Italian immigrants; all around, the aroma of freshly baked bread drifts out of the small specialty bakeries that share the area with one-room grocery stores, delis and a host of restaurants specializing in meaty pasta dishes and the city's signature appetizer, toasted ravioli.

Just east of the Hill in lovely Tower Grove Park, the 79-acre **Missouri Botanical Garden** (daily 9am–5pm; $8; ⓣ314/577-5100, ⓦwww.mobot.org) is a haven of peace and tranquillity. The grounds contain everything from a magnificent Japanese garden, scented rose and English woodland gardens to the Climatron, a huge greenhouse that recreates a tropical rainforest, complete with waterfalls and cliffs. Just off the southeast edge of the park, a stretch of **Tower Grove**'s South Grand Avenue is outfitted with pleasant shops and restaurants.

Eating

Thanks to heavy Italian immigration in the early twentieth century, **Italian food** predominates in St Louis, from humble salami sellers upwards. Otherwise, there are many friendly **Irish pubs**, serving beef sandwiches and stew, while University City's **Delmar Boulevard** offers a full slate of global options, from African and Middle Eastern to all sorts of Asian cuisine.

Baileys' Chocolate Bar 1915 Park Ave ⓣ314/241-8100. This combination café-bar just off Lafayette Square offers cheese plates, pizzettas, a raft of chocolate martinis and note-perfect desserts (try the milk chocolate bread pudding) inside its dusky main room and out on its patio.

Blues City Deli 2438 McNair Ave ⓣ314/773-8225. Blues memorabilia line the walls from floor to ceiling at this immensely popular deli on a Benton Park corner, adjacent to Soulard; it's tough to go wrong with any of the two dozen sandwich choices on the menu.

John D. McGurk's Irish Pub and Garden 1200 Russell Blvd ⓣ314/776-8309. Soulard's premier Irish tavern offers freshly baked soda bread, corned beef and cabbage, Irish stew and imported Guinness. There's live Irish music nightly and plentiful outdoor seating.

LoRusso's 3121 Watson Rd ⓣ314/647-6222. The house specialties at this colourfully curtained dining room on the Hill are pepper-fuelled dishes such as *ziti con vodka* and *fettucine pollo asiago*. The wine list is equally robust.

Ted Drewes Frozen Custard 4224 S Grand Blvd (summer only) ⓣ314/352-7376; also 6726 Chippewa Ave (closed Jan) ⓣ314/481-2652. A legendary slice of Americana, especially on a warm evening. Try a "concrete" – an ice cream so thick it won't budge if you turn your cup upside down. Closed Jan & Feb.

Nightlife and the arts

A sharp concentration of tourist-oriented **bars** and **clubs** can be found in Laclede's Landing, with nightly live music of all stripes; the Loop in U City, however, is where local students and thirty-something adults often head out for the evening. The slightly more upmarket **cafés and wine bars** of Central West End are also worth a look, while dressed-down Soulard is the place to go for good jazz and blues. Elsewhere in town, the **St Louis Symphony Orchestra** (ⓣ314/534-1700, ⓦwww.slso.org) calls 718 North Grand Ave in Grand Center home. Complete **listings** can be found in the free local weekly *Riverfront Times*.

1860 Saloon 1860 S 9th St ⓣ314/231-1860. One of the liveliest bars in Soulard, with dancing to blues, R&B and soul bands. Also serves good Cajun and fish dishes.

Blueberry Hill 6504 Delmar Blvd ⓣ314/727-4444. Crammed full of memorabilia, this local shrine includes a downstairs space called the Elvis Room, dedicated to the King himself. There's live music every weekend, and Chuck Berry drops in for monthly cameos.

Soulard Bastille 1027 Russell Blvd ⓣ314/664-4408. Built by Anheuser-Busch during prohibition, every square inch of this gay bar's walls is plastered in random bric-a-brac. There's a wide complement of cocktails to go along with a full pub fare menu.

Hannibal

HANNIBAL likely would have been just another medium-sized river settlement, had not one Samuel Langhorne Clemens spent his boyhood here (Clemens renamed himself **Mark Twain**, after the depth-marking cry of pilots on the Mississippi). Today, Hannibal's downtown is little more than a Twain-themed collection of museums, period buildings and wax displays, generally geared toward Midwestern weekenders and the *Tom Sawyer* enthusiast.

Twain wrote surprisingly little about his hometown in his extensive nonfiction works; you could say he spoke with his feet when he left for good at eighteen to become a journeyman printer, steamboat pilot and, of course, writer. Still, although he calls the rowdy frontier river port "St Petersburg" in *The Adventures of Tom Sawyer* and its sequel *The Adventures of Huckleberry Finn*, Hannibal is the inspiration for the novels.

The Town

Squeezed between two steep bluffs – *Tom Sawyer*'s lighthouse-topped **Cardiff Hill** to the north (accessible by stairs) and **Lover's Leap** to the south – once-vibrant Hannibal is a fairly quiet affair these days. Get an intimate look at the river's chugging, muddy waters aboard a sightseeing or dinner cruise on the **Mark Twain riverboat** (departure times vary seasonally; $14–37; ⓣ573/221-3222, ⓦwww.marktwainriverboat.com).

Twain's youthful stomping ground was the short, cobbled incline of **Hill Street** at the north end of downtown, where you'll find the restored **Mark Twain Boyhood Home**, a simple, white clapboard house where Twain lived between 1844 and 1853. Adjoining the house at the corner of Hill and Main streets is the **Original Mark Twain Museum** (June–Aug daily 8am–6pm; till 5pm rest of year, opening times vary seasonally; $9; ⓣ573/221-9010, ⓦwww.marktwainmuseum.org), which includes such memorabilia as first editions, letters, photos, original artwork and one of the author's trademark white coats. Antique, souvenir and gift stores stretch down Main Street, which also holds the **New Mark Twain Museum** (same information as above) at no. 120. Included in the admission price to the original museum and home, exhibits here re-create scenes from Twain's books, with the cave and Huck Finn's raft among them.

About two miles south of town at 300 Cave Hollow Rd is the **Mark Twain Cave** (June–Aug daily 9am–8pm, times vary slightly in other months; $15.95; ⓣ573/221-1656, ⓦwww.marktwaincave.com), where one-hour tours recall Tom Sawyer and Becky Thatcher's frightening misadventure in the dark. Further south, Hwy-79 towards St Louis offers one of the most **scenic drives** along the Mississippi, continually broken by thickly wooded islands and bounded by towering limestone bluffs.

Practicalities

Drop into Hannibal's **visitor centre**, 505 N Third St (Mon–Fri 8am–5pm, Sat 9am–5pm, Sun 10am–5pm; ⓣ573/221-2477, ⓦwww.visithannibal.com) for plenty of local information. If you're looking for a place to **stay** right in town, the *Best Western on the River* at 401 N Third St (ⓣ573/248-1150, ⓦwww.bestwestern.com; ❹–❺) was remodelled in 2009 and is one short block from Main Street; otherwise, try the clean and comfortable *Quality Inn & Suites* (ⓣ573/221-4001, ⓦwww.qualityinn.com; ❹) a few miles west of town along Hwy-36. About a mile south of town on Hwy-79, you can **camp** at the shaded *Mark Twain State Park Campground* (ⓣ573/565-3440, ⓦwww.mostateparks.com; $11–13). The best **food** option in downtown Hannibal is *The Brick Oven* at 205 Center St, where hearty Italian dishes are the main order, as well as pizzas baked in the cosy restaurant's namesake oven.

Western Missouri

Just as the Mississippi River defines Eastern Missouri, its tributary the Missouri (which gave the state its name) dominates the northwest border. Here along the river, jazz, blues and BBQ flourish in **Kansas City**, while upriver in St Joseph, the Pony Express Museum provides a glimpse at the earliest days of express mail delivery. Further south in the **Ozark Mountains**, cool lakes, forested hills and the hokey family-entertainment centre of **Branson** await.

Kansas City

KANSAS CITY straddles Missouri and Kansas 250 miles due west of St Louis, although the state line creates two fairly distinct – and governmentally separate – cities. Virtually all major points of interest sit on the Missouri side (known as "KC MO"), while the Kansas section ("KCK") maintains a much lower profile. Cool fountains, broad boulevards and Art Deco architecture make this a unique place, though one that's still resolutely Midwestern at heart.

Kansas City was a convenient staging post for 1830s wagon trains heading west. Its consequent prosperity – and rough-and-tumble "sin city" image – was brought to an abrupt end by the **Civil War**. However, its fortunes revived in the 1870s, when railroads supplied the meatpacking boom responsible for the development of the huge stockyards, which ultimately shut in 1992.

Thanks to political boss **Tom Pendergast**, an outrageous figure with whom the city had a love-hate relationship, Kansas City's many jazz clubs continued to sell alcohol during **Prohibition**. As in Chicago and New Orleans, speakeasies, brothels and gambling dens went hand in hand with superlative **jazz** – and, to a lesser extent, **blues** – spawning the careers of a handful of important artists, most notably bop pioneer Charlie Parker.

Arrival, information and city transport

From the **Kansas City International Airport**, twenty miles northwest of downtown, **shuttle buses** regularly head to downtown hotels; try SuperShuttle ($17;

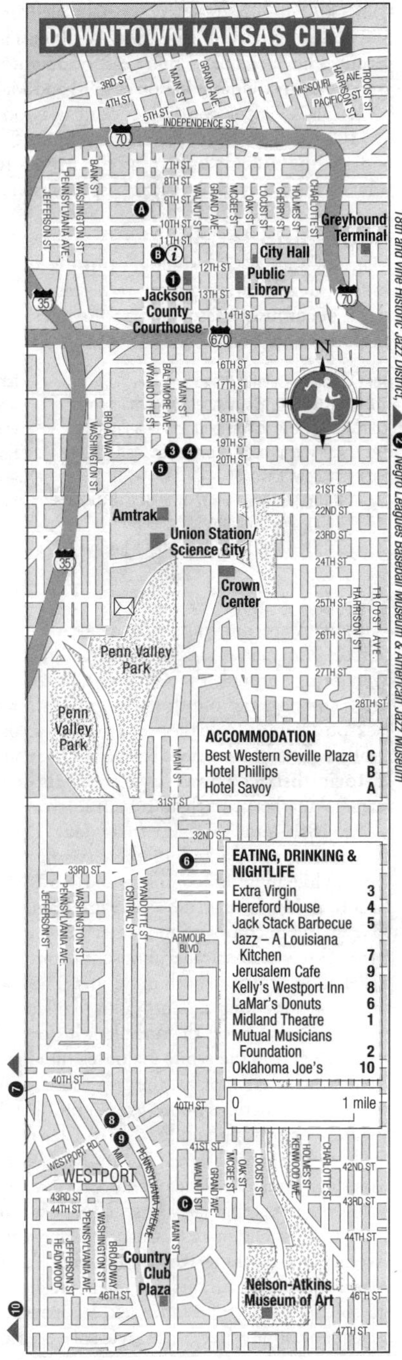

Ⓣ1-800/258-3826, Ⓦwww.supershuttle.com). The equivalent taxi ride costs around $50; call Yellow Cab (Ⓣ816/471-5000). The somewhat isolated Greyhound **bus** terminal lies a couple of miles east of downtown at 1101 Troost Ave, while Amtrak **trains** call in at Union Station at 23rd and Main streets, opposite Crown Center.

The city's **visitor centre** is tucked away on the 22nd floor of City Center Square at 1100 Main St (Mon–Fri 8.30am–5pm; Ⓣ816/221-5242, Ⓦwww.visitkc.com), and its **bus** system, known as the **Metro** (Ⓣ816/221-0660, Ⓦwww.kcata.org), offers a three-day, $10 visitor pass exclusively through its website.

Accommodation

Many of Kansas City's budget **motels** are found along I-70 heading east toward Independence, although you're better off staying more centrally considering the city's generously reasonable room rates. The visitor centre is a good place to enquire about **B&Bs**.

Best Western Seville Plaza 4309 Main St Ⓣ816/561-9600, Ⓦwww.bestwesternmissouri.com. Fairly close to Westport and Country Club Plaza, with rooms costing even less than what you'll find downtown. ④

Hotel Phillips 106 W 12th St Ⓣ816/221-7000, Ⓦwww.hotelphillips.com. Gorgeously restored downtown 1930s luxury hotel. Rooms are spacious and relaxing, while the mezzanine above the lobby is decked out in wonderful Art Deco touches. ⑤–⑥

Hotel Savoy 219 W 9th St Ⓣ816/842-3575, Ⓦwww.savoyhotel.net. Opened in 1888, this Garment District landmark has been beautifully renovated into a boutique B&B offering gourmet breakfasts. ⑤

The City

With many sparkling projects already completed and a riverfront in the early stages of redevelopment, Kansas City is working hard to invigorate its relaxed **downtown**. Wandering through the **Garment District**'s restored lofts and small businesses, between Sixth and Ninth streets, makes for a pleasant route to **City Hall** and the Jackson County Courthouse, a pair of striking Art Deco buildings that face one another across 12th Street between Oak and Locust streets. Also downtown is the **historic district** known as **River Market**, where colourful shops, cafés and a farmers' market at Fifth and Walnut streets liven up the river-adjacent area.

The **18th and Vine Historic Jazz District**, a couple of miles southeast of downtown, was the hub of the city's flourishing jazz scene through the 1940s. A worthwhile museum complex, at 1616 E 18th St, containing the **Negro Leagues Baseball Museum** (Tues–Sat 9am–6pm, Sun noon–6pm; $8; Ⓣ816/221-1920, Ⓦwww.nlbm.com) and the American Jazz Museum (same hours; $8; Ⓣ816/474-8463, Ⓦwww.americanjazzmuseum.com), now anchors the neighbourhood; a $10 ticket allows entry to both museums. The baseball museum is the more complete of the two, presenting an enthralling collection of photographs, exhibits and game equipment that traces the turbulent history of black baseball in America, which was segregated from the white major leagues for the first half of the twentieth century. Across the interior plaza, the jazz museum offers an introduction to the first half-century of America's home-grown music, taking close looks at early pioneers such as Louis Armstrong and local hero Charlie Parker but ignoring any developments made in the genre after 1955. Its *Blue Room* functions as a working jazz bar each Monday, Thursday, Friday and Saturday night, while the *Gem Theater* it operates across the street regularly hosts larger-scale performances.

Owned by Hallmark Cards, the sprawling concrete **Crown Center**, at Grand Avenue and Pershing Road, calls itself "a city within a city" and contains apartments, shops, restaurants, offices, a hotel, cinemas and even an ice rink. Displays in its splendidly awful **Hallmark Visitors Center** (Mon–Fri 10am–4.30pm, Sat 9.30am–4.30pm; free) trace styles of greeting cards alongside political and cultural changes; designs from the 1940s, for example, feature stars and stripes and Uncle Sam. **Westport**, an attractive quarter of boutiques, cafés and restaurants (including an inordinate number of pizzerias), is west of Main Street between 39th and 45th streets and was the original jumping-off point for the Santa Fe Trail. A little further south along Main, beginning at 47th Street, you'll find elegant **Country Club Plaza**, which looks amazingly fresh despite dating from the early 1920s. Several blocks of upmarket shops and restaurants sit amid lovely tiling and mosaics, grand fountains, shade trees and even a canal, all evoking a Mediterranean feel in the middle of North America.

Just to the east, highlights at the extensive **Nelson-Atkins Museum of Art**, 4525 Oak St (Wed 10am–4pm, Thurs & Fri 10am–9pm, Sat 10am–5pm, Sun noon–5pm; museum and grounds free, parking $5; Ⓣ816/561-4000, Ⓦwww.nelson-atkins.org), include superb Oriental exhibits and Monet canvases. Outside, a sculpture park is set amid immaculately landscaped grounds, where lawns stretch into the distance and provide scale for the stately museum.

Eating

BBQ, once the unfashionable food of the poor, is now a big deal in Kansas City, from lowbrow joints flourishing on word-of-mouth popularity to fine-dining restaurants where saucy meats and white tablecloths make for peculiar company. Still, as much as meat rules the scene, this is a major city, so a variety of dining options are available.

Extra Virgin 1900 Main St Ⓣ816/842-2202. Excellent spot for tapas in the Crossroads art district; its patio is a choice spot on a warm evening. Small plates such as crispy pork belly ($11) and potatoes bravas ($6) squarely hit the mark, with a far-reaching wine list.

Hereford House 100 E 20th St Ⓣ816/842-1080. Known for its prime rib, this steakhouse south of downtown has been a local staple for decades.

Jack Stack Barbecue 101 W 22nd St Ⓣ816/472-7427. Widely regarded as the finest of Kansas City's upmarket BBQ restaurants, with three other locations scattered around the metro area. Dinner platters of pork and beef slabs for two are roughly $26.

Jerusalem Cafe 431 Westport Rd Ⓣ816/756-2770. Small Middle Eastern restaurant serving superb falafel and kebabs.

LaMar's Donuts 3395 Main St Ⓣ816/561-7176. A KC institution, now with branches in several states; this one is the original. Closes at 2pm.

Oklahoma Joe's 3002 W 47th Ave Ⓣ913/722-3366. Cross the state line into Kansas and hit this rightfully popular meatery at a corner gas station. Everything's hot off the grill (even the meat-topped salads) and priced to please, with reasonable portion sizes that won't send you scurrying for the nearest sofa. The perfectly smoky BBQ beans alone are worth a visit.

Nightlife

Consult the Friday and Sunday editions of the *Kansas City Star* for **entertainment listings**, as well as *The Pitch,* a free weekly which covers the entire metropolitan area, including the nearby college town of Lawrence, Kansas.

Jazz – A Louisiana Kitchen 1823 W 39th St Ⓣ816/531-5556. Live jazz or blues performances nightly at this Cajun restaurant and watering hole.

Kelly's Westport Inn 500 Westport Rd Ⓣ816/561-5800. Shabby but friendly bar inside Kansas City's oldest structure.

Midland Theatre 1228 Main St Ⓣ816/283-9900. Lovingly restored music hall that's Kansas City's primary mid-level concert venue.

Mutual Musicians Foundation 1823 Highland Ave Ⓣ816/471-5212. National historic landmark in the somewhat rough 18th and Vine district. Jazz jam sessions run Fri & Sat 1.30–5.30am.

St Joseph

Sixty miles north of Kansas City, **ST JOSEPH** boomed as a supply depot during California's gold rush. These days, it's a fairly sleepy riverside town, but for a brief eighteen months, beginning in 1860, it was the home of the legendary **Pony Express**, which delivered mail to Sacramento, California, in ten days via continuous horseback relay. The Pony Express was soon made irrelevant by the completion of the transcontinental telegraph, but riders such as Buffalo Bill Cody went on to become legends. The full story is told in dioramas and a short introductory film at the **Pony Express Museum**, 914 Penn St (Mon–Sat 9am–5pm, Sun 1–5pm; $5; ⓣ816/279-5059, ⓦwww.ponyexpress.org), set in the company's original stables.

St Joseph's other claim to fame is that it was the site of **Jesse James**' death on April 3, 1882, when the notorious outlaw was shot in the back by Robert Ford, a 20-year-old member of his own gang who had negotiated a $10,000 reward from the governor. The **Jesse James Home Museum** (April–Oct: Mon–Sat 10am–5pm, Sun 1–5pm; call for hours rest of year; $3; ⓣ816/232-8206, ⓦwww.ponyexpressjessejames.com), the one-storey frame cottage where James was living incognito while he planned his next bank job, now stands at 1202 Penn St, having been moved closer to the Pony Express Museum to attract more visitors. A ragged hole in the wall is pointed out as the spot where the bullet supposedly hit, after striking James as he was hanging a picture; you can also see where bloodstained splinters were chiselled from the floor to be sold as souvenirs.

You'll find plenty of rock-bottom rates at several **motels** along I-29 as it passes east of downtown, including a *Days Inn* at the Frederick Boulevard exit (ⓣ816/279-1671, ⓦwww.daysinn.com; ❷).

Southwestern Missouri and the Ozarks

South of Kansas City, there's little to see before the **Ozark Mountains**. Occupying most of southern Missouri and northern Arkansas, the area remained frontier territory until timber companies moved in at the end of the nineteenth century. When they moved on, the hill-dwellers were left to eke out a living from the denuded terrain; severe droughts forced many to leave for the cities. For those who stayed, fishing resorts and tourist attractions supply some work, though the region remains poor. None of the Ozark peaks are particularly high, though the roads through them switch, dip, climb and swerve to provide **views** of steep hillsides thick with oak, elm, hickory and redbud, particularly resplendent in autumn. **Springfield** is the region's main city, 130 miles south of Kansas City, but the toothless resort and entertainment town of **Branson** is more popular by far.

Branson

Nestled among beautiful lakes, **BRANSON**, forty miles south of Springfield, has become one of the top tourist destinations in the United States. Millions of visitors each year are attracted to what's become known as the "Ozark Disneyland" for its fifty or so music venues (almost all of a country or nostalgia bent), a handful of theme parks, and shows exclusively geared toward families – if you're looking for anything remotely edgy or avant-garde, you've veered far off path.

The newly constructed **Branson Landing** offers waterfront shopping, dining and entertainment highlighted (weather permitting) by an impressive hourly water and light show (noon–10pm; free). Elsewhere in town, **the Strip** is populated by a wide range of neon-licked tourist traps and entertainment venues, where the spectrum ranges from Japanese fiddler-singer Shoji Tabuchi, Russian comedian Yakov Smirnoff and ancient crooner Andy Williams to superb acts such as Alison Krauss. **Tickets** for a two-hour show are fairly priced ($20–30 is typical) and there's no shortage of takers, especially in summer.

Once you've had it with Branson, escape by driving thirty miles west to **Table Rock Lake**, a scenic area offering hiking, biking, camping, waterskiing and world-class fishing.

Practicalities

Greyhound **buses** connect Branson with Springfield, Kansas City and Memphis. Visit Ⓦwww.explorebranson.com for a wealth of information of local lodging, dining and entertainment options, or drop in at the **North Welcome Center** (Mon–Sat 8am–5pm, Sun 10am–4pm; Ⓣ417/334-4084) at 4910 Hwy-65.

If you're looking for **lodging** in Branson, *Best Western Music Capital Inn* (Ⓣ417/334-8378, Ⓦwww.bestwesternmissouri.com; ❺), at 3257 Shepherd of the Hills Expressway, offers adequate lodging at fairly reasonable rates. Alternately, you can stay on the campus of **College of the Ozarks** in either a standard motel room or a rustically luxurious suite at the *Keeter Center Lodge* (Ⓣ417/239-1900, Ⓦwww.keetercenter.edu; ❸–❼). If it's rusticity you're after, try **camping** at nearby Table Rock State Park (Ⓣ417/334-4704; $10–13).

Calorific eats abound in Branson: *Joe's Crab Shack* at Branson Landing (Ⓣ417/337-7373) and the unpretentious cooking at *Farmhouse Restaurant* (Ⓣ417/334-9701), 119 W Main St, are each reliable choices.

Oklahoma

Wedged between gargantuan Texas to the south and the gently rolling farmland of Kansas to the north, **OKLAHOMA** has experienced a singularly traumatic history. In the 1830s, all this land, held to be useless, was set aside as **Indian Territory** – a convenient dumping ground for the so-called Five Civilized Tribes who, for a time, had blocked white settlement in the southern states. The Choctaw and Chickasaw of Mississippi, the Seminole of Florida and the Creek of Alabama were each assigned a share, while the rest (though already inhabited by Native Americans) was given to the Cherokee from Carolina, Tennessee and Georgia, who followed in 1838 on the notorious four-month trek known as "the Trail of Tears" (see p.450). Today, the state claims a large Native American population – "oklahoma" is the Choctaw word for "red man" – and many of its towns host museums devoted to Native American history.

Once white settlers realized that Indian Territory was, in fact, well worth farming, they decided to stay. The Native Americans were relocated once more, and in a series of manic free-for-all scrambles starting in 1889, entire towns sprang up literally overnight. Those who jumped the gun and claimed land illegally were known as Sooners; hence Oklahoma's nickname, the "**Sooner State**".

White settlers didn't have an easy life, however. They faced, after great oil prosperity in the 1920s, an era of unthinkable hardship in the 1930s. The desperate migration, when whole communities fled the state's blinding dust bowl for California, has come to encapsulate the worst horrors of the Depression, most famously in John Steinbeck's novel (and John Ford's film) **The Grapes of Wrath**, but also in Dorothea Lange's haunting photos of itinerant families hitching and camping on the road, and in the sad yet hopeful songs of Woody Guthrie. Improved farming techniques in the post-World War II era eventually brought life back to Oklahoma.

Many of the state's places of interest, including **Tulsa**, lie in the hilly and wooded northeast, while the Tornado Alley grassland of central Oklahoma holds the revitalized capital, **Oklahoma City**. The lakes and parks of Oklahoma's southern reaches have helped make tourism the state's second leading industry after oil.

Eastern Oklahoma

Eastern Oklahoma includes the "Green Country" of the northeast, patterned with the foothills of the Ozarks, as well as woods, streams, lakes and rivers that make it a popular camping destination. **Tulsa** is its cultural centre, while the towns of **Bartlesville** and **Muskogee** also hold attractions worth visiting.

Tulsa

TULSA had its heyday as a wealthy oil town in the 1920s, and today its sedate downtown merits a tour for its Art Deco architecture alone. Despite – or possibly because of – its liveable atmosphere and excellent art museums, the city tends towards complacency.

Downtown Tulsa's most obvious Art Deco landmark is the ornate **Union Depot train station,** 3 S Boston Ave, built in the early 1930s and now housing offices. One distinctive 1920s skyscraper, the **Philtower** at 427 S Boston Ave, features a red-tiled sloping roof and crouching gargoyles, while at 1301 S Boston Ave, the huge and gloriously exuberant Art Deco **Boston Avenue Methodist Church** offers terrific views of the city from its 258ft-high tower.

The **Greenwood Historic District**, a small section of narrow streets north of downtown, is where most of the town's black population once lived. In 1921, a brutal race riot erupted after a black man was accused of assaulting a white woman in a downtown elevator; houses, businesses and churches in Greenwood were burned to the ground in the ensuing melee. Other Greenwood properties fell victim to urban renewal in the mid-1960s, but a small group of original buildings remains along Greenwood Avenue and Archer Street.

The airy and stylish **Philbrook Museum of Art**, 2727 S Rockford Rd (Tues, Wed & Fri–Sun 10am–5pm, Thurs 10am–8pm; $7.50; Ⓣ918/749-7941, Ⓦwww.philbrook.org), in the well-heeled suburb of Mapleridge, is housed in a Florentine-style mansion amid an oasis of fountains and greenery. Though displays include Native American pottery, African sculpture and Renaissance paintings, the building itself is every bit as decorative as the art, with ostentatious marble floors, indoor fountains and sweeping staircases.

Just northwest of downtown Tulsa, the **Gilcrease Museum**, 1400 N Gilcrease Museum Rd (Tues–Sun 10am–5pm; $8; Ⓣ918/596-2700, Ⓦwww.gilcrease.org), is set in the verdant, gently rolling Osage Hills. Thomas Gilcrease, of Native American heritage, grew very rich once oil was discovered under his land. His private collection of Western art includes Native American works, as well as excellent Remingtons, Russells and Morans.

If you're looking to balance local history and art museums with quirky Americana, head out to the neighbouring community of Catoosa for a picnic at the **Blue Whale** sculpture, an old **Route 66** mainstay restored to its original glory. If you're interested in other sights along the Oklahoma section of the erstwhile national highway, contact the Oklahoma Route 66 Association (Ⓣ 405/258-0008, Ⓦwww.oklahomaroute66.com).

Practicalities

Tulsa International Airport lies eight miles northeast of downtown. Greyhound **buses** arrive and depart downtown at 317 S Detroit Ave. Tulsa Transit, the city's **bus** service, operates between 5am and 8.30pm, with no Sunday service ($1.50). The **Tulsa Convention & Visitors Bureau**, 2 W Second St, Suite 150 (Mon–Fri 8am–5pm; ⓣ1-800/558-3311, ⓦwww.visittulsa.com), provides information on a self-guided **walking tour** of downtown.

Most of Tulsa's budget **hotels** are adjacent to the interstates and along W Skelly Drive, forking southwest from I-44. If you're feeling flush, try the tastefully restored *Hotel Ambassador* downtown at 1324 S Main St (ⓣ1-888/408-8282, ⓦwww.hotelambassador-tulsa.com; ❽). Otherwise, a few **B&Bs** dot Tulsa, including *McBirney Mansion* at 1414 S Galveston Ave (ⓣ918/585-3234, ⓦwww.mcbirneymansion.com; ❻), perched overlooking the Arkansas River.

Tulsa's **restaurants** are diverse and scattered, and several good options can be found along S Peoria Avenue in the Brookside district and, north from there a couple of miles, along E 15th Street. For inexpensive and tasty pasta dishes with a heavy carnivorous bent, head over to *Camerelli's Ristorante*, 1536 E 15th St (ⓣ918/582-8900).

Bartlesville

For forty miles north of Tulsa, the monotony of the plains is relieved only by clumps of spindly scrub oaks. Then comes quiet **BARTLESVILLE**, dominated by the extraordinary, anachronistic **Price Tower** (Tues–Sat 10am–5pm, Sun noon–5pm; call or check website for tour times; ⓣ918/336-4949, ⓦwww.pricetower.org). This cantilevered green oddity, at Sixth Street and Dewey Avenue, was designed by Frank Lloyd Wright and completed in 1956; judge for yourself if it resembles a very tall tree, as many believe. The tower was the only Wright-designed skyscraper the famed architect saw built, and today it holds the Price Tower Art Center and stylish *Copper Bar* (Tues–Sat 4–9pm) on its top floors, and the modern *Inn at Price Tower*, an Arts and Crafts-style hotel (ⓣ1-877/424-2424; ❻), in between.

The **Frank Phillips Home**, 1107 Cherokee Ave (Wed–Sat 10am–5pm, second Sun of each month 1–5pm; $3 suggested donation; ⓣ918/336-2491, ⓦwww.frankphillipshome.org), built in 1908 by the founder of Phillips Oil, displays wealth at its gaudiest, with gold faucets, mirrored ceilings and marble floors. More impressive is Phillips' former ranch, now known as the **Woolaroc Museum & Wildlife Preserve** (Tues–Sun 10am–5pm; Sept–May closed Tues; $8; ⓣ1-888/966-5276, ⓦwww.woolaroc.org), twelve miles southwest in the Osage Hills, where over sixty thousand Western art and history artefacts are scattered throughout seven huge rooms. Paintings and decorative art, from Native American works to the epic Western scenes of Remington and Russell, line the walls, while items belonging to various tribes, pioneers and cowboys are gathered in too great an abundance to take in. Look for the 95-million-year-old dinosaur egg, exquisite Navajo blankets, scalps taken by Native Americans and Buffalo Bill's weathered saddle.

If you linger in Bartlesville and the *Inn at Price Tower* is out of your **lodging** budget, opt for no-frills lodging at *Travelers Motel*, 3105 E Frank Phillips Blvd (ⓣ918/333-1900; ❷).

Muskogee

In 1834, the Creek tribe trudged along "the Trail of Tears" (see p.450), ultimately ending up in **MUSKOGEE**, fifty miles southeast of Tulsa. After establishing the town as the central meeting place of the Five Civilized Tribes, Native American

Storm chasing around Tornado Alley

Given the Great Plains' violently unpredictable weather, it's no surprise that **storm chasing** has become big business in Oklahoma and its neighbouring Tornado Alley states. If you're either very brave or simply foolhardy, you can spend a week or two driving around the prairies tracking tornadoes and all sorts of other wicked weather. Companies such as Cloud 9 Tours (ⓣ405/323-1145, ⓦwww.cloud9tours.com) and Storm Chasing Adventure Tours (ⓣ303/888-8629, ⓦwww.stormchasing.com) claim their operations are perfectly safe and all but guarantee you an up-close encounter with a tornado. Tours cover many Midwestern states and will set you back $2600–2800; be sure to book well in advance.

leaders gathered here in 1905 to draw up a plan for their own separate state, which was never to be – the arrival of the railroad in the 1870s and the discovery of oil in 1903 guaranteed that white settlers would usurp the town. The **Five Civilized Tribes Museum** (Mon–Fri 10am–5pm, Sat 10am–2pm; $3; ⓣ918/683-1701, ⓦwww.fivetribes.org), 1101 Honor Heights Drive, tells the Native Americans' story through costumes, documents, photographs and jewellery.

Oklahoma City

OKLAHOMA CITY was created in a matter of hours on April 22, 1889, after a single gunshot signalled the opening of the land to white settlement; what was barren prairie at dawn had by nightfall become a city of ten thousand. In 1911, the capital was moved here from nearby Guthrie, and in 1928 oil was discovered. Sitting on one of the nation's largest oil fields, the city has found that its fortunes are all too closely tied to those of the oil industry over the decades, although tourism development, its enormous cattle market and an inflated sales tax that has funded redevelopment in run-down neighbourhoods all continue to help diversify its portfolio.

The devastating **bombing** of the Alfred P. Murrah Federal Building on April 19, 1995 – which killed 168 people, 19 of them children – tore the heart out of the city in the most painful of literal terms. However, the massive community rescue effort has since helped Oklahoma City regain some of its self-confidence, while a solemnly landscaped memorial has been constructed at the buildings' former site.

Arrival, information and city transport

Will Rogers World Airport lies southwest of the city and is connected to downtown by both Oklahoma City Metro Transit and Airport Express ($20; ⓣ405/681-3311). The city's **Visitor Information Center** (Mon–Fri 9am–6pm; ⓣ405/602-5141, ⓦwww.visitokc.com) is downtown at the Cox Convention Center, at the corner of Sheridan Ave and E.K. Gaylord Blvd. Greyhound **buses** call in at the Union Bus Depot at 427 W Sheridan, while Amtrak's *Heartland Flyer* **train** arrives and departs at Santa Fe Station, directly across the street from the convention centre.

Oklahoma City's public transportation system, Metro Transit (ⓣ405/235-7433, ⓦwww.gometro.org), operates Monday to Saturday; fares are $1.25 for **buses** and 25¢–$1 for **Oklahoma Spirit Trolleys**, the latter linking downtown attractions with Bricktown and, in summer, Regatta Park.

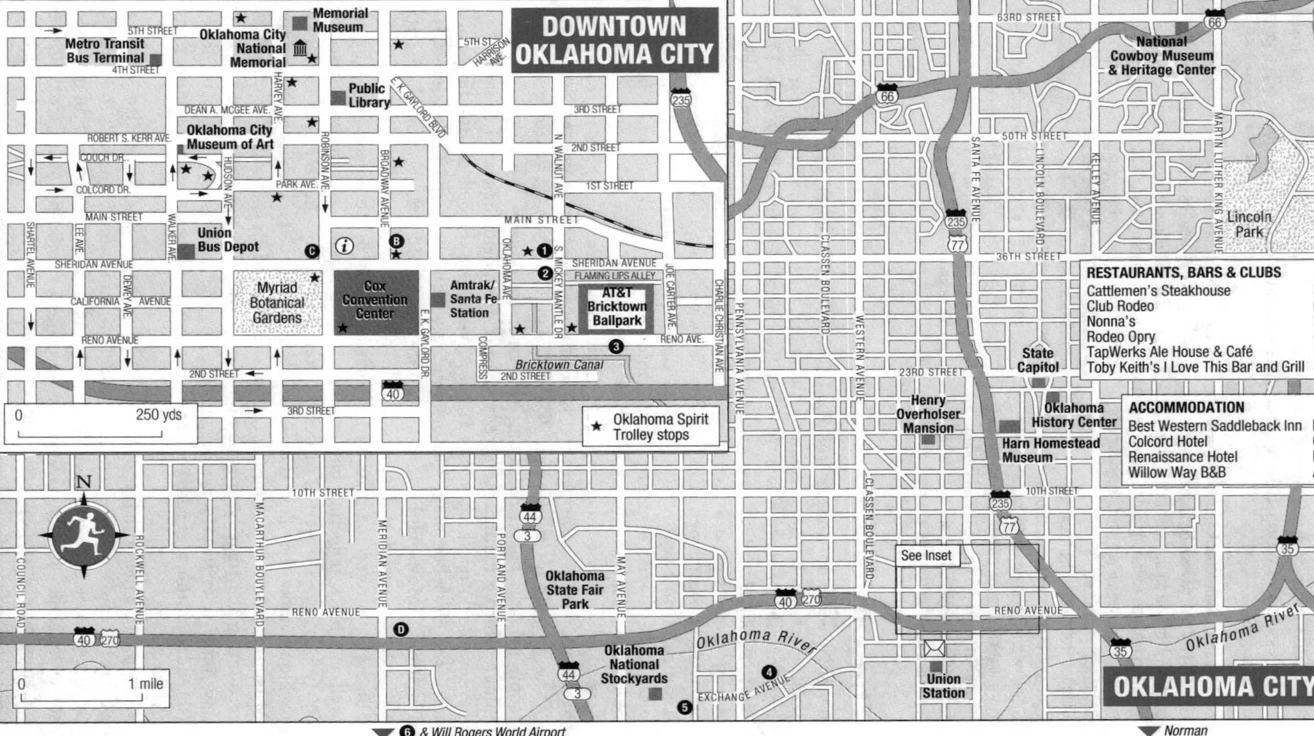
OKLAHOMA CITY
DOWNTOWN OKLAHOMA CITY
RESTAURANTS, BARS & CLUBS
Cattlemen's Steakhouse 5
Club Rodeo 6
Nonna's 2
Rodeo Opry 4
TapWerks Ale House & Café 1
Toby Keith's I Love This Bar and Grill 3
ACCOMMODATION
Best Western Saddleback Inn D
Colcord Hotel C
Renaissance Hotel B
Willow Way B&B A
Oklahoma Spirit Trolley stops
0 250 yds
0 1 mile
A, Tulsa, Wichita (KS) & Guthrie
6 & Will Rogers World Airport
Norman
Amarillo (TX)
National Cowboy Museum & Heritage Center
Lincoln Park
State Capitol
Oklahoma History Center
Harn Homestead Museum
Henry Overholser Mansion
Union Station
See Inset
Oklahoma State Fair Park
Oklahoma National Stockyards
Oklahoma River
Metro Transit Bus Terminal
Oklahoma City National Memorial
Memorial Museum
Public Library
Oklahoma City Museum of Art
Union Bus Depot
Myriad Botanical Gardens
Cox Convention Center
Amtrak/ Santa Fe Station
AT&T Bricktown Ballpark
Bricktown Canal
63RD STREET
50TH STREET
36TH STREET
23RD STREET
10TH STREET
MARTIN LUTHER KING AVENUE
KELLEY AVENUE
LINCOLN BOULEVARD
SANTA FE AVENUE
CLASSEN BOULEVARD
WESTERN AVENUE
PENNSYLVANIA AVENUE
MAY AVENUE
PORTLAND AVENUE
MERIDIAN AVENUE
MACARTHUR BOULEVARD
ROCKWELL AVENUE
COUNCIL ROAD
RENO AVENUE
EXCHANGE AVENUE
5TH STREET
4TH STREET
5TH ST
HARRISON AVE.
3RD STREET
2ND STREET
1ST STREET
MAIN STREET
DEAN A. MCGEE AVE.
ROBERT S. KERR AVE.
COUCH DR.
COLCORD DR.
PARK AVE.
SHERIDAN AVENUE
CALIFORNIA AVENUE
RENO AVENUE
2ND STREET
3RD STREET
SHARTEL AVENUE
LEE AVE.
DEWEY AVE.
WALKER AVE.
HUDSON AVE.
HARVEY AVE.
ROBINSON AVE.
BROADWAY AVENUE
E. K. GAYLORD BLVD
E. K. GAYLORD DR.
COMPRESS
N WALNUT AVE
OKLAHOMA AVE
S. MICKEY MANTLE DR
FLAMING LIPS ALLEY
JOE CARTER AVE.
CHARLIE CHRISTIAN AVE
RENO AVE.
N

Accommodation

The usual array of **budget motels** are scattered along Oklahoma City's interstates, especially along I-40 at Meridian Avenue; local **B&Bs** often offer good deals as well.

Best Western Saddleback Inn 4300 SW 3rd St ⓣ405/947-7000, ⓦwww.bwsaddleback.com. One block north of I-40 on the west side of town, this tidy hotel features an inviting outdoor pool and an on-site bar and restaurant where everything is Southwestern-themed. ④

Colcord Hotel 15 N Robinson Ave ⓣ405/601-4300, ⓦwww.colcordhotel.com. Sleek, relaxing boutique hotel housed in the city's first skyscraper. Spacious rooms with downtown views are outfitted with modern furnishings and glass-tiled showers, while the lobby is a marbled feast for the eyes. ⑥–⑦

Renaissance Hotel 10 N Broadway Ave ⓣ405/228-8000, ⓦwww.renaissanceoklahomacity.com. Very centrally located high-rise a short walk or trolley ride from Bricktown. Rooms and suites are sizeable and boast views across the Oklahoma prairie. ⑦

Willow Way B&B 27 Oakwood Drive ⓣ405/427-2133, ⓦwww.willowwaybb.com. Cosy, English-style B&B about seven miles northeast of the city centre, set amid two acres of gardens and ponds. ⑤

The City

Tumbleweeds no longer roll by downtown Oklahoma City's low-key skyscrapers, but the area remains a bit muted, with little to detain most visitors for more than a day or two. **Myriad Botanical Gardens** (daily 6am–11pm; free; ⓣ405/297-3995, ⓦwww.myriadgardens.com), at Reno and Robinson Avenues, offers great views of the brick-towered downtown skyline from its attractively landscaped hills, gardens and waterways. The **Crystal Bridge Tropical Conservatory** (Mon–Sat 9am–6pm, Sun noon–6pm; $6), set in a glass, tube-shaped structure in the middle of the park, abounds in exotic blooms. Both are scheduled to reopen in spring 2011 after a year-long overhaul. Several blocks east ducks ply calm **Bricktown Canal**, which is crossed by numerous pedestrian bridges as it winds through the tourist quarter. Bricktown Water Taxi ($8 for all-day pass; ⓣ405/234-8263, ⓦwww.bricktownwatertaxi.com) operates boat rides along the canal continually every ten to fifteen minutes during summer; service is weather dependent the rest of the year.

A few blocks north, at 620 N Harvey Ave, where the Federal Building stood until the 1995 bombing, visitors sombrely mill about the **Oklahoma City National Memorial** (free; ⓣ405/235-3313, ⓦwww.oklahomacitynationalmemorial.org). Dominating the city's core, the site includes a field of 168 empty bronze and glass chairs (each strikingly lit from below at night), as well as a black reflecting pool flanked by two massive gold barriers marking 9.01–9.03am – the period of destruction. Nearby, an elm tree that continued to bloom after the blast stands as a lone sentinel. The adjacent **Memorial Museum** (Mon–Sat 9am–6pm, Sun 1–6pm; $10) is also worth a visit, recounting the tragedy in gruesome detail, with TV news coverage from the day, interviews with survivors, tributes to the victims and poignant debris (shredded clothing, cracked coffee mugs, twisted filing cabinets) all pulled from the wreckage.

Close to the memorial, at 415 Couch Drive, is the **Oklahoma City Museum of Art** (Tues–Sat 10am–5pm, Thurs till 9pm, Sun noon–5pm; $12; ⓣ405/236-3100, ⓦwww.okcmoa.com). The lobby is host to a 55ft-tall blown-glass tower by Dale Chihuly, as well as a permanent exhibition of his work. Other galleries hold European and American art, as well as numerous travelling exhibitions.

Just northeast of downtown, the **Oklahoma State Capitol** at 2300 N Lincoln Blvd (Mon–Fri 8am–4.30pm; free) is unique among government buildings for its working oil wells pumping crude from below. The complex also includes the **Oklahoma History Center** (Mon–Sat 10am–5pm; $7; ⓣ405/522-5248, ⓦwww.okhistorycenter.org), across from the Governor's Mansion.

Sitting atop Persimmon Hill overlooking old Route 66, the **National Cowboy Museum and Heritage Center**, 1700 NE 63rd St (daily 10am–5pm; $12.50; ⓣ405/478-2250, ⓦwww.nationalcowboymuseum.org), is a real treat, combining high and popular art in one loving collection. Examining the works of Remington and Russell, the link between Western art and Western movies becomes clear: the paintings look like film stills, while titles such as *Waiting for Trouble* evoke cinema's endlessly reworked myths of the West. Large exhibitions focus on contemporary Native American work, much of it colourful, bitter and subversive. John Wayne's collection is a delight for the cowboy fetishist, and the Western Performers Gallery pays homage to movie cowboys and cowgirls via overly reverent oil paintings and memorabilia.

Finally, the **Oklahoma National Stockyards**, at 2501 Exchange Ave, a few miles southwest of downtown, touts itself as the biggest stocker/feeder cattle market the world over. Although vegetarians and animal-lovers should steer clear, the place is well worth a visit for some. This is the real thing: free to visit, defiantly un-touristy and full of stomping and snorting cattle being shunted in and out of smelly, cramped pens for auction. The roughnecks who spend their lives here – smoking, chatting, even sleeping – take no apparent notice of the quick-fire auctioneer, but it can make for addictive entertainment. Sales begin at 6am (Mon & Tues only) and reach a fever pitch in mid-morning before fizzling out by late afternoon.

Eating

Although it's known for meat-and-potatoes grub, Oklahoma City's **restaurant scene** holds a surprise or two. The renovated-warehouse restaurants of Bricktown, along Sheridan and Reno avenues east of the Santa Fe Station, are popular with visitors and locals alike.

Cattlemen's Steakhouse 1309 S Agnew Ave ⓣ405/236-0416. Regulars from the adjacent stockyards populate this evocatively dark restaurant from another era – expect burgundy booths, juicy steaks and lots of chatter about the cattle trade.

Nonna's 1 Mickey Mantle Way ⓣ405/235-4410. High-end American eats with European flair. Diners delight in choice cuisine such as pan-seared sea scallops and bacon-wrapped filet mignon.

TapWerks Ale House and Cafe 121 E Sheridan Ave ⓣ405/319-9599. This popular Bricktown spot features a British-influenced menu and lays claim to the largest beer selection in the state, with hundreds available.

Nightlife and entertainment

If you're into **country music**, Oklahoma City will set you right, with quite a few live-music and dance venues. Wednesday's *Oklahoma Gazette* carries helpful **listings**.

Club Rodeo 2301 S Meridian Ave ⓣ405/686-1191. Located several miles southwest of downtown, this popular dance hall and saloon can be hit and miss – a little cheesy some nights, rollicking fun on others.

Rodeo Opry 221 Exchange Ave ⓣ405/297-9773. Nonprofit venue devoted to authentic country music shows in the style of Nashville's Grand Ole Opry. One show a week: Sat 7.30pm ($6–12).

Toby Keith's I Love This Bar And Grill 310 Johnny Bench Drive ⓣ405/231-0254. The country crooner's down-to-earth joint in Bricktown is a good place for a beer and live country music.

Kansas

KANSAS may be associated with quaint, gingham-pinafore images from *Little House on the Prairie* and *The Wizard of Oz*, but the region was at one time known as "bleeding Kansas". The 1854 **Kansas-Nebraska Act**, which gave both territories the right to self-determination over slavery, led to fierce clashes between Free Staters and pro-slavery forces. Runaway slaves from the South were given passage through the area, aided by abolitionist John Brown, and Kansas eventually joined the Union as a free state.

After the Civil War, the mighty cattle drives from Texas made towns like Abilene, Wichita and Dodge City centres of the "**Wild West**". The debauched, masculine image of the West, spawning such "heroes" as Wyatt Earp and Wild Bill Hickok, is challenged in Kansas, however, which along with being the first state to give women the vote in municipal elections, also boasts claims to having the nation's first female mayor and senator. Despite all this, its politics have taken a decidedly conservative turn in recent years.

In 1874, Russian Mennonites brought the grain that was to transform the state into the bountiful "breadbasket" that now harvests much of the nation's wheat. However, only in the west do miles of golden stalks sway in Kansas's perennial prairie wind. The green and hilly northeast, patterned with woods and lakes, is home to the unattractive, industrial capital city of **Topeka**, vibrant college town of **Lawrence** and the dull suburbs of Kansas City (whose downtown lies across the state line in Missouri). The once-wicked cowtown of **Dodge City** is in the southwest, while **Wichita**, the state's largest city, lies in the south-central area.

Eastern Kansas

Undulating east Kansas is laced with a surprising number of lakes, streams and rivers. The **northeast**, once crossed by the Oregon, Santa Fe and Smoky Hill trails, and now home to both Topeka and **Lawrence**, is more heavily visited than the **southeast**, where the major attraction is the *Little House on the Prairie* historical site, located thirteen miles southwest of Independence on Hwy-75. The heritage of Kansas's four Native American tribes comes alive in annual powwows, held in major towns as well as on northwestern reservations.

Lawrence

Collegiate **LAWRENCE** lies on the Kansas River, roughly halfway between Kansas City and Topeka. Tree-lined streets, a welcoming historic downtown and an aura of artiness make it an appealing destination, with a cultural energy owed in part to the **University of Kansas** and a long liberal and intellectual history.

Founded by the New England Emigrant Aid Company in 1854, and a centre of Free State activities, Lawrence was the site of a violent Civil War skirmish in 1863, when it was set ablaze by Confederate guerillas. Rebuilding was quick, however, as evidenced by the limestone and brick buildings of today's downtown, centred on Massachusetts Street and the KU campus, which stands on a steep, tree-covered grassy bank known as Mount Oread.

Arrival, information and accommodation

Amtrak **trains** arrive in Lawrence at 413 E 7th St, and Greyhound **buses** come in at 2447 W 6th St. The **visitor centre** is north of downtown in the renovated Union Pacific Depot, at 402 N 2nd St (Mon–Sat 8.30am–5.30pm, Sun 1–5pm; ⓣ785/865-4499, ⓦwww.visitlawrence.com).

Comfortable **rooms** can be found at the lovely, all-suite *Eldridge Hotel*, at 7th and Massachusetts streets (ⓣ785/749-5011, ⓦwww.eldridgehotel.com; ❻). Twice burned down by pro-slavery forces, it has been restored to an evocative elegance and now houses the stylish *Ten* restaurant (ⓣ785/749-5011), which specializes in New American cuisine; the atmospheric *Jayhawker* bar and its extensive Martini menu is just off the lobby. Alternately, you can **camp** four miles out of town at Clinton Lake State Park (ⓣ785/842-8562; $8.50).

The Town

Studded with cafés and eclectic shops, downtown Lawrence is a delight to walk around – and just as busy outside of university term time, when day-trippers flock in from less congenial Kansas towns. However, most of the town's formal attractions are clustered on campus. The **University of Kansas Natural History Museum**, inside Dyche Hall at 1345 Jayhawk Blvd (Tues–Sat 9am–5pm, Sun noon–5pm; $5; ⓣ785/864-4450, ⓦwww.nhm.ku.edu), holds a chronological panorama of North American flora and fauna, as well as the stuffed horse Comanche, the lone survivor of Custer's cavalry at the Battle of Little Bighorn. The **Spencer Museum of Art**, 1301 Mississippi St (Tues–Sat 10am–4pm, Thurs till 8pm, Sun noon–4pm; free; ⓣ785/864-4710, ⓦwww.spencerart.ku.edu), specializes in world art, with an Oriental gallery, Old Masters and a pre-Raphaelite masterpiece.

Eating, drinking and entertainment

As befits a college town, the **restaurant** scene in Lawrence is dominated by inexpensive options. Try *La Parrilla*, 814 Massachusetts St (ⓣ785/841-1100), where there's frequently a line out the door for plates of enchiladas and tacos. If cheap eats aren't your scene, indulge in some fine dining at *Pachamama's* at 800 New Hampshire (ⓣ785/841-0990), where an ever-changing seasonal menu includes delectable specialties such as paprika-cured beef fillet and chili-raspberry BBQ duck breast.

Unsurprisingly, Lawrence's **nightlife** is defined by students, who can be found in droves along Massachusetts Street – the *Free State Brewing Company* at no. 636 (ⓣ785/843-4555) pulls pints of its award-winning amber beer. As for **performing arts**, one of the better places in town is Liberty Hall at no. 644 (ⓣ785/749-1972), which presents arthouse films, plays and concerts.

West through Kansas

Further west across Kansas, three towns recreate the state's Wild West heritage, although only in the westernmost, **Dodge City**, does the scrubby landscape conform to the cowboy-movie image. **Abilene**, if less famous than Dodge City, boasts as many outlaw and gunslinger stories, and **Wichita**, about two hundred miles southwest of Kansas City, holds an excellent, authentic reconstruction of frontier days in its Old Cowtown Museum.

Abilene

Like all the old cattle-trail towns, **ABILENE**, 115 miles west of Lawrence on I-70, claims to have been the most rip-roaring of the lot. By the time legendary lawman

Wild Bill Hickok became its marshal in 1871, local unruly behaviour was already dying down. Today, little remains to remind you of those raucous days; rather, Abilene prefers to stress its connections with the man who led the US through the 1950s. The **Dwight D. Eisenhower Presidential Library and Museum**, 200 SE Fourth St (daily 9am–4.45pm; $8; ⓣ785/263-6700, ⓦwww.eisenhower.archives.gov), encompasses his boyhood home, with its original furnishings, the obligatory film and many photos and papers on display in the spacious museum. The former president and his wife are buried in the meditation chapel.

Abilene's **visitor centre** is at 201 NW Second St (Mon–Sat 9am–6pm, Sun noon–6pm; ⓣ785/263-2231, ⓦwww.abilenekansas.org). Most of the town's budget **motels** are off I-70 at Hwy-15, with the *Holiday Inn Express* (ⓣ1-785/263-4049, ⓦwww.hiexpress.com; ❺), 110 E Lafayette, offering comfortable rooms near the freeway. The American and Southwest dishes at *Kirby House* (ⓣ785/263-7336), 205 NE Third St, are your best bet for **food**.

Wichita

WICHITA, about 165 miles southwest of Lawrence on I-35, is the largest city in Kansas, split by the Arkansas River, which forks just north of downtown into the Big and Little Arkansas rivers (incidentally, Kansans take umbrage if you pronounce it "Arkansaw"; pronounce it here the way it is spelled). Originally settled by the Wichita, who by 1865 had been relocated to Oklahoma Indian Territory, the city grew up as a stop on the Chisholm Trail, a Texas to Kansas cattle route. Its glory days were to be short-lived, however, as farmers, angry about the damage done by stampeding cattle, erected fences that forced the drives onto different trails further west, creating new cowtowns such as Dodge City. Today, the city, a global centre of aircraft construction and the home of a rich arts scene, has been invigorated with a downtown revival.

The City

Downtown Wichita is enlivened mainly by the public art and sculpture that pops up unexpectedly – in empty lots and even in tree stumps. The exceptional **Wichita-Sedgwick County Historical Museum**, 204 S Main St (Tues–Fri 11am–4pm, Sat & Sun 1–5pm; $4; ⓣ316/265-9314, ⓦwww.wichitahistory.org), is in **Old City Hall**, a heavy stone building decorated with turrets, gargoyles and arches. One mile north, a stately church with vivid stained-glass windows at 601 N Water St houses the **Kansas African American Museum** (Mon–Fri 10am–5pm, weekends by appointment; $5.50; ⓣ316/262-7651), where details on Buffalo Soldiers, inventors from across the country and early black Wichitans present a less-told side of Great Plains history.

The **riverside parks** are home to a fine walking- and biking-trail system, as well as the 44ft-tall *Keeper of the Plains* statue, which faces east at the confluence of the Little and Big Arkansas rivers. It was designed in the 1970s by Kiowa-Comanche artist Blackbear Bosin; Native Americans and city officials smoked the peace pipe at its dedication ceremony.

Nearby, the **Wichita Art Museum**, 1400 West Museum Blvd (Tues–Sat 10am–5pm, Sun noon–5pm; $7, Sat free; ⓣ316/268-4921, ⓦwww.wichitaartmuseum.org), is well worth a visit. The three-storey space goes far in redefining "American art" to include not only the work of famed Western painter C.M. Russell (which commands its own room here) but also Aztec artefacts and pieces from Central America. Also nearby is the fun **Old Cowtown Museum**, 1865 W Museum Blvd (mid-April to mid-Dec Wed–Sat 9.30am–4.30pm, Sun noon–4.30pm; mid-Dec to mid-April days & hours vary; $7.75; ⓣ316/219-1871,

The great outdoors

From the otherworldly outcrops of Monument Valley to the churning surf of California's Big Sur shoreline, the USA abounds in stupendous scenery. Many first-time visitors are staggered by the immensity and diversity of the country's wide-open spaces. Whether you're a hiker, climber, skier or even a "city person", you should seize the opportunity to venture into the spectacular wilderness. While not all of the USA's finest landscapes lie within their boundaries, its fifty-plus national parks, which combine practical amenities with environmental stewardship, make the obvious focus for an unforgettable outdoors itinerary.

Antelope Canyon, Navajo Nation ▲

Hiking in Mount Rainier National Park ▼

Hiking

America's national parks offer the perfect opportunity to experience the thrills of hiking in genuine wilderness while minimizing the risks. Almost all can be explored on networks of maintained trails, on which you can escape the crowds and face real physical challenges.

Rather than simply ticking off the hardest trails at the biggest-name parks, hiking is all about taking the time to engage with the landscape, and to appreciate where you are. That said, certain truly fabulous trails are worth seeking out. At the Grand Canyon, clear time for the two-day hike down to the Colorado River and back. Set off before dawn on the steep, exposed South Kaibab Trail, to avoid the midday heat; spend the night at Phantom Ranch on the canyon floor; and climb back the next day along the gentler, shadier Bright Angel Trail. Spellbinding Zion National Park, further north, offers a wider range of trails, from the easy but spectacular Riverside Walk to the more demanding West Rim Trail, up to the awesome Angel's Landing viewpoint. Great mountain hikes include the Skyline Trail in Washington's Mount Rainier National Park, and the Hidden Lake Trail through the wildflowers of Glacier National Park. Hikers on Maui in Hawaii descend the Sliding Sands Trail into the multicoloured volcanic crater in Haleakala National Park, while fearless adventurers in California's Yosemite climb the amazing Half Dome, for vertiginous views over the awesome valley below.

Before you attempt any long trail, ask park rangers about current conditions. Don't underestimate the difficulties posed by desert or mountain terrain, or adverse weather, but don't let them put you off either. Just be sure to take all the proper precautions.

Scenic drives

While the ideal way to experience the American wilderness is on foot, plan carefully and you can have just as much fun on the road. Time your trip to coincide with the autumn colours, for example, and you won't regret it.

Great scenic drives can be found all over the US. The serpentine Blue Ridge Parkway crests the Appalachian mountains for hundreds of forested miles through Virginia and North Carolina, with barely a sign of human habitation. Similarly, the Natchez Trace Parkway follows a Native American trail from Tennessee down to the Mississippi, through dense woodland scattered with ancient settlements. Up near the Canadian border the Pictured Rocks National Lakeshore skirts the dramatic cliffs of Michigan's Upper Peninsula.

The further west you go, the more spectacular the scenery. Even the interstates can serve up stupendous views, while on lesser roads like US-14 through Wyoming's Wapiti Valley you may spot bighorn sheep or even grizzlies. In Idaho, Hwy-75 heads north from Ketchum through the stunning serrated peaks of the Sawtooth National Recreation Area; further south in Utah, Scenic Hwy-12 spends a hundred miles dipping into the red-rock wonderland of Grand Staircase-Escalante National Monument. Colorado's Million Dollar Highway connects a string of atmospheric old mining towns via 11,000ft mountain passes, while down in Texas the River Road parallels the Rio Grande along the Mexican border, passing through quirky ghost towns like Terlingua. And in California, Hwy-1 makes a superb coastal drive from San Francisco south towards Los Angeles, with the sublime canyon-cut landscape of the Big Sur Coast as its undisputed highlight.

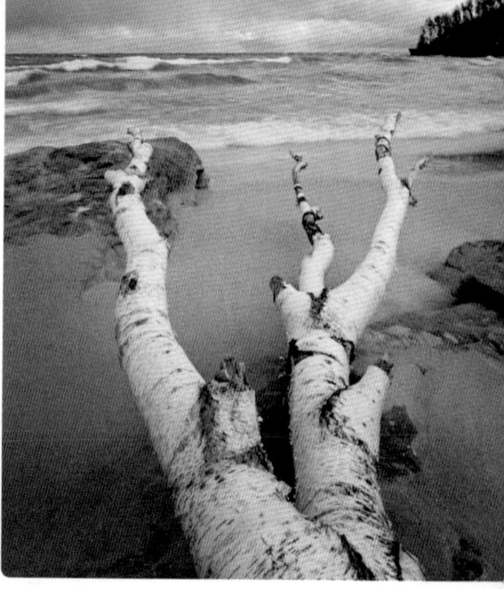

▲ Lake Superior, Pictured Rocks National Lakeshore

▼ Bighorn ram

▼ Blue Ridge Parkway National Park

Chisos Mountains, Big Bend National Park ▲

Glacier National Park ▼

Hawaii Volcanoes National Park ▼

Top ten national parks

▸▸ **Acadia**, Maine. Tiny Mount Desert Island, just off northern New England, is where the sun first hits the US each morning. A narrow fjord teems with wildlife, while rugged hills offer fine hiking. p.239

▸▸ **Big Bend**, Texas. A colourful, high-desert wilderness on the Mexican border, cradled within a sweeping curve of the Rio Grande that's a whitewater rafter's paradise. p.627

▸▸ **Bryce Canyon**, Utah. A totally bizarre sight: a throng of sandstone pinnacles, glowing red, yellow and orange, and burning like flames into a remote Utah hillside. p.808

▸▸ **Canyonlands**, Utah. The Colorado and Green rivers thread through this mind-boggling labyrinth of contorted canyons and desiccated plateaus, explored by hundreds of miles of hiking trails. p.811

▸▸ **Crater Lake**, Oregon. A staggeringly beautiful blue lake, filling a collapsed volcanic caldera – with another cinder cone rising from its depths. p.993

▸▸ **Denali**, Alaska. Visitors flock to America's highest peak, Mount McKinley, for rafting, skiing, hiking and the virtual certainty of seeing a bear. p.1022

▸▸ **Glacier**, Montana. With its spectacular waterfalls, lush alpine meadows and mighty massifs, Glacier is the crown jewel of the Rockies. p.740

▸▸ **Hawaii Volcanoes**, Hawaii. Where the Big Island grows bigger before your very eyes, as torrents of incandescent lava explode into the steaming Pacific. p.1043

▸▸ **Yellowstone**, Wyoming. A true natural wonder, best known for its spurting geysers and bubbling mud pots, but also filled with lakes and mountains, wolves and bison. p.718

▸▸ **Yosemite**, California. Whether you stroll the valley floor or climb its soaring cliffs, this geological wonderland is a must-see for any California visitor. p.889

www.oldcowtown.org), where a seventeen-acre riverside exhibit recreates the buildings of 1870s Wichita. Looking and feeling like a movie set, the area includes – along with some docile longhorns – the city's first one-room jail, a schoolroom, a store, a smithy, churches, stables and old homes.

Practicalities

Domestic **flights** arrive at the Mid-Continent Airport, five miles southwest of downtown on W Kellogg Drive; call Best Cabs (316/838-2233) for a ride into the city centre. Amtrak **trains** stop at Newton, a small Mennonite town 25 miles to the north, with a local bus connection to Wichita throughout the day. Greyhound **buses** come in to 312 S Broadway Ave, two blocks east of Main Street. The resourceful **Wichita Convention & Visitors Bureau** is in the heart of downtown at Douglas Avenue and Main Street (Mon–Fri 7.45am–5.30pm; 316/265-2800, www.visitwichita.com), where you can hop aboard a ninety-minute **trolley tour** (Thurs–Sat 10am; $10; 316/773-1931, www.rctrolley.com).

Comfortable budget **lodging** in Wichita is plentiful, especially near the airport on W Kellogg Drive. For something more upmarket, two choice hotels anchor the city's Old Town entertainment and dining district: the *Hotel at Old Town*, at First and Mosley streets (316/267-4800, www.hotelatoldtown.com; 5–6), has a stylish turn-of-the-twentieth-century flavour, while the *Courtyard Wichita at Old Town*, a block north at E Second and Mosley streets, was recently converted from a grocer's warehouse to feature modern amenities galore (316/264-5300, www.marriott.com; 5–7).

Top-notch **pizzas** and own-brewed ales are available at Old Town's *River City Brewing Co*, 150 N Mosley St (316/263-2739), which hosts local bands every weekend, while *Old Mill Tasty Shop*, a nostalgic soda fountain at 604 E Douglas Ave (316/264-6500), is popular for great sandwiches. Just across the river, cowboy entertainers hoot and holler at Old Cowtown's *Diamond W Chuck-wagon Supper* (check website for schedule; $30, reservations recommended; 316/729-4825, www.diamondwchuckwagon.com), where you can fill up on baked beans, honey cornbread, peach cobbler and limitless quantities of smoked beef brisket.

Dodge City

Portrayed in a handful of 1930s Westerns, **DODGE CITY**, about 150 miles west of Wichita, is perhaps the most famous of all America's frontier towns. However, this wildest of Wild West cities had a relatively brief heyday, from 1875 until 1886. Established in 1872 along with the Santa Fe Railroad, which transported millions of buffalo hides, by 1875 the town of traders, trappers and hunters had to find a new economic base – the buffalo had been practically exterminated. The era of the great cattle drives was already underway and Dodge City became a den of iniquity where gambling, drinking and general lawlessness were the norm. Such wickedness led to gunfights galore, and the notorious Boot Hill cemetery (where villains were buried with their boots on) was kept busy by charismatic, if morally suspect, lawmen such as Bat Masterson and Wyatt Earp.

The Town

Today, Dodge City's old **downtown** area is enveloped by a hinterland of railroad tracks and giant silos, and aside from the city's main annual event, July and August's **Dodge City Days and Rodeo** (www.dodgecitydays.com), the town is content to replay its movie image in the **Boot Hill Museum**, 400 Front St (June–Aug daily 8am–8pm; Sept–May Mon–Sat 9am–5pm, Sun 1–5pm; $7, $8 in summer). **Boot Hill Cemetery** looms above, although there's just a sorry little patch of lawn on one corner of the original site, which was abandoned in 1879 after just six years and thirty-four burials. The bodies were re-interred elsewhere, and as the graves were never marked in the first place, the wooden markers seen today are more than a little bogus.

A more true-to-life sight is **El Capitan**, a massive bronze longhorn at Second Street and Wyatt Earp Boulevard. The stoic beast faces south towards an identical north-facing statue in Abilene, Texas, together marking the beginning and end of the old cattle-drive trail.

Practicalities

Amtrak trains come right into downtown at the sharply renovated Santa Fe Station, at Central Avenue and Wyatt Earp Boulevard. The **Convention & Visitors Bureau** at 400 W Wyatt Earp Blvd (summer daily 8.30am–6.30pm; winter Mon–Fri 8.30am–5pm; ⓣ620/225-8186, ⓦwww.visitdodgecity.org) can offer advice on activities, lodging and dining around town. The Dodge City Trolley runs narrated town **tours** ($7) four times daily in summer only, from a booth in the Boot Hill car park.

Accommodation is affordable here, and most of Dodge City's motels are spread roughly a mile west of downtown along US-50 (West Wyatt Earp Boulevard); the *Dodge House* at no. 2408 (ⓣ620/225-9900, ⓦwww.dodgehousehotel.com; ❹) is pleasant enough and also has an on-site restaurant. Another **dining** choice is *Beatty & Kelley's* inside the Boot Hill Museum (ⓣ620/227-8188), where specialities include saucy beef brisket and buffalo sandwiches.

Nebraska

Though modern transcontinental travellers tend to see **NEBRASKA** in much the same way westward settlers did during the pioneer era – as a dreary expanse of prairie to slog through – this sparsely populated state in fact holds a few places of interest. Still, it doesn't help that three hundred miles of underwhelming, livestock-rearing flatlands separate its principal cities – commercial **Omaha** and its livelier counterpart, state government and university centre **Lincoln** – from the dramatic landscapes of its western region. This little-known area contains giant sand hills and valleys broken by towering rocky columns, all hemmed in by sheer-faced buttes, and is well worth the diversion from I-80's seemingly endless tedium.

Western Nebraska was still embroiled in bloody battles between the American military and Native Americans long after its eastern lands had been settled; from the first serious uprising in 1854, it was thirty-six years before the US Army could make American control unchallengeable. In the far northwest of the state, **Fort Robinson**, an old Army post where Crazy Horse was murdered, remains one of the West's most crucial historic sites.

Without navigable rivers, Nebraska had to rely on the **railroads** to help populate the land. During the 1870s and 1880s, rail companies, encouraged by grants that allowed them to accumulate one-sixth of the state's land, laid down such a comprehensive network of tracks that virtually every farmer was within a day's cattle drive of the nearest halt. Thus the buffalo-hunting country of the Sioux and Pawnee was turned into high-yield farmland, which today has few rivals in terms of beef production.

Eastern Nebraska

The silt-laden Missouri River separates Nebraska from Iowa and Missouri to the east. There are few natural ports on this stretch, and **Omaha** remains the only riverfront community of any size. **Lincoln**, about 55 miles southwest, is the state's capital and home to the University of Nebraska.

Omaha

OMAHA, Nebraska's largest and most easterly city, claims a great zoo, several museums and a lively entertainment district. As a major terminus on the first transcontinental railroad, Omaha made a logical alternative to distant Chicago as a marketplace for Wyoming and Nebraska ranchers to sell their herds of **cattle**. By 1900, massive stockyards had spread along the southern edge of town, although their rise and fall – from the world's largest livestock centre in the 1960s to shuttered and derelict by 1999 – was precipitous.

In downtown Omaha, you'll find good bars and cafés along the cobbled streets of the **Old Market district**. Rail buffs will enjoy the **Durham Museum**, converted from the Art Deco Union Pacific Railroad station, at 801 S 10th St (Tues 10am–8pm, Wed–Sat till 5pm, Sun 1–5pm; extended hours in summer; $7; ⓣ402/444-5071, ⓦwww.durhammuseum.org), where old train cars and huge model train sets are featured alongside a gallery of Omaha history.

The **Henry Doorly Zoo**, 3701 S 10th St (daily: June–Aug 8.30am–5pm; Sept–May 9.30am–5pm; $11.50; ⓣ402/733-8400, ⓦwww.omahazoo.com), rightfully considers itself one of the best zoos in America. It opened in 1894 with two bison borrowed from Buffalo Bill; today, it features a sizeable aviary, a magnificent bear canyon and a huge aquarium, as well as a towering IMAX screen.

Practicalities

Omaha's Greyhound **bus** station is at 1601 Jackson St; Amtrak **trains** inconveniently roll through well after hours at 1003 S Ninth St. Both depots are well placed for downtown; however, the city's **public transportation** is poor, so try Happy Cab (ⓣ402/339-8294) or Safeway Cabs (ⓣ402/342-7474). The **Omaha Convention & Visitors Bureau** is right downtown at 1001 Farnam St (Mon–Sat 9am–4.30pm; ⓣ402/444-4660, ⓦwww.visitomaha.com).

Hotel rates are generally reasonable, except when baseball's College World Series happens here each June. Rooms at the downtown *Hilton Garden Inn*, 1005 Dodge St (ⓣ402/341-4400, ⓦhiltongardeninn.hilton.com; ❺–❼), fit the bill cleanly and comfortably. Thirty miles southwest of town, family-oriented Eugene T. Mahoney State Park (ⓣ402/944-2523) has **camping** ($19–23), as well as **cabins** (❺) and a **lodge** (❸).

The Old Market, centred on Tenth and Howard streets, contains Omaha's most vibrant **restaurants** and **bars**. The menu at *Vivace*, 1108 Howard St (ⓣ402/342-2050), focuses on contemporary Italian cuisine, while *Upstream Brewing Company*, at 514 S 11th St (ⓣ402/344-0200), makes fine ales and lagers to pair with its standard American fare. *The Slowdown*, 729 N 14th St (ⓣ402/345-7569), is the epicentre of Omaha's stalwart **indie rock** scene.

Lincoln

Tiny Rochester was selected to be state capital in 1867 – on the condition that it change its name to **LINCOLN** in honour of the recently assassinated president. Such was the rabid disappointment in the territorial seat of government, Omaha, that officials smuggled documents, books and office furniture out of the city in the middle of the night to avoid armed gangs.

Dwarfing the rest of **downtown**, the central tower of the 1932 Nebraska **State Capitol**, 1445 K St (Mon–Fri 8am–5pm, Sat 10am–5pm, Sun 1–5pm; hourly free tours), protrudes 400ft into the sky and is topped by a statue of a seed sower on a pedestal of wheat and corn. The superb iridescent murals in the foyer are a welcome alternative in a government building, and from the fourteenth-floor observation deck you can survey the tracts of farmland that surround the city.

Twelve thousand years of life on the Plains are covered at the **Museum of Nebraska History**, 131 Centennial Mall North (Tues–Fri 9am–4.30pm, Sat & Sun 1–4.30pm; $2 suggested donation; ⓣ402/471-4754, ⓦwww.nebraskahistory.org), where displays focus on anthropology rather than history. The highlight of the **University of Nebraska State Museum**, at 14th and U streets (Mon–Wed & Fri–Sat 9.30am–4.30pm, Thurs till 8pm, Sun 1.30–4.30pm; $5; ⓣ402/472-2642, ⓦwww-museum.unl.edu), is the Elephant Hall, a gallery of towering mammoth, mastodon and four-tusker skeletons. A few blocks away, the **Sheldon Memorial Art Gallery**, 12th and R streets (Tues 10am–8pm, Wed–Sat 10am–5pm, Sun noon–5pm; free; ⓣ402/472-2461, ⓦwww.sheldon//art//gallery.org), traces the development of American art and also features a twenty-piece sculpture garden.

Practicalities

Lincoln's Greyhound **bus** station is at 5250 Superior St, while **Amtrak** trains pass through 201 N 7th St at uncomfortably early-morning hours; StarTran (ⓣ402/476-1234) operates **local buses** ($1.75). The city's **visitor centre** is in Lincoln Station, right next to Amtrak (Mon–Fri 9am–8pm, Sat 8am–2pm, Sun noon–4pm; ⓣ402/434-5348, ⓦwww.lincoln.org).

If you plan to **stay** overnight, try the very affordable *New Victorian Suites*, 216 N 48th St (ⓣ402/464-4400, ⓦwww.newvictoriansuites.com; ❸), three miles east of downtown. Pricier but closer to Lincoln's entertainment district is the *Holiday Inn*, 141 N St (ⓣ402/475-4011, ⓦwww.holidayinn.com; ❻–❼).

Lincoln's restaurant scene is anchored by grills, pizzerias and family diners, but a terrific alternative is the highly regarded Northern Indian cuisine at *The Oven*, 201 N 8th St (ⓣ402/475-6118). Lincoln's compact, student-thronged downtown comes into its own after dark. Among its alphabetical array of broad boulevards, **O Street** (the subject of Allen Ginsberg's poem *Zero Street*) is the main drag; 13th and 14th streets are packed with bars and places to eat. *Zoo Bar*, at 136 N 14th St (ⓣ402/435-8754), attracts both local and national **jazz** and **blues** acts; another Lincoln mainstay, *Duffy's Tavern* at 1412 O St (ⓣ402/474-3543), pulls in a younger crowd and good **rock bands**.

Western Nebraska

After the unerringly flat journey across Nebraska, the state's western sections come as a refreshing change – the terrain here clearly has more in common with the rugged West than it does the rest of the state. This is windmill country, where wave upon wave of gusty and sandy hills, thinly coated with prairie grass, repeat towards the horizon like a sea in constant turmoil. Early pioneers wrote the area off as unproductive, and it remained barren until massive irrigation work at the start of the twentieth century enabled agricultural settlement. In the **Panhandle region**, as it's often called, the sand hills yield to classic, John Ford-style Western scenery: pancake-flat valleys, crisscrossed by meandering river washes and corralled by contorted bluffs, all under the perpetual shadow of chugging clouds. Emigrants on the **Oregon Trail** used bizarrely crusted outcrops such as Chimney Rock and Scotts Bluff as road signs of sorts.

Hwy-2 toward Alliance

A particularly scenic section of Hwy-2 meanders and dips for well over three hundred miles from Grand Island toward South Dakota's Black Hills. It passes through the **Sandhills**, an otherworldly landscape carpeted with short-grass prairie and softened by delicate wildflowers and shiny ponds. Apart from a few farmsteads, grain silos and tiny churches, all you're likely to see along this open road are lazing cattle, a few sluggish rivers and mile-long coal trains weaving their way through the hills. It's a long, desolate, yet strangely beautiful drive through an anachronistic region.

The road dawdles for miles through scattered villages before drifting into **ALLIANCE** and its brick downtown streets, which pulls in visitors from far and wide for its one big attraction, **Carhenge** and its adjacent Car Art Reserve, three miles north on Hwy-87 (daily dawn – dusk; free; Ⓦwww.carhenge.com). The site is a rough replica of Stonehenge, with old cars swapped in for Salisbury Plain's famous stones. Erected next to a cornfield during a family reunion, this intriguing collection of Chevys, Cadillacs and Plymouths, painted a brooding battleship grey and tilted at unusual angles, is an ingenious piece of pop art to most; upon its 1987 construction, however, Nebraska's Department of Roads rapidly declared it a junkyard, and ordered the city of Alliance to remove it. Locals soon formed **Friends of Carhenge**, whose efforts have secured the monument's future.

There's no other compelling reason to linger in or near Alliance, but if you need a place to **stay**, there's a serviceable *Days Inn* at 117 Cody Ave (Ⓣ308/762-8000, Ⓦwww.daysinn.com; ❹).

The Oregon Trail landmarks

Two of the first landmarks encountered by travellers on the **Oregon Trail**, which in western Nebraska paralleled the route of modern US-26 between Ogallala and the Wyoming border, were the lumpy **Courthouse** and **Jail rocks**, noticeable outcrops that lie four miles south of the little town of **Bridgeport**. A short drive west, **Chimney Rock National Historic Site** (daily 9am–5pm; $3; Ⓣ308/586-2581) rises almost 500ft above the North Platte River. Chipped away by erosion and lightning since the era of westward migration, it remains one of the most recognizable and memorable landmarks in the area.

The twin towns of **GERING** and **SCOTTSBLUFF**, twenty or so miles further west, form the commercial centre of western Nebraska's farmlands. Nearby is the 800ft rampart of **Scotts Bluff National Monument** (daily: summer 8am–7pm; rest of year 8am–5pm; $5; Ⓣ308/436-4340), which stands like a Nebraskan Gibraltar. Trips to the top (by foot or free shuttle bus) are rewarded with a magnificent view, and the entrance fee includes the absorbing **Oregon Trail Museum**, which relates the experiences of the early emigrants.

Follow the ruts of bygone wagon trains to the inviting **B&B** at *Barn Anew*, 170549 County Rd L (Ⓣ308/632-8647, Ⓦwww.barnanew.com; ❺), four miles west of Scottsbluff. The converted nineteenth-century farmstead sits on the Oregon Trail in a choice spot with sweeping views of the monument as it erupts from the prairie floor. If you'd rather stay in town, *Hampton Inn & Suites*

The life and death of Crazy Horse

The life of Oglala Sioux leader **Crazy Horse** is shrouded in confusion, misinterpretation and controversy. So thoroughly did the most enigmatic figure in Plains Indian history avoid contact with whites (outside battle, at least) that no photograph or even sketch of him exists; unlike other Indian chiefs, he refused to visit Washinfgton DC or speak with reporters.

Crazy Horse earned his title as a youth after he single-handedly charged the rival Arapahoe and took two scalps. His finest moment came in June 1876, when he led a thousand warriors in inflicting a stinging defeat on the superior forces of General George Crook at the **Battle of the Rosebud River**. Just eight days later, Crazy Horse headed the attack at the **Battle of Little Bighorn** in today's Montana, where Custer and his entire company were killed (see p.729).

After Little Bighorn, US Army efforts to round up the Native Americans were redoubled. In May 1877, Crazy Horse surprised friend and foe alike by leading nine hundred of his people into Fort Robinson. They gave up their weapons, and Crazy Horse, keen to stay in his native land (unlike Sitting Bull, who had retreated to Canada), demanded that the buffalo grounds along the Powder River remain in Sioux hands. Tensions at the army camp rose after a rumour went around the barracks that the Sioux chief had come to murder General Crook and Crazy Horse was arrested on September 5, 1877; during a tussle outside the fort jail, he was bayoneted three times and died the next morning.

Quite why this undefeated warrior should have surrendered without a fight, and whether he fell victim to a deliberate assassination, remains unclear. What is certain is that his death signalled the closing chapter of the Indian Wars. The Oglala Sioux were forcibly moved to the poor hunting country of Missouri as white settlers immediately swept into western Nebraska, South Dakota, Wyoming and Montana.

Crazy Horse, so one story goes, was buried by his family in an unmarked grave in an out-of-the-way creek called **Wounded Knee** – the very place where, thirteen years later, three hundred Sioux men, women and children were slaughtered in the bloody finale to over half a century of barbarism (see p.669).

at 301 W Hwy-26 (ⓣ308/635-5200, ⓦhamptoninn.hilton.com; ❺) is a solid option; breakfast is included. Also in Scottsbluff itself, grab **dinner** at the *Emporium Coffeehouse & Cafe,* 1818 1st Ave (ⓣ308/632-6222), where you can enjoy dishes such as ricotta-stuffed ravioli and flaky pot pie.

Fort Robinson State Park

A ninety-mile drive north of Scottsbluff, just west of the tiny town of Crawford, **Fort Robinson State Park** (open 24hr/day in summer, call for hours rest of year; $4; ⓣ308/665-2900) preserves the spot where the US Army coordinated its campaign to rid the gold-rich Badlands of the native Sioux. Today, it's a cross between a dude ranch and a living history village – a smoothing-over that makes the memories of the obliteration of an entire way of life all the more poignant.

Restored fort buildings contain period furnishings and there are two small museums: the **State Historical Society Museum** traces the fort's history from 1874–1946, while the **Trailside Museum** interprets the geology and natural history of the region. A simple stone marks the spot where **Crazy Horse** was killed (see box, above), while the **horse-drawn tour** (six daily; $4) acknowledges it with a brief halt. Elsewhere in the park, **horseback rides** pass wondrously weird rock formations.

Fort Robinson Lodge (same contact number as park; ❷) has nice **rooms** as well as bargain cottages; **camping** is also available for $12. The *Lodge*'s **restaurant** serves a range of meaty items.

Iowa

Boasting undulating hills and acre upon acre of verdant pastures, **IOWA** lacks the glitz and glamour of America's more widely visited states. While nothing about the state truly stands out, Iowa represents as vivid a portrait of quintessential small-town America as you're likely to find.

Iowa's history, too, has been relatively uneventful since it was opened for settlement after the **Black Hawk Treaty** of 1832, a one-sided exercise in negotiation with the Sauk Indians conducted after many of them had been chased down and slaughtered in neighbouring Wisconsin and Illinois. The Northern European immigrants who soon flowed in made agricultural development their prime concern, turning the Iowa countryside into the quilt of rolling corn farms that blanket the state today.

Eastern Iowa

Eastern Iowa, in the Mississippi River hinterland, is liberally sprinkled with agribusiness towns that display the continuing influence of their Central and Northern European pioneers; **religious communities** such as the Amana Colonies, along with those based around Amish and Mennonite cultures, also call the region home. All are easily accessible from **Iowa City**, home to a huge university and one of the state's livelier centres. River towns such as northerly **Dubuque** and Burlington, near the Missouri state line in the southeast, have been enlivened in recent decades by **gambling**, though so far casinos are only allowed onboard Mississippi paddle-wheelers, each of which is invariably decked out in less-than-authentic Mark Twain-era trimmings. The blufftop views and riverside meanderings of the **Great River Road**, which traces the Mississippi River along the state's eastern border, offer an enjoyable driving tour.

Dubuque and around

The riverside town of **DUBUQUE**, set amid rocky bluffs on the Mississippi River 180 miles west of Chicago, was founded as the first white settlement in Iowa by French-Canadian lead miners in 1788; in the nineteenth century, it became a booming river port and logging centre. Today, the recently expanded **National Mississippi River Museum & Aquarium** (daily: summer 9am–6pm; rest of year 10am–5pm; $10.50; Ⓣ563/557-9545, Ⓦwww.rivermuseum.com), in the old Ice Harbor area, tells the story of Mississippi navigation from the days of Robert Fulton's first commercial steamboat in 1807 to the floods of 1993.

Once your river appetite has been whetted, travel along the high-banked Mississippi on a *Spirit of Dubuque* **paddle-wheeler cruise** (May–Oct; $21–71; Ⓣ563/583-8093, Ⓦwww.dubuqueriverrides.com); cruises depart daily from Ice Harbor. Those who prefer terra firma can ride the **Fenelon Place Elevator**, said to be the world's shortest and steepest cable-car railway (April–Nov daily 8am–10pm; $1 one-way, $2 return; Ⓦwww.dbq.com). The brief but fun ride lifts passengers 296ft up a sharp bluff to a sweeping view across downtown Dubuque and over the great river to Illinois and Wisconsin.

Film buffs who enjoyed the 1989 baseball fantasy **Field of Dreams** can meet like-minded souls in surprising numbers at the movie's original location (April–Nov daily

9am–6pm; free; ⓣ563/875-8404, ⓦwww.fieldofdreamsmoviesite.com) near Dyersville, 25 miles west of Dubuque on US-20. True to the movie's catchphrase – "If you build it, they will come" – crowds still gather on the bleachers to watch phantom games at the edge of the cornfields.

Practicalities

The **Iowa Welcome Center** at 300 Main St (daily 9am–5pm; ⓣ1-800/798-8844, ⓦwww.traveldubuque.com) is the best place to pick up information on Dubuque. As for places to **stay**, try the homey *Redstone Inn & Suites*, 504 Bluff St (ⓣ563/582-1894, ⓦwww.theredstoneinn.com; ❸–❹), a mansion constructed by early Dubuque benefactor A.A. Cooper and now a fifteen-room B&B. The 150-year-old, freshly restored *Hotel Julien*, 200 Main St (ⓣ1-800/798-7098, ⓦwww.hoteljuliendubuque.com; ❺), was once owned by mobster Al Capone; he used his personal suite as his safe house when trouble was brewing in Chicago. Local **camping** is available at *Miller Riverview Park*, set in the middle of the Mississippi River northeast of downtown (ⓣ563/589-4238; $10 per tent).

For **food**, head to *The Bank Bar & Grille*, 342 Main St (ⓣ563/584-1729) for hearty meat and fish fare, or quieter *Café Manna Java* at 269 Main St (ⓣ563/588-3105) for good salads and sandwiches. If you're in the mood for a **drink**, head downstairs to the subterranean, unsigned *Busted Lift* at 180 Main St for local colour and fun bar games.

Cedar Rapids

Seventy-five miles southwest of Dubuque, **CEDAR RAPIDS**, home of Quaker Oats, is Iowa's industrial leader. The city is still in recovery from the devastating Iowa River flood of 2008, a disaster that forced nearly a quarter of the city's residents to evacuate. Still, its very modern **Museum of Art** at 410 Third Ave SE (Tues–Sat 10am–4pm, Thurs till 8pm, Sun noon–4pm; $5; ⓣ319/366-7503, ⓦwww.crma.org) is notable for its comprehensive collection of works by regionalist painter Grant Wood, best known for *American Gothic* and other evocative depictions of 1930s Midwest farm life.

The city's **Cedar Rapids Area Convention & Visitors Bureau** is based at 119 First Ave SE (Mon–Fri 8am–5pm; ⓣ1-800/735-5557, ⓦwww.cedar-rapids.com). For reasonably priced **rooms**, there's the straightforward *Best Western Cooper's Mill Hotel*, 100 F Ave NW (ⓣ319/366-5323; ❹).

The Amana Colonies

Less than twenty miles southwest of Cedar Rapids, the **AMANA COLONIES** were founded in 1855 by the Community of True Inspiration, a group of pacifist German refugees (not linked to the Amish or Mennonites) who believed that God spoke through prophets – themselves, for example – rather than ordained ministers. Members led a simple, collective lifestyle, and while each family lived in their own home, they all ate together and shared profits from the farms. During the Great Depression, communal ownership became increasingly difficult to maintain, and in 1932 stock was redistributed among all the community's adults. However, members of the Colonies have retained their commitment to close family ties and a sense of community, as well as their religious principles.

Today, the Amana Colonies consist of seven separate villages set in an immaculate, serene valley. Their prosperity is very evident, with tasteful clapboard houses standing on well-groomed lawns and neat plank fences dividing rolling meadows. As a place to visit, they're geared less toward families and more toward senior Midwestern couples on a weekend getaway. The streets of the largest village, **Amana**, are lined with restaurants, craft shops, a brewery, a woollen mill and several wineries – although don't get your hopes up about the sweet, medicinal concoctions, since grapes are largely eschewed in favour of berries and dandelions.

Amana's **visitor centre** at 622 46th Ave (Mon–Sat 9am–5pm, Sun 10am–5pm; ⓣ1-800/579-2294, ⓦwww.amanacolonies.com) has details on the many local **B&Bs**. Probably the most compelling reason to visit the Colonies is their undeniably excellent, old-style **German food** – the *Ox Yoke Inn* (ⓣ319/622-3441), at 4420 220th Trail in Amana, dishes up family-style meals of wiener schnitzel, *spatzle* (egg noodles), *kasseler rippchen* (smoked pork with apple sauce) and similarly diet-busting plates.

Iowa City

The collegiate heart of Iowa beats strongest in **IOWA CITY**, where residents rally around the University of Iowa and its student body of over 30,000. Since the state is without a major professional sports franchise, the school's black and gold colours are a *de facto* uniform among supporters all over the state.

Iowa City's gold-domed **Old Capitol** is a reminder of its days as state capital, before government was transferred to more central Des Moines in 1857; today, it remains the centrepiece of the university's campus. Shops and street cafés dot the inviting, compact downtown area immediately east of campus, while the university's red and grey buildings are cloistered by tall dark trees.

Greyhound **buses** stop at 170 E Court St, right downtown. The **Coralville Area Convention & Visitors Bureau** is at 900 First Ave in Coralville, a little over a mile northeast of downtown (Mon–Fri 8am–5pm; ⓣ1-800/283-6592, ⓦwww.iowacitycoralville.org); check their website for B&Bs and hotels. *Iowa House Hotel* provides comfortable **lodging** in the student union building adjacent to the Iowa River (ⓣ319/335-3513, ⓦwww.iowahousehotel.com; ❹). Local **dining** options abound, from hot sandwiches at friendly (if dimly lit) *Micky's Irish Pub*, 11 S Dubuque St (ⓣ319/338-6860), to the eclectic menu at upmarket *Atlas* at 127 Iowa Ave (ⓣ319/341-7700), which offers everything from macaroni and cheese to Jamaican jerked chicken.

Des Moines

The steel-and-glass skyline of downtown **DES MOINES** (pronounced da-MOYN), most of which shot up during the 1980s, is testimony to the town's ever-growing insurance business. For such a fast-track financial centre, the streets are conspicuously empty; pedestrians instead often use the **Skywalk**, a three-mile network of temperature-controlled corridors linking twenty blocks of offices, banks, car parks, restaurants, hotels and movie theatres.

Most businesses stand on the west bank of the Des Moines River, which slashes downtown in two. In 1857, a group of speculators attempted to shift the commercial hub to the east side by bribing commissioners to site the **State Capitol** at E Ninth Street and Grand Avenue; their hopes of huge spin-offs were dashed when a nationwide financial crash later that same year saw property prices collapse. As a result, the five-domed Italian Renaissance-style mass, on the crest of a steep hill, is now detached from the heart of the city (Mon–Fri 8am–4.30pm, Sat 9am–4pm, closed Sun, call for tour times; free; ⓣ515/281-5591).

Ten miles west of downtown Des Moines in Urbandale, at 2600 111th St via I-80's exit 125, **Living History Farms** (May–Oct Mon–Sat 9am–5pm, Sun noon–5pm; $11.50; ⓣ515/278-5286, ⓦwww.lhf.org) traces the evolution of agriculture on the Plains. Self-guided tours progress through five historic sites, from the oval bark homes of an eighteenth-century Iowa settlement, through an 1850s homestead, to a look at today's technology-reliant farming methods.

While an extended **stay** in Des Moines is an unlikely proposition – its main sights can easily be taken in during the course of an afternoon – if you do find yourself in town overnight, try the *Hotel Fort Des Moines* at 1000 Walnut Ave (ⓣ1-800/532-1466, ⓦwww.hotelfortdesmoines.com; ❺). Otherwise, a handful of budget-friendly options line I-35 north of downtown in the suburb of Ankeny.

The fact that Iowans eat well is reflected in the quantity of food on offer in Des Moines' **restaurants**. *Iowa Beef Steakhouse*, 1201 E Euclid Ave (ⓣ515/262-1138), delivers massive slabs of beef supplemented with a salad bar, baked potatoes and generous helpings of garlic bread. *Stella's Blue Sky Diner*, under pink neon at 3281 100th St (ⓣ515/727-4408) in Urbandale, has an interior that might assault your eyes, but its 1950s-style menu graciously lets you pair the usual burgers and fries with cleverly flavoured malts: chocolate, peanut butter and banana, among them.

South Dakota

The wide-open spaces of the Great Plains seemingly roll away to infinity on either side of I-90 in **SOUTH DAKOTA**. The land may be more green and fertile east of the Missouri River, but vast numbers of high-season visitors speed straight to the spectacular southwest, home of the **Badlands** and the adjacent **Black Hills** – two of the most dramatic, mysterious and legend-impacted tracts of land in the US. For certain whites, they encapsulate a wagonload of American notions about heritage and the taming of the West; to some Native Americans, they are ancient, spiritually resonant places.

The science-fiction severity of the Badlands resists fitting into easy tourist tastes. The bigger, more user-friendly Black Hills, home of that most patriotic of icons, **Mount Rushmore**, have been subjected to greater exploitation (dozens of physical, historical and downright commercial attractions, as well as the mining of gold and other metals), but encourage more active exploration via hiking trails, mountain lakes and streams and memorably scenic highways.

Time and Hollywood have mythologized the larger-than-life personalities for whom the Dakota Territory served as a stomping ground: **Custer** and **Crazy Horse** battled here for supremacy over the Plains, while **Wild Bill Hickok** and **Calamity Jane** were denizens of the once-notorious Gold Rush town of **Deadwood**.

Sioux tribes dominated South Dakota's plains from the eighteenth century onward, having gradually been pushed westwards from the Great Lakes by encroaching white settlement. To these nomadic hunters, the concept of owning the earth was utterly alien, a belief that ran contrary to those of gun-toting Christian settlers and federal politicians. The Sioux fought hard to stay free and theirs was the sole Native American nation to defeat the United States in war and force it to sign a favourable treaty (in 1868). Even so, they were forced to relinquish the sacred Black Hills in the face of a gung-ho gold rush; ultimately, their choice lay between death or confinement on reservations.

For decades, Sioux history and culture were outlawed; until the 1940s, it was illegal to teach or even speak their language, Lakota. Today, more Sioux live on South Dakota's six reservations than dwelled in the whole state during pioneer days, but their prospects are often grim. Nowhere is the legacy of injustice better symbolized than at **Wounded Knee**, on the Oglala Sioux **Pine Ridge Reservation** – scene of the infamous 1890 massacre by the US Army, and also of a prolonged "civil disturbance" by the radical American Indian Movement in 1973.

Today, Native American traditions are celebrated by music, dance and socializing at **powwows**, held in summer on the reservations; local tourism offices offer annual dates and locations.

East of the Missouri

For tourists, little in eastern or central South Dakota can be considered essential. **Sioux Falls**, the state's biggest city, is faceless but handy. As one of the country's quietest and smallest capitals, **Pierre** has its minor charms, while **Mitchell** boasts the palatial Corn Palace, an arena adorned with the cash crop reconstructed on an annual basis. About sixty miles northwest of Sioux Falls, **De Smet** is known as "Little Town on the Prairie" thanks to the autobiographical books of Laura Ingalls Wilder; you can visit several sites the author mentions for smatterings of history, pretty scenery and homely pride, including Silver Lake and the Big Slough. Finally, **Yankton** in the far southeast has the excellent Lewis and Clark Recreation Area on its doorstep.

Pierre

Straggling along the east bank of the Missouri River at the centre of South Dakota, **PIERRE** (rhymes with "deer") is the second-smallest and certainly the least sophisticated of all US state capitals. It's very much a typical South Dakota town, home to thirteen thousand residents who remain unimpressed that it's the seat of state government.

Apart from the black-domed **capitol building** itself (daily 8am–10pm; free), which sits in a pleasant park at the northeast edge of downtown, don't expect Pierre to detain you for long. One exception is the worthwhile **Cultural Heritage Center** (hours vary seasonally; $4; ⓣ605/773-3458), located on the hill at 900 Governors Drive, half a mile north of the capitol. This repository of Native American objects, pioneer implements and prehistoric artefacts is the state's largest museum; it's also one of only a few places that does more than pay lip service to the state's significant Native American cultures.

Pierre's **visitor centre** is at 800 W Dakota Ave (ⓣ605/224-7361, ⓦwww.pierre.org). The bulk of the town's **motels** line up along Sioux Avenue, including the reliable *Governor's Inn*, 700 W Sioux Ave (ⓣ605/224-4200, ⓦwww.govinn.com; ④). Dining is predictably understated here, but *Pier 347*, 347 S Pierre St (ⓣ605/224-2400), offers good bagels and coffee drinks.

The Badlands

South Dakota's White River **BADLANDS** could be considered a pocket-sized relative of Arizona's Grand Canyon, or even a grass-swathed cousin to Death Valley in California. More than 35 million years ago, there was an ancient saltwater sea here, which subsequently dried up; over the last few million years, erosion has slowly eaten away at the terrain revealing rippling gradations of earth tones and pastel colours and unearthing the remains of prehistoric mammals such as sabre-toothed cats and three-toed horses. The crumbly earth is carved into all manner of shapes: pinnacles, precipices, pyramids, knobs, cones, ridges, gorges – or, if you're feeling poetic, lunar sandcastles and cathedrals. The Sioux cherished these incredible contortions of nature for harbouring bighorn sheep, mule, deer and other prairie fare, but early French trappers didn't share the natives' enthusiasm, dubbing them the *Mauvaises Terres à Traverser* ("Bad Lands to Travel Across"); they have also been described in more brutal terms as simply "hell with the fires out".

Spectacular formations can be found within the northern section of **Badlands National Park**, where the state's "White Hills" seem to dominate every vista. Elsewhere nearby, the enormous, impoverished Pine Ridge Indian Reservation encompasses the park's supremely remote southern stretches, while clean-cut **Wall**, along heavily travelled I-90, is the region's most visited commercial centre.

Badlands National Park

The spectacularly eroded layers of sand, silt, ash, mud and gravel on display in **BADLANDS NATIONAL PARK** are most accessible via I-90, which skirts Badlands' northern edge; a paved forty-mile road through the park is peppered with scenic overlooks. The rainbow hues that colour these formations are most striking at dawn, dusk and just after rainfall (heaviest in May & June).

Among the best of the park's marked **hiking trails** is the Door Trail, a less than one mile excursion from the large car park about two miles north of the Ben Reifel Visitor Center that enters the eerie wasteland through a natural "doorway" in the rock pinnacles. A longer hike along the gently undulating Castle Trail, which winds through buttes and grassy prairies for five miles, begins from the same parking area. Visitors are permitted to amble just about anywhere, although remember to carry more than enough water (particularly if you venture into the back country), as none is available beyond developed areas.

Adjoining the **Ben Reifel Visitor Center**, five miles from the northeast entrance (daily 8am–4pm, extended summer hours; $15 park admission; ⓣ605/433-5361, ⓦwww.nps.gov/badl), is *Cedar Pass Lodge* (ⓣ605/433-5460, ⓦwww.cedarpasslodge.com; cabins ❹–❺, cottages ❺; closed Nov–March), the only **accommodation** option within the park; the lodge also operates its own **restaurant**. If *Cedar Pass Lodge* is full, try the basic but clean *Badlands Inn* (same details; ❹), less than two miles away just past the park's Interior Entrance. A pair of **campgrounds** are also available: *Cedar Pass* ($14) and primitive *Sage Creek* (free).

A second visitor centre, White River (summer only daily 10am–4pm; ⓣ605/455-2878), stands on Hwy-27 in the park's South Unit and is staffed by tribal rangers familiar with this far less-visited section of the park.

Wall

The adjacent town of **WALL** owes its notoriety to massive **Wall Drug**, which began modestly in 1931 as a pharmacy and veterinary supplies shop on Main Street; it's now one of the most visited tourist traps in the world. By the time you reach the 85ft-tall Wall Drug dinosaur at I-90's exit 110, expect to have been worn down by over five hundred billboards along the freeway touting the store's wares – including the free ice water that was its original sales gimmick.

Behind the hype lies a kitschy emporium that serves up to twenty thousand visitors daily. You can fill up on a wide range of food ranging from buffalo hot dogs to freshly fried doughnuts in the 520-seat café-cum-Western art gallery; alternately, you're free to enjoy the wall-to-wall collection of photos, memorabilia, animal trophies and mechanical automata like the Cowboy Orchestra and the Chuckwagon Quartet.

For **lodging** in Wall, try the rough-hewn *Frontier Cabins* at 1101 S Glenn St (Ⓣ605/279-2619, Ⓦwww.frontiercabins.net; ❸–❺), right off the freeway. *Cactus Café and Lounge*, 519 Main St (Ⓣ605/279-2561), offers a mixed menu of reasonably priced Mexican, Italian and American **food**.

Wounded Knee

No other place represents nineteenth-century atrocities against Native Americans as potently as **WOUNDED KNEE**. It was here on December 29, 1890, that the US Army delivered a *coup de grâce* to the vestiges of Native American resistance on the Plains, killing over three hundred unarmed Sioux men, women and children. The massacre was triggered by a misunderstanding during a tribal round-up: a deaf Native American, asked to surrender his rifle along with his peers, instead held it above his head, shouting that he'd paid a lot for it; an officer grabbed at the gun, it went off and the troops started firing.

Today, the site, near the junction of highways 27 and 28 in Pine Ridge Indian Reservation, is a naked tribute to the tragic event. A simple **marker** – on which "Massacre" has been tellingly laid over the original "Battle" – details the hour of mass death in sordid detail, while a commemorative stone **monument**, surrounded by a chain-link fence on a nearby hill, marks the victims' collective gravesite. Tribal leaders have so far refused federal funds to turn the site into a national monument, wanting instead to leave it uncommercialized, apart from a few local vendors selling handmade jewellery and dream catchers.

The Black Hills

Our people knew there was yellow metal in little chunks up there, but they did not bother with it, because it was not good for anything.

Black Elk, Oglala Sioux holy man

The timbered, rocky **BLACK HILLS** rise like an island from a sea of rolling hills and grain-growing plains, stretching for a hundred miles between the Belle Fourche River in the north and the Cheyenne to the south. For generations of Sioux, their value was and still is immeasurable, a kind of spiritual safe place where warriors went to speak with Wakan Tanka (the Great Spirit) and await visions. Even though they're mountains in the classic sense – the highest of the lot, Harney Peak, rises 7242ft – they were dubbed *Paha Sapa*, or Black Hills, and the blue spruce and Norway pine trees blanketing them only appear black from a distance.

Assuming the Black Hills to be worthless, the United States government drew up a treaty in the mid-nineteenth century that gave these mountains (along with most of South Dakota's land west of the Missouri River) to the Native Americans. All such treaties were eventually broken once the discovery of **gold** turned the natives' Eden into the white explorers' El Dorado, and it wasn't long before fortune-hunters came pouring in.

These days, the Hills are a major tourist destination, but despite the T-shirt stores, pseudo-historical wax museums, cowboy supper shows and water slides, they have not been robbed of all their beauty and dignity. No place here is much farther than a ninety-minute drive from the four presidential heads carved into **Mount Rushmore**, or its ambitious work-in-progress counterpart, the **Crazy Horse Memorial**. The mostly unspoiled southern hills are home to the bison of **Custer State Park** and **Wind Cave National Park**, along with the town of **Hot Springs**.

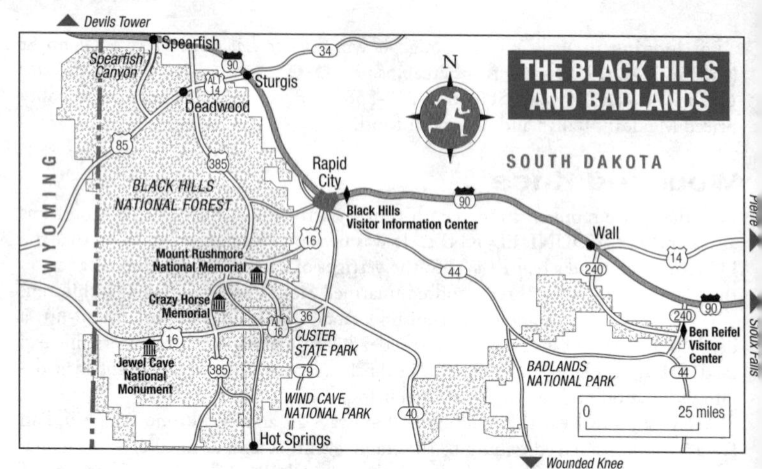

The northern hills

Far more commercialized than their southern siblings, the **northern Black Hills** beckon visitors with a trio of small towns – motorcycle-happy **Sturgis**, subdued **Spearfish** and rowdy **Deadwood** with its Wild West revivalism – that flank (and overshadow) regional hub **Rapid City**. Certain backroads, especially in the **Spearfish Canyon** area, form a network of prime driving and cycling country. The excellent **Black Hills Visitor Information Center**, at exit 61 off I-90 (May–Sept: daily 8am–7pm; Oct–April: daily till 5pm; ⓣ605/355-3700), is just outside Rapid City.

Rapid City

South Dakota's second-largest settlement, **RAPID CITY** – the "City of Presidents", so called for its 39 life-size statues of US leaders found at most of its downtown street corners, as well as for its proximity to Mount Rushmore – makes a convenient base for exploring the Black Hills. Greyhound **buses** pull into town at 333 Sixth St. If you're looking for somewhere to **stay**, it's hard to top the delightful *Alex Johnson Hotel*, 523 Sixth St (ⓣ605/342-1210, ⓦwww.alexjohnson.com; ④); a recent renovation project installed a bar atop the ten-storey, c.1928 building. Downtown Rapid City has a number of inviting **restaurants**, including *Firehouse Brewing Co.*, 610 Main St (ⓣ605/348-1915), where pub grub, craft beer and outdoor dining help make it a local favourite. Around the corner and fronted by a statue of a grinning, ruggedly dressed Ronald Reagan, *Tally's Silver Spoon*, at the corner of Sixth and St Joseph streets (ⓣ605/342-7621), features unique mains like waffled Dijon chicken and blueberry bison.

Sturgis

The hamlet of **STURGIS**, about thirty miles northwest of Rapid City, comes to life in a big way each August when the **Sturgis Motorcycle Rally** (ⓣ605/720-0800, ⓦwww.sturgismotorcyclerally.com) packs the otherwise sleepy town. Throughout the week, pasties and chaps pass for formal attire as virtually every square foot of the town is inundated with motorcycle enthusiasts. An abundance of Harley souvenirs stock the downtown stores year-round, and even if you've rolled into Sturgis on four wheels, the **Sturgis Motorcycle Museum & Hall of Fame**, 999 Main St (daily 10am–4pm; $5; ⓣ605/347-2001, ⓦwww.sturgismuseum.com) is worth a visit.

The Sturgis **visitor centre** (Ⓣ605/347-2556, Ⓦwww.sturgis-sd.org) is right off I-90 at exits 30 and 32. For a taste of the biker culture that defines the town, head to the *Full Throttle Saloon*, 12997 Hwy-34 (Ⓣ605/423-4584), a raucous indoor-outdoor tavern full of dubious diversions such as mechanical bull-riding.

Deadwood

One of the West's wildest Gold Rush towns, **DEADWOOD**, in a deep gulch 42 miles northwest of Rapid City, has the rare accolade of being a **National Historic Landmark** in its entirety, although you'd never know it for the liberal assortment of gambling halls and souvenir shops strung along Main Street. Within a year of the discovery of **gold** here in 1876, six thousand diggers swarmed in to stake their claims; the usual array of con artists, outlaws and other dodgy frontier types trailed closely. Among them was James Butler, aka **Wild Bill Hickok**, a spy, scout, bullwhacker, stagecoach driver, sheriff and gambler who spent only a few weeks in Deadwood prior to his murder here by a young drifter in 1876. Martha "**Calamity Jane**" Canary Burke, an illiterate alcoholic whose chequered career included stints as scout, prostitute, nurse and even stage performer, arrived around the same time as Hickok; despite barely knowing him, she was buried 27 years later beside Hickok in nearby **Mount Moriah Cemetery**.

For an overview of Deadwood's past and present, visit the **History and Information Center**, in the heart of town at 3 Siever St (daily 9am–5pm; Ⓣ605/578-9749). Boisterous Main Street – complete with corny, scripted "gunfights" and, late on weekend nights, seemingly scripted hoots and hollers from drunken tourists – boasts several grand old **hotels**, including the Victorian *Bullock Hotel* at no. 633 (Ⓣ1-800/336-1876, Ⓦwww.historicbullock.com; ❺). Up Main Street at no. 657, grab a **beer** at the sawdust-floored *Saloon #10* (Ⓣ1-800/952-9398), where above the door is the chair in which Hickok was sitting when he was shot dead while holding two aces, a pair of eights and the nine of diamonds – forever after christened the Dead Man's Hand. While the *Saloon* represents the wilder side of town, the elegant **dining** upstairs at the *Deadwood Social Club* (same phone) affords an opportunity to enjoy a Kobe ribeye or filet mignon.

Spearfish Canyon

Aspen, birch and white spruce spread over the towering limestone cliffs above the nineteen-mile **Spearfish Canyon National Scenic Highway**, which begins on Hwy-14A west of Deadwood and threads past sights such as Bridal Veil and Roughlock falls. At the southern mouth of the canyon where Hwy-14A and Hwy-85 intersect, drop in at the *Stage Stop Cafe* (Ⓣ605/584-3510) inside Cheyenne Crossing Store, where hearty breakfast mains (served until 3pm) practically overflow off the hot skillets on which they're served. Also be sure to try a plate of *wojapi*, a delicious traditional Sioux fry bread served with warm strawberry sauce.

Marking the canyon's north end, the reserved community of **SPEARFISH** has affordable and charming **lodging** at *Yesterday's Inn B&B*, 735 N Eighth St (Ⓣ605/644-0210; ❹), which has classically decorated rooms in a restored 1889 Victorian home. For **dinner**, *Roma's Ristorante*, 701 N Fifth St (Ⓣ605/722-0715), offers modern Italian cuisine often paired with live piano music.

The southern hills

The **southern Black Hills** encompass lower foothills and wooded pastureland, drawing visitors for their scenery and wildlife rather than kitsch or gambling. The **Mount Rushmore** and **Crazy Horse memorials** mark the northern end of the region; **Custer State Park** and **Wind Cave National Park** account for much of the central zone; while the pleasant town of **Hot Springs** sits on the southern edge.

Mount Rushmore National Memorial

America's two largest stone carvings are a mere seventeen miles apart – no more than spitting distance when you consider the scale on which they're conceived. The better-known **Mount Rushmore National Memorial** (summer: daily 8am–9pm, check website for hours rest of year; free admission, parking $10; ⓣ605/574-2523, ⓦwww.nps.gov/moru), originally dubbed "The Shrine of Democracy", is the unarguable linchpin of the Hills' tourist circuit. It's an easy 24-mile drive southwest of Rapid City, though by far the most impressive approach is to follow **Iron Mountain Road** (US-16A) from Custer State Park (see opposite). The gorgeous route runs seventeen miles up and over Iron Mountain and features three slender tunnels, along with three curly twists in the road called "pigtail bridges", each an engineering and design triumph.

In 1923, South Dakota historian Doane Robinson and sculptor **Gutzon Borglum**, known for carvings such as the leaders of the Confederacy in Stone Mountain, Georgia, discussed the possibility of turning the imposing fingers of granite known as the Needles into a dramatic patriotic sculpture. Borglum eventually opted for a nearby mountain named after New York attorney Charles E. Rushmore, upon which he would fashion the faces and heads of four certifiably great American presidents: **George Washington**, **Thomas Jefferson**, **Abraham Lincoln** and Borglum's buddy, **Theodore Roosevelt**.

Sixty years old when the project began in 1927, Borglum died shortly prior to the dedication of the last head – Roosevelt's – in 1941. Inclement weather

The bison of the Great Plains

In the fifteenth century, the Great Plains were roamed by one hundred million shaggy, short-sighted American **bison** (popularly known as buffalo, a corruption of the French *boeuf*). Apart from eating bison's flesh, Native Americans used the animals' fur and hide for clothing and shelter; their bones for weapons, utensils and toys; and even their droppings for fuel. The US Army and the flood of ensuing settlers correctly figured that eliminating the bison en masse was a mercilessly effective way to deplete the Native Americans as well; by 1900, there were fewer than one thousand of the short-horned beasts left in North America.

Custer State Park was instrumental in helping to raise that meagre number to a current head count in the hundreds of thousands in the US and Canada. The park's own 1200 bison constitute the country's second largest publicly owned herd, surpassed only by Yellowstone National Park (see p.718). However, over ninety percent of bison in the US are now privately owned – the meat, higher in protein and lower in cholesterol than either chicken or tuna, has become a regular item on restaurant menus throughout the Dakotas, Montana and Wyoming, and is something between novelty and delicacy in other parts of the US and Canada.

The Custer State Park bison are free to roam where they please until either the last Monday of September or the first Monday in October, when the park stages its annual **roundup**. From selected viewing points, you can watch one of the region's most thrilling events, as helicopters, ground vehicles and horseback riders steer the often recalcitrant herds down a six-mile "corridor" and into a series of pens. There the calves are branded and vaccinated, with the whole lot sorted to determine which five hundred will be auctioned off on the third Saturday in November. Proceeds from this sale account for twenty percent of the park's annual revenue.

Don't let the tranquil, easy-going appearance of North America's largest mammal lull you into a false sense of security – these are famously unpredictable animals. An average bison can stand over 6ft-high at the hump, weigh more than a ton, outrun a horse, turn on a dime and gore a human most efficiently.

and uncertain funding had meant that the actual sculpting took far longer than originally anticipated, at a total cost just short of $1 million.

The Big Four gaze out impassively, cheek by jowl, arguably a greater engineering feat than an artistic one. Each head is about 60ft from chin to crown – by way of comparison, the Statue of Liberty's head is only 17ft. The best times to view Rushmore are at dawn or dusk, when there are fewer people and better natural lighting. *Carver's Cafe* (Ⓣ605/574-2515), complete with panoramic windows as portrayed in Alfred Hitchcock's *North by Northwest*, serves full **meals** – robust eaters should opt for the "Monumental Breakfast", consisting of hash browns, eggs, country-fried steak with gravy and a biscuit piled on a plate sagging from the weight.

Crazy Horse Memorial

In 1939, prompted by the sight of the Rushmore monument, Sioux leader Henry Standing Bear wrote to **Korczak Ziolkowski**, who had just won first prize for sculpture at the New York World's Fair, telling him that Native Americans "would like the white man to know that the red man has great heroes, too". The chief invited Ziolkowski to take on a similar project – and, less than a decade later, pushing forty and with only $174 to his name, the New Englander moved permanently to the Black Hills to undertake a vastly more ambitious mission than Rushmore: the **Crazy Horse Memorial**, on US-16, five miles north of Custer.

The subject, the revered warrior Crazy Horse on horseback, so appealed to Ziolkowski that he set out to make his monument the biggest statue in the world, taller even than Egypt's Great Pyramid of Giza. The work he began on **Thunderhead Mountain** in 1948 – five Native American survivors of the Battle of Little Bighorn attended the dedication ceremony – didn't stop with his death in 1982; his widow, children and grandchildren continue to realize his vision. Ziolkowski himself raised and spent $4 million on the nonprofit project, refusing to accept federal or state funds, instead relying entirely on admissions and contributions, a practice the memorial's foundation continues to this day. National and international interest has greatly increased as the monument has finally started to take recognizable shape: the 90ft-high face was completed in time for the fiftieth anniversary celebrations in 1998, although it will easily be another half-century before the project is completed.

The main viewing terrace at the **visitor centre** (May–Oct: daily 8am–dusk, check website for hours rest of year; Ⓣ605/673-4681, Ⓦwww.crazyhorsememorial.org) is nearly a mile from the carving itself; its 20ft scale model on display is 34 times smaller than the end result, which will be 563ft high and 641ft long. The site, open dawn to dusk year-round (and illuminated for an hour each night), is free to Native Americans. Otherwise, **admission** costs $10 per person or $27 per carload, though many consider it a donation of sorts since the face is just as visible from the highway. The premises include exhibits of Native American artefacts and crafts, the *Laughing Water Restaurant* and a gift shop.

Custer State Park

The 71,000 billboard-free acres of **Custer State Park** fill much of the southern-central Black Hills; the park acts as nature's antidote to the commercial crassness found to the north. The **Needles Highway** (Hwy-87; closed mid-Oct to mid-April) winds for fourteen miles through pine forests and past the eponymous jagged granite spires in the park's northwestern corner, between Sylvan and Legion lakes; a few miles along the road past Sylvan Lake, look for the **Needle's Eye**, a slender gap in one of the pinnacles. In the southeastern reaches of the park, the eighteen-mile **Wildlife Loop** undulates through rolling meadows rich with Rocky Mountain elk, bighorn sheep, pronghorn antelope, deer and begging burros (tame and disarming four-legged panhandlers who'll stick their snouts through the windows of slow-moving vehicles in search of snack handouts), as well as the bison for which the park is known.

For a fuller appreciation of the beauty of Custer State Park, set out on one of its myriad **hiking** and **biking trails**. Rangers at the park entrances – where you're required to purchase an "**entrance license**" of $6 (valid for one week) – can advise on various park activities, from trail exploration to fishing; various firms also offer horseback rides, boat rentals and cross-country drives in open-topped jeeps. A good, short introductory hike is the three-mile **Lovers Leap Trail**, which begins near the park's main **visitor centre** (daily: summer 8am–8pm; rest of year 9am–5pm, closed Dec–March; ⓣ605/255-4464), on Hwy-16A in the park's eastern section. One of the park's most prominent hikes is the six-mile trek from Sylvan Lake up **Harney Peak**, where the payoff is expansive views from the stone lookout tower perched atop the summit; at 7242ft, the peak stands as the tallest point between the Rockies and the Pyrenees.

The park's four state-run resorts make it a splendid **place to stay**. The finest is the *State Game Lodge* (ⓣ605/255-4772), on Hwy-16A not far from the visitor centre, which operates a motel-style lodge and also has some lovely individual cabins (both ❻) at the edge of the woods; its *Pheasant Dining Room* offers hearty meals, including exceptional flapjacks and French toast for breakfast. Tucked in the park's northwest corner, the *Sylvan Lake Resort* (same phone; ❺–❻) similarly offers comfy cabins, more traditional rooms in its tasteful main building and the upscale *Lakota Dining Room*. Custer State Park also has eight **campgrounds** (ⓣ1-800/710-2267), four of which feature camping cabins ($45); all have standard tent sites ($16–18).

Wind Cave National Park

Beneath wide-open rangelands, **Wind Cave National Park**, directly south of Custer State Park, comprises over one hundred miles of mapped underground passages etched out of limestone. One of the largest caves in the US, it was discovered in 1881 when a loud whistling noise on the plains led a settler to a hole in the ground – the cave's only natural opening. Nowadays, rangers lead a variety of cave **tours** ($7–23 depending on length of tour) from the **visitor centre** (June–Aug: daily 8am–7pm, check website for hours rest of year; ⓣ605/745-4600, ⓦwww.nps.gov/wica), pointing out delicate features such as frostwork and boxwork along the way. If you come in summer, forget the standard walking tours and opt for the ones that allow you to crawl around in the smaller passages, or explore the caves by candlelight – call ahead for reservations.

If you lack the inclination to delve into the Dakotas' dank bowels, **driving** through the park is another quintessential Black Hills experience. Its native grass prairies are home to deer, antelope, elk, coyote, prairie dogs and a sizeable herd of bison; it's likely you'll see at least a few of these species along the sublime, five-mile Lookout Point Loop **hiking** trail, which begins at the Centennial Trailhead two miles north of the visitor centre. For **camping** in the park, try *Elk Mountain Campground* ($12).

Hot Springs

The Black Hills' southern anchor, **HOT SPRINGS**, differs from other regional towns in that it hasn't tarted up its downtown to look like a movie set. It doesn't need to – several dozen utilitarian yet handsome sandstone structures dominate its centre, through which flows the sprightly Fall River.

Battles over the town's thermal pools caused as much grief as the clamour for gold, although they ceased in 1890 once local entrepreneur Fred Evans incorporated numerous small springs and one mammoth hot-water pool into a spa centre. Today, **Evans Plunge**, on the north edge of town at 1145 N River St (May–Aug: Mon–Fri 8am–9pm, Sat & Sun 10am–9pm, check website for hours rest of year;

$11; ⓣ605/745-5165, ⓦwww.evansplunge.com), is a popular waterpark, where three great slides zoom down into invitingly warm waters.

The unique **Mammoth Site** on the Hwy-18 bypass is the only *in situ* display of mammoth fossils in the US (May–Aug: daily 8am–8pm, check website for hours rest of year; $8; ⓣ605/745-6017, ⓦwww.mammothsite.com). Inside its dome, fascinating guided **tours** explain how these ten-ton mammoths (along with camels, bears and rodents) were trapped in a steep-sided sinkhole and gradually became covered by sediment; complete skeletons are easy to pick out in the excavation site.

Information for visitors to Hot Springs is available at the old train depot (June–Aug only Mon–Fri 8am–5pm; ⓣ605/745-4140, ⓦwww.hotsprings-sd.com) at 630 N River St. The *Super 8*, 800 Mammoth St (ⓣ605/745-3888 or 1-800/800-8000; ❹), offers comfortable rooms adjacent to the mammoth site.

North Dakota

Like a quiet afterthought, **NORTH DAKOTA** has no nationally recognizable landmarks, nor is the state's history particularly lurid or glamorous; to some, this constitutes much of its understated charm. Grain silos and grassy prairies stretch to the horizon, haystacks resemble oversized loaves of bread, and the wind rakes strong fingers through tall fields of golden wheat and flax. As in South Dakota, the fertile east is more thickly settled than the wilder west, where vast livestock ranges predominate. North Dakota epitomizes all things rural American: it's friendly, simple and picturesque, with a highly localized speech pattern drawn from neighboring Minnesota, Manitoba and Saskatchewan.

From where it crosses the state's eastern boundary, the Red River of the North, I-94 passes through the central capital of **Bismarck** and on into the **Badlands** of the west; its less travelled northern counterpart, US-2, makes for a pleasant east–west alternative. Though the national park bearing his name is the state's key tourist destination, President Theodore Roosevelt would surely not be pleased about the continuing disfiguration of western North Dakota by strip-mining and oil operations.

Eastern and central North Dakota

The **Red River Valley**, North Dakota's furthest eastern strip, is home to two sizeable cities, easygoing **Grand Forks** and less attractive **Fargo**, best known to many for the eponymous 1996 Coen brothers' film. Waterfowl live off the sloughs and potholes of the rolling, glaciated prairie of the state's south-central section, while lakes and woodlands dominate the north and the Canadian border. Also in the north, you'll find the low **Turtle Mountains**, along with lovely **Lake Metigoshe** and the **International Peace Garden** (more a political symbol than a compelling sight).

The **Missouri River** wriggles like a giant worm out of Montana, down past North Dakota's capital, **Bismarck**, and into South Dakota. En route to Bismarck, it's transformed into **Lake Sakakawea**, a virtual inland sea that's the state's premier water playground.

Grand Forks

GRAND FORKS sits along the north-flowing Red River of the North, closer to Canada than it is to I-94. Even before its 1870 founding, fur traders had used the area to rest and barter during travels between Winnipeg and Minneapolis. It's a friendly and outdoorsy city, with scores of parks and several tree-lined avenues of attractive homes. Along with its cross-river counterpart of East Grand Forks, Minnesota, the city was ravaged by ruinous floodwaters in the spring of 1997, which precipitated the largest natural disaster evacuation in US history before Hurricane Katrina in 2005. The fresh appearance of the city's downtown today is due to the swift and smart reconstruction that ensued, which has resulted in a smattering of inviting shops and restaurants, as well as extensively redeveloped parkland on both sides of the river.

The city's most captivating distractions can be found on the red-brick campus of the **University of North Dakota**, where the **North Dakota Museum of Art** (Mon–Fri 9am–5pm, Sat & Sun 1–5pm; donation requested; ⓣ701/777-4195, ⓦwww.ndmoa.com) features an eclectic assortment of contemporary art and touring exhibits. Also on campus, fascinating tours are offered of the **John D. Odegard School of Aerospace Sciences** (call ahead for tour appointment; ⓣ701/777-2791), one of the largest civilian pilot-training schools in the world, where you can take in flight simulators, an air-traffic control room and even an altitude chamber.

Grand Forks' **visitor centre** is at 4251 Gateway Drive (ⓣ701/746-0444, ⓦwww.visitgrandforks.com). Greyhound buses stop where US-81 and Hwy-2 intersect, as well as on the UND campus; Amtrak trains pull into town at 5555 W Demers Ave. Within walking distance of downtown is the *GuestHouse International Inn*, 710 First Ave N (ⓣ701/746-5411, ⓦwww.guesthouseintl.com; ❸), a comfortable and nicely situated, if low-slung **hotel**, complete with indoor pool. The most serene place to **camp** nearby is pretty Turtle River State Park (ⓣ701/594-4445; vehicle fee $5, woodland cabin ❷, $12 for campsite), 22 miles west of town on US-2. As for **dining**, two options along downtown's North Third Street beckon: *Dakota Harvest Bakers* at no. 17 (ⓣ701/772-2100), serves good soups, sandwiches and baked goods, while *The Toasted Frog* (ⓣ701/772-3764) at no. 124 offers a festive atmosphere and more extensive menu, with items such as wood-fired pizzas and New York strip steaks.

Bismarck and Mandan

Named in honour of German Chancellor Otto von Bismarck in the hope of attracting Germanic settlers, North Dakota's government centre, **BISMARCK**, survived a colourfully lawless period early in its history – its present-day Fourth Street was once known as "Murderers' Gulch". Today, the capital city retains a mellow mood, where locals are proud of the nineteen-storey limestone **capitol building**, 600 E Boulevard Ave, dating from the mid 1930s and set at the crest of a public park. The interior, a model of spatial economy and marbled Art Deco elegance, is open for guided **tours** (hourly Mon–Fri 9–11am & 1–3pm, more frequent in summer; free; ⓣ701/328-2480). Across the street, the superb **Heritage Center** (Mon–Fri 8am–5pm, Sat & Sun 10am–5pm; donation suggested; ⓣ701/328-2666) divides the state's past into six sections, from the dinosaur era onward. Look for Sitting Bull's painted robe and the bison "smell box", which offers the olfactorily brave a whiff of buffalo dung. A few miles west of downtown at the **Port of Bismarck**, the *Lewis & Clark Riverboat* runs one-hour **historical cruises** (daily; $12–16; ⓣ701/255-4233, ⓦwww.lewisandclarkriverboat.com); longer cruises with meals ($20–40) are also available.

The state's western region seems to begin as soon as you cross the Missouri River from **Bismarck** over to neighboring **MANDAN**. The major reason to venture across the water is **Fort Abraham Lincoln State Park** ($5; ⓣ701/667-6380), seven miles south of downtown via Hwy-1806, where the centrepiece is the **Custer House** (daily tours every half-hour, 9am–5pm, $6), an admirable reconstruction of the 1874 original designed by US Army officer George Custer. The forty-minute guided tour supplies nuggets of quirky information about the brutally ambitious, indefatigable horseman (for example, he liked to eat raw onions), his wife and their household. Nearer to the river, four earth lodge reconstructions stand on the site of the once-vast **On-A-Slant village**, occupied by the Mandan (or River-Dweller) tribe during most of the sixteenth and seventeenth centuries. After the Mandan abandoned On-A-Slant, they moved upstream and settled on the site that became Fort Mandan, where in 1804 the explorers Lewis and Clark came into contact with **Sakakawea** (aka Sacajawea), who helped guide them west towards the Pacific. The site and adjacent **historical museum** (May–Oct: daily 9am–5pm, closed rest of year; free with Custer House ticket) sit below a bluff topped with replicas of the Fort Lincoln infantry post.

Practicalities

Bismarck's Greyhound **bus** terminal is at 3750 E Rosser Ave, while the Bismarck-Mandan **visitor centre** is at 1600 Burnt Boat Drive (Mon–Fri 7.30am–7pm, Sat 8am–6pm, Sun 10am–5pm; ⓣ1-800/767-3555, ⓦwww.bismarckmandancvb.com). Near downtown, a good and affordable place to **stay** is the *Expressway Inn*, 200 E Bismarck Expressway (ⓣ701/222-2900, ⓦwww.expresswayhotels.com; ❸). For **camping**, try the excellent Cross Ranch State Park, thirty minutes north of Bismarck on Hwy-1806 (ⓣ701/794-3731; vehicle fee $5, $12 for campsite, log cabin ❸); overlapped by a six-thousand-acre nature reserve, the park features sixteen miles of **trails**. Closer to Bismarck, you can sleep at Fort Abraham Lincoln State Park ($12 for campsite, camping cabin ❷).

Bismarck's small-town feel comes through in its limited **dining** and **nightlife**; try *Peacock Alley*, 422 E Main St (ⓣ701/255-7917), which serves pasta, American cuisine and flown-in seafood.

Western North Dakota

With clouds whipping past its colourful, pyramid-like landforms, the **Badlands** of North Dakota's western region is a somewhat gentler-looking version of its better-known South Dakota sibling, although it's clearly no less rugged once you set boot to trail. **Theodore Roosevelt** declared, "I never would have been president if it had not been for my experiences in North Dakota", but you may find the modern comforts of neighbouring town of **Medora** more welcome than the physically strenuous ranching lifestyle Roosevelt so appreciated.

Theodore Roosevelt National Park

A huge tract of multi-hued rock formations, rough grassland and brackish streams, **Theodore Roosevelt National Park** ($10/car) is split into north and south units approximately seventy miles apart. The park's seventy thousand acres encompass desert, woods and mountains, and both units are at their most beautiful at sunrise or sundown – the best times to observe such fauna as elk, antelope, ever-present bison and closely knit prairie dog communities.

Your first taste of the larger, more popular **southern unit** is likely to be at the breathtaking **Painted Canyon**, seven miles east of Medora off I-94. Here and elsewhere in the park, the land is like a sedimentary layer cake that for millions of years has been beaten by hard rains, baked by the sun into a kaleidoscope of colours and cut through to its base by the erosive Little Missouri River and lesser streams. A mile-long **nature hike**, accessible in the summer months, begins at the end of the canyon's boardwalk.

The southern unit's main **visitor centre** in Medora (daily: summer 8am–6pm, rest of year 8am–4.30pm; ⓣ701/623-4466, ⓦwww.nps.gov/thro) acts as park headquarters; it also offers tours, nature walks and lectures by campfire during the summer season. Behind it sits the simple Maltese Cross Cabin that served as Roosevelt's first home in North Dakota during his early ranching days; also worth seeking out is the view from **Wind Canyon**, ten miles out of Medora along the park's remarkably scenic 36-mile loop road. Peaceful Valley Ranch (ⓣ701/623-4568), one mile from the park's *Cottonwood Campground* ($10/tent site), arranges horseback tours between May and September; a ninety-minute ride is $30.

The park's smaller **northern unit**, off Hwy-85 fifteen miles south of Watford City, receives only a fraction of the southern unit's visitors, though it's arguably more spectacular. Two highlights are **River Bend Overlook**, along the park's fourteen-mile scenic drive, and **Oxbow Overlook**, at that same road's end, while the demanding twelve-mile **Buckhorn Trail** winds through sage-filled terrain before following steep gulches up into lofty prairies full of grazing bison; look for the trailhead directly across from the *Juniper Campground* ($10) turn-off.

The northern unit's **visitor centre** is open daily (April–Oct 9am–5.30pm, limited hours rest of year; ⓣ701/842-2333). In an odd twist of raggedly-drawn **time zones**, the park's northern unit is on Central time, while the southern unit is on Mountain time (see p.58).

Medora

Tiny **MEDORA**, the southern gateway to Theodore Roosevelt National Park, languished in obscurity until a local wealthy philanthropist pumped new life into it in the 1960s. In the decades since, it has become one of North Dakota's principal attractions, an agreeable hamlet primarily geared toward wholesome family fun, albeit much more in step with its beautiful surroundings than the incongruent waterslides and theme parks of South Dakota's Black Hills. The community's biggest draw by far is the long-running **Medora Musical** (May–Sept daily 8.30pm; $30–34; ⓣ1-800/633-6721, ⓦwww.medora.com), a super-Americana song-and-dance and variety show staged beneath the stars in a marvellously sited amphitheatre on a hillside just outside of town. The extravaganza, which runs nearly one hundred consecutive nights each summer, is preceded two hours prior by a fantastic feed for which hundreds of steaks are simultaneously fondued on pitchforks inside giant oil vats.

As for local **lodging**, the town's original *Rough Riders Hotel* (ⓣ1-800/633-6721; ❼) at 301 Third Ave, dating back to Roosevelt's era and so named for his Army brigade, received a major expansion and remodelling in 2010. Its equally sparkling **dining** room, *Theodore's*, just off the hotel lobby, specializes in buffalo kabobs and prime rib, as well as unique appetizers such as walleye cheeks. If you're on a budget but don't feel like camping at the national park next door, rest your head at the utilitarian *Badlands Motel* (ⓣ1-800/633-6721; ❸–❻; closed Nov–March), 501 Pacific Ave, and take breakfast, lunch or dinner at the serviceable *Chuckwagon Buffet* (closed Oct–April). **Information** on these and other Medora inns and restaurants is available at ⓣ1-800/633-6721 and ⓦwww.medora.com.

The Rockies

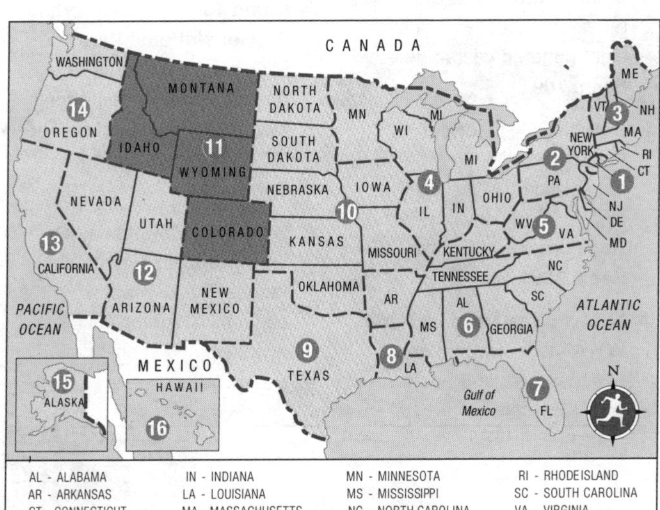

CANADA
WASHINGTON
MONTANA
NORTH DAKOTA
MN
ME
VT
NH
MA
RI
CT
14
OREGON
IDAHO
11
WYOMING
SOUTH DAKOTA
WI
MI
NEW YORK
2
3
1
PA
NEBRASKA
IOWA
4
IL
IN
OHIO
NJ
DE
MD
NEVADA
UTAH
COLORADO
10
KANSAS
MISSOURI
KENTUCKY
WV
5
VA
13
CALIFORNIA
12
TENNESSEE
NC
ARIZONA
NEW MEXICO
OKLAHOMA
AR
SC
PACIFIC OCEAN
AL
MS
6
GEORGIA
ATLANTIC OCEAN
9
TEXAS
8
LA
MEXICO
15
ALASKA
HAWAII
16
Gulf of Mexico
7
FL
N
AL - ALABAMA
AR - ARKANSAS
CT - CONNECTICUT
DE - DELAWARE
FL- FLORIDA
IL - ILLINOIS
IN - INDIANA
LA - LOUISIANA
MA - MASSACHUSETTS
MD - MARYLAND
ME - MAINE
MI - MICHIGAN
MN - MINNESOTA
MS - MISSISSIPPI
NC - NORTH CAROLINA
NH - NEW HAMPSHIRE
NJ - NEW JERSEY
PA - PENNSYLVANIA
RI - RHODE ISLAND
SC - SOUTH CAROLINA
VA - VIRGINIA
VT - VERMONT
WI - WISCONSIN
WV - WEST VIRGINIA

CHAPTER 11

Highlights

* **Durango & Silverton Narrow Gauge Railroad, CO** This steam-train ride corkscrews through spectacular mountains to the mining town of Silverton. See p.707

* **Mesa Verde National Park, CO** Explore the extraordinary cliffside dwellings, abandoned by the Ancestral Puebloans eight hundred years ago. See p.709

* **Buffalo Bill Historical Center, WY** Centring on an extraordinary museum, the town of Cody celebrates the life and times of Buffalo Bill. See p.716

* **Yellowstone National Park, WY** A thermal wonderland, where wolves and bears prowl, and shaggy bison wander past towering geysers. See p.718

* **Gates of the Mountains, MT** Lewis and Clark were awestruck floating past these huge limestone cliffs, and you will be, too. See p.736

* **Going-to-the-Sun Road, Glacier National Park, MT** The hairpin turns along this fifty-mile stretch offer staggering views near the Continental Divide. See p.740

* **Sawtooth Mountains, ID** Of all Idaho's 81 mountain ranges, the Sawtooth summits make for the most awe-inspiring scenic drive. See p.745

▲ Durango & Silverton Narrow Gauge Railroad

11

The Rockies

Exploring the **Rocky Mountain** states of **Colorado**, **Wyoming**, **Montana** and **Idaho** could literally take a lifetime. Stretching over one thousand miles from the virgin forests on the Canadian border to the deserts of New Mexico, America's rugged spine encompasses an astonishing array of **landscapes** – geyser basins, lava flows, arid valleys and huge sand dunes – each in its own way as dramatic as the region's magnificent white-topped peaks. All that geological grandeur is enhanced by wildlife such as bison, bear, moose and elk, and the conspicuous legacy of the miners, cowboys, outlaws and Native Americans who fought over the area's rich resources during the nineteenth century.

Apart from the **Ancestral Puebloan** cliff-dwellers, who lived in southern Colorado until around 1300 AD, most **Native Americans** in this region were nomadic hunters. They inhabited the western extremities of the Great Plains, the richest buffalo-grazing land in the continent. Only after the territory was sold to the US in 1803 as part of the **Louisiana Purchase** was it thoroughly charted, starting with the **Lewis and Clark expedition** that traversed Montana and Idaho in 1805. As a result of the team's reports of abundant game, the fabled "**mountain men**" had soon trapped the beavers here to the point of virtual extinction. They left as soon as the pelt boom was over, however, and permanent white settlement did not begin until gold was discovered near Denver in 1858. Within a decade, speculators were plundering every accessible gorge and creek in the four states in the search for valuable ores. The construction of transcontinental rail lines and the establishment of vast cattle ranches to feed the mining camps led to the slaughter of millions of buffalo, and conflict with the Native Americans became inevitable. The **Sioux** and **Cheyenne**, led by brilliant strategists like Sitting Bull and Crazy Horse, achieved decisive victories over the US Army, most notably at Little Bighorn – "**Custer's Last Stand**". By the late 1870s, a massive military operation had cleared the region of all warring tribes.

Most of those who followed saw the Rockies strictly in terms of profit: they took what they wanted and left. Small communities in this isolated terrain remain exclusively dedicated to coal, oil or some other single commodity, and all too often the uncertain tightrope walk between boom and bust is evident in their run-down facades.

Each of the four states has its own distinct character. **Colorado**, with fifty peaks over 14,000ft, is the most mountainous and populated, as well as the economic leader of the region. Friendly, sophisticated **Denver**, the Rockies' only major metropolis, is also the most visited city, in part because it serves as gateway to some of the best ski resorts in the country. Less touched by the tourist circus is vast, brawny **Montana**, where the "Big Sky" looks down on a glorious verdant manuscript scribbled over with gushing streams, lakes and tiny communities.

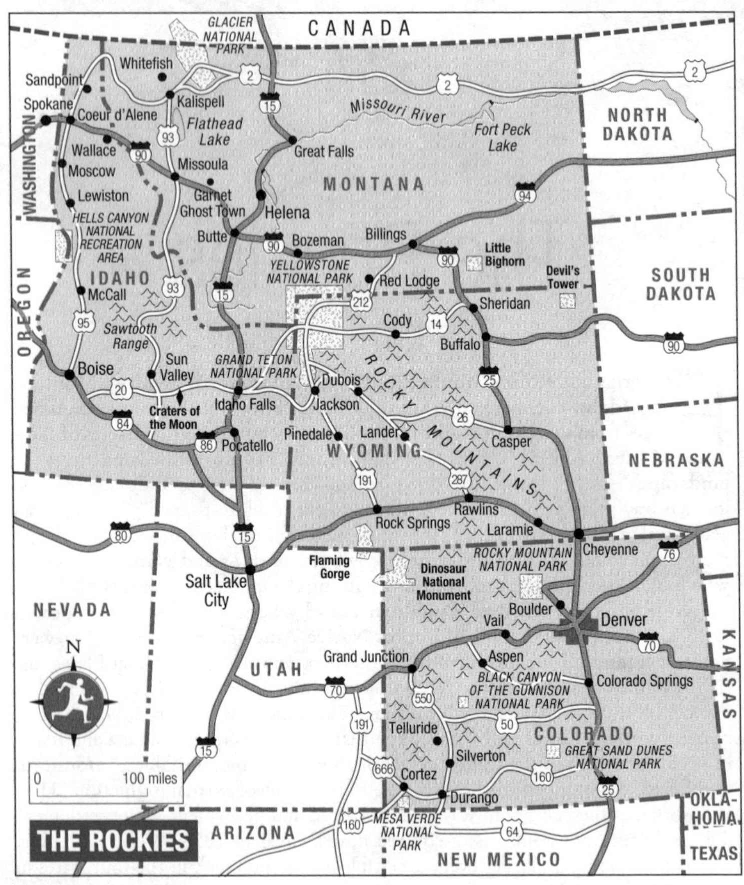

Vast stretches of scrubland fill **Wyoming**, the country's least populous state, best known for gurgling, spitting **Yellowstone**, adjacent **Grand Teton National Park**, and the nearby **Bighorn Mountains**. Rugged, remote, and desolate **Idaho** holds some of the Rocky Mountains' last unexplored wildernesses, most notably the mighty **Sawtooth** range.

Between early June and early September you can expect **temperatures** in the high sixties all the way up to a hundred degrees Fahrenheit, depending on whether you are in the high desert of Wyoming, the plains of Idaho or the mountains of Colorado. Be prepared for wild variations in the mountains – and, of course, the higher you go the colder it gets. The altitude is high enough to warrant a period of acclimatization, while the sun at these elevations can be uncomfortably fierce. In fact, parts of Wyoming and Colorado bask in more hours of sunshine per year than San Diego or Miami Beach. Spring, when the snow melts, is the least attractive time to visit, and while the delicate golds of quaking aspen trees light up the mountainsides in early autumn, by October things are generally a bit cold for enjoyable hiking or sports. Most **ski** runs are open by late November and operate well into March – or even June, depending on snow conditions. The coldest month is January, when temperatures below 0°F are common.

Attempt to rush around every national park and major town and you'll miss out on one of the Rockies' real delights – coaxing your car along the tight switchback roads that wind up and over precipitous mountain passes, especially through the majestic **Continental Divide**. Remember to check in the rear-view mirror as you go, though – you might be missing that perfect photo. At some point it's worth forsaking motorized transport, to see at least some of the area by **bike**; the Rockies contain some of the most challenging and rewarding cycling terrain on the continent. And of course, you cannot really claim to have seen the area unless you embark on a hike or two.

Getting around the Rockies

By far the largest **airport** in the Rockies is in **Denver**, Colorado, though **Salt Lake City** in neighbouring Utah also offers useful access to the Yellowstone area. Otherwise, ski resorts such as Jackson and Aspen have their own airports, and commuter airlines serve lesser regional hubs like Cheyenne, Billings, Bozeman and Boise.

Denver is also the major hub for Greyhound **buses** to all neighbouring states – the busiest bus routes follow the cross-country interstates, I-70 through Colorado and I-90 through Wyoming and Montana. Amtrak **trains** too run straight across central Colorado – they can be frustratingly slow, but at least they pass through magnificent Glenwood Canyon in daylight hours – and also across Montana, stopping at Whitefish and east and west of Glacier National Park, and at Essex in the summer.

As ever, though, public transport is only really useful for reaching towns and cities. The only way to explore the true majesty of the Rockies, and the national parks in particular, is by **car**.

Colorado

The diverse state of **COLORADO** veers from the outstretched flats of the east and the colossal mountains of its central region to the arid canyons and plateaus of the west. In the north, **Native Americans** hunted and trapped in lush mountain valleys in summer, and returned to the prairies for the winter; in the south, the Ancestral Puebloans of Mesa Verde grew corn on their isolated mesas and shared in the great early civilization of the Southwest.

Parts of what is now Colorado accrued to the US at different times: the east and north were acquired under the **Louisiana Purchase** in 1803, while the south was won 45 years later in the war with **Mexico**. Gold-hungry Spaniards came through in the sixteenth century, and US Army Colonel Zebulon Pike ventured into the mountains on an exploratory expedition in 1806, but the Native American way of life only became seriously threatened with the actual discovery of **gold** west of Denver in 1858. At that time, Colorado was still part of Kansas Territory; it became a territory in its own right in 1861, and a state in 1876. The distractions of the Civil War gave the Native Americans the opportunity to fight back, but they were soon overwhelmed. From then until the end of the century, Colorado boomed; the quantities of gold and silver extracted from the mountains did not compare with the riches found in California, but were sufficient to fuel a rip-roaring frontier lifestyle.

For the modern visitor, the obvious first stop is **Denver,** at the eastern edge of the Rockies and the biggest city for several hundred miles around. Outside Denver, the northern half of the state holds many popular destinations, starting with the dynamic college town of **Boulder** and spectacular **Rocky Mountain National Park**. Most of the resorts that make Colorado the continent's foremost **skiing** destination snuggle into the mountains west of Denver: **Summit County** attracts the most visitors, **Vail** is best for terrain, and **Aspen** boasts the glitziest après-ski scene. The far west of the state stretches onto the red-rock deserts of the Colorado Plateau, where the dry climate has preserved the extraordinary natural sculptures of **Colorado National Monument**. **Pikes Peak** towers over the state's second-largest city, **Colorado Springs**, but beyond that, the state's **southeast** quarter is mostly agricultural plains. In the southwest, **Mesa Verde National Park** preserves remarkable cliff cities left by the ancient Ancestral Puebloans, while the former mining towns of **Durango** and **Crested Butte** stand revitalized in the mountains.

Denver

Its skyscrapers marking the final transition between the Great Plains and the American West, **DENVER** stands at the threshold of the **Rocky Mountains**. Though clearly visible from downtown, the majestic peaks of the Front Range start to rise roughly fifteen miles west, and the **"Mile High City"** is itself uniformly flat, with abundant room to spread out.

Denver was founded in 1858, on a riverless spot that happened to be the site of Colorado's first **gold** strike. Prospectors swiftly moved on to the more substantial deposits at Central City and beyond, but Denver has remained the state's most important commercial and transportation nexus ever since. When the first railroads bypassed it – the death knell for so many other communities – its citizens simply banded together and built their own connecting spur.

These days, Denver is a welcoming and enjoyable place to visit, with a liberal, go-ahead spirit. Tourism is based on getting out into the great outdoors rather than on sightseeing in town, but somehow the city's isolation gives its 2.8-million population a refreshing friendliness; and in a city that is used to providing its own entertainment, there always seems to be something going on.

Arrival, information and getting around

The gigantic, state-of-the-art **Denver International Airport** (Ⓦwww.flydenver.com) lies 24 miles northeast of downtown; if you rent a car and are heading for Rocky Mountains National Park or Boulder, there's no need to go anywhere near the city centre. All **taxi** companies, including Metro (Ⓣ303/333-3333) charge a flat rate of $54.50 to downtown, while RTD SkyRide **buses** (Ⓦwww.rtd-denver.com) serve downtown ($10) and Boulder ($12). Various independent **shuttles**, like Big Sky (Ⓣ303/300-2626, Ⓦwww.bigskyshuttle.com), drop passengers at downtown hotels for around $25, and also serve the ski resorts further afield.

Amtrak **trains** arrive on the northwest edge of downtown Denver at the beautiful old **Union Station** on Wynkoop Street; the Greyhound **bus terminal** is just as close to the action at 1055 19th St.

For **information**, stop by the city's main Visitor Center, downtown at 1600 California St and entered via the pedestrian-only 16th Street (Mon–Fri 9am–6pm, Sat till 5pm, Sun 11am–3pm; Ⓣ303/892-1505 or 1-800/233-6837, Ⓦwww.denver.org).

Downtown Denver is small enough to explore **on foot**, aided perhaps by the free **buses** (daily 6am–1am) that run for a mile up and down the central 16th Street Mall.

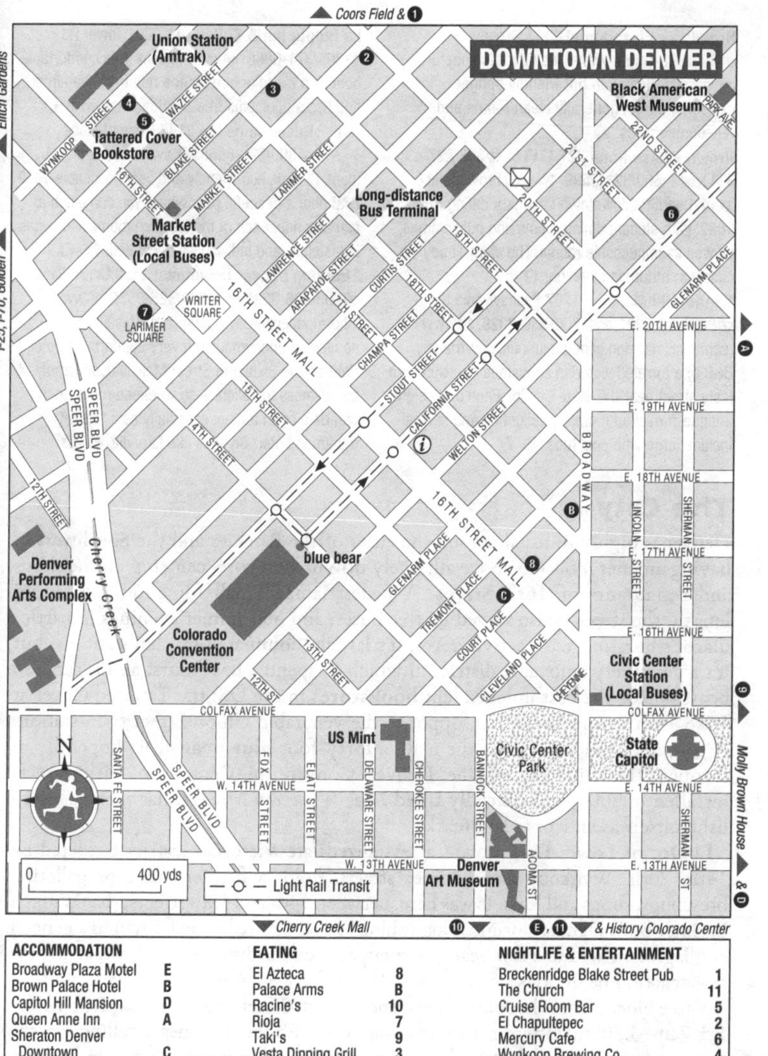

RTD also run pay-to-ride buses throughout the city ($2; ⓣ303/229-6000, ⓦwww.rtd-denver.com); frequent services to local sports venues and the airport leave from the underground **Market Street Station** at Market and 16th. All RTD services can carry bikes (free) and wheelchair users, and there's also a **light railway** (same fares).

Accommodation

Although plenty of **accommodation** is available in central Denver, ranging from homey B&Bs to grand historic hotels, it's notably short these days of inexpensive options. Chain motels are located further out on Colfax Avenue and along the major cross-town highways.

Broadway Plaza Motel 1111 Broadway ☎303/893-0303. Within walking distance of downtown, this plain but friendly budget motel has large, generally clean rooms and reasonable rates. ❸

Brown Palace Hotel 321 17th St ☎303/297-3111 or 1-800/321-2599, Ⓦwww.brownpalace.com. Beautiful downtown landmark dating from 1892, with elegant dining rooms and public areas, as well as impeccable rooms. The eight-storey cast-iron atrium is stunning. ❽

Capitol Hill Mansion 1207 Pennsylvania St ☎303/839-5221 or 1-800-839-9329, Ⓦwww.capitolhillmansion.com. Luxurious, gay-friendly B&B in a turreted Victorian sandstone mansion on a leafy street near the State Capitol. Each of its eight antique-furnished rooms is delightful, and several include large whirlpool tubs. ❺–❼

La Quinta Inn & Suites DIA 6801 Tower Rd ☎303/371-0888, Ⓦwww.lq.com. This comfortable hotel is a six-mile free shuttle ride from the airport, and has a pool, plus free breakfast and wi-fi. ❹

Queen Anne Inn 2147 Tremont Place ☎303/296-6666, Ⓦwww.queenannebnb.com. Central, eco-friendly and very hospitable 1879 B&B near a peaceful park where you can catch a carriage ride; each of the fourteen rooms and suites is tastefully and individually decorated. ❻–❽

Sheraton Denver Downtown 1550 Court Place ☎303/893-3333 or 1-800/325-3555, Ⓦwww.sheratondenverdowntown.com. This sizeable, somewhat anonymous but very comfortable hotel, right on the Sixteenth Street Mall, is used largely by business travellers – so weekend room rates can be a real bargain, especially as a "secret unnamed hotel" on sites like Expedia. ❹–❼

The City

Denver is highly unusual among the cities of the Rockies and the Southwest in having an energetic and above all, lively **downtown** core, centring on the shops and restaurants of **16th Street**. A pedestrianized mall for almost its entire length, the street is also served by free buses, and on summer evenings in particular it's bursting with activity. Yes, it's largely dominated by chain outlets, but it's a genuinely enjoyable district in which to spend a few hours, and it can also boast one of the best independent **bookstores** in the US: the Tattered Cover at 1628 16th St and Wynkoop, opposite the venerable Union Street train station. A couple of blocks west of the mall, a forty-foot **blue bear** peers hopefully in through the windows of the Denver Convention Center on 14th Street; installed in 2005, and officially titled *I See What You Mean*, it has rapidly established itself as an iconic landmark.

LoDo, or Lower Downtown, a revitalized late-Victorian district bordered by 14th, 20th, Wynkoop and Larimer streets, holds a further range of galleries, brewpubs, shops and lofts. It was here, between 14th and 15th streets, that William Larimer built Denver's original log cabin. The structure burned down in a general conflagration within a few years, whereupon a city ordinance decreed that all new construction be in brick.

Three blocks from the southeastern end of 16th Street, the **State Capitol** (Mon–Fri 7am–5.30pm) offers a commanding view of the Rockies swelling on the western horizon; the thirteenth step up to its entrance is exactly one mile above sea level. The Capitol is a rather predictable copy of that in Washington DC, but the free tours (every 45min; June–Aug Mon–Fri 9am–3.30pm, Sept–May 9.15am–2.30pm) are pleasantly informal, and you can climb its dome for an even better view.

Civic Center Park, right in front of the Capitol, is flanked by two of Denver's finest museums. The splendidly eclectic collections of the **Denver Art Museum** spread through two separate modern buildings, either side of W 13th Ave (Tues–Sat 10am–5pm, Sun noon–5pm; $13; Ⓦwww.denverartmuseum.org). The Hamilton Building (which stays open until 10pm on Fri) holds contemporary artworks, including Sandy Skoglund's spooky installation *Fox Games*, as well as galleries of African and Oceanic works, while the North Building has a spectacular array of Native American and pre-Columbian artefacts of all kinds – its Olmec miniatures are truly extraordinary. The **Colorado History Museum** nearby has closed, pending a move to the **History Colorado Center** currently under construction at 12th and Broadway (see Ⓦwww.coloradohistory.org for news).

Denver's black community is most prominent in the old **Five Points** district, northeast of LoDo, created to house black railroad workers in the 1870s. The **Black American West Museum** at 3091 California St (Tues–Sat 10am–2pm; $8; Ⓦwww.blackamericanwestmuseum.com) has intriguing details on black pioneers and outlaws, and debunks Western myths: one-third of all nineteenth-century cowboys were black, and many were former slaves who left the South after the Civil War.

A few miles east of downtown, in the enormous **City Park**, exhibits at the **Denver Museum of Nature and Science** (daily 9am–5pm; museum $11, IMAX $8, museum plus IMAX or planetarium $16, all three $21; Ⓦwww.dmns.org) extend beyond the very good dinosaur and wildlife displays to include material on Native Americans. There's also a large **zoo** nearby (daily: March–Oct 9am–6pm, last admission 5pm, $13; Nov–Feb 10am–5pm, last admission 4pm, $10; Ⓦwww.denverzoo.org), whose four thousand inmates include huge lowland gorillas and orang-utans in a large, thickly wooded sanctuary.

On the western edge of downtown at 2000 Elitch Circle, just ten minutes' walk from the city centre along the Cherry Creek cycle path, the **Elitch Gardens** theme park has some great white-knuckle rides, as well as **waterslides** (late April to Oct only, hours vary enormously, from daily 10am–9pm for most of summer down to weekends in Oct; $39, parking $10; Ⓦwww.elitchgardens.com).

Finally, the town of **Golden**, twenty miles west of downtown but essentially a Denver suburb, is served by regular buses from Market Street Station. Ever since the 1860s, Golden has been virtually synonymous with beer giant **Coors**, the world's largest brewery, which is based three blocks east of its main thoroughfare, Washington Avenue. Ninety-minute tours, heavy on the corporate hard-sell, include a tasting session of such products as the much-maligned low-cal Coors Light (Mon–Sat 10am–4pm; free; Ⓦwww.coors.com). Among the peaks that rise sharply on the opposite side of downtown Golden is Lookout Mountain, the final resting place of Buffalo Bill Cody, the famed frontiersman and showman who died in Denver in 1915 (see also p.717). Though surrounded by huge electricity pylons, the gravesite offers great views over the city and out to the mountains. Gruesome artefacts in the comprehensive adjacent **Buffalo Bill Museum** (May–Oct daily 9am–5pm, Nov–April Tues–Sun 9am–4pm; $5; Ⓦwww.buffalobill.org) include a pistol with a handle fashioned from human bone.

Eating

Besides the expected Western-themed steak and barbecue places, Denver holds a good array of restaurants of all kinds. While the Sixteen Street Mall is dominated by unremarkable chains, the streets to all sides – especially in the **Larimer Square** area – boast some much more interesting alternatives. Several of the city's famed **brewpubs** serve good-quality meals as well.

El Azteca 301 16th St Ⓣ303/534-4222. Lunching office workers arrive en masse for authentic, top-notch Mexican food served in this small restaurant in the basement of a dreary food-court. Prices are low, service quick and the food – particularly the *carne asada* – excellent. Breakfast and lunch only.

Palace Arms 321 17th St Ⓣ303/297-3111. This intimate, classy restaurant tucked in the *Brown Palace* (see opposite) is the ultimate splurge in town, with a menu of mostly seasonal game specialties and Napoleonic decor including a pair of the emperor's duelling pistols. Closed Mon eve & all Sun.

Racine's 650 Sherman St Ⓣ303/595-0418. Housed in a former auto showroom, this large, laidback place is a Denver institution. The inexpensive menu features excellent egg-based breakfasts, with imaginative pastas, reliably good sandwiches and serviceable Mexican entrees later in the day.

Rioja 1431 Larimer St ⓣ303/820-2282, ⓦwww.riojadenver.com. Creative and hugely enjoyable Mediterranean cuisine, with robust meat, fish and pasta entrees from around $20, and some tables outside. Dinner daily, lunch Wed–Sun.

Taki's 341 E Colfax Ave ⓣ303/832-4440. Friendly family business, with cafeteria-style ordering for giant, inexpensive portions of Japanese food. The miso soup is too good to miss and the salmon bowl – a sizeable piece of salmon smothered in a mustard sauce, with rice – is exceptional.

Vesta Dipping Grill 1822 Blake St ⓣ303/296-1970, ⓦwww.vestagrill.com. Attractive dinner-only restaurant in a renovated LoDo warehouse serving tasty food in unusual combinations; the basic concept is to dip meat or veggies in a wide spectrum of flavours (Mediterranean, Asian and Mexican).

Nightlife and entertainment

Denver's liveliest **nightlife** is concentrated in the LoDo district, which runs the gamut from brewpubs and sports bars (especially near baseball park Coors Field) to upmarket cocktail bars. For **music** listings, see the free weekly *Denver Westword* (ⓦwww.westword.com).

The remarkable, 9000-capacity **Red Rocks Amphitheater** (ⓦwww.redrocksonline.com), squeezed between two glowing 400ft red-sandstone rocks fifteen miles west of downtown Denver, has been the setting for thousands of rock and classical concerts; U2 filmed the landmark *Under a Blood Red Sky* here in 1983. The surrounding Red Rocks Park is open to visitors free of charge during the day.

Denver's other pride and joy, the modern **Denver Performing Arts Complex** on 14th and Curtis streets (ⓣ303/893-4100, ⓦwww.artscomplex.com), is home to the Denver Center Theater Company, Colorado Symphony Orchestra, Opera Colorado and the Colorado Ballet. Facilities include eight **theatres**, as well as the acoustically superb, in-the-round **Symphony Hall**.

Breckenridge Blake Street Pub 2220 Blake St ⓣ303/297-3644. Cosy and lively brewpub opposite Coors Field, with quality craft beer and a terrific range of delicious barbecue plates.

The Church 1160 Lincoln St ⓣ303/832-3528. A dance club inside a gutted cathedral that combines a downtown nightlife landmark, wine bar, sushi bar and three invariably busy dancefloors. Programming varies from hard house to garage to hip-hop, and the crowd can be equally eclectic. $5–15 cover. Thurs–Sun only.

Cruise Room Bar *Oxford Hotel*, 1600 17th St ⓣ303/628-5400. This replica of the Art Deco bar on the *Queen Mary* ocean liner, is worth a stop for its great atmosphere.

El Chapultepec 1962 Market St ⓣ303/295-9126. Tiny but popular LoDo stalwart with nightly live jazz and occasional big names. No cover, but two-drink minimum.

Grizzly Rose 5450 N Valley Hwy ⓣ303/295-1330, ⓦwww.grizzlyrose.com. Huge, legendary country-music venue, 10min drive north of downtown on I-25, where nightly bands include some famous names, and there's even a mechanical bull. Cover $5–20.

Mercury Cafe 2199 California St ⓣ303/294-9281, ⓦwww.mercurycafe.com. When the *Merc*'s not hosting jazz, you'll find tango dance classes, poetry readings or some other form of entertainment. A good-value restaurant serves healthy choices (many vegetarian) as well as high tea.

Wynkoop Brewing Co 1634 18th St ⓣ303/297-2700. Opposite Union Station, the state's oldest brewpub, set up by current mayor John Hickenlooper, serves up solid home-brewed beers and great bar food; there's an elegant pool hall upstairs.

Northern Colorado

Rocky Mountain National Park, northwest of Denver, is too large to see as a day-trip from the city. Segments of its loop drive can be very slow and laborious, and in a single day it's more realistic just to dip a few miles into the park's eastern fringes.

The dynamic foothill town of **Boulder** makes a good base, though smaller mountain towns can give you more time in the wilds: **Estes Park**, near the park's eastern entrance, is a less attractive stopover than either **Grand Lake** or the affordable, enjoyable ski resort of **Winter Park** on the west side. Further west, midway across Colorado on either side of the I-70 freeway, lie more famous ski resorts such as **Vail** and **Aspen**, as well as the evocative mining town of **Leadville**. Continuing toward the Utah border, the landscape dips and rises in a patchwork of granite peaks, raging rivers and red-sandstone canyons, through **Glenwood Springs** and winding up at **Grand Junction** and the striking scenery of **Colorado National Monument**.

Boulder

The lively college town of **BOULDER**, just 27 miles northwest of Denver on US-36, is home to a youthful population that seems to divide its time between phenomenally healthy daytime pursuits and almost equally unhealthy night-time activities. Sometimes referred to as "seven miles surrounded by reality", Boulder was founded in 1858 by a prospecting party who felt that the nearby Flatiron Mountains "looked right for gold"; they found little, but the community grew anyway.

With its easy-going, forward-looking vibe and abundance of great places to eat and drink, Boulder makes an excellent overnight base after long days in the mountains. Downtown centres on the leafy pedestrian mall of **Pearl Street**, lined with bustling cafés, galleries and stores – including several places where you can rent **mountain bikes**. The most obvious short excursion is to drive or hike up nearby **Flagstaff Mountain** for views over town and further into the Rockies; any road west joins up with the Peak to Peak Highway, which heads through spectacular scenery towards Rocky Mountain National Park. For rock climbing, **Eldorado Canyon State Park** offers many opportunities; the excellent Neptune Mountaineering, south of town at 633 S Broadway (Ⓣ303/499-8866, Ⓦwww.neptunemountaineering.com), can answer questions and provide gear.

The adventurous **University of Colorado** offers regular **arts events**, including the classical-focused Colorado Music Festival (Ⓦwww.coloradomusicfest.org), held each summer in the Chautauqua Auditorium; two campus theatres also host the six-week Colorado Shakespeare Festival (Ⓦwww.coloradoshakes.org). Another notable local presence is the small **Naropa University** (Ⓦwww.naropa.edu), founded in 1974 as a meeting point for Eastern and Western intellectual traditions, which sponsors events throughout the year.

Practicalities

Most local and long-distance **buses**, including services from Denver ($5) and its airport ($12), use the Transit Center, 14th and Walnut streets (Ⓣ303/299-6000). Boulder's hospitable, low-key **visitor centre** is at 2440 Pearl St (Mon–Fri 9am–5pm; Ⓣ303/442-2911, Ⓦwww.bouldercoloradousa.com).

Even if you're not **staying** in the historic *Hotel Boulderado*, located near Pearl Street at 2115 13th St (Ⓣ303/442-4344 or 1-800/433-4344, Ⓦwww.boulderado.com; ❼), wander in for a drink and free evening jazz. The *Foot of the Mountain Motel*, 200 W Arapahoe Ave (Ⓣ303/442-5688 or 1-866/773-5489, Ⓦwww.footofthemountainmotel.com; ❹), is a friendly, log-cabin-style motel, nine blocks west of downtown beside Boulder Creek, while the *Boulder International Hostel* near the campus at 1107 12th St (Ⓣ303/442-0522, Ⓦwww.boulderhostel.com), offers both dorm beds ($34) and private rooms (❷).

Bars and **restaurants** abound in the Pearl Street area. *Sunflower*, 1701 Pearl St (Ⓣ303/440-0220), serves a healthy menu of organic and free-range items, while the *Laughing Goat Coffee House* is nearby at 1709 Pearl St (Ⓣ303/440-4628). Student favourite *Tra-Ling's Oriental Cafe*, 1305 Broadway (Ⓣ303/449-0400), is a grungy canteen-style restaurant with tasty and amazingly cheap Chinese food. The *Hotel Boulderado* (see p.689) also houses two popular **nightspots**: the *Corner Bar*, offering reasonably priced dishes until late at night on the patio, and the more casual *Catacombs Bar*, which features nightly live music. *West End Tavern*, 926 Pearl St (ⓣ303/444-3535), is a nice spot for roots music, locally brewed beer and spectacular views of the Flatirons from the roof terrace.

Rocky Mountain National Park

You don't have to go to **ROCKY MOUNTAIN NATIONAL PARK** to appreciate the full splendour of the Rockies; it's simply one small section of the mighty range, measuring roughly twenty-five by fifteen miles. However, it's undeniably beautiful, straddling the Continental Divide at elevations often well in excess of ten thousand feet. A tenth of the size of Yellowstone, it attracts a similar number of visitors – over three million per year, the bulk of whom come in high summer, meaning that the one main road through the mountains can get incredibly congested. A full third of the park is above the tree line, and large areas of snow never melt; the name of the **Never Summer Mountains** speaks volumes about the long, empty expanses of arctic-style tundra. The park's lower reaches, among the rich forests, hold patches of lush greenery; you never know when you may stumble upon a sheltered mountain meadow flecked with flowers. Parallels with the European Alps spring to mind – helped, of course, by the heavy-handed Swiss and Bavarian themes of so many local motels and restaurants.

Approaching the park

Coming from the **east**, you barely penetrate the foothills of the Rockies before arriving at the unattractive but bustling gateway town of **Estes Park**, 65 miles northwest of Denver. At the end of the nineteenth century, Estes Park was the private hunting preserve of the Irish Earl of Dunraven; once he was squeezed out, the town took on the more democratic function it still serves: providing visitors with food, lodging and other services. The **park headquarters** and **Beaver Meadows Visitor Center** is a couple of miles north, on US-36 (daily: mid-June to Aug 8am–9pm, late Oct to late April till 4.30pm, otherwise till 5pm; park admission $20/vehicle, good for seven days; ⓦwww.nps.gov/romo).

To reach the **western** entrance, 85 miles from Denver, turn north off I-70 onto US-40, which negotiates **Berthoud Pass** en route to **Grand Lake**. This unlikely yachting centre, high in the mountains, is much more likeable than Estes Park, consisting of one main boardwalk-lined street featuring family amusements, lodgings and restaurants beside the lake. The park's **Kawuneeche Visitor Center** stands a mile north (daily: late June to early Sept 8am–6pm, late Sept to April till 4.30pm, otherwise till 5pm).

Exploring the park

The showpiece of the park is **Trail Ridge Road** (generally open late May to mid-October), the 45-mile stretch of US-34 that connects Estes Park with Grand Lake. The highest-elevation paved road in any US national park, it affords a succession of tremendous views, and several short trails start from car parks along the way. Majestic peaks and alpine tundra are at their most breathtaking to either side of the **Alpine Visitor Center** (late May to early Oct only, daily: late June to early Sept 9am–5pm, otherwise 10.30am–4.30pm), halfway along at Fall River Pass. If you're generally happy simply to admire the scenery from your car, the visitor centre is really the only requisite stop along the way, for its **exhibits** explaining the flora and fauna of the tundra and also its simple, good-value **cafeteria**. Good areas for wildlife viewing lie a little further east along Trail Ridge Road.

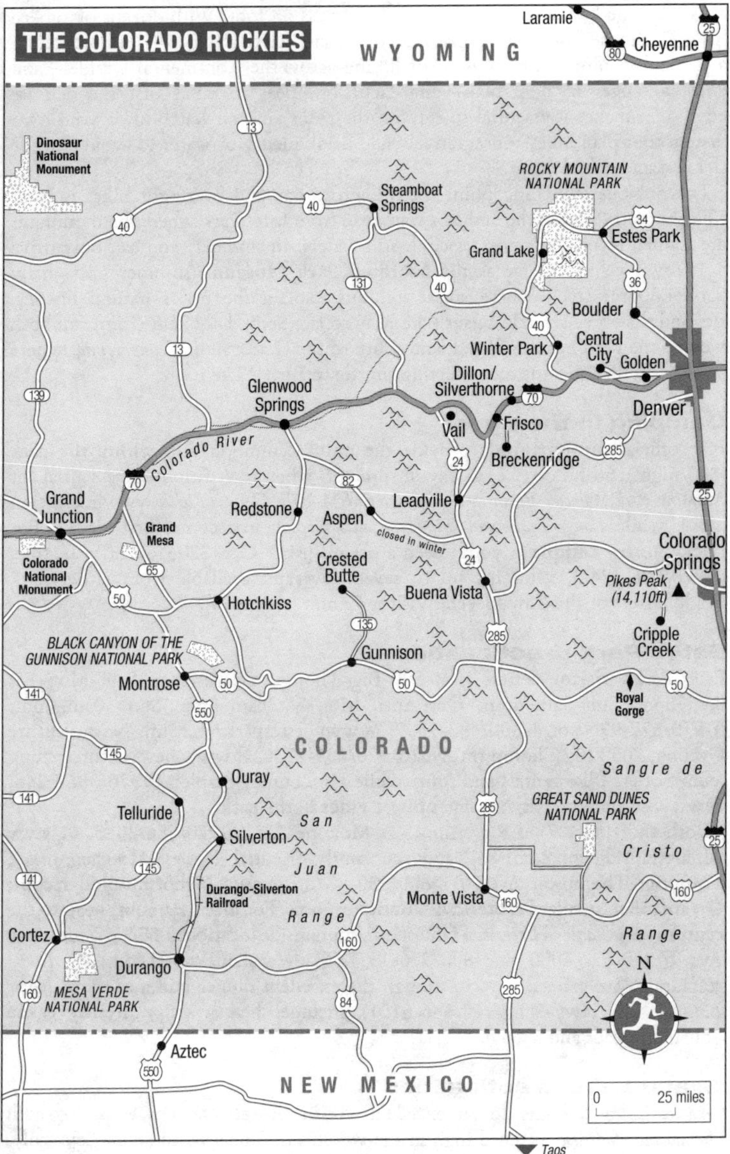

An alternative scenic drive follows the unpaved, summer-only **Old Fall River Road**, which was the park's first road, completed in 1920. Running east–west along the bed of a U-shaped glacial valley, it doesn't have open mountain vistas, but it's much quieter than its paved counterpart, and there's far more chance of spotting **wildlife**: roaming the area are moose, coyote, mountain lions and black bears, which with the park's plentiful natural food supply, tend to avoid contact with humans.

As ever, the best way to appreciate the park is on foot. With dozens of superb **hikes** to choose from, think what kind of experience you're after – photographing a particular animal, for instance, or hiking across the Continental Divide – and enlist a ranger to help plan your excursion. Bear in mind that the delicate ecosystem makes it essential to stay on the paths, and be watchful of your own system too; plan hikes conservatively and drink plenty of water to avoid altitude sickness and dehydration.

The obvious launching point for numerous day and overnight hikes is **Bear Lake**, a pretty spot at the end of a spur road from Estes Park where the mountains are framed to perfection in its cool, still waters. In summer, you can only drive your own vehicle as far as the **Moraine Park Museum** (summer only, daily 9am–4.30pm; free), where smart exhibits explain the park's natural history. Beyond that, free **shuttle buses** (late May to late Sept, daily 7am–7pm) run both west to the Fern Lake trailhead, and south to the *Glacier Basin Campground*, where you can in turn pick up a connecting shuttle to **Bear Lake** itself.

Camping in the park

Five official **campgrounds** provide the only accommodation within the park ($20/night); all fill early each day in summer, when reservations are essential for *Moraine Park*, *Glacier Basin* and *Aspenglen* (Ⓣ1-877/444-6777, Ⓦwww.recreation.gov), while *Longs Peak* and *Timber Creek* remain first-come, first-served. For **backcountry camping**, you'll need a permit (May–Oct, $20; rest of year, free; Ⓣ970/586-1242), valid for up to seven days and available from either park headquarters or the Kawuneeche Visitor Center (see p.690).

Estes Park practicalities

Estes Park's **visitor centre** is at 500 Big Thompson Ave (May–Sept Mon–Sat 8am–8pm, Sun 9am–5pm; Oct–April Mon–Sat 8am–5pm, Sun 10am–4pm; Ⓣ970/577-9900 or 1-800/443-7837, Ⓦwww.estesparkcvb.com). New Venture Cycling, 2050 Big Thompson Ave (Ⓣ970/231-2736, Ⓦwww.newventurecycling.com), offers **bike** rentals and tours while Hi Country Stables (Ⓣ970/586-3244, Ⓦwww.sombrero.com), arranges **horse rides** in the park.

Both the *Alpine Trail Ridge Inn*, 927 Moraine Ave (Ⓣ970/586-4585, Ⓦwww.alpinetrailridgeinn.com; ❹), and the family-oriented *Bighorn Mountain Lodge*, 1340 Big Thompson Ave (Ⓣ1-800/530-8822, Ⓦwww.bighornmtnlodge.com; ❺), are clean, standard motels with outdoor pools. For more glamour, head to the century-old *Stanley Hotel*, in a fantastic mountainside location at 333 Wonderview Ave (Ⓣ970/577-4000 or 1-800/976-1377, Ⓦwww.stanleyhotel.com; ❽). Local restaurants are generally poor, though the excellent dinner buffet at the *Baldpate Inn*, 4900 S Hwy-7 (Ⓣ970/586-6151), includes hearty soups, freshly baked gourmet breads and a range of salads.

Grand Lake practicalities

Grand Lake is home to an excellent **youth hostel**: the gorgeous, log-built ★ *Shadowcliff Lodge*, perched high in the woods on Tunnel Road (June–Sept only; Ⓣ970/627-9220, Ⓦwww.shadowcliff.org; ❷), which has dorm rooms for $27 and clean and comfortable doubles (❷), and also hosts residential workshops on environmental themes. Moderately priced **motels**, many of which insist on a minimum two-night stay in summer, include the attractive lakeside *Western Riviera Motel and Cabins*, 419 Garfield St (Ⓣ970/627-3580, Ⓦwww.westernriv.com; ❺–❻). Right next door, the *Blue Water Bakery Café*, 928 Grand Ave (Ⓣ970/627-8404), serves fine coffee, pastries and sandwiches until 5pm daily; for a full dinner, *Caroline's Cuisine*, 9921 Hwy-34 (Ⓣ970/627-9404), serves excellent Mediterranean specialities.

Winter Park

The former railroad centre of **WINTER PARK**, 67 miles northwest of Denver, may not be Colorado's trendiest resort, but its wide, ever-expanding variety of ski and bike terrain, friendly atmosphere, family attractions and good-value lodgings draw over one million visitors a year. Its namesake **ski resort** (lift ticket $93, various passes available; Ⓦwww.winterparkresort.com) also has exceptional facilities for kids and disabled skiers, as well as the 200-acre Discovery Park, an excellent, economical area for beginners. Experienced skiers, in turn, relish mogul runs on Mary Jane Mountain, the fluffy snows of the Parsenn Bowl and the backcountry idyll of Vasquez Cirque.

In addition to skiing, you can **snowmobile** the Continental Divide on a two-hour tour with Trailblazers in Fraser ($100, other tours available; Ⓦwww.trailblazersnowmobile.com); Mountain Madness also offer snowmobile trips ($50/hr; Ⓣ970/726-4529). Summer visitors enjoy six hundred miles of excellent **mountain-biking** trails, the best of which are accessible from the chairlift, in addition to the exhilarating mile-and-a-half-long **Alpine Slide** sled ride ($15), and several contemporary music festivals.

Practicalities

Year-round service to Winter Park is provided by **Amtrak**, five miles north in Fraser, and by Home James **shuttles** from Denver airport ($65 one-way; Ⓣ1-800/359-7503, Ⓦwww.homejamestransportation.com). An excellent network of free **shuttle buses** means you don't need a car in town. Trail maps and local **information** are available at the Chamber of Commerce, 151 W Lyman Ave (Mon–Fri 8.30am–5pm, Sat 9am–3pm; Ⓣ407/644-8281, Ⓦwww.winterpark.org).

Hotels and **condos** near the ski area can be booked through Winter Park Central Reservations (Ⓣ1-800/979-0332, Ⓦwww.winterparkresort.com; ❺ and up), while **motels** line the main street of Winter Park itself, including the basic *Viking Lodge* (Ⓣ1-800/421-4013, Ⓦwww.skiwp.com/vikinglodge.html; ❷–❸). Good places to **eat** downtown include lively *Deno's*, across from Copper Creek Square (Ⓣ970/726-5332), which offers a large choice of beers and wines, Mediterranean-inspired pasta dishes, salads and daily specials.

Steamboat Springs

Surrounded by wide valleys, **STEAMBOAT SPRINGS**, 65 miles north of I-70 via Hwy-131, looks like no other Colorado mountain resort. Its roots are in ranching rather than mining, and its downtown area still evokes a pioneer feel – until you spot the upmarket boutiques. In this ski-mad town, ranchers judge the quality of snowfall by the number of fence wires it covers; they're usually satisfied with a three-wire winter, which roughly corresponds to Steamboat's average annual snowfall of 334 inches.

The town's namesake, top-notch **ski resort** (one-day lift ticket $93, various saver passes available; Ⓦwww.steamboat.com), snuggled into Mount Werner four miles south of downtown, is boosted by dogsled expeditions, hot-air ballooning and snowmobiling, available in and around town. The town also benefits from its hot springs: you can soak year-round in the secluded 105°F **Strawberry Park Hot Springs** (Sun–Thurs 10am–10.30pm, Fri & Sat till midnight; $10; Ⓦwww.strawberryhotsprings.com), seven miles north of town and only accessible by four-wheel-drive in winter; various shuttles, detailed on the website, make the trip from town. In town, the **Old Town Hot Springs** (Mon–Fri 5.30am–9.45pm, Sat 7am–8.45pm, Sun 8am–8.45pm; pools $15, waterslides $5, fitness centre $15; Ⓦsteamboathotsprings.org) has more of a water-park feel, offering water-based attractions and childcare facilities in addition to its healing mineral waters. During Steamboat Springs' summer season, opportunities for **mountain biking**, **whitewater rafting** and **horseback riding** abound; outfitters in town can assist with gear and guides.

Practicalities

Most winter visitors fly into **Yampa Valley Airport**, 26 miles from Steamboat Springs in Hayden, though it's possible to drive, weather permitting, from Denver on Hwy-40 over scenic Rabbit Ears Pass. Visitor **information** can be found at 125 Anglers Drive, (winter Mon–Fri 8am–5pm, Sat 10am–3pm, Sun 9am–6pm; summer Mon–Sat 8am–6pm, Sun 10am–4pm; ⓣ970/879-0880, ⓦwww.steamboat-chamber.com). From town, free SST **buses** (ⓣ970/879-3717) run the four miles to and from the ski resort. *Strawberry Park Hot Springs* offers characterful **accommodation** in bare-bones cabins (❸), converted wagons (❷) or a two-storey train carriage (❺) by the springs; camping is also available (ⓣ970/879-0342, ⓦwww.strawberryhotsprings.com). Staying **slopeside** tends to cost more than downtown, though the comfortable *Ptarmigan Inn* (ⓣ1-800/538-7519, ⓦwww.steamboat-lodging.com; winter ❺–❽, summer ❺–❻) offers good rates. Downtown, the *Rabbit Ears Motel*, 201 Lincoln Ave (ⓣ970/879-1150, ⓦwww.rabbitearsmotel.com; winter ❻–❼, summer ❺–❻) is a good, friendly choice.

Café Diva, 1855 Ski Time Square Drive (ⓣ970/871-0508), is a fine **restaurant**, serving sophisticated fusion food. For dining with a view, *Hazie's* on the mountain (ⓣ970/871-5150), throws in a free gondola ride up the slope with the price of a meal; Sunday's brunch buffet (9.30am–1.30pm) is great value. Microbrews and decent pub food are available near the ski area at the cheery *Tugboat Grill and Pub,* 1860 Mt Werner Rd (ⓣ970/879-7070).

Summit County

The purpose-built ski resorts, old mining towns, snow-covered peaks, alpine meadows and crystal lakes that make up **Summit County** lie alongside I-70, arrayed around large, pretty **Lake Dillon** roughly seventy miles west of Denver. Before white settlement, the Ute hunted here every summer: the swanky Keystone Ranch Golf Club now occupies a meadow where they once pitched their tepees. During the late nineteenth century, the county witnessed several gold-mining booms; today, dilapidated **ghost towns** cling to the mountainsides, but one settlement that has survived is **BRECKENRIDGE**, where streets are lined with brightly painted Victorian houses, shops and cafés. This is the liveliest of Summit County's four towns; **FRISCO**, stretching sedately along a quiet valley, appeals to those looking for a less hectic pace, while both **DILLON** and **SILVERTHORNE** are frankly dull. The formulaic ski-resort villages of **Keystone** and **Copper Mountain** are also unexciting unless you're here for snowsports.

Arrival and information

By **car**, Summit County is less than two hours from Denver. Greyhound **buses** stop at the Frisco Transit Center, 1010 Meadow Drive from where free buses radiate to the surrounding ski resorts. **Shuttles** from Denver airport include Colorado Mountain Express, which serves the county's ski resorts ($82; ⓣ970/926-9800, ⓦwww.cmex.com). Summit Stage (6.30am–1.30am; ⓣ970/668-0999, ⓦwww.summitstage.com) provides free **local transportation** around the county, while Town Trolley (ⓣ970/547-3140) runs through Breckenridge and up to the resort every 20 minutes during ski season. The main local

visitor centres are at 300 Main St in Frisco (daily 9am–5pm; Ⓣ970/668-2051, Ⓦwww.townoffrisco.com), and 203 S Main St in Breckenridge (Ⓣ970/453-5579, Ⓦwww.townofbreckenridge.com).

Accommodation

Lodging rates in Summit County double in winter. Frisco generally has the best-priced inns and **motels**, while Breckenridge holds a few downtown **B&Bs** and a large number of expensive slopeside condos; the Breckenridge Resort Chamber (Ⓣ970/453-2918 or 1-888/251-2417, Ⓦwww.gobreck.com) has details of package deals. Resort accommodation at both Copper Mountain and Keystone (see below) is first class, and so too are the prices.

Best Western Ptarmigan Lodge 625 Lake Drive, Dillon Ⓣ970/468-2341, Ⓦwww.ptarmiganlodge.com. Friendly, quiet, good-value motel, in a nice lakeside setting on the southern fringes of Dillon, with a steakhouse next door. ❹

Fireside Inn 114 N French St, Breckenridge Ⓣ970/453-6456, Ⓦwww.firesideinn.com. Homey little B&B with floral, antique-filled bedrooms (all with private bath), plus several cramped dorm rooms ($28–45) that share a TV lounge and kitchenette. Winter ❺, summer ❹

Frisco Lodge 321 Main St, Frisco Ⓣ970/668-0195 or 1-800/279-6000, Ⓦwww.friscolodge.com. Creaky B&B in a very central old railroad inn. Units have kitchenettes and access to an outdoor hot tub, and cooked buffet breakfast and teatime snacks are served in the cluttered lounge. ❹

Ridge Street Inn 212 N Ridge St, Breckenridge Ⓣ970/453-4680. Comfortable, comparatively affordable B&B in the heart of Breckenridge's lively downtown. ❺

Outdoor activities

Winter is still the busiest time in Summit County. **Breckenridge Ski Resort** (Ⓣ970/453-5000, Ⓦwww.breckenridge.com), the oldest of the area's four top-class resorts, spans four peaks and offers ideal terrain for all skiers and snowboarders, as does the plush **Keystone** (Ⓣ1-888/222-9285, Ⓦwww.keystoneresort.com), where the biggest night-ski operation in the US permits skiing until 8.30pm. The smallest resort in the county, **Arapahoe Basin** ("A-Basin"; Ⓣ1-888/272-7246, Ⓦwww.arapahoebasin.com), offers great above-tree-line bowl skiing. The slopes at **Copper Mountain** (Ⓣ1-888/219-2441, Ⓦwww.coppercolorado.com), are divided into three clear sections to separate beginners, intermediates and experts.

In **summer**, mountain-bikers and road-racers alike especially relish **cycling** the stretch between Frisco and Breckenridge; Colorado Freeride at 114 N Main St in Breckenridge (Ⓣ970/453-0995) is good for rental bikes. Each resort runs a chairlift or **gondola** to the top of the mountains for access to great **hiking** and cycling trails. Keystone is particularly outstanding for its mountain-bike trails with world-class downhill and cross-country trails accessed by its lifts (mid-June to early Sept, Sun–Thurs 10am–5pm, Fri & Sat till 7pm; day pass $36). Breckenridge offers its Peak 8 Fun Park (mid-June to early Sept, daily 9am–5pm; all-day pass $60), featuring toboggan rides down the dry **Superslide** (single ride $15), as well as trampolining, miniature golf and a giant maze.

Eating and drinking

Summit County has no great reputation for fine **dining**, though there's no end of good-value places to eat, especially in Breckenridge. Après-ski **drinking** is alive and well at the slopeside bars of all four resorts, while Frisco also has some good options.

Alpenglow Stube Keystone Ⓣ970/496-4386. The best dining experience in Summit County – take the free gondola ride to the top of 11,444ft North Peak and feast in beautiful surroundings on New American cuisine with a Bavarian edge. It doesn't come cheaply, though: multi-course meals run $90 and up.

Backcountry Brewery 710 Main St, Frisco Ⓣ970/668-2337. Sizeable brewpub where the upstairs deck – with its choice view of the nearby peaks – is the best spot to kick back. Own-brewed beers and dishes such as porter beer-braised ribs ($18) anchor the ample menu.

Breckenridge Brewery 600 S Main St, Breckenridge ⓣ970/453-1550. This huge brewpub, a landmark at the southern edge of town, serves good-quality microbrews and hearty pub food.

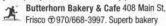

Butterhorn Bakery & Cafe 408 Main St, Frisco ⓣ970/668-3997. Superb bakery churning out huge and delicious breads, bagels, cookies and cakes. It's also well known for its breakfast burrito, frittatas and good range of sandwiches or soup lunches (all well under $10). Daily until 2.30pm.

Denzaemon 216 S Main St, Breckenridge ⓣ970/453-9809. Basement Japanese noodle bar across from the visitor centre; inexpensive rice and noodle bowls, and friendly service.

Leadville

Ringed by snowcapped mountains at an elevation of over ten thousand feet, south of I-70 eighty miles west of Denver, the atmospheric old mining town of **LEADVILLE** (officially the highest city in the US), enjoys a magnificent view across to broad-shouldered mounts **Elbert** (14,440ft) and **Massive** (14,421ft), Colorado's two highest peaks. If you approach "Cloud City" from the south, don't let the giant slag heaps and disused mining sheds put you off: Leadville is rich in character and history, its old red-brick streets abounding with tales of gunfights, miners dying of exposure and graveyards being excavated to get at the seams.

For an illuminating romp through the town's grim early history, head for the **Heritage Museum**, 102 E Ninth St (summer daily 10am–4pm; $6). Glass cases hold snippets on local fraternal organizations, quack doctors, music-hall stars and the like, while smoky photographs portray the lawless boomtown that in two years grew from a mining camp of two hundred people to become (briefly) Colorado's second largest city.

In 1878, **Horace Tabor**, a storekeeper who grubstaked prospectors in exchange for potential profits, hit the jackpot when two prospectors developed a silver mine that produced $20 million within a year. Collecting his one-third share, Tabor left his wife to marry waitress "**Baby Doe**" McCourt. However, by the time of his death in 1899, Tabor was financially ruined. Baby Doe survived him by 36 years, living a hermit-like existence in the godforsaken wooden shacks on his only remaining mine – the **Matchless Mine**. The buildings still stand, two miles out on Seventh Street, and in the crude wooden shack in which she died, emaciated and frostbitten, guides recount Baby Doe's bizarre saga in full, fascinating detail (May–Sept 9am–4.15pm, Oct–April call for hours; $4; ⓣ719/486-4918, ⓦwww.matchlessmine.com).

Back in town, self-guided tours of the **Tabor Opera House**, 308 Harrison Ave (summer Mon–Sat 10am–5pm; $5; ⓦwww.taboroperahouse.net), enable you to wander onto the stage, through the ranks of red velvet and gilt seats, and around the eerie, dusty old dressing rooms. Recorded oral histories tell tales of the theatre's golden days. In 1882, garbed in black velvet knee britches and diamonds, Oscar Wilde addressed a host of dozing miners here on the "Practical Application of the Aesthetic Theory to Exterior and Interior House Decoration with Observations on Dress and Personal Ornament".

Practicalities

Leadville's **visitor centre** is at 809 Harrison Ave (June–Sept daily 10am–5pm; ⓣ719/486-3900, ⓦwww.leadvilleusa.com). Rates at the town's historic landmark **hotel**, the *Delaware,* 700 Harrison Ave (ⓣ719/486-1418 or 1-800/748-2004, ⓦwww.delawarehotel.com; ❹), include continental breakfast. **Food** and **drink** options are surprisingly limited. *Manuelita's*, 311 Harrison Ave (ⓣ719/486-0292), serves simple, spicy Mexican standards, while the *Proving Grounds Coffee and Bakery*, 508 Harrison Ave (ⓣ719/486-0797), serves espresso, pastries and sandwiches from early morning. Leadville's finest **bar** is the wood-paneled *Silver Dollar Saloon*, 315 Harrison Ave (☎719/486-9914), a welcoming watering hole filled with Irish memorabilia.

Aspen

While there's more than a grain of truth to the image of **ASPEN**, 160 miles west of Denver, as a celebrity hangout – Jack Nicholson is among those who own second homes here – it's a perfectly accessible and appealing place for ordinary folks to visit, and in summer at least the room rates are affordable for all but those on shoestring budgets. Visiting in winter requires more cash, though you can save money by commuting to the slopes from Glenwood Springs (see p.701), less than fifty miles away.

From inauspicious beginnings in 1879, this pristine, remote and mountain-locked town established itself as one of the world's top **silver** producers. By the time the silver market crashed fourteen years later, it had acquired tasteful residential palaces, grand hotels and an opera house. Ironically enough, during the 1930s, when Aspen's population had slumped below seven hundred, the anti-poverty WPA programme gave the struggling community the cash to build its first crude ski lift. Entrepreneurs seized the opportunity presented by the varied terrain and

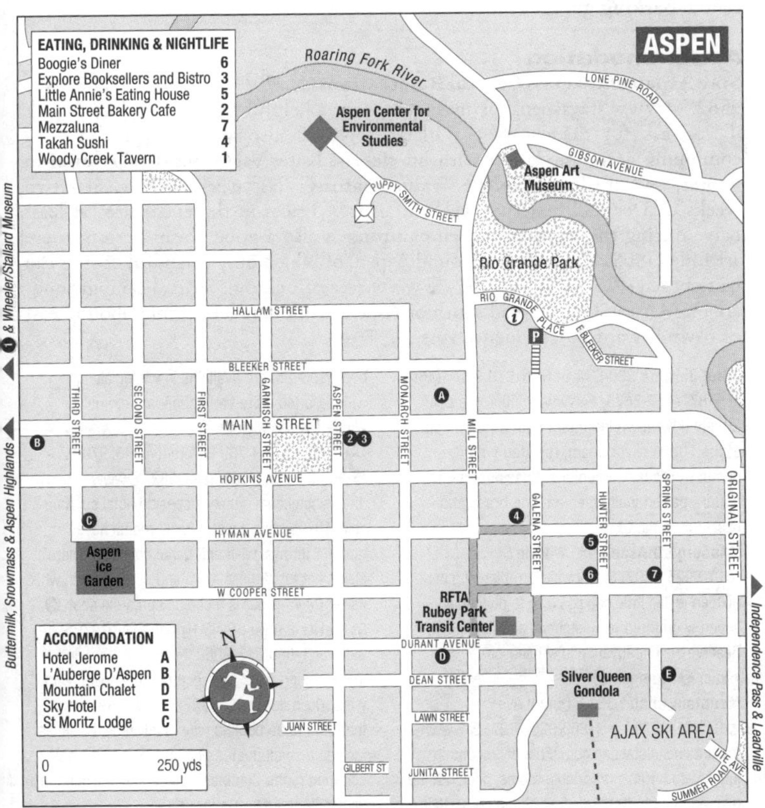

plentiful snow, and the first chairlift was dedicated on Aspen Mountain in 1947. Skiing has since spread to three more mountains – Aspen Highlands, Snowmass and Buttermilk, and the jet set arrived in force during the 1960s. While **development** is a burning political issue, and subject to tight architectural constraints, the vicinity continues to fill with ever more Scandinavian-style lodges, condo blocks and giant houses that remain empty for most of the year.

Arrival and information

Towering **Independence Pass**, which provides the most direct access to Aspen via Hwy-82, is generally closed between November and late May; the detour through Glenwood Springs adds an extra seventy miles to the trip from Denver. Many instead choose to fly into tiny **Aspen–Pitkin County Airport** (Ⓦwww.aspenairport.com), four miles north of town. If you fly into Denver, connecting flights may only cost another $100 or so, much the same price as a **shuttle** from Denver airport with Colorado Mountain Express (Ⓣ970/926-9800, Ⓦwww.cmex.com), who also run shuttles from Eagle County Airport near Vail, an eighty-minute drive away.

Once in Aspen, **free buses** (Ⓣ970/925-8484, Ⓦwww.rfta.com), centred on the **Rubey Park transit center** on Durant Avenue in the heart of town, connect the four mountains with each other, plus the airport and outlying areas.

The local **visitor centre** is at 425 Rio Grande Place (Mon–Fri 8.30am–5pm; Ⓣ970/925-1940, Ⓦwww.aspenchamber.org), alongside the most convenient central **parking garage**.

Accommodation

Stay Aspen Snowmass Central Reservations (Ⓣ970/925-9000 or 1-888/649-9582, Ⓦwww.stayaspensnowmass.com) runs a helpful service and doesn't balk if you ask for the cheapest available room; it also arranges package deals combining accommodation with lift tickets. Rates vary considerably even in winter, and are lowest in the "**value seasons**" (last week in Nov, first two weeks of Dec and first two weeks of April). Prices in the entire area at least halve during the **summer**, when **camping** is also a good cheap option; there are nine USFS campgrounds around Aspen, of which only a handful of sites can be reserved (Ⓣ1-877/444-6777, Ⓦwww.recreation.gov). Several campgrounds are on Maroon Creek Road south of Aspen, while smaller options abound east of town toward Independence Pass.

Hotel Jerome 330 E Main St Ⓣ970/920-1000 or 1-877/417-7625, Ⓦwww.hoteljerome.com. Stately downtown landmark built at the height of the 1880s silver boom, re-fitted with the gamut of modern amenities. Spacious rooms feature period wallpaper, antique brass and cast-iron beds. ❾

L'Auberge D'Aspen 435 W Main St Ⓣ970/925-8297, Ⓦwww.preferredlodging.com. Sixteen idyllic little cabins close to downtown, superbly outfitted with kitchens and fireplaces. Reserve well in advance in ski season. Winter ❼, summer ❻

Mountain Chalet 333 E Durant Ave Ⓣ970/925-7797 or 1-800/925-7797, Ⓦwww.mountainchaletaspen.com. Friendly mountain lodge with large, comfortable rooms, pool, hot tub, gym and fine buffet breakfast. Some dorm-style beds ($55–95) are available in winter, along with assorted more straightforward rooms. Winter ❽, summer ❺

Sky Hotel 709 E Durant Ave Ⓣ970/925-6760 or 1-800/882-2582, Ⓦwww.theskyhotel.com. Funky slopeside hotel sporting chic, 1970s-style decor; playful rooms have faux-fur throws, wi-fi and game consoles. There's also a hot tub, fitness room and outdoor pool, while its *39 Degrees* bar is a choice après-ski spot. ❽

St Moritz Lodge 334 W Hyman Ave Ⓣ970/925-3220 or 1-800/817-2069, Ⓦwww.stmoritzlodge.com. A short walk from central downtown, with well-priced dorms ($33–57) and private rooms that tend to be booked way in advance. Facilities include a small heated pool and a comfortable common room. Continental breakfast included in winter. Winter ❼, summer ❺

The town and the mountains

While spending too much time in Aspen itself is something of a waste in view of the virtually limitless recreation opportunities in the neighbouring mountains, hanging out on benches around the town's leafy pedestrianized streets or browsing in the chichi stores and galleries makes a pleasant way to spend a couple of hours.

In summer, the Aspen Historical Society, which runs the excellent **Wheeler/ Stallard Museum**, 620 W Bleeker St (Tues–Sat 1–5pm; $6; Ⓦwww.heritageaspen.org), offers **walking tours** ($10) of Aspen and nearby ghost towns. The free **Aspen Art Museum** at 590 N Mill St (Tues–Wed & Fri–Sat 10am–6pm, Thurs till 7pm, Sun noon–6pm; Ⓦwww.aspenartmuseum.org) holds changing exhibits and puts on lectures and special events, while the **Aspen Center for Environmental Studies (ACES)**, 100 Puppy Smith St (May–Nov Mon–Sat 9am–5pm; Dec–April Mon–Fri till 5pm; Ⓦwww.aspennature.org), is a wildlife sanctuary at nearby Hallam Lake that offers guided hikes, and ski and snowshoe tours (bring your own gear), including nature programmes designed for kids.

Aspen's four mountains are run by the **Aspen Skiing Company** (Ⓣ970/925-1220 or 1-800/525-6200, Ⓦwww.aspensnowmass.com; snow report Ⓣ1-888/277-3676). The mogul-packed monster of **Aspen Mountain**, looming over downtown, is for experienced skiers only. On the other hand, **Buttermilk** is great for beginners, with an excellent ski school that offers a three-day guaranteed "Learn to Snowboard" programme; the wide-open runs of **Snowmass**, though mostly for intermediate skiers, feature some testing routes. **Aspen Highlands** has high-speed lifts and offers excellent extreme skiing terrain. The town's best value has to be its fifty miles of groomed **Nordic ski trails** – one of the most extensive free cross-country trail networks in the US.

Cycling is the main **summer** pursuit around Aspen; Timberline Bike Tours, 730 E Cooper Ave (Ⓣ970/274-6076, Ⓦwww.timberlinebike.com), offers mountain bikes to rent, organized tours including multi-night trips and guidance on routes and difficulty levels. The Roaring Fork River, surging out of the Sawatch Range, is excellent for **kayaking** and **rafting** during a short season that's typically over by early to mid-July. Beware, though, as sections of Class V rapids here are dangerous and every summer sees fatalities. Aspen Whitewater Rafting, 520 Durant St (Ⓣ970/920-3511, Ⓦwww.aspenwhitewater.com), offers guided trips.

If you fancy **walking** in the mountains, an easy way to get your bearings and enjoy great valley views is to take the Silver Queen **gondola** from 601 Dean St to the summit of **Aspen Mountain** (mid-June to early Sept daily 10am–4pm; $24; Ⓣ970/925-1220), where ACES regularly offers guided nature walks. Occasional free lunchtime concerts and talks are also held, and there's a good restaurant, the *Sundeck*, as well.

Even more alluring is the landscape around the twin purple-grey peaks of the **Maroon Bells**, fifteen miles southwest, soaring above dark blue Maroon Lake. The Bells are reached via the eleven-mile-long Maroon Creek Road, accessible to only overnight campers with permits, disabled travellers, bikers, in-line skaters and RFTA buses (8.30am–5pm); buses depart from the Aspen Highlands Ski Area (mid-June to Sept 9am–4.30pm; $6 return). A combination ticket ($26) covers both the Maroon Bells bus and the Silver Queen gondola.

Eating, drinking and nightlife

While many of Aspen's classy **cafés** and **restaurants** charge over $25 for a main course, good budget places exist and competition can be keen. Nightlife is at its peak in the **après-ski** winter season, but there's always something going on year-round. In summer, downtown hosts several top-notch festivals, including the summer-long **Aspen Music Festival** (Ⓣ970/925-9042, Ⓦwww.aspenmusicfestival.com), when orchestras and operas feature well-known international performers, as well as promising students. The Wheeler Opera House, 320 E Hyman Ave (Ⓣ970/920-5570, Ⓦwww.wheeleroperahouse.com), puts on concerts, plays and dance performances.

Boogie's Diner 534 E Cooper Ave Ⓣ970/925-6610. Inexpensive 1950s-style diner occupying an airy second-floor atrium lined with vinyl and chrome. The menu includes great meatloaf, thick shakes and even a one-pound burger, as well as a few imaginative tofu options.

Explore Booksellers and Bistro 221 E Main St Ⓣ970/925-5338. Fantastic bookstore with a shady roof terrace and a quiet, light café serving creative vegetarian dishes, and $14 set lunches.

Little Annie's Eating House 517 E Hyman Ave Ⓣ970/925-1098. Lively, popular and unpretentious saloon-style restaurant serving potato pancakes, hearty stews and salads at lunch, and huge trout, chicken, beef or rib dinner platters for just over $20.

Main Street Bakery Cafe 201 E Main St Ⓣ970/925-6446. Inventive New American cuisine in a casual, chatty setting, plus massive, fresh fruit-packed breakfasts.

Mezzaluna 624 E Cooper Ave Ⓣ970/925-5882. Mid-priced Northern Italian dishes (including wood-fired pizzas), served in a vivacious setting with patio seating.

Takah Sushi 320 S Mill St Ⓣ970/925-8588. Phenomenally good sushi and pan-Asian cuisine in a cheerful atmosphere, with some outdoor seating. Highly recommended, but quite expensive.

Woody Creek Tavern 1858 Woody Creek Rd, Woody Creek Ⓣ970/923-4585, Ⓦwww.woodycreektavern.com. Rustic tavern in tiny Woody Creek, seven miles northwest along Hwy-82, where ranch hands, Aspen visitors and the occasional celebrity local (Hunter S. Thompson was a frequent patron) shoot pool, guzzle fresh lime-juice margaritas and eat good Tex-Mex. Daily until 10pm.

Vail

Compared to most other Colorado ski towns, **VAIL**, 97 miles west of Denver on I-70, is a new creation: only a handful of farmers lived here before the resort opened in 1952. An uninspiring collection of Tyrolean-style chalets and concrete-block condos, pockmarked by pricey fashion boutiques and often painfully pretentious restaurants, at least the town is a compact and pedestrian-friendly place. Vail Resorts, which operates the ski area at Vail, also owns an even more exclusive gated resort, **Beaver Creek**, eleven miles further west on I-70; given the exceptional quality of the snow, and the sheer size and variety of terrain available, the two together produce a formidable winter sport destination. In summer, you can use the lifts at both resorts to go **mountain biking**, best at Vail, and **hiking**, best at the quieter Beaver Creek.

Practicalities

From Denver International Airport, several companies offer **shuttles** to Vail and Beaver Creek, including Colorado Mountain Express ($89; Ⓣ970/926-9800, Ⓦwww.cmex.com). More convenient (and therefore, more expensive) flights are available to **Eagle County Regional Airport** (Ⓦwww.eaglecounty.us/airport), 35 miles west of Vail. Ground transport from the airport to either resort is just $4 on Eagle County Transit (Ⓦwww.eaglecounty.us/Transit/).

Vail sprawls eight miles or so along the narrow valley floor, with nuclei from east to west at Vail Village – the area's main social centre – Lionshead, Cascade Village and West Vail. Each is pedestrianized and linked by free shuttle buses between them and the lifts. For information on skiing and accommodation, contact the **Vail Valley Tourism Bureau** (Ⓣ970/476-1000, Ⓦwww.visitvailvalley.com). **Accommodation** in and around **Vail Village** is pricey; good bets include the cosy *Tivoli Lodge*, 386 Hanson Ranch Rd (Ⓣ970/476-5615, Ⓦwww.tivolilodge.com; winter ❽, summer ❻), with pool, whirlpool and sauna; rates include a continental breakfast, and you can find bargains online. The sumptuous *Sonnenalp Resort,* 20 Vail Rd Village (Ⓣ1-866/284-4411, Ⓦwww.sonnenalp.com; winter ❾, summer ❽) is a luxury hotel bang in the centre of Vail with an excellent spa. Simpler lodging is available at the nearby hamlet of **Minturn**, seven miles south on US-24, where the *Eagle River Inn*, 145 N Main St (ⓣ303/827-5761; winter ❼, summer ❻), offers tasteful Southwestern-style rooms, nice views and a good breakfast. **Eating** well in Vail can prove expensive. *Vendetta's*, 291 Bridge St (ⓣ970/476-5070), is an established place offering Italian lunch specials, pizza and pasta dinners, mostly for under $20. For an upmarket evening meal, *Kelly Liken*, 12 Vail Rd (ⓣ970/479-0175) is winning accolades for its seasonally changing, locally sourced food; try the elk carpaccio and the sticky bun sundae. **Nightlife** revolves around Vail Village's Bridge Street; *The Tap Room*, no. 333 (ⓣ970/479-0500), has an outdoor deck, while *The Club* (ⓣ970/479-0556, ⓦwww.theclubvail.com), no. 304, is a lively basement bar hosting boisterous rock bands.

Glenwood Springs

Bustling, touristy **GLENWOOD SPRINGS** sits at the western end of impressive Glenwood Canyon, 157 miles west of Denver on I-70 and within striking distance of both Vail and Aspen; as such, it offers those with their own vehicle a budget base for either destination. Just north of the confluence of the Roaring Fork and Colorado rivers, the town was long used by the Ute people as a place of relaxation thanks to its **hot springs,** which became the target for unscrupulous speculators who broke treaties and established resort facilities in the 1880s. North from downtown and across the Eagle River is the town's main attraction, the huge **Hot Springs Pool**, 410 N River St (daily: summer 7.30am–10pm; rest of year 9am–10pm; $13.25–18.25; ⓦwww.hotspringspool.com), offering spa services in addition to two large pools, waterslides and a humble, mini-golf course. More intimate are the natural, subterranean steam baths of the nearby **Yampah Spa Vapor Caves**, 709 E 6th St (daily 9am–9pm; from $12; ⓦwww.yampahspa.com), where you can relax on cool marble benches set deep in ancient caves and enjoy a variety of classy spa treatments. Also on the north side of town is the **Glenwood Caverns Adventure Park**, 508 Pine St (summer daily 9am–9pm, hours vary at other times; $39; ⓦwww.glenwoodcaverns.com), with thrill rides, horseback rides and caverns that extend for two miles, with chambers reaching as high as 50ft ($5 in addition to day pass; special tours $30–60).

Some of the West's most colourful characters came to Glenwood Springs in the early days, including Dr John R. **"Doc" Holliday**, a dentist better known as a gambler, gunslinger and shooter in the gunfight at the OK Corral (see p.781). A chronic tuberculosis sufferer, Holliday came to the springs for a cure but died just a few months later in November 1887, at the age of 35; he's buried on a bluff overlooking the town in the picturesque **Linwood Cemetery**. In the paupers' section lies the grave of Harvey Logan, alias bank robber Kid Curry, a member of Butch Cassidy's notorious Hole-in-the-Wall gang.

Practicalities

Amtrak **trains** arrive at 413 7th St, at the end of a scenic route through central Colorado. Greyhound **buses**, travelling along a stunning, riverside stretch of I-70, stop close to downtown at the Phillips 66 station at 51171 US-6. The **visitor centre**, 1102 Grand Ave (summer Mon–Fri 9am–5pm, Sat & Sun 10am–3pm, rest of year Mon–Fri 9am–5pm; ⓣ970/945-6589, ⓦwww.glenwoodchamber.com) is in the middle of town. RFTA provides free **bus** service in town (ⓦwww.rfta.com).

The good-value, family-owned *Glenwood Motor Inn*, 141 W 6th St, has clean, comfortable **rooms** a couple of blocks away from the hot springs (ⓣ970/945-5438, ⓦwww.glenwoodmotorinn.com; ❸), while the funky *HI-Glenwood Springs Hostel*, near downtown at 1021 Grand Ave (closed 10am–4pm; ⓣ970/945-8545, ⓦwww.hostelcolorado.com), has spacious dorms ($16), less-good private rooms (❶), kitchen facilities and a giant record collection. Staff can also arrange tours and whitewater trips. For **food and drink**, the *Daily Bread Cafe and Bakery*, downtown at 729 Grand Ave (Ⓣ970/945-6253), has tasty breakfasts, soups and salads – but no espresso drinks. Inside the nearby *Hotel Denver*, the *Glenwood Canyon Brewing Company*, 402 7th St (Ⓣ970/945-1276), does reliable pub grub and excellent handcrafted microbrews.

Grand Junction

The immediate environs of **GRAND JUNCTION**, 244 miles west of Denver on I-70, are awash in outdoor opportunities, and within a fifty-mile stretch you can trace the transition from fertile alpine valley to full-blown desert. Another town that sprang into life in the 1880s with the arrival of the railroad, Grand Junction now makes its living primarily through the oil and gas industries. Although initial impressions are unfavourable – a sprawl of factory units and sales yards lines the I-70 Business Loop – the tiny downtown is much nicer, with leafy boulevards hemming in a small, tree-lined historic district dotted with sculptures and stores.

Although the Colorado section of Dinosaur National Monument is 90 miles north of Grand Junction, the town of **Fruita**, 12 miles west of town, holds the intriguing **Dinosaur Journey Museum**, 550 Jurassic Court (daily 9am–5pm; $7; Ⓦwww.dinosaurjourney.org). The interactive museum features robotic displays of several kinds of dinosaurs, as well as a collection of giant, locally excavated bones – all helping to create a vivid picture of these prehistoric beasts. Their Dino Digs programme (Ⓦwww.dinodigs.org) offers half- to five-day **digs** nearby.

Grand Junction's main attraction, though, is its splendid **hiking and biking trails** and **rock-climbing sites**, in and through parched, rugged and spectacular high desert country. All are possible year-round, and generally more pleasant in the winter, given the area's often suffocating summer heat. Particularly enticing for hikers is the remarkable scenery of **Colorado National Monument**, just west of Grand Junction. More than two hundred million years of wind and water erosion have gouged out rock spires, domes, arches, pedestals and balanced rocks along a line of cliffs; the colourful result makes for an enthralling painted desert of warm reds, stunning purples, burnt oranges and rich browns. The park has two entrances ($7, good for one week) at either end of twisting, 23-mile **Rim Rock Drive**, which links a string of spectacular overlooks with the **visitor centre** at the north end of the park (daily: summer 8am–6pm, Dec–Feb 9am–4pm, rest of year till 5pm; Ⓦwww.nps.gov/colm). Short hikes along the way afford views of several monoliths, while longer treks get right down to the canyon floor. Nearby but outside the park, rock climbers should investigate excellent **Unaweep Canyon**, southeast of Grand Junction on Hwy-141; back in Grand Junction itself, Summit Canyon Mountaineering, 461 Main St (Ⓣ970/243-2847, Ⓦwww.summitcanyon.com), can supply information and gear. **Mountain bikers** make for Fruita and the many smooth, rolling single-track trails nearby; Over the Edge Sports, 202 E Aspen Ave (Ⓣ970/858-7220, Ⓦwww.otefruita.com), in the centre of town, has trail information and rental bikes (from $49/day).

The only truly **seasonal activity** in Grand Junction is the sampling of Colorado **wine** and the excellent local peaches; contact the visitor centre (see below) for information on touring the wineries in the surrounding Grand Valley.

Practicalities

Amtrak **trains** stop at 2nd St and Pitkin Ave; Greyhound **buses** serve Durango, Denver and Salt Lake City from 230 S 5th St. The town's friendly **visitor centre** is at 740 Horizon Drive (Ⓣ1-800/962-2547, Ⓦwww.visitgrandjunction.com). **Accommodation** near the interstate includes the dependable *Best Western Sandman Motel*, 708 Horizon Drive (Ⓣ970/243-4150, Ⓦwww.bestwesterncolorado.com;

❹), with pool and a nice continental breakfast. Colorado National Monument's sole **campground**, *Saddlehorn*, high above Grand Junction, offers sites for $10; there is usually plenty of space. You can **dine** inexpensively at *Kannah Creek Brewing Company*, 1960 N 12th St (ⓣ970/263-0111), which serves gourmet pizza, pub grub and craft beers; tasty breakfasts and lunches are available at the retro *Main St Cafe*, 504 Main St (ⓣ970/242-7225), a 1950s-nostalgic diner with a few outside tables.

Southern Colorado

The richly varied landscape of **southern Colorado** ranges from the grassy, farm-rich plains of the sparsely populated southeast to the **San Juan Mountains** in the southwest, where vibrant **Durango** is the beating heart. Subdued **Colorado Springs** sits beside the I-85 Denver–Albuquerque interstate, at the foot of towering **Pikes Peak**; to the west, lofty mountain passes lead into deep, river-cut valleys and classic mining territory. Mineral riches brought in the land's original white settlers, who drove the Ute people away into the poorer **Four Corners** region of Colorado's far southwest.

North of Durango, the dramatic **San Juan Skyway** loops over two hundred miles through the mountains. The stretch of road north of Durango, negotiating its way through stunning alpine scenery, is known as the **Million Dollar Highway** for the supposedly gold-laden gravel used in its construction; it passes over multiple 10,000ft-plus summits and through the picturesque villages of **Silverton** and **Ouray**. West of Durango, **Mesa Verde National Park** is home to some extraordinary Ancestral Puebloan dwellings, while remote **Crested Butte**, north of the San Juans, is a gorgeously preserved late-Victorian frontier town reborn as a ski resort.

Colorado Springs and around

Sprawling for ten miles alongside I-25, **COLORADO SPRINGS** was developed as a vacation spot in 1871 by railroad tycoon William Jackson Palmer. He attracted so many English gentry to the town that it earned the nickname "Little London". Today the town, a bastion of conservatism compared to liberal Denver, still retains much of Palmer's vision, thanks to a high military presence (most notably the US Air Force Academy), fundamentalist religious organizations, exclusive Colorado College and an affluent Anglo-American community.

West of town and off US-24 W is the incredible **Garden of the Gods**, where a gnarled and warped red sandstone rockery was lifted up at the same time as the nearby mountains (around 65 million years ago), and has since eroded into finely balanced overhangs, jagged pinnacles, massive pedestals and mushroom formations. The **visitor centre** (daily: summer 8am–8pm, rest of year 9am–5pm; free; ⓦwww.gardenofgods.com) at the park's eastern border has details on hiking and mountain-biking **trails**, as well as **rock-climbing** routes. The most entertaining man-made attraction in the area is the **Pro Rodeo Hall of Fame**, 101 Pro Rodeo Drive (summer daily 9am–5pm, rest of year Wed–Sun same hours; $6; ⓦwww.prorodeohalloffame.com), where videos and displays explain the sport's various disciplines – calf roping, barrel racing and the like.

Pikes Peak and the Royal Gorge Bridge

Though there are thirty taller mountains in Colorado alone, **PIKES PEAK**, just west of Colorado Springs, is probably the best known – largely because the view from its crest inspired Katharine Lee Bates to write the words to "America The Beautiful". The 14,110ft peak was first mapped by American soldier and explorer Zebulon Pike in 1806, who never climbed it himself. By the end of the nineteenth century, gondola trails had been built to carry wealthy tourists like Ms Bates to the top; its unlikeliest summit, however, came in 1929, when a Texan named Bill Williams spent twenty days (and made 170 trouser changes) scaling the mountain, all the while pushing a peanut with his nose.

Less insane souls can reach the peak by a long **hike**, or via a difficult **toll road** (daily: May to early Sept 7.30am–8pm; rest of Sept till 7pm; Oct–April 9am–5pm; May–Nov $12/person up to $40/car, Dec–April $10/person up to $35/car; Ⓦwww.pikespeakcolorado.com) that becomes unpaved halfway up the mountain. The thrilling **Pikes Peak Cog Railway** ($33, reservations advised; Ⓣ719/685-5401, Ⓦwww.cograilway.com) runs year-round and grinds its way up an average of 847ft per mile on its ninety-minute journey to the summit; from 11,500ft onward it crosses a barren expanse of alpine tundra, scarred by giant scree flows. From the bleak and windswept peak, it's possible to see Denver seventy miles north and the endless prairie to the east, while to the west, mile upon mile of snowcapped Rockies peaks soar into the distance. The train leaves from 515 Ruxton Ave in **Manitou Springs**, a time-warped little town six miles west of Colorado Springs.

About 45 miles south of Pikes Peak, beside the town of Cañon City – via Hwy-115 and US-50 from Colorado Springs – is the rather rickety **ROYAL GORGE BRIDGE** (daily 7am–dusk; $23; Ⓦwww.royalgorgebridge.com), the world's highest wooden suspension bridge, spanning a vertiginous 1053ft crack over the roaring Arkansas River. The gorge is the focus of a park offering several other attractions, which though quite commercialized, can still terrify you; these include an aerial tram, an incline railway and the Royal Rush Skycoaster – a bungee swing (mid-March to mid-Oct) that for $25 will send you reeling over the canyon.

Colorado Springs practicalities

From **Denver International Airport** there are a number of inexpensive **flights**, or you can book a ride on Colorado Springs Shuttle ($50; Ⓣ719/687-3456, Ⓦwww.coloradoshuttle.com). Greyhound **buses** stop at 120 S Weber St downtown. Colorado Springs' **visitor centre** is at 515 S Cascade Ave (Mon–Fri 8.30am–5pm, Sat 9am–1pm; Ⓣ719/635-7506, Ⓦwww.experiencecoloradosprings.com).

The rustically elegant *Old Town GuestHouse*, 115 S 26th St (Ⓣ719/632-9194, Ⓦwww.oldtown-guesthouse.com; ❺), offers flower-themed B&B **rooms** and an evening guest reception, while the *Sunflower Lodge*, not far from Manitou Springs at 3703 W Colorado Ave, provides cosy budget accommodation in retro motel units (Ⓣ719/520-1864, Ⓦwww.sunflowerlodge.com; ❸). Nearby, the busy *Garden of the Gods Campground*, 3704 W Colorado Ave (Ⓣ719/475-9450, Ⓦwww.coloradocampground.com), has **cabins** (❶) – far better value than the overpriced tent sites ($42).

For **food**, *Marigold Café*, a little north of downtown at 4605 Centennial Blvd (Ⓣ719/599-4776; closed Sun) serves good lunchtime sandwiches, patisserie and, in the evenings, delicious French-inspired bistro food that belies the drab exterior. Downtown, the *Phantom Canyon Brewing Co.*, 2 E Pikes Peak Ave (Ⓣ719/635-2800), is a great place for own-brewed beer and filling pub food. Colorado Springs is not much of a party town, but the area known as the Tejon Strip, between Platte and Colorado aves, is the best bet for **bars**.

Great Sand Dunes National Park

Your first sight of **GREAT SAND DUNES NATIONAL PARK** comes as a shock; far from being tucked away in crevices or sheltered in a valley, the dunes are simply a colossal pile of sand that appears to have been dumped alongside the craggy Sangre de Cristo Mountains, 170 miles southwest of Colorado Springs. Over millions of years, these fine glacial grains have eroded from the San Juan Mountains and blown east until they could drift no further; the result is an eerie and deeply incongruous fifty-square-mile area of silky, shifting trackless desert.

The park's **visitor centre** (daily: summer 9am–6pm, rest of year till 4.30pm; ⓣ719/378-6399, ⓦwww.nps.gov/grsa) is three miles beyond the park entrance ($3/vehicle, good for one week). Shortly beyond that lies the goal for most visitors, the "**beach**" beside Medano Creek, which flows along the eastern and southern side of the dune mass. To reach the dunes themselves, you'll have to wade across the shallow creek, but be sure to take shoes – the sand can get incredibly hot. The dunes loom very large from the moment you start walking, but depending on current drifting they may take ten minutes or so to reach, which can be hugely tiring, especially when the often-high winds swirl grit into your eyes at every step. Your reward is the sheer fun of climbing up the actual dunes, and, especially, sliding back down again (bring your own dune board). The scenery is spectacular, but few visitors venture out of sight of the stream.

With a free **backcountry permit**, you can **camp** in the park's seven primitive backcountry sites; the large *Pinyon Flats Campground* (first-come, first-served; $14), however, is accessible by car, and much more popular, usually filling with tents and RVs alike in summer. *Great Sand Dunes Oasis* (April–Oct; ⓣ719/378-2222, ⓦwww.greatdunes.com), just south of the park entrance, has the only **restaurant** for miles around, serving burgers, frybread and Mexican specialties, and also offers showers, laundry and tent sites ($18), as well as a small number of basic **cabins** (❹). Behind the store, *Great Sand Dunes Lodge* (mid-March to late Oct; ⓣ719/378-2900, ⓦwww.gsdlodge.com; ❹), has pleasant rooms with dunes views, an indoor pool and outdoor gas grills.

Black Canyon of the Gunnison National Park

More than living up to its bleak-sounding name, **BLACK CANYON OF THE GUNNISON NATIONAL PARK**, seventy miles southeast of Grand Junction, can be reached via US-50 to the south or Hwy-92 from the north. The view down into the fearsome, black rock canyon to the foaming Gunnison River below is as foreboding as mountain scenery gets. Over two million years, the river has eroded a deep, narrow gorge, leaving exposed cliffs and jagged spires of crystalline rock more than 1.7 billion years old. The aspen-lined road leading to the top of the canyon winds uphill until the trees abruptly come to an end, the road levels out and the scenery takes a dramatic turn – stark black cliffs, with the odd pine clinging to a tiny ledge in desperation. Snowshoeing and cross-country skiing are possibilities in winter, while summer sees opportunities for fishing, hiking and advanced-level climbing and kayaking.

The park's **entrance fee**, good for one week, is $15 per vehicle. The **visitor centre** (daily: summer 8am–6pm, rest of year 8.30am–4pm; ⓣ970/249-1914, ⓦwww.nps.gov/blca) on the south rim has details on the two first-come, first-served **campgrounds**, one on each side of the canyon.

Crested Butte

The beautiful Victorian mining village of **CRESTED BUTTE**, 150 miles northeast of Telluride and 230 miles southwest of Denver, almost died off in the 1950s after its coal deposits were exhausted. However, the development of 11,875ft **Mount Crested Butte** into a world-class **ski resort** in the 1960s, and a **mountain-biker's** paradise two decades later, means that today it can claim to be the top year-round resort in Colorado. The old town is resplendent with gaily painted clapboard homes and businesses, while zoning laws ensure that condos and chalets are confined to the resort area, three miles up the road behind the foothills.

In skiing and snowboarding circles, **Crested Butte Mountain Resort** (one-day lift tickets late Nov to mid-Dec $59, mid-Dec to early April $87; ⓣ970/349-2333, ⓦwww.skicb.com) is best known for its extreme terrain, with lifts serving out-of-the-way bowls and faces that would only be accessible by helicopter at other resorts; unsurprisingly, the resort hosts both the US extreme skiing and snowboarding championships. That said, plenty of long beginner runs are mixed in over the mountain's one thousand skiable acres, with sixteen chairlifts linking 121 usually uncrowded runs.

In summer, **mountain bikes** all but outnumber cars around the town, especially during **Fat Tire Week** in late June, one of the oldest festivals in the young sport and one that, according to local legend, evolved from a race over the rocky 21-mile **Pearl Pass** to Aspen in the 1970s. You can still ride this route – 190 miles shorter than the road – but some of the most exciting trails are much nearer the town and include the gorgeous 401 trail with its wide-open vistas; the thickly wooded Dyke Trail; and the long, varied and occasionally challenging Deadman's Gulch. The Alpineer, 419 Sixth St (ⓣ970/349-5210, ⓦwww.alpineer.com), rents bikes.

Practicalities

Five hours' drive southwest from Denver along mostly minor highways, Crested Butte is not easy to reach, though the roads are almost always open. Many skiers **fly** from Denver to Gunnison Airport, 28 miles south, a forty-minute trip to Crested Butte via the Alpine Express Shuttle ($34 single; ⓣ1-800/822-4844, ⓦwww.alpineexpressshuttle.com). Free **buses** ply the three miles between the town and resort every fifteen minutes 7.10am–midnight. The **visitor centre** is at 601 Elk Ave (daily 9am–5pm; ⓣ970/349-6438 or 1-800/545-4505, ⓦwww.visitcrestedbutte.com).

The choice of **accommodation** is between the ski area or downtown; in season, you're likely to flit between the two areas every day, so it's only worth staying at the generally more expensive mountainside lodgings if you're obsessed with getting first tracks. *Crested Butte Mountain Resort* (see above) can book rooms and advise on package deals – reserve well in advance during winter. Down in town, the *Purple Mountain*, 714 Gothic Ave (ⓣ1-877/349-5888, ⓦwww.purplemountainlodge.com; ❺), is a very comfortable (and very purple) **B&B** with its own day spa, while *Old Town Inn*, 708 Sixth St (ⓣ1-888/349-6184, ⓦwww.oldtowninn.net; ❺), offers standard **motel** rooms. The *Crested Butte International Lodge and Hostel*, 615 Teocalli Ave (ⓣ970/349-0588 or 1-888/389-0588 ⓦwww.crestedbuttehostel.com; ❹), offers dorm beds for $25–38, but very poor-value private rooms.

Crested Butte lays claim to several gourmet **restaurants**. The inviting *Bacchanale*, 209 Elk Ave (ⓣ970/349-5257), serves espresso from 7am, then later on features two-tiered dining and a varied Northern Italian menu, including good veal and cannelloni. There's tasty Thai, Indian and Vietnamese food, including vegetarian options, at the *Ginger Cafe*, 425 Elk Ave (ⓣ970/349-7291), while *Pitas In Paradise*, 212 Elk Ave (ⓣ970/349-0897), serves inexpensive wraps and salads. Elk Avenue is also lined with no-nonsense **bars**, such as *Kochevars* at no. 127 (ⓣ970/349-6745) and *Talk of the Town* at no. 230 (ⓣ970/349-6809).

Durango

Thanks to a splendid setting amid the San Juan Mountains, **DURANGO**, southwest Colorado's largest town, has boomed in recent years. A friendly, ebullient, place, it's now home to a mixed population of teleworkers and outdoor enthusiasts, who enjoy its year-round range of activities, excellent restaurants and flourishing arts scene.

Durango was founded in 1880 as a refining town and rail junction for Silverton, 45 miles north. Steam trains continue to run along the spectacular old mining route through the Animas Valley, though nowadays tourists, not sacks of gold, are the money-making cargo. **The Durango & Silverton Narrow Gauge Railroad** runs up to three round-trips daily ($81–169 return; ⓣ970/247-2733, ⓦwww.durangotrain.com) between May and October, from the depot at 479 Main Ave at the south end of town. The views from the train are spectacular as it chugs by rocky cliffs and through huddles of lush aspen, framed by the rugged Animas River below (the trains are slow, however; if you need to save time, you can return by bus).

It's also possible to combine the train ride with a day's **zip-lining** at remote **Soaring Tree Top Adventures** (daily, mid-May to mid-Oct; $429 inc train fare & lunch; ⓣ970/769-2357, ⓦwww.soaringtreetopadventures.com), only accessible via the railroad. Alternatively, several operators run **river-rafting** excursions on the Animas River; Mild to Wild Rafting (ⓣ970/247-4789, ⓦwww.mild2wildrafting.com), charge from $79 for a full-day expedition.

Practicalities

Durango's **tourism office** is at 111 S Camino del Rio by the train station (June–Sept Mon–Fri 8am–6pm, Sat 9am–5pm, Sun 11am–4pm; Oct–May Mon–Fri 8am–5pm; ⓣ970/247-3500, ⓦwww.durango.org). Greyhound **buses** arrive at 275 E Eighth Ave.

The finest of many **accommodation** options is the stalwart *Strater Hotel* at 699 Main Ave (ⓣ970/247-4431 or 1-800/247-4431, ⓦwww.strater.com; ❼), which has a hundred tasteful antique-furnished rooms. *Durango Lodge*, 150 East Fifth St ⓣ970/247-0955 or 1-888/440-4489), is a convenient downtown **motel**, close to the railroad station, though you can find cheaper rates a couple of miles north at the *Siesta Motel* at 3475 Main Ave (ⓣ970/247-0741, ⓦwww.durangosiestamotel.com; ❸).

Downtown Durango also holds a multitude of good **restaurants**, such as *East by Southwest*, a ravishing "pan-Asian bistro" a block up from Main Avenue at 160 E College Drive (ⓣ970/247-5533). The fun *Carver's Bakery & Brewpub*, 1022 Main Ave (ⓣ970/259-2545) opens early for breakfast, serves Southwestern lunches and dinners, and buzzes late into the night in its brewpub role.

Silverton

The turnaround point for the narrow gauge railroad from Durango comes at **SILVERTON**: "silver by the ton", allegedly. Spread across a small flat valley and hemmed in entirely by the tall peaks of the San Juan Mountains, it's one of Colorado's most evocative (and secluded) mountain towns, where wide, dirt-paved streets lead off toward the surrounding heights. Silverton's zinc- and copper-mining days only came to an end in 1991, and the population has dropped since then, with those who remain generally relying on the seasonal tourist train – winters here are harsh and largely quiet. Although the false-fronted stores along "Notorious Blair Street" may remind one of the days when **Wyatt Earp** dealt cards here, the town is defined by the restaurants and gift shops that fill up between 11am and 2pm, when train passengers are in town.

Practicalities

Silverton offers inexpensive **accommodation** at the *Triangle Motel*, 848 Greene St (ⓣ970/387-5780, ⓦwww.trianglemotel.com; ❸), at the south end of town, which also offers good-value two-room suites and jeep rental. For a little extra cash, you can enjoy one of the forty creaky, antique-furnished rooms at the *Grand Imperial Hotel*, 1219 Greene St (ⓣ970/387-5527, ⓦwww.grandimperialhotel.com; ❹). The thin-walled *Silverton Inn & Hostel*, 1025 Blair St (ⓣ970/387-0115; ❷), has dorm beds for $26 and private rooms (❷). As for **food and drink**, *Romero's*, 1151 Greene St (ⓣ970/387-5501), is an enjoyable Mexican *cantina*.

Ouray

The equally attractive mining community of **OURAY** lies 23 miles north of Silverton, on the far side of 11,018ft **Red Mountain Pass**, where the bare rock beneath the snow really is red, thanks to mineral deposits. The Million Dollar Highway twists and turns to get here, passing abandoned mine workings and rusting machinery in the most unlikely and inaccessible spots; trails and backroads into the San Juans offer rich pickings for hikers or drivers with four-wheel-drive vehicles.

Ouray itself is squeezed into a verdant sliver of a valley, with the commercially run **Ouray Hot Springs** beside the Uncompahgre River at the north end of town. A mile or so south, a one-way-loop dirt road leads to Box Canyon Falls Park (daily 8am–dusk; $3), where a straightforward 500ft trail, partly along a swaying wooden parapet, leads into narrow Box Canyon and the namesake falls that thunder through a tiny cleft in the mountain at the far end.

Practicalities

The local **visitor centre** (mid-June to Aug Mon–Wed 9am–5pm, Thurs–Sat till 7pm, Sun 10am–4pm; Sept to mid-June Mon–Sat 10am–5pm, Sun till 3pm; ⓣ970/325-4746, ⓦwww.ouraycolorado.com) is on the northern edge of town, beside the local hot springs. At *Box Canyon Lodge*, an old-style timber **motel** at 45 Third Ave below the park (ⓣ970/325-4981 or 1-800/327-5080, ⓦwww.boxcanyonouray.com; ❹–❻), you can soak in natural hot tubs. The luxurious *St Elmo Hotel*, 426 Main St (ⓣ970/325-4951 or 1-866/243-1502, ⓦwww.stelmohotel.com; ❹–❼), features a good **restaurant** (the *Bon Ton*), while the *Grounds Keeper Coffee House*, 524 Main St (ⓣ970/325-0550), is a central café serving espresso drinks and healthy and light lunches.

Telluride

Set in a picturesque valley, at the flat base of a bowl of vast steep-sided mountains, **TELLURIDE** lies 120 miles northwest of Durango via an indirect highway route. The former mining village was briefly home to the young Butch Cassidy, who robbed his first bank here in 1889. These days, it's better known as a top-class **ski resort** that rivals Aspen for celebrity allure. Happily, it has achieved its status without losing its character, exemplified by the beautifully preserved low-slung buildings along its wide main street. Healthy young bohemians with few visible means of support but top-notch ski equipment seem to form the bulk of the twelve hundred inhabitants, while most visitors tend to stay two miles up from town in **Mountain Village**, served by a free, year-round gondola service. Summer **hiking** opportunities are excellent; one three-mile round-trip walk leads from the head of the valley, where the highway ends at Pioneer Mill, up to the 431ft **Bridal Veil Falls**, the tallest in Colorado. Come winter, nearly half the ski terrain in Telluride is geared for experts, with its steep mogul fields particular favourites.

Practicalities

Telluride's extremely helpful **visitor centre** is on the edge of downtown at 630 W Colorado Ave (Mon–Fri 8am–8pm, Sat & Sun 10am–8pm; ⓣ970/728-3401 or

1-888/355-8743, Ⓦwww.visittelluride.com). **Accommodation** is much less expensive in summer than during ski season, though prices do go up for the Bluegrass Festival in June, the Jazz Festival in early August and the Film Festival in early September. The landmark 1895 *New Sheridan Hotel*, 231 W Colorado Ave (Ⓣ970/728-4351 or 1-800/200-1891, Ⓦwww.newsheridan.com; ❻), has handsome rooms and a cosy library, as well as an in-house bar and restaurant, while the *Victorian Inn*, 401 W Pacific Ave (Ⓣ970/728-6601 Ⓦwww.tellurideinn.com; ❺), is a smart motel with its own sauna. Contemporary Southwestern entrees at the dinner-only *Cosmopolitan*, 300 W San Juan Ave (Ⓣ970/728-1292; closed Sun), the fanciest **restaurant** in town, cost from $20, while *Smugglers Brewpub and Grille*, San Juan and Pine (Ⓣ970/728-0919), is a lively evening hangout with a wide-ranging menu. *Baked in Telluride*, 127 S Fir St (Ⓣ970/728-4705), is a takeaway deli that has a nice little terrace where you can enjoy soup, sandwiches or pizza.

Mesa Verde National Park

The only national park in the US devoted exclusively to archeological remains, **MESA VERDE NATIONAL PARK** is set high on a densely wooded plateau south of US-160, around fifty miles west of Durango. It lies so far off the beaten path that its extensive **Ancestral Puebloan ruins** were not fully explored until 1888, when a local rancher discovered them on his land.

During the thousand or so years up to 1300 AD, Ancestral Puebloan peoples expanded to cover much of the area now known as the **"Four Corners"**. While their earliest dwellings were simple pits in the ground, they ultimately developed the architectural sophistication needed to build the spectacular multistorey apartments that characterize Mesa Verde, nestled in rocky alcoves high above the sheer canyons that bisect the southern edge of the Mesa Verde plateau. Why such remote and inaccessible structures were necessary remains unclear, but it suggests that Ancestral Puebloan culture was not as peaceful as it's often depicted; in any event, the soil at Mesa Verde ultimately appears to have been depleted, and the region's inhabitants migrated into what's now New Mexico to establish the pueblos where their descendants still live.

Touring the park

The access road to Mesa Verde climbs south from US-160, ten miles east of Cortez. Once past the entrance station ($15 in summer, $10 rest of year, good for one week), the road climbs and twists for fifteen miles to the **Far View Visitor Center** (late April to mid-Oct daily 8am–5pm; Ⓣ970/529-4465, Ⓦwww.nps.gov/meve), where exhibits cover Navajo, Hopi and Pueblo crafts and jewellery. You can also buy the tickets here necessary to **tour** any of the major ruins ($3; see below); at busy periods you can't tour both Balcony House and Cliff Palace on the same day.

Immediately beyond the visitor centre, the road forks to the two main constellations of remains: **Chapin Mesa** to the south, and **Wetherill Mesa** to the west, which is only accessible in summer. Six miles along the road toward Chapin Mesa, the **Chapin Mesa Archeological Museum** (daily: April to mid-Oct 8am–6.30pm; mid-Oct to March till 5pm) holds informative displays on Ancestral Puebloans. It's also the starting point for the short, steep hike down to **Spruce Tree House**, the only ruin open in winter (via guided tour) – a neat little village of three-storey structures, snugly moulded into a rocky alcove and fronted by plazas.

Beyond the museum, **Ruins Road** (April to early Nov, daily 8am–dusk) consists of two one-way, six-mile loops. If you're pressed for time, follow the eastern one to reach **Cliff Palace**, the largest Ancestral Puebloan cliff dwelling to survive anywhere. Tucked one hundred feet below an overhanging ledge of pale rock, its

217 rooms once housed over two hundred people. Even if you haven't bought a ticket for a tour (daily, early April to early Nov; hours range from 9am–4pm, up to 6pm in midsummer), you can get a great view from the promontory where tour groups gather, beside the car park. Entering the ruin itself, especially on a quieter day, provides a haunting evocation of a lost and little-known world, as you walk through the empty plazas, peer down into the mysterious *kivas* (circular, stone-lined ceremonial pits) and glimpse fading murals inside some of the structures.

Balcony House, a little further on, is one of the few Mesa Verde complexes clearly geared towards defence; access is very difficult and it's not visible from above. Guided tours (late April to mid-Oct, daily 9am–5pm) involve scrambling up three hair-raising ladders and crawling through a narrow tunnel, teetering all the while above a steep drop into Soda Canyon. If you lack a head for heights, consider giving it a miss.

At the end of the twisting twelve-mile drive onto **Wetherill Mesa** (daily late May to early Sept 8am–4.30pm; no RVs), you can catch a free miniature train around the tip of the mesa to the **Long House**, the park's second largest ruin, set in its largest cave. Hour-long tours (daily 9am–4pm) descend sixty or so steps to reach its central plaza, then scramble around its 150 rooms and 21 *kivas*.

Park practicalities

Mesa Verde gets very crowded in high summer; the best months to visit are May, September and October. The park is open all year, but most structures are inaccessible in winter, and services such as gas, food and lodging only operate between late April and mid-October. Most visitors stay in nearby towns; the only **rooms** in the park itself are at the visitor centre-adjacent *Far View Motor Lodge* (late April to late Oct; Ⓣ1-800/449-2288, Ⓦwww.visitmesaverde.com; ❺), where the balconies have superb views and the absence of phones and TVs makes for a tranquil stay. The gigantic *Morefield Campground*, four miles up from the park entrance (early May to early Oct; $20 and up), holds 435 **camping pitches**, and there are several commercial campgrounds nearby. The lodge's upmarket *Metate Room* provides fabulous **meals** incorporating buffalo and elk meat into main courses, and sides such as beans, flat-bread and roasted corn. Food is also available year-round at *Spruce Tree Terrace* cafeteria near the Chapin Mesa museum.

Wyoming

Pronghorn antelope all but outnumber people in wide-open **WYOMING**, the ninth largest but least populous state in the union, with just 570,000 residents. Above all, this is classic **cowboy country** – the inspiration behind *Shane*, *The Virginian* and countless other Western novels – replete with open range, rodeos and country-music dance halls. The state emblem, seen everywhere, is a hat-waving cowboy astride a bucking bronco, and the spurious "Code of the West", signed into state law in 2010 and urging residents to follow such maxims as "ride for the brand", illustrates Wyoming's ongoing attachment to the myths of the Wild West.

Well over three million tourists per year head to Wyoming's northwest corner to admire the simmering geothermal landscape of **Yellowstone National Park**, and the craggy mountain vistas of adjacent **Grand Teton National Park**. Between Yellowstone and South Dakota to the east are the helter-skelter **Bighorn Mountains**, likeable Old West towns such as **Cody** and **Buffalo**, and the otherworldly outcrop of **Devils Tower**.

Unlikely as it may seem, this rowdy state was the first to grant women the right to vote in 1869 – a full half-century before the rest of the country, on the grounds that the enfranchisement of women would attract settlers and increase the population, thereby hastening statehood. A year later Wyoming appointed the country's first women jurors, and the "Equality State" elected the first female US governor in 1924.

The absence of rivers to irrigate farmland has put a lid on agricultural growth. Any weather-beaten, denim-clad stranger is just as likely to be an oil roustabout as a genuine cowboy, with **mineral extraction** having replaced livestock as the mainstay of the state's economy in the early twentieth century; today, Wyoming's coffers depend on profits from the coal, oil and natural gas industries.

South and central Wyoming

State capital **Cheyenne** is one of the few towns of real note in the lower two-thirds of Wyoming. Set in the heart of rich prairie – a surprise after the scrubland, mountain and desert of most of the region – it has closer economic ties with Omaha or Denver than with the rest of Wyoming. West of Cheyenne, beyond energetic little **Laramie**, lies the spectacular wilderness of the **Wind River Range**, accessible from **Lander** and **Pinedale**.

Cheyenne

The eastern approach into **CHEYENNE**, dropping into a wide dip in the plains, leaves enduring memories for most travellers. With the snow-crested Rockies looming in the distance and short, sun-bleached grass encircling the town, the sky appears gargantuan, dwarfing the city's outlying neighbourhoods. Even a quick exploration reveals a diverse community shaped by railroads, state politics and even nuclear arms. Union Pacific's sprawling yards and fine old terminus now mark the eastern edge of downtown, while to the west, the city's long-standing military installation was expanded in 1957 to house the first US intercontinental ballistic missile base.

Cowboy culture is big here, too, as the ranchwear stores and honky-tonks attest. In late July, the ten-day **Cheyenne Frontier Days** festival (Ⓦwww.cfdrodeo.com) attracts thousands to its huge outdoor rodeo, big-name C&W concerts, parades, chuckwagon races, air shows and cook-outs. The rest of the year, things are pretty quiet. The **Wyoming State Museum**, 2301 Central Ave, takes a sober look at Wild West history (May–Oct Mon–Sat 9am–4.30pm; Nov–April Mon–Fri same hours, Sat 10am–2pm; free; Ⓦwyomuseum.state.wy.us), while the more light-hearted **Cheyenne Frontier Days Old West Museum**, five minutes' drive from downtown at 4610 Carey Ave (Mon–Fri 9am–5pm, Sat & Sun 10am–5pm; $7; Ⓦwww.oldwestmuseum.org), tells how the railroad came to town, with some great old engines and lots on the Frontier Days celebrations.

Practicalities

Greyhound **buses** run east and west along I-80 and south to Denver; the local station is at 5401 Walker Rd. Cheyenne's **visitor centre**, at Depot Square, 121 W 15th St (May–Sept Mon–Fri 10am–6pm, Sat 9am–6pm, Sun 10am–4pm; Oct–April

Mon–Fri 8am–5pm; ⓣ1-800/426-5009, ⓦwww.cheyenne.org), has lots of local information. **Accommodation** prices increase sharply during the Frontier Days festival. For budget motels try West Lincolnway; homier surroundings are found at the friendly *Nagle Warren Mansion*, 222 E 17th St (ⓣ307/637-3333, ⓦwww.naglewarrenmansion.com; ❻), a historic B&B. Many of Cheyenne's **restaurants** serve cowboy-sized meals; among them, *Sanford's*, 115 E 17th St (ⓣ307/634-3381), is a lively local brewpub with good pub food. *The Bread Basket*, 1819 Maxwell Ave (ⓣ307/432-2525; closed Sun), serves light lunches including simple sandwiches, home-made soups, fresh pies and cookies, in a cosy little spot.

Laramie and around

LARAMIE lies fifty miles west of Cheyenne via either I-80 or the spectacular Hwy-210 (Happy Jack Road), the latter slicing through plains studded with bizarrely shaped boulders and outcrops. At first Laramie seems typical of rural Wyoming, but behind downtown's Victorian facades lurk vegetarian cafés, day spas and secondhand bookstores – unusual for rodeo land, and a direct by-product of the **University of Wyoming**, whose campus spreads east from the town centre. Tensions between the differing cultures were highlighted by the notorious murder of gay student Matthew Shepard in 1998, which directly led to a change in US hate crime laws to cover sexual orientation.

The centrepiece of the ambitious **Wyoming Territorial Prison State Park**, west of town at 975 Snowy Range Rd (May–Sept daily 9am–6pm, winter hours vary; $5, ⓦwww.wyomingterritorialprison.com), is the old **prison** itself. A touch over-restored, it nonetheless holds informative displays on the Old West and women in Wyoming, as well as huge mugshots of ex-convicts – among them Butch Cassidy, incarcerated here for eighteen months in 1896 for the common crime of cattle-rustling.

Practicalities

Greyhound **buses** pull into Laramie at 1300 S Third St; the **visitor centre** is at 210 Custer St (Mon–Fri 8am–5pm; ⓣ1-800/445-5303, ⓦwww.laramie-tourism.org). **Rooms** are clean and rates are reasonable at the downtown *Travelodge*, 165 N Third St (ⓣ307/742-6671, ⓦwww.travelodge.com; ❸). If you're looking for a more rural place to lay your head, travel about 20 miles west out of Laramie on Hwy-130 to the *Vee Bar Guest Ranch*, 2091 Hwy-130 (three-night minimum in summer; ⓣ307/745-7036 or 1-800/483-3227, ⓦwww.veebar.com; ❻), where you can relax in a cosy creekside cabin overnight and enjoy a hearty cooked breakfast in the morning, and they offer week-long riding and ranching vacations in summer. For **dining**, buzzing *Lovejoy's Bar and Grill*, 101 E Grand Ave (ⓣ307/745-0141), is a busy diner/bar, while student hangout *Coal Creek Coffee Co*, opposite at 110 E Grand Ave (ⓣ307/745-7737), serves good espresso, smoothies and sandwiches.

The Medicine Bow Mountains and Saratoga

West of Laramie, **Hwy-130** dips into the huge wind-gouged bowl of **Big Hollow**. Beyond the tiny foothill community of **Centennial**, home to the rustic *Old Corral Hotel & Steak House*, 2750 Hwy-130 (ⓣ370/745-5918, ⓦwww.oldcorral.com; ❹), it starts the steady climb up through the **MEDICINE BOW MOUNTAINS**, one of Wyoming's most picturesque drives. Overlooks at the top of the 10,847ft Snowy Range Pass (closed in winter) reveal alpine lakes and meadows set tightly against steep mountain faces.

Butch Cassidy and the Sundance Kid

Two of the most engaging characters to roam the Rocky Mountains, **Butch Cassidy and the Sundance Kid**, remain legends not only of the Old West, but of a romantic outlaw existence in which breaking the law became an expression of personal freedom. Thanks in large part to the 1969 movie (starring Paul Newman and Robert Redford), these two former thieves and cattle rustlers continue to cast a long shadow across the Rockies.

Butch Cassidy was born **George LeRoy Parker** in Beaver, Utah, on 6 April, 1866. Taught the art of cattle-rustling by ranch-hand Mike Cassidy, he borrowed his mentor's last name, and picked up the handle "Butch" while working as a butcher in Rock Springs, Wyoming. Having pulled his first bank job in Telluride, Colorado, in 1889, he threw in his lot with a like-minded group of outlaws known as the **Wild Bunch**. Among them was one **Harry Longabaugh** – the Sundance Kid – who picked up his nickname following a jail stint in Sundance, Wyoming. Eclectic in their criminal pursuits, the Wild Bunch's resumé would include horse-rustling as well as the robbing of trains, banks and mine payrolls; between them, they gave away a fortune in gold to friends and even strangers in need.

The gang took to laying low through the winter months in **Brown's Hole**, a broad river valley in remote northwest Colorado, and were also known to visit the southern Wyoming towns of Baggs, Rock Springs and Green River. Their saloon excesses were tolerated, however, because at the end of a spree they would meticulously account for every broken chair and bullet hole, making generous restitution in gold. The gang, however, was eventually undone by their own vanity and love of a good time: during a visit to Fort Worth, Texas, five of the men posed for a photo in smart suits and derby hats, looking so dapper that the photographer proudly placed the photo in his shop window, where it was seen the following day by a detective from the famous Pinkerton agency.

Wearying of life on the run, Butch and Sundance sailed for **South America** in 1902, and were soon trying their hand at gold-mining, while robbing the occasional bank or train. The Hollywood version was true enough to this point, but Butch Cassidy did not die in a hail of bullets at the hands of Bolivian soldiers in 1909 as depicted in the film – although it seems that Harry Longabaugh did. The last say belongs to Josie Morris, an old girlfriend from Butch's Brown's Hole days, who insisted that he came to see her on his return from South America, and claimed furthermore that he died an old man in Johnny, Nevada, sometime in the 1940s.

Across the mountains, 49 miles west of Centennial, sleepy **Saratoga** sits at a valley crossroads between the Snowy and Sierra Madre ranges. Though not much to look at, **Hobo Hot Springs** on Walnut Avenue is a free outdoor pool fed by natural hot springs, available 24 hours a day. Saratoga's most evocative **hotel** is the slightly musty, but antique-furnished *Wolf Hotel*, 101 E Bridge St (Ⓣ307/326-5525, Ⓦwww.wolfhotel.com; ❸), which also has a restaurant and bar (closed Sun).

Rawlins

There would be little reason to stop at the tiny prairie town of **RAWLINS**, 100 miles west of Laramie on I-80, but for the unmissable **Wyoming Frontier Prison**, 500 W Walnut St (hourly tours 8.30am–4.30pm; $7; Ⓦwww.wyomingfrontierprison.org). In service until 1981, this huge jail with dingy cells, peeling walls and echoing corridors can make for a creepy experience – not least due to the fascinating anecdotes told with aplomb by the exceptional guides. The darkest moment comes as the gas chamber (in use from 1937 until 1965) is revealed.

Just west, the Continental Divide briefly splits into two in the **Great Divide Basin**. Theoretically, rain that falls here should remain here, unable to flow toward either ocean; in reality, virtually all of it evaporates, as the brick-red dirt of the **Red Desert** stretches implacably away toward the horizon.

The Wind River Range

Roads to Grand Teton and Yellowstone national parks from southern Wyoming skirt the **WIND RIVER RANGE**, the state's longest and highest mountain range; beautiful and challenging hiking terrain is found in the **Bridger Wilderness** area, accessible from the west. No roads cross the mountains; you can either see them from the east by driving through the Wind River Indian Reservation on US-26/287, or from the less accessible west, by taking US-191 up from I-80 at Rock Springs.

Wind River Indian Reservation and Lander

The 1.7 million acres of **WIND RIVER INDIAN RESERVATION** occupy a largely forgotten swath of west-central Wyoming, overshadowed by the high snowcapped peaks to the west and south. Wyoming's only Native American reservation, it extends roughly seventy miles from the natural spa town of **Thermopolis** in the east, through arid grasslands and desiccated uranium-rich badlands, to **Dubois** in the west, with the rich fishing grounds of the cottonwood-lined Wind River at its heart.

Near **Fort Washakie** – named for the centenarian Chief Washakie, who held the Shoshone together throughout the period of white expansion – is the likely grave of **Sacagawea**, the guide of Lewis and Clark's expedition. **Powwows** – gatherings of both spiritual and social significance to Native Americans – are held mainly in summer, and are open to the public. Contact the Shoshone Tribal Cultural Center in Fort Washakie (Mon–Fri 9am–4pm; ⓣ307/332-9106) or check ⓦwww.easternshoshone.net for details.

The friendly one-horse town of **LANDER** on US-287 makes an appealing base, with a string of cheap **motels** along Main Street and a couple of rural cabins with lovely views at the *Outlaw B&B*, a working ranch a few miles out of town at 2415 Squaw Creek Rd (ⓣ307/332-9655; ⓦwww.outlawcabins.com; ❹). The *Gannett Grill*, 126 Main St (ⓣ307/332-8228), serves deliciously fresh half-pound burgers (including buffalo burgers), interesting salads, craft beers and New York-style pizza.

Dubois

The former logging town of **DUBOIS** ("dew-BOYS"), squeezed into the northern tip of the Wind River valley and an oasis among the badlands, turned to tourism after its final sawmill closed in 1987; it doesn't hurt that it's located sixty miles southeast of Grand Teton National Park via dramatic **Togwotee Pass**. Home to the biggest herd of bighorn sheep in the lower 48 states, Dubois celebrates that fact with the impressive **National Bighorn Sheep Interpretative Center**, a half-mile northwest of town on US-26/287 (summer Mon–Sat 9am–7pm, Sun 9am–5pm, rest of year Mon–Sat same hours, closed for part of winter; $2.50; ⓦwww.bighorn.org). Along with running 4WD sheep-spotting tours ($25, reservations required), the centre provides self-guided tours and has exhibits on the majestic mascot of the Rockies.

Dubois has lots of clean and affordable **lodging**, including the historic *Twin Pines Lodge*, 218 Ramshorn St (ⓣ1-800/550-6332, ⓦwww.twinpineslodge.com; ❸), which holds some rustic cabins, and the immaculate, peaceful *Trail's End*, 511 W Ramshorn St, with a riverside deck (ⓣ307/455-2540, ⓦwww.trailsendmotel.com; ❸). The *Cowboy Café*, 115 E Ramshorn St (ⓣ307/455-2595), is great for a country breakfast or a fresh, juicy **burger**; after dark you can enjoy country crooners in classic Western **bars** like the venerable *Rustic Pine Tavern*, 119 E Ramshorn St (ⓣ307/455-2430), where the menu includes pork ribs and ribeye chili.

Pinedale

On the west side of the Wind River Range, a lovely 77-mile drive from Jackson on US-189/191 along the Hoback River, tiny well-to-do **PINEDALE** offers excellent access to outdoor pursuits. Once a major logging centre, it now attracts second home-owners and hikers. The **Museum of the Mountain Man**, 700 E Hennick Rd (May–Sept daily 9am–5pm, Oct Mon–Fri till 4pm; $5; ⓦwww.museumofthemountainman.com), commemorates its role as a rendezvous for fur trappers in the 1830s, as well as the legacy of the Native American trappers.

A sixteen-mile road winds east from Pinedale past Fremont Lake to **Elkhart Park Trailhead**, from where horse-worn paths lead past beautiful **Seneca Lake** and up rugged Indian Pass to glaciers and 13,000ft peaks; the Pinedale Ranger Station office at 29 E Fremont Lake Rd (ⓣ307/367-4326; ⓦwww.pinedaleonline.com/TrailInfo.HTM) has maps to help you plan a hiking route. More so even than in most areas of the Rockies, mosquito repellent is a necessity in the Wind River Range in summer.

The best place to **stay**, the cosy *Log Cabin Motel*, 49 E Magnolia St (ⓣ370/367-4579, ⓦwww.thelogcabinmotel.com; summer ❹, rest of year ❸), maintains several 1920s cabins, many with kitchens. When it comes to **dining**, the friendly *Wind River Brewery*, 402 Pine St (ⓣ307/367-2337) serves interesting beers, cooks up good, fresh Western burgers and hosts occasional live local music. *Café on Pine*, 27 E Pine (ⓣ370/367-3111), prepares lighter lunch salads and Italian dishes.

Northeast and north central Wyoming

There's more to Northern Wyoming than just a handy route between the Black Hills and Yellowstone: the surreal volcanic outcrop of **Devils Tower**, the massive **Bighorn Mountains** and the desertscape of the **Bighorn Basin** are notable natural attractions in a land steeped in the history of Native American wars, outlaw activity and pioneer hardships. The striking Bighorns soar abruptly from the plains to over 9000ft; the loftiest peaks, protruding well above the timber line, seem bald beside their dark-coated neighbours. Small **Cody**, eighty miles east of the heart of Yellowstone, is well worth a stopover for its Western-themed museums.

Devils Tower National Monument

Though Congress designated **DEVILS TOWER**, in far northeastern Wyoming, as the country's first national monument in 1906, it took Steven Spielberg's inspired use of it as the alien landing spot in *Close Encounters of the Third Kind* to make this eerie 1267ft volcanic outcrop a true national icon. Plonked on top of a thickly forested hill above the peaceful Belle Fourche River, it resembles a giant wizened tree stump; however, it can be hauntingly beautiful when painted ever-changing hues by the sun and moon.

Four short trails loop the tower, beginning from the **visitor centre** (early April to late Nov, hours vary; ⓣ307/467-5283, ⓦwww.nps.gov/deto) at its base, three miles from the main gate. The **entrance fee** is $10 per car (good for one week), and until late October you can **camp** for $12 per night – arrive early or you'll end up paying more than twice that at one of the nearby commercial campgrounds.

Buffalo

Snuggled among the southeastern foothills of the Bighorn Mountains, easy-going **BUFFALO** remains largely unaffected by the bustle of the nearby I-90/I-25 junction; winters here are mild compared to other areas of Wyoming, thus prompting locals to refer to the town as the state's "banana belt". Although Main Street, now lined with frontier-style stores, used to be an old buffalo trail, the place was actually named after Buffalo, New York. The **Jim Gatchell Museum**, 100 Fort St (June–Aug Mon–Sat 9am–6pm, Sun noon–6pm; Sept Mon–Fri 9am–5pm; May & Oct Mon–Fri till 4pm; $5; Ⓦwww.jimgatchell.com), houses a fine collection of Old West curiosities pertaining to soldiers, ranchers and Native Americans.

Pick up information from the **visitor centre**, 55 N Main St (Mon–Fri 9am–5pm; Ⓣ307/684-5544, Ⓦwww.buffalowyo.com). At the wonderfully restored historic *Occidental Hotel*, an old Western bordello at 10 N Main St (Ⓣ370/684-0451, Ⓦwww.occidentalwyoming.com; summer ❸–❼, rest of year ❷–❻), you can **stay** in the Owen Wister Suite, where the writer wrote a chunk of *The Virginian*. The sumptuous lobby is a sight in itself, and many rooms feature vintage radios tuned to old-time music on the hotel's own micro-frequency. There's also bluegrass music in the bar on some nights.

The Bighorn Mountains and Bighorn Basin

Of the three scenic highways that wind through the **Bighorn Mountains**, US-14A from **Burgess Junction**, fifty miles west of **Sheridan**, is the most spectacular. The road, typically closed November to May due to snow, edges its way up **Medicine Mountain**, on whose windswept western peak the mysterious **Medicine Wheel** – the largest such monument still intact – stands protected behind a wire fence. Local Native American legends offer no clues as to the original purpose of these flat stones, arranged in a circular "wheel" shape with 28 spokes and a circumference of 245ft – though the pattern suggests sun worship or early astronomy. For more information, drop into the **Burgess Junction Visitor Center** (late May to mid-Sept 9am–5.30pm; Ⓣ307/548-6541), half a mile east of Burgess Junction on US-14.

The route down the highway's west side, with gradients of ten to twenty percent, is said to have cost more to build per mile than any other road in America. Tight hairpin bends will keep drivers' eyes off the magnificent overlooks down into the **Bighorn Basin**, a sparsely vegetated valley walled in by mighty mountains on three sides and ragged foothills to the north. North of here up Hwy-37 is **Bighorn Canyon National Recreation Area** and its Yellowtail Reservoir, a favourite of watersports enthusiasts.

Cody

CODY, the "rodeo capital of the world", located along US-14 and the North Fork of the Shoshone River, was the brainchild of investors who, in 1896, persuaded "Buffalo Bill" Cody to become involved in their development company, knowing his approval would attract homesteaders and visitors alike. During summer, tourism is huge business here, but underneath all the Buffalo Bill-connected attractions and paraphernalia, Cody manages to retain the feel of a rural Western settlement.

By far the biggest year-round attraction in town is the superb **Buffalo Bill Historical Center** at 720 Sheridan Ave (March to mid-April & Nov daily 10am–5pm; second half of April and mid-Sept to Oct daily 8am–5pm; May to mid-Sept daily till 6pm; Dec–Feb Thurs–Sun 10am–5pm; $15; Ⓣ307/587-4771, Ⓦwww.bbhc.org). Home to the nation's most comprehensive collection of Western Americana, and never afraid to shatter prevailing myths about the West

Buffalo Bill

The much-mythologized exploits of **William Frederick "Buffalo Bill" Cody**, born in Iowa in 1846, began at the age of just eleven, when the murder of his father forced him to take a job on a wagon train. An early escape from ambush brought Cody fame as the "Youngest Indian Slayer of the Plains"; four years later, he became the youngest rider on the **Pony Express**, averaging a blazing 15mph on his leg of the legendary mail route. After a stint fighting for the Union in the Civil War, Cody found work – and a lifelong nickname – supplying buffalo meat to workers laying the transcontinental railroad. He claimed to have killed over 4200 animals in just eighteen months, before rejoining the army in 1868 as its chief scout.

By the 1870s, exaggerated accounts of Cody's adventures were appearing back east in the "dime novels" of Ned Buntline, and with the Indian Wars all but over he took to guiding Yankee and European gentry on buffalo hunts; the theatrical productions he laid on for his rich guests developed into his world-famous **Wild West Show**. First staged in 1883, these spectacular outdoor carnivals usually consisted of a re-enactment of an Indian battle such as Custer's Last Stand (featuring Sioux who had been present at Little Bighorn), trick riders, buffalo, clowns and exhibition shooting and riding by the man himself. A tremendous logistical operation, the show spent ten of its thirty years in Europe. Dressed in the finest silks and sporting a well-groomed goatee, Cody stayed in the grandest hotels and dined with heads of state; Queen Victoria was so enthusiastic in her admiration that rumours circulated of an affair between them.

Later in life, a mellower Cody played down his past activities, to the point of urging the government to respect all Native American treaties and put an end to the wanton slaughter of buffalo and game. Although the Wild West Show was reckoned to have brought in as much as one million dollars per year, many of his investments failed badly, and, in January 1915, a penniless 69-year-old Buffalo Bill died at his sister's home in Denver. His grave can be found atop Lookout Mountain, outside Golden, Colorado (see p.687).

and its peoples, the centre comprises five distinct museums, all of which are accessed via a common entrance hall. At the **Buffalo Bill Museum**, artefacts trace William Cody's life through his years involved with the Pony Express, Civil War, Indian Wars and his own Wild West shows. The lives of western Native Americans are celebrated in the **Plains Indian Museum**, where many of the ceremonial garments – adorned with everything from cowrie shells from the Pacific to glass beads from Venice – remain in stunning condition. In the **Whitney Gallery of Western Art**, plenty of stimulating new works serve as counterpoints to the more traditional canvases of Frederic Remington and Charles M. Russell. The largest known collection of American-made firearms in the world is housed in the **Cody Firearms Museum**, while the **Draper Museum of Natural History** is lined with interactive exhibits and beautiful taxidermy displays, all of which highlight the geology, wildlife and human history of the Greater Yellowstone region.

Cody's wide main thoroughfare, **Sheridan Avenue**, holds souvenir and ranchwear shops and hosts parades during early July's annual **Cody Stampede Rodeo** (Ⓣ307/587-5155, Ⓦwww.codystampederodeo.com). In summer, the **Cody Nite Rodeo** takes place nightly at the open-air arena on the western edge of town (June–Aug daily 8pm; $18; same contact info); there's a $5 shuttle bus from town.

Just east of the rodeo grounds off US-14, the late-nineteenth-century buildings gathered at **Old Trail Town** (mid-May to mid-Sept, 8am–8pm; $8; Ⓦwww.museumoftheoldwest.org), include cabins and saloons frequented by Butch Cassidy and the Sundance Kid.

Practicalities

Cody's **visitor centre** is at 836 Sheridan Ave (late May to Sept Mon–Fri 8am–6pm, Sat 9am–5pm, Sun 10am–3pm; Oct to late May Mon–Fri 8am–5pm; ⓣ307/587-2777, ⓦwww.codychamber.org). Wyoming River Trips offer **whitewater rafting** and **kayak** trips on the Shoshone ($27–67; ⓣ307/587-6661 or 1-800/586-6661, ⓦwww.wyomingrivertrips.com).

The showpiece *Irma* **hotel**, 1192 Sheridan Ave (ⓣ307/587-4221 or 1-800/745-4762, ⓦwww.irmahotel.com; ❺), was named for Buffalo Bill's daughter in 1902, and retains a superb original cherrywood bar (a gift to Buffalo Bill from Queen Victoria) in its namesake downstairs restaurant. With almost all the local **motels** charging over $100 per night in summer, the clean and comfortable *Buffalo Bill's Antlers Inn*, 1213 17th St (ⓣ1-800/388-2084, ⓦwww.antlersinncody.com; ❹) stands out as good value. Sheridan Avenue holds abundant **eating** and **drinking** options; after a stout meal at the *Irma Hotel* (see above), call in for a drink at the *Proud Cut Saloon* (ⓣ307/527-6905) at no. 1227.

Yellowstone National Park

Millions of visitors arrive yearly at **YELLOWSTONE NATIONAL PARK**, America's oldest national park, to glory in its magnificent mountain scenery and abundant wildlife, and to witness hydrothermal phenomena on a grand scale. Measuring roughly sixty by fifty miles, and overlapping slightly from Wyoming's northwestern corner into Idaho and Montana, the park centres on a 7500ft-high plateau, the caldera of a vast volcanic eruption that occurred a mere 600,000 years ago. Into it are crammed more than half the world's **geysers**, plus thousands of **fumaroles** jetting plumes of steam, **mud pots** gurgling with acid-dissolved muds and clays, and of course, **hot springs**. All this activity is on such a scale that the entire region is often characterized as a **supervolcano**, a full-force eruption of which might be capable of destroying the human species.

A visit to Yellowstone offers an extraordinary experience, combining the **colours** of the Grand Canyon of the Yellowstone, massive and deep-azure Yellowstone Lake, wildflower-filled meadows and rainbow-hued geyser pools; the **sounds** of subterranean rumblings, belching mud pools and steam hissing from the mountainsides; the constant **smells** of drifting sulphurous fumes; and, in the closest US equivalent to a safari park, the **sights** of shambling bears, heavy-bearded bison, herds of elk and more than a dozen elusive wolf packs on the prowl. The key to appreciating the park is to take your time, plan carefully and – particularly if you visit in summer – exercise patience with the inevitable crowds and traffic. While you can explore a representative proportion in a day-trip, allow for a stay of at least three days to see the park fully.

Arrival and information

Two of the five main **entrances** to Yellowstone are in Wyoming, via **Cody** to the east and **Grand Teton National Park** to the south. The others are in Montana: **West Yellowstone** (west), **Gardiner** (north) and **Cooke City** (northeast). Due to winter snow, most roads are open from early May to October only (see p.720). **Admission** ($25/car, good for one week) includes entry to adjacent Grand Teton National Park (p.724).

The free park newspaper *Yellowstone Today*, handed out at entrance stations, details activities and current regulations. **Albright Visitor Center** at **Mammoth**

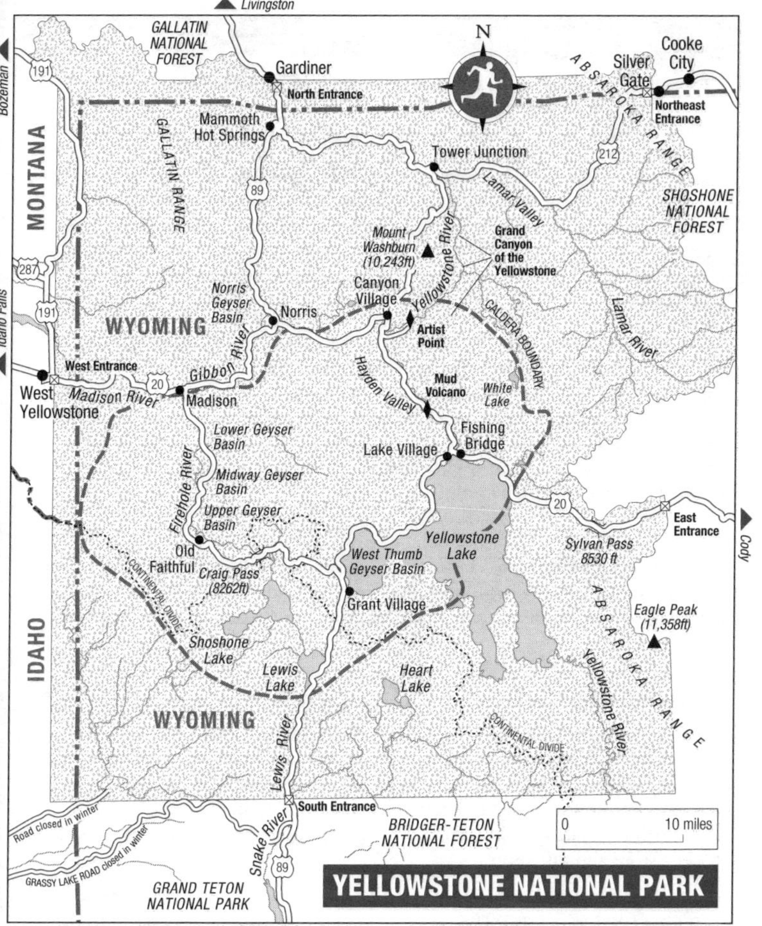

is the sole year-round information centre, near the north entrance (daily late May to Sept 8am–7pm, Oct to late May 9am–5pm; ⓣ307/344-2263, ⓦwww.nps.gov/yell). Other, summer-only **visitor centres** along the main **Loop Road** include the Canyon Visitor Education Center (daily May 9am–5pm, June–Sept 8am–8pm; ⓣ307/344-2550) in the east, and the new Old Faithful Visitor Education Center (daily mid-April to late May 9am–6pm, late May to Sept 8am–7pm; ⓣ307/344-2750). Each hosts an exhibit on a different aspect of the park, and issues backcountry hiking permits.

Although a **car** is virtually essential to explore Yellowstone, Karst Stage (ⓣ406/556-3500 or 1-800/845-2778, ⓦwww.karststage.com) operates expensive shuttle **buses** to West Yellowstone and Mammoth from the Bozeman, Montana airport. Companies that offer **park tours**, at over $100 for a full day, include Xanterra (ⓣ1-866/439-7375, ⓦwww.travelyellowstone.com), West Yellowstone's Buffalo Bus Tours (ⓣ1-800/426-7669, ⓦwww.yellowstonevacations.com) and Jackson's Gray Line (ⓣ307/733-4325, ⓦwww.graylinejh.com).

Winter in Yellowstone

Blanketed in several feet of snow between November and April, Yellowstone takes on a new appearance in **winter**: a silent and bizarre world where waterfalls freeze in mid-plunge, geysers blast towering plumes of steam and water into the crisp air and bison – beards matted with ice – stand in huddles. It's undeniably cold, and transport can require some hefty pre-planning, but crowds are nonexistent and wildlife-spotting opportunities are superb. Only the fifty-mile road from Gardiner to Cooke City via Mammoth Hot Springs is kept open (although beyond that, the Beartooth Highway is closed). The park's sole winter lodging is available at *Mammoth Hot Springs Hotel* or *Old Faithful Snow Lodge & Cabins* (both accessible only by snowcoach and snowmobile, and closed for Nov and much of Dec).

Xanterra (Ⓣ1-866/439-7375, Ⓦwww.travelyellowstone.com) operates **snowcoach** trips and tours of the park over the closed roads from West Yellowstone, Flagg Ranch to the south, Old Faithful and Mammoth Hot Springs ($55–70). **Snowmobile** rental, generally cheapest in West Yellowstone, costs around $150 a day; only a limited number of snowmobiles are allowed in the park at any one time, so reserve ahead. Much less expensive is **cross-country skiing** and **snowshoeing**, with groomed or blazed trails throughout the park.

The invaluable, nonprofit Yellowstone Association (Ⓣ406/848-2400, Ⓦwww.yellowstoneassociation.org), founded in 1933, organizes excellent **courses** that range from wolf watching and backcountry excursions to science-and-nature writing.

Accommodation in the park

All indoor **lodging** within Yellowstone is run by Xanterra (Ⓣ1-866/439-7375, Ⓦwww.travelyellowstone.com). Unless otherwise indicated, all the properties listed below are open in summer only. **Reservations**, always strongly recommended, are essential over holiday weekends. Every major location has a lodge offering dining facilities (most close by 9.30pm), and sometimes a laundromat, grocery store and gift shop.

Canyon Lodge & Cabins Plain hotel rooms and simple frame cabins, all en suite and located half a mile from Grand Canyon of the Yellowstone. Cabins ❸, rooms ❼

Grant Village Spartan en-suite motel rooms on the southwest shore of Yellowstone Lake – the southernmost indoor lodging in the park. ❻

Lake Lodge Cabins Nearly two hundred en-suite cabins, at Lake Village on the park's east side. The cheapest with one double bed; others have two doubles and can accommodate four people. ❸–❼

Lake Yellowstone Hotel & Cabins Alarmingly yellow, this Grand Colonial-style hotel features ordinary rooms and dark, dingy en-suite cabins. Its *Sun Room*, overlooking the lake, is a terrific spot for an evening drink. ❻

Mammoth Hot Springs Hotel & Cabins Circa 1930s lodging at the north end of the park, offering a range of cabins and hotel rooms. Open mid-April to mid-Oct & Xmas to early March. Cabins ❹, rooms ❻

Old Faithful Inn & Lodge Cabins One of the most beautiful lodges around, this magnificent 1904 inn – said to be the world's largest log building – has a wide range of rooms, in addition to budget and en-suite cabins. You can watch Old Faithful erupt from the terrace bar. Cabins ❸, rooms ❺

Old Faithful Snow Lodge & Cabins This comparatively new lodge holds modern rooms, alongside attractive slightly older cabins that are well sealed against the cold. Open May to late Oct & Xmas to early March. Cabins ❹, rooms ❼

Roosevelt Lodge Cabins Over eighty cabins a short drive from the Lamar Valley, from sparsely furnished to motel-like. ❸–❺

Accommodation in gateway towns

In addition to **Jackson** (see p.727) and **Cody** (p.716) in Wyoming, the small towns just outside the park's western and two northern gates offer somewhat cheaper lodging. **West Yellowstone**, the largest town, is somewhat disfigured by gift stores and fast-food joints but manages to retain a certain charm, and its surrounding national forest lands are well worth exploring. Friendly **Gardiner** lies just five miles from Mammoth Hot Springs. Less developed, the one-street town of **Cooke City** is three miles from the isolated northeast entrance on US-212, which stops just east of town in winter.

Elk Horn Lodge 103 Main St, Cooke City ⓣ406/838-2332, ⓦwww.elkhornlodgemt.com. Two cabins and six motel rooms, all with full bath, TV, mini-fridges, microwaves and coffeemakers. Cabins ❹, rooms ❺

Headwaters of the Yellowstone Bed & Breakfast Hwy-89, Gardiner ⓣ406/848-7073 or 1-888/848-7220, ⓦwww.headwatersbandb.com. A fantastic B&B on the banks of the Yellowstone River, less than four miles north of Gardiner. All five guest rooms have their own private bathroom, while the two cabins – one sleeping up to four, the other up to six – enjoy amazing views. ❻

Madison Hotel 139 Yellowstone Ave, West Yellowstone ⓣ406/646-7745 or 1-800/838-7745, ⓦwww.madisonhotelmotel.com. This historic 1912 hotel includes an adjacent motel (with cabin-themed rooms) and one of the few hostels in the region; the attractive, log-hewn main building includes single-sex dorm rooms ($30/person) that sleep up to four. Open late May to early Oct. Hotel ❷, motel ❺

Three Bear Lodge 217 Yellowstone Ave, West Yellowstone ⓣ406/646-7353 or 1-800/646-7353, ⓦwww.three-bear-lodge.com. Large motel housing 75 sizeable rooms and two-bedroom family units that sleep six. On-site amenities include a friendly diner, and snowmobile packages are usually available. ❻

Yellowstone Village Inn 1102 Scott St, Gardiner ⓣ1-800/228-8158, ⓦwww.yellowstonevinn.com. On the edge of town, this high-end motel has 43 tidy rooms, most themed around wildlife or Western Americana, including a John Wayne room. Substantially lower rates off-season. ❺

Camping

Of Yellowstone's twelve **campgrounds**, Xanterra operates five – *Bridge Bay*, *Canyon*, *Grant Village*, *Madison* and *Fishing Bridge* (RVs only), all of which can be reserved in advance (ⓣ1-866/439-7375, ⓦwww.travelyellowstone.com) – while the park service runs the other seven on a first-come, first-served basis; arrive early in the day to get a site during summer months, as most are full by 11am. **Fees** for tent camping range $14–28 per night. Only *Mammoth* campground is open year-round; the rest open any time from early May until late June and start closing in mid-September. All have toilet facilities, but few have showers.

To camp in the **backcountry**, you'll need a permit – free from visitor centres, information stations and ranger stations; these can be collected no earlier than 48 hours in advance of your camping trip. You can also camp at commercial grounds in the gateway towns, and in neighbouring national forests Gallatin (ⓣ406/587-6701) to the northwest and Shoshone (ⓣ307/527-6241) to the east.

Touring the park

The majority of Yellowstone's top sights are signposted within a few hundred yards of the 142-mile **Loop Road**, a figure-of-eight circuit fed by roads from the park's five entrances. Although the **speed limit** is a radar-enforced 45mph – important, given the number of bison and other oversize mammals that regularly cross the roads – journey times are very difficult to predict, and you'd do well to average even 30mph. **Wildlife traffic jams**, usually caused by stubborn herds of bison parking themselves on the pavement, are not unusual and should be expected; also for this reason, it's advisable to avoid night driving in Yellowstone.

To get the most out of a visit, even if you're short of time, choose one or two areas of the park to explore. Only in the early morning is **cycling** bearable or safe; there are only a few mountain-bike trails, and all are accessible to hikers and horses as well. Of course, no trip to Yellowstone is complete without at least one **hike**, be it to a waterfall or geyser; each visitor centre has free day-hiking handouts for their areas.

The following account runs clockwise around the Loop Road, from Old Faithful to the Yellowstone Lake area.

Geyser country: from Old Faithful to Mammoth Hot Springs

For well over a century, the dependable **Old Faithful** has erupted more frequently than any of its higher or larger rivals, making it the most popular geyser in the park. As a result, a half-moon of concentric benches, backed by a host of visitor facilities, now surround it at a respectful distance on the side away from the Firehole River. On average, it "performs" for expectant crowds every 78 minutes; approximate schedules are displayed nearby. The first sign of activity is a soft hissing as water splashes repeatedly over the rim; after several minutes, a column of water shoots to a height of 100 to 180ft as the geyser spurts out a total of eleven thousand gallons. As soon as it stops, everyone leaves, and you'll suddenly have the place to yourself.

Two miles of boardwalks lead from Old Faithful to dozens of other geysers in the Upper Basin. If possible, try to arrive when **Grand Geyser** is due to explode. This colossus blows its top on average just twice daily, for twelve to twenty minutes, in a series of four powerful bursts that can reach 200ft. Other highlights along the banks of the Firehole River, usually lined with browsing bison, include the fluorescent intensity of the **Grand Prismatic Spring** at **Midway Geyser Basin**, particularly breathtaking in early evening when human figures and bison herds are silhouetted against plumes of mineral spray.

Thirty miles north of Old Faithful in the less crowded **Norris Geyser Basin**, two separate trails explore a pallid landscape of whistling vents and fumaroles. **Steamboat** is the world's tallest geyser, capable of forcing near-boiling water over 300ft into the air; full eruptions are entirely unpredictable. The **Echinus Geyser** is the largest acid-water geyser known; every 35 to 75 minutes it spews crowd-pleasing, vinegary eruptions of forty to sixty feet.

At **Mammoth Hot Springs**, at the northern tip of the Loop Road, terraces of barnacle-like deposits cascade down a vapour-shrouded mountainside. Tinted a marvellous array of greys, greens, yellows, browns and oranges by algae, they are composed of travertine, a form of limestone which, having been dissolved and carried to the surface by boiling water, is deposited as tier upon tier of steaming stone.

Tower and the Lamar Valley

The main landmark of Yellowstone's **Tower** and **Roosevelt** areas, east of Mammoth Hot Springs, is the high peak of **Mount Washburn**; its lookout tower can be reached by an enjoyable hike (five or six miles round-trip, depending on which trailhead you use) or a gruelling cycle ride. For an easier hike, take the trail that leads down to the spray-drenched base of **Tower Fall**. From Tower Junction, the Northeast Entrance highway wanders east through the meadows of serene **Lamar Valley** – often called "North America's Serengeti" for its **abundant wildlife**, where life-and-death struggles between predators (grizzlies, wolves, mountain lions) and prey (elk, bison, pronghorn, mule deer) play out daily. Beyond Lamar Valley tower the classic, icy peaks of the **Absaroka** (pronounced "ab-SORE-kuh") **Mountains**.

The Grand Canyon of the Yellowstone

The Yellowstone River roars and tumbles for twenty miles between the sheer golden-hued cliffs of the **Grand Canyon of the Yellowstone**, its course punctuated by two powerful **waterfalls**: 109ft **Upper Falls** and its downstream counterpart, thunderous 308ft **Lower Falls**. On the south rim, **Artist Point** looks down hundreds of feet to the river canyon, where frothing water swirls between mineral-stained walls. Nearby, **Uncle Tom's Trail** descends steeply to a spray-covered platform in the canyon, gently vibrating in the face of the pounding Lower Falls. A few miles south, the river widens to meander through tranquil **Hayden Valley**, one of the finest spots in Yellowstone to view wildlife from the road.

Yellowstone Lake

North America's largest alpine lake, deep and deceptively calm **Yellowstone Lake** fills a sizeable chunk of the eastern half of the Yellowstone caldera. At 7733ft above sea level, it's high enough to be frozen half the year, and its waters remain perilously cold through summer. Rowboats ($10/hour), along with larger motorboats and powerboats, can be rented from the Bridge Bay Marina (May–Sept; ⓣ307/242-3876) near Lake Village.

At **West Thumb Geyser Basin**, where hot pools empty into the lake's tranquil waters and fizz away into nothing, it's easy to see why early tourists would have made use of the so-called **Fishing Cone** by cooking freshly caught fish in its boiling waters. To the south, the highway leads towards Grand Teton past **Lewis Lake**, the third largest lake in the park, with **Shoshone Lake** and **Heart Lake** hidden in the backcountry to the west and east respectively; both lakes are well worth a hike.

A brief human history of Yellowstone

Although Native Americans had long hunted in what is now **Yellowstone National Park**, they were present only in limited numbers by the 1807 arrival of the first white man – **John Colter**, a veteran of the Lewis and Clark expedition (see also p.733). Colter's account of the exploding geysers and seething cauldrons of "Colter's Hell" (located east of Yellowstone, near Cody) was widely ridiculed at the time. However, as ever more trappers, scouts and prospectors told similar tales, three increasingly larger expeditions set out to chart the region each year beginning in 1869. In 1872, Yellowstone was set aside as the first **national park**, in part to ensure that its assets were not entirely stripped by hunters and miners, and also to appease railroad interests looking for a new destination to which they could shuttle visitors.

At first, management of the park was beset by problems, and Congress devoted enthusiasm, but little funding, toward its protection. Irresponsible tourists stuck soap down the geysers, damaging their intricate plumbing; bandits preyed on stage-coaches carrying rich excursionists; and, the Nez Percé even killed two tourists as they were chased through the park (see p.748). By 1886, Congress had taken the park out of civilian hands and put the army in charge.

When the army handed Yellowstone over to the newly created **National Park Service** in 1917, automobiles were already a prevalent presence. Conflict between tourism and wilderness preservation has raged ever since. Ecologists now warn that the park cannot stand alone as some pristine paradise; rather, it must be seen as part of a much larger "Greater Yellowstone Ecosystem" encompassing Yellowstone, the Tetons, the Snake River Valley (which stretches south of Jackson to just over the Idaho border) and the northern reaches of the Wind River Mountains. In 1995, amid vociferous complaints from local ranchers fearing a loss of livestock, **grey wolves** were reintroduced. From the original fourteen animals released, there are now around 150 wolves comprising some fifteen packs roaming the Greater Yellowstone area.

Eating in the park

There's little menu variation among Yellowstone's several **restaurants**, but those at *Old Faithful Inn*, *Old Faithful Snow Lodge* and *Lake Yellowstone Hotel* stand out for location, mood and ambience; entrees ($15–32) typically range from salmon and steak to pasta and Caesar salads. All are also open for **breakfast** – usually a buffet that includes fresh fruit, cereals, pastries and standard cooked items, for a little over $10 – and **lunch**. Reasonably priced **snack bars** and workaday **cafeterias** are **scattered** throughout the park as well, as are **soda fountains** inside several general stores, where burgers and fries along with ice cream and shakes are served to rows of customers on stools.

Eating in the gateway towns

While Yellowstone's gateway towns hold few culinary delights, they do offer cheaper prices and more variety. In **West Yellowstone**, *Running Bear Pancake House*, 538 Madison Ave (ⓣ406/646-7703), serves an enjoyable breakfast, while *Bullwinkles* at 19 Madison Ave (ⓣ406/646-7974) is tops for lunch and dinner, with huge salads and delicious pan-fried fish. **Gardiner**'s *Sawtooth Deli*, 220 Park St (ⓣ406/848-7600), serves breakfasts and BBQ, while the *Corral Drive-Inn*, 711 Scott St (ⓣ406/848-7627) makes a terrific burger. The impossible-to-miss *Beartooth Cafe* (ⓣ406/838-2475) is **Cooke City**'s best eatery throughout the day.

Grand Teton National Park and Jackson Hole

The classic triangular peaks of **GRAND TETON NATIONAL PARK**, stretching for fifty miles south from Yellowstone to Jackson, are more dramatic than the mountains of its superstar neighbour park to the north. These sheer-faced cliffs make a magnificent spectacle, rising abruptly to tower 7000ft above the valley floor. A string of gem-like lakes is set tight at the foot of the mountains; beyond them lies the broad, sagebrush-covered **Jackson Hole** river basin (a "hole" was a pioneer term for a flat, mountain-ringed valley), broken by the gently winding Snake River.

Though the Shoshone people knew the mountains as the *Teewinot* ("many pinnacles"), their present name, meaning "large breast", was bestowed by over-imaginative French-Canadian trappers in the 1830s. After Congress set the mountains aside as a national park in 1929, it took another 21 years of legal wrangling for Grand Teton to attain its current size – local ranchers protested that the economy of Jackson Hole would be ruined if further land was surrendered to tourism. During this time, John D. Rockefeller Jr bought up large parts of Jackson Hole and presented them to the government for conversion to parklands, on condition that his Grand Teton Lodge Company be the park's primary concessionaire, which it remains today.

Seeing the park

While no road crosses the Tetons, those that run along their eastern flank were designed with an eye to the mountains, affording stunning views at every bend. Two excellent side-trips are the **Jenny Lake Scenic Loop**, leading to a face-to-face encounter with towering, partly hunchbacked 13,770ft **Grand Teton**, and the narrow track up **Signal Mountain**, which offers a breathtaking panorama including the Tetons and Jackson Hole.

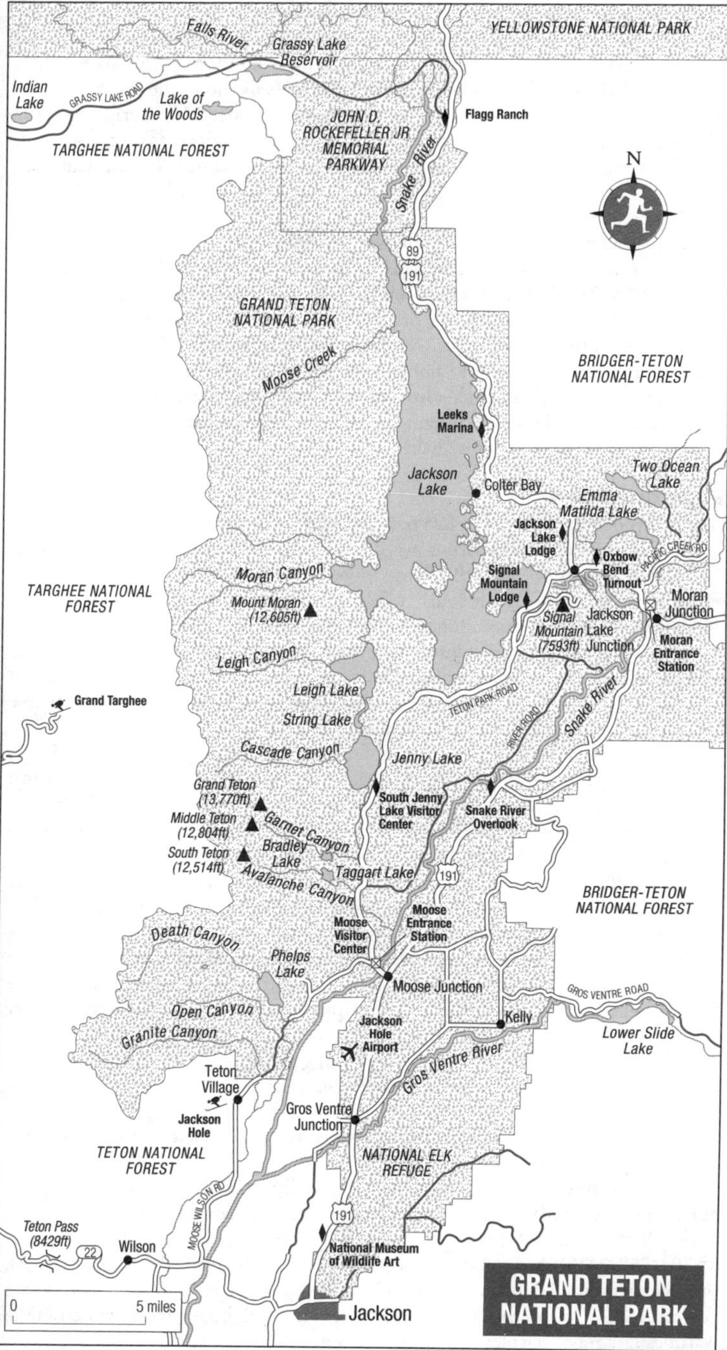

YELLOWSTONE NATIONAL PARK
Falls River
Grassy Lake Reservoir
Indian Lake
GRASSY LAKE ROAD
Lake of the Woods
JOHN D. ROCKEFELLER JR MEMORIAL PARKWAY
Flagg Ranch
TARGHEE NATIONAL FOREST
Snake River
N
89
191
GRAND TETON NATIONAL PARK
Moose Creek
BRIDGER-TETON NATIONAL FOREST
Leeks Marina
Jackson Lake
Colter Bay
Two Ocean Lake
Emma Matilda Lake
Jackson Lake Lodge
Oxbow Bend Turnout
PACIFIC CREEK RD
Moran Canyon
Signal Mountain Lodge
TARGHEE NATIONAL FOREST
Mount Moran (12,605ft)
Signal Mountain (7593ft)
Jackson Lake Junction
Moran Junction
Moran Entrance Station
Leigh Canyon
Leigh Lake
TETON PARK ROAD
Grand Targhee
String Lake
RIVER ROAD
Snake River
Cascade Canyon
Jenny Lake
Grand Teton (13,770ft)
South Jenny Lake Visitor Center
Snake River Overlook
Middle Teton (12,804ft)
Garnet Canyon
Bradley Lake
South Teton (12,514ft)
Avalanche Canyon
Taggart Lake
191
BRIDGER-TETON NATIONAL FOREST
Moose Entrance Station
Death Canyon
Moose Visitor Center
Phelps Lake
Moose Junction
GROS VENTRE ROAD
Open Canyon
Kelly
Jackson Hole Airport
Lower Slide Lake
Granite Canyon
Gros Ventre River
Teton Village
Jackson Hole
Gros Ventre Junction
TETON NATIONAL FOREST
NATIONAL ELK REFUGE
MOOSE WILSON RD
191
Teton Pass (8429ft)
22
Wilson
National Museum of Wildlife Art
0
5 miles
Jackson
GRAND TETON NATIONAL PARK

Hiking trails waste no time in getting to the highlights. One easy and popular walk follows the sandy beaches of **Leigh Lake**, where the imposing 12,605ft **Mount Moran** bursts out dramatically from the lake shores. Also accessible is cascading **Hidden Falls**, reachable by a two-mile walk along the south shore of Jenny Lake; an even easier option is to take the shuttle boat ($10 return) across the lake and walk the remaining eight hundred yards. A more adventurous, but suitably rewarding amble heads up the macabrely named **Death Canyon**, reaching a verdant plateau after four miles on a well-graded trail adjacent to crashing creek waters.

Cycling the flat roads of the Hole is a joy; bikes can be rented at Adventure Sports within the Dornan's complex in Moose Junction ($12/hour, $36/day; ⓣ307/733-3307, ⓦwww.dornans.com). To admire the Tetons from **water**, take a float trip along the Snake River or rent a **canoe** or **kayak** from the marinas at Jenny Lake, Colter Bay or *Signal Mountain Lodge*. In winter, all hiking trails are open to **cross-country skiers**, and **snowmobiles** can be rented in Jackson. The Tetons also offer excellent **rock-climbing** opportunities; Exum Mountain Guides (ⓣ307/733-2297, ⓦwww.exumguides.com) runs classes and guided trips from a summer office steps from Jenny Lake.

Practicalities

Grand Teton's **entrance fee** of $25 per car (good for one week) also covers Yellowstone. The main **visitor centre** is just off the main road in **Moose** (daily: May & Oct 8am–5pm, June–Sept till 7pm, Nov–April 9am–5pm; ⓣ307/739-3399, ⓦwww.nps.gov/grte), in the south; others include **Jenny Lake** (daily: second half of May & all Sept 8am–5pm, June–Aug till 7pm; ⓣ307/739-3392) near the park's centre, **Flagg Ranch** (daily June–Aug 9am–3.30pm; ⓣ307/543-2327) at the park's northern end and **Colter Bay** (daily: May & Sept 8am–5pm, June–Aug till 7pm; ⓣ307/739-3594) halfway up the east shore of Jackson Lake, where the free **Indian Arts Museum** has an extensive collection of native craftwork.

Most **rooms** and **activities** within the park are managed by Grand Teton Lodge Company (ⓣ307/543-2811 or 1-800/628-9988, ⓦwww.gtlc.com); reservations are absolutely essential in summer. Prices for the comfortable rooms and cottages at *Jackson Lake Lodge* (❽) depend on whether or not you want a mountain view. *Colter Bay Village Cabins* (❸) are more utilitarian; in high summer, $50 "tent cabins" – canvas cabins with bunk beds (bed linen available for hire), wood-burning stove and outdoor BBQ grill – are also available. The independently run *Signal Mountain Lodge*, in a great location beside Jackson Lake (ⓣ307/543-2831, ⓦwww.signalmountainlodge.com; ❻–❼) has a wide range of lodging, from somewhat bland motel-style units to much nicer rustic one- or two-room log cabins. All five park **campgrounds** are only open in summer (dates vary between mid-May and mid-Oct) and operate on a first-come, first-served basis ($17–19/site). Individual campgrounds tend to fill in July and August in roughly the following order: *Jenny Lake* (49 tents; no RVs), *Signal Mountain* (86 pitches), *Colter Bay* (350 pitches), *Lizard Creek* (60 pitches) and *Gros Ventre* (355 pitches). For **backcountry camping**, you'll need a permit, available free from park visitor centres.

The park **restaurants and snack bars**, especially at *Jackson Lake Lodge*, are good but a little pricey; *Signal Mountain Lodge* offers well-priced lake-view dining in *The Peaks*. Within the Dornan's complex in Moose, the *Pizza Pasta Company* (ⓣ307/733-2415) serves good pizzas, salads and sandwiches. Be sure to earmark time for an evening **drink** at the *Blue Heron Lounge* inside *Jackson Lake Lodge*, where you can recline in comfortable chairs and ogle through huge picture windows the warm blues, greys, purples and pinks of a Teton sunset.

Jackson

More Mild West than Wild West thanks to an overflow of art galleries and high-end lodging, **JACKSON** makes for an enjoyable base, tucked in at the end of **Jackson Hole**, five miles from Grand Teton National Park's southern boundary. Centred around a tree-shaded square marked by an arch of tangled elk antlers at each corner, the Old West-style boardwalks of **downtown** front boutiques, galleries, restaurants and bars. In winter, time is best spent visiting the 25,000-acre **National Elk Refuge** on the north edge of town, where you can take a horse-drawn sleigh ride among a 7000-strong herd of elk (daily early Dec to early April 10am–4pm; $18; ⓣ307/733-9212, ⓦwww.fws.gov/nationalelkrefuge); buy tickets at Jackson Hole's Visitor Center (see below), and you'll be taken by shuttle bus to the departure point. Across the highway from the elk refuge, the **National Museum of Wildlife Art** (daily 9am–5pm; $12; ⓦwww.wildlifeart.org) houses an impressive collection from all over the world.

While busiest in summer with road-tripping national park visitors, Jackson remains a year-round draw thanks to **Jackson Hole Mountain Resort** (lift tickets $91; ⓣ1-888/333-7669, ⓦwww.jacksonhole.com), a twenty-minute drive from downtown to **Teton Village** at its base, where the 2500 acres of terrain are among the finest in the US for confident intermediates and advanced skiers and boarders. Within town, **Snow King** ($45; ⓣ 1-800/522-5464, ⓦwww.snowking.com) is an affordable, family-friendly hill that's also lit for night skiing, while **Grand Targhee Resort** ($72; ⓣ 1-800/827-4433, ⓦwww.grandtarghee.com), an hour's drive away on the Wyoming/Idaho border, is renowned for fresh powder. Come summer, all three resorts offer limited lift-accessed mountain biking, along with outdoor activities including hiking and paragliding.

Arrival, information and activities

The excellent **Jackson Hole & Greater Yellowstone Visitor Center** is at 532 N Cache St (daily: late May to late September 8am–7pm, rest of year 9am–5pm; ⓣ307/733-3316, ⓦwww.jacksonholechamber.com). Jackson's **airport**, eight miles north in Grand Teton National Park, is linked to town by AllTrans **shuttle service** ($16 one-way to Jackson, $26 to Teton Village; ⓣ307/733-3135, ⓦwww.jacksonholealltrans.com), and $25–30 **taxis**.

START **buses** (daily 6.30am–10pm, ⓦwww.startbus.com), provide free **transport** within Jackson Hole, and charge $3 for trips to Teton Village. Guided **bike tours** with Teton Mountain Bike Tours (ⓣ1-800/733-0788, ⓦwww.tetonmtbike.com) start at $60 for half a day. Dozens of **rafting** companies, including Charlie Sands Wild Water (ⓣ307/733-4410, ⓦwww.sandswhitewater.com), offer float trips within Grand Teton and whitewater trips on the Snake River south of town; expect to pay about $55 for a half-day trip, including transportation and outerwear. You can even take a **dogsled** tour, costing from $180 for half a day, with Continental Divide Dogsled Adventures (ⓣ307/455-30522, ⓦwww.dogsledadventures.com).

Accommodation

Accommodation in Jackson is fairly expensive in summer; rates drop by around 25 percent in winter and are good value for a ski vacation. In Teton Village, on the other hand, the ski-in ski-out accommodation is at a premium come winter. Explore possibilities quickly using Jackson Hole Central Reservations (ⓣ307/733-4005, ⓦwww.jacksonholewy.com). If **camping** is your goal, you're best off staying at Grand Teton's enormous *Gros Ventre Campground* a few miles to the north (see opposite).

The Alpine House 285 N Glenwood St ⓣ307/739-1570, ⓦwww.alpinehouse.com. You won't receive better service at five-star resorts than you'll get at this cosy, 22-room B&B on a quiet street a few blocks from the town square. Breakfasts are equally extraordinary. ❼

Anvil Motel 215 N Cache St ⓣ307/733-3668, or 1-800/234-4507, ⓦwww.anvilmotel.com. Situated at one of Jackson's busier intersections, it's not the quietest spot, but the smallish rooms are in good shape. ❹

The Hostel 3315 Village Drive, Teton Village ⓣ307/733-3415, ⓦwww.thehostel.us. Excellent slopeside hostel featuring a lounge with fireplace, TV and games room, and laundry, as well as ping pong and pool tables. Dorm beds from $32, and private rooms, either with king bed or four twin beds, which sometimes requires a five-night minimum stay. Winter ❺, summer ❹

The Inn at Jackson Hole 3345 W Village Drive, Teton Village ⓣ307/733-2311 or 1-800/842-7666, ⓦwww.innatjh.com. 83 mid-size rooms, along with a few lofts. Amenities include heated outdoor pool and hot tub, laundry and a popular restaurant, *Masa Sushi*. Winter ❼, summer ❻

The Wort Hotel 50 N Glenwood St ⓣ307/733-2190 or 1-800/322-2727, ⓦwww.worthotel.com. Built in 1941, the *Wort* is the most venerable high-end property in town, combining old-world style with modern facilities that include two large hot tubs, a grill-bistro and the attractive *Silver Dollar Bar & Grill*. ❾

Eating and nightlife

The year-round tourist trade makes Jackson the best town in Wyoming for nightlife, with its ever-changing roster of **restaurants** and **bars**.

Jackson Hole Roasters Coffee House 145 E Broadway ⓣ307/690-9318. Popular morning rendezvous for fresh pastries and coffee, plus free wi-fi.

Mangy Moose Teton Village ⓣ307/733-4913, ⓦwww.mangymoose.net. Legendary ski-bum hangout, famed for its après-ski sessions that segue into evenings of live rock or reggae. The bustling upstairs dining room serves decent burgers, chicken and pasta. Cover charge for live music $5–25.

Nani's Cucina Italia 242 N Glenwood St ⓣ307/733-3888. Charming, if overpriced Italian restaurant serving up enormous platters of pasta. Red and white chequered tablecloths and a pleasant outdoor patio add to the ambience.

Rendezvous Bistro 380 S Broadway ⓣ307/739-1100. Moderately priced dinner-only bistro on the outskirts of town, where a clever menu of main courses includes chili-rubbed pork chops and crispy risotto cake, and there's an impressive wine list.

Shades Cafe 82 S King St ⓣ307/733-2015. Unpretentious and affordable spot, with excellent breakfasts early and light, and healthy lunches (soups, sandwiches, burritos) come afternoon. The lovely deck is a popular hangout on mild-weather days. Closed evenings.

Snake River Brewing Co 265 South Millward St ⓣ307/739-2337. Great locals' brewpub a few blocks southwest of the town square. Reasonably priced pastas and wood-fired pizzas are well worth trying, but it's the award-winning beers that pack 'em in.

Montana

MONTANA's wondrous Big Sky country, along the northernmost edge of the US portion of the Rocky Mountains, is a region of snowcapped summits, turbulent rivers, spectacular glacial valleys, heavily wooded forests and sparkling blue lakes. The scenery is at its most dramatic and heavily trafficked in the **western** side of the state, especially the phenomenal **Glacier National Park**. By contrast, the **eastern** two-thirds is dusty high prairie – sun-parched in summer and wracked by blizzards in winter – that attracts far fewer visitors. Grizzly bears, elk and bighorn sheep are found in greater numbers in Montana than just about anywhere else on the continent.

Each of Montana's small cities has its own proud identity. The enjoyable town of **Missoula** is a laidback college town, a glimmer of liberalism in this otherwise libertarian state; the historic copper-mining hamlet of **Butte** was once a barren union stronghold; the elegant state capital **Helena** harkens back to its prosperous gold-mining years; and **Bozeman**, just to the south, is one of the hippest mountain towns in the US, buzzing with out-of-towners in the peak months.

Wheat, lumber and mining form the contemporary base of Montana's economy. Tourism is the state's second biggest earner; however, apart from skiing, the harsh climate generally restricts many outdoor activities to the summer months.

Eastern Montana

Before ranchers and farmers settled the flat prairie of **eastern Montana**, it was prime **buffalo** territory: one early traveller waited three nights while a massive herd crossed his path. Native Americans fought hard to hold onto their land; the crushing defeats they inflicted on the US Army include the legendary victory at **Little Bighorn**. However, the ongoing spectre of white colonization was enforced with heartless martial rigour – the military nearly wiped out the buffalo by the 1870s, thus depleting the natives' major food source. The result ensured that by the end of the nineteenth century the native peoples would be marginalized, ultimately confined to reservations and without a voice (or often, a stake) in the lucrative mineral exploitation of the land.

The plains are intermittently broken by mountains, of which the most impressive are the icy **Beartooth Range**, crammed between the town of Red Lodge and Yellowstone National Park. Other than that and a few other exceptions, there's not too much to see. Most of the region's towns are sleepy agricultural centres, stopovers on the way to outlying historical or natural attractions. Even **Billings**, Montana's largest city, would feel like a small town anywhere else.

Little Bighorn Battlefield National Monument

By the middle of the 1870s, the bloody and exhausting **Indian Wars** had been going on for decades in the American West, fuelled by white colonists' desires for land and, increasingly, **gold**. Unfortunately for the native Lakota and Cheyenne, the valuable ore was discovered on their Black Hills land, and the predictable onrush occurred. With tensions mounting, in June 1876, massive army detachments were sent to southeastern Montana led by the crack **Seventh Cavalry** and, at its head, flamboyant **General George Custer** – who had first commanded the exploratory expedition that discovered the gold. This time, he then led the military to one of its most enduring defeats at **Little Bighorn** (see box, p.730).

Located on the current Crow Indian Reservation in the Little Bighorn Valley, the **monument** is 56 miles southeast of Billings, with the entrance one mile east of I-90 on US-212. You can trace the course of the battle on a five-mile, self-guided driving tour through the grasslands (daily 8am–6pm; $10/car, $5 for pedestrians and motorcycles; Ⓦwww.nps.gov/libi), below the high ridge overlooking the valley, or on a narrated bus tour (spring–autumn daily on the hour 10am–3pm except 1pm; $8, kids $2). White-marble tablets mark where individual soldiers fell, and a sandstone obelisk stands above their mass grave on "Last Stand Hill" (Custer himself was buried at the West Point Military Academy in New York). Dioramas in the **visitor centre** and **museum** (same hours as monument) outline the battle, while the US military **cemetery** nearby holds soldiers from all of America's wars.

Custer's Last Stand

During an erratic career, **George Armstrong Custer** was one of the central American military icons of the mid- to late nineteenth century. Though he graduated last in his class at West Point in 1861, he became the army's youngest-ever brigadier general, seeing action at Gettysburg and national fame through his presence at the ultimate Union victory at Appomattox, with his own troops blocking the Confederate retreat. However, he was also suspended for ordering the execution of deserters from a forced march he led through Kansas, and found notoriety for allowing the murder in 1868 of almost one hundred Cheyenne women and children. His most (in)famous moment, though, came on June 25, 1876, at the **Battle of the Little Bighorn**, known to native tribes as the **Battle of the Greasy Grass**.

Custer's was the first unit to arrive in the **Little Bighorn Valley**. Disdaining to await reinforcements, he set out to raze a village along the Little Bighorn River – which turned out to be the largest-ever gathering of Plains Indians. As a party of his men pursued fleeing women and children, they were encircled by two thousand Lakota and Cheyenne warriors emerging from either side of a ravine. The soldiers dismounted to attempt to shoot their way out, but were soon overwhelmed; simultaneously, Custer's command post on a nearby hill was wiped out. Although American myth up to the 1960s established Custer as an unquestioned hero, archeologists and historians have since discounted the idea of **Custer's Last Stand** as a heroic act of defiance in which Custer was the last cavalryman left standing; the battle lasted less than an hour, with the white soldiers being systematically and effortlessly picked off. This most decisive Native American victory in the West – led by Sitting Bull – was also their final great show of resistance. An incensed President Grant piled maximum resources into a military campaign that brought about the effective defeat of all Plains Indians by the end of the decade.

Hardin, thirteen miles northwest, makes its living from tourists seeking native artefacts and Western mementos. Each year, on the weekend closest to the battle's anniversary, the **Little Bighorn Days** festival centres on re-enactments of the battle at a site eight miles west of the town (*not* the original battlefield; Ⓦwww.custerslaststand.org). Other activities include tribal dancing, downtown parades, dinner dances and a rodeo.

A reasonable place to **stay** is the *American Inn,* 1324 N Crawford Ave (Ⓣ406/665-1870, Ⓦwww.hardinamericaninn.com; ❸), a motel with clean and simple rooms, and the *Kendrick House Inn*, 206 N Custer Ave (Ⓣ406/665-3035; ❺), is a worthwhile B&B offering five rooms rich with old-time antique decor.

Billings

By Montana standards, **BILLINGS** is a big city. It has a dramatic setting, bounded on its north and east sides by the 400ft crumpled sandstone cliffs of the **Rimrock**, and sports an attractive and lively row of galleries, bars and restaurants along Montana Avenue. The most prominent historical gem is the **Moss Mansion**, 914 Division St (June–Sept Mon–Sat 9am–4pm, Sun 1–3pm; Oct–May daily same hours; $7; Ⓦwww.mossmansion.com), a sturdy 1903 red-sandstone manse that appeals for its late-Victorian decor and glimpse at how comfortably an industrialist could live a century ago. Another striking structure, a former Romanesque Revival library at 2822 Montana Ave, now houses the **Western Heritage Center** (Tues–Sat 10am–5pm; $3; Ⓦwww.ywhc.org), where you can bone up on antique documents, relics and photographs. Also worth a stop, the **Yellowstone Art Museum**, 401 N 27th St (Tues–Sat 11am–6pm, Thurs & Fri till 8pm, Sun till 4pm; $5; Ⓦyellowstone.artmuseum.org), partly housed in the town's 1910 jail, specializes in Western books, paintings and posters by cowboy illustrator Will James, as well as the latest contemporary works from regional artists.A half-hour north of Billings on I-94, **Pompeys Pillar** (May to early Sept 8am–8pm, early Sept to early Oct 9am–4pm; $7; ⓣ406/875-2400) is something of a minor tourist draw: a giant sandstone monolith and national monument whose one claim to fame – other than its huge size – is that explorer William Clark added his graffiti to it some two centuries ago. Six miles south of Billings, **Pictograph Cave State Park**, 2300 Lake Elmo Drive (May–Sept daily dawn–dusk; free; ⓦwww.pictographcave.org), is an evocative sight that houses early native rock paintings that you can view on a short path around a hundred images of animals, warriors and plants that still decorate the rocks after more than 2,000 years.

Billings' **bus station** is at 2502 First Ave N. For **accommodation**, try the cheery *C'mon Inn*, 2020 Overland Ave S (ⓣ1-800/655-1170, ⓦwww.cmoninn.com; ❺), an agreeable spot whose rooms variously offer fireplaces, jacuzzis and fridges, plus continental breakfast; or the five cosy rooms and suites of the *Josephine B&B*, 514 N 29th St (ⓣ406/248-5898, ⓦwww.thejosephine.com; ❹), which has the added draw of free wi-fi and passes to a nearby gym. For **eating**, *Stella's Kitchen and Bakery*, 110 N 29th St (ⓣ406/248-3060), is a local favourite for its hearty breakfasts and pastries, while the *Chalet Market*, 327 24th St W (ⓣ406/656-6600), is a deli with good subs, croissant sandwiches and soups.

Red Lodge and the Beartooth Scenic Highway

The atmospheric town of **RED LODGE** is sixty miles south of Billings at the foot of the awe-inspiring **Beartooth Mountains** – whose jagged peaks and outcrops contain some of the oldest rocks on earth – and in winter acts as a base for skiers using the popular **Red Lodge Mountain**, six miles west on US-212 (lift tickets $47; ⓣ1-800/444-8977, ⓦwww.redlodgemountain.com). Originally founded to mine coal for the transcontinental railroads, Red Lodge's future was secured by the construction of the 65-mile **Beartooth Scenic Highway**, connecting to Cooke City at the northeastern entrance to Yellowstone National Park (see p.718), a striking series of tight switchbacks, steep grades and vertiginous overlooks. Even in summer the springy tundra turf of the 10,940ft **Beartooth Pass** is covered with snow that (due to algae) turns pink when crushed. All around are gem-like corries, deeply gouged granite walls and huge blocks of roadside ice. Contact the **Beartooth Ranger District** of Custer National Forest (office in Billings at 1310 Main St, ⓣ406/657-6200, ⓦwww.fs.fed.us/r1/custer), for more information on the rugged options for hiking and **camping** (most sites free or $9–14) in this chilly, wind-scoured terrain, and taking in the fine views of the Beartooth area and the abundant bighorn sheep, elk and bear.

Though Red Lodge has plenty of cheap motels south of town, the nicest **place to stay** is the lovely *Pollard Hotel*, 2 N Broadway (ⓣ406/446-0001 or 1-800/POLLARD, ⓦthepollard.com; ❹–❽), a historic 1893 brick building with some rooms offering jacuzzis and balconies, plus pool, sauna and a comfortable old library. Much cheaper, the *Yodeler Motel*, 601 S Broadway (ⓣ406/446-1435, ⓦwww.yodelermotel.com; ❸), offers a quirky alpine theme to go with its clean and basic motel rooms. Some of the best **food** in town is served in *Pollard*'s dining room, which offers fresh, local, expensive fare – leaning toward beef and fish – while on Broadway, *Bridge Creek Backcountry Kitchen*, no. 116 S (ⓣ406/446-9900), serves fine clam chowder alongside steak and burgers, and *Carbon County Steakhouse*, no. 121 S (ⓣ406/446-4025), has hearty pasta, ribs, steak and seafood as well as Rocky Mountain Oysters – bull's testicles, to the unaware.

Fort Peck Lake

Some two hundred miles north of Billings, lonely Hwy-2 is an isolated, both bleak and beautiful stretch that runs from Glacier National Park to North Dakota, peppered with remote villages, Indian Wars battlefields and striking vistas. The highlight is the irregular expanse of 130-mile-long **Fort Peck Lake**, with 1500 miles of shoreline, which the New Deal created in the 1930s by damming the Missouri River. The main draw is **fishing** for trout, bass and pike (licences $15, see ⓦfwp.mt.gov/fishing). In the adjacent million-acre **Charles M. Russell Wildlife Refuge** (ⓣ406/438-8706, ⓦwww.fws.gov/cmr) you can spot pronghorn antelope, elk, deer and bighorn sheep. Fossils – among them *T.rex* and *Triceratops* bones discovered around the site – are on view in the dam's **interpretive centre** (May–Sept daily 9am–5pm, Oct–April Mon–Fri 10am–4pm; free; ⓣ406/526-3493). On the lake's south side, about 25 miles north of Jordan, off Hwy-200, **Hell Creek State Park** ($5 day-use fee) is a popular, serviceable spot for **camping** ($13–15; ⓣ406/234-0900, ⓦwww.recreation.gov), and has some of the best walleye fishing in the country. As with the other campgrounds in the area, this one is quite remote and only accessible by a rugged country road. Use a four-wheel-drive vehicle to explore.

Western Montana

Western Montana offers a beautifully expansive setting where the big skies must be seen to be believed, and you'll encounter entirely different weather from one horizon to the next. The region is replete with outdoor adventures, from the natural delights around **Bozeman** to glorious **Glacier National Park**, one of America's scenic wonders. The only old-time mining camps that have grown into substantial settlements are the genteel state capital **Helena** and rough, copper-mining **Butte**.

Bozeman and around

Fetching **BOZEMAN** lies at the north end of the lush Gallatin Valley, 142 miles west of Billings and ninety miles north of Yellowstone – well placed as a base for exploring many kinds of outdoor adventures in the region. The stately Victorian storefronts along **Main Street** are some of the most historic in the West, and it's here where you can find many good choices for dining, drinking and shopping.

South of downtown, the huge **Museum of the Rockies** 600 W Kagy Blvd at S Seventh Avenue (summer daily 9am–8pm; rest of year Mon–Sat till 5pm, Sun 12.30–5pm; $10; ⓦwww.museumoftherockies.org) features Native American weapons, biology exhibits, a planetarium, Western landscape paintings and a well-preserved, walk-in 1889 farmhouse constructed from logs and built from a catalogue design. The collection is best known, though, for its stunning dinosaur finds — among them the world's largest-known skull of a *T.rex*, one of the museum's dozen sets of bones from that species. Smaller in scale, the **Pioneer Museum**, 317 W Main St (June–Aug Mon–Sat 10am–5pm, rest of year Tues–Sat 11am–4pm; $5; ⓦwww.pioneermuseum.org), is housed in a crenellated 1911 jail, with an intriguing selection of historic objects, including a replica log cabin, scale-model pioneer wagons and army forts, and a gallows for hanging town miscreants. From the museum you can take **walking tours** (brochures from visitor centre, below) of Main Street's elegant structures, its districts strewn with grand nineteenth-century mansions, and even the local cemetery where the town's bigwigs are buried. More unexpectedly, the **American Computer Museum**, Bridger Park Mall, 2304 N 7th Ave, suite B (June–Aug daily 10am–4pm; March, April & May Tues–Sat noon–4pm, Thurs tills 8pm;

donation; Ⓦwww.compustory.org), follows the evolution of computers, from their bulky, awkward beginnings to today's tiny, lightning-fast marvels.

Practicalities

Greyhound stops at 1205 E Main St, and the **visitor centre** is at 224 E Main St (Ⓣ406/586-4008, Ⓦwww.downtownbozeman.org). **Hotels** in Bozeman tend toward the familiar chain variety, so you may be better off at a distinctive **B&B** like *Lehrkind Mansion*, 719 N Wallace Ave (Ⓣ1-800/992-6932, Ⓦwww.bozemanbedandbreakfast.com; ❻), which occupies a delightful Queen Anne home and nearby garden house, offering nine rooms and suites richly appointed with Victorian antiques and Old West-styled furniture. Alternatively, the *Howlers Inn*, 3185 Jackson Creek Rd (Ⓣ1-888/469-5377, Ⓦwww.howlersinn.com; ❺), true to its name, sits next to a small wolf sanctuary and features a jacuzzi, sauna and modern rooms with DVD players and microwaves. Another reliable choice is the *Voss Inn*, 319 S Willson Ave (Ⓣ406/587-0982, Ⓦwww.bozeman-vossinn.com; ❺), a handsome 1883 Victorian estate with six lace-and-chintz guest rooms and an excellent morning breakfast.

Bozeman boasts plenty of good **places to eat**. The *Community Co-op*, 908 W Main St (Ⓣ406/587-4039), serves terrific vegetarian dishes, deli sandwiches and mouth-watering desserts. Other favourites include the *MacKenzie River Pizza Co.*, 232 E Main St (Ⓣ406/587-0055) and eight other Montana locations, which has 22 different kinds of pizza – try the chili-laden Branding Iron for a kick, and, for fine dining, *Looie's Downunder*, 101 E Main St (Ⓣ406/522-8814), a terrific choice for its steak and seafood (with a sushi bar), as well as inventive entrees such as vanilla-roasted chicken and bison ribeye steak. For **drinking** *Montana Ale Works*, 611 E Main St (Ⓣ406/587-7700), has dozens of regional microbrews along with solid steaks and burgers.

Outdoor activities

There are many **outdoor activities** in the vicinity, particularly in rugged Hyalite Canyon just south of town, which has top-notch hiking and mountain biking in summer and excellent ice climbing in winter, or at the challenging ski area, **Bridger Bowl** (lift tickets $48; Ⓣ406/587-2111, Ⓦwww.bridgerbowl.com). An hour's drive south down the beautiful Gallatin Valley is the much pricier **Big Sky Resort** (lift tickets $80; Ⓣ1-800/548-4486, Ⓦwww.bigskyresort.com; hotel rooms ❺–❾), popular for its top-quality powder and steep slopes on 11,166ft Lone Mountain.

Three miles north of I-90, thirty miles west of Bozeman, **Missouri Headwaters State Park** ($5 day-use fee; camping $13–15; Ⓣ406/994-4042), marks the place where the Missouri River begins its circuitous journey to the Mississippi. Its marshy grasslands beneath a shallow bluff were seen by Lewis and Clark in July 1805; fur trappers who followed in their wake included Kit Carson, and traces remain of the nineteenth-century town they created. These days the park has plenty of good fishing, hiking and birdwatching. Another fifteen miles west, **Lewis & Clark Caverns State Park** (tours May–Sept daily 9am–4.30pm; $10; Ⓣ406/287-3541) offers a fascinating underworld of limestone spires and pillars, which you can see on rugged two-hour, two-mile **walking tours**; bring sturdy shoes and a jacket – the temperature is a consistent 50°F. To stay in the park, three **cabins** ($30–45) are available. For details on more outdoor activities, check with the **ranger office**, in Bozeman at 3710 Fallon St (Mon–Fri 8am–4.30pm; Ⓣ406/522-2520, Ⓦwww.fs.fed.us/r1/gallatin), which also provides information on hiking trails.

Butte and around

Eighty miles west of Bozeman, the former copper-mining colossus of **BUTTE** (pronounced "mute") sits on a steep hillside where massive black headframes

– "gallows frames" to miners – of long-abandoned pits soar up among dirty-yellow slag heaps, making it one of the most polluted parts of the US. Still, at dusk it's oddly compelling, when the golden light casts a glow on the mine-pocked hillsides, and the old neon signs illuminate historic brick buildings. Among immigrants to leave their mark here were miners from **Ireland** – Butte still puts on a formidable St Patrick's Day celebrations – and **Cornwall**, which gave Butte the traditional meat-and-potato pasty (*PASS-tee*) that's still served in many cafés, and tough enough to survive being dropped for lunch to miners in their shafts.

Butte was once a pillar of union activism, as miners obtained a minimum wage and an eight-hour day, and it became impossible to get work without a union card. By the 1950s the focus had switched from traditional mining in shafts to ugly open pits. Today only the Continental Pit mine is in use. To take a look at the ecological disaster that is the 1800ft-deep, 5600ft-wide and 7000ft-long **Berkeley Pit**, head for Continental Drive. Here, a viewing platform surveys the most toxic stretch of water in the United States (more information at ⓦwww.pitwatch.org).

Butte is also rich with Victorian architecture, with some six thousand preserved buildings. On West Park Street at Mining Museum Road, the excellent **World Museum of Mining** (April–Oct daily 9am–5pm; $8.50; ⓦwww.miningmuseum.org) is packed with fascinating memorabilia, and outside, beyond the scattered collection of rusting machinery – from jackhammers to mine carts – the museum's 50-building **Hell Roarin' Gulch** re-creates a cobbled-street mining camp, complete with saloon, bordello, church, schoolhouse and Chinese laundry. Above it all looms the 100ft headframe of the 3200ft-deep **Orphan Girl** mineshaft; below it all you can take in an **underground tour** ($5) of some of the rickety old facilities. For more on the town's colourful history, take a 90min **walking tour** with Old Butte Historical Adventures, 117 N Main St (April–Oct daily 10am–4pm; $10; ⓣ406/498-3424, ⓦwww.buttetours.info), which covers the area's architecture, mines, railway lines, a speakeasy and even journeys to the region's ghost towns (prices vary; by appointment only).

Few mining baron estates are grander than the 34-room **Copper King Mansion**, 219 W Granite St (tours May–Sept daily 9am–4pm; $7.50; ⓣ406/782-7580, ⓦwww.thecopperkingmansion.com). Along with frescoed ceilings, handcrafted woodwork, and chandeliers and fireplaces, the mansion also has the draw of being a B&B, where you can **stay** amid tasteful old-time luxury for as little as $65 a night. Another curiosity is the 26-room **Charles W Clark Chateau**, 321 W Broadway (June–Sept, hours vary, often Mon–Sat 9am–4pm; $6; ⓣ406/491-5636), a mock-French castle splendid for its spiral staircase, exotic-wood-inlaid rooms and wrought-iron decor. It now holds Victorian furniture and antiques, as well as a rotating selection of contemporary regional art. By contrast, in an old noodle parlour at 17 W Mercury St, the **Mai Wah Museum** (June–Sept Tues–Sat 11am–5pm; $3; ⓦwww.maiwah.org) focuses on the history of the Chinese community with photos, cooking implements, toys, fireworks, menus and books. The community was six hundred strong at the end of the nineteenth century, but by the 1940s rampant racism had reduced it to just a few families.

At night the 90ft **Our Lady of the Rockies** statue, 3100 Harrison Ave (ⓦwww.ourladyoftherockies.org), is illuminated by floodlights. Built entirely by voluntary labour, it was set in place on top of the Continental Divide, some 3500ft above Butte, by helicopter.

Practicalities

Greyhound **buses** drop off downtown at 1324 Harrison Ave. From June to August, 2-hour **trolley tours** of town (Mon–Fri 8am–6pm, Sat & Sun 9am–4pm; $7) leave from the **Chamber of Commerce**, 1000 George St (ⓣ406/723-3177, ⓦwww.buttecvb.com). Good **accommodation** (along with *Copper King Mansion*;

see above) includes the 1924 *Finlen Hotel*, 100 E Broadway (ⓣ406/723-5461, ⓦwww.finlen.com; ❸), which has basic but functional motel-style rooms, as well as more upmarket hotel units in a classic 1924 building; and *Toad Hall Manor*, 1 Green Lane (ⓣ406/494-2625, ⓦwww.toadhallmanor.com; ❺), a quite stylish B&B in a stately neo-Georgian house, whose four units variously come with jacuzzis, fridges, microwaves and courtyards.

Butte has plenty of good places to **eat and drink**, most of them uptown. *Joe's Pasty Shop*, 1641 Grand Ave (ⓣ406/723-9071), serves up the hearty, meat-and-potato-filled Cornish dish with vigour, while the smarter *Uptown Café*, 47 E Broadway (ⓣ406/723-4735), serves pizza, pasta and sandwiches, but is best known for its steak-and-seafood dinner entrees and inexpensive, fixed ($13.50) five-course meals. For more rib-stuffing, lunch-bucket fare, head to *Pork Chop John's*, 8 W Mercury (ⓣ406/782-0812), an old-time favourite for its cheap pork and fried-ham sandwiches, burgers and grilled-cheese sandwiches.

The Grant-Kohrs Ranch

The National Historic Site of **GRANT-KOHRS RANCH**, 266 Warren Lane in the town of Deer Lodge (June–Aug 9am–5.30pm, Sept–May till 4.30pm; free; ⓦwww.nps.gov/grko), lies forty miles west of Butte on I-90. In operation since 1860, this Western cattle ranch, under the guidance of "Montana Cattle King" **Conrad Kohrs**, was once the hub of ten million acres of range property and many thousands of Hereford and Shorthorn cows. Though its holdings are substantially reduced these days, the ranch still has its share of cows and draft horses on view. It also displays authentic buggies and wagons around its preserved old barns, and **wagon tours** around the site are available in the summer (June–Aug Thurs–Mon 9am–5pm on the hour; $5). Compare the pleasant Victorian environs of the house of the first owner, John Grant, with the much humbler conditions the ranch hands tolerated in Bunkhouse Row.

Helena and around

An hour north of Butte on I-15, **HELENA** offers a fine view over the golden-brown **Prickly Pear Valley**, and was founded in 1864 when a party of prospectors hit the jackpot at what is now **Last Chance Gulch**, the town's attractive main street, whose stately Romanesque Revival and Neoclassical buildings are now home to gift shops, diners and bars. Above it all looms the **Old Fire Tower**, also known as the "Guardian of the Gulch", off-limits to interlopers but still worth a short walk to see the latest in fire prevention, circa 1876.

During the boom years, more than $20 million of gold was extracted from the gulch, and fifty successful prospectors remained here as millionaires. Their palatial residences grace the west side of town in the **Mansion District**. Contrast this with the far more modest digs southwest of town in **Reeder's Alley** (ⓦwww.reedersalley.com), a collection of miners' cabins, wooden storehouses and other humble working-class structures, now refurbished into smart shops and restaurants. Helena has an unexpected Hollywood connection, too: Gary Cooper was born and raised here, and Myrna Loy lived here as a child. Honouring the actress is the **Myrna Loy Center for the Performing Arts**, based in a former jail at 15 N Ewing St (ⓣ406/443-0287, ⓦwww.myrnaloycenter.com), which screens indie films and presents concerts, plays, comedy and more.

Another worthwhile stop is the **Original Governor's Mansion**, 304 N Ewing St (May–Sept Tues–Sat noon–3pm on the hour, rest of year Sat only; $4; ⓣ406/444-4789), which housed the state's chief executive during the first half of the twentieth century and still impresses with its Queen Anne style and broad decorative-arts collection. The legislative branch has worked since 1902 out of the massive Neoclassical **State Capitol**, 1301 E Sixth Ave (Mon–Sat 8am–5pm; free), covered with a copper-clad dome and featuring, in the House chamber, a huge mural by "cowboy artist" Charles M. Russell depicting a dramatic encounter between native tribes and Lewis and Clark. You can see more of Russell's work at the excellent **Montana Historical Society Museum**, 225 N Roberts St (Mon–Sat 9am–5pm, Thurs closes 8pm; $5; Ⓦmontanahistoricalsociety.org), as well as early photographs of Montana life, pioneer and tribal artefacts, and an array of costumes and textiles.

Elsewhere, the majestic red spires of the **Cathedral of St Helena** rise 230ft at 530 N Ewing St (Ⓣ406/442-5825, Ⓦwww.sthelenas.org); the inside is adorned with elaborate Bavarian stained glass, white-marble altars and gold leaf. Also interesting are the **Holter Museum of Art**, 12 E Lawrence St (Tues–Sat 10am–5.30pm, Sun noon–4pm; free; Ⓦholtermuseum.org), most notable for its contemporary sculpture and decorative works, and west of downtown, the **Archie Bray Foundation**, 2915 Country Club Ave (Mon–Sat 10am–5pm, also summer Sun 1–5pm; free; Ⓦarchiebray.org), which hosts world-renowned ceramic artists who work while you watch, and displays a broad variety of pottery.

Practicalities

Greyhound connects at Helena's **transit centre** at 630 N Last Chance Gulch. In the summer the Historical Society runs hour-long **tours** in an imitation steam train (actually a tram) from the corner of Sixth and Roberts (June to mid-Sept daily, hours vary; $7.50; Ⓦwww.lctours.com). The **visitor centre** is at 225 Cruse Ave (Ⓣ406/447-1530, Ⓦwww.gohelena.com), where you can pick up a free map. Information and maps on local hiking trails are available from **Helena National Forest Ranger Station**, 2001 Poplar St (Mon–Fri 8am–4.30pm; Ⓣ406/449-5490, Ⓦwww.fs.fed.us/r1/helena), which can also direct you to first-come, first-served **campgrounds** (summer only; free or $5–8) near the Continental Divide. Beyond camping and its many chain motels, Helena's most stylish **lodging** is its B&Bs, including *Barrister Bed & Breakfast*, 416 N Ewing St (Ⓣ406/443-7330 or 1-800/823-1148, Ⓦthebarristermt.tripod.com; ❺), a lovely 1874 Victorian mansion near the cathedral and originally used as priest's quarters, now offering five graceful rooms; and *Sanders B&B*, 328 N Ewing St (Ⓣ406/442-3309, Ⓦwww.sandersbb.com; ❻), whose seven old-fashioned rooms come with Western decor and antiques, some with claw-footed tubs and fireplaces. Decent places to **eat** include *Bert and Ernie's*, 361 N Last Chance Gulch (Ⓣ406/443-5680), for its deli sandwiches and nice array of pizzas, plus mid-priced seafood and pasta; the *Windbag Saloon*, 19 S Last Chance Gulch (Ⓣ406/443-9669), a big old barn of a place – and former brothel – that serves rib-stuffing seafood, burgers and steaks; and *Miller's Crossing*, 52 S Park Ave (Ⓣ406/442-3290), which has microbrews and eclectic live music.

Gates of the Mountains

One of the region's more worthwhile excursions is on a two-hour **boat tour** through the stunning **Gates of the Mountains**, 25 miles north of Helena off Hwy-287 (June–Sept hours vary, generally hourly Mon–Fri 11am–2pm or 3pm, Sat & Sun 10am–4pm; $14; Ⓣ406/458-5241, Ⓦwww.gatesofthemountains.com). This dramatic stretch of the Missouri River, which enters a gorge between sheer 1200ft-tall limestone cliffs that rise abruptly from the northern shores of a tranquil lake, was named by explorer Meriwether Lewis. The area offers unmatched scenic splendour and plenty of excellent hiking and backpacking opportunities, not to mention an eye-opening array of wildlife, including black bears, eagles, bighorn sheep, beavers and mountain lions.

Missoula

Framed by the striking Bitterroot and Sapphire mountains, vibrant and friendly **MISSOULA** is full of contrasts – bookstores, continental cafés and gun shops – a place where students from the local University of Montana provide much of the town's energy. One sign of Missoula's dynamism is its **Missoula Art Museum**, 335 N Pattee St (Wed–Fri 10am–5pm, Sat & Sun till 3pm; free; ⓦwww.missoulaartmuseum.org), which shows challenging work in digital photography, modern painting and sculpture, and a range of eye-opening pieces by contemporary Native American artists. Elsewhere, on the university campus at Main Hall, the **Montana Museum of Art & Culture** (Sept–May Tues–Thurs 11am–3pm, Fri & Sat 4–8.30pm; June–Aug Wed–Sat 11am–3pm; donation; ⓦwww.umt.edu/montanamuseum), has a mixed collection of art highlighted by interesting Renaissance-era Flemish tapestries, modern ceramics and prints by Chagall, Delacroix, Picasso, Toulouse-Lautrec and Ed Ruscha, among others. For more natural appeal, the **Elk Country Visitor Center**, 5705 Grant Creek Rd (May–Dec Mon–Fri 8am–6pm, Sat & Sun 9am–6pm; free; ⓣ1-800/CALL-ELK, ⓦwww.rmef.org), provides exhibits about the prodigious, especially horned, creatures in the region, with a short walking trail providing on-site examples of a few of the creatures you can expect to see on more rugged hikes.

For another interesting experience, the 1914 **Fort Missoula**, off Hwy-93 S, holds a worthwhile **Historical Museum** in building 322 (summer Tues–Sun noon–5pm, rest of year Mon–Sat 10am–5pm, Sun noon–5pm; $3; ⓦwww.fortmissoulamuseum.org). Amid the mostly dry displays on military and agricultural history is a small collection of buildings relocated here that date from the Old West era, including a railroad depot, church and schoolhouse. More unexpected are the World War II internment barracks for Italian nationals and Japanese-Americans, recalling the days when the fort was used for confining perceived "enemies", many of whom were US citizens.

Finally, the Forest Service **Smokejumper Center**, ten miles out of town on US-93 at 5765 W Broadway, discusses methods used to train smokejumpers – highly skilled firefighters who parachute into forested areas to stop the spread of wildfires. Fires are common in this part of the country during the dry season. A small **visitor centre** further explains their work (summer 8.30am–5pm; ⓣ406/329-4934).

Practicalities

Greyhound pulls in at 1660 W Broadway, and the **visitor centre** is across the river from the campus, at 825 E Front St (ⓣ406/543-6623, ⓦwww.missoulachamber.com). The more distinctive **accommodation** choices include *Goldsmith's Inn*, 809 E Front St (ⓣ406/728-1585, ⓦwww.goldsmithsinn.com; ❺), a quaint 1911 Victorian B&B with nice riverside views, whose seven rooms and suites variously offer balconies and fireplaces; the *Doubletree Missoula Edgewater*, 100 Madison St (ⓣ406/728-3100, ⓦwww.doubletree.com; ❻), near the university right on the Clark Fork River – on which you can conveniently fly-fish – with nice rooms and suites and gym, pool and hot tub; and *Ruby's Inn*, 4825 N Reserve St (ⓣ406/721-0990, ⓦrubys.montana.com; ❹), which has simple rooms plus free high-speed internet, pool, spa and laundry.

You can **eat** well in Missoula: *The Shack*, 222 W Main St (ⓣ406/549-9903), has moderately priced Mexican fare, pasta and sandwiches, plus some tasty omelets for breakfast; the *Staggering Ox*, 123 E Main St (ⓣ406/327-9400), offers the most bizarre take on conventional fare – sub sandwiches baked in a can and presented vertically – but does it very well; and if for some reason you want to go fancy in this most casual of towns, try the *Red Bird*, 111 N Higgins St (ⓣ406/549-2906), for its delicious, and pricey, nouveau Western eats, such as local lamb with apple couscous and chilli-rubbed bison tenderloin.

Outdoor activities

Missoula is a particularly good base for outdoor activities. The **visitor centre** can provide details on **trails**, such as the gruelling two-mile one leading from its office up **Mount Sentinel**, embellished by the huge concrete letter "M". The top gives a great view of the area, especially the rugged Hellgate River Canyon. Other worthwhile hikes traverse the 60,000 acres of the **Rattlesnake National Recreation Area**, which, despite the name, claims to be serpent-free; find more information at the local **ranger station**, at Fort Missoula, Building 24 (Mon–Fri 7.30am–4pm; ⓣ406/329-3750, ⓦfs.usda.gov/lolo). Missoula is excellent for cycling, too, and another good source of information and **trail maps** is the Adventure Cycling Association, 150 E Pine St (ⓣ406/721-1776, ⓦwww.adventurecycling.org); the Bicycle Hangar, 1801 Brooks St (ⓣ406/728-9537), rents out good-quality bikes.

The most developed of the city's small ski areas is **Montana Snowbowl**, twelve miles northwest, which has a range of slopes for all abilities (lift tickets $39) and boasts a summer **chairlift** (July to early Sept daily noon–5pm; $7, kids free, $2 for bikes; ⓣ406/549-9777, ⓦwww.montanasnowbowl.com). For state-park **camping** you'll need to backtrack east, either 25 miles on I-90 to small **Beavertail Hill** (May–Sept; day-use fee $5, camping $15; ⓣ406/542-5500), which also has replica tepees to stay in ($25), or forty miles on Hwy-200 and a brief jog on Hwy-83 north to **Salmon Lake** (same info and phone), which is great for its fishing and swimming in the Clearwater River.

Garnet Ghost Town

To get a more in-depth look at the rugged days of the Old West, travel east from Missoula some forty miles on I-90, then another ten bumpy miles by single-lane gravel road, to **Garnet Ghost Town** (road open May–Dec; summer daily 10am–5pm, rest of year Sat & Sun 11am–3pm; $3; ⓦwww.garnetghosttown.net), a slice of Industrial Age history that rewards a long look. A century ago, the site was home to hundreds of hard-rock gold miners doing a tough, perilous job. Since the buildings have been kept in their semi-decayed state, the atmosphere is quite arresting: the quiet and lonely spectre of vacant, wood-framed saloons, cabins, stores and a jail, set amid acres of rolling hills that invite a leisurely stroll. Most intriguing are the three evocative, creaky levels of the **Wells Hotel**, where you can contrast the once-chic parlour and dining area on the ground floor with the bare, spartan floors of the unheated top level, where miners would lay out their bedrolls and bodies in lined, human-sized parking spaces.

Flathead Lake and around

Awe-inspiring, 28-mile-long **Flathead Lake** is the largest freshwater lake west of the Mississippi, and it provides a welcome diversion on the long route north toward Glacier National Park, reached by following US-93 north from I-90. Before getting to the lake, stop off and view the five hundred residents of the 18,500-acre **National Bison Range**, accessible near the town of Moiese, twenty miles west of St Ignatius off Hwy-212 (visitor centre: May to mid-Oct daily 8am–6pm, opens 9am on weekends, mid-Oct to April Mon–Fri 8am–4pm; driving concourse: daily 7am–dusk; $5; ⓦwww.fws.gov/bisonrange). You drive through the striking mountainside scenery past the great horned beasts travelling in herds – however, getting out to pet these irascible creatures is a bad idea, so observe from the safety of your slow-moving car.

Once you get to the south lakeshore, **boats** can be rented in **Polson** at Flathead Lake Boat Co, 4 8th Ave (ⓣ406/883-0999), while summertime **lake cruises** ($17–23; ⓣ406/883-3636) are offered by *Best Western KwaTaqNuk Resort*, 49708 Hwy-93 E in Polson (ⓣ406/883-3636 or 1-800/882-6363, ⓦwww.kwataqnuk.com; ❺), which has rooms with flat-screen TVs and wi-fi, and a marina with boat rentals, as well as a grubby casino. As alternate digs, the *Swan Hill B&B*, 39407 Kings Point Rd (ⓣ406/883-1450, ⓦwww.swanhillbedandbreakfast.com; ❻), has fetching B&B accommodation in a modern cabin setting with five rooms offering lakefront access plus a pool, sauna and wi-fi.

Between Polson in the south and Somers in the north, US-93 follows the lake's curving western shore, while the smaller Hwy-36 runs up the east below the **Mission Mountains**, and is the summer home to countless roadside cherry and berry vendors. Both routes offer superb views of the deep alpine waters, though US-93 is closest to **Wild Horse Island** (daily dawn – dusk; free), the lake's largest island, which you can reach by boat. Hiking on its terrific range of moderate-to-steep trails, which lead past knolls and buttes up to fine lookouts over the lake, you're apt to see the odd group of bighorn sheep – though the eponymous untamed equines are few and rarely visible.

Bigfork

Fishing and pleasure boats also launch at the small resort of **Bigfork** in the northeast, and you can **stay** in town at the smart and cosy *Grand Hotel Bigfork*, 425 Grand Drive (ⓣ406/837-7377, ⓦwww.grandhotelbigfork.com; ❻), which is best for its central location, or at the *Candlewycke Inn*, 311 Aero Lane (ⓣ406/837-6406, ⓦwww.candlewyckeinn.com; ❻), an antique-laden B&B whose five pleasant units variously come with jacuzzis, skylights and fridges. For **dining**, there's fine nouveau-French fare at *La Provence*, 408 Bridge St (ⓣ406/837-2923), or the adequate bars and diners along Electric Avenue; a little way outside of town, the *Echo Lake Cafe*, 1195 Hwy-83 (ⓣ406/837-4252), serves up solid omelets, scrambles and burgers, with some veggie options, too. Don't miss the sugary temptations at *Eva Gates*, 456 Electric Ave (ⓣ406/837-4356), the town's prime draw for its fudges, jams and sweets made with **huckleberries**, which show up in everything locally from ice cream to beer.

Kalispell

Fifteen miles north of the lake, drab **Kalispell** is out of sight of the water, but is a good jumping-off point for trips around the lake or up to Glacier National Park. **Accommodation** options include the stylish 1912 *Kalispell Grand Hotel*, 100 Main St (ⓣ406/755-8100, ⓦwww.kalispellgrand.com; ❺), whose rooms have free high-speed internet access and continental breakfast, with the fancier suites offering jacuzzis; and the *Garrison Inn*, five miles west of Kalispell off Hwy-2 (ⓣ406/752-5103, ⓦwww.thegarrisoninn.com; ❺), with three cosy log-cabin-type rooms with rustic decor and nice views. For decent **food**, try *MacKenzie River Pizza*, 2230 Hwy-93 S (ⓣ406/756-0060), for its range of tasty, savoury pies, while *Capers*, 121 Main St (ⓣ406/755-7687), is a reliable choice for its upmarket steak, seafood and scrumptious lasagnes.

Whitefish

The enjoyable resort of **WHITEFISH**, seventeen miles north of Kalispell, lies on the south shore of beautiful **Whitefish Lake** in the shade of the Whitefish Mountain Ski Resort (lift tickets $61; ⓣ406/862-2900, ⓦwww.skiwhitefish.com), also known as "Big Mountain". As one of the area's big-name winter-sports draws, it's also excellent for its **hiking** in summer months, when you can trudge four hard miles up to a restaurant on top of the mountain and take a free chair-lift ride for the descent (uphill it's $10), or **cycle** the roads around the lake and foothills – bikes can be rented from Glacier Cyclery, 326 E 2nd St ($30/day; ⓣ406/862-6446).

Amtrak **trains** drop off downtown, off Central Avenue at 500 Depot St, en route to and from Glacier National Park. There's a useful tourist **information** counter in the depot; the local **Chamber of Commerce** is at 520 E 2nd St (Ⓣ406/862-3501, Ⓦwww.whitefishchamber.com). Try **staying** at one of the 22 homey log cabins of the *North Forty Resort*, 3765 Hwy-40 W (Ⓣ406/862-7740, Ⓦwww.northfortyresort.com; ❼), which come equipped with fireplaces, kitchens, DVD players, free wi-fi and outdoor BBQs, or one of the nicer **B&Bs**, such as the timber-chic *Hidden Moose Lodge*, 1735 E Lakeshore Drive (Ⓣ1-888/733-6667, Ⓦwww.hiddenmooselodge.com; ❻), excellent for its outdoor hot tub, hearty breakfasts and rooms with jacuzzis or private decks, or, at Whitefish Mountain, *Kandahar, The Lodge* (Ⓣ406/862-6094, Ⓦwww.kandaharlodge.com; ❻), a stylish affair with spa, sauna, gym and jacuzzi, and wide range of rooms, suites, lofts and studios.

For **dining**, the *Tupelo Grille*, 17 Central Ave (Ⓣ406/862-6136), is probably the most esteemed place around, giving your stomach a (pricey) Southern spin with crawfish cakes, creole chicken and good ol' shrimp and grits. You can power down cheaper, but still tasty, burgers and pasta at the *Craggy Range Bar & Grill*, 10 Central Ave (Ⓣ406/862-7550), or the *Hellroaring Saloon & Eatery* (Ⓣ406/862-6364) at Whitefish Mountain, with similar entrees, as well as buffalo ribeye steak and beef brisket. *Great Northern Brewing*, 2 Central Ave (Ⓣ406/863-1000), is Whitefish's finest craft brewer, with its own tasting room.

Glacier National Park

Two thousand lakes, a thousand miles of rivers, thick forests, breezy meadows and awe-inspiring peaks make up one of America's finest attractions, **GLACIER NATIONAL PARK** – a haven for bighorn sheep, mountain goats, black and grizzly bears, wolves and mountain lions. Although the park does hold 25 small glaciers, it takes its name from the huge flows of ice that carved these immense valleys 20,000 years ago. Outside of summer, the crisp air, icy-cold waterfalls and copious snowfall give the impression of being close to the Arctic Circle; in fact, the latitude here is lower than that of London.

Arrival and information

There are several **visitor centres**. One centre is at the park's main, **western entrance** at **Apgar**, on the shores of gorgeous McDonald Lake, twenty miles east of Whitefish and just 35 miles south of the Canadian border (mid-May to Sept hours vary, often daily 9am–4.30pm, till 8pm in summer), and another at the **east gate** at **St Mary**, seventy miles west of Shelby (daily: mid-May to late June & early Sept to mid-Oct 8am–5pm; late June to early July till 9pm; early July to early Sept 7am–8pm). **Logan Pass** (mid-June to mid-Sept; hours vary, often daily 10am–5pm) visitor centre stands at the top of the Going-to-the-Sun Road – the one through-road between the two entrances, usually passable between early June and mid-October, though in recent years road closures for constructions have made travel more intermittent. The park itself is **open year-round**, however, and it's well worth trekking as far as Lake McDonald or St Mary's Lake even when the road is blocked and the visitor centres are closed (the lower-elevation roads are often ploughed in winter). In summer, the **entrance fee** is $25 per vehicle (or $12/individual on foot, bike or motorcycle), and the winter rate is $15 per car ($10 for other visitors); both are good for seven days. For **park information** call Ⓣ406/888-7800 or go to Ⓦwww.nps.gov/glac.

Glacier, together with the adjacent, much smaller Waterton Lakes National Park (May to early Oct; $8; Ⓣ403/859-2224) in Canada, is part of **Waterton-Glacier International Peace Park**, though Going-to-the-Sun Road does not enter

Canada. Both parks operate their own fees and regulations, and to get to Waterton's separate entrance, north of St Mary, you have to pass through customs (camping is $15–38/night).

Getting around

The southern border of Glacier is skirted by US-2, which remains open all year and is an attractive alternative drive. Amtrak **trains** follow the same route, stopping at West Glacier, a short walk from the west gate; East Glacier, thirty miles south of St Mary; and Essex (summer only), in between.

Travellers arriving by **public transportation** can travel around the park via the bright-red vintage "**jammer**" buses (so called because of the need to jam the gears into place) that provide narrated sightseeing tours from the main lodges (June–Sept; ⓣ406/892-2525, ⓦwww.glacierparkinc.com; 2–8hr $30–90). Free **Glacier Shuttles** operate on two routes: one between **Apgar Transit Center**, several miles from the park gate, and Logan Pass (7am–7pm, 90min–2hr trip), and one between Logan Pass and St Mary Visitor Center (same hours, 1hr); both run at least every 30min, and July to early Sept only. **Sun Tours** (June–Sept; ⓣ406/226-9220 or 1-800/786-9220, ⓦwww.glaciersuntours.com) offers guided tours led by members of the Blackfeet tribe.

Accommodation within the park

Accommodation within the park is run by Glacier Park Inc. (all reservations at ⓣ406/892-2525, ⓦwww.glacierparkinc.com), and most of the lodges are open from June into September. The striking, century-old *Glacier Park Lodge* in East Glacier (❻) is known for the massive Douglas-fir pillars in its huge lobby, while near West Glacier, the lovely *Lake McDonald Lodge* has an ideal shoreline location with a Swiss chalet design, offering simple motel rooms (❻), more spacious lodge rooms (❼) or small rustic cottages outside the complex (❺). More upscale are the *Prince of Wales Hotel* in Waterton, resembling a gargantuan Swiss chalet, which has fetching mountain-view and lake-view units (❽) and luxurious suites for $799. The *Many Glacier Hotel* is another grand lodge, on Swiftcurrent Lake, with pricey suites (❽), with value rooms for half that price (❻). The park's cheapest accommodation is the *Swiftcurrent Motor Inn* at Many Glacier, featuring cabins with or without bathrooms (❸–❹), and good for its access to trails on the northeast side. A bit nicer is the lakeside *Rising Sun Motor Inn* (❺), seven miles in from the east gate at St Mary, as well as the *Village Inn at Apgar* (❻), fronting Lake McDonald with great views.

The park's thirteen **campgrounds** – ranging from $10 to $23 – often fill up by late morning during July and August; ask at any visitor centre for locations and availability or call ⓣ406/888-7800. Most are open from June to mid-September, though there are also several cheap **primitive campgrounds** ($10) at Apgar and St Mary, which may not include water but do tend to be open longer, usually April to November. All sites are first-come, first-served, though you can reserve *Fish Creek* and *St Mary* six months in advance (ⓣ1-800/365-CAMP, ⓦwww.recreation.gov). For overnight backpacking, get a permit from any visitor centre.

Accommodation outside the park

The places to **stay** outside Glacier are a bit removed from the park. The quaint 1910 *Belton Chalet*, two miles outside the western entrance (June–Oct; ⓣ406/888-5000, ⓦwww.beltonchalet.com; ❻), offers simple yet elegant digs, though the three-bedroom cottages (❾) have fireplaces and balconies; no phone or TV. One- and two-bedroom cabins are rented by the *Glacier Outdoor Center*, off Hwy-2 a half-mile from the west entrance (ⓣ406/888-5454, ⓦwww.glacierraftco.com; ❾), with decks, kitchens and fireplaces, at some of the steepest prices in the area.

Halfway between the east and west park gates is **Essex**, where the atmospheric 1939 *Izaak Walton Inn* (ⓣ406/888-5700, ⓦwww.izaakwaltoninn.com) is the site of the Amtrak stop. Beside cosy wood-panelled rooms (❻), the inn provides four fun, remodelled train cabins (both ❽), and has a serviceable restaurant for fish and burgers. In the village of **East Glacier Park**, near another Amtrak station, the simple *Backpacker's Inn* hostel (May–Sept; ⓣ406/226-9392), behind *Serrano's Mexican Restaurant* at 29 Dawson Ave, has three cabins: two are private with bathrooms ($30) and a third offers shared dorm space ($12/person). Up in **Polebridge**, 28 miles north of the park's west entrance, largely via gravel road, the *Northfork Hostel* (ⓣ406/888-5241, ⓦwww.nfhostel.com) is extremely cosy. Camping pitches go for $10, dorm beds cost $20 and small private cabins start at $45, while log cabins are $80.

Information on other **lodging** in the park's vicinity is available from Glacier Country (ⓣ1-800/338-5072, ⓦwww.glaciermt.com), while Whitefish and Kalispell are alternative bases west of the park (see p.739).

Exploring the park

The fifty-mile **Going-to-the-Sun Road** is one of the most awe-inspiring scenic drives in the country, and driving it from west to east can take several hours, creating the illusion that you'll be climbing forever – with each successive hairpin bringing a new colossus into view. At the east end of ten-mile **Lake McDonald**, the road starts to climb, as snowmelt from waterfalls gushes across the road, and the winding route nudges over the **Continental Divide** at **Logan Pass** (6680ft) – a good spot to step out and enjoy the views. Four miles on, there's an overlook at **Jackson Glacier**, one of the few glaciers visible from the roadside. Once you get to the east gate, continue about five miles southeast on US-89 for an expansive view of the Great Plains.

Glacier is a true hiker's paradise, with beautiful views at every turn. Good short **trails** start from **Avalanche Creek** on the west flank of the Divide. The mile-long **Trail of the Cedars** loop leads through dark forest to a wall of contoured vivid red sandstone, from where a four-mile path continues gently uphill, past several waterfalls, to glacier-fed **Avalanche Lake**. The most popular trail in the park begins at Logan Pass, following a boardwalk for a mile and a half across wildflower-strewn alpine meadows framed by towering craggy peaks, en route to serene **Hidden Lake**.

At **Swiftcurrent Lake**, north of the east entrance and reached by the Many Glacier entrance, an easy two-mile loop trail runs along the lakeshore, and an exciting five-mile, one-way trail heads to **Iceberg Lake**, so called for the blocks of ice that float on its surface even in midsummer.

From **St Mary Lake**, you can weave a mile and a half up through fir forest to the crashing, frothing **St Mary Falls** and on to the taller **Virginia Falls**; combined with an early-morning boat trip from the Rising Sun launch to the trailhead (see below), this can be a sublime experience.

Down in the quiet southeastern end of the park, the two-mile **Aster Park** trail starts at Two Medicine Lake, framed by the majestic massifs, and leads through spruce forest into flower-filled meadows, passing a couple of beaver ponds and a nice waterfall before ascending steeply for half a mile through the forest to a small outcrop. From here there are fantastic views of the mighty Sinopah and Rising Wolf mountains, and the calm lakes below.

Tour boats explore all of the large lakes, starting at $10–15 for one-hour trips, including sunset cruises on Lake McDonald and St Mary Lake. You can also rent canoes, rowboats and outboards. The lakes, teeming with cut-throat trout, are excellent for **fishing**; information on outfitters and regulations are available from visitor centres.

Finally, pay heed to the signs marking most of the trails as **grizzly bear** country – there's no guarantee of your safety, especially if you wander off the main trails. Don't travel alone, be unnecessarily quiet or wear perfume. Avoid hiking at dusk or in the early morning (prime time for bear activity) and carry bear spray (available from gun dealers).

Eating and drinking

Food in the park, served in hotel dining rooms, is nothing special. You have to hit the *Izaak Walton Inn* in Essex (see opposite) for something tastier, but the best place to head is **East Glacier Park**, where *Serrano's*, 29 Dawson Ave (May–Sept; ⓣ406/226-9392), serves decent Mexican food and microbrews, and the *Whistle Stop*, 1024 Hwy-49 (ⓣ406/226-9292), is worth a stop for its famous huckleberry pie, with adequate meaty dinners and even better breakfasts. *Glacier Village*, 306 Hwy-2 (ⓣ406/226-4464), is the place to come for all things huckleberry, in traditional jams and pancakes, or even ladled on BBQ chicken, along with buffalo ribs, meatloaf, steaks and burgers, and a solid selection of regional beers. On the northeast side of Glacier, the *Two Sisters Café* on Hwy-89 in **Babb** (June–Sept; ⓣ406/732-5535) is a funky roadhouse famous for its outlandish decor, as well as its breakfasts, burgers, chili and desserts.

Idaho

IDAHO was the last of the states to be penetrated by white settlers, and in 1805, **Lewis and Clark** declared central Idaho's bewildering labyrinth of razor-edged peaks and wild waterways the most difficult leg of their epic trek. Though much of its scenery deserves national-park status, its citizens have long been suspicious of the government. It remains one of the country's most environmentally compelling places, despite widespread anti-environmental attitudes. Indeed, the name "Idaho" was promoted by a mining lobbyist, who claimed it was a Shoshone word meaning "gem of the mountains"; he later admitted to making it up.

Idaho is a great destination for the outdoors enthusiast: natural wonders in its five-hundred-mile stretch include **Hells Canyon**, America's deepest river gorge, the dramatic **Sawtooth National Recreation Area**, and the black, barren **Craters of the Moon** – not to mention the skiing mecca of **Sun Valley**. Beyond these, hikers and backpackers have the choice of some eighty mountain ranges, interspersed with virgin forest and lava plateaus, while the mighty **Snake** and **Salmon rivers** offer endless **fishing** and **whitewater rafting**.

To this day, there is no east–west road across the heart of the state, and the central wilderness divides the state in half. The heavily forested **north** is interspersed with glacial lakes fronted by resorts like **Sandpoint** and **Coeur d'Alene**; in the **south**, irrigation begun in the 1880s has transformed the scrubland along the Snake River into the fertile fields responsible for the state's license-plate tag of "Famous Potatoes".

Southern Idaho

Dropping down into **southern Idaho** from western Montana can be dispiriting: Though the initial leg on I-15 is visually compelling, with the magnificent **Mesa Falls** as a worthwhile detour along Hwy-47 and Yellowstone only a short distance east, the scenery along the interstate soon offers little more than farming plots and a few deserted stretches of sand and rocks. Only state capital **Boise** provides any urban interest, as Idaho Falls and Pocatello are both drab. However, a trip into the interior along US-20 brings you to the spectacular ragged outcrops of the **Sawtooth Mountains**, and an hour away is the forbidding landscape of **Craters of the Moon**. Also, during summer, the much-hyped **Sun Valley** ski resort is a good base for outdoor activity, with many fine bars and restaurants.

Craters of the Moon National Monument

The eerie, 83-square-mile **Craters of the Moon National Monument**, ninety miles west of Idaho Falls, comprises a surreal cornucopia of lava cones, tubes, buttes, craters, caves and splatter cones, with trees battered by the fierce winds into bonsai-like contortions. The Monument arose from successive waves of lava pouring from wounds in the earth's crust throughout the millennia; the most recent event occurred 2,000 years ago.

The park **visitor centre** is on US-20 (daily summer 8am–6pm, rest of year till 4.30pm; Ⓣ208/527-1300, Ⓦwww.nps.gov/crmo); entrance for seven days is $8 per car, or $4 per bicycle and pedestrian, and spaces at first-come, first-served *Lava Flow* **campground** cost $10 (May–Oct). A seven-mile **loop road**, open late April to mid-November, takes you around myriad lava fields, where trails of varying difficulty lead past assorted cones and monoliths – don't stray from the paths, as the rocks are razor-sharp and can reach ovenlike temperatures. Highlights include the one-mile trail past hollow **tree moulds** where the ancient wood ignited, leaving craggy holes; the steep half-mile trek to the top of the **Inferno Cone**, with commanding views of the region; and the eight-mile **Wilderness Trail** (wilderness permit required, from the visitor centre), which leads deep into the back-country past cinder cones, ropy lava flows and the blown-out expanse of **Echo Crater**. In winter, the road is open for groomed **cross-country skiing**; for a conditions report, call Ⓣ208/527-3257.

There are also caves here and elsewhere in the monument, molten lava tubes that can be explored alone or on ranger-led tours. The short Cave Trail takes you past four of them, notably the lengthy and spacious Indian Cave and the innocent-sounding Boy Scout Cave – involving an entry crawl over broken rock and a wet, icy floor that invites at least a twisted ankle.

Sun Valley

East of Boise and 150 miles west of Idaho Falls, **Sun Valley** is the common label for the entire Wood River Valley area – though technically it is just the name of a **ski resort** (Ⓦwww.sunvalley.com). Here in the gentle foothills of the Sawtooths near the old sheep-ranching village of **KETCHUM**, the Sun Valley name was chosen because the snow withstood even the brightest winter sun. The world's first chairlift was built here in 1936, and the resort was an instant success, attracting the likes of Clark Gable and Gary Cooper, who came to hunt and fish. **Ernest Hemingway** completed *For Whom the Bell Tolls* as a guest of the resort in 1939, and lived in Ketchum for the last two years of his life before his shotgun suicide (his simple grave can be found in the town cemetery). The resort has information on events commemorating him in late summer.

Sun Valley is based around **Bald Mountain**, the excellent 9100ft peak on which most of the serious skiing occurs, and **Dollar Mountain**, the 6600ft peak with easier runs for beginner skiers. The **season** runs from late November to April; as well as downhill skiing (daily lift pass $56–85 by season at Bald Mountain, $30–42 at Dollar Mountain), you can also set off cross country. Ketchum itself is a lively little town with plenty of accommodation, and even a bit of nightlife. Among **summer** outdoor activities are **cycling** along thirty miles of excellent trails, as well as **mountain biking** on the superb lift-accessed trails on Bald Mountain (lift ticket $20/day), and **rafting** on the rivers to the north.

Practicalities

There's **transport** on the Mountain Rides bus system (rides free or $3; ⓣ208/788-RIDE, ⓦmountainrides.org), and Ketchum's **visitor centre** is at 491 Sun Valley Rd E (ⓣ1-866/305-0408 or 1-800/234-0599, ⓦvisitsunvalley.com).

Room rates are highest in summer and winter, but you can save a bundle by staying in nearby Hailey, twelve miles south. The luxurious 600-room *Sun Valley Lodge* resort is as expensive as you'd expect (ⓣ208/622-4111 or 1-800/786-8259, ⓦwww.sunvalley.com; ❽), with in-room flat-screen TVs, high-speed internet access and DVD players, and suites with parlours and fireplaces. For similar prices, the resort's *Sun Valley Inn* (same contact; ❼) offers a mock-Swiss Alps design but rather plain rooms. Most spots in Ketchum are pricey, though the simple and functional *Lift Tower Lodge*, 703 S Main St (ⓣ208/726-5163; ❹), has basic motel units that include complimentary breakfast. Another option, in **Hailey**, is the *Inn at Ellsworth Estate*, 702 Third Ave S (ⓣ1-866/788-6354, ⓦwww.ellsworthestate.com; ❺), with nine clean and tasteful B&B rooms with smart modern furnishings, some with fireplaces and DVD players.

There's a range of **dining** options at the Sun Valley resort, many serving quality breakfasts and lunches, such as the après-ski *Roundhouse* (ⓣ208/622-2800), though some are only accessible by gondola or chairlift. In Ketchum the mid-priced *Ketchum Grill*, 520 East Ave (ⓣ208/726-4460), has tasty, eclectic options, from pasta and hamburgers to lamb shank and duck breast. More expensive is the breakfast-and-lunch hangout *Cristina's*, 520 Second St E (ⓣ208/726-4499), which also offers a nice Sunday brunch and good omelets. *Whiskey Jacques*, 251 N Main St (ⓣ208/726-5297), is a fun local bar, with **live music** by mid-level national acts, and a solid range of pizzas and burgers.

The Sawtooth Mountains and around

North of Ketchum and Sun Valley, Hwy-75 climbs through rising tracts of forests and mountains to top out after twenty miles at the spectacular panorama of **Galena Summit**. Spreading out far below, the meadows of the Sawtooth Valley stretch northward. The simple road meanders beside the young **Salmon River**, whose headwaters rise in the forbidding icy peaks to the south, as the serrated ridge of the **Sawtooth Mountains** forms an impenetrable barrier along the western horizon. Backpackers are guaranteed solitude in these climes, dotted with some five hundred remote alpine lakes – pick up details of **camping** sites and hiking trails at the **Sawtooth National Recreation Area headquarters**, eight miles north of Ketchum at 5 North Fork Canyon Rd (daily 8.30am–5pm; ⓣ208-727-5000, ⓦwww.fs.fed.us/r4/sawtooth). Fly-fishing for brown trout, steelhead and salmon is a popular pastime here as well.

At tiny **STANLEY**, a few miles north, there are assorted **motels** around the junction of Hwy-75 and Hwy-21, the better of which include the Western-flavoured *Valley Creek Motel* (ⓣ208/774-3606, ⓦwww.stanleyidaho.com; ❹), whose rooms have kitchenettes and wi-fi; and the *High Country Inn*, 21 Ace of Diamonds St (ⓣ208/774-7000, ⓦwww.highcountryinn.biz; ❺), whose rooms and suites offer kitchenettes, with a free breakfast buffet to boot. There isn't much in Stanley to **eat**, but the *Stanley Baking Company*, along Wall St (ⓣ208/774-2981), offers good breakfasts and lunches to begin the day. In summer, Stanley's main activity is organizing **rafting trips**. Operators include The River Company (ⓣ208/788-5775, ⓦwww.therivercompany.com), which charges $75–89.

Twelve miles west of Stanley at the town of **Sunbeam**, you begin the 45-mile scenic drive that leads into the historic settings preserved at the **Land of the Yankee Fork State Park**, whose **interpretive centre** (summer daily 9am–5pm; free; ⓣ208/879-5244) at the park's eastern junction, near Challis at the intersection of highways 75 and 93, gives you the opportunity to try your luck panning gold. Along the way you can find opportunities for camping, rafting, fishing and cross-country skiing, or exploring the preserved ghost towns of **Custer** and **Bonanza**. Also worth a look is the **Yankee Fork Gold Dredge**, a 112-foot, nearly thousand-ton barge that mined gold from stream gravel, and the **Custer Motorway** (also known as Forest Road 070), an old, rustic toll road, curving northwest away from Hwy-75, with numerous historic attractions and rugged trails leading off from it.

Boise

The verdant, likeable community of **BOISE** (pronounced *BOY-see*) straddles I-84 some 350 miles from Salt Lake City, and was established in 1862 for the benefit of pioneers using the Oregon Trail. After adapting (or misspelling) the name originally given to the area by French trappers – *les bois* (the woods) – the earliest residents boosted the town's appearance by planting hundreds more trees.

The centrepiece of town is the **State Capitol**, Jefferson Street and Capitol Boulevard (Mon–Fri 6am–6pm, Sat & Sun 9am–5pm; ⓣ208/332-1970), a stately Neoclassical structure that exhibits gemstones such as the star garnet, found only in southeast Asia and Idaho. Nearby, **Old Boise Historic District** (ⓦwww.oldboise.com) is an elegant area of stone-trimmed brick restaurants and shops built in the tasteful commercial Victorian style of the time. The **Basque Museum and Cultural Center**, 611 Grove St (Tues–Fri 10am–4pm, Sat 11am–3pm; $4; ⓦwww.basquemuseum.com), traces the heritage of the Basque shepherds of mountainous central Idaho through illuminating antiques, relics, photographs and key manuscripts.

Perhaps Boise's best attraction is its **Greenbelt**, some nineteen miles of paths that crisscross the tranquil **Boise River** to link various parks. In **Julia Davis Park**, the **Idaho Historical Museum** (May–Sept Tues–Sat 9am–5pm, Sun 1–5pm; Oct–April Tues–Fri 9am–5pm, Sat 11am–5pm; $5; ⓦhistory.idaha.gov) displays artefacts from Native American and Basque peoples, details the difficult experience of the Chinese miners of the 1870s and 1880s, and describe the lives of Idahoans from furriers to gold miners and ranchers. Also, the **Pioneer Village** preserves cabins and houses dating from as early as 1863, among them an adobe that belonged to the mayor in the 1870s. Nearby, the Discovery Center of Idaho, 131 W Myrtle St (Mon–Thurs 9am–5pm, Fri till 7pm, Sat 10am–5pm, Sun noon–5pm, winter closed Mon; $6.50; ⓦscidaho.org), has a wealth of kid-friendly science exhibits that include robots, telescopes and a 7ft-high tornado you can control.

The **Old Idaho Penitentiary**, at 2445 Old Penitentiary Rd, off Warm Springs Avenue (daily summer 10am–5pm; rest of year noon–5pm; $5; ⓦwww.idahohistory.net/oldpen.html), is an imposing 1870 sandstone citadel that remained open until 1974. Self-guided tours take you through the cramped solitary-confinement unit, and the gallows where the last hanging in Idaho was carried out a half-century ago. A small museum displays confiscated weapons and mugshots of former inmates, including one Harry Orchard, who murdered the state governor in 1905. Oddly situated beside the prison, the **Idaho Botanical Gardens** (Mon–Fri 9am–5pm, also summer Sat & Sun 10am–6pm; $4; Ⓦwww.idahobotanicalgarden.org) has a dozen themed gardens adorned with irises, roses, herbs and cacti, with one of them based around native plants that Meriwether Lewis reported in his 1805 explorer's journal.

Practicalities

Greyhound **buses** stop at 1212 W Bannock St, and Valley Ride (tickets $1; Ⓣ208/345-7433, Ⓦwww.valleyride.org) runs a fairly extensive **local bus** service. The **visitor centre** is at 312 S 9th St, suite 100 (April–Sept Mon–Sat 10am–6pm; Oct–March Mon–Fri till 3pm; Ⓣ208/344-7777, Ⓦwww.boise.org). Appealing **hotels** include *The Grove*, 245 S Capitol Blvd (Ⓣ208/333-8000 or 1-888/961-5000, Ⓦwww.grovehotelboise.com; ❸), offering good-value, well-appointed rooms, many with great views of the city and mountains, and *The Modern*, 1314 W Grove St (Ⓣ866/780-6012, Ⓦwww.themodernhotel.com; ❹), a revamped chain motel turned boutique hotel, which has a smart mid-century modern design and rooms with designer decor and HDTVs. The nicest **B&B** is the *Idaho Heritage Inn B&B*, 109 W Idaho St (Ⓣ208/342-8066, Ⓦwww.idheritageinn.com; ❸), a lovely Victorian building that was once the residence of Governor Chase Clark and later Senator Frank Church, with four agreeable rooms and suites.

Good options for **eating** in Boise include *Goldy's*, 108 S Capitol Blvd (Ⓣ208/345-4100), serving up a range of savoury items from salmon cakes to biscuits 'n gravy, and where you can create your own excellent breakfast combos for less than $12, and the *Grape Escape*, 800 W Idaho St (Ⓣ208/368-0200), a fine bistro offering gourmet cheeses, sandwiches, quiches, salads and wine tastings. *Bar Gernika*, 202 Capitol Blvd (Ⓣ208/344-2175), is excellent for its authentic Basque specialties – particularly the range of stews and lamb dishes. Appealing downtown **bars** include the bustling *Bittercreek Alehouse*, 246 N 8th St (Ⓣ208/345-1813), with its dozens of microbrews and decent burgers, and *Bardenay Restaurant & Distillery*, 610 Grove St (Ⓣ208/426-0538), which distils its spirits and features a nice range of affordable, tasty beef and seafood.

Finally, at the **Idaho Shakespeare Festival**, 5657 Warm Springs Ave (June–Sept; most tickets $29–39; Ⓣ208/336-9221, Ⓦwww.idahoshakespeare.org), performances can be inspired and tickets are usually cheap and available. Around five plays are presented per season, with two or three of them penned by the Bard.

Northern Idaho

The stark wilderness of the Sawtooth, Salmon River and Clearwater mountains makes travelling through the heart of Idaho impossible. There are only two routes between south and north: up the eastern fringe from Idaho Falls, or, more enjoyably, along US-95 via Hwy-55 out of Boise. The **Nez Percé** hunted buffalo, gathered berries and fished here for hundreds of years, until gold was discovered and they were forced to beat a bloody retreat. The heavily forested far north of the Idaho Panhandle is broken by hundreds of deep glacial lakes, the largest of which host resort towns such as **Coeur d'Alene** and **Sandpoint** – more stopovers than major destinations.

Hells Canyon region

From the busy little watersports and ski resort of **McCALL**, 110 miles north of Boise, Hwy-55 climbs steadily to merge with US-95 and follow the turbulent **Little Salmon River**. Just south of the hamlet of Riggins, thirty miles on, comes a good opportunity to see **Hells Canyon** from Idaho. With an average depth of 5500ft this is the deepest river gorge in the US, though you wouldn't guess so due to its broad expanse and lack of sheer walls. Nevertheless, it is impressive, with Oregon's Wallowa and Eagle Cap ranges rising behind it and the river glimmering far down below. Hwy-241 leads toward the overlooks; the final few miles of dirt road require a four-wheel-drive vehicle and permission from the Riggins forest ranger office on Hwy-95 (Mon–Fri 8am–5pm; Ⓣ208/628-3916, Ⓦwww.fs.fed.us/hellscanyon). The canyon is also accessible by road from Oregon (see p.996) and by boat from Lewiston.

The hamlet of **RIGGINS** sits in a steeply rising T-shaped canyon, and is prime **whitewater-rafting** and **kayaking** country, as outfitters, spread along a one-mile stretch of the one-street village, outnumber cafés and shops. The **Chamber of Commerce** (Ⓣ208/628-3778 or 1-866/221-3901, Ⓦwww.rigginsidaho.com) has details. From Riggins, US-95 heads north along the Salmon River Valley for thirty miles to the rumpled terrain around even smaller **White Bird**, the start of Nez Percé country.

Industrial **LEWISTON**, 110 miles north of Riggins, is best known for its **Lewiston Roundup**, a massive rodeo held in early September (Ⓣ208/746-6324, Ⓦwww.lewistonroundup.org), and as a starting point for journeys through Hells

The Nez Percé

The first whites to encounter the **Nez Percé** people were the weak, hungry and disease-ridden Lewis and Clark expedition in 1805. The natives gave them food and shelter, and cared for their animals until the party was ready to carry on westward.

Relations between the Nez Percé (so called by French-Canadian trappers because of their shell-pierced noses) and whites remained agreeable for over fifty years – until the discovery of gold, and white pressure for property ownership led the government to persuade some renegade Nez Percé to sign a treaty in 1863 that took away three-quarters of tribal land. As settlers started to move into the hunting grounds of the Wallowa Valley in the early 1870s, the majority of the Nez Percé, under **Chief Joseph**, refused to recognize the agreement. In 1877, after much vacillation, the government decided to enact its terms and gave the tribe thirty days to leave.

Ensuing skirmishes resulted in the deaths of a handful of settlers, and a large army force began to gather to round up the tribe. Chief Joseph then embarked upon the famous **Retreat of the Nez Percé**. Around 250 warriors (protecting twice as many women, children and old people) outmanoeuvred army columns many times their size, launching frequent guerrilla attacks in a series of narrow escapes. After four months and 1700 miles, the Nez Percé were cornered just thirty miles from the safety of the Canadian border. Chief Joseph then (reportedly) made his legendary speech of surrender, "From where the sun now stands I will fight no more forever". Today some 1500 live in a reservation between Lewiston and Grangeville – a minute fraction of their original territory.

Nez Percé National Historic Park, with 38 separate sites, is spread over a huge range of north-central Idaho, eastern Oregon and western Montana. At the visitor centre in Spalding, ten miles east of Lewiston (daily 8am–4.30pm, summer closes 5pm; free; Ⓣ208/843-7001, Ⓦwww.nps.gov/nepe), the Museum of Nez Percé Culture focuses on tribal arts and crafts, while the White Bird Battlefield, seventy miles further south on US-95, was where the tribe inflicted 34 deaths on the US Army, in the first major battle of the Retreat.

Canyon on the Salmon River. Boats sail past abandoned mineshafts and tribal caves, with mountain goats, bobcats, snakes and birds of prey adding further interest. Contact the Lewiston **Chamber of Commerce**, 111 Main St, Suite 120 (Mon–Fri 8am–4.30pm, ⓣ208/743-3531, ⓦwww.lewistonchamber.org) for information on the various outfitters.

Moscow

The thirty miles of US-95 between Lewiston and **MOSCOW** wind through the beautiful rolling hillsides of the fertile Palouse Valley. Moscow itself is a fun, friendly town that makes a good overnight stop, and is the site of the **University of Idaho**. Bookstores, galleries, bars and cafés line the tree-shaded **Main Street**, while theatre, music and independent cinema are on offer throughout the year, along with a sprinkling of arts festivals: the **Moscow Artwalk** (ⓣ208/883-7036) brings together dozens of artists, galleries and the public for diverting summertime exhibits, and the **Lionel Hampton Jazz Festival** (ⓣ208/885-6765, ⓦwww.uidaho.edu/jazzfest) showcases big names new and old.

Moscow's **visitor centre** is at 411 S Main St (ⓣ208/882-1800, ⓦwww.moscowchamber.com). Greyhound **buses** stop at the bare-bones *Royal Motor Inn*, 120 W Sixth St, though you're better off **staying** at the more reliable *Best Western*, 1516 Pullman Rd (ⓣ208/882-0550, ⓦwww.bestwesternidaho.com; ❺), which has a pool, clean rooms and a few serviceable restaurants. Alternatively, *Mary Jane's Farm*, 1000 Wild Iris Lane (ⓣ1-888/750-6004, ⓦwww.maryjanesfarm.org/bb; ❻), is a pleasant **B&B** with primitive facilities, where you're expected to get in touch with your pastoral side by working the farm like an authentic rustic. Good places to **eat** include *Wheatberries Bake Shop*, 531 S Main St (ⓣ208/882-4618), which has nice sandwiches, espresso drinks, soups and panini, and the stylish *Red Door*, 215 S Main St (ⓣ208/882-7830), excellent for its cocktails and upmarket seafood, game and steak.

Coeur d'Alene

No longer strictly identified with the neo-Nazis who made their home in nearby Hayden Lake, **COEUR D'ALENE**, fifty miles north of Moscow on US-95, is the site of the lovely 25-mile-long **Lake Coeur d'Alene**, which stretches into the mountains with evocative scenery that makes a great backdrop for boating, hiking and other activities. Poised on the lake is the expensive **Coeur d'Alene Resort**, which dominates the unremarkable downtown and is well worth the money if you want to spend most of your time golfing (ⓣ208/765-4000, ⓦwww.cdaresort.com; ❽). West of the resort at Independence Point, **cruises** ($20–44; ⓣ208/765-2300) range from ninety-minute jaunts that give you a closer view of the lake to six-hour journeys through the scenic St Joe River corridor, where all kinds of wildlife are on view.

Greyhound **buses** stop at 137 E Spruce St, and free local **transit** is available on Idaho City Link (ⓣ1-877/941-RIDE, ⓦwww.idahocitylink.com). The **visitor centre** is at 105 N First St (Mon–Fri 8am–5pm; ⓣ1-877/782-9232, ⓦwww.coeurdalene.org), which has a good range of information of outdoor outfitters, cruise operators, area parks, bike rentals and the like. Aside from the resort, you can **stay** at the cheap and clean *Flamingo Motel*, 718 E Sharman Ave (ⓣ1-800/955-2159, ⓦwww.flamingomotelidaho.com; ❺), which, along with its fridges and wi-fi, offers kitschy theme rooms kitted out in classic cowboy, tropical cabana and ultra-patriotic stylings, among other choices. By contrast, the *McFarland Inn*, 601 E Foster Ave (ⓣ208/667-1232, ⓦwww.mcfarlandinn.com; ❻), offers a more tasteful, though much less fun, B&B setting with DVD players and wi-fi. For **eating** out, the delights of *Beverly's* make a chic choice for seafood and beef in the *Coeur d'Alene Resort* (ⓣ208/765-4000), serving up the likes of king crab and bison carpaccio, and the *Bistro on Spruce*, 1710 N 4th St (ⓣ208/664-1774), has mid-priced, scrumptious items such as seared ahi tuna, duck confit and wild salmon, and huckleberry crème brûlée for dessert.

Silver Mountain and Wallace

About forty miles east of Coeur d'Alene on I-90, you'll come to Kellogg and the surprisingly good ski hill of **SILVER MOUNTAIN** (ⓣ208/783-1111 or 1-866/344-2675, ⓦwww.silvermt.com). It has the world's longest single-stage **gondola** (3.1 miles; rides $18), and is open year-round for fine skiing in winter (lift tickets $50–55), and some good mountain biking (rental $30–50/day) and hiking in summer; there's also lodging (❼), rates for which include use of the sizeable indoor **waterpark** facility (otherwise $27 for non-guests).

A further ten miles east are the authentic Western streets of **WALLACE**, where the town's buildings evoke strong images of silver-mining days. A fun, 75-minute trolley-car ride, the **Sierra Silver Mine Tour**, leaves from 420 N Fifth St (June–Aug daily tours on the half-hour 10am–4pm, May & Sept till 2pm; $12.50; ⓣ208/752-5151, ⓦwww.silverminetour.org), lets you descend a thousand feet to appreciate the hard labour endured by miners a century ago. To find out more about how they dug for shiny metal, drop by the **Wallace District Mining Museum**, 590 Bank St (daily: May–Sept 9am–5pm, Oct–April 10am–5pm, Nov–March till 3pm on Sat & Sun; $3; ⓦwallaceminingmuseum.org), which has replicas, photos and artefacts from the golden and silvery days; to find out what they did on their days off, visit the **Bordello Museum**, 605 Cedar St (tours on the half-hour Mon–Sat 9.30am–6.30pm, Sun 10am–5pm; $5; ⓣ208/753-0801), giving the hundred-year history of a certain local "institution". Wallace isn't a place to linger for long, but if you want to **stay** here, the *Wallace Inn*, 100 Front St (ⓣ208/752-1252, ⓦwww.wallaceinn.net; ❹), has a pool, hot tub, sauna and gym, though pretty basic rooms. For **dining**, the *Jameson*, 304 6th St (ⓣ208/556-6000), has mid-priced seafood and steak, and you can eat surrounded by vintage decor.

Sandpoint

Forty-four miles north of Coeur d'Alene, little **SANDPOINT** lies at the northwestern end of **Lake Pend Oreille** (pronounced "PON-duh-ray"), with its downtown overlooking placid Sandy Creek but its main attractions somewhat further out. At the south end of the lake, **Farragut State Park,** 13400 Ranger Rd (ⓣ208/683-2425), has 4,000 acres for boating, hiking, camping ($20–22) and the like. To the northeast, the spiky Selkirk Mountains hold the **Schweitzer Mountain Resort**, northern Idaho's best ski resort, with plenty of spacious, comfortable lodging (ⓣ208/263-9555, ⓦwww.schweitzer.com; ❻). Lift tickets are $60–65 and night skiing is $20; in summer you can use one of the lifts for hiking and mountain biking, $10 per ride or all day for $20.

Amtrak **trains** on the *Empire Builder* line pass through late at night in Sandpoint – the only stop in Idaho – at 450 Railroad Ave. Aside from the resort, **accommodation** includes the *Church Street House*, 401 Church St (ⓣ208/255-7094, ⓦwww.churchstreethouse.com; ❹), a fetching Arts and Crafts bungalow with a pair of pleasant rooms with some antique furnishings; and the handsome forest lodge of the *Talus Rock Retreat*, 291 Syringa Heights Rd (ⓣ208/255-8458, ⓦwww.sandpointretreat.com), whose capacious suites variously offer flat-screen TVs, kitchens, balconies, lofts and fireplaces. Good **dining** can be found at the *Sand Creek Grill,* 105 1st Ave (ⓣ208/255-5736), which serves upscale Northwest cuisine. For **drinking**, *Eichardts*, 212 Cedar St (ⓣ208/263-4005), has microbrews on tap and rock bands on weekends.

The Southwest

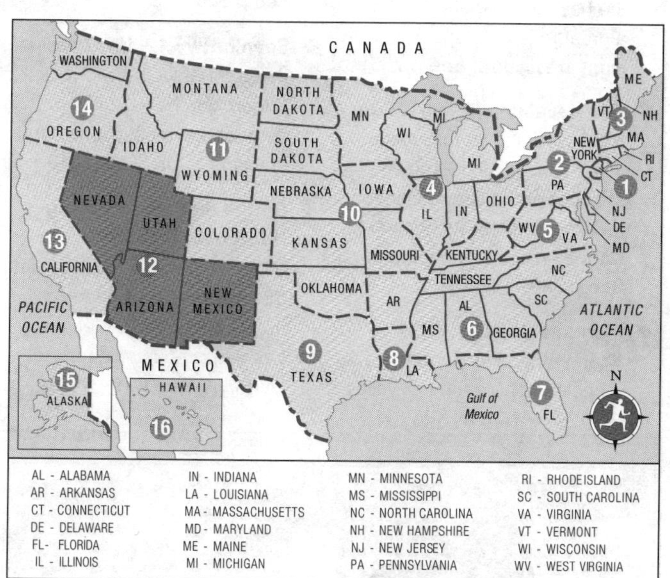

CHAPTER 12

Highlights

* **Santa Fe, NM** Great museums, fascinating history, atmospheric hotels – New Mexico's capital is a must on any Southwest itinerary. See p.757
* **La Posada** Glorious old restored hotel, straight from the heyday of Route 66, that's a great reason to spend a night in Winslow. See p.786
* **The Havasupai Reservation, AZ** Glorying in its turquoise waterfalls, this little-known offshoot of the Grand Canyon remains home to its original Native American inhabitants. See p.796
* **Monument Valley, AZ** Though the eerie sandstone monoliths of Monument Valley are familiar the world over, they still take every visitor's breath away. See p.800
* **Canyon de Chelly, AZ** Ancestral Puebloan "cliff dwellings" pepper every twist and turn of this stupendous sheer-walled canyon. See p.800
* **Scenic Hwy-12, UT** Crossing the heart of Utah's red-rock wilderness, Hwy-12 is perhaps the most exhilarating drive in the US. See p.810
* **Cirque du Soleil, Las Vegas, NV** Choose from seven different, dazzling shows from this postmodern Canadian troupe which has redefined Las Vegas spectacle for the century. See p.831

▲ John Ford Point, Monument Valley

12

The Southwest

The Southwestern desert states of **New Mexico**, **Arizona**, **Utah** and **Nevada** stretch from Texas to California, across an elemental landscape ranging from towering monoliths of red sandstone to snowcapped mountains, on a high desert plateau that repeatedly splits open to reveal yawning canyons. This overwhelming scenery is complemented by the emphatic presence of Native American cultures and the palpable legacy of America's Wild West frontier.

Among the region's earliest inhabitants were the **Ancestral Puebloans**. While their settlements and cliff palaces, abandoned seven centuries ago, are now evocative ruins, their descendants, the **Pueblo** peoples of New Mexico and the **Hopi** in Arizona, still lead similar lifestyles. Arriving from the fourteenth century onwards and adopting local agricultural and craft techniques, the **Navajo** and the **Apache** appropriated vast tracts of territory, which they in turn were soon defending against European immigrants. The first such, in 1540, were Coronado's **Spanish** explorers who spent two years fruitlessly searching for cities of gold. Sixty years later, Hispanic colonists founded **New Mexico**, an ill-defined province that extended into much of modern California and Colorado. Not until 1848 was the region forcibly taken over by the **United States**. Almost immediately, large numbers of outsiders began to pass through on their way to Gold Rush California.

Thereafter, violent confrontations increased between the US government and the Native Americans. The entire **Navajo** population was rounded up and forcibly removed to barren eastern New Mexico in 1864 (though they were soon allowed to return to northeastern Arizona), while the **Apache**, under warrior chiefs Cochise and Geronimo, fought extended battles with the US cavalry. Though the nominal intention was to open up lands to newly American settlers, few ever succeeded in extracting a living from this harsh terrain.

One exception were the **Mormons**, whose flight from persecution brought them by the late 1840s to the alkaline basin of Utah's **Great Salt Lake**. Through sheer hard work, they established what amounted to an independent country, with outlying communities all over the Southwest. They still constitute over sixty percent of Utah's population and control the state's government.

Each of the four Southwestern states remains distinct. New Mexico bears the most obvious traces of long-term settlement, the Native American pueblos of the north coexisting alongside former Spanish colonial towns like **Santa Fe**, **Albuquerque** and **Taos**. In Arizona, the history of the Wild West is more conspicuous, in towns such as **Tombstone**, site of the OK Corral. Over a third of the state belongs to Native American tribes, including the Apache, Hopi and Navajo; most live in the red-rock lands of the northeast, notably amid the splendour typified by the **Canyon de Chelly** and **Monument Valley**.

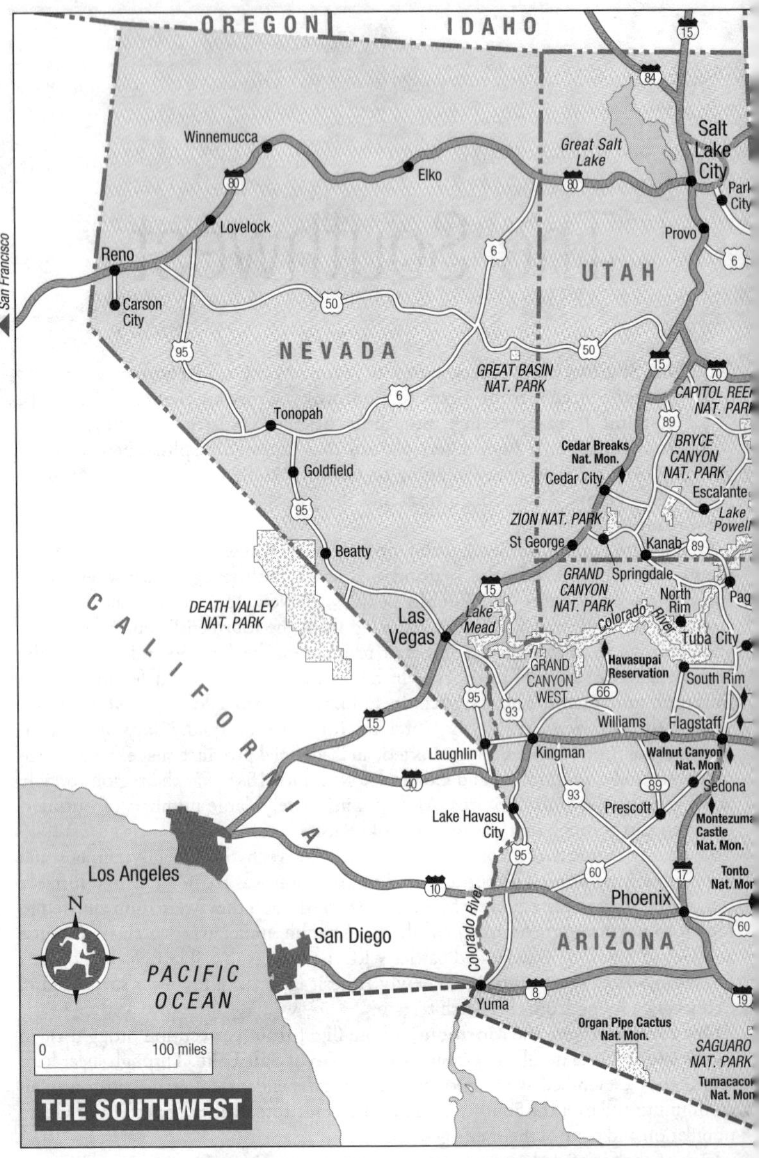

The canyon country of northern Arizona – even the immense **Grand Canyon** – won't prepare you for the uninhabited but compelling landscape of southern Utah, where **Zion** and **Bryce** canyons are the best known of a string of national parks and monuments. **Moab**, between majestic **Canyonlands** and surreal **Arches** in the east, is the top destination for outdoors enthusiasts. Nevada, on the other hand, is nothing short of desolate; gamblers are lured by the bright lights of **Las Vegas**, but away from the casinos there's little to see or do.

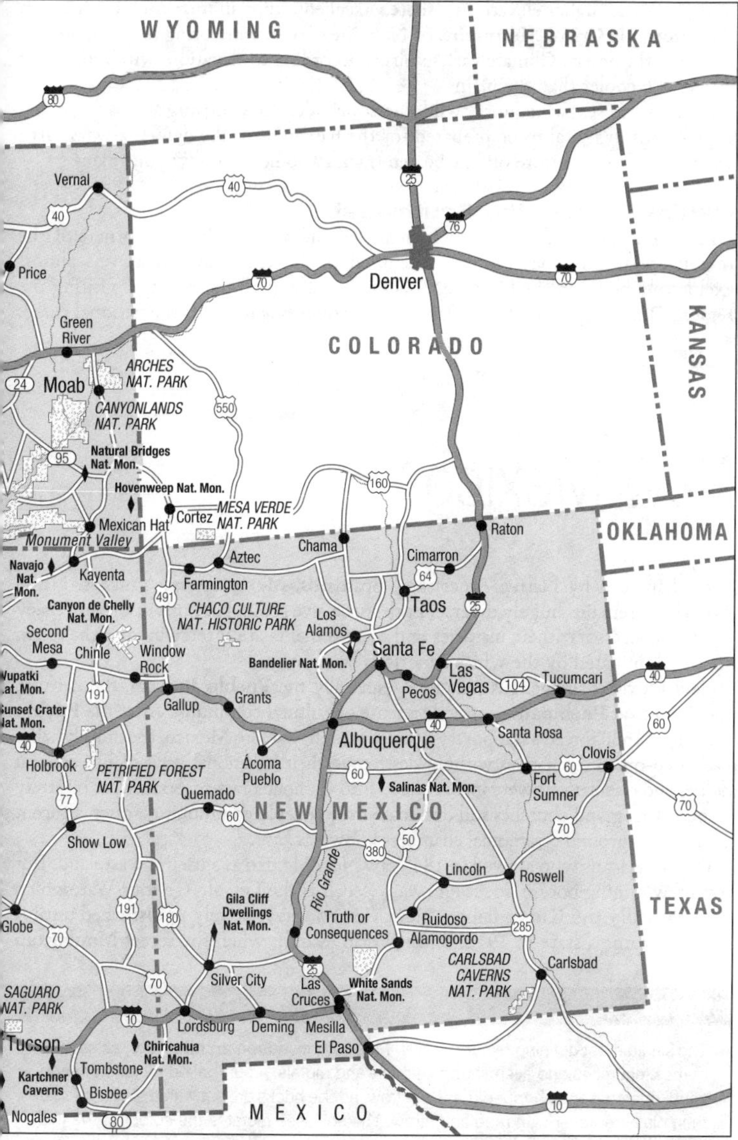

You can count on warm sunshine anywhere in the Southwest for nine months of the year, with incredible sunsets most evenings. Although "snowbirds" flock to southern Arizona in winter, elsewhere summer is the peak tourist season, for no good reason – air temperatures topping 100°F can make the outdoors unbearable, while in late summer awesome thunderstorms sweep in without warning, causing flash floods and forest fires. By October, perhaps the best time to come, the crowds are gone and in the mountains and canyons the leaves turn red and gold. Winter brings snow to higher elevations – there's excellent skiing in **northern Utah** and in the **Sangre de Cristo Mountains** of New Mexico – while spring sees wildflowers bloom in the desert. Climate varies sharply according to elevation, with mountains often 30°F cooler than the plains.

The Southwest's backcountry wildernesses are ideal for **camping** and backpacking expeditions. It's vital to be prepared for the harshness of the desert: always carry water and if you venture off the beaten track let someone know your plans.

Getting around the Southwest

Unless you have your own vehicle, many of the most fascinating corners of the region are utterly inaccessible. Scheduled public **transportation** runs almost exclusively between the big cities – which are not at all the point of visiting the region. One exception is Utah; various firms offer **bus tours** of the national parks.

New Mexico

Settled in turn by Native Americans, Spaniards, Mexicans and Yankees, **NEW MEXICO** remains hugely diverse. Each successive group has built upon the legacy of its predecessors; their histories and achievements are intertwined, rather than simply dominated by the white American latecomers.

New Mexico's indigenous peoples – especially the **Pueblo Indians**, the heirs of the **Ancestral Puebloans** – provide a sense of cultural continuity. After the **Pueblo Revolt** of 1680 forced a temporary Spanish withdrawal into Mexico, the proselytizing padres co-opted the natives without destroying their traditional ways of life, as local deities and celebrations were incorporated into Catholic practice. Somewhat bizarrely to outsiders, grand churches still dominate many Pueblo communities, often adjacent to the underground ceremonial chambers known as *kivas*.

The Americans who arrived in 1848 saw New Mexico as a useless wasteland. But for a few mining booms and range wars – such as the Lincoln County War, which brought **Billy the Kid** to fame – New Mexico was relatively undisturbed until it finally became a state in 1912. Since World War II, when the secret **Manhattan**

Adobe

The single most defining feature of New Mexico is its **adobe architecture**, as seen on homes, churches and even shopping malls and motels. A sun-baked mixture of earth, sand, charcoal and chopped grass or straw, adobe bricks are set with a similar mortar, then plastered over with mud and straw. The soil used dictates the colour of the final building, so subtle variations are apparent everywhere. However, adobe is a far from convenient material: it needs replastering every few years and turns to mud when water seeps up from the ground. These days, most of what looks like adobe is actually painted cement or concrete, but even this looks attractive enough in its own semi-kitsch way, while hunting out such superb genuine adobes as the remote **Santuario de Chimayó** on the **"High Road"** between Taos and Santa Fe, the formidable church of **San Francisco de Asis** in Ranchos de Taos or the multi-tiered dwellings of **Taos Pueblo**, can provide the focus of an enjoyable New Mexico tour.

Project built the first atomic bomb here, it has been home to America's premier weapons research outposts. By and large, people work close to the land, mining, farming and ranching.

In **northern New Mexico**, the magnificent **Rio Grande Valley** cradles both **Santa Fe**, the adobe-fronted capital and the artists' colony of **Taos**, with its nearby pueblo. The broad swath of **central New Mexico** along I-40 – which succeeded the old **Route 66** – pivots around the state's biggest city, **Albuquerque**, with the mesa-top Pueblo village of **Ácoma** ("Sky City") an hour's drive west. In wild, wide-open **southern New Mexico**, deep **Carlsbad Caverns** are the main attraction, while you can still stumble upon mining and cattle-ranching towns barely changed since the end of the Wild West.

Northern New Mexico

The mountainous north is the New Mexico of popular imagination, with its pastel colours, vivid desert landscape and adobe architecture. Even **Santa Fe**, the one real city, is hardly metropolitan in scale and the narrow streets of its small historic centre retain the feel of bygone days. The amiable frontier town of **Taos**, 75 miles northeast, is remarkable chiefly for the stacked dwellings of neighbouring **Taos Pueblo**.

An hour's drive west from Taos or Santa Fe brings you to **Bandelier National Monument**, where ancient cliff dwellings were carved out of the volcanic plateau that now holds the laboratories of **Los Alamos**. Alternatively, the hills east of the Rio Grande hold characterful Hispanic hamlets, threaded along the scenic mountain **High Road**.

Santa Fe

One of America's **oldest** and most **beautiful** cities, **SANTA FE** was founded by Spanish adventurers and missionaries a decade before the Pilgrims reached Plymouth Rock. Spread across a high plateau at the foot of the stunning **Sangre de Cristo** mountains, New Mexico's capital still glories in the adobe houses and baroque churches of its original architects, while its newer museums and galleries attract art-lovers from all over the world. The busiest season is **summer**, when temperatures usually reach into the eighties Fahrenheit; in winter, the average daytime high is a mere 42°F, though with snow on the mountains the city looks more ravishing than ever.

As upward of a million and a half tourists descend yearly upon a town of just seventy thousand inhabitants, Santa Fe has inevitably grown somewhat overblown. There's still a lot to like about Santa Fe, however. Despite the summer crowds, the downtown area – clustered around its venerable **plaza** – still has the peaceful ambience of a small country town, while holding an extraordinary array of cultural and historic treasures. The rigorous insistence that every building should look like a seventeenth-century Spanish colonial palace takes a bit of getting used to, but above all else, it's rare indeed for it to be such fun simply to stroll around a Southwestern city.

Arrival and information

A handful of **flights** from Dallas and LA serve Santa Fe's tiny municipal airport, but most visitors arrive by **car**, driving an hour north on I-25 from **Albuquerque**. The new Rail Runner **train** line connects Albuquerque, both the airport and downtown, with Santa Fe's Railyard district, half a mile southwest of downtown (journey time 1 hr 30min; $7 one-way, $9 all-day pass; Ⓣ 1-866/795-7245, Ⓦ www.nmrailrunner.com).

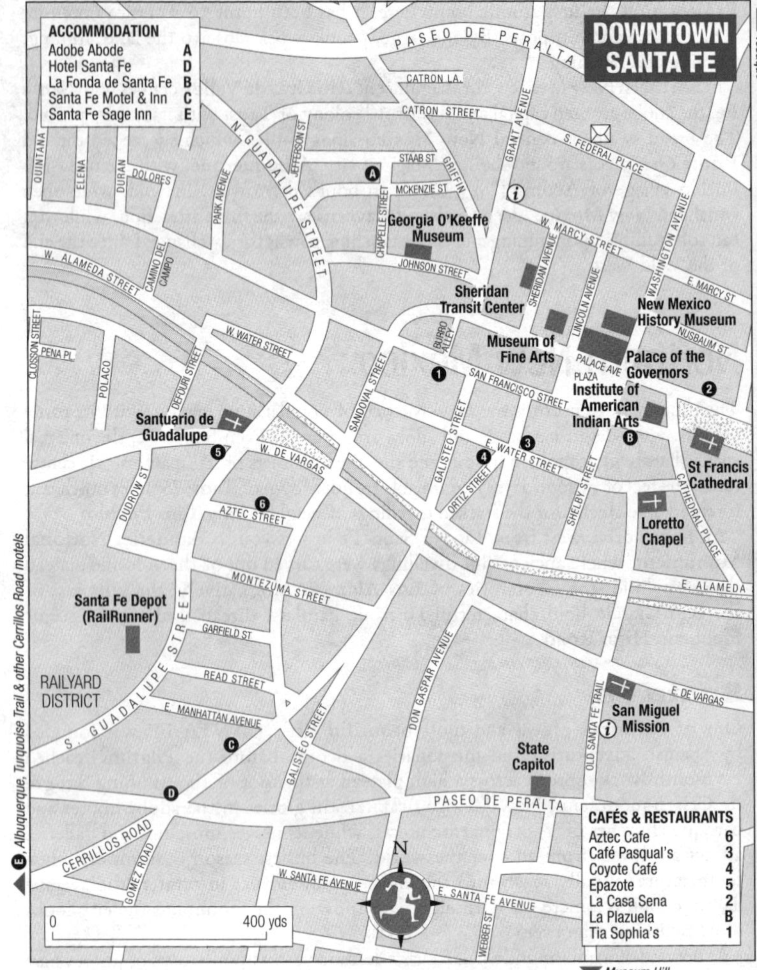

Amtrak trains do not serve Santa Fe, though arrivals at **Lamy**, 17 miles southeast, are met by Lamy Shuttle vans ($20 one-way; ⓣ505/982-8829). **Buses** from all over the Southwest call at the Greyhound terminal at 858 St Michael's Drive (ⓣ505/471-0008), a long way from the plaza.

By far the most useful **visitor centre** is run by the New Mexico Department of Tourism, at 491 Old Santa Fe Trail (daily: June–Aug 8am–7pm; Sept–May 8am–5pm; ⓣ505/827-7336 or 1-800/545-2040, ⓦwww.newmexico.org).

Most of what there is to see lies within walking distance of the central plaza, but to get there from your hotel or to see the farther-flung attractions, you may need to use the Santa Fe Trails **bus** #2, which connects with the motels on Cerrillos Road, while route #M loops between the plaza and the outlying museums (flat fare $1, all-day pass $2; ⓣ505/955-2001, ⓦsantafenm.gov). Santa Fe's only **taxi** company is Capital City Cabs (ⓣ505/438-0000). Two-hour **walking tours** of town set off from the blue gate of the Palace of the Governors on Lincoln Avenue (April–Oct Mon–Sat 10.15am; $10; ⓣ505/476-5100).

Accommodation

Even in winter, you won't find a **room** within walking distance of downtown for under $80 and in summer – when every bed is frequently taken – there's little under $125. The main road in from I-25, Cerrillos Road, holds most of the motels and the one hostel.

The most appealing **campgrounds** nearby are in the Santa Fe National Forest, starting seven miles up Hwy-475, northeast of town (summer only; ⓣ1-877/444-6777, ⓦwww.recreation.gov).

Adobe Abode 202 Chapelle St ⓣ505/983-3133, ⓦwww.adobeabode.com. Small, playfully themed, central B&B, offering folk-art-filled rooms both in a century-old house and in a separate newer building. ❻

El Rey Inn 1862 Cerrillos Rd at St Michael's Drive ⓣ505/982-1931 or 1-800/521-1349, ⓦwww.elreyinnsantafe.com. Great-value white-painted 1930s adobe motel, with stylish and distinctive Southwestern rooms, free breakfasts and pool. ❺

Hotel Santa Fe 1501 Paseo de Peralta at Cerillos Rd ⓣ505/982-1200 or 1-800/825-9876, ⓦwww.hotelsantafe.com. Attractive, elegant and very comfortable adobe hotel, within walking distance of the plaza, owned and run by Picuris Pueblo Indians and holding a good restaurant, *Amaya*. ❼

La Fonda de Santa Fe 100 E San Francisco St; ⓣ505/982-5511 or 1-800/523-5002, ⓦwww.lafondasantafe.com. Gorgeous old inn on the plaza, which features hand-painted murals and stained glass throughout. Each lavishly furnished room is different and there's a good restaurant, plus a lounge with live entertainment and a rooftop bar. ❾

Santa Fe International Hostel 1412 Cerrillos Rd at Alta Vista ⓣ505/988-1153, ⓦwww.hostelsantafe.com. This old-fashioned hostel, in a ramshackle former motel a couple of miles southwest of the plaza, is one of those love-it-or-hate-it places. Some travellers find the staff unfriendly and the rooms poorly furnished and dirty; others seem totally satisfied, say there's a good atmosphere and don't mind the compulsory chores. Dorms beds cost $18, en-suite rooms $35 single, $45 double. In winter the whole place can be damp and cold. ❷

Santa Fe Motel & Inn 510 Cerrillos Rd ⓣ505/982-1039 or 1-800/930-5002, ⓦwww.santafemotel.com. Delightfully stylish little adobe complex where even the most conventional rooms are appealingly furnished. Some have their own kitchens, while there are also several gorgeous little *casitas*. The staff are very friendly and rates – great for such a quiet, central location – include cooked breakfast. ❺

Santa Fe Sage Inn 725 Cerrillos Rd at Don Diego; ⓣ505/982-5952 or 1-866/433-0335, ⓦwww.santafesageinn.com. Large, clean, motel, on the edge of the Railyard District with good rates and very helpful staff. Rates include free breakfast and local shuttle. ❹

Downtown Santa Fe: around the plaza

Even if it's not always easy to tell genuine historic buildings from modern counterfeits, there's a romantic continuity between today's Santa Fe and the Spanish settlement of four centuries ago. Once you've got your bearings, the best places to get a sense of local history and culture are the **Palace of the Governors** and the **Museum of Fine Arts** downtown and the museums of **Indian Arts and Culture** and **Folk Art** a couple of miles southeast. Two private museums, the **Museum of Spanish Colonial Art** and the **Georgia O'Keeffe Museum**, are also well worth seeing. Alternatively, set about exploring Santa Fe's distinct neighbourhoods, such as the old **Barrio Analco** just southeast of downtown, home to the **San Miguel Mission**; the **Canyon Road** arts district, just beyond; and funkier **Guadalupe Street** to the west, with its new **Railyard** development.

The main focus of life in Santa Fe, however, is still the central **plaza** – especially when filled with buyers and craftspeople during the annual **Indian Market**, on the weekend after the third Thursday in August and during the first weekend in September for the **Fiestas de Santa Fe**. Apart from an influx of art galleries and restaurants, the surrounding web of narrow streets has changed little. When the US took over in 1848, the new settlers chose to build in wood, but many of the finer adobe houses have survived. Since the 1930s, almost every non-adobe structure in sight of the plaza has been designed or redecorated to suit the Pueblo Revival mode, with rounded, mud-coloured plaster walls supporting roof beams made of thick pine logs. Central Santa Fe today, in fact, looks much more like its original Spanish self than it did a hundred years ago.

The low-slung, initially unprepossessing **Palace of the Governors**, set behind an arcaded veranda that serves as a market for Native American crafts-sellers, fills the entire northern side of the plaza (Mon–Thurs, Sat, & Sun 10am–5pm, Fri 10am–8pm; closed Mon in winter; $9, free Fri 5–8pm; Ⓦwww.palaceofthe governors.org). Originally sod-roofed, the oldest public building in the US was constructed in 1610 as the headquarters of Spanish colonial administration. Until 1913, it looked like a typical, formal, territorial building, with a square tower at each corner; its subsequent adobe "reconstruction" was based on pure conjecture. The well-preserved interior, organized around an open-air courtyard, holds excellent historical displays and a well-stocked bookstore. A new but sensitively integrated extension immediately behind the palace holds the very visual exhibits of the **New Mexico History Museum** (same hours and ticket), including some fascinating letters from Billy the Kid.

Just west of the palace, the **Museum of Fine Arts** (same hours and prices; Ⓦwww.mfasantafe.org) is housed in a particularly attractive adobe, with ornamental beams and a cool central courtyard and focuses on changing exhibits of contemporary painting and sculpture by mostly local artists. A block northwest at 217 Johnson St, the **Georgia O'Keeffe Museum** (June–Aug Sun–Wed 10am–5pm, Thurs–Sat 10am–8pm; Sept–May daily 10am–5pm; $10; Ⓦwww.okeeffemuseum.org) boasts the largest collection of O'Keeffes in the world, including many of the desert landscapes she painted near **Abiquiu**, forty miles northwest of Santa Fe, where she lived from 1946 until her death in 1986. In its permanent collection, some New York cityscapes make a surprising contrast to her trademark sun-bleached skulls and iconic flowers.

Across the tiny Santa Fe River to the southwest, three blocks along **Guadalupe Street**, an attractive little district centres around the small eighteenth-century **Santuario de Guadalupe** (May–Oct Mon–Sat 9am–4pm; Nov–April Mon–Fri 9am–4pm; donation). Former warehouses and factories in the **Railyard** nearby house boutiques, art galleries and restaurants, plus a Farmers Market (Tues & Sat 7am–noon, Thurs 3–7pm, Sun 10am–4pm).

Two blocks south of the plaza along the Old Santa Fe Trail stands the ancient **San Miguel Mission** (Mon–Sat 9am–5pm, Sun 1.30–4pm; $1). Only a few of the massive adobe internal walls survive from the original 1610 building, most of which was destroyed in the 1680 Pueblo Revolt.

Not far east, gallery-lined **Canyon Road** – which claims to be the oldest street in the US, dating from Pueblo days – climbs a steady but shallow incline along the riverbed, with plenty of fine adobes along the way.

The Museums of New Mexico

A combination ticket, costing $20 and valid for four days, grants admission to five leading **Santa Fe museums**: the Palace of the Governors (which also incorporates the New Mexico History Museum), the Museum of Fine Arts, the Museum of Indian Arts and Culture, the Museum of International Folk Art and the Museum of Spanish Colonial Art. You can also buy a one-day pass to any two museums for $15.

The outlying museums

On a plateau two miles southeast of the town centre, with extensive views of the surrounding hills and mountains, stands Santa Fe's other museum cluster. The delightful **Museum of International Folk Art** (daily 10am–5pm; closed Mon in winter; $9; Ⓦwww.moifa.org), focuses on a huge collection of clay figurines and models from around the world, arranged in colourful dioramas that include a Pueblo Feast Day with dancing *kachinas* and camera-clicking tourists. Its Hispanic Heritage Wing is an engaging reminder of just how close New Mexico's ties have always been with Mexico itself, while the gift shop sells unusual ethnic souvenirs from all over the world, such as miniature cars made from bottle-tops in Ghana. The neighbouring **Museum of Indian Arts and Culture** (same hours and prices; Ⓦwww.miaclab.org) holds superb Native American pottery, ranging from **Ancestral Puebloan** pieces up to the works of twentieth-century revivalists and covers contemporary Southwestern cultures in fascinating detail.

In the same complex, the **Museum of Spanish Colonial Art** displays traditional Hispanic religious artworks, such as the *santos* (naïve painted images) and *bultos* (carved wooden statues of saints) that are so pervasive in the iconography of Santa Fe (daily 10am–5pm; closed Mon in winter; $6; Ⓦwww.spanishcolonial.org).

Eating

Long renowned as a culinary hot spot, Santa Fe is bursting with high-quality **restaurants** per head, most of which lie within walking distance of the plaza.

Aztec Cafe 317 Aztec St Ⓣ505/820-0025. Counterculture hangout in the Galisteo St district, serving coffees, pastries and light meals until 7pm nightly, with occasional live music.

Café Pasqual's 121 Don Gaspar Ave Ⓣ505/983-9340. Lovely, lively Old/New Mexican restaurant, serving top-quality food (including breakfast) in an attractive tiled dining room a block south of the plaza. Entrees include vegetarian enchiladas ($23) and chile-rubbed filet mignon ($38); as an appetizer, try warm brie with whole roasted garlic ($16).

Coyote Café 132 W Water St Ⓣ505/983-1615, Ⓦwww.coyotecafe.com. Celebrity chef Mark Miller sold his showcase restaurant, just off the plaza, in 2007, but under new owners it remains as trendy as ever. The à la carte prices can be ferocious, with entrees like pan-seared white miso sea bass or elk tenderloin costing $40 or more and appetizers like chilled Hawaiian fish for $18. Lunch, especially at the rooftop *Cantina* upstairs, is a better deal.

Epazote 416 Agua Fria Ⓣ505/988-5991. Absolutely wonderful, very stylish Mexican restaurant, housed in a former convent. The chef takes an infectious delight in good food; forget the menu and let him cook whatever he fancies – whether it's spiced corn truffles with cheese, or even *chapulines* (grilled grasshoppers) – it all tastes wonderful. A full dinner should cost under $30/head. Dinner only, closed Sun.

La Casa Sena 125 E Palace Ave Ⓣ505/988-9232. Charming courtyard restaurant, a block from the plaza; zestful Southwestern lunches, with entrees around $11–15, are the best deal, though the set dinners are consistently good. *La Cantina*, adjoining, is a little cheaper and its staff performs Broadway show songs.

La Plazuela *La Fonda de Santa Fe*, 100 E San Francisco St Ⓣ505/982-5511. Delightful, beautifully decorated Mexican restaurant in the heart of *La Fonda*, open daily for all meals and with an open-air feel despite the glass ceiling. All the usual Mexican dishes are nicely prepared and sold for $12–16 at lunchtime, though dinner entrees, like filet mignon, can cost up to $44.

Tia Sophia's 210 W San Francisco St Ⓣ505/983-9880. Spicy, very inexpensive Mexican diner west of the plaza that's a huge hit with lunching locals. Daily except Mon 7am–2pm.

Nightlife and entertainment

Unlike its abundance of restaurants, Santa Fe has the limited **nightlife** you'd expect in a small city, though its cultural scene livens up in summer. For full listings, check the free weekly *Reporter* (Ⓦsfreporter.com). Year-round, musical and theatrical performances take place downtown at the **Lensic Performing Arts Centre**, a striking former movie theatre at 211 W San Francisco St (Ⓣ505/988-1234, Ⓦwww.lensic.org). The much-anticipated Santa Fe Opera season runs through July and

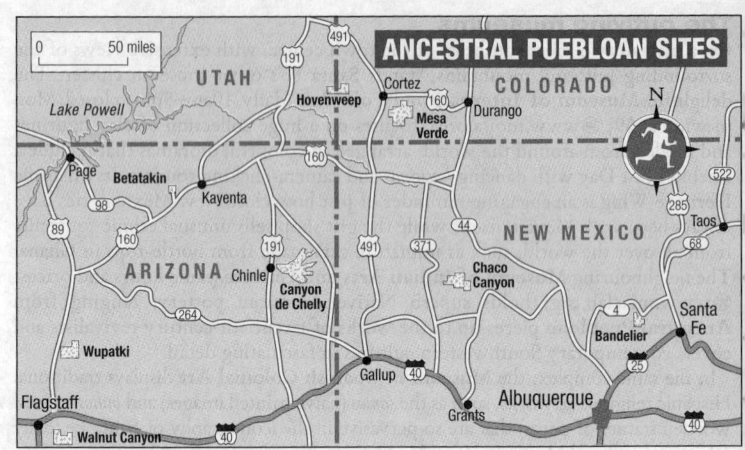

The Ancestral Puebloans

Few visitors to the Southwest are prepared for the awesome scale and beauty of the desert cities and cliff palaces left by the **Ancestral Puebloans**, as seen all over the high plateaus of the "**Four Corners**" district, where Colorado, New Mexico, Arizona and Utah now meet.

Although the earliest humans reached the Southwest around 10,000 BC, the Ancestral Puebloans first appeared as the **Basketmakers**, near the San Juan River, two thousand years ago. Named for their woven sandals and bowls, they lived in pits in the earth, roofed with logs and mud. Over time, the Ancestral Puebloans adopted an increasingly settled lifestyle, becoming expert farmers and potters. Their first freestanding houses on the plains were followed by multistoreyed **pueblos**, in which hundreds of families lived in complexes of contiguous "apartments". The astonishing **cliff dwellings**, perched on precarious ledges high above remote canyons, which they began to build around 1100 AD, were the first Ancestral Puebloan settlements to show signs of defensive fortifications. Competition for scarce resources became even fiercer toward the end of the thirteenth century and it's thought that warfare and even cannibalism played a role in their ultimate dispersal. Moving eastward, they joined forces with other displaced groups in a coming-together that eventually produced the modern **Pueblo Indians**. Hence the recent change of name, away from "Anasazi", a Navajo word meaning "ancient enemies", in favour of "Ancestral Puebloan".

Among the most significant **Ancestral Puebloan sites** are:

Mesa Verde Magnificent cliff palaces, high in the canyons of Colorado; see p.709.

Bandelier National Monument Large riverside pueblos and cave-like homes hollowed from volcanic rock; see opposite.

Chaco Canyon The largest and most sophisticated freestanding pueblos, far out in the desert; see p.771.

Wupatki Several small pueblo communities, built by assorted tribal groups; see p.788.

Walnut Canyon Numerous canyon-wall houses above lush Walnut Creek; see p.788.

Betatakin Canyon-side community set in a vast rocky alcove in Navajo National Monument; see p.798.

Canyon de Chelly Superbly dramatic cliff dwellings in a glowing sandstone canyon now owned and farmed by the Navajo; see p.800.

Hovenweep Enigmatic towers poised above a canyon; see p.817.

August in a magnificent amphitheatre seven miles north of town (Ⓣ505/986-5900, Ⓦwww.santafeopera.org).

Some of the most atmospheric places to **drink** in town are in the old hotels – such as the downstairs lounge and rooftop bar of *La Fonda* on the plaza (see p.759) – but otherwise conventional bars are few and far between.

Catamount Bar 125 E Water St Ⓣ505/988-7222. Downtown bar with plenty of microbrews on tap and live rock or blues most nights.

Cowgirl Hall of Fame 319 S Guadalupe St Ⓣ505/982-2565. Very busy country-themed restaurant and bar, with regular live music.

El Farol 808 Canyon Rd Ⓣ505/983-9912. Historic bar-cum-restaurant that serves Spanish tapas to musical accompaniment from blues to flamenco.

Evangelo's 200 W San Francisco St Ⓣ505/982-9014. The only good bare-bones bar in easy walking range of the plaza, with a pool table, a jukebox and occasional live music.

Bandelier National Monument

The Ancestral Puebloan ruins of **Bandelier National Monument** cut into the forested mesas of the Pajarito Plateau, 35 miles northwest of Santa Fe. Around 1300 AD, itinerant groups, seeking sanctuary from drought and invasion, gathered here to build a community that amalgamated their assorted cultures.

A paved 1.5-mile trail through the prime site, **Frijoles Canyon**, starts from the **visitor centre**, at the end of the narrow switchbacking road down from Hwy-4 (daily: June–Aug 8am–6pm; March–May, Sept & Oct 9am–5.30pm; Nov–Feb 9am–4.30pm; $12/vehicle; Ⓣ505/672-3861, Ⓦwww.nps.gov/band). Not far along, a side path from the circular, multistorey village of **Tyuonyi** leads up to dozens of **cave dwellings**, their rounded chambers scooped out of the soft volcanic rock; you can scramble up to and even enter, some, to peer out across the valley. The main trail continues to the **Long House**, an 800-foot series of two- and three-storey houses built against the canyon wall. Rows of petroglyphs are visible, carved above the holes that held the roof beams. Half a mile beyond, protected by a rock overhang 150ft above the canyon floor and accessible only via rickety ladders and steep stairs, a reconstructed *kiva* sits in **Alcove House**.

Los Alamos

Immediately east of Bandelier, **Los Alamos National Laboratory** is the main US centre for the research and development of **nuclear weapons** (as well as neurobiology, computer science and solar and geothermal energy). Apart from the small and oversimplified **Bradbury Science Museum** (Tues–Fri 10am–5pm, Sat–Mon 1–5pm; free; Ⓦlanl.gov/museum), where guides glow with excitement as they describe their weapons' devastating power, most of the complex is off-limits.

From Santa Fe to Taos: the High Road

The quickest route between Santa Fe and Taos follows US-84 as far as the Rio Grande, then follows the river northeast on Hwy-68. US-84 passes through the heartland of the **northern pueblos**, a cluster of tiny Tewa-speaking communities, but unless your visit coincides with a feast day (see box, p.764), there's little to see.

However, a circuitous route known as the **"High Road"** leaves US-68/84 a dozen miles north of Santa Fe, near Nambe Pueblo. Leading high into the wooded **Sangre de Cristo Mountains**, it passes a number of pueblos and Hispanic villages.

Chimayó

The quaint mountain village of **CHIMAYÓ**, 25 miles north of Santa Fe at the junction of Hwy-503 and Hwy-76, is the site of the 1816 **Santuario de Chimayó**

The Rio Grande Pueblos

The first Spaniards to explore what's now New Mexico encountered one hundred thousand so-called **Pueblo Indians**, living in a hundred villages and towns (*pueblo* is Spanish for "village"). Resenting the imposition of Catholicism and their virtual enslavement, the various tribes banded together in the 1680 **Pueblo Revolt** and ousted the entire colonial regime, killing scores of priests and soldiers and sending hundreds more south to Mexico. After the Spanish returned in 1693, the Pueblos showed little further resistance and they have coexisted ever since, accepting aspects of Catholicism – most pueblos hold a large adobe church – without giving up their traditional beliefs and practices. New Mexico is now home to around forty thousand Pueblo Indians; each of its nineteen autonomous pueblos has its own laws and system of government.

The Pueblos celebrate Saints' days, major Catholic holidays such as Easter and the Epiphany and even the Fourth of July with a combination of Native American traditions and Catholic rituals, featuring elaborately costumed dances and massive communal feasts. The spectacle of hundreds of costumed, body-painted tribal members of all ages, performing elaborate dances in such timeless surroundings, is hugely impressive.

However, few pueblos are quite the tourist attractions they're touted to be. While the best known, **Taos** and **Ácoma**, retain their ancient defensive architecture, the rest tend to be dusty adobe hamlets scattered around a windblown plaza. Unless you arrive on a feast day or are a knowledgeable shopper in search of Pueblo crafts, visits are liable to prove disappointing. In addition, you'll be made very unwelcome if you fail to behave respectfully – don't "explore" places that are off-limits to outsiders, such as shrines, *kivas* or private homes.

Fifteen of the pueblos are concentrated along the Rio Grande north of Albuquerque, with a long-standing division between the seven **southern pueblos**, south of Santa Fe, most of which speak Keresan and the group to the north, which mostly speak Tewa (pronounced *tay-wah*). Visitors to each are required to register at a visitor centre; some charge an admission fee of $3 to $10 and those that permit such activities typically charge additional fees of $5 for still photography, $10–15 for video cameras and up to $100 for sketching. There's no extra charge for feast days or dances, but photography is usually forbidden on special occasions.

(daily: May–Sept 9am–6pm; Oct–April 9am–4pm). Known as the "Lourdes of America" for the devotion of its many pilgrims, this round-shouldered, twin-towered adobe beauty sits behind an enclosed courtyard; a pit in the floor of a side room holds the "holy dirt" for which the site is venerated.

Half a mile further north on Hwy-503, the *Rancho de Chimayó*, a traditional New Mexican **restaurant**, serves superb *flautas* (filled rolled tortillas) and a mouthwatering *sopaipilla*, a fluffy pastry parcel stuffed with meat and chilies, on a lovely sun-drenched outdoor patio and offers reasonable **rooms** in a separate building (closed Mon Nov–April; ⓣ505/351-2222; ⓦwww.ranchodechimayo.com; ④).

Taos

Still home to one of the longest-established Native American populations in the US, though transformed by becoming first a Spanish colonial outpost and more recently a hangout for bohemian artists, Hollywood exiles and New Age dropouts **TAOS** (which rhymes with "mouse") is famous out of all proportion to its size. Just seven thousand people live in its three component parts: **Taos** itself, around the plaza; sprawling **Ranchos de Taos**, three miles to the south; and the Native American community of **Taos Pueblo**, two miles north.

Beyond the usual unsightly highway sprawl, Taos is a delight to visit. Besides museums, galleries and stores, it still offers an unhurried pace and charm and the sense of a meeting place between Pueblo, Hispanic and American cultures. Its reputation as an **artists' colony** began at the end of the nineteenth century. English novelist **D.H. Lawrence** visited three times in the 1920s and his widow Frieda later made her home in Taos. New generations of artists and writers have "discovered" Taos ever since, the most famous of all, **Georgia O'Keeffe**, stayed for a few years later in the 1920s.

Arrival and information

The Taos Express **shuttle bus** provides quick connections between Taos and the RailRunner station in Santa Fe ($7 one way; ⓣ575/551-4459, ⓦwww.taosexpress.com). Greyhound buses arrive at **Taos Bus Centre** (ⓣ575/758-1144), opposite the well-equipped local **visitor centre**, two miles south of the plaza at the intersection of Hwy-68 and US-64 (daily 9am–5pm, closed Sun in winter; ⓣ575/758-3873 or 1-800/732-8267, ⓦwww.taosvacationguide.com).

Accommodation

Taos has **accommodation** to meet all needs, at prices well below those of Santa Fe (though thanks to ski season, rates don't drop in winter). The best places to **camp** are the nine summer-only campgrounds in **Carson National Forest** (ⓣ575/758-6200, ⓦwww.fs.fed.us/r3/carson), reached by following Kit Carson Road east until it becomes US-64.

Abominable Snowmansion Hostel/HI-Taos Taos Ski Valley Rd, Arroyo Seco ⓣ575/776-8298, ⓦwww.snowmansion.com. Pleasant, friendly HI hostel-cum-ski lodge, on a tight curve in the road up to the Ski Valley, five miles north of downtown. Office open daily 8–11am & 4–10pm. Dorm beds $19 in summer, $22 in winter, when rates include breakfast; teepees and camping space outside, plus private rooms and cabins, with and without en-suite facilities. ❷

Best Western Kachina Lodge de Taos 413 Paseo del Pueblo Norte ⓣ575/758-2275 or 1-800/522-4462, ⓦwww.kachinalodge.com. Large, tasteful, family motel at the Taos Pueblo turn-off, with Southwestern art, a reasonable restaurant, a pool, live music and small-scale Pueblo dances every summer night. ❹

Historic Taos Inn 125 Paseo del Pueblo Norte ⓣ575/758-2233 or 1-888/518-8267, ⓦwww.taosinn.com. Rambling, ravishing – and very Southwestern – central hotel. Each of its 44 rooms plays a variation on the Pueblo theme, while *Doc Martin's* restaurant (see p.767) and the *Adobe Bar* are packed nightly. ❺–❾

Indian Hills Inn 233 Paseo del Pueblo Sur ⓣ575/758-4293 or 1-800/444-2346, ⓦwww.newmex.com/indianhillsinn. The only cheapish highway motel within walking distance of the plaza; be sure to get a room away from the street. ❹

La Fonda de Taos 108 South Plaza ⓣ575/758-2211 or 1-800/833-2211, ⓦwww.lafondataos.com. Vintage 1930s hotel on the plaza that's been revamped to hold 24 luxurious suites, with Southwestern furnishings and tiled bathrooms. ❺

Mabel Dodge Luhan House 240 Morada Lane ⓣ575/751-9686 or 1-800/846-2235, ⓦwww.mabeldodgeluhan.com. Gorgeous 200-year-old adobe B&B complex, not far northeast of the plaza, where the lovely guest rooms are named for former guests like Willa Cather and Ansel Adams. Two rooms, including the light-filled solarium, share a bathroom painted by D.H. Lawrence; a cheaper lodge annexe has more modern fittings. ❺

Taos plaza and the museums

The old Spanish **plaza** at the heart of Taos is now ringed by jewellery stores, art galleries and restaurants; all conform to the predominant Pueblo motif of rounded brown adobe. Specific sights are few – a small **gallery** in the *Fonda de Taos* holds a collection of sexy but amateurish paintings by D.H. Lawrence and the tree-filled square itself is often animated by guitar-toting buskers – but the surrounding streets are perfect for an aimless stroll. **Bent Street**, a block north of the plaza, takes its name from the first American governor of New Mexico, Charles Bent; his house here, in which he was murdered in 1847, has been preserved as a ramshackle little museum of frontier life (daily April–Oct 9.30am–5pm, Nov–March 10am–4pm; $2).

Just east of the plaza, across the highway at the end of Taos's sole surviving stretch of wooden boardwalk, the mid-1800s adobe home of mountain man, mason and part-time US cavalry officer **Kit Carson** (see opposite) is now a small **museum**, commemorating his many adventures (daily 9am–6pm; $5).

Two miles north of the Taos Pueblo turn-off, reached by a dirt road that angles into a tricky five-way intersection, the **Millicent Rogers Museum** (daily 10am–5pm; closed Mon Nov–March; $10; Ⓦwww.millicentrogers.org) holds the collections of the Standard Oil heiress, who died in 1953, including superb Ancestral Puebloan and Mimbres pottery; the more recent black-on-black ceramics of San Ildefonso Pueblo potter Maria Martínez; and beautiful Navajo blankets.

Ranchos de Taos

South of the plaza, **Ranchos de Taos** was originally a separate farming community. Each *rancho* had its own main house or *hacienda*; the 1804 **Hacienda Martínez** (daily April–Oct 9am–5pm, Nov–March 10am–4pm; $7), two miles southwest on Ranchitos Road, is now a **museum** of colonial life. Within its fortress-like, windowless, adobe walls, two dozen rooms are wrapped around two patios, holding animal pens and a well. Trade goods of the kind its first owner, Taos mayor Don Antonio Martínez, carried south along the Rio Grande are displayed alongside tools, looms and simple furnishings.

In Ranchos' own small plaza, the mission church of **San Francisco de Asis** squares its broad shoulders or more accurately its massive adobe buttresses, to the passing traffic. Built around 1776, it's among colonial New Mexico's most splendid architectural achievements, with subtly rounded walls and corners disguising its underlying structural strength. Though the ever-changing interplay of light and shade across its golden exterior has fascinated painters from Georgia O'Keeffe onward, the interior is equally intriguing, with a magnificently ornate green-and-red reredos framing several naïve paintings.

Taos Pueblo

Continuously inhabited for nearly one thousand years, the two multistorey adobes at **Taos Pueblo**, two miles north of Taos plaza and half a mile east of Hwy-68, jointly constitute the most impressive Native American dwelling place still in use. Hlauuma, the north house and Hlaukwima, the south house, are separated by the Rio Pueblo de Taos, which flows down from the sacred Blue Lake, inaccessible to outsiders. Pueblo residents make few concessions to the modern world, living without toilets, running water or electricity.

The pueblo is generally open to visitors daily from 8am until 4.30pm, but it often closes for tribal events such as festivals or funerals and remains closed between mid-February and early April (Ⓣ575/758-1028, Ⓦwww.taospueblo.com). Assuming the pueblo is open, park at the edge of the plaza and pay an **entrance fee** ($10/person, plus $5/still or video camera), that entitles you to join guided **walking tours** led by Pueblo residents.

For most of the year, Pueblo life continues with scant regard for the intrusion of tourists, but summer feast days and dances, like the **Corn Dances** in June and July and the **Feast of San Gerónimo** at the end of September, can be spectacular.

Taos Ski Valley

Fifteen miles north of Taos, the challenging slopes of **Taos Ski Valley** are reached via an attractive road that winds up from the village of Arroyo Seco. Located on the north flank of **Wheeler Peak**, the highest point in New Mexico at 13,161ft, the demanding runs are usually open to skiers and snowboarders between late November and early April (daily lift tickets late Nov to mid-Dec and late March to early April $48, mid-Dec to late March $71; ⓣ1-800/238-2829, ⓦwww.skitaos.org).

Eating, drinking and nightlife

Taos is too small to offer much **nightlife**, but it does have a fine selection of **restaurants** in all price ranges and several coffeehouses. If your main priority is to **drink**, the *Adobe Bar* in the *Historic Taos Inn* (see p.765) is the cosiest spot in town.

Bent Street Deli & Cafe 120 Bent St ⓣ575/758-5787. Airy, partly outdoor place, just north of the plaza with good-value breakfasts, sandwich lunches and tasty dinners for under $20.

Caffè Tazza 122 Kit Carson Rd ⓣ575/758-8706. Ramshackle central café with nice sunlit terrace, selling coffees and light veggie meals to students and assorted eccentrics.

Doc Martin's *Taos Inn*, 125 Paseo del Pueblo Norte ⓣ575/758-1977. Delicious, inventive New Mexican food in a romantic adobe inn, just east of the plaza. All meals daily; a *prix-fixe* dinner featuring dishes like piñon-crusted salmon or roast chicken, costs $40.

Taos Pizza Outback 712 Paseo del Pueblo Norte ⓣ575/748-3112. Hard-to-find pizzeria, a mile north of town, with a welcoming, youthful ambience and huge portions of great food – the $12 veggie calzones are amazing.

Albuquerque and central New Mexico

Most travellers simply race through **central New Mexico**, but it does hold isolated pockets of interest. Dozens of small towns hang on to remnants of the winding old "Chicago-to-LA" **Route 66**, long since superseded by I-40. **Albuquerque**, New Mexico's largest city, sits dead centre, where I-40 and I-25 meet. The area to the **east**, stretching toward Texas, is largely desolate, but the mountainous region **west** offers more – above all **Ácoma Pueblo**, the mesa-top "Sky City".

Tucumcari and Fort Sumner

A long line of truck stops, diners and motels makes **TUCUMCARI**, 175 miles **east** of Albuquerque, a favourite I-40 pit stop. To enjoy one of the world's greatest collections of barbed wire, drop in at the **Tucumcari Historical Museum**, housed in a former schoolhouse at 416 S Adams St (Tues–Sat 10am–5pm; $2). Literally hundreds of inexpensive **rooms** lie along this stretch of old Route 66, including the classic *Blue Swallow* **motel**, 815 E Route 66 (closed Dec–Feb; ⓣ505/461-9849, ⓦwww.blueswallowmotel.com; ❷). *Del's Restaurant*, 1202 E Route 66 (ⓣ505/461-1740; closed Sun), is as good a **diner** as you're going to find.

FORT SUMNER, southwest of Tucumcari, is where frontiersman and US Army colonel **Kit Carson** dragged the Navajo from Arizona in 1864 (see p.798). At **Fort Sumner State Monument**, seven miles southeast of the modern town on their former reservation, the **Bosque Redondo Memorial** honours the Navajo and Apache who died during their imprisonment (daily 8.30am–5pm; $5; ⓦwww.nmmonuments.org). The grave of **Billy the Kid**, gunned down in Fort Sumner by Pat Garrett in 1881, stands behind the jumbled **Old Fort Sumner Museum** (daily 9am–5pm; $4), his tombstone shielded from memento-seekers by a steel cage.

Albuquerque

Sprawling at the heart of New Mexico, where the east–west road and rail routes cross both the Rio Grande and the old road south to Mexico, **ALBUQUERQUE**

Route 66

If you do ever plan to motor west, there's still one definitive highway that's the best. Eighty years since it was first completed, seventy since John Steinbeck called it "the mother road, the road of flight" in *The Grapes of Wrath* and sixty since songwriter Bobby Troup set it all down in rhyme, what better reason to visit the Southwest could there be than to get hip to this timely tip and get your kicks on **Route 66**?

The heyday of Route 66 as the nation's premier cross-country route – winding from Chicago to LA – lasted barely twenty years, from its being paved in 1937 until it began to be superseded by freeways in 1957. It was officially rendered defunct in 1984, when Williams, Arizona, became the last town to be bypassed. Nonetheless, substantial stretches of the original Route 66 survive, complete with the motels and drive-ins that became icons of vernacular American architecture. Restored 1950s roadsters and the latest Harley Davisons alike flock to cruise along the atmospheric, neon-lit frontages of towns such as Albuquerque and Flagstaff, or through such empty desertscapes as those between Grants and Gallup in New Mexico or Seligman and Kingman in Arizona.

is, with half a million people, the state's only major metropolis. The "**Duke City**" may have grown a bit fast for comfort, but the original Hispanic settlement is still discernible at its core and its diverse population gives it a rare cultural vibrancy. Even if its architecture is often uninspired, the setting is magnificent, sandwiched between the Rio Grande and the glowing **Sandia Mountains**. Specific highlights include the intact **Spanish plaza**, the neon-lit **Route 66** frontage of Central Avenue and the excellent **Indian Pueblo Cultural Centre**, while every October Albuquerque hosts the nation's largest **hot-air balloon** rally.

Arrival and information

Public transportation in Albuquerque has been transformed by the **Rail Runner** light-rail system (fares from $1; ⓣ1-866/795-7245, ⓦwww.nmrailrunner.com). Commuter trains from its downtown Albuquerque station, in the **Alvarado Transportation Centre** at First and Central, run south to Belen and north all the way to Santa Fe (see p.757). The first Rail Runner stop south of downtown, the Bernalillo County/International Sunport station at 113 Rio Bravo SE, is a short ride from the **airport** on ABQ Ride bus #222.

Besides being a stop for cross-country Amtrak trains, the Alvarado Transportation Centre is also the hub of the ABQ Ride **city bus** network (ⓣ505/843-9200, ⓦwww.cabq.gov/transit). Its free D-Ride route circles downtown, while commuter buses further afield cost $1 a ride.

Accommodation

The twenty-mile length of **Central Avenue**, the old Route 66, is lined with the flashing neon signs of $40-per-night **motels**. You'll have to pay a little extra to stay in the heart of Old Town or downtown. Larger convention **hotels** are congregated along the interstates and near the airport.

Ambassador Inn 7407 Central Ave NE ⓣ505/265-1161. There's nothing fancy or exciting about the *Ambassador*, east of the liveliest part of Central Avenue, but for a clean, presentable ordinary motel room, the price is great. ❷

Andaluz 125 Second St NW ⓣ505/242-9090 or 1-800/777-5732, ⓦwww.hotelandaluz.com. Historic, elegant hotel, built as *La Posada* by Conrad Hilton in 1939 and now exquisitely re-vamped as downtown's most appealing upscale option. ❼

Casas de Sueños 310 Rio Grande Blvd SW ⓣ505/247-4560 or 1-800/665-7002, ⓦwww.casasdesuenos.com. Beautifully furnished, exotic and friendly B&B, very close to Old Town, with themed cottages and smaller rooms. ❺

La Quinta Inn Albuquerque Airport 2116 Yale Blvd SE ⓣ505/243-5500, ⓦwww.lq.com. Large, upscale motel, served by frequent shuttles from the nearby airport and offering safe, good-value accommodation. ❹

Monterey Nonsmokers Motel 2402 Central Ave SW ⓣ505/243-3554 or 1-877/666-8379, ⓦwww.nonsmokersmotel.com. Clean, fifteen-room motel, two blocks west of Old Town, with pool, laundry and a strict nonsmoking policy. ❷

Route 66 Hostel 1012 Central Ave SW ⓣ505/247-1813, ⓦwww.rt66hostel.com. Albuquerque's only hostel, a friendly place between Old Town and downtown, offers dorm beds for $20, kitchen facilities and very plain private doubles from $30 or $35 en suite. Rates include breakfast. ❶

Old Town

Once you've cruised up and down **Central Avenue**, looking at the flashing neon and 1940s architecture of this twenty-mile stretch of Route 66, most of what's interesting about Albuquerque is concentrated in **Old Town**, the heart of the Spanish city. As the interstate billboards rightly proclaim, "it's darned old and historic". The tree-filled **main plaza** is overlooked by the twin-towered adobe facade of **San Felipe de Neri church**; it's a pleasant place to wander or have a meal, even if there's not a whole lot to do.

Five minutes northeast of the plaza, the **Albuquerque Museum of Art and History**, 2000 Mountain Rd (daily except Mon 9am–5pm; $4, free Sun 9am–1pm; ⓦwww.cabq.gov/museum), holds impressive weapons carried by the Spanish conquistadors as well as delicate religious artefacts and paintings and photos depicting Albuquerque through the centuries.

Nearby, the **New Mexico Museum of Natural History**, 1801 Mountain Rd NW (daily 9am–5pm; $7; ⓦwww.nmnaturalhistory.org), has full-scale models of dinosaurs and a replica of a Carlsbad-like snow cave. Its fascinating "Start Up" exhibition uses Microsoft's origins in Albuquerque in 1977 as the springboard for a history of the computer revolution.

The riverfront

The Rio Grande being an unruly river, which repeatedly shifts its course, much of the land immediately west of Old Town has perforce been left undeveloped. Along the wooded eastern riverbank, the **Bio Park** holds two attractions. The **Albuquerque Aquarium** (June–Aug Mon–Fri 9am–5pm, Sat & Sun 9am–6pm; Sept–May daily 9am–5pm; $7; ⓦwww.cabq.gov/biopark) offers the chance to dine beside a glass-walled tank filled with live sharks or walk through a tunnel surrounded by fierce-eyed moray eels. Across the way, the **Rio Grande Botanic Garden** (same hours; same ticket) consists of two large conservatories – one holding rare plants from the Sonoran and Chihuahua deserts, the other more temperate Mediterranean species – plus a series of walled gardens.

Indian Pueblo Cultural Centre

The **Indian Pueblo Cultural Centre**, at 2401 12th St NW, one block north of I-40, is a stunning museum (daily 9am–5pm; $6; ⓦwww.indianpueblo.org) and crafts market (daily 9am–5.30pm; free), cooperatively owned and run by the diverse Pueblo Indians of New Mexico.

As well as explaining the shared Ancestral Puebloan heritage at the root of Pueblo culture, the museum explores the impact of the Spanish conquistadors. There's also a good explanation of a topic Pueblo Indians rarely discuss with outsiders: how indigenous religion has managed to coexist with imported Catholicism. Videos illustrate modern Pueblo life and the stores upstairs sell outstanding pottery and jewellery, while a good-quality **café** serves Pueblo specialties.

Sandia Crest

The forested 10,500-foot peaks of the **Sandia Crest** soar east of Albuquerque, affording beautiful views during and after sunset. In summer it's a good 25°F cooler up here than in the valley, while in winter you can go downhill or cross-country **skiing** (mid-Dec to mid-March; lift tickets $50; ⓣ505/242-9052, ⓦwww.sandiapeak.com). If you don't want to drive the scenic but twisting twenty-mile route from Albuquerque, take the stunning **Sandia Peak Tramway** (summer daily 9am–9pm; winter Mon & Wed–Sun 9am–8pm, Tues 5–8pm; $20), the world's longest single-span tramway at 2.7 miles; it leaves from the end of Tramway Road at the city's northeast edge.

Eating

Albuquerque is the place to get to grips with what real New Mexico food is all about. Family diners all over the city compete to create the spiciest *chiles rellenos* (stuffed chilies) and enchiladas.

Artichoke Café 424 Central Ave SE ⓣ505/243-0200. Simple but classy restaurant in the heart of downtown, serving a good, varied menu of California-influenced modern American cuisine; typical entrees cost $18–30. Dinner only on weekends.

Flying Star 3416 Central Ave SE ⓣ505/255-6633. Lively, crowded University District café serving eclectic international cuisine to a largely student clientele. The vast menu ranges through breakfast specialties, salads and blue-plate specials such as Vietnamese noodles or pasta pomodoro for $10. Daily 6am until late.

Frontier 2400 Central Ave SE ⓣ505/266-0550. Legendary 24-hour diner across from the university, where an unceasing parade of characters chow down on burgers, burritos and great vegetarian enchiladas.

Pueblo Harvest Cafe Indian Pueblo Cultural Centre, 2401 12th St NW ⓣ505/843-7270. Unusual Native American restaurant, serving Pueblo specialties like fry-bread at lunchtime, plus fine dinners, with braised bison ribs among the tasty $20–30 entrees.

66 Diner 1405 Central Ave NE ⓣ505/247-1421, ⓦwww.66diner.com. Classic Fifties diner near the university, with white-capped waiting staff, a soda fountain and a lively late-night clientele. Mon–Fri 11am–11pm, Sat 8am–11pm, Sun 8am–10pm.

Village Coffee Roaster 519 Central Ave NW ⓣ505/242-4781. Very funky downtown coffee bar, which also serves great sandwiches.

Drinking and nightlife

Many of downtown Albuquerque's **bars** and **nightclubs** double as small theatres or music venues. The free weekly *Alibi* magazine (ⓦwww.alibi.com) carries full listings of what's coming up or going down.

Burt's Tiki Lounge 313 Gold Ave SW ⓣ505/247-2878, ⓦwww.burtstikilounge.com. Tuesday is the big tiki-bar cocktail night here, though the Polynesian decor makes a good backdrop for no-cover live bands for the rest of the week. Mon–Sat 8pm–2am.

Caravan East 7605 Central Ave NE ⓣ505/265-7877, ⓦwww.caravaneast.com. Enormous honky-tonk, where tenderfeet can do the two-step with throngs of urban cowboys. Closed Mon.

KiMo Theatre 423 Central Ave NW ⓣ505/768-3522, ⓦwww.cabq.gov/kimo. Gorgeous, city-owned "Pueblo Deco" theatre, dating from the late 1920s, which puts on an eclectic programme of opera, dance and theatre performances, kids' movies and also regular live bands.

The Launchpad 618 Central Ave SW ⓣ505/764-8887, ⓦwww.launchpadrocks.com. Dance and live music space that showcases touring indie and world music bands; there's also a cluster of pool tables.

West of Albuquerque: I-40 to Arizona

As you drive between Albuquerque and Arizona, don't let the tacky parade of billboards and hoardings cause you to miss such interesting side-trips as **Ácoma Pueblo** and **Chaco Canyon**, respectively south and north of I-40.

Ácoma Pueblo

The amazing **Ácoma Pueblo**, a dozen miles south of I-40 fifty miles west of Albuquerque, encapsulates a thousand years of Native American history. Its focus is the ancient village known as **"Sky City"**, perched 367ft high atop a magnificent isolated mesa. Probably occupied by Chacoan migrants between 1100 and 1200 AD, when the great pueblos of Chaco Canyon were still in use, Ácoma has adapted to repeated waves of invaders ever since, while retaining its own strong identity. Although visitors seldom feel the awkwardness possible at other pueblo communities, Ácoma is the real thing and its sense of unbroken tradition can reduce even the least culturally sensitive traveller to awestruck silence.

To visit Sky City, you have to join one of the hour-long guided **tours** (April–Oct daily 9.30am–5pm, closed Nov–March; $20 or $12 for shorter 5pm tour; no camcorders or video; ⓣ505/470-0181 or 1-800/747-0181, ⓦwww.skycity.com), which leave regularly from the excellent visitor centre and museum at the base of the mesa. The main stop is at the striking **San Esteban del Rey** mission, a thick-walled adobe church completed in 1640. Rather than follow its architectural example, the Ácomans went on constructing the multistorey stone and adobe houses around which the tour then proceeds. Only thirteen families live permanently on the mesa; most Ácomans reside down below, where they can get electricity, running water and jobs. Villagers do, however, come up here during the day to sell pottery and fry-bread.

Grants

The old Route 66 town of **GRANTS**, fifteen miles west of Ácoma, holds half a dozen budget motels, including a good *Super 8*, 1604 E Santa Fe Ave (ⓣ505/287-8811; ❸). *El Cafecito*, 820 E Santa Fe Ave (ⓣ505/285-6229; closed Sun), is a bright, clean New Mexican **diner**, serving delicious local specialties. The enjoyable **New Mexico Museum of Mining**, 100 N Iron Ave (Mon–Sat 9am–4pm; $3; ⓦwww.grants.org), offers a chance to make a virtual descent into a mock-up **uranium mine** and doubles as a regional **visitor centre**.

El Morro National Monument

Hidden away on Hwy-53 south of the Zuni Mountains, 42 miles west of Grants, **El Morro National Monument** feels far off the beaten track. Incredibly, however, this pale-pink sandstone cliff was a regular rest stop for international travellers before the Pilgrims landed at Plymouth Rock, thanks to a perennial pool of water that collects beneath a tumbling waterfall. This spot was first recorded by Spanish explorers in 1583 and in 1605, Don Juan de Oñate, the founder of New Mexico, carved the first of many messages that earned it the American name of **Inscription Rock**.

Translations of El Morro's graffiti are displayed in the **visitor centre** (daily: summer 8am–7pm; spring & autumn 9am–6pm; winter 9am–5pm; $3/person; ⓦwww.nps.gov/elmo), while you can see the real thing on a half-mile trail.

Chaco Canyon

Few visitors brave the long, bumpy ride to **Chaco Canyon**, north of I-40 between Grant and Gallup. Although **Chaco Culture NHP** holds North America's **largest pre-Columbian city**, for beauty and drama it can't match such sites as Canyon de Chelly (see p.800) and the low-walled canyon itself is a mere scratch in the scrubby high-desert plains.

However, Chaco still holds plenty to take your breath away. Thirteen separate sites are open to visitors. Six, arrayed along the canyon's north wall, are so-called **Great Houses** – self-contained pueblos, three or four storeys high, whose fortress-like walls concealed up to eight hundred rooms.

Both routes to Chaco Canyon entail driving twenty miles over rough but passable dirt roads, not to be attempted in poor weather. Whether you approach from the south, by following Hwy-57 up from **Seven Lakes**, eighteen miles northeast of **Crownpoint** or from the north or east, by turning off US-550 at **Nageezi**, 36 miles south of **Bloomfield,** you enter the park at its southeast corner, close to the **visitor centre** (daily 8am–5pm; $8/vehicle; Ⓦwww.nps.gov/chcu). The basic first-come, first-served *Gallo* **campground** ($10), a short way east, usually fills by 3pm.

The major stop along the canyon's eight-mile one-way **loop road** (daily dawn–dusk) is at the far end, where **Pueblo Bonito** ("beautiful town") can be explored on an easy half-mile trail. Work on this four-storey D-shaped structure started in 850 AD and continued for three hundred years; it remained the largest building in America until 1898. Entering the ruin via its lowest levels, the path reaches its central plaza, which held at least three **Great Kivas** – ceremonial chambers used by entire communities rather than individual clans or families.

Gallup

Half an hour from Arizona, 65 miles west of Grants, the famous Route 66 town of **GALLUP** is a handy but uninteresting I-40 pit stop. Though the former Route 66 frontage contains some incredibly inexpensive **motels** and Native American jewellery is also at its cheapest here, the main reason to stop is to sleep or at least eat in the lovely *El Rancho Hotel*, 1000 E 66 Ave (Ⓣ505/863-9311 or 1-800/543-6351, Ⓦwww.elrancho hotel.com; ❹), built in 1937 to serve the many Hollywood stars filming nearby.

The Navajo and other Native Americans come together in **Red Rock State Park**, four miles east of Gallup, on the second weekend in August for the **Inter-Tribal Indian Ceremonial**, the largest such gathering anywhere (Ⓣ505/863-3896; Ⓦwww.theceremonial.com). Four days of dances and craft shows have as their highlight a Saturday morning parade through the town.

Southern New Mexico

Most travellers who come to **southern New Mexico** are here to visit the amazing if over-commercialized **Carlsbad Caverns National Park**. Northwest of Carlsbad, the **Sacramento** and **Jicarilla mountains** are home to the **Mescalero Apache** reservation as well as some rough-and-ready resorts. The desolate dunes of the **White Sands** monument spread west, with the rolling hills of the **Rio Grande Valley** beyond.

Carlsbad Caverns National Park

In **CARLSBAD CAVERNS NATIONAL PARK**, the Guadalupe Mountains are so riddled with underground caves and tunnels as to be virtually hollow. Tamed in classic park service style with concrete trails and electric lighting, this subterranean wonderland is now a walk-in gallery, where tourists flock to marvel at its intricate limestone tracery. Summer crowds can get intense, but that's part of the fun – Carlsbad feels like a throwback to the great 1950s boom in mass tourism. It is however a *long* way from anywhere else – three hundred miles southeast of Albuquerque and 150 miles northeast of El Paso, Texas.

A narrow, twisting seven-mile road climbs from US-62/180 at **White's City**, twenty miles southwest of **CARLSBAD** itself, to the park **visitor centre** (daily: June to late Aug 8am–7pm; late Aug to May 8am–5pm; Ⓣ505/785-2232, Ⓦwww .nps.gov/cave).

Almost all visitors confine their attention to **Carlsbad Cavern** itself, the only cave covered by the park fee of $6 per person for three days. Direct elevators drop to the

Cavern's centrepiece, the **Big Room**, 750 feet below the visitor centre, but you can walk down instead via the **Natural Entrance Route** (last entry summer 3.30pm; rest of year 2pm). This steep footpath switchbacks into the guano-encrusted maw of the cave, taking fifteen minutes to reach the first formation and another fifteen to reach the Big Room. All visitors must ride the elevator back out.

Measuring up to 1800ft long and 250ft high, the Big Room is festooned with stalactites, stalagmites and countless unnameable shapes of swirling liquid rock. All are a uniform stone grey; rare touches of colour are provided by slight red or brown mineral-rich tinges, improved with pastel lighting. It takes an hour to complete the level trail around the perimeter. Whatever the weather up top – summer highs exceed 100°F – the temperature down here is always a cool 56°F.

Adjoining the Big Room, the **Underground Lunchroom** is a vast formation-free side cave, paved in the 1950s to create a diner-cum-souvenir-shop that sells indigestible lunches in polystyrene containers, plus Eisenhower-era souvenirs like giant pencils and Viewmaster reels.

Guided tours explore beautiful side caves such as the **King's Palace**, filled with translucent "draperies" of limestone (daily summer 10am, 11am, noon, 2pm & 3pm; winter 10am & 2pm; $8). Additional tours can take you along the **Left Hand Tunnel** route down from the visitor centre ($7), or on a much more demanding descent into either **Spider Cave** or the **Hall of the White Giant** (both $20). All tours can be **reserved** on ⓣ1-877/444-6777 or ⓦwww.recreation.gov.

Practicalities

WHITE'S CITY is not a town but a privately owned tourist complex, which holds the closest **accommodation** and **camping** to the park, including the mock-adobe *Cavern Inn* (ⓣ505/785-2291, ⓦwww.whitescitycaverninn.com; ❸), plus an RV park, campground and steakhouse (all same number and website). There's little to **CARLSBAD** itself, 25 miles north of White's City, beyond its many motels, such as the large *Best Western Stevens Inn*, 1829 S Canal St (ⓣ505/887-2851 or 1-800/730-2851, ⓦwww.stevensinn.com; ❹), where the *Flume Room* is the best **restaurant** in town.

Roswell

Seventy-five miles north of Carlsbad, an alien spaceship supposedly crash-landed outside the small ranching town of **ROSWELL** on July 4, 1947. The commander of the local air-force base announced that they had retrieved the wreckage of a flying saucer and despite a follow-up denial the story has kept running, with TV series like *X-Files*, *Roswell* and *Taken* stoking the imaginations of UFO theorists.

Despite the wishful thinking of the truly weird clientele who drift in from the plains, the **International UFO Museum**, 114 N Main St (daily 9am–5pm; $5; ⓦwww.roswellufomuseum.com), inadvertently exposes the whole tawdry business as transparent nonsense. By way of contrast, the **Roswell Museum**, 100 W 11th St (Mon–Sat 9am–5pm, Sun 1–5pm; free), boasts an excellent, multifaceted collection, with a section celebrating pioneer rocket scientist Robert Goddard (1882–1945).

Roswell's **visitor centre** is at 912 N Main St (Mon–Sat 9am–5pm; ⓣ505/624-6860, ⓦwww.roswellnm.org). The finest **motel**, the *Best Western Sally Port Inn*, 2000 N Main St (ⓣ505/622-6430 or 1-800/548-5221, ⓦwww.bestwestern.com; ❸), also has a good **restaurant**.

Lincoln

Better known as **Billy the Kid**, Brooklyn-born William Bonney first came to fame as an 18-year-old in 1878, when the **Lincoln County War** erupted between rival groups of ranchers and merchants in the frontier town of **LINCOLN**, on Hwy-380 halfway between Carlsbad and Albuquerque. Since those days, no new buildings have joined the venerable false-fronted structures that line Main Street and the entire town is now the **Lincoln State Monument**. Visitors can stroll its length at any time and visit various historical sites (each site $3.50, joint admission to all sites $5; not all sites remain open in winter; ⓣ505/653-4372, ⓦwww.nmmonuments.org).

Displays in the **Historic Lincoln Visitors Centre** (daily 8.30am–5pm), cover Hispanics, cowboys and Apaches, as well as the Lincoln County War. Billy the Kid's most famous jailbreak is commemorated at the **Lincoln County Courthouse** (daily 8.30am–5pm), at the other end of the street; waiting here under sentence of death, he shot his way out and fled to Fort Sumner, where Sheriff Pat Garrett eventually caught up with him (see p.767). On the first weekend of August the streets echo with gunfire once again, during the three-day **Old Lincoln Days** festival.

Near the courthouse, the *Wortley Hotel* – once owned by Pat Garrett – offers seven simple but appealing **hotel** rooms (ⓣ505/653-4300, ⓦwww.wortleyhotel.com; closed mid-Oct to March; ❹) and its **dining room** serves simple stews and sandwiches at lunchtime only.

Ruidoso

The **Sacramento, Capitan and Jicarilla mountains**, which rise 85 miles northwest of Carlsbad, form a rare respite from the prevailing scrubby flatness. Spread out along winding roads that cut through dense groves of pine, fir and aspen, the main town here is the fast-growing resort of **RUIDOSO**.

Alongside, the **Ruidoso Downs** racetrack east of town, which hosts a 77-day racing season, the **Hubbard Museum of the American West** (daily 9am–5pm; $6; ⓦwww.hubbardmuseum.org) explores all aspects of Western history, with an especial emphasis on horses. In winter, attention turns to the 12,000-foot slopes of **Ski Apache** (ⓦwww.skiapache.com), a downhill ski area northwest of town on Hwy-532 where lift tickets cost around $54 per day.

Ruidoso's **visitor centre** is at 720 Sudderth Ave (Mon–Sat 9am–5pm, Sun 1–4pm; ⓦwww.ruidoso.net), while **motels** include the inexpensive *Apache*, 344 Sudderth Ave (ⓣ505/257-2986 or 1-800/426-0616, ⓦwww.ruidoso.net/apache; ❷). The glitzy *Inn of the Mountain Gods*, three miles southwest (ⓣ505/257-5141 or 1-800/545-9011, ⓦwww.innofthemountaingods.com; ❻) is, like the ski resort, owned by the Mescalero Apache and holds a casino as well as fine dining and luxury accommodation.

White Sands National Monument

Filling a broad valley west of Ruidoso and the Sacramento Mountains, the **White Sands** are 250 square miles of glistening, three-storey-high dunes, not of sand, but of finely ground gypsum eroded from the nearby peaks. Most of the desert valley is used as a missile range and training ground; only the southern half of the dunes is protected within **White Sands National Monument** (and even that is often closed for an hour or two at a time while missile tests are under way). The **visitor centre**, just off US-70, illuminates the unique local plants and animals (daily: late May to early Sept 8am–7pm; early Sept to late May 8am–6pm; ⓣ505/479-6124, ⓦwww.nps.gov/whsa). An eight-mile paved road ($3/person) stretches into the heart of the dunes, where you can scramble and slide in the sheer white landscape.

ALAMOGORDO, at the base of the Sacramento Mountains, sixteen miles east, holds the nearest food and lodging.

Las Cruces

From White Sands, US-70 heads southwest across the Tularosa Valley to **LAS CRUCES** – "the Crosses" – a large, modern farming community on the Rio Grande at the junction of I-10 and I-25. The town takes its name from the white crosses set up in the sands to mark the graves of early travellers killed by the Apache, but any sense of its history is pretty well buried by motels and fast-food franchises. It's a prosperous place, though and may become more so if and when **Spaceport America**, currently approaching completion in the empty desert roughly 45 miles northeast, becomes the base for the first-ever passenger spaceflights, due to be operated by Virgin Galactic (Ⓦ www.virgingalactic.com).

The cream of Las Cruces' **motels** is the ★ *Best Western Mission Inn*, 1765 S Main St (Ⓣ575/524-8591 or 1-800/390-1440; ❸); it may not look all that special from the outside, but the large rooms are surprisingly attractive, featuring lovely Mexican tilework and murals.

The southwest corner

I-10 heads west from Las Cruces across southwestern New Mexico, also known as the "**Boot heel**" for the way it steps down toward Mexico. Towns in this wide-open rangeland are few and far between. Both **DEMING**, sixty miles west of Las Cruces and **LORDSBURG**, on I-10 twenty miles short of Arizona, hold Amtrak stations, plus a string of gas stations, cafés and motels, but little else.

Silver City

Almost entirely wilderness, the semi-arid, forested, volcanic **Mogollon** and **Mimbres mountains** soar to ten thousand feet above the high desert plains and remain little altered since Apache warrior **Geronimo** was born at the headwaters of the Gila River.

Halfway up the mountains, the biggest settlement, **SILVER CITY**, lies 45 miles north of I-10. The Spanish came here in 1804, sold the Mimbreño Indians into slavery and opened the **Santa Rita copper mine**, just east of town below the Kneeling Nun monolith. The town was re-established in 1870 as a rough-and-tumble silver camp – **Billy the Kid** spent most of his childhood here. Ornate old buildings stand scattered along elm-lined avenues and across the hills. The **Western New Mexico University Museum**, 12th and Alabama (Mon–Fri 9am–4.30pm, Sat & Sun 10am–4pm; free), holds the world's finest collection of beautiful **Mimbres pottery**, produced locally around 1100 AD.

In downtown Silver City, the *Palace Hotel*, 106 W Broadway (Ⓣ575/388-1811, Ⓦ www.zianet.com/palacehotel; ❷), is a small, nicely restored nineteenth-century hotel. Nearby Bullard Street holds **saloons and cafés** like the *Diane's Restaurant and Bakery* at no. 510 (Ⓣ575/538-8722; closed Mon).

Arizona

The tourism industry in **ARIZONA** has, literally, one colossal advantage – the **Grand Canyon** of the Colorado River, the single most awe-inspiring spectacle in a land of unforgettable geology. Several other Arizona destinations have a similarly abiding emotional impact, however, thanks to the sheer drama of human involvement in this forbidding but deeply resonant desert landscape.

Over a third of the state still belongs to **Native Americans**, who outside the cities form the majority of the population. In the so-called **Indian Country** of northeastern Arizona, the **Navajo Nation** holds the stupendous **Canyon de Chelly** and dozens of other **Ancestral Puebloan ruins**, as well as the stark rocks of **Monument Valley**. The Navajo surround the homeland of the stoutly traditional **Hopi**, who live in remote **mesa-top villages**. The third main group, the **Apache**, in the harshly beautiful southeastern mountains, were the last Native Americans to give in to the overwhelming power of the American invaders.

Away from the reservations, **Wild West** towns like **Tombstone** give a clear sense of Arizona's rough-and-ready, pioneer mentality; this was the last of the lower 48 states to join the Union, in 1912. The **cities**, however, are not nearly so much fun. In **Phoenix**, the capital, well over a million souls are scattered over a five-hundred-square-mile morass of shopping malls and tract-house suburbs; **Tucson** is rather more appealing, but can still wear thin after a couple of days.

Though the open spaces of southern Arizona can be harsh, the bleakness is balanced somewhat by the many reserves that protect its amazing flora and fauna, such as **Saguaro National Park**, just outside Tucson, with its giant cactuses, real-life roadrunners and rare Gila monsters.

Tucson, Phoenix and southern Arizona

While most of Arizona's compelling natural attractions are in its northern reaches, the **southern** half of the state holds ninety percent of its people and all its significant cities. State capital **Phoenix** is larger and duller than lively **Tucson** and there's some great frontier Americana in the southeast corner, especially in **Tombstone**.

Tucson and around

The former Spanish and Mexican outpost of **TUCSON** (pronounced *too-sonn*), a mere sixty miles north of Mexico, has grown into a modern metropolis of 900,000-plus people without entirely sacrificing its historic quarters. Equal parts college town and retirement community, it suffers from the same Sunbelt sprawl as Albuquerque and Phoenix, but has a compact centre, some enjoyable restaurants and pretty good nightlife. Some superb landscape lies within easy reach, from the forested flanks of **Mount Lemmon** to the rolling foothills of **Saguaro National Park**.

Arrival and information

Tucson International Airport, eight miles south of downtown, receives far fewer long-distance flights than Phoenix. It's connected to central Tucson by the $25 shuttle vans of Arizona Stagecoach (Ⓣ1-877/782-4355, Ⓦwww.azstagecoach.com). For **taxi** service, call Allstate Cab (Ⓣ520/798-1111). The Amtrak station, downtown at 400 E Toole Ave, is served by **trains** between Los Angeles and points east, with connecting buses running north to Phoenix. Greyhound **buses** also stop centrally, at 471 W Congress St.

Tucson's **visitor centre** is downtown at 100 S Church Ave (Mon–Fri 9am–5pm, Sat & Sun 9am–4pm; Ⓣ520/624-1817 or 1-800/638-8350, Ⓦwww.visittucson.org).

Accommodation

Tucson has reasonably priced downtown **hotels** and **motels**, as well as atmospheric **B&Bs** both in the historic centre and out in the desert. It also holds its fair share of **resorts** and **dude ranches**. Rates drop when the mercury rises.

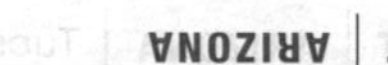

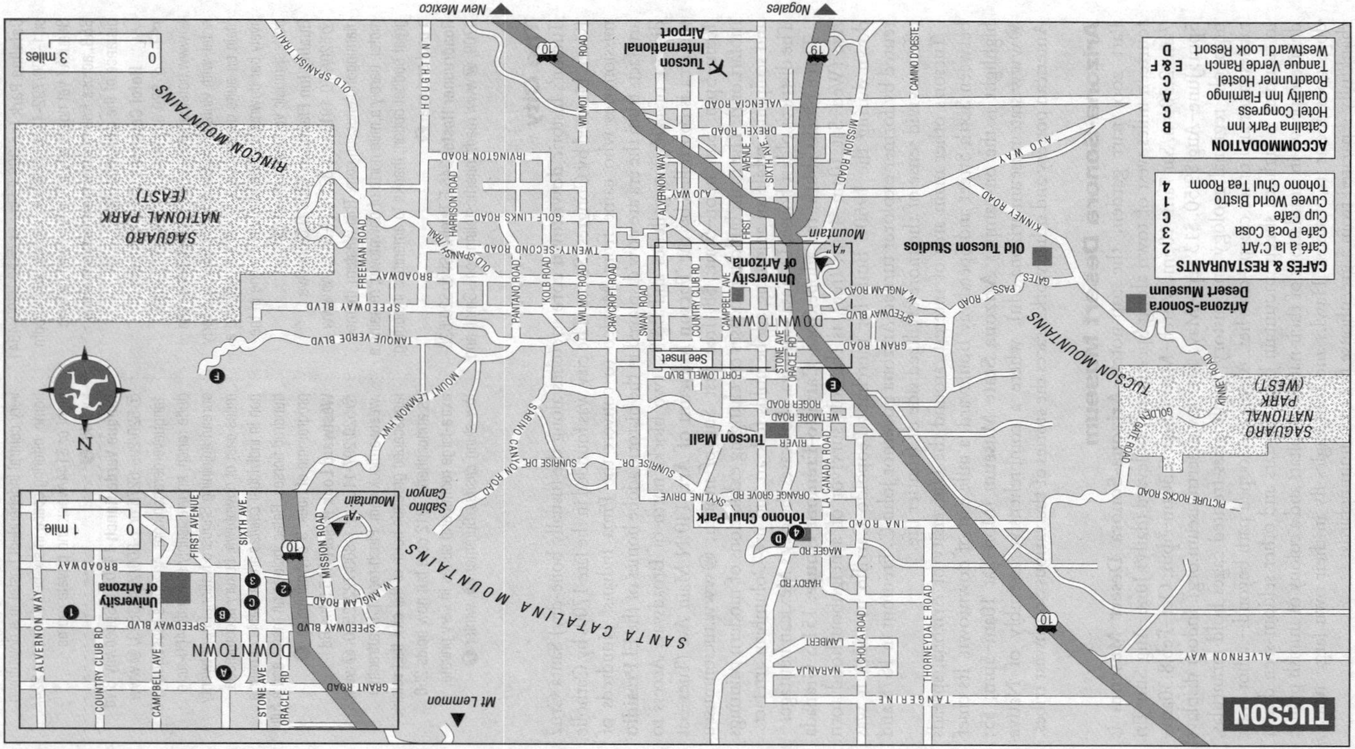

TUCSON
CAFÉS & RESTAURANTS
Café à la C'Art 2
Cafe Poca Cosa 3
Cup Cafe C
Cuvee World Bistro 1
Tohono Chul Tea Room 4
ACCOMMODATION
Catalina Park Inn B
Hotel Congress C
Quality Inn Flamingo A
Roadrunner Hostel C
Tanque Verde Ranch E & F
Westward Look Resort D
Phoenix
New Mexico
Nogales
Mt Lemmon
SANTA CATALINA MOUNTAINS
RINCON MOUNTAINS
TUCSON MOUNTAINS
SAGUARO NATIONAL PARK (EAST)
SAGUARO NATIONAL PARK (WEST)
Sabino Canyon
Tohono Chul Park
Tucson Mall
University of Arizona
DOWNTOWN
"A" Mountain
Old Tucson Studios
Arizona-Sonora Desert Museum
Tucson International Airport
See Inset
0 3 miles
0 1 mile
N

Catalina Park Inn 309 E First St ⓣ520/792-4541 or 1-800/792-4885, ⓦwww.catalinaparkinn.com. Beautiful yet not overly fussy six-room historic B&B, across from a quiet park within walking distance of the university. ❼

Hotel Congress 311 E Congress St ⓣ520/622-8848 or 1-800/722-8848, ⓦwww.hotelcongress.com. Central, bohemian hotel, with vintage Art Deco furnishings and forty plain en-suite guest rooms. There's a café and a lively bar downstairs and at night it's one of the hottest music venues in town. ❹

Quality Inn Flamingo 1300 N Stone Ave ⓣ520/770-1910 or 1-877/424-6423, ⓦwww.flamingohoteltucson.com. This Western-themed motel, barely a mile north of downtown, remains a great budget option, thanks to amenities including a pool and spa. ❷

Roadrunner Hostel 346 E Twelfth St ⓣ520/628-4709, ⓦwww.roadrunnerhostelinn.com. Small and very central independent hostel in a downtown home, offering space in six-bed dorms for $24/night or $144/week and private rooms for $48. ❷

Tanque Verde Ranch 14301 E Speedway Blvd ⓣ520/296-6275 or 1-800/234-3833, ⓦwww.tanqueverderanch.com. Arizona's most authentic dude ranch, an irresistibly romantic 400-acre spread adjoining Saguaro National Park twenty miles east of downtown. Luxury accommodation in individual *casitas* and a stable of over a hundred horses. Rates include all meals and a full programme of rides. 3-day minimum. ❾

Westward Look Resort 245 E Ina Rd ⓣ520/297-1151 or 1-800/722-2500, ⓦwww.westwardlook.com. Plush resort, in attractive landscaped grounds north of the city, that retains its atmospheric 1912 core but now holds 250 extra-large rooms and suites in very private, low-slung *casitas*. Summer ❹, winter ❼

The City

Tucson's historic **downtown core** stretches along the (usually bone-dry) Santa Cruz River, bisected by Congress Street. The city was founded in the late 1700s by Catholic missionaries who came from Mexico to convert the Pima Indians. Hundreds of artefacts from the era are now displayed in the historic adobe homes of the **El Presidio** district of cafés, art galleries and B&Bs, two blocks north of Broadway. Access to the area is controlled by the **Tucson Museum of Art**, 140 N Main Ave (Tues–Sat 10am–5pm, Sun noon–5pm; $8, free first Sun of month; ⓦwww.tucsonmuseumofart.org). The main building focuses on changing exhibitions of modern paintings and sculpture, while an adjoining adobe holds folk art and pre-Columbian artefacts. The district's oldest house, La Casa Cordova, showcases the city's Mexican heritage.

Three blocks south, the adobe **Sosa-Carrillo-Frémont House**, 151 S Granada Ave (Wed–Sat 10am–4pm; free), is the sole survivor of a neighbourhood torn down during the 1960s. Built for merchant Leopoldo Carrillo in 1858, it was rented by former explorer turned Arizona governor John C. Frémont in 1878 and offers a vivid sense of the more civilized side of frontier life.

Tucson's other main area of interest, around the University of Arizona, spreads between Sixth Street and Speedway Boulevard, a mile east of downtown. Its chief highlight is the on-campus **Arizona State Museum** (Mon–Sat 10am–5pm; $5; ⓦwww.statemuseum.arizona.edu), where a comprehensive assembly of Native American pottery and other works traces the stories of the various Southwest tribes.

Arizona-Sonora Desert Museum

Part zoo, part garden, the top-notch **Arizona-Sonora Desert Museum** is fourteen miles west of town along Speedway Boulevard (daily: June–Aug Sun–Fri 7am–2.30pm, Sat 7am–10pm; March–May & Sept 7.30am–5pm; Oct–Feb 8.30am–5pm; June–Aug $9.50, $13 Sept–May; ⓦwww.desertmuseum.org). Indoor displays highlight regional geology and history, while glass-fronted cages hold tarantulas, rattlesnakes and other creepy-crawlies. Along the looped path beyond – a hot walk in summer – bighorn sheep, mountain lions, jaguars and other seldom-seen desert denizens prowl in simulations of their natural habitats and a colony of impish prairie dogs goes about its business. Hawks and bald eagles fly in their own large aviary, thankfully separated from a greenhouse full of hummingbirds.

Saguaro National Park

Flanking Tucson to either side, the two sections of **Saguaro National Park** offer visitors a rare opportunity to stroll through desert "forests" of monumental, multi-limbed **saguaro** (*sa-wah-row*) cactuses. Each saguaro can grow fifty feet tall and weigh eight tons, but takes around 150 years to do so. They're unique to the Sonora Desert and encountering them en masse is a real thrill. Both segments of the park can be seen on short forays from the city: in summer, it's far too hot to do more than pose for photographs and there is no lodging or even permanent campground. **Admission** to either or both sections, valid for a week, costs $10 per vehicle. **Backcountry camping** is by permit only.

The **Tucson Mountain District** stretches north from the Desert Museum fifteen miles west of downtown Tucson, on the far side of the mountains. Beyond the **visitor centre** (daily 8am–5pm; Ⓣ520/733-5158, Ⓦwww.nps.gov/sagu), the nine-mile **Bajada Loop Drive** loops through a wonderland of weird saguaro, offering plentiful short hiking trails. Signal Hill is especially recommended, for its petroglyphs and superb sunset views.

In the **Rincon Mountain District** (Ⓣ520/733-5153), seventeen miles east of town along first Broadway Boulevard and then Old Spanish Trail, short trails such as the quarter-mile Desert Ecology Trail lead off the eight-mile **Cactus Forest Drive** (daily: April–Oct 7am–7pm; Nov–March 7am–5pm). The saguaro cactuses thin out almost as soon as you start climbing the Tanque Verde Ridge Trail, which leads in due course to a hundred-mile network of remote footpaths through thickly forested canyons.

Eating and drinking

Though downtown Tucson shuts down pretty early each evening – it's hard to find anywhere to eat after 9pm – the city has a fine selection of **restaurants**. Mexican joints and cowboy-style Wild West steakhouses abound in the central districts, while fancier places congregate further north in the foothills.

Café à la C'Art Tucson Museum of Art, 150 N Main Ave Ⓣ520/628-8533. With such a good café in the art museum courtyard, serving sandwiches, salads and daily specials, there's no need to look further afield. Lunch only, closed Sat & Sun.

Cafe Poca Cosa 110 E Pennington St Ⓣ520/622-6400. Popular and stylish downtown café that serves tasty, inexpensive Mexican – or to be more precise, Sonoran – cuisine with contemporary Southwestern flair. Typical menu highlights include shredded beef or cod with clams. Lunch entrees cost around $10; at dinner they're more like $20. Closed Sun & Mon.

Cup Cafe *Hotel Congress*, 311 E Congress St Ⓣ520/798-1618. Jazzy downtown café, straight out of the 1930s, updated to include an espresso bar. A good breakfast rendezvous, it also stays open late nightly.

Cuvee World Bistro 3352 E Speedway Blvd Ⓣ520/881-7577. The eclectic menu at this playfully opulent yet casual bistro samples pretty much any tasty world cuisine. Entrees from crispy sea bass to mahogany roasted duck are priced at $21–26 and there's live music at weekends. Closed Sun.

Tohono Chul Tea Room Tohono Chul Park, 7366 N Paseo del Norte Ⓣ520/797-1222. Attractive adobe café in a small desert park on the northern fringes of town that's ideal for breakfast, a $10 lunch special or a scones-and-jam afternoon tea.

Nightlife

Most of the arty **cafés** and **nightclubs** on Congress Street downtown double as bars and restaurants, while the university area holds lots of student-oriented places and half a dozen country-and-western saloons are scattered around the outskirts. For listings, see the free *Tucson Weekly* (Ⓦwww.tucsonweekly.com).

Choice options include *Club Congress*, inside *Hotel Congress* at 311 E Congress St (Ⓣ520/622-8848), a hectic, late-opening bar with live music a couple of nights each week. For microbrews and simple food, head for *Gentle Ben's Brewing Co*, 865 E University Blvd (Ⓣ520/624-4177), usually packed with students. A 1920s vaudeville palace, the Rialto Theatre, 318 E Congress St (ⓣ520/740-0126, ⓦwww.rialtotheatre.com), is the hottest venue for touring bands.

South to the border: the Mission Trail

South from Tucson, I-19 heads straight for the Mexican border, 65 miles away, passing reminders of the region's Spanish and Mexican heritage. The **Mission San Xavier del Bac** – the best-preserved mission church in the US – lies just west of the freeway, nine miles south of downtown Tucson on the fringe of the vast arid San Xavier Indian Reservation, home to the Akimel O'odham people (daily 9am–6pm; donation suggested). It was built for the Franciscans between 1783 and 1797 and even today its white-plastered walls and towers seem like a dazzling desert mirage. No one can name the architect responsible for its Spanish Baroque, even Moorish lines – it consists almost entirely of domes and arches, making only minimal use of timber – let alone the O'odham craftsmen who embellished its every feature. Sunday morning masses draw large congregations from the reservation.

Forty miles further south, the evocative ruin of another eighteenth-century mission church is preserved as **Tumacácori National Historical Park** (daily 9am–5pm; $3/person). Topped by a restored whitewashed dome, the mission is home only to the birds that fly down from the Patagonia Mountains. Behind its red-tinged, weather-beaten facade, the plaster has crumbled from the interior walls to reveal bare adobe bricks.

Nogales, Arizona and Nogales, Mexico

Twenty miles south of Tumacácori, an hour from Tucson, sits the largest of the Arizona–Mexico border towns, **NOGALES** – in effect two towns, one in the US and one in Mexico, known jointly as *Ambos Nogales* (both Nogales). There's nothing particular to see, either side, though the contrast between the orderly streets of the dreary little American town and the jumbled whitewashed houses that cling to the slopes in Nogales, Mexico, which is basically a large-scale street market, is striking.

Crossing the border is straightforward, as only travellers heading further south of the border require Mexican visas. US citizens should, however, carry their passports, while foreign visitors should check that their visa status entitles them to re-enter the US; if you're on or eligible for the Visa Waiver Scheme (see p.53), you're fine. If driving, leave your car on the US side. There's no need to change money: businesses across the border accept US dollars.

None of the Arizona-side **motels** stands within a mile of the border; the closest is the *Best Western Siesta Motel*, 673 N Grand Ave (ⓣ520/287-4671; ④). Most visitors prefer to **eat** in Mexico, where abundant cafés and diners line the busy central streets. Classier dining is offered by *La Roca*, hollowed into the rocky hillside just east of the railroad, a couple of blocks from the border at *Calle Elias 91*, where a full meal still costs under $20.

The southeast corner

Amid copious acreage of unspoiled and magnificent wilderness, southeast Arizona contains numerous well-preserved and highly atmospheric **ghost towns**. I-10 buzzes east towards New Mexico; to enjoy a grand tour, detour south instead along the more scenic US-80.

Tombstone

The legendary Wild West town of **TOMBSTONE** lies 22 miles south of I-10 on US-80, 67 miles southeast of Tucson. Over a century has passed since its mining heyday, but "The Town Too Tough to Die" clings to an afterlife as a tourist theme park. With its dusty streets, wooden sidewalks and swinging saloon doors, it's barely unchanged. While it's much more commercialized than its counterpart in New Mexico, Lincoln (see p.773), it's also more fun. The moody gunslingers who stroll the streets these days are merely rounding up customers to watch them fight, but there's enough genuine rivalry between groups to give the place an oddly appealing edge. The ideal time to visit is during **Helldorado Days** in late October (Ⓦ www.helldoradodays.com), a bonanza of parades and shoot-outs, when the air is cooler and the sun less harsh.

Tombstone began life as a silver boomtown in 1877 and by the end of the 1880s it was all but deserted again. On October 26, 1881, however, its population stood at more than ten thousand. At 2pm that day, **Doc Holliday**, along with sheriff **Wyatt Earp** and his brothers Virgil and Morgan, confronted a band of suspected cattle rustlers, the Clantons, in the **Gunfight at the OK Corral**. Within a few minutes, three of the rustlers were dead. The Earps were accused of murder, but charges were eventually dropped.

Although the gunfight in fact took place on Fremont Street, the **OK Corral** itself remains the major attraction (daily 8.30am–5pm; gunfights Tues–Thurs 2pm & 4pm, Fri–Mon 2pm & 5pm; $5.50 or $9 with gunfight; Ⓦ www.ok-corral.com). In a baking-hot adobe-walled courtyard, crude dummies show the supposed locations of the Earps and the Clantons.

Just off the main drag at Toughnut and Third, the **Tombstone Courthouse State Historic Park** (daily 9am–5pm; $3; Ⓦ www.pr.state.az.us/parks/TOCO/), holds displays on the Apache and early outlaws and documents several rough episodes of frontier justice.

Central **motels** include the *Tombstone Motel*, 502 E Fremont St (Ⓣ 520/457-3478 or 1-888/455-3478, Ⓦ www.tombstonemotel.com; ❸), while the classier *Holiday Inn Express* is a mile north on US-80 W (Ⓣ 520/457-9507 or 1-800/465-4329; Ⓦ www.ichotelsgroup.com; ❹). Among raucous old-style beer-and-burger **saloons** are the *Crystal Palace* at Fifth and Allen and *Big Nose Kate's* at 417 E Allen St.

Bisbee

Crammed into a narrow gorge 25 miles south of Tombstone, the town of **BISBEE** is rivalled only by Jerome as Arizona's most atmospheric Victorian relic. Like Jerome, its fortunes were built on a century of mining mundane copper from the mountains, rather than a few ephemeral years of gold and silver. Its solid brick buildings testify to the days when Bisbee's population of twenty thousand made it the largest city between New Orleans and San Francisco. Phelps Dodge mining company finally ceased operations in 1975, having extracted over six billion dollars' worth of metals. As the miners moved away, however, artists and retirees moved in, preserving Bisbee's architecture while turning it into a thriving, friendly little community that caters to tourists without being overwhelmed by them.

Walking Bisbee's narrow central streets, lined with galleries and antiques stores, is a pleasure in itself. If you'd like to know more of the background, call in at the **Bisbee Mining and Historical Museum**, 5 Copper Queen Plaza (daily 10am–4pm; $7.50; Ⓦ www.bisbeemuseum.org).

The fanciest **place to stay**, the venerable *Copper Queen Hotel*, 11 Howell Ave (Ⓣ 520/432-2216, Ⓦ www.copperqueen.com; ❺), has a plush bar and a good **restaurant** with terrace seating. On the southern outskirts, the *Shady Dell RV Park*, 1 Douglas Rd (Ⓣ 520/432-3567, Ⓦ www.theshadydell.com; ❷–❺), offers a unique opportunity to sleep in one of eleven beautifully restored, irresistibly kitsch 1950s trailers.

Southwest Arizona: Yuma

There's virtually nothing in the vast desert plain of southwest Arizona to tempt you off the twin freeways that sprint to California. The largest town, **YUMA**, is little more than an oversized pit stop for freight trains and cross-country truckers. **Yuma Territorial Prison** (Thurs–Mon 8am–3pm; $5) beside the Colorado River, was known a century ago as the "Hell Hole of Arizona", holding over a hundred of the Wild West's most violent criminals. Its first inmates were forced to build the adobe walls that later contained them; visitors can wander around the grounds and cell blocks at will.

Neon-lit budget **motels** along the main drag include the good-value *Yuma Cabana*, 2151 S Fourth Ave (Ⓣ928/783-8311 or 1-800/874-0811, Ⓦwww.yumacabana.com; ❷), while the **River City Grill**, downtown at 600 W Third St (Ⓣ928/782-7988), is a bright "international" restaurant.

Phoenix

Arizona's state capital and largest city, **PHOENIX** holds minimal appeal for tourists. It began life in the 1860s, as a sweltering little farming town in the heart of the Salt River Valley, with a ready-made irrigation system left by ancient Native Americans (the name Phoenix honours the fact that the city rose from the ashes of a long-vanished **Hohokam** community). Within a century, however, Phoenix had turned into what Edward Abbey called "the blob that is eating Arizona", acquiring the money and political clout to defy the self-evident absurdity of building a huge city in a waterless desert. Now the fifth largest city in the US, it has filled the entire valley; over 1.5 million people live within its boundaries, while four million people inhabit the twenty separate incorporated cities, such as **Scottsdale, Tempe** and **Mesa**, which make up the metropolitan area.

Above all, Phoenix is hot; summer daytime highs average over 100°F, making it the hottest city outside the Middle East. Even in winter, temperatures rarely drop below 65°F, making the Phoenix/Scottsdale area popular with snowbirds looking to warm their bones in the luxury resorts and spas, play a round of golf in top-class courses or hike through the mountain and desert preserves.

Apart from the **Heard Museum**'s excellent Native American displays, the cactuses at the **Desert Botanical Garden** and Frank Lloyd Wright's winter home and architecture studio at **Taliesin West**, Phoenix is short of must-see attractions.

Arrival, information and getting around

Phoenix's **Sky Harbor International Airport** (Ⓣ602/273-3300, Ⓦwww.phxskyharbor.com) is three miles east of downtown. Door-to-door **shuttle buses** cost around $10 for downtown destinations, more like $20 for Scottsdale, (SuperShuttle; Ⓣ602/244-9000 or 1-800/258-3826,Ⓦwww.supershuttle.com).

The city is so vast that it's much easier to drive than to use **public transport** – even driving, it can take hours to get across town. However, the **Metro Light Rail System** (Ⓣ602/253-5000, Ⓦwww.valleymetro.org; flat fare $1.25) runs a twenty-mile route, from Camelback Road north of downtown Phoenix to Apache Boulevard in Mesa and there's a station close to the airport at 44th and Washington. Tourists are more likely to use the blue/green DASH buses, which ply two extravagant loops around downtown (Mon–Fri 6.30am–8pm; free). Local **cab** companies include Checker Cab (Ⓣ602/257-1818).

Arizona Shuttle Services runs frequent buses south to **Tucson** (daily 6.30am–11.30pm; single $30 with 7-day advance reservation; Ⓣ520/795-6772 or 1-800/888-2749, Ⓦwww.arizonashuttle.com). There's no Amtrak train service, but Greyhound buses arrive at 2115 E Buckeye Rd (Ⓣ602/389-4200), close to the airport.

Phoenix's main **visitor centre** is downtown at 125 N Second St (Mon–Fri 8am–5pm; ⓣ602/254-6500 or 1-877/225-5749, ⓦwww.visitphoenix.com), while **Scottsdale** has its own visitor centre at 4343 N Scottsdale Rd (Mon–Fri 8am–5pm; ⓣ480/421-1004 or 1-800/782-1117, ⓦwww.scottsdalecvb.com).

Accommodation

Downtown Phoenix is among the least expensive districts in the vast Metropolitan area; cheap motels line run-down W Van Buren Street a few blocks north of the centre. The summer room rates given below rise significantly in winter.

Best Western Central Phoenix Inn & Suites 1100 N Central Ave ⓣ602/252-2100 or 1-800/780-7234; ⓦwww.bestwestern.com. Rates remain constant year-round at this good-value business-oriented hotel, close to downtown a quarter-mile north of the Heard Museum. ❺

Budget Lodge Motel 402 W Van Buren St ⓣ602/254-7247 or 1-800/780-5733; ⓦwww.budgetinn.com. Reasonably attractive rooms at very attractive rates, in an unexciting motel close to the downtown core. ❸

Days Inn Scottsdale Resort at Fashion Square Mall 4710 N Scottsdale Rd ⓣ480/947-5411 or 1-800/329-7466, ⓦwww.scottsdaledaysinn.com. Though not all that prepossessing, this two-storey motel, immediately north of Fashion Square Mall – just stroll across the street – has perfectly acceptable rooms, plus an outdoor pool. ❺

Hotel San Carlos 202 N Central Ave ⓣ602/253-4121 or 1-866/253-4121, ⓦwww.hotelsancarlos.com. To appreciate this historic, very central 1920s hotel, you have to prefer an old-fashioned, frazzled and often noisy downtown hotel to a crisp, new deathly-quiet motel. That said, rooms are very tastefully furnished and there's a nice café and a rooftop pool. ⑦

Metcalf House Hostel 1026 N Ninth St above Roosevelt ⓣ602/254-9803, ⓦhome.earthlink.net/~phxhostel/. Dorm beds at $18 for HI/AYH members, $25 non-members, in a slightly rundown location in a residential district, 15min walk north of downtown. No phone reservations, but space is usually available. No curfew. Check-in 5–10pm or, usually but not always, 7–10am. Closed July & Aug. ①

Sleep Inn Airport 2621 S 47th Place ⓣ480/967-7100 or 1-800/631-3054, ⓦwww.sleepinn.com. Above-average chain motel, three miles south of the airport but served by 24hr free shuttles; breakfast is free. ⑥

Tempe Mission Palms Hotel 60 E Fifth St ⓣ480/894-1400 or 1-800/547-8705, ⓦwww.missionpalms.com. Very comfortable Southwestern-themed, largely business-oriented hotel in Tempe's revitalized Mill Avenue district, with a rooftop swimming pool. Good value in summer, but pricier in winter. ⑨

Central Phoenix

Despite determined and in many ways successful revitalization efforts, **Downtown Phoenix** – the few blocks east and west of Central Avenue and north and south of **Washington Street** – remains too hot and too spread out to walk around in any comfort. A ninety-block district, focusing on two massive side-by-side sports stadiums, the **US Airways Centre** and **Chase Field** (home respectively to the Phoenix Suns and Arizona Diamondbacks; see opposite), even has a new name – **Copper Square**.

What little remains of Phoenix's nineteenth-century architecture now constitutes **Heritage Square**, at 115 N Sixth St. Rather than original adobe ranch houses, however, it preserves quaint Victorian homes, converted into tearooms and toy museums.

A mile north of downtown, the huge – and hugely rewarding – **Phoenix Art Museum**, 1625 N Central Ave (Wed 10am–9pm, Thurs–Sat 10am–5pm, Sun noon–5pm; $10; ⓦwww.phxart.org), is rooted in an extensive array of Western art, though temporary exhibitions range through all eras and styles. Three blocks north, the similarly enormous **Heard Museum**, centring on a lovely group of original buildings at 2301 N Central Ave (Mon–Sat 9.30am–5pm, Sun 11am–5pm; $12; ⓦwww.heard.org), offers a good introduction to the culture of the Native Americans of the Southwest. Its superb pottery collection ranges from stunning Mimbres bowls to modern Hopi ceramics, but best of all is a wonderful array of Hopi kachina dolls.

In **Papago Park** at the south end of Scottsdale, the fascinating **Desert Botanical Garden** (daily: May–Sept 7am–8pm; Oct–April 8am–8pm; adults $15; ⓦwww.dbg.org), is filled with amazing cactuses and desert flora from around the world. Prime specimens include spineless "totem pole" cactuses from the Galápagos Islands and "living stone" plants from South Africa. Separate enclaves are devoted to **butterflies** – at their best in August and September – and **hummingbirds**, of which Arizona boasts fifteen indigenous species.

Taliesin West

Visionary architect **Frank Lloyd Wright** came to Phoenix to work on the *Biltmore Hotel* and stayed for most of the 25 years before his death in 1959. His winter studio, **Taliesin West** – at 114th Street and Frank Lloyd Wright Boulevard, at Scottsdale's northeastern edge – is now an architecture school and a working design studio, with multimedia exhibits of his life and work (Oct–May daily 10am–4pm, June & Sept daily 9am–4pm, July & Aug Mon & Thurs–Sun 9am–4pm; ⓣ480/860-2700; ⓦwww.franklloydwright.org). It's still a splendidly isolated spot and one where his trademark "organic architecture" makes perfect sense. The site can only be seen on **guided tours**; you can join either an hour-long

"Panorama Tour" ($24) or a ninety-minute "Insight Tour" ($32), which are offered at frequent intervals. Thanks to the expertise and enthusiasm of the guides, the experience is well worth the price.

Eating

Unless you're prepared to pay resort prices, it's hard to find a good **restaurant** in Phoenix with much atmosphere. Apart from a block or two in central Scottsdale and Tempe's lively Mill Avenue, no areas of the metropolis are small enough to explore on foot, but if you're happy to drive, neighbourhood diners – especially Mexican – can still be found.

Alice Cooper'stown 101 E Jackson St ⓣ602/253-7337. Barbecue restaurant-cum-sports bar, owned by the rock star and alongside downtown's US Airways Centre. While far from fine dining, the food's better than you might expect and the atmosphere is fun, with waiters in full Alice make-up. Lunch and dinner daily.

Bandera 3821 N Scottsdale Rd, Scottsdale ⓣ480/994-3524. Chicken cooked in the wood-burning oven is the specialty in this busy, inexpensive rotisserie in downtown Scottsdale, but other meats and fish are almost as good. Daily, dinner only.

Barrio Café 2814 N 16th St ⓣ602/636-0240, ⓦwww.barriocafe.com. Reservations are not taken at this popular little place, but it's worth the wait to enjoy authentic southern Mexican food. Closed Mon.

Coup des Tartes 4626 N 16th St ⓣ602/212-1082, ⓦwww.nicetartes.com. Unassuming 1930s farmhouse that conceals a romantic little dinner-only restaurant, serving classic French cuisine. Bring your own wine, corkage $9/bottle. Closed Sun & Mon.

Cowboy Ciao 7133 E Stetson Drive at Sixth, Scottsdale ⓣ480/946-3111, ⓦwww.cowboyciao.com. Hip Scottsdale roadhouse serving "modern American food with global influences". Lunchtime burgers, salads or sandwiches cost around $13; dinner entrees like stuffed pork rib chop or lamb loin $27–32.

Fuego Bistro 713 E Palo Verde Rd ⓣ602/277-1151, ⓦwww.fuegobistro.com. Delicious contemporary Latin American food, in a hard-to-find spot five miles north of downtown; dinner entrees cost around $24, but lunch is less than half that. Closed Sun & Mon.

House of Tricks 114 E Seventh St, Tempe ⓣ480/968-1114. Tiny, romantic modern-American place in the university district, with lots of vegetarian options. Closed Sun.

Pizzeria Bianco Heritage Square, 623 E Adams St ⓣ602/258-8300. High-quality pizzas in a very convenient downtown location; no wonder it's so popular. Dinner only, Tues–Sat.

Nightlife, entertainment and sports

For a rundown of what's on musically, pick up the free weekly *New Times* (ⓦwww.phoenixnewtimes.com). Both the **Phoenix Symphony Hall**, 225 E Adams St (ⓣ602/495-1999; ⓦwww.phoenixsymphony.org) and the **Scottsdale Centre for the Arts**, 7380 E Second St (ⓣ480/994-2787, ⓦwww.scottsdalearts.org), put on classical music, theatre and ballet. The **Arizona Diamondbacks** play major league baseball beneath the retractable roof of air-conditioned Chase Field (ⓦwww.azdiamondbacks.com), while the **Phoenix Suns** play NBA basketball at the US Airways Centre, 201 E Jefferson St (ⓦwww.suns.com) and football's **Arizona Cardinals** are based at Glendale's state-of-the-art University of Phoenix Stadium (ⓣ602/379-0102, ⓦwww.azcardinals.com).

Bar Smith 130 E Washington St, Phoenix ⓣ602/229-1265, ⓦwww.barsmithphoenix.com. The best thing about this stylish downtown bar and lounge is its fabulous outdoor dancefloor, upstairs. Closed Sun.

Bikini Lounge 1502 Grand Ave, Phoenix ⓣ602/252-0472. A real gem of a dive bar, this veteran tiki joint attracts a fascinating, eclectic mix of local characters.

Last Exit Bar & Grill 1425 W Southern Ave, Tempe ⓣ480/557-6656, ⓦwww.lastexitlive.com. Rock-oriented live music venue in an unpromising mall, where acts range from country-rock to local punks.

Marquee Theatre 730 N Mill Ave, Tempe ⓣ480/829-0607, ⓦwww.luckymanonline.com. The best venue to see big-name touring acts, with an open floor rather than seating and good beer.

Central Arizona

The I-40 interstate crosses the centre of Arizona, skirting the **Navajo Reservation** in the northeast. Though the narrow strip of land to either side can be extraordinarily beautiful, it holds few specific places worth stopping. The main exception is the pleasant town of Flagstaff, an ideal base for visits to the Grand Canyon as well as excursions to ancient Native American sites and the New Age centre of Sedona.

East of Flagstaff: Holbrook and Winslow

East of Flagstaff, two old Route 66 towns, **WINSLOW** and **HOLBROOK**, are kept alive by transcontinental truckers. Each town consists of little more than a strip of motels, such as the concrete teepees of the *Wigwam Motel* at 811 W Hopi Drive in Holbrook (ⓣ928/524-3048, ⓦwww.galerie-kokopelli.com/wigwam; ❷). However, Winslow is also graced by the restored splendour of *La Posada Hotel*, 303 E Second St (ⓣ928/289-4366, ⓦwww.laposada.org; ❺), which is so totally magnificent that it's worth a very long detour to spend a night here. A glorious fake, it was designed as a railroad hotel by Mary Jane Colter, of Grand Canyon fame, in the 1920s to emulate an 1860s hacienda; it still doubles as the local Amtrak stop. It also holds a great **restaurant**, the *Turquoise Room* (ⓣ928/289-2888), open for all meals daily.

Petrified Forest National Park

At **Petrified Forest National Park**, which straddles I-40 a dozen miles east of Holbrook, erosion continues to unearth a fossilized prehistoric forest of gigantic trees. The original cells of the wood have been replaced by multicoloured crystals of quartz. Cross sections, cut through and polished, look stunning and can be seen in the two **visitor centres**, thirty miles apart at the north and south entrances. On the ground, however, along the trails that set off from the park's **27-mile Scenic Drive**, the trees are not always all that exciting. Segmented, crumbling and very dark, they can seem like a bunch of logs lying in the sand; the best viewing is when the setting sun brings out rich red and orange hues.

The park's northern section – site of the main visitor centre (daily: summer 7am–7pm; winter 8am–5pm; $10/vehicle; ⓣ928/524-6228, ⓦwww.nps.gov/pefo) – is renowned for its views of the **Painted Desert**, an undulating expanse of solidified sand dunes, which at different times of day take on different colours (predominantly bluish shades of grey and reddish shades of brown).

Flagstaff

Northern Arizona's liveliest and most attractive town, **FLAGSTAFF** occupies a dramatic location beneath the San Francisco Peaks. Poised halfway between New Mexico and California, it's much more than just a way station for tourists en route to the Grand Canyon, eighty miles northwest.

Downtown, where barely a building rises more than three storeys, oozes Wild West charm. Its main thoroughfare, Santa Fe Avenue, used to be **Route 66** and before that the pioneer trail west. The tracks of the Santa Fe Railroad still cut downtown in two, so life remains punctuated by the mournful wail of passing trains.

Ever since it was founded, in 1876, Flagstaff has been a diverse place, with a strong black and Hispanic population and Navajo and Hopi heading in from the nearby reservations. Now home to just over fifty thousand, it makes an ideal base for travellers.

Arrival and information

Daily Amtrak **trains** stop in the centre of town, where the station doubles as a helpful **visitor centre** (Mon–Sat 8am–5pm, Sun 9am–4pm; ⓣ928/774-9541 or 1-800/379-0065, ⓦwww.flagstaffarizona.org).

Arizona Shuttle (ⓣ928/226-8060 or 1-800/766-7117, ⓦwww.arizonashuttle.com), based at the station, runs twice-daily **bus services** via Williams to the Grand Canyon (8am & 3.45pm; $28), as well as routes to Sedona and Phoenix. Greyhound is a few blocks south of downtown at 399 S Malpais Lane (ⓣ928/774-4573).

Accommodation

A brace of restored historic hotels make staying in downtown Flagstaff a real pleasure, while budget travellers can benefit from a couple of even cheaper high-quality **hostels** and there are dozens of well-priced **motels** further out.

DuBeau International Hostel 19 W Phoenix Ave ⓣ928/774-6731 or 1-800/398-7112, ⓦwww.dubeauhostel.com. Welcoming independent hostel just south of the tracks, whose converted en-suite motel rooms serve as four-person dorms at $20/bed or private doubles from $45. ❷

Grand Canyon International Hostel 19 S San Francisco St ⓣ928/779-9421 or 1-888/442-2696, ⓦwww.grandcanyonhostel.com. Independent hostel, under the same friendly management as the *DuBeau*. Dorm beds $20, private rooms $42–45. Free pick-up from Greyhound, car rental discounts and Grand Canyon tours (Mon, Wed, & Sat, plus Fri March–Oct; $75). ❷

Hotel Weatherford 23 N Leroux St ⓣ928/779-1919, ⓦwww.weatherfordhotel.com. Attractive old downtown hotel, with elegant wooden fittings; tasteful accommodation in restored rooms, not all en suite. Can be noisy. ❷–❻

Monte Vista 100 N San Francisco St ⓣ928/779-6971 or 1-800/545-3068, ⓦwww.hotelmontevista.com. Similarly atmospheric and appealing 1920s downtown landmark. Rooms, not all en suite, are named for celebrity guests; Paul McCartney stayed here in 2008. Weekend rates rise by up to $20. ❸–❻

Super 8 Flagstaff Downtown 602 W Route 66 ⓣ928/774-4581 or 1-800/800-8000, ⓦwww.super8.com. Pleasant chain motel centred on an enclosed swimming pool, adjacent to a Barnes & Noble bookstore less than a mile southwest of downtown. ❹

The Town

Flagstaff's appealing **downtown** stretches for a few red-brick blocks north of the railroad. Filled with cafés, bars and stores selling Route 66 souvenirs and Native American crafts, as well as outdoors outfitters, it's a fun place to stroll around, but holds no significant tourist attractions. Your most lasting impression may well be of the magnificent San Francisco Peaks on the northern horizon, topped by a jagged ridge.

The exceptional **Museum of Northern Arizona**, however, is three miles northwest of downtown on US-180 (daily 9am–5pm; $7; ⓦwww.musnaz.org). Its main emphasis is on documenting Native American life, with an excellent run-through of the Ancestral Puebloan past and contemporary Navajo, Havasupai and Hopi cultures, but it also actively encourages modern Native American craftworkers.

Eating and nightlife

While short of high-end **restaurants**, central Flagstaff holds a lively assortment of both old-style Western **diners** and eclectic **budget** options. Thanks to the students of Northern Arizona University, San Francisco Street, both north and south of the tracks, is filled with vegetarian cafés and espresso bars.

Beaver Street Brewery 11 S Beaver St ⓣ928/779-0079. Inventive sandwiches and salads, wood-fired pizza and outdoor beer garden.

Dara Thai 14 S San Francisco St ⓣ928/774-0047. Large Thai place just south of the tracks, where the service is great and a plate of delicious pad Thai noodles costs just $8 for lunch, $10 for dinner.

Diablo Burger 120 N Leroux St ⓣ928/774-3274. Stylish joint in the centre of town, where the $8–10 burgers feature exclusively local ingredients, most obviously free-range hormone-free cattle. Closed Sun.

Downtown Diner 7 E Aspen Ave ⓣ928/774-3492. Classic Route 66 diner a block north of the main drag, featuring leatherette booths and hefty burgers and sandwiches.

Macy's European Coffee House & Bakery 14 S Beaver St ⓣ928/774-2243. Not merely superb coffee, but heavenly pastries to go with it, plus more substantial vegetarian dishes such as black bean pizza and even couscous for breakfast.

The Museum Club 3404 E Route 66 ⓣ928/526-9434, ⓦwww.museumclub.com. A real oddity; this log-cabin taxidermy museum, somehow transmogrified into a classic Route 66 roadhouse, saloon and country-music venue, is a second home to hordes of dancing cowboys.

Sunset Crater and Wupatki national monuments

North of Flagstaff, the **San Francisco Volcanic Field** holds four hundred volcanoes. The most recent eruption took place in 1066 AD at **Sunset Crater**, twelve miles from Flagstaff. Its cone swells from a black base through reds and oranges to a yellow-tinged crest; walkers are not allowed onto the rim, but a trail passes through lava tubes around its base (daily 8am–5pm; ⓦwww.nps.gov/sucr; $5/person).

A dozen miles further north stand the ancient ruins of **Wupatki National Monument** (daily: summer 8am–7pm; winter 8am–5pm; $5/person, including Sunset Crater; ⓦwww.nps.gov/wupa). The **Sinagua** were joined by many others, including the **Ancestral Puebloans**, after the Sunset Crater explosion deposited a rich new layer of topsoil. The specific site known as Wupatki ("big house"), set proud on its natural foundations of red sandstone, is the largest of numerous ruins.

Walnut Canyon National Monument

Between 1100 and 1250 AD, **Walnut Canyon**, ten miles east of Flagstaff just south of I-40, was home to a thriving Sinagua community. Hundreds of their **cliff dwellings** nestle beneath overhangs in the canyon sides. They simply walled off natural alcoves and put up partitions to make separate rooms. No single dwelling is on the same scale as at Wupatki and only a handful are accessible, but cumulatively they make an impressive spectacle.

A scenic window in the **visitor centre** (daily: June–Aug 8am–6pm; March–May & Sept–Nov 8am–5pm; Dec–Feb 9am–5pm; $5/person; ⓦwww.nps.gov/waca) gives an excellent overall view. No accommodation and only minimal snack food, is available.

Sedona and Red Rock Country

US-89A threads south from Flagstaff through spectacular **Oak Creek Canyon** to emerge after 28 miles at **Sedona**, on the threshold of the extraordinary **Red Rock Country**, where giant mesas and buttes of stark red sandstone soar from the valley floor. The boom-and-bust mining town of **Jerome** looks down from a mountainside to the south.

Sedona

There's no disputing that the New Age resort of **SEDONA** enjoys a magnificent setting, amid definitive Southwestern canyon scenery. Sadly, however, the town adds nothing to the beauty of its surroundings, with mile upon mile of ugly red-brick sprawl interrupted only by hideous malls. While Europeans tend to be turned off by Sedona, many American travellers love its luxurious accommodation, fancy restaurants and almost limitless opportunities for active outdoor vacationing.

Since author Page Bryant "channelled" the information in 1981 that Sedona is in fact "the heart *chakra* of the planet" and pinpointed her first **vortex** – a point at which psychic and electromagnetic energies can supposedly be channelled for personal and planetary harmony – the town has achieved its own personal growth and blossomed as a focus for **New Age** practitioners of all kinds. Whether you love it or hate it may depend on whether you share their wide-eyed awe for angels, crystals and all matters mystical – and whether you're prepared to pay over-the-odds prices for the privilege of joining them.

You can see most of the sights, albeit from a distance, from US-89A; the best parts are south along Hwy-179 within Coconino National Forest. The closest **vortex** to town is on **Airport Mesa**; turn left up Airport Road from US-89A as you head south, a mile past the downtown junction known as the "**Y**" and it's at the junction of the second and third peaks. Further up, beyond the precariously sited airport, the **Shrine of the Red Rocks** looks out across the entire valley.

Sedona's **visitor centre** is just north of the "Y" (Mon–Sat 8.30am–5pm, Sun 9am–3pm; ⓣ928/282-7722 or 1-800/288-7336, ⓦwww.visitsedona.com). This is an expensive place to **stay**; cheaper options include the *Sedona Motel*, close to the "Y" at 218 Hwy-179 (ⓣ928/282-7187, ⓦwww.thesedonamotel.com; ❸) and the *Quality Inn King's Ransom*, further south at 771 Hwy-179 (ⓣ928/282-7151 or 1-800/846-6164, ⓦwww.kingsransomsedona.com; ❺).

Heartline, 1610 W Hwy-89A (ⓣ928/282-0785), is a health-conscious courtyard Southwestern **restaurant**, open for dinner only; the *Coffee Pot Restaurant*, 2050 W Hwy-89A (ⓣ928/282-6626; daily 6am–2.15pm), on the other hand, is a large old-style diner, serving all the burgers, Mexican dishes and fried specials you could hope for.

Jerome

The former mining town of **JEROME**, high above the Verde Valley on US-89A thirty miles south of Sedona, is conspicuous from far and wide: an enormous letter "J" is etched deep into the hillside above it, while a large chunk of that hillside is missing altogether, having been blown apart for **opencast copper mining**.

From the 1950s, when the mines closed down, until the 1970s, Jerome was a **ghost town**. Many of those who simply moved into its empty houses are still here, making a living from arts and crafts, while the town itself has made a dramatic recovery. The hillside is so steep that many houses have two storeys at the front and four or five at the back. Under the concussion of two hundred miles of tunnels being blasted into the mountainside, the whole town used to slip downhill at the rate of five inches per year; the **Sliding Jail** on Hull Avenue came to rest 225ft from where it was built.

At the highest point in town, the *Jerome Grand Hotel*, 200 Hill St (ⓣ928/634-8200 or 1-888/817-6788; ⓦwww.jeromegrandhotel.com; ❺), is a restored Spanish Mission hotel with fabulous views. The rooms are atmospheric rather than particularly luxurious and there's a good on-site restaurant, *The Asylum*.

Montezuma Castle National Monument

In an idyllic setting just above Beaver Creek and just east of I-17, 25 miles from Sedona, **Montezuma Castle National Monument** preserves a superb Sinagua **cliff dwelling** (daily: summer 8am–6pm; winter 8am–5pm; $5; ⓦwww.nps.gov/moca). Filling a hillside alcove with a wall of pink adobe, its five storeys taper to fit the contours of the rock. Apparently, the fingerprints of the masons are still visible on the bricks and the sycamore beams remain firmly in place, but visitors can't climb up.

West of Flagstaff: I-40 to California

Everything along I-40 west of Flagstaff is dominated by the road's function as the main route between Las Vegas and the Grand Canyon. The first town you reach, **WILLIAMS**, seems to exist solely to capture the passing tourist trade, with a historic **railroad** running north to the Canyon (see p.792). From **SELIGMAN**, 45 miles further west, a long stretch of the old Route 66 loops northward through the **Hualapai Indian Reservation** and a dozen fading towns, **PEACH SPRINGS** in particular, that look straight out of *The Grapes of Wrath*. As well as making a great detour on what can be a very dull drive; it provides the only access to **Havasu Canyon** (see p.796).

There's little reason to stop at **KINGMAN**, the largest town in western Arizona, from where US-93 branches north to Las Vegas and I-40 continues to Los Angeles.

Lake Havasu City

Forty miles southwest of Kingman, ten miles from California, a detour south leads to the bizarre sight of the old grey **London Bridge**, reaching across the dammed Colorado River to an artificial island at **LAKE HAVASU CITY**. The resort's developer, Robert P. McCulloch, bought the bridge (under the impression it was Tower Bridge – or so the story goes) for $2.4 million in the 1960s, shipped it across the Atlantic chunk by chunk and reassembled it over a channel dug to divert water from Lake Havasu. Lake Havasu City holds an undeniable attraction for the parched urbanites of Phoenix, who fish on the lake or race on jet-skis, but minimal appeal for travellers from further afield. Moreover, between March and June, it's filled with students on **spring break**, drinking and partying around the clock.

Motels abound, ranging from the surprisingly hip *Agave Inn*, 1420 W McCulloch Blvd (Ⓣ928/854-2833 or 1-888/898-4328; ❹), to the extravagant riverfront *London Bridge Resort*, 1477 Queen's Bay Rd (Ⓣ928/855-0888 or 1-866/331-9231, Ⓦlondonbridgeresort.com; ❻).

The Grand Canyon

Although almost five million people visit **GRAND CANYON NATIONAL PARK** every year, the canyon itself remains beyond the grasp of the human imagination. No photograph, no statistics, can prepare you for such vastness. At more than one mile deep, it's an inconceivable abyss; varying between four and eighteen miles wide, it's an endless expanse of bewildering shapes and colours, glaring desert brightness and impenetrable shadow, stark promontories and soaring sandstone pinnacles. Somehow it's so impassive, so remote – you could never call it a disappointment, but at the same time many visitors are left feeling peculiarly flat. In a sense, none of the available activities can quite live up to that first stunning sight of the chasm. The **overlooks** along the rim all offer views that shift unceasingly from dawn to sunset; you can **hike** down into the depths on foot or by mule, hover above in a **helicopter** or raft through the **whitewater rapids** of the river itself; you can spend a night at **Phantom Ranch** on the canyon floor or swim in the waterfalls of the idyllic **Havasupai Reservation**. And yet that distance always remains – the Grand Canyon stands apart.

The vast majority of visitors come to the **South Rim** – it's much easier to get to, it holds far more facilities (mainly at **Grand Canyon Village**) and it's open year round. There is another lodge and campground at the **North Rim**, which by virtue of its isolation can be a lot more evocative, but at one thousand feet higher

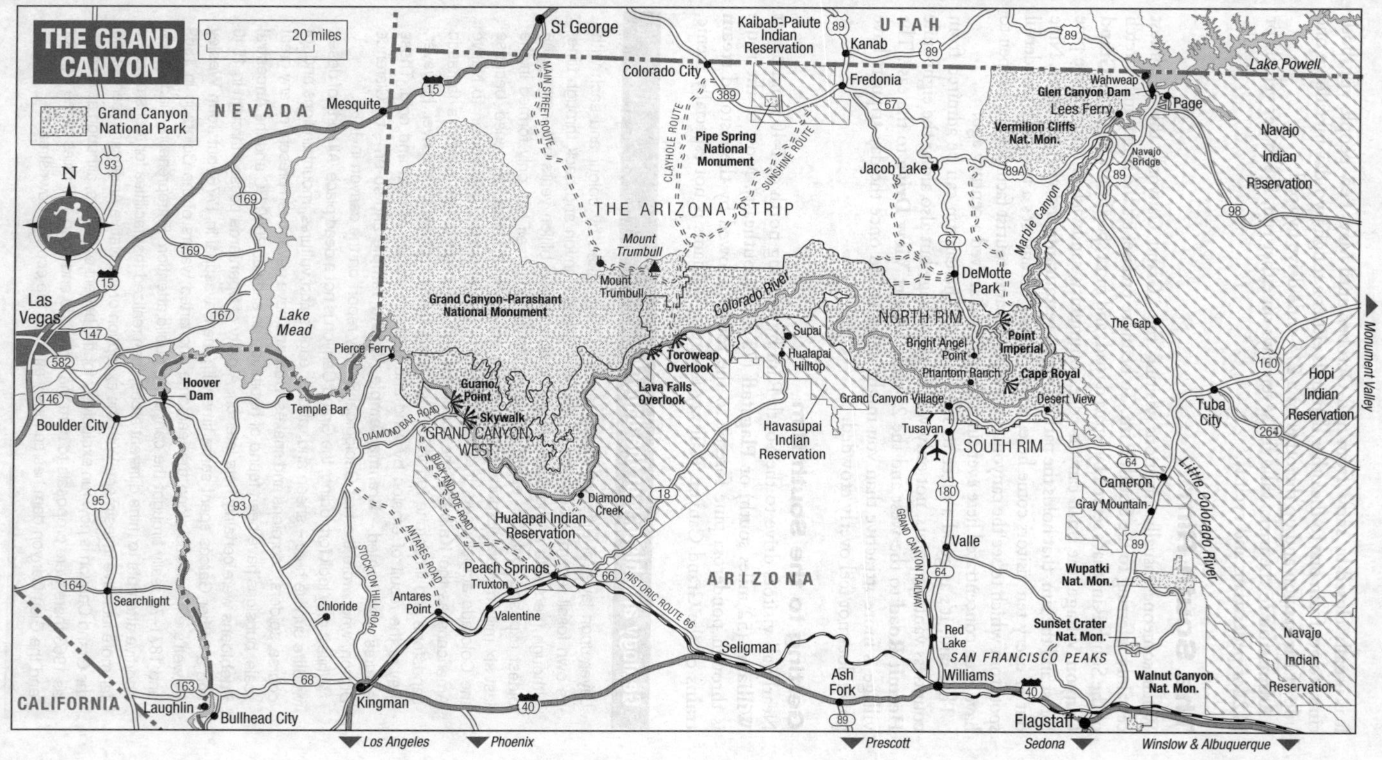
THE GRAND CANYON
0 20 miles
Grand Canyon National Park
N
NEVADA
UTAH
ARIZONA
CALIFORNIA
THE ARIZONA STRIP
St George
Mesquite
Las Vegas
Boulder City
Hoover Dam
Lake Mead
Temple Bar
Pierce Ferry
Searchlight
Laughlin
Bullhead City
Kingman
Chloride
Colorado City
Kaibab-Paiute Indian Reservation
Kanab
Fredonia
Pipe Spring National Monument
Jacob Lake
DeMotte Park
Vermilion Cliffs Nat. Mon.
Lees Ferry
Wahweap
Glen Canyon Dam
Page
Lake Powell
Navajo Bridge
Navajo Indian Reservation
Marble Canyon
Mount Trumbull
Grand Canyon-Parashant National Monument
Colorado River
Toroweap Overlook
Lava Falls Overlook
Supai
Hualapai Hilltop
Havasupai Indian Reservation
NORTH RIM
Point Imperial
Bright Angel Point
Phantom Ranch
Cape Royal
Grand Canyon Village
Desert View
Tusayan
SOUTH RIM
The Gap
Tuba City
Hopi Indian Reservation
Cameron
Gray Mountain
Little Colorado River
Valle
Wupatki Nat. Mon.
Sunset Crater Nat. Mon.
Walnut Canyon Nat. Mon.
Red Lake
SAN FRANCISCO PEAKS
Williams
Flagstaff
Ash Fork
Seligman
Peach Springs
Truxton
Valentine
Antares Point
Guano Point
Skywalk
GRAND CANYON WEST
Hualapai Indian Reservation
Diamond Creek
MAIN STREET ROUTE
CLAYHOLE ROUTE
SUNSHINE ROUTE
DIAMOND BAR ROAD
BUCK AND DOE ROAD
ANTARES ROAD
STOCKTON HILL ROAD
HISTORIC ROUTE 66
GRAND CANYON RAILWAY
Monument Valley
Los Angeles
Phoenix
Prescott
Sedona
Winslow & Albuquerque

it is usually closed by snow from mid-October until May. Few people visit both rims; to get from one to the other demands either a tough two-day hike down one side of the canyon and up the other or a 215-mile drive by road.

Admission to the park, valid for seven days on either rim, is $25 per vehicle or $12 for pedestrians and cyclists.

The South Rim

When someone casually mentions visiting the "Grand Canyon", they're almost certainly referring to the **South Rim**. To be more precise, it's the thirty-mile stretch of the South Rim that's served by a paved road; and most specifically of all, it's **Grand Canyon Village**, the small canyon-edge community, sandwiched between the pine forest and the rim, that holds the park's **lodges**, **restaurants** and **visitor centre**. Nine out of every ten visitors come here, however, not because it's a uniquely wonderful spot from which to see the canyon, but simply because tourist facilities just happen to have been concentrated here ever since the railroad arrived a century ago.

That said, it's as good a place to start as any. The canyon can be admired from countless vantage points, not only within the village but also along the eight-mile **Hermit Road** to the west and the 23-mile **Desert View Drive** to the east. The village is more attractive than you might imagine and once the day-trippers have gone, does not feel overly crowded.

Getting to the South Rim

Nearly all visitors drive to the South Rim by heading north of I-40 from either **Williams** (52 miles south) or **Flagstaff** (75 miles southeast). Most of the route is through ponderosa pine forests, so the route followed by the restored **steam trains** of the Grand Canyon Railway up from Williams is not especially scenic,

Geology and history of the canyon

Layer upon layer of different rocks, readily distinguished by colour and each with its own fossil record, recede down into the Grand Canyon and back through time. Although the strata at the riverbed are, at almost two billion years old, among the oldest exposed rocks on earth, however, the canyon itself has only formed in the last six million years, Experts cannot agree quite how that has happened, because the Colorado actually cuts through the heart of an enormous hill (known to Native Americans as the **Kaibab**, "the mountain with no peak"). The canyon's fantastic sandstone and limestone formations were not literally carved by the river, however; they're the result of erosion by wind and extreme cycles of heat and cold. These features were named – **Brahma Temple**, **Vishnu Temple** and so on – by Clarence Dutton, who wrote the first Geological Survey report on the canyon in 1881.

While it may look forbidding, the Grand Canyon is not a dead place. All sorts of desert **wildlife** survive here – sheep and rabbits, eagles and vultures, mountain lions and, of course, spiders, scorpions and snakes. **Humans** have never been present on any great scale, but signs have been found of habitation as early as 2000 BC and the **Ancestral Puebloans** were certainly here later on. A party of **Spaniards** passed through in 1540 and a Father Garcés spent some time with the Havasupai in 1776, but **John Wesley Powell**'s expeditions along the fearsome uncharted waters of the Colorado in 1869 and 1871–72 really brought the canyon to public attention. Entrepreneurs made a few abortive attempts to mine different areas, then realized that facilities for tourism were a far more lucrative investment. With the exception of the Native American reservations, the Grand Canyon is now run exclusively for the benefit of visitors, although as recently as 1963 there were proposals to dam the Colorado and flood 150 miles of the Canyon and the Glen Canyon dam has seriously affected the ecology downstream.

even if it does make a fun ride (departs Williams daily 9.30am; from $70 return; ⓣ303/843-8724 or 1-800/843-8724, ⓦwww.thetrain.com). For details of buses from Flagstaff, see p.787.

The small **airport** at Tusayan, six miles from the South Rim and used primarily by "flight-seeing" companies (see p.794), also welcomes daily tours from Las Vegas, with operators such as Scenic Airlines (from $190 return; ⓣ702/638-3300 or 1-800/634-6801, ⓦwww.scenic.com).

Arrival and information

Massive car parks alongside the **Canyon View Information Plaza**, a couple of miles east of the village centre, enable visitors both to get a first view of the canyon itself from nearby Mather Point and also to call in at the park's main **visitor centre** (daily: May to mid-Oct 7.30am–6pm; mid-Oct to April 8am–5pm; ⓣ928/638-7888, ⓦwww.nps.gov/grca), where the open-air displays and trail guides are complemented by a good bookstore. Inexpensive **bike rental** is also available here (ⓣ928/914-8704, ⓦwww.bikegrandcanyon.com); a bike shuttle service out to Hopi Point (daily 9am–4pm, on the hour; $9 return) makes a great way to escape the crowds.

Grand Canyon Village is accessible to private vehicles, as is the road east from the village to Desert View. Both the road west from the village to **Hermit's Rest**, however, and the short access road to **Yaki Point** – the first overlook east of Mather Point and the trailhead for the **South Kaibab Trail** – are only open to private vehicles during December, January and February. Free **shuttle buses** run on four routes: the ponderous **Village Route**, which loops between Grand Canyon Village and the information plaza; the **Kaibab Trail Route** between the plaza and Yaki Point; the eight-mile **Hermit's Rest Route**, which heads west to eight canyon overlooks; and the **Tusayan Route**, to the gateway community of Tusayan seven miles south of the rim.

South Rim accommodation

All the "lodges" in Grand Canyon Village are operated by Xanterra Parks & Resorts (same-day ⓣ928/638-2631, advance ⓣ303/297-2757 or 1-888/297-2757, ⓦwww.grandcanyonlodges.com). Much the best of the bunch are the magnificent 1905 *El Tovar Hotel* (❼) and the *Bright Angel*, which has some great rustic cabins (rooms ❹, rim-side cabins ❻), but even in those and the other "rim-edge" places – the more mundane *Thunderbird* and *Kachina* lodges (both ❼) – very few rooms have actual canyon views and in any case it's always dark by 8pm. Unless you reserve months in advance, any rooms that may be available are most likely to be further back, in *Maswik Lodge* (❹) or the two-part *Yavapai Lodge* (❺), not far from the information plaza.

Tent and RV camping (without hook-ups) is available at the year-round **Mather Campground**, south of the main road through Grand Canyon Village. Sites for up to two vehicles and six people cost $18 per night between March and mid-November, when it's possible and strongly recommended, to make a reservation (ⓣ1-877/444-6777, ⓦwww.recreation.gov). Between mid-November and February, sites are first-come, first-served and the fee drops to $15 per night. The adjacent **Trailer Village** consists exclusively of RV sites with hook-ups, costing $34 per site per night for two people; reserve through Xanterra (see above).

The summer-only *Desert View* campground, 26 miles east, is first-come, first-served, costs $12 and has no hook-ups. You can also camp inside the canyon itself, with a permit from the **Backcountry Reservations Office** near *Maswik Lodge* (daily 8am–noon & 1–5pm; see ⓦwww.nps.gov/grca/backcountry); permits cost $10, plus $5 per person per night.

If all the park accommodation is full, the nearest alternative is the underwhelming service village of **Tusayan**. *Seven Mile Lodge* (Ⓣ928/638-2291; no advance reservations; ❹) offers the least expensive rooms, while the *Holiday Inn Express* (Ⓣ928/638-3000 or 1-888/473-2269, Ⓦwww.gcanyon.com; ❺) is more stylish.

South Rim eating

Grand Canyon Village holds a reasonably wide range of places to **eat**. Both *Yavapai* and *Maswik* lodges have basic cafeterias, open until 9pm and 10pm respectively. *Bright Angel Lodge* has its own **restaurant**, as well as the *Arizona Steakhouse*; both are open until 10pm and offer entrees costing $15–25. At *El Tovar*, where the dining room looks right out over the canyon, the sumptuous menu is enormously expensive, though breakfast is relatively affordable meal. Most of the hotels in **Tusayan** have their own dining rooms.

Exploring the South Rim

Most South Rim visits start at **Mather Point** near the Canyon View Information Plaza, where the canyon panorama is more comprehensive than any obtainable from Grand Canyon Village. The views to the east in particular are consistently stupendous; it's hard to imagine a more perfect position from which to watch the **sunrise** over the canyon.

Various vantage points along the rim-edge footpath nearby offer glimpses of the Colorado River. Walk west for around ten minutes – turn left along the rim from the information plaza – and you'll come to **Yavapai Point**. From here, you can see two tiny segments of the river, one of which happens to include both the suspension footbridge across the Colorado and *Phantom Ranch* (see p.796). Nearby, the **Yavapai Observation Station** (daily: summer 8am–8pm, winter 8am–5pm; free) has illuminating displays on how the canyon may have formed.

South Rim tours

Xanterra (contact the "transportation desk" in any lodge or call Ⓣ928/638-2631) runs at least two short daily **coach tours** along the **rim** to the west ($25) and east ($44) of the village, **sunrise** and **sunset** trips to Yavapai Point ($20) and **mule** rides to Abyss Overlook, at rim level ($110) and *Phantom Ranch* down by the river (from $447; see p.796).

Multi-day **whitewater rafting trips** in the canyon proper – such as those run by Western River Expeditions (Ⓦwww.westernriver.com) or Canyoneers (Ⓦwww.canyoneers.com) – are often booked up years in advance, while no **one-day** raft trips are available within Grand Canyon National Park. For a trip along the river at short notice, there are, however, two alternatives, at either end of the canyon. Colorado River Discovery, based in Page, Arizona, offers one-day trips that start below **Glen Canyon Dam** and take out at **Lees Ferry** ($78; Ⓣ928/645-9175 or 1-888/522-6644; Ⓦwww.raftthecanyon.com), while further west, the tribal-run Hualapai River Runners arrange pricey one-day trips on the Hualapai Reservation, starting at Diamond Creek (March–Oct, $328; Ⓣ928/769-2636 or 1-888/868-9378, Ⓦwww.grandcanyonwest.com).

Airplane tours cost from around $100 for 30min up to as long as you like for as much as you've got. Operators include Air Grand Canyon (Ⓣ928/638-3300 or 1-800/634-6801, Ⓦwww.airgrandcanyon.com) and Grand Canyon Airlines (Ⓣ928/638-2359 or 1-866/235-9422, Ⓦwww.grandcanyonairlines.com). **Helicopter tours**, from more like $150 for 30min, are offered by Maverick (Ⓣ928/638-2622 or 1-888/261-4414, Ⓦwww.maverickhelicopter.com) and Papillon (Ⓣ702/736-7243 or 1-888/635-7272, Ⓦwww.papillon.com). All the companies are in **Tusayan**.

Two separate roads extend along the South Rim for several miles in either direction from the information plaza and Grand Canyon Village, paralleled to the west in particular by the **Rim Trail** on the very lip of the canyon. Along **Hermit Road** to the west, accessible only by shuttle bus or bike for most of the year, no single overlook can be said to be the "best", but there are far too many to stop at them all. **Sunset** is particularly magical at Hopi Point, to the west.

Driving or taking a shuttle bus along Desert View Drive to the east opens up further dramatic views. **Desert View** itself, 23 miles out from the village, is, at 7500ft, the highest point on the South Rim. Visible to the east are the vast flatlands of the **Navajo Nation**; to the northeast, **Vermillion** and **Echo Cliffs** and the grey bulk of **Navajo Mountain** ninety miles away; to the west, the gigantic peaks of **Vishnu** and **Buddha temples**, while through the plains comes the narrow gorge of the **Little Colorado**. The odd-looking construction on the very lip of the canyon is **Desert View Watchtower**, built by Mary Jane Colter in 1932 in a conglomeration of Native American styles and decorated with Hopi pictographs.

Into the canyon

Hiking any of the trails that descend **into the Grand Canyon** allows you to pass through successive different landscapes, each with its own climate, wildlife and topography. While the canyon offers a wonderful wilderness experience, however, it can be a hostile and very unforgiving environment, gruelling even for expert hikers.

That the South Rim is 7000ft above sea level is for most people fatiguing in itself. Furthermore, all hikes start with a long, steep descent and unless you camp overnight you'll have to climb all the way back up again when you're hotter and wearier.

For day-hikers, the golden rule is to keep track of how much time you spend hiking down and allow twice that much to get back up again. Average summer temperatures inside the canyon exceed 100°F; to hike for eight hours in that sort of heat, you have to drink an incredible thirty pints of water. Always carry at least a quart per person and much more if there are no water sources along your chosen trail. You must have food as well, as drinking large quantities without also eating can cause deadly water intoxication.

Bright Angel Trail

The **Bright Angel Trail**, which starts from the wooden shack in the village that was once the Kolb photographic studio, switchbacks for 9.6 miles down to **Phantom Ranch**. Under no circumstances should you try to hike down and back in a single day – it might not look far on the map, but it's harder than running a marathon. Instead, the longest feasible day-hike is to go as far as **Plateau Point** on the edge of the arid Tonto Plateau, an overlook above the Inner Gorge from which it is not possible to descend any further. That twelve-mile round trip usually takes at least eight hours. In summer, water can be obtained along the way.

Miners laid out the first section of the trail a century ago, along an old Havasupai route. It has two short tunnels in its first mile. After another mile, the **wildlife** starts to increase (deer, rodents and ravens) and there are a few **pictographs,** all but obscured by graffiti.

At the lush **Indian Gardens** almost five miles down, site of a ranger station and campground with water, the trails split to Plateau Point or down to the river via the **Devil's Corkscrew**. The latter route leads through sand dunes scattered with cactuses and down beside **Garden Creek** to the Colorado, which you then follow for more than a mile to *Phantom Ranch*.

Phantom Ranch

It's a real thrill to spend a night at the very bottom of the canyon, at the 1922 **Phantom Ranch**. The **cabins** are reserved exclusively for the use of excursionists on two-day mule trips ($448/person for one night, $627 for the winter-only two-night trips), booked through Xanterra (see p.793). Beds in the four ten-bunk **dorms** ($39) are usually reserved way in advance, also through Xanterra; check for cancellations at the *Bright Angel* transportation desk as soon as you reach the South Rim. All supplies reach *Phantom Ranch* the same way you do (an all-day hike on foot or mule), so **meals** are expensive, a minimum of $18.50 for breakfast and up to $39 for dinner. **Camping** at the beautiful *Bright Angel Campground*, a little closer to the Colorado River, is by **permit** only, as detailed on p.793. Do not hike down without a reservation at either the ranch or campground and even if you do have one, reconfirm it the day before you set off.

Grandview Trail

The **Grandview Trail**, down from Grandview Point, was built during the 1890s to aid copper mining on **Horseshoe Mesa**, still littered with abandoned mine workings. Although it's possible by connecting with other trails to make your way down to the Tonto Platform and thus, eventually, the Colorado River, the Grandview itself is not a rim-to-river route. Instead, going down to the mesa and back is a popular **day-hike**, though that doesn't mean it's easy; now officially "unmaintained", it's a very demanding trail. Several of its switchbacks were constructed by inserting metal rods deep into the canyon wall, then covering them with juniper logs, stones and dirt. At times it can be a little hair-raising, but it has stayed surprisingly sturdy for over a century. Reckon on six hours for the round trip.

The Havasupai Reservation

The **Havasupai Reservation** really is another world. Things have changed a little since a 1930s anthropologist called it "the only spot in the United States where native culture has remained in anything like its pristine condition", but the sheer magic of its turquoise waterfalls and canyon scenery makes this a very special place.

Havasu Canyon is a side canyon of the Grand Canyon, 35 miles as the raven flies from Grand Canyon Village, but almost two hundred miles by road. Turn off the interstate at Seligman or Kingman, onto AZ-66 (which curves north between the two), stock up with food, water and gas and then follow Arrowhead Hwy-18 to **Hualapai Hilltop**. An eight-mile trail zigzags down a bluff from there, leading through the stunning waterless Hualapai Canyon to the village of **SUPAI**. Riding down on horseback with a Havasupai guide costs $70 one-way, $120 return and there's often a helicopter service as well ($85 one-way; ⓣ623/516-2790). Hiking is free, but all visitors pay a $35 entry fee on arrival at Supai.

Beyond Supai the trail leads to a succession of spectacular waterfalls, starting with a dramatic and as yet unnamed cascade created by a flash flood in 2008. Beyond that lie **Havasu Falls**, which is great for swimming and **Mooney Falls**, where a precarious chain-ladder descent leads to another glorious pool.

For all practical details, see the tribe's helpful **website**, ⓦwww.havasupaitribe .com. Supai itself holds the **motel**-like *Havasupai Lodge* (ⓣ928/448-2111; ❻), along with a **café**, a **general store** and the only **post office** in the US still to receive its mail by pack train. Fuirther down and looking rather dilapidated since the latest flood, a **campground** (ⓣ928/448-2141; $17) stretches between Havasu and Mooney Falls.

The Hualapai Reservation: the "West Rim"

Immediately west of the Havasupai reservation and also inhabited by descendants of the Pai people, the **Hualapai Indian reservation** spreads across almost a million acres, bounded to the north by a 108-mile stretch of the Colorado River.

Fifty miles northwest of the reservation's only town, **PEACH SPRINGS**, itself 35 miles northwest of **Seligman** on Route 66, a cluster of overlooks above the Colorado river is cannily promoted as **Grand Canyon West** or the "**West Rim**" of the Grand Canyon. This is the closest spot to Las Vegas where it's possible to see the canyon and most of its visitors are day-trippers who fly here unaware that they're not seeing the canyon at its best. The massive Hualapai programme to attract tourists culminated in 2007 in the unveiling of the **Skywalk** (Ⓣ928/769-2636 or 1-888/868-8378, Ⓦwww.grandcanyonwest.com) a horseshoe-shaped glass walkway which despite the hype does not extend out over the canyon itself, but above a side arm, with a vertical drop of just 1200 feet immediately below. It's so extraordinarily expensive, limited in scope and time-consuming to visit – unless you pay for an air tour from Las Vegas (from $170; Scenic Airlines, Ⓣ1-800/634-6801, Ⓦwww.scenic.com), you have to drive a minimum of forty miles on rough remote roads from the nearest highway and pay $20 to park at the end, plus at least $68 per person to reach and walk on the Skywalk – that it can't be recommended over a trip to the national park.

To the North Rim

The 215-mile route by road from Grand Canyon Village to the **North Rim** follows AZ-64 along the East Rim Drive to Desert View, then passes an overlook into the gorge of the Little Colorado, before joining US-89 fifty miles later at **CAMERON**. The Cameron Trading Post, still a trading centre for the Navajo Nation, holds a good **motel** and **restaurant** (Ⓣ928/679-2231 or 1-800/338-7385, Ⓦwww.camerontradingpost.com; ❺).

Lees Ferry

The direct route to the North Rim, now US-89A, crosses **Navajo Bridge** seventy barren miles north of Cameron, five hundred feet above the Colorado River. There are in fact two Navajo Bridges, the 1929 original, now reserved for pedestrians, having been supplanted by a wider facsimile in 1995. Until the first was built, a ferry service operated six miles north at **LEES FERRY**. Established in 1872 by Mormon pioneer John D. Lee, it was the only spot within hundreds of miles to offer easy access to the banks of the river on both sides. Lee himself was on the run after the **Mountain Meadows Massacre** in Utah in 1857, in which he led a white band clumsily disguised as Native Americans in their slaughter of a wagon train of would-be settlers.

Lees Ferry is the sole launching point for **whitewater rafting** trips into the Grand Canyon – the first point where boats can get out again is at Diamond Creek, twelve days away by muscle power. The ferry site still holds the atmospheric remains of Lee's Lonely Dell ranch, as well as a basic **campground** (Ⓣ928/355-2334; $12). Back on US-89A, beneath the red of the **Vermilion Cliffs**, a succession of **motels** all have their own restaurants – *Marble Canyon Lodge* (Ⓣ928/355-2225 or 1-800/726-1789; Ⓦwww.leesferryflyfishing.com; ❸), *Lees Ferry Lodge* (Ⓣ928/355-2231 or 1-800/451-2231, Ⓦwww.vermilioncliffs.com; ❸) and *Cliff Dweller's Lodge* (Ⓣ928/355-2261 or 1-800/962-9755; Ⓦwww.cliffdwellerslodge.com; ❹).

The turning south to get to the North Rim, off US-89A onto AZ-67, comes at **JACOB LAKE**, home to the welcoming *Jacob Lake Inn* (Ⓣ928/643-7232, Ⓦwww.jacoblake.com; ❺) and the lovely *Jacob Lake Campground*, open to tent campers only (Ⓣ928/643-7395; $17; mid-May to Oct), but not much else. From here – along a road that's closed in winter – it's 41 miles to the canyon itself.

The North Rim

Higher, more exposed and far less accessible than the South Rim, the **NORTH RIM** of the Grand Canyon receives less than a tenth as many visitors. A cluster of venerable Park Service buildings stand where the main highway reaches the canyon and a handful of rim-edge roads allow drivers to take their pick from additional lookouts. Only one hiking trail sees much use, the **North Kaibab Trail**, which follows Bright Angel Creek down to *Phantom Ranch*.

Tourist facilities on the North Rim, concentrated at **Bright Angel Point**, open for the season in mid-May and close in mid-October. **Accommodation** at *Grand Canyon Lodge* is in cabins and motel-like structures that spread back along the ridge from the lodge entrance, very few of which have canyon views; advance reservations are essential (Ⓣ480/337-1320 or 1-877/386-4383, Ⓦwww.grandcanyonlodgenorth.com; ❺). The *Lodge* also holds a good **restaurant** (Ⓣ928/638-2612), plus a saloon and an espresso bar and arranges **mule rides** (1hr $40, half-day $75; Ⓣ435/679-8665, Ⓦwww.canyonrides.com). Just over a mile north is the *North Rim Campground*, where space is usually available to backpackers, but can be reserved (Ⓣ1-877/444-6777; Ⓦwww.recreation.gov; $18).

The park itself remains open for day-use only after mid-October, but no food, lodging or gas is available and visitors must be prepared to leave at a moment's notice. It's shut down altogether by the first major snowfall of winter.

Northeastern Arizona: Indian Country

The astonishing desert landscapes of northeastern Arizona, popularly known as **INDIAN COUNTRY**, are home to some of the greatest architectural achievements of the **Ancestral Puebloans**. The cliff palaces of **Canyon de Chelly** and **Betatakin** and **Keet Seel** in the Navajo National Monument are that much more special for standing on lands still occupied by their heirs, the Hopi and Navajo.

The **NAVAJO NATION**, the largest Native American reservation in the US, extends into both western New Mexico and Monument Valley in southernmost Utah. Everyone can speak English, but Navajo, a language so complex that it served as a secret code during World War II, is still the lingua franca. The reservation follows its own rules over Daylight Savings; in frontier-style towns like Tuba City, the time varies according to whether you're in an American or a Navajo district.

When the Americans took over this region from the Mexicans in the mid-nineteenth century, the Navajo – who call themselves *Dineh*, "The People" – almost lost everything. In 1864, Kit Carson rounded up every Navajo he could find and packed them off to Fort Sumner in desolate eastern New Mexico (see p.767). A few years later, however, the Navajo were allowed to return. Most of the 300,000-plus Navajo today work as shepherds and farmers on widely scattered smallholdings, though craftspeople also sell their wares from roadside stands and tourist stops.

As you travel in this region, respect its people and places. Though the Ancestral Puebloans are no longer present, many of the relics they left behind are on land that holds spiritual significance to their modern counterparts. Similarly, it is offensive to photograph or intrude upon people's lives without permission.

On a practical note, don't expect extensive **tourist facilities**. Most towns are bureaucratic outposts that only come alive for tribal fairs and rodeos and hold few places to eat and even fewer hotels and motels. For information online, visit Ⓦwww.discovernavajo.com and www.explorenavajo.com.

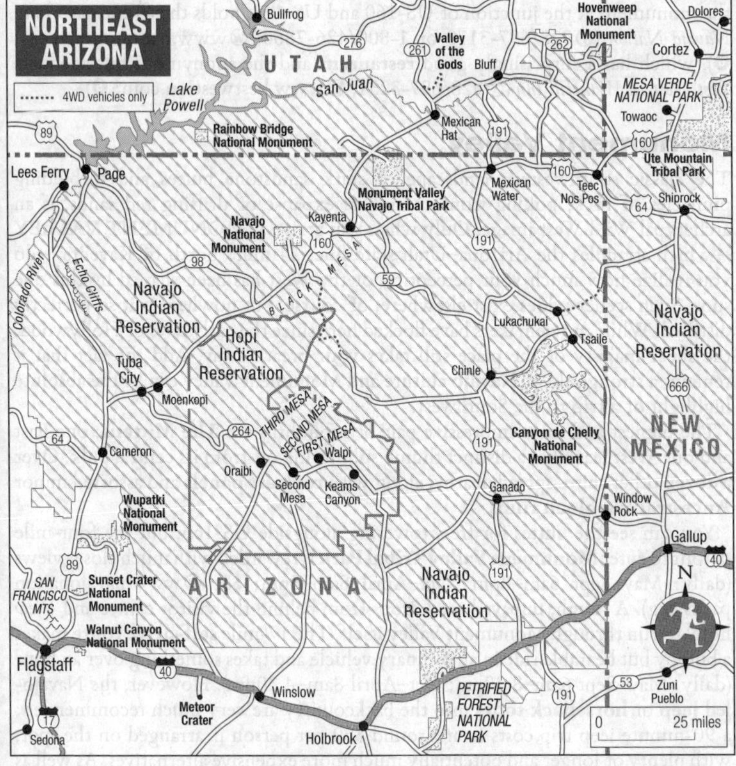

Navajo National Monument

Navajo National Monument, in the northwest quarter of the reservation, protects two beautifully sited cliff dwellings. You'll find the useful **visitor centre** (daily 8am–5pm; free; Ⓣ928/672-2700, Ⓦwww.nps.gov/nava) at the end of paved Hwy-564, ten miles north of US-160. Behind it, a ten-minute trail leads to a viewpoint overlooking **Betatakin**, an exceptionally well-preserved 135-room masonry structure tucked in a large alcove halfway up the 700-foot-high, brilliant-red sandstone cliff on the far side of a canyon. It's only possible to hike down to Betatakin – which feels as though it was abandoned seven years, not seven centuries, ago – by joining one of the unforgettable five-hour ranger-guided hikes (typically summer daily 8.15am & 10am, winter daily 10am). Numbers are limited, so call ahead and get to the visitor centre as early as possible on the day – or stay the previous night at the attractive free **campground** alongside.

In summer, you can also visit the even larger Ancestral Puebloan site of **Keet Seel**. However, the seventeen-mile round-trip hike from the visitor centre is too gruelling to attempt in a single day, so you'll have to stay in the small **campground** near the site; get a permit from the visitor centre at least a day in advance.

There are few **places to stay** nearby. However, **TUBA CITY**, west of the monument, has the large, modern *Quality Inn Navajo Nation* (Ⓣ928/283-4545; Ⓦwww.qualityinntubacity.com; ⑤), while **KAYENTA**, 22 miles northeast of the monument at the junction of US-160 and US-163, holds the *Hampton Inn–Navajo Nation* (ⓣ928/697-3170 or 1-800/426-7866, ⓦwww.hamptoninn.com; ❻), which has a surprisingly good **restaurant** and the anonymous but adequate *Best Western Wetherill Inn* (ⓣ928/697-3231, ⓦwww.bestwestern.com; ❺).

Monument Valley

The classic southwestern landscape of stark sandstone buttes and forbidding pinnacles of rock, poking from an endless expanse of drifting red sands, is an archetypal Wild West image. Only when you arrive at **MONUMENT VALLEY** – which straddles the Arizona–Utah state line, 24 miles north of Kayenta – do you realize how much your perception of the West has been shaped by this one spot. Such scenery does exist elsewhere, of course, but nowhere is it so perfectly distilled. While moviemakers have flocked here since the early days of Hollywood, the sheer majesty of the place still takes your breath away. Add the fact that it remains a stronghold of **Navajo** culture and Monument Valley can be the absolute highlight of a trip to the Southwest.

The biggest and most impressive pair of monoliths are **The Mittens**; one East and one West, each has a distinct thumb splintering off from its central bulk. Over a dozen other spires spread nearby, along with **rock art panels** and assorted minor **Ancestral Puebloan ruins**.

You can see the buttes for free, towering alongside US-163, but the four-mile detour to enter **Monument Valley Tribal Park** is rewarded with much closer views (daily: May–Sept 6am–8pm; Oct–April 8am–5pm; $5; ⓦwww.navajonationparks.org). A rough, unpaved road drops from behind the visitor centre and *View* hotel to run through Monument Valley itself. The 17-mile **self-drive route** makes a bumpy but bearable ride in an ordinary vehicle and takes something over an hour (daily: May–Sept 6am–8.30pm; Oct–April 8am–4.30pm). However, the Navajo-led **jeep** or **horseback tours** into the backcountry are very much recommended; a 90-minute jeep trip costs from around $50 per person if arranged on the spot, with plenty of longer and potentially much more expensive alternatives. As well as stopping at such movie locations as the **Totem Pole**, most tours call in at a Navajo *hogan* (eight-sided dwelling) to watch weavers at work.

A stunning Navajo-owned **hotel** alongside the main viewpoint, appropriately named *The View* (ⓣ435/727-5555, ⓦwww.monumentvalleyview.com; ❼), offers luxurious rooms with absolutely magnificent views, plus a reasonable **restaurant** and its own extensive programme of well-priced tours. Nearby, the exposed *Mitten View* **campground** is first-come, first-served, with water available in summer only (summer $10, winter $5). Just outside the park, six miles west in Utah but still with good views, the veteran *Goulding's Lodge* (ⓣ435/727-3231, ⓦwww.gouldings.com; ❼), is a 1920s trading post that offers pricey motel rooms and an unexceptional restaurant, plus its own campground ($25).

Canyon de Chelly National Monument

A short distance east of **CHINLE**, sixty miles southwest of Kayenta and seventy miles north of I-40, twin sandstone walls emerge abruptly from the desert floor, climbing at a phenomenal rate to become the awesome thousand-foot cliffs of **CANYON DE CHELLY NATIONAL MONUMENT**. Between these sheer sides, the meandering cottonwood-fringed Chinle Wash winds through grasslands and planted fields. Here and there a Navajo *hogan* stands in a grove of fruit trees, a straggle of sheep is penned in by a crude wooden fence or ponies drink at the water's edge. And everywhere, perched on ledges in the canyon walls and dwarfed by the towering cliffs, are the long-abandoned adobe dwellings of the **Ancestral Puebloans**.

Into the canyons

Tours of the canyon floor, organized by *Thunderbird Lodge* (see overleaf), zigzag along the washes, which vary from two or three feet deep during the spring thaw to completely dry in summer. For most of the year, the bone-shaking tours are in open-top flatbed trucks that lurch over the rutted earth and the heat can be incredible; in winter they carry on in glass-roofed army vehicles with caterpillar tracks. To reach as far as Spider Rock, you have to take the full-day tour ($79; no reductions for children), but the half-day trip at $49 (under-13s $38) still enables you to see a wide variety of sites and terrain, including the White House Ruins.

Other tour operators can be contacted via the visitor centre, which also arranges highly recommended 4.5-mile, four-hour **group hikes** ($15/person). The precise schedule varies, but usually includes a morning trip via the White House Trail and an afternoon hike in the Canyon del Muerto; separate **night hikes** last just two hours but cost slightly more. Tsotsonii Ranch (Ⓣ928/220-5204, Ⓦwww.totsoniiranch.com) organize horseback trips for $15 per person per hour, plus $15 an hour for a guide.

Two main canyons branch apart a few miles upstream: **Canyon de Chelly** (pronounced *de shay*) to the south and **Canyon del Muerto** to the north. Each twists and turns in all directions, scattered with vast rock monoliths, while several smaller canyons break away. The whole labyrinth threads its way northward for thirty miles into the Chuska Mountains.

Canyon de Chelly is a magnificent place, on a par with the best of the Southwest's national parks. Its relative lack of fame owes much to the continuing presence of the **Navajo**, for whom the canyon retains enormous symbolic significance (although they did not build its cliff dwellings). Visitors are largely restricted to peering into the canyon from above, from overlooks along the two "rim drives". There's no road in and, apart from one short trail, you can only enter the canyons with a Navajo guide.

The view from above: the rim drives

Each of the two "rim drives" is a forty-mile round-trip, with a succession of spectacular overlooks that takes two to three hours to complete.

Junction Overlook, four miles along the **South Rim Drive**, stands far above the point where the two main canyons branch apart; as you scramble across the bare rocks you can see Canyon de Chelly narrowing away, with a *hogan* immediately below. Two miles further on, by which time the canyon is 550ft deep, **White House Overlook** looks down on the highly photogenic **White House Ruins**. This is the only point from which unguided hikers can descend to the canyon floor, taking perhaps 30 to 45 minutes to get down and a good hour to get back up. The beautiful if precarious trail, at times running along ledges chiselled into the slick rock, culminates with a close-up view of the ruins; the most dramatic dwellings, squeezed into a tiny alcove sixty feet up a majestic cliff, were once reached via the rooftops of now-vanished structures. Visitors can only walk a hundred yards or so in either direction beyond the site. Back up on the South Rim Drive, twelve miles along, the view from **Sliding House Overlook** reveals more Ancestral Puebloan ruins seemingly slipping down the canyon walls toward the ploughed Navajo fields below, while eight miles further on the road ends above the astonishing **Spider Rock**, where twin 800-foot pinnacles of rock come to within 200ft of the canyon rim.

The **North Rim Drive** runs twenty miles up Canyon del Muerto to **Massacre Cave** – really just a pitifully exposed ledge – where a Spanish expedition of 1805 killed a hundred Navajo women, children and old men. Visible from the nearby **Mummy Cave Overlook**, is the striking **House Under The Rock**, with its central tower in the Mesa Verde style. Of the two viewpoints at **Antelope House Overlook**, one is opposite Navajo Fortress, an isolated eminence atop which the Navajo were besieged by US troops for three months in 1863, while the other looks down on the twin ruined square towers of Antelope House. In the **Tomb of the Weaver** across the wash, the embalmed body of an old man was found wrapped in golden eagle feathers.

Practicalities

The Canyon de Chelly **visitor centre**, on the road from Chinle (daily 8am–5pm; no entrance fee; ⓣ928/674-5500, ⓦwww.nps.gov/cach), has informative displays and provides guides for unorthodox hiking or motorized expeditions. Facilities nearby are overstretched, so it's essential to book your **accommodation** well in advance. The most appealing options are the *Thunderbird Lodge* (ⓣ928/674-5841 or 1-800/679-2473, ⓦwww.tbirdlodge.com; ❺), very near the canyon entrance, which arranges the standard sightseeing tours and has an adequate cafeteria and the *Chinle Holiday Inn* (ⓣ928/674-5000, ⓦwww.holiday-inn.com/chinle-garcia; ❺), slightly further back toward Chinle, where the food is a lot better. The free, minimally equipped *Cottonwood* **campground** has pleasant sites among the trees alongside *Thunderbird Lodge*.

Window Rock

The reservation's governing body, the Navajo Tribal Council, has its seat at **WINDOW ROCK** near the New Mexico border. Named for the natural stone arch on its northern side, it's not a great place to get a grasp of Navajo culture, but it does at least have gas stations, shops and a **motel**, the showpiece *Quality Inn Navajo Nation Capital*, at 48 W Hwy-264 (ⓣ928/871-4108; ⓦwww.qualityinnwindowrock.com; ❹). The nearby **Navajo Nation Museum and Visitor Centre** (summer Mon & Sat 8am–5pm, Tues–Fri 8am–8pm; winter Mon–Fri 8am–5pm; donation; ⓣ928/871-7941) gives the background on tribal history and displays high-quality crafts.

The Hopi Mesas

Almost uniquely in the United States, the **Hopi** people have lived continuously in the same place for over eight hundred years. Some invaders have come and gone in that time, others have stayed; but the villages on **First**, **Second** and **Third mesas** have endured, if not exactly undisturbed then at least unmoved.

To outsiders, it's not immediately obvious why the Hopi chose to live on three barren and unprepossessing fingers of rock poking from the southern flanks of **Black Mesa** in the depths of northeast Arizona. There are two simple answers. The first lies within the mesa itself: its rocks are tilted to deliver a tiny but dependable trickle of water and also hold vast reserves of coal. The second is that the Hopi used to farm and hunt across a much wider area and were only restricted to their mesa-top villages when their Navajo neighbours encroached. While the Hopi are celebrated for their skill at "**dry farming**", preserving enough precious liquid to grow corn, beans and squash on hand-tilled terraces, this precarious and difficult way of life has nonetheless been forced upon them.

By their very survival and the persistence of their ancient beliefs and ceremonies, the Hopi have long fascinated outsiders. While visitors are welcome, the Hopi have no desire to turn themselves into a tourist attraction. Although stores and galleries make it easy to buy crafts such as pottery, basketwork, silver overlay jewellery and hand-carved *kachina* dolls, tourists who hope for extensive sightseeing – let alone spiritual revelations – are likely to leave disappointed and quite possibly dismayed by what they perceive as conspicuous poverty.

Visiting the Hopi Mesas

The modern, mock-Pueblo **Hopi Cultural Centre** below Second Mesa holds a **museum** (summer Mon–Sat 8am–5pm, Sun 9am–4pm; winter Mon–Fri 8am–5pm; $3; ⓣ928/734-6650), as well as a **cafeteria** and **motel** (ⓣ928/734-2401, ⓦwww.hopiculturalcentre.com; ❹). In summer, its plain but adequate rooms are usually booked a week or more in advance.

Unless your visit coincides with one of the very few social events that's open to tourists (ask at the cultural centre), the only way to see the mesa-top villages is on a **guided tour**. These are currently available at **WALPI** on First Mesa, where visitors assemble at the road's-end community centre in nearby **SICHOMOVI** (daily: winter 10am–4pm, summer 9.30am–6pm; $8; ⓣ928/737-2262) and at **SIPAULOVI** on Second Mesa, which has its own small visitor centre (Mon–Fri 9am–4pm; tours $15/person; ⓣ928/737-5426, ⓦwww.sipaulovihopiinformationcentre.org). All tours offer plenty of opportunity to ask questions and to buy pottery, *kachina* dolls and fresh-baked *piiki*, a flatbread made with blue cornflour.

Utah

With the biggest and most beautiful landscapes in North America, **UTAH** has something for everyone: from brilliantly coloured canyons, across desert plains, to thickly wooded and snow-covered mountains. Almost all of this unmatched range of terrain is public land, making Utah *the* place to come for **outdoor pursuits**, whether your tastes run to hiking, mountain biking, whitewater rafting or skiing.

Southern Utah has so many **national parks**, it has often been suggested that the entire area should become one vast national park. The most accessible parts – such as **Zion** and **Bryce Canyon** – are by far the most visited, but lesser-known parks like **Arches** and **Canyonlands** are every bit as dramatic. Huge tracts of this empty desert, in which fascinating pre-Columbian pictographs and Ancestral Puebloan ruins lie hidden, are all but unexplored; seeing them requires self-sufficiency and considerable planning.

Though **northwestern** Utah is predominantly flat and dry, the granite mountains of the **Wasatch Front** tower over state capital **Salt Lake City** – an attractive and enjoyable stopover – while the resorts around **Park City** offer fine **skiing**.

Led by Brigham Young, Utah's earliest white settlers – the **Mormons** or Latter Day Saints (LDS) – arrived in the Salt Lake area, which then lay outside the US, in 1847 and embarked on massive irrigation projects. At first they provoked great suspicion and hostility back East. The Republican Convention of 1856 railed against slavery and polygamy in equal measure; had the Civil War not intervened, a war against the Mormons was a real possibility. Relations eased when the Mormon Church dropped polygamy in 1890 and statehood followed in 1896; to this day, well over sixty percent of Utah's two-million-strong population are Mormons. The Mormon influence is responsible for the layout of Utah's towns, where residential streets are as wide as interstates and all are numbered block by block according to the same logical if ponderous system.

Mormon businessmen became renowned as fiercely pro-mining and anti-conservation. Only since the 1980s has tourism been appreciated as a major industry and former mining towns such as **Moab** developed facilities for wide-eyed travellers smitten by the allure of the desert. Increased tourism has also led to a relaxation of Utah's notorious **drinking laws**. In most towns, at least one restaurant is licensed to serve beer, wine and mixed drinks to diners and maybe even to sell beer in its bar.

Southern Utah: the national parks

Southern Utah is a peculiar combination of the mind-boggling and the mundane. Its **scenery** is stupendous, a stunning geological freakshow where the earth is ripped bare to expose cliffs and canyons of every imaginable colour, unseen rivers gouge mighty furrows into endless desert plateaus and strange sandstone towers thrust from the sagebrush. By contrast, however, almost all the tiny **Mormon towns** scattered across this epic landscape are boring in the extreme, so most visitors spend as much time as possible **outdoors**.

The most obvious targets for travellers are the five national parks. In the southwest, **Zion National Park** centres on an awe-inspiring canyon, backed by barren highlands of white sandstone, while **Bryce Canyon** is a blaze of orange pinnacles. To the east, **Arches** holds an eroded desertscape of graceful red-rock fins and spurs, all on a more manageable scale than the astonishing hundred-mile vistas of neighbouring **Canyonlands**. Both lie within easy reach of **Moab**, Utah's hippest destination. The fifth park, **Capitol Reef**, stretches through the middle of the state, pierced by slender, ravishing canyons.

Named by pioneer river-runner John Wesley Powell, the **Grand Staircase** in southwest Utah consists of a series of plateaus, stacked tier upon tier, that climb from the North Rim of the Grand Canyon. The **Chocolate Cliffs**, nearest Arizona, are followed by the dazzling **Vermilion Cliffs**, then the **White Cliffs** – a 2000-foot wall of Navajo sandstone, best seen at Zion – the **Grey Cliffs** and finally the **Pink Cliffs** of Bryce. Although these rocks took a billion years to form, the staircase itself has only been created in the last dozen million years by the general upthrust of the **Colorado Plateau**.

St George

Set beneath a broad, reddish-brown sandstone cliff just off 1-15 in Utah's southwest corner, pretty **ST GEORGE** was the winter home of Brigham Young and other early Mormon leaders. At its centre, the fine 1877 LDS **Temple** is the oldest still in use anywhere. The rest of the town holds quaint pioneer homes, including Brigham Young's much-restored **adobe house** at 200 North First West (daily: summer 9am–8pm, winter 9am–5pm; free).

Travellers driving up I-15 can call in at the **Utah Visitor Centre**, just inside the state line (daily: summer 8am–9pm; winter 8am–5pm; ⓣ435/673-4542, ⓦwww.utah.com). Virtually all St George's commercial life takes place along the main drag, St George Boulevard, where the twenty or so **motels** include the veteran *Dixie Palm* at no. 185 E (ⓣ435/673-3531; ❷). Decent **restaurants** in the lively Ancestor Square mall, at 1 W St George Blvd, include the *Pizza Factory* (ⓣ435/628-1234; closed Sun).

Cedar City

CEDAR CITY, 53 miles north of St George and half its size, was founded by iron miners in the 1850s. It's now kept alive by the Southern Utah State College on its western fringe, which stages the **Utah Shakespeare Festival** each summer (late June to Oct; ⓣ435/586-7878, ⓦwww.bard.org).

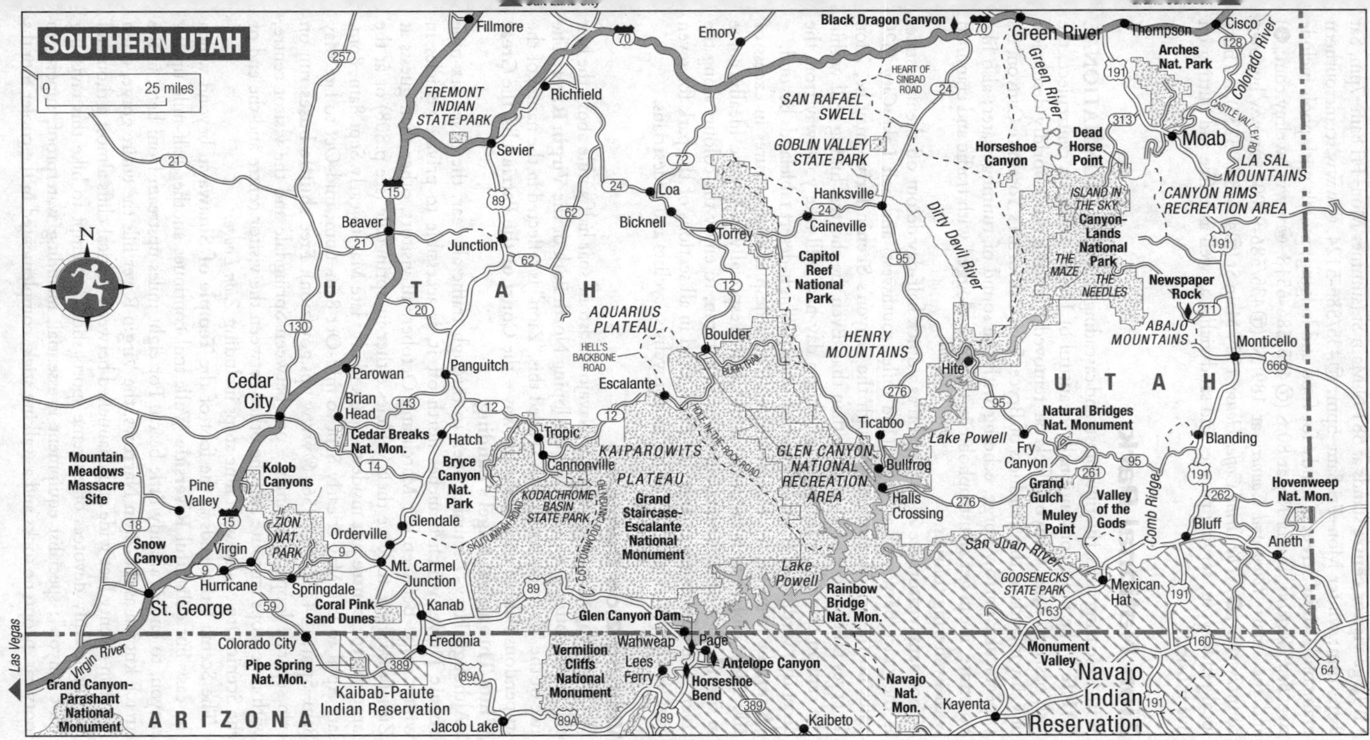
SOUTHERN UTAH
0
25 miles
N
U T A H
A R I Z O N A
Fillmore
Emory
Black Dragon Canyon
Green River
Thompson
Cisco
Arches Nat. Park
Colorado River
Castle Valley Rd
Moab
La Sal Mountains
Canyon Rims Recreation Area
Dead Horse Point
Island in the Sky
Canyon-Lands National Park
The Maze
The Needles
Newspaper Rock
Abajo Mountains
Monticello
Richfield
Fremont Indian State Park
Sevier
Heart of Sinbad Road
San Rafael Swell
Goblin Valley State Park
Horseshoe Canyon
Green River
Dirty Devil River
Hanksville
Caineville
Loa
Bicknell
Torrey
Capitol Reef National Park
Henry Mountains
Beaver
Junction
Aquarius Plateau
Hell's Backbone Road
Boulder
Burr Trail
Escalante
Hite
Lake Powell
Natural Bridges Nat. Monument
Blanding
Fry Canyon
Ticaboo
Bullfrog
Halls Crossing
Glen Canyon National Recreation Area
Hole-in-the-Rock Road
Cedar City
Parowan
Brian Head
Panguitch
Cedar Breaks Nat. Mon.
Hatch
Tropic
Cannonville
Kaiparowits Plateau
Bryce Canyon Nat. Park
Kodachrome Basin State Park
Cottonwood Canyon Rd
Skutumpah Road
Grand Staircase-Escalante National Monument
Grand Gulch
Muley Point
Valley of the Gods
Comb Ridge
Hovenweep Nat. Mon.
Bluff
Aneth
San Juan River
Goosenecks State Park
Mexican Hat
Mountain Meadows Massacre Site
Pine Valley
Kolob Canyons
Zion Nat. Park
Glendale
Orderville
Mt. Carmel Junction
Snow Canyon
Virgin
Hurricane
Springdale
Coral Pink Sand Dunes
Kanab
St. George
Glen Canyon Dam
Lake Powell
Rainbow Bridge Nat. Mon.
Colorado City
Fredonia
Wahweap
Page
Antelope Canyon
Lees Ferry
Horseshoe Bend
Vermilion Cliffs National Monument
Monument Valley
Navajo Indian Reservation
Pipe Spring Nat. Mon.
Kaibab-Paiute Indian Reservation
Jacob Lake
Kaibeto
Navajo Nat. Mon.
Kayenta
Virgin River
Las Vegas
Grand Canyon-Parashant National Monument
Flagstaff
15
70
257
21
24
72
62
89
20
130
143
12
14
18
9
59
389
89A
95
276
261
191
313
128
211
666
262
163
160
64

A large **visitor centre** stands at 581 N Main St (summer Mon–Fri 8am–7pm, Sat 9am–1pm; winter Mon–Fri 8am–5pm; ⓣ435/586-5124, ⓦwww.scenicsouthernutah.com). **Main Street** is handy for food and lodging; motels with pools include two *Best Westerns*, the *El Rey* at 80 S (ⓣ435/586-6518, ⓦwww.bwelrey.com; ❹) and the smart *Town and Country* at 189 N (ⓣ435/586-9900, ⓦwww.bwtowncountry.com; ❹). *The Grind Coffee House*, 19 N Main St (ⓣ435/867-5333), is a busy local rendezvous, serving pastries and sandwiches as well as coffee and putting on live music.

Zion National Park

With its soaring cliffs, riverine forests and cascading waterfalls, **ZION NATIONAL PARK** is the most conventionally beautiful of Utah's parks. Its centrepiece, the lush oasis of **Zion Canyon**, feels far removed from the otherworldly desolation of Canyonlands or the weirdness of Bryce. Like California's Yosemite Canyon, it's a spectacular narrow gorge, echoing with the sound of running water; also like Yosemite, it can get claustrophobic in summer, clogged with traffic and crammed with sweltering tourists.

Too many visitors see Zion Canyon as a quick half-day detour off the interstate, as they race between Las Vegas (158 miles southwest) and Salt Lake City (320 miles northeast). Magnificent though the canyon's **Scenic Drive** may be, Zion deserves much more of your time than that. Even the shortest hiking trail within the canyon can escape the crowds, while a day-hike will take you away from the deceptive verdure of the valley and up onto the high-desert tablelands beyond.

Summer is by far the busiest season. That's despite temperatures in excess of 100°F and violent thunderstorms concentrated especially in August. Ideally, come in spring, to see the flowers bloom or in autumn, to enjoy the colours along the river. The **admission charge** for Zion, valid in all sections of the park for seven days, is $25 per vehicle or $12 for motorcyclists, cyclists and pedestrians.

Visiting Zion Canyon

In **Zion Canyon**, mighty walls of Navajo sandstone soar half a mile above the box elders and cottonwoods that line the loping North Fork of the **Virgin River**. The awe of the Mormon settlers who called this "Zion" is reflected in the names of the stupendous slabs of rock along the way – the **Court of the Patriarchs**, the **Great White Throne** and **Angel's Landing**.

Although Hwy-9 remains open to through traffic all year, the paved six-mile **Scenic Drive**, which branches north off it, is accessible to private vehicles in winter only. Between late March and October, all visitors, other than guests at *Zion Lodge*, have to leave their vehicles either in Springdale (see p.808) or at the large **visitor centre** just inside the park (daily: late May to early Sept 8am–8pm, late April to late May & early Sept to mid-Oct 8am–6pm; mid-Oct to late May 8am–5pm; ⓣ435/772-3256, ⓦwww.nps.gov/zion). Free **shuttle buses** run on two separate loops in summer – one between Springdale and the visitor centre, with nine stops en route and the other between the visitor centre and the end of the Scenic Drive, also with nine stops including *Zion Lodge*.

The Scenic Drive ends at the foot of the **Temple of Sinawava**, beyond which the easy but delightful **Riverside Walk** trail continues another half-mile up the canyon, to end at a sandy little beach. For eight miles upstream from here, in the stretch known as the **Zion Narrows**, the Virgin River fills the entire gorge, often less than twenty feet wide and channelled between vertical cliffs almost a thousand feet high. Only devotees of extreme sports should attempt to hike this ravishing "slot canyon"; specialist equipment is essential, including waterproof, super-grip footwear, neoprene socks and a walking stick, complemented in the cooler months

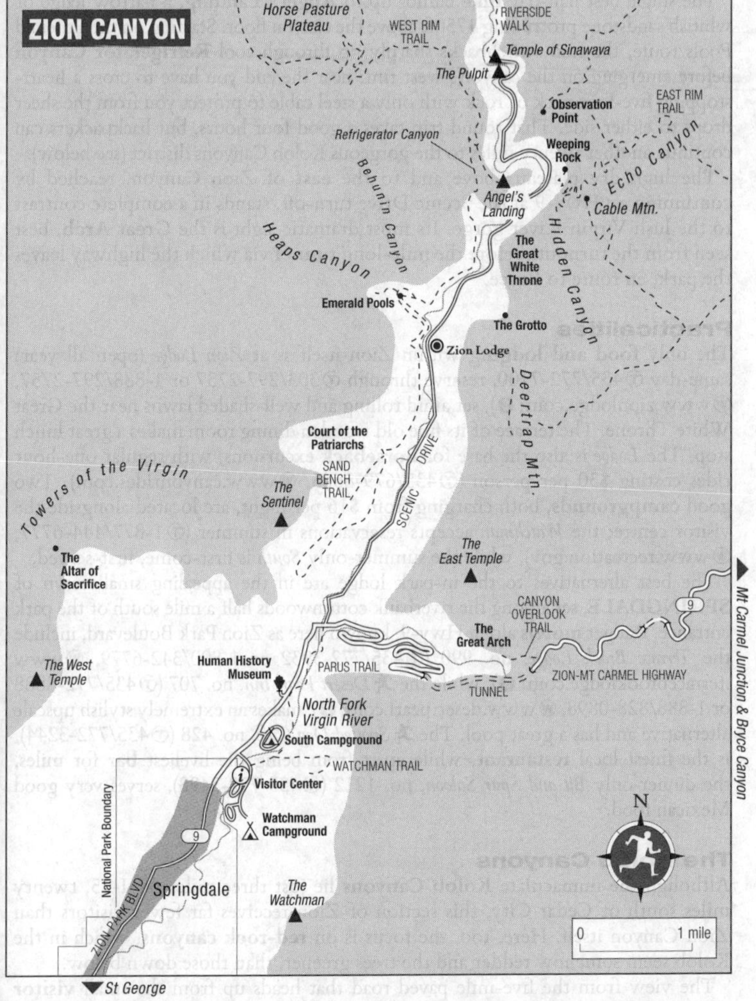

by a drysuit, plus all the water you need to drink. You can only hike its full length downstream, a total of sixteen miles from remote Chamberlain's Ranch, twenty miles north of the park's East Entrance. Commercial companies based in Springfield, such as Zion Adventure Company (ⓣ435/772-1001, ⓦwww.zionadventures.com), rent out equipment and offer early-morning rides to the trailhead; you also need a permit from the visitor centre.

A much less demanding hike leads up to **Weeping Rock**, an easy half-hour round trip from the road to a gorgeous spring-fed garden dangling from a rocky alcove. From the same trailhead, a mile beyond *Zion Lodge*, a more strenuous and exciting route cuts through narrow **Hidden Canyon**, whose mouth turns into a waterfall after a good rain. Directly across from the lodge a short and fairly flat trail (two-mile round trip) winds up at the **Emerald Pools**, a series of three clearwater pools, the best (and furthest) of which has a small sandy beach at the foot of a gigantic cliff.

The single best half-day **hike** climbs up to **Angel's Landing**, a narrow ledge of whitish sandstone protruding 1750ft above the canyon floor. Starting on the Emerald Pools route, the trail switchbacks sharply up through cool **Refrigerator Canyon** before emerging on the canyon's west rim; near the end you have to cross a heart-stopping five-foot neck of rock with only a steel cable to protect you from the sheer drops to either side. That round trip takes a good four hours, but backpackers can continue another twenty miles to the gorgeous Kolob Canyons district (see below).

The high dry plateau above and to the **east** of Zion Canyon, reached by continuing on Hwy-9 at the Scenic Drive turn-off, stands in a complete contrast to the lush Virgin River gorge. Its most dramatic sight is the **Great Arch**, best seen from the turnouts before the mile-long **tunnel** via which the highway leaves the park, en route to Bryce.

Practicalities

The only **food and lodging** within Zion itself is at *Zion Lodge* (open all year; same-day ⓣ435/772-7700, reserve through ⓣ303/297-2757 or 1-888/297-2757, ⓦwww.zionlodge.com; ❻), set amid rolling and well-shaded lawns near the Great White Throne. The terrace of its fine old wooden dining room makes a great lunch stop. The *Lodge* is also the base for **horseback** excursions, with regular one-hour rides costing $30 per person (ⓣ435/679-8665, ⓦwww.canyonrides.com). Two good **campgrounds**, both charging from $16 per night, are located alongside the visitor centre; the *Watchman* accepts reservations in summer (ⓣ1-877/444-6777, ⓦwww.recreation.gov), while the summer-only *South* is first-come, first-served.

The best alternatives to the in-park lodge are in the appealing small town of **SPRINGDALE**, set among the riverbank cottonwoods half a mile south of the park entrance. Budget **motels** along Hwy-9, known here as Zion Park Boulevard, include the *Terrace Brook Lodge*, no. 990 (ⓣ435/772-3932 or 1-800/342-6779, ⓦwww.terracebrooklodge.com; ❸), while the *Desert Pearl Inn*, no. 707 (ⓣ435/772-8888 or 1-888/828-0898, ⓦwww.desertpearl.com; ❼), makes an extremely stylish upscale alternative and has a great pool. The *Spotted Dog Café*, no. 428 (ⓣ435/772-3244), is the finest local **restaurant**, while apart from being the liveliest **bar** for miles, the dinner-only *Bit and Spur Saloon*, no. 1212 (ⓣ435/772-3498), serves very good Mexican food.

The Kolob Canyons

Although the immaculate **Kolob Canyons** lie just three miles off I-15, twenty miles south of Cedar City, this section of Zion receives far fewer visitors than Zion Canyon itself. Here, too, the focus is on **red-rock canyons**, which in the Kolob seem somehow redder and the trees greener, than those down below.

The view from the five-mile paved road that heads up from the small **visitor centre** (daily: late April to mid-Oct 8am–5pm, mid-Oct to late April 8am–4.30pm; ⓣ435/772-3256) is amazing, while the two main hiking trails are highly recommended. One starts two miles from the visitor centre and follows Taylor Creek on a five-mile round trip to **Double Arch Alcove**, a spectacular natural amphitheatre roofed by twin sandstone arches. The other trail sets off from the north side of the parking area at Lee Pass, four miles beyond the visitor centre and follows a well-marked route for seven miles past LaVerkin Falls to **Kolob Arch**, which at over 300ft across rivals Landscape Arch in Arches (see p.808) as the world's longest natural rock span.

Bryce Canyon National Park

The surface of the earth can hold few weirder-looking spots than **BRYCE CANYON**, a two-hour, 86-mile drive northeast of Zion. Named for Mormon settler Ebenezer Bryce, who declared that it was "a helluva place to lose a cow", it is not in fact a canyon at all. Along a twenty-mile shelf on the eastern edge of the thickly forested **Paunsaugunt Plateau**, 8000ft above sea level, successive strata of dazzlingly coloured rock have slipped and slid and washed away to leave a menagerie of multi-hued and contorted **stone pinnacles**.

In hues of yellow, red and flaming orange, the formations here have been eroded out of the muddy sandstone by a combination of icy winters and summer rains. The top-heavy pinnacles known as "**hoodoos**" form when the harder upper layers of rock stay firm as the lower levels wear away beneath them. **Thor's Hammer**, visible from Sunset Point, is the most alarmingly precarious. These hoodoos look down into technicolour ravines, all far more vivid than the Grand Canyon and much more human in scale. The whole place is at its most inspiring in winter, when the figures stand out from a blanket of snow.

The park approach road runs south from Hwy-12 about twenty miles east of the small town of Panguitch; the **entrance fee** is $25 per vehicle, per week. There's a free (summer-only) **shuttle bus** system, but visitors can drive to all the scenic overlooks year-round.

The two most popular viewpoints into **Bryce Amphitheatre**, at the heart of the park, are on either side of *Bryce Canyon Lodge*: the more northerly, **Sunrise Point**, is slightly less crowded than **Sunset Point**, where most of the bus tours stop. **Hiking trails** drop abruptly from the rim down into the amphitheatre. One good three-mile trek switchbacks steeply from Sunset Point through the cool 200-foot canyons of **Wall Street**, where a pair of 800-year-old fir trees stretch to reach daylight. It then cuts across the surreal landscape into the **Queen's Garden** basin, where the stout likeness of Queen Victoria sits in majestic condescension, before climbing back up to Sunrise Point. A dozen trails crisscross the amphitheatre, but it's surprisingly easy to get lost, so don't stray from the marked routes.

Sunrise and Sunset points notwithstanding, the best view at both sunset and dawn (the best time for taking pictures) is from **Bryce Point**, at the southern end of the amphitheatre. From here, you can look down not only at the Bryce Canyon formations but also take in the grand sweep of the whole region, east to the **Henry Mountains** and north to the Escalante range. The park road then climbs another twenty miles south, by way of the intensely coloured **Natural Bridge**, an 85-foot rock arch spanning a steep gully, en route to its dead end at **Rainbow Point**.

Practicalities

The **visitor centre**, just past the entrance, carries information on current weather and hiking conditions (daily: May–Sept 8am–8pm; April & Oct 8am–6pm; Nov–March 8am–4.30pm; Ⓣ435/834-5322, Ⓦwww.nps.gov/brca). Much the best place to **stay** is the venerable *Bryce Canyon Lodge*, 100 yards from the rim between Sunrise and Sunset points (April–Oct only; Ⓣ435/834-8700 or 1-877/386-4383, Ⓦwww.brycecanyonforever.com; ❼), where rustic cabins cost a few dollars more than basic doubles. It also has a **dining room**, a grocery store, a laundry and public showers.

A number of ugly year-round **motels** guard the approach to the park, on and just off Hwy-12, including the large *Ruby's Inn* (Ⓣ435/834-5341 or 1-866/866-6616, Ⓦwww.rubysinn.com; ❺) and the cheaper *Foster's Motel* (Ⓣ435/834-5227, Ⓦwww.fostersmotel.com; ❸), both of which have pretty dreadful restaurants. *Ruby's Inn* has its own **campground** ($24) and there are also two first-come, first-served campgrounds within the park ($15): *Sunset Campground*, close to Sunset Point and *North Campground*, near the visitor centre. To camp below the rim, backpackers require permits from the visitor centre.

Bryce Canyon to Capitol Reef: Highway 12

Turning its back on the grand amphitheatre of Bryce Canyon, tiny **TROPIC**, straggling along Hwy-12 eight miles east of the park entrance, seems almost embarrassed by the flamboyant geological phenomena ranged above it. As well as a few motels, this Mormon farming community holds Ebenezer Bryce's restored log cabin, alongside the **Bryce Pioneer Village** motel-cum-restaurant (ⓣ435/679-8546 or 1-866/657-8414, ⓦwww.bpvillage.com; ❸).

Hwy-12 next curves along the edge of the Table Cliff Plateau before dropping into the remote canyons of the **Escalante River**, the last river system discovered within the continental US and site of some wonderful **backpacking** routes.

At the west end of **ESCALANTE**, 38 miles east of Tropic, a **visitor centre** holds information on the vast **Grand Staircase-Escalante National Monument** (mid-March to mid-Nov daily 7.30am–5.30pm; mid-Nov to mid-March Mon–Fri 8am–4.30pm; ⓣ435/826-5499, ⓦwww.ut.blm.gov/monument). The most accessible highlight is **Calf Creek**, sixteen miles east, where a trail leads just under three miles upstream from a nice undeveloped **campground** ($7) to a gorgeous shaded dell replete with a 125-foot waterfall. More ambitious trips start from trailheads along the dusty but usually passable **Hole-in-the-Rock Road**, which turns south from Hwy-12 five miles east of Escalante. A trio of slender, storm-gouged **slot canyons**, including the delicate, graceful Peek-a-Boo Canyon and the downright intimidating Spooky Canyon, can be reached by a mile-long hike from the end of Dry Fork Road, 26 miles along. From **Hurricane Wash**, 34 miles along, you can hike five miles to reach Coyote Gulch and then a further five miles, passing sandstone bridges and arches, to the Escalante River. Under normal conditions, two-wheel-drive vehicles should go no further than **Dance Hall Rock**, 36 miles down the road, a superb natural amphitheatre sculpted out of the slickrock hills. The pick of Escalante's **motels** is the *Prospector Inn*, 380 W Main St (ⓣ435/826-4653, ⓦwww.prospectorinn.com; ❸).

Thirty miles beyond Escalante, at **BOULDER**, the Burr Trail, almost all of which is paved, heads east through the southern reaches of **Capitol Reef National Park** and down to **Lake Powell**. Where it leaves Hwy-12, the modern *Boulder Mountain Lodge* (ⓣ435/335-7460 or 1-800/556-3446, ⓦwww.boulder-utah.com; ❺) holds twenty comfortable rooms. It also has a reasonable **restaurant**, but a few yards further east, the spotless *Boulder Mesa Restaurant* (ⓣ435/335-7447) is better.

North of Boulder, Hwy-12 makes a gorgeous drive up onto the Aquarius Plateau, with marvellous vistas to the east across waves of gold and red sandstone outcrops; the lovely Oak Creek **campground** is fifteen miles along (ⓣ435/425-3702; $9).

Capitol Reef National Park

CAPITOL REEF might sound like something you'd find off the coast of Australia, but its towering ochre, white and **red-rock walls** and deep **river canyons** are of a piece with the rest of the Utah desert. The outstanding feature is a multilayered, 1000-foot-high reef-like wall of uplifted sedimentary rock. Stretching over a hundred miles north to south, but only a few miles across, the seemingly impenetrable barrier of the **Waterpocket Fold** was warped upward by the same process that lifted the Colorado Plateau and its sharply defined sedimentary layers display two hundred million years of geological activity. The Fold is repeatedly sliced through by deeply incised river canyons – some only twenty feet wide, but hundreds of feet deep – often accessible only on foot.

Motorists who stick to the park's paved through road, Hwy-24, which follows the canyon of the **Fremont River** across the northern half of the Fold, do not incur an entrance fee. Beneath the **Castle**, an enormous rock outcrop, you'll find the **visitor centre** (daily: June–Sept 8am–7pm; Oct–May 8am–4.30pm; Ⓣ435/425-3791, Ⓦwww.nps.gov/care) and an irresistible campground ($10), set amid the cherry, apple and peach orchards of the abandoned Mormon community of **FRUITA**. To the west, the **Goosenecks Overlook** gazes down 500ft into the entrenched canyons cut by Sulphur Creek. Further east, beyond Fruita's former schoolhouse, some extraordinary **Fremont petroglyphs** of bighorn sheep and stylized space-people were chipped into the varnished red rock a thousand years ago. Another four and a half miles along, a beautiful **day-hike** heads up along the gravelly riverbed through **Grand Wash** – a cool canyon where Butch Cassidy and his gang used to hide out.

Alternatively, the paved **Scenic Drive** ($5/vehicle) heads twelve miles south from the visitor centre, past the top of Grand Wash, to **Capitol Gorge** and back. A more adventurous sixty-mile loop trip explores **Cathedral Valley** in the north, while a 125-mile southern route starts at the foot of the volcanic **Henry Mountains**, then follows the Burr Trail through **Muley Twist Canyon** and continues west to Boulder.

The nearest **food and lodging** to Capitol Reef is eleven miles west, around **TORREY**. The *Capitol Reef Inn & Café*, in the heart of town at 360 W Main St (Ⓣ435/425-3271, Ⓦwww.capitolreefinn.com; ❸), is a crisply maintained little motel with a nice café, while the *Rim Rock Inn*, three miles east at 2523 E Hwy-24 (March–Nov; Ⓣ435/425-3388 or 1-888/447-4676, Ⓦwww.therimrock.net; ❸) is a newer, wood-built hotel, with a good dining room.

Goblin Valley

Fifty desolate miles east of Capitol Reef along Hwy-24, you reach the tiny cross-roads of **Hanksville**. Twenty miles north on Hwy-24, a right turn takes you onto a 32-mile dirt road to the rock art of **Horseshoe Canyon**, a remote subsection of Canyonlands National Park (see below).

Half a mile further north on Hwy-24, a side road veers off west to **Goblin Valley State Park** (open 24hr; $7), where thousands of gnome-like figures loom out of the soft Entrada sandstone. The **Carmel Canyon** trail loops through a throng of misshapen rock pillars, many of which seem to have eyes and other human features. To see the place at its spookiest, by moonlight, stay at the well-equipped **campground** (Ⓣ1-800/322-3770; $16) if you want.

Green River

The uneventful riverside town of **GREEN RIVER**, just east of the Hwy-24 junction on I-70, is the largest community on a 200-mile stretch of interstate. Its **John Wesley Powell River History Museum**, 885 E Main St, doubles as the local visitor centre (April–Oct daily 8am–7pm, Nov–March Tues–Sat 9am–5pm; $4; Ⓣ435/564-3427; Ⓦwww.johnwesleypowell.com).

As well as various cheap **motels**, Green River holds a few classier options, including the *Best Western River Terrace*, 880 E Main St (Ⓣ435/564-3401 or 1-800/780-7234, Ⓦwww.bestwestern.com; ❺), which has a pool, river views and a decent restaurant.

Canyonlands National Park

The largest and most magnificent of Utah's national parks, **CANYONLANDS NATIONAL PARK** is as hard to define as it is to map. Its closest equivalent, the Grand Canyon, is by comparison simply an almighty crack in a relatively flat plain; Canyonlands is a bewildering tangle of canyons, plateaus, fissures and faults, scattered with buttes and monoliths, pierced by arches and caverns and penetrated only by a paltry handful of dead-end roads.

Canyonlands fees and permits

Canyonlands National Park charges an **entry fee** of $10 per vehicle, $5 for cyclists or hikers, valid for seven days in all sections of the park. **Backpacking** permits, covering a maximum seven persons in the Needles and Island In The Sky districts, or five in the Maze, cost $15. Permits for **four-wheel-drive** or **mountain-biking** expeditions that involve backcountry camping, issued for groups of up to three vehicles with a total of fifteen people in the Island In The Sky, ten in the Needles, or nine in the Maze, are $30. **Reservations** are essential for the most popular areas, especially in spring and autumn. Permits must be picked up in person – with every group member present – from the appropriate park visitor centre. For full details, see ⓦwww.nps.gov/cany.

Canyonlands focuses on the Y-shaped confluence of the **Green** and **Colorado rivers**, buried deep in the desert forty miles southwest of Moab. The only spot from which you can see the rivers meet, however, is a five-mile hike from the nearest road. With no road down to the rivers, let alone across them, the park therefore splits into three major sections. The **Needles**, east of the Colorado, is a red-rock wonderland of sandstone pinnacles and hidden meadows that's a favourite with hardy hikers and four-wheel-drive enthusiasts, while the **Maze**, west of both the Colorado and the Green, is a virtually inaccessible labyrinth of tortuous, waterless canyons. In the wedge of the "Y" between the two, the high, dry mesa of the **Island In The Sky** commands astonishing views, with several overlooks that can easily be toured by car. Getting from any one of these sections to the others involves a drive of at least a hundred miles.

Canyonlands does not lend itself to a short visit. With no lodging and little camping, inside the park, it takes a full day to have even a cursory look at a single segment. Considering that summer temperatures regularly exceed 100°F and most trails have no water and little shade, the Island In The Sky is the most immediately rewarding option. On the other hand, for a long day-hike you'd do better to set off into the Needles.

Island In The Sky and Dead Horse Point State Park

Reached by a good road that climbs steadily from US-191, 21 miles south of I-70, the **Island In The Sky** district looks out over hundreds of miles of flat-topped mesas that drop in 2000-foot steps to the river. Four miles along from its **visitor centre** (daily: March–Oct 8am–6pm; Nov–Feb 9am–4.30pm; ⓣ435/259-4712), the enjoyable **Mesa Arch Trail** loops for a mile around the mesa-top hillocks to the edge of the abyss, where long, shallow Mesa Arch frames an extraordinary view of the **La Sal Mountains**, 35 miles northeast. The definitive vantage point, however, is **Grand View Point Overlook**, another five miles on at the southern end of the road. An agoraphobic's nightmare, it commands an endless prospect of layer upon layer of bare sandstone, here stacked thousands of feet high, there fractured into bottomless canyons. The Island In The Sky's only developed **campground**, the first-come, first-served and waterless *Willow Flat* ($10), is just back from the **Green River Overlook**, along the right fork shortly after the Mesa Arch trailhead.

A turn-off long before the Island In The Sky visitor centre cuts south to the smaller but equally breathtaking **Dead Horse Point**, located at the tip of a narrow mesa, which looks straight down 2000ft to the twisting Colorado River. Cowboys used the mesa as a natural corral, herding up wild horses then blocking them in behind a piñon pine fence that still marks its 90-foot neck. One band of horses was left here too long and died – hence the name. As a Utah state park, Dead Horse Point charges its own $10 admission fee. The **visitor centre** (daily: summer 8am–6pm; winter 8am–5pm; ⓣ435/259-2614) stands two miles short of the point itself and there's also a **campground** ($20).

The Needles and Newspaper Rock

Taking its name from the colourful sandstone pillars, knobs and hoodoos that punctuate its many lush canyons and basins, the **Needles** district allows a more intimate look at the Canyonlands environment, where you're not always gazing thousands of feet downward or scanning the distant horizon.

A demanding eleven-mile round-trip hike from mushroom-shaped hoodoos at the road's-end **Big Spring Canyon Overlook** offers the only access to the **Confluence Overlook**, 1000ft above the point where the Green River joins the muddy waters of the Colorado, to flow together toward fearsome **Cataract Canyon**. Among the best of the shorter walks that head away from the road is **Pothole Point**, a mile earlier. A longer day-trip or a good overnight hike leaves from near the *Squaw Flat* **campground** ($15) to the green meadow of **Chesler Park**, cutting through the narrow cleft of the Joint Trail. Pick up information and backcountry permits at the **visitor centre** (daily: March–Oct 8am–5pm; Nov–Feb 9am–4.30pm; ⓣ435/259-4711).

The pretty 35-mile drive into the Needles from US-191 winds along Indian Creek through deep red-rock canyons lined by pines and cottonwoods. At **Newspaper Rock**, twelve miles in, hundreds of tiny **petroglyphs**, many of which show deer, antelope, bear claws and helmeted human figures, have been etched in the jet-black desert varnish of a red-sandstone boulder. There's a lovely if basic (free) streamside **campground** just across the road.

The Maze and Horseshoe Canyon

Filling the western third of Canyonlands, on the far side of the Colorado and Green rivers, the harsh and remote **Maze** district is noted for its many-fingered box canyons, accessible only by jeep or by long, dry hiking trails. Tree-lined **Horseshoe Canyon**, reached halfway down a long, long dirt road that loops south from Green River itself to join Hwy-24 just south of Goblin Valley, contains some fabulous **ancient rock art**. Allowing at least an hour's driving from the highway both before and after, plus five hours for the six-mile round-trip hike into the canyon itself, you'll need to set aside a full day, but it's well worth the effort, both for the joy of the walk and for the **"Great Gallery"** at the far end. Hundreds of mysterious, haunting pictographs – mostly life-sized human figures, albeit weirdly elongated or draped in robes and adorned with strange, staring eyes – were painted onto these red-sandstone walls, probably between 500 BC and 500 AD. Contact the Hans Flat **ranger station**, 46 miles east of Hwy-24 (daily 8am–4.30pm; ⓣ435/259-2652), for details of occasional guided hikes into Horseshoe Canyon.

Arches National Park

The writer Edward Abbey, who spent a year as a ranger at **ARCHES NATIONAL PARK** in the 1950s, wrote that its arid landscape was as "naked, monolithic, austere and unadorned as the sculpture of the moon". Apart from the single ribbon of black asphalt that snakes through the park, there's nothing even vaguely human about it. Massive fins of red and golden sandstone stand to attention out of the bare desert plain and over eighteen hundred natural arches of various shapes and sizes have been cut into the rock by eons of erosion. The narrow, hunching ridges are more like dinosaurs' backbones than solid rock and under a full moon, you can't help but imagine that the landscape has a life of its own.

While you could race through in a couple of hours, it takes at least a day to do Arches justice. A twenty-mile road cuts uphill sharply from US-191 and the **visitor centre** (daily: April–Oct 7.30am–6.30pm; Nov–March 8am–4.30pm; $10/vehicle; ⓣ435/719-2299, ⓦwww.nps.gov/arch). The first possible stop is the south trailhead for **Park Avenue**, an easy trail leading one mile down a scoured, rock-bottomed wash. If you stay on the road, the **La Sal Mountains Viewpoint** provides a grandstand look at the distant 12,000ft peaks, as well as the huge red chunk of **Courthouse Towers** closer at hand.

From **Balanced Rock** beyond – a 50-foot boulder atop a slender 75-foot pedestal – a right turn winds two miles through the **Windows** section, where a half-mile trail loops through a dense concentration of massive arches, some over

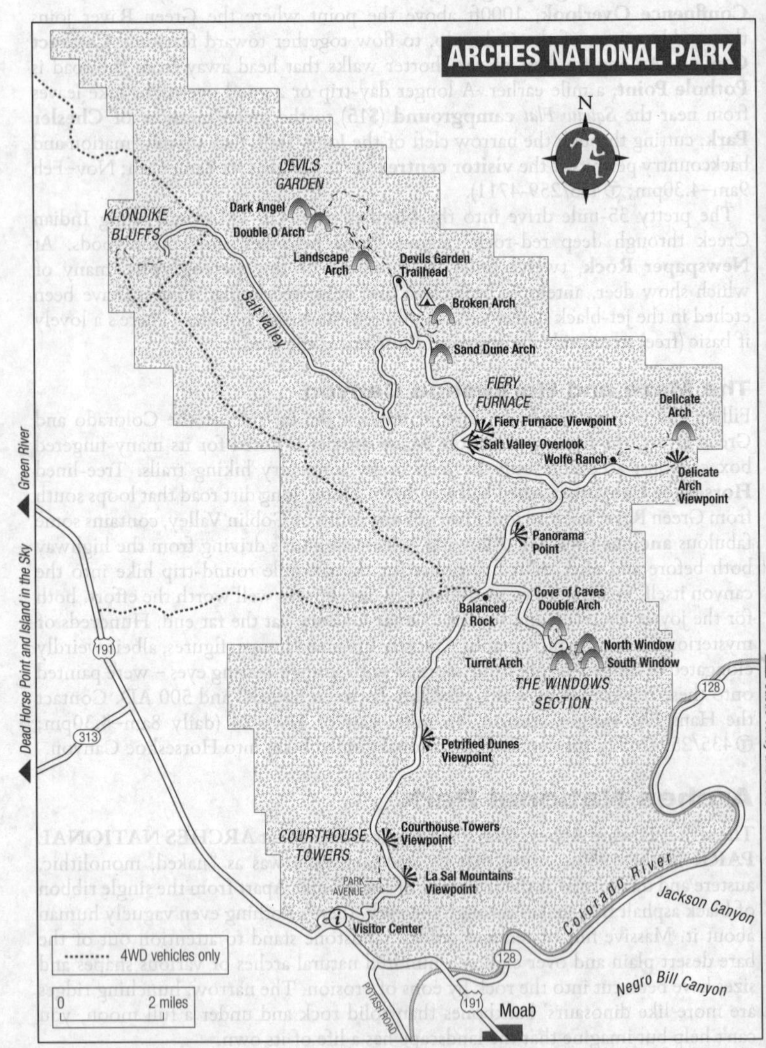

100ft high and 150ft across. A second trail, fifty yards beyond, leads to **Double Arch**, a staunch pair of arches that together support another.

Further on, the main road drops downhill for two miles past Panorama Point and the turn-off to **Wolfe Ranch**, where a century-old log cabin serves as the trailhead for the wonderful three-mile round-trip hike up to **Delicate Arch**. Crowds congregate each evening beside the arch, a freestanding crescent of rock perched at the brink of a deep canyon, for the superb sunset views; coming back down in the dark can be a little hair-raising, though. Three miles beyond the Wolfe Ranch turn-off, the deep, sharp-sided mini-canyons of the **Fiery Furnace** section form a labyrinth through which rangers lead regular hikes in spring, summer and autumn ($10; reserve at the visitor centre or via Ⓦwww.recreation.gov).

From the **Devil's Garden** trailhead at the end of the road, an easy one-mile walk leads to a view of the astonishing 306-foot span of **Landscape Arch**, now too perilously slender to approach more closely. Several other arches lie along short spur trails off the route, though one, Wall Arch, finally collapsed in 2008. Seeing them all and returning from **Double O Arch** via the longer primitive trail, requires a total hike of just over seven miles. Arches' only **campground** ($20; water only available mid-March to Oct) is across from the trailhead; sites can be reserved March–Oct only, between four and 180 days in advance (Ⓣ1-877/444-6777, Ⓦwww.recreation.gov).

Moab

Founded in the late 1800s, **MOAB** was hardly a speck until the 1950s, when prospector Charlie Steen discovered uranium nearby. When the mining boom finally waned, the town threw in its lot with tourism, to become the Southwest's number one adventure-vacation destination.

Moab still isn't a large town, though – the population has yet to reach ten thousand – and neither is it attractive. The setting is what matters. With two national parks on its doorstep, plus millions more acres of public land, Moab is an ideal base for outdoors enthusiasts. At first, it was a haven for **mountain bikers** lured by the legendary **Slickrock Bike Trail**. Then the **jeep** drivers began to turn up and the **whitewater-rafting** companies moved in, too. These days it's almost literally bursting, all year, with legions of Lycra-clad vacationers from all over the world.

Perhaps the main reason Moab has grown so fast is that out-of-state visitors tend to find Utah's other rural communities so boring. As soon as Moab emerged from the pack, it became a beacon in the desert, attracting tourists ecstatic to find a town that stayed up after dark – even if it does amount to little more than a few miles of motels, restaurants and bars.

Arrival and information

Moab's superb **visitor centre** is at Centre and Main (April–Sept Mon–Sat 8am–8pm, Sun 9am–7pm; Nov–March daily 9am–1pm & 2–5pm; Ⓣ435/259-8825 or 1-800/635-6622, Ⓦwww.discovermoab.com).

Accommodation

Though Moab holds around thirty **motels** and a dozen **B&Bs**, all of its 1500-plus rooms are frequently taken between mid-March and October – when you'd be lucky to find anything below $80 – so reservations are strongly recommended.

Commercial **campgrounds** nearby include the shaded *Slickrock Campground*, 1301 N Hwy-191 (Ⓣ435/259-7660 or 1-800/448-8873, Ⓦwww.slickrockcampground.com; $23), a mile north of town; if you're happy to put up with far more primitive facilities to escape the crowds, head for the BLM's **Sand Flats Recreation Area**, along the top of the mesa east of town, near the Slickrock Bike Trail, at 1924 S Roadrunner Hill (Ⓣ435/259-6111; $10).

Adobe Abode 778 W Kane Creek Blvd ☎435/259-7716, ⓦwww.adobeabodemoab.com. Attractive, Pueblo-style home not far from downtown, offering six tastefully furnished B&B rooms. ❺
Best Western Greenwell Inn 105 S Main St ☎435/259-6151 or 1-800/780-7234, ⓦwww.bestwesternmoab.com. Central, modern hotel that offers spacious, tasteful rooms. ❺
Gonzo Inn 100 W 200 South ☎435/259-2515 or 1-800/791-4044, ⓦwww.gonzoinn.com. Luxurious if rather self-consciously hip inn, complete with kitsch-retro furnishings, quirky artworks and an espresso bar. ❻
Inca Inn Motel 570 N Main St ☎435/259-7261 or 1-866/462-2466, ⓦwww.incainn.com. Clean, minimally equipped but adequate budget motel, with pool. Closed Dec & Jan. ❸
Lazy Lizard International Hostel 1213 S Hwy-191 ☎435/259-6057, ⓦwww.lazylizardhostel.com. Amiable, very laidback independent hostel, a mile south of the centre, with $10 beds in six-person dorms, $7 camping and private cabins for $30-plus, plus hot tub, kitchen and internet access. ❶
Red Rock Lodge 51 North 100 West ☎435/259-5431 or 1-877/253-5431, ⓦwww.red-rocklodge.com. Though lacking the flair of Moab's fancier inns, this simple traditional motel offers clean rooms in a supremely central location. ❸

Eating and drinking

Moab offers the greatest range of **restaurants** in southern Utah, most of which cater to vegetarians. With two pubs and a winery, there's also no problem getting a **drink**, while **coffee bars** are ubiquitous.

Buck's Grill House 1393 N Hwy-191 ☎435/259-5201. Belying its stockade-like exterior, this dinner-only "American Western Food" joint is actually a sophisticated affair, serving rich, classy Southwestern food, such as game hen or pork ribs, at very reasonable prices.
Desert Bistro 1266 N Main St ☎435/259-0756. Top-notch dinner-only restaurant, set in a ranch home with a patio that's perfect for summer nights. On the modern bistro menu, entrees like venison medallions or smoked rabbit agnolotti cost up to $40.
Eddie McStiff's 57 S Main St ☎435/259-2337. Central pub that serves interesting beers, including raspberry and blueberry varieties and inexpensive salads, pizzas and pasta.
Jailhouse Café 101 N Main St ☎435/259-3900. Very popular central café, open for breakfast only. Indoor and outdoor seating year-round and great specials like ginger pancakes and eggs Benedict. Daily except Tues 7am–noon.
The Peace Tree 20 S Main St ☎435/259-8503. Very central juice bar and café that serves good sandwiches, wraps and smoothies to take away or eat on the small outdoor patio, until 6.30pm daily.

Natural Bridges National Monument

Hwy-95 runs a hundred miles southeast from Capitol Reef, through dozens of red-rock canyons and across the Dirty Devil and Colorado rivers, before topping out on the sagebrush plains of San Juan County. En route it gives access to the marvellous sandstone spans at **Natural Bridges National Monument**, forty miles west of US-191. The **visitor centre** is four miles off Hwy-95 (daily 9am–5.30pm; $6/vehicle; ☎435/692-1234, ⓦwww.nps.gov/nabr), near a small **campground** ($10).

Wherever the monument's three separate canyons intersect, the streams that carved them have also formed sandstone bridges. The largest, **Sipapu Bridge**, is 268ft across and over 200ft high and can be seen from the nine-mile paved loop road; hike less than a mile down into the canyon for a closer look. **Kachina Bridge**, the next along, is nearly as high but twice as thick and has Ancestral Puebloan pictographs at its base. The oldest, slimmest and most fragile bridge – **Owachomo**, a mile and a half up Armstrong Canyon – spans 180ft but is only nine feet thick at its thinnest point.

Monticello

The small town of **MONTICELLO** stands 56 miles south of Moab on US-191, sixteen miles beyond the turn-off for the Needles section of Canyonlands. The

visitor centre at 232 S Main St doubles as a small frontier **museum** (daily except Tues 9am–6pm; ⓣ435/587-3235, ⓦwww.southeastutah.org). **Motels** include a smart *Days Inn*, 549 N Main St (ⓣ435/587-2458, ⓦwww.daysinn.com; ❸). Good, large **meals** can be had at the *MD Ranch Cookhouse*, 380 S Main St (ⓣ435/587-3299).

The San Juan River, Mexican Hat and Bluff

From Natural Bridges, Hwy-261 runs south for 25 miles to the edge of Cedar Mesa, high above the eerie sandstone towers of the **Valley of the Gods**. It then turns to gravel and drops over a thousand feet in little over two twisting, hairpin-turning miles down the "**Moki Dugway**". Six miles from the foot of the switchbacks, the barely marked Hwy-316 branches off to the aptly named **Goosenecks State Reserve** (open 24hr; free), high above the **San Juan River**. A thousand feet below, the river snakes in such convoluted twists and turns that it flows six miles in total for every one mile west.

Back on Hwy-261, sleepy **MEXICAN HAT**, just twenty miles north of Monument Valley, takes its name from a riverside **sandstone hoodoo** that looks like a south-of-the-border sombrero. Right on the river, the *San Juan Inn* (ⓣ435/535-2210 or 1-800/447-2022; ⓦwww.sanjuaninn.net; ❹), holds a grocery store, restaurant, bar and trading post.

The rafts you may see emerging from the water at Mexican Hat went in at **BLUFF**, twenty miles upstream. US-163 connects the two towns, well away from the river but still an enthralling drive, while the backstreets of Bluff hold **Mormon pioneer houses**. Places to **eat** include the friendly outdoor *Cottonwood Steakhouse* (ⓣ435/672-2282), while an excellent **motel**, the *Desert Rose Inn*, 701 W Hwy-191 (ⓣ435/672-2303 or 1-888/475-7673, ⓦwww.desertroseinn.com; ❹), holds thirty attractively decorated rooms.

Hovenweep National Monument

Hidden in the no-man's-land that straddles the Utah–Colorado border, the remote **Ancestral Puebloan ruins** at **Hovenweep National Monument** offer a haunting sense of timeless isolation. Located 25 miles east of US-191 along Hwy-262, which branches off between Bluff and Blanding and 35 miles west of Cortez, Colorado, Hovenweep preserves six distinct conglomerations of ruins sprouting from the rims of shallow desert canyons. Easy access is restricted to **Little Ruin Canyon**, behind the **visitor centre** (daily: April–Sept 8am–6pm; Oct–March 8am–5pm; $6; ⓣ970/562-4282, ⓦwww.nps.gov/hove). A mile-long loop trail offers good views of the largest ruins, including the grandly named **Hovenweep Castle**, constructed around 1200 AD. No accommodation, gasoline or food is available, but a **campground** remains open all year ($10; no reservations).

Lake Powell and Glen Canyon Dam

The mighty rivers and canyons of southern Utah come to an abrupt and ignoble end at the Arizona border, where the **Glen Canyon Dam** stops them dead in the stagnant waters of **Lake Powell**. Ironically, the lake is named for John Wesley Powell, the first person to run the Colorado River through the Grand Canyon. The roaring torrents that he battled, along with magnificent Glen Canyon itself, are now lost beneath these placid blue waters and the blocked-up Colorado, Green, Dirty Devil, San Juan and Escalante rivers have become a playground for houseboaters and waterskiers. The construction of the dam in the early 1960s outraged environmentalists and archeologists and created a peculiar and utterly unnatural landscape, the deep and tranquil lake a surreal contrast with the surrounding dry slickrock and sandstone buttes.

Lake Powell has 1960 miles of shoreline – more than the entire US Pacific coast – and 96 water-filled side canyons. The water level fluctuates considerably, so for much of the time the rocks to all sides are bleached for many feet above the waterline, with a dirty-bath tidemark sullying the golden sandstone. Many summer visitors bring their own boats or rent a vessel from one of the marinas that fringe the lake.

At **Wahweap Marina**, just off US-89 on the way between Zion and the Grand Canyon, the plush *Lake Powell Resort* (ⓣ928/645-2433 or 1-888/896-3829, ⓦwww.lakepowell.com; ❻) has comfortable lakeside rooms and good food. The same company arranges **houseboat rental** from Wahweap and other Lake Powell marinas and there's **camping** at each marina. Otherwise, the nearest **accommodation** is across the Arizona border in the motels of **PAGE**, like the tiny, very welcoming *LuLu's Sleep Ezze Motel*, 208 N Lake Powell Blvd (ⓣ928/608-0273 or 1-800/553-6211; ❸).

GLEN CANYON DAM itself, in between Page and Wahweap, can be seen from the **Carl Hayden Visitor Centre** (daily: March–Oct 8am–6pm; Nov–Feb 8.30am–4.30pm; ⓣ928/608-6404, ⓦwww.nps.gov/glca) on the west bank, which also arranges free 45-minute dam tours.

The cheapest way to get out on the waters of Lake Powell is to take the **ferry** ($20/car) between **Halls Crossing** and **Bullfrog** marinas, two-thirds of the way up the lake, from where the Burr Trail heads west toward Capitol Reef, while Hwy-276 runs northeast to Natural Bridges.

Northern Utah

Although northern Utah holds less appeal for tourists, **Salt Lake City**, the capital, is by far the state's largest and most cosmopolitan urban centre. The **northeast corner** has coal mines, old railroad towns and, along the Wyoming border, the **Uinta Mountains**, uncrossed by road and showing hardly a sign of civilization. From the **northwest**, the harshly alkaline **Great Basin** plain stretches uneventfully west across Nevada to California.

Salt Lake City

Disarmingly pleasant and easy-going, **SALT LAKE CITY** is well worth a stopover of a couple of days. Its setting is superb, towered over by the **Wasatch Front**, which marks the dividing line between the comparatively lush eastern and the bone-dry western halves of northern Utah. The area offers great hiking and cycling in summer and autumn and, in winter, superb **skiing**. Outsiders still tend to imagine Salt Lake City as decidedly short on fun, but so long as you're willing to switch gears and slow down, its unhurried pace and the positive energy of its people, can make for an enjoyable experience.

Arrival, information and getting around

Salt Lake City International Airport is a mere four miles west of downtown. A **taxi** into town costs around $20; cheaper **shuttle vans** are run by Xpress Shuttles (ⓣ801/596-1600 or 1-800/397-0773, ⓦwww.xpressshuttleutah.com), while Canyon Transportation (ⓣ1-800/255-1841, ⓦwww.canyontransport.com) serves the ski areas. Greyhound-Trailways **buses** arrive downtown, at 300 S 600 West (ⓣ801/355-9579), as do Amtrak **trains**, at 320 S Rio Grande Ave. Local buses and also TRAX trams, are operated by the Utah Transit Authority (ⓣ801/743-3882, ⓦwww.rideuta.com); journeys within the immediate downtown area are free.

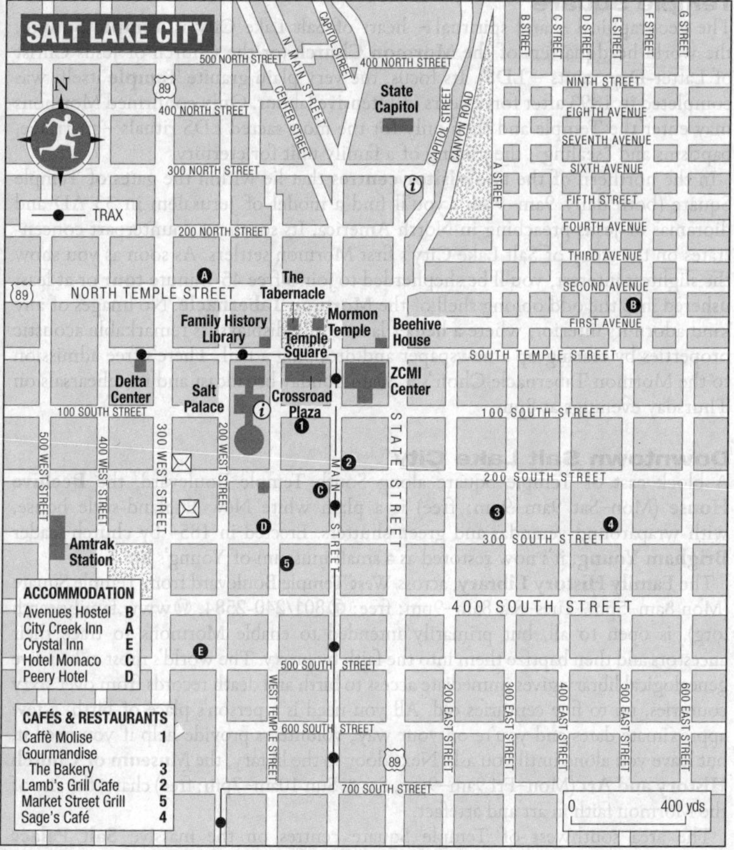

The **visitor centre** is downtown at 90 S West Temple Blvd (daily 9am–5pm; ⓣ801/534-4490, ⓦwww.visitsaltlake.com).

Accommodation

Salt Lake City is well equipped with **accommodation**, with downtown options from budget motels on upwards and the usual mid-range places near the airport and along the interstates. Weekend rates can be real bargains.

Avenues Hostel 107 F St ⓣ801/539-3855, ⓦwww.saltlakehostel.com. Simple hostel a short way east of downtown, with $15 dorm beds and $35 private rooms. ❷

Crystal Inn 230 W 500 South ⓣ801/328-4466 or 1-800/366-4466, ⓦwww.crystalinnsaltlake.com. Spacious, well-equipped and very reasonably priced hotel close to downtown, with large buffet breakfasts included and free airport shuttle.

City Creek Inn 230 W North Temple Blvd ⓣ801/533-9100 or 1-866/533-4898, ⓦwww.citycreekinn.com. Family-owned budget motor court, old-fashioned but spruced up, offering good-value rooms very close to downtown. ❸

Hotel Monaco 15 W 200 South ⓣ801/595-0000 or 1-800/805-1801, ⓦwww.monaco-saltlakecity.com. Stylish, very upscale downtown hotel, housed in a former bank. ❽

Peery Hotel 110 W 300 South St ⓣ801/521-4300 or 1-800/331-0073, ⓦwww.peeryhotel.com. Renovated 1910 downtown landmark, offering very tasteful, comfortable rooms. ❻

Temple Square

The geographical – and spiritual – heart of Salt Lake City is **Temple Square**, the world headquarters of the **Mormon Church** (or the Church of Jesus Christ of Latter-Day Saints – LDS). Its focus, the very plain granite **Temple** itself, was completed in 1893 after forty years of intensive labour. Only confirmed Mormons may enter the Temple and then only for the most sacred LDS rituals – marriage, baptisms and "sealing", the joining of a family unit for eternity.

In the northern of the two **visitor centres** that lie within the gates of Temple Square (both daily 9am–9pm), you'll find a model of Jerusalem in 33 AD and dioramas of Jesus preaching in North America. Its southern counterpart concentrates on the story of Salt Lake City's first Mormon settlers. As soon as you show the slightest interest, you'll be shepherded to join a free 45-minute **tour** or at least ushered into the odd oblong shell of the **Mormon Tabernacle**. No images of any kind adorn its interior, where a helper laconically displays its remarkable acoustic properties by tearing up a newspaper and dropping a nail. There's free admission to the Mormon Tabernacle Choir's 9.30am Sunday broadcast and its rehearsals on Thursday evenings at 8pm.

Downtown Salt Lake City

A block east of Temple Square along South Temple Boulevard, the **Beehive House** (Mon–Sat 9am–9pm; free) is a plain white New England-style house, with wraparound verandas and green shutters. Erected in 1854 by church leader **Brigham Young**, it's now restored as a small museum of Young's life.

The **Family History Library**, across West Temple Boulevard from Temple Square (Mon 8am–5pm, Tues–Sat 8am–9pm; free; Ⓣ801/240-2584, Ⓦwww.familysearch.org), is open to all, but primarily intended to enable Mormons to trace their ancestors and then baptize them into the faith by proxy. The world's most exhaustive genealogical library gives immediate access to birth and death records from over sixty countries, up to five centuries old. All you need is a person's place of birth, a few approximate dates and you're on your way; volunteers provide help if you need it, but leave you alone until you ask. Next door to the library, the **Museum of Church History and Art** (Mon–Fri 9am–9pm, Sat & Sun 10am–7pm; free) charts the rise of the Mormon faith in art and artefact.

The area southwest of Temple Square centres on the massive **Salt Palace** convention centre and sports arena (home of the Utah Jazz basketball team). The surrounding district of brick warehouses around the Union Pacific railroad tracks is filled with designer shops and art galleries, signs that even Mormons can be yuppies.

The **Capitol Hill** neighbourhood, around the imposing, domed **Utah State Capitol** (summer Mon–Sat 8am–8pm; rest of year Mon–Sat 8am–6pm; free) on the gentle hill above Temple Square, holds some of Salt Lake City's grandest Victorian homes.

Eating

Though it has perfectly good **restaurants**, Salt Lake City lacks an atmospheric – let alone hip – dining district. The only downtown area with much potential is the block or two to either side of West Temple Street, south and east of the Salt Palace.

Caffè Molise 55 W 100 South Ⓣ801/364-8833, Ⓦwww.caffemolise.com. Authentic, high-quality, great-value Italian food downtown, with tables in a nice little courtyard in summer and jazz on Fridays.

Gourmandise The Bakery 250 S 300 East Ⓣ801/328-3330. It's the pastries that draw downtown devotees in droves, but this café also does great, cheap, lunchtime salads, sandwiches and specials. Closed Sun.

Lamb's Grill Cafe 169 S Main St Ⓣ801/364-7166, Ⓦlambsgrill.com. Great breakfasts, best eaten at the long shiny counter and excellent-value set meals later on; a full dinner typically costs $20. Closed Sun.

Market Street Grill 48 W Market St ⓣ801/322-4668, ⓦwww.marketstreetgrill.com. As close as Salt Lake City comes to a New York City bar and grill, with fresh seafood, especially oysters, plus steaks in all shapes and sizes. $13 lunch specials, full dinners $20 and up.

Ruth's Diner 2100 Emigration Canyon Rd ⓣ801/582-5807, ⓦwww.ruthsdiner.com. Good-value indoor and patio dining, often with live music, set in and around old railroad carriages in a narrow canyon three miles east of town. A wide selection of fresh dishes, great salads and Utah's best breakfasts.

Sage's Café 473 E 300 South ⓣ801/322-3790, ⓦwww.sagescafe.com. Salt Lake's finest vegetarian restaurant, with an all-organic menu that ranges from pizza to raw salads. Closed Sun.

Drinking and nightlife

Salt Lake City doesn't roll up the sidewalks when the sun goes down. To find out about the broad range of **fringe** art, music and clubland happenings, pick up the free *City Weekly* (ⓦwww.slweekly.com). A handful of **brewpubs**, for which membership is not required, includes the casual, friendly *Squatters Pub*, 147 W 300 South (ⓣ801/363-2739).

The best place to hear **live music** is, surprisingly enough, *The Depot*, in the Union Pacific Station at 400 W South Temple Blvd (ⓣ801/456-2888, ⓦwww.depotslc.com), where you can expect to hear anything from jazz to reggae and most points in between, though *The Urban Lounge*, 241 S 500 East (ⓣ801/746-05570, ⓦwww.theurbanlounge.com), also programmes a wide range of indie bands.

Park City

Despite Brigham Young's strictures against prospecting for precious metals – he feared a Gentile Gold Rush – the first mining camp at **PARK CITY**, thirty miles east of downtown Salt Lake City along I-80 through the mountains, was established in the 1860s. In 1872 George Hearst laid the foundations of the Hearst media empire by paying $27,000 for a claim that became the Ontario Silver Mine, worth $50 million.

These days, the **Park City Mountain Resort** (ⓣ435/649-8111 or 1-800/222-7275, ⓦwww.parkcitymountain.com) and the nearby **The Canyons** (ⓣ435/615-3410, ⓦwww.thecanyons.com) and (skiers-only) **Deer Valley** (ⓣ435/649-1000 or 1-800/424-3337, ⓦwww.deervalley.com) resorts constitute Utah's largest **ski area**. Daily lift passes for each resort cost around $100; equipment rental outlets include Park City Sport (ⓣ1-800/523-3922, ⓦwww.parkcitysport.com).

In addition, Park City hosts the prestigious **Sundance Film Festival**, a major showcase for independent movies from the US and all over the world, which is held during the second half of January each year (ⓣ435/658-3456, ⓦwww.sundance.org).

Practicalities

Park City has an information kiosk at 333 Main St (Mon–Fri 10am–7pm, Sat & Sun noon–6pm; ⓣ435/615-9559, ⓦwww.parkcityinfo.com). Lewis Bros Stages (ⓣ801/359-8677 or 1-800/826-5844, ⓦwww.lewisstages.com) runs scheduled **shuttles** from Salt Lake City ($37).

Accommodation rates double in ski season. The down-to-earth *Chateau Apres*, 1299 Norfolk Ave (ⓣ435/649-9372 or 1-800/357-3556, ⓦwww.chateauapres.com; ❺), a cosy lodge motel, also offers $40 dorm rooms. *Café Terigo*, 424 Main St (ⓣ435/645-9555), is a good, central Mediterranean restaurant, while the *Windy Ridge Cafe*, 1250 Iron Horse Drive (ⓣ435/647-0880), offers deli snacks and sandwiches. The *Wasatch Brew Pub*, 250 Main St (ⓣ435/649-0900), is open until midnight daily and serves good food as well as microbrewed beer.

Nevada

Desolate **NEVADA** consists largely of endless tracts of bleak, empty desert, its flat sagebrush plains cut intermittently by angular mountain ranges. Apart from the huge acreages given over to mining and grazing, much of Nevada is used by the **military** to test aircraft and weapons systems.

By far the most compelling reason to visit Nevada is to see the surreal oasis of **Las Vegas**. While its eye-popping architecture, lavish restaurants, decadent nightclubs and amazing shows offer an unforgettable sensory overload, the experience remains rooted in **gambling**. Even the smaller and more down-to-earth settlements of **Reno** and state capital **Carson City** revolve around the casino trade.

Las Vegas

Shimmering from the desert haze of Nevada like a latter-day El Dorado, **LAS VEGAS** is the most dynamic, spectacular city on earth. At the start of the twentieth century, it didn't even exist; now home to two million people, it boasts eighteen of the world's twenty-five largest hotels, holding flamboyant, no-expense-spared **casinos** that lure over thirty-five-million tourists each year.

Las Vegas has been stockpiling superlatives since the 1950s, but never rests on its laurels. Many first-time visitors expect the city to be kitsch, but the casino owners are far too canny to be sentimental. Yes, there are a few Elvis impersonators around, but what characterizes the city far more is its endless quest for **novelty**. Long before they lose their sparkle, yesterday's showpieces are blasted into rubble, to make way for ever more extravagant replacements. A few years ago, when the fashion was for fantasy, Arthurian castles and Egyptian pyramids mushroomed along the Strip; next came a craze for constructing entire replica cities, like New York, Paris, Monte Carlo and Venice; and the current trend is for high-end properties that attempt to straddle the line between screaming ostentation and "elegant" sophistication.

While the city has cleaned up its act since the days of Mob domination, it certainly hasn't become a **family** destination. Hit hard by the recession, however, just as the massive new **CityCenter** development increased its capacity yet again, it is perforce becoming a **cheap** destination once again. Two main companies, MGM Resorts and Harrah's control colossal swathes of the Strip and much as they'd like to keep room rates at their former levels they've had to let them drop. The fact that you can get a high-quality room on the Strip for well under $50, at least on weekdays, means there's less to gain than ever in spending your time in the ailing downtown and dining and entertainment prices too are more reasonable than they've been for years.

Although Las Vegas is an unmissable destination, it's one that palls for most visitors after a couple of (hectic) days. If you've come solely to gamble, there's not much to say beyond the fact that all the casinos are free and open 24 hours per day, with acres of floor space packed with ways to lose money: million-dollar slots, video poker, blackjack, craps, roulette wheels and much, much more.

A brief history

The name Las Vegas – "the meadows" – originally referred to natural springs that served as a way-station for travellers on the Old Spanish Trail. In 1900, the valley had a population of just thirty people. Things changed in 1905, with the completion of the now-defunct rail link between Salt Lake City and Los Angeles.

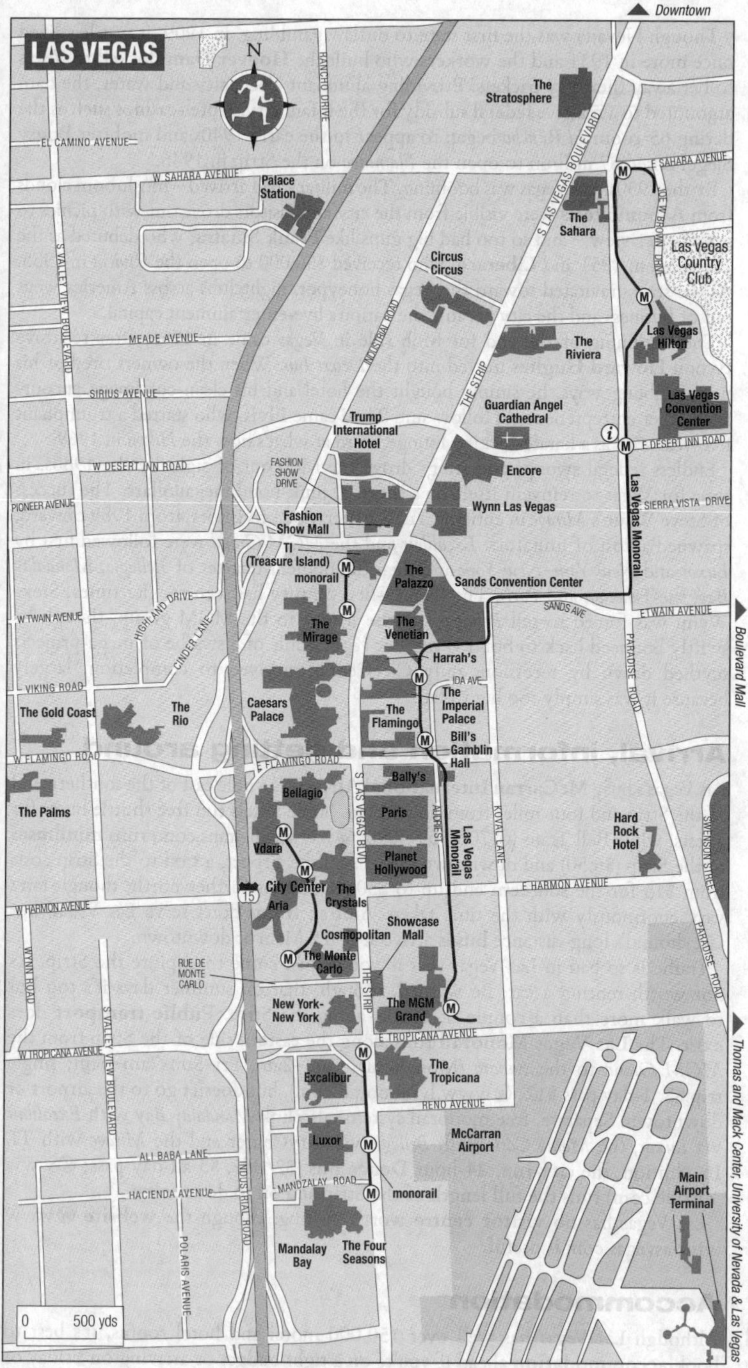

LAS VEGAS

Downtown
N
The Stratosphere
EL CAMINO AVENUE
W SAHARA AVENUE
E SAHARA AVENUE
RANCHO DRIVE
S LAS VEGAS BOULEVARD
Palace Station
The Sahara
JOE W BROWN DRIVE
Las Vegas Country Club
Circus Circus
INDUSTRIAL ROAD
S VALLEY VIEW BOULEVARD
Las Vegas Hilton
MEADE AVENUE
The Riviera
THE STRIP
SIRIUS AVENUE
Las Vegas Convention Center
Trump International Hotel
Guardian Angel Cathedral
E DESERT INN ROAD
W DESERT INN ROAD
FASHION SHOW DRIVE
Encore
Las Vegas Monorail
PIONEER AVENUE
Wynn Las Vegas
SIERRA VISTA DRIVE
Fashion Show Mall
TI (Treasure Island)
monorail
The Palazzo
Sands Convention Center
HIGHLAND DRIVE
SANDS AVE
E TWAIN AVENUE
W TWAIN AVENUE
The Mirage
The Venetian
CINDER LANE
PARADISE ROAD
Harrah's
VIKING ROAD
IDA AVE
The Imperial Palace
The Gold Coast
The Rio
Caesars Palace
The Flamingo
Bill's Gamblin Hall
W FLAMINGO ROAD
E FLAMINGO ROAD
Bally's
Bellagio
S LAS VEGAS BLVD
The Palms
Paris
AUDREST
KOVAL LANE
Hard Rock Hotel
SWENSON STREET
Vdara
Las Vegas Monorail
Planet Hollywood
City Center
15
The Crystals
E HARMON AVENUE
Aria
W HARMON AVENUE
Showcase Mall
Cosmopolitan
WYNN ROAD
The Monte Carlo
RUE DE MONTE CARLO
PARADISE ROAD
New York-New York
THE STRIP
The MGM Grand
E TROPICANA AVENUE
W TROPICANA AVENUE
S VALLEY VIEW BOULEVARD
Excalibur
The Tropicana
RENO AVENUE
Luxor
McCarran Airport
ALI BABA LANE
MANDZALAY ROAD
monorail
HACIENDA AVENUE
INDUSTRIAL ROAD
Main Airport Terminal
POLARIS AVENUE
Mandalay Bay
The Four Seasons
0 500 yds

Though Nevada was the first state to outlaw gambling, in 1909, it was legalized once more in 1931 and the workers who built the **Hoover Dam** flocked to Vegas to bet away their pay packets. Providing abundant electricity and water, the dam amounted to a massive federal subsidy for the infant city. Hotel-casinos such as the daring 65-room *El Rancho* began to appear in the early 1940s and mobster Bugsy Siegel raised $7 million to open the *Flamingo* on the Strip in 1946.

By the 1950s, Las Vegas was booming. The military had arrived – mushroom clouds from **A-bomb tests** were visible from the city and visitors drove out with picnics to get a better view – and so too had big guns like **Frank Sinatra**, who debuted at the *Desert Inn* in 1951 and **Liberace**, who received $50,000 to open the *Riviera* in 1955. As the stars gravitated toward the Vegas honeypot, nightclubs across America went out of business and the city became the nation's live-entertainment capital.

The beginning of the end for Mob rule in Vegas came in 1966, after reclusive tycoon **Howard Hughes** moved into the *Desert Inn*. When the owners tired of his non-gambling ways, he simply bought the hotel and his clean-cut image encouraged other entrepreneurs to follow suit. Then came **Elvis**, who started a triumphant five-year stint as a karate-kicking lounge lizard at what's now the *Hilton* in 1969.

Endless federal swoops and stings drove the Mob out of sight by the 1980s, in time for Vegas to reinvent itself on a surge of junk-bond megadollars. The success of Steve Wynn's *Mirage* in enticing a new generation of visitors, from 1989 onward, spawned a host of imitators. *Excalibur* and the *MGM Grand* were followed first by *Luxor* and *New York–New York* and then the opulent quartet of *Bellagio*, *Mandalay Bay*, the *Venetian* and *Paris*. The twenty-first century has seen rockier times; Steve Wynn was forced to sell *Bellagio* and the *Mirage* to the MGM group, though he swiftly bounced back to build *Wynn Las Vegas*, while of a swathe of mega-projects scythed down by recession, only CityCenter survived to completion, largely because it was simply too big to fail.

Arrival, information and getting around

Las Vegas's busy **McCarran International Airport** is a mile east of the southern end of the Strip and four miles from downtown. Some hotels run free shuttle buses for guests, while Bell Trans (Ⓣ702/739-7990, Ⓦwww.bell-trans.com) runs **minibuses** to the Strip ($6.50) and downtown ($8). From the airport, a **taxi** to the Strip costs from $15 for the southern end up to $30 for casinos further north, though fares vary enormously with the time taken. Amtrak **trains** don't serve Las Vegas, but Greyhound's long-distance **buses** arrive at 200 S Main St downtown.

Traffic is so bad in Las Vegas that if you've just come to explore the Strip, it's not worth renting a car. Be warned, though, that on summer days it's too hot to walk more than a couple of blocks along the Strip. **Public transport** does exist. The **Las Vegas Monorail** runs along the eastern side of the Strip from the *MGM Grand* to the *Sahara* (Mon–Thurs 7am–2am, Fri–Sun 7am–3am; single trip $5, 1-day pass $12; Ⓦwww.lvmonorail.com), but doesn't go to the airport or downtown. Separate, free monorail systems also link *Mandalay Bay* with *Excalibur* via *Luxor*, the *Monte Carlo* with *Bellagio* via CityCenter and the *Mirage* with *TI*. In addition, the city-run, 24-hour **Deuce bus** ($2/ride, $3 all-day pass; Ⓦwww.catride.com) runs the full length of the Strip and on to downtown.

Las Vegas has no **visitor centre** worth visiting, though the **website** Ⓦwww.visitlasvegas.com is useful.

Accommodation

Although Las Vegas has well over 150,000 motel and hotel rooms, it's best to book **accommodation** ahead if you're on a tight budget or arriving on Friday or

Saturday; upwards of two hundred thousand people descend upon the city every weekend. Since the recession hit, room rates have dropped to such low levels that there's no need to seek out downtown or other off-Strip alternatives.

All hotels charge different rates for each specific day you stay, depending on the day of the week and what's going on in town. To keep costs down, aim to **visit during the week** rather than on the weekend. Rates rise enormously on Friday or Saturday, by at least $50 extra in a lower-end property and often over $100 in the big-name casinos. On top of that, many hotels won't accept Saturday arrivals. Note also that many charge compulsory **resort fees** of $5–20 per day, supposedly to cover internet and phone access and other amenities, on top of their nominal room rates.

Aria 3730 Las Vegas Blvd S ⓣ866/359-7757 or 702/590-7111, ⓦarialasvegas.com. Albeit subdued by Las Vegas standards, *Aria*'s stylish contemporary rooms, with their high-end, high-tech amenities, can be a real bargain, especially if you have the time – and the weather – to enjoy the superb pool complex. Sun–Thurs ❺, Fri & Sat ❽.

Bellagio 3600 Las Vegas Blvd S ⓣ888/987-6667 or 702/693-7111, ⓦbellagio.com. The opulent *Bellagio* remains at the top end of the Vegas spectrum, with its plush European furnishings and marble bathrooms now giving it a slightly retro feel. Sun–Thurs ❺, Fri & Sat ❽

Caesars Palace 3570 Las Vegas Blvd S ⓣ866/227-5938, ⓦcaesarspalace.com. Long the epitome of Las Vegas luxury, *Caesars Palace* can feel like a baffling labyrinth, but matches its newer rivals for both size and amenities. The pseudo-Roman splendour of its older rooms is a joy; the newer towers are more conventionally elegant. Sun–Thurs ❻, Fri & Sat ❽

Circus Circus 2880 Las Vegas Blvd S ⓣ800/634-3450 or 702/734-0410, ⓦcircuscircus.com. With Las Vegas rates so low these days, *Circus Circus* feels inconveniently far from the main Strip action and its low prices are only really worth it if you're bringing kids to its theme park. Sun–Thurs ❶, Fri & Sat ❷

El Cortez 600 E Fremont St ⓣ800/634-6703 or 702/385-5200, ⓦecvegas.com. Veteran downtown casino, transformed by a face-lift, with cut-price "vintage" rooms, great-value mini-suites in a newer tower and the very stylish new Cabana Suites for around $20 extra across the street. Sun–Thurs ❶ Fri & Sat ❷

Excalibur 3850 Las Vegas Blvd S ⓣ877/750-5464 or 702/597-7777, ⓦexcalibur.com.So long as you stay in the much nicer "wide-screen rooms", typically costing $10 extra, this garish fake castle, while often uncomfortably crowded, can be excellent value. Sun–Thurs ❶, Fri & Sat ❸

Imperial Palace 3535 Las Vegas Blvd S ⓣ800/351-7400 or 702/731-3311, ⓦimperialpalace.com. Great value in the heart of the Strip. Standard rooms are more than adequate, with balconies overlooking the pool, while the irresistible "luv tub" suites, at about $40 extra, offer huge beds, even bigger sunken baths and mirrors everywhere you can imagine. Sun–Thurs ❶, Fri & Sat ❹

Luxor 3900 Las Vegas Blvd S ⓣ877/386-4658 or 262-4444, ⓦluxor.com. All two thousand rooms in this vast smoked-glass pyramid have tremendous views – and they're much larger than usual. Unlike the extra two thousand rooms in the *Luxor*'s newer tower next door, however, most have showers, not baths. Sun–Thurs ❷, Fri & Sat ❺

Mandalay Bay 3950 Las Vegas Blvd S ⓣ877/632-7800 or 702/632-7777, ⓦmandalaybay.com. This upscale, young-adult playground is a long way south of the central Strip, but all its luxurious rooms have both bath and walk-in shower and as well as great dining there's a spectacular wave pool. Mon–Thurs & Sun ❺, Fri & Sat ❽

MGM Grand 3799 Las Vegas Blvd S ⓣ877/880-0880 or 891-7777, ⓦmgmgrand.com. Waiting for any kind of service, especially check-in, in this behemoth – 5044 rooms and counting – can be horrendous, but you get a great standard of accommodation for the price. The spacious rooms in the main tower have a fun 1930s Hollywood feel; in the funkier, more contemporary West Wing, they're smaller and only have showers. Sun–Thurs ❹, Fri & Sat ❼

New York-New York 3790 Las Vegas Blvd S ⓣ888/696-9887 or 740/6969, ⓦnynyhotelcasino.com. Toned down but still among the most enjoyable Strip casinos, *New York–New York* is refreshingly small, offering nice if somewhat cramped rooms at good rates. Sun–Thurs ❸, Fri & Sat ❺

Paris 3655 Las Vegas Blvd S ⓣ877/796-2096 or 877/603-4386, ⓦparislasvegas.com. For location, views and ambience the flamboyant *Paris* more than holds its own. Its standard rooms are pretty good, while the plush Red Rooms, at $40 extra, have an irresistible French flair. Sun–Thurs ❹, Fri & Sat ❼

Planet Hollywood 3667 Las Vegas Blvd S ⓣ866/919-7472 or 785-5555, ⓦplanethollywoodresort.com. Some of the nicest mid-rate rooms in town – spacious, with separate bath and shower and quirkily remodelled with original movie memorabilia.

They're an awful long way from the self-park garage though. Sun–Thurs ❺, Fri & Sat ❽

The Stratosphere 2000 Las Vegas Blvd S ⓣ800/998-6937 or 702/380-7777, ⓦstratospherehotel.com. Despite its unfashionable location north of the Strip, the *Stratosphere* survives thanks to rock-bottom rates and a steady flow of budget tour groups. No accommodation is in the hundred-storey tower, so don't expect amazing views, just large, plain rooms. Sun–Thurs ❶, Fri & Sat ❷

USA Hostels Las Vegas 1322 E Fremont St ⓣ702/385-1150 or 1-800/550-8958, ⓦwww.usahostels.com. Price-wise, there's no point staying in a hostel in Las Vegas and this former motel is in an inconvenient, forbidding neighbourhood ten blocks east of downtown. That said, it's much the best in town, with dorm beds from $22 and private double rooms from $44. Rates include free breakfast; cheap dinners are also available. The friendly staff arrange city and national-park tours. ❷

The Venetian 3355 Las Vegas Blvd S ⓣ866/659-9643 or 702/414-1000, ⓦvenetian.com. Even the standard rooms in this colossal and hugely luxurious resort are split-level suites, with decadently comfortable canopied beds. Downstairs there's a mind-blowing array of shops and restaurants and it has a magnificent rooftop pool. Sun–Thurs ❼, Fri & Sat ❽

Wynn Las Vegas 3131 Las Vegas Blvd S ⓣ877/321-9966 or 702/770-7000, ⓦwynnlasvegas.com. Las Vegas' highest standard of luxury; exceptionally large guest rooms with wonderful beds and fabulous linens, plus super-sized bathtubs. ❽

The City

Though the Las Vegas sprawl measures fifteen miles wide by fifteen miles long, the only area of interest to tourists is the six-mile stretch of **Las Vegas Boulevard** that includes both the **Strip**, home to the major casinos and, separated by two seedy and best avoided miles, **downtown**, near where I-15 meets US-95.

The Strip

For its razor-edge finesse in harnessing sheer, magnificent excess to the serious business of making money, there's no place like the **Las Vegas Strip**. It's hard to imagine that Las Vegas was once an ordinary city and Las Vegas Boulevard a dusty thoroughfare scattered with edge-of-town motels. After seven decades of capitalism run riot, with every new casino-hotel setting out to surpass anything its neighbours ever dreamed of, the Strip remains locked into a hyperactive craving for thrills and glamour, forever discarding its latest toy in its frenzied pursuit of the next jackpot.

Mandalay Bay

The Strip's southern end kicks off with the glowing gilded towers of the upmarket, vaguely Asian-themed **Mandalay Bay**, whose excellent restaurants, as well as the *House of Blues* music venue, keep it lively at night. During the day, all it has to offer the casual sightseer is the **Shark Reef** aquarium, right at the back of the property (Sun–Thurs 10am–8pm, Fri & Sat 10am–11pm; $17), a small mock-up of a steamy, half-submerged temple complex, inhabited by crocodiles, jellyfish and, of course, sharks.

Luxor

A block north of *Mandalay Bay*, the 36-storey **Luxor** pyramid remains an astonishing building, despite losing most of its ancient-Egyptian trappings in its rebranding as the sort of "hip", upscale casino resort that now dominates the Strip. It now houses two expensive permanent exhibitions: **Bodies** (daily 10am–10pm; $34), a sobering collection of genuine "plastinated" human corpses and **Titanic**, featuring not merely artefacts but a huge piece of the doomed liner, recovered from two miles down in the Atlantic Ocean (same hours, $27).

Excalibur and the MGM Grand

Excalibur, immediately north of *Luxor*, is a mock medieval castle, complete with drawbridge, crenellated towers and a basement stuffed with fairground-style sideshows, that's usually packed out with low-budget tour groups. Its brief reign as the world's largest hotel, from 1990 to 1993, ended when the five-thousand-room **MGM Grand** opened across the street. In the **Lion Habitat**, a walk-through glass-walled zoo near the front entrance, real lions lounge around a ruined temple (daily 11am–10pm; free).

New York–New York

Opposite the *MGM Grand*, **New York–New York** is an exuberantly meticulous recreation of the Big Apple. This miniature Manhattan boasts a skyline featuring twelve separate skyscrapers and is fronted, naturally, by the Statue of Liberty. The interior has some nice touches too, with bars clustered around its central rendition of Central Park at dusk. In one respect, it even surpasses New York itself: for $14 you can swoop around the whole thing at 65mph on the hair-raising Manhattan Express **roller coaster**.

Planet Hollywood

Planet Hollywood is a remodelled version of the former *Aladdin*, which hit the rocks in 2004. In keeping with the latest generation of casinos, it's all geared towards a young crowd, with a screaming loud decor it calls "Hollywood Hip". The mile-long **Miracle Mile Shops**, wrapped in a figure-eight around the casino and its theatre, is under different ownership and is looking quite a mess, having attracted some frankly tacky stores, diners and bars.

City Centre

The enormous **CityCenter** complex, unveiled in 2009 and readily accessible on foot or by tram from the *Monte Carlo* to the south and *Bellagio* to the north, is a bold attempt by MGM Resorts to reshape Las Vegas's urban landscape. The exciting new theme here is that there is no theme; CityCenter is supposedly the kind of project that might be built in any city. Whether it proves to be a disastrous blunder in the face of impending recession still remains to be seen. Its twin centrepieces are the huge **Aria** casino, where the rather dark but undeniably cutting-edge architecture is adorned with some stunning contemporary sculpture and the quirky **Crystals** shopping mall, a showpiece of playful design that's aimed at such high-end shoppers that it may well have difficulty surviving.

Paris

Paris was the 1999 handiwork of the same designers as *New York–New York*. With a half-size Eiffel Tower straddling the Arc de Triomphe and the Opera, it's all rather compressed, but the attention to detail is a joy. There's also a fine assortment of top-notch French restaurants. Elevators soar through the roof of the casino and up to the summit of the Eiffel Tower, for stunning views of the city, at their best after dark (daily 9.30am–midnight; $10 daytime, $15 evening).

Bellagio

Paris' Eiffel Tower was cheekily positioned to enjoy a perfect prospect of **Bellagio,** opposite. Unveiled by Steve Wynn in 1998 as his attempt to build the best hotel in world history, *Bellagio* is undeniably a breathtaking achievement, even if, unlike the original town on Lake Como, it's not in Italy, but Las Vegas and it's stuffed full of slot machines. The main hotel block, a stately curve of blue and cream pastels, stands aloof from the Strip behind an eight-acre artificial lake in which submerged fountains erupt every half-hour in Busby-Berkeley water-ballets, choreographed with booming music and coloured lights.

Otherwise, *Bellagio*'s proudest boast is its opulent Conservatory, where a network of flowerbeds beneath a Belle Époque canopy of copper-framed glass is replanted every few weeks with gorgeous and hugely imaginative seasonal displays.

Caesars Palace

Despite approaching its fiftieth birthday – making it virtually prehistoric by Las Vegas standards – **Caesars Palace** remains the most famous name in the casino business. In the last few years, it has comprehensively overhauled itself to meet the challenge of upstart rivals and with its statues, Roman centurions and grand marble staircases it's once again a must-see for every visitor. Above the stores and restaurants of the Forum, the blue-domed ceiling dims and glows as it endlessly cycles from dawn to dusk and back again. The mall itself is now three storeys tall, but gloriously kitsch "living statues" still populate its various fountains.

The Mirage and TI

Night-time crowds jostle for space outside the glittering **Mirage**, beyond *Caesars*, to watch the recently rebuilt volcano that erupts every fifteen minutes, spewing water and fire into the lagoon below. Although veteran magicians Siegfried and Roy were finally driven into retirement by Roy's near-fatal accident in 2003, their trademark white tigers can still be seen in the **Secret Garden & Dolphin Habitat** (Mon–Fri 11am–6.30pm, Sat & Sun 10am–6.30pm; $15).

Next door, a pirate galleon and a British frigate, crewed by actors, continue to do noisy battle outside **TI**, the former *Treasure Island*, though ludicrously enough the sailors these days are no longer gnarled buccaneers but the scantily-clad **Sirens of TI** (every 90min after dark; free). *Treasure Island* used to be pirate-themed throughout, but having abandoned all thoughts of appealing to children, its lovingly crafted fripperies have been stripped away.

The Venetian and the Palazzo

Across the Strip from *TI*, the facade of the **Venetian** includes loving facsimiles of six major Venice buildings, as well as the Rialto Bridge and the Bridge of Sighs. Once inside, climb a staircase topped by vivid frescoes to reach the ludicrous **Grand Canal**. This luxury shopping mall, complete with gondolas and singing gondoliers ($15 a ride), is quintessential Las Vegas and as such utterly irresistible – it's *upstairs*, for God's sake. The *Venetian* also holds an overpriced branch of **Madame Tussaud's** waxwork museum (daily 10am–10pm; $25), while the adjoining **Palazzo**, entered either via the Grand Canal or directly from the Strip, is officially a resort in its own right, but just feels like a big, bland mall.

Wynn Las Vegas

Wynn Las Vegas, next door to the *Venetian*, was built by Steve Wynn on the site of the vanished *Desert Inn*, using all the fortune he accrued by building and selling the *Mirage* and *Bellagio*. In a nutshell, it's *Bellagio* reimagined for a younger, hipper and even richer crowd, with a shift away from European elegance in favour of contemporary Asian design. The resort is partly obscured behind an artificial tree-covered mountain; once you find your way inside, you find that's the backdrop for the enormous **Lake of Dreams**, an "environmental theatre" in which ethereal sculpted figures emerge from a large expanse of water, in front of a massive waterfall that continually changes colour.

The interior of *Wynn Las Vegas* is a riot of colour, with spectacular patterns and motifs sprawling all over carpets, mosaics and tiles and a central atrium filled with sparkling trees and dazzling flowers. It has all proved profitable enough to be complemented by the similar **Encore**, clad in the same glossy "Wynn Bronze" and filled with dazzling red furnishings.

The North Strip: Circus Circus and the Stratosphere

North of *Wynn Las Vegas*, the long-neglected northern segment of the Strip was, until the recession hit, widely expected to be the city's next growth area. While the veteran *New Frontier* and *Stardust* casinos have been demolished, the promised *Echelon* and *Fontainebleau* mega-resorts seem unlikely to materialize and it's all looking more derelict than ever.

Instead, the main landmarks are the family-oriented **Circus Circus**, which holds an indoor theme park, the **Adventuredome** (Mon–Thurs 11am–6pm, Fri & Sat 10am–midnight, Sun 10am–9pm; all-day pass adults $25, kids $15; Ⓦadventuredome.com) and the **Stratosphere**, at 1149ft the tallest building west of the Mississippi. The outdoor deck near its summit offers amazing panoramas across the city ($16), while three wonderfully demented thrill rides can take you even closer to heaven (Sun–Thurs 11am–1am, Fri & Sat 11am–2am; $36 all-day rides). Insanity and X-Scream dangle riders over the edge, strapped into individual seats and in a precarious gondola respectively; and the terrifying Big Shot is an open-air couch that shunts to the top of an additional 160-foot spire, then free-falls down again. In addition, the **SkyJump**, unveiled in 2010, is a "controlled free-fall", more like a zip line than a bungee jump, in which you simply jump off the top and plummet 855 feet (same hours; $100; minimum age 14).

Downtown

As the Strip has evolved from strength to strength, **downtown** Las Vegas, the city's original core, has been neglected. Long known as "Glitter Gulch", it never really was a "downtown" in the conventional sense, having never held many stores or businesses apart from its few compact blocks of lower-key casinos. It has, however, repeatedly attempted to revive itself. In the **Fremont Street Experience**, five entire blocks of its central street have been roofed over to form a "Celestial Vault", studded with over twelve million LED nodules to create a screen that's illuminated in dazzling nightly displays (hourly, sunset–midnight; free).

Eating

With the casinos competing to attract culinary superstars from all over the country, many tourists now come to Las Vegas specifically to sample the best restaurants in the US. The choice on the Strip is overwhelming and every hotel seems to have at least one good restaurant.

Buffets

The Buffet at Aria *Aria*, 3730 Las Vegas Blvd S ⓣ702/590-7111. CityCenter's only buffet, upstairs at *Aria*, is among the best in town. Each cuisine is represented by just a couple of dishes, but they're invariably good and the Indian station, with its fresh-baked naan bread and tasty curries, is exceptional. Breakfast $15; lunch Mon–Fri $20; Sat & Sun champagne brunch 7am–4pm, $29; dinner Sun–Thurs $28, Fri & Sat $36.

The Buffet at Wynn *Wynn Las Vegas*, 3131 Las Vegas Blvd S ⓣ702/770-7000. The best buffet food on the Strip. It's the sheer variety that makes it exceptional, with traditional buffet staples like Alaskan crab legs and peeled shrimp plus unusual specials like baba ganoush, clams in black bean sauce or a salad of pears, walnuts, grapes and blue cheese. Breakfast $20; lunch Mon–Fri $23; brunch Sat & Sun $32; dinner Sun–Thurs $35, Fri & Sat $39.

Studio B Buffet *M Resort*, 12300 Las Vegas Blvd S ⓣ702/797-1000. New off-Strip buffet, ten miles south of *Mandalay Bay* along Las Vegas Blvd, that has created a real sensation. Selections along the all but endless serving counter range from Thai curries and Asian barbecued pork to paella, stuffed vine leaves and all-American mac and cheese and it's all fresh and flavourful. Rates include unlimited wine and beer. Lunch $15; dinner Mon–Thurs $23; Seafood buffet Fri eve and all day Sat & Sun, $30.

Todai Seafood Buffet Miracle Mile Shops, *Planet Hollywood*, 3663 Las Vegas Blvd S ⓣ702/892-0021. *Todai* specializes in magnificent all-you-can-eat Japanese spreads. It's seafood heaven, with unlimited sushi and sashimi plus hot entrees, noodles and barbecued and teriyaki meats. Lunch Mon–Fri $20, Sat & Sun $22; dinner Mon–Thurs $30, Fri–Sun $32.

Le Village Buffet *Paris*, 3655 Las Vegas Blvd S ⓣ702/946-7000. Superb French cuisine, with great seafood, succulent roast chicken and super-fresh vegetables. The setting is a little cramped, squeezed into a very Disney-esque French village, but the food is *magnifique*. Breakfast is $16, lunch $18, dinner and weekend brunch $25.

Restaurants

Beijing Noodle No. 9 *Caesars Palace*, 3570 Las Vegas Blvd S ⓣ877/346-4642. Supposedly casual noodle shop, with delightful, dizzyingly white decor, fabulously dressed staff and great Chinese food. "Single" portions at around $20 are very substantial.

Bouchon Venezia Tower, *The Venetian*, 3355 Las Vegas Blvd S ⓣ702/414-6200. Despite its sky-high reputation and exclusive setting, Thomas Keller's spacious French bistro is friendly and affordable. A delicious French onion soup costs $10 and a roast chicken with onions and lentils costs $29.50. Breakfast is a Francophile's dream of croissants, pastries, yogurt and coffee and sitting outside on the huge piazza is a real joy. Breakfast and dinner daily.

Dos Caminos Mexican Kitchen *The Palazzo*, 3355 Las Vegas Blvd S ⓣ702/577-9600. For flair as well as food, this huge, beautifully designed Mexican restaurant is highly recommended, from the deliciously creamy guacamole onwards. Dinner might start with roasted plantain empanada ($10) followed by avocado-leaf-crusted big-eye tuna ($25); at weekends, lunch is replaced by a well-priced, relaxed brunch. Lunch and dinner daily.

Il Fornaio *New York–New York*, 3790 Las Vegas Blvd S ⓣ702/650-6500. The nicest place to enjoy the atmosphere of the casino, this rural-Italian restaurant is a real joy. Choose from pizzas ($13–16), or entrees like seafood linguini ($24) or rotisserie chicken ($20). Delicious olive breads, pastries and espresso coffees are also sold in a separate deli nearby.

Julian Serrano *Aria*, 3730 Las Vegas Blvd S ⓣ877/230-2742. Superb and very stylish tapas restaurant, where almost everything comes from different regions of Spain. It sounds inexpensive, at $8–14 per plate, but dishes like the balls of cocoa butter filled with chilled gazpacho are so delicious you can quickly eat $100 worth. Lunch and dinner daily.

Mon Ami Gabi *Paris*, 3655 Las Vegas Blvd S ⓣ702/944-4224. The first and the finest casino restaurant to offer open-air seating right on the Strip has the feel of a proper French pavement bistro. At lunch, try the gloriously authentic onion soup ($9), the mussels ($11) or the thin-cut steak frites ($24). Dinner features more expensive steak cuts and fish entrees. Lunch and dinner daily.

Silk Road *Vdara*, 2600 W Harmon Ave ⓣ702/590-2800. Daily 7am–2pm. This beautiful, futuristic space is only open in daylight hours, so it's always seen at its best. Set breakfasts and lunches cost just over $20; both food and setting are so exquisite it's worth every cent. Breakfast and lunch daily.

Bars and clubs

All the casinos hold plenty of bars, but if you want a drink, there's no need to look for one; instead, a tray-toting waitress will come and find you. The old-fashioned **Las Vegas lounge** has returned in force, whether knowingly retro-styled for twenty-something rockers, glammed up as an "ultra-lounge" or lovingly recreated for older visitors looking to recapture the decadent flavour of the Rat-Pack era. The success of **nightclubs** at hipper casinos like the *Hard Rock* and *Mandalay Bay* has prompted all their major rivals to follow suit, often with spectacular results; the latest trend is for open-air "beach" or at least pool clubs. Be warned that prices can be very, very high; ordering bottle service to a club table can cost $500 or more.

The Beatles Revolution Lounge *Mirage*, 3400 Las Vegas Blvd S ⓣ702-692-8300, ⓦwww.thebeatlesrevolutionlounge.com. Once you get past the somewhat silly claim that this ultra-lounge truly reflects an artistic collaboration between the Beatles and the Cirque du Soleil, you can enjoy the psychedelic light show and fab 1960's decor. DJ sets most nights, some live indie bands. Closed Tues.

Horse-a-Round Bar *Circus Circus*, 2880 Las Vegas Blvd S ⓣ702/734-0410. Tiny but truly bizarre, this perfect replica of a children's merry-go-round overlooks the clowns and acrobats of *Circus Circus*'s Midway. Fri & Sat 4.30pm–midnight.

House of Blues *Mandalay Bay*, 3950 Las Vegas Blvd S ⓣ702/632-7600, ⓦwww.hob.com. The Strip's premier live-music venue, the voodoo-tinged, folk-art-decorated *House of Blues* has a definite, but not exclusive, emphasis toward blues, R&B and the like. Typical prices range from $35 up to $100 for stars like Aretha Franklin.

Liquidity *Luxor*, 3900 Las Vegas Blvd S ⓣ702/262-4591. Very blue, very modern, water-themed ultra-lounge in the centre of *Luxor*, with waterfalls both real and virtual cascading from the ceiling.

Nine Fine Irishmen *New York–New York*, 3790 Las Vegas Blvd S ⓣ702/740-6463. Wood-panelled pub, shipped from Ireland and featuring Irish musicians, singers and dancers nightly.

Tao *The Venetian*, 3355 Las Vegas Blvd S ⓣ702/388-8588, ⓦwww.taolasvegas.com. Attached to by far the highest grossing independent restaurant in the US, this opulent, very Asian-influenced nightclub is filled with glowing golden Buddhas and big-spending beautiful people; it attracts very big names indeed.Thurs–Sat 10pm–5am. Cover Thurs & Fri $20, Sat $30.

Entertainment

In the early 1960s, when Frank Sinatra's Rat Pack were shooting *Ocean's 11* during the day then singing the night away at the *Sands*, the city could claim to be the capital of the international entertainment industry. After that, the world moved on, but in the last few years, Las Vegas has come back into its own. Almost all the cheesy, feathers-and-tassels revues have closed down, to be replaced by surprisingly stimulating, postmodern shows by the likes of the **Cirque du Soleil** – who currently run seven only-in-Vegas shows in purpose-built theatres in the city, making this the worldwide epicentre of their operations – and the **Blue Man Group**. A new generation of big-name stars are taking up the kind of long-term residencies we all thought had vanished with Elvis. **Cher**, **Bette Midler**, **Celine Dion** and **Elton John** at *Caesars*' huge Colosseum have been the most conspicuous, but more are expected to follow.

Blue Man Group *The Venetian*, 3355 Las Vegas Blvd S ⓣ1-866/641-7469, ⓦwww.blueman.com. Enter a strange and unfamiliar world, in which three bald, blue performance artists sell out a 1750-seat theatre every night. Don't expect stars or a plot or even words; instead, you get synchronized eating of breakfast cereal and live endoscopies on audience members, plus deafening, exhilarating drumming from the Men themselves and some stunning special effects. Daily 7pm & 10pm. $65–149.

Kà *MGM Grand*, 3799 Las Vegas Blvd S ⓣ702/769-9999, ⓦwww.ka.com. Cirque du Soleil's *Kà* is an absolute must-see. The most expensive theatrical production ever staged, it boasts an extraordinary set; the stage floor not only rises, but can swivel and pivot in every direction. Although *Kà* is basically a succession of breathtaking stunts, with extraordinary puppetry and sumptuous costumes, its complex plot, about two Asian twins separated by enemy kidnappers, allows scope for darkness and emotional impact alongside the usual whimsy. Tues–Sat 7pm & 9:30pm. $69–150.

Jubilee *Bally's*, 3645 Las Vegas Blvd S ⓣ877/374-7469. If you've never been to a Las Vegas show, *Jubilee* is probably what you think they're all like. In fact, it's the last survivor of the camp old tits'n'tassels tradition, a lumbering great thing that after its first few jaw-dropping moments – just how bad is this going to be? – really grows on you. Roman soldiers in leather codpieces cavort with Arabian-Nights maidens across the stage, thirty dancing showgirls quick-change from turquoise pantsuits to huge ostrich-feather extravaganzas and for a finale they even raise the *Titanic*. Daily except Fri 7.30pm & 10.30pm (topless); $73–93.

Love *The Mirage*, 3400 Las Vegas Blvd S ⓣ702/792-7777, ⓦwww.cirquedusoleil.com. The Cirque du Soleil do their stuff to a remixed Beatles soundtrack, in an auditorium that's intimate at some moments and exuberantly all-embracing at others. Nostalgic and visionary in equal measure, *Love* celebrates the Beatles' achievement while avoiding anything too literal. The costumes, lighting and staging are all magnificent and some set-pieces are astonishing. When all's said and done, it's a dance show, but don't let that put you off. Daily except Tues & Wed 7pm & 9.30pm. $94–150.

Mystère *TI*, 3300 Las Vegas Blvd S ⓣ702/894-7722, ⓦwww.cirquedusoleil.com. Cirque du Soleil's original showcase remains as captivating as ever, with tumblers, acrobats, trapeze artists, pole climbers, clowns and strongmen, but no animals apart from fantastic costumed apparitions. Sat–Wed 7pm & 9.30pm. $60–109.

O *Bellagio*, 3600 Las Vegas Blvd S ⓣ702/796-9999, ⓦwww.cirquedusoleil.com. From the synchronized swimmers onward, the Cirque du Soleil display their magnificent skills to maximum advantage. Any part of the stage at any time may be submerged in water – one moment a performer walks across a particular spot, the next someone may dive headfirst into it from the high wire. Wed–Sun 7.30pm & 10pm. $94–150.

Terry Fator & His Cast Of Thousands *The Mirage*, 3400 Las Vegas Blvd S ⓣ702/792-7777. If you saw Terry Fator win *America's Got Talent* in 2007, you'll know what to expect of this amazing ventriloquist impressionist. If you didn't, you're in for a huge and very enjoyable surprise. The man is quite extraordinary; while manipulating animal puppets, he delivers note-perfect imitations of anyone from Marvin Gaye and Roy Orbison to Gary Numan and Gnarls Barkley – without moving his lips. And even if his humor is hardly cutting-edge, at least it's funny. Tues–Sat 7.30pm. $59–129.

Lake Mead and the Hoover Dam

The vast reservoir thirty miles southeast of the city, **LAKE MEAD**, was created by the construction of the Hoover Dam. A bizarre spectacle, its blue waters a vivid counterpoint to the surrounding desert, it gets excruciatingly crowded all year round. Though the Lake Mead National Recreation Area straddles the border between Nevada and Arizona, the best views come from the Nevada side. For details on how to sail, scuba-dive, waterski or fish from the marinas along the five-hundred-mile shoreline, call in at the Alan Bible **visitor centre** (daily 8.30am–4.30pm; ⓣ702/293-8990, ⓦwww.nps.gov/lame), four miles northeast of Boulder City on US-93.

Eight miles on, US-93 reaches the **Hoover Dam** itself, completed in 1935. Designed to block the Colorado River and provide low-cost electricity for the Southwest, it's among the tallest dams ever built (760ft high) and used enough concrete to build a two-lane highway from the West Coast to New York. Three levels of visit are possible; you can simply explore the **Hoover Dam Visitor Centre** (daily April–Sept 8.30am–5.45pm, Oct–March 9.15am–4.15pm) for $8, or take a half-hour ($11) or two-hour **guided tour** ($30).

Crossing Nevada

The bulk of Nevada is made up of dry plains, sliced by knife-edge volcanic mountain ranges. In the so-called **Great Basin**, where the rivers and streams have no outlet to the ocean, the land has an eerie beauty. The main cross-state route, **I-80**, shoots from Salt Lake City to Reno, skirting dozens of bizarrely named small towns packed with casinos, bars, brothels, motels and little else. The other main route, **US-50**, has a reputation as the loneliest highway in America. Older and slower, it follows much the same route as the Pony Express of the 1860s, but many towns have faded away altogether.

Great Basin National Park

Just across the border from Utah, **Great Basin National Park** encapsulates the scenery of the Nevada desert, from angular peaks to high mountain meadows cut by fast-flowing streams. Guided tours from the **Lehman Caves visitor centre** (daily: summer 8.30am–4pm; winter 9.30am–3pm; ⓣ775/234-7331, ⓦwww.nps.gov/grba), five miles west of tiny **Baker**, explore limestone caves that are densely packed with intriguing formations (1hr $8, 1hr 30min $10). Beyond the caves, a twelve-mile road climbs the east flank of the bald, usually snowcapped **Wheeler Peak**, where trails lead past alpine lakes and through a grove of gnarled, ancient bristlecone pines to the 13,063ft summit. Off-track cross-country skiing is excellent in winter.

Burning Man

Nevada's legendary **Burning Man Festival** is celebrated in a temporary, vehicle-free community known as **Black Rock City**, way out in the Black Rock Desert, twelve miles north of tiny Gerlach, which is itself a hundred miles north of Reno. It takes place at the end of August each year, in the week leading up to Labor Day. That's a very, very hot time to be out in the Nevada desert, particularly if, like approaching half of the fifty thousand revellers, you're completely naked.

The festival takes on a different theme each year, always with a strong emphasis on spontaneity and mass participation. An exhilarating range of performances, happenings and art installations culminates in the burning of a giant human effigy on the final Saturday. After that, in theory at least, Black Rock City simply disappears without trace.

For full information and the latest ticket prices, which start at $210 for the week, access Ⓦwww.burningman.com. All visitors must buy tickets in advance; you can't pay at the gate. Only those who can prove total self-sufficiency are admitted; that means you have to bring all your water, food and shelter. The site holds no public showers or pools and its economy is almost entirely based on barter. No money can change hands, with the single exception of the sale of coffee and ice.

The nearest real town, **ELY**, an hour's drive away, has two worthwhile museums – the entertaining **Nevada Northern Railway Museum** (Mon & Wed–Sat 8am–5pm, Sun 8am–4pm; $4; Ⓦnevadanorthernrailway.net), which offers $24 rides on a restored steam train and the **County Museum** (daily 9am–4pm; free) – as well as a dozen **motels**, including the *Bristlecone*, 700 Avenue I (Ⓣ775/289-8838, Ⓦbristleconemotelelynv.com; ❸), plus a handful of casinos and restaurants.

Elko

ELKO, the self-proclaimed last real cowtown in the West, straggles alongside I-80 a hundred miles west of Utah. Amid huge open cattle ranges, it's a fitting home for January's annual **Cowboy Poetry Gathering** (Ⓦwww.westernfolklife.org), a get-together to celebrate folk culture and keep alive the traditions and tales of the Wild West.

This area having been extensively settled by Basque shepherds in the nineteenth century, each Fourth of July weekend sees the 72-hour **National Basque Festival** (Ⓦwww.elkobasque.com), in which hulking men throw huge logs at each other amid a whole lot of carousing and downing of platefuls of Basque food. Northern Spanish food is available year-round in **restaurants** like the *Star Hotel*, two blocks south of the main drag at 246 Silver St (Ⓣ775/753-8696), while the many **motels** include the *Thunderbird*, 345 Idaho St (Ⓣ775/738-7115, Ⓦwww.thunderbirdmotelelko.com; ❸).

Reno and around

The "biggest little city in the world", **RENO**, on I-80 near the California border, is a somewhat downmarket version of Las Vegas, with miles of gleaming slot machines and poker tables, along with tacky wedding chapels and quickie divorce courts. While the town itself may not be much to look at, its setting – at the foot of the snowcapped **Sierra Nevada**, with the Truckee River winding through the centre – is superb. The **casinos** are concentrated downtown, along Virginia Street on either side of the railroad tracks.

Practicalities

Reno's **Cannon International Airport** is a couple of miles southeast of downtown. Greyhound **buses** arrive at 155 Stevenson St, while daily Amtrak **trains** between San Francisco and Salt Lake City call at 280 N Centre St downtown.

All the big casinos offer **accommodation** – rates double at weekends – as well as all-you-can-eat **buffets**. The best are the *Atlantis*, 3800 S Virginia St (ⓣ775/825-4700 or 1-800/723-6500, ⓦwww.atlantiscasino.com; ❷) and the *Silver Legacy*, 407 N Virginia St (ⓣ775/325-7401 or 1-800/687-8733, ⓦwww.silverlegacyreno.com; ❷).

Carson City

US-395 heads south from Reno along the jagged spires of the **High Sierra**, en route to **Death Valley**. After just thirty miles, state capital **CARSON CITY** – named after frontier explorer Kit Carson in 1858 – holds a number of elegant buildings and a handful of world-weary casinos. The excellent **Nevada State Museum**, 600 N Carson St (Wed–Sat 8.30am–4.30pm; $8), covers the geology and natural history of the Great Basin.

Bliss Bungalow is a luxurious **B&B** in a restored Arts and Crafts house, downtown at 408 W Robinson St (ⓣ775/883-6129, ⓦwww.blissbungalow.com; ❹), while *Hardman House* at 917 N Carson St (ⓣ775/882-7744; ❹) is an attractive, well-priced **hotel**.

Virginia City

Much of the wealth on which Carson City – and indeed San Francisco – was built came from the silver mines of the **Comstock Lode**, a solid seam of pure silver discovered in 1859 beneath Mount Hamilton, fourteen miles northeast of Carson City. Along with his brother, the acting Secretary to the Governor of the Nevada Territory, a young writer named Samuel Clemens made his way to raucous **VIRGINIA CITY**, which grew up on the steep slopes above the mines. As **Mark Twain**, he published his descriptions of the wild life of the mining camp in the hilarious *Roughing It*. There's not much to Virginia City nowadays, as all the old storefronts have been taken over by hot-dog vendors and tacky souvenir stands, but the surrounding arid mountains still feel remote and undisturbed.

13

California

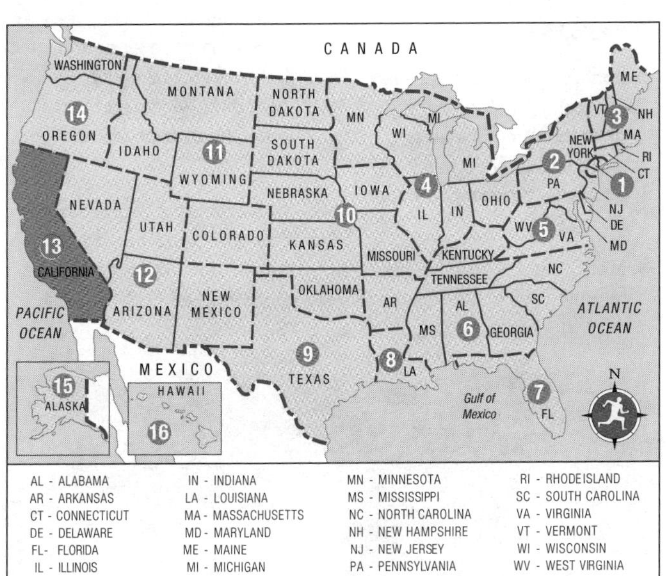

CHAPTER 13 Highlights

✱ **San Diego Zoo** About as humane and "natural" as a zoo can get, with a vast collection of rare species. See p.844

✱ **Disney Hall** LA's foremost example of modern sculpture – which also happens to be a terrific symphony hall. See p.856

✱ **Joshua Tree National Park** The eerily twisted "arms" of Joshua trees beckon visitors to explore this long-abandoned mining country. See p.879

✱ **Mono Lake** A strange and remote sight that's well worth the trip – prime birdwatching territory amid blue waters and gnarled tufa columns. See p.884

✱ **Yosemite National Park** Giant sequoias, towering waterfalls, the sheer face of Half Dome – your eyes will hardly get a rest. See p.889

✱ **Highway 1** A thrilling, circuitous drive along the US's West Coast, with pounding Pacific surf and dramatic cliffside vistas. See p.897

✱ **Alcatraz** Eerie, legendary one-time maximum-security prison stuck out on "the Rock" in San Francisco Bay. See p.912

▲ Joshua Tree National Park

13

California

Publicized and idealized all over the world, **CALIFORNIA** has a formidable reputation as a terrestrial paradise of sun, sand and surf, added to fast-paced, glitzy cities, primeval old-growth forests and vast stretches of deserts. Despite its great appeal, though, the state also lies under the constant threat of the **Big One** – a massive earthquake of unimaginable destruction – along with the floods, fires, droughts and other disasters. While it's been the source of some of the country's most **progressive movements**, from the protests of the Sixties to modern environmentalist, civil rights and various reform activities, its **economy** has been sputtering in recent years, with the possibility of state bankruptcy looming ever larger, thanks to an antiquated tax system. Nonetheless, the state is crucial to the American economy as a whole, whether in film, music, finance, shipping or the hard-hit real-estate sector.

California is far too large to be fully explored in a single trip – much will depend on what you're looking for. **Los Angeles** is far and away the biggest and most stimulating city: a maddening collection of freeways, beaches, suburbs and extreme lifestyles, and to many minds the polar opposite of New York City. To the south, the more conservative metropolis of **San Diego** has broad, welcoming beaches and a renowned zoo, while further inland, the **deserts**, most notably **Death Valley**, make up a barren and inhospitable landscape of volcanic craters and saltpans that in summer becomes the hottest place on earth. Heading north, the **central coast** is a gorgeous run that takes in lively small towns such as **Santa Barbara** and **Santa Cruz**.

California's second city, **San Francisco**, is a European-styled jewel whose wooden Victorian houses and steep hills make it one of the world's most distinctive and appealing cities. To the east, excellent national parks include **Yosemite**, where waterfalls cascade into a sheer glacial valley, and **Sequoia/Kings Canyon** with its gigantic trees, as well as the ghost towns of the **Gold Country**. North of San Francisco the countryside becomes wilder, wetter and greener, peppered with volcanic tablelands and verdant mountains.

The **climate** in **southern California** features seemingly endless days of sunshine and warm, dry nights, with occasional bouts of winter flooding. **Coastal** mornings can be hazy or overcast, especially in May and June; in the Bay Area around San Francisco it can be chilly all year, and fog rolls in to spoil many a sunny day. Much more so than in the south, winter in **northern California** can bring rain for weeks on end. Most hiking trails in the **mountains** are blocked between October and June by the snow that keeps California's ski slopes among the busiest in the nation.

Some history

Spaniard **Juan Cabrillo** first sighted San Diego harbour in 1542, naming it **California** after an imaginary island inhabited by Amazons, from a Spanish

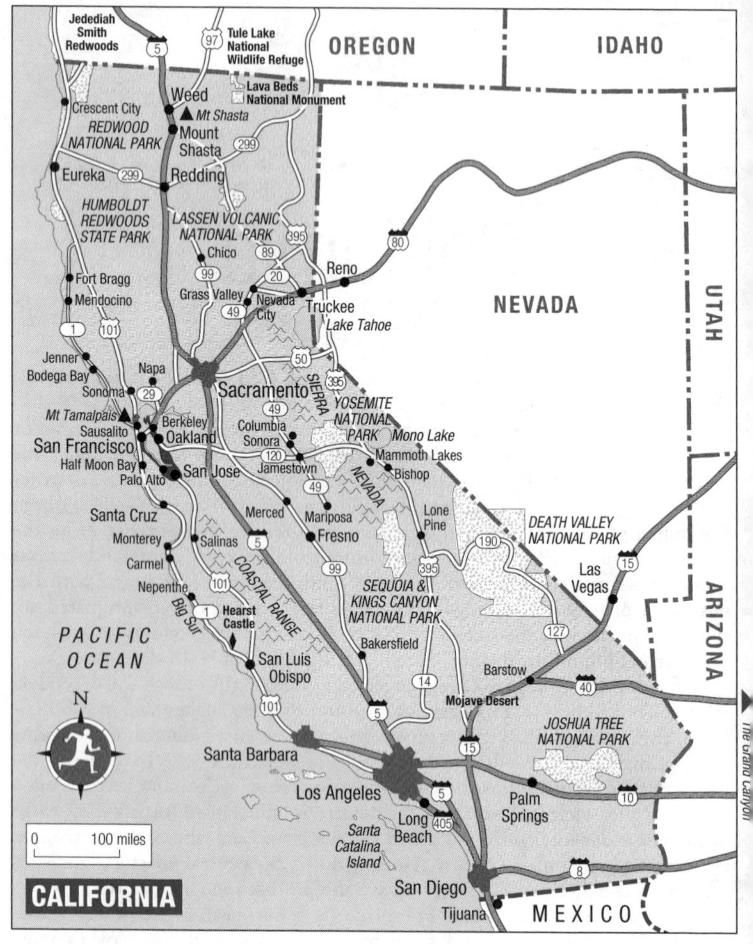

The Grand Canyon

novel. **Sir Francis Drake** landed near Point Reyes, north of San Francisco, in 1579, where the "white bancks and cliffes" reminded him of Dover, and in 1602 **Sebastián Vizcáino** bestowed most of the place names that still survive; his exaggerated description of **Monterey** as a perfect harbour led later colonizers to make it the region's military and administrative centre. The Spanish occupation began in earnest in 1769, combining military rule with **missionary** zeal. Father **Junípero Serra** first established a small mission and *presidio* (fort) at San Diego, and by 1804 a chain of 21 missions, each a long day's walk from the next along the dirt path of *El Camino Real* (The Royal Road), ran from San Diego to San Francisco. Native Americans were either forcibly converted into Catholicism or executed, with disease killing off those who managed to survive the Spanish onslaught.

Mexico gained its independence in 1821, taking control of California, but **Americans** were already starting to arrive, despite the immense difficulty of getting to the Mexican state – three months by sea or four months by covered wagon. The growing belief that it was the **Manifest Destiny** of the United States to cover the continent from coast to coast, evident in the imperialist policies of President James K. Polk, soon led to the brief **Mexican–American War**. By January 1847 the Americans controlled the entire West Coast.

A mere nine days before the signing of the treaty that ended the war, flakes of **gold** were discovered in the Sierra Nevada, leading to a rush of prospectors from all parts of the world and California's 1850 entry into the US as the **31st state**. It took just fifteen years to pick the land clean of visible gold, and the **transcontinental railroad** was completed in 1869, linking the gold fields to the rest of the US. Due to cut-rate rail prices and the lure of a dry, toasty climate and bountiful citrus groves, hordes of newcomers came from the Great Plains to Southern California and helped make Los Angeles the state's biggest city. Thanks to this migration, along with periodic real-estate booms and the rise of the **film industry**, California became the nation's fastest-growing state. Heavy industry followed during **World War II**, in the form of shipyards and areoplane factories.

As home to the **Beats** in the 1950s and the **hippies** in the 1960s, California was at the leading edge of cultural change. The Vietnam-era protests ended with the abolition of the draft, followed by the rise of the indulgent, cocained-fuelled "Me Generation" of the 1970s. The economic counterpart of this shift also developed when **Proposition 13**, in 1978, augured a national trend to dramatically cut taxes at the cost of government solvency – and which is still crippling the state a third of a century later. The 1980s saw further right-wing gains, with a string of laissez-faire Republican governors, and the 1990s crash-landed in economic scandal, a depressed real-estate market, rising unemployment, gang violence and race riots in LA – compounded by **earthquakes**, **drought** and **flooding**.

Some of the glow has further come off the golden state in the twenty-first century, but countless new **migrants** continue to arrive – many from Latin America. One of these immigrants, Austrian **Arnold Schwarzenegger**, had the good fortune to become a well-paid action movie hero before taking his place as 38th California governor, and the misfortune to rule during the recent, severe economic recession, which helped weaken the state's economy and pop the unemployment rate above 12 percent. Nonetheless, despite its struggles in recovering from these trying times, the state continues to wear a brave face, and with reduced demand for goods and services, lower travel costs make California a very affordable and attractive option for vacationers – who are needed by the state tourism industry now more than ever.

Getting around California

As you might expect, a **car** is necessary for exploring much of California. A city such as Los Angeles couldn't exist without the automobile, and in any case driving down the coastal freeways in a sleek convertible is too fun to resist.

Amtrak **trains** link **San Diego** and **LA** (and up to San Luis Obispo), with a stop at Fullerton, southeast of central Los Angeles, for buses to Disneyland; they also run up the coast from LA, stopping at **Oakland** and **Emeryville**, the nearest stations to San Francisco with other routes continuing on to Sacramento and Seattle. Greyhound **buses** link all the main towns, too. Keep in mind that in some cases, depending on route, **flying** may be a better bet between the major cities.

If you plan to do any **long-distance cycling**, travelling from north to south can make all the difference – the wind blows this way in the summer, and the ocean side of the road offers the best views. Be careful if you cycle along the coast on Hwy-1: despite the stunning views, the highway has heavy traffic, tight curves and is prone to fog.

San Diego

Relatively free from smog and overbuilt freeways, **SAN DIEGO**, set around a gracefully curving bay, is the second most populous city in California – affluent and libertarian, but also easy-going and friendly. Although it was the site of the first mission in California, the city only really took off with the arrival of the Santa Fe Railroad in the 1880s, and has long been in the shadow of Los Angeles. However, during World War II the US Navy made San Diego its Pacific Command Center, and the military continues to dominate the local economy, alongside tourism. Understandably, the long white beaches, sunny weather and bronzed bodies give rise to the city's well-deserved nickname, "Sandy Ego".

Arrival, information and city transport

Amtrak **trains** on the Pacific Surfliner route between LA and San Diego use the Santa Fe Railroad Depot, 1050 Kettner Blvd, while the Greyhound **bus** terminal is six blocks east at Broadway and First Avenue. Lindbergh Field **airport** (also called San Diego International; ⓣ619/400-2400, ⓦwww.san.org) is only two miles from downtown, and is connected to it by bus #992, which also links to the railroad depot and stops for the San Diego Trolley (see below). By car, San Diego is two hours south via the I-5 freeway from central Los Angeles.

The **International Visitor Information Center** is downtown at 1040 W Broadway (daily 9am–4pm, summer until 5pm; ⓣ619/236-1212, ⓦwww.seeyouinsandiego.com). **Getting around** the downtown core without a car is comparatively easy, though travelling to outlying areas requires more planning. **Buses** (ⓦwww.transit511sd.com), charge typical one-way fares from $2.25–2.50, $5 for express routes and $5–10 for the most lengthy journeys into rural terrain; the exact fare is required when boarding. The **Transit Store**, at First and Broadway (Mon–Sat 9am–5pm; ⓣ619/234-1060), has detailed timetables and sells a **Day Tripper Transit Pass** for one- to four-day visits ($5–15). The passes apply also to the tram-like **San Diego Trolley**, which runs throughout the area (single tickets $2.50) and covers the sixteen miles from the Santa Fe Depot to the Mexican border-crossing at San Ysidro. North San Diego County is linked to downtown via a simple commuter light-rail system called **The Coaster**. Fares range from $5–6.50 (ⓣ760/966-6500, ⓦwww.gonctd.com). For **taxi** services, try Yellow Cab (ⓣ619/234-6161); for **bicycle** rentals, try Cheap Rentals, 3695 Mission Blvd, Mission Beach (ⓣ858/488-9070, ⓦwww.cheap-rentals.com).

Accommodation

Accommodation is plentiful throughout San Diego, with the highest prices near the downtown business core and in the more resort-oriented beach towns. The best-placed, though rather mall-like, **campground** is **Campland on the Bay**, 2211 Pacific Beach Drive (ⓣ1-800/422-9386, ⓦwww.campland.com), where a basic pitch starts at $60, with more elaborate resort-style digs running up to $400. For a more serene camping option, there's **San Elijo Beach State Park**, Rte-21 south of Cardiff-by-the-Sea ($35–55; ⓣ1-800/444-7275, ⓦwww.reserveamerica.com).

Hotels, motels and B&Bs

Bahia Resort 998 West Mission Bay Drive, Mission Bay ⓣ1-800/576-4229 or 858/488-0551, ⓦwww.bahiahotel.com. Beachside accommodation with expansive ocean views, watersport rentals, pool and jacuzzi. Rooms have wi-fi and fridges, and range from cosy but pleasant rooms in a palm-garden setting to pricier bayside suites ❼

Balboa Park Inn 3402 Park Blvd, Hillcrest ⓣ619/298-0823, ⓦwww.balboaparkinn.com. Spanish Colonial, gay-oriented B&B, within walking distance of Balboa Park and museums. Offers 26 romantic themed suites (with Parisian, Impressionist and jungle motifs, to name a few) with complimentary breakfast, microwaves and mini-fridges ❺–❻

Bed and Breakfast Inn at La Jolla 7753 Draper Ave ⓣ1-888/988-8481, ⓦwww.innlajolla.com. An elegant collection of fifteen themed rooms with copious antiques, tranquil gardens, great service and nice proximity to the beach and art museum ❽

Bristol 1055 First Ave, downtown ⓣ619/232-6141, ⓦwww.thebristolsandiego.com. Excellent value at this friendly boutique hotel with stylish modern decor and tasteful amenities, plus iPod docks, flat-screen TVs and wi-fi ❻

El Cordova 1351 Orange Ave, Coronado ⓣ1-800/229-2032, ⓦwww.elcordovahotel.com. One of the better deals in pricey Coronado, comprising Spanish Colonial buildings arranged around lovely gardens. There's a pool, and many rooms have kitchenettes. Large price spread, from cheap and ultra-basic units without a/c to grand suites. ❼

Horton Grand 311 Island Ave at 3rd Ave, downtown ⓣ619/544-1886 or 1-800/542-1886, ⓦwww.hortongrand.comd One of the more prominent and imposing San Diego hotels, with fireplaces in most of the rooms (some also have balconies), an on-site restaurant and piano bar. Somewhat minimal amenities for such a historic spot, though. ❼

Hotel del Coronado 1500 Orange Ave, Coronado ⓣ619/522-8000 or 1-800/468-3533, ⓦwww.hoteldel.com. The luxurious place that put Coronado on the map in 1888 and is still the area's major tourist sight (see p.844). The striking rooms and suites, expansive bay views and old-fashioned Victorian charm give the place much appeal. ❾

Park Manor Suites 525 Spruce St, near Balboa Park ⓣ1-800/874-2649, ⓦwww.parkmanorsuites.com. Stately old pile that's a hundred years old, now a tasteful hotel whose suites feature wi-fi access, kitchens and nice sitting areas with sofas. Continental breakfast included ❻

Solamar 435 6th Ave, downtown ⓣ619/531-8740, ⓦwww.hotelsolamar.com. Very tasteful and modern boutique hotel central to the Gaslamp District, whose rooms have wi-fi, flat-screen TVs, CD and DVD players. The site also offers spa and gym facilities, plus in-room yoga accessories. Suites with jetted tubs add to the hip appeal. ❼

Tower23 4551 Ocean Blvd, Pacific Beach ⓣ1-866/TOWER-23, ⓦwww.tower23hotel.com. Despite being named for a lifeguard tower, this is among the most chic of the local boutique hotels, offering clean modern designs in stylish rooms with flat-screen TVs, wi-fi and designer furnishings. The suites variously come with balconies, cabanas and whirlpool tubs. ❽

US Grant 326 Broadway, downtown ⓣ619/232-3121 or 1-800/237-5029, ⓦwww.usgrant.net. Downtown's poshest address since 1910, with a grand Neoclassical design, chandeliers, marble floors, and cosy but comfortable guest rooms and more capacious suites. The elegant ballrooms and swanky conference rooms are worth a peek. ❽

Hostels

Banana Bungalow 707 Reed Ave, Pacific Beach ⓣ858/273-3060 or 1-800/5-HOSTEL, ⓦwww.bananabungalowsandiego.com. Friendly, if scruffy place, with access to the beach, offering volleyball, BBQ cookouts and a lively atmosphere. Free breakfast, wi-fi and a communal kitchen are included. Take bus #30, then it's a five-minute walk. Dorm beds $20–25, private rooms. ❸–❺

HI-Pt Loma 3790 Udall St, Ocean Beach ⓣ619/223-4778, ⓦwww.sandiegohostels.org. A couple of miles back from the beach and offering free breakfast, personal lockers, patio and weekly bonfires. Well run and friendly, with dorms for $20–31 and private rooms. ❷–❸

HI-San Diego Downtown 521 Market St at 5th Ave, downtown ⓣ619/525-1531, ⓦwww.sandiegohostels.org. Handy for the Gaslamp District, with free breakfast and high-speed wi-fi access, plus a library, kitchen and various organized trips. Dorm beds $28–31, private doubles. ❷–❸

Ocean Beach International Backpacker Hostel 4961 Newport Ave, Ocean Beach ⓣ619/223-7873 or 1-800/339-7263, ⓦwww.californiahostel.com. Lively spot a block from the beach, offering barbecues, bike and surfboard rentals, airport transport and nightly movies. Dorm beds $16–24, with free wi-fi, sheets, showers and continental breakfast.

USA Hostels – San Diego 726 5th Ave, downtown ⓣ619/232-3100 or 1-800/438-8622, ⓦwww.usahostels.com/sandiego. Well-placed hostel on the edge of the Gaslamp District. Converted 1890s building, with six to eight beds per room, sheets and continental breakfast, for $28–31. Private rooms ❸. Free breakfast, free wi-fi and organized tours to Tijuana make this one of the city's best hostels.

The City

With its assertively libertarian vibe, San Diego embodies a work-hard, play-hard ethic, although it leans more towards the latter. Featuring an easily navigable downtown, scenic bay, 42 miles of beaches and plentiful parks and museums, the city is hard not to like from the moment you arrive.

Downtown San Diego

Loosely bordered by the curve of San Diego Bay and the I-5 freeway, **downtown** is, for those not headed straight to the beach, the inevitable nexus of San Diego and the best place to start a tour of the city. Various preservation and restoration projects have improved many of the older buildings, resulting in several pockets of stylish turn-of-the-century architecture. The tall Moorish archways of the **Santa Fe Railroad Depot**, at the western end of Broadway, built in 1915 for the Panama-California Exposition, still evoke a sense of grandeur, as the station continues to operate as a functional Amtrak depot. The depot is contiguous with the downtown branch of the **Museum of Contemporary Art**, or MCA San Diego, 1001 Kettner Blvd (Thurs–Tues 11am–5pm; $10; ⓣ858/454-3541, ⓦwww.mcasd.org), a fine first-stop for anyone interested in contemporary art with a California twist. Further east,

Broadway slices through the middle of downtown, at its most colourful between Fourth and Fifth avenues. Many visitors linger around the fountains on the square outside **Horton Plaza**, between First and Fourth avenues, south of Broadway (Mon–Sat 10am–9pm, Sun 11am–7pm; Ⓦwww.westfield.com/hortonplaza), a giant roofless mall of some 140 stores and, for better or worse, San Diego's de facto city centre. The complex's whimsical, colourful postmodern style, loaded with quasi-Art Deco and southwestern motifs, is inevitably a colossal tourist draw. A half-mile north of Broadway along India Street is the **Little Italy** district (Ⓦwww.littleitalysd.com), mostly worth visiting for its restaurants and occasional festivals such as the late-May Sicilian Festival (Ⓦwww.sicilianfesta.com) and mid-October Festa.

Gaslamp District

South of Broadway, a few blocks from Horton Plaza, lies the sixteen-block **Gaslamp District**, San Diego's original city centre, which later became a notorious red-light district, but is now filled with charming cafés, antique stores, art galleries and, of course, "gas lamps" – powered by electricity. A tad touristy it may be, but its late-nineteenth-century buildings are intriguing to examine, especially the grandiose **Louis Bank of Commerce**, 835 Fifth Ave, an eye-popping Victorian confection from 1888 replete with carved wooden and terracotta bay windows, a sheet-metal frieze across the front and a pair of squat, colourful little towers on top. This classic building is best approached – and the area's general history gleaned – during the two-hour **walking tour** (Sat 11am; $10; Ⓣ619/233-4692, Ⓦwww.gaslampquarter.org/tours) that begins from the small cobbled square at Fourth and Island avenues. The square is within the grounds of the **William Heath Davis House**, 410 Island Ave (Tues–Sat 10am–6pm, Sun 9am–3pm; $5), whose owner founded modern San Diego and in 1850 built this saltbox-styled home – copious with photographs, with each room commemorating a different historical period.

Nearer the waterline, the focus of San Diego sporting activity, especially at the weekend, is **Petco Park**, Seventh Avenue at Harbor Drive (tickets $10–63; Ⓣ619/795-5000, Ⓦsandiego.padres.mlb.com), which draws plenty of Padres baseball fans.

The bayfront

Along San Diego's curving, enjoyable **bayfront**, the pathway of the **Embarcadero** runs a mile or so along the bay, curling around to the western end of downtown; along this stretch, the expansive green lawn of **Embarcadero Marina Park South** provides some summertime amusement with its mainstream concerts. Beyond this, if you can't get enough of the US military on your TV set at home, clamber aboard for a tour of the **USS Midway**, 910 N Harbor Drive (daily 10am–5pm, last admission 4pm; $18; Ⓦwww.midway.org), which shows off its formidable collection of naval hardware and weapons to the public, along with flight simulators and various old-time planes. More vintage ships can be visited further north at the **Maritime Museum**, 1492 Harbor Drive (daily 9am–8pm; $12; Ⓦwww.sdmaritime.org), which has a collection of nine floating vessels that occasionally take to the seas, highlighted by the 1863 **Star of India**, the world's oldest iron sailing ship still afloat; the **Californian**, a modern replica of an 1847 cutter; the **HMS Surprise**, a replica of an eighteenth-century, 24-gun frigate; and an actual Soviet diesel submarine, the creaky old **B-39**.

Coronado

Across San Diego Bay from downtown, the isthmus of **Coronado** is a well-scrubbed resort community with a major naval station occupying its western end. It's reached by the majestically modern **Coronado Bay Bridge**, a curving

11,000ft span that's one of the area's signature images, or on the **San Diego Bay ferry** (daily 9am–10pm; $3.50 each way; ⓣ619/234-1111, ⓦwww.sdhe.com), which leaves Broadway Pier on the hour, returning on the half-hour. The town of Coronado grew up around the **Hotel del Coronado** (see p.841), a glorious Victorian whirl of turrets and towers erected as a health resort in 1888, and still best known as the spot where **Some Like It Hot** was filmed in 1958, posing as a Miami Beach hotel. A less grandiose place to explore Coronado's past is the **Coronado Museum of History and Art**, 1100 Orange Ave (Mon–Fri 9am–5pm, Sat & Sun 10am–5pm; $4; ⓦwww.coronadohistory.org), which chronicles the town's early pioneers and naval aviators, as well as its yachting and architecture. For a look at the historical importance of the various buildings in town, the museum offers hour-long **tours** (Wed 2pm, $10; reservations required).

Balboa Park and the San Diego Zoo

Northeast of downtown, sumptuous **Balboa Park** is one of the largest **museum enclaves** in the US, as well as a delight for its landscaping, traffic-free promenades, and stately Spanish Colonial-style buildings. The park is large but easy to get around **on foot** – if you get tired, there's always the free tram. The **Balboa Park Passport**, a week-long pass that allows one-time admission to all fourteen of the park's museums and its Japanese garden (plus the San Diego Zoo, for an extra $25), is available for $45 from the **visitor information centre** (daily 9.30am–4.30pm; ⓣ619/239-0512, ⓦwww.balboapark.org), inside the on-site House of Hospitality. Near the centre, the **Spreckels Organ Pavilion** (concerts Sun 2pm; free; ⓦwww.sosorgan.com), is worth a look as the home of one of the world's largest organs, with some 4500 pipes.

Most of the major museums flank El Prado, the pedestrian-oriented road that bisects the park. Highlights include the stirring collection of Russian icons and other Old World art at the **Timkin Museum of Art** (Tues–Sat 10am–4.30pm, Sun 1.30–4.30pm; closed Sept; free; ⓦwww.timkenmuseum.org); the **San Diego Museum of Art**'s (Tues–Sat 10am–5pm, Sun noon–5pm; $12; ⓦwww.sdmart.org) solid stock of European paintings, from the Renaissance to the nineteenth century, highlighted by Hals and Rembrandt; the anthropological exhibitions of the **Museum of Man** (daily 10am–4.30pm; $10; ⓦwww.museumofman.org), which may include replicas of huge Mayan stones, Native American artefacts and Egyptian relics; the child-oriented science-lite amusements and IMAX theatre of the **Reuben H. Fleet Science Center** (hours vary, often Mon–Thurs 9.30am–5pm, Fri & Sat 9.30am–8pm, Sun 9.30am–6pm; $10, kids $8.75, or $14.50 and $11.75 including an IMAX film; ⓦwww.rhfleet.org); the **Natural History Museum** (daily 10am–5pm; $16; ⓦwww.sdnhm.org) and its great collection of fossils, hands-on displays of minerals and exhibits on dinosaurs and crocodiles; and the classic motorcycles and cars of the **Automotive Museum** (daily 10am–5pm; $8; ⓦwww.sdautomuseum.org), among them a 1948 Tucker Torpedo – one of only fifty left.

Immediately north of the main museums, the enormous **San Diego Zoo** (daily mid-June to early Sept 9am–9pm; early Sept to mid-June 9am–5pm; ⓦwww.sandiegozoo.org) is one of the world's most renowned, with hundreds of different species, among them rare Chinese pheasants, Mhorr gazelles and a freakish two-headed corn snake. It's an enormous place, and you can easily spend a full day here, soaking in the major sections devoted to the likes of chimps and gorillas, panda and polar bears, lizards and lions, and African and Asian elephants. Regular **admission** ($37, kids $27) covers entry to the main zoo and children's zoo, plus a short bus tour and a return ticket on the Skyfari aerial tram. A $70 ticket (kids $50) also admits you to the San Diego Wild Animal Park near Escondido (hours vary, often daily 9am–4pm, summer closes 8pm; $37, $27 kids), a two-thousand-acre preserve for big cats, rhinos, giraffes, and the like, which roam about outside your car windows.

On the border of Balboa Park, **Hillcrest** is a lively and artsy area at the centre of the city's **gay community**. Go there either for something to eat – there's a selection of interesting cafés and restaurants around University and Fifth streets – or simply to stroll around the fine gathering of Victorian homes.

Old Town San Diego and Presidio Hill

In 1769, Spanish settlers chose **Presidio Hill** as the site of the first of California's missions. **Old Town San Diego**, reachable from downtown via the northbound Trolley, is now a state historical park and the site of several dozen original dwellings. These are generally open 10am to 5pm and have free admission, but most things in the park that aren't historical – shops and restaurants – open around 10am and close at 9–10pm. Highlights include **La Casa de Estudillo** on Mason Street, built by the commander of the **presidio**, José Maria de Estudillo, in 1827, one of the poshest of the original adobes. There's also a blacksmith's shop, stables with antique wagons and an early school and print shop. Details on the many structures here are available from the **visitor centre**, inside the Robinson-Rose House, near Taylor and Congress streets (daily 10am–5pm, free Old Town tours daily 11am & 2pm; Ⓦ www.oldtownsandiego.org).

The Spanish-style building now atop Presidio Hill is only a rough approximation of the original mission – moved in 1774 – but its **Junípero Serra Museum**, 2727 Presidio Dr (Sat & Sun 10am–5pm; $5), offers an intriguing examination of Junípero Serra, the padre who led the aggressive Spanish colonization and Catholic conversion of California. The **Mission San Diego de Alcalá** itself was relocated six miles north to 10818 San Diego Mission Rd (daily 9am–4.45pm; donation; Ⓦ www.missionsandiego.com), to be near a water source and fertile soils – and to be safer from attack. The present building is still a working parish church, with a small **museum**; among the craft objects and artefacts from the mission is the crucifix held by Serra at his death in 1834.

Ocean Beach and Point Loma

OCEAN BEACH, six miles northwest of downtown, is a fun and relaxed beach town whose quaint, old-time streets and shops have preserved some of their funky 1960s character, though ongoing development has worn away some of their ramshackle appeal. The two big hangouts include **Newport Street**, where backpackers slack around at snack bars, surf and skate rental shops, and **Voltaire Street**, which true to its name has a good range of independent-minded local businesses. There is often good surf, and the beach itself can be quite fun – especially on weekends, when the local party scene gets cranking. South from the pier rise the dramatic **Sunset Cliffs**, a prime spot for twilight vistas.

South of Ocean Beach, at the southern end of the hilly green peninsula of **Point Loma**, the **Cabrillo National Monument** (daily 9am–5pm; seven-day pass $5/car, pedestrians and cyclists $3; Ⓦ www.nps.gov/cabr) marks the spot where Juan Cabrillo and crew became the first Europeans to land in California, albeit briefly, in 1542. The startling views from this high spot, across San Diego Bay to downtown and down the coast to Mexico, easily repay a trip here. A platform atop the western cliffs of the park makes it easy to view the November to March **whale migration**, when scores of grey whales pass by en route to their breeding grounds off Baja California, Mexico. The nearby visitor centre (same as park hours) contains more information, and lies near the **Old Point Loma Lighthouse** (daily 9am–5pm; free), which offers tours that showcase replica Victorian furnishings and equipment from the 1880s.

Sea World, Mission Beach and Pacific Beach

North of Ocean Beach, **Mission Bay** is the site of San Diego's most popular tourist attraction: **SeaWorld** (hours vary, often mid-June to Labor Day 9am–dusk; rest of year 10am–dusk; $69, children $59; Ⓦwww.seaworld.com), part of a national chain of marine theme parks. For children it offers an undeniable, if very expensive, appeal. Along with various thrill rides, some of its spectacles include Shamu's SkySplash (orcas paired with music and fireworks); Forbidden Reef, stocked with moray eels and stingrays; the Wild Arctic, populated by walruses, beluga whales and polar bears; and the Shark Encounter, where sharks circle menacingly around visitors walking through a viewing tunnel.

The biggest-name public beaches in San Diego are **Mission Beach**, the peninsula that separates Mission Bay from the ocean, and its northern extension, **Pacific Beach** – nightlife central for coastal San Diego. Enjoy nursing a beer at one of the many beachfront bars, rollerblade or bike down **Ocean Front Walk**, the concrete boardwalk running the length of both beaches, or observe the toasty sands overrun with scantily clad beach babes and high-fiving surfer dudes. A mile north of Pacific Beach's Crystal Pier, **Tourmaline Surfing Park**, La Jolla Boulevard at Tourmaline Street, is reserved exclusively for the sport, as well as windsurfing – but no swimmers are allowed. If you don't have a board, a good alternative is a few miles north at **Windansea Beach**, a favourite surfing hotspot that's also fine for swimming and hiking alongside the oceanside rocks and reefs.

Near the southern end of Ocean Front Walk at 3146 Mission Blvd (hours vary, often Mon–Thurs 11am–8pm, Fri–Sun 11am–10pm; most rides $2–6, or full park pass for $20; Ⓦwww.belmontpark.com), once-derelict **Belmont Park** has been renovated with modern rides, though the two main attractions are both from 1925: the **Giant Dipper** roller coaster, one of the few of its era still around, and the **Plunge**, once the largest saltwater plunge in the world, and a regular film set for old-time Hollywood swim spectaculars.

La Jolla and farther north

A more pretentious air prevails in **La Jolla** (pronounced "La Hoya"), an elegant beach community just north. Stroll its immaculate, gallery-filled streets, fuel up on some California cuisine at one of the many street cafés, or visit the local site of the **Museum of Contemporary Art**, 700 Prospect St (Thurs–Tues 11am–5pm; $10; Ⓦwww.mcasd.org), which has a huge, regularly changing stock of paintings and sculptures from 1955 onwards, highlighted by California pop and minimalism. Nearby is the popular **La Jolla Cove**, much of it an ecological reserve whose clear waters make it perfect for snorkelling (if you can find a parking space).

Just up the road, architecture fans won't want to miss a chance to tour one of the citadels of high modernism in the US, the **Salk Institute for Biological Studies**, 10010 N Torrey Pines Rd (Mon–Fri 8.30am–5pm; free tours Mon–Fri noon; reserve two days ahead at Ⓣ858/453-4100 ext 1287, Ⓦwww.salk.edu), a collection of rigid geometric concrete blocks and walls featuring stark vistas that look out over the Pacific Ocean. Further north, the **Stephen Birch Aquarium and Museum**, 2300 Expedition Way (daily 9am–5pm; $12; Ⓦaquarium.ucsd.edu), has a wide range of highlights including the Hall of Fishes, a huge kelp forest home to countless sea creatures, and the Shark Reef, displaying a nice range of fearsome creatures.

Farther north, Torrey Pines Scenic Drive provides the main access (via a steep path) to **Black's Beach** (Ⓦwww.blacksbeach.com) – the region's premier clothing-optional beach and one of the best and most daunting surfing beaches in Southern California, known for its huge barrelling waves during big swells. The beach lies within the southern part of the **Torrey Pines State Preserve** (daily 8am–sunset; Ⓣ858/755-2063, Ⓦwww.torreypine.org), which protects the country's rarest species of pine, the Torrey Pine – one of two surviving stands. Thanks to salty conditions and stiff ocean breezes, the pines contort their ten-foot frames into a variety of tortured, twisted shapes.

Eating

Wherever you are in San Diego, you'll have few problems finding something good to **eat**. Everything from funky coffeeshops to stylish ethnic eateries are in copious supply here, with seafood at its best around the beaches and the Gaslamp District, and the latter also home to the greatest concentration of restaurants, of widely varying quality.

Berta's 3928 Twiggs St, Old Town Ⓣ619/295-2343. Solid south-of-the-border restaurant, offering well-priced, authentic cooking from all over Latin America. The affordable and savoury dishes include empanadas, seafood soups and paella.

Café 222 222 Island Ave, downtown Ⓣ619/236-9902. Hip café serving great breakfasts and lunches, with excellent pancakes, French toast, and cornbread, pumpkin and peanut butter waffles. Also has inventive sandwiches and burgers (including veggie), at reasonable prices.

Caffé Calabria 3933 30th St, Hillcrest Ⓣ619/291-1759. Serious coffee drinks for serious coffee drinkers, serving up some fine espresso, and French and Italian roasts from their own roasted beans, which you can buy to take home. Also offers good pastries and panini.

Candelas 416 3rd Ave, downtown Ⓣ619/702-4455. Gaslamp District restaurant offering pricey Mexican fare with flavourful combinations of seafood and meat dishes with a California-cuisine influence. Try the ceviche, prawns with sashimi or Serrano ham-stuffed chicken breast.

Chez Loma 1132 Loma Ave, Coronado Ⓣ619/435-0661. Delicious and dear French cuisine; especially strong on old-line favourites, though with nouvelle influences too. Good for its roasted duck, sea scallops, lobster crepes and filet mignon tartare.

Chilango's Mexican Grill 142 University Ave, Hillcrest Ⓣ619/294-8646. Regional, mid-priced Mexican food, highlighted by tasty shrimp, ceviche, enchiladas, tortilla soup and pork with tamarind sauce.

Cody's La Jolla 8030 Girard Ave, La Jolla Ⓣ858/459-0040. Innovative California cuisine with good buttermilk pancakes, sage sausages, eggplant sandwiches and scrumptious burgers. A little more expensive than comparable breakfast and lunch spots, but worth it.

Confidential 901 4th Ave, downtown Ⓣ619/696-8888. Curious Gaslamp choice for tapas in a trendy, modern setting; the small plates are intriguing, if pricey, from lobster-bisque "shooters", to honey-rum-glazed duck and "deconstructed" pizza, broken down to its bare elements.

Filippi's Pizza Grotto 1747 India St, Little Italy Ⓣ619/232-5094. A good spot for devouring affordable favourites like thick, chewy pizzas and various pasta dishes, including a fine lasagne. Meals are served in a small room at the back of an Italian grocery.

Karinya 4475 Mission Blvd, Pacific Beach Ⓣ858/270-5050. Hot and spicy soups, firecracker shrimp and volcano chicken to set your mouth ablaze, with a good range of Thai staples such as noodle dishes and satays as well. A tasty, inexpensive bet.

Kono's 704 Garnet Ave, Pacific Beach Ⓣ858/483-1669. Crowded, touristy place for a cheap breakfast or lunch on the boardwalk, with hefty burritos, sandwiches, hamburgers and other favourites.

The Mission 3795 Mission Blvd, Mission Beach Ⓣ858/488-9060. With all the delicious blackberry pancakes, roast-beef hash and steak quesadillas on the menu at this lunch-and-breakfast spot, your wallet won't end up busted, but your belt might.

Old Town Mexican Café 2489 San Diego Ave, Old Town Ⓣ619/297-4330. Among the better Mexican diners in the Old Town, where the crowds queue up for the likes of *pozole* soup and *carne asada* tacos; you are only unlikely to wait for a table at breakfast.

Point Loma Seafoods 2805 Emerson St, Ocean Beach ⓣ619/223-1109. Fast, cheap counter serving up San Diego's freshest fish in a basket, along with a mean crab-cake sandwich.
Primavera 932 Orange Ave, Coronado ⓣ619/435-0454. Swanky Italian cuisine that's among the best in town. There's pasta and risotto for those a little lighter in the wallet and fine osso bucco, steak and lamb chops for the big spenders.
Sportsmen's Seafood 1617 Quivira Rd, Mission Beach ⓣ619/224-3551. A combo diner/market offering cheap and delicious fare – highlighted by great fish and chips, *cioppino* and fish sandwiches.
Upstart Crow 835 W Harbor Drive, downtown ⓣ619/232-4855. This coffee bar fused with a bookstore offers a lively cross section of customers, primo java, well-chosen reading material and free Saturday-night jazz performances.
Taste of Thai 527 University Ave, Hillcrest ⓣ619/291-7525. Terrific Thai staples – spicy soups, curries, drunken noodles, pad thai and so on – for reasonable prices; expect a wait on weekends.

Nightlife

San Diego's upscale cultural focus is **classical music** and **opera**, the big names of which are downtown: the **San Diego Opera**, based at the Civic Theatre, 1200 Third Ave (ⓣ619/533-7000, ⓦwww.sdopera.com), and the **San Diego Symphony**, Copley Symphony Hall, 750 B St (ⓣ619/235-0804, ⓦwww.sandiegosymphony.com). **Tickets** range widely for both, from $20–210. Half-priced tickets and information are at the **Arts Tix** booth, Broadway at Third Avenue (Tues–Thurs 11am–6pm, Fri & Sat 10am–6pm, Sun 10am–5pm; ⓣ619/497-5000, ⓦwww.sandiegoperforms.com). Elsewhere, the crowds flock to beachside **dance clubs** and boozy Gaslamp District **music venues** for evening amusement. For full listings, pick up the free **San Diego Reader** (ⓦwww.sandiegoreader.com), the Thursday edition of the **San Diego Union-Tribune** (ⓦwww.signonsandiego.com), or the youth-oriented **San Diego CityBeat** ⓦwww.sdcitybeat.com).

Bars and clubs

Bitter End 770 5th Ave, Gaslamp District ⓣ619/338-9300. Three-storey venue in the Gaslamp, complete with dancefloor, martini bar and upstairs, a private VIP lounge for sophisticated poseurs.
Live Wire 2103 El Cajon Blvd, just east of Hillcrest ⓣ619/291-7450. A solid place to groove with the rocking jukebox and get hammered on imported and local beers. There's also pinball, pool and a funky sub-bohemian atmosphere to wet your whistle.
Onyx Room 852 5th Ave, Gaslamp District ⓣ619/235-6699. Groovy bar with lush decor, where you can knock back a few cocktails, then hit the back room for live jazz and dance tunes. The chic lounge upstairs has pricier drinks and bigger attitudes.
Ruby Room 1271 University Ave ⓣ619/299-7372. Good-time Hillcrest dive bar that serves up cheap brews and convivial company, and presents the odd rock'n'roll or burlesque show.
Whistle Stop Bar 2236 Fern St, South Park ⓣ619/284-6784. Sited on the east side of Balboa Park, this hip and lively bar presents a wide range of theme nights, from weekend DJs to Sunday "knitting jams" and movie matinees.

Live music venues

4th and B 345 B St, downtown ⓣ619/231-4343. One of the city's more notable venues for metal, funk, hip-hop and other music, with good sightlines if a bare-bones atmosphere, and a mix of local up-and-comers and old-timers.
Belly Up Tavern 143 S Cedros Ave, Solana Beach ⓣ858/481-9022. Mid-sized hall that plays host nightly to an eclectic range of live music – anything from grizzled rockers to salsa spectaculars and tub-thumping DJs.
Brick by Brick 1130 Buenos Ave, Mission Bay ⓣ619/275-5483. Lounge standby serving up a mix of indie rock, metal, hip-hop and burlesque acts.
Casbah 2501 Kettner Blvd, downtown ⓣ619/232-4355. A grungy joint that nevertheless has a solid reputation for its blues, funk, reggae, rock and indie bands. Local popularity contrasts with cramped environs.
Dizzy's At Harbor Club Towers, J St at 2nd, downtown ⓣ858/270-7467. As the name suggests, this spot is devoted to straight-up jazz and little else – in a dark, intimate brick-walled environment.
Humphrey's by the Bay 2241 Shelter Island Drive, Point Loma ⓣ619/220-8497. Mainstream

concert venue draws a range of mellow, agreeable pop, blues, jazz, country, folk and lite-rock acts, and its restaurant is a solid choice for seafood. **Kensington Club** 4079 Adams Ave, Kensington District, north of Hillcrest ⓣ619/284-2848. Also called "The Ken" – a great divey joint for beer, wine and cocktails, but also for wide-ranging live music selections from thumping-dance DJs to head-banging rockers.

Los Angeles

The rambling metropolis of **LOS ANGELES** sprawls across the thousand square miles of its great desert basin, knitted together by an intricate network of freeways between the Pacific Ocean and snowcapped mountains. Its colourful melange of shopping malls, palm trees and swimming pools is both surreal and familiar, thanks to the potent celluloid self-image it has spread all over the world.

Los Angeles is thrilling and threatening in equal proportions – a place that picks you up and sweeps you along whether you like it or not. While it has its fine-art museums, unexpected swaths of parkland and quintessential fun-in-the-sun beach life, what people really come here for is to experience the fantasy worlds of **Disneyland** and **Hollywood**, as well as the gilded opulence of **Beverly Hills** and **Malibu**. And as you might expect, if you want to experience as much as possible, you'll need a set of wheels.

Arrival

All European and most domestic **flights** use LA International Airport – almost always **LAX** – sixteen miles southwest of downtown along Santa Monica Bay (ⓣ310/646-5252, ⓦwww.los-angeles-lax.com). Shuttle bus C goes to carpark C, the place to board city buses. Minibuses such as SuperShuttle (ⓣ1-800/BLUE-VAN, ⓦwww.supershuttle.com) and Prime Time Shuttle (ⓣ1-800/RED-VANS, ⓦwww.primetimeshuttle.com), run all over town; fares depend on your destination but start around $15 for travel to downtown and the Westside (or up to $40 for more outlying areas), with a journey time of between thirty and sixty minutes. **Taxis** charge at least $35 to West LA or $40 to Hollywood, $100 to Disneyland, and a flat $46.50 to downtown; a $2.50 surcharge applies for all trips starting from LAX. For more information, check out ⓦwww.taxicabsla.org.

If you're arriving from elsewhere in the US, or from Mexico, you might just land at one of the **other airports** in the LA area – at Burbank, Long Beach, Ontario or Orange County's John Wayne Airport in Costa Mesa. Burbank's Bob Hope Airport is by far the most convenient alternative to LAX, if you happen to be on one of the seven domestic carriers that land there (see ⓦwww.burbankairport.com for details). **MTA buses** (ⓣ1-800/COMMUTE, ⓦwww.mta.net) serve all the major airports – phone on arrival and tell them where you are and want to go.

The main **Greyhound** bus terminal, at 1716 E Seventh St (24hr; ⓣ213/629-8401, ⓦwww.greyhound.com), is in a seedy section of downtown, but access is restricted to ticket-holders, so it's safe enough inside. If arriving in LA by **train** you'll be greeted with the Mission Revival architecture of Union Station, 800 N Alameda St (ⓣ213/624-0171), on the north side of downtown, from which you can easily access the city's MTA bus lines.

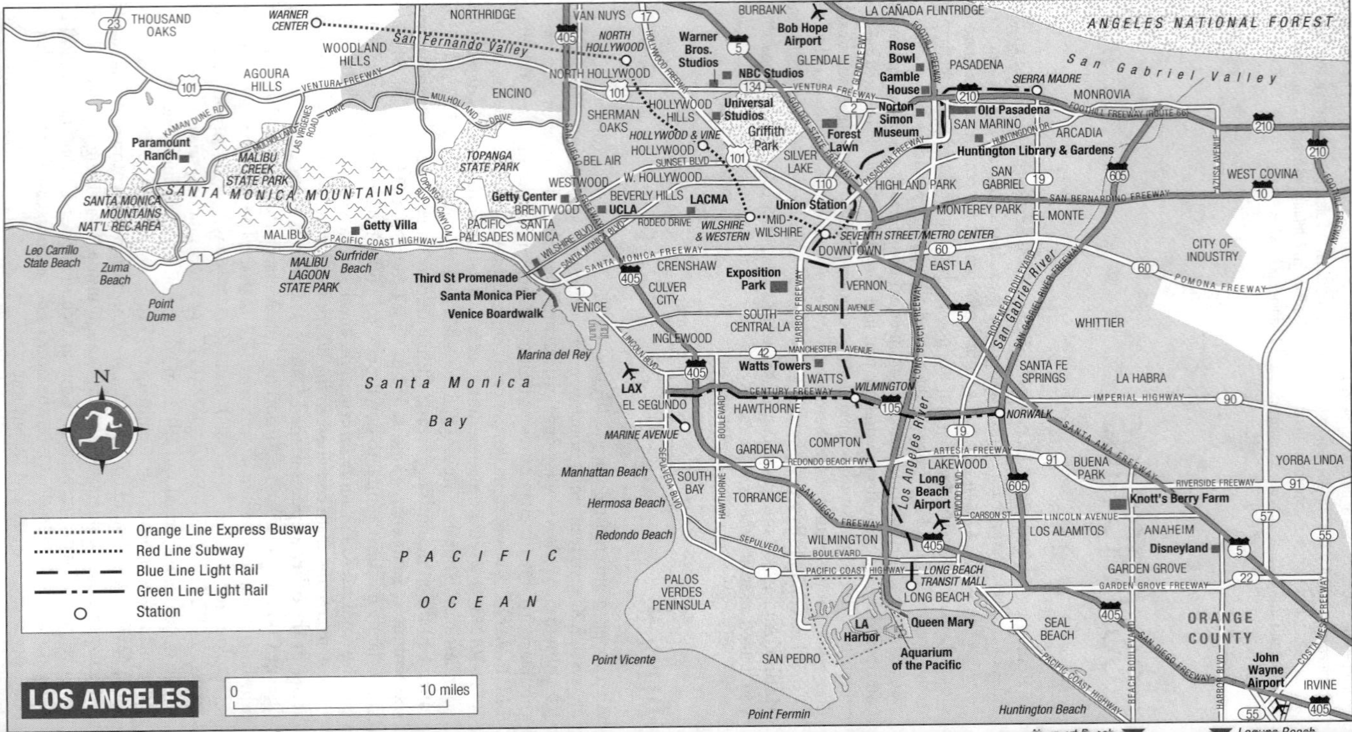
LOS ANGELES
Santa Clarita & Magic Mountain
Palm Springs
San Juan Capistrano
Santa Barbara
ANGELES NATIONAL FOREST
San Gabriel Valley
San Fernando Valley
SANTA MONICA MOUNTAINS
THOUSAND OAKS
WARNER CENTER
WOODLAND HILLS
AGOURA HILLS
NORTHRIDGE
VAN NUYS
NORTH HOLLYWOOD
ENCINO
SHERMAN OAKS
BURBANK
Bob Hope Airport
Warner Bros. Studios
NBC Studios
Universal Studios
GLENDALE
LA CAÑADA FLINTRIDGE
Rose Bowl
Gamble House
Norton Simon Museum
Forest Lawn
PASADENA
SIERRA MADRE
MONROVIA
Old Pasadena
SAN MARINO
ARCADIA
Huntington Library & Gardens
WEST COVINA
Paramount Ranch
MALIBU CREEK STATE PARK
SANTA MONICA MOUNTAINS NAT'L REC.AREA
TOPANGA STATE PARK
Getty Center
Getty Villa
MALIBU
Leo Carrillo State Beach
Zuma Beach
Point Dume
MALIBU LAGOON STATE PARK
Surfrider Beach
HOLLYWOOD HILLS
HOLLYWOOD & VINE
HOLLYWOOD
Griffith Park
SILVER LAKE
BEL AIR
WESTWOOD
W. HOLLYWOOD
BEVERLY HILLS
LACMA
UCLA
BRENTWOOD
PACIFIC PALISADES
SANTA MONICA
WILSHIRE & WESTERN
MID WILSHIRE
Union Station
SEVENTH STREET/METRO CENTER
DOWNTOWN
HIGHLAND PARK
SAN GABRIEL
MONTEREY PARK
EL MONTE
CITY OF INDUSTRY
EAST LA
Third St Promenade
Santa Monica Pier
Venice Boardwalk
VENICE
CRENSHAW
CULVER CITY
Exposition Park
VERNON
SOUTH CENTRAL LA
INGLEWOOD
WHITTIER
Marina del Rey
Watts Towers
WATTS
LAX
EL SEGUNDO
WILMINGTON
HAWTHORNE
SANTA FE SPRINGS
LA HABRA
NORWALK
MARINE AVENUE
COMPTON
GARDENA
LAKEWOOD
BUENA PARK
YORBA LINDA
Manhattan Beach
Hermosa Beach
Redondo Beach
SOUTH BAY
TORRANCE
Long Beach Airport
Knott's Berry Farm
LOS ALAMITOS
ANAHEIM
Disneyland
WILMINGTON
LONG BEACH TRANSIT MALL
LONG BEACH
GARDEN GROVE
PALOS VERDES PENINSULA
LA Harbor
Queen Mary
Aquarium of the Pacific
SEAL BEACH
ORANGE COUNTY
John Wayne Airport
IRVINE
SAN PEDRO
Point Vicente
Point Fermin
Huntington Beach
Santa Monica Bay
PACIFIC OCEAN
Los Angeles River
San Gabriel River
VENTURA FREEWAY
MULHOLLAND DRIVE
PACIFIC COAST HIGHWAY
SANTA MONICA FREEWAY
SAN DIEGO FREEWAY
HOLLYWOOD FREEWAY
GOLDEN STATE FREEWAY
FOOTHILL FREEWAY
PASADENA FREEWAY
SAN BERNARDINO FREEWAY
POMONA FREEWAY
HARBOR FREEWAY
LONG BEACH FREEWAY
CENTURY FREEWAY
IMPERIAL HIGHWAY
SANTA ANA FREEWAY
ARTESIA FREEWAY
RIVERSIDE FREEWAY
GARDEN GROVE FREEWAY
COSTA MESA FREEWAY
SEPULVEDA BLVD
LINCOLN BLVD
WILSHIRE BLVD
SUNSET BLVD
RODEO DRIVE
N
Orange Line Express Busway
Red Line Subway
Blue Line Light Rail
Green Line Light Rail
Station
0
10 miles

Guided tours

Some of your best bets for touring downtown and other spots are the **walking tours** offered by the **LA Conservancy** (Sat 10am; 2hr 30min; $10; ⓣ213/623-CITY, ⓦlaconservancy.org), which typically set off from Pershing Square downtown and concentrate on various aspects of the city's architecture, history and culture. More expensive, **Architours** (ⓣ323/294-5821, ⓦwww.architours.com) offers walking, driving and custom tours of the art and architecture highlights of the city, with most running 2–3 hr for $68–75. Also appealing, **Neon Cruises,** 501 W Olympic Blvd, downtown (June–Nov; $55; ⓣ213/489-9918, ⓦwww.neonmona.org), are three-hour-long, eye-popping evening tours of LA's best remaining neon art, once a month on Saturdays, sponsored by the Museum of Neon Art. One type of trek to avoid, however, are the uninspired bus tours that focus on the **homes of the stars** (ie, their ivy-covered security gates) and advertise their overpriced services around Hollywood's Chinese Theatre.

Information

Most **visitor centres** are open Monday to Friday 9am–5pm and Saturday 9am–1pm, except in summer, when they may be open daily from 8 or 9am until 6pm or later. Details are as follows: **Anaheim/Disneyland**, 800 W Katella Ave, ⓣ714/991-8963, ⓦwww.anaheimoc.org; **Beverly Hills**, 239 S Beverly Drive, ⓣ1-800/345-2210, ⓦwww.beverlyhillscvb.com; **Downtown LA**, 685 S Figueroa St, ⓣ213/689-8822, ⓦwww.discoverlosangeles.com; **Hollywood** at Hollywood & Highland mall, 6801 Hollywood Blvd, ⓣ323/467-6412; **Long Beach**, 1 World Trade Center, 3rd Floor, ⓣ562/436-3645, ⓦwww.visitlongbeach.com; **Pasadena**, 300 E Green St, ⓣ626/795-9311, ⓦwww.pasadenacal.com; **Santa Monica**, 1920 Main St, ⓣ310/393-7593, ⓦwww.santamonica.com; **West Hollywood**, in the Pacific Design Center, 8687 Melrose Ave #M38, ⓣ310/289-2525, ⓦwww.visitwesthollywood.com.

City transport

Los Angeles covers 500 square miles in the central city, and more than 2600 square miles in the metropolitan area. The sheer scale of the metroplex, therefore, means it really is difficult to get around without a car (unless you're sticking to more centralized towns such as Santa Monica or Pasadena). Even though the traffic is often bumper-to-bumper, the freeways are the only way to cover long distances quickly. Otherwise, try the fastest alternative, **express buses**.

Metrorail and Metrolink

LA's **Metrorail** system (same info as for MTA, below) comprises seven colour-coded lines. The **Red Line** subway stretches from Union Station through Hollywood, to North Hollywood in the San Fernando Valley – and from North Hollywood on to the western Valley, where the **Orange Line** takes over with express buses. The three light rails include the **Green Line**, from Hawthorne to Norwalk along the Century Freeway (stopping short of LAX); the **Blue Line**, connecting downtown via Watts to downtown Long Beach; and the **Gold Line**, linking downtown to the San Gabriel Valley through Old Pasadena. Smaller lines are the **Purple Line** subway that links Union Station with Western Avenue, and the **Silver Line** express buses to the San Gabriel Valley. Tickets cost $1.25 single, or $5 for a day pass, and trains run every five to fifteen minutes (more infrequently at night). By contrast, **Metrolink** commuter trains ($5–14 one-way; ⓣ1-800/371-LINK, ⓦwww.metrolinktrains.com) operate inter-suburban routes on weekdays, but can be useful if you find yourself at the fringes of the metropolis (for example, Anaheim to LA Union Station is $7.75).

Buses and taxis

Car-less Angelenos are still best served by **buses**, most of which are run by the LA County Metropolitan Transit Authority (MTA or Metro; ⓣ1-800/COMMUTE, ⓦwww.mta.net). Information can also be obtained in person at downtown's Gateway Transit Center, Chavez Avenue at Vignes Street (Mon–Fri 6am–6.30pm), and 5301 Wilshire Blvd, Mid-Wilshire (Mon–Fri 9am–5pm). Buses on the major streets between downtown and the coast run roughly every fifteen minutes between 5am and 2am; other routes, and the **all-night services** along the major streets, are less frequent. At night, be careful not to get stranded alone downtown waiting for a connection.

The standard one-way **fare** is $1.25; **transfers** cost 30¢ more, but must be made within an hour; **express buses**, and any others using the freeway, are $1.85 up to $2.45 (and usually run 6–8.30am & 4–7pm, every 20–60min). If you're staying a while, you can save some money with a **daily**, **weekly** or **monthly pass**, which cost $5, $17 and $62, respectively. There are also the mini **DASH** buses (ⓣ808-2273 for area codes 213, 310, 323 and 818, ⓦwww.ladottransit.com) with a flat fare of 25¢ and broad coverage throughout downtown and very limited routes elsewhere. You'll be hard-pressed to find an available **taxi** cruising the streets, so call ahead; among the more reliable companies are Independent Taxi (ⓣ1-800/521-8294), Yellow Cab (ⓣ1-800/200-1085) and United Independent Taxi (ⓣ1-800/411-0303). Fares include a base charge of $2.85; add $2.70 per mile, and tack on another $2.50 if you're getting picked up from LAX. (For car rental information, see Basics, "Getting Around", p.34.)

Cycling

Cycling in LA may sound perverse, but in some areas it can be one of the better ways of getting around. There are beachside bike paths between Santa Monica and Redondo Beach, and from Long Beach to Newport Beach, and many equally enjoyable inland routes, notably around Griffith Park and Pasadena. For maps and information, contact the LA Department of Transportation, 100 S Main St, 9th Floor (ⓣ213/972-4962, ⓦwww.bicyclela.org); AAA, 2601 S Figueroa St (Mon–Fri 9am–5pm; ⓣ213/741-3686); or the California Department of Transportation, known as CalTrans, 100 S Main St (Mon–Fri 8am–5pm; ⓣ213/897-3656, ⓦwww.dot.ca.gov). The best place to **rent a bike** for the beaches is around the Venice Boardwalk. Prices range from $10 a day for a clunker, to $20 a day or more for a mountain bike. Many beachside stores also rent roller skates and rollerblades.

Accommodation

There's a huge range of **places to stay** in LA: downtown has both upscale and mid-range hotels (along with numerous fleabag dives), Hollywood has plenty of

Camping in LA

The best **campgrounds** in the LA area are along the Orange County coast, such as Bolsa Chica in Huntington Beach (ⓣ714/846-3460) and the state parks at San Clemente (ⓣ949/492-3156) and Crystal Cove (ⓣ949/492-0802), and in the mountains and beaches around Malibu, notably Malibu Creek State Park (ⓣ818/880-0367) and Leo Carrillo State Beach (ⓣ1-818/880-0363). Campgrounds run around $25, though some may cost as much as $50 in the high season. Reserve America handles most park camping **reservations** (ⓣ1-800/444-7275, ⓦwww.reserveamerica.com).

cheap motels, West Hollywood is a swanky boutique zone, and the Westside and Malibu are mid- to upper-range territory. If you're not driving, choose your base carefully to avoid lengthy cross-town journeys.

Hotels, motels and B&Bs

Hotels and **motels** are listed by neighbourhood. If you're arriving on a late flight, or leaving on an early one, hotels near LAX are blandly similar and generally cost around $75–100 a night, but do offer complimentary shuttle service to and from the terminals. Prices increase at many tourist-oriented establishments during peak travel periods, especially those near major attractions like Disneyland and Universal Studios. However, weekday rates at business-oriented hotels, especially during conventions, can be just as expensive, or even more so, than weekend prices.

Downtown and around

Hilton Checkers 535 S Grand Ave ⓣ213/624-0000 or 1-800/HILTONS, ⓦwww.hiltoncheckers.com. One of the great LA hotels, with sleek modern appointments in historic 1920s architecture, and nicely furnished rooms, rooftop pool and spa, and sleek *Checkers* restaurant. Good value, too. ❼

Millennium Biltmore 506 S Grand Ave ⓣ213/624-1011 or 1-800/222-8888, ⓦwww.thebiltmore.com. Renaissance Revival architecture from 1923, with a health club modelled on a Roman bathhouse, cherub and angel decor, and a view overlooking Pershing Square. The well-appointed rooms match the stateliness of the design. ❼

Miyako Inn 328 E 1st St ⓣ213/617-2000, ⓦwww.miyakoinn.com. Despite the concrete-box exterior, this basic hotel offers comfortable rooms with fridges, plus on-site gym, spa, massage room and free internet access. ❻

Omni 251 S Olive St at Fourth St ⓣ213/617-3300, ⓦwww.omnilosangeles.com. Fancy Bunker Hill hotel with plush, elegant rooms, swimming pool and weight room. Adjacent to MOCA and the Music Center. One of the best deals in LA. ❻

Westin Bonaventure 404 S Figueroa St ⓣ213/624-1000, ⓦwww.westin.com. High-modernist hotel with five glass towers that resemble cocktail shakers, a six-storey atrium with a "lake" and elegant, conic-shaped rooms. A breathtaking exterior elevator ride ascends to a rotating cocktail lounge. ❻

Hollywood and West Hollywood

Chamberlain 1000 Westmount Drive ⓣ310/657-7400, ⓦwww.chamberlainwesthollywood.com. Sumptuous hotel just off the Strip, within easy walking distance of major attractions. The impressive suites include sunken living rooms, internet access, DVD players, fireplaces, balconies and refrigerators. ❽

Grafton on Sunset 8462 Sunset Blvd ⓣ323/654-4600, ⓦwww.graftononsunset.com. Fun boutique hotel with rooms offering trendy furnishings, CD and DVD players, iPod docks and flat-screen TVs, plus a pool and fitness centre. ❼

Hollywood Celebrity 1775 Orchid Ave ⓣ323/850-6464 or 1-800/222-7017, ⓦwww.hotelcelebrity.com. Good choice on the affordable boutique scene, with great location in central Hollywood and rooms with charming furnishings, free breakfast and free high-speed wi-fi . ❻

Hollywood Roosevelt 7000 Hollywood Blvd ⓣ323/466-7000, ⓦwww.hollywoodroosevelt.com. The first hotel built for the movie greats in 1927. The place reeks of atmosphere, with cabanas and suites, plus a jacuzzi, fitness room and swimming pool. However, many of the old-fashioned rooms can be a bit cramped for modern travellers. ❽

Orchid Suites 1753 Orchid Ave ⓣ323/874-9678 or 1-800/537-3052, ⓦwww.orchidsuites.com. Roomy if spartan suites with cable TV, kitchenettes and heated pool, plus free breakfast. Very close to the most popular parts of Hollywood – good value all round. ❺

Renaissance Hollywood 1755 N Highland Blvd ⓣ323/856-1200, ⓦwww.renaissancehollywood.com. The hotel centrepiece of the Hollywood & Highland mall complex, with arty flair in the overall design, upscale rooms and suites, and a prime location in the heart of tourist central.❽

West LA and Beverly Hills

Avalon 9400 W Olympic Blvd ⓣ310/277-5221, ⓦwww.avalonbeverlyhills.com. Located in south Beverly Hills, this hipster hotel boasts mid-modern furnishings with in-room CD players, internet access and balconies. The chic poolside bar is where *Entourage* types pose and cut actual Hollywood deals. ❼

Best Western Royal Palace 2528 S Sepulveda Blvd ⓣ310/477-9066, ⓦwww.bestwesternroyalpalace.com. If you want a cheap room and don't mind staying near the junction of the 405 and 10 freeways, this is the place: with microwaves and a pool, hot tub, and fitness centre. Westside Pavilion shopping mall is a mile away. ❹

Beverly Hills Hotel 9641 Sunset Blvd ⓣ310/276-2251, ⓦwww.beverlyhillshotel.com. The classic Hollywood resort, surrounded by its own exotic gardens. Rooms feature marbled bathrooms, hot tubs and other such luxuries, and the famed *Polo Lounge* restaurant is also on site. ❾

Hotel Angeleno 170 N Church Lane at Sunset Blvd ⓣ310/476-6411, ⓦwww.jdvhotels.com/angeleno. Cylindrical eyesore poking out of a hillside under the Getty Center, but with good comfort and boutique furnishings, plus pool, spa, weight room and rooftop restaurant. All rooms have balconies, some with terrific views. ❼

Santa Monica and Malibu

Ambrose 1255 20th St, Santa Monica ⓣ310/315-1555, ⓦwww.ambrosehotel.com. Excellent choice for inland Santa Monica, with Craftsman-styled decor and boutique rooms that have wi-fi and include continental breakfast. ❽

Cal Mar 220 California St, Santa Monica ⓣ310/395-5555, ⓦwww.calmarhotel.com. Good for its central location, plus garden suites have CD/DVD players, dining rooms, kitchens and balconies, and there's a heated pool, fitness room and airport shuttle. ❼

Casa Malibu Inn 22752 PCH ⓣ310/456-2219. Located opposite Carbon Beach and featuring superb, well-appointed rooms – facing a courtyard garden or right on the beach – with great modern design and some in-room fireplaces, jacuzzis and balconies. ❼

Channel Road Inn 219 W Channel Rd, Pacific Palisades ⓣ310/459-1920, ⓦwww.channelroadinn.com. Romantic getaway nestled in lower Santa Monica Canyon, with ocean views, hot tub and free bike rental. Enjoy complimentary grapes and champagne in the sumptuous rooms, each priced according to its view. ❽

The LA suburbs

Beach House at Hermosa 1300 Strand, Hermosa Beach ⓣ310/374-3001, ⓦwww.Beach-House.com. The height of South Bay luxury, offering two-room suites with fireplaces, in-room bars, balconies, hot tubs, stereos and fridges, with many rooms overlooking the sea. ❾

Disneyland Hotel 1150 W Cerritos Ave, Anaheim ⓣ714/956-6400, ⓦdisneyland.disney.go.com. Cookie-cutter rooms with little charm, but still an irresistible lure for many. The Disneyland monorail does stop outside (theme park admission is separate). ❾

Safari Inn 1911 W Olive St, Burbank ⓣ818/845-8586, ⓦwww.safariburbank.com. A classic mid-century motel, renovated but still loaded with pop-architecture touches. Features a pool, fitness room, Burbank airport shuttle and in-room fridges, plus free breakfast. ❹

Stovall's Inn 1110 W Katella Ave, Anaheim ⓣ714/778-1880, ⓦwww.stovallsinn.com. Tasteful, clean chain accommodation near Disneyland, with fitness centre, two pools, two spas and in-room fridges and microwaves. ❸

Hostels

Hostels are dotted all over the city, many of them also offering cut-rate single and double rooms. Some hostels also offer tours of theme parks, shopping malls and stars' homes, while others organize events, such as sports and pizza parties.

Banana Bungalow 5920 Hollywood Blvd ⓣ323/469-2500 or 1-877/977-5077, ⓦwww.bananabungalow.com. Popular hostel just east of the main Hollywood action, with airport shuttles, internet, tours to Venice Beach and theme parks, and in-room kitchens and many other amenities. Dorms $25–27, private doubles ❸–❹. Also a similarly priced branch in West Hollywood at 603 N Fairfax Ave ⓣ323/655-2002.

HI-Anaheim/Fullerton 1700 N Harbor Blvd, Fullerton ⓣ714/738-3721, ⓦwww.hihostels.com. Convenient and comfortable, five miles north of Disneyland, with kitchen, laundry and internet access. There are only twenty dorm beds, so reservations are a must. Dorms $25.

HI-LA/Santa Monica 1436 2nd St, Santa Monica ⓣ310/393-9913, ⓦwww.hilosangeles.org. A few blocks from the beach and pier, this was LA's Town Hall from 1887 to 1889, now renovated with pleasant inner courtyard, internet café and free wi-fi, movie room and 260 beds. Reservations essential in summer. Dorms $39.

HI-LA/South Bay 3601 S Gaffey St #613 ⓣ310/831-8109, ⓦwww.hihostels.com. Sixty beds in an old US Army barracks, with a panoramic view of the Pacific Ocean. Ideal for seeing San Pedro, Palos Verdes and the whole LA Harbor area. Dorms $25, private rooms ❷.

Hollywood International 6820 Hollywood Blvd, Hollywood ⓣ323/463-2770 or 1-800/557-7038, ⓦwww.hollywoodhostels.com. Centrally located with

game room, gymnasium, patio garden, kitchen and laundry. Offers tours of Hollywood, theme parks, Las Vegas and Tijuana. Dorms $17, private rooms ❷.
Orbit Hotel 7950 Melrose Ave, West Hollywood ⓣ323/655-1510 or 1-877/ORBIT-US, ⓦwww.orbithotel.com. Retro-1960s hotel and hostel with sleek furnishings and modern decor, offering complimentary breakfast, movie screening room, patio, café, private baths in all rooms and shuttle tours. Dorms $22–28, private rooms ❷–❹.
Stay Hotel 636 S Main St ⓣ213/213-7829, ⓦwww.stayhotels.com. Rock-bottom-priced lodging in central downtown LA, offering internet access and some rooms with DVD players, but mostly small, no-frills accommodation. Shared rooms $25, private rooms ❷.

The City

Los Angeles spreads out in so many directions, getting a handle on it is almost impossible for newcomers – though you can try. **Downtown** is still largely a financial zone, but also includes upscale and underground art galleries as well as cheap and buzzing commercial districts. West from downtown, **Hollywood** has streets imbued with movie myths and legends – and adjoining **West LA** is home to the city's newest money, shown off in Beverly Hills and along the Sunset Strip. **Santa Monica** and **Venice** further west are the quintessential seafront LA of palm trees, white sands and laidback living, while twenty miles northwest, **Malibu** is home to the movieland elite.

Suburban **Orange County** to the southeast, holds little of interest apart from **Disneyland**, a few museums and a handful of libertine beach towns. On the far side of the northern hills lie the **San Gabriel and San Fernando valleys**, or simply "the Valley", tract homes and strip malls enlivened by occasional sights of interest, many of them in genteel **Pasadena**.

Downtown LA

Downtown LA embraces the city's every social, economic and ethnic division, and the whole area can easily be seen in a day on foot. LA's original settlement at **The Plaza** is the obvious first stop, before crossing into the corporate zone of **Bunker Hill** and continuing through the free-spirited chaos along **Broadway**.

The Plaza

The several dozen extant buildings of El Pueblo de Los Angeles Historic Park, 845 N Alameda St (daily 9am–5pm; free; ⓣ213/625-3800, ⓦwww.ci.la.ca.us/ELP), make for an essential stop on any history trek through LA. The square known as **the Plaza** was roughly the site of the city's original 1781 settlement, and the plaza church **La Placita**, 535 N Main St (daily 6.30am–8pm; ⓦwww.laplacita.org), is the city's oldest, a small adobe structure with a gabled roof, though from 1861 to 1923 it was remodelled or reconstructed four times. **Olvera Street**, which runs north from the plaza (daily 10am–7pm; free; ⓦwww.olvera-street.com), contrived in part as a pseudo-Mexican village market, offers a cheery collection of food and craft stalls. Among the historic structures here is **Avila Adobe** (daily 9am–4pm; free), technically the city's oldest building, though it's been completely rebuilt in the last thirty years. Other worthwhile sights include the **Sepulveda House** (daily 9am–4pm; free), an 1887 Eastlake Victorian structure that houses the visitor centre and has rooms highlighting different periods in Mexican-American history and the **Garnier Building**, now the **Chinese American Museum**, 425 N Los Angeles St (Tues–Sun 10am–3pm; $5; ⓦwww.camla.org). Inside, local Chinese history, society and culture is detailed, including revealing letters, photos and documents, as well as a smattering of contemporary art and the

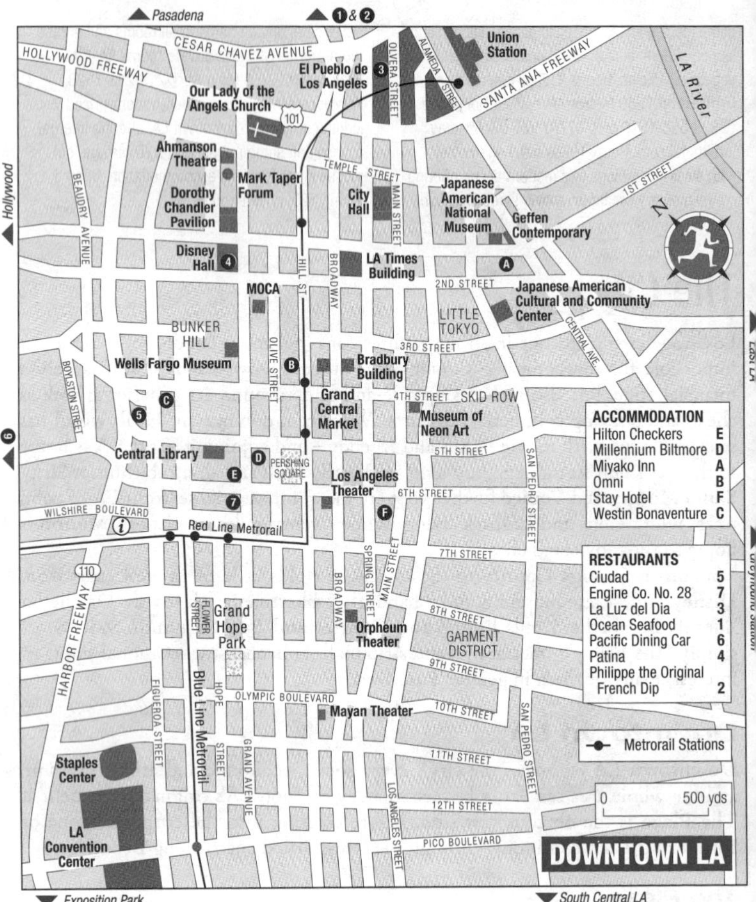

re-creation of a Chinese herb shop c.1900. To get a sense of everything in the historic park, take a free **tour** (Tues–Sat 10am, 11am & noon; ⓣ213/628-1274, ⓦwww.lasangelitas.org), which begins at the business office next to the Old Plaza Firehouse on the Plaza's south end.

Civic Center

South from the Plaza, across the Santa Ana Freeway, the municipal-government core of the **Civic Center** offers three of the city's most notable buildings. **City Hall**, 200 N Spring St, is an iconic, classically styled tower that's been visible in media from *Dragnet* to *Superman*. You can get a good look at the inside of the building on free **tours**, which include its 28th-storey 360-degree observation deck (Mon–Fri 9am–4pm; free). To the west, **Disney Hall**, First Street at Grand Avenue, is Frank Gehry's grand spectacle of modern architecture, a 2300-seat acoustic showpiece with a curvaceous, stainless-steel exterior and an interior with rich, warm acoustics and a mammoth, intricate pipe organ. It's one of the best places to hear music in the country, which you can do courtesy of the LA Philharmonic (ⓦwww.laphil.com; see p.873) during the music season. A long block north, the **Our Lady of the Angels** Catholic church (Mon–Fri 6.30am–6pm, Sat 9am–6pm, Sun 7am–6pm; tours Mon–Fri 1pm; free; Ⓦwww.olacathedral.org) is a concrete fortress on the outside, but features exquisite decor inside, such as a grand marble altar and ultra-thin alabaster screens for diffusing light.

Bunker Hill

Until a century ago the area south of the Civic Center, **Bunker Hill**, was LA's most elegant neighbourhood, but after a half-century of decay, 1960s urban renewal transformed it into the imperious **Financial District**, with colossal new towers. The main highlight is the **Museum of Contemporary Art** (MOCA), 250 S Grand Ave (Mon & Fri 11am–5pm, Thurs 11am–8pm, Sat & Sun 11am–6pm; $10, free Thurs 5–8pm; Ⓦwww.moca.org), which was designed by showman architect Arata Isozaki as a vivid array of reddish geometric blocks. In addition to work by Mark Rothko, Robert Rauschenberg and Claes Oldenburg, and some eye-opening temporary exhibits, it features an impressive selection of **Southern California artists**, ranging from Lari Pittman's spooky, sexualized silhouettes to Robert Williams' feverishly violent and satiric comic-book-styled paintings.

Opposite MOCA, the diverting **Wells Fargo Museum**, 333 S Grand Ave (Mon–Fri 9am–5pm; free; Ⓦwww.wellsfargohistory.com) displays old mining equipment, antiques, photographs, a two-pound chunk of gold, a re-created assay office from the nineteenth century and a simulated stagecoach journey from St Louis to San Francisco. A short distance away, the **Richard J. Riordan Central Library**, 630 W 5th St (Mon–Thurs 10am–8pm, Fri & Sat 10am–6pm, Sun 1–5pm; Ⓦwww.lapl.org/central), dates back to 1926, when its striking, angular lines set the tone for many LA buildings, most obviously City Hall.

Little Tokyo and around

East of Bunker Hill, **Little Tokyo** is an appealing collection of historic sites, restaurants and galleries, centred around the **Yagura Tower**, Street at Central Avenue, a small canopy sitting atop slender wooden beams, built in the style of a traditional Japanese fire tower used to spot forest fires. Nearby, the comprehensive **Japanese American National Museum**, 369 E First St (Tues–Sun 11am–5pm, Thurs closes at 8pm; $9; Ⓦwww.janm.org), offers everything from origami to traditional furniture and folk craftwork to the story of the internment of Japanese-Americans during World War II. Just north along a pedestrian plaza, **The Geffen Contemporary**, 152 N Central Ave (Ⓣ213/621-1745), is used for the edgier temporary shows of the Museum of Contemporary Art (same hours as above), for which a ticket also entitles you to same-day entry. Finally, a few blocks away, the latest home for the ever-itinerant **Museum of Neon Art**, 136 W 4th St (Thurs–Sat noon–6pm, Sun noon–5pm; $7; Ⓦwww.neonmona.org), is worth a stop to check out some enchanting neon signs, kinetic displays and an array of oddball artworks that glow, move, sparkle and otherwise behave in ways foreign to most conventional galleries.

Broadway

Broadway was once LA's most fashionable shopping and entertainment district, but today it's largely taken over by the hustle and bustle of Hispanic clothing and trinket stores, all to a soundtrack of blaring salsa music. You can sample a vivid taste of the area at the **Grand Central Market**, between Third and Fourth streets (daily 9am–6pm; Ⓦwww.grandcentralsquare.com), where you'll find everything from apples and oranges, to pickled pig's feet and ice cream. Right alongside, the whimsical terracotta facade of the 1918 **Million Dollar Theater** mixes buffalo heads with bald eagles and was seen in the film *Blade Runner*, as was the neighbouring 1893 **Bradbury Building**, no. 304 (lobby open Mon–Sat 9am–5pm; free), featuring a magnificent sunlit atrium surrounded by stylish wrought-iron balconies and open-cage elevators. While the moviehouse has since closed, it, along with the extravagant arches and marble columns of the **Los Angeles Theater**, 615 S Broadway and the **Orpheum**'s neo-French Renaissance grand staircases and chandeliers, at no. 630, are still on view during the annual "Last Remaining Seats" film festival in June (tickets $20/show; details at Ⓦwww.laconservancy.org).

Around downtown

The LA sprawl begins as soon as you leave downtown, diverse environs cut through by freeways and boulevards, with large distances separating the points of interest. As such, it makes little sense to see them consecutively.

Exposition Park

South of downtown, across Exposition Boulevard from the fortress-like USC campus, **Exposition Park** is one of the better parks in LA, incorporating lush gardens and several modest museums. The kid-oriented **California Science Center**, off Figueroa Street at 700 State Drive (daily 10am–5pm; free; Ⓦwww.californiasciencecenter.org), contains enjoyable working models and thousands of gadgets to keep the children distracted, with an **IMAX Theater** ($8.25, kids $5) and an **Air and Space Gallery** marked by a sleek jet stuck to its facade and showcasing satellites, telescopes, aeroplanes and rockets. To the south, the **California African American Museum**, 600 State Drive (Tues–Sat 10am–5pm, Sun 11am–5pm; free; Ⓦwww.caamuseum.org), has stimulating exhibits on the history and culture of America's black communities.

The **Natural History Museum of Los Angeles County**, 900 Exposition Blvd (daily 9.30am–5pm; $9; Ⓦwww.nhm.org), with its echoey domes and travertine columns, has a tremendous stock of dinosaur skeletons, which include the skull of a Tyrannosaurus rex and the frame of a huge flightless bird. Other fascinating displays include Mayan pyramid murals, the reconstructed contents of a Mexican tomb and several roomfuls of opulent crystals.

The Watts Towers

Now more Hispanic than black, **WATTS** provides only one compelling reason to visit, and only during the day: the Gaudí-esque **Watts Towers**, sometimes called the Rodia Towers, at 1765 E 107th St, a half-mile north off the 105 freeway on Wilmington Avenue. Constructed from iron, stainless steel, old bed frames and cement, and adorned with bottle fragments and some 70,000 crushed seashells, these striking pieces of folk art are shrouded in mystery. Their maker, Italian immigrant **Simon Rodia**, had no artistic background or training, but laboured over the towers' construction from 1921 to 1954, refusing offers of help and unable to explain their meaning or why he was building them. Unfortunately, the 30-minute **tours** (every half-hour Fri 11am–3pm, Sat 10.30am–3pm, Sun 12.30–3pm; $7; Ⓣ213/847-4646) don't let you get too close, but can be interesting for the full story of the site.

Hollywood

Hollywood encapsulates the LA dream of glamour, money and overnight success, with millions of tourists arriving on pilgrimages every year. Although many of the big film companies long ago relocated to blander digs in Burbank, and you're still more likely to see a homeless person than a movie star, recent attempts at renovation have added a bit of the old glitz to a downtrodden scene.

Central Hollywood

The hub of **Central Hollywood** is the corner of Hollywood Boulevard and Highland Avenue, where, amid the flashy neon tourist traps, the **Hollywood and Highland** mall (Mon–Sat 10am–10pm, Sun 10am–7pm, Ⓦwww.hollywoodandhighland.com) hosts a major hotel and chic restaurants, plus colossal pseudo-film-set architecture and the **Kodak Theater,** where the Oscars are held annually. Also incorporated in the complex is the historic **Chinese Theatre**, 6925 Hollywood Blvd (Ⓣ323/464-8111, Ⓦwww.manntheatres.com/chinese), a curious version of a classical Chinese temple, replete with dubious Asian motifs and upturned dragon-tail flanks. You can take in a mainstream film in the theatre and afterwards, on the street outside, see the famous forecourt (free access) adorned with the hand- and footprints of Hollywood bigwigs from the silent era to the present. While there, you can linger with hundreds of other sightseers amid the celebrity impersonators – Elvis, Marilyn and Darth Vader among them – and the low-rent magicians and assorted oddballs vying for your amusement and money.

The most legendary intersection, however, isn't at Highland, but just east at the junction of **Hollywood and Vine** – the mythical place for budding stars to be "spotted" by big-shot directors and whisked off to fame and fortune – in the shadow of the iconic "record stack" of the **Capitol Records Tower**. Few aspiring stars actually loiter in this gritty environment, but many visitors do come to trace the **Walk of Fame**, which officially begins here with a series of gold-inset stars honouring famous and forgotten names of radio, TV and movies.

Several blocks west, another grand design, the **Egyptian Theater**, at no. 6708, was built in a modest attempt to re-create the Temple of Thebes and the very first Hollywood premiere (*Robin Hood*) took place here in 1922. Movie-lovers should make a special trip here to view an art, foreign or indie film (tickets $11), or to take a brief tour and watch a documentary chronicling the rise of Hollywood (Sat & Sun 11.40am; $10; Ⓣ323/461-2020 ext 3, Ⓦwww.egyptiantheatre.com); you can also take a 60-minute tour of the facility (Tues–Sun 10.30am–4pm; $7; by reservation only; Ⓣ323/461-2020 ext 121). A few blocks west, across from the Hollywood and Highland mall, the similarly impressive **El Capitan Theater**, no. 6834 (see p.876), is a colourful 1926 movie palace, with Baroque and Moorish details and a wild South Seas–themed interior of sculpted angels and garlands, while a few doors down, at no. 7000, the **Hollywood Roosevelt** was movieland's first luxury hotel (see p.853). Just south of Hollywood and Highland, the **Hollywood Museum**, 1660 Highland Blvd (Wed–Sun 10am–5pm; $15; Ⓦwww.thehollywoodmuseum.com), has four floors of fashion, sets, make-up and other artefacts taken from movie history, though it has less the feel of a museum than a hodgepodge of castoffs in an overstuffed attic.

Further south, near Santa Monica Boulevard and Gower Street, **Hollywood Forever Cemetery** (daily dawn–dusk; free; Ⓦwww.hollywoodforever.com) is the district's most famous graveyard and features all manner of buried stars, such as Rudolph Valentino and Douglas Fairbanks Sr, as well as more unexpected grave markers, such as Johnny Ramone playing one last guitar riff. South of the cemetery, **Paramount Studios**, 5555 Melrose Ave (2hr tour, on the hour Mon–Fri 10am & 2pm; $35; by reservation; Ⓣ323/956-1777), is famous for its grand **gate**, though the original studio entrance – which Gloria Swanson rode through in *Sunset Boulevard* – is now inaccessible. The tour isn't quite up to the standard of other studio tours, but if you want to poke around empty soundstages and a mildly interesting backlot, it may be worth it.

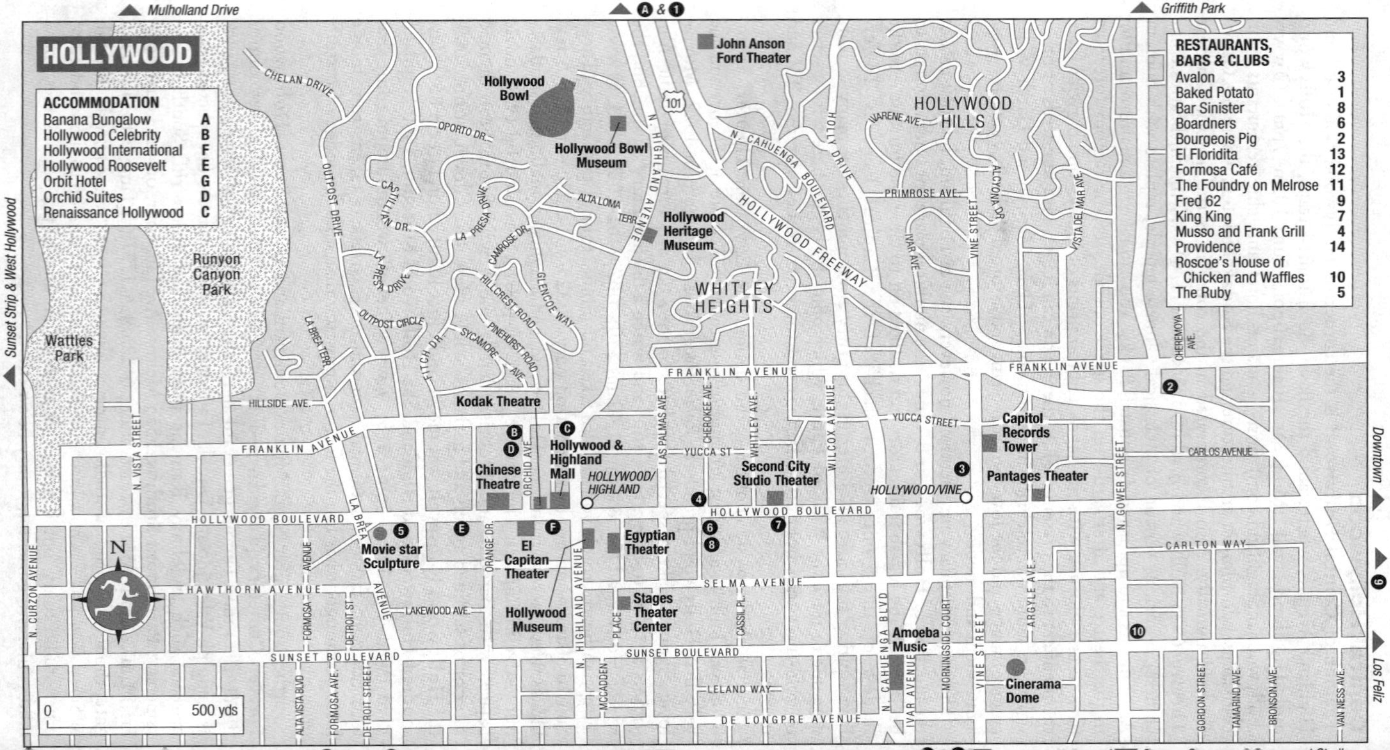

HOLLYWOOD

ACCOMMODATION

Banana Bungalow	A
Hollywood Celebrity	B
Hollywood International	F
Hollywood Roosevelt	E
Orbit Hotel	G
Orchid Suites	D
Renaissance Hollywood	C

RESTAURANTS, BARS & CLUBS

Avalon	3
Baked Potato	1
Bar Sinister	8
Boardners	6
Bourgeois Pig	2
El Floridita	13
Formosa Café	12
The Foundry on Melrose	11
Fred 62	9
King King	7
Musso and Frank Grill	4
Providence	14
Roscoe's House of Chicken and Waffles	10
The Ruby	5

Mulholland Drive
A & 1
Griffith Park
Sunset Strip & West Hollywood
Downtown
9
Los Feliz

Hollywood Bowl
Hollywood Bowl Museum
John Anson Ford Theater
Hollywood Heritage Museum
HOLLYWOOD HILLS
WHITLEY HEIGHTS
Runyon Canyon Park
Wattles Park
Kodak Theatre
Chinese Theatre
Hollywood & Highland Mall
HOLLYWOOD/HIGHLAND
El Capitan Theater
Hollywood Museum
Egyptian Theater
Stages Theater Center
Second City Studio Theater
Capitol Records Tower
Pantages Theater
HOLLYWOOD/VINE
Amoeba Music
Cinerama Dome
Movie star Sculpture

0 500 yds

Griffith Park

The greenery and mountain slopes that make up vast **Griffith Park**, northeast of Hollywood (daily 6am–dusk; ⓣ323/913-4688), offer lush gardens, splendid views and many miles of fine trails – though if you come at the wrong time, you might just find the park on fire. Hillside conflagrations regularly menace the park during the summer, when it may remain closed for weeks to visitors. Otherwise, it's a great place for a long stroll, hike or bike ride. One notable sight here, the **LA Zoo**, 5333 Zoo Drive (daily 10am–5pm; $13; ⓦwww.lazoo.org), pales in comparison to its San Diego counterpart (see p.844), though the landmark Art Deco **Griffith Observatory**, 2800 E Observatory Rd (Tues–Fri noon–10pm, Sat & Sun 10am–10pm; free; ⓦwww.griffithobservatory.org), is well worth a visit, highlighted by the twelve-inch Zeiss refracting telescope, solar telescopes for viewing sunspots and solar storms, and modern exhibits covering the history of astronomy and human observation. The observatory has been used as a backdrop in innumerable Hollywood films, most famously *Rebel Without a Cause*, and the site offers great views over the LA basin and out to sea (provided the smog isn't too thick). Also meriting a stop is the **Museum of the American West**, near the junction of the Ventura and Golden State freeways at 4700 Western Heritage Way (Tues–Fri 10am–4pm, Sat & Sun 11am–5pm; $9; ⓦwww.theautry.org), whose comprehensive collection of artefacts includes sections on native peoples, European exploration, nineteenth-century pioneers, the Wild West, Asian immigrants and, of course, Hollywood's versions of all of the above.

The Hollywood Hills

The canyons and slopes of the **Hollywood Hills**, which run from Hollywood west to the canyons above Beverly Hills, are best seen from the winding concourse of **Mulholland Drive**, threading the crest of the mountains. With its striking panorama after dark of the illuminated city-grid stretching nearly to the horizon, the road is a prime axis for the LA good life, with mansions so commonplace that only the half-dozen fully-blown castles really stand out. For a more up-close look at landmark architecture, take in a concert at the **Hollywood Bowl**, 2301 N Highland Ave (ⓣ323/850-2000, ⓦwww.hollywoodbowl.org), the massive concrete bandshell whose summer music offerings tend toward the crowd-pleasing variety – it's as good a spot as any to hear the festive roar of the *1812 Overture*.

Throughout Hollywood, you can see the **Hollywood Sign**, erected as a property advertisement in 1923 (when it spelled "Hollywoodland", until 1949) and illuminated with four thousand light bulbs. Nowadays, infrared cameras and radar-activated zoom lenses have been installed to catch graffiti writers. Curious tourists who can't resist a close look are liable for a steep fine.

West LA

LA's Westside begins immediately beyond Hollywood, known also as **West LA** and roughly bordered by the foothills of the Hollywood Hills to the north and the Santa Monica Freeway (I-10) to the south. West LA is the place where the city's nouveau riche flaunt their fortunes most conspicuously, from the trendy confines of West Hollywood and shadowy wealth of Bel Air to the high-priced shopping strips of Beverly Hills.

Museum Row

On the commercial axis of Wilshire Boulevard, the **Miracle Mile**, between La Brea and Fairfax avenues, was the premier property development of the 1930s, although recent public investment has created a "**Museum Mile**" in its place, also known as **Museum Row**. The first is sited at the **La Brea Tar Pits**, where for thousands of years, animals who tried to drink from the thin layer of water covering this rank pool of tar became stuck fast and preserved for posterity. It's now surrounded by life-sized replicas of such victims as mastodons and sabre-toothed tigers, some of them reconstructed next door at the impressive **George C. Page Museum**, 5801 Wilshire Blvd (daily 9.30am–5pm; $7; Ⓦwww.tarpits.org). Across the street, the **Craft and Folk Art Museum**, 5814 Wilshire Blvd (Tues–Fri 11am–5pm, Sat & Sun noon–6pm; $5; Ⓦwww.cafam.org), has a small selection of handmade objects – rugs, pottery, clothing and so on – with rotating exhibitions featuring the likes of handmade tarot cards, ceramic folk art and highly detailed Asian textiles. At the intersection with Fairfax Avenue, the **Petersen Automotive Museum**, 6060 Wilshire Blvd (Tues–Sun 10am–6pm; $10; Ⓦwww.petersen.org), pays homage to motorized vehicles of all kinds on three floors, with rotating exhibits such as the Golden Age of customizing, Hollywood prop cars and "million-dollar" vehicles.

Los Angeles County Museum of Art

On the west side of the La Brea Tar Pits, the enormous **LA County Museum of Art (LACMA)**, 5905 Wilshire Blvd (Mon, Tues & Thurs noon–8pm, Fri noon–9pm, Sat & Sun 11am–8pm; $12, pay what you wish after 5pm; Ⓦwww.lacma.org), is one of the least known of the important museums in the US, but, in fact, one of the largest west of the Mississippi. The **Art of the Americas Building** is home to the museum's somewhat spotty collection of **American art**; highlights include the work of John Singleton Copley (the regal *Portrait of a Lady*), Winslow Homer (the dusty realism of the *Cotton Pickers*), Albert Pinkham Ryder (the murky, alluring landscape of *The River*) and Thomas Eakins (the writhing, nude *Wrestlers*).

The adjacent **Ahmanson Building** has a broad array of exquisite and priceless works of **Asian art** from China and Korea to India and Tibet, as well as an assortment of American **costumes** and **textiles**, occasionally with a nod to Hollywood. However, its central attractions are undoubtedly the **European art rooms**, which begin with a good overview of Greek and Roman art and continue into the medieval era with religious sculptures and various shards of ecclesiastical architecture such as Romanesque capitals, Gothic reliefs and so on. Aficionados of Rodin will also delight in a room full of his small, vigorous sculptures, and elsewhere the likes of Rembrandt, Degas, Renoir and others make their appearances.

On its eastern end LACMA offers the **Pavilion for Japanese Art**, elegant with its sloping ramp and walls styled after shoji screens, and at its western end **LACMA West**, featuring kids' art and temporary shows, but it's in the centre building – the **Broad Museum for Contemporary Art** – that LACMA has really come into its own. This four-level creation houses some of the best modern art in town, much of it by LA stalwarts such as John Baldessari, Mike Kelley and Chris Burden. Some of the building is given over to space for rotating exhibitions, which are also on view at the new **Resnick Pavilion**, a huge, glass-and-marble showpiece designed by Renzo Piano that houses flexible open galleries to accommodate works of any size.

West Hollywood

North along Fairfax Avenue from the Museum Mile, **West Hollywood** is home to Los Angeles's most prominent – and affluent – gay community, seen most prominently along the chic blocks of **Santa Monica Boulevard**, from Doheny Drive to La Cienega Boulevard. Just south, **Melrose Avenue** is LA's trendiest shopping street and one of the unmistakable symbols of Southern California, where neon and flashy signs abound among a fluorescent rash of designer and secondhand boutiques, antique shops and high-end diners. **La Brea Avenue** runs perpendicular to the east side of the Melrose district, offering more space, fewer tourists, chic clothiers, upscale restaurants and even trendier galleries.

On the north edge of West Hollywood, on either side of La Cienega Boulevard, is the two-mile-odd amalgam of restaurants, hotels, billboards and nightclubs on Sunset Boulevard known as the **Sunset Strip**, one of LA's best areas for nightlife. The scene hit its stride in the 1960s around the landmark **Whisky-a-Go-Go** club, no. 8901, which featured seminal psychedelic rock bands such as The Doors, Love and Buffalo Springfield. The music venues (see p.873 for more choices) are still worth a visit, whether you want to rock, headbang or just dance, and, like the streets noted above, Sunset Boulevard makes for a lively night-time walk.

Beverly Hills and around

Beverly Hills is one of the world's wealthiest residential areas, patrolled by more cops per capita than anywhere else in the US. Glorified by the elite shops of **Rodeo Drive**, squeaky-clean streets, and ostentatious displays of wealth, the city is undoubtedly the height of LA pretension. Some of the bigger retail names include Barney's, 9570 Wilshire Blvd, and, all on Rodeo itself, Christian Dior, no. 309; Prada, no. 343; Gucci, no. 347; Chanel, no. 400; Hermes, no. 434; and Giorgio Armani, no. 436. Luckily, there are a number of decent and unassuming spots for visitors interested in things other than commodities. The **Paley Center for Media**, 465 N Beverly Drive (Wed–Sun noon–5pm; $10, kids $5; Ⓦwww.mtr.org), is one such place, vividly chronicling eighty years of our media-saturated age, and best for its voluminous library of shows, where you can take in everything from *I Love Lucy* to *The Simpsons*, and many more obscure offerings as well. For an overview of Beverly Hills' shopping and the area's art and architecture, take a trip on the **Beverly Hills Trolley** (40min ride; year-round Sat & Sun 11am–4pm; July–Aug & Dec Tues–Sun same hours; $5; Ⓣ310/285-2442), departing hourly from the corner of Rodeo and Dayton Way.

In the northern hills and canyons, curvaceous roads head into the hills and become narrower and more upmarket. A number of well-concealed gardens and parks offer a nice respite. One such place, the wooded **Virginia Robinson Gardens**, 1008 Elden Way (tours Tues–Fri 10am & 1pm; $10; by appointment only; Ⓣ310/276-5367), spreads across six acres of flora, with more than a thousand varieties, including some impressive Australian King Palm trees. To the east, the grounds of the biggest house in Beverly Hills, **Greystone Mansion**, 905 Loma Vista Drive, are now maintained as a public **park** by the city (daily 10am–5pm; free; Ⓦwww.greystonemansion.org). The fifty-thousand-square-foot manor was once the property of oil titan Edward Doheny. You can't go inside, but you can admire the mansion's limestone facade and intricate chimneys, then stroll through the sixteen-acre park, with its koi-filled ponds and expansive views of the LA sprawl.

Westwood and UCLA

West of Beverly Hills and the drab corporate box-towers of Century City, and north of Wilshire Boulevard, **Westwood** is the home of the **University of California at Los Angeles (UCLA)**, and is known to many as "Westwood Village". Once LA's prime movie-going district, Westwood has lost some of its eminence due to a lack of parking, but remains the most densely packed movie-theatre district in town and its 1931 **Westwood Village Theater**, crowned with a grand neon spire at 961 Broxton Ave, is still used for Hollywood premieres and "sneak previews" to gauge audience reactions. Art lovers shouldn't miss a trip to the **UCLA Hammer Museum**, 10899 Wilshire Blvd (Tues–Sat 11am–7pm, Thurs closes 9pm, Sun 11am–5pm; $7, kids free, Thurs free to all; Ⓦwww.hammer.ucla.edu), where there are some impressive early-American works from Gilbert Stuart, Thomas Eakins and John Singer Sargent, and insightful, sometimes risk-taking contemporary and avant-garde exhibits.

The university's highlights include the central **quadrangle**, a greenspace bordered by UCLA's most graceful buildings, including **Royce Hall**, modelled on Milan's Church of St Ambrosio, with high bell towers, rib vaulting and grand archways; and the **Powell Library**, featuring a spellbinding interior with lovely Romanesque arches, columns and stairwell. The **Fowler Museum of Cultural History**, Bruin Walk at Westwood Plaza (Wed–Sun noon–5pm, Thurs closes 8pm; free; Ⓦwww.fowler.ucla.edu), offers an immense range of multicultural art – including ceramics, religious icons, paintings and musical instruments. The **Franklin Murphy Sculpture Garden**, in the northeast corner of campus (open 24hr; free; for tours call Ⓣ310/443-7041), is LA's best outdoor display of modern sculpture, featuring pieces by Henry Moore, Barbara Hepworth, Henri Matisse, Jacques Lipchitz and Isamu Noguchi; while the **Hannah Carter Japanese Garden**, 10619 Bellagio Rd (Tues, Wed & Fri 10am–2pm; free; by appointment only; Ⓣ310/794-0320; Ⓦwww.japanesegarden.ucla.edu), is an idyllic spot featuring magnolias and Japanese maples, and traditional structures and river rocks brought directly from Japan.

The Getty Center

Towering over the surrounding area, the **Getty Center** (Tues–Thurs & Sun 10am–5.30pm, Fri & Sat 10am–9pm; free, parking $15; Ⓦwww.getty.edu), near the Sepulveda Pass north of Wilshire Boulevard, is Richard Meier's towering modernist temple to high art, clad in acres of travertine, its various buildings devoted to conservation, acquisition and other philanthropic tasks, and its surrounding gardens arranged with geometric precision. You can get here by MTA bus #761, on its route from UCLA, stopping on Sepulveda Boulevard, near the car park.

The quality of the **exhibits** is extraordinary. In the rooms devoted to decorative arts, you can see a formidable array of ornate French furniture from the reign of Louis XIV, with clocks, chandeliers, tapestries and gilt-edged commodes filling several overwhelmingly opulent chambers. The painting collection features all the major names from the thirteenth century on, including Van Gogh's **Irises** and a trio of evocative Rembrandts: *Daniel and Cyrus before the Idol Bel*, in which the Persian king tries foolishly to feed the bronze statue he worships; *An Old Man in Military Costume*, the exhausted, uncertain face of an old soldier; and *Saint Bartholomew*, showing the martyred saint as a quiet, thoughtful Dutchman – the knife that will soon kill him visible in the corner of the frame. Elsewhere in the museum, photography is well represented by Man Ray, Moholy-Nagy and other notables, and there's also a rich assortment of classical, Renaissance and Baroque sculpture – highlighted by Bernini's **Boy with a Dragon**, depicting a plump, possibly angelic toddler bending back the jaw of a dragon with surprising ease.

Venice, Santa Monica and Malibu

Set along an unbroken twenty-mile stretch of beaches, the cosy communities that line **Santa Monica Bay** feature some of the best vistas LA has to offer, with little of the smog or searing heat that can make the rest of the metropolis unpleasant. The entire area is well served by public transportation, and a wide choice of accommodation makes it a good base for seeing the rest of the city.

Venice

Venice was laid out in 1905 by developer Abbot Kinney as a romantic replica of the northern Italian city, complete with a twenty-mile network of canals. Over the decades it then became an amusement-park zone, grungy oil-drilling site, ground zero for hippies, drugs and crime, and finally today's arty district drawing a mix of hipsters, yuppies and real-estate speculators – as well as a few thugs and homeless people. The town's main artery, **Windward Avenue**, runs from the sands into what was the Grand Circle of the canal system – now only visible with the block-long fragment of a Neoclassical **arcade**, around the intersection with Pacific Avenue. Nearby, the few remaining **canals** display renovated white bridges and pedestrian-friendly footpaths (best accessed northbound on Dell Avenue from Washington Boulevard).

Nowhere else does LA parade itself quite so openly as along the wide pathway of **Venice Boardwalk**, packed year-round at weekends and every day in summer with musicians, street performers, trinket vendors and many others; it's lively and fun during the day, but strictly avoid the place after dark, when shades of the creepy old Venice appear. South of Windward is **Muscle Beach**, a legendary outdoor weight-lifting centre where serious-looking dudes (and a few muscularized women) pump serious iron, and budding basketballers hold court on the concrete.

Santa Monica

North of Venice, **Santa Monica** is perched on palm-tree-shaded bluffs above the blue Pacific. Once a wild beachfront playground, it's now a self-consciously healthy and very liberal community with a large expatriate British and Irish contingent.

Santa Monica reaches nearly three miles inland, but most spots of interest are within a few blocks of the beach, notably **Palisades Park**, the pleasant, cypress-tree-lined strip along the top of the bluffs which makes for striking views of the surf below. Two blocks east of Ocean Avenue, the **Third Street Promenade**, a pedestrianized stretch with street vendors, buskers and itinerant evangelists, is the closest LA comes to having a dynamic urban energy, and by far the best place to come for alfresco dining, beer-drinking and people-watching, especially after dark. Further south, another good stretch is **Main Street**, where the visitor centre is located (see p.851) and which boasts a serviceable array of fine restaurants, bars, shops and a few galleries.

Down below Palisades Park, the crowded **beach** is better for sunbathing than swimming, and the refurbished **Santa Monica pier** boasts a well-restored 1922 wooden **carousel** (late March to Sept Mon–Thurs 11am–5pm, Fri–Sun 11am–7pm; Oct to early March Thurs–Mon only; adults $2, kids 50¢, per ride) and crowds of tourists, teenagers and anyone else seeking a mild carnival thrill by the water. Although the tired rides of **Pacific Park** (hours vary, often summer daily 11am–11pm, Sat & Sun closes 12.30am; unlimited rides $21; Ⓦwww.pacpark.com) may catch your eye, save your money for the **Santa Monica Pier Aquarium** (Tues–Fri 2–6pm, Sat & Sun 12.30–6pm; $5, kids 12 and under free; Ⓦwww.healthebay.org/smpa), below the pier at 1600 Ocean Front Walk, where you can get your fingers wet touching sea anemones and starfish.

Getty Villa

If you really want to indulge in some serious (ancient) art, head five miles north along the beautiful, curving **Pacific Coast Highway (PCH)**, to the opulent **Getty Villa**, 17985 PCH (Wed–Mon 10am–5pm; free; parking $15; by reservation only at Ⓣ310/440-7300, Ⓦwww.getty.edu), modelled after a Roman country house buried by Mount Vesuvius in 79 AD, and built around its own fetching gardens. Inside, the museum is based around a two-storey peristyle and courtyard. Athenian vases are well represented, many of them the red-ground variety, as are ancient *kylikes*, or drinking vessels, and ceremonial amphorae, or vases, given as prizes in athletic contests. Not to be missed is a wondrous Roman *skyphos*, a fragile-looking blue vase decorated with white cameos of Bacchus and his friends, properly preparing for a bacchanalia.

Malibu and the Santa Monica Mountains

Twenty miles north of Santa Monica at the top of the bay, **Malibu** is synonymous with luxurious celebrity isolation, along with hillside wildfires, which routinely smoke those same celebrities out of their gilded confines. **Surfrider Beach** here was the surfing capital of the world in the 1950s and early 1960s, and is still a big attraction (the surf is best in late summer; check the surfing report at Ⓦwww.surfrider.org). Just beyond is **Malibu Lagoon State Park** (daily 8am–dusk), a nature reserve and bird refuge, and nearby is the **Adamson House**, 23200 PCH (grounds 8am–sunset, house tours Wed–Sat 11am–3pm; $5; Ⓦwww.adamsonhouse.org), a stunning, historic Spanish Colonial-style home featuring opulent decor and colourful tilework.

Downtown Malibu isn't much to look at, and most of the fancier homes are tucked away in the narrow canyons on the fringes of town – and typically accessible only by private drive. You'd do better to explore the huge **Santa Monica Mountains National Recreation Area** (Ⓦwww.lamountains.com), north of town, which is wilderness in many places, and you can still spot a variety of deer and coyotes, and even the odd mountain lion. If you'd like to find out more about this marvellous protected area, the Santa Monica Mountains **visitor centre**, over the hills in Thousand Oaks, 401 W Hillcrest Drive (daily 9am–5pm; Ⓣ805/370-2301, Ⓦwww.nps.gov/samo), has maps and information. Other good spots here include the 4000-acre **Malibu Creek State Park**, on Las Virgenes Road near Mulholland Drive, where 20th Century-Fox filmed many Tarzan pictures, as well as the TV show **M★A★S★H**, and the park includes a large lake, waterfalls and nearly fifteen miles of hiking trails. Further west, the **Paramount Ranch**, 2813 Cornell Rd, is another studio backlot with a phony rail crossing and cemetery, and Western movie set used in countless productions.

Five miles up the coast from Malibu Pier, **Zuma Beach** is the largest and most crowded of the Los Angeles County beaches, but adjacent **Point Dume State Beach**, below the imposing promontory of Point Dume, is a lot more relaxed, and the rocks at its southern tip, **Pirate's Cove**, are a good place to view seals and migrating grey whales in winter. At the northwestern edge of LA County, **Leo Carrillo** ("ca-REE-oh") **State Beach Park**, 35000 PCH, has a mile-long sandy beach divided by Sequit Point, a bluff with underwater caves and a tunnel you can pass through at low tide, and is also one of LA's best campgrounds (see p.852).

The South Bay and LA Harbor

South from LA along PCH is an eight-mile coastal strip of quiet South Bay beach towns: **Manhattan Beach**, **Hermosa Beach** and **Redondo Beach**. Each has a beckoning strip of white sand, and Manhattan and Hermosa are especially well equipped for surfing and beach sports; a good time to come is during the **Fiesta Hermosa** (Ⓦwww.fiestahermosa.com), a three-day event held on Memorial Day and Labor Day. They're also well connected by the regular bus lines to downtown LA. To the south are **Long Beach** – site of the LA Harbor – and the natural gem of **Santa Catalina Island**.

Long Beach

The massive port of **Long Beach** is part of the biggest such complex in the US and largest in the world outside of China. As a huge industrial site, it's well off the tourist trail, though its downtown section does offer an enjoyable stretch of restored architecture and antique stores around **Pine Avenue** (linked by the Blue Line light rail to downtown LA; see p.851). The one big draw is unquestionably the **Queen Mary**, docked in the bay at 1126 Queen's Hwy (daily 10am–6pm; $25 self-guided tours, $12 parking for 1–12 hr; Ⓦwww.queenmary.com), the Cunard flagship from the 1930s until the 1960s, and now a hotel chock-full of Art Deco amenities, decor and fixtures. The guided tours ($3–8 extra) are mostly oriented around ghosts that supposedly haunt the ship. Across the bay along Shoreline Drive, the **Aquarium of the Pacific** (daily 9am–6pm; $24, children $12; Ⓦwww.aquariumofpacific.org) is a terrific exploration of aquatic flora and fauna from geographic and climatic zones around the world, featuring more than 500 species in all, from sea lions and otters, to tide-pool creatures, exotic leopard sharks and giant Japanese spider crabs.

Orange County

Throughout the US, **Orange County** is synonymous with anodyne, white suburbia – most famously as the site of **Disneyland** – but in recent years it's begun to change, with many new Hispanic arrivals and more cultural (and culinary) diversity. Still, most tourists come just for the theme parks and for the easy-going, upscale beach towns of the **Orange County Coast**.

Disneyland

The pop-culture colossus of **Disneyland**, in Anaheim at 1313 Harbor Blvd (summer daily 8am–midnight; rest of year Mon–Fri 10am–6pm, Sat 9am–midnight, Sun 9am–10pm; $72, kids 3–9 $62, parking $14; Ⓦwww.disneyland.com), is one of America's most iconic sights, as well as one of its most expensive – most of the park's hotels are ridiculously overpriced (see p.854) and there's little quality cuisine in the area. The park is 45 minutes by **car** from downtown LA on the Santa Ana Freeway. Arrive early, as traffic and rides quickly become nightmarishly busy, especially in the summer.

Disneyland's best **rides** are in **Adventureland**: the Indiana Jones Adventure, an interactive archeological dig and 1930s-style newsreel show leading up to a giddy journey along 2500ft of skull-encrusted corridors; the Pirates of the Caribbean, a boat trip through underground caverns full of singing rogues; and the Haunted Mansion, a riotous "doom buggy" tour in the company of the house spooks. By contrast, **Frontierland** has mainly lower-end Wild West–themed carnival attractions, **Fantasyland** low-tech fairy-tale rides, notably the treacly It's a Small World; and **Toontown**, a cartoonish zone aimed at the kindergarten set. It's more worthwhile to zip right through to **Tomorrowland**, Disney's vision of the future, where the Space Mountain roller coaster plunges through the darkness of outer space.

Technically a separate park, the **California Adventure** is a lot less worthwhile. Aside from its slightly more exciting roller coasters and better food, the Adventure is really just another "land" to visit on your Disney trek, albeit a much more expensive one: you'll have to shell out $97 for a one-day pass that covers both this and the main park, or a jaw-dropping $151 for a two-day pass for both. Avoid visiting here until later in 2011, when the Adventure is due for a long-needed renovation.

Knott's Berry Farm

If you're a bit fazed by the excesses of Disneyland, you might prefer **Knott's Berry Farm**, four miles northwest, off the Santa Ana Freeway at 8039 Beach Blvd (hours vary, often summer Sun–Thurs 9am–11pm, Fri & Sat 9am–midnight; rest of year Mon–Fri 10am–6pm, Sat 10am–10pm, Sun 10am–7pm; $54, kids $20; Ⓦwww.knotts.com), whose roller coasters are far more exciting than anything at its rival. Knott's also has its own adjacent water park, **Soak City USA** (June–Sept only, hours vary but generally daily 10am–5pm or 6pm; $32, $20 for children or adult entry after 3pm), offering dozens of drenching rides of various heights and speeds.

Orange County Coast

Stretching from the edge of the LA Harbor to the border of San Diego County 35 miles south, the **Orange County Coast** is chic suburbia with a shoreline, the ambience easy-going, libertarian and affluent. As the names of the main towns suggest – **Huntington Beach**, **Newport Beach** and **Laguna Beach** – most of the good reasons to come here involve sea and sand, though a handful of other sights can also make for an interesting trip. Check out the **International Surfing Museum**, 411 Olive Ave, Huntington Beach (Mon–Fri noon–5pm; Sat & Sun 11am–6pm; $3; Ⓦwww.surfingmuseum.org), loaded with famous legends of the waves; Newport Beach's excellent **Orange County Museum of Art**, 850 San Clemente Drive (Wed–Sun 11am–5pm, Thurs closes 8pm; $12; Ⓦwww.ocma.net), focusing on modern California art and presenting regular lectures, events and art and architecture tours; and Laguna Beach's incredibly popular **Pageant of the Masters** (July & Aug daily shows begin at 8.30pm; tickets $20–150; Ⓣ1-800/487-3378, Ⓦwww.foapom.com), a strangely compelling spectacle in which participants dress up as characters from famous paintings. To the far south, **San Juan Capistrano** merits a stop as the site of the best kept of all the Californian **missions**, at Ortega Highway and Camino Capistrano (daily 8.30am–5pm; $9; Ⓦwww.missionsjc.com). It's also noted for its **swallows**, popularly thought to return here from their winter migration every March 19 (though they can actually arrive several weeks before or after).

The San Gabriel and San Fernando valleys

The northern limit of LA is defined by two long stretches, the **San Gabriel and San Fernando valleys**, lying over the hills from the central basin. Starting close to one another a few miles north of downtown, spanning outwardly in opposite directions – east to the deserts, west to the Central Coast – they feature a few worthwhile points of interest at considerable distance from each other, the highlight of which is undoubtedly the old-money hamlet of **Pasadena**.

The San Gabriel Valley

Ten miles northeast of downtown LA, the **San Gabriel Valley**'s main appeal is **Pasadena**, best known for its **Rose Parade** in January and **Rose Bowl** stadium west of town. Particularly distinctive is the historic shopping precinct of **Old Pasadena** along Colorado Boulevard, now fashionable for its restaurants and boutiques (and accessible on the Gold Line light rail), but also worthy for its century-old architecture in various historic-revival styles.

Pasadena's other best offerings are the splendid collection of the **Norton Simon Museum**, 411 W Colorado Blvd (Wed–Mon noon–6pm, Fri closes 9pm; $8, students free; Ⓦwww.nortonsimon.org), one of LA's best and most little-known art institutions, with a prime selection of Old Masters like Rubens and Rembrandt and modern works by Klee and Picasso – works that match up to anything at the Getty Center, though the crowds here are much more manageable; and the **Gamble House**, 4 Westmoreland Place (hour-long tours every 20–30min Thurs–Sun noon–3pm; $10; Ⓦwww.gamblehouse.org), a famed Craftsman mansion with striking Arts and Crafts decor and Japanese-inspired design elements – one of many works in the vicinity built by Craftsman masters Charles and Henry Greene. The engaging **Pacific Asia Museum**, a mile east at 46 N Los Robles Ave (Wed–Sun 10am–6pm; $9; Ⓦwww.pacificasiamuseum.org), is modelled after a Chinese imperial palace, showcasing historical treasures from Korea, China and Japan, including decorative jade and porcelain, swords and spears, and a large amount of paintings and drawings.

South of Pasadena, in dull, upper-crust **San Marino**, the **Huntington Museum and Library**, off Huntington Drive at 1151 Oxford Rd (Mon & Wed–Fri noon–4.30pm, Sat & Sun 10.30am–4.30pm; $15 weekdays, $20 weekends; Ⓦwww.huntington.org), is a lovely complex set off by many acres of themed gardens and handsome buildings. It definitely deserves a visit, as it contains some key historic documents and rare books, such as a Gutenberg Bible and the Ellesmere Chaucer – the latter an illuminated manuscript of **The Canterbury Tales** dating from around 1410. Notable paintings include Gainsborough's **Blue Boy** and Reynolds' **Mrs Siddons as the Tragic Muse**, and a few signature works of Constable, Turner, Blake and van Dyck.

The San Fernando Valley and Magic Mountain

The **San Fernando Valley**, spreading west, is a vast, uninspiring sprawl of tract homes, mini-malls and fast-food diners, but merits a trip to see **Forest Lawn Cemetery**, in Glendale at 1712 S Glendale Ave (daily 8am–5pm; free; Ⓦwww.forestlawn.org), a fascinating, often kitschy, display of death Hollywood-style. Those buried here include Errol Flynn, Walt Disney, Clara Bow, Nat King Cole, Chico Marx, Clark Gable and Jean Harlow, among other notables, many under grave markers so garish and tacky they must be seen to be believed.

North of the San Fernando Valley, the three-hundred-acre theme park of **Magic Mountain**, Magic Mountain Parkway at I-5 (hours vary, often summer daily 10am–10pm; rest of year Sat & Sun only 10am–8pm; $55, kids $27, $15 parking; Ⓦwww.sixflags.com), holds the region's wildest roller coasters, with a new fright-ride unleashed nearly every summer.

Burbank and the studios

Miles from Hollywood proper, the nitty-gritty business of actually making films goes on over the hills in otherwise boring **BURBANK**. The studio tours include a peek inside **NBC**, 3000 W Alameda Blvd (box office open Mon–Fri 9am–4pm; $8; reserve at Ⓣ818/840-3537), which also allows you the chance to get a free seat in the audience of *The Tonight Show*, though call ahead for details. Not far away, you can take a fun, two-hour trek into the soundstages and studio lots of **Warner Brothers**, 3400 Riverside Drive (Mon–Fri 8.30am–4pm; $45, parking $7; Ⓦwww.wbstudiotour.com), but elsewhere, Disney's fortress-like compound, at 500 S Buena Vista St, is strictly off-limits.

The largest of the backlots belongs to **Universal Studios**, whose lengthy tours (hours vary, often summer daily 9am–8pm or 9pm; rest of year 10am–6pm; minimum two-day ticket $69, kids $59; Ⓦwww.universalstudioshollywood.com) are more like a trip around an amusement park, with high-tech thrill rides and "evening spectaculars" based on current movies. The shows are without exception cheesy, but for fans of explosions and hijinks, they're an absolute must.

Eating

Eating in LA covers every extreme, whatever you want to eat and however much you want to spend. Try to take at least a few meals in the higher-end restaurants, many of which serve superb California cuisine in chic surroundings. At the cheaper end of the scale, the options are almost endless, and include terrific burger stands where you can scarf down mountains of fries, outstanding ethnic diners, and free food available for the price of a drink at **happy hours**.

Downtown and around

Ciudad 445 S Figueroa St ⓣ213/486-5171. Ceviche, empanadas and rabbit paella are some of the highlights at this colourful, if pricey, Mexican-influenced spot, where the live Latin music competes with the delicious food for your attention.

Engine Co. No. 28 644 S Figueroa St ⓣ213/624-6996. Longtime favourite for all-American fare, featuring expensive grilled steaks and seafood, plus lamb shank and chicken pot pie, served with great fries in a renovated 1912 fire station.

La Luz del Dia 107 Paseo de la Plaza ⓣ213/628-7495. Authentic Mexican eatery on Olvera Street, worth seeking out for the fiery burritos, enchiladas and tacos carnitas, all served in sizeable portions.

Ocean Seafood 750 N Hill St ⓣ213/687-3088. Busy Cantonese restaurant serving cheap and excellent food – dim sum, crab, shrimp and duck among many standout choices.

Pacific Dining Car 1310 W 6th St, west of downtown ⓣ213/483-6000. Since 1921, this would-be English supper club located inside an old railroad carriage has been the spot for very expensive and delicious steaks. Open 24hr.

Patina 141 S Grand Ave ⓣ213/972-3331. Ultra-swanky spot in Disney Hall, where you can devour Maine lobster, Jidori chicken and foie-gras ravioli, among other supreme items on the menu, if you're prepared to drop a wad of cash.

Philippe the Original French Dip 1001 N Alameda St ⓣ213/628-3781. Renowned 1908 cafeteria that invented the French dip, and keeps patrons loaded with succulent turkey, pork, beef or lamb.

Hollywood

Bourgeois Pig 5931 Franklin Ave, Hollywood ⓣ323/464-6008. Self-consciously hip environment and overpriced cappuccinos – you pay a bit more for the artsy atmosphere, but the agreeable java and colourful people-watching make it worthwhile.

The Foundry on Melrose 7465 Melrose Ave ⓣ323/651-0915. Expensive Cal-cuisine served with aplomb, whether its the tuna tartare, caramelized scallops, monkfish or green-tea brûlée.

Fred 62 1850 N Vermont Ave ⓣ323/667-0062. Tasty modern twists on 1950s staples like salads, burgers and fries, and a tempting array of pancakes and omelets, too.

Guelaguetza 3014 Olympic Blvd ⓣ213/427-0608. Primo eatery south of Hollywood that appeals for its cheap, authentic Mexican fare from Oaxaca – delicious *moles*, savoury stews and soups, and all manner of south-of-the-border staples, from *chile rellenos* to *horchata*.

Intelligentsia 3922 W Sunset Blvd, Silver Lake ⓣ323/663-6173. A new arrival that's more stylish than your average coffeehouse and its beans come in many varieties and from many places. Part of a local chain.

Mario's Peruvian & Seafood 5786 Melrose Ave ⓣ323/466-4181. Top-notch Peruvian fare that's well worth seeking out: supremely tender squid, rich and flavourful mussels, and fine ceviche, for affordable prices.

Providence 5955 Melrose Ave ⓣ323/460-4170. In price and quality, near the top of the LA foodie heap, and for good reason: the place has fantastic black sea bass, lobster risotto, oysters and plenty of other memorable choices.

Roscoe's House of Chicken and Waffles 1514 N Gower St ⓣ323/466-7453. This diner attracts all sorts for its fried chicken, greens, goopy gravy and thick waffles. One of five locations in the city.

West LA

Apple Pan 10801 W Pico Blvd ⓣ310/475-3585. Grab a spot at the counter and enjoy apple pie, baked ham and steakburgers at an old-time joint that opened just after World War II.

Campanile 624 S La Brea Ave ⓣ323/938-1447. Fine but expensive Northern Italian food, highlighted by pan-roasted veal chop and seared tuna. Adjacent *La Brea Bakery* has some of the city's best bread, too.

Canter's Deli 419 N Fairfax Ave ⓣ323/651-2030. Old-time favourite for kosher soup and sandwiches in a kitschy diner setting, with its own bizarre cabaret.

Grace 7360 Beverly Blvd ⓣ323/934-4400. Upper-end but delicious Cal-cuisine that inspires confidence for its pork shank, wild-boar tenderloin and inventive desserts, from pecan brown-sugar doughnuts to salted-caramel ice cream.

Hatfield's 6703 Melrose Ave ⓣ323/935-2977. Fine elite restaurant with a solid reputation for California cuisine, such as Japanese mackerel, smoked pork belly and outstanding desserts.

Il Pastaio 400 N Canon Drive ⓣ310/205-5444. Ever-popular Beverly Hills fave serving fine, affordable food – tasty Northern Italian offerings such as risotto (prepared in a range of ways), many traditional pastas and veal, pork and seafood entrees.

Mishima 8474 W 3rd St ⓣ323/782-0181. Great miso soup, soft-shell crab salad, and udon and soba noodles, at very affordable prices, at this popular Westside eatery.

Nate 'n' Al's 414 N Beverly Drive ⓣ310/274-0101. The best-known deli in Beverly Hills, popular with movie people and one of the few reasonable places for dining in the vicinity. Get there early to grab a booth.

Santa Monica, Venice and Malibu

Benito's Taco Shop 11614 Santa Monica Blvd ⓣ310/442-9924. Beef, pork or fish rolled up in a flour tortilla, for just a few bucks. Most combos are also under $6, making this a good spot to gobble and run. One of three 24-hour joints in the area.

Chaya Venice 110 Navy St ⓣ310/396-1179. Elegant mix of Japanese and Mediterranean foods in an arty sushi bar, with plenty of Cal-cuisine elements and a suitably snazzy clientele. One of Santa Monica's best eateries. Two other citywide branches.

Chinois on Main 2709 Main St, Santa Monica ⓣ310/392-9025. One of LA's most renowned and most expensive, restaurants, serving esteemed Asian dishes such as Kurobota pork, Cantonese duck and catfish in ginger sauce.

Hal's 1349 Abbot Kinney Blvd, Venice ⓣ310/396-3105. Popular restaurant in a hip shopping zone in Venice, with mid- to upper-end offerings including marinated steaks, Kobe beef ravioli and pan-roasted cod. Regular live jazz, too.

Valentino 3115 Pico Blvd, Santa Monica ⓣ310/829-4313. Some call it the finest Italian restaurant in the US – traditional Northern Italian dishes, with an infusion of Cal-cuisine, including a fine veal scallopini and osso bucco. Expect to max out your credit card.

South Bay and LA Harbor

El Pollo Inka 1100 PCH, Hermosa Beach ⓣ310/372-1433. Cheap Peruvian-style chicken, catfish, and hot and spicy soups to make your mouth water. The most convenient of several South Bay locations.

George's Greek Café 135 Pine Ave, Long Beach ⓣ562/437-1184. Centrally located and affordable eatery where you can indulge in tasty gyros, dolmas and souvlaki, as well as several fine combo plates.

Johnny Reb's 4663 N Long Beach Blvd ⓣ562/423-7327. The waft of BBQ ribs, catfish and hush puppies alone may draw you to this prime Southern spot, where the portions are large and the prices are cheap.

Lasher's 3441 E Broadway, Long Beach ⓣ562/433-0153. Set in a little house east of downtown, a New American choice for steak, rack of lamb, seafood and pasta, at the upper end of what you'll pay in this port town.

Orange County

Angelo's 511 S State College Blvd, Anaheim ⓣ714/533-1401. Straight out of TV's *Happy Days*, a drive-in complete with roller-skating car-hops (waiting staff), vintage cars and juicy burgers.

Claes Seafood In the *Hotel Laguna*, 425 S Coast Hwy, Laguna Beach ⓣ949/376-9283. Fine seafood eatery where you can sample pricey and delicious short ribs, prawns and lobster pot pie, all with a Cal-cuisine spin, with a fine view of the Pacific.

Mimi's Café 1400 S Harbor Blvd, Anaheim ⓣ714/956-2223. Huge servings, low prices and solid breakfasts and lunches. Part of a sizeable chain in Los Angeles and Orange counties, and popular in both.

Sage 2531 Eastbluff Drive, Newport Beach ⓣ949/718-9650. Fancy eatery catering to Cal-cuisine lovers, featuring tasty delights like blue crab cakes, steelhead trout, flatiron steak and roasted duck breast. Also a branch at 7862 E Coast Hwy, Newport Beach ⓣ949/715-7243.

The San Gabriel and San Fernando valleys

Fair Oaks Pharmacy and Soda Fountain 1526 Mission St, South Pasadena ⓣ626/799-1414. A grand old soda fountain with many old-fashioned drinks, from lime rickeys to egg creams – a historic 1915 highlight along the former Route 66.

Porto's Bakery 315 N Brand Blvd, Glendale ⓣ818/956-5996. Popular and cheap café serving flaky Cuban pastries, scrumptious sandwiches, cheesecake soaked in rum, croissants, tarts and tortes, and cappuccino. Also at 3614 W Magnolia Blvd, Burbank ⓣ818/846-9100.

Saladang 363 S Fair Oaks Ave, Pasadena ⓣ626/793-8123. Don't miss out on the pad thai, curry and salmon at this chic and delicious spot, or the spicy noodles that would pass muster anywhere. The annexe, *Saladang Song*, offers even spicier Thai concoctions.

Shiro 1505 Mission St ⓣ626/799-4774. One of the few top-notch restaurants in South Pasadena: perhaps the only one. The seafood is excellent – particularly the catfish in ponzu sauce and shrimp with curry champagne sauce.

Nightlife and entertainment

Exploring the jungle of LA **nightlife** can be great fun. Even the quietest venue offers a chance to eavesdrop on the doings of the city's clubkids and hipsters; the most raucous ones will take your breath away. In all the bars, clubs and discos, you'll need to be 21 and will be asked for ID. The best sources of **listings** are **LA Weekly** (ⓦ www.laweekly.com) and Friday's **LA Times** (ⓦ www.latimes.com).

Bars

LA's **bars** provide a wide range of choices, from the funky dives of Hollywood to the chic enclaves of West LA and Santa Monica. As elsewhere along the West Coast, **coffeehouses** are established all over the city as popular meeting places.

Barney's Beanery 8447 Santa Monica Blvd, West Hollywood ⓣ 310/654-2287. Well-worn pool room/bar, good for its beer and rib-stuffing food and its solid, rock'n'roll-hedonist history. For many, a key stop on the bar-hopping trail.

Boardners 1652 N Cherokee Ave, Hollywood ⓣ 323/462-9621. Formerly one of Hollywood's premier dive bars, now remade into more yuppie-friendly digs, with a fairly good late-night pub grub menu.

Formosa Café 7156 Santa Monica Blvd, Hollywood ⓣ 323/850-9050. Started in 1925 as a watering hole for Charlie Chaplin's adjacent United Artists studios, this creaky spot is still alive with old Hollywood ghosts. Imbibe the spirits; stay away from the food.

Good Luck Bar 1514 Hillhurst Ave, Hollywood ⓣ 323/666-3524. A hip Los Feliz retro-dive, this hangout is popular for its chinoiserie decor and tropical drinks straight from the heyday of *Trader Vic's*. Worth a look for the art design alone.

Library Alehouse 2911 Main St, Santa Monica ⓣ 310/314-4855. Presenting the choicest brews from West Coast microbreweries and beyond, this is a good spot to select from a nice range of well-known and obscure labels.

Molly Malone's Irish Pub 575 S Fairfax Ave, mid-Wilshire ⓣ 323/935-1577. One of LA's drinking staples: a good-time Irish bar, with a crowd of regulars who look like they've been there for ages, plus nightly music and the requisite pints of thick Guinness.

Musso and Frank Grill 6667 Hollywood Blvd ⓣ 323/467-7788. Simply put, if you haven't had a drink in this landmark 1919 bar, you haven't been to Hollywood. The pricey diner food leaves something to be desired, though.

Tom Bergin's 840 S Fairfax Ave, West LA ⓣ 323/936-7151. Old-time drinking joint from 1936 – a great place for Irish coffee (supposedly invented here). You can spot the regulars from the pictures on the walls.

Ye Olde Kings Head 116 Santa Monica Blvd, Santa Monica ⓣ 310/451-1402. British pub heavy with expats, offering familiar olde beers, a jukebox and dartboards; don't miss the steak-and-kidney pie, afternoon tea or the fish and chips.

Clubs and discos

LA's **clubs** range from posy hangouts to industrial noise cellars. The trendier side of the club scene is, as always, elusive, with some venues changing names and clientele every six months, but listed below are some of the more established names. **Gay and lesbian clubs** are centred around West Hollywood and are noted below. Check the **LA Weekly** before setting out.

The Abbey 692 N Robertson Blvd, West Hollywood ⓣ 310/289-8410. One-time coffeeshop that's outgrown its humble origins and is now a sprawling, multi-room complex buzzing with straight and gay action, go-go dancers, video bar and packed Sunday-night party scene.

Avalon 1735 N Vine St, Hollywood ⓣ 323/462-8900. Major dance club spinning old-school faves, along with the usual techno and house, with the occasional big-name DJ dropping in. Prices are among the most expensive in town.

Bar Sinister 1652 N Cherokee, Hollywood ⓣ 323/462-1934. A collection of sprightly dance beats most nights of the week, then spooky goth music and anaemic-looking vampire types on Saturdays. Connected to *Boardners* bar (see above).

Bordello 901 E First St, downtown ⓣ 213/687-3766. An extravagantly decorated, plush setting – in the style of an old-time brothel – where the nightly entertainment might be anything from an up-and-coming indie band to a burlesque event or cabaret freakshow.

El Floridita 1253 N Vine St, Hollywood ⓣ323/871-8612. Quality Mexican and Cuban food plus a fine mix of Cuban and salsa music, played to a mostly local, lively crowd.

Jewel's Catch One 4067 W Pico Blvd, Mid-Wilshire ⓣ323/734-8849. Sweaty barn catering to a mixed crowd of gays and straights and covering two wild dancefloors. A longtime LA favourite, located in the middle of nowhere.

King King 6555 Hollywood Blvd ⓣ323/960-5765. A crowd of lively regulars hits this prime Hollywood spot for live dance music, with house, funk, rap and retro-pop all on the DJ docket.

Little Temple 4519 Santa Monica Blvd ⓣ323/660-4540. East Hollywood club scene themed around moody Asian decor, with tasty beverages like coconut martini; an expressive, schmoozy clientele, and tunes ranging from hip-hop to reggae, soul and funk.

Mayan 1038 S Hill St, downtown ⓣ213/746-4287. Formerly a pre-Columbian-styled movie palace, now hosting Latin rhythms and nonstop disco and house tunes on three dancefloors. One of the city's most eye-opening clubs.

Mother Lode 8944 Santa Monica Blvd, West Hollywood ⓣ310/659-9700. Strong drinks, wild dancing to house and "hi-NRG" music, karaoke and periodic drag antics make this one of the liveliest WeHo gay clubs.

The Ruby 7070 Hollywood Blvd ⓣ323/467-7070. A wide range of feverish dance nights take turns Thurs–Sun, covering everything from modern electronica and grinding industrial to perky house and retro-80s cheese.

Live music

LA has an overwhelming choice for **live music**: ever since the 1960s, the local **rock** scene has been excellent, with up-and-comers in mainstream or indie rock getting their first break here; **jazz** is played in a few authentic locales; and **salsa** is quite popular. Cover charges can vary widely, so call ahead.

Babe and Ricky's Inn 4339 Leimert Blvd, South Central LA ⓣ323/295-9112. One of LA's top spots for blues, offering plenty of quality, nationally known acts as well as fun weekly jam sessions.

Baked Potato 3787 Cahuenga Blvd West, North Hollywood ⓣ818/980-1615. A small but legendary jazz spot, where many reputations have been forged. Don't come looking for bland lounge jazz/muzak – instead, expect to be surprised.

Catalina Bar & Grill 6725 W Sunset Blvd ⓣ323/466-2210. Central Hollywood jazz institution with many big-name performers, as well as good acoustics, filling meals and potent drinks. It can get pricey, though.

Harvelle's 1432 4th St, Santa Monica ⓣ310/395-1676. Near the Promenade, a stellar blues joint for more than seven decades offering different performers nightly and a little funk, R&B and burlesque to boot.

McCabe's 3101 Pico Blvd, Santa Monica ⓣ310/828-4497. LA's premier acoustic guitar shop; long the scene of some excellent and unusual folk and country shows, with the occasional alternative act.

The Roxy 9009 Sunset Blvd, West Hollywood ⓣ310/278-9457. The showcase of the rock industry's new signings, intimate and with a great sound system.

Spaceland 1717 Silver Lake Blvd, Hollywood ⓣ323/661-4380. Excellent East Hollywood spot to catch local and national rockers and other acts, including punk, folk and alternative.

The Troubadour 9081 Santa Monica Blvd, West Hollywood ⓣ310/276-6168. An old 1960s mainstay that's been through a lot of incarnations. Used to be known for folk and country rock, then metal, now for various flavours of indie rock.

Viper Room 8852 Sunset Blvd, West Hollywood ⓣ310/358-1881. Intense live rockers and a headline-grabbing past have helped boost this club's hip aura. A much flashier reputation than the gloomy confines would suggest.

Whisky-a-Go-Go 8901 Sunset Blvd, West Hollywood ⓣ310/652-4202. For many years LA's most famous rock'n'roll club, nowadays featuring lesser-known hard rock, metal and alternative acts.

Classical music, opera and dance

LA has a number of choices for **classical music** and, in the last two decades, has surprisingly established itself as an international force in highbrow music. The Los Angeles Philharmonic (ⓣ323/850-2000, ⓦwww.laphil.org), now led by wunderkind Gustavo Dudamel, and Los Angeles Master Chorale (ⓣ213/972-7282,

Ⓦwww.lamc.org) perform regularly during the year at Disney Hall; the Los Angeles Chamber Orchestra (Ⓣ213/622-7001, Ⓦwww.laco.org) performs at assorted venues; and the Da Camera Society (Ⓣ213/477-2929, Ⓦwww.dacamera.org) offers chamber works in stunning settings, from grand churches to legendary modernist homes to renovated movie palaces.

As for **opera**, LA Opera (Ⓣ213/972-8001, Ⓦwww.losangelesopera.com), led by general director Placido Domingo, stages productions at Downtown's Music Center, but the region's most exciting company is Long Beach Opera (Ⓣ562/432-5934, Ⓦwww.longbeachopera.org), which puts on challenging but well-regarded performances of modern and lesser-known operas, at rotating venues. Finally, Los Angeles Ballet (Ⓣ310/998-7782, Ⓦwww.losangelesballet.org) is a recent attempt to fill a serious hole in the LA cultural scene, also performing at rotating venues.

Bing Theater 5905 Wilshire Blvd, Mid-Wilshire Ⓣ213/473-8493 or 0625, Ⓦwww.lacma.org. When it isn't hosting movie revivals, this auditorium at the LA County Museum of Art provides a fine space for classical concerts, which occur periodically during the year. Plus, free Friday-night jazz in the courtyard April–Nov.

Disney Hall 1st St at Grand Ave, downtown Ⓣ213/850-2000. Home of the LA Philharmonic, a striking Frank Gehry design (see p.856) with superb sound and visual design, hosting many kinds of arts groups.

Dorothy Chandler Pavilion In the Music Center, 135 N Grand Ave, downtown Ⓣ213/972-7211, Ⓦwww.musiccenter.org. Warhorse of the arts world, dating from the 1960s, used by LA Opera and other top names.

Greek Theatre 2700 N Vermont Ave, Griffith Park Ⓣ323/665-5857 Ⓦwww.greektheatrela.com. A broad range of mainstream music acts – often classical, jazz and Latin – at this outdoor, summer-only venue.

Hollywood Bowl 2301 N Highland Ave, Hollywood Ⓣ323/850-2000, Ⓦwww.hollywoodbowl.org. Hosts LA Philharmonic concerts, usually of the toe-tapping pops variety, and jazz and world-beat groups, for open-air concerts during the summer.

John Anson Ford Theatre 2850 Cahuenga Blvd, Hollywood Ⓣ323/461-3673, Ⓦwww.fordamphitheatre.org. An open-air venue that has eclectic productions by local classical and operatic groups as well as sporadic pop and rock concerts.

Comedy

The **comedy** scene in LA has long been a national proving ground for aspiring jokesters and inspired clowns, and it's also a good place to catch live performances by established names as well as up-and-comers. The better-known places are open nightly, but are often solidly booked on weekends. Cover typically ranges from $10–30.

Comedy & Magic Club 1018 Hermosa Ave, Hermosa Beach Ⓣ310/372-1193, Ⓦwww.comedyandmagicclub.com. Strange couplings of magic acts and comedians, but you're as likely to see a hilarious up-and-comer as a big name. Tickets can run up to $30.

Comedy Store 8433 W Sunset Blvd, West Hollywood Ⓣ323/650-6268, Ⓦwww.thecomedystore.com. LA's premier comedy showcase and popular enough to be spread over three rooms – which means there's usually space, even at weekends.

Groundlings Theatre 7307 Melrose Ave, Hollywood Ⓣ323/934-4747, Ⓦwww.groundlings.com. Only the gifted survive at this pioneering improv venue, where Pee Wee Herman and many past and future *Saturday Night Live* cast members got their start.

The Improv 8162 Melrose Ave, West Hollywood Ⓣ323/651-2583, Ⓦwww.improv.com. Long-standing brick-walled joint known for hosting some of the best acts working. One of LA's top comedy spots, and the forerunner of a large national chain.

iO West 6366 Santa Monica Blvd, Hollywood Ⓣ323/962-7560, Ⓦwest.ioimprov.com. Cheap and frequently riotous, this is a spot for those who like their improv drawn out, with comedy routines more like short theatre pieces than wacky one-liners.

Second City Studio Theatre 6560 Hollywood Blvd, Hollywood Ⓣ323/464-8542, Ⓦwww.secondcity.com. Groundbreaking comedy troupe with numerous branches in LA, hosting nightly improv and sketch comedy, sometimes built around lengthy routines.

Pro sports in LA

Baseball The **LA Dodgers** (Ⓣ323/224-1500, Ⓦwww.dodgers.com) play at Dodger Stadium near downtown; the **LA Angels of Anaheim** (Ⓣ1-888/796-4256, Ⓦwww.angelsbaseball.com) at Anaheim Stadium in Orange County; seats for both $10–150.

Basketball The **Lakers** (tickets $20–260; Ⓣ213/480-3232, Ⓦwww.lakers.com), **Clippers** ($18–250; Ⓣ213/742-7430, Ⓦwww.clippers.com), and women's **Sparks** ($10–55; Ⓣ1-877/44-SPARKS, Ⓦwww.wnba.com/sparks) all play at the Staples Center, south of downtown.

Football The 102,000-seat **Rose Bowl** (Ⓣ626/577-3100, Ⓦwww.rosebowlstadium.com) is the site of Pasadena's New Year's Day college football game, but LA hasn't had a pro franchise in 17 years.

Hockey The **Kings** are based at Staples Center ($25–135; Ⓣ1-888/KINGS-LA, Ⓦwww.lakings.com), and Orange County's **Anaheim Ducks** play at Honda Center ($20–175; Ⓣ714/704-2500, Ⓦducks.nhl.com).

Soccer The **Galaxy** ($20–125; Ⓣ1-877/3-GALAXY, Ⓦwww.lagalaxy.com) and **CD Chivas** ($15–100; Ⓣ1-877/CHIVAS-1, Ⓦweb.mlsnet.com/t120) both play at the Home Depot Center in the South Bay city of Carson.

Theatre

Not surprisingly for a place loaded with actors, LA has a very active **theatre** scene, with countless venues spread all over town; ticket services like LA Stage Alliance (Ⓣ213/614-0556, Ⓦwww.lastagealliance.com) have discount tickets for given shows, under its LA Stage programme. The **LA Weekly** and the Friday **LA Times** both offer listings and reviews.

Ahmanson Theatre/Mark Taper Forum In the Music Center, 135 N Grand Ave, Downtown Ⓣ213/972-0700, Ⓦwww.taperahmanson.com. Institutional, mainstream theatre, with agreeable classics and less frequently, new plays. Kirk Douglas Theatre, Culver City, 9820 Washington Blvd (same phone), is part of the same organization.

The Complex 6476 Santa Monica Blvd, Hollywood Ⓣ323/465-0383, Ⓦwww.complexhollywood.com. An association of five small theatres and five studios putting on innovative works with lesser-known actors you may not see anywhere else.

Matrix Theatre 7657 Melrose Ave Ⓣ323/852-1445, Ⓦwww.matrixtheatre.com. Lower Hollywood theatre offering uncompromising productions that often feature some of LA's better young actors and playwrights.

Odyssey Theatre Ensemble 2055 S Sepulveda Blvd, West LA Ⓣ310/477-2055, Ⓦwww.odysseytheatre.com. Respected Westside theatre company with a bent for the modernist and avant-garde, showing a range of quality productions on three stages for good prices.

Pantages Theatre 6233 Hollywood Blvd Ⓣ1-800/982-ARTS, Ⓦwww.broadwayla.org. An exquisite, atmospheric Art Deco theatre in the heart of historic Hollywood, hosting major touring Broadway productions and some musical acts.

Stages Theatre Center 1540 N McCadden Place, Hollywood Ⓣ323/465-1010, Ⓦwww.stagestheatrecenter.com. With three stages offering twenty to one hundred seats, this is an excellent place to catch a wide range of comedies and dramas.

Theatre West 3333 Cahuenga Blvd W, Hollywood Ⓣ323/851-7977, Ⓦwww.theatrewest.org. A classic venue with a lengthy track record that's always a good spot to see inventive, or odd, productions with a troupe of excellent up-and-comers.

Film

Many films are often released in LA months (or years) before they play anywhere else. You can catch **mainstream releases** in any mall-based multiplex, but if you're after a golden-age-of-film **atmosphere**, head for one of the historic moviehouses or evocative second-run houses listed below – or check out the excellent Last Remaining Seats festival in June (tickets $20; Ⓦwww.laconservancy.org) in classic movie palaces.

ArcLight 6360 Sunset Blvd, Hollywood ⓣ323/464-4226. ⓦwww.arclightcinemas.com. All-reserved seating in 14 theatres, top-of-the-line projection, good sightlines and the iconic Cinerama Dome, a white hemisphere that has the biggest screen in California.

Bing at the LA County Art Museum 5905 Wilshire Blvd, Mid-Wilshire ⓣ323/857-6010. Offers engaging retrospectives of famed actors and directors, as well as full-priced evening programmes of classic, independent, foreign, arthouse and revival cinema.

Chinese 6925 Hollywood Blvd, Hollywood ⓣ323/464-8111. Landmark cinema showing mainstream fare, with a large main screen, six-track stereo sound, and wild chinoiserie interior (see p.859), plus the famed forecourt where celebrities have laid down countless handprints.

Egyptian 6712 Hollywood Blvd ⓣ323/466-FILM. Wonderfully renovated showcase for classic and foreign films, in the middle of historic Hollywood (see p.859).

El Capitan 6834 Hollywood Blvd, Hollywood ⓣ323/467-7674. Legendary Hollywood venue restored to full glory and renovated several times. Expect to see plenty of animated and live-action Disney fare.

Nuart 11272 Santa Monica Blvd, West LA ⓣ310/281-8223. Classics, documentaries and foreign-language films, and the main option for independent film-makers testing their work. Sometimes offers brief Dec previews of Oscar contenders.

Village 961 Broxton Ave, Westwood ⓣ310/248-6266. One of the best places to watch a movie in LA, equipped with a giant screen, fine seats and modern sound system, and a frequent spot for Hollywood premieres.

Shopping

Not surprisingly for a city identified with mass consumerism, you can **buy** virtually anything in LA. The big department stores and exclusive **Rodeo Drive** are the first options for many tourists, along with the city's massive **malls**. Big names in central LA include West Hollywood's **Beverly Center**, at Beverly and La Cienega boulevards (ⓣ310/854-0070, ⓦwww.beverlycenter.com); **Westside Pavilion**, Pico and Westwood boulevards, West LA (ⓣ310/474-6255, ⓦwww.westsidepavilion.com); the **Century City Marketplace**, 10250 Santa Monica Blvd, West LA (ⓣ310/553-5300, ⓦwestfield.com/centurycity); **The Grove**, 6301 W 3rd St, West LA (ⓣ323/900-8080, ⓦwww.thegrovela.com) and **Hollywood and Highland**, at the eponymous Hollywood intersection (ⓣ323/960-2331, ⓦwww.hollywoodandhighland.com). Many chic boutiques line **Melrose Avenue** between La Brea and Fairfax avenues.

Books

Book Soup 8818 Sunset Blvd, West Hollywood ⓣ323/659-3110. You can't miss this prominent bookstore on the Sunset Strip, nor should you. Great, wide-ranging selection and celebs are sometimes known to drop by, attempting to look studious.

Hennessey and Ingalls 214 Wilshire Blvd, Santa Monica ⓣ310/458-9074. An impressive range of coffee-table art and architecture books makes this among the best of its kind in LA. Also in Hollywood at 1520 N Cahuenga Blvd ⓣ323/466-1256.

Samuel French Theatre & Film Bookshop 7623 Sunset Blvd, Hollywood ⓣ323/876-0570. LA's broadest selection of theatre books is found in this local institution, along with a good collection of movie and media-related titles.

Taschen 354 N Beverly Drive, Beverly Hills ⓣ310/274-4300. A publisher's own outlet with fun, weird and edifying titles that focus on everything from Renaissance art to kitsch Americana and fetish photography.

Wacko 4633 Hollywood Blvd, Hollywood ⓣ323/663-0122. East Hollywood favourite that stocks anything from alternative art and architecture to bizarre fetishes, music guides and conspiracy rants. Also with oddball adult toys.

Music

Amoeba Music 6400 W Sunset Blvd, Hollywood ⓣ323/245-6400. You'd never know the record industry was dying, at this huge music emporium with a vast selection of titles on CD, tape and vinyl. Also presents occasional in-store live music.

Counterpoint 5911 Franklin Ave, Hollywood ⓣ323/957-7965. Provides a terrific smorgasbord of used vinyl, CDs, movies on cassette and DVD, books and even antique 78 records. Also connected to its own underground art gallery.

Fingerprints 4612 E Second St, Long Beach ⓣ562/433-4996. A formidable indie outfit in the South Bay, offering alternative-leaning CDs and vinyl, plus in-store performances from local rockers.

Record Surplus 11609 W Pico Blvd, West LA ⓣ310/478-4217. The best spot for used music in LA (or anywhere for that matter), loaded with ancient LPs, out-of-print CDs, new releases and all manner of assorted junk you strangely want to own.

The Deserts

The hot and forbidding landscape of California's **deserts** exerts a powerful fascination for venturesome travellers. The two distinct regions are the **Low Desert** in the south, the most easily reached from LA, containing the opulent oasis of **Palm Springs** and the primeval expanse of **Joshua Tree National Park**; and the **Mojave** or **High Desert**, dominated by **Death Valley** and stretching along Hwy-395 to the sparsely populated **Owens Valley**, infamous as the place from which LA stole its water a hundred years ago.

It is impossible to do justice to this area without a car. Palm Springs can be reached on public transit from LA, but only the periphery of Joshua Tree is accessible and it's a long hot walk to anywhere worth seeing. You can get as far as dreary Barstow on Greyhound and Amtrak, but no transportation traverses Death Valley, understandably so in the summer.

The Low Desert

Most visitors to the **Low Desert** head straight for its capital, that sun-scorched refuge of the Hollywood and golfing elite, **Palm Springs**. It's the first major town east from LA on I-10, at the centre of the **Coachella Valley**, an agricultural empire that grows dates and citrus fruits in vast quantities and is the toasty location of one of the country's best outdoor music festivals, **Coachella** (ⓦwww.coachella.com), in the spring. Even more compelling, an hour's drive east of Palm Springs is the eerily sublime landscape of **Joshua Tree National Park**.

Palm Springs

Amid farmland replete with golf courses, condos and millionaires, **PALM SPRINGS** embodies a strange mix of Spanish Colonial and mid-twentieth-century modernist architecture. Massive Mount San Jacinto looms over its low-slung buildings, casting a welcome shadow over the town in the late-afternoon heat. In recent years, the city has also become a major **gay and lesbian** resort (ⓦwww.gaypalmspringsca.com has a list of options).

Arrival, information and getting around

Arriving by car, you drive into town on N Palm Canyon Drive, passing the **visitor centre** at no. 2901 (daily 9am–5pm, Sun closes 4pm; ⓣ1-800/347-7746, ⓦwww.palm-springs.org), a classic piece of pop architecture with an upswept roof and boomerang design. Greyhound **buses** (4 daily from LA; 2hr 30min–3hr) pull in downtown at 311 N Indian Canyon Drive, while Amtrak **trains** from LA (2 daily;

2hr 30min) stop just south of I-10 at N Indian Avenue, about ten minutes from downtown. The local operator SunBus (6am–8pm; tickets $1, day passes $3; ⓣ760/343-3456, ⓦwww.sunline.org) circulates in all the local resort towns. Guided tours of Palm Springs' stash of notable **modernist architecture** are organized by PS Modern Tours (2hr 30min; $75; ⓣ760/318-6118).

Accommodation

Luxury **hotels** outnumber the cheaper variety in Palm Springs, but prices drop by as much as seventy percent as temperatures soar in the summer. The north end of town, along Hwy-111, holds many of the lower-priced places, including countless motels, virtually all of which have pools and air conditioning. The prices below are **spring** and **autumn rates**; expect to pay about $20–50 more or less for winter and summer, respectively.

Casa Cody 175 S Cahuilla Rd ⓣ760/320-9346, ⓦwww.casacody.com. Built in the 1920s, this historic Southwestern-style B&B offers attractive rooms and a shady garden. A bit more comfortable than higher-priced retro-motels. ❹

Ingleside Inn 200 W Ramon Rd ⓣ760/325-0046 or 1-800/772-6655, ⓦwww.inglesideinn.com. Compelling downtown option with a star-studded guest list and rooms with antiques, fireplaces, whirlpool tubs and patios (for double the price of a standard room). Two-night minimum stay. ❼

Orbit In 562 W Arenas Rd ⓣ1-877/996-7248, ⓦwww.orbitin.com. Old-style 1957 motel remade into a suave, yuppie-friendly hotel – drink cutely-named cocktails by the pool and enjoy plush amenities in stylish, arch-modern rooms. ❼

Rendezvous 1420 N Indian Canyon Drive ⓣ1-800/485-2808, ⓦwww.palmspringsrendezvous.com. Motel remodelled into a chic B&B with modern luxuries and retro-1950s designs in its themed rooms (Rat Pack, Marilyn, surfing, etc). ❻

Villa Royale Inn 1620 S Indian Trail ⓣ1-800/245-2314, ⓦwww.villaroyale.com. Elegant inn with two pools, nicely furnished rooms and suites, as well as in-room jacuzzis and a good restaurant. ❺

The Willows 412 W Tahquitz Canyon ⓣ760/320-0771, ⓦwww.thewillowspalmsprings.com. The reason celebrities were first attracted to Palm Springs in the 1930s: a stunning hangout for the Hollywood elite that provides great views and opulent rooms. ❾

Downtown Palm Springs

Downtown Palm Springs stretches for half a mile along **Palm Canyon Drive** from Tamarisk to Ramon roads, much of it a wide, bright and modern strip of chain stores that has engulfed the town's quaint Spanish Colonial-style buildings. In the vicinity you'll find the **Agua Caliente Cultural Museum**, 219 S Palm Canyon Drive (Wed–Sat 10am–5pm, Sun noon–5pm; summer Fri–Sun only; free; ⓣ760/323-0151, ⓦwww.accmuseum.org), with a fine selection of native baskets and pottery craftwork, as well as household objects from the local Cahuilla tribe, such as tools and utensils made from bone, reeds and stone.

Another attraction, the **Palm Springs Art Museum**, 101 Museum Drive (Tues, Wed, & Fri–Sun 10am–5pm, Thurs noon–8pm; summer Fri–Sun only, 10am–5pm; $12.50, children $5; ⓦwww.psmuseum.org), is strong on Native American and Southwestern art, as well as grand American landscape painting from the nineteenth century. There is a modern art gallery and some lovely sculpture courts in the grounds, and the museum hosts performances of music, theatre, comedy and dance in the 450-seat **Annenberg Theater** (tickets ⓣ760/325-4490).

There's an eye-catching bit of gardening at **Moorten Botanical Gardens**, 1701 S Palm Canyon Drive (Mon–Sat 9am–4.30pm, Sun 10am–4pm; $3; ⓦwww.palmsprings.com/moorten), a cornucopia of desert plants including native agaves, barrel cacti and other succulents, plus regional plants from as far away as South Africa and South America.

Around Palm Springs

More intrepid visitors to Palm Springs often light out for the **Indian Canyons** (daily 8am–5pm, summer Fri–Sun only; $8; ⓦwww.indian-canyons.com), three miles southeast of downtown along S Palm Canyon Drive, where centuries ago, ancestors of the Cahuilla developed extensive agricultural communities. The Palm Canyon Trading Post, 380 N Palm Canyon Drive (same hours as canyons; ⓣ760/323-6018), is a gift shop that serves as the visitor centre, from which mile-long guided hikes (90min; $3) leave during regular canyon hours. The canyons can be toured by car, although it's worth walking at least a few miles; the easiest trails lead past the waterfalls, rocky gorges and copious palm trees of **Palm Canyon** and **Andreas Canyon**.

If the desert heat becomes too much to bear, large cable cars grind and sway over eight thousand feet up the **Palm Springs Aerial Tramway**, Tramway Road, just off Hwy-111 north of Palm Springs (Mon–Fri 10am–8pm, Sat & Sun 8am–8pm; $23, kids $16; ⓦwww.pstramway.com), heading to the striking 10,815ft summit of Mount San Jacinto – one of the area's signature sights. In the opposite direction from Palm Springs, a few miles east of town, **PALM DESERT** is, like the sun-baked towns further east, littered with golf courses and elite resorts, with the added treat of the mile-long **El Paseo**, a boutique-rich strip known for its kitschy Halloween golf-cart parade (ⓦwww.golfcartparade.com). Palm Desert is also home to the **Living Desert**, a combination garden and zoo at 47900 Portola Ave, Palm Desert (daily: summer 8.30am–1pm; rest of year 9am–5pm; $12.50, summer $9.50; ⓦwww.livingdesert.org), rich with cactus and palm gardens, but throwing in incongruous African desert animals such as giraffes, zebras, cheetahs and warthogs.

Eating and drinking

The better **restaurants** in Palm Springs are ultra-expensive, but more reasonable options can be found with a little effort; the spots preferred by locals are, as ever, to be favoured over the slick, often banal cuisine served up by places catering to the tourist trade.

Copley's on Palm Canyon 621 N Palm Canyon Drive ⓣ760/327-9555. Hang out in Cary Grant's old digs while you sup on upscale California cuisine, which may include Scottish salmon with Thai curry, lobster pot pie and ahi tacos.

Europa 1620 S Indian Trail ⓣ1-800/245-2314. Located in the *Villa Royale Inn* (see p.878), a romantic, upscale French and Italian eatery, serving splendid dishes from duck confit, to osso bucco and *escargots royale*.

Las Casuelas Viejas 368 N Palm Canyon Drive ⓣ760/325-3213. Predictable, affordable Mexican favourite that's been around since 1958 and remains popular for its hefty portions and laidback atmosphere.

Le Vallauris 385 W Tahquitz Canyon Way ⓣ760/325-5059. Fine California-Mediterranean cuisine in a gorgeous setting, with high prices for temptations such as Russian caviar, Dover sole and port-glazed squab. Reservations only.

Native Foods 1775 E Palm Canyon Drive ⓣ760/416-0070. One of the town's better choices for cheap vegetarian cuisine – with veggie chili, chicken wings, pizzas, burgers and tacos, plus bean soups, rice bowls and tempeh burgers. Part of a regional chain.

Shame on the Moon 69950 Frank Sinatra Drive, Rancho Mirage ⓣ760/324-5515. Mid- to upper-end California cuisine is the draw here, highlighted by Long Island duck, sautéed calf's liver and ahi tuna steaks. Located eight miles east of downtown Palm Springs.

Tyler's 149 S Indian Canyon Drive ⓣ760/325-2990. The tasty burgers are what send residents tramping out here, but the potato salad, fries and sandwiches aren't bad either.

Joshua Tree National Park

Where the low Colorado Desert meets the high Mojave northeast of Palm Springs, **JOSHUA TREE NATIONAL PARK** (ⓦwww.nps.gov/jotr) protects 1250 square miles of grotesquely gnarled plants, which aren't trees at all, but a type of **yucca**, similar to an agave. Named by Mormons in the 1850s, who saw in their craggy branches the arms of Joshua pointing to the promised land, Joshua trees can rise up to forty feet tall, and somehow manage to flourish despite the extreme aridity and rocky soil.

This unearthly landscape is ethereal at sunrise or sunset, when the desert floor is bathed in red light; at noon it can be a furnace, with temperatures topping 125°F in summer. Still, the park attracts campers, day-trippers and rock-climbers for its unspoiled beauty, gold-mine ruins, ancient petroglyphs and striking rock formations. A half-mile guided tour of **Keys Ranch** (Oct–May Sat & Sun 10am & 1pm; $5; see park website for details) provides a testament to the difficulty of making a life in such a difficult environment, but if you'd rather wander around the national park by yourself, there are many options: one of the easiest hikes (3 miles, foot-travel only) starts one and a half miles from Canyon Road, six miles from the visitor centre at Twentynine Palms, at **Fortynine Palms Oasis**. West of the oasis, quartz boulders tower around the **Indian Cove** campground; a trail from the eastern branch of the campground road heads to **Rattlesnake Canyon**, where, after rainfall, the streams and waterfalls break an otherwise eerie silence among the monoliths.

Moving south into the main body of the park, the **Wonderland of Rocks** features rounded granite boulders that draw rock-climbers from around the world. One fascinating trail climbs four miles past abandoned mines to the antiquated foundations and equipment of **Lost Horse Mine**, which once produced around $20,000 in gold a week. You can find a brilliant desert panorama of badlands and mountains at the 5185ft **Keys View** nearby, from where Geology Tour Road leads down to the east through the best of Joshua Tree's **rock formations** and, further on, to the **Cholla Cactus Garden**.

Practicalities

Less than an hour's drive northeast from Palm Springs, Joshua Tree National Park (always open; $15/vehicle for 7 days, $5/cyclist or hiker) is best approached along Hwy-62, which branches off I-10. You can enter the park via the **west entrance**, on Park Boulevard in the town of Joshua Tree (daily 8am–5pm; ⓣ760/366-1855); the **north entrance** at Twentynine Palms, where you'll also find the **Oasis Visitor Center**, 74485 National Park Drive (daily 8am–5pm; ⓣ760/367-5500); or, if you're coming from the south, the **Cottonwood Visitor Center** (daily 9am–3pm; ⓣ760/367-5500), seven miles north of I-10.

The park has nine established **campgrounds**, all in the northwest except for one at Cottonwood. Only two have water – *Black Rock Canyon* ($15) and *Cottonwood* ($15–30) – and except for *Indian Cove* ($15), all the others are $10. You can reserve sites at *Black Rock* and *Indian Cove* by contacting the park reservation centre (ⓣ1-877/444-6777, ⓦwww.recreation.gov). The rest are operated on a first-come, first-served basis. Come prepared – gathering firewood is not allowed, and you should stock up on water. **TWENTYNINE PALMS**, a small desert town two minutes' drive from the park, has low-grade motels aplenty, but more pleasant is the historic *Twentynine Palms Inn*, 73950 Inn Ave (ⓣ760/367-3505, ⓦwww.29palmsinn.com; ⑤), with its nice wooden cabins and adobe bungalows, and a fine **restaurant** where the bread is home-made and the vegetables are fresh from an on-site garden. Morongo Basin Transit Authority **buses** (ⓣ760/366-2395, ⓦwww.mbtabus.com) run between Palm Springs and Twentynine Palms (1 hr 15min; $7–10 one-way, $11–15 return), but not into the park itself.

The High Desert

The stretches of the **Mojave Desert** that most people see from the road are bleak and desolate. However, if you explore further, you'll find this **High Desert** – sited above 2000ft – offers some of the most dramatic scenery in Southern California, rolling with lush grasses, startling volcanic formations, large stands of Joshua trees and, even in spots, piñon pines.

Death Valley National Park

DEATH VALLEY – the hottest place on earth – is a place where sculpted rock layers form deeply shadowed, eroded crevices at the foot of silhouetted hills, their exotic minerals turning ancient mud flats into rainbows of sunlit iridescence. Throughout the summer, the **temperature** averages 112°F and the hot ground can reach near boiling. Better to come during the spring, when wildflowers are in bloom and it's generally mild and dry. Still, the area is almost entirely devoid of shade, much less water, so carry plenty for both car and body. The central north–south valley contains two main outposts, **Stovepipe Wells** and **Furnace Creek**, site of the **visitor centre** (daily 9am–5pm; seven-day park pass $20/vehicle, $10/pedestrian or cyclist; ⓣ760/786-3200, ⓦwww.nps.gov/deva).

Dante's View, twenty-one miles south on 190 and ten miles along a very steep access road, offers a fine morning vista in which the pink-and-gold Panamint Mountains are highlighted by the rising sun. Near Stovepipe Wells, some thirty miles northwest of Furnace Creek, spread fifteen rippled and contoured square miles of ever-changing **sand dunes**. The most popular site, though, is the surreal luxury of **Scotty's Castle** (50min tours daily 9.30am–4pm, winter 8.30am–5pm; $11; reservations ⓣ760/786-2392), forty miles north of Stovepipe Wells, built in the 1920s as a desert retreat, tours of which take in the decorative wooden ceilings, indoor waterfalls and a remote-controlled player piano.

Practicalities

If you plan to **stay**, you must reserve ahead. Furnace Creek Resort (ⓣ760/786-2345, ⓦwww.furnacecreekresort.com) operates two hotels on natural oases – the gorgeous 1920s adobe *Furnace Creek Inn* (❽) and the ordinary *Furnace Creek Ranch* (❺), which has two **restaurants** and a nice bar. An alternative is *Stovepipe Wells Village* (ⓣ760/786-2387, ⓦwww.stovepipewells.com; ❹) on Hwy-190 about thirty miles northwest of Furnace Creek, offering its own mineral-water pool and restaurant. **Camping** in one of the many Park Service campgrounds costs $12–14, depending on facilities and location, or is free if you don't mind being up in the Panamint Range, far from the valley's sights: the only campground that takes reservations is *Furnace Creek* (seasonal $12–18; ⓣ1-877/444-6777, ⓦwww.recreation.gov), just north of town. As ever when travelling to these desiccated parts, be careful about heading out in the middle of the day when the danger of heatstroke is at its worst and always carry plenty of water.

The High Sierra and Owens Valley

The towering **eastern** peaks of the **HIGH SIERRA** drop abruptly to the barren landscape of the **OWENS VALLEY**, sixty miles west of Death Valley. Almost this entire section of the Sierra Nevada is wilderness: well-maintained roads lead to trailheads at over eight thousand feet, providing access to the stark terrain of spires, glaciers and clear mountain lakes. US-395 is the lifeline of the area connecting several small towns, all with plenty of budget motels. As there is virtually **no public transportation** in this area (except for CREST and YARTS; see p.883), you'll really need a **car** to get around.

Mount Whitney and Lone Pine

Rising out of the northern Mojave Desert, the mountainous backbone of the Sierra Nevada announces itself with a bang two hundred miles north of Los Angeles at 14,505ft **Whitney**, the highest point in the lower 48 states. A silver-grey ridge of pinnacles forms a nearly sheer wall of granite, dominating the small roadside town of **LONE PINE** nearly eleven thousand feet below. The best **motel** choice is the *Dow Villa*, 310 S Main St (ⓣ760/876-5521 or 1-800/824-9317, ⓦwww.dowvillamotel.com; ❺), where John Wayne always stayed when filming in the area, and which offers a pool and spa. Those headed north might want to push on sixteen miles to Independence, where you'll find the appealing *Ray's Den*, 405 N Edwards St (ⓣ760/878-2122; ❹), a simple strip motel that offers clean rooms, free internet access and complimentary breakfast. You can **camp** at *Tuttle Creek* campground ($5; no water) on Horseshoe Meadow Road in the shadow of mountain peaks some four miles west of Lone Pine beyond the Alabama Hills (see below). You can **eat** at the surprisingly delicious French bistro of the *Still Life Cafe*, 135 S Edwards St (ⓣ760/878-2555), or the diner-style *Mt Whitney Restaurant*, 227 S Main St (ⓣ760/876-5751), which has adequate burgers and comfort food. The **Eastern Sierra Interagency Visitor Center**, a mile south of town on US-395 at the junction of Hwy-136 (daily 8am–5pm; ⓣ760/876-6222), is a great source of information about the Owens Valley.

Many early Westerns were filmed in the **Alabama Hills** to the west, named after Confederate sympathizers during the Civil War, a rugged expanse of bizarrely eroded sedimentary rock. Some of the oddest formations are linked by the **Picture Rocks Circle**, a paved road that loops around from Whitney Portal Road, passing rocks shaped like bullfrogs, walruses and baboons.

Two thousand eager souls make the strenuous 22-mile round-trip **hike** (12–16hr; 6100ft ascent) to the summit of Mount Whitney each summer and autumn (generally snow-free June–Oct), some doing it in a very long day, others sleeping along the way at one of two trail camps. The excellent **Mount Whitney Trail** passes a few lakes before following roughly one hundred switchbacks up to 13,600ft Trail Crest Pass; it then weaves its way through an often-windy landscape of jagged boulders to the epic summit. Trail permits are awarded by lottery, and you're required to carry bear spray to ward off the (occasionally) venturesome beasts: applications (ⓦwww.fs.fed.us/r5/inyo or ⓦwww.whitneyzone.com) are only accepted in February. Any permits left after the lottery are available from the Wilderness Permit Office, Inyo National Forest, 351 Pacu Lane, Suite 200, Bishop, CA 93514 (ⓣ760/873-2400). All hikers pay a $15 fee.

One-day ascents start well before dawn from near the excellent *Whitney Portal* **campground** (late May to mid-Oct; ⓣ1-877/444-6777; $19); another nearby camping option is the one-night-only first-come, first-served *Whitney Trailhead* site ($10) at the end of twisting Whitney Portal Road.

Big Pine and the White Mountains

Nearly fifty miles north, hikes lead from the end of Glacier Lodge Road, ten miles west of nondescript **BIG PINE**, up to the **Palisades Glacier**, the southernmost glacier in the northern hemisphere. Along the opposite wall of the five-mile-wide Owens Valley, the ancient, bald and dry **White Mountains** are home to the gnarled **bristlecone pines**, the oldest living things on earth, some first sprouting over four thousand years ago.

The most accessible trees are in 10,000ft **Schulman Grove**, 24 miles east of Big Pine in **Ancient Bristlecone Pine Forest** (late May to Oct; $3/person or $5/vehicle; recorded info on ⓣ760/873-2500), where two trails radiate out from the former site of the visitor centre, which burned in 2008. The mile-long **Discovery Trail** passes some photogenic examples, while the four-mile **Methuselah Trail** loops by but (intentionally) fails to identify the oldest tree, the 4750-year-old Methuselah.

In the White Mountains there's the waterless *Grandview* **campground** (year-round; $5/night), or you can **stay** back in Big Pine at the *Big Pine Motel*, 370 S Main St (ⓣ760/938-2282; ❸).

Bishop

The largest town (population 3500) in the Owens Valley, **BISHOP** is an excellent base for cross-country skiing, fly-fishing and especially rock climbing. The best **motel** choice is the *Thunderbird*, 190 W Pine St (ⓣ760/873-4215; ❸). For **eating**, grab a sandwich and any of a number of delicious cakes and breads at *Erick Schat's Bakkerÿ*, 763 N Main St (ⓣ760/873-7156); a half-mile south through town on US-395, try the serviceable meats on offer at *Bar-B-Q Bill's*, 187 S Main St (ⓣ760/872-5535). The **visitor centre** at 690 N Main St (Mon–Fri 10am–5pm, Sat & Sun 10am–4pm; ⓣ760/873-8405 or 1-800/395-3952, ⓦwww.bishopvisitor.com) can provide details of the many **adventure travel specialists** based in town, including Sierra Mountain Center at 174 W Line St (ⓣ760/873-8526; ⓦwww.sierramountaincenter.com). If you are interested in **hiking** and **camping**, the White Mountain Ranger Station, 798 N Main St (May–Oct daily 8am–5pm; rest of year Mon–Fri hours vary; ⓣ760/873-2500), will be of more use.

Mammoth Lakes

Forty miles north along US-395 from Bishop, then three miles west on Hwy-203, the resort town of **MAMMOTH LAKES** offers the state's premier ski slopes outside the Lake Tahoe basin, and in summer hosts on- and off-road bike races. To ski **Mammoth Mountain** (ⓣ1-800/MAMMOTH, ⓦwww.mammothmountain.com), which looms up behind the resort, pick up **lift tickets** ($87 a day) from the Main Lodge on Minaret Road, where you can also rent **equipment** and book **lessons.** In summer, fifty miles of snow-free slopes transform into the 3500-acre **Mammoth Mountain Bike Park** (one-day pass with unlimited rides on the bike shuttle and gondola $39; $78 with bike rental).

One appealing summer-only destination is **Devil's Postpile National Monument**, seven miles southwest of Mammoth Mountain ($7, includes shuttle bus; ⓦwww.nps.gov/depo). This collection of slender, blue-grey basaltic columns, some as tall as sixty feet, was formed as lava from a volcanic eruption cooled and fractured into columnar forms. From here, a two-mile hike along the San Joaquin River leads to the 101ft **Rainbow Falls**, which refract the midday sun perfectly.

Practicalities

Year-round CREST **buses** (ⓣ760/872-1901 or ⓣ1-800/922-1930, ⓦeasternsierratransitauthority.com) offer a range of fares, depending on where you're going, for $7–34. For summer visitors travelling to or from Yosemite, YARTS (ⓣ1-877/989-2787, ⓦwww.yarts.com) operates buses daily from **Mammoth Mountain Inn** in July and August, and on weekends only in June and September; a single fare between Mammoth and Yosemite Valley is $15. For information, go to the combined US Forest Service **ranger station** and Mammoth Lakes **visitor centre**, 2520 Main St, half a mile east of the town centre (daily 8am–5pm; ⓣ760/924-5500, ⓦwww.visitmammoth.com).

Mammoth's plentiful **accommodation** is cheapest in summer; during ski season, expect one price range higher than that noted below. For a reasonable B&B close to downtown, visit the rambling *Cinnamon Bear Inn*, 113 Center St (ⓣ1-800/845-2873, ⓦwww.cinnamonbearinn.com; midweek ❺, weekends ❻), which offers a spa and the usual quaint decor. The *Swiss Chalet Lodge*, 3776 Viewpoint Rd (ⓣ1-800/937-9477, ⓦwww.mammoth-swisschalet.com; ❹) offers more basic digs but with striking mountain views. There are developed **campgrounds** ($14–19/person) close to Devil's Postpile National Monument, and a number of free water-less campgrounds in the Crestview region of Inyo National Forest about ten miles north of Mammoth.

Mammoth has the most **restaurants** in the Eastern Sierra, so you'll be able to find a good meal without too much effort. The *Good Life Cafe*, 126 Old Mammoth Rd (ⓣ760/934-1734), has tasty and filling American breakfasts; *Whiskey Creek*, Main at Minaret (ⓣ760/934-2555), is a lively **bar** and restaurant pouring its own beer; and, for a fancy night out, *The Lakefront Restaurant* at Tamarack Lodge, off Lake Mary Road (ⓣ760/934-2442), offers superb views and sublime French-Californian dishes for mid to high prices.

Mono Lake, Lee Vining and Bodie

The vitreous blue expanse of **Mono Lake** sits in the midst of a volcanic desert tableland at the north end of the valley. This science-fiction landscape holds two large islands, one light-coloured, the other black, surrounded by salty, alkaline water. Strange sandcastle-like formations of **tufa** – calcium deposited from springs – were exposed after Los Angeles extended an aqueduct (which carries water diverted from the lake's feeder streams) into the Mono Basin through an eleven-mile tunnel. Mono Lake is the primary nesting ground for the state's **California gull** population – twenty percent of the world total – and a prime stopover for hundreds of thousands of grebes and phalaropes.

For more details about Mono Lake, stop by the **Mono Lake Committee Information Center**, Hwy 395 at 3rd Street (daily: late Jun to Aug 8am–9pm; rest of year 9am–5pm; ⓣ760/647-6595, ⓦwww.monolake.org), in the small town of **LEE VINING** on US-395, or a mile north at the excellent **Mono Basin Scenic Area Visitor Center** (May–Oct daily 9am–5pm; ⓣ760/647-3044). The most accommodating **motel** is the *El Mono*, 51 Hwy-395 (open late April to late autumn; ⓣ760/647-6310, ⓦwww.elmonomotel.com; ❹), and decent places to **eat** include the *Whoa Nellie Deli*, US-395 at Hwy-120 just south of Lee Vining (ⓣ760/647-1088), for fish tacos, ribs, pizza and breakfast fare; and *Bodie Mike's* (open summer only; ⓣ760/647-6432) along Lee Vining's brief business strip, for gut-stuffing barbecue lunches and dinners.

Northeast of Lee Vining, in a remote, high desert valley accessed by hardscrabble road, stands a well-preserved relic of the gold-mining 1870s. **Bodie State Park** (open all year but often inaccessible in winter; summer daily 9am–6pm, winter daily 10am–3pm; $3/person; ⓣ760/647-6445) is perhaps the most evocative **ghost town** in the US, with most of its structures preserved in their decay, but not renovated. Boasting sixty saloons and dance halls and a population of nearly ten thousand at its peak, it was among the wildest of Western mining camps; over 150 wooden buildings survive around the town centre, littered with old bottles, bits of machinery and old stagecoaches. Note that the last three miles of the 13-mile drive east from US-395 are unpaved, and, even outside of winter, this is one of the coldest spots in the state.

The San Joaquin Valley

The vast **interior** of California is split down the middle by the **Sierra Nevada** (Spanish for "snowy range"), or High Sierra, a sawtooth range of snowcapped peaks that stands high above the semi-desert of the Owens Valley. The wide **San Joaquin Valley** in the west was made fertile by irrigation projects during the 1940s, and is now almost totally agricultural. The real reason to come here is for the grand **national parks** of **Sequoia** and **Kings Canyon** – and **Yosemite**, where waterfalls cascade down towering walls of silvery granite. Few roads penetrate the hundreds of square miles of wilderness, but the entire pristine alpine backcountry is crisscrossed by hiking trails.

The I-5 freeway barrels through the valley on a course so flat, straight and dull it's almost hypnotic. Three to six daily **trains** on the San Joaquin line – connecting Oakland and Bakersfield, but not LA – and frequent Greyhound **buses** run through the valley, calling at the towns along Hwy-99, in particular Merced, which has bus connections to Yosemite but otherwise doesn't merit a look-in.

Bakersfield

The flat and colourless oil town of **BAKERSFIELD** is the unlikely home of one of the liveliest **country music** scenes in the nation. In the mid-1960s, the gutsy honky-tonk of Bakersfield artists such as Merle Haggard and Buck Owens challenged the slick commercial output of Nashville, and even today the city serves as something of an alternative to the glossy country pop coming from Tennessee.

Bakersfield's honky-tonks are jumping every weekend night, when Stetson hats and fringy shirts are the required apparel, and audiences span generations. Most venues are hotel lounges or restaurant backrooms; don't miss the country bar *Trouts*, 805 N Chester Ave (ⓣ661/399-6700), which throws in swing and rockabilly with its honky-tonk fixins, or *Ethel's Old Corral Café*, 4310 Alfred Harrel Hwy (ⓣ661/873-7613), a roadside staple that's as good a spot as any for a country hoedown. Closer to town, *Buck Owens Crystal Palace*, 2800 Buck Owens Blvd (ⓣ661/328-7560, ⓦwww.buckowens.com; closed Sun evenings & Mon), offers live shows for under $10, plus access to a museum of Buck Owens memorabilia. Legendary guitarist Owens died in 2006, but his band, The Buckaroos, continue to play on Friday and Saturday nights.

Practicalities

From LA, the Amtrak Thruway bus goes to Bakersfield, where you can catch the train through the valley toward Oakland and northern California. Several Greyhound **bus** routes require changes here too, calling at 1820 18th St. The **Bakersfield Convention & Visitors Bureau** is at 515 Truxtun Ave (Mon–Fri 8.30am–5pm; ⓣ661/852-7282; ⓦwww.visitbakersfield.com). You can **stay** at the clean chain rooms of *La Quinta*, 8858 Spectrum Parkway (ⓣ661/393-7775; ❸), which offers a pool and free in-room wi-fi, or pay a little more for a suite and amenities like flat-screen TVs at the *Wyndham Garden Bakersfield*, 3001 Buck Owens Rd (ⓣ661/395-9800; ❹). For **food**, *Ethel's Old Corral Café* (see above) has rib-stuffing pork chops and country-fried steak, while *Zingo's*, 3201 Buck Owen

Blvd (Ⓣ661/321-0627), is a 24-hour truckstop where frilly-aproned waitresses deliver big plates of fried chicken and biscuits 'n gravy. The *Noriega Hotel*, 525 Sumner St (Ⓣ661/322-8419), isn't much of a place to stay, but does offer excellent all-you-can-eat Basque meals at long communal tables.

Sequoia and Kings Canyon

The southernmost of the Sierra Nevada national parks, preserving ancient forests of giant sequoia trees, are Sequoia and Kings Canyon. As you might expect, **Sequoia National Park** contains the thickest concentration – and the biggest specimens – of sequoias to be found anywhere, tending (literally) to overshadow its assortment of meadows, peaks, canyons and caves. **Kings Canyon National Park** has few big trees but compensates with a gaping canyon gored out of the rock by the Kings River as it cascades down from the High Sierra.

Arrival and information

A summer **shuttle bus** (late May to Aug, $15 return, Ⓦwww.sequoiashuttle.com) runs into Sequoia National Park from the transit centre, 425 E Oak St, in the Central Valley town of **Visalia**, where there are Greyhound and Amtrak Thruway connections. The two-hour, fifty-mile journey along Hwy-198 ends at Giant Forest from where two free shuttle services call at Sequoia's main sights. There's no **public transportation** into Kings Canyon, though both parks are easily reached by **car** either from **Visalia**, or on a slightly longer but faster route along Hwy-180 from Fresno: note that there is **no gas** available in the parks. The **entrance fee** ($20/car, $10/cyclist, free for bus passengers; valid seven days) entitles you to a detailed map of the paired parks, which are separate but jointly run; for **information** call Ⓣ559/565-3341 or visit Ⓦwww.nps.gov/seki.

Accommodation and eating

The least expensive **rooms** are in the anonymous motels near the park entrances, but it's better to stay inside the parks, where all facilities are managed by SKC Park Services (Ⓣ1-866/522-6966, Ⓦwww.sequoia-kingscanyon.com; ❸–❼), who operate handsome cabins and hotel units at Stony Creek, Grant Grove, Montecito Sequoia, Cedar Grove and the *John Muir Lodge*; and DNC (Ⓣ1-866/807-3598, Ⓦwww.visitsequoia.com; ❻–❼) who run the upmarket *Wuksachi Lodge* in Sequoia. Space is at a premium during the high season (May to mid-Oct), but you can usually pick up cancellations on the day. In winter you can still camp, but the cheapest roofed accommodation is at the *John Muir Lodge* for $69.

Campgrounds are dotted all over both parks, most charging $18–20 a pitch, though a few are $12. In **Sequoia**, the busiest campground is *Lodgepole*, which you can reserve up to five months in advance through the National Park Reservation System (Ⓣ1-800/444-6777, Ⓦwww.recreation.gov). In **Kings Canyon**, the bulk of the sites are around Grant Grove, with another at Cedar Grove. For **backcountry** camping, pick up a free permit from a visitor centre or ranger station. And remember these parks are busy with **black bears**: in established campgrounds use the bear-proof food boxes; in the backcountry rent bear canisters from the stores in Cedar Grove, Grant Grove and Lodgepole.

There are pricey **food** markets in the various villages and a couple of restaurants, including the *Montecito-Sequoia Lodge*, which serves notably bargain buffets, in the national forest between the two parks. Three Rivers, on the southern approach to

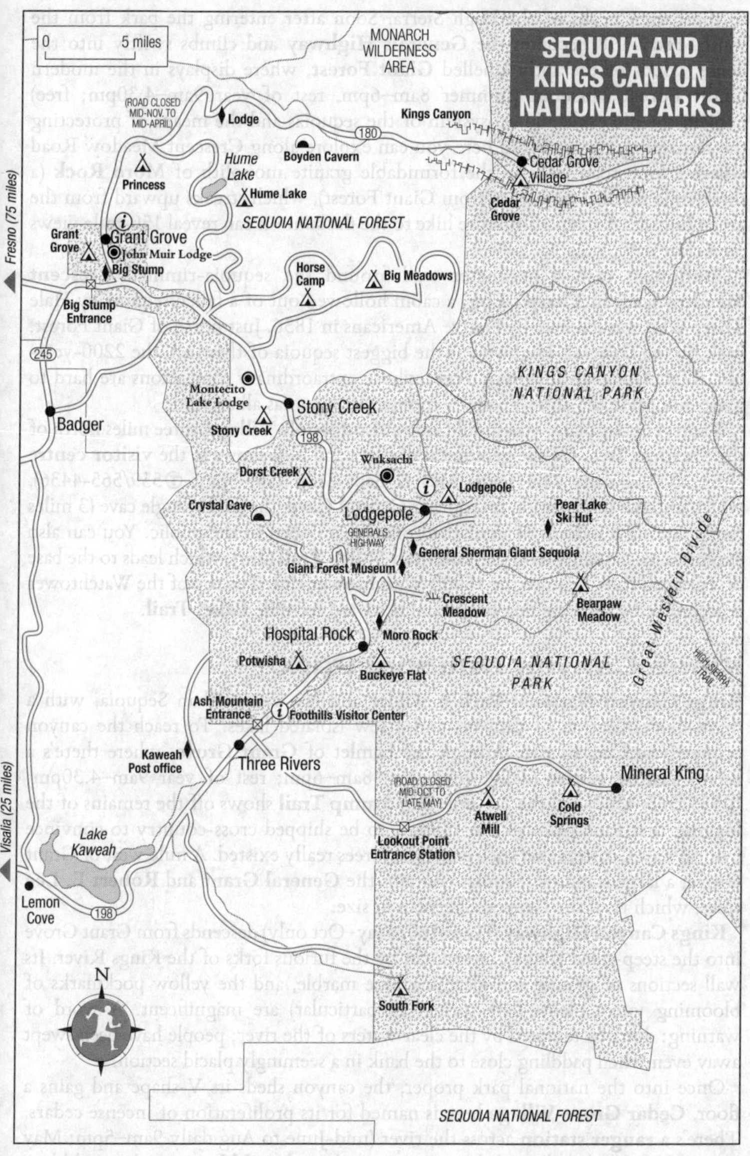

Sequoia, has the best range of places to eat nearby, with the *Pizza Factory*, 40915 Sierra Drive (☎559/561-1018), among the more reliable choices.

Sequoia National Park

The scenery is quite varied in **SEQUOIA NATIONAL PARK** – paths lead through copious forests and meadows, while longer treks rise above the tree line to the barren peaks of the High Sierra. Soon after entering the park from the south, Hwy-198 becomes the **Generals Highway** and climbs swiftly into the dense woods of the aptly labelled **Giant Forest**, where displays in the modern **Giant Forest Museum** (summer 8am–6pm, rest of year 9am–4.30pm; free) explain the life cycle and ecosystem of the sequoias and the means of protecting the remaining groves. From here you can explore along Crescent Meadow Road where a loop road leads to the formidable granite monolith of **Moro Rock** (a three-mile marked trail leads from Giant Forest), which streaks upward from the green hillside. A steep 15-minute hike to the flat summit can reveal 150-mile views on a clear day.

Continuing east, a perimeter trail around the sequoia-rimmed **Crescent Meadow** leads to **Tharp's Log**, a cabin hollowed out of a fallen sequoia by Hale Tharp who was led here by Native Americans in 1856. Just north of Giant Forest, back on the Generals Highway, is the biggest sequoia of them all, the 2200-year-old, 275ft **General Sherman Tree**, whose extraordinary dimensions are hard to grasp alongside the almost equally monstrous sequoias all around.

Whatever your plans, you should stop at **Lodgepole Village**, three miles north of the Sherman Tree, for the geological displays and film shows at the **visitor centre** (June to Aug daily 7am–6pm; May & Sept daily 7am–5pm; ⓣ559/565-4436), which also has information on touring **Crystal Cave**, the park's single cave (3 miles long), among hundreds of unmarked ones, that's open to the public. You can also explore a glacial canyon on the **Tokopah Valley Trail** (2hr), which leads to the base of Tokopah Falls, beneath the 1600ft **Watchtower** cliff. The top of the Watchtower is accessible by the fatiguing but straightforward six-mile **Lakes Trail**.

Kings Canyon National Park

Kings Canyon National Park is wilder and less visited than Sequoia, with a maze-like collection of canyons and a few isolated lakes. To reach the canyon proper, you have to pass through the hamlet of **Grant Grove**, where there's a useful **visitor centre** (daily: June–Aug 8am–6pm; rest of year 9am–4.30pm; ⓣ559/565-4307) and the 2.5-mile **Big Stump Trail** shows off the remains of the logging that took place in the 1880s – to be shipped cross-country to convince cynical East Coasters that such enormous trees really existed. A mile west of Grant Grove, a large stand of sequoias contains the **General Grant** and **Robert E. Lee** trees, which rival the General Sherman in size.

Kings Canyon Highway (Hwy-180; May–Oct only) descends from Grant Grove into the steep-sided Kings Canyon, cut by the furious forks of the Kings River. Its wall sections of granite and gleaming blue marble, and the yellow pockmarks of blooming yucca plants (late spring, in particular) are magnificent. A word of warning: don't be tempted by the clear waters of the river; people have been swept away even when paddling close to the bank in a seemingly placid section.

Once into the national park proper, the canyon sheds its V-shape and gains a floor. **Cedar Grove Village** here is named for its proliferation of incense cedars. There's a **ranger station** across the river (mid-June to Aug daily 9am–5pm; May & Sept hours reduced), and the scenery is rich with **wildflowers** – leopard lilies, shooting stars, violets, lupins and others – and **birdlife**, too. Wander around the green **Zumwalt Meadow**, four miles from Cedar Grove Village, which spreads beneath the forbidding grey walls of Grand Sentinel and North Dome.

Just a mile further on, Kings Canyon Road comes to an end at **Copper Creek**. Beyond, the multitude of canyons and peaks that constitute the Kings River Sierra are networked by **hiking paths**, almost all best enjoyed armed with a tent, provisions and a wilderness permit from the trailhead ranger station.

The Sierra National Forest

The Sierra National Forest, sited between Kings Canyon and Yosemite, offers a chance to hike and camp in near-complete solitude. Planning is essential, though – public transportation is nonexistent, and roads and trails are often closed due to bad weather. The best-placed source for free backcountry permits, and camping and wilderness information is the **ranger station** (daily 8am–4.30pm; ⓣ559/855-5360), on Hwy-168 at Prather, five miles west of the forest entrance.

The popular Shaver Lake and Huntington Lake area, rich in campgrounds (reserve in summer on ⓣ1-877/444-6777), soon give way to the isolated alpine landscapes beyond the 9200ft Kaiser Pass. The sheer challenge posed by the rugged, unspoiled terrain of the adjoining **John Muir Wilderness** can make the national parks look like holiday camps, though the area can get surprisingly busy (for a wilderness) in the summer; permits are required from May to November and for overnight stays (contact an area ranger station or visitor centre for information.) You can bathe outdoors at the nearby **Mono Hot Springs**, or head for the *Mono Hot Springs Resort*, near Edison Lake (mid-May to Oct; ⓣ559/325-1710, ⓦwww.monohotsprings.com; ❹–❺), which has indoor mineral baths along with primitive cabins.

Yosemite National Park

Simply put, **YOSEMITE NATIONAL PARK** (ⓦwww.nps.gov/yose), nestled in the picturesque **Yosemite Valley**, is one of the world's most dramatic geological spectacles. Just seven miles long and less than one mile across, it is walled by near-vertical three-thousand-foot cliffs, streaked by tumbling waterfalls and topped by domes and pinnacles that form a jagged silhouette against the sky. At ground level, grassy meadows are framed by oak, cedar and fir trees; deer, coyotes and even black bears abound. You can visit at any time of year, even in winter when the waterfalls ice over and the trails are blocked by snow, and, excepting summer, the valley itself is rarely overcrowded. **Park entry** costs $20 per vehicle, $10 per pedestrian or cyclist, and is valid for seven days (an annual pass is only $40). Bus passengers get in free.

Yosemite Valley was created by glaciers gouging through the canyon of the Merced River: the ice scraped away the softer granite leaving soaring cliffs. Thanks to the campaigning work of naturalist **John Muir**, in 1864 Yosemite Valley and Mariposa Grove were set aside as America's first protected wilderness. A Scottish immigrant who travelled the entire area on foot, Muir spearheaded the conservation movement that led to the founding of the Sierra Club, with the express aim of preserving Yosemite.

Getting there

Getting to Yosemite by **car** is straightforward, and the park is open 24hr, every day of the year – though the only road in from the east, Hwy-120 from Lee Vining, is closed from early November to around the beginning of June. **Gas** is not available in Yosemite Valley. **Public transportation** into the park centres on the Amtrak-accessible Central Valley town of Merced, from where YARTS **buses** (ⓣ1-877/989-2787, ⓦwww.yarts.com) make the two-hour run to Yosemite Valley five or six times a day, charging $18 one-way, $25 return. All services call at Merced Transport, 710 W 16th St (ⓦwww.mercedthebus.com), for Greyhound connections, and at the Amtrak station, 324 W 24th St (ⓦwww.amtrak.com), whose San Joaquin line connects with Oakland and Sacramento. YARTS also runs a once-daily summer-only service over

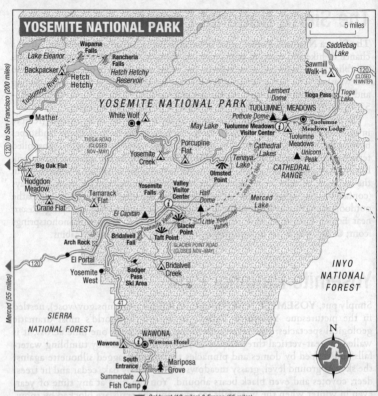

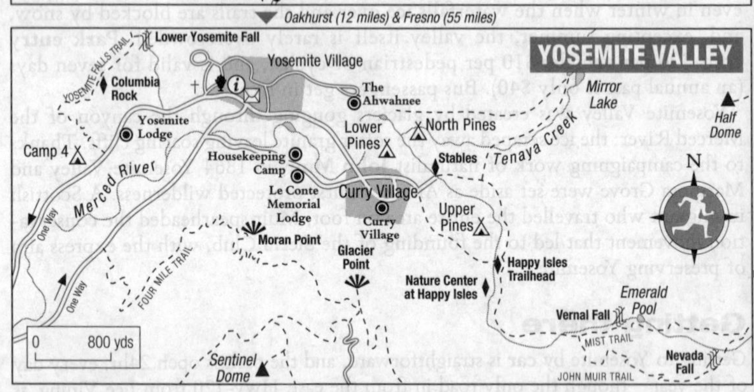

the Tioga Pass road from Mammoth Lakes and Lee Vining ($15 each way; see p.883) to the Yosemite Valley Visitor Center.

There's also the Yosemite Bug Bus (Ⓦ www.yosemitebugbus.com), which picks up from San Francisco hostels and hotels (Mon, Wed, Fri) for two-day-two-night tours to Yosemite with nights at the *Yosemite Bug* (see below) in a dorm ($205 total), tent cabin ($270) or private room ($314). Bus fares are inclusive of park entry and meals.

If you need somewhere to stay in Merced before heading to Yosemite, consider the adequate *HI-Merced Home Hostel* (ⓣ209/725-0407; members $16, others $19), where the staff pick you up from the train or bus and drop you off the following morning, or the clean chain rooms of the *Hampton Inn*, 225 S Parsons Ave (ⓣ209/386-1210; ⓦwww.hamptoninn.com; ❺). If you'd rather be closer to the park, try the lively *Yosemite Bug Rustic Mountain Resort*, 6979 Hwy-140 (ⓣ1-866/826-7108, ⓦwww.YosemiteBug.com); without bus fare, private rooms are ❸, tent cabins ❷, and bunks ❶. It's located at **Midpines**, on the YARTS bus route, where there's a wide range of accommodation and an excellent bar and café.

Yosemite Valley

The three roads from the Central Valley converge on **Yosemite Valley**, roughly in the centre of the park's 1200 square miles, and home to its most dramatic scenery. This is the busiest part of Yosemite, with **Yosemite Village** holding the main shops and the useful **visitor centre** (daily: June–Sept 9am–7pm; Oct – May 9am–5pm; ⓣ209/372-0299).

The main reason to come here is to explore the major cliffs that dominate Yosemite Valley. The 3600ft **El Capitan** is one of the world's biggest pieces of exposed granite, so large that rock-climbers on its face are virtually invisible to the naked eye. The truncated face of **Half Dome** is the sheerest cliff in North America, just seven degrees off the vertical. It attracts a lot of interest, though you'll need a permit if you want to hike to the top during the high season (May–Oct; $1.50; reserve at ⓣ1-877/444-6777 or ⓦwww.recreation.gov).

You can hike to the rounded summit of Half Dome by initially following the popular **Mist Trail to Vernal Fall** (3 mile round trip; 2–3hr; 1100ft ascent), which winds up so close to the sensual waterfall that during the late-spring snowmelt period hikers are drenched by the spray, but rewarded by vivid rainbows. Continuing on the Mist Trail past Vernal Fall, it's a strenuous ascent, the final section aided by a steel staircase hooked on to Half Dome's curving back; if you plan a one-day assault, you'll need to start at the crack of dawn.

An early start is also recommended for the trail to **Upper Yosemite Fall** (7 miles round trip; 4–7hr; 2700ft ascent), which leads up along a steep switchback path from behind the *Camp 4* campground, near *Yosemite Lodge*. This almost continuous ascent provides fine views over the valley on the way up, and after about two miles, a chance to appreciate the power of the water as it crashes almost 1500ft in a single cascade.

The most spectacular views of Yosemite Valley are from **Glacier Point**, the top of a 3200ft almost-sheer cliff, 32 miles by road from the valley. It's possible to get there on foot using the vertiginous **Four-Mile Trail** (4.8 miles one way; 3–4hr; 3200ft ascent) though slackers prefer to take the bus up (details below) and the trail down. The valley floor lies directly beneath the viewing point, and there are tremendous views across to Half Dome and the distant snowcapped summits of the High Sierra.

Practicalities

Prices within Yosemite are higher than outside the park, but not unaffordable. Of the **hotels** in the valley, try *Yosemite Lodge* (❽) or *Curry Village*, a mile from Yosemite Village, which has similarly priced rooms, plus fixed tent cabins (❺) and cabins (❻); it also offers showers for non-guests ($3). For hotel information and reservations, call ⓣ801/559-4884 or visit ⓦwww.yosemitepark.com.

Camping in the valley is only permitted in campgrounds, such as *Camp 4 Walk-in* ($5/person), just west of *Yosemite Lodge*, which is popular with rock-climbers and has a bohemian reputation; it lacks showers and can only be reserved on the day at the kiosk on site. Other valley campgrounds cost $10–20 per site, and you can reserve up to five months ahead in summer (ⓣ1-877/444-6777; ⓦwww.recreation.gov) – always a good idea.

Food in Yosemite is expensive for what you get, though there is reasonable choice. Yosemite Village has a small supermarket and snack bars, the best of which is *Degnan's Deli*, where you can sip an espresso and the massive sandwiches cost around $7. The *Curry Village Pavilion* has solid pastas, tacos and comfort food for low to mid-prices. The baronial-style *Ahwahnee Dining Room* (ⓣ209/372-1489) has the best (and most expensive) food in Yosemite and an appealing Grand Brunch on Sunday.

Once in Yosemite Valley, **getting around** is easy. If you drive in for the day, park at Yosemite Village and ride the frequent, free **shuttle buses** that loop around the valley in summer (daily 7am–10pm), calling at all points of interest. A number of bicycle paths cross the valley floor but **bike rental** is limited to outlets at *Yosemite Lodge* and *Curry Village* ($25.50 a day). There are also six **guided bus tours** ($25–82; ⓣ209/372-4386), countless hikes and rambling trips on horseback. Pick up a copy of *Yosemite Today* or browse ⓦwww.yosemitepark.com for details.

Outside the valley

Mariposa Grove, close to the park's southern entrance, is the biggest and best of Yosemite's groves of **giant sequoia** trees, accessed by a 2.5-mile loop trail. The most renowned of the grouping is the **Grizzly Giant**, thought to be over 2700 years old. Though the access road is closed Nov–April, you can hike here at any time of the year; in fact, that's the only way to get into the other sequoia stands, at Tuolumne and Merced groves, near Crane Flat – via 2–3 miles on foot.

On the eastern edge of the park, **Tuolumne Meadows** (June–Oct only) has an atmosphere quite different from the valley; here, at 8600ft, you almost seem to be level with the tops of the surrounding snow-covered mountains. Early summer reveals a plethora of colourful wildflowers. It's a better starting point than the valley for backcountry hiking into the High Sierra, with eight hundred miles of trails, both long and short, crisscrossing their way along the Sierra Nevada ridges. To spend a night in the backcountry, you must get a **wilderness permit**. You can obtain one up to 24 hour in advance (free) at the nearest visitor centre, but places are limited so it is best to reserve online (ⓦwww.nps.gov/yose/wilderness; $5/person, plus $5/reservation) up to 24 weeks in advance. There are tent cabins at *Tuolumne Meadows Lodge* (ⓣ801/559-4884, ⓦwww.yosemitepark.com; ❺) and camping at the *Tuolumne Meadows* campground for $20 per site if you have a vehicle, or $5 per person if you're hiking and have a wilderness permit.

The Central Coast

Between LA and San Francisco, the four hundred miles of the **Central Coast** are home to just a few modestly sized cities and lined by clean sandy beaches and dramatic stretches of cliffs and capes. Of the various highlights, **Big Sur** is one of the most rugged and beautiful stretches of coastline in the world, **Santa Barbara** is a wealthy resort full of old and new money, and **Santa Cruz** is a coastal town still redolent of the Sixties. In between, languorous **San Luis Obispo** makes a good base for visiting **Hearst Castle**, the hilltop palace of publishing magnate William Randolph Hearst. Almost all of the towns grew up around the original Spanish Catholic **missions**, many of which feature their original architecture – **Monterey**, a hundred miles south of San Francisco, was California's capital under Spain and Mexico, and briefly the state capital in 1850.

Amtrak's **Coast Starlight** and **Pacific Surfliner trains** run along the coast up to San Luis Obispo, with the former continuing on to the Bay Area and up to Seattle. Greyhound **buses** stop at most coastal towns, especially along the main highway, US-101.

Santa Barbara

Beautifully sited on gently sloping hills above the Pacific, **SANTA BARBARA**'s low-slung Spanish Revival buildings feature red-tiled roofs and white stucco walls, while its wide golden beaches are lined by palm trees along a curving bay. **State Street**, the main drag, is home to an appealing assortment of diners, bookshops, coffeehouses and nightclubs.

The few remaining genuine mission structures are preserved as **El Presidio de Santa Barbara**, two blocks east of State Street at 123 E Canon Perdido St (daily 10.30am–4.30pm; $5; Ⓦwww.sbthp.org/presidio.htm), at the centre of which are the barracks of the old fortress **El Cuartel**, the second-oldest building in California, and now housing historical exhibits and a scale model of the small Spanish colony. Nearby, the **Santa Barbara Historical Museum**, 136 E De la Guerra St (Tues–Sat 10am–5pm, Sun noon–5pm; donation; Ⓦwww.santabarbaramuseum.com), is built around an 1817 adobe, presenting aspects of the city's past, from native settlements to modern photo studies.

Three blocks north of El Presidio, the still-functional **County Courthouse**, 1100 Anacapa St (Mon–Fri 8.30am–5pm, Sat & Sun 10am–4.30pm; free; Ⓦwww.santabarbaracourthouse.org), is a Spanish Revival gem, an idiosyncratic 1929 variation on the Mission theme with striking murals, tilework and fountain. Enjoy a free tour (daily 2pm, also Mon, Tues & Fri 10.30am) or take a break in the sunken gardens, explore the quirky staircases, or climb the seventy-foot-high "**El Mirador**" clock tower for a nice view out over the town. Afterwards, drop by the nearby **Santa Barbara Museum of Art**, 1130 State St (Tues–Sun 11am–5pm; $9; Ⓦwww.sbmuseart.org), which features some classical Greek and Egyptian statuary, a smattering of French Impressionists, an Asian collection of note and a wide-ranging **American collection**. Also engaging, the beautifully decorated **Karpeles Manuscript Library**, 21 W Anapamu St (Wed–Sun 10am–4pm; free; Ⓦwww.rain.org/~karpeles), is home to a diverse array of important documents, which display in rotating exhibitions, such as Napoleon's battle plans for his Russian invasion and manuscripts by figures such as Twain, Edison, Locke and Borges.

State Street leads half a mile down from the town centre to **Stearns Wharf** (Ⓦwww.stearnswharf.org), the oldest wooden pier in the state, built in 1872, home to shopping stalls, food vendors and the **Ty Warner Sea Center** (daily 10am–5pm; $8), which showcases whale bones and tot-friendly tide pools.

In the hills above the town is the engaging **Museum of Natural History**, 2559 Puesta del Sol Rd (daily 10am–5pm; $10; Ⓦwww.sbnature.org), which showcases intriguing artefacts from native culture, various dioramas of mammals, birds, reptiles and insects, a planetarium and actual skeletons of such extinct creatures as the pygmy mammoth. Nearby at 2201 Laguna St, **Mission Santa Barbara** (daily

9am–4.30pm; $5; Ⓦwww.sbmission.org), dating from 1820, has a colourful twin-towered facade facing out over a perfectly manicured garden towards the sea, combining Romanesque and Spanish Mission styles in a formidable manner. If you continue on into the hills from the mission, you come to the splendid **Botanic Garden**, 1212 Mission Canyon Rd (daily 9am–6pm, Nov–Feb closes 5pm; $8; Ⓦwww.sbbg.org), whose 65 acres of hillside meadows and glades are laced with endemic cacti, manzanita, trees and wildflowers.

Arrival, information and accommodation

Greyhound **buses** stop every few hours downtown at 34 W Carrillo St; Amtrak **trains** arrive at the old Southern Pacific station at 209 State St, right by US-101. A few blocks away is the **visitor centre**, 1 Garden St, (Mon–Sat 9am–5pm, Sun 10am–5pm; Ⓣ805/965-3021, Ⓦwww.santabarbara.com). You can walk to most places, although a frequent **shuttle bus** (25¢) loops around Santa Barbara during the day, with regional buses ($1.75; Ⓣ805/963-3366, Ⓦwww.sbmtd.gov) covering the outlying areas into the evening.

While there are no **campgrounds** in Santa Barbara proper, there are several spots along the coast to the north, including El Capitan and Refugio state beaches, and to the south, Carpinteria State Beach; all are accessible via Reserve America (Ⓣ1-800/444-7275, Ⓦwww.reserveamerica.com) and fees are $35 per car, or $10 if you come by bicycle or on foot.

Blue Sands Motel 421 S Milpas St Ⓣ805/965-1624, Ⓦwww.bluesandsmotel.com. A great bet for accommodation: clean rooms with gas fireplaces, free wireless internet, kitchenettes and flat-screen TVs – along with a heated pool. ❺

Cheshire Cat 36 W Valerio St Ⓣ805/569-1610, Ⓦwww.cheshirecat.com. Loaded with precious Victorian decor, this B&B has twelve rooms, three cottages and a coach house, and features a hot tub, bikes for guests' use and an *Alice in Wonderland* theme. ❻

Inn at East Beach 1029 Orilla del Mar Ⓣ805/965-0546, Ⓦwww.innateastbeach.com. Clean, modern rooms with free wi-fi, microwaves and fridges, and some suites with kitchens. ❻

Inn of the Spanish Garden 915 Garden St Ⓣ805/564-4700, Ⓦwww.spanishgardeninn.com. Elegant boutique rooms in a chic Mediterranean complex with designer decor, fireplaces, high-speed wi-fi and on-site fitness centre. ❾

Marina Beach Motel 21 Bath St Ⓣ1-877/627-4621, Ⓦwww.marinabeachmotel.com. Clean motel rooms with continental breakfast and options for bike rentals, kitchenettes and jacuzzis. A pleasant getaway. ❺, summer ❼

Santa Barbara Tourist Hostel 134 Chapala St Ⓣ805/963-0154, Ⓦwww.sbhostel.com. Centrally located hostel near the beach and State St, with bicycle and surfboard rentals, complimentary breakfast and internet access. Dorm rooms go for $22–35, depending on the season, with private rooms also available ($59–95), some with private bath.

Eating, drinking and nightlife

Although Santa Barbara has plenty of places for devouring comfort food and swilling beer, the unquestioned centre for local and tourist activity is **State Street**, lined with a number of good **restaurants**, **bars** and **clubs**.

Arigato Sushi 1225 State St Ⓣ805/965-6074. The main draw for sushi fans in town, this boutique spot is a bit on the pricey side, but the fresh, delicious fish justifies the expense.

Bouchon 9 W Victoria St Ⓣ805/730-1160. Elite California cuisine favourite, presenting a rotating menu of scrumptious dishes such as *escargots*, rack of lamb, maple-glazed duck breast and a full selection of fresh seafood.

Ca' Dario 37 E Victoria St Ⓣ805/884-9419. An upscale Italian haunt that lives up to its prices, with fine cheeses and pasta, and dishes such as roasted quail, veal chops, crepes and plenty of fish.

Natural Café 508 State St Ⓣ805/962-9494. Good and cheap veggie meals – with pasta, sandwiches, salads, falafel and desserts – and meat entrees such as tacos and enchiladas, in a prime spot for people-watching. Part of a regional chain.

Tupelo Junction Cafe 1218 State St ⓣ805/899-3100. One of the town's best spots for breakfast, focusing on mid-priced items like mushroom-and-truffle scrambles, crab cake and potato hash, vanilla French toast and Maine lobster chowder. Also serves lunch and dinner.

Velvet Jones 423 State St ⓣ805/965-8676. Among the few good places in town to catch a rock show, typically of the indie variety, from Thurs–Sat, and the odd comedy and reggae show at other times.

Wildcat Lounge 15 W Ortega St ⓣ805/962-7970. A good spot for seeing electronica DJs and various bands, in a chic atmosphere with a mix of locals, students and out-of-towners.

San Luis Obispo

SAN LUIS OBISPO, 160 miles north of Santa Barbara and halfway between LA and San Francisco, is a few miles inland, but makes a good base for exploring the coast. Still mainly an agricultural centre, it holds a smattering of nineteenth-century architecture, especially around **Buchon Street**, as well as good restaurants, pubs and accommodation.

The compact core of San Luis is eminently walkable, centred on the late-eighteenth-century **Mission San Luis Obispo de Tolosa**, 751 Palm St (daily 9am–5pm; donation; ⓦwww.missionsanluisobispo.org), which was the prototype for the now-ubiquitous red-tile-roof church. Between the mission and the visitor centre, **Mission Plaza**'s terraces step down along San Luis creek, along which footpaths meander, crisscrossed by bridges every hundred feet, and overlooked by shops and outdoor restaurants on the south bank. **Higuera Street**, a block south of Mission Plaza, is the main drag, and springs to life on Thursday nights for the **Farmers' Market**, (6–9pm; free) when the street is closed to cars and filled with vegetable stalls, barbecues and street musicians. Another highlight, the **Dallidet Adobe and Gardens**, 1185 Pacific St (gardens Fri 10am–1pm, adobe summer-only Sun 1–4pm; donation; ⓣ805/544-2303), is a handsome 1860s residence and one of the area's oldest buildings, with a pleasant garden sitting in the shadow of a pair of 125ft-tall redwoods.

Arrival, information and accommodation

The Greyhound **bus** depot is at 345 Marsh St, while Amtrak **trains** stop at 1011 Railroad Ave, at the end of Santa Rosa Street. The **Chamber of Commerce**, 1039 Chorro St (ⓣ805/781-2777, ⓦwww.visitslo.com), provides brochures for self-guided walking tours of town. The local transit company, San Luis Obispo Regional Rideshare (ⓣ805/541-2277, ⓦwww.rideshare.org), has information on transit options in the region, including shuttles and taxis; area **bus** rides cost $1–3.

Rates for **accommodation** are generally low, though if you want a nice view of the ocean, you're better off taking a short drive south to **Pismo Beach**, a beach town that makes a pleasant stopover.

Garden Street Inn B&B 1212 Garden St ⓣ1-800/488-2045, ⓦwww.gardenstreetinn.com. B&B in a restored 1887 Victorian building, with nine comfortable themed rooms and four suites. There's wine and hors d'oeuvres on arrival and gourmet cooked breakfasts. ❼

Hostel Obispo 1617 Santa Rosa St ⓣ805/544-4678, ⓦwww.hostelobispo.com. Good-value hostel, though amenities are a bit meagre and the place closes in the afternoon. Still, it has a central location and cheap bike rentals. Dorm rooms $27, private rooms $45–85.

Madonna Inn 100 Madonna Rd ⓣ1-800/543-9666, ⓦwww.madonnainn.com. Legendary roadside attraction that explodes with kitsch in each of its 110 variously themed rooms (desert, jungle, Wild West, the list goes on). Memorable in a freakish sort of way. ❼

Petit Soleil 1473 Monterey St ⓣ805/549-0321, ⓦwww.petitsoleilslo.com. Very stylish French-themed

B&B offering modish decor in each uniquely designed room, and truly continental breakfasts that can be quite tasty. ❽

San Luis Creek Lodge 1941 Monterey St ⓣ1-800/593-0333, ⓦwww.sanluiscreeklodge.com. Offers 25 smart rooms in three buildings, each in a Greek Revival, Tudor Revival and Craftsman style, with microwaves and wi-fi access. Some units have fireplaces, jacuzzis or balconies. ❻, but rates jump by $70 on summer weekends.

Eating and drinking

Higuera Street is the prime place to **eat**, with a nice range of unassuming restaurants and **bars**. Other good dining choices can also be found throughout town, along with a few microbreweries.

Downtown Brewing Company 1119 Garden St ⓣ805/543-1843. The major venue on the SLO nightlife scene, featuring two bars on different floors and hosting regular performances by Southern California bands and DJs. Also brews its own savoury ales.

Koberl at Blue 998 Monterey St ⓣ805/783-1135. Swanky lounge/bar/restaurant with chic modern decor and delicious seafood (including a caviar martini) and other tasty items such as beef carpaccio, duck confit and rack of lamb.

Linnaea's Cafe 1110 Garden St ⓣ805/541-5888. Café that serves good espresso and desserts, and offers live music, from indie rock and acoustic to variety shows, on its small stage on weekend nights.

Mondeo 893 Higuera St ⓣ805/544-2956. Asian-styled fast-food joint with inventive wraps and bowls, some of the better ones served with swordfish and kung pao chicken.

Oasis 675 Higuera St ⓣ805/543-1155. Delicious, inexpensive Middle Eastern eatery that features weekend belly dancing – and the set lunches are especially good value.

Hearst Castle

Forty-five miles northwest of San Luis Obispo, the hilltop **Hearst Castle** is one of the most extravagant estates in the world. The former holiday home of publisher **William Randolph Hearst** brings in more than a million visitors a year. Its interior combines walls, floors and ceilings torn from European churches and castles, with Gothic fireplaces and Moorish tiles – Hearst's buying sprees were legendary for their cost and breadth, and nearly every room is bursting with Greek vases and medieval tapestries. Even the extravagant pools are lined with works of art.

Work on Hearst's nearly four-hundred-square-mile ranch began in 1919, but the castle was never truly completed: rooms were torn out as soon as they were finished to accommodate more booty. The main facade, a twin-towered copy of a Mudejar cathedral, stands atop steps curving up from the world's most photographed swimming pool, the **Neptune Pool**, which is lined by a Greek colonnade and marble statues – the height of aesthetic glory, or irredeemably vulgar, depending on your taste.

The most dramatic time to visit is in the morning, when coastal fog often enshrouds the slopes below the castle, making it resemble **Citizen Kane**'s eerily evocative Xanadu, which was modelled on the estate. Five different, two-hour guided **tours** – which are essential, as are reservations – leave from the visitor centre just off Hwy-1 (daily 8.20am–3.20pm; ⓣ1-916/414-8400 ext 4100, ⓦwww.hearstcastle.com) and showcase different aspects of the estate, from an introductory Experience Tour ($24), to a Garden Tour ($24) that encompasses the castle's blooms, as well as the wine cellar, to an Evening Tour ($30), in which docents in period dress speak of Master Hearst in the present tense.

Building America

Architecture has helped to define America's cultural and political life since the country's inception, and still provides many of its most iconic images, from the neon spectacles on the Las Vegas strip to the soaring skyscrapers of Chicago and New York City. But beyond these showstoppers, there are many important structures of the country's native and immigrant populations – from the starkly beautiful adobe homes of Taos Pueblo in New Mexico to the stunning Spanish missions along the California coast.

Log cabins, Cody ▲

Mercer House, Savannah ▼

Chrysler Building, New York ▼

Rise of a national style

The **National Mall** in Washington DC was envisioned according to Masonic principles of balance and geometric order, with Neoclassical buildings, grand boulevards and radial axes. Though the city took 150 years to fully realize, its imperial design was prescient. But far removed from the budding capital and a handful of key East Coast cities, the early US was still an undeveloped country of frontier log cabins, wooden forts and clapboard farmhouses.

In the nineteenth century, the US was awash in imported designs. The stately **Georgian manors** of the northeast gave the impression of British gentry, the neo-Gothic cathedrals suggested an old Catholic order and mock Egyptian temples, Swiss chalets and Tudor mansions were conspicuous sights on a Midwest prairie or New England township.

The greatest influence, of course, was the colourful **Victorian** style, which defined the cityscape of places from San Francisco and Boston to Butte, Montana. By 1900, though, the growing ambitions of the US brought forth the imperious effect of the Beaux Arts movement: stunning banks and libraries modelled as temples, robber baron mansions as imperial palaces and train stations like the old Penn Station as the Baths of Caracalla.

Native invention

The 1920s and 30s were a peak of American architectural creativity – best exemplified by the **Art Deco** towers of the Empire State and Chrysler buildings, descendants of the work done in Chicago by Louis Sullivan, credited with inventing the skyscraper. Elsewhere, **Frank Lloyd Wright** had a long career and Europeans like Mies van der Rohe and Eero Saarinen did some of their best work here. Although architectural trends can change like haute couture, the greatest builders have preserved their individuality. The concrete austerity of Louis Kahn, the sharp white angles of Richard Meier, and the sculptural fantasies of Frank Gehry are just a few of the homegrown creations that have had a distinct and lingering impact on the wide American landscape.

Frank Lloyd Wright

Possibly the greatest American architect, Frank Lloyd Wright enjoyed a career spanning more than seven decades. His influence was huge: with his use of horizontal volumes he evoked the native landscape; with his inventive materials like glass brick, Pyrex tubes and precast concrete "knit-blocks", he gave rise to architecture as sculpture; with his "Usonian" homes, he hoped to devise affordable housing. The most familiar of his landmarks are:

Oak Park, IL (see p.298). His most concentrated collection of early-modern gems, including the stunning Unity Temple and his own house and studio.

The Robie House (see p.299). The single most important signpost for the coming suburban ranch home, as well as a lovely piece of design.

Fallingwater (see p.153). Innovative environmental architecture built around an enchanting site of forested beauty and cascading water.

Taliesin (see p.315 & p.784). Two buildings, same name: his marvellous Wisconsin studio and home, and his Scottsdale architecture and design school.

Guggenheim Museum (see p.91). A piece of abstract design in the form of a circular beehive, with a famous sloping interior ramp.

▲ Experience Music Project, Seattle

▼ Fallingwater, Pennsylvania

▼ Guggenheim Museum, New York

Victorian houses, San Francisco ▲

Old Mission Santa Barbara, California ▼

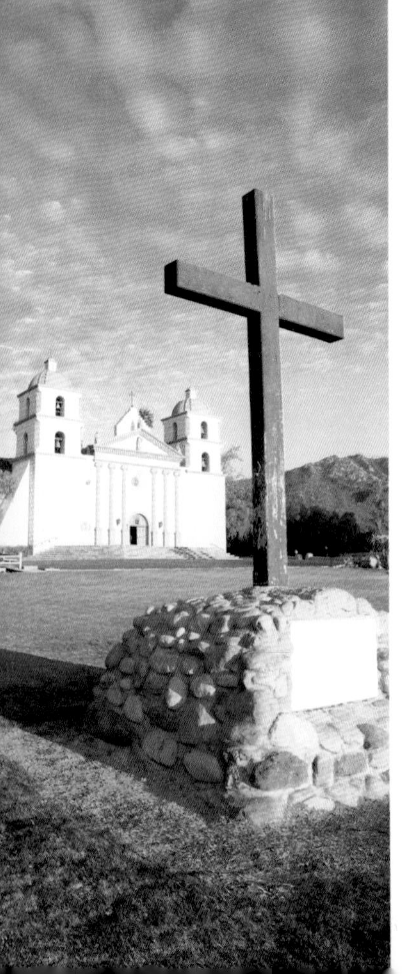

Architectural field trips

If you're really into seeing the variety of designs the US has on offer, these enclaves of architectural form, function and style are a good start.

▸▸ **The Painted Ladies, CA** From Haight-Ashbury to Pacific Heights and Alamo Square, a resplendent reminder of the good old Victorian days of the Italianate, Queen Anne and Eastlake styles.

▸▸ **Charlottesville, VA** Thomas Jefferson's work as the founder and builder of the University of Virginia and Monticello is the classical style at its most refined and elegant.

▸▸ **Anasazi Country, in the Southwest** America's indigenous peoples were some of its most inventive architects – none more so than the Anasazi, whose cliff dwellings, kivas and Great Houses are easily accessible in the Four Corners region of the Southwest.

▸▸ **South Beach, FL** In Miami's fabulous Art Deco District, oceanfront buildings are alive with zigzag lines, neon-rimmed curves and zesty letters.

▸▸ **The Serra Missions, CA** Father Junipero Serra and his Catholic missionaries left behind a chain of 21 striking, late-eighteenth-century Spanish missions along the coast of California.

▸▸ **Boston, MA** The cauldron of the American Revolution, the city's most eye-catching attractions are the gilded-dome-topped Massachusetts State House and H.H. Richardson's rusticated-stone Romanesque Trinity Church.

▸▸ **Charleston, SC and Savannah, GA** Two ideal towns to see the comfort and gentility of the Old South as well as its darker aspects, from fetching town squares and grand plantations, to grim slave quarters and auction blocks.

▸▸ **Las Vegas, NV** Sin City has long been an icon of pop architecture, with its ersatz castles, pyramids, tropical islands and pint-sized versions of Paris, Venice and New York.

The Big Sur Coast

Starting just north of Hearst Castle, the ninety wild and undeveloped miles of rocky cliffs along the **Big Sur Coast** feature grand redwood groves lining river canyons in the shadow of the Santa Lucia Mountains. Running through this striking terrain is the exhilarating route of **Hwy-1**, carved out of bedrock cliffs 500ft above the ocean, though **public transport** is limited to the Monterey-Salinas Transit (MST) bus (Ⓣ1-888/MST-BUS1, Ⓦwww.mst.org), which runs between Monterey to Nepenthe two to four times daily (Rte-22; $4.50 each way). Summer weekends are sunny and winters turbulent, but the southern coastline of Big Sur is comparatively gentle, with sandy beaches hiding below crumbling ochre cliffs. Contact the regional **Chamber of Commerce** (Ⓣ831/667-2100, Ⓦwww.bigsurcalifornia.org) for additional information.

Heading north on Hwy-1, the acreage on the east side of the highway by **Julia Pfeiffer Burns State Park** (daily dawn–dusk; Ⓣ831/667-2315) was damaged by fire and its trails are still closed, but closer to the shore the park offers some of the best day-hikes in the Big Sur area, including a short walk along the cliffs to an overlook of McWay Falls, which crash onto a beach below. A less-travelled path leads down from Hwy-1 two miles north of the 80ft waterfall, through a 200ft-long tunnel to the remains of a small wharf at **Partington Cove**, one of the few places in Big Sur where you can get to the sea. Once you get there, check out the fascinating, 1700-acre **underwater preserve** where scuba divers can explore the rich marine life. As with other Big Sur parks, Pfeiffer Burns provides campgrounds for $20–35 per night (reserve at Ⓣ831/667-2315, Ⓦwww.reserveamerica.com). Seven miles north of Pfeiffer Burns, lovely old *Deetjen's Big Sur Inn*, 48865 Hwy-1 (Ⓣ831/667-2377; Ⓦwww.deetjens.com; $80–220 ❹–❽), has a range of log cabins with rooms hand-crafted from thick redwood planks, and some with in-room fireplaces, plus fine breakfasts and dinners on site.

Further north at **NEPENTHE**, the rooftop *Nepenthe* restaurant, 48510 Hwy-1 (Ⓣ831/667-2345), offers pricey but good steaks, duck and seafood, while on the terrace below you can find similarly striking views at *Café Kevah* (Ⓣ831/667-2344), which serves affordable organic breakfasts and lunches. Across the highway, the **Henry Miller Library** (daily 11am–6pm; donation; Ⓦwww.henrymiller.org), displays and sells books by the author, who lived elsewhere in the area intermittently until the 1960s, and offers concerts by musical acts you might have even heard of. Two miles north along Hwy-1, unmarked Sycamore Canyon Road leads a mile west to Big Sur's best strip of coast, **Pfeiffer Beach** (daily dawn–dusk; $5/car; Ⓣ831/667-2315), a white sandy stretch dominated by a large rock whose earth-tone colours vary in the changing light.

Big Sur River Valley

Immediately north of the Pfeiffer Beach turn-off, Hwy-1 drops into the valley of the Big Sur River. The area is still recovering from fires in 2008, especially the outlying trails, so contact the **ranger station** (daily dawn–dusk; Ⓣ831/667-2315) for current information and for wilderness permits. When fully open, sheltered **Pfeiffer Big Sur State Park** features deep, clear swimming holes that form in the steep-walled river gorge during late spring and summer, and a hiking trail that leads half a mile up a canyon shaded by redwoods to the 60ft **Pfeiffer Falls**. The **campgrounds** here charge $25–35 and are often full on summer weekends (Ⓣ831/667-2315 or 1-800/444-7275, Ⓦwww.reserveamerica.com).

Just north of Pfeiffer Big Sur, the cluster of shops, lodgings and restaurants known as **The Village** is the most feasible base for seeing the area. **Accommodation** fills up in summer, and is mostly limited to the assorted motels lining the highway and a handful of overpriced resorts. As an alternative, try the rustic cabins at *Ripplewood Resort*, 47047 Hwy-1 (ⓣ831/667-2242, ⓦwww.ripplewoodresort.com; ❺), which variously come with kitchens and fireplaces. There are also basic cabins in the *Big Sur Lodge* (ⓣ831/667-3100, ⓦwww.bigsurlodge.com; ❼), though amenities are spare and the place has no air conditioning. There are additional regular cabins ($125), tent cabins ($88) and campgrounds ($40) at *Big Sur Campgrounds and Cabins*, a mile north of Pfeiffer Big Sur State Park (ⓣ831/667-2322; ⓦwww.bigsurcamp.com).

The Monterey Peninsula

At the northern edge of the Big Sur coast, a hundred miles south of San Francisco, are the rocky headlands of the **Monterey Peninsula**, where gnarled cypress trees mark the collision between the cliffs and the sea. The lively harbour town of **Monterey** was the capital of California under the Spanish, and briefly under the Mexicans and Americans, and retains many old adobes and historic structures alongside the usual tourist traps. **Carmel**, on the other hand, three miles to the south, is a self-consciously quaint village of million-dollar holiday homes and art galleries, while pleasant **Pacific Grove** is known mainly for its lighthouse and resident butterflies.

Arrival, information and getting around

Amtrak and Greyhound avoid the peninsula entirely, so you'll have to arrive by bus at the sprawling agricultural town of **Salinas** inland, then take a further hour-long trip on local bus #20 or #21 on Monterey-Salinas Transit buses ($4.50; ⓣ1-888/MST-BUS1, ⓦwww.mst.org); fares closer to Monterey are $2.25. Pick up information on Monterey and the entire peninsula at the **visitor centre**, near downtown at 401 Camino El Estero at Franklin Street (ⓣ1-877/MONTEREY, ⓦwww.seemonterey.com).

Accommodation

Hotels and **B&Bs** can get pricey, but cheap, fairly colourless **motels** are clustered along Fremont Street and Munras Avenue, two miles west of the centre. The nearest **camping** is in Veterans Memorial Park ($5/pedestrian or bicycle, $25/vehicle; ⓣ831/646-3865), site of Steinbeck's fictional **Tortilla Flat**, in the hills above town.

Bide-a-Wee Inn and Cottages 221 Asilomar Ave, Pacific Grove ⓣ831/372-2330, ⓦwww.bideaweeinn.com. Good value for the area, with some units featuring kitchenettes, fridges and microwaves. Short walk to the ocean. Two-night minimum at summer peak. ❻

Carmel River Inn Hwy-1 at Carmel River Bridge, Carmel ⓣ831/624-1575 or 1-800/966-6490, ⓦwww.carmelriverinn.com. A mix of hotel rooms and charming cottages, some of which come with patios or private decks, and some with kitchenettes and fireplaces, plus a heated pool and riverside location. $139 ❻

Green Gables Inn 104 5th St, Pacific Grove ⓣ831/375-2095 or 1-800/722-1774, ⓦwww.greengablesinnpg.com. Plush B&B doubles in one of the prettiest homes in a town of fine houses, on the waterfront a few blocks from the Aquarium. Some rooms have fireplaces and spas. Most units $185 and up ❼

HI-Monterey Hostel 778 Hawthorne St, Monterey ⓣ831/649-0375, ⓦwww.montereyhostel.org. Located downtown near Cannery Row, a fairly standard hostel with dorms for $26 and private rooms for $62 (two or more guests only). No alcohol allowed. Closed in the afternoon.

Horizon Inn and Ocean View Lodge 3rd St at Junipero, Carmel ⓣ1-800/350-7723, ⓦwww.horizoninncarmel.com. An enjoyable stopover in Carmel with stylish modern units, some of which have balconies, jacuzzis, flat-screen TVs and microwaves. ❼

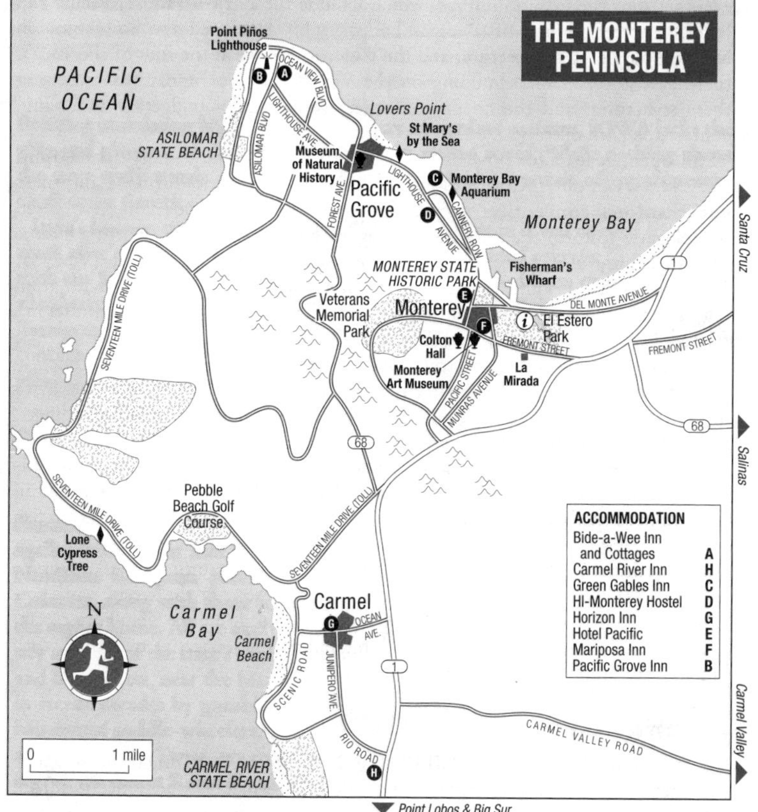

Hotel Pacific 300 Pacific St, Monterey ⓣ831/373-5700, ⓦwww.hotelpacific.com. All-suite digs with luxury to spare, including continental breakfast, stylish decor, fireplaces, high-speed net access and patios and/or balconies. ❽

Mariposa Inn 1386 Munras Ave, Monterey ⓣ831/649-1414, ⓦwww.mariposamonterey.com. Chic modern rooms with fireplaces, plus flat-screen TVs, wi-fi, a hot tub and continental breakfast. ❼

Pacific Grove Inn 581 Pine Ave, Pacific Grove ⓣ1-800/732-2825, ⓦwww.pacificgrove-inn.com. Classic 1904 Victorian inn boasting 17 rooms with wi-fi, and some with ocean views and fireplaces. A good deal, considering the proximity to the sea. ❽

Monterey

Named by the Spanish merchant and explorer Sebastian Vizcaíno in 1602, **MONTEREY** went from a Spanish and Mexican military and administrative centre to, after the US took over in 1846, the site of the negotiating and writing of the state constitution, and then became the first capital of California – before being superseded by Sacramento.

The compact centre still features some of the best vernacular **buildings** of California's Hispanic past, most sitting within a few blocks of the waterfront. A loosely organized **Path of History** connects the numerous sites of **Monterey State Historic Park**, though unfortunately **walking tours** have been suspended thanks to California's seemingly intractable budget problems. For now you can't even get into the main buildings, which include the **Larkin House**, Pacific and Jefferson streets, home of Thomas Larkin, who developed the now-common Monterey style of architecture; and the **Custom House** at the foot of the wharf, the oldest governmental building on the West Coast. For updates on accessing these structures, and the dozens of others shuttered by budgetary bumbling, contact the park office at ⓣ831/649-7118.

Still open, at least for now, is **Colton Hall** 570 Pacific St (daily 10am–4pm; free; ⓦwww.monterey.org/museum), furnished as it was during California's **constitutional convention**, with an early map of the West Coast on view – used by delegates to form the long boundaries of the 31st state. Also worth a look is the **Monterey Art Museum**, across the street at 559 Pacific St (Wed–Sat 11am–5pm, Sun 1–4pm; $5; ⓦwww.montereyart.org), which along with good regional photography and painting has excellent rose gardens. The museum's related **La Mirada** house, 720 Via Mirada (same hours and admission), is a charming nineteenth-century stone adobe furnished in the decor of the time.

More well known, tacky **Fisherman's Wharf** is a tourist trap loaded with disused wharves and canneries, some of them converted into boutiques and diners. Heading north from the wharf, a **bike path** runs two miles to Pacific Grove along **Cannery Row** – named after John Steinbeck's literary portrait of the rough-and-ready workers of its seafood plants. Since abandoned, the canneries reopened in the 1970s as malls and restaurants, and now teem with tourists instead of fish (more info at ⓦwww.canneryrow.com). Along the route, the engaging **Monterey Bay Aquarium**, 886 Cannery Row (daily 10am–5pm, summer 9.30am–6pm; $30, kids $18; ⓦwww.montereybayaquarium.org), is one of the West Coast's best aquariums, with a spectacular display of sealife, including a huge Kelp Forest tank, a touch pool, a two-storey sea-otter exhibit and a large, evocative tank filled with bluefin tuna and hammerhead sharks.

Pacific Grove

Just north of Monterey, **PACIFIC GROVE** began as a nineteenth-century campground and Methodist retreat, and still holds ornate wooden **cottages** from those long-forgotten days, along 16th and 17th streets, and a good number of preserved Victorian homes throughout town. One other reminder of that pious era is the deep-red wooden Gothic church **St Mary's by the Sea**, Central Avenue at 12th Street (Mon–Fri 8.30am–4.30pm; ⓦwww.stmarysbythesea.org), with a simple interior of polished redwood beams and an authentic signed Tiffany stained-glass window.

Ocean View Boulevard circles the coast around the town, passing the headland of **Lovers Point** (originally called Lovers of Jesus Point), where preachers used to hold sunrise services – indeed, it's one of the peninsula's best **beaches**. Every year, from October through to early March, hundreds of thousands of golden Monarch **butterflies** come here from Canada to escape the winter chill, forming orange and black blankets on the **Butterfly Trees**, on Ridge Road, a quarter of a mile inland on Lighthouse Avenue. At the end of the avenue, near the tip of Monterey Peninsula, stands the 150-year-old **Point Piños** lighthouse (Thurs–Mon 1–4pm; $2), the oldest continuously operating lighthouse on the California coast, though basically a quaint farmhouse with a revolving light poking out of its roof. To find out more about the area's stunning topography and biology, head to the **Pacific Grove Museum of Natural History**, downtown at Forest Street and Central Avenue (Tues–Sun 10am–5pm; free; ⓦwww.pgmuseum.org), where you can learn all about the area's flora and fauna, and cultural artefacts of the peninsula's native tribes.

If you have time, take the **Seventeen Mile Drive** (daily dawn–dusk; $9.25/car), a privately owned, scenic toll road that loops along the coast south to Carmel and provides beautiful vistas of rugged headlands and the glistening shore, as well as famed Pebble Beach golf course. One other highlight along the way is the **Lone Cypress Tree**, whose solitary silhouette has been the subject of many a postcard in these parts.

Carmel

Set on gently rising bluffs above a rocky shore, the boutique town of **CARMEL** is well known for its genteel air, inflated real-estate prices, neat rows of quaint shops and miniature homes along Ocean Avenue, and a largely untouched coastline. Don't expect to see street addresses, mail delivery, street lights, parking meters or franchise businesses in town: they're all officially banned. For all its charm, the town offers little to do, other than to purchase baubles and artworks from one of its boutiques.

The town's best feature is the largely untouched nearby coastline. **Carmel River State Beach**, west of town, is a tranquil cove of blue water near a bird sanctuary, bordered by soft white sand and cypress-covered cliffs, though the tides are deceptively strong and dangerous, so be careful if you chance a swim. **Point Lobos State Natural Reserve**, just south of town on Hwy-1 (daily 8am–dusk; $10/vehicle; ⓣ831/624-4909), is spread over two square miles, and has more than 250 bird and animal species along its hiking trails, and the sea here is one of the richest underwater habitats in California. Grey whales are often seen offshore, migrating south in January and returning with young calves in April and early May.

Eating

There are many excellent places to **eat** on the peninsula. However, if you're on a tight budget, the best cheap eats are on the north side of Monterey, along Fremont Street and just south of Cannery Row on and around Lighthouse Avenue.

Akaoni 6th St at Mission, Carmel ⓣ831/620-1516. All your favourite sushi and sashimi choices, plus prawn and crab, make this upper-end sushi joint a good stop for lovers of Japanese fare.

Fishwife 1996 Sunset Drive at Asilomar Blvd, Pacific Grove ⓣ831/375-7107. Long-standing fixture on the seafood scene, where the dishes come at reasonable prices (around $16 a plate) and range from mahi-mahi to swordfish.

Little Napoli Dolores St between Ocean and 7th St, Carmel ⓣ831/626-6335. Solid mid-priced Italian eatery that offers fresh pasta in sizeable portions and is also good for its pizza.

Old Monterey Café 489 Alvarado St, Monterey ⓣ831/646-1021. Hearty breakfasts with solid pancakes and omelets, plus a rib-stuffing corned beef hash. Breakfast and lunch only.

Papa Chano's 462 Alvarado St, Monterey ⓣ831/646-9587. Affordable Mexican fare with juicy, authentic south-of-the-border specialties, highlighted by some mean burritos.

Sardine Factory 701 Wave St, Monterey ⓣ831/373-3775. Dreadful name but prime California seafood – from oysters to crab cakes to abalone bisque – served in French chateau splendour, with entrees starting at $30.

The Works 667 Lighthouse Ave, Pacific Grove ⓣ831/372-2242. Decent café where you can pick up information about the area while snacking on pastries and drinking coffee or tea.

Drinking and nightlife

Pacific Grove and Carmel offer few decent **nightlife** options, so all listings below are for Monterey. Mid-September's **Monterey Jazz Festival** ($35 and up; ⓣ1-800/307-3378, ⓦwww.montereyjazzfestival.org) is the oldest of its kind in the world, dating from 1958 – though 1967's even more famous Monterey Pop

Festival was unfortunately only a one-time event. Check out the **Monterey County Weekly** (ⓦwww.montereycountyweekly.com) for **listings**.

The Bulldog 611 Lighthouse Ave ⓣ831/658-0686. British pub with a range of hearty food on offer – bangers and mash to fish and chips, and burgers – along with darts and plenty of beers on tap.

Crown and Anchor 150 W Franklin St ⓣ831/649-6496. All your favourite English cuisine at this unpreten tious local pub, best known for its wide array of brews.

The Hippodrome 321 Alvarado St, suite D ⓣ831/646-9244. Trendy nightclub spread over three floors and boasting a variety of club nights and a young, pulsing crowd.

Lallapalooza 474 Alvarado St ⓣ831/645-9036. Swanky martini bar – also serving mid-priced surf 'n' turf and pasta – for relaxed social-climbing, with well-mixed, trendy drinks with names like "Water Moccasin" and "Purple Haze".

Lounge Underground 638 Wave St ⓣ831/655-4419. Prime spot for checking out what's happening on the indie-rock music scene, with some electronica and jazz thrown in for good measure. Near Cannery Row.

Santa Cruz

The quintessential California beach town, **SANTA CRUZ**, 75 miles south of San Francisco, is sited at the foot of thickly wooded mountains beside a clean sandy beach. With a strong leftover 1960s vibe, it's not too touristy and roadside stands are more likely to sell apples or sprouts than postcards and trinkets. The highlight, the **Santa Cruz Boardwalk**, 400 Beach St (June–Aug open daily, rest of year Sat & Sun only; hours vary, often 11am–7pm; $3–5/ride, unlimited rides $37; ⓦwww.beachboardwalk.com), is one of the last surviving beachfront amusement parks on the West Coast, and features the 1924 **Giant Dipper**, a wild wooden roller coaster that doubles in the movies as a Coney Island ride.

The **beach** next to the boardwalk is popular, but can get rowdy and dirty. For more peace and quiet, follow the coast out of town to one of the smaller beaches such as Capitola or New Brighton. From **West Cliff Drive**, you'll see some of the biggest waves in California, not least at **Steamer Lane**, beyond the Municipal Pier, where surfing in California allegedly began in the nineteenth century. **Cowell's Beach**, just north of the Municipal Pier, is the best place to give the sport a try. The ghosts of surfers past are animated at the **Surfing Museum**, in the old Abbott Memorial lighthouse on the point (Thurs–Mon noon–4pm; free; ⓦwww.santacruzsurfingmuseum.org), where the boards on display range from early 12ft redwood planks to modern high-tech multi-finned cutters. A clifftop cycle path runs two miles out from here to **Natural Bridges State Beach** (daily 8am–dusk; $10/car; ⓦwww.santacruzstateparks.org), where waves once cut holes through the cliffs and formed delicate stone arches – though only one remains.

In the hills above town, the **University of California Santa Cruz** famously has as its mascot the **banana slug**, but is best for its **Arboretum**, near Bay and High streets (daily 9am–5pm; $5; ⓦarboretum.ucsc.edu), world famous for its experimental techniques of cultivation and stocked with numerous plants, including gardens showcasing conifers, rare fruits and aromatic blossoms.

Arrival, information and accommodation

Greyhound **buses** stop five times a day at 425 Front St, and Santa Cruz has an excellent public transit system known as the **Metro** (tickets $1.50; day pass $4.50; ⓣ831/426-6080, ⓦwww.scmtd.com). Electric Sierra Cycles, 302 Pacific Ave (ⓣ831/425-1593), rents **bikes** for $8/hr or $25/day. The **visitor centre** is at 1211 Ocean St (ⓣ831/425-1234, ⓦwww.santacruz.org).

Santa Cruz has plenty of places to **stay**, though rates can be much higher on summer weekends. Of the many **campgrounds** in the area, the best is at **New Brighton State Beach** (Ⓣ831/464-6330, Ⓦwww.reserveamerica.com; $35) three miles south at 1500 Park Ave, near the town of Capitola.

Capitola Venetian 1500 Wharf Rd, Capitola Ⓣ831/476-6471, Ⓦwww.capitolavenetian.com. Appealing though ageing beach hotel with one- to three-bed rooms, some with kitchens, fireplaces and ocean views. Rates vary from ❹ on a winter weekday to ❾ on a summer weekend.

HI-Santa Cruz 321 Main St, Santa Cruz Ⓣ831/423-8304, Ⓦwww.hi-santacruz.org. Well-situated hostel set in 1870s cottages, offering dorm beds from $25–28, private rooms for $58–93. Often booked up well in advance.

Pleasure Point Inn 2-3665 E Cliff Drive, Santa Cruz Ⓣ408/291-0299, Ⓦwww.pleasurepointinn.com. Stylishly modern B&B boasting four rooms with clifftop views, a roof sundeck and hot tub; rooms have stereos and jacuzzis. ❽ year-round.

Terrace Court Motel 125 Beach St Ⓣ831/423-3031. Quality accommodation offering some oceanside rooms with kitchenettes and free wi-fi. One of the better deals in town. ❾, though rates drop by $40 in winter.

Eating, drinking and nightlife

The main drag of **Pacific Avenue** is peppered with many relaxed **restaurants** and **bars**, while the town itself has the Central Coast's rowdiest **nightlife**, ranging from laidback coffeehouses to raucous nightclubs. Consult *Good Times* magazine (free; Ⓦwww.gtweekly.com) for listings.

The Catalyst 1011 Pacific Ave Ⓣ831/423-1336. Happening club with nightly entertainment and one of the best bets for catching mid-level touring artists and up-and-coming locals.

The Crepe Place 1134 Soquel Ave Ⓣ831/429-6994. Serving up mid-priced crepes with a tasty assortment of savoury and sweet fillings, including a few surprises, like smoked-salmon and jambalaya.

Kuumbwa Jazz Center 320 Cedar St Ⓣ831/427-2227. Friendly and intimate spot in a garden setting showcasing both traditional and modern jazz, and some rock shows, too. Cover anywhere from $5–25.

Rio Theatre 1205 Soquel Ave Ⓣ831/423-8209, Ⓦwww.riotheatre.com. Historic theatre that presents cult films, oddball performances and eclectic music concerts, some from big names.

Saturn Café 145 Laurel St Ⓣ831/429-8505. Vegetarian diner serving tasty items like faux burgers and chicken breasts – a good place to enjoy the (self-consciously) eccentric flair of Santa Cruz. Open till 3am.

San Francisco

SAN FRANCISCO proper occupies just 48 hilly square miles at the tip of a slender peninsula along the Northern California coast. Arguably the most beautiful, and likely the most liberal major city in the US, it remains true to itself: an individualistic place whose residents pride themselves on being the cultured counterparts to their cousins in LA. It's a surprisingly compact and approachable city, where downtown streets rise on impossible gradients to reveal stunning views of the city, the bay and beyond, and where **fog** rolls in on a moment's notice to envelop the city in mist. This is not the California of monotonous blue skies and slothful warmth – the temperature rarely exceeds 80°F and usually hovers in the 60s between May and August, until summer weather finally arrives in autumn's early weeks.

The original inhabitants of this area, the **Ohlone Indians**, were all but wiped out within a few years of the establishment in 1776 of the **Mission Dolores**, the sixth in the chain of Spanish Catholic missions that ran the length of California. Two years after the Americans replaced the Mexicans in 1846, the discovery of gold in the Sierra foothills precipitated the rip-roaring **Gold Rush**. Within a year, fifty thousand pioneers had come from the Midwest and East Coast (or from China), turning San Francisco from a muddy village and wasteland of sand dunes into a thriving supply centre and transit town. By the time the **transcontinental railroad** was completed in 1869, San Francisco was a lawless, rowdy boomtown of bordellos and drinking dens, something the moneyed elite – who hit it big on the much more dependable silver Comstock Lode in Nevada – worked hard to mend by constructing wide boulevards, parks, a cable-car system and elaborate Victorian redwood mansions by century's end.

In the midst of the city's golden age, however, a massive **earthquake**, followed by three days of fire, wiped out most of the town in 1906. Rebuilding began immediately and resulted in another magnificent city; in the decades that followed, many of the city's landmarks were built, including both local **bridges** (the Golden Gate and the Bay). By World War II, San Francisco had been eclipsed by Los Angeles as the West Coast's most populous city, but it achieved a new cultural eminence with the emergence of the Beats in the 1950s and the hippies in the 1960s, when the fusion of music, protest, rebellion and, of course, drugs, made international headlines.

It's estimated that over half of San Francisco's population originates from somewhere else. It is a city in a constant state of evolution, quickly gentrifying itself into one of the most high-end towns on earth – thanks, in part, to the disposable incomes pumped into its coffers from its sizeable singles and gay contingents. San Francisco has also been the scene of the dot-com revolution's meteoric rise, fall and slow recovery; the resultant wealth has pushed housing prices sky-high. Despite all its economic ebbs and flows, your impression of the city will be that of a proudly singular place.

Arrival and information

All international and most domestic flights arrive at **San Francisco International Airport** (SFO), located about fifteen miles south of downtown San Francisco. Regular BART (see p.905) trains get you downtown in about thirty minutes ($8.10). San Mateo County Transit (SamTrans) **buses** (ⓣ1-800/660-4287, ⓦwww.samtrans.org) leave every hour from the lower level of the airport; the KX express ($5) takes around twenty-five minutes to reach the Transbay Terminal downtown. A number of private **minibus shuttles** depart every five to ten minutes from the lower level of the circular road and take passengers to any San Francisco destination; try SuperShuttle (ⓣ1-800/258-3826, ⓦwww.supershuttle.com), which charges $17 per person but only $10 for each additional person in your party. **Taxis** from the airport cost $35–50 (plus tip) for any downtown location, more for the East Bay and Marin County – only worth considering if you can split the charges with others. If you're planning to drive, the usual **car rental** agencies operate free shuttle buses from the upper level to their car parks.

United and several domestic airlines (such as JetBlue and Southwest) fly into **Oakland International Airport** (see p.924), across the bay.

By bus and train

All of San Francisco's **Greyhound** services (Ⓣ1-800/231-2222, Ⓦwww.greyhound.com) use the new temporary **Transbay Terminal**, bound by Main, Folsom, Beale and Howard Streets, two blocks south of Market Street; the gleaming new Terminal is scheduled to open a few blocks away by 2015. **Amtrak** trains stop across the bay in **Richmond** (the most efficient BART transfer point) and continue to **Emeryville**, from where free shuttle buses run across the Bay Bridge to downtown San Francisco.

Information

The **San Francisco Visitor Information Center**, on the lower level of Hallidie Plaza, adjacent to the end of the cable-car line at 900 Market St at Powell (Mon–Fri 9am–5pm, Sat & Sun 9am–3pm, Nov–April closed Sun; Ⓣ415/391-2000, Ⓦwww.onlyinsanfrancisco.com) has free maps of the city and the Bay Area, and can help with lodging and travel plans. Its free **San Francisco Book** provides detailed, if a little selective, information about accommodation, entertainment, exhibitions and stores. The good value **City Pass** ($59; Ⓦwww.citypass.com), which allows entry into various attractions, free Muni rides, and other discounts for nine days, is also available here.

Two convenient post offices near downtown are Sutter Street Station, 150 Sutter St at Kearny (Mon–Fri 8am–5pm) in the Financial District, and Rincon Finance Station, 180 Steuart St at Mission (Mon–Fri 7am–6pm, Sat 9am–2pm), SoMa.

City transport

San Francisco is the rare American city where you don't need a car to see everything. In fact, given the difficult parking, dense traffic, zealous meter attendants and treacherous hills, going car-less makes sense. The public transportation system, **Muni**, though maligned by locals for its sometimes unpredictable schedule, covers every neighbourhood.

Despite constant car traffic, **cycling** is a popular form of transportation here, with marked routes to all major points of interest. if you have the time, however, **walking** the compact metropolis is your best bet. Wear comfortable shoes for the killer hills, some of them angled at a steep 30 degrees.

For a wealth of information on all forms of Bay Area transportation, including real-time traffic maps, visit Ⓦwww.511.org.

Muni and BART

San Francisco's public transportation is its beleaguered **Muni** (Ⓣ415/673-6864, Ⓦwww.sfmta.com), which operates a comprehensive network of buses, streetcars and cable cars that trundle up and around the city's hills. The flat **fare** is $2 on buses and trains (exact change only), with a possible increase on the horizon; with each ticket you buy, make sure you get a **free transfer** – good on all lines (except cable cars) for at least ninety minutes from the time you receive it. Muni streetcars run until about 1am nightly; after that, owl **buses** run sporadically between 1am–5am. A single **cable car** fare is as steep as the hills the vessels climb: $5, with no free transfers.

If you're staying a few days, the Muni **Passport** is available in one-day, three-day and seven-day denominations ($13, $20, $26, respectively) and is valid for unlimited travel on both Muni and BART within San Francisco. A **Fast Pass** costs $70 for a full calendar month and is also accepted by both Muni and BART within city limits; a Muni-only monthly pass ($60) is also available. Buy passes in baggage claim areas at SFO or at select locations around the city – visit Ⓦwww.sfmta.com for **more information**. You can also purchase a handy Muni map ($3) from the Visitor Information Center.

BART (Bay Area Rapid Transit; Mon–Fri 4am–midnight, Sat 6am–midnight, Sun 8am–midnight; $1.75–10.90; ⓣ415/989-2278, Ⓦwww.bart.gov) is the Bay Area region's electric rail transport system. Although access is limited within San Francisco to Market and Mission streets and a few neighbourhoods in the southern part of the city, it does a good job of connecting the city with myriad Easy Bay communities and airports on both sides of the bay. Trains are generally timely, clean and comfortable. Finally, bikes are allowed on **Muni** buses equipped with bicycle racks (on the front of the bus) and on BART, except during peak hours.

Other transport services

Taxis ply the streets, although they can be quite expensive and difficult to find outside of downtown, especially on weekends. If you're phoning ahead, try Veterans Cab (ⓣ415/552-1300) or Yellow Cab (ⓣ415/333-3333). Fares within the city are roughly $5 for the first mile, plus a customary fifteen-percent tip.

If you fancy **cycling**, the handiest option for rentals is Blazing Saddles (ⓣ415/202-8888, Ⓦwww.blazingsaddles.com), which has several locations – two of the most convenient are at 1095 Columbus Ave at Francisco Street in North Beach, and Pier 41 at Fisherman's Wharf. Rates for a standard bike are $28 per day, but check the company's website for coupons.

Organized tours

One-hour **bay cruises** are operated by Blue & Gold Fleet (ⓣ415/705-8200, Ⓦwww.blueandgoldfleet.com) from Pier 39, though be warned that everything may be shrouded in fog, making the price ($24; online bookings $19) less than worth it.

The best of San Francisco's considerable choices of **walking tours** include City Guides; (free, but small donation requested ⓣ415/557-4266, Ⓦwww.sfcityguides.org), which features a sprawling roster of fun ambles; Cruisin' the Castro ($35–45; ⓣ415/255-1821, Ⓦwww.cruisinthecastro.com), offering absorbing and witty tours of the gay community; Victorian Home Walk ($25; ⓣ415/252-9485, Ⓦwww.victorianwalk.com), which swings past the pick of the city's posh old homes; and the free, self-guided Barbary Coast Trail (ⓣ415/454-2355, Ⓦwww.sfhistory.org), highlighting the oldest parts of the city and marked by bronze medallions set in the street. There are also two-hour tours of the Mission's murals (see p.914 for details) that take in the district's distinctive street art.

Accommodation

San Francisco certainly isn't short on lodging, but to get the best pick be sure to reserve well in advance, especially in summer and autumn; expect to pay over $100 per room in any decent **hotel** or **motel** in high season. For **B&Bs**, the city's fastest-growing source of accommodation, contact a specialist agency such as Bed & Breakfast San Francisco (ⓣ1-800/452-8249, Ⓦwww.bbsf.com). If funds are tight, look into one of the many excellent **hostels**, where beds start at around $20.

San Francisco Reservations (Mon–Fri 6am–11pm, Sat–Sun 8am–11pm; ⓣ1-800/737-2060, Ⓦwww.hotelres.com) features fairly priced package options and will book you a room, sometimes for under $100. Bear in mind that all quoted room rates are subject to a **fourteen-percent lodging tax**.

Hotels, motels and B&Bs

The Fairmont San Francisco 950 Mason St at California, Nob Hill ⓣ1-866/540-4491, ⓦwww.fairmont.com/sanfrancisco. The most famous of the city's five-star hotels, decked out with several lounges, fantastic views from the rooms, a lovely terrace garden and the splendour of the *Tonga Room* in the basement (see p.920). ❽

Golden Gate Hotel 775 Bush St at Mason, Union Square ⓣ1-800/835-1118, ⓦwww.goldengatehotel.com. Friendly, European-style B&B with warmly furnished rooms, some with shared baths. Beautiful original iron elevator and Edwardian interior. ❼

Good Hotel 112 7th St at Mission, SoMa ⓣ415/621-7001, ⓦwww.jdvhotels.com. New, eco-aware hotel within walking distance of several museums, features pet-friendly accommodation and free bicycle rentals for all guests. ❺

Hotel Adagio 550 Geary St at Jones, Union Square ⓣ415/775-5000, ⓦwww.jdvhotels.com. The decor at this hotel echoes its ornate Spanish Revival facade with deep reds and ochres. Rooms are spacious and exude a calming feng shui vibe. ❾

Hotel Bohème 444 Columbus Ave at Vallejo, North Beach ⓣ415/433-9111, ⓦwww.hotelboheme.com. Located amid the city's Italian quarter, this small, fifteen-room hotel has tiny but dramatic rooms, with canopied beds. Columbus Ave can be noisy, so light sleepers should ask for a room at the back. ❼

Hotel Del Sol 3100 Webster St at Lombard, Cow Hollow ⓣ415/921-5520, ⓦwww.jdvhotels.com. Funky updated motor lodge with a tropical theme and a swimming pool. ❻

Hotel Diva 440 Geary St at Mason, Union Square ⓣ1-800/553-1900, ⓦwww.hoteldiva.com. Trendy modern art hotel with spacious rooms, as well as sleek metal and leather furniture. Particularly well positioned if you're planning to see theatre, with A.C.T. and the Curran directly across the street. ❺–❼, depending on season.

Ocean Park Motel 2690 46th Ave at Wawona, Parkside ⓣ415/566-7020, ⓦwww.oceanparkmotel.com. Fully across the city from downtown, San Francisco's oldest Art Deco motel is convenient for the coast and the zoo. The outdoor hot tub and pleasant garden courtyard are nice touches. ❺

Phoenix Hotel 601 Eddy St at Larkin, Tenderloin ⓣ415/776-1380, ⓦwww.thephoenixhotel.com. This raucous hipster-retro motor lodge feels more like Los Angeles than San Francisco, and is a favourite with touring rock bands. There's a small pool and the rooms are decorated in tropical colours and rotating local artwork. ❺

The Queen Anne Hotel 1590 Sutter St at Octavia, Western Addition ⓣ1-800/227-3970, ⓦwww.queenanne.com. Gloriously restored Victorian building enjoying its second life as a boutique B&B. Each room is stuffed with gold-accented Rococo furniture and bunches of silk flowers: the parlour (where afternoon tea and sherry is served) is stuffed with museum-quality period furniture. ❻

Stanyan Park Hotel 750 Stanyan St at Waller, Haight-Ashbury ⓣ415/751-1000, ⓦwww.stanyanpark.com. Adjacent to Golden Gate Park, this small hotel has 35 sumptuous rooms busily decorated in country florals, heavy drapes and junior four-poster beds. ❼

Hostels

Adelaide Hostel 51 Isadora Duncan Lane off Taylor St at Geary, Union Square ⓣ877/359-1915, ⓦwww.adelaidehostel.com. 100-bed hostel that includes both multi-person dorm ($25) and private rooms (❸). There's a big, sofa-filled lounge, backyard deck, clean kitchen and free wi-fi. Also hefty continental breakfasts and cheap laundry. Open 24hr.

Green Tortoise 494 Broadway at Montgomery St, North Beach ⓣ1-800/867-8647, ⓦwww.greentortoise.com. Laidback destination with dorm beds for $25–30 and private rooms with shared bath (❸). Both options include free internet and luggage storage, complimentary breakfast daily (and dinner three nights a week) and use of the small sauna. No curfew. Dorm and private rooms both available.

USA Hostel 711 Post St at Jones, Tenderloin ⓣ415/440-5600, ⓦwww.usahostels.com. A friendly and fun place on a safe edge of a gritty neighbourhood. There's a new 45-seat movie theatre (with complimentary popcorn) on site, along with free all-you-can-make pancakes and oatmeal in the morning. Large lockers and wi-fi included. Dorms go for $40 and there are also private rooms (❹).

Gay and lesbian accommodation

Inn on Castro 321 Castro St at Market, Castro ⓣ415/861-0321, ⓦwww.innoncastro.com. This luxurious B&B is spread across two nearby houses: It has eight rooms and three apartments available, all of which are brightly decorated in individual styles and have private baths. ❺

The Parker House 520 Church St at 18th, Castro ⓣ1-888/520-7275, ⓦwww.parkerguesthouse.com. This 21-room converted mansion is set in beautiful gardens and features ample common areas, a sunny breakfast room and a sauna. ❻

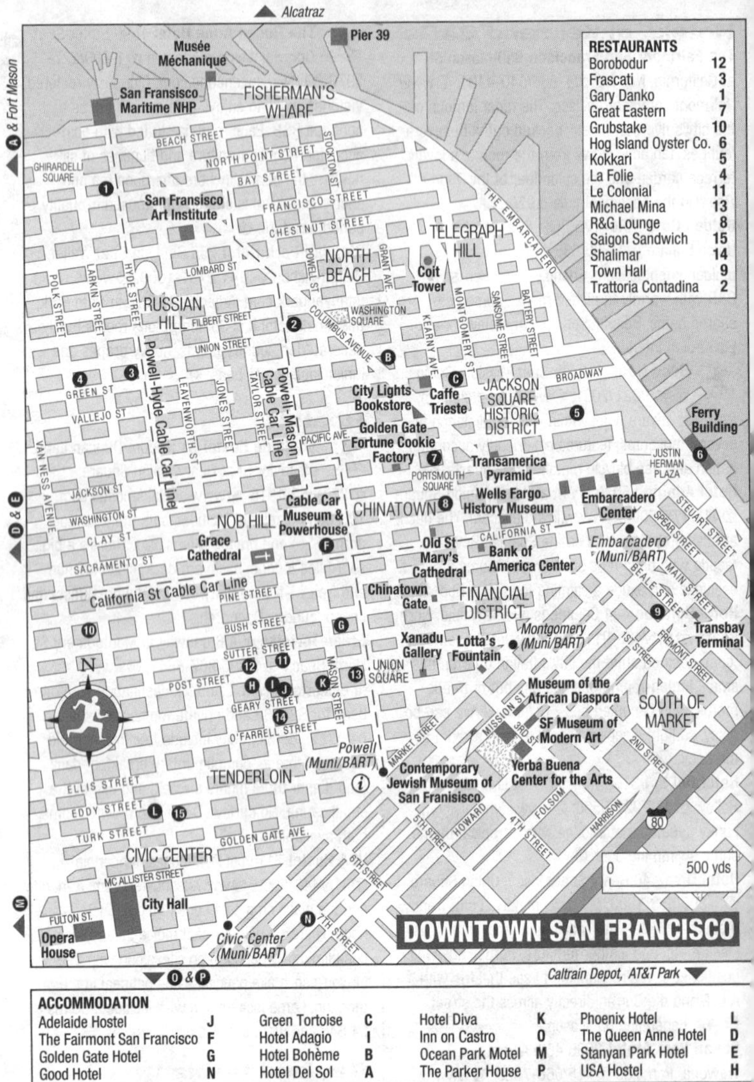

ACCOMMODATION

Adelaide Hostel	J	Green Tortoise	C	Hotel Diva	K	Phoenix Hotel	L
The Fairmont San Francisco	F	Hotel Adagio	I	Inn on Castro	O	The Queen Anne Hotel	D
Golden Gate Hotel	G	Hotel Bohème	B	Ocean Park Motel	M	Stanyan Park Hotel	E
Good Hotel	N	Hotel Del Sol	A	The Parker House	P	USA Hostel	H

The City

San Francisco is a city of distinct neighbourhoods. It's second in the US to only New York in terms of population density – commercial square-footage is surprisingly small and mostly confined to the downtown area and the rest of the city is made up of primarily residential neighbourhoods with street-level shopping districts easily explored on foot. Armed with a good map and strong legs, you could plough through much of the city in a day or two, but the best way to get to know San Francisco is to dawdle.

Union Square

The city's heart can be found around recently redesigned **Union Square**, located north of Market Street and bordered by Powell and Stockton streets; it takes its name from its role as gathering place for stumping speechmakers during the US Civil War. Cable cars clank past throngs who gravitate to the district's many upscale hotels, department stores, boutiques and theatres. The square witnessed the attempted assassination of President Gerald Ford outside the **Westin St Francis Hotel** in 1975 and was also the location of Francis Ford Coppola's film *The Conversation*, where Gene Hackman spied on strolling lovers. Many of **Dashiell Hammett**'s detective stories are set partly in the *St Francis*; in fact, during the 1920s, he worked there as a Pinkerton detective.

Along Geary Street, not far from the south side of the square, the **Theater District** is a pint-sized Broadway of restaurants, tourist hotels and naturally, stage theatres. On the eastern side of the square, **Maiden Lane** is a chic urban walkway that before the 1906 earthquake and fire was one of the city's roughest areas, where prostitution ran rampant and homicides averaged around ten a month. Nowadays, aside from some prohibitively expensive boutiques, the main feature is San Francisco's only **Frank Lloyd Wright-designed building**, an intriguing circular space at no. 140 that, when it opened in 1948, was a prototype for the Guggenheim Museum in New York. Today it's occupied by Xanadu Gallery, which specializes in premium Asian art pieces.

The Financial District and the Embarcadero

North of the city's main artery, Market Street, the glass-and-steel skyscrapers of the **Financial District** have sprung up in recent decades to form the city's only real high-rise area. Sharp-suited workers clog the streets and coffee kiosks during business hours, but the area's canyons of skyscrapers quieten down considerably by evening. Along Montgomery Street, grand pillared entrances and banking halls of the post-1906 earthquake buildings era jostle for attention with a mixed bag of modern towers. The best known is undoubtedly the **Bank of America Center** monolith, 555 California St at Kearny; this broad-shouldered hulk was hugely unpopular when completed in 1969, and continues to divide the city into fans and those who would like to see it razed to the ground. The **Wells Fargo History**

Cable cars

It was the invention of the **cable car** that put the high in San Francisco's high society, as it made life on the hills both possible and practical. Since 1873, these little trolleys have been an integral part of life in the city, supposedly thanks to Scotland-born Andrew Hallidie's concern for horses. Having watched a team struggle and fall, breaking their legs on a steep San Franciscan street, Hallidie designed a **pulley system** around the thick wire rope his father had patented for use in the California mines (the Gold Rush was slowing, so the Hallidies needed a new market for their product). Despite locals' initial doubts, a transportation revolution followed. At their peak, just before the 1906 earthquake, hundreds of cable cars travelled 110 miles of track throughout the city; over the years, usage dwindled and, in 1964, nostalgic citizens voted to preserve the last seventeen miles (now just ten) as a moving historic landmark.

The cars fasten onto a moving two-inch cable which runs beneath the streets, gripping on the ascent then releasing at the top and gliding down the other side. You can see the huge motors that still power these cables at the fun **Cable Car Museum and Powerhouse**, 1201 Mason St at Washington (daily: April–Sept 10am–6pm; Oct–March 10am–5pm; free; ⓣ415/474-1887, ⓦwww.cablecarmuseum.org).

Museum, 420 Montgomery St at California (Mon–Fri 9am–5pm; free; ⓣ415/396-2619, ⓦwww.wellsfargo.com), traces the far-from-slick origins of San Francisco's big money right from the days of the Gold Rush, with mining equipment, gold nuggets, photographs and a genuine retired stagecoach.

Once cut off from the rest of San Francisco by the double-decker Embarcadero Freeway – damaged in the 1989 earthquake and torn down two years later – the **Ferry Building**, at the foot of Market Street, was modelled on the cathedral tower in Seville, Spain. Before the bridges were built in the 1930s, it was the arrival point for fifty thousand cross-bay commuters daily. After decades of misguided modifications that resulted in colourless workspaces and a dwindling emphasis on ferry service, it has emerged immaculately restored, now boasting deluxe offices, an airy gourmet marketplace in its grand nave and an increasingly revitalized commuter service. The best time to stop by is during the **Ferry Plaza Farmers Market** (year-round Sat 8am–2pm, April–Nov Tues 10am–2pm; ⓣ415/291-3276, ⓦwww.ferryplazafarmersmarket.com), with local produce sold from numerous stalls around the building. Since the freeway was pulled down, the **Embarcadero** (the boulevard the Ferry Building fronts) has experienced a dramatic renaissance, from an area of charmless office blocks into a swanky waterfront district with fine restaurants and hotels making the most of the bay views. Its wide bayside promenade is one of the city's most popular paths for walking, running and skating.

Jackson Square and around

At the turn of the twentieth century, the eastern flank of the Financial District formed part of the **Barbary Coast**. This area of landfill appeared thanks to the hundreds of ships that lay abandoned by sailors heading for the Gold Rush; enterprising San Franciscans repurposed the dry ships as hotels, bars and stores. At the time, the district was a rough-and-tumble place that gave San Francisco an unsavoury reputation as **Baghdad by the Bay**, packed with saloons and brothels, where hapless young males were forcibly taken aboard merchant ships and pressed into involuntary servitude. William Randolph Hearst's *Examiner* newspaper lobbied frantically to shut down the quarter, resulting in a 1917 California law prohibiting prostitution.

Remains of this tumultuous era can be seen in the **Jackson Square Historic District**, not an actual square but an area bordered by Washington, Columbus, Sansome and Pacific streets. These were the only buildings downtown to escape the catastrophic 1906 fire unharmed, and today Jackson Street and Pacific Avenue in particular provide a hint of what early San Francisco looked like.

Chinatown

The oldest such enclave in the US, bustling and noisy **Chinatown** is shoehorned into several densely populated blocks and is home to one of the largest Chinese communities outside Asia. It has its roots in the arrival of Chinese sailors keen to benefit from the Gold Rush, and the migration of Chinese labourers to the city after the completion of the transcontinental railroad less than twenty years later. The city didn't extend much of a welcome: they were met by a tide of vicious racial attacks and the 1882 Chinese Exclusion Act (the only law in American history aimed at a single racial group), which prevented Chinese immigration and naturalization. Nowadays, Chinatown boasts some of the tackiest stores in the city, making it more akin to shopping in a tasteless part of Hong Kong than in Beijing. Nonetheless, it bristles with activity despite its increasingly elderly population base and, in sharp contrast to the districts that surround it, a clear lack of wealth.

Enter through **Chinatown Gate** at the intersection of **Grant Avenue** (the district's tourist thoroughfare) and Bush Street. Gold-ornamented portals and brightly painted balconies sit above Grant's crass souvenir stores. A few blocks up, **Old St Mary's Cathedral**, 660 California St at Grant, was one of the few San Francisco buildings to survive the 1906 earthquake and fire, and there's a good photo display of the damage to the city in its entranceway.

A half-block east of Grant between Washington, Clay and Kearny streets stands **Portsmouth Square**, San Francisco's first real city centre in the mid 1800s and now, for all intents and purposes, Chinatown's living room. When John Montgomery came ashore in 1846 to claim the land for the United States, he raised his flag here and named the square after his ship; the spot where he first planted the US flag is marked today by the one often flying in the square. The plaza is primarily worth visiting to simply absorb everyday Chinatown life, with spirited card games played atop cardboard boxes and other makeshift tables, and neighbourhood children letting off steam in the playground.

Parallel to Grant Avenue, **Stockton Street** is the commercial artery for Chinatown locals, its public housing tenements looming overhead and streets full to bursting with locals on the hunt for that day's meat, fish and produce. **Ellison Enterprises**, 805 Stockton St at Sacramento, is known as Chinatown's best-stocked herbal pharmacy, where you'll find clerks filling orders the ancient Chinese way – with hand-held scales and abaci – from drug cases filled with dried bark, roots, cicadas, ginseng and other restorative staples. Down adjacent Ross Alley, anyone with even a moderate sweet tooth will want to duck into the fragrant **Golden Gate Fortune Cookie Factory** (daily 7am–8.30pm; ⓣ415/781-3956; free) at no. 56. True to its name, the cramped plant has been churning out 20,000 fresh fortune cookies a day since 1962 – by hand.

North Beach

Resting in the hollow between Russian and Telegraph hills, and bisected by busy Columbus Avenue, **North Beach** has always been a gateway for immigrants, especially Italians who flocked here during the Gold Rush. It became the centre of alternative culture in 1953, after the opening of the **City Lights Bookstore**, 261 Columbus Ave at Broadway, the first paperback bookstore in the US and still owned by poet and novelist Lawrence Ferlinghetti. The **Beat Generation** briefly made the store (and the city) the literary capital of America, achieving overnight notoriety when charges of obscenity were levelled at Allen Ginsberg's epic poem *Howl* in 1957. It was the hedonistic antics of the Beats as much as their literary merits that struck a chord, and North Beach came to symbolize a wild and subversive lifestyle.

Next to City Lights, **Vesuvio**, an old North Beach bar where the likes of Dylan Thomas and Jack Kerouac would drink, remains a haven for lesser-knowns to pontificate on the state of the arts. At the crossroads of Columbus and Broadway, poetry meets porn in a neon-lit assembly of strip joints, the most famous of these being the **Condor Club**, 300 Columbus Ave, where a well-endowed waitress named Carol Doda slipped out of her top one night and kickstarted the concept of topless waitressing in the summer of 1964.

As you continue north on Columbus Avenue, you enter the heart of the old Italian neighbourhood, an enclave of narrow streets and leafy enclosures. Brief exploration leads to small landmarks like **Caffè Trieste**, 609 Vallejo St at Kearny (ⓣ415/982-2605, ⓦwww.caffetrieste.com), where the jukebox often blasts opera classics to cappuccino-sipping artists and other neighbourhood denizens; legend has it that Francis Ford Coppola wrote the screenplay for *The Godfather* here. Two

Alcatraz

Before the rocky islet of **Alcatraz** became America's most dreaded **high-security prison** in 1934, it had already served as a fortress and military jail. Surrounded by the bone-chilling water of San Francisco Bay, it made an ideal place to hold the nation's most wanted criminals – men such as Al Capone and Machine Gun Kelly. The conditions were inhumane: inmates were kept in solitary confinement, in cells no larger than nine by five feet, most without light. They were not allowed to eat together, read newspapers, play cards, or even talk; relatives could visit for only two hours each month. Escape really was impossible: nine men managed to get off "The Rock", but none gained his freedom, and the only two to reach the mainland (using a jacket stuffed with inflated surgical rings as a raft) were soon apprehended.

Due to its massive running costs, the prison finally closed in 1963. The island remained abandoned until 1969, when a group of Native Americans staged an occupation as part of a peaceful attempt to claim the island for their people, citing treaties that designated all federal land not in use as automatically reverting to their ownership. Using all the bureaucratic trickery it could muster, the US government finally ousted them two years later, claiming the operative lighthouse qualified it as active.

At least 750,000 tourists each year take the excellent hour-long, self-guided audio **tour** of the abandoned prison, which includes sharp anecdotal commentary as well as re-enactments of prison life featuring improvised voices of the likes of Capone and Kelly. Note that the island's name is a corruption of the Spanish word for pelicans (*alcatraces*), although the only reason the current islet is known as Alcatraz is thanks to a muddle-headed English mapmaker and captain who confused the names of several outcrops in the bay in 1826 – what we know as Yerba Buena Island was in fact the original Alcatraz.

Ferries to Alcatraz leave from Pier 33 (frequent departures from 9am–3.55pm, last ferry returns at 6.15pm; night tour departs at 5.55pm and 6.45pm; day tour $26, night tour $33; ⓣ415/981-7625, ⓦwww.alcatrazcruises.com); allow at least three hours for a visit, including cruise time. Advance reservations are essential – in peak season, it's nearly impossible to snag a ticket for a same-day visit.

blocks north, dawdle in **Washington Square**, where dozens of older, local Chinese practice tai chi on the expansive lawn each morning. From there, head east up the very steep steps on Filbert Street to reach **Telegraph Hill** and **Coit Tower**, which affords grand views of the city and beyond (daily 10am–5pm; lobby free, $4.50 for elevator to top; ⓣ415/362-0808). Also worth a stroll are the **Greenwich and Filbert steps**, a pair of beautifully lush pedestrian paths that cling to Telegraph Hill's steep eastern flank.

Back across North Beach and rising a few blocks west of Columbus, **Russian Hill** was named for six unknown Russian sailors who died here on an expedition in the early 1800s. In the summer, there's always a long line of cars waiting to drive down the tight curves of **Lombard Street** from the precipitous perch on Hyde Street. Surrounded by palatial dwellings and herbaceous borders, Lombard is an especially thrilling drive at night, when most visitors are gone and the city lights twinkle below.

Fisherman's Wharf

If the districts of San Francisco are a family, then **Fisherman's Wharf** is the boisterous uncle who showed up at the reunion in a ghastly shirt, put a lampshade on his head and never left. The city doesn't go dramatically out of its way to court and fleece tourists, but the scores of tacky souvenir shops and overpriced restaurants that crowd Fisherman's Wharf expose this area's mission of raking in disposable tourist dollars. The district flourished as a serious fishing port well into the twentieth century, although these days, the few fishermen that can afford the exorbitant mooring charges have usually finished their trawling by early morning and are gone by the time most visitors arrive.

The most endearing sight here is the large colony of barking **sea lions** that often take over a number of floating platforms between piers 39 and 41. However, one recent winter saw them head north to the Oregon coast for more abundant food, so if the packs of charmingly noisy pinnipeds have gone missing during your visit, another entertaining pick is the **Musée Mécanique** on Pier 45 (Mon–Fri 10am–7pm, Sat & Sun 10am–8pm; free; ⓣ415/346-2000, ⓦwww.museemechanique.org), which houses an extensive collection of vintage arcade machines and 1980s video games.

Immediately west of the Wharf is **San Francisco Maritime National Historic Park**, a low-key complex that includes restored sailing vessels, curving jetties, impressive nautical architecture and a sandy spit. Drop into the fine Visitor Center, 499 Jefferson St at Hyde (summer 9.30am–6pm; rest of year 9.30am–5pm; ⓣ415/447-5000, ⓦwww.nps.gov/safr), which sells tickets for touring the park's docked ships.

Civic Center, SoMa and the Tenderloin

While parts of San Francisco can almost seem like an urban utopia, the adjoining districts of **the Tenderloin** and **Civic Center** are gritty reminders that not everybody has it so easy. **SoMa**, the district south of Market Street, meanwhile, was transformed by the dot-com boom of the 1990s from an industrial wasteland to a hive of loft offices and granite-walled eateries. The internet business crash of the early twenty-first century ended much of its economic upswing, though the area has revived in recent years.

The majestic federal and municipal buildings of **Civic Center** can't help but look strangely out of sync, both with their immediate neighbours and with San Francisco as a whole. Their grand Beaux Arts style is at odds with the quirky wooden architecture of much of the rest of the city – little wonder, as they're the sole remnant of a grand architectural plan to transform the city's downtown into a boulevard-dotted, Paris-inspired place after the original buildings were levelled by the 1906 earthquake. It was at the huge, domed **City Hall**, across from grassy **Civic Center Plaza**, that Mayor George Moscone and Supervisor Harvey Milk were assassinated in 1978. The recently restored gold plate dome is an impressive relic of Gold Rush-era largesse. If you want to take one of the free 45-minute tours around its extraordinary interior, sign up at the Docent Tour kiosk on the Van Ness Avenue side of the building (tours Mon–Fri 10am, noon & 2pm, ⓣ415/554-4799, ⓦwww.ci.sf.ca.us/cityhall).

Formerly one of San Francisco's least desirable neighbourhoods, SoMa is now anchored by the lovely (and free) Yerba Buena Gardens and a host of nearby museums, including the **SF Museum of Modern Art**, 151 Third St at Mission (Mon, Tues & Fri–Sun 11am–5.45pm, Thurs 11am–8.45pm, closed Wed; $15, $7.50 Thurs 6–8.45pm, free first Tues of each month; ⓣ415/357-4000, ⓦwww.sfmoma.org). Major works include paintings by Jackson Pollock, Frida Kahlo and Diego Rivera, though the temporary exhibitions are the museum's strongest suit. The building, designed by Swiss architect Mario Botta, is flooded with natural light from a striking cylindrical skylight, while the upper galleries are connected by a vertigo-inducing metal catwalk.

Also nearby is the **Museum of the African Diaspora**, 685 Mission St at Third (Wed–Sat 11am–6pm, closed Sun–Tues; $10; ⓣ415/358-7200, ⓦwww.moadsf.org), which spotlights traditional African art, work inspired by the horrors of slavery and modern pieces in a range of media. One block away, you'll see a striking askew blue cube: the atrium gallery attached to the **Contemporary Jewish Museum of San Francisco**, 736 Mission St (Thurs 1–8pm, Fri–Tues 11am–5pm, closed Wed; $10; ⓣ415/655-7800, ⓦwww.thecjm.org). The museum has no permanent collection; instead, it hosts smartly curated exhibitions spanning Jewish history and culture, such as retrospectives of Gertrude Stein and *Shrek* creator William Steig.

The Mission

Vibrant, hip and ethnically mixed, the **Mission** is one of San Francisco's most intriguing neighbourhoods. Beginning a few miles southwest of downtown, nestled in a basin, it's also one of the warmest (all things relative). The district was initially predominantly Scandinavian, then Irish, before becoming a sizeable Latino settlement. Though white hipsters have in recent decades swarmed to its old buildings and affordable (by San Francisco standards) rents, it's still a Hispanic neighbourhood at its core and one of the unmissable sights of the city.

The area takes its name from the old **Mission Dolores**, 3321 16th St at Dolores (daily 9am–4.30pm; $5 donation; ⓣ415/621-8203, ⓦwww.missiondolores.org), the oldest building to survive the 1906 earthquake and fire. It was founded in 1776 as Spain staked its claim to California; the graves of the Native Americans it tried to "civilize" can be seen in the atmospheric cemetery next door, along with those of white pioneers.

The heart of the residential Mission lies east of Mission Street between 16th and Cesar Chavez streets. Here you'll absorb the district's original Latino flavour among a bevy of stores and salons, as well as taquerias cooking hearty Mexican (and Cal-Mex) fare, markets selling tropical fruits and panaderias baking traditional pastries. Head over to the same stretch along Valencia Street, one block west of Mission, where a profusion of bookstores, boutiques and thrift stores makes for a fun afternoon of browsing.

What really sets the Mission apart from the city's other neighbourhoods are its **murals** – there are over two hundred in all, though many are more heartfelt than skilled or beautiful. The densest concentration is along **Balmy Alley**, between Folsom and Harrison streets off 24th Street, which is especially known for its politically charged paintings depicting the agonies of many Central American countries. For a more detailed recap join one of the **tours** run by mural arts organization Precita Eyes, 2981 24th St at Harrison (tours Sat & Sun 11am and 1.30pm; $12–15; ⓣ415/285-2287, ⓦwww.precitaeyes.org).

The Castro

Progressive and celebratory, but also increasingly comfortable and wealthy, the **Castro** is the city's centre of gay culture. Some people maintain it's still the wildest place in town, while others insist it's a shadow of its former self. Many of the same hangouts still stand from its 1970s heyday as portrayed in the 2009 film *Milk*, but these days they're host to a slightly more conservative breed as cute shops and restaurants lend a boutique-like feel to the place. A visit to the district is a must if you're to get any idea of just what San Francisco is all about – the liveliest time to stroll around is on Sunday afternoons, when the streetside cafés are packed.

The neighbourhood's major sight is the **Castro Theater**, 429 Castro St at Market (ⓣ415/621-6120, ⓦwww.thecastrotheatre.com), a stunning example of the Mediterranean Revival style, and flagged by the neon sign that towers above surrounding buildings. Inside, its foamy balconies, wall-mounted busts of heroic figures and massive ceiling ornamentation lend an air of affirmed glamour, though you'll have to come for a movie showing to get in.

The junction of **Castro and 18th Street**, known as the "gayest four corners of the earth", marks the Castro's centre, cluttered with bookstores, clothing shops, cafés and bars. Walk a few blocks in most any direction and you're sure to see exotic delicatessens, fine wine shops and fancy florists amid steep, manicured residential streets.

Haight-Ashbury

The fame of **Haight-Ashbury**, a few miles west of downtown San Francisco, is synonymous with the hippie movement of the 1960s, an era that brought the area the notoriety it has capitalized on ever since. Centred on the junction of Haight and Ashbury streets, "The Haight" (as locals call it) was a run-down Victorian neighbourhood until being transformed into the hub of counterculture cool in the mid-1960s. These days, it's as overtly capitalistic as anywhere else in town, a sort of boho theme-park where shops sell hippie memorabilia like tie-dye clothing, hand-blown hookahs and Grateful Dead Beanie Babies, with a number of brightly coloured, youthful clothing boutiques interspersed. It also remains a mecca for runaway youths, so expect to be repeatedly hit up for spare change as you roam Haight Street's increasingly menacing streets.

Toward the eastern end of Haight Street, around Fillmore Street, is the area known as the **Lower Haight**. Primarily an African-American neighbourhood since World War II, it's become more vibrant (but no less edgy) over the past decade-plus, largely due to a profusion of popular bars and ethnic restaurants.

Golden Gate Park

The largest and most diverse greenspace in a city rich in parklands, **Golden Gate Park** is the one above all that's not to be missed. Stretching three miles west from the Haight all the way to the Pacific Ocean, it was constructed in the late 1800s on what was then an area of wild sand dunes buffeted by sea spray. Today, despite throngs of daily visitors, you can always find some solitude here among its hidden meadows and quiet paths.

Of the park's museums, the best is the **M. H. de Young Museum**, 50 Tea Garden Drive (Tues–Thurs, Sat & Sun 9.30am–5.15pm, Fri 9.30am–8.45pm; $10, free first Tues of each month; ⓣ415/750-3600, ⓦwww.thinker.org), which hosts temporary exhibits and a hit-and-miss collection of American art from colonial times up to the present day, although the copper-coloured building's alluring interior and twisting tower are the real stars on display. Across the Music Concourse from the de Young, the immensely popular **California Academy of Sciences**' (Mon–Sat 9.30am–5pm, Sun 11am–5pm; $24.95, free third Wed of each month; ⓣ415/379-8000, ⓦwww.calacademy.org) grass-roofed structure is a nod toward twenty-first-century sustainable building practices. Inside the grand, glass-walled entrance, exhibits from the planetarium, natural history museum and aquarium are smartly intertwined and make for an entertainingly educational day's visit.

Next to the de Young, the **Japanese Tea Garden** (March–Oct daily 9am–6pm, Nov–Feb daily 9am–4.45pm; $5, free daily before 10am; ⓣ415/666-3232, ⓦwww.japaneseteagardensf.com) features carp-filled ponds, bonsai and cherry trees, and sloping bridges that all lend a tranquil feel. Nearby, the immaculately restored **Conservatory of Flowers** (Tues–Sun 9am–5pm, closed Mon; $7; ⓣ415/831-2090, ⓦwww.conservatoryofflowers.org) and 75-acre **Strybing Arboretum** (Mon–Fri 8am–4.30pm, Sat & Sun 10am–5pm; free; ⓣ415/661-1316, ⓦwww.sfbotanicalgarden.org) are each worthwhile destinations for quiet reflection and examining exotic foliage.

The Golden Gate Bridge

The orange towers of the **Golden Gate Bridge**, arguably the best-loved symbol of San Francisco, are visible from almost every high point in the city. Its colour was originally intended as a temporary undercoat before a grey topcoat was to be applied, but locals liked the primer so much upon the bridge's 1937 opening that it's remained ever since. Driving or bicycling across it is a real thrill, while the walk across its 1.7-mile span allows you to take in its enormous size and absorb the views of the Marin headlands, as well as those of the city itself. The view is especially beautiful at sunset, when the waning glow paints the city a delicate pink – unless of course everything's shrouded in fog, when the bridge takes on a patently eerie quality.

Eating

San Francisco has long been known for its fine-dining **restaurants**, and more recently for its wealth of low-end marvels like **taquerias, dim-sum eateries** and **street food carts**. Indeed, the greatest asset of the city's food scene is its staggering variety – not only in types of cuisine, but in price ranges and overall experiences. These listings reflect the city's dining diversity, from gourmet **vegetarian** restaurants, **steakhouses** and **oyster** bars, to **Spanish tapas** joints, **Japanese sushi** bars and **Czech fare**, for everyone from big spenders to budget-minded visitors.

Downtown and around

Borobudur 700 Post St at Jones, Tenderloin ⓣ415/775-1512. This Indonesian powerhouse fuses Indian and Thai influences with often extraordinary results. Don't pass up the *roti prata* (grilled, flaky bread) and curry dipping sauce appetizer. Mains about $10.

Frascati 1901 Hyde St at Green, Russian Hill ⓣ415/928-1406. Vividly romantic, bi-level bistro on a prime corner. Uniquely paired California dishes such as maple-leaf duck breast with herb *spaetzle* and huckleberry sauce retain a level of comfort, and the wine list is impressive. Dinner only. Mains $20–30.

Gary Danko 800 North Point St at Hyde, Fisherman's Wharf ⓣ415/749-2060. This understated California cuisine oasis regularly vies for the title of best restaurant in town. Granted, this is performance food served with a flourish, but it's utterly splurge-worthy. Arrange well ahead for a reservation. Dinner only. The three-course *prix-fixe* option is $68, the five-course $102.

Great Eastern 649 Jackson St at Kearny, Chinatown ⓣ415/986-2500. Elegant and traditional restaurant serving favourites such as sautéed squab with Chinese broccoli. Open late. Mains over $20.

Greens Building A, Fort Mason Center ⓣ415/771-6222. San Francisco's original vegetarian restaurant remains popular thanks to its continually inventive menu, picturesque pier setting and airy interior. It's surprisingly casual, given the quality and price of the food. Mains over $20.

Grubstake 1525 Pine St at Polk, Polk Gulch ⓣ415/673-8268. Its dining counter set in an old railcar, this classic diner dishes out all the American basics (and breakfast all night!). What really sets it apart, however, are all the Portuguese specialties on the menu, including *caldo verde* soup. Open 5pm–4am. Mains $8–15.

Hog Island Oyster Co. 1 Ferry Building, Embarcadero ⓣ415/391-7117. This outpost of the Tomales Bay (Marin County) farm hosts mollusk devotees who sit elbow to elbow at the 25-seat wraparound granite bar. Mains $10–25.

Kokkari 200 Jackson St at Front, Jackson Square ⓣ415/981-0983. This bustling restaurant's Greek influence runs deep, relying as it does on Hellenic staples such as lamb and eggplant. Its huge open fireplace heats two bedazzling dining rooms decorated with Oriental rugs and goatskin lampshades. Mains $20–30.

La Folie 2316 Polk St at Green, Russian Hill ⓣ415/776-5577. Magnificent Provençal food served sans attitude or pretension. There are typically several five-course *prix-fixe* options to choose from; worth it if you fancy a gourmet treat. Dinner only. $75–105/person.

Le Colonial 20 Cosmo Place at Taylor, Union Square ⓣ415/931-3600. Upscale Vietnamese restaurant with a quiet French influence. It boasts

San Francisco's super burrito

Philadelphia has its cheesesteaks, New York its pastrami sandwiches and Texas its barbecue. In San Francisco, the super burrito is not only the premier bargain food, but truly a local phenomenon. The city is home to well over 150 taquerias – informal Mexican restaurants specializing in tacos, quesadillas, tortas and, of course, burritos – and locals are often heard debating their favourites effusively. San Francisco's take on the burrito differs from its Southern California cousin not only in its comparatively gargantuan size, but also in its ingredient list. Whereas a San Diego-style burrito can be an austere meal of meat, cheese and salsa scattered about a standard-size tortilla, the San Francisco version stuffs a jumbo tortilla with any number of grilled or barbecued meats, Spanish rice, beans (choices include whole pinto, black, or refried), melted cheese, *pico de gallo* (a splashy mix of diced tomato, onion, jalapeño and cilantro), guacamole or slices of avocado, a splatter of salsa and even sour cream.

And with its emphasis on vegetables, grains and legumes, the burrito also easily lends itself to vegetarian and vegan variants. Most San Francisco taquerias wrap their goods in aluminum foil for easy handling, as the majority of locals eat burritos by hand. Expect to pay $5–8 for a super burrito and to not have much of an appetite for hours afterward. Forego the utensils, order a Mexican beer or non-alcoholic *agua fresca* (fruit drink) with your foiled meal, and you'll fit right in.

lush, 1920s-themed dining quarters decked out with tile floors, palm fronds and ceiling fans, while the upstairs lounge is a salon with rattan couches and faded rugs. Dinner only. Mains over $30.

Liverpool Lil's 2942 Lyon St at Lombard, Cow Hollow ⓣ415/921-6664. One of the few pub-restaurants in San Francisco to offer a bracingly British menu: liver and onions, lamb shepherd's pie, fish and chips. Open late. Mains $15–25.

Michael Mina Westin St Francis, 335 Powell St at Geary, Union Square ⓣ415/397-9222. Postpone the diet and pack your credit card if you want to enjoy the adventurous New American menu at this grandly columned restaurant run by the namesake local chef. Dinner only. Expect to fork out $90–135 per person.

R&G Lounge 631 Kearny St at Commercial, Chinatown ⓣ415/982-7877. Behind frosted windows looms this enormous restaurant, where the family-style Cantonese dishes lean heavily toward seafood. Mains under $20.

Saigon Sandwich 560 Larkin St at Eddy, Tenderloin ⓣ415/474-5698. Closet-sized, lunch-only shop selling sizeable, made-to-order *bahn mi* (Vietnamese sandwiches). Expect a line out the door every afternoon. Cash only. Sandwiches well under $5.

Shalimar 532 Jones St at O'Farrell, Tenderloin ⓣ415/928-0333. The chicken tikka masala is the main attraction at this austere South Asian joint, although the lamb saag is just as exceptional (and generous in its portion). Afterward, expect to smell as if you yourself have been doused in spices and baked in the tandoor oven. Mains under $10.

Trattoria Contadina 1800 Mason St at Union, North Beach ⓣ415/982-5728. Family-owned, warm, and charming, with white-cloth-swathed tables and photograph-covered walls. The rigatoni with eggplant and smoked mozzarella is a top option, and the Powell-Mason cable car will drop you off steps from the front door. Mains under $20.

SoMa, the Mission and around

Asia SF 201 Ninth St at Howard, SoMa ⓣ415/255-2742. Notorious hotspot where gender-illusionist servers perform cheeky dance routines on the bar, while the equally crossbred pan-Asian food is surprisingly successful. Popular with large groups; best avoided by quiet types. Dinner only. Entrees under $20.

Bi-Rite Creamery 3692 18th St at Dolores, Mission ⓣ415/626-5600. Tiny ice-cream shop that hits all the right notes with its artisanal flavours. Usual suspects like mint chip and chocolate share freezer space with unique concoctions such as toasted coconut and honey lavender. Inexpensive.

Delfina 3621 18th St at Guerrero, Mission ⓣ415/552-4055. Continually buzzing, dinner-only restaurant that attracts nearly every sort of San Franciscan. The light, Cal-Ital dishes rarely miss the mark, while its pizzeria next door (open for lunch and dinner) is just as terrific. Mains over $20.

Dosa 995 Valencia St at 21st St, Mission ⓣ415/642-3672. *Dosa*'s crepe-like namesake item – and its close cousin, the thicker *uttapam* – dominate its South Indian menu, while the terra-cotta dining room is welcoming and not too noisy. Dinner only. Mains $10–20.

Goood Frikin Chicken 10 29th St at Mission, Mission ☎415/970-2428. Superbly seasoned poultry that warrants the extra 'o' in this airy restaurant's goofy name. The dining room is cast in various earthtones, with the ceiling and walls covered in soothing landscape murals. Mains under $10.

Just for You 732 22nd St at Third St., Potrero Hill ☎415/647-3033. Out-of-the-way gem produces some of the finest, fluffiest (and largest!) beignets outside of New Orleans. All breads are home-made (try the raisin cinnamon toast), while the enormous pancakes are the stuff of legend. Open for dinner on weeknights. Mains about $10.

Le P'tit Laurent 699 Chenery St at Diamond, Glen Park ☎415/334-3235. Carnivores won't want to miss the meaty cassoulet (complete with full leg of duck) and memorable desserts; service and overall vibe are equally warm. Conveniently, it's steps from the Glen Park BART station. Dinner only. Mains over $20.

Papalote 3409 24th St at Valencia, Mission ☎415/970-8815. Peerless Cal-Mex cuisine – there's nary a poor menu choice to be made, from the marinated tofu burrito to anything that includes the perfectly grilled *carne asada*. The warm chips and otherworldly chipotle salsa is the real *piecè de résistance*. Burritos and plate meals under $10.

Taqueria San Francisco 2794 24th St at York, Mission ☎415/641-1770. The quintessential San Francisco taqueria (look no further than its name), characterized by weighty burritos, flaky grilled tortillas and rustic meats like *al pastor* (rotisserie-grilled pork) – and for the especially adventurous, *lengua* (tongue) and *sesos* (brain). Expect bouncy tuba-pop from the jukebox. Cash only. Burritos and plate meals under $10.

Town Hall 342 Howard St at Fremont, SoMa ☎415/908-3900. An old ship engine manufacturing building hosts this roomy, vibrant restaurant, where New Orleans-inspired dishes such as grilled gulf shrimp are tempered by California cuisine's lighter influence. Mains $16–20.

Walzwerk 381 S Van Ness Ave at 15th St, Mission ☎415/551-7181. Cramped German eatery serving hearty comfort food. Framed East German pop records and large portraits of twentieth-century Eastern Bloc industry evoke past eras behind the Iron Curtain. Dinner only. Mains under $20.

Western Addition, Haight-Ashbury and around

Burgermeister 86 Carl St at Cole, Cole Valley ☎415/566-1274. Increasingly popular spot that broils excellent gourmet half-pound burgers. All the mainstream choices are available, as well as a handful of unusual options (like the mango burger) for the adventurous. Burgers under $10.

Frankie's Bohemian Cafe 1862 Divisadero St at Pine, Western Addition ☎415/921-4725. Amber wood-lined bar-restaurant where the house specialty is a burly Czech mess called *brambory*, which piles meat and/or veggies atop a pan-fried bed of potato and zucchini. Burgers, salads and 20oz beers fill out the menu. Mains $10–15.

The Little Chihuahua 292 Divisadero St at Page, Lower Haight ☎415/255-8225. Not your garden variety taqueria at all – look for utterly unique menu items such as Mexican French toast and fried plantain burritos alongside standard favourites like tortilla soup and enchiladas. Burritos and plate meals under $10.

Little Star Pizza 846 Divisadero St at McAllister, Western Addition ☎415/441-1118. One of San Francisco's top pizzerias, dimly lit and packed nightly with hipsters enjoying its lively bar and jukebox blasting American and British indie rock. The kitchen bakes deep-dish and thin-crust pizzas with equal aplomb. Dinner only. Large pizzas $15–23.

Massawa 1538 Haight St at Ashbury, Haight-Ashbury ☎415/621-4129. Terrific East African eatery where you shouldn't expect to keep your hands clean as you stab at delicious dishes served with spongy *injera* bread, presented family-style on a gigantic platter. Mains $10–15.

Nopa 560 Divisadero St at Hayes, Western Addition ☎415/864-8643. Buzzing, impossibly popular hotspot leans on a number of cuisine styles, from New American (country pork chop, rotisserie herbed chicken) to further afield (Moroccan vegetable tagine, baked pastas). Reserve ahead. Dinner only. Mains under $20.

Rosamunde Sausage Grill 545 Haight St at Fillmore, Lower Haight ☎415/437-6851. Tiny storefront serving top-grade grilled sausages on sesame rolls. Savvy customers place their order, head next door to *Toronado* (see p.920), and await their sausage's delivery over a beer. Queue up early for top-notch burgers, only available on Tuesday afternoons. Inexpensive.

Sociale 3665 Sacramento St at Spruce, Presidio Heights ☎415/921-3200. Intimate Italian bistro worth seeking out at the end of its verdant pedestrian lane. Go for the heated dining courtyard, cosy atmosphere, fontina-cheese-crammed fried olives appetizer and Italian-leaning wine list. Mains $20–30.

The Sunset and the Richmond

Arizmendi 1331 Ninth Ave at Irving, Inner Sunset ☎415/566-3117. The artisanal breads and pastries are reason enough to head to this small, earthy bakery, but its regular rotation of gourmet pizza is the true surprise treat. Baked goods and pizzas vary daily. Inexpensive.

Aziza 5800 Geary Blvd at 22nd Ave, Outer Richmond ⓣ415/752-2222. Moroccan fine-dining destination with opulent decor, a superb wine list and fun touches like a rose-water-filled pewter basin presented for pre-meal handwashing. The menu's packed with California-accented North African specialties. Dinner only. Mains $20–30.

Brothers Korean BBQ 4128 Geary Blvd at Sixth Ave, Inner Richmond ⓣ415/387-7991. The decor here is nothing to get excited about, but the moderately priced feasts of marinated meats and myriad, pungent side dishes are worth the visit. Certain tables have sunken *hibachis* on which you can cook your own meats. Mains $12–20.

Gordo Taqueria 1233 Ninth Ave at Lincoln, Inner Sunset ⓣ415/566-6011. Efficient burrito shop that lives up to its name (which translates to "fat" in English) by specializing in hefty, stumpy slabs on par with any in town. The menu's as simple as can be, including only tacos, burritos and quesadillas. Cash only. Mains under $6.

Koo 408 Irving St at Fifth Ave, Inner Sunset ⓣ415/731-7077. Japanese fusion restaurant featuring a combination of cooked plates designed to be shared, as well as plenty of sushi, sashimi and specialty rolls. Dinner only. Mains under $20.

Marnee Thai 1243 Ninth Ave at Lincoln, Inner Sunset ⓣ415/731-9999. Humming spot where the kitchen's home-style central Thai cooking rolls with the seasons – winter visitors may see a markedly different menu than those in summer. Mains about $10.

Park Chow 1240 Ninth Ave at Lincoln, Inner Sunset ⓣ415/665-9912. Surprisingly huge space with a menu that's all over the globe, from salads, American comfort food, pizzas and pastas, to artisan cheese plates and even a handful of Asian noodle dishes. Mains $10–15.

Pluto's 627 Irving St at Seventh Ave, Inner Sunset ⓣ415/753-8867. Custom salads are the big draw here, as they're among the biggest, best and cheapest in town. The turkey and stuffing is a soul-warming option any day of the year. Mains under $10.

Nightlife and entertainment

Compared to **nightlife** in other major cities, where you need money and attitude in equal measure, San Francisco's scene demands little of either. This is no 24-hour city, however, and the approach to socializing is often surprisingly low-key, with little of the pandering to fads and fashions that goes on elsewhere. The club scene may be less than cutting-edge, but it's inexpensive compared to those elsewhere: a decent night out might run to a mere $40–50, including cover charges and a few drinks. As is the case in San Francisco restaurants, smoking is illegal in local bars and clubs.

The Sunday *Chronicle*'s Datebook pull-out supplement (ⓦwww.sfgate.com), along with the free weeklies *San Francisco Bay Guardian* (ⓦwww.sfbg.com) and *SF Weekly* (ⓦwww.sfweekly.com), are the best sources of **listings**.

Bars

While justly famous for its restaurants, San Francisco also boasts an inordinately huge number of **bars**, ranging from comfortably scruffy jukebox joints to chic watering holes and everything in between.

111 Minna 111 Minna St at Second St, SoMa ⓣ415/974-1719. Loft space that's a combination bar, art gallery and performance venue, located in a vibrant area of SoMa. Free–$5.

The Alembic 1725 Haight St at Cole, Haight-Ashbury ⓣ415/666-0822. With its wooden bar and mustard-yellow walls, this classy spot has perhaps the best alcohol selection in the city, with a vast range of spirits as well as locally brewed beer and clever cocktails.

The Attic 3336 24th St at Mission, Mission ⓣ415/643-3376. Beloved dive that's so dark, it takes your eyes time to adjust to the low lighting. Sure enough, the decor is clearly inspired by a vintage attic, with oddball antiques in random places.

Bambuddha Lounge *Phoenix Hotel*, 601 Eddy St at Larkin, Tenderloin ⓣ415/885-5088. Sleek, South Pacific-inspired cocktail lounge with regular DJs and strong drinks. Skip the overly self-aware interior and head outside for drinks by the pool.

Edinburgh Castle 950 Geary Blvd at Polk, Tenderloin ⓣ415/885-4074. Evocative Scottish bar filled with heraldic Highland memorabilia. The room upstairs regularly hosts live performances, while the pub food comes straight from co-owned chippie *The Old Chelsea*, right around the corner. Arrive early on Tues for trivia night.

Latin American Club 3286 22nd St at Valencia, Mission ⓣ415/647-2732. Cosy place with a neighbourhood feel, great for an early chat over drinks before the crowds arrive later in the evening. The ceiling space above is crammed with piñatas, Mexican streamers and assorted trinkets.

Li Po Cocktail Lounge 916 Grant Ave at Jackson, Chinatown ⓣ415/982-0072. Named after the Chinese poet, this narrow haunt is a little grotty, although that's part of its charm.

Lucky 13 2140 Market St at Church, Castro ⓣ415/487-1313. Straight bar on the outskirts of the Castro with an extensive selection of international beers. It's filled with pool-players chomping on free popcorn; there's a loud jukebox inside and a humble patio outside.

Mad Dog in the Fog 530 Haight St at Fillmore, Lower Haight ⓣ415/626-7279. Aptly named pub that's one of the Lower Haight's most loyally patronized bars, with darts, English beer and footie on TV. Trivia night each Thurs.

Place Pigalle 520 Hayes St at Gough, Hayes Valley ⓣ415/552-2671. Decorated in plush, deep reds, this friendly lounge boasts rotating art on the walls and the neighbourhood's most popular pool table.

Spec's Twelve Adler Museum Café 12 Saroyan Place off Columbus at Broadway, North Beach ⓣ415/421-4112. Amiable, anachronistic watering hole packed with an eccentric local crowd and known for its chatty bar staff.

Tonga Room *Fairmont Hotel*, 950 Mason St at California, Nob Hill ⓣ415/772-5278. Ultra-campy bar styled like a Polynesian village, complete with pond, simulated rainstorms and grass-skirted band strangling jazz and pop covers to death upon a floating raft. Cocktails are outrageously overpriced, but the happy hour buffet (under $10) makes up for it.

Toronado 547 Haight St at Fillmore, Lower Haight ⓣ415/863-2276. Renowned for its vast selection of international beers, this cacophonous tavern should be the first stop on any beer aficionado's itinerary.

Trad'r Sam 6150 Geary Blvd at 26th Ave, Outer Richmond ⓣ415/221-0773. San Francisco's original tiki bar is a bit of a trek from the central neighbourhoods, but go for the enormous, colourful, and occasionally flaming cocktails such as the $14 Scorpion Bowl.

Tunnel Top 601 Bush St at Stockton, Union Square ⓣ415/722-6620. Fun spot atop the Stockton Tunnel that boasts stiff drinks, a terrific balcony and DJs.

Zeitgeist 199 Valencia St at Duboce, Mission ⓣ415/255-7505. San Francisco's version of a biker bar (it's particularly popular with bicycle messengers) with a huge backyard adjacent to the Central Freeway that's a smoker's dream. There's also a short food menu consisting mostly of barbecue chicken and burgers.

Gay and lesbian bars

San Francisco's **gay and lesbian bars** are many and varied, and although the scene may no longer be quite as wild as its reputation would have you believe, at its best it can still be tough to beat.

The Café 2369 Market St at 17th St, Castro ⓣ415/861-3846. Longtime staple of the local club scene that remains a crowd-pleaser. It's classic out-and-proud Castro, from the thumping beats to the rainbow-coloured socks strategically placed on male dancers.

Eagle Tavern 398 12th St at Harrison, SoMa ⓣ415/626-0880. A good old-fashioned biker bar (with a terrific patio) that's mostly popular with 30-somethings and older. Expect a mud wrestling night here and there.

Pilsner Inn 225 Church St at Market, Castro ⓣ415/621-7058. Mature watering hole filled with a diverse crowd playing pool and darts. There's a large patio outside, and a generally welcoming, open vibe.

The Stud 399 Folsom St at Ninth St, SoMa ⓣ415/252-7883. Legendary club that's been on the scene since the mid-1960s. It's still as popular as ever, attracting an energetic and uninhibited crowd.

Wild Side West 424 Cortland Ave at Andover, Bernal Heights ⓣ415/647-3099. Unpretentious and friendly tavern at the centre of the Bernal Heights lesbian scene, with plenty of kitsch Americana to gaze at. There's a lovely garden outside, but without heatlamps, you'd be well advised to stay inside on a cold evening.

Live music: rock, blues and jazz

San Francisco's **live music scene** reflects the character of the city: laidback, eclectic and not a little nostalgic. Options for shows are wide and the scene is strong, with the city regularly spawning good young bands.

Boom Boom Room 1601 Fillmore St at Geary, Western Addition ⓣ415/673-8000, ⓦwww.boomboomblues.com. Once owned by late blues legend John Lee Hooker, this small, intimate bar with a chequeboard floor delivers blues and roots acts nightly. $7–20.

Bottom of the Hill 1233 17th St at Missouri, Potrero Hill ⓣ415/621-4455, ⓦwww.bottomofthehill.com. Well off the beaten path, San Francisco's celebrated indie rock stronghold draws loyal crowds nightly for local and nationally touring acts. $8–15.

Café du Nord 2170 Market St at Sanchez, Castro ⓣ415/861-5016, ⓦwww.cafedunord.com. This old subterranean speakeasy is a terrific place to enjoy touring or local rock bands, with the occasional swing and folk act booked for good measure. The amber-walled Swedish American Hall upstairs also regularly features shows. $10–20.

Elbo Room 647 Valencia St at 17th St, Mission ⓣ415/552-7788, ⓦwww.elbo.com. A local cradle of acid jazz in the early 1990s, this neighbourhood spot now hosts a smorgasbord of bands and DJs, from rock to reggae to soul. $6–10.

The Fillmore 1805 Geary St at Fillmore, Western Addition ⓣ415/346-6000, ⓦwww.thefillmore.com. This landmark auditorium was the musical heart of 1960s national counterculture. Today, it continues to draw loads of touring acts to its large ballroom, and there's a free apple and commemorative poster for every showgoer. Ticket prices vary wildly, depending on the headliner.

Great American Music Hall 859 O'Farrell St at Polk, Tenderloin ⓣ415/885-0750, ⓦwww.musichallsf.com. A former bordello converted long ago into a beloved (by locals and performers alike) venue for rock, blues and international acts. The ornately moulded balcony offers seats with terrific views for those who arrive early. $14–25.

The Independent 628 Divisadero St at Hayes, Western Addition ⓣ415/771-1421, ⓦwww.theindependentsf.com. This mid-sized club with disarmingly friendly staff and exceptional sound specializes in booking acts from near (Rogue Wave) and far (Vieux Farka Toure). $10–20.

Yoshi's 1330 Fillmore St at Eddy, Western Addition ⓣ415/655-5600, ⓦwww.yoshis.com. With a round stage, balcony, sizeable dancefloor and supreme sound system, Oakland's fabled jazz club has expanded across the bay to draw big names across a variety of genres. $12–32.

Clubbing

San Francisco's **nightclub scene** may not be recognized the world over, but it's unlikely you'll have to endure high cover charges, ridiculously priced drinks, feverish posing or long lines here. Also, many local clubs have to close at 2am during the week, so expect things to get underway earlier.

Cat Club 1190 Folsom St at Eighth St, SoMa ⓣ415/703-8965, ⓦwww.sfcatclub.com. This dark, loud space remains one of the city's hotspots; popular throwback parties throughout the month include *Hot Pants* and *1984*. $5–7.

The Endup 401 Sixth St at Harrison, SoMa ⓣ415/646-0999, ⓦwww.theendup.com. Longtime favourite attracts hardcore clubbers of all sexual walks for after-hours dancing on its cramped dancefloor. It's best known as the home of Sunday's all-day *T-Dance* party (6am–8pm); if you want a break from the beats, there's an outdoor patio with plenty of seating. $6–10.

Skylark 3089 16th St at Valencia, Mission ⓣ415/621-9294, ⓦwww.skylarkbar.com. Popular for its intimate vibe, low lighting, strong drinks and varied DJs, this spot makes for an inexpensive night out. No cover.

Ballet, opera and symphony

San Francisco rightfully has a reputation for embracing the performing arts. The top-form **San Francisco Ballet** ($26–275; ⓣ415/865-2000, ⓦwww.sfballet.org), the oldest such troupe in the US, performs January to May, with *The Nutcracker* showing each holiday season. The Ballet shares its stage at **War Memorial Opera House**, 301 Van Ness Ave at Grove, with the **San Francisco**

Opera ($25–200; ⓣ415/864-3330, ⓦwww.sfopera.org), whose season runs September to December, with a short summer season in June and July.

Adjacent to the War Memorial, the **Louise M. Davies Symphony Hall**, 201 Van Ness Ave at Hayes, is the permanent home of the **San Francisco Symphony** ($35–125; ⓣ415/864-6000, ⓦwww.sfsymphony.org), a once-musty institution that has catapulted to the first rank of American symphonies in recent years. Its season runs September to May.

If you visit San Francisco between June and August, check the schedule of the annual **Stern Grove Festival** (ⓣ415/252-6252, ⓦwww.sterngrove.org), which presents free symphony, opera and ballet performances every summer at its namesake park at 19th Avenue and Sloat Boulevard in the city's outlying Parkside district.

Theatre

Theatre is plentiful in San Francisco, though many of the larger venues often fall prey to a schedule of Broadway reruns. The bolder **fringe circuit** stages new plays with greater frequency, and while quality can be uneven, these smaller productions are more interesting than the crowd-pleasers staged at the major houses. For half-price bargains, try the **Tix Bay Area** booth (Tues–Fri 11am–6pm, Sat 11am–6pm, Sun 11am–3pm; ⓣ415/430-1140, ⓦwww.tixbayarea.com) in Union Square.

American Conservatory Theater (A.C.T.) 415 Geary St at Taylor, Union Square ⓣ415/749-2228, ⓦwww.act-sf.org. Leading resident group that mixes newly commissioned works and innovative renditions of the classics, with inventive set design and staging. Tickets can cost as little as $10 for a preview show, though you'll pay $17–67 for most other performances.

BATS Improv Bayfront Theater, Fort Mason Center ⓣ415/474-6776, ⓦwww.improv.org. Celebrated long-form improv company (its titular acronym stands for Bay Area Theatresports) that stages shows such as *Improvised Elvis: The Musical* year-round. Tickets $17–20.

Beach Blanket Babylon *Club Fugazi*, 678 Green St at Powell, North Beach ⓣ415/421-4222, ⓦwww.beachblanketbabylon.com. This legendary musical revue has been running continuously since 1974, though it regularly incorporated new spoofs of current events. Expect celebrity impersonations and towering hats, and be sure to reserve in advance. Tickets $25–56.

Exit Theatre 156 Eddy St at Taylor, Tenderloin ⓣ415/673-3847, ⓦwww.theexit.org. One of the best spots in town for cutting-edge theatre. It's known for women-centric plays and performances, as well as being an anchor venue for the local Fringe Festival each Sept. Tickets $10–30.

Magic Theatre Building D, Fort Mason Center ⓣ415/441-8822, ⓦwww.magictheatre.org. The busiest and largest local company after A.C.T. specializes in the works of contemporary playwrights, as well as those by emerging new talents. Tickets $25–55.

The Marsh 1062 Valencia St at 22nd St, Mission ⓣ1-800/838-3006, ⓦwww.themarsh.org. This long-standing alternative space hosts fine solo shows, many with an offbeat bent. Monday nights are test nights ($7) for works in progress; other nights typically run $15–30.

Theatre Rhinoceros Eureka Theatre, 215 Jackson at Battery, Jackson Square ⓣ1-800/838-3006, ⓦwww.therhino.org. The city's prime LGBT company presents productions that range from heartfelt political drama to raunchy cabaret acts. Formerly based in the Mission, it's currently in search of a new permanent home. Tickets $15–25.

The Bay Area

Of the nearly seven million people who live in the vicinity of San Francisco, only one in eight lives in the city itself. Everyone else is spread around the **Bay Area**, a sharply contrasting patchwork of mostly rich and some poor towns dotted down the peninsula or across one of the three impressive bridges that span the chilly waters of

Sports in San Francisco and the Bay Area

San Francisco's dedication to its **professional sports** teams can verge on the obsessive. Advance tickets for all Bay Area sports events are available through Ticketmaster (Ⓣ415/421-8497, Ⓦwww.ticketmaster.com) or direct from the teams, although you can get often get one on the day, at least for baseball.

Baseball The **Oakland A's** play at the usually sunny Coliseum (Ⓣ510/638-4900, Ⓦwww.oaklandathletics.com), which has a BART stop in front. The **San Francisco Giants** play at AT&T Park, where home runs sometimes land in the bay (Ⓣ415/972-2000, Ⓦwww.sfgiants.com).

Football The **San Francisco 49ers**, five-time Super Bowl champions, bash heads at 3Com Park (Ⓣ415/656-4900, Ⓦwww.sf49ers.com), where you may have to pay around $100 per seat, while the **Oakland Raiders** share the Coliseum (Ⓣ510/864-5000, Ⓦwww.raiders.com) with the A's.

Basketball The gradually resurgent **Golden State Warriors** play at the Oracle Arena (Ⓣ510/986-2200, Ⓦwww.nba.com/warriors).

Ice hockey The always competitive **San Jose Sharks** (Ⓣ408/287-7070, Ⓦsharks.nhl.com) play at the HP Pavilion in San Jose.

Soccer The **San Jose Earthquakes** (Ⓣ408/985-4625, Ⓦwww.sjearthquakes.com), MLS champs in 2001, draw large crowds at collegiate Buck Shaw Stadium in Santa Clara.

the exquisite natural harbour. In the **East Bay** are hard-working Oakland and intellectual Berkeley, while south of the city, the **Peninsula** holds the gloating wealth of Silicon Valley. To the north across the Golden Gate Bridge is the woody, leafy landscape and rugged coastline of **Marin County**, a combination of ostentatious luxury and copious natural beauty.

The East Bay

The largest and the second-most-travelled bridge in the US, the **Bay Bridge** connects downtown San Francisco to the East Bay. Currently being replaced along half its span, a hundred million vehicles cross it each year. The heart of the East Bay is **Oakland**, a resolutely blue-collar city that spreads north to the progressive university town of **Berkeley**; the two communities merge into one conurbation, and the hills above them are topped by a twenty-mile string of forested **regional parks**.

Arrival, information and getting around

Flights direct to the East Bay touch down at **Oakland Airport**, just outside town (Ⓣ510/563-3300 or 1-800/992-7433 for automated flight info, Ⓦwww.oaklandairport.com). The AirBART shuttle van (every 15min; $3; Ⓣ510/569-8300) runs to the Coliseum BART station from where you can hop on the line (see below) to Berkeley, Oakland or San Francisco. There are numerous door-to-door **shuttle buses** from the airport, such as A1 American (Ⓣ1-877/378-3596, Ⓦwww.a1americanshuttle.com) – expect to pay around $20 to downtown Oakland, $30–40 to San Francisco. Note that the Greyhound **bus** station is in a dodgy part of northern Oakland on San Pablo Avenue at 21st Street. Amtrak **trains** terminate at 2nd Street near Jack London Square, after stopping in Richmond and Emeryville.

There are two main **visitor centres**: Oakland CVB is at 463 11th St (Mon–Fri 8.30am–5pm; Ⓣ510/839-9000, Ⓦwww.oaklandcvb.com), while Berkeley's office is at 2030 Addison St (Mon–Fri 9am–1pm & 2–5pm; Ⓣ510/549-7040, Ⓦwww.visitberkeley.com).

The underground **BART** system links the East Bay with San Francisco (see p.905). **AC Transit** ($2 one-way; ⓣ510/891-4777, ⓦwww.actransit.org) buses cover the entire East Bay area, with a more limited service running to Oakland and Berkeley from the Transbay Terminal in San Francisco; they're the only option for crossing the Bay when BART shuts down for the night.

East Bay accommodation

The East Bay's **motels** and **hotels**, which cost from $55 a night, are barely better value for money than their San Francisco counterparts.

Bancroft Hotel 2680 Bancroft Way, Berkeley ⓣ510/549-1000 or 1-800/549-1002, ⓦwww.bancrofthotel.com. Small hotel – just 22 rooms – with good location and service. Breakfast included. 6

The Claremont Resort & Spa 41 Tunnel Rd, Berkeley ⓣ510/843-3000 or 1-800/551-7266, ⓦwww.claremontresort.com. The lap of luxury among Berkeley hotels in a 1915 building. Even the basic rooms are a treat, but you'll pay for the privilege. Spa sessions start around $100/hour for facials or massages. 8

Downtown Berkeley YMCA 2001 Allston Way at Milvia St, Berkeley ⓣ510/848-9622, ⓦwww.baymca.org. Berkeley's best bargain accommodation, just one block from the Berkeley BART stop. Rates, including singles from $45, include use of gym and pool. 3

The French Hotel 1538 Shattuck Ave, North Berkeley ⓣ510/548-9930. There's a touch of European class about this small and comfortable hotel with 18 simple but pleasant rooms in the heart of Berkeley's Gourmet Ghetto. 4

Jack London Inn 444 Embarcadero West, Oakland ⓣ510/444-2032 or 1-800/549-8780, ⓦwww.jacklondoninn.com. Kitschy but great value 1950s-style motor lodge next to Jack London Square. 2

Rose Garden Inn 2740 Telegraph Ave, Berkeley ⓣ1-800/992-9005, ⓦwww.rosegardeninn.com. Forty stylishly decorated rooms with fireplaces in a mock-Tudor mansion near the university. 5

Waterfront Plaza Hotel 10 Washington St, Oakland ⓣ510/836-3800 or 1-800/738-7477, ⓦwww.jdvhotels.com. Plush, modern hotel moored on the best stretch of the Oakland waterfront. 4

Oakland

OAKLAND, the workhorse of the Bay Area, is one of the largest ports on the West Coast. It has also been the breeding ground of revolutionary **political movements.** In the Sixties, the city's fifty-percent black population found a voice through the militant Black Panthers and in the Seventies the Symbionese Liberation Army, kidnappers of heiress Patty Hearst, obtained a ransom of free food for the city's poor. It's not all hard graft, though: the climate is often sunny and mild when San Francisco is cold and dreary, and there's great hiking in the redwood- and eucalyptus-covered hills above the city.

There's not much to see within Oakland itself. The major concession to the tourist trade is the waterfront Jack London Square, an aseptic cluster of chains that have nothing to do with the writer. At the far eastern end of the promenade, however, you will find **Heinhold's First and Last Chance Saloon**, a tiny slanting bar built in 1883 from the hull of a whaling ship (see p.926). Jack London really did drink here and the collection of yellowed portraits of him on the wall are the only genuine thing about the writer you'll find on the square. A half-mile north up Broadway from the waterfront, Oakland's restored downtown is anchored by chain stores and the gargantuan open-air **City Center** complex of offices and fast-food outlets. Beside it, at Broadway and 14th Street, **Frank Ogawa Plaza** is a pleasant place to eat lunch outdoors, while further east on 10th and Oak streets, the **Oakland Museum of California** (Wed, Sat & Sun 11am–5pm, Thurs & Fri till 8pm; $12, free first Sun of month; ⓣ510/238-2200, ⓦwww.museumca.org) has good exhibits of California's ecology and history, including the Beat Generation.

Writer **Gertrude Stein** was born in Oakland at around the same time as the macho and adventurous London, but she's barely commemorated anywhere because she harshly criticized her home town. Oakland residents cite in its defence the small, trendy community of **Rockridge** and the lively neighbourhoods around Piedmont and Grand avenues, the latter near pleasant **Lake Merrit**.

Joaquin Miller Park, the most easily accessible of Oakland's hilltop parks, stands above East Oakland (take AC Transit bus #64 from downtown) and includes a small white cabin called The Abbey, former abode of the "Poet of the Sierras", Joaquin Miller. Also in the nearby hills but reached by AC Transit bus #53, the **Chabot Space & Science Center**, 10000 Skyline Blvd (Wed & Thurs 10am–5pm, Fri & Sat till 10pm, Sun 11am–5pm; $14.95; ⓣ510/336-7300, ⓦwww.chabotspace.org) features excellent interactive displays and a fine planetarium.

Berkeley

BERKELEY (named after the English philosopher-theologian George Berkeley) is dominated by the **University of California**, one of America's most famous places of learning, especially known for progressive politics. Its grand buildings and thirty thousand students give off an energy that spills south down raucous **Telegraph Avenue**, where dishevelled vendors peddle rainbow bracelets in front of vegetarian restaurants, music stores and pizza joints. The very name of Berkeley conjures up images of dissent and it remains a solidly left-wing oasis. **Sproul Plaza**, in front of the school's entranceway, Sather Gate, is where the Free Speech Movement began. Among the sites of the almost-daily pitched battles of the Sixties and early Seventies, part of the broad campus revolt against the Vietnam War, is the now-quiet **People's Park**. Today the campus prides itself on its high academic rankings and Nobel-laureate-laden faculty. Stroll the campus's tree-shaded pathways or join the free student-led **tours** that leave from the visitor centre, 101 Sproul Hall (Mon–Sat 10am, Sun 1pm; ⓣ510/642-5215, ⓦberkeley.edu).

Telegraph Avenue holds most of the student hangouts, and several excellent bookstores. Older academics congregate in **Northside**, popping down from their woodsy hillside homes to partake of goodies from Gourmet Ghetto – the restaurants, delis and bakeries on Shattuck Avenue, including the renowned *Chez Panisse* (see below). North of here, on the hills, **Tilden Regional Park** has good trails and a fine rose garden. Along the bay itself, at the **Berkeley Marina**, you can rent windsurfing boards and sailboats, or just watch the sun set behind the Golden Gate.

Eating

As befits the birthplace of California cuisine, the East Bay offers a choice of good **restaurants**. Berkeley is both an upmarket diner's paradise and a student town where you can eat cheaply and well, especially on and around Telegraph Avenue.

Bay Wolf 3853 Piedmont Ave, North Oakland ⓣ510/655-6004. Chic restaurant whose menu is influenced by the cuisine of Tuscany, Provence and the Basque country. Entrees like double mustard-tarragon chicken cost mostly over $20. Closed Mon.

Brennan's 700 University Ave, West Berkeley ⓣ510/841-0960. Great simple self-service meals like roast beef and mash. Also a solidly blue-collar hangout that's a great place for drinking inexpensive beers and watching sports on TV, including European soccer.

Cha-Am 1543 Shattuck Ave, North Berkeley ⓣ510/848-9664. Climb the stairs to this unlikely, always crowded small restaurant for deliciously spicy Thai food at bargain prices.

Cheeseboard Pizza 1512 Shattuck Ave, North Berkeley ⓣ510/549-3055. Incredibly good gourmet pizza at $2.50 a slice. Irregular hours, but usually open for lunch and dinner Tues–Sun.

Chez Panisse 1517 Shattuck Ave, North Berkeley ⓣ510/548-5525. First and still the best of the California cuisine restaurants, overseen by legendary chef Alice Waters. Dinner is served at two sittings, 6pm and 8.30pm; the *prix-fixe* menu costs $65–95 depending on the day of the week. The café upstairs is comparatively inexpensive. Reservations recommended for the café, essential for the main restaurant.

Kirala 2100 Ward St, Berkeley ⓣ510/549-3486. Many argue that *Kirala* serves the best sushi in the

Bay Area, if not the whole USA. Moderate pricing, too – expect to pay around $20 to get your fill.

La Note 2377 Shattuck Ave, Berkeley ⓣ510/843-1535. The appropriately sunny, light cuisine of Provence isn't the only flavour you'll find in this petite dining room: students and teachers from the jazz school next door routinely stop in for casual jam sessions.

Le Cheval 1007 Clay St, Oakland ⓣ510/763-8595. Huge downtown Vietnamese place serving exquisitely spiced food at reasonable prices in comfortable, stylishly decorated surroundings.

Revival 2102 Shattuck Ave, Berkeley ⓣ510/549-9950. Trendy new restaurant serving entirely local organic produce. Dishes such as zatar-braised McCormick ranch goat go for $22–24. Closed Mon.

Tropix Backyard Café 3814 Piedmont Ave, North Oakland ⓣ510/653-2444. Large portions of fruity Caribbean delicacies at reasonable prices, with authentic jerk sauce and thirst-quenching mango juice. Outside seating on the patio.

Vik's Chaat Corner 2390 4th St, West Berkeley ⓣ510/644-4432. Fantastic daytime spot (until 6pm weekdays, 8pm weekends), where you can feast cheaply on authentic South Indian dishes such as *masala dosa* in a huge, saffron-coloured self-service canteen. Closed Mon.

Cafés and bars

The many bohemian **cafés** in Berkeley are full from dawn to near midnight with earnest characters wearing their intellects on their sleeves; if you're not after a caffeine fix, you can generally get a glass of beer or wine. For serious drinking you're better off in one of the many **bars**, particularly in rough-hewn Oakland.

The Alley 3325 Grand Ave, Oakland ⓣ510/444-8505. Ramshackle old-timers' piano bar where locals come specifically to sing. Music starts at 9pm. Closed Mon.

Caffè Mediterraneum 2475 Telegraph Ave, Berkeley ⓣ510/841-5634. Berkeley's oldest café, straight out of the Beat Generation archives: beards and berets optional, books de rigueur.

Coffee Mill 3363 Grand Ave, Oakland ⓣ 510/465-4224. This café near Lake Merritt doubles as an art gallery and often hosts poetry readings, too.

Heinhold's First and Last Chance Saloon 56 Jack London Square, Oakland ⓣ510/839-6761. Tiny and authentic waterfront bar whose interior has hardly changed since around 1900, when Jack London drank here. Small oudoor patio too.

Pacific Coast Brewing Co 906 Washington St, Oakland ⓣ510/836-2739. The only real microbrewery downtown, where you can also get decent grub to wash down with your ale.

Pub (Schmidt's Tobacco & Trading Co) 1492 Solano Ave, North Berkeley ⓣ510/525-1900. This small, relaxed bar lures a mixture of bookworms and game players with a good selection of beers. They even get away with a semi-open smoking area outside, perhaps because their other speciality is selling the evil weed.

Triple Rock Brewery 1920 Shattuck Ave, Berkeley ⓣ510/843-2739. Lively student bar with fine burgers and beers, including cask-conditioned ales at weekends.

The White Horse Inn 6551 Telegraph Ave at 66th St, North Oakland ⓣ510/652-3820. Oakland's oldest gay bar – a small, friendly place with mixed dancing for men and women, plus comedy nights.

Live music and entertainment

Nightlife is where the East Bay really comes into its own. Though traditional **clubs** are virtually nonexistent, there are plenty of **live music venues**. The range of **films** screened here is also top-notch. Berkeley's **Pacific Film Archives** at 2575 Bancroft Ave ($9.50; ⓣ510/642-5249, ⓦwww.bampfa.berkeley.edu for tickets) is one of the finest film libraries in California. The free *East Bay Express* has the most comprehensive listings of what's on.

924 Gilman 924 Gilman St, West Berkeley ⓣ510/525-9926, ⓦwww.924gilman.org. On the outer edge of the hardcore punk, indie and experimental scene, this institution helped launch Green Day and Sleater-Kinney. No alcohol, all ages. Weekends only; cover $5–10.

Ashkenaz 1317 San Pablo Ave, Berkeley ⓣ510/525-5054, ⓦwww.ashkenaz.com. World music and dance café hosting acts from modern Afro-beat to the best of the Balkans. Kids and under-21s welcome. Cover $10–20.

Blake's on Telegraph 2367 Telegraph Ave, Berkeley ⓣ510/848-0886, ⓦwww.blakesontelegraph.com. No-nonsense student club featuring a variety of live acts from blues and soul through rock to punk and rap. $5–15.

Freight and Salvage 2020 Addison St, West Berkeley ⓣ510/644-2020, ⓦwww.freightandsalvage.org. Singer-songwriters perform in a smooth coffeehouse setting. Tickets mostly under $20, open-mic nights $5.

Yoshi's World Class Jazz House 510 Embarcadero W, Oakland ⓣ510/238-9200, ⓦwww.yoshis.com. The centrepiece of Oakland's revived Jack London Square, this combination jazz club and sushi bar routinely attracts the biggest names in jazz. Cover $10–50.

The Peninsula

The city of San Francisco sits at the tip of a neck of land commonly referred to as the **Peninsula**. Home of old money and new technology, the Peninsula stretches south from San Francisco through fifty miles of relentless suburbia along the Bay side, winding up in the futuristic roadside landscape of Silicon Valley near **San Jose**. There was a time when the region was largely agricultural, but the computer boom – spurred by Stanford University in **Palo Alto** – has replaced the orange groves and fig trees with office complexes and car parks. Most of the land along the **coast** – separated from the bayfront sprawl by a ridge of redwood-covered peaks – remains rural; it also contains some of the best **beaches** in the Bay Area.

Palo Alto

Palo Alto, home of preppy, conservative **Stanford University** (ⓣ650/723-2560, ⓦwww.stanford.edu), has become somewhat of a social centre for Silicon Valley's nouveau riche and wealthy students, as evidenced by the trendy cafés and chic new restaurants along its main drag, **University Avenue**. The town doesn't offer much to see other than Spanish Colonial homes, but it's a great place for a lazy stroll and a gourmet meal. Wash down a California-style Greek dish from *Evvia*, 420 Emerson St (ⓣ650/326-0983), or Parisian cuisine from *La Cheminée*, 530 Bryant St (ⓣ650/329-0695), with a microbrewed beer from the *Gordon Biersch Brewery*, 640 Emerson St (ⓣ650/323-7723). Cheaper but still delicious ethnic fare can be enjoyed at the Thai *Krung Siam* (ⓣ650/322-5900) and Indian *Hyderabad House* (ⓣ650/327-3455) restaurants, located at nos. 423 and 448 University Ave, respectively. Reasonably affordable **rooms**, some with shared bathrooms, are available at the *Cardinal Hotel*, 235 Hamilton Ave, in the heart of downtown (ⓣ650/323-5101, ⓦwww.cardinalhotel.com; ❹–❻).

San Jose

Burt Bacharach could easily find **SAN JOSE** today by heading south from San Francisco and following the heat and smog that collects below the Bay. Although one of the fastest-growing cities in California, it is not strong on identity – though in area and population it's close to twice the size of San Francisco. Sitting at the southern end of the peninsula, San Jose has over the last three decades emerged as the civic heart of Silicon Valley. Ironically, it's also acknowledged as the first city in California, though the only sign of this is the unremarkable eighteenth-century **Mission Santa Clara de Asis**, on the pleasant campus of the Jesuit-run Santa Clara University.

The area's most famous landmark is the relentlessly hyped **Winchester Mystery House**, 525 S Winchester Blvd, just off I-280 near Hwy-17 (daily 9am–5pm, till 7pm in summer; various tours $25–33; ⓣ408/247-1313, ⓦwww.winchestermysteryhouse.com), a folly of a mansion built by Sarah Winchester, heiress to the Winchester rifle fortune following her husband's death in 1884, to appease the spirits of those killed with the weapons. The **Rosicrucian Museum**, 1342 Naglee Ave (Mon–Thurs 9am–5pm, Fri till 8pm, Sat & Sun 11am–6pm; $9; ⓣ408/947-3636, ⓦwww.rosicrucian.org), houses a brilliant collection of Assyrian and Babylonian artefacts, while the revamped **Tech Museum of**

Innovation (Mon–Wed 10am–5pm, Thurs–Sun till 8pm; $10; ⓣ408/294-8224, ⓦwww.thetech.org), downtown at 201 S Market St, contains hands-on displays of high-tech engineering as well as an IMAX theatre (one show included in admission; extra show $5).

San Jose's **visitor centre** is inside the huge Convention Center complex at 408 S Almaden Blvd (Mon–Fri 8am–5pm, Sat & Sun 11am–5pm; ⓣ408/295-9600 or 1-800/726-5673, ⓦwww.sanjose.org), though it is geared more to business people than travellers. Downtown **accommodation** is grossly overpriced, so it's best to try further out. Options include the budget *Valley Inn*, 2155 The Alameda (ⓣ408/241-8500, ⓦwww.valleyinnsanjose.com; ❸), and the equally simple *Howard Johnson Express*, 1215 S 1st St (ⓣ408/280-5300 or 1-800/509-7666, ⓦwww.hojo.com; ❸). Good old-fashioned American **food** is dished up at *Original Joe's*, 301 S First St (ⓣ408/292-7030). Grab a stool at the counter or settle into one of the comfy booths at this San Jose institution, where $10 still goes a long way. For a snack and a touch of hubbly-bubbly, head to *Hookah Nites*, 371 S 1st St (ⓣ408/286-0800). The same stretch of S 1st Street is also home to most of the city's bustling **nightlife**.

The coast

The **coastline** of the Peninsula south from San Francisco is a world away from the bayside: mostly undeveloped, with a few small towns, and countless beaches that run 75 miles down to the mellow cities of Santa Cruz and Capitola. Just south of San Francisco, Hwy-1 hugs the precipitous cliffs of Devil's Slide, passing the decent mini-resort of **Pacifica** en route to the clothing-optional sands of **Gray Whale Cove State Beach** (daily 8am–sunset; ⓣ650/728-5336, ⓦwww.parks.ca.gov). Two miles further on Hwy-1, the red-roofed buildings of the 1875 **Point Montara Lighthouse**, set among the windswept Monterey pine trees at the top of a steep cliff, have been converted into a **youth hostel** (ⓣ650/728-7177, ⓦwww.norcalhostels.org; dorm $23–28; private rooms ❸). Just beyond the hostel, down California Street, the **Fitzgerald Marine Reserve** (free; ⓣ650/728-3584) has three miles of diverse oceanic habitat, peaceful trails and, at low tide, the best tidal pools. But continue a tiny bit further for the historic *Moss Beach Distillery* (ⓣ650/728-5595), a great place to grab a snack and a beer on its windswept patio – they provide enormous blankets to help brave the fog.

A few miles further south on Hwy-1 is **Princeton-by-the-Sea**, where you can wash down a full meal or cheaper bar snack with the finely crafted ales of the excellent *Half Moon Bay Brewing Company*, 390 Capistrano Ave (ⓣ650/728-2739). Next up is the wonderful strand of **Miramar**, also the unlikely location of the *Douglass Beach House* (ⓣ650/726-4143, ⓦwww.bachddsoc.org), an informal jazz pub that attracts some big names. The next town, constantly expanding **Half Moon Bay**, offers camping behind its eponymous state beach (ⓣ650/726-8820; $35, hike/bike in $7), as well as fancier accommodation such as the *Old Thyme Inn*, 779 Main St (ⓣ650/726-1616 or 1-800/720-4277, ⓦwww.oldthymeinn.com; ❻), and a few eating options – try *Cetrella*, 845 Main St (ⓣ650/726-4090), a large and snazzy Mediterranean place that serves delicious upmarket fare. Fill your car here; fuel stations are rare for the next fifty miles to Santa Cruz.

Marin County

Across the Golden Gate from San Francisco, **Marin County** is an unabashed introduction to Californian self-indulgence in wonderful natural surroundings: a pleasure zone of conspicuous luxury and abundant natural beauty, with sunshine or fog, sandy beaches, high mountains and thick redwood forests. Though in the past the region served as logging headquarters, the county is now one of the wealthiest in the US, attracting young professionals to its swanky waterside towns.

The modern **ferries** that travel across the bay from San Francisco can make a great start to a day out. Boats to the chic bayside settlement of **Sausalito** leave from the Ferry Building on the Embarcadero, run by Golden Gate Ferry (Mon–Fri 7.40am–7.55pm, frequency varies; reduced timetable at weekends; $8.25 each way; ⓣ415/455-2000, ⓦwww.goldengate.org) or Pier 39 at Fisherman's Wharf, run by Blue & Gold Fleet ferries (6–7 trips daily; $10 each way; ⓣ415/705-8200, ⓦwww.blueandgoldfleet.com). **Biking** over here means a beautiful ride over the Golden Gate Bridge (unless there's fog) and allows you to explore the headlands freely. Golden Gate Ferries accommodate up to 25 bikes, first-come, first-served.

The Marin Headlands

The largely undeveloped **Marin Headlands**, across the Golden Gate Bridge from San Francisco and far more rugged, afford some of the most impressive views of the bridge and the city behind. Heading west on Bunker Hill Road takes you up to the brink of the headlands before the road snakes down to Fort Barry and wide, sandy **Rodeo Beach**, from which numerous hiking trails branch out. Check in at the Marin Headlands **Visitor Center** (daily 9.30am–4.30pm; ⓣ415/331-1540, ⓦwww.nps.gov/goga) above Rodeo Lagoon for free maps. The largest of the fort's old buildings has been converted into the spacious but homely *HI-Marin Headlands* **hostel** (ⓣ415/331-2777 or 1-800/979-4776 ext 168, ⓦwww.norcalhostels.org; dorm from $24; ❸), an excellent base for more extended explorations of the inland ridges and valleys.

Sausalito

Attractive, smug little **SAUSALITO**, along the Bay below US-101, was once a gritty community of fishermen and sea traders, full of bars and bordellos. Now exclusive restaurants and pricey boutiques line its picturesque waterfront promenade and expensive, quirky houses climb the ridges above central Bridgeway Avenue.

The town has a one-of-a-kind exhibit in the **Bay Model Visitor Center**, 2100 Bridgeway (Tues–Sat 9am–4pm, summer also Sat & Sun 10am–5pm; donation; ⓣ415/332-3870, ⓦwww.spn.usace.army.mil/bmvc), where elevated walkways in a huge building lead you around a scale model of the entire bay, surrounding deltas and its aquatic inhabitants, offering insight on the enormity and diversity of this area.

If you decide **to stay**, *Casa Madrona* at 801 Bridgeway Ave (ⓣ415/332-0502 or 1-800/288-0502, ⓦwww.casamadrona.com; ❽) is a deluxe **hotel** that climbs up the hill opposite the bay and also houses *Mikayla*, a delectable seafood **restaurant** (ⓣ415/331-5888). For less expensive food, head for *Tommy's Wok*, 3001 Bridgeway Ave (ⓣ415/332-1683), a largely organic Chinese restaurant, or try terrific, low-cost curries at *Sartaj India Cafe*, 43 Caledonia St (ⓣ415/332-7103). The *Bar With No Name*, 757 Bridgeway Ave (ⓣ415/332-1392), is an ex-haunt of the Beats, hosting frequent live jazz.

Mount Tamalpais and Muir Woods

Mount Tamalpais dominates the skyline of the Marin peninsula, looming over the cool canyons of the rest of the county and dividing it into two distinct parts: the wild western slopes above the Pacific Coast and the suburban communities along the calmer bay frontage. The Panoramic Highway branches off from Hwy-1 along the crest above Mill Valley, taking ten miles to reach the centre of **Mount Tamalpais State Park** (daily 8am–sunset; parking $8; ⓣ415/388-2070, ⓦwww.mttam.net), which has some thirty miles of hiking trails and many campgrounds. While most of the redwood trees that once covered its slopes have long since been chopped down, one towering grove remains, protected as the **Muir Woods National Monument** (daily 8am–sunset; $5; ⓣ415/388-2595, ⓦwww.nps.gov/muwo). It's a tranquil and majestic spot, with sunlight filtering three hundred feet down from the treetops to the laurel- and fern-covered canyon below. Being so close to San Francisco, Muir Woods is often packed with coach-tour hordes; more secluded hiking paths include the Matt Davis Trail, leading south to Stinson Beach and north to Mount Tamalpais.

Mill Valley

From the east peak of Mount Tamalpais, a quick two-mile downhill hike follows the Temelpa Trail through velvety shrubs of chaparral to the town of **MILL VALLEY**, the oldest and most enticing of the inland towns of Marin County. For many years the town has made a healthy living out of tourism and October's annual **Mill Valley Film Festival**, a world-class event that draws Bay Area stars and up-and-coming directors alike.

The restored town centres on the redwood-shaded square of the *Depot Bookstore and Café* (ⓣ415/383-2665), a popular meeting place at 87 Throckmorton Ave. The **Chamber of Commerce** is next door at 85 Throckmorton Ave (Mon–Fri 10am–noon and 1–4pm; ⓣ415/388-9700, ⓦwww.cityofmillvalley.org). Far and away the best place to **stay** is the *Mill Valley Inn*, 165 Throckmorton Ave (ⓣ415/389-6608 or 1-800/595-2100, ⓦwww.millvalleyinn.com; ❼), a gorgeous European-style inn with elegant rooms and two private cottages. *Avatar's Punjabi Burritos*, at 15 Madrona St (ⓣ415/381-8293), serves a unique range of burritos with spicy curry fillings, while the *Toast Café*, 31 Sunnyside Ave (ⓣ415/388-2500), serves large, affordable breakfasts and lunches.

Point Reyes National Seashore

The westernmost tip of Marin County comes at the end of the **Point Reyes National Seashore**, a near-island of wilderness bordered on three sides by over fifty miles of isolated coastline – pine forests and sunny meadows hemmed in by rocky cliffs and sandy, windswept beaches. This wing-shaped landmass is a rogue piece of the earth's crust that has been drifting steadily northward along the San Andreas Fault, having started out some six million years ago as a suburb of Los Angeles. This was the epicentre of the great earthquake of 1906, when the land here shifted over sixteen feet in an instant.

The **Bear Valley visitor centre** (Mon–Fri 9am–5pm, Sat & Sun 8am–5pm; ⓣ415/464-5100, ⓦwww.nps.gov/pore), two miles southwest of Point Reyes Station in Olema, has engaging displays on local geology and natural history, plus details of hiking trails. Just to the north, Limantour Road heads six miles west to the *HI-Point Reyes* **hostel** (closed 10am–4.30pm; ⓣ415/663-8811, ⓦwww.norcalhostels.org; dorms from $22; private rooms ❸) in an old ranch house. Nearby **Limantour Beach** is good for a chilly dip.

Eight miles west of Inverness, a small road leads down to **Drake's Beach**, the presumed landing spot of Sir Francis Drake in 1579. Appropriately, the coastline resembles the southern coast of England – cold, wet and windy, with chalk-white cliffs rising above the wide sandy beach. The road continues southwest another four miles to the very tip of Point Reyes, where a precarious-looking **lighthouse** (Thurs–Sun 10am–4.30pm, tours first and third Sat of each month; free; ⓣ415/669-1534) is an excellent spot for watching sea lions and, from mid-March to April and late December to early February, migrating grey whales.

The Gold Country

Around 150 years before techies from all over the world rushed to California in search of Silicon gold, rough-and-ready "forty-niners" invaded the **GOLD COUNTRY** of the Sierra Nevada, about 150 miles east of San Francisco, in search of the real thing. The area ranges from the foothills near Yosemite to the deep gorge of the Yuba River two hundred miles north, with **Sacramento** as its largest city. Many of the mining camps that sprang up around the Gold Country vanished as quickly as they appeared but about half still survive. Some are bustling resorts, standing on the banks of whitewater rivers in the midst of thick pine forests; others are just eerie ghost towns, all but abandoned on the grassy rolling hills. Most of the mountainous forests along the Sierra crest are preserved as near-pristine wilderness, with excellent hiking and camping. There's also great skiing in winter, around the mountainous rim of **Lake Tahoe** on the border between California and Nevada.

Sacramento

California's state capital, **SACRAMENTO**, in the flatlands of the Central Valley, was founded in 1839 by the Swiss John Sutter. He worked hard for ten years to build a busy trading centre and cattle ranch, only to be thwarted by the discovery of gold at a nearby sawmill in 1848. His workers quit their jobs to go prospecting and thousands more flocked to the goldfields of the Central Mother Lode, without any respect for Sutter's claims to the land. Sacramento became the main supply point for the miners and remained important as the western headquarters of the transcontinental railroad. Flashy office towers and hotel complexes have now sprung from its rather suburban streetscape, enlivening the flat grid of leafy, tree-lined blocks.

There's not a great deal to see, though the wharves, warehouses, saloons and stores of the historic core along the **riverfront** have been restored and converted into the touristy shops and restaurants of **Old Sacramento**. On the northern edge of the old town, the **California State Railroad Museum** (daily 10am–5pm; $9; ⓣ916/445-6645, ⓦwww.csrmf.org) brings together a range of lavishly restored 1860s locomotives, with "cow-catcher" front grilles and bulbous smokestacks.

A mile or so east of downtown, the dome of the **State Capitol** (ⓣ916/324-0333, ⓦwww.capitolmuseum.ca.gov) stands proudly in a spacious green park. Restored to its original elegance, the luxurious building brims over with finely crafted details. There are free hourly **tours** (daily 10am–4pm); ID is required to enter the building. Further east at 27th and L streets, **Sutter's Fort State Historic Park** (daily 10am–5pm; $5; ⓣ916/445-4422) is a re-creation of Sacramento's original settlement. An adobe house displays relics from the Gold Rush, and on summer weekends costumed volunteers act out scenes from the 1850s.

Practicalities

Trains come in at 4th and I streets, near Old Sacramento, while Greyhound **buses** arrive at 7th and L streets. The **airport** is twelve miles northwest of the city: SuperShuttle Sacramento vans ($15; ⓣ1-800/258-3826, ⓦwww.supershuttle.com) take you directly to your downtown destination.

Sacramento's most accessible **visitor information centre** is at 1002 2nd St (daily 10am–5pm; Ⓣ916/442-7644, Ⓦwww.sacramento365.com). Besides the central *HI-Sacramento Hostel*, 900 H St (Ⓣ916/443-1691, Ⓦwww.norcalhostels.org; dorms from $28; private rooms ❸), there are plenty of **places to stay** within walking distance of the city centre – the best value being the *Econo Lodge*, 711 16th St (Ⓣ916/443-6631 or 1-800/553-2666, Ⓦwww.econolodge.com; ❷). Further away, the *Vizcaya Pavilion & Mansion*, 2019 21st St (Ⓣ916/455-5243, Ⓦwww.viscayapavilion.com; ❹), offers good deals on historic luxury in a quiet residential area. *Paesano's*, at 1806 Capitol Ave (Ⓣ916/447-8646), is a deservedly popular pizza **restaurant**; *Tapa the World*, at 2115 J St (Ⓣ916/442-4353), serves delicious tapas until midnight, often accompanied by live flamenco guitar; and *Centro Cocina Mexicana*, 2730 J St (Ⓣ916/442-2552), offers innovative Californian-Mexican fusion cuisine. For alternative **live music** try *Old Ironsides*, 1901 10th St (Ⓣ916/443-9751, Ⓦwww.theoldironsides.com). Pick up the free weekly *Sacramento News & Review* (Ⓦwww.newsreview.com) for more entertainment details.

The Mines

In the romantically rugged landscape of the Gold Country, overshadowed by the 10,000ft granite peaks of the Sierra Nevada, fast-flowing rivers cascade through steeply walled canyons. During the autumn, the flaming reds and golds of poplars and sugar maples stand out against an evergreen background of pine and fir. The camps of the **southern mines** were the liveliest and most uproarious of all the Gold Rush settlements: Wild West towns full of gambling halls, saloons and gunfights in the streets. Freebooting prospectors in these "placer" mines sometimes panned for nuggets of gold in the streams and rivers; further **north**, the diggings were far richer and more successful, but the gold was (and still is) buried deep underground, so had to be pounded out of hardrock ore.

Sonora, Columbia and Jamestown

The hub of the southern mining district is **SONORA**, set on steep ravines roughly a hundred miles east of San Francisco. This friendly and animated logging town boasts Victorian houses and false-fronted buildings on its main Washington Street. The **Tuolumne County Visitors Bureau**, 542 West Stockton St off Hwy-49 (April–Sept Mon–Fri 9am–7pm, Sat 10am–6pm, Sun till 5pm; Oct–March Mon–Fri 9am–6pm, Sat 10am–6pm; Ⓣ209/533-4420 or 1-800/446-1333, Ⓦwww.thegreatunfenced.com), is the best source of information.

Sonora's onetime arch-rival, **COLUMBIA**, three miles north on Parrots Ferry Road, is now a ghost town designated as a state historic park, with a carefully restored Main Street that gives an excellent idea of what Gold Rush life might have been like. In 1854 it was California's second largest city and missed becoming the state capital by two votes, but by 1870 the gold had run out and it was abandoned.

In **JAMESTOWN**, three miles south of Sonora, the **Railtown 1897 State Historic Park** (daily April–Oct 9.30am–4.30pm, Nov–March 10am–3pm; $5; Ⓣ209/984-3953, Ⓦwww.railtown1897.org), on the corner of 5th and Reservoir streets, holds an impressive collection of old steam trains, including the one used in *High Noon*, and offers rides some weekends (April–Oct; $13).

Practicalities

In downtown Columbia, the best **place to stay** is right on the historic Main Street in the balconied *City Hotel* (Ⓣ1-800/532-1479, Ⓦwww.cityhotel.com; ❻); in Sonora, the well-placed *Gunn House Hotel* (Ⓣ209/532-3421, Ⓦwww.gunnhousehotel.com; ③) is right in town at 286 S Washington St; motels on Hwy-49 between Sonora and Jamestown include the good-value *Miner's Motel* (Ⓣ209/532-7850 or 1-800/451-4176; ③). Jamestown's Main Street is lined by old Gold Rush hotels such as the fantastic *Jamestown Hotel* at no. 18153 (Ⓣ209/984-3902 or 1-800/205-4901, Ⓦwww.jamestownhotel.com; ④), which boasts an impressive restaurant while being close to other good options, including *Morelia Mexican* (Ⓣ209/984-1432), across the street at no. 18148. Sonora has a wide variety of places to **eat or drink** along Washington Street, such as the *Diamondback Grill* at no. 110 (Ⓣ209/532-6661), which has tapas and Mediterranean dishes. Among the bars, the retro *Iron Horse Lounge* at no. 97 (Ⓣ209/532-4482) maintains a Wild West saloon image.

Grass Valley and Nevada City

The compact communities of **GRASS VALLEY** and **NEVADA CITY**, four miles apart in the Sierra Nevada Mountains, were the most prosperous and substantial of the gold-mining towns. Since the 1960s, artists and craftspeople have settled in the elaborate Victorian homes of the surrounding hills. In Grass Valley, the **North Star Mining Museum** (May–Oct daily 10am–5pm; donation; Ⓣ530/273-4255) at the south end of Mill Street is housed in what used to be the power station for the North Star Mine. Its giant water-driven **Pelton wheel**, fitted with a hundred or so iron buckets, once powered the drills and hoists of the mine.

The last mine in California to shut down was its richest, the **Empire Mine** (July to early Sept 9am–6pm; Sept–April 10am–5pm; $5; Ⓣ530/273-8522, Ⓦwww.empiremine.org), now preserved as a pine-forested state park a mile southeast of Grass Valley off Rte-49. It closed in 1956, after more than six million ounces of gold had been recovered, when the cost of getting the gold out of the ground exceeded $35 an ounce, the government-controlled price at the time. Machinery sold off when the mine closed has been replaced from other disused workings and now augments the excellent **museum** at the entrance.

The excellent Grass Valley **visitor centre** at 248 Mill St (Mon–Fri 9am–5pm, Sat 10am–3pm; Ⓣ530/273-4667 or 1-800/655-4667, Ⓦwww.grassvalleychamber.com) is housed in a replica of the original home of Lola Montez, an Irish entertainer and former mistress of Ludwig of Bavaria, who retired here after touring America with her provocative "Spider Dance" and kept a grizzly bear in her front yard.

Towns don't get much quainter than **Nevada City**. Amid all its shops and restaurants, the lacy-balconied and bell-towered **Old Firehouse** at 214 Main St houses a small **museum** of social history of the region (May–Oct daily 11am–4pm; Nov–April Fri–Sun noon–3pm; donation).

Both towns are very compact and connected every thirty minutes by the Gold Country Stage **minibus** (Mon–Fri 7am–6pm, Sat 10am–5pm; $1.50, $4.50 for a day pass; Ⓣ1-888/660-7433, Ⓦwww.goldcountrystage.com).

Accommodation

Accommodation in the revamped old Gold Rush **hotels** and **B&Bs** is solidly mid-range and there are some excellent options, as well as humbler **motels**.

Coach'N'Four Motel 628 S Auburn St, Grass Valley Ⓣ530/273-8009, Ⓕ0827. Handy for the Empire Mine, this simple but clean motel has unbeatable rates. ②

Holbrooke Hotel 212 W Main St, Grass Valley Ⓣ530/273-1353 or 1-800/933-7077, Ⓦwww.holbrooke.com. Historic hotel, once visited by Mark Twain, and right in the centre of town. Breakfast included. ⑤

National Hotel 211 Broad St, Nevada City Ⓣ530/265-4551, Ⓦwww.thenationalhotel.com. Oozing faded glory, this historic landmark is the oldest continuously operating hotel in the West and still provides decent rooms. ④

Outside Inn 575 E Broad St, Nevada City ⓣ530/265-2233, ⓦwww.outsideinn.com. Quiet, 1940s motel with swimming pool, and only a 10min walk from the centre of town. ❸

Swan-Levine House 328 S Church St, Grass Valley ⓣ530/272-1873, ⓦwww.swanlevinehouse.com. Attractively decorated, sunny rooms in an old Victorian hospital run by two artists. ❺

Eating and drinking

Both Grass Valley and Nevada City have numerous good places to **eat**, as well as quite a few **bars** and **saloons**, where you'll often be treated to free live music.

Cirino's 309 Broad St, Nevada City ⓣ530/265-2246 and 213 W Main St, Grass Valley ⓣ530/477-6000. Casual Italian place serving filling deli sandwiches and a range of tasty entrees.

Friar Tuck's 111 N Pinel St, Nevada City ⓣ530/265-9093. A good mixture of American, European and Pacific Rim cuisine is on offer at this high-quality but fairly pricey restaurant. Main courses over $20.

Marshall's Pasties 203 Mill St, Grass Valley ⓣ530/272-2844. Stunning array of freshly filled Cornish-style pasties, a tradition brought over by British miners. Takeaway only.

Sopa Thai 312 Commercial St, Nevada City ⓣ530/470-0101. Beautifully decorated place that dishes up authentic Siamese fare and has become a local favourite.

Swiss House 535 Mill St, Grass Valley ⓣ530/273-8272. The central European decor seems out of place here but the hearty food, such as schnitzel and apple strudel, will fill you up.

Lake Tahoe

One of the highest, deepest, cleanest and coldest lakes in the world, **Lake Tahoe** is perched high above the Gold Country in an alpine bowl of forested granite peaks. Longer than the English Channel is wide, and more than a thousand feet deep, it's so cold that perfectly preserved cowboys who drowned over a century ago have been recovered from its depths. The lake straddles the Nevada stateline as well and lures weekenders with sunny beaches in the summer, snow-covered slopes in the winter and bustling casinos year-round.

Arrival, information and getting around

The nearest you can get to Lake Tahoe on Greyhound or Amtrak from San Francisco and Sacramento is Truckee, fifteen miles north (see p.937). From there, local TART **buses** (ⓣ530/581-3922 or 1-800/736-6365, ⓦwww.laketahoetransit.com) run to Tahoe City and around but, frustratingly, not onwards to South Lake Tahoe. Transport around the south shore is provided by BlueGo buses and trolleys (ⓣ530/541-7149, ⓦwww.bluego.org). There are shuttles from both ends of the lake to Reno airport: North Lake Tahoe Express (ⓣ530/541-4892, ⓦwww.laketahoetransit.com) and South Tahoe Express (ⓣ1-866/898-2463, ⓦwww.southtahoeexpress.com); prices vary according to the number of passengers. You can rent **bicycles** from numerous outlets, including the Mountain Sports Center in South Lake Tahoe's *Camp Richardson Resort* (see below) and from Olympic Bike Shop (ⓣ530/581-2500) in Tahoe City.

There are four official **visitor centres** around the lake: the two in California are at 3066 US-50, South Lake Tahoe (daily 9am–5pm; ⓣ530/541-5255 or 1-800/288-2463, ⓦwww.tahoesouth.com) and 380 North Lake Blvd, Tahoe City (daily 9am–5pm; ⓣ530/581-6900 or 1-800/824-6348, ⓦwww.gotahoenorth.com).

Accommodation

There are dozens of bargain **motels** along the Southshore, though weekday rates from $50 can easily more than double on weekends and in summer. In

Tahoe City, there are fewer budget choices. If you're stuck, any of the visitor centres will try to help.

Camp Richardson Resort Hwy-89 towards Emerald Bay, South Lake Tahoe ⓣ1-800/544-1801, ⓦwww.camprichardson.com. Occupying a huge chunk of prime lakeside with its own beach, this established resort includes hotel rooms, spacious cabins and camping spaces. Fine restaurant too. ❹

Inn by the Lake 3300 Lake Tahoe Blvd, South Lake Tahoe ⓣ1-800/877-1466, ⓦwww.innbythelake.com. Nicely furnished rooms and suites, a heated swimming pool and jacuzzi, free breakfast, and use of bicycles render this a relaxing spot; good value for money too. Free shuttle bus to the casinos. ❺

River Ranch Lodge Hwy-89 and Alpine Meadows Rd, Tahoe City ⓣ530/583-4264 or 1-866/991-9912, ⓦwww.riverranchlodge.com. Historic lodge on the Truckee River with a casual atmosphere and one of the lake's best restaurants. Great value for the north lake. ❹

Royal Valhalla 4104 Lakeshore Blvd, South Lake Tahoe ⓣ530/544-2233 or 1-866/493-4603, ⓦwww.tahoeroyalvalhalla.com. Not exactly regal but one of the better motels, with balconies overlooking the lake and kitchenettes. ❺

Tahoma Meadows B&B 6821 W Lake Blvd, Tahoma ⓣ1-866/525-1553, ⓦwww.tahomameadows.com. Well-furnished cottages in a lovely setting at this friendly place on the west shore, 7 miles south of Tahoe City. ❹

Tamarack Lodge 2311 North Lake Blvd, Tahoe City ⓣ530/583-3350 or 1-888/824-6323, ⓦwww.tamarackattahoe.com. One of the best deals anywhere on the lake, with comfortable and clean cabins and rooms. ❸

South Lake Tahoe and around

In **South Lake Tahoe**, the lakeside's largest community, ranks of restaurants, modest motels and pine-bound cottages stand cheek by jowl with the high-rise gambling dens of **Stateline**, just across the border in Nevada. If you happen to lose your money at the tables and slot machines, you can always explore the beautiful hiking trails, parks and beaches in the surrounding area.

The **Heavenly Gondola**, in the heart of town, rises to an elevation of 9136ft (summer daily 10am–5pm; $32). From there, enjoy breathtaking views from East Peak Lake, East Peak Lookout or Sky Meadows. Hikes are graded from easy to strenuous. Closer to the water, the prettiest part of the lake is along the southwest shore, at **Emerald Bay State Park**, ten miles from South Lake Tahoe, which has a number of good shoreline **campgrounds**. A mile from the car park, **Vikingsholm** is a reproduction of a Viking castle, built as a summer home in 1929 and open for hourly tours (summer daily 10am–4pm; $8). In **Sugar Pine Point State Park**, two miles north, the huge **Ehrman Mansion** (daily 11am–4pm; $8) is decorated in Thirties-era furnishings; the extensive lakefront grounds were used as a location in *The Godfather II*.

The rest of the 75-mile **drive** is lovely enough, though certainly not the "most beautiful drive in America", as locally produced brochures claim. Another way to see the lake is to take a paddlewheel **boat cruise** on the MS *Dixie II* from Zephyr Cove in Nevada, reached on a free shuttle from South Lake Tahoe, or *Tahoe Queen* from Ski Run Marina in South Lake Tahoe itself (timetable varies; $39–75; ⓣ775/589-4906, ⓦwww.zephyrcove.com). The more expensive cruises include dinner.

Tahoe City

Tahoe City, the hub on the lake's northwestern shore manages to retain a more relaxed small-town attitude than South Lake Tahoe. Hwy-89 meets Hwy-28 at Lake Tahoe's only outlet, the **Truckee River**. At the mouth of the river, the **Gatekeeper's Museum** (May–Sep Wed–Mon 10am–5pm; Oct–April Sat & Sun 11am–3pm; $5; ⓣ530/583-1762, ⓦwww.northtahoemuseums.org), contains a well-presented hodgepodge of artefacts from the nineteenth century, and a good collection of native basketware. **Rafting** down the Truckee is a common activity

Lake Tahoe skiing

Lake Tahoe rivals the Rocky Mountains in offering some of the best **downhill skiing** and **snowboarding** in North America. Although skiing is not cheap – lift passes can cost well over $60 per day and ski/snowboard rental $30–35 – most resorts offer decent-value pass/rental/lesson packages or multi-day discounts, especially if booked in advance online. **Cross-country skiing** is also popular, with rentals around $20 and trail passes in the region of $15–30.

Downhill skiing

Heavenly reachable by shuttle from Southshore, two miles from the casinos, or via the gondola on Hwy-50, next to the state line (ⓣ775/586-7000 or 1-800/243-2836, ⓦwww.skiheavenly.com). Prime location and sheer scale (85 runs and 29 lifts) make this one of the lake's most frequented resorts, and it also offers the highest vertical skiing served by a lift in the area.

Kirkwood Ski Resort 35 miles south of South Lake Tahoe on Hwy-88 (ⓣ209/258-6000, ⓦwww.kirkwood.com). A bit out of the way if you're in Tahoe but worth the trip as a destination in itself for its recreational possibilities, including excellent hiking and biking trails.

Squaw Valley USA Squaw Valley Road, halfway between Truckee and Tahoe City (ⓣ530/583-6955 or 1-888/766-9321, ⓦwww.squaw.com). Thirty-three lifts service over four thousand acres of unbeatable terrain at the site of the 1960 Winter Olympics. Non-skiers can take the cable lift and use the ice-skating/swimming pool complex for the day.

Cross-country skiing

Royal Gorge in Soda Springs, ten miles west of Truckee (ⓣ530/426-3871 or 1-800/666-3871, ⓦwww.royalgorge.com). The largest and best of Tahoe's cross-country resorts has 204 miles of groomed trails.

Spooner Lake in Nevada at the intersection of Hwy-50 and Hwy-28 (ⓣ775/749-5349, ⓦwww.spoonerlake.com). The closest cross-country resort to South Lake Tahoe has lake views and 63 miles of groomed trails.

in summer, with raft rental companies (prices start around $35/person) clustered at the junction of highways 28 and 89.

Squaw Valley, the site of the 1960 Winter Olympics, is situated five miles west of Tahoe City off Hwy-89, although the original facilities (except the flame and the Olympic rings) are now swamped by the rampant development that has made this California's largest ski resort (see box above).

Eating and drinking

Fast food and casino all-you-care-to-eat buffets are standard in Southshore, while Tahoe City has a better range of moderately priced **restaurants** and a couple of good **bars**, all within a few minutes of each other.

Blue Agave 423 North Lake Blvd, Tahoe City ⓣ530/583-8113. Ample portions of fine Mexican food like fish tacos in colourful surroundings, as well as a range of margaritas.

The Brewery at Lake Tahoe 3542 Lake Tahoe Blvd, South Lake Tahoe ⓣ530/544-2739. Microbrewery with decent ales ranging from pale to porter, and food specials such as beer-steamed shrimp and quality steaks.

Bridgetender Bar & Grill 30 West Lake Blvd, Tahoe City ⓣ530/583-3342. Friendly rustic bar with good music, a fine range of beers and huge portions of ribs and burgers.

River Ranch Hwy-89 and Alpine Meadows Rd, Tahoe City ⓣ530/583-4264 or 1-800/535-9900. Historic lodge on the Truckee River serving excellent New American cuisine in a relaxed atmosphere.

Sprouts 3123 Lake Tahoe Blvd near Alameda Ave, South Lake Tahoe ⓣ530/541-6969. Almost, but not completely, vegetarian, with good organic sandwiches, burritos and smoothies.

Sunnyside 1850 West Lake Blvd, near Tahoe City ⓣ530/583-7200. One of the most popular places to have cocktails at sunset on the deck overlooking the lake.

Tahoe House Bakery Hwy-89, half a mile south of Hwy-28, Tahoe City ⓣ530/583-1377. Family-style bakery and deli, popular with locals.

Tep's Villa Roma 3450 Hwy-50, South Lake Tahoe ⓣ530/541-8227. Long-standing South-shore institution that serves large portions of hearty Italian food.

Truckee and Donner Lake

Fifteen miles north of Tahoe City, the pleasant town of **TRUCKEE** is not only a jumping-off point for Lake Tahoe, but a developing tourist destination in its own right. It is well placed for outdoor excursions and it retains a fair amount of nineteenth-century wooden architecture along its main drag, Donner Pass Road, still referred to as Commercial Row by locals. This strip holds a good choice of **eating** and **drinking** joints, such as *Dragonfly* (ⓣ530/587-0557), a Pacific Rim and Asian fusion restaurant at no. 10118, and *OB's* (ⓣ530/587-4164), a relaxed pub with decent food at no. 10046. Around the corner at 10007 Bridge St, the *Truckee Hotel* (ⓣ530/587-4444 or 1-800/659-6921, ⓦwww.truckeehotel.com; ③) is a central **place to stay** with a wide range of rooms. The California Welcome Center, 10065 Donner Pass Rd (daily 9am–5.30pm; ⓣ530/587-2757, ⓦwww.truckee.com) is very helpful and friendly.

Several miles west of Truckee, **DONNER LAKE**, surrounded by alpine cliffs of silver-grey granite, was the site of a gruesome tragedy in 1846, when the **Donner Party**, heading for the Gold Rush, found their route blocked by early snowfall. They stopped and built crude shelters, hoping that the snow would melt; it didn't. Fifteen of their number braved the mountains in search of help from Sutter's Fort in Sacramento; only two men and five women made it, surviving by eating the bodies of the men who died. The horrific tale is recounted in the small **Emigrant Trail Museum** (daily 9am–4pm; free; ⓣ530/582-7892), just off Donner Pass Road in Donner State Park (parking $8 and camping May–Sept; $35, hike/bike in $7; ⓣ1-800/444-7275, ⓦwww.parks.ca.gov).

Northern California

The massive and eerily silent volcanic lands of **northern California** have more in common with Oregon and Washington than with the rest of the state. Its inhabitants live by farming and an ever-decreasing number by logging and fishing, augmented in recent years by New Agers, ex-hippies and a growing contingent of tourists. Once you're past the atypically lush valleys of the **Wine Country**, the coast stretches for three hundred miles of rugged bluffs and forests. Aside from the beautiful deserted beaches that stripe the coast, trees are the big attraction, thousands of years old and hundreds of feet high, dominating a landscape swathed in swirling mists. The **Redwood National Park** teems with campers and hikers in summer, but out of season it can be idyllic. The remote wildernesses of the interior can be enchanting, especially around the **Shasta Cascade** and **Lassen Volcanic National Park**.

Public transport is, not surprisingly, scarce, though Greyhound buses run from San Francisco and Sacramento up and down I-5 into Oregon and US-101 as far as Arcata.

The Wine Country

The warm and sunny hills of **Napa** and **Sonoma valleys**, an hour north of San Francisco, are by reputation at the centre of the American wine industry. In truth, less than five percent of California's wine comes from the region, but what it does produce is America's best. In summer, cars jam the main arteries, as visitors embark on a day's hectic tasting.

The Napa Valley

Thirty miles of gently landscaped hillsides, the **Napa Valley** looks more like southern France than a near-neighbour of the Pacific Ocean. The one anomaly is the town of **Napa** itself, a sprawling, ungainly city of 60,000, best avoided in favour of the wineries and small towns north on Hwy-29. Nine miles north is **YOUNTVILLE**, anchored by **Vintage 1870**, 6525 Washington St (daily 10.30am–5.30pm; ⓣ1-800/946-3487, ⓦwww.vintagewinecellar.com), a shopping and wine complex in a converted winery that's home to Napa Valley Aloft (ⓣ1-800/627-2759, ⓦwww.nvaloft.com), which specializes in sunrise hot-air balloon tours from $225 per person.

Of the large wineries at the valley's southern end, **Robert Mondavi**, at 7801 St Helena Hwy in Oakville (daily 10am–5pm; ⓣ1-888/766-6328, ⓦwww.robertmondavi.com) offers the most informative and least sales-driven tours ($25) and tastings (from $15). Up the valley past the pretty village of **ST HELENA**, **Beringer Vineyards**, at 2000 Main St (daily 10am–5pm; tasting $10, tours $10–35; ⓣ707/963-7115, ⓦwww.beringer.com), is modelled on a German Gothic mansion, whose spacious lawns and grand tasting room heavy with dark wood make for quite a regal experience.

Homey **CALISTOGA**, at the very northern tip of the valley, is as well known for its mud baths, whirlpools and mineral water as its wineries. South of town, **Clos Pegase**, 1060 Dunaweal Lane (daily 10.30am–5pm; $10; ⓣ707/942-4981, ⓦwww.clospegase.com), is a flamboyant, high-profile winery that draws a link between fine wine and fine art, with an excellent sculpture garden; there are tours at 11am and 2pm. **Chateau Montelena**, 1429 Tubbs Lane (daily 9.30am–4pm; $15–25; ⓣ707/942-5105, ⓦwww.montelena.com), just north of town, is one of the valley's oldest and smallest wineries, with an impressive medieval facade and a reputation for first-class chardonnays. A mile further up the road, the **Old Faithful Geyser** (daily summer 9am–6pm, winter till 5pm; $10; ⓣ707/942-6463), discovered during oil drilling here in the 1920s, spurts boiling water sixty feet into the air at forty-minute intervals.

Practicalities

From San Francisco there are daily Gray Line **bus tours** ($68; ⓣ1-888/428-6937, ⓦwww.grayline.com) to the Wine Country; otherwise you will need a car. The main **Visitors Bureau** (daily 9am–5pm; ⓣ707/226-7459, ⓦwww.napavalley.com) is at 1310 Napa Town Center, off First Street in Napa itself, but most towns have their own information outlet.

In **St Helena**, the *El Bonita Motel*, 195 Main St (ⓣ707/963-3216 or 1-800/541-3284, ⓦwww.elbonita.com; ❺), is a smart Art Deco hotel on the south side of town, while the nearby *Ambrose Bierce Inn* (ⓣ707/963-3003, ⓦwww.ambrosebiercehouse.com; ❼), is a luxury B&B at 1515 Main St. St Helena's **restaurants** range from the inexpensive Mexican *Armadillo's*, 1304 Main St (ⓣ707/963-8082), to the haute cuisine and four-hundred-plus wine list at the gigantic *Wine Spectator Greystone Restaurant*, 2555 Main St (ⓣ707/967-1010), owned by the Culinary Institute of America.

In **Calistoga**, *Dr Wilkinson's Hot Springs*, 1507 Lincoln Ave (ⓣ707/942-4102, ⓦwww.drwilkinson.com; ❻), is a legendary health spa and hotel, while less expensive lodgings lining the main drag, Lincoln Avenue, include the quiet, modern *Comfort Inn* at no. 1865 (ⓣ707/942-9400, ⓦwww.comfortinn.com; ❸). Downtown's most enticing hotel, with some fancy cottages, can be found at 1457 Lincoln Ave in the historic *Mount View Hotel and Spa* (ⓣ707/942-6877 or 1-800/816-6877, ⓦwww.mountviewhotel.com; ❼). Creative cuisine, featuring unheard-of combinations such as *chile rellenos* with walnut pomegranate sauce, makes **dining** at the *Wappo Bar & Bistro*, 1226 Washington St (ⓣ707/942-4712), a delicious adventure. *Brannan's Grill*, 1374 Lincoln Ave (ⓣ707/942-2233), serves fresh oysters, salmon and pecan-stuffed quail in an airy wood-interior bistro. The less expensive *Calistoga Inn*, 1250 Lincoln Ave (ⓣ707/942-4101), offers great seafood appetizers, including wheat-ale steamed clams and mussels, plus a wide range of wines, microbrewed beers and excellent desserts.

The Sonoma Valley

On looks alone, the crescent-shaped **Sonoma Valley** beats Napa hands down. This altogether more rustic valley curves between oak-covered mountain ranges from the Spanish Colonial town of **SONOMA** to Glen Ellen, a few miles north along Hwy-12. It's far smaller than Napa, and many of its wineries are less formal, family-run businesses.

The restored **Mission San Francisco Solano de Sonoma** in Sonoma State Historic Park (daily 10am–5pm; $3), just east of the spacious plaza in Sonoma, was the last and northernmost of the California missions. The plaza was also the site of the Bear Flag Revolt, the 1846 action that propelled California into independence from Mexico and then statehood. Many of Sonoma's wineries are concentrated a mile east and include the grand old **Buena Vista Carneros**, 18000 Old Winery Rd (daily 10am–5pm; tasting $5–10; various tours free–$50; ⓣ1-800/678-8504, ⓦwww.buenavistacarneros.com). A ten-minute drive further north, in charming Glen Ellen, is the **Benziger Family Winery**, 1883 London Ranch Rd (daily 10am–5pm; tasting $10–15; ⓣ1-888/490-2739, ⓦwww.benziger.com), where a tram tour (9 daily; $15) takes you around the vineyard along the side of Mount Sonoma. A half-mile up London Ranch Road, **Jack London State Park** (daily 9.30am–5pm, till 7pm in summer; $8/car) sits on the 140 acres of ranchland owned by the famed author of *The Call of the Wild*. Here you'll find the author's final resting place, along with a decent museum that houses a collection of souvenirs.

Practicalities

Public transportation to the valley is available through Golden Gate Transit's bus services from San Francisco to Petaluma and Santa Rosa (ⓣ707/541-2000, ⓦwww.goldengate.org). For useful **info**, head for the Visitors Bureau (daily summer 9am–6pm, winter till 5pm; ⓣ707/996-1090, ⓦwww.sonomavalley.com), in a cute building right on Sonoma's plaza. **Accommodation** is pricey, though the *Sonoma Hotel*, 110 W Spain St (ⓣ1-800/468-6016, ⓦwww.sonomahotel.com; ❺), has French-country-style doubles, while the *Swiss Hotel*, 18 W Spain

St (Ⓣ707/938-2884, Ⓦwww.swisshotelsonoma.com; ❻), is in a landmark building on the plaza with four-poster beds in each room; both places have excellent **restaurants**. Another fine place to eat is *The General's Daughter*, 400 W Spain St (Ⓣ707/938-4004), which offers creative California cuisine, while at 400 E First St, *Cucina Viansa* (Ⓣ707/935-5656) serves tasty Italian dishes at reasonable prices.

The northern coast

The fog-bound towns and windswept, craggy beaches of the **northern coast** that stretches to the Oregon border is better suited for hiking and camping than sunbathing, with cool temperatures year-round and a huge network of national, state and regional parks preserving magnificent **redwoods**, the tallest and among the oldest trees on earth.

The Sonoma Coast and Russian River Valley

Despite the weekend influx from San Francisco, the villages of the **Sonoma Coast** and **Russian River Valley** seem all but asleep for most of the year. Tucked along the slow, snaking Hwy-1, towns include **BODEGA BAY**, where Hitchcock filmed *The Birds*. From here, a great thirteen-mile hike leads along the rugged cliffs to a prime seal- and whale-watching spot, **Goat Rock Beach**, where the Russian River joins the ocean.

About ten miles inland on Hwy-116, along the warm and pastoral Russian River Valley, **GUERNEVILLE** is a well-established gay resort. It offers plenty of **places to stay** – though many are expensive. The *New Dynamic Inn*, 14030 Mill St (Ⓣ707/869-1563, Ⓦwww.newdynamicinn.com; ❹), is one of the more modest places, while the **campground** at *Johnson's Resort* (Ⓣ707/869-2022, Ⓦwww.johnsonsbeach.com; $20) on 1st Street also has cabins (❷), rentable by the week. *Main St Station*, 16280 Main St (Ⓣ707/869-0501), is a great Italian **restaurant** with nightly live jazz, while *Wild Jane's*, 16440 Main St (Ⓣ707/869-3600), serves reliable food and also has live music. The **Armstrong Redwoods State Reserve** ($8/car), two miles north, contains 750 very dense acres of enormous redwoods interspersed by trails. Guided expeditions run by Horseback Adventures (Ⓣ707/887-2939, Ⓦwww.redwoodhorses.com) vary in length from half a day ($80) to overnight pack trips (from $400) with tented accommodation.

The Mendocino coast

The coast of **Mendocino County**, 150 miles north of San Francisco, is an even more dramatic extension of the Sonoma coastline. **MENDOCINO** itself looks like a transplanted New England fishing village: weathered and charming, with plenty of art galleries and boutiques. Just south of town, hiking and cycling trails weave through the unusual **Van Damme State Park**, on Hwy-1 ($8/car; Ⓣ707/937-5804), where the ancient trees of the Pygmy Forest are stunted to waist height because of poor drainage and soil chemicals. Two-hour sea cave tours through the park are available through Kayak Mendocino (three times daily; $50; Ⓣ707/964-7480, Ⓦwww.kayakmendocino.com).

The most affordable **accommodation** in the centre of town is the *Sea Gull Inn*, 44960 Albion St (Ⓣ707/937-5204 or 1-888/937-5204, Ⓦwww.seagullbb.com; ❺), though the antique-filled *The Mendocino Hotel*, 45080 Main St (Ⓣ707/937-0511 or 1-800/548-0513, Ⓦwww.mendocinohotel.com; ❺), offers some rooms with shared baths and more luxurious suites. The town's oldest **bar** is *Dick's Place*

Bigfoot Country

Willow Creek, forty miles east of Arcata, is the self-proclaimed gateway to "**Bigfoot Country**". Reports of giant 350- to 800-pound humanoids wandering the forests of northwestern California have circulated since the late nineteenth century, fuelled by long-established Native American legends, but weren't taken seriously until 1958, when a road maintenance crew found giant footprints. Thanks to their photos, the Bigfoot story went worldwide. However, in 2002, the bereaved family of Ray L. Wallace claimed he made the 1958 footprints, a hoax they had promised to keep secret until after his death. But the number and variety of prints (over forty, since 1958) still points to a Bigfoot mystery, and the small **visitor centre** (summer daily 9am–5pm; ⓣ530/629-6293, ⓦwww.willowcreekchamber.com) in Willow Creek has details of Bigfoot's alleged activities.

on Main Street, while the most famous **restaurant** is *Café Beaujolais*, 961 Ukiah St (ⓣ707/937-5614), which specializes in organic California cuisine. *955 Ukiah Street* (ⓣ707/937-1955; closed Tues) serves some of the best food in town. For slightly cheaper fare with a great view, try the *Mendocino Café*, 10451 Lancing St (ⓣ707/937-4197), which serves sandwiches, salads and pasta.

The Humboldt coast

Humboldt is by far the most beautiful of the coastal counties: almost entirely forest, overwhelmingly peaceful in places, in others plain eerie. The impassable cliffs of **Kings Range** prevent even the sinuous Hwy-1 from reaching the "Lost Coast" of its southern reaches. To get there you have to detour inland via US-101 through the deepest redwood territory as far as **GARBERVILLE**, a one-street town with a few good bars that is the centre of the "Emerald Triangle", which produces the majority of California's largest cash crop, marijuana.

Redwood country begins in earnest a few miles north, at the **Humboldt Redwoods State Park** (ⓣ707/946-2409, ⓦwww.humboldtredwoods.org), California's largest redwood park. The serpentine **Avenue of the Giants** weaves for 33 miles through trees that block all but a few strands of sunlight, with numerous access points to US-101. This is the habitat of *Sequoia sempervirens*, the coastal redwood, with ancestors dating back to the days of the dinosaurs, and some are over 360ft tall. Three campgrounds fill up quickly in summertime (ⓣ1-800/444-7275, ⓦwww.parks.ca.gov; $35–55).

Tiny **SAMOA**, a few minutes by car over the bay from sprawling Eureka, holds the last remaining cookhouse in the West. Lumbermen came to the *Samoa Cookhouse* (ⓣ707/442-1659) to eat gargantuan portions of red meat on long trestle tables after a day of felling redwoods, a dining experience now available to visitors. Many people bypass **EUREKA** itself but the Old Town is worth a wander, especially during the Arts Alive! nights on the first Saturday of each month, when almost a hundred businesses open their doors for arts – much of it performing – along with plenty of drinking and frivolity. The *Carter House Inns*, an enclave of several buildings at the corner of L and 3rd streets (ⓣ1-800/404-1390; ⓦwww.carterhouse.com; ❼), offers luxurious **accommodation** and a top-quality **restaurant**.

ARCATA, seven miles north of Eureka, a small college town with an earthy, mellow pace, has a grassy central plaza surrounded by good restaurants, and some excellent white sand, windswept beaches to the north. The *Fairwinds Motel*, 1674 G St (ⓣ707/822-4824 or 1-866/352-5518, ⓦwww.fairwindsmotelarcata.com; ❸), is probably the best deal in town. More upmarket, the *Hotel Arcata*, 708 Ninth St (ⓣ707/826-0217 or 1-800/344-1221, ⓦwww.hotelarcata.com; ❹), is central and offers standard rooms and nicer suites. *Humboldt Brewery*, 856 10th St, stocks a good range of ale, has low-priced food and often hosts live music.

Redwood National Park

Thirty miles north of Arcata, the small town of **ORICK** marks the southern limit and busiest section of the **Redwood National Park**. **Tall Trees Grove** here is home to one of the world's tallest trees – a mighty 367-footer. Many visitors hike to it on the 8.5-mile trail from Bald Hill Road near Orick, but make sure to visit the **Kuchel information centre** (daily summer 9am–6pm, winter till 4pm; ⓣ707/464-6101), from which you can obtain the necessary free permit to drive along the access road to the trailhead.

Of the three state parks within the Redwood National Park area, **Prairie Creek**, is the most varied and popular. Highlights include the meadows of **Elk Prairie** in front of the **ranger station** (daily: summer 9am–6pm; rest of year till 5pm; ⓣ707/464-6101), where herds of Roosevelt Elk – massive beasts weighing up to twelve hundred pounds – wander freely.

Spectacular coastal views can be had from trails in the Klamath area, especially the **Klamath Overlook**, two miles up Requa Road and about three-quarters of a mile above the sea. You can jump over, lumber under or glide through all the naturally contorted and sculpted **Trees of Mystery** (daily: summer 8am–7pm; winter 9am–5pm; $14; ⓣ1-800/638-3389, ⓦwww.treesofmystery.net), except the impressive **Cathedral Tree**, where nine trees have grown from one root structure to form a spooky circle.

The park headquarters are in otherwise missable **Crescent City** at 1111 Second St (summer daily 9am–5pm, winter Mon–Sat same hours; ⓣ707/464-6101, ⓦwww.nps.gov/redw), but you can pick up information all over the park. There are **campgrounds** everywhere; three that have showers and water are *Prairie Creek* on US-101, *Mill Creek*, five miles south of Crescent City and *Jedediah Smith*, eight miles north of Crescent City on the Smith River. If you do come in summer, make reservations through ReserveAmerica (ⓣ1-800/444-7275, ⓦwww.parks.ca.gov). If they are full, there are numerous **motels** around Crescent City.

The northern interior

The remote **northern interior** of California, cut off from the coast by the **Shasta Cascade** range and dominated by forests, lakes and mountains, is largely uninhabited. Interstate 5 leads through the heart of this near-wilderness, forging straight through the unspectacular farmland of **Sacramento Valley** to **Redding** – the region's only buses follow this route. Redding makes a good base for the **Whiskeytown-Shasta-Trinity area** and the more demanding **Lassen Volcanic National Park**. Mountaineers and the spiritually minded flock to **Mount Shasta**, which is close enough to the volcanic **Lava Beds** at the very northeastern tip of the state for them to be a long but feasible day's car trip.

Redding and Shasta

With strip malls lining the I-5 that bisects it, **REDDING** appears to be an anomaly amid the natural splendour of the northern interior. The region's largest city, with over 70,000 people, it has acted as a northern nexus since the late nineteenth century. Today it remains a crossroads but the superb **Turtle Bay Exploration Park**, 800 Auditorium Drive (mid-March to mid-Sep daily 9am–5pm; mid-Sep to mid-March Wed–Sat till 4pm, Sun 10am–4pm; $14; ⓣ530/243-8850, ⓦwww.turtlebay.org), full of fascinating interactive exhibits, and stunning Sundial Bridge, designed by Spanish architect Santiago Calatreva, have greatly enhanced the town's image. If you need to **stay** and have a car, try the *Best Western Hilltop Inn*, 2300 Hilltop Drive (ⓣ530/221-6100 or 1-800/336-4880, ⓦwww.bestwestern.com; ④); the *Bridgehouse B&B*, 1455 Riverside Drive (ⓣ530/247-7177, ⓦwww.reddingbridgehouse.com; ⑤), in contrast, is only a short walk from downtown. *Buz's Crab* (ⓣ530/243-2120), 2159 East St, is a local institution, serving a huge range of moderately-priced fish and **seafood**.

SHASTA, four miles west of Redding and not to be confused with Mount Shasta, is somewhat a ghost town. The row of half-ruined brick buildings here represent a once booming gold-mining town. The **Courthouse** has been turned into a museum (Thurs–Sun 10am–5pm; $3), full of historical California artwork and mining paraphernalia, while the gallows and prison cells are a grim reminder of the daily executions that went on here.

Lassen Volcanic National Park

About fifty miles over gently-sloping plains east from Red Bluff on Hwy-36, or forty miles east from Redding on Hwy-44, the 106,000 acres that make up the pine forests, crystal-green lakes and boiling thermal pools of the **LASSEN VOLCANIC NATIONAL PARK** are one of the most unearthly parts of northern California's forbidding landscape, which receives up to fifty feet of snowfall each year, keeping the area pretty much uninhabited outside the brief summer season. **Mount Lassen** itself last erupted in 1915, when the peak blew an enormous mushroom cloud some seven miles skyward, tearing the summit into chunks that landed as far away as Reno; scientists predict that it is the likeliest of all the West Coast volcanoes to blow again.

The thirty-mile tour of the park along Hwy-89 from **Manzanita Lake** in the north should take no more than a few hours but is often not fully open until the snows have melted in June. There is a $10 access fee per vehicle to the park, valid for seven days. The Mount Lassen explosion denuded the devastated area, ripping out every tree and patch of grass, and a large area of desolation remains amid the reforestation. Marking the halfway point, **Summit Lake** is a busy camping area set around a beautiful icy lake, close to the most manageable hiking trails. From a parking area to the south (8000ft up), the steep, five-mile ascent to Lassen Peak begins. Experienced hikers can do it in four hours, but wilderness seekers will have a better time pushing east to the steep trails of the **Juniper Lake** area.

Continuing south along Hwy-89, Lassen's indisputable show-stealers are **Bumpass Hell** and **Emerald Lake**, the former (named after a man who lost a leg trying to cross it), a steaming valley of active pools and vents that bubble away at a low rumble. The trails are sturdy and easy to manage, but you should never venture off them; the crusts over the thermal features are often brittle, and breaking through could plunge you into very hot water. From **Sulphur Works**, an acrid cauldron of steam vents near the south entrance, a magnificent but gruelling trail leads for a mile around the site to the avalanche-prone summit at **Diamond Peak**, which affords great views over the entire park and forest beyond.

The main **visitor centre** is at the southern entrance on Hwy-89 (daily: summer 9am–6pm, winter till 5pm; ⓣ530/595-4480, ⓦwww.nps.gov/lavo), where you can get free maps and information, including the *Lassen Park Guide*. There is also a smart café. Another visitor centre (summer daily 9am–5pm; ⓣ530/595-4444 ext 5180) is at Manzanita Lake, just inside the northern entrance, and includes the Loomis Museum, which documents the park's eruption cycle. There is a general store (ⓣ530/595-4422) nearby, which runs cabins beside the lake.

Mount Shasta City and Mount Shasta

Roughly sixty miles north of Redding, a scenic road branches off I-5 to **MOUNT SHASTA CITY**, hard under the enormous bulk of the 14,162-foot **Mount Shasta**. Still considered active despite not having erupted for two hundred years, this lone peak dominates the landscape for a hundred miles around, and its "energies" attract New Agers by the score. If you want to climb to the summit (10hr; crampons and ice axe needed most of the year), or simply to explore the flanks of the mountain along the many trails, you must obtain a free permit from the **ranger district office**, 204 W Alma St (April–Oct Mon–Sat 8am–4.30pm; rest of year Mon–Fri same hours; ⓣ530/926-4511), or you can self-issue one at the main trailheads.

The nearest Greyhound stop is at Weed, nine miles north, whence local STAGE **buses** (ⓣ530/842-8295 or 1-800/247-8243) connect to Mount Shasta City. The **Chamber of Commerce** is at 300 Pine St (daily: summer 9am–5.30pm, winter 10am–4pm; ⓣ530/926-3696 or 1-800/926-4865, ⓦwww.mtshastachamber.com). There's friendly **accommodation** at the excellent *Alpenrose Cottage Guest House*, 204 E Hinkley St (ⓣ530/926-6724, ⓦwww.snowcrest.net/alpenrose; ❸), among other choices. Within ten miles to the southeast and south respectively, the *McCloud B&B Hotel*, 408 Main St, McCloud (ⓣ530/964-2822 or 1-800/964-2823, ⓦwww.mccloudhotel.com; ❺), has some rooms with jacuzzis, while *Cave Springs*, 4727 Dunsmuir Ave, Dunsmuir (ⓣ530/235-2721, ⓦwww.cavesprings.com; ❷), has a unique range of rooms and cabins by a river. *Lake Siskiyou Campground* (ⓣ530/926-2618; $25) is four miles west of town and the most picturesque in the area.

Some of the town's best **meals** can be had at *Trinity Café*, 622 N Mount Shasta Blvd (ⓣ530/926-3372; closed Sun & Mon), which serves quality California cuisine, and *Vivify* (ⓣ530/926-1345), an upmarket Japanese restaurant at 531 Chestnut St.

Lava Beds National Monument

Lava Beds National Monument ($10/vehicle for seven days), in the far north of the state, is one of the most remote and alluring of California's parks. The human history of these volcanic caves and huge black lava flows is as violent as the natural forces that created them. Before the Gold Rush the area was home to the **Modoc** Indians, but repeated bloody confrontations with miners led to them being forced into a reservation with the Klamath, their traditional enemy. When the Modocs drifted back to the area in 1872, the army was sent in. Fifty-five Modoc warriors, under the leadership of "Captain Jack", held back an army ten times the size for five months from a natural fortress of passageways now known as **Captain Jack's Stronghold**, at the park's northern tip.

The bulk of the lava tube caves are close to the **visitor centre** (daily: summer 8am–6pm; rest of year till 5pm; ⓣ530/667-8113, ⓦwww.nps.gov/labe), where you can take the free ranger tours (times vary) or borrow a torch for free to explore the caves alone. You can camp near the visitor centre for $10 but there are no shops nearby. Immediately north and west of Lava Beds, the **Klamath Basin National Wildlife Refuge** hosts millions of birds migrating along the Pacific Flyway. The **visitor centre** (Mon–Fri 8am–4.30pm, Sat & Sun 10am–4pm; ⓣ530/667-2231) is off Hill Road, near the northwest entrance for the Lava Beds. Surprisingly, the best way of spotting the wildlife is by driving along designated routes. If you want to **stay** in the area, the best place is *Fe's B&B* (ⓣ1-877/478-0184, ⓦwww.fesbandb.com; ❸) at 660 Main St in Tulelake, fourteen miles north of the main park entrance.

14

The Pacific Northwest

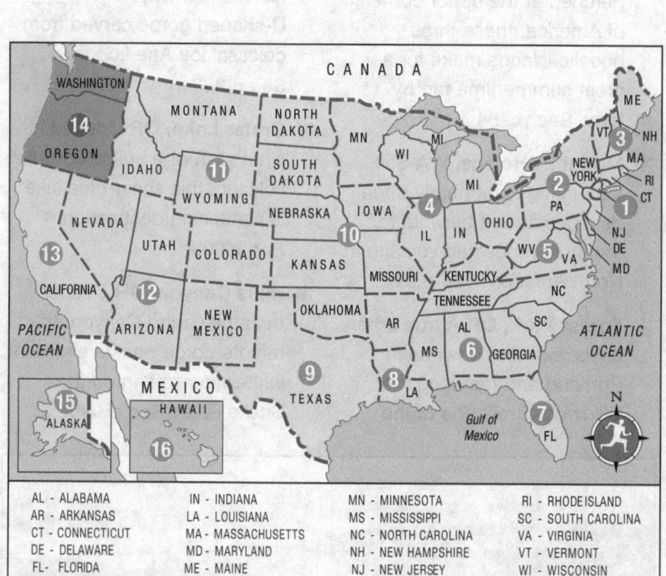

CHAPTER 14

Highlights

* **Pike Place Market, Seattle, WA** Seattle's lively urban market is loaded with fine restaurants, seafood and produce vendors, and street entertainers. See p.953

* **San Juan Islands, WA** Perched at the upper corner of America, these three bucolic islands make for a great summertime trip by ferry. See p.964

* **Mount St Helens, WA** Still a haunting sight nearly three decades after it blew its top, the most renowned volcano in North America. See p.972

* **Forest Park, OR** A true urban oasis, set near downtown Portland and featuring the Wildwood Trail, one of the Northwest's best routes for a walk, jog or simple wandering. See p.980

* **Columbia River Gorge, WA and OR** One of the USA's best natural attractions, home to precipitous waterfalls, historic highways and a huge, U-shaped gorge carved from colossal Ice Age floods. See p.983

* **Crater Lake, OR** Cradled in what's left of a hollowed-out volcano, this sheer-blue lake is a stunning destination. See p.993

* **Hells Canyon, OR** Deeper than the Grand Canyon, this remote gorge boasts excellent whitewater rafting on the Snake River. See p.996

▲ Roche Harbor, San Juan Island

14

The Pacific Northwest

The **Pacific Northwest** states of **Washington** and **Oregon** are well known as the wet green pocket in America's upper-left corner, similar in climate, topography and environmental politics, but quite different in their attitudes toward growth. Washington's sprawling development, bustling military bases and notorious freeway gridlock contrast dramatically with Oregon's low-scaled design and easy-going lifestyle, thanks in no small measure to the latter's stringent land-use laws and "urban-growth boundaries" around its larger cities.

Cooler and wetter than California to the south, both states are split by the great north–south spine of the **Cascade Mountains**, where regular rainfall and a moist climate create a verdant landscape thick with woodlands. In the adjoining Olympic Mountains of Washington's **Olympic Peninsula** the woods have even become small rainforests. Both **Seattle** and **Portland** lie roughly fifty miles from the Pacific Ocean along the I-5 freeway. Seattle, the commercial and cultural capital of the Northwest, is a major port known for its high-tech and aerospace industries, and location along the beautiful islands of the **Puget Sound**. Portland offers much historic appeal for its old-time terracotta architecture and ten stately bridges crossing the scenic Willamette River, along with its nationally regarded culture of bicycling.

Beyond the Cascades, the land to the **east** is far drier, peppered with desert and scrubland, as well as bleak stretches of lava beds and cinder cones. Of the towns, only **Spokane** in Washington is of any appreciable size, though Oregon's resort town of **Bend** has a location just east of the Cascades that makes it a useful base for exploring mountains, deserts, and especially the beautiful **Columbia River Gorge** to the north. Of great interest also is the scarred territory between Seattle and Portland around **Mount St Helens**, which erupted with devastating effect in 1980.

Some history

The **first inhabitants** of the Pacific Northwest may have reached the continent 12,000 to 20,000 years ago by crossing a land bridge over what is now the Bering Strait between Siberia and Alaska. By the late eighteenth century, European sea captains such as James Cook and George Vancouver came in search of the fabled **Northwest Passage**, an ice-free route between the Atlantic and the Pacific. Explorers Meriwether Lewis and William Clark, who reached the Oregon coast near present-day Astoria in 1804, were the first whites to cross the interior of the continent, and within forty years American settlers were streaming in along the **Oregon Trail**. This legendary period of immigration gave de facto control of the region to the United States, and official title followed in 1846 with the signing of a land pact with Britain that established a territorial boundary for the US and Canada at the 49th Parallel. In 1859 Oregon became the second **American state**

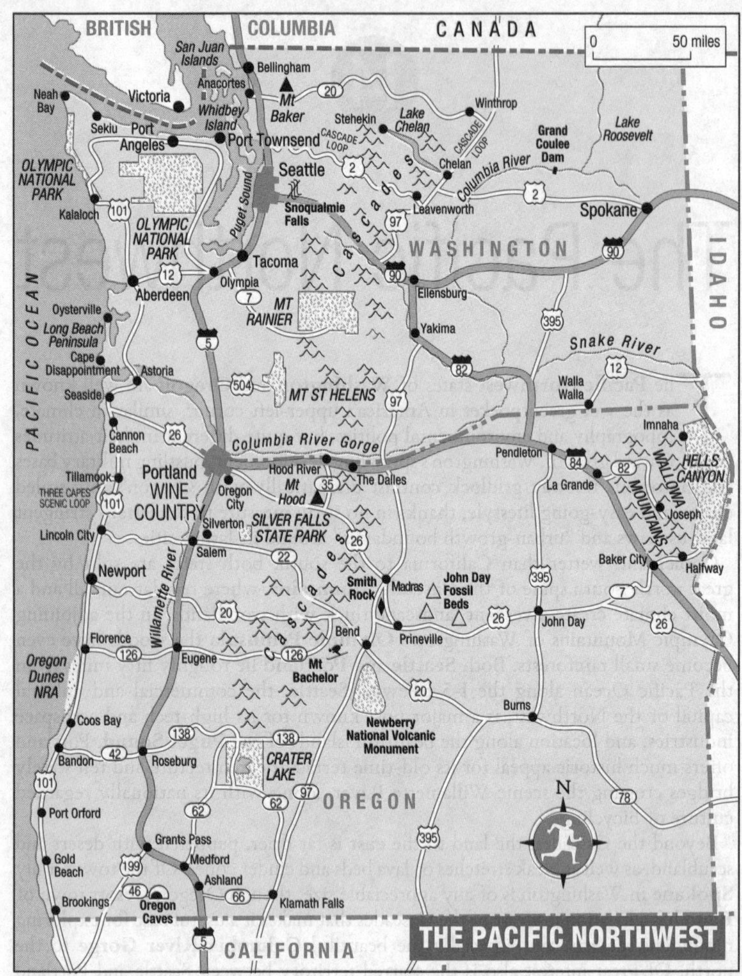

west of the Great Plains (after California). Thirty more years would pass before Washington state entered the Union.

When the railroads reached Portland and Seattle, Oregon and Washington began their economic ascent, aided by timber sales and, in the case of Seattle, the booming trade supplying prospectors on their way to Alaska's Klondike Gold Rush. Later decades would see the rise and fall of the lumber market and the emergence of computer software as a major local product. Outdoor adventuring and nature tourism have since become big attractions, especially from late May through to September, when the region's rains abate enough for the sun to illuminate the striking mountain and forest scenery.

Getting around the Pacific Northwest

Amtrak's *Coast Starlight* **train** runs once daily between Seattle and Portland and down to Los Angeles; the *Cascades* line runs four times per day from Seattle to

Eugene, Oregon, and twice daily from Seattle to Bellingham and Vancouver, BC; and the daily *Empire Builder* route heads east to Chicago, with separate lines originating from both Seattle and Portland. Greyhound provides **bus** service from Seattle east across the Cascades to **Spokane** and beyond, and north–south routes along I-5 linking Bellingham and Portland. In Oregon bus routes radiate from Portland through the Willamette Valley and across southern and central Oregon and to the coast. Having your own **vehicle** can facilitate access to many of the state's more remote spots, particularly if you're planning to sample the many great hiking and camping options on hand (see Ⓦwww.oregon.gov/OPRD).

Getting around Puget Sound is difficult and requires planning. **Washington State Ferries** (Ⓣ206/464-6400 or 1-800/84-FERRY; Ⓦwww.wsdot.wa.gov/ferries) run between the islands and major stops on the Sound (check each section for details). Finally, **cycling** throughout both states, and especially Oregon, is a popular endeavour, notably along majestic stretches of coastal Hwy-101.

Washington

Likeable and vibrant, Seattle's greatest asset may be its proximity to the glorious **Puget Sound**, the deep-water inlet around which much of the population of Washington lives, and which hosts the metropolis on its eastern shore. To the west is the **Olympic Peninsula**, whose mountains are home to rare elk and lush vegetation that merges into rainforest, and whose rustic beaches have remained pristine and protected. Not quite as rainy as the mountains to its north, the **southern coast** is flatter and more accessible but not as appealing. The nearest real attraction lies a few hours south, where you can marvel at the eye-opening volcanic scenery of **Mount St Helens**.

Dry and desolate, the sprawling prairie-plateau and flood-scoured "channeled scablands" that make up most of **eastern Washington** are a great, bleak expanse enlivened by the pleasant city of **Spokane** and the colossal **Grand Coulee Dam**. Otherwise you're only likely to come out here if you're travelling the Cascade loop, a memorable four-hundred-mile round-trip drive through the stunning **Cascade Mountains**.

Seattle

Located on the shore of sparkling Elliott Bay, with the snowy peak of Mount Rainier in the distance and a modern skyline of glass skyscrapers, **SEATTLE** has a famously picturesque setting, as well as a friendly charm, and plenty of fun coffeehouses, good restaurants and engaging clubs, making a lengthy visit worthwhile, especially during the summer.

Flooded out of its first location on Alki Point in what is now the suburb of West Seattle, the town in the 1850s shifted to Pioneer Square (south of the downtown core), renaming itself after the Native American **Chief Sealth**, who helped reduce violent tensions between whites and local tribes. As the surrounding forest was gradually felled and the lumber shipped out, Seattle grew slowly until the Klondike Gold Rush of 1897 put it firmly on the national map as a transport and commercial hub. From the beginning of the twentieth century, the **Boeing** corporation was crucial to the city's economic strength, and more recent success stories have included **Microsoft**, **Starbucks** and **Amazon.com**, the boom times interrupted only by the occasional dot-com bust or housing crunch.

Despite the changes wrought by Seattle's solid economy as the city grows into an international destination, its more established neighbourhoods remain distinctive, and it has a pleasantly down-to-earth ambience, whether you come here during peak season, or make like the locals and brave the steady rains (with many fewer visitors) from October to May.

Arrival and information

Seattle-Tacoma International Airport, or **Sea-Tac** (ⓣ206/787-5388 or 1-800/544-1965, ⓦwww.portseattle.org/seatac/), is fourteen miles south of downtown Seattle. **Gray Line Airport Express** bus (daily 6.30am–9pm every 30min; $11, $18 return ⓣ206/624-5077 or 1-800/426-7532, ⓦwww.graylineseattle.com) drops off at eight major hotels downtown. Shuttle Express has door-to-door service (daily 24hr; ⓣ425/981-7000 or 1-800/487-RIDE, ⓦwww.shuttleexpress.com) for $30–35 to downtown. **Taxis** charge $40 to go downtown and leave from the third floor of the parking garage. Much cheaper, and the best option overall, the recently opened **Link Light Rail** connects the airport with the central Westlake station downtown ($2.50; ⓣ206/398-5000, ⓦwww.soundtransit.org), a journey that takes less than 40 minutes.

Trains arrive at the Amtrak terminal in King Street Station at Third Avenue and Jackson Street (ⓣ206/382-4125 or 1-800/872-7245, ⓦwww.amtrak.com); just to the east along Jackson Street, the International District Station is a hub for frequent Metro buses going downtown (see below). Greyhound **buses** (ⓣ206/628-5526 or 1-800/231-2222, ⓦwww.greyhound.com) arrive at Eighth Avenue and Stewart Street, on the eastern edge of downtown, as well as at King Street Station. Located inside the Washington State Convention and Trade Center, Seventh Avenue at Pike Street (daily 9am–5pm; ⓣ206/461-5840, ⓦwww.visitseattle.org), the Seattle Convention and Visitors Bureau can provide directions, **information**, bus schedules and help with accommodation. The free official travellers' brochure, *Washington State Visitors' Guide* (call ⓣ1-800/544-1800 for a copy, or visit ⓦwww.experiencewa.com), has a comprehensive list of hotels, motels, B&Bs and the like.

City transport

Seattle's mass transit system, known as the **Metro** (ⓣ206/553-3000, ⓦmetro.kingcounty.gov), runs **bus** routes throughout the city, extending into the Eastside suburbs across Lake Washington. Customer service stations are available at King Street Station, 201 S Jackson St (Mon–Fri 8am–5pm), and at Westlake Station, near Fourth Avenue and Pike Street (Mon–Fri 9am–5.30pm); both offer maps and schedules and sell daily passes (you can purchase passes online at ⓦbuypass.kingcounty.gov). The Metro's best feature is its **Downtown Ride Free Area**, bounded by Battery Street, South Jackson Street, 6th Avenue and the waterfront. From 6am to 7pm daily, bus trips beginning and ending within this zone are free; cross out of the free zone and you pay the driver as you get off; come back in and you pay as you enter. Buses run weekdays from 5am or 5.30am to midnight or 1am, though some routes may end service as early as 7pm; typically, weekend hours start an hour or two later and end an hour earlier; fares are $2, or up to $2.75 during rush hour.

Washington State **ferries** (ⓣ206/464-6400 or 1-800/84-FERRY; ⓦwww.wsdot.wa.gov/ferries) dock at Pier 52 (Colman Dock) on downtown's waterfront. Other ferry routes connect at Fauntleroy in West Seattle, at 4829 SW Barton St. Gray Line

(☎206/626-5208, Ⓦwww.graylineseattle.com) organizes three-hour **bus tours** ($35) and two-hour **Segway tours** ($125) of the city, as well as combination **bus-and-boat tours** ($61; 6hr) on an Argosy sightseeing cruise (more boat tours at ☎206/623-1445, Ⓦwww.argosycruises.com).

Accommodation

When it comes to **hotels** in Seattle, the best, though most expensive, choices are downtown. Of better value are the city's **hostels** and **B&Bs**, the latter of which are abundant on Capitol Hill. Specialist **B&B agencies** include A Pacific Reservation Service (☎206/439-7677 or 1-800/684-2932, Ⓦwww.seattlebedandbreakfast.com) and Seattle Bed and Breakfast Association (☎206/547-1020 or 1-800/348-5630, Ⓦwww.lodginginseattle.com).

Ace 2423 First Ave ☎206/448-4721, Ⓦwww.theacehotel.com. A Seattle favourite with modern white minimalist rooms in the heart of Belltown. Hardwood floors, lofty ceilings and shared bathrooms for $99; double that price for more comfortable and well-appointed suites. 5

Alexis 1007 1st Ave, downtown ☎206/624-4844 or 1-800/426-7033, Ⓦwww.alexishotel.com. Plush decor at this top-notch hotel, as well as a spa and steam room, just south of Pike Place Market. Nearly half the rooms are suites which, at their largest, have luxurious touches like fireplaces and dining rooms. 8

Bacon Mansion 959 Broadway E, Capitol Hill ☎206/329-1864 or 1-800/240-1864, Ⓦwww.baconmansion.com. Eleven elegant rooms and suites in a grand 1909 Tudor Revival structure. Well decorated if a bit small, the least expensive rooms are cheap for the area, although the price doubles at the high end. Two-night minimum stay on summer weekends. 5

Green Tortoise 105 Pike St, downtown ☎206/340-1222, Ⓦwww.greentortoise.net. Conveniently located hostel right across from Pike Place Market, with ($29–33) steeping from four to eight and some private doubles ($54–56). Free breakfast, wi-fi and pick-ups at Amtrak, Greyhound or ferries; also summer walking tours of the city. 1

Hotel Andra 2000 Fourth Ave ☎206/448-8600 or 1-877/448-8600, Ⓦwww.hotelandra.com. An intimate boutique hotel in the Belltown neighbourhood, with chic, modern units featuring designer furnishings – more than half of them suites. Gym, restaurant and wi-fi, too. 8

Hotel Max 620 Stewart St ☎206/441-4200 or 1-800/426-0670, Ⓦwww.hotelmaxseattle.com. Located in a renovated 1920s building a block from the monorail, a stylish hotel whose smallish rooms are kitted out with vaguely aesthetic themes – with original art in each room. 7

Hotel Vintage Park 1100 Fifth Ave ☎206/624-8000, Ⓦwww.hotelvintagepark.com. Stylish boutique hotel with rooms themed around wine-drinking and vineyards; amenities may include fireplaces, jacuzzis, flat-screen TVs, stereos and, of course, nightly tastings of vino. 7

Inn at the Market 86 Pine St ☎1-800/446-4484, Ⓦwww.innatthemarket.com. If you want close proximity to Pike Place Market, this top-notch boutique spot is a good choice for its fine views of the market, city or bay, and its tasteful decor, free wi-fi and rooftop deck. 8

Monaco 1101 4th Ave, downtown ☎206/621-1770 or 1-800/715-6513, Ⓦwww.monaco-seattle.com. Luxurious boutique hotel with designer furnishings, plus a striking lobby, gym and elegant suites with CD players and flat-screen TVs – some with jacuzzis, too. 8

Pan Pacific 2125 Terry Ave ☎206/264-8111, Ⓦwww.panpacific.com. Affordable luxury with stylish boutique appointments in a smart modern tower, offering in-room HDTVs and free wi-fi, and a central location north of Belltown. 7

Pensione Nichols 1923 1st Ave, Belltown ☎206/441-7125, Ⓦwww.pensionenichols.com. Classy little B&B with small but clean rooms, shared baths and simple, tasteful decor in a classic 1904 building (though lacking an elevator). Only $99 for single travellers; add $31 for another person. Two-night minimum during summer. 5

Shafer-Baillie Mansion 907 14th Ave E, Capitol Hill ☎1-800/985-4654, Ⓦsbmansion.com. Oak-panelled 1914 Tudor Revival mansion-turned-B&B that offers three rooms and two suites (plus three units in a subdivided ballroom) with antique tubs and refrigerators, plus DVD players and flat-screen TVs. 6

Sorrento 900 Madison St, First Hill ☎206/622-4400 or 1-800/426-1265, Ⓦwww.hotelsorrento.com. Modern edifice with a European flair, stylish decor, and posh on-site restaurant, on the east side of I-5 by downtown. The regal exterior surrounds a circular courtyard with palm trees, and some units have views of Puget Sound. 8

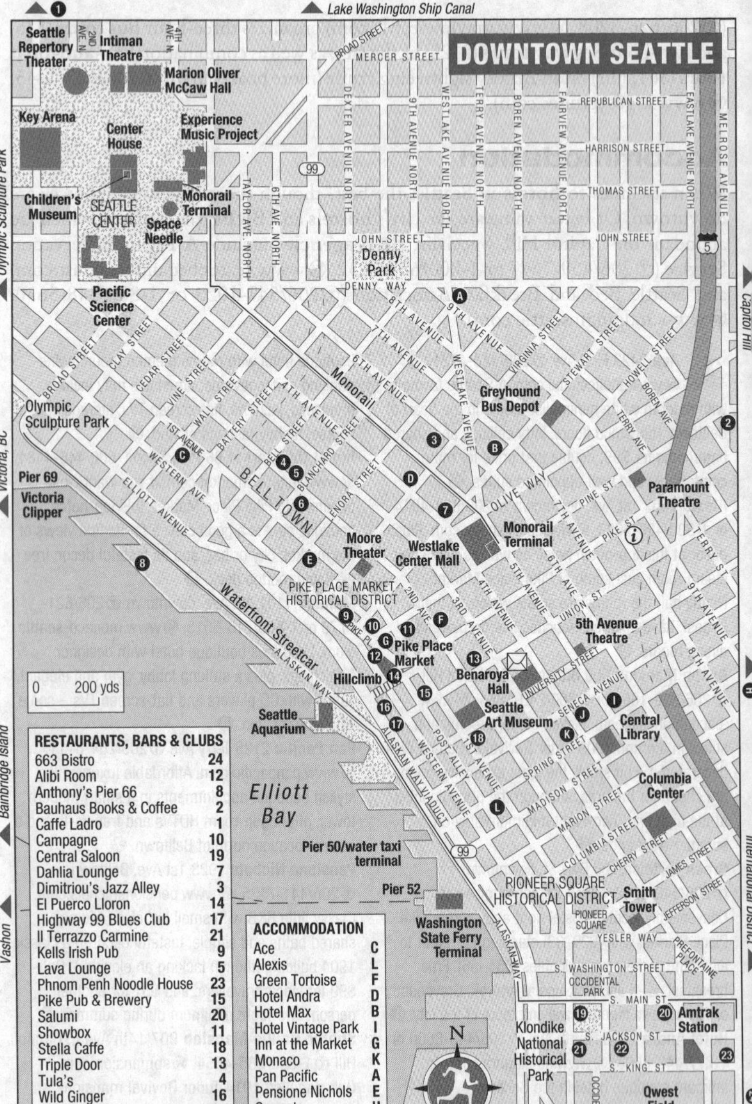

University Inn 4140 Roosevelt Way NE, University District ⓣ 206/632-5055 or 1-800/733-3855, ⓦ www.universityinnseattle.com. Business-oriented hotel close to the University of Washington. Some rooms have kitchens, all have complimentary breakfast; there's also a pool and spa and free wi-fi. 6

W Seattle 1112 4th Ave, downtown ⓣ 206/264-6000, ⓦ www.whotels.com. Stylish modern tower with a staff of beautiful people and smart rooms in high style. An even better draw is the ambience: there's a chic lobby bar with often packed "cocktail couches". 8

The City

Downtown Seattle sits alongside the sweeping curve of Elliott Bay just off the I-5 freeway. Though it offers plenty of attractions, none is more popular than **Pike Place Market** and its engaging array of produce stalls and cafés. Further south, the nineteenth-century Victorian townsite of **Pioneer Square** is lined with funky bars and clubs, while at the **Seattle Center** in the north, the **Space Needle** presides over museums and carnival rides, as well as the **Experience Music Project**. Several outlying districts are often livelier than downtown: **Capitol Hill**'s cafés and bars are the heart of the city's hipster and gay scene, and the **University District** is a student area with inexpensive cafés and up-tempo nightlife.

Pike Place Market and the Seattle Art Museum

Centrally located at Pike Street and First Avenue, **Pike Place Market** (daily Mon–Sat 10am–6pm, Sun 11am–5pm; ⓣ206/682-7453, ⓦwww.pikeplacemarket.org) began in the early twentieth century and is the oldest continuously working public market in the US. Now undergoing an extensive, multi-year renovation (while still open to the public), it comprises thirteen buildings on a triangular lot covering nine acres, holding three hundred produce and fish vendors, bakeries, craft stalls and small retailers. Fishmongers hurl the catch of the day back and forth, street entertainers play to rapt crowds, the aroma of organic coffee drifts from cafés, and countless stalls offer piles of lobsters, crabs, salmon, vegetables, fruit and flowers. Near the entrance, a favourite meeting place is the **brass pig** – a large, actual piggy bank, with receipts going to charity. Since the market is also threaded with many worthwhile restaurants, bars and live music venues, you might find yourself here after-hours, even if you have no interest in buying salmon or apples during the day.

Close to Pike Place Market at 1300 First Ave, the **Seattle Art Museum** (Wed & Sat–Sun 10am–5pm, Thurs & Fri till 9pm; $15, free first Thurs of month; ⓣ206/654-3100, ⓦwww.seattleartmuseum.org), is one of the top cultural institutions in the Pacific Northwest, occupying four floors of a corporate tower. Highlights include the **Art Ladder**, a stairway featuring numerous large-scale installation and sculptural pieces; important monumental **nineteenth-century American** works by landscape masters Frederic Church and Albert Bierstadt; and notable **twentieth-century works** like Andy Warhol's *Double Elvis*, Bruce Nauman's neon wall-piece *Double Poke in the Eye II* and Roy Lichtenstein's cartoonish *Study for Vicki!*. However, it's best for its ethnic art, such as **Native American** totem poles, rattles and canoes, along with colourful headdresses, masks, baskets and woven fabrics; and contemporary and traditional **African art**, with surprising pieces like *Mercedes-Benz Shaped Coffin* by Ghana's Kane Kwei, a mix of tradition and postmodernism.

The Business District

Between Second and Seventh avenues, most of downtown is given over to the steel-and-glass office towers of Seattle's **Business District**. Here, the multistorey **Westlake Center** mall, 400 Pine St (Mon–Sat 10am–8pm, Sun 11am–6pm), is notable for being the southern terminus of the 1.3-mile **monorail** (Sun–Thurs 8am–8pm, Fri–Sat 9am–11pm; return fare $4, kids $1.50; ⓦwww.seattlemonorail.com), a holdover from the 1962 Seattle World's Fair that connects to the Seattle Center and provides the city with one of its prime emblems. The mall is also a transit hub that hosts Link Light Rail trains from Sea-Tac (see p.950). Further south, the darkly looming **Columbia Center**, 701 Fifth Ave, has three concave walls that give the structure an oddly curving silhouette. At nearly a thousand feet high, it's the second tallest building west of the Mississippi River. Head to the 73rd-floor **observation deck** (Mon–Fri 8.30am–4.30pm; $5, kids $3) for a predictably good panoramic view.

Just north, the **Central Library**, 1000 Fourth Ave (Mon–Thurs 10am–8pm, Fri–Sat till 6pm, Sun noon–6pm; ⓣ206/386-4636, ⓦwww.spl.org), is a colossal Rem Koolhaas creation that resembles few other libraries in America, with a facade composed of brilliantly reflective glass panels, unexpected angles and cantilevered storeys looming above. Other curious features are the **Spiral**, with its myriad ramps, escalators and cramped geometry, and conference rooms linked by an eerie, blood-red **tunnel** that more closely resembles something out of *The Shining* than it does a public library.

The waterfront

West from Pike Place Market, stairs in the complex lead down to the steep staircase of the **Hillclimb**, heading to the **waterfront** below. Almost opposite the stairway, **Pier 59**, an old wooden jetty that once served tall ships, now houses the **Seattle Aquarium** (daily 9.30am–5pm; $17, kids $11; ⓣ206/386-4300, ⓦwww.seattleaquarium.org), which has recently undergone a considerable expansion to showcase its hundreds of species of fish, birds, plants and mammals. A 400,000-gallon underwater dome recreates life in Puget Sound, its highlights including black-tip sharks; electric eels; octopuses; a functional salmon hatchery and fish ladder, which displays the life cycle of the threatened Pacific salmon.

On the opposite end of the waterfront, at 2901 Western Ave, the 8.5-acre **Olympic Sculpture Park** (daily 7am–8pm; free; ⓦwww.seattleartmuseum.org/visit/osp) is a showpiece for contemporary sculpture set around a zigzagging pathway that passes over road and railway before leading down to the water's edge. On the way are notable items such as Alexander Calder's 39ft tall *Eagle*, a jagged array of red steel arcs; Louise Bourgeois' disembodied black-granite *Eye Benches*; Richard Serra's undulating rusty-steel *Wake* slabs; and a Claes Oldenburg typewriter eraser, among other arch-modern pieces – but the greatest piece of sculpture may be the park itself, a bravura example of landscape art.

Pioneer Square

A few blocks inland from the ferry terminal, **Pioneer Square** is Seattle's oldest district, rich with appealing bookshops and galleries amid the old red-brick and wrought-iron buildings. There are also a number of rough-around-the-edges clubs and bars, and more than a few homeless people adding to the diverse environs.

The city's seamy past is on display in a 90-minute **Underground Tour**, 608 First Ave (hours vary, often daily on the hour 11am–5pm; $15, kids $7; ⓣ206/682-4646, ⓦwww.undergroundtour.com), which details how, after a disastrous 1889 fire, this area was rebuilt with the street level raised by one storey, so what used to be storefronts are now underground, linked by subterranean passageways. One long block east, the 1914 white-terracotta **Smith Tower**, 506 Second Ave, was the city's first skyscraper, as well as its longtime visual icon well before the 1960s arrival of the Space Needle. These days, it's best for the prime views from its 35th-floor **observation deck** (April–Oct daily 10am–dusk, rest of year Sat & Sun till–4pm; $7.50; ⓦwww.smithtower.com).

A few blocks south at 117 S Main St, **Klondike Gold Rush National Historical Park** (daily 9am–5pm; free; ⓦwww.nps.gov/klse) houses a small museum recalling the days when Seattle was the gateway to Alaskan gold, and prospectors streamed in and traders – and con artists – made their fortunes. In the streets around, highbrow culture finds a place on the first Thursday of the month at the **Gallery Walk** (6–8pm; free), while **Art in the Park** (3–9pm; free) features a broad range of visual and performance-art pieces in nearby Occidental Park.

Seattle Center

North of downtown, the **Seattle Center** (ⓦwww.seattlecenter.com) dates from the 1962 Seattle World's Fair and since then the 74-acre complex has become the city's cultural hub, the site of museums, sporting events, concerts and festivals. The **monorail** from Westlake Center (see p.953) drops you close to the **Space Needle**, the Space Age-modernist city icon, which is most appealing at night when it's lit up. The panoramic view from the observation deck is always a major draw (Mon–Thurs 10am–9.30pm, Fri & Sat till 10.30pm, Sun 9.30am–9.30pm; $17, two trips in 24hr $22; ⓦwww.spaceneedle.com).

Throughout the complex, there are numerous performing-arts and cultural venues (see "Performing Arts", p.959, for a rundown). Otherwise, the most prominent sights are the **Pacific Science Center** 200 2nd Ave N (Mon–Fri 10am–5pm, Sat & Sun till 6pm; $14, kids $9; ⓣ206/443-2001, ⓦwww.pacsci.org); which is full of science-related exhibits for children, and includes a planetarium and IMAX theatre; the **Children's Museum**, in the Center House complex (Mon–Fri 10am–5pm, Sat & Sun till 6pm; $7.50; ⓦwww.thechildrensmuseum.org), offering attractions like an artificial mountain forest, where kids crawl through logs or simulate a rock climb; and the Frank Gehry-designed **Experience Music Project**, 325 5th Ave N (daily 10am–7pm, winter closes 5pm; $15, kids $12; ⓦwww.empsfm.org), a giant burst of coloured aluminium – into which the monorail passes – that houses a giant collection of rock memorabilia divided up into exhibits on different phases of popular music history, as well as rotating exhibits on subjects from folk rock to hip-hop.

Capitol Hill and around

A fifteen-minute bus ride east of downtown takes you to the mildly counterculture flavoured **Capitol Hill**, whose **Broadway** axis offers a solid choice for dining, buying music, clubbing and drinking coffee from espresso carts. On the northern end of Broadway, between E Roy Street and E Highland Drive, the **Harvard-Belmont Historic District**, is rich with huge Neoclassical mansions and sprawling period-revival homes; for a tour, contact the Seattle Architectural Foundation ($15; ⓣ206/667-9184, ⓦwww.seattlearchitecture.org). East of Broadway from Twelfth to Ninth avenues, the **Pike/Pine Corridor** is filled with all-night coffeehouses, live music venues and trendy bars. Near its southern end, the **Frye Art Museum**, 704 Terry Ave (Tues–Sat 10am–5pm, Sun noon–5pm, Thurs 8pm; free; ⓣ206/622-9250, ⓦfryemuseum.org), holds works by Winslow Homer, John Singer Sargent and Thomas Eakins, as well as a fine selection of the **Munich school**, focusing on the Belle Epoque between 1870 and 1900. Recent exhibits have broadened the museum's focus to include more contemporary work, including multimedia, performance and installation art.

The northern end of Capitol Hill is highlighted by **Volunteer Park** 1247 15th Ave (daily 6am–11pm), where you'll find the 1912 **Conservatory**'s hothouses, home to flowers, shrubs and orchids from jungle, desert and rainforest habitatsy (Tues–Sun 10am–4pm, summer till 6pm; free; ⓣ206/322-4112), as well as the old **Water Tower** that provides a free, sweeping view of Seattle, albeit through wire mesh. Also located within the park is the **Seattle Asian Art Museum** (Wed–Sun 10am–5pm, Thurs till 9pm; $7; ⓣ206/654-3100, ⓦwww.seattleartmusem.org), home to one of the most extensive collections of Asian art in the US, encompassing Japanese, Korean, Vietnamese, Chinese and Southeast Asian art, spread across many centuries and dynasties, and highlighted by meticulously crafted Japanese landscape scrolls and the grim, early Chinese statues of tomb guardians, court attendants and warriors.

Ten blocks east, on the other side of Capitol Hill, **Washington Park Arboretum** (daily dawn–dusk; free; ⓣ206/543-8800) is a lush showcase for indigenous vegetation, with many charming footpaths and regional trees, plus the immaculately designed **Japanese Gardens**, where banks of pink flowers sit beside neat little pools with brightly coloured carp (hours vary, often daily 10am–7pm; $5).

The University District

Across the Lake Washington Ship Canal from Washington Park, the **University District**, or the "U" District, is a busy hodgepodge of coffeehouses, cinemas and boutiques catering to the University of Washington's 43,000 students. The area centres on University Way, known as **"The Ave"**, and is lined with inexpensive ethnic restaurants and a handful of decent book and record stores.

On campus, the **Henry Art Gallery**, 15th Avenue NE and NE 41st Street (Thurs & Fri 11am–9pm, Sat & Sun till 4pm; $10, free for students with ID; Ⓦwww.henryart.org), houses American and European paintings and photography from the last two centuries, and imaginative contemporary exhibits, while the **Burke Memorial Museum**, 17th Ave NE and NE 45th St (daily 10am–5pm; $9.50; Ⓦwww.washington.edu/burkemuseum), holds the US's largest collection of Native American art and artefacts west of the Mississippi – and presents selections from its huge collection of 2.75 million fossils and Ice Age skeletons, including the remains of a 12,000-year-old sloth.

Along the Lake Washington Ship Canal

As with the "U" District, Seattle's northern neighbourhoods are divided from the rest of town by the **Lake Washington Ship Canal**, which connects Lake Union with Elliott Bay to the west and Lake Washington to the east. On the north shore of Lake Union, **Gas Works Park**, 2101 N Northlake Way (daily 4am–11.30pm; free), is a former gas plant turned postmodern park, where children now play on grassy hills that were once slag heaps amid decaying, graffiti-covered machines. Further west, a procession of boats passes through the **Hiram M. Chittenden Locks** (daily 7am–9pm; free; Ⓣ206/783-7059), and a **fish ladder** is laid out with viewing windows, through which you can see enormous fish leaping up). On the northern side of Salmon Bay, blue-collar **Ballard** appeals for its historic **Ballard Avenue**, between 17th and 22nd avenues NW, home to galleries, bars and restaurants behind the stately facades of hundred-year-old buildings.

Fremont and the Woodland Park Zoo

East of Ballard, **Fremont** is a self-consciously hip area with a spate of boutiques, bookshops and cafés, with its hub around Fremont Avenue N from N 34th to N 37th streets. Just off N 34th Street, the **Fremont Sunday Market** (summer 10am–5pm, rest of year till 4pm; free; Ⓦwww.fremontmarket.com) hosts 150 vendors of secondhand jewellery, furniture, clothing, trinkets and music. Fremont's other main draws are its quirky **public artworks**, most notably the **Fremont Troll** lurking under the Aurora Bridge, 36th St and Aurora Ave, emerging from the gloom with an actual VW Bug in its clutches, and, at the triangular corner of N 36th Street and Fremont Place, a colossal, Slovakia-built statue of **Vladimir Lenin** thrusting forth toward passing motorists, surrounded by blocky flames. The **Fremont Fair & Solstice Parade** (Ⓣ206/297-6801, Ⓦwww.fremontfair.org), in mid-June, is Seattle's jolliest celebration, with hundreds of food stalls and arts vendors, plus a parade of naked bicyclists and human-powered floats, followed by a pageant at the end of the route in Gasworks Park.

A bit further north, Aurora Avenue leads toward the **Woodland Park Zoo**, N 55th St and Phinney Ave N (daily 9.30am–4pm, summer till 6pm; summer $16.50, rest of year $11; Ⓦwww.zoo.org), a sleek facility whose spacious layout and botanical garden-quality trees and plants make it attractive to anyone with a love of nature. Most of the engaging exhibits are arranged to reflect different climates and terrains – Northern Trail, Tropical Asia, Tropical Forest, Temperate Forest and so on.

The Museum of Flight

The biggest of Seattle's museums, the **Museum of Flight**, a twenty-minute bus ride (#124 or #174) south of downtown at 9404 E Marginal Way (daily 10am–5pm; $15, kids $8; ⓦwww.museumofflight.org), is partly housed in the restored 1909 **"Red Barn"** that was the original Boeing manufacturing plant, now displaying relics from the early days of flight. Elsewhere, the **Great Gallery** features more than fifty full-sized aeroplanes, from ancient prototypes to a replica of John Glenn's 1962 Mercury space capsule, to an SR-71 Blackbird spy plane, which once flew 80,000ft above the jungles of Vietnam. More icons are on display outside in the museum's expansive **Airpark** (daily 11am–3.30pm, summer till 4.30pm; free with museum admission), which has a walk-in collection of planes that include the 727, 737 and 747, as well as, a Concorde and an original model of Air Force One.

Boeing Tour Center

Thirty miles north of Seattle, the last major suburb along I-5, **Everett**, is home to the manufacturing plant for **Boeing**, site of the popular **Boeing Tour Center**, whose entrance is on Hwy 526, a few miles west of Exit 189 off I-5 (daily tours 8.30am–5.30pm; $15.50 for same-day tickets, $18 in advance; tickets at ⓣ1-800/464-1476, ⓦwww.futureofflight.org). The 98-acre **factory** is listed in the *Guinness Book of World Records* as the largest building in the world by volume (472 million cubic feet). Overhead platforms afford views of much of the floor space, cluttered by new planes in various phases of gestation, and the tour concludes with a bus ride on the "flight line", where finished models are tested.

Eating

Seattle has many fine **restaurants**, from the funky diners of Capitol Hill and ethnic restaurants of the University District to the delicious seafood of Pike Place Market. Moreover, local **coffeehouses** host an engaging cultural scene, and are inexpensive choices for whiling away the time or surfing the internet). Corporate giant *Starbucks* started here in the early 1970s (in an extant location in the Pike Place Market), though you're better off sampling a local brew that you can't find in your hometown mini-mall. Better yet, check out one of the 200-plus **espresso carts** scattered about town, each colourfully styled and uniquely designed.

Restaurants and cafés

The 5 Spot 1502 Queen Anne Ave N, north of Seattle Center ⓣ206/285-SPOT. Southern-style diner whose affordable meals may include red beans & rice, fried chicken dipped in buttermilk and honey, and brisket with Coca-Cola marinade. Open daily 'til midnight.

663 Bistro 663 S Weller St, south of Pioneer Square ⓣ206/667-8760. Located in Seattle's Chinatown (aka "International District") this is among the best Asian diners in the area, chock-full of favourites such as barbequed pork, roasted duck, curry seafood and lots of cheap noodles.

Anthony's Pier 66 2201 Alaskan Way ⓣ206/448-6688. Waterfront restaurant with expensive seafood – such as tuna, crab, octopus and salmon fillets – but best for its excellent bayside views.

Café Flora 2901 E Madison St, Capitol Hill ⓣ206/325-9100. One of the city's best vegetarian restaurants, attracting even devout carnivores for its creative soups, salads and entrees, like yam fries and white-bean pizza, for moderate prices.

Campagne 1600 Post Alley, downtown ⓣ206/728-2800. Superb French cooking near the Pike Place Market, with excellent beef entrees, steak tartare, squab and the ever-tasty *pommes* *frites*, fried in duck fat. A less expensive branch, *Café Campagne*, can be found downstairs.

Canlis 2576 Aurora Ave N, south of Fremont ⓣ206/283-3313. Delicious, memorable spot for nouveau Northwest cuisine, highlighted by wild-nettle pasta, Kobe tenderloin and Maine lobster – for some of the highest prices in town.

Dahlia Lounge 2001 4th Ave, Belltown ⓣ206/682-4142. Upmarket restaurant best known for its seafood, featuring delicious main courses like five-spice duck and roasted saddle of lamb. If you can't afford to drop a wad on dinner, try the adjoining, excellent *Dahlia Bakery*.

Dick's Drive-In 115 Broadway Ave E, Capitol Hill ⓣ206/323-1300. Long-standing fast-food institution serving up sloppy but serviceable burgers, rich shakes and fries with just the right crunch. One of six citywide locations, all open daily until 2am.

El Puerco Lloron 1501 Western Ave ⓣ206/624-0541. "The Crying Pig", a rare authentic Mexican restaurant in Seattle – including traditional decor – serving affordable tamales, tostadas and excellent *chiles rellenos*. Located on the Hillclimb behind the market.

Il Terrazzo Carmine 411 First Ave S, Pioneer Square ⓣ206/467-7797. The height of Italian chic in the city, with splendid risotto, osso bucco, squid, rack of lamb, gnocchi and a fine range of pastas, for steep prices.

Monsoon 615 19th Ave E, Capitol Hill ⓣ206/325-2111. Upper-end pan-Asian restaurant that's popular for delicious, though rotating, items like drunken chicken, flat-iron steak with ginger, Idaho catfish and prawn salad.

Phnom Penh Noodle House 660 S King St, south of Pioneer Square ⓣ206/748-9825. Like the name says, an honest-to-God Cambodian noodle joint that doles out rich helpings of noodles in various sauces, as well as traditional favourites like spicy soups and fishcakes.

Piecora's 1401 E Madison St, Capitol Hill ⓣ206/322-9411. One of the better pizza parlours in a city not known for its pizza, leaning toward the New York style with rich, flavourful and gooey pizzas served in a friendly neighbourhood environment.

Salumi 309 Third Ave S, Pioneer Square ⓣ206/621-8772. Old-fashioned sausages served on delicious home-made bread, featuring oxtail, prosciutto, lamb and assorted hog parts. Open Tues–Fri 11am–4pm, so expect long waits during peak hours.

Wild Ginger 1401 Third Ave, downtown ⓣ206/623-4450. Upmarket restaurant with fiery dishes from Southeast Asia, India and China. Try the Bangkok Boar, fragrant duck, Dungeness crab or Angkor Wat chicken.

Zo 2137 Second Ave, Belltown ⓣ206/256-2060. Somewhat pricey Northwest cuisine eatery that appeals for its range of inventive entrees such as wild boar bolognese, veal sweetbreads, lamb loin and other enterprising choices.

Coffeehouses

Bauhaus Books & Coffee 301 E Pine St, Capitol Hill ⓣ206/625-1600. A stylish hangout for the hipster set with large tables, a used-book section – focusing on art and architecture volumes – and good coffee and tea.

Caffè Ladro 600 Queen Anne Ave N ⓣ206/282-1549. Near the Seattle Center, this "coffee thief" has an arty flair, with a range of light meals (and some veggie options) in addition to hearty coffees that many swear by. Seven other citywide branches.

Online Coffee Company 1720 E Olive Way, Capitol Hill ⓣ206/328-3731. Spacious and relaxed internet café with coffee, beer, wine, and baked goods — plus free wi-fi. The outside patio has a view of Puget Sound. Open until 1am. Also downtown at 1111 First Ave, ⓣ206/381-1911.

Stella Caffe 1224 First Ave, downtown ⓣ206/624-1299. Seattle coffee bars come in all styles, and this one's devoted to matching the top-notch quality of Italian espresso. Overall, it does a good job at making you forget just how far away Rome is.

Vivace Espresso 532 Broadway E, Capitol Hill ⓣ206/860-2722. A fine haunt for serious java-drinkers and truly run by "espresso roasting and preparation specialists"; their street café at 321 Broadway E is the prime people-watching perch in the area.

Zeitgeist Coffee 171 S Jackson St ⓣ206/583-0497. Mostly coffee, some sandwiches and pastries, and copious modern art are found at this pleasant haunt in the heart of Pioneer Square's gallery scene.

Drinking and nightlife

Seattle's **nightlife** revolves around its pounding **live music** venues and convivial **bars**, which pour an excellent selection of microbrewed beers. The tavern scene is at its most frenetic in **Pioneer Square**, but other prime turf for hearing music can be found in **Capitol Hill** and, here and there, downtown and Belltown.

Bars and clubs

Alibi Room 85 Pike St ⓣ206/623-3180. Swanky bar tucked in an alley behind the Pike Street Market. Excellent food in café-type rooms upstairs, DJs spinning tunes on the dancefloor downstairs and a happy hour that starts in the middle of the afternoon.

Central Saloon 207 First Ave S, Pioneer Square ⓣ206/622-0209. Seattle's oldest (dive) saloon was established in 1892, and is consistently crowded, filled with a mix of slumming tourists and slumming scenesters. Live music ranges from alt-rock to blues and metal.

Comet Tavern 922 E Pike St, Capitol Hill ⓣ206/323-9853. The oldest bar on Capitol Hill and a grunge institution – not surprisingly a smoky dive and a rocker's hangout, too, with regular shows by hard-rockers and head-bangers.

Elysian Brewing 1221 E Pike St, Capitol Hill ⓣ206/860-1920. Brewpub of one of the best local microbreweries, with flavourful oddities like the Immortal IPA, Zepyrus Pilsner and Dragonstooth Stout. The menu is pretty good, too, including sandwiches and tacos.

Kells Irish Pub 1916 Post Alley, Pike Place Market ⓣ206/728-1916. Spirited Irish bar and restaurant in a central location, with patio seating and performances by Irish-oriented folk and rock groups. Crowd is mostly tourists and business-district types.

Lava Lounge 2226 2nd Ave, Belltown ⓣ206/441-5660. 1950s lounge-revival kitsch, with a tiki-inspired decor and eclectic live music and DJs at night, happy hour from 3 to 7pm, and shuffleboard to pass the time.

Linda's Tavern 707 E Pine St, Capitol Hill ⓣ206/325-1220. Good old tub-thumping watering hole that's popular for its jukebox stocked with classics and indie rock, and quintessential Seattle hedonist vibe.

Pike Pub & Brewery 1415 1st Ave, downtown ⓣ206/622-6044. Small craft brewery serving its own beers, as well as numerous bottled brands; however, only adequate food and a touristy atmosphere (near Pike Place Market).

Music venues

Dimitriou's Jazz Alley 2033 6th Ave, Belltown ⓣ206/441-9729. Best big-name jazz spot in town, showcasing international acts across a range of styles, as well as up-and-coming brilliants. Tickets start around $20.

Highway 99 Blues Club 1414 Alaskan Way, downtown ⓣ206/382-2171. Rootsy joint showcasing regional and national performers in blues, rockabilly and R&B, in a fun, convivial atmosphere with a dancefloor.

Moore Theater 1932 2nd Ave, Belltown ⓣ206/467-5510. This 1907 former vaudeville auditorium sometimes hosts exciting up-and-coming bands, but more often you'll find established names in pop and rock, along with comedians, dancers, kids' shows and so on.

Neumo's 925 E Pike St, Capitol Hill ⓣ206/709-9467. A hard-thrashing venue that has clawed its way up (almost) to the top of the rawk heap. The bands are of the punk, goth, rock and alt-anything variety, and the crowd will mosh you into oblivion if you let them.

Showbox 1426 1st Ave, downtown ⓣ206/628-3151. This thousand-person hall across from Pike Place Market is the best place to catch touring acts that have yet to make the bigger arenas, along with well-regarded regional bands, usually with an indie slant.

Sunset Tavern 5433 Ballard Ave NW, Ballard ⓣ206/784-4880. Along with being a colourful bar and karaoke spot, the *Sunset's* also a good venue for catching aggressive young rockers and various eclectic acts in cheap nightly performances.

Tractor Tavern 5213 Ballard Ave NW, Ballard ⓣ206/789-3599. Solid joint in Ballard with great character, stuffed with a mix of hipsters and burnouts, good microbrewed beers and roots music of all kinds – zydeco, Irish, blues, bluegrass, alt-country.

Triple Door 216 Union St, downtown ⓣ206/838-4333. Attractive complex that's good for folk, roots, alt-country and blues; the Mainstage has major players and up-and-comers, while the Musicquarium mixes things up with DJs and more experimental fare – it's also free.

Tula's 2214 2nd Ave, Belltown ⓣ206/443-4221. Jazz of all stripes every evening, mostly from regional unknowns, with regular live jams.

Performing arts and festivals

Many of Seattle's **performing arts** venues are based around the Seattle Center; the most prominent of these is **Marion Oliver McCaw Hall**, a sleek, modern facility that hosts the **Seattle Opera** (ⓣ206/389-7676, ⓦwww.seattleopera.org). In the same complex, **Pacific Northwest Ballet** (ⓣ206/441-2424, ⓦwww.pnb.org) puts on around ten programmes from September to June. Away from Seattle Center, **Seattle Symphony Orchestra** performs downtown in the glass-walled

Day-trips to Bainbridge and Vashon islands

For a brief escape from Seattle, the **ferry ride** across Elliott Bay to **Bainbridge Island** provides a relaxing, scenic experience. Washington State Ferries leave from Pier 52 (hourly 5.30am–1.35am; foot passengers $6.90 (collected westbound only in peak season); vehicle and driver $11.85 non-peak, $14.85 peak season; ⓣ206/464-6400 or 1-800/84-FERRY, ⓦwww.wsdot.wa.gov/ferries) for the 35-minute trip to the island, a green and rural spot occupying less than fifty square miles. The island's only conventional attraction, the **Bloedel Reserve**, 7571 NE Dolphin Drive, off the Agatewood Road exit of Hwy-305 (Wed–Sun 10am–4pm; $12; ⓣ206/842-7631, ⓦwww.bloedelreserve.org), is a conservatory containing nearly 150 acres of gardens, ponds, meadows and wildlife habitats. If you want to pitch a tent on the island, there's **camping** at the far end in Fay Bainbridge State Park ($14–28; ⓣ206/842-3931, ⓦwww.parks.wa.gov). Area accommodation is limited to **B&Bs**, details of which can be obtained from the **visitor centre** in the town of **WINSLOW**, 395 Winslow Way E (ⓣ206/842-3700, ⓦwww.bainbridgechamber.com). Decent choices for eating in Winslow are the *Harbour Public House*, 231 Parfitt Way SW (ⓣ206/842-0969), for its seafood, salads, burgers and microbrews and *Café Nola*, 101 Winslow Way (ⓣ206/842-3822), for its tasty pastries and breakfasts, and agreeable Sunday brunch.

Other routes from Seattle and West Seattle make the short trip to easy-going, bicycle-friendly **Vashon Island**. King County **water taxis** from downtown Seattle's Pier 50 are passenger-only (Mon–Fri 5.40–7.40am & 4.30–6.30pm; 35min trip; $4.50; ⓣ206/684-1551), while trips from the West Seattle Fauntleroy terminal are by ferry and also for vehicles (daily 5.20am–2am; 20min; foot passengers $4.45, vehicle and driver $15.20, $19 peak season). A few nice beaches lie along the coast of this island, where the community of **VASHON** is little more than a simple hamlet. The *AYH Ranch Hostel*, 12119 SW Cove Rd (May–Sept; ⓣ206/463-2592, ⓦwww.vashonhostel.com; ❸), six miles from the Seattle–Vashon ferry dock at the north end of the island, offers log-cabin dorm beds for $23, or private rooms (❸). There are also a number of good **B&Bs**, among them *Artist's Studio Loft,* 16592 91st Ave SW (ⓣ206/463-2583, ⓦwww.asl-bnb.com; ❺), and the *Swallow's Nest Guest Cottages*, 6030 SW 248th St (ⓣ206/463-2646, ⓦwww.vashonislandcottages.com; ❺).

Benaroya Concert Hall, 3rd and Union streets (ⓣ206/215-4747, ⓦwww.seattlesymphony.org).

For **theatre**, Seattle's longest-established small troupe is the **Seattle Repertory Company** (ⓣ206/443-2222, ⓦwww.seattlerep.org) at the Seattle Center, while next door, the **Intiman Theater** (ⓣ206/269-1900, ⓦwww.intiman.org) performs classics and premieres of innovative works. A bit to the north at 100 W Roy St, **On the Boards** presents modern **dance** performances (ⓣ206/217-9888, ⓦwww.ontheboards.org), while big-name musicals open downtown at the **Fifth Avenue Theatre**, 1308 5th Ave (ⓣ206/625-1900, ⓦwww.5thavenue.org), or the **Paramount**, 911 Pine St (ⓣ206/682-1414, ⓦwww.stgpresents.org), a large 1928 movie palace hosting lectures, films, comedians, concerts and more.

Seattle's biggest events are **Bumbershoot**, hosting hundreds of artists on dozens of stages around town on Labor Day weekend (ⓣ206/281-7788, ⓦwww.bumbershoot.org), and the **Northwest Folklife Festival** (ⓣ206/684-7300, ⓦwww.nwfolklife.org), a Memorial Day event at the Seattle Center drawing folk musicians from around the world. In late May and early June, the Seattle **International Film Festival** (ⓣ206/464-5830, ⓦwww.siff.net) centres on classic moviehouses in Capitol Hill, and in July and early August, **Seafair** (ⓣ206/728-0123, ⓦwww.seafair.com), is a colourful celebration held all over town with airplane spectacles, hydroplane events and milk-carton boat races.

For **listings**, the free *Seattle Weekly* (Ⓦwww.seattleweekly.com) and *The Stranger* (Ⓦwww.thestranger.com) are good for reviews of theatre, cinema and the arts, as is the Friday edition of the *Seattle Times* newspaper (Ⓦwww.seattletimes.com).

Puget Sound

The grand waterway of **Puget Sound** hooks far into western Washington, its array of islands and peninsulas the dramatic setting for passing yachts, oceangoing ships, fishing trawlers and even nuclear submarines. The southern edge of the Sound is strongly urban, where the formerly industrial **Tacoma** and the small state capital of **Olympia** are worthwhile stopovers, while the waterway itself surrounds many appealing mountains, forests and lakes. Popular escapes include rural **Whidbey Island** and the beautiful **San Juan Islands** further north.

Tacoma

Sitting on the Seattle–Portland axis of I-5, **TACOMA** is an old industrial town that has somewhat transformed itself with new museums, theatres and restaurants. Its centrepiece is the massive blue-and-white **Tacoma Dome**, a major concert venue just off the freeway (Ⓣ253/272-3663, Ⓦwww.tacomadome.org), if something of an eyesore.

Most of Tacoma's attractions lie on **Pacific Avenue**, just south of downtown. The most notable of these is art celebrity Dale Chihuly's glittering pedestrian overpass, the **Bridge of Glass** (daily dawn–dusk; free; Ⓦwww.chihuly.com/bridgeofglass), chock-a-block with crystalline blue spires, glass vases and other vitreous curiosities. It leads to the **Museum of Glass**, 1801 E Dock St (Wed–Sat 10am–5pm, Sun noon–5pm; $12; Ⓣ1-866/4-MUSEUM, Ⓦwww.museumofglass.org), which resembles a giant kiln and presents Chihuly's work and that of other glassblowers, veering between quality museum art and workaday industrial design. On the west side of the bridge is the copper-domed 1911 **Union Station** (Mon–Fri 8am–5pm; Ⓣ253/863-5173 ext. 223), redesigned as a courthouse and display space for some of Chihuly's more extravagant works – especially the orange-hued glass butterflies of the **Monarch Window**. On the south side of Union Station, the excellent **Washington State History Museum**, 1911 Pacific Ave (Wed–Fri 10am–4pm, Sat & Sun till 5pm; $8; Ⓦwww.wshs.org/wshm), has large galleries nicely recreating the milieu of frontier towns and the early logging industry, as well as a replica general store and native plank house. On the north side of the Station is the **Tacoma Art Museum**, 1701 Pacific Ave (Wed–Sun 10am–5pm; $9; Ⓦwww.tacomaartmuseum.org), whose temporary exhibits are wide-ranging, from native tribal works to photography to installation art.

Further north, the historic core of Tacoma is centred around the **Broadway Center for the Performing Arts**, 901 Broadway (Ⓣ253/591-5890, Ⓦwww.broadwaycenter.org), whose two stunning former moviehouses are landmarks with terracotta facades and much historic-revival decor. If you have time, wander about eight blocks northwest of the Theater District to stately **Wright Park**, Sixth Avenue and S G Street, highlighted by the **Seymour Botanical Conservatory**, 316 S G St (Tues–Sun 10am–4.30pm; $4; Ⓣ253/591-5330), a 1908 glass-and-steel structure that holds some two hundred different species, from orchids and lilies to ferns and bromeliads, and, across the street, the Neoclassical **Karpeles Manuscript Museum**, 407 S G St (Tues–Sun 10am–4pm; free; Ⓣ253/383-2575, Ⓦwww.karpeles.com), which holds an immense collection of manuscripts, among them the concluding page of Darwin's *Origin of Species* and a study page for Karl Marx's *Das Kapital*, and some excellent temporary exhibits as well.

Finally, four miles north of downtown is picturesque **Point Defiance Park**, Pearl Street off Ruston Way, which at seven hundred acres is one of the largest urban parks in the USA. Its **Five-Mile-Drive** loop has fine vistas of Puget Sound and many appealing trails. Also diverting are an on-site zoo, aquarium and logging museum, but especially **Fort Nisqually** (hours vary, often Wed–Sun 11am–5pm; $4; Ⓦwww.fortnisqually.org), a reconstruction of the fur-trading post Hudson's Bay Company set up in 1833, with homes and storehouses that illustrate the stark lifestyles of denizens of the original fort.

Practicalities

The **Amtrak** station is at 1001 Puyallup Ave, where Greyhound **buses** also pick up. You can easily get around the downtown core on the free **Link Light Rail** system (daily 5.30am–10pm; Ⓣ206/398-5000, Ⓦwww.soundtransit.org).

Hotels in Tacoma are less expensive than their counterparts in Seattle. If you're sufficiently fired up by all the glass art in town, make a night of it with a stay at the *Hotel Murano*, 1320 Broadway Plaza (Ⓣ253/986-8083, Ⓦwww.hotelmuranotacoma.com; ❽), which, apart from its designer digs, flat-screen TVs, and the like, has corridors and public spaces loaded with shimmery artworks. Tacoma's better **B&B** choices include *Geiger Victorian*, 912 North I St (Ⓣ253/383-3504, Ⓦwww.geigervictorian.com; ❻), loaded with all the chintz and antiques you'd expect, plus a fireplace and claw-footed tubs in the rooms. If you want to splurge, the *Thornewood Castle Inn*, south of Tacoma at 8601 N Thorne Lane SW (Ⓣ253/584-4393, Ⓦwww.thornewoodcastle.com; ❾), more than lives up to its name, as a mock-English country estate with eight B&B suites with gracious designs rich with antiques, plus DVD players and wi-fi. For a bite to **eat**, try the *Southern Kitchen*, 1716 6th Ave (Ⓣ253/627-4282), whose delicious gumbo, catfish, hush puppies, candied yams and fried okra are about as close to Dixie as you're going to get in the Pacific Northwest; the *Primo Grill*, 601 S Pine St (Ⓣ253/383-7000), a reliable option for its mid-priced pizza and pasta, and pricier steak and seafood; and *Harmon Pub & Brewery*, 1938 Pacific Ave (Ⓣ253/383-2739), a solid choice for quaffing primo microbrews that also has serviceable burgers, salads and pizza.

Olympia

Picked as Washington's territorial capital in 1853 and state capital in 1889, **OLYMPIA's** compact downtown area is presided over by the **Old Capitol**, Washington Steet at 7th Avenue (Mon–Fri 8am–5pm; free), an 1892 jewel with Gothic turrets and arched windows, while the area around **East Fourth Avenue** is one of the prime strips for hearing Northwest rock and drinking yourself into cheerful oblivion (try *Le Voyeur*, no. 404, Ⓣ360/943-5710; or *Brotherhood Lounge*, 119 Capitol Way N Ⓣ360/352-4153). There's also the waterfront **Olympia Farmers Market**, 700 N Capitol Way (April–Oct Thurs–Sun 10am–3pm; Nov–Dec Sat & Sun only; Ⓦwww.olympiafarmersmarket.com), with a nice selection of fruits, vegetables, herbs and handicrafts.

Just south of downtown, the neat lawns of the **Capitol Campus** are the setting for the grand Neoclassical **Legislative Building** (tours daily on the hour 10am–3pm; self-guided visits daily 10am–4pm; free; Ⓣ360/902-8880, Ⓦwww.ga.wa.gov/visitor), which merits a look for its six gargantuan bronze entry-doors decorated with scenes from state history; a rotunda with a five-ton Tiffany chandelier; and a large circular walnut table in the State Reception Room, whose base was carved from a single tree trunk in the shape of eagles' legs.

Finally, ten miles south of Olympia along Old Highway 99, **Wolf Haven International** (1hr tours on the hour, April–Sept Mon & Wed–Sat 10am–3pm, Sun noon–3pm; $9; Ⓦwww.wolfhaven.org) is a nonprofit organization offering sanctuary to wolves unable to survive in the wild. Not to be missed is the famed "**howl-in**" (summer only, Sat 6–9pm; $17–19), a storytelling and music event that draws upon wolf myths and legends and involves howling at the wolves until they respond in kind.

Practicalities

The Greyhound **bus** station is at 107 Seventh Ave SE at Capitol Way (ⓣ360/357-5541), just north of the Capitol Campus, and the Amtrak **train** station is eight miles southeast, at 6600 Yelm Hwy SE in the town of Lacey. Intercity Transit runs local **buses** ($1 ticket, one-day pass $2; ⓣ360/786-1881, ⓦwww.intercitytransit.com), also providing a free DASH shuttle service between downtown, the Farmers Market and the Capitol Campus. Olympia's **visitor centre** (Mon–Fri 10am–4pm, till 2pm in winter; ⓣ360/704-7544) is near the Capitol Campus, at 103 Sid Snyder Ave SW.

Beyond the typical chain motels, distinctive **accommodation** includes the *Swantown Inn*, 1431 11th Ave SE (ⓣ360/753-9123, ⓦwww.swantowninn.com; ❺), four rooms in a striking 1887 Eastlake Victorian, with wi-fi, CD players, savoury breakfast and views of the Capitol; the *Phoenix Inn*, 415 Capitol Way (ⓣ1-877/570-0555, ⓦwww.phoenixinnsuites.com; ❻), with fridges and microwaves in each room, plus an on-site pool, jacuzzi and gym; and the *Inn at Mallard Cove*, 5025 Meridian Rd NE (ⓣ360/491-9795, ⓦwww.theinnatmallardcove.com; ❻), a half-timbered Tudor Revival estate whose three lovely rooms variously come with fireplaces, private decks and jacuzzis. There's also **camping** at forested Millersylvania State Park, 12245 Tilley Rd ($21–28; ⓣ360/753-1519), south of Olympia, two miles east of I-5, exit 99. Of places to **eat and drink**, the *New Moon Cafe*, 113 Fourth Ave W (ⓣ360/357-3452), features great pancakes and scrambles for breakfast, and burgers, sandwiches and biscuits & gravy for lunch; *Acqua Via*, 500 Capitol Way S (ⓣ360/357-6677), presents moderately priced Italian fare, including duck prosciutto and lamb-ragu penne; and the *Eastside Club Tavern*, 410 E Fourth Ave (ⓣ360/357-9985), is tops for its wide beer selection, pool, pinball and kick-ass jukebox.

Whidbey Island

With its sheer cliffs and craggy outcrops, rocky beaches and rambling countryside, **WHIDBEY ISLAND** is the second-largest island in the continental US – nearly fifty miles in length from north to south. Although it's possible to reach the island by road – Hwy-20 off I-5 drops into the north end of Whidbey, 85 miles north of Seattle – the **ferry** is a better option. The quickest route from Seattle is to head thirty miles north to Mukilteo and catch the ferry to **Clinton** on Whidbey's southern tip (daily 5am–12.30am; 20min trip; foot passengers $4.10, vehicle and driver $7). From Port Townsend on the Olympic Peninsula (see p.967) another ferry goes to **Keystone**, in the middle of the island (6.30am–8.30pm; 30min; foot passengers $2.65, vehicle and driver $9.15; ⓦwww.wsdot.wa.gov/ferries). Whidbey's **bus** system, Island Transit (most routes Mon–Fri only; ⓣ360/321-6688, ⓦwww.islandtransit.org), offers ten free routes that collectively run along the length of the island.

Just a few miles away from where the ferry docks in Clinton, the town of **Langley** is a well-heeled seaside village with a stretch of wooden storefronts set on a picturesque bluff overlooking the water. The town's charm is based on its antique stores and galleries. Good places to **stay** are the ✱ *Country Cottage of Langley*, 215 6th St (ⓣ360/221-8709 or 1-800/718-3860, ⓦwww.acountrycottage.com; ❻), which has six cottages set around in a restored 1920s farmhouse, all units with CD players and fridges, some with jacuzzis and fireplaces; and *The Inn at Langley*, 400 First St (ⓣ360/221-3033, ⓦwww.innatlangley.com; ❽), whose posh rooms have porches, balconies and waterfront views. Among the limited **food** options in town, *The Braeburn*, 197 2nd Street (ⓣ360/221-3211), has old-fashioned meatloaf and coleslaw, pot roast, pancakes and omelets; and *Cafe Langley*, 113 First St (ⓣ360/221-3090), has a nice blend of local seafood and Mediterranean stews, rack of lamb and kabobs.

The middle part of the island contains **Ebey's Landing National Historic Reserve** (daily 8am–dusk; free; ⓦwww.nps.gov/ebla), whose late-nineteenth-century military garrisons Fort Casey and Fort Ebey have been converted into evocative state parks, peppered with haunting gun batteries and eerie, bomb-shelter-like bunkers. Fort Ebey is also a good spot to camp (closed Nov–Feb; ⓣ1-888/226-7688; $19–26). Nearby, charming little **Coupeville** features several preserved Victorian mansions, and its Front Street is where you'll find most of the shops and eateries. Good **accommodation** includes *Captain Whidbey Inn*, 2072 W Captain Whidbey Inn Rd, two miles west of town at Penn Cove (ⓣ360/678-4097, ⓦwww.captainwhidbey.com; ❹), a nautical-themed hotel whose simple rooms have shared bathrooms and with more elaborate cabins for twice the price; and the *Anchorage Inn*, 807 N Main St (ⓣ1-877/230-1313, ⓦwww.anchorage-inn.com; ❹), with seven pleasant B&B units with wi-fi. For **eating**, try *Knead & Feed*, 4 Front St (ⓣ360/678-5431), offering fine home-made bread, soups, sandwiches, pies and cinnamon rolls; and *Christopher's*, 103 NW Coveland St (ⓣ360/678-5480), with its savoury mid-priced pasta, pork tenderloin and hearty stews.

On the northern edge of the island, **Deception Pass State Park**, 5175 N Hwy-20 (daily 8am–dusk; ⓣ360/675-2417) is not to be missed, sprawling over four thousand acres of rugged land and sea that's great for hiking, fishing, bird-watching and scuba diving. You can **camp** here, as it has around 300 sites ($21–28; ⓣ1-888/226-7688), though it fills up quickly in the summer months, so call ahead.

The San Juan Islands

North and west of Whidbey Island, midway between Seattle and Vancouver, BC, the beautiful **SAN JUAN ISLANDS** are scattered across the northern reaches of Puget Sound and are some of nature's high points along the West Coast. Every summer brings plenty of visitors, especially on the largest ones, San Juan and Orcas, so you're well advised to book your stay and transport in advance.

Arrival and getting around

Washington State Ferries sails to the islands from the harbour a few miles west of **Anacortes**, a gritty port 75 miles north of Seattle at the end of Hwy-20. The town is reachable via **Airporter Shuttle** (6am–11.30pm; 3hr trip; $33 one-way, $61 return; ⓣ1-866/235-5247, ⓦwww.airporter.com), which runs 11 buses daily from Sea-Tac Airport and three from downtown Seattle. The ferry runs 12–18 times daily and stops at Lopez, Shaw, Orcas and San Juan islands (5.30am–10.45pm; ⓣ1-888/808-7977, ⓦwww.wsdot.wa.gov/ferries), and the slow cruise through the archipelago is a delight. Motorists should get to the port early, as there's often an hour's wait or more to get vehicles onto a summer crossing. Return **fares** to the islands – $11.20 for foot passengers and $27–52 for a car and driver, depending on the destination and season – are collected only on the westbound journey, and there is no charge for foot passengers on inter-island trips (bringing a bike is an extra $2).

If you want to catch an early ferry from Anacortes, Commercial Avenue is lined with numerous budget **hotels**, the least generic of which is the hot-tub-equipped *Islands Inn*, no. 3401 (ⓣ360/293-4644, ⓦwww.islandsinn.com; ❹), offering bayside views, wi-fi and fireplaces, while the *Majestic Hotel*, no. 419 (ⓣ360/299-1400, ⓦwww.majesticinnandspa.com; ❻), is an 1889 edifice offering studios to suites, with a spa and a decent restaurant and bar.

As an alternative to ferry travel, Kenmore Air (ⓣ1-866/435-9524, ⓦwww.kenmoreair.com) has **seaplane flights** from Seattle's Lake Union to seven stops in the San Juans ($129 one-way). A passenger-only alternative is the *Victoria Clipper* (ⓣ206/448-5000 or 1-800/888-2535, ⓦwww.clippervacations.com), which runs twice daily from Seattle to San Juan's Friday Harbor ($47–52 one-way, $80 return), with a 5-hour layover.

Orcas Island

Horseshoe-shaped **ORCAS ISLAND** offers a nice bucolic getaway with rugged hills and leafy timbers that tower over its fetching farm country, craggy beaches and abundant wildlife. The ferry lands in tiny **Orcas**, and in the summer you can get around the island on the **Orcas Island Shuttle** ($6/ride; ⓣ360/376-RIDE, ⓦwww.orcasislandshuttle.com). The best spot to stay near the ferry landing is the *Orcas Hotel* (ⓣ1-888/672-2792, ⓦwww.orcashotel.com; ❺–❼), a restored Victorian inn whose plushest rooms have jacuzzis, balconies and harbour views, though not the cheaper ones. You can rent **bicycles** from Dolphin Bay Bicycles, just up from the dock ($30/day; by reservation only at ⓣ360/376-4157, ⓦwww.rockisland.com/~dolphin).

Ten miles north, in the drab town of **Eastsound**, you can also rent bikes from Wildlife Cycles, 350 N Beach Rd at A Street ($30/day; ⓣ360/376-4708, ⓦwww.wildlifecycles.com). The Chamber of Commerce, 65 N Beach Rd (ⓣ360/376-2273, ⓦwww.orcasislandchamber.com), provides maps and information. *Kingfish Inn*, 4362 Crow Valley Rd (ⓣ360/376-4440, ⓦwww.kingfishinn.com; ❻), is one of the best places to **stay** in the vicinity, with an elegant array of rooms and suites, and a superb **restaurant** that features delicious Northwest cuisine such as Thai curry halibut, fish tacos and grilled salmon. Also worthwhile, nestled at the end of West Beach Road, is the *Beach Haven Resort* (ⓣ360/376-2288, ⓦwww.beach-haven.com; ❺) its beachfront apartments and log cabins lining a densely wooded, sunset-facing cove; in summer they're only available by the week. Another solid dining choice, *Portofino Pizzeria*, 274 A St (ⓣ360/376-2085), has tasty pizzas and calzones.

The island's highlight is **Moran State Park**, off Horseshoe Highway southeast of Eastsound (ⓦwww.orcasisle.com/~elc), where more than thirty miles of hiking trails wind through dense forest and open fields to freshwater lakes, to the summit of **Mount Constitution** – the San Juans' highest point – crowned with a rugged stone observation tower. The park's four **campgrounds** (ⓣ1-888/226-7688; $21–28) fill up early in summer, so book ahead. Further along, lovely *Doe Bay Village & Resort*, Doe Bay Road, 18 miles east of Eastsound (ⓣ360/376-2291, ⓦwww.doebay.com), is tucked into a secluded bay and offers everything from hostel beds (❶) to basic campsites (❶), modern cabins (❹–❼) and yurts (❹–❺); whatever your choice, there's a minimum stay of two to three nights. Their on-site **restaurant** (ⓣ360/376-8059) provides organic meals of seafood and pizza, and in nearby **Olga**, *Café Olga*, 11 Point Lawrence Rd (ⓣ360/376-5862) also serves tasty **breakfasts** and fruit pies and has an adjoining art gallery.

San Juan Island

SAN JUAN ISLAND is the ferry's last stop before Canada, best known as the site of, at the southern tip, **San Juan Island National Historical Park**, where the **American Camp** (hours vary, often daily 8am–4.30pm; free; ⓣ360/378-2902, ⓦwww.nps.gov/sajh), once played a role in the so-called "Pig War", a rather absurd 1859 border conflict between the US and Britain. More appealing is **English Camp**, to the west (same entry as American Camp), where forests overlook pleasant fields and maple trees near the shore, and four buildings from the 1860s and a small formal garden have been restored.

Friday Harbor is a small and pleasant resort village with cafés, shops and a waterfront that make for pleasant wandering. Its small **Whale Museum**, 62 First St N (daily: June–Aug 9am–6pm, rest of year 10am–5pm; $6; Ⓦwww.whalemuseum.org), has a set of whale skeletons and displays explaining their migration and growth cycles, as well as a listening booth for whale and other cetacean songs. To see the real thing, head past the coves and bays on the island's west side to **Lime Kiln Point State Park**, 6158 Lighthouse Rd (daily 8am–dusk), named after the site's former lime quarry. Orca ("killer") whales come here in summer to feed on migrating salmon, and there's usually at least one close sighting a day. San Juan Safaris (Ⓣ360/378-1323 or 1-800/450-6858, Ⓦwww.sanjuansafaris.com) is one of several companies offering three-hour **whale-watching cruises** (April–Oct only; $75), plus sea-kayaking trips (June–Sept) for the same price.

From April to September, **San Juan Shuttle** stops at most of the island's principal attractions ($5/one-way, $15/day pass; Ⓣ360/378-8887 or 1-800/887-8387, Ⓦwww.sanjuantransit.com), and **bikes** can be rented at Island Bicycles, 380 Argyle St ($10–12/hr, $38–50/day; summer daily, Wed–Sat rest of year; Ⓣ360/378-4941, Ⓦwww.islandbicycles.com). You can also pick up information and **maps** of the island's irregular main roads at the **Chamber of Commerce** at 135 Spring St (daily 10am–4pm; Ⓣ360/378-5240, Ⓦwww.sanjuanisland.org).

Choices to **stay** include *Bird Rock Hotel*, 35 First St (Ⓣ1-800/352-2632, Ⓦwww.birdrockhotel.com; ❻), a boutique location with designer furnishings, flat-screen HDTVs, free wi-fi, iPod docks and some units with jacuzzis (the cheapest rooms have shared bath); *Lakedale Resort* (Ⓣ1-800/617-2267, Ⓦwww.lakedale.com), six miles from the ferry on Roche Harbor Road (accessible by bus), which has everything from simple campsites (❶) to elegant lodge rooms (❽), to canvas-walled (❻) and log-framed cabins (❾); and *Harrison House*, 235 C St (Ⓣ360/378-3587, Ⓦwww.harrisonhousesuites.com; ❼), a popular B&B in a verdant setting, whose five sizeable suites may include jacuzzis, kitchens, fireplaces and one to three bedrooms each. The local Bed & Breakfast Association (Ⓣ360/378-3030, Ⓦwww.san-juan-island.net) can also hook you up with a room, though it's essential to reserve ahead. Of Friday Harbor's plentiful places to **eat**, *Downriggers*, 10 Front St (Ⓣ360/378-2700), has moderate to expensive seafood and pasta – everything from lobster quesadillas to crab cakes – while *Rocky Bay Cafe*, 225 Spring St (Ⓣ360/378-5051), is quite good for its all-American breakfasts of omelets, eggs Benedict and biscuits & gravy, and *Duck Soup Inn*, 50 Duck Soup Lane, near *Lakedale Resort* (Ⓣ360/378-4878), is among the most expensive restaurants in the islands, but worth it for its excellent fresh fish, stews, rack of lamb and other prime Northwest cuisine.

At the northwest tip of the island is **Roche Harbor**, established in the 1880s around the limestone trade, and highlighted by the elegant *Hotel de Haro*, 248 Reuben Memorial Drive (Ⓣ1-800/451-8910, Ⓦwww.rocheharbor.com; ❻–❾), an 1886 complex with standard rooms featuring bathrooms, as well as upmarket suites and quaint cottages with antique decor. At the hotel there are several places to eat. The best is *McMillin's* (Ⓣ360/378-5757), with good, if pricey, steak and seafood entrees and waterside vistas.

The Olympic Peninsula

West of Puget Sound lies the great **Olympic Peninsula**, accessible by US-101, which loops around its coastal perimeter. Rugged peaks dominate the peninsular core, which rises high above lush subalpine vegetation, giving way to the tangled rainforests of the western valleys, and the pristine beaches of the Pacific edge.

Fringed with logging communities, the peninsula's most magnificent parts are protected within **Olympic National Park**, with its superb hiking trails, campsites and lodges.

Port Townsend

With its colourful mansions, convivial cafés and compact scale, **PORT TOWNSEND** is a fetching relic from the 1890s that's a great place to spend a day or two before venturing on to the mountains. There are few "official" sights, but there is plenty in the way of charm in this attractive little town, largely isolated and perched on the peninsula's northeastern tip across from Keystone on Whidbey Island. Port Townsend's physical split – half on a bluff, half at sea level – reflects nineteenth-century social divisions, when wealthy merchants built their houses uptown, far above the clamour of the working-class port below.

The downtown area lies at the base of the hill on **Water Street**, which sports an attractive medley of Victorian brick and stone commercial buildings, now home to restaurants, boutiques and especially, art galleries. The area's rich history is detailed in the museum of the **Jefferson County Historical Society**, 540 Water St (March–Dec daily 11am–4pm; $4; Ⓦwww.jchsmuseum.org), based in the old City Hall, which has an eclectic assortment of items, from a photographer's chair draped with bear and buffalo skins, to antique farm and nautical implements, to unusual late-nineteenth- and early-twentieth-century two-necked harp guitars.

Though bustling year-round, the town is busiest during its **summer festivals** – principally American Fiddle Tunes in early July and Jazz Port Townsend in late July (see Ⓦwww.centrum.org for information on both), and the Wooden Boat Festival in early September (Ⓣ360/385-4742, Ⓦwww.woodenboat.org). Some of these take place at the state park at **Fort Worden** (Ⓣ360/344-4400, Ⓦwww.fortworden.org), the remains of a military garrison two miles north of town. It offers a wide range of accommodation from dorm beds ($28–30) to campsites ($22–42) and former officers' houses ($182–415), as well as several museums, a science centre and a lighthouse – not to mention dozens of good hiking trails at the edge of Puget Sound, one of which leads to the massive concrete gun emplacements of the 1890s **Kinzie Battery**.

Practicalities

Although Port Townsend is easily accessed by road, you can also get there by **ferry** from Keystone (see p.963). The ferry terminal is just south of downtown, off Water Street. Get maps and information on town history and notable buildings at the helpful **visitor centre**, 440 12th St (Mon–Fri 9am–5pm, Sat 10am–4pm, Sun 11am–4pm; Ⓣ360/385-2722, Ⓦwww.enjoypt.com).

There's a good choice of places to **stay**, and the most central is the *Palace Hotel*, 1004 Water St (Ⓣ360/385-0773, Ⓦwww.palacehotelpt.com; ❸), a Victorian charmer that's seen better days, but still has antique decor, claw-footed tubs and excellent views of the Sound (the cheapest rooms have shared bathrooms). The town's specialty, though, is its **B&Bs**, the best of which occupy grand Victorian mansions uptown, such as the *Old Consulate Inn*, 313 Walker St (Ⓣ360/385-6753 or 1-800/300-6753, Ⓦwww.oldconsulateinn.com; ❺), an 1889 villa with spiky tower and wraparound veranda, and seven plush suites (plus one rather small room), and *Manresa Castle*, Seventh and Sheridan streets (Ⓣ360/385-5750 or 1-800/732-1281, Ⓦwww.manresacastle.com), a quasi-French castle from 1892 that has thirty rooms ranging from affordable cosy single units to swanky suites in the tower (❺–❽).

Port Townsend has many fine places to **eat**, among them *Fountain Café*, 920 Washington St (ⓣ360/385-1364), with seafood and pasta specialties a short distance from the waterfront; the *Silverwater Café*, 237 Taylor St (ⓣ360/385-6448), with fresh seafood such as lavender-pepper ahi tuna, prawns alfredo and pan-fried oysters; and *Sweet Laurette Patisserie*, 1029 Lawrence St (ⓣ360/385-4886), the best French-style bakery in town, featuring elaborate cakes that resemble artworks, and cheaper scones, pies and pastries, plus good breakfasts and lunches.

Port Angeles

PORT ANGELES is the most popular point of entry into Olympic National Park, a few miles to the south. Its harbour is backed by striking mountains, but there are few reasons to linger at this workaday stopover – other than the town's having the peninsula's best transport links. If you do want to **stay** here (instead of the more compelling option of the park lodges), there are inexpensive **motels** near its main drags, First Street and Front Street. But the best choice is *Domaine Madeleine*, 146 Wildflower Lane (ⓣ360/457-4174, ⓦwww.domainemadeleine.com; ❼), a B&B with a lovely five-acre garden and five art-themed rooms, which variously come with jetted tubs, fireplaces and balconies. For **eating**, *Michael's Fresh Northwest Seafood & Steakhouse*, 117-B E 1st St (ⓣ360/417-6929), is a moderate to expensive spot that has paella, oysters, pizza, pasta and especially steak, while *Olympic Bagel Company*, 802 E 1st St (ⓣ360/452-9100), serves the town's best bagels, omelets and panini.

The **bus** depot is beside the waterfront at W Front and Oak streets, and from there it's only a couple of minutes' walk to the main **ferry** terminal. Olympic Bus Lines (ⓣ360/417-0700, ⓦwww.olympicbuslines.com) offers daily trips to Amtrak and Greyhound stations in Seattle ($39) and to Sea-Tac Airport ($49). Black Ball Transport (ⓣ360/457-4491, ⓦwww.cohoferry.com) **car ferries** cross to and from Victoria, BC (March–Dec two to four ferries daily; 90min trip; one-way fares $14.50 walk-on, $53/car and driver). Arriving at a neighbouring pier at the foot of Lincoln Street, the **passenger ferries** of Victoria Express (late May to mid-Sept; ⓣ360/452-8088 or 1-800/633-1589, ⓦwww.victoriaexpress.com) operate a faster service (2–4 daily) for $20 return. Port Angeles' **visitor centre**, 121 E Railroad St, beside the ferry terminal (ⓣ360/452-2363, ⓦwww.portangeles.org), has information on the entire peninsula and can put you in touch with river-rafting and sea-kayaking operators.

Olympic National Park

Magnificent **OLYMPIC NATIONAL PARK**, comprising the colossal Olympic Mountains in the heart of the peninsula plus a separate, isolated sixty-mile strip of Pacific coastline farther west, is one of Washington's prime wilderness destinations, with boundless opportunities for spectacular hiking and wildlife watching. Created in 1938 by Franklin D. Roosevelt, it features more than two hundred miles of wild rivers, while the river valleys contain sizeable tracts of **temperate rainforest**.

Natural highlights, which are numerous, include **Hurricane Ridge**, with its jagged peaks and sparkling mountain glaciers; glacially carved **Lake Crescent**, popular for trout fishing and hiking on shoreline trails; and the 73 miles of wild **beaches** of the Pacific coast, where black rocks jut out of the sea, and appealing **Ruby Beach** is named for its red-and-black-pebbled sand. Meanwhile, the **Queets River Rainforest** is worth a visit for its rustic trails, and for the luxuriant flora and fauna, highlighted by the world's tallest Douglas fir – 220ft tall and 45ft around; and **Quinault Rainforest**, the most beautiful of all the peninsula's rainforests, around the shores of glacier-carved **Lake Quinault**.

Practicalities

The main **visitor centre**, in Port Angeles at 600 E Park Ave (hours vary, often daily 9am–4pm, summer till 6pm; seven-day park pass $5 for individuals, or $15/car; ⓣ360/565-3100, ⓦwww.nps.gov/olym), has useful brochures and trail maps, while the **Wilderness Information Center**, 3002 Mount Angeles Rd (hours vary, often daily 8am–4pm; ⓣ360/565-3100), supplies information on trail conditions in the area; smaller visitor centres are located at Hurricane Ridge and Hoh Rainforest. The **weather** is often rainy – there's even a fair amount of snow as late as June.

You can stay inside the park at any of the sixteen excellent **campgrounds** ($10–18; ⓣ360/565-3130); try *Heart o' the Hills*, six miles south of Port Angeles, along Hurricane Ridge Road, or further west, *Altair* – though this is closed from November to mid May along with several others. Other good places to stay are *Lake Crescent Lodge* (May–Oct; ⓣ1-866/875-8456, ⓦwww.olympicnationalparks.com), well placed among dense forest on the lake's south shore, offering simple rooms (5) to elegant cottages (8); and *Sol Duc Hot Springs Resort* (March–Oct; ⓣ1-866/4SOLDUC; 6–9), set deep in the park twelve miles off US-101, whose 26 basic cabins come with spartan but adequate amenities, though the pricier ones are three-bedroom suites with kitchens. The resort provides free guest access to **Sol Duc Hot Springs** (otherwise $12) – three pools with mineral-rich waters bubbling up at 99 to 104°F. Elsewhere, impressive *Kalaloch Lodge* (ⓣ360/962-2271, ⓦwww.visitkalaloch.com), has basic lodge rooms (5) and more upmarket cabins (6); and the charming 1926 *Lake Quinault Lodge* (ⓣ360/288-2900 or 1-800/562-6672, ⓦwww.visitlakequinault.com; 4–5), on the shores of Lake Quinault, offers rooms with fireplaces or lakeside views, and an on-site pool and sauna.

The southwest coast

Heading south on US-101 from Lake Quinault, leaving the national park, it's about forty hilly miles to industrial **Aberdeen**, from where there's a choice of routes: US-12/Hwy-8 lead east towards Olympia (see p.962), while Hwy-101 pushes south over the hills, threading along the shore of muddy Willapa Bay and the **southwest coast** of Washington. Here, the bay is home to the 15,000-acre **Willapa National Wildlife Refuge** (ⓦwww.fws.gov/willapa), whose various dunes, forests, marshes and mudflats shelter some two hundred species of migrating shorebirds. Continuing on, the **Long Beach Peninsula** is something of a low-rent resort area, but merits a trip to the northern tip, where **OYSTERVILLE** is a forested collection of rusting old buildings that's the home of **Oysterville Sea Farms** (ⓣ360/665-6585), recognizable by its piles of discarded shells and renowned for its fresh smoked oysters. Also tasty is the **Pacific Coast Cranberry Museum**, 2907 Pioneer Rd in the town of Long Beach (April to mid-Dec 10am–5pm; ⓣ360/642-5553, ⓦwww.cranberrymuseum.com), where you can wander through a cranberry bog and purchase berry-flavoured treats.

Down at the far southwestern tip of Washington, near the mouth of the Columbia River on a craggy headland, is scenic **Cape Disappointment State Park** (daily 6.30am–dusk; ⓦwww.parks.wa.gov). You can camp in these windswept environs ($21–28; ⓣ1-888/226-7688), take in the evocative 1856 **North Head Lighthouse** (summer daily 11am–3pm; $2.50) or visit the **Lewis and Clark Interpretive Center** (daily 10am–5pm; $5), which can tell you all about the historical hazards of navigating the Columbia River. Fortunately, you'll be spared any such difficulty as you travel south on Hwy-101 over the sweeping 1966 span of the **Astoria Bridge**, crossing the state boundary into Oregon (see p.988).

The Cascade Mountains

The **Cascade Mountains** offer mile upon mile of dense forested wilderness, traversed by a dense web of beautiful trails and spectacular vistas. The most popular access point is **Mount Rainier**, set in its own national park ninety miles southeast of Seattle, while the haunting scenery around volcanic **Mount St Helens** compels visitors internationally. Further north, Hwy-20, the high mountain road that crosses the Cascades, is by far the most spectacular route to eastern Washington, traversing the snowcapped wonder of **North Cascades National Park**.

The North Cascades and the Cascade Loop

The magnificent **Cascade Loop** (ⓣ509/662-3888, ⓦwww.cascadeloop.com) offers a 400-mile round trip along highways 20, 153, 97 and 2 – though the full trip is only feasible during the summer, since at other times snow closes the mountain passes; take a few selected treks through the gorgeous environs unless you have at least three days to explore the territory in full. You can find out more information at **North Cascades National Park Headquarters**, 2105 Hwy-20 near Sedro Woolley, located just east of where Hwy-20 begins its journey inland at Burlington (daily 8am–4.30pm; ⓣ360/854-7200, ⓦwww.nps.gov/noca).

Winthrop

From the information centre, the highway threads through high mountain passes to tiny **WINTHROP**, an old mining town decked out in a Wild West get-up. While the effect is more than a bit cheesy, the false-fronted "saloons" and "dance halls" do make for some good snapshots, and the town can serve as a base for further exploration in the mountains.

If you'd like to **stay**, one good choice is the *Hotel Rio Vista*, 285 Riverside Ave (ⓣ509/996-3535 or 1-800/398-0911, ⓦwww.hotelriovista.com; ❺), designed to resemble something out of the 1880s, and which offers nice suites with hot tubs, kitchenettes and DVD players in a fine riverside setting; or the luxurious ★ *Sun Mountain Lodge* (ⓣ509/996-2211 or 1-800/572-0493, ⓦwww.sunmountainlodge.com; ❼), with cabins and lodge rooms in a grand spot on the edge of the Cascades, nine miles southwest of town along Twin Lakes and then Patterson Lake Road.

As for **eating** options, *Arrowleaf Bistro*, 253 Riverside Ave (ⓣ509/996-3919), is good for its moderate to expensive Northwest cuisine featuring items such as venison tenderloin and crawfish étouffée, and the *Duck Brand Cantina*, 248 Riverside Ave (ⓣ509/996-2192, ⓦwww.methownet.com/duck), serves up cheap and tasty Mexican fare and has six simple, Western-themed rooms in its on-site B&B (❸). The nearby **visitor centre**, 202 Riverside Ave (ⓣ509/996-2125, ⓦwww.winthropwashington.com), offers information and backcountry permits for hiking and camping.

Chelan and Stehekin

The fetching resort of **CHELAN**, sixty miles south of Winthrop, nestles at the foot of **Lake Chelan**, whose spectacularly deep waters fill a glacially carved trough nestled in the mountains. Of several good **lodging options,** *Grandview on the Lake*, 322 W Woodin Ave (ⓣ509/682-2582, ⓦwww.grandviewonthelake.com; ❻), is a reliable spot for its rooms and suites with lakeside views, fireplaces, balconies and some with jacuzzis, while cheaper digs are available at the *Midtowner Motel*, 721 E Woodin Ave (ⓣ509/682-4051, ⓦwww.midtowner.com; ❹), which has simple rooms with microwaves and an on-site pool and jacuzzi. The **ranger station** at 428 W Woodin Ave (daily 8.30am–4.30pm; ⓣ509/682-4900) can ply you with hiking maps when you're ready to hit the trails, while the **visitor centre** is near the waterfront at 102 E Johnson Ave (Mon–Sat 9am–5pm; ⓣ509/682-3503, ⓦwww.lakechelan.com).

The Lake Chelan Boat Company, 1418 W Woodin Ave (ⓣ509/682-4584 reservations, ⓦwww.ladyofthelake.com), runs a passenger ferry service to the head of Lake Chelan. Leaving from the jetty a mile west of town on Woodin Avenue, the *Lady of the Lake II* takes four hours to cruise the 55 miles of the nation's deepest gorge (May to mid-Oct; $23.25 one-way, $39 return); the year-round *Lady Express* (May–Oct $35.75 one-way, $59 return; Nov–April $39 return) reaches Lake Chelan's mountainous western tip in half the time. All cruises feature 60- to 90-minute layovers at **STEHEKIN**, a tiny, isolated village otherwise accessible only by a Chelan Airways **seaplane** ($79 one-way, $158 return; ⓣ509/682-5555, ⓦwww.chelanairways.com), which is also available for airborne **tours** of the region ($49–99/person; minimum four people). Stehekin makes an excellent base for **hiking** in the North Cascades, where, in every direction, trails strike into the mountains, nudging up along bubbling creeks through the thinning alpine forest, with easier trails along the lakeshore. Bikes and canoes are available from the *Stehekin Landing Resort* (ⓣ509/682-4494, ⓦwww.stehekinlanding.com; ❺–❼), where the lakeside rooms are a bit pricier than standard units. For camping and hiking information, visit the **Golden West Visitor Center** near the Stehekin jetty (hours vary, summer daily 8.30am–5pm; ⓣ360/854-7365).

Wenatchee to Snoqualmie Falls

Several miles south of Chelan, the Cascade Loop turns west along US-2 just north of the apple-producing town of **Wenatchee**, where you can munch away on various varieties and guzzle apple juice at the **Washington Apple Commission Visitor Center**, on the northern edge of town at 2900 Euclid Ave (Mon–Fri 8am–5pm; free; ⓦwww.bestapples.com). Afterwards, head back to US-2 for pocket-sized **Leavenworth**, a pseudo-Bavarian theme town decked out in high gables and half-timbered woodwork. It's best as a base for taking in the outdoor activities in the spectacular mountain surroundings. The **ranger station**, just off US-2 at 600 Sherbourne St (Mon–Sat 8am–4.30pm; ⓣ509/782-1413), provides trail guides and hiking information, and River Rider (ⓣ1-800/448-RAFT, ⓦwww.riverrider.com) is one of the more prominent guides offering tubing on the Wenatchee River ($15/person) and kayaking and rafting excursions ($55–70) on a range of Cascade rivers.

The **visitor centre**, 940 Hwy-2 (ⓣ509/548-5807, ⓦwww.leavenworth.org), has copious listings of places to **stay** and **eat**. The rooms of the *Hotel Pension Anna*, 926 Commercial St (ⓣ1-800/509-ANNA, ⓦwww.pensionanna.com; ❻), are decked out in cheerful Teutonic kitsch, with its suites holding fireplaces and jacuzzis, but the rooms at the stylish *Enzian Motor Inn*, 590 Hwy-2 (ⓣ509/548-5269 or 1-800/223-8511, ⓦwww.enzianinn.com; ❺), are more tasteful, and feature free breakfast buffets and decor imported from the Old World. The *Andreas Keller*, 829 Front St (ⓣ509/548-6000), doles out hefty helpings of hearty German cuisine like pickled herring, schnitzel and spatzele. You can get much the same thing, for more expensive prices, at *King Ludwig's*, 921 Front St (ⓣ509/548-6625), which also features "Schweinshax'n", a formidable platter of pork hocks.

West of Leavenworth, US-2 crosses the mountains over Stevens Pass, but the principal east–west highway, I-90, lies further south, connecting Seattle with the Yakima Valley. Near I-90 is the strikingly beautiful, 270ft-tall torrent of **Snoqualmie Falls** (ⓦwww.snoqualmiefalls.com), and behind it the luxurious *Salish Lodge*, 6501 Railroad Ave SE (ⓣ425/888-2556 or 1-800/2-SALISH, ⓦwww.salishlodge.com; ❾), still best known as the stately lodge location in the David Lynch TV series *Twin Peaks*.

Mount Rainier National Park

Set in its own national park, glacier-clad **MOUNT RAINIER** is the highest (14,410ft) peak in the Cascades, and a major Washington landmark. Not until June does the snow melt enough for roads to open, and then the deer and mountain goats appear, dazzling wildflowers illuminate the alpine meadows and the mountain makes for some perfect hiking. More than three hundred miles of **trails** crisscross the park, ranging from short walks, such as the 1.2-mile Nisqually Vista Trail loop, to the five-mile Skyline Trail up to Glacier Overlook, to the 93-mile Wonderland Trail that encircles the mountain. If you only have a day to explore , visit the south and east sides from the Nisqually entrance to **Paradise**, with a side-trip to **Sunrise** – a stunning eighty-mile drive winding through river valleys and lowland forests with glaciated peaks and stunning vistas (climbing Mount Rainier, however, is hazardous and should only be undertaken by experienced climbers).

Practicalities

The park is **located** some seventy miles southeast of Tacoma by way of Hwy-7 and a transfer onto minor route 706. Admission to the park is $15 per vehicle, $5 per person, for a one-week pass. The park has four **entrances**: Nisqually in the southwest corner, Stephen's Canyon in the southeast, White River in the northeast and Carbon River in the northwest. Only the Nisqually entrance is open year-round (for cross-country skiing; the others open June–Sept) and it is also the only one serviced by public **transportation** – a ten-hour day-trip with Gray Line from Seattle (May–Sept; $65; ⓣ1-800/426-7505, ⓦwww.graylineseattle.com). For map and trail conditions, stop by the **visitor centres** at Longmire, Ohanapecosh, Sunrise, White River and, the most useful, Paradise (May–Sept daily 9am–5pm; ⓣ360/569-2211, ⓦwww.nps.gov/mora).

For official park **accommodation** (ⓣ360/569-2275, ⓦwww.mtrainierguest services.com; ❺, plus $38 for private bath), the classic lodge of the *National Park Inn* is open year-round with 25 guest rooms and a restaurant, while the *Paradise Inn* (late May to Sept), appeals for its 1916 rustic charm amid fields of hillside wildflowers. Make reservations well in advance. Outside the park, in the town of Ashford, *Whittaker's Bunkhouse*, 30205 SR 706 E (ⓣ360/569-2439, ⓦwww .whittakersbunkhouse.com), is an old loggers' bunkhouse with dorm beds (❶) and small double rooms with private baths (❹); and *Mounthaven*, 38210 SR 706 E (ⓣ360/569-2594 or 1-800/456-9380, ⓦwww.mounthaven.com; ❺), has eight cabins, some with fireplaces, kitchenettes, fridges, wood stoves and porches. The park's five **campgrounds** require reservations (ⓣ1-877-444-6777, ⓦwww .recreation.gov; $12–15), which you can obtain up to 24 hours in advance from any hiking centre in the park.

Mount St Helens

The looming volcanic mound of **MOUNT ST HELENS** erupted on May 18, 1980, its blast wave flattening 230 square miles of surrounding forests, a massive mudflow sending an avalanche of debris down the river valleys. Since then, the forests and animals have re-emerged through the scarred landscape, which still testifies to the awesome force of nature.

The area around the mountain has three entry routes. Many visitors arrive along Hwy-504, off I-5 roughly halfway between Olympia and Portland, which snakes through dark green forests until bald, spiky trees give way to thousands of lifeless grey trees lying in combed-down rows. At the end is the **Johnson Ridge Observatory** (May–Oct daily 10am–6pm; ⓣ360/274-2140, ⓦwww.fs.fed.us/gpnf/mshnvm), which offers fine views of the still-steaming lava dome, a film of the eruption and testimony by survivors. One alternative is to take Hwy-503 from Portland (via I-5) to **Cougar**, on the mountain's southern side – dotted with ravines and lava caves, as well as ashen lahars – from where the summer-only forest roads USFS-90, -25 and -99 wind along its flanks to **Windy Ridge** on the northeast side of the mountain, where entire slopes are denuded of foliage, and colossal tree husks lie scattered like twigs. Windy Ridge can also be accessed from the north from **Randle** along USFS-25 and -99, passing through lava flows with numerous viewpoints en route.

Practicalities

The one-day **Monument Pass** ($8) allows entry to the Coldwater Lake Recreation Area and the Johnston Ridge Observatory; the **Northwest Forest Pass** ($5) is good for other sites, and is available through putting money in drop boxes at site car parks. En route to Windy Ridge from Hwy-503 is **Mount St Helens Volcanic Monument Headquarters** (daily 8am–5pm; ⓣ360/449-7800) in Amboy, which has maps and information. Near Silver Lake on Hwy-504 is the **Mount St Helens Visitor Center** (daily 9am–4pm, summer closes 5pm; $3; ⓣ360/274-0962, ⓦwww.parks.wa.gov/mountsthelens.asp), complete with informative exhibits and a small-scale model of the volcano.

Though there aren't any **campgrounds** within the national monument, but there are some private ones in the vicinity of Cougar (June–Aug only; $17–20; ⓣ503/813-6666 for information and reservations). Mountain **permits** are required for those interested in climbing above 4800ft. From April to October, the time you'll most likely want to make the effort, only one hundred permits per day are given out, a fee is charged ($22), and you must reserve your permit ahead of time online at ⓦwww.mshinstitute.org. You're required to pick up your permit at *Lone Fir Resort*, 16806 Lewis River Rd in Cougar (ⓣ360/238-5210, ⓦwww.lonefirresort.com; ❸).

Eastern Washington

Olive-collared sagebrush covers many acres of **eastern Washington** and massive red rocks loom over the prairies, while huge bare patches of basalt and torn-away groundcover testify to the enduring effect of ancient Ice Age floods. To the south lies the lower Yakima Valley, with miles of orchards and farms, which make it one of the largest producers of apples in the world. Of eastern Washington's major towns, only **Spokane** has any degree of cultural life, but some are decent bases for outdoor activities such as fishing, hiking and skiing.

Ellensburg

East of the mountains along I-90, 130 miles from Seattle, **ELLENSBURG** is a dusty little city of fetching nineteenth-century red-brick architecture, mainly known for its **Ellensburg Rodeo** (tickets $15–23; ⓣ509/962-7831 or 1-800/637-2444, ⓦwww.ellensburgrodeo.com), held over Labor Day weekend, with Stetson-clad cowhands roping steers, riding bulls and braving bucking broncos; and the **Clymer Museum of Art**, 416 N Pearl St at 4th Ave (Mon–Fri 10am–5pm, Sat till 4pm, Sun noon–4pm; free; ⓣ509/962-6416), which displays Old West paintings alongside exhibitions of everything from patchwork quilts to cowboy poetry.

Greyhound stops at 1512 Hwy-97. The **visitor centre**, 609 N Main St (Mon–Fri 8am–5pm, Sat 10am–2pm, also summer Sun same hours; ⓣ509/925-2002, ⓦwww.visitellen.com), provides maps and **hotel** options; one good choice is the *Inn at Goose Creek*, 1720 Canyon Rd (ⓣ509/962-8030, ⓦwww.innatgoosecreek.com; ❺), whose ten twee rooms are themed around hunting, sports, Christmas, the rodeo and so on, each with internet access. For something more conventional, the *Best Western Lincoln Inn*, 211 W Umptanum Rd (ⓣ509/925-4244, ⓦwww.bestwestern.com; ❺), has rooms with microwaves and fridges, plus a pool, gym and hot tub. The best pit stop for **food** is the *Yellow Church Cafe*, 111 S Pearl St (ⓣ509/933-2233), which has good chili, sandwiches and salads for lunch, and pricier steak and seafood for dinner.

Walla Walla

About 120 miles southeast of Yakima along I-82 and US-12, **WALLA WALLA** is becoming known for its terrific wines, but is otherwise best known for its sweet onions – eaten raw like apples. This was the place where the missionary **Marcus Whitman** arrived from the East Coast in 1836, only to be martyred eleven years later when a band of natives murdered him, his wife and eleven others. This was followed by swift action by the US Army to deal harshly with the local tribes. The site where the **Whitman Mission** was burned down (daily 8am–4.30pm, summer until 6pm; $3; ⓣ509/522-6360, ⓦwww.nps.gov/whmi), seven miles west of town off US-12, has basic marks on the ground to illustrate its layout.

Greyhound stops at 108 W Main. Contact the **Walla Walla Wine Alliance** (ⓣ509/526-3117, ⓦwww.wallawallawine.com) for locations and opening hours of most area wineries, as well as maps. Walla Walla's **visitor centre** is at 29 E Sumach St (Mon–Fri 8.30am–5pm; ⓣ509/525-0850, ⓦwww.wwvchamber.com). The most prominent place to **stay** is the 1927 tower of the *Marcus Whitman Hotel*, 6 W Rose St (ⓣ509/525-2200, ⓦwww.marcuswhitmanhotel.com; ❻), with a grand lobby, complimentary breakfast, and rooms and suites that variously come with HDTVs and jacuzzis. The best **B&B** is the *Inn at Blackberry Creek*, 1126 Pleasant St (ⓣ1-877/522-5233, ⓦwww.innatblackberrycreek.com; ❻), whose three, artist-themed rooms have flat-screen TVs, DVD players, and, in selected rooms, a wood stove and/or jacuzzi. **Dining** is best enjoyed at the *CreekTown Cafe*, 1129 S 2nd Ave (ⓣ509/522-4777), with tasty sandwiches, pasta and burgers for lunch, and top-shelf oysters, salmon and duck for dinner – plus a good selection of Walla Walla wine.

Spokane

A few miles from Idaho on I-90, **SPOKANE** ("spo-CAN"), eastern Washington's only real city of any size, has some grandiose late-nineteenth-century buildings and pleasant parks. The town's hub, hundred-acre **Riverfront Park**, was the site of the 1974 World's Fair and sprawls over two islands in the middle of the Spokane River, which tumbles down the rocky shelves of **Spokane Falls**. The **attractions** (hours vary, often daily 11am–6pm, Sat & Sun until 8pm; day passes $16.25; ⓦwww.spokaneriverfrontpark.com) include an ice-skating rink, carousel and the **Spokane Falls Skyride** ($7), which rises above the falls to take in a commanding view of the area.

Most of the relics of Spokane's early grandeur can be found several blocks southwest on West Riverside Avenue, where Neoclassical facades cluster around Jefferson Street. One highlight is the **Clark Mansion**, 2208 W Second Ave, an 1897 marvel of lovely classical arcades and red-tiled roofs. Also check out the **Northwest Museum of Art and Culture**, 2316 W 1st Ave (Wed–Sat 10am–6pm; $7; ⓦwww.northwestmuseum.org), which focuses on regional history and artwork, Native American culture and fine arts from WPA-era paintings to items from nineteenth-century Japan and seventeenth-century Holland. Make sure to drop by the adjacent **Campbell House** (tours on the hour Wed–Sat noon–3pm; free with museum admission), a Tudor Revival confection dreamed up for a silver baron in 1898.

Practicalities

Amtrak and Greyhound share the **transit centre** at 221 W First St, and the **visitor centre** is at 201 W Main St (Mon–Fri 9am–5pm, also summer Sat & Sun; ⓣ509/747-3230 or 1-800/776-5263, ⓦwww.visitspokane.com). Appealing **accommodation** includes the 1914 *Davenport Hotel*, 10 S Post St (ⓣ1-800/899-1482, ⓦwww.thedavenporthotel.com; ❼), a stately 1914 treasure with a wildly ornate lobby and spacious, well-designed suites; and the stylish *Hotel Lusso*, N One Post St (ⓣ509/747-9750, ⓦwww.hotellusso.com; ❺), whose well-appointed rooms have HDTVs and free wi-fi access. For **eating**, *Luna*, 5620 S Perry St (ⓣ509/448-2383), serves up delicious, pricey Northwest cuisine such as wild salmon and seafood risotto, while *Milford's Fish House*, 719 N Monroe St (ⓣ509/326-7251), has chic seafood like pan-fried oysters, lobster tail, Thai catfish and Manila clams.

Grand Coulee Dam

Eighty miles west of Spokane, the vast **Grand Coulee Dam** is the country's largest concrete structure and was one of the cornerstones of FDR's New Deal, and remains one of the world's top generators of **hydroelectricity**. Heroic tales of power production are detailed in the **visitor centre**, on Hwy-155 on the west side of the dam (daily 9am–5pm; free; ⓦwww.grandcouleedam.com), which also runs free tours of the dam and one of its massive generating plants. The area offers little in the way of notable accommodation or food, but more than thirty **campgrounds** lie around the 150-mile-long, spindly reservoir of **Lake Roosevelt**, which becomes more woody and secluded as you get further north. Some noteworthy spots include *Spring Canyon Campground*, on the lakeshore (ⓣ1-877/444-6777, $10 May–Sept, rest of year $5; ⓦwww.nps.gov/laro), and *Steamboat Rock State Park*, twelve miles south of Grand Coulee (ⓣ509/633-1304; $21–28).

Oregon

For nineteenth-century pioneers on the arduous Oregon Trail, the rich and fertile **Willamette Valley** was the promised land of Oregon (OR-uh-gun), and it's still the heart of the state's social, political and cultural life. **Portland**, the biggest city, is centralized and walkable, with a cosy European feel; **Salem**, the state capital, maintains a small-town air; and **Eugene** is a likeable college community.

East of Portland, waterfalls cascade down mossy cliffs along the **beautiful Columbia River Gorge**, south of which looms the imposing silhouette of **Mount Hood**. Central Oregon is based around the popular recreation hub of **Bend**, while further south around **Grants Pass**, the major rivers carve steep gorges and make for some excellent whitewater rafting, and the liberal hamlet of **Ashland** offers a splash of culture with its annual Shakespeare Festival.

The **Oregon Coast**'s most northerly town, **Astoria**, enjoys a magnificent setting strewn with imposing Victorian homes, while farther south, wide expanses of pristine sand are broken by jagged black monoliths, and pale lighthouses look out from stark headlands over sheltered coves. Finally, the rugged deserts and lava fields of **Eastern Oregon** are much more remote, and some small towns still celebrate their cowboy roots with annual rodeos.

Portland

With few major attractions and an unpretentious bohemian flavour, **PORTLAND** makes for an excellent spot to slow down and relax in the wealth of good diners, microbreweries, clubs and coffeehouses. Though sporting grand Beaux Arts architecture, Portland has a small-city feel thanks to a walkable urban core of short city blocks and attractions that cluster close together. The city is also internationally famous for its **bicycling** culture, with two-wheeled commuting a rising trend and major streets losing their auto lanes to make way for more prominent bike lanes.

The city was named after Portland, Maine, following a coin toss between its two East Coast founders in 1845 ("Boston" was the other option). Its location on the **Willamette River**, just 78 miles from the Pacific, made it a perfect lumber and trading port, and it grew quickly, replacing its clapboard houses with ornate facades and Gothic gables. Though the heroic age of timber is long gone, as a reminder of that era, the town's quirky downtown "**Benson Bubblers**" – four-headed drinking fountains funded by a lumber baron – are constantly flowing.

Arrival and information

Portland International Airport (PDX) is a twenty-minute drive from downtown, also accessed from Terminal C by the **MAX Red Line** light rail (every 5–20min, 5am–midnight; $2.30), which shuttles passengers on a 40-minute trip downtown. A **cab** from the airport into town costs $30–40. Greyhound **buses**, 550 NW 6th Ave (ⓣ503/243-2361), and Amtrak **trains**, close by at 800 NW 6th Ave (ⓣ503/273-4865), are within walking distance of the centre; if you arrive at night, take a cab – this part of town can be dicey after dark.

The **visitor centre**, in Pioneer Square at 701 SW 6th Ave (Mon–Fri 8.30am–5.30pm, Sat 10am–4pm; ⓣ503/275-8355, ⓦwww.travelportland.com), has maps and information on the city and the state. Portland's main **post office** is at 715 NW Hoyt St (ⓣ503/294-2124; zip code 97205). Unlike most US states, Oregon has **no sales tax**, so buying goods here is cheaper than in neighbouring states.

City transport

You can see much of the compact city centre on **foot**, or along the city's impressive, extensive network of **cycling** paths and trails (visit ⓦwww.portlandonline.com/transportation for maps and information); the most central place to **rent** a bike is at Waterfront Bicycles, 10 SW Ash St ($9/hr or $28/half-day; ⓣ503/227-1719). Portland also has an excellent public transit network. Its **MAX light rail** system (see Tri-Met fares below) channels riders around central downtown and Old Town, connecting to the western and eastern suburbs on the **Red and Blue lines**; north Portland on the **Yellow Line**; and the far eastern and southern suburbs on the **Green Line**. Tri-Met **buses** are based at the downtown **transit mall** along Fifth and Sixth avenues. The **Tri-Met Ticket Office** in Pioneer Square (Mon–Fri 8.30am–5.30pm, unstaffed Sat 10am–4pm; ⓣ503/238-7433, ⓦwww.trimet.org) offers free transit maps and sells all-zone day tickets ($4.75), regular fares ($2–2.30) and other passes.

The colourful **Portland Streetcar** line runs between the south waterfront, Pearl District and Northwest Portland, covering many downtown sights on NW and SW 10th and 11th streets – and will connect to the Eastside in coming years. As with buses, **fares** are free inside Fareless Square – basically the downtown core – otherwise $2 (ⓦwww.portlandstreetcar.org). At the streetcar's southern terminus, at SW Moody Avenue and Gibbs Street, the sleek **Aerial Tram** (Mon–Fri 5.30am–9.30pm, Sat 9am–5pm, Sun 1–5pm; $4 return; ⓦwww.portlandtram.org) connects the south waterfront to OHSU hospital 500ft up – a 3-minute ride that's great for viewing the beautiful landscape of trees, skyscrapers and, on a clear day, Mount Hood. Finally, **taxis** don't stop in the street; get one at a hotel or call Broadway Cab (ⓣ503/227-1234) or Portland Taxi Co. (ⓣ503/256-5400).

Accommodation

Flavourless **motels** line the interstates, but for a few dollars more you're far better staying downtown, where you'll find **hostels**, **B&Bs** and a good range of **hotels**, the pick of which occupy grand and elegantly restored old buildings.

Hotels, motels and B&Bs

Ace 1022 SW Stark St ⓣ503/228-2277, ⓦwww.acehotel.com. Affordable boutique hotel with amenities like flat-screen TVs, in-room murals and other fun art, wi-fi, a photo booth and convenient location two blocks from Powell's Books. ❹

Benson 309 SW Broadway ⓣ503/228-2000 or 1-888/523-6766, ⓦwww.bensonhotel.com. The spot for visiting dignitaries and celebs, this classy hotel has a superb walnut-panelled 1912 lobby, and a wide range of rooms, suites and penthouses with modern appointments. ❻

Edgefield 2126 SW Halsey St ⓣ503/669-8610 or 1-800/669-8610, ⓦwww.mcmenamins.com. East of town in the suburb of Troutdale, this unique brewery-resort has restaurants, bars, winery and tasting room, distillery, movie theatre and golf course. Also with its own hostel, at $30/dorm bed. The cheapest doubles have shared baths. ❸

Governor 611 SW 10th Ave ⓣ1-800/554-3456 or 503/224-3400, ⓦwww.governorhotel.com. Stylish 1909 pile rich with elegant rooms and suites with fireplaces, spas, sofas and stylish decor, plus an on-site pool and fitness centre. A block from MAX and streetcar lines. ❻

Heathman 1001 SW Broadway ⓣ503/241-4100 or 1-800/551-0011, ⓦwww.heathmanhotel.com. This lovely Neoclassical building, with an elegant, teak-panelled interior and much marble and brass, has splendid rooms and suites, HDTV, excellent restaurant and popular lobby-lounge where you can swill among the swells. ❼

Heron Haus 2545 NW Westover Rd ⓣ503/274-1846, ⓦwww.heronhaus.com. Stylish 1904 Tudor B&B, with some large suites featuring fireplaces, spas and cosy sitting areas. Excellent continental breakfast and close hiking access to Portland's expansive Forest Park. ❻

Hotel DeLuxe 729 SW 15th Ave ⓣ1-866/986-8085, ⓦwww.hoteldeluxeportland.com. Boutique treasure with smart decor and on-site gym, plus in-room wi-fi, iPod stations and HDTVs – plus outdoor movies on the roof every Thurs night in summer. Well placed along the MAX tracks, just west of downtown. ❻

Inn at Northrup Station 2025 NW Northrup St ⓣ503/224-0543, ⓦwww.northrupstation.com. Cute boutique hotel on the trolley line in Northwest Portland, offering colourful suites with splashy designs, some with kitchens, patios and in-room bars. ❻

Jupiter 800 E Burnside ⓣ503/230-9200, ⓦwww.jupiterhotel.com. Youth-oriented motel flush with arty minimalism, a party atmosphere and quirky rooms. The uber-cool presence of the adjoining *Doug Fir Lounge* (see p.983) makes it worthwhile. ❺

Kennedy School 5736 NE 33rd Ave ⓣ503/249-3983 or 1-888/249-3983, ⓦwww.mcmenamins.com. Unique rooms in a refurbished 1915 schoolhouse with chalkboards and cloakrooms, plus modern appointments. Multiple on-site brewpubs, movie theatre, outdoor bathing pool and "detention bar." ❹

Monaco 506 SW Washington St ⓣ503/222-0001 ⓦwww.monaco-portland.com. Primo luxury spot that appeals for its designer decor, free wi-fi, flat-panel TVs and DVD players, and central location in the downtown core. ❼

The Nines 525 SW Morrison ⓣ1-877/229-9995, ⓦwww.thenines.com. The most central hotel in Portland, hovering above Pioneer Courthouse Square and offering visitors upmarket designer furnishings, DVD players, iPod docks and an on-site ballroom and gym. ❼

White Eagle 836 N Russell St ⓣ503/335-8900, ⓦwww.mcmenamins.com. Ultra-cheap 1905 hotel and hip brewpub north of downtown. Rooms are clean and simple, with shared baths. Live music nightly downstairs – so early sleepers beware. ❶–❷

Hostels

HI-Portland Hawthorne 3031 SE Hawthorne Blvd ⓣ503/236-3380 or 1-866/447-3031, ⓦwww.portlandhostel.org. Nice Victorian house in the Hawthorne District, offering free wi-fi, tours of local sights, cheap bike rental and occasional live music. Dorms $22–26, private rooms ❷

HI-Portland Northwest 425 NW 18th Ave ⓣ503/241-2783, ⓦwww.nwportlandhostel.com. Located in a nineteenth-century home in Northwest Portland. Contains espresso bar, free wi-fi, kitchen and fireplace. Dorms $25–28, private rooms ❷–❸

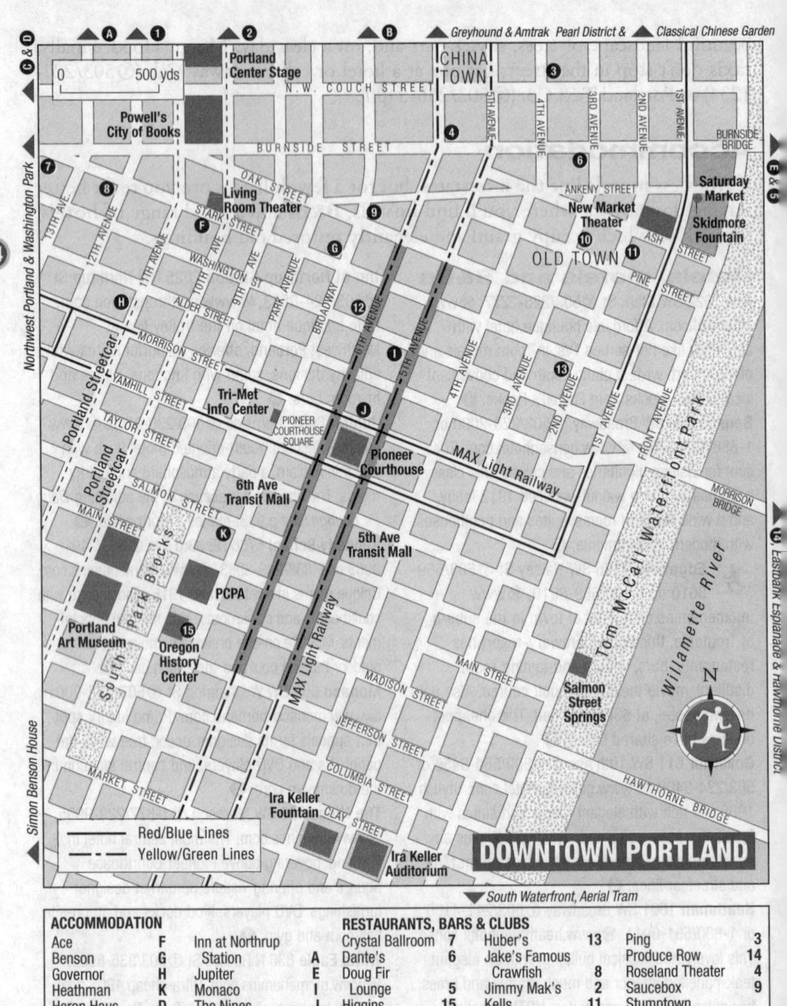

The City

The **Willamette** (pronounced "wuh-LAM-it") **River** bisects Portland into its east and west sides, with **Burnside Street** delineating north from south; each street address describes its relation to these dividers – SE, NW, SW and NE (there's also N, which is everything east of the river and roughly west of I-5). The **downtown core** lies between the river's west bank and the I-405 freeway, in the city's southwest section.

Downtown

Named after the adjacent **Pioneer Courthouse**, a Neoclassical 1868 structure that still maintains its judicial function, **Pioneer Courthouse Square** is the indisputable centre of Portland. Surrounded by **downtown**'s historic white terracotta buildings, the square's curving brick terraces are regularly filled with music and people. Just south of the square, at SW Broadway and Salmon, you can take a two-and-a-half-hour **walking tour** of city highlights (daily 10am; $19; Ⓦwww.portlandwalkingtours.com), a good introduction for first-time visitors.

Broadway epitomizes Portland's mix of early grandeur and new wealth – prestigious hotels share space with cultural institutions, such as the grand old Paramount movie theatre, restored as part of the impressive **Portland Center for the Performing Arts**, 1111 SW Broadway (Ⓣ503/248-4335, Ⓦwww.pcpa.com). One block west, the **South Park Blocks** are a twelve-block green belt and favourite Portland hangout, under the shadow of statues of Teddy Roosevelt riding on to victory at San Juan Hill and a dour Abe Lincoln. The park hosts a popular **farmers' market** (mid-March to mid-Dec Sat 8.30am–2pm; Ⓦwww.portlandfarmersmarket.org) that draws fruit and vegetable growers, and other vendors of bread, pastries, candles and handicrafts. Sitting nearby is the grand **Simon Benson House**, Park at Montgomery Street (Mon–Fri 9am–5pm; Ⓣ503/725-4948), a Queen Anne mansion once owned by a famous timber baron, featuring graceful moon windows and horseshoe arches, and a lovely wraparound veranda.

Several blocks north, the **Portland Art Museum**, 1219 SW Park Ave (Tues, Wed & Sat 10am–5pm, Thurs & Fri till 8pm, Sun noon–5pm; $12; Ⓦwww.pam.org), has a wide-ranging collection of Northwest Native American masks, Mexican statues and ancient Chinese figures. In its **Mark Building**, it holds a fine array of modern and postmodern works in various media, with part of the top floor reserved for temporary shows. Across the park, decorated with huge trompe l'oeil pioneer murals, the **Oregon History Center**, 1200 SW Park Ave (Tues–Sat 10am–5pm, Sun noon–5pm; $11; Ⓦwww.ohs.org), presents imaginative exhibits exploring different facets of the state's history.

A half-mile east is a favourite urban oasis, the two-mile-long **Tom McCall Waterfront Park**, where flocks of Canadian geese abound on the grass, and young and old alike dash through the fountains of **Salmon Street Springs**. As a cheap and fun way to get wet, the springs are second only in popularity to the user-friendly **Ira Keller Fountain**, SW 3rd and Clay, a huge water sculpture just west of the riverfront, where you can clamber around and get drenched on huge concrete blocks and pillars.

Old Town and Chinatown

Old Town, the area around and just south of the **Burnside Bridge**, is where Portland was founded in 1843, and where hapless drunks were once regularly kidnapped, or "shanghaiied", to be indentured servants on Asia-bound ships. These days, missions for the homeless coexist with galleries, brewpubs, boutiques and, especially, clubs. The **Saturday Market** (March–Dec Sat 10am–5pm, Sun 11am–4.30pm; Ⓦwww.portlandsaturdaymarket.com) packs the area around the Burnside Bridge with arts and crafts stalls, eclectic street musicians, spicy foods and lively crowds, all right by the MAX tracks.

North of Burnside, the ornamental gate at Fourth Avenue marks **Chinatown**, once the second-largest Chinese community in the US until the 1880s, when racist attacks forced most to leave. There's still enough of a community here to support a range of cheap ethnic restaurants and the enticing **Classical Chinese Garden**, NW 3rd Avenue at Everett (daily: April–Oct 10am–6pm; Nov–March till 5pm; $8.50; Ⓦwww.portlandchinesegarden.org), a Suzhou-styled garden with traditional vegetation, ponds and walkways.

Pearl District and Northwest Portland

Northwest of Chinatown lies the chic **Pearl District**, a gentrified zone thick with lofts, galleries, restaurants and boutiques, at its swankiest between NW 10th and 12th avenues, and Glisan and Northrup streets. Nearby at 10th and Johnson, **Jamison Park**'s terraced fountain is popular with countless children, while a few blocks north, **Tanner Springs Park** has an odd design of metal girders bordering sloping, marshy turf peppered with benches and indigenous plants. On the southern edge of the Pearl is Portland's biggest draw, the famed **Powell's City of Books**, 1005 W Burnside St (daily 9am–11pm; ⓦwww.powells.com). With more than a million new, used and rare books on four floors, Powell's occupies an entire block, as well as separate branches around town, and provides free colour-coded maps so customers don't get lost.

Further west, what's known in travel brochures as Nob Hill is called **Northwest Portland** by locals. Stretching between Burnside and Pettygrove streets along NW 23rd and 21st avenues, the neighbourhood is thick with fine restaurants and boutiques, the assortment of handsomely restored Victorian homes adding an old-fashioned tinge.

Forest Park and Washington Park

A few miles west of Northwest Portland, the 5000-acre **Forest Park** (ⓦwww.forestparkconservancy.org) is Portland's best feature – the country's largest urban green space, interlaced with countless hiking routes, including the thirty-mile **Wildwood Trail**, which can be accessed around NW 31st Avenue and Upshur Street; otherwise, follow NW Thurman until it dead-ends and take **Leif Erickson Drive** (closed to traffic) deep into the hills. South of Forest Park, the elegant houses of the wealthy include **Pittock Mansion**, 3229 NW Pittock Drive (Feb–Dec daily 11am–4pm, opens 10am July & Aug; $8; ⓦwww.pittockmansion.org), a 1914 French Renaissance Revival gem with a stunning – and free – view of the city from its front lawn.

Beyond the mansion, the 130-acre **Washington Park** is home to a number of Portland's top attractions. These include the lovely **International Rose Test Garden** (daily 7.30am–9pm; free), featuring a huge array of bright early-summer blooms; the tranquil **Japanese Garden** (daily: April–Sept 10am–7pm; Oct–March till 4pm; opens at noon on Mon; $9.50; ⓦwww.japanesegarden.com), actually a collection of five traditional gardens with ponds, bridges, foliage and sand designs; and the **Oregon Zoo** (daily: May–Sept 8am–6pm; Oct–April 9am–4pm; $10.50; ⓦwww.oregonzoo.org), with the requisite primates, penguins, elephants and, this being the Northwest, beavers.

Most park attractions have easy access to **MAX light rail** ($2 from downtown), whose station is buried deep underground and accessible only by elevator. Once you get here, you can hop on a summertime **shuttle** (every 15min daily: June–Sept 10am–7pm; $2) and access all the park's major sights on a day-pass ticket.

The Eastside

Since the end of the nineteenth century, most of the city's population has lived on the **Eastside**. Perhaps the best reason to venture across the river is to walk or bike the three-mile loop of the **Eastbank Esplanade**, which connects from the Hawthorne to the Steel bridges on floating walkways and cantilevered footpaths, offering striking views of downtown. Near the loop's south end, the interactive exhibits and high-tech toys of the **Oregon Museum of Science and Industry (OMSI)**, 1945 SE Water Ave (Tues–Sun 9.30am–5.30pm; $11; ⓦwww.omsi.edu), are bright and kinetic, though primarily geared toward children and adults with only a sketchy knowledge of science. South of here, at SE Ivon Street, is another of Portland's outdoor delights, the **Springwater Corridor** (info at ⓦwww.40mileloop.org), a former rail corridor now redesigned as a lovely bucolic path leading 21 miles to the outskirts of the suburb of Gresham, with ample space for cyclists, runners and strollers – but no motorized vehicles.

Two miles further east, the **Hawthorne District** is Portland's best alternative culture zone. With Hawthorne Boulevard as its axis between 34th and 45th streets, and dominated by the quasi-Moorish 1927 *Bagdad Theater & Pub* at no. 3702 (☎503/236-9234), the area teems with bookstores, hip cafés, dive bars and cheap restaurants. Six blocks north, **Belmont Avenue** is a short historic corridor thick with boutiques, novelty shops and ethnic diners, cantered around 34th Street, while a mile southwest around 26th Avenue, the pocket of **Clinton Street** is home to a few good restaurants, funky bars and vintage clothiers.

Finally, intrepid Eastside explorers may wish to venture up to **NE Broadway**, between 12th and 20th streets, good for its ethnic and upmarket restaurants; the galleries and diners of the gentrifying **North Mississippi District**, between Beech and Skidmore streets; the gallery- and boutique-rich stretch of **NE Alberta Street**, between 20th and 30th avenues (at its most frenetic during the monthly Last Thursday art event; 6–9pm); or the antique-buying centre of **Sellwood**, several miles south of OMSI along Tacoma Street.

Eating

Portland's Northwest cuisine provides a mix of international cooking and fresh regional produce, and the city is becoming nationally famous for its many excellent **dining** options – especially the **"food cart pods"** (notably at SW 5th at Oak, SW 9th at Alder and SE 12th at Hawthorne) where vendors congregate in trailers and sell all manner of prime, sometimes gourmet meals for less than $10. Elsewhere, downtown, the Pearl District and Northwest Portland have swank cocktail bars, upscale bistros, and fun brewpubs, while the Eastside has many of the city's best new restaurants.

Beast 5425 NE 30th Ave ☎503/841-6968. Located near the Alberta District, a top showcase for all things beef, and anything from pork-trotters osso bucco to chicken-liver mousse and quail-egg toast. There are only two seatings per night, Wed–Sat only, so reserve ahead.

Country Cat 7937 SE Stark, Eastside ☎503/408-1414. Solid Southern-style cuisine that's great for its molasses-and-hickory duck leg, bacon-wrapped trout and other nouveau, moderately priced spins on traditional cooking.

Higgins 1239 SW Broadway, downtown ☎503/222-9070. Fine, expensive Northwest cuisine restaurant, whose menu rotates, but watch for the Alaskan halibut, salmon risotto and "whole pig" plate that features a festival of pork.

Hot Lips Pizza 721 NW 10th Ave, Pearl District ☎503/595-2342. A pizza joint serving the city's best organic pizzas – complex, delicious concoctions that use locally grown ingredients and include vegan options. Also at 2211 SE Hawthorne Blvd, Eastside (☎503/234-9999).

Jake's Famous Crawfish 401 SW 12th Ave, downtown ☎503/226-1419. A landmark for more than a hundred years, with a staggering, expensive choice of fresh local seafood like sturgeon and Dungeness crab, and spicy crawfish cakes. Terrific desserts, too.

Lauro Kitchen 3377 Division St, Eastside ☎503/239-7000. A local favourite that's one of the best value in town – great Northwest cuisine such as smoked-salmon ravioli, wine-braised short ribs and terrific desserts, with most entrees $15–18. No reservations, so expect a wait.

Le Pigeon 738 E Burnside St, Eastside ☎503/546-8796. Locals argue constantly about whether this is Portland's – or the Northwest's – best eatery. For its pricey but outstanding French-influenced beef-cheek Bourguignon, duck crepes and sweetbreads, you be the judge.

Los Gorditos SE Division at 50th St, Eastside ☎503/875-2615. One of countless taco trucks around Portland, but easily the best – and perhaps the best Mexican fare overall – for its cheap, delicious and huge burritos, quesadillas and fajitas (with some vegan options, too).

Lovely's Fifty-Fifty 4039 N Mississippi Ave, Eastside ☎503/281-4060. Odd name for a terrific gourmet pizza haunt, offering rotating toppings that may include hedgehog mushrooms, wild nettles, squid or an over-easy egg, for moderate prices.

Pazzo 621 SW Washington St, downtown ☎503/228-1515. Top-notch Italian and Northwest cuisine with a solid selection of fresh seafood and inventive pasta, on the expensive side for most items. The bar can make for good people-watching.

Ping 102 NW 4th Ave, Chinatown ☎503/229-7464. Looks like nouveau Chinese fare, but is actually based on Asian street-vendor cooking – including fried pork knuckles, stewed duck leg and many different, very tasty skewers – though for higher-end prices.

Pix Patisserie 3402 SE Division, Eastside ⓣ503/232-4407. Local hotspot with a colourful range of French desserts made by a Parisian-trained chef known as the "Pixie". Good for its international beers. Also at 3901 N Williams Ave, North Portland (ⓣ503/282-6539).

Pok Pok 3226 SE Division St, Eastside ⓣ503/232-1387. One of the city's best spots for Thai food – scrumptious curry noodles, green papaya salad and pad thai – though portions can be small. The Vietnamese fish-sauce wings are legendary.

Nightlife

Portland is a beer-drinker's paradise, with dozens of small-scale **craft** and **microbreweries**, including *Rogue Ales Public House*, 1339 NW Flanders St (ⓣ503/222-5910); *Bridgeport Brewing*, 1313 NW Marshall St (ⓣ503/241-3612); and *Widmer Gasthaus*, 929 N Russell St (ⓣ503/281-3333). McMenamins "concept" brewpubs sell their own locally brewed ales in unique settings, such as former schoolhouses and renovated hotels (ⓦwww.mcmenamins.com), and Belmont Station, 4500 SE Stark St (ⓣ503/232-8538), is the town's greatest retail beer seller, featuring labels from around the world. For **music**, Portland maintains a small but vital presence on the national map, with countless alternative bands. The coolest venues are located around east and west Burnside.

Bars, brewpubs and coffeehouses

Amnesia Brewing 832 N Beech St ⓣ503/281-7708. Terrific summertime people-watching in this microbrewer's beer garden, set on a happening stretch of the North Mississippi District.

Dot's Café 2521 SE Clinton St, Eastside ⓣ503/235-0203. Funky late-night spot decked out in garage-sale decor, offering good brews, classic burgers, cheese and jalapeno fries, and a helluva grilled-cheese sandwich.

Green Dragon 928 SE 9th Ave, Eastside ⓣ503/517-0660. Fine place to eat Northwest cuisine, but an even better place to drink – with dozens of choices scrawled on the chalkboard and a wide range of national and international taps.

Horse Brass Pub 4534 SE Belmont St, Eastside ⓣ503/232-2202. Offers a voluminous beer list loaded with micro- and Eurobrews – considered one of the best around – and a savoury British pub menu of Scotch eggs, bangers and mash, and the like. Fun atmosphere, too.

Huber's 411 SW 3rd Ave, downtown ⓣ503/228-5686. Portland's oldest bar is an elegant spot with an arched stained-glass skylight, mahogany panelling and terrazzo floor. Famous for roast turkey sandwiches and flaming Spanish coffees.

Kells 112 SW 2nd Ave, downtown ⓣ503/227-4057. Long-standing Irish bar, with fine authentic eats and a range of microbrews, imported beers and of course, Irish (and Scotch) whiskey. Expect loud, drunken hijinks on weekends.

Pied Cow 3244 SE Belmont Ave ⓣ503/230-4866. An Eastside favourite for its coffee, tea and dessert. Set in a stately Victorian house, it offers late-night hours, garden seating and the chance to puff fruit-flavoured tobacco from a hookah pipe.

Produce Row 204 SE Oak St ⓣ503/232-8355. An unglamorous spot by the railroad tracks but ideal for beer lovers, with dozens of taps and bottled brews. Also has a nice range of live music.

Saucebox 214 SW Broadway, downtown ⓣ503/241-3393. Great pan-Asian cuisine, colourful cocktails and nightly music that attracts black-clad poseurs and serious hipsters in the loft, and more serious diners in the front room.

Stumptown Roasters 128 SW 3rd Ave, downtown ⓣ503/295-6144. Widely acknowledged as the city's best coffee, made from a blend of seven different types and organically certified. The most convivial and central branch of a local chain.

Live music and clubs

Blue Monk 3341 SE Belmont St, Eastside ⓣ503/595-0575. A hip little spot where you can devour serviceable Italian food upstairs and hear the sounds of jazz performers downstairs.

Crystal Ballroom 1332 W Burnside St, downtown ⓣ503/225-0047. Two levels above the *Ringlers* bar, a nineteenth-century dance hall with a "floating" floor on springs. Bands tend toward great national indie rockers; also retro-DJs in "Lola's Room" on the floor in between.

Dante's 1 SW 3rd Ave, downtown ⓣ503/226-6630. Cabaret acts and live music mix with the club's signature "Sinferno" Sunday strip shows and "Karaoke from Hell" Mondays.

Doug Fir Lounge 830 E Burnside, Eastside ⓣ503/231-WOOD. One of the city's prime venues for alt-country, dance and indie rock. The adjacent *Jupiter* hotel (see p.977) can be handy for passing out afterwards.

Goodfoot 2845 SE Stark St, Eastside ⓣ503/239-9292. Frenetic live-music joint and dance club, always sweaty, smoky and packed on weekends – but worth it to hear top-notch DJs spinning funk and retro-soul.

Holocene 1001 SE Morrison St, Eastside ⓣ503/239-7639. Packed with hipsters posing at point-blank range and an essential stop for local DJs and bands, *Holocene* mixes a range of cocktails and even broader spectrum of musical styles.

Jimmy Mak's 221 NW 10th Ave, downtown ⓣ503/295-6542. One of the few choices for nightly jazz in a town not known to swing. Come by to hear local Mel Brown or visiting name acts.

Roseland Theater 8 NW 6th Ave, downtown ⓣ503/224-2038. Located in one of the city's dicier corners, but a top spot for rock and alternative acts – often the last affordable venue for fans before the groups start touring stadiums.

Wonder Ballroom 128 NE Russell St, Eastside ⓣ503/284-8686. A specially renovated old ballroom that plays host to some of the more intriguing national and international acts in indie rock and other alternative styles. Just off a gritty stretch of MLK Blvd, so drive or take a cab.

Performing arts

The **performing arts** scene revolves around the **Portland Center for the Performing Arts**, 1111 SW Broadway (ⓣ503/248-4335, ⓦwww.pcpa.com), which includes the **Arlene Schnitzer Concert Hall**. The "Schnitz" is a sumptuously restored 1928 vaudeville and movie house that presents musical extravaganzas, dance and theatre, hosting performances by the **Oregon Symphony** (ⓣ503/228-1353, ⓦwww.orsymphony.org) and **Oregon Ballet Theater** (ⓣ503/222-5538, ⓦwww.obt.org), among others. Several blocks away at SW 3rd Avenue, between Market and Clay, the **Ira Keller Auditorium** is home to travelling musicals and the **Portland Opera** (ⓣ503/241-1407, ⓦwww.portlandopera.org). **Portland Center Stage**, 128 NW 11th Ave (ⓣ503/445-3700, ⓦwww.pcs.org), is a premier theatre that offers new and classic works in the stylishly renovated space of an old armoury.

During the summer, some **free concerts** are held at Pioneer Courthouse Square, Waterfront Park, the zoo and the International Rose Test Garden. The free *Willamette Week* (ⓦwww.wweek.com) carries **listings** of what's on, as does the free *Portland Mercury* (ⓦwww.portlandmercury.com), and the Friday edition of the main local newspaper, *The Oregonian* (ⓦwww.oregonian.com).

Around Portland: the Columbia River Gorge and Mount Hood

East of Portland along the I-84 freeway, the **Columbia River Gorge** is a striking geological setting with gusty winds, craggy rocks and incredible views. Scoured into a wide U-shape by huge Ice Age-era floods, the gorge is a nationally protected scenic area (ⓦwww.fs.fed.us/r6/columbia), where waterfalls tumble down sheer cliffs, and fir and maple trees turn fabulous shades of gold and red in the autumn.

The most dramatic part of the gorge is around the town of **Hood River**, where colourful windsurfers in the summer bound over the white-capped waves, while rising to the south, the snowy peak of Mount Hood provides a romantic, mist-shrouded backdrop. The narrow, winding **Historic Columbia River Highway** (accessible at exits 22 or 35 off I-84) boasts several excellent vantage points, particularly at **Crown Point**, where the 1915 **Vista House** lookout – perched high above the gorge about ten miles east of Troutdale – has been restored to its original rustic charm (May–Oct daily 10am–4pm; free; ⓦwww.vistahouse.com). Further east, some old highway sections are closed to automotive traffic, but open to hikers and cyclists, while down on the Columbia River itself (I-84 exit 25) is **Rooster Rock State Park** ($5; ⓣ503/695-2261), popular with windsurfers but best known for offering one of the few clothing-optional beaches in the region.

The most spectacular of the waterfalls in the vicinity is the hugely popular **Multnomah Falls** (daily dawn–dusk; free; ⓣ503/695-2372), the second-tallest year-round waterfall in the US, whose waters plunge 530ft down a rock face, collect in a pool, and then drop another seventy feet. Further east, **Bonneville Dam** (daily 9am–5pm; free; ⓣ541/374-8820) is a colossal New Deal project that generates regional electricity and offers a chamber where you can see salmon making their way upstream.

Mount Hood

To the south along Highway 35, **Mount Hood** is a dormant volcano rising about eleven thousand feet – the tallest peak in the Oregon Cascades. The **Mount Hood Loop** – a combination of highways 35 and 26 – takes in both the mountain and the gorge and connects to numerous orchards along the way, which in the spring and summer offer great opportunities to sample fresh fruit, juice and desserts (see ⓦwww.hoodriverfruitloop.com). One of the other joys of the area is to explore the mountain via trails radiating out from its slopes; contact Mount Hood Information Center (see below) for information. The highest point on the loop at some 4000ft, **Barlow Pass** is named after Sam Barlow, a wagon-train leader who blazed the Oregon Trail's first "road" around the mountain, which became the unpleasant, precipitous alternative to the even more dangerous route rafting down the (undammed) Columbia River.

Near the intersection of highways 35 and 26, a turn-off leads to the grand, New Deal-era *Timberline Lodge* (ⓣ1-800/547-1406, ⓦwww.timberlinelodge.com; ❻), solidly built in rough-hewn stone and timber, and featuring an interior loaded with Arts and Crafts-style wooden furniture and antique fittings. It's also a popular ski resort (lift tickets $59; ⓣ503/272-3158), and was the exterior set for Stanley Kubrick's **The Shining**. Two other downhill ski areas – Mount Hood Meadows ($57; ⓦwww.skihood.com) and Mount Hood SkiBowl ($44; ⓦwww.skibowl.com) – are good alternatives, though without the handsome lodge. There are also many miles of cross-country skiing trails throughout the **Mount Hood National Forest**. For more information on mountain activities and lodging, contact Mount Hood Information Center (Mon–Fri 9am–5pm; ⓣ1-888/622-4822, ⓦwww.mthood.info).

Hood River

Adjacent to the Columbia River, north of Mount Hood, charming little **HOOD RIVER** is great for outdoor activities, with cycling shops lining the hillside streets and **Port Marina Park** to take in the windsurfers traversing the waves. One of the best **places to stay** is the *Columbia Gorge Hotel*, just off I-84 at the far west end of town, at 4000 Westcliff Drive (ⓣ1-800/345-1921, ⓦwww.columbiagorgehotel.com; ❼), where hacienda-style buildings perch on a clifftop right above the gorge, and the hotel's exquisite gardens even have their own waterfalls. More central, *Inn at the Gorge*, 1113 Eugene St (ⓣ541/386-4429, ⓦwww.innatthegorge.com; ❻), is a stately 1908 Colonial Revival B&B with minimal Victorian kitsch, but with DVD players and wi-fi. For **eating** and **drinking**, *Full Sail Brewing*, 506 Columbia St (ⓣ541/386-2247), is a fine local microbrewery; the *Sixth Street Bistro*, 509 Cascade Ave (ⓣ541/386-5737), has some reliable burgers and American fare; and *Mike's Ice Cream*, 504 Oak St (ⓣ541/386-6260), is known for its marionberry milkshakes. The **visitor centre**, 720 E Port Marina Drive (ⓣ1-800/366-3530, ⓦwww.hoodriver.org), provides information on all the regional attractions. The antique blue-and-red trains of the **Mount Hood**

Railroad (Ⓣ541/386-3556 or 1-800/872-4661, Ⓦwww.mthoodrr.com), offer avariety of sightseeing trips (2–4hr) along the Hood River Valley, using a railway that was built in 1906 to service the valley's agricultural communities. Trains depart from the old railway station at 110 Railroad Ave, just off Second Street (April–Dec; 2–6 weekly; $25–30).

The Willamette Valley

South of Portland, the **WILLAMETTE VALLEY** has a diverse agricultural scene, but is best known for its grapes. The scenic route through wine country, Hwy-99 W, accesses dozens of acclaimed **wineries**, most of which pour superb Cabernets, Rieslings and pinot noirs. Pick up a wine-country tour map from any local visitor centre (or visit Ⓦwww.oregonwine.org). In **Dayton**, the renowned *Joel Palmer House*, 600 Ferry St (Ⓣ503/864-2995, Ⓦwww.joelpalmerhouse.com), draws Portlanders for its delicious, if expensive, **Northwest cuisine**; in tiny **Dundee,** the same applies for *Tina's*, 760 N Hwy 99W (Ⓣ503/538-8880), and *Red Hills Provincial Dining*, 276 N Hwy 99W (Ⓣ503/538-8224). Solid choices for **accommodation** include *Lobenhaus*, 6975 NE Abbey Rd near Lafayette (Ⓣ1-888/339-3375, Ⓦwww.lobenhaus.com; ❻), with six modern B&B rooms, some with views of gardens, a pond and woods, and *Springbrook Hazelnut Farm*, 30295 N Hwy 99W, Newberg (Ⓣ1-800/793-8528 or 503/538-4606, Ⓦwww.nutfarm.com; ❽), a grand 1912 estate built around a restored farmhouse with a cottage and carriage house among orchards and vineyards.

Closer to Portland, Highway 99W passes historic **Oregon City**, the first state capital, at the end of the Oregon Trail. Today, with its trail museums closed due to budget cuts, the only reason to stop in town is the **John McLoughlin House**, 713 Center St (Wed–Sat 10am–4pm, Sun 1–4pm; donation; Ⓦwww.mcloughlinhouse.org), the 1846 dwelling of a pioneer that's loaded with artefacts and details on local history.

If you're headed through the valley on I-5, the main reasons to stop in **SALEM** are the modern, white Vermont-marble **State Capitol**, 900 Court St NE (Mon–Fri 7.30am–5pm; free; tours at Ⓣ503/986-1388), whose cupola is topped by a large gold-leaf pioneer, axe in hand, eyes to the West, and **Mission Mill Village**, 1313 Mill St SE (Mon–Sat 10am–5pm; $6; Ⓦwww.missionmill.org), a collection of well-preserved pioneer buildings and a gloomy, nineteenth-century woollen mill. If you're **camping**, head for the huge waterfalls and lush forests of **Silver Falls State Park** (Ⓣ503/873-8681; $16–39), 26 miles east of Salem, the state's most popular park – so reserve well in advance. In the general area, the valley also has some of the best examples of **covered bridges**, with thirty-four in the state spanning creeks from Albany to Cottage Grove (see Ⓦcoveredbridges.stateoforegon.com for a list).

Eugene

Student and hippie central, **EUGENE** is a liberal enclave and energetic cultural centre, to which the **University of Oregon** in the city's southeast corner lends a youthful bohemian feel, especially along 13th Avenue just west of campus. The campus is most worth visiting for its **Jordan Schnitzer Museum of Art** (Tues–Sun 11am–5pm, Wed closes 8pm; $5; Ⓦuoma.uoregon.edu), the jewels of which are a Cézanne watercolour, Asian art and artefacts (among them Japanese ceramics, lacquerware, textiles and gowns), and Russian Orthodox icons. Another major attraction is the **Saturday Market**, Eighth Ave and Oak St (April–Nov

10am–5pm; ⓦwww.eugenesaturdaymarket.org), a countercultural carnival with live folk music, plenty of handicrafts and oddball performers. Eugene is also a prime spot for **sports**, and trails abound in the city centre, along the river banks and up imposing **Spencer's Butte**, a huge basalt monolith south of town. Especially appealing, north of the Willamette River from downtown and the university, is four-hundred-acre **Alton Baker Park**, with running and BMX tracks, rock and other gardens, an amphitheatre for hosting seasonal events and concerts, and a science museum.

Ten miles west of Eugene on US-126, little **Veneta** hosts the **Oregon Country Fair** (tickets $20–28; ⓣ541/343-4298, ⓦwww.oregoncountryfair.org) in July, a long-standing hippie festival of music, art, food and dancing. Traffic can be heavy, and even if you have a car it's easier to go by bus – the LTD (see below) has special services.

Practicalities

Greyhound **buses** stop at 987 Pearl St, and Amtrak **trains** at Fourth Ave and Willamette St. Eugene has a terrific **bus** system, the LTD ($1.50; ⓣ541/687-5555, ⓦwww.ltd.org), offering day passes for $3. The **visitor centre** is at 754 Olive St (Mon–Fri 9am–5pm, Sat 10am–4pm; ⓣ541/484-5307, ⓦwww.travellanecounty.org).

The best **places to stay** include the *Campbell House*, 252 Pearl St (ⓣ541/343-1119 or 1-800/264-2519, ⓦwww.campbellhouse.com; ❻), an elegant 1892 Victorian home with 17 handsome rooms; and *Excelsior Inn*, 754 E 13th Ave (ⓣ541/342-6963 or 1-800/321-6963, ⓦwww.excelsiorinn.com; ❺), a small hotel with fourteen rooms and suites themed around classical music, plus a fine, on-site Northwest cuisine restaurant. Other good places to **eat** include *Café Zenon*, 898 Pearl St (ⓣ541/684-4000), with an eclectic, mid-priced menu rich with pasta, steak and international fare; and *Newman's Fish Company*, 1545 Willamette St (ⓣ541/344-2371), a fine seafood house where you can fill up on fish 'n' chips, clam chowder and shrimp skewers for less than $10. Funky *WOW Hall*, 291 W 8th Ave (ⓣ541/687-2746, ⓦwww.wowhall.org), showcases up-and-coming rockers; for a taste of the **music** scene near the university, stroll along **13th Avenue** and hear the indie rock and punk wafting out from the bars and clubs.

South to California

South of Eugene along I-5, unenticing **Grants Pass** is a great base for **white-water rafting** – the visitor centre, just off I-5 at 1995 NW Vine St (ⓣ541/476-5510, ⓦwww.visitgrantspass.org), provides brochures from more than a dozen licensed river guides. Beyond Grants Pass, I-5 dips southeast through **Ashland** (see opposite), taking a mountainous inland route to California, while thirty miles southwest of Grants Pass along US-199, at the dull city of **Cave Junction**, Hwy-46 veers east twenty miles to the **Oregon Caves National Monument** (90min tours daily April–Nov: hours vary, often 9am–5pm; $8.50; ⓣ541/592-2100, ⓦwww.nps.gov/orca). Tucked into a wooded canyon at a constant temperature of 41°F, it's actually one enormous cave, where the marble walls are covered with elaborate limestone formations. Close to the cave entrance is the appealing *Oregon Caves Chateau*, 2000 Caves Hwy (May–Oct; ⓣ1-877/245-9022, ⓦwww.oregoncaves.com; ❹–❻), an elegant 1930s lodge with grand public rooms. You can also try one of the **campgrounds** along Hwy-46, with *Grayback* and *Cave Creek* being the closest to the monument (ⓣ541/592-2166 for reservations; $10–18).

Ashland and the Shakespeare Festival

The progressive hamlet of **ASHLAND**, forty miles southeast of Grants Pass, has a magnificent Rogue River Valley setting, with good skiing in the winter and rafting in summer. However, it's mainly known for its **Oregon Shakespeare Festival**, held between February and October, packing audiences into the half-timbered **Elizabethan Theatre**. Adjacent to it, the **Angus Bowmer Theatre** stages both classical and more recent works, while the austere **New Theatre** has a mostly modern repertoire. The three theatres share the same box office, 15 S Pioneer St (tickets $20–96; ⓣ541/482-4331, ⓦwww.osfashland.org). There are also some pleasant cafés, galleries and boutiques around the **Historic Railroad District** (ⓦwww.ashlandrrdistrict.com), a few blocks north of the festival. For a dose of musical comedy to relieve the drama, try the **Oregon Cabaret Theater**, in a renovated pink church at First and Hargadine ($19–33; ⓣ541/488-2902, ⓦwww.oregoncabaret.com).

Practicalities

The **visitor centre** is at 110 E Main St (Mon–Fri 9am–5pm; ⓣ541/482-3486, ⓦwww.ashlandchamber.com). Greyhound **buses** drop passengers on the edge of town near the I-5 freeway exit. Ashland has more than sixty **B&Bs**, many of which are in charming Victorian homes; the Ashland B&B Network (ⓣ1-800/944-0329, ⓦwww.abbnet.com) has information on most of them. The best **hotel** is the grand and centrally located ★ *Ashland Springs*, 212 E Main St (ⓣ1-888/795-4545, ⓦwww.ashlandspringshotel.com; ❻), with its charming two-storey lobby, day spa and small but nicely appointed rooms; the *Winchester Inn*, 35 S 2nd St (ⓣ541/488-1113, ⓦwww.winchesterinn.com; ❻), has fetching en-suite rooms, attractive gardens and an excellent, expensive Northwest cuisine restaurant; and the top budget option is the well-placed *Ashland Hostel*, 150 N Main St (ⓣ541/482-9217, ⓦwww.theashlandhostel.com; $28 dorm beds, private rooms ❷). The main choices for **eating** are found along **Main Street**, near the entrance to Lithia Park. The choices vary from the eclectic entrees of the upmarket French *Chateaulin*, 50 E Main St (ⓣ503/482-2264), to the terrific Latin American dishes of *Agave*, 92 N Main St (ⓣ541/488-1770), and the elite Northwest cuisine fare of ★ *Larks*, 212 E Main St in the *Ashland Springs Hotel* (ⓣ1-888/795-4545). If you come in the summer, head twenty miles northwest to the preserved Old West hamlet of **Jacksonville** for the annual **Britt Festival** (June–Aug; most tickets $18–38; ⓣ541/773-6077; ⓦwww.brittfest.org), to hear the top names in jazz, pop, rock and country music.

The Oregon coast

The **Oregon coast** offers four hundred beautiful, moody and often secluded miles of stunning terrain, almost all of it public land, where parks and campgrounds abound, and the extensive beaches are open for hiking, beachcombing, shell fishing and whale-watching. A number of coastal state parks offer accommodation in the form of seaside **cabins** and **yurts** – domed circular tents with wooden floors, electricity and lockable doors, as well as bunk beds and a futon (ⓣ1-800/452-5687, ⓦwww.oregonstateparks.org; yurts $36–41/night, cabins $39–43). Alternatively, you can **camp** for $16–22 at various sites on the coast. For the most scenic transportation alongside the waves, **cycling** is always a good option, whether within the state parks, along US-101 (following the coast to California) or on the many smaller "scenic loop" roads. Pick up a coastal bike route map from any major visitor centre.

Astoria

Set near the mouth of the Columbia River, the port of **ASTORIA** was founded in 1811 as a base for exporting furs to Asia by John Jacob Astor, but nowadays many of Astoria's rusty canneries and nautical facilities have vanished, and what remains are a few dozen good boutiques, restaurants and antique stores. From the east, the main road, **Marine Drive**, runs parallel to the waterfront, about eight miles from the Pacific Ocean. Exhibits from Astoria's seafaring past are on display at the **Columbia River Maritime Museum**, 1792 Marine Drive (daily 9.30am–5pm; $10; ⓦwww.crmm.org), which also has impressive displays of native artefacts and reconstructed ships, as well as walrus-tusk Inuit sculptures once sold to sailors as scrimshaw.

From Marine Drive, numbered streets climb up towards fancy Victorian mansions, leading to the top of Coxcomb Hill, where the **Astoria Column** (daily dawn–dusk; $1; ⓦwww.astoriacolumn.org) is decorated with a winding mural depicting pioneer history, and offers stunning views for anyone willing to climb its 164 cramped spiral stairs. Back in town, the **Flavel House**, 441 8th St (daily: summer 10am–5pm; rest of the year 11am–4pm; $5; ⓣ503/325-2203), is the grand 1886 Queen Anne home of sea captain George Flavel, featuring main rooms set up as dioramas with period furniture and decor.

Less than ten miles south of Astoria, reached by a turn-off on Hwy-101, **Fort Clatsop National Memorial** (daily: summer 9am–6pm; rest of the year till 5pm; $3; ⓦwww.nps.gov/lewi) is a replica of Lewis and Clark's winter camp – the various exhibits, reconstructions and activities make it well worth seeking out, though in the summer, off-site parking (to accommodate all the visitors) is often necessary, at the water launch at Netul Landing, a mile south of the site off Fort Clatsop Road, where you can ride a **shuttle** back to the visitor centre. Further west, off US-101, **Fort Stevens State Park** (day-use fee $3; ⓣ1-800/452-5687) offers many good trails and miles of beaches, with the hundred-year-old iron carcass of the **Peter Iredale**, slowly sinking into the sand, one of the few shipwrecks you can actually crawl around on.

Practicalities

Bus or train access to this part of the coast is limited, but Amtrak operates a once-daily **bus** service that drops off near the **visitor centre** at 111 W Marine Drive (summer daily 8am–6pm; winter Mon–Fri 9am–5pm; ⓣ503/325-6311, ⓦwww.oldoregon.com), near the base of the US-101 bridge over the Columbia, which leads into southwest Washington (see p.969). To make a leisurely trip along the waterfront, hop aboard the **Astoria Trolley** (summer daily noon–7pm; rest of year Fri–Sun, hours vary; $1), historic rail cars that ply a tourist-oriented route. Many of Astoria's distinctive offerings are **B&Bs** – plenty of them in Victorian mansions. Among the best is the *Astoria Inn*, 3391 Irving Ave (ⓣ503/325-8153, ⓦwww.astoriainnbb.com; ❹), a charming 1890 Eastlake Victorian establishment with four comfy rooms, the requisite chintz and close access to nature trails into the hills. For fancier digs, the *Hotel Elliott*, 357 12th St (ⓣ1-877/EST-1924, ⓦwww.hotelelliott.com; ❼), is a historic 1924 structure with upmarket amenities in its rooms and suites, some with fireplaces and jacuzzis, while *Cannery Pier*, 10 Basin St, near the Astoria Bridge (ⓣ503/325-4996 or 1-888/325-4996, ⓦwww.cannerypierhotel.com; ❾), is a boutique property housed on a waterfront pier, whose sleek modern rooms have high-speed internet access, fireplaces and balconies.

Good places to **eat** include *Baked Alaska*, 1 12th St (ⓣ503/325-7414), which has fine, moderate to expensive entrees like halibut with applejack brandy, oysters and Dungeness crab, as well as the delicious eponymous dessert; *T Paul's Urban Cafe*, 1119 Commercial St (ⓣ503/338-5133), good for its fish tacos, clam chowder, pasta and sandwiches; and *Rogue Ales*, 100 39th St (ⓣ503/325-5964), which serves up its signature microbrews and burgers and seafood right on the water a bit east of town.

Cannon Beach

Seventeen miles south of Astoria, **Seaside** is a drab resort of carnival rides and chain motels, but another nine miles south, more upmarket and pleasant **CANNON BEACH** is best known for its 240ft-tall **Haystack Rock**, a black monolith crowned with nesting seagulls – accessible at low tide, though definitely not climbable. The place is at its liveliest during the mid-June **Sandcastle Competition**, a one-day event that draws inspired sand artists and hapless muck-shovellers from around the region. You're apt to see anything from sandy dinosaurs and sphinxes to mermaids and monkeys, with Jesus and Elvis also rising from the beach. To escape the tourists, head four miles north to **Ecola State Park**, where dense conifer forests decorate the basaltic cliffs of Tillamook Head, or south to **Oswald West State Park** (dawn–dusk; free; ⓣ1-800/551-6949), named after the pioneering governor who helped preserve most of the state's beaches, where there's a beautiful beach, rocky headland and coastal rainforest.

The **visitor centre** is at 207 N Spruce St (ⓣ503/436-2623, ⓦwww.cannonbeach.org). In town, **accommodation** is sparse, especially in the summer. *The Inn at Haystock Rock*, 487 S Hemlock St (ⓣ1-800/507-2714, ⓦwww.haystacklodgings.com; ⑤), is good value for its pleasant cottages that variously come with kitchenettes, fireplaces and jetted tubs, while the *Waves Motel*, 188 W Second St (ⓣ503/436-2205 or 1-800/822-2468, ⓦwww.thewavescannonbeach.com; ⑥), has agreeable studios and suites, some sited right on the seafront. For **food**, *Newman's at 988*, 988 S Hemlock (ⓣ503/436-1151), provides pricey continental fare that's fresh and succulent, from duck comfit and the catch of the day to beef medallions and mushroom polenta, and *Bill's Tavern & Brewhouse*, 188 N Hemlock St (ⓣ503/436-2202), is the town's busiest **bar**, offering decent bar fare along with its own handcrafted brews.

Tillamook to Newport

Forty-four miles south of Cannon Beach, **TILLAMOOK** is famous mainly for its **Tillamook Cheese Factory**, just north of town on US-101 (daily 8am–6pm, summer till 8pm; free; ⓦwww.tillamookcheese.com), where on a self-guided tour you can watch cheese evolve from milky liquid in huge vats to yellow bricks on conveyor belts, and sample quality ice cream in the process. South of Tillamook, Hwy-101 curves around bucolic inland valleys, but better is the lengthier alternative of the **Three Capes Scenic Loop**, which leads you on a circuitous trip lurching around picturesque bays and jagged promontories, across lowlands and around hillsides, until the road merges with Hwy-101 west of the coastal **Siuslaw National Forest**.

Further south, there's no avoiding **Lincoln City**, the ugliest town on the Oregon coast, sprawling along the highway for seven congested, dreadful miles, but hold out for another thirty miles and you'll reach **NEWPORT**, which makes a fine base for visiting the central coast. The **Historic Bayfront** along Bay Boulevard is the obvious first stop for many – with its souvenir shops, seafood diners and sea lions wallowing on the wharves – along with pleasant **Nye Beach**, a quiet oceanside gem further west. To the south, across the bridge at 2820 SE Ferry Slip Rd, the impressive **Oregon Coast Aquarium** (daily summer 9am–6pm; rest of year 10am–5pm; $15.45; ⓦwww.aquarium.org) is home to marine mammals like the sea otter and seal, seabirds like the tufted puffin, and a whopping octopus in a glass-framed sea grotto, but its highlight is Passages of the Deep, a shark-surrounded underwater tunnel. Just north of town, Newport's other top attraction is **Yaquina Head** (daily dawn–dusk; three-day pass $7), a deservedly decreed "Outstanding Scenic Area" with an informative marine biology centre, striking cape lighthouse, man-made tidepools, and jaunty seals and sea lions playing on the shoreline rocks.

Newport practicalities

Newport's Greyhound bus station is at 956 SW 10th St, and the chamber of commerce is at 555 SW Coast Hwy (Ⓣ541/265-8801, Ⓦwww.newportchamber.org). The best-known place to **stay** is the well-worn *Sylvia Beach Hotel*, on Nye Beach at 267 NW Cliff St (Ⓣ541/265-5428, Ⓦwww.sylviabeachhotel.com; ⑤), whose twenty rooms each bear the name of a famous writer, from Melville to Dickinson, but better is the town's wide range of **B&Bs** (details at Ⓦwww.moriah.com/npbba), with charming amenities set in historic houses and estates. Among the finest are the *Tyee Lodge*, 4925 NW Woody Way (Ⓣ1-888/553-8933, Ⓦwww.tyeelodge.com; ⑥), where six comfortable and modern B&B units have expansive oceanfront views, and *Elizabeth Street Inn*, 232 Elizabeth St (Ⓣ1-877/265-9400, Ⓦwww.elizabethstreetinn.com; ⑥), whose sizeable rooms have kitchenettes, microwaves, fireplaces and sea-facing balconies, and there's an on-site spa, gym and pool.

There's a cluster of serviceable **cafés** and **restaurants** on Bay Boulevard at the bayfront. *Mo's Original*, in the 600 block (Ⓣ541/265-2979), is the most conspicuous chowder house, but better is *Chowder Bowl*, on Nye Beach at 728 NW Beach Drive (Ⓣ541/265-7477), which, despite its unexceptional look, does serve the best bowl in town. *Rogue Ales Public House*, no. 748 (Ⓣ541/265-3188), is the liveliest spot for food and beer, and also offers one- and two-bedroom "Bed and Beer" hotel units (④–⑤, plus two complimentary bottles; Ⓣ541/961-0142) so you don't have to risk driving away drunk. Near Nye Beach, *Cafe Stephanie*, 411 NW Coast St (Ⓣ541/265-8082), is a good place to go for sandwiches, fish tacos and salmon chowder, with filling breakfasts, too.

Oregon Dunes National Recreation Area

Beginning at the town of Florence, colossal sand dunes dominate the coast for 45 miles, punctuated with dramatic pockets of forest and lake, and rise up to an incredible 180ft high, but are infrequently visible from Hwy-101. About half of them, however, are accessible to the public in the **Oregon Dunes National Recreation Area**, part of the Siuslaw National Forest ($5 day-use fee; Ⓦwww.fs.fed.us/r6/siuslaw). The US Forest Service, which manages the dunes, maintains evocative **hiking trails** that are, for the most part, free of ATVs and proceed through a variety of terrains. More information is available from local visitor centres and the **Oregon Dunes National Recreation Area Visitor Center**, 855 Highway Ave (summer daily 8am–4.30pm, rest of the year Mon–Fri same hours; Ⓣ541/271-6000), at the junction of Hwy-101 and Hwy-38, twenty miles south of Florence.

Bandon

At the mouth of the Coquille River along US-101, easy-going **BANDON** is a quaint beach town that has the usual souvenir shops, chain stores and motels, as well as a rugged **beach** strewn with unusual rock formations and magnificent in stormy weather. In calmer conditions, clam-diggers head off to the river's mudflats and crabbers gather at the town dock, and the whole scene makes for a nice stroll. The **visitor centre** is at 300 SE 2nd St (Ⓣ541/347-9616, Ⓦwww.bandon.com), and there's oceanfront **accommodation** just south of town at the *Sunset Motel*, 1865 Beach Loop Drive (Ⓣ541/347-2453 or 1-800/842-2407, Ⓦwww.sunsetmotel.com; ③–⑥), which offers a wide range of oceanfront rooms, condos and seafront cabins. In town, the place to stay is the harbourfront *Sea Star Guest House*, 370 1st St (Ⓣ541/347-9632, Ⓦwww.seastarbandon.com; ④), offering kitchenettes and wi-fi, suites and a penthouse, plus a harbour and sunset view from a deck. You can **camp** just north of town at **Bullards Beach State Park** ($24; ⓣ541/347-2209), where the disused Coquille River Lighthouse casts a romantic silhouette over miles of windswept sands. For **dining**, you can wolf down the crustacean catch of the day at *Tony's Crabshack*, 155 First St (ⓣ541/347-2875), which also has tasty shrimp cocktails, chowder and crab sandwiches, and *Wild Rose Bistro*, 130 Chicago Ave SE (ⓣ541/347-4428), which has fine pasta and steak, too, as well as good home-made bread and desserts.

Port Orford to the California border

Towns are fewer and farther apart going south on US-101 from Bandon, with the coastline at its prettiest beyond **Port Orford**, where forested mountains sweep smoothly down to the sea. These mountains mark the western limit of the **Siskiyou National Forest**, a vast slab of remote wilderness best explored by boat along the turbulent Rogue River from workaday **GOLD BEACH**. Here, the **visitor centre**, on the main road at 29795 Ellensburg Ave (ⓣ541/247-0923, ⓦwww.goldbeachchamber.com), has details of rafting and powerboat excursions plus details for the town's basic motels and hotels. Starting seven miles south of Gold Beach are a trio of very appealing state parks: **Cape Sebastian**, which has a fine viewpoint perched two hundred feet above the surging waves, as well as trails through flowery meadows and ocean bluffs; **Pistol River**, best known for its fabulous collection of sea stacks – monstrous, gnarled behemoths scattered amid the waters – and regular **windsurfing** competitions; and **Samuel H. Boardman**, a twelve-mile coastal strip rich with viewpoints, picnic areas and scenic paths. Finally, at the state's far southwestern corner, **Brookings** is a retirement-oriented town with a warm climate, and is best used as a base for exploring northern California's **Redwood National Park**, with the park's headquarters just 25 miles south in Crescent City (see p.942). Contact the Brookings **visitor centre** (ⓣ541/469-3181, ⓦwww.brookingsor.com) for more details.

Central Oregon

East of the Cascades, Oregon grows warmer and drier, as green mountains and valleys give way to the high desert, with sagebrush, juniper trees, craggy hills and stark rock formations broken up by the occasional tract of pine forest. **Central Oregon**'s eye-catching volcanic landscape also features cracked lava beds, towering cone-like hills and deep craters such as beautiful **Crater Lake** in the south.

Bend and around

BEND is the most useful base for visiting central Oregon, giving access to prime outdoor activities, and packed with good restaurants, microbreweries and sports shops. Bracketing the west side of downtown along the river, **Drake Park** is a popular half-mile stretch with pleasant paths, an outdoor stage and a setting near fetching **Mirror Pond**, the most picturesque sight in the city. Beyond recreation, the area's main attraction is the **High Desert Museum**, 59800 US-97 (daily: May–Oct 9am–5pm, $15; Nov–March 10am–4pm, $10; ⓦwww.highdesertmuseum.org), a fascinating collection of artefacts from Native American and pioneer history, along with displays of regional flora and fauna – river otters, porcupines and so forth – and a reconstructed pioneer homestead and sawmill. There are panoramic views over Bend and the Cascades from **Pilot Butte**, the remains of a small volcano a mile east of downtown off US-20; you can drive or walk to the top. Also worth a visit is **Smith Rock**, about 25 miles north (day use $5, primitive camping $5; ⓦwww.smithrock.com), a state park whose towering basalt cliffs draw thousands of rock climbers; the deep gorge also creates an ideal landscape for horseback riding, cycling and hiking.

Practicalities

Greyhound **buses** stop at 1555 NE Forbes Rd and the **visitor centre** is at 917 NW Harriman (ⓣ541/382-8048, ⓦwww.visitbend.com) – it and the **Central Oregon Welcome Center**, 661 SW Powerhouse Drive (ⓣ1-800/800-8334, ⓦwww.covisitors.com), have brochures and accommodation listings. The best **accommodation** can be found in several smart **B&Bs**, such as the trim and elegant ranch-style digs of the *Cabin Creek*, 22035 Hwy-30 East (ⓣ541/318-4798, ⓦwww.cabincreekbedandbreakfast.com; ❻), which has the added appeal of horses out the back, and the fancier *Lara House*, 640 NW Congress St (ⓣ541/388-4064, ⓦlarahouse.com; ❼), six nice rooms in a 1910 Craftsman estate, with flat-screen TVs and wi-fi. Alternatively, the most central is the *St Francis Hotel*, 700 NW Bond St (ⓣ541/382-5174, ⓦwww.mcmenamins.com; ❺–❼), a charming former Catholic school that offers rooms with wi-fi and free on-site movie-theatre admission, and the chance to stay in a nunnery, friary or parish house (❽). You can also camp ($17) or stay in a **yurt** ($29) in **Tumalo State Park** (ⓣ541/388-6055), near the Deschutes River five miles northwest along US-20.

For **eating** and **drinking**, *Pine Tavern*, 967 NW Brooks St (ⓣ541/382-5581), serves microbrewed ales, moderately priced seafood, steak and sandwiches, while the *Deschutes Brewery and Public House*, 1044 NW Bond St (ⓣ541/382-9242), serves some of the Northwest's best beers. Upmarket diners may enjoy *The Blacksmith*, 211 NW Greenwood Ave (ⓣ541/318-0588), with pricey but delicious Northwest cuisine such as BBQ ribeye steak, Idaho trout and king salmon filiets.

Mount Bachelor and the Cascades Lake Highway

The Northwest's largest ski resort, **Mount Bachelor**, 22 miles southwest of Bend (mid-Nov to late May; lift tickets $49–69; ⓣ1-800/829-2442, ⓦwww.mtbachelor.com), caters to intrepid downhill and cross-country skiers and snowboarders alike, with twelve ski lifts and no fewer than seventy runs. It's also the first stop on the **Cascade Lakes Highway**, a hundred-mile mountain loop road giving access to trailheads into the **Three Sisters** – a trio of spiky peaks visible throughout central Oregon – and passing dense forests and deep-blue lakes, crumbly lava flows and craggy peaks. Further south is the **Diamond Peak** wilderness area and a sprinkling of campgrounds (see ⓦwww.oregonstateparks.org for information). Get details from **Deschutes National Forest Ranger Station**, in Bend at 1001 SW Emkay Drive (ⓣ541/383-5300, ⓦwww.fs.fed.us/r6/centraloregon).

Newberry National Volcanic Monument

The so-called **Lava Lands** cover a huge area of central Oregon, but especially in the Bend area at **Newberry National Volcanic Monument** (dawn–dusk; day pass $5). Dating back seven thousand years to the eruption of Mount Newberry, the monument is actually a caldera – a huge, gently sloping crater laced with hiking paths, nature trails, campgrounds and prime fishing spots. Some of the highlights (most free with monument admission) include the chilly, mile-long **Lava River Cave** (May & June Wed–Sun 9am–5pm, July to mid-Sept daily till 5pm; $4 for a lamp), an eerie subterranean passage made from a hollow lava tube that remains a steady 42°F; the **Lava Cast Forest** – circular, basalt holes of tree trunks burnt by lava before they could fall; and the surreal landscape of the **Big Obsidian Flow**, huge hills of volcanic black glass that native tribes throughout the area once used to make arrowheads – be careful not to drag your hands across them as you stroll through. The **Lava Lands visitor centre** (hours vary, often Wed–Sun 9am–5pm; ⓣ541/593-2421), eleven miles south of Bend on US-97, is an excellent source of maps and information on hiking trails, and provides access to the monument's other major sight, **Lava Butte**, a massive 500ft-tall cinder cone, whose narrow rim you can reach by car and traverse in a short walk. There are several seasonal **campgrounds** here, too, mostly around the lakes (generally May–Oct; $14–18; reservations from visitor centre or US Forest Service office in Bend; see p.991).

Crater Lake National Park

Just over a hundred miles south of Bend, the blown-out shell of Mount Mazama holds the resoundingly beautiful **CRATER LAKE** (seven-day pass $10; ⓦwww.nps.gov/crla), the deepest lake in the Western hemisphere, formed after an explosion 42 times greater than that of Mount St Helens. The biggest island on the lake, **Wizard Island**, is actually the tip of a still-rising cinder cone, and the so-called **Phantom Ship** is a jagged volcanic dyke that, in dim light or fog, resembles a mysterious clipper on the water. In its snowy isolation, the lake, at a depth of nearly two thousand feet, is awe-inspiring; in summer, wildflowers bloom along its high rim; the waters host a small population of rainbow trout and kokanee (landlocked) salmon, but these were introduced in the early 1900s.

Practicalities

You'll need a **car** to get to the park, though only the southern route (US-62 from Medford) is open year-round. The northern access road (via Hwy-138) is more exciting, emerging from the forests to cut across a bleak pumice desert, though it's closed from mid-October to June, as is the spectacular, 33-mile "Rim Drive" around the crater's edge. Regular **boats** cruise the lake (mid-July to mid-Sept daily 10am–3pm; 1hr 45min; $27), reached via the sheer, mile-long **Cleetwood Cove trail**, which provides the only access to the lake surface. The trail is on the north edge, but visitor facilities are clustered on the south edge at tiny **Rim Village**, where the **visitor centre** (June–Sept daily 9.30am–5pm) is a few steps from *Crater Lake Lodge* (late May to mid-Oct; ⓣ541/830-8700, ⓦwww.craterlakelodges.com; ❻), a 1915 hotel on the lake's south side, with a magnificent Great Hall, complete with Art Deco flourishes and pleasant rooms – get either a corner room or one overlooking the lake. Operated by the same company, the *Cabins at Mazama Village* (June–Oct; same phone; ❺) are seven miles from the crater, offering private baths but few other amenities. Park **campgrounds** include the large *Mazama Village* (mid-June to early Oct; $21; reserve at ⓣ1-888/774-2728) and the much smaller *Lost Creek* (mid-July to early Oct; $21). The **park headquarters** is at the Steel Visitors Center, located three miles south of Crater Lake on Hwy-62 (daily: April–Oct 9am–5pm; rest of year 10am–4pm; ⓣ541/594-3100), where you can enquire about the activities on offer, including taking a **scuba dive** (June–Sept; free permits) into the depths of the deep blue lake.

Eastern Oregon

The sage scrubland, spartan hills and stark rock formations of **Eastern Oregon** have an austere beauty that's frequently inspiring, and there is a real sense of adventure in exploring this vast, sparsely populated land. Much of it is classic **cowboy country**, familiar from some of the Hollywood films not made in the Southwest. The unexpected colours of the **John Day Fossil Beds**, the remote, snowcapped **Wallowa Mountains**, and the wide chasm of **Hells Canyon** are all very dramatic landscapes, and not to be missed if you have the time to explore them. Eastbound on Hwy-126/26 from Redmond, you'll emerge from a brief passage through the **Ochoco National Forest** – also worth a look for its wooded slopes, craggy canyons and rocky pillars.

John Day Fossil Beds

John Jacob Astor's fur-trapping employee **John Day** provided the moniker for the **John Day Fossil Beds**, preserved in a layer of volcanic ash while the Cascades formed, just after the extinction of the dinosaurs 65 million years ago. There are three fossil sites, the first of which is the **Painted Hills Unit**, nine miles northwest of Mitchell, just off US-26. Striped in shades of beige, rust and brown, the surfaces of these evocative, sandcastle-like hills are quilted with rivulets worn by draining water. Thirty miles east is the **Sheep Rock Unit**, on Hwy-19, two miles from its junction with US-26. Here, the **Condon Paleontology Center** (hours vary, often daily 9am–5pm; free; Ⓣ541/987-2333, Ⓦwww.nps.gov/joda) provides a good introduction to the local geology and the world of fossils. A mile north is the **Blue Basin**, a natural amphitheatre where a mile-long trail leads past various fossil replicas, like that of a sabre-toothed cat and a tortoise that hurtled to its death millions of years ago. The last site, the **Clarno Unit**, is twenty miles west of the town of Fossil. It doesn't have a visitor centre, but does offer the **Trail of the Fossils**, where you can see up-close impressions of the plants and creatures that lived in the jungle-like forest conditions, along with huge **palisades** that loom over the setting – massive pillars of rock created by volcanic mudflows some 44 million years ago.

The Oregon Trail

Between the 1840s and 1870s, more than a quarter of a million Americans journeyed by wagon train from the Midwest on the **Oregon Trail**, fuelled by an idea of "Manifest Destiny" to see their country expand from coast to coast, regardless of who or what might be in the way. The first migrants were further inspired by the **missionaries** who went west to try to Christianize Native Americans in the 1830s, and who sent back glowing reports of the region's temperate climate, fertile soil, dense forests, fish-rich rivers and absence of malaria.

In spring 1843, more than a thousand would-be migrants gathered at Independence and Westport on the banks of the Missouri, preparing for the "**Great Migration**". Nearly all were experienced farmers, using ox-pulled wagons with flimsy canvas roofs to transport supplies and often walking alongside their vehicles, instead of riding and adding extra weight to them, as Hollywood would have it.

Traversing almost two thousand miles, the migrants forced their wagons across pristine rivers, forests and mountains, pausing at the occasional army fort or missionary station to recuperate. After three months on the trail, they arrived at what is now the town of The Dalles. From here the group faced an uneasy choice before reaching the lush Willamette Valley just beyond: build rafts and risk the treacherous currents and whirlpools of the Columbia River or take the equally perilous Barlow Road around Mount Hood (see p.984), notorious for its swiftly changing weather and steep hillsides.

Over the next thirty years, fifty thousand more settlers arrived in the Willamette Valley, with others moving into California and (what would become) Washington State. Along with helping Oregon to become a state in 1859, the migration spawned a cottage industry of specialist suppliers and wagon-builders. Inevitably, except for some isolated wagon-wheel ruts here and there, there are few surviving signs of the migrants, other than the considerable lore of their journey that continues to this day.

Baker City

In the forested hills east of John Day, US-26 turns southeast for the long run down to Idaho. More enjoyable is the far shorter drive on Hwy-7 through the southern reaches of the **Wallowa-Whitman National Forest** to the former Gold Rush boomtown of **BAKER CITY**, whose **Main Street** features stylish old piles mostly built of local stone in a potpourri of European styles – from Gothic through to Renaissance revivals. The **Oregon Trail Regional Museum**, 2480 Grove St (late March to Oct daily 9am–5pm; $5), showcases artefacts from pioneer days, but is most notable for its fine collection of rocks, petrified wood and fluorescent geodes. More expansive, the **Oregon Trail Interpretative Center**, five well-signposted miles east of town at Flagstaff Hill (daily: April–Oct 9am–6pm, $8; Nov–March till 4pm, $5; Ⓦoregontrail.blm.gov), features dioramas, replicas, relics and audiovisual displays, and four miles of trails revealing wagon ruts and other points of interest from that historic route (see box).

Greyhound **buses** connect to Portland at 515 Campbell St. The most prominent **hotel** is the 1889 *Geiser Grand*, 1996 Main St (Ⓣ1-888/434-7374, Ⓦwww.geisergrand.com; ❺), but somewhat better value is the *Bridge Street Inn*, 134 Bridge St (Ⓣ541/523-6571, Ⓦwww.bridgestreetinn.net; ❸), whose clean and simple motel rooms offer kitchenettes and microwaves. Otherwise, the surrounding Wallowa-Whitman National Forest has many **campgrounds**; get details from the **visitor centre**, 490 Campbell St, beside exit 304 on I-84 (Ⓣ541/523-5855, Ⓦwww.visitbaker.com). Among the limited choices for **eating**, try *Barley Brown's Brewpub*, 2190 Main St (Ⓣ541/523-4266), for its dependable pub fare and good microbrews; or the *Baker City Cafe*, 1840 Main St (Ⓣ541/523-6099), for its affordable pizza, pasta and sandwiches.

Pendleton

The large, flat **Grande Ronde Valley**, north of Baker City on I-84, is based around the dusty city of **La Grande**, but for local colour and history you're better off pushing northwest on I-84, following the route of the Oregon Trail, to **PENDLETON**. It's best known as the home of the popular, week-long **Pendleton Round-Up** in September ($15–20/event; Ⓣ1-800/45-RODEO, Ⓦwww.pendletonroundup.com), combining traditional rodeo with extravagant pageantry; the **Round-Up Hall of Fame**, 1205 SW Court Ave (June–Sept Mon–Sat 10am–4pm; $5), is stuffed with memorabilia, and around town you can pick up a cowboy hat or fringy shirt at one of the many Western boutiques. Elsewhere, the famed **Pendleton Woolen Mills**, 1307 SE Court Place (tours Mon–Fri 9am–3pm; free; Ⓣ541/276-6911, Ⓦwww.pendleton-usa.com), will mainly appeal to textile fans fascinated by the intricacies of carding, spinning, warp dressing and weaving, although you can always pick up a sweater, too. The town's star turn, though, is the **Pendleton Underground**, 37 SW Emigrant Ave (March–Oct Mon–Sat 9.30am–3pm, rest of year varies; 90min tours; $15; Ⓦwww.pendletonundergroundtours.org), which lets you tour the town's subterranean passageways, initially built for shelter from the inclement climate, but used during Prohibition as saloons, card rooms and brothels, as well as housing, laundries and opium dens.

Practicalities

Greyhound **buses** pull in at 801 SE Court Ave, and the **visitor centre** at 501 S Main St (Mon–Fri 9am–5pm; Ⓣ541/276-7411 or 1-800/547-8911, Ⓦwww.pendletonchamber.com), issues free town maps and has details of local attractions and accommodation. For **accommodation**, *Rugged Country Lodge*, 1807 SE Court Ave (Ⓣ1-877/7-RUGGED, Ⓦwww.ruggedcountrylodge.com; ❸), has affordable suites with wi-fi and complimentary breakfast; more unusual is the *Working Girls Hotel*, 17 SW Emigrant Ave (June–Oct; ⓣ1-800/226-6398; ❸), where four guest rooms and one suite are housed up in what was once – until the 1950s, in fact – a brothel. Most **restaurants** dole out hefty portions of all-American fare. The best of the lot are the *Rainbow Café and Lounge*, 209 S Main St (ⓣ541/276-4120), with Round-Up memorabilia plastered over the walls, and doling out hearty burgers, omelets and chicken-fried steak; and *Raphael's*, 233 SE 4th St (ⓣ541/276-8500), for its innovative Northwest cuisine, from elk medallions and huckleberry salmon to BBQ rattlesnake.

Hells Canyon

East of Joseph, marking the Idaho border, the **Snake River** has cut the deepest chasm on the continent – **Hells Canyon**, a 130-mile-long gorge that's a thousand feet deeper than the Grand Canyon, though it doesn't really look it, since it spreads out wider and lacks the sheer cliffs of its Arizona counterpart. With the **Seven Devils** mountains rising above it, the area is preserved as **Hells Canyon National Recreation Area** (day pass $5; ⓦwww.fs.fed.us/hellscanyon), where otters, mink and elk live, along with rattlesnakes, black bears and mountain lions. Motor vehicles are banned in much of the canyon, so you can only explore by foot or on horseback. Many of the forest roads that skirt the area are closed by snow much of the year. When open, if you intend to use them, first check with the **rangers** in Enterprise, 88401 Hwy-82 (ⓣ541/426-5546), or Baker City, 1550 Dewey Ave (ⓣ541/523-6391). Also available is information on the US Forest Service's twenty scattered primitive **campgrounds** (first-come, first-served; free or $5) – eleven in Oregon, nine in Idaho.

From Joseph, Little Sheep Creek Highway leads to **Imnaha**, where a narrow and perilous gravelled Forest Service road leads to a great view from **Hat Point**, site of a campground and lookout tower. The easier approach is at the south end of the canyon, along Hwy-86 east from Baker City. Another approach into the canyon, from the town of Halfway on Hwy-86, meets the Snake River at Oxbow Dam, where a rough Forest Service road leads to **Hells Canyon Dam**, the launching point for jet-boat and rafting trips in the canyon. Hells Canyon Adventures (reserve at ⓣ1-800/422-3568; ⓦwww.hellscanyonadventures.com) and other companies run these and other **tours** in the summer (2–3hr; $55–75/person).

15

Alaska

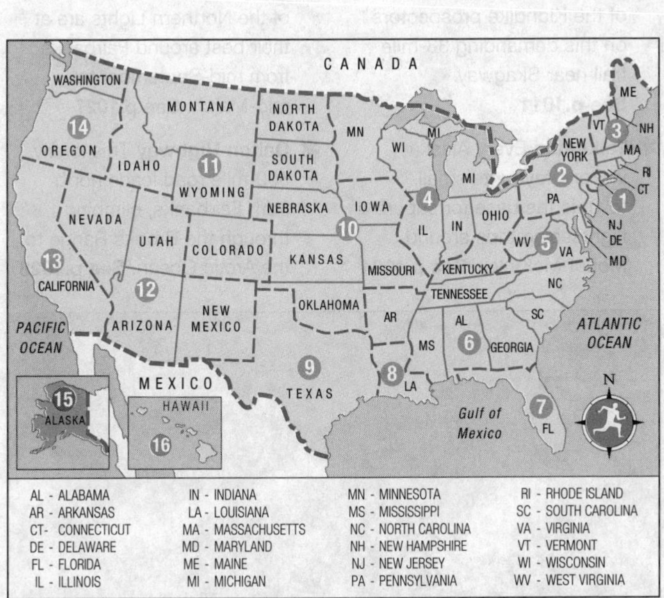

CANADA
WASHINGTON
MONTANA
NORTH DAKOTA
MN
MI
ME
VT
NH
NEW YORK
MA
RI
CT
OREGON
IDAHO
WYOMING
SOUTH DAKOTA
WI
MI
PA
NJ
DE
MD
NEVADA
NEBRASKA
IOWA
IL
IN
OHIO
WV
VA
UTAH
COLORADO
KANSAS
MISSOURI
KENTUCKY
CALIFORNIA
NC
TENNESSEE
OKLAHOMA
SC
ARIZONA
NEW MEXICO
AR
AL
PACIFIC OCEAN
ATLANTIC OCEAN
MS
GEORGIA
TEXAS
LA
MEXICO
HAWAII
ALASKA
Gulf of Mexico
FL
N
14
11
3
2
1
4
10
5
13
12
6
9
8
7
15
16
AL - ALABAMA
AR - ARKANSAS
CT- CONNECTICUT
DE - DELAWARE
FL - FLORIDA
IL - ILLINOIS
IN - INDIANA
LA - LOUISIANA
MA - MASSACHUSETTS
MD - MARYLAND
ME - MAINE
MI - MICHIGAN
MN - MINNESOTA
MS - MISSISSIPPI
NC - NORTH CAROLINA
NH - NEW HAMPSHIRE
NJ - NEW JERSEY
PA - PENNSYLVANIA
RI - RHODE ISLAND
SC - SOUTH CAROLINA
VA - VIRGINIA
VT - VERMONT
WI - WISCONSIN
WV - WEST VIRGINIA

CHAPTER 15 Highlights

* **Sitka** Russian influence blended with Native heritage and fabulous coastal scenery, make this one of Alaska's most diverting towns. See p.1005
* **The Chilkoot Trail** Follow in the (frozen) footsteps of the Klondike prospectors on this demanding 33-mile trail near Skagway. See p.1011
* **Talkeetna** Every Alaska visitor's favourite small town is the base for superb flightseeing trips around Mount McKinley. See p.1021
* **Denali National Park** Alaska's finest park offers superb mountain scenery and incomparable wildlife-spotting around the highest peak in North America. See p.1022
* **Aurora borealis** The spectacular after-dark displays of the Northern Lights are at their best around Fairbanks from mid-September to mid-March. See p.1027
* **Dalton Highway** This lonely 500-mile road leads north from Fairbanks, climbing through the Brooks Range to the Arctic Ocean. See p.1028

▲ Caribou stag, Denali National Park

15

Alaska

No other region in North America fires the imagination like **ALASKA** – derivation of *Alayeska*, an Athabascan word meaning "great land of the west". Few who see this land of gargantuan ice fields, sweeping tundra, lush rainforests, deep fjords and occasionally smoking volcanoes leave unimpressed. **Wildlife** may be under threat elsewhere, but here it is abundant, with bears standing twelve feet tall, moose stopping traffic in downtown Anchorage, wolves prowling national parks, bald eagles circling over the trees and rivers solid with fifty-plus-pound salmon.

Alaska's sheer size is hard to grasp. Superimposed onto the Lower 48 states, it would stretch from the Atlantic to the Pacific, while its coastline is longer than that of the rest of the US combined. All but three of the nation's twenty highest peaks are found here and one glacier alone is twice the size of Wales. In addition, not only does it contain America's **northernmost** and **westernmost** points, but because the Aleutian Islands stretch across the 180th meridian, it contains the **easternmost** point as well.

Perhaps surprisingly then, a mere 670,000 people live in Alaska, of whom only one-fifth were born in the state: as a rule of thumb the more winters you have endured, the more Alaskan you are. Often referred to as the **"Last Frontier"**, Alaska in many ways mirrors the American West of the nineteenth century: an endless, undeveloped space in which to stake one's claim and live without interference – or at least that's how Alaskans would like it to be. Since the late nineteenth century tens of thousands have been lured by the promise of wealth, first by gold and then by fishing, logging and most recently, oil. However, this has led to the marginalization of Alaska's 100,000 Native peoples, though Native corporations set up as a result of pre-oil boom land deals have increasing economic clout.

Travelling around Alaska still demands a spirit of adventure and to make the most of the state you need to enjoy striking out on your own and roughing it a bit. Binoculars are an absolute must, as is bug spray; the **mosquito** is referred to as "Alaska's state bird" and only industrial-strength repellent keeps it away. On top of that, there's the **climate** – though Alaska is far from the great big icebox people imagine. While winter temperatures of -40°F are commonplace in Fairbanks, the most touristed areas – the southeast and the Kenai Peninsula – enjoy a maritime climate (45–65°F in summer) similar to that of the Pacific Northwest, meaning much more rain (in some towns 180-plus inches per year) than snow. Remarkably, the summer temperature in the Interior often reaches 80°F.

Alaska is more expensive than most other states and major cities. There's little budget accommodation and **eating** and **drinking** will set you back at least twenty percent more than in the Lower 48 (perhaps fifty percent in more remote regions). Still, experiencing Alaska on a **low budget** is possible though it requires planning

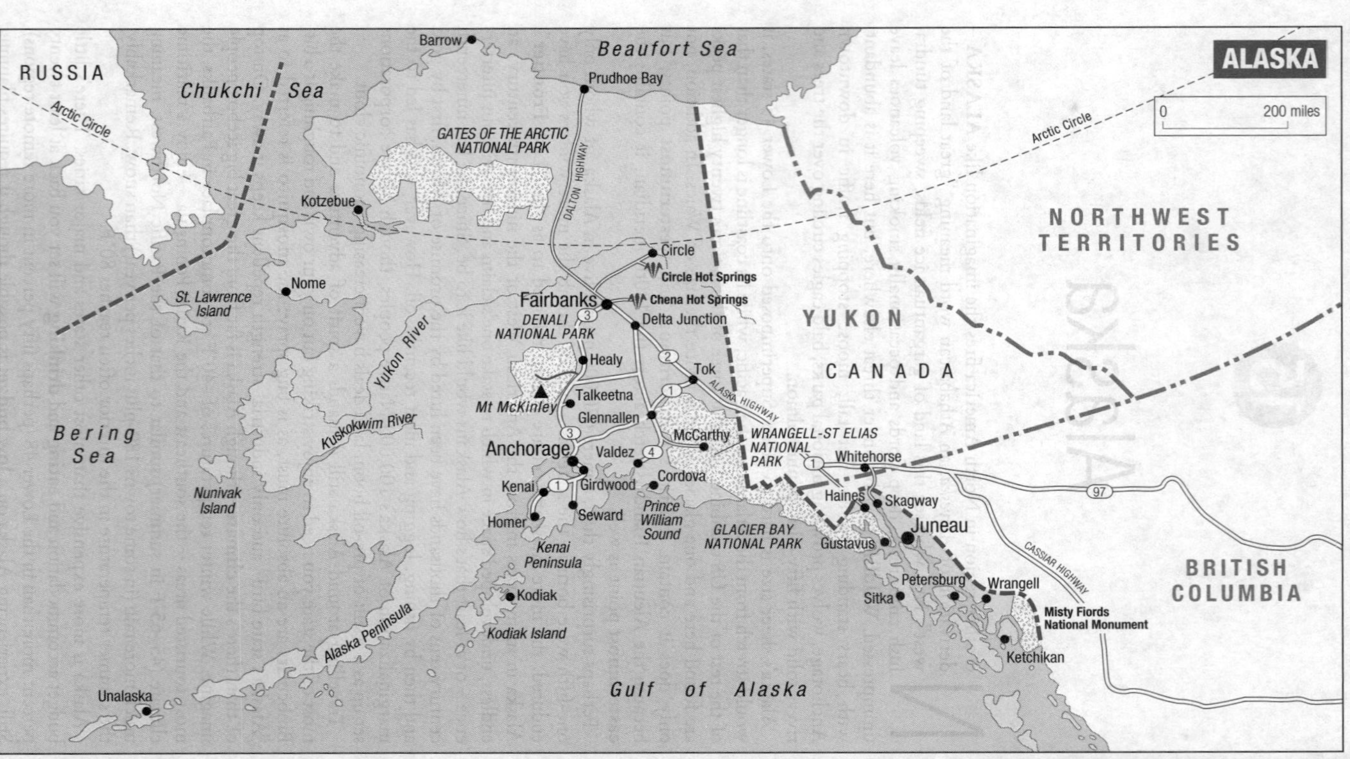
ALASKA
0
200 miles
RUSSIA
Chukchi Sea
Beaufort Sea
Arctic Circle
Arctic Circle
Barrow
Prudhoe Bay
GATES OF THE ARCTIC NATIONAL PARK
DALTON HIGHWAY
Kotzebue
Nome
St. Lawrence Island
Circle
Circle Hot Springs
Chena Hot Springs
Fairbanks
Delta Junction
DENALI NATIONAL PARK
Healy
Tok
ALASKA HIGHWAY
Talkeetna
Mt McKinley
Glennallen
McCarthy
WRANGELL-ST ELIAS NATIONAL PARK
Anchorage
Valdez
Cordova
Girdwood
Kenai
Seward
Homer
Kenai Peninsula
Prince William Sound
GLACIER BAY NATIONAL PARK
Whitehorse
Haines
Skagway
Juneau
Gustavus
Petersburg
Sitka
Wrangell
Misty Fiords National Monument
Ketchikan
CASSIAR HIGHWAY
97
Yukon River
Kuskokwim River
Bering Sea
Nunivak Island
Kodiak
Kodiak Island
Alaska Peninsula
Unalaska
Gulf of Alaska
YUKON
CANADA
NORTHWEST TERRITORIES
BRITISH COLUMBIA

and off-peak travel. From June to August room prices are crazy; May and September, when tariffs are relaxed and the weather only slightly chillier, are just as good times to go, and in April or October you'll have the place to yourself, albeit with a smaller range of places to stay and eat. Ground **transportation**, despite the long distances, is reasonable, with backpacker shuttles between major centres, although it is often easier to do combine a car rental with flights. **Winter**, when hotels drop their prices by as much as half, is becoming an increasingly popular time to visit, particularly for the dazzling **aurora borealis** (see box, p.1028).

Some history

Alaska has been inhabited for longer than anywhere else in the Americas; it was here that humans first reached the "New World" from eastern Russia, at least fourteen thousand years ago. Their descendants can be classified into four groups. The **Aleut**, in the inhospitable Aleutian Islands, built underground homes and hunted sea mammals such as walrus for food and clothing, while the nomadic **Athabascan** hunted caribou in the Interior. The warrior **Tlingit** lived in the warmer coastal regions of the southeast, where food was plentiful, while the **Eskimos** (or, more correctly, the Yup'ik and Iñupiat), inhabiting the northwestern coast, lived off fish and larger marine life.

In 1741, Danish explorer **Vitus Bering**, working for the Tzar of Russia, became the first Caucasian to set foot on Alaskan soil and found huge numbers of fur seals and **sea otters**, whose treasured pelts were made into hats. Russians, and later British and Spaniards, joined in the ensuing slaughter, with the Aleut forced to nearly wipe out the otters on behalf of the fur traders. By the end of the century, the Russians had established their Alaskan capital at present-day **Sitka** and pushed down the coast as far as Northern California.

Ultimately, declining sea otter stocks led Russia to sell its lands to America. On October 18, 1867, Secretary of State William Seward purchased what was disparagingly known as "**Seward's Folly**" or "Seward's Icebox" for $7.2 million – less than 2¢ per acre. Alaska soon turned out to be a literal **gold mine** with major discoveries at Juneau (1880), Nome (1898), and Fairbanks (1902). With logging companies and commercial fishing operations soon descending upon the territory, the government began to take a more active interest in its affairs and in 1959 Alaska became the **49th state**.

Fortune-seekers headed to Alaska again in the mid-1970s to build the **trans-Alaska pipeline** running south from Prudhoe Bay to the ice-free port of Valdez on Prince William Sound. Today, Alaska still derives the majority of its wealth from oil and gas and consequently, is prone to extreme boom-and-bust cycles. Once-lucrative fishing and lumber industries are fast giving way to tourism as a source of income and the ethical question of how best to use Alaska lands in the future has led to bitter controversy. Nowhere is this more apparent than in the case of the **Arctic National Wildlife Refuge**, a vast tract of tundra in Alaska's northeast that has some degree of protection, but is constantly under threat from the oil industry.

Getting to Alaska

Alaska is a long way from the rest of the United States, and however you get there it is going to be **expensive**. Having accepted that, however, there is no question as to the most **enjoyable** method – the memorable ferry trip on the Alaska Marine Highway, which runs 3500 miles from Alaska to Washington. Almost entirely in sheltered waters, you'll see plenty of marine wildlife and spend at least two nights on board bonding with fellow passengers.

By air

Most **flights** from the Lower 48 are routed via Seattle. The most frequent service is operated by Alaska Airlines (Ⓣ1-800/252-7522, Ⓦwww.alaskaair.com), who charge $500–600 return to Anchorage with optional stop-offs at Ketchikan, Juneau, Sitka and Cordova at little extra cost.

By sea

The **ferries** of the state-run **Alaska Marine Highway System** (Ⓣ1-800/642-0066, Ⓦwww.ferryalaska.com) reaching many places that cars can't, operate in two separate regions with only an occasional link. The popular **southeast** route runs a thousand miles from Bellingham, north of Seattle, through a wonderland of pristine waters, narrow fjords and untouched forests to Skagway, at the northern end of the **Inside Passage**, stopping at Ketchikan, Wrangell, Sitka, Juneau and Haines. The whole trip takes three days and costs $363 for walk-on passengers, $478 for a small car, $58 for a bicycle and $89 for kayaks. It is possible to sleep – and even to pitch a tent – on the "solarium", a covered, heated upper deck, while a two-berth cabin costs from $337. The **southwest** ferry system connects the Kenai Peninsula and Prince William Sound to Kodiak and the Aleutians and the two systems are linked by "Cross-Gulf" ferries from Juneau to Whittier and Kodiak twice a month in summer. Intermediate fares vary with distance: $45 from Sitka to Juneau; $83 from Sitka to Ketchikan; or $221 from Juneau to Whittier. While it's a bargain for foot passengers prepared to rough it, an extended voyage with vehicle and a cabin (both of which should be reserved in advance) becomes expensive. If you're driving up from the Lower 48, consider boarding a ferry at Prince Rupert in British Columbia, two days' drive north of Seattle. This saves one day at sea without missing much of the natural spectacle.

By road

For many people the drive up through Canada is one of the major highlights of a visit to Alaska. The only road is the 1500-mile **Alaska Highway** from Dawson Creek in British Columbia to Fairbanks, which was built by the military in just eight months. It has a fearsome reputation but is now fully paved with gas stations, campgrounds and hotels along the way. It remains as beautiful as ever, and still demands a spirit of adventure from drivers who attempt it.

No direct **buses** run to Alaska, though for around $150 (booking 21 days ahead) you can hop on a Greyhound in Seattle and after a few transfers over two gruelling days, reach Whitehorse in the Yukon, from where Alaska Direct (Ⓣ1-800/770-6652, Ⓦwww.alaskadirectbusline.com) make the run to Anchorage ($220) or Fairbanks ($200).

The AlaskaPass

Foot passengers planning to travel up the Inside Passage to Anchorage, Denali, and Fairbanks may make considerable savings by purchasing the **AlaskaPass** (Ⓦwww.alaskapass.com), covering the Alaska Marine Highway ferries, the Alaska Railroad, and the White Pass & Yukon Railroad. There are three passes: 15 consecutive days of travel ($879); 8 travel days out of 12 ($749); and 12 days out of 21 ($899). Kids (2 to 11) travel half-price. Add on a $85 booking fee, which is charged per itinerary (not per person).

Getting around Alaska

Getting around Alaska on the cheap can be tough; **public transportation** is limited and many areas are only accessible by boat or plane which is invariably pricey. With the exception of the ferry system (see above), **Anchorage** is very much the hub of Alaska, with several **bus** companies running to major destinations: Seward with The Park Connection ($55; ⓣ1-800/266-8625, ⓦwww.alaskacoach.com); Homer with Stage Line ($78; ⓣ907/868-2607, ⓦwww.thestageline.net); Talkeetna with Denali Overland ($85; ⓣ1-800/651-5221, ⓦwww.denalioverland.com) and Denali ($75) and Fairbanks ($99) with Alaska/Yukon Trails (ⓣ1-800/770-7275, ⓦwww.alaskashuttle.com). The **Alaska Railroad** (ⓦwww.akrr.com) runs nearly five hundred miles from Seward north through Anchorage to Fairbanks, with a spur to Whittier for cruise liners and ferries to Valdez and Juneau. One-way summer **fares** from Anchorage are: Denali $117–146, Fairbanks $167–210, Whittier $65 and Seward $75.

Driving around Alaska in summer requires no special skills, though minor routes are often gravel, requiring caution. Wildlife, especially moose, can be a danger any time, even on city streets. In spring and autumn you should be prepared for snow, and it is wise to carry a **survival kit**, particularly in winter, as traffic can be sparse even on major routes. Road conditions can change rapidly – call ⓣ511 or 1-866/282-7577 or see ⓦ511.alaska.gov.

Travel by **plane** is not always more expensive than other methods. Alaska Airlines (see opposite) flies to most major communities and uses partners such as ERA Aviation (ⓣ1-800/866-8394, ⓦwww.flyera.com) and PenAir (ⓣ1-800/448-4226, ⓦwww.penair.com) to get to smaller towns. **Chartering a plane** might sound extravagant but can be inexpensive for groups of four or more and may be the crowning glory of an Alaska vacation. To arrange this contact any "bush plane" operator (every town has at least one). ERA Aviation and PenAir are good starting points, though they may refer you to another company.

Southeast Alaska

Southeast Alaska is archetypal Alaska: an awesome four-hundred-mile-long tableau of fjords, mountains, glaciers, a thousand islands and thick conifer forests lining the **Inside Passage**. The area's first settlers were the **Tlingit** (*thling-get*), and it was not until the end of the eighteenth century that Russian expansionists burst into the region. Today, southeast Alaska's small communities resound with tales of endurance, folly and cruelty.

The state's southernmost town, **Ketchikan**, rich in Native heritage, makes a pretty introduction, while **Sitka** retains a Russian influence. Further north are swanky **Juneau**, the capital; **Haines**, with its mix of old-timers and arty newcomers; and **Skagway**, thoroughly redolent of the old gold-rush days. You could spend months exploring here, but most are content to focus on the towns of Sitka and Skagway, and **Glacier Bay National Park**, an expensive side-trip from Juneau that penetrates one of Alaska's most stunning regions.

With no roads connecting towns, by far the best way to travel is by **ferry**, though at some stage make sure you take a **floatplane** ride. For a true outdoor adventure, you can rent a **cabin** in the huge Tongass National Forest – which encompasses most of southeast Alaska – for around $35 per night; details from the visitor centres in Juneau (see p.1006) and Ketchikan (see p.1004) or through ⓦwww.recreation.gov.

Ketchikan and around

KETCHIKAN, almost seven hundred miles north of Seattle, is the first port of call for cruise ships and ferries and its historic downtown, wedged between water and forested mountains, becomes saturated in summer. Beyond the souvenir shops it's delightful, built into steep hills and partly propped on wooden pilings, dotted with boardwalks, wooden staircases and totem poles.

By 1886, the town's numerous canneries made it the "salmon capital of the world", while forests of cedar, hemlock and spruce fed its sawmills. Ketchikan now looks to tourism as its saviour, with the nearby **Misty Fiords National Monument** as the prime draw.

The state's fourth largest city is a strong contender for the nation's wettest; annual precipitation averages 165 inches, but the perennial drizzle and sporadic showers won't spoil your visit.

Arrival and information

Ferries dock two miles north of downtown on Tongass Highway; city **buses** stop hourly. Alaska Airlines serves the **airport**, which is on an island reached by half-hourly ferries ($5 return). The **visitor centre** is downtown at 131 Front St (daily 8am–5pm; ⓣ1-800/770-3300, ⓦwww.visit-ketchikan.com), and for information about the surrounding Tongass forests visit the **Southeast Alaska Discovery Center**, 50 Main St (summer 8am–5pm daily; ⓣ907/228-6220, ⓦwww.fs.fed.us/r10/tongass), a striking cedar-framed building which houses absorbing displays ($5) of the region's natural habitats and native culture.

Accommodation

The closest **campgrounds** to town ($10) are in the attractive Ward Lake Recreation Area, five miles northwest of the ferry terminal.

Alderhouse 420 Alder St ⓣ907/247-2537, ⓦwww.alderhousebnb.com. Very welcoming B&B close to the AMHS ferry dock and to buses running between downtown and Totem Bight. Attention to detail makes everything, especially the breakfast, a treat. Open June–Sept; 2-night minimum. ❺

Eagle View Hostel 2305 5th Ave ⓣ907/225-5461, ⓦwww.eagleviewhostel.com. Suburban house with great views of the Narrows. Single-sex dorm beds (as well as one double room) cost $25 (plus tax) including bed linen, towel and use of kitchen and barbecue. No lockout or curfew. Take Jefferson off Tongass Hwy then right onto 5th. Open April–Oct.

Ketchikan Youth Hostel United Methodist Church, 400 Main St ⓣ907/225-3319, ⓔketchikanhostel@gmail.com. Very basic hostel with beds for $20, June–Aug only.

The New York Hotel 207 Stedman St ⓣ1-866/225-0246, ⓦwww.thenewyorkhotel.com. Tastefully refurbished hotel by the small boat harbour with cosy rooms and a good café. ❺

The Town

The bulk of Ketchikan's historic buildings lie on **Creek Street**, a picturesque boardwalk along Ketchikan Creek. This was a red-light district until 1954; the bordellos now house gift shops and galleries. **Dolly's House**, 24 Creek St, once the home and workplace of Dolly Arthur, the town's most famous madam, is now a preserved brothel stuffed with saucy memorabilia (generally daily 8am–5pm; $5).

Most of the totem poles around town are authentic replicas, but the **Totem Heritage Center**, 601 Deermount St (daily 8am–5pm; $5) exhibits the US's largest collection of original totem poles: 33 mostly nineteenth-century examples recovered from abandoned Native villages. The Tlingit-run **Saxman Totem Park**, two miles south of town (hourly bus) displays the world's largest standing collection of poles and an authentic tribal house. For $3 you can see the poles and exterior of the buildings, but you'll need to join the **Saxman Native Village Tour** (May–Sept daily; 1hr; $40; Ⓔinfo@capefoxtours.com; no phone) to see sculptors at work and a dance performance in the clan house.

Fourteen of the best replica totem poles and a rebuilt tribal house stand in **Totem Bight State Park**, breathtakingly set between the forest and the Tongass Narrows, an arm of the sea/channel, ten miles north of town on the Tongass Highway. On the way back take some time out to walk the easy but enjoyable boardwalk up to **Perseverance Lake**, starting on Ward Lake Road, four miles north of town.

Eating and drinking

Inexpensive **food** in Ketchikan tends to be rather good, a rare combination in Alaska. The town is also renowned for its hard **drinking**.

Chico's 435 Dock St ⓣ907/225-2833. Bargain authentic Mexican food and pizza with dinners starting at $10 or just grab a $7 burrito to eat in or take away.

Diaz Café 335 Stedman St ⓣ907/225-2257. Great inexpensive diner food with some tasty Filipino dishes. Closed Mon.

First City Saloon 830 Water St. Straightforward boozing bar (though with free wi-fi) occasionally featuring bands and shows. The likeliest place for a little dancing.

Ketchikan Coffee Company 211 Stedman St ⓣ907/247-2326. Attractive coffeeshop with a daytime menu loaded with excellent soups, sandwiches and salads (mostly $9–13), plus desserts and microbrews. Breakfast and lunch daily, dinner Thurs–Sun.

Misty Fjords National Monument

Twenty-two miles east of Ketchikan on the mainland, the awe-inspiring **MISTY FJORDS NATIONAL MONUMENT** consists of 2.3 million acres of deep fjords flanked by sheer 3000ft glacially scoured walls topped by dense rainforest. As befits its name, the monument is at its most atmospheric when swathed in low-lying mists. The best access is with Alaska Cruises (ⓣ1-800/860-3845) who offer a six-hour cruise ($159) and an excellent four-hour cruise/fly combo ($329). Fourteen rustic cabins ($25–45) are rented out by the Forest Service (ⓣ1-877/444-6777; Ⓦwww.reserveusa.com). Access is either by floatplane with Taquan Air (ⓣ1-800/770-8800, Ⓦwww.taquanair.com), or kayak with Southeast Sea Kayaks (ⓣ1-800/287-1607, Ⓦwww.kayakketchikan.com).

Sitka

Shielded by islands from the Pacific Ocean, **SITKA** is one of Alaska's prettiest and most historic towns. The Russians established a fort here in 1799 and Sitka subsequently became the capital of Russian America, witnessing transfer of ownership to the US in 1867. Sitka today earns its keep mostly from fishing and tourism and offers a wealth of great outdoor activities.

Arrival and information

Traditional and fast **ferries** jointly visit Sitka around five times per week, docking seven miles northwest of town. Sitka Tours **shuttles** ($8 each way; ⓣ907/747-8443) run downtown and offer two-hour town tours ($12). They also serve the airport, a half-hour walk from downtown. You can rent **kayaks** from Sitka Sound Ocean Adventures ($45 a half-day, double $60; ⓣ907/747-6375, Ⓦwww.ssoceanadventures.com), who also organize day-long guided trips on the Sound ($199). The **visitor centre** is in the Centennial Building, 330 Harbor Drive (daily 8am–5pm; ⓣ907/747-3220, Ⓦwww.sitka.org).

Accommodation

Sitka's **accommodation** includes the historic ✱ *Sitka Hotel*, 118 Lincoln St (ⓣ907/747-3288, ⓦwww.sitkahotel.net; ❸–❹) which offers a touch of old-fashioned style, some rooms without bathrooms; and the *Sitka International Hostel*, 109 Jeff Davis St ⓣ907/747-8661; ⓦwww.sitkahostel.org), with bunks for $24. The gorgeous *Starrigavan* campground is less than a mile north of the ferry dock on Halibut Point Road ($12; ⓣ1-877/444-6777).

The Town

The best place to get a grasp of Sitka's Russian past is diminutive **Castle Hill**, where Alaska was officially transferred to the US on October 18, 1867. It's a two-minute stroll to **St Michael's Orthodox Cathedral**, a typically Russian church completed in 1848 and rebuilt after a disastrous fire in 1966 (Mon–Fri 9am–4pm; $2). Nearby is the large, mustard-coloured 1842 **Russian Bishop's House** (daily 9am–5pm; $4). Guided tours take in the restored chapel, schoolroom and living quarters. Four blocks east at 104 College Drive, the **Sheldon Jackson Museum** (daily 9am–5pm; $4) houses a compact but extensive display of Native artefacts accumulated by missionary and educationalist Sheldon Jackson.

Nearby, the site of a decisive battle between the Tlingit and the Russians is now the **Sitka National Historic Park** with its evocative collection of vividly painted **totem poles**, copies of nineteenth-century originals. A **visitor centre** (summer daily 8am–5pm; $4) features good displays plus working craftspeople.

Sitka's **trail system** ranges from coastal strolls to harder climbs up Gavan Hill and steep Mount Verstovia: for more information visit the **Forest Service office**, 204 Siganaka Way (ⓣ907/747-6671).

Eating and drinking

Sitka's **restaurants** aren't exactly going to set gourmet tongues wagging, though there are several decent places to dine out. Coffee and light lunches are best at ✱ *Backdoor*, 104 Barracks St (ⓣ907/747-8856; closed Sun). For more upmarket dining, try ✱ *Ludvig's Bistro*, 256 Katlian St (ⓣ907/966-3663; ⓦwww.ludvigsbistro.com), offering expensive but excellent Spanish- and Moroccan-influenced dishes; closed Sun & Mon. *Pioneer Bar*, 212 Katlian St (ⓣ907/747-3456), is a down-to-earth boozing spot lined with hundreds of black-and-white photographs of fishing boats.

Juneau and around

The sophisticated and vibrant city of **JUNEAU** is the only state capital in the nation not accessible by road. It is exceptionally picturesque, wedged between the **Gastineau Channel** and the rainforested hills behind. In 1880, Joe Juneau made **Alaska's first gold strike** here, and until the last mine closed in 1944 this was the world's largest producer of low-grade ore – all the flat land in Juneau, stretching from downtown to the airport, is waste rock from the mines. Today, state government provides much of the employment, and tourism plays its part with the drive-to **Mendenhall Glacier** and the watery charms of **Tracy Arm fjord** as temptation.

Arrival, information and getting around

Ferries dock fourteen miles northwest of downtown at Auke Bay; they often arrive at unearthly hours, so getting into town can be a problem. The only alternative to a $35 taxi ride (sharing encouraged) is walking a mile and a half south to DeHarts grocery, served by Capital Transit **buses** (Mon–Sat hourly 8am–10.30pm, Sun 9am–5pm; $1.50 ⓣ907/789-6901). Buses also pick up near the busy airport, nine miles north of downtown.

The **visitor centre**, Centennial Hall, 101 Egan Drive (Mon–Fri 8.30am–5pm, Sat & Sun 9am–5pm; ⓣ1-888/581-2201, ⓦwww.traveljuneau.com) has stacks of brochures about the Tongass National Forest, Glacier Bay and around. Popular easy **hikes** from Juneau include the Perseverance Trail and over the bridge on Douglas Island, the Treadwell Mine Historic Trail. *Driftwood Lodge* (ⓣ907/586-2280), rents out **mountain bikes** for $25 a day.

Accommodation

Juneau has the widest range of accommodation in Southeast Alaska, as well as some fine camping.

Alaskan Hotel and Bar 167 S Franklin St ⓣ1-800/327-9374, ⓦwww.thealaskanhotel.com. Pleasant old hotel with a salacious past. Doubles with shared or private bath ❸–❹, suites ❺

Juneau Hostel 614 Harris St ⓣ907/586-9559, ⓦwww.juneauhostel.net. Clean, comfortable and relaxed hostel, in an old home near downtown, with dorm beds ($10) and a family room, but an inconvenient daytime lockout (9am–5pm) and a midnight curfew.

Mendenhall Lake Campground Montana Creek Rd, 13 miles from downtown. A gorgeous Forest Service campground within sight of the Mendenhall Glacier and with space for RVs ($26) and some lovely lakeside walk-in tent sites ($10). Mid-May to Sept.

Silverbow Inn 120 2nd St, downtown ⓣ1-800/586-4146, ⓦwww.silverbowinn.com. Attractive little hotel with smallish but nicely furnished rooms, each with TV, phone and wi-fi and with a good continental breakfast included. ❻

The Town

Many original buildings stand in the **South Franklin Street Historic District** – Juneau managed to avoid the fires that destroyed many other gold towns in Alaska. The onion-domed **St Nicholas Russian Orthodox Church**, 326 Fifth St (Mon 9am–6pm, Tues & Thurs 9am–5pm, Fri 10am–noon & 3–5pm, Sat 11am–3pm, Sun 1–5pm; $2 suggested donation), contains icons and religious treasures, while the well-presented **Alaska State Museum**, 395 Whittier St (daily 8.30am–5.30pm; $5), covers Native culture, Russian heritage and the first gold strikes. Its pride and joy is the logbook in which Bering reported his first sighting of Alaska. The smaller **City Museum**, at Main and Fourth streets (Mon–Fri 9am–5pm, Sat & Sun 10am–5pm; $4), displays relics from the mining era. The best views of town are from the top of the **Mount Roberts Tramway** (summer daily 9am–9pm; $27), which rises 1800 feet from the cruise-ship dock to a nature centre and some easy trails.

Eating and drinking

Downtown has a reasonable selection of places to **eat and drink**, but most fill up very quickly when cruise ships are in town.

Alaskan Hotel Bar 167 S Franklin St. Great old bar with live music most nights, especially toward the weekend.

The Hanger on the Wharf Merchants Wharf ⓣ907/586-5018. Former floatplane hangar with great waterfront views. There are over twenty beers on tap, plus pool tables and live music on weekends. Serves wraps and burgers at lunch and the likes of jambalaya and halibut tacos ($13–14) at dinner.

Paradise Café 245 Marine Way. Stylish little café and bakery with excellent soups, salads and wraps. A little pricey but worth it. Open 7am–3pm daily.

Rainbow Foods 224 4th St ⓣ907/586-6476. Wholefood and organic grocery serving a limited selection of light lunches (Mon–Fri), plus a salad bar. Try the home-made cookies and espresso.

Silverbow Bakery 120 2nd St ⓣ907/586-4146. Relaxed eat-in bakery and coffee bar with bagels, hot and cold deli sandwiches ($7–11), soups and superb pastries.

Mendenhall Glacier and Tracy Arm Fjord

The mile-and-a-half-wide **Mendenhall Glacier**, 13 miles north of downtown, is the state's most accessible. Capital Transit **buses** leave you a mile away or MGT's

Glacier Express ($7 each way; ⓣ907/789-5460) runs half-hourly to the **visitor centre** (daily 8am–7.30pm; $3), built on a point occupied by the glacier as recently as 1940. Hiking **trails** include the West Glacier Trail, on which, with extreme caution and without official approval you can explore the ice caves.

One of the best day-trips from Juneau is up the narrow, twisting **Tracy Arm fjord**, with waterfall-fringed cliffs and common sightings of whales and seals. Take a day-**cruise** with Adventure Bound Alaska ($150; ⓣ1-800/228-3875, ⓦwww.adventureboundalaska.com).

Glacier Bay National Park

Sixteen glaciers spill into the 65-mile-long **Glacier Bay**, northwest of Juneau. Brown and black bears, moose, mountain goats, sea otters, humpback whales, porpoise, seals and a colourful array of birds call the area home. It is an expensive trip, requiring an Alaska Airlines flight from Juneau to Gustavus, 65 miles northwest of Juneau (about $100 each way). Visit the glacier by **day-cruise** (8hr; $185) from Bartlett Cove, 9 miles north, and you'll also need at least one night's **accommodation**. At Bartlett Cove you can camp for free or stay at *Glacier Bay Lodge* (ⓣ1-888/229 8687, ⓦwww.visitglacierbay.com; ❼), with tasteful rooms and a good restaurant. In central Gustavus there's accommodation at *Homestead B&B* (ⓣ907/697-2777, ⓦwww.homesteadbedbreakfast.com; ❺–❻).

Haines

Tiny **HAINES** sits on a peninsula at the northern end of the longest and deepest fjord in the US, Lynn Canal. Somewhat overshadowed by its brasher neighbour, Skagway, it remains a slice of real Alaska with an interesting mix of locals and urban escapees.

The Tlingit fished and traded here for years before 1881, when the first missionaries arrived. Today, the town survives on fishing and tourism, hosting in mid-August the cookouts, crafts and log-rolling of the **Southeast Alaska Fair**.

Arrival and information

Haines' AMHS **ferry** terminal is five miles north of town, with daily services to and from Juneau and Skagway. A convenient passenger-only fast ferry ($35 one-way; ⓣ1-888/766-2103, ⓦwww.hainesskagwayfastferry.com) runs between Haines and Skagway from a dock near Fort Seward. The **visitor centre**, 122 Second St (Mon–Fri 8am–6pm, Sat & Sun 9am–5pm; ⓣ1-800/458-3579, ⓦwww.haines.ak.us), has all kinds of maps and information.

Accommodation

As well as the usual mid-range **accommodation**, Haines has half a dozen handy **campgrounds.**

Bear Creek Cabins and Hostel Small Tracts Rd ⓣ907/766-2259, ⓦbearcreekcabinsalaska.com. Good hostel over a mile south of Fort Seward with coin-op laundry and no lockout or curfew. Campers ($14 for two) can use hostel facilities. Dorms $20, cabins $68.

Port Chilkoot Campground Mud Bay Rd ⓣ1-800/542-6363, ⓦwww.hotelhalsingland.com. Central campground with pay-showers and a laundromat on site. Full hookup $25, dry RV $16, tents $10.

Portage Cove State Recreation Site Beach Rd, half a mile southeast of Fort Seward. A small site for backpackers and cyclists only, by the beach with great views and potable water. No overnight parking. $5.

Summer Inn B&B 117 2nd Ave ⓣ907/766-2970, ⓦwww.summerinnbnb.com. Immaculate downtown B&B with shared bathrooms and a good cooked breakfast. It has a very homey feel with claw-foot baths, quilts and fresh flowers. ❹

The Town

The **Sheldon Museum & Cultural Center**, 11 Main St (Mon–Fri 10am–5pm, Wed to 9pm, Sat & Sun 1–4pm; $5 ⓦwww.sheldonmuseum.org), shows how Haines fits into its Chilkat environment and the wider Tlingit world, exhibiting fine examples of woodwork, clothing and the distinctive yellow and black Chilkat blanket in wolf, raven and killer whale designs.

Half a mile away, grassy **Fort William H. Seward** was established in 1903 to contain Gold Rush lawlessness and territorial disputes with Canada. It is now home to **Alaska Indian Arts** (Mon–Fri 9am–5pm; free), where you can meet carvers working on huge totem poles.

Nearby, the stuffed birds of the **American Bald Eagle Foundation**, 113 Haines Hwy at Second Avenue (daily 10am–6pm; $3), make a poor substitute for seeing the world's largest gathering of **bald eagles**, each November in the **Chilkat Bald Eagle Preserve**. Over three thousand birds – as many as two dozen to a tree – gather along a five-mile stretch of the Chilkat River, starting nineteen miles from town on the Haines Highway.

Haines is also a popular starting point for **rafting trips**: Chilkat Guides on Beach Road (ⓣ1-888/292-7789, ⓦwww.raftalaska.com) run four-hour **float trips** ($89) down the Chilkat River, ideal for viewing eagles and other wildlife.

Eating and drinking

Haines' best **bars** and **restaurants** can be found in the Fort Seward area, notably at the *Hotel Halsingland*.

Bamboo Room 11 2nd St near Main ⓣ907/766-2800. Standard diner popular for its well-prepared meals (especially the dinner of local halibut and chips, $21), and fresh-baked pies.

Chilkat Restaurant and Bakery 5th Ave & Dalton St ⓣ907/766-3653. A great spot for baked goods with an espresso coffee, or more substantial fare – everything from tasty breakfasts, salads and halibut sandwiches to Thai lunches for $11, all beautifully cooked.

Mountain Market 151 3rd Ave at Haines Hwy ⓣ907/766-3340. Combined natural-food grocery and espresso bar that's one of the best places in town for a $6 bagel breakfast, a $7 tortilla wrap, or just a muffin with your mocha.

Skagway and around

SKAGWAY, the northern terminal of the southeast ferry route, sprang up overnight in 1897 as a trading post serving **Klondike Gold Rush** pioneers setting off on the five-hundred-mile ordeal. Having grown from one cabin to a town of twenty thousand in three months, Skagway, rife with disease and desperado violence was reported to be "hell on earth". It boasted over seventy bars and hundreds of prostitutes and was controlled by criminals, including **Jefferson "Soapy" Smith**, notorious for cheating hapless prospectors out of their gold.

By 1899, the Gold Rush was over but the completion in 1900 of the White Pass and Yukon Route railway from Skagway to Whitehorse, the Yukon capital, ensured Skagway's survival. Today the town's eight hundred residents have gone to great lengths to maintain (or recreate) the original appearance of their home, much of which lies in the **Klondike Gold Rush National Historic Park** and in summer as many as five cruise ships a day call in to appreciate the effort.

Arrival, information and getting around

AMHS ferries and an independent operator (see opposite) arrive daily from Haines and Juneau on the edge of downtown just a block from the WP & YR **train station** (see p.1010). Yukon Alaska Tourist Tours (reservations essential ⓣ1-866/626-7383, ⓦwww.yatt.ca), run a bus from Skagway to Whitehorse ($60) and a train – bus combo ($131).

Skagway is very compact, and most of the sights can easily be seen on foot. The Klondike Gold Rush National Historic Park **visitor centre**, Broadway at Second Avenue (daily 8am–6pm; ⓣ907/983-2223, ⓦwww.nps.gov/klgo), offers historical displays, talks, walking tours and an impressive movie about the Gold Rush, as well as maps and information on the Chilkoot Trail. Skagway's **visitor centre** (daily 8am–6pm; ⓣ1-888/762-1898, ⓦwww.skagway.com) is on Broadway between Second and Third Avenues in the Arctic Brotherhood Hall.

Accommodation

Being a touristy little town, **accommodation** prices run slightly high and rooms are often reserved far in advance.

At the White House 475 8th Ave at Main St ⓣ907/983-9000, ⓦwww.atthewhitehouse.com. High-standard B&B in a restored historic home with modernized rooms and substantial breakfasts. ❺

Cindy's Place Mile 0.2 Dyea Rd ⓣ1-800/831-8095, ⓦwww.alaska.net/~croland. Three log cabins in the woods two miles from downtown, one budget, two more luxurious affairs with private bathrooms (one with a wood-burning stove), phone and cooking equipment. There's free use of the hot tub plus thoughtful touches like a dozen varieties of tea and coffee in the cabins, fresh baking and home-made jams. Deluxe ❺, budget ❷

Skagway Home Hostel 3rd Ave and Main St ⓣ907/983-2131, ⓦwww.skagwayhostel.com. In-with-the-family hostel in a century-old building with single-sex dorms ($20) and mixed dorms ($15). There's a communal feel, ample supplies for cooking (honesty box) and an 11pm curfew.

Skagway Mountain View RV Park Broadway at 12th Ave ⓣ1-888/323-5757, ⓦwww.bestofalaskatravel.com. Large RV-dominated spot with all the expected facilities, water and electricity hookup ($47) and a few wooded tent sites ($26) that are in high demand.

The Town

Strolling up Broadway you can't miss the eye-catching facade of the 1899 **Arctic Brotherhood Hall**, decorated with almost nine thousand pieces of driftwood and housing the Skagway Visitor Center. Many of the other buildings hereabouts form part of the **Klondike Gold Rush National Historic Park**, notably the **Mascot Saloon** on Broadway (daily 8am–6pm; free), and **Moore Homestead**, Fifth Avenue at Spring Street (daily 10am–5pm; free), a museum **devoted to** Skagway's founder with photos of the Gold Rush. There's further detail in the **City of Skagway Museum** (Mon–Fri 9am–5pm, Sat 10am–5pm, Sun noon–4pm; $2), which contains Soapy's Derringer pistol and good Tlingit artefacts.

The *Skagway Trail Map*, available from the visitor centre and at ⓦwww.skagway.com/skagwaytrailmap.pdf, details local **hikes**, including the Dewey Lakes trails, which pass pretty subalpine lakes and tumbling waterfalls, and the tougher scramble up AB Mountain. Sockeye Cycles, Fifth Avenue and Broadway (ⓣ907/983-2851, ⓦwww.cyclealaska.com), rents out well-maintained **mountain bikes** for $25 for 4 hours, and the Mountain Shop, 4th Avenue and State (ⓣ907/983-2544, ⓦwww.packerexpeditions.com) rents and sells backpacking supplies.

A lazier way to take in the scenery is on the **White Pass and Yukon Route** railway (early May to late Sept; 2–3 departures daily; ⓣ1-800/343-7373, ⓦwpyr.com), which follows the gushing Skagway River past waterfalls and ice-packed gorges and over a 1000ft-high bridge, stopping at the White Pass summit ($110 return). There's no shortage of riders, so get there early and grab a seat on the left-hand side going up. The company also offers a bus connection to Whitehorse.

Eating and drinking

Most of Skagway's **bars** and **restaurants** line the touristy part of Broadway.

Corner Café State St at 4th Ave ⓣ907/983-2155. A daytime diner (6am–4pm) that's popular with locals for its salads, soups, sandwiches and pizza.

Red Onion Saloon Broadway at 2nd Ave ⓣ907/983-2222. An 1898 bar and former bordello with heaps of character, draft beers and excellent pizza.

Skagway Brewing Company Broadway at 7th Ave ⓣ907/983-2739. Good brews and a varied menu of sandwiches, "Alaskan tapas" and (after 5pm) more substantial fare.

Stowaway Café 205 Congress Way ⓣ907/983-3463. Stop by in the evening for the likes of king crab ($33), smoked ribs ($22) and peach bread pudding ($8), all served in a congenial atmosphere with views of the small boat harbour. Open nightly 4–10pm.

The Chilkoot Trail

Alaska's most famous hike, the 33-mile **CHILKOOT TRAIL**, is one huge wilderness museum following the footsteps of the original Klondike prospectors. Starting in **Dyea**, nine miles from Skagway and ending in **Bennett** in Canada, the trail climbs through rainforest to tundra strewn with haunting reminders of the past, including ancient boilers that once drove aerial tramways and several collapsed huts.

The three- to five-day hike is strenuous, especially the ascent from Sheep Camp (1000ft) to Chilkoot Pass (3550ft). You must carry food, fuel and a tent and be prepared for foul weather. Campgrounds along the trail have shelters with stoves and firewood; not all have bear-proof lockers for food. Shuttles run to Dyea, and the White Pass and Yukon Railway runs a service for hikers returning to Skagway (Mon, Tues, Fri; $95).

The hiking season runs from July to early September, with a quota system administered by Parks Canada (ⓦwww.pc.gc.ca/chilkoot). First visit the Skagway **Trail Center**, Broadway at 1st Avenue (early June to early Sept daily 8.30am–4.30pm), where rangers brief you on the challenges and dangers, and can advise on weather conditions and bus and train schedules for the trip back to Skagway. While here, you must also pay CAN $50 for a permit.

Anchorage

Wedged between Cook Inlet and the imposing Chugach Mountains, **ANCHORAGE** is home to over forty percent of Alaska's population and is the state's transport hub. A sprawling city on the edge of one of the world's great wildernesses, it is often derided as "just half an hour from Alaska". However, it has its attractions and, with its beautiful setting, can make a pleasant one- or two-day stopover.

Anchorage was born in 1915 as a tent city for Alaska Railroad construction workers. During the 1930s, hopefuls fleeing the Depression poured in from the Lower 48 and World War II – and construction of the Alaska Highway – further boosted the city. The opening of the airport established Anchorage – midway between New York and Tokyo – as the "Crossroads of the World", and statehood in 1959 and the 1970s oil boom brought in yet more optimistic adventurers.

Arrival and information

Anchorage International Airport, five miles southwest of town, is served by the city's People Mover bus #7A ($1.75 flat fare or $4 day pass from the driver). Alaska Shuttle (ⓣ907/388-8888) charges $10 to take you downtown and taxis cost around $25. The **train station** is downtown at 411 W 1st Ave (ⓣ1-800/544-0552, ⓦwww.akrr.com) and the major sights are easily reached on foot.

ANCHORAGE

See "Downtown Anchorage" map

Fairbanks (355 miles)

Girdwood (25 miles) & Seward (115 miles)

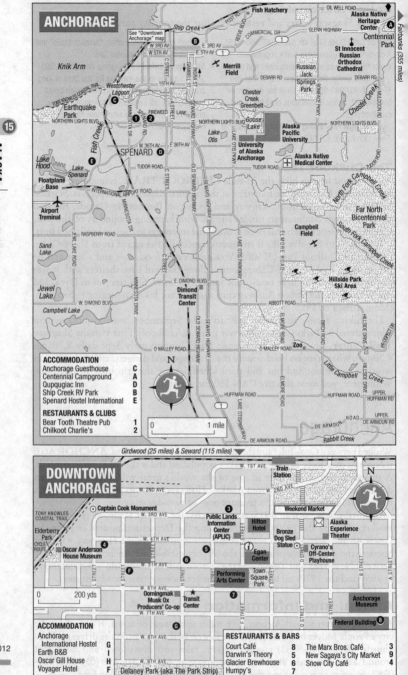

Knik Arm · Ship Creek · Fish Hatchery · Alaska Native Heritage Center · Centennial Park · St Innocent Russian Orthodox Cathedral · Merrill Field · Russian Jack Springs Park · Chester Creek Greenbelt · Westchester Lagoon · Earthquake Park · Goose Lake · Alaska Pacific University · University of Alaska Anchorage · Lake Otis · SPENARD · Alaska Native Medical Center · Lake Hood · Lake Spenard · Floatplane Base · Airport Treminal · Far North Bicentennial Park · Campbell Field · Hillside Park Ski Area · Sand Lake · Jewel Lake · Campbell Lake · Dimond Transit Center · Zoo · Rabbit Creek

ACCOMMODATION	
Anchorage Guesthouse	C
Centennial Campground	A
Qupqugiac Inn	D
Ship Creek RV Park	B
Spenard Hostel International	E

RESTAURANTS & CLUBS	
Bear Tooth Theatre Pub	1
Chilkoot Charlie's	2

0 — 1 mile

DOWNTOWN ANCHORAGE

ACCOMMODATION	
Anchorage International Hostel	G
Earth B&B	I
Oscar Gill House	H
Voyager Hotel	F

RESTAURANTS & BARS			
Court Café	8	The Marx Bros. Café	3
Darwin's Theory	5	New Sagaya's City Market	9
Glacier Brewhouse	6	Snow City Café	4
Humpy's	7		

H (50yds)   I & 9 (200yds)

The **Log Cabin Visitor Center**, downtown at 4th and F (daily 8am–6pm; ⓣ907/274-3531, ⓦwww.anchorage.net), is across the street from the **Alaska Public Lands Information Center** (daily 9am–5pm; ⓣ907/271-2737, ⓦwww.nps.gov/aplic) which has excellent natural history displays plus maps and brochures. It'll help plan back-country trips, and make reservations both for accommodation and shuttle buses in Denali National Park – vital in summer.

Accommodation

Inexpensive **accommodation** in Anchorage can be hard to find, especially in summer. **Campers** should head for the central *Ship Creek RV Park*, 150 N Ingra (ⓣ1-800/323-5757, ⓦwww.alaskarv.com; $16–24 (tents $16 in May & Sept, $26 June–Aug; RVs $18–26 to $37–47)).

Anchorage Guesthouse 2001 Hillcrest Drive ⓣ907/274-0408, ⓦwww.akhouse.com. Upscale hostel, just over a mile from downtown and handy for the Coastal Trail (bikes $8/hr). Free perks include sheets, towels, breakfast, use of kitchen, gear storage, local calls and wi-fi. Dorm beds cost $30 and there are private doubles and kings. ④

Anchorage International Hostel 700 H St ⓣ907/276-3635, ⓦwww.anchoragehostel.org. Functional and very central hostel with daytime lockout and evening curfew; reserve well ahead in summer. Dorm beds $25, private rooms. ③

Earth B&B 1001 W 12th Ave ⓣ907/279-9907, ⓦwww.earthbb.com. Enthusiastically and liberally run, this is home away from home for Denali-bound climbers. It's simple but very accommodating, with a barbecue outside. ⑤

Oscar Gill House 1344 W 10th Ave ⓣ907/279-1344, ⓦwww.oscargill.com. Lovely B&B in a 1913 house, restored with understated elegance. Two rooms share a bath while one has its own jacuzzi, all tastefully done and managed by very welcoming hosts. Private bath ⑥, shared ⑤

Qupqugiac Inn 640 W 36th Ave, midtown ⓣ907/563-5633, ⓦwww.qupq.com. Great budget hotel with clean, simple rooms with phone and satellite TV, and a communal lounge with kitchen and free internet. Bus #9 from downtown passes a block away on Arctic Blvd. Private bath ④, shared ③

Spenard Hostel International 2845 W 42nd Place ⓣ907/248-5036, ⓦwww.alaskahostel.org. Friendly suburban hostel with nearby mall just a mile and a half from the airport (bus #7A). Cheap bike rental, free wi-fi, no curfew or lockout and dorm beds for $25.

Rodeway Inn 501 K St at 5th Ave ⓣ1-800/424-6423, ⓦwww.rodewayinn.com. The best of the mid- to upper-range hotels featuring spacious rooms (with kitchenette) and most of the facilities of a business hotel at much lower cost. Reserve well ahead in summer. ⑦

The City

Travellers eager to rush off into the "real" Alaska tend to overlook cosmopolitan Anchorage – a blend of old and new, urban blight and rural parks – but there is plenty to see, and it's worth spending some time experiencing it.

Your first stop should be the **Anchorage Museum**, 6th Avenue at C Street (summer daily 9am–6pm, Thurs to 9pm; $10), providing an excellent overview of the state and its history alongside beautiful examples of carved ivory and basketware. There's a fine collection of art, including the iconic painting of Mount McKinley by Alaska's best-known painter, Sydney Laurence, and contemporary works. A new extension houses the Smithsonian's Arctic Studies Center, a superb collection of native artefacts with touch-screen interpretation.

Other downtown sights are more modest: the 1915 **Oscar Anderson House Museum**, 420 M St (June–Sept Mon–Fri noon–5pm; $3), illustrates early Anchorage life, and the **Alaska Experience Theatre**, 333 West 4th Ave (daily 10am–6pm), presents films of the Northern Lights and of Alaska's best scenery, (every 30 min, $10), and of the devastating 1964 Good Friday **earthquake** that levelled much of downtown – North America's strongest-ever quake at Magnitude 9.2 (every 20 min, $6; combined $13).

Seven miles east on the edge of town lies the **Alaska Native Heritage Center**, off the Glenn Highway at Muldoon Road (May–Sept daily 9am–5pm; $25 ⓦwww.alaskanative.net). Although pricey, it gives an excellent introduction to the state's five main ethnic groups, each represented by a typical house where Native guides interpret their culture. There are also performances and films in the auditorium. A free shuttle runs four times a day from the Anchorage Museum and the Visitor Center.

On long summer days it is better to stay outside, perhaps strolling (or biking) along the **Tony Knowles Coastal Trail**, which offers restorative views of Turnagain Arm, or exploring the mountains and lakes of the 495,000-acre **Chugach State Park**, just fifteen minutes' drive east from Anchorage. Challenging trails include the scramble up 4500ft Flattop Mountain, giving spectacular views of the city and Cook Inlet.

Eating, drinking and nightlife

Nowhere in Alaska will you find a more diverse range of places to **eat** than in Anchorage. You wouldn't make a special journey for its culinary wonders, but after weeks in the wilds the city can seem like heaven. Carr's supermarket at the junction of Northern Lights Boulevard and Minnesota Drive (bus #3 or #36) has groceries and a strong deli section.

Good **bars** abound, both downtown and in the lively (and somewhat edgy) strip of Spenard Road between Northern Lights Boulevard and International Airport Road. Shows, plays, opera and concerts take place at the **Center for Performing Arts** (ⓣ907/263-2787).

Bear Tooth Theatre Pub 1230 W 27th Ave ⓣ907/276-4200, ⓦwww.beartooththeatre.net. Splendid cinema with attached restaurant, where pizzas ($14–22), Caesar salads ($7), burritos and tacos ($11–14) are served as you watch arthouse movies ($3); the microbrews are excellent.

Chilkoot Charlie's 2435 Spenard Rd ⓣ907/272-1010, ⓦwww.koots.com. Sawdust-strewn barn that packs them in nightly for pricey drinks, pool, foosball, two floors of DJ-led dance, and live music from 9.30pm.

Court Café 222 W 7th at C St ⓣ907/277-6736. Breakfast and lunch cafeteria in the Federal Building (photo ID required) that's about the best budget value downtown, certainly a cut above the fast-food joints and more filling. Steaming clam chowder or an entree will cost around $8.

Darwin's Theory 426 G St at 4th Ave ⓣ907/277-5322. Straightforward bar for inexpensive boozing and encounters with colourful local characters.

Glacier Brewhouse 737 W 5th St ⓣ907/274-2739 ⓦwww.glacierbrewhouse.com. Hugely popular restaurant, bar and microbrewery serving wonderful food and drink. Half a dozen toothsome house-brewed beers accompany alderwood-baked pizza ($11), wood-grilled New York steak ($30), or steamed king crab legs ($37).

Humpy's 610 W 6th Ave ⓣ907/276-2337, ⓦwww.humpys.com. Popular watering hole with live music and a strong college-bar feel. The likes of charbroiled salmon ($19), burgers ($10–15), soups, and salads ($5–15) slip down with local microbrews plus English and Belgian bottled beers, and over thirty single malts.

The Marx Bros. Café 627 W 3rd Ave ⓣ907/278-2133, ⓦwww.marxcafe.com. The best all-round fine dining downtown served up in a historic house with views of the water. Start with Alaskan oysters with pepper vodka and ginger sorbet ($14.50) or Neapolitan seafood mousse ($15), followed by baked halibut in macadamia-nut crust ($38). Dinner only.

New Sagaya's City Market 900 W 13th Ave at I St ⓣ907/274-6173. Trendy and expensive grocery, deli and café with a great selection ranging from organic vegetables and great cheeses to pizza, wraps, Thai dishes and good coffee.

Snow City Café1034 W 4th Ave ⓣ907/272-2489, ⓦwww.snowcitycafe.com. The best place for breakfast – eggs Benedict or Florentine for $12, yogurt, fruit and granola for $6 – or relaxing over a pot of Earl Grey and a slice of cake. Lunch options include soups, salads, pesto chicken pasta ($13), and meatloaf with mac and cheese ($13). Mon–Fri to 4pm, Sat/Sun to 3pm.

Kenai Peninsula

South of Anchorage, the Seward Highway hugs the shore of **Turnagain Arm** past **Girdwood** and the **Alyeska ski resort**. Just beyond, a side road heads past the ever-popular **Portage Glacier** and through a tunnel to **Whittier**, little more than a ferry dock giving access to Prince William Sound (see p.1018). Beyond Portage, the Seward Highway enters the **Kenai Peninsula**, "Anchorage's playground", which at over nine thousand square miles is larger than some states. It offers an endless diversity of activities and scenery, based around communities such as **Seward**, the base for cruises into the inspirational **Kenai Fjords National Park** and artsy **Homer**, where the waters and shorelines of the glorious **Kachemak Bay State Park** are the main destination. Most Alaskans come to the peninsula to **fish**: the Kenai, Russian and Kasilof rivers host "combat fishing", thousands of anglers standing elbow to elbow using strength and know-how to pull in thirty-pound-plus king salmon. **Campgrounds** along the rivers fill up fast, especially in July and August.

Girdwood and Portage Glacier

GIRDWOOD, 37 miles south of Anchorage, lies two miles inland in the shade of the **Alyeska Resort**, Alaska's largest winter sports complex and the world's lowest-elevation ski resort, starting just 270 feet above sea level. Downhill runs (some lit at night) are open from November to mid-April (lifts $60 a day), and in summer you can ride the Alyeska Tramway ($18) up to stunning views and good hiking territory. Girdwood Ski and Cyclery, Mile 1.5 Alyeska Hwy (10am–7pm Wed–Sun ⓣ907/783-2453, ⓦwww.girdwood-ski-and-cyclery.com), rents **bikes** ($25/day) to explore the town and coastal cycle path.

Stay at the grand *Alyeska Hotel* (ⓣ907/754-1111 or 1-800/880-3880, ⓦwww.alyeskaresort.com; ❽), *Carriage House B&B*, Mile 0.2 Crow Creek Rd (ⓣ1-888/961-9464, ⓦwww.thecarriagehousebandb.com; ❺), or *Alyeska Hostel* (ⓣ907/783-2222, ⓦwww.alyeskahostel.com; $50), with $20 bunks and rooms ($50 double). There's tasty, inexpensive **food** at *The Bake Shop* (ⓣ907/783-2831; ⓦwww.thebakeshop.com) on Olympic Circle Drive at the base of the ski lifts and at the unmissable Cajun-influenced *Double Musky Inn* on Crow Creek Road (ⓣ907/783-2822; ⓦwww.doublemuskyinn.com; Tues–Sun evenings): budget on $50 a head and a meal to remember.

Eleven miles south of Girdwood, a road leads to Whittier, past **Portage Glacier**, a popular day-tour from Anchorage. Frustratingly, you can no longer see the glacier from the visitor centre (9am–6pm daily); instead you must pay $29 for a one-hour cruise. Two USFS **campgrounds** ($14–28) can be found two or three miles back down the road.

Seward and Kenai Fjords National Park

SEWARD, 127 miles south of Anchorage, sprang to life in 1903 after this ice-free port was declared the ideal starting point for a railroad to the Interior. It's still a key freight terminal, but tourism – particularly cruises into Kenai Fjords National Park – is now its most conspicuous business.

Seward's main activities are enjoying the scenery and visiting the waterfront **SeaLife Center** (summer daily 9am–7pm; $20 ⓦwww.alaskasealife.org), a successful marriage of research, education and tourism partly funded by the Exxon Valdez oil spill settlement. It offers the chance to watch ongoing research and marvel at the underwater antics of Steller sea lions, harbour seals and puffins. Also tackle the trail to Race Point on **Mount Marathon** (4hr round-trip), scene of an annual Fourth of July race, thanks to two pioneers who, in 1909, bet each other to run up and down the 3022-foot climb – the current record is 43 minutes 23 seconds.

Most visitors also drive thirteen miles out to **Exit Glacier** (24hr; free), one of the few in the state you can approach on land. From the **nature centre** at the end of the road (summer daily 9am–8pm; free), it's under a mile to the still-active glacier, though signs warn you back from the ice wall and its inviting blue clefts. Exit Glacier is part of **KENAI FJORDS NATIONAL PARK**, a magnificent 669,983-acre region of peaks, glaciers and craggy coastline. The prodigious three-hundred-square-mile Harding Icefield feeds three dozen glaciers, now retreating and exposing more of the dramatic fjords after which the park is named. Eight "tidewater" glaciers "calve" icebergs into the sea with thunderous booms and the fjords also hold a wealth of **marine wildlife** – sea otters, porpoises, orcas, seals, Steller sea lions, plus grey, humpback and minke whales – as well as the sea-bird rookeries of the Chiswell Islands. Fast catamaran **cruises** ($59–189) are operated by Major Marine Tours (ⓣ1-800/764-7300, ⓦwww.majormarine.com) and Kenai Fjords Tours (ⓣ1-888/478-3346, ⓦwww.kenaifjords.com); pay out for the longer day-tours that go right up to the calving glaciers.

The park's **visitor centre**, 1212 Fourth Ave by Seward's small boat harbour (summer daily 8.30am–7pm; ⓣ907/224-2125), provides maps, film shows and details on regional hikes.

Practicalities

Get here from Anchorage by **train** (a lovely journey; $75 one-way, $119 return; ⓣ1-800/544-0552) or Seward Bus Lines (ⓣ907/224-3608; $50 one-way). Seward's two hubs of activity, the small boat harbour and downtown, are joined by the mile-long Fourth Avenue, while the main **visitor centre** is inconveniently situated at Mile 2 Seward Hwy (summer daily 8am–6pm; ⓣ907/224-8051, ⓦwww.seward.com). A shuttle bus (ⓣ907/224-5569; $10 return) runs hourly from the small boat harbour to Exit Glacier.

For budget **accommodation** downtown, go to the slightly cramped *Moby Dick Hostel*, 432 3rd Ave (mid-April to Sept; ⓣ907/224-7072, ⓦwww.mobydickhostel.com; ❸) with bunks ($20), kitchen and small private rooms, or *Murphy's Motel*, 911 Fourth Ave (ⓣ1-800/886-8191, ⓦwww.murphysmotel.com; ❺–❼), near the small boat harbour. Alternatively, head out to the lovely *Alaska's Treehouse* (ⓣ907/224-3867, ⓦwww.virtualcities.com/ak/treehouse.htm; ❹) a large timber house with a hot tub on the deck in the forest seven miles north on the Seward Highway (take Timber Lane Drive then Forest Rd). Campers can almost fish from their tent at the excellent *Waterfront Park* (mid-April to Sept; tents $10, RVs $15–30), downtown off Ballaine Boulevard.

Food in Seward is fairly reasonably priced: for good coffee or light meals, head to *Resurrect Art*, 320 3rd Ave, a converted church with board games, wi-fi, art and events. For fine dining (mains around $25), try the *Resurrection Roadhouse*, Mile 0.5 Exit Glacier Rd (ⓣ907/224-716, ⓦwww.sewardwindsong.com). For a good range of beers, stop at the boisterous *Yukon Bar*, 201 4th Ave at Washington Street, with live music in summer, usually with a set or two from Kenai legend Hobo Jim on Sunday.

Homer and around

HOMER is the end of the road, 226 miles south of Anchorage. The town sits beneath low bluffs with a four-mile finger of land – **The Spit** – slinking out into Kachemak Bay, framed by dense black forest and crystalline glaciers. With plenty of outdoor activities, spirited nightlife and a busy arts community, you'll probably want to linger a few days.

Russians, in pursuit of sea otters, were the first whites to reach the area; at the end of the 1800s coal mining and fish-salting brought American settlers. In 1896, **Homer Pennock**, a gold-seeker from Michigan, set up the community that still bears his name. In summer hordes of young people arrive from the Lower 48 to work on the halibut boats, many living in an impromptu tent city on the Spit.

Arrival, information and getting around

The Stage Line (Ⓣ907/399-4429, Ⓦwww.homerstageline.com) runs **buses** between Anchorage and Homer for $78 each way. Most hotels, restaurants and shops are in town, while fishing charter and tour operators can be found along the twee boardwalks of the Spit. There is no public transport between the town and The Spit so hitch, grab a cab or rent a bike from Homer Saw & Cycle, 1532 Ocean Drive; $25/day (Ⓣ907/235-8406). The main **visitor centre** is at 201 Sterling Hwy (summer Mon–Fri 9am–7pm, Sat & Sun 10am–5pm; Ⓣ907/235-7740, Ⓦhomeralaska.org).

Accommodation

Homer's good-value **hotels** and **B&Bs** are often fully booked in summer.

Driftwood Inn 135 W Bunnell Ave Ⓣ1-800/478-8019, Ⓦwww.thedriftwoodinn.com. Rambling older hotel with an extensive and varied range of rooms, RV parking and a communal TV lounge with video library. There is free tea and coffee and breakfast is available for a fee. Shared bath ❹, private bath ❹–❼

Homer Hostel 304 W Pioneer Ave Ⓣ907/235-1463, Ⓦwww.homerhostel.com. Central hostel with mixed and single-sex dorms (5- to 6-beds; $27) and two private rooms, and a big lounge with a great view. There's no curfew or lockout and they have cheap bike and rod rental. Rooms ❸

Homer Spit Campground Ⓣ907/235-8206. The classic Homer experience, in various sites with washblocks and fish-cleaning tables nearby. Tent $8, RV $15.

Old Town B&B 106 W Bunnell Ave Ⓣ907/235-7558, Ⓦwww.oldtownbedandbreakfast.com. Three-room B&B in a 1936 building with wooden floors, antiques, quilted bed covers and old-fashioned bathroom fittings; two have tremendous sea views. Shared bath ❹, private ❺

Seaside Farm Hostel Mile 5 East End Rd Ⓣ907/235-7850, Ⓦwww.xyz.net/~seaside. Small farm hostel with slightly cramped bunks ($20) and a lovely range of rooms, plus small cabins dotted around the property. Open May–Sept. Camping $10, rooms & cabins. ❷

The town and around

Stop first at the new **Alaska Islands & Ocean Visitor Center**, 95 Sterling Hwy (summer daily 9am–6pm; free; Ⓣ907/235-6961, Ⓦwww.islandsandocean.org), showcasing the Alaska Maritime National Wildlife Refuge through dioramas and interactive exhibits. Not far away, the excellent **Pratt Museum**, 3779 Bartlett St (daily 10am–6pm; $8), covers the people and history of Kachemak Bay, along with cameras trained on nesting sea birds and the salmon-feeding bears. Many of Homer's most popular activities, however, revolve around the Spit. To Alaska anglers, Homer is "**Halibut Central**": a day's fishing excursion with any of the charter companies begins at around $220. If you don't mind the crowds, it's cheaper and simpler to visit the **Fishing Hole**, on the Spit, which is stocked with salmon and offers good fishing from mid-May to mid-September.

The prime tourist attraction in the Homer area is **Kachemak Bay State Park**, directly across the bay, with nearly 400,000 acres of forested mountains, glaciers and fjords. Birds here include puffin, auklets, kittiwakes and storm petrels, and marine mammals such as seals, sea otters and whales are also plentiful. The most popular destination is the gorgeous hamlet of **Halibut Cove**, where boardwalks link art galleries and *The Saltry* restaurant: the *Danny J* **ferry** (Ⓣ907/235-7847) makes two daily trips via Gull Island rookery, for $50 return, $30 if you book in for an evening meal.

Pick up the park's hiking-trails leaflet ($2) and other information from the visitor centre in Homer. The most-travelled route, up to **Grewingk Glacier**, is an easy three-and-a-half-mile trek above the forest to the foot of the glacier, from where you get splendid views of the bay.

Eating and drinking

Not surprisingly, Homer's culinary scene focuses mostly on fresh fish. For **nightlife**, head out to the Spit for colourful bars or the **Pier One Theatre** (June–Aug; ⓣ907/235-7333), next to the fishing hole.

Café Cups 162 Pioneer Ave ⓣ907/235-8330. Relaxing yet vibrant café serving great coffee, sandwiches and salads.

Fresh Sourdough Express 1316 Ocean Drive ⓣ907/235-7571, ⓦwww.freshsourdoughexpress.com. Fine local and organic produce at this friendly bakery-restaurant, noted for its breakfasts ($9), burgers and seafood dinners.

Salty Dawg The Spit ⓣ907/235-6718. No self-respecting drinker should pass up a few jars in the *Dawg* with its dark interior, life preservers pinned to the wall, and what seems to be the only surveyor's benchmark located in a bar in the US.

Two Sisters Bakery 233 E Bunnell Ave ⓣ907/235-2280. Great little spot for that morning coffee either inside or at tables out on the deck. Also pizza, soups and quiches at moderate prices.

Prince William Sound

Prince William Sound, a largely unspoiled wilderness of steep fjords and mountains, glaciers and rainforest, sits between the Kenai Peninsula to the west and the Chugach Mountains to the north and east. Teeming with marine mammals, the Sound has a relatively low-key tourist industry. The only significant settlements, spectacular **Valdez**, at the end of the trans-Alaska pipeline, and **Cordova**, a fishing community only accessible by sea or air, are the respective bases for visiting the **Columbia** and **Childs glaciers**.

The Chugach and Eyak people were displaced by Russian trappers in search of sea otter pelts, and then by American miners and fishers. The whole glorious show was very nearly spoiled forever on Good Friday 1989, when the **Exxon Valdez** spilled eleven million gallons of crude oil. Although 1400 miles of coast were befouled and a quarter- of-a-million birds died, and the long-term effects are still unclear, today no surface pollution is visible.

Valdez

VALDEZ (pronounced *val-Deez*), 300 road miles from Anchorage and the Western Hemisphere's northernmost ice-free port, has a stunning backdrop of mountains, glaciers and waterfalls and a record annual snowfall of over forty feet. It offers great hiking, rafting, sea kayaking, wildlife-viewing and, of course, fishing.

In the 1890s **Gold Rush** Valdez became a base for prospectors crossing the deadly Valdez and Klutina glaciers to the Yukon. Only three hundred of the 3500 miners who set out on the Valdez Trail made it to the goldmines – those that did not perish from frostbite and starvation gave up. Valdez came to depend on fish canneries, logging and the military for its survival, but nature conspired to finish it off on Good Friday 1964: the epicentre of North America's largest **earthquake** was just 45 miles away. The ground turned to quivering jelly, shattering roads and buildings and killing 33 residents. Refusing to be intimidated, the survivors moved sixty-odd buildings four miles to the more stable present site.

The town's fortunes rose again during the 1970s, when oil was found beneath Prudhoe Bay, and Valdez became the southern terminus of the 800-mile **trans-Alaska pipeline**, carrying close to a million barrels of oil per day. Winds and tides kept the *Exxon Valdez*'s oil away from Valdez in 1989, and in fact the city profited as base for the massive **cleanup.** The operation cost Exxon three billion dollars, with eleven thousand workers in over one thousand boats and three hundred planes scouring the beaches. All seems pristine now, though many species have still not fully recovered their former numbers.

Arrival and information

One of the most exciting things about Valdez is getting here; both car and ferry rides are unforgettable. The **Richardson Highway** holds epic scenery: alpine meadows, mountain glaciers, icy **Thompson Pass** and waterfall-fringed **Keystone Canyon**. There is no regular bus service, but **ferries** from Cordova or Whittier dock at the end of Hazelet Avenue (ⓣ907/835-4436). ERA Aviation (ⓣ1-800/866-8394, ⓦwww.flyera.com) flies twice daily from Anchorage (from $190 return) to the **airport** four miles east, from where **taxis** (ⓣ907/835-2500) downtown cost around $10. The **visitor centre** (summer Mon–Fri 8am–7pm, Sat 9am–6pm, Sun 10am–5pm; ⓣ907/835-4636, ⓦwww.valdezalaska.org) is on Fairbanks at Chenega Street.

Accommodation

Valdez's **accommodation** gets snapped up pretty quickly and there's no hostel, but a free phone outside the visitor centre connects with some of the fifty-plus **B&Bs,** or see ⓦwww.valdezbnbnetwork.com. **Campers** can choose between the central but busy *Bear Paw RV Park* (ⓣ907/835-2530, ⓦwww.bearpawrvpark.com; $25), and the inconvenient *Valdez Glacier Campground* (ⓣ907/873-4058; $10), five miles from town past the airport. The cheapest rooms are at *L&L's B&B*, 533 W Hanagita St (ⓣ907/835-4447, ⓦwww.lnlalaska.com; ❸), with five comfortable shared bathrooms ten minutes' walk from the centre, free bikes and a good breakfast. Upscale, there's the *Valdez Harbor Inn*, 100 N Harbor Drive (ⓣ1-888/222-3440, ⓦwww.valdezharborinn.com; ❻), a renovated Best Western, with a great waterside location, where rooms have cable TV, DVD player, microwave, fridge and free wi-fi.

The town and around

The **Valdez Museum**, 217 Egan Drive (summer daily 9am–5pm; $7), carries just enough detail on the Gold Rush, oil terminal, glaciation and *Exxon Valdez* oil spill. The entry price covers you for its **annexe**, at 436 S Hazelet Ave (same hours), which covers the 1964 earthquake at length.

The **Maxine & Jesse Whitney Museum** at the Community College, 303 Lowe St (summer daily 9am–7pm; free) has an astounding collection of carved ivory and an assortment of dead beasts, including a couple of moose hides with Alaskan scenes burned into them by an early pioneer. There's also an instructive documentary on the Alaska Pipeline.

If you fancy something more active, Pangaea Adventures, 107 N Harbor Drive (ⓣ1-800/660-9637, ⓦwww.alaskasummer.com) offer **sea-kayaking** trips to Duck Flats; $60 (3–4hr), or a more ambitious coastal paddle to Gold Creek; $99 (6–7hr). It is worth making the effort to reach distant paddling destinations, (accessed by water taxi), principally Shoup Glacier; $180 (8hr) and Columbia Glacier; $230 (10hr). They also offer **kayak rentals** (single $45/day, double $65, $5/day less after the first day), and glacier hikes (half-day $99).

You should also take a cruise out into Prince William Sound, principally to see the spectacular **Columbia Glacier**, three miles wide at its face and towering three hundred feet above the sea. Unfortunately it is receding rapidly and the fjord is now so choked with ice that you can't get close to the face. Weather permitting, you can see it at long range from the AMHS **ferries** between Valdez and Whittier, but for a closer look go with Stan Stephens Glacier & Wildlife Cruises (ⓣ1-866/867-1297, ⓦwww.stanstephenscruises.com), who pick their way through a floating ice field and point out such sights as Bligh Reef, where the *Exxon Valdez* grounded. Choose between a six-hour cruise at $115 and the nine-hour cruise that also visits the Meares Glacier ($150).

Eating

Valdez's restaurants, while nothing special, should satisfy for a night or two. The *Alaska Halibut House*, 208 Meals Ave (ⓣ907/835-2788) serves budget halibut sandwiches and salmon wedges. Oil-boom survivor *The Pipeline Club*, 136 Egan Drive (ⓣ907/835-4332), is also worth a try for top-quality steak and seafood, as well as for its lively dark bar.

Cordova and the Copper River Delta

Far quieter than Valdez, and only accessible by sea or air, **CORDOVA** is an unpretentious fishing community on the southeastern edge of the Sound. In 1906 Cordova was chosen as the port for the copper mined in Kennicott, a hundred miles northeast, gambling on cutting a path between two active glaciers for the proposed Copper River and Northwestern Railroad – the CR&NW – ridiculed at the time as the "Can't Run & Never Will". Nonetheless, in 1911 it was completed when the "**Million Dollar Bridge**" spanned the Copper River. However the mines lasted just 27 years and Cordova shifted its dependency to fishing, in turn dealt a potentially fatal blow by the *Exxon Valdez* in 1989. For the next two seasons, the community reeled from the effects of the **oil spill**; since then fortunes have slowly improved.

Today the "Million Dollar Bridge", battered by the 1964 earthquake, cuts a lonely figure at the end of the Copper River Highway, a 48-mile gravel road across the wetlands of the **Copper River Delta**, a major stopover for migratory birds backed by the Chugach Mountains. It is a tranquil spot for fishing, birdwatching or **hiking** along excellent trails, such as the one to Saddlebag Glacier. The road ends just over the bridge beside the incredibly active **Childs Glacier**.

Copper River and Northwest Tours (ⓣ907/424-5356) run occasional day-trips to the Million Dollar Bridge ($85 including lunch), but by far the best way to make the journey is in a **rental car** (from around $80/day, unlimited mileage) from Chinook Auto Rentals, in the Airport Depot Diner or at the *Northern Nights Inn* (ⓣ1-877/424-5279, ⓦwww.chinookautorentals.com).

Cordova itself has few sights; the **small boat harbour** is the core of the town's activity, particularly in summer. The **Cordova Museum**, 620 First St (summer Mon–Sat 10am–6pm, Sun 2–4pm; $1 suggested donation), has quirky exhibits on local history, including the tiny **ice worm** that lives in the glaciers and the funky festival that celebrates its existence each February. The **Ilanka Cultural Center**, by the harbour at 110 Nicholoff Way (ⓣ907/424-7903; summer Mon–Fri 10am–5pm; donation), has a complete orca skeleton hanging over the entrance, plus local native arts and crafts and a fine bookshop.

Practicalities

There is no road access to Cordova; daily **flights** from Anchorage and Juneau land at the airport twelve miles down the Copper River Highway, to be met by a **shuttle** ($12). Near-daily **ferries** from Valdez and Whittier dock a mile north of town. For information, contact the **Chamber of Commerce** at 404 First St (Mon–Fri 9am–5pm; ⓣ907/424-7260, ⓦwww.cordovachamber.com). Cordova has no **hostel** and the only tent **camping** close to town is at the scruffy *Odiak Campground and RV Park* on Whitshed Road, half a mile south of town (ⓣ907/424-6200; $20), so you might want to rent a car and camp out along the Copper River Delta. The cheapest option in town is the basic *Alaskan Hotel*, 600 First St (ⓣ907/424-3299, ⓔhotelak@ctcak.net; shared bath ❷, private ❸), though you may prefer the revamped *Reluctant Fisherman*, 407 Railroad Ave (ⓣ1-877/424-3272, ⓦwww.reluctantfisherman.com; ❻), or the cosy *Cordova Lighthouse Inn*, Nicholoff Way (ⓣ907/424-7080, ⓦwww.cordovalighthouseinn.com; ❻), both overlooking the small boat harbour. For **food**, try the *Reluctant Fisherman* or the *Killer Whale Cafe*, 507 First St (ⓣ907/424-7733). Wash it down afterwards with a drink at the *Alaskan Hotel*'s **bar**.

Interior and northern Alaska

Interior and northern Alaska is the quintessential "great land". It's mostly a rolling plateau divided by the glacier-studded Alaska and Brooks ranges, criss-crossed by rivers and with views of imposing peaks, above all Mount McKinley, the nation's highest. Even in high summer, when RVs clog the George Parks Highway, people are still hugely outnumbered by game: moose, Dall sheep, grizzly bears, and herds of caribou sweep over seemingly endless swathes of taiga (sparse birch woodland) and tundra.

Heading north from Anchorage the first essential stop is tiny **Talkeetna**, which has great views of Mount McKinley and the opportunity to fly around it. The mountain is at the heart of **Denali National Park**, the jewel of the Interior. If you prefer your wilderness with fewer people and regulations, head east to the untrammelled vastness of **Wrangell-St Elias National Park**. Alternatively, **Fairbanks**, Alaska's diverting second city, serves as the hub of the North, with roads fanning out to **hot springs** and five hundred miles north to the Arctic Ocean at **Prudhoe Bay**.

Weather here can vary enormously from day to day, with even greater seasonal variations: in winter temperatures can drop to -50°F for days at a time, while summer days reach a sweltering 90°F. However, the major problem in summer is huge mosquitoes; don't forget the insect repellent.

Talkeetna

A hundred miles from Anchorage, the eclectic hamlet of **TALKEETNA** has a palpable small-town Alaska feel, but is lent an international flavour by the world's mountaineers, who come here to scale the 20,320ft **Mount McKinley**, usually referred to in Alaska by its Athabascan name **Denali**, "the Great One". Whatever you choose to call it, North America's highest peak rises from 2000ft lowlands, making it the world's tallest from base to peak (other major peaks such as Everest rise from high terrain). The mountain is best seen from the **overlook** just south of Talkeetna, which reveals the peak's transcendent white glow, in sharp contrast to the warm colours all around.

From mid-April to mid-July, climbers mass in Talkeetna to be flown to the mountain: only half of the 1200 attempting the climb each year succeed, usually due to extreme weather. Air-taxi companies such as K2 Aviation (ⓣ1-800/764-2291, ⓦwww.flyk2.com) also run **flightseeing** trips ranging from a spectacular one-hour ($195) flight to the full ninety-minute grand tour ($285) all around the mountain. Add half an hour and $75 for a glacier landing in a plane fitted with skis.

Talkeetna's famed **Moose Dropping Festival** falls on the second weekend of July; little brown balls sell fast (with a sanitary coat of varnish) for use in earrings or necklaces. In addition to these highly desirable lumps of Alaskana, the festival features dancing, drinking, a moose-dropping throwing competition and some more drinking.

Practicalities

Talkeetna is at the end of a fourteen-mile spur off the George Parks Highway, which can usually be hitched. Bus services avoid Talkeetna except for Alaska Park Connection (daily from Anchorage; $65; ⓣ1-800/266-8625, ⓦwww.alaskacoach.com); daily **trains** from Anchorage to Denali and Fairbanks stop half a mile south of town. Information is available from the **Talkeetna Ranger Station**, on B Street (summer daily 8am–5.30pm; ⓣ907/733-2231).

For a town of just three hundred, Talkeetna teems with good **accommodation**, including the welcoming *Talkeetna Hostel* on I Street (ⓣ907/733-4678, ⓦwww.talkeetnahostel.com; bunks $22, rooms ❸). Dating from 1917, the central *Talkeetna Roadhouse* (ⓣ907/733-1351, ⓦwww.talkeetnaroadhouse.com; ❸–❺) bolsters its old-style atmosphere with great home-cooking, bunks ($21), rooms with shared bathrooms ❻–❽ and cabins ($110–125). Easily the fanciest hotel is the *Talkeetna Alaskan Lodge* (ⓣ1-877/777-4067, ⓦwww.talkeetnalodge.com; ❼) on the hill to the south of town. **Campers** can stay at the *Talkeetna River Park* ($10), at the western end of Main Street, but many stroll another hundred yards west and (unofficially) pitch by the river.

Good places to **eat** include the bakery/diner at the *Talkeetna Roadhouse* (see above), and the *West Rib Pub & Grill*, Main Street (ⓣ907/733-3354), which has good burgers and sandwiches. And make sure you stop for a **drink** in the wonderfully ancient *Fairview Inn* on Main Street.

Denali National Park

The six-million-acre **DENALI NATIONAL PARK**, 240 miles north of Anchorage, is home to **Mount McKinley**, which is often shrouded in cloud. The mountain is far from the park's only attraction, however. Shuttle buses offer a glimpse of a vast world of tundra and taiga, glaciers, huge mountains and abundant wildlife – the Park Service reports that 95 percent of visitors see **bears**, **caribou** and **Dall sheep**, 82 percent moose, and over one-fifth **wolves**, along with porcupine, snowshoe hare, red foxes and over 160 bird species. Visiting Alaska without trying to see Denali is unthinkable for most travellers, and therein lies a problem. In high summer, the visitor centre and service areas out on the Parks Highway are a stream of RVs, tour buses and the like. Things pick up in the park itself, and back-country hiking, undertaken by only a tiny fraction of visitors, remains a wonderfully solitary experience.

In **winter**, Denali is transformed into a ghostly, snow-covered world. Motorized vehicles are banned and travel, even for park personnel, is by snowshoe, skis or dogsled as temperatures dive and northern lights glitter over the snows.

Getting to the park

Driving to Denali Park takes about five hours from Anchorage or three from Fairbanks; **hitching** is quite easy with twenty hours of summer daylight. **Bus** services from Anchorage are run by The Park Connection (ⓣ1-800/266-8625, ⓦwww.alaskacoach.com) and Alaska/Yukon Trails (ⓣ1-800/770-2267, ⓦwww.alaskashuttle.com), charging $75–90, with the latter continuing to Fairbanks ($55). **Trains** (daily in summer) leave at 8.15am from both Anchorage ($117) and Fairbanks ($51), depositing you at 3.45pm and 12.15pm respectively at the train station a mile and a half inside the park entrance. Free shuttles run from the hotels outside the park gate to the Denali Visitor Center (8am–6pm daily) opposite the train station. **Park entry** costs $10 per person or $20 per carload and is valid for a week.

Sightseeing, hiking and other activities

The only vehicles allowed on Denali's narrow, unpaved ninety-mile road are a few tour buses and green **shuttle buses**, which you should book well in advance (Ⓣ1-800/622-7275, Ⓦwww.nps.gov/dena) or up to two days ahead at the **wilderness access centre** (May–Sept daily 5am–8pm; Ⓣ907/683-9274), just inside the park entrance. You can pick up a free copy of the *Alpenglow* paper and a wide range of literature here or at the visitor centre, near the train station, or join ranger-led activities including short hikes and the popular, and free, dogsled demonstration held daily at 10am, 2pm and 4pm.

Shuttle buses run to the Savage River at Mile 15 (free), **Toklat River** at Mile 53 ($24), where rangers lead one-hour tundra tours each day at 1.30pm, the Eielson Visitor Center at Mile 67 ($31) or to the aptly named **Wonder Lake** at Mile 84 ($42); round-trips take two, six, eight and eleven hours, respectively. The shuttle drivers don't give guided tours, but with forty pairs of watchful eyes on board, you're almost guaranteed to see the big mammals. You can also hop off at any point for a day-hike (no permits required), returning to the road to flag down the next bus back, if it has room. Buses run at least hourly in season, with more to pick up stragglers at day's end.

Back-country camping is the best way to appreciate Denali's scenery and its inhabitants. Don't expect it to be easy though, as there are no formal trails and with thick spongy tundra and frequent river crossings even hardy hikers find themselves limited to five miles a day. The park is divided into 87 units with only a limited number of campers allowed in 41 of them. Free permits are available one day in advance from the **Backcountry Information Center** (daily 9am–6pm), facing the Wilderness Access Center, though high demand means you should be prepared to hike in the less popular areas. The BIC will also teach you about avoiding run-ins with bears and issue you with bear-resistant food containers. Camper buses reserved for those with campground or back-country permits cost $31. These also carry bikes; cyclists can be dropped anywhere, but are obliged to keep to the road. Another option is to join a **narrated tour** (Ⓣ1-800/622-7275) along the park road: either the five-hour Natural History Tour ($61) or the full-day Tundra Wilderness Tour ($103), which reaches at least Mile 53, stopping frequently to observe wildlife.

Just outside the park entrance, several **rafting** companies offer two-hour trips down the Nenana River: all offer a gentle "scenic float" and an eleven-mile "Canyon Run" through Class III and IV rapids – they cost around $80 individually and $112 for a joint run. Denali Outdoor Center (Ⓣ1-888/303-1925, Ⓦwww.denalioutdoorcenter.com) charges a few dollars more than some others, but offers a quality experience.

Practicalities

With the exception of several exclusive lodges deep in the heart of the park, there are no hotels in Denali, so your choice is between camping, the $160-a-night gaggle of summer-only hotels a mile north of the park entrance or the cheaper offerings either ten miles further north in the little coal-mining town of **HEALY**, or spots a few miles south along the highway. The only cheap option by the park entrance is to camp at *Denali Rainbow Village RV Park* (Mile 238.6, Ⓣ907/683-7777, Ⓦwww.denalirv.com; $25–41) or *Denali Riverside RV Park* (Mile 240.5, Ⓣ1-866/583-2696,

Ⓦwww.denaliriversiderv.com; $22–36), while the only real hostel hereabouts is the excellent *Denali Mountain Morning Hostel*, Mile 224.5 (Ⓣ907/683-7503, Ⓦwww.hostelalaska.com), in the woods thirteen miles south with a free shuttle to the park. There are spacious dorms and fixed tents (both $32/person), one room ($80 double) and cabins ($80–160), there's an efficient kitchen, all manner of games and friendly hosts. In Healy there's the high-quality *Motel Nord Haven*, Mile 249.5 Parks Hwy (Ⓣ1-800/683-4501, Ⓦwww.motelnordhaven.com; ❻), and the lovely *Earth Song Lodge*, Mile 4 Stampede Rd (Ⓣ907/683-2863, Ⓦwww.earthsonglodge.com; ❻), with a cluster of cabins with great views and a café on site.

Camping is the best way to experience Denali up close, with most of the park's six campgrounds open from mid-May to mid-September. The best is **Wonder Lake** ($16), with a stunning view of McKinley; failing that, **Igloo Creek** ($9) is good for spotting Dall sheep, while **Riley Creek** ($14–28), near the entrance, is open year-round. All sites are bookable at the main visitor centre or via phone or the web (Ⓣ1-800/622-7275, Ⓦwww.reservedenali.com). If you don't do this you may have to wait a day or two to get a spot. The best alternative is *Denali Grizzly Bear Resort*, Mile 231.1, seven miles south (Ⓣ1-866/583-2696, Ⓦwww.denaligrizzlybear.com; ❶–❼), with $24 campsites set in the trees close to the Nenana River with a wide variety of attractive cabins all around.

Eating is expensive, with only a limited range of grocery stores and a small selection of fairly pricey restaurants close to the park entrance, such as the *Black Bear Coffee House* (Ⓣ907/683-1656), serving light meals and *Lynx Creek Pizza and Pub* (Ⓣ907/683-2547), offering salads and sandwiches as well as pizza and draft microbrews.

Wrangell-St Elias National Park

As Denali becomes more crowded, people are increasingly making the trip to remoter **WRANGELL-ST ELIAS NATIONAL PARK** in the extreme southeast corner of the Interior, where four of the continent's great mountain ranges – the Wrangell, St Elias, Chugach and Alaska – cramp up against each other. Everything is writ large: glacier after enormous glacier, canyon after dizzying canyon, and nine of the sixteen highest peaks in the US, all laced together by braided rivers and idyllic lakes where mountain goats, Dall sheep, bears, moose and caribou roam.

The first whites in the area came in search of gold but instead hit upon one of the continent's richest copper deposits. The mines closed in 1938, after 27 frantic years of production, and today **Kennicott**, with over thirty creaking, disused buildings, is a ghost town. You can visit the mill complex on fascinating two-hour **walking tours** run by St Elias Alpine Guides ($25; Ⓣ1-888/933-5427, Ⓦwww.steliasguides.com), who also run a number of hikes, ice-climbing trips, mountain-bike rides, raft trips and even glacier skiing adventures out into the virtually trailless park.

Practicalities

Half the fun is getting to McCarthy along 58 rugged miles of the **McCarthy Road**, following the abandoned railroad that once linked the Kennicott mill to the port at Cordova. Take it slow and stop often to admire the scenery and abandoned trestle bridges. At the end of the road you cross the Kennicott River on a footbridge and continue half a mile to the village of McCarthy on foot, from where a shuttle bus runs along four miles of dirt road to Kennicott. Hitching along the McCarthy Road can be a hit-or-miss affair; if you haven't got a vehicle you can go with Backcountry Connection (Ⓣ1-866/582-5292, Ⓦwww.kennicottshuttle.com), who charge $139 return from Glennallen. The park's **visitor centre** is just south of Glennallen at Mile 107 on the Richardson Highway (summer daily 9am–7pm; Ⓣ907/822-5234, Ⓦwww.nps.gov/wrst).

Accommodation around McCarthy and Kennicott isn't cheap, though the *Kennicott River Lodge and Hostel* (Ⓣ907/554-4441, Ⓦwww.kennicottriverlodge.com; (❹–❻)), near the road end, has four-bunk cabins ($30 pp) and nice common areas. The atmospheric *Lancaster's Backpacking Hotel*, in McCarthy (Ⓣ907/554-4402, Ⓦwww.mccarthylodge.com) has simple rooms with shared bathrooms ($68 single, $98 double), and the associated *Ma Johnson's Hotel* (❻) is also very pleasant, with good food across the road at the *McCarthy Lodge*. In Kennicott there's the upmarket *Kennicott Glacier Lodge* (Ⓣ1-800/582-5128, Ⓦwww.kennicottlodge.com; ❼), which also has the town's one restaurant (reserve for dinner).

Fairbanks

FAIRBANKS, 360 miles north of Anchorage and at the end of the Alaska Highway from Canada, is somewhat bland but makes a great base for exploring a hinterland of gold mines, hot springs and limitless wilderness and for journeys along the **Dalton Highway** to the Arctic Ocean oilfield of **Prudhoe Bay**.

Alaska's second largest town was founded accidentally, in 1901, when a steamship carrying trader E.T. Barnette ran aground in the shallows of the Chena River, a tributary of the Yukon. Unable to move his supplies any further, he set up shop in the wilderness, catering to the few trappers and prospectors in the area. The following year **gold** was found, a tent city sprang up and Barnette made a mint. In 1908, at the height of the rush, Fairbanks had a population of 18,500, but by 1920 it had dwindled to only 1100. During World War II several huge **military bases** were built and the population rebounded getting a further boost in the mid-1970s when it became the construction centre for the **trans-Alaska pipeline**.

The spectacular **aurora borealis** is a major winter attraction, as is the **Ice Alaska Festival** in mid-March, with its ice-sculpting competition and dogsled racing on frozen downtown streets. Summer visitors should try to catch the three-day **World Eskimo-Indian Olympics** (Ⓦwww.weio.org) in mid-July when contestants from around the state compete in dance, art and sports competitions, as well as some unusual ones like ear-pulling, knuckle hop, high kick and the blanket toss.

Fairbanks suffers remarkable extremes of climate, with winter temperatures dropping to -70°F and summer highs topping 90°F. Proximity to the Arctic Circle means over 21 hours of sunlight in midsummer, when midnight baseball games take place under natural light, and 2am bar evacuees are confronted by bright sunshine.

Arrival, information and getting around

Alaska Airlines flies frequently from Anchorage to **Fairbanks Airport**, four miles southwest; the MACS Yellow Line **bus** (Mon–Sat; $1.50) runs downtown, but the long wait between services means you'll probably want to grab a **taxi** (around $15). Most hotels offer shuttles to the airport or rail depot. The airport is also a gateway for flights into the bush; Era Aviation (Ⓣ1-800/478-6779, Ⓦwww.flyera.com) operates a reliable service. **Trains** from Anchorage (daily in summer, weekly in winter) stop beside the Johansen Expressway inconveniently far from downtown. It's cheaper to get here by bus with Alaska/Yukon Trails (Ⓣ1-800/770-7275, Ⓦwww.alaskashuttle.com; daily May–Sept), who charge $99 from Anchorage, drop off at the airport and major hostels and hotels. The best way to get around town is by car, but there's a good riverside cycle trail and the six MACS **bus lines** (Ⓣ907/459-1011), provide a reasonable service. Among the companies that can whisk you off into the surrounding bush and fly you to the **Arctic Circle**, the widest choice is with the Northern Alaska Tour Company (Ⓣ1-800/474-1986, Ⓦwww.northernalaska.com).

The new Morris Thompson Cultural and **Visitor Center**, at 101 Dunkel St (summer daily 8am–9pm; Ⓣ1-800/459-3701, Ⓦwww.explorefairbanks.com), dispenses information on lodging and activities, with free films, cultural events, internet access and an excellent historical display. It also houses the **Alaska Public Land Information Center** (APLIC; Ⓣ907/459-3730, Ⓦwww.alaskacenters.gov/fairbanks.cfm; 9am–6pm daily) for information on back-country activities and the area's parks, including Denali.

Accommodation

Downtown motels and hotels tend to be either quite pricey or pretty dodgy. **B&B**s are plentiful, with rooms from $80 a night; the visitor centre offers free phone calls and all the brochures. Thankfully there are a couple of good hostels, and for campers there's the tranquil and convenient *Tanana Valley Campground*, 1800 College Rd at Aurora Drive (mid-May to mid-Sept; Ⓣ907/456-7956; $16–24), on the MACS bus Red line.

Ah, Rose Marie 302 Cowles St Ⓣ907/456-2040, Ⓦwww.akpub.com/akbbrv/ahrose.html. Small but justly popular B&B where a hearty breakfast is served on the glassed-in porch. ❹

Backpacker Hostel 2895 Mack Blvd Ⓣ907/479-2034, Ⓦwww.alaskahostel.com. Welcoming though somewhat cramped hostel, in a nice area and handily placed on the bus routes between downtown and the university. Free internet access, kitchen and bikes. Bunks $30, camping $15.

Golden North Motel 4888 Old Airport Way Ⓣ1-800/447-1910, Ⓦwww.goldennorthmotel.com. Friendly and spotlessly clean motel near the airport with cable TV and free wi-fi. Free pick-ups are available and the Yellow and Blue buses pass nearby. ❹

GoNorth Base Camp 3500 Davis Rd Ⓣ907/479-7272, Ⓦwww.gonorthalaska.com. A kind of outdoors hostel in a forested area with large fixed tents with five beds ($28; $25 with own sleeping bag). There's also camping ($12–18), space in a tipi ($20) and reasonably priced bike rental.

Minnie Street B&B Inn 345 Minnie St Ⓣ1-888/456-1849, Ⓦwww.minniestreetbandb.com. Top-line B&B with every luxury, including free wi-fi and a spacious deck with a hot tub. Some rooms have a jacuzzi and there's a full breakfast. Shared bath ❻, private bath ❼, jacuzzi ❽

The Town

The main point of interest **downtown** is the small **Fairbanks Community Museum**, 410 Cushman St at 5th Avenue (Mon–Fri 10am–4pm; free), displaying trapping, mining and dogsled racing equipment. A similarly wintry theme is pursued at the **Ice Museum**, 500 2nd Ave at Lacey Street (summer daily 10am–8pm; $12), a year-round taster of the Ice Sculpting competition by way of a slide show and walk-in refrigerators housing some small carvings. A couple of miles west on the banks of the Chena River, the touristy **Pioneer Park** (mostly free) celebrates Alaskan history though various pioneer museums, the only large wooden sternwheeler left in the US, and a miniature railway encircling the entire park; there's plenty to amuse the kids. College Road heads west past **Creamer's Field**, thick with sandhill cranes and Canada geese, especially in spring and autumn, to the University of Alaska Fairbanks' attractive campus. Here UAF's superb modern **Museum of the North** (summer daily 9am–9pm; $10; Ⓦwww.uaf.edu/museum) displays eclectic collections of native and contemporary art, as well as natural and human history displays.

Unashamedly touristy but fun and very popular is a four-hour **cruise** down the Chena River on the "Riverboat Discovery" ($55; Ⓣ1-866/479-6673, Ⓦwww.riverboatdiscovery.com), which includes a visit to a mock Native village.

Eating and nightlife

Fairbanks' **eating** options are varied, with good Thai particularly prevalent. They're also well scattered, with downtown and College Road, toward the university, having the greatest concentrations. Nowhere downtown sells groceries: the closest are Safeway and Fred Meyer at the eastern end of College Road. Fairbanks has its decent **nightspots** though none lie in hard-drinking downtown.

Alaska Coffee Roasting Co. West Valley Plaza, 4001 Geist Rd ⓣ907/457-5282. Fairbanks' best coffee, roasted daily on the premises, served in a cosy café hung with local art. There's a good selection of wraps, cakes and muffins, too.

Blue Loon Mile 353.5 Parks Hwy ⓣ907/457-5666, ⓦwww.theblueloon.com. Late-closing hotspot five miles west of Fairbanks that's always good for a convivial drink. Hosts local and touring bands (sometimes a DJ) several nights a week, as well as movies. Closed Sun/Mon.

The Diner 244 Illinois St ⓣ907/451-0613. Reliable diner fare at good prices.

Gambardella's Pasta Bella 706 2nd Ave, downtown ⓣ907/457-4992, ⓦwww.gambardellas.com. Fairbanks' best Italian and not wildly expensive, with a pleasant outdoor area for those endless summer evenings.

Howling Dog Saloon Mile 11 Old Steese Hwy, Fox ⓣ907/456-4695, ⓦwww.howlingdogsaloon.com. Eleven miles north of town, but perhaps the north's best bar – unassuming, unpretentious and fun. Live rock and R&B bands perform.

The Marlin 3412 College Rd ⓣ907/479-4646. Poky wood-panelled cellar bar with cutting-edge bands – blues, jazz, and rock – most evenings from around 9pm and only a small cover charge, if any.

Pump House Mile 1.3 Chena Pump Rd ⓣ907/479-8452, ⓦwww.pumphouse.com. A local favourite in a historic pumphouse, stuffed with gold-mining paraphernalia and with a deck by the Chena River. Great for steak, seafood and burgers, and also pulls in a substantial drinking crowd.

Second Story Café 3525 College Rd ⓣ907/474-9574. Pleasant spot above Gulliver's Bookstore, serving wraps, sandwiches, bagels, biscotti and coffee all at reasonable prices. Free internet access as well.

Thai House 412 5th Ave, downtown ⓣ907/452-6123. A small but ever-popular restaurant serving the usual range of Thai dishes, but all done to perfection and modestly priced at around $11. Closed Sun.

Around Fairbanks: Chena hot springs

Chena Hot Springs, the most accessible and developed resort in the area, stands sixty miles east of Fairbanks amid a bucolic swath of **muskeg** (grassy swampland) and forest traversed by good hiking trails and teeming with moose. For $10 a day non-guests can use the hot pools and large outdoor "rock pool", which are free for those staying at the fully equipped resort (ⓣ1-800/478-4681, ⓦwww.chenahotsprings.com; ❼–❽), where camping costs $20 and yurts $65. The resort also rents out canoes and mountain bikes, as well as offering rafting float trips.

The Northern Lights

The **aurora borealis**, or "Northern Lights", an ethereal display of light in the uppermost atmosphere, give their brightest and most colourful displays in the sky above Fairbanks. For up to one hundred winter nights, the sky appears to shimmer with dancing curtains of colour ranging from luminescent greens to fantastic veils that run the full spectrum. Named after the Roman goddess of dawn, the aurora is caused by an interaction between the earth's magnetic field and the **solar wind**, an invisible stream of charged electrons and protons continually blown out into space from the sun. The earth deflects the solar wind like a rock in a stream, with the energy released at the magnetic poles – much like a neon sign.

The Northern Lights are at their most dazzling from December to March, when nights are longest and the sky darkest, but late September can be good for summer visitors. They are visible pretty much everywhere, but the further north the better, especially around Fairbanks.

The Dalton Highway

Built in the 1970s to service the **trans-Alaska pipeline**, the mostly gravel **Dalton Highway**, or Haul Road, runs from Fairbanks five hundred miles to the oil facility of Prudhoe Bay on Alaska's north coast, some three hundred miles beyond the Arctic Circle. It is a long, bumpy and demanding drive, so take spare tyres, gas, provisions and, ideally, a sturdy four-wheel-drive vehicle: most regular rentals aren't permitted up here. Not far from Fairbanks you start to parallel the pipeline, snaking up hills and in and out of the ground. At 188 miles, a sign announces that you've just crossed the **Arctic Circle**. The **Northern Alaska Tour Company** (Ⓣ1-800/474-1986, Ⓦwww.northernalaska.com) will drive you up in a minibus and either drive you back to Fairbanks ($189; a long arduous day) or fly you back ($359).

The highway plugs on north through increasingly barren territory, finally dispensing with trees as you climb through the wilderness of the **Brooks Range**, a 9000ft chain mostly held within the **Gates of the Arctic National Park**. From Atigun Pass you descend through two hundred miles of grand glaciated valleys and blasted Arctic plains to the end of the road at dead-boring **Deadhorse**. You can't stroll by the ocean or camp here, so your choices are confined to staying in one of the $190-per-night hotels and taking a $39 tour past the adjacent – and off-limits – **Prudhoe Bay** oil facility to dip a toe (or your full body) into the Arctic Ocean. By far the best way to do it is with Northern Alaska, who run a three-day fly/drive tour to Prudhoe Bay for $989.

16 Hawaii

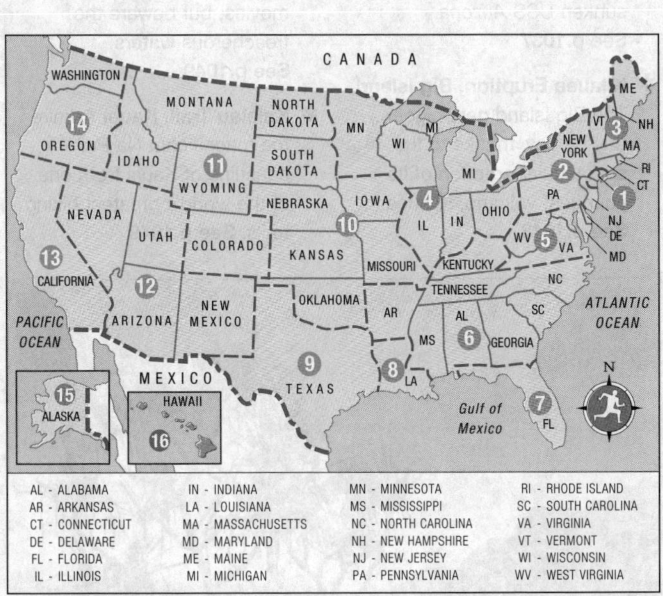
CANADA
WASHINGTON
MONTANA
NORTH DAKOTA
MN
WI
MI
ME
VT
NH
NEW YORK
MA
RI
CT
OREGON
IDAHO
WYOMING
SOUTH DAKOTA
MI
PA
NJ
DE
MD
NEBRASKA
IOWA
IL
IN
OHIO
WV
VA
NEVADA
UTAH
COLORADO
KANSAS
MISSOURI
KENTUCKY
CALIFORNIA
NC
TENNESSEE
OKLAHOMA
ARIZONA
NEW MEXICO
AR
AL
SC
ATLANTIC OCEAN
PACIFIC OCEAN
MS
GEORGIA
TEXAS
LA
MEXICO
ALASKA
HAWAII
Gulf of Mexico
FL
N
1
2
3
4
5
6
7
8
9
10
11
12
13
14
15
16
AL - ALABAMA
AR - ARKANSAS
CT - CONNECTICUT
DE - DELAWARE
FL - FLORIDA
IL - ILLINOIS
IN - INDIANA
LA - LOUISIANA
MA - MASSACHUSETTS
MD - MARYLAND
ME - MAINE
MI - MICHIGAN
MN - MINNESOTA
MS - MISSISSIPPI
NC - NORTH CAROLINA
NH - NEW HAMPSHIRE
NJ - NEW JERSEY
PA - PENNSYLVANIA
RI - RHODE ISLAND
SC - SOUTH CAROLINA
VA - VIRGINIA
VT - VERMONT
WI - WISCONSIN
WV - WEST VIRGINIA

CHAPTER 16 Highlights

* **Waikiki Beach, Oahu** Learn to surf, or just sip a cocktail, on the world's most famous beach. **See p.1036**

* **Pearl Harbor, Oahu** View a reminder of December 7, 1941 – the "date that will live in infamy" – by visiting the sunken USS *Arizona*. **See p.1037**

* **Kilauea Eruption, Big Island** The Big Island gets bigger day by day, thanks to the spectacular eruption of its youngest volcano, Kilauea. **See p.1043**

* **Lahaina, Maui** This early-nineteenth-century whaling port ranks among the most historic towns in Hawaii. **See p.1045**

* **Lumahai Beach, Kauai** This superb beach has been featured in countless movies, but beware the treacherous waters. **See p.1049**

* **Kalalau Trail, Kauai** Admire the magnificent Na Pali coastline of Kauai from one of the world's greatest hiking trails. **See p.1049**

▲ The Kalalau Trail, Kauai

16 Hawaii

With their fiery volcanoes, palm-fringed beaches, verdant valleys, glorious rainbows and awesome cliffs, the islands of **HAWAII** boast some of the most spectacularly beautiful scenery on earth. Despite their isolation, two thousand miles out in the Pacific, they belong very definitely to the United States. Pulling in 6.5 million tourists per year, the fiftieth state can seem at times like a gigantic theme park.

Honolulu, on **Oahu**, is by far the largest city in Hawaii, while Waikiki, its resort annexe, is the main tourist centre. Three other islands attract sizeable numbers of visitors: **Hawaii** itself, also known as the **Big Island** in a vain attempt to avoid confusion, **Maui** and **Kauai**. All the islands share a similar topography and **climate**. Ocean winds shed their rain on their northeast, **windward** coasts, keeping them wet and green; the southwest, **leeward** (or "Kona") coasts can be almost barren, and so make ideal locations for big resorts. While temperatures remain consistent all year at between 70°F and 85°F, rainfall is heaviest from December to March, which nonetheless remains the most popular time to visit. Although a visit to Hawaii doesn't have to cost a fortune, the one major expense you can't avoid, except possibly on Oahu, is car rental.

Some history

Each of the Hawaiian islands was forced up like a vast mass of candle drippings by submarine volcanic action, all fuelled by the same "hot spot", which has remained stationary as the Pacific plate drifted above. The process continues at Kilauea on the Big Island, where lava explodes into the sea to add new land day by day, while the oldest islands are now mere atolls way to the northwest. Until two thousand years ago, these unknown specks were populated only by the few plants, birds and animals carried here by wind or wave. The first known human inhabitants were the **Polynesians**, who arrived in two principal migrations: from the Marquesas from around 200 AD, and another from Tahiti several centuries later.

No western ship chanced upon Hawaii until **Captain Cook** reached Kauai in 1778. He was amazed to find a civilization sharing a culture – and language – with the peoples of the South Pacific. Although Cook himself was killed in Hawaii in 1779, his visit started an irreversible process of change. In reshaping the islands to suit their needs, Westerners decimated the indigenous flora and fauna – as well as the Hawaiians themselves. Cook's men estimated that there were a million islanders; the population today is roughly the same, but barely eight thousand **pure-blood Hawaiians** are left.

Within a few years of Cook's arrival, **Kamehameha** became the first king to unite all the islands. However, exposure to the world economy swiftly

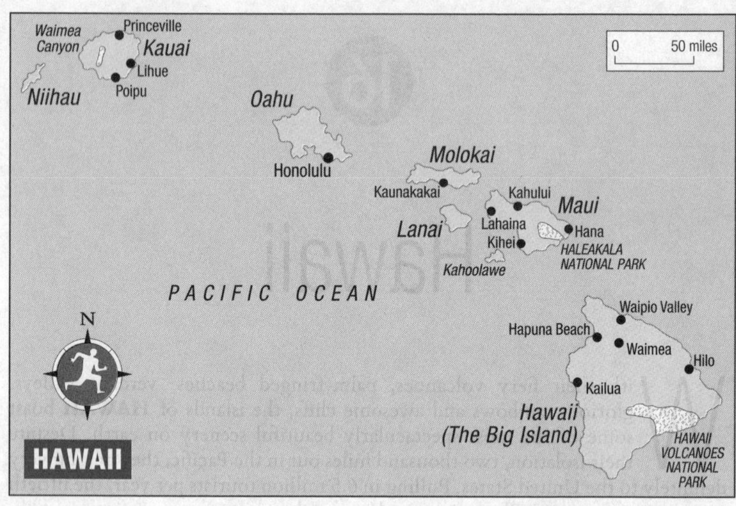

devastated Hawaii's traditional way of life. White advisers and ministers soon dominated the government, and the descendants of the first missionaries from New England became Hawaii's most powerful class. As the US grew increasingly reliant on Hawaiian-grown **sugar**, Hawaii moved inexorably towards annexation. In 1887 an all-white group of "concerned businessmen" forced King David Kalakaua to surrender power, and subsequently called in a US warship and declared a provisional republican government. US President Cleveland (a Democrat) responded that "Hawaii was taken possession of by the United States forces without the consent or wish of the government of the islands…(It) was wholly without justification…not merely a wrong but a disgrace".

On August 12, 1898, Hawaii was formally **annexed** as a territory of the United States. Its ultimate integration into the American mainstream was hastened by its crucial role in the war against Japan, and the expansion of tourism thereafter. The islands finally became the fiftieth of the United States in 1959, after a plebiscite showed a seventeen-to-one majority in favour. The only group to oppose statehood were the few remaining native Hawaiians.

Modern Hawaii

Roughly sixty percent of the million-plus modern Hawaiians were born here. Around one-third are Caucasian, one-third Japanese and one-sixth Filipino, with 200,000 claiming at least some Hawaiian ancestry. With agriculture in decline, the need to import virtually all the basics of life results in a high **cost of living**.

Few vestiges of **ancient Hawaii** remain. What is presented as "historic" usually postdates the missionary impact. Ruined temples (**heiaus**) to the old gods still stand in some places, but Hawaii's "old towns" are pure nineteenth-century Americana, with false-front stores and raised wooden boardwalks. While authentic **hula** dancing is a powerful art form, you're most likely to encounter it bastardized in a **luau**. Primarily tourist money-spinners, these "traditional feasts" provide an opportunity to sample Hawaiian **foods** such as **kalua** pig, baked underground, and local fish such as **ono**, **ahi**, **mahi-mahi** and **lomi-lomi** (raw salmon).

The Hawaiian **language** endures primarily in place names and music. At first glance it looks unpronounceable – especially as its written form uses just twelve letters (the five vowels, plus **h**, **k**, **l**, **m**, **n**, **p**, and **w**) – but each letter is enunciated individually, and long words break down into repeated sounds, such as "**meha-meha**" in "Kamehameha".

Getting to and around Hawaii

Honolulu, just under six hours by plane from the West Coast, is one of the world's busiest centres for air traffic; return fares from **LA**, **San Francisco** and **Seattle** start at around $350. Direct flights from the mainland also serve Maui, the Big Island and Kauai.

Hawaiian Airlines (Ⓣ1-800/367-5320, Ⓦwww.hawaiianair.com), connects all the major islands several times per day, with standard one-way fares of around $80. A budget competitor, Go! (Ⓣ1-888/435-9462, Ⓦwww.iflygo.com), offers less frequent services at lower rates. There are no ferry services between the major islands.

All the airports have **car rental** outlets; with the exception of Oahu, however, **bus** services on the islands barely exist.

Oahu

Three-quarters of Hawaii's population live on **OAHU**, which has monopolized the islands' trade and tourism since European sailors realized that **Honolulu** offered the safest in-shore anchorage for thousands of miles. Eighty percent of visitors to Hawaii arrive in Honolulu and many remain for their entire vacation. Oahu effectively confines tourists to the tower-block enclave of **Waikiki**, just east of downtown Honolulu; there are few rooms anywhere else.

While overcrowding and development make it hard to recommend Oahu over its neighbours, it can still give a real flavour of Hawaii. Oahu has some excellent **beaches**, with those on the North Shore a haven for **surfers** and campers, and the **cliffs** of the windward side are awesome.

Honolulu

Until the Europeans came, there was no significant settlement on the site of modern **HONOLULU**; soon so many foreign ships were frequenting its waters that it had become Kamehameha's capital, and it remains the economic centre of the archipelago. While the city covers a long (if narrow) strip of southern Oahu, **downtown** is a manageable size, and a lot quieter than its glamorous image might suggest. The tourist hotels are concentrated in the skyscrapers of the distinct suburb of **Waikiki**, a couple of miles east.

While its setting is beautiful, right on the Pacific and backed by dramatic cliffs and extinct volcanoes, most visitors are here simply to enjoy the sheer **hedonism** of shopping, eating and generally hanging out in the sun. It's also the centre of an exemplary **public transportation** system that covers the whole island.

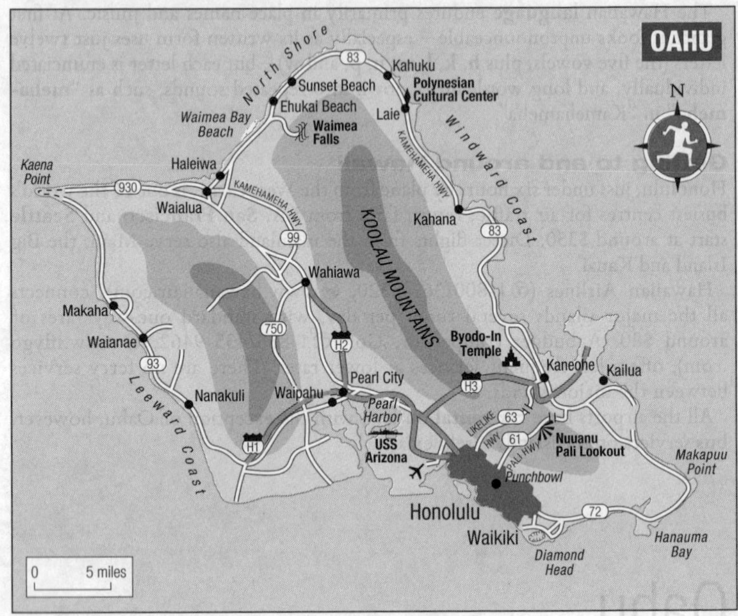

Arrival, information and getting around

Honolulu's **International Airport** is west of downtown. **Car rental** outlets abound, but a car is not especially desirable, what with city traffic and hefty parking fees in Waikiki. The nine-mile (not at all scenic) drive to Waikiki takes anything from 25 to 75 minutes; Airport Waikiki Express (one-way $9, return $15; ⓣ808/944-1879, ⓦislandexpresstransport.com) is a **shuttle service** to any Waikiki hotel. Regular **buses #19** and **#20** also head to Waikiki, but don't allow large bags, cases or backpacks. A **taxi** will cost around $25.

Information

The **Hawaii Visitors Bureau** maintains a strong online presence at ⓦwww.gohawaii.com. Free listings magazines and leaflets are everywhere you turn, and all the hotels have information desks. Kiosks around Waikiki offer greatly discounted rates for island tours, helicopter rides, dinner cruises, surfing lessons and so on.

Getting around

Sixty **bus** routes, collectively named TheBus, cover the whole of Oahu (ⓣ808/848-5555, ⓦwww.thebus.org). All journeys cost $2.25, with free transfers onto any connecting route; a 4-day pass is $25. The most popular routes with Waikiki-based tourists are **#2** to downtown, **#8** to Ala Moana, **#20** to Pearl Harbor, **#22** to Hanauma Bay, and the bargain "Circle Island" buses (**#52** clockwise and **#55** counterclockwise), which take four hours to loop around the central valley and the east coast, passing the legendary North Shore surf spots.

Among companies running **city and island bus tours**, for anything from $30 up to $100 for a full day, as well as off-island packages, are Polynesian Adventure Tours (ⓣ808/833-3000 or 1-800/622-3011, ⓦwww.polyad.com).

Accommodation

All the accommodation listed below is in or near **Waikiki**; very little is available in central Honolulu. Waikiki accommodation covers a wide range and the highest rates will bring absolute luxury, but it's possible to find comfortable lodging for much less. Though an ocean view costs at least $50 extra, nothing is far from the Pacific.

Aloha Punawai 305 Saratoga Rd ⓣ808/923-5211 or 1-866/713-9694, ⓦwww.alternative-hawaii.com/alohapunawai. This Japanese-style hotel offers 19 clean, a/c apartments and studios, all with kitchenettes. ❺

Aston Waikiki Joy 320 Lewers St ⓣ808/923-2300 or 1-877/997-6667, ⓦwww.astonhotels.com. Good-value little hotel, with quirky pastel decor, from the airy garden lobby through to the faded but adequate rooms, all of which have whirlpool baths. ❺

The Breakers 250 Beach Walk ⓣ808/923-3181 or 1-800/426-0494, ⓦwww.breakers-hawaii.com. Small, old-fashioned Polynesian hotel on the western edge of central Waikiki; all rooms have kitchenettes and TV, and there's a bar and grill beside the pool. ❺

New Otani Kaimana Beach Hotel 2863 Kalakaua Ave ⓣ808/923-1555 or 1-800/356-8264, ⓦwww.kaimana.com. Intimate, Japanese-toned beach-front hotel half a mile east of central Waikiki. ❼

Outrigger and **Ohana** Linked hotel chains with numerous Waikiki locations, mostly high-rises (*Outrigger* ⓣ1-866/956-4262, ⓦwww.outrigger.com; *Ohana* ⓣ1-866/968-8744, ⓦwww.ohanahotels.com; both also on ⓣ303/369-7777). *Ohana* hotels like the *Ohana Waikiki East*, 150 Kaiulani Ave (❺), or the slightly more luxurious *Ohana Waikiki Beachcomber*, 2300 Kalakaua Ave (❺), are generally cheaper than the *Outriggers*, such as the all-condo *Luana Waikiki*, 2045 Kalakaua Ave (❻), and the flagship *Waikiki on the Beach*, 2335 Kalakaua Ave (❻). ❺–❾

Polynesian Hostel Beach Club 2584 Lemon Rd ⓣ808/922-1340, ⓦwww.polynesianbeachclub.com. Clean, safe and efficient hostel, a block from the sea. All the a/c dorms have en-suite bathrooms; some hold four bunk beds ($25/person), some six ($23/person). "Semi-private" rooms, sharing a bathroom, cost $40 single, $50 double, and a studio is $70. Van tours offered. Free wi-fi and use of snorkel gear and boogie boards. ❶–❸

The Royal Hawaiian 2259 Kalakaua Ave ⓣ808/923-7311 or 1-866/716-8110, ⓦwww.royal-hawaiian.com. The 1920s "Pink Palace", commanding the beach, is one of Waikiki's best-loved landmarks. Its original building, looking out across terrace gardens to the sea, remains irresistible. ❾

Waikiki Beachside Hostel 2556 Lemon Rd ⓣ808/923-9566, ⓦwww.waikikibeachsidehostel.com. Small hotel block near the park in eastern Waikiki – not literally "beachside" – that has been converted into a popular, lively private hostel, with dorm beds from $20, plus pricier double rooms and free wi-fi. ❶–❸

The City

Downtown Honolulu is surprisingly small, set back a little from the sea and focused around a spacious plaza on King Street that includes **Iolani Palace** and the **state capitol**. The imposing palace, built for King David Kalakaua in 1882, can be visited on guided tours (by reservation, ⓣ808/522-0832; ⓦwww.iolanipalace.org; Tues–Sat 9–11.15am; $20) or self-guided audio tours (Tues–Sat 11.45am–3pm; $13); there's an impressive collection of ancient artefacts in the basement, including feathered royal cloaks. Across the road stands a flower-bedecked, gilt statue of Kamehameha the Great.

To reach the nearby ocean, pedestrians have to negotiate fearsome traffic. The **Aloha Tower** on Pier 9 used to be the city's tallest building; the surrounding area is now a mall, fronting onto the docks and better for dining than it is for shopping. Climb to the top of the tower for an enjoyable overview (daily 9am–5pm; free).

Honolulu residents take great pride in the stunning fine art at the **Academy of Arts**, half a mile east of the capitol at 900 S Beretania St (Tues–Sat 10am–4.30pm, Sun 1–5pm; $10, under-13s free; ⓣ808/532-8700, ⓦwww.honoluluacademy.org). As well as paintings including Van Gogh's **Wheat**

Field, Gauguin's **Two Nudes on a Tahitian Beach** and one of Monet's **Water Lilies**, the Academy also holds fascinating depictions of Hawaii by visiting artists, including vivid, stylized studies of Maui's Iao Valley and Hana coast by Georgia O'Keeffe, plus magnificent ancient **Chinese** ceramics and bronzes.

Chinatown

Just five minutes' walk west of downtown Honolulu, the faded green-clapboard storefronts of **Chinatown**, lining the narrow streets that lead down to Nuuanu Stream, seem like another world. Some of Chinatown's old walled courtyards are now malls, but the businesses remain much the same as ever, and you can still find herbalists weighing out dried leaves in front of vast arrays of bottles. Pig snouts and salmon heads are among the food specialties at **Oahu Market**, on N King and Kekaulike streets.

Bishop Museum

The anthropological collection at the **Bishop Museum** at 1525 Bernice St (daily except Tues 9am–5pm; $18; ⓣ808/847-3511, ⓦwww.bishopmuseum.org) – well away from the ocean and downtown, near the foot of the Likelike Highway – showcases real Polynesian culture. Three floors of its beautifully restored Hawaian Hall display ancient carved stone and wooden images of gods, magnificent feather **leis** and cloaks, and a full-sized **hale** (traditional hut) from Kauai, in addition to a full-sized sperm whale. There are also excellent exhibitions for kids and a planetarium. TheBus #2 from Waikiki stops two blocks away on Kapalama Street.

Punchbowl

High above Honolulu, lush lawns in the caldera of an extinct volcano are the setting for the **National Memorial Cemetery of the Pacific** (daily: March–Sept 8am–6.30pm; Oct–Feb 8am–5.30pm), which holds casualties from all US Pacific wars, including Vietnam. Once home to an ancient sacrificial temple, it's on TheBus route #15.

Waikiki

Built on a reclaimed swamp, **Waikiki** is very nearly an island, all but separated from Honolulu between the sea and the Ala Wai canal. The site may be venerable, but these days its *raison d'être* is rampant commercialism. You could, just about, survive here with very little money, but there would be no point – there's nothing to see, and the only thing to do apart from surf and sunbathe is to stroll along the seafront **Kalakaua Avenue** and shop.

In places, the parallel **Waikiki Beach** narrows to just a thin strip of sand, but it's still a wonderful place to spend a lazy day, and there's always something going on, from surf lessons to outrigger canoe rides. The pedestrian walkway along its edge, lined with pleasant gardens, makes it a refuge from the frenzy nearby, and usually you only have to walk a little west of the centre to find a more secluded spot.

Diamond Head

Waikiki's most famous landmark is the pinnacle of **Diamond Head**, another extinct volcano just to the east. The lawns of the crater interior are oddly bland, but a straightforward hiking trail, passing through a network of tunnels built during World War II, leads up a mile or so to the summit, and a panorama of the whole coast. TheBus #22 and #58 stop on the road nearby.

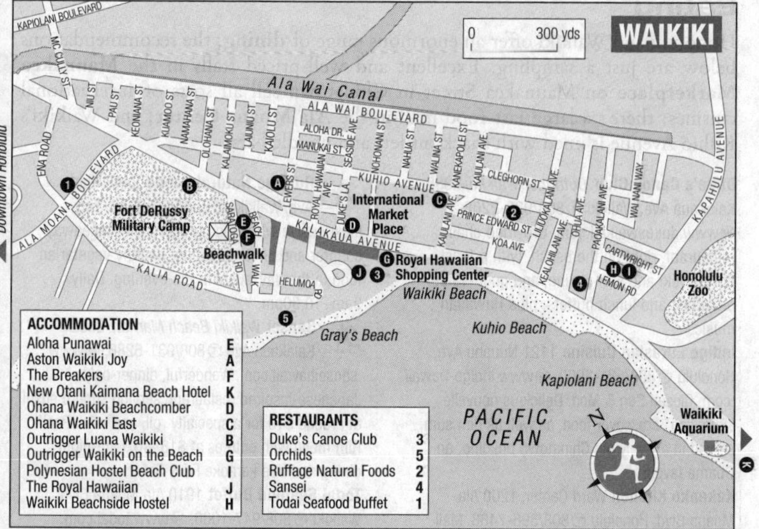

Hanauma Bay

A few miles east, the magnificent crescent-shaped **Hanauma Bay**, formed when the wall of a crater collapsed and let in the sea, is Oahu's best place to **snorkel** (summer daily except Tues 6am–7pm, 2nd and 4th Sat of month 6am–10pm; winter daily except Tues 6am–6pm, 2nd Sat of month 6am–10pm; $7.50, under-13s free; ⓣ808/396-4229). Thanks to strict conservation measures, the sea abounds in brightly coloured fish. The hourly #22 bus from Waikiki drop passengers at the visitor centre.

Pearl Harbor

Almost the whole of **Pearl Harbor**, the principal base for the US Pacific fleet (just over an hour west of Waikiki on TheBus #20), is off-limits to visitors. However, the surprise Japanese attack of December 7, 1941, which an official US inquiry called "the greatest military and naval disaster in our nation's history", is commemorated by a simple white memorial set above the wreck of the battleship **USS Arizona**, still discernible in the clear blue waters. More than 1100 of its crew lie entombed there.

Free tours of the memorial operate between 8am and 3pm each day, but it can be two or three hours after you pick up your numbered ticket at the **Pearl Harbor visitor centre** (daily 7am–5pm; ⓣ808/422-0561; ⓦwww.nps.gov/usar) before you're called to board the ferry that takes you there. The visitor centre does at least offer long-range views of the memorial, which was partly financed by Elvis Presley's 1961 Honolulu concert, his first show after leaving the army. The huge **USS Missouri**, which survived the attack and was used four years later for the ceremony in Tokyo Harbor that ended World War II, is moored alongside the *Arizona*. Guided visits, by bus from alongside the Pearl Harbor visitor centre, include the actual surrender site as well as sweeping views of the harbour from the **Missouri**'s bridge (daily 9am–5pm, tickets sold 8am–4pm; tours $20–65; ⓣ1-877/644-4489, ⓦwww.ussmissouri.com).

Eating

Honolulu and Waikiki offer an enormous range of **dining**; the recommendations below are just a sampling. Excellent and well-priced stalls in the **Maunakea Marketplace** on Maunakea Street in Chinatown sell all sorts of international cuisines; there's a large fast-food mall in the **Ala Moana Center**; and Waikiki's Kuhio Avenue is lined with snack outlets and noodle bars.

Duke's Canoe Club *Outrigger Waikiki*, 2335 Kalakaua Ave, Waikiki ⓣ808/922-2268, ⓦwww.dukeswaikiki.com. Crowded chain restaurant, right on the beach, with a feast of retro tiki and surf styling, and good-value breakfast and lunch buffets, plus Hawaiian music.

Indigo Eurasian Cuisine 1121 Nuuanu Ave, Honolulu ⓣ808/521-2900, ⓦwww.indigo-hawaii.com. Closed Sun & Mon. Delicious nouvelle "Eurasian" crossover food, as well as dim sum, served in a lovely old Chinatown building; an Obama favourite.

Kakaako Kitchen Ward Center, 1200 Ala Moana Blvd, Honolulu ⓣ808/596-7488. Mall diner that dishes up high-quality fast food; pretty much everything, from the hamburger stew to the signature dish chicken linguine, costs $9–13, and there's a menu of daily specials like meat loaf or pot roast.

Orchids *Halekulani*, 2199 Kalia Rd, Waikiki ⓣ808/923-2311. Waikiki's finest gourmet restaurant, facing the beach in the gorgeous, peaceful *Halekulani* hotel and offering scintillating contemporary Hawaiian cuisine. Open for all meals daily.

Ruffage Natural Foods 2443 Kuhio Ave, Waikiki ⓣ808/922-2042. Tiny, inexpensive wholefood grocery with takeaway counter and limited seating; healthy vegetarian food in the day, sushi in the evening. Daily 9am–10.30pm.

Sansei *Waikiki Beach Marriott*, 2552 Kalakaua Ave ⓣ808/931-6286, ⓦwww.sanseihawaii.com. Wonderful, dinner-only Japanese-inspired restaurant, serving superb sushi at around $10 for a specialty roll, and a full Pacific Rim menu with entrees at $18–40. Late-night dining and free karaoke Fri & Sat.

Todai Seafood Buffet 1910 Ala Moana Blvd, Waikiki ⓣ808/947-1000, ⓦwww.todai.com. Stylish all-you-care-to-eat Japanese buffet in western Waikiki. Lunch costs $15 and dinner $29, but the range and quality of the food, including sushi, shrimp, crab and lobster, makes it a real bargain.

Yakiniku Camellia 2494 S Beretania St ⓣ808/946-7955. Korean buffet restaurant a mile north of Waikiki, where you select slices of marinated beef, chicken, or pork and grill it yourself at the gas-fired burners set into each table. Open daily for lunch ($14) and dinner ($21).

Nightlife

Honolulu's **nightlife** is concentrated in Waikiki, where fun-seeking tourists set the tone. On the whole, the available entertainment is on the bland side. Hawaii tends to be off the circuit for touring musicians, so if you enjoy live music you'll probably have to settle for lesser-known local performers. Look out for special events at downtown's beautifully restored Hawaii Theatre, 1130 Bethel St (ⓣ808/528-0506, ⓦwww.hawaiitheatre.com).

Chai's Island Bistro Aloha Tower Marketplace, 101 Ala Moana Blvd, Honolulu ⓣ808/585-0011, ⓦwww.chaisislandbistro.com. Sumptuous and very expensive Thai restaurant, where the very finest Hawaiian musicians perform for diners nightly 7–8.30pm.

House Without A Key *Halekulani*, 2199 Kalia Rd, Waikiki ⓣ808/923-2311. Romantic open-air beach bar, blessed with spectacular ocean sunsets, where the no-cover evening cocktail hour features gentle, old-time Hawaiian classics performed by top-notch musicians and hula dancers.

La Mariana Sailing Club 50 Sand Island Access Rd ⓣ808/848-2800. An extremely quirky waterfront restaurant with an authentic 1950s ambience, hidden away amid Honolulu's docks, with classic Hawaiian music on Friday evenings and live piano nightly except Mon 5–9pm.

Pipeline 805 Pohukaina St, Honolulu ⓣ808/589-1999, ⓦwww.pipelinecafehawaii.com. Mon–Thurs 9pm–4am, Fri & Sat 10pm–4am. Nightclub, behind the Ala Moana mall, that's a favourite with the surf set. DJs most nights, cover charge for weekly rock or reggae gigs.

Sea sports and safety

The nation that invented **surfing** remains its greatest arena. The sport was popularized early in the twentieth century by Olympic swimmer Duke Kahanamoku, using a 20ft board; these days most are around six feet. As a rule, the best surfing beaches are on the north shore of each island. **Windsurfing and kitesurfing**, too, are hugely popular, in similar locations, while smaller **boogie boards** make an exhilarating initiation. **Snorkelling** and **diving** are top-quality, although Hawaii's **coral** has fewer brilliant hues than those seen in warmer equatorial waters.

Bear in mind, however, that **drownings** in Hawaii are all too common. Waves can sweep in from two thousand miles of open ocean onto beaches that are unprotected by any reef. Not all beaches have lifeguards and warning flags, and unattended beaches are not necessarily safe. Watch the sea carefully before going in, and never take your eyes off it thereafter. If you get swept out, don't fight the big waves; allow yourself to be carried out of the danger zone, then when the current dies down swim back to shore.

Windward Oahu

The most spectacular moment on a tour of Oahu comes as you leave Honolulu on the **Pali Highway** (Hwy-61), and cross the Koolau Mountains to see the sheer green cliffs of the windward side, veiled by swirling mists. The highest spot, four miles northeast of Honolulu, is the **Nuuanu Pali Lookout**. Kamehameha the Great finalized his conquest of Oahu here in 1795, forcing hundreds of enemy warriors over the edge of the cliffs.

Kailua, the main windward town, has a beautiful beach; President Obama vacations here each winter. Oahu's leading paying attraction, with one million annual visitors, is further north: the **Polynesian Cultural Center**, ten miles short of the island's northernmost tip (Mon–Sat 12.30–9pm; \$45–225; ⓣ808/293-3333, ⓦwww.polynesia.com). This haphazard mixture of real and bogus Polynesia – in which the history veers firmly towards the latter – is owned and run by the Mormon Church. After touring "villages" modelled on the various islands of Polynesia, you can stay into the evening for a luau and/or dance performances. TheBus #52 takes roughly two hours to get this far.

North Shore Oahu

The **surfing beaches** of northern Oahu are famous the world over, but they're minimally equipped for tourists. **Waimea**, **Sunset** and **Ehukai** beach parks are all laidback roadside stretches of sand, where you can usually find a quiet spot to yourself. In summer, the tame waves may leave you wondering what all the fuss is about; see them at full tilt in the winter and you'll have no doubts.

HALEIWA, the main surfers' hangout, combines alternative shops and cafés with upfront tourist traps. Much of the **food** around is vegetarian; the *Paradise Found Café*, 66-443 Kamehameha Hwy (ⓣ808/637-4540), serves breakfast and lunch, both for under \$10, while *Haleiwa Eats*, nearer the ocean at 66-011 Kamehameha Hwy (closed Mon; ⓣ808/637-4247), is a simple, well-priced Thai joint.

For **accommodation**, you'll have to head five miles northeast to the *Backpacker's Vacation Inn*, at 59-788 Kamehameha Hwy by Waimea Bay (ⓣ808/638-7838, ⓦwww.backpackers-hawaii.com; ❶–❸), which has dorm beds for \$27–30 per night, as well as some great-value ocean-view private rooms and studios.

The Big Island

Although the **Big Island of Hawaii** could hold all the other islands with room to spare, it has the population of a medium-sized town, with just 176,000 people (half what it was in Captain Cook's day). Visitation remains lower than Oahu and Maui; despite its fair share of restaurants, bars and facilities, this is basically a rural community, where sleepy old towns have remained unchanged for a century. The few resorts are built on the barren lava flows of the **Kona** coast to catch maximum sunshine.

Thanks to the **Kilauea** volcano, which has destroyed roads and even towns, and spews out pristine beaches of jet-black sand, the Big Island is still growing, its southern shore inching ever further out to sea. **Hawaii Volcanoes National Park**, which includes **Mauna Loa** as well as Kilauea (though not **Mauna Kea**, further to the north and higher than either), is absolutely compelling; you can explore steaming craters and cinder cones, venture into the rainforest, and at times approach within feet of the eruption itself.

As befits the birthplace of King Kamehameha, more of the ancient Hawaii survives on the Big Island than anywhere else. **Puuhonua O Honaunau** preserves a "place of refuge" for defeated warriors and those who ran afoul of society's rules, and there are further temples along the island's northwest coastline, while **Waipio Valley**, where Kamehameha spent his youth, remains as lush and green as ever.

Flights to the Big Island arrive both near **Kailua** on the west coast and at **Hilo** on the rainy east. Public transportation is all but nonexistent.

The Kona coast

Hawaii's leeward **Kona coast** divides into two distinct areas. North of its only sizeable community, **Kailua**, barren lava trails down to the sea from the third-highest Big Island volcano, Hualalai. Thanks to the relentless sun on its superb beaches, luxury hotels dot the shoreline as incongruous green patches. To the south, the hillsides are more fertile, and although the condos are spreading, you can still get a real feel for the old Hawaii in the land where Captain Cook met his end.

North Kona and the resorts

The best of the spectacular sandy **beaches** along the Kona coast – safe for summer swimming, though with tempestuous winter surf – lie north of Kailua. **Hapuna Beach**, almost forty miles up the coast, is deservedly the most famous, despite being overshadowed by the giant *Hapuna Beach Prince Hotel* (Ⓣ808/880-1111 or 1-866/774-6236, Ⓦwww.hapunabeachprincehotel; ❽).

Several more luxurious **resort hotels** lie in the district of South Kohala, thirty miles north of Kailua. Three separate enclaves – Waikoloa, Mauna Kea and Mauna Lani – have been landscaped out of this inhospitable lava desert, each one a self-contained oasis holding two or three hotels, a beach or two, and nothing else. Although **Waikoloa** is the least exclusive of the three, it's home to the ostentatious, mile-long *Hilton Waikoloa Village* (Ⓣ808/886-1234 or 1-800/445-8667, Ⓦwww.hiltonwaikoloavillage.com; ❽), where guests travel to and from their rooms by electric boats or monorail.

For idyllic seclusion, head a few miles south, to the turquoise lagoons of **Kiholo Bay**, reached via an unmarked and very bumpy dirt road halfway between mileposts 82 and 83 on Kamehemeha Highway.

Kailua (Kona)

Although the Big Island's main resort is officially called **KAILUA**, it's much more commonly referred to as **Kona**. An attractive little town that has played a major part in Hawaiian history, it's more affected by tourism than any other Big Island community, and its seafront row of fast-food restaurants and souvenir shops could be almost anywhere.

King Kamehameha's funeral rites were performed in the ancient temple of **Ahuena Heiau**, poised beside a little beach at the northern end of the bay. A short way south, **Hulihee Palace** (Wed–Sat 10am–3pm; $6) faces out to sea from the centre of Kailua. Built as the governor's residence in 1838, it was damaged in an earthquake in 2006, but you can still inspect the massive **koa**-wood furnishings inside, made to fit the considerable girth of its royal Hawaiian residents.

Practicalities

The largely open-air **Kona International Airport**, situated on a field of black lava nine miles north of Kailua, has the usual car rental places; otherwise Speedi Shuttle **buses** into town cost around $25 per person (Ⓣ808/329-5433, Ⓦwww.speedishuttle.com).

Accommodation options in Kailua start in the north with the landmark King *Kamehameha's Kona Beach Hotel*, 75-5660 Palani Rd (Ⓣ808/329-2911 or 1-800/367-2111, Ⓦwww.konabeachhotel.com; ❺), set around a picturesque little beach. Further hotels line the oceanfront Alii Drive for about five miles south; the pick for budget travellers is the simple, three-storey *Kona Tiki* motel, 75-5968 Alii Drive (Ⓣ808/329-1425, Ⓦwww.konatiki.com; ❸). Recommended **restaurants** in town include the sea-view *Island Lava Java*, 75-5799 Alii Drive (Ⓣ808/327-2161), and the *Kona Brewing Co*, 75-5629 Kuakini Hwy (Ⓣ808/334-2739).

Kealakekua Bay

Kealakekua Bay, a dozen miles south of Kailua, was where Captain Cook was killed on February 14, 1779, during his second visit to Hawaii. Once a major population centre, it's now barely inhabited, and the white **obelisk** on the death site – legally a small piece of England – is all but inaccessible. You can only get to within a mile of the obelisk by car, at **Napoopoo Beach**. The bay itself is the best place on the Big Island for **snorkelling**, even if there are sharks further out. The catamaran **Fair Wind** offers snorkelling cruises here from Keauhou Bay, just south of Kailua (daily: 9am departure $125, shorter 2pm departure $109; Ⓣ808/345-0268, Ⓦwww.fair-wind.com).

This region, South Kona, is the prime source of **Kona coffee**. The town of **CAPTAIN COOK**, on the verdant slopes high above Kealakekua, is home to the bargain *Manago Hotel* (Ⓣ808/323-2642, Ⓦwww.managohotel.com; ❶–❸), which offers comfortable ocean-view rooms amid flowering Japanese gardens. A mile south, the *Coffee Shack* (daily 7.30am–3pm; Ⓣ808/328-9555) serves wonderfully fresh coffee and smoothies on a terrace that enjoys staggering views all the way down to the bay.

Puuhonua O Honaunau

Puuhonua O Honaunau National Historical Park (daily 7.30am–5.30pm; $5), four miles on from Kealakekua, is the single most evocative historical site in all of the Hawaiian islands, jutting into the Pacific on a small peninsula of jagged black lava. The grounds include a lovely little beach, backed by a fishpond and three **heiaus** (places of worship), guarded by large carved effigies of gods. An ancient "**place of refuge**" lies firmly protected behind the mortarless masonry of the sixteenth-century **Great Wall**. Those who broke ancient Hawaii's intricate system of **kapu** (taboo) – perhaps by treading on the shadow of a chief or fishing in the wrong season – could expect summary execution unless they fled to such a sanctuary. As chiefs lived on the surrounding land, transgressors had to swim through shark-infested seas. If successful, they would be absolved and released overnight.

Windward Hawaii

Almost all the rain that falls on Mauna Kea flows down the eastern side of the Big Island. As a result, myriad streams and waterfalls nourish dense jungle-like vegetation, so the main road north along the coast from Hilo is alive with flowering trees and orchids.

Hilo

Although it's the Big Island's capital and largest town, just 45,000 people live in **HILO**, which remains endearing and unpressured. Mass tourism has never taken off here, mainly because it rains too much. However, the rain falls mostly at night and America's wettest city blazes with tropical blooms against a backdrop of rainbows.

With its modest streets and wooden stores, Hilo's **downtown** looks appealingly low-key. Sadly, that's largely because all the buildings that stood on the seaward side of Kamehameha Avenue were destroyed by two tsunami, in 1946 and 1960. The story is told in the **Pacific Tsunami Museum**, on Kamehameha Avenue (Mon–Sat 9am–4pm; $8; Ⓦwww.tsunami.org). A scale model shows how the city looked before 1946; contemporary footage and letters bring home the impact of the tragedy.

The **Lyman Museum**, based in the 1830s home of early missionaries at 276 Haili St (Mon–Sat 10am–4.30pm; $10; Ⓦwww.lymanmuseum.org), holds a fascinating display of ancient weapons and documents Hawaii's various ethnic groups, including the Portuguese who arrived in 1878 from the volcanic Azores.

Five minutes' drive from downtown brings you to the **'Imiloa Astronomy Center of Hawaii**, 600 'Imiloa Place (daily except Mon 9am–4pm; $17.50; Ⓦwww.imiloahawaii.org). This explains the work of the international scientists who use the astronomical observatories at the summit of Mauna Kea, while also outlining traditional Hawaiian beliefs about the site's spiritual importance.

Practicalities

A taxi into town from Hilo International **Airport**, on the eastern outskirts, costs around $12. From Kamehameha Avenue, Hilo's Hele-On **bus** (Ⓣ808/961-8744, Ⓦwww.heleonbus.org) operates services to Kailua and Hawaii Volcanoes National Park.

Two good **hostels** offer reasonably priced private rooms and dorms; the attractive *Hilo Bay Hostel* is downtown at 101 Waianuenue Ave (Ⓣ808/933-2771, Ⓦwww.hawaiihostel.net; dorms $25, private rooms ❸), while *Arnott's Lodge* is in the woods two miles southeast at 98 Apapane Rd (Ⓣ808/969-7097, Ⓦwww.arnottslodge.com; dorms $25, private rooms ❸), and also offers tent spots for $10, plus island tours. Otherwise, the *Dolphin Bay*, 333 Iliahi St (Ⓣ808/935-1466 or 1-877/935-1466, Ⓦwww.dolphinbayhilo.com; ❺), is a friendly little **hotel**. The *Seaside Restaurant*, 1790 Kalanianaole Ave (Ⓣ808/935-8825; closed Mon) is a great local fish **restaurant** with its own aquafarm.

North from Hilo

The **Belt Road** (Hwy-19) follows the **Hamakua coast** north of Hilo, clinging to the hillsides and crossing ravines on slender bridges. For a glimpse into the interior, head into the mountains after fifteen miles to the 450ft **Akaka Falls**. A short loop trail through the forest, festooned with wild orchids, offers views of Akaka and other waterfalls.

Waipio Valley

Highway 240, which turns north off the Belt Road at **HONOKAA,** comes to an abrupt end after nine miles at the edge of **Waipio Valley**. As the southernmost of six successive sheer-walled valleys, this is the only one accessible by land. It's as close as Hawaii comes to the classic South Seas image of an isolated and self-sufficient valley, dense with fruit trees and laced by footpaths leading down to the sea.

It's perfectly possible to walk down the steep, mile-long track into Waipio, but most visitors take tours, either in the four-wheel-drive vehicles of the Waipio Valley Shuttle (Mon–Sat 9am, 11am, 1pm & 3pm; ⓣ808/775-7121; $55), or on horseback (ⓣ808/775-1007; $85).

Hawaii Volcanoes National Park

The Big Island's southernmost volcanoes, **Mauna Loa** and **Kilauea**, jointly constitute **HAWAII VOLCANOES NATIONAL PARK**, thirty miles from Hilo and eighty from Kailua. Its dramatic landscapes include desert, arctic tundra and rainforest, besides two active volcanoes.

Evidence is everywhere of the awesome power of the volcanoes to create and destroy; no map can keep up with the latest whims of the lava flow. Whole towns have been engulfed, and once-prized beachfront properties lie buried hundreds of yards back from the sea.

Kilauea Caldera

The main focus of the park is **Kilauea Caldera**, the summit crater of Kilauea, twenty miles up from the ocean. Close to the rim, on the eleven-mile **Crater Rim Drive**, both the **visitor centre** (daily 7.45am–5pm; $10/vehicle; ⓣ808/967-7311, ⓦwww.nps.gov/havo) and the fascinating **Jaggar Museum** of geology (daily 8.30am–5pm; free) offer basic orientation. Kilauea is said to be the home of the volcano goddess **Pele**, who has followed the "hot spot" from island to island. When Mark Twain came here in 1866, he observed a dazzling lake of liquid fire; after a huge explosion in 1924 it became shallower and quieter, a black dusty expanse dotted with hissing steam vents. Volcanic activity resumed in 2008, however, and as of 2010 access to the caldera floor is forbidden.

It's still possible to **hike** nearby. The five-mile **Kilauea Iki Trail** explores an adjoining crater, where you pick your way from cairn to cairn across an eerie landscape of cracked and jagged lava, while the mile-long **Devastation Trail** is a boardwalk laid across the scene of a 1959 eruption.

Chain of Craters Road

Chain of Craters Road winds down to the sea from Crater Rim Drive, sweeping around cones and vents in an empty landscape where the occasional dead white tree trunk or flowering shrub pokes up. Fresh sheets of lava constantly ooze down the slopes to cover the road. When a new road is built on top of the flow, more lava covers it. Along the coast, the scale of the damage since 1983 has been too great to repair – over seven miles have been lost – so now the road is a dead end, and getting shorter year by year.

Check current conditions at the **visitor centre** when you arrive, and make sure you have enough gas. The end of the road is a fifty-mile round-trip from the park entrance and there are no facilities along the way. Depending on where current volcanic activity is concentrated, it is possible at times to walk across the congealed lava blocking Chain of Craters Road to see molten rock gush from the earth – sometimes directly into the sea. The **Volcano Update** (Ⓣ808/985-6000, Ⓦhvo.wr.usgs.gov) has the latest details.

Practicalities

The national park operates two free **campgrounds** on a first-come, first-served basis, while the recently renovated *Volcano House*, close to the edge of the crater within the park (Ⓣ808/967-7321, Ⓦwww.volcanohousehotel.com; cabins ❸, rooms ❺–❽), has spectacular views, and good food in the evening. Otherwise, the small and inconspicuous town of **VOLCANO**, just before the park entrance on the Hilo side, provides the best places to **stay** in the vicinity, with B&Bs such as the lovely *Hale Ohia* (Ⓣ808/967-7986, Ⓦwww.haleohia.com; ❺), south of the highway across from the village. *Kilauea Lodge*, on the leafy main street (Ⓣ808/967-7366, Ⓦwww.kilauealodge.com; ❼), is a comfortable inn with a very good **restaurant**.

Maui

The island of **MAUI**, the second largest in the Hawaiian chain, is Oahu's principal rival, attracting roughly a third of all visitors to the state. Some say that things have gone too far, with formerly remote, unspoiled beaches, around **Kaanapali** (north of Lahaina) and **Kihei** for example, now swamped by sprawling resorts. On the other hand, the crowds come to Maui for the good reason that it's still beautiful. This is the best equipped of all the islands for **activity** holidays – whale-watching, windsurfing, diving, sailing, snorkelling and cycling. Temperatures along the coast can be searing, but it's always possible to escape to somewhere cooler. **Upcountry Maui**, on the slopes of the mighty **Haleakala** volcano, is a delight, while the waterfalls and ravines along the tortuous road out east to **Hana** outclass anything on Oahu.

Kahului and Wailuku

Almost half of Maui's 150,000 inhabitants live in the twin towns of **KAHULUI** and **WAILUKU**, north of the "neck" connecting its two mountainous sections. Kahului is the main commercial centre; Wailuku is one of the few towns on Maui that feels like a genuine community, with budget accommodation and restaurants to make it a good central base.

Although there's no sightseeing to speak of in either Kahului or Wailuku, Wailuku's Main Street heads straight into the **West Maui Mountains**, stopping three miles in at **Iao Needle**, a stunning 1200ft pinnacle of green-clad lava that stands, head usually in the clouds, at the intersection of two lush valleys. Kamehameha won control of Maui here in 1790, in a battle determined by a cannonade directed by two European gunners.

Molokini Snorkel Cruises

Maui's best-known **snorkelling** and **diving** spot is the tiny crescent of **Molokini**, poking above the sea – all that's left of a once-great volcano. There's no beach or landfall, but you do see a lot of fish, including deep-water species. Countless cruises leave early each morning (to avoid the heat) from Maalea Harbor on the south shore of the central isthmus; snorkellers can pay anything from $60 to $120 for a morning trip, and from $40 for a shorter afternoon jaunt. Recommended boats include *Four Winds II* (Ⓣ808/879-8188, Ⓦwww.mauicharters.com) and the smaller *Paragon II* (Ⓣ808/244-2087, Ⓦwww.sailmaui.com).

Practicalities

Virtually all visitors to Maui arrive at **Kahului Airport**. Speedi Shuttle (Ⓣ808/661-6667 or 1-877/242-5777, Ⓦwww.speedishuttle.com) run vans to resorts around the island.

Although Wailuku is nowhere near Maui's main resort areas, and lacks hotels, two lively, friendly **hostels** make it popular with budget travellers. Both *Banana Bungalow,* 310 N Market St (Ⓣ808/244-5090 or 1-800/846-7835, Ⓦwww.mauihostel.com; ❶–❸) and the *Northshore Hostel*, 2080 Vineyard St (Ⓣ808/986-8095 or 1-866/946-7835, Ⓦwww.northshorehostel.com; ❶–❸) offer dorm beds for $25 and simple private rooms, with free airport shuttles.

Neither Kahului and Wailuku offers much in the way of fine **dining**, but *AK's Cafe*, at 1237 L Main St in Wailuku (Ⓣ808/244-8774) is a bright, health-oriented little restaurant, while *Maui Coffee Roasters*, at 444 Hana Hwy, Kahului (Ⓣ808/877-2877) is a relaxed espresso bar that serves good lunch specials.

Lahaina

The only real town along the green but sunny shoreline of West Maui, **LAHAINA** is one of Hawaii's prettiest communities. Back in the nineteenth century it was capital of the entire Kingdom of Hawaii, but it has barely grown since then, and still resembles a peaceful tropical village. Its main oceanfront street is lined with timber-frame buildings; coconut palms sway to either side of the mighty central banyan tree; surfers swirl into the thin fringe of beach to the south; and the mountains of West Maui dominate the skyline.

The view out to sea from Lahaina, towards the island of **Lanai**, is superb. There's little to see on Lanai, but its main beach, at Hulopoe Bay, is a delight, and day-trips offer a great chance to see whales in winter. Expeditions provides five sailings daily, from Lahaina Harbor ($30 each way; Ⓣ808/661-3756, Ⓦwww.go-lanai.com).

Practicalities

Lahaina's only budget **accommodation** is *Lahaina's Last Resort*, 252 Lahainaluna Rd (Ⓣ808/661-6655, Ⓦwww.lahainaslastresort.com; ❶–❹), a friendly, well-run hostel beside the main highway, which has co-ed six-bed dorms and some nicer private rooms, with and without en-suite facilities. Otherwise, the *Pioneer Inn*, 658 Wharf St (Ⓣ808/661-3636 or 1-800/457-5457, Ⓦwww.pioneerinnmaui.com; ❻) is a lively old historic hotel.

Good places to **eat** include *Cilantro Fresh Mexican Grill*, in the Old Lahaina Center mall at 170 Papalaua Ave (Ⓣ808/667-5444), but for a gourmet treat you can't beat *The Feast at Lele*, 505 Front St (Ⓣ808/667-5353, Ⓦwww.feastatlele.com), where $110 buys a magnificent Polynesian banquet, served right on the beach and accompanied with live music and hula.

Whale-hunting and whale-watching

Whaling ships first arrived in Hawaii in 1820, the same year as the missionaries – and had an equally dramatic impact. Whales were never actually hunted here, but Hawaii swiftly became the centre of the industry and was such a paradise that up to fifty percent of each crew deserted here, to be replaced by native Hawaiians. Decline came with the Civil War – when many ships were deliberately sunk to blockade Confederate ports – and an 1871 disaster, when 31 vessels lingered in the Arctic too long, became frozen in, and had to be abandoned. Ironically, the waters off western Maui now rate among the world's best areas for whale-watching and between roughly December and April, **humpback whales** are often visible from the shore, although whale-watching trips can take you much closer. Operators include the nonprofit Pacific Whale Foundation ($30; ⓣ808/249-8811 or 1-800/942-5311, ⓦwww.pacificwhale.org).

Kihei and Wailea

Maui's other main resort area is south of Kahului, across the isthmus. The long strip of hotels, malls and condos begins at **KIHEI**, with the road heavily built-up on both sides, but thins out beyond the manicured lawns of **WAILEA**, near some superb beaches. **Paluea Beach** is ideal for families, while **Little Beach**, reached by a trail from the gorgeous, enormous **Makena (Big) Beach**, is famous for (illegal) nudism.

Few of the **accommodation** options are particularly affordable, though inexpensive condos are available at *Koa Lagoon*, 800 S Kihei Rd ⓣ808/879-3002 or 1-800/367-8030, ⓦwww.koalagoon.com; ⑤). For **food**, *Sansei*, 1881 S Kihei Rd (ⓣ808/669-6286), offers great-value sushi and Pacific Rim concoctions.

Upcountry Maui

Hawaii is not always a land tarnished by civilization. **Central Maui** has been turned into a pastoral idyll, thanks to an ingenious system of irrigation channels. The highway to the top of **Haleakala** climbs higher, at a faster rate, than any road on earth. Starting in rich meadows, it climbs past purple-blossoming jacaranda, firs and eucalyptus to reach open ranching land, and then ascends in huge curves to the volcanic desert and the crater itself.

Haleakala

Though **HALEAKALA** – "the House of the Sun" – is the world's largest dormant volcano, you may not appreciate its full ten-thousand-foot majesty until you're at the top. Shield volcanoes are not as dramatic as the classic cones, as lava oozes from fissures along broad flanks to create a long, low profile and the summit is often obscured by clouds. That it hasn't erupted for two hundred years doesn't necessarily mean it won't ever again.

The higher reaches of the mountain are a **national park**, which never closes (admission $10/vehicle). Manhattan would fit comfortably into the awe-inspiring **crater**, almost eight miles across, which was for the ancient Hawaiians a site of deep spiritual power. The most popular time to come is for the **sunrise**; the **visitor centre** at the top operates from just before dawn until 3pm (ⓣ808/572-4400, ⓦwww.nps.gov/hale). Hiking trails cross the crater floor, where **camping** is permitted in three remote cabins that can be reserved up to ninety days in advance ($75 per night; ⓣ808/572-4400, ⓦfhnp.org). In addition, 25 free tent sites outside the crater are available every day (first-come, first-served).

Makawao and Paia

Coming down from Haleakala, Hwy-365 leads north to two laidback little country towns populated mainly by alternative Californian types: **MAKAWAO**, five miles up from the ocean, and **PAIA**, Maui's first plantation town, near the great windsurfing beach of **Hookipa**.

Right in the middle of Paia, the *Paia Inn*, 93 Hana Hwy (808/579-6000 or 1-800/721-4000, www.paiainn.com; 7) is a lovely little boutique **hotel**. Vegetarians will be glad of the top-quality Vietnamese **food** at *Fresh Mint*, 115 Baldwin Ave (808/579-9144), while fresh fish is the specialty at the oceanfront *Mama's*, a mile east at 799 Poho Place (808/579-8488).

The road to Hana

The rains that fall on Haleakala cascade down Maui's long windward flank, covering it in thick, jungle-like vegetation. Convicts in the 1920s hacked out a road along the coast that has become a major tourist attraction, twisting in and out of gorges, past innumerable waterfalls and across more than fifty tiny one-lane bridges. All year round, and especially in June, the route is ablaze with colour from orchids, rainbow eucalyptus and orange-blossomed African tulip trees.

The former sugar town of Hana at the far end of the road is a pleasant enough little community that isn't especially interested in attracting tourists. The usual day's excursion continues ten miles further to gorgeous **Oheo Gulch**, where waterfalls tumble down the hillside to oceanfront meadows. That makes a total of roughly fifty miles (three hours) each way from Paia.

There's **camping** beside the black-sand beach at gorgeous Waianapanapa State Park, four miles short of Hana (808/984-8109; $18).

Kauai

Although no point on the tiny island of **KAUAI** is as much as a dozen miles from the sea, the variety of its landscapes is quite incredible. This is the oldest of the major islands, and erosion has had more than six million years to sculpt it into fantastic shapes. The mist-shrouded extinct volcano **Mount Waialeale** at its heart is the world's wettest spot, draining into a high landlocked swamp. Nearby is the chasm of **Waimea Canyon**, while the north shore holds the vertiginous green cliffs of the awe-inspiring **Na Pali** coast, familiar from films such as **Jurassic Park** and **South Pacific**, but the sole preserve of adventurous **hikers**. Kauai is a place to be active, on sea and land; if you only take one **helicopter** flight in your life, this is the place to do it.

Lihue

Flights arrive at the capital, **LIHUE**, which stands slightly inland of little Nawiliwili Harbor at Kauai's southeast corner. Roughly at the midpoint of the one main road that encircles the island (prevented from completing a loop by the Na Pali cliffs), as a base it's undistinguished. The population is just five thousand, and downtown consists of a few tired plantation-town streets set well back from the sea.

The small **Kauai Museum** at 4428 Rice St (Mon–Sat 10am–5pm; $10) traces the island's history from the mythical **menehune** (dwarfs said to have been here before the Polynesians arrived) through Captain Cook's 1778 landfall and on to its sugar-growing heyday.

Practicalities

Lihue's **airport** is only two miles from downtown ($10 by **taxi**; Wailua or Kapaa cost closer to $20). Along with the usual **car** rental outlets, it also has **helicopters** – Blue Hawaiian (Ⓣ808/245-5800, Ⓦwww.bluehawaiian.com) is typical, offering tours from $200. The **Hawaii Visitors Bureau** is in town at 4334 Rice St (Mon–Fri 8am–4.30pm; Ⓣ808/245-3971, Ⓦwww.kauaidiscovery.com).

There's no great point staying in Lihue rather than along the coast. However, the *Garden Island Inn*, near the harbour at 3445 Wilcox Rd (Ⓣ808/245-7227 or 1-800/648-0154, Ⓦwww.gardenislandinn.com; ❹), is a lovely refurbished three-storey motel, dripping with purple bougainvillea. For a **quick meal** in the heart of town, call in at *Hamura Saimin*, 2956 Kress St (Ⓣ808/245-3271), a family-run Japanese food counter which specializes in bowls of *saimin* (noodles) for $5. A mile or two east, the *Hanamaulu Restaurant and Tea House*, 3-4253 Kuhio Hwy (closed Mon; Ⓣ808/245-2511) is a delightful old place, complete with fishponds, that serves both Chinese and Japanese food.

East Kauai

Most Kauaians live between Lihue and the overlapping communities of **WAILUA**, **WAIPOULI** and **KAPAA**, whose malls, condos and hotels blend into each other a few miles north of the capital. All the way along there's an exposed thin strip of beach; only Wailua is especially scenic, and you have to go further north for snorkelling.

Accommodation

While most East Shore **hotels** are expensive by any other than Hawaiian standards, possibilities on a more affordable scale do exist.

Aston Aloha Beach Hotel 3-5920 Kuhio Hwy, Wailua Ⓣ808/823-6000 or 1-877/997-6667, Ⓦwww.abrkauai.com. Lively much-remodelled oceanfront hotel, with a welcoming feel, immediately south of Wailua River. ❹

Hotel Coral Reef 1516 Kuhio Hwy, Kapaa Ⓣ808/822-4481 or 1-800/843-4659, Ⓦwww.hotelcoralreefresort.com. This simple little hotel, facing the beach, offers some of Kauai's best rates. ❹

Lae Nani 410 Papaloa Rd, Wailua Ⓣ808/822-4938 or 1-877/523-6264, Ⓦwww.outrigger.com. Irresistible complex of luxurious oceanfront apartments and condos, with lovely swimming alongside. ❼

Eating

Kapaa is the only town in East Kauai with anything like a centre; you can windowshop for **restaurants** along its street of wooden stores, which are fronted by a beach park.

Caffè Coco 4-369 Kuhio Hwy, Wailua Ⓣ808/822-7990. Attractively ramshackle café, serving cheap and wholesome, if not entirely vegetarian, breakfasts and lunches for under $10, plus changing dinner specials. Closed Mon.

Lemongrass Grill 4-885 Kuhio Hwy, Kapaa Ⓣ808/821-2288. Smart, lively, upmarket restaurant, serving a predominantly Japanese and seafood menu with entrees at $15–28. Dinner only.

Mermaids Cafe 1384 Kuhio Hwy, Kapaa Ⓣ808/821-2026. Small, partly vegetarian café in central Kapaa, serving wholesome breakfasts and bargain Asian-flavoured lunches and dinners.

Kauai's North Shore

Despite the development elsewhere on the island, the astonishing valleys of Kauai's **Na Pali coast** remain inviolate – though accessible enough by canoe to sustain large Hawaiian populations, their awesome walls shield them from any attempt to build roads.

To reach long, golden **Secret Beach** – where swimming is usually unsafe – drive up Hwy-56 from the south, pass **Kilauea**, and then turn right at Kalihiwai. Take the second right onto a dirt track and the beach is a ten-minute walk down through the woods. At the far end, a waterfall of beautiful fresh mountain water cascades down the cliffs, and there are often spinner dolphins just offshore, especially around the picturesque 1913 Kilauea **lighthouse**. The cliffs above are a bird sanctuary.

Hanalei

Major development stops beyond the resort of **Princeville**, mainly because the road then crosses seven successive one-lane bridges. The first is over the Hanalei River, where endangered Hawaiian ducks, coots and stilts are protected by the preservation of their major habitats – natural wetlands and taro ponds.

The small town of **HANALEI**, set around a magnificent bay, has some low-key apartments for rent, but otherwise little formal accommodation. Of local **restaurants**, the busy *Hanalei Gourmet* in the Hanalei Center mall (Ⓣ808/826-2524) makes an ideal stop for breakfast or a sandwich lunch, and also has live music most nights.

Gorgeous **Lumahai Beach**, at the western edge of Hanalei Bay, has starred in countless movies, among them **South Pacific**, but is too treacherous for swimming. All the roadside beaches from here on, however, are good for snorkelling. Just two miles from the start of the Na Pali coast (see below), the *Hanalei Colony Resort* (Ⓣ808/826-6235 or 1-800/628-3004, Ⓦwww.hcr.com; ⑧) is Kauai's most dramatic waterfront property, within a few feet of the pounding surf; all its units have two bedrooms. The road finally comes to an end at **Kee Beach**, perhaps the most delightful spot of all, with safe inshore swimming.

The Na Pali coast

The lush valleys of the **Na Pali coast**, separated by knife-edge ridges of rock thousands of feet high but just a few feet thick, make Kauai one of the world's great hiking destinations. Although many of the best views (other than from a helicopter) are from the trails in Kokee State Park (see below) or boat trips out to sea, the **Kalalau Trail** along the shore is unforgettable. The full eleven miles to Kalalau Valley is arduous and gets progressively more dangerous; in places you have to scramble along a precipitous (and shadeless) wall of crumbly red rock.

However, the first two miles of the trail, to **Hanakapiai Beach**, are the most beautiful. They're steep but straightforward, passing through patches of dense vegetation where you clamber over the gnarled root systems of the splay-footed **hala** (pandanus) tree. From the beach, a further hour's arduous hike (off the main trail) leads inland to the natural amphitheatre of the towering **Hanakapiai Falls**. It takes at least four and a half hours to get to the falls and back from the trailhead at Kee Beach. Hikers and campers doing anything more than a day-hike must obtain **permits**, costing $20 per person per night (Ⓣ808/274-3444, Ⓦwww.hawaiistateparks.org/camping).

South Kauai

POIPU, Kauai's principal beach resort, lies on the south coast roughly ten miles west of Lihue, where sunshine is more consistent and there's great surfing and snorkelling. Its finest **hotel** is the sumptuous *Grand Hyatt Kauai*, 1571

Poipu Rd (ⓣ808/742-1234 or 1-800/492-8804, ⓦwww.kauai-hyatt.com; ❾), while *Parrish Collection Kauai* (ⓣ808/742-2000 or 1-800/325-5701, ⓦwww.parrishkauai.com; ❺–❾) quotes lower prices for local condos than you'll be offered by individual properties. The best **restaurants** are two upmarket Pacific Rim options: *Casa di Amici*, 2301 Nalo Rd (ⓣ808/742-1555), and *Roy's Poipu Bar & Grill* (ⓣ808/742-5000), in the Poipu Shopping Village.

West Kauai

Two of Hawaii's major scenic attractions – the gorge of **Waimea Canyon** and **Kokee State Park** (with its views of the Na Pali cliffs to one side and the sodden Alakai Swamp to the other) – can only be reached from the **west coast** of Kauai. The coast itself, however, is nondescript. **WAIMEA**, the largest town, is just one short street at the foot of the poorly marked road up to the canyon. The statue of **Captain Cook**, which commemorates his "discovery" of Hawaii here on January 20, 1778, is an exact replica of one in Cook's home town of Whitby, England. Western Kauai's only **accommodation** option is *Waimea Plantation Cottages* (ⓣ808/338-1625 or 1-866/774-2924, ⓦwww.waimea-plantation.com; ❼), set in an attractive coconut grove, and with a good restaurant in the main plantation house.

Waimea Canyon and Kokee State Park

It's not unreasonable to call **Waimea Canyon** the "Grand Canyon of the Pacific". At three thousand feet, it may not be quite as deep as its Arizona rival, but the colours – all shades of green against the bare red earth – are absolutely breathtaking. The road from Waimea climbs beside the widening gorge, until after eight miles the mile-wide canyon can be seen in all its splendour.

Explore **Kokee State Park**, higher up, as early in the day as possible; by late morning the valleys may be filled with mist and clouds. Although the ranger station at **KOKEE**, the park headquarters, is often unstaffed, you can pick up trail information from the small but informative **Kokee Natural History Museum** nearby (daily 10am–4pm; $1 donation), where displays centre on the indigenous wildlife. Kauai is the only island where mongooses have not killed off most native **birds**, and at this height mosquitoes are no threat either, so some of the world's rarest species survive here and nowhere else.

Kokee Lodge Housekeeping Cabins, next to the park headquarters, are rented by the day (ⓣ808/335-6061, ⓦwww.thelodgeatkokee.net; ❹), and there's also **camping** (ⓦwww.hawaiistateparks.org/camping). For **food**, *Kokee Lodge* has lunch specials for around $7.

A few miles further up, **Kalalau Lookout** stands over the valley where the Kalalau Trail ends. The **Pihea Trail** follows the course of a lunatic attempt to extend the road beyond its current end. At times it narrows to a few feet, with precipitous drops to either side, and visibility can drop to nothing as the clouds siphon across the ridges. Inland lies the **Alakai Swamp**, where the heaviest rainfall on earth collects in the rock; the few humans who manage to penetrate the mists are assailed on all sides by the shrills, whistles and buzzes of a jungle without mammals or snakes. The trail running through the swamp consists of a boardwalk for almost its entire six-mile length, though in places the planks just rest on cloying black mud. Giant ferns dangle above the trail and orchids gleam from the undergrowth. If you make it all the way to the end, you're rewarded with a stupendous panorama of Hanalei Bay.

Contexts

Contexts

History

There is much more to the history of North America than the history of the United States alone. In these few pages, however, there's little room to do more than survey the peopling and political development of the disparate regions that now form the USA. Many of the topics discussed below are covered in more detail in the relevant chapters.

First peoples

The true pioneers of North America, nomadic hunter-gatherers from Siberia, are thought to have reached what's now **Alaska** just 14,000 years ago. Thanks to the last ice age, when sea levels were three hundred feet lower, a **"land-bridge"** – actually a vast plain, measuring six hundred miles north to south – connected Eurasia to America.

At that time, Alaska was effectively part of Asia rather than North America, being separated by glacier fields from what is now Canada and points south. Like an air lock, the region has "opened" in different directions at different times; migrants reaching it from the west, unaware that they were leaving Asia, would at first have found their way blocked to the east. Several generations might pass, and the connection back towards Asia be severed, before an eastward passage appeared. When thawing ice did clear a route into North America, it was not along the Pacific coast but via a corridor that led east of the Rockies and out onto the Great Plains.

This migration was almost certainly spurred by the pursuit of large mammal species, and especially **mammoth**, which had already been harried to extinction throughout almost all of Eurasia. A huge bonanza awaited the hunters when they finally encountered America's own indigenous **"megafauna"**, such as mammoths, mastodons, giant ground sloths and enormous long-horned bison, all of which had evolved with no protection against human predation.

Within a thousand years, ten million people were living throughout both North and South America. Although that sounds like a phenomenally rapid spread, a band of just one hundred individuals could have entered the continent, and then advanced a mere eight miles per year, with an annual population growth of 1.1 percent, to achieve that impact. The mass **extinction** of the American megafauna was so precisely simultaneous that humans must surely have been responsible, eliminating the giant beasts in each locality in one fell swoop, before pressing on in search of the next kill.

The elimination of large land mammals precluded future American civilizations from domesticating any of the animal species that were crucial to Old World economies. Without cattle, horses, sheep or goats, or significant equivalents, they lacked the resources to supply food and clothing to large settlements, provide draft power to haul ploughs or wheeled vehicles, or increase mobility and the potential for conquest. What's more, most of the human diseases later introduced from the rest of the world evolved in association with domesticated animals; the first Americans developed neither immunity to such diseases, nor any indigenous diseases of their own that might have attacked the invaders.

At least three distinct waves of **migrants** arrived via Alaska, each of whom settled in, and adapted to, a more marginal environment than its predecessors. The second, five thousand years on, were the **"Nadene"** or Athapascans – the ancestors of the Haida of the Northwest, and the Navajo and Apache of the Southwest – while the third, another two thousand years later, found their niche in the frozen Arctic and became the **Aleuts** and the **Inuits**.

The earliest known settlement site in the modern United States, dating back 12,000 years, has been uncovered at Meadowcroft in southwest Pennsylvania. Five hundred years later, the Southwest was dominated by the so-called **Clovis** culture, while subsequent subgroups ranged from the Algonquin farmers of what's now New England to peoples such as the Chumash and Macah, who lived by catching fish, otters and even whales along the coasts of the Pacific Northwest.

Nowhere did a civilization emerge to rival the wealth and sophistication of the great cities of ancient Mexico. However, the influence of those far-off cultures did filter north; the cultivation of crops such as beans, squash and maize facilitated the development of large communities, while northern religious cults, some of which performed human sacrifice, owed much to Central American beliefs. The **Mound-builders** of the **Ohio** and **Mississippi** valleys developed sites such as the Great Serpent Mound in modern Ohio and Poverty Point in Louisiana. The most prominent of these early societies, now known as the **Hopewell** culture, flourished in the first four centuries AD. Later on, **Cahokia**, just outside present-day St Louis, became the largest pre-Columbian city in North America, centred on a huge temple-topped mound, and peaking between 1050 and 1250 AD.

In the deserts of the **Southwest**, the **Hohokam** settlement of Snaketown, near what's now Phoenix, grappled with the same problems of water management that plague the region today. Nearby, the **Ancestral Puebloan** "Basketmakers" developed pottery around 200 AD, and began to gather into the walled villages later known as pueblos, possibly for protection against Athapascan invaders, such as the Apache, who were arriving from the north. Ancestral Puebloan "cities", such as Pueblo Bonito in New Mexico's Chaco Canyon – a centre for the turquoise trade with the mighty Aztec – and the "Cliff Palace" at Mesa Verde in Colorado, are the most impressive monuments to survive from ancient North America. Although the Ancestral Puebloans dispersed after a devastating drought in the twelfth century, many of the settlements created by their immediate descendants have remained in use ever since. Despite centuries of migration and war, the desert farmers of the **Hopi Mesas** in Arizona (see p.802), and the pueblos of **Taos** and **Ácoma** in New Mexico, have never been dispossessed of their homes.

Although estimates of the total indigenous population before the arrival of the Europeans vary widely, an acceptable median figure suggests around fifty million people in the Americas as a whole; perhaps five million of those were in North America, speaking around four hundred different languages.

European contacts

The greatest seafarers of early medieval Europe, the **Vikings**, established a colony in Greenland around 982 AD. Under the energetic leadership of Eirik the Red, this became a base for voyages along the mysterious coastline to the west. **Leif Eiriksson** – also known as Leif the Lucky – spent the winter of 1001–02 at a site that has been identified with L'Anse aux Meadows in northern Newfoundland. Climatic conditions may well have been much better than today, though it remains unclear what "grapes" led him to call it **Vinland**. Expeditions returned over the next dozen years, and may have ventured as far south as Maine. However, repeated clashes with the people the Vikings knew as **Skraelings** or "wretches" – probably Inuit, also recent newcomers – led them to abandon plans for permanent settlement.

Five more centuries passed before the crucial moment of contact with the rest of the world came on October 12, 1492, when **Christopher Columbus**, sailing on behalf of the Spanish, reached the Bahamas. A mere four years later the English navigator John Cabot officially "discovered" Newfoundland, and soon British fishermen were setting up makeshift encampments in what became **New England**, to spend the winter curing their catch.

Over the next few years various expeditions mapped the eastern seaboard. In 1524, the Italian **Giovanni Verrazano** sailed past Maine, which he characterized as the "Land of Bad People" thanks to the inhospitable and contemptuous behavior of its natives, and reached the mouth of the Hudson River. The great hope was to find a sea route in the Northeast that would lead to China – the fabled **Northwest Passage**. To the French **Jacques Cartier**, the St Lawrence Seaway seemed a distinct possibility, and unsuccessful attempts were made to settle the northern areas of the Great Lakes from the 1530s onwards. Intrepid trappers and traders ventured ever further west.

To the south, the Spaniards started to nose their way up from the Caribbean in 1513, when **Ponce de Leon**'s expedition in search of the Fountain of Youth landed at what's now Palm Beach, and named **Florida**. Following the lucrative conquest of Mexico, the Spanish returned in 1528 under Panfilo de Narvaez, who was shipwrecked somewhere in the Gulf. A junior officer, **Cabeza de Vaca**, survived, and with three shipmates spent the next six years on an extraordinary odyssey across Texas into the Southwest. Sometimes held as slaves, sometimes revered as seers, they finally got back to Mexico in 1534, bringing tales of golden cities deep in the desert, known as the **Seven Cities of Cibola**.

One of Cabeza de Vaca's companions was a giant black African slave called **Estevanico the Moor**. Rather than re-submit to slavery, he volunteered to map the route for a new expedition; racing alone into the interior, with two colossal greyhounds at his side, he was killed in Zuni Pueblo in 1539. The following year, **Francisco Vázquez de Coronado**'s full party proved to everyone's intense dissatisfaction that the Seven Cities of Cibola did not exist. They reached as far as the Grand Canyon, encountering the Hopi along the way. Hernán Cortés, the conqueror of the Aztec, had meanwhile traced the outline of Baja California, and in 1542 Juan Cabrillo sailed up the coast of California, failing to spot San Francisco Bay in the usual mists.

Although no treasures were found to match the vast riches plundered from the Aztec and Inca empires, a steady stream of less spectacular discoveries – whether new foodstuffs such as potatoes, or access to the cod fisheries of the northern Atlantic – boosted economies throughout Europe. The Spanish established the first permanent settlement in the present United States when they founded **St Augustine** on the coast of Florida in 1565, only for Sir Francis Drake to burn it to the ground in 1586. In 1598 the Spanish also succeeded in subjugating the Pueblo peoples, and founded **New Mexico** along the Rio Grande. More of a missionary than a military enterprise, the colony's survival was always precarious due to the vast tracts of empty desert that separated it from the rest of Mexico. Nonetheless, the construction of a new capital, **Santa Fe**, began in 1609 (see p.757).

The growth of the colonies

The great rivalry between the English and the Spanish in the late sixteenth century extended right around the world. Freebooting English adventurers-cum-pirates contested Spanish hegemony along both coasts of North America.

Sir Francis Drake staked a claim to California in 1579, five years before **Sir Walter Raleigh** claimed **Virginia** in the east, in the name of his Virgin Queen, Elizabeth I. The party of colonists he sent out in 1585 established the short-lived settlement of **Roanoke**, now remembered as the mysterious "Lost Colony" (see p.372).

The Native Americans encountered by the earliest settlers were seldom hostile at the outset. To some extent the European newcomers were obliged to make friends with the locals; most had crossed the Atlantic to find religious freedom or to make their fortunes, and lacked the skills to make a success of mundane subsistence farming. Virginia's first enduring colony, **Jamestown**, was founded by Captain John Smith on May 24, 1607. He bemoaned "though there be Fish in the Sea, and Foules in the ayre, and Beasts in the woods, their bounds are so large, they are so wilde, and we so weake and ignorant, we cannot much trouble them"; six in every seven colonists died within a year of reaching the New World.

Gradually, however, the settlers learned to cultivate the strange crops of this unfamiliar terrain. As far as the English government was concerned, the colonies were commercial ventures, intended to produce crops that could not be grown at home, and the colonists were not supposed to have goals of their own. Following failures with sugar and rice, Virginia finally found its feet with its first **tobacco** harvest in 1615 (the man responsible, John Rolfe, is better known as the husband of Pocahontas). A successful tobacco plantation requires two things in abundance: land and labour. No self-respecting Englishman came to America to work for others; when the first **slave** ship called at Jamestown in 1619, the captain found an eager market for his cargo of twenty African slaves. By that time there were already a million slaves in South America.

The 102 **Puritans** remembered as the "**Pilgrim Fathers**" were deposited on Cape Cod by the *Mayflower* in late 1620, and soon moved on to set up their own colony at Plymouth (see p.185). Fifty died that winter, and the whole party might have perished but for their fortuitous encounter with the extraordinary **Squanto**. This Native American had twice been kidnapped and taken to Europe, only to make his way home; he had spent four years working as a merchant in the City of London, and had also lived in Spain. Having recently come home to find his entire tribe exterminated by smallpox, he threw in his lot with the English. With his guidance, they finally managed to reap their first harvest, celebrated with a mighty feast of **Thanksgiving**.

Of greater significance to New England was the founding in 1630 of a new colony, further up the coast at Naumkeag (later Salem), by the Massachusetts Bay Company. Its governor, **John Winthrop**, soon moved to establish a new capital on the Shawmut peninsula – the city of **Boston**, complete with its own university of Harvard. His vision of a Utopian "City on a Hill" did not extend to sharing Paradise with the Native Americans; he argued that they had not "subdued" the land, which was therefore a "vacuum" for the Puritans to use as they saw fit. While their faith helped individual colonists to endure the early hardships, the colony as a whole failed to maintain a strong religious identity (the Salem witch trials of 1692 did much to discredit the notion that the New World had any moral superiority to the Old), and breakaway groups left to create the rival settlements of Providence and Connecticut.

Between 1620 and 1642, sixty thousand migrants – 1.5 percent of the population – left England for America. Many in pursuit of economic opportunities joined the longer-established colonies, thereby serving to dilute the religious zeal of the Puritans. Groups hoping to find spiritual freedom were more inclined to start afresh; thus **Maryland** was created as a haven for Catholics in 1632, and fifty years later **Pennsylvania** was founded by the Quakers.

The English were not alone, however. After Sir Henry Hudson rediscovered Manhattan in 1609, it was "bought" by the **Dutch** in 1624 – though the Native

Americans who took their money were passing nomads with no claim to it either. The Dutch colony of New Amsterdam, founded in 1625, lasted less than forty years before being captured by the English and renamed **New York**; by that time, a strong Dutch presence dominated the lower reaches of the Hudson River.

From their foothold in the Great Lakes region, meanwhile, the **French** sent the explorers Joliet and Marquette to map the Mississippi in 1673. Upon establishing that the river did indeed flow into the Gulf of Mexico, they turned back, but they'd cleared the way for the foundation of the huge and ill-defined colony of **Louisiana** in 1699. The city of **New Orleans**, at the mouth of the Mississippi, was created in 1718.

While the Spanish remained ensconced in Florida, things were going less smoothly in the Southwest. The bloody **Pueblo Revolt** of 1680 drove the Spanish out of New Mexico altogether, though they returned in force a dozen years later. Thereafter, a curious synthesis of traditional and Hispanic religion and culture began to evolve, and, but for hostile raids from the north, the Spanish presence was not seriously challenged.

Things were also changing in the unknown hinterland. The frontier was pushing steadily eastwards, as colonists seized Native American land, with or without the excuse of an "uprising" or "rebellion" to provoke them into bloodshed. The major killer of indigenous peoples, however, was **smallpox**, which worked its way deep into the interior of the continent long before the Europeans. As populations were decimated, great migrations took place. The original inhabitants of the region had been sedentary farmers, who also hunted buffalo by driving them over rocky bluffs. With the arrival of **horses** on the Great Plains (probably captured from the Spanish, and known at first as "mystery dogs"), an entirely new, nomadic lifestyle emerged. Groups such as the Cheyenne and the Apache swept their rivals aside to dominate vast territories, and eagerly seized the potential offered by the later introduction of firearms. Increasing dependence on trade with Europeans created a very dynamic, but fundamentally unstable culture.

The American Revolution

The American colonies prospered during the **eighteenth century**. Boston, New York and Philadelphia in particular became home to a wealthy, well-educated and highly articulate middle class, as frustration mounted at the inequities of the colonies' relationship with Britain. While allowed to trade among themselves, the Americans could otherwise only sell their produce to the British, and all transatlantic commerce had to be undertaken in British ships.

Although full-scale independence was not an explicit goal until late in the century, the main factor that made it possible was the economic impact of the pan-European **Seven Years' War**. Officially, war in Europe lasted from 1756 to 1763, but fighting in North America broke out a little earlier. Beginning in 1755 with the mass expulsion of French settlers from Acadia in Nova Scotia (triggering their epic migration to Louisiana, where the **Cajuns** remain to this day), the British went on to conquer all of Canada. In forcing the **surrender of Québec** in 1759, General Wolfe brought the war to a close; the French ceded Louisiana to the Spanish rather than let it fall to the British, while Florida passed briefly into British control before reverting to the Spanish. All the European monarchs were left hamstrung by debts, and the British realized that colonialism in America was not as profitable as in those parts of the world where the native populations could be coerced into working for their overseas masters.

There was one other major player on the scene – the **Iroquois Confederacy**. Iroquois culture in the Great Lakes region, characterized by military expansionism and even human sacrifice, dates back around a thousand years. Forever in competition with the Algonquin and the Huron, the southern Iroquois had by the eighteenth century formed a League of Five Nations – the Seneca, Cayuga, Onondaga, Oneida and Mohawk, all in what's now upstate New York. Wooed by both the French and British, the Iroquois charted an independent course. Impressed by witnessing negotiations between the Iroquois and the squabbling representatives of Pennsylvania, Virginia and Maryland, Benjamin Franklin wrote in 1751 that "It would be a very strange thing if …ignorant savages should be capable of forming a scheme for such a union…that has subsisted ages and appears indissoluble; and yet that a like union should be impracticable for ten or a dozen English colonies".

An unsuccessful insurrection by the Ottawa in 1763, led by their chief **Pontiac**, led the cash-strapped British to conclude that, while America needed its own standing army, it was reasonable to expect the colonists to pay for it. In 1765, they introduced the **Stamp Act**, requiring duty on all legal transactions and printed matter in the colonies to be paid to the British Crown. Firm in the belief that there should be "no taxation without representation", delegates from nine colonies met in the Stamp Act Congress that October. By then, however, the British prime minister responsible had already been dismissed by King George III, and the Act was repealed in 1766.

However, in 1767, Chancellor Townshend made political capital at home by proclaiming "I dare tax America", as he introduced legislation including the broadly similar Revenue Act. That led Massachusetts merchants, inspired by **Samuel Adams**, to vote to boycott English goods; they were subsequently joined by all the other colonies except New Hampshire. Townshend's Acts were repealed in turn by a new prime minister, Lord North, on March 5, 1770. By chance, on that same day a stone-throwing mob surrounded the Customs House in Boston; five people were shot in what became known as the **Boston Massacre**. Even so, most of the colonies resumed trading with Britain, and the crisis was postponed for a few more years.

In May 1773, Lord North's **Tea Act** relieved the debt-ridden East India Company of the need to pay duties on exports to America, while still requiring the Americans to pay duty on tea. Massachusetts called the colonies to action, and its citizens took the lead on December 16 in the **Boston Tea Party**, when three tea ships were boarded and 342 chests thrown into the sea.

The infuriated British Parliament thereupon began to pass legislation collectively known as both the "Coercive" and the "Intolerable" Acts, which included closing the port of Boston and disbanding the government of Massachusetts. Thomas Jefferson argued that the acts amounted to "a deliberate and systematical plan of reducing us to slavery". To discuss a response, the first **Continental Congress** was held in Philadelphia on May 5, 1774, and attended by representatives of all the colonies except Georgia.

War finally broke out on April 18, 1775, when General Gage, the governor of Massachusetts, dispatched four hundred British soldiers to destroy the arms depot at **Concord**, and prevent weapons from falling into rebel hands. Silversmith **Paul Revere** was dispatched on his legendary ride to warn the rebels, and the British were confronted en route at Lexington by 77 American "Minutemen". The resulting skirmish led to the "shot heard 'round the world".

Congress set about forming an army at Boston, and decided for the sake of unity to appoint a Southern commander, **George Washington**. One by one, as the war raged, the colonies set up their own governments and declared themselves to be states, and the politicians set about defining the society they wished to create. The

The Constitution

As signed in 1787 and ratified in 1788, the **Constitution** stipulated the following form of government:

All **legislative** powers were granted to the **Congress of the United States.** The lower of its two distinct houses, the **House of Representatives**, was to be elected every two years, with its members in proportion to the number of each state's "free Persons" plus "three fifths of all other persons" (meaning slaves). The upper house, the **Senate**, would hold two Senators from each state, chosen by state legislatures rather than by direct elections. Each Senator was to serve for six years, with a third of them to be elected every two years.

Executive power was vested in the **President**, who was also Commander in Chief of the Army and Navy. He would be chosen every four years, by as many **"Electors"** from each individual state as it had Senators and Representatives. Each state could decide how to appoint those Electors; almost all chose to have direct popular elections. Nonetheless, the distinction has remained ever since between the number of "popular votes", across the whole country, received by a presidential candidate, and the number of state-by-state "electoral votes", which determines the actual result. Originally, whoever came second in the voting automatically became **Vice President**.

The President could **veto** acts of Congress, but that veto could be overruled by a two-thirds vote in both houses. The House of Representatives could **impeach** the President for treason, bribery or "other high crimes and misdemeanors". in which instance the Senate could remove him from office with a two-thirds majority.

Judicial power was invested in a **Supreme Court**, and as many "inferior Courts" as Congress should decide.

The Constitution has so far been altered by 27 **Amendments**. Numbers **14** and **15** extended the vote to black males in 1868 and 1870; **17** made Senators subject to election by direct popular vote in 1913; **18** introduced women's suffrage in 1920; **22** restricted the president to two terms in 1951; **24** stopped states using poll taxes to disenfranchise black voters, in 1964; and **26** reduced the minimum voting age to 18 in 1971.

writings of pamphleteer Thomas Paine – especially *Common Sense* – were, together with the Confederacy of the Iroquois, a great influence on the **Declaration of Independence**. Drafted by Thomas Jefferson, this was adopted by the Continental Congress in Philadelphia on July 4, 1776. Anti-slavery clauses originally included by Jefferson – himself a slave-owner – were omitted to spare the feelings of the Southern states, though the section that denounced the King's dealings with "merciless Indian Savages" was left in.

At first, the **Revolutionary War** went well for the British. General Howe crossed the Atlantic with twenty thousand men, took New York and New Jersey, and ensconced himself in Philadelphia for the winter of 1777–78. Washington's army was encamped not far away at Valley Forge, freezing cold and all but starving to death. It soon became clear, however, that the longer the Americans could avoid losing an all-out battle, the more likely the British were to over-extend their lines as they advanced through the vast and unfamiliar continent. Thus, General Burgoyne's expedition, which set out from Canada to march on New England, was so harried by rebel guerrillas that he had to surrender at Saratoga in October 1777. Other European powers took delight in coming to the aid of the Americans. Benjamin Franklin led a wildly successful delegation to France to request support, and soon the nascent American fleet was being assisted in its bid to cut British naval communications by both the French and the Spanish. The end came when Cornwallis, who had replaced Howe, was instructed to dig in at Yorktown and wait for the Royal Navy to come to his aid, only for the French to seal off Chesapeake Bay and prevent reinforcement. Cornwallis surrendered to Washington on October 17, 1781.

The ensuing **Treaty of Paris** granted the Americans their independence on generous terms – the British completely abandoned their Native American allies, including the Iroquois, to the vengeance of the victors – and Washington entered New York as the British left in November 1783. The Spanish were confirmed in possession of Florida.

The victorious US Congress met for the first time in 1789, and the tradition of awarding political power to the nation's most successful generals was instigated by the election of George Washington as the first **president**. He was further honoured when his name was given to the new capital city of **Washington DC**, deliberately sited between the North and the South.

The nineteenth century

During its first century, the territories and population of the new **United States of America** expanded at a phenomenal rate. The white population of North America in 1800 stood at around five million, and there were another one million African slaves (of whom thirty thousand were in the North). Of that total, 86 percent lived within fifty miles of the Atlantic, but no US city could rival Mexico City, whose population approached 100,000 inhabitants (both New York and Philadelphia reached that figure within twenty years, however, and New York had passed a million fifty years later).

It had suited the British to discourage settlers from venturing west of the Appalachians, where they would be far beyond the reach of British power. However, adventurers such as **Daniel Boone** started to cross the mountains into Tennessee and Kentucky during the 1770s. Soon makeshift rafts, made from the planks that were later assembled to make log cabins, were careering west along the Ohio River (the only westward-flowing river on the continent).

In 1801, the Spanish handed Louisiana back to the French, on condition that the French would keep it forever. However, Napoleon swiftly realized that attempting to hang on to his American possessions would spread his armies too thinly, and chose instead to sell them to the United States for $15 million, in the **Louisiana Purchase** of 1803. President Thomas Jefferson swiftly sent the explorers **Lewis and Clark** to map out the new territories, which extended far beyond the boundaries of present-day Louisiana. With the help of Sacagawea, their female Shoshone guide, they followed the Missouri and Columbia rivers all the way to the Pacific; in their wake, trappers and "mountain men" came to hunt in the wilderness of the Rockies. The **Russians** had already reached the Pacific Northwest, and established fortified outposts to trade in beaver and otter pelts.

British attempts to blockade the Atlantic, primarily targeted against Napoleon, gave the new nation a chance to flex its military muscles. British raiders succeeded in capturing Washington DC, and burned the White House, but the **War of 1812** provided the US with a cover for aggression against the Native American allies of the British. Thus **Tecumseh** of the Shawnee was defeated near Detroit, and **Andrew Jackson** moved against the Creek of the southern Mississippi. Jackson's campaign against the Seminole won the US possession of Florida from the Spanish; he was rewarded first with the governorship of the new state, and later by his election to the presidency. While in office, in the 1830s, Jackson went even further, and set about clearing all states east of the Mississippi of their native

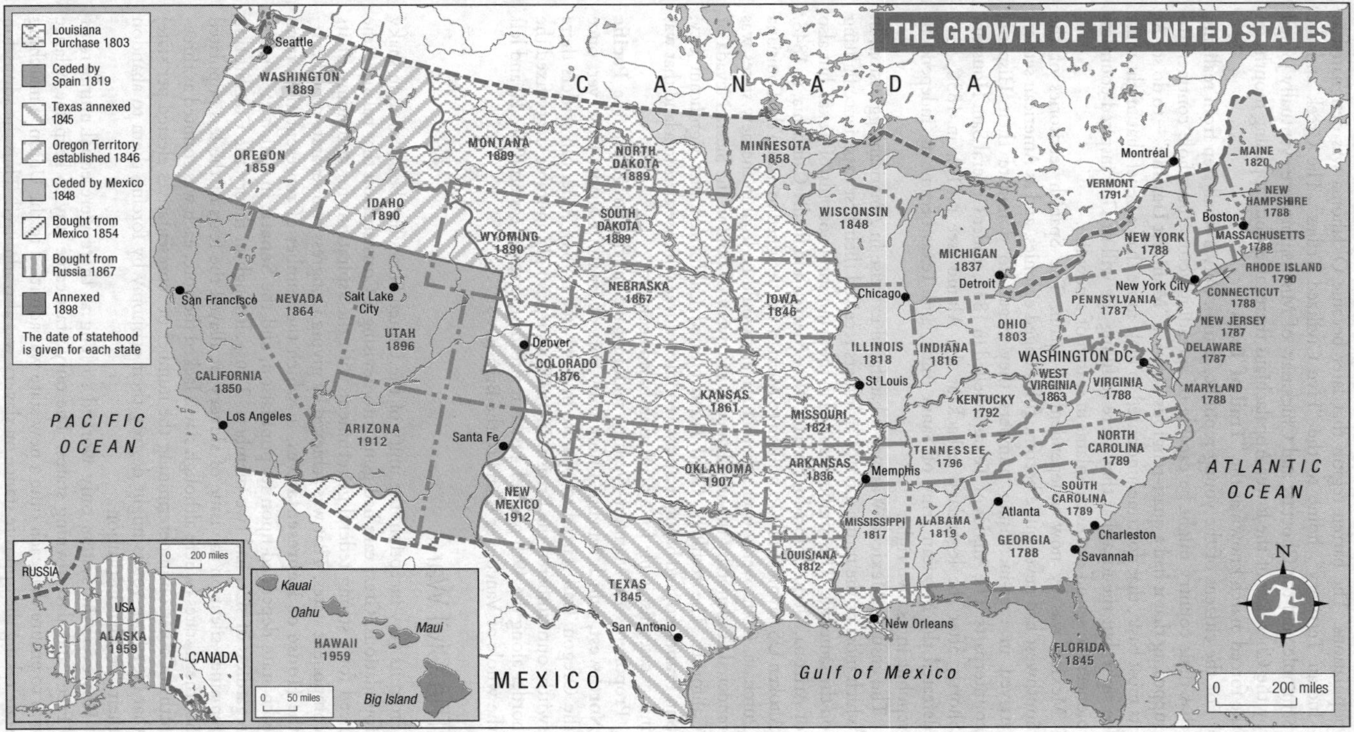

THE GROWTH OF THE UNITED STATES

Louisiana Purchase 1803
Ceded by Spain 1819
Texas annexed 1845
Oregon Territory established 1846
Ceded by Mexico 1848
Bought from Mexico 1854
Bought from Russia 1867
Annexed 1898
The date of statehood is given for each state

CANADA
WASHINGTON 1889
OREGON 1859
IDAHO 1890
MONTANA 1889
WYOMING 1890
NORTH DAKOTA 1889
SOUTH DAKOTA 1889
NEBRASKA 1867
MINNESOTA 1858
WISCONSIN 1848
IOWA 1846
MICHIGAN 1837
CALIFORNIA 1850
NEVADA 1864
UTAH 1896
COLORADO 1876
KANSAS 1861
MISSOURI 1821
ILLINOIS 1818
INDIANA 1816
OHIO 1803
ARIZONA 1912
NEW MEXICO 1912
OKLAHOMA 1907
ARKANSAS 1836
TEXAS 1845
LOUISIANA 1812
MISSISSIPPI 1817
ALABAMA 1819
TENNESSEE 1796
KENTUCKY 1792
GEORGIA 1788
FLORIDA 1845
SOUTH CAROLINA 1789
NORTH CAROLINA 1789
VIRGINIA 1788
WEST VIRGINIA 1863
MARYLAND 1788
DELAWARE 1787
NEW JERSEY 1787
PENNSYLVANIA 1787
NEW YORK 1788
CONNECTICUT 1788
RHODE ISLAND 1790
MASSACHUSETTS 1788
NEW HAMPSHIRE 1788
VERMONT 1791
MAINE 1820
Seattle
San Francisco
Los Angeles
Salt Lake City
Denver
Santa Fe
San Antonio
St Louis
Chicago
Detroit
Memphis
New Orleans
Atlanta
Savannah
Charleston
WASHINGTON DC
New York City
Boston
Montréal
PACIFIC OCEAN
ATLANTIC OCEAN
Gulf of Mexico
MEXICO
N
0 200 miles

RUSSIA
USA
ALASKA 1959
CANADA
0 200 miles

Kauai
Oahu
Maui
HAWAII 1959
Big Island
0 50 miles

populations. The barren region that later became Oklahoma was designated as "Indian Territory", home to the "Five Civilized Tribes". The Creek and the Seminole, and the Choctaw and Chickasaw of Mississippi were eventually joined by the Cherokee of the lower Appalachians there, after four appalling months on the forced march known as the "**Trail of Tears**".

For the citizens of the young republic, it took only a small step from realizing that their country might be capable of spreading across the whole continent to supposing that it had a quasi-religious duty – a "**Manifest Destiny**" – to do so. At its most basic, that doctrine amounted to little more than a belief that might must be right, but the idea that they were fulfilling the will of God inspired countless pioneers to set off across the plains in search of a new life.

Mexico was by now independent of Spain. The Spanish territories of the Southwest had never quite become full-fledged colonies, and as American settlers arrived in ever-increasing numbers they began to dominate their Hispanic counterparts. The Anglos of **Texas** rebelled in 1833, under General Sam Houston. Shortly after the legendary setback at the **Alamo** (see p.610), in 1836, they defeated the Mexican army of Santa Anna, and Texas became an independent republic in its own right.

The ensuing **Mexican War** was a barefaced exercise in American aggression, in which most of the future Civil War leaders received their first experience fighting on the same side. The conflict resulted in the acquisition not only of Texas, but also of Arizona, Utah, Colorado, Nevada, New Mexico and finally California, in 1848. A token US payment of $15 million to Mexico was designed to match the Louisiana Purchase. Controversy over whether slavery would be legal in the new states was rendered academic by the simultaneous discovery of gold in the Sierra Nevada of California. The resultant **Gold Rush** created California's first significant city, **San Francisco**, and brought a massive influx of free white settlers to a land that was in any case unsuitable for a plantation-based economy.

Proponents of Manifest Destiny seldom gave much thought to the **Pacific Northwest**, which remained nominally part of British Canada. However, once the Oregon Trail started to operate in 1841 (see p.984), American settlers there swiftly outnumbered the British. In 1846, a surprisingly amicable treaty fixed the border along the 49th parallel, just as it already did across eastern Canada, and left the whole of Vancouver Island to the British.

The Civil War

From its very inception, the unity of the United States had been based on shaky foundations. Great care had gone into devising a **Constitution** that balanced the need for a strong federal government with the aspirations for autonomy of its component states. That was achieved by giving Congress two separate chambers – the **House of Representatives**, in which the number of representatives from each state depended upon its population, and the **Senate**, in which each state, regardless of size, had two members. Thus, although in theory the Constitution remained silent on the issue of **slavery**, it allayed the fears of the less populated Southern states (where although slaves lacked the vote, each was counted as three-fifths of a person in determining the number of representatives elected per state) that Northern voters might destroy their economy by forcing them to abandon their "peculiar institution".

However, the system only worked so long as there were equal numbers of "Free" and slave-owning states. The only practicable way to keep the balance was to ensure that each time a new state was admitted to the Union, a matching state taking the opposite stance on slavery was also admitted. Thus the admission of every new state became subject to endless intrigue. The 1820 **Missouri Compromise**, under which Missouri joined as a slave-owning state and Maine as a Free one, was straightforward in comparison to the prevarication and chest-beating that surrounded the admission of Texas, while the Mexican War was widely seen in the North as a naked land grab for new slave states.

Abolitionist sentiment in the North was not all that great before the middle of the nineteenth century. At best, after the importation of slaves from Africa ended in 1808, Northerners vaguely hoped slavery was an anachronism that might simply wither away. As it turned out, Southern plantations were rendered much more profitable by the development of the cotton gin, and the increased demand for manufactured cotton goods triggered by the **Industrial Revolution**. However, the rapid growth of the nation as a whole made it ever more difficult to maintain a political balance between North and South.

Matters came to a head in 1854, when the **Kansas–Nebraska Act** sparked guerrilla raids and mini-wars between rival settlers by allowing both prospective states self-determination on the issue. That same year, the **Republican Party** was founded to resist the further expansion of slavery. Escaped former slaves such as Frederick Douglass were by now inspiring Northern audiences to moral outrage, and Harriet Beecher Stowe's *Uncle Tom's Cabin* found unprecedented readership.

In October 1859, **John Brown** – a white-bearded, wild-eyed veteran of Kansas's bloodiest infighting – led a dramatic raid on the US Armory at Harpers Ferry, West Virginia, intending to secure arms for a slave insurrection (see p.373). Swiftly captured by forces under Robert E. Lee, he was hanged within a few weeks, proclaiming that "I am now quite certain that the crimes of this guilty land will never be purged away but with blood".

Although the Republican candidate for the presidency in 1860, the little-known **Abraham Lincoln** from Kentucky, won no Southern states, with the Democrats split into Northern and Southern factions he was elected with 39 percent of the popular vote. Within weeks, on December 20, South Carolina became the first state to secede from the Union; the **Confederacy** was declared on February 4, 1861, when it was joined by Mississippi, Florida, Alabama, Georgia, Louisiana and Texas. Its first (and only) president was **Jefferson Davis**, also from Kentucky; at their inauguration, his new vice president remarked that their government was "the first in the history of the world based upon the great physical and moral truth that the negro is not equal to the white man". Lincoln was inaugurated in turn in March 1861, proclaiming that "I have no purpose, directly or indirectly, to interfere with the institution of slavery in the States where it exists. I believe I have no lawful right to do so, and I have no inclination to do so". He was completely inflexible, however, on one paramount issue: the survival of the Union.

The **Civil War** began just a few weeks later. The first shots were fired on April 12, when a federal attempt to resupply Fort Sumter, off Charleston, South Carolina, was greeted by a Confederate bombardment that forced its surrender. Lincoln's immediate call to raise an army against the South was greeted by the further secession of Virginia, Arkansas, Tennessee and North Carolina. Within a year, both armies had amassed 600,000 men; Robert E. Lee had been offered command of both and opted for the Confederacy, while George McLellan became the first leader of the Union forces. Although the rival capitals of Washington DC, and Richmond, Virginia, were a mere one hundred miles apart, over the next four years operations reached almost everywhere south of Washington and east of the Mississippi.

Tracing the ebb and flow of the military campaigns – from the early Confederate victories, via Grant's successful siege of Vicksburg in 1863 and Sherman's devastating March to the Sea in 1864, to Lee's eventual surrender at Appomattox in April 1865 – it's easy to forget that it was not so much generalship as sheer economic (and man) power that won the war. The **Union** of 23 Northern states, holding over 22 million people, wore down the **Confederacy** of 11 Southern states, with 9 million people. As for potential combatants, the North initially drew upon 3.5 million white males aged between 18 and 45 – and later recruited blacks as well – whereas the South had more like one million. In the end, around 2.1 million men fought for the Union, and 900,000 for the Confederacy. Of the 620,000 soldiers who died during the conflict, a disproportionate 258,000 came from the South – one quarter of its white men of military age. Meanwhile, not only did the North continue trading with the rest of the world while maintaining its industrial and agricultural output, it also stifled the Confederacy with a devastating **naval blockade**. The Southern war effort was primarily financed by printing $1.5 billion of paper currency, which was so eroded by inflation that it became worthless.

Even so, the Confederacy came much closer to victory than is usually appreciated. The repeated out-manoeuvring of federal forces by General **Robert E. Lee**, and his incursions into Union territory, meant that in each of three successive years, from 1862 to 1864, there was a genuine possibility that Northern morale would collapse, allowing opponents of the war to be elected to power and agree to peace. After all, the Revolutionary War had shown how such a war could be won: for the Union to triumph, it had to invade and occupy the South, and destroy its armies, but for the South to win it only had to survive until the North wearied of the struggle.

The dashing tactics of Confederate generals Lee and Jackson, forever counter-attacking and carrying the fight to the enemy, arguably contributed to the Southern defeat. The grim, relentless total-war campaigning of Grant and Sherman eventually ground the South down. Ironically, had the Confederacy sued for peace before Lee gave it fresh hope, a negotiated settlement might not have included the abolition of slavery. In the event, as the war went on, with Southern slaves flocking to the Union flag and black soldiers fighting on the front line, emancipation did indeed become inevitable. Lincoln took the political decision to match his moral conviction by issuing his **Emancipation Proclamation** in 1862, though the **Thirteenth Amendment** outlawing slavery only took effect in 1865.

Lincoln himself was assassinated within a few days of the end of the war, a mark of the deep bitterness that would almost certainly have precluded successful **Reconstruction** even if he had lived. For a brief period, after black men were granted the vote in 1870, Southern states elected black political representatives, but without a sustained effort to enable former slaves to acquire land, racial relations in the South swiftly deteriorated. Thanks to white supremacist organizations such as the Ku Klux Klan, nominally clandestine but brazenly public, Southern blacks were soon effectively disenfranchised once more. Anyone working to transform the South came under attack either as a "carpetbagger" (a Northern opportunist heading South for personal profit) or a treacherous "scalawag" (a Southern collaborator).

The aftermath of the Civil War can almost be said to have lasted for a hundred years. While the South condemned itself to a century as a backwater, the rest of the re-United States embarked on a period of expansionism and prosperity.

The Indian Wars

With the completion of the transcontinental railroad in 1867, Manifest Destiny became an undeniable reality. Among the first to head west were the troops of the federal army, with Union and Confederate veterans marching under the same flag to battle the remaining Native Americans. Treaty after treaty was signed, only to be broken as soon as expedient (usually upon the discovery of gold or precious metals). When the whites overreached themselves, or when driven to desperation, the Native Americans fought back. The defeat of **General George Custer** at Little Bighorn in 1876, by **Sitting Bull** and his Sioux and Cheyenne warriors (see p.729), provoked the full wrath of the government. Within a few years, leaders such as **Crazy Horse** of the Oglala Sioux and **Geronimo** of the Apache had been forced to surrender, and their people confined to reservations. One last act of resistance was the visionary, messianic cult of the **Ghost Dance**, whose practitioners hoped that by ritual observance they could win back their lost way of life, in a land miraculously free of white intruders. Such aspirations were regarded as hostile, and military harassment of the movement culminated in the massacre at **Wounded Knee** in South Dakota in 1890.

A major tactic in the campaign against the Plains Indians was to starve them into submission, by eliminating the vast herds of bison that were their primary source of food. As General Philip Sheridan put it, "For the sake of a lasting peace … kill, skin and sell until the buffalo are exterminated. Then your prairies can be covered by the speckled cow and the festive cowboy". More significant than the activities of the much-mythologized cowboys, however, was the back-breaking toil of the miners up in the mountains, and the homesteading families out on the Plains.

Industry and immigration

The late nineteenth century saw massive **immigration** to North America, with influxes from Europe to the East Coast paralleled by those from Asia to the West. As in colonial times, national groups tended to form enclaves in specific areas – from the Scandinavian farmers of Minnesota and the northern Plains, to the Basque shepherds of Idaho and the Cornish miners of Colorado. In the Southwest, where individual hard work counted for less than shared communal effort, the **Mormons** of Utah had fled persecution to become the first white settlers to eke a living from the unforgiving desert.

The fastest growth of all was in the nation's greatest **cities**, especially New York, Chicago and Boston. Their industrial and commercial strength enabled them to attract and absorb migrants not only from throughout Europe but also from the Old South – particularly ex-slaves, who could now at least vote with their feet.

Stretching "from sea to shining sea", the territorial boundaries of the US had almost reached their current limits. In 1867, however, Secretary of State William Seward agreed to buy **Alaska** from the crisis-torn Russian government for $7.2 million. The purchase was at first derided as "Seward's Folly", but soon gold was discovered there as well.

The various presidents of the day, from the victorious General Grant onwards, now seem anonymous figures compared to the industrialists and financiers who manipulated the national economy. These "**robber barons**" included such men as John D. Rockefeller, who controlled seventy percent of the world's oil almost before anyone else had realized it was worth controlling; Andrew Carnegie, who made his fortune introducing the Bessemer process of steel manufacture; and J.P. Morgan, who went for the most basic commodity of all – money. Their success was predicated on the willingness of the government to cooperate in resisting the development of a strong labour movement. Strikes on the railroads in 1877, in the mines of Tennessee in 1891 and in the steel mills of Pittsburgh in 1892, were forcibly crushed.

The nineteenth century had also seen the development of a distinctive American voice in **literature**, which rendered increasingly superfluous the efforts of passing English visitors to "explain" the United States. From the 1830s onwards, writers explored new ways to describe their new world, with results as varied as the introspective essays of Henry Thoreau, the morbid visions of

Edgar Allan Poe, the all-embracing novels of Herman Melville and the irrepressible poetry of Walt Whitman, whose endlessly revised *Leaves of Grass* was an exultant hymn to the young republic. Virtually every leading participant in the Civil War wrote at least one highly readable volume of memoirs, while public figures as disparate as Buffalo Bill Cody and the showman P.T. Barnum produced lively autobiographies. The boundless national self-confidence found its greatest expression in the vigorous vernacular style of **Mark Twain**, whose depictions of frontier life, fictionalized for example in *Huckleberry Finn*, gave the rest of the world an abiding impression of the American character.

Many Americans saw the official "closure" of the Western frontier, announced by the Census Bureau in 1890, as tantamount to depriving the country of the Manifest Destiny that was its *raison d'être*, and sought new frontiers further afield. Such **imperialist ventures** reached a crescendo in 1898, with the annexation of the Kingdom of **Hawaii** – which even then-President Cleveland condemned as "wholly without justification… not merely wrong but a disgrace" – and the double seizure of Cuba and the Philippines in the **Spanish–American War**, which catapulted **Theodore Roosevelt** to the presidency. Though he took the African proverb "speak softly and carry a big stick" as his motto – and was hardly, if truth be told, noted for being soft-spoken – Roosevelt in office did much to heal the divisions within the nation. While new legislation reined in the worst excesses of the Robber Barons, and of rampant capitalism in general, it alleviated popular discontent without substantially threatening the business community, or empowering the labour movement. A decade into the twentieth century, the United States had advanced to the point that it knew, even if the rest of the world wasn't yet altogether sure, that it was the strongest, wealthiest country on earth.

The twentieth century

While not necessarily apparent to everyone at the time, the first few years of the twentieth century witnessed the emergence of many features that came to characterize modern America. In 1903 alone, Wilbur and Orville Wright achieved the first successful powered **flight**, and Henry Ford established his Ford Motor Company. Ford's enthusiastic adoption of the latest technology in mass production – the assembly line – gave Detroit a head start in the new **automobile** industry, which swiftly became the most important business in America. Both **jazz** and **blues** music first reached a national audience during that same period, while Hollywood acquired its first **movie** studio in 1911, and its first major hit in 1915 with D.W. Griffith's unabashed glorification of the Ku Klux Klan in *Birth of a Nation*.

This was also a time of growing **radicalism**. Both the NAACP (National Association for the Advancement of Colored People) and the socialist International Workers of the World ("the Wobblies") were founded in the early 1900s, while the campaign for women's suffrage also came to the forefront. Writers such as Upton Sinclair, whose *The Jungle* exposed conditions in Chicago's stockyards, and Jack London proselytized to the masses.

Though President Wilson kept the US out of the **Great War** for several years, American intervention was, when it came, decisive. With the Russian Revolution illustrating the dangers of anarchy, the US also took charge of supervising the peace. However, while Wilson presided over the negotiations that produced the Treaty of Versailles in 1919, isolationist sentiment at home prevented the US from joining his pet scheme to preserve future world peace, the League of Nations.

Back home, the 18th Amendment, in 1920, forbade the sale and distribution of alcohol, while the 19th finally gave all American women the vote. Quite how **Prohibition** ever became the law of the land remains a mystery; certainly, in the buzzing metropolises of the Roaring Twenties, it enjoyed little conspicuous support. There was no noticeable elevation in the moral tone of the country, and Chicago in particular became renowned for the street wars between bootlegging gangsters such as Al Capone and his rivals.

The two Republican presidents who followed Wilson did little more than sit back and watch the Roaring Twenties unfold. Until his premature death, **Warren Harding** enjoyed considerable public affection, but he's now remembered as probably the worst US president of all, thanks to the cronyism and corruption of his associates. It's hard to say quite whether **Calvin Coolidge** did anything at all; his laissez-faire attitude extended to working a typical four-hour day, and announcing shortly after his inauguration that "four-fifths of our troubles would disappear if we would sit down and keep still".

The Depression and the New Deal

By the middle of the 1920s, the US was an industrial powerhouse, responsible for more than half the world's output of manufactured goods. Having led the way into a new era of prosperity, however, it suddenly dragged the rest of the world down into economic collapse. The consequences of the **Great Depression** were out of all proportion to any one specific cause. Possible factors include American overinvestment in the floundering economy of postwar Europe, combined with high tariffs on imports that effectively precluded European recovery. Conservative commentators at the time chose to interpret the calamitous **Wall Street Crash** of October 1929 as a symptom of impending depression rather than a contributory cause, but the quasi-superstitious faith in the stock market that preceded it showed all the characteristics of classic speculative booms. On "Black Tuesday" alone, enough stocks were sold to produce a total loss of ten thousand million dollars – more than twice the total amount of money in circulation in the US. Within the next three years, industrial production was cut by half, the national income dropped by 38 percent, and, above all, unemployment rose from 1.5 million to 13 million.

National self-confidence, however shaky its foundations, has always played a crucial role in US history, and President Hoover was not the man to restore it. Matters only began to improve in 1932, when the patrician figure of **Franklin Delano Roosevelt** accepted the Democratic nomination for president with the words "I pledge myself to a new deal for America", and went on to win a landslide victory. At the time of his inauguration, early in 1933, the banking system had all but closed down; it took Roosevelt the now-proverbial "Hundred Days" of vigorous legislation to turn around the mood of the country.

Taking advantage of the new medium of radio, he used his "Fireside Chats" to cajole America out of crisis; among his earliest observations was that it was a good time for a beer, and that the experiment of Prohibition was therefore over. The **New Deal** took many forms, but was marked throughout by a massive growth in the power of the federal government. Among its accomplishments were the National Recovery Administration, which created two million jobs; the Social Security Act, of which Roosevelt declared "no damn politician can ever scrap my social security program"; the Public Works Administration, which built dams and highways the length and breadth of the country; the Tennessee Valley Authority, which by generating electricity under public ownership for the common good was probably the closest the US has ever come to institutionalized socialism; and measures to legitimize the role of the unions and revitalize the "Dust Bowl" farmers out on the plains.

Roosevelt originally saw himself as a populist who could draw support from every sector of society. By 1936, however, business leaders – and the Supreme Court – were making their opinion clear that he had done more than enough already to kick-start the economy. From then on, as he secured an unprecedented four consecutive terms as president, he was firmly cast as the champion of the little man.

After the work-creation programmes of the New Deal had put America back on its feet, the deadly pressure to achieve victory in **World War II** spurred industrial production and know-how to new heights. Once again the US stayed out of the war at first, until it was finally forced in when the Japanese launched a pre-emptive strike on Hawaii's Pearl Harbor in 1941. In both the Pacific and in Europe, American manpower and economic muscle eventually carried all before it. By dying early in 1945, having laid the foundations for the postwar carve-up with Stalin and Churchill at Yalta, Roosevelt was spared the fateful decision, made by his successor Harry Truman, to use the newly developed atomic bomb on Hiroshima and Nagasaki.

The coming of the Cold War

With the war won, Americans were in no mood to revert back to the isolationism of the 1930s. Amid much hopeful rhetoric, Truman enthusiastically participated in the creation of the **United Nations**, and set up the **Marshall Plan** to speed the recovery of Europe. However, as Winston Churchill announced in Missouri in 1946, an "**Iron Curtain**" had descended upon Europe, and Joseph Stalin was transformed from ally to enemy almost overnight.

The ensuing **Cold War** lasted for more than four decades, at times fought in ferocious combat (albeit often by proxy) in scattered corners of the globe, and during the intervals diverting colossal economic resources towards the stockpiling of ever more destructive arsenals. Some of its ugliest moments came in its earliest years; Truman was still in office in 1950 when war broke out in **Korea**. A dispute over the arbitrary division of the Korean peninsula into two separate nations, North and South, soon turned into a stand-off between the US and China (with Russia lurking in the shadows). Two years of bloody stalemate ended with little to show for it, except that Truman had by now been replaced by the genial **Dwight D. Eisenhower**, the latest war hero to turn president.

The Eisenhower years are often seen as characterized by bland complacency. Once Senator **Joseph McCarthy**, the "witch-hunting" anti-Communist scourge of the State Department and Hollywood, had finally discredited himself by attacking the army as well, middle-class America seemed to lapse into a wilful suburban stupor. Great social changes were taking shape, however. World War II had introduced vast numbers of women and members of ethnic minorities to the rewards of factory work, and shown many Americans from less prosperous regions the lifestyle attainable elsewhere in their own country. The development of a **national highway system**, and a huge increase in automobile ownership, encouraged people to pursue the American Dream wherever they chose. Combined with increasing mechanization on the cotton plantations of the South, this led to another **mass exodus** of blacks from the rural South to the cities of the North, and to a lesser extent the West. **California** entered a period of rapid growth, with the aeronautical industries of Los Angeles in particular attracting thousands of prospective workers.

Also during the 1950s, **television** reached every home in the country. Together with the LP record, it created an entertainment industry that swiftly showed itself capable of addressing the needs of consumers who had previously been barely identified. **Youth culture** burst into public prominence from 1954 onwards, with Elvis Presley's recording of "*That's Alright Mama*" appearing within a few months of Marlon Brando's moody starring role in *On the Waterfront* and James Dean's in *Rebel Without a Cause*.

The civil rights years

Racial segregation of public facilities, which had remained the norm in the South ever since Reconstruction, was finally declared illegal in 1954 by the Supreme Court ruling on *Brown v. Topeka Board of Education*. Just as a century before, however, the Southern states saw the issue more in terms of states' rights than of human rights, and attempting to implement the law, or even to challenge the failure to implement it, required immense courage. The action of Rosa Parks in refusing to give up her seat on a bus in Montgomery, Alabama, in 1955, triggered a successful mass boycott (see p.473), and pushed the 27-year-old **Rev Dr Martin Luther King Jr** to the forefront of the civil rights campaign. Further confrontation took place at the Central High School in Little Rock, Arkansas, in 1957 (see p.486), when the reluctant Eisenhower had to call in federal troops to counter the state's unwillingness to integrate its education system.

The election of **John F. Kennedy** to the presidency in 1960, by the narrowest of margins, marked a sea-change in American politics, even if in retrospect his policies do not seem exactly radical. At 43 the youngest man ever to be elected president, and the first Catholic, he was prepared literally to reach for the moon, urging the US to victory in the Space Race in which it had thus far lagged humiliatingly behind the Soviet Union. The two decades that lay ahead, however, were to be characterized by disillusion, defeat and despair. If the Eisenhower years had been dull, the 1960s in particular were far too interesting for almost everybody's liking.

Kennedy's sheer glamour made him a popular president during his lifetime, while his assassination suffused his administration with the romantic glow of "Camelot". His one undisputed triumph, however, came with the **Cuban missile crisis** of 1962, when the US military fortunately spotted Russian bases in Cuba before any actual missiles were ready for use, and Kennedy faced down premier Khrushchev to insist they be withdrawn. On the other hand, he'd had rather less success the previous year, in launching the abortive **Bay of Pigs** invasion of Cuba, and he also managed to embroil America deeper in the ongoing war against Communism in Vietnam, by sending more "advisers" to Saigon.

Although a much-publicized call to the wife of Rev Martin Luther King Jr, during one of King's many sojourns in Southern jails, was a factor in Kennedy's election success, he was rarely identified himself with the **civil rights** movement. The campaign nonetheless made headway, lent momentum by television coverage of such horrific confrontations as the onslaught by Birmingham police on peaceful demonstrators in 1963. The movement's defining moment came when Rev King delivered his electrifying "I Have a Dream" speech later that summer. King was subsequently awarded the Nobel Peace Prize for his unwavering espousal of Gandhian principles of nonviolence. Perhaps an equally powerful factor in middle America's recognition that the time had come to address racial inequalities, however, was the not-so-implicit threat in the rhetoric of **Malcolm X**, who argued that black people had the right to defend themselves against aggression.

After Kennedy's assassination in November 1963, his successor, **Lyndon B. Johnson**, pushed through legislation that enacted most of the civil rights campaigners' key demands. Even then, violent white resistance in the South continued, and only the long, painstaking and dangerous work of registering Southern black voters en masse eventually forced Southern politicians to mend their ways.

Johnson won election by a landslide in 1964, but his vision of a "**Great Society**" soon foundered. Instead, he was brought low by the war in **Vietnam**, where US involvement escalated beyond all reason or apparent control. Broad-based popular opposition to the conflict grew in proportion to the American death toll, and the threat of the draft heightened youthful rebellion. San Francisco in particular responded to psychedelic prophet Timothy Leary's call to "turn on, tune in, drop out"; 1967's "Summer of Love" saw the lone beatniks of the 1950s transmogrify into an entire generation of hippies.

Dr King's long-standing message that social justice could only be achieved through economic equality was given a new urgency by riots in the ghettoes of Los Angeles in 1965 and Detroit in 1967, and the emergence of the Black Panthers, an armed defence force in the tradition of the now-dead Malcolm X. King also began to denounce the Vietnam War; meanwhile, after refusing the draft with the words "No Vietcong ever called me nigger", **Muhammad Ali** was stripped of his title as world heavyweight boxing champion.

In 1968, the social fabric of the US reached the brink of collapse. Shortly after Johnson was forced by his plummeting popularity to withdraw from the year-end elections, Martin Luther King was gunned down in a Memphis motel. Next, JFK's brother **Robert Kennedy**, now redefined as spokesman for the dispossessed, was fatally shot just as he emerged as Democratic frontrunner. It didn't take a conspiracy theorist to see that the spate of deaths reflected a malaise in the soul of America.

Richard Nixon to Jimmy Carter

Somehow – perhaps because the brutally suppressed riots at the Chicago Democratic Convention raised the spectre of anarchy – the misery of 1968 resulted in the election of Republican **Richard Nixon** as president. Eisenhower's vice president while in his thirties, Nixon had told the press after his failed bid for the governorship of California in 1962 that "you won't have Nixon to kick around any more". Now he was back, with plenty of scores to settle with his perceived enemies, above all in the media. Nixon's conservative credentials enabled him to bring the US to a rapport with China, but the war in Vietnam dragged on, to claim a total of 57,000 American lives. Attempts to win it included the secret and illegal bombing of Cambodia, which raised opposition at home to a new peak, but ultimately it was simpler to abandon the original goals in the name of "peace with honor". The end came either in 1972 – when Henry Kissinger and Le Duc Tho were awarded the Nobel Peace Prize for negotiating a treaty, and Tho at least had the grace to decline – or in 1975, when the Americans finally withdrew from Saigon.

During Nixon's first term, many of the disparate individuals politicized during the 1960s coalesced into **activist groupings**. Feminists united to campaign for abortion rights and an Equal Rights Amendment; gay men in New York's *Stonewall* bar fought back after one police raid too many; Native Americans formed the American Indian Movement; and even prisoners attempted to organize themselves, resulting in such bloody debacles as the storming of Attica prison in 1971. Nixon directed various federal agencies to monitor the new radicalism, but his real bugbear was the antiwar protesters. Increasingly ludicrous covert operations against real and potential opponents culminated in a botched attempt to burgle Democratic National Headquarters in the **Watergate** complex in 1972. It took two years of investigation for Nixon's role in the subsequent cover-up to be proved, but in 1974 he **resigned**, one step ahead of impeachment by the Senate, to be succeeded by **Gerald Ford**, his own appointee as vice president.

With the Republicans momentarily discredited, former Georgia governor **Jimmy Carter** was elected president as a clean-handed outsider in the bicentennial year of 1976, supported by the recently enfranchised black population of the South. However, Carter's enthusiastic attempts to put his Baptist principles into practice on such issues as global human rights were soon perceived as naive, if not un-American. Misfortune followed misfortune. He had to break the news that the nation was facing an **energy crisis**, while after the Shah of Iran was overthrown, staff at the US embassy in Tehran were taken hostage by Islamic revolutionaries. Carter's failed attempts to arrange their release all but destroyed his hopes of winning re-election in 1980. Instead he was replaced by a very different figure, the former Hollywood movie actor **Ronald Reagan**.

From Reagan to Clinton

Reagan was a new kind of president. Unlike his workaholic predecessor, he made a virtue of his hands-off approach to the job, joking that "they say hard work never killed anybody, but I figured why take the risk"? That laissez-faire attitude was especially apparent in his domestic economic policies, under which the rich were left to get as rich as they could. The common perception that Reagan was barely aware of what went on around him allowed his popularity to remain undented by a succession of scandals, including the labyrinthine **Iran-Contra** affair.

Reagan's most enduring achievement came during his second term, when, with his credentials as a Cold Warrior beyond question, the electorate allowed him greater leeway than a Democrat might have received to negotiate **arms-control** agreements with **Mikhail Gorbachev**, the new leader of what he had previously called the "Evil Empire".

In 1988, **George Bush** became the first vice president in 150 years to be immediately elected to the presidency. Despite his unusually broad experience in foreign policy, Bush did little more than sit back and watch in amazement as the domino theory suddenly went into reverse. One after another, the Communist regimes of eastern Europe collapsed, until finally even the Soviet Union crumbled away. Bush was also president when **Operation Desert Storm** drove the Iraqis out of Kuwait in 1991, an undertaking that lasted 100 hours and in which virtually no American lives were lost.

However, the much-anticipated "**peace dividend**" – the dramatic injection of cash into the economy that voters expected to follow the end of the arms race – never materialized. With the 1992 campaign focusing on domestic affairs rather than what was happening overseas, twelve years of Republican government were ended by the election of Arkansas Governor **Bill Clinton**.

Clinton's initial failure to deliver on specific promises – most obviously, to reform the health-care system – enabled the Republicans to capture control of Congress in 1994, prompting two years of legislative gridlock. The "Comeback Kid" nevertheless managed to assign the blame for the government's ineffectiveness to the Republicans, and was elected to a second term. Holding on to office proved more of a challenge, when his affair with White House intern Monica Lewinsky led to the disgrace of **impeachment**, but the Senate ultimately failed to convict, sensing perhaps that the American people did not feel Clinton's indiscretions were serious enough to merit removal.

The Twenty-First Century

When Clinton left the presidency, the economy was **booming**. His former vice president, however, **Al Gore**, contrived to throw away the 2000 presidential election. Both Gore and his Republican opponent, **George W. Bush**, so adeptly followed Clinton's trademark tactic of "**triangulation**" – targeting the centre of the political spectrum by adopting elements of their opponents' agenda – that the result was inevitable: a **tie**. With the final conclusion depending on a mandatory re-counting of votes in Florida, where various irregularities and mistakes complicated the issue, the impasse was ultimately decided in Bush's favour by the conservative **Supreme Court**. At the time, the charge that he had "stolen" the election was expected to seriously overshadow his presidency, while the authority of the Supreme Court was also threatened by the perception of its ruling as partisan.

Within a year, however, the atrocity of September 11, 2001 drove such concerns into the background, inflicting a devastating blow to both the nation's economy and its pride. Over three thousand people were killed in the worst terrorist attack in US history, when two hijacked planes were flown into the World Trade Center in New York City, and one into the Pentagon. The attacks were quickly linked to the al-Qaeda network of Saudi Arabian terrorist Osama bin Laden, and within weeks President Bush declared an open-ended "War on Terror".

Confronting a new, changed world, Bush set about re-writing the traditional rule-book of diplomacy and international law. In 2002, he declared that the US has a right to launch pre-emptive attacks: "If we wait for threats to fully materialize, we will have waited too long… We must take the battle to the enemy, disrupt his plans, and confront the worst threats before they emerge."

A US-led invasion of **Afghanistan** in 2001 was followed by a similar incursion into **Iraq** in 2003, ostensibly on the grounds that Iraqi dictator Saddam Hussein was developing "weapons of mass destruction". Although Saddam was deposed, apprehended, and in due course executed, it became universally acknowledged that no such weapons existed. Iraq both degenerated into civil war and became a major recruiting ground for international terrorism, while bin Laden himself remained unfound.

Despite a wave of financial scandals, spearheaded by the collapse of the mighty energy firm Enron, Bush defeated Massachusetts Senator John Kerry in 2004 to win a second term. That election did little to suggest the country had become any less polarized, however, and the Bush administration was lambasted for its appalling failure to respond promptly or adequately when **Hurricane Katrina** and consequent floods devastated New Orleans and the Gulf Coast in 2005.

That the Democrats regained control of both Senate and House in 2006 was due largely to the deteriorating situation in Iraq. Similarly, the meteoric rise of Illinois Senator **Barack Obama** – and his hard-fought victory over Hillary Clinton in the 2008 Democratic primaries – owed much to his being almost unique among national politicians in his consistent opposition to the Iraq war. However, while Obama's message of change and optimism, coupled with his oratorical gifts and embrace of new technologies, especially resonated with young and minority voters, his ultimate triumph over John McCain in the presidential election later that year was triggered by the abrupt impact of a new **recession**. After bankers Lehmann Brothers filed for bankruptcy in September 2008 – the largest bankruptcy in US history – it was clear that no element of the economy was safe from the consequences of reckless "subprime" mortgage lending.

The national exhilaration over Obama's astonishing achievement in becoming the first black US president had long since faded when this book went to press. Despite finally achieving at least some measure of reform of the **healthcare** system, Obama was otherwise seen as having failed to deliver on many crucial campaign pledges. In particular, the military involvement in the Middle East has dragged on to the point that the Afghanistan war is now the longest conflict in US history. However unfairly, the longer the recession continued on his watch, the more Obama was being blamed for failing to nurse the economy back to health – and he was even, despite his championing of environmental causes, being held responsible for failing to prevent, or at least rectify, the calamitous **Gulf oil spill** of May 2010.

Books

It would be futile to attempt to provide a comprehensive overview of American literature in the limited space available. The following bibliography is, therefore, an idiosyncratic selection of books intended as a starting point for interested readers. Books tagged with the symbol are particularly recommended.

Non-fiction

History and society

Dee Brown *Bury My Heart at Wounded Knee*. Approaching forty years on from its first publication, this remains the best narrative of the impact of white settlement and expansion on Native Americans across the continent.

Bill Bryson *Made in America*. A compulsively readable history of the American language, packed with bizarre snippets, which does much to illuminate the history of the nation.

Mike Davis *City of Quartz*. City politics, neighbourhood gangs, unions, film noir and religion are drawn together in this award-winning, leftist, hyperbolic history of Los Angeles.

John Demos *The Unredeemed Captive*. This story of the aftermath of a combined French and Native American attack on Deerfield, Massachusetts, in 1704 illuminates frontier life in the eighteenth century.

W.E.B. DuBois *The Souls of Black Folk*. Seminal collection of largely autobiographical essays examining racial separation at the start of the twentieth century.

Brian Fagan *Ancient North America*. Archeological history of America's native peoples, from the first hunters to cross the Bering Strait up to initial contact with Europeans.

Tim Flannery *The Eternal Frontier*. "Ecological" history of North America that reveals how the continent's physical environment has shaped the destinies of all its inhabitants, from horses to humans.

Shelby Foote *The Civil War: a Narrative*. Epic, three-volume account containing anything you could possibly want to know about the "War Between the States".

John Kenneth Galbraith *The Great Crash 1929*. An elegant and authoritative interpretation of the Wall Street Crash and its implications.

David Halberstam *The Best and the Brightest*. Still-relevant, gut-wrenching examination of how America's finest, most brilliant Ivy Leaguers plunged the nation into the first war it ever lost, disastrously.

Tony Horwitz *Confederates in the Attic: Dispatches from the Unfinished Civil War*. Strange meld of past and present, as journalist Horwitz explores the places in the South where die-hards keep the Civil War very much alive.

Meriwether Lewis and William Clark *The Original Journals of the Lewis and Clark Expedition, 1804–1806*. Eight volumes of meticulous jottings by the Northwest's first inland explorers, scrupulously following President Jefferson's orders to record every detail of flora, fauna and native inhabitant.

Magnus Magnusson and Herman Pálsson (trans) *The Vinland Sagas*. If you imagine stories that the Vikings reached America to be no more than myths, here's the day-to-day minutiae to convince you otherwise.

James M. McPherson *Battle Cry of Freedom*. Extremely readable history of the Civil War, which integrates and explains the complex social, economic, political and military factors in one concise volume.

Clyde A. Milner II, Carol A. O'Connor and Martha A. Sandweiss *The Oxford History of the American West*. Fascinating collection of essays on Western history, covering topics ranging from myths and movies to art and religion.

James Mooney *The Ghost Dance Religion and The Sioux Outbreak of 1890*. An extraordinary Bureau of Ethnology report, first published in 1890 but still available in paperback. Mooney persuaded his Washington superiors to allow him to roam the West in search of first-hand evidence and even interviewed Wovoka, the Ghost Dance prophet, in person.

Edmund Morgan *American Slavery, American Freedom*. Complex and far-reaching historical account of the cunning means by which white working-class conflict was averted by rich Virginia planters through the spread of black slavery.

Roderick Frazier Nash *Wilderness and the American Mind*. Classic study of the American take on environmental and conservation issues over the past couple of hundred years. Especially good sections on John Muir and his battles to preserve Yosemite.

Stephen Plog *Ancient Peoples of the Southwest*. Much the best single-volume history of the pre-Hispanic Southwest, packed with diagrams and colour photographs.

Marc Reisner *Cadillac Desert*. Concise, engaging account of the environmental and political impact on the West of the twentieth-century mania for dam-building and huge irrigation projects.

David Reynolds *Waking Giant: America in the Age of Jackson*. Rousing new portrait of America in the first half of the nineteenth century, from its clumsy attempt to take Canada in the War of 1812 to its successful Mexican land grab three decades later, with the figure of Andrew Jackson providing the touchstone throughout.

Billy Sothern *Down in New Orleans: Reflections from a Drowned City*. Death penalty lawyer/activist Sothern's personal account of Katrina is moving, but it is his uncompromising report of the dirty secrets the floods revealed that truly shock. Yet he miraculously manages to imbue the horror with humanism and hope.

Alan Taylor *American Colonies*. Perhaps the best book on any single era of American history – a superb account of every aspect of the peopling of the continent, from remote antiquity until the Declaration of Independence.

Henry David Thoreau *Walden*. Few modern writers are more relevant than this nineteenth-century stalwart, whose Walden imagined environmentalism 100 years early, and whose *Civil Disobedience* provided the template for modern activism.

Mark Twain *Roughing It*, *Life on the Mississippi*, and many others. Mark Twain was by far the funniest and most vivid chronicler of nineteenth-century America. *Roughing It*, which covers his early wanderings across the continent, all the way to Hawaii, is absolutely compelling.

Geoffrey C. Ward, with Ric and Ken Burns *The Civil War*. Illustrated history of the Civil War, designed to accompany the TV series and using hundreds of the same photographs.

Richard White *It's Your Misfortune And None of My Own*. Dense, authoritative and all-embracing history of the American West, which debunks the notion of the rugged pioneer by stressing the role of the federal government.

Juan Williams *Eyes on the Prize*. Informative and detailed account of the civil rights years from the early 1950s up to 1966, with lots of rare and some very familiar, photos.

Edmund Wilson *Patriotic Gore*. Fascinating eight-hundred-page survey of the literature of the Civil War, which serves in its own right as an immensely readable narrative of the conflict.

Bob Woodward and Carl Bernstein *All the President's Men* and *The Final Days*. Although Woodward continues to crank out Washington exposés, his Nixon-era books still can't be beaten for their portrait of diligent young journalists bringing down a corrupt president, and that president's own unique mania.

Biography and oral history

Muhammad Ali, with Hana Yasmeen Ali *The Soul of a Butterfly: Reflections on Life's Journey*. Thought-provoking and moving autobiography, in the course of which the iconic boxer's third daughter helps him describe his career and embrace of Sufi Islam.

Maya Angelou *I Know Why the Caged Bird Sings*. First of a five-volume autobiography that provides an ultimately uplifting account of how a black girl transcended her traumatic childhood in 1930s Arkansas.

Donald A. Barclay, James H. Maguire and Peter Wild (eds) *Into the Wilderness Dream*. Gripping collection of Western exploration narratives written between 1500 and 1800; thanks to any number of little-known gems, the best of many such anthologies.

Taylor Branch *America in the King Years*. Brilliant three-volume series showing the immense and long-overdue changes that enveloped America in the civil rights struggle of the 1950s and 60s through the lens of Martin Luther King Jr.

William F. Cody *The Life of Hon. William F. Cody, Known as Buffalo Bill*. Larger-than-life autobiography of one of the great characters of the Wild West. Particularly treasurable for the moment when he refers to himself more formally as "Bison William".

Jill Ker Conway (ed) *Written by Herself*. Splendid anthology of women's autobiographies from the mid-1800s to the present, including sections on African-Americans, scientists, artists and pioneers.

Frederick Douglass, et al *The Classic Slave Narratives*. Compilation of ex-slaves' autobiographies, ranging from Olaudah Equíano's kidnapping in Africa and global wanderings, to Frederick Douglass's eloquent denunciation of slavery. Includes Harriet Jacobs' story of her escape from Edenton, North Carolina.

U.S. Grant *Personal Memoirs*. Encouraged by Mark Twain, the Union general and subsequent president wrote his autobiography just before his death, in a (successful) bid to recoup his horrendous debts. At first the book feels oddly downbeat, but the man's down-to-earth modesty grows on you.

Edmund Morris *The Rise of Theodore Roosevelt* and *Theodore Rex*. Thoroughly engaging and superbly researched two-volume biography of Theodore Roosevelt, tracing the energetic and controversial president's astonishing trajectory to the White House and his far-reaching achievements.

Ron Powers *Mark Twain*. Definitive recent biography of America's most compelling literary figure.

Luc Sante *Low Life*. Rip-roaring look at New York vice in the nineteenth century, and how gangsters, prostitutes, machine politicians and saloon thugs all contributed to the colour and character of the city.

Joanna L. Stratton *Pioneer Women*. Original memoirs of women – mothers, teachers, homesteaders and circuit riders – who ventured across the Plains from 1854 to 1890. Lively, superbly detailed accounts, with chapters on journeys, homebuilding, daily domestic life, the church, the cowtown, temperance and suffrage.

Studs Terkel *American Dreams Lost and Found*. Interviews with ordinary American citizens. As illuminating a guide to US life as you could hope for.

Frank Waters *Book of the Hopi*. Extraordinary insight into the traditions and beliefs of the Hopi, prepared through years of interviews and approved by tribal elders.

Malcolm X, with Alex Haley *The Autobiography of Malcolm X*. Searingly honest and moving account of Malcolm's progress from street hoodlum to political leadership. Written over a period of years, it traces the development of Malcolm X's thinking before, during and after his split from the Nation of Islam. The conclusion, when he talks about his impending assassination, is extremely painful.

Gary Younge *Stranger In A Strange Land* and *No Place Like Home*. Black British journalist Gary Younge is one of the most acute observers of contemporary America; his experiences in the self-proclaimed New South, chronicled in *No Place Like Home*, make fascinating reading.

Entertainment and culture

Kenneth Anger *Hollywood Babylon*. A vicious yet high-spirited romp through Tinseltown's greatest scandals, amply illustrated with gory and repulsive photographs, and always inclined to bend the facts for the sake of a good story. A shoddily researched second volume covers more recent times.

Thomas Brothers *Louis Armstrong's New Orleans*. Published in 2006, this is the best of the single volumes on Armstrong, a vivid account not only of the wildly talented trumpeter but also of his contemporaries and their cultural context. A brilliant evocation of the exciting hotbed of creativity that fired early-twentieth-century New Orleans.

Bob Dylan *Chronicles: Volume One*. Far from the kind of endless stream-of-consciousness he wrote in his younger days, Dylan chose in this long-awaited autobiography to focus in almost microscopic detail on three distinct moments in his life, including Greenwich Village in the early 1960s, and New Orleans in the 1980s. The result is a compelling testament to his place at the epicentre of America's cultural life.

Robert Evans *The Kid Stays in the Picture*. Spellbinding insider's view of the machinations of Hollywood after the demise of the studio system, written with verve by one of LA's biggest egos, the head of Paramount at its peak.

Peter Guralnick *Lost Highways*, *Feel Like Going Home* and *Sweet Soul Music*. Thoroughly researched personal histories of black popular music, packed with obsessive detail on all the great names. His twin Elvis biographies, *Last Train to Memphis* and *Careless Love*, trace the rise and fall of the iconic star in an unsensational but nonetheless gripping manner, while also managing to evaluate him seriously as a musician.

Gerri Hershey *Nowhere to Run: the History of Soul Music*. Definitive rundown on the evolution of soul music from the gospel heyday of the 1940s through the Memphis, Motown, and Philly scenes to the sounds of the early 1980s. Strong on social commentary and political background and studded with anecdotes and interviews.

Michael Ondaatje *Coming through Slaughter*. Extraordinary, dream-like fictionalization of the life of doomed New Orleans cornet player Buddy Bolden, written in a lyrical style that evokes the rhythms and pace of jazz improvisation.

Robert Palmer *Deep Blues*. Readable history of the development and personalities of the Delta Blues.

Geoffrey C. Ward, Ken Burns, et al *Jazz: a History of America's Music*. While the story peters out somewhat after bebop, this highly readable volume (linked to the TV series) boasts hundreds of illustrations and rare photographs, first-hand accounts and lively essays to provide a beautifully drawn picture of America's home-grown music and its icons.

Travel writing

Edward Abbey *The Journey Home*. Hilarious accounts of whitewater rafting and desert hiking trips alternate with essays by the man who inspired the radical environmentalist movement Earth First! All of Abbey's books, especially *Desert Solitaire*, a journal of time spent as a ranger in Arches National Park, make great travelling companions.

James Agee and Walker Evans *Let Us Now Praise Famous Men*. A deeply personal but also richly evocative journal of travels through the rural lands of the Depression-era Deep South, complemented by Evans' powerful photographs.

Bill Bryson *The Lost Continent*. Using his boyhood home of Des Moines in Iowa as a benchmark, the author travels the length and breadth of America to find the perfect small town. Hilarious, if occasionally a bit smug.

Alistair Cooke *Alistair Cooke's America*. The author's thorough, eloquent overview of American life and customs touches on the complexity of its culture and politics. Also worth a look are any of Cooke's other volumes on the American experience.

J. Hector St-John de Crèvecoeur *Letters from an American Farmer and Sketches of Eighteenth-Century America*. A remarkable account of the complexities of Revolutionary America, first published in 1782.

Charles Dickens *American Notes*. Amusing satirical commentary about the US from a jaded British perspective that's still lighter in tone than the author's later, more scabrous *Martin Chuzzlewit*.

Robert Frank *The Americans*. The Swiss photographer's brilliantly evocative portrait of mid-century American life from coast to coast, with striking images contextualized by an introductory essay from Jack Kerouac.

Ian Frazier *Great Plains*. An immaculately researched and well-written travelogue containing a wealth of information on the people of the American prairielands from Native Americans to the soldiers who staff the region's nuclear installations.

William Least Heat-Moon *Blue Highways*. Account of a mammoth loop tour of the US by backroads, in which the author interviews ordinary people in ordinary places. A good overview of rural America, with lots of interesting details on Native Americans.

Jack Kerouac *On the Road*. Definitive account of transcontinental Beatnik wanderings, which now reads as a curiously dated period piece. Not as incoherent as you might expect.

James A. MacMahon (ed) *Audubon Society Nature Guides*. Attractively produced, fully illustrated and easy-to-use guides to the flora and fauna of seven different US regional ecosystems, covering the entire country from coast to coast and from grasslands to glaciers.

Virginia and Lee McAlester *A Field Guide to American Houses*. Well-illustrated and engaging guide to America's rich variety of domestic architecture, from pre-colonial to postmodern.

John McPhee *Encounters with the Arch Druid*. In three interlinked narratives, the late environmental activist and Friends of the Earth founder David Brower confronts developers, miners and dam-builders, while trying to protect three different American wilderness areas – the Atlantic shoreline, the Grand Canyon and the Cascades of the Pacific Northwest.

Jonathan Raban *Old Glory*. A somewhat pompous though always interesting account of Raban's journey on a small craft down the Mississippi River from the head-waters in Minnesota to the bayous of Louisiana.

Bernard A. Weisberger (ed) *The WPA Guide to America*. Prepared during the New Deal as part of a make-work programme for writers, these guides paint a fairly comprehensive portrait of 1930s and earlier America.

Edmund White *States of Desire: Travels in Gay America*. A revealing account of life in gay communities across the country, focusing heavily on San Francisco and New York.

Fiction

General Americana

Raymond Carver *Will You Please Be Quiet Please?* Stories of the American working class, written in a distinctive, sparse style that perhaps owes something to Hemingway and certainly influenced untold numbers of contemporary American writers. The stories served as the basis for Robert Altman's film *Short Cuts*.

Don DeLillo *White Noise*; *Underworld*. The former is his best, a funny and penetrating pop culture exploration, while the latter is one of those typically flawed attempts to pack the twentieth-century American experience into a great big novel. Worthwhile, though.

William Kennedy *Ironweed*. Terse, affecting tale of a couple of down-on-their-luck drunks haunted by ghosts from a chequered past; excellent evocation of 1930s America, specifically working-class Albany, New York.

Herman Melville *Moby-Dick*. Compendious and compelling account of nineteenth-century whaling, packed with details on American life from New England to the Pacific.

John Dos Passos *USA*. Hugely ambitious novel (originally a trilogy) that grapples with the US in the early decades of the twentieth century from every possible angle. Gripping human stories with a strong political and historical point of view.

E. Annie Proulx *Accordion Crimes*. Proulx's masterly book comes as close to being the fabled "Great American Novel" as anyone could reasonably ask, tracing a fascinating history of immigrants in all parts of North America through the fortunes of a battered old Sicilian accordion.

New York City

Paul Auster *New York Trilogy*. Three Borgesian investigations into the mystery and madness of contemporary New York. Using the conventions of the detective novel, Auster unfolds a disturbed and disturbing picture of the city.

Truman Capote *Breakfast at Tiffany's* and *In Cold Blood*. The first story is about a fictional social climber in New York called Holly Golightly; the second concerns the true-life stories of two serial killers in the heartland. The subject matter of these two uniquely American stories could hardly be more different, but they display an equally high degree of insight.

Michael Chabon *The Amazing Adventures of Kavalier & Clay*. Pulitzer Prize-winning novel charting the rise and fall of comic-book-writing cousins in New York City – one a refugee from World War II Prague, the other a closeted Brooklynite.

Chester Himes *Cotton Comes to Harlem*, *Blind Man with a Pistol* and many others. Action-packed and uproariously violent novels set in New York's Harlem, starring the much-feared detectives Coffin Ed Johnson and Grave Digger Jones.

Grace Paley *Collected Stories*. Shrewd love-hate stories written over a lifetime by the daughter of Russian-Jewish immigrants, who published dead-on accounts of New York life in three instalments, which came out in the 1950s, the early 1970s and the late 1980s respectively.

J.D. Salinger *The Catcher in the Rye*. Classic novel of adolescence, tracing Holden Caulfield's sardonic journey through the streets of New York.

New England

Emily Dickinson *The Cambridge Companion*. Rightfully considered one of the pre-eminent poets of her age, though it took many decades for her innovative work, touching on dark emotional themes, to be recognized. This anthology is a good place to start.

Nathaniel Hawthorne *The House of the Seven Gables*. This quintessential US novelist's entire oeuvre is worth pursuing, especially this gloomy Gothic tale of Puritan misdeeds coming back to haunt the denizens of a cursed mansion.

John Irving *The Cider House Rules*. One of Irving's more successful sprawling novels, weaving themes of love, suffering and the many facets of the abortion debate against a Maine backdrop.

H.P. Lovecraft *The Best of H.P. Lovecraft: Bloodcurdling Tales of Horror and the Macabre*. Creepy New England stories from the author Stephen King called "the twentieth century's greatest practitioner of the classic horror tale".

The South

William Faulkner *The Reivers*. The last and most humourous work of this celebrated Southern author. *The Sound and the Fury*, a fascinating study of prejudice, set like most of his books in the fictional Yoknatapawpha County in Mississippi, is a much more difficult read.

Zora Neale Hurston *Spunk*. Short stories celebrating black culture and experience from around the country, by a writer from Florida who became one of the bright stars of the Harlem cultural renaissance in the 1920s.

Harper Lee *To Kill a Mockingbird*. Classic tale of racial conflict and society's view of an outsider, Boo Radley, as seen through the eyes of children.

Cormac McCarthy *Suttree*. McCarthy is better known for his "modern Western" works like *Blood Meridian* and *All the Pretty Horses*, but this beautifully written tale, of a Knoxville, Tennessee, scion opting for a hard-scrabble life among a band of vagrants on the Tennessee River, is his best.

Carson McCullers *The Heart is a Lonely Hunter*. McCullers is unrivalled in her sensitive treatment of misfits, in this case the attitude of a small Southern community to a deaf-mute.

Margaret Mitchell *Gone With the Wind*. Worth a read even if you know the lines of Scarlett and Rhett by heart.

Toni Morrison *Beloved*. Exquisitely written ghost story by the Nobel Prize-winning novelist, which recounts the painful lives of a group of freed slaves after Reconstruction, and the obsession a mother develops after murdering her baby daughter to spare her a life of slavery.

Flannery O'Connor *A Good Man is Hard to Find*. Short stories, featuring strong, obsessed characters, that explore religious tensions and racial conflicts in the Deep South.

Alice Walker *In Love and Trouble*. Moving and powerful stories of black women in the South, from the author of the much-acclaimed *The Color Purple*.

Eudora Welty *The Ponder Heart*. Quirky, humorous evocation of life in a backwater Mississippi town. Her most critically acclaimed work, *The Optimist's Daughter*, explores the tensions between a judge's daughter and her stepmother.

Louisiana

James Lee Burke *The Tin Roof Blowdown*. Louisiana resident Burke's 27th crime novel, written in the immediate aftermath of Katrina, is a bleak, angry and miserable vision of the flood-ravaged and lawless city of New Orleans. Not always an easy read, it ripples with the author's personal pain.

George Washington Cable *The Grandissimes*. Romantic saga of Creole family feuds, written c.1900 but set during the Louisiana Purchase. Superb evocation of steamy Louisiana elite, the Creole lifestyle and the resistance of New Orleans to its Americanization. Apparently shocking at the time for its sympathetic portrayal of blacks.

Kate Chopin *The Awakening*. Subversive story of a bourgeois married woman whose fight for independence ends in tragedy. The swampy Louisiana of a century ago is portrayed as both a sensual hotbed for her sexual awakening and as her eventual nemesis.

Valerie Martin *Property*. A bleak but wonderfully written tale of the brutalizing effects, on both mistress and slave, of slavery on a Louisiana sugar plantation.

Anne Rice *Feast Of All Saints*. Rice's vampire novels are great fun, but her finest portrait of nineteenth-century New Orleans comes in this sensitive examination of race, sexuality and gender issues in the antebellum period.

John Kennedy Toole *A Confederacy of Dunces*. Anarchic black tragicomedy in which the pompous and repulsive anti-hero Ignatius J. Reilly wreaks havoc through an insalubrious and surreal New Orleans.

Robert Penn Warren *All The King's Men*. This fascinating fictionalized saga of Louisiana's legendary "Kingfish", Huey Long, is a truly great American novel.

The Great Lakes and the Great Plains

Willa Cather *My Ántonia*. Stunning book set in Nebraska that provides a great sense of the pioneer hardships on the Plains.

Louise Erdrich *The Beet Queen*. Offbeat tale of passion and obsession among poor white North Dakota folk – particularly women – against the backdrop of an economy and culture changing with the introduction of sugar beet as a crop in the 1940s.

Garrison Keillor *Lake Wobegon Days*. Wry, witty tales about a mythical Minnesota small town, poking gentle fun at the rural Midwest.

Mari Sandoz *Old Jules*. Written in 1935, this fictionalized biography gives a wonderful insight into the life of the author's pioneer Swiss father on the Nebraskan plains.

Upton Sinclair *The Jungle*. Documenting the horrific unsanitary conditions in Chicago's meat-packing industry, Sinclair's compelling Socialist-tract-cum-novel, first serialized in 1905, ranks among the most influential books in US history.

Richard Wright *Native Son*. The harrowing story of Bigger Thomas, a black chauffeur who accidentally kills his employer's daughter. The story develops his relationship with his lawyer, the closest he has ever come to being on an equal footing with a white.

The Rockies and the Southwest

A.B. Guthrie Jr *Big Sky*. When first published in the Thirties it shattered the image of the mythical West peddled by Hollywood. Realistic historical fiction at its very best, following desperate mountain man and fugitive Boone Caudill, whose idyllic life in Montana was ended by the arrival of white settlers.

Tony Hillerman *The Dark Wind*, and many others. The adventures of Jim Chee of the Navajo Tribal Police on the reservations of northern Arizona, forever dabbling in dark and mysterious forces churned up from the Ancestral Puebloan past.

Barbara Kingsolver *Pigs in Heaven*. A magnificent evocation of tensions and realities in the contemporary Southwest, by a Tucson-based writer who ranks among America's finest stylists.

Norman MacLean *A River Runs Through It*. Unputdownable – the best ever novel about fly-fishing, set in beautiful Montana lake country.

California and the West

Raymond Chandler *The Big Sleep* and *Farewell My Lovely*. The original incarnations of archetypal tough guy and iconic private eye Philip Marlowe are far more complex and beautifully written than the related movies lead you to expect. Pulp fiction at its finest – written by an American raised in London.

David Guterson *Snow Falling on Cedars* and *East Of the Mountains*. Two gripping novels that capture the flavour of the Pacific Northwest; the first is an atmospheric mystery centring on postwar interracial tensions, the second features a dying man looking back on his life.

Jack London *The Call of the Wild and Other Stories*. London's classic tale, of a family pet discovering the ways of the wilderness while forced to pull sleds across Alaska's Gold Rush trails, still makes essential reading before a trip to the far north.

Armistead Maupin *Tales of the City*. Long-running saga comprising sympathetic and entertaining tales of life in San Francisco, that also work surprisingly well as suspenseful stand-alone novels. That many of its key characters are gay meant that over the years the series became a chronicle of the impact of AIDS on the city.

Thomas Pynchon *The Crying of Lot 49*. Shorter, funnier and more accessible than *Gravity's Rainbow*, this novel of techno-freaks and potheads in Sixties California reveals, among other things, the sexy side of stamp collecting.

John Steinbeck *The Grapes of Wrath*. The classic account of a migrant family forsaking the Midwest for the Promised Land. Steinbeck's light-hearted but crisply observed novella *Cannery Row* captures daily life on the prewar Monterey waterfront. The epic *East of Eden* updates and resets the Bible in the Salinas Valley and details three generations of familial feuding.

Nathanael West *The Day of the Locust*. West wrote dark novels wholly vested in the American experience; this one, set in LA, is an apocalyptic story of fringe characters at the edge of the film industry.

Film

The list below focuses on key films in certain genres that have helped define the American experience – both the light and the dark. Films tagged with the symbol are particularly recommended.

Music/musicals

Calamity Jane (David Butler, 1953). The Western gets a rumbustious musical twist with tomboy Doris Day bringing thigh-slapping gusto to the title role and Howard Keel as the rugged hero who (almost) tames her.

Gimme Shelter (Albert and David Maysles, 1969). Excellent documentary about the ill-fated Rolling Stones concert at Altamont. Its searing look at homegrown American violence and Vietnam-era chaos at the end of the 1960s also includes an on-camera stabbing.

The Girl Can't Help It (Frank Tashlin, 1956). Pneumatic, pouting Jayne Mansfield defined the blonde bombshell for the Atomic generation. And Tashlin, who spent years as a madcap Looney Tunes animator, knew just how best to display her cartoonish, candy-sweet charms. The rock'n'roll plot delivers some fab musical moments, too, with numbers from Eddie Cochran, Little Richard and the wonderful Julie London.

Gold Diggers of 1933 (Mervyn LeRoy/Busby Berkeley, 1933). In which genius choreographer Berkeley pioneered his trademark overhead-crane shots of flamboyantly trompe l'oeil dance numbers featuring lines of glamorous chorines. See also *42nd Street* and *Footlight Parade*.

Meet Me in St Louis (Vincente Minnelli, 1944). Most famous for its Judy Garland number "The Trolley Song", this charming piece of nostalgia celebrates turn-of-the-century America through the ups and downs of a St Louis family during the 1903 World's Fair.

Singin' in the Rain (Stanley Donen/Gene Kelly, 1952). Beloved musical comedy about Hollywood at the dawn of the sound era, featuring memorable tunes like "Make 'Em Laugh" and the title song, along with energetic performances by star Kelly, sidekick Donald O'Connor and a pixieish Debbie Reynolds.

Viva Las Vegas (George Sidney, 1964). One of Elvis's finer musicals, partly due to the effervescent presence of Ann-Margret – of all the King's co-stars only she could match him for sheer animal sexuality. The two were having an affair during the shoot, and the chemistry drips from the screen.

Woodstock (Michael Wadleigh, 1969). *Gimme Shelter*'s upbeat counterpart, documenting the musical pinnacle of the hippie era, showing half a million flower children peacefully grooving to Jimi Hendrix, The Who and Sly and the Family Stone while getting stoned, muddy and wild on an upstate New York farm.

Silent era

Birth of a Nation (D.W. Griffith, 1915). Possibly the most influential film in American history, both for its pioneering film technique (close-ups, cross-cutting and so on) and appalling racist propaganda, which led to a revival of the KKK.

The General (Buster Keaton, 1926). A fine introduction to Keaton's acrobatic brand of slapstick and his inventive cinematic approach, in which the Great Stone Face chases down a stolen locomotive during the Civil War.

The Gold Rush (Charlie Chaplin, 1925). Chaplin's finest film: the Little Tramp gets trapped in a cabin during an Alaska blizzard in an affecting story that mixes sentiment and high comedy in near-perfect balance.

Greed (Erich von Stroheim, 1923). An audacious scene-by-scene adaptation of Frank Norris's novel *McTeague*, a tragic tale of love and revenge in San Francisco at the end of the nineteenth century. Slashed from ten to two and a half hours by MGM, the film remains a cinematic triumph for its striking compositions, epic drama and truly bleak ending.

Sunrise (F.W. Murnau, 1927). Among the most beautiful Hollywood productions of any era. *Sunrise*'s German émigré director employed striking lighting effects, complex travelling shots and emotionally compelling performances in a tale of a country boy led astray by a big-city vamp.

Westerns

McCabe and Mrs Miller (Robert Altman, 1971). Entrepreneur Warren Beatty brings prostitution to a Washington town and tries to reinvent himself as a gunslinger in this now-classic anti-Western.

Once Upon a Time in the West (Sergio Leone, 1968). The quintessential spaghetti Western, actually filmed in Spain by an Italian director, steeped in mythic American themes of Manifest Destiny and rugged individualism.

Red River (Howard Hawks, 1948). Upstart Montgomery Clift battles beef-baron John Wayne on a momentous cattle drive through the Midwest. Prototypical Hawks tale of clashing tough-guy egos and no-nonsense professionals on the range.

The Searchers (John Ford, 1956). Perhaps the most iconic of Ford's many Westerns; a highly influential production with vivid cinematography and epic scale, in which John Wayne relentlessly hunts down the Native American chief who massacred his friends and family.

The Wild Bunch (Sam Peckinpah, 1969). A movie that says as much about the chaotic end of the 1960s as it does about the West, featuring a band of killers who hunt for women and treasure and wind up in a bloodbath unprecedented in film history.

Americana

Breakfast at Tiffany's (Blake Edwards, 1961). Manhattan never looked more chic, and Audrey Hepburn, dressed in Givenchy, gives a quintessentially stylish performance as vulnerable kept woman Holly Golightly. The theme tune, too, "Moon River", penned by Henry Mancini, shines. Based on a racy novella by Truman Capote (see p.1080), who originally wanted Marilyn Monroe to play Golightly.

Citizen Kane (Orson Welles, 1941). Often called the greatest American movie ever, and one that subverts the rags-to-riches American Dream: a poor country boy finds nothing but misery when he inherits a fortune.

The Color Purple (Steven Spielberg, 1985). Spielberg translates Alice Walker's Pulitzer Prize-winning epistolary novel about an African-American woman's triumph over adversity in the segregated south into a huge, visually rich experience. Splendid performances and a delicious dose of shameless heart-tugging.

E.T. The Extra-Terrestrial (Steven Spielberg, 1982). Reagan-era block-buster and sentimental variation on 1950s monster flicks, imbued with the director's ongoing interest in absentee fathers, suburban fantasies and other-worldly saviours. A fine example of American cinema's never-ending quest for lost innocence.

Gone with the Wind (Victor Fleming, 1939). Possibly the most popular movie of all time, this lush, affecting and elegiac look at the Old South provides three hours of expertly wrought historical melodrama. Vivien Leigh dazzles as rebellious Southern belle Scarlett O'Hara, while Hattie McDaniel, as her mammy, won the first Oscar ever to be awarded to an African-American.

Mr. Smith Goes to Washington (Frank Capra, 1939). Tub-thumping populist film that still resonates for its rosy belief in the goodness of the common man, dark view of political elites and earnest hope for America's future. Though less familiar, the director's *Meet John Doe* offers a grimmer variation on the tale, while the enduring tearjerker *It's A Wonderful Life* provides a Christmas take on the same themes.

North by Northwest (Alfred Hitchcock, 1959). Not only an exciting chase film, in which international criminal James Mason hunts down ad-man Cary Grant, but also a fun travelogue that starts on New York's Madison Avenue and ends on the cliff-face of Mount Rushmore in South Dakota.

Prairie Home Companion (Robert Altman, 2006). It's fitting that Altman, no stranger to nostalgia, came up with this impeccable movie as his swansong: a musical about the (fictional) final broadcast of the (real-life) down-home radio show from author Garrison Keillor. Altman's typically star-studded ensemble cast, and a smart screenplay from Keillor – who plays himself – create a wry, melancholy and beautiful tribute to lost dreams.

Rebel Without a Cause (Nicholas Ray, 1955). The apotheosis of adolescent angst, with James Dean lamenting the hypocrisies of family life and engaging in all manner of fisticuffs, deadly drag races and night-time battles with the cops.

There Will Be Blood (Paul Thomas Anderson, 2007). This unsettling epic saga of America's turn-of-the-century oil boom differs from Upton Sinclair's novel, *Oil!* in unexpected ways to become dominated by its lead, Daniel Day-Lewis. His magisterial performance as the monstrous prospector Daniel Plainview raises many disturbing questions about the American Dream.

The Way We Were (Sidney Pollack, 1973). The kind of Hollywood movie they don't make any more – a political film made by political people about a political time. Barbra Streisand is superb as the fiery left-wing intellectual who falls hard for Robert Redford's blonde WASP in the 1930s; the desperately romantic film then follows their relationship against decades of huge social and cultural change.

The Wizard of Oz (Victor Fleming, 1939). A cinematic institution and Technicolor extravaganza that shows Hollywood at its zenith, romanticizing small-town life in the Midwest and offering eye-popping fantasies of good and evil witches, scary flying monkeys and a wide-eyed Judy Garland sporting ruby slippers on a yellow-brick road.

Road movies

Badlands (Terrence Malick, 1973). Midwest loner-loser Martin Sheen and girlfriend Sissy Spacek take a spellbinding tour of the heartland while on a random murder spree. A dark view of life on the road as a synonym for existential futility.

Easy Rider (Dennis Hopper, 1969). Hippies Peter Fonda and director Hopper take to the road while riding a groovy set of wheels, pick up nerdy Jack Nicholson on the way, have a bad trip in a New Orleans cemetery and meet a futile fate. Melancholy and yearning, it's a haunting piece of cinema, with something real to say about American disillusionment and despair.

Thelma and Louise (Ridley Scott, 1991). The road movie as feminist manifesto, in which two friends (Susan Sarandon and Geena Davis) wind up on the run after one of them kills a would-be rapist. At last it's the girls who get to tote the guns and swig the whisky – and director Scott provides plenty of stunning images of the American Southwest.

Film noir and gangster films

Bonnie and Clyde (Arthur Penn, 1967). Warren Beatty and Faye Dunaway play Depression-era gangsters in a film that did much to destroy Hollywood's censorship code by ushering in an era of open sexuality and unmitigated blood and violence.

Chinatown (Roman Polanski, 1974). Film noir seventies-style, with Jack Nicholson as Jake Gittes, a morally aloof private eye whose dogged investigations reveal municipal corruption, racism and incest in LA.

Double Indemnity (Billy Wilder, 1944). In many ways the quintessential film noir: insurance salesman Fred MacMurray is corrupted by femme fatale Barbara Stanwyck, with stylishly dark photography and a memorably fatalistic ending.

The Godfather (Francis Ford Coppola, 1972). The film that revived the gangster genre for modern times, avoiding the cartoonish mobsters and no-nonsense G-men of its predecessors and focusing instead on the family hierarchy of organized crime and its deep connections to all levels of American society. *The Godfather II* is if anything, an even better movie, tracing both the genesis of the Corleone family and moving towards its inevitable decline.

Klute (Alan J Pakula, 1971). A feminist film noir, which marked the transformation of Jane Fonda from sex kitten into radical firebrand. She offers a nuanced portrayal of a fiercely independent New York hooker who refuses to be rescued by Donald Sutherland's PI.

Mildred Pierce (Michael Curtiz, 1945). Half film noir, half mother-daughter melodrama, with a barnstorming performance from arch diva Joan Crawford in the title role. Both femme fatale and long-suffering heroine, she's as ambiguous as any character you'll find in the noir canon.

Independent and cult movies

Be Kind Rewind (Michel Gondry, 2008). With his back catalogue of pop music, MTV videos and Levi's commercials, Gondry is sometimes accused of pretension, but despite its quirks this hilarious film, about a

On location

Although many memorable sights are off-limits to the public or exist only on the backlot tours of movie-studio theme parks, there are still countless film-making locations that widely advertise their Tinseltown appearances or make quiet efforts to accommodate visitors. This list provides an overview of notable films; you could conceivably make an entire vacation out of travelling from spot to spot.

2001: A Space Odyssey (Stanley Kubrick, 1968). Monument Valley, Arizona, p.800.

Back to the Future (Robert Zemeckis, 1985). Gamble House, Pasadena, p.868.

Badlands (Terrence Malick, 1973). Badlands National Park, South Dakota, p.668.

Being There (Hal Ashby, 1979). Biltmore Estate, Asheville, North Carolina, p.416.

The Birds (Alfred Hitchcock, 1963). Bodega Bay, California, p.940.

Blade Runner (Ridley Scott, 1982). Los Angeles: Union Station, Bradbury Building, p.851.

The Bridges of Madison County (Clint Eastwood, 1995). Winterset, Iowa. p.663

Chinatown (Roman Polanski, 1974). Los Angeles: Santa Catalina Island, p.866, *Biltmore Hotel*.

Citizen Kane (Orson Welles, 1941). Hearst Castle, California, p.896 – inspiration for film's "Xanadu".

Close Encounters of the Third Kind (Steven Spielberg, 1978). Devils Tower, Wyoming, p.715.

Easy Rider (Dennis Hopper, 1969). New Orleans p.555; Sunset Crater, Arizona, p.788.

Five Easy Pieces (Bob Rafelson, 1970). San Juan Islands, Washington, p.964.

Galaxy Quest (Dean Parisot, 1999). Goblin Valley, Utah, p.811.

Grapes of Wrath (John Ford, 1940). Petrified Forest, Arizona, p.786.

Greed (Erich von Stroheim, 1923). Death Valley, California, p.881.

High Plains Drifter (Clint Eastwood, 1972). Mono Lake, California, p.884.

Intolerance (D.W. Griffith, 1916). "Babylon" set, Hollywood, California, p.859.

Jaws (Steven Spielberg, 1975). Martha's Vineyard, Massachusetts, p.194.

Little Big Man (Arthur Penn, 1970). Custer State Park, South Dakota, p.673.

Manhattan (Woody Allen, 1978). Central Park, p.89, Brooklyn Bridge, p.77.

Midnight in the Garden of Good and Evil (Clint Eastwood, 1998). Savannah, Georgia, p.436.

Mr. Smith Goes to Washington (Frank Capra, 1939). Lincoln Memorial, p.340.

Mystery Train (Jim Jarmusch, 1989). *Arcade*, Memphis, Tennessee, p.459.

Nashville (Robert Altman, 1975). Parthenon, p.464, Grand Ole Opry, p.463.

group of misfits who accidentally wipe all the videos in their store and have to remake them – is a yearning hymn to cinephilia, community and popular memory.

Blue Velvet (David Lynch, 1986). A young man (Kyle Maclachlan) peers under the cheery facade of apple-pie America and finds a sinister netherworld of tortured lounge singers, vicious sex games and nitrous-inhaling perverts.

Bowling for Columbine (Michael Moore, 2002). Maverick director Moore bagged an Oscar for this eye-opening documentary into US gun culture.

Fargo (Joel Coen, 1996). Set amid the snowy landscapes of northern Minnesota and North Dakota, a quirky tale of a scheming car salesman whose plan to kidnap his own wife and keep the ransom money goes terribly wrong. See also *Raising Arizona*, *O Brother, Where Art Thou* and

North by Northwest (Alfred Hitchcock, 1959). United Nations, New York City, p.87; Mount Rushmore, South Dakota, p.633.

On the Town (Stanley Donen/Gene Kelly, 1949). American Museum of Natural History, New York City, p.92.

Paper Moon (Peter Bogdanovich, 1973). St Joseph, Missouri, p.645.

The Parallax View (Alan J. Pakula, 1974). Space Needle, Seattle, p.955.

Planet of the Apes (Franklin J. Schaffner, 1968). Page, Arizona: p.818, Lake Powell, Utah, p.817.

Poseidon Adventure (Ronald Neame, 1972). *Queen Mary*, Long Beach, California p.867.

Rebel Without a Cause (Nicholas Ray, 1955). Griffith Observatory, Los Angeles, California p.861.

Return of the Jedi (Richard Marquand, 1983). Redwood National Park, California, p.942.

Rocky (John G. Avildsen, 1976). Philadelphia Museum of Art, Pennsylvania p.151.

The Searchers (John Ford, 1956). Monument Valley, Arizona, p.800.

Shane (George Stevens, 1953). Wyoming: Grand Teton National Park, p.724, Jackson Hole, p.727.

The Shining (Stanley Kubrick, 1980). *Timberline Lodge*, Oregon, p.984.

Singin' in the Rain (Stanley Donen/Gene Kelly, 1952). Chinese Theatre, Hollywood, p.859.

Some Like It Hot (Billy Wilder, 1959). *Coronado Hotel*, San Diego, p.844.

The Sting (George Roy Hill, 1973). Santa Monica Pier, California, p.865.

A Streetcar Named Desire (Elia Kazan, 1951). New Orleans, Louisiana, p.555.

Sunset Boulevard (Billy Wilder, 1950). Hollywood: Paramount Studios, p.859, Sunset Boulevard, p.863.

Thelma and Louise (Ridley Scott, 1991). Arches National Park, Utah, p.813.

The Thing (Christian Nyby/Howard Hawks, 1951). Glacier National Park, Montana, p.740.

Touch of Evil (Orson Welles, 1958). Venice, California, p.865.

Twin Peaks (David Lynch/ABC-TV, 1990–1991). Snoqualmie Falls/*Salish Lodge*, Washington, p.971.

Vertigo (Alfred Hitchcock, 1958). San Francisco: Golden Gate Bridge, p.916, *Fairmont Hotel*, Nob Hill, p.907.

Witness (Peter Weir, 1985). Lancaster County, Pennsylvania, p.141.

Zabriskie Point (Michelangelo Antonioni, 1969). Death Valley, California, p.881.

A Serious Man for more strange and twisted Coen brother visions.

Mystery Train (Jim Jarmusch, 1989). Shock-haired indie darling Jarmusch offers a deeply atmospheric and typically skewed portrayal of the crumbling, melancholic music city of Memphis, with four stories revolving around different guests in a Gothic motel. Includes cameos from musical icons Rufus Thomas, Screamin Jay Hawkins and Tom Waits.

Pulp Fiction (Quentin Tarantino, 1994). A touchstone for American independent cinema, composed of three interlocking vignettes and directed with stylish verve and audacity.

Slacker (Richard Linklater, 1990). Emblematic of Generation X ennui in the 1990s, this indie great also manages to highlight 96 characters with episodic monologues over the course of 24 hours in Austin, Texas.

Memorable alone for its collection of paranoid conspiracy rants.

Taxi Driver (Martin Scorsese, 1976). Robert De Niro does a memorable turn as Travis Bickle, a psychotic loner and would-be assassin whose infatuation with a teen prostitute (Jodie Foster) inspired a real-life assassination attempt on Ronald Reagan five years later.

When the Levees Broke (Spike Lee, 2006). No one does righteous anger like Spike Lee, and this powerful documentary – the full four hours of it – was the first to ram the point home that the catastrophe that hit New Orleans in 2005 was not a natural disaster, but a man-made, entirely preventable event. Telling the story via news footage, interviews, home movies and punditry, and with a haunting jazz soundtrack, this is an intense and brave work of art.

Small print and

Index

A Rough Guide to Rough Guides

Published in 1982, the first Rough Guide – to Greece – was a student scheme that became a publishing phenomenon. Mark Ellingham, a recent graduate in English from Bristol University, had been travelling in Greece the previous summer and couldn't find the right guidebook. With a small group of friends he wrote his own guide, combining a highly contemporary, journalistic style with a thoroughly practical approach to travellers' needs.

The immediate success of the book spawned a series that rapidly covered dozens of destinations. And, in addition to impecunious backpackers, Rough Guides soon acquired a much broader and older readership that relished the guides' wit and inquisitiveness as much as their enthusiastic, critical approach and value-for-money ethos.

These days, Rough Guides include recommendations from shoestring to luxury and cover more than 200 destinations around the globe, including almost every country in the Americas and Europe, more than half of Africa and most of Asia and Australasia. Our ever-growing team of authors and photographers is spread all over the world, particularly in Europe, the US and Australia.

In the early 1990s, Rough Guides branched out of travel, with the publication of Rough Guides to World Music, Classical Music and the Internet. All three have become benchmark titles in their fields, spearheading the publication of a wide range of books under the Rough Guide name.

Including the travel series, Rough Guides now number more than 350 titles, covering: phrasebooks, waterproof maps, music guides from Opera to Heavy Metal, reference works as diverse as Conspiracy Theories and Shakespeare, and popular culture books from iPods to Poker. Rough Guides also produce a series of more than 120 World Music CDs in partnership with World Music Network.

Visit www.roughguides.com to see our latest publications.

Rough Guide credits

Text editor: Alison Roberts
Additional editor: Christina Valhouli
Layout: Sachin Gupta
Cartography: Animesh Pathak
Picture editor: Chloë Roberts
Production: Erika Pepe
Proofreader: Karen Parker
Cover design: Nicole Newman, Dan May, Jess Carter
Photographers: Dan Bannister, Curtis Hamilton, Nelson Hancock, Angus Oborn, Anthony Pidgeon, Greg Roden, Susannah Sayler, Greg Ward, Paul Whitfield
Editorial: **London** Andy Turner, Keith Drew, Edward Aves, Alice Park, Lucy White, Jo Kirby, James Smart, Natasha Foges, Róisín Cameron, James Rice, Emma Beatson, Emma Gibbs, Kathryn Lane, Monica Woods, Mani Ramaswamy, Harry Wilson, Lucy Cowie, Lara Kavanagh, Eleanor Aldridge, Ian Blenkinsop, Joe Staines, Matthew Milton, Tracy Hopkins; **Delhi** Madhavi Singh, Jalpreen Kaur Chhatwal, Jubbi Francis
Design & Pictures: **London** Scott Stickland, Dan May, Diana Jarvis, Mark Thomas, Nicole Newman, Sarah Cummins, Emily Taylor; **Delhi** Umesh Aggarwal, Ajay Verma, Jessica Subramanian, Ankur Guha, Pradeep Thapliyal, Sachin Tanwar, Anita Singh, Nikhil Agarwal
Production: Rebecca Short, Liz Cherry, Louise Daly
Cartography: **London** Ed Wright, Katie Lloyd-Jones; **Delhi** Rajesh Chhibber, Ashutosh Bharti, Rajesh Mishra, Jasbir Sandhu, Swati Handoo, Deshpal Dabas, Lokamata Sahu
Marketing, Publicity & roughguides.com: Liz Statham
Digital Travel Publisher: Peter Buckley
Reference Director: Andrew Lockett
Operations Assistant: Becky Doyle
Operations Manager: Helen Atkinson
Publishing Director (Travel): Clare Currie
Commercial Manager: Gino Magnotta
Managing Director: John Duhigg

Publishing information

This tenth edition published March 2011 by

Rough Guides Ltd,
80 Strand, London WC2R 0RL
11, Community Centre, Panchsheel Park,
New Delhi 110017, India

Distributed by the Penguin Group

Penguin Books Ltd,
80 Strand, London WC2R 0RL

Penguin Group (USA)
375 Hudson Street, NY 10014, USA

Penguin Group (Australia)
250 Camberwell Road, Camberwell,
Victoria 3124, Australia

Penguin Group (NZ)
67 Apollo Drive, Mairangi Bay, Auckland 1310,
New Zealand

Rough Guides is represented in Canada by Tourmaline Editions Inc. 662 King Street West, Suite 304, Toronto, Ontario M5V 1M7

Cover concept by Peter Dyer.
Typeset in Bembo and Helvetica to an original design by Henry Iles.

Printed in Malaysia by Vivar Printing Sdn. Bhd.

1112pp includes index
A catalogue record for this book is available from the British Library
ISBN: 978-1-84836-581-0
The publishers and authors have done their best to ensure the accuracy and currency of all the information in **The Rough Guide to USA**, however, they can accept no responsibility for any loss, injury, or inconvenience sustained by any traveller as a result of information or advice contained in the guide.
1 3 5 7 9 8 6 4 2

Help us update

We've gone to a lot of effort to ensure that the tenth edition of **The Rough Guide to USA** is accurate and up-to-date. However, things change – places get "discovered", opening hours are notoriously fickle, restaurants and rooms raise prices or lower standards. If you feel we've got it wrong or left something out, we'd like to know, and if you can remember the address, the price, the hours, the phone number, so much the better.

Please send your comments with the subject line **"Rough Guide USA Update"** to ⓔmail @uk.roughguides.com. We'll credit all contributions and send a copy of the next edition (or any other Rough Guide if you prefer) for the very best emails.

Find more travel information, connect with fellow travellers and book your trip on ⓦwww .roughguides.com

SMALL PRINT

Acknowledgements

Sam: Thanks to eagle-eyed editor Alison Roberts for steering the guide through with such grace and efficiency; Christina Valhouli; Sal and everyone at the *Napoleon House*; David Nicholson; Peter Hannaford; Jenny Steuber in Nashville; Jackie Reed in Memphis; Amanda Latson in Atlanta; Erica Backus in Savannah; co-authors Jeff and Nick; and above all co-author and husband Greg Ward, for a long and very happy journey.

J.D. would like to thank his co-authors, and his editor Alison Roberts for expertly handling all aspects of this considerable volume. Thanks also to all those who have provided current and ongoing help in the research of this book. Some of these names include Marcia Murphy, Sarah Crocker, Allison Goldstein, Lisa Scarpelli, Peter Moskos, Leopoldo Marino, Aaron Wong, Brenna Dickey, Gray Nieland, Eric Macey, Dennis Holifena, Kim Partlow, David Cohen, Lauren Zelisko, David Rodriguez, Doug Camp, Jane Vorwig and Thomas Blasczcyk. Also, the assistance of Convention and Visitors Center staff of numerous cities is much appreciated, but especially those of Baltimore, Washington DC, Los Angeles, San Diego, Richmond and Seattle. Finally, thanks to everyone on the Rough Guide staff who have worked so assiduously.

Nick would like to thank all the staff of the various tourist authorities, especially Ed McMasters & Jackie Reau in Cincinnati, Jessica Wagner of Ohio, Pete Burakowski in Buffalo, Patti Donahue in Rochester, Lisa Berger of Ulster Co NY, Ellen Kornfield in Philadelphia, Barbara Hillman in Berkeley, Kelly Chamberlin of Half Moon Bay, Emily Polsby of Mendocino, Bob Warren & Karen Whitaker of Shasta Cascades and my good friend Richard Stenger of Humboldt Co. Thanks also to Keith Drew, Mani Ramaswamy, Alison Roberts and all the RG editing team for fine guidance. Personal thanks for hospitality and excellent company to old Pittsburgh friends Nick Poulos, Brendan Wiant, Pam Scott, Minette & Ken, Marguerite, the Littlefields and deeksha brother Nicholas Vukmanic, also Christine & Todd of Gettysburg, Charles & Heather Duncan in Fairfax VA, the merry fellows of Bonita Hollow in Berkeley and Nikki & Eric in them thar hills. Thanks to Danny Rose for that goal, which raised the roof of a NYC bar. Finally, as ever, heartfelt thanks for support from afar to my dearest Maria.

Greg would like to thank Sam for all the good times on the road and back home, and for her hard work, help, and support on this edition; Nick and Jeff; and, at Rough Guides, Alison Roberts for pulling the whole thing together so efficiently, and Christina Valhouli for her text editing. And thanks to everyone in the US who helped this time around, including Allan Affeldt, Hannah Allen, Darla Cook, David Gonzalez, Robert Graff, Daisy Hobbs, Jacki Lenners, Steve Lewis, Robin Palmer and Jessica Stephens.

Readers' letters

Thanks to all the readers who have taken the time to write in with comments and suggestions (and apologies if we've inadvertently omitted or misspelt anyone's name):

Maria Argyropoulos, Paul Cavanagh, Carole Dane, Jenn Huntoon, Alfred Jacobsen, Mohammad Javidnia, Jim Jirik, Jerry Metzger, Alexandra Pharmakidis, Alison Rowlings, Rob Waslin and Carol Wilson.

Photo credits

All photos © Rough Guides except the following:

Full page

Grand Prismatic Spring, Yellowstone National Park © Werner Van Steen/Getty

Introduction

Lincoln Memorial statue © Bill Heinsohn/Getty
The choir of Mount Gideon Baptist Missionary Church, St Louis © Greenblatt Bill/Corbis Sygma
I-40, near Meteor Crator, Arizona © Walter Bibikow/AWL Images Ltd
Major General G.K. Warren Statue at Gettysburg National Military Park © Wolfgang Kaehler/Corbis
Milwaukee Art Museum, Wisconsin © Don Klumpp/Getty
Bulldogging cowboy, Apache Junction, Arizona © Richard Hamilton Smith/Corbis
Grizzly bearcub in Denali National Park © Momatiuk - Eastcott/Corbis
Cloud Gate by Anish Kapoor, Chicago, Illinois © Michael Robinson/Corbis
The Temple of Joy, Burning Man Festival © Craig Lovell/Corbis

Things not to miss

03 Skier, Sun Valley © Karl Weatherly/Corbis
04 Pink Floyd exhibit, Rock and Roll Hall of Fame © Rock and Roll Hall of Fame and Museum
05 Pike Place Market © Atlantide Phototravel/Corbis

06 Hugh Mercer House, Savannah, Georgia © Lee Snider/Photo Images/Corbis
07 Mesa Verde National Park, Colorado © Jose Fuste Raga/Corbis
08 Yellowstone Park © Momatiuk - Eastcott/Corbis
09 Fenway Park baseball stadium, Boston © David Madison/Getty
10 Messages for Elvis outside Graceland, Memphis © Terry Eggers/Corbis
11 Ebenezer Baptist Church © Robert W. Ginn/Alamy
12 Niagara Falls © Free Agents Limited/Corbis
13 Highway 1, Big Sur coast © Blaine Harrington III/Corbis
14 Crater Lake, Oregon © Roger Ressmeyer/Corbis
15 Detail of Crazy Horse Memorial © Blaine Harrington III/Corbis
18 Astro Orbiter Ride, Walt Disney World © Blaine Harrington III/Corbis
19 Roky Erickson and Okkervil River, South by Southwest festival © Laure Lea Nalle/South by Southwest
20 Baltimore's National Aquarium © Kevin Fleming/Corbis
21 Grinnell Lake, Glacier National Park © Ian Shive/Corbis
22 View from Kearny Street in San Francisco © Raimund Koch/Corbis
23 Exploding lava, Kilauea © Roger Ressmeyer/Corbis
26 Marching Band in Mardi Gras parade © Bob Sacha/Corbis
28 Baxter State Park, Lake Millinocket © Alan Copson/Corbis
29 Art Deco hotel in Miami © PictureNet/Corbis

From burger bars to bistros colour section

Vintage diner sign, Coos Bay, Oregon © Robert Landau/Corbis
Hamburger on diner table © Ian O'Leary/Getty
Chicken BBQ sign © Envision/Corbis
Lobsters © Nicho Sodling/Johnér Images/Corbis
Cajun signs, New Orleans © Randy Faris/Corbis
Chicken and chocolate *mole* tacos © Thomas Barwick/Getty
Katz's Deli, New York City © JL Photography/Alamy
Maui Wowie Salad, *Roy's* © John Blais/Roy's
Chez Panisse, California © Danita Delimont/Alamy

American music colour section

Jazz musician performing in nightclub, LA © Hill Street Studios/Blend Images/Corbis
Fiddler, Smithville Jamboree, Tennessee © offiwent.com/Alamy
Tim Hadler outside *Tootsie's Orchid Lounge*, Nashville © Catherine Karnow/Corbis
Patsy Cline © Michael Ochs Archives/Corbis
Jazz musician Miles Davis © Pictorial Press Ltd/Alamy
Bob Dylan at the All for the Sea concert, Southampton College © Gordon M. Grant/Alamy
Yeasayer play the Guggenheim, New York © Jen Maler/Retna Ltd./Corbis
Red Rocks Amphitheatre, Colorado © Blaine Harrington III/Alamy
Walter "Wolfman" Washington, *Maple Leaf* bar © Lee Celano/Reuters/Corbis
Rosa's Lounge, Chicago © Sarah Hadley/Alamy

The great outdoors colour section

Female hiker, Antelope Canyon © Keith Ladzinski/Getty
Hikers at foot of Mount Rainier, Washington © Stuart Westmorland/Getty
Lake Superior, Pictured Rocks National Lakeshore, Michigan © Carr Clifton/Getty
Bighorn ram, Yellowstone National Park © Kennan Ward/Corbis
Blue Ridge Parkway National Park © Yves Marcoux/Getty
Chisos Mountains, Big Bend National Park, Texas © Ian Shive/Aurora Photos/Corbis
The Rocky Mountains, Saint Mary Lake, Glacier National Park, Montana © Adam Jones/Visuals Unlimited/Corbis
Molten lava, Hawaii Volcanoes National Park © Gavriel Jecan/Corbis

Building America colour section

Cliff Palace in Mesa Verde National Park © Nik Wheeler/Corbis
Log cabins, Old Trail Town, Cody, Wyoming © Kevin R. Morris/Corbis
Facade of Mercer House in Savannah © Bob Krist/Corbis
Experience Music Project, Seattle, Washington © Peter Carroll/First Light/Corbis
Exterior View of Fallingwater, Pennsylvania © Catherine Karnow/Corbis
Interior of the Guggenheim Museum, New York © Christian Kober/Robert Harding World Imagery/Corbis
Victorian Houses, Alamo Square, San Francisco © Richard Cummins/Corbis
Santa Barbara Mission © Macduff Everton/Corbis

Black and whites

p.112 Pittsburgh, Pennsylvania © Stephen Simpson/Corbis
p.328 New River Gorge National River, West Virginia © Richard T. Nowitz/Corbis
p.392 Pier, Islamorada, Florida Keys © jonarnoldimages
p.396 Stax in Memphis © Jerome De Perlinghi/Corbis
p.552 *Napoleon House*, French Quarter, New Orleans © Greg Ward
p.586 Cowboys at indoor rodeo, Fort Worth © Walter Bibikow/JAI/Corbis
p.632 Mount Rushmore National Memorial, South Dakota © Blaine Harrington III/Corbis
p.680 Durango and Silverton Narrow Gauge Railroad © Nik Wheeler/Corbis
p.946 Roche Harbor, San Juan Island, Washington © Kevin Schafer/Corbis
p.998 Caribou stag on ridge, Alaska © Kim Heacox/Getty

Index

Map entries are in colour.

Rough Guide favourites

Americana

The Boardwalk, Atlantic City, NJ p.159
Carhenge, NE..p.661
Coney Island, NY p.96
Crazy Horse Memorial, SD p.20, 673
Dollywood, TN p.467
Graceland, Memphis, TN p.19, 456
The Strip, Las Vegas, NV p.21, 826
Watts Towers, Los Angeles, CA...................... p.858

C

Rough Guide favourites

College towns

Ann Arbor, MI p.273
Athens, GA........ p.434
Berkeley, CA p.925
Boulder, CO p.689
Burlington, VT ... p.227
Chapel Hill, NC... p.412
Madison, WI...... p.313
Missoula, MT..... p.737

I

Rough Guide favourites

Historic sites

The Alamo, San Antonio, TX....................p. 610
Fort Sumter, SC p.423
Ground Zero, NY....................p.76
Harpers Ferry, WV....................p.373
Lexington, MA....................p.183
Lincoln Memorial....................p.340
Little Bighorn Battlefield, MT p.729
Mesa Verde, CO....................p.709
MLK Jr National Historic Site, Atlanta, GA........p.429
Pearl Harbor, HI p.1037
Roanoke Island, NC....................p.407
St Augustine, FL p.521
The Sixth Floor Museum, Dallas, TX p.616

J

K

L

Rough Guide favourites

Movie locations

The Birds..........p.940
Close Encounters of the Third Kind..........p.715
Giant..........p.626
Mystery Train..........p.459
Mystic Pizza..........p.208
Rocky..........p.151
The Shining..........p.984
Thelma and Louise..........p.813
Witness..........p.141

O

P

INDEX

S

Rough Guide favourites

Ski resorts

Rough Guide favourites

Small towns

Rough Guide favourites

Sports

Rough Guide favourites

The Wild West

Canyon de Chelly, AZ....p.800
Cody, WY....p.716
Fort Robinson State Park, NE....p.662
Fort Worth, TX....p.618
Monument Valley, AZ/UT....p.800
OK Corral, AZ....p.753
Silver City, NM....p.775
Silverton, CO....p.707
Wounded Knee, SD....p.669

X

Y

Z

Map symbols

maps are listed in the full index using coloured text

- International border
- State border
- Chapter boundary
- Interstate highway
- US highway
- State highway
- Pedestrianized road
- Steps
- Unpaved road
- 4WD road
- Tunnel
- Path/trail
- Railroad
- Ferry route
- River
- Wall
- Cave
- Mountain range
- Mountain peak
- Waterfall
- Spring
- Marshland/swamp
- Gorge
- Battlefield
- Point of interest
- Airport
- Airfield
- Bridge
- Lighthouse
- Museum
- Monument/memorial
- Ski area
- Restaurant
- Accommodation
- Campsite
- Viewpoint/lookout
- Parking
- Bus stop
- Metro
- Hospital/medical center
- Information center
- Post office
- Statue
- Fountain/gardens
- Arch
- Park entrance
- Hindu/jain temple
- Church (regional maps)
- Building
- Church (town maps)
- Stadium
- Cemetery
- Park/forest
- Beach
- Indian reservation